PEÑÍN GUIDE TO SPANISH WINE 2012

Team:

Supervising editor: José Peñín
Technical director: Carlos González
Tasting team: José Peñín, Carlos González, Javier Luengo and Pablo Vecilla
Texts: José Peñín, Carlos González and Javier Luengo
Editor-in-chief: Javier Luengo
Database manager: Erika Laymuns
Commercial director: Carlos del Hoyo
Advertising: Luna Castañeda
Cover design, layout and desktop publishing: Javier Herrán
Photographs: PI&ERRE

PUBLISHED BY: PI&ERRE
Arga, 11
28002 – MADRID
SPAIN
Tel.: 0034 914 119 464 - Fax: 0034 915 159 499
comunicacion@pi-erre.com
www.pi-erre.com ~ www.guiapenin.com

ISBN: 978-84-95203-77-9
Copyright library: M-45854-2011
Printed by: PrinterMan

DISTRIBUTED BY: GRUPO COMERCIAL ANAYA
Juan Ignacio Luca de Tena, 15
Tel: 0034 913 938 800
28027 MADRID
SPAIN

WELCOME to the future

Well over two decades tasting annually thousands and thousands of samples for this unique Guide have given me the opportunity to correct and improve this product all along. The new generations that landed in this publishing house guided me through the amazing universe of computers, something which has allowed me to implement a tasting model which I deem simply infallible, able to regulate and optimize the results in an independent fashion based on the historical scoring and tasting record and perfectly away from any bias, surely the most precise quality assessment imaginable for any wine. This more or less innovative method has permitted the tasting team that I have willingly selected in the past eight years to face the assessment of a whole diversity of styles and wine regions with minimal judgement deviation.

Today, the goal has been achieved with a bunch of young people, still in their thirties, knowledgeable and capable of achieving the finest possible balance between illusion and responsibility when they face the paramount task of rating the most phenomenal number of Spanish wines one could imagine.

The Penín Guide has always been a teamwork affair, in the beginning pretty much –I shall admit– under the shadow of my persona, but an almost independent thing nowadays. There is not a single annual wine guide in the world containing almost 10.000 samples that is not the result of teamwork, and the Peñín Wine Guide is no exception. I never felt that my name and professional work was above this huge project, as proved by the fact that in the beginning it was called "Guía de los Vinos de España" (Spanish Wines Guide), until someone convinced me that a kind of personal seal was starting to be necessary from a entrepreneurial point of view. Believe me, then, if I tell you that it all happened out of marketing plans rather that a more self-centered approach.

NEW TIMES

It is true nonetheless that the Guía Peñín has won over the years the sort of reputation that makes us the only –so far– international reference for the Spanish wines. There is no wonder, then, that my humble editorial experience, the alliance with a young and excellent team has taken us all to the core of the digital era: thus, the "green" (our corporative colour) Guide of the Spanish wines has become a vast (also the most comprehensive) database for Spanish wineries, brands, wine regions, prices, grape varieties and type of wines imaginable. A multi-channel guide available for every reader in this planet, compatible with the "physical" green-guide of old that will still be bearing the flag of our commitment. Along with it, the wine page www.guiapenin.com will remain a sort of formidable catwalk for landscape and wine resources alike: videos, forums, real-time tasting events, wineries and winemakers' latest, markets… and even my own blog, a kind of nothing-if-not-critical spot to know the latest on this millenary drink.

To end, I would like you to announce that Guía Peñín has spread its critical reach beyond the seas and we will shortly come up with a brand-new guide on wines from Argentina, Chile and México that follows the same scoring format as the original one.

The future is already present.

José Peñín

PEÑÍN GUIDE 2012 novelties update

Once again, like every single year, a long and arduous time travelling to practically every corner of Spain allowed us to gauge the current shape of all of the Spanish wine regions. After tasting almost 9800 samples, the conclusions are varied, but almost all of them put the accent on the price/quality ratio. Probably the first one would be that in this country there is hardly any bad wine any more. The very few that fall under the 70-point mark had evident faults, no redeeming features whatsoever and were simply impossible to enjoy.

A second conclusion is the overall, unstoppable quality increase, in parallel with the upward trend of the scores of the tasted samples. Five years ago, the average score of the wines assessed by our Guide was 83,6 points, while today is 87,3 points, a valuable data in any case and particularly if we consider that the average retail price is 10 €. Their formidable price/quality ratio is surely known to all national and foreign buyers.

A special mention deserves the outstanding quality of the 2010 vintage (up to 3,200 wines have improved their scores on those from 2009), a year of a cool and fresher character in almost every wine region, which has afforded fresh fruit notes even in those areas where the excessive exposure to sunlight during the last part of the maturation cycle has left its trace, achieving rich wines of the dullest quality.

With all this data in hand, we come up with another conclusion, the fact that young wines with wood ageing (the so called "joven roble" label) or without it are preferred over the crianza and reserva typologies. To prove the point, there is no better way than to confront the 3,200 young wine renderings, 1,083 crianzas and 1,200 reservas to realize that consumer's perception of wood-aged wines is changing. We are still the world's leading country in terms of oak casks consumption, but evidently what matters is the length of that ageing, and what has changed is the way the producers in Spain seem to care for overall balance between fruit an oak rather than legal ageing time requirements. It also matters the fact that younger wines are usually cheaper, and therefore more apt for modern markets.

All in all, the overall picture that this year's edition of our Guide is painting up altogether is the increasing harmony between varietal expression and oak creaminess, i.e., richer and more complex wines and therefore a broader catalogue of styles.

Carlos González
Technical Manager

From left to right: ***Javier Luengo*** *(editor-in-chief, taster),* ***Pablo Vecilla*** *(taster),* ***Carlos González*** *(technical director) and* ***Érika Laymuns*** *(database manager).*

TASTINGTEAM

commercialteam

From left to right: ***Carlos del Hoyo*** *(commercial director),* ***Luna Castañeda*** *(advertising), and* ***Mª Carmen Hernández****, label-hiring manager.*

SUMMARY

ACKNOWLEDGMENTS

To all the **Consejos Reguladores** that have so readily collaborated with the Guide, providing their buildings and professional staff to make the tastings possible. In other cases it was not their fault but problems on our part that did not make them happen in the end. We have to thank also –and very especially– **José Matás** from **Enoteca Casa Bernal**, in El Palmar (Murcia); **Juan Luis Pérez de Eulate** from **La Vinoteca**, a wine shop in Palma de Mallorca; Quim Vila from **Vila Viniteca**, a wine shop in Barcelona; **Casa del Vino La Baranda** from El Sauzal, and particularly **José Alfonso González Lorente**, as well as the **Casa del Vino of Gran Canaria; the Parque Tecnológico del Vino (VITEC)**, in Falset (Tarragona), and **Vinatería Pámpano** in Almendralejo (Badajoz).

WINE-REGIONS

IIn Spain there are currently 82 designations of origin, including the sole thirteen "Vinos de Pago" designations that there have been granted so far: Calzadilla, Campo Laguardia, Casa del Blanco, Dehesa del Carrizal, Dominio de Valdepusa, Finca Élez, Pago Florentino, Pago del Guijoso, Prado de Irache, Señorío de Arínzano, Vinos de Pago de Otazu, El Terrerazo and Pago Los Balagueses.

In a way, the "pago" label seems to complicate the wine map even further, but it is being driven –albeit in a less revolutionary fashion– by highly influential Consejos Reguladores such as Rioja, in line with the concept proposed by the Wine Law (Ley del Vino) of 2003, which defines "pago" as a rural location with its own unique and differentiated characteristics, and at least a five-year market record under the same name to be granted the status.

As for the Guide, all the DOs are listed in alphabetical order, whilst the rest of the labels under the "Vino de la Tierra" label, as well as the VCPRD wines and "Vino de Mesa labels" are also listed in strictly alphabetical order. The latter has also been listed by autonomous region: Andalucía, Aragón, Baleares, Castilla-La Mancha, Castilla-León, Cataluña, Extremadura, La Rioja, Navarra and Valencia. Finally, the section "Sparkling Wines–Traditional Method" comprises the sparkling wines made in the same way as cava –by the method of inducing a second fermentation in the bottle– but within wine regions outside the DO Cava or any other designation of origin.

The following sections are found in each chapter:

- A map of the DO and the largest vineyard areas.
- An overview of the region with a brief commentary on its current situation and foreseeable future.
- The general characteristics of the wines of every region.
- A rating (excellent, very good, good, average and mediocre) of the vintage according to our wine-tasting team, and the evaluation of the final products as they are ready to hit the market, a much more realistic approach to quality than the official one, which bases primarily the assessment of the wines in their post-fermentative state, when they show abundant notes directly derived from the winemaking process, either fermentative or else.
- A list of wineries and tasting notes.

WINERIES

They are listed in alphabetical order within the wine region they belong to. Of each winery, we have detailed name and address, telephone and fax numbers, e-mail and web page. All the basic information (address, telephone numbers and brand names of the different wines) was provided by the producers themselves, with a deadline on the 30th of June 2011, and has been updated practically to the full in this year's edition. Those wineries that did not provide any samples for our assessment have not been included in the Guide.

If a single producer makes wine in different wine regions or designations of origin, he will be included in each one of them, and in the winery index he will have as many entries as the number of wineries he owns. The most frequent case would be that of cava and still wine producers in Penedès.

HOW TO USE THIS GUIDE

In all the different categories (designation of origin, vino de la tierra, vino de calidad, etc.), we have included all the producers that make, bottle and market at least one wine with the back-label of any given DO, regardless of the fact that they are inscribed within it or not. Today, it has become more and more common to find in any particular region wines that have been made "by" local producers ascribed to the DO "for" a company outside that specific territory.

Usually, consumers are looking for wines within a particular region, and once they spot it, it is easy for them to get in contact with the winery that owns the brand label to buy it, or to find related information of any kind.

WINES

The wines and their corresponding tasting notes make up the bulk of the text. They are always displayed just after the information on the winery that makes them, according to the following specifications:

- Brand name, type of ageing (crianza, etc.) and vintage (if supplied by the producer), as well as its specific type (red, white, etc.), the DO it belongs to and retail price as provided by the winery.

- Given our peremptory necessity to keep the number of pages of our Guide as low as possible to make of it an easy-to-handle book, we have only included the tasting notes of those wines that scored 80 points and above; of those that did not hit that mark, only the brand name and the score will be shown, although we will keep their tasting notes in our database for future reference.

- Tasting notes try to convey the samples main characteristics.

- Whenever a winery decides not to send the wines that they fear may not reach the 80-point mark, we would try to get the samples in any other way. Obviously, producers who deem their wines are susceptible of higher scores are more than keen to send them in for our assessment.

- The labels reproduced in our Guide are not in any case an indication of quality, but merely advertising space paid by those producers who think the labels would help costumers to spot their wines more easily, since they follow an alphabetical order within their pages.

EQUIVALENCE CHART

Every now and then, the wineries complain about the difficulty to find the equivalences between the different scoring systems that wine critics (or writers) use in magazines and wine guides. The Guía Peñín adopted, back in 1992, the American scoring system simply because it started to have a real impact on the market and appeared to be a bit above the most common icon systems (wine-glasses, stars, grape-bunches, etc.) or the 0 to 20 one, this latter highly generalized between European wine critics. The real colophon was the worldwide –and particularly in Spain– relevance rapidly acquired by Robert Parker's Wine Advocate. Our goal was to become the first independent catalogue of Spanish wines, a comprehensive vademecum to properly assess the price/quality ratio, something that drove us away necessarily from the most traditional Spanish academic scoring system of 0 to 10.

Our Guide has had in mind right from the start to disentangle the different scoring systems' equivalences and put forward our own ratings.

Guías de Vinos Gourmets, Anuario de Vinos El País	0-10	0	1	2	3	4	5	6	7	8	9	10
Jancis Robinson, Bettane et Desseauve, Vinum, elmundovino.com, Revista Vinho, Wine "Esencia deo Vinho"	0-20	0	2	4	6	8	10	12	14	16	18	20
Sobremesa, Guía Proensa	0-100	0	10	20	30	40	50	60	70	80	90	100
Wine Enthusiast, Wine Spectator, Wine Advocate (Robert Parker), Vino y Gastronomía, Wine Cellar (Stephen Tanzer s), Guía Peñín	50-100	50	55	60	65	70	75	80	85	90	95	100

INDEXES

As well as the more usual alphabetical indexes listing wine brands and wineries, there is a "Best wines by wine region" index that includes all those within the 90-point mark, except for those areas where this sort of high scores are too difficult to get, and where lower ratings will be included instead.

In this 2012 edition and due to the great number of wines that have reached the 90-point mark (what we usually call the "Podium"), we have upped the lintel to those between 95 and 100 (both included), under the tag of EXCEPTIONAL WINES. Those from 90 to 95 will be just EXCELLENT.

There are also a DO, a VT, and a "Wine group" list that includes all the wineries within a single owner.

The utter goal of this book is to inform fast and efficiently of all of the wines available in the Spanish market during the last three months of 2011 and the whole of 2012. Our assessments are entirely under the responsibility of Guía Peñín and its tasting team, and therefore are only to be judged in the light of the team's rating ability and the confidence the reader may have in it. However, judgments would have a 6% deviation margin.

Except for the wines with a prominent character, the tasting has been simplified by highlighting the most significant aspects as well as those most easily detected by the average consumer. Very detailed and technical descriptions have therefore been avoided altogether, for we believe them to be decidedly confusing for the average consumer. However, there is a glossary with the terms that may appear a little too technical.

HOW THE WINES ARE SAMPLED

The majority of the tasting takes place from the end of January to June the 30th. Therefore, any samples received after that time will not be included in our Guide. We carefully schedule all the wine regions' tastings so that we can conduct them systematically in a relatively short time.

NOTE: Since we deem unacceptable the absence in our Guide of wines of outstanding notoriety and quality, in case they miss the deadline (June the 30th), we would proceed to purchase them, as long as the producers agree on the necessity of it, given their reputation. However, our team will not take any responsibilities as to the storing conditions and quality of the samples acquired in –as a rule– well-established merchants.

WHEN ARE THE SAMPLES TASTED?

HOW THE SAMPLES WERE RECEIVED

We have not set out in search of wines that missed the deadline, except for those we knew from previous years would be susceptible to achieve high scores. The producers have realized by now the prestige our Guide is gaining year after year, so the number of samples has steadily increased with every new edition.

Samples of nearly all of the most notorious Spanish wines were submitted by the producers themselves. Whenever a notorious absence happened, it was out of fear on the part of the producers that their wines may not reach high scores. In other cases the reason could be that a particular winery has sold out the whole of its production, either because of high demand or a shortage of grapes in a given vintage. Occasionally, the absence of important brand names was due to a totally unintentional error attributable exclusively to our organization. Whenever the winery is solely responsible for the absence, we would resort to purchasing that particular sample, provided the brand is a well-known one, commercially or else.

SCORING SYSTEM

We have chosen the American scoring system (in which 0 equals 50), given the international reach our Guide has acquired in recent years. That system expresses the different quality levels in a very general way, somehow segmenting the overall assessment in five different 10-point fractions. We would like to point out at the fact that there is no correspondence whatsoever between this system and the 0-10 academic scale traditionally used in Spain and broadly adopted by wine critics in our country. In view of this, the reader must go to the chart in page 15 to find the equivalences. However, a most specific description of the wine in our Guide adheres to the following scale:

95-100 EXCEPTIONAL

The wine excels among those of the same type, vintage and origin. It is in every sense extraordinary. It is full of complexity, with abundant sensory elements both on the nose and on the palate that arise from the combination of soil, grape variety, winemaking and ageing methods; elegant and utterly outstanding, it exceeds average commercial standards and in some cases it may still be unknown to the general public.

90-94 EXCELLENT

A wine with the same attributes as those indicated above but with less exceptional or significant characteristics.

85-89 VERY GOOD

The wine stands out thanks to features acquired through great winemaking and/or ageing standards, or an exceptional varietal character. It is a wine with unique features, although it may lack soil or terroir expression.

80-84 GOOD

Although not as distinctive, the wine expresses the basic characteristics of both its type and region of origin.

70-79 AVERAGE

The wine has no defects, but no virtues either.

60-69 NOT RECOMMENDED

It is a non-acceptable wine in which some faults are evident, although they may not spoil the overall flavour.

50-59 FAULTY

A non-acceptable wine from a sensory point of view that may be oxidised or have defects due to bad ageing or late racking; it may be an old wine past its best or a young wine with unfavourable fermentation off-odours.

THE TOTAL NUMBER OF SAMPLES TASTED

It is difficult to give a precise figure, since many of the wines over the 80-point mark were re-tasted, sometimes more than once. To the number of wines sampled and commented, one should have to add approximately some 1500 more.

HOW THE WINES ARE RATED

Our tasting team is no particularly prone to numerical ratings. However, pure and simple tasting notes with no scores do not give the average consumer sufficient indication of the differences in quality between brands, particularly when they happen to have similar writing descriptions.

Evidently, both positive and negative elements that are used to describe wines have limits of their own, with or without the scores. Somehow, it seems that it probably would be enough to use just three categories, good, very good and excellent, but we judge we should go beyond that mere classification in order to point out the differences between wines within each category.

HOW THE TASTING IS CARRIED OUT

The Guide's tasting team is partial to conduct the tasting of the samples knowing their identity rather than using the comparative and blind tasting forms. There are two reasons for it:

1.- To be able to establish the typicity of the different wines: region, climate, grape varieties, vintage, etc. help to define their character and eventually provide a pattern for all the wines that come from a specific area.
2.- A matter of feasibility: it would simply be impossible from a practical point of view to blind taste the huge amount of wines that we sample every year.

The experience of our tasters helps them to elude the influence that watching the label may exert on their judgement. On the other hand, their knowledge on each particular producer's quality progress allow them the opportunity to come up with fairer assessments, since generally the differences between vintages, beyond the natural factors affecting each particular vintage, tend to be smaller every year.

Unless the tastings of the same wines are conducted by different tasting commissions in also different flights, the results obtained by blind tasting a whole annual guide will never be fair; only when the tasting notes are confronted with those from an "open label" session, the tasters know the historic record of the winery and the features to look for in a specific area can we assure the validity of the assessment.

HERE IS THE WAY WE CONDUCT OUR TASTING:

- We take a general impression derived both from various tastings in different places and situations, and the knowledge we have on the style and overall quality of the producers.

It is unusual for two samples of the same brand, type and ageing category (crianza, reserva or gran reserva) to get scores with a difference of more than three points, even for different vintages; however, it is much more common for those variations to happen upwards in scoring terms, thanks to significant changes in vine growing or winemaking practises.

- Our tasting team's knowledge on the style (generally consistent over the years) of each producer minimizes the possibility of mistakes associated, for instance, to a particular bottle, not to be confused with bad winemaking practises that should in every case be penalized.

In the case of new wineries, or new brands included in our Guide for the first time that may show a style totally out of step with the most traditional renderings of a particular winery, our tasters can compare their opinions and even carry out a survey amongst other colleagues.

- On the other hand, we are aware that in Spain, due to relatively consistent climatic conditions within the regions and the skilful –verging on tricky– traditional blending of different wines, a long-standing practise in most of the country, the variations between vintages are less evident than the changes in style, the latter a common feature in recent times normally declared by the producers, but also very easy to detect through tasting.

TASTING OF PREMATURELY-BOTTLED WINES

In previous editions of our Guide we found that some high quality wines that had been bottled just up to three months before our tasting averaged lower scores. It was also evident that six months later (correction already an impossible issue until the following edition) those same wines deserved higher scores, for they had improved both in the nose and in the palate.

We know of the negative notes that arise when we taste samples bottled within such a short time (underdeveloped fruit character, poor balance between oak and wine, harsh tannins), but even when we try to disregard them, it becomes a high-risk task to rate the samples higher than what we perceive with our senses there and then. That is why our tasting team recommends producers not to send their samples until they totally sure of the optimal development of their sensory character, to avoid the risk of discrediting both the wine and our tasting team. In those cases, we rather advise them to send a sample from the previous vintage –a fully developed wine– even when it has been sold out, for there may still be some bottles available in the market, which surely renders its publication in our Guide still a most interesting issue.

HOW TO INTERPRET OUR TASTING NOTES

Each wine description comprises two different concepts:

OBJECTIVE

These are the "measurable" and more reliable qualities that do not depend on the personal idiosyncrasies of the taster, and therefore may be easily compared and understood by a non-professional taster.

- **Colour:** both intensity and clarity; for example, if the wines is intense, open, pale, cloudy, limpid, etc.
- **Aroma:** intensity, as well as any possible fault or excessive pre-eminence of a particular element contained in the sample (e.g. wood, grape variety, fruit notes, type of ageing and its length, etc.)
- **Taste:** both intensity and structure; whether it is meaty or not, its body, roundness, the basic flavours (acidity, bitterness –tannins–, sweet, acidic, saline) as well as the notes already described for the aroma.

SUBJECTIVE

These are the "non-measurable" qualities of a more personal nature, related to other elements that the experienced taster may know and which could serve as a sort of sensory guide for the reader. For example, in terms of colour, to speak of "golden, cherry, old gold, mahogany, straw, etc"; or "roasted coffee, jam, cherry, attic, etc." when referring to both aroma and flavour. For another taster, for instance "roasted coffee" could be equivalent to a toasted hint, and "attic" would rather be "dust" or "seasoned wood".

We would like to draw your attention to many Spanish oak-aged wines that reach the market with no indication (crianza, roble, barrica, etc.) of that ageing whatsoever. However, we can assure you that it has become increasingly more common to age them for a short period (3-4 months) with the aim of making them more finished and refined.

In this sense, in our Guide we inform the reader that the wine has been aged in oak, even when we do not specify the number of months. Whenever the word "roble" (oak) stands on the label, we will mention it as such, along with the brand name and other information.

Likewise, we have used different abbreviations to identify the different type of wines included in our Guide, and they should be read as follows:

B	**WHITE**
BC	**AGED WHITE**
BFB	**BARREL-FERMENTED WHITE**
RD	**ROSÉ**
T	**RED**
TC	**AGED (CRIANZA) RED**
TR	**AGED (RESERVA) RED**
TGR	**AGED (GRAN RESERVA) RED**
FI	**FINO**
MZ	**MANZANILLA**
OL	**OLOROSO**
OLV	**OLOROSO VIEJO (OLD OLOROSO)**
AM	**AMONTILLADO**
PX	**PEDRO XIMÉNEZ (SWEET)**
PC	**PALO CORTADO**
CR	**CREAM**
PCR	**PALE CREAM**
GE	**GENEROSO (FORTIFIED)**
ESP	**SPARKLING**
BR	**BRUT**
BN	**BRUT NATURE**
SC	**DRY**
SS	**SEMI-DRY**
S/C	**SIN COSECHA (NON-VINTAGE)**

HOW THE WINES WERE TASTED?

NON-TASTED WINES

There are two groups of non-tasted wines*:

A) THOSE BELONGING TO WINERIES THAT HAVE SUBMITTED FOR OUR ASSESSMENT ONLY PART OF THEIR CATALOGUE.
The absence can be due either to the wine being sold out at the winery (an absurd reason, for the wine could still be available in the market –shops, restaurants…), or to the producer's belief that, in the case of some of his lower quality brands, they would be awarded lower scores. In this latter case, we can simply deduce that they are in fact of a poorer quality and, since we already have had the chance to assess the "top" wines of that particular winery to have an approximate idea or its style, we will not try to get them to send us the missing samples.

B) WINES BELONGING TO WINERIES THAT HAVE NOT SUBMITTED ANY SAMPLES.
We know for certain that, save for a few rare exceptions, these wines would not reach easily the 80-point mark. Still, we will be trying to get samples of them for the next editions of our Guide. Even when they surely would not be getting the greatest scores, some of them may have a good price/quality ratio, and therefore would be really interesting buys for the international market.

**In none of these cases the wines will be included in our Guide.*

EXCEPTIONAL WINES

One more year, our tasting brings some new, surprising names to the fore, as well as ratifying some traditionally great brands. We want to remind our readers that this outstanding part of our Podium that we have named "Exceptional Wines" includes those rated 95 points or above, given that, as well as their indisputable quality, they show sheer singularity and a unique style.

In the red wine front, it is surprising to see that the Dalmau 2007 has been rated as highly as its –so far– "untouchable" brother Castillo de Ygay 2001, in line with the modernity that a most traditional house like Marqués de Murrieta has been showing of late. Artadi has gone even beyond this with two novelties: Valdeginés and La Poza de Ballesteros, both from the 2009 vintage. Bernabé Navarro with its Curro 2009, Mano a Mano with Venta la Ossa TNT 2009 or Bodegas Ribas with Sió 300 Aniversario –a truly unique wine–, have all reached for the first time the most outstanding part our Podium; we should not forget either the outstanding novelty of Rumbo al Norte 2010, Comando G (Daniel Jiménez-Landi, Fernando García and Marc Isart), who have brought the *garnacha* from Gredos to the top echelons of winemaking prominence in this country. We have also discovered the greatness behind Artuke K4, from La Rioja, an another great novelty like Viñedos Culturales, a winery that have managed to bring two new renderings from Alicante (VC Metal and VC Madera) to the selected group of Spain's most outstanding wines.

In regard to white wines, the biggest surprise has been that of the winery Naia, from Rueda, that has managed yet another turn of the screw winemaking-wise with its Naiades 2008, making of it the best barrel-fermented white in the whole of Spain. Besides it, we should keep a close eye on Pedrouzos Magnum 2008, from Bodegas Valdesil, a novelty in our Guide that has become the top rated wine in Valdeorras.

In Jerez, the key issues being power and uniqueness, Equipo Navazos keeps solidly ahead, since there seems to be nobody so capable of extracting the "soul" out of the finest fino and manzanilla soleras of the wineries they choose. Besides, they have been able to bring a sparkling from outside the DO Cava, Colet Navazos Extra Brut, to a level of quality equal to the leading houses within it, like Gramona with their Celler Batlle, a wine that it is again leading the rankings along with a total novelty, Raventós i Blanc Gran Reserva Personal M.R.N.

Yet again, the throne of the Spanish sweet wines is occupied by the Malvasía Dulce 2001 from Bodegas Carballo, from the island of La Palma, a wine that somehow bring us back to the greatness of those 18th century canary sacks exported to England.

And here is the list of exceptional wines by typology:

EXCEPTIONAL WINES/GENEROSOS)

WINE	WINERY
La Bota de Fino (Bota nº 27) FI	Equipo Navazos
La Bota de Manzanilla Pasada (Bota nº 30 "Capataz Rivas") MZ	Equipo Navazos
La Bota de Amontillado (Bota nº 31) AM	Equipo Navazos
Alvear PX 1830 PX Reserva	Alvear
Malvasía Dulce Carballo 2001 B	Bodegas Carballo
Moscatel Viejísimo Toneles Moscatel	Valdespino
Osborne Rare Sherry Solera BC 200 OL	Bodegas Osborne
Venerable VORS PX	Bodegas Osborne
Osborne Rare Sherry AOS AM	Bodegas Osborne
Molino Real 2007 B	Compañía de Vinos de Telmo Rodríguez
Jorge Ordóñez & Co Nº 2 Victoria 2008 Blanco dulce	Bodegas Jorge Ordóñez & Co
La Ina FI	Emilio Lustau
La Bota de Manzanilla (Bota nª 32) MZ	Equipo Navazos
Manzanilla en Rama Saca de Invierno MZ	Bodegas Barbadillo
Don Gonzalo VOS OL	Valdespino
La Bota de Oloroso "Bota punta Nº 28" OL	Equipo Navazos
Solera Su Majestad VORS OL	Valdespino
Cardenal VORS PC	Valdespino
Colección Roberto Amillo Palo Cortado PC	Espíritus de Jerez
Reliquia PX	Bodegas Barbadillo
Casa del Inca 2010 PX	Equipo Navazos
La Bota de Pedro Ximenez nº25 Bota NO PX	Equipo Navazos
La Cañada PX	Pérez Barquero S.A.
Barbadillo Amontillado VORS AM	Bodegas Barbadillo
Colección Roberto Amillo Amontillado AM	Espíritus de Jerez
Reliquia AM	Bodegas Barbadillo
El Grifo Canari Dulce de Licor B	El Grifo
Jorge Ordóñez & Co Nº 1 Selección Especial 2008 B	Bodegas Jorge Ordóñez & Co
Chivite Colección 125 Vendimia Tardía 2008 B	Bodegas Chivite
Alma de Reboreda Tostado 2005 B	Bodegas Campante
Humboldt 1997 Blanco dulce	Bodegas Insulares Tenerife
La Panesa Especial Fino S/C FI	Hidalgo
Pastrana Manzanilla Pasada MZ	Bodegas Hidalgo-La Gitana
Colección Roberto Amillo Oloroso OL	Espíritus de Jerez
Sibarita V.O.R.S. OL	Bodegas Osborne
Gonzalez Byass Añada 1982 1982 PC	González Byass Jerez
Colección Roberto Amillo Pedro Ximénez PX	Espíritus de Jerez
Fernando de Castilla "P.X. Antique" PX	Fernando de Castilla
Humboldt 2001 Tinto dulce	Bodegas Insulares Tenerife

POINTS	TYPE	DO
99	Fino	Jerez
99	Manzanilla	Jerez
98	Amontillado	Jerez
98	Pedro Ximénez	Montilla-Moriles
97	White	La Palma
97	Moscatel	Jerez
97	Oloroso	Jerez
97	Pedro Ximénez	Jerez
96	Amontillado	Jerez
96	White	Málaga y Sierras de Málaga
96	Sweet White	Málaga y Sierras de Málaga
96	Fino	Jerez
96	Manzanilla	Jerez
96	Manzanilla	Jerez
96	Oloroso	Jerez
96	Oloroso	Jerez
96	Oloroso	Jerez
96	Palo Cortado	Jerez
96	Palo Cortado	Jerez
96	Pedro ximénez	Jerez
96	Pedro Ximénez	Montilla-Moriles
96	Pedro Ximénez	Montilla-Moriles
96	Pedro ximénez	Montilla-Moriles
95	Amontillado	Jerez
95	Amontillado	Jerez
95	Amontillado	Jerez
95	White	Lanzarote
95	White	Málaga y Sierras de Málaga
95	White	Navarra
95	White	Ribeiro
95	Sweet White	Tacoronte-Acentejo
95	Fino	Jerez
95	Manzanilla	Jerez
95	Oloroso	Jerez
95	Oloroso	Jerez
95	Palo Cortado	Jerez
95	Pedro Ximénez	Jerez
95	Pedro Ximénez	Jerez
95	Sweet Red	Tacoronte-Acentejo

EXCEPTIONAL WINES/RED WINES)

WINE	WINERY
Contador 2009 T	Bodega Contador
Aquilón 2008 T	Bodegas Alto Moncayo
Vega Sicilia Reserva Especial 91/94/99 T	Bodegas Vega Sicilia
Castillo Ygay 2001 TGR	Marqués de Murrieta
Dalmau 2007 TR	Marqués de Murrieta
Viña El Pisón 2009 T	Bodegas y Viñedos Artadi
Victorino 2008 T	Teso la Monja
La Faraona 2008 T	Descendientes de J. Palacios
Espectacle 2007 T	Espectacle Vins
Espectacle 2008 T	Espectacle Vins
L'Ermita 2008 TC	Alvaro Palacios
Dominio de Atauta Valdegatiles 2008 T	Dominio de Atauta
Pingus 2009 T	Dominio de Pingus S.L.
Valbuena 5º 2007 T	Bodegas Vega Sicilia
Viña Sastre Pesus 2007 T	Bodegas Hermanos Sastre
Artadi Pagos Viejos 2009 T	Bodegas y Viñedos Artadi
Artuke K4 2009 T	Artuke Bodegas y Viñedos
Cirsion 2009 T	Bodegas Roda
Dalmau 2005 TR	Marqués de Murrieta
La Nieta 2008 T	Viñedos de Páganos
San Vicente 2008 T	Señorío de San Vicente
Sierra Cantabria Colección Privada 2008 T	Sierra Cantabria
Cenit 2007 T	Viñas del Cénit
Alabaster 2008 T	Teso la Monja
Alabaster 2009 T	Teso la Monja
Pintia 2008 T	Bodegas y Viñedos Pintia
Victorino 2009 T	Teso la Monja
Rumbo al Norte 2010 T	Comando G
Curro 2009 T	Bodegas Bernabé Navarro
VC Madera 2009 T	Viñedos Culturales
VC Metal 2009 T	Viñedos Culturales
Moncerbal 2008 T	Descendientes de J. Palacios
Ultreia 2009 T	Raul Pérez Bodegas y Viñedos
Villa de Corullón 2008 T	Descendientes de J. Palacios
Alto Moncayo 2008 T	Bodegas Alto Moncayo
Casa Castillo Pie Franco 2008 T	Propiedad Vitícola Casa Castillo
El Nido 2008 T	Bodegas El Nido
Finca Sandoval Cuvee TNS Magnum 2007 T	Finca Sandoval
Ataulfos 2009 T	Bodegas Jiménez Landi
Malpaso 2008 T	Bodegas Canopy
Piélago 2009 T	Bodegas Jiménez Landi
Trossos Tros 2008 T	Portal del Priorat
Les Manyes 2008 T	Terroir al Limit
Perinet + Plus 2006 T	Mas Perinet

POINTS	TYPE	DO
98	Red	Rioja
97	Red	Campo de Borja
97	Red	Ribera del Duero
97	Red	Rioja
97	Red	Rioja
97	Red	Rioja
97	Red	Toro
96	Red	Bierzo
96	Red	Montsant
96	Red	Montsant
96	Red	Priorat
96	Red	Ribera del Duero
96	Red	Ribera del Duero
96	Red	Ribera del Duero
96	Red	Ribera del Duero
96	Red	Rioja
96	Red	Rioja
96	Red	Rioja
96	Red	Rioja
96	Red	Rioja
96	Red	Rioja
96	Red	Rioja
96	Red	Tierra del Vino de Zamora
96	Red	Toro
96	Red	Toro
96	Red	Toro
96	Red	Toro
96	Red	VT CastyLe
95	Red	Alicante
95	Red	Alicante
95	Red	Alicante
95	Red	Bierzo
95	Red	Bierzo
95	Red	Bierzo
95	Red	Campo de Borja
95	Red	Jumilla
95	Red	Jumilla
95	Red	Manchuela
95	Red	Méntrida
95	Red	Méntrida
95	Red	Méntrida
95	Red	Montsant
95	Red	Priorat
95	Red	Priorat

EXCEPTIONAL WINES/RED WINES]

WINE	WINERY
Torroja Vi de la Vila 2008 T	Terroir al Limit
Dominio do Bibei 2007 T	Dominio do Bibei
Lacima 2008 T	Dominio do Bibei
Moure de Autor 2010 T	Adegas Moure
Pago de Carraovejas "Cuesta de las Liebres" Vendimia Seleccionada 2007 TR	Pago de Carraovejas
Pago de los Capellanes Parcela El Picón 2005 T	Pago de los Capellanes
Protos Selección Finca el Grajo Viejo 2009 T	Protos Bodegas Ribera Duero de Peñafiel
Regina Vides 2006 T	Bodegas Hermanos Sastre
Valbuena 5º 2006 T	Bodegas Vega Sicilia
Vega Sicilia Único 2002 T	Bodegas Vega Sicilia
Vizcarra Torralvo 2009 T	Bodegas Vizcarra
Salitre 2009 T	Pago los Balancines
Artadi El Carretil 2009 T	Bodegas y Viñedos Artadi
Artadi La Poza de Ballesteros 2009 T	Bodegas y Viñedos Artadi
Artadi Valdeginés 2009 T	Bodegas y Viñedos Artadi
Artuke Finca de los Locos 2009 T	Artuke Bodegas y Viñedos
Avrvs 2008 T	Finca Allende
Castillo Ygay 2004 TGR	Marqués de Murrieta
El Puntido 2008 T	Viñedos de Páganos
Finca El Bosque 2008 T	Sierra Cantabria
Finca Torrea 2007 TR	Bodegas de los Herederos del Marqués de
Gran Reserva 904 Rioja Alta 1998 TGR	La Rioja Alta
La Nieta 2009 T	Viñedos de Páganos
La Vicalanda 2004 TGR	Bodegas Bilbaínas
La Viña de Andrés Romeo 2009 T	Bodega Contador
Malpuesto 2009 T	Bodegas Orben
Remírez de Ganuza 2006 TR	Bodegas Remírez de Ganuza
Roda I 2006 TR	Bodegas Roda
San Vicente 2007 T	Señorío de San Vicente
Sierra Cantabria Colección Privada 2009 T	Sierra Cantabria
Magma de Cráter 2006 TC	Bodegas Buten
El Titán del Bendito 2008 T	Dominio del Bendito
Numanthia 2008 T	Bodega Numanthia
Termanthia 2008 T	Bodega Numanthia
Termanthia 2009 T	Bodega Numanthia
Almendros 2009 T	Bodegas El Angosto
Quincha Corral 2009 T	Mustiguillo Viñedos y Bodega
Señorío de Otazu 2007 T	Bodega Otazu
Señorío de Otazu Altar 2006 T	Bodega Otazu
Venta la Ossa TNT 2009 T	Bodegas Mano a Mano
Abadía Retuerta Petit Verdot PV 2009 T	Abadía Retuerta
El Reventón 2009 T	Daniel El Travieso S.L.
Pegaso "Granito" 2008 T	Compañía de Vinos de Telmo Rodríguez
Sió 300 Aniversario 2009 T	Bodegas Ribas

POINTS	TYPE	DO
95	Red	Priorat
95	Red	Ribeira Sacra
95	Red	Ribeira Sacra
95	Red	Ribeira Sacra
95	Red	Ribera del Duero
95	Red	Ribera del Duero
95	Red	Ribera del Duero
95	Red	Ribera del Duero
95	Red	Ribera del Duero
95	Red	Ribera del Duero
95	Red	Ribera del Duero
95	Red	Ribera del Guadiana
95	Red	Rioja
95	Red	Rioja
95	Red	Rioja
95	Red	Rioja
95	Red	Rioja
95	Red	Rioja
95	Red	Rioja
95	Red	Rioja
95	Red	Rioja
95	Red	Rioja
95	Red	Rioja
95	Red	Rioja
95	Red	Rioja
95	Red	Rioja
95	Red	Rioja
95	Red	Rioja
95	Red	Rioja
95	Red	Rioja
95	Red	Tacoronte-Acentejo
95	Red	Toro
95	Red	Toro
95	Red	Toro
95	Red	Toro
95	Red	Valencia
95	Red	Vino de Pago El Terrerazo
95	Red	Vinos de Pago de Otazu
95	Red	Vinos de Pago de Otazu
95	Red	VT Castilla
95	Red	VT CastyLe
95	Red	VT CastyLe
95	Red	VT CastyLe
95	Red	VT Mallorca

EXCEPTIONAL WINES/WHITE WINES)

WINE	WINERY
Naiades 2008 BFB	Bodegas Naia
Enate Uno Chardonnay 2006 BFB	Enate
Pedrouzos Magnum 2008 B	Bodegas Valdesil
Trossos Tros 2009 B	Portal del Priorat
Nora da Neve 2008 BFB	Viña Nora
Pazo de Piñeiro 2010 B	Pazos de Lusco
Mártires 2010 B	Finca Allende
Belondrade y Lurton 2009 BFB	Belondrade
El Transistor 2009 B	Compañía de Vinos de Telmo Rodríguez
Edetària 2005 BFB	Edetària
Pedrouzos Magnum 2009 B	Bodegas Valdesil

EXCEPTIONAL WINES/SPARKLING WINES)

WINE	WINERY
Gramona Celler Batlle 2000 BR Gran Reserva	Gramona
Raventós i Blanc Gran Reserva Personal M.R.N. 1999 BN	Josep Mª Raventós Blanc
Castell Sant Antoni	
Torre de L'Homenatge 1999 BN Gran Reserva	Castell Sant Antoni
Recaredo Reserva Particular 2002 BN Gran Reserva	Cava Recaredo
Colet Navazos Extra Brut 2007 Extra Brut Reserva	Colet Vinos

EXCEPTIONAL WINES/WHITE WINES)

POINTS	TYPE	DO
97	White	Rueda
96	White	Somontano
96	White	Valdeorras
95	White	Montsant
95	White	Rias Baixas
95	White	Rias Baixas
95	White	Rioja
95	White	Rueda
95	White	Rueda
95	White	Terra Alta
95	White	Valdeorras

EXCEPTIONAL WINES/SPARKLING WINES)

POINTS	TYPE	DO
97	Brut	Cava
96	Brut Nature	Cava
95	Brut Nature	Cava
95	Brut Nature	Cava
95	Extra Brut	Penedès

VARIETIES, TERROIR and CLIMATES and MICROCLIMATES

VARIETIES

THE MAIN SPANISH WHITE VARIETIES

~ **Airén.** It is the main white grape in La Mancha producing the largest single variety volume of wine in the world. When grown on a large scale without proper care it provides very uninteresting wines. However, with good care, it offers white wines of a pale colour and a fruity nose that are smooth and pleasant on the palate, although lacking remarkable features.

~ **Albarín.** Grown mainly in Asturias, in Cangas de Narcea. Its characteristic flavour falls somewhere between sweet and herbaceous, with the latter feature more pronounced when yields are high. In recent years it has been increasingly grown in the VT León region to an overwhelming quality. Given its short ripening cycle, even when grown in high and relatively sunny regions –as it is the case of that part of León–, it easily achieves an alcohol content of 14%, retaining a fresh acidity with hints of herbs and white fruits.

~ **Albariño.** Mainly produced on the Atlantic coast of Galicia, it is a high quality grape typical of humid and not too sunny regions, and therefore thought to have its origins in central Europe. Its wines are fruity and floral, with a characteristically fat, fleshy, lingering taste.

~ **Albillo.** A considerably neutral variety, low in acidity and with a tendency to oxidise, it produces smooth wines with high glycerine content but no remarkable features. Once the main table wine grape throughout Castile, its early-ripening cycle and high sugar levels afforded its reputation in historic wines such as those of San Martín de Valdeiglesias, known as 'blancos pardillos', slightly coloured –oxidized– whites. Albillo is the dominant variety in San Martín de Valdeiglesias, a sub-region in the DO Vinos de Madrid, and is also grown in higher areas of La Palma –in the Canary Islands– and in Ribera del Duero.

~ **Cayetana blanca.** Grown in Extremadura, mainly in Tierra de Barros, it adapts easily to clay soils and hot climates, yielding light wines with some singular herbal –not herbaceous– notes. It has a pleasant freshness, which is easily lost after the first year in the bottle.

~ **Dona Blanca.** Grown mainly in the DO Monterrei, in the province of Orense. Also known as moza fresca and valenciana in Bierzo, some experts identify it as the merseguera from the Mediterranean coast of Valencia. It is characterized by some fine herbal nuances and good acidity, and it performs well when blended with *godello*.

~ **Forastera Gomera.** Found predominantly in La Gomera along with listán (in both the white and red versions) and the indigenous negramoll, it was one of the grape varieties considered "of interest" when the former vinos de la tierra (VT) designation became DO. Particularly interesting are its colour intensity (lemony yellow), aroma (ripe white fruit) and acidity, all of them characteristics that can be found in the best young wines.

~ **Garnacha blanca.** Considered the Mediterranean white grape par excellence, it is grown mainly in Catalonia (Empordà, Priorat, and above all Terra Alta), and characterised by pleasant herb, hay and scrubland nuances, some warm, alcoholic notes on the palate and its capacity to age wonderfully in the rancio style when aged in wood and winemakers resort to lee-stirring practices.

~ **Godello.** Another high quality Galician white grape cultivated in Valdeorras and Monterrei –in the province of Ourense– as well as in the Bierzo region, in León. Its high glycerol level and acidity provides pleasant bittersweet notes along with high alcohol content.

~ **Hondarrabi Zuri.** This variety is used to produce txakoli in the Basque provinces of Vizcaya and Guipúzcoa. Perfectly adapted to a cool and humid climate, it yields fresh and fruity wines with lovely green grass and apple notes and a refreshing acidity.

~ **Jaén.** Grown mainly in Andalusia, jaén is an old grape variety, already mentioned by Alonso de Herrera in 1513. Another ampelographer of the XVIII century, García de la Leña, mentions two types of jaén: jaén blanco and jaén doradillo. About the latter he recalls: "The grape has a somewhat golden colour, after which it is named: its skin is a little harder than that of the blanco and ripens later". Herbaceousness is the main feature of the wines made from jaén, along with some mineral nuances, although there has been little research on its performance with selected yeasts.

~ Lado. This variety, as subtle as it is scarce, is found in DO Ribeiro. The white wines in that region are made by blending different grape varieties, a way to add complexity and nuances to the renderings. Lado is added to provide lightness, aromatic intensity and acidity.

~ Listán blanca. Cultivated in the Canary Islands, it provides wines with a singular character that falls between ripe grape and mountain herbs notes. It is balsamic and even more so if grown in vineyards on dry and difficult terrains (Valle de Güímar), whereas in more humid regions such as Tacoronte-Acentejo, Valle de la Orotava and –to a lesser extent– Ycoden-Daute-Isora, this variety shows herbal notes and some sweetness.

~ Loureiro. Another Galician variety used to add complexity and round wines off. It is a highly aromatic grape, although it is used in blends in only tiny proportions. There is also a red loureiro, which is very scarce. The white one is best known for an aroma reminiscent of bay leaf (loureiro in Galician language).

~ Macabeo (or viura). It is the main variety for quality white Rioja wines and also cavas. Its slow oxidation pattern makes it ideal for barrel ageing. The wine is pale and light, with hints of green fruits when yields are high. Recent research has proved macabeo cultivated in poor soils and under low-yield growing patterns –just the opposite to current practices in Penedès and La Rioja– yields grapes of higher quality.

~ Malvar. The main white grape variety in the region of Madrid, it has a smooth texture, a good fruity character and some sweetness that combines brilliantly with airén, as well as being an ideal grape to make wines with sobremadre (with the skins), the most popular winemaking practice within the region.

~ Malvasía. It gave name to the most famous sweet wine of the Middle Ages and, although it reigned throughout the Mediterranean region, it is now relegated to Italy, Portugal (it is the main grape variety in Madeira) and Spain. Considered nobler than moscatel, it produces very aromatic whites with a highly original taste that falls somewhere between musky and bitter. In the Mediterranean basin there are many clones and types of this age-old grape variety. The best-known examples in Spain are the malvasías from the Canary Islands and the town of Sitges in Catalonia, and it is also produced in smaller quantities in Navarra and La Rioja. Aromatic and historic as it gets (its Greek provenance links it to the oldest winemaking in the Western world), known in Catalonia as subirat parent, its huge character is promoting its renaissance in the Mediterranean coast as well as in the inland regions.

~ Merseguera. A variety cultivated in Valencia, basically in the Alto Turia and on a lesser scale in Utiel-Requena. It provides whites with a grassy character, dry mountain herbs and a light almondy background; it has a little more body than cayetana blanca and airén. So far there is no evidence of any improvement in its quality with the application of new winemaking methods.

~ Moscatel. Generally used in the production o sweet mistela wines, it yields aromatic, neat wines that are very fragrant and fresh when young. It is grown in Levante, Cádiz, Málaga and the Ebro valley, the latter an area where they grow mainly the type known as moscatel de grano menudo, used in the production of high quality sweet wines.

~ Palomino. This is the grape variety par excellence in the region of Jerez. Its fast evolution makes it ideal for the production of 'vinos generosos' (fortified wines). It has little body and a fresh pungent flavour with bitter almond nuances. Palomino is also grown in the provinces of Galicia, León and Valladolid.

~ Pardina. Is the most characteristic white grape in Extremadura, particularly abundant in the regions of Tierra de Barros and Ribera Baja. New winemaking methods are helping to reveal a lovely character of mountain herbs and white ripe fruit, and it also shows a lovely character on the palate.

~ Parellada. lGrown in the higher regions of Catalonia. It is a delicate grape and therefore very difficult to grow. Its low-alcoholic wines are pale, with delicate aromas and a light body. It is also a complementary variety in cava production.

~ Pedro Ximénez. Mainly grown in the provinces of Córdoba and Málaga. The wines from Montilla-Moriles are made from this grape and its fast evolution makes it suitable for the production of dry and sweet fortified wines, as well as ¬blended with moscatel, for the sweet wines of Málaga. When made into dry wines, it shows a pleasant, easy palate with a slight sweetness.

~ **Picapoll.** A grape native to the Catalonian region of Pla de Bages, and it is also grown in the Languedoc in France. According to some theories its name comes from the spots I has on the skin and according to others from its sharp acidity. Although it is traditionally used blended with other varieties (mainly macabeo and parellada), new wave producers such as Abadal have used it in single-varietal wines given its intense, fruity aromas of flowers and herbs.

~ **Torrontés.** It is used blended –along with godello, albariño, treixadura and loureiro– in modern Ribeiro wines, and gives musts of a somewhat neutral taste –partly to high-yielding production patterns–, and therefore less intense and more acidic than its white counterparts. Outside Spain, it is the most popular grape for white wine production in Argentina.

~ **Treixadura.** The main grape variety from Ribeiro, it is similar to albariño but not as refined and with less glycerol content. Its taste is reminiscent of ripe apples and it blends beautifully with the albariño. Floral and fruity in character, it is a good quality grape; however, it does have a limited production.

~ **Verdejo.** This is perhaps the Spanish white variety most integrated with the ecosystem of the plateau and, therefore, best adapted to the continental climate of Castile. When selected yeasts are not used, its wines are characterized by flavours that are both pleasantly herbal and fruity, with some structure on the palate, leading to a typically bitter finish, but with a background of sweetness that provides a lot of character. It grows well when planted in alluvial soils and areas with strong day-night temperature contrast.

~ **Vijariego.** It is one of the oldest indigenous Spanish grape varieties, grown exclusively in the Canary Islands and Andalusia (mainly in the provinces of Granada and Almería). It has a fruity character with some pleasant herbal and balsamic nuances. A very interesting white grape, even when barrel-fermented.

~ **Xarel.lo.** A very harmonious, balanced grape variety, but with more body than the other characteristic Catalonian grapes, parellada and macabeo. It shows a splendid character when is grown under low-yield production patterns and manages to ripen properly.

~ **Zalema.** The name stems from the Arabic "salem", meaning peace. This variety, exclusive to the DO Condado de Huelva, is full, fruity and fresh on the nose, characterised by fruit notes bordering on exotic. On the

GEOGRAPHICAL DISTRIBUTION OF THE MAIN WHITE GRAPES

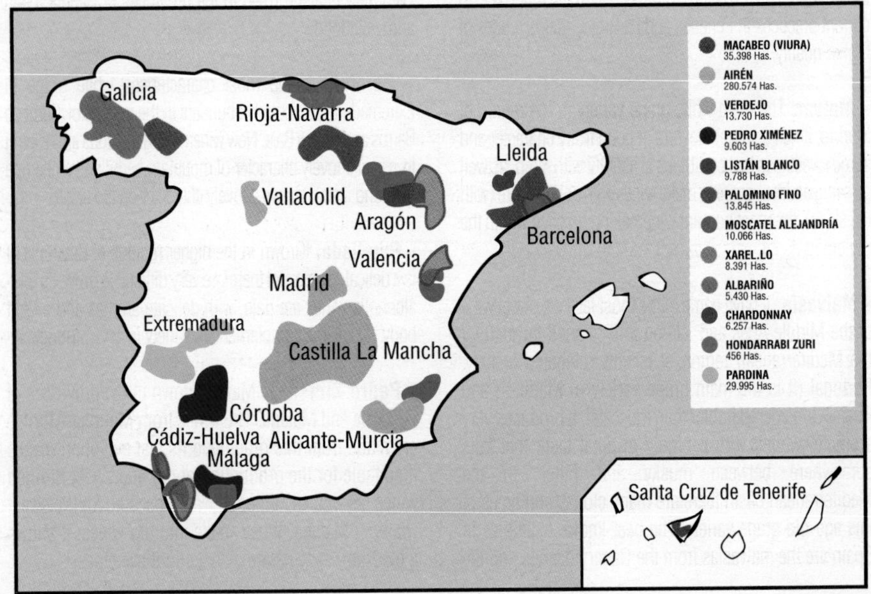

palate, in addition to freshness, its more prominent feature is a smooth, ripe aftertaste with hints of flowers and apple peel.

THE MAIN SPANISH RED VARIETIES

~ **Bobal.** A typical grape of the high areas of Levante, and particularly abundant in Utiel-Requena. Very intense in terms of colour, with brilliant reflections thanks to its high acidity, it has generally low alcohol content, though. It has also a fresh, not too intense nose, and makes good rosé wines. When the grape comes from old vines, a more pronounced wild-berry character appears. An improved knowledge on low-yield viticulture is giving rise to meatier and more tannic reds with excellent ageing potential.

~ **Brancellao.** A variety characterised by small to medium-size bunches and light-coloured flesh, it provides structure. It is grown in Ribeira Sacra along with merenzao, although to a much lesser extent than mencía.

~ **Caíño.**Found in both white and red versions, the former authorised in Rías Baixas, the latter one of the main varieties in Ribeiro.

~ **Callet.** Native to Mallorca, for years it has been considered a second-rate grape, producing musts with very little colour due to high-yield production patterns. However, young wine growers from around the town of Felanitx have given it a new lease of life over the last few years thanks to selective work on old vines and low yields, producing wines with good colour and high alcohol content. It is usually blended with cabernet sauvignon, manto negro or tempranillo to improve the wines ageing potential and add complexity. The skin needs to fully ripen to avoid its typical herbaceous notes.

~ **Cariñena.** Perhaps the Spanish variety more capable to stand overripeness. With old vines and in warm dry soils it can be obtained a good fruit expression of great freshness and dry and lively tannins, although only above 14 % alcohol content. It generally shows hints of wild red berries that are fresher than those related to monastrell and garnacha. It is usually blended with garnacha, which has a somewhat weaker tannic structure. It is grown mainly in Tarragona (Priorat and Montsant).

~ **Garnacha.** For many decades this has been the main Spanish grape variety in terms of production. In recent times its wines have improved in colour, character and depth, thanks to a considerable average reduction in yield. As it tends, like monastrell, to oxidize easily, to keep a good colour is crucial, but it does have an enormous fruit expression with a certain touch of sweetness, maybe not as pronounced as monastrell. It is grown mainly in the warm regions of La Rioja, Navarra, Aragón and Catalonia, i.e., along the Ebro River Valley. In Toledo and to the west of Madrid there is a clone of garnacha with slightly less colour and tannins.

~ **Garnacha tintorera.** The main characteristic of this grape is that its pulp is coloured, which makes it a very sought after grape to give colour to bulk wines. Traditionally known as the alicante bouschet hybrid, some authors say it is grape variety on its own right native from Alicante, Toledo and Ciudad Real. Some recent single-varietal renderings in the DO Almansa have proved its great aromatic and fruity character, as well as its capability to provide body and structure on the palate.

~ **Graciano.** This is a classic Rioja grape, which, as it was grown in less accessible areas of La Rioja, was used only in small proportions and mainly to improve both the acidity and the fruit expression of tempranillo. As soon as it was discovered that planted in warmer areas the grape grew richer in fruit and colour expression, single-varietal wines began to emerge. It has a great aromatic character with hints of blueberries and is fresher and more vigorous than the tempranillo grown in warmer regions. Most of the graciano is planted in La Rioja and in the hottest parts of Valencia and Extremadura.

~ **Hondarribi Beltza.** The red txakoli variety has its origins –and it is cultivated exclusively– within the geographical boundaries of the Basque Country. It is characterised by a high acidity and strong fruit and wild herbs aromas. As well as being made into varietal wines, it is also part of rosé blends along with its white counterpart, hondarribi zuri. Some French experts maintain that it is very similar to cabernet franc as it is also grown in the French region of Irulegui.

~ **Juan García.** Native to the region of Fermoselle, in the province of Zamora (Castilla-León), where it is the main variety. It can provide interesting young wines of moderate alcoholic content. However, its thin skin makes it a fragile variety in areas of high humidity or when it comes to lengthy ageing periods.

~ **Listán Negra.** This grape is grown in the Canary Islands and yields brilliant red wines with a marked balsamic nose, hints of eucalyptus and some fresh, juicy red fruit notes. Its average low tannic level makes it more suitable for the production of young wines.

~ **Manto negro.** Native to the Balearic Islands, it is especially abundant in the DO Binissalem, in Mallorca, although is also found in Pla i Llevant. It yields typical ripe fruit aromas along with hints of caramel. On the palate it is quite balanced, although it is normally blended with another local grape –callet– or some other international varieties.

~ **Marselan.** A fairly new variety (just under a decade old), it is a hybrid or crossbreed of cabernet sauvignon and garnacha and it first went on the market in 2002. Its aromatic and sensory profile is characterised by a stimulating opposition between a high concentration of fruity and spicy notes and the subtlety of its tannins, which makes it one of the grapes with the greatest potential in the Mediterranean area. Its tendency to ripen very quickly makes it prone to over-maturation.

~ **Mencía.** The cultivation of this grape is limited to the northeast of the Iberian Peninsula, and it is abundant in the border of the provinces of León and Zamora with the region of Galicia. Quite similar to cabernet franc, it yields fruity wines, rich in colour and acidity when grown in cooler regions with sufficient water. Recently, deeper, more concentrated reds are being made thanks to more careful winemaking and lower yields.

~ **Monastrell.** Of Spanish provenance and known in France as mourvèdre, the monastrell is characterised by its suitability to regions with little rainfall and high temperatures. It is almost entirely grown in the limestone soils of the provinces of Alicante and Murcia. It has a lot of fruit expression, though of a candied-fruit kind, as well as sweet and soft tannins. It is prone to oxidation, and therefore excellent for sweet and rancio wines. It needs to reach 13.5º of potential alcohol and the wine should not age for more than 10 months for the fruit to achieve full expression. Except in the areas already mentioned, where monastrell is vinified on its own, in cooler regions like Catalonia it is usually blended with other varieties.

~ **Moristel.** It is grown within the geographical boundaries of Somontano, like parraleta, although from a sensory point of view it is slightly sweeter, with certain rusticity, some candied-fruit notes and cherry preserve.

GEOGRAPHICAL DISTRIBUTION OF THE MAIN RED GRAPES

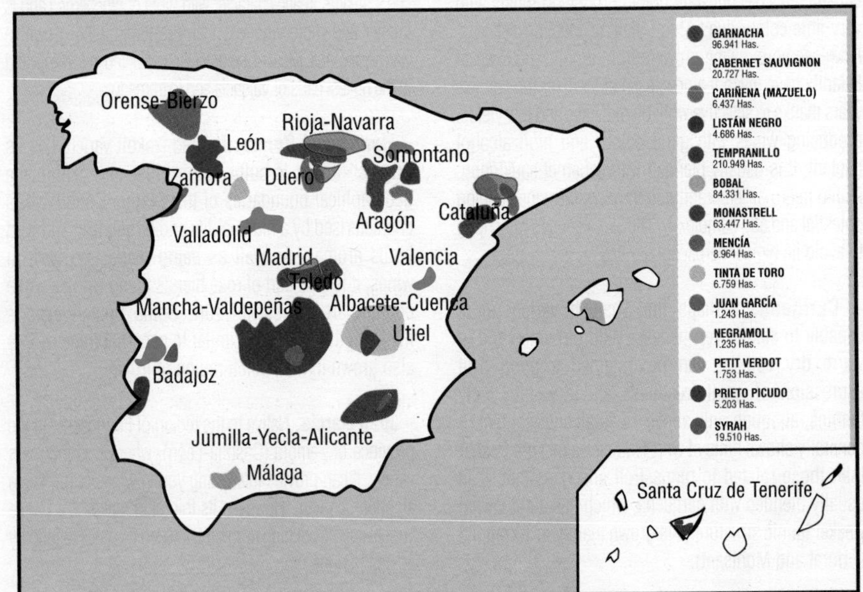

~ **Negramoll.** A grape cultivated in the Canary Islands, particularly in the island of La Palma. It has less character than listán, but more structure and tannins. When harvested late, it sometimes shows a juicy blackcurrant character.

~ **Parraleta.** A grape variety indigenous to Somontano region and not found anywhere else, its main characteristic is a lovely rusticity; it also shows some balsamic (herbal) character derived from its typical notes of wild berries –mainly strawberries and raspberries– as well as spices.

~ **Prieto picudo.** Grown in the area comprised between the towns of Benavente (Zamora) and Astorga (León), and from there to the border of the province of Palencia. Its main characteristic is to grow even in extreme climatic conditions. Its wines have usually a dark cherry colour and shows intense red fruit notes similar to those made of mencía, but with some added, pleasant herbal hints and more tannins, given it has a thicker skin. It is also similar to graciano.

~ **Rufete**. Grown exclusively in the Sierra de Salamanca and therefore the flagship of the wine region of Arribes del Duero, it generally provides wines light in both colour and body. Its tendency to oxidization asks for careful winemaking, but the best examples keep some singular characteristics: herbs, spices, and blackthorn berry notes both on the palate and on the nose.

~ **Sumoll.** Its indigenous character is still a matter of dispute between different Catalonian regions, although Conca de Barberà acts as the most vehement defender. Easy to grow and therefore a very popular choice at the end of the 19th Century to produce "vinos de pasto" (bulk wines) in a region, Catalonia, that was leading back then Spanish red wine production.

~ **Tempranillo.** The most widely grown grape variety in Spain as a result of two factors: its adaptability to extreme continental climate and its tannic structure, which allows for longer wood-ageing periods. Its general characteristics can be summed up in a fruity aroma and a flavour that is less "virile" than those of cabernet sauvignon or syrah, as well as smoother tannins. It prefers continental climates with a sharp temperature contrast and lots of sunshine hours, therefore it is grown in almost all continental zones of Spain and hardly found in coastal regions or humid areas under Atlantic rainfall patterns.

~ **Tinta de Toro.** An old clone of tempranillo, which manages in a hot region like Toro to achieve the same acidity levels as in Ribera del Duero, only with a higher alcohol content. The best red wines come from rocky and sandy areas, and shows more similarities with the Portuguese tinta roriz for its fine herbal background than with the tempranillo from Ribera del Duero. It has the same fruit potential as garnacha, with just a touch drier character. Its palate is generally one of ripe black fruit with abundant dry tannins capable to balance out sweetness beautifully.

~ **Trepat.** An early variety in terms of bud-break and late in terms of harvesting, it is vigorous, with large berries, plenty of seeds, thick skin and compact bunches. It yields rosé wines very light in colour and body, with moderate alcoholic content and a well-balanced acidity. It is grown mainly in DO Costers del Segre and DO Conca de Barberá, its native soil and where it has traditionally been made into single-varietal rosé wines through a light maceration process.

THE MAIN FOREIGN VARIETIES CULTIVATED IN SPAIN

RED:

~ **Cabernet Franc.** Like cabernet sauvignon it comes from the Bordeaux region, although it gives more supple and fruitier wines. It is thought to be related to mencía –a grape abundantly grown in regions like Galicia and Castile–, and it is mainly grown in Catalonia.

~ **Cabernet Sauvignon.** Originally from France and typical the Bordeaux region, its wines are ideal for ageing, very intense in colour, with strong tannins and a penetrating aroma of violets and berries. In Spain it has acclimatised perfectly to areas such as Penedès, Navarra and Ribera del Duero, and it is difficult to find a red wine producing area in which this champion variety has not been planted in recent years.

~ **Merlot.** Again of French origin, this grape variety has a dark blue colour and a very thick skin. Although it ripens earlier than cabernet sauvignon, it grows well in hot-climate regions. It is widely grown in Spain in Somontano and Catalonia, and to a lesser extent in Alicante and Murcia.

~ Petit Verdot. Again originally from Bordeaux, it is hardly found in that region and is relatively new to Spain, where it is associated more to the whims of some producers (Marqués de Griñón, Abadía Retuerta) than to an specific geographical area, although the best results are achieved in continental regions with lots of annual sunshine hours (Jumilla, Alicante, Toledo and Ronda). The existing Spanish examples yield aromatic notes of fresh, ripe berries, have good intensity both on the palate and the nose –thanks to their late ripening pattern– and achieve high alcohol levels.

~ Pinot Noir. The classic grape variety from Burgundy and Champagne, its fruit has a small size and a dark violet skin that provides a lot of colour. However, its wines lose colour faster, turning orangey. In warm climates it loses its complexity and elegance. It is mainly grown in Catalonia.

~ Syrah. This is the grape of the Rhône valley and Australia par excellence and, ideally suited to warm regions it is becoming very fashionable in Spain. The grapes are ovoid and small with a very pleasant flavour. Its wine has a characteristic aroma of violets and very ripe black fruit. At present it has become a very popular grape in Jumilla (the first place in Spain where it was grown), where it is blended with monastrell, as well as other parts of Spain that enjoy a Mediterranean–continental climate.

WHITE:

~ Chardonnay. Originally from Burgundy (France), it has become the most valuable white grape in the world. The wines, characterised by a slight smoky nose and –given its high dry extract, glycerine levels and low oxidation tendency– achieve good results when aged in wood. Perfectly adapted to different Spanish regions (Penedès, Costers del Segre, Navarra, Somontano, etc.), it is being authorised in numerous DOs.

~ Gewürztraminer. One of the varieties of the "traminer" species, of a spicy flavour and originally from the Alsace region (France) and Germany, it is grown in Spain on a limited scale in Somontano and Penedès, but the wines produced are not obviously as famous as the ones produced in the above mentioned European regions. In Spain its musky character is more prominent than the spicy one.

~ Marsanne. Part of the great varietal trio –along with viognier and roussane– from the Rhône valley and originally from the region of Montélimar, it is characterised by mineral and exotic fruit (melon) notes and a lovely, unctuous palate. It is hard to find in single-varietal form, since it requires the aromatic contribution of more intense varieties from that region like viognier.

~ Riesling. The most famous white wines from Alsace, the Moselle an the Rhine regions, are produced from this grape. The berry is small, yellowish in colour and low yielding. In Spain, where is mainly grown in Catalonia, produces fresh, fruity and floral dry wines, which are not as great and complex as those from the European regions mentioned above.

~ Roussane. Like marsanne, it comes from the Rhône river valley wine region. It is present in the best wines from the most significant appellations such as Hermitage, Saint Joseph, Çotes du Rhône, Châteauneuf du Pape and Corbières. Despite its tendency to oxidise it can provide subtle wines that age magnificently in the bottle. Its aromas are reminiscent of apricot, with floral (narcissus), citric and sometimes honey notes. It has a somewhat unctuous character making it very attractive on the palate. At present we can find some examples of it in Catalonia.

~ Sauvignon blanc. A quality white grape with small berries and a lovely golden colour when properly ripe. It is mainly grown in Bordeaux (Graves) and the Loire region, although it has acclimatised to other countries such as Argentina, Chile, Uruguay, California and above all New Zealand. In Spain it is mainly grown in the DO Rueda and to a lesser extent in Catalonia. It has a taste of tropical fruits and a slight floral nuance.

~ Viognier. The jewel of the Rhone valley is growing fast in popularity all over the world and has acclimatised well in Spain thanks to the similarity of the Mediterranean climate with its region of origin. Considered a noble grape, it ages with grace, has a floral and fruity character with hints of herbs and lots of depth, and in the best renderings it shows also great complexity. Mainly grown in Catalonia, Teruel, and Toledo.

THE INFLUENCE OF THE DIFFERENT VARIETES ON THE COLOUR OF WINES

RED WINES

Tempranillo. When young it has a garnet red cherry colour, with an intense velvet rim that gives a sense of immaturity.

Garnacha. Violet rim and a slightly orangey cherry tone at the core. .

Cabernet Sauvignon. Pronounced red colour, with a swift change from solid ripe cherry in the centre to purple at the rim.

Garnacha Tintorera (called alicante in Galicia and León) has high pigmentation levels both in the skin and in the must, the reason why it is grown in regions with little sunlight –such as Galicia– to compensate for the lack of colour typical of cooler climates. However the finest quality is found in Almansa, where more of it is grown.

ROSÉ WINES

Cariñena. Pomegranate notes at the rim.

Cabernet Sauvignon. Raspberry notes.

Garnacha. Purple with a shade of mauve.

WHITE WINES

Xarel-lo. It yields wines that are usually straw-coloured with yellow reflections, very similar to albariño.

Parellada. It usually yields pale wines, given that is generally grown in higher regions and hardly manage to complete its ripening cycle. When blended with xarel-lo, wines tend to have higher alcohol levels and a moderate acidity, which makes a good blend for cava production.

Chardonnay. It yields a more yellow hue thanks to the colour of its skin.

TERROIR

This is the magical term used by the French to express the intimate association between a soil of homogeneous characteristics, a variable microclimate and the grape varieties adapted to them, therefore a key element to produce a wine with its own personality and able to stand out from the rest.

The origin

Terroir is in France the cornerstone of both their vine-growing philosophy and their appellation system. It is used not only to define regions of a certain entity and size, but also to delimit small areas of just a few hectares, as it is the case of the cru in Bordeaux and the even smaller clos in Burgundy.

The concept in Spain

Although the system of designations of origin is similar to that of the French appellations, the geographical demarcations were created in Spain on a much larger scale, either due to the influence of a group of growers, historical or even political reasons, and only occasionally in attention to soil and climate. The designation Vinos de Pago has not been a serious option until recently and only as the result of an increased interest in the singularity of vineyards, and it is being used mainly for commercial purposes to identify a higher status in the vineyard hierarchy. However, it is important to make a distinction between the French cru, which identifies a soil of very defined and similar characteristics transferred to the bottle, from the Spanish pago, which refers to an undivided estate with different types of soils where wines are blended together before being bottled.

The concept in the New World

The New World has made of the grape variety the real star of their system, and branded the concept of terroir as unrealistically poetic or even as a mere marketing strategy. The New World has also promoted high-yields policies to a point where the grape variety completely loses its character, and therefore the soil and climate (terroir) expression is lost likewise. But there is a point of contradiction in the respect most Australian, Californian and even Chilean growers show for their old vineyards and use this concept –deeper and more abundant roots absorb mineral minerals from the soil much better– as a way to produce wines of greater complexity. At present, some exceptional single estate wines are also being produced in these countries.

How to manage *terroir*?

Perhaps the most important practical philosophy associated with terroir is the respect for all the natural elements (climate, soil, etc.) which, by definition, cannot be manipulated. On the other hand, to achieve the greatest possible expression from the land demands quality practices: to limit yields, and to use the best available training and watering methods to appropriately manage the vigour of the vines.

Are some terroirs better than others?

There is no democracy when it comes to wines and terroirs. Therefore there are terroirs that, given the nature of their soil and climate, produce finer wines than others and even wines with a greater complexity and the ability to age much better, for no apparent reason.

What are the main types of soil that produce quality wines?

Neither age, geological composition or texture of the soil are determinant quality factors. We can find that excellent wines can come from all sorts of soils (clay, slate, alluvial, limestone, etc.). The only common factors seem to be that these soils are very poor and almost in every case unable to grow any other plant but vines, and that they have an excellent natural drainage, which may even be improved by man if necessary, in a way that water supply to the plant is strictly controlled; in other words, the soil has the necessary mechanisms to balance shortage or surplus of water, depending on rainfall and latitude.

Is an ideal soil enough?

A typical soil cross-section found in many parts of Spain is that of a vineyard with a top layer of stones (gravel, pebbles, slate), which helps to increase temperature and therefore ensures a better ripening cycle, followed by a second layer of sand that drains the water, and below that a third layer of clay to retain the humidity in the subsoil, but this optimal soil pattern must also have environmental and climatic factors in harmony with it. For example, a red wine from Priorat with the same soil pattern at a higher altitude would be entirely different. And the same would happen if we had the same poor slate soil but without the fresh breezes coming off the Sierra del Montsant. In addition, we must remember that the better a given variety is adapted to the soil and climate, the more character it will be able to extract from the soil.

THE BEST TERROIRS IN SPAIN

The terroirs listed below (more or less in order of importance) are the predominant ones in Spain:

~ **Slate soils.** Priorat, some areas of Cebreros (Ávila), Arribes del Duero, Ribeira Sacra, La Axarquía (Málaga), highest areas in Valle de Güímar (Tenerife), some areas in Calatayud and the northeast part of Empordà.

~ **Stony soils.** The best estates of Toro, certain estates in Tarragona (Falset, Conca de Barberà and Terra Alta), some areas in Ribera de Navarra, areas close to the Duero river in Rueda and some areas in Rioja Baja.

~ **Predominantly limestone soils with some clay.** Rioja Alavesa and surrounding regions, Sonsierra, Rioja Alta, in Ribera del Duero the area closer to Valladolid, Calatayud, Jumilla, Yecla, Jerez, Montilla-Moriles, Terra Alta, Alicante, Cigales, Costers del Segre and Somontano.

~ **Sandy (siliceous) and granite soils.** Rías Baixas, Valdeorras, Ribeiro, Ribeira Sacra, Fermoselle, the area north of Méntrida and the western area of Vinos de Madrid.

~ **Volcanic soils.** Lanzarote, Hierro, Valle de Güímar, Gran Canaria, Monte de Lentiscal, La Palma, Ycoden-Daute-Isora and Abona.

THE INFLUENCE OF THE SOIL ON THE AROMA OF WINES

The type of soil subtly modifies the aroma of wine.

~ **Granite and sandy soils.** They produce neat wines with pure, well-defined aromas that perfectly identify the grape variety, although they may at times show a high alcohol content due to the excessive drainage of the soil, which promotes concentration, as it is the case of the wines from Galicia or the red Garnachas from San Martín de Valdeiglesias, made from grapes grown on soils with low moisture retention.

~ **Gravel or stony vineyards** (as found in some parts of Rueda and Toro). They yield wines with earthy aromas and flinty notes, which merge well with ripe grape nuances achieved thanks to the stones being warmed up by sunlight.

~ **Slate soils and mineral-rich soils.** In Priorat, Arribes del Duero, Cebreros and La Axarquía the wines always have slight hints of mineral, roasted coffee and overall toasty aromas, the same notes found in the Portuguese wines from the Upper Duero valley, the birthplace of Port.

~ **Volcanic soils.** These soils are found in Lanzarote, Hierro, La Palma, and certain areas of Tenerife. Their wines have slightly burnt and iodised nuances.

~ **Clay soils** (the majority within Spain). By retaining water, they provide higher yields and necessarily lower quality grapes. The wines have therefore less expression and, especially in white wines, there can appear some herbaceous notes if the vineyard is located on flat and humid areas. Clay is needed deep down in the subsoil to retain the moisture and to ensure an adequate feeding of the vine through the roots.

~ **Ferruginous soils.** They are difficult soils to produce quality wines. In general, ferruginous clay soils give the grapes a high level of iron, which should be eliminated, and a somewhat rustic and slightly burnt note.

~ **Limestone-rich soils** (found in Burgundy –Côtes de Nuits–, Champagne, Jumilla, Jerez or Rioja Alavesa). These soils add a note of elegance to the wines, which are overall better, richer and more complex.

CLIMATES AND MICROCLIMATES

The climate plays a decisive role in vine growing. Factors such as temperature, rainfall or the amount of sunshine will determine winemaking and the differences in style. Spain, which occupies a territory where both the Atlantic and the Mediterranean climate merge, is therefore subject to a great variety of climatic conditions within a limited area.

THE COMPLEXITY OF SPANISH OROGRAPHY.

High plateaus, river valleys, terraces, plots and ravines outline the real backbone of the peninsular geographic profile, mountain ranges that, curiously enough, run from northeast to southwest, and make up large catchment areas open to the west where 80% of the humid currents from the southwest come and manage to make up for mild temperatures; rains which appear precisely when the grape has not formed in the plant, but are nevertheless necessary to feed the roots, which is what really matters. The low rainfall in the mainland (due to a permanent and dominant high pressure zone over the Azore Islands during the growing period of the vine) considerably reduces humidity in comparison with a large part of Italy and the rest of Europe. This accounts for poor organic levels in the soil but a richer mineral content, which greatly favours vine growing.

Descriptions of all the climatic patterns found in Spain are listed below.

ATLANTIC CLIMATE

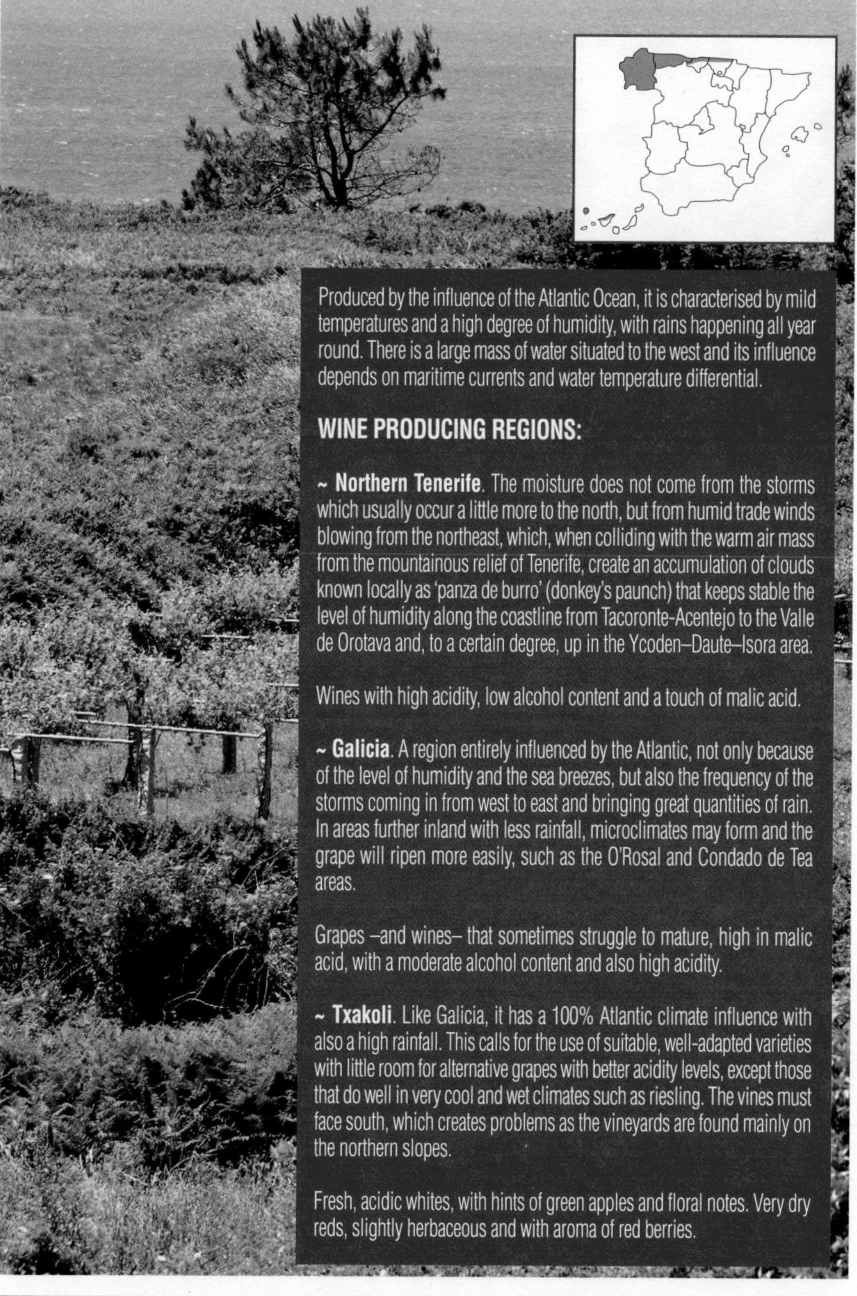

Produced by the influence of the Atlantic Ocean, it is characterised by mild temperatures and a high degree of humidity, with rains happening all year round. There is a large mass of water situated to the west and its influence depends on maritime currents and water temperature differential.

WINE PRODUCING REGIONS:

~ **Northern Tenerife**. The moisture does not come from the storms which usually occur a little more to the north, but from humid trade winds blowing from the northeast, which, when colliding with the warm air mass from the mountainous relief of Tenerife, create an accumulation of clouds known locally as 'panza de burro' (donkey's paunch) that keeps stable the level of humidity along the coastline from Tacoronte-Acentejo to the Valle de Orotava and, to a certain degree, up in the Ycoden–Daute–Isora area.

Wines with high acidity, low alcohol content and a touch of malic acid.

~ **Galicia**. A region entirely influenced by the Atlantic, not only because of the level of humidity and the sea breezes, but also the frequency of the storms coming in from west to east and bringing great quantities of rain. In areas further inland with less rainfall, microclimates may form and the grape will ripen more easily, such as the O'Rosal and Condado de Tea areas.

Grapes –and wines– that sometimes struggle to mature, high in malic acid, with a moderate alcohol content and also high acidity.

~ **Txakoli**. Like Galicia, it has a 100% Atlantic climate influence with also a high rainfall. This calls for the use of suitable, well-adapted varieties with little room for alternative grapes with better acidity levels, except those that do well in very cool and wet climates such as riesling. The vines must face south, which creates problems as the vineyards are found mainly on the northern slopes.

Fresh, acidic whites, with hints of green apples and floral notes. Very dry reds, slightly herbaceous and with aroma of red berries.

ATLANTIC-CONTINENTAL CLIMATE

These are regions up on the high plateau right in the middle of the Iberian Peninsula with less rainfall (around 600 mm.) but still under Atlantic influence and characterised by lower night temperatures.

WINE PRODUCING REGIONS:

~ **El Bierzo**. This is a transitional region between Castile and Galicia found at a lower altitude than the Castilian plateau. Because of its proximity to the Atlantic Ocean it enjoys an Atlantic climate with traces of the continental climatic pattern. It has a lower rainfall than Galicia, night temperatures are also lower and therefore the grape ripens more slowly and steadier.

~ **Navarra**. There we find a better balance between the Atlantic and continental climates in the northern regions (Valdizarbe and Tierra Estella), where the mountains hinders the sea influence.

~ **Rioja Alta.** As its name suggests, it is the highest area within La Rioja. And again, it enjoys a similar climatic pattern to that of the western part of northern Navarre.

Well-balanced wines, between 12% and 13% alcohol from good-ripened grapes –achieved with not a lot of sunshine–, just elegant without further character.

CONTINENTAL–ATLANTIC CLIMATE

Mainly characterised by a huge contrast between day and night temperatures. The sunlight during the day provides good ripening, slowed down by cool night temperatures that ultimately help to preserve good acidity levels. The Atlantic influence comes from the rains that arrive from the ocean during spring and autumn.

WINE PRODUCING REGIONS

~ **Castilla–León**. Includes the DO Ribera del Duero, located in the Duero river valley and partly influenced by altitude; Rueda –to the southwest, at a lower altitude, enjoying a milder climate–, Toro and Cigales.

Wines with good colour and alcohol content and with a great acid structure.

ATLANTIC-MEDITERRANEAN CLIMATE

This might seem a strange combination, but the area is very close to both seas and is therefore influenced by both climates, perhaps a little more Mediterranean and just moderated by the Atlantic.

WINE PRODUCING REGIONS:

~ **Jerez**. When the cool western wind blows, the climate is sufficiently Atlantic to form heavy condensation at night. But in summer, when the drier easterly wind blows, the climate becomes clearly Mediterranean.

~ **Huelva**. The Atlantic influence is not as obvious since, in spite of its western location, the southern exposure give it a more Mediterranean influence.

Wines with moderate alcohol and acidity, although in the case of generoso (fortified) wines, particularly common in this area, this is irrelevant as there is alcohol addition.

CONTINENTAL–MEDITERRANEAN CLIMATE

The rainfall is similar to a Continental–Atlantic climatic pattern; the vineyards are located at a lower altitude and therefore are closer to the sea, in spite of its situation on a plateau.

WINE PRODUCING REGIONS

Castilla-La Mancha, Montilla-Moriles and Ribera del Guadiana; Campo de Borja, Cariñena and Calatayud in Aragón; Costers del Segre, southern part of Navarra, Rioja Baja and Rioja Alavesa.

Wines with higher alcohol content and lower acidity.

MEDITERRANEAN CLIMATE

It is characterised by low rainfall and altitude.

WINE PRODUCING REGIONS:

Valencia, Clariano, Alto Turia, Alicante, Murcia with two of its three winegrowing regions (Yecla and Jumilla); practically all the wine regions in Catalonia but especially the coastal one. The vines are capable of enduring longer ageing periods, a circumstance that yields wines with higher alcohol levels, even though these are vines with a long vegetative cycle more suited to warmer climates.

Full-bodied wines, slightly warm nose, notes of dry earth and very ripe, jammy black fruit.

VITICULTURAL MICROCLIMATES

These are climates that occur in very small areas, such as a single town, vineyard or even just a vine. In this section we will concentrate on those microclimates that affect small plots and are more common in Spanish vineyards.

MOUNTAIN MICROCLIMATES

It affects vineyards surrounded by forest, located on uneven slopes and which have different expositions (north, south, east, or west). The grapes ripen unevenly as the sun does not shine homogenously on the vineyard. There are even microclimates within the microclimate. However, the common factor is that they are 'enclosed' areas.

Where to find them? In San Martin de Valdeiglesias (Madrid), La Axarquía (Málaga), Alto Turia (Valencia), Sierra de Francia (Salamanca), Cebreros (Ávila) or the extraordinarily qualitative Catalonian Priorat.

VALLEY MICROCLIMATES

These are usually found north of the 40° latitude line. Normally, we have a river running through a valley acting as a hinge between the two slopes, which are partially or completely protected by mountains. The vines grown on the slopes will have shorter growing cycles than those on the plain, but they will also have different alcohol levels depending on the exposition and the incline.

Two sides of the valley. The southern bank of a river means more sunlight, as the sun rays fall almost perpendicularly, while on the northern slope the rays are oblique which means a longer ripening period and consequently more acidic wines and greater ageing potential. This is what happens in Ribera del Duero with vineyards like Vega Sicilia and Viña Mayor, located on the north-facing slopes and able to produce grapes with same sugar levels as those on the opposite side (Pesquera, Dehesa de los Canónigos, Hacienda Monasterio).

When the orientation of the valley is north–south and the slopes go east to west, ripening is also different. An east or southwest orientation in a northern latitude such as Côte de Nuits in Burgundy means they can take advantage of the sun from daybreak. But the same situation in Spain does not have any special advantages. The worst orientation is west, as high temperatures during the day are capped with an excess of sunlight in the afternoon, the hottest time of the day.

The altitude factor. Ripening improves with an increase in altitude, as vines get away from the humidity and cooler climate of the lower areas. Only when we go 100 metres above the valley do cold night temperatures make ripening difficult. Equally, the vineyard on a plain will be more productive and therefore grapes would be of inferior quality.

Where to find them? In extreme growing-conditions areas such as Ribera del Duero, Lerma river valley (a more exposed area with a harsher climate which produces lighter wines), Rioja Alavesa (when we add the foehn effect, rainfall gets lower on the opposite side of the mountain range there and the wines have deeper colour and a higher alcohol content) and Rioja Alta (vineyards with less sunlight and higher rainfall levels, which slow down ripening patterns giving wines with less colour and more acidity).

FLUVIAL MICROCLIMATE

It is given in areas close to a river, which benefit from valley climate. However, there is an element of risk in being at such low altitude and near a mass of water, for ground temperature is lower than in areas higher up, more evaporation takes place generating mists and a greater risk of frost and vine diseases. The only positive side of it happens in stony, alluvial areas, when heat accumulated in the stones helps ripening.

Where to find it? Some Rueda vineyards near the Duero as well as the vineyards of Vega Sicilia and Abadia Retuerta, also located along that river.

MARITIME MICROCLIMATE

Determined by the positive influence that the sea has on very hot, sunny areas to slow down the growing cycle. It is very common in southern areas where they grow varieties that require a lot of sunshine and benefit from the alternating temperatures regime provided by the sea breezes.

Its influence on ageing. The influence of the sea also brings about a slower and less oxidative wood-ageing period, as it happens in El Puerto de Santa María and Sanlúcar de Barrameda. It used to be compulsory for the wines from Málaga (at its very port) and Oporto (in Vila Nova de Gaia, near the coast).

Where to find it? In the area of La Marina in Alicante and La Axarquía in Málaga, where the moscatel grape needs a certain amount of humidity but also lots of sunshine. In Jerez, the best vineyards are found on the highest hills open to westerly sea breezes. In the north of Tenerife, the trade winds from the northeast moderate the alcohol content of the grape and keep acidity levels high.

THE INFLUENCE OF THE CLIMATE ON THE COLOUR OF WINES

The climate can have a definitive influence on the colour of wines as proved by the following examples.

Pedro Ximénez wines. The grapes are dehydrated after the harvest. They are placed on esparto grass mats and sunned until they turn to raisins and take on a brownish, ochre colour. The resulting wine is dark. This is due to a process similar to caramelization, as the sun burns the grapes and concentrates the sugar by reducing the volume of water. Also, oxidation takes place during ageing under the solera system, darkening the wine even further. Depending on the length of the ageing period the colour will be lighter or darker

Sunning in glass bonbonnes. This is only done in Rueda and Catalonia. As a way to accelerate ageing, the wine is put in glass containers and left in the open; day-night temperature differences provide a similar effect to that of more common summer-winter annual ageing. The sun causes the white whine to turn a yellow-reddish colour after just a few months.

The colour of red wines. It is clear that the pigmentation of grapes is produced by the sun. But a very dark grape is not necessarily ready to be made into wine. Although very unlikely in sunny climates, its sugar level may not be sufficient. However, it is also quite common for the colour and the sugars to be right and the skin still unripe. This often happens in warm regions where, as well as testing sugar and acid levels with a refractometer, the skins and pips are checked for ripeness since, occasionally, sugars form and pigmentation takes place before the skin has fully ripened. Therefore, paradoxically, there are reds from very sunny regions with herbaceous notes although the colour is deep and the alcohol content is above 12.5%.

* A cabernet sauvignon wine from Lérida is exposed to more sunlight than a cabernet sauvignon from Bordeaux. The wines from the French region have a lively violet rim, while the ones from Lérida tend to have light ochre tones, although they still keep a good balance thanks to modern winemaking methods.

* Monastrell wines from Catalonia, Provence, Jumilla or Alicante also differ. In the latter two areas, sunlight hours and the high alcohol content gives them a bluish-coppery hue, while those to the north show a redder, more lively colour.

THE INFLUENCE OF THE CLIMATE ON THE AROMA OF WINES

In cold and humid regions (such as txakoli in the Basque Country, Galicia, and the north of Portugal), high rainfall makes it difficult for the grape to fully ripen, and therefore wines are low in alcohol and high in acidity. Given their high malic acid content, white wines from those areas show a slight note of cider or apple, even when malolactic fermentation is induced to help reduce acidity.

However, the same variety can show a whole new character under different climates. The Mediterranean varieties, which are the most common in Spain, tend to lose a lot of their aromatic expression in higher, more humid regions.

This is what happens to garnacha grown in Rioja Alta, as opposed to that of Rioja Baja. The wine of the former will have less colour intensity, but it will be more elegant and suitable for ageing thanks to a greater acidity that, on the other hand, may mask its aromatic expression.

A similar thing happens to parellada, a fine, classy white grape which needs the cool temperatures of the higher regions of Penedès, in Catalonia, to show at its best, while it loses some of its finesse in warmer climates.

As to the tempranillo, while it will typically, with a slow and balanced ripening cycle, display red mulberry notes, it will show a blackberry jam, slightly "cooked" character with a faster and deeper maturation, brought usually about by higher temperatures.

WINERIES and the TASTING of the WINES by DESIGNATION of ORIGIN

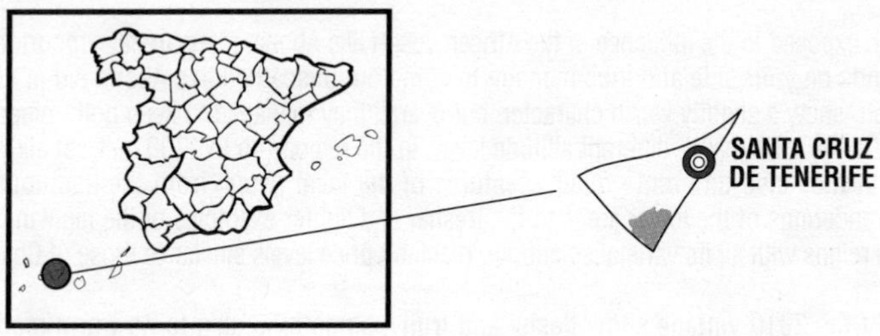

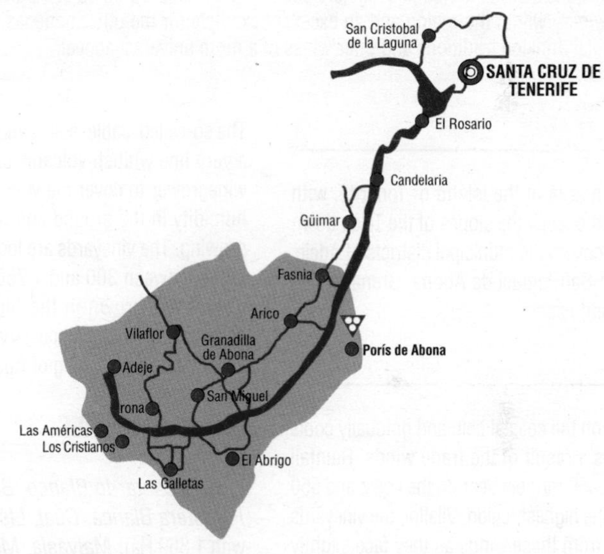

Consejo Regulador
DO Boundary

DO ABONA

NEWS ABOUT THE VINTAGE:

In a region so exposed to the influence of the African desert like Abona, there are few opportunities to get the trade winds on your side and thus manage to come out unscathed like Abona did in 2010. White wines, though, show a slightly warm character, but overall they managed to keep both mineral and fruit expression. On the other hand, different altitude levels in the region (up to 1700 metres) allow us have a closer look at the –also different– quality features of the local *listán*, from the unctuous and even voluptuous renderings of the lower areas to the fresher and lighter examples of the highlands. All in all, the *malvasía* reigns with all its varietal splendour, reaching price levels similar to those of Champagne.

Red wines of the 2010 vintage show fleshy and fruity, something akin to its warm mediterranean climate character, but the most important feature is the fact that the region's winemakers are progressively eliminating overripe notes, something which has afforded wines of a fresher and fruitier character, while still carrying those slightly confected notes typical of low acidity wines. A whole different issue are barrel-aged renderings, which rely heavily on the quality of the wood and thus offer the customer quite a broad although irregular spectrum. The coop Cumbres de Abona is by far the most interesting winery within the region and an excellent example for the other bodegas, given its ability to jump over local drinking traditions and offer wines of a more universal appeal.

LOCATION:

In the southern area of the island of Tenerife, with vineyards which occupy the slopes of the Teide down to the coast. It covers the municipal districts of Adeje, Arona, Vilaflor, San Miguel de Abona, Granadilla de Abona, Arico and Fasnia.

CLIMATE:

Mediterranean on the coastal belt, and gradually cools down inland as a result of the trade winds. Rainfall varies between 350 mm per year on the coast and 550 mm inland. In the highest region, Vilaflor, the vineyards do not benefit from these winds as they face slightly west. Nevertheless, the more than 200 Ha of this small plateau produce wines with an acidity of 8 g/l due to the altitude, but with an alcohol content of 13%, as this area of the island has the longest hours of sunshine.

SOIL:

Distinction can be made between the sandy and calcareous soil inland and the more clayey, well drained soil of the higher regions, seeing as they are volcanic. The so-called 'Jable' soil is very typical, and is simply a very fine whitish volcanic sand, used by the local winegrower to cover the vineyards in order to retain humidity in the ground and to prevent weeds from growing. The vineyards are located at altitudes which range between 300 and 1,750 m (the better quality grapes are grown in the higher regions), which determines different grape harvesting dates in a period spanning the beginning of August up to October.

GRAPE VARIETIES:

WHITE: *Bastardo Blanco, Bermejuela, Forastera Blanca, Güal, Listán Blanca* (majority with 1,869 Ha), *Malvasía, Moscatel, Pedro Ximénez, Sabro, Torrontés, Verdello, Vijariego.* The white varieties make up the majority of the vineyards.

RED: *Bastardo Negro, Cabernet Sauvignon, Castellana Negra, Listán Negro, Listán Prieto, Malvasía Rosada, Moscatel Negro, Negramoll, Pinot Noir, Rubí Cabernet, Syrah, Tempranillo, Tintilla, Vijariego Negro.*

FIGURES:

Vineyard surface: 1,033 – **Wine-Growers:** 1,236 – **Wineries:** 18 – **2010 Harvest rating:** Very Good – **Production:** 675,000 litres – **Market percentages:** 100% domestic

CONSEJO REGULADOR
Martín Rodríguez, 9
38588 Porís de Abona - Arico (Santa Cruz de Tenerife)
☎: +34 922 164 241 - Fax: +34 922 164 135
@ vinosdeabona@vinosdeabona.com
www.vinosdeabona.com

GENERAL CHARACTERISTICS OF THE WINES

WHITES	They have a pale yellow colour with a fruity and sometimes floral nose and are dry, pleasant and well-balanced on the palate.
ROSÉS	They are characterised by their pink colour and are light and pleasant to drink, although less fragrant than those from Tacoronte.
REDS	Although less representative than the white wines, they have a deep cherry-red, with a red berries and bramble nose and a somewhat light structure.

VINTAGE RATING PEÑÍNGUIDE

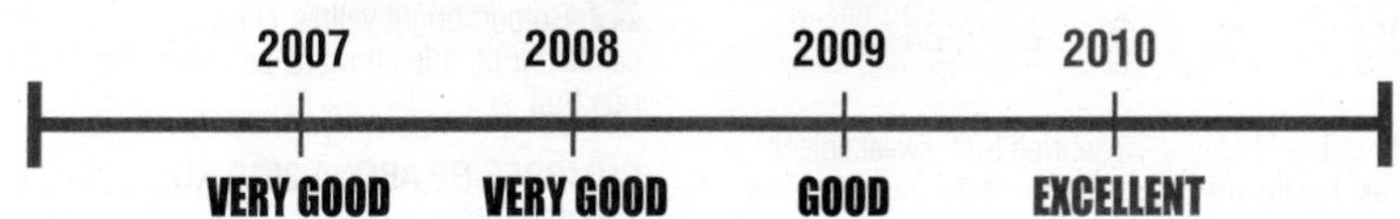

BODEGA SAN MIGUEL

Ctra. General del Sur, 5
38620 San Miguel de Abona (Santa Cruz de Tenerife)
☎: +34 922 700 300 - Fax: +34 922 700 301
bodega@casanmiguel.com
www.sanmiguelappis.com

CHASNERO ACACIA 2010 B
listán blanco.

86 Colour: bright straw. Nose: powerfull, ripe fruit, fruit liqueur notes, spicy. Palate: flavourful, good acidity, fine bitter notes.

MARQUÉS DE FUENTE 2010 B
malvasía, gual, albillo, moscatel.

85 Colour: bright straw, greenish rim. Nose: medium intensity, citrus fruit. Palate: light-bodied, easy to drink.

MARQUÉS DE FUENTE 2010 B BARRICA
listán blanco, albillo.

84 Colour: bright straw, greenish rim. Nose: dried herbs, medium intensity, fresh. Palate: flavourful, spicy, easy to drink.

CHASNERO NEGREMOLL 2010 B
negramoll.

84 Colour: bright straw. Nose: expressive, ripe fruit, citrus fruit, white flowers. Palate: flavourful, fine bitter notes, sweetness.

CHASNERO 2010 T
listán negro, listán prieto, castellana.

84 Colour: cherry, garnet rim. Nose: balsamic herbs, ripe fruit. Palate: spicy, good acidity, fine bitter notes.

MARQUÉS DE FUENTE 2009 T BARRICA
merlot.

87 Colour: bright cherry. Nose: ripe fruit, sweet spices, creamy oak. Palate: flavourful, fruity, toasty, round tannins.

CUMBRES DE ABONA

Bajada El Vizo, s/n
38580 Arico (Santa Cruz de Tenerife)
☎: +34 922 768 604 - Fax: +34 922 768 234
bodega@cumbresdeabona.es
www.cumbresabona.com

TESTAMENTO MALVASÍA 2010 BFB
100% malvasía.

89 Colour: bright yellow. Nose: white flowers, fresh fruit, tropical fruit, citrus fruit, sweet spices, cocoa bean. Palate: fruity, flavourful, balanced.

FLOR DE CHASNA NATURALMENTE DULCE 2010 B
listán blanco.

89 Colour: golden. Nose: powerfull, floral, honeyed notes, candied fruit. Palate: flavourful, sweet, fresh, long.

TESTAMENTO MALVASÍA DRY 2010 B
100% malvasía.

87 Colour: bright straw, greenish rim. Nose: ripe fruit, balanced, jasmine. Palate: fruity, fine bitter notes, flavourful, ripe fruit.

FLOR DE CHASNA AFRUTADO 2010 B
100% listán blanco.

84 Colour: bright straw. Nose: fresh fruit, citrus fruit, white flowers. Palate: flavourful, fruity, fresh.

FLOR DE CHASNA 2010 B
100% listán blanco.

83 Colour: bright yellow. Nose: ripe fruit, white flowers, balanced. Palate: flavourful, ripe fruit.

TESTAMENTO MALVASÍA 2009 BFB
100% malvasía.

90 Colour: bright yellow. Nose: powerfull, ripe fruit, spicy, cocoa bean, honeyed notes. Palate: rich, smoky aftertaste, flavourful, fresh, good acidity.

TESTAMENTO MALVASÍA ESENCIA 2008 B
100% malvasía.

90 Colour: golden. Nose: powerfull, floral, honeyed notes, candied fruit. Palate: flavourful, sweet, fresh, fruity, good acidity, long.

TESTAMENTO MALVASÍA 2008 BFB
100% malvasía.

87 Colour: bright yellow. Nose: medium intensity, candied fruit, dried flowers, pattiserie. Palate: flavourful, ripe fruit, spicy.

CUMBRES DE ABONA 2010 RD
100% listán negro.

80 Colour: onion pink. Nose: powerfull, ripe fruit, red berry notes. Palate: sweetness, fine bitter notes.

FLOR DE CHASNA 2010 T BARRICA
40% listán negro, 30% tempranillo, 30% zalema.

91 Colour: bright cherry. Nose: ripe fruit, creamy oak, expressive. Palate: flavourful, fruity, toasty, round tannins.

CUMBRES DE ABONA 2010 T
100% listán negro.

87 Colour: cherry, purple rim. Nose: fresh fruit, red berry notes, floral. Palate: flavourful, fruity, good acidity, round tannins.

FLOR DE CHASNA 2010 T MACERACIÓN CARBÓNICA
100% listán negro.

86 Colour: cherry, garnet rim. Nose: ripe fruit, red berry notes. Palate: flavourful, fruity, fresh.

FLOR DE CHASNA 2010 T
40% listán negro, 30% tempranillo, 30% syrah.

85 Colour: deep cherry. Nose: ripe fruit, earthy notes, floral. Palate: spicy, ripe fruit, good acidity.

FLOR DE CHASNA NATURALMENTE DULCE 2009 T
listán negro, tempranillo, syrah.

85 Colour: cherry, garnet rim. Nose: balsamic herbs, dried fruit, fruit liqueur notes. Palate: fine bitter notes, confected, long.

TESTAMENTO MALVASÍA DULCE 2010 BLANCO DULCE
100% malvasía.

88 Colour: bright straw. Nose: ripe fruit, citrus fruit, tropical fruit, lactic notes. Palate: powerful, flavourful, sweet.

FRONTOS

Lomo Grande, 1- Los Blanquitos
38616 Granadilla de Abona (Santa Cruz de Tenerife)
☎: +34 922 777 253 - Fax: +34 922 777 246
bodega@tierradefrontos.com
www.tierradefrontos.com

FRONTOS SEMISECO ECOLÓGICO 2010 B
100% listán blanco.

87 Colour: bright straw. Nose: balsamic herbs, grassy, ripe fruit. Palate: flavourful, fruity, fresh.

FRONTOS 2010 B
40% verdejo, 30% marmajuelo, 20% malvasía, 5% albillo, 5% gual.

86 Colour: bright straw. Nose: ripe fruit, citrus fruit, earthy notes. Palate: powerful, flavourful, fleshy.

FRONTOS BLANCO SECO ECOLÓGICO 2010 B
100% listán blanco.

85 Colour: bright yellow, greenish rim. Nose: white flowers, citrus fruit. Palate: fruity, flavourful.

FRONTOS 2010 RD
100% syrah.

83 Colour: rose, purple rim. Nose: red berry notes, ripe fruit, faded flowers. Palate: flavourful, ripe fruit, good acidity.

FRONTOS 2010 T BARRICA
100% baboso negro.

89 Color bright cherry. Aroma ripe fruit, sweet spices, creamy oak, expressive. Taste flavourful, fruity, toasty, round tannins.

FRONTOS 2010 T
70% baboso, 30% listán prieto.

88 Colour: deep cherry. Nose: powerfull, ripe fruit, sweet spices. Palate: fruity, flavourful, fresh.

HIMACOPASA

Avda. Reyes Católicos, 23
38005 Santa Cruz de Tenerife (Santa Cruz de Tenerife)
☎: +34 922 218 155 - Fax: +34 922 215 666
sofusa@gruposocas.com

LOMO BERMEJO AFRUTADO 2010 B

84 Colour: bright straw. Nose: ripe fruit, white flowers. Palate: flavourful, fruity, fresh.

JOTTOCAR

Marta, 3 Chimiche
38594 Granadilla de Abona (Santa Cruz de Tenerife)
☎: +34 922 777 285 - Fax: +34 922 777 259
ventas@menceychasna.com
www.menceychasna.es

LOS TABLEROS 2010 B BARRICA
listán blanco.

87 Colour: bright straw. Nose: ripe fruit, citrus fruit, jasmine. Palate: flavourful, fruity, fresh.

MENCEY DE CHASNA AFRUTADO 2010 B
listán blanco.

86 Colour: bright straw. Nose: expressive, fresh fruit, citrus fruit. Palate: flavourful, fruity, fresh.

MENCEY DE CHASNA 2010 B
listán blanco.

85 Colour: bright straw, greenish rim. Nose: wild herbs, citrus fruit. Palate: flavourful, fruity, easy to drink.

LOS TABLEROS 2010 B
listán blanco, moscatel.

84 Colour: bright straw. Nose: white flowers, powerfull, fresh fruit, citrus fruit. Palate: flavourful, fruity, good acidity.

MENCEY DE CHASNA 2010 RD
listán negro.

80 Colour: coppery red. Nose: medium intensity, candied fruit, citrus fruit. Palate: fine bitter notes, fleshy.

LOS TABLEROS 2010 T BARRICA
syrah, vijariego negro , rubi, listán negro.

84 Colour: deep cherry. Nose: ripe fruit, red berry notes, spicy. Palate: flavourful, fruity, fleshy, round tannins.

MENCEY DE CHASNA 2010 T
listán negro, rubi, tempranillo, syrah.

83 Colour: deep cherry. Nose: ripe fruit, raspberry, balsamic herbs, scrubland. Palate: fruity, spicy.

PEDRO HERNÁNDEZ TEJERA

Ctra. Archifira, s/n
38570 Fasnia (Santa Cruz de Tenerife)
☎: +34 616 920 832

VIÑA ARESE 2010 B

87 Colour: bright straw. Nose: fresh, fresh fruit, white flowers, lactic notes. Palate: flavourful, fruity, good acidity, balanced.

VIÑA ARESE 2010 T

82 Colour: cherry, garnet rim. Nose: ripe fruit, spicy, scrubland. Palate: flavourful, fine bitter notes, spicy.

VIÑA ARESE T BARRICA

86 Colour: cherry, garnet rim. Nose: ripe fruit, spicy, toasty. Palate: fine bitter notes, fruity.

S.A.T. REVERÓN E HIJOS

Los Quemados, s/n
38620 Vilaflor (Santa Cruz de Tenerife)
☎: +34 607 867 206

PAGOS REVERÓN AFRUTADO 2010 B
listán blanco.

85 Colour: bright straw. Nose: fresh, fresh fruit, white flowers, expressive. Palate: flavourful, fruity, balanced.

LOS QUEMADOS 2010 B
albillo.

84 Colour: bright yellow. Nose: wild herbs, white flowers. Palate: fruity, flavourful, fine bitter notes.

PAGOS REVERÓN 2010 B
listán blanco.

77

PAGOS REVERÓN B

88 Colour: bright golden. Nose: candied fruit, overripe fruit, citrus fruit, honeyed notes. Palate: spicy, creamy, sweet.

PAGOS REVERÓN 2010 RD

75

PAGO REVERÓN 2010 T

83 Colour: cherry, garnet rim. Nose: fruit expression, ripe fruit. Palate: balsamic, flavourful, powerful.

PAGOS REVERÓN 2009 T BARRICA
listán negro, tempranillo, rubí cabernet, prieto picudo.

86 Colour: cherry, garnet rim. Nose: spicy, cocoa bean, ripe fruit. Palate: flavourful, good acidity, ripe fruit.

TOMÁS FRÍAS GONZÁLEZ

Los Cazadores, s/n
38570 Fasnia (Santa Cruz de Tenerife)
☎: +34 922 164 301
ivanfriasperez@hotmail.com

VIJARIEGO NEGRO 2010 T
vijariego negro.

83 Colour: bright cherry. Nose: medium intensity, spicy, warm. Palate: spicy, ripe fruit.

VERA DE LA FUENTE BABOSO 2009 T
baboso negro.

82 Colour: deep cherry. Nose: fruit liqueur notes, grassy, scrubland. Palate: sweetness, fine bitter notes.

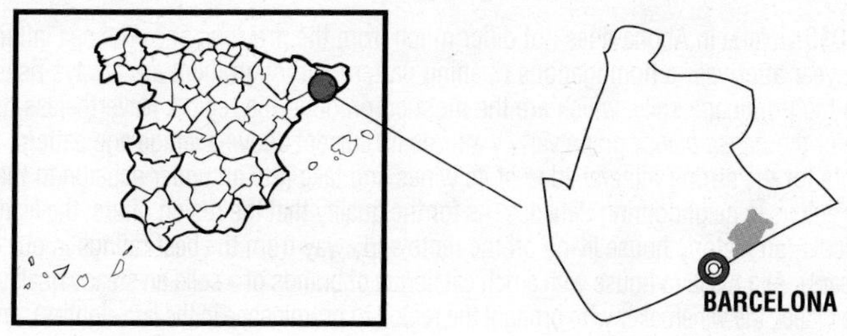
BARCELONA

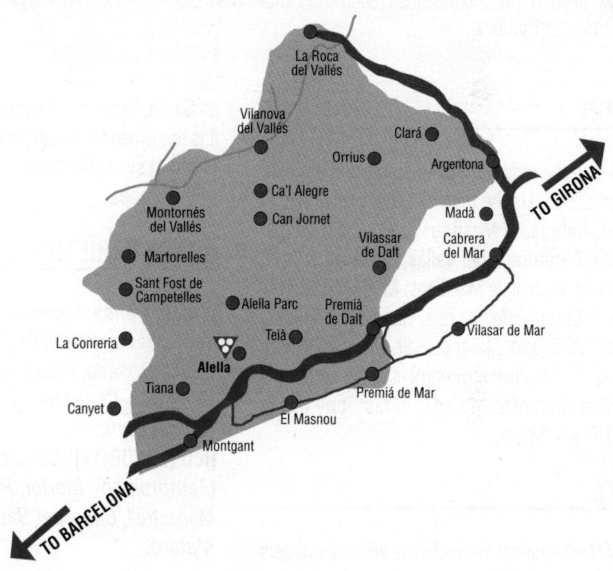
La Roca
del Vallés
Vilanova
del Vallés
Clará
Orrius
Argentona
TO GIRONA
Ca'l Alegre
Can Jornet
Montornés
del Vallés
Madà
Vilassar
de Dalt
Cabrera
del Mar
Martorelles
Sant Fost de
Campetelles
Alella Parc
Premià
de Dalt
Vilasar de Mar
La Conreria
Teià
Alella
Tiana
Premiá de Mar
Canyet
El Masnou
Montgant
TO BARCELONA

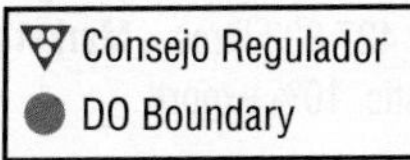
Consejo Regulador
DO Boundary

NEWS ABOUT THE VINTAGE:

The current 2010 vintage in Abona does not differ much from the previous one. The sea influence in the region allows year after year a homogenous ripening pattern, although there are always risks involved, particularly in high-drainage soils, which are the most common in the region. Nevertheless, the historic pre-eminence of the *pansa blanca* grape variety affords its current above-average age pattern, something which accounts for the strong mineral edge of its wines and take it to an upper echelon to that its sister grape *xarel.lo* enjoys in neighbouring Penedès. As for the quality that the region offers, the leading names are Alella Vinícola (an historic house living off the rents and away from the best ratings in our Guide over the last few years), Alta Alella (a house with a rich catalogue of brands of a solid an steady quality with Pujol Busquet at the wheel, the winemaker who brought the region to prominence in the late eighties), and Marqués de Alella, the makers of Marqués de Alella Allier, a white wine rated at 92 points which has gained three points on its score in the 2011 edition of our Guide. To these three wineries we have to add a new name, that of Castillo de Sajazarra, a group that has come up strongly in this small region with its In Vita 2010, a white wine that has gained two points on previous vintage's score. Another noteworthy feature within the region is the way Bodegas Roura, also an historic name in Alella, is proving unable year after year to express anything beyond a far too obvious French edge, thus ducking all likely local (terroir) expression and therefore away from our Podium.

LOCATION:

It extends over the regions of El Maresme and el Vallès in Barcelona. It covers the municipal districts of Alella, Argentona, Cabrils, El Masnou, La Roca del Vallès, Martorelles, Montornès del Vallès, Montgat, Orrius, Premià de Dalt, Premià de Mar, Santa Mª de Martorelles, Sant Fost de Campsentelles, Teià, Tiana, Vallromanes, Vilanova del Vallès and Vilasar de Salt. The main feature of this region is the urban environment which surrounds this small stretch of vineyards; in fact, one of the smallest DO's in Spain.

CLIMATE:

A typically Mediterranean microclimate with mild winters and hot dry summers. The coastal hills play an important role, as they protect the vines from cold winds and condense the humidity from the sea.

SOIL:

Distinction can be made between the clayey soils of the interior slope of the coastal mountain range and the soil situated along the coastline. The latter, known as Sauló, is the most typical. Almost white in colour, it is renowned for it high permeability and great capacity to retain sunlight, which makes for a better ripening of the grapes.

GRAPE VARIETIES:

WHITE: *Pansa Blanca* (similar to the *Xarel·lo* from other regions in Catalonia), *Garnatxa Blanca, Pansa Rosada, Picapoll, Malvasía, Macabeo, Parellada, Chardonnay, Sauvignon Blanc* and *Chenin Blanc.*
RED (MINORITY): *Garnatxa Negra, Ull de Llebre* (*Tempranillo*), *Merlot, Pinot Noir, Syrah, Monastrell, Cabernet Sauvignon, Sumoll and Mataró.*

FIGURES:

Vineyard surface: 320 – **Wine-Growers:** 92 – **Wineries:** 8 – **2010 Harvest rating:** Good – **Production:** 427,803 litres – **Market percentages:** 90% domestic. 10% export

CONSEJO REGULADOR
Masía Can Magarola, s/n
08328 Alella (Barcelona)
☎: +34 935 559 153 - Fax: +34 935 405 249
@ doalella@doalella.org
www.doalella.org

GENERAL CHARACTERISTICS OF THE WINES

WHITES	These are the most characteristic of the region. One can distinguish between the traditional Alella, light, fruity and quite supple (although not sweet), and the other dry wines with a pale straw colour which are fresh, fruity, well-balanced, slightly supple with a persistent nose. There are also examples of white wines fermented in barrels.
ROSÉS	These are not the most abundant, although very good rosé wines are produced which are very flavourful on the palate.
REDS	The most interesting examples in the region are those that include foreign varieties in the blend, especially *merlot* and *cabernet sauvignon*, which stand out for their unique fruity character

VINTAGE RATING PEÑÍNGUIDE

ALELLA VINÍCOLA

Angel Guimerà, 62
08328 Alella (Barcelona)
☎: +34 935 403 842 - Fax: +34 935 401 648
comercial@alellavinicola.com
www.alellavinicola.com

MARFIL CLÀSSIC 2010 B
100% pansa blanca.

84 Colour: bright straw. Nose: dried herbs, floral, tropical fruit. Palate: light-bodied, fresh, sweetness.

MARFIL BLANCO SECO 2010 B
100% pansa blanca.

83 Colour: bright straw. Nose: white flowers, citrus fruit, medium intensity. Palate: light-bodied, fresh, fruity.

IVORI 2009 B
60% pansa blanca, 20% chardonnay, 10% sauvignon blanc, 10% moscatel.

83 Colour: bright golden. Nose: floral, fragrant herbs, slightly evolved. Palate: fresh, flavourful, fleshy.

MARFIL MOT DOLÇ 2003 B
100% pansa blanca.

93 Colour: old gold, amber rim. Nose: honeyed notes, sweet spices, pattiserie, expressive. Palate: rich, fruity, flavourful, unctuous.

MARFIL GENEROSO SEMI 1976 B
100% pansa blanca.

91 Colour: old gold, amber rim. Nose: sweet spices, caramel, acetaldehyde. Palate: rich, flavourful, fleshy, long, spirituous, sweetness.

MARFIL GENEROSO SEC 1976 B
100% pansa blanca.

89 Colour: old gold, amber rim. Nose: dry nuts, sweet spices, candied fruit, fruit liqueur notes, caramel. Palate: creamy, powerful, flavourful, great length.

MARFIL ROSAT 2010 RD
50% garnacha, 50% syrah.

85 Colour: raspberry rose. Nose: fresh fruit, white flowers, fresh, expressive. Palate: easy to drink, fruity, light-bodied.

MAYLA ROSADO DE AGUJA NATURAL 2010 RD
60% garnacha, 40% syrah.

84 Colour: brilliant rose. Nose: fresh fruit, violet drops, floral, fresh. Palate: easy to drink, light-bodied, fruity.

MARFIL 2008 TC
40% garnacha, 40% cabernet sauvignon, 15% syrah, 5% merlot.

86 Colour: cherry, garnet rim. Nose: cocoa bean, spicy, toasty, ripe fruit. Palate: flavourful, fleshy, round tannins.

VALLMORA 2008 T
100% garnacha.

85 Colour: cherry, garnet rim. Nose: cocoa bean, spicy, ripe fruit. Palate: flavourful, powerful, toasty, fleshy.

MARFIL VIOLETA 2003 T
100% garnacha.

91 Colour: black cherry. Nose: floral, mineral, dried fruit, powerfull, complex. Palate: good acidity, unctuous, balanced, flavourful, fleshy.

MARFIL BLANC DE NOIRS 2008 BR
100% garnacha.

88 Colour: bright straw. Nose: fresh fruit, white flowers, fragrant herbs, fresh. Palate: easy to drink, light-bodied, fruity, fresh, fleshy.

MARFIL ROSAT 2008 BR ESPUMOSO
100% garnacha.

87 Colour: rose, purple rim. Nose: red berry notes, white flowers, fresh, expressive. Palate: good acidity, fine bead, flavourful, fleshy.

MARFIL 2008 BN
50% chardonnay, 50% pansa blanca.

86 Colour: bright straw. Nose: fresh fruit, floral, fine lees. Palate: fine bitter notes, fresh, flavourful.

MARFIL MOSCATEL 2008 ESP
100% moscatel.

90 Colour: bright straw. Nose: scrubland, ripe fruit, tropical fruit, expressive, complex. Palate: good structure, flavourful, fleshy, fresh, fruity. Personality.

ALTA ALELLA

Can Genis, s/n
08391 Tiana (Barcelona)
☎: +34 934 693 720 - Fax: +34 934 691 343
altaalella@altaalella.cat
www.altaalella.cat

ALTA ALELLA PARVUS CHARDONNAY 2010 BFB
chardonnay, pansa blanca.

89 Colour: bright golden. Nose: white flowers, creamy oak, fragrant herbs. Palate: good acidity, powerful, flavourful, fleshy.

ALTA ALELLA PANSA BLANCA 2010 B
100% pansa blanca.

89 Colour: bright straw. Nose: fragrant herbs, white flowers, fresh, expressive. Palate: balanced, good acidity, powerful, flavourful, fleshy.

ALTA ALELLA LANIUS 2009 BFB
pansa blanca, chardonnay, sauvignon blanc, viognier, moscatel.

90 Colour: bright golden. Nose: creamy oak, sweet spices, ripe fruit, complex. Palate: rich, flavourful, fleshy, toasty, good acidity, complex.

ALTA ALELLA BLANC DE NEU 2009 BFB
chardonnay, pansa blanca, viognier.

90 Colour: bright golden. Nose: complex, candied fruit, dry nuts, citrus fruit, varnish. Palate: complex, light-bodied, fruity, flavourful, creamy.

ALTA ALELLA EXEO 2009 BFB
chardonnay, viognier.

86 Colour: bright golden. Nose: sweet spices, cocoa bean, creamy oak, fragrant herbs. Palate: complex, powerful, fleshy, toasty.

ALTA ALELLA PARVUS 2010 RD
100% cabernet sauvignon.

83 Colour: rose, purple rim. Nose: slightly evolved, red berry notes, herbaceous. Palate: light-bodied, fresh, fleshy.

ALTA ALELLA PARVUS SYRAH 2009 T
100% syrah.

89 Colour: cherry, garnet rim. Nose: red berry notes, expressive, cocoa bean, sweet spices. Palate: good acidity, fresh, fruity, fleshy.

ALTA ALELLA SYRAH 2008 T
100% syrah.

89 Colour: cherry, purple rim. Nose: red berry notes, fragrant herbs, expressive, complex. Palate: good acidity, fruity, flavourful.

ALTA ALELLA DOLÇ MATARÓ 2009 TINTO DULCE
100% monastrell.

90 Colour: cherry, purple rim. Nose: red berry notes, ripe fruit, sweet spices. Palate: good acidity, rich, fruity, fleshy, complex.

BODEGAS CASTILLO DE SAJAZARRA

Del Río, s/n
26212 Sajazarra (La Rioja)
☎: +34 941 320 066 -
Fax: +34 941 320 251
bodega@castillo-de-sajazarra.com
www.castillo-de-sajazarra.com

IN VITA 2009 B
60% pansa blanca, 40% sauvignon blanc.

91 Colour: bright golden, bright straw. Nose: fragrant herbs, fresh, expressive, complex, white flowers, floral. Palate: powerful, flavourful, long, slightly acidic, fresh. Personality.

IN VITA 2010 B
60% sauvignon blanc, 40% pansa blanca.

92 Colour: bright straw. Nose: white flowers, citrus fruit, fruit expression, macerated fruit, complex, expressive, fresh, varietal, fragrant herbs. Palate: good acidity, fruity, fresh, powerful, flavourful, complex. Personality.

BODEGAS ROURA

Valls de Rials
08328 Alella (Barcelona)
☎: +34 933 527 456 - Fax: +34 933 524 339
roura@roura.es
www.roura.es

ROURA XAREL.LO 2010 B
100% xarel.lo.

87 Colour: bright straw. Nose: white flowers, tropical fruit, citrus fruit. Palate: fruity, flavourful, fleshy, good acidity.

ROURA SAUVIGNON BLANC 2010 B
100% sauvignon blanc.

85 Colour: bright golden. Nose: citrus fruit, expressive, floral, fragrant herbs. Palate: fresh, fruity, light-bodied.

ROURA 2010 RD
100% merlot.

85 Colour: rose, purple rim. Nose: red berry notes, fresh fruit, lactic notes. Palate: fruity, flavourful, light-bodied, fleshy.

ROURA COUPAGE 2008 T
50% merlot, 30% garnacha, 20% cabernet sauvignon.

85 Colour: cherry, garnet rim. Nose: caramel, spicy, roasted coffee, ripe fruit. Palate: fleshy, powerful, complex, balanced.

ROURA CRIANZA TRES CEPS 2007 TC
50% cabernet sauvignon, 30% merlot, 20% syrah.

87 Colour: bright cherry, orangey edge. Nose: old leather, spicy, toasty. Palate: fleshy, flavourful, good acidity, unctuous.

ROURA MERLOT 2007 T
100% merlot.

87 Colour: cherry, garnet rim. Nose: ripe fruit, sweet spices, cocoa bean, toasty. Palate: powerful, flavourful, fleshy, round.

JOAQUIM BATLLE PONCE

Masía La Sentiu, s/n
08391 Tiana (Barcelona)
☎: +34 933 954 527 - Fax: +34 933 954 534
celler@joaquimbatlle.com
www.joaquimbatlle.com

FORANELL 2009 B
40% pansa blanca, 40% garnacha blanca, 20% picapoll.

85 Colour: bright golden. Nose: dried flowers, fragrant herbs, creamy oak. Palate: good acidity, rich, flavourful.

MARQUÉS DE ALELLA

Torrente, 38
08391 Tiana (Barcelona)
☎: +34 933 950 811 - Fax: +34 933 955 500
info@parxet.es
www.parxet.es

MARQUÉS DE ALELLA 2010 B
100% pansa blanca.

89 Colour: bright straw. Nose: fresh, expressive, fresh fruit, white flowers, fragrant herbs. Palate: light-bodied, fresh, fruity, flavourful.

MARQUÉS DE ALELLA ALLIER 2009 BFB
100% chardonnay.

92 Colour: bright golden. Nose: dried flowers, ripe fruit, dried herbs, creamy oak, mineral. Palate: rich, flavourful, complex, fleshy, long.

PERFUM DE PANSA 2009 B
100% pansa blanca.

90 Colour: golden. Nose: candied fruit, scrubland, dry nuts, slightly evolved. Palate: fruity, complex, sweetness.

MARQUÉS DE ALELLA PANSA BLANCA 2009 B
100% pansa blanca.

87 Colour: bright straw. Nose: fragrant herbs, dried flowers, fresh fruit, fresh. Palate: good structure, fresh, fruity, rich, flavourful.

MARQUÉS DE ALELLA VGR 2009 B
100% viognier.

87 Colour: bright golden. Nose: floral, ripe fruit, fresh, expressive. Palate: good structure, rich, fruity, flavourful.

ACOT 2009 RD
100% syrah.

88 Colour: onion pink. Nose: complex, fresh, ripe fruit, dried flowers. Palate: powerful, flavourful, fruity, complex, fleshy.

NEWS ABOUT THE VINTAGE:

It has been six years since DO Alicante started to abandon its former reputation of cheap table wines, shaping up a new one based on the singularity of its rancio and generoso wines, as well as more modern renderings partial to terroir expression given the excellent quality of the region's soils, mostly limestone where *monastrell* –well escorted by some foreign grape varieties that have been abundantly planted–, simply thrives. The leading names are Beryna, El Sequé, Sierra Salinas, Enrique Mendoza and Gutiérrez de la Vega, all of them splendid references for the other wineries, and working in unison with an equally forward-minded Consejo Regulador.

In tasting terms, the 2010 wines show the relatively low rainfall levels of that year, which accounts for higher alcohol and some overripe notes. The more sophisticated face of the *monastrell* –the best-performing grape variety in the region, along with *moscatel*– is perceived in wines like Curro 2009, from Bodegas Bernabé Navarro; Estrecho Monastrell 2006, from Bodegas Eduardo Mendoza, and in VC Tierra de Viñedos Culturales, all of them high quality products and a formidable reference for the rest of the region's wineries.

Nevertheless, some of the old-style wines are still to be found, with traditionally long-ageing spells in old wood casks and a prominent ripe, mediterranean accent historically cherished by local consumers.

Young whites of the 2010 vintage show as easy-drinking wines, quite fruity and fresh and altogether better than the red and rosé renderings. The increasing demand for white wines and their scarcity have forced the Consejo Regulador to resort to buying wines made from the *merseguera* grape variety in Titagua, a well known white wine region within the neighbouring province of Valencia.

LOCATION:

In the province of Alicante (covering 51 municipal districts), and a small part of the province of Murcia. The vineyards extend over areas close to the coast (in the surroundings of the capital city of Alicante, and especially in the area of La Marina, a traditional producer of Moscatel), as well as in the interior of the province.

CLIMATE:

Distinction must be made between the vineyards situated closer to the coastline, where the climate is clearly Mediterranean and somewhat more humid, and those inland, which receive continental influences and have a lower level of rainfall.

SOIL:

In general, the majority of the soils in the region are of a dun limestone type, with little clay and hardly any organic matter.

GRAPE VARIETIES:

WHITE: *Merseguera, Moscatel de Alejandría, Macabeo, Planta Fina, Verdil, Airén, Chardonnay* and *Sauvignon Blanc.*
RED: *Monastrell, Garnacha Tinta* (*Alicante* or *Giró*), *Garnacha Tintorera, Bobal, Tempranillo, Cabernet Sauvignon, Merlot, Pinot Noir*, *Syrah* and *Petit Verdot.*

FIGURES:

Vineyard surface: 8,785 – **Wine-Growers:** 2,500 – **Wineries:** 54 – **2010 Harvest rating:** Very Good – **Production:** 174,190,71 litres – **Market percentages:** 76% domestic. 24% export

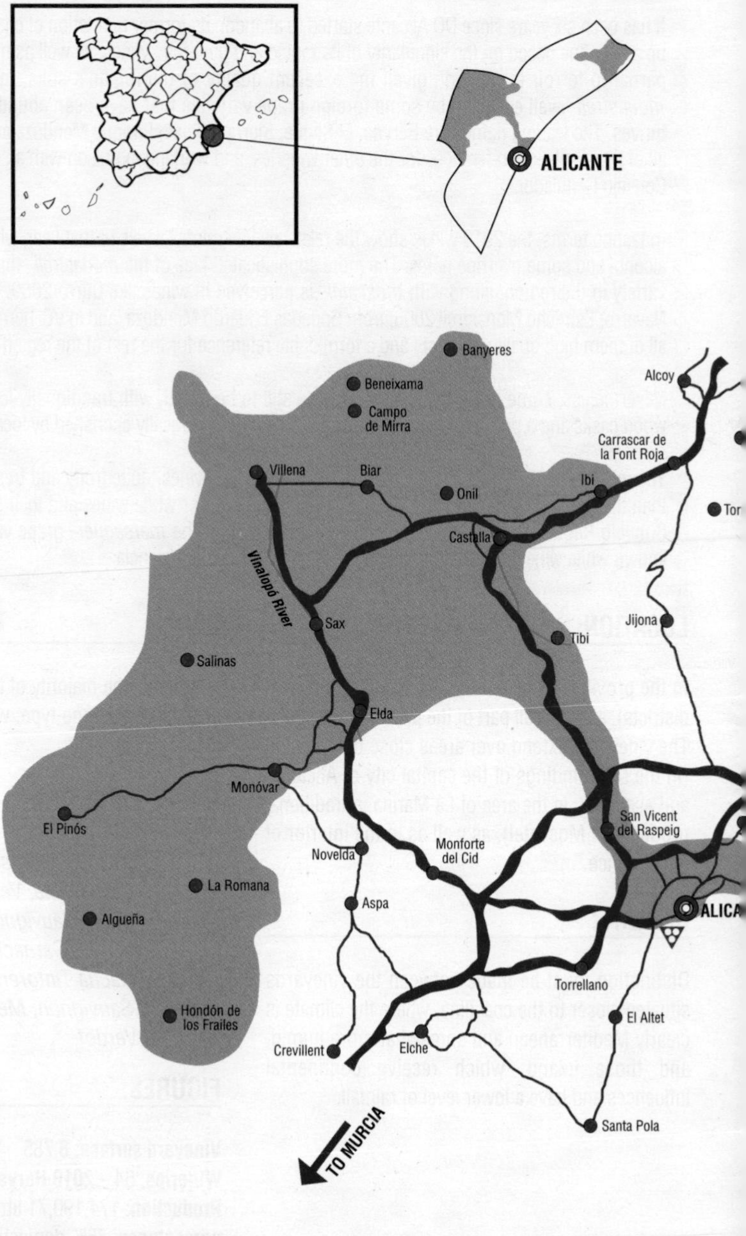

DO ALICANTE

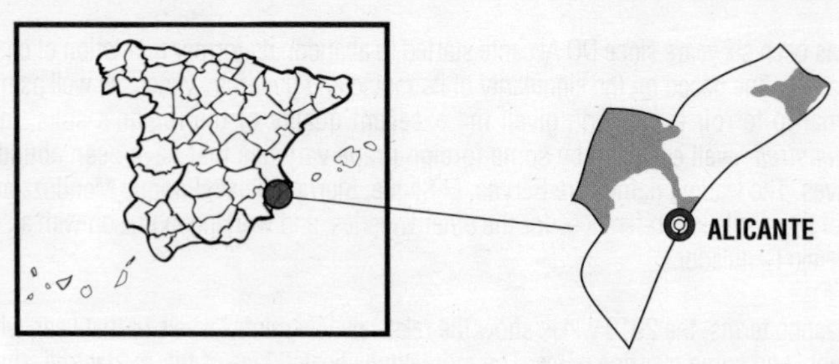
ALICANTE
Banyeres
Beneixama
Campo de Mirra
Alcoy
Carrascar de la Font Roja
Villena
Biar
Onil
Ibi
Tor
Castalla
Vinalopó River
Sax
Jijona
Tibi
Salinas
Elda
Monóvar
El Pinós
San Vicent del Raspeig
Novelda
Monforte del Cid
La Romana
Aspa
Algueña
ALICA
Torrellano
Hondón de los Frailes
El Altet
Crevillent
Elche
Santa Pola
TO MURCIA

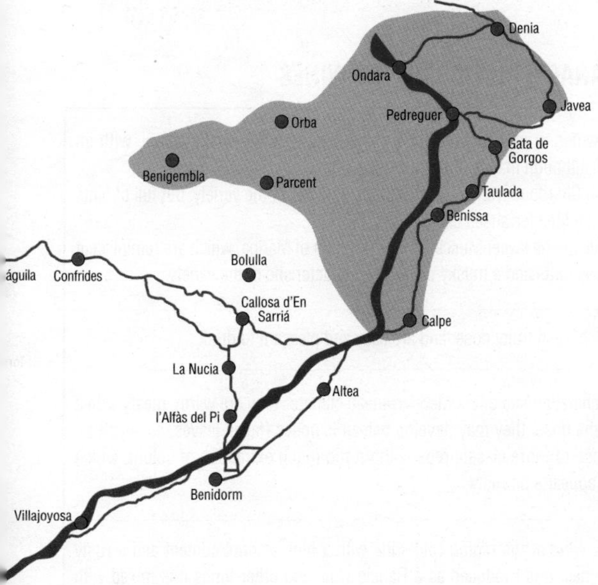
Denia
Ondara
Javea
Pedreguer
Orba
Gata de Gorgos
Benigembla
Parcent
Taulada
Benissa
águila
Confrides
Bolulla
Callosa d'En Sarriá
Calpe
La Nucia
Altea
l'Alfàs del Pi
Benidorm
Villajoyosa

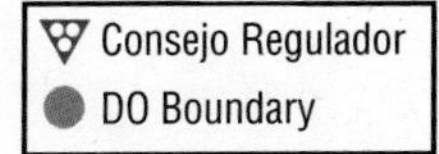
Consejo Regulador
DO Boundary

CONSEJO REGULADOR
Orense, 3, Entlo. Dcha.
03003 Alicante
☎: +34 965 984 478 - Fax: +34 965 229 295
@ crdo.alicante@crdo-alicante.org
www.crdo-alicante.org

GENERAL CHARACTERISTICS OF THE WINES

WHITES	The young white wines produced from local varieties are usually pale yellow, with an honest, fruity nose, although maybe not too intense, and are pleasant to drink. There are also some Chardonnays which reflect the character of the variety, but full of hints of ripe fruit due to the Mediterranean climate. More significant still are the sweet Muscatels of the region of Marina, which are reminiscent of honey, with grapey hints and a musky character characteristic of the variety.
ROSÉS	These are pink with a fresh fruity nose: and are easy and pleasant to drink.
REDS	The red wines are characteristic of the Mediterranean climate. They are warm, meaty with a fine structure; on the nose: they may develop balsamic noses (fallen leaves, eucalyptus). There is also a range of more classic reds without too much extraction of colour, which unfortunately may appear a bit rusty.
FONDILLÓN	This is the historic wine of the region (old wine with a high alcohol content and a rusty character). Sometimes, it is produced as a Rancio wine and other times it is mixed with Mistelas.

VINTAGE RATING PEÑÍNGUIDE

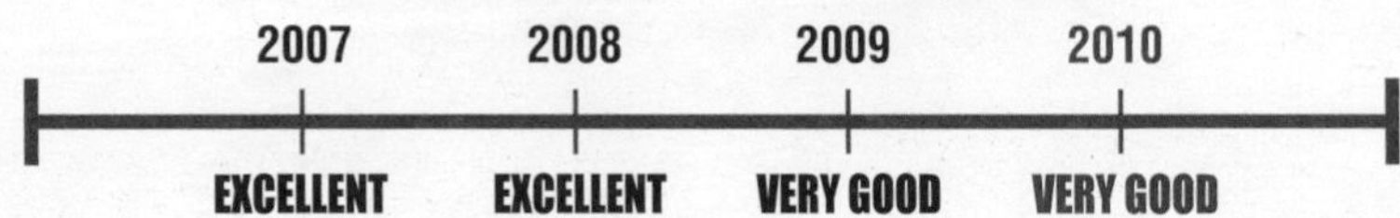

BODEGA COOPERATIVA DE ALGUEÑA COOP. V.

Ctra. Rodriguillo, Km. 29.500
03668 Algueña (Alicante)
☎: +34 965 476 113 - Fax: +34 965 476 229
bodega@vinosdealguenya.es

TORREVIÑAS 2010 B
50% chardonnay, 50% sauvignon blanc.

86 Color bright straw. Aroma fresh, fresh fruit, white flowers, expressive. Taste flavourful, fruity, good acidity, balanced.

TORREVIÑAS LÁGRIMA 2010 RD
100% monastrell.

85 Colour: rose, purple rim. Nose: red berry notes, floral, fresh. Palate: fleshy, powerful, fruity, fresh.

TORREVIÑAS DOBLE PASTA 2009 T
100% monastrell.

85 Colour: cherry, garnet rim. Nose: powerfull, ripe fruit. Palate: powerful, concentrated, sweetness.

ALHENIA 2009 T
100% monastrell.

83 Colour: bright cherry. Nose: ripe fruit, sweet spices, creamy oak, fine reductive notes. Palate: flavourful, fruity, toasty, round tannins.

CASA JIMÉNEZ 2008 TC
100% monastrell.

85 Colour: cherry, garnet rim. Nose: ripe fruit, creamy oak, complex. Palate: flavourful, toasty, round tannins.

FONDONET 2008 T
100% monastrell.

85 Colour: black cherry. Nose: powerfull, fruit preserve, dried fruit. Palate: powerful, sweet, fine bitter notes.

FONDILLÓN 1980 FONDILLÓN
100% monastrell.

88 Color iodine, amber rim. Aroma powerfull, complex, elegant, dry nuts, toasty. Taste rich, fine bitter notes, fine solera notes, long, spicy.

BODEGA COOPERATIVA SANT VICENTE FERRER

Avda. Las Palmas, 32
03725 Teulada (Alicante)
☎: +34 965 740 051 - Fax: +34 965 740 489
bodega@coop-santvicent.com
www.coop-santvicent.com

PITÁGORA 2010 ESP
100% moscatel.

85 Colour: pale. Nose: fresh fruit, tropical fruit, white flowers, fresh, expressive. Palate: fresh, fruity, flavourful.

BODEGA J. BELDA

Ctra. Benirrama s/n
46635 Fontanars dels Alforins (Valencia)
☎: +34 962 222 278 - Fax: +34 962 222 245
info@danielbelda.com
www.danielbelda.com

MIGJORN 2007 T
merlot, cabernet sauvignon, tintorera.

80 Colour: pale ruby, brick rim edge. Nose: ripe fruit, slightly evolved, short. Palate: dry wood, reductive nuances.

BODEGA NUESTRA SEÑORA DE LAS VIRTUDES COOP. V.

Ctra. de Yecla, 9
03400 Villena (Alicante)
☎: +34 965 802 187
coopvillena@coopvillena.com
www.coopvillena.com

VINALOPÓ ESENCIA DEL MEDITERRÁNEO 2010 B
50% moscatel, 50% sauvignon blanc.

87 Colour: bright straw. Nose: fresh, white flowers. Palate: flavourful, fruity, good acidity, balanced.

VINALOPÓ MACABEO 2010 B
100% macabeo.

87 Colour: bright straw. Nose: fresh, white flowers, grassy. Palate: flavourful, fruity, good acidity, balanced.

VINALOPÓ SAUVIGNON BLANC 2010 B
100% sauvignon blanc.

82 Colour: bright straw. Nose: citrus fruit, ripe fruit, dried herbs. Palate: flavourful, fruity, fresh.

VINALOPÓ 2010 T
50% monastrell, 50% merlot.

84 Colour: cherry, purple rim. Nose: medium intensity, floral, ripe fruit. Palate: flavourful, fruity, fleshy.

VINALOPÓ MONASTRELL 2009 T
100% monastrell.

85 Colour: cherry, purple rim. Nose: red berry notes, balsamic herbs, balanced. Palate: flavourful, fruity, fleshy, easy to drink.

VINALOPÓ PETIT VERDOT 2009 T
100% petit verdot.

82 Colour: cherry, garnet rim. Nose: ripe fruit, creamy oak, floral. Palate: fruity, flavourful, spicy.

VINALOPÓ 2008 TC
50% monastrell, 50% cabernet sauvignon.

88 Colour: cherry, garnet rim. Nose: sweet spices, creamy oak, scrubland. Palate: powerful, flavourful, rich, spicy, round tannins.

VINALOPÓ SELECCIÓN 2008 T
50% monastrell, 50% syrah.

87 Colour: cherry, garnet rim. Nose: ripe fruit, expressive, spicy, toasty. Palate: fruity, flavourful, long.

VINALOPÓ 2005 TR
monastrell, cabernet sauvignon.

84 Colour: bright cherry, orangey edge. Nose: old leather, fruit liqueur notes, roasted coffee. Palate: spirituous, flavourful, fleshy.

TESORO DE VILLENA RESERVA ESPECIAL FONDILLÓN 1972 FONDILLÓN SOLERA
100% monastrell.

85 Color iodine, amber rim. Aroma powerfull, complex, elegant, dry nuts, toasty. Taste rich, fine bitter notes, fine solera notes, long, spicy.

BODEGA SANTA CATALINA DEL MAÑÁN

Ctra. Monóvar-Pinoso, Km. 10,5
03649 Mañán Monóvar (Alicante)
☎: +34 966 960 096 - Fax: +34 966 960 096
bodegamanan@terra.es

MAÑÁ CHARDONNAY 2010 B
100% chardonnay.

86 Colour: bright straw. Nose: fresh, white flowers, expressive, tropical fruit. Palate: flavourful, fruity, good acidity, balanced.

MAÑÁ MARISQUERO 2010 B
moscatel, macabeo, airén.

85 Colour: bright straw. Nose: fresh, fresh fruit, white flowers, expressive. Palate: flavourful, fruity, good acidity.

TORRENT DEL MAÑÁ 2010 B
50% merseguera, 50% airén.

83 Colour: bright straw. Nose: fresh, fresh fruit, white flowers. Palate: flavourful, fruity, good acidity, balanced.

TERRA DEL MAÑÁ CHARDONNAY 2010 B
100% chardonnay.

81 Colour: bright straw. Nose: candied fruit, citrus fruit. Palate: fresh, fruity, light-bodied.

TERRA DEL MAÑÁ SYRAH 2010 RD
100% syrah.

82 Colour: rose, purple rim. Nose: powerfull, red berry notes, fruit preserve. Palate: fleshy, powerful, fruity, fresh.

TERRA DEL MAÑÁ MONASTRELL 2010 T MACERACIÓN CARBÓNICA
100% monastrell.

86 Colour: cherry, purple rim. Nose: expressive, fresh fruit, floral. Palate: flavourful, fruity, good acidity, round tannins.

TORRENT DEL MAÑÁ 2009 T
85% monastrell, 15% merlot.

86 Colour: cherry, purple rim. Nose: fresh fruit, red berry notes, floral. Palate: flavourful, fruity, good acidity, round tannins.

TERRA DEL MAÑÁ SELECCIÓN DE BARRICAS 2009 T
40% monastrell, 30% syrah, 30% merlot.

86 Colour: cherry, purple rim. Nose: red berry notes, ripe fruit, sweet spices. Palate: flavourful, fruity, fleshy, round tannins.

MAÑÁ MERLOT 2009 T
100% merlot.

83 Colour: cherry, purple rim. Nose: red berry notes, floral, fresh. Palate: fruity, easy to drink.

TERRA DEL MAÑÁ 2007 TC
40% monastrell, 30% cabernet sauvignon, 30% tempranillo.

84 Colour: cherry, garnet rim. Nose: ripe fruit, fruit liqueur notes, toasty, sweet spices. Palate: flavourful, fleshy, spirituous.

TORRENT DEL MAÑÁ 2007 TC
70% monastrell, 15% merlot, 15% syrah.

84 Colour: cherry, garnet rim. Nose: spicy, toasty, aromatic coffee, reduction off-odours. Palate: flavourful, spicy, ripe fruit.

MAÑA RUSTIC 2005 TC
100% cabernet sauvignon.

87 Colour: cherry, garnet rim. Nose: spicy, creamy oak, toasty, ripe fruit. Palate: powerful, flavourful, toasty, round tannins.

TORRENT DEL MAÑÁ 2005 TR
90% monastrell, 10% cabernet sauvignon.

80 Colour: pale ruby, brick rim edge. Nose: ripe fruit, toasty, aromatic coffee. Palate: creamy, round tannins, long.

GRAN MAÑÁN FONDILLÓN
100% monastrell.

86 Colour: iodine, amber rim. Nose: aged wood nuances, sweet spices, pattiserie. Palate: balanced, spirituous, flavourful, sweetness.

GRAN MAÑÁN MOSCATEL
moscatel.

87 Colour: bright straw. Nose: powerfull, candied fruit, citrus fruit, honeyed notes, warm. Palate: rich, sweet, fruity.

BODEGA VINESSENS

Ctra. de Caudete, Km. 1
03400 Villena (Alicante)
☎: +34 965 800 265
comercial@vinessens.es
www.vinessens.es

ESSENS 2010 B
100% chardonnay.

91 Colour: bright yellow. Nose: ripe fruit, sweet spices, creamy oak, fragrant herbs. Palate: rich, smoky aftertaste, flavourful, fresh, good acidity.

SEIN 2009 T
50% monastrell, 40% syrah, 10% cabernet sauvignon.

91 Colour: cherry, garnet rim. Nose: powerfull, ripe fruit, creamy oak, toasty. Palate: flavourful, powerful, fleshy, spicy, ripe fruit.

BODEGA XALÓ

Ctra. Xaló Alcalali, s/n
03727 Xaló (Alicante)
☎: +34 966 480 034 - Fax: +34 966 480 808
comercial@bodegasxalo.com
www.bodegasxalo.com

BAHÍA DE DENIA 2010 B JOVEN
100% moscatel.

90 Nose: white flowers, tropical fruit, fragrant herbs, expressive, powerfull. Palate: complex, fruity, flavourful, creamy.

VALL DE XALÓ 2010 B JOVEN
100% moscatel.

85 Colour: bright straw. Nose: expressive, fresh, floral, fruit expression. Palate: good acidity, balanced, flavourful.

VALL DE XALÓ 2010 RD
garnacha.

88 Colour: rose, purple rim. Nose: ripe fruit, red berry notes, floral, expressive. Palate: fleshy, powerful, fruity, fresh.

VALL DE XALÓ 2010 T
50% garnacha, 50% tempranillo.

85 Colour: cherry, purple rim. Nose: fresh fruit, red berry notes, fresh. Palate: fleshy, light-bodied, easy to drink.

SERRA DE BERNIA 2008 T ROBLE
80% garnacha, 20% cabernet sauvignon.

87 Colour: cherry, garnet rim. Nose: expressive, red berry notes, floral, creamy oak. Palate: fruity, good acidity, round tannins.

BAHÍA DE DENIA BN
100% moscatel.

80 Colour: bright straw. Nose: medium intensity, dried herbs, fine lees, floral. Palate: fresh, fruity, flavourful, good acidity.

VALL DE XALÓ 2009 MISTELA
100% moscatel.

85 Colour: bright golden. Nose: expressive, honeyed notes, citrus fruit, pattiserie. Palate: flavourful, rich, correct.

VALL DE XALÓ GIRÓ 2009 MISTELA
100% garnacha.

83 Colour: cherry, garnet rim. Nose: powerfull, fruit preserve, candied fruit, fruit liqueur notes. Palate: flavourful, powerful, fleshy, sweet.

VALL DE XALÓ 2008 MISTELA ROBLE
100% moscatel.

85 Colour: golden. Nose: honeyed notes, candied fruit, fragrant herbs, toasty. Palate: flavourful, sweet, fresh, fruity, good acidity, long.

BODEGAS ALEJANDRO PÉREZ MARTÍNEZ

El Mañán, HJ10
03640 Monóvar (Alicante)
☎: +34 966 960 291
bodegasalejandro@gmail.com

VEGA CUYAR 2010 B
50% merseguera, 50% sauvignon blanc.

85 Colour: bright straw. Nose: fresh, fresh fruit, expressive, floral. Palate: flavourful, fruity, good acidity.

VEGA CUYAR 2010 T
100% monastrell.

86 Colour: cherry, purple rim. Nose: fresh fruit, red berry notes, fresh. Palate: fruity, good acidity, easy to drink.

VEGA CUYAR 2008 TC
50% tempranillo, 50% cabernet sauvignon.

88 Colour: bright cherry. Nose: sweet spices, ripe fruit. Palate: flavourful, fruity, toasty, round tannins.

BODEGAS BERNABÉ NAVARRO

Ctra. Villena-Cañada, Km. 3- Finca Casa Balaguer
03400 Villena (Alicante)
☎: +34 966 770 353 - Fax: +34 966 770 353
info@bodegasbernabenavarro.com
www.bodegasbernabenavarro.com

BERYNA 10º ANIVERSARIO 2009 T
70% monastrell, 15% tempranillo, 5% syrah, 5% merlot, 5% cabernet sauvignon.

94 Colour: cherry, garnet rim. Nose: spicy, creamy oak, toasty, complex, ripe fruit, mineral. Palate: powerful, flavourful, toasty, round tannins.

CASA BALAGUER 2007 T
60% monastrell, 15% syrah, 10% merlot, 10% tempranillo, 5% cabernet sauvignon.

91 Colour: cherry, garnet rim. Nose: fruit preserve, sweet spices, creamy oak. Palate: powerful, fleshy, sweetness.

CURRO 2009 T
70% monastrell, 30% tempranillo.

95 Colour: bright cherry. Nose: creamy oak, expressive, ripe fruit, mineral. Palate: fruity, toasty, flavourful, powerful tannins.

BODEGAS BOCOPA

Paraje Les Pedreres, Autovía A-31, km. 200 - 201
03610 Petrer (Alicante)
☎: +34 966 950 489 - Fax: +34 966 950 406
info@bocopa.com
www.bocopa.com

MARINA ALTA 2010 B
100% moscatel.

88 Colour: bright straw. Nose: fresh, fresh fruit, white flowers. Palate: flavourful, fruity, good acidity, balanced.

TERRETA ROSÉ 2010 RD
100% monastrell.

88 Colour: rose, purple rim. Nose: powerfull, ripe fruit, red berry notes, floral. Palate: fleshy, powerful, fruity, fresh.

ALCANTA MONASTRELL 2010 T
100% monastrell.

87 Colour: cherry, purple rim. Nose: fresh fruit, red berry notes, floral. Palate: flavourful, fruity, good acidity, round tannins.

LAUDUM PETIT VERDOT 2008 T
100% petit verdot.

82 Colour: cherry, garnet rim. Nose: herbaceous, ripe fruit, toasty. Palate: good acidity, spicy, grainy tannins.

LAUDUM MONASTRELL ESPECIAL 2006 T
100% monastrell.

88 Colour: cherry, garnet rim. Nose: sweet spices, ripe fruit, creamy oak. Palate: fruity, flavourful, balanced, round tannins.

MARINA ESPUMANTE 2010 B
100% moscatel.

85 Colour: bright straw. Nose: citrus fruit, candied fruit, expressive. Palate: fresh, fruity, flavourful.

LAUDUM CABERNET SAUVIGNON 2006 T
100% cabernet sauvignon.

85 Colour: cherry, garnet rim. Nose: toasty, overripe fruit, aromatic coffee. Palate: powerful, flavourful, toasty, round tannins.

LAUDUM GARNACHA SYRAH 2006 T
50% garnacha, 50% syrah.

84 Colour: cherry, garnet rim. Nose: ripe fruit, spicy, caramel. Palate: powerful, flavourful, toasty, round tannins.

SOL DE ALICANTE DULCENEGRA T
100% monastrell.

88 Colour: black cherry. Nose: powerfull, fruit liqueur notes, fruit liqueur notes, varnish, tar, dark chocolate. Palate: powerful, sweet, fine bitter notes.

ALCANTA MONASTRELL 2007 TC
50% monastrell, 50% tempranillo.

85 Colour: cherry, garnet rim. Nose: spicy, creamy oak, toasty. Palate: powerful, flavourful, toasty, round tannins.

LAUDUM 2007 TC
70% monastrell, 15% cabernet sauvignon, 15% merlot.

82 Colour: cherry, garnet rim. Nose: old leather, toasty, ripe fruit. Palate: fleshy, ripe fruit, toasty.

BODEGAS E. MENDOZA

Partida El Romeral, s/n
03580 Alfás del Pi (Alicante)
☎: +34 965 888 639 - Fax: +34 965 889 232
bodegas-mendoza@bodegasmendoza.com
www.bodegasmendoza.com

ENRIQUE MENDOZA MOSCATEL DE MENDOZA 2008 B
100% moscatel.

93 Colour: golden. Nose: powerfull, floral, honeyed notes, candied fruit, sweet spices. Palate: flavourful, sweet, fresh, fruity, good acidity, long.

ENRIQUE MENDOZA SHIRAZ 2008 TC
100% syrah.

93 Colour: cherry, garnet rim. Nose: spicy, creamy oak, toasty, complex, red berry notes. Palate: powerful, flavourful, toasty, round tannins.

ENRIQUE MENDOZA CABERNET SAUVIGNON 2007 TC
100% cabernet sauvignon.

91 Colour: cherry, garnet rim. Nose: creamy oak, sweet spices, ripe fruit, characterful, complex. Palate: flavourful, fleshy, good structure.

ENRIQUE MENDOZA CABERNET SAUVIGNON - SHIRAZ 2007 TR
50% cabernet sauvignon, 50% syrah.

90 Color cherry, garnet rim. Aroma ripe fruit, spicy, creamy oak, toasty, complex. Taste powerful, flavourful, toasty, round tannins.

ENRIQUE MENDOZA MERLOT 2007 TC
100% merlot.

89 Colour: cherry, garnet rim. Nose: overripe fruit, sweet spices, toasty. Palate: flavourful, powerful, fleshy, complex.

ENRIQUE MENDOZA PINOT NOIR 2007 TC
100% pinot noir.

88 Colour: cherry, garnet rim. Nose: expressive, ripe fruit, warm, toasty, aromatic coffee. Palate: flavourful, fine bitter notes, good acidity.

ESTRECHO MONASTRELL 2006 T
100% monastrell.

94 Colour: cherry, garnet rim. Nose: spicy, creamy oak, toasty, complex, mineral, ripe fruit. Palate: powerful, flavourful, toasty, round tannins.

ENRIQUE MENDOZA SANTA ROSA 2006 TR
70% cabernet sauvignon, 15% merlot, 15% syrah.

93 Colour: bright cherry. Nose: sweet spices, creamy oak, ripe fruit. Palate: flavourful, fruity, toasty, round tannins.

BODEGAS FAELO

Poeta Miguel Hernández, 60
03201 Elche (Alicante)
☎: +34 655 856 898
info@vinosladama.com
www.vinosladama.com

PALMA BLANCA 2010 B
100% moscatel.

88 Color golden. Aroma powerfull, floral, honeyed notes, candied fruit, fragrant herbs. Taste flavourful, sweet, fresh, fruity, good acidity, long.

L'ALBA 2010 RD
100% syrah.

87 Colour: rose, purple rim. Nose: ripe fruit, red berry notes, floral. Palate: fleshy, powerful, fruity, fresh.

LA DAMA 2007 TC
60% cabernet sauvignon, 30% monastrell, 10% petit verdot.HHHH8€

88 Colour: cherry, garnet rim. Nose: overripe fruit, warm, powerfull, toasty, dark chocolate. Palate: powerful, fleshy, spicy, ripe fruit.

BODEGAS FONDARIUM

03760 Ondara (Alicante)
☎: +34 675 960 754
info@bodegasfondarium.es
www.bodegasfondarium.es

FONDARIUM BLANC SELECCIÓ FRUTAL 2010 B
100% moscatel.

88 Color bright straw. Aroma fresh, fresh fruit, white flowers, expressive. Taste flavourful, fruity, good acidity, balanced.

FONDARIUM 2010 B
moscatel.

87 Colour: bright straw. Nose: fresh, white flowers, expressive, tropical fruit. Palate: flavourful, fruity, good acidity, balanced, easy to drink.

FONDARIUM 2007 TC
merlot, cabernet sauvignon, monastrell, tempranillo, giró.

84 Colour: pale ruby, brick rim edge. Nose: fruit liqueur notes, fruit liqueur notes, aromatic coffee. Palate: flavourful, ripe fruit.

BODEGAS FRANCISCO GÓMEZ

Ctra. Villena - Pinoso, Km. 8,8
03400 Villena (Alicante)
☎: +34 965 979 195 - Fax: +34 965 979 196
info@bodegasfranciscogomez.es
www.bodegasfranciscogomez.es

FRUTO NOBLE 2010 B
sauvignon blanc.

85 Colour: bright straw. Nose: fragrant herbs, white flowers, tropical fruit. Palate: light-bodied, easy to drink.

BOCA NEGRA DULCE S/C T
monastrell.

87 Colour: cherry, garnet rim. Nose: balsamic herbs, scrubland, aromatic coffee, pattiserie. Palate: sweetness, flavourful, fleshy.

BOCA NEGRA 2007 TC
monastrell.

90 Colour: cherry, garnet rim. Nose: spicy, creamy oak, expressive, complex. Palate: rich, flavourful, complex, fleshy.

MORATILLAS 2007 TC
monastrell, merlot, cabernet sauvignon.

87 Colour: cherry, garnet rim. Nose: balsamic herbs, spicy, toasty, powerfull. Palate: flavourful, fleshy, spicy.

SERRATA 2006 TR
merlot, petit verdot, cabernet sauvignon, monastrell.

89 Colour: cherry, garnet rim. Nose: aromatic coffee, sweet spices, toasty, expressive. Palate: balanced, fleshy, long, soft tannins.

FRUTO NOBLE 2006 TC
cabernet franc, monastrell, syrah.

87 Colour: cherry, garnet rim. Nose: spicy, toasty, balsamic herbs. Palate: flavourful, complex, fleshy, toasty.

QUO VADIS S/C FONDILLÓN
monastrell.

90 Colour: light mahogany. Nose: sweet spices, creamy oak, dark chocolate, aged wood nuances, acetaldehyde. Palate: unctuous, flavourful, complex.

SERRATA S/C MOSCATEL
moscatel.

86 Colour: bright golden. Nose: candied fruit, honeyed notes, citrus fruit. Palate: creamy, rich, flavourful.

BODEGAS GUTIÉRREZ DE LA VEGA

Les Quintanes, 1
03792 Parcent (Alicante)
☎: +34 966 403 871 - Fax: +34 966 405 257
info@castadiva.es
www.castadiva.es

FURTIVA LÁGRIMA 2010 B
moscatel.

93 Colour: bright straw. Nose: honeyed notes, fragrant herbs, elegant, white flowers, citrus fruit. Palate: flavourful, sweet, fresh, fruity, good acidity, long.

LA DIVA 2010 BC
moscatel.

92 Colour: golden. Nose: powerfull, floral, honeyed notes, candied fruit, scrubland. Palate: flavourful, sweet, fresh, fruity, good acidity, long.

CASTA DIVA RESERVA REAL 2002 B RESERVA
moscatel.

94 Color golden. Aroma powerfull, floral, honeyed notes, candied fruit, fragrant herbs. Taste flavourful, sweet, fresh, fruity, good acidity, long.

CASTA DIVA RECÓNDITA ARMONÍA T
monastrell.

91 Colour: cherry, garnet rim. Nose: spicy, toasty, complex, overripe fruit, honeyed notes, dried fruit, sweet spices. Palate: powerful, flavourful, toasty, round tannins, sweet.

BODEGAS MURVIEDRO

Ampliación Pol. El Romeral, s/n
46340 Requena (Valencia)
☎: +34 962 329 003 - Fax: +34 962 329 002
murviedro@murviedro.es
www.murviedro.es

DULCE DE MURVIEDRO 2008 B
100% moscatel.

85 Colour: golden. Nose: honeyed notes, candied fruit, fragrant herbs. Palate: flavourful, sweet, fresh, fruity, good acidity, long.

CUEVA DEL PERDÓN 2008 T
60% monastrell, 40% syrah.

87 Colour: cherry, garnet rim. Nose: ripe fruit, spicy, toasty, sweet spices. Palate: powerful, flavourful, toasty, round tannins.

BODEGAS PARCENT

Avda. Denia, 15 (Ctra. Parcent Alcalali)
03792 Parcent (Alicante)
☎: +34 636 536 693 - Fax: +34 966 405 467
armando@bodegasparcent.com
www.bodegasparcent.com

GRÀ D'OR BLANCO SECO 2010 B
100% moscatel.

84 Colour: bright straw. Nose: fresh, fresh fruit, white flowers, expressive. Palate: flavourful, fruity, light-bodied.

ROSAT 2010 RD
syrah.

85 Colour: rose, purple rim. Nose: ripe fruit, red berry notes, floral. Palate: fleshy, powerful, fruity, fresh.

PARCENT MERLOT 2008 TC
merlot.

78

BODEGAS PORSELLANES

Avda. País Valencia, 4
03720 Benissa (Alicante)
☎: +34 965 730 200 - Fax: +34 965 732 609
info@bodegasporsellanes.com
www.bodegasporsellanes.com

LA MERINA 2008 B
50% macabeo, 50% malvasía.

78

MAS DE CARAITA 2009 RD
50% garnacha, 50% monastrell.

78

MAS DE CARAITA 2008 T
tempranillo, garnacha, syrah.

80 Colour: cherry, garnet rim. Nose: ripe fruit, spicy, toasty, cedar wood. Palate: powerful, flavourful, toasty, round tannins.

AGULLÓ 2007 T
80% tempranillo, 20% cabernet sauvignon.

90 Colour: cherry, garnet rim. Nose: powerfull, ripe fruit, raspberry, creamy oak, toasty. Palate: flavourful, powerful, fleshy.

ENTREPINS 2007 T
82% merlot, 18% cabernet sauvignon.

86 Colour: cherry, garnet rim. Nose: spicy, creamy oak, toasty, overripe fruit. Palate: powerful, flavourful, toasty, round tannins.

LA SORT 2008 MOSCATEL
100% moscatel.

82 Colour: old gold. Nose: fruit liqueur notes, honeyed notes, fresh. Palate: easy to drink, fruity, flavourful.

BODEGAS SANBERT

Ctra. Pinoso - Fortuna, s/n
03650 Pinoso (Alicante)
☎: +34 965 978 603 - Fax: +34 965 978 274
bodegasanbert@yahoo.es

CAMPS DE GLORIA 2010 B
moscatel, merseguera.

86 Colour: pale. Nose: fresh, fresh fruit, white flowers, expressive. Palate: flavourful, fruity, good acidity, balanced, fine bitter notes.

RODRIGUILLO 2010 T ROBLE
monastrell.

85 Colour: cherry, purple rim. Nose: fresh, creamy oak, spicy. Palate: fruity, flavourful, balsamic.

RODRIGUILLO MONASTRELL 2010 T
monastrell.

84 Colour: cherry, purple rim. Nose: expressive, fresh fruit, floral. Palate: flavourful, fruity, easy to drink.

RODRIGUILLO 2006 TC
monastrell.

87 Color cherry, garnet rim. Aroma ripe fruit, spicy, creamy oak, toasty, complex. Taste powerful, flavourful, toasty, round tannins.

DOCTUS 2006 TC
monastrell, syrah.

80 Colour: cherry, garnet rim. Nose: ripe fruit, spicy, creamy oak, balsamic herbs. Palate: flavourful, toasty, round tannins.

BODEGAS SIERRA SALINAS

Paraje del Puerto, s/n
03400 Villena (Alicante)
☎: +34 968 791 271 - Fax: +34 968 791 900
office@sierrasalinas.com
www.sierrasalinas.com

MO SALINAS MOSCATEL CHARDONNAY 2010 B
moscatel, chardonnay.

87 Colour: bright straw. Nose: fresh fruit, white flowers, expressive. Palate: flavourful, fruity, good acidity, balanced.

MO DE MONASTRELL 2009 T
95% monastrell, 5% garnacha tintorera.

88 Colour: bright cherry. Nose: sweet spices, ripe fruit, creamy oak. Palate: flavourful, fruity, toasty, round tannins.

SALINAS 1237 2007 T
30% garnacha tintorera, 40% cabernet sauvignon, 30% petit verdot.

94 Colour: cherry, garnet rim. Nose: creamy oak, toasty, complex, overripe fruit, sweet spices, earthy notes. Palate: powerful, flavourful, toasty, round tannins.

MIRA SALINAS 2007 T
65% mira, 20% cabernet sauvignon, 15% garnacha.

93 Colour: cherry, garnet rim. Nose: ripe fruit, spicy, creamy oak, toasty, mineral. Palate: powerful, flavourful, toasty, round tannins.

PUERTO SALINAS 2007 T
60% monastrell, 22% cabernet sauvignon, 18% garnacha.

91 Color bright cherry. Aroma ripe fruit, sweet spices, creamy oak, expressive. Taste flavourful, fruity, toasty, round tannins.

BODEGAS TERRA NATURA

Pintor Juan Gris, 26
03400 Villena (Alicante)
☎: +34 965 801 486 - Fax: +34 965 800 978
comercial@aymnavarro.com
www.bodegasterranatura.com

MIGUEL NAVARRO 2010 B
moscatel.

91 Colour: bright straw. Nose: fresh, white flowers, expressive, honeyed notes, citrus fruit. Palate: flavourful, fruity, good acidity, balanced.

TERRA NATURA 2010 B
macabeo.

88 Colour: bright straw. Nose: fresh, fresh fruit, white flowers. Palate: flavourful, fruity, good acidity, balanced.

TERRA NATURA 2010 RD
monastrell.

86 Colour: rose, purple rim. Nose: fruit preserve, red berry notes, floral. Palate: flavourful, fruity, fresh.

MIGUEL NAVARRO MONASTRELL TEMPRANILLO 2010 T BARRICA
tempranillo, monastrell.

90 Colour: bright cherry. Nose: ripe fruit, sweet spices, creamy oak, expressive, red berry notes. Palate: flavourful, fruity, toasty, round tannins.

TERRA NATURA 2010 T
monastrell.

88 Colour: cherry, purple rim. Nose: fresh fruit, red berry notes, floral. Palate: flavourful, fruity, good acidity, round tannins.

MIGUEL NAVARRO SELECCIÓN SYRAH MERLOT 2009 T
syrah, merlot.

86 Colour: cherry, purple rim. Nose: powerfull, characterful, overripe fruit, warm, sweet spices. Palate: powerful, spirituous, sweetness.

MIGUEL NAVARRO 2007 TC
monastrell, syrah.

88 Colour: cherry, garnet rim. Nose: spicy, toasty, overripe fruit. Palate: powerful, flavourful, toasty, round tannins.

TERRA NATURA CLÁSICO 2006 TC
merlot.

90 Colour: cherry, garnet rim. Nose: toasty, sweet spices, cocoa bean. Palate: flavourful, sweetness, fleshy, powerful.

BODEGAS VICENTE GANDÍA PLA

Ctra. Cheste a Godelleta, s/n
46370 Chiva (Valencia)
☎: +34 962 524 242 - Fax: +34 962 524 243
sgandia@vicentegandia.com
www.vicentegandia.com

PUERTO ALICANTE CHARDONNAY 2010 B
100% chardonnay.

88 Colour: bright yellow. Nose: powerfull, fresh, fruit expression, tropical fruit. Palate: flavourful, powerful, good acidity.

EL MIRACLE FUSIÓN 2009 B
70% chardonnay, 20% sauvignon blanc, 10% moscatel.

86 Colour: bright straw. Nose: ripe fruit, earthy notes, floral. Palate: fruity, fleshy, sweetness.

EL MIRACLE MUSIC 2010 RD
syrah, garnacha.

85 Colour: rose, purple rim. Nose: fresh, neat, fruit expression. Palate: flavourful, fruity, fresh.

EL MIRACLE PLANET VINO ORGÁNICO 2009 T
100% monastrell.

83 Colour: cherry, garnet rim. Nose: powerfull, scrubland, medium intensity, spicy, fruit preserve. Palate: flavourful, fleshy, sweetness.

EL MIRACLE ART 2008 T
25% monastrell, 20% pinot noir, 20% syrah, 20% merlot, 15% tempranillo.

88 Colour: dark-red cherry. Nose: expressive, ripe fruit, sweet spices, creamy oak, cocoa bean. Palate: flavourful, fleshy, fruity, balanced.

PUERTO ALICANTE SYRAH 2008 T
100% syrah.

88 Colour: cherry, garnet rim. Nose: spicy, creamy oak, toasty, overripe fruit, medium intensity. Palate: powerful, flavourful, toasty, round tannins.

BODEGAS VIVANZA

Ctra. Pinoso Jumilla, Km. 13 La Alberquilla
30520 Jumilla (Murcia)
☎: +34 966 678 686 - Fax: +34 965 215 651
agomez@domka.es
www.vivanza.es

LASCALA 2010 B
50% sauvignon blanc, 50% chardonnay.

88 Colour: bright straw. Nose: fresh fruit. Palate: flavourful, fruity, good acidity, balanced.

VIVANZA 2010 B
40% verdil, 40% sauvignon blanc, 20% chardonnay.

85 Colour: bright straw. Nose: fresh, fresh fruit, floral. Palate: flavourful, fruity, good acidity, balanced.

VIVANZA 2010 RD
50% syrah, 50% merlot.

84 Colour: rose, purple rim. Nose: powerfull, ripe fruit, red berry notes. Palate: fleshy, powerful, fruity, fresh.

VIVANZA 2009 T
merlot, syrah, pinot noir.

84 Colour: cherry, garnet rim. Nose: powerfull, characterful, ripe fruit, fruit liqueur notes. Palate: flavourful, sweetness, fleshy.

LASCALA 2009 T
50% monastrell, 50% cabernet sauvignon.

81 Colour: cherry, garnet rim. Nose: overripe fruit, warm, balsamic herbs. Palate: sweetness, fine bitter notes.

BODEGAS VOLVER

Pza. de Grecia, 1
45005 Toledo (Toledo)
☎: +34 690 818 509 - Fax: +34 976 852 764
rafa@bodegasvolver.com
www.orowines.com

TARIMA MONASTREL 2010 T
monastrell.

90 Colour: cherry, purple rim. Nose: powerfull, expressive, red berry notes, raspberry, medium intensity. Palate: fruity, fresh, flavourful, fleshy, unctuous.

TARIMA HILL 2009 T
monastrell.

90 Colour: cherry, purple rim. Nose: red berry notes, balanced, sweet spices, creamy oak, cocoa bean. Palate: long, flavourful, fleshy.

BODEGAS Y VIÑEDOS EL SEQUÉ

El Sequé, 59
03650 Pinoso (Alicante)
☎: +34 945 600 119 - Fax: +34 945 600 850
elseque@artadi.com

EL SEQUÉ 2009 T
100% monastrell.

94 Colour: cherry, garnet rim. Nose: powerfull, varietal, ripe fruit, fruit expression, scrubland. Palate: flavourful, powerful, fleshy, spicy, round tannins.

COMPAÑIA DE VINOS TELMO RODRÍGUEZ

El Monte, s/n
01308 Lanciego (Álava)
☎: +34 945 628 315 - Fax: +34 945 628 314
contact@telmorodriguez.com
www.telmorodriguez.com

AL MUVEDRE 2009 T JOVEN
100% monastrell.

87 Colour: cherry, garnet rim. Nose: ripe fruit, balsamic herbs, spicy. Palate: flavourful, powerful, fleshy.

FINCA COLLADO

Ctra. Villena Salinas, s/n
03638 (Alicante)
☎: +34 962 871 241
maricaramen@fincacollado.com
www.fincacollado.com

FINCA COLLADO 2010 BFB
50% chardonnay, 50% moscatel.

86 Colour: bright straw. Nose: fresh fruit, white flowers. Palate: flavourful, fruity, good acidity, balanced.

FINCA COLLADO 2010 RD
100% merlot.

84 Colour: rose, purple rim. Nose: red berry notes, fresh fruit. Palate: flavourful, fruity.

FINCA COLLADO MERLOT 2009 T BARRICA
100% merlot.

84 Colour: cherry, garnet rim. Nose: fruit liqueur notes, fruit preserve, creamy oak. Palate: sweetness, powerful.

FINCA COLLADO 2008 T
50% cabernet sauvignon, 50% merlot.

87 Colour: bright cherry. Nose: sweet spices, creamy oak, ripe fruit. Palate: flavourful, fruity, toasty, round tannins.

LA BODEGA DE PINOSO

Paseo de la Constitución, 82
03650 Pinoso (Alicante)
☎: +34 965 477 040 - Fax: +34 966 970 149
labodega@labodegadepinoso.com
www.labodegadepinoso.com

VERMADOR ECOLÓGICO 2010 B
macabeo, airén.

88 Color bright straw. Aroma fresh, fresh fruit, white flowers, expressive. Taste flavourful, fruity, good acidity, balanced.

LA TORRE DEL RELOJ MACABEO 2010 B
macabeo, airén.

83 Colour: bright straw. Nose: fresh, expressive, floral. Palate: light-bodied, flavourful, easy to drink.

VERGEL 2010 RD
monastrell.

88 Color onion pink. Aroma elegant, candied fruit, dried flowers, fragrant herbs, red berry notes. Taste light-bodied, flavourful, good acidity, long, spicy.

VERMADOR 2010 RD
monastrell.

86 Colour: rose, purple rim. Nose: powerfull, floral, expressive, violet drops, fresh fruit. Palate: fleshy, powerful, fruity, flavourful, light-bodied.

LA TORRE DEL RELOJ 2010 RD
monastrell, tempranillo, syrah.

85 Colour: rose, purple rim. Nose: powerfull, floral, expressive, fresh fruit. Palate: fleshy, powerful, fruity, fresh, easy to drink.

VERGEL 2009 T
garnacha, merlot, monastrell.

89 Colour: bright cherry. Nose: sweet spices, creamy oak, red berry notes. Palate: flavourful, fruity, toasty, round tannins.

LA TORRE DEL RELOJ MONASTRELL 2009 T
monastrell, merlot, tempranillo.

87 Colour: cherry, purple rim. Nose: ripe fruit, red berry notes, varietal, neat. Palate: correct, fruity, flavourful.

VERMADOR ECOLÓGICO MONASTRELL 2009 T BARRICA
monastrell, syrah.

86 Colour: cherry, purple rim. Nose: red berry notes, floral, sweet spices. Palate: flavourful, fruity, good acidity, round tannins.

VERMADOR ECOLÓGICO 2009 T
monastrell.

85 Colour: cherry, purple rim. Nose: floral, fresh fruit, fresh. Palate: flavourful, fruity, good acidity, easy to drink.

VERGEL SELECCIÓN BARRICAS 2008 T
syrah, merlot, monastrell.

88 Colour: cherry, purple rim. Nose: neat, creamy oak, ripe fruit, red berry notes. Palate: round tannins, toasty, flavourful.

PONTOS 1932 ALTA EXPRESIÓN 2008 TC
monastrell.

87 Colour: cherry, garnet rim. Nose: ripe fruit, balanced, creamy oak. Palate: fruity, flavourful, long, round tannins.

PONTOS CLASI 2006 TC
monastrell, merlot, cabernet sauvignon.

86 Colour: cherry, garnet rim. Nose: ripe fruit, creamy oak, neat. Palate: powerful, toasty, round tannins, long.

PRIMITIVO QUILES

Mayor, 4
03640 Monóvar (Alicante)
☎: +34 965 470 099 - Fax: +34 966 960 235
info@primitivoquiles.com
www.primitivoquiles.com

PRIMITIVO QUILES MONASTRELL-MERLOT 2008 T ROBLE
60% monastrell, 40% merlot.

84 Colour: cherry, garnet rim. Nose: overripe fruit, warm, roasted coffee, aromatic coffee. Palate: fine bitter notes, spirituous, round tannins.

RASPAY 2004 T RESERVA ESPECIAL
100% monastrell.

83 Colour: pale ruby, brick rim edge. Nose: ripe fruit, spicy, creamy oak, toasty, complex. Palate: toasty, slightly evolved, balsamic.

GRAN IMPERIAL GE RESERVA ESPECIAL
100% moscatel.

92 Colour: dark mahogany. Nose: powerfull, fruit liqueur notes, fruit liqueur notes, varnish, tar, honeyed notes.* Palate: powerful, sweet, concentrated, long, spicy.

PRIMITIVO QUILES FONDILLÓN 1948 GE
100% monastrell.

88 Colour: iodine, amber rim. Nose: acetaldehyde, dry nuts, expressive. Palate: balanced, spirituous, flavourful.

PRIMITIVO QUILES MONASTRELL 2006 TC
100% monastrell.

82 Colour: cherry, garnet rim. Nose: ripe fruit, spicy. Palate: flavourful, toasty, round tannins.

PRIMITIVO QUILES MOSCATEL EXTRA VINO DE LICOR
100% moscatel.

86 Colour: light mahogany. Nose: characterful, varietal, candied fruit, acetaldehyde, toasty, dark chocolate. Palate: powerful, flavourful, fleshy.

SALVADOR POVEDA

CV 830 Ctra. Salinas, Km. 3
03640 Monóvar (Alicante)
☎: +34 966 960 180 - Fax: +34 965 473 389
salvadorpoveda@salvadorpoveda.com
www.salvadorpoveda.com

MOSCATEL B
100% moscatel.

88 Colour: golden. Nose: powerfull, honeyed notes, candied fruit, fragrant herbs. Palate: flavourful, sweet, fresh, fruity, good acidity, long.

TOSCAR MONASTRELL 2008 T
100% monastrell.

88 Colour: cherry, garnet rim. Nose: spicy, toasty, powerfull, ripe fruit. Palate: powerful, flavourful, toasty, round tannins.

POVEDA CABERNET-MERLOT 2008 TC
60% cabernet sauvignon, 40% merlot.

86 Colour: cherry, garnet rim. Nose: ripe fruit, toasty, complex. Palate: powerful, flavourful, toasty, round tannins, fruity.

TOSCAR SYRAH 2008 T
100% syrah.

86 Colour: cherry, garnet rim. Nose: ripe fruit, fruit expression, fresh, expressive. Palate: correct, light-bodied, flavourful.

TOSCAR MERLOT 2008 TC
100% merlot.

86 Colour: cherry, garnet rim. Nose: ripe fruit, toasty, complex, powerfull. Palate: powerful, flavourful, toasty, round tannins.

VIÑA VERMETA 2007 TC
85% monastrell, 15% tempranillo.

86 Color cherry, garnet rim. Aroma ripe fruit, spicy, creamy oak, toasty, complex. Taste powerful, flavourful, toasty, round tannins.

BORRASCA 2004 T
100% monastrell.

85 Color cherry, garnet rim. Aroma ripe fruit, spicy, creamy oak, toasty, complex. Taste powerful, flavourful, toasty, round tannins.

VIÑA VERMETA 2004 TR
85% monastrell, 15% otras.

83 Colour: pale ruby, brick rim edge. Nose: spicy, fine reductive notes, wet leather, aged wood nuances, fruit liqueur notes. Palate: spicy, fine tannins, elegant.

FONDILLÓN 1987 S/C FONDILLÓN GRAN RESERVA
100% monastrell.

90 Color dark mahogany. Aroma complex, fruit liqueur notes, dried fruit, pattiserie, toasty. Taste sweet, rich, unctuous, powerful.

VINS DEL COMTAT

Turballos, 1 - 3
03820 Cocentaina (Alicante)
☎: +34 965 593 194 - Fax: +34 965 593 590
vinsdelcomtat@gmail.com
www.vinsdelcomtat.com

CRISTAL.LI 2009 B
100% moscatel.

91 Colour: golden. Nose: powerfull, floral, candied fruit, fragrant herbs, tropical fruit. Palate: flavourful, sweet, fresh, fruity, good acidity, long.

PEÑA CADIELLA 2007 T ROBLE
20% cabernet sauvignon, 40% monastrell, 20% merlot, 10% tempranillo, 10% giró.

87 Colour: bright cherry. Nose: ripe fruit, sweet spices. Palate: flavourful, fruity, toasty, round tannins.

SERRELLA 2007 T
33% pinot noir, 33% petit verdot, 33% monastrell.

86 Colour: bright cherry. Nose: spicy, ripe fruit, creamy oak. Palate: flavourful, fleshy, round tannins.

MAIGMÓ 2007 T
100% monastrell.

85 Colour: black cherry. Nose: expressive, ripe fruit, neat. Palate: spirituous, fruity, flavourful.

PENYA CADIELLA SELECCIÓ 2006 T
30% monastrell, 30% cabernet sauvignon, 20% merlot, 10% syrah, 10% tempranillo, 10% giró.

91 Colour: cherry, garnet rim. Nose: spicy, creamy oak, ripe fruit, woody. Palate: powerful, flavourful, toasty, round tannins.

MONTCABRER 2006 T BARRICA
100% cabernet sauvignon.

88 Colour: cherry, garnet rim. Nose: spicy, creamy oak, toasty, ripe fruit. Palate: powerful, flavourful, toasty, round tannins.

VIÑEDOS CULTURALES

Purísima, 15 Bajo
03380 Bigastro (Alicante)
☎: +34 966 770 353 - Fax: +34 966 770 353
vinedosculturales@gmail.com

LOS CIPRESES DE USALDÓN 2010 T
100% garnacha peluda.

91 Colour: cherry, purple rim. Nose: expressive, red berry notes, fruit expression, scrubland. Palate: flavourful, balsamic, spicy.

LA AMISTAD 2010 T
rojal.

87 Colour: light cherry, garnet rim. Nose: ripe fruit, mineral, scrubland. Palate: light-bodied, flavourful, sweetness.

VC MADERA 2009 T
100% syrah.

95 Colour: bright cherry. Nose: sweet spices, creamy oak, expressive, red berry notes, ripe fruit. Palate: flavourful, fruity, toasty, round tannins.

VC METAL 2009 T
80% monastrell, 20% syrah.

95 Colour: bright cherry. Nose: sweet spices, expressive, new oak, ripe fruit, aromatic coffee, dark chocolate. Palate: flavourful, fruity, toasty, round tannins.

VC TIERRA 2009 T
80% tempranillo, 20% tempranillo.

94 Colour: cherry, garnet rim. Nose: toasty, complex, overripe fruit, fruit expression, cocoa bean. Palate: powerful, flavourful, toasty, round tannins.

VC FUEGO 2009 T
90% merlot, 10% cabernet sauvignon.

92 Colour: cherry, garnet rim. Nose: toasty, complex, overripe fruit, sweet spices. Palate: powerful, flavourful, toasty, round tannins.

VC AGUA 2009 T
80% cabernet sauvignon, 20% tempranillo.

92 Color cherry, garnet rim. Aroma ripe fruit, spicy, creamy oak, toasty, complex. Taste powerful, flavourful, toasty, round tannins.

VC FUSIÓN 2009 T
70% cabernet sauvignon, 15% merlot, 10% tempranillo, 2,5% syrah, 2,5% monastrell.

92 Colour: bright cherry. Nose: ripe fruit, sweet spices, creamy oak, mineral. Palate: flavourful, fruity, toasty, round tannins.

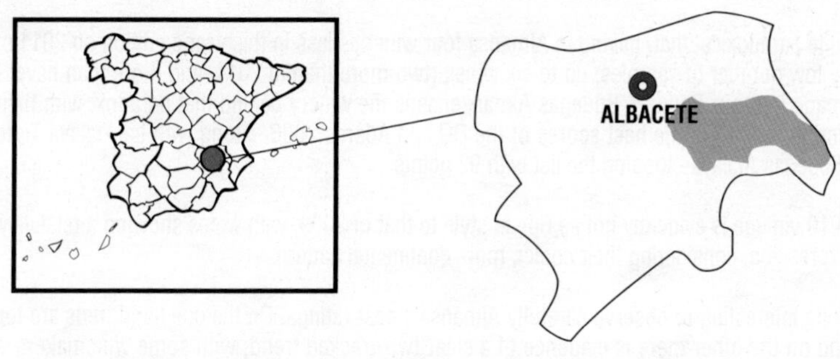

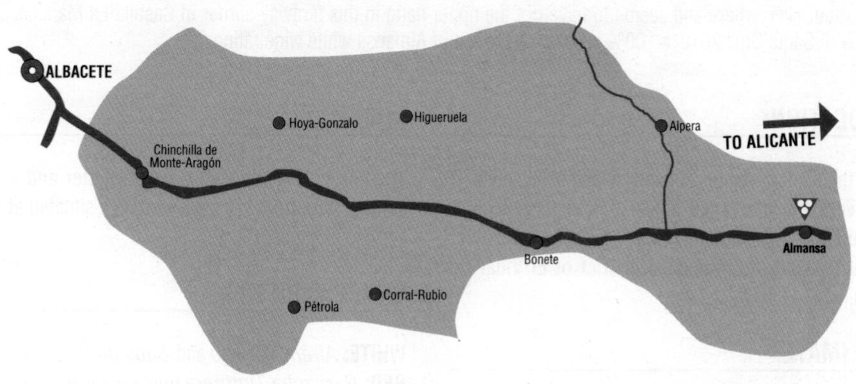

Consejo Regulador
DO Boundary

DO ALMANSA

NEWS ABOUT THE VINTAGE:

It is quite paradoxical that, having in Almansa four wineries less in this year's edition on 2011's and an equally low number of samples, up to six wines (two more than in 2011, and more than never before) have made it to our Podium. Bodegas Almanseñas is the winery behind that paradox, with their wines accounting for half of the best scores of the DO and Adarás 2006 –along with La Atalaya Tinto 2009, from Bodegas Atalaya– topping the list with 92 points.

The 2010 vintage is evidently not as ripe in style to that of 2009, with wines showing a relatively higher fruit expression, considering their cooler, more continental pattern.

It is quite interesting to observe carefully Almansa's best ratings. On the one hand, reds are top of the list, and on the other there is evidence of a clear two-tracked trend, with some winemakers working exclusively with *garnacha tintorera* to try and exact that grape variety's singularity and potential, and those whose bet is on blending it with the local *monastrell* and sometimes even *syrah*. In any case, the use of *garnacha tintorera* by the young generation of winemakers instead of *cencibel* (*tempranillo*) is just common sense –for the former is better adapted to the extreme climate of the region– and ultimately means glad tidings for the DO.

We just managed to taste three white wines from Almansa, and curiously enough not a single one of them has any airén in it. Instead of that most traditional white grape variety in the region, *verdejo* is just about everywhere and seems to have got the upper hand in this faraway corner of Castilla-La Mancha, with Santa Cruz 2010, a 100% *verdejo*, at the top of Almansa white wine ratings.

LOCATION:

In the eastern region of the province of Albacete. It covers the municipal areas of Almansa, Alpera, Bonete, Corral Rubio, Higueruela, Hoya Gonzalo, Pétrola and the municipal district of El Villar de Chinchilla.

CLIMATE:

Of a continental type, somewhat less extreme than the climate of La Mancha, although the summers are very hot, with temperatures which easily reach 40 °C. Rainfall, on the other hand, is scant, an average of about 350 mm a year. The majority of the vineyards are situated on the plains, although there are a few situated on the slopes.

SOIL:

The soil is limy, poor in organic matter and with some clayey areas. The vineyards are situated at an altitude of about 700 m.

GRAPE VARIETIES:

WHITE: *Airén, Verdejo* and *Sauvignon Blanc.*
RED: *Garnacha Tintorera* (most popular), *Cencibel* (*Tempranillo*), *Monastrell* (second most popular), *Syrah.*

FIGURES:

Vineyard surface: 7,600 – **Wine-Growers:** 760 – **Wineries:** 12 – **2010 Harvest rating:** Very Good – **Production:** 2,909,000 litres – **Market percentages:** 25% domestic. 75% export

CONSEJO REGULADOR
Méndez Núñez, 5. Apdo. 158
02640 Almansa (Albacete)
☎: +34 967 340 258. Fax: +34 967 310 842
@ crdo@tvalmansa.es
www.vinosdealmansa.com

GENERAL CHARACTERISTICS OF THE WINES

WHITES	These are produced mainly from the *Airén* variety. They are pale yellow, light, fruity and pleasant, in line with the wines from La Mancha.
ROSÉS	These are pink or salmon pink; fresh and fruity with an honest nose and are usually full - bodied and easy drinking.
REDS	The *Garnacha Tintorera* has over the past few years recovered the prominence of the DO, producing strong, fruity, fresh and meaty wines, especially since it is now bottled more selectively instead of being sold in bulk. Up to then, the most characteristic reds were the young wines of *Cencibel*, with an intense cherry colour and a fruity character. All of them stand out for a certain acidity on the palate due to the altitude of the vineyards.

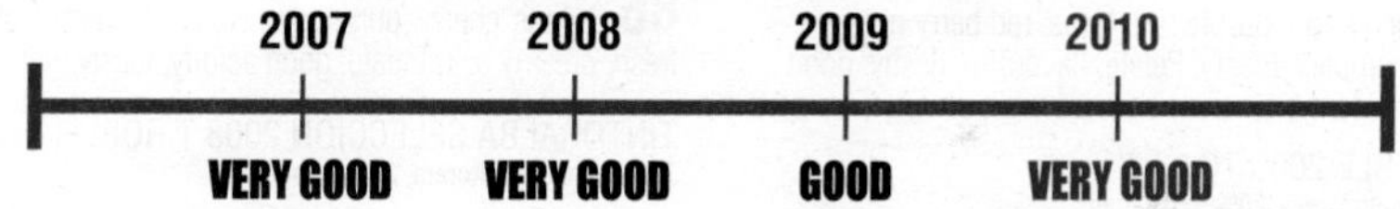

BODEGA SANTA CRUZ DE ALPERA

Cooperativa, s/n
02690 Alpera (Albacete)
☎: +34 967 330 108 - Fax: +34 967 330 903
comercial@bodegassantacruz.com
www.bodegasantacruz.com

SANTA CRUZ 2010 B
100% verdejo.

89 Colour: bright straw. Nose: complex, floral, tropical fruit, citrus fruit. Palate: good acidity, balanced, fruity, flavourful.

SANTA CRUZ 2010 RD
100% syrah.

84 Colour: rose, purple rim. Nose: floral, raspberry, fresh fruit, grassy. Palate: good acidity, fresh, light-bodied.

SANTA CRUZ 2010 T
100% garnacha tintorera.

90 Colour: cherry, purple rim. Nose: violet drops, raspberry, fresh fruit, expressive. Palate: fruity, powerful, flavourful, fleshy.

SANTA CRUZ (MOSTO PARCIALMENTE FERMENTADO) 2010 T
100% syrah.

84 Colour: cherry, purple rim. Nose: raspberry, ripe fruit, fresh. Palate: sweet, fruity, flavourful.

RUPESTRE 2009 T ROBLE
100% garnacha tintorera.

89 Colour: cherry, purple rim. Nose: red berry notes, powerfull, complex, toasty. Palate: flavourful, fleshy, good acidity, round tannins.

ALBARROBLE 2009 TC
80% garnacha tintorera, 20% monastrell.

87 Colour: cherry, garnet rim. Nose: toasty, ripe fruit, balanced. Palate: good acidity, flavourful, powerful, fleshy.

BODEGA TINTORALBA, COOPERATIVA AGRARIA SANTA QUITERIA

Baltasar González Sáez, 34
02694 Higueruela (Albacete)
☎: +34 967 287 012 - Fax: +34 967 287 031
direccion@tintoralba.com
www.tintoralba.com

DULCE TINTORALBA 2010 T
100% garnacha tintorera.

84 Colour: cherry, purple rim. Nose: dark chocolate, cocoa bean, sweet spices, ripe fruit. Palate: good acidity, concentrated, rich, flavourful.

HIGUERUELA 2010 T
100% garnacha tintorera.

89 Colour: cherry, purple rim. Nose: fresh fruit, red berry notes, expressive, floral. Palate: flavourful, fruity, fleshy, easy to drink.

TINTORALBA 2009 T ROBLE
65% garnacha tintorera, 35% syrah.

86 Colour: cherry, purple rim. Nose: red berry notes, fresh, creamy oak. Palate: good acidity, toasty, rich.

TINTORALBA SELECCIÓN 2008 T ROBLE
70% garnacha tintorera, 30% syrah.

88 Colour: cherry, garnet rim. Nose: aromatic coffee, creamy oak, ripe fruit, powerfull. Palate: powerful, flavourful, fleshy, toasty.

BODEGAS ALMANSEÑAS

Ctra. de Alpera, CM 3201 Km. 96,6
02640 Almansa (Albacete)
☎: +34 967 098 116 - Fax: +34 967 098 121
adaras@ventalavega.com
www.ventalavega.com

ADARAS SELECCIÓN 2010 BFB
sauvignon blanc, verdejo.

88 Colour: bright straw. Nose: balanced, creamy oak, fine lees, spicy. Palate: unctuous, flavourful, complex, creamy.

ALDEA DE ADARAS 2010 T
100% monastrell.

88 Colour: deep cherry. Nose: red berry notes, fresh fruit, expressive, floral. Palate: correct, fruity, flavourful, fleshy.

LA HUELLA DE ADARAS 2008 T
garnacha, monastrell, syrah.

90 Colour: cherry, purple rim. Nose: ripe fruit, dark chocolate, cocoa bean, expressive, scrubland. Palate: fruity, flavourful, round tannins, complex.

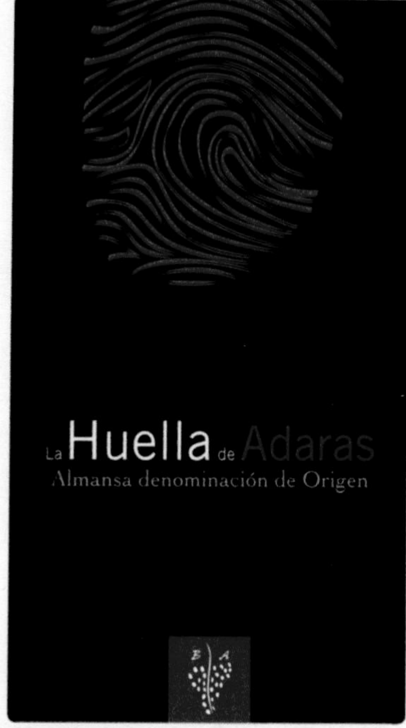

CALIZO DE ADARAS 2010 T
garnacha tintorera, monastrell, petit verdot, syrah.

90 Colour: cherry, purple rim. Nose: mineral, red berry notes, raspberry, complex. Palate: balanced, good acidity, fruity, fleshy, mineral.

LA HUELLA DE ADARAS 2010 B
verdejo, sauvignon blanc, monastrell.

85 Colour: bright straw. Nose: white flowers, fresh fruit, fragrant herbs. Palate: good acidity, balanced, fruity.

LA VEGA DE ADARAS 2008 T
garnacha tintorera, monastrell.

89 Colour: cherry, garnet rim. Nose: mineral, earthy notes, spicy, toasty. Palate: balsamic, spicy, fleshy, powerful, flavourful.

ADARAS 2006 T
garnacha tintorera.

92 Colour: cherry, garnet rim. Nose: ripe fruit, expressive, complex, cocoa bean, creamy oak. Palate: good acidity, flavourful, complex, fleshy, soft tannins.

BODEGAS ATALAYA

Ctra. Almansa - Ayora, Km. 1
02640 Almansa (Albacete)
☎: +34 968 435 022 - Fax: +34 968 716 051
info@orowines.com
www.orowines.com

LA ATALAYA 2009 T
85% garnacha tintorera, 15% monastrell.

92 Colour: black cherry, garnet rim. Nose: spicy, cocoa bean, red berry notes, balanced, mineral. Palate: powerful, fleshy, concentrated, flavourful, creamy.

ALAYA 2009 T
100% garnacha tintorera.

91 Colour: cherry, garnet rim. Nose: red berry notes, candied fruit, expressive. Palate: creamy, rich, flavourful, fruity, sweetness.

LAYA 2009 T
70% garnacha tintorera, 30% monastrell.

90 Colour: cherry, garnet rim. Nose: powerfull, expressive, red berry notes, cocoa bean, creamy oak. Palate: spicy, fleshy, concentrated, flavourful.

SANTA ROSA

Valle Inclan, 2 4ºG
02640 Almansa (Albacete)
☎: +34 967 342 296 - Fax: +34 967 310 481
cristobal@agricolassantarosa.com
www.matamangos.com

MATAMANGOS SYRAH 2007 T
syrah.

88 Colour: cherry, garnet rim. Nose: ripe fruit, dark chocolate, sweet spices, aromatic coffee, toasty. Palate: good acidity, round, powerful, flavourful, fleshy.

MATAMANGOS 2006 TC
monastrell, garnacha.

86 Colour: cherry, garnet rim. Nose: ripe fruit, creamy oak, toasty, sweet spices. Palate: powerful, flavourful, toasty, round tannins.

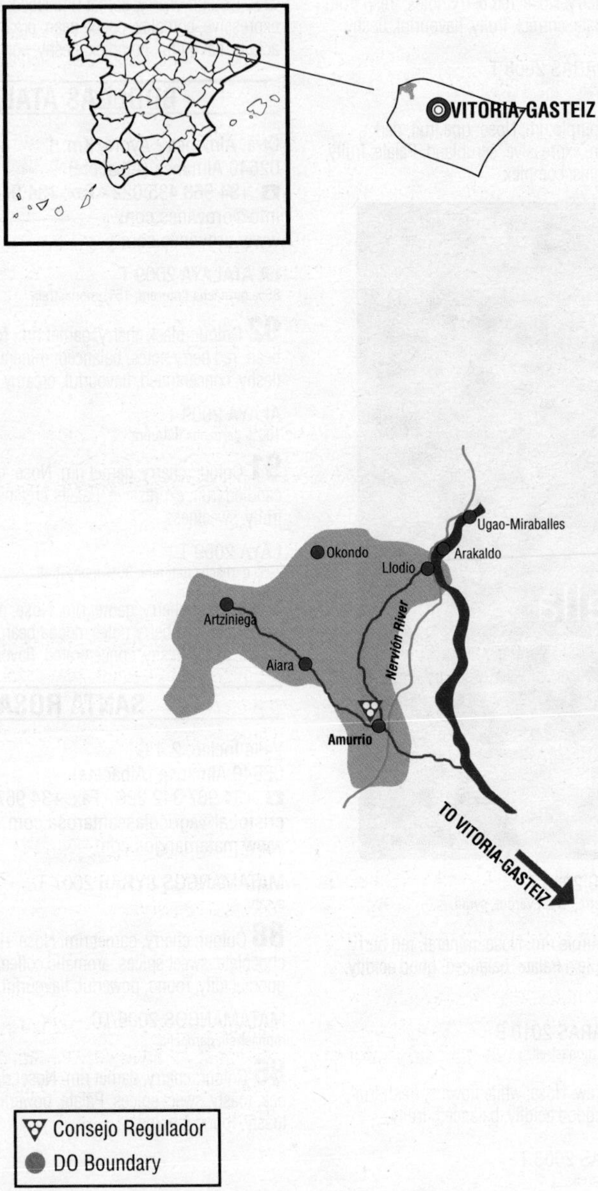

VITORIA-GASTEIZ
Ugao-Miraballes
Arakaldo
Okondo
Llodio
Nervión River
Artziniega
Aiara
Amurrio
TO VITORIA-GASTEIZ
Consejo Regulador
DO Boundary

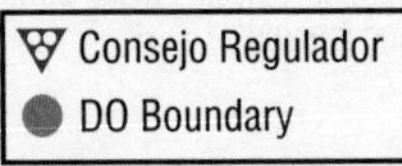

NEWS ABOUT THE VINTAGE:

In the light of the number of registered wineries, the DO Arabako Txakolina is going through a growing phase, from only two wineries in 2005 to seven in 2011, having doubled as well its vineyard surface in just twelve years. As it is usually the case in small wine regions, changes happen slowly but surely.

Arabako Txakolina seems to remain focused on the local market rather than in foreign ones. We deem that is just a political issue, related to the way that the province of Álava wants to have its own txakoli label –same as the neighbouring Basque provinces of Vizcaya and Guipúzcoa– and obviously with its eye set on the subsidies promised by the Basque government. So far, Arabako Txakolina is evidently lagging behind its sister designations, Bizkaiko Txakolina and Getariako Txakolina (from Vizcaya and Guipúzcoa, respectively), at least in regard to its markets, pre-eminently local, as we have already mentioned above. The DO's aspirations are as big as its own size, i.e., quite small both in terms of vineyard surface and total production, so it is no surprising to find no prominent brands or wineries. We only managed to taste two wines, a figure which does not allow us to come up with any quality assessment for the 2010 vintage.

From the climatic point o view, 2010 has not been a bad year in the region, in spite of heavy rainfall during springtime, late flowering and the resulting abnormal fruit set and production loss for early varieties. The absence of rains in the last part of the cycle allowed a good ripening pattern and healthy grapes, at least in the light of the two sampled wines.

LOCATION:

It covers the region of Aiara (Ayala), situated in the north west of the province of Alava on the banks of the Nervion river basin. Specifically, it is made up of the municipalities of Amurrio, Artziniega, Aiara (Ayala), Laudio (Llodio) and Okondo.

CLIMATE:

Similar to that of the DO Bizkaiko Txakolina, determined by the influence of the Bay of Biscay, although somewhat less humid and slightly drier and fresher. In fact, the greatest risk in the region stems from frost in the spring. However, it should not be forgotten that part of its vineyards borders on the innermost plantations of the DO Bizkaiko Txakolina.

SOIL:

A great variety of formations are found, ranging from clayey to fundamentally stony, precisely those which to date are producing the best results and where fairly stable grape ripening is achieved.

GRAPE VARIETIES:

MAIN: *Hondarrabi Zuri* (80%).
AUTHORIZED: *Petit Manseng, Petit Corbu* and *Gross Manseng*.

FIGURES:

Vineyard surface: 100 – **Wine-Growers:** 52 – **Wineries:** 7 – **2010 Harvest rating:** Very Good – **Production:** 301,034 litres – **Market percentages:** 80% domestic. 20% export

DO ARABAKO TXAKOLINA

CONSEJO REGULADOR

Dionisio Aldama, 7- 1ºD Apdo. 36

01470 Amurrio (Álava)

☎: +34 945 393 786 / 656 789 372 - Fax: +34 945 891 211

@ merino@txakolidealava.com

www.txakolidealava.com

GENERAL CHARACTERISTICS OF THE WINES

WHITES	Produced mainly from the autochthonous variety *Hondarrabi Zuri*, the Txakoli from Álava is very similar to those from the other two provinces of the Basque Country, especially those from Bizkaia. They are pale steely or greenish, with hints of fresh herbs and a fruity character slightly more aged than their neighbours. On the palate, they are slightly more round and full-bodied thanks to a slightly higher alcohol content and, although fresh, they are less acidic on the palate.

BODEGA SEÑORÍO DE ASTOBIZA, OKENDO TXAKOLINA

Barrio Jandiola, 16 (Caserío Aretxabala)
01409 Okondo (Álava)
☎: +34 945 898 516 - Fax: +34 945 898 447
comercial@senoriodeastobiza.com
www.senoriodeastobiza.com

SEÑORÍO DE ASTOBIZA 2010 B
55% hondarrabi zuri, 35% gros manseng, 15% petit corbu. HHHH8€

87 Colour: bright straw. Nose: white flowers, fresh fruit, fragrant herbs, expressive. Palate: fresh, fruity, easy to drink.

MALKOA TXAKOLI 2009 B
100% hondarrabi zuri.

89 Colour: bright straw. Nose: fresh, white flowers, expressive, mineral. Palate: flavourful, fruity, good acidity, balanced.

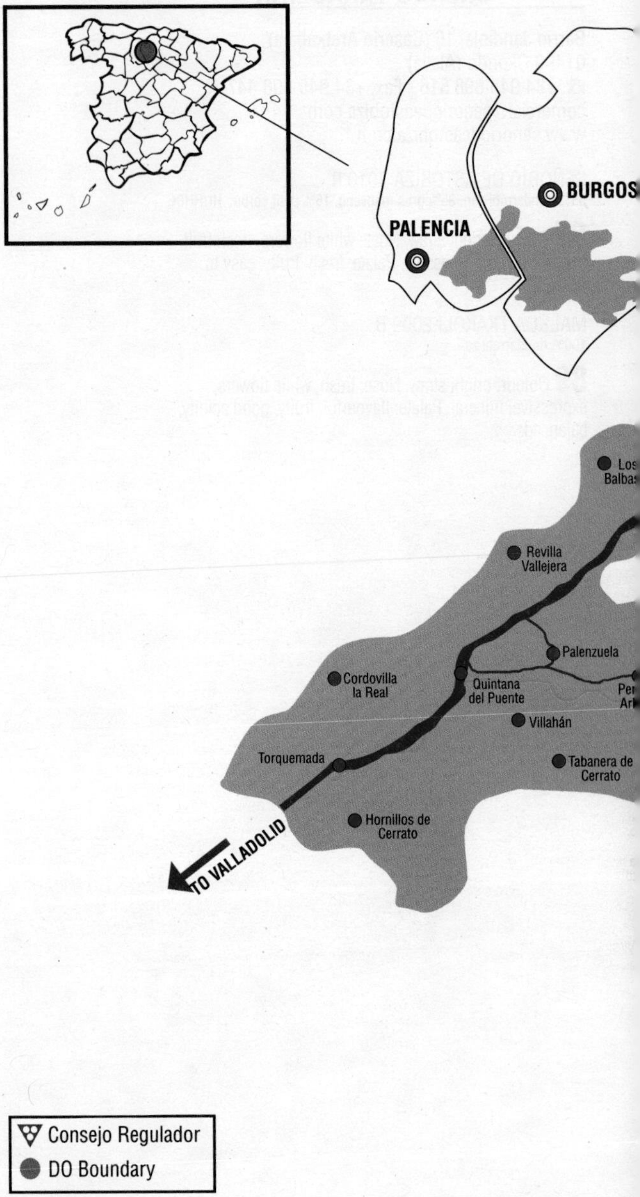
BURGOS
PALENCIA
Revilla Vallejera
Palenzuela
Cordovilla la Real
Quintana del Puente
Villahán
Torquemada
Tabanera de Cerrato
Hornillos de Cerrato
TO VALLADOLID
Consejo Regulador
DO Boundary

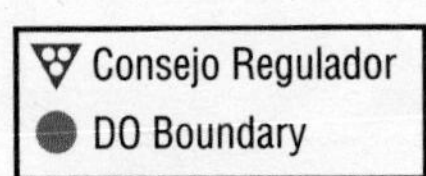

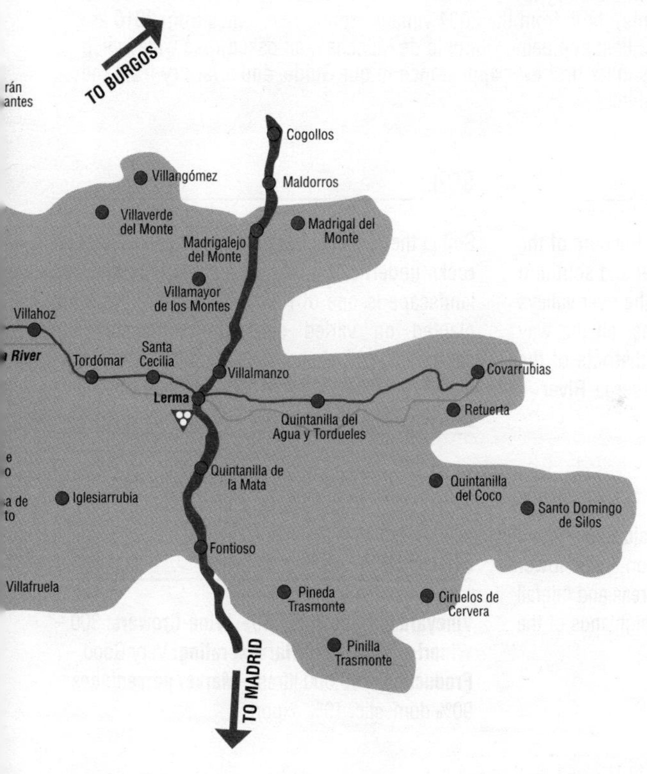
TO BURGOS
Cogollos
Maldorros
Villangómez
Villaverde del Monte
Madrigal del Monte
Madrigalejo del Monte
Villamayor de los Montes
Villahoz
River
Tordómar
Santa Cecilia
Villalmanzo
Covarrubias
Lerma
Retuerta
Quintanilla del Agua y Tordueles
Quintanilla de la Mata
Iglesiarrubia
Quintanilla del Coco
Santo Domingo de Silos
Fontioso
Villafruela
Pineda Trasmonte
Ciruelos de Cervera
Pinilla Trasmonte
TO MADRID

DO ARLANZA

NEWS ABOUT THE VINTAGE:

Arlanza has many similarities with neighbouring DO Ribera del Duero. They share the same continental climate with strong Atlantic influence and limestone soils, so the differences between them in terms of quality rest only on altitude. In Ribera del Duero the management of frost risks is the key factor to obtain a good or a bad harvest, and in Arlanza that is even more crucial, so in cooler years it is quite common to find strong herbaceous (green) notes and higher acidity levels. This year we have tasted 12 more samples on last year's figures, and up to 8 wines reached 90 points or above, compared to just three in 2011.

The 2010 vintage was generally cooler than 2009, but grapes reach good maturity levels in spite of spring frost and heavy rainfall during flowering, all of which meant lower production. In terms of tasting, red wines are pretty similar to those of 2009, with good balance and acidity, and fresh balsamic notes. The best wines from Arlanza, though, are crianza wines mainly from Bodegas Buezo –50% of the wines above 89 points belong to this winery–: Buezo Nattan (92 points) and Buezo Petit Verdot-Tempranillo (91 points), both from the 2004 vintage. Young rosé wines from 2010 are better than those from 2009, the best one being Dominio de Manciles, an oaked rosé wine which has managed to reach 90 points in its first ever appearance in our Guide, and a far cry from the poorer performances of young whites.

LOCATION:

With the medieval city of Lerma at the core of the region, Arlanza occupies the central and southern part of the province of Burgos, on the river valleys of the Arlanza and its subsidiaries, all the way westwards through 13 municipal districts of the province of Palencia until the Pisuerga River is reached.

CLIMATE:

The climate of this wine region is said to be one of the harshest within Castilla y León, with lower temperatures towards the western areas and rainfall higher on the eastern parts, in the highlands of the province of Soria.

SOIL:

Soil in the region is not particularly deep, with soft rocks underneath and good humidity levels. The landscape is one of rolling hills where vines are planted on varied soils, from limestone to calcareous, with abundant granite on certain areas.

GRAPE VARIETIES:

RED: *Tempranillo, Garnacha* and *Mencía.*
WHITE: *Albillo* and *Viura.*

FIGURES:

Vineyard surface: 445,560 – **Wine-Growers:** 300 – **Wineries:** 14 – **2010 Harvest rating:** Very Good – **Production:** 740,000 litres – **Market percentages:** 90% domestic. 10% export

CONSEJO REGULADOR
Ronda de la Cárcel, 4
09340 Lerma (Burgos)
☎: +34 947 171 046 - Fax: +34 947 171 046
@ info@arlanza.org
www.arlanza.org

GENERAL CHARACTERISTICS OF THE WINES

REDS	Mostly made from *Tempranillo* grapes, they keep certain similarities with those from Ribera de Duero -both regions enjoy an extreme Atlantic climate-, although they have a stronger roasted character, fresher fruit and softer tannins. As we travel westwards and the altitude gets lower, wines get more powerful and increase their alcohol content, but probably the greatest potential still to be achieved is related to acidity levels.

VINTAGE RATING PEÑÍNGUIDE

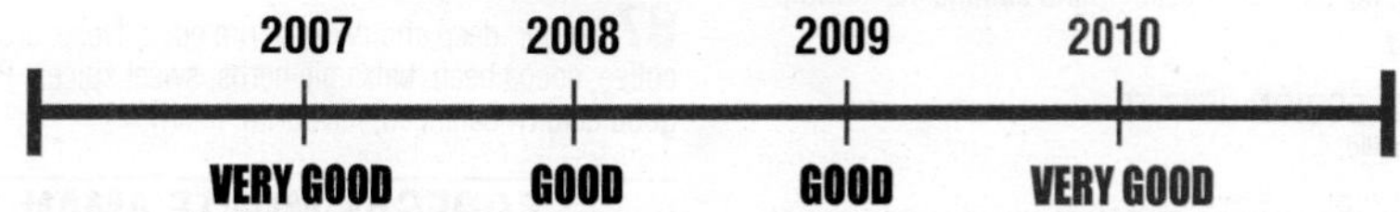

BODEGA LA COLEGIADA

Ctra. Madrid-Irún, Km. 202,5
09340 Lerma (Burgos)
☎: +34 947 177 030 - Fax: +34 947 177 004
info@tintolerma.com
www.tintolerma.com

RISCO 2010 RD
75% tempranillo, 15% garnacha, 10% viura.

86 Colour: rose, purple rim. Nose: raspberry, fresh fruit, floral, expressive. Palate: easy to drink, light-bodied, fresh, fruity.

NABAL 2008 TC
100% tempranillo.

89 Colour: cherry, garnet rim. Nose: red berry notes, caramel, sweet spices, creamy oak. Palate: flavourful, fleshy, long.

TINTO LERMA 2008 TC
100% tempranillo.

87 Colour: cherry, garnet rim. Nose: ripe fruit, spicy, creamy oak, cocoa bean. Palate: round tannins, flavourful, fleshy, spicy.

LERMA SELECCIÓN 2007 TR
100% tempranillo.

87 Colour: cherry, garnet rim. Nose: sweet spices, cocoa bean, toasty, ripe fruit. Palate: balsamic, spicy, fleshy, long.

BODEGAS ARLANZA

Ctra. Madrid-Irún km 203, 800
09390 Villalmanzo (Burgos)
☎: +34 947 172 070 - Fax: +34 947 170 259
comercial@bodegasarlanza.com
www.bodegasarlanza.com

DOMINIO DE MANCILES 2010 B
50% viura, 50% albillo.

84 Colour: bright straw. Nose: citrus fruit, white flowers, fragrant herbs. Palate: fresh, light-bodied, flavourful.

DOMINIO DE MANCILES 2010 RD BARRICA
60% tempranillo, 40% garnacha.

90 Colour: brilliant rose. Nose: red berry notes, ripe fruit, sweet spices, creamy oak. Palate: long, flavourful, fruity, fleshy. Personality.

DOMINIO DE MANCILES 2010 RD
60% tempranillo, 40% garnacha.

86 Colour: rose, purple rim. Nose: fresh, raspberry, fresh fruit, floral. Palate: flavourful, light-bodied, fruity.

DOMINIO DE MANCILES 2010 T
80% tempranillo, 15% cabernet sauvignon, 5% mencía.

85 Colour: cherry, purple rim. Nose: red berry notes, fresh, floral. Palate: fruity, fresh, flavourful, easy to drink.

DOMINIO DE MANCILES 2009 T ROBLE
80% tempranillo, 15% cabernet sauvignon, 5% mencía.

82 Colour: cherry, garnet rim. Nose: tar, roasted coffee, aromatic coffee. Palate: good acidity, fleshy, toasty.

DOMINIO DE MANCILES SELECCIÓN 2007 TC
100% tempranillo.

85 Colour: cherry, garnet rim. Nose: aromatic coffee, caramel, red berry notes, ripe fruit. Palate: good acidity, flavourful, fleshy.

DOMINIO DE MANCILES 2005 TC
100% tempranillo.

86 Colour: cherry, garnet rim. Nose: red berry notes, ripe fruit, spicy, creamy oak. Palate: flavourful, fleshy, toasty, round tannins.

DOMINIO DE MANCILES 2004 TR
100% tempranillo.

87 Colour: deep cherry, brick rim edge. Nose: aromatic coffee, cocoa bean, balsamic herbs, sweet spices. Palate: good acidity, balanced, flavourful, fleshy.

BODEGAS MONTE AMÁN

Ctra. Santo Domingo de Silos, s/n
09348 Castrillo de Solarana (Burgos)
☎: +34 947 173 304 - Fax: +34 947 173 308
bodegas@monteaman.com
www.monteaman.com

MONTE AMÁN 2010 RD
100% tempranillo.

82 Colour: rose, purple rim. Nose: fresh, fresh fruit, medium intensity. Palate: fresh, light-bodied, easy to drink.

MONTE AMÁN 5 MESES DE BARRICA 2009 T ROBLE
100% tempranillo.

85 Colour: cherry, garnet rim. Nose: ripe fruit, creamy oak, sweet spices. Palate: flavourful, fleshy, toasty, good acidity.

MONTE AMÁN 2006 TC
100% tempranillo.

85 Colour: cherry, garnet rim. Nose: cocoa bean, spicy, toasty, ripe fruit. Palate: good acidity, flavourful, fleshy.

MONTE AMÁN PAGO DE VALDEÁGUEDA VIÑAS VIEJAS 2004 T
100% tempranillo.

87 Colour: light cherry, orangey edge. Nose: ripe fruit, cocoa bean, sweet spices, dark chocolate, creamy oak. Palate: good acidity, flavourful, fleshy.

MONTE AMÁN 2003 TR
100% tempranillo.

86 Colour: pale ruby, brick rim edge. Nose: red berry notes, ripe fruit, cocoa bean, spicy. Palate: balanced, unctuous, long, spicy.

BODEGAS SIERRA

Ctra. Madrid-Irún km 203,700
09390 Villalmanzo (Burgos)
☎: +34 947 170 083
info@bodegassierra.com
www.bodegassierra.com

CASTILLO DE URA 2010 B
verdejo.

87 Colour: bright straw. Nose: fragrant herbs, white flowers, expressive, tropical fruit. Palate: rich, flavourful, fruity, creamy.

CASCAJUELO 2009 T ROBLE
100% tempranillo.

90 Colour: cherry, garnet rim. Nose: red berry notes, cocoa bean, dark chocolate, toasty, expressive. Palate: fresh, light-bodied, flavourful, creamy.

CASTILLO DE URA TR

85 Colour: cherry, garnet rim. Nose: ripe fruit, cocoa bean, aromatic coffee, dark chocolate. Palate: good acidity, correct, toasty.

BUEZO

Paraje Valdeazadón, s/n
09342 Mahamud (Burgos)
☎: +34 947 616 899 - Fax: +34 947 616 885
rfranco@buezo.com
www.buezo.com

BUEZO NATTAN 2005 TC
tannat, tempranillo.

90 Colour: bright cherry, garnet rim. Nose: red berry notes, ripe fruit, spicy, toasty. Palate: fleshy, good structure, round tannins.

BUEZO VARIETALES 2004 TC
50% tempranillo, 25% merlot, 25% cabernet sauvignon.

89 Colour: cherry, garnet rim. Nose: ripe fruit, wild herbs, balanced. Palate: full, flavourful, fruity, good acidity.

BUEZO PETIT VERDOT TEMPRANILLO 2005 TC
50% petit verdot, 50% tempranillo.

89 Colour: cherry, garnet rim. Nose: candied fruit, sweet spices, mineral, aged wood nuances. Palate: flavourful, fruity, balanced.

BUEZO NATTAN 2004 TR
tempranillo, tannat.

92 Colour: bright cherry, garnet rim. Nose: elegant, medium intensity, balanced, red berry notes, sweet spices. Palate: good structure, fruity, spicy, round tannins, good acidity.

BUEZO PETIT VERDOT TEMPRANILLO 2004 T
50% petit verdot, 50% tempranillo.

91 Colour: bright cherry, garnet rim. Nose: medium intensity, balanced, red berry notes, spicy, mineral. Palate: flavourful, ripe fruit, great length, fruity aftestaste.

BUEZO TEMPRANILLO 2004 TC
100% tempranillo.

90 Colour: bright cherry, garnet rim. Nose: fresh, varietal, red berry notes, spicy. Palate: fruity, easy to drink, good acidity, spicy.

GARMENDIA VIÑEDOS Y BODEGA

Finca Santa Rosalia, s/n
34260 Vizmalo (Burgos)
☎: +34 947 166 171 - Fax: +34 947 166 147
info@bodegasgarmendia.com
www.bodegasgarmendia.com

GARMENDIA 2010 RD
garnacha, tempranillo.

88 Colour: rose, purple rim. Nose: floral, red berry notes, fresh fruit, lactic notes, expressive. Palate: fresh, fruity, rich, flavourful, fleshy.

GARMENDIA 2010 T
tempranillo.

90 Colour: cherry, purple rim. Nose: red berry notes, fresh fruit, lactic notes, expressive. Palate: fruity, flavourful, fleshy, easy to drink.

GARMENDIA 2009 T ROBLE
tinta del país.

87 Colour: cherry, purple rim. Nose: fruit liqueur notes, grassy, medium intensity. Palate: flavourful, fleshy, green.

PAGOS DE NEGREDO VIÑEDOS

Avda. Casado del Alisal, 26
34001 Palencia (Palencia)
☎: +34 979 700 450 - Fax: +34 979 702 171
administracion@pagosdenegredo.com
www.pagosdenegredo.com

PAGOS DE NEGREDO MAGNUM 2006 TC
100% tempranillo.

90 Colour: cherry, garnet rim. Nose: red berry notes, ripe fruit, balanced, expressive, spicy, toasty. Palate: powerful, flavourful, fruity, fleshy, good acidity, round tannins.

PALACIO DE LERMA

Ctra. Madrid-Irún, Km. 203
09340 Lerma (Burgos)
☎: +34 947 240 880 - Fax: +34 947 222 905
info@palaciodelerma.com
www.palaciodelerma.com

PALACIO DE LERMA 2006 TC
100% tempranillo.

84 Colour: cherry, garnet rim. Nose: candied fruit, spicy, creamy oak, expressive. Palate: flavourful, fleshy, toasty.

VITIVINÍCOLA LADRERO S.L.

Avda. de la Paz, 4
34230 Torquemada (Palencia)
☎: +34 979 800 545 - Fax: +34 979 800 545
bodega@ladrero.e.telefonica.net
www.bodegasladrero.es

SEÑORÍO DE VALDESNEROS 2010 RD
100% tempranillo.

85 Colour: rose, purple rim. Nose: raspberry, red berry notes, white flowers, fresh, expressive. Palate: fresh, fruity, flavourful.

SEÑORÍO DE VALDESNEROS 2008 T ROBLE
100% tempranillo.

86 Colour: cherry, purple rim. Nose: powerfull, ripe fruit, grassy. Palate: balsamic, lacks balance, easy to drink.

AMANTIA 2007 TC
100% tempranillo.

85 Colour: cherry, garnet rim. Nose: red berry notes, spicy, creamy oak. Palate: good acidity, unctuous, flavourful.

SEÑORÍO DE VALDESNEROS 2006 TC
100% tempranillo.

85 Colour: cherry, garnet rim. Nose: ripe fruit, red berry notes, creamy oak. Palate: fleshy, fruity, flavourful.

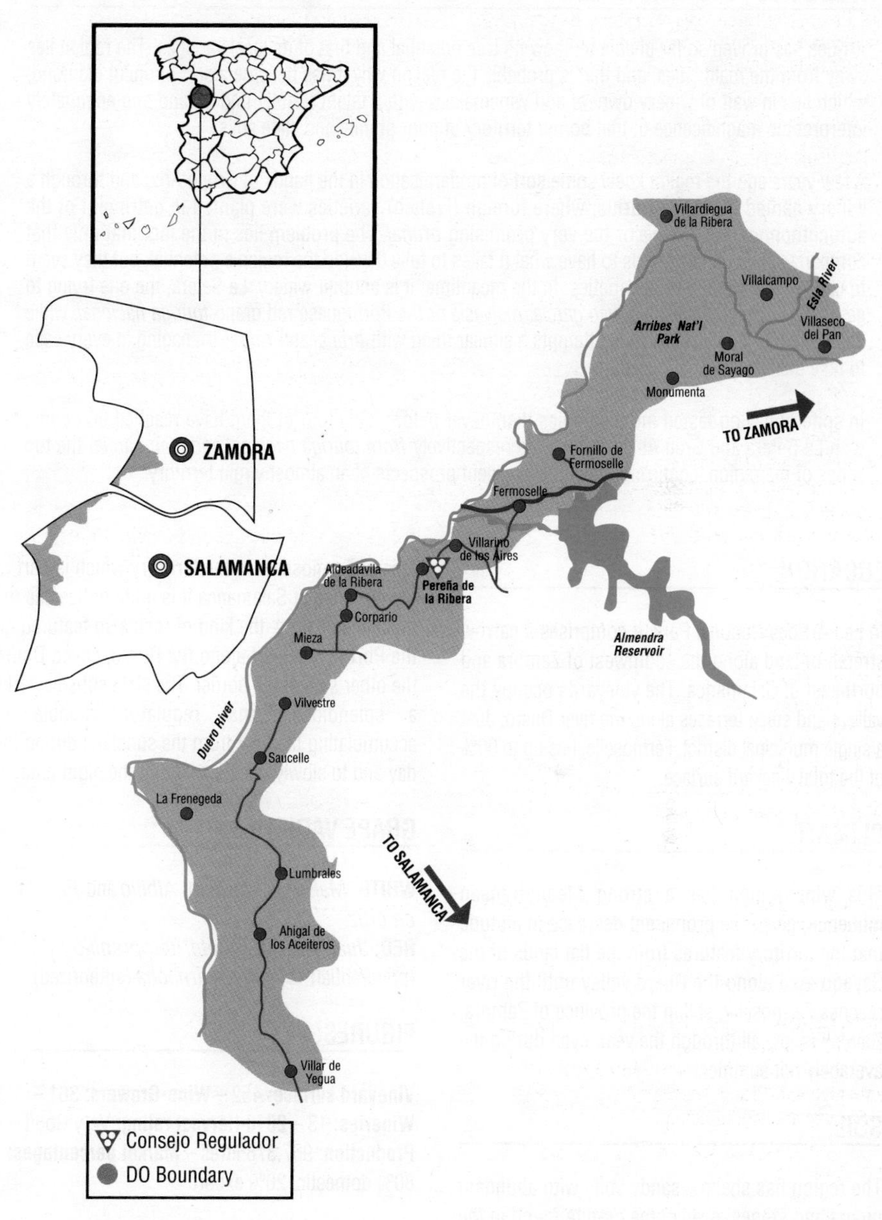
ZAMORA
SALAMANCA
Villardiegua de la Ribera
Villalcampo
Esla River
Villaseco del Pan
Arribes Nat'l Park
Moral de Sayago
Monumenta
TO ZAMORA
Fornillo de Fermoselle
Fermoselle
Villarino de los Aires
Aldeadávila de la Ribera
Pereña de la Ribera
Corpario
Mieza
Almendra Reservoir
Vilvestre
Duero River
Saucelle
La Frenegeda
TO SALAMANCA
Lumbrales
Ahigal de los Aceiteros
Villar de Yegua
Consejo Regulador
DO Boundary

DO ARRIBES

NEWS ABOUT THE VINTAGE:

Arribes has proved so far unable to show its true potential and that of its local varieties. The region lies away from the main cities, and that is probably the reason why it has become a sort of uncut diamond, which lies in wait of winery owners and winemakers with a talent to fully understand and adequately interpret the magnificence of that border territory of poor granite and slate soils.

A few years ago the region knew some sort of modernisation in the hands of Grupo Arco and through a winery named Hacienda Durius, where foreign (French) varieties were planted in detriment of the autochthonous *juan garcía* or the very promising *bruñal*. The problem lies in the fact that only that company (Grupo Arco) seems to have what it takes to fully develop the region's potential, but they seem to care little about the local varieties. In the meantime, it is another winery, La Setera, the one trying to get the best out varieties like *juan garcía*, *malvasía* or the Portuguese red grape *touriga nacional*, while another winery, Ocellvum Durii, attempts a similar thing with *bruñal* and *rufete*, managing in every case to take their wines to our Podium.

In spite of having tasted more samples than never before, only four of them have reached 90 points, with La Setera and Gran Abadengo (made respectively *from touriga nacional and juan garcía*) the top wines of the region, confirming thus the excellent prospects of an almost virgin territory.

LOCATION:

In Las Arribes National Park, it comprises a narrow stretch of land along the southwest of Zamora and northeast of Salamanca. The vineyards occupy the valleys and steep terraces along the river Duero. Just a single municipal district, Fermoselle, has up to 90% of the total vineyard surface.

CLIMATE:

This wine region has a strong Mediterranean influence, given the prominent decrease in altitude that the territory features from the flat lands of the Sáyago area along the Duero valley until the river reaches Fermoselle, still in the province of Zamora. Rainfall is low all through the year, even during the averagely hot summer.

SOIL:

The region has shallow sandy soils with abundant quartz and stones, even some granite found in the area of Fermoselle. In the territory which is part of the province of Salamanca it is quite noticeable the presence of slate, the kind of rock also featured on the Portuguese part along the Duero, called Douro the other side of the border. The slate subsoil works a splendid thermal regulator capable of accumulating the heat from the sunshine during the day and to slowly release it during the night time.

GRAPE VARIETIES:

WHITE: *Malvasía, Verdejo, Albillo* and *Puesta en cruz.*
RED: *Juan García, Rufete, Tempranillo* (preferential); *Mencía, Garnacha* (authorized).

FIGURES:

Vineyard surface: 452 – **Wine-Growers:** 361 – **Wineries:** 13 – **2010 Harvest rating:** Very Good – **Production:** 957,378 litres – **Market percentages:** 80% domestic. 20% export

CONSEJO REGULADOR
La Almofea, 95
37175 Pereña de la Ribera (Salamanca)
☎: +34 923 573 413 - Fax: +34 923 573 209
@ info@doarribes.com
www.vinoarribesduero.com

GENERAL CHARACTERISTICS OF THE WINES

WHITES	Very rare and made from *Malvasía*, they get all the benefits from sunshine and altitude as well as the mineral notes derived from the slate subsoil
REDS	Wines made with *Juan García* or *Rufete* are lighter both in colour and body and oxidize easily, although they can show an eminently fruity character when the grapes get the appropriate sunshine hours or the blend with other grape varieties is also adequate. Nevertheless, proper vineyard management is achieving a smaller grape size and thus stronger colour for the final wines made from these two varieties. Also quite noticeable are the strong mineral nuances provided by the slate subsoil that renders these wines very similar to those from the Douro, the name that the river Duero gets once it has got over the Portuguese border.

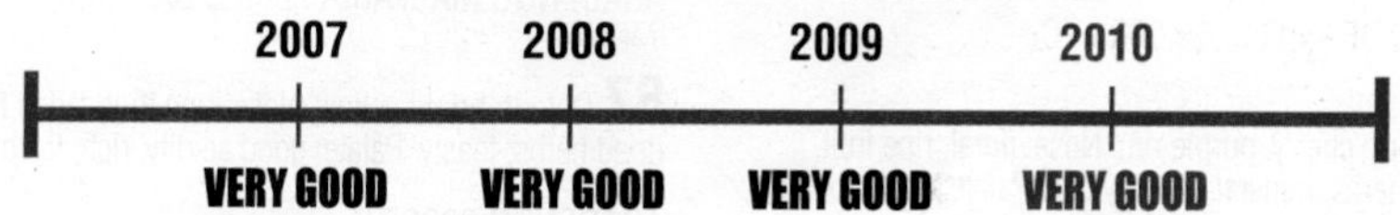

BODEGAS ARRIBES DE DUERO

Ctra. Masueco, s/n
37251 Corporario (Aldeadavila) (Salamanca)
☎: +34 923 169 195 - Fax: +34 923 169 019
secretaria@bodegasarribesdelduero.com
www.bodegasarribesdelduero.com

ARRIBES DE VETTONIA 2010 B
malvasía.

84 Colour: bright straw. Nose: fresh, faded flowers, ripe fruit. Palate: flavourful, fruity, easy to drink.

ARRIBES DE VETTONIA SEMI-DULCE 2010 B
malvasía.

83 Colour: bright straw. Nose: fresh, fresh fruit, white flowers, expressive. Palate: flavourful, fruity.

ARRIBES DE VETTONIA 2007 BFB
malvasía.

85 Colour: bright golden. Nose: ripe fruit, citrus fruit, balsamic herbs, creamy oak. Palate: warm, powerful, flavourful.

ARRIBES DE VETTONIA 2010 RD
juan garcía.

85 Colour: raspberry rose. Nose: red berry notes, raspberry, floral, fresh, expressive. Palate: good acidity, flavourful, fruity, easy to drink.

ARRIBES DE VETTONIA 2008 TC
juan garcía.

88 Colour: cherry, purple rim. Nose: floral, ripe fruit, balsamic herbs, mineral, creamy oak. Palate: light-bodied, flavourful, fleshy.

ARRIBES DE VETTONIA 2004 TR
juan garcía.

89 Colour: cherry, garnet rim. Nose: ripe fruit, balsamic herbs, fine reductive notes, spicy, creamy oak. Palate: ripe fruit, flavourful, fleshy.

BODEGAS LAS GAVIAS

Avda. Constitución, 2
37175 Pereña de la Ribera (Salamanca)
☎: +34 902 108 031 - Fax: +34 987 218 751
info@bodegaslasgavias.com
www.bodegaslasgavias.com

POZO DE LOS HUMOS 2010 B
malvasía.

75

POZO DE LOS HUMOS 2010 RD
juan garcía.

82 Colour: raspberry rose. Nose: floral, ripe fruit, medium intensity. Palate: good acidity, light-bodied, fresh.

POZO DE LOS HUMOS 2010 T
juan garcía.

85 Colour: deep cherry. Nose: ripe fruit, scrubland. Palate: fruity, flavourful, sweetness.

ALDANA T ROBLE
juan garcía.

85 Colour: light cherry, garnet rim. Nose: dried flowers, ripe fruit, sweet spices, creamy oak. Palate: correct, powerful, flavourful.

BODEGAS RIBERA DE PELAZAS

Camino de la Ermita, s/n
37175 Pereña de la Ribera (Salamanca)
☎: +34 902 108 031 - Fax: +34 987 218 751
bodega@bodegasriberadepelazas.com
www.bodegasriberadepelazas.com

ABADENGO 2010 B
malvasía.

88 Colour: pale. Nose: fresh fruit, floral, dried herbs, expressive. Palate: light-bodied, fresh, fruity, fleshy.

ABADENGO MALVASÍA 2009 B BARRICA
malvasía.

87 Colour: bright yellow. Nose: ripe fruit, faded flowers, dried herbs, toasty. Palate: good acidity, rich, flavourful.

ABADENGO 2006 TC
juan garcía.

88 Colour: cherry, garnet rim. Nose: ripe fruit, floral, cocoa bean, sweet spices, toasty. Palate: good acidity, round, flavourful.

GRAN ABADENGO 2005 TR
juan garcía.

91 Colour: cherry, garnet rim. Nose: ripe fruit, spicy, toasty, complex, aromatic coffee, earthy notes. Palate: powerful, flavourful, toasty, round tannins, complex.

BRUÑAL 2005 T
bruñal.

89 Colour: bright cherry. Nose: ripe fruit, sweet spices, creamy oak, fine reductive notes, mineral. Palate: flavourful, fruity, toasty, round tannins.

ABADENGO 2004 TR
juan garcía.

87 Colour: cherry, garnet rim. Nose: ripe fruit, toasty, fine reductive notes. Palate: spicy, powerful, fleshy, complex.

LA SETERA

Calzada, 7
49232 Fornillos de Fermoselle (Zamora)
☎: +34 980 612 925 - Fax: +34 980 612 925
lasetera@lasetera.com
www.lasetera.com

LA SETERA 2010 B
malvasía.

85 Colour: bright straw. Nose: citrus fruit, white flowers, dried herbs, mineral. Palate: light-bodied, fresh, flavourful.

LA SETERA ROSADO DE LÁGRIMA 2010 RD
verdejo colorado.

85 Colour: onion pink. Nose: white flowers, red berry notes, ripe fruit, medium intensity. Palate: good acidity, fruity, fresh.

LA SETERA 2010 T
juan garcía.

87 Colour: cherry, purple rim. Nose: ripe fruit, scrubland, earthy notes. Palate: good acidity, flavourful, fruity, sweetness.

LA SETERA 2008 T ROBLE
touriga.

92 Colour: bright cherry. Nose: ripe fruit, sweet spices, creamy oak, expressive, complex. Palate: flavourful, fruity, toasty, round tannins. Personality.

LA SETERA 2008 TC
juan garcía.

88 Colour: cherry, garnet rim. Nose: ripe fruit, spicy, complex, balsamic herbs. Palate: powerful, flavourful, toasty, long.

MARQUÉS DE LA CONCORDIA FAMILY OF WINES

Hacienda Zorita, Ctra. Ledesma, Km. 12
37115 Valverdón (Salamanca)
☎: +34 914 365 924
comunicacion@arcoinvest-group.com
www.haciendas-espana.com

HACIENDA ZORITA (MARQUÉS DE LA CONCORDIA) 2009 TC
100% tempranillo.

86 Colour: cherry, garnet rim. Nose: ripe fruit, scrubland, spicy, earthy notes, toasty. Palate: fleshy, complex, flavourful, ripe fruit, balanced.

OCELLUM DURII

San Juan 56 - 58
49220 Fermoselle (Zamora)
☎: +34 983 390 606
ocellumdurii@hotmail.com

CONDADO DE FERMOSEL 2010 T
juan garcía, garnacha, tempranillo, rufete, bruñal.

85 Colour: cherry, purple rim. Nose: ripe fruit, caramel, aromatic coffee, roasted coffee. Palate: powerful, flavourful, fruity.

TRANSITIUM DURII 2007 T
juan garcía, tempranillo, rufete, bruñal, garnacha.

91 Colour: black cherry, garnet rim. Nose: red berry notes, ripe fruit, dark chocolate, aromatic coffee, toasty, mineral. Palate: balanced, round, powerful, flavourful.

CONDADO DE FERMOSEL VENDIMIA SELECCIONADA 2006 TC
juan garcía, tempranillo.

90 Colour: black cherry, cherry, garnet rim. Nose: ripe fruit, complex, earthy notes, mineral, sweet spices, toasty. Palate: powerful, flavourful, fleshy, long.

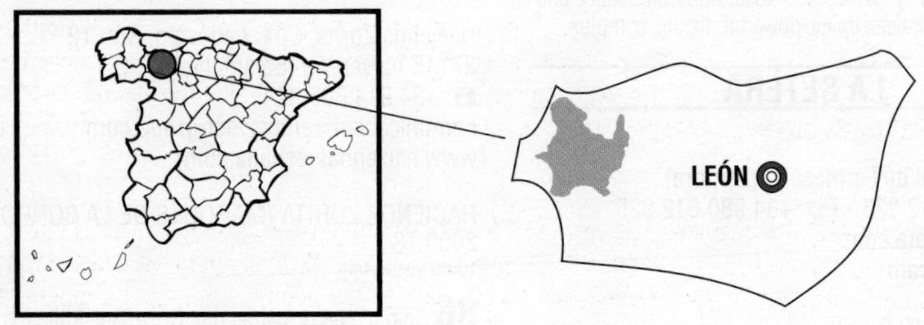

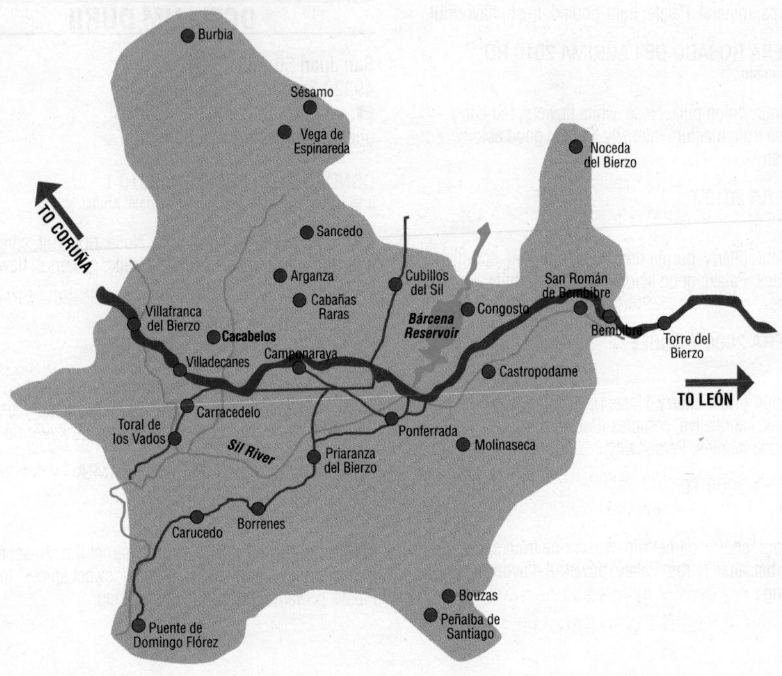

Consejo Regulador
DO Boundary

NEWS ABOUT THE VINTAGE:

Compared to 2009, 2010 seems to be a cooler vintage, though we are still missing the best signs of a truly great *mencía*, possibly due to uneven maturation of the bunches, and the way that most winemakers merrily mix underripe and overripe produce. This year's edition confirms the excellent prospects that white *godello* has kept showing over the years, with an overall 15% increase in the number of samples.

Also of note is the fact that five new wineries have registered in the DO over the last year, in spite of crisis, and the way *mencía* has become one of the most sough-after Spanish grape varieties abroad –probably thanks to its solid Atlantic rather than Mediterranean character–, although the region only exports around 17% of its total production. Nevertheless, we should remember that *mencía*, as an early variety, is always risking –given the relative low altitude of the region– both overripeness and the loss of varietal character. The portrait of Bierzo as a truly Atlantic vineyard with earlier, cooler maturation patterns lies almost entirely in the hands of Descendientes de J. Palacios, at the top of the region's rating with wines that convey the traditional red fruit *mencía* notes, along with lovely floral hints.

LOCATION:

In the north west of the province of León. It covers 23 municipal areas and occupies several valleys in mountainous terrain and a flat plain at a lower altitude than the plateau of León, with higher temperatures accompanied by more rainfall. It may be considered an area of transition between Galicia, León and Asturias.

CLIMATE:

Quite mild and benign, with a certain degree of humidity due to Galician influence, although somewhat dry like Castilla. Thanks to the low altitude, late frost is avoided quite successfully and the grapes are usually harvested one month before the rest of Castilla. The average rainfall per year is 721 mm.

SOIL:

In the mountain regions, it is made up of a mixture of fine elements, quartzite and slate. In general, the soil of the DO is humid, dun and slightly acidic. The greater quality indices are associated with the slightly sloped terraces close to the rivers, the half - terraced or steep slopes situated at an altitude of between 450 and 1,000 m.

GRAPE VARIETIES:

WHITE: *Godello, Palomino* and *Dona Blanca.*
RED: *Mencía* or *Negra* and *Garnacha Tintorera.*

FIGURES:

Vineyard surface: 3,683 – **Wine-Growers:** 4,210 – **Wineries:** 55 – **2010 Harvest rating:** S/C – **Production:** 9,170,600 litres – **Market percentages:** 83,3% domestic. 16,7% export

CONSEJO REGULADOR
Mencía, 1
24540 Cacabelos (León)
☎: +34 987 549 408 - Fax: +34 987 547 077
@ info@crdobierzo.es
@ comunicacion@crdobierzo.es
www.crdobierzo.es

GENERAL CHARACTERISTICS OF THE WINES

WHITES	These are pale yellow, light, fresh and fruity, although not too defined. The ones with most character are those that contain the *Godello* variety.
ROSÉS	The colour can range from onion skin to pink tones; on the nose, strawberry and raspberry noses dominate, typical of the *Mencía* variety, which must make up at least 50% of the blend. In general, they are light and supple.
REDS	These are the most characteristic wines of the denomination. Those that most stand out are the young wines of normal vinification or produced using the carbonic maceration procedure. Sometimes there is a risk of a slightly low acidity due to the fast ripening of the *Mencía* in such a mild climate. They have an intense cherry colour with a brilliant violet edge and are fruity with a very robust nose (strawberries, blackberries) typical of the variety; on the palate they are dry, light and fruity with a great varietal character. Barrel - aged red wines are also produced.

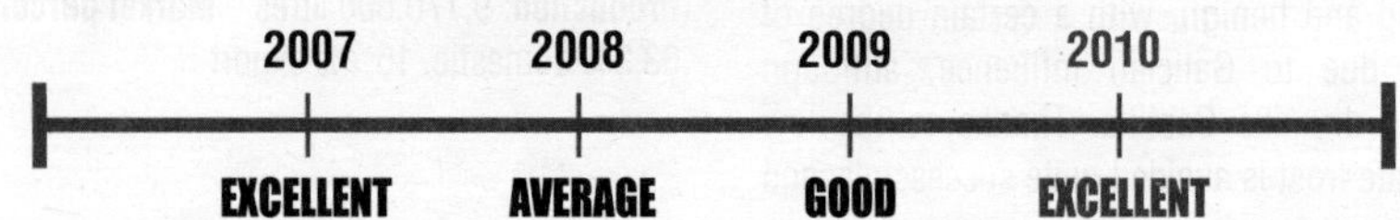

ÁLVAREZ DE TOLEDO VIÑEDOS Y GRUPO BODEGAS

Río Selmo, 8
24560 Toral de los Vados (León)
☎: +34 987 563 551 - Fax: +34 987 563 551
admon@bodegasalvarezdetoledo.com
www.bodegasalvarezdetoledo.com

ÁLVAREZ DE TOLEDO 2009 T

87 Colour: very deep cherry. Nose: spicy, aromatic coffee, characterful, powerfull, ripe fruit. Palate: fleshy, fruity, creamy, spicy.

ÁLVAREZ DE TOLEDO 2008 T
mencía.

87 Colour: deep cherry. Nose: candied fruit, powerfull, spicy, creamy oak. Palate: fleshy, good structure, powerful, flavourful.

ARTURO GARCÍA VIÑEDOS Y BODEGAS

La Escuela, 3
24516 Perandones (León)
☎: +34 987 553 000 - Fax: +34 987 553 001
info@bodegarturo.com
www.bodegarturo.com

HACIENDA SAEL GODELLO 2010 B
godello.

90 Colour: bright straw. Nose: fresh, white flowers, expressive, varietal. Palate: flavourful, fruity, good acidity, balanced.

HACIENDA SAEL MENCÍA 2010 T
mencía.

88 Colour: cherry, purple rim. Nose: red berry notes, floral, ripe fruit. Palate: flavourful, fruity, good acidity, round tannins.

SOLAR DE SAEL 2007 TC
mencía.

90 Colour: bright cherry. Nose: sweet spices, creamy oak, expressive, varietal, ripe fruit. Palate: flavourful, fruity, toasty, round tannins.

SOLAR DE SAEL 2005 TR
mencía.

85 Colour: cherry, garnet rim. Nose: spicy, creamy oak, toasty. Palate: powerful, flavourful, toasty, round tannins.

SOLAR DE SAEL 2003 TGR
mencía.

85 Colour: cherry, garnet rim. Nose: powerfull, ripe fruit, dark chocolate, creamy oak, wet leather. Palate: flavourful, powerful, fleshy.

BERNARDO ÁLVAREZ

San Pedro, 75
24430 Villadecanes (León)
☎: +34 987 562 129 - Fax: +34 987 562 129
migarron@bodegasbernardoalvarez.e.telefonica.net

CAMPO REDONDO GODELLO 2010 B
100% godello.

91 Color bright straw. Aroma fresh, fresh fruit, white flowers, expressive. Taste flavourful, fruity, good acidity, balanced.

VIÑA MIGARRÓN 2010 B
60% valenciana, 20% jerez, 20% godello.

85 Colour: straw. Nose: white flowers, fresh fruit, fragrant herbs. Palate: complex, fresh, fruity, full, powerful, flavourful.

VIÑA MIGARRÓN 2010 RD
100% mencía.

86 Colour: rose, purple rim. Nose: expressive, fresh, varietal. Palate: sweetness, flavourful.

VIÑA MIGARRÓN 2010 T
100% mencía.

86 Colour: dark-red cherry. Nose: earthy notes, damp earth, macerated fruit, wild herbs. Palate: sweetness, powerful, flavourful, fruity.

CAMPO REDONDO 2009 T ROBLE
100% mencía.

90 Colour: cherry, garnet rim. Nose: varietal, expressive, ripe fruit, toasty. Palate: powerful, flavourful, fleshy, spicy.

VIÑA MIGARRÓN 2008 TC
100% mencía.

86 Colour: cherry, garnet rim. Nose: powerfull, ripe fruit, toasty, dark chocolate. Palate: powerful, spicy, ripe fruit.

BODEGA ALBERTO LEDO

Estación, 6
24500 Villafranca del Bierzo (León)
☎: +34 636 023 676
aallrs@msn.com
www.albertoledo.com

LEDO. 8 2007 T
100% mencía.

92 Colour: cherry, garnet rim. Nose: spicy, creamy oak, toasty, ripe fruit, characterful. Palate: powerful, flavourful, toasty, round tannins.

LEDO CLUB DE BARRICAS 2007 T
100% mencía.

90 Colour: cherry, garnet rim. Nose: powerfull, characterful, varietal, ripe fruit, spicy, toasty. Palate: flavourful, spicy, ripe fruit, round tannins.

LEDO SELECCIÓN 2007 T
100% mencía.

89 Colour: cherry, garnet rim. Nose: characterful, balsamic herbs, ripe fruit. Palate: spicy, fine bitter notes, round tannins.

BODEGA DEL ABAD

Ctra. N-VI, km. 396
24549 Carracedelo (León)
☎: +34 987 562 417 - Fax: +34 987 562 428
vinos@bodegadelabad.com
www.bodegadelabad.com

ABAD DOM BUENO GODELLO 2010 B
100% godello.

87 Colour: bright straw. Nose: expressive, varietal, fresh fruit, floral. Palate: flavourful, fruity, fresh.

ABAD DOM BUENO MENCÍA 2009 T ROBLE
100% mencía.

88 Colour: cherry, garnet rim. Nose: powerfull, characterful, ripe fruit, roasted coffee. Palate: powerful, fleshy, complex.

GOTÍN DEL RISC MENCÍA 2008 T
100% mencía.

89 Colour: black cherry. Nose: powerfull, ripe fruit, dark chocolate, sweet spices. Palate: powerful, sweetness, fleshy.

CARRACEDO 2007 T
100% mencía.

90 Colour: deep cherry. Nose: expressive, powerfull, aromatic coffee, spicy, creamy oak. Palate: fruity, powerful, flavourful, fleshy.

GOTÍN DEL RISC ESSENCIA 2007 T ROBLE
100% mencía.

90 Colour: cherry, garnet rim. Nose: ripe fruit, spicy, creamy oak, toasty, varietal. Palate: powerful, flavourful, toasty, round tannins.

BODEGA LUZDIVINA AMIGO

Ctra. Villafranca, 10
24516 Parandones (León)
☎: +34 987 544 826 - Fax: +34 987 544 826
info@bodegaluz.com
www.bodegaluz.com

VIÑADEMOYA 2010 T
100% mencía.

85 Colour: cherry, purple rim. Nose: ripe fruit, varietal, powerfull. Palate: fleshy, powerful, flavourful.

BALOIRO 2008 TC
100% mencía.

90 Colour: cherry, garnet rim. Nose: powerfull, ripe fruit, mineral, toasty, aromatic coffee. Palate: flavourful, powerful, spicy.

BODEGA SILVA BROCO

Ctra. Villafranca, 4
24516 Parandones (León)
☎: +34 987 553 043 - Fax: +34 987 553 043
antoniosilvabroco@hotmail.com

LAGAR DE CAXÁN 2009 T
mencía.

86 Colour: deep cherry. Nose: ripe fruit, damp earth, varietal, reduction notes. Palate: spirituous, powerful, flavourful, fruity.

LAGAR DE CAXÁN 2008 TC
mencía.

88 Colour: cherry, garnet rim. Nose: powerfull, ripe fruit, toasty, sweet spices, dark chocolate. Palate: powerful, flavourful, fleshy, complex.

BODEGA Y VIÑEDOS LUNA BEBERIDE

Ant. Ctra. Madrid - Coruña, Km. 402
24540 Cacabelos (León)
☎: +34 987 549 002 - Fax: +34 987 549 214
info@lunabeberide.es
www.lunabeberide.es

MENCÍA LUNA BEBERIDE 2009 T
mencía.

93 Colour: cherry, purple rim. Nose: powerfull, varietal, mineral, balsamic herbs. Palate: flavourful, fleshy, spicy, balsamic.

LUNA BEBERIDE ART 2009 T
100% mencía.

92 Colour: cherry, garnet rim. Nose: ripe fruit, creamy oak, toasty, mineral, balsamic herbs. Palate: powerful, toasty, round tannins.

LUNA BEBERIDE "FINCA LA CUESTA" 2009 T ROBLE
mencía.

88 Colour: cherry, garnet rim. Nose: ripe fruit, toasty, creamy oak, powerfull. Palate: flavourful, fruity, fleshy, spicy.

BODEGAS ADRIÁ

Antigua Ctra. Madrid - Coruña, Km. 408
24500 Villafranca del Bierzo (León)
☎: +34 987 540 907 - Fax: +34 987 540 347
export@bodegasadria.com
www.vegamontan.com

VEGA MONTÁN VM GODELLO SOBRE LÍAS 2010 B
100% godello.

89 Colour: bright yellow. Nose: mineral, citrus fruit, fresh fruit, fragrant herbs. Palate: fresh, fruity, powerful, flavourful, complex.

VEGA MONTÁN GODELLO DOÑA BLANCA 2010 B
50% godello, 50% dona blanca.

86 Colour: bright straw. Nose: white flowers, ripe fruit. Palate: flavourful, fruity, fresh.

VEGA MONTÁN 2010 RD
100% mencía.

87 Colour: rose. Nose: raspberry, fresh fruit, fruit expression. Palate: flavourful, powerful, fruity, fresh.

VEGA MONTÁN MENCÍA 2010 T
100% mencía.

86 Colour: dark-red cherry. Nose: varietal, fresh, red berry notes, earthy notes. Palate: ripe fruit, lacks expression, easy to drink.

VEGA MONTÁN VM SILK 2009 T
100% mencía.

85 Colour: very deep cherry. Nose: powerfull, varietal, ripe fruit, aged wood nuances, sweet spices.

VEGA MONTÁN VM VELVET 2008 T
100% mencía.

90 Color cherry, purple rim. Aroma expressive, fresh fruit, red berry notes, floral. Taste flavourful, fruity, good acidity, round tannins.

BODEGAS ALMÁZCARA MAJARA

Las Eras, 5
24398 Almázcara (León)
☎: +34 609 322 194 - Fax: +34 937 952 859
javier.alvarez@alvarezmiras.com
www.almazcaramajara.com

DEMASIADO CORAZÓN 2009 BFB
godello.

91 Colour: bright yellow. Nose: white flowers, creamy oak, spicy, smoky. Palate: fresh, powerful, flavourful, complex, smoky aftertaste.

JARABE DE ALMÁZCARA MAJARA 2008 T
mencía.

87 Colour: cherry, garnet rim. Nose: spicy, creamy oak, toasty, fruit expression. Palate: powerful, flavourful, toasty, round tannins.

ALMÁZCARA MAJARA 2007 T
mencía.

85 Colour: cherry, garnet rim. Nose: warm, spicy, aromatic coffee, fruit liqueur notes. Palate: spicy, ripe fruit, fine bitter notes.

BODEGAS CUATRO PASOS

Santa María, 45
24540 Cacabelos (León)
☎: +34 987 548 089 - Fax: +34 987 548 089
comercial@martincodax.com
www.cuatropasos.es

CUATRO PASOS 2010 RD
mencía.

88 Colour: rose, purple rim. Nose: floral, fruit expression, red berry notes. Palate: flavourful, powerful, fleshy.

CUATRO PASOS 2009 T
mencía.

88 Colour: bright cherry. Nose: sweet spices, creamy oak, varietal, red berry notes. Palate: flavourful, fruity, toasty, round tannins.

MARTÍN SARMIENTO 2006 T
mencía.

91 Color cherry, garnet rim. Aroma ripe fruit, spicy, creamy oak, toasty, complex. Taste powerful, flavourful, toasty, round tannins.

BODEGAS MADAI

Avda. Marina, 4 2 Dª
15160 Sada (A Coruña)
☎: +34 620 867 398
madaibodegas@gmail.com
www.bodegasmadai.com

MADAI GODELLO SOBRE LÍAS 2009 B
godello.

83 Colour: bright straw. Nose: ripe fruit, citrus fruit, dried flowers. Palate: flavourful, fleshy, fine bitter notes.

MADAI MENCÍA SOBRE LÍAS 2008 T
mencía.

89 Colour: dark-red cherry. Nose: varietal, powerfull, ripe fruit, sweet spices, cedar wood. Palate: full, powerful, fruity, flavourful, creamy, toasty.

BODEGAS PEIQUE

El Bierzo, s/n
24530 Valtuille de Abajo (León)
☎: +34 987 562 044 - Fax: +34 987 562 044
bodega@bodegaspeique.com
www.bodegaspeique.com

PEIQUE GODELLO 2010 B
godello.

88 Colour: bright straw. Nose: candied fruit, citrus fruit, white flowers. Palate: flavourful, powerful, fleshy.

PEIQUE 2010 RD
mencía.

86 Colour: rose, purple rim. Nose: powerfull, ripe fruit, red berry notes. Palate: fleshy, powerful, fruity, fresh.

PEIQUE TINTO MENCÍA 2010 T
mencía.

87 Colour: cherry, garnet rim. Nose: powerfull, ripe fruit, red berry notes. Palate: flavourful, powerful, fleshy.

RAMÓN VALLE 2009 T
mencía.

89 Colour: bright cherry. Nose: sweet spices, creamy oak, fruit expression. Palate: flavourful, fruity, toasty, round tannins.

PEIQUE VIÑEDOS VIEJOS 2007 T ROBLE
mencía.

92 Colour: cherry, garnet rim. Nose: powerfull, ripe fruit, creamy oak, toasty, mineral. Palate: powerful, fleshy, spicy, ripe fruit.

PEIQUE SELECCIÓN FAMILIAR 2006 T
mencía.

93 Colour: cherry, garnet rim. Nose: ripe fruit, characterful, complex, undergrowth, earthy notes. Palate: powerful, flavourful, concentrated.

BODEGAS Y VIÑEDO MENGOBA

Ctra. de Cacabelos, 11
24540 Sorribas (León)
☎: +34 649 940 800
gregory@mengoba.com
www.mengoba.com

BREZO GODELLO Y DOÑA BLANCA 2010 B
godello, dona blanca.

88 Colour: bright straw. Nose: ripe fruit, candied fruit, citrus fruit. Palate: flavourful, fruity, light-bodied.

MENGOBA GODELLO SOBRE LÍAS 2009 B
godello.

91 Colour: bright yellow. Nose: powerfull, ripe fruit, sweet spices, fragrant herbs. Palate: rich, smoky aftertaste, flavourful, fresh, good acidity.

MENGOBA DE ESPANILLO 2009 T
mencía.

92 Colour: bright cherry. Nose: ripe fruit, sweet spices, creamy oak, balsamic herbs, earthy notes. Palate: flavourful, fruity, toasty, round tannins.

BREZO MENCÍA 2009 T
mencía.

90 Colour: cherry, garnet rim. Nose: powerfull, ripe fruit, creamy oak. Palate: powerful, flavourful, fleshy, complex.

BODEGAS Y VIÑEDOS CASTRO VENTOSA

Finca El Barredo, s/n
24530 Valtuille de Abajo (León)
☎: +34 987 562 148 - Fax: +34 987 562 191
info@castroventosa.com
www.castroventosa.com

CASTRO VENTOSA 2010 T

85 Colour: dark-red cherry. Nose: dry stone, fresh fruit, short. Palate: easy to drink, balsamic, fresh, fruity, flavourful.

EL CASTRO DE VALTUILLE JOVEN 2009 T
mencía.

91 Colour: cherry, purple rim. Nose: expressive, red berry notes, floral, varietal, balsamic herbs. Palate: fruity, good acidity, round tannins.

EL CASTRO DE VALTUILLE 2008 T
mencía.

91 Colour: cherry, garnet rim. Nose: spicy, creamy oak, toasty, ripe fruit, balsamic herbs. Palate: powerful, flavourful, toasty, round tannins.

CASTRO VENTOSA"VINTAGE" 2008 T
mencía.

90 Colour: cherry, garnet rim. Nose: spicy, aromatic coffee, ripe fruit, toasty. Palate: flavourful, powerful, fleshy, round tannins.

VALTUILLE CEPAS CENTENARIAS 2007 T ROBLE
mencía.

94 Colour: cherry, garnet rim. Nose: spicy, creamy oak, toasty, complex, varietal, balsamic herbs. Palate: powerful, flavourful, toasty, long.

BODEGAS Y VIÑEDOS GANCEDO

Vistalegre, s/n
24548 Quilós (León)
☎: +34 987 134 980 - Fax: +34 987 563 278
info@bodegasgancedo.com
www.bodegasgancedo.com

VAL DE PAXARIÑAS "CAPRICHO" 2010 B
85% godello, 15% dona blanca.

92 Colour: bright straw. Nose: fresh, fresh fruit, white flowers, expressive, mineral, spicy. Palate: flavourful, fruity, good acidity, balanced.

HERENCIA DEL CAPRICHO 2008 BFB
90% godello, 10% dona blanca.

94 Colour: bright yellow. Nose: powerfull, sweet spices, creamy oak. Palate: rich, smoky aftertaste, flavourful, fresh, good acidity.

GANCEDO 2010 T
mencía.

89 Colour: cherry, purple rim. Nose: red berry notes, floral, ripe fruit. Palate: flavourful, fruity, round tannins.

XESTAL 2007 T
mencía.

93 Colour: black cherry. Nose: powerfull, ripe fruit, creamy oak, toasty, earthy notes. Palate: ripe fruit, long, balsamic, round tannins.

GANCEDO 2006 TR
mencía.

92 Colour: deep cherry. Nose: cocoa bean, creamy oak, fruit expression, mineral. Palate: flavourful, powerful, full, fruity, complex, spicy, balsamic.

BODEGAS Y VIÑEDOS NEO

Ctra. N-122, Km. 274,5
09391 Castrillo de la Vega (Burgos)
☎: +34 947 514 393 - Fax: +34 947 515 445
info@bodegasconde.com
www.bodegasneo.com

TERCER MOTIVO 2008 T ROBLE
100% mencía.

86 Colour: cherry, purple rim. Nose: ripe fruit, earthy notes, fine reductive notes, spicy. Palate: good acidity, flavourful, complex, toasty.

BODEGAS Y VIÑEDOS PAIXAR

Ribadeo, 56
24500 Villafranca del Bierzo (León)
☎: +34 987 549 002 - Fax: +34 987 549 214
info@lunabeberide.es

PAIXAR MENCÍA 2008 T
100% mencía.

93 Colour: cherry, garnet rim. Nose: earthy notes, mineral, fruit expression, sweet spices, creamy oak. Palate: balanced, fleshy, complex, flavourful.

CASAR DE BURBIA

Travesía la Constitución s/n
24459 Carracedelo (León)
☎: +34 987 562 910 - Fax: +34 987 562 850
info@casardeburbia.com
www.casardeburbia.com

CASAR DE BURBIA 2009 T
97% mencía, 3% garnacha.

92 Colour: cherry, garnet rim. Nose: powerfull, varietal, raspberry, scrubland, new oak. Palate: flavourful, fruity, fleshy, harsh oak tannins.

TEBAIDA 2009 T
100% mencía.

91 Colour: very deep cherry. Nose: dark chocolate, sweet spices, aromatic coffee, ripe fruit. Palate: powerful, fleshy, concentrated, sweetness, round tannins.

HOMBROS 2008 T
100% mencía.

94 Colour: cherry, garnet rim. Nose: spicy, creamy oak, toasty, complex, mineral, earthy notes, raspberry. Palate: powerful, flavourful, toasty, round tannins.

CEPAS DEL BIERZO

Ctra. de Sanabria, 111
24400 Ponferrada (León)
☎: +34 987 412 333 - Fax: +34 987 412 912
coocebier@coocebier.e.telefonica.net

DON OSMUNDO 2008 T
mencía.

90 Colour: dark-red cherry. Nose: varietal, powerfull, violet drops, fresh fruit, balsamic herbs. Palate: powerful, flavourful, fruity, fresh, balsamic, creamy.

DON OSMUNDO 2007 T ROBLE
mencía.

85 Colour: cherry, garnet rim. Nose: spicy, balsamic herbs, wet leather. Palate: flavourful, spicy.

COMPAÑIA SANTA TRINIDAD XXI

24530 Villadecanes (León)
☎: +34 987 418 595
asesores@asofi.es

CORRO DAS XANAS 2010 T
mencía.

89 Colour: dark-red cherry. Nose: balanced, elegant, characterful. Palate: flavourful, fruity, mineral, fruity aftestaste.

CORRO DAS XANAS 2009 T
100% mencía.

88 Colour: deep cherry. Nose: powerfull, ripe fruit, expressive. Palate: fleshy, fresh, fruity, full, powerful.

DESCENDIENTES DE J. PALACIOS

Avda. Calvo Sotelo, 6
24500 Villafranca del Bierzo (León)
☎: +34 987 540 821 - Fax: +34 987 540 851
info@djpalacios.com

PÉTALOS DEL BIERZO 2009 T
100% mencía.

94 Colour: cherry, garnet rim. Nose: powerfull, ripe fruit, fruit expression, scrubland, spicy. Palate: flavourful, fruity, fine bitter notes, mineral.

LA FARAONA 2008 T
mencía.

96 Colour: dark-red cherry. Nose: fragrant herbs, complex, varietal, fresh, balsamic herbs, fruit expression, elegant. Palate: elegant, fruity, mineral, balsamic.

VILLA DE CORULLÓN 2008 T
mencía.

95 Colour: cherry, garnet rim. Nose: cocoa bean, mineral, balsamic herbs, fresh fruit. Palate: elegant, complex, fresh, flavourful, balsamic, mineral.

MONCERBAL 2008 T
mencía.

95 Colour: deep cherry. Nose: expressive, varietal, ripe fruit, fruit expression, balsamic herbs, spicy. Palate: flavourful, spicy, fine bitter notes, long, fine tannins.

LAS LAMAS 2008 T
mencía.

94 Colour: cherry, garnet rim. Nose: fruit preserve, sweet spices, creamy oak, balsamic herbs. Palate: ripe fruit, spicy, round tannins, fleshy.

ESTEFANÍA

Ctra. Dehesas - Posada, s/n
24390 Ponferrada (León)
☎: +34 987 420 015 - Fax: +34 987 420 015
info@tilenus.com
www.tilenus.com

CASTILLO DE ULVER 2010 T
mencía.

87 Colour: dark-red cherry. Nose: damp earth, fresh fruit, red berry notes, varietal. Palate: fruity, powerful, flavourful, easy to drink.

TILENUS 2010 T
mencía.

86 Colour: dark-red cherry. Nose: fruit expression, red berry notes, dried fruit, fresh, neat, varietal.

TILENUS ENVEJECIDO EN ROBLE 2007 T ROBLE
100% mencía.

90 Colour: cherry, garnet rim. Nose: powerfull, ripe fruit, balsamic herbs, toasty. Palate: flavourful, spicy, ripe fruit.

TILENUS 2005 TC
100% mencía.

90 Colour: cherry, garnet rim. Nose: powerfull, ripe fruit, aromatic coffee, toasty. Palate: powerful, flavourful, fleshy, round tannins.

TILENUS PAGOS DE POSADA 2003 TR
100% mencía.

91 Colour: deep cherry. Nose: sweet spices, cedar wood, cocoa bean, elegant. Palate: elegant, round, flavourful, rich, fruity.

TILENUS PIEROS 2002 T
100% mencía.

91 Colour: deep cherry, orangey edge. Nose: sweet spices, aromatic coffee, fruit liqueur notes. Palate: flavourful, fruity, spicy, ripe fruit.

GODELIA

Antigua Ctra. N-VI, Km. 403,5
24547 Pieros Cacabelos (León)
☎: +34 987 546 279 - Fax: +34 987 548 026
export@godelia.es
www.godelia.es

GODELIA BLANCO SOBRE LÍAS 2010 B
80% godello, 20% dona blanca.

90 Colour: bright straw. Nose: white flowers, ripe fruit, citrus fruit. Palate: flavourful, fruity, fresh, fine bitter notes.

GODELIA BLANCO SELECCIÓN 2009 B
100% godello.

90 Colour: bright straw. Nose: expressive, varietal, ripe fruit, citrus fruit, white flowers. Palate: flavourful, fleshy, ripe fruit.

VIERNES 2010 T
100% mencía.

88 Colour: cherry, purple rim. Nose: fresh fruit, red berry notes, floral, varietal. Palate: flavourful, fruity, good acidity, round tannins.

GODELIA 12 MESES 2009 T ROBLE
100% mencía.

93 Colour: cherry, garnet rim. Nose: powerfull, ripe fruit, fruit expression, creamy oak, aged wood nuances. Palate: flavourful, fleshy, ripe fruit, toasty.

LOSADA VINOS DE FINCA

Ctra. LE-713, Km. 12
24540 Cacabelos (León)
☎: +34 987 548 053 - Fax: +34 987 548 069
bodega@losadavinosdefinca.com
www.losadavinosdefinca.com

LOSADA 2008 T
100% mencía.

90 Colour: deep cherry. Nose: aromatic coffee, spicy, toasty, ripe fruit. Palate: balsamic, creamy, roasted-coffee aftertaste, powerful, flavourful, ripe fruit.

ALTOS DE LOSADA 2007 T
100% mencía.

93 Colour: deep cherry. Nose: spicy, creamy oak, aromatic coffee, ripe fruit, fruit expression. Palate: fleshy, complex, good structure, rich, powerful, flavourful.

LA BIENQUERIDA 2007 T
95% mencía, 5% otras.

91 Colour: dark-red cherry. Nose: expressive, powerfull, sweet spices, creamy oak, ripe fruit. Palate: fruity, powerful, flavourful, slightly dry, soft tannins, spicy, mineral.

MENCÍAS DE DOS

Cuatro Calles, s/n
47491 La Seca (Valladolid)
☎: +34 983 103 223 - Fax: +34 983 816 561
info@sitiosdebodega.com
www.sitiosdebodega.com

OLLO DE GALO 2009 B
100% godello.

88 Colour: bright straw. Nose: characterful, candied fruit, citrus fruit. Palate: flavourful, powerful, fleshy.

DE 2 2010 T
100% mencía.

84 Colour: dark-red cherry. Nose: short, medium intensity, ripe fruit. Palate: fresh, fruity, balsamic.

AMBOS MENCÍA 2007 T
100% mencía.

90 Colour: bright cherry. Nose: sweet spices, creamy oak, ripe fruit, varietal. Palate: flavourful, fruity, toasty, round tannins..

OTERO SANTÍN

Ortega y Gasset, 10
24400 Ponferrada (León)
☎: +34 987 410 101 - Fax: +34 987 418 544
oterobenito@gmail.com

OTERO SANTÍN 2010 B
godello.

88 Colour: pale. Nose: powerfull, varietal, ripe fruit. Palate: flavourful, fruity, fresh.

OTERO SANTÍN 2010 RD
mencía.

85 Colour: brilliant rose. Nose: candied fruit, ripe fruit. Palate: flavourful, fruity, fresh.

VALDECAMPO 2010 T
mencía.

87 Colour: dark-red cherry. Nose: fresh fruit, medium intensity, mineral, earthy notes, toasty. Palate: flavourful, fleshy, fine bitter notes.

OTERO SANTÍN 2009 T
mencía.

80 Colour: cherry, garnet rim. Nose: candied fruit, toasty, aromatic coffee. Palate: toasty, fine bitter notes, correct.

PÉREZ CARAMÉS

Peña Picón, s/n
24500 Villafranca del Bierzo (León)
☎: +34 987 540 197 - Fax: +34 987 540 314
info@perezcarames.com
www.perezcarames.com

VALDAIGA X 2010 T
mencía.

90 Colour: dark-red cherry. Nose: complex, characterful, powerfull, undergrowth, truffle notes. Palate: powerful, flavourful, rich, complex.

VALDAIGA 2009 T
mencía.

84 Colour: bright cherry. Nose: sweet spices, creamy oak, ripe fruit. Palate: flavourful, fruity, toasty, round tannins.

VALDAIGA CUSTOM X 2005 T
mencía.

85 Colour: deep cherry. Nose: reduction notes, ripe fruit, creamy oak, spicy. Palate: good structure, powerful, flavourful, fleshy.

PRADA A TOPE

La Iglesia, s/n
24546 Canedo (León)
☎: +34 902 400 101 - Fax: +34 987 567 000
info@pradaatope.es
www.pradaatope.es

PALACIO DE CANEDO GODELLO 2009 B
godello.

88 Colour: bright yellow. Nose: ripe fruit, sweet spices, creamy oak, fragrant herbs, elegant. Palate: rich, flavourful, fresh, good acidity.

PALACIO DE CANEDO 2010 T MACERACIÓN CARBÓNICA
mencía.

87 Colour: cherry, purple rim. Nose: expressive, fresh, varietal, red berry notes. Palate: flavourful, fruity, fresh.

PICANTAL 2008 T
mencía.

90 Colour: deep cherry. Nose: aromatic coffee, sweet spices, toasty, ripe fruit. Palate: spirituous, powerful, flavourful, roasted-coffee aftertaste.

PALACIO DE CANEDO 2007 TR
mencía.

90 Colour: deep cherry. Nose: expressive, varietal, damp undergrowth, herbaceous. Palate: complex, fresh, fruity, powerful, flavourful.

PRADA A TOPE 2006 TR
mencía.

90 Colour: dark-red cherry. Nose: varietal, powerfull, expressive, cocoa bean, aged wood nuances, creamy oak. Palate: powerful, flavourful, fruity, complex, fleshy.

RAUL PÉREZ BODEGAS Y VIÑEDOS

Bulevar Rey Juan Carlos 1º Rey de España, 11 B
24400 Ponferrada (León)
raulperez@raulperezbodegas.es
www.raulperezbodegas.es

ULTREIA 2009 T
100% mencía.

95 Colour: bright cherry. Nose: fresh, complex, balsamic herbs, fruit expression, mineral. Palate: flavourful, good acidity, fine bitter notes, mineral, fine tannins.

ULTREIA "SAINT JACQUES" 2009 T
100% mencía.

89 Colour: cherry, garnet rim. Nose: ripe fruit, fragrant herbs, mineral, spicy, creamy oak. Palate: good acidity, flavourful, fleshy.

RIBAS DEL CÚA

Finca Robledo, Apdo. Correos 83
24540 Cacabelos (León)
☎: +34 987 971 018 - Fax: +34 987 971 016
bodega@ribasdelcua.com
www.ribasdelcua.com

RIBAS DEL CÚA PRIVILEGIO 2008 T
mencía.

89 Colour: deep cherry, orangey edge. Nose: candied fruit, fruit liqueur notes, toasty. Palate: flavourful, spicy, ripe fruit.

SAT FERBE Nº 8451

Avda. de España, 25 entreplanta Izquierda
24400 Ponferrada (León)
☎: +34 987 562 910 - Fax: +34 987 562 850
info@liaran.com
www.liaran.com

LIARÁN 2009 T
85% mencía, 15% garnacha.

86 Colour: bright cherry. Nose: sweet spices, creamy oak, characterful, ripe fruit. Palate: flavourful, fruity, toasty, round tannins.

SOTO DEL VICARIO

Ctra. Cacabelos- San Clemente, Pol. Ind. 908
Parcela 155
24547 San Clemente (León)
☎: +34 670 983 534 - Fax: +34 926 666 029
sandra.luque@pagodelvicario.com
www.sotodelvicario.com

SOTO DEL VICARIO GO DE GODELLO 2009 BFB
100% godello.

92 Colour: bright yellow. Nose: powerfull, sweet spices, creamy oak, fragrant herbs, candied fruit. Palate: rich, smoky aftertaste, flavourful, fresh, good acidity.

SOTO DEL VICARIO MEN SELECCIÓN 2008 T
100% mencía.

91 Colour: black cherry. Nose: powerfull, candied fruit, ripe fruit, warm, creamy oak, toasty. Palate: powerful, fleshy, concentrated.

SOTO DEL VICARIO MEN 2008 T
100% mencía.

90 Colour: cherry, garnet rim. Nose: powerfull, ripe fruit, toasty, dark chocolate, sweet spices. Palate: flavourful, powerful, fleshy, good acidity, balsamic.

VINOS DE ARGANZA

Río Ancares, 2
24560 Toral de los Vados (León)
☎: +34 987 544 831 - Fax: +34 987 563 532
admon@vinosdearganza.com
www.vinosdearganza.com

SÉCULO 2010 B
godello, dona blanca.

86 Colour: bright straw. Nose: ripe fruit, fruit expression, citrus fruit. Palate: flavourful, fruity, fresh.

FLAVIUM 2010 B
godello, dona blanca.

85 Colour: bright straw. Nose: ripe fruit, citrus fruit, grassy. Palate: flavourful, fruity, fresh.

FLAVIUM 2010 T
mencía.

85 Colour: dark-red cherry. Nose: fresh fruit, red clay notes, varietal, expressive. Palate: fresh, fruity, flavourful, lacks expression.

FLAVIUM 2009 T ROBLE
mencía.

91 Colour: deep cherry. Nose: fruit expression, ripe fruit, powerfull, expressive, spicy, creamy oak, toasty. Palate: fleshy, fruity, flavourful, powerful, creamy.

SÉCULO 2009 T
mencía.

86 Colour: dark-red cherry. Nose: varietal, powerfull, expressive, violet drops, balsamic herbs. Palate: powerful, flavourful, fruity, fleshy.

FLAVIUM 2008 TC
mencía.

90 Colour: bright cherry. Nose: sweet spices, creamy oak, ripe fruit. Palate: flavourful, fruity, toasty, round tannins.

SÉCULO 2008 TC
mencía.

88 Colour: cherry, garnet rim. Nose: spicy, creamy oak, toasty, fruit expression, red berry notes. Palate: powerful, flavourful, toasty, round tannins.

CANEIROS 2007 T ROBLE
mencía.

91 Colour: bright cherry. Nose: sweet spices, creamy oak, red berry notes, fresh fruit. Palate: flavourful, fruity, toasty, round tannins.

FLAVIUM 2005 TR
mencía.

88 Colour: cherry, garnet rim. Nose: creamy oak, sweet spices, fruit expression, red berry notes. Palate: flavourful, fleshy, fruity.

SÉCULO 2003 TR
mencía.

88 Colour: dark-red cherry. Nose: fine reductive notes, macerated fruit, spicy, cedar wood. Palate: soft tannins, powerful, full, complex.

VINOS DEL BIERZO S. COOP.

Avda. Constitución, 106
24540 Cacabelos (León)
☎: +34 987 546 150 - Fax: +34 987 549 236
info@vinosdelbierzo.com
www.vinosdelbierzo.com

VINICIO GODELLO 2010 B
godello.

84 Colour: bright straw. Nose: fresh, white flowers, fresh fruit. Palate: flavourful, fruity, good acidity, balanced.

VIÑA ORO 2010 B
dona blanca, godello.

83 Colour: pale. Nose: floral, fresh fruit. Palate: flavourful, light-bodied, fruity.

VIÑA ORO 2010 RD
mencía.

77

VIÑA ORO 2010 T
mencía.

82 Colour: cherry, garnet rim. Nose: medium intensity, grassy. Palate: flavourful, fine bitter notes.

GUERRA 2009 T
mencía.

78

GUERRA SELECCIÓN 2008 T
mencía.

82 Colour: cherry, garnet rim. Nose: balsamic herbs, ripe fruit. Palate: flavourful, fleshy, spicy.

CARRALERO 2007 T
mencía.

85 Colour: cherry, garnet rim. Nose: powerfull, fruit liqueur notes, candied fruit, toasty, aromatic coffee. Palate: powerful, spicy, ripe fruit.

VINICIO 2005 TC
mencía.

80 Colour: dark-red cherry. Nose: medium intensity, earthy notes, mineral, ripe fruit, balsamic herbs. Palate: ripe fruit, creamy, balsamic.

GUERRA 2004 TC
mencía.

84 Colour: cherry, garnet rim. Nose: powerfull, characterful, ripe fruit. Palate: spicy, ripe fruit.

VINICIO 2001 TR
mencía.

87 Colour: deep cherry, orangey edge. Nose: fruit liqueur notes, spicy, toasty. Palate: flavourful, powerful, fleshy, easy to drink.

SEÑORÍO DEL BIERZO TR
mencía.

86 Colour: pale ruby, brick rim edge. Nose: elegant, spicy, fine reductive notes, wet leather, aged wood nuances, fruit liqueur notes. Palate: spicy, fine tannins, elegant, long.

VINOS VALTUILLE

La Fragua, s/n
24530 Valtuille de Abajo (León)
☎: +34 987 562 165 - Fax: +34 987 549 425
pagodevaldoneje@yahoo.es

PAGO DE VALDONEJE 2010 T
100% mencía.

87 Colour: cherry, garnet rim. Nose: powerfull, ripe fruit, raspberry. Palate: powerful, fleshy, spicy, long.

PAGO DE VALDONEJE VIÑAS VIEJAS 2008 T
100% mencía.

90 Colour: deep cherry. Nose: medium intensity, expressive, closed, fresh fruit, fruit expression, spicy, cedar wood, aromatic coffee. Palate: complex, powerful, fruity, creamy, mineral.

VIÑA ALBARES

Camino Rea,l s/n
24310 Albares de la Ribera (León)
☎: +34 987 519 147 - Fax: +34 987 519 152
info@vinaalbareswine.com
www.vinaalbareswine.com

TIERRAS DE ALBARES 2010 T
mencía.

86 Colour: cherry, purple rim. Nose: powerfull, varietal, fruit expression, fresh fruit. Palate: fruity, light-bodied, powerful, flavourful.

TIERRAS DE ALBARES 2007 TC
mencía.

90 Colour: cherry, garnet rim. Nose: ripe fruit, spicy, creamy oak, toasty, balsamic herbs, varietal. Palate: powerful, flavourful, toasty, round tannins.

VIÑAS DEL BIERZO

Ctra. Ponferrada a Cacabelos, s/n
24410 Camponaraya (León)
☎: +34 987 463 009 - Fax: +34 987 450 323
vdelbierzo@granbierzo.com
www.granbierzo.com

MARQUÉS DE CORNATEL 2010 B
godello.

84 Colour: bright straw. Nose: ripe fruit, citrus fruit, dried herbs. Palate: flavourful, light-bodied, fruity.

VALMAGAZ 2010 B
godello, dona blanca.

81 Colour: bright straw. Nose: candied fruit, citrus fruit, floral. Palate: flavourful, fruity.

VALMAGAZ 2010 RD
mencía.

78

VALMAGAZ MENCÍA 2010 T
mencía.

78

MARQUÉS DE CORNATEL 2009 T ROBLE
mencía.

85 Colour: cherry, garnet rim. Nose: powerfull, creamy oak, aged wood nuances, cocoa bean, ripe fruit. Palate: powerful, fleshy, fine bitter notes, roasted-coffee aftertaste.

FUNDACIÓN 1963 2005 TR

86 Colour: cherry, garnet rim. Nose: powerfull, ripe fruit, sweet spices, toasty. Palate: powerful, flavourful, fleshy.

GRAN BIERZO 2003 TR
mencía.

83 Colour: deep cherry, orangey edge. Nose: candied fruit, fruit liqueur notes, spicy. Palate: easy to drink, spicy, fine bitter notes.

VIÑEDOS SINGULARES

Llorer, 31
08905 Hospitalet de Llobregat (Barcelona)
☎: +34 934 807 041 - Fax: +34 934 807 076
info@vinedossingulares.com
www.vinedossingulares.com

CORRAL DEL OBISPO 2009 T
mencía.

89 Colour: cherry, garnet rim. Nose: characterful, complex, red berry notes, mineral. Palate: flavourful, powerful, fleshy, fruity, fresh.

VIÑEDOS Y BODEGAS DOMINIO DE TARES

P.I. Bierzo Alto, Los Barredos, 4
24318 San Román de Bembibre (León)
☎: +34 987 514 550 - Fax: +34 987 514 570
info@dominiodetares.com
www.dominiodetares.com

DOMINIO DE TARES GODELLO 2010 BFB
100% godello.

91 Color bright yellow. Aroma powerfull, ripe fruit, sweet spices, creamy oak, fragrant herbs. Taste rich, smoky aftertaste, flavourful, fresh, good acidity.

BALTOS 2009 T
100% mencía.

89 Colour: bright cherry. Nose: sweet spices, creamy oak, fruit expression. Palate: flavourful, fruity, toasty, round tannins.

TARES P. 3 2007 T ROBLE
100% mencía.

92 Colour: cherry, garnet rim. Nose: creamy oak, toasty, candied fruit, mineral. Palate: powerful, flavourful, toasty, round tannins.

DOMINIO DE TARES CEPAS VIEJAS 2008 TC
100% mencía.

91 Colour: cherry, garnet rim. Nose: ripe fruit, spicy, toasty, complex. Palate: powerful, flavourful, toasty, round tannins, rich.

BEMBIBRE 2007 T
100% mencía.

90 Colour: bright cherry. Nose: sweet spices, creamy oak, ripe fruit. Palate: flavourful, fruity, toasty, round tannins.

VIÑEDOS Y BODEGAS PITTACUM

De la Iglesia, 11
24546 Arganza, El Bierzo (León)
☎: +34 987 548 054 - Fax: +34 987 548 028
pittacum@pittacum.com
www.pittacum.com

TRES OBISPOS 2010 RD
100% mencía.

80 Colour: rose, purple rim. Nose: fresh fruit, reduction notes, varietal. Palate: flavourful, powerful, fresh.

PITTACUM 2007 TC
100% mencía.

93 Colour: cherry, garnet rim. Nose: ripe fruit, toasty, sweet spices. Palate: fine bitter notes, flavourful, powerful, fleshy.

PITTACUM AUREA 2007 TC
100% mencía.

94 Colour: cherry, garnet rim. Nose: powerfull, ripe fruit, fruit expression, creamy oak, toasty. Palate: flavourful, powerful, fleshy, ripe fruit, spicy, round tannins.

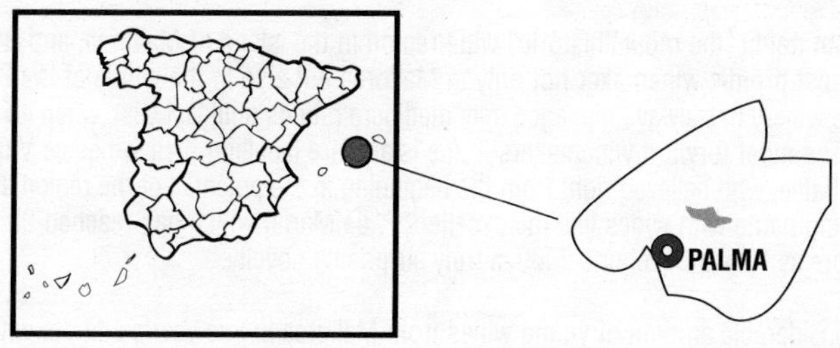

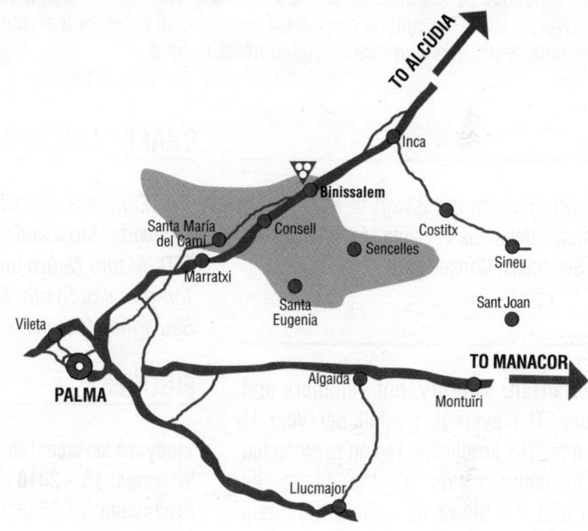

Consejo Regulador
DO Boundary

NEWS ABOUT THE VINTAGE:

Binissalem is, without doubt, the most "historic" wine region in the island of Mallorca, and Bodegas José L. Ferrer the most prolific winemaker not only in Mallorca but also in the whole of the Balearic Islands, although the winery has always managed only mediocre ratings until last year, when its crianza reached 91 points. The most forward winemakers in the island are labelling their wines as Vino de la Tierra except Macía Batlle, who believed right from the beginning in the potential of the region as such, and is now the leading name with wines like the excellent P. de María, which has reached 93 points, exactly the same score as Tianna Bocchoris 2009, a truly surprising novelty.

We have tasted a considerable amount of young wines from Mallorca in this year's edition, which has led us to believe winemakers are adjusting formidably wood-ageing times for their wines in such way these show much more expression without losing their primary notes. We must bear in mind that the region is the hottest one within the island given its location just under the Sierra Norte and therefore off the cooling influence of sea breezes. Being also the oldest wine region means it has a broader local following. Overall, the 2010 vintage has been a cool one, so it seems that more white wines were made than in previous years, and with neater, fruitier notes to boot.

LOCATION:

In the central region on the island of Majorca. It covers the municipal areas of Santa María del Camí, Binissalem, Sencelles, Consell and Santa Eugenia.

CLIMATE:

Mild Mediterranean, with dry, hot summers and short winters. The average rainfall per year is around 450 mm. The production region is protected from the northerly winds by the Sierra de Tramuntana and the Sierra de Alfabia mountain ranges.

SOIL:

The soil is of a brownish - grey or dun limey type, with limestone crusts on occasions. The slopes are quite gentle, and the vineyards are situated at an altitude ranging from 75 to 200 m.

GRAPE VARIETIES:

WHITE: *Moll* or *Prensal Blanc* (46 Ha), *Macabeo, Parellada, Moscatel* and *Chardonnay.*
RED: *Manto Negro* (majority 229 Ha), *Callet, Tempranillo, Syrah, Monastrell, Cabernet Sauvignon* (second red variety 56 Ha) and *Merlot.*

FIGURES:

Vineyard surface: 600 – **Wine-Growers:** 138 – **Wineries:** 15 – **2010 Harvest rating:** S/C – **Production:** 2,036,083 litres – **Market percentages:** 90% domestic. 10% export

CONSEJO REGULADOR
Concepció, 7
07350 Binissalem (Illes Balears)
☎: +34 971 512 191 - Fax: +34 971 886 522
@ info@binissalemdo.com
www.binissalemdo.com

GENERAL CHARACTERISTICS OF THE WINES

WHITES	These are straw yellow in colour. They are characterised by their wild, fruity traits, with hints of mountain herbs and a very Mediterranean character; the best, in which the personality of the local *Prensal* grapes stands out, provide a great complexity of nuances and excellent balance on the palate..
ROSÉS	These are pink and are characterised by their hints of aged wood, typical of the vineyards that receive a lot of sunshine
REDS	These are the most characteristic of the region and represent almost three quarters of the production of the denomination. There are young and, especially, aged wines. Their character is determined by the peculiarities of the *Manto Negro* autochthonous variety, which provides an essence of ripe fruits and hints of caramel; on the palate, the wines are well - balanced and persistent.

VINTAGE RATING PEÑÍNGUIDE

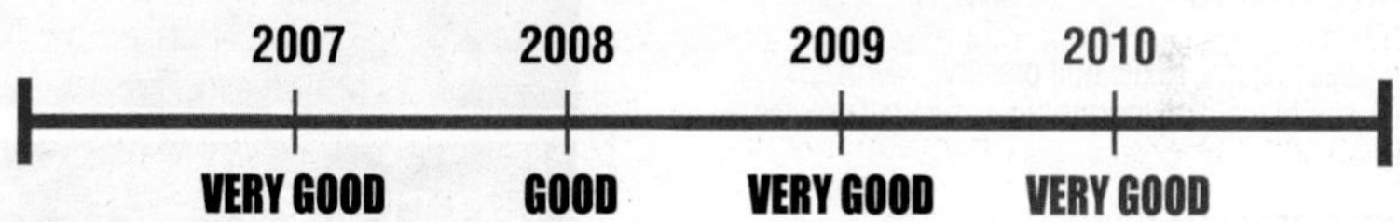

BODEGUES MACIÀ BATLE

Camí Coanegra, s/n
07320 Santa María del Camí (Illes Balears)
☎: +34 971 140 014 - Fax: +34 971 140 086
bodega@maciabatle.com
www.maciabatle.com

EL VINO DEL LLAÜT 2010 B
prensal, chardonnay.

90 Colour: bright straw. Nose: fresh, fresh fruit, white flowers, mineral. Palate: flavourful, fruity, good acidity.

LLUM 2010 B
prensal.

89 Colour: bright straw. Nose: ripe fruit, citrus fruit, white flowers. Palate: flavourful, fruity, fresh.

MACIÀ BATLE BLANC DE BLANCS 2010 B

88 Colour: bright straw. Nose: powerfull, ripe fruit, spicy, dried herbs. Palate: flavourful, powerful, fleshy.

DOS MARIAS 2010 T

89 Colour: cherry, purple rim. Nose: fresh fruit, red berry notes, floral, creamy oak, sweet spices. Palate: flavourful, fruity, good acidity, round tannins.

P. DE MARÌA 2008 T
manto negro, cabernet sauvignon, syrah, merlot.

93 Colour: bright cherry. Nose: ripe fruit, sweet spices, creamy oak, expressive, balsamic herbs. Palate: flavourful, fruity, toasty, round tannins.

MACIÀ BATLE 2008 TC

88 Colour: deep cherry. Nose: fruit preserve, warm, toasty, spicy, scrubland. Palate: spirituous, fine bitter notes, fine tannins.

MACIÀ BATLE RESERVA PRIVADA 2007 TR
manto negro, callet, cabernet sauvignon, merlot.

91 Color cherry, garnet rim. Aroma ripe fruit, spicy, creamy oak, toasty, complex. Taste powerful, flavourful, toasty, round tannins.

CELLER TIANNA NEGRE

Camí des Mitjans. Desvio a la izquierda en el km. 1,5 de la Ctra. Binissalem-Inca
07350 Binissalem (Illes Balears)
☎: +34 971 886 826 - Fax: +34 971 226 201
info@tiannanegre.com
www.tiannanegre.com

SES NINES BLANC SELECCIÓ 2010 B
prensal, chardonnay, moscatel de frontignan.

85 Colour: bright straw. Nose: fresh, ripe fruit, medium intensity. Palate: flavourful, fruity, good acidity, balanced.

SES NINES SELECCIÓ 07/9 2009 T
manto negro, cabernet sauvignon, syrah, merlot, callet.

88 Colour: bright cherry. Nose: sweet spices, creamy oak, fruit liqueur notes. Palate: flavourful, toasty, round tannins.

RANDEMAR BLANC 2010 B
prensal, chardonnay, moscatel de frontignan.

84 Colour: bright straw. Nose: fresh, white flowers, candied fruit. Palate: flavourful, fruity, good acidity, balanced.

SES NINES ROSAT 2010 RD
syrah, manto negro, cabernet sauvignon.

87 Color rose, purple rim. Aroma powerfull, ripe fruit, red berry notes, floral, expressive. Taste fleshy, powerful, fruity, fresh.

SES NINES NEGRE 2010 T
manto negro, cabernet sauvignon, callet, syrah, monastrell.

89 Colour: cherry, garnet rim. Nose: scrubland, warm, complex. Palate: flavourful, spicy, balsamic.

RANDEMAR NEGRE 2010 T
callet, manto negro, monastrell, cabernet sauvignon, syrah, merlot.

86 Colour: cherry, garnet rim. Nose: medium intensity, ripe fruit, warm. Palate: flavourful, round tannins, good acidity.

TIANNA NEGRE 2009 T
manto negro, cabernet sauvignon, syrah, callet, merlot.

90 Colour: cherry, garnet rim. Nose: spicy, creamy oak, toasty, fruit expression, earthy notes. Palate: powerful, toasty, round tannins, fleshy, fine bitter notes.

TIANNA NEGRE "BOCCHORIS" 2009 T
manto negro, cabernet sauvignon, syrah, callet, merlot.

93 Colour: cherry, garnet rim. Nose: spicy, creamy oak, toasty, complex, fruit expression, characterful, mineral. Palate: powerful, flavourful, toasty, round tannins.

JAUME DE PUNTIRÓ

Pza. Nova, 23
07320 Santa María del Camí (Illes Balears)
☎: +34 971 620 023 - Fax: +34 971 620 023
pere@vinsjaumedepuntiro.com
www.vinsjaumedepuntiro.com

DAURAT 2010 BFB
100% prensal.

90 Colour: bright straw. Nose: fresh fruit, citrus fruit, grassy, spicy. Palate: flavourful, fruity, spicy.

JAUME DE PUNTIRÓ BLANC 2010 B
100% prensal.

87 Colour: bright straw. Nose: powerfull, characterful, fresh fruit, citrus fruit. Palate: flavourful, fruity, fresh.

BUC 2006 TC
55% manto negro, 45% cabernet sauvignon.

90 Colour: cherry, garnet rim. Nose: spicy, creamy oak, toasty, balsamic herbs, fruit liqueur notes. Palate: powerful, flavourful, toasty, round tannins.

J.P. 2006 TC
50% manto negro, 50% cabernet sauvignon.

89 Colour: cherry, garnet rim. Nose: spicy, creamy oak, toasty, complex, fruit preserve, warm. Palate: powerful, flavourful, toasty, round tannins.

JOSÉ L. FERRER

Conquistador, 103
07350 Binissalem (Illes Balears)
☎: +34 971 511 050 - Fax: +34 971 870 084
info@vinosferrer.com
www.vinosferrer.com

JOSÉ L. FERRER VERITAS 2010 B
60% moll, 40% chardonnay.

87 Colour: bright straw. Nose: ripe fruit, citrus fruit, sweet spices. Palate: fine bitter notes, good acidity, flavourful.

JOSÉ L. FERRER BLANC DE BLANCS 2010 B
moll, chardonnay, moscatel.

82 Colour: bright straw. Nose: ripe fruit, grassy, citrus fruit. Palate: flavourful, fruity, fresh, fleshy.

JOSÉ L. FERRER 2010 RD
manto negro, callet, tempranillo, cabernet sauvignon, syrah.

84 Colour: rose, purple rim. Nose: powerfull, red berry notes, floral. Palate: fleshy, powerful, fruity, fresh.

JOSÉ L. FERRER PEDRA DE BINISSALEM ROSAT 2010 RD
manto negro, cabernet sauvignon.

83 Colour: rose. Nose: powerfull, warm, ripe fruit. Palate: flavourful, powerful.

JOSÉ L. FERRER D2UES SYRAH CALLET 2009 T
50% syrah, 50% callet.

88 Colour: cherry, garnet rim. Nose: powerfull, ripe fruit, fruit expression, toasty, sweet spices. Palate: flavourful, powerful, fleshy, round tannins.

JOSÉ L. FERRER 2008 TC
manto negro, tempranillo, cabernet sauvignon, callet, syrah.

90 Colour: cherry, garnet rim. Nose: spicy, creamy oak, toasty, fruit liqueur notes. Palate: powerful, flavourful, toasty, round tannins.

JOSÉ L. FERRER PEDRA DE BINISSALEM 2009 T
manto negro, cabernet sauvignon.

88 Color bright cherry. Aroma ripe fruit, sweet spices, creamy oak, expressive. Taste flavourful, fruity, toasty, round tannins.

JOSÉ L. FERRER D2UES CABERNET SAUVIGNON MANTONEGRO 2009 T
50% cabernet sauvignon, 50% manto negro.

87 Colour: cherry, garnet rim. Nose: powerfull, fruit liqueur notes, fruit liqueur notes, toasty, spicy. Palate: flavourful, powerful, spicy, sweetness.

JOSÉ L. FERRER 2005 TR
manto negro, callet, cabernet sauvignon.

90 Colour: cherry, garnet rim. Nose: mineral, toasty, spicy. Palate: flavourful, spicy, ripe fruit, long.

JOSÉ L. FERRER BRUT VERITAS 2009 ESP
moll, moscatel, parellada.

85 Colour: bright straw. Nose: white flowers, fine lees, candied fruit. Palate: powerful, sweetness, fine bitter notes.

JOSÉ L. FERRER BRUT ROSADO VERITAS 2009 ESP
manto negro, tempranillo, cabernet sauvignon.

84 Colour: light cherry. Nose: fruit expression, raspberry, characterful. Palate: fleshy, concentrated, fruity.

JOSÉ L. FERRER VERITAS DOLÇ 2010 MOSCATEL
100% moscatel grano menudo.

87 Colour: bright straw. Nose: candied fruit, fruit liqueur notes, citrus fruit. Palate: flavourful, sweetness, light-bodied.

VINS NADAL

Ramón Llull, 2
07350 Binissalem (Illes Balears)
☎: +34 971 511 058 - Fax: +34 971 870 150
albaflor@vinsnadal.com
www.vinsnadal.com

ALBAFLOR 2010 RD
45% manto negro, 44% merlot, 11% cabernet sauvignon.

88 Color rose, purple rim. Aroma powerfull, ripe fruit, red berry notes, floral, expressive. Taste fleshy, powerful, fruity, fresh.

ALBAFLOR 2007 TC
71% manto negro, 20% cabernet sauvignon, 9% merlot.

87 Colour: cherry, garnet rim. Nose: medium intensity, ripe fruit, spicy, aromatic coffee. Palate: fine bitter notes, spicy, ripe fruit.

ALBAFLOR 2006 TR
50% manto negro, 30% cabernet sauvignon, 20% merlot.

84 Colour: cherry, garnet rim. Nose: fruit preserve, fruit liqueur notes, toasty, wet leather. Palate: fine bitter notes, good acidity, easy to drink.

VINYA TAUJANA

Balanguera, 40
07142 Santa Eugenia (Illes Balears)
☎: +34 971 144 494 - Fax: +34 971 144 494
vinyataujana@gmail.com

VINYA TAUJANA BLANC DE BLANC 2010 B
100% moll.

89 Colour: bright straw. Nose: powerfull, candied fruit, citrus fruit, sweet spices. Palate: flavourful, fruity, spicy, round tannins.

VINYA TAUJANA ROSAT 2010 RD
100% manto negro.

81 Colour: coppery red. Nose: medium intensity, warm, fruit liqueur notes. Palate: fine bitter notes, warm.

TORRENT FALS 2007 TC
manto negro, cabernet sauvignon, syrah.

88 Colour: bright cherry. Nose: fruit liqueur notes, fruit expression, creamy oak, sweet spices. Palate: flavourful, spicy, ripe fruit.

VINYES I VINS CA SA PADRINA

Camí dels Horts, s/n
07140 Sencelles (Illes Balears)
☎: +34 660 211 939 - Fax: +34 971 874 370
cellermantonegro@gmail.com

MOLLET GONZÁLEZ SUÑER 2010 B JOVEN
50% prensal, 50% chardonnay.

90 Colour: bright straw. Nose: fresh, fresh fruit, white flowers, mineral, complex. Palate: flavourful, fruity, good acidity, balanced.

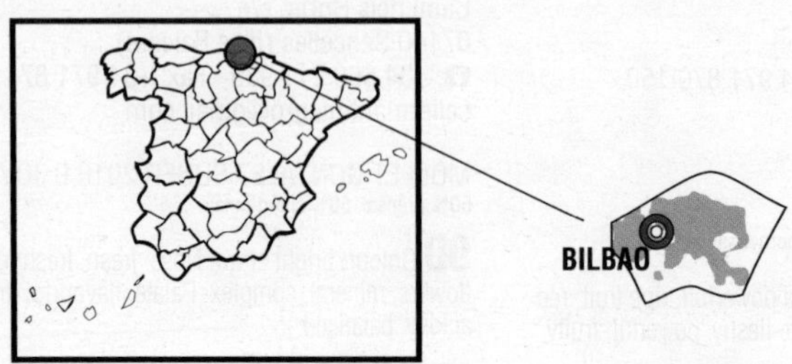

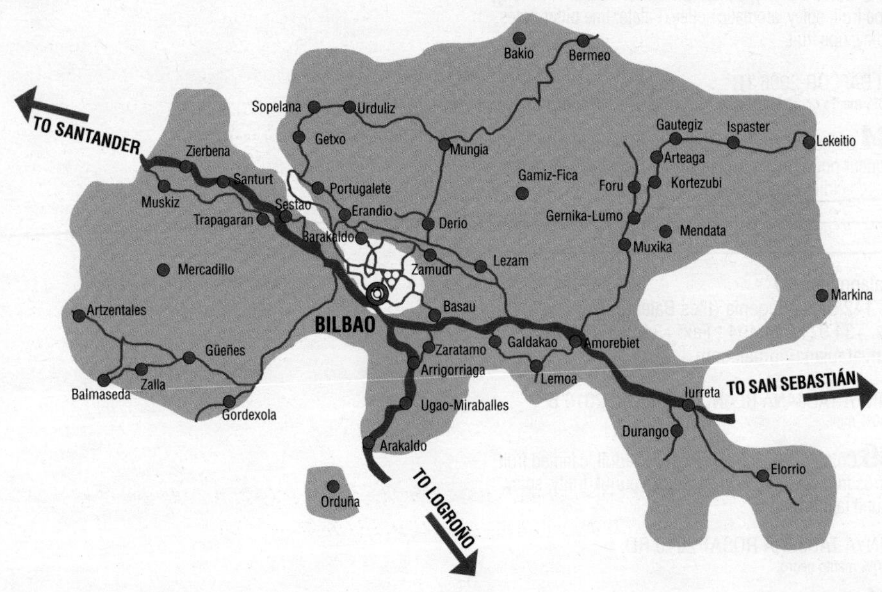

Consejo Regulador
DO Boundary

NEWS ABOUT THE VINTAGE:

Leaving aside all sorts of controversies over the use of the word txakoli (or chacolí) for wines made outside the Basque Country, Bizkaiko Txakolina is steadily keeping its leading role within txakoli's realm, as well as its attributes as a prominent and qualitative wine region both within the Spanish and international contexts, not in vain it was the first designation of origin of txakoli to undertake research and development not only on the local grape varieties, but also on foreign ones such as *sauvignon blanc* and *folle blanche*. Technology and technical qualification of the region's winemakers has taken the quality of txakoli wines from Vizcaya well beyond their former status as local "tavern wines". In the last year the DO has focused on foreign markets in an attempt to diversify a demand deemed to be excessively local and has managed to open new markets in places like USA (88% of the DO's total exports), the Netherlands, Australia and China.

And they have good grounds for such success. The 2010 vintage is excellent, in spite of heavy winds and heavy rainfall during flowering, which meant a production fall of around 5% on 2009. A hot and dry summer did a lot of good to the vines and allowed vine growers the get the best out of *hondarribi zuri*, the star variety of the DO. Thus, white wines of 2010 show lots of freshness, plus the added complexity and richness that derives from harvesting grapes a bit riper than in other years. Altogether, the wines are full of aromas and typicity, fresh, fruity, with a riper character that brings in white drupe and slightly confected notes, and take them ultimately to higher scores.

Of all the samples tasted, 8 of them reach the 90-point boundary, for just 5 the previous year. Also the DO manages to bring the number of wines with 88 points or more from just 15 to 25 in this year's edition, an important increase in any case. Señorío de Otxaran 2010, Itsas Mendi Urezti 2008 and Uriondo Fermentado en Barrica 2009 get the top scores of the DO, something which tells us as well of the potential not only of the young wines but also of the barrel-fermented and on-the-lees renderings from previous vintages.

There is also a small red wine production in the region, wines made from *hondarrabi beltza*, with a fierce and fresh Atlantic character and some green nuances typical of that grape variety, which should not in any case be confused with underripe notes.

LOCATION:

In the province of Vizcaya. The production region covers both coastal areas and other areas inland.

CLIMATE:

Quite humid and mild due to the influence of the Bay of Biscay which tempers the temperatures. Fairly abundant rainfall, with an average of 1,000 to 1,300 mm per year.

SOIL:

Mainly clayey, although slightly acidic on occasions, with a fairly high organic matter content.

GRAPE VARIETIES:

WHITE: *Hondarrabi Zuri, Folle Blanche.*
RED: *Hondarrabi Beltza.*

FIGURES:

Vineyard surface: 342,86 – **Wine-Growers:** 235 – **Wineries:** 52 – **2010 Harvest rating:** Very Good – **Production:** 1,170,378 litres – **Market percentages:** 96,6% domestic. 3,4% export

DO BIZKAIKO TXAKOLINA

CONSEJO REGULADOR

Bº Mendibile, 42

48940 Leioa (Bizkaia)

☎: +34 946 076 071 - Fax: +34 946 076 072

@ info@bizkaikotxacolina.org

www.bizkaikotxakolina.org

GENERAL CHARACTERISTICS OF THE WINES

WHITES	These are the most characteristic of the denomination. They are characterised by their dull, straw yellow with, on occasions, green glimmer; their nose combines floral and fruity notes, although they have a more herbaceous character than those of Getaria due to the *Folle Blanche* variety, together with the *Hondarrabi* Zuri variety. on the palate they are light, easy drinking and have a freshness that gives them their high acidity.
ROSÉS	This type of wine is known in the region as "ojo de gallo" (i.e., cock's eye), although very few litres are made. They are light, fresh wines with pronounced acidity.
REDS	As with the rosé wines they are also a minority product; in fact, they are only produced in regions with a certain tradition. In general, they are excessively acidic.

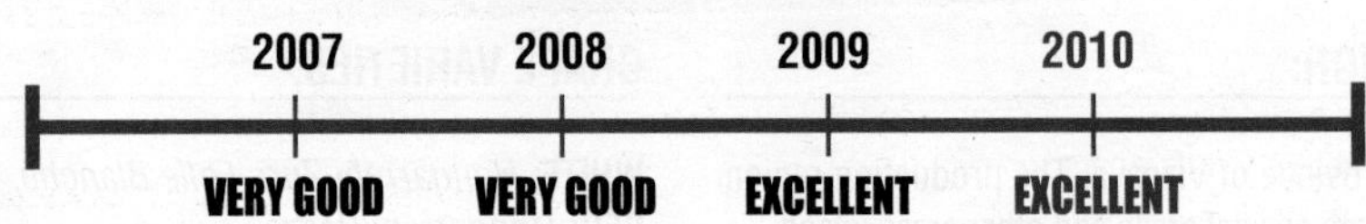

ABIO TXAKOLINA

Barrio Elexalde, 5 Caserío Basigo
48130 Bakio (Bizkaia)
☎: +34 946 194 345

ABIO TXACOLINA 2010 B

88 Colour: bright straw. Nose: white flowers, ripe fruit, varietal, grassy. Palate: good acidity, balanced, fine bitter notes.

ABIOGORRIA 2010 RD

82 Colour: rose, purple rim. Nose: red berry notes, ripe fruit. Palate: flavourful, fruity, sweetness.

ABIO BELTZA 2010 T

78

BASARTE

Urkitzaurrealde, 4
48130 Bakio (Bizkaia)
☎: +34 605 026 115
basarte@basarte.net
www.basarte.net

ADOS 2010 B
hondarrabi zuri.

86 Colour: pale. Nose: fresh fruit, citrus fruit, grassy. Palate: flavourful, light-bodied, fresh.

BIKANDI TXAKOLINA

Eguzkitza, 6A
48200 Durango (Bizkaia)
☎: +34 616 292 436 - Fax: +34 946 816 519
miren@bikanditxakolina.com
www.bikanditxakolina.com

BIKANDI TXACOLINA 2010 B
hondarrabi zuri zerratia, riesling, grand mansel.

88 Colour: bright straw. Nose: expressive, ripe fruit, citrus fruit, white flowers. Palate: flavourful, powerful, fresh.

BODEGA AMUNATEGI

San Bartolomé, 57
48350 Busturia (Bizkaia)
☎: +34 685 737 398
info@amunategi.eu
www.amunategi.eu

AMUNATEGI 2010 B
60% hondarrabi zuri, 35% hondarrabi zuri zerratia, 5% hondarrabi beltza.

88 Colour: bright straw. Nose: fresh, fresh fruit, white flowers, fine lees. Palate: flavourful, fruity, good acidity, balanced.

AMUNATEGI 2009 B
60% hondarrabi zuri, 35% hondarrabi zuri zerratia, 5% hondarrabi beltza.

87 Colour: pale. Nose: scrubland, balsamic herbs, citrus fruit, fresh fruit. Palate: flavourful, fine bitter notes, good acidity.

BODEGA BERROJA

Ctra. de Zugastieta al Balcón de Bizkaia. Ajuria Barrio Berroja
48392 Muxika (Bizkaia)
☎: +34 944 106 254 - Fax: +34 946 309 390
txakoli@bodegaberroja.com
www.bodegaberroja.com

AGUIRREBEKO 2010 B
85% hondarrabi zuri, 5% folle blanch, 10% riesling.

88 Colour: pale. Nose: balsamic herbs, citrus fruit, grassy, powerfull. Palate: flavourful, light-bodied, fruity.

BERROJA 2009 B
80% hondarrabi zuri, 20% riesling.

87 Colour: bright straw. Nose: white flowers, ripe fruit. Palate: flavourful, fruity, good acidity, balanced.

BODEGA ELIZALDE

Barrio Mendraka, 1
48230 Elorrio (Bizkaia)
☎: +34 946 820 000 - Fax: +34 946 820 000
kerixa@gmail.com

MENDRAKA 2010 B
95% hondarrabi zuri, 5% otras.

87 Colour: bright straw. Nose: fresh fruit, white flowers, powerfull, varietal. Palate: flavourful, fruity, good acidity.

BODEGA MERRUTXU

Caserío Merrutxu, Arboliz 15
48311 Ibarrangelu (Bizkaia)
☎: +34 946 276 435
koldo@merrutxu.com
www.casaruralpaisvasco.net

MERRUTXU 2010 B
55% hondarrabi zuri, 25% mune mahatsa, 20% chardonnay.

87 Colour: bright straw. Nose: ripe fruit, white flowers, tropical fruit. Palate: flavourful, fruity, fresh.

BODEGA VIÑA SULIBARRIA

El Bentorro, 4
48191 Galdames (Bizkaia)
☎: +34 946 100 107 - Fax: +34 946 100 107
info@vinasulibarria.com
www.viñasulibarria.com

TORRE DE LOIZAGA BIGARREN 2010 B

85 Colour: bright straw. Nose: fresh, white flowers, varietal. Palate: flavourful, fruity, good acidity, balanced.

BODEGAS GURRUTXAGA

Baurdo Auzoa, s/n
48289 Mendexa ()
☎: +34 946 844 937
www.bodegasgurrutxaga.com

GURRUTXAGA 2010 B

83 Colour: straw. Nose: fresh fruit, citrus fruit, scrubland, balsamic herbs. Palate: flavourful, fruity, fresh.

DONIENE GORRONDONA TXAKOLINA

Gibelorratzagako San Pelaio, 1
48130 Bakio (Bizkaia)
☎: +34 946 194 795 - Fax: +34 946 195 831
gorrondona@donienegorrondona.com
www.donienegorrondona.com

DONIENE 2010 BFB
100% hondarrabi zuri.

92 Colour: bright yellow. Nose: powerfull, ripe fruit, sweet spices, creamy oak, fragrant herbs. Palate: rich, flavourful, fresh, round, elegant.

DONIENE 2010 B
100% hondarrabi zuri.

90 Colour: bright straw. Nose: fresh, fresh fruit, white flowers, balsamic herbs, grassy. Palate: flavourful, fruity, good acidity.

ARTXANDA 2010 B
85% hondarrabi zuri, 15% otras.

90 Colour: bright straw. Nose: fresh, fresh fruit, white flowers, varietal. Palate: flavourful, fruity, good acidity, balanced.

GORRONDONA 2010 B
85% hondarrabi zuri, 5% hondarrabi beltza, 10% otras.

87 Colour: bright straw. Nose: fresh, white flowers, fruit expression, grassy. Palate: flavourful, fruity, good acidity, balanced.

GORRONDONA 2010 T
100% hondarrabi beltza.

87 Colour: cherry, purple rim. Nose: red berry notes, floral, fragrant herbs, complex, mineral. Palate: powerful, fruity, flavourful, easy to drink.

ERDIKOETXE LANDETXEA

Goitioltza, 38
48196 Lezama (Bizkaia)
☎: +34 944 573 285 - Fax: +34 944 573 285
erdikoetxelandetxea@hotmail.com
www.nekatur.net

ERDIKOETXE 2010 B
hondarrabi zuri, folle blanch.

88 Colour: bright straw. Nose: fresh fruit, white flowers. Palate: flavourful, fruity, good acidity, balanced.

ERDIKOETXE 2010 T

83 Colour: cherry, purple rim. Nose: fresh fruit, red berry notes, grassy. Palate: flavourful, fruity, fine bitter notes.

GARKALDE TXAKOLINA

Barrio Goitioltza, 8 - Caserio Garkalde
48196 Lezama (Bizkaia)
☎: +34 944 556 412
garkaldetxakolina@hotmail.com

GARKALDE TXACOLINA 2010 B
hondarrabi zuri.

86 Colour: bright straw. Nose: fresh, white flowers, grassy, tropical fruit. Palate: flavourful, fruity, good acidity, balanced.

ITSASMENDI

Barrio Arane, 3
48300 Gernika (Bizkaia)
☎: +34 946 270 316 - Fax: +34 946 251 032
info@bodegasitsasmendi.com
www.bodegasitsasmendi.com

ITSAS MENDI 2010 B
hondarrabi zuri.

89 Colour: bright straw. Nose: white flowers, ripe fruit, grassy. Palate: flavourful, fruity, good acidity, fine bitter notes.

ITSASMENDI Nº 7 2009 B
hondarrabi zuri, riesling.

87 Colour: bright straw. Nose: fresh, white flowers, medium intensity, ripe fruit. Palate: fruity, good acidity, balanced.

ITSAS MENDI UREZTI 2008 B
hondarrabi zuri.

91 Colour: bright straw. Nose: fresh, candied fruit, citrus fruit, white flowers. Palate: flavourful, fruity, good acidity, sweetness.

ITSASMENDI Nº 7 2008 B
hondarrabi zuri, riesling.

88 Colour: bright straw. Nose: candied fruit, citrus fruit, mineral. Palate: flavourful, fruity, good acidity.

ITURRIALDE

Barrio Legina, s/n
48195 Larrabetzu (Bizkaia)
☎: +34 946 742 706 - Fax: +34 946 741 221
txakoli@gorkaizagirre.com
www.gorkaizagirre.com

MARKO 2010 B

91 Colour: bright straw. Nose: white flowers, citrus fruit, fragrant herbs. Palate: powerful, flavourful, fruity, fleshy, creamy.

UIXAR 2010 B
hondarrabi zerratia.

90 Colour: bright straw. Nose: fresh, white flowers, citrus fruit, dry stone, mineral. Palate: flavourful, fruity, balanced, fine bitter notes.

SARATSU 2010 B

89 Colour: bright straw. Nose: fresh, balsamic herbs, ripe fruit. Palate: flavourful, fruity, good acidity, balanced.

NEKESOLO 2010 B

88 Colour: bright straw. Nose: fresh, white flowers, ripe fruit. Palate: flavourful, fruity, good acidity, balanced.

GORKA IZAGIRRE 2010 B

88 Colour: bright straw. Nose: fresh, white flowers, grassy, balsamic herbs. Palate: fruity, good acidity, balanced.

TORREKO 2010 B

87 Colour: bright straw. Nose: white flowers, fresh fruit, fruit expression, balsamic herbs. Palate: flavourful, fruity, light-bodied.

MUNETABERRI 2010 B

87 Colour: pale. Nose: grassy, fresh fruit, balsamic herbs. Palate: flavourful, light-bodied, fruity.

EGIA ENEA 2010 B
hondarrabi zuri.

86 Colour: bright straw. Nose: white flowers, ripe fruit, dried herbs. Palate: good acidity, fresh, flavourful.

E-GALA 2010 B

86 Colour: bright straw. Nose: fresh, fresh fruit, white flowers. Palate: flavourful, fruity, good acidity, balanced.

GORKA IZAGIRRE ARIMA 2009 B
hondarrabi zerratia, hondarrabi zuri.

90 Color golden. Aroma powerfull, floral, honeyed notes, candied fruit, fragrant herbs. Taste flavourful, sweet, fresh, fruity, good acidity, long.

MAGALARTE LEZAMA

B. Garaioltza, 92 B
48196 Lezama (Bizkaia)
☎: +34 944 556 508 - Fax: +34 944 556 508
magalarteinaki@yahoo.es

MAGALARTE IÑAKI ARETXABALETA 2010 B
hondarrabi zuri.

88 Colour: bright straw. Nose: balsamic herbs, scrubland, fruit expression, ripe fruit. Palate: fine bitter notes, balanced, good acidity.

SAGASTIBELTZA KARRANTZA 2010 B
hondarrabi zuri.

88 Colour: bright straw. Nose: fresh fruit, white flowers, expressive. Palate: flavourful, fruity, good acidity, balanced.

MAGALARTE ZAMUDIO

Arteaga Auzoa, 107
48170 Zamudio (Bizkaia)
☎: +34 944 521 431 - Fax: +34 944 521 431
magalarte@hotmail.com

MAGALARTE JABI ARETXABALETA 2010 B

88 Colour: bright straw. Nose: fresh, white flowers, varietal, ripe fruit. Palate: flavourful, fruity, good acidity, fine bitter notes.

ARTEBAKARRA 2010 B

86 Colour: bright straw. Nose: fresh, expressive, ripe fruit. Palate: flavourful, fruity, fine bitter notes.

OTXANDURI TXAKOLINA

Otxanduri, 41
48498 Arrankudiaga (Bizkaia)
☎: +34 946 481 769
otxanduri@euskalnet.net

OTXANDURI 2010 B

89 Colour: bright straw. Nose: white flowers, ripe fruit, citrus fruit. Palate: flavourful, fruity, good acidity, balanced.

ARTZAI 2009 B
hondarrabi zuri.

90 Colour: bright straw. Nose: fresh fruit, white flowers, sweet spices. Palate: flavourful, fruity, good acidity.

ARTZAI 2008 B
hondarrabi zuri.

88 Colour: bright yellow. Nose: powerfull, sweet spices, fragrant herbs, toasty. Palate: rich, smoky aftertaste, flavourful, fresh, fine bitter notes.

TXAKOLI LLARENA

Eras de Polankos, 13
48460 Orduña (Bizkaia)
☎: +34 945 384 300

TXAKOLI LLARENA 2010 B

83 Colour: bright straw. Nose: fresh fruit, citrus fruit, grassy. Palate: flavourful, fruity, fresh.

TXAKOLI OXINBALTZA

Olleria 7 5ºA
48200 Durango (Bizkaia)
☎: +34 686 345 131
oxinbaltza@oxinbaltza.com
www.oxinbaltza.com

OXINBALTZA 2010 B
hondarrabi zuri.

88 Colour: bright yellow. Nose: ripe fruit, sweet spices, creamy oak, fragrant herbs. Palate: rich, smoky aftertaste, flavourful, fresh, good acidity.

MAIORA 2010 B

87 Colour: bright straw. Nose: grassy, citrus fruit, fruit expression. Palate: flavourful, fruity, fresh.

KATAN 2010 B
hondarrabi zuri.

86 Colour: bright straw. Nose: balsamic herbs, scrubland, citrus fruit, fresh fruit. Palate: flavourful, fruity, fresh.

MAUMA 2010 T
hondarrabi beltza.

82 Colour: cherry, purple rim. Nose: fresh fruit, grassy. Palate: flavourful, fruity.

TXAKOLI TXABARRI

Juan Antonio del Yelmo, 1 4C
48860 Zalla (Bizkaia)
☎: +34 946 390 947 - Fax: +34 946 390 947
itxasa@yahoo.es

TXABARRI 2010 B
hondarrabi zuri, riesling, sauvignon blanc.

87 Colour: bright straw. Nose: fresh, white flowers, ripe fruit. Palate: flavourful, fruity, good acidity, balanced.

TXABARRI 2010 RD
hondarrabi beltza.

86 Colour: onion pink. Nose: elegant, candied fruit, dried flowers, red berry notes. Palate: light-bodied, flavourful, good acidity, long, spicy.

TXABARRI 2010 T
hondarrabi beltza.

84 Colour: cherry, purple rim. Nose: fresh fruit, red berry notes. Palate: flavourful, fruity, good acidity.

URIONDO

Barrio Urriondo, 2
48480 Zaratamo (Bizkaia)
☎: +34 946 711 870
uriondo.txakoli@gmail.com

URIONDO CUVÉE 2010 B
hondarrabi zuri, mune matja.

86 Colour: bright straw. Nose: ripe fruit, citrus fruit, white flowers. Palate: flavourful, fruity.

URIONDO 2009 BFB
hondarrabi zuri, mune matja.

91 Colour: bright yellow. Nose: sweet spices, creamy oak, fragrant herbs, expressive, ripe fruit. Palate: rich, flavourful, fresh, good acidity.

VIRGEN DE LOREA

Barrio de Lorea
48860 Otxaran-Zalla (Bizkaia)
☎: +34 946 390 296 - Fax: +34 946 670 521
espancor@cnb.informail.es
bodegasvirgendelorea.com

SEÑORÍO DE OTXARAN 2010 B
hondarrabi zuri, folle blanch.

91 Colour: bright straw. Nose: fresh, fresh fruit, white flowers, dry stone. Palate: flavourful, fruity, good acidity, balanced.

ARETXAGA 2010 B
hondarrabi zuri.

88 Colour: bright straw. Nose: fresh, white flowers, expressive. Palate: flavourful, fruity, good acidity, balanced.

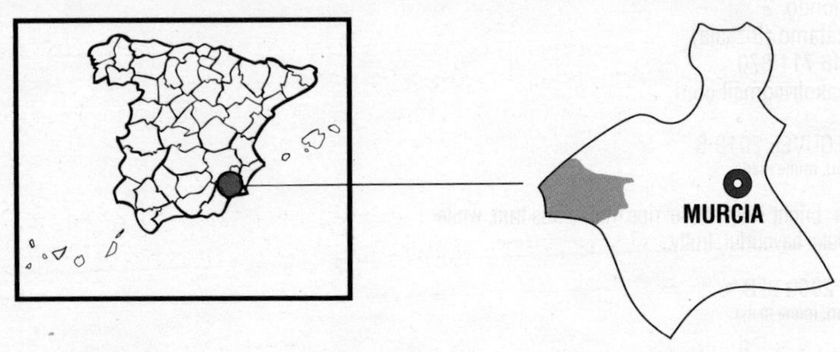
MURCIA

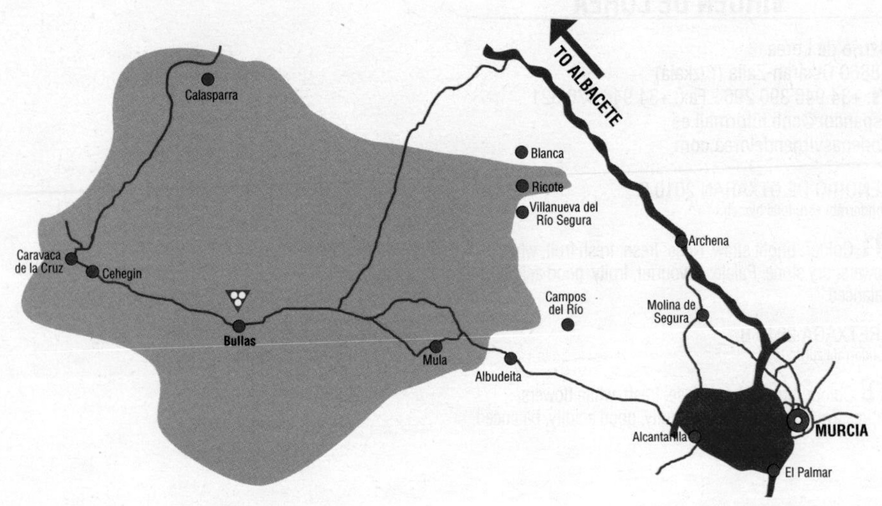
TO ALBACETE
Calasparra
Blanca
Ricote
Villanueva del Río Segura
Archena
Caravaca de la Cruz
Cehegin
Campos del Río
Molina de Segura
Bullas
Mula
Albudeita
Alcantarilla
MURCIA
El Palmar

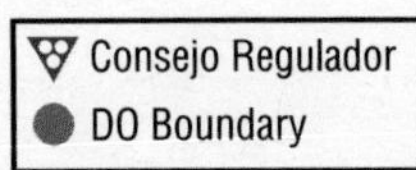
Consejo Regulador
DO Boundary

NEWS ABOUT THE VINTAGE:

Bullas is likely to be the territory to find the best varietal expression of *monastrell*. Having a higher altitude than regions like Alicante or Jumilla –where *monastrell* is also widely planted–, allows Bullas to harvest grapes with optimal maturity levels, the likes of which are only to be found in foreign places like Bandol, in Provenze.

Wine in Bullas is made from 100% *monastrell* almost in every case, so that is obviously the star grape within the DO and gets the best ratings. Two different vintages of Lavia+ Monastrell Cepas Viejas are top of the ranking.

There are some plantings of *syrah* in Bullas. The French grape is sometimes blended with *monastrell* in wines like 3000 Años, from Bodegas del Rosario, a 50% *syrah* and 50% *monastrell* rendering that got 92 points.

Apart from these examples, we are still missing the kind of fresher and cooler wines we understand this micro-zone in the province of Murcia ought to be able to make, as it proved indeed in years like 2008 and 2009. For, overall, we get the feeling that their wines are nowadays too similar to those from Yecla and Jumilla, only just slightly more confected. On the other hand, we are also missing a little more pre-eminence on the part of Bodegas Balcona, the one-time leading house in the region, when José Luis Pérez (Clos Martinet) designed for them Partal, a red wine of note that a few years back lead us straight to the discovery of this far away corner in the mountains of Murcia.

LOCATION:

In the province of Murcia. It covers the municipal areas of Bullas, Cehegín, Mula and Ricote, and several vineyards in the vicinity of Calasparra, Moratalla and Lorca.

CLIMATE:

Mediterranean, with an average annual temperature of 15.6 °C and low rainfall (average of 300 mm per year). The heavy showers and storms which occur in the region are another defining element.

SOIL:

Brownish - grey limey soil, with limestone crusts, and alluvial. The terrain is rugged and determined by the layout of the little valleys, each with their own microclimate. Distinction can be made between 3 areas: one to the north north - east with an altitude of 400 – 500 m; another in the central region, situated at an altitude of 500 – 600 m; and the third in the western and north - western region, with the highest altitude (500 – 810 m), the highest concentration of vineyards and the best potential for quality.

GRAPE VARIETIES:

WHITE: *Macabeo* (main), *Airén, Chardonnay, Malvasía, Moscatel de Grano Menudo* and *Sauvignon Blanc*.
RED: *Monastrell* (main), *Petit Verdot, Tempranillo, Cabernet Sauvignon, Syrah, Merlot* and *Garnacha*.

FIGURES:

Vineyard surface: 2,563 – **Wine-Growers:** 609 – **Wineries:** 13 – **2010 Harvest rating:** S/C – **Production:** 1,390,000 litres – **Market percentages:** 70% domestic. 30% export

CONSEJO REGULADOR
Avda. de Murcia, 4
30180 Bullas (Murcia)
☎: +34 968 652 601 - Fax: +34 968 652 601
@ consejoregulador@vinosdebullas.es
www.vinosdebullas.es

GENERAL CHARACTERISTICS OF THE WINES

WHITES	Produced with *Macabeo* and *Airén*, they are pale yellow and have pleasant fruity notes.
ROSÉS	The varietal character of those produced with *Monastrell* stands out. They are light, pleasant and easy drinking. Those produced from *Garnacha* are full - bodied on the palate.
REDS	Those produced from *Monastrell* and *Tempranillo* stand out for their Mediterranean character, sun - drenched fruit and fruity character, although they are less rounded than those of Jumilla and Alicante. On the other hand, their inclusion in the blend of the new varieties recently approved by the Council should afford greater structure and longevity to the red wines.

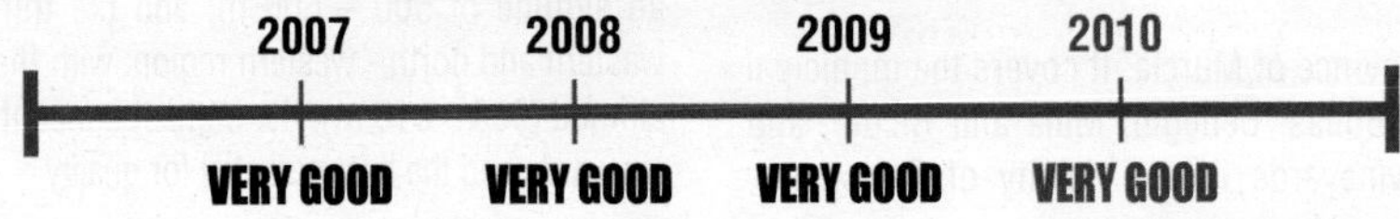

BODEGA BALCONA

Ctra. Bullas-Avilés, Km. 10 Valle del Aceniche
30180 Bullas (Murcia)
☎: +34 968 652 891
info@partal-vinos.com
www.partal-vinos.com

PARTAL DE AUTOR 2006 T
50% monastrell, 25% syrah, 15% merlot, 10% cabernet sauvignon.

88 Colour: cherry, garnet rim. Nose: spicy, creamy oak, toasty, overripe fruit. Palate: powerful, flavourful, toasty, round tannins.

37 BARRICAS DE PARTAL 2006 TC
60% monastrell, 20% syrah, 10% tempranillo, 10% cabernet sauvignon.

84 Colour: cherry, garnet rim. Nose: complex, fruit liqueur notes, overripe fruit. Palate: powerful, toasty, round tannins, sweetness.

BODEGA MONASTRELL

Paraje El Aceniche
30430 Cemejín (Murcia)
☎: +34 968 653 708 - Fax: +34 968 653 708
info@bodegamonastrell.com
www.bodegamonastrell.com

CHAVEO DULCE 2008 T FERMENTADO EN BARRICA
100% monastrell.

82 Colour: cherry, garnet rim. Nose: sweet spices, pattiserie, fresh. Palate: spicy, easy to drink.

VALCHE 2007 TC
100% monastrell.

90 Colour: cherry, garnet rim. Nose: ripe fruit, spicy, complex, new oak, roasted coffee. Palate: powerful, flavourful, toasty, round tannins.

ALMUDÍ UNO 2007 TC
100% petit verdot.

88 Colour: bright cherry. Nose: ripe fruit, sweet spices. Palate: flavourful, fruity, toasty, round tannins.

ALMUDÍ TRES 2007 TC
76% monastrell, 12% tempranillo, 12% petit verdot.

88 Colour: bright cherry. Nose: sweet spices, creamy oak, macerated fruit. Palate: flavourful, fruity, toasty, round tannins.

CHAVEO 2007 TC
100% monastrell.

88 Colour: bright cherry. Nose: sweet spices, expressive, ripe fruit, toasty. Palate: flavourful, fruity, toasty, round tannins.

VALCHE 2006 TC
100% monastrell.

92 Colour: cherry, garnet rim. Nose: mineral, ripe fruit, toasty, creamy oak. Palate: flavourful, fleshy, spicy.

CHAVEO 2006 TC
100% monastrell.

89 Color cherry, garnet rim. Aroma ripe fruit, spicy, creamy oak, toasty, complex. Taste powerful, flavourful, toasty, round tannins.

BODEGA TERCIA DE ULEA

Tercia de Ulea, s/n. Ctra. B-35 Km. 3,5
30440 Moratalla (Murcia)
☎: +34 968 433 213 - Fax: +34 968 433 965
druiz@terciadeulea.com
www.terciadeulea.com

ADIVINA 2010 RD
64% monastrell, 18% syrah, 18% tempranillo.

86 Colour: brilliant rose. Nose: elegant, candied fruit, dried flowers, red berry notes. Palate: light-bodied, flavourful, good acidity, long, sweetness.

REBELDÍA 2010 RD
80% monastrell, 15% syrah, 5% tempranillo.

83 Colour: rose, purple rim. Nose: red berry notes, floral, medium intensity, candied fruit. Palate: fleshy, fruity, fresh.

TERCIA DE ULEA 2009 T
monastrell, tempranillo.

87 Colour: bright cherry. Nose: expressive, overripe fruit. Palate: flavourful, fruity, toasty, round tannins.

VIÑA BOTIAL 2009 T ROBLE
monastrell, tempranillo.

87 Colour: cherry, purple rim. Nose: expressive, floral, ripe fruit. Palate: flavourful, fruity, good acidity.

TERCIA DE ULEA 2008 TC
monastrell, tempranillo.

88 Colour: cherry, purple rim. Nose: expressive, fresh fruit, red berry notes, floral. Palate: fruity, good acidity, good finish.

BODEGAS CONTRERAS

Los Ríos, 2
30812 Avilés de Lorca (Murcia)
☎: +34 685 874 593 - Fax: +34 968 492 836
info@bodegas-contreras.com
www.bodegas-contreras.com

SORTIUS SYRAH 2009 T ROBLE
100% monastrell.

90 Colour: cherry, purple rim. Nose: fresh fruit, red berry notes, floral, balanced, violet drops. Palate: flavourful, fruity, good acidity, fleshy.

UVIO C 07 2007 TC
65% monastrell, 20% syrah, 15% cabernet franc.

84 Colour: cherry, garnet rim. Nose: creamy oak, toasty, overripe fruit. Palate: powerful, flavourful, toasty, round tannins.

BODEGAS DEL ROSARIO

Avda. de la Libertad, s/n
30180 Bullas (Murcia)
☎: +34 968 652 075 - Fax: +34 968 653 765
info@bodegasdelrosario.com
www.bodegasdelrosario.com

LAS REÑAS MACABEO 2010 B
macabeo.

84 Colour: bright straw. Nose: fresh, fresh fruit, medium intensity. Palate: fruity, good acidity, balanced.

LAS REÑAS MONASTRELL 2010 RD
100% monastrell.

86 Colour: rose, purple rim. Nose: ripe fruit, red berry notes, floral. Palate: fleshy, powerful, fruity, fresh.

LAS REÑAS MONASTRELL 2010 T
monastrell, tempranillo.

90 Colour: cherry, purple rim. Nose: fresh fruit, aromatic coffee, expressive. Palate: long, fleshy, flavourful.

LAS REÑAS 2008 T BARRICA
monastrell, syrah.

88 Colour: cherry, garnet rim. Nose: ripe fruit, spicy, toasty. Palate: fleshy, flavourful, toasty.

LAS REÑAS MONASTRELL - SHIRAZ 2007 TC
monastrell, syrah.

87 Colour: cherry, garnet rim. Nose: ripe fruit, spicy, creamy oak, toasty. Palate: powerful, flavourful, round tannins, ripe fruit.

3000 AÑOS 2006 T
50% monastrell, 50% syrah.

92 Colour: cherry, garnet rim. Nose: ripe fruit, spicy, creamy oak, toasty, mineral. Palate: powerful, flavourful, toasty, round tannins.

BODEGAS MADROÑAL

Partal, 6
30180 Bullas (Murcia)
☎: +34 968 655 183 - Fax: +34 968 654 479
info@bodegasmadronal.com
www.bodegasmadronal.com

MADROÑAL 2006 TC
monastrell, syrah.

83 Colour: bright cherry. Nose: sweet spices, creamy oak, overripe fruit, warm. Palate: flavourful, fruity, toasty, round tannins.

MADROÑAL 2005 TC
monastrell, syrah.

85 Colour: cherry, garnet rim. Nose: ripe fruit, spicy, toasty, complex. Palate: powerful, flavourful, toasty, round tannins.

MADROÑAL DE LA FAMILIA 2004 TC
monastrell, syrah.

87 Colour: bright cherry. Nose: sweet spices, creamy oak, expressive, overripe fruit. Palate: flavourful, fruity, toasty, round tannins.

SISCAR T
monastrell.

89 Color cherry, purple rim. Aroma expressive, fresh fruit, red berry notes, floral. Taste flavourful, fruity, good acidity, round tannins.

BODEGAS MERCADER-QUESADA

Herrera, 22
30180 Bullas (Murcia)
☎: +34 968 654 205 - Fax: +34 968 654 205
pilarquesadagil@yahoo.es
www.mundoenologico.com

MERCADER QUESADA VENDIMIA 2010 T

86 Colour: cherry, purple rim. Nose: red berry notes, floral, ripe fruit. Palate: flavourful, fruity, good acidity, round tannins.

MERCADER QUESADA SELECCIÓN MONASTRELL ECOLÓGICO 2007 T

83 Colour: cherry, garnet rim. Nose: creamy oak, toasty, complex, overripe fruit, fruit preserve. Palate: powerful, flavourful, toasty, round tannins.

CARRASCALEJO

Finca El Carrascalejo, s/n
30180 Bullas (Murcia)
☎: +34 968 652 003 - Fax: +34 968 652 003
carrascalejo@carrascalejo.com
www.carrascalejo.com

CARRASCALEJO 2010 RD
100% monastrell.

82 Colour: rose, purple rim. Nose: red berry notes, floral, medium intensity. Palate: fleshy, powerful, fruity, fresh.

CARRASCALEJO 2010 T
100% monastrell.

89 Color cherry, purple rim. Aroma expressive, fresh fruit, red berry notes, floral. Taste flavourful, fruity, good acidity, round tannins.

COOPERATIVA VINÍCOLA AGRARIA SAN ISIDRO

Pol. Ind. Marimingo- Altiplano, s/n
30180 Bullas (Murcia)
☎: +34 968 654 991 - Fax: +34 968 652 160
bodegasanisidro@terra.es

CEPAS DEL ZORRO MACABEO 2010 B
100% macabeo.

85 Colour: bright straw. Nose: fresh, fresh fruit, floral. Palate: flavourful, fruity, good acidity.

CEPAS DEL ZORRO 2010 RD
80% monastrell, 20% garnacha.

86 Colour: rose, purple rim. Nose: ripe fruit, floral, expressive. Palate: fleshy, powerful, fruity, fresh.

CEPAS DEL ZORRO 2008 TC
85% monastrell, 15% syrah.

84 Color cherry, garnet rim. Aroma ripe fruit, spicy, creamy oak, toasty, complex. Taste powerful, flavourful, toasty, round tannins.

MOLINO Y LAGARES DE BULLAS

Paraje Venta del Pino, Ctra. Portugales, Km. 12
30180 Bullas (Murcia)
☎: +34 638 046 694
lavia@bodegaslavia.com
www.bodegaslavia.com

LAVIA MONASTRELL SYRAH 2007 TC
70% monastrell, 30% syrah.

92 Colour: cherry, garnet rim. Nose: fragrant herbs, balsamic herbs, candied fruit. Palate: flavourful, spicy, good acidity, ripe fruit.

LAVIA+ MONASTRELL VIÑA VIEJA 2007 TC
100% monastrell.

92 Colour: cherry, garnet rim. Nose: ripe fruit, spicy, creamy oak, toasty, complex, earthy notes, balsamic herbs. Palate: powerful, flavourful, toasty, round tannins.

LAVIA+ MONASTRELL VIÑA VIEJA 2006 TC
100% monastrell.

93 Colour: cherry, garnet rim. Nose: ripe fruit, toasty, sweet spices, scrubland. Palate: powerful, flavourful, toasty, round tannins.

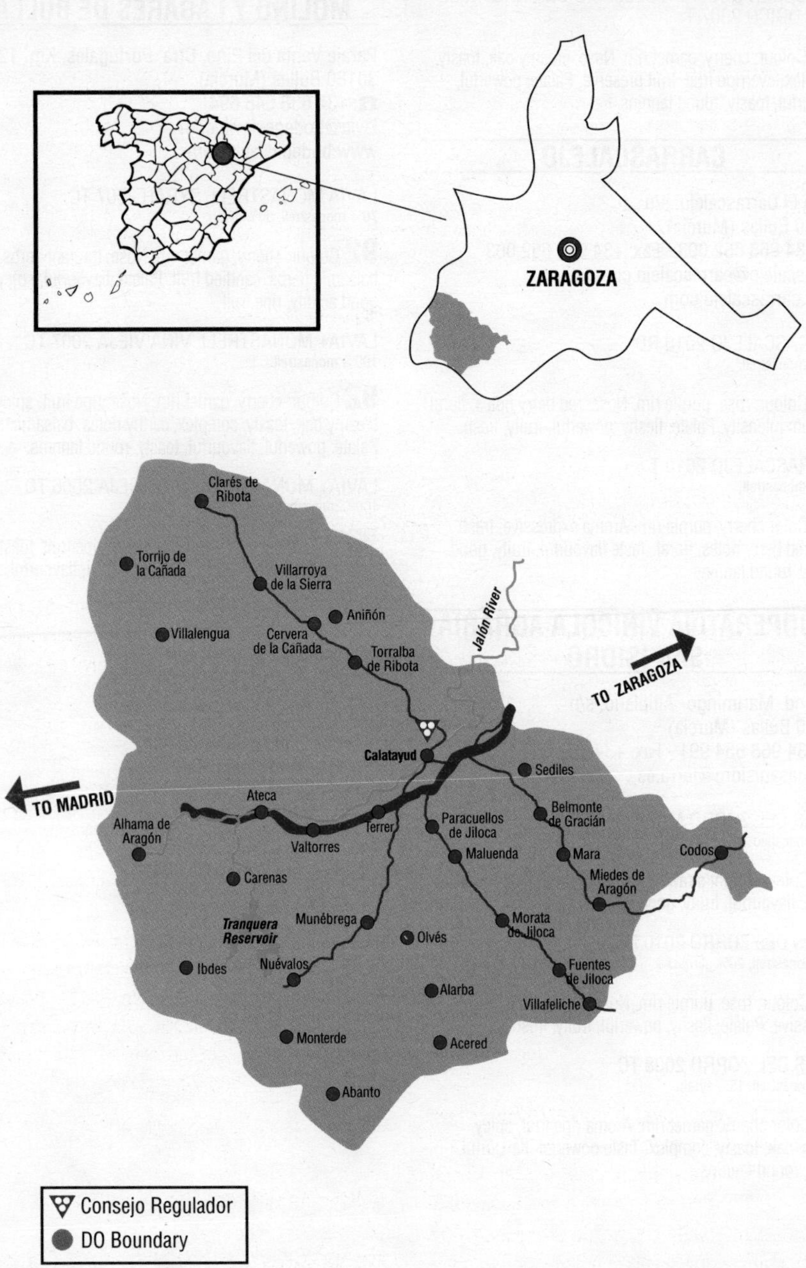
ZARAGOZA
Jalón River
TO ZARAGOZA
TO MADRID
Clarés de Ribota
Torrijo de la Cañada
Villarroya de la Sierra
Aniñón
Villalengua
Cervera de la Cañada
Torralba de Ribota
Calatayud
Sediles
Ateca
Terrer
Belmonte de Gracián
Alhama de Aragón
Valtorres
Paracuellos de Jiloca
Maluenda
Mara
Codos
Carenas
Miedes de Aragón
Tranquera Reservoir
Munébrega
Olvés
Morata de Jiloca
Nuévalos
Ibdes
Fuentes de Jiloca
Alarba
Villafeliche
Monterde
Acered
Abanto
Consejo Regulador
DO Boundary

NEWS ABOUT THE VINTAGE:

Spain, with all its vine-growing and winemaking diversity, is capable of generating great paradoxes such as the one that Calatayud is currently living. An area with wines of an excellent average quality, a well-defined style and a broad catalogue of brands is proving unable to reach the Spanish consumer, so they have resorted to exporting their products (up to 85% of their production). What we have then is that their wines are better known abroad, particularly in the English market –whose critics wax-lyrical about them– where they are bought at bargain prices. In the meantime, in Spain, they are perfectly unknown. Soils diversity, slope orientations and altitude are surely the region's best assets, along with judicious winemaking that does not go for "over-the-top" wines, not for lack the knowledge but simply because it does not match their winemakers character, or else out of fear that that sort of attitude may lead their wines to reach higher prices out of tune with the average prices in Aragón.

The best wines from Calatayud are those made from *garnacha*. It could not be otherwise, for diversity of soils and the region's star grape variety is a next to perfect marriage. The best of these "inner land" *garnachas* in this year's edition are Las Rocas de San Alejandro 2009, Las Rocas Viñas Viejas 2009 and Lajas 2008, up in our Podium with 93 points. We have hardly had any white wine samples, just seven of them, made mainly from *macabeo*, with some fresh, mineral and balsamic notes, wines that –overall– carry the same basic feature that characterize red wines from Calatayud, i.e., terroir. It is a pity, though, that the cooperative past of the region have brought grape prices down to unsustainable limits: nearly 800 hectares –mainly old vines– have been uprooted in the past three years.

In the light of the scores given to the wines from Calatayud, we can ascertain that there is not such a thing as a bad wine in the whole of the region; what is more, they have a magnificent terroir expression –a sense of territory, to put it differently–, a fact that the politicians should bear in mind when they think of Aragón –the autonomous region– as a whole, and therefore to try and promote these wonderful wines in Zaragoza (the region's capital) to start with!

LOCATION:

It is situated in the western region of the province of Zaragoza, along the foothills of the Sistema Ibérico, outlined by the network of rivers woven by the different tributaries of the Ebro: Jalón, Jiloca, Manubles, Mesa, Piedra and Ribota, and covers 46 municipal areas of the Ebro Valley.

CLIMATE:

Semi - arid and dry, although somewhat cooler than Cariñena and Borja, with cold winters, an average annual temperature which ranges between 12 and 14 °C, and a period of frost of between 5 and 7 months which greatly affects the production. The average rainfall ranges between 300 – 550 mm per year, with great day/night temperature contrasts during the ripening season.

SOIL:

In general, the soil has a high limestone content. It is formed by rugged stony materials from the nearby mountain ranges and is on many occasions accompanied by reddish clay. The region is the most rugged in Aragón, and the vineyards are situated at an altitude of between 550 and 880 m.

GRAPE VARIETIES:

WHITE: PREFERRED: *Macabeo* (25%) and *Malvasía*.
AUTHORIZED: *Moscatel de Alejandría, Garnacha*

Blanca, Sauvignon Blanc, Gewurztraiminer and *Chardonnay.*
RED: PREFERRED: *Garnacha Tinta* (61.9%), *Tempranillo* (10%) and *Mazuela.*
AUTHORIZED: *Monastrell, Cabernet Sauvignon, Merlot, Bobal* and *Syrah.*

FIGURES:

Vineyard surface: 3,594 – **Wine-Growers:** 992 – **Wineries:** 16 – **2010 Harvest rating:** S/C – **Production:** 8,290,000 litres – **Market percentages:** 15% domestic. 85% export

CONSEJO REGULADOR
Ctra. de Valencia, 8
50300 Calatayud (Zaragoza)
☎: +34 976 884 260 - Fax: +34 976 885 912
@ administracion@docalatayud.com
www.docalatayud.com

GENERAL CHARACTERISTICS OF THE WINES

WHITES	These are pale yellow and are characterised by their fresh, fruity style. There is some experience with fermentation in barrels.
ROSÉS	These constitute the most characteristic product of the region and are excellent value for money. Produced mainly from *Garnacha*, they stand out for their fine varietal expression, their brilliant raspberry colour, their freshness, their strong nose and their full-bodiedness, typical of the variety..
REDS	The *Garnacha* grapes give these wines a lively dark colour. The finest examples have quite a strong nose, with notes of ripe black fruit; on the palate they are full-bodied and sometimes somewhat warm.

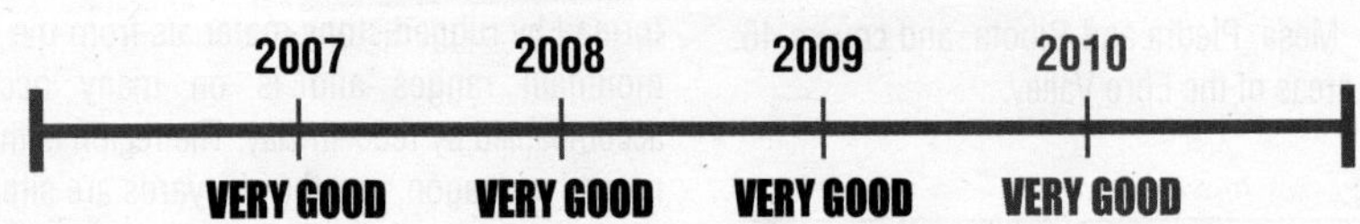

AGUSTÍN CUBERO

La Charluca
50300 Calatayud (Zaragoza)
☎: +34 976 882 332 - Fax: +34 976 887 245
calatayud@bodegascubero.com
www.bodegascubero.com

STYLO 2010 T
100% garnacha.

89 Colour: black cherry. Nose: ripe fruit, cocoa bean, wild herbs, sweet spices. Palate: flavourful, fruity, good structure.

NIETRO 2010 T
100% garnacha.

89 Colour: black cherry, purple rim. Nose: ripe fruit, powerfull, sweet spices. Palate: flavourful, good structure, long, good acidity, round tannins.

UNUS 2009 T
100% syrah.

90 Colour: black cherry, garnet rim. Nose: violets, ripe fruit, sweet spices, complex. Palate: balanced, long, round tannins.

STYLO 2009 T
100% garnacha.

90 Colour: deep cherry, garnet rim. Nose: creamy oak, sweet spices, cocoa bean, candied fruit. Palate: good structure, fleshy.

ALQUEZ 2009 T
100% garnacha.

89 Colour: bright cherry. Nose: ripe fruit, sweet spices, creamy oak, violets. Palate: flavourful, fruity, toasty, round tannins.

CASTILLO DEL MAGO 2008 T
75% garnacha, 25% tempranillo.

87 Colour: deep cherry, garnet rim. Nose: ripe fruit, warm, powerfull, sweet spices. Palate: fruity, varietal, balanced.

BODEGA COOPERATIVA VIRGEN DE LA SIERRA

Avda. de la Cooperativa, 21-23
50310 Villarroya de la Sierra (Zaragoza)
☎: +34 976 899 015 - Fax: +34 976 899 032
oficina@bodegavirgendelasierra.com
www.bodegavirgendelasierra.com

CRUZ DE PIEDRA 2010 B
macabeo.

86 Colour: bright straw, greenish rim. Nose: fresh fruit, wild herbs, fresh. Palate: fruity, fine bitter notes, good acidity.

ALBADA 2010 B
macabeo.

86 Colour: bright straw, greenish rim. Nose: medium intensity, fresh, wild herbs. Palate: powerful, flavourful.

CRUZ DE PIEDRA 2010 RD
garnacha.

86 Colour: raspberry rose. Nose: floral, red berry notes, wild herbs. Palate: flavourful, fruity, easy to drink, good acidity.

ALBADA S/C T
garnacha.

89 Colour: black cherry. Nose: varietal, balsamic herbs, ripe fruit, expressive. Palate: flavourful, balanced, fine bitter notes, balsamic, long.

CRUZ DE PIEDRA 2010 T
garnacha.

88 Colour: cherry, purple rim. Nose: red berry notes, wild herbs, varietal. Palate: balanced, good structure, fruity.

CRUZ DE PIEDRA CAPRICHO 2008 T
garnacha.

87 Colour: deep cherry, garnet rim. Nose: ripe fruit, varietal, powerfull, wild herbs. Palate: fruity, balanced, spicy.

ALBADA 2007 TR
garnacha.

87 Colour: deep cherry, garnet rim. Nose: balanced, varietal, medium intensity. Palate: ripe fruit, correct.

BODEGA SAN GREGORIO

Ctra. Villalengua, s/n
50312 Cervera de la Cañada (Zaragoza)
☎: +34 976 899 206 - Fax: +34 976 896 240
tresojos@bodegasangregorio.com
www.bodegasangregorio.com

ARMANTES 2010 B
100% macabeo.

85 Colour: bright straw, greenish rim. Nose: medium intensity, dried flowers, wild herbs. Palate: correct, good acidity, easy to drink.

ARMANTES 2010 RD
50% garnacha, 50% tempranillo.

87 Colour: brilliant rose. Nose: fruit expression, violets, balanced, fresh. Palate: flavourful, fruity, fresh, fruity aftestaste.

ARMANTES 2010 T
50% garnacha, 50% tempranillo.

88 Colour: very deep cherry. Nose: ripe fruit, spicy, dried herbs. Palate: fleshy, good structure, round tannins.

TRES OJOS TEMPRANILLO 2010 T
100% tempranillo.

88 Colour: very deep cherry, purple rim. Nose: ripe fruit, powerfull, balanced. Palate: good structure, ripe fruit, long.

TRES OJOS GARNACHA 2010 T
100% garnacha.

87 Colour: deep cherry, purple rim. Nose: ripe fruit, warm, powerfull. Palate: fleshy, ripe fruit, round tannins, warm.

ARMANTES SELECCIÓN ESPECIAL 2009 T
60% garnacha, 22% tempranillo, 6% syrah, 6% merlot, 6% cabernet sauvignon.

89 Colour: cherry, garnet rim. Nose: ripe fruit, powerfull, dried herbs, mineral. Palate: good structure, complex, fleshy, spicy.

TRES OJOS SHIRAZ MERLOT 2009 T
40% syrah, 40% merlot, 20% tempranillo.

87 Colour: bright cherry. Nose: ripe fruit, spicy. Palate: good acidity, correct, fruity, easy to drink.

ARMANTES SELECCIÓN ESPECIAL 2008 T
60% garnacha, 22% tempranillo, 6% syrah, 6% merlot, 6% cabernet sauvignon.

90 Colour: cherry, garnet rim. Nose: balanced, ripe fruit, spicy. Palate: flavourful, full, round tannins, long.

MONTE ARMANTES CARMESÍ 2008 T
50% garnacha, 50% tempranillo.

87 Colour: cherry, garnet rim. Nose: medium intensity, ripe fruit, dried herbs, spicy. Palate: fruity, balanced.

ARMANTES 2007 TC
36% garnacha, 35% tempranillo, 12% cabernet sauvignon, 11% syrah, 6% merlot.

88 Colour: cherry, garnet rim. Nose: ripe fruit, spicy, complex, warm, cocoa bean. Palate: powerful, flavourful, toasty, round tannins.

ARMANTES SELECCIÓN 20 BARRICAS 2007 TR
55% garnacha, 28% tempranillo, 7% syrah, 5% cabernet sauvignon, 5% merlot.

88 Colour: bright cherry. Nose: ripe fruit, spicy, toasty, complex. Palate: powerful, flavourful, toasty, round tannins.

BODEGA VIRGEN DEL MAR Y DE LA CUESTA

Ctra. Monasterio de la Piedra, s/n
50219 Munebrega (Zaragoza)
☎: +34 976 895 071 - Fax: +34 976 895 171
bodegamunebrega@hotmail.com

MUZARES 2010 RD
100% garnacha.

86 Colour: brilliant rose. Nose: medium intensity, red berry notes, ripe fruit. Palate: fruity, flavourful, fleshy.

MUZARES 2010 T
55% tempranillo, 30% garnacha, 15% syrah.

90 Colour: black cherry, cherry, purple rim. Nose: ripe fruit, mineral, undergrowth, complex, warm. Palate: good structure, fruity, fruity aftestaste.

MUZARES GARNACHA VIÑAS VIEJAS 2009
100% garnacha.

86 Colour: deep cherry, garnet rim. Nose: fruit preserve, spicy, warm, powerfull. Palate: fleshy, flavourful, spicy.

BODEGAS ATECA

Ctra.-Nac. II, s/n
50200 Ateca (Zaragoza)
☎: +34 968 435 022 - Fax: +34 968 716 051
info@orowines.com
www.orowines.com

HONORO VERA GARNACHA 2010 T
100% garnacha.

90 Colour: deep cherry, purple rim. Nose: complex, ripe fruit, spicy, smoky, mineral. Palate: good structure, complex, fruity, ripe fruit.

ATTECA 2009 T
100% garnacha.

90 Colour: bright cherry. Nose: toasty, smoky, ripe fruit, spicy. Palate: flavourful, fruity, good acidity, fine bitter notes, round tannins.

ATTECA ARMAS 2007 T
100% garnacha.

92 Colour: very deep cherry, garnet rim. Nose: creamy oak, sweet spices, dark chocolate, candied fruit, mineral. Palate: balanced, spirituous, round, round tannins.

BODEGAS AUGUSTA BILBILIS

Carramiedes, s/n
50331 Mara (Zaragoza)
☎: +34 677 547 127
bodegasaugustabilbilis@hotmail.com
www.bodegasaugustabilbilis.com

SAMITIER 2008 T
100% garnacha.

88 Colour: deep cherry. Nose: ripe fruit, mineral, balsamic herbs, fruit liqueur notes, sweet spices. Palate: balanced, fine bitter notes, round tannins.

BODEGAS LANGA

Ctra. Nacional II, Km. 241,700
50300 Calatayud (Zaragoza)
☎: +34 976 881 818 - Fax: +34 976 884 463
info@bodegas-langa.com
www.bodegas-langa.com

LANGA 2010 B
100% chardonnay.

85 Colour: bright yellow. Nose: wild herbs, faded flowers, ripe fruit. Palate: flavourful, fruity, fine bitter notes, good acidity.

LANGA EMOCIÓN 2009 T
50% cabernet sauvignon, 50% syrah.

90 Colour: very deep cherry, purple rim. Nose: creamy oak, sweet spices, dark chocolate, ripe fruit. Palate: long, fruity, round tannins.

LANGA TRADICIÓN 2009 T
100% garnacha.

88 Colour: deep cherry, garnet rim. Nose: fruit preserve, balanced, expressive, varietal, sweet spices. Palate: fleshy, flavourful, long.

LANGA MERLOT 2009 T
merlot.

88 Colour: bright cherry. Nose: fruit expression, wild herbs, sweet spices. Palate: fruity, balanced, round tannins.

REAL DE ARAGÓN CENTENARIA 2008 T
garnacha.

92 Colour: dark-red cherry. Nose: complex, balanced, varietal, balsamic herbs, earthy notes, sweet spices. Palate: long, spicy, fruity.

REYES DE ARAGÓN MERLOT SYRAH ECOLÓGICO 2008 T
merlot, syrah.

88 Colour: very deep cherry. Nose: warm, powerfull, ripe fruit, creamy oak. Palate: fleshy, fruity, long, spicy, good structure.

REYES DE ARAGÓN GARNACHA CABERNET 2008 TC
garnacha, cabernet sauvignon.

87 Colour: cherry, garnet rim. Nose: ripe fruit, spicy, creamy oak, toasty. Palate: powerful, flavourful, toasty, round tannins, spirituous.

REYES DE ARAGÓN 2006 TR
garnacha, merlot.

87 Colour: cherry, garnet rim. Nose: spicy, medium intensity, ripe fruit. Palate: good structure, ripe fruit.

BODEGAS SAN ALEJANDRO

Ctra. Calatayud - Cariñena, Km. 16
50330 Miedes de Aragón (Zaragoza)
☎: +34 976 892 205 - Fax: +34 976 890 540
contacto@san-alejandro.com
www.san-alejandro.com

BALTASAR GRACIÁN VENDIMIA SELECCIONADA 2010 B
macabeo.

86 Colour: bright straw, greenish rim. Nose: powerfull, balsamic herbs, wild herbs, dry nuts. Palate: flavourful, fruity.

BALTASAR GRACIÁN VENDIMIA SELECCIONADA 2010 RD
garnacha.

87 Colour: brilliant rose. Nose: expressive, balanced, wild herbs, varietal. Palate: flavourful, ripe fruit, balanced, good acidity, fine bitter notes, balsamic.

BALTASAR GRACIÁN VENDIMIA SELECCIONADA 2010 T
garnacha.

90 Colour: very deep cherry, purple rim. Nose: dried herbs, fruit expression, complex, balanced. Palate: long, good acidity.

LAS ROCAS DE SAN ALEJANDRO 2009 T
garnacha.

93 Colour: deep cherry, garnet rim. Nose: varietal, balsamic herbs, ripe fruit, dry stone. Palate: flavourful, good structure, complex.

LAS ROCAS VIÑAS VIEJAS 2009 T
garnacha.

93 Colour: cherry, garnet rim. Nose: complex, elegant, ripe fruit, closed. Palate: full, complex, flavourful, fine bitter notes, mineral.

BALTASAR GRACIÁN GARNACHA VIÑAS VIEJAS 2009 T
garnacha.

91 Colour: cherry, purple rim. Nose: red berry notes, ripe fruit, wild herbs, spicy. Palate: balanced, fine bitter notes, round tannins.

BALTASAR GRACIÁN 2007 TC
garnacha, tempranillo, syrah.

90 Colour: deep cherry, garnet rim. Nose: varietal, balanced, wild herbs, ripe fruit. Palate: spicy, ripe fruit, fleshy.

BALTASAR GRACIÁN EXPRESIÓN 2007 T
53% garnacha, 19% tempranillo, 28% syrah.

88 Colour: cherry, garnet rim. Nose: warm, ripe fruit, spicy, dry stone. Palate: good structure, flavourful, spicy, ripe fruit.

BALTASAR GRACIÁN 2006 TR
garnacha, tempranillo, cabernet sauvignon.

90 Colour: deep cherry, garnet rim. Nose: medium intensity, warm, ripe fruit, closed. Palate: good structure, flavourful, balanced, fine bitter notes.

BODEGAS Y VIÑEDOS DEL JALÓN

Avda. José Antonio, 61
50340 Maluenda (Zaragoza)
☎: +34 976 893 017 - Fax: +34 976 546 969
info@castillodemaluenda.com
www.castillodemaluenda.com

CASTILLO DE MALUENDA 2010 RD
100% garnacha.

83 Colour: brilliant rose. Nose: fresh, red berry notes, medium intensity. Palate: flavourful, fruity, balanced, ripe fruit.

CASTILLO DE MALUENDA 2010 T
100% syrah.

89 Colour: deep cherry, purple rim. Nose: varietal, balsamic herbs, red berry notes, ripe fruit, earthy notes. Palate: balanced, fleshy.

VIÑA ALARBA VOLCÁN 2010 T MACERACIÓN CARBÓNICA
100% tempranillo.

88 Colour: bright cherry, cherry, purple rim. Nose: medium intensity, red berry notes. Palate: fruity, easy to drink, balanced.

TEOREMA 2009 T
100% garnacha.

90 Colour: bright cherry. Nose: medium intensity, wild herbs, ripe fruit, fruit preserve, earthy notes. Palate: varietal, flavourful.

SIOSY 2009 T
100% syrah.

87 Colour: bright cherry. Nose: ripe fruit, spicy. Palate: correct, good acidity, ripe fruit, round tannins.

ALTO LAS PIZARRAS 2008 T
100% garnacha.

91 Colour: bright cherry, garnet rim. Nose: complex, balanced, expressive, toasty, spicy, mineral. Palate: flavourful, full, balanced.

FABLA GARNACHA ESPECIAL 2008 T
100% garnacha.

90 Colour: deep cherry, garnet rim. Nose: mineral, varietal, spicy, candied fruit. Palate: good structure, ripe fruit.

CLARAVAL 2008 T
50% garnacha, 20% tempranillo, 20% cabernet sauvignon, 10% syrah.

88 Colour: deep cherry, garnet rim. Nose: ripe fruit, earthy notes, sweet spices, creamy oak. Palate: balanced, round tannins.

LAS PIZARRAS 2008 T
100% garnacha.

88 Colour: very deep cherry. Nose: fruit preserve, powerfull, complex, spicy. Palate: ripe fruit, balsamic, fleshy, full, spirituous.

EL ESCOCÉS VOLANTE

Barrio La Rosa Bajo, 16
50300 Calatayud (Zaragoza)
☎: +34 637 511 133
norrelrobertson@hotmail.com
www.escocesvolante.es

MANGA DEL BRUJO 2009 T
65% garnacha, 15% syrah, 15% tempranillo, 2,5% mazuelo, 2,5% monastrell.

90 Colour: bright cherry. Nose: ripe fruit, expressive, spicy, cocoa bean. Palate: flavourful, fruity, toasty, round tannins.

EL PUÑO PEGAJOSO 2009 T
50% syrah, 50% cabernet sauvignon.

89 Colour: deep cherry. Nose: candied fruit, warm, balanced, powerfull. Palate: good structure, fruity, sweet, rich.

LA MULTA GARNACHA VIÑAS VIEJAS 2009 T
100% garnacha.

88 Colour: bright cherry. Nose: ripe fruit, expressive, warm, spicy. Palate: flavourful, toasty, round tannins, spicy.

DOS DEDOS DE FRENTE 2009 T
93% syrah, 7% viognier.

87 Colour: bright cherry. Nose: sweet spices, creamy oak, expressive, cocoa bean, toasty, warm. Palate: toasty, round tannins, fruity.

EL PUÑO GARNACHA 2007 T
100% garnacha.

91 Colour: bright cherry, garnet rim. Nose: medium intensity, ripe fruit, earthy notes, spicy. Palate: good structure, rich, mineral, spicy.

LOBBAN WINES

Creueta, 24
08784 St. Jaume Sesoliveres (Barcelona)
☎: +34 667 551 695
info@lapamelita.com
www.lapamelita.com

EL GORDITO 2007 T
garnacha, syrah.

86 Colour: cherry, garnet rim. Nose: medium intensity, old leather, ripe fruit. Palate: fruity, spicy, easy to drink.

EL GORDITO 2005 T
garnacha, syrah.

86 Colour: bright cherry, orangey edge. Nose: candied fruit, spicy. Palate: balanced, fine bitter notes, easy to drink, spicy.

NIÑO JESÚS

Las Tablas, s/n
50313 Aniñón (Zaragoza)
☎: +34 976 899 150 - Fax: +34 976 896 160
gerencia@satninojesus.com
www.satninojesus.com

ESTECILLO 2010 B
100% macabeo.

87 Colour: straw. Nose: ripe fruit, jasmine, wild herbs. Palate: fruity, ripe fruit, easy to drink.

ESTECILLO 2010 BFB
100% macabeo.

86 Colour: straw. Nose: dried herbs, medium intensity, candied fruit, spicy. Palate: fruity, flavourful, ripe fruit.

ESTECILLO 2009 RD
100% garnacha.

85 Colour: light cherry. Nose: candied fruit, medium intensity, dried herbs. Palate: fruity, easy to drink.

ESTECILLO 2010 T
75% garnacha, 25% tempranillo.

87 Colour: cherry, purple rim. Nose: fruit expression, balanced. Palate: fruity, easy to drink, good acidity.

ESTECILLO LEGADO VIÑAS VIEJAS 2009 T
100% garnacha.

87 Colour: bright cherry. Nose: fruit expression, sweet spices, cocoa bean, balanced. Palate: fruity, good acidity.

ESTECILLO 2009 T
85% garnacha, 15% tempranillo.

87 Colour: cherry, garnet rim. Nose: fruit preserve, sweet spices, powerfull. Palate: fruity, easy to drink, balanced.

ESTECILLO GARNACHA & SYRAH 2009 T
50% garnacha, 50% syrah.

86 Colour: deep cherry, garnet rim. Nose: red berry notes, ripe fruit, fruit liqueur notes. Palate: powerful, spicy, long.

PAGOS ALTOS DE ACERED

Avda. Río Jalón, 62
50300 Calatayud (Zaragoza)
☎: +34 976 887 496

LAJAS 2008 T
100% garnacha.

93 Colour: cherry, garnet rim. Nose: sweet spices, dark chocolate, spicy, candied fruit, earthy notes. Palate: fleshy, powerful, round tannins.

LAJAS 2007 T
100% garnacha.

92 Colour: cherry, garnet rim. Nose: complex, mineral, warm, sweet spices, cocoa bean. Palate: concentrated, fleshy, complex, long.

PROYECTO GARNACHAS DE ESPAÑA

Gral. Vara del Rey, 7 1º Dcha.
26003 Logroño (La Rioja)
☎: +34 941 271 217 - Fax: +34 941 272 911
info@garnachasdeespana.com
www.garnachasdeespana.com

LA GARNACHA OLVIDADA DE ARAGÓN 2009 T
100% garnacha.

90 Colour: cherry, garnet rim. Nose: red berry notes, ripe fruit, earthy notes, expressive, sweet spices, toasty. Palate: powerful, flavourful, complex, fleshy.

TERRA SIGILATA

Ctra. Nacional II, s/n
50200 Ateca (Zaragoza)
☎: +34 682 471 916
ircata@avanteselecta.com

FILÓN 2010 T ROBLE
garnacha.

91 Colour: dark-red cherry. Nose: ripe fruit, powerfull, mineral, roasted coffee, varietal. Palate: powerful, flavourful, fleshy, grainy tannins.

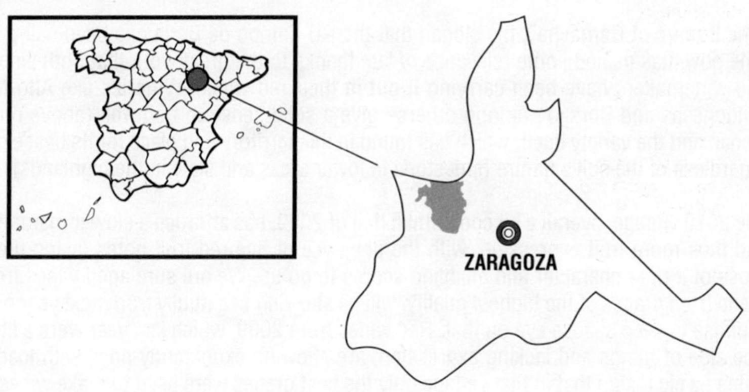
ZARAGOZA

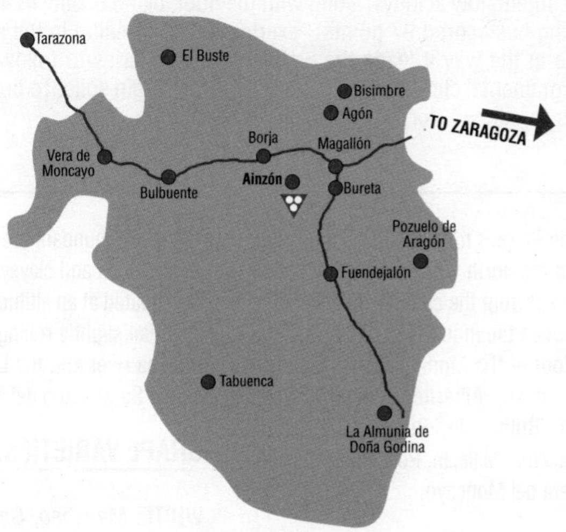
Tarazona
El Buste
Bisimbre
Agón
TO ZARAGOZA
Borja
Magallón
Vera de Moncayo
Bulbuente
Ainzón
Bureta
Pozuelo de Aragón
Fuendejalón
Tabuenca
La Almunia de Doña Godina

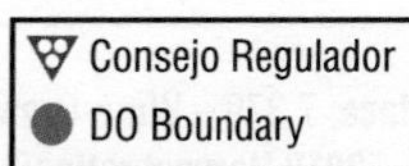
Consejo Regulador
DO Boundary

DO CAMPO DE BORJA

NEWS ABOUT THE VINTAGE:

"The Empire of Garnacha", the slogan that the DO Campo de Borja has been using for some time now, has gained some relevance of late thanks to the great work that both vine growers and winemakers have been carrying it out in their red wines. Wineries like Alto Moncayo, Aragonesas and Borsao –among others– give a solid sense to both the (above mentioned) slogan and the variety itself, which has found in this territory a fit place for its best expression, regardless of the soil's nature (limestone in lower areas and slate in the highlands).

The 2010 vintage, overall a bit cooler than that of 2009, has afforded a slower maturation cycle and thus more fruit expression, with the presence of fine red fruit notes taking the place of those of a riper character and enabling scores to go up. We are sure aged wines from 2010, made from grapes of the highest quality, will be showing beautifully from next year on, and we promise to keep a close eye on that. Red wines from 2009, which last year were a little on the ripe side of things and lacking expression, are showing exuberantly now, with loads of fruit notes –a clear sign that in that vintage only the best grapes were used to make wines destined for wood-ageing– and a great balance between fruit and wood. Nevertheless, this does not apply to previous vintages we remember having tasted, were wood predominated and there was a more than evident lack of fruit character, probably as a consequence of using overripe grapes (high sugar content, low acidity), along with the poor, bland quality of the tannins. Aquilón (its 2008 rendering has scored 97 points!) exerts a total dominion in the region, not only score-wise but also in the way it leads the way for other wineries to follow, revealing the infinite potential of continental climate, old vines, and almost virgin soils. To prove the point, 20 wines got 90 points (or above), for just 13 in last year's edition.

LOCATION:

The DO Campo de Borja is made up of 16 municipal areas, situated in the north west of the province of Zaragoza and 60 km from the capital city, in an area of transition between the mountains of the Sistema Ibérico (at the foot of the Moncayo) and the Ebro Valley: Agón, Ainzón, Alberite, Albeta, Ambel, Bisimbre, Borja, Bulbuente, Burueta, El Buste, Fuendejalón, Magallón, Malejan, Pozuelo de Aragón, Tabuenca and Vera del Moncayo.

CLIMATE:

A rather extreme continental climate, with cold winters and dry, hot summers. One of its main characteristics is the influence of the 'Cierzo', a cold and dry north - westerly wind. Rainfall is rather scarce, with an average of between 350 and 450 mm per year.

SOIL:

The most abundant are brownish - grey limey soils, terrace soils and clayey ferrous soils. The vineyards are situated at an altitude of between 350 and 700 m on small slightly rolling hillsides, on terraces of the Huecha river and the Llanos de Plasencia, making up the Somontano del Moncayo.

GRAPE VARIETIES:

WHITE: *Macabeo, Garnacha Blanca, Moscatel, Chardonnay, Sauvignon Blanc* and *Verdejo.*
RED: *Garnacha* (majority with 75%), *Tempranillo, Mazuela, Cabernet Sauvignon, Merlot* and *Syrah.*

FIGURES:

Vineyard surface: 7,379 – **Wine-Growers:** 1,650 – **Wineries:** 17 – **2010 Harvest rating:** Very Good – **Production:** 21,182,632 litres – **Market percentages:** 37% domestic. 63% export

CONSEJO REGULADOR
Subida de San Andrés, 6
50570 Ainzón (Zaragoza)
☎: +34 976 852 122 - Fax: +34 976 868 806
@ vinos@docampodeborja.com
www.docampodeborja.com

GENERAL CHARACTERISTICS OF THE WINES

WHITES	Mainly produced from *Macabeo*, they are light, fresh and pleasant. There is also experience with white wines fermented in barrels.
ROSÉS	With notably fine quality, they are produced mainly from *Garnacha*; they are somewhat fresher than those of Cariñena and stand out for the full-bodied character that the variety provides..
REDS	Also based on the *Garnacha*, they are the most important type of wine in the region. In their youth, dark cherry coloured, they have a fine intense nose and offer notes of ripe black fruit; they are flavourful, fruity and meaty. The Crianza reds are somewhat lighter and more round; the Reservas and Gran Reservas produced in the traditional manner, however, may have animal nuances and hints of reduced fruit with the rusty character of the *Garnacha*.

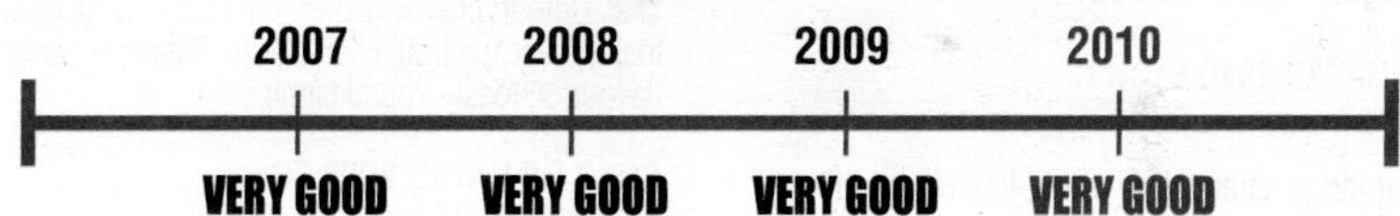

BODEGAS ALTO MONCAYO

Ctra. CV-606 Borja - El Buste, Km. 1,700
50540 Borja (Zaragoza)
☎: +34 976 867 807 - Fax: +34 976 868 147
info@bodegasaltomoncayo.com

AQUILÓN 2008 T
garnacha.

97 Colour: black cherry, garnet rim. Nose: fruit expression, cocoa bean, dark chocolate, sweet spices, creamy oak, aromatic coffee. Palate: concentrated, powerful, flavourful, fleshy, complex, long, round tannins.

ALTO MONCAYO 2008 T
garnacha.

95 Colour: black cherry, garnet rim. Nose: mineral, sweet spices, creamy oak, fruit expression. Palate: good acidity, powerful, flavourful, fleshy, toasty, round tannins.

ALTO MONCAYO VERATÓN 2008 T
garnacha.

93 Colour: cherry, garnet rim. Nose: red berry notes, ripe fruit, expressive, spicy, toasty, mineral. Palate: fleshy, complex, flavourful, mineral, toasty, round tannins.

BODEGAS ARAGONESAS

Ctra. Magallón, s/n
50529 Fuendejalón (Zaragoza)
☎: +34 976 862 153 - Fax: +34 976 862 363
fcura@bodegasaragonesas.com
www.bodegasaragonesas.com

COTO DE HAYAS 2010 B
100% chardonnay.

88 Colour: bright straw. Nose: fresh, fresh fruit, white flowers. Palate: flavourful, fruity, good acidity, balanced.

COTO DE HAYAS 2009 BFB
80% chardonnay, 17% macabeo, 3% moscatel.

88 Color bright yellow. Aroma powerfull, ripe fruit, sweet spices, creamy oak, fragrant herbs. Taste rich, smoky aftertaste, flavourful, fresh, good acidity.

COTO DE HAYAS 2010 RD
90% garnacha, 10% cabernet sauvignon.

88 Colour: brilliant rose. Nose: powerfull, ripe fruit, red berry notes, floral, expressive. Palate: fleshy, powerful, fruity, fresh.

COTO DE HAYAS SOLO 10 2010 T
syrah.

92 Colour: bright cherry. Nose: sweet spices, creamy oak, expressive, fruit expression. Palate: flavourful, fruity, toasty, round tannins.

COTO DE HAYAS GARNACHA CENTENARIA 2010 T
100% garnacha.

91 Colour: bright cherry. Nose: ripe fruit, sweet spices, expressive. Palate: flavourful, fruity, toasty, round tannins.

ARAGUS ECOLÓGICO 2010 T
90% garnacha, 10% syrah.

91 Colour: cherry, purple rim. Nose: fresh fruit, red berry notes, floral, balsamic herbs, scrubland. Palate: flavourful, fruity, good acidity.

COTO DE HAYAS TEMPRANILLO CABERNET 2010 T ROBLE
70% tempranillo, 30% cabernet sauvignon.

90 Colour: bright cherry. Nose: sweet spices, creamy oak, fruit expression. Palate: flavourful, fruity, toasty, round tannins.

COTO DE HAYAS GARNACHA SYRAH 2010 T
85% garnacha, 15% syrah.

89 Color cherry, purple rim. Aroma expressive, fresh fruit, red berry notes, floral. Taste flavourful, fruity, good acidity, round tannins.

FAGUS DE COTO DE HAYAS 2009 T
100% garnacha.

92 Colour: cherry, garnet rim. Nose: spicy, creamy oak, toasty, overripe fruit, characterful. Palate: powerful, flavourful, toasty, round tannins.

COTO DE HAYAS 2008 TC
60% garnacha, 40% tempranillo.

89 Colour: bright cherry. Nose: ripe fruit, sweet spices, earthy notes. Palate: flavourful, fruity, toasty, round tannins.

ARAGONIA SELECCIÓN ESPECIAL 2008 T
100% garnacha.

89 Colour: cherry, garnet rim. Nose: toasty, cocoa bean, aromatic coffee, ripe fruit. Palate: flavourful, ripe fruit, fine bitter notes.

DON RAMÓN 2008 TC
75% garnacha, 25% tempranillo.

87 Colour: cherry, garnet rim. Nose: scrubland, fruit liqueur notes, spicy, aromatic coffee. Palate: spicy, ripe fruit, fine bitter notes.

COTO DE HAYAS 2007 TR
100% garnacha.

90 Colour: deep cherry, orangey edge. Nose: overripe fruit, powerfull, warm, toasty, spicy. Palate: flavourful, sweetness, spicy, long.

OXIA 2006 TC
100% garnacha.

93 Colour: cherry, garnet rim. Nose: spicy, creamy oak, toasty, complex, earthy notes, mineral, ripe fruit. Palate: powerful, toasty, round tannins, balsamic.

COTO DE HAYAS MISTELA 2010 VINO DULCE NATURAL
100% garnacha.

88 Colour: cherry, garnet rim. Nose: candied fruit, fruit preserve, sweet spices, cocoa bean. Palate: flavourful, powerful, sweetness, good acidity.

BODEGAS BORDEJÉ

Ctra. Borja a Rueda, Km. 3
50570 Ainzón (Zaragoza)
☎: +34 976 868 080 - Fax: +34 976 868 989
ainzon@bodegasbordeje.com
www.bodegasbordeje.com

MARI DULCIS VINO DE LICOR 2010 B
100% moscatel.

88 Color golden. Aroma powerfull, floral, honeyed notes, candied fruit, fragrant herbs. Taste flavourful, sweet, fresh, fruity, good acidity, long.

LIDIA 2008 B
100% chardonnay.

87 Colour: bright golden. Nose: ripe fruit, dry nuts, toasty, aged wood nuances. Palate: flavourful, spicy, toasty, long.

CRISTINA VINO DE LICOR 2010 T
100% garnacha.

87 Colour: deep cherry. Nose: expressive, varietal, raspberry, candied fruit. Palate: flavourful, fruity, sweetness.

ABUELO NICOLÁS 2008 T
100% merlot.

83 Colour: deep cherry, orangey edge. Nose: warm, overripe fruit, aromatic coffee. Palate: ripe fruit, spicy, warm.

PAGO DE ROMEROSO 2007 TR
100% tempranillo.

89 Colour: bright cherry. Nose: ripe fruit, sweet spices, creamy oak, lactic notes. Palate: flavourful, toasty, round tannins.

LELES DE BORDEJE 2007 T
100% garnacha.

88 Colour: cherry, garnet rim. Nose: warm, fruit preserve, caramel. Palate: fine bitter notes, sweetness, toasty.

BORDEJÉ DON PABLO 2006 TR
50% tempranillo, 50% garnacha.

86 Colour: cherry, garnet rim. Nose: creamy oak, toasty, wet leather. Palate: powerful, toasty, round tannins.

BORDEJÉ 2005 TR
50% tempranillo, 50% garnacha.

87 Colour: cherry, garnet rim. Nose: ripe fruit, spicy, creamy oak, toasty, complex. Palate: toasty, fine bitter notes.

PAGO DE HUECHASECA 2005 T
45% tempranillo, 40% merlot, 15% cabernet sauvignon.

87 Colour: cherry, garnet rim. Nose: ripe fruit, spicy, toasty, wet leather. Palate: powerful, toasty, round tannins.

BODEGAS BORSAO

Ctra. N- 122, Km. 63
50540 Borja (Zaragoza)
☎: +34 976 867 116 - Fax: +34 976 867 752
info@bodegasborsao.com
www.bodegasborsao.com

BORSAO SELECCIÓN 2010 B
macabeo.

84 Colour: bright straw. Nose: fresh, candied fruit, citrus fruit, dried herbs. Palate: flavourful, fruity, good acidity.

BORSAO SELECCIÓN 2010 RD
100% garnacha.

88 Colour: brilliant rose. Nose: powerfull, ripe fruit, red berry notes, floral. Palate: fleshy, powerful, fruity, fresh.

BORSAO SELECCIÓN 2010 T
70% garnacha, 20% syrah, 10% tempranillo.

91 Colour: cherry, purple rim. Nose: red berry notes, floral, fresh, ripe fruit. Palate: flavourful, fruity, good acidity.

BORSAO TRES PICOS 2009 T
100% garnacha.

92 Colour: cherry, garnet rim. Nose: candied fruit, fruit liqueur notes, sweet spices, toasty, aromatic coffee, fragrant herbs. Palate: flavourful, spicy, ripe fruit, long.

BORSAO BOLE 2008 T
70% garnacha, 30% syrah.

90 Colour: cherry, garnet rim. Nose: powerfull, fruit liqueur notes, toasty, spicy, aromatic coffee. Palate: flavourful, spirituous, spicy.

BORSAO BEROLA 2007 T
80% garnacha, 20% syrah.

92 Colour: cherry, garnet rim. Nose: creamy oak, toasty, fruit preserve. Palate: powerful, flavourful, toasty, round tannins.

BORSAO SELECCIÓN 2007 TC
60% garnacha, 20% tempranillo, 20% merlot.

88 Colour: cherry, garnet rim. Nose: ripe fruit, red berry notes, toasty. Palate: spicy, ripe fruit, long.

CRIANZAS Y VIÑEDOS SANTO CRISTO

Ctra. Tabuenca, s/n
50570 Ainzón (Zaragoza)
☎: +34 976 869 696 - Fax: +34 976 868 097
info@bodegas-santo-cristo.com
www.bodegas-santo-cristo.com

MOSCATEL AINZÓN 90 DÍAS 2010 B BARRICA
100% moscatel grano menudo.

92 Colour: golden. Nose: floral, honeyed notes, candied fruit, fragrant herbs, expressive, varietal. Palate: flavourful, sweet, fresh, fruity, good acidity, long.

SANTO CRISTO 2010 T ROBLE
60% tempranillo, 30% cabernet sauvignon, 10% garnacha.

89 Colour: cherry, purple rim. Nose: powerfull, ripe fruit, red berry notes. Palate: flavourful, fleshy.

VIÑA COLLADO 2010 T
100% garnacha.

89 Colour: cherry, purple rim. Nose: powerfull, ripe fruit, red berry notes, violet drops. Palate: flavourful, good acidity, long.

CAYUS SELECCIÓN 2009 T
100% garnacha.

91 Colour: cherry, garnet rim. Nose: ripe fruit, spicy, creamy oak, toasty, mineral. Palate: powerful, flavourful, toasty, round tannins.

TERRAZAS DEL MONCAYO GARNACHA 2008 T ROBLE
100% garnacha.

91 Colour: cherry, garnet rim. Nose: spicy, creamy oak, toasty, complex, mineral, fruit preserve. Palate: powerful, flavourful, toasty, round tannins.

PEÑAZUELA SELECCIÓN 2008 T ROBLE
100% garnacha.

88 Colour: cherry, garnet rim. Nose: candied fruit, warm, scrubland, balsamic herbs. Palate: flavourful, powerful, sweetness.

VIÑA AINZÓN 2008 TC
70% garnacha, 20% tempranillo, 10% cabernet sauvignon.

87 Colour: bright cherry. Nose: ripe fruit, sweet spices, caramel, toasty. Palate: flavourful, fruity, round tannins.

VIÑA AINZÓN 2006 TR
garnacha, tempranillo.

86 Colour: cherry, garnet rim. Nose: spicy, creamy oak, toasty, ripe fruit. Palate: powerful, flavourful, toasty, round tannins.

MOSCATEL AINZÓN 2010 VINO DE LICOR
70% moscatel grano menudo, 30% moscatel romano.

87 Colour: bright straw. Nose: powerfull, citrus fruit, honeyed notes. Palate: good acidity, round, fine bitter notes.

PAGOS DEL MONCAYO

Ctra. Z-372, Km. 1,6
50580 Vera de Moncayo (Zaragoza)
☎: +34 687 992 660 - Fax: +34 976 900 257
info@pagosdelmoncayo.com
www.pagosdelmoncayo.com

PAGOS DEL MONCAYO 2010 T
65% garnacha, 35% syrah.

91 Colour: cherry, purple rim. Nose: floral, expressive, balsamic herbs, scrubland. Palate: long, good acidity, fine bitter notes.

PAGOS DEL MONCAYO GARNACHA 2009 T
100% garnacha.

93 Colour: cherry, garnet rim. Nose: candied fruit, warm, complex, mineral. Palate: flavourful, spicy, long, elegant.

PAGOS DEL MONCAYO SYRAH 2009 T
100% syrah.

92 Colour: cherry, purple rim. Nose: candied fruit, fruit expression, red berry notes, creamy oak, new oak. Palate: long, creamy, spicy, fleshy.

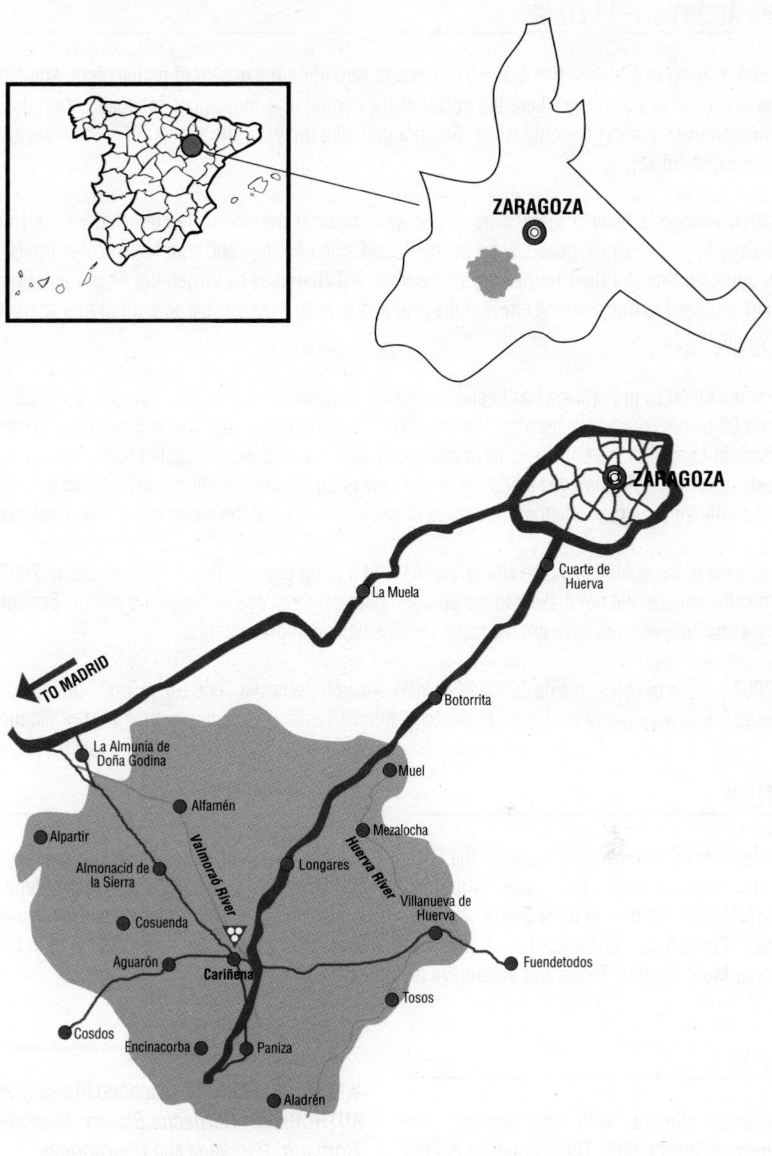
ZARAGOZA
ZARAGOZA
Cuarte de
Huerva
La Muela
TO MADRID
Botorrita
La Almunia de
Doña Godina
Muel
Alfamén
Mezalocha
Alpartir
Valmoraó River
Huerva River
Almonacid de
la Sierra
Longares
Villanueva de
Huerva
Cosuenda
Aguarón
Cariñena
Fuendetodos
Tosos
Cosdos
Encinacorba
Paniza
Aladrén
Consejo Regulador
DO Boundary

DO CARIÑENA

NEWS ABOUT THE VINTAGE:

Cariñena is living in a constant to and fro movement regarding the quality of its harvests. And harvest quality is crucial in a territory where the power of the cooperative movement has made of productivity (production over quality) the only issue. So, in a bad climatic year, the problems in the vineyard will increase exponentially.

The 2010 vintage is heavily marked by a heat wave right at the end of August that left its trace in particularly in young wines, generally on the confected side of things and with high alcohol levels. Still, those wineries that did their homework in the vineyard (the likes of Virgen del Águila and Solar de Urbezo) managed to minimize the effect of the heat and to keep a reasonable amount of fruit character in their young wines.

The scores increase in Cariñena has happened thanks to wines from previous vintages. Up to 25 wines reached 89 points (or above), for just 19 in the 2011 edition of our Guide. This is mainly due to samples that have aged well in the bottle and have integrated well fruit and wood (toasted oak) nuances. In this respect, surely the 2008 vintage stands out. In the case of 2009, wood is still too evident, so we will have to wait a little longer to see whether the excess of oak integrates and the wines reach a finer balance.

Also evident is the quality increase within the DO, and a good proof of that is the fact that in 2007 well over twenty samples did not make it to the 80-point range, for just one in this year's edition. Both private wineries and cooperatives have put the focus on winemaking improvements.

The 2007 vintage of Aylés Tres de 3000 (94 points), Anayón Garnacha 2008 (92 points) –both reds– and the sweet white wine Sierra del Viento Moscatel Vendimia Tardía (92 points), are the best within the DO.

LOCATION:

In the province of Zaragoza, and occupies the Ebro valley covering 14 municipal areas: Aguarón, Aladrén, Alfamén, Almonacid de la Sierra, Alpartir, Cariñena, Cosuenda, Encinacorba, Longares, Mezalocha, Muel, Paniza, Tosos and Villanueva de Huerva.

CLIMATE:

A continental climate, with cold winters, hot summers and low rainfall. The viticulture is also influenced by the effect of the 'Cierzo'.

SOIL:

Mainly poor; either brownish - grey limey soil, or reddish dun soil settled on rocky deposits, or brownish - grey soil settled on alluvial deposits. The vineyards are situated at an altitude of between 400 and 800 m.

GRAPE VARIETIES:

WHITE: PREFERRED: *Macabeo* (majority 20%).
AUTHORIZED: *Garnacha Blanca, Moscatel Romano, Parellada* and *Chardonnay.*
RED: PREFERRED: *Garnacha Tinta* (majority 55%), *Tempranillo, Mazuela* (or *Cariñena*).
AUTHORIZED: *Juan Ibáñez, Cabernet Sauvignon, Syrah, Monastrell, Vidadillo* and *Merlot.*

FIGURES:

Vineyard surface: 14,624 – **Wine-Growers:** 1,954 – **Wineries:** 45 – **2010 Harvest rating:** Excellent – **Production:** 56,844,200 litres – **Market percentages:** 41% domestic. 59% export

CONSEJO REGULADOR
Camino de la Platera, 7
50400 Cariñena (Zaragoza)
☎: +34 902 190 713 / +34 976 793 031 - Fax: +34 976 621 107
@ consejoregulador@docarinena.com
@ promocion@docarinena.com
www.docarinena.com

GENERAL CHARACTERISTICS OF THE WINES

WHITES	These are not the most important of the region. They are characterised by their straw yellow colour, notes of ripe fruit and fruity character..
ROSÉS	Most are the result of new technology: they are pink, with fine fruit intensity and flavourful on the palate, thanks to the intervention of the *Garnacha*.
REDS	These are the wines par excellence of the region, quite robust with a warm character. The young wines have a dark cherry colour with hints of violet and noses of ripe fruit reminiscent of blackberries and plums; thanks to the *Garnacha*, they are also very flavourful on the palate. The Crianza wines maintain these characteristics, although they are more supple due to being aged in barrels; these may display balsamic notes and dark-roasted flavours; on the palate they are supple and warm. These long-aged wines, if only produced from *Garnacha*, may have rough notes due to the fact that this grape variety does not age very well.

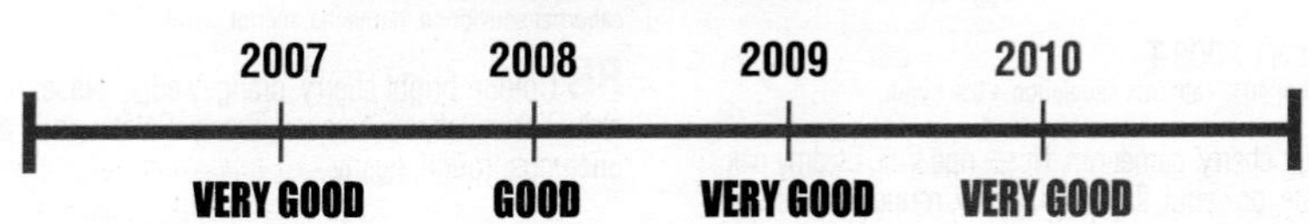

BIOENOS

Mayor, 88
50400 Cariñena (Zaragoza)
☎: +34 976 620 045 - Fax: +34 976 622 082
bioenos@bioenos.com
www.bioenos.com

PULCHRUM CRESPIELLO 2006 T
100% vidadillo.

90 Colour: cherry, garnet rim. Nose: spicy, creamy oak, toasty, fruit preserve, balsamic herbs, scrubland. Palate: powerful, flavourful, toasty, round tannins, sweetness.

PULCHRUM CRESPIELLO 2004 T
100% vidadillo.

87 Colour: cherry, garnet rim. Nose: powerfull, characterful, fruit preserve, roasted coffee. Palate: powerful, concentrated, sweetness, powerful tannins.

BODEGAS AÑADAS

Ctra. Aguarón, km 47,100
50400 Cariñena (Zaragoza)
☎: +34 976 793 016 - Fax: +34 976 620 448
bodega@carewines.com
www.carewines.com

CARE CHARDONNAY 2010 B
chardonnay.

89 Color bright straw. Aroma fresh, fresh fruit, white flowers, expressive. Taste flavourful, fruity, good acidity, balanced.

CARE 2010 RD
cabernet sauvignon, tempranillo.

88 Colour: rose, purple rim. Nose: powerfull, ripe fruit, red berry notes, floral. Palate: fleshy, powerful, fruity, fresh.

CARE 2010 T ROBLE
syrah, tempranillo.

90 Colour: bright cherry. Nose: ripe fruit, sweet spices, creamy oak. Palate: flavourful, fruity, toasty, round tannins.

CARE XCLNT 2008 T
40% garnacha, 40% cabernet sauvignon, 20% syrah.

90 Colour: cherry, garnet rim. Nose: ripe fruit, creamy oak, toasty. Palate: powerful, flavourful, toasty, round tannins.

CARE GARNACHA CABERNET SAUVIGNON 2008 TR
80% garnacha, 20% cabernet sauvignon.

90 Colour: cherry, garnet rim. Nose: spicy, creamy oak, toasty. Palate: powerful, flavourful, toasty, round tannins, fine bitter notes, long.

CARE 2008 TC
50% merlot, 50% tempranillo.

89 Colour: bright cherry. Nose: ripe fruit, sweet spices, creamy oak. Palate: fruity, round tannins, powerful.

BODEGAS ESTEBAN MARTÍN

Camino Virgen de Lagunas, s/n
50461 Alfamén (Zaragoza)
☎: +34 976 628 490 - Fax: +34 976 628 488
info@estebanmartin.es
www.estebanmartin.com

VINEM 2010 B
chardonnay, macabeo.

87 Colour: bright straw. Nose: lactic notes, citrus fruit, tropical fruit. Palate: flavourful, fruity, fleshy, good acidity.

ESTEBAN MARTÍN 2010 B
chardonnay, macabeo.

85 Colour: bright straw. Nose: fresh, fresh fruit, expressive, citrus fruit. Palate: flavourful, fruity, good acidity, balanced.

ESTEBAN MARTÍN 2010 RD
garnacha, syrah.

87 Colour: rose, purple rim. Nose: powerfull, red berry notes, floral, expressive, raspberry. Palate: fleshy, powerful, fruity, fresh.

ESTEBAN MARTÍN 2010 T
syrah, merlot, garnacha.

86 Colour: cherry, purple rim. Nose: ripe fruit, fruit preserve, raspberry, warm, powerfull. Palate: powerful, concentrated, fine bitter notes.

VINEM 2010 T
garnacha, syrah.

84 Colour: cherry, purple rim. Nose: powerfull, ripe fruit, grassy. Palate: powerful, concentrated, fruity.

ESTEBAN MARTÍN 2007 TR
cabernet sauvignon, garnacha, merlot, syrah.

86 Colour: bright cherry, orangey edge. Nose: ripe fruit, reduction notes, cocoa bean, toasty. Palate: good acidity, unctuous, round, fleshy.

ESTEBAN MARTÍN 2008 TC
cabernet sauvignon, garnacha, merlot.

88 Colour: cherry, garnet rim. Nose: ripe fruit, creamy oak, toasty, characterful. Palate: powerful, flavourful, toasty, round tannins.

BODEGAS IGNACIO MARÍN

San Valero, 1
50400 Cariñena (Zaragoza)
☎: +34 976 621 129 - Fax: +34 976 621 031
comercial@ignaciomarin.com
www.ignaciomarin.com

DUQUE DE MEDINA 2010 T
garnacha, tempranillo, cariñena.

86 Colour: cherry, purple rim. Nose: red berry notes, fresh, powerfull, medium intensity. Palate: fresh, light-bodied, flavourful.

MARÍN GARNACHA 2008 T
garnacha.

86 Colour: cherry, garnet rim. Nose: ripe fruit, cocoa bean, dark chocolate, toasty. Palate: flavourful, fleshy, rich.

MARÍN MERLOT 2008 T
merlot.

83 Colour: cherry, garnet rim. Nose: ripe fruit, old leather, woody. Palate: powerful, flavourful, slightly evolved.

CAMPO MARÍN 2003 TR
tempranillo, garnacha, cariñena.

83 Colour: ruby red, orangey edge. Nose: ripe fruit, slightly evolved, spicy, toasty. Palate: toasty, flavourful.

BARÓN DE LAJOYOSA TGR
garnacha, tempranillo, cariñena.

82 Colour: deep cherry. Nose: fruit preserve, powerfull, ripe fruit, toasty. Palate: flavourful, powerful, sweetness.

BARÓN DE LAJOYOSA MOSCATEL MISTELA
moscatel.

90 Colour: golden. Nose: powerfull, floral, honeyed notes, candied fruit. Palate: flavourful, sweet, fruity, good acidity, long.

BODEGAS LALAGUNA GARCÍA

Ctra. A-1304 de Longares a Alfamés, Km. 1,28
50460 Longares (Zaragoza)
☎: +34 657 804 783 - Fax: +34 976 369 980
bodegaslalaguna@bodegaslalaguna.com
www.bodegaslalaguna.com

LALAGUNA 2010 B
macabeo.

83 Colour: bright straw. Nose: fresh, fresh fruit, expressive. Palate: flavourful, fruity, good acidity, balanced.

LALAGUNA 2010 RD
garnacha.

85 Colour: rose, purple rim. Nose: powerfull, expressive, fresh fruit. Palate: fleshy, powerful, fruity, fresh.

LALAGUNA 2010 T
garnacha.

85 Colour: cherry, purple rim. Nose: ripe fruit, fresh, medium intensity. Palate: powerful, flavourful, fleshy.

BODEGAS LOMABLANCA

Ctra. de Valencia, Km. 459
50460 Longarés (Zaragoza)
☎: +34 976 145 100 - Fax: +34 976 142 621
info@bodegaslomablanca.com
www.bodegaslomablanca.com

GABARDA IV 2004 TC
garnacha, cabernet sauvignon, merlot.

87 Colour: cherry, garnet rim. Nose: powerfull, characterful, fruit preserve, overripe fruit. Palate: powerful, concentrated, fine bitter notes.

BODEGAS MANUEL MONEVA E HIJOS

Avda. Zaragoza, 10
50108 Almonacid de la Sierra (Zaragoza)
☎: +34 976 627 020 - Fax: +34 976 627 334
monevahijos@terra.es
www.bodegasmanuelmonevaehijos.com

VIÑA VADINA GARNACHA 2010 T
100% garnacha.

85 Colour: cherry, purple rim. Nose: ripe fruit, balsamic herbs, fresh. Palate: fruity, flavourful, fresh.

VIÑA VADINA TEMPRANILLO GARNACHA 2010 T
tempranillo, garnacha.

85 Colour: cherry, purple rim. Nose: powerfull, ripe fruit, raspberry. Palate: powerful, fleshy.

BODEGAS PRINUR

Ctra. N-330, Km. 449,150
50400 Cariñena (Zaragoza)
☎: +34 976 621 039 - Fax: +34 976 620 714
ivan@bodegasprinur.com
www.bodegasprinur.com

PRINUR CHARDONNAY 2010 B
100% chardonnay.

86 Colour: bright straw. Nose: white flowers, tropical fruit, fragrant herbs. Palate: light-bodied, fresh, fruity, easy to drink.

PRINUR MACABEO 2010 B
100% macabeo.

83 Colour: bright straw. Nose: citrus fruit, fragrant herbs, fresh. Palate: good acidity, fresh, fruity.

PRINUR MOSCATEL 2009 B
moscatel.

92 Colour: bright yellow. Nose: citrus fruit, honeyed notes, tropical fruit, expressive. Palate: powerful, fruity, flavourful, fleshy, creamy.

PRINUR RED PASSION 2010 RD
100% tempranillo.

84 Colour: rose, purple rim. Nose: ripe fruit, red berry notes, floral. Palate: fleshy, powerful, fruity, fresh.

PRINUR VIÑAS VIEJAS 2005 T
tempranillo, cabernet sauvignon, garnacha, cariñena, vidadilo.

91 Colour: cherry, garnet rim. Nose: earthy notes, scrubland, ripe fruit, spicy, creamy oak. Palate: powerful, flavourful, balanced, fleshy, round tannins.

PRINUR SELECCIÓN CALAR 2005 T
tempranillo, cabernet sauvignon, garnacha.

90 Colour: cherry, garnet rim. Nose: mineral, red berry notes, ripe fruit, balsamic herbs, expressive, toasty. Palate: light-bodied, powerful, flavourful, fleshy, ripe fruit.

BODEGAS SAN VALERO

Ctra. Nacional 330, Km. 450
50400 Cariñena (Zaragoza)
☎: +34 976 620 400 - Fax: +34 976 620 398
bsv@sanvalero.com
www.sanvalero.com

CARINVS 2008 T ROBLE
20% garnacha, 20% tempranillo, 20% cabernet sauvignon, 20% merlot, 20% syrah.

87 Colour: cherry, garnet rim. Nose: powerfull, complex, ripe fruit, grassy. Palate: spicy, fine bitter notes, good acidity.

MONTE DUCAY 2010 RD
garnacha, cabernet sauvignon.

87 Colour: rose, purple rim. Nose: red berry notes, fresh, lactic notes. Palate: fruity, fresh, good acidity, round.

MONTE DUCAY 2010 T
tempranillo, garnacha, cabernet sauvignon.

84 Colour: cherry, purple rim. Nose: fruit expression, red berry notes, balanced. Palate: correct, easy to drink, balsamic.

SIERRA DE VIENTO TEMPRANILLO 2009 T
100% tempranillo.

89 Colour: cherry, garnet rim. Nose: ripe fruit, fruit expression, red berry notes. Palate: flavourful, fruity, fleshy.

CARINVS MUSCAT 2010 B
100% moscatel.

87 Colour: pale. Nose: white flowers, varietal, citrus fruit, ripe fruit. Palate: flavourful, fruity, easy to drink.

SIERRA DE VIENTO GARNACHA 2008 T
100% garnacha.

90 Colour: bright cherry. Nose: ripe fruit, sweet spices, creamy oak, balsamic herbs, scrubland. Palate: flavourful, fruity, toasty, round tannins.

MONTE DUCAY 2002 TGR
tempranillo, garnacha, cabernet sauvignon.

86 Colour: pale ruby, brick rim edge. Nose: spicy, wet leather, aged wood nuances, fruit liqueur notes, tobacco. Palate: spicy, fine tannins, elegant, long.

SIERRA DE VIENTO MOSCATEL VENDIMIA TARDÍA B
100% moscatel.

92 Colour: light mahogany. Nose: powerfull, floral, honeyed notes, candied fruit, balsamic herbs. Palate: flavourful, sweet, fresh, fruity, good acidity, easy to drink.

CARINVS CHARDONNAY 2010 B
100% chardonnay.

85 Colour: bright straw. Nose: medium intensity, ripe fruit, citrus fruit. Palate: flavourful, fruity.

MONTE DUCAY 2010 B
macabeo.

83 Colour: straw, pale. Nose: white flowers, tropical fruit, medium intensity. Palate: fresh, light-bodied.

MARQUÉS DE TOSOS 2005 TR
tempranillo, garnacha, cabernet sauvignon.

86 Colour: cherry, garnet rim. Nose: old leather, tobacco, spicy, powerfull. Palate: flavourful, balanced, round tannins, spicy.

SIERRA DE VIENTO GARNACHA GRAN SELECCIÓN 2006 T
100% garnacha.

91 Colour: deep cherry. Nose: overripe fruit, fruit liqueur notes, toasty, creamy oak, earthy notes, mineral. Palate: flavourful, powerful, fleshy, warm, spirituous.

BODEGAS VICTORIA

Camino Virgen de Lagunas, s/n Apdo. Correos 47
50400 Cariñena (Zaragoza)
☎: +34 976 621 007 - Fax: +34 976 621 106
comercial@bodegasvictoria.com
www.bodegasvictoria.com

LONGUS 2006 T
40% cabernet sauvignon, 30% merlot, 30% syrah.

91 Colour: cherry, garnet rim. Nose: ripe fruit, powerfull, spicy, cocoa bean, dark chocolate. Palate: flavourful, complex, fleshy, balanced.

DOMINIO DE LONGAZ PREMIUM 2006 T
40% syrah, 30% merlot, 30% cabernet sauvignon.

90 Colour: cherry, garnet rim. Nose: ripe fruit, powerfull, mineral, spicy, toasty. Palate: good acidity, unctuous, fleshy.

BODEGAS VIRGEN DEL ÁGUILA

Ctra. Valencia, Km. 53
50480 Paniza (Zaragoza)
☎: +34 976 622 515 - Fax: +34 976 622 958
info@bodegasaguila.com
www.bodegasvirgenaguila.com

VAL DE PANIZA 2010 B
viura, chardonnay.

87 Colour: bright straw. Nose: fresh, fresh fruit, white flowers, citrus fruit. Palate: flavourful, fruity, good acidity, sweetness.

JABALÍ VIURA & CHARDONNAY 2010 B
50% viura, 50% chardonnay.

86 Colour: bright straw. Nose: fresh, fresh fruit, white flowers. Palate: flavourful, fruity, good acidity, balanced.

JABALÍ GARNACHA-CABERNET 2010 RD
75% garnacha, 25% cabernet sauvignon.

86 Colour: rose. Nose: ripe fruit, fruit expression, raspberry. Palate: flavourful, fruity, light-bodied.

JABALÍ GARNACHA-SYRAH 2010 T
50% garnacha, 50% syrah.

91 Colour: cherry, purple rim. Nose: floral, fresh fruit, balanced. Palate: fresh, fruity, flavourful, easy to drink.

JABALÍ TEMPRANILLO - CABERNET 2010 T
50% tempranillo, 50% cabernet sauvignon.

90 Colour: cherry, purple rim. Nose: red berry notes, floral, expressive, grassy. Palate: fruity, flavourful, fleshy.

VAL DE PANIZA 2010 T
50% tempranillo, 30% garnacha, 20% syrah.

88 Colour: cherry, purple rim. Nose: raspberry, red berry notes, fresh, expressive. Palate: fruity, powerful, flavourful, fleshy.

SEÑORÍO DEL ÁGUILA 2008 TC
40% garnacha, 40% tempranillo, 20% syrah.

84 Colour: cherry, garnet rim. Nose: fruit preserve, overripe fruit, roasted coffee. Palate: powerful, sweetness, concentrated.

SEÑORÍO DEL ÁGUILA 2007 TR
40% tempranillo, 30% syrah, 30% cabernet sauvignon.

85 Colour: cherry, garnet rim. Nose: spicy, cocoa bean, dark chocolate, toasty, ripe fruit. Palate: powerful, flavourful, fleshy.

SEÑORÍO DEL ÁGUILA 2006 TGR
40% tempranillo, 40% cabernet sauvignon, 20% garnacha.

87 Colour: pale ruby, brick rim edge. Nose: spicy, aromatic coffee, old leather. Palate: powerful, flavourful, fleshy.

CAMPOS DE LUZ

Avda. Diagonal, 590, 5º - 1
08021 Barcelona (Barcelona)
☎: +34 660 445 464
info@vinergia.com
www.vinergia.com

CAMPOS DE LUZ 2010 B
viura, chardonnay, moscatel.

84 Colour: bright straw. Nose: fresh, fresh fruit, white flowers, expressive, tropical fruit. Palate: flavourful, fruity, good acidity.

CAMPOS DE LUZ 2010 RD
100% garnacha.

83 Color rose, purple rim. Aroma powerfull, ripe fruit, red berry notes, floral, expressive. Taste fleshy, powerful, fruity, fresh.

CAMPOS DE LUZ GARNACHA 2010 T
100% garnacha.

85 Colour: cherry, purple rim. Nose: red berry notes, ripe fruit. Palate: flavourful, good acidity, round tannins, ripe fruit.

CAMPOS DE LUZ GARNACHA 2008 TC
100% garnacha.

86 Colour: cherry, garnet rim. Nose: ripe fruit, spicy, creamy oak. Palate: powerful, flavourful, round.

CAMPOS DE LUZ GARNACHA 2005 TR
100% garnacha.

87 Colour: cherry, garnet rim. Nose: creamy oak, toasty, overripe fruit. Palate: powerful, flavourful, toasty, round tannins.

COVINCA S. COOP.

Ctra, Valencia, s/n
50460 Longares (Zaragoza)
☎: +34 976 142 653 - Fax: +34 976 142 402
info@covinca.es
www.covinca.es

TORRELONGARES MACABEO 2010 B
100% macabeo.

85 Color bright straw. Aroma fresh, fresh fruit, white flowers, expressive. Taste flavourful, fruity, good acidity, balanced.

TORRELONGARES GARNACHA 2010 T
100% garnacha.

85 Colour: cherry, purple rim. Nose: red berry notes, ripe fruit. Palate: flavourful, good acidity, round tannins.

TERRAI M08 2008 T
100% mazuelo.

89 Colour: cherry, garnet rim. Nose: earthy notes, scrubland, balanced, creamy oak. Palate: flavourful, powerful, fleshy.

TORRELONGARES GARNACHA SELECCIÓN 50 2007 T
100% garnacha.

88 Color bright cherry. Aroma ripe fruit, sweet spices, creamy oak, expressive. Taste flavourful, fruity, toasty, round tannins.

TERRAI G06 2006 T
100% garnacha.

88 Colour: cherry, garnet rim. Nose: powerfull, characterful, mineral, balsamic herbs. Palate: powerful, concentrated, spicy.

TORRELONGARES LICOR DE GARNACHA 2006 VINO DE LICOR
100% garnacha.

91 Colour: cherry, garnet rim. Nose: candied fruit, fruit liqueur notes, warm. Palate: flavourful, powerful, spirituous, sweet.

GRANDES VINOS Y VIÑEDOS

Ctra. Valencia Km 45,700
50400 Cariñena (Zaragoza)
☎: +34 976 621 261 - Fax: +34 976 621 253
info@grandesvinos.com
www.grandesvinos.com

ANAYÓN CHARDONNAY 2010 BFB
chardonnay.

90 Colour: bright yellow. Nose: powerfull, ripe fruit, sweet spices, creamy oak. Palate: rich, smoky aftertaste, flavourful, fresh, good acidity.

MONASTERIO DE LAS VIÑAS 2010 B
macabeo.

85 Color bright straw. Aroma fresh, fresh fruit, white flowers, expressive. Taste flavourful, fruity, good acidity, balanced.

CORONA DE ARAGÓN 2010 B
macabeo, chardonnay.

84 Colour: straw. Nose: medium intensity, fresh fruit, grassy. Palate: flavourful, fruity, light-bodied.

BESO DE VINO 2010 B
macabeo.

82 Colour: bright straw. Nose: candied fruit, citrus fruit, medium intensity. Palate: fresh, fruity, light-bodied.

MONASTERIO DE LAS VIÑAS 2010 RD
garnacha.

89 Colour: rose, purple rim. Nose: powerfull, ripe fruit, red berry notes, floral, fresh. Palate: fleshy, fruity, flavourful.

CORONA DE ARAGÓN 2010 RD
garnacha, syrah.

86 Colour: rose, purple rim. Nose: ripe fruit, red berry notes, floral. Palate: fleshy, fruity, fresh.

CORONA DE ARAGÓN 111 EDICIÓN ESPECIAL LUIS BUÑUEL C.V.C. T
tempranillo, cabernet sauvignon, cariñena.

88 Colour: bright cherry. Nose: ripe fruit, sweet spices, creamy oak. Palate: fruity, toasty, round tannins, sweetness.

CORONA DE ARAGÓN GARNACHA 2010 T
garnacha.

87 Colour: cherry, purple rim. Nose: ripe fruit, raspberry, powerfull. Palate: flavourful, concentrated, fleshy.

ANAYÓN 2006 T BARRICA
tempranillo, cabernet sauvignon, syrah.

90 Colour: cherry, garnet rim. Nose: ripe fruit, spicy, toasty, characterful, aromatic coffee. Palate: powerful, flavourful, toasty, round tannins, fine bitter notes.

CORONA DE ARAGÓN SPECIAL SELECTION GARNACHA CARIÑENA 2009 T
garnacha, cariñena.

88 Colour: cherry, purple rim. Nose: ripe fruit, varietal, balanced, complex. Palate: good structure, flavourful, balanced.

BESO DE VINO 2010 RD
garnacha.

86 Colour: rose, purple rim. Nose: red berry notes, floral, fruit preserve. Palate: fleshy, powerful, fruity, fresh.

MONASTERIO DE LAS VIÑAS 2010 T
garnacha, tempranillo, cariñena.

87 Colour: cherry, purple rim. Nose: powerfull, warm, overripe fruit. Palate: powerful, fleshy, concentrated.

BESO DE VINO SELECCIÓN 2009 T
syrah, garnacha.

90 Color bright cherry. Aroma ripe fruit, sweet spices, creamy oak, expressive. Taste flavourful, fruity, toasty, round tannins.

BESO DE VINO GARNACHA 2009 T
garnacha.

88 Colour: cherry, garnet rim. Nose: sweet spices, ripe fruit, scrubland, grassy. Palate: flavourful, fleshy, fruity.

CORONA DE ARAGÓN OLD VINE GARNACHA 2009 T
garnacha.

88 Colour: bright cherry. Nose: sweet spices, creamy oak, mineral, ripe fruit. Palate: flavourful, fruity, toasty, round tannins.

ANAYÓN GARNACHA 2008 T
garnacha.

92 Colour: cherry, garnet rim. Nose: ripe fruit, spicy, creamy oak, toasty, complex, mineral, scrubland. Palate: powerful, flavourful, toasty, round tannins.

MONASTERIO DE LAS VIÑAS 2008 TC
garnacha, tempranillo, cariñena.

85 Colour: cherry, garnet rim. Nose: fruit preserve, medium intensity, toasty. Palate: powerful, flavourful, fleshy.

CORONA DE ARAGÓN 2007 TC
tempranillo, cabernet sauvignon, garnacha, cariñena.

88 Colour: cherry, garnet rim. Nose: ripe fruit, spicy, creamy oak, toasty. Palate: powerful, flavourful, toasty, round tannins, spicy.

MONASTERIO DE LAS VIÑAS 2006 TR
garnacha, tempranillo, cariñena.

87 Colour: cherry, garnet rim. Nose: ripe fruit, creamy oak, dark chocolate. Palate: powerful, flavourful, toasty, round tannins.

CORONA DE ARAGÓN 2005 TR
tempranillo, cabernet sauvignon, garnacha, cariñena.

88 Colour: pale ruby, brick rim edge. Nose: powerfull, candied fruit, wet leather, fine reductive notes, aromatic coffee. Palate: toasty, spicy, fine bitter notes.

CORONA DE ARAGÓN 2004 TGR
tempranillo, cabernet sauvignon, cariñena, garnacha.

86 Colour: pale ruby, brick rim edge. Nose: old leather, spicy, aromatic coffee. Palate: good acidity, flavourful, fleshy.

MONASTERIO DE LAS VIÑAS 2004 TGR
garnacha, tempranillo, cabernet sauvignon, cariñena.

85 Colour: pale ruby, brick rim edge. Nose: old leather, tobacco, waxy notes, aromatic coffee. Palate: powerful, flavourful, aged character.

HACIENDA MOLLEDA

Ctra. Belchite, km 29,3
50154 Tosos (Zaragoza)
☎: +34 976 620 702 - Fax: +34 976 620 102
hm@haciendamolleda.com
www.haciendamolleda.com

HACIENDA MOLLEDA 2010 T
50% garnacha, 50% tempranillo.

83 Colour: cherry, purple rim. Nose: ripe fruit, warm, fresh. Palate: correct, flavourful, easy to drink.

GHM GRAN HACIENDA MOLLEDA 2009 TC
100% mazuelo.

90 Colour: cherry, garnet rim. Nose: spicy, creamy oak, overripe fruit, roasted coffee. Palate: powerful, flavourful, toasty, round tannins. Personality.

GHM GARNACHA HACIENDA MOLLEDA 2006 T ROBLE
100% garnacha.

90 Colour: bright cherry. Nose: ripe fruit, expressive, mineral. Palate: flavourful, fruity, toasty, round tannins.

HACIENDA MOLLEDA 2004 T ROBLE
45% tempranillo, 40% garnacha, 5% cabernet sauvignon, 10% syrah.

84 Colour: pale ruby, brick rim edge. Nose: old leather, cigar, spicy. Palate: fleshy, flavourful, balsamic.

HACIENDA MOLLEDA 2002 TR
100% tempranillo.

78

HEREDAD ANSÓN

Camino Eras Altas, s/n
50450 Muel (Zaragoza)
☎: +34 976 141 133 - Fax: +34 976 141 133
info@bodegasheredadanson.com
www.bodegasheredadanson.com

ANSÓN 2010 B
macabeo.

83 Colour: bright straw. Nose: fresh, fresh fruit, medium intensity. Palate: fruity, flavourful.

HEREDAD DE ANSÓN 2010 RD
100% garnacha.

85 Colour: rose, purple rim. Nose: powerfull, red berry notes, floral, expressive. Palate: fleshy, powerful, fruity, fresh.

HEREDAD DE ANSÓN MERLOT SYRAH 2010 T
50% merlot, 50% syrah.

87 Colour: cherry, purple rim. Nose: powerfull, characterful, warm, ripe fruit. Palate: concentrated, sweetness, fine bitter notes, fruity.

LEGUM 2007 T ROBLE
100% garnacha.

88 Colour: cherry, garnet rim. Nose: spicy, cocoa bean, creamy oak, ripe fruit. Palate: fleshy, flavourful, long.

HEREDAD DE ANSÓN 2005 TC
80% garnacha, 10% syrah, 10% tempranillo.

80 Colour: ruby red, orangey edge. Nose: cocoa bean, sweet spices, reduction off-odours, slightly evolved. Palate: flavourful, short.

JORDÁN DE ASSO

Cariñena, 55
50408 Aguarón (Zaragoza)
☎: +34 976 620 291 - Fax: +34 976 230 270
info@jordandeasso.com
www.jordandeasso.com

JORDÁN DE ASSO 2006 TC
35% garnacha, 35% cariñena, 30% cabernet sauvignon.

87 Colour: cherry, garnet rim. Nose: ripe fruit, spicy, creamy oak. Palate: flavourful, toasty, round tannins.

JORDÁN DE ASSO 2006 TR
40% tempranillo, 30% syrah, 30% cabernet sauvignon.

85 Colour: cherry, garnet rim. Nose: ripe fruit, spicy, creamy oak. Palate: powerful, flavourful, toasty.

PAGO DE AYLÉS

Finca Aylés. Ctra. A-1101, Km. 24
50152 (Zaragoza)
☎: +34 976 140 473 - Fax: +34 976 140 268
info@bodegasayles.com
www.bodegasayles.com

DORONDÓN CHARDONNAY DE AYLÉS 2010 B
100% chardonnay.

88 Colour: bright straw. Nose: fresh, white flowers, citrus fruit, ripe fruit. Palate: flavourful, fruity, good acidity, balanced.

AYLÉS 2010 RD
garnacha, syrah.

86 Colour: rose, purple rim. Nose: powerfull, red berry notes, floral, expressive. Palate: fleshy, powerful, fruity, fresh.

AYLÉS 4 VARIEDADES 2010 T
merlot, tempranillo, syrah, garnacha.

84 Colour: cherry, purple rim. Nose: ripe fruit, warm, fresh. Palate: good acidity, light-bodied, fruity.

AYLÉS GARNACHA 2009 T
garnacha.

87 Colour: cherry, purple rim. Nose: powerfull, varietal, grassy, fruit expression. Palate: flavourful, good acidity, spicy, round tannins.

AYLÉS GARNACHA 2009 T
100% garnacha.

86 Colour: cherry, garnet rim. Nose: spicy, ripe fruit, medium intensity. Palate: good acidity, flavourful, fresh.

AYLÉS MERLOT-TEMPRANILLO 2008 T
50% merlot, 50% tempranillo.

88 Colour: cherry, garnet rim. Nose: ripe fruit, spicy, toasty, characterful. Palate: flavourful, toasty, round tannins.

AYLÉS 2008 TC
cabernet sauvignon, merlot, tempranillo.

85 Colour: cherry, garnet rim. Nose: ripe fruit, old leather, spicy, toasty. Palate: good acidity, flavourful, fleshy.

AYLÉS "TRES DE 3000" 2007 T
garnacha, merlot, cabernet sauvignon.

94 Colour: cherry, garnet rim. Nose: spicy, creamy oak, toasty, characterful, ripe fruit, fruit expression. Palate: powerful, flavourful, toasty, round tannins.

SOLAR DE URBEZO

San Valero, 14
50400 Cariñena (Zaragoza)
☎: +34 976 621 968 - Fax: +34 976 620 549
info@solardeurbezo.es
www.solardeurbezo.es

ALTIUS MERLOT 2010 RD
100% merlot.

89 Colour: rose, purple rim. Nose: faded flowers, red berry notes, fruit expression. Palate: elegant, flavourful, light-bodied.

URBEZO CHARDONNAY 2010 B
100% chardonnay.

90 Colour: bright straw. Nose: white flowers, jasmine, ripe fruit, balsamic herbs, grassy. Palate: flavourful, fruity, fine bitter notes, long.

URBEZO MERLOT 2010 RD
100% merlot.

88 Colour: onion pink. Nose: candied fruit, dried flowers, fragrant herbs, red berry notes. Palate: light-bodied, good acidity, long, spicy.

ALTIUS GARNACHA 2010 T
100% garnacha.

90 Colour: cherry, purple rim. Nose: fresh fruit, red berry notes, floral, varietal, scrubland. Palate: flavourful, fruity, good acidity, round tannins.

DANCE DEL MAR 2010 T
tempranillo, merlot.

88 Colour: cherry, purple rim. Nose: balsamic herbs, grassy, fresh fruit. Palate: good acidity, fine bitter notes, fruity.

ALTIUS SYRAH CABERNET 2010 T
85% syrah, 15% cabernet sauvignon.

88 Colour: cherry, purple rim. Nose: fresh fruit, red berry notes, floral, grassy. Palate: flavourful, fruity, good acidity, round tannins.

ALTIUS 2008 TC
merlot, cabernet sauvignon, syrah.

91 Colour: bright cherry. Nose: sweet spices, creamy oak, expressive, fragrant herbs, balsamic herbs, fruit expression. Palate: flavourful, fruity, toasty, round tannins.

URBEZO 2008 TC
tempranillo, cabernet sauvignon, syrah.

88 Colour: bright cherry. Nose: sweet spices, creamy oak, ripe fruit, balsamic herbs. Palate: flavourful, fruity, round tannins, mineral.

URBEZO 2006 TR
syrah, cabernet sauvignon, merlot.

86 Colour: pale ruby, brick rim edge. Nose: aromatic coffee, spicy, wet leather. Palate: spirituous, powerful, sweetness.

VIÑA URBEZO 2010 T MACERACIÓN CARBÓNICA
40% garnacha, 30% tempranillo, 30% syrah.

90 Colour: cherry, purple rim. Nose: fresh fruit, floral, lactic notes, raspberry. Palate: flavourful, fruity, good acidity.

URBEZO GARNACHA 2010 T
100% garnacha.

90 Colour: cherry, purple rim. Nose: fresh fruit, red berry notes, floral, balsamic herbs. Palate: flavourful, fruity, good acidity, round tannins.

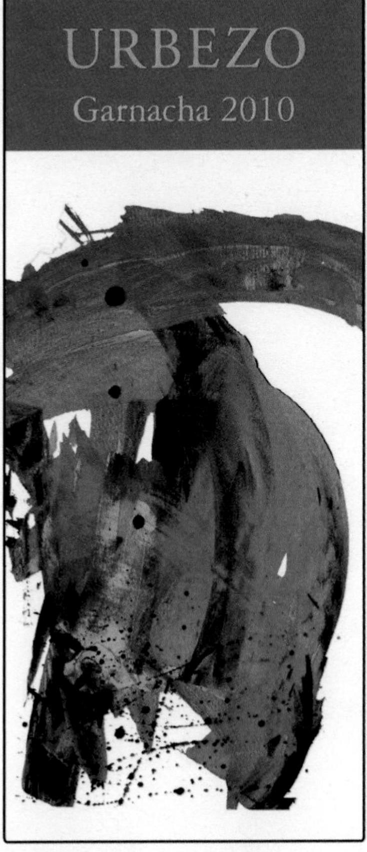

URBEZO 2005 TGR
50% garnacha, 50% cabernet sauvignon.

85 Colour: pale ruby, brick rim edge. Nose: medium intensity, fruit liqueur notes, spicy, toasty. Palate: powerful, spirituous, fine bitter notes.

VINNICO EXPORT

Muela, 16
03730 Jávea (Alicante)
☎: +34 965 791 967 - Fax: +34 966 461 471
info@vinnico.com
www.vinnico.com

ALMEZ 2010 T
100% garnacha.

87 Colour: cherry, purple rim. Nose: ripe fruit, fresh, balsamic herbs. Palate: flavourful, fruity, fleshy, easy to drink.

FLOR DEL MONTGÓ OLD VINES GARNACHA 2010 T
100% garnacha.

83 Colour: cherry, purple rim. Nose: ripe fruit, medium intensity, short. Palate: correct, good acidity.

VIÑEDOS Y BODEGAS PABLO

Avda. Zaragoza, 16
50108 Almonacid de la Sierra (Zaragoza)
☎: +34 976 627 037 - Fax: +34 976 627 102
granviu@granviu.com
www.granviu.com

MENGUANTE GARNACHA BLANCA 2010 B
garnacha blanca.

90 Colour: bright straw. Nose: white flowers, ripe fruit, citrus fruit, varietal, mineral. Palate: flavourful, fruity, good acidity, balanced.

MENGUANTE GARNACHA 2010 T
garnacha.

83 Colour: cherry, purple rim. Nose: ripe fruit, grassy, fresh. Palate: fresh, flavourful, fleshy.

GRAN VÍU SELECCIÓN 2008 T
garnacha, cabernet sauvignon, tempranillo, syrah.

90 Colour: bright cherry. Nose: ripe fruit, sweet spices, creamy oak, toasty. Palate: flavourful, fruity, toasty, round tannins.

MENGUANTE VIDADILLO 2008 T
vidadillo.

90 Colour: cherry, garnet rim. Nose: ripe fruit, creamy oak, toasty, complex, mineral, balsamic herbs. Palate: powerful, flavourful, toasty, round tannins.

MENGUANTE SELECCIÓN GARNACHA 2007 T
garnacha.

88 Colour: cherry, garnet rim. Nose: red berry notes, powerfull, creamy oak, balsamic herbs. Palate: powerful, flavourful, fruity, fleshy.

GIRONA
LLEIDA
BARCELONA
Reus
TARRAGONA
Consejo Regulador
DO Boundary

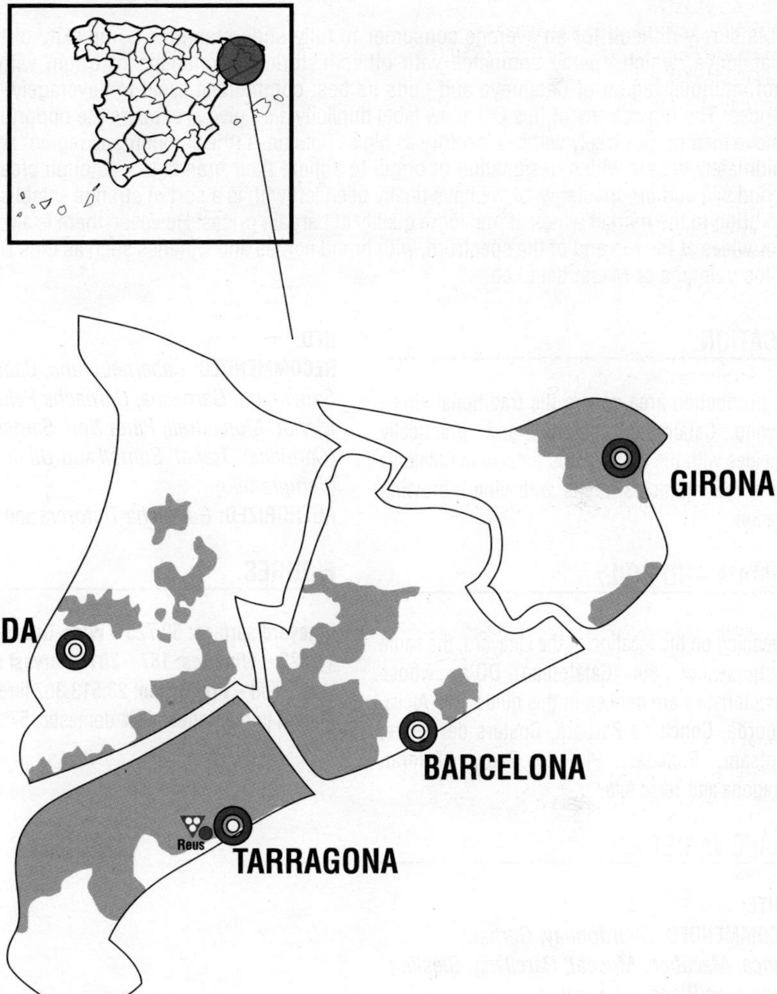

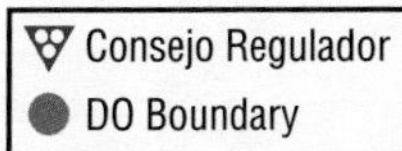

DO CATALUNYA

NEWS ABOUT THE VINTAGE:

It is surely difficult for an average consumer to fully understand the complexity of the DO Catalunya, which openly competes with other historic designations of origin within the autonomous region of Catalunya and finds its best commercial asset in –averagely– lower prices. The regulations of this DO allow label duplicity, i.e., give producers the opportunity to move their grapes freely within a territory as big as Catalunya (the autonomous region) and only ultimately decide which designation of origin to adhere their brands to. Although created on good will and prospects, what we have finally been left with is a sort of strange establishment to bring to the market wines of mediocre quality at bargain prices. However, there is also room for wines at the top end of the spectrum, with brand names and wineries such as Clos D'Agon, Clos Valmaña or Maset del LLeó.

LOCATION:

The production area covers the traditional vine - growing Catalonian regions, and practically coincides with the current DOs present in Catalonia plus a few municipal areas with vine - growing vocation.

CLIMATE AND SOIL:

Depending on the location of the vineyard, the same as those of the Catalonian DO's, whose characteristics are defined in this guide. See Alella, Empordà, Conca de Barberà, Costers del Segre, Montsant, Penedès, Pla de Bages, Priorat, Tarragona and Terra Alta.

GRAPE VARIETIES:

WHITE:
RECOMMENDED: *Chardonnay, Garnacha Blanca, Macabeo, Muscat, Parellada, Riesling, Sauvignon Blanc* and *Xarel·lo.*
AUTHORIZED: *Gewürztraminer, Subirat Parent* (*Malvasía*), *Malvasía de Sitges, Picapoll, Pedro Ximénez, Chenin, Riesling* and *Sauvignon Blanc*

RED:
RECOMMENDED: *Cabernet Franc, Cabernet Sauvignon, Garnacha, Garnacha Peluda, Merlot, Monastrell, Pinot Noir, Samsó* (*Cariñena*), *Trepat, Sumoll* and *Ull de Llebre* (*Tempranillo*).
AUTHORIZED: *Garnacha Tintorera* and *Syrah.*

FIGURES:

Vineyard surface: 50,725 – **Wine-Growers:** 11,522 – **Wineries:** 187 – **2010 Harvest rating:** Very Good – **Production:** 23,513,367 litres – **Market percentages:** 43% domestic. 57% export

CONSEJO REGULADOR
Passeig Sunyer 4-6 - 1º
43202 Reus (Tarragona)
☎: +34 977 328 103 - Fax: +34 977 321 357
@ info@do-catalunya.com
www.do-catalunya.com

GENERAL CHARACTERISTICS OF THE WINES

WHITES	In general, the autochtonous varieties from Catalonia predominate, *Macabeo, Xarel·lo* and *Parellada*. They are straw yellow and have a fresh and fruity nose; on the palate they are light and easy drinking. One can also find some *Chardonnay*, which are somewhat fruitier, typical of the variety, although not excessively, as they come from high-yield vineyards..
ROSÉS	These are quite modern; most are pink or raspberry pink in colour and the nose is fresh and fruity with hints of red berries; on the palate they are light and correct.
REDS	These may be produced from autochtonous grapes, especially *Ull de Llebre* (*Tempranillo*) and *Garnacha*. Cherry-coloured, they tend to be fruity on the nose with notes of wild berries; on the palate they are fruity, without too much body, although easy drinking. There are also examples of foreign varieties, especially, which can have balsamic and, on occasions, vegetative notes and which have a greater structure on the palate.

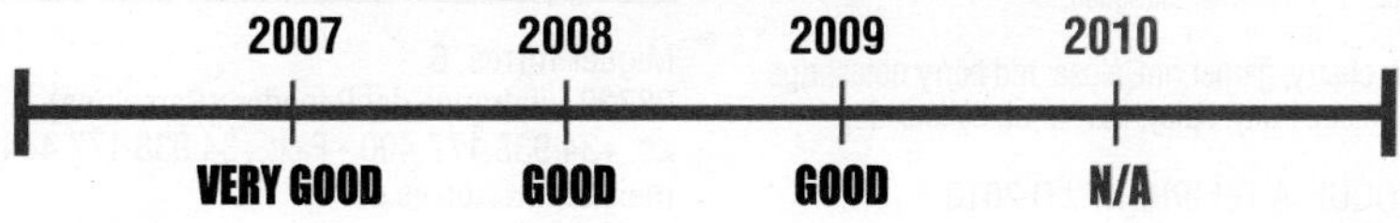

ALBET I NOYA

Can Vendrell de la Codina, s/n
08739 Sant Pau D'Ordal (Barcelona)
☎: +34 938 994 812 - Fax: +34 938 994 930
albetinoya@albetinoya.cat
www.albetinoya.cat

ALBET I NOYA PETIT ALBET NEGRE 2010 T
tempranillo, garnacha.

87 Colour: bright cherry, purple rim. Nose: red berry notes, balanced, medium intensity. Palate: flavourful, fruity, easy to drink.

BODEGAS 1898

Ctra. de Vic, 81
08241 Manresa (Barcelona)
☎: +34 938 743 511 - Fax: +34 938 737 204
info@bodegas1898.com
www.abadal.net

SYNERA 2010 B
85% macabeo, 15% moscatel.

84 Colour: bright straw. Nose: varietal, white flowers, fresh fruit. Palate: fruity, fresh, good acidity.

SYNERA 2010 RD
50% garnacha, 50% tempranillo.

86 Colour: brilliant rose. Nose: floral, red berry notes, fresh, balanced. Palate: fruity, fresh, correct, balanced.

SYNERA 2010 T BARRICA
75% tempranillo, 25% cabernet sauvignon.

87 Colour: cherry, garnet rim. Nose: red berry notes, ripe fruit, spicy. Palate: fruity, spicy, flavourful, balanced.

RAMÓN ROQUETA TEMPRANILLO 2010 T
100% tempranillo.

86 Colour: deep cherry, purple rim. Nose: red berry notes, varietal, spicy. Palate: fruity, flavourful, easy to drink.

RAMÓN ROQUETA CABERNET SAUVIGNON 2009 T
100% cabernet sauvignon.

85 Colour: cherry, garnet rim. Nose: medium intensity, ripe fruit, scrubland, spicy. Palate: flavourful, ripe fruit, great length.

BODEGAS PUIGGRÒS

Ctra. de Manresa, Km. 13
08711 Odena (Barcelona)
☎: +34 629 853 587
bodegaspuiggros@telefonica.net
www.bodegaspuiggros.com

SENTITS BLANCS 2010 B
100% garnacha blanca.

91 Colour: bright yellow. Nose: ripe fruit, sweet spices, creamy oak, fragrant herbs. Palate: rich, smoky aftertaste, flavourful, fresh, good acidity.

SENTITS NEGRES 2009 T
100% garnacha.

91 Colour: deep cherry. Nose: expressive, ripe fruit, sweet spices, scrubland. Palate: flavourful, fine bitter notes, good acidity, long.

SIGNES 2009 T
sumoll, garnacha.

91 Colour: bright cherry. Nose: expressive, earthy notes, mineral, scrubland, ripe fruit. Palate: flavourful, spicy, good acidity, fine bitter notes.

MESTRE VILA VELL VINYES VELLES 2009 T
100% sumoll.

88 Colour: cherry, garnet rim. Nose: ripe fruit, scrubland, spicy, creamy oak. Palate: powerful, flavourful, fleshy, complex.

BODEGAS TORRES

Miguel Torres, 6
08720 Vilafranca del Penedès (Barcelona)
☎: +34 938 177 400 - Fax: +34 938 177 444
mailadmin@torres.es
www.torres.es

VIÑA ESMERALDA 2010 B
moscatel, gewürztraminer.

87 Colour: bright straw. Nose: varietal, ripe fruit, honeyed notes, jasmine, white flowers. Palate: fruity, flavourful, good acidity.

SAN VALENTÍN 2010 B
parellada.

84 Colour: bright straw. Nose: dried herbs, dried flowers, ripe fruit. Palate: fruity, sweetness, easy to drink.

NEROLA 2009 B
xarel.lo, garnacha blanca.

88 Colour: bright straw. Nose: ripe fruit, floral, fragrant herbs, balanced. Palate: balanced, fine bitter notes, good acidity.

VIÑA SOL 2009 B
100% parellada.

88 Colour: bright straw. Nose: fragrant herbs, ripe fruit, faded flowers, balanced. Palate: flavourful, fruity, balanced.

DECASTA 2010 RD
65% garnacha, 35% cariñena.

87 Colour: brilliant rose. Nose: fresh, red berry notes, floral, dried herbs. Palate: flavourful, fruity, fine bitter notes, good acidity.

SANGRE DE TORO 2010 T
65% garnacha, 35% cariñena.

87 Colour: bright cherry, purple rim. Nose: balanced, medium intensity, red berry notes, ripe fruit. Palate: flavourful, fruity.

NEROLA 2009 T
syrah, garnacha, tempranillo, merlot.

89 Colour: deep cherry, purple rim. Nose: red berry notes, balanced, neat. Palate: fruity, full, flavourful, great length, spicy.

GRAN SANGRE DE TORO 2008 TR
60% garnacha, 25% cariñena, 15% syrah.

86 Colour: cherry, garnet rim. Nose: ripe fruit, spicy, toasty, warm. Palate: ripe fruit, spicy.

CA N'ESTRUC

Ctra. C-1414, Km. 1,05
08292 Esparreguera (Barcelona)
☎: +34 937 777 017 - Fax: +34 937 771 108
canestruc@vilaviniteca.es
www.canestruc.com

L'EQUILIBRISTA 2010 B
100% xaxarel.lo.

94 Colour: bright straw. Nose: fresh fruit, complex, balanced, varietal, fruit expression. Palate: powerful, complex, good structure, fruity, flavourful, creamy.

CA N'ESTRUC BLANC 2010 B

88 Colour: bright straw. Nose: fresh, fresh fruit, white flowers. Palate: flavourful, fruity, good acidity, balanced.

IDOIA BLANC 2009 BFB
xarel.lo, chardonnay, macabeo.

93 Colour: bright straw. Nose: white flowers, citrus fruit, candied fruit, creamy oak. Palate: flavourful, powerful, fleshy, fine bitter notes, long.

CA N'ESTRUC 2010 RD

85 Colour: rose, purple rim. Nose: fruit expression, raspberry, ripe fruit. Palate: flavourful, fruity, sweetness.

CA N'ESTRUC 2010 T
syrah, garnacha, cariñena.

89 Colour: very deep cherry. Nose: spicy, ripe fruit, sweet spices. Palate: flavourful, spicy, ripe fruit.

L'EQUILIBRISTA 2009 T
50% syrah, 25% garnacha, 25% cariñena.

93 Colour: cherry, garnet rim. Nose: creamy oak, sweet spices, raspberry. Palate: fine bitter notes, flavourful, powerful, round tannins.

L'EQUILIBRISTA GARNATXA 2009 T
garnacha.

92 Colour: cherry, garnet rim. Nose: scrubland, fruit expression, sweet spices, cocoa bean. Palate: flavourful, spicy, ripe fruit, round tannins.

IDOIA 2009 T

89 Colour: dark-red cherry. Nose: fruit expression, ripe fruit, cocoa bean. Palate: balanced, powerful, mineral, spicy.

CAN BONASTRE WINE RESORT

Ctra. B 224, Km. 13,2
08783 Masquefa (Barcelona)
☎: +34 937 726 167 - Fax: +34 937 727 929
bodega@canbonastre.com
www.canbonastre.com

ERUMIR 2010 B
45% sauvignon blanc, 35% macabeo, 20% riesling.

88 Colour: bright straw. Nose: fresh, fresh fruit, white flowers, expressive, fragrant herbs. Palate: flavourful, fruity, good acidity, balanced, light-bodied.

CAN BONASTRE PINOT NOIR 2009 T
100% pinot noir.

88 Colour: light cherry. Nose: red berry notes, ripe fruit, medium intensity, balanced, sweet spices. Palate: flavourful, fruity, balanced, easy to drink.

CASTELL D'OR

Mare Rafols, 3- 1r 4a
08720 Vilafranca del Penedès (Barcelona)
☎: +34 938 905 385 - Fax: +34 938 905 446
castelldor@castelldor.com
www.castelldor.com

FLAMA D'OR 2010 B
60% macabeo, 40% xarel.lo.

84 Colour: bright straw. Nose: ripe fruit, tropical fruit, white flowers. Palate: fruity, easy to drink.

PUIG DE SOLIVELLA 2010 B
80% macabeo, 20% parellada.

83 Colour: bright straw. Nose: medium intensity, dried flowers, citrus fruit, ripe fruit. Palate: fruity, easy to drink.

FLAMA D'OR 2010 RD
100% tempranillo.

86 Colour: rose, purple rim. Nose: medium intensity, red berry notes, ripe fruit, wild herbs. Palate: correct, easy to drink, fine bitter notes.

PUIG DE SOLIVELLA 2010 RD
80% trepat, 20% garnacha.

84 Colour: brilliant rose. Nose: red berry notes, medium intensity, floral. Palate: light-bodied, fruity, easy to drink.

FLAMA D'OR 2008 T
100% tempranillo.

82 Colour: cherry, garnet rim. Nose: grassy, ripe fruit, warm. Palate: light-bodied, easy to drink, correct.

PUIG DE SOLIVELLA 2007 T
75% tempranillo, 25% garnacha.

86 Colour: bright cherry, garnet rim. Nose: medium intensity, red berry notes, spicy, fresh. Palate: fruity, easy to drink, good finish.

FLAMA D'OR OAKED 2004 T
100% tempranillo.

84 Colour: cherry, garnet rim. Nose: medium intensity, ripe fruit, spicy, toasty. Palate: light-bodied, good finish.

FLAMA D'OR 2002 TR
60% tempranillo, 40% cabernet sauvignon.

85 Colour: cherry, garnet rim. Nose: ripe fruit, spicy, toasty, candied fruit, warm. Palate: powerful, toasty, round tannins.

FLAMA D'OR 2001 TGR
100% cabernet sauvignon.

86 Colour: cherry, garnet rim. Nose: candied fruit, sweet spices, creamy oak, cocoa bean. Palate: flavourful, fine bitter notes.

CAVAS DEL AMPURDÁN

Pza. del Carme, 1
17491 Perelada (Girona)
☎: +34 972 538 011 - Fax: +34 972 538 277
perelada@castilloperelada.com
www.blancpescador.com

MASIA PERELADA 2010 B
70% macabeo, 30% garnacha blanca.

85 Colour: bright straw. Nose: jasmine, white flowers, ripe fruit, medium intensity. Palate: fruity, fine bitter notes.

BLANC PESCADOR SEGUNDA GENERACIÓN 2010 B
80% garnacha blanca, 20% sauvignon blanc.

85 Colour: bright straw. Nose: white flowers, citrus fruit, balanced. Palate: fruity, flavourful, fine bitter notes, good acidity.

CRESTA ROSA SEGUNDA GENERACIÓN 2010 RD
70% garnacha, 30% cabernet sauvignon.

80 Colour: rose. Nose: ripe fruit, candied fruit, warm, dried herbs. Palate: ripe fruit, good finish.

MASIA PERELADA 2010 T
65% garnacha, 25% tempranillo, 10% syrah.

84 Colour: cherry, purple rim. Nose: medium intensity, fresh fruit, lactic notes. Palate: fruity, correct.

CAVES CONDE DE CARALT S.A.

Ctra. Sant Sadurní-Sant Pere de Riudebitlles, Km. 5
08775 Torrelavit (Barcelona)
☎: +34 938 917 070 - Fax: +34 938 996 006
seguraviudas@seguraviudas.es
www.freixenet.es

CONDE DE CARALT BLANC DE BLANCS 2010 B
40% xarel.lo, 30% macabeo, 30% parellada.

84 Colour: bright straw. Nose: fresh, ripe fruit, dried flowers. Palate: flavourful, fruity, good acidity, balanced.

CONDE DE CARALT 2010 RD
35% tempranillo, 45% garnacha, 20% cariñena.

84 Colour: brilliant rose. Nose: faded flowers, dried herbs, citrus fruit, medium intensity. Palate: fruity, fresh, light-bodied.

CONDE DE CARALT 2007 TC
80% tempranillo, 10% cabernet sauvignon, 10% merlot. HHHH5,5€

88 Colour: deep cherry, garnet rim. Nose: ripe fruit, toasty, sweet spices, dark chocolate. Palate: powerful, fleshy, spicy, ripe fruit.

CELLER PASCONA

Camí dels Fontals, s/n
43730 Falset (Tarragona)
☎: +34 609 291 770 - Fax: +34 977 117 098
info@pascona.com
www.pascona.com

991'N MACABEVS 2010 B
macabeo.

87 Colour: bright yellow. Nose: candied fruit, ripe fruit, faded flowers. Palate: rich, ripe fruit, flavourful, balanced.

992'S MONASTRELLS 2010 T
monastrell.

81 Colour: deep cherry, purple rim. Nose: medium intensity, red berry notes, slightly evolved. Palate: light-bodied, correct.

CELLERS UNIÓ

Joan Oliver, 16-24
43206 Reus (Tarragona)
☎: +34 977 330 055 - Fax: +34 977 330 070
info@cellersunio.com
www.cellersunio.com

MASIA PUBILL S/C B
40% garnacha blanca, 40% macabeo, 20% chardonnay.

84 Colour: bright straw. Nose: medium intensity, fresh, dried flowers, citrus fruit. Palate: flavourful, fruity, good acidity.

MASIA PUBILL S/C RD
75% garnacha, 25% merlot.

83 Colour: rose. Nose: candied fruit, red berry notes, floral, lactic notes. Palate: fruity, sweetness.

MASIA PUBILL S/C T
50% garnacha, 50% ull de llebre.

84 Colour: light cherry, purple rim. Nose: medium intensity, red berry notes, ripe fruit. Palate: light-bodied, easy to drink, correct.

CLOS D'AGON

Afores, s/n
17251 Calonge (Girona)
☎: +34 972 661 486 - Fax: +34 972 661 462
info@closdagon.com
www.closdagon.com

AMIC DE CLOS D'AGON 2010 T
64% garnacha, 17% merlot, 11% cabernet sauvignon, 8% syrah.

89 Colour: bright cherry, purple rim. Nose: red berry notes, elegant, violets. Palate: flavourful, good structure, fine bitter notes, easy to drink.

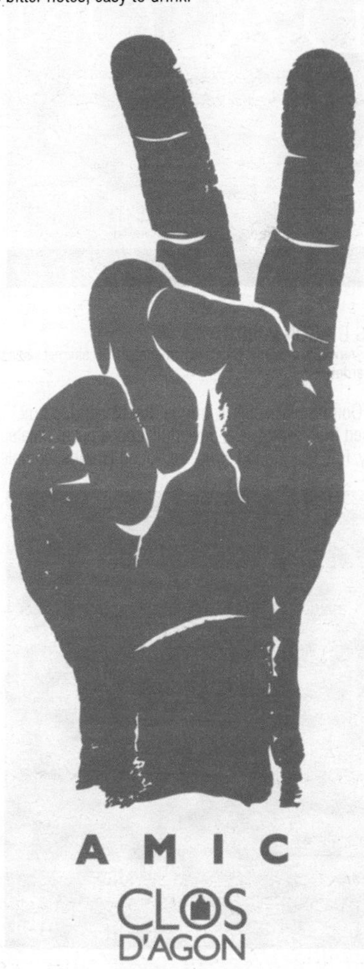

CLOS D'AGON 2010 B
roussanne, viognier, maesanne.

92 Colour: bright straw. Nose: elegant, balanced, wild herbs, white flowers. Palate: fruity, flavourful, fine bitter notes, good acidity.

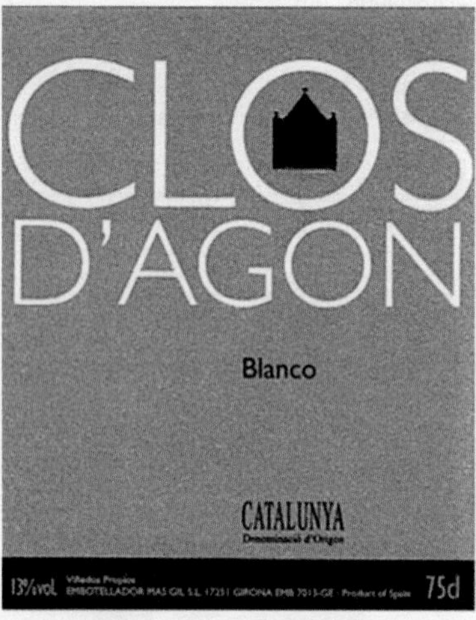

CLOS D'AGON 2009 T
35% syrah, 32% cabernet franc, 13% merlot, 10% cabernet sauvignon, petit verdot.

94 Colour: black cherry, purple rim. Nose: ripe fruit, candied fruit, expressive, powerfull, cocoa bean. Palate: fleshy, full, fruity, good structure, round tannins, complex.

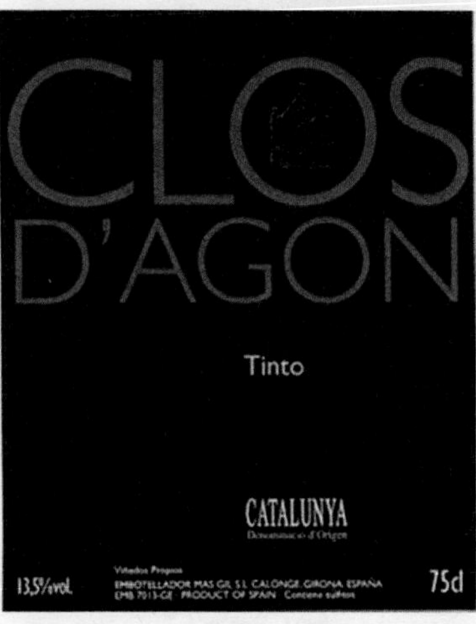

CLOS VALMAÑA 2009 TC
61% merlot, 20% cabernet sauvignon, 8% petit verdot, 7% cabernet sauvignon, 4% syrah.

93 Colour: black cherry, purple rim. Nose: complex, cocoa bean, creamy oak, sweet spices, candied fruit. Palate: complex, fleshy, good structure, round tannins.

CLOS MONTBLANC

Ctra. Montblanc-Barbera, s/n
43422 Barberà de la Conca (Tarragona)
☎: +34 977 887 030 - Fax: +34 977 887 032
info@closmontblanc.com
www.closmontblanc.com

PROYECTO CU4TRO 2010 B
macabeo, parellada, xarel.lo, garnacha blanca.

87 Colour: bright straw. Nose: fresh, white flowers, expressive. Palate: flavourful, fruity, good acidity, balanced, ripe fruit, fine bitter notes.

PROYECTO CU4TRO 2007 T
merlot, tempranillo, cabernet sauvignon, samsó.

89 Colour: deep cherry, garnet rim. Nose: balanced, complex, powerfull, ripe fruit, sweet spices, creamy oak. Palate: fruity, round tannins.

FERMÍ BOHIGAS

Finca Can Maciá
08711 Ódena (Barcelona)
☎: +34 938 048 100 - Fax: +34 938 032 366
tecnic@bohigas.es
www.bohigas.es

UDINA DE FERMÍ BOHIGAS 2010 B
garnacha blanca, chenin blanc, xarel.lo.

88 Colour: bright straw. Nose: white flowers, medium intensity, ripe fruit, jasmine. Palate: fresh, flavourful, good acidity, fine bitter notes.

BOHIGAS BLANC DE BLANCS 2010 B
xarel.lo.

87 Colour: bright straw. Nose: fresh, floral, wild herbs, ripe fruit, balanced. Palate: flavourful, ripe fruit, great length, good acidity.

FERMÍ DE FERMÍ BOHIGAS 2008 TR
syrah.

89 Colour: very deep cherry, purple rim. Nose: red berry notes, lactic notes, violets, medium intensity. Palate: fruity, flavourful, balanced, round tannins.

BOHIGAS CABERNET SAUVIGNON 2008 TC
cabernet sauvignon.

87 Colour: very deep cherry, garnet rim. Nose: ripe fruit, sweet spices, cocoa bean, medium intensity. Palate: flavourful, balanced, fine bitter notes, toasty.

FINCA VALLDOSERA

Pol. Ind. Clot de Moja- Merlot, 11
08734 Moja (Barcelona)
☎: +34 938 904 353 - Fax: +34 938 904 334
euroseleccio@euroseleccio.com
www.fincavalldosera.com

FINCA VALLDOSERA 2010 RD
60% syrah, 40% merlot.

84 Colour: rose, purple rim. Nose: fruit expression, raspberry. Palate: good acidity, flavourful.

GRAU VELL

Can Grau Vell, s/n
08784 Hostalets de Pierola (Barcelona)
☎: +34 676 586 933 - Fax: +34 932 684 965
info@grauvell.cat

ALCOR 2008 T
monastrell, garnacha, cabernet sauvignon.

93 Colour: cherry, garnet rim. Nose: spicy, creamy oak, toasty, earthy notes. Palate: powerful, flavourful, toasty, round tannins.

ALCOR 2007 T
monastrell, garnacha, cabernet sauvignon.

93 Colour: deep cherry. Nose: complex, expressive, varietal, cocoa bean, dark chocolate, creamy oak. Palate: powerful, full, fruity, rich, flavourful.

JAUME GRAU - VINS GRAU

Ctra. C-37 de Igualada a Manresa, Km. 75,5
08255 Maians (Barcelona)
☎: +34 938 356 002 - Fax: +34 938 356 812
info@vinsgrau.com
www.vinsgrau.com

CLOS DEL RECÓ 2010 B
macabeo, xarel.lo, parellada.

81 Colour: pale. Nose: white flowers, tropical fruit, fresh. Palate: light-bodied, fresh, easy to drink.

CLOS DEL RECÓ 2010 RD
merlot, tempranillo.

85 Colour: rose, purple rim. Nose: fresh, fresh fruit, medium intensity. Palate: easy to drink, light-bodied, fresh.

CLOS DEL RECÓ 2010 T
tempranillo, merlot.

83 Colour: cherry, purple rim. Nose: candied fruit, fresh, short. Palate: light-bodied, fresh, easy to drink.

JAUME SERRA (J. GARCÍA CARRIÓN)

Ctra. de Vilanova, Km. 2,5
08800 Vilanova i la Geltru (Barcelona)
☎: +34 938 936 404 - Fax: +34 938 142 262
jaumeserra@jgc.es
www.garciacarrion.es

VIÑA DEL MAR SEMIDULCE 2010 B
60% macabeo, 40% xarel.lo.

80 Colour: bright straw. Nose: candied fruit, white flowers. Palate: easy to drink, ripe fruit.

VIÑA DEL MAR SECO 2010 B
40% macabeo, 40% xarel.lo, 20% parellada.

78

VIÑA DEL MAR 2010 RD
80% tempranillo, 20% cariñena.

82 Colour: rose. Nose: red berry notes, medium intensity, floral. Palate: good finish, easy to drink.

VIÑA DEL MAR 2009 T
80% tempranillo, 20% cariñena.

80 Colour: cherry, purple rim. Nose: ripe fruit, spicy, dried herbs. Palate: easy to drink, ripe fruit.

LA XARMADA

Hisenda Casa Llivi, s/n
08796 Pacs del Penedès (Barcelona)
☎: +34 938 171 237 - Fax: +34 938 171 546
laxarmada@laxarmada.com
www.laxarmada.com

LA XARMADA BLANC DE BLANCS 2010 B
chardonnay, chenin blanc.

84 Colour: bright straw. Nose: ripe fruit, dried flowers, slightly evolved. Palate: light-bodied, fresh, flavourful.

LA XARMADA 2010 RD
70% merlot, 30% cabernet sauvignon.

72

LA XARMADA 2009 T
60% merlot, 40% syrah.

81 Colour: deep cherry, purple rim. Nose: fruit preserve, overripe fruit. Palate: correct.

PETIT CLOS CABANA 2008 T
100% merlot.

85 Colour: dark-red cherry, garnet rim. Nose: candied fruit, warm, spicy. Palate: ripe fruit, sweetness, good finish.

LONG WINES

Avda. Monte, 46
28723 Algete (Madrid)
☎: +34 916 221 305 - Fax: +34 916 220 029
raquel@longwines.com
www.longwines.com

ALTOS D'OLIVA 2010 B
100% garnacha blanca.

86 Colour: bright straw. Nose: fresh, medium intensity, wild herbs, dried flowers. Palate: flavourful, good acidity, fine bitter notes.

ALTOS D'OLIVA 2004 TGR
40% cabernet sauvignon, 30% tempranillo, 30% garnacha.

85 Colour: bright cherry, brick rim edge. Nose: macerated fruit, spicy. Palate: flavourful, fruity, spicy, great length.

MASET DEL LLEÓ

C-244, Km. 32,5
08792 La Granada del Penedès (Barcelona)
☎: +34 902 200 250 - Fax: +34 938 921 333
info@maset.com
www.maset.com

VIÑA SELENA 2010 B
parellada, macabeo, xarel.lo.

84 Colour: bright straw. Nose: medium intensity, ripe fruit. Palate: fruity, balanced, correct.

VIÑA SELENA RD
cariñena, tempranillo.

82 Colour: rose, purple rim. Nose: red berry notes, ripe fruit, floral. Palate: fruity, good finish.

MASET DEL LLEÓ SYRAH 2006 TR
syrah.

92 Colour: very deep cherry, garnet rim. Nose: complex, elegant, ripe fruit, cocoa bean, sweet spices. Palate: good structure, complex, flavourful, round tannins.

MASET DEL LLEÓ GRAN ROBLE 2005 TR
tempranillo.

87 Colour: deep cherry, garnet rim. Nose: ripe fruit, spicy, creamy oak. Palate: fruity, balanced, good acidity.

PORTAL DEL MONTSANT

Mas Parxet, Torren, 38
08391 Tiana (Barcelona)
☎: +34 933 950 811 - Fax: +34 933 955 500
info@parxet.com
www.parxet.es

SANTES 2009 B
100% macabeo.

88 Colour: bright straw. Nose: expressive, ripe fruit, complex, floral, balanced. Palate: fruity, flavourful, good acidity, ripe fruit.

SANTES 2009 RD
50% merlot, 50% cabernet sauvignon.

90 Colour: rose, purple rim. Nose: expressive, complex, red berry notes, citrus fruit, floral, fragrant herbs. Palate: fleshy, flavourful, long, spicy.

SANTES 2009 T
100% tempranillo.

88 Colour: black cherry, purple rim. Nose: ripe fruit, spicy. Palate: balanced, fruity, flavourful, great length, round tannins.

ROCAMAR

Major, 80
08755 Castellbisbal (Barcelona)
☎: +34 937 720 900 - Fax: +34 937 721 495
info@rocamar.net
www.rocamar.net

BLANC DE PALANGRE S/C B
macabeo, parellada.

79

MASIA RIBOT 2010 B
macabeo, parellada.

82 Colour: bright straw. Nose: medium intensity, dried herbs, ripe fruit. Palate: easy to drink, fruity.

ROSAT DE PALANGRE S/C RD
trepat.

78

MASIA RIBOT 2009 T
50% tempranillo, 50% garnacha.

77

VEGA AIXALÀ WINUM

De la Font, 11
43439 Vilanova de Prades (Tarragona)
☎: +34 609 336 825 - Fax: +34 977 869 019
info@vegaaixala.com
www.winum.cat

PONT DE PEDRA S/C B
garnacha blanca, macabeo.

86 Colour: bright straw. Nose: fresh fruit, citrus fruit, dried herbs. Palate: fruity, good acidity, easy to drink.

PONT DE PEDRA S/C RD
trepat.

85 Colour: light cherry, bright. Nose: red berry notes, ripe fruit, faded flowers, medium intensity. Palate: light-bodied, fruity, easy to drink.

PONT DE PEDRA S/C T
garnacha, samsó, syrah.

86 Colour: cherry, purple rim. Nose: red berry notes, violets, lactic notes, fruit expression. Palate: fruity, easy to drink, correct.

DHUODA 2008 T
garnacha, samsó.

86 Colour: cherry, garnet rim. Nose: ripe fruit, warm, spicy. Palate: flavourful, ripe fruit, spicy.

VINS DEL MASSIS

Ctra. de Gava - Avimyonet, Km. 18,7
08795 Olesa de Bonesvails (Barcelona)
☎: 606 784 036
benjamin@bodegacontador.com

MACIZO 2010 B
xarel.lo, garnacha blanca.

91 Colour: bright straw. Nose: dried flowers, ripe fruit, fragrant herbs, mineral, sweet spices. Palate: round, unctuous, powerful, flavourful.

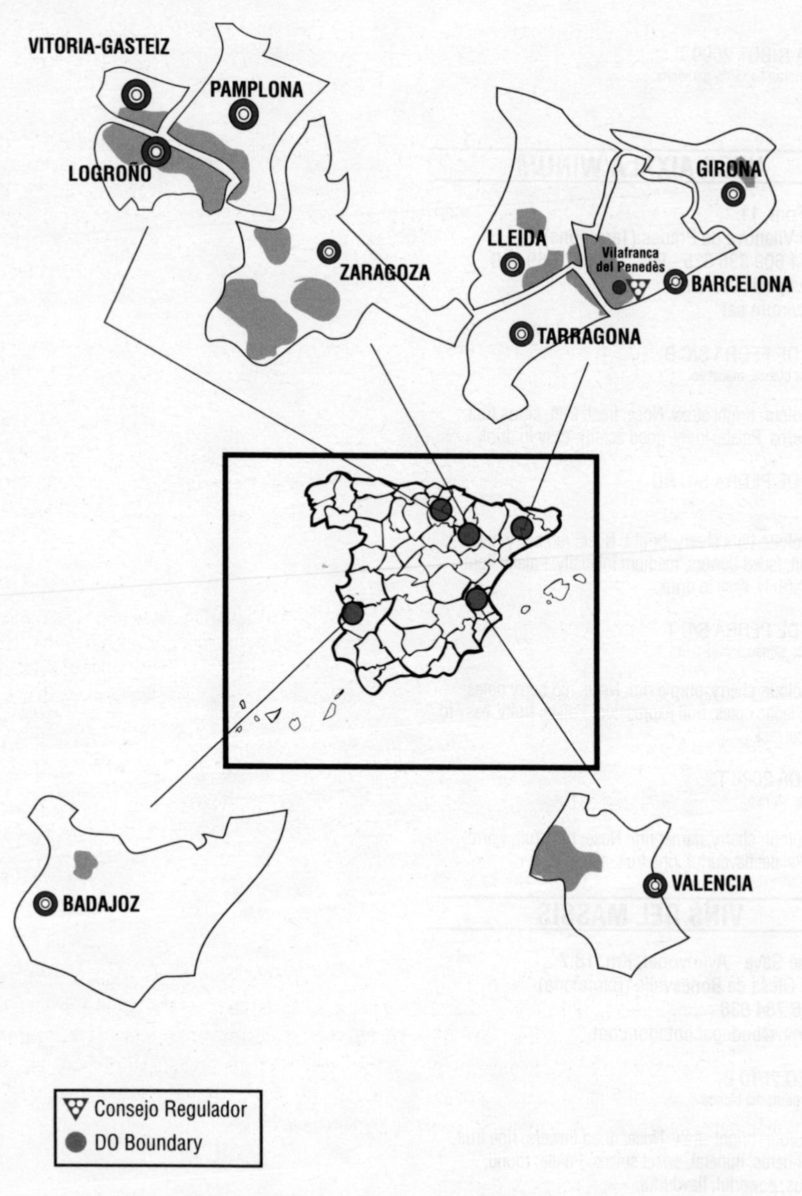
VITORIA-GASTEIZ
PAMPLONA
LOGROÑO
ZARAGOZA
LLEIDA
Vilafranca del Penedès
BARCELONA
GIRONA
TARRAGONA
BADAJOZ
VALENCIA
Consejo Regulador
DO Boundary

NEWS ABOUT THE VINTAGE:

This year we have beaten every record as to the number of samples tasted. We are talking about 695 references for just 600 in last year's edition, and an increase of 3% on those wines scoring 90 points or above, a sign that producers are coming up with finer and more balanced products.

In the last seven years most of the Cava producers have abandoned the traditional method of "tricking" the bottling liquor (French "liqueur de tiràge" and Spanish "licor de tiraje") with old wines and some other secret additions in order to achieve a "crianza express" effect, a sort of practice that Champagne left behind some 35 years ago and that in Catalunya has been maintained until recently. Nowadays, producers tend to rather rely on the reductive effect of the lees and the addition of just base wine as dosage, which helps to obtain Cava wines with a lighter, more elegant colour, less body, a fine herbal character and smaller and more integrated bubbles.

As for the typology, we have witnessed a slight change in the last couple of years: "brut nature" is no longer considered the "prima donna", and "brut" has come to steal the limelight, probably as a result of both the strong bitter notes and acidity of the former type and its higher price. While some producers still advocate for "brut nature" waving the flag of pure, unadulterated winemaking, some other experienced cavistas, who have usually reaped high scores for their wines, just "retouch" them with a bit of sugar when they disgorge them to minimize the sensation of any herbaceous or acidic notes that may arise from the use of underripe grapes. As we have already mentioned, we finally get wines which are paler in colour and lighter in body, as well as much more elegant and creamier (thanks to the positive reductive effect of the lees) and showing overall a fine herbal aftertaste.

It is also noticeable in Cava the way the whole of the DO is somewhat split in two different sides, those producers who believe they will manage to get some results from the use of *pinot noir* and *chardonnay* in their blends, and those who try to defend the singularity of their wines through the exclusive use of the local varieties. Logically, there are great houses in each side but we think we should single out those that are going places giving another turn of the screw to the local triad, macabeo, xarel.lo and parellada, an interesting bet that also seems in tune with the international market, avid for singular products able to express the essence of a particular territory without losing the elegance and finesse typical of sparkling wines made by the "méthode champenoise" of a second fermentation in the bottle. Two giants dominate Cava rankings: Gramona, with its Celler Batlle 2000 Brut Gran Reserva; and Raventós i Blanc with its Gran Reserva Personal 1999 Brut Nature, wines that got 97 and 96 points respectively.

LOCATION:

The defined Cava region covers the sparkling wines produced according to the traditional method of a second fermentation in the bottle of 63 municipalities in the province of Barcelona, 52 in Tarragona, 12 in Lleida and 5 in Girona, as well as those of the municipal areas of Laguardia, Moreda de Álava and Oyón in Álava, Almendralejo in Badajoz, Mendavia and Viana in Navarra, Requena in Valencia, Ainzón and Cariñena in Zaragoza, and a further 18 municipalities of La Rioja.

CLIMATE:

That of each producing region stated in the previous epigraph. Nevertheless, the region in which the largest part of the production is concentrated (Penedès) has a Mediterranean climate, with some production areas being cooler and situated at a higher altitude.

SOIL:

This also depends on each producing region.

GRAPE VARIETIES:

WHITE: *Macabeo* (*Viura*), *Xarel.lo, Parellada, Subirat* (*Malvasía Riojana*) and *Chardonnay*.
RED: *Garnacha Tinta, Monastrell, Trepat* and *Pinot Noir*.

FIGURES:

Vineyard surface: 30,654 – **Wine-Growers:** 6,686 – **Wineries:** 256 – **2010 Harvest rating:** Good – **Production:** 194,000,000 litres – **Market percentages:** 39,1% domestic. 60,9% export

CONSEJO REGULADOR
Avinguda Tarragona, 24
08720 Vilafranca del Penedès (Barcelona)
☎: +34 938 903 104 - Fax: +34 938 901 567
@ consejo@crcava.es
www.crcava.es

GENERAL CHARACTERISTICS OF THE WINES

YOUNG CAVAS	Their youth is due to a shorter ageing period in the bottle (the minimum stipulated by the Consejo is nine months). They are somewhat lighter, fresher and easier to drink; they have notes of fruit and vegetables..
WITH LONGER AGEING PERIODS	(For the Gran Reserva, the wines have to be aged for a minimum of 30 months in the bottle). They have more complex notes due to the longer time that the yeasts remain in the bottles. There is a distinction between the more traditional styles, normally with noses of dried fruit and bitter almonds, sometimes also due to the inclusion of old wine in the expedition liqueur, although this custom is gradually dying out. The more modern styles combine slightly fruity and floral notes, even herbs, with hints of toast and nuts; they are also characterised by their refinement and elegance, typical of champagne.
CHARDONNAY BASED	These are characterised by their greater body on the palate and a light oily mouthfeel; on the nose they may sometimes develop noses of tropical fruit.

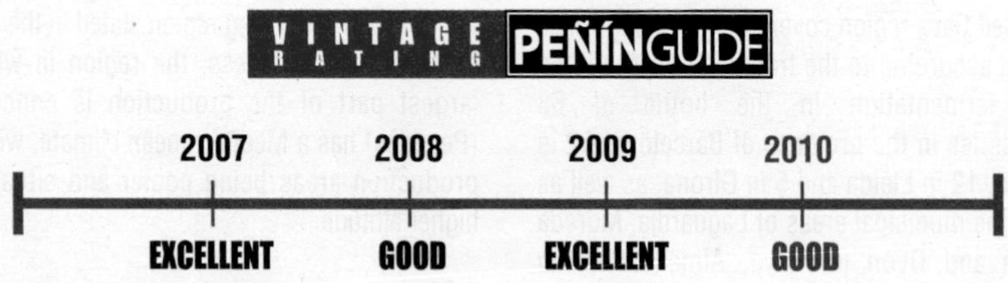

AGRÍCOLA DE BARBERÀ

Comercio, 40
43422 Barberà de la Conca (Tarragona)
☎: +34 977 887 035 - Fax: +34 977 887 035
cobarbera@doconcadebarbera.com

CASTELL DE LA COMANDA 2008 BR RESERVA
50% macabeo, 50% parellada.

85 Colour: bright straw. Nose: medium intensity, fresh fruit, dried herbs, fine lees, dried flowers. Palate: fresh, fruity, flavourful, correct.

CASTELL DE LA COMANDA 2008 BN RESERVA
50% macabeo, 50% parellada.

87 Colour: bright straw. Nose: medium intensity, fresh fruit, floral. Palate: fresh, fruity, flavourful.

AGUSTÍ TORELLÓ MATA

La Serra, s/n
08770 Sant Sadurní D'Anoia (Barcelona)
☎: +34 938 911 173 - Fax: +34 938 912 616
info@agustitorellomata.com
www.agustitorellomata.com

AGUSTÍ TORELLÓ MATA ROSAT 2009 RD RESERVA
100% trepat.

88 Colour: rose. Nose: ripe fruit, red berry notes. Palate: flavourful, fruity, fresh.

AGUSTÍ TORELLÓ MATA 2008 BR RESERVA
39% macabeo, 25% xarel.lo, 36% parellada.

88 Colour: bright straw. Nose: fresh fruit, dried herbs, fine lees, floral. Palate: fresh, fruity, flavourful, good acidity.

BAYANUS ROSAT 375 2009 BN RESERVA
100% trepat.

87 Colour: coppery red. Nose: fresh, red berry notes, ripe fruit, rose petals. Palate: flavourful, fruity, fresh.

BAYANUS 375ML 2008 BN RESERVA
40% macabeo, 30% xarel.lo, 30% parellada.

90 Colour: bright straw. Nose: dried herbs, fine lees, floral, ripe fruit. Palate: fresh, fruity, flavourful, good acidity.

AGUSTÍ TORELLÓ MATA GRAN RESERVA BARRICA 2007 BN
100% macabeo.

92 Colour: bright golden. Nose: dry nuts, fragrant herbs. Palate: powerful, flavourful, good acidity, fine bead, fine bitter notes.

AGUSTÍ TORELLÓ MATA 2007 BN GRAN RESERVA
39% macabeo, 30% xarel.lo, 31% parellada.

90 Colour: bright golden. Nose: dry nuts, fragrant herbs. Palate: powerful, flavourful, good acidity, fine bead, fine bitter notes.

KRIPTA 2006 BN GRAN RESERVA
45% macabeo, 20% xarel.lo, 35% parellada.

91 Colour: bright straw. Nose: powerfull, ripe fruit, grassy, spicy. Palate: good acidity, fine bead, long.

AGUSTÍ TORELLÓ MATA MAGNUM 2005 BN GRAN RESERVA
45% macabeo, 25% xarel.lo, 30% parellada.

90 Colour: bright golden. Nose: dry nuts, fragrant herbs, complex. Palate: powerful, flavourful, good acidity, fine bead, fine bitter notes.

ALBET I NOYA

Can Vendrell de la Codina, s/n
08739 Sant Pau D'Ordal (Barcelona)
☎: +34 938 994 812 - Fax: +34 938 994 930
albetinoya@albetinoya.cat
www.albetinoya.cat

ALBET I NOYA BRUT 21 BARRICA 2006 BR
pinot noir.

91 Colour: bright straw. Nose: expressive, powerfull, creamy oak, sweet spices, cocoa bean, ripe fruit, fragrant herbs. Palate: flavourful, fruity, fleshy, sweetness, long.

ALBET I NOYA DOLÇ DE POSTRES RESERVA
chardonnay, macabeo, parellada, xarel.lo.

87 Colour: bright straw. Nose: powerfull, candied fruit, citrus fruit, dried herbs, floral. Palate: round, sweet, flavourful.

ALBET I NOYA BRUT 21 BR
57% chardonnay, 43% parellada.

90 Colour: bright straw. Nose: fresh fruit, fine lees, floral, fragrant herbs. Palate: fresh, fruity, flavourful, good acidity, fine bead.

ALBET I NOYA BRUT ROSAT PINOT NOIR BR
pinot noir.

88 Colour: rose. Nose: red berry notes, powerfull, complex. Palate: flavourful, powerful, fleshy.

ALBET I NOYA BR
chardonnay, macabeo, parellada, xarel.lo.

88 Colour: bright straw. Nose: fresh fruit, dried herbs, fine lees, floral. Palate: fresh, fruity, good acidity.

PETIT ALBET BR
xarel.lo, macabeo, parellada.

88 Colour: bright straw. Nose: fresh fruit, dried herbs, fine lees, floral. Palate: fresh, fruity, flavourful, good acidity.

ALBET I NOYA 2007 BN GRAN RESERVA
chardonnay, macabeo, parellada, xarel.lo.

92 Color bright golden. Aroma fine lees, dry nuts, fragrant herbs, complex. Taste powerful, flavourful, good acidity, fine bead, fine bitter notes.

ALSINA & SARDÁ

Barrio Les Tarumbas, s/n
08733 Pla del Penedès (Barcelona)
☎: +34 938 988 132 - Fax: +34 938 988 671
alsina@alsinasarda.com
www.alsinasarda.com

ALSINA & SARDÁ 2005 BR GRAN RESERVA
50% xarel.lo, 25% parellada, 25% macabeo.

85 Colour: bright golden. Nose: lees reduction notes, dry nuts, expressive. Palate: correct, fine bitter notes, good acidity.

ALSINA & SARDÁ BR RESERVA
34% parellada, 33% xarel.lo, 33% macabeo.

87 Colour: bright straw. Nose: expressive, fresh, fine lees, fruit expression. Palate: light-bodied, fresh, flavourful.

ALSINA & SARDÁ 2008 BN RESERVA
34% parellada, 33% xarel.lo, 33% macabeo.

87 Colour: bright straw. Nose: dried flowers, fine lees, complex. Palate: long, spicy, fine bitter notes, correct.

ALSINA & SARDÁ GRAN RESERVA ESPECIAL 2007 BN
50% chardonnay, 50% xarel.lo.

87 Colour: bright golden. Nose: dry nuts, fruit expression, neat, complex. Palate: balanced, fine bead, fine bitter notes.

ALSINA & SARDÁ SELLO 2007 BN GRAN RESERVA
50% xarel.lo, 25% macabeo, 25% parellada.

85 Colour: bright golden. Nose: ripe fruit, faded flowers, short. Palate: slightly evolved, fleshy, long.

ALSINA & SARDÁ MAS D'ALSINA BN RESERVA
65% chardonnay, 35% xarel.lo, macabeo, parellada.

90 Colour: bright straw. Nose: dry nuts, floral, expressive, complex. Palate: good acidity, unctuous, powerful, flavourful.

PINOT NOIR ROSAT DE ALSINA & SARDA BN
100% pinot noir.

87 Colour: raspberry rose. Nose: floral, red berry notes, fresh, expressive. Palate: good acidity, balanced, correct.

ALTA ALELLA

Can Genis, s/n
08391 Tiana (Barcelona)
☎: +34 934 693 720 - Fax: +34 934 691 343
altaalella@altaalella.cat
www.altaalella.cat

PRIVAT NU 2008 BN
100% xarel.lo.

85 Colour: bright straw. Nose: wild herbs, ripe fruit, medium intensity. Palate: flavourful.

ALTA ALELLA MIRGIN BLANC 2007 BN GRAN RESERVA
chardonnay, pinot noir.

90 Colour: bright yellow. Nose: ripe fruit, expressive, complex, fine lees, spicy. Palate: flavourful, great length, good acidity.

ALTA ALELLA MATARÓ ROSÉ 2007 BN RESERVA
100% monastrell.

87 Colour: salmon. Nose: candied fruit, ripe fruit, powerfull, fine lees. Palate: fruity, flavourful, long.

ALTA ALELLA MIRGIN ROSÉ 2007 BN GRAN RESERVA
100% pinot noir.

87 Colour: coppery red. Nose: rose petals, candied fruit, fine lees. Palate: fruity, good acidity, great length.

PRIVAT OPUS EVOLUTIUM BN GRAN RESERVA
chardonnay, pinot noir.

91 Colour: bright straw. Nose: medium intensity, dried herbs, fine lees, complex, balanced. Palate: fresh, fruity, flavourful, good acidity.

PRIVAT LAIETÀ BN RESERVA
chardonnay, pinot noir.

89 Colour: bright yellow. Nose: ripe fruit, fragrant herbs, fine lees, balanced. Palate: flavourful, fruity, great length.

PRIVAT EVOLUCIÓ CHARDONNAY BN RESERVA
100% chardonnay.

88 Colour: bright straw. Nose: balanced, varietal, grassy. Palate: fruity, good acidity, fresh.

PRIVAT LAIETÀ ILURO ROSÉ BN RESERVA
100% monastrell.

86 Colour: rose. Nose: rose petals, red berry notes, balanced. Palate: fruity, great length.

AVINYÓ CAVAS

Masia Can Fontanals
08793 Avinyonet del Penedès (Barcelona)
☎: +34 938 970 055 - Fax: +34 938 970 691
avinyo@avinyo.com
www.avinyo.com

AVINYÓ ROSÉ SUBLIM RD RESERVA
100% pinot noir.

85 Colour: rose. Nose: red berry notes, fruit expression. Palate: flavourful, fruity, sweetness.

AVINYÓ BR RESERVA
60% macabeo, 25% xarel.lo, 15% parellada.

88 Colour: bright straw. Nose: fine lees, floral, citrus fruit, fresh. Palate: balanced, fresh, light-bodied, easy to drink.

AVINYÓ SELECCIÓ LA TICOTA 2006 BN GRAN RESERVA
65% xarel.lo, 35% macabeo.

90 Colour: bright straw. Nose: dried herbs, fine lees, floral, neat, ripe fruit. Palate: fresh, fruity, flavourful, good acidity.

AVINYÓ BN RESERVA
55% macabeo, 35% xarel.lo, 10% parellada.

87 Colour: bright straw. Nose: dried herbs, fine lees, floral, ripe fruit. Palate: fresh, fruity, flavourful, good acidity.

BLANCHER-CAPDEVILA PUJOL

Plaça Pont Romà, Edificio Blancher
08770 Sant Sadurní D'Anoia (Barcelona)
☎: +34 938 183 286 - Fax: +34 938 911 961
blancher@blancher.es
www.blancher.es

BLANCHER 2007 BR RESERVA ESPECIAL
xarel.lo, macabeo, parellada.

85 Colour: bright straw. Nose: medium intensity, fine lees, floral, fruit expression. Palate: fresh, flavourful, good acidity.

OBRAC 2006 BR GRAN RESERVA
35% xarel.lo, 40% macabeo, 25% parellada.

88 Colour: bright straw. Nose: fine lees, fragrant herbs, expressive, neat. Palate: good acidity, balanced, fine bitter notes.

MAGNUM CAPDEVILA PUJOL 2008 BN RESERVA
xarel.lo, macabeo, parellada.

88 Colour: bright straw. Nose: fresh fruit, white flowers, neat. Palate: good acidity, fine bead, correct, flavourful.

CAPDEVILA PUJOL 2008 BN RESERVA
35% xarel.lo, 35% macabeo, 30% parellada.

87 Colour: bright straw. Nose: dried herbs, fine lees, floral. Palate: fresh, fruity, flavourful, good acidity, balanced.

TERESA BLANCHER DE LA TIETA 2006 BN GRAN RESERVA
35% xarel.lo, 35% macabeo, 30% parellada.

89 Colour: bright straw. Nose: fruit expression, fine lees, expressive, fresh. Palate: fleshy, fruity, light-bodied, flavourful.

BLANCHER 2006 BN GRAN RESERVA
xarel.lo, macabeo, parellada.

81 Color bright golden. Aroma fine lees, dry nuts, fragrant herbs, complex. Taste powerful, flavourful, good acidity, fine bead, fine bitter notes.

BODEGA SEBIRAN

Pérez Galdos, 1
46352 Campo Arcis - Requena (Valencia)
☎: +34 962 301 326 - Fax: +34 962 303 966
info@bodegasebiran.com
www.bodegasebiran.com

COTO D'ARCIS ESPECIAL BR
100% macabeo.

88 Color bright straw. Aroma medium intensity, fresh fruit, dried herbs, fine lees, floral. Taste fresh, fruity, flavourful, good acidity.

COTO D'ARCIS BR
100% macabeo.

85 Colour: bright yellow. Nose: medium intensity, dry nuts, fine lees. Palate: flavourful, fruity, good acidity.

COTO D'ARCIS BN
100% macabeo.

84 Colour: bright yellow. Nose: medium intensity, dried herbs. Palate: correct, fresh, fine bitter notes, good acidity.

BODEGAS BORDEJÉ

Ctra. Borja a Rueda, Km. 3
50570 Ainzón (Zaragoza)
☎: +34 976 868 080 - Fax: +34 976 868 989
ainzon@bodegasbordeje.com
www.bodegasbordeje.com

CAVA BORDEJÉ MACABEO 2008 B
100% macabeo.

80 Colour: bright straw. Nose: white flowers, fresh. Palate: flavourful, fruity, fresh.

CAVA BORDEJÉ ROSADO DE GARNACHA 2008 BN
100% garnacha.

84 Colour: rose. Nose: expressive, varietal, red berry notes, ripe fruit. Palate: flavourful, sweetness, long.

CAVA BORDEJÉ CHARDONNAY 2008 BN
100% chardonnay.

83 Colour: bright straw. Nose: ripe fruit, citrus fruit, white flowers. Palate: flavourful, fruity, fresh.

BODEGAS CA N'ESTELLA

Masia Ca N'Estella, s/n
08635 Sant Esteve Sesrovires (Barcelona)
☎: +34 934 161 387 - Fax: +34 934 161 620
canestella@fincacanestella.com
www.fincacanestella.com

RABETLLAT I VIDAL BRUT CA N'ESTELLA 2008 BR
70% macabeo, 30% xarel.lo.

88 Colour: bright straw. Nose: medium intensity, fresh fruit, dried herbs, fine lees, floral. Palate: fresh, flavourful, good acidity.

RABETLLAT I VIDAL 2008 BN
80% chardonnay, 20% macabeo.

87 Colour: bright straw. Nose: medium intensity, dried herbs, floral. Palate: fresh, fruity, flavourful, good acidity.

RABETLLAT I VIDAL CHARDONNAY RESERVA DE LA FINCA 2006 BN
chardonnay.

86 Colour: bright yellow. Nose: powerfull, varietal, ripe fruit, spicy, fine lees. Palate: fruity, flavourful, great length.

RABETLLAT I VIDAL 2008 BRUT ROSADO
trepat.

85 Colour: light cherry. Nose: red berry notes, ripe fruit, dried flowers. Palate: fruity, easy to drink, good finish.

BODEGAS CAPITÀ VIDAL

Ctra. Villafranca-Igualada, Km. 30
08733 Pla del Penedès (Barcelona)
☎: +34 938 988 630 - Fax: +34 938 988 625
capitavidal@capitavidal.com
www.capitavidal.com

FUCHS DE VIDAL CUVÉE BN RESERVA
40% xarel.lo, 35% macabeo, 25% parellada.

90 Colour: bright straw. Nose: dried herbs, fine lees, floral, powerfull, expressive, fresh fruit. Palate: fresh, fruity, flavourful, good acidity.

FUCHS DE VIDAL UNIC BN
50% chardonnay, 35% pinot noir, 15% macabeo, xarel.lo, parellada.

85 Colour: bright straw. Nose: fresh fruit, dried herbs, fine lees, floral. Palate: fresh, fruity, flavourful, good acidity.

PALAU SOLÁ BN
40% xarel.lo, 35% macabeo, 25% parellada.

84 Colour: bright straw. Nose: ripe fruit, citrus fruit, white flowers. Palate: flavourful, fine bitter notes.

FUCHS DE VIDAL ROSÉ PINOT NOIR BN
100% pinot noir.

84 Colour: rose, purple rim. Nose: fresh fruit, red berry notes. Palate: flavourful, fruity, fresh.

BODEGAS FAUSTINO

Ctra. de Logroño, s/n
01320 Oyón (Álava)
☎: +34 945 622 500 - Fax: +34 945 622 511
info@bodegasfaustino.es
www.bodegasfaustino.es

CAVA FAUSTINO BR
viura, chardonnay.

84 Colour: bright straw. Nose: citrus fruit, fine lees, fresh, medium intensity. Palate: fresh, light-bodied, flavourful.

CAVA FAUSTINO ROSADO BR RESERVA
garnacha.

84 Colour: raspberry rose. Nose: floral, red berry notes, raspberry, fresh. Palate: fine bitter notes, good acidity, balanced.

BODEGAS HISPANO SUIZAS

Ctra. N-322, Km. 451,7
46357 El Pontón (Valencia)
☎: +34 962 138 318 - Fax: +34 962 138 318
info@bodegashispanosuizas.com
www.bodegashispanosuizas.com

TANTUM ERGO PINOT NOIR ROSÉ 2009 BN
100% pinot noir.

92 Colour: salmon. Nose: red berry notes, fruit preserve, fine lees, lactic notes, ripe fruit. Palate: flavourful, sweetness, fruity, good acidity.

TANTUM ERGO CHARDONNAY PINOT NOIR 2008 BN
chardonnay, pinot noir.

93 Colour: bright straw. Nose: powerfull, ripe fruit, fruit expression, citrus fruit, fragrant herbs. Palate: balanced, long, flavourful, fruity.

BODEGAS LA ESPERANZA

Brisol, 16 bis
28230 Las Rozas (Madrid)
☎: +34 917 104 880 - Fax: +34 917 104 881
anap@swd.es
www.swd.es

NOCHE Y DÍA (GREEN LABEL) BR
40% macabeo, 40% xarel.lo, 20% parellada.

87 Colour: bright straw. Nose: fresh fruit, dried herbs, fine lees, floral. Palate: fresh, fruity, flavourful, good acidity.

NOCHE Y DÍA ROSÉ (PINK LABEL) BR
100% trepat.

87 Colour: onion pink. Nose: powerfull, ripe fruit, red berry notes, floral, expressive. Palate: powerful, fruity, fresh.

NOCHE Y DÍA (YELLOW LABEL) BN
40% macabeo, 40% xarel.lo, 20% parellada.

85 Colour: bright straw. Nose: medium intensity, dried herbs, fine lees, citrus fruit. Palate: fresh, good acidity, fine bitter notes, light-bodied.

NOCHE Y DÍA (BLUE LABEL) SS
40% macabeo, 40% xarel.lo, 20% parellada.

87 Colour: bright straw. Nose: medium intensity, fresh fruit, dried herbs, floral. Palate: fresh, fruity, good acidity, sweetness.

BODEGAS LANGA

Ctra. Nacional II, Km. 241,700
50300 Calatayud (Zaragoza)
☎: +34 976 881 818 - Fax: +34 976 884 463
info@bodegas-langa.com
www.bodegas-langa.com

REYES DE ARAGÓN BR RESERVA
macabeo, chardonnay.

85 Colour: bright straw. Nose: fresh fruit, floral, fine lees. Palate: fruity, fresh, fine bitter notes, good acidity.

REYES DE ARAGÓN BN RESERVA
chardonnay, macabeo.

86 Colour: bright straw. Nose: dry nuts, faded flowers, scrubland, fine lees. Palate: flavourful, good acidity, fine bitter notes.

REYES DE ARAGÓN BN GRAN RESERVA
chardonnay, macabeo.

84 Colour: bright yellow. Nose: fragrant herbs, complex, medium intensity. Palate: powerful, flavourful, fine bitter notes.

REYES DE ARAGÓN SELECCIÓN FAMILIAR BN
chardonnay, macabeo.

82 Colour: bright straw. Nose: medium intensity, fresh. Palate: correct, fine bitter notes, good acidity.

BODEGAS LAR DE BARROS INVIOSA

Apdo. Correos 291
06200 Almendralejo (Badajoz)
☎: +34 924 671 235 - Fax: +34 924 687 231
sophia@lardebarros.com
www.lardebarros.com

MARQUÉS DE LARES BR
100% macabeo.

82 Colour: bright straw. Nose: medium intensity, dried herbs, lees reduction notes, fruit liqueur notes. Palate: fresh, fruity, sweetness, fine bitter notes.

BONAVAL BR
100% macabeo.

82 Colour: bright straw. Nose: medium intensity, dried herbs, floral, candied fruit. Palate: fresh, fruity, flavourful, good acidity.

LAR DE PLATA BR
100% macabeo.

80 Colour: bright golden. Nose: fruit liqueur notes, fragrant herbs, powerfull. Palate: easy to drink, sweetness, flavourful.

BONAVAL 37,5 CL. BR
macabeo.

78

EXTREM DE BONAVAL BN RESERVA
100% macabeo.

85 Colour: bright golden. Nose: fruit liqueur notes, fresh, neat. Palate: light-bodied, flavourful, easy to drink.

BONAVAL BN
100% macabeo.

85 Color bright straw. Aroma medium intensity, fresh fruit, dried herbs, fine lees, floral. Taste fresh, fruity, flavourful, good acidity.

BONAVAL MAGNUM BN
100% macabeo.

85 Colour: bright straw. Nose: dried herbs, fine lees, floral, fresh fruit. Palate: fresh, fruity, flavourful, good acidity.

BONAVAL ROSADO BN RESERVA
100% garnacha.

82 Colour: coppery red. Nose: powerfull, fruit liqueur notes, reduction notes. Palate: powerful, fine bitter notes.

BONAVAL NUEVO MILENIO 37,5 CL. BN
100% macabeo.

82 Colour: bright straw. Nose: candied fruit, fruit liqueur notes, faded flowers. Palate: sweetness, fine bitter notes.

LAR DE PLATA BN
100% macabeo.

72

BONAVAL SC
100% macabeo.

84 Colour: bright straw. Nose: medium intensity, dried herbs, fine lees, ripe fruit. Palate: fruity, good acidity, sweetness.

LAR DE PLATA SS
100% macabeo.

78

BODEGAS LUIS ALEGRE

Ctra. Navaridas, s/n
01300 Laguardia (Álava)
☎: +34 945 600 089 - Fax: +34 945 600 729
luisalegre@bodegasluisalegre.com
www.luisalegre.com

FINCALEGRE BR
40% macabeo, 40% xarel.lo, 20% chardonnay.

87 Colour: bright straw. Nose: citrus fruit, floral, fresh fruit. Palate: flavourful, fruity, fresh.

FINCALEGRE BN
40% macabeo, 40% xarel.lo, 20% chardonnay.

88 Color bright straw. Aroma medium intensity, fresh fruit, dried herbs, fine lees, floral. Taste fresh, fruity, flavourful, good acidity.

BODEGAS MUGA

Barrio de la Estación, s/n
26200 Haro (La Rioja)
☎: +34 941 310 498 - Fax: +34 941 312 867
info@bodegasmuga.com
www.bodegasmuga.com

MUGA CONDE DE HARO BR

88 Color bright straw. Aroma medium intensity, fresh fruit, dried herbs, fine lees, floral. Taste fresh, fruity, flavourful, good acidity.

BODEGAS MUR BARCELONA

Rambla de la Generalitat, 1-9
08770 Sant Sąduri D'Anoia (Barcelona)
☎: +34 938 183 641 - Fax: +34 938 914 366
info@mur-barcelona.com
www.mur-barcelona.com

MOST DORÉ 2009 BN
35% xarel.lo, 35% parellada, 30% macabeo.

86 Colour: bright straw. Nose: fine lees, white flowers, tropical fruit, expressive. Palate: fine bead, fruity, flavourful, easy to drink.

GRAN MONTESQUIUS 2009 BN RESERVA
35% xarel.lo, 35% parellada, 30% macabeo.

85 Colour: bright straw. Nose: fine lees, citrus fruit, medium intensity. Palate: fresh, light-bodied, easy to drink.

ROBERT J. MUR ESPECIAL TRADICIÓ 2008 BN RESERVA
60% xarel.lo, 20% macabeo, 20% parellada.

85 Colour: bright yellow. Nose: fine lees, citrus fruit, dry nuts. Palate: powerful, flavourful, fruity, rich, fine bead, good acidity.

GRAN MONTESQUIUS MAGNUM 2002 BN RESERVA
30% macabeo, 35% xarel.lo, 35% parellada.

87 Colour: bright golden. Nose: lees reduction notes, ripe fruit, dry nuts, pattiserie, toasty. Palate: fresh, powerful, flavourful, toasty.

BODEGAS MURVIEDRO

Ampliación Pol. El Romeral, s/n
46340 Requena (Valencia)
☎: +34 962 329 003 - Fax: +34 962 329 002
murviedro@murviedro.es
www.murviedro.es

LUNA DE MURVIEDRO RD
100% garnacha.

83 Colour: raspberry rose. Nose: powerfull, candied fruit, red berry notes. Palate: powerful, fine bitter notes, ripe fruit.

LUNA DE MURVIEDRO BR
100% macabeo.

87 Colour: bright straw. Nose: fresh fruit, dried herbs, fine lees, floral. Palate: fresh, fruity, flavourful, good acidity.

EXPRESIÓN SOLIDARITY CUVÉE BN
100% chardonnay.

88 Colour: bright straw. Nose: fresh fruit, dried herbs, fine lees, faded flowers. Palate: fresh, flavourful, good acidity.

BODEGAS OLARRA

Avda. de Mendavia, 30
26009 Logroño (La Rioja)
☎: +34 941 235 299 - Fax: +34 941 253 703
bodegasolarra@bodegasolarra.es
www.bodegasolarra.es

AÑARES BR
viura.

85 Colour: bright straw. Nose: medium intensity, fresh fruit, fine lees. Palate: fresh, fruity, good acidity, light-bodied, powerful.

AÑARES BN
100% viura.

85 Colour: bright straw. Nose: jasmine, fine lees, fruit expression. Palate: fresh, light-bodied, flavourful.

BODEGAS ONDARRE

Ctra. de Aras, s/n
31230 Viana (Navarra)
☎: +34 948 645 300 - Fax: +34 948 646 002
bodegasondarre@bodegasondarre.es
www.bodegasondarre.es

ONDARRE MILLENNIUM BR
100% viura.

87 Colour: bright straw. Nose: fine lees, floral, candied fruit. Palate: fresh, fruity, good acidity.

ONDARRE BN RESERVA
100% viura.

84 Colour: bright straw. Nose: medium intensity, fresh fruit, fine lees, citrus fruit. Palate: fresh, good acidity, light-bodied.

BODEGAS PATROCINIO

Ctra. Cenicero
26313 Uruñuela (La Rioja)
☎: +34 941 371 319 - Fax: +34 941 371 435
info@bodegaspatrocinio.com

GRAN ZINIO BR

83 Colour: bright straw. Nose: candied fruit, citrus fruit. Palate: flavourful, fine bitter notes.

BODEGAS ROMALE

Pol. Ind. Parc. 6, Manz. D
06200 Almendralejo (Badajoz)
☎: +34 924 667 255 - Fax: +34 924 665 877
romale@romale.com
www.romale.com

VIÑA ROMALE 2006 BN
60% macabeo, 40% parellada.

84 Colour: golden. Nose: lees reduction notes, floral, expressive. Palate: correct, fine bitter notes, reductive nuances.

VIÑA ROMALE 2009 BRUT NATURE ROSADO
100% garnacha.

83 Colour: raspberry rose. Nose: ripe fruit, red berry notes. Palate: sweetness, easy to drink, fruity.

BODEGAS ROURA

Valls de Rials
08328 Alella (Barcelona)
☎: +34 933 527 456 - Fax: +34 933 524 339
roura@roura.es
www.roura.es

ROURA ROSAT BR
100% pinot noir.

83 Colour: onion pink. Nose: sweet spices, ripe fruit, fresh. Palate: light-bodied, flavourful, easy to drink.

ROURA BR
75% xarel.lo, 25% chardonnay.

76

ROURA BN
70% xarel.lo, 30% chardonnay.

85 Colour: bright straw. Nose: medium intensity, fine lees, floral. Palate: flavourful, rich, light-bodied.

ROURA BRUT NATURE 5 * BN RESERVA
50% xarel.lo, 50% chardonnay.

85 Colour: bright straw. Nose: lees reduction notes, dry nuts, dried herbs, expressive. Palate: fresh, flavourful, reductive nuances.

BODEGAS TRIAS BATLLE

Comerç, 6
08720 Vilafranca del Penedès (Barcelona)
☎: +34 938 902 627 - Fax: +34 938 901 724
bodegas@jtrias.com
www.jtrias.com

TRIAS BATLLE ROSADO BR
100% trepat.

88 Colour: raspberry rose. Nose: expressive, fresh fruit, floral. Palate: powerful, light-bodied, flavourful, fresh.

TRIAS BR RESERVA
45% macabeo, 30% xarel.lo, 25% parellada.

88 Colour: bright straw. Nose: citrus fruit, floral, expressive. Palate: fruity, light-bodied, fresh.

TRIAS BATLLE 2005 BN GRAN RESERVA
40% xarel.lo, 30% macabeo, 20% parellada, 10% chardonnay.

88 Colour: bright straw. Nose: fine lees, fragrant herbs, complex. Palate: powerful, flavourful, good acidity, fine bitter notes, balanced.

TRIAS BN RESERVA
45% macabeo, 30% xarel.lo, 25% parellada.

88 Colour: bright straw. Nose: fresh fruit, dried herbs, fine lees, floral. Palate: fresh, fruity, flavourful.

BODEGAS TROBAT

Castelló, 10
17780 Garriguella (Girona)
☎: +34 972 530 092 - Fax: +34 972 552 530
bodegas.trobat@bmark.es
www.bodegastrobat.com

CELLER TROBAT ROSAT 2010 BR
garnacha, monastrell.

83 Colour: raspberry rose. Nose: red berry notes, fresh, expressive. Palate: fine bitter notes, correct, fresh, light-bodied.

GRAN AMAT 2010 BN
macabeo, xarel.lo, parellada.

83 Colour: bright straw. Nose: medium intensity, dried herbs, fine lees. Palate: fresh, fruity, light-bodied.

CELLER TROBAT 2008 BN RESERVA
macabeo, xarel.lo, parellada.

87 Colour: bright straw. Nose: fresh fruit, dried herbs, dried flowers, neat. Palate: fresh, fruity, flavourful.

CELLER TROBAT 2005 BN GRAN RESERVA
macabeo, xarel.lo, parellada.

85 Colour: bright golden. Nose: dried flowers, dry nuts, neat. Palate: balanced, flavourful, correct.

BODEGAS VICENTE GANDÍA PLA

Ctra. Cheste a Godelleta, s/n
46370 Chiva (Valencia)
☎: +34 962 524 242 - Fax: +34 962 524 243
sgandia@vicentegandia.com
www.vicentegandia.com

EL MIRACLE S/C BR
macabeo, chardonnay.

86 Colour: bright straw. Nose: fresh fruit, dried herbs, floral. Palate: fresh, fruity, flavourful.

HOYA DE CADENAS S/C BN
100% macabeo.

88 Colour: bright straw. Nose: white flowers, dried herbs, sweet spices, expressive. Palate: good acidity, fine bead, flavourful, fleshy.

BODEGUES SUMARROCA

Barrio El Rebato, s/n
08739 Subirats (Barcelona)
☎: +34 938 911 092 - Fax: +34 938 911 778
tpuig@sumarroca.es
www.sumarroca.es

SUMARROCA GRAN BRUT 2009 RD
100% pinot noir.

88 Colour: rose. Nose: elegant, balanced, ripe fruit, powerfull. Palate: flavourful, powerful, fleshy.

SUMARROCA 2008 BR RESERVA
parellada, macabeo, xarel.lo, chardonnay.

90 Colour: bright straw. Nose: fine lees, floral, ripe fruit. Palate: fresh, fruity, flavourful, good acidity.

NÚRIA CLAVEROL 2007 BR RESERVA
xarel.lo, chardonnay, parellada.

94 Colour: bright straw. Nose: elegant, fresh fruit, fine lees, jasmine. Palate: flavourful, fruity, fresh, long, good acidity.

SUMARROCA GRAN BRUT 2007 BR GRAN RESERVA
pinot noir blanco, chardonnay.

91 Colour: bright straw. Nose: dried herbs, fine lees, floral, ripe fruit, sweet spices. Palate: fresh, fruity, flavourful, good acidity.

SUMARROCA GRAN BRUT ALLIER 2006 BR
pinot noir blanco, chardonnay, parellada.

93 Colour: bright golden. Nose: fine lees, fragrant herbs, complex, sweet spices. Palate: flavourful, good acidity, fine bead, fine bitter notes.

CAVA SUMARROCA CUVÉE 2007 BN GRAN RESERVA
chardonnay, parellada.

90 Colour: bright golden. Nose: fine lees, dry nuts, fragrant herbs. Palate: good acidity, fine bead, fine bitter notes.

SUMARROCA 2006 BN GRAN RESERVA
parellada, macabeo, xarel.lo, chardonnay.

90 Color bright golden. Aroma fine lees, dry nuts, fragrant herbs, complex. Taste powerful, flavourful, good acidity, fine bead, fine bitter notes.

CAVA SUMARROCA 2009 BRUT ROSADO
90% pinot noir, 10% garnacha.

89 Colour: rose. Nose: red berry notes, ripe fruit, rose petals. Palate: flavourful, fleshy, sweetness.

CAN DESCREGUT

Masia Can Descregut s/n
08735 Vilobi del Penedès (Barcelona)
☎: +34 938 978 273 - Fax: +34 938 170 786
info@descregut.com
www.montdarac.com

MEMORIA 2007 BN GRAN RESERVA
xarel.lo, chardonnay.

88 Colour: bright straw. Nose: fine lees, floral, citrus fruit. Palate: fresh, fruity, flavourful, good acidity.

MONT D'ARAC BN
macabeo, xarel.lo, parellada.

87 Colour: bright straw. Nose: candied fruit, citrus fruit, fresh fruit. Palate: flavourful, fruity, good acidity.

CAN FEIXES (HUGUET)

Finca Can Feixes, s/n
08718 Cabrera D'Anoia (Barcelona)
☎: +34 937 718 227 - Fax: +34 937 718 031
canfeixes@canfeixes.com
www.canfeixes.com

HUGUET 2007 BR GRAN RESERVA
56% parellada, 24% macabeo, 20% pinot noir.

88 Colour: bright straw. Nose: fresh fruit, dried herbs, fine lees. Palate: fresh, fruity, flavourful, good acidity.

HUGUET 2006 BN GRAN RESERVA
59% parellada, 22% macabeo, 19% pinot noir.

89 Colour: bright straw. Nose: dried herbs, fine lees, floral, ripe fruit. Palate: fresh, fruity, flavourful, good acidity.

CAN RÀFOLS DELS CAUS

Can Rafols del Caus s/n
08793 Avinyonet del Penedès (Barcelona)
☎: +34 938 970 013 - Fax: +34 938 970 370
canrafolsdelscaus@canrafolsdelscaus.com
www.canrafolsdelscaus.com

PARISAD 2003 BRUT EXTRA GRAN RESERVA
80% chardonnay, 15% xarel.lo, 5% macabeo.

92 Colour: bright golden. Nose: dry nuts, fragrant herbs, complex, lees reduction notes. Palate: powerful, flavourful, good acidity, fine bead, fine bitter notes, long.

GRAN CAUS 2006 BN GRAN RESERVA
50% xarel.lo, 45% macabeo, 5% chardonnay.

86 Colour: bright golden. Nose: fine lees, dry nuts, fragrant herbs, complex, fruit liqueur notes. Palate: powerful, flavourful, good acidity, fine bitter notes.

GRAN CAUS CAVA ROSADO BN GRAN RESERVA
pinot noir.

79

CANALS & MUNNÉ

Pl. Pau Casals, 6
08770 Sant Sadurní D'Anoia (Barcelona)
☎: +34 938 910 318 - Fax: +34 938 911 945
info@canalsimunne.com
www.canalsimunne.com

CANALS & MUNNÉ ROSÉ 2007 BR RESERVA
75% monastrell, 25% garnacha.

84 Colour: rose. Nose: medium intensity, candied fruit, rose petals. Palate: flavourful, fruity, fresh.

CANALS & MUNNÉ INSUPERABLE 2004 BR GRAN RESERVA
40% macabeo, 30% xarel.lo, 30% parellada.

88 Colour: bright straw. Nose: dried herbs, fine lees, floral, candied fruit. Palate: fresh, fruity, flavourful, good acidity.

CANALS & MUNNÉ 2004 BR GRAN RESERVA
50% xarel.lo, 30% macabeo, 20% parellada.

86 Colour: bright straw. Nose: dried herbs, fine lees, floral, ripe fruit. Palate: fresh, fruity, flavourful, good acidity.

CANALS & MUNNÉ RESERVA DE L'AVI 3 LITROS 2008 BN RESERVA
50% chardonnay, 15% macabeo, 20% xarel.lo, 15% parellada.

88 Colour: bright straw. Nose: fresh fruit, dried herbs, balanced. Palate: fruity, fresh, great length, flavourful.

CANALS & MUNNÉ GRAN DUC XXI 2006 BN GRAN RESERVA
60% chardonnay, 25% xarel.lo, 15% macabeo.

90 Color bright golden. Aroma fine lees, dry nuts, fragrant herbs, complex. Taste powerful, flavourful, good acidity, fine bead, fine bitter notes.

CANALS & MUNNÉ 2006 BN GRAN RESERVA
40% macabeo, 30% chardonnay, 30% parellada.

88 Colour: bright golden. Nose: dry nuts, fragrant herbs, lees reduction notes. Palate: powerful, flavourful, good acidity, fine bead, fine bitter notes.

CANALS & MUNNÉ (37,5 CL.) 2006 BN GRAN RESERVA
40% macabeo, 30% chardonnay, 30% parellada.

87 Colour: bright straw. Nose: powerfull, ripe fruit, characterful, grassy. Palate: sweetness, flavourful, good acidity, fine bitter notes.

CANALS & MUNNÉ MAGNUM 2004 BN GRAN RESERVA
40% macabeo, 30% chardonnay, 30% parellada.

90 Colour: bright golden. Nose: dry nuts, powerfull, complex, fragrant herbs. Palate: fleshy, flavourful, good acidity, fine bitter notes.

CANALS & MUNNÉ RESERVA DE L'AVI 2004 BN GRAN RESERVA
50% chardonnay, 15% macabeo, 20% xarel.lo, 15% parellada.

90 Color bright golden. Aroma fine lees, dry nuts, fragrant herbs, complex. Taste powerful, flavourful, good acidity, fine bead, fine bitter notes.

CANALS CANALS

Avda. Mare de Deu Montserrat, 7-9
08769 Castellví de Rosanes (Barcelona)
☎: +34 937 755 446 - Fax: +34 937 741 719
cava@canalscanals.com
www.canalscanals.com

CANALS CANALS RESERVA ESPECIAL 2009 BR
30% xarel.lo, 30% macabeo, 35% parellada.

88 Colour: bright straw. Nose: white flowers, fragrant herbs, fresh fruit. Palate: fruity, fresh, easy to drink.

CANALS CANALS CLÀSSIC 2010 BN
45% parellada, 30% xarel.lo, 25% macabeo.

88 Colour: bright straw. Nose: medium intensity, fresh fruit, floral, balanced. Palate: fresh, fruity, flavourful, good acidity.

MARTA DELUXE 2007 BN GRAN RESERVA
50% parellada, 25% xarel.lo, 25% macabeo.

89 Colour: bright straw, greenish rim. Nose: dry nuts, complex, spicy, fine lees, dried herbs. Palate: fresh, good acidity.

RAMÓN CANALS GRAN RESERVA LIMITADA 2007 BN
50% xarel.lo, 25% macabeo, 25% parellada.

88 Colour: bright yellow. Nose: lees reduction notes, candied fruit, spicy, dry nuts. Palate: flavourful, ripe fruit, balanced.

CANALS CANALS 2006 BN GRAN RESERVA
35% xarel.lo, 35% macabeo, 30% parellada.

91 Colour: bright golden. Nose: dry nuts, fragrant herbs, fine lees. Palate: powerful, flavourful, good acidity, fine bead, fine bitter notes.

CANALS CANALS RESERVA BN
xarel.lo, macabeo, parellada.

88 Color bright straw. Aroma medium intensity, fresh fruit, dried herbs, fine lees, floral. Taste fresh, fruity, flavourful, good acidity.

CANALS NADAL

Ponent, 2
08733 El Pla del Penedès (Barcelona)
☎: +34 938 988 081 - Fax: +34 938 989 050
cava@canalsnadal.com
www.canalsnadal.com

ANTONI CANALS NADAL CUPADA SELECCIÓ 2008 RESERVA
50% macabeo, 40% xarel.lo, 10% parellada.

86 Colour: bright yellow. Nose: slightly evolved, floral, grassy. Palate: fruity, flavourful.

CANALS NADAL 2009 BR
40% macabeo, 40% xarel.lo, 20% parellada.

87 Colour: bright straw. Nose: medium intensity, fresh fruit, dried herbs, dry nuts. Palate: fresh, fruity, flavourful, good acidity.

CANALS NADAL GRAN VINTAGE 2008 BR RESERVA
40% chardonnay, 30% macabeo, 20% xarel.lo, 10% parellada.

90 Colour: bright straw. Nose: medium intensity, dried flowers, fine lees, complex, elegant. Palate: fresh, good acidity, easy to drink.

CANALS NADAL 2008 BR RESERVA
45% macabeo, 40% xarel.lo, 15% parellada.

89 Colour: bright straw. Nose: medium intensity, fresh fruit, dried herbs. Palate: fresh, fruity, flavourful, good acidity.

ANTONI ÇANALS NADAL CUPADA MAGNUM SELECCIÓ 2008 BN FERMENTADO EN BARRICA
50% macabeo, 40% xarel.lo, 10% parellada.

89 Colour: bright straw. Nose: fruit expression, floral, fragrant herbs, neat. Palate: good acidity, fine bitter notes, fine bead, powerful, flavourful.

CANALS NADAL MAGNUM 2007 BN RESERVA
45% macabeo, 40% xarel.lo, 15% parellada.

90 Colour: bright golden. Nose: dry nuts, fragrant herbs. Palate: powerful, flavourful, good acidity, fine bead, fine bitter notes.

CANALS NADAL 2007 BN RESERVA
45% macabeo, 40% xarel.lo, 15% parellada.

88 Colour: bright straw. Nose: medium intensity, dried herbs, fine lees, floral, sweet spices. Palate: fresh, fruity, flavourful, good acidity.

CANALS NADAL 2006 BN GRAN RESERVA
50% macabeo, 40% xarel.lo, 10% parellada.

88 Colour: bright yellow. Nose: candied fruit, lees reduction notes, dry nuts, balanced. Palate: fruity, fine bitter notes, good acidity.

CASTELL D'AGE

Ctra.de Martorell a Capellades, 6-8
08782 La Beguda Baixa (Barcelona)
☎: +34 937 725 181 - Fax: +34 937 727 061
info@castelldage.com
www.castelldage.com

CASTELL D'AGE ROSADO 2009 BR RESERVA
pinot noir.

86 Colour: raspberry rose. Nose: fine lees, fruit expression, fresh. Palate: good acidity, fine bitter notes, correct.

CASTELL D'AGE 2008 BN RESERVA
xarel.lo, macabeo, parellada, chardonnay.

85 Colour: straw. Nose: dry nuts, fresh, dried herbs. Palate: fine bitter notes, fresh, flavourful.

CASTELL D'AGE CHARDONNAY 2008 BN
chardonnay.

85 Colour: bright straw. Nose: fine lees, floral, medium intensity. Palate: fresh, flavourful, easy to drink.

ANNE MARIE COMTESSE 2008 BN RESERVA
xarel.lo, macabeo, parellada.

85 Colour: pale. Nose: fine lees, citrus fruit, fresh. Palate: balanced, fine bitter notes, light-bodied, easy to drink.

CASTELL D'AGE POCULUM BONI GENI 2006 BN GRAN RESERVA
chardonnay, pinot noir.

87 Colour: bright straw. Nose: fine lees, dry nuts, fragrant herbs, complex. Palate: powerful, flavourful, good acidity, fine bead, fine bitter notes.

POCULUM BONI GENI 2006 BN GRAN RESERVA
chardonnay, pinot noir.

86 Colour: bright straw. Nose: fresh fruit, fine lees, floral, fragrant herbs. Palate: fresh, flavourful, good acidity, fine bitter notes.

CASTELL D'OR

Mare Rafols, 3- 1r 4a
08720 Vilafranca del Penedès (Barcelona)
☎: +34 938 905 385 - Fax: +34 938 905 446
castelldor@castelldor.com
www.castelldor.com

FLAMA D'OR BRUT ROSÉ RD
100% trepat.

88 Colour: salmon. Nose: medium intensity, faded flowers, candied fruit. Palate: flavourful, fruity, great length, good acidity.

FRANCOLÍ BR RESERVA
50% macabeo, 50% parellada.

87 Colour: bright straw. Nose: dried herbs, floral, ripe fruit. Palate: fresh, fruity, good acidity.

CASTELL COMANDA BR
50% macabeo, 50% parellada.

87 Colour: bright straw. Nose: medium intensity, floral, tropical fruit, dry nuts. Palate: fresh, fruity, flavourful, good acidity.

PUPITRE BR
40% xarel.lo, 40% macabeo, 20% parellada.

87 Color bright straw. Aroma medium intensity, fresh fruit, dried herbs, fine lees, floral. Taste fresh, fruity, flavourful, good acidity.

COSSETÀNIA ROSADO BR
100% trepat.

85 Colour: rose. Nose: red berry notes, medium intensity, dried flowers. Palate: fruity, flavourful, good acidity.

FRANCOLI ROSAT BR
100% trepat.

84 Colour: rose. Nose: medium intensity, fresh fruit, red berry notes. Palate: flavourful, fruity, good acidity.

FLAMA D'OR BR
40% xarel.lo, 40% macabeo, 20% parellada.

84 Colour: bright straw. Nose: fresh fruit, dried herbs, floral. Palate: fresh, fruity, flavourful, good acidity.

COSSETÀNIA BR RESERVA
50% xarel.lo, 30% macabeo, 20% parellada.

84 Colour: bright straw. Nose: fine lees, fresh fruit, white flowers. Palate: flavourful, fruity, fresh.

PUIG SOLIVELLA BR
60% macabeo, 40% parellada.

83 Color bright straw. Aroma medium intensity, fresh fruit, dried herbs, fine lees, floral. Taste fresh, fruity, flavourful, good acidity.

FRANCOLI BN
50% macabeo, 50% parellada.

86 Colour: bright straw. Nose: fresh fruit, fine lees, floral. Palate: fresh, fruity, flavourful, good acidity.

FLAMA D'OR BN
35% macabeo, 40% xarel.lo, 25% parellada.

86 Colour: bright straw. Nose: fragrant herbs, ripe fruit, citrus fruit, floral. Palate: flavourful, fresh, fruity.

COSSETÀNIA BN
50% xarel.lo, 20% parellada, 30% macabeo.

85 Colour: bright straw. Nose: fresh fruit, dried herbs, floral. Palate: fresh, fruity, flavourful, good acidity.

PUPITRE BN
40% xarel.lo, 25% parellada, 35% macabeo.

84 Colour: bright straw. Nose: medium intensity, dried herbs, floral. Palate: fresh, fruity, flavourful, good acidity.

CASTELL COMANDA BRUT ROSÉ
100% trepat.

85 Colour: rose. Nose: red berry notes, dried flowers, balanced. Palate: fruity, sweetness, good acidity.

CASTELL DELS SORELLS

Partida de Calabarra, 1100
46389 Turís (Valencia)
☎: +34 962 527 257 - Fax: +34 962 528 260
info@castelldelssorells.com
www.castelldelssorells.com

CASTELL DELS SORELLS 2006 BR RESERVA
30% macabeo, 30% xarel.lo, 30% parellada, 10% chardonnay.

84 Colour: bright straw. Nose: medium intensity, dried herbs, floral. Palate: fresh, fruity, flavourful, good acidity.

CASTELL DELS SORELLS ROSADO 2006 BN RESERVA
100% trepat.

86 Color rose, purple rim. Aroma powerfull, ripe fruit, red berry notes, floral, expressive. Taste fleshy, powerful, fruity, fresh.

CASTELL DELS SORELLS 2005 BN RESERVA
30% macabeo, 30% xarel.lo, 30% parellada, 10% chardonnay.

87 Colour: bright straw. Nose: medium intensity, dried herbs, fine lees, floral, ripe fruit. Palate: fresh, fruity, flavourful, good acidity.

CASTELL DELS SORELLS 2004 BN GRAN RESERVA
30% macabeo, 30% xarel.lo, 30% parellada, 10% chardonnay.

86 Colour: bright golden. Nose: dry nuts, fragrant herbs, lees reduction notes. Palate: powerful, flavourful, good acidity, fine bitter notes.

CASTELL DELS SORELLS CUVÉE SATÉN 2003 BN GRAN RESERVA
30% macabeo, 30% xarel.lo, 30% parellada, 10% chardonnay.

88 Color bright golden. Aroma fine lees, dry nuts, fragrant herbs, complex. Taste powerful, flavourful, good acidity, fine bead, fine bitter notes.

CASTELL DELS SORELLS CUVÉE MAGENTA 2003 BN
100% trepat.

78

CASTELL SANT ANTONI

Passeig del Parc, 13
08770 Sant Sadurní D'Anoia (Barcelona)
☎: +34 938 183 099 - Fax: +34 938 184 451
cava@castellsantantoni.com
www.castellsantantoni.com

CASTELL SANT ANTONI GRAN BRUT MAGNUM BR RESERVA
macabeo, xarel.lo, parellada, chardonnay.

92 Colour: bright straw. Nose: dried herbs, floral, elegant, fresh fruit. Palate: fresh, fruity, flavourful, good acidity.

CASTELL SANT ANTONI GRAN BRUT BR GRAN RESERVA
macabeo, xarel.lo, parellada, chardonnay.

92 Colour: bright golden. Nose: dry nuts, complex, ripe fruit, expressive. Palate: powerful, flavourful, good acidity, fine bead, fine bitter notes.

CASTELL SANT ANTONI 37.5 BRUT BR
macabeo, xarel.lo, parellada, chardonnay.

91 Colour: bright straw. Nose: dried herbs, fine lees, white flowers, ripe fruit. Palate: fresh, fruity, flavourful, good acidity.

CASTELL SANT ANTONI BRUT DE POSTRE BR
macabeo, xarel.lo, parellada, chardonnay.

88 Colour: bright straw. Nose: medium intensity, dried herbs, fine lees, floral, candied fruit, fruit preserve. Palate: fresh, fruity, flavourful, sweetness.

CASTELL SANT ANTONI GRAN BARRICA 2006 BN GRAN RESERVA
chardonnay, xarel.lo, parellada, macabeo.

90 Colour: bright straw. Nose: dried herbs, fine lees, floral, toasty, candied fruit, citrus fruit. Palate: fruity, flavourful, good acidity, spicy, creamy, long.

CASTELL SANT ANTONI GRAN RESERVA MAGNUM 2005 BN
macabeo, xarel.lo, parellada.

94 Colour: bright straw. Nose: fresh fruit, dried herbs, fine lees, floral, dry nuts. Palate: fresh, fruity, flavourful, good acidity.

CASTELL SANT ANTONI GRAN RESERVA 2005 BN GRAN RESERVA
macabeo, xarel.lo, parellada.

93 Colour: bright golden. Nose: fine lees, dry nuts, fragrant herbs, expressive, fresh, neat. Palate: powerful, flavourful, good acidity, fine bead, fine bitter notes.

CASTELL SANT ANTONI TORRE DE L'HOMENATGE 1999 BN GRAN RESERVA
50% xarel.lo, 25% parellada, 25% macabeo.

95 Colour: bright golden. Nose: dry nuts, fragrant herbs, fine lees. Palate: powerful, flavourful, good acidity, fine bead, fine bitter notes, elegant.

CASTELL SANT ANTONI CAMÍ DEL SOT BN RESERVA
macabeo, xarel.lo, parellada.

92 Colour: bright straw. Nose: powerfull, candied fruit, citrus fruit, sweet spices. Palate: flavourful, spicy, fleshy, good acidity.

CASTELL SANT ANTONI GRAN ROSAT PINOT NOIR BN
pinot noir.

91 Colour: rose, purple rim. Nose: powerfull, ripe fruit, red berry notes, expressive, candied fruit. Palate: fleshy, powerful, fruity, fresh.

CASTELL SANT ANTONI CAMÍ DEL SOT MAGNUM BN RESERVA
xarel.lo, macabeo, parellada, chardonnay.

91 Colour: bright straw. Nose: fresh fruit, dried herbs, fine lees, floral, neat, fresh, expressive. Palate: fresh, fruity, good acidity, long.

CASTELL SANT ANTONI 37.5 BRUT NATURE BN
macabeo, xarel.lo, parellada, chardonnay.

90 Colour: bright straw. Nose: fresh fruit, dried herbs, fine lees, floral. Palate: fresh, fruity, flavourful, good acidity.

CASTELLROIG FINCA SABATÉ I COCA

Ctra. Sant Sadurní d'Anoia a Vilafranca del Penedès, Km. 1
08739 Subirats (Barcelona)
☎: +34 938 911 927 - Fax: +34 938 914 055
info@castellroig.com
www.castellroig.com

CASTELLROIG ROSAT 2009 BR
trepat.

86 Colour: light cherry. Nose: red berry notes, ripe fruit, faded flowers. Palate: fruity, good finish, correct.

CASTELLROIG 2009 BN
macabeo, xarel.lo, parellada.

87 Colour: bright straw. Nose: fresh fruit, tropical fruit, floral, fragrant herbs. Palate: fruity, fresh, good acidity.

CASTELLROIG 2008 BN RESERVA
xarel.lo, macabeo.

89 Colour: bright yellow, greenish rim. Nose: dried flowers, wild herbs, fine lees. Palate: flavourful, good acidity, fine bead.

SABATÉ I COCA RESERVA FAMILIAR 2007 BN RESERVA
xarel.lo, chardonnay.

89 Colour: bright straw. Nose: medium intensity, fresh fruit, dried herbs, fine lees. Palate: fresh, fruity, flavourful, good acidity.

CASTELLROIG 2007 BN GRAN RESERVA
xarel.lo, macabeo.

88 Color bright golden. Aroma fine lees, dry nuts, fragrant herbs, complex. Taste powerful, flavourful, good acidity, fine bead, fine bitter notes.

CASTILLO PERELADA VINOS Y CAVAS

Avda. Barcelona, 78
08720 Vilafranca del Penedès (Barcelona)
☎: +34 938 180 676 - Fax: +34 938 180 926
perelada@castilloperalada.com
www.castilloperelada.com

CASTILLO PERELADA CUVÉE ESPECIAL ROSADO 2008 BR
trepat.

87 Colour: coppery red. Nose: red berry notes, fresh fruit, dried herbs, fine lees, dry nuts. Palate: flavourful, fruity, good acidity.

CASTILLO PERELADA BR RESERVA
macabeo, xarel.lo, parellada.

87 Color bright straw. Aroma medium intensity, fresh fruit, dried herbs, fine lees, floral. Taste fresh, fruity, flavourful, good acidity.

TORRE GALATEA BR
pinot noir, trepat, monastrell.

87 Colour: rose, purple rim. Nose: powerfull, ripe fruit, red berry notes, floral. Palate: fleshy, powerful, fruity, fresh.

CASTILLO PERELADA CUVÉE ESPECIAL 2008 BN
macabeo, parellada, xarel.lo, chardonnay.

92 Colour: bright straw. Nose: dried herbs, fine lees, floral, complex, expressive, fresh fruit. Palate: fresh, fruity, flavourful, good acidity.

GRAN CLAUSTRO DE CASTILLO PERELADA 2008 BN RESERVA
chardonnay, pinot noir, parellada.

89 Color bright straw. Aroma medium intensity, fresh fruit, dried herbs, fine lees, floral. Taste fresh, fruity, flavourful, good acidity.

CASTILLO PERELADA 2008 BN
parellada, xarel.lo, macabeo.

88 Colour: bright straw. Nose: dried herbs, fine lees, floral, ripe fruit. Palate: fresh, fruity, flavourful, good acidity.

CASTILLO PERELADA CHARDONNAY 2007 BN
chardonnay.

88 Colour: bright straw. Nose: dried herbs, fine lees, floral, ripe fruit, citrus fruit. Palate: fresh, fruity, flavourful, good acidity.

GRAN CLAUSTRO CUVÉE ESPECIAL DE CASTILLO PERELADA 2006 BN GRAN RESERVA
chardonnay, pinot noir, parellada.

90 Color bright golden. Aroma fine lees, dry nuts, fragrant herbs, complex. Taste powerful, flavourful, good acidity, fine bead, fine bitter notes.

CASTILLO PERELADA BRUT ROSADO
trepat, garnacha, pinot noir.

86 Colour: light cherry. Nose: medium intensity, dry nuts, dried herbs, red berry notes. Palate: flavourful, fine bitter notes.

CAVA BERDIÉ

Les Conilleres (La Conillera Gran)
08732 Castellví de la Marca (Barcelona)
☎: +34 902 800 229 - Fax: +34 938 919 735
info@cavaberdie.com
www.cavaberdie.com

BERDIÉ RUPESTRE 2008 BR RESERVA
macabeo, xarel.lo, parellada.

88 Colour: bright straw. Nose: medium intensity, fresh fruit, dried herbs, fine lees, floral. Palate: fresh, flavourful, good acidity, fine bitter notes.

BERDIÉ ROMAGOSA ROSÉ BR
macabeo, xarel.lo, parellada.

86 Colour: rose. Nose: fresh, red berry notes, medium intensity, floral. Palate: powerful, good acidity, fine bitter notes.

BERDIÉ GRAN RUPESTRE 2006 BRUT EXTRA GRAN RESERVA
macabeo, xarel.lo, parellada.

85 Colour: bright straw. Nose: medium intensity, dried herbs, floral. Palate: fresh, fruity, flavourful, good acidity.

BERDIÉ 2008 BN RESERVA
macabeo, xarel.lo, parellada.

87 Colour: bright straw. Nose: fresh fruit, dried herbs, fine lees, floral. Palate: fresh, fruity, flavourful, good acidity.

BERDIÉ 2007 BN GRAN RESERVA
macabeo, xarel.lo, parellada.

89 Colour: bright straw. Nose: balanced, fresh fruit, fine lees, sweet spices. Palate: fruity, flavourful, good acidity, fine bead.

CAVA CONDE DE VALICOURT

Sant Antoni, 33-39
08770 Sant Sadurní D'Anoia (Barcelona)
☎: +34 938 910 036 - Fax: +34 938 910 696
cavas@condedevalicourt.com
www.condedevalicourt.com

ROSÉ DE VALICOURT 2009 BR RESERVA
100% garnacha.

83 Colour: raspberry rose. Nose: floral, fruit expression, fresh. Palate: light-bodied, flavourful, correct.

COUPAGE DE ALICIA 2008 BR RESERVA
40% parellada, 30% macabeo, 30% parellada.

84 Colour: bright straw. Nose: dried flowers, fresh, slightly evolved. Palate: good finish, light-bodied, fine bitter notes.

PERMONT'S 2009 BN
40% macabeo, 40% xarel.lo, 20% parellada.

85 Colour: bright straw. Nose: fine lees, floral, citrus fruit, fresh. Palate: easy to drink, fine bitter notes, correct.

COUPAGE DE ALICIA 2007 BN GRAN RESERVA
40% parellada, 30% xarel.lo, 30% macabeo.

84 Colour: bright straw. Nose: floral, citrus fruit, neat. Palate: lacks balance, fresh, light-bodied.

GRAND PAS DE SUCRE MAGNUM 2006 BN GRAN RESERVA
40% parellada, 30% macabeo, 30% xarel.lo.

89 Colour: bright straw. Nose: fresh fruit, white flowers, balanced, neat. Palate: powerful, flavourful, fruity.

MAJESTUOSO 2006 BN GRAN RESERVA
40% macabeo, 40% xarel.lo, 20% parellada.

87 Colour: bright straw. Nose: fine lees, citrus fruit, neat. Palate: easy to drink, good acidity, correct.

PAS DE SUCRE 2006 BN GRAN RESERVA
40% parellada, 30% macabeo, 30% xarel.lo.

86 Colour: bright straw. Nose: medium intensity, fresh fruit, dried herbs, fine lees, floral. Palate: fresh, flavourful, good acidity.

CAVA CRISTINA COLOMER BERNAT

Diputació, 58-60
08770 Sant Sadurní D'Anoia (Barcelona)
☎: +34 938 910 804 - Fax: +34 938 913 034
ccolomer@cavescolomer.com
www.cavescolomer.com

COLOMER HOMENATGE A GAUDÍ PINOT NOIR ROSÉ 2006 BR GRAN RESERVA
pinot noir.

87 Colour: brilliant rose. Nose: ripe fruit, red berry notes, sweet spices, floral. Palate: light-bodied, fresh, flavourful, easy to drink.

COLOMER COSTA BN RESERVA
xarel.lo, macabeo, parellada.

91 Colour: bright straw. Nose: floral, ripe fruit, fine lees, sweet spices. Palate: flavourful, fleshy, fine bead, balanced.

COLOMER COSTA MAGNUM 2007 BN RESERVA
xarel.lo, macabeo, parellada.

89 Colour: bright straw. Nose: fresh fruit, dried herbs, fine lees, floral. Palate: fresh, fruity, flavourful, good acidity.

COLOMER PRESTIGE 2006 BN GRAN RESERVA
xarel.lo, macabeo, parellada, chardonnay, pinot noir.

90 Colour: bright straw. Nose: fine lees, sweet spices, ripe fruit, dry nuts. Palate: fresh, fruity, flavourful, good acidity.

COLOMER "ER" 2004 BN GRAN RESERVA
xarel.lo, macabeo, parellada, chardonnay, pinot noir.

87 Colour: bright golden. Nose: candied fruit, fine lees, pattiserie, honeyed notes. Palate: fine bead, flavourful, good finish.

CAVA GUILERA

Masia Artigas, s/n
08734 Lavern-Subirats (Barcelona)
☎: +34 938 993 085 - Fax: +34 938 993 491
info@cavaguilera.com
www.cavaguilera.com

GUILERA BR RESERVA
xarel.lo, macabeo, parellada.

83 Colour: bright yellow. Nose: medium intensity, dried flowers, dried herbs. Palate: correct, fine bitter notes.

GUILERA BN GRAN RESERVA
xarel.lo, macabeo, parellada.

85 Colour: bright straw. Nose: medium intensity, dried herbs, floral. Palate: fresh, fruity, flavourful, good acidity.

GUILERA EXTRA BRUT GRAN RESERVA
xarel.lo, macabeo, parellada.

86 Colour: bright yellow. Nose: candied fruit, powerfull, lees reduction notes, fragrant herbs. Palate: fruity, flavourful.

CAVA M. BOSCH

Ctra. San Martí Sarroca s/n
08737 Torroella de Foix (Barcelona)
☎: +34 938 405 488 - Fax: +34 938 403 026
info@grupombosch.com
www.cavesmbosch.com

M. BOSCH RESERVA FAMILIAR BN RESERVA
macabeo, xarel.lo, parellada.

83 Colour: bright straw. Nose: medium intensity, dried herbs, fine lees. Palate: fresh, fruity, good acidity, fine bitter notes, slightly evolved.

CAVA MARÍA CASANOVAS

Montserrat, 117
08770 Sant Sadurní D'Anoia (Barcelona)
☎: +34 938 910 812 - Fax: +34 938 911 572
mariacasanovas@brutnature.com
www.mariacasanovas.com

MARÍA CASANOVAS GLAÇ 2009 BN
xarel.lo, macabeo, parellada, pinot noir.

86 Colour: bright straw. Nose: dried herbs, fine lees, candied fruit. Palate: fresh, fruity, flavourful, good acidity.

MARÍA CASANOVAS 2008 BN GRAN RESERVA
chardonnay, xarel.lo, parellada, pinot noir, macabeo.

90 Colour: bright golden. Nose: dry nuts, fragrant herbs, expressive, characterful, fine lees. Palate: powerful, flavourful, good acidity, fine bead, fine bitter notes.

MARÍA CASANOVAS BRUT DE BRUT BN RESERVA
xarel.lo, macabeo, parellada.

85 Colour: bright straw. Nose: dried herbs, fine lees, floral, ripe fruit. Palate: fresh, fruity, flavourful, good acidity.

CAVA MONT-FERRANT

Mont Ferrant, 1- Esquina Abat Escarré
17300 Blanes (Girona)
☎: +34 934 191 000 - Fax: +34 934 193 170
jcivit@montferrant.com
www.montferrant.com

AGUSTÍ VILARET 2006 GRAN RESERVA
70% chardonnay, 10% macabeo, 10% xarel.lo, 10% parellada.

90 Colour: bright golden. Nose: fragrant herbs, ripe fruit, dry nuts, toasty. Palate: good acidity, fine bead, fresh, fleshy, flavourful.

BERTA BOUZY 2007 BR RESERVA
40% xarel.lo, 27% macabeo, 22% parellada, 5% chardonnay.

91 Colour: bright straw. Nose: fresh fruit, fine lees, complex, characterful. Palate: spicy, flavourful, powerful, fruity.

MONT FERRANT L AMERICANO 2007 BR RESERVA
40% xarel.lo, 29% macabeo, 26% parellada, 5% chardonnay.

88 Colour: bright straw. Nose: fresh, expressive, fruit expression, fine lees. Palate: good acidity, balanced, fine bitter notes.

MONT FERRANT TRADICIÓ 2007 BR RESERVA
40% xarel.lo, 32% macabeo, 23% parellada, 5% chardonnay.

86 Colour: bright straw. Nose: fresh fruit, balanced, neat. Palate: good acidity, correct, unctuous, easy to drink.

MONT FERRANT 2006 BR GRAN RESERVA
23% macabeo, 26% xarel.lo, 18% parellada, 18% chardonnay, 15% pinot noir.

89 Colour: bright straw. Nose: fine lees, fruit expression, spicy, expressive. Palate: good acidity, fine bead, fine bitter notes, flavourful.

MONT-FERRANT PINOT NOIR 2006 BR
100% pinot noir.

85 Colour: rose. Nose: ripe fruit, raspberry, fresh, expressive. Palate: good acidity, fleshy, fruity, easy to drink.

BLANES NATURE 2006 BN GRAN RESERVA
37% xarel.lo, 33% macabeo, 25% parellada, 5% chardonnay.

87 Colour: bright straw. Nose: floral, candied fruit, balanced, expressive. Palate: rich, powerful, flavourful.

BLANES & BLANES 2006 BN GRAN RESERVA
5% chardonnay, 37% xarel.lo, 33% macabeo, 25% parellada.

87 Colour: bright straw. Nose: fragrant herbs, candied fruit, expressive, fresh. Palate: fruity, flavourful, full.

CAVA RECAREDO

Tamarit, 10
08770 Sant Sadurní D'Anoia (Barcelona)
☎: +34 938 910 214 - Fax: +34 938 911 697
cava@recaredo.es
www.recaredo.com

RECAREDO 2007 BN GRAN RESERVA
50% xarel.lo, 38% macabeo, 12% parellada.

92 Colour: bright golden. Nose: fine lees, dry nuts, fragrant herbs. Palate: flavourful, good acidity, fine bead, fine bitter notes.

RECAREDO SUBTIL 2006 BN GRAN RESERVA
44% xarel.lo, 44% macabeo, 12% chardonnay.

91 Colour: bright golden. Nose: fine lees, dry nuts, fragrant herbs. Palate: powerful, flavourful, good acidity, fine bead, fine bitter notes.

RECAREDO BRUT DE BRUTS 2004 BN GRAN RESERVA
33% xarel.lo, 67% parellada.

92 Colour: bright straw. Nose: fresh fruit, dried herbs, floral, fine lees, dry nuts. Palate: fresh, fruity, flavourful, good acidity.

RECAREDO RESERVA PARTICULAR 2002 BN GRAN RESERVA
72% macabeo, 28% xarel.lo.

95 Colour: bright golden. Nose: dry nuts, fragrant herbs, complex, lees reduction notes, pattiserie, aromatic coffee. Palate: powerful, flavourful, good acidity, fine bead, fine bitter notes, long.

TURO D'EN MOTA 2000 BN RESERVA
100% xarel.lo.

92 Colour: bright straw. Nose: expressive, candied fruit, citrus fruit, aromatic coffee, sweet spices. Palate: flavourful, powerful, fleshy, long.

CAVA ROGER GOULART

Major, 6
08635 Sant Esteve Sesrovires (Barcelona)
☎: +34 934 191 000 - Fax: +34 934 193 170
jcivit@montferrant.com
www.rogergoulart.com

ROGER GOULART GRAN CUVÉE 2005 GRAN RESERVA
35% xarel.lo, 30% chardonnay, 20% macabeo, 15% parellada.

87 Colour: bright straw. Nose: fine lees, dry nuts, fruit expression, balanced, expressive. Palate: spicy, correct, fine bitter notes.

ROGER GOULART ROSÉ 2007 BR
60% garnacha, 40% monastrell.

85 Colour: brilliant rose. Nose: expressive, fruit expression, floral. Palate: fleshy, fruity, light-bodied.

ROGER GOULART BR RESERVA
40% xarel.lo, 30% macabeo, 30% parellada.

88 Colour: bright straw. Nose: neat, fresh, expressive, fresh fruit. Palate: fine bead, good acidity, fine bitter notes, correct.

ROGER GOULART BN RESERVA
40% xarel.lo, 30% macabeo, 25% parellada, 5% chardonnay.

88 Colour: bright straw. Nose: complex, expressive, fresh fruit, floral. Palate: good acidity, fine bead, flavourful.

ROGER GOULART EXTRA BRUT GRAN RESERVA
35% xarel.lo, 30% macabeo, 30% parellada, 5% chardonnay.

87 Colour: bright straw. Nose: lees reduction notes, candied fruit, fresh, complex. Palate: good acidity, unctuous, fruity.

CAVA VIDAL I FERRÉ

Nou, 2
43815 Les Pobles (Tarragona)
☎: +34 977 638 554 - Fax: +34 977 638 554
vidaliferre@terra.es

VIDAL I FERRÉ BR RESERVA
macabeo, xarel.lo, parellada.

90 Colour: bright straw. Nose: fresh fruit, dried herbs, fine lees, floral, balanced, expressive. Palate: fresh, fruity, flavourful, good acidity, fine bead.

VIDAL I FERRÉ 2006 BN GRAN RESERVA
macabeo, xarel.lo, parellada.

91 Colour: bright straw. Nose: complex, neat, expressive, floral, fruit expression. Palate: good acidity, fine bead, elegant, fine bitter notes.

VIDAL I FERRÉ BN RESERVA
macabeo, xarel.lo, parellada.

85 Colour: bright golden. Nose: fine lees, citrus fruit, fragrant herbs, expressive. Palate: fine bitter notes, fruity, correct.

VIDAL I FERRÉ SS
macabeo, xarel.lo, parellada.

86 Colour: bright straw. Nose: fruit liqueur notes, floral, fresh, neat. Palate: fruity, light-bodied, flavourful.

CAVAS BOLET

Finca Mas Lluet, s/n
08732 Castellvi de la Marca (Barcelona)
☎: +34 938 918 153
cavasbolet@cavasbolet.com
www.cavasbolet.com

BOLET PINOT NOIR 2007 RD
pinot noir.

83 Colour: rose. Nose: fresh, balanced, neat, red berry notes. Palate: fruity, light-bodied, flavourful.

BOLET ECO 2007 BR RESERVA
macabeo, xarel.lo, parellada.

86 Colour: bright straw. Nose: candied fruit, fine lees, fresh. Palate: fresh, light-bodied, flavourful.

BOLET ECO 2007 BN RESERVA
macabeo, xarel.lo, parellada.

85 Colour: bright straw. Nose: medium intensity, fine lees, floral, fruit liqueur notes. Palate: fresh, fruity, flavourful, good acidity.

BOLET ECO 2003 BN GRAN RESERVA
macabeo, xarel.lo, parellada.

86 Colour: bright straw. Nose: candied fruit, floral, expressive. Palate: fruity, powerful, flavourful.

BOLET SELECCIÓN FAMILIAR 2003 BN
macabeo, xarel.lo, parellada.

80 Colour: bright golden. Nose: lees reduction notes, sweet spices, petrol notes. Palate: lacks balance, powerful, reductive nuances.

CAVAS EL MAS FERRER

S. Sebastia, 25 C'al Avi
08739 Subirats (Barcelona)
☎: +34 938 988 292 - Fax: +34 938 988 545
info@elmasferrer.com
www.elmasferrer.com

EL MAS FERRER SEGLE XXI 2005 B GRAN RESERVA
30% macabeo, 37% xarel.lo, 33% parellada.

89 Colour: straw. Nose: fine lees, floral, fruit expression, neat, expressive. Palate: balanced, round, good acidity.

EL MAS FERRER 2009 BR
39% macabeo, 35% xarel.lo, 31% parellada.

89 Colour: bright straw. Nose: fresh fruit, dried herbs, fine lees, floral. Palate: fresh, fruity, flavourful, fine bead.

EL MAS FERRER 2008 BR RESERVA
35% macabeo, 37% parellada, 28% xarel.lo.

88 Colour: bright straw. Nose: ripe fruit, fine lees. Palate: balanced, fine bead, good acidity.

EL MAS FERRER 2007 BN RESERVA
32% macabeo, 35% xarel.lo, 33% parellada.

87 Colour: bright straw. Nose: fine lees, citrus fruit, fresh. Palate: fresh, light-bodied, flavourful.

EL MAS FERRER FAMILIAR 2005 BN GRAN RESERVA
30% macabeo, 32,5% xarel.lo, 32,5% parellada.

89 Colour: bright straw. Nose: dried herbs, fine lees, floral, ripe fruit. Palate: fresh, fruity, flavourful, good acidity.

CAVAS FERRET

Avda. de Catalunya, 36
08736 Guardiola de Font-Rubí (Barcelona)
☎: +34 938 979 148 - Fax: +34 938 979 285
ferret@cavasferret.com
www.cavasferret.com

FERRET BR RESERVA
40% parellada, 40% macabeo, 20% xarel.lo.

90 Colour: bright straw. Nose: medium intensity, fresh fruit, dried herbs, floral, dry nuts. Palate: fresh, good acidity, balanced.

FERRET ROSADO BR RESERVA
trepat, garnacha, monastrell.

90 Colour: raspberry rose. Nose: red berry notes, rose petals, expressive, fresh. Palate: balanced, fruity, flavourful, powerful.

FERRET 2006 BN GRAN RESERVA
40% macabeo, 35% parellada, 25% xarel.lo.

90 Colour: bright yellow. Nose: fine lees, dry nuts, fragrant herbs, complex. Palate: powerful, flavourful, good acidity, fine bead, fine bitter notes.

FERRET BARRICA 2005 BN GRAN RESERVA
parellada, xarel.lo, macabeo, chardonnay.

88 Colour: bright yellow. Nose: expressive, toasty, pattiserie, dry nuts. Palate: flavourful, good structure, good acidity.

CELIA DE FERRET ROSADO 2003 BN GRAN RESERVA
80% pinot noir, 20% garnacha.

88 Colour: onion pink. Nose: candied fruit, fine lees, faded flowers. Palate: fruity, flavourful, good acidity.

EZEQUIEL FERRET 2002 BN GRAN RESERVA
50% xarel.lo, 30% parellada, 20% macabeo.

87 Colour: bright yellow. Nose: lees reduction notes, candied fruit, pattiserie. Palate: flavourful, good finish, fine bead.

FERRET BN RESERVA
40% parellada, 40% macabeo, 20% xarel.lo.

89 Colour: bright yellow. Nose: fine lees, dry nuts, fragrant herbs, complex. Palate: powerful, flavourful, good acidity, fine bead, fine bitter notes.

FERRET MAGNUM BN

88 Color bright straw. Aroma medium intensity, fresh fruit, dried herbs, fine lees, floral. Taste fresh, fruity, flavourful, good acidity.

CAVAS HILL

Bonavista, 2
08734 Moja (Barcelona)
☎: +34 938 900 588 - Fax: +34 938 170 246
cavashill@cavashill.com
www.cavashill.com

CAVA 1887 BR
50% xarel.lo, 35% macabeo, 15% parellada.

85 Colour: bright straw. Nose: medium intensity, fresh fruit, floral. Palate: fresh, fruity, flavourful, good acidity.

CAVAS HILL ROSADO ARTESANÍA BR
60% garnacha, 40% monastrell.

83 Colour: light cherry. Nose: scrubland, dried flowers, medium intensity. Palate: easy to drink.

BRUTÍSIMO 2007 BN GRAN RESERVA
40% xarel.lo, 30% chardonnay, 20% macabeo, 10% parellada.

88 Colour: bright straw. Nose: fresh fruit, dried herbs, floral. Palate: fresh, fruity, flavourful, good acidity, fine bitter notes.

HILLIUM 2005 BN GRAN RESERVA
55% xarel.lo, 30% chardonnay, 10% macabeo, 5% parellada.

91 Color bright golden. Aroma fine lees, dry nuts, fragrant herbs, complex. Taste powerful, flavourful, good acidity, fine bead, fine bitter notes.

CAVAS HILL BRUT DE BRUT BN RESERVA
40% xarel.lo, 25% macabeo, 25% parellada, 10% chardonnay.

87 Colour: bright straw. Nose: medium intensity, fresh fruit, fine lees, floral. Palate: fresh, fruity, flavourful, good acidity.

CAVAS HILL ARTESANÍA BN
40% xarel.lo, 25% macabeo, 25% parellada, 10% chardonnay.

85 Colour: bright straw. Nose: dried herbs, dried flowers, medium intensity. Palate: fresh, fruity, good acidity.

CAVAS LAVERNOYA

Finca La Porxada
08729 Sant Marçal (Barcelona)
☎: +34 938 912 202 - Fax: +34 938 919 948
lavernoya@lavernoya.com
www.lavernoya.com

LÁCRIMA BACCUS HERETAT 2009 BR
macabeo, xarel.lo, parellada, chardonnay.

90 Colour: bright straw. Nose: candied fruit, expressive, floral. Palate: good acidity, fine bitter notes, fresh, light-bodied.

LÁCRIMA BACCUS 2009 BR
macabeo, xarel.lo, parellada.

85 Colour: bright straw. Nose: candied fruit, citrus fruit, fragrant herbs. Palate: flavourful, sweetness, good acidity.

LÁCRIMA BACCUS PRIMERÍSIMO 2008 BR GRAN RESERVA
macabeo, xarel.lo, parellada, chardonnay.

87 Colour: bright straw. Nose: candied fruit, fine lees, expressive. Palate: fine bitter notes, good acidity, fresh.

LÁCRIMA BACCUS 2009 BN
xarel.lo, macabeo, parellada.

88 Colour: bright straw. Nose: fresh fruit, dried herbs, fine lees, floral. Palate: fresh, fruity, flavourful, good acidity.

LÁCRIMA BACCUS HERETAT 2008 BN
macabeo, xarel.lo, parellada, chardonnay.

87 Colour: bright straw. Nose: fine lees, white flowers, citrus fruit. Palate: fine bitter notes, correct, fresh.

LÁCRIMA BACCUS SUMMUM 2007 BN GRAN RESERVA
macabeo, xarel.lo, parellada, chardonnay.

91 Colour: bright straw. Nose: fragrant herbs, lees reduction notes, dry nuts, expressive, powerfull. Palate: fine bitter notes, good acidity, fleshy, fine bead, smoky aftertaste.

LAVERNOYA BN RESERVA
xarel.lo, macabeo, parellada.

89 Colour: bright straw. Nose: fresh fruit, dried herbs, fine lees, floral. Palate: fresh, fruity, flavourful, good acidity.

CAVAS MESTRES

Plaça Ajuntament, 8
08770 Sant Sadurní D'Anoia (Barcelona)
☎: +34 938 910 043 - Fax: +34 938 911 611
cava@mestres.es
www.mestres.es

MESTRES 1312 2007 BR RESERVA
40% parellada, 30% macabeo, 30% xarel.lo.

88 Colour: bright straw. Nose: floral, fragrant herbs, ripe fruit. Palate: fruity, fresh, flavourful, sweetness.

MESTRES CUPAGE ROSÉ 2007 BR RESERVA
50% trepat, 30% monastrell, 20% pinot noir.

84 Colour: cherry, purple rim. Nose: ripe fruit, faded flowers, medium intensity. Palate: light-bodied, fresh, easy to drink.

MESTRES CUPAGE BARCELONA 2006 BR RESERVA
40% xarel.lo, 35% macabeo, 25% parellada.

91 Colour: bright straw. Nose: sweet spices, caramel, dry nuts, toasty. Palate: fleshy, powerful, flavourful, rich, toasty.

MESTRES CUPAGE 50 AÑOS DE "CAVA" 2006 BR RESERVA
55% xarel.lo, 25% macabeo, 20% parellada.

90 Colour: bright straw. Nose: ripe fruit, fine lees, dried herbs, floral. Palate: fruity, fresh, flavourful, long, good acidity, fine bead.

MESTRES CUPATGE PIT LANE 2006 BR RESERVA
40% xarel.lo, 35% macabeo, 25% parellada.

87 Colour: bright golden. Nose: candied fruit, fine lees, dried herbs, sweet spices. Palate: fresh, fruity, flavourful.

MESTRES CUPAGE 80 ANIVERSARIO 2004 BR RESERVA
60% xarel.lo, 25% macabeo, 15% parellada.

90 Colour: bright golden. Nose: white flowers, fragrant herbs, citrus fruit, ripe fruit. Palate: fruity, fresh, powerful, flavourful, fleshy, good acidity, fine bead.

MESTRES MAS VÍA 2000 BR GRAN RESERVA
75% xarel.lo, 15% macabeo, 10% parellada.

90 Colour: bright golden. Nose: ripe fruit, dried flowers, sweet spices, expressive. Palate: powerful, rich, fleshy, good acidity, fine bead, long.

ELENA DE MESTRES ROSADO 2007 BN
60% trepat, 40% monastrell.

81 Colour: rose, purple rim. Nose: overripe fruit, medium intensity, floral. Palate: light-bodied, fresh, short.

MESTRES COQUET 2006 BN RESERVA
45% xarel.lo, 30% macabeo, 25% parellada.

88 Colour: bright straw. Nose: fine lees, white flowers, ripe fruit, expressive. Palate: long, flavourful, powerful, fleshy, fine bead.

MESTRES VISOL 2005 BN RESERVA
40% xarel.lo, 35% macabeo, 25% parellada.

89 Colour: bright golden. Nose: fresh fruit, citrus fruit, white flowers, fine lees. Palate: fruity, powerful, flavourful, good acidity, fine bead.

MESTRE CLOS NOSTRE SENYOR 2002 BN RESERVA
60% xarel.lo, 20% macabeo, 20% parellada.

89 Colour: bright straw. Nose: fine lees, ripe fruit, fragrant herbs, toasty. Palate: good acidity, fine bead, flavourful, toasty.

CAVAS SANSTRAVÉ

De la Conca, 10
43412 Solivella (Tarragona)
☎: +34 977 892 165 - Fax: +34 977 892 073
bodega@sanstrave.com
www.sanstrave.com

SANSTRAVÉ BN GRAN RESERVA
macabeo, xarel.lo, parellada, chardonnay.

87 Colour: bright straw. Nose: dried herbs, fine lees, floral. Palate: fresh, fruity, flavourful, good acidity.

CAVAS SIGNAT

Escultor Llimona, s/n
08328 Alella (Barcelona)
☎: +34 935 403 400 - Fax: +34 935 401 471
signat@signat.es
www.signat.es

SIGNAT 5 ESTRELLAS BR RESERVA
macabeo, xarel.lo, parellada, chardonnay.

91 Colour: bright straw. Nose: fresh fruit, dried herbs, fine lees, floral, powerfull, expressive. Palate: fresh, fruity, flavourful, good acidity.

CAVES CONDE DE CARALT S.A.

Ctra. Sant Sadurní-Sant Pere de Riudebitlles, Km. 5
08775 Torrelavit (Barcelona)
☎: +34 938 917 070 - Fax: +34 938 996 006
seguraviudas@seguraviudas.es
www.freixenet.es

CONDE DE CARALT BLANC DE BLANCS BR
60% macabeo, 20% xarel.lo, 20% parellada.

90 Colour: bright straw. Nose: medium intensity, fresh fruit, dried herbs, floral, tropical fruit. Palate: fresh, flavourful, good acidity.

CONDE DE CARALT BR
50% macabeo, 30% parellada, 20% xarel.lo.

87 Colour: bright straw. Nose: medium intensity, fresh fruit, dried herbs, floral. Palate: fresh, fruity, flavourful, good acidity.

CAVES MONASTELL

Girona, 30
08770 Sant Sadurní D'Anoia (Barcelona)
☎: +34 938 910 396 - Fax: +34 938 911 070
ferrangirones@terra.es
www.cavesmonastell.com

ROCA GIBERT BRUT 2009 RD
93% trepat, 7% pinot noir.

85 Colour: raspberry rose. Nose: floral, raspberry, fresh, neat. Palate: correct, good acidity, fine bitter notes.

MONTSANT ARTESA 2008 BN RESERVA
45% macabeo, 35% xarel.lo, 20% parellada.

86 Colour: bright straw. Nose: medium intensity, dried herbs, fine lees, white flowers, citrus fruit. Palate: fresh, fruity, good acidity.

ROCA GIBERT 2008 BN RESERVA
40% macabeo, 40% xarel.lo, 20% parellada.

85 Colour: bright straw. Nose: fine lees, white flowers, fruit expression. Palate: good acidity, correct, balanced.

CAVES MUNGUST

San Josep, 10-12
08784 Sant Jaume Sesoliveres Piera (Barcelona)
☎: +34 937 763 016
info@cavesmungust.com
www.cavesmungust.com

PERE MUNNÉ DURÁN ROSAT BR
garnacha, trepat, pinot noir.

86 Colour: rose. Nose: ripe fruit, red berry notes. Palate: flavourful, fruity, fleshy.

MUNGUST BR RESERVA
xarel.lo, parellada.

85 Colour: bright straw. Nose: medium intensity, dried herbs, fine lees, candied fruit. Palate: fresh, fruity, flavourful, good acidity, sweetness.

PERE MUNNÉ DURÁN BR
xarel.lo, macabeo, parellada.

84 Colour: bright straw. Nose: fresh fruit, dried herbs, fine lees. Palate: fresh, fruity, good acidity.

MUNGUST BN RESERVA
xarel.lo, macabeo, parellada.

85 Colour: bright straw. Nose: fresh fruit, dried herbs, floral, pungent, lees reduction notes. Palate: fresh, fruity, flavourful, good acidity.

PERE MUNNÉ DURÁN BN RESERVA
xarel.lo, macabeo, parellada.

84 Colour: bright straw. Nose: floral, fruit expression, fresh, expressive. Palate: correct, fine bitter notes, fresh.

PERE MUNNÉ DURÁN BN
xarel.lo, macabeo, parellada.

82 Colour: bright straw. Nose: medium intensity, fresh fruit, floral. Palate: fresh, fruity, flavourful, good acidity.

CAVES NADAL

Escultor Limona, s/n
08328 Alella (Barcelona)
☎: +34 935 403 400 - Fax: +34 935 401 471
signat@signat.es
www.signat.es

R.N.G. BR GRAN RESERVA
68% xarel.lo, 32% parellada.

86 Colour: bright golden. Nose: dry nuts, lees reduction notes. Palate: powerful, flavourful, good acidity, fine bitter notes.

SALVATGE ROSÉ 2008 RD RESERVA
100% pinot noir.

90 Colour: salmon. Nose: red berry notes, ripe fruit, complex, elegant, faded flowers. Palate: complex, fruity, good acidity.

NADAL ESPECIAL 2006 BN GRAN RESERVA
58% parellada, 32% macabeo, 10% xarel.lo.

89 Colour: bright straw. Nose: medium intensity, dried herbs, fine lees, floral. Palate: fresh, fruity, flavourful, good acidity.

CAVES NAVERÁN

Masia Can Parellada - Sant Martí Sadevesa - Ctra. Sitges a Igualada, Km. 25,1
08775 Torrelavit (Barcelona)
☎: +34 938 988 400 - Fax: +34 938 989 027
sadeve@naveran.com
www.naveran.com

NAVERÁN PERLES ROSES PINOT NOIR RD
100% pinot noir.

89 Colour: onion pink. Nose: medium intensity, ripe fruit, fine lees. Palate: good structure, fruity, flavourful, good acidity.

CAVA NAVERAN PERLES BLANQUES 2007 BR
65% pinot noir, 35% chardonnay.

91 Colour: bright yellow. Nose: spicy, ripe fruit, dry nuts, faded flowers, fine lees. Palate: ripe fruit, great length, fine bitter notes.

ODISEA NAVERÁN BN
65% chardonnay, 25% parellada, 10% xarel.lo.

91 Colour: bright yellow. Nose: ripe fruit, fine lees, pattiserie. Palate: flavourful, fleshy, spicy, good acidity.

CAVES ORIOL ROSSELL

Propietat Can Cassanyes, s/n
08732 St. Marçal (Barcelona)
☎: +34 977 671 061 - Fax: +34 977 671 050
oriolrossell@oriolrossell.com
www.oriolrossell.com

ORIOL ROSSELL 2008 BN RESERVA
macabeo, xarel.lo, parellada.

86 Colour: bright straw. Nose: fine lees, expressive, fresh, neat, candied fruit. Palate: fleshy, fruity, light-bodied.

ORIOL ROSSELL 2007 BN GRAN RESERVA
macabeo, xarel.lo, parellada.

88 Colour: bright golden. Nose: fragrant herbs, dried flowers, fine lees, neat. Palate: good acidity, flavourful, great length.

ORIOL ROSSELL RESERVA DE LA PROPIETAT 2007 BN GRAN RESERVA
xarel.lo, macabeo, parellada.

85 Colour: bright straw. Nose: dried flowers, lees reduction notes, expressive. Palate: great length, powerful, flavourful.

ORIOL ROSSELL BRUT ROSÉ
trepat.

89 Colour: raspberry rose. Nose: red berry notes, complex, expressive. Palate: fleshy, fresh, fruity, flavourful.

CELLER CARLES ANDREU

Sant Sebastià, 19
43423 Pira (Tarragona)
☎: +34 977 887 404 - Fax: +34 977 887 427
info@cavandreu.com
www.cavandreu.com

CAVA ROSADO BRUT CARLES ANDREU 2009
100% trepat.

87 Colour: light cherry. Nose: red berry notes, ripe fruit, floral, dried herbs. Palate: fruity, good finish, fine bitter notes.

CAVA RESERVA BARRICA BRUT NATURE CARLES ANDREU 2008
parellada, macabeo, chardonnay.

90 Colour: bright yellow. Nose: balanced, complex, spicy, fine lees, fragrant herbs. Palate: fruity, flavourful, good acidity.

CAVA ROSADO RESERVA BARRICA BRUT CARLES ANDREU 2008
100% trepat.

90 Colour: raspberry rose. Nose: elegant, complex, fine lees, candied fruit, spicy. Palate: fruity, flavourful, fine bead.

BRUT CARLES ANDREU 2008 BR
parellada, macabeo.

88 Colour: bright straw. Nose: fresh fruit, tropical fruit, floral. Palate: fruity, good acidity, fine bitter notes.

CAVA BRUT NATURE CARLES ANDREU 2008 BN
parellada, macabeo.

88 Colour: bright yellow. Nose: fresh fruit, fragrant herbs, medium intensity. Palate: flavourful, good acidity, fresh.

CAVA RESERVA BRUT NATURE CARLES ANDREU 2008 BN
parellada, macabeo, chardonnay.

88 Colour: bright straw. Nose: dried flowers, fresh, fine lees, medium intensity. Palate: fresh, fruity, good finish, easy to drink.

CELLER COOPERATIU D'ARTÉS SCCL - CAVES ARTIUM

Cr. Rocafort, 44
08271 Artés (Barcelona)
☎: +34 938 305 325 - Fax: +34 938 306 289
artium@cavesartium.com
www.cavesartium.com

ARTIUM ROSAT 2009 BR RESERVA
100% trepat.

87 Colour: rose. Nose: red berry notes, candied fruit, characterful. Palate: flavourful, powerful, fleshy.

ARTIUM 2007 BR RESERVA
40% macabeo, 30% xarel.lo, 30% parellada.

87 Colour: bright straw. Nose: medium intensity, fine lees, floral, ripe fruit. Palate: fresh, fruity, flavourful, good acidity.

LLUÍS GUITART BR
xarel.lo, macabeo, parellada.

83 Colour: bright straw. Nose: dried herbs, fine lees, floral, candied fruit. Palate: fresh, fruity, flavourful, good acidity.

ARTIUM 2007 BN RESERVA
40% macabeo, 40% xarel.lo, 20% parellada.

87 Colour: bright straw. Nose: medium intensity, fresh fruit, dried herbs. Palate: fresh, fruity, flavourful, good acidity.

ARTIUM 1908 BN GRAN RESERVA
50% macabeo, 30% xarel.lo, 20% parellada.

88 Colour: bright golden. Nose: dry nuts, fragrant herbs, complex, lees reduction notes. Palate: powerful, flavourful, good acidity, fine bitter notes.

CELLER DEL RAVAL

Vinyals, 161
08223 Terrassa (Barcelona)
☎: +34 937 330 695 - Fax: +34 937 333 605
jcernuda@asociadis.com
www.angelcava.com

ÀNGEL NOIR 2008
pinot noir, garnacha, trepat.

82 Colour: light cherry. Nose: red berry notes, ripe fruit, medium intensity, short. Palate: easy to drink, good acidity.

ÀNGEL BRUT DE BRUTS 2009 BR
xarel.lo, macabeo, parellada.

86 Colour: bright straw. Nose: medium intensity, fresh fruit, dried herbs, fine lees. Palate: fresh, flavourful, good acidity.

ÀNGEL CUPATGE 2010 BN
chardonnay, xarel.lo, macabeo, parellada.

90 Colour: bright straw. Nose: fruit expression, citrus fruit, white flowers, expressive. Palate: good structure, good acidity, great length.

CELLER JORDI LLUCH

Barrio Les Casetes, s/n
08777 Sant Quinti de Mediona (Barcelona)
☎: +34 938 988 138 - Fax: +34 938 988 138
vinyaescude@vinyaescude.com
www.vinyaescude.com

VINYA ESCUDÉ 523 RESERVA
macabeo, parellada, xarel.lo.

88 Colour: bright yellow. Nose: ripe fruit, fine lees, dried herbs. Palate: good acidity, fine bitter notes, balanced.

VINYA ESCUDÉ ROSAT PINOT NOIR BN
100% pinot noir.

82 Colour: brilliant rose. Nose: dry nuts, dried herbs, overripe fruit. Palate: light-bodied, fruity.

CELLER MARIOL

Rosselló, 442 - Bajos
08025 (Barcelona)
☎: +34 934 367 628 - Fax: +34 934 500 281
celler@cellermariol.es
www.cellermariol.es

CASA MARIOL ARTESANAL 36 MESOS 2008 BR RESERVA
40% macabeo, 40% xarel.lo, 20% parellada.

85 Colour: bright straw. Nose: white flowers, candied fruit, characterful. Palate: good acidity, fine bitter notes, correct.

CASA MARIOL ROSADO 2007 BR RESERVA
100% trepat.

85 Colour: raspberry rose. Nose: raspberry, fresh, balanced. Palate: fresh, fruity, flavourful.

CASA MARIOL ARTESANAL 18 MESES 2009 BN
macabeo, xarel.lo, parellada.

84 Colour: bright straw. Nose: fine lees, candied fruit, fresh. Palate: fresh, light-bodied, flavourful.

CASA MARIOL CAVA ARTESANAL 48 MESES 2007 BN RESERVA
macabeo, xarel.lo, parellada.

86 Colour: bright straw. Nose: floral, fruit expression, fresh, expressive. Palate: good acidity, balanced, fine bitter notes, flavourful.

CASA MARIOL 2004 BN GRAN RESERVA
60% xarel.lo, 20% macabeo, 20% parellada.

87 Colour: bright golden. Nose: dried flowers, neat, spicy. Palate: good structure, powerful, good finish.

CASA MARIOL ARTESANAL 18 MESOS SS
macabeo, xarel.lo, parellada.

81 Colour: bright straw. Nose: fresh, expressive, dry nuts. Palate: fine bitter notes, correct, good acidity.

CELLER VELL

Partida Mas Solanes, s/n
08770 Sant Sadurní D'Anoia (Barcelona)
☎: +34 938 910 290 - Fax: +34 938 183 246
info@cellervell.com
www.cellervell.com

CELLER VELL EXTRA BRUT 2007 EXTRA BRUT GRAN RESERVA
xarel.lo, macabeo, parellada, chardonnay.

87 Colour: bright straw. Nose: ripe fruit, fine lees, grassy. Palate: fine bitter notes, good acidity, flavourful.

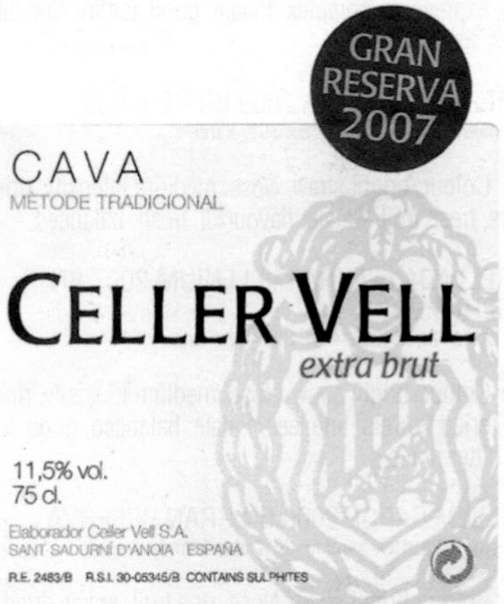

CELLER VELL 2008 BN RESERVA
xarel.lo, macabeo, parellada.

87 Color bright straw. Aroma medium intensity, fresh fruit, dried herbs, fine lees, floral. Taste fresh, fruity, flavourful, good acidity.

CELLER VELL CUVÈE LES SOLANES 2007 BN RESERVA
xarel.lo, chardonnay, pinot noir.

87 Colour: bright straw. Nose: dried herbs, fine lees, floral, dry nuts. Palate: fresh, fruity, flavourful, good acidity.

CELLERS CAROL VALLÈS

Can Parellada, s/n - Corral del Mestre
08739 Subirats (Barcelona)
☎: +34 938 989 078 - Fax: +34 938 988 413
info@cellerscarol.com
www.cellerscarol.com

GUILLEM CAROL CHARDONNAY PINOT NOIR 2008 BR RESERVA
60% chardonnay, 40% pinot noir.

85 Colour: straw. Nose: candied fruit, fine lees, medium intensity. Palate: easy to drink, spicy, fine bitter notes.

GUILLEM CAROL MILLENIUM 2003 BR GRAN RESERVA
35% parellada, 30% xarel.lo, 20% macabeo, 15% chardonnay.

86 Colour: bright golden. Nose: lees reduction notes, dry nuts, expressive, complex. Palate: good acidity, fine bitter notes, flavourful.

PARELLADA I FAURA 2009 BN RESERVA
40% parellada, 30% macabeo, 30% xarel.lo.

87 Colour: bright straw. Nose: medium intensity, dried herbs, fresh fruit. Palate: flavourful, fresh, balanced.

PARELLADA I FAURA MILLENIUM 2007 BN RESERVA
40% macabeo, 30% xarel.lo, 30% parellada.

88 Colour: bright straw. Nose: medium intensity, ripe fruit, dried flowers, fine lees. Palate: balanced, good acidity, fine bitter notes.

GUILLEM CAROL 2005 BN GRAN RESERVA
40% parellada, 40% xarel.lo, 20% chardonnay.

86 Colour: bright straw. Nose: ripe fruit, spicy, dried herbs. Palate: flavourful, good acidity, fine bitter notes.

GUILLEM CAROL PINOT NOIR ROSAT 2005 BN RESERVA
100% pinot noir.

80 Colour: raspberry rose. Nose: dried fruit, overripe fruit, lees reduction notes, fresh. Palate: easy to drink, powerful, flavourful.

GUILLEM CAROL 2005 EXTRA BRUT GRAN RESERVA
40% parellada, 36% xarel.lo, 24% chardonnay.

84 Colour: bright straw. Nose: candied fruit, dried herbs. Palate: sweetness, easy to drink.

CELLERS DE CAN SURIOL DEL CASTELL

Castell de Grabuac
08736 Font-Rubí (Barcelona)
☎: +34 938 978 426 - Fax: +34 938 978 426
cansuriol@suriol.com
www.suriol.com

SURIOL 2006 BR RESERVA
40% xarel.lo, 40% parellada, 20% macabeo.

85 Colour: bright golden. Nose: lees reduction notes, fragrant herbs, expressive. Palate: correct, flavourful, fine bitter notes.

CASTELL DE GRABUAC 2006 BN FERMENTADO EN BARRICA
80% macabeo, 20% xarel.lo.

87 Colour: bright golden. Nose: dried flowers, dry nuts, fragrant herbs. Palate: good acidity, balanced, flavourful.

SURIOL BN
50% xarel.lo, 30% macabeo, 20% parellada.

85 Colour: bright straw. Nose: dried flowers, candied fruit, fresh. Palate: slightly acidic, fine bitter notes, good finish.

SURIOL 2007 BRUT ROSÉ
pinot noir, garnacha.

85 Colour: raspberry rose. Nose: floral, fresh fruit, neat. Palate: fine bitter notes, correct, flavourful.

CELLERS PLANAS ALBAREDA

Ctra. Guardiola, Km. 3
08735 Vilobí del Penedès (Barcelona)
☎: +34 938 922 143 - Fax: +34 938 922 143
planasalbareda@yahoo.es
www.planas-albareda.com

PLANAS ALBAREDA ROSAT 2009 BR
trepat.

84 Colour: raspberry rose. Nose: fruit expression, fresh, expressive. Palate: fleshy, fruity, light-bodied.

PLANAS ALBAREDA 2008 BN
macabeo, xarel.lo, parellada.

82 Colour: bright straw. Nose: medium intensity, dried herbs, fine lees, citrus fruit. Palate: fresh, fine bitter notes, easy to drink.

PLANAS ALBAREDA RESERVA DE L'AVI 2007 BN RESERVA
macabeo, xarel.lo, parellada, chardonnay.

87 Colour: bright straw. Nose: lees reduction notes, dried flowers, expressive. Palate: unctuous, fine bitter notes, flavourful.

PLANAS ALBAREDA 2007 BN RESERVA
macabeo, xarel.lo, parellada.

85 Colour: bright straw. Nose: fresh fruit, fine lees, floral. Palate: fresh, flavourful, good acidity, easy to drink.

CHOZAS CARRASCAL

Vereda San Antonio Pol. Ind. Catastral, 16 Parcelas 136-138
46340 San Antonio de Requena (Valencia)
☎: +34 963 410 395 - Fax: +34 963 168 067
chozas@chozascarrascal.es
www.chozascarrascal.es

CHOZAS CARRASCAL BN RESERVA
chardonnay, macabeo.

93 Colour: bright yellow. Nose: ripe fruit, powerfull, dry nuts. Palate: complex, fruity, good structure, good acidity.

CODORNÍU

Avda. Jaume Codorníu, s/n
08770 Sant Sadurní D'Anoia (Barcelona)
☎: +34 938 183 232 - Fax: +34 938 910 822
s.martin@codorniu.es
www.codorniu.com

REINA Mª CRISTINA BLANC DE NOIRS 2008 BR RESERVA
87% pinot noir, 13% chardonnay.

91 Colour: bright straw. Nose: powerfull, fresh fruit, citrus fruit, grassy. Palate: flavourful, fruity, fresh.

JAUME CODORNÍU BR
chardonnay, pinot noir.

92 Colour: bright straw. Nose: powerfull, fresh fruit, citrus fruit, grassy. Palate: flavourful, fruity, fleshy, good acidity.

NON PLUS ULTRA BR
xarel.lo, macabeo, parellada.

90 Colour: bright straw. Nose: dried herbs, fine lees, floral, fresh fruit, grassy. Palate: fresh, fruity, flavourful, good acidity, sweetness.

ANNA DE CODORNÍU BR
70% chardonnay, 15% parellada, 15% xarel.lo, macabeo.

89 Colour: bright straw. Nose: fresh fruit, dried herbs, fine lees, floral, citrus fruit. Palate: fresh, fruity, flavourful, good acidity.

ANNA DE CODORNÍU ROSÉ BR
70% pinot noir, 30% chardonnay.

88 Colour: rose. Nose: fine lees, ripe fruit, red berry notes, violet drops. Palate: flavourful, fruity, fresh, fleshy.

GRAN PLUS ULTRA BN
chardonnay, parellada.

91 Colour: bright straw. Nose: complex, expressive, ripe fruit. Palate: good acidity, fine bitter notes, flavourful.

CODORNÍU PINOT NOIR EXTRA BRUT ESPUMOSO
100% pinot noir.

89 Colour: rose. Nose: red berry notes, ripe fruit, fine lees, rose petals. Palate: flavourful, fruity, fresh.

COVIDES VINYES CELLERS

Rambla Nostra Senyora, 45 - 1er
08720 Vilafranca del Penedès (Barcelona)
☎: +34 938 172 552 - Fax: +34 938 171 798
covides@covides.com
www.covides.com

DUC DE FOIX BR RESERVA ESPECIAL
chardonnay, macabeo, xarel.lo, parellada.

88 Colour: bright straw. Nose: powerfull, fresh fruit, citrus fruit. Palate: flavourful, sweetness, fine bitter notes.

DUC DE FOIX BR
macabeo, xarel.lo, parellada.

86 Colour: bright straw. Nose: powerfull, fresh, expressive, fresh fruit. Palate: flavourful, fruity, fresh.

COVIÑAS COOP. V.

Avda. Rafael Duyos, s/n
46340 Requena (Valencia)
☎: +34 962 300 680 - Fax: +34 962 302 651
covinas@covinas.com
www.covinas.com

COVIÑAS BR
75% macabeo, 12,5% xarel.lo, 12,5% parellada.

86 Colour: bright straw. Nose: fragrant herbs, fresh fruit, expressive. Palate: fresh, fruity, light-bodied.

MARQUÉS DE PLATA BR
75% macabeo, 12,5% xarel.lo, 12,5% parellada.

82 Colour: bright straw. Nose: medium intensity, fresh fruit, fine lees. Palate: fresh, fruity, flavourful.

MARQUÉS DE PLATA BN
75% macabeo, 12,5% xarel.lo, 12,5% parellada.

86 Colour: bright straw. Nose: medium intensity, fine lees, floral. Palate: fresh, flavourful, good acidity.

DOMINIO DE LA VEGA

Ctra. Madrid - Valencia, Km. 270,6
46390 San Antonio. (Valencia)
☎: +34 962 320 570 - Fax: +34 962 320 330
info@dominiodelavega.com
www.dominiodelavega.com

DOMINIO DE LA VEGA BR RESERVA
70% macabeo, 30% chardonnay.

89 Colour: bright golden. Nose: powerfull, fine lees, dried herbs, fruit liqueur notes. Palate: flavourful, sweetness, good acidity, fine bead.

DOMINIO DE LA VEGA PINOT NOIR BR
pinot noir.

88 Colour: rose. Nose: powerfull, ripe fruit, red berry notes. Palate: flavourful, sweetness, fleshy.

DOMINIO DE LA VEGA BR
macabeo.

87 Colour: bright straw. Nose: fresh fruit, dried herbs, floral. Palate: fresh, flavourful, good acidity.

ARTEMAYOR IV CAVA BN
50% chardonnay, 50% macabeo.

92 Color bright golden. Aroma fine lees, dry nuts, fragrant herbs, complex. Taste powerful, flavourful, good acidity, fine bead, fine bitter notes.

DOMINIO DE LA VEGA BN RESERVA
70% macabeo, 30% chardonnay.

90 Colour: bright straw. Nose: fresh fruit, fine lees, floral, expressive, neat. Palate: fresh, fruity, flavourful, good acidity.

DOMINIO DE LA VEGA BN
macabeo.

89 Colour: bright straw. Nose: medium intensity, fresh fruit, fine lees, floral, grassy. Palate: fresh, flavourful, good acidity.

DURAN

Font, 2
08769 Castellví de Rosanes (Barcelona)
☎: +34 937 755 446
info@cavaduran.com
www.cavaduran.com

DURAN 5V 2008 BR GRAN RESERVA
chardonnay, xarel.lo, macabeo, parellada, pinot noir.

87 Colour: bright straw. Nose: medium intensity, dried herbs, fine lees, floral. Palate: fresh, fruity, flavourful, good acidity.

DURAN ROSÉ 2008 BR GRAN RESERVA
80% pinot noir, 20% trepat.

84 Colour: light cherry. Nose: ripe fruit, floral. Palate: fruity, flavourful, good acidity, ripe fruit.

DURAN 2007 BR GRAN RESERVA
35% xarel.lo, 20% macabeo, 25% chardonnay, 20% parellada.

88 Colour: bright straw. Nose: medium intensity, dried herbs, fine lees, floral, candied fruit. Palate: fruity, flavourful, good acidity, ripe fruit, spicy.

EL XAMFRÀ - F. DOMÍNGUEZ

Lavernó, 25-27
08770 Sant Sadurní D'Anoia (Barcelona)
☎: +34 938 910 182 - Fax: +34 938 910 176
info@elxamfra.com
www.elxamfra.com

EL XAMFRÀ 2009 RD
trepat.

86 Colour: rose, purple rim. Nose: red berry notes, expressive, sweet spices, ripe fruit. Palate: correct, good acidity, fine bead.

EL XAMFRÀ 2004 BR GRAN RESERVA
xarel.lo, macabeo.

89 Colour: bright golden. Nose: fine lees, dried flowers, fresh, expressive. Palate: fine bead, good acidity, flavourful, fleshy.

EL XAMFRÀ 2007 BN RESERVA
xarel.lo, parellada, macabeo.

87 Colour: bright golden. Nose: fresh, fine lees, candied fruit. Palate: light-bodied, fresh, flavourful, easy to drink.

EL XAMFRÀ MAGNUM 2006 BN RESERVA
xarel.lo, parellada, macabeo.

90 Colour: bright straw. Nose: fine lees, white flowers, fruit expression. Palate: good acidity, fruity, fine bead, flavourful

EMENDIS

Barrio de Sant Marçal, 67
08732 Castellet i La Gornal (Barcelona)
☎: +34 938 186 119 - Fax: +34 938 918 169
avalles@emendis.es
www.emendis.es

EMENDIS BR
xarel.lo, macabeo, parellada.

88 Colour: bright straw. Nose: fresh fruit, floral, fragrant herbs. Palate: fresh, fruity, easy to drink, good acidity.

EMENDIS IMUM BN RESERVA
50% xarel.lo, 25% macabeo, 25% parellada.

90 Colour: bright straw. Nose: fresh fruit, fine lees, dried flowers, dried herbs, elegant. Palate: complex, fresh, good acidity.

EMENDIS BN GRAN RESERVA
xarel.lo, macabeo, parellada, chardonnay.

88 Colour: bright straw. Nose: medium intensity, fresh fruit, dried herbs, fine lees, floral. Palate: fresh, fruity, flavourful, good acidity.

EMENDIS BRUT ROSÉ
trepat.

86 Colour: raspberry rose. Nose: red berry notes, fragrant herbs, medium intensity, floral. Palate: fruity, flavourful, good acidity.

EUDALD MASSANA NOYA

Finca El Maset, s/n
08739 Sant Pau D'Ordal (Subirats) (Barcelona)
☎: +34 938 994 124 - Fax: +34 938 994 139
bodega@massananoya.com
www.massananoya.com

EUDALD MASSANA NOYA BN RESERVA
xarel.lo, macabeo, parellada, chardonnay.

85 Colour: bright straw. Nose: citrus fruit, fine lees, fresh. Palate: flavourful, light-bodied, easy to drink.

EUDALD MASSANA NOYA FAMÍLIA BN
xarel.lo, macabeo, parellada.

83 Colour: pale. Nose: fine lees, citrus fruit, medium intensity. Palate: fresh, light-bodied, fruity.

EUDALD MASSANA NOYA MIL.LENNI BN
xarel.lo, macabeo, chardonnay.

82 Colour: bright yellow. Nose: candied fruit, dried flowers, spicy, slightly evolved. Palate: flavourful, fruity.

FERMÍ BOHIGAS

Finca Can Maciá
08711 Ódena (Barcelona)
☎: +34 938 048 100 - Fax: +34 938 032 366
tecnic@bohigas.es
www.bohigas.es

BOHIGAS BR RESERVA
xarel.lo, macabeo, parellada.

87 Colour: bright straw. Nose: balanced, medium intensity, dried flowers, fresh fruit. Palate: flavourful, fresh, fruity, fine bitter notes.

MAS MACIÀ BR
macabeo, xarel.lo, parellada.

79

NOA DE BOHIGAS 2009 BN RESERVA
pinot noir, xarel.lo.

88 Colour: bright straw. Nose: medium intensity, fresh fruit, dried herbs, floral. Palate: fresh, fruity, flavourful, good acidity.

BOHIGAS BN GRAN RESERVA
xarel.lo, chardonnay, macabeo, parellada.

85 Colour: bright straw. Nose: medium intensity, fine lees, candied fruit. Palate: fresh, fruity, flavourful, good acidity.

FERRE I CATASUS

Ctra. de Sant Sadurní, Km. 8- Masía Can Gustems
08792 La Granada (Barcelona)
☎: +34 938 974 558 - Fax: +34 938 974 708
maracalvo@ferreicatasus.com
www.castelldelmirall.com

FERRÉ I CATASÚS 2007 BR RESERVA
55% xarel.lo, 35% macabeo, 10% parellada.

88 Colour: bright straw. Nose: fragrant herbs, powerfull, characterful, fruit liqueur notes. Palate: powerful, spirituous, good acidity, long.

CAVA ROSÉ 2007 BR
100% pinot noir.

83 Colour: rose. Nose: powerfull, ripe fruit, red berry notes. Palate: powerful, sweetness, fleshy.

MAS SUAU ROSÉ 2007 BR CRIANZA
60% monastrell, 40% trepat.

81 Colour: rose. Nose: ripe fruit, red berry notes. Palate: powerful, sweetness, good acidity.

FERRÉ I CATASÚS 2007 BN RESERVA
35% macabeo, 55% xarel.lo, 10% parellada.

90 Colour: bright golden. Nose: fine lees, dry nuts, fragrant herbs. Palate: flavourful, good acidity, fine bead, fine bitter notes.

FERRÉ I CATASÚS CLÀSSIC 2007 BN RESERVA
35% macabeo, 50% xarel.lo, 10% parellada, 5% chardonnay.

90 Colour: bright straw. Nose: fresh fruit, dried herbs, fine lees, floral. Palate: fresh, fruity, flavourful, good acidity.

MAS SUAU 2007 BN CRIANZA
40% macabeo, 30% xarel.lo, 30% parellada.

89 Colour: bright straw. Nose: medium intensity, dried herbs, fine lees, ripe fruit. Palate: fresh, fruity, flavourful, good acidity.

FINCA TORREMILANOS BODEGAS PEÑALBA LÓPEZ

Finca Torremilanos
09400 Aranda de Duero (Burgos)
☎: +34 947 512 852 - Fax: +34 947 508 044
nacional@torremilanos.com
www.torremilanos.com

PEÑALBA-LÓPEZ BN
80% viura, 20% chardonnay.

87 Colour: bright straw. Nose: medium intensity, fresh fruit, dried herbs, fine lees. Palate: fresh, fruity, flavourful, good acidity.

FINCA VALLDOSERA

Pol. Ind. Clot de Moja- Merlot, 11
08734 Moja (Barcelona)
☎: +34 938 904 353 - Fax: +34 938 904 334
www.fincavalldosera.com

VALLDOSERA BN
45% xarel.lo, 30% macabeo, 10% parellada, 10% chardonnay, 5% subirat parent.

89 Colour: bright straw. Nose: acacia flower, fine lees, dry stone, dried herbs. Palate: fine bead, fine bitter notes, fresh.

MS 4.7 BN
45% xarel.lo, 30% macabeo, 10% parellada, 10% chardonnay, 5% subirat parent.

88 Color bright straw. Aroma medium intensity, fresh fruit, dried herbs, fine lees, floral. Taste fresh, fruity, flavourful, good acidity.

VALLDOSERA SUBIRAT PARENT BN
xarel.lo, macabeo, parellada, chardonnay, subirat parent.

82 Colour: bright yellow. Nose: complex, faded flowers, honeyed notes. Palate: fine bead, powerful, lacks expression.

FREIXA RIGAU

Santa Llucía, 15
17750 Capmany (Girona)
☎: +34 972 549 012 - Fax: +34 972 549 106
comercial@grupoliveda.com
www.grupoliveda.com

FAMILIA OLIVEDA 2009 BR
50% macabeo, 30% xarel.lo, 20% parellada.

85 Colour: bright straw. Nose: medium intensity, dried herbs, candied fruit. Palate: fruity, flavourful, good acidity.

GRAN RIGAU BRUT DE BRUTS 2006 BR
40% xarel.lo, 30% macabeo, 30% parellada.

86 Colour: bright straw. Nose: fine lees, white flowers, fruit expression, neat. Palate: easy to drink, good acidity, fine bitter notes.

GRAN RIGAU ROSADO 2006 BR RESERVA
100% pinot noir.

82 Colour: light cherry. Nose: overripe fruit, medium intensity. Palate: correct, easy to drink.

FAMILIA OLIVEDA 2008 BN RESERVA
60% macabeo, 40% xarel.lo.

87 Colour: bright straw. Nose: medium intensity, fresh fruit, dried herbs, floral. Palate: fresh, fruity, good acidity.

FREIXA RIGAU NATURE MIL.LÈSSIMA RESERVA FAMILIAR 2007 BN
40% macabeo, 30% xarel.lo, 30% parellada.

88 Colour: bright straw. Nose: medium intensity, dried herbs, fine lees, ripe fruit, dried flowers. Palate: fruity, flavourful, good acidity.

GRAN RIGAU CHARDONNAY 2006 BN
100% chardonnay.

86 Colour: bright straw. Nose: medium intensity, fresh fruit, citrus fruit, fragrant herbs. Palate: easy to drink.

FREIXENET

Joan Sala, 2
08770 Sant Sadurní D'Anoia (Barcelona)
☎: +34 938 917 000 - Fax: +34 938 183 095
freixenet@freixenet.es
www.freixenet.es

FREIXENET MALVASÍA 2001 B
malvasía.

87 Colour: bright golden. Nose: candied fruit, dry nuts, toasty, honeyed notes. Palate: good acidity, rich, fruity, sweet.

TREPAT 2006 BR
100% trepat.

90 Colour: coppery red. Nose: ripe fruit, red berry notes, rose petals. Palate: flavourful, fruity, fresh, balanced.

CUVÉE D.S. 2006 BR GRAN RESERVA
40% macabeo, 40% xarel.lo, 20% parellada.

89 Colour: bright golden. Nose: dry nuts, fragrant herbs, complex. Palate: powerful, flavourful, good acidity, fine bead, fine bitter notes.

RESERVA REAL BR RESERVA
macabeo, xarel.lo, parellada, vins reserva.

94 Colour: bright golden. Nose: complex, fine lees, neat, fresh, fragrant herbs. Palate: powerful, flavourful, good acidity, fine bead, fine bitter notes, long.

BRUT BARROCO BR RESERVA
40% parellada, 30% macabeo, 30% xarel.lo.

90 Colour: bright golden. Nose: fine lees, fragrant herbs, white flowers. Palate: powerful, flavourful, good acidity, fine bead, fine bitter notes.

MERITUM BR GRAN RESERVA
40% xarel.lo, 30% macabeo, 30% parellada.

90 Colour: bright golden. Nose: fine lees, dry nuts, fragrant herbs. Palate: powerful, flavourful, fine bitter notes.

ELYSSIA PINOT NOIR BR
pinot noir, trepat.

89 Colour: rose. Nose: ripe fruit, rose petals, dried herbs. Palate: flavourful, fruity, fresh, fine bitter notes.

ELYSSIA GRAN CUVÉE BR
chardonnay, macabeo, pinot noir.

87 Colour: bright straw. Nose: fresh fruit, dried herbs, fine lees, floral. Palate: fresh, fruity, flavourful, good acidity.

CORDÓN NEGRO BR RESERVA
40% parellada, 35% macabeo, 25% xarel.lo.

86 Colour: bright straw. Nose: fresh fruit, citrus fruit, grassy. Palate: flavourful, fruity.

FREIXENET CARTA NEVADA BR RESERVA
33% macabeo, 33% xarel.lo, 33% parellada.

85 Colour: bright straw. Nose: medium intensity, dried herbs, floral. Palate: fresh, fruity, flavourful, good acidity.

FREIXENET 2006 BN RESERVA
40% macabeo, 30% xarel.lo, 30% parellada.

87 Colour: bright straw. Nose: dried herbs, fine lees, floral. Palate: fresh, fruity, flavourful, good acidity.

GIRÓ DEL GORNER

Finca Giró del Gorner, s/n
08797 Puigdálber (Barcelona)
☎: +34 938 988 032 - Fax: +34 938 988 032
gorner@girodelgorner.com
www.girodelgorner.com

GORNER 2008 BR RESERVA
macabeo, xarel.lo, parellada.

89 Colour: bright straw. Nose: fresh fruit, dried herbs, fine lees, floral. Palate: fresh, fruity, flavourful, good acidity.

GORNER 2007 BN RESERVA
macabeo, xarel.lo, parellada.

86 Colour: bright straw. Nose: fresh, ripe fruit, citrus fruit. Palate: flavourful, fruity.

GORNER 2004 BN GRAN RESERVA
macabeo, xarel.lo, parellada.

86 Colour: bright golden. Nose: dry nuts, fragrant herbs. Palate: flavourful, good acidity, fine bead.

GIRÓ RIBOT

Finca El Pont, s/n
08792 Santa Fe del Penedès (Barcelona)
☎: +34 938 974 050 - Fax: +34 938 974 311
comercial@giroribot.es
www.giroribot.es

GIRÓ RIBOT AVANT BR RESERVA
50% xarel.lo, 25% chardonnay, 15% macabeo, 10% parellada.

91 Colour: bright straw. Nose: fine lees, floral, neat, powerfull. Palate: good acidity, fine bead, unctuous, flavourful.

PAUL CHENEAU BLANC DE BLANCS BR RESERVA
47% macabeo, 33% xarel.lo, 20% parellada.

89 Colour: bright straw. Nose: medium intensity, dried herbs, fine lees, floral. Palate: fresh, fruity, flavourful, good acidity.

GIRÓ RIBOT AB ORIGINE BR RESERVA
50% macabeo, 30% xarel.lo, 20% parellada.

86 Colour: bright straw. Nose: medium intensity, dried herbs, fine lees. Palate: fresh, fruity, flavourful, good acidity.

GIRÓ RIBOT MARE 2006 BN GRAN RESERVA
50% xarel.lo, 30% macabeo, 20% parellada.

91 Colour: bright yellow. Nose: fine lees, dry nuts, fragrant herbs, complex. Palate: powerful, flavourful, good acidity, fine bead, fine bitter notes.

GIRÓ RIBOT AB ORIGINE 2006 BN GRAN RESERVA
50% macabeo, 30% xarel.lo, 20% parellada.

87 Colour: bright golden. Nose: dry nuts, fragrant herbs. Palate: powerful, flavourful, good acidity, fine bead, fine bitter notes.

GIRÓ RIBOT AB ORIGINE BRUT ROSADO
85% trepat, 15% pinot noir.

86 Colour: light cherry. Nose: red berry notes, dried flowers, balanced. Palate: fruity, fresh, flavourful, good acidity.

GIRÓ RIBOT TENDENCIAS EXTRA BRUT
50% macabeo, 30% xarel.lo, 20% macabeo.

85 Colour: bright straw. Nose: medium intensity, fresh fruit, dried herbs. Palate: fresh, fruity, flavourful.

GRAMONA

Industria, 34-36
08770 Sant Sadurní D'Anoia (Barcelona)
☎: +34 938 910 113 - Fax: +34 938 183 284
comunicacion@gramona.com
www.gramona.com

GRAMONA ARGENT 2007 BR RESERVA
100% chardonnay.

92 Colour: bright straw. Nose: powerfull, ripe fruit, citrus fruit, cocoa bean, sweet spices. Palate: flavourful, powerful, long, good acidity.

GRAMONA ALLEGRO BR
33% chardonnay, 33% macabeo, 33% xarel.lo.

90 Colour: bright straw. Nose: fresh fruit, dried herbs, fine lees, floral. Palate: fresh, fruity, flavourful, good acidity.

GRAMONA CELLER BATLLE 2001 BR GRAN RESERVA
70% xarel.lo, 30% macabeo.

94 Colour: bright golden. Nose: fine lees, dry nuts, fragrant herbs, complex, creamy oak. Palate: powerful, flavourful, good acidity, fine bead, fine bitter notes.

GRAMONA CELLER BATLLE 2000 BR GRAN RESERVA
70% xarel.lo, 30% macabeo.

97 Colour: bright yellow. Nose: expressive, characterful, complex, candied fruit. Palate: flavourful, good acidity, fine bitter notes, spicy, round.

GRAMONA IMPERIAL 2006 BR GRAN RESERVA
50% xarel.lo, 40% macabeo, 10% chardonnay.

93 Colour: bright golden. Nose: dry nuts, fragrant herbs, complex. Palate: powerful, flavourful, good acidity, fine bead.

GRAMONA ROSÉ BR
pinot noir.

87 Colour: onion pink. Nose: ripe fruit, fresh, expressive, floral. Palate: spicy, good acidity, fine bitter notes, correct.

GRAMONA III LUSTROS 2004 BN GRAN RESERVA
70% xarel.lo, 30% macabeo.

91 Colour: bright golden. Nose: fragrant herbs, complex, lees reduction notes, dry nuts. Palate: flavourful, good acidity, fine bead, fine bitter notes.

GRAMONA GRAN CUVÉE DE POSTRE ESP GRAN RESERVA
xarel.lo, macabeo, parellada.

88 Colour: bright straw. Nose: fruit expression, expressive, sweet spices, pattiserie. Palate: easy to drink, good acidity, correct.

GRAMONA LA SUITE SC RESERVA
xarel.lo, macabeo, parellada.

89 Colour: bright straw. Nose: fresh fruit, expressive, fragrant herbs. Palate: good acidity, fine bitter notes, complex, flavourful.

GRAN DUCAY BODEGAS

Ctra. N-330, Km. 450
50400 Cariñena (Zaragoza)
☎: +34 976 620 400 - Fax: +34 976 620 398
bsv@sanvalero.com
www.sanvalero.com

GRAN DUCAY BN
macabeo, xarel.lo, parellada.

85 Colour: bright straw. Nose: fresh, fresh fruit, floral. Palate: flavourful, fine bitter notes, dry.

GRAN DUCAY ROSÉ BN
100% garnacha.

82 Colour: coppery red. Nose: fruit liqueur notes, warm. Palate: sweetness, good finish.

GRIMAU DE PUJADES

Castell de Les Pujades, s/n
08732 La Munia (Barcelona)
☎: +34 938 918 031 - Fax: +34 938 918 427
grimau@grimau.com
www.grimau.com

GRIMAU BR
macabeo, xarel.lo, parellada.

88 Colour: bright straw. Nose: fresh fruit, citrus fruit, white flowers, elegant. Palate: fresh, good acidity, fine bitter notes.

GRIMAU BN
macabeo, xarel.lo, parellada.

88 Colour: pale. Nose: fine lees, citrus fruit, white flowers, expressive, fresh. Palate: good acidity, balanced, light-bodied, flavourful.

TRENCADÍS BN
macabeo, xarel.lo, parellada, chardonnay.

87 Colour: bright straw. Nose: fresh fruit, dried herbs, fine lees, floral. Palate: fresh, fruity, flavourful, good acidity.

GRIMAU RESERVA FAMILIAR BN
macabeo, xarel.lo, parellada, chardonnay.

86 Colour: bright straw. Nose: candied fruit, fine lees, fresh. Palate: spicy, flavourful, fine bitter notes.

TRENCADÍS ROSAT BN
garnacha, pinot noir.

82 Colour: rose. Nose: fruit preserve, short. Palate: sweetness, easy to drink.

HERETAT MAS TINELL

Ctra. de Vilafranca a St. Martí Sarroca, Km. 0,5
08720 Vilafranca del Penedès (Barcelona)
☎: +34 938 170 586 - Fax: +34 938 170 500
info@mastinell.com
www.mastinell.com

MAS TINELL BRUT ROSÉ 2007 BR RESERVA
100% trepat.

90 Colour: onion pink. Nose: complex, expressive, red berry notes, floral. Palate: good acidity, fine bead, fine bitter notes, fruity.

MAS TINELL BRUT REAL 2007 BR RESERVA
35% macabeo, 30% xarel.lo, 35% parellada.

88 Colour: bright straw. Nose: fine lees, white flowers, expressive, neat. Palate: good acidity, fruity, flavourful.

MAS TINELL BRUT REAL MAGNUM 2006 BR RESERVA
35% macabeo, 30% xarel.lo, 35% parellada.

89 Colour: bright straw. Nose: complex, fresh, expressive, fresh fruit. Palate: fine bead, good acidity, easy to drink, flavourful.

MAS TINELL NATURE REAL 2005 BN GRAN RESERVA
30% macabeo, 40% xarel.lo, 25% parellada, 5% chardonnay.

85 Colour: bright straw. Nose: lees reduction notes, fruit liqueur notes, fresh. Palate: flavourful, fleshy, correct.

MAS TINELL CRISTINA VINTAGE 2006 EXTRA BRUT GRAN RESERVA
10% macabeo, 35% xarel.lo, 35% parellada, 20% chardonnay.

88 Colour: bright straw. Nose: fine lees, fragrant herbs, complex, floral. Palate: flavourful, good acidity, fine bead.

MAS TINELL CARPE DIEM RESERVA ESPECIAL 2005 BN RESERVA
30% xarel.lo, 30% parellada, 40% chardonnay.

88 Colour: bright straw. Nose: fine lees, floral, fragrant herbs, expressive, complex. Palate: fruity, flavourful, great length.

J. M. SOGAS MASCARÓ

Amalia Soler, 35
08720 Vilafranca del Penedès (Barcelona)
☎: +34 931 184 107
info@sogasmascaro.com

SOGAS MASCARÓ BR
macabeo, xarel.lo, parellada.

85 Colour: bright straw. Nose: citrus fruit, white flowers, fragrant herbs. Palate: flavourful, spicy, fine bitter notes.

SOGAS MASCARÓ 2007 BN
macabeo, xarel.lo, parellada.

85 Colour: bright straw. Nose: fresh fruit, dried herbs, floral. Palate: fresh, fruity, good acidity.

SOGAS MASCARÓ BN RESERVA
macabeo, xarel.lo, parellada.

85 Colour: bright straw. Nose: fresh fruit, dried herbs, floral. Palate: fresh, fruity, flavourful, good acidity.

JANÉ VENTURA

Ctra. Calafell, 2
43700 El Vendrell (Tarragona)
☎: +34 977 660 118 - Fax: +34 977 661 239
janeventura@janeventura.com
www.janeventura.com

JANÉ VENTURA RESERVA DE LA MÚSICA 2008 BR RESERVA
macabeo, xarel.lo, parellada.

90 Colour: bright straw. Nose: fresh, elegant, fragrant herbs, faded flowers. Palate: elegant, correct, good acidity, fresh, flavourful.

JANÉ VENTURA RESERVA DE LA MÚSICA ROSÉ 2008 BR RESERVA

89 Colour: rose. Nose: varietal, fresh, neat, red berry notes, powerfull. Palate: good acidity, fine bead, fruity, fresh.

JANÉ VENTURA RESERVA DE LA MÚSICA 2007 BR
xarel.lo, macabeo, parellada.

89 Colour: bright straw. Nose: fresh fruit, dried herbs, fine lees, floral. Palate: fresh, fruity, flavourful, good acidity.

JANÉ VENTURA VINTAGE 2007 BN GRAN RESERVA
51% xarel.lo, 29% macabeo, 20% parellada.

90 Colour: bright straw. Nose: fragrant herbs, white flowers, ripe fruit, citrus fruit, fine lees. Palate: flavourful, fruity, fleshy, full.

JANÉ VENTURA RESERVA DE LA MÚSICA 2007 BN RESERVA
38% xarel.lo, 32% macabeo, 30% parellada.

89 Colour: bright straw. Nose: dried herbs, fresh fruit, citrus fruit, white flowers. Palate: flavourful, fruity, fresh, fleshy.

JANÉ VENTURA DE L'ORGUE BN
xarel.lo, macabeo, parellada.

92 Colour: bright straw. Nose: fine lees, ripe fruit, citrus fruit, expressive, neat, elegant. Palate: flavourful, fruity, fresh, fleshy.

JAUME GIRÓ I GIRÓ

Montaner i Oller, 5
08770 Sant Sadurní D'Anoia (Barcelona)
☎: +34 938 910 165 - Fax: +34 938 911 271
cavagiro@cavagiro.com
www.cavagiro.com

JAUME GIRÓ I GIRÓ CAL REI 2005 BR GRAN RESERVA
40% parellada, 40% xarel.lo, 20% chardonnay.

89 Color bright golden. Aroma fine lees, dry nuts, fragrant herbs, complex. Taste powerful, flavourful, good acidity, fine bead, fine bitter notes.

JAUME GIRÓ I GIRÓ BOMBONETTA 2005 BR GRAN RESERVA
40% parellada, 40% xarel.lo, 20% chardonnay.

89 Colour: yellow. Nose: ripe fruit, balanced, fine lees, dried flowers. Palate: balanced, good acidity, flavourful.

JAUME GIRÓ I GIRÓ GRANDALLA 2004 BR GRAN RESERVA
40% parellada, 45% xarel.lo, 15% chardonnay.

89 Colour: bright yellow. Nose: ripe fruit, elegant, expressive, floral. Palate: fruity, good acidity, fine bead, fine bitter notes.

JAUME GIRÓ I GIRÓ DE CAL REI BR RESERVA
40% xarel.lo, 40% parellada, 20% chardonnay.

86 Colour: bright straw. Nose: medium intensity, fresh fruit, dried herbs. Palate: fresh, fruity, flavourful, good acidity.

JAUME GIRÓ I GIRÓ MONTANER 2007 BN GRAN RESERVA
40% parellada, 32,5% xarel.lo, 25% macabeo, 2,5% chardonnay.

87 Colour: bright straw. Nose: fragrant herbs, dried flowers, fine lees, medium intensity. Palate: fruity, good acidity.

JAUME GIRÓ I GIRÓ SELECTE 2006 BN GRAN RESERVA
40% parellada, 35% macabeo, 20% xarel.lo, 10% chardonnay.

90 Colour: bright straw. Nose: medium intensity, fresh fruit, dried herbs, fine lees, floral, complex. Palate: fresh, fruity, flavourful, good acidity.

JAUME GIRÓ I GIRÓ 2005 BN GRAN RESERVA
40% parellada, 40% xarel.lo, 20% chardonnay.

89 Colour: bright yellow. Nose: fine lees, ripe fruit, spicy, dried herbs, complex. Palate: flavourful, fruity, good acidity, fine bitter notes.

JAUME LLOPART ALEMANY

Font Rubí, 9
08736 Font-Rubí (Barcelona)
☎: +34 938 979 133 - Fax: +34 938 979 133
info@jaumellopartalemany.com
www.jaumellopartalemany.com

JAUME LLOPART ALEMANY 2007 BR RESERVA
macabeo, parellada, xarel.lo.

88 Colour: bright straw. Nose: fresh fruit, dried herbs, fine lees, floral. Palate: fruity, flavourful, good acidity.

JAUME LLOPART ALEMANY ROSADO 2008 BN RESERVA
pinot noir.

87 Colour: rose, purple rim. Nose: red berry notes, ripe fruit, expressive. Palate: flavourful, fruity, fresh.

JAUME LLOPART ALEMANY 2007 BN RESERVA
macabeo, parellada, xarel.lo.

85 Colour: bright straw. Nose: medium intensity, dried herbs, fine lees. Palate: fruity, flavourful, good acidity.

JAUME LLOPART ALEMANY VINYA D'EN FERRAN 2006 BN GRAN RESERVA
pinot noir, chardonnay.

92 Colour: bright golden. Nose: fragrant herbs, complex, expressive, dry nuts. Palate: powerful, flavourful, good acidity, fine bead, fine bitter notes.

JAUME LLOPART ALEMANY 2006 BN GRAN RESERVA
macabeo, parellada, xarel.lo.

90 Colour: bright straw. Nose: fine lees, floral, ripe fruit, grassy. Palate: fresh, fruity, flavourful, good acidity, fine bead.

JAUME SERRA

Ctra. de Vilanova, Km. 2,5
08800 Vilanova i la Geltrú (Barcelona)
☎: +34 938 936 404 - Fax: +34 938 142 262
jaumeserra@jgc.es
www.garciacarrion.es

JAUME SERRA CHARDONNAY 2006
100% chardonnay.

83 Colour: bright straw. Nose: expressive, candied fruit, neat. Palate: easy to drink, light-bodied, flavourful.

JAUME SERRA ROSADO BR
80% trepat, 20% pinot noir.

85 Colour: rose, purple rim. Nose: fruit expression, fresh, neat. Palate: correct, unctuous, light-bodied, flavourful.

JAUME SERRA VINTAGE 2007 BN
30% macabeo, 30% chardonnay, 25% parellada, 15% xarel.lo.

80 Colour: bright straw. Nose: floral, citrus fruit, fresh. Palate: fresh, slightly acidic, fine bitter notes.

JAUME SERRA BN RESERVA
45% macabeo, 25% parellada, 15% xarel.lo, 15% chardonnay.

82 Colour: bright straw. Nose: fine lees, dried flowers, citrus fruit, fresh. Palate: fine bitter notes, fresh, light-bodied.

JAUME SERRA BN
50% macabeo, 25% xarel.lo, 25% parellada.

80 Colour: bright straw. Nose: fine lees, floral, overripe fruit. Palate: light-bodied, fresh, slightly evolved.

JOAN RAVENTÓS ROSELL

Ctra. Sant Sadurní a Masquefa, Km. 6,5
08783 Masquefa (Barcelona)
☎: +34 937 725 251 - Fax: +34 937 727 191
export@raventosrosell.com
www.raventosrosell.com

JOAN RAVENTÓS ROSELL 2009 BR
chardonnay, macabeo, parellada, xarel.lo.

85 Colour: bright golden. Nose: spicy, roasted almonds, dry nuts. Palate: fine bitter notes, good acidity, correct.

MARIEN 2008 BR RESERVA
chardonnay, macabeo, parellada.

85 Colour: bright straw. Nose: fine lees, floral, expressive. Palate: light-bodied, fresh, flavourful.

JOAN RAVENTÒS ROSELL 2008 BR RESERVA
chardonnay, macabeo, parellada.

78

JOAN RAVENTÓS ROSELL 2009 BN
chardonnay, macabeo, parellada, xarel.lo.

85 Colour: bright straw. Nose: spicy, dried herbs, dry nuts. Palate: good acidity, fine bitter notes, flavourful.

GRADIVA 2008 BN
chardonnay, macabeo, parellada, xarel.lo, pinot noir.

85 Colour: bright straw. Nose: fine lees, spicy, dry nuts, expressive. Palate: balanced, fine bitter notes, flavourful.

GRAN HERETAT VALL-VENTÓS 2008 BN
chardonnay, macabeo, parellada, pinot noir.

84 Colour: bright golden. Nose: fragrant herbs, lees reduction notes, expressive. Palate: fine bitter notes, correct, spicy.

HERETAT VALL-VENTOS DONE'S ROSÉ 2009 BRUT ROSADO
pinot noir.

78

JOAN SARDÀ

Ctra. Vilafranca a St. Jaume dels Domenys, Km. 8,1
08732 Castellvi de la Marca (Barcelona)
☎: +34 937 720 900 - Fax: +34 937 721 495
joansarda@joansarda.com
www.joansarda.com

JOAN SARDÀ BR RESERVA
macabeo, xarel.lo, parellada.

88 Colour: bright straw. Nose: fresh fruit, dried herbs, floral. Palate: fresh, fruity, flavourful, good acidity.

JOAN SARDÁ ROSÉ BR RESERVA
monastrell, garnacha.

86 Colour: rose. Nose: ripe fruit, red berry notes, floral. Palate: ripe fruit, good acidity.

JOAN SARDÀ MILLENIUM BN RESERVA
macabeo, xarel.lo, parellada.

88 Colour: bright straw. Nose: fresh fruit, citrus fruit, jasmine. Palate: flavourful, fresh, fleshy.

JOAN SARDÀ BN RESERVA
macabeo, xarel.lo, parellada.

87 Colour: bright straw. Nose: fresh fruit, fine lees, floral, fragrant herbs. Palate: fresh, fruity, flavourful, good acidity.

JOSEP Mª RAVENTÓS BLANC

Plaça del Roure, s/n
08770 Sant Sadurní D'Anoia (Barcelona)
☎: +34 938 183 262 - Fax: +34 938 912 500
raventos@raventos.com
www.raventos.com

L'HEREU BR
macabeo, xarel.lo, parellada.

90 Colour: bright straw. Nose: fresh fruit, dried herbs, fine lees, white flowers. Palate: fresh, fruity, good acidity.

RAVENTÓS I BLANC DE NIT BR
macabeo, xarel.lo, parellada, monastrell.

90 Colour: coppery red. Nose: ripe fruit, red berry notes, violet drops, expressive. Palate: flavourful, fruity, fresh, good acidity.

ELISABET RAVENTÓS BR
xarel.lo, chardonnay, monastrell.

89 Color bright straw. Aroma medium intensity, fresh fruit, dried herbs, fine lees, floral. Taste fresh, fruity, flavourful, good acidity.

RAVENTÓS I BLANC GRAN RESERVA PERSONAL M.R.N. 1999 BN
40% parellada, 25% xarel.lo, 25% macabeo, 10% chardonnay.

96 Colour: bright golden. Nose: dry nuts, fragrant herbs, expressive, lactic notes. Palate: powerful, good acidity, fine bead, fine bitter notes, flavourful.

MAGNUM LA FINCA BN GRAN RESERVA
xarel.lo, macabeo, parellada, chardonnay, pinot noir.

93 Colour: bright golden. Nose: fine lees, dry nuts, fragrant herbs. Palate: powerful, flavourful, good acidity, fine bead, fine bitter notes.

RAVENTÓS I BLANC GRAN RESERVA DE LA FINCA BN GRAN RESERVA
xarel.lo, macabeo, parellada, chardonnay, pinot noir.

89 Colour: bright straw. Nose: fresh fruit, dried herbs, fine lees, floral, citrus fruit. Palate: fresh, fruity, flavourful, good acidity.

JUVÉ Y CAMPS

Sant Venat, 1
08770 Sant Sadurní D'Anoia (Barcelona)
☎: +34 938 911 000 - Fax: +34 938 912 100
juveycamps@juveycamps.com
www.juveycamps.com

JUVÉ & CAMPS BLANC DE NOIRS 2008
50% pinot noir, 30% chardonnay, 20% xarel.lo.

90 Colour: bright straw. Nose: white flowers, ripe fruit, citrus fruit, fragrant herbs. Palate: ripe fruit, flavourful, fruity.

GRAN JUVÉ CAMPS 2007 BR GRAN RESERVA
25% macabeo, 25% xarel.lo, 25% parellada, 25% chardonnay.

92 Color bright golden. Aroma fine lees, dry nuts, fragrant herbs, complex. Taste powerful, flavourful, good acidity, fine bead, fine bitter notes.

JUVÉ & CAMPS MILESIMÉ CHARDONNAY 2007 BR RESERVA
100% chardonnay.

91 Colour: bright golden. Nose: dry nuts, fragrant herbs, complex, ripe fruit, fine lees. Palate: powerful, flavourful, good acidity, fine bead, fine bitter notes.

JUVÉ & CAMPS CINTA PÚRPURA BR RESERVA
47% macabeo, 32% parellada, 21% xarel.lo.

89 Colour: bright straw. Nose: ripe fruit, citrus fruit, white flowers. Palate: flavourful, fruity, fleshy, long.

JUVÉ & CAMPS ROSÉ BR
100% pinot noir.

87 Colour: rose. Nose: ripe fruit, red berry notes, expressive, rose petals. Palate: flavourful, powerful, fleshy, ripe fruit.

JUVÉ & CAMPS RESERVA DE LA FAMILIA MAGNUM 2008 BN RESERVA
macabeo, xarel.lo, parellada.

93 Colour: bright straw. Nose: dried herbs, fine lees, floral, fresh fruit. Palate: fresh, fruity, flavourful, good acidity.

JUVÉ & CAMPS RESERVA DE LA FAMILIA 2008 BN GRAN RESERVA
45% xarel.lo, 30% macabeo, 15% parellada, 10% chardonnay.

91 Colour: bright golden. Nose: dry nuts, fragrant herbs, complex, dried flowers. Palate: powerful, flavourful, good acidity, fine bead, fine bitter notes.

L'ORIGAN

Avernó, 28
08770 Sant Sadurní D'Anoia (Barcelona)
☎: +34 938 183 602 - Fax: +34 938 913 461
lorigan@lorigancava.com
www.lorigancava.com

L'O DE L'ORIGAN MAGNUM BN
xarel.lo, macabeo, parellada, chardonnay.

91 Color bright golden. Aroma fine lees, dry nuts, fragrant herbs, complex. Taste powerful, flavourful, good acidity, fine bead, fine bitter notes.

AIRE DE L'O DE L'ORIGAN BN
macabeo, xarel.lo, parellada, chardonnay.

90 Colour: bright straw. Nose: fresh fruit, dried herbs, fine lees, floral. Palate: fresh, fruity, flavourful, good acidity.

L'O DE L'ORIGAN BN
xarel.lo, macabeo, parellada, chardonnay.

88 Colour: bright straw. Nose: dried herbs, floral, lees reduction notes, ripe fruit. Palate: fresh, fruity, flavourful, good acidity.

LLOPART CAVA

Ctra. de Sant Sadurni - Ordal, Km. 4
08739 Subirats (Barcelona)
☎: +34 938 993 125 - Fax: +34 938 993 038
llopart@llopart.es
www.llopart.es

LLOPART ROSÉ 2008 BR RESERVA
60% monastrell, 20% garnacha, 20% pinot noir.

87 Colour: rose. Nose: ripe fruit, red berry notes, sweet spices. Palate: flavourful, fruity, fleshy.

LLOPART IMPERIAL 2007 BR GRAN RESERVA
45% xarel.lo, 40% macabeo, 5% parellada.

87 Colour: bright straw. Nose: medium intensity, fresh fruit, floral, grassy. Palate: fresh, fruity, flavourful, good acidity.

LLOPART EX-VITE 2005 BR GRAN RESERVA
60% xarel.lo, 40% macabeo.

91 Color bright golden. Aroma fine lees, dry nuts, fragrant herbs, complex. Taste powerful, flavourful, good acidity, fine bead, fine bitter notes.

LLOPART LEOPARDI 2006 BN GRAN RESERVA
40% macabeo, 40% xarel.lo, 10% parellada, 10% chardonnay.

92 Colour: bright golden. Nose: fine lees, complex, fresh fruit. Palate: powerful, flavourful, good acidity, fine bead, fine bitter notes.

LLOPART INTEGRAL 2009 BN RESERVA
45% parellada, 30% chardonnay, 25% xarel.lo.

87 Colour: bright straw. Nose: powerfull, fresh fruit, grassy, white flowers. Palate: flavourful, fruity, fleshy, good acidity.

LLOPART 2008 BN RESERVA
35% macabeo, 30% xarel.lo, 25% parellada, 10% chardonnay.

87 Colour: bright straw. Nose: medium intensity, fresh fruit, dried herbs, floral, fine lees. Palate: fresh, fruity, flavourful, good acidity.

LLOPART MICROCOSMOS ROSÉ 2007 BN RESERVA
85% pinot noir, 15% monastrell.

87 Colour: rose, purple rim. Nose: powerfull, ripe fruit, sweet spices, floral. Palate: flavourful, fruity, balanced.

LLOPART NÉCTAR TERRENAL 2008 SEMIDULCE RESERVA
70% xarel.lo, 30% parellada.

85 Colour: bright straw. Nose: powerfull, candied fruit, sweet spices, white flowers. Palate: flavourful, fruity, sweet.

LOXAREL

Masia Can Mayol, s/n
08735 Vilobí del Penedès (Barcelona)
☎: +34 938 978 001 - Fax: +34 938 978 111
loxarel@loxarel.com
www.loxarel.com

LOXAREL VINTAGE 2008 BN
xarel.lo, chardonnay, macabeo.

89 Colour: bright straw. Nose: fresh fruit, dried herbs, fine lees, floral. Palate: fresh, fruity, flavourful, good acidity.

MM DE LOXAREL 2007 BN
pinot noir, xarel.lo, chardonnay.

88 Color bright golden. Aroma fine lees, dry nuts, fragrant herbs, complex. Taste powerful, flavourful, good acidity, fine bead, fine bitter notes.

REFUGI DE LOXAREL 2007 BN RESERVA
xarel.lo, chardonnay, macabeo.

87 Color bright golden. Aroma fine lees, dry nuts, fragrant herbs, complex. Taste powerful, flavourful, good acidity, fine bead, fine bitter notes.

LOXAREL RESERVA FAMILIA 2006 BN
xarel.lo, chardonnay, macabeo.

90 Colour: bright golden. Nose: dry nuts, fragrant herbs, complex, pattiserie. Palate: powerful, flavourful, good acidity, fine bead, fine bitter notes.

LOXAREL 2006 BN GRAN RESERVA
xarel.lo, chardonnay, macabeo.

85 Colour: bright golden. Nose: dry nuts, fragrant herbs. Palate: powerful, flavourful, good acidity, fine bead, fine bitter notes.

999 DE LOXAREL BRUT ROSADO
pinot noir, xarel.lo.

87 Colour: coppery red. Nose: floral, red berry notes, ripe fruit. Palate: flavourful, fruity, sweetness.

MARCELINO DÍAZ

Mecánica, s/n
06200 Almendralejo (Badajoz)
☎: +34 924 677 548 - Fax: +34 924 660 977
bodega@madiaz.com
www.madiaz.com

PUERTA PALMA BR
100% macabeo.

80 Colour: bright yellow. Nose: dried herbs, lees reduction notes, medium intensity. Palate: fleshy, easy to drink, slightly overripe.

PUERTA PALMA BN RESERVA
80% macabeo, 20% parellada.

81 Colour: bright straw. Nose: ripe fruit, dry nuts. Palate: fine bitter notes, correct, easy to drink.

MARQUÉS DE LA CONCORDIA FAMILY OF WINES

Monistrol D'Anoia, s/n
08770 Sant Sadurní D'Anoia (Barcelona)
☎: +34 914 365 900
www.haciendas-espana.com

MM BRUT VINTAGE 2008 BR
35% xarel.lo, 25% chardonnay, 25% parellada, 15% macabeo.

89 Color bright straw. Aroma medium intensity, fresh fruit, dried herbs, fine lees, floral. Taste fresh, fruity, flavourful, good acidity.

MM PREMIUM CUVÉE MILLESIME 2007 BR
35% chardonnay, 25% macabeo, 15% xarel.lo, 25% parellada.

90 Colour: bright straw. Nose: dried herbs, fine lees, floral, expressive, fresh fruit. Palate: fresh, fruity, flavourful, good acidity.

MM PREMIUM CUVÉE ROSÉ BRUT MILLESIME 2007 BR
70% pinot noir, 30% monastrell.

88 Colour: brilliant rose. Nose: red berry notes, fresh fruit, fruit expression. Palate: flavourful, fruity, fresh.

MARQUÉS DE MONISTROL

Monistrol d'Anoia, s/n
08770 Sant Sadurní D'Anoia (Barcelona)
☎: +34 914 365 900

MARQUÉS DE MONISTROL PREMIUM CUVÉE 2008 BN
15% xarel.lo, 30% parellada, 25% chardonnay, 30% macabeo.

85 Colour: bright straw. Nose: white flowers, fresh fruit, citrus fruit, grassy. Palate: flavourful, fruity, fresh, fleshy.

MARQUÉS DE MONISTROL BN
30% macabeo, 30% parellada, 25% chardonnay, 15% xarel.lo.

88 Colour: bright straw. Nose: dried herbs, fine lees, floral, ripe fruit. Palate: fresh, fruity, flavourful, good acidity.

MARQUÉS DE MONISTROL PREMIUM CUVÉE 2007 BRUT ROSÉ
70% pinot noir, 30% monastrell.

86 Colour: rose, purple rim. Nose: red berry notes, fresh fruit, rose petals. Palate: flavourful, fruity, fresh.

CLOS MONISTROL 2008 EXTRA BRUT
35% xarel.lo, 25% chardonnay, 20% macabeo, 20% parellada.

87 Colour: bright straw. Nose: fresh fruit, dried herbs, fine lees. Palate: fresh, fruity, flavourful, good acidity.

MARRUGAT

Doctor Pasteur, 6
08720 Vilafranca del Penedès (Barcelona)
☎: +34 938 903 066 - Fax: +34 938 170 979
pinord@pinord.es
www.pinord.es

MARRUGAT 2009 BR
xarel.lo, macabeo, parellada.

87 Colour: bright straw. Nose: medium intensity, ripe fruit, citrus fruit. Palate: flavourful, fruity, fresh.

MARRUGAT ROSADO 2007 BR RESERVA
trepat.

91 Colour: rose, purple rim. Nose: red berry notes, fresh fruit, fine lees. Palate: flavourful, sweetness, fine bitter notes, good acidity.

MARRUGAT GRAN BRUT 2007 BR RESERVA
xarel.lo, macabeo, parellada.

86 Colour: bright straw. Nose: fresh fruit, dried herbs, fine lees, floral. Palate: fresh, fruity, flavourful, good acidity.

MARRUGAT CHARDONNAY 2006 BR RESERVA
chardonnay.

85 Colour: bright straw. Nose: grassy, fresh fruit, citrus fruit, white flowers. Palate: powerful, complex, balanced.

MARRUGAT 2005 BN GRAN RESERVA
xarel.lo, macabeo, parellada.

87 Colour: bright straw. Nose: powerfull, fresh fruit, grassy, white flowers. Palate: flavourful, fruity, fresh, ripe fruit.

MARRUGAT SUSPIRUM 2005 BN
xarel.lo, macabeo, parellada, chardonnay.

85 Colour: bright straw. Nose: medium intensity, dried herbs, floral. Palate: fresh, fruity, flavourful.

MARRUGAT RIMA 32 BN RESERVA
pinot noir, chardonnay.

90 Colour: bright straw. Nose: white flowers, fresh fruit, citrus fruit, grassy. Palate: flavourful, good acidity, fine bitter notes, long.

MARRUGAT 2009 SS
xarel.lo, macabeo, parellada.

86 Colour: bright straw. Nose: candied fruit, citrus fruit, expressive. Palate: flavourful, sweet, good acidity.

MARTÍ SERDÀ

Ctra. de Igualada a Vilafranca, Km. 31,300
08792 Santa Fe del Penedès (Barcelona)
☎: +34 938 974 411 - Fax: +34 938 974 405
info@martiserda.com
www.martiserda.com

MARTÍ SERDÀ XAREL.LO 2010 B
100% xarel.lo.

87 Colour: bright straw, greenish rim. Nose: white flowers, medium intensity, balanced. Palate: flavourful, full, good acidity.

MARTÍ SERDÀ CHARDONNAY BR
100% chardonnay.

86 Colour: bright straw. Nose: fresh, expressive, fragrant herbs. Palate: fruity, flavourful, light-bodied.

MARTÍ SERDÀ BR
35% macabeo, 35% parellada, 30% xarel.lo.

86 Colour: bright straw. Nose: medium intensity, dried herbs, fine lees, floral. Palate: fresh, fruity, flavourful, good acidity.

MARTÍ SERDÀ CUVÉE REAL BN GRAN RESERVA
50% macabeo, 25% xarel.lo, 25% vino reserva.

90 Colour: bright straw. Nose: complex, medium intensity, elegant, floral. Palate: fruity, flavourful, good acidity, fine bead.

MARTÍ SERDÀ BN RESERVA
40% xarel.lo, 35% chardonnay, 25% macabeo.

88 Colour: bright straw. Nose: medium intensity, fresh fruit, dried herbs, floral, lees reduction notes. Palate: fresh, fruity, flavourful, good acidity.

MARTÍ SERDÀ BRUT ROSÉ
35% garnacha, 35% pinot noir, 30% trepat.

87 Colour: rose. Nose: red berry notes, candied fruit, expressive. Palate: flavourful, powerful, fleshy, sweetness.

MAS BERTRAN VITICULTORS

Avda. Josep Anselm Clavé, 25
08731 St. Martí Sarroca (Barcelona)
☎: +34 938 990 859 - Fax: +34 938 990 859
info@masbertranviticultors.com
www.masbertranviticultors.com

BALMA 2007 BN RESERVA
55% macabeo, 45% xarel.lo.

88 Colour: bright yellow. Nose: balanced, medium intensity, dry nuts, dried flowers. Palate: fresh, fruity, good acidity.

ARGILA 2007 BN GRAN RESERVA
100% xarel.lo.

88 Colour: bright yellow. Nose: candied fruit, fine lees, fragrant herbs, dried flowers. Palate: flavourful, good acidity.

MAS CODINA

Barri El Gorner, s/n - Mas Codina
08797 Puigdalber (Barcelona)
☎: +34 938 988 166 - Fax: +34 938 988 166
info@mascodina.com
www.mascodina.com

MAS CODINA 2007 BR
50% macabeo, 35% xarel.lo, 10% chardonnay, 5% pinot noir.

85 Colour: bright straw. Nose: medium intensity, dried herbs, floral, ripe fruit. Palate: fresh, fruity, flavourful, good acidity.

MAS CODINA 2007 BN RESERVA
50% macabeo, 35% xarel.lo, 10% chardonnay, 5% pinot noir.

89 Colour: bright straw. Nose: fresh fruit, dried herbs, fine lees, floral, expressive. Palate: fresh, fruity, flavourful, good acidity.

MAS CODINA 2006 BN RESERVA ESPECIAL
47% chardonnay, 38% macabeo, 10% xarel.lo, 5% parellada.

88 Color bright straw. Aroma medium intensity, fresh fruit, dried herbs, fine lees, floral. Taste fresh, fruity, flavourful, good acidity.

MAS ROMANI

Mas Romaní
08736 Font-Rubí (Barcelona)
☎: +34 938 988 027 - Fax: +34 938 974 486
masromani@hotmail.com
www.masromani.com

MAS ROMANI BR RESERVA
40% parellada, 30% xarel.lo, 30% macabeo.

86 Colour: bright straw. Nose: fine lees, candied fruit, expressive. Palate: fine bitter notes, correct, fresh, light-bodied.

MAS ROMANI BR GRAN RESERVA
40% macabeo, 33% xarel.lo, 20% parellada, 7% chardonnay.

86 Colour: bright straw. Nose: lees reduction notes, candied fruit, fresh. Palate: fine bitter notes, confected, correct.

MASCARÓ

Casal, 9
08720 Vilafranca del Penedès (Barcelona)
☎: +34 938 901 628 - Fax: +34 938 901 358
mascaro@mascaro.es
www.mascaro.es

MASCARÓ NIGRUM BR RESERVA
60% parellada, 30% macabeo, 10% xarel.lo.

88 Colour: bright straw. Nose: fresh fruit, fragrant herbs, fine lees. Palate: fresh, fruity, good acidity, fine bitter notes.

MASCARÓ ROSADO "RUBOR AURORAE" BR
100% trepat.

88 Colour: light cherry. Nose: red berry notes, fresh, medium intensity. Palate: fruity, good acidity, fine bitter notes.

MASCARÓ PURE BN RESERVA
80% parellada, 20% macabeo.

87 Colour: bright straw. Nose: fresh fruit, dried herbs, fine lees, floral. Palate: fresh, fruity, flavourful, good acidity.

CUVÉE ANTONIO MASCARÓ EXTRA BRUT GRAN RESERVA
50% parellada, 35% macabeo, 15% chardonnay.

89 Colour: bright yellow. Nose: dry nuts, floral, lees reduction notes, ripe fruit. Palate: good structure, flavourful, fine bitter notes.

MASCARÓ "AMBROSIA" SS RESERVA
60% parellada, 30% macabeo, 10% xarel.lo.

85 Colour: bright straw. Nose: medium intensity, fresh fruit, dried herbs, fine lees, floral. Palate: flavourful, good acidity, sweetness.

MASET DEL LLEÓ

C-244, Km. 32,5
08792 La Granada del Penedès (Barcelona)
☎: +34 902 200 250 - Fax: +34 938 921 333
info@maset.com
www.maset.com

MASET DEL LLEÓ ROSÉ RD
tempranillo, trepat.

84 Colour: rose. Nose: ripe fruit, red berry notes, violet drops. Palate: fine bitter notes, good acidity, flavourful.

MASET DEL LLEÓ (NU) BR RESERVA
50% xarel.lo, 30% macabeo, 20% parellada.

88 Color bright straw. Aroma medium intensity, fresh fruit, dried herbs, fine lees, floral. Taste fresh, fruity, flavourful, good acidity.

MASET DEL LLEÓ BR RESERVA
macabeo, xarel.lo, parellada.

87 Colour: bright straw. Nose: powerfull, fresh fruit, citrus fruit, grassy. Palate: flavourful, fruity.

MASET DEL LLEÓ COUVÉE L'AVI PAU BN RESERVA
macabeo, xarel.lo, parellada, chardonnay.

88 Colour: bright straw. Nose: fresh fruit, dried herbs, fine lees, floral. Palate: fresh, fruity, flavourful, good acidity.

MASET DEL LLEÓ BN RESERVA
macabeo, xarel.lo, parellada.

87 Colour: bright straw. Nose: powerfull, characterful, ripe fruit, citrus fruit. Palate: good acidity, fine bitter notes.

MASET DEL LLEÓ VINTAGE BN RESERVA
macabeo, xarel.lo, parellada.

83 Colour: bright straw. Nose: dried herbs, candied fruit, citrus fruit. Palate: fruity, fresh.

MASIA VALLFORMOSA

La Sala, 45
08735 Vilobi del Penedès (Barcelona)
☎: +34 938 978 286 - Fax: +34 938 978 355
vallformosa@vallformosa.es
www.vallformosa.com

VALLFORMOSA CLASIC 2009 BR
40% xarel.lo, 30% macabeo, 30% parellada.

85 Colour: bright straw. Nose: medium intensity, fresh fruit, grassy. Palate: fresh, fruity, flavourful, good acidity.

CARLA DE VALLFORMOSA 2007 BR RESERVA
40% xarel.lo, 30% macabeo, 30% parellada.

88 Colour: bright yellow. Nose: medium intensity, fragrant herbs, balanced. Palate: fresh, good acidity, fine bead.

GALA DE VALLFORMOSA 2006 BR GRAN RESERVA
macabeo, xarel.lo, parellada, chardonnay.

87 Colour: bright yellow. Nose: ripe fruit, lees reduction notes, dried herbs, powerfull. Palate: flavourful, fruity, spicy.

ERIC DE VALLFORMOSA 2007 BN RESERVA
55% parellada, 45% chardonnay.

88 Colour: bright golden. Nose: dry nuts, fragrant herbs, complex, lees reduction notes. Palate: flavourful, fine bead, fine bitter notes.

MATA I COLOMA

Montserrat, 73
08770 Sant Sadurní D'Anoia (Barcelona)
☎: +34 938 183 968 - Fax: +34 938 183 968
info@matacoloma.com
www.matacoloma.com

PERE MATA RESERVA FAMILIA 2007 BN GRAN RESERVA
macabeo, xarel.lo, parellada.

89 Colour: bright golden. Nose: fine lees, fragrant herbs, complex. Palate: powerful, flavourful, good acidity, fine bead, fine bitter notes.

PERE MATA L'ENSAMBLATGE 2007 BN GRAN RESERVA
macabeo, xarel.lo, parellada.

88 Colour: bright golden. Nose: dry nuts, fragrant herbs. Palate: powerful, flavourful, good acidity, fine bead.

PERE MATA CUPADA Nº 3 BN RESERVA
40% macabeo, 30% xarel.lo, 30% parellada, 15% vino de reserva.

84 Colour: bright straw. Nose: neat, ripe fruit, citrus fruit. Palate: flavourful, powerful, ripe fruit.

MONT MARÇAL

Finca Manlleu
08732 Castellví de la Marca (Barcelona)
☎: +34 938 918 281 - Fax: +34 938 919 045
mrivas@mont-marcal.com
www.mont-marcal.com

MONT MARÇAL GRAN CUVÉE BR
40% xarel.lo, 25% macabeo, 20% chardonnay, 15% parellada.

90 Colour: bright straw. Nose: dried herbs, fine lees, floral, ripe fruit. Palate: fresh, fruity, flavourful, good acidity.

MONT MARÇAL EXTREMARIUM BR
35% xarel.lo, 25% macabeo, 20% parellada, 20% chardonnay.

87 Colour: bright straw. Nose: fresh fruit, dried herbs, fine lees, floral. Palate: fresh, fruity, flavourful, good acidity.

MONT MARÇAL BR
40% xarel.lo, 30% macabeo, 20% parellada, 10% chardonnay.

85 Colour: bright straw. Nose: dried herbs, fine lees, ripe fruit, floral. Palate: fresh, fruity, flavourful, good acidity.

AUREUM DE MONT MARÇAL BN RESERVA
50% xarel.lo, 30% chardonnay, 10% pinot noir, 10% parellada.

90 Colour: bright straw. Nose: medium intensity, fresh fruit, dried herbs, fine lees, floral. Palate: fresh, fruity, flavourful, good acidity, fine bead.

MONT MALÇAL BRUT ROSADO
100% trepat.

82 Colour: rose. Nose: candied fruit, red berry notes, floral. Palate: flavourful, fruity, fleshy, sweetness.

PAGO DE THARSYS

Ctra. Nacional III, km. 274
46340 Requena (Valencia)
☎: +34 962 303 354 - Fax: +34 962 329 000
pagodetharsys@pagodetharsys.com
www.pagodetharsys.com

PAGO DE THARSYS MILLÉSIME ROSÉ RESERVA 2007 BR
garnacha.

90 Colour: salmon. Nose: red berry notes, fruit expression, floral, expressive, elegant. Palate: flavourful, fruity, good acidity.

PAGO DE THARSYS MILLESIME 2007 BR RESERVA
macabeo, chardonnay, parellada.

88 Colour: bright yellow. Nose: dried herbs, medium intensity, ripe fruit. Palate: good structure, fruity, flavourful.

PAGO DE THARSYS BRUT ROSADO BR RESERVA
garnacha.

86 Colour: light cherry. Nose: red berry notes, medium intensity, dry nuts, fruit liqueur notes. Palate: fruity, fine bitter notes, great length.

PAGO DE THARSYS MILLÉSIME 2005 BN GRAN RESERVA
macabeo, parellada.

90 Colour: bright yellow. Nose: lees reduction notes, candied fruit, powerfull. Palate: flavourful, ripe fruit, good acidity, fine bead.

CARLOTA SURIA BN
macabeo, parellada.

88 Colour: bright straw. Nose: expressive, candied fruit, lees reduction notes, floral. Palate: ripe fruit, fine bitter notes, flavourful.

PAGO DE THARSYS BN
macabeo, chardonnay.

86 Colour: bright yellow. Nose: slightly evolved. Palate: powerful, flavourful, great length, good acidity.

PARATÓ

Can Respall de Renardes
08733 (Barcelona)
☎: +34 938 988 182 - Fax: +34 938 988 510
info@parato.es
www.parato.es

ÁTICA PINOT NOIR 2008
100% pinot noir.

87 Colour: raspberry rose. Nose: fruit liqueur notes, powerfull. Palate: fruity, flavourful, easy to drink, good acidity.

PARATÓ 2009 BR
macabeo, xarel.lo, parellada, chardonnay.

88 Colour: bright straw. Nose: fragrant herbs, floral, fine lees, neat. Palate: correct, fine bitter notes, powerful, flavourful.

RENARDES CUVÉE ESPECIAL 2009 BN
macabeo, xarel.lo, parellada.

86 Colour: bright straw. Nose: medium intensity, fresh fruit, dried herbs. Palate: fresh, fruity, flavourful, good acidity.

PARATÓ 2008 BN RESERVA
macabeo, xarel.lo, parellada, chardonnay.

86 Colour: bright straw. Nose: fresh fruit, fragrant herbs, dried flowers. Palate: fresh, fruity, flavourful, good acidity, fine bitter notes.

ELIAS I TERNS 2004 BN
macabeo, xarel.lo, parellada, chardonnay.

90 Colour: bright golden. Nose: dry nuts, dried flowers, fragrant herbs, spicy. Palate: balanced, unctuous, fine bitter notes, flavourful.

ÁTICA 2007 EXTRA BRUT GRAN RESERVA
macabeo, xarel.lo, parellada, chardonnay.

86 Colour: bright straw. Nose: fresh, balanced, candied fruit. Palate: fruity, flavourful, easy to drink.

PARÉS BALTÀ

Masía Can Baltá, s/n
08796 Pacs del Penedès (Barcelona)
☎: +34 938 901 399 - Fax: +34 938 901 143
paresbalta@paresbalta.com
www.paresbalta.com

ROSA CUSINE 2007 RD
garnacha.

90 Colour: coppery red. Nose: powerfull, fresh fruit, red berry notes, sweet spices, fine lees. Palate: flavourful, fleshy, sweetness.

BLANCA CUSINÉ 2008 BR
chardonnay, pinot noir.

92 Colour: bright golden. Nose: powerfull, expressive, candied fruit, citrus fruit, dry nuts. Palate: flavourful, fruity, fleshy, fine bitter notes.

PARÉS BALTÀ SELECTIO BR
macabeo, xarel.lo, parellada, chardonnay.

90 Colour: bright straw. Nose: dried herbs, floral, ripe fruit, fragrant herbs. Palate: fresh, fruity, flavourful, good acidity.

PARÉS BALTÀ BN
macabeo, xarel.lo, parellada.

87 Colour: bright straw. Nose: fresh fruit, dried herbs, fine lees, floral. Palate: fresh, fruity, flavourful, good acidity.

PARXET

Mas Parxet, s/n
08391 Tiana (Barcelona)
☎: +34 933 950 811 - Fax: +34 933 955 500
info@parxet.es
www.parxet.es

PARXET CUVÉE DESSERT RD
pinot noir.

85 Colour: onion pink. Nose: candied fruit, fruit liqueur notes, faded flowers. Palate: flavourful, sweet.

PARXET PANSA BLANCA BARRICA 2008 BR
pansa blanca.

90 Colour: bright straw. Nose: balanced, expressive, fragrant herbs, fine lees, elegant. Palate: fresh, light-bodied, great length, varietal.

PARXET CHARDONNAY 1986 BR
chardonnay.

82 Colour: golden. Nose: candied fruit, spicy, dry nuts, honeyed notes, fine lees, slightly evolved. Palate: fine bitter notes, pruney, short.

PARXET BR RESERVA
macabeo, parellada, pansa blanca.

88 Colour: bright straw. Nose: fresh fruit, dried herbs, fine lees, floral. Palate: fresh, flavourful, good acidity.

PARXET BR
macabeo, parellada, pansa blanca.

88 Colour: bright straw. Nose: medium intensity, dried herbs, fine lees, ripe fruit. Palate: fresh, fruity, flavourful, good acidity.

TITIANA PINOT NOIR ROSÉ BR
100% pinot noir.

87 Colour: rose. Nose: faded flowers, rose petals, candied fruit. Palate: flavourful, sweetness, spirituous.

PARXET 2008 BN
macabeo, parellada, pansa blanca, chardonnay.

86 Colour: bright straw. Nose: medium intensity, floral, grassy, ripe fruit. Palate: fresh, fruity, fine bead.

PARXET ANIVERSARIO BN
coupage especial.

92 Colour: bright golden. Nose: fine lees, dry nuts, fragrant herbs. Palate: powerful, flavourful, good acidity, fine bead, fine bitter notes.

TITIANA VINTAGE BN
chardonnay.

88 Colour: bright straw. Nose: medium intensity, dried herbs, fine lees, ripe fruit. Palate: fresh, fruity, flavourful, good acidity.

PARXET PINOT NOIR EN BLANC 2008 EXTRA BRUT

88 Colour: pale, coppery red. Nose: balanced, fresh, fine lees, fragrant herbs, white flowers. Palate: fresh, light-bodied, fine bead, fruity.

GRAN RESERVA MARÍA CABANE EXTRA BRUT
macabeo, parellada, pansa blanca.

91 Colour: bright golden. Nose: fine lees, fragrant herbs, complex, fresh fruit. Palate: powerful, flavourful, good acidity, fine bead, fine bitter notes.

PARXET SS RESERVA
macabeo, parellada, pansa blanca.

88 Colour: bright straw. Nose: medium intensity, dried herbs, fine lees, floral, candied fruit, dry nuts. Palate: flavourful, sweetness, fine bitter notes.

PERE VENTURA

Ctra. de Vilafranca, Km. 0,4
08770 Sant Sadurní D'Anoia (Barcelona)
☎: +34 938 183 371 - Fax: +34 938 912 679
info@pereventura.com
www.pereventura.com

PERE VENTURA TRESOR BR
40% xarel.lo, 40% macabeo, 20% parellada.

87 Color bright straw. Aroma medium intensity, fresh fruit, dried herbs, fine lees, floral. Taste fresh, fruity, flavourful, good acidity.

PERE VENTURA PRIMER BRUT BR
35% xarel.lo, 35% macabeo, 30% parellada.

86 Colour: bright straw. Nose: dried herbs, fine lees, floral, ripe fruit. Palate: fresh, fruity, good acidity.

PERE VENTURA CUVÉE MARÍA DEL MAR BN
30% macabeo, 25% xarel.lo, 15% parellada, 15% chardonnay, xarel.lo fermentado en barrica.

88 Colour: bright straw. Nose: ripe fruit, white flowers, dried herbs. Palate: flavourful, fruity, fleshy, complex.

PERE VENTURA CUPATGE D'HONOR BN RESERVA
70% xarel.lo, 30% chardonnay.

84 Colour: bright straw. Nose: medium intensity, fresh fruit, dried herbs, fine lees, floral. Palate: fruity, good acidity.

RIMARTS

Avda. Cal Mir, 44
08770 Sant Sadurní D'Anoia (Barcelona)
☎: +34 938 912 775 - Fax: +34 938 912 775
rimarts@rimarts.net
www.rimarts.net

RIMARTS BR RESERVA
xarel.lo, macabeo, parellada.

87 Colour: bright straw. Nose: fresh fruit, dried herbs, fine lees, floral. Palate: fresh, fruity, flavourful, good acidity.

RIMARTS 2008 BN RESERVA
xarel.lo, macabeo, parellada.

89 Colour: bright straw. Nose: fresh fruit, dried herbs, fine lees, floral. Palate: fresh, fruity, flavourful, good acidity.

RIMARTS 2007 BN GRAN RESERVA
xarel.lo, macabeo, parellada, chardonnay.

90 Color bright golden. Aroma fine lees, dry nuts, fragrant herbs, complex. Taste powerful, flavourful, good acidity, fine bead, fine bitter notes.

RIMARTS CHARDONNAY 2007 BN RESERVA ESPECIAL
chardonnay.

88 Colour: bright straw. Nose: dried herbs, fine lees, floral, ripe fruit. Palate: fresh, fruity, flavourful, good acidity.

RIMARTS MAGNUM 2007 BN GRAN RESERVA
xarel.lo, macabeo, parellada, chardonnay.

88 Colour: bright golden. Nose: fine lees, dry nuts, fragrant herbs. Palate: powerful, flavourful, good acidity, fine bead, fine bitter notes.

RIMARTS UVAE 2006 BN GRAN RESERVA
xarel.lo, chardonnay.

83 Colour: bright straw. Nose: fragrant herbs, candied fruit, honeyed notes. Palate: fine bitter notes, fine bead, sweetness.

ROCAMAR

Major, 80
08755 Castellbisbal (Barcelona)
☎: +34 937 720 900 - Fax: +34 937 721 495
info@rocamar.net
www.rocamar.net

CASTELL DE RIBES BR
macabeo, xarel.lo, parellada.

84 Colour: bright straw. Nose: fine lees, floral, short. Palate: fresh, light-bodied, flavourful.

ROSELL & FORMOSA

Rambla de la Generalitat, 14
08770 Sant Sadurní D'Anoia (Barcelona)
☎: +34 938 911 013 - Fax: +34 938 911 967
rformosa@roselliformosa.com
www.roselliformosa.com

ROSELL I FORMOSA 2007 BR
40% macabeo, 25% parellada, 35% xarel.lo.

86 Colour: bright straw. Nose: dried herbs, fine lees, floral, fresh. Palate: fresh, fruity, light-bodied.

ROSELL I FORMOSA ROSAT 2007 BR
50% garnacha, 50% monastrell.

85 Colour: rose. Nose: white flowers, red berry notes, fresh. Palate: correct, unctuous, good acidity.

DAURAT "BRUT DE BRUTS" 2005 BR GRAN RESERVA
45% macabeo, 30% xarel.lo, 25% parellada.

84 Colour: bright straw. Nose: citrus fruit, fresh, fine lees. Palate: fine bitter notes, correct, good acidity.

ROSELL I FORMOSA 2006 BN GRAN RESERVA
45% macabeo, 30% xarel.lo, 25% parellada.

87 Colour: bright straw. Nose: citrus fruit, expressive, fragrant herbs. Palate: fine bitter notes, correct, good acidity.

ROSELL GALLART

Montserrat, 56
08770 Sant Sadurní D'Anoia (Barcelona)
☎: +34 938 912 073 - Fax: +34 938 183 539
info@rosellgallart.com
www.cavarosellgallart.com

TERESA MATA GARRIGA 2008 BN
macabeo, xarel.lo, parellada, chardonnay.

87 Colour: bright straw. Nose: dried herbs, fine lees, floral, ripe fruit. Palate: fresh, fruity, flavourful, good acidity.

ROSELL GALLART 2007 BN
macabeo, xarel.lo, parellada, chardonnay.

87 Colour: bright yellow. Nose: ripe fruit, citrus fruit, fine lees. Palate: flavourful, sweetness, fruity.

ROSELL RAVENTÓS CRISTAL 2003 BN RESERVA
macabeo, xarel.lo, parellada, chardonnay.

85 Colour: bright golden. Nose: dry nuts, fragrant herbs, complex, lees reduction notes. Palate: powerful, flavourful, good acidity, fine bead, fine bitter notes.

ROVELLATS

Finca Rovellats Bº La Bleda
08731 Sant Marti Sarroca (Barcelona)
☎: +34 934 880 575 - Fax: +34 934 880 819
rovellats@cavasrovellats.com
www.cavasrovellats.com

ROVELLATS IMPERIAL 2008 BR RESERVA
60% macabeo, 25% parellada, 15% xarel.lo.

88 Color bright straw. Aroma medium intensity, fresh fruit, dried herbs, fine lees, floral. Taste fresh, fruity, flavourful, good acidity.

ROVELLATS ROSÉ 2008 BR RESERVA
80% garnacha, 20% monastrell.

86 Colour: rose. Nose: red berry notes, medium intensity, rose petals. Palate: fruity, fresh, good acidity.

ROVELLATS COL.LECCIÓ 2006 BRUT EXTRA GRAN RESERVA
58% xarel.lo, 42% parellada.

90 Colour: bright golden. Nose: fine lees, dry nuts, fragrant herbs, complex. Palate: powerful, flavourful, good acidity, fine bead.

ROVELLATS PREMIER 2009 BN RESERVA
77% parellada, 12% macabeo, 11% xarel.lo.

87 Colour: bright straw. Nose: floral, fresh, balanced, fresh fruit. Palate: fruity, fresh, good acidity.

ROVELLATS MAGNUM 2006 BN
55% xarel.lo, 29% macabeo, 16% parellada.

90 Colour: bright straw. Nose: dried herbs, fine lees, floral, fresh fruit. Palate: fresh, fruity, flavourful, good acidity.

ROVELLATS 2006 BN GRAN RESERVA
55% xarel.lo, 29% macabeo, 16% parellada.

88 Colour: bright straw. Nose: balanced, elegant, fresh, scrubland, fine lees. Palate: good structure, fruity, fine bitter notes.

ROVELLATS MASIA S. XV MILLESIMEE 2004 BN GRAN RESERVA
50% xarel.lo, 30% macabeo, 12% parellada, 8% chardonnay.

87 Colour: bright yellow. Nose: ripe fruit, scrubland, balanced, medium intensity. Palate: fruity, good acidity.

SEGURA VIUDAS

Ctra. Sant Sadurní a St. Pere de Riudebitlles, Km. 5
08775 Torrelavit (Barcelona)
☎: +34 938 917 070 - Fax: +34 938 996 006
seguraviudas@seguraviudas.es
www.seguraviudas.com

SEGURA VIUDAS BRUT VINTAGE 2007 BR
67% macabeo, 33% parellada.

88 Colour: bright straw. Nose: wild herbs, dried flowers, fresh. Palate: fruity, flavourful, balanced, good acidity.

SEGURA VIUDAS RESERVA HEREDAD BR GRAN RESERVA
67% macabeo, 33% parellada.

91 Colour: bright yellow. Nose: complex, ripe fruit, floral, fine lees, balanced. Palate: flavourful, good structure, fine bitter notes.

LAVIT ROSADO BR
80% trepat, 10% monastrell, 10% garnacha.

88 Colour: raspberry rose. Nose: red berry notes, rose petals, medium intensity. Palate: good structure, flavourful, easy to drink, good acidity.

SEGURA VIUDAS BR RESERVA
50% macabeo, 35% parellada, 15% xarel.lo.

85 Colour: bright straw. Nose: balanced, fresh fruit, fragrant herbs. Palate: correct, fresh, fruity.

TORRE GALIMANY 2007 BN GRAN RESERVA
xarel.lo.

90 Colour: bright straw, greenish rim. Nose: fine lees, floral, complex, balanced. Palate: fruity, flavourful, good structure.

LAVIT 2007 BN
60% macabeo, 40% parellada.

89 Colour: bright straw. Nose: medium intensity, floral, fresh, fresh fruit. Palate: fruity, good acidity.

ARIA BN
60% macabeo, 20% xarel.lo, 20% parellada.

87 Colour: bright straw. Nose: dried herbs, fresh fruit, white flowers. Palate: fruity, fresh, great length, good acidity.

TORELLÓ

Can Martí de Baix, Ctra. de Sant Sadurni a Gélida - Apdo. Correos 8
08770 Sant Sadurní D'Anoia (Barcelona)
☎: +34 938 910 793 - Fax: +34 938 910 877
torello@torello.es
www.torello.es

TORELLÓ DOLÇ 2008 RESERVA
macabeo, xarel.lo, parellada.

86 Colour: bright golden. Nose: candied fruit, white flowers, dried herbs. Palate: flavourful, good acidity, sweet.

TORELLÓ PETIT DOLÇ 2008 RESERVA
macabeo, xarel.lo, parellada.

85 Colour: bright straw. Nose: powerfull, white flowers, fruit preserve. Palate: powerful, sweet.

TORELLÓ 2008 BR RESERVA
macabeo, xarel.lo, parellada.

88 Colour: bright straw. Nose: ripe fruit, citrus fruit, spicy. Palate: flavourful, powerful, fruity.

TORELLÓ ROSÉ 2008 BR RESERVA
monastrell, garnacha.

87 Colour: rose. Nose: ripe fruit, red berry notes, rose petals. Palate: flavourful, fleshy, good acidity, balanced.

TORELLÓ ROSÉ MAGNUM 2007 BR RESERVA
monastrell, garnacha.

88 Colour: rose, purple rim. Nose: fresh fruit, expressive, powerfull, floral. Palate: good acidity, balanced, unctuous, great length.

TORELLÓ PETIT ROSÉ 2007 BR RESERVA
monastrell, garnacha.

87 Colour: rose. Nose: powerfull, ripe fruit, red berry notes, violet drops. Palate: flavourful, fruity, sweet.

TORELLÓ BY CUSTO BARCELONA 2006 BR GRAN RESERVA
macabeo, xarel.lo, parellada.

92 Colour: bright golden. Nose: dry nuts, fragrant herbs, fine lees. Palate: powerful, flavourful, good acidity, fine bead.

TORELLÓ 225 2007 BN GRAN RESERVA
macabeo, xarel.lo, parellada.

91 Colour: bright straw. Nose: elegant, expressive, balanced, toasty, sweet spices. Palate: flavourful, fruity, fresh.

GRAN TORELLÓ 2007 BN GRAN RESERVA
macabeo, xarel.lo, parellada.

91 Colour: bright golden. Nose: dry nuts, fragrant herbs. Palate: powerful, flavourful, good acidity, fine bead, fine bitter notes.

GRAN TORELLÓ MAGNUM 2007 BN GRAN RESERVA
macabeo, xarel.lo, parellada.

89 Colour: bright straw. Nose: fresh fruit, dried herbs, fine lees, floral. Palate: fresh, fruity, flavourful, good acidity.

JEROBOAM TORELLÓ 2005 BN GRAN RESERVA
macabeo, xarel.lo, parellada.

94 Colour: bright straw. Nose: powerfull, characterful, complex, fresh fruit, citrus fruit, fine lees, grassy. Palate: flavourful, powerful, fruity, good acidity, fine bead.

TORELLÓ PETIT BRUT NATURE 2008 BN RESERVA
macabeo, xarel.lo, parellada.

88 Colour: bright straw. Nose: ripe fruit, candied fruit, citrus fruit. Palate: flavourful, fleshy, complex.

TORELLÓ 2007 BN
macabeo, xarel.lo, parellada.

90 Colour: bright straw. Nose: dried herbs, fine lees, floral, fresh fruit. Palate: fresh, fruity, flavourful, good acidity.

TORRE ORIA

Ctra. Pontón - Utiel, Km. 3
46390 El Derramador (Valencia)
☎: +34 962 320 289 - Fax: +34 962 320 311
santiago.sancho@natra.es
www.torreoria.com

MARQUÉS DE REQUENA BR
macabeo, parellada.

86 Colour: bright straw. Nose: medium intensity, fresh fruit, dried herbs, fine lees. Palate: fresh, fruity, flavourful, good acidity.

MARQUÉS DE REQUENA BN
90% macabeo, 10% parellada.

88 Colour: bright straw. Nose: medium intensity, fresh fruit, dried herbs, floral. Palate: fresh, fruity, flavourful, fine bitter notes, dry.

TORRENS MOLINER

Ctra Sant Sadurni - Piera BV-2242, - km 10,5
08784 La Fortesa (Barcelona)
☎: +34 938 911 033 - Fax: +34 938 911 761
tormol@torrensmoliner.com
www.torrensmoliner.com

TORRENS & MOLINER GRAN SELECCIÓ BN GRAN RESERVA
macabeo, xarel.lo, parellada, chardonnay.

87 Colour: bright yellow. Nose: ripe fruit, pattiserie. Palate: powerful, flavourful, good acidity, spicy.

U MÉS U FAN TRES

Masía Navinés Bº Els Pujols
08736 Font-Rubí (Barcelona)
☎: +34 938 974 069 - Fax: +34 938 974 724
umesu@umesufan3.com
www.umesufan3.com

1 + 1 = 3 PINOT NOIR 2007 BN
pinot noir.

87 Colour: rose. Nose: powerfull, ripe fruit, red berry notes. Palate: flavourful, fruity, ripe fruit.

1 + 1 = 3 2007 BN
macabeo, xarel.lo, parellada.

88 Colour: bright straw. Nose: dried herbs, fine lees, floral, fresh fruit. Palate: fresh, fruity, flavourful, good acidity.

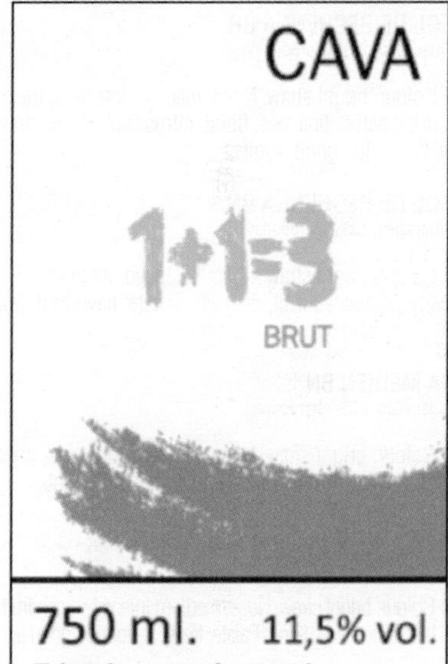

1 + 1 = 3 GRAN RESERVA ESPECIAL 2005 BN
xarel.lo, pinot noir.

90 Colour: bright golden. Nose: dry nuts, fragrant herbs, complex. Palate: powerful, flavourful, good acidity, fine bead, fine bitter notes.

1 + 1 = 3 2005 BN FERMENTADO EN BARRICA
xarel.lo, chardonnay.

88 Colour: bright golden. Nose: fine lees, fragrant herbs, complex, sweet spices, cocoa bean. Palate: powerful, flavourful, good acidity, fine bead, fine bitter notes.

1 + 1 = 3 2008 BR
macabeo, xarel.lo, parellada.

86 Colour: bright straw. Nose: dried herbs, fine lees, floral. Palate: fresh, fruity, flavourful, good acidity.

CYGNUS 1 + 1 = 3 2007 BN
macabeo, xarel.lo, parellada.

89 Colour: bright straw. Nose: expressive, ripe fruit, fresh fruit, citrus fruit. Palate: flavourful, fruity, fresh.

UNIÓN VINÍCOLA DEL ESTE

Pl. El Romeral- Construcción, 74
46340 Requena (Valencia)
☎: +34 962 323 343 - Fax: +34 962 349 413
cava@uveste.es

NASOL DE RECHENNA BR
90% macabeo, 10% chardonnay.

90 Colour: bright straw. Nose: medium intensity, fresh fruit, dried herbs, fine lees, floral, citrus fruit. Palate: fresh, fruity, flavourful, good acidity.

NASOL DE RECHENNA BN
90% macabeo, 10% chardonnay.

88 Colour: bright straw. Nose: balanced, medium intensity, macerated fruit, dry nuts. Palate: flavourful, fruity, spicy, good acidity.

VEGA MEDIEN BN
80% macabeo, 20% chardonnay.

87 Colour: bright straw. Nose: fine lees, dry nuts, dried flowers. Palate: correct, good acidity, fine bitter notes.

DOMINIO DE CALLES BN
80% macabeo, 20% chardonnay.

86 Colour: bright straw. Nose: medium intensity, fresh fruit, dried herbs, fine lees, floral. Palate: fresh, flavourful, good acidity.

BESO DE RECHENNA BN RESERVA
80% macabeo, 20% chardonnay.

83 Colour: bright straw. Nose: medium intensity, citrus fruit, floral. Palate: fresh, good acidity, fine bead.

VALL DOLINA

Plaça de la Creu, 1
08795 Olesa de Bonesvalls (Barcelona)
☎: +34 938 984 181 - Fax: +34 938 984 181
info@valldolina.com
www.valldolina.com

VALL DOLINA 2008 BN RESERVA
macabeo, xarel.lo, parellada, chardonnay.

90 Colour: bright straw. Nose: fresh fruit, dried herbs, fine lees, floral. Palate: fresh, fruity, flavourful, good acidity.

TUTUSAUS ECO 2007 BN GRAN RESERVA
macabeo, xarel.lo, parellada, chardonnay.

87 Color bright golden. Aroma fine lees, dry nuts, fragrant herbs, complex. Taste powerful, flavourful, good acidity, fine bead, fine bitter notes.

VERA DE ESTENAS

Junto N-III, km. 266 - Paraje La Cabezuela
46300 Utiel (Valencia)
☎: +34 962 171 141 - Fax: +34 962 174 352
estenas@estenas.es
www.estenas.es

ESTENAS BN
macabeo, chardonnay.

88 Colour: bright straw. Nose: fresh fruit, dried herbs, fine lees, floral. Palate: fresh, fruity, flavourful, good acidity.

VILARNAU

Ctra. d'Espiells, Km. 1,4 Finca "Can Petit"
08770 Sant Sadurní D'Anoia (Barcelona)
☎: +34 938 912 361 - Fax: +34 938 912 913
vilarnau@vilarnau.es
www.gonzalezbyass.com

ALBERT DE VILARNAU 2007 BR FERMENTADO EN BARRICA
60% chardonnay, 20% macabeo, 20% parellada.

92 Colour: bright golden. Nose: dry nuts, fragrant herbs, complex, sweet spices, cocoa bean. Palate: powerful, flavourful, good acidity, fine bead, fine bitter notes.

VILARNAU VINTAGE 2007 BR GRAN RESERVA
35% macabeo, 35% parellada, 30% chardonnay.

90 Colour: bright golden. Nose: fine lees, fragrant herbs, complex. Palate: powerful, flavourful, good acidity, fine bead, fine bitter notes.

VILARNAU 2008 BN RESERVA
50% macabeo, 35% parellada, 15% chardonnay.

87 Color bright straw. Aroma medium intensity, fresh fruit, dried herbs, fine lees, floral. Taste fresh, fruity, flavourful, good acidity.

ALBERT DE VILARNAU CHARDONNAY 2007 BN GRAN RESERVA
60% chardonnay, 40% pinot noir.

91 Colour: bright straw. Nose: dried herbs, fine lees, floral, fresh fruit. Palate: fresh, fruity, flavourful, good acidity.

VILARNAU BRUT ROSÉ BRUT ROSADO
85% trepat, 15% pinot noir.

86 Colour: rose. Nose: expressive, ripe fruit, red berry notes. Palate: flavourful, good acidity, fine bitter notes, round.

VINÍCOLA I SECCIÓ DE CRÉDIT SANT ISIDRE DE NULLES

Estació, s/n
43887 Nulles (Tarragona)
☎: +34 977 614 965 - Fax: +34 977 602 622
casinulles@casinulles.com
www.vinicoladenulles.com

ADERNATS DOLÇ 2008
50% macabeo, 25% xarel.lo, 25% parellada.

86 Colour: bright straw. Nose: ripe fruit, citrus fruit, jasmine. Palate: sweet, easy to drink.

ADERNATS XC 2006 GRAN RESERVA
100% xarel.lo.

92 Colour: bright yellow. Nose: sweet spices, fine lees, candied fruit, complex. Palate: flavourful, good acidity, fine bitter notes.

ADERNATS ROSAT 2009 BR
100% trepat.

88 Colour: light cherry. Nose: red berry notes, balanced, rose petals. Palate: flavourful, fruity, good acidity, easy to drink.

ADERNATS 2008 BR
50% macabeo, 25% xarel.lo, 25% parellada.

88 Colour: bright straw. Nose: fresh fruit, citrus fruit, floral. Palate: flavourful, great length, good acidity.

ADERNATS 2006 BR GRAN RESERVA
40% macabeo, 30% xarel.lo, 30% chardonnay.

89 Colour: bright yellow. Nose: fine lees, dry nuts, fragrant herbs, ripe fruit. Palate: powerful, flavourful, good acidity, fine bead.

ADERNATS RESERVA 2008 BN
50% macabeo, 25% xarel.lo, 25% parellada.

89 Colour: bright straw. Nose: medium intensity, fresh fruit, dried herbs, floral. Palate: fresh, fruity, flavourful, good acidity.

CAMPASSOS 2008 BN
82% macabeo, 8% xarel.lo, 10% parellada.

87 Colour: bright straw. Nose: medium intensity, fresh fruit, dried herbs, citrus fruit. Palate: fresh, fruity, flavourful, good acidity.

ADERNATS 2006 BN GRAN RESERVA
40% macabeo, 30% xarel.lo, 30% chardonnay.

89 Colour: bright straw. Nose: dried herbs, fine lees, floral. Palate: fresh, fruity, flavourful, good acidity.

VINÍCOLA DE SARRAL Í SELECCIÓ DE CREDIT

Avda. de la Conca, 33
43424 Sarral (Tarragona)
☎: +34 977 890 031 - Fax: +34 977 890 136
cavaportell@covisal.es
www.cava_portell.com

PORTELL 2009 BR
70% macabeo, 30% parellada.

88 Colour: bright straw. Nose: fresh fruit, fine lees, floral, citrus fruit. Palate: fresh, fruity, flavourful, good acidity.

PORTELL ROSAT 2009 BR
100% trepat.

85 Colour: raspberry rose. Nose: raspberry, red berry notes, fresh. Palate: fresh, light-bodied, flavourful.

PORTELL 2008 BN
80% macabeo, 20% parellada.

85 Color bright straw. Aroma medium intensity, fresh fruit, dried herbs, fine lees, floral. Taste fresh, fruity, flavourful, good acidity.

PORTELL VINTAGE 2007 BN
75% macabeo, 25% parellada.

88 Colour: bright straw. Nose: dried herbs, fine lees, floral, fresh fruit. Palate: fresh, fruity, flavourful, good acidity.

PORTELL SUBLIM BN
100% trepat.

89 Colour: salmon. Nose: sweet spices, red berry notes, expressive, complex. Palate: powerful, fleshy, good acidity, elegant.

PORTELL ROSAT 2009 SS
100% trepat.

83 Colour: brilliant rose. Nose: powerfull, ripe fruit, red berry notes, floral. Palate: flavourful, sweet, fruity.

VINS EL CEP

Can Llopart de Les Alzines
08770 Sant Sadurní D'Anoia (Barcelona)
☎: +34 938 912 353 - Fax: +34 938 183 956
info@elcep.com
www.elcep.com

MARQUÉS DE GELIDA A. ECOLÓGICA 2008 BR RESERVA
35% xarel.lo, 30% macabeo, 25% parellada, 10% chardonnay.

88 Colour: bright straw. Nose: ripe fruit, dry nuts, floral, fine lees. Palate: light-bodied, fresh, flavourful, fruity, fleshy.

L'ALZINAR 2008 BR RESERVA
35% xarel.lo, 35% macabeo, 20% parellada, 10% chardonnay.

86 Colour: bright straw. Nose: fine lees, dried flowers, dried herbs, ripe fruit. Palate: good acidity, correct, sweetness, light-bodied.

MARQUÉS DE GELIDA PINOT NOIR 2008 BR RESERVA
100% pinot noir.

85 Colour: raspberry rose. Nose: ripe fruit, dried flowers, fine lees. Palate: easy to drink, fresh, fruity.

MARQUÉS DE GELIDA BRUT EXCLUSIVE 2007 BR RESERVA
35% xarel.lo, 30% macabeo, 25% parellada, 10% chardonnay.

86 Colour: bright straw. Nose: medium intensity, dried herbs, fine lees, candied fruit. Palate: fresh, fruity, flavourful, good acidity.

L'ALZINAR 2007 BN RESERVA
40% xarel.lo, 30% macabeo, 30% parellada.

87 Colour: bright straw. Nose: fresh, fine lees, ripe fruit. Palate: good acidity, fine bead, light-bodied, flavourful.

MARQUÉS DE GELIDA CLAROR 2006 BN GRAN RESERVA
45% xarel.lo, 35% macabeo, 20% parellada.

86 Colour: bright golden. Nose: dried flowers, dry nuts, macerated fruit, fine lees. Palate: good acidity, fleshy, flavourful, fruity.

MARQUÉS DE GELIDA 2004 BN GRAN RESERVA
35% xarel.lo, 25% macabeo, 20% parellada, 20% chardonnay.

90 Colour: bright golden. Nose: fragrant herbs, dried flowers, sweet spices, expressive. Palate: balanced, fine bead, good acidity, flavourful.

VINS I CAVES CUSCÓ BERGA

Esplugues, 7
08793 Avinyonet del Penedès (Barcelona)
☎: +34 938 970 164
cuscoberga@cuscoberga.com
www.cuscoberga.com

CUSCÓ BERGA 2009 BR
100% trepat.

86 Color rose, purple rim. Aroma powerfull, ripe fruit, red berry notes, floral, expressive. Taste fleshy, powerful, fruity, fresh.

CUSCÓ BERGA 2008 BR
40% xarel.lo, 30% macabeo, 30% parellada.

82 Colour: bright straw. Nose: medium intensity, ripe fruit, floral. Palate: fine bitter notes, ripe fruit, great length.

CUSCÓ BERGA 2006 BR GRAN RESERVA
40% xarel.lo, 30% macabeo, 30% parellada.

87 Colour: bright golden. Nose: fine lees, dry nuts, fragrant herbs. Palate: flavourful, good acidity, fine bead, fine bitter notes.

CUSCÓ BERGA 2007 BN
40% xarel.lo, 30% macabeo, 30% parellada.

82 Colour: bright yellow. Nose: ripe fruit, honeyed notes. Palate: fruity, powerful, good finish.

VINYA NATURA

Herrero, 32- Sº 12
12005 Castellón (Castellón)
☎: +34 678 126 449
eloy@winestatus.com
www.vinyanatura.com

BABEL DE VINYA NATURA BR
macabeo.

83 Colour: bright yellow. Nose: medium intensity, ripe fruit. Palate: flavourful, good finish, good acidity.

VIÑEDOS Y BODEGAS VEGALFARO

Ctra. Pontón - Utiel, Km. 3
46340 Requena (Valencia)
☎: +34 962 320 680 - Fax: +34 962 321 126
rodolfo@vegalfaro.com
www.vegalfaro.com

VEGALFARO BN
chardonnay, macabeo.

89 Colour: bright straw. Nose: dried herbs, fine lees, floral, candied fruit. Palate: fresh, fruity, flavourful, good acidity.

VIVES AMBRÒS, CAVA

Mayor, 39
43812 Montferri (Tarragona)
☎: +34 639 521 652 - Fax: +34 977 606 579
covives@tinet.org
www.vivesambros.com

VIVES AMBRÒS 2008 BR
40% xarel.lo, 35% macabeo, 25% parellada.

87 Colour: bright straw. Nose: medium intensity, dried herbs, fine lees, floral, fruit expression. Palate: fresh, fruity, flavourful, good acidity, fine bitter notes.

VIVES AMBRÒS 2006 BN GRAN RESERVA
40% xarel.lo, 35% macabeo, 25% chardonnay.

85 Colour: bright golden. Nose: expressive, fresh, candied fruit, fragrant herbs. Palate: good acidity, correct, fine bitter notes.

VIVES AMBRÒS SALVATGE 2006 BN
60% xarel.lo, 40% macabeo.

85 Colour: bright yellow. Nose: scrubland, medium intensity, white flowers, ripe fruit, fine lees. Palate: powerful, flavourful, fleshy.

WINNER WINES

Avda. del Mediterráneo, 38
28007 Madrid (Madrid)
☎: +34 915 019 042 - Fax: +34 915 017 794
winnerwines@ibernoble.com
www.ibernoble.com

JUVENALS BR RESERVA
macabeo, xarel.lo, parellada.

86 Colour: bright straw. Nose: medium intensity, dried flowers, fine lees, fresh. Palate: easy to drink, good finish.

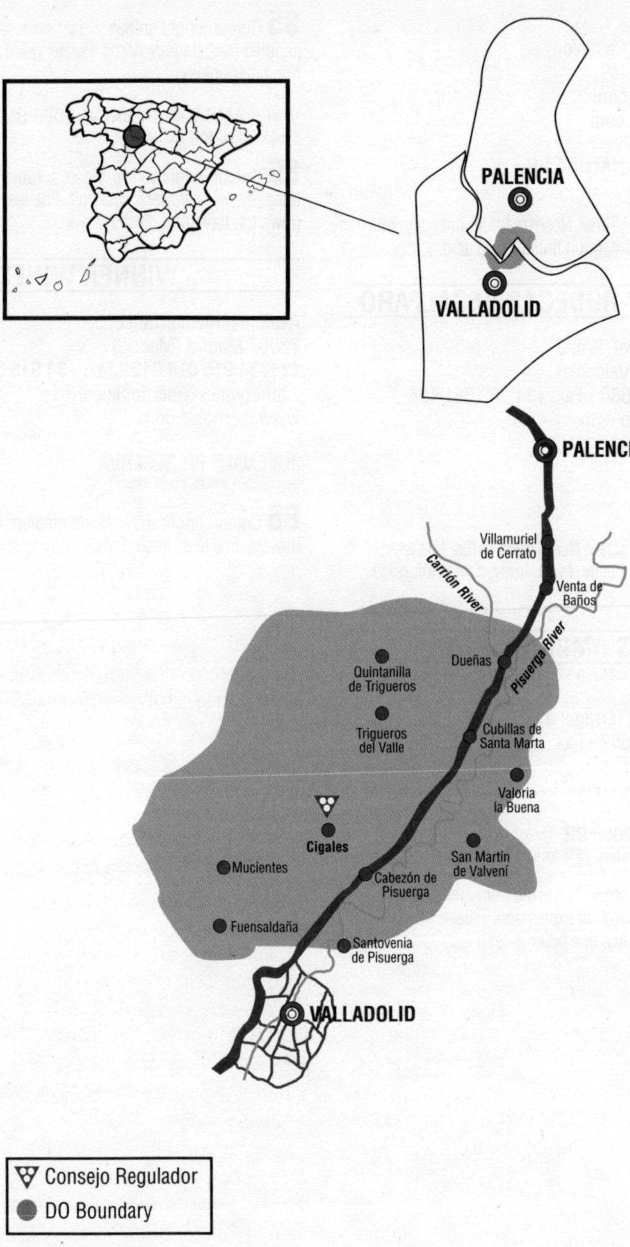

PALENCIA
VALLADOLID
PALENCIA
Villamuriel de Cerrato
Carrión River
Venta de Baños
Pisuerga River
Dueñas
Quintanilla de Trigueros
Trigueros del Valle
Cubillas de Santa Marta
Valoria la Buena
Cigales
San Martín de Valvení
Mucientes
Cabezón de Pisuerga
Fuensaldaña
Santovenia de Pisuerga
VALLADOLID
Consejo Regulador
DO Boundary

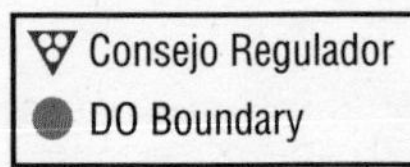

NEWS ABOUT THE VINTAGE:

Some twenty years ago Cigales decided to change its winemaking tradition and started making red wines instead of claretes, the light rosé wines of old which had managed in the past a reputation equal to rosé wines from Navarra by mixing red and white grapes and through very slow fermentations in underground caves more than 25 meters deep. Today, red wines from the region are struggling to get a defined style and lack altogether the elegance of those from neighbouring Ribera del Duero, or the powerful character of those from Toro. The problem lies in the fact that that lack of definition is putting off foreign investors, and only through modernization of the long-time family producers can we foresee a better future for the region.

If there is a product that identifies Cigales, that is their rosé renderings, which have managed good ratings in this year's edition thanks to milder (without being cool) climatic conditions. Besides the traditional claretes, there are modern rosé wines with some wood ageing –or barrel fermentation in some cases– that adds a fine spicy complexity. It has been also a good year for red wines –overall fresher and subtler than those from the 2009 vintage–, which promise even higher excellence when they complete their crianza. Their relatively good ratings are somehow eclipsed by those from the 2006 vintage, wines with a long ageing period made from excellent grapes that show fine red fruit notes finely blended with creamy oak. As always, César Príncipe and Balvinar are the best reds from the region.

LOCATION:

The region stretches to the north of the Duero depression and on both sides of the Pisuerga, bordered by the Cérvalos and the Torozos hills. The vineyards are situated at an altitude of 750 m; the DO extends from part of the municipal area of Valladolid (the wine estate known as 'El Berrocal') to the municipality of Dueñas in Palencia, also including Cabezón de Pisuerga, Cigales, Corcos del Valle, Cubillas de Santa Marte, Fuensaldaña, Mucientes, Quintanilla de Trigueros, San Martín de Valvení, Santovenia de Pisuerga, Trigueros del Valle and Valoria la Buena.

CLIMATE:

The climate is continental with Atlantic influences, and is marked by great contrasts in temperature, both yearly and day/night. The summers are extremely dry; the winters are harsh and prolonged, with frequent frost and fog; rainfall is irregular.

SOIL:

The soil is sandy and limy with clay loam which is settled on clay and marl. It has an extremely variable limestone content which, depending on the different regions, ranges between 1% and 35%.

TYPES OF WINE:

ROSÉS:
Cigales Nuevo. Produced with at least 60% of the *Tinta del País* variety and at least 20% of white varieties. The vintage must be displayed on the label.
Cigales. Elaborado con un mínimo del 60% de la varieProduced with at least 60% of the *Tinta del País* variety and at least 20% of white varieties. Marketed from 31st December of the following year.
REDS: Produced with at least 85% of the Tinta del País and the *Garnacha Tinta* varieties.

GRAPE VARIETIES:

WHITE: *Verdejo, Albillo* and *Viura.*
RED: *Tinta del País* (*Tempranillo*), *Garnacha Tinta* and *Garnacha Gris.*

DO CIGALES

FIGURES:

Vineyard surface: 2,300 – **Wine-Growers:** 501 – **Wineries:** 35 – **2010 Harvest rating:** N/A – **Production:** 5,612,884 litres – **Market percentages:** 75% domestic. 25% export

CONSEJO REGULADOR

Pza. Corro Vaca, 5

47270 Cigales (Valladolid)

☎: +34 983 580 074 - Fax: +34 983 586 590

@ consejo@do-cigales.es

www.do-cigales.es

GENERAL CHARACTERISTICS OF THE WINES

ROSÉS	There is a distinction between the more traditional rosé wines, with the classic onion skin colour, fresh, fruity, with medium-intensity, roasted and light and supple on the palate; and the more modern rosé wines: raspberry-coloured with more powerful noses and greater fruitiness on the palate. There are also Crianza rosé wines aged for a minimum of six months in barrel and one year in the bottle.
REDS	Young and Crianza wines are produced. The first are typical fresh, fruity red wines that are pleasant and easy drinking. Those that are aged in barrels are quite correct and well-balanced. The best stand out for having obtained more colour and greater concentration, thanks to the use of finer wood and a greater fruity expression and to the Terroir.

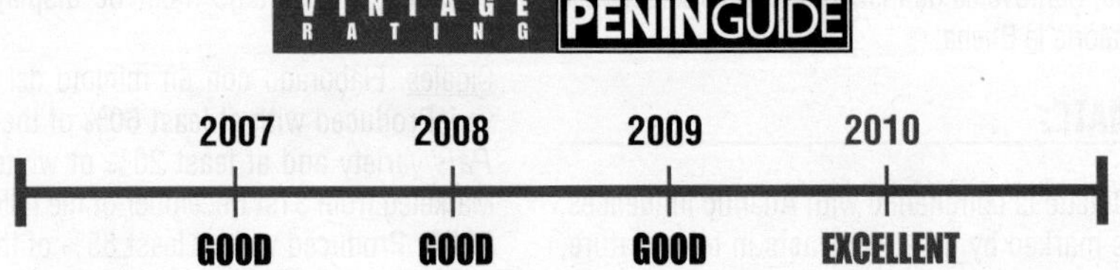

AURELIO PINACHO

Ronda Las Huertas, 17
47194 Mucientes (Valladolid)
☎: +34 983 587 859 - Fax: +34 983 586 954
lpigo@hotmail.com

PINACHO 2010 RD
80% tempranillo, 20% verdejo, viura.

83 Colour: rose, purple rim. Nose: ripe fruit, red berry notes, floral. Palate: fleshy, fruity, fresh.

PINACHO 2009 T ROBLE
100% tempranillo.

85 Colour: cherry, garnet rim. Nose: overripe fruit, toasty, dark chocolate, cocoa bean. Palate: powerful, sweetness, spicy.

AVELINO VEGAS

Real del Pino, 36
40460 Santiuste (Segovia)
☎: +34 921 596 002 - Fax: +34 921 596 035
ana@avelinovegas.com
www.avelinovegas.com

VEGA LOS ZARZALES 2010 RD
70% tempranillo, 15% garnacha, 15% albillo.

85 Colour: rose, purple rim. Nose: dried flowers, red berry notes, medium intensity. Palate: good acidity, fruity, fresh, flavourful.

BODEGA CÉSAR PRÍNCIPE

Ronda, 22
47194 Fuensaldaña (Valladolid)
☎: +34 983 663 123 - Fax: +34 983 108 018
cesarprincipe@cesarprincipe.es
www.cesarprincipe.es

CÉSAR PRÍNCIPE 2008 TC
100% tempranillo.

93 Colour: cherry, garnet rim. Nose: spicy, complex, roasted coffee, new oak, cocoa bean, ripe fruit. Palate: powerful, flavourful, toasty, round tannins.

BODEGA COOPERATIVA DE CIGALES

Las Bodegas, s/n
47270 Cigales (Valladolid)
☎: +34 983 580 135 - Fax: +34 983 580 682
bcc@bodegacooperativacigales.com
www.bodegacooperativacigales.com

TORONDOS CIGALES 2010 RD

88 Colour: rose, purple rim. Nose: ripe fruit, red berry notes, floral, powerfull. Palate: fleshy, powerful, fruity, fresh.

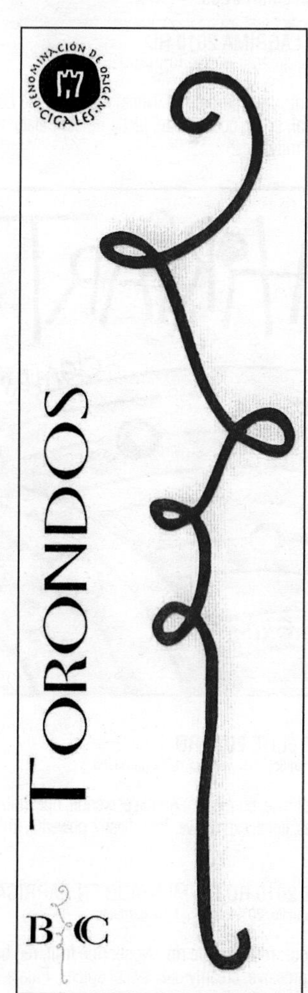

COMPROMISO 2010 RD
tinta del país, garnacha, verdejo, albillo.

87 Colour: light cherry. Nose: fresh, expressive, white flowers, ripe fruit. Palate: flavourful, fruity, fresh.

BODEGA HIRIART

Los Cortijos, 38
47270 Cigales (Valladolid)
☎: +34 983 580 094 - Fax: +34 983 100 701
ines@bodegahiriart.es
www.bodegahiriart.es

HIRIART LÁGRIMA 2010 RD
70% tempranillo, 20% verdejo, 10% garnacha.

90 Colour: rose, purple rim. Nose: ripe fruit, red berry notes, floral, spicy, cocoa bean, lactic notes. Palate: fleshy, powerful, fruity, fresh.

HIRIART ÉLITE 2010 RD
70% tempranillo, 20% verdejo, 10% garnacha.

88 Color rose, purple rim. Aroma powerfull, ripe fruit, red berry notes, floral, expressive. Taste fleshy, powerful, fruity, fresh.

HIRIART 2010 RD FERMENTADO EN BARRICA
70% tempranillo, 20% verdejo, 10% garnacha.

88 Colour: rose, purple rim. Nose: ripe fruit, red berry notes, expressive, creamy oak, sweet spices. Palate: fleshy, powerful, fruity, fresh.

HIRIART 2010 T ROBLE
100% tempranillo.

89 Colour: bright cherry. Nose: ripe fruit, sweet spices, creamy oak. Palate: flavourful, fruity, toasty, round tannins.

HIRIART 2009 T ROBLE
tempranillo.

88 Colour: cherry, garnet rim. Nose: spicy, creamy oak, toasty, complex, ripe fruit, warm. Palate: powerful, flavourful, toasty, round tannins.

HIRIART 2008 TC
100% tempranillo.

90 Colour: cherry, garnet rim. Nose: ripe fruit, spicy, creamy oak, toasty. Palate: powerful, flavourful, toasty, round tannins.

BODEGA VALDELOSFRAILES

Camino de Cubillas, s/n
47290 Cubillas de Santa Marta (Valladolid)
☎: +34 983 485 028 - Fax: +34 983 485 028
valdelosfrailes@matarromera.es
www.valdelosfrailes.es

VALDELOSFRAILES 2010 RD
80% tinta del país, 20% verdejo.

88 Colour: rose, purple rim. Nose: ripe fruit, red berry notes, floral. Palate: fleshy, powerful, fruity, fresh.

VALDELOSFRAILES 2010 T
tempranillo.

88 Colour: cherry, purple rim. Nose: red berry notes, floral, ripe fruit, dark chocolate. Palate: flavourful, fruity, good acidity, round tannins.

SELECCIÓN PERSONAL CARLOS MORO VALDELOSFRAILES 2006 T
100% tinta del país.

91 Colour: cherry, garnet rim. Nose: spicy, creamy oak, toasty, overripe fruit, powerfull. Palate: powerful, flavourful, toasty, round tannins.

VALDELOSFRAILES VENDIMIA SELECCIONADA 2006 T
tempranillo.

91 Colour: bright cherry. Nose: ripe fruit, sweet spices, creamy oak, expressive, toasty, aromatic coffee, dark chocolate, mineral. Palate: flavourful, toasty, round tannins, spicy.

VALDELOSFRAILES PRESTIGIO 2006 TR
tempranillo.

90 Colour: cherry, garnet rim. Nose: ripe fruit, spicy, creamy oak, toasty. Palate: powerful, flavourful, toasty, round tannins.

VALDELOSFRAILES PAGO DE LAS COSTANAS 2005 T
tempranillo.

88 Colour: cherry, garnet rim. Nose: powerfull, fruit liqueur notes, premature reduction notes. Palate: powerful, fine bitter notes, spicy.

BODEGAS FERNÁNDEZ CAMARERO

Condes de Torreanaz, 45- 1ºA
28028 Madrid (Madrid)
☎: +34 677 682 426
javier.fernandez@balvinar.com
www.balvinar.com

BALVINAR PAGOS SELECCIONADOS 2007 TC
100% tempranillo.

90 Colour: cherry, garnet rim. Nose: ripe fruit, spicy, complex, roasted coffee, new oak, cocoa bean. Palate: flavourful, toasty, harsh oak tannins.

BALVINAR PAGOS SELECCIONADOS 2006 TC
100% tempranillo.

92 Colour: cherry, garnet rim. Nose: ripe fruit, spicy, creamy oak, toasty, complex, earthy notes. Palate: powerful, flavourful, toasty, round tannins.

BODEGAS HIJOS DE FÉLIX SALAS

Corrales, s/n
47280 Corcos del Valle (Valladolid)
☎: +34 983 580 378 - Fax: +34 983 580 262
bodega@bodegasfelixsalas.com
www.bodegasfelixsalas.com

VIÑA PICOTA 2010 RD
tempranillo, albillo, verdejo, garnacha.

86 Colour: light cherry. Nose: elegant, candied fruit, dried flowers, red berry notes. Palate: light-bodied, flavourful, good acidity, long, spicy.

FÉLIX SALAS 2010 T
tempranillo.

84 Colour: cherry, purple rim. Nose: medium intensity, ripe fruit, red berry notes. Palate: fine bitter notes, spicy, ripe fruit.

BODEGAS LEZCANO-LACALLE

Ctra. Valoria, s/n
47282 Trigueros del Valle (Valladolid)
☎: +34 629 280 515
oficina@bodegaslezcano.es
www.bodegaslezcano.es

DOCETAÑIDOS 2010 RD
80% tempranillo, 10% albillo, 5% verdejo, 5% sauvignon blanc.

85 Colour: rose, purple rim. Nose: ripe fruit, red berry notes, dried flowers. Palate: fleshy, powerful, fruity, fresh.

MAUDES 2008 TC
80% tempranillo, 15% merlot, 5% cabernet sauvignon.

86 Colour: cherry, garnet rim. Nose: ripe fruit, spicy, sweet spices, pattiserie, premature reduction notes. Palate: powerful, flavourful, round tannins, roasted-coffee aftertaste.

LEZCANO-LACALLE DÚ 2004 T
80% tempranillo, 15% merlot, 5% cabernet sauvignon.

91 Colour: pale ruby, brick rim edge. Nose: elegant, fine reductive notes, aged wood nuances, fruit liqueur notes, aromatic coffee. Palate: spicy, fine tannins, elegant, long.

LEZCANO-LACALLE 2004 TR
80% tempranillo, 15% merlot, 5% cabernet sauvignon.

89 Colour: pale ruby, brick rim edge. Nose: elegant, spicy, fine reductive notes, wet leather, aged wood nuances. Palate: spicy, fine tannins, elegant, long.

BODEGAS REMIGIO DE SALAS JALÓN

Carril de Vinateras, s/n
34210 Dueñas (Palencia)
☎: +34 979 780 056 - Fax: +34 979 780 056
amada@remigiodesalasjalon.com
www.remigiodesalasjalon.com

LAS LUCERAS 2010 RD
tempranillo.

90 Colour: rose, purple rim. Nose: powerfull, red berry notes, floral. Palate: fleshy, fruity, fresh.

LAS LUCERAS 2009 T
tempranillo.

88 Colour: bright cherry. Nose: ripe fruit, sweet spices, varietal, toasty. Palate: flavourful, fruity, toasty, round tannins.

BODEGAS RODRÍGUEZ SANZ S.L.

Santa María, 6
47270 Cigales (Valladolid)
☎: +34 983 580 006 - Fax: +34 983 580 006
rodriguezsanz@telefonica.net

ROSAN 2010 RD

87 Colour: brilliant rose. Nose: elegant, candied fruit, dried flowers, red berry notes. Palate: light-bodied, flavourful, good acidity, long, spicy.

BODEGAS SANTA RUFINA

Pago Fuente La Teja. Pol. Ind. 3 - Parcela 102
47290 Cubillas de Santa Marta (Valladolid)
☎: +34 983 585 202 - Fax: +34 983 585 202
info@bodegassantarufina.com
www.bodegassantarufina.com

VIÑA RUFINA VENDIMIA SELECCIONADA 2010 RD

88 Colour: brilliant rose. Nose: candied fruit, dried flowers, fragrant herbs, red berry notes. Palate: light-bodied, flavourful, good acidity, long, spicy.

VIÑA RUFINA 2009 T ROBLE
tempranillo.

86 Colour: bright cherry. Nose: sweet spices, creamy oak, fruit expression. Palate: flavourful, fruity, toasty, round tannins.

BODEGAS SINFORIANO

Ctra. Villalba, Km. 1 Dcha.
47194 Mucientes (Valladolid)
☎: +34 983 663 008
sinfo@sinforianobodegas.com
www.sinforianobodegas.com

SINFO 2010 T ROBLE
100% tempranillo.

88 Colour: bright cherry. Nose: ripe fruit, sweet spices, creamy oak. Palate: flavourful, fruity, toasty, round tannins.

SINFORIANO 2008 TC
100% tempranillo.

91 Colour: cherry, garnet rim. Nose: ripe fruit, spicy, creamy oak, roasted coffee, mineral. Palate: powerful, flavourful, toasty, round tannins.

SINFORIANO 2006 TR
100% tempranillo.

89 Colour: pale ruby, brick rim edge. Nose: sweet spices, aromatic coffee, ripe fruit, dark chocolate. Palate: flavourful, fleshy, sweetness, long.

BODEGAS Y VIÑEDOS ALFREDO SANTAMARÍA

Poniente, 18
47290 Cubillas de Santa Marta (Valladolid)
☎: +34 983 585 006 - Fax: +34 983 440 770
info@bodega-santamaria.com
www.bodega-santamaria.com

VALVINOSO 2010 RD

81 Colour: rose. Nose: sulphur notes, ripe fruit. Palate: flavourful.

TRASCASAS 2007 TR
tempranillo.

90 Colour: cherry, garnet rim. Nose: ripe fruit, spicy, creamy oak, sweet spices, mineral. Palate: powerful, toasty, round tannins, ripe fruit, spicy.

ALFREDO SANTAMARÍA 2007 TC
tempranillo.

87 Colour: cherry, garnet rim. Nose: fruit preserve, warm, toasty, spicy. Palate: powerful, sweetness, spicy.

BODEGAS Y VIÑEDOS VALERIANO

Camino de las Bodegas, s/n
47290 Cubillas de Santa Marta (Valladolid)
☎: +34 983 585 085 - Fax: +34 983 585 186
bodegasvaleriano@wanadoo.es
www.bodegasvaleriano.com

EL BERROJO 2010 RD

82 Colour: rose. Nose: powerfull, ripe fruit, red berry notes. Palate: flavourful, ripe fruit.

VIÑA SESMERO 2010 RD

80 Colour: rose. Nose: faded flowers, warm. Palate: easy to drink.

VALERIANO JOVEN 2010 T

85 Colour: cherry, purple rim. Nose: red berry notes, floral, ripe fruit. Palate: flavourful, fruity, good acidity, round tannins.

VALERIANO 2007 TC

86 Colour: cherry, garnet rim. Nose: creamy oak, dark chocolate, aromatic coffee, ripe fruit. Palate: fine bitter notes, flavourful, fleshy.

C.H. VINOS DE CUBILLAS

Paseo Fuente la teja nº 31
47290 Cubillas de Santa Marta (Valladolid)
☎: +34 983 585 203 - Fax: +34 983 585 093
info@valdecabado.com

VALDECABADO 2008 T BARRICA
tempranillo.

88 Color bright cherry. Aroma ripe fruit, sweet spices, creamy oak, expressive. Taste flavourful, fruity, toasty, round tannins.

SELECCIÓN VIÑEDOS VIEJOS VALDECABADO 2006 T
tempranillo.

88 Colour: cherry, garnet rim. Nose: spicy, creamy oak, toasty, fruit liqueur notes. Palate: powerful, flavourful, round tannins.

VALCABADO 2004 TC
tempranillo.

87 Colour: cherry, garnet rim. Nose: ripe fruit, spicy, creamy oak, aromatic coffee, dark chocolate. Palate: powerful, flavourful, toasty, round tannins.

COMPAÑÍA DE VINOS MIGUEL MARTÍN

Ctra. Burgos - Portugal, Km. 101
47290 Cubillas de Santa María (Valladolid)
☎: +34 983 250 319 - Fax: +34 983 250 329
exportacion@ciadevinos.com
www.ciadevinos.com

VIÑA GOY 2010 RD
tempranillo.

85 Colour: raspberry rose. Nose: ripe fruit, dried flowers, medium intensity. Palate: fleshy, flavourful, fruity.

CONSEJO BODEGAS

Ctra. Valoria, Km. 3.6
47200 Valoria La Buena (Valladolid)
☎: +34 +34 983 502263 - Fax: +34 +34 983 502253
info@concejobodegas.com
www.concejobodegas.com

CARREDUEÑAS 2010 RD FERMENTADO EN BARRICA
tempranillo.

90 Colour: rose, purple rim. Nose: ripe fruit, red berry notes, sweet spices. Palate: fleshy, powerful, fruity, fresh.

CARREDUEÑAS 2010 RD
tempranillo.

89 Colour: rose, purple rim. Nose: powerfull, ripe fruit, red berry notes, floral. Palate: fleshy, powerful, fruity, fresh.

CARREDUEÑAS 2009 T ROBLE
tempranillo.

84 Colour: cherry, garnet rim. Nose: powerfull, fruit preserve, creamy oak, dark chocolate. Palate: sweetness, powerful, full.

VIÑA CONCEJO 2007 T
tempranillo.

88 Colour: cherry, garnet rim. Nose: toasty, candied fruit, fruit liqueur notes. Palate: powerful, flavourful, toasty, fleshy.

FINCA MUSEUM

Ctra. Cigales - Corcos, Km. 3
47270 Cigales (Valladolid)
☎: +34 983 581 029 - Fax: +34 983 581 030
info@bodegasmuseum.com
www.bodegasmuseum.com

VINEA 2009 TC
100% tinta del país.

87 Colour: cherry, garnet rim. Nose: ripe fruit, spicy, creamy oak, toasty, complex, balsamic herbs. Palate: powerful, flavourful, toasty, round tannins.

MUSEUM 2008 TC
100% tinta del país.

86 Colour: bright cherry. Nose: ripe fruit, sweet spices, creamy oak, fine reductive notes. Palate: flavourful, fruity, round tannins.

MUSEUM REAL 2005 TR
100% tinta del país.

89 Colour: deep cherry, orangey edge. Nose: wet leather, powerfull, fruit liqueur notes, toasty, sweet spices. Palate: powerful, spirituous, good structure.

FRUTOS VILLAR

Camino Los Barreros, s/n
47270 Cigales (Valladolid)
☎: +34 983 586 868 - Fax: +34 983 580 180
bodegasfrutosvillar@bodegasfrutosvillar.com
www.bodegasfrutosvillar.com

VIÑA CALDERONA 2010 RD
tinta del país, variedades blancas.

87 Colour: rose, purple rim. Nose: ripe fruit, red berry notes, floral. Palate: fleshy, powerful, fruity, fresh.

CONDE ANSÚREZ 2010 RD
tinta del país, variedades blancas.

84 Colour: brilliant rose. Nose: fresh fruit, red berry notes. Palate: flavourful, fruity, easy to drink.

CALDERONA 2010 T
100% tinta del país.

87 Colour: cherry, purple rim. Nose: fresh fruit, red berry notes. Palate: flavourful, fruity, good acidity, round tannins.

CONDE ANSÚREZ 2010 T
100% tinta del país.

86 Colour: cherry, purple rim. Nose: medium intensity, ripe fruit, balsamic herbs. Palate: good acidity, fine bitter notes, fruity.

CALDERONA 2006 TC
100% tinta del país.

88 Colour: bright cherry. Nose: ripe fruit, sweet spices, toasty. Palate: flavourful, fruity, toasty, round tannins.

CONDE ANSÚREZ 2006 TC
100% tinta del país.

88 Colour: deep cherry. Nose: sweet spices, dark chocolate, fruit preserve. Palate: fleshy, powerful.

CALDERONA 2005 TR
100% tinta del país.

90 Colour: cherry, garnet rim. Nose: ripe fruit, spicy, creamy oak, complex, dark chocolate, aromatic coffee. Palate: powerful, flavourful, toasty, round tannins.

HIJOS DE CRESCENCIA MERINO

Mayor, 15
47280 Corcos del Valle (Valladolid)
☎: +34 983 580 118 - Fax: +34 983 580 118
eugenio@bodegashcmerino.com
www.bodegashcmerino.com

VIÑA CATAJARROS 2010 RD
80% tempranillo, 10% verdejo, 10% otras.

85 Colour: light cherry. Nose: balsamic herbs, powerfull, ripe fruit. Palate: flavourful, ripe fruit, easy to drink.

HIJOS DE MARCOS GÓMEZ S.L.

Cuarto San Pedro s/n
47194 Mucientes (Valladolid)
☎: +34 983 587 764 - Fax: +34 983 587 764
bodegas@salvueros.com

SALVUEROS 2010 RD
80% tempranillo, 10% verdejo, 10% albillo.

86 Colour: rose, purple rim. Nose: ripe fruit, red berry notes, floral. Palate: fleshy, powerful, fruity, fresh.

HIJOS DE RUFINO IGLESIAS

La Canoniga, 25
47194 Mucientes (Valladolid)
☎: +34 983 587 778 - Fax: +34 983 587 778
bodega@hijosderufinoiglesias.com

CARRATRAVIESA 2010 RD
80% tempranillo, 10% garnacha, 10% albillo, verdejo.

87 Colour: rose, purple rim. Nose: ripe fruit, red berry notes, expressive, faded flowers. Palate: fleshy, fruity, fresh.

LA LEGUA

Ctra. Cigales, km. 1
47194 Fuensaldaña (Valladolid)
☎: +34 983 583 244 - Fax: +34 983 583 172
lalegua@lalegua.com
www.lalegua.com

LA LEGUA 2010 T
96% tempranillo, 4% garnacha.

83 Colour: cherry, garnet rim. Nose: ripe fruit, spicy, floral. Palate: flavourful, powerful, fleshy.

LA LEGUA 2009 T ROBLE
100% tempranillo.

87 Colour: bright cherry. Nose: sweet spices, expressive, ripe fruit, warm, new oak, cocoa bean. Palate: flavourful, fruity, toasty, round tannins.

LA LEGUA 2008 TC
100% tempranillo.

87 Colour: cherry, garnet rim. Nose: powerfull, fruit liqueur notes, toasty, spicy. Palate: flavourful, spicy, fine bitter notes.

LA LEGUA CAPRICHO 2007 T
100% tempranillo.

91 Colour: cherry, garnet rim. Nose: spicy, creamy oak, toasty, powerfull, mineral, overripe fruit. Palate: powerful, flavourful, toasty, round tannins, long.

LA LEGUA 2007 TR
100% tempranillo.

82 Colour: deep cherry. Nose: fruit liqueur notes, overripe fruit, aromatic coffee. Palate: easy to drink, spicy.

MAS FERRANT MARXANTS DE VINS

Córsega, 73- 1º
08029 (Barcelona)
☎: +34 934 191 000 - Fax: +34 934 193 170
jcivit@montferrant.com

MAS FERRANT SANG NOVA 2004 TR
100% tempranillo.

78

OVIDIO GARCÍA

Malpique, s/n
47012 Cigales (Valladolid)
☎: +34 628 509 475 - Fax: +34 983 474 085
info@ovidiogarcia.com
www.ovidiogarcia.com

OVIDIO GARCÍA ESENCIA 2008 TC
100% tempranillo.

88 Colour: cherry, garnet rim. Nose: spicy, toasty, sweet spices, characterful, overripe fruit. Palate: powerful, flavourful, toasty, round tannins.

OVIDIO GARCÍA ESENCIA 2006 TC
100% tempranillo.

90 Colour: cherry, garnet rim. Nose: ripe fruit, spicy, creamy oak, toasty. Palate: powerful, flavourful, toasty, round tannins.

OVIDIO GARCÍA 2005 TR
100% tempranillo.

90 Colour: cherry, garnet rim. Nose: ripe fruit, spicy, creamy oak, characterful, pattiserie. Palate: powerful, flavourful, toasty, sweetness, powerful tannins.

PINEDO MENESES

Picón del Rollo, s/n
47280 Corcos del Valle (Valladolid)
☎: +34 983 586 877 - Fax: +34 983 586 877
www.lubolrosado.com

LUBOL 2010 RD

88 Colour: rose, purple rim. Nose: powerfull, ripe fruit, red berry notes. Palate: fleshy, powerful, fruity, fresh.

TRASLANZAS

Barrio de las Bodegas, s/n
47194 Mucientes (Valladolid)
☎: +34 639 641 123
traslanzas@traslanzas.com
www.traslanzas.com

TRASLANZAS 2008 T
100% tempranillo.

90 Colour: cherry, garnet rim. Nose: spicy, new oak, overripe fruit. Palate: powerful, flavourful, toasty, round tannins.

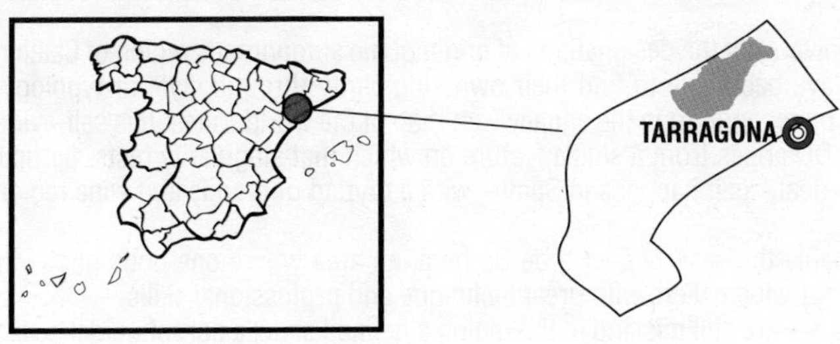

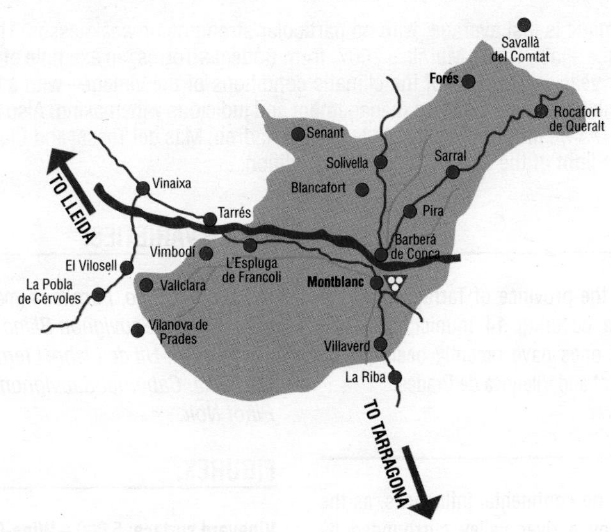

Consejo Regulador
DO Boundary

DO CONCA DE BARBERÀ

NEWS ABOUT THE VINTAGE:

In the vast universe of the designations of origin of the autonomous region of Catalunya we find some that have been able to find their own singularity through style or typology, and have managed to be recognised in the equally vast map of the world wines. It is self-evident that the identity of a DO arises from a single feature on which that singularity rests, particularly when they have to deal –as it happens in Spain– with a myriad of brands and wine regions.

That is probably the case of Conca de Barberá, an area where one finds good vine growers and equally apt winemakers with great technique and professional skills.
Nonetheless, we are still missing in the region a defined style, a sort of guideline that could be followed by all the wineries in order to characterize their wines and make them more easily recognizable and unique. Their local grape variety, *trepat*, seems a good starting point in that search of singularity for Conca de Barberá. In general terms, quality is pretty good in the region, at least in the light of the scores: a 23% of the samples tasted got 88 and 89 points.

The 2010 vintage is just average, with no particular strengths or weaknesses. The flagship of the DO is, once again, Grans Muralles 2007, from Bodegas Torres, an example of how to come up year after year –regardless of the climatic conditions of the vintage– with a homogenous product, thanks to careful vineyard management and judicious winemaking. Also in the leading group of the DO we find Escoda Sanahuja, Carles Andreu, Mas del Tossal and Clos Montblanc, at least in the light of the scores in this year's edition.

LOCATION:

In the north of the province of Tarragona with a production area covering 14 municipalities, to which two new ones have recently been added: Savallà del Comtat and Vilanova de Prades.

CLIMATE:

Mediterranean and continental influences, as the vineyards occupy a river valley surrounded by mountain ranges without direct contact with the sea.

SOIL:

The soil is mainly brownish-grey and limy. The vines are cultivated on slopes protected by woodland. An important aspect is the altitude which gives the wines a fresh, light character.

GRAPE VARIETIES:

WHITE: *Macabeo, Parellada* (majority 3,300 Ha) *Chardonnay, Sauvignon Blanc.*
RED: *Trepat, Ull de Llebre* (*Tempranillo*), *Garnatxa, Cabernet Sauvignon, Merlot, Syrah, Pinot Noir.*

FIGURES:

Vineyard surface: 5,000 – **Wine-Growers:** 1,100 – **Wineries:** 24 – **2010 Harvest rating:** N/A – **Production:** 278,800 litres – **Market percentages:** 71,7% domestic. 28,3% export

CONSEJO REGULADOR
Torre del Portal de Sant Antoni
C/ de la Volta, 2
43400 Montblanc
☎: +34 977 926 905 / +34 692 596 044 -Fax: +34 977 926 906
@ cr@doconcadebarbera.com
www.doconcadebarbera.com

GENERAL CHARACTERISTICS OF THE WINES

WHITES	Pale and brilliant, they are fruity, pleasant to drink and very light, although not excessively roasted.
ROSÉS	Raspberry-pink coloured, quite modern in their production style, with red fruit noses, slightly fresh, flavourful and well-balanced.
REDS	These are quite light and easy drinking, for the moment, with characteristics more adapted to producing young wines than for Crianza wines, except in the case of the most experienced producers who produce powerful, meaty and concentrated red wines.

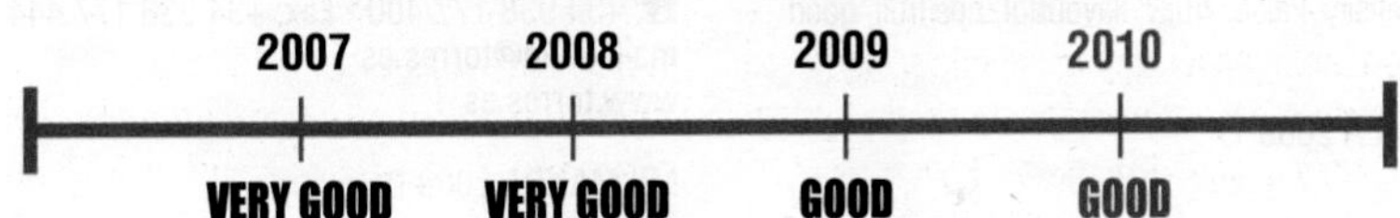

AGRÍCOLA DE BARBERÀ

Comercio, 40
43422 Barberà de la Conca (Tarragona)
☎: +34 977 887 035 - Fax: +34 977 887 035
cobarbera@doconcadebarbera.com

CABANAL TREPAT 2009 T
100% trepat.

85 Colour: light cherry, garnet rim. Nose: scrubland, ripe fruit, medium intensity, balanced, toasty. Palate: balanced, good acidity.

CABANAL TREPAT 2008 T
100% trepat.

86 Colour: cherry, garnet rim. Nose: ripe fruit, spicy, old leather. Palate: light-bodied, fruity, easy to drink.

BODEGA VEGA AIXALÁ

De la Font, 11
43439 Vilanova de Prades (Tarragona)
☎: +34 636 519 821 - Fax: +34 977 869 019
info@vegaaixala.com
www.vegaaixala.com

VEGA AIXALÁ 2009 B
garnacha blanca.

83 Colour: bright yellow. Nose: white flowers, ripe fruit, medium intensity. Palate: fruity, flavourful, ripe fruit, good finish.

VEGA AIXALÁ 2009 T
tempranillo.

87 Colour: bright cherry, purple rim. Nose: fruit expression, fresh fruit, violets. Palate: flavourful, fruity, easy to drink.

VEGA AIXALÁ 2008 TC
cabernet sauvignon, tempranillo, garnacha, syrah, cariñena, merlot.

86 Colour: bright cherry. Nose: ripe fruit, sweet spices, creamy oak, red berry notes. Palate: flavourful, fruity, toasty, round tannins, long.

BODEGAS BELLOD

Avda. Mare de Déu de Montserrat, 6
08970 Sant Joan Despí (Barcelona)
☎: +34 933 731 151 - Fax: +34 933 731 354
bodegasbellod@bodegasbellod.com
www.bodegasbellod.com

PRINCIPAT S/C RD
garnacha.

85 Colour: rose, purple rim. Nose: red berry notes, fresh, floral. Palate: fruity, good acidity, fine bitter notes.

MAS DEL NEN 2009 T
50% cabernet sauvignon, 50% syrah.

88 Colour: bright cherry, purple rim. Nose: sweet spices, creamy oak, ripe fruit, balanced. Palate: fruity, flavourful, fruity aftestaste.

CEP D'ART 2008 TC
50% tempranillo, 30% cabernet sauvignon, 20% syrah.

87 Colour: cherry, garnet rim. Nose: ripe fruit, balanced, sweet spices. Palate: flavourful, fruity, ripe fruit, spicy, soft tannins.

BODEGAS TORRES

Miguel Torres, 6
08720 Vilafranca del Penedès (Barcelona)
☎: +34 938 177 400 - Fax: +34 938 177 444
mailadmin@torres.es
www.torres.es

MILMANDA 2009 B
100% chardonnay.

90 Colour: bright yellow. Nose: ripe fruit, jasmine, white flowers, sweet spices. Palate: good structure, toasty, good acidity.

GRANS MURALLES 2008 T
monastrell, garnacha, garro, samso, mazuelo.

94 Colour: cherry, purple rim. Nose: powerfull, fruit expression, raspberry, toasty, creamy oak. Palate: flavourful, powerful, fleshy, spicy.

GRANS MURALLES 2007 TGR
monastrell, garnacha, garró, samsó, mazuelo.

94 Colour: very deep cherry, garnet rim. Nose: ripe fruit, mineral, complex, balanced, expressive. Palate: fleshy, flavourful, fine bitter notes, round tannins.

CARLANIA CELLER

Polígono 23, Parcela 93
43422 Barberà de la Conca (Tarragona)
☎: +34 977 887 375
info@carlania.com
www.carlania.com

CARLANIA 2009 B
80% macabeo, 20% trepat.

84 Colour: bright straw. Nose: toasty, spicy, overripe fruit, honeyed notes. Palate: toasty, flavourful.

CARLANIA 2009 RD
100% trepat.

82 Colour: raspberry rose. Nose: candied fruit, dried flowers, powerfull. Palate: fine bitter notes, correct.

CARLANIA 2009 T
60% ull de llebre, 40% trepat.

87 Colour: bright cherry, purple rim. Nose: ripe fruit, scrubland, spicy, medium intensity. Palate: powerful, fruity.

CARLANIA 2007 T
90% merlot, 10% trepat.

88 Colour: cherry, garnet rim. Nose: ripe fruit, candied fruit, sweet spices, complex. Palate: flavourful, good structure, round tannins, good acidity.

CASTELL D'OR

Mare Rafols, 3- 1r 4a
08720 Vilafranca del Penedès (Barcelona)
☎: +34 938 905 385 - Fax: +34 938 905 446
castelldor@castelldor.com
www.castelldor.com

FRANCOLI 2010 B
80% macabeo, 20% parellada.

82 Colour: bright straw. Nose: jasmine, ripe fruit, honeyed notes. Palate: fruity, rich, ripe fruit.

CASTELL DE LA COMANDA 2010 B
80% macabeo, 20% parellada.

82 Colour: bright straw. Nose: jasmine, white flowers, ripe fruit, dried herbs, citrus fruit. Palate: easy to drink, good finish.

CASTELL DE LA COMANDA 2010 RD
100% trepat.

86 Colour: rose, purple rim. Nose: raspberry, fruit expression, faded flowers.

FRANCOLI 2010 RD
100% trepat.

85 Colour: brilliant rose. Nose: red berry notes, violets, floral. Palate: correct, easy to drink, fruity.

FRANCOLI 2009 T
50% trepat, 50% tempranillo.

86 Colour: cherry, garnet rim. Nose: red berry notes, ripe fruit, spicy, medium intensity. Palate: flavourful, fruity, round tannins.

CASTELL DE LA COMANDA 2008 T
100% tempranillo.

87 Colour: bright cherry. Nose: red berry notes, medium intensity, fruit expression, balanced. Palate: fruity, flavourful, fruity aftestaste.

FRANCOLI 2008 TC
60% cabernet sauvignon, 40% tempranillo.

85 Colour: cherry, garnet rim. Nose: macerated fruit, ripe fruit, toasty, spicy. Palate: easy to drink, ripe fruit, spicy.

FRANCOLI 2006 TR
60% cabernet sauvignon, 40% tempranillo.

88 Colour: cherry, garnet rim. Nose: spicy, ripe fruit, balanced. Palate: fleshy, powerful, spicy.

CASTELL DE LA COMANDA OAKED 2006 T
100% tempranillo.

82 Colour: cherry, garnet rim. Nose: candied fruit, spicy, toasty. Palate: fruity, easy to drink, good finish.

CASTELL DE LA COMANDA 2004 TR
100% cabernet sauvignon.

88 Colour: light cherry, garnet rim. Nose: sweet spices, balanced, ripe fruit, candied fruit. Palate: fruity, easy to drink.

CAVAS SANSTRAVÉ

De la Conca, 10
43412 Solivella (Tarragona)
☎: +34 977 892 165 - Fax: +34 977 892 073
bodega@sanstrave.com
www.sanstrave.com

SANSTRAVÉ FINCA GASSET MOSCATEL 2009 BFB
100% moscatel.

88 Colour: yellow. Nose: jasmine, white flowers, ripe fruit, varietal. Palate: fruity, flavourful, good acidity, good finish.

SANSTRAVÉ FINCA GASSET CREPUSCLE 2009 T FERMENTADO EN BARRICA
90% syrah, 10% merlot.

87 Colour: bright cherry, purple rim. Nose: ripe fruit, old leather, spicy. Palate: good structure, flavourful, fruity.

SANSTRAVÉ PARTIDA DELS JUEUS 2008 TC
80% merlot, 10% tempranillo, 5% cabernet sauvignon, 2% trepat, 3% garnacha.

87 Colour: cherry, garnet rim. Nose: red berry notes, ripe fruit, dried herbs, spicy. Palate: flavourful, fruity, good structure.

SANSTRAVÉ FINCA GASSET SYRAH 2005 TR
100% syrah.

84 Colour: cherry, garnet rim. Nose: grassy, spicy, balsamic herbs. Palate: flavourful, fruity.

CELLER CAL JOAN

Església, 4
43425 Montbrió de la Marca (Tarragona)
☎: +34 977 898 150
ccaljoan@gmail.com

TROS D'ENYOR 2010 RD
merlot, garnacha.

86 Colour: brilliant rose. Nose: fruit expression, wild herbs, red berry notes. Palate: fresh, correct, good acidity.

TROS D'ENYOR 2008 T
merlot, ull de llebre.

86 Colour: cherry, garnet rim. Nose: old leather, warm, ripe fruit, spicy. Palate: flavourful, fruity.

CELLER CARLES ANDREU

Sant Sebastià, 19
43423 Pira (Tarragona)
☎: +34 977 887 404 - Fax: +34 977 887 427
info@cavandreu.com
www.cavandreu.com

CARLES ANDREU PARELLADA 2010 B
100% parellada.

89 Colour: bright straw. Nose: fresh fruit, dried flowers, scrubland, neat. Palate: fresh, fruity, good acidity.

VINO TINTO TREPAT CARLES ANDREU 2009 T
100% trepat.

90 Colour: light cherry, garnet rim. Nose: fruit expression, balanced, medium intensity, expressive, wild herbs. Palate: fruity, flavourful, elegant.

CELLER ESCODA SANAHUJA

Camí de Lilla a Prenafeta, s/n
43400 Montblanc (Tarragona)
☎: +34 659 478 198 - Fax: +34 977 314 897
jre@celler-escodasanahuja.com
www.celler-escodasanahuja.com

ELS BASSOTS 2008 B
100% chenin blanc.

89 Colour: golden. Nose: balanced, complex, expressive, warm, white flowers, spicy. Palate: good structure, fruity, toasty, ripe fruit, flavourful.

TORRE DEL MORO 2009 T
garnacha, cariñena, merlot, cabernet franc.

91 Colour: deep cherry, garnet rim. Nose: scrubland, earthy notes, spicy, red berry notes. Palate: flavourful, good structure, round tannins, good acidity.

LA LLOPETERA 2008 TC
pinot noir.

90 Colour: cherry, garnet rim. Nose: ripe fruit, creamy oak, sweet spices, complex. Palate: good structure, fleshy, round tannins, good acidity.

LES PARADETES 2006 TC
garnacha, cariñena.

89 Colour: cherry, garnet rim. Nose: ripe fruit, complex, expressive, spicy. Palate: balanced, elegant, good acidity, round tannins.

COLL DEL SABATER 2006 TC
cabernet franc, merlot.

87 Colour: cherry, garnet rim. Nose: candied fruit, sweet spices, cocoa bean, warm. Palate: good structure, fruity, good acidity.

CELLER GUSPÍ

Avda. Arnau de Ponç, 10
43423 Pira (Tarragona)
☎: +34 636 816 724
josep.guspi@hotmail.com
www.viverdecelleristes.concadebarbera.cat

GUSPI BLANCTRESC 2010 B
50% macabeo, 30% chardonnay, 20% sauvignon blanc.

84 Colour: bright straw. Nose: white flowers, medium intensity. Palate: flavourful, fruity, good acidity, balanced.

GUSPI EMBIGATS DE LA MARÍA 2008 T
100% tempranillo.

88 Colour: bright cherry, garnet rim. Nose: balanced, spicy, creamy oak, wild herbs. Palate: good structure, ripe fruit, good acidity.

GUSPI PINETELL 2008 T
100% merlot.

87 Colour: cherry, garnet rim. Nose: ripe fruit, scrubland, spicy. Palate: balanced, spicy, fruity, round tannins, good acidity.

CELLER JORDI LLORENS

Prim, 5-7
43411 Blancafort (Tarragona)
☎: +34 629 204 672
cellerjll@gmail.com

CELLER JORDI LLORENS PARELLADA 2010 B
100% parellada.

81 Colour: yellow. Nose: ripe fruit, slightly evolved, dried flowers. Palate: flavourful, good acidity.

CELLER JORDI LLORENS CABERNET SAUVIGNON 2010 T
100% cabernet sauvignon.

86 Colour: bright cherry, purple rim. Nose: scrubland, ripe fruit. Palate: flavourful, fruity, fruity aftestaste, round tannins.

ATIQETE CABERNET 2009 T BARRICA
100% cabernet sauvignon.

87 Colour: cherry, garnet rim. Nose: ripe fruit, powerfull, scrubland, warm, spicy. Palate: fleshy, sweetness, good structure, great length.

CELLER MAS FORASTER

Camino Ermita de Sant Josep, s/n
43400 Montblanc (Tarragona)
☎: +34 977 860 229 - Fax: +34 977 875 037
info@josepforaster.com
www.josepforaster.com

JOSEP FORASTER BLANC SELECCIÓ 2010 BFB
50% garnacha blanca, 40% macabeo, 10% chardonnay.

85 Colour: bright straw. Nose: ripe fruit, toasty, spicy. Palate: flavourful, toasty, spicy, light-bodied.

JOSEP FORASTER COLLITA 2010 T
90% tempranillo, 10% cabernet sauvignon.

87 Colour: cherry, purple rim. Nose: red berry notes, ripe fruit. Palate: good structure, fruity, easy to drink, good acidity.

JOSEP FORASTER TREPAT 2010 T
100% trepat.

84 Colour: bright cherry. Nose: faded flowers, ripe fruit, grassy, mineral, toasty. Palate: flavourful, fleshy, ripe fruit.

JOSEP FORASTER TREPAT 2009 T
100% trepat.

83 Colour: light cherry. Nose: toasty, spicy. Palate: ripe fruit, spicy, easy to drink, good finish.

JOSEP FORASTER 2008 TC
40% cabernet sauvignon, 30% tempranillo, 30% syrah.

88 Colour: cherry, garnet rim. Nose: wild herbs, candied fruit, ripe fruit, spicy. Palate: fleshy, fruity, round tannins.

JOSEP FORASTER SELECCIÓ 2006 TR
90% cabernet sauvignon, 10% tempranillo.

89 Colour: cherry, garnet rim. Nose: balanced, spicy, ripe fruit. Palate: good structure, fruity, round tannins, great length.

CELLER MOLÍ DELS CAPELLANS

Avenir, 24 3 - 5
43800 Valls (Tarragona)
☎: +34 651 034 221
info@molidelscapellans.com
www.molidelscapellans.com

MOLÍ DELS CAPELLANS 2010 B
parellada, moscatel.

88 Color bright straw. Aroma fresh, fresh fruit, white flowers, expressive. Taste flavourful, fruity, good acidity, balanced.

MOLÍ DELS CAPELLANS 2009 BFB
chardonnay.

85 Colour: yellow. Nose: ripe fruit, sweet spices, floral. Palate: powerful, toasty, great length.

CELLERS ROSET

Finca de Sant Feliu - Ctra. Tàrrega, s/n
43410 La Guardia del Prats (Tarragona)
☎: +34 937 369 690 - Fax: +34 937 361 303
info@brescat.com
www.brescat.com

BRESCAT 2006 TC
cabernet sauvignon, merlot, syrah.

87 Colour: cherry, garnet rim. Nose: ripe fruit, spicy, creamy oak, toasty, complex, cocoa bean. Palate: powerful, flavourful, toasty, round tannins.

CLOS MONTBLANC

Ctra. Montblanc-Barbera, s/n
43422 Barberà de la Conca (Tarragona)
☎: +34 977 887 030 - Fax: +34 977 887 032
info@closmontblanc.com
www.closmontblanc.com

CLOS MONTBLANC XIPELLA BLANC 2010 B
macabeo, parellada.

90 Colour: bright straw. Nose: jasmine, white flowers, ripe fruit, citrus fruit. Palate: flavourful, ripe fruit, good acidity, fine bitter notes.

CASTILLO DE MONTBLANC MACABEO/CHARDONNAY 2010 B
macabeo, chardonnay.

88 Colour: yellow. Nose: wild herbs, dried flowers, ripe fruit, varietal, citrus fruit. Palate: fruity, flavourful, good acidity.

CLOS MONTBLANC SAUVIGNON BLANC PREMIUM 2010 B
sauvignon blanc.

87 Colour: bright straw. Nose: fresh fruit, citrus fruit, wild herbs, dried flowers. Palate: flavourful, fruity, good acidity.

CLOS MONTBLANC CHARDONNAY 2010 BFB
chardonnay.

86 Colour: bright yellow. Nose: ripe fruit, candied fruit, floral. Palate: toasty, ripe fruit, flavourful.

CASTILLO DE MONTBLANC 2010 RD
syrah, trepat, tempranillo, cariñena, garnacha, monastrell.

86 Colour: rose, purple rim. Nose: candied fruit, dried flowers, fragrant herbs, medium intensity. Palate: flavourful, good acidity, long, spicy.

CLOS MONTBLANC SYRAH PREMIUM 2009 T
syrah.

88 Colour: deep cherry, purple rim. Nose: balanced, ripe fruit, dried herbs, spicy, expressive. Palate: fruity, good structure, easy to drink.

CLOS MONTBLANC XIPELLA PREMIUM 2009 T
garnacha, monastrell, syrah, samsó.

88 Colour: very deep cherry, garnet rim. Nose: ripe fruit, candied fruit, sweet spices, creamy oak. Palate: fruity, full.

CLOS MONTBLANC PINOT NOIR PREMIUM 2009 TC
pinot noir.

87 Colour: cherry, purple rim. Nose: toasty, sweet spices, red berry notes, ripe fruit. Palate: flavourful, spicy, great length.

CLOS MONTBLANC MASÍA LES COMES 2006 TR
cabernet sauvignon, merlot.

90 Colour: cherry, garnet rim. Nose: ripe fruit, candied fruit, sweet spices, balanced, complex. Palate: good structure, flavourful, full.

CLOS MONTBLANC MERLOT PREMIUM 2006 TC
merlot.

89 Colour: cherry, garnet rim. Nose: medium intensity, ripe fruit, spicy, balanced. Palate: fruity, flavourful, good acidity, spicy.

GATZARA VINS

Josep M. Tossas, 47. 1º-2º
43400 Montblanc (Tarragona)
☎: +34 977 861 175 - Fax: +34 977 861 175
info@gatzaravins.com
http://viverdecelleristes.concadebarbera.cat

GATZARA 2010 B
macabeo, chardonnay.

88 Colour: bright straw. Nose: fresh, fresh fruit, white flowers, fragrant herbs. Palate: flavourful, fruity, good acidity, balanced.

GATZARA 2010 T
trepat.

92 Colour: bright cherry. Nose: fresh fruit, red berry notes, balsamic herbs, scrubland. Palate: flavourful, fruity, fresh. Personality.

GATZARA 2008 TC
48% cabernet sauvignon, 52% merlot.

90 Colour: cherry, garnet rim. Nose: sweet spices, dark chocolate, creamy oak, ripe fruit, balanced. Palate: flavourful, fruity, good structure, round tannins.

HEREDAD PALLARÉS

Ctra. Montblanc Prenafeta km 4
43415 Montblanc (Tarragona)
☎: +34 639 168 514 - Fax: +34 977 252 729
alosada@heredad-pallares.com
www.heredad-pallares.com

ARRELS DE LA CONCA 2010 B
chardonnay.

87 Colour: bright straw. Nose: tropical fruit, citrus fruit, fresh, expressive. Palate: good acidity, fresh, fruity.

MAS DE LA SABATERA 2008 T
70% cabernet sauvignon, 15% tempranillo, 15% merlot.

88 Colour: cherry, garnet rim. Nose: ripe fruit, fresh, spicy, creamy oak. Palate: good acidity, balanced, fruity, flavourful.

MAS DE LA SABATERA 2007 T
80% cabernet sauvignon, 20% merlot.

87 Colour: cherry, garnet rim. Nose: cocoa bean, creamy oak, ripe fruit. Palate: flavourful, balsamic, balanced.

MAS DEL TOSSAL

Comerç, 2
43422 Barberà de la Conca (Tarragona)
☎: +34 618 546 050
pepburguera@yahoo.es

ESPURNA 2008 T
60% cabernet franc, 35% syrah, 5% trepat.

90 Colour: very deep cherry, garnet rim. Nose: complex, spicy, toasty, mineral, dark chocolate. Palate: fleshy, good structure, ripe fruit.

ESPURNA 2007 T
65% cabernet franc, 35% syrah.

90 Colour: very deep cherry, garnet rim. Nose: sweet spices, cocoa bean, ripe fruit, mineral. Palate: flavourful, fleshy, fruity, round tannins.

RENDÉ MASDÉU

Avda. Catalunya, 44
43440 L'Espluga de Francolí (Tarragona)
☎: +34 977 871 361 - Fax: +34 977 871 361
rendemasdeu@terra.es
www.rendemasdeu.com

RENDÉ MASDEU 2010 RD
syrah.

88 Colour: brilliant rose. Nose: floral, balanced, red berry notes, wild herbs, ripe fruit. Palate: fruity, flavourful, great length.

ARNAU 2009 T
syrah.

87 Colour: deep cherry, purple rim. Nose: red berry notes, ripe fruit, sweet spices. Palate: flavourful, fruity, balanced, easy to drink, good finish.

MANUELA VENTOSA 2008 T
70% cabernet sauvignon, 30% syrah.

90 Colour: deep cherry, garnet rim. Nose: complex, ripe fruit, cocoa bean, sweet spices. Palate: balanced, good acidity, round tannins, spicy, fleshy.

RENDÉ MASDEU 2008 TC
90% cabernet sauvignon, 10% syrah.

87 Color bright cherry. Aroma ripe fruit, sweet spices, creamy oak, expressive. Taste flavourful, fruity, toasty, round tannins.

RENDÉ MASDEU 2006 TR
85% cabernet sauvignon, 15% syrah.

89 Colour: bright cherry, garnet rim. Nose: red berry notes, ripe fruit, cocoa bean, medium intensity, balanced, expressive. Palate: ripe fruit, flavourful, good acidity.

ROSA MARÍA TORRES

Avda. Anguera, 2
43424 Sarral (Tarragona)
☎: +34 977 890 013 - Fax: +34 977 890 173
info@rosamariatorres.com
www.rosamariatorres.com

VIOGNIER 2009 BFB
viognier.

86 Colour: bright straw. Nose: white flowers, jasmine, fruit expression, dried herbs. Palate: fruity, flavourful, spicy, ripe fruit.

RD ROURE 2009 T
cabernet sauvignon, syrah.

86 Colour: cherry, garnet rim. Nose: wild herbs, red berry notes, ripe fruit, balanced. Palate: flavourful, fruity, easy to drink, spicy.

VINYA PLANS 2008 TC
cabernet franc, cabernet sauvignon, syrah.

88 Colour: cherry, garnet rim. Nose: balanced, medium intensity, expressive, red berry notes, spicy. Palate: good structure, flavourful, easy to drink, fruity aftestaste.

VINÍCOLA DE SARRAL Í SELECCIÓ DE CREDIT

Avda. de la Conca, 33
43424 Sarral (Tarragona)
☎: +34 977 890 031 - Fax: +34 977 890 136
cavaportell@covisal.es
www.cava_portell.com

PORTELL BLANC DE BLANCS 2010 B
80% macabeo, 20% parraleta.

85 Colour: bright straw. Nose: fresh fruit, citrus fruit, white flowers. Palate: fruity, fine bitter notes.

PORTELL TREPAT 2010 RD
100% trepat.

87 Colour: light cherry. Nose: red berry notes, ripe fruit, floral, balanced, powerfull. Palate: fruity, fresh, good acidity.

PORTELL MERLOT 2009 T
100% merlot.

87 Colour: cherry, purple rim. Nose: ripe fruit, candied fruit, spicy, scrubland. Palate: balanced, fruity.

PORTELL SELECCIÓ 2 ANY 2008 T
70% tempranillo, 15% merlot, 15% cabernet sauvignon.

87 Colour: bright cherry. Nose: expressive, spicy, ripe fruit. Palate: flavourful, fruity, toasty, round tannins.

PORTELL 2006 TC
40% cabernet sauvignon, 40% merlot, 20% tempranillo.

84 Colour: cherry, garnet rim. Nose: spicy, ripe fruit, fruit liqueur notes. Palate: fruity, easy to drink.

PORTELL 2005 TR
50% merlot, 40% cabernet sauvignon, 10% ull de llebre.

88 Colour: cherry, garnet rim. Nose: ripe fruit, balanced, expressive, spicy. Palate: ripe fruit, good acidity, balanced.

PORTELL 2010 BLANCO DE AGUJA
80% macabeo, 20% parellada.

78

PORTELL TREPAT 2010 ROSADO DE AGUJA
100% trepat.

82 Colour: brilliant rose. Nose: red berry notes, ripe fruit, wild herbs. Palate: correct, good acidity, easy to drink.

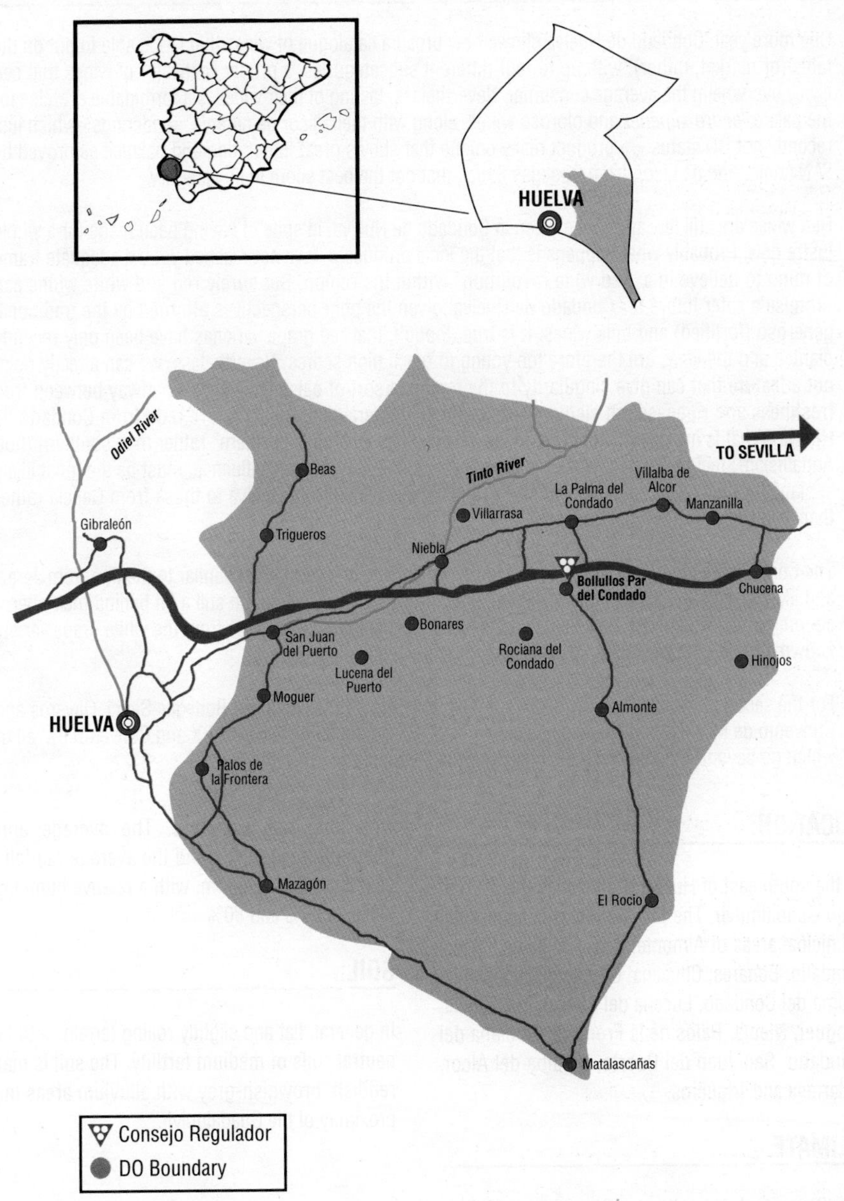
HUELVA
Odiel River
Beas
Gibraleón
Trigueros
Tinto River
TO SEVILLA
La Palma del Condado
Villalba de Alcor
Manzanilla
Villarrasa
Niebla
Bollullos Par del Condado
Chucena
Bonares
San Juan del Puerto
Lucena del Puerto
Rociana del Condado
Hinojos
Moguer
Almonte
HUELVA
Palos de la Frontera
Mazagón
El Rocío
Matalascañas
Consejo Regulador
DO Boundary

NEWS ABOUT THE VINTAGE:

One more year, Condado de Huelva shows how broad a catalogue of wines that DO is able to put on the table (or market, rather), with up to four different subcategories, a proper "catwalk" of wines that can easily overwhelm the average consumer. Nevertheless, tasting of their wines is a formidable exercise for the palate: *pedro ximénez* and oloroso wines, along with their "licor de naranja" renderings –which just recently got DO status–, a product really unique that shows great integration and balance as proved by S' Naranja Vino de Licor, from Bodegas Sauci, that got the best score in its category.

Red wines are still few and far between in Condado de Huelva, in spite of having been made for a whole lustre now. Probably what happens is that the local producers have not reached yet the adequate frame of mind to believe in a "red wine revolution" within the region. But surely red and white wines can promise a safer future for Condado de Huelva, given the poor perspectives afforded by the traditional generoso (fortified) and bulk wines. It is true, though, that red grape varieties have been only recently planted and the vines are therefore too young to reach high scores. Nevertheless, we can already point out a feature that can give singularity to the region, a sort of balsamic element halfway between fruit freshness and ripeness, an element that could characterize the (near) future reds from Condado de Huelva. What is interesting about that note is that it has a certain "northern" rather than southern (hot, Andalusian!) feel to it. The climate of the region, with a heavy Atlantic influence, must be the most likely explanation for a phenomenon that seem to relate the wines from Huelva to those from Galicia rather than to those from Códoba or Málaga.

The Condado Pálido (the category refers to the wine made in Huelva most similar to the fino from Jerez, and likewise made from *palomino* grapes) show pretty balanced, although still a bit behind their sherry counterparts. Young wines labelled as Condado de Huelva Joven and made from the white grape variety known as *zalema* show in the 2010 vintage quite fresh and easy to drink.

For the second year in a row, the best scores in Condado de Huelva go for Bodegas Sauci, Oliveros and Convento de Morañina with –respectively– their S' PX Solera 1989, Oliveros PX and Convento PX, all of which go beyond the 89-points boundary and thus verging on excellence.

LOCATION:

In the south east of Huelva. It occupies the plain of Bajo Guadalquivir. The production area covers the municipal areas of Almonte, Beas, Bollullos Par del Condado, Bonares, Chucena, Gibraleón, Hinojos, La Palma del Condado, Lucena del Puerto, Manzanilla, Moguer, Niebla, Palos de la Frontera, Rociana del Condado, San Juan del Puerto, Villalba del Alcor, Villarrasa and Trigueros.

CLIMATE:

Mediterranean in nature, with certain Atlantic influences. The winters and springs are fairly mild, with long hot summers. The average annual temperature is 18 °C, and the average rainfall per year is around 550 mm, with a relative humidity of between 60% and 80%.

SOIL:

In general, flat and slightly rolling terrain, with fairly neutral soils of medium fertility. The soil is mainly reddish, brownish-grey with alluvium areas in the proximity of the Guadalquivir.

GRAPE VARIETIES:

WHITE: *Zalema* (majority with 86% of vineyards), *Palomino, Listán de Huelva, Garrido Fino, Moscatel de Alejandría* and *Pedro Ximénez.*
RED: *Merlot, Syrah, Tempranillo, Cabernet Sauvignon* and *Cabernet Franc.*

FIGURES:

Vineyard surface: 3,008 – **Wine-Growers:** 1,747 – **Wineries:** 36 – **2010 Harvest rating:** N/A – **Production:** 10,742,991 litres – **Market percentages:** 90% domestic. 10% export

CONSEJO REGULADOR
Plaza Ildefonso Pinto, s/n.
21710 Bollullos Par del Condado (Huelva)
☎: +34 959 410 322 - Fax: +34 959 413 859
@ cr@condadodehuelva.es
www.condadodehuelva.es

GENERAL CHARACTERISTICS OF THE WINES

YOUNG WHITES	Produced from the autochtonous *Zalema* variety, they are characterised by their slightly vegetative notes with hints of scrubland; they are pleasant and easy drinking.
CONDADO PÁLIDO	These are quite similar to the other Finos of Andalusia (Jerezanos and Montillanos). *Palomino* grapes are used in their production, the same as those used for Jerez, although they have somewhat less biological character.
CONDADO VIEJO	These are the most traditional wines of the region, although now only produced in a few cellars, and come from the oldest Soleras.

VINTAGE RATING PEÑÍNGUIDE

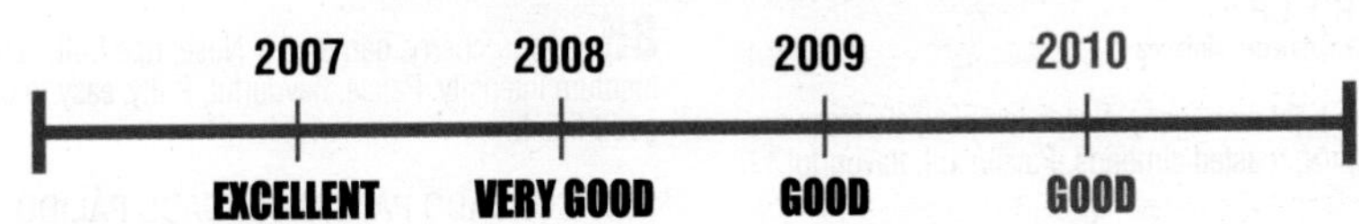

AGROALIMENTARIA VIRGEN DEL ROCÍO

Avda. de Cabezudos, s/n
21730 Almonte (Huelva)
☎: +34 959 406 146 - Fax: +34 959 407 052
administracion@raigal.com
www.raigal.com

RAIGAL S/C B
100% zalema.

79

TEJARES CONDADO DULCE GE
100% zalema.

80 Colour: light mahogany. Nose: dried fruit, candied fruit, powerfull, pattiserie. Palate: sweet, flavourful, toasty.

BODEGAS ANDRADE

Avda. Coronación, 35
21710 Bollullos del Condado (Huelva)
☎: +34 959 410 106 - Fax: +34 959 411 305
bodegas_andrade@hsoft.es
www.bodegasandrade.es

CASTILLO DE ANDRADE 2010 B
100% zalema.

82 Colour: bright yellow. Nose: ripe fruit, honeyed notes, tropical fruit. Palate: ripe fruit, flavourful.

DOCEAÑERO OLOROSO CONDADO VIEJO
palomino, zalema.

87 Colour: old gold. Nose: acetaldehyde, roasted almonds, pattiserie, candied fruit, complex. Palate: powerful, flavourful.

DOCEAÑERO CR
palomino, zalema, pedro ximénez.

88 Colour: light mahogany. Nose: complex, expressive, balanced, spicy, roasted almonds. Palate: full, flavourful, sweet.

BODEGAS DEL DIEZMO NUEVO

Sor Ángela de la Cruz, 56
21800 Moguer (Huelva)
☎: +34 959 370 004 - Fax: +34 959 370 004
info@bodegadiezmonuevo.com
www.bodegadiezmonuevo.com

MELQUIADES SAENZ "VINO DE NARANJA" B

86 Colour: light mahogany. Nose: candied fruit, citrus fruit, balanced. Palate: correct, flavourful, sweet, easy to drink.

MELQUÍADES SÁENZ B

85 Colour: mahogany. Nose: candied fruit, powerfull, sweet spices. Palate: sweet, fruity, flavourful, great length.

MELQUIADES SAENZ "VINO DE FRESA" T

85 Colour: old gold. Nose: citrus fruit, candied fruit, macerated fruit. Palate: sweet, rich, concentrated, balanced.

BODEGAS DÍAZ

Pol. Ind. El Lirio Toneleros, 6
21710 Bollullos del Condado (Huelva)
☎: +34 959 410 340 - Fax: +34 959 408 095
diaz@bodegasdiaz.com
www.bodegasdiaz.com

VADO DEL QUEMA S/C B
100% zalema.

86 Colour: bright yellow. Nose: fresh, balanced, medium intensity, dried flowers, dried herbs. Palate: flavourful, balanced.

DAIZ S/C T
syrah.

85 Colour: cherry, garnet rim. Nose: ripe fruit, scrubland, medium intensity. Palate: flavourful, fruity, easy to drink, good finish.

1955 CONDADO PÁLIDO CONDADO PÁLIDO
palomino.

86 Colour: bright straw. Nose: expressive, saline, dry nuts, ripe fruit. Palate: flavourful, powerful.

ONUBIS GE
100% moscatel.

86 Colour: mahogany. Nose: candied fruit, grapey, pattiserie. Palate: rich, flavourful, sweet.

1955 GE
zalema, listán blanco.

86 Colour: iodine, amber rim. Nose: powerfull, fruit liqueur notes, spicy, dry nuts. Palate: flavourful, good structure.

NARANJA DE ORO VINO NARANJA
zalema.

86 Colour: old gold, amber rim. Nose: citrus fruit, macerated fruit, powerfull. Palate: spirituous, unctuous, great length.

BODEGAS DOÑANA

Labradores, 2
21710 Bollulos del Condado (Huelva)
☎: +34 959 411 513
bodegasdonana@terra.es
www.bodegasdoñana.es

VIÑA DOÑANA S/C B
100% zalema.

85 Colour: bright straw. Nose: wild herbs, dried flowers, fresh. Palate: flavourful, fruity, correct.

VIÑA DOÑANA 2008 B ROBLE

86 Colour: bright yellow. Nose: candied fruit, creamy oak, sweet spices, toasty. Palate: powerful, rich, spicy, toasty.

VIÑA DOÑANA VINO NARANJA B

87 Colour: mahogany. Nose: macerated fruit, fruit liqueur notes, citrus fruit, balanced. Palate: rich, sweet, complex, great length.

VIÑA DOÑANA 2009 T ROBLE
100% syrah.

84 Colour: cherry, garnet rim. Nose: ripe fruit, spicy, earthy notes, wild herbs. Palate: correct, good finish.

VIÑA DOÑANA 2007 TC
100% syrah.

84 Colour: deep cherry, garnet rim. Nose: creamy oak, sweet spices, cocoa bean, candied fruit. Palate: easy to drink, fruity, good structure.

BODEGAS IGLESIAS

Teniente Merchante, 2
21710 Bollullos del Condado (Huelva)
☎: +34 959 410 439 - Fax: +34 959 410 463
bodegasiglesias@bodegasiglesias.com
www.bodegasiglesias.com

RICAHEMBRA SOLERA 1980 GE
85% zalema, 15% pedro ximénez.

86 Colour: dark mahogany. Nose: candied fruit, fruit liqueur notes, fruit liqueur notes, toasty. Palate: good structure, flavourful, great length, unctuous.

LETRADO SOLERA 1992 GE SOLERA
100% zalema.

84 Colour: mahogany. Nose: candied fruit, overripe fruit, sweet spices, roasted almonds. Palate: powerful, sweetness, spirituous.

PAR VINO NARANJA VINO DE LICOR
85% zalema, 15% pedro ximénez.

88 Colour: old gold, amber rim. Nose: fruit liqueur notes, fruit liqueur notes, powerfull, wild herbs. Palate: ripe fruit, long, creamy.

BODEGAS OLIVEROS

Rábida, 12
21710 Bollullos Par del Condado (Huelva)
☎: +34 959 410 057 - Fax: +34 959 410 057
oliveros@bodegasoliveros.com
www.bodegasoliveros.com

OLIVEROS OLOROSO OL

76

OLIVEROS PEDRO XIMÉNEZ PX
100% pedro ximénez.

90 Colour: light mahogany. Nose: powerfull, complex, candied fruit, honeyed notes, pattiserie. Palate: flavourful, creamy, long.

BODEGAS RAPOSO (JOSÉ ANTONIO RAPOSO)

Miguel Hernández, 31
21710 Bollullos Par del Condado (Huelva)
☎: +34 959 410 565 - Fax: +34 959 413 821
bodegas-raposo@terra.es

M.F. LA NUEZ CONDADO PÁLIDO
100% palomino.

87 Colour: bright straw. Nose: balanced, wild herbs, medium intensity, faded flowers. Palate: complex, flavourful.

AVELLANERO CREAM GE
100% listán blanco.

87 Colour: old gold, amber rim. Nose: toasty, spicy, candied fruit. Palate: sweet, balanced, unctuous, great length.

RAPOSO MOSCATEL PASAS GE
100% zalema.

85 Colour: dark mahogany. Nose: pattiserie, dried fruit, sun-drenched nuances. Palate: spicy, long, toasty, unctuous.

BODEGAS SAUCI

Doctor Fleming, 1
21710 Bollullos del Condado (Huelva)
☎: +34 959 410 524 - Fax: +34 959 410 331
sauci@bodegassauci.es
www.bodegassauci.es

SAUCI VENDIMIA TARDÍA 2010 B JOVEN
100% zalema.

82 Colour: bright yellow. Nose: macerated fruit, candied fruit, medium intensity, floral. Palate: fruity, sweetness, light-bodied.

ESPINAPURA CONDADO PÁLIDO
100% palomino.

86 Colour: bright yellow. Nose: wild herbs, balanced, saline. Palate: balanced, flavourful.

SAUCI CREAM SOLERA 1980 CR
75% palomino, 25% pedro ximénez.

85 Colour: old gold. Nose: candied fruit, fruit preserve, pattiserie, caramel. Palate: unctuous, powerful, flavourful.

S' PX SOLERA 1989 VINO DE LICOR
100% pedro ximénez.

91 Colour: mahogany. Nose: expressive, varietal, complex, candied fruit, fruit liqueur notes, sweet spices, pattiserie. Palate: unctuous, spirituous, spicy, long.

S' NARANJA VINO DE LICOR
80% pedro ximénez, 20% palomino.

89 Colour: mahogany. Nose: elegant, expressive, macerated fruit, citrus fruit, honeyed notes. Palate: fruity, flavourful, long, complex, sweet.

S' PX DULCE NATURAL VINO DE LICOR
100% pedro ximénez.

88 Colour: light mahogany. Nose: overripe fruit, grapey, balanced, powerfull. Palate: good structure, sweet, concentrated, complex, flavourful.

SAUCI VINO DULCE VINO DE LICOR
palomino, pedro ximénez.

85 Colour: mahogany. Nose: pattiserie, sweet spices, candied fruit, fruit liqueur notes. Palate: balanced, sweet, rich.

CONVENTO DE MORAÑINA

Avda. de la Paz, 43
21710 Bollullos Par del Condado (Huelva)
☎: +34 959 412 250 - Fax: +34 959 412 250
bodega@bodegasconvento.com
www.bodegasconvento.com

CONVENTO DE MORAÑINA 2010 B
100% zalema.

86 Colour: bright yellow. Nose: balanced, ripe fruit, tropical fruit. Palate: flavourful, fruity, good acidity.

AMARANTO GENEROSO DE LICOR DULCE
moscatel.

87 Colour: dark mahogany. Nose: balanced, powerfull, dried fruit, fruit liqueur notes, pattiserie. Palate: flavourful, unctuous, spirituous.

CONVENTO SUREÑO CONDÁDO PÁLIDO
palomino, listán blanco.

85 Colour: bright straw. Nose: medium intensity, fruit expression. Palate: fresh, fruity, easy to drink.

CONVENTO SUREÑO VIEJO CONDADO VIEJO OLOROSO
palomino, zalema.

85 Colour: light mahogany. Nose: balanced, dry nuts, pattiserie, sweet spices. Palate: good finish, powerful, flavourful, good structure.

CONVENTO PX
100% pedro ximénez.

90 Colour: dark mahogany. Nose: balanced, complex, candied fruit, caramel, pattiserie. Palate: flavourful, concentrated, sweet.

CONVENTO NARANJA 2008 SEMIDULCE
100% zalema.

88 Colour: old gold, amber rim. Nose: macerated fruit, citrus fruit, expressive, wild herbs. Palate: flavourful, sweet, fruity.

MARQUÉS DE VILLALÚA

Ctra. A-472, Km. 25,2
21860 Villalba del Alcor (Huelva)
☎: +34 959 420 905 - Fax: +34 959 421 141
bodega@marquesdevillalua.com
www.marquesdevillalua.com

MARQUÉS DE VILLALÚA 2010 B
80% zalema, 20% otras.

86 Colour: bright straw. Nose: floral, ripe fruit, wild herbs. Palate: flavourful, good acidity, fine bitter notes.

MARQUÉS DE VILLALÚA COLECCIÓN 2009 B
70% zalema, 30% moscatel.

87 Colour: bright yellow. Nose: balanced, ripe fruit, fine lees, expressive. Palate: flavourful, good structure, great length.

NUESTRA SEÑORA DEL SOCORRO

Carril de los Moriscos, 72
21720 Rociana del Condado (Huelva)
☎: +34 959 416 108 - Fax: +34 959 416 108
jl63@nuestrasenoradelsocorro.com

VIÑAGAMO S/C B
zalema.

84 Colour: bright straw. Nose: fresh, wild herbs, ripe fruit, floral. Palate: fruity, flavourful.

DON FREDE S/C RD
100% tempranillo.

84 Colour: light cherry. Nose: red berry notes, balanced, fresh, medium intensity. Palate: correct, ripe fruit.

DON FREDE 2010 T
70% tempranillo, 30% syrah.

82 Colour: cherry, garnet rim. Nose: wild herbs, fresh fruit, medium intensity, grassy. Palate: fruity, easy to drink.

DON FREDE 2008 TC
70% tempranillo, 30% syrah.

82 Colour: cherry, garnet rim. Nose: ripe fruit, grassy, wild herbs. Palate: ripe fruit, spicy.

VINÍCOLA DEL CONDADO

San José, 2
21710 Bollullos del Condado (Huelva)
☎: +34 959 410 261 - Fax: +34 959 410 171
comercial@vinicoladelcondado.com
www.vinicoladelcondado.com

MIORO 2010 B
100% zalema.

82 Colour: bright straw. Nose: fresh fruit, tropical fruit, white flowers. Palate: fresh, easy to drink.

MIORO GRAN SELECCIÓN 2009 B
75% zalema, 25% moscatel.

86 Colour: bright straw. Nose: balanced, expressive, ripe fruit, fine lees, floral. Palate: fresh, easy to drink.

LANTERO 2009 RD
100% syrah.

82 Colour: light cherry. Nose: fresh, wild herbs. Palate: ripe fruit, easy to drink.

LANTERO SYRAH 2009 T
100% syrah.

83 Colour: cherry, garnet rim. Nose: medium intensity, ripe fruit, wild herbs. Palate: light-bodied, fruity, good finish.

VDM ORANGE
50% zalema, 50% moscatel.

88 Colour: old gold. Nose: complex, powerfull, citrus fruit, macerated fruit. Palate: good structure, sweet, flavourful, spicy, great length.

MISTERIO DULCE GE
100% zalema.

84 Colour: light mahogany. Nose: dried fruit, candied fruit, pattiserie. Palate: sweet, rich, correct, great length.

MISTERIO OLOROSO SECO OL
100% zalema.

89 Colour: old gold. Nose: pattiserie, roasted almonds, dry nuts, complex. Palate: powerful, flavourful, fine bitter notes.

LANTERO ROBLE SYRAH 2008 T ROBLE
100% syrah.

80 Colour: cherry, garnet rim. Nose: fruit preserve, toasty, slightly evolved, sweet spices. Palate: light-bodied, easy to drink.

VINÍCOLA VALVERDEJO

Ctra. Gibraleón - Trigueros, km. 2
21500 Gibraleón (Huelva)
☎: +34 959 240 215 - Fax: +34 959 240 900
mateobarba@vinicolavalverdejo.com
www.vinicolavalverdejo.com

TORREUMBRÍA 2010 B
palomino.

82 Colour: bright straw. Nose: wild herbs, short. Palate: light-bodied, easy to drink.

TORRECANALES GENEROSO B

84 Colour: light mahogany. Nose: toasty, cocoa bean, sweet spices, candied fruit. Palate: flavourful, toasty, great length.

TORREUMBRÍA 2008 T
tempranillo, cabernet sauvignon, merlot.

86 Colour: cherry, garnet rim. Nose: balanced, fruit expression, elegant. Palate: fruity, good structure, soft tannins.

TORRECANALES NARANJA OL

86 Colour: old gold. Nose: citrus fruit, fruit expression, jasmine, powerfull. Palate: powerful, flavourful, sweet, spicy, spirituous.

NEWS ABOUT THE VINTAGE:

The producers in Costers del Segre are putting a lot of effort, particularly when facing the current difficulty of changing climatic conditions. It is simply the only way ahead when you work in an area with a heavy continental influence, with low rainfall, and where most of the growers have to do also with a relatively low altitude –between 260 meters in Balaguer and 480 in Vinaixa– that promises little or no cooling conditions for your vines. If we add a judicious use of oak, common between most of the producers, it is no wonder the wines from the region have plenty of fruit and balance. The DO has managed to keep the same philosophy it had when if was first created, based on the use of commercial –back then– varieties, grapes that nowadays may not have such great appeal and could be a commercial burden. It should be ideal for producers to start using medium to long-cycled varieties, more suitable for the region's climate and with a more efficient water management that will enable them to withstand the frequent heat waves that occur in the region.

At the top of the ranking of Costers del Segre we find Auzells 2010, from Tomás Cusiné, a white wine that blends numerous varieties; and Thalarn 2009 (100% *syrah*), from Castell D'Encus, both with 94 points.

LOCATION:

In the southern regions of Lleida, and a few municipal areas of Tarragona. It covers the sub-regions of: Artesa de Segre, Garrigues, Pallars Jussà, Raimat, Segrià and Valls del Riu Corb.

CLIMATE:

Rather dry continental climate in all the sub-regions, with minimum temperatures often dropping below zero in winter, summers with maximum temperatures in excess of 35° on occasions, and fairly low rainfall figures: 385 mm/year in Lleida and 450 mm/year in the remaining regions.

SOIL:

The soil is mainly calcareous and granitic in nature. Most of the vineyards are situated on soils with a poor organic matter content, brownish-grey limestone, with a high percentage of limestone and very little clay.

GRAPE VARIETIES:

WHITE: PREFERRED: *Macabeo, Xarel·lo, Parellada, Chardonnay, Garnacha Blanca, Moscatel de Grano Menudo, Malvasía, Gewürztraminer, Albariño, Riesling* and *Sauvignon Blanc.*

RED: PREFERRED: *Garnacha Negra, Ull de Llebre* (*Tempranillo*), *Cabernet Sauvignon, Merlot, Monastrell, Trepat, Samsó, Pinot Noir* and *Syrah.*

SUB-REGIONS:

Artesa de Segre: Located on the foothills of the Sierra de Montsec, just north of the Noguera region, it has mainly limestone soils.

Urgell: Located in the central part of the province of Lleida, at an average altitude of 350 meters, its climate is a mix of mediterranean and continental features.

Garrigues: To the southeast of the province of Lleida, it is a region with a complex topography and marl soils. Its higher altitude is near 700 meters.

Pallars Jussà: Located in the Pyrinees, it is the northernmost sub-zone. Soils are predominantly

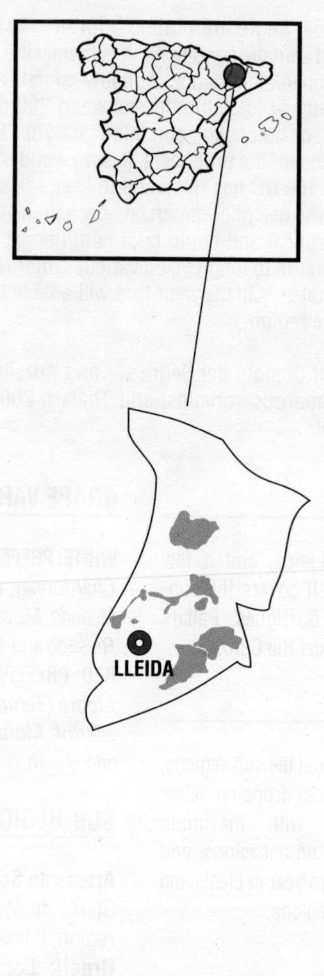

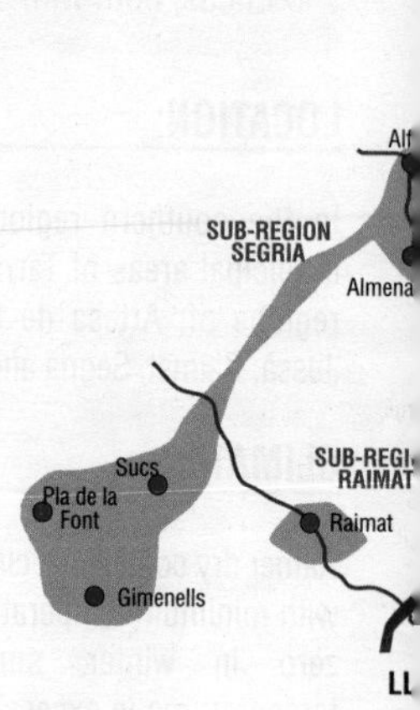

▽ Consejo Regulador

● DO Boundary

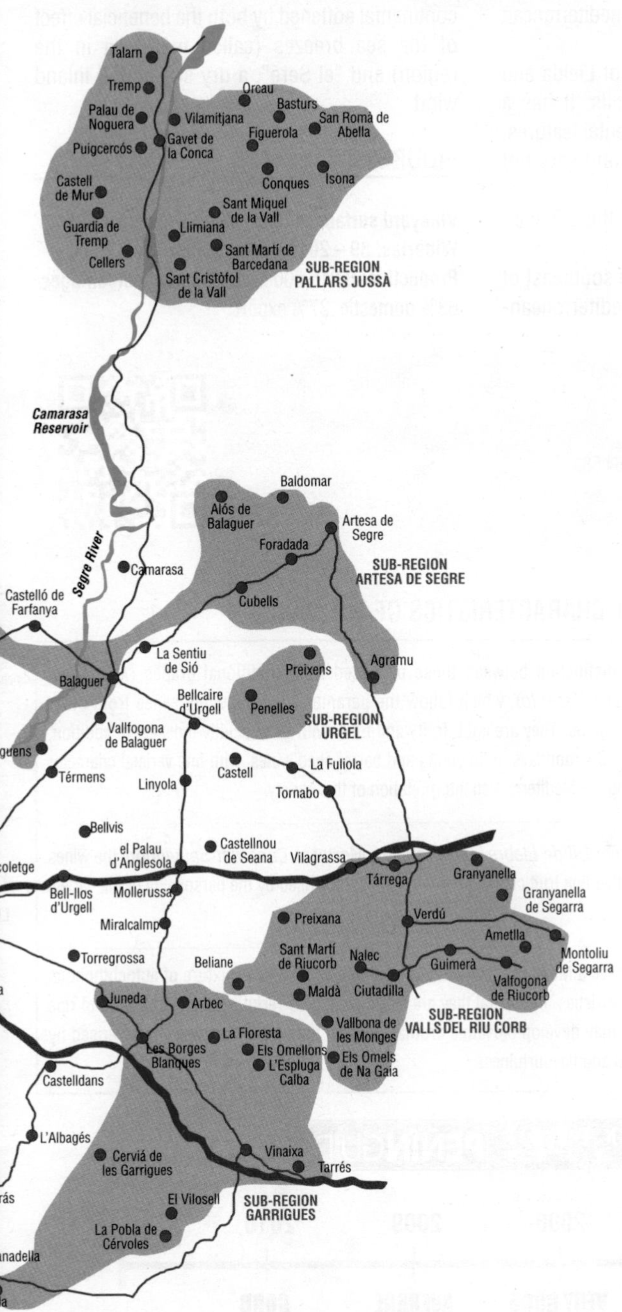
Talarn
Tremp
Palau de Noguera
Vilamitjana
Orcau
Basturs
San Romà de Abella
Figuerola
Puigcercós
Gavet de la Conca
Castell de Mur
Conques
Isona
Sant Miquel de la Vall
Guardia de Tremp
Llimiana
Sant Martí de Barcedana
Cellers
Sant Cristòfol de la Vall
SUB-REGION PALLARS JUSSÀ
Camarasa Reservoir
Baldomar
Alós de Balaguer
Artesa de Segre
Foradada
Segre River
Camarasa
SUB-REGION ARTESA DE SEGRE
Castelló de Farfanya
Cubells
La Sentiu de Sió
Preixens
Agramu
Balaguer
Bellcaire d'Urgell
Penelles
SUB-REGION URGEL
Vallfogona de Balaguer
La Fuliola
Castell
Térmens
Linyola
Tornabo
Bellvis
Castellnou de Seana
el Palau d'Anglesola
Vilagrassa
Tárrega
Granyanella
Bell-lloc d'Urgell
Mollerussa
Granyanella de Segarra
Preixana
Verdú
Miralcalmp
Ametlla
Montoliu de Segarra
Torregrossa
Beliane
Sant Martí de Riucorb
Nalec
Guimerà
Ciutadilla
Maldà
Valfogona de Riucorb
Juneda
Arbec
Vallbona de les Monges
SUB-REGION VALLS DEL RIU CORB
La Floresta
Les Borges Blanques
Els Omellons
L'Espluga Calba
Els Omels de Na Gaia
Castelldans
L'Albagés
Cerviá de les Garrigues
Vinaixa
Tarrés
El Vilosell
SUB-REGION GARRIGUES
La Pobla de Cérvoles

limestone and its type of climate mediterranean with strong continental influence.

Raimat: Located in the province of Lleida and with predominantly limestone soils, it has a mediterranean climate with continental features, with predominantly cold winters and very hot summers.

Segrià: Is the central sub-zone of the DO, with limestone soils.

Valls del Riu Corb: Located in the southeast of the DO, its climate is primarily mediterranean-continental softened by both the beneficial effect of the sea breezes (called marinada in the region) and "el Seré", a dry sea-bound inland wind.

FIGURES:

Vineyard surface: 4,688 – **Wine-Growers:** 629 – **Wineries:** 39 – **2010 Harvest rating:** Very Good – **Production:** 8,915,000 litres – **Market percentages:** 63% domestic. 37% export

CONSEJO REGULADOR
Complex de la Caparrella, 97
25192 Lleida
☎: +34 973 264 583 - Fax: +34 973 264 583
@ secretari@costersdelsegre.es
www.costersdelsegre.es

GENERAL CHARACTERISTICS OF THE WINES

WHITES	There is a distinction between those produced from traditional grapes (*Macabeo, Parellada* and *Xarel·lo*), which follow the parameters of the white wines from other Catalonian regions. They are light, fruity and fresh with good acidity indexes. In addition, there are the Chardonnays, both young and barrel-aged wines, with fine varietal character and following the Mediterranean interpretation of this variety.
ROSÉS	Produced from *Ull de Llebre* (*Tempranillo*), *Merlot* or *Cabernet Sauvignon*, the wines are pink, with a fine fruit character, fresh and characterised by the personality of the variety used.
REDS	The wines have a Mediterranean character, single varietal or a mixture of autochthonous and foreign varieties. In general they are warm, with a powerful nose and character of ripe fruit. Some may develop balsamic aromas and, on the palate, they are characterised by their warmth and flavourfulness.

VINTAGE RATING PEÑÍNGUIDE

2007	2008	2009	2010
VERY GOOD	VERY GOOD	AVERAGE	GOOD

BODEGAS COSTERS DEL SIÓ

Ctra. de Agramunt, Km. 4,2
25600 Balaguer (Lleida)
☎: +34 973 424 062 - Fax: +34 973 424 112
comunicacio@costersio.com
www.costersio.com

VIÑA DEL SIÓS 2010 B
85% sauvignon blanc, 15% chardonnay.

84 Colour: bright straw. Nose: wild herbs, ripe fruit, citrus fruit. Palate: fruity, easy to drink.

VIÑA DEL SIÓS 2010 RD
80% garnacha, 20% syrah.

87 Colour: rose, purple rim. Nose: violets, red berry notes, ripe fruit. Palate: fruity, easy to drink, fine bitter notes.

SIÓS SELECCIÓN 2008 T
90% syrah, 10% experimentales.

90 Colour: cherry, garnet rim. Nose: ripe fruit, balanced, expressive, complex, warm, spicy. Palate: good structure, full, good acidity, round tannins.

VIÑA DEL SIÓS 2008 T
75% tempranillo, 20% merlot, 5% syrah.

88 Colour: cherry, garnet rim. Nose: ripe fruit, spicy, warm. Palate: fruity, concentrated, round tannins, great length.

ALTO SIÓS 2007 T
60% syrah, 40% tempranillo.

90 Colour: cherry, garnet rim. Nose: ripe fruit, creamy oak, cocoa bean, sweet spices. Palate: complex, good structure, spicy, long.

CAR VINÍCOLAS REUNIDAS

Ctra. , 19
25340 Verdú (Lleida)
☎: +34 973 310 732 - Fax: +34 973 310 616
carviresa@carviresa.com
www.carviresa.com

VALLCORB 2009 B
100% macabeo.

87 Colour: bright straw. Nose: wild herbs, spicy, citrus fruit. Palate: balanced, fruity, ripe fruit, great length.

VALLCORB 2008 T
100% ull de llebre.

85 Colour: cherry, garnet rim. Nose: ripe fruit, warm, spicy, scrubland. Palate: fruity, good structure, correct.

CASTELL D'ENCUS

Ctra. Tremp a Santa Engracia, Km. 5
25630 Talarn (Lleida)
☎: +34 973 252 974
celler@encus.org
www.encus.org

TALEIA 2010 B
100% sauvignon blanc.

94 Colour: bright straw. Nose: jasmine, dried flowers, ripe fruit, complex, balanced. Palate: flavourful, powerful, good structure, ripe fruit, long.

EKAM ESSÈNCIA 2010 B
100% riesling.

90 Colour: bright straw, greenish rim. Nose: dried flowers, dried herbs, ripe fruit, balanced, powerfull. Palate: fruity, rich, sweetness, ripe fruit.

EKAM 2010 B
100% riesling.

88 Colour: bright straw. Nose: white flowers, balanced, powerfull. Palate: fruity, good acidity, balanced, full, rich.

THALARN 2009 T
syrah.

94 Colour: cherry, garnet rim. Nose: expressive, balanced, elegant, ripe fruit, mineral, creamy oak, spicy, aromatic coffee. Palate: elegant, round, fruity, flavourful, spicy, fine tannins.

ACUSP 2009 T
100% pinot noir.

91 Colour: cherry, garnet rim. Nose: medium intensity, elegant, balanced, ripe fruit. Palate: good structure, complex, long, fruity.

QUEST 2009 T
87% cabernet sauvignon, 10% cabernet franc, 3% petit verdot.

90 Colour: deep cherry, purple rim. Nose: scrubland, ripe fruit, spicy. Palate: fruity, good structure, balanced, spicy, round tannins.

CASTELL DEL REMEI

Finca Castell del Remei, s/n
25300 Castell del Remei (Lleida)
☎: +34 973 580 200 - Fax: +34 973 718 312
info@castelldelremei.com
www.castelldelremei.com

CASTELL DEL REMEI 1780 2006 T
55% cabernet sauvignon, 20% tempranillo, 15% garnacha, 5% syrah, 5% merlot.

90 Colour: cherry, garnet rim. Nose: powerfull, ripe fruit, warm, toasty, sweet spices. Palate: powerful, fleshy, complex, full.

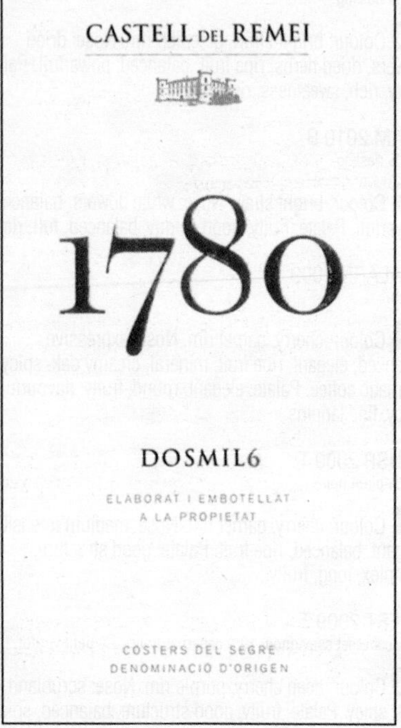

CASTELL DEL REMEI ODA BLANC 2010 BFB
50% macabeo, 50% chardonnay.

91 Color bright yellow. Aroma powerfull, ripe fruit, sweet spices, creamy oak, fragrant herbs. Taste rich, smoky aftertaste, flavourful, fresh, good acidity.

CASTELL DEL REMEI BLANC PLANELL 2010 B
55% macabeo, 45% sauvignon blanc.

88 Colour: bright straw. Nose: powerfull, candied fruit, citrus fruit, fragrant herbs. Palate: flavourful, fleshy, fine bitter notes.

CASTELL DEL REMEI GOTIM BRU 2009 T
35% tempranillo, 30% garnacha, 20% cabernet sauvignon, 10% merlot, 5% syrah.

87 Colour: dark-red cherry. Nose: short, fresh, fruit preserve. Palate: powerful, flavourful, sweetness, pruney, spicy.

CASTELL DEL REMEI ODA 2008 T
50% merlot, 25% cabernet sauvignon, 15% tempranillo, 10% syrah.

90 Colour: cherry, garnet rim. Nose: powerfull, ripe fruit, scrubland, creamy oak, sweet spices. Palate: powerful, concentrated, flavourful.

CELLER ANALEC

Ctra. a Analec, s/n
25341 Nalec (Lleida)
☎: +34 973 303 190 - Fax: +34 973 303 190
info@analec.net
www.analec.net

LA CREU 2009 RD
cabernet sauvignon, tempranillo, syrah.

84 Colour: rose, purple rim. Nose: ripe fruit, dried herbs, lactic notes. Palate: flavourful, ripe fruit, correct.

LA CREU NEGRO 2009 T
100% tempranillo.

85 Colour: cherry, garnet rim. Nose: toasty, ripe fruit, warm. Palate: flavourful, fruity, good structure, spicy.

LA ROMIGUERA 2008 T
cabernet sauvignon, tempranillo, syrah.

87 Colour: cherry, garnet rim. Nose: toasty, spicy, ripe fruit. Palate: good structure, fruity, flavourful, spicy.

ANALEC 2008 BN
macabeo, parellada.

84 Colour: bright yellow. Nose: toasty, spicy, roasted almonds. Palate: flavourful, ripe fruit, toasty.

ANALEC BRUT ROSAT 2009 ESP
trepat.

85 Colour: rose. Nose: candied fruit, dry nuts, faded flowers, dried herbs. Palate: flavourful, fruity, easy to drink.

ANALEC SORT ABRIL 2007 ESP RESERVA
macabeo, parellada.

84 Colour: bright yellow. Nose: medium intensity, dried herbs, spicy, ripe fruit. Palate: correct, easy to drink, good acidity.

CELLER LAGRAVERA

Ctra. de Tamarite, 9
25120 Alfarrás (Lleida)
☎: +34 973 761 374 - Fax: +34 973 760 218
info@lagravera.com
www.lagravera.com

ÒNRA 2009 T
garnacha, merlot, cabernet sauvignon.

89 Colour: deep cherry, purple rim. Nose: ripe fruit, wild herbs, balanced, warm. Palate: good structure, flavourful.

ÓNRA MOLTA HONRA 2010 B
garnacha blanca, sauvignon blanc.

87 Colour: bright straw, greenish rim. Nose: ripe fruit, fine lees, jasmine, dried flowers. Palate: fruity, easy to drink, good finish.

ÒNRA 2010 B
sauvignon blanc, garnacha blanca, chenin blanc.

84 Colour: bright straw, greenish rim. Nose: wild herbs, ripe fruit, candied fruit. Palate: fruity, flavourful, correct.

LALTRE 2010 T
monastrell, garnacha, merlot.

85 Colour: purple rim. Nose: violets, red berry notes. Palate: flavourful, easy to drink, fruity, good finish.

ÓNRA MOLTA HONRA 2009 T
garnacha, cabernet sauvignon.

91 Colour: deep cherry, purple rim. Nose: complex, ripe fruit, candied fruit, cocoa bean, sweet spices. Palate: good structure, flavourful, spicy, balanced.

CELLER TORRES DE SANUI

Camí Torres de Sanui - La Cerdera, s/n
25193 (Lleida)
☎: +34 973 050 202 - Fax: +34 973 050 202
celler@desanui.com
www.desanui.com

DE SANUI BLANC JOVE 2009 B
60% macabeo, 30% riesling, 10% moscatel.

82 Colour: yellow. Nose: candied fruit, wild herbs, honeyed notes. Palate: ripe fruit, fine bitter notes.

DE SANUI BLANC BARRICA 2008 B BARRICA
50% macabeo, 40% riesling, 10% moscatel.

88 Colour: bright yellow. Nose: powerfull, ripe fruit, sweet spices, creamy oak. Palate: rich, smoky aftertaste, flavourful, fresh, good acidity.

DE SANUI NEGRE JOVE 2009 T
30% syrah, 40% garnacha, 30% tempranillo.

84 Colour: cherry, purple rim. Nose: medium intensity, red berry notes, ripe fruit, spicy. Palate: fruity, easy to drink.

DE SANUI NEGRE 2008 T BARRICA
35% syrah, 40% garnacha, 25% tempranillo.

84 Colour: cherry, garnet rim. Nose: medium intensity, red berry notes, ripe fruit, spicy, grassy, wild herbs. Palate: fruity, easy to drink.

DE SANUI MERLOT 2006 TC
100% merlot.

87 Colour: bright cherry, garnet rim. Nose: ripe fruit, red berry notes, balanced, spicy. Palate: flavourful, fruity, ripe fruit, great length.

DE SANUI SYRAH 2006 TC
100% syrah.

86 Colour: cherry, garnet rim. Nose: ripe fruit, spicy, toasty, cocoa bean. Palate: powerful, flavourful, toasty, round tannins, fruity.

DE SANUI NEGRE 2006 TC
42% syrah, 40% garnacha, 18% tempranillo.

84 Colour: deep cherry, garnet rim. Nose: candied fruit, warm, powerfull, dark chocolate. Palate: rich, fruity, round tannins.

CELLER VILA CORONA

Camí els Nerets, s/n
25654 Vilamitjana (Lleida)
☎: +34 973 652 638 - Fax: +34 973 652 638
vila-corona@avired.com
www.vilacorona.cat

LLABUSTES RIESLING 2010 B
100% riesling.

88 Colour: bright straw, greenish rim. Nose: jasmine, white flowers, ripe fruit, honeyed notes. Palate: fruity, flavourful, fine bitter notes, long.

LLABUSTES CHARDONNAY 2009 B
100% chardonnay.

86 Colour: bright straw. Nose: white flowers, expressive, dried herbs. Palate: flavourful, fruity, good acidity, balanced, rich.

LLABUSTES ULL DE LLEBRE 2009 T
100% ull de llebre.

85 Colour: cherry, garnet rim. Nose: ripe fruit, warm, spicy. Palate: flavourful, fleshy, balanced.

LLABUSTES MERLOT 2007 T
100% merlot.

86 Colour: light cherry, garnet rim. Nose: medium intensity, ripe fruit, warm. Palate: correct, spicy, toasty, easy to drink.

LLABUSTES CABERNET SAUVIGNON 2006 TC
100% cabernet sauvignon.

88 Colour: cherry, garnet rim. Nose: candied fruit, spicy, balanced, wild herbs. Palate: good structure, flavourful, ripe fruit, spicy.

CÉRVOLES CELLER

Avda. Les Garrigues, 26
25471 La Pobla de Cèrvoles (Lleida)
☎: +34 973 175 101 - Fax: +34 973 718 312
info@cervoles.com
www.cervoles.com

CÉRVOLES 2010 BFB
50% chardonnay, 50% macabeo.

92 Colour: bright straw. Nose: scrubland, ripe fruit, fine lees, lactic notes. Palate: round, powerful, spirituous, mineral, creamy.

CÉRVOLES COLORS 2010 B
75% macabeo, 25% chardonnay.

90 Colour: bright straw. Nose: scrubland, fruit expression, fine lees. Palate: elegant, complex, fresh, flavourful, rich.

CÉRVOLES COLORS 2009 T
45% tempranillo, 20% garnacha, 15% cabernet sauvignon, 10% merlot, 10% syrah.

87 Colour: dark-red cherry. Nose: cocoa bean, expressive, elegant, varietal, macerated fruit, ripe fruit. Palate: fresh, powerful, flavourful, creamy.

CÉRVOLES NEGRE 2007 T
44% cabernet sauvignon, 32% tempranillo, 16% garnacha, 8% merlot

90 Colour: deep cherry. Nose: roasted coffee, cedar wood, macerated fruit, varietal. Palate: flavourful, powerful, fruity, fleshy, smoky aftertaste, spicy.

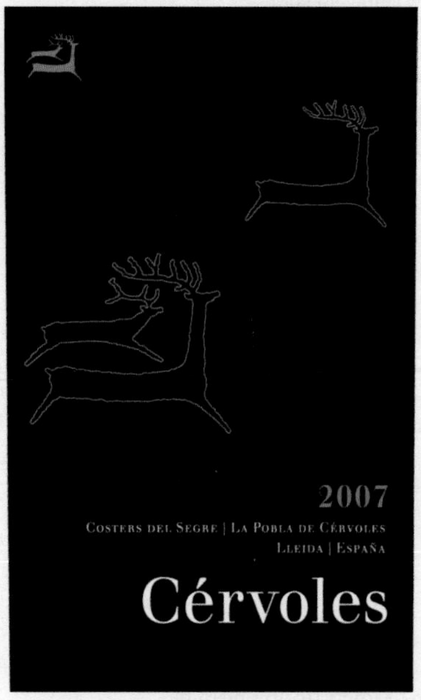

CÉRVOLES ESTRATS 2006 T
42% cabernet sauvignon, 36% tempranillo, 17% garnacha, 5% merlot.

93 Colour: cherry, garnet rim. Nose: mineral, ripe fruit, creamy oak, toasty, sweet spices. Palate: powerful, spicy, long, mineral.

CLOS PONS

Avda. Garrigues, 16
25155 L'Albagés (Lleida)
☎: +34 973 730 525 - Fax: +34 973 730 515
clospons@grup-pons.com
www.grup-pons.com

CLOS PONS SISQUELLA 2010 B
garnacha blanca, albariño, moscatel.

87 Colour: bright yellow. Nose: balanced, jasmine, white flowers, ripe fruit, honeyed notes. Palate: fruity, rich, flavourful.

CLOS PONS ALGES 2009 TC
tempranillo, garnacha, syrah.

87 Colour: bright cherry, purple rim. Nose: balanced, medium intensity, ripe fruit. Palate: good structure, fruity, flavourful, great length.

CLOS PONS ROC NU 2008 TC
tempranillo, garnacha, cabernet sauvignon.

90 Colour: cherry, garnet rim. Nose: ripe fruit, spicy, earthy notes. Palate: good structure, complex, flavourful, spicy, round tannins.

MAS BLANCH I JOVÉ

Paratge Llinars. Pol. Ind. 9- Parc. 129
25471 La Pobla de Cérvoles (Lleida)
☎: +34 973 050 018 - Fax: +34 973 391 151
sara@masblanchijove.com
www.masblanchijove.com

SAÓ BLANC 2009 B
macabeo.

90 Colour: bright straw, greenish rim. Nose: floral, expressive, ripe fruit, dried flowers. Palate: complex, fruity, good structure, flavourful.

SAÓ ROSAT 2010 RD
60% syrah, 40% garnacha.

85 Colour: rose, purple rim. Nose: macerated fruit, wild herbs, dried flowers. Palate: fruity, flavourful, great length.

SAÓ ABRIVAT 2008 T
40% tempranillo, 35% garnacha, 15% cabernet sauvignon.

90 Colour: cherry, garnet rim. Nose: balanced, ripe fruit, cocoa bean, sweet spices, creamy oak. Palate: good structure, fruity, full, spicy, fruity aftestaste.

SAÓ EXPRESSIU 2007 T
55% garnacha, 25% cabernet sauvignon, 20% tempranillo.

92 Colour: bright cherry, garnet rim. Nose: ripe fruit, mineral, spicy, creamy oak, complex. Palate: good structure, fruity, flavourful, good acidity, balanced.

OLIVERA

La Plana, s/n
25268 Vallbona de les Monges (Lleida)
☎: +34 973 330 276 - Fax: +34 973 330 276
olivera@olivera.org
www.olivera.org

BLANC DE SERÈ 2010 B
macabeo, parellada, chardonnay.

87 Colour: bright straw. Nose: citrus fruit, ripe fruit, white flowers. Palate: fruity, fine bitter notes, easy to drink.

VALLISBONA 89 2009 B
90% chardonnay, 10% malvasía.

92 Colour: bright yellow. Nose: balanced, complex, spicy, creamy oak, ripe fruit, floral, mineral. Palate: flavourful, toasty, ripe fruit, great length.

MISSENYORA 2009 BFB
100% macabeo.

91 Colour: yellow. Nose: ripe fruit, tropical fruit, jasmine, complex, spicy. Palate: rich, flavourful, balanced, fruity, spicy.

RASIM VI PANSIT 2009 B
malvasía, xarel.lo, chardonnay.

89 Colour: golden. Nose: candied fruit, honeyed notes, balanced, expressive. Palate: ripe fruit, unctuous, balanced. Personality.

BLANC DE MARGES 2009 BFB
parellada, sauvignon blanc, chardonnay, moscatel.

88 Colour: bright yellow. Nose: fruit expression, dried herbs, dried flowers. Palate: good structure, fruity, flavourful, spicy.

BLANC DE ROURE 2009 B
macabeo, parellada, chardonnay.

88 Colour: bright yellow. Nose: powerfull, ripe fruit, sweet spices, creamy oak. Palate: rich, smoky aftertaste, flavourful, good acidity.

EIXADERS 2008 BFB
100% chardonnay.

90 Colour: bright yellow. Nose: ripe fruit, expressive, complex, sweet spices, creamy oak, varietal. Palate: fruity, rich.

AGALIU BFB
100% macabeo.

88 Colour: bright yellow. Nose: floral, fruit expression, balanced, dried herbs, spicy. Palate: fruity, flavourful, good finish.

RASIM VIMADUR 2009 T BARRICA
garnacha, touriga.

88 Colour: black cherry. Nose: overripe fruit, macerated fruit. Palate: flavourful, rich, good structure, sweet, spicy.

RAIMAT

Ctra. Lleida, s/n
25111 (Lleida)
☎: +34 973 724 000 - Fax: +34 935 051 567
info@raimat.es
www.raimat.es

CASTELL DE RAIMAT CHARDONNAY 2010 B
100% chardonnay.

89 Colour: bright straw, greenish rim. Nose: floral, ripe fruit, varietal, balanced, expressive. Palate: fruity, flavourful, long.

RAIMAT TERRA 2010 B
100% chardonnay.

88 Colour: bright yellow. Nose: ripe fruit, citrus fruit, floral. Palate: ripe fruit, flavourful, good structure, good acidity, balanced.

CASTELL DE RAIMAT CHARDONNAY BARRICAS 2010 B
100% chardonnay.

88 Colour: bright yellow. Nose: faded flowers, ripe fruit, sweet spices, creamy oak. Palate: fleshy, complex, powerful, flavourful.

CASTELL DE RAIMAT XAREL.LO CHARDONNAY 2010 B
50% xarel.lo, 50% chardonnay.

87 Colour: bright straw. Nose: citrus fruit, fruit expression, dried herbs, floral. Palate: flavourful, light-bodied, fresh, fruity.

CASTELL DE RAIMAT CABERNET SAUVIGNON 2007 TC
100% cabernet sauvignon.

87 Colour: cherry, garnet rim. Nose: ripe fruit, spicy, toasty, fruit liqueur notes. Palate: powerful, flavourful, toasty, round tannins.

CASTELL DE RAIMAT TEMPRANILLO 2006 TC
100% tempranillo.

86 Colour: light cherry, garnet rim. Nose: medium intensity, ripe fruit, warm. Palate: fruity, easy to drink.

RAIMAT GRAN BRUT BR
60% chardonnay, 40% pinot noir.

90 Colour: bright yellow. Nose: fine lees, dry nuts, fragrant herbs, complex. Palate: powerful, flavourful, good acidity, fine bead, fine bitter notes.

RAIMAT CHARDONNAY BR
95% chardonnay, 5% pinot noir.

88 Colour: bright straw. Nose: ripe fruit, dried herbs, fine lees. Palate: flavourful, good acidity, balanced.

TOMÁS CUSINÉ

Plaça Sant Sebastià, 13
25457 El Vilosell (Lleida)
☎: +34 973 176 029 - Fax: +34 973 175 945
info@tomascusine.com
www.tomascusine.com

AUZELLS 2010 B
41% macabeo, 18% chardonnay, 16% sauvignon blanc, 10% müller thurgau, 10% albariño, 5% otras.

93 Colour: bright straw. Nose: dried herbs, fresh fruit, citrus fruit, cocoa bean, expressive. Palate: flavourful, fruity, fine bitter notes, long, mineral.

FINCA RACONS 2010 B
macabeo.

92 Colour: straw. Nose: faded flowers, fruit expression, ripe fruit, scrubland. Palate: elegant, fine bitter notes, mineral, fruity, powerful, flavourful.

VILOSELL 2008 T
43% tempranillo, 18% syrah, 16% cabernet sauvignon, 14% merlot, 6% cariñena, 3% garnacha.

92 Colour: bright cherry. Nose: sweet spices, expressive, fruit expression, creamy oak. Palate: flavourful, fruity, toasty, round tannins.

GEOL 2007 T
45% merlot, 35% cabernet sauvignon, 6% marselan, 5% cabernet franc, 5% syrah, 4% cariñena.

92 Colour: deep cherry. Nose: truffle notes, damp earth, ripe fruit, varietal, spicy, cocoa bean. Palate: powerful, fruity, fleshy, mineral, spicy.

VALL DE BALDOMAR

Ctra. de Alós de Balaguer, s/n
25737 Baldomar (Lleida)
☎: +34 973 402 205 - Fax: +34 932 104 040
info@cristiari.com
www.cristiari.com

CRISTIARI 2010 B
müller thurgau.

88 Colour: straw, greenish rim. Nose: scrubland, dried flowers, powerfull. Palate: balanced, good structure, fruity, flavourful.

CRISTIARI 2010 RD
merlot, cabernet sauvignon.

84 Colour: rose, purple rim. Nose: floral, red berry notes, ripe fruit, grassy. Palate: correct, sweetness.

PETIT BALDOMA 2010 T
merlot, cabernet sauvignon.

84 Colour: cherry, purple rim. Nose: wild herbs, varietal, grassy, red berry notes, ripe fruit. Palate: fruity, easy to drink.

BALDOMÀ SELECCIÓ 2009 T
merlot, cabernet sauvignon, tempranillo, bobal.

86 Colour: bright cherry, garnet rim. Nose: ripe fruit, balanced, scrubland. Palate: ripe fruit, flavourful.

CRISTIARI D'ALÒS MERLOT 2009 T ROBLE
merlot.

86 Colour: cherry, garnet rim. Nose: medium intensity, ripe fruit, spicy. Palate: fruity, easy to drink.

VINYA L'HEREU DE SERÓ

Molí, s/n
25739 Sero (Artesa de Segre) (Lleida)
☎: +34 973 400 472 - Fax: +34 973 400 472
vinyalhereu@vinyalhereu.com
www.vinyalhereu.com

PETIT GREALÓ 2007 T
40% syrah, 30% merlot, 30% cabernet sauvignon.

87 Colour: cherry, garnet rim. Nose: candied fruit, wild herbs, spicy. Palate: flavourful, ripe fruit, good structure.

FLOR DE GREALÓ 2006 T
40% merlot, 30% syrah, 30% cabernet sauvignon.

87 Colour: deep cherry, brick rim edge. Nose: candied fruit, wild herbs. Palate: fleshy, concentrated, rich, fruity.

VINYA VILARS

Camí de Puiggrós, s/n
25140 Arbeca (Lleida)
☎: +34 973 149 144 - Fax: +34 973 321 600
vinyaelsvilars@vinyaelsvilars.com
www.vinyaelsvilars.com

LEIX 2008 T
100% syrah.

89 Colour: deep cherry, garnet rim. Nose: ripe fruit, spicy, mineral, candied fruit. Palate: balanced, ripe fruit, round tannins.

TALLAT DE LLUNA 2008 T
100% syrah.

88 Colour: cherry, garnet rim. Nose: ripe fruit, wild herbs, spicy. Palate: powerful, fleshy, long, round tannins, toasty.

VILARS 2008 T
50% syrah, 50% merlot.

87 Colour: cherry, garnet rim. Nose: balsamic herbs, scrubland, fruit preserve. Palate: correct, fine bitter notes.

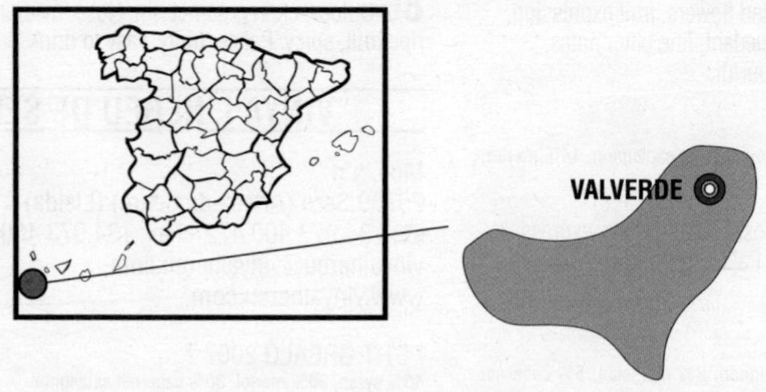

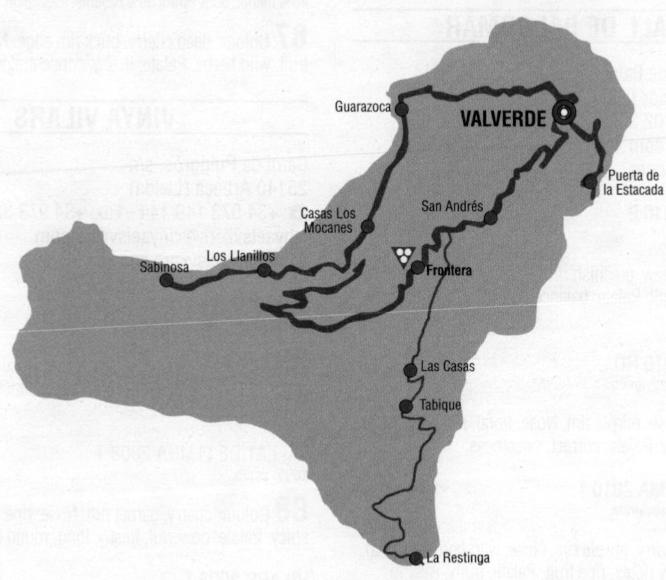

Consejo Regulador

DO Boundary

NEWS ABOUT THE VINTAGE:

With just 200 hectares of vineyard lost in the middle of this Atlantic paradise of an island and 7 wineries –of which only the Cooperativa Campo Frontera looks like a proper company, the rest of them being no more than a bunch of romantics–, it is hardly surprising that the market does not hear often of El Hierro wines.

The singularity of this island lies on the fact that its vineyards are less affected by trade winds than those of the other Canary Islands. The climate is Atlantic, rains usually arriving at this island before they hit the rest of the Canary's. In vine growing terms, the differences rest on altitude and slope orientation. The best vineyards are located in the central part of the island, a sort of low mountain range –reaching higher altitude levels between the towns of Frontera and Valverde– that ultimately yield wines with some wild herbal and saline notes, made from grape varieties well adapted to the region's characteristics like *tinta baboso* and the white *verijadiego.*

The 2010 vintage is going down in history, since it is the first time ever a wine from Viña Frontera makes it to our Podium with 90 points, thanks to a carbonic maceration blend of listán (90%) and 10% negramoll. It is a pity, though, that two wines from Tanajara (a vijariego white and a red made entirely from baboso) were not ready for tasting, for we are sure they would have completed a wonderful triad.

LOCATION:

On the island of El Hierro, part of the Canary Islands. The production area covers the whole island, although the main growing regions are Valle del Golfo, Sabinosa, El Pinar and Echedo.

CLIMATE:

Fairly mild in general, although higher levels of humidity are recorded in high mountainous regions. Rainfall is relatively low.

SOIL:

Volcanic in origin, with a good water retention and storage capacity. Although the vineyards were traditionally cultivated in the higher regions, at present most of them are found at low altitudes, resulting in an early ripening of the grapes.

GRAPE VARIETIES:

WHITE: *Verijadiego* (majority with 50% of all white varieties), *Listán Blanca, Bremajuelo, Uval* (*Gual*), *Pedro Ximénez, Baboso* and *Moscatel.*
RED: *Listán Negro, Negramoll, Baboso Negro* and *Verijadiego Negro.*

FIGURES:

Vineyard surface: 191 – **Wine-Growers:** 246 – **Wineries:** 7 – **2010 Harvest rating:** Very Good – **Production:** 180,000 litres – **Market percentages:** 99% domestic. 1% export

CONSEJO REGULADOR
Oficina de Agricultura. El Matorral, s/n
38911 Frontera (Santa Cruz de Tenerife)
☎: +34 922 556 064 / +34 922 559 744 - Fax: +34 922 559 691
@ doelhierro@hotmail.com
www.elhierro.tv

GENERAL CHARACTERISTICS OF THE WINES

WHITES	These are the most characteristic wines of the island. They are produced mainly from the *Vijariego* and *Listán Blanco* varieties. They are straw yellow, quite fresh and fruity and, on occasions, they have notes of tropical fruit.
ROSÉS	These are characterised by their orangey raspberry colour and are quite fresh and fruity.
REDS	These are characterised by their good quality. Likewise, they are quite full-bodied and fruity.

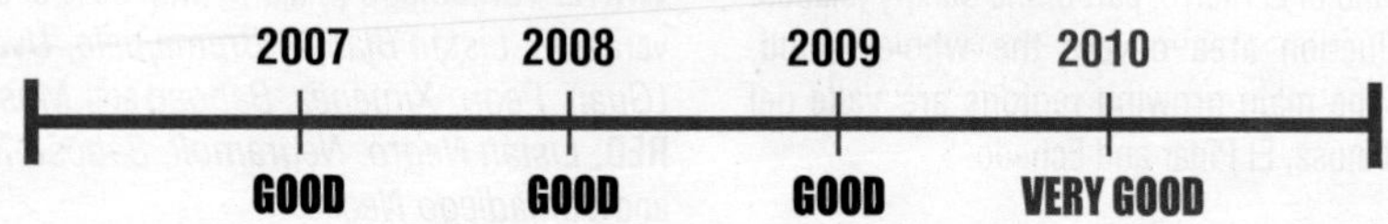

SDAD. COOPERATIVA DEL CAMPO FRONTERA VINÍCOLA INSULAR

El Matorral, 55
38911 Frontera (Santa Cruz de Tenerife)
☎: +34 922 556 016 - Fax: +34 922 556 042
coopfrontera@cooperativafrontera.com
www.cooperativafrontera.com

VIÑA FRONTERA 2010 B
verijadiego, listán blanco.

86 Colour: bright straw. Nose: powerfull, ripe fruit, citrus fruit. Palate: flavourful, fruity, fresh.

VIÑA FRONTERA AFRUTADO 2010 B
verijadiego, listán blanco, vidueño.

82 Colour: bright straw. Nose: medium intensity, citrus fruit, fresh fruit, jasmine. Palate: flavourful, fruity, fresh.

VIÑA FRONTERA 2010 RD
listán negro, negramoll.

79

VIÑA FRONTERA 2010 T MACERACIÓN CARBÓNICA
listán negro.

90 Colour: light cherry, garnet rim. Nose: scrubland, ripe fruit, medium intensity, mineral. Palate: fruity, flavourful.

VIÑA FRONTERA BABOSO 2009 T
100% baboso.

83 Colour: bright cherry. Nose: candied fruit, fruit liqueur notes, sweet spices, toasty. Palate: fine bitter notes, good acidity, spicy.

VIÑA FRONTERA VERIJADIEGO 2009 T
100% verijadiego.

79

VIÑA FRONTERA 2009 T
listán negro, negramoll.

68

VIÑA FRONTERA 2008 T BARRICA
100% verijadiego negro.

80 Colour: deep cherry. Nose: candied fruit, overripe fruit, toasty. Palate: powerful, fine bitter notes.

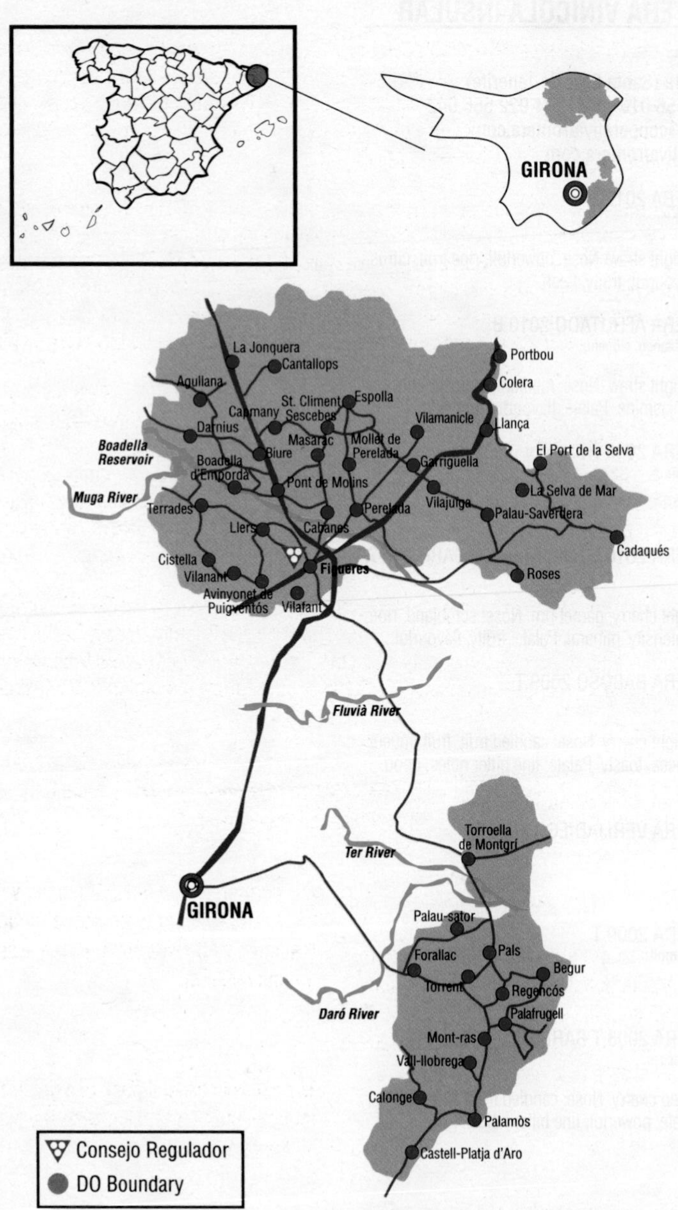
GIRONA
La Jonquera
Cantallops
Agullana
St. Climent Sescebes
Espolla
Capmany
Darnius
Masarac
Mollet de Perelada
Vilamanicle
Portbou
Colera
Llançà
Boadella Reservoir
Biure
Boadella d'Empordà
Garriguella
El Port de la Selva
Muga River
Pont de Molins
La Selva de Mar
Terrades
Vilajuïga
Peralada
Palau-Saverdera
Llers
Cabanes
Cadaqués
Cistella
Figueres
Vilanant
Roses
Avinyonet de Puigventós
Vilafant
Fluvià River
Torroella de Montgrí
Ter River
GIRONA
Palau-sator
Pals
Forallac
Begur
Torrent
Regencós
Daró River
Palafrugell
Mont-ras
Vall-llobrega
Calonge
Palamòs
Castell-Platja d'Aro
Consejo Regulador
DO Boundary

NEWS ABOUT THE VINTAGE:

The wines from this north-eastern part of Catalunya are becoming a bench-mark for wines from mild-mediterranean climate. If the 2009 vintage became a difficult one for Empordà given the heat-waves and the impossible blend of green and overripe notes, the 2010's shows a much fresher character and therefore wines which are far more loyal to the traditional style of the region: truly Mediterranean in style, but with an elegant, fresh European touch.

After tasting more than 160 wines from the 2002 vintage up to 2010, we appreciate scores for Empordà wines are going up, thanks to the care and exigency of most of the region's producers. In the last few years the DO is showing an excellent ability for both regeneration and succession: many of the local family wineries have accomplished their generational changes and new blood is holding now the reins and showing a touch of new vigour and originality in their products. It may well be that there is still a few things in Empordà that could be improved, but in general lines its trend is definitely upward, and a promising one to boot.

Red wines are the real stars of the DO, wines which manage to show Mediterranean notes along the cooler character afforded by the proximity of the Pyrenees and the northerly wind called here "Tramontana". This wind, when blowing slowly (something that hardly ever happens) exerts a truly benefitial effect in the vineyard, helping to dry up humidity. The "bad" side of the Tramontana is its fierce character, as it happened in April 2010, when an important part of the vineyard was heavily affected by it. Aged crianza wines show quite balanced, with elegant mediterranean notes.

Rosé wines have improved an average of two points, something that translates into more abundant red fruit notes and a fresher character. Also white wines have slightly improved their ratings, but overall they struggle to escape mediocrity, probably because most producers tend to focus on red winemaking, leaving young whites unattended. The best red from the region is Castillo de Perelada Ex Ex 8, with 95 points.

Sweet wines, a traditional product of the region, show pretty irregular in quality. On the one hand we find some exceptional examples, complex wines with good structure and lots of identity, while some others brands are mere sugar bombs, with no balance whatsoever.

LOCATION:

In the far north west of Catalonia, in the province of Girona. The production area covers 40 municipal areas and is situated the slopes of the Rodes and Alberes mountain ranges forming an arch which leads from Cape Creus to what is known as the Garrotxa d'Empordà.

CLIMATE:

The climatology is conditioned by the 'Tramontana', a strong north wind which affects the vineyards. Furthermore, the winters are mild, with hardly any frost, and the summers hot, although somewhat tempered by the sea breezes. The average rainfall is around 600 mm.

SOIL:

The soil is in general poor, of a granitic nature in the mountainous areas, alluvial in the plains and slaty on the coastal belt.

GRAPE VARIETIES:

WHITE:
PREFERRED: *Garnacha Blanca, Macabeo (Viura)* and *Moscatel de Alejandría.*
AUTHORIZED: *Xarel.lo, Chardonnay, Gewürztraminer, Malvasía, Moscatel de Gra Petit, Picapoll Blanc* and *Sauvignon Blanc.*
RED:
PREFERRED: *Cariñena* and *Garnacha Tinta.*
AUTHORIZED: *Cabernet Sauvignon, Cabernet Franc, Merlot, Monastrell, Tempranillo, Syrah, Garnacha Roja (lledoner roig)* and *Garnacha Peluda.*

FIGURES:

Vineyard surface: 1,826 – **Wine-Growers:** 362 – **Wineries:** 49 – **2010 Harvest rating:** Very Good – **Production:** 5,440,000 litres – **Market percentages:** 79% domestic. 21% export

CONSEJO REGULADOR
Avda. Marignane, 2
Apdo. de Correos 186
17600 Figueres (Girona)
☎: +34 972 507 513 - Fax: +34 972 510 058
@ info@doemporda.com
www.doemporda.com

GENERAL CHARACTERISTICS OF THE WINES

WHITES	Those produced from autochthonous varieties are fresh and flavourful on the palate and persistent; their nose is reminiscent of hay and apples. Single variety wines from Chardonnay are also produced.
ROSÉS	These are pink-raspberry coloured with a fruity nose and are relatively intense, fresh and light.
REDS	Novell red wines are produced (they are marketed immediately after the harvest to be consumed within the year) with a deep cherry-red colour, easy drinking with good acidity levels and a red berry nose. The Crianza wines are aromatic with notes of spices; on the palate they are flavourful and pleasant to drink.
LICOROSOS	Traditional wines of the region produced from *Garnacha.* Red amber in colour, the nose has notes of Mistela and Rancio; on the palate they stand out for their sweetness and stickiness.

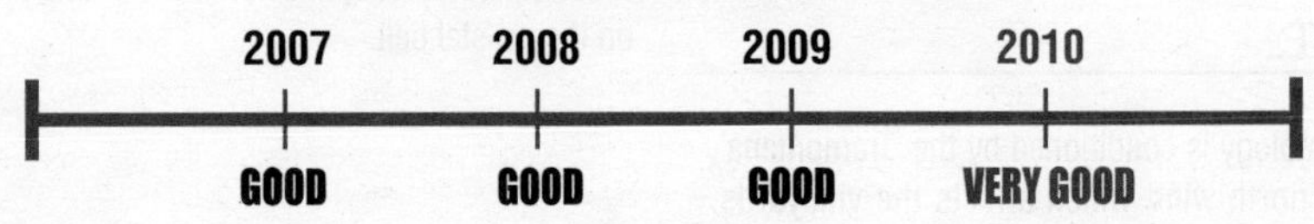

AGRÍCOLA DE GARRIGUELLA

Ctra. de Roses, s/n
17780 Garriguella (Girona)
☎: +34 972 530 002 - Fax: +34 972 531 747
info@cooperativagarriguella.com
www.cooperativagarriguella.com

PUNTILS BLANC GARNACHA 2010 B
100% garnacha blanca.

86 Colour: bright straw. Nose: white flowers, ripe fruit, expressive. Palate: light-bodied, fresh, flavourful.

DINARELLS 2010 B
65% macabeo, 35% garnacha blanca.

84 Colour: bright straw. Nose: citrus fruit, white flowers, fragrant herbs. Palate: flavourful, fruity, easy to drink.

PUNTILS 2010 B
75% garnacha blanca, 25% moscatel.

84 Colour: bright straw. Nose: fresh, fresh fruit, white flowers, honeyed notes. Palate: flavourful, fruity, good acidity, balanced.

PUNTILS BLANC MACABEO 2010 B
100% macabeo.

83 Colour: bright straw, greenish rim. Nose: medium intensity, dried flowers. Palate: flavourful, fine bitter notes, correct.

PUNTILS CARINYENA 2010 B
cariñena blanca.

83 Colour: bright straw. Nose: fresh, white flowers, medium intensity, grassy. Palate: flavourful, fruity, good acidity, balanced.

PUNTILS GARNACHA 2010 RD
100% garnacha.

87 Colour: rose, purple rim. Nose: powerfull, red berry notes, expressive, white flowers. Palate: fleshy, powerful, fruity, fresh.

DINARELLS 2010 RD
50% garnacha, 30% mazuelo, 20% tempranillo.

86 Color rose, purple rim. Aroma powerfull, ripe fruit, red berry notes, floral, expressive. Taste fleshy, powerful, fruity, fresh.

PUNTILS 2010 RD
50% garnacha, 30% mazuelo, 20% tempranillo.

85 Colour: rose, purple rim. Nose: red berry notes, floral, expressive. Palate: fleshy, powerful, fruity, easy to drink.

GARRIGUELLA NOVELL 2010 T
40% merlot, 40% tempranillo, 20% garnacha.

89 Colour: cherry, purple rim. Nose: floral, red berry notes, fresh fruit, expressive. Palate: good acidity, fresh, fruity, powerful, fleshy.

DINARELLS NEGRE 2009 T
50% garnacha, 35% cabernet sauvignon, 15% merlot.

84 Colour: cherry, garnet rim. Nose: ripe fruit, powerfull, medium intensity, warm. Palate: powerful, flavourful, fleshy.

GARRIGUELLA 2008 TC
60% mazuelo, 15% cabernet sauvignon, 15% garnacha, 10% merlot.

86 Colour: cherry, garnet rim. Nose: sweet spices, cocoa bean, aromatic coffee. Palate: light-bodied, fresh, toasty.

PUNTILS 2007 T
cariñena, merlot, garnacha.

86 Colour: cherry, garnet rim. Nose: balsamic herbs, scrubland, creamy oak. Palate: good acidity, flavourful, fleshy.

GARRIGUELLA GARNATXA D'EMPORDÁ NEGRA 2005 T
100% garnacha.

85 Colour: deep cherry, garnet rim. Nose: dried fruit, candied fruit, powerfull. Palate: flavourful, sweet.

DOLÇ DE GERISENA 2005 VINO DE LICOR
75% garnacha, 25% mazuelo.

91 Colour: deep cherry, orangey edge. Nose: toasty, caramel, acetaldehyde. Palate: good structure, fruity, full, spirituous.

GARRIGUELLA GARNATXA D'EMPORDÁ ROJA 2007 VINO DEL LICOR
100% garnacha roja.

85 Colour: light mahogany. Nose: candied fruit, warm, sweet spices. Palate: correct, good acidity, unctuous, fleshy.

ALCONVEST S.L.

Camí de Fitor s/n
17110 Forallac (Girona)
☎: +34 972 640 093 - Fax: +34
masanglada@masangrada.e.telefonica.es

RAIMS DE FONTETA 2009 T
merlot, cabernet sauvignon.

85 Colour: bright cherry. Nose: ripe fruit, sweet spices. Palate: flavourful, fruity, toasty, round tannins, easy to drink.

ALDEA DE BUSCARÓS

Ctra. de Darnius, Km. 2,5
17750 Capmany (Girona)
☎: +34 972 531 765 - Fax: +34 972 531 766

BROC 2006 T
cabernet sauvignon, merlot, garnacha.

87 Colour: cherry, garnet rim. Nose: ripe fruit, spicy, toasty. Palate: powerful, flavourful, toasty, round tannins.

BODEGAS MAS VIDA S.L.

Afuera s/n
17741 Cistella (Girona)
☎: +34 972 546 384 - Fax: +34 932 037 541
info@bodegasmasvida.com
www.bodegasmasvida.com

MAS VIDA 17 2010 B
chardonnay.

86 Colour: bright straw. Nose: white flowers, fresh fruit, varietal. Palate: balanced, flavourful, fresh.

MAS VIDA 32 2009 T ROBLE
100% merlot.

86 Colour: cherry, garnet rim. Nose: candied fruit, wild herbs. Palate: flavourful, spicy.

BODEGAS TROBAT

Castelló, 10
17780 Garriguella (Girona)
☎: +34 972 530 092 - Fax: +34 972 552 530
bodegas.trobat@bmark.es
www.bodegastrobat.com

AMAT SAUVIGNON BLANC 2010 B
sauvignon blanc.

85 Colour: bright straw. Nose: floral, wild herbs. Palate: correct, fruity, easy to drink.

NOBLE CHARDONNAY BLANC DE BLANCS 2010 B
chardonnay.

85 Colour: bright straw. Nose: citrus fruit, fresh fruit, fragrant herbs. Palate: fruity, powerful, flavourful.

AMAT MERLOT 2010 RD
merlot, garnacha.

86 Colour: rose, purple rim. Nose: powerfull, red berry notes, floral, lactic notes. Palate: fleshy, powerful, fruity, fresh, easy to drink.

TROBAT VI NOVELL 2010 T
syrah.

86 Colour: cherry, purple rim. Nose: red berry notes, fresh, expressive. Palate: fruity, powerful, flavourful, good acidity.

AMAT NEGRE 2010 T
merlot, syrah, garnacha.

83 Colour: cherry, purple rim. Nose: ripe fruit, balsamic herbs, medium intensity. Palate: correct, light-bodied, fresh.

AMAT ULL DE LLEBRE 2008 TC
ull de llebre.

85 Colour: light cherry. Nose: balsamic herbs, ripe fruit, old leather, toasty. Palate: balsamic, fleshy, toasty.

NOBLE CABERNET SAUVIGNON 2005 TC
cabernet sauvignon, garnacha.

84 Colour: ruby red, brick rim edge. Nose: fruit preserve, sweet spices, toasty. Palate: spicy, flavourful, fleshy.

CASTILLO DE CAPMANY

Fort, 5
17750 Capmany (Girona)
☎: +34 972 549 043 - Fax: +34 972 549 043
jlmoll@terra.es
www.castillodecapmany.com

CASTILLO OLIVARES 2005 T
cabernet sauvignon, merlot, syrah, garnacha.

83 Colour: bright cherry, garnet rim. Nose: slightly evolved, candied fruit. Palate: fruity, great length.

MOLL DE ALBA 2003 TR
cabernet sauvignon, merlot, garnacha, syrah.

84 Colour: pale ruby, brick rim edge. Nose: aromatic coffee, green pepper, scrubland. Palate: spicy, balsamic, toasty.

CASTILLO PERELADA VINOS Y CAVAS

Pl. del Carmen, 1
17491 Perelada (Girona)
☎: +34 972 538 011 - Fax: +34 972 538 277
perelada@castilloperelada.com
www.castilloperelada.com

CASTILLO PERELADA CHARDONNAY 2010 B
100% chardonnay.

91 Colour: bright straw. Nose: fresh fruit, expressive, jasmine, complex, fine lees. Palate: flavourful, fruity, good acidity, balanced.

CASTILLO DE PERELADA 5 FINCAS 2006 TR
40% merlot, 20% cabernet sauvignon, 20% garnacha, 15% syrah, 5% samsó.

92 Colour: cherry, garnet rim. Nose: ripe fruit, cocoa bean, creamy oak. Palate: balanced, ripe fruit, creamy, round tannins.

CASTILLO PERELADA LA GARRIGA 2010 B
50% cariñena blanca, 25% chardonnay, 15% sauvignon blanc, 10% marsanne.

90 Colour: bright yellow. Nose: powerfull, ripe fruit, fragrant herbs, fine lees, spicy. Palate: rich, flavourful, good acidity.

CASTILLO PERELADA GARNATXA BLANCA 2010 B
100% garnacha blanca.

89 Colour: bright straw. Nose: white flowers, fragrant herbs, complex. Palate: light-bodied, fresh, flavourful, fruity.

CIGONYES 2010 B
90% macabeo, 10% sauvignon blanc.

89 Colour: pale. Nose: white flowers, fresh fruit, expressive, mineral. Palate: powerful, flavourful, fruity, easy to drink.

CASTILLO PERELADA BLANC DE BLANCS 2010 B
50% macabeo, 20% garnacha blanca, 20% chardonnay, 10% sauvignon blanc.

87 Colour: bright straw. Nose: fresh fruit, citrus fruit, white flowers, balanced. Palate: flavourful, fruity, fresh, fleshy, long.

CASTILLO PERELADA SAUVIGNON BLANC 2010 B
100% sauvignon blanc.

85 Colour: bright straw. Nose: fresh, white flowers, citrus fruit. Palate: flavourful, fruity, good acidity, balanced, fine bitter notes.

CASTILLO PERELADA GARNATXA DE L'EMPORDÀ B
80% garnacha roja, 20% garnacha blanca.

92 Colour: light mahogany. Nose: acetaldehyde, iodine notes, cocoa bean, dark chocolate, sweet spices, creamy oak. Palate: good acidity, unctuous, flavourful, fleshy. Personality.

CASTILLO PERELADA CABERNET SAUVIGNON 2010 RD
100% cabernet sauvignon.

88 Colour: rose, purple rim. Nose: powerfull, red berry notes, floral, expressive, violet drops. Palate: fleshy, powerful, fruity, fresh, complex.

CASTILLO PERELADA 2010 RD
45% garnacha, 45% samso, 10% ull de llebre.

86 Colour: rose, purple rim. Nose: powerfull, ripe fruit, red berry notes, floral, expressive. Palate: fleshy, powerful, fruity, fresh, long.

CIGONYES 2010 T
90% garnacha, 10% syrah.

89 Colour: cherry, purple rim. Nose: expressive, red berry notes, floral, warm. Palate: flavourful, fruity, good acidity, round tannins, spirituous.

CASTILLO PERELADA FINCA ESPOLLA 2008 T
60% monastrell, 40% syrah.

90 Colour: black cherry, garnet rim. Nose: complex, balanced, cocoa bean, sweet spices. Palate: good structure, spicy, creamy.

CASTILLO PERELADA FINCA MALAVEÏNA 2008 T
50% merlot, 30% cabernet sauvignon, 10% syrah, 10% garnacha.

90 Colour: cherry, garnet rim. Nose: ripe fruit, spicy, creamy oak, wild herbs. Palate: powerful, flavourful, toasty, round tannins.

CASTILLO DE PERELADA 3 FINCAS 2008 TC
35% garnacha, 33% samso, 15% cabernet sauvignon, 15% merlot.

87 Colour: cherry, garnet rim. Nose: ripe fruit, grassy, wild herbs, sweet spices. Palate: flavourful, good structure, round tannins.

CASTILLO PERELADA LA GARRIGA 2007 T
100% samsó.

89 Colour: cherry, garnet rim. Nose: spicy, aromatic coffee, cocoa bean, candied fruit. Palate: rich, powerful, flavourful, fleshy, toasty.

CASTILLO DE PERELADA EX EX 8 2006 T
100% marselan.

94 Colour: black cherry, garnet rim. Nose: complex, elegant, expressive, fragrant herbs, spicy. Palate: good structure, full, ripe fruit, mineral.

CASTILLO PERELADA FINCA MALAVEÏNA 2007 T
50% merlot, 30% cabernet sauvignon, 10% syrah, 10% garnacha.

90 Colour: cherry, garnet rim. Nose: earthy notes, mineral, cocoa bean, dark chocolate, spicy, balsamic herbs. Palate: long, spicy, powerful, complex, fleshy.

FINCA GARBET 2006 T
90% syrah, 10% cabernet sauvignon.

92 Colour: cherry, garnet rim. Nose: ripe fruit, spicy, creamy oak, complex, earthy notes. Palate: powerful, flavourful, long.

CASTILLO PERELADA CABERNET SAUVIGNON 2006 T
100% cabernet sauvignon.

87 Colour: light cherry, garnet rim. Nose: varietal, ripe fruit, old leather, grassy. Palate: easy to drink, ripe fruit.

CASTILLO PERELADA GRAN CLAUSTRO 2005 T
50% cabernet sauvignon, 20% merlot, 15% garnacha, 15% samsó.

91 Colour: very deep cherry, garnet rim. Nose: spicy, ripe fruit, expressive, complex, toasty. Palate: good structure, fruity, toasty.

FINCA GARBET 2005 T
40% syrah, 60% cabernet sauvignon.

90 Colour: deep cherry. Nose: creamy oak, cocoa bean, varietal, aromatic coffee. Palate: ripe fruit, balanced, spicy, round tannins.

CELLER ARCHÉ PAGÈS

Sant Climent, 31
17750 Capmany (Girona)
☎: +34 626 647 251 - Fax: +34 972 549 229
bonfill@capmany.com
www.cellerarchepages.com

SÀTIRS 2010 B
100% macabeo.

86 Colour: bright straw. Nose: fresh fruit, medium intensity, wild herbs, dried flowers. Palate: easy to drink, great length.

BONFILL 2006 T
65% garnacha, 30% samsó, 5% cabernet sauvignon.

90 Colour: cherry, garnet rim. Nose: ripe fruit, creamy oak, toasty. Palate: powerful, flavourful, toasty, round tannins, mineral.

CARTESIUS 2006 T
55% garnacha, 24% merlot, 21% cabernet sauvignon.

88 Colour: cherry, garnet rim. Nose: ripe fruit, spicy, toasty, complex. Palate: powerful, flavourful, round tannins.

SÀTIRS 2006 T
46% garnacha, 28% cabernet sauvignon, 26% samsó.

82 Colour: deep cherry, brick rim edge. Nose: ripe fruit, slightly evolved. Palate: flavourful, ripe fruit.

CELLER CAN SAIS

Raval de Dalt, 10
17253 Vall-Llobrega (Girona)
☎: +34 647 443 873
correu@cellercansais.com
www.cellercansais.com

CAN SAIS MESTRAL 2010 B
65% macabeo, 20% malvasía, 15% garnacha blanca.

86 Colour: bright yellow. Nose: medium intensity, ripe fruit, honeyed notes, jasmine. Palate: flavourful, good structure, great length.

CAN SAIS ENCANTERI 2003 B
100% malvasía.

85 Colour: light mahogany. Nose: powerfull, floral, honeyed notes, candied fruit, acetaldehyde. Palate: flavourful, sweet, long.

CAN SAIS GREGAL 2010 RD
70% garnacha, 30% merlot.

84 Colour: rose, purple rim. Nose: ripe fruit, red berry notes, floral, expressive. Palate: fleshy, powerful, fruity, fresh, easy to drink.

CAN SAIS MIGJORN 2009 T
100% samsó.

82 Colour: bright cherry, purple rim. Nose: ripe fruit, fruit preserve, wild herbs. Palate: fleshy, great length.

CAN SAIS EXPRESSIÓ ZERO SULFITS 2008 T
100% garnacha.

88 Colour: cherry, garnet rim. Nose: spicy, creamy oak, toasty, complex, candied fruit. Palate: powerful, flavourful, toasty.

CELLER COOPERATIU D'ESPOLLA

Ctra. Roses, s/n
17753 Espolla (Girona)
☎: +34 972 563 049 - Fax: +34 972 563 178
ccdespolla@telefonica.es
www.cellerespolla.com

CASTELL DE PANISSARS 2010 B
40% lledoner blanc, 25% macabeo, 20% chardonnay, 15% moscatel.

86 Colour: bright straw. Nose: fresh fruit, white flowers, fragrant herbs. Palate: good acidity, fresh, flavourful.

MUSCAT D'EMPORDÀ ESPOLLA 2009 B
100% moscatel.

80 Colour: bright yellow. Nose: ripe fruit, medium intensity, short. Palate: light-bodied, fresh, sweetness.

CASTELL DE PANISSARS 2007 BFB
100% moscatel.

83 Colour: bright yellow. Nose: candied fruit, spicy. Palate: toasty, ripe fruit, great length.

NEGRE JOVE 2010 T
80% lledoner, 20% merlot.

88 Colour: bright cherry, purple rim. Nose: red berry notes, violets, fresh, balanced. Palate: fruity, good structure.

CASTELL DE PANISSARS 2008 TC
40% cariñena, 30% lledoner, 30% merlot.

85 Colour: cherry, garnet rim. Nose: ripe fruit, warm, spicy. Palate: correct, rich, fleshy.

CLOS DE LES DÒMINES 2007 TR
45% merlot, 30% cabernet sauvignon, cariñena.

88 Colour: cherry, garnet rim. Nose: candied fruit, spicy, balanced. Palate: fruity, fleshy, flavourful, round tannins.

GARNATXA D'EMPORDÀ ESPOLLA S/C DULCE NATURAL GRAN RESERVA
65% lledoner blanc, 35% lledoner roig.

89 Colour: light mahogany. Nose: acetaldehyde, caramel, cocoa bean, sweet spices. Palate: powerful, flavourful, fleshy, toasty, creamy.

CELLER MARIÀ PAGÈS

Pujada, 6
17750 Capmany (Girona)
☎: +34 972 549 160 - Fax: +34 972 549 160
info@cellermpages.com
www.cellermpages.com

CELLER MARÍÀ PAGÈS GARNACHA S/C B
garnacha tinta, garnacha blanca.

91 Colour: old gold, amber rim. Nose: citrus fruit, honeyed notes, acetaldehyde, creamy oak, sweet spices. Palate: creamy, flavourful, fruity, toasty.

SERRASAGUÉ VINYA DE HORT 2010 B
garnacha blanca, chardonnay, moscatel.

82 Colour: bright straw. Nose: medium intensity, white flowers, tropical fruit, honeyed notes. Palate: powerful, fruity.

CELLER MARÍÀ PAGÈS MOSCAT B
moscatel.

89 Colour: bright golden. Nose: candied fruit, pattiserie, honeyed notes, jasmine. Palate: sweet, flavourful, fleshy.

SERRASAGUÉ ROSA - T 2010 RD
garnacha, merlot.

87 Colour: rose, purple rim. Nose: powerfull, red berry notes, floral, expressive. Palate: fleshy, powerful, fruity, fresh.

SERRASAGUÉ 2010 T
garnacha, tempranillo, merlot.

87 Colour: cherry, purple rim. Nose: ripe fruit, red berry notes, wild herbs. Palate: fruity, flavourful, fleshy.

SERRASAGUÉ 2005 TC
garnacha, cabernet sauvignon, merlot.

85 Colour: cherry, garnet rim. Nose: spicy, balsamic herbs, old leather. Palate: spicy, balsamic, flavourful.

MARÍÀ PAGÈS GARNATXA TR
garnacha tinta, garnacha blanca.

88 Colour: light mahogany. Nose: caramel, acetaldehyde, fruit liqueur notes. Palate: good structure, sweet, rich.

CELLER MARTÍ FABRA

Barrio Vic, 26
17751 Sant Climent Sescebes (Girona)
☎: +34 972 563 011 - Fax: +34 972 563 867
info@cellermartifabra.com

VERD ALBERA 2010 B
70% garnacha blanca, 20% moscatel, chardonnay.

89 Colour: bright straw. Nose: ripe fruit, white flowers, fragrant herbs, expressive. Palate: good acidity, powerful, flavourful.

MASÍA CARRERAS 2009 BFB
40% cariñena blanca, 30% cariñena rosada, 10% garnacha blanca, 10% garnacha rosada, 10% picapoll.

90 Color bright yellow. Aroma powerfull, ripe fruit, sweet spices, creamy oak, fragrant herbs. Taste rich, smoky aftertaste, flavourful, fresh, good acidity.

MASÍA PAIRAL CAN CARRERAS MOSCAT B
100% moscatel.

89 Colour: golden. Nose: powerfull, floral, honeyed notes, candied fruit. Palate: flavourful, sweet, fresh, fruity, good acidity, long.

MASÍA PAIRAL CAN CARRERAS GARNATXA DE L'EMPORDÀ B
garnacha blanca, garnacha rosada.

86 Colour: dark mahogany. Nose: dry nuts, candied fruit, aromatic coffee, spicy, aged wood nuances. Palate: spirituous, flavourful, fleshy, toasty.

LLADONER 2010 RD
100% garnacha.

82 Colour: rose, purple rim. Nose: ripe fruit, candied fruit, floral, grassy. Palate: fine bitter notes, flavourful, stalky.

L'ORATORI 2008 T
50% garnacha, 30% cabernet sauvignon, 20% cariñena.

86 Colour: cherry, garnet rim. Nose: ripe fruit, wild herbs, mineral, spicy. Palate: good acidity, round, flavourful.

MASÍA CARRERAS NEGRE 2007 T
80% cariñena, 20% merlot.

88 Colour: cherry, garnet rim. Nose: ripe fruit, spicy, creamy oak, toasty, complex. Palate: powerful, flavourful, toasty, harsh oak tannins.

MARTÍ FABRA SELECCIÓ VINYES VELLES 2007 T ROBLE
60% garnacha, 25% cariñena, 8% syrah, 5% cabernet sauvignon, 2% tempranillo.

86 Colour: cherry, garnet rim. Nose: fruit preserve, faded flowers, spicy, toasty. Palate: powerful, flavourful, fleshy.

CELLER MAS PATIRÀS

Jardins de l'Empordà- Jardin botànic
17110 Fonteta (Girona)
☎: +34 972 642 687
info@jardinsemporda.com
www.jardinsemporda.com.com

BLAU DE TRAMUNTANA 2007 T ROBLE
syrah, garnacha, samsó.

82 Colour: cherry, garnet rim. Nose: warm, overripe fruit, medium intensity. Palate: lacks balance, fresh, light-bodied.

BLAU DE TRAMUNTANA 2006 T
garnacha, syrah, samsó.

83 Colour: cherry, garnet rim. Nose: grassy, ripe fruit, spicy. Palate: light-bodied, fruity.

DOLÇ TRAMUNTANA 2006 MISTELA
garnacha, syrah.

83 Colour: black cherry, garnet rim. Nose: dried fruit, honeyed notes. Palate: rich, flavourful, fleshy, sweet.

CELLERS SANTAMARÍA

Pza. Mayor, 6
17750 Capmany (Girona)
☎: +34 972 549 033 - Fax: +34 972 549 022
info@granrecosind.com
www.granrecosind.com

GRAN RECOSIND 2008 BC
macabeo, chardonnay.

83 Colour: bright golden. Nose: ripe fruit, medium intensity, creamy oak. Palate: ripe fruit, reductive nuances.

GRAN RECOSIND 2005 TR
merlot.

86 Colour: dark-red cherry, orangey edge. Nose: candied fruit, sweet spices. Palate: flavourful, ripe fruit.

GRAN RECOSIND 2005 TC
garnacha, tempranillo, cabernet sauvignon, merlot.

82 Colour: light cherry, brick rim edge. Nose: aromatic coffee, old leather, powerfull. Palate: powerful, dry wood, smoky aftertaste.

GRAN RECOSIND 2002 TR
cabernet sauvignon.

89 Colour: pale ruby, brick rim edge. Nose: elegant, spicy, fine reductive notes, wet leather, earthy notes. Palate: spicy, fine tannins.

COMERCIAL VINÍCOLA DEL NORDEST

Empolla, 9
17752 Mollet de Peralada (Girona)
☎: +34 972 563 150 - Fax: +34 972 545 134
vinicola@vinicoladelnordest.com
www.vinicoladelnordest.com

COVEST CHARDONNAY 2010 B
100% chardonnay.

85 Colour: bright straw. Nose: ripe fruit, medium intensity. Palate: flavourful, fruity, great length.

COVEST 2010 B
70% macabeo, 30% garnacha blanca.

83 Colour: bright straw. Nose: white flowers, medium intensity. Palate: flavourful, fruity, good acidity.

VINYA FARRIOL SEMIDULCE 2009 B
60% macabeo, 40% garnacha blanca.

81 Colour: bright straw. Nose: medium intensity, wild herbs. Palate: flavourful, sweet.

ANUBIS MOSCATEL DE L'EMPORDÀ B
moscatel.

89 Colour: bright golden. Nose: candied fruit, pattiserie, sweet spices, complex, powerfull. Palate: flavourful, long, creamy.

COVEST 2010 RD
65% cariñena, 35% garnacha.

84 Colour: rose, purple rim. Nose: floral, fresh fruit, red berry notes, fresh. Palate: fruity, flavourful, correct.

COVEST 2010 T
garnacha, cariñena.

88 Colour: bright cherry. Nose: red berry notes, wild herbs, earthy notes. Palate: flavourful, great length, good acidity.

GARRIGAL 2007 TC
80% garnacha, 20% cariñena.

84 Colour: cherry, garnet rim. Nose: ripe fruit, sweet spices. Palate: fruity, easy to drink.

ANUBIS 2004 TR
60% garnacha, 25% merlot, 15% cabernet sauvignon.

86 Colour: light cherry, orangey edge. Nose: medium intensity, ripe fruit, spicy, old leather. Palate: easy to drink, fine tannins.

ANUBIS GARNATXA DE L'EMPORDÀ 1996 DULCE NATURAL GRAN RESERVA
garnacha rosada.

90 Colour: mahogany. Nose: dry nuts, expressive, sweet spices, creamy oak, aromatic coffee. Palate: powerful, flavourful, fleshy, rich, creamy.

EMPORDÀLIA

Ctra. Roses, s/n
17494 Pau (Girona)
☎: +34 972 530 140 - Fax: +34 972 530 528
info@empordalia.com
www.empordalia.com

EMPORDÀLIA SAMSÓ 2009 T
cariñena.

88 Colour: cherry, garnet rim. Nose: powerfull, red berry notes, ripe fruit, expressive. Palate: rich, powerful, fleshy, balanced.

SINOLS 2007 TC
mazuelo, garnacha, cabernet sauvignon, syrah.

88 Colour: cherry, garnet rim. Nose: ripe fruit, toasty, complex, balanced, sweet spices. Palate: powerful, flavourful, round tannins.

SINOLS 2005 TR
cabernet sauvignon, mazuelo, garnacha.

86 Colour: bright cherry. Nose: ripe fruit, spicy. Palate: powerful, fruity, round tannins.

SINOLS COROMINA 2005 T
mazuelo, garnacha.

86 Colour: pale ruby, brick rim edge. Nose: ripe fruit, balsamic herbs, cocoa bean. Palate: flavourful, fleshy, toasty.

SINOLS MOSCATELL 2009 BLANCO DULCE
moscatel.

85 Colour: bright yellow. Nose: pattiserie, caramel, roasted almonds, candied fruit. Palate: sweet, flavourful.

EMPORDÀLIA BR
macabeo, garnacha blanca.

83 Color bright straw. Aroma medium intensity, fresh fruit, dried herbs, fine lees, floral. Taste fresh, fruity, flavourful, good acidity.

ESPELT VITICULTORS

Mas Espelt
17493 Vilajuiga (Girona)
☎: +34 972 531 727 - Fax: +34 972 531 741
info@espeltviticultors.com
www.espeltviticultors.com

ESPELT MARENY 2010 B
sauvignon blanc, moscatel.

85 Colour: bright straw. Nose: fresh, fresh fruit, white flowers. Palate: flavourful, fruity, good acidity, balanced.

ESPELT VAILET 2010 B
garnacha blanca, macabeo.

82 Colour: bright straw. Nose: fresh fruit, white flowers. Palate: fruity, good acidity, balanced, easy to drink.

ESPELT QUINZE ROURES 2009 BFB
garnacha gris, garnacha blanca.

83 Colour: bright yellow. Nose: ripe fruit, toasty. Palate: rich, smoky aftertaste, flavourful, good acidity.

ESPELT LLEDONER 2010 RD
garnacha.

83 Colour: onion pink. Nose: fresh fruit, floral, medium intensity. Palate: easy to drink, flavourful, fresh.

ESPELT SAULÓ 2010 T
garnacha, cariñena.

87 Colour: cherry, purple rim. Nose: medium intensity, ripe fruit, dried herbs. Palate: fruity, spicy.

ESPELT VIDIVÍ 2009 T
garnacha, merlot.

85 Colour: cherry, purple rim. Nose: ripe fruit, wild herbs, sweet spices, candied fruit. Palate: spicy, flavourful.

ESPELT COMABRUNA 2008 T
syrah, cariñena.

88 Colour: cherry, purple rim. Nose: cocoa bean, spicy, creamy oak, ripe fruit. Palate: balanced, fleshy, flavourful.

ESPELT TERRES NEGRES 2008 T
cariñena.

87 Colour: cherry, garnet rim. Nose: ripe fruit, cocoa bean, aromatic coffee, toasty. Palate: rich, flavourful.

ESPELT GARNACHA AIRAM VINO DE LICOR
garnacha tinta, garnacha rosada.

87 Colour: coppery red. Nose: acetaldehyde, fruit liqueur notes, pattiserie, roasted almonds. Palate: flavourful, rich, good structure, sweet.

JOAN SARDÀ

Ctra. Vilafranca a St. Jaume dels Domenys, Km. 8,1
08732 Castellvi de la Marca (Barcelona)
☎: +34 937 720 900 - Fax: +34 937 721 495
joansarda@joansarda.com
www.joansarda.com

CAP DE CREUS NACRE 2010 B
lledoner roig, lledoner blanc.

83 Colour: bright straw. Nose: white flowers, medium intensity. Palate: flavourful, fruity, good acidity, balanced.

FEIXES DEL PORT 2008 T
lledoner, samsó, cabernet sauvignon.

85 Colour: cherry, garnet rim. Nose: ripe fruit, scrubland, toasty. Palate: correct, flavourful, toasty.

LAVINYETA

Ctra. de Mollet de Peralada a Masarac, s/n
17752 Mollet de Peralada (Girona)
☎: +34 647 748 809 - Fax: +34 972 505 323
celler@lavinyeta.es
www.lavinyeta.es

HEUS BLANC 2010 B
59% macabeo, 12% garnacha blanca, 18% moscatel, 11% xarel.lo.

84 Colour: bright straw. Nose: fresh fruit, tropical fruit, honeyed notes. Palate: fruity, flavourful, fleshy.

HEUS ROSAT 2010 RD
38% garnacha, 34% samsó, 20% merlot, 8% syrah.

85 Colour: rose, purple rim. Nose: floral, red berry notes, fresh, lactic notes. Palate: good acidity, fruity, flavourful.

HEUS 2010 T
51% samsó, 20% garnacha, 19% syrah, 10% merlot.

91 Colour: bright cherry, purple rim. Nose: medium intensity, expressive, red berry notes. Palate: good structure, fruity, flavourful.

LLAVORS 2009 T
33% samsó, 29% merlot, 16% cabernet franc, 14% cabernet sauvignon, 8% syrah.

85 Colour: cherry, garnet rim. Nose: fruit preserve, balsamic herbs, medium intensity. Palate: rich, powerful, flavourful, fleshy, round tannins.

PUNTIAPART 2008 T
85% cabernet sauvignon, 15% samsó.

88 Colour: cherry, garnet rim. Nose: cocoa bean, spicy, red berry notes, expressive. Palate: fleshy, flavourful, creamy, balsamic.

SOLS 2008 DULCE
50% garnacha roja, 50% garnacha blanca.

85 Colour: coppery red. Nose: ripe fruit, candied fruit, sweet spices, varnish, acetaldehyde. Palate: good acidity, easy to drink, creamy, flavourful.

LORDINA

Ctra. de Roses, Km. 9,5
17493 Vilajuiga (Girona)
☎: +34 629 578 001 - Fax: +34 934 340 480
lordina7@gmail.com
www.lordina.net

LORDINA MESSAGE 2010 B
sauvignon blanc, moscatel.

87 Colour: bright straw, greenish rim. Nose: floral, wild herbs. Palate: flavourful, balanced, great length.

LORDINA MESSAGE 2010 RD
garnacha.

82 Colour: onion pink. Nose: fresh, slightly evolved, ripe fruit. Palate: flavourful, fruity, fleshy.

LORDINA MESSAGE 2010 T
garnacha, cariñena.

87 Colour: bright cherry, purple rim. Nose: red berry notes, ripe fruit, medium intensity, balanced. Palate: flavourful, fruity, good acidity.

LORDINA GRANIT 2008 T
cariñena, cabernet sauvignon.

88 Colour: cherry, garnet rim. Nose: spicy, ripe fruit, medium intensity, balanced. Palate: flavourful, mineral, great length.

LORDINA "AMPHORA" 2008 T
70% syrah, 30% garnacha.

87 Colour: bright cherry, garnet rim. Nose: ripe fruit, powerfull, balanced. Palate: fruity, round tannins, great length.

MAS LLUNES

Ctra. de Roses, s/n
17780 Garriguela (Girona)
☎: +34 972 552 684 - Fax: +34 972 530 112
masllunes@masllunes.es
www.masllunes.es

MARAGDA 2010 B
80% garnacha blanca, 10% macabeo, 10% roussane.

85 Colour: bright yellow. Nose: floral, ripe fruit, fragrant herbs. Palate: balanced, fruity.

NIVIA 2009 BFB
90% garnacha blanca, 10% samsó blanca.

88 Colour: bright straw. Nose: expressive, spicy, candied fruit, complex. Palate: flavourful, fruity, good acidity, balanced, elegant.

MARAGDA 2010 RD
90% garnacha, 10% cabernet franc.

87 Colour: raspberry rose. Nose: elegant, dried flowers, fragrant herbs, red berry notes. Palate: light-bodied, flavourful, good acidity, long, spicy.

CERCIUM 2009 T
50% garnacha, 40% syrah, 10% samsó.

85 Colour: cherry, garnet rim. Nose: spicy, fresh, candied fruit, ripe fruit. Palate: fresh, flavourful, long.

RHODES 2007 T
63% samsó, 37% syrah.

90 Colour: bright cherry. Nose: mineral, ripe fruit, complex, expressive. Palate: fruity, flavourful, balanced.

EMPÓRION 2005 T
70% cabernet sauvignon, 15% merlot, 15% syrah.

86 Colour: deep cherry, garnet rim. Nose: ripe fruit, spicy, cocoa bean. Palate: long, balanced, ripe fruit.

MAS OLLER

Ctra. GI-652, Km. 0,23
17123 Torrent (Girona)
☎: +34 972 300 001
mas_oller@yahoo.es

MAS OLLER 2010 B
80% picapoll, 20% malvasía.

92 Colour: bright straw. Nose: white flowers, fresh fruit, tropical fruit, fragrant herbs, expressive. Palate: rich, flavourful, long, balanced.

MAS OLLER PUR 2010 T
garnacha, syrah, cabernet sauvignon.

91 Colour: cherry, garnet rim. Nose: mineral, ripe fruit, red berry notes, spicy. Palate: flavourful, fruity, fleshy.

MAS OLLER BLAU 2010 T
syrah, garnacha.

90 Colour: bright cherry. Nose: ripe fruit, sweet spices, neat, fruit expression. Palate: flavourful, fruity, round tannins.

MAS OLLER PLUS 2008 T
syrah, garnacha.

93 Colour: cherry, garnet rim. Nose: spicy, creamy oak, toasty, earthy notes, characterful. Palate: powerful, flavourful, round tannins.

MAS POLIT

Raval de la Font, 1
17781 Vilamaniscle (Girona)
☎: +34 636 482 472
celler@maspolit.com
www.maspolit.com

SAMSO BLANC 2010 B
100% cariñena blanca.

80 Colour: bright straw. Nose: faded flowers, dried herbs, spicy. Palate: good acidity, correct, balanced.

MAS POLIT NEGRE 2008 T
45% garnacha, 35% cabernet sauvignon, 20% syrah.

88 Colour: cherry, garnet rim. Nose: creamy oak, sweet spices, candied fruit. Palate: good structure, flavourful, spicy, round tannins.

CLOS D'ILLA 2008 T
75% syrah, 25% garnacha.

86 Colour: bright cherry, purple rim. Nose: sweet spices, cocoa bean, ripe fruit. Palate: flavourful, spicy.

MASIA SERRA

Dels Solés, 20
17708 Cantallops (Girona)
☎: +34 972 531 765
masiaserra@masiaserra.com
www.masiaserra.com

CTÒNIA 2010 BFB
100% garnacha blanca.

91 Colour: bright straw. Nose: white flowers, ripe fruit, citrus fruit, fruit expression. Palate: flavourful, good acidity, ripe fruit, long.

AROA 2006 T
72% garnacha, 28% marselan.

87 Colour: deep cherry. Nose: toasty, spicy, ripe fruit. Palate: powerful, flavourful, spirituous, pruney.

GNEIS 2003 T
43% merlot, 31% cabernet sauvignon, 26% garnacha.

89 Colour: cherry, garnet rim. Nose: toasty, fruit liqueur notes, aromatic coffee, cigar. Palate: sweetness, fine bitter notes, spicy.

OLIVEDA

La Roca, 3
17750 Capmany (Girona)
☎: +34 972 549 012 - Fax: +34 972 549 106
comercial@grupoliveda.com
www.grupoliveda.com

RIGAU ROS CHARDONNAY 2010 BFB
100% chardonnay.

88 Color bright yellow. Aroma powerfull, ripe fruit, sweet spices, creamy oak, fragrant herbs. Taste rich, smoky aftertaste, flavourful, fresh, good acidity.

RIGAU ROS BLANCO DE FLOR 2010 B
60% chardonnay, 30% macabeo, 10% sauvignon blanc.

85 Colour: bright straw. Nose: ripe fruit, fresh, white flowers. Palate: flavourful, fruity, easy to drink.

FINCA FUROT SAUVIGNON BLANC 2010 B
100% sauvignon blanc.

85 Colour: bright straw. Nose: fresh fruit, citrus fruit, fragrant herbs. Palate: fresh, fruity, light-bodied.

RIGAU ROS 2010 RD
50% merlot, 30% garnacha, 20% samso.

87 Colour: rose, purple rim. Nose: powerfull, red berry notes, floral, expressive. Palate: fleshy, powerful, fruity, fresh, easy to drink.

FINCA FUROT 2007 TC
100% samso.

87 Colour: cherry, garnet rim. Nose: spicy, cocoa bean, balsamic herbs, ripe fruit, red berry notes. Palate: flavourful, fleshy, long, toasty.

FINCA FUROT 2004 TR
80% garnacha, 10% cabernet sauvignon, 10% merlot.

87 Colour: cherry, garnet rim. Nose: ripe fruit, spicy, old leather. Palate: powerful, flavourful, toasty, round tannins.

RIGAU ROS 2004 TGR
50% cabernet sauvignon, 30% garnacha, 20% samso.

86 Colour: pale ruby, brick rim edge. Nose: elegant, spicy, wet leather, aged wood nuances. Palate: spicy, long.

RIGAU ROS CABERNET SAUVIGNON 2003 TGR
100% cabernet sauvignon.

86 Colour: bright cherry, garnet rim. Nose: medium intensity, old leather, spicy. Palate: flavourful, fine tannins.

OLIVER CONTI

Puignau, s/n
17750 Capmany (Girona)
☎: +34 972 193 161 - Fax: +34 972 193 040
dolors@oliverconti.com
www.oliverconti.com

OLIVER CONTI TREYU 2010 B
50% gewürztraminer, 50% macabeo.

87 Colour: bright yellow. Nose: white flowers, fragrant herbs, fresh fruit. Palate: light-bodied, fruity, fleshy.

OLIVER CONTI 2008 B BARRICA
gewürztraminer, sauvignon blanc.

88 Colour: bright golden. Nose: fragrant herbs, dried flowers, expressive, creamy oak. Palate: ripe fruit, flavourful, fruity.

OLIVER CONTI CARLOTA 2009 T
75% cabernet franc, 25% cabernet sauvignon.

91 Colour: black cherry, garnet rim. Nose: powerfull, complex, red berry notes, earthy notes, mineral. Palate: good acidity, balanced, powerful, fleshy, complex.

OLIVER CONTI ARA 2009 T
55% cabernet sauvignon, 20% garnacha, 20% cabernet franc, 5% merlot.

89 Colour: cherry, purple rim. Nose: red berry notes, balsamic herbs, earthy notes. Palate: long, fruity, powerful, fleshy, spicy, round tannins.

OLIVER CONTI 2007 TR
70% cabernet sauvignon, 20% merlot, 10% cabernet franc.

90 Colour: cherry, garnet rim. Nose: scrubland, ripe fruit, mineral, balsamic herbs. Palate: complex, flavourful, fruity.

PERE GUARDIOLA

Ctra. GI-602, Km. 2,9
17750 Capmany (Girona)
☎: +34 972 549 096 - Fax: +34 972 549 097
vins@pereguardiola.com
www.pereguardiola.com

FLORESTA 2010 B
macabeo, chardonnay, garnacha blanca.

84 Colour: bright straw. Nose: ripe fruit, white flowers, citrus fruit. Palate: good acidity, fresh, fruity.

TORRE DE CAPMANY MOSCATEL B
moscatel.

87 Colour: bright golden. Nose: candied fruit, honeyed notes, citrus fruit, expressive. Palate: fresh, flavourful, rich, creamy.

FLORESTA 2010 RD
garnacha, mazuelo, merlot, syrah.

86 Colour: rose, purple rim. Nose: powerfull, red berry notes, floral, expressive. Palate: fleshy, fruity, fresh, flavourful.

FLORESTA 2006 TC
merlot, syrah, garnacha, cabernet sauvignon.

87 Colour: cherry, garnet rim. Nose: ripe fruit, aromatic coffee, cocoa bean, balsamic herbs. Palate: long, fleshy, complex, flavourful.

CLOS FLORESTA 2004 TR
cabernet sauvignon, merlot, syrah, garnacha.

87 Colour: very deep cherry. Nose: varietal, medium intensity, ripe fruit, old leather. Palate: spicy, easy to drink.

JONCARIA MERLOT 2003 TR
merlot.

87 Colour: cherry, garnet rim. Nose: ripe fruit, spicy, toasty, old leather. Palate: powerful, flavourful, toasty, round tannins.

ROIG PARALS

Garriguella, 8
17752 Mollet de Peralada (Girona)
☎: +34 972 634 320 - Fax: +34 972 306 209
info@roigparals.cat
www.roigparals.com

ROIG PARALS 2009 T
samsó, merlot.

88 Colour: cherry, garnet rim. Nose: balsamic herbs, red berry notes, ripe fruit, expressive. Palate: powerful, flavourful, fleshy, long.

LA BOTERA 2008 T
80% samsó, 20% merlot.

81 Colour: cherry, garnet rim. Nose: fruit preserve, dried herbs. Palate: fruity, easy to drink, good finish.

CAMÍ DE CORMES 2007 T
100% samsó.

86 Colour: cherry, garnet rim. Nose: sweet spices, aromatic coffee, ripe fruit, earthy notes. Palate: balsamic, rich, fleshy.

SOTA ELS ÀNGELS

Apdo. Correos 27
17100 La Bisbal (Girona)
☎: +34 972 006 976
info@sotaelsangels.com
www.sotaelsangels.com

SOTA ELS ÀNGELS 2009 B
picapoll, viognier.

90 Colour: bright yellow. Nose: powerfull, ripe fruit, creamy oak, fragrant herbs. Palate: rich, smoky aftertaste, flavourful, good acidity, unctuous.

DESEA 2008 T
merlot, samsó, syrah.

87 Colour: cherry, garnet rim. Nose: ripe fruit, toasty, complex, wet leather. Palate: flavourful, round tannins, fruity.

SOTA ELS ÀNGELS 2007 T
cabernet sauvignon, carmenere, merlot, samsó, syrah.

88 Colour: cherry, garnet rim. Nose: ripe fruit, spicy, complex, old leather, toasty. Palate: powerful, flavourful, toasty, round tannins, mineral.

VINYES D'OLIVARDOTS

Paratge Olivadots, s/n
17750 Capmany (Girona)
☎: +34 650 395 627
vdo@olivardots.com
www.olivardots.com

BLANC DE GRESA 2010 BFB
garnacha blanca, garnacha rosada, cariñena blanca.

90 Colour: bright straw, greenish rim. Nose: complex, expressive, ripe fruit, spicy. Palate: good structure, flavourful, great length, fine bitter notes.

VD'O 3.08 2008 T
100% syrah.

92 Colour: cherry, garnet rim. Nose: red berry notes, spicy, cocoa bean, creamy oak, mineral. Palate: powerful, flavourful, fleshy, mineral, roasted-coffee aftertaste.

GRESA 2008 T
30% garnacha, 30% syrah, 30% cariñena, 10% cabernet sauvignon.

89 Colour: dark-red cherry, garnet rim. Nose: ripe fruit, spicy, balanced, complex. Palate: flavourful, fruity, balanced.

GRESA 2007 T
30% garnacha, 30% cariñena, 20% syrah, 20% cabernet sauvignon.

93 Colour: cherry, garnet rim. Nose: mineral, ripe fruit, dark chocolate, cocoa bean, creamy oak. Palate: rich, fleshy, long, balanced.

VD'O 1.07 2007 T
100% cariñena.

92 Colour: black cherry, garnet rim. Nose: earthy notes, mineral, ripe fruit, cocoa bean, creamy oak. Palate: powerful, flavourful, fleshy, complex, mineral, great length.

VINYES DELS ASPRES

Requesens, 7
17708 Cantallops (Girona)
☎: +34 972 463 146 - Fax: +34 972 420 662
vinyesdelsaspres@vinyesdelsaspres.cat
www.vinyesdelsaspres.cat

BLANC DELS ASPRES 2009 BC
100% garnacha blanca.

83 Colour: bright golden. Nose: ripe fruit, faded flowers, medium intensity. Palate: powerful, flavourful, fleshy.

ORIOL 2009 T
40% cariñena, 30% garnacha, 10% merlot, 10% cabernet sauvignon, 10% tempranillo.

85 Colour: cherry, garnet rim. Nose: wild herbs, ripe fruit, warm. Palate: flavourful, spicy, great length, sweet tannins.

S'ALOU 2007 TC
60% garnacha, 13% cariñena, 13% syrah, 13% cabernet sauvignon.

89 Colour: cherry, garnet rim. Nose: balanced, expressive, ripe fruit, sweet spices, mineral. Palate: long, round tannins.

XAVIER MASET ISACH

Paratge - Pedreguers, s/n
17780 Garriguella (Alt Empordà)
☎: +34 972 505 455 - Fax: +34 972 501 948
jmaset@masetplana.com
www.masetplana.com

A21 MASETPLANA 2010 B
100% garnacha blanca.

83 Colour: yellow, pale. Nose: floral, wild herbs, medium intensity. Palate: easy to drink, good finish, fresh.

A21 MASETPLANA 2010 RD
cariñena.

85 Colour: brilliant rose. Nose: white flowers, fresh fruit, red berry notes, expressive. Palate: correct, good acidity, flavourful.

A21 MASETPLANA 2010 T
100% monastrell.

84 Colour: cherry, purple rim. Nose: fresh, fruit preserve, balsamic herbs. Palate: light-bodied, fresh, fruity.

A21 MASETPLANA 2006 TC
mazuelo.

84 Colour: cherry, garnet rim. Nose: spicy, ripe fruit, balsamic herbs. Palate: fleshy, flavourful, spicy, toasty.

MASETPLANA S/C BN RESERVA

85 Colour: bright straw. Nose: medium intensity, fresh fruit, dried herbs, fine lees, floral, citrus fruit. Palate: fresh, fruity, flavourful, good acidity.

MASETPLANA ROSAT S/C BN

85 Colour: rose, purple rim. Nose: red berry notes, ripe fruit, fine lees. Palate: flavourful, fruity, good acidity, fine bead.

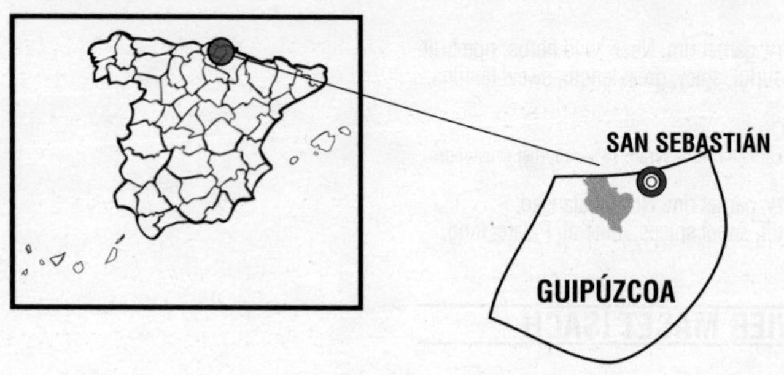

Consejo Regulador
DO Boundary

NEWS ABOUT THE VINTAGE:

The model of the DO Getariako Txakolina is almost at the opposite end of the one from Vizcaya, the reason being that in the town of Getaria, txakoli has always been a more down-to-earth, popular product, abundantly served in small glasses in the local taverns. They should basically have a fresh, clean character, even with a slight carbonic touch to ease the palate, and should altogether be an easy-drinking product. And that is exactly the way they have shown in our tasting, with the added bonus of a great vintage (2010) to make txakoli. Thus, we have seven wines with 88 points or more, for just two in last year's edition. This increase is due mainly to the quality of the 2010 vintage, which, as stated above, shows much more complex than that of 2009, although with a marked acidity, a common trait in these wines in any case. The 2010 harvest was one of the latest-ripening ones in recent years; besides, there happened an abnormal flowering in June, which was about the only negative note during the whole cycle. This obviously thwarted fruit set as well, but thanks to the absence of rains during the summer and judicious winemaking, the wine finally bottled was of an excellent quality.

The best ratings (89 points) of the DO go for Aialle 2009, Txomin Etxaniz Berezia 2009, and a formidable novelty, the K-5, from the ineffable TV chef Karlos Arguiñano, who, along with some other shareholders, has created a modern and up-to-date winery on a lovely west-facing hill.

Since 2007, when wine planting in the DO was made available for the whole of the Guipúzcoa province, the wine region has grown in both vineyard surface and production figures –in 2010 the DO has reached a production record–, a situation that will force producers to try and increase their sales, and therefore go beyond the traditional "local" market.

LOCATION:

On the coastal belt of the province of Guipuzcoa, covering the vineyards situated in the municipal areas of Aia, Getaria and Zarauz, at a distance of about 25 km from San Sebastián.

CLIMATE:

Fairly mild, thanks to the influence of the Bay of Biscay. The average annual temperature is 13°C, and the rainfall is plentiful with an average of 1,600 mm per year.

SOIL:

The vineyards are situated in small valleys and gradual hillsides at altitudes of up to 200 m. They are found on humid brownish-grey limy soil, which are rich in organic matter.

GRAPE VARIETIES:

WHITE: *Hondarrabi Zuri* (majority with 90% of all vineyards), *Gros Manseng* and *Riesling*.
RED: *Hondarrabi Beltza*.

FIGURES:

Vineyard surface: 402 – **Wine-Growers:** 96 – **Wineries:** 24 – **2010 Harvest rating:** Very Good – **Production:** 1,740,600 litres – **Market percentages:** 95% domestic. 5% export

DO GETARIAKO TXAKOLINA

CONSEJO REGULADOR
Parque Aldamar, 4 bajo
20808 Getaria (Gipuzkoa)
☎: +34 943 140 383 - Fax: +34 943 896 030
@ info@getariakotxakolina.com
www.getariakotxakolina.com

GENERAL CHARACTERISTICS OF THE WINES

WHITES	Produced from the autochtonous variety Hondarrabi Zuri; nevertheless, they may include a small percentage of red grapes (*Hondarrabi Beltza*) in the blend. The Txakoli from Getaria is characterised by its pale steely colour; the clean and frank nose of the wine, with pleasant herby notes and, in the best case, with floral traits; on the palate it is very fresh due to its high acidity, and light; it may also seem a bit carbonic.

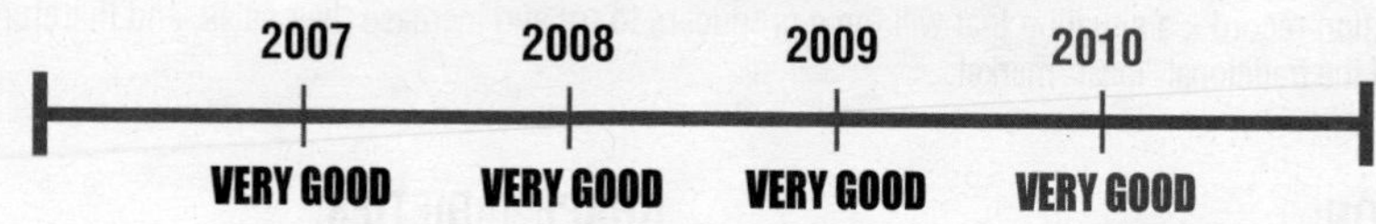

AGERRE

Agerre Baserria - Bº Askizu
20808 Getaria (Gipuzkoa)
☎: +34 943 140 446 - Fax: +34 943 140 446
txakaguerre@terra.es

AGERRE 2010 B
hondarrabi zuri.

86 Colour: bright straw. Nose: fresh, fresh fruit, white flowers. Palate: flavourful, fruity, balanced.

AKARREGI TXIKI

Akarregi Txiki Baserria
20808 Guetaria (Gipuzkoa)
☎: +34 689 035 789 - Fax: +34 943 140 726

AKARREGI TXIKI 2010 B
hondarrabi zuri.

87 Colour: bright straw. Nose: fresh, fresh fruit, white flowers. Palate: flavourful, fruity, good acidity, balanced.

AMEZTOI

Barrio Eitzaga, 10
20808 Getaria (Gipuzkoa)
☎: +34 943 140 918 - Fax: +34 940 250 320
ameztoi@txakoliameztoi.com
www.txakoliameztoi.com

AMEZTOI 2010 B
hondarrabi zuri.

87 Colour: bright straw. Nose: fresh, fresh fruit, dried flowers. Palate: flavourful, fruity, good acidity, balanced.

ARREGI

Talaimendi, 727- Bajo
20800 Zarautz (Gipuzkoa)
☎: +34 943 580 835
info@txakoliarregi.com
www.txakoliarregi.com

ARREGI 2010 B
hondarrabi zuri.

85 Colour: bright straw. Nose: fresh fruit, white flowers. Palate: flavourful, fruity, good acidity, fine bitter notes.

BASA LORE

Santa Bárbara Auzoa
Buzón 1
20800 Zarautz (Gipuzkoa)
☎: +34 943 132 231 - Fax: +34 943 834 747
basa-lore@mixmail.com

BASA LORE 2010 B
hondarrabi zuri.

85 Colour: bright straw. Nose: fresh fruit, white flowers, varietal, grassy. Palate: flavourful, fruity, good acidity, balanced.

BODEGA REZABAL

Itsas Begi Etxea, 628
20800 Zarautz (Gipuzkoa)
☎: +34 943 580 899 - Fax: +34 943 580 775
info@txakolirezabal.com
www.txakolirezabal.com

TXAKOLI REZABAL 2010 B
hondarrabi zuri.

88 Colour: bright straw. Nose: fresh fruit, white flowers, varietal. Palate: flavourful, fruity, good acidity, balanced.

BODEGAS JUAN CELAYA

Upaingoa-Barrio Zañartuko
20560 Oñati (Gipuzkoa)
☎: +34 948 782 255 - Fax: +34 948 401 182
administracion@naparralde.com
www.upain.es

UPAINGOA 2010 B
hondarrabi zuri, riesling.

87 Colour: bright straw. Nose: white flowers, fragrant herbs, citrus fruit, expressive. Palate: correct, powerful, flavourful, fruity.

UPAINGOA 2009 B
hondarrabi zuri, riesling.

86 Colour: bright straw. Nose: dried flowers, citrus fruit, fresh, expressive. Palate: light-bodied, flavourful, fruity.

BODEGAS SANTARBA

Santa Bárbara, 7- buzón Nº 8
20800 Zarautz (Gipuzkoa)
☎: +34 943 140 452

SANTARBA 2010 B
hondarrabi zuri.

85 Colour: bright straw. Nose: fresh fruit, white flowers. Palate: fruity, good acidity, balanced.

EIZAGUIRRE

Azpeiti Bidea, 18
20800 Zarautz (Gipuzkoa)
☎: +34 943 130 303 - Fax: +34 943 130 303
eizagirre@hotmail.com

EIZAGUIRRE 2010 B
hondarrabi zuri.

80 Colour: straw. Nose: medium intensity, sulphur notes, fresh fruit, grassy. Palate: fruity, fresh.

EMETERIO AIZPURUA

San Prudentzio Auzoa, 36
20808 Getaria (Gipuzkoa)
☎: +34 943 580 922
bodegaaizpurua@txakoli.com

AIZPURUA. B 2010 B
hondarrabi zuri.

87 Colour: bright straw. Nose: fresh, fresh fruit, white flowers. Palate: flavourful, fruity, good acidity, fine bitter notes, fine bead.

AIALLE 2009 B
hondarrabi zuri, hondarrabi beltza.

89 Colour: bright straw. Nose: fresh, fresh fruit, white flowers, fine lees. Palate: flavourful, fruity, good acidity, balanced.

ETXETXO

Etxetxo Baserria
20808 Getaria (Gipuzkoa)
☎: +34 943 140 085 - Fax: +34 943 140 146
etxetxo@euskalnet.net

ETXETXO 2010 B
hondarrabi zuri.

85 Colour: bright straw. Nose: fresh, white flowers. Palate: flavourful, fruity, good acidity.

GAÑETA

Agerre Goikoa Baserria
20808 Getaria (Gipuzkoa)
☎: +34 943 140 174 - Fax: +34 943 140 174

GAÑETA 2010 B
hondarrabi zuri.

86 Colour: pale. Nose: floral, fresh fruit, grassy. Palate: flavourful, fruity, fresh.

GAÑETA BEREZIA 2009 B
hondarrabi zuri.

87 Colour: bright straw. Nose: fresh, white flowers, ripe fruit. Palate: flavourful, fruity, balanced, sweetness.

J.I. ETXEBERRIA ZUBIZARRETA Y OTRO

Cs Bengoetxe
20212 Olaberria (Gipuzkoa)
☎: +34 619 977 019 - Fax: +34 943 884 955
inakietxeberria@hotmail.es

BENGOETXE 2010 B
82% hondarrabi zuri, 13% petit corbu, 5% gross mansen.

84 Colour: bright straw. Nose: balsamic herbs, ripe fruit, grassy. Palate: flavourful, fine bitter notes, ripe fruit.

K5

Apdo. Correos 258
20800 Zarautz (Gipuzkoa)
☎: +34 943 240 005
bodega@txakolina-k5.com
www.txakolina-k5.com

K5 ARGIÑANO 2010 B
100% hondarrabi zuri.

89 Colour: bright straw. Nose: grassy, fresh fruit, citrus fruit. Palate: flavourful, fruity, fresh, good acidity.

MOKOROA

Urteta Auzoa Kortaburu Baserria
20800 Zarautz (Gipuzkoa)
☎: +34 630 222 653 - Fax: +34 943 833 925
bodega@txakolimokoroa.com

MOKOROA 2010 B
hondarrabi zuri.

88 Colour: bright straw. Nose: grassy, white flowers, fresh fruit, floral. Palate: flavourful, fruity, fresh.

TXAKOLI TALAI BERRI

Talaimendi, 728
20800 Zarautz (Gipuzkoa)
☎: +34 943 132 750 - Fax: +34 943 132 750
info@talaiberri.com
www.talaiberri.com

TALAI BERRI 2010 B
90% hondarrabi zuri, 10% hondarrabi beltza.

88 Colour: bright straw. Nose: fresh, white flowers, elegant. Palate: flavourful, fruity, good acidity, fine bead.

TXAKOLI ULACIA

Ctra. Meagas
20808 Getaria (Gipuzkoa)
☎: +34 943 140 893 - Fax: +34 943 140 893

ULACIA 2010 B
90% hondarrabi zuri, 10% hondarrabi beltza.

86 Colour: bright straw. Nose: fresh fruit, white flowers, dried flowers. Palate: flavourful, fruity, good acidity, fine bitter notes.

TXAKOLI ZUDUGARAI

Ctra. Zarautz - Aia Bº Laurgain
20809 Aia (Gipuzkoa)
☎: +34 943 134 625 - Fax: +34 943 835 952
txakolizudugarai@euskalnet.net
www.txakolizudugarai.com

ZUDUGARAI 2010 B
90% hondarrabi zuri, 10% hondarrabi beltza.

86 Colour: bright straw. Nose: fresh, fresh fruit, ripe fruit, medium intensity. Palate: flavourful, fruity, good acidity, balanced.

AMATS 2010 B
90% hondarrabi zuri, 10% hondarrabi beltza.

82 Colour: pale. Nose: ripe fruit, candied fruit, dried flowers. Palate: sweetness, flavourful.

TXOMIN ETXANIZ

Txomin Etxaniz
20808 Getaria (Gipuzkoa)
☎: +34 943 140 702 - Fax: +34 943 140 462
txakoli@txominetxaniz.com
www.txominetxaniz.com

TXOMÍN ETXANÍZ BEREZIA 2010 B
100% hondarrabi zuri.

89 Colour: bright straw. Nose: fresh fruit, white flowers, grassy, varietal. Palate: flavourful, fruity, good acidity, balanced.

TXOMÍN ETXANÍZ 2010 B
90% hondarrabi zuri, 10% hondarrabi beltza.

88 Colour: bright straw. Nose: fresh, white flowers, varietal, ripe fruit. Palate: flavourful, fruity, good acidity, balanced.

TXOMÍN ETXANÍZ WHITE WINE 2010 B
80% hondarrabi zuri, 20% chardonnay.

87 Colour: bright straw. Nose: fresh, white flowers, expressive, candied fruit, tropical fruit. Palate: flavourful, fruity, good acidity, balanced.

EUGENIA TXOMÍN ETXANÍZ 2009 ESP
100% hondarrabi zuri.

88 Colour: bright straw. Nose: medium intensity, fresh fruit, fine lees, floral, grassy. Palate: fresh, fruity, flavourful, good acidity.

URKI

Urki Txakolina
20808 Getaria (Gipuzcoa)
☎: +34 943 140 049 - Fax: +34 943 140 049
info@urkitxakolina.com
www.urkitxakolina.com

URKI 2010 B
100% hondarrabi zuri.

87 Colour: bright straw. Nose: fresh fruit, white flowers, varietal. Palate: flavourful, fruity, good acidity, balanced.

URKI II 2010 B
100% hondarrabi zuri.

86 Colour: bright straw. Nose: fresh fruit, characterful, medium intensity, dried flowers. Palate: flavourful, fruity, good acidity, fine bitter notes.

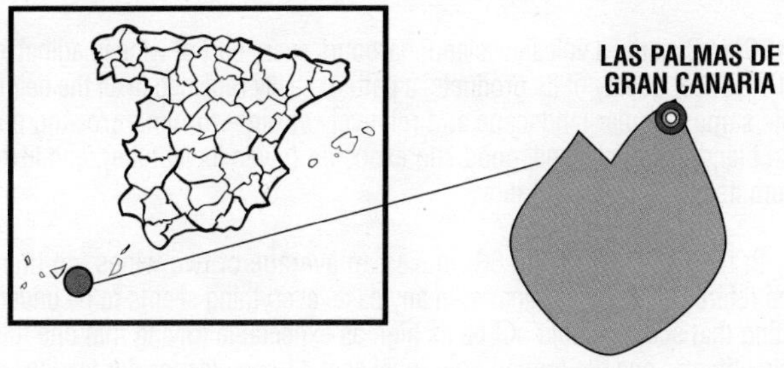

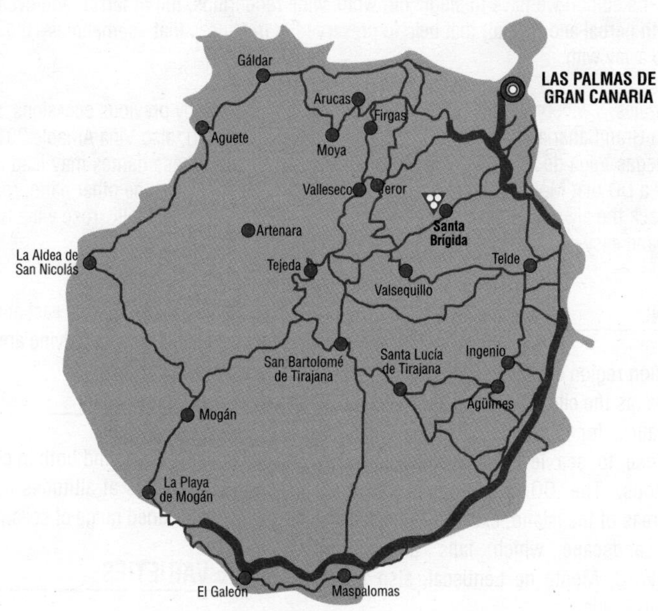

Consejo Regulador
DO Boundary

DO GRAN CANARIA

NEWS ABOUT THE VINTAGE:

We know pretty well that Gran Canaria, a volcanic island, harbours every sort of wine imaginable, thanks to its telluric nature and the sheer quality of its products, a pattern easily repeated in all the neighbouring islands, which share the same singular landscape and relatively virgin – for vine-growing purposes–soils. Mineral wines that blend beautifully soil, good sun exposure (given its latitude), and lovely acidic freshness that arises from its imposing topography.

Each and every winery in the island (totalling 66) makes an average of two wines, so there are an amazing number of wine references in Gran Canaria. In any case, everything seems to be under control. The producers, suspecting that scores would not be as high as expectable (giving that one thing is the local market and a whole different one the foreign one), only sent 11 samples for our tasting, obviously the best of them, of which three reached the 90-point boundary for the first time in the whole history of the region, something totally unaccounted for in a territory where the local market seems to have a lot of influence in the final, traditional style of the wines.

In this year's edition we have to single out white wine renderings, full of terroir and even some "wild" notes (both herbal and animal) that help to preserve the freshness that –sometimes– the African winds tend to do away with.

Los Berrazales, a winery that had failed to send its samples on many previous occasions, seems to lead the way in Gran Canaria with two white wines (one of them sweet); also Viña Amable 2010, a red wine from Bodegas Vega de Gáldar gets good ratings. We hope that these names may lead to even better things for a DO that Mother Nature seems to permanently pamper. On the other hand, rosé renderings seem to lack the always necessary and expectable fruit expression. Locally, rosé wine is drunk for its lightness and easy-drinking character.

LOCATION:

The production region covers 99% of the island of Gran Canaria, as the climate and the conditions of the terrain allow for the cultivation of grapes at altitudes close to sea level up to the highest mountain tops. The DO incorporates all the municipal areas of the island, except for the Tafira Protected Landscape which falls under an independent DO, Monte de Lentiscal, also fully covered in this Guide.

CLIMATE:

As with the other islands of the archipelago, the differences in altitude give rise to several microclimates which create specific characteristics for the cultivation of the vine. Nevertheless, the climate is conditioned by the influence of the trade winds which blow from the east and whose effect is more evident in the higher-lying areas.

SOIL:

The vineyards are found both in coastal areas and on higher grounds at altitudes of up to 1500 m, resulting in a varied range of soils.

GRAPE VARIETIES:

WHITE:
PREFERRED: *Malvasía, Güal, Marmajuelo* (*Bermejuela*), *Vijariego, Albillo* and *Moscatel.*
AUTHORIZED: *Listán Blanco, Burrablanca, Torrontés, Pedro Ximénez, Brebal* and *Bastardo Blanco.*

RED:
PREFERRED: *Listán Negro, Negramoll, Tintilla, Malvasía Rosada.*
AUTHORIZED: *Moscatel Negra, Bastardo Negro, Listán Prieto, Vijariego Negro, Bastardo Negro, Listón Prieto* und *Vijariego Negro.*

FIGURES:

Vineyard surface: 236 – **Wine-Growers:** 343 – **Wineries:** 66 – **2010 Harvest rating:** N/A – **Production:** 234,000 litres – **Market percentages:** 97% domestic. 3% export

CONSEJO REGULADOR
Calvo Sotelo nº 26
35300 Santa Brígida (Las Palmas)
☎: +34 928 640 462
@ crdogc@yahoo.es
www.vinosdegrancanaria.es

GENERAL CHARACTERISTICS OF THE WINES

WHITES	Yellow straw, the nose tends to be of herbs with fruity notes. Sweet wines from *Moscatel* are also produced with the characteristic musky nuance of the variety, with honey and herb notes
ROSÉS	These have an onion skin colour; they are fruity, but with a character still to be defined.
REDS	With a deep cherry-red colour, they offer some fruity notes and characteristic balsamic hints, without too much body on the palate.

VINTAGE RATING PEÑÍNGUIDE

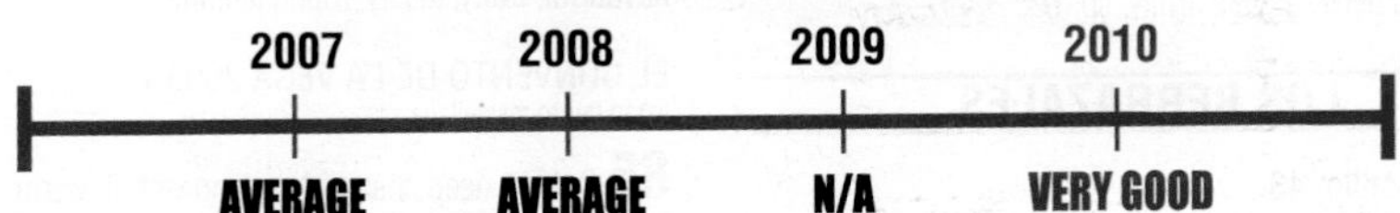

BENTAYGA

El Alberconcillo, s/n
35360 Tejeda (Las Palmas)
☎: +34 928 426 047 - Fax: +34 928 418 795
info@bodegasbentayga.com
www.bodegasbentayga.com

AGALA DULCELENA DULCE 2010 B

88 Colour: bright straw. Nose: candied fruit, citrus fruit, white flowers. Palate: flavourful, sweet, good acidity.

AGALA 2010 B
75% vijariego, 20% moscatel, 5% listán blanco.

86 Colour: bright straw. Nose: white flowers, powerfull, expressive, fresh fruit. Palate: flavourful, fruity, fresh.

AGALA VENDIMIA NOCTURNA 2010 BLANCO SEMIDULCE

87 Colour: bright straw. Nose: powerfull, expressive, fresh fruit, citrus fruit. Palate: flavourful, fruity, fresh.

LA HIGUERA MAYOR

El Palmital Ctra. de Teldes a Santa Brígida, GC 80, Pto. Km., 7,5
35218 Telde (Las Palmas)
☎: +34 630 285 454
lahigueramayor@telefonica.net
www.lahigueramayor.com

LA HIGUERA MAYOR 2008 T
listán negro, castellana, negramoll, tintilla.

84 Colour: deep cherry, garnet rim. Nose: ripe fruit, spicy, dried herbs. Palate: fruity, spicy.

LOS BERRAZALES

León y Castillo, 43
35480 Agaete (Las Palmas)
☎: +34 628 922 588 - Fax: +34 928 898 154
lugojorge3@hotmail.com

LOS BERRAZALES SEMISECO 2010 B
moscatel, malvasía.

90 Colour: bright straw. Nose: fresh, fresh fruit, white flowers. Palate: flavourful, fruity, good acidity, balanced.

LOS BERRAZALES DULCE NATURAL 2010 B
moscatel, malvasía.

90 Color golden. Aroma powerfull, floral, honeyed notes, candied fruit, fragrant herbs. Taste flavourful, sweet, fresh, fruity, good acidity, long.

LOS BERRAZALES SECO 2010 B
moscatel, malvasía.

87 Colour: bright straw. Nose: ripe fruit, honeyed notes, citrus fruit, powerfull. Palate: flavourful, powerful, good acidity.

LOS BERRAZALES DULCE 2009 B BARRICA
moscatel, malvasía.

88 Colour: bright straw. Nose: tropical fruit, ripe fruit, lactic notes, fine lees. Palate: flavourful, fleshy, sweetness.

VEGA DE GÁLDAR

Camino de La Longuera - La Vega de Gáldar
35460 Gáldar (Las Palmas)
☎: +34 605 043 047
vinoamable@gmail.com

NUBIA 2010 B
malvasía.

88 Colour: bright straw. Nose: fresh, fresh fruit, white flowers, earthy notes, mineral. Palate: flavourful, fruity, good acidity, balanced.

VIÑA AMABLE 2010 T
listán negro, castellana.

90 Colour: bright cherry. Nose: ripe fruit, sweet spices, creamy oak, expressive, balsamic herbs, scrubland. Palate: flavourful, fruity, toasty, round tannins.

EL CONVENTO DE LA VEGA 2009 T
listán negro, castellana.

85 Colour: deep cherry. Nose: powerfull, warm, ripe fruit, sweet spices. Palate: powerful, sweetness, fleshy.

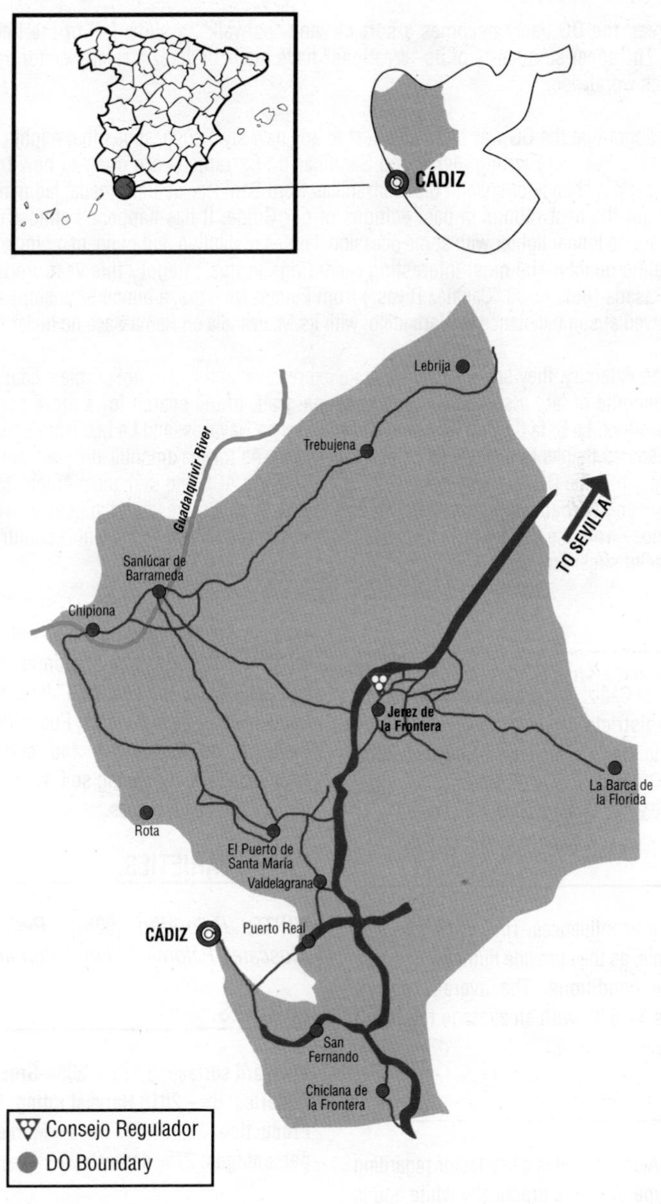
CÁDIZ
Lebrija
Trebujena
Guadalquivir River
TO SEVILLA
Sanlúcar de Barrameda
Chipiona
Jerez de la Frontera
La Barca de la Florida
Rota
El Puerto de Santa María
Valdelagrana
CÁDIZ
Puerto Real
San Fernando
Chiclana de la Frontera
Consejo Regulador
DO Boundary

NEWS ABOUT THE VINTAGE:

Year after year, the DO Jerez becomes a sort of wine "catwalk", a show full of the finest wines imaginable. The sheer singularity of its "creations" have made of Jerez a reference for special and singular wines worldwide.

If we ever thought that the DO was blind and deaf to any new style suggestions that might come from foreign markets, we were wrong: Jerez and Sanlúcar de Barrameda are open to new trends. We appreciate a certain change of style in the manzanillas from Sanlúcar de Barrameda, led mainly by the brands that got the best ratings in past editions of our Guide. It has happened almost overnight: manzanillas are no longer lighter with some occasional notes of dilution, but pungent, complex and with a marked saline quality. The most interesting renderings in this category this year are La Bota de Manzanilla Pasada (Bota nº 30 "Capataz Rivas") from Equipo Navazos, a bunch of unstoppable trend-setters, followed at some distance by Barbadillo, with its Manzanilla en Rama Saca de Invierno.

As for the fino category, they show powerful, quite expressive, and with a noticeable oxidative quality, which has become of late a sort of totally intentional trait, in the search for a more complex and expressive product. La Bota de Fino (Bota nº 27) from Equipo Navazos, and La Ina, from Emilio Lustau, get the best scores thanks to their elegance and expression. As for the amontillados, without doubt the star category within the DO, the best examples are Rare Sherry AOS and Barbadillo Amontillado VORS, from Osborne and Barbadillo, respectively. *PX* and *moscatel* wines are, as it happens every year and along with those from the Canary Islands, the best sweet wines available in the whole country, with the finest balance of sugar and acidity.

LOCATION:

In the province of Cádiz. The production area covers the municipal districts of Jerez de la Frontera, El Puerto de Santa María, Chipiona, Trebujena, Rota, Puerto Real, Chiclana de la Frontera and some estates in Lebrija.

CLIMATE:

Warm with Atlantic influences. The west winds play an important role, as they provide humidity and help to temper the conditions. The average annual temperature is 17.5°C, with an average rainfall of 600 mm per year.

SOIL:

The so-called 'Albariza' soil is a key factor regarding quality. This type of soil is practically white and is rich in calcium carbonate, clay and silica. It is excellent for retaining humidity and storing winter rainfall for the dry summer months. Moreover, this soil determines the so-called 'Jerez superior'. It is found in Jerez de la Frontera, Puerto de Santa María, Sanlúcar de Barrameda and certain areas of Trebujena. The remaining soil, known as 'Zona', is muddy and sandy.arenas.

GRAPE VARIETIES:

WHITE: *Palomino* (90%), *Pedro Ximénez, Moscatel, Palomino Fino, Palomino de Jerez.*

FIGURES:

Vineyard surface: 8,771 – **Wine-Growers:** 2,044 – **Wineries:** 88 – **2010 Harvest rating:** N/A – **Production:** 46,470,637 litres – **Market percentages:** 27% domestic. 73% export

CONSEJO REGULADOR
Avda. Álvaro Domecq, 2
11405 Jerez de la Frontera (Cádiz)
☎: +34 956 332 050 - Fax: +34 956 338 908
@ vinjerez@sherry.org
@ prensa@sherry.org
www.sherry.org

GENERAL CHARACTERISTICS OF THE WINES

MANZANILLA Y FINO	These are straw yellow in colour. They are characterised by their salty notes, typical of the biological ageing under the Velo en Flor (more pronounced in the case of the Manzanilla), and by the bitter notes conferred by ageing.
OLOROSO	With completely oxidative ageing, the range can be varied depending on the higher or lower scale level (i.e. the number of sacas of Solera wine to be bottled) and, consequently, the greater or lesser refreshing with unaged wine for the first criadera. In the very old wines, it is customary to tone them down with Mistela of *Pedro Ximénez* which provide notes of sweetness to mitigate the bitter tannins of the oak.
PEDRO XIMÉNEZ	These are characterised by their marked palate of raisin, although some have a small percentage of Oloroso to reduce the sweetness. On the palate they are flavourful and sweet.
CREAM	These combine the bitter notes of the Olorosos with hints of toast and the sweetness of the *Pedro Ximénez*.
AMONTILLADOS	They are fino wines that end up loosing their "velo de flor "(veil of yeast) and start oxidizing. They are wines with pungent and saline notes, and a slightly more unctuous palate, with fine toasted notes and complexity derived from the cask.
PALOS CORTADOS	They are wines born out accidentally; with a nature that somewhat escapes the winemaker's will. The style combines the fine nose of an amontillado and the more structured and unctuous palate of an oloroso.

VINTAGE RATING PEÑÍNGUIDE

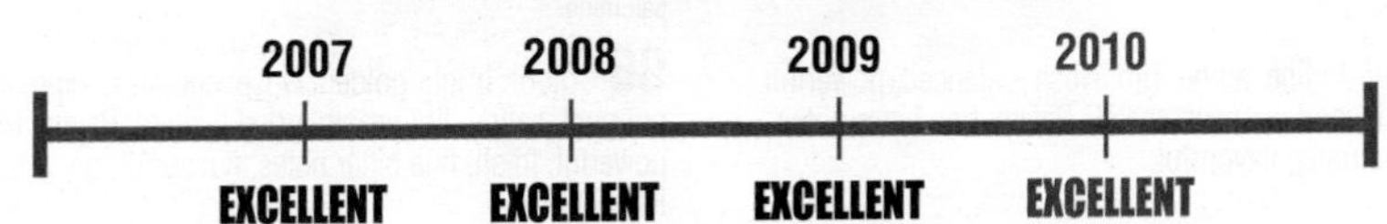

AECOVI-JEREZ

Urb. Pie de Rey, 3- LOCAL IZQUIERDA
11407 Jerez de la Frontera (Cádiz)
☎: +34 956 180 873 - Fax: +34 956 180 301
info@aecovi-jerez.com
www.aecovi-jerez.com

MIRA LA MAR MZ
palomino.

90 Color bright yellow. Aroma complex, expressive, pungent, saline. Taste rich, powerful, fresh, fine bitter notes.

ALFARAZ MOSCATEL DE PASAS MOSCATEL
moscatel.

85 Colour: light mahogany. Nose: powerfull, varietal, acetaldehyde, honeyed notes, toasty, dark chocolate. Palate: flavourful, spirituous, spicy.

ALFARAZ PX
pedro ximénez.

92 Colour: dark mahogany. Nose: smoky, sweet spices, roasted coffee, complex, powerfull, acetaldehyde. Palate: fleshy, complex, powerful, flavourful, long.

ALVARO DOMECQ

Alamos, 23
11401 Jerez de la Frontera (Cádiz)
☎: +34 956 339 664 - Fax: +34 956 340 402
alvarodomecqsl@alvarodomecq.com
www.alvarodomecq.com

LA JANDA FI
palomino.

86 Colour: bright yellow. Nose: pungent, saline, short. Palate: fresh, fine bitter notes, correct, light-bodied.

LA JACA MZ
palomino.

85 Colour: bright yellow. Nose: pungent, saline, short. Palate: fine bitter notes, light-bodied, fresh.

ALBUREJO OL
palomino.

90 Colour: iodine, amber rim. Nose: balanced, powerfull, spicy, aged wood nuances, toasty. Palate: fine bitter notes, correct, unctuous, flavourful.

ARANDA CREAM OL
palomino, pedro ximénez.

87 Colour: iodine, amber rim. Nose: medium intensity, pattiserie, aged wood nuances. Palate: burning notes, spirituous, fine bitter notes.

1730 PX
pedro ximénez.

92 Colour: dark mahogany. Nose: dried fruit, pattiserie, toasty, characterful, dark chocolate. Palate: sweet, rich, unctuous, powerful.

BODEGAS BARBADILLO

Luis de Eguilaz, 11
11540 Sanlúcar de Barrameda (Cádiz)
☎: +34 956 385 500 - Fax: +34 956 385 501
barbadillo@barbadillo.com
www.barbadillo.com

BARBADILLO AMONTILLADO VORS AM
palomino.

95 Colour: iodine, amber rim. Nose: powerfull, complex, elegant, toasty, roasted almonds. Palate: rich, fine bitter notes, , long, spicy.

RELIQUIA AM
palomino.

95 Colour: light mahogany. Nose: varnish, aged wood nuances, pattiserie, fruit liqueur notes, dry nuts, toasty. Palate: flavourful, powerful, fleshy, spicy, long, warm.

PRÍNCIPE AM
palomino.

92 Colour: iodine, amber rim. Nose: acetaldehyde, pungent, dry nuts, varnish, sweet spices, pattiserie. Palate: spicy, long, fleshy, complex.

EVA CREAM CR
palomino.

90 Colour: iodine, amber rim. Nose: caramel, pattiserie, expressive, complex. Palate: sweetness, flavourful, balanced, fine bitter notes.

MANZANILLA EN RAMA SACA DE INVIERNO MZ
palomino.

96 Colour: bright golden. Nose: complex, expressive, pungent, saline, flor yeasts, dried flowers. Palate: rich, powerful, fresh, fine bitter notes, flavourful, good structure. Personality.

MANZANILLA EN RAMA SACA DE PRIMAVERA MZ
palomino.

94 Colour: bright straw. Nose: powerfull, complex, expressive, faded flowers, pungent, iodine notes, saline. Palate: powerful, rich, flavourful, complex, dry.

SOLEAR MZ
palomino.

90 Colour: bright yellow. Nose: complex, expressive, pungent, saline, dried herbs. Palate: rich, powerful, fresh, fine bitter notes, long.

MUYFINA MZ
palomino.

87 Colour: bright yellow. Nose: expressive, pungent, saline, fresh, medium intensity. Palate: fresh, fine bitter notes, light-bodied.

LAURA MOSCATEL
moscatel.

87 Colour: mahogany. Nose: overripe fruit, sweet spices, pattiserie, acetaldehyde. Palate: ripe fruit, balanced, fine bitter notes.

BARBADILLO OLOROSO SECO VORS OL
palomino.

90 Colour: old gold, amber rim. Nose: dry nuts, fruit liqueur notes, aged wood nuances, sweet spices. Palate: correct, fleshy, powerful, flavourful.

RELIQUIA OL
palomino.

90 Colour: iodine, amber rim. Nose: powerfull, warm, toasty, sweet spices, varnish. Palate: fine bitter notes, good acidity, spirituous.

BARBADILLO OLOROSO DULCE VORS OL
palomino.

89 Colour: light mahogany. Nose: powerfull, toasty, aromatic coffee, sweet spices, dark chocolate, acetaldehyde. Palate: long, spicy, sweetness.

SAN RAFAEL OL
palomino.

88 Colour: light mahogany. Nose: powerfull, fruit preserve, dry nuts, toasty. Palate: good acidity, fine bitter notes, sweetness.

CUCO OLOROSO SECO OL
palomino.

88 Colour: iodine, amber rim. Nose: powerfull, sweet spices, toasty, dark chocolate. Palate: flavourful, sweetness, fleshy.

RELIQUIA PC
palomino.

94 Colour: light mahogany. Nose: acetaldehyde, saline, expressive, powerfull, characterful. Palate: flavourful, powerful, sweetness, long.

BARBADILLO PALO CORTADO VORS PC
palomino.

93 Colour: light mahogany. Nose: powerfull, dry nuts, pattiserie, acetaldehyde, pungent. Palate: flavourful, fleshy, sweetness, spicy, long.

OBISPO GASCÓN PC
palomino.

92 Colour: iodine, amber rim. Nose: sweet spices, pattiserie, toasty, powerfull. Palate: fine bitter notes, spirituous, correct.

RELIQUIA PX
pedro ximénez.

96 Colour: dark mahogany. Nose: complex, pattiserie, toasty, fruit liqueur notes, acetaldehyde. Palate: sweet, rich, powerful, unctuous, round, spicy, great length.

LA CILLA PX
pedro ximénez.

88 Colour: mahogany. Nose: dried fruit, medium intensity, expressive. Palate: unctuous, rich, flavourful.

BODEGAS GARVEY JEREZ

Ctra. Circunvalación, s/n
11407 Jerez de la Frontera (Cádiz)
☎: +34 956 319 650 - Fax: +34 956 319 824
marketing@grupogarvey.com
www.bodegasgarvey.com

ASALTO AMOROSO B
palomino, pedro ximénez.

90 Colour: light mahogany. Nose: powerfull, dry nuts, dried fruit, toasty. Palate: sweetness, powerful, balanced.

OÑANA AM
palomino.

93 Color iodine, amber rim. Aroma powerfull, complex, elegant, dry nuts, toasty. Taste rich, fine bitter notes, fine solera notes, long, spicy.

TIO GUILLERMO AM
palomino.

84 Colour: iodine, amber rim. Nose: candied fruit, fruit liqueur notes, caramel. Palate: spicy, long, fine bitter notes.

FLOR DEL MUSEO CR
palomino, pedro ximénez.

90 Colour: light mahogany. Nose: characterful, expressive, sweet spices, toasty. Palate: flavourful, sweetness, concentrated.

FLOR DE JEREZ CR
palomino, pedro ximénez.

86 Colour: mahogany. Nose: fruit liqueur notes, dried fruit, expressive, caramel. Palate: flavourful, light-bodied, fine bitter notes, correct, confected.

SAN PATRICIO FI
palomino.

92 Color bright yellow. Aroma complex, expressive, pungent, saline. Taste rich, powerful, fresh, fine bitter notes.

JUNCAL MZ
palomino.

88 Colour: bright yellow. Nose: complex, pungent, saline, medium intensity. Palate: rich, fresh, fine bitter notes.

GARVEY 1780 VORS OL
palomino.

92 Color iodine, amber rim. Aroma powerfull, complex, elegant, dry nuts, toasty. Taste rich, fine bitter notes, fine solera notes, long, spicy.

GARVEY 1780 VOS OL
palomino.

89 Colour: iodine, amber rim. Nose: sweet spices, caramel, aged wood nuances, powerfull, expressive. Palate: creamy, long, spirituous, powerful, flavourful.

OCHAVICO OL
palomino.

87 Colour: light mahogany. Nose: dried fruit, dry nuts, powerfull, medium intensity. Palate: spicy, fine bitter notes, correct.

JAUNA PC
palomino.

91 Colour: light mahogany. Nose: powerfull, candied fruit, fruit liqueur notes, pattiserie, toasty. Palate: flavourful, sweetness, fine bitter notes.

GRAN ORDEN PX
pedro ximénez.

94 Colour: dark mahogany. Nose: acetaldehyde, dried fruit, honeyed notes, complex, balanced. Palate: long, balanced, unctuous, toasty.

GARVEY 1780 VOS PX
pedro ximénez.

92 Colour: dark mahogany. Nose: dried fruit, pattiserie, toasty, tar, dark chocolate. Palate: sweet, rich, unctuous, powerful, fine bitter notes.

GARVEY 1780 VORS PX
pedro ximénez.

91 Colour: dark mahogany. Nose: fruit liqueur notes, dried fruit, pattiserie, toasty, tar, smoky. Palate: sweet, rich, unctuous, powerful.

GARVEY PX
pedro ximénez.

88 Colour: dark mahogany. Nose: fruit liqueur notes, overripe fruit, caramel, balanced, expressive. Palate: balanced, unctuous, fleshy, flavourful.

BODEGAS GUTIÉRREZ COLOSÍA

Avda. Bajamar, 40
11500 El Puerto de Santa María (Cádiz)
☎: +34 956 852 852 - Fax: +34 956 542 936
info@gutierrezcolosia.com
www.gutierrezcolosia.com

GUTIÉRREZ COLOSÍA SOLERA FAMILIAR AM
100% palomino.

90 Colour: dark mahogany. Nose: smoky, spicy, aged wood nuances, pattiserie. Palate: spirituous, complex, flavourful.

GUTIÉRREZ COLOSÍA AM
100% palomino.

88 Colour: iodine, amber rim. Nose: acetaldehyde, powerfull, dry nuts, fruit liqueur notes. Palate: powerful, fleshy, flavourful, spicy, fine bitter notes.

MARI PEPA CR
palomino, pedro ximénez.

87 Colour: mahogany. Nose: powerfull, aged wood nuances, sweet spices, caramel. Palate: fleshy, powerful, sweetness, good finish.

GUTIÉRREZ COLOSÍA CR
palomino, pedro ximénez.

86 Colour: light mahogany. Nose: powerfull, overripe fruit, fruit liqueur notes, toasty, sweet spices. Palate: flavourful, sweetness, pruney.

GUTIÉRREZ COLOSÍA FINO EN RAMA FI
100% palomino.

92 Colour: bright yellow. Nose: powerfull, expressive, characterful, dry nuts, warm, complex. Palate: powerful, sweetness, fleshy, fine bitter notes, round.

GUTIÉRREZ COLOSÍA FI
palomino.

91 Colour: bright straw. Nose: powerfull, iodine notes, pungent. Palate: flavourful, powerful, fleshy, fine bitter notes.

CAMPO DE GUÍA FI
100% palomino.

88 Colour: bright straw. Nose: saline, pungent, white flowers. Palate: flavourful, powerful, fleshy.

GUTIÉRREZ COLOSÍA MZ
palomino.

91 Colour: bright yellow. Nose: expressive, pungent, saline, candied fruit. Palate: rich, powerful, fresh, fine bitter notes.

GUTIÉRREZ COLOSÍA MOSCATEL SOLEADO MOSCATEL
moscatel.

88 Colour: iodine, amber rim. Nose: powerfull, varietal, honeyed notes, caramel, acetaldehyde. Palate: unctuous, round, fine bitter notes.

GUTIÉRREZ COLOSÍA SOLERA FAMILIAR OL
100% palomino.

92 Color iodine, amber rim. Aroma powerfull, complex, elegant, dry nuts, toasty. Taste rich, fine bitter notes, fine solera notes, long, spicy.

GUTIÉRREZ COLOSÍA OL
100% palomino.

86 Colour: light mahogany. Nose: aged wood nuances, warm, toasty, dried fruit, dry nuts. Palate: fine bitter notes, spirituous, correct.

SANGRE Y TRABAJADERO OL
palomino.

85 Colour: light mahogany. Nose: fruit liqueur notes, aged wood nuances, sweet spices, toasty. Palate: fleshy, powerful, flavourful.

GUTIÉRREZ COLOSÍA SOLERA FAMILIAR PC
100% palomino.

90 Colour: iodine, amber rim. Nose: dry nuts, expressive, pattiserie, sweet spices. Palate: creamy, long, spirituous, correct.

GUTIÉRREZ COLOSÍA SOLERA FAMILIAR PX
pedro ximénez.

88 Color dark mahogany. Aroma complex, fruit liqueur notes, dried fruit, pattiserie, toasty. Taste sweet, rich, unctuous, powerful.

GUTIÉRREZ COLOSÍA PX
100% pedro ximénez.

88 Colour: mahogany. Nose: pattiserie, sweet spices, caramel, expressive. Palate: fleshy, sweetness, flavourful, correct.

BODEGAS HARVEYS

Pintor Muñoz Cebrián, s/n
11402 Jerez de la Frontera (Cádiz)
☎: +34 956 346 000 - Fax: +34 956 349 427
visitas@bodegasharveys.com
www.bodegasharveys.com

HARVEYS VORS AM
100% palomino.

92 Colour: old gold, amber rim. Nose: aged wood nuances, sweet spices, pattiserie, dry nuts. Palate: spirituous, powerful, flavourful, fine bitter notes, long.

HARVEYS BRISTOL CREAM CR
palomino, pedro ximénez.

85 Colour: light mahogany. Nose: powerfull, fruit liqueur notes, dry nuts, toasty, sweet spices. Palate: creamy, flavourful, sweetness.

HARVEYS FI
100% palomino.

91 Colour: bright golden. Nose: fragrant herbs, saline, complex, fresh. Palate: balsamic, balanced, unctuous, long.

HARVEYS VORS RICH OLD OL
90% palomino, 10% pedro ximénez.

94 Colour: mahogany. Nose: sweet spices, caramel, aged wood nuances, characterful, powerfull. Palate: fleshy, complex, rich, flavourful, balanced.

HARVEYS VORS PC
98% palomino, 2% pedro ximénez.

93 Colour: mahogany. Nose: complex, powerfull, sweet spices, pattiserie, aged wood nuances. Palate: fine bitter notes, unctuous, spirituous, flavourful.

HARVEYS VORS PX
100% palomino.

90 Colour: dark mahogany. Nose: dried fruit, pattiserie, toasty, complex, aromatic coffee, dark chocolate. Palate: sweet, rich, unctuous, powerful.

BODEGAS HIDALGO-LA GITANA

Banda de Playa, 42
11540 Sanlúcar de Barrameda (Cádiz)
☎: +34 956 385 304 - Fax: +34 956 363 844
bodegashidalgo@lagitana.es
www.lagitana.es

NAPOLEÓN 30 AÑOS VORS 50 CL. AM
100% palomino.

94 Colour: iodine, amber rim. Nose: powerfull, complex, dry nuts, toasty, expressive. Palate: rich, fine bitter notes, , long, toasty.

NAPOLEÓN AM
100% palomino.

89 Colour: old gold, amber rim. Nose: acetaldehyde, complex, spicy, toasty, dry nuts. Palate: correct, flavourful, rich.

ALAMEDA CR
75% palomino, 25% pedro ximénez.

87 Colour: iodine, amber rim. Nose: acetaldehyde, characterful, overripe fruit, toasty, pattiserie.

PASTRANA MANZANILLA PASADA MZ
100% palomino.

95 Colour: bright golden. Nose: expressive, pungent, saline, dry nuts, characterful. Palate: rich, powerful, fresh, fine bitter notes, fleshy, great length.

LA GITANA MZ
100% palomino.

91 Colour: bright yellow. Nose: pungent, saline, expressive. Palate: rich, powerful, fresh, fine bitter notes, dry.

FARAÓN 30 AÑOS VORS 50 CL. OL
100% palomino.

91 Colour: iodine, amber rim. Nose: aged wood nuances, sweet spices, toasty, balanced. Palate: good structure, light-bodied, flavourful, long.

FARAÓN OL
100% palomino.

86 Colour: old gold. Nose: pattiserie, sweet spices, medium intensity. Palate: fine bitter notes, spirituous, sweetness.

JEREZ CORTADO WELLINGTON 20 AÑOS VOS PC
palomino.

91 Colour: iodine, amber rim. Nose: flor yeasts, expressive, pattiserie, sweet spices. Palate: complex, spirituous, flavourful, rich.

WELLINGTON 30 AÑOS VORS PC
100% palomino.

90 Colour: iodine, amber rim. Nose: pattiserie, sweet spices, aged wood nuances, balanced. Palate: flavourful, rich, long, correct.

TRIANA 30 AÑOS VORS PX
100% pedro ximénez.

92 Colour: dark mahogany. Nose: fruit liqueur notes, dried fruit, pattiserie, toasty, complex, characterful, dark chocolate. Palate: sweet, rich, unctuous, powerful.

TRIANA PX
100% pedro ximénez.

90 Color dark mahogany. Aroma complex, fruit liqueur notes, dried fruit, pattiserie, toasty. Taste sweet, rich, unctuous, powerful.

BODEGAS LA CIGARRERA

Pza. Madre de Dios, s/n
11540 Sanlúcar de Barrameda (Cádiz)
☎: +34 956 381 285 - Fax: +34 956 383 824
lacigarrera@bodegaslacigarrera.com
www.bodegaslacigarrera.com

LA CIGARRERA AM
100% palomino.

91 Colour: iodine, amber rim. Nose: powerfull, complex, pungent, iodine notes. Palate: flavourful, powerful, fleshy, spicy.

LA CIGARRERA MZ
palomino.

88 Colour: bright straw. Nose: flor yeasts, candied fruit, white flowers. Palate: flavourful, sweetness, fleshy.

LA CIGARRERA MOSCATEL
moscatel.

92 Colour: light mahogany. Nose: powerfull, fruit preserve, citrus fruit, fruit liqueur notes, toasty, aged wood nuances, caramel. Palate: powerful, sweetness, fine bitter notes.

LA CIGARRERA OL
palomino.

90 Colour: iodine, amber rim. Nose: powerfull, candied fruit, toasty, sweet spices. Palate: flavourful, powerful, fleshy, long.

LA CIGARRERA PX
pedro ximénez.

89 Colour: dark mahogany. Nose: dried fruit, acetaldehyde, cocoa bean, sweet spices, complex, expressive. Palate: good structure, sweetness, flavourful, creamy.

BODEGAS OSBORNE

Fernán Caballero, 7
11500 El Puerto de Santa María (Cádiz)
☎: +34 925 860 990 - Fax: +34 925 860 905
carolina.cerrato@osborne.es
www.osborne.es

OSBORNE RARE SHERRY AOS AM
palomino.

96 Colour: iodine, amber rim. Nose: powerfull, complex, elegant, dry nuts, toasty, acetaldehyde, sweet spices, aged wood nuances. Palate: rich, fine bitter notes, , long, spicy.

AMONTILLADO 51-1ª V.O.R.S AM
palomino.

93 Colour: old gold, amber rim. Nose: roasted almonds, aged wood nuances, spicy, balanced, expressive. Palate: spirituous, good structure, powerful, flavourful.

COQUINERO AM
palomino.

92 Colour: bright yellow. Nose: iodine notes, pungent, saline, dry nuts. Palate: flavourful, fleshy, long.

SANTA MARÍA CREAM CR
palomino, pedro ximénez.

87 Colour: iodine, amber rim. Nose: toasty, caramel, sweet spices, acetaldehyde. Palate: powerful, sweetness, concentrated, fine bitter notes.

FINO QUINTA FI
palomino.

94 Colour: bright yellow. Nose: complex, expressive, pungent, iodine notes. Palate: rich, powerful, fresh, fine bitter notes.

OSBORNE RARE SHERRY SOLERA BC 200 OL
palomino.

97 Color iodine, amber rim. Aroma powerfull, complex, elegant, dry nuts, toasty. Taste rich, fine bitter notes, fine solera notes, long, spicy.

SIBARITA V.O.R.S. OL
palomino.

95 Colour: iodine, amber rim. Nose: powerfull, complex, elegant, dry nuts, toasty. Palate: rich, fine bitter notes, , long, spicy, flavourful. Personality.

OSBORNE SOLERA INDIA OL
palomino.

94 Colour: light mahogany. Nose: powerfull, warm, expressive, pattiserie. Palate: flavourful, powerful, fleshy, concentrated, spicy, long, creamy.

10 RF OL
palomino.

88 Colour: iodine, amber rim. Nose: powerfull, warm, sweet spices, caramel. Palate: fleshy, powerful, flavourful, good finish.

BAILÉN OL
palomino.

88 Color iodine, amber rim. Aroma powerfull, complex, elegant, dry nuts, toasty. Taste rich, fine bitter notes, fine solera notes, long, spicy.

CAPUCHINO V.O.R.S PC
palomino.

93 Colour: old gold, amber rim. Nose: roasted almonds, expressive, aged wood nuances, spicy. Palate: balanced, spirituous, flavourful, fine bitter notes.

OSBORNE RARE SHERRY SOLERA PAP PC
palomino.

93 Colour: light mahogany. Nose: sweet spices, pattiserie, cocoa bean, roasted almonds, acetaldehyde. Palate: flavourful, powerful, concentrated, fleshy, long.

VENERABLE VORS PX
100% pedro ximénez.

97 Colour: dark mahogany. Nose: dried fruit, powerfull, expressive, aromatic coffee, caramel, sweet spices. Palate: complex, rich, flavourful, long, unctuous.

OSBORNE RARE SHERRY PX PX
pedro ximénez.

93 Colour: dark mahogany. Nose: complex, fruit liqueur notes, dried fruit, pattiserie, toasty, dark chocolate. Palate: sweet, rich, unctuous, powerful.

OSBORNE 1827 PX
pedro ximénez.

91 Colour: dark mahogany. Nose: dried fruit, pattiserie, toasty, fruit liqueur notes. Palate: sweet, rich, unctuous, powerful.

BODEGAS PEDRO ROMERO

Trasbolsa, 84
11540 Sanlúcar de Barrameda (Cádiz)
☎: +34 956 360 736 - Fax: +34 956 361 027
pedroromero@pedroromero.es
www.pedroromero.es

VIÑA EL ÁLAMO AM
palomino.

87 Colour: iodine, amber rim. Nose: aged wood nuances, sweet spices, pattiserie, toasty, medium intensity. Palate: fine bitter notes, correct, good finish.

PEDRO ROMERO MZ
palomino.

91 Colour: bright yellow. Nose: complex, expressive, pungent, saline, dry nuts. Palate: rich, powerful, fresh, fine bitter notes, elegant.

AURORA MZ
palomino.

88 Colour: bright straw. Nose: dried herbs, fresh, medium intensity. Palate: light-bodied, correct, easy to drink.

GASPAR FLORIDO MOSCATEL
moscatel.

88 Colour: light mahogany. Nose: powerfull, fruit preserve, citrus fruit, dry nuts, toasty, dark chocolate. Palate: flavourful, sweetness, spirituous.

TRES ÁLAMOS PX
pedro ximénez.

85 Colour: mahogany. Nose: honeyed notes, dried fruit, expressive. Palate: fleshy, sweetness, flavourful.

BODEGAS TERESA RIVERO

Puerto, 21
11540 Sanlúcar de Barrameda (Cádiz)
☎: +34 956 361 491 - Fax: +34 956 368 379
info@bodegascaydsa.com

LA SANLUQUEÑA MZ
palomino.

90 Color bright yellow. Aroma complex, expressive, pungent, saline. Taste rich, powerful, fresh, fine bitter notes.

BODEGAS TERRY

Toneleros, s/n
11500 El Puerto de Santa María (Cádiz)
☎: +34 956 151 500 - Fax: +34 956 858 474
visitas@bodegasterry.com
www.bodegasterry.com

TERRY AMONTILLADO AM
100% palomino.

90 Colour: old gold, amber rim. Nose: aged wood nuances, pattiserie, sweet spices. Palate: fine bitter notes, unctuous, flavourful.

TERRY FINO FI
100% palomino.

91 Colour: bright straw. Nose: powerfull, candied fruit, fine lees, flor yeasts. Palate: powerful, flavourful, fleshy, full.

TERRY MANZANILLA MZ
100% palomino.

88 Colour: bright straw. Nose: floral, balanced, dried herbs. Palate: fresh, flavourful, confected, great length.

TERRY OLOROSO OL
100% palomino.

89 Colour: iodine, amber rim. Nose: candied fruit, powerfull, pattiserie, sweet spices. Palate: toasty, sweetness, flavourful, fine bitter notes.

TERRY PEDRO XIMÉNEZ PX
100% pedro ximénez.

90 Colour: dark mahogany. Nose: complex, dried fruit, pattiserie, toasty. Palate: sweet, rich, unctuous, powerful.

BODEGAS TRADICIÓN

Pza. Cordobeses, 3
11408 Jerez de la Frontera (Cádiz)
☎: +34 915 104 134 - Fax: +34 915 104 135
jerez@bodegastradicion.com
www.bodegastradicion.com

AMONTILLADO TRADICIÓN VORS AM
palomino.

92 Colour: old gold, amber rim. Nose: sweet spices, pattiserie, toasty, aromatic coffee, acetaldehyde. Palate: flavourful, spirituous, sweetness, fine bitter notes.

OLOROSO TRADICIÓN VORS OL
palomino.

93 Color iodine, amber rim. Aroma powerfull, complex, elegant, dry nuts, toasty. Taste rich, fine bitter notes, fine solera notes, long, spicy.

PALO CORTADO TRADICIÓN VORS PC
palomino.

90 Colour: light mahogany. Nose: powerfull, fruit liqueur notes, toasty, sweet spices, varnish, acetaldehyde. Palate: flavourful, powerful, fleshy, long.

PEDRO XIMÉNEZ TRADICIÓN VOS PX
pedro ximénez.

91 Colour: dark mahogany. Nose: acetaldehyde, dried fruit, dry nuts, balanced, expressive. Palate: balanced, unctuous, sweetness, powerful, flavourful, long.

BODEGAS VALDIVIA

Zoilo Ruiz Mateo Camacho, s/n
11408 Jerez de la Frontera (Cádiz)
☎: +34 956 314 358 - Fax: +34 956 169 657
info@bodegasvaldivia.com
www.bodegasvaldivia.com

SACROMONTE 15 AÑOS AM
palomino.

90 Colour: iodine, amber rim. Nose: expressive, powerfull, pattiserie, aged wood nuances, sweet spices. Palate: correct, flavourful, fresh, long.

VALDIVIA DORIUS AM
palomino.

89 Colour: bright golden. Nose: sweet spices, pattiserie, iodine notes, toasty. Palate: flavourful, light-bodied, fine bitter notes.

VALDIVIA ATRUM CR
palomino.

90 Colour: iodine, amber rim. Nose: dark chocolate, aromatic coffee, dry nuts. Palate: powerful, sweetness, spicy, long.

SACROMONTE 15 AÑOS OL
palomino.

93 Colour: iodine, amber rim. Nose: powerfull, warm, candied fruit, toasty, sweet spices. Palate: flavourful, powerful, sweetness.

VALDIVIA PRUNE OL
palomino.

90 Colour: iodine, amber rim. Nose: caramel, pattiserie, sweet spices, powerfull, balanced. Palate: fine bitter notes, spirituous, unctuous, sweetness.

VALDIVIA SUN PALE CREAM PCR
palomino.

91 Colour: bright straw. Nose: pungent, saline, flor yeasts, medium intensity. Palate: flavourful, sweetness, balanced.

SACROMONTE 15 AÑOS PX
palomino.

91 Color dark mahogany. Aroma complex, fruit liqueur notes, dried fruit, pattiserie, toasty. Taste sweet, rich, unctuous, powerful.

VALDIVIA PX
pedro ximénez.

88 Colour: dark mahogany. Nose: acetaldehyde, dried fruit, honeyed notes, expressive. Palate: creamy, spirituous, unctuous, correct.

CÉSAR L. FLORIDO ROMERO

Padre Lerchundi, 35-37
11550 Chipiona (Cádiz)
☎: +34 956 371 285 - Fax: +34 956 370 222
florido@bodegasflorido.com
www.bodegasflorido.com

CRUZ DEL MAR CR
75% palomino, 25% moscatel.

85 Colour: iodine, amber rim. Nose: citrus fruit, caramel, pattiserie, expressive. Palate: fleshy, spirituous, flavourful.

FINO CÉSAR FI
100% palomino.

87 Color bright yellow. Aroma complex, expressive, pungent, saline. Taste rich, powerful, fresh, fine bitter notes.

CÉSAR FLORIDO MOSCATEL ESPECIAL MOSCATEL
100% moscatel.

90 Colour: dark mahogany. Nose: sweet spices, pattiserie, citrus fruit, overripe fruit, expressive. Palate: complex, good structure, flavourful, ripe fruit.

CÉSAR FLORIDO MOSCATEL PASAS MOSCATEL
100% moscatel.

88 Colour: light mahogany. Nose: citrus fruit, fruit liqueur notes, toasty, spicy, honeyed notes. Palate: flavourful, fleshy, sweet.

CÉSAR FLORIDO MOSCATEL DORADO MOSCATEL
100% moscatel.

87 Colour: iodine, amber rim. Nose: powerfull, candied fruit, honeyed notes, citrus fruit. Palate: flavourful, concentrated, sweetness.

CRUZ DEL MAR OL
100% palomino.

90 Colour: iodine, amber rim. Nose: powerfull, complex, dry nuts, toasty, sweet spices. Palate: rich, fine bitter notes, long, spicy.

DELGADO ZULETA

Avda. de Rocío Jurado, s/n
11540 Sanlúcar de Barrameda (Cádiz)
☎: +34 956 360 133 - Fax: +34 956 360 780
comercial@delgadozuleta.com
www.delgadozuleta.com

QUO VADIS AM
100% palomino.

92 Color iodine, amber rim. Aroma powerfull, complex, elegant, dry nuts, toasty. Taste rich, fine bitter notes, fine solera notes, long, spicy.

MONTEAGUDO MEDIUM CR
95% palomino, 5% pedro ximénez.

88 Colour: iodine, amber rim. Nose: aged wood nuances, sweet spices, pattiserie, expressive, powerfull. Palate: fine bitter notes, unctuous, sweetness, flavourful.

MONTEAGUDO CR
80% palomino, 20% pedro ximénez.

85 Colour: light mahogany. Nose: pattiserie, caramel, varnish, overripe fruit, fruit preserve. Palate: fine bitter notes, unctuous.

LA GOYA MZ
100% palomino.

91 Colour: bright yellow. Nose: expressive, saline, balsamic herbs, dry nuts. Palate: rich, powerful, fine bitter notes.

ZULETA BARBIANA MZ
100% palomino.

88 Color bright yellow. Aroma complex, expressive, pungent, saline. Taste rich, powerful, fresh, fine bitter notes.

LAS SEÑORAS OL
palomino.

83 Colour: iodine, amber rim. Nose: fruit liqueur notes, overripe fruit, caramel. Palate: spicy, sweetness, flavourful.

DIOS BACO

Tecnología, parcela A-14 (Parque empresarial de Jerez)
11402 Jerez de la Frontera (Cádiz)
☎: +34 956 333 337 - Fax: +34 956 333 825
info@bodegasdiosbaco.com
www.bodegasdiosbaco.com

DIOS BACO AM
100% palomino.

88 Colour: iodine, amber rim. Nose: powerfull, dried fruit, fruit liqueur notes, pattiserie, toasty. Palate: flavourful, fleshy, sweetness, fine bitter notes.

BULERÍA FI
100% palomino.

88 Colour: bright golden. Nose: complex, pungent, flor yeasts. Palate: rich, powerful, fresh, fine bitter notes.

BACO DE ÉLITE MEDIUM DRY OL
95% palomino, 5% pedro ximénez.

90 Colour: iodine, amber rim. Nose: caramel, pattiserie, expressive, powerfull. Palate: spirituous, fine bitter notes, unctuous, rich, flavourful.

BACO IMPERIAL 30 AÑOS VORS PC
100% palomino.

88 Colour: iodine, amber rim. Nose: pungent, sweet spices, toasty. Palate: fine bitter notes, spirituous, rich.

OXFORD 1970 PX
100% pedro ximénez.

91 Colour: dark mahogany. Nose: aromatic coffee, sweet spices, roasted coffee, honeyed notes, complex, acetaldehyde. Palate: balanced, unctuous, flavourful, fleshy.

EL MAESTRO SIERRA

Pza. de Silos, 5
11403 Jerez de la Frontera (Cádiz)
☎: +34 956 342 433 - Fax: +34 956 342 433
info@maestrosierra.com
www.maestrosierra.com

EL MAESTRO SIERRA VIEJO 1830 AM
palomino.

89 Colour: old gold. Nose: caramel, pattiserie. Palate: flavourful, complex, long, sweetness.

EL MAESTRO SIERRA FI
palomino.

91 Colour: bright yellow. Nose: balanced, expressive, fresh fruit, wild herbs, pungent. Palate: flavourful, powerful.

EL MAESTRO SIERRA OLOROSO EXTRAVIEJO 1/7 OL
palomino.

92 Colour: light mahogany. Nose: pungent, acetaldehyde, varnish, balanced. Palate: powerful, complex, fine bitter notes, great length.

EL MAESTRO SIERRA VIEJÍSIMO PX
pedro ximénez.

91 Colour: dark mahogany. Nose: fruit liqueur notes, dark chocolate, pattiserie. Palate: creamy, powerful, varietal, sweet.

EMILIO LUSTAU

Arcos, 53
11402 Jerez de la Frontera (Cádiz)
☎: +34 956 341 597 - Fax: +34 956 859 204
lustau@lustau.es
www.lustau.es

LUSTAU ESCUADRILLA AM
palomino.

90 Colour: iodine, amber rim. Nose: powerfull, complex, dry nuts, toasty, iodine notes, pungent. Palate: rich, fine bitter notes, long, spicy.

EAST INDIA CR
palomino, pedro ximénez.

90 Colour: mahogany. Nose: dried fruit, caramel, aromatic coffee, expressive, powerfull. Palate: great length, complex, sweetness, flavourful.

CANDELA CR
palomino, pedro ximénez.

85 Colour: iodine, amber rim. Nose: powerfull, fruit liqueur notes, honeyed notes. Palate: flavourful, sweetness, concentrated.

LA INA FI
palomino.

96 Colour: bright straw. Nose: flor yeasts, elegant, complex, expressive, powerfull, saline. Palate: powerful, fleshy, long, great length, fine bitter notes.

PAPIRUSA MZ SOLERA
palomino.

94 Colour: bright straw. Nose: powerfull, characterful, complex, iodine notes, saline. Palate: flavourful, powerful, fleshy.

MACARENA MZ
palomino.

89 Colour: bright yellow. Nose: expressive, saline. Palate: rich, fresh, fine bitter notes.

EMILÍN MOSCATEL
moscatel.

91 Colour: iodine, amber rim. Nose: expressive, characterful, overripe fruit, citrus fruit, honeyed notes, acetaldehyde. Palate: flavourful, sweetness, fleshy.

RÍO VIEJO OL
palomino.

92 Color iodine, amber rim. Aroma powerfull, complex, elegant, dry nuts, toasty. Taste rich, fine bitter notes, fine solera notes, long, spicy.

AÑADA 1997 OLOROSO ABOCADO OL
palomino.

92 Colour: iodine, amber rim. Nose: balanced, powerfull, sweet spices, pattiserie. Palate: long, flavourful, fleshy, complex, sweetness.

SAN EMILIO PX
pedro ximénez.

93 Color dark mahogany. Aroma complex, fruit liqueur notes, dried fruit, pattiserie, toasty. Taste sweet, rich, unctuous, powerful.

EQUIPO NAVAZOS

Cartuja, 1 - módulo 6
11401 Jerez de la Frontera (Cádiz)
☎: +34 649 435 979
equipo@navazos.com
www.equiponavazos.com

LA BOTA DE AMONTILLADO (BOTA Nº 31) AM
palomino.

98 Colour: iodine, amber rim. Nose: saline, fresh, dry nuts, candied fruit, cocoa bean, pattiserie. Palate: powerful, flavourful, fleshy, elegant, good acidity, long, great length.

LA BOTA DE FINO (BOTA Nº 27) FI
palomino.

99 Colour: bright golden. Nose: complex, expressive, dry nuts, saline, pungent, balsamic herbs. Palate: fleshy, complex, rich, flavourful, powerful, great length.

MANZANILLA I THINK S/C MZ
palomino.

92 Colour: old gold. Nose: pungent, dry nuts, expressive, elegant, complex, fruit liqueur notes. Palate: flavourful, correct, fine bitter notes, good finish.

LA BOTA DE MANZANILLA PASADA (BOTA Nº 30 "CAPATAZ RIVAS") MZ
palomino.

99 Colour: old gold. Nose: powerfull, acetaldehyde, pungent, dry nuts, candied fruit, pattiserie, slightly evolved. Palate: flavourful, fleshy, powerful, fine bitter notes, concentrated, dry wood.

LA BOTA DE MANZANILLA (BOTA Nª 32) MZ
palomino.

96 Colour: bright golden. Nose: acetaldehyde, pungent, iodine notes, saline, powerfull. Palate: powerful, flavourful, fleshy, complex, spicy, long.

LA BOTA DE OLOROSO "BOTA PUNTA Nº 28" OL
palomino.

96 Colour: light mahogany. Nose: expressive, reduction notes, acetaldehyde, dry nuts, caramel, pattiserie. Palate: powerful, flavourful, fleshy, good acidity, fine bitter notes, toasty, great length, long.

ESPÍRITUS DE JEREZ

Pza. Cocheras, 3
11403 Jerez de la Frontera (Cádiz)
☎: +34 649 456 990
direccion@espiritusdejerez.com

COLECCIÓN ROBERTO AMILLO AMONTILLADO AM
palomino.

95 Colour: iodine, amber rim. Nose: complex, dry nuts, toasty, acetaldehyde, pungent, expressive. Palate: rich, fine bitter notes, long, spicy.

COLECCIÓN ROBERTO AMILLO OLOROSO OL
palomino.

95 Colour: iodine, amber rim. Nose: dry nuts, toasty, pattiserie, expressive. Palate: rich, fine bitter notes, long, spicy.

COLECCIÓN ROBERTO AMILLO PALO CORTADO PC
palomino.

96 Colour: iodine, amber rim. Nose: elegant, dry nuts, toasty, expressive, warm, varnish, acetaldehyde. Palate: rich, fine bitter notes, long, spicy.

COLECCIÓN ROBERTO AMILLO PEDRO XIMÉNEZ PX
pedro ximénez.

95 Colour: dark mahogany. Nose: fruit liqueur notes, dried fruit, pattiserie, toasty, tar, varnish, characterful. Palate: rich, unctuous, powerful, spicy, long, spirituous.

FEDERICO PATERNINA

Ctra. Morabita, Km. 2
11407 Jerez de la Frontera (Cádiz)
☎: +34 956 186 112 - Fax: +34 956 303 500
paternina@paternina.com
www.paternina.com

FINO IMPERIAL 30 AÑOS VORS AM
palomino.

92 Colour: old gold, amber rim. Nose: dry nuts, complex, characterful, sweet spices, toasty. Palate: flavourful, powerful, sweetness, long.

BERTOLA 12 AÑOS AM
palomino.

91 Colour: iodine, amber rim. Nose: powerfull, complex, aged wood nuances, pattiserie. Palate: balanced, fine bitter notes, long, spicy.

BERTOLA CR
palomino, pedro ximénez.

85 Colour: light mahogany. Nose: sweet spices, dark chocolate, toasty, fruit preserve. Palate: sweetness, fine bitter notes, spicy.

BERTOLA FI
palomino.

92 Colour: bright golden. Nose: fragrant herbs, flor yeasts, saline, powerfull, expressive. Palate: complex, powerful, flavourful, fleshy, fine bitter notes.

VICTORIA REGINA VORS OL
palomino.

88 Colour: iodine, amber rim. Nose: dry nuts, sweet spices, aged wood nuances, toasty. Palate: fine bitter notes, spirituous, unctuous, good finish.

BERTOLA 12 AÑOS OL
palomino.

87 Colour: iodine, amber rim. Nose: dry nuts, honeyed notes, expressive, medium intensity. Palate: fine bitter notes, spirituous, warm, correct.

VIEJA SOLERA 30 AÑOS VORS PX
pedro ximénez.

92 Colour: dark mahogany. Nose: acetaldehyde, dried fruit, dry nuts, sweet spices, pattiserie, balanced, complex. Palate: flavourful, powerful, sweetness, long, creamy.

BERTOLA 12 AÑOS PX
pedro ximénez.

88 Colour: dark mahogany. Nose: fruit liqueur notes, overripe fruit, honeyed notes, balanced. Palate: unctuous, balanced, fleshy, flavourful.

FERNANDO DE CASTILLA

San Fco. Javier, 3
11404 Jerez de la Frontera (Cádiz)
☎: +34 956 182 454 - Fax: +34 956 182 222
bodegas@fernandodecastilla.com
www.fernandodecastilla.com

FERNANDO DE CASTILLA "AMONTILLADO ANTIQUE" AM
100% palomino.

92 Colour: iodine, amber rim. Nose: complex, elegant, dry nuts, toasty, powerfull, aged wood nuances. Palate: rich, fine bitter notes, long, spicy.

FERNANDO DE CASTILLA "FINO ANTIQUE" FI
100% palomino.

91 Colour: bright golden. Nose: acetaldehyde, iodine notes, expressive, powerfull. Palate: fleshy, flavourful, great length.

FERNANDO DE CASTILLA FINO CLASSIC FI
100% palomino.

90 Colour: bright straw. Nose: powerfull, white flowers, saline, pungent, iodine notes. Palate: flavourful, powerful, fleshy.

FERNANDO DE CASTILLA MANZANILLA CLASSIC MZ
100% palomino.

88 Colour: bright straw. Nose: pungent, medium intensity. Palate: correct, fine bitter notes.

FERNANDO DE CASTILLA "OLOROSO ANTIQUE" OL
100% palomino.

92 Colour: light mahogany. Nose: expressive, characterful, acetaldehyde, pattiserie, toasty. Palate: powerful, flavourful, fleshy, complex, sweetness, long.

FERNANDO DE CASTILLA "PALO CORTADO ANTIQUE" PC
100% palomino.

94 Colour: iodine, amber rim. Nose: elegant, expressive, aged wood nuances, sweet spices, toasty. Palate: flavourful, powerful, fleshy, long.

FERNANDO DE CASTILLA "P.X. ANTIQUE" PX
100% pedro ximénez.

95 Colour: dark mahogany. Nose: fruit liqueur notes, dried fruit, pattiserie, toasty, dark chocolate, aromatic coffee, tar. Palate: sweet, rich, unctuous, powerful, round, fine bitter notes.

FERNANDO DE CASTILLA "PX PREMIUM" PX
100% pedro ximénez.

92 Color dark mahogany. Aroma complex, fruit liqueur notes, dried fruit, pattiserie, toasty. Taste sweet, rich, unctuous, powerful.

GONZÁLEZ BYASS JEREZ

Manuel María González, 12
11403 Jerez de la Frontera (Cádiz)
☎: +34 956 357 000 - Fax: +34 956 357 043
atencion@gonzalezbyass.es
www.gonzalezbyass.es

AMONTILLADO DEL DUQUE VORS AM
palomino.

93 Colour: iodine, amber rim. Nose: complex, elegant, dry nuts, toasty. Palate: rich, fine bitter notes, , long, spicy, spirituous.

VIÑA AB AM
palomino.

91 Colour: bright golden. Nose: acetaldehyde, iodine notes, dry nuts, toasty, sweet spices. Palate: round, fleshy, complex, rich. Personality.

MATUSALEM VORS CR
palomino, pedro ximénez.

92 Colour: dark mahogany. Nose: powerfull, characterful, dark chocolate, pattiserie, aged wood nuances. Palate: powerful, fleshy, sweetness, spicy.

TÍO PEPE FI
100% palomino.

93 Colour: bright yellow. Nose: expressive, pungent, saline, characterful, fresh. Palate: rich, powerful, fresh, fine bitter notes.

ALFONSO OL
palomino.

89 Colour: iodine, amber rim. Nose: powerfull, complex, dry nuts, toasty. Palate: rich, fine bitter notes, , long, spicy.

SOLERA 1847 OL
palomino.

86 Colour: light mahogany. Nose: powerfull, characterful, dried fruit, dry nuts, acetaldehyde. Palate: sweetness, pruney, unctuous, fine bitter notes.

CROFT ORIGINAL PCR
palomino.

89 Colour: bright straw. Nose: flor yeasts, pungent, powerfull. Palate: flavourful, powerful, fleshy, sweet.

GONZALEZ BYASS AÑADA 1982 1982 PC
palomino.

95 Colour: iodine, amber rim. Nose: powerfull, complex, elegant, dry nuts, toasty, acetaldehyde. Palate: rich, fine bitter notes, long, spicy.

APÓSTOLES VORS PC
palomino.

93 Colour: light mahogany. Nose: powerfull, toasty, sweet spices, dark chocolate, roasted almonds, pungent. Palate: spicy, sweetness, warm.

LEONOR PC
palomino.

90 Colour: iodine, amber rim. Nose: acetaldehyde, saline, roasted almonds, caramel. Palate: flavourful, powerful, fleshy, spicy, long.

NOÉ PX
pedro ximénez.

94 Colour: dark mahogany. Nose: fruit liqueur notes, dried fruit, pattiserie, toasty, dark chocolate, characterful. Palate: sweet, rich, unctuous, powerful.

NÉCTAR PX
pedro ximénez.

89 Colour: dark mahogany. Nose: dried fruit, expressive, powerfull, aromatic coffee, toasty. Palate: unctuous, fleshy, rich, sweetness.

HEREDEROS DE ARGÜESO S.A.

Mar, 8
11540 Sanlúcar de Barrameda (Cádiz)
☎: +34 956 385 116 - Fax: +34 956 368 169
argueso@argueso.es
www.argueso.es

ARGÜESO AMONTILLADO VIEJO VORS AM
100% palomino.

90 Colour: old gold, amber rim. Nose: spicy, toasty, aged wood nuances, powerfull. Palate: toasty, smoky aftertaste, long.

ARGÜESO AM
100% palomino.

90 Colour: iodine, amber rim. Nose: pungent, wild herbs, sweet spices, aged wood nuances, dry nuts. Palate: unctuous, correct, flavourful, spicy.

ARGÜESO CREAM CR
80% palomino, 20% pedro ximénez.

86 Colour: iodine, amber rim. Nose: candied fruit, sweet spices, pattiserie, toasty. Palate: spirituous, fine bitter notes, sweetness, flavourful.

SAN LEÓN RESERVA DE FAMILIA MZ
100% palomino.

94 Colour: bright yellow. Nose: complex, pungent, saline, characterful. Palate: rich, powerful, fresh, fine bitter notes, fleshy.

SAN LEÓN "CLÁSICA" MZ
100% palomino.

93 Colour: bright straw. Nose: pungent, saline, powerfull, expressive. Palate: flavourful, powerful, fleshy, complex, full, long.

LAS MEDALLAS DE ARGÜESO MZ
100% palomino.

91 Colour: bright straw. Nose: characterful, saline, pungent, flor yeasts. Palate: flavourful, fresh, good acidity, fine bitter notes.

ARGÜESO MZ
100% palomino.

89 Colour: bright straw. Nose: fragrant herbs, saline, pungent. Palate: flavourful, fresh, long, good acidity, fine bitter notes.

ARGÜESO MOSCATEL
100% moscatel.

86 Colour: iodine, amber rim. Nose: caramel, pattiserie, honeyed notes. Palate: sweetness, rich, flavourful.

ARGÜESO PX
100% pedro ximénez.

84 Colour: mahogany. Nose: caramel, sweet spices, medium intensity. Palate: creamy, spirituous, unctuous.

HIDALGO

Clavel, 29
11402 Jerez de la Frontera (Cádiz)
☎: +34 956 341 078 - Fax: +34 956 320 922
emiliohidalgo@emiliohidalgo.es
www.hidalgo.com

EL TRESILLO AMONTILLADO VIEJO S/C AM
palomino.

94 Colour: old gold, amber rim. Nose: acetaldehyde, roasted almonds, sweet spices, expressive. Palate: balanced, elegant, complex, flavourful, fleshy.

LA PANESA ESPECIAL FINO S/C FI
100% palomino.

95 Colour: bright golden. Nose: dry nuts, pungent, saline, iodine notes, aged wood nuances, spicy. Palate: balanced, powerful, flavourful, fleshy, long.

VILLAPANÉS S/C OL
100% palomino.

94 Colour: light mahogany. Nose: acetaldehyde, pungent, dry nuts, roasted almonds, sweet spices. Palate: balanced, fine bitter notes, fleshy, powerful, flavourful.

GOBERNADOR S/C OL
palomino.

90 Colour: old gold, amber rim. Nose: acetaldehyde, dry nuts, roasted almonds, aged wood nuances. Palate: warm, powerful, flavourful.

MARQUÉS DE RODIL S/C PC
palomino.

90 Colour: bright golden. Nose: acetaldehyde, flor yeasts, pungent, roasted almonds, spicy. Palate: powerful, fleshy, flavourful.

HIDALGO PEDRO XIMÉNEZ S/C PX
pedro ximénez.

88 Colour: dark mahogany. Nose: caramel, sweet spices, pattiserie, acetaldehyde. Palate: correct, flavourful, fleshy.

HIJOS DE RAINERA PÉREZ MARÍN

Ctra. Nacional IV, Km. 640
11406 Jerez de la Frontera (Cádiz)
☎: +34 956 321 004 - Fax: +34 956 340 829
visitas@grupoestevez.com
www.grupoestevez.com

LA GUITA MZ
palomino.

90 Colour: bright yellow. Nose: complex, pungent, saline, fresh, fragrant herbs. Palate: rich, powerful, fresh, fine bitter notes.

LA ALACENA DE CARLOS HERRERA

Amapola, 2- Local 14 Edificio Notaria
41950 Castilleja de la Cuesta (Sevilla)
☎: +34 954 169 128 - Fax: +34 954 164 288
info@alacenach.com
www.laalacenadecarlosherrera.com

ALACENA DE CARLOS HERRERA MZ
palomino.

89 Colour: bright straw. Nose: balanced, medium intensity, fresh. Palate: correct, balanced, fine bitter notes.

LUIS CABALLERO

San Francisco, 32
11500 El Puerto de Santa María (Cádiz)
☎: +34 956 851 751 - Fax: +34 956 859 204
marketing@caballero.es
www.caballero.es

PAVÓN PUERTO FINO FI SOLERA
palomino.

87 Colour: bright yellow. Nose: flor yeasts, fresh, medium intensity, mineral. Palate: correct, unctuous, smoky aftertaste, easy to drink.

MANUEL ARAGÓN

Olivo, 1
11130 Chiclana de la Frontera (Cádiz)
☎: +34 956 400 756 - Fax: +34 956 532 907
administracion@bodegamanuelaragon.com
www.bodegamanuelaragon.com

FINO GRANERO 2004 FI
100% palomino.

80 Colour: bright yellow. Nose: medium intensity, short, fresh. Palate: lacks balance, light-bodied, short, dry.

GLORIA 2007 MOSCATEL
100% moscatel.

83 Colour: bright golden. Nose: citrus fruit, fresh, short. Palate: good finish, easy to drink, sweetness, light-bodied.

TÍO ALEJANDRO OL
palomino.

85 Colour: dark mahogany, light mahogany. Nose: dried fruit, warm, medium intensity, varnish. Palate: fine bitter notes, warm, good finish.

VIEJO ARRUMBAO OL
80% palomino, 20% moscatel.

80 Colour: dark mahogany. Nose: dried fruit, honeyed notes, powerfull. Palate: spirituous, flavourful, sweetness.

REAL TESORO

Ctra. Nacional IV, Km. 640
11406 Jerez de la Frontera (Cádiz)
☎: +34 956 321 004 - Fax: +34 956 340 829
visitas@grupoestevez.com
www.grupoestevez.es

TÍO MATEO FI
palomino.

93 Colour: bright yellow. Nose: powerfull, pungent, iodine notes, flor yeasts. Palate: flavourful, fleshy, complex, fine bitter notes, round.

SÁNCHEZ ROMATE HERMANOS

Lealas, 26-30
11403 Jerez de la Frontera (Cádiz)
☎: +34 956 182 212 - Fax: +34 956 185 276
comercial@romate.com
www.romate.com

OLD & PLUS AMONTILLADO VORS AM
palomino.

94 Colour: iodine, amber rim. Nose: sweet spices, pattiserie, powerfull, expressive, acetaldehyde, pungent. Palate: powerful, flavourful, fleshy, complex.

NPU AM
palomino.

92 Colour: iodine, amber rim. Nose: complex, dry nuts, toasty, pungent. Palate: rich, fine bitter notes, , long, spicy.

IBERIA CR
palomino, pedro ximénez.

89 Colour: light mahogany. Nose: candied fruit, dried fruit, aromatic coffee, caramel. Palate: powerful, sweetness, pruney.

MARISMEÑO FI
palomino.

87 Colour: bright yellow. Nose: fresh, short, medium intensity. Palate: light-bodied, good finish, easy to drink.

ROMATE VIVA LA PEPA MZ
palomino.

89 Colour: bright golden. Nose: flor yeasts, dried flowers, dry nuts. Palate: rich, flavourful, balsamic.

AMBROSÍA MOSCATEL
moscatel.

90 Colour: mahogany. Nose: acetaldehyde, overripe fruit, citrus fruit, complex. Palate: spirituous, fine bitter notes, fleshy, good structure, flavourful.

OLD & PLUS OLOROSO OL
palomino.

93 Colour: mahogany. Nose: expressive, powerfull, complex, aged wood nuances, sweet spices. Palate: fleshy, good structure, rich, spirituous, flavourful.

DON JOSÉ OL
palomino.

91 Colour: light mahogany. Nose: powerfull, characterful, complex, candied fruit, toasty, sweet spices. Palate: flavourful, powerful, fleshy, complex.

REGENTE PC
palomino.

90 Colour: iodine, amber rim. Nose: sweet spices, aged wood nuances, toasty, iodine notes, pungent. Palate: long, great length, toasty, spirituous, flavourful.

OLD & PLUS PX
pedro ximénez.

93 Colour: dark mahogany. Nose: fruit liqueur notes, dried fruit, pattiserie, toasty, warm, tar, dark chocolate. Palate: sweet, rich, unctuous, powerful.

CARDENAL CISNEROS PX
pedro ximénez.

91 Colour: dark mahogany. Nose: fruit liqueur notes, dried fruit, pattiserie, toasty, dark chocolate. Palate: sweet, rich, unctuous, powerful.

DUQUESA PX
pedro ximénez.

89 Colour: dark mahogany. Nose: dried fruit, pattiserie, toasty, fruit liqueur notes. Palate: sweet, rich, unctuous, powerful.

SANDEMAN JEREZ

Pizarro, 10
11403 Jerez de la Frontera (Cádiz)
☎: +34 956 151 700 - Fax: +34 956 300 007
visitors.jerez@sandeman.eu
www.sandeman.eu

ROYAL ESMERALDA VOS AMONTILLADO 20 AÑOS AM
100% palomino.

92 Color iodine, amber rim. Aroma powerfull, complex, elegant, dry nuts, toasty. Taste rich, fine bitter notes, fine solera notes, long, spicy.

ROYAL CORREGIDOR 20 AÑOS VOS OL
palomino, pedro ximénez.

91 Color iodine, amber rim. Aroma powerfull, complex, elegant, dry nuts, toasty. Taste rich, fine bitter notes, fine solera notes, long, spicy.

ROYAL AMBROSANTE 20 AÑOS PX
100% pedro ximénez.

93 Colour: dark mahogany. Nose: powerfull, characterful, fruit liqueur notes, dark chocolate, smoky. Palate: powerful, sweet, concentrated.

VALDESPINO

Ctra. Nacional IV, Km.640
11406 Jerez de la Frontera (Cádiz)
☎: +34 956 321 004 - Fax: +34 956 340 829
visitas@grupoestevez.com
www.grupoestevez.es

COLISEO VORS AM
palomino.

94 Colour: old gold, amber rim. Nose: powerfull, fruit liqueur notes, candied fruit, acetaldehyde, pattiserie. Palate: flavourful, powerful, fleshy, fine bitter notes.

TÍO DIEGO AM
palomino.

88 Colour: iodine, amber rim. Nose: medium intensity, dry nuts, fruit liqueur notes, creamy oak, toasty. Palate: powerful, fleshy, sweetness.

YNOCENTE FI
palomino.

93 Colour: bright yellow. Nose: pungent, iodine notes, powerfull, characterful. Palate: flavourful, fleshy, long.

MOSCATEL VIEJÍSIMO TONELES MOSCATEL
moscatel.

97 Colour: dark mahogany. Nose: powerfull, expressive, characterful, acetaldehyde, dark chocolate. Palate: powerful, spirituous, fine bitter notes, long.

DON GONZALO VOS OL
palomino.

96 Color iodine, amber rim. Aroma powerfull, complex, elegant, dry nuts, toasty. Taste rich, fine bitter notes, fine solera notes, long, spicy.

SOLERA SU MAJESTAD VORS OL
palomino.

96 Colour: iodine, amber rim. Nose: complex, elegant, dry nuts, toasty, expressive. Palate: rich, fine bitter notes, , spicy, long.

SOLERA 1842 VOS OL
palomino.

94 Colour: dark mahogany. Nose: aromatic coffee, dark chocolate, sweet spices, acetaldehyde. Palate: powerful, concentrated, sweetness, spirituous, long.

CARDENAL VORS PC
palomino.

96 Colour: dark mahogany. Nose: aged wood nuances, dark chocolate, varnish, pattiserie, acetaldehyde, iodine notes. Palate: flavourful, powerful, fleshy, complex, spicy.

EL CANDADO PX
pedro ximénez.

89 Colour: dark mahogany. Nose: acetaldehyde, dried fruit, honeyed notes, balanced. Palate: fleshy, flavourful, spirituous, long.

VINÍCOLA SOTO

Finca Cerro Viejo Cañada de la Loba, s/n
11407 Jerez de la Frontera (Cádiz)
☎: +34 956 319 650
www.vinicolasoto.com

DON JOSÉ MARÍA AM
palomino.

88 Colour: old gold, amber rim. Nose: sweet spices, pattiserie, toasty. Palate: fine bitter notes, spirituous, warm, flavourful.

DON JOSÉ MARÍA CR
palomino, pedro ximénez.

90 Colour: mahogany. Nose: dried fruit, honeyed notes, expressive, powerfull. Palate: spirituous, balanced, fleshy, sweetness.

DON JOSÉ MARÍA FI
palomino.

91 Colour: bright golden. Nose: complex, expressive, pungent, saline, flor yeasts. Palate: rich, powerful, fresh, flavourful, fine bitter notes.

DON JOSÉ MARÍA MZ
palomino.

90 Colour: bright golden. Nose: complex, powerfull, dried flowers, toasty, saline. Palate: correct, balanced, rich, flavourful.

DON JOSÉ MARÍA OL
palomino.

91 Colour: iodine, amber rim. Nose: powerfull, complex, dry nuts, toasty. Palate: rich, fine bitter notes, , long.

WILLIAMS & HUMBERT S.A.

Ctra. N-IV, Km. 641,75
11408 Jerez de la Frontera (Cádiz)
☎: +34 956 353 400 - Fax: +34 956 353 412
secretaria@williams-humbert.com
www.williams-humbert.com

CANASTA CR
palomino, pedro ximénez.

85 Colour: light mahogany. Nose: aged wood nuances, sweet spices, neat. Palate: rich, flavourful, easy to drink.

DRY SACK FINO FI
palomino.

86 Colour: bright yellow. Nose: expressive, pungent. Palate: fresh, fine bitter notes, light-bodied, sweetness.

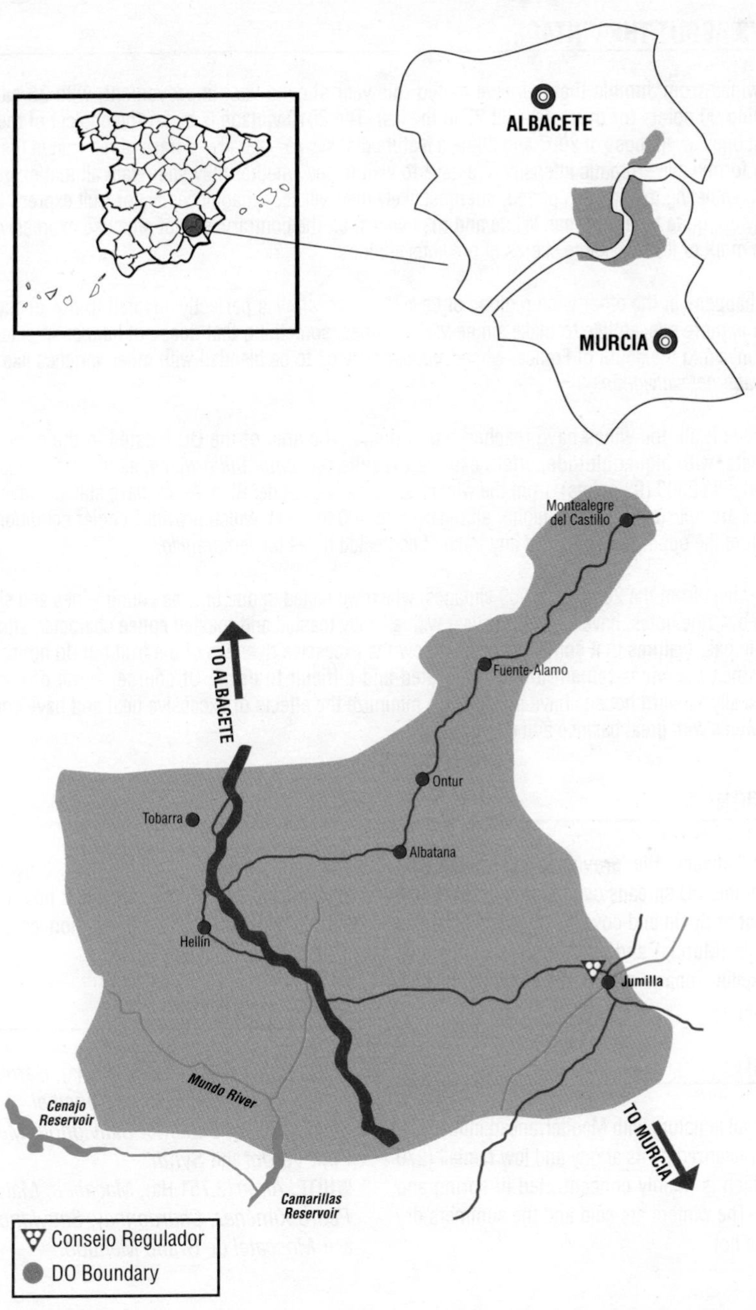

ALBACETE
MURCIA
Montealegre del Castillo
Fuente-Alamo
TO ALBACETE
Ontur
Tobarra
Albatana
Hellín
Jumilla
Mundo River
Cenajo Reservoir
Camarillas Reservoir
TO MURCIA
Consejo Regulador
DO Boundary

NEWS ABOUT THE VINTAGE:

The wines from Jumilla that we have tasted this year show a vast improvement, with 35 samples reaching 90 points (or over), for just 27 in the last. The 2010 vintage is by far the coolest of the most recent ones, even those of 2007 and 2008, a feature that leaves –literally– a trace of red fruit in the wines and a formidable aromatic intensity. We have to wait to see whether they still retain all that expression after completing their ageing period, but most likely they will keep magnificently, for fruit expression and acidity are quite high this year. White and rosé wines, on the contrary, do not show so expressive, and retain more or less the same scores of previous editions.

As it happens in the other wine regions of Levante, *monastrell* is perfectly adapted to this ecosystem, and it is more susceptible to make single-variety wines, something that does not happen in places like Catalunya and the south of France, where *monastrell* need to be blended with other varieties like *syrah* and *cabernet sauvignon.*

To prove it all, the wines have reached high ratings. The area of the DO located in the province of Albacete, with higher altitude, offers excellent results for *tempranillo* wines, as proved by Gorgocil Tempranillo 2008 (93 points), from the winery Viñas de la Casa del Rico. As we have stated above, good ratings are possible thanks to higher altitude (up to 800 meters), which provides cooler conditions and therefore the opportunity to avoid any trace of confected notes for *tempranillo.*

Aged wines from the 2008 and 2009 vintages, which we tasted in due time as young wines and showed some overripe notes, have shown this year with a heavy toasted and roasted coffee character, after their spell in oak, features that somehow overshadow the excessive ripeness of the fruit but do not save the day, since the wines remain too concentrated and difficult to drink. Of course, some of the most technically forward houses have managed to minimize the effects of excessive heat and have come up with wines with great balance and complexity.

LOCATION:

Midway between the provinces of Murcia and Albacete, this DO spreads over a large region in the southeast of Spain and covers the municipal areas of Jumilla (Murcia) and Fuente Álamo, Albatana, Ontur, Hellín, Tobarra and Montealegre del Castillo (Albacete).

CLIMATE:

Continental in nature with Mediterranean influences. It is characterized by its aridity and low rainfall (270 mm) which is mainly concentrated in spring and autumn. The winters are cold and the summers dry and quite hot.

SOIL:

The soil is mainly brownish-grey, brownish-grey limestone and limy. In general, it is poor in organic matter, with great water retention capacity and medium permeability.

GRAPE VARIETIES:

RED: *Monastrell* (main 35,373 Ha), *Garnacha Tinta, Garnacha Tintorera, Cencibel* (*Tempranillo*), *Cabernet Sauvignon, Merlot, Petit Verdot* and *Syrah.*
WHITE: *Airén* (3,751 Ha), *Macabeo, Malvasía, Pedro Ximénez, Chardonnay, Sauvignon Blanc* and *Moscatel de Grano Menudo.*

FIGURES:

Vineyard surface: 26,240 – **Wine-Growers:** 2,560 – **Wineries:** 44 – **2010 Harvest rating:** Very Good – **Production:** 25,000,000 litres – **Market percentages:** 55% domestic. 45% export

CONSEJO REGULADOR
San Roque, 15, Apdo. 66
30520 Jumilla (Murcia)
☎: +34 968 781 761 - Fax: +34 968 781 900
@ info@vinosdejumilla.org
www.vinosdejumilla.org

GENERAL CHARACTERISTICS OF THE WINES

WHITES	Although they are not the most characteristic of the region, those produced from *Macabeo* are superior to those produced from Airen. In general, the white wines of Jumilla are straw yellow in colour; they have a moderate fruity character and a certain body on the palate; moreover, they are balanced and flavourful.
ROSÉS	These tend have a salmon pink colour; the nose is quite fruity and has a good aromatic intensity; on the palate they are flavourful, some with slightly more body and a bit warmer.
REDS	These are the region's wines par excellence, based on a variety, the *Monastrell* that, subject to the production techniques, provides wines with a lot of intense colour, with characteristic aromas of ripe black fruit and occasionally dried fruit; on the palate the best are very powerful with excellent tannin structure, flavourful and meaty. The Crianzas combine this fruity character with the contributions of the wood, and in the case of the older wines, although oxidation notes may still appear, the evolutionary trend of the variety is controlled more and more.

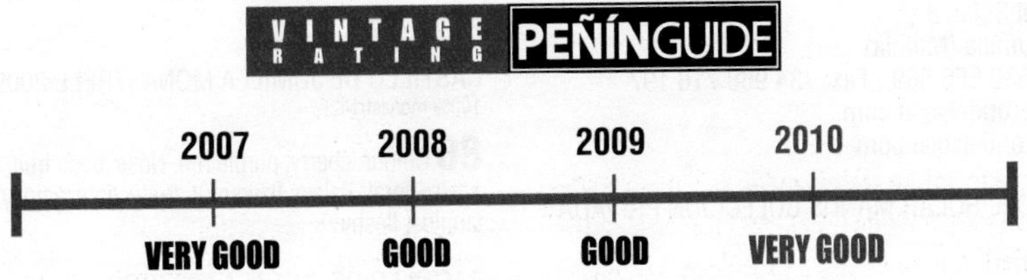

ALTOS DEL CUADRADO

Pío Baroja, 3- Apdo. Correos 120
30510 Yecla (Murcia)
☎: +34 968 791 115 - Fax: +34 968 791 900
info@altosdelcuadrado.com
www.altosdelcuadrado.com

ALTOS DEL CUADRADO 2009 T
85% monastrell, 10% petit verdot, 5% cabernet sauvignon.

89 Color bright cherry. Aroma ripe fruit, sweet spices, creamy oak, expressive. Taste flavourful, fruity, toasty, round tannins.

ALTOS DEL CUADRADO VVV 2008 T
85% monastrell, 15% petit verdot.

88 Colour: cherry, garnet rim. Nose: creamy oak, toasty, complex, red berry notes. Palate: powerful, flavourful, toasty, round tannins.

ASENSIO CARCELÉN N.C.R.

Ctra. Comarcal 3314, Km. 8
30520 Jumilla (Murcia)
☎: +34 968 435 543 - Fax: +34 968 435 542
bodegascarcelen@terra.es

100 X 100 SYRAH 2009 T
syrah.

84 Colour: cherry, garnet rim. Nose: warm, characterful, powerfull, ripe fruit. Palate: powerful, concentrated, warm.

PURA SANGRE 2006 TR
monastrell.

83 Colour: cherry, garnet rim. Nose: spicy, toasty, overripe fruit. Palate: powerful, flavourful, toasty, round tannins.

BARÓN DEL SOLAR

Barón del Solar, 8
30520 Jumilla (Murcia)
☎: +34 630 566 889 - Fax: +34 968 716 197
juani@barondelsolar.com
www.barondelsolar.com

BARÓN DEL SOLAR MANOS COLECCIÓN PRIVADA 2008 T
100% monastrell.

92 Colour: deep cherry. Nose: ripe fruit, sweet spices, toasty. Palate: flavourful, powerful, fleshy.

BARÓN DEL SOLAR 2008 T
80% monastrell, 20% cabernet sauvignon.

85 Colour: cherry, garnet rim. Nose: fruit liqueur notes, aromatic coffee, varnish. Palate: sweetness, spirituous, fleshy.

BLEDA

Ctra. de Ontur, Km. 2. Apdo. Correos 62
30520 Jumilla (Murcia)
☎: +34 968 780 012 - Fax: +34 968 782 699
vinos@bodegasbleda.com
www.bodegasbleda.com

CASTILLO DE JUMILLA 2010 B
40% airén, 25% macabeo, 35% sauvignon blanc.

85 Colour: bright straw. Nose: fresh, fresh fruit, expressive, floral. Palate: flavourful, fruity, good acidity, balanced.

CASTILLO DE JUMILLA MONASTRELL 2010 RD
100% monastrell.

87 Colour: rose, purple rim. Nose: powerfull, ripe fruit, red berry notes, floral, expressive. Palate: fleshy, powerful, fruity, easy to drink.

CASTILLO DE JUMILLA MONASTRELL - TEMPRANILLO 2010 T
50% monastrell, 50% tempranillo.

88 Colour: cherry, garnet rim. Nose: fresh fruit, red berry notes, scrubland. Palate: flavourful, fruity, fresh.

DIVUS 2009 T
100% monastrell.

91 Colour: bright cherry. Nose: sweet spices, expressive, toasty, dark chocolate, overripe fruit. Palate: flavourful, fruity, toasty, round tannins.

AMATUS DULCE 2009 T
85% monastrell, 15% syrah.

89 Colour: cherry, purple rim. Nose: expressive, red berry notes, fruit preserve. Palate: flavourful, fruity, good acidity, sweet.

CASTILLO DE JUMILLA MONASTRELL 2009 T
100% monastrell.

86 Colour: cherry, purple rim. Nose: fresh fruit, red berry notes, floral. Palate: flavourful, fruity, good acidity, round tannins, fleshy.

CASTILLO DE JUMILLA 2007 TC
90% monastrell, 10% tempranillo.

87 Color cherry, garnet rim. Aroma ripe fruit, spicy, creamy oak, toasty, complex. Taste powerful, flavourful, toasty, round tannins.

CASTILLO DE JUMILLA 2005 TR
90% monastrell, 10% tempranillo.

85 Colour: pale ruby, brick rim edge. Nose: elegant, spicy, fine reductive notes, wet leather, fruit liqueur notes. Palate: spicy, fine tannins, elegant.

ORO VIEJO T
100% monastrell.

87 Colour: pale ruby, brick rim edge. Nose: acetaldehyde, balanced, aged wood nuances, varnish. Palate: easy to drink, sweetness, warm.

BODEGA ARTESANAL VIÑA CAMPANERO

Ctra. de Murcia, s/n- Apdo. 346
30520 Jumilla (Murcia)
☎: +34 968 780 754 - Fax: +34 968 780 754
bodegas@vinacampanero.com
www.vinacampanero.com

VEGARDAL MONASTRELL CEPAS VIEJAS 2010 T
100% monastrell.

87 Colour: cherry, purple rim. Nose: expressive, fresh fruit, red berry notes, floral. Palate: flavourful, fruity, good acidity, fleshy.

VEGARDAL CUCO DEL ARDAL SELECCIÓN 2009 T
100% monastrell.

86 Colour: cherry, garnet rim. Nose: fruit preserve, toasty, creamy oak. Palate: powerful, flavourful, round tannins.

VEGARDAL CUCO DEL ARDAL 2008 TC
100% monastrell.

85 Colour: bright cherry. Nose: overripe fruit, creamy oak. Palate: flavourful, fruity, toasty, round tannins.

BODEGA SAN JOSÉ

Camino de Hellín, s/n
02652 Ontur (Albacete)
☎: +34 967 324 212 - Fax: +34 967 324 186
comercial@bodegasanjose.com
www.bodegasanjose.com

VILLA DE ONTUR 2010 B
airén.

85 Colour: bright straw. Nose: fresh, fresh fruit, white flowers. Palate: flavourful, fruity, good acidity, balanced.

DOMINIO DE ONTUR MERLOT 2010 T
merlot.

88 Colour: cherry, purple rim. Nose: red berry notes, ripe fruit, sweet spices. Palate: flavourful, fruity, good acidity, round tannins.

DOMINIO DE ONTUR SYRAH 2010 T
syrah.

88 Colour: cherry, purple rim. Nose: red berry notes, violet drops. Palate: flavourful, fruity, good acidity, round tannins.

DOMINIO DE ONTUR MONASTRELL 2010 T
monastrell.

86 Colour: cherry, purple rim. Nose: expressive, fresh fruit, red berry notes. Palate: flavourful, fruity, good acidity, easy to drink.

DOMINIO DE ONTUR SELECCIÓN 2009 T
syrah.

87 Colour: cherry, garnet rim. Nose: red berry notes, floral, fresh. Palate: good acidity, balanced, fruity.

PATRE 2009 T
garnacha.

85 Colour: bright cherry. Nose: sweet spices, creamy oak, fruit preserve. Palate: fruity, toasty, round tannins.

BODEGA TORRECASTILLO

Ctra. de Bonete, s/n
02650 Montealegre del Castillo (Albacete)
☎: +34 967 582 188 - Fax: +34 967 582 339
bodega@torrecastillo.com
www.torrecastillo.com

TORRECASTILLO 2010 B
100% sauvignon blanc.

88 Colour: bright straw. Nose: fresh, fresh fruit, white flowers, tropical fruit. Palate: flavourful, fruity, good acidity, fine bitter notes.

TORRECASTILLO 2010 RD
100% monastrell.

86 Colour: rose, purple rim. Nose: ripe fruit, red berry notes, floral, expressive. Palate: fleshy, powerful, fruity, fresh.

TORRECASTILLO 2010 T
100% monastrell.

87 Colour: cherry, purple rim. Nose: fresh fruit, red berry notes, violet drops. Palate: flavourful, fruity, good acidity.

TORRECASTILLO ELLO 2007 T
80% monastrell, 10% cabernet sauvignon, 10% syrah.

87 Colour: cherry, garnet rim. Nose: spicy, toasty, overripe fruit. Palate: powerful, flavourful, toasty, round tannins.

BODEGAS 1890

Ctra. Venta del Olivo, Km. 2,5
30520 Jumilla (Murcia)
☎: +34 968 757 099 - Fax: +34 968 757 099
elisam@jgc.es
www.vinosdefamilia.com

MAYORAL 2010 T JOVEN
70% monastrell, 20% syrah, 10% cabernet sauvignon.

88 Colour: cherry, purple rim. Nose: fresh fruit, red berry notes, floral. Palate: flavourful, fruity, good acidity, round tannins.

MAYORAL 2007 TC
70% monastrell, 30% tempranillo.

87 Colour: cherry, garnet rim. Nose: roasted coffee, overripe fruit. Palate: fine bitter notes, spicy, round tannins.

BODEGAS CARCHELO

Casas de la Hoya, s/n
30520 Jumilla (Murcia)
☎: +34 968 435 137 - Fax: +34 968 435 200
administracion@carchelo.com
www.carchelo.com

CARCHELO 2009 T
40% monastrell, 40% tempranillo, 20% cabernet sauvignon.

89 Colour: cherry, garnet rim. Nose: spicy, complex, roasted coffee. Palate: powerful, flavourful, toasty, round tannins.

ALTICO SYRAH 2008 T
100% syrah.

91 Colour: bright cherry. Nose: expressive, red berry notes, toasty, cocoa bean. Palate: flavourful, fruity, toasty, round tannins.

SIERVA 2008 TC
40% monastrell, 30% cabernet sauvignon, 30% syrah.

90 Colour: bright cherry. Nose: sweet spices, creamy oak, expressive, overripe fruit. Palate: flavourful, fruity, toasty, round tannins.

CANALIZO 2007 TC
40% monastrell, 40% syrah, 20% tempranillo.

90 Colour: cherry, garnet rim. Nose: spicy, creamy oak, toasty, overripe fruit. Palate: powerful, flavourful, toasty, round tannins.

AUTISTA 2007 TC
monastrell, tempranillo, syrah.

89 Colour: cherry, garnet rim. Nose: roasted coffee, spicy, overripe fruit. Palate: powerful, concentrated, sweetness, fruity.

BODEGAS EL NIDO

Paraje de la Aragona, s/n
30520 Jumilla (Murcia)
☎: +34 968 435 022 - Fax: +34 968 435 653
info@bodegaselnido.com
www.bodegaselnido.com

EL NIDO 2008 T
70% cabernet sauvignon, 30% monastrell.

95 Colour: cherry, garnet rim. Nose: spicy, toasty, complex, fruit expression, dark chocolate, cocoa bean. Palate: powerful, flavourful, toasty, powerful tannins, long.

CLÍO 2008 T
70% monastrell, 30% cabernet sauvignon.

94 Colour: cherry, garnet rim. Nose: spicy, toasty, complex, fruit expression, dark chocolate. Palate: powerful, flavourful, toasty, round tannins, complex, fleshy, powerful tannins.

BODEGAS HACIENDA DEL CARCHE

Ctra. del Carche, Km. 8,3- Apdo. Correos 257
30520 Jumilla (Murcia)
☎: +34 968 108 248 - Fax: +34 968 975 935
info@haciendadelcarche.com
www.haciendadelcarche.com

HACIENDA DEL CARCHE 2010 B
40% sauvignon blanc, 30% airén, 30% macabeo.

86 Colour: bright straw. Nose: fresh, fresh fruit, floral. Palate: flavourful, fruity, good acidity, balanced.

HACIENDA DEL CARCHE 2010 RD
80% monastrell, 20% syrah.

87 Colour: rose, purple rim. Nose: ripe fruit, red berry notes, floral. Palate: fleshy, powerful, fruity, fresh.

TAVS 2010 T
80% monastrell, 20% syrah.

88 Colour: cherry, purple rim. Nose: expressive, fresh, red berry notes. Palate: flavourful, fruity, fresh.

TAVS SELECCIÓN 2009 T
50% monastrell, 25% cabernet sauvignon, 25% syrah.

91 Colour: cherry, garnet rim. Nose: ripe fruit, spicy, complex, sweet spices, mineral. Palate: powerful, flavourful, toasty, round tannins.

HACIENDA DEL CARCHE CEPAS VIEJAS 2008 TC
50% cabernet sauvignon, 50% monastrell.

88 Colour: bright cherry. Nose: sweet spices, expressive, overripe fruit, new oak. Palate: fruity, toasty, harsh oak tannins.

BODEGAS HUERTAS

Avda. de Murcia, s/n
30520 Jumilla (Murcia)
☎: +34 968 783 061 - Fax: +34 968 781 180
vinos@bodegashuertas.es
www.bodegashuertas.es

RODREJO 2009 T
monastrell, tempranillo.

85 Colour: cherry, purple rim. Nose: expressive, fresh fruit, red berry notes. Palate: flavourful, fruity, good acidity.

BODEGAS JUAN GIL

Paraje de la Aragona
30520 Jumilla (Murcia)
☎: +34 968 435 022 - Fax: +34 968 716 051
info@juangil.es
www.juangil.es

JUAN GIL 4 MESES 2010 T
100% monastrell.

91 Colour: bright cherry. Nose: ripe fruit, sweet spices, roasted coffee. Palate: flavourful, fruity, toasty, round tannins.

HONORO VERA ORGANIC 2010 T
85% monastrell, 15% syrah.

87 Colour: bright cherry. Nose: scrubland, toasty, overripe fruit. Palate: ripe fruit, oaky.

JUAN GIL 12 MESES 2009 T
100% monastrell.

92 Colour: bright cherry. Nose: sweet spices, creamy oak, expressive, complex, fruit expression. Palate: flavourful, fruity, toasty, round tannins, fleshy, complex.

JUAN GIL 18 MESES 2009 T
60% monastrell, 30% cabernet sauvignon, 10% syrah.

91 Colour: cherry, garnet rim. Nose: ripe fruit, spicy, roasted coffee. Palate: powerful, flavourful, toasty, round tannins, fleshy, long.

JUAN GIL DULCE T
100% monastrell.

87 Colour: black cherry. Nose: powerfull, warm, fruit preserve, dried fruit, aromatic coffee, roasted coffee. Palate: powerful, sweet, unctuous.

BODEGAS LA ESPERANZA

Brisol, 16 bis
28230 Las Rozas (Madrid)
☎: +34 917 104 880 - Fax: +34 917 104 881
anap@swd.es
www.swd.es

NUDO SAUVIGNON BLANC 2010 B
100% sauvignon blanc.

78

NUDO MACABEO 2010 B
100% macabeo.

77

NUDO 2009 RD
100% syrah.

75

NUDO CABERNET SAUVIGNON 2010 T
100% cabernet sauvignon.

86 Colour: bright cherry. Nose: sweet spices, creamy oak, ripe fruit. Palate: flavourful, fruity, toasty, round tannins.

NUDO SYRAH 2009 T
100% syrah.

87 Colour: bright cherry. Nose: ripe fruit, sweet spices. Palate: flavourful, fruity, round tannins, ripe fruit.

NUDO MONASTRELL 2009 T
100% monastrell.

82 Colour: bright cherry. Nose: ripe fruit, sweet spices, aromatic coffee. Palate: flavourful, fruity, toasty, round tannins.

NUDO PETIT VERDOT 2008 T
100% petit verdot.

86 Colour: bright cherry. Nose: ripe fruit, creamy oak, expressive, toasty, new oak. Palate: flavourful, fruity, toasty, round tannins.

NUDO GARNACHA 2008 T
100% garnacha.

85 Colour: bright cherry. Nose: sweet spices, overripe fruit, toasty. Palate: flavourful, fruity, toasty, harsh oak tannins.

NUDO SELECCIÓN MONASTRELL SYRAH 2008 T ROBLE
monastrell, syrah.

84 Colour: bright cherry. Nose: sweet spices, creamy oak, ripe fruit. Palate: flavourful, fruity, toasty, round tannins.

NUDO MERLOT 2007 TR
100% merlot.

87 Colour: cherry, garnet rim. Nose: ripe fruit, spicy, toasty, mineral. Palate: powerful, flavourful, toasty, round tannins.

NUDO PETIT VERDOT PRIVATE COLLECTION 2007 T
100% petit verdot.

85 Colour: cherry, garnet rim. Nose: creamy oak, toasty, sweet spices. Palate: powerful, flavourful, toasty, round tannins.

NUDO SELECCIÓN MONASTRELL SYRAH 2007 T ROBLE
monastrell, syrah.

85 Colour: cherry, garnet rim. Nose: ripe fruit, spicy, aromatic coffee. Palate: powerful, flavourful, toasty, round tannins.

BODEGAS LUZÓN

Ctra. Jumilla-Calasparra, Km. 3,100
30520 Jumilla (Murcia)
☎: +34 968 784 135 - Fax: +34 968 781 911
info@bodegasluzon.com
www.bodegasluzon.com

LUZÓN 2010 T
70% monastrell, 30% syrah.

92 Colour: bright cherry. Nose: sweet spices, creamy oak, expressive, ripe fruit. Palate: flavourful, fruity, toasty, round tannins.

PORTÚ 2008 T
80% monastrell, 20% cabernet sauvignon.

93 Colour: bright cherry. Nose: sweet spices, creamy oak, expressive, ripe fruit, earthy notes. Palate: flavourful, fruity, toasty, round tannins.

LUZÓN 2008 TC
50% monastrell, 20% tempranillo, 20% cabernet sauvignon, 10% merlot.

90 Colour: cherry, garnet rim. Nose: spicy, creamy oak, toasty, mineral, ripe fruit. Palate: powerful, flavourful, toasty, round tannins.

ALMA DE LUZÓN 2007 T
70% monastrell, 20% cabernet sauvignon, 10% syrah.

93 Colour: cherry, garnet rim. Nose: spicy, creamy oak, toasty, complex, dark chocolate, ripe fruit. Palate: powerful, flavourful, toasty, round tannins.

PORTÚ 2007 T
monastrell, cabernet sauvignon.

93 Colour: black cherry. Nose: expressive, balanced, characterful, ripe fruit, spicy, cocoa bean, toasty. Palate: long, fruity, flavourful, ripe fruit, round tannins, balanced.

ALTOS DE LUZÓN 2007 T
50% monastrell, 25% tempranillo, 25% cabernet sauvignon.

90 Colour: cherry, garnet rim. Nose: ripe fruit, spicy, toasty. Palate: powerful, flavourful, toasty, round tannins.

BODEGAS PÍO DEL RAMO

Ctra. Almanza, s/n
02652 Ontur (Albacete)
☎: +34 967 323 230 - Fax: +34 967 323 604
info@piodelramo.com
www.piodelramo.com

CHARDONNAY PÍO DEL RAMO 2009 B BARRICA
100% chardonnay.

90 Colour: bright yellow. Nose: ripe fruit, sweet spices, creamy oak, fragrant herbs. Palate: rich, smoky aftertaste, flavourful, fresh, good acidity.

PÍO DEL RAMO 2009 T ROBLE
60% monastrell, 25% syrah, 15% cabernet sauvignon.

86 Colour: cherry, purple rim. Nose: expressive, fresh fruit, red berry notes, floral. Palate: flavourful, fruity, good acidity.

PÍO DEL RAMO 2008 TC
60% monastrell, 15% petit verdot, 15% syrah, 10% cabernet sauvignon.

88 Colour: deep cherry. Nose: ripe fruit, spicy, creamy oak, toasty, complex. Palate: powerful, flavourful, toasty, round tannins.

BODEGAS SALZILLO

Ctra. Nacional 344, km 57,2
30520 Jumilla (Murcia)
☎: +34 968 846 705 - Fax: +34 968 843 604
salzillo@bodegassalzillo.com
www.bodegassalzillo.com

MATIUS 2008 TC
monastrell.

84 Colour: cherry, garnet rim. Nose: fruit preserve, dark chocolate, balsamic herbs. Palate: flavourful, fleshy, toasty.

CAMELOT DULCE MONASTRELL S/C TINTO DULCE
monastrell.

82 Colour: cherry, garnet rim. Nose: fruit liqueur notes, rancio notes, sweet spices. Palate: fresh, fruity, flavourful.

BODEGAS SAN DIONISIO

Ctra. Higuera, s/n
02651 Fuenteálamo (Albacete)
☎: +34 967 543 032 - Fax: +34 967 543 136
sandionisio@bodegassandionisio.es
www.bodegassandinisio.es

SEÑORÍO DE FUENTEÁLAMO MACABEO SELECCIÓN 2010 B
85% macabeo, 15% airén.

86 Colour: bright straw. Nose: white flowers, medium intensity, ripe fruit. Palate: flavourful, fruity, good acidity, fine bitter notes.

SEÑORÍO DE FUENTEÁLAMO SYRAH 2010 RD
100% syrah.

85 Colour: rose, purple rim. Nose: ripe fruit, red berry notes, floral. Palate: fleshy, powerful, fruity, fresh.

SEÑORIO DE FUENTEÁLAMO SELECCIÓN 2010 T
100% monastrell.

75

SEÑORÍO DE FUENTEÁLAMO MONASTRELL SYRAH 2007 TC
60% monastrell, 40% syrah.

85 Colour: bright cherry. Nose: ripe fruit, sweet spices. Palate: flavourful, fruity, toasty, round tannins.

BODEGAS SAN ISIDRO BSI

Ctra. Murcia, s/n
30520 Jumilla (Murcia)
☎: +34 968 780 700 - Fax: +34 968 782 351
bsi@bsi.es
www.bsi.es

SABATACHA 2009 BFB
100% airén.

82 Colour: bright yellow. Nose: sweet spices, creamy oak, candied fruit. Palate: rich, smoky aftertaste, good acidity.

SABATACHA MONASTRELL 2010 T
100% monastrell.

87 Colour: cherry, purple rim. Nose: expressive, fresh fruit, floral. Palate: flavourful, fruity, good acidity.

SABATACHA SYRAH 2010 T
100% syrah.

85 Colour: cherry, purple rim. Nose: fresh fruit, red berry notes, floral. Palate: flavourful, fruity, round tannins, balanced, good acidity.

SABATACHA PETIT VERDOT 2008 T
100% petit verdot.

85 Color bright cherry. Aroma ripe fruit, sweet spices, creamy oak, expressive. Taste flavourful, fruity, toasty, round tannins.

GENUS MONASTRELL SYRAH 2008 T
80% monastrell, 20% syrah.

84 Colour: bright cherry. Nose: ripe fruit, sweet spices, creamy oak. Palate: flavourful, fruity, toasty.

SABATACHA 2007 TC
100% monastrell.

82 Colour: pale ruby, brick rim edge. Nose: ripe fruit, spicy, complex, roasted coffee. Palate: powerful, toasty, round tannins.

GÉMINA CUVÉE SELECCIÓN 2006 T
100% monastrell.

85 Colour: cherry, garnet rim. Nose: ripe fruit, spicy, complex. Palate: powerful, flavourful, toasty, round tannins.

GÉMINA PREMIUM 2003 TR
100% monastrell.

88 Color bright cherry. Aroma ripe fruit, sweet spices, creamy oak, expressive. Taste flavourful, fruity, toasty, round tannins.

SABATACHA 2002 TR
100% monastrell.

86 Colour: cherry, garnet rim. Nose: ripe fruit, spicy, toasty. Palate: powerful, flavourful, toasty, round tannins.

LACRIMA CHRISTI T
100% monastrell.

87 Colour: iodine, amber rim. Nose: powerfull, complex, dry nuts, toasty, acetaldehyde. Palate: rich, fine bitter notes, long, spicy.

BODEGAS SILVANO GARCÍA

Avda. de Murcia, 29
30520 Jumilla (Murcia)
☎: +34 968 780 767 - Fax: +34 968 916 125
bodegas@silvanogarcia.com
www.silvanogarcia.com

VIÑAHONDA 2010 B
macabeo.

88 Colour: bright straw. Nose: powerfull, ripe fruit, citrus fruit, tropical fruit. Palate: flavourful, fleshy, fruity.

SILVANO GARCÍA MOSCATEL 2009 B
moscatel.

90 Color golden. Aroma powerfull, floral, honeyed notes, candied fruit, fragrant herbs. Taste flavourful, sweet, fresh, fruity, good acidity, long.

VIÑAHONDA 2010 RD
monastrell.

84 Colour: coppery red. Nose: candied fruit, powerfull. Palate: powerful, sweetness, fleshy.

SILVANO GARCÍA DULCE MONASTRELL 2009 T
monastrell.

87 Colour: cherry, purple rim. Nose: aromatic coffee, sweet spices, pattiserie, dried fruit. Palate: spicy, unctuous, sweetness.

VIÑAHONDA 2007 TC
monastrell, tempranillo, cabernet sauvignon.

85 Colour: cherry, garnet rim. Nose: ripe fruit, spicy, creamy oak, toasty. Palate: powerful, flavourful, toasty.

BODEGAS SIMÓN

Madrid, 15
02653 Albatana (Albacete)
☎: +34 967 323 340 - Fax: +34 967 323 340
info@bodegassimon.com
www.bodegassimon.com

GALÁN DEL SIGLO MONASTRELL SYRAH 2009 T
60% monastrell, 40% syrah.

84 Colour: cherry, garnet rim. Nose: ripe fruit, spicy, complex. Palate: powerful, easy to drink.

GALÁN DEL SIGLO PETIT VERDOT 2008 T
100% petit verdot.

87 Colour: bright cherry. Nose: sweet spices, expressive, ripe fruit. Palate: flavourful, fruity, toasty, round tannins.

BODEGAS VIÑA ELENA

Estrecho de Marín, s/n
30520 Jumilla (Murcia)
☎: +34 968 781 340 - Fax: +34 968 435 275
info@vinaelena.com
www.vinaelena.com

PACHECO 2010 T
monastrell.

90 Colour: cherry, purple rim. Nose: red berry notes, fresh fruit. Palate: flavourful, fruity, good acidity, round tannins.

FAMILIA PACHECO 2009 T ROBLE
monastrell, cabernet sauvignon, syrah.

88 Colour: bright cherry. Nose: sweet spices, creamy oak, overripe fruit. Palate: flavourful, fruity, toasty, round tannins.

FAMILIA PACHECO CUVÉE ELENA 2009 T
cabernet sauvignon, monastrell.

88 Color bright cherry. Aroma ripe fruit, sweet spices, creamy oak, expressive. Taste flavourful, fruity, toasty, round tannins.

LOS CUCOS DE LA ALBERQUILLA 2009 T
cabernet sauvignon.

88 Color bright cherry. Aroma ripe fruit, sweet spices, creamy oak, expressive. Taste flavourful, fruity, toasty, round tannins.

FAMILIA PACHECO SELECCIÓN 2008 T
monastrell, cabernet sauvignon, syrah.

91 Color cherry, garnet rim. Aroma ripe fruit, spicy, creamy oak, toasty, complex. Taste powerful, flavourful, toasty, round tannins.

BODEGAS VOLVER

Pza. de Grecia, 1
45005 Toledo (Toledo)
☎: +34 690 818 509 - Fax: +34 976 852 764
rafa@bodegasvolver.com
www.orowines.com

WRONGO DONGO 2010 T
monastrell.

89 Colour: cherry, purple rim. Nose: red berry notes, raspberry, expressive. Palate: good acidity, balanced, fruity, flavourful.

BODEGAS Y VIÑEDOS CASA DE LA ERMITA

Ctra. El Carche, Km. 11,5
30520 Jumilla (Murcia)
☎: +34 968 783 035 - Fax: +34 968 716 063
bodega@casadelaermita.com
www.casadelaermita.com

CASA DE LA ERMITA 2010 B

87 Colour: bright straw. Nose: fresh, fresh fruit, white flowers. Palate: flavourful, fruity, good acidity, balanced.

CASA DE LA ERMITA 2010 B

82 Colour: bright straw. Nose: white flowers, candied fruit, citrus fruit. Palate: fruity, good acidity, sweetness.

MONASTERIO DE SANTA ANA MONASTRELL 2010 T
monastrell, tempranillo.

87 Colour: cherry, garnet rim. Nose: ripe fruit, spicy, creamy oak, toasty. Palate: powerful, flavourful, toasty, round tannins.

CASA DE LA ERMITA 2010 T ROBLE
monastrell, petit verdot.

87 Colour: bright cherry. Nose: fruit expression, toasty, sweet spices. Palate: flavourful, fruity, toasty, round tannins.

CASA DE LA ERMITA 2010 T
monastrell.

86 Colour: cherry, purple rim. Nose: floral, ripe fruit, fragrant herbs. Palate: flavourful, fruity, good acidity, round tannins.

CASA DE LA ERMITA 2008 TC
monastrell, syrah.

90 Color bright cherry. Aroma ripe fruit, sweet spices, creamy oak, expressive. Taste flavourful, fruity, toasty, round tannins.

IDÍLICO 2007 TC
monastrell, syrah.

88 Colour: bright cherry. Nose: sweet spices, creamy oak, expressive, overripe fruit, fragrant herbs. Palate: fruity, round tannins.

CASA DE LA ERMITA PETIT VERDOT 2007 T
petit verdot.

87 Colour: bright cherry. Nose: expressive, new oak, dark chocolate, ripe fruit. Palate: flavourful, fruity, toasty, round tannins.

CASA DE LA ERMITA 2007 TC

87 Colour: cherry, garnet rim. Nose: toasty, complex, fruit liqueur notes, scrubland. Palate: powerful, flavourful, toasty, round tannins.

CASA DE LA ERMITA DULCE MONASTRELL T
monastrell.

85 Colour: cherry, garnet rim. Nose: spicy, creamy oak, toasty, dried fruit. Palate: powerful, flavourful, toasty, round tannins, sweet.

CAMPOS DE RISCA

Avda. Diagonal, 590, 5 1
08021 Barcelona (Barcelona)
☎: +34 660 445 464
info@vinergia.com
www.vinergia.es

CAMPOS DE RISCA 2010 T
90% monastrell, 10% syrah.

87 Colour: cherry, purple rim. Nose: fresh fruit, red berry notes, scrubland. Palate: flavourful, fruity, good acidity, round tannins.

COOP. NTRA. SRA. DE LA ENCARNACIÓN

Avda. Guardia Civil, 106
02500 Tobarra (Albacete)
☎: +34 967 325 033 - Fax: +34 967 328 410
riberaalta.enolog@hotmail.com

RA RIBERA ALTA DEL MUNDO 2010 B
60% chardonnay, 40% moscatel.

85 Color bright straw. Aroma fresh, fresh fruit, white flowers, expressive. Taste flavourful, fruity, good acidity, balanced.

RA RIBERA ALTA DEL MUNDO SELECCIÓN 2009 T
100% monastrell.

85 Colour: bright cherry. Nose: sweet spices, creamy oak, expressive, overripe fruit. Palate: toasty, round tannins, fleshy.

RIBERA ALTA DEL MUNDO 2009 T
100% monastrell.

83 Colour: cherry, garnet rim. Nose: sweet spices, fresh, ripe fruit. Palate: fruity, toasty, easy to drink.

FINCA OMBLANCAS

Ctra. Jumilla-Ontur, Km. 3,3
30520 Jumilla (Murcia)
☎: +34 968 780 850 - Fax: +34 968 780 850
omblancas@fincaomblancas.com
www.fincaomblancas.com

OMBLANCAS DENUÑO SYRAH 2010 T
syrah.

90 Colour: cherry, purple rim. Nose: fresh fruit, red berry notes, floral, violet drops. Palate: flavourful, fruity, good acidity, round tannins.

GLM ESTRATEGIAS DE VINOS

Avda. Nuestra Señora de la Asunción, 42 Plt. 2
30520 Jumilla (Murcia)
☎: +34 968 781 855
gmartinez@vinocrapula.com

CÁRMINE 2009 T
monastrell, syrah.

91 Colour: cherry, purple rim. Nose: expressive, fresh fruit, red berry notes, floral. Palate: flavourful, fruity, good acidity, round tannins, round.

CRÁPULA 2009 T
85% monastrell, 15% otras.

90 Colour: bright cherry. Nose: sweet spices, creamy oak, expressive, red berry notes, fruit expression. Palate: flavourful, fruity, toasty, round tannins.

NDQ (NACIDO DEL QUORUM) 2009 T
monastrell, syrah.

85 Colour: black cherry. Nose: fruit preserve, warm, toasty, dark chocolate. Palate: powerful, flavourful, spicy, ripe fruit.

NDQ (NACIDO DEL QUORUM) 2008 T
monastrell, syrah.

88 Colour: dark-red cherry. Nose: fruit preserve, warm, characterful, tar, dark chocolate. Palate: powerful, concentrated, round tannins.

HACIENDA PINARES

San Juan Bautista, 18
02513 Santiago Tubarra (Albacete)
☎: +34 609 108 393
haciendapinar@gmail.com

HACIENDA PINARES 2010 T
syrah, monastrell.

87 Colour: cherry, garnet rim. Nose: pattiserie, aromatic coffee, sweet spices. Palate: spicy, creamy, flavourful.

HACIENDA PINARES 2009 T
monastrell.

85 Colour: bright cherry. Nose: ripe fruit, sweet spices, expressive. Palate: flavourful, fruity, toasty, round tannins.

HACIENDA PINARES PIE FRANCO 2008 T
syrah, monastrell.

88 Colour: bright cherry. Nose: sweet spices, overripe fruit, toasty, dark chocolate. Palate: flavourful, fruity, toasty, round tannins.

ORO WINES JUMILLA

Paraje de la Aragona
30520 Jumilla (Murcia)
☎: +34 968 435 022 - Fax: +34 968 716 051
info@orowines.com
www.orowines.com

ANIMIC 2010 B
moscatel.

90 Colour: bright straw. Nose: fresh, fresh fruit, white flowers, varietal. Palate: flavourful, fruity, good acidity, balanced.

COMOLOCO 2010 T
100% monastrell.

86 Colour: cherry, garnet rim. Nose: overripe fruit, varietal, expressive, spicy. Palate: flavourful, fleshy, complex, concentrated.

PEDRO LUIS MARTÍNEZ

Barrio Iglesias, 55
30520 Jumilla (Murcia)
☎: +34 968 780 142 - Fax: +34 968 716 256
plmsa@alceno.com
www.alceno.com

ALCEÑO 2010 B
macabeo, airén.

85 Colour: bright straw. Nose: fresh fruit, white flowers, medium intensity, floral. Palate: flavourful, fruity, good acidity, balanced.

ALCEÑO 2010 RD
monastrell, tempranillo, syrah.

86 Colour: rose, purple rim. Nose: ripe fruit, red berry notes, floral, expressive. Palate: fleshy, powerful, fruity, fresh, easy to drink.

ALCEÑO MONASTRELL 2010 T JOVEN
100% monastrell.

87 Colour: cherry, purple rim. Nose: expressive, fresh fruit, red berry notes, floral. Palate: flavourful, fruity, good acidity.

ALCEÑO 2010 T
monastrell, tempranillo, syrah.

85 Colour: cherry, purple rim. Nose: fresh fruit, red berry notes, fresh. Palate: flavourful, fruity, good acidity, easy to drink.

ALCEÑO SYRAH PREMIUM 2009 T
syrah, monastrell.

92 Colour: cherry, garnet rim. Nose: spicy, toasty, complex, mineral, ripe fruit, aged wood nuances. Palate: powerful, flavourful, toasty, round tannins.

ALCEÑO 4 MESES 2009 T ROBLE
monastrell, syrah.

91 Colour: bright cherry. Nose: ripe fruit, sweet spices, creamy oak, expressive, aromatic coffee. Palate: flavourful, fruity, toasty, round tannins.

ALCEÑO MONASTRELL 2009 T ROBLE
monastrell, syrah.

87 Colour: bright cherry. Nose: sweet spices, creamy oak, roasted coffee, ripe fruit. Palate: flavourful, fruity, toasty, round tannins.

ALCEÑO MONASTRELL 2008 T ROBLE
monastrell, syrah.

89 Colour: bright cherry, garnet rim. Nose: balanced, lactic notes, fruit liqueur notes. Palate: balanced, soft tannins, easy to drink.

ALCEÑO DULCE 2007 T
monastrell.

91 Colour: bright cherry. Nose: sweet spices, creamy oak, expressive, raspberry, fruit expression. Palate: flavourful, fruity, toasty, round tannins, sweet, concentrated.

ALCEÑO SELECCIÓN 2007 TC
monastrell, tempranillo, syrah.

86 Colour: cherry, garnet rim. Nose: creamy oak, toasty, characterful, overripe fruit. Palate: powerful, flavourful, toasty, round tannins.

ALCEÑO 12 MESES AUTOR 2006 T
monastrell.

90 Colour: cherry, garnet rim. Nose: ripe fruit, spicy, toasty, complex. Palate: powerful, flavourful, toasty, fleshy.

PROPIEDAD VITÍCOLA CASA CASTILLO

Ctra. Jumilla - Hellín, RM-428, Km. 8
30520 Jumilla (Murcia)
☎: +34 968 781 691 - Fax: +34 968 716 238
info@casacastillo.es
www.casacastillo.es

CASA CASTILLO MONASTRELL 2010 T
100% monastrell.

91 Colour: cherry, purple rim. Nose: red berry notes, floral, complex. Palate: flavourful, fruity, good acidity, round tannins.

VALTOSCA 2009 T
100% syrah.

94 Colour: bright cherry. Nose: sweet spices, creamy oak, expressive, red berry notes, fruit expression, mineral. Palate: flavourful, fruity, toasty, round tannins, long.

CASA CASTILLO PIE FRANCO 2008 T
100% monastrell.

95 Colour: cherry, garnet rim. Nose: spicy, toasty, complex, earthy notes, fruit expression. Palate: powerful, flavourful, toasty, round tannins, long, elegant.

LAS GRAVAS 2008 T
80% monastrell, 10% syrah, 10% garnacha.

93 Colour: deep cherry. Nose: earthy notes, mineral, ripe fruit, spicy, aromatic coffee, complex. Palate: flavourful, spicy, ripe fruit, long.

RED BOTTLE INTERNATIONAL

Rosales, 6
09400 Aranda de Duero (Burgos)
☎: +34 947 515 884 - Fax: +34 947 515 886
rbi@redbottleint.com

CASPER 2008 T BARRICA
100% monastrell.

87 Color cherry, garnet rim. Aroma ripe fruit, spicy, creamy oak, toasty, complex. Taste powerful, flavourful, toasty, round tannins.

VIÑAS DE LA CASA DEL RICO

Poeta Andrés Bolarin, 1- 5ºB
30011 Murcia (Murcia)
☎: +34 639 957 687
vino@gorgocil.com
www.casadelrico.com

GORGOCIL TEMPRANILLO 2008 T
100% tempranillo.

93 Colour: bright cherry. Nose: sweet spices, creamy oak, expressive, red berry notes, fragrant herbs. Palate: flavourful, fruity, toasty, round tannins.

GORGOCIL MONASTRELL 2008 T
100% monastrell.

91 Color cherry, garnet rim. Aroma ripe fruit, spicy, creamy oak, toasty, complex. Taste powerful, flavourful, toasty, round tannins.

VIÑEDOS Y BODEGAS JM MARTÍNEZ VERDÚ

Valle Hoya de Torres
30520 Jumilla (Murcia)
☎: +34 968 756 240 - Fax: +34 968 756 240
info@xenysel.com
www.xenysel.com

XENYSEL 6 2009 T
monastrell.

84 Colour: bright cherry. Nose: sweet spices, fruit liqueur notes, roasted coffee. Palate: flavourful, fruity, toasty, round tannins.

XENYSEL PIE FRANCO 2009 T
monastrell.

83 Colour: cherry, purple rim. Nose: fresh fruit, red berry notes, floral. Palate: flavourful, fruity, round tannins.

CALZÁS PIE FRANCO 2008 T
monastrell.

89 Colour: bright cherry. Nose: sweet spices, creamy oak, overripe fruit. Palate: flavourful, fruity, toasty, round tannins.

XENYSEL 12 2008 T
monastrell.

85 Colour: cherry, garnet rim. Nose: balanced, fresh, ripe fruit. Palate: toasty, flavourful.

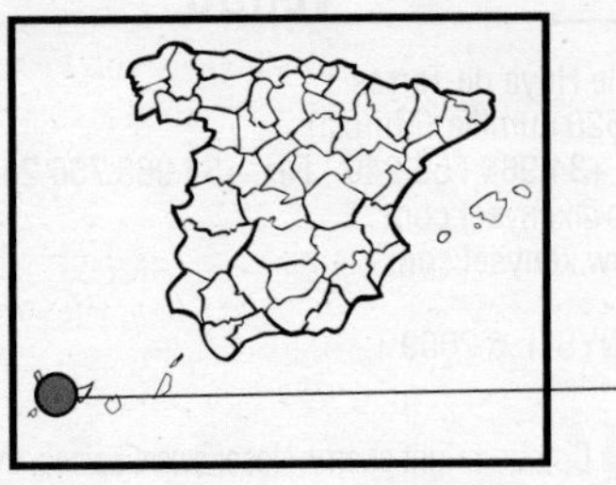

SAN SEBASTIÁN DE
LA GOMERA

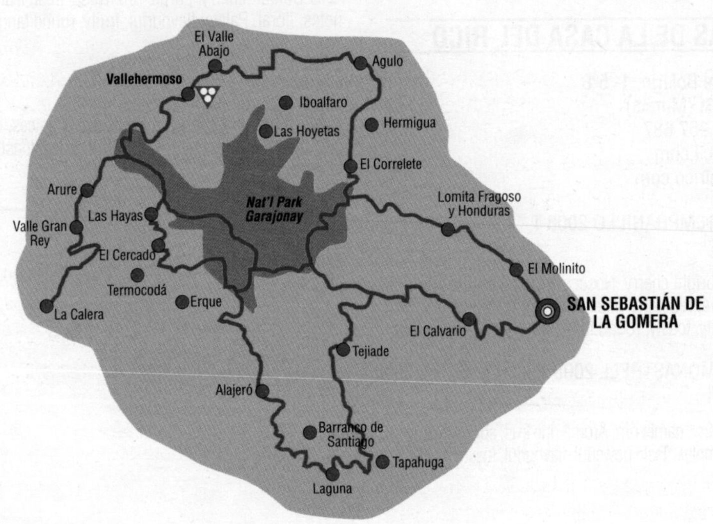
El Valle
Abajo
Vallehermoso
Agulo
Iboalfaro
Las Hoyetas
Hermigua
El Correlete
Nat'l Park
Garajonay
Arure
Las Hayas
Valle Gran
Rey
El Cercado
Termocodá
Erque
La Calera
Lomita Fragoso
y Honduras
El Molinito
SAN SEBASTIÁN DE
LA GOMERA
El Calvario
Tejiade
Alajeró
Barranco de
Santiago
Tapahuga
Laguna

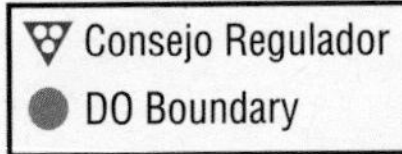
Consejo Regulador
DO Boundary

NEWS ABOUT THE VINTAGE:

Every three to four years our tasting team travels to that almost unknown wine territory of La Gomera, wines partial to a most traditional style faithfully modelled after the local taste, but certanly one that the modern global consumers would dislike. We know what they taste like and we know that there are no relevant names that would entice us to board the ferry from Tenerife to arrive (and that is surely the most exciting thing about the trip) to one of the most beautiful landscapes in the whole of the Canary Islands, with vineyards climbing up the hills until they reach the "wuthering" heights of Garajonay National Park. We do not want the reader to think that this may not be the most suitable territory to produce great wines. We are probably talking of a land destined to be in the future a "terroirists" paradise, full of a singularity equal to its landscape. Trade winds, mild temperatures and varied soils are there ready to be challenged and exploited. This year we did not make the trip to La Gomera, but the next one we will surely go there as part of our commitment to reflect in our Guide as many samples as possible from the vast map of Spanish wine regions.

LOCATION:

The majority of the vineyards are found in the north of the island, in the vicinity of the towns of Vallehermoso (some 385 Ha) and Hermigua. The remaining vineyards are spread out over Agulo, Valle Gran Rey –near the capital city of La Gomera, San Sebastián– and Alajeró, on the slopes of the Garajonay peak.

CLIMATE:

The island benefits from a subtropical climate together with, as one approaches the higher altitudes of the Garajonay peak, a phenomenon of permanent humidity known as 'mar de nubes' (sea of clouds) caused by the trade winds. This humid air from the north collides with the mountain range, thereby creating a kind of horizontal rain resulting in a specific ecosystem made up of luxuriant valleys. The average temperature is 20°C all year round.

SOIL:

The most common soil in the higher mountain regions is deep and clayey, while, as one approaches lower altitudes towards the scrubland, the soil is more Mediterranean with a good many stones and terraces similar to those of the Priorat.

GRAPE VARIETIES:

WHITE: *Forastera* (90%), *Gomera Blanca, Listán Blanca, Marmajuelo, Malvasía* and *Pedro Ximenez.*
RED: *Listán Negra* (5%), *Negramoll* (2%);
Experimental: *Tintilla Castellana, Cabernet Sauvignon* and *Rubí Cabernet.*

FIGURES:

Vineyard surface: 125 – **Wine-Growers:** 220 – **Wineries:** 13 – **2010 Harvest rating:** -- – **Production:** -- – **Market percentages:** 96% domestic. 4% export

CONSEJO REGULADOR
Avda. Guillermo Ascanio,16, 1º
Vallehermoso 38840 La Gomera
☎: +34 922 800 801 - Fax: +34 922 801 146
@ crdolagomera@mixmail.com
www.vinosdelagomera.es

GENERAL CHARACTERISTICS OF THE WINES

WHITES	Almost all the wines are based on the *Forastera*, and are produced according to traditional methods: they are usually a little overripe and have rustic and warm notes. The best examples are from the higher and less humid areas, with wild and scrubland notes.
REDS	The warm climate leaves its mark on most of the young red wines of the island, with a somewhat sweet taste with balsamic notes. The greenness that can be seen in many of them is the result of the high production that on occasions the varietal pattern of the *Listán Negra* and the *Negramoll* have, from which they are produced.

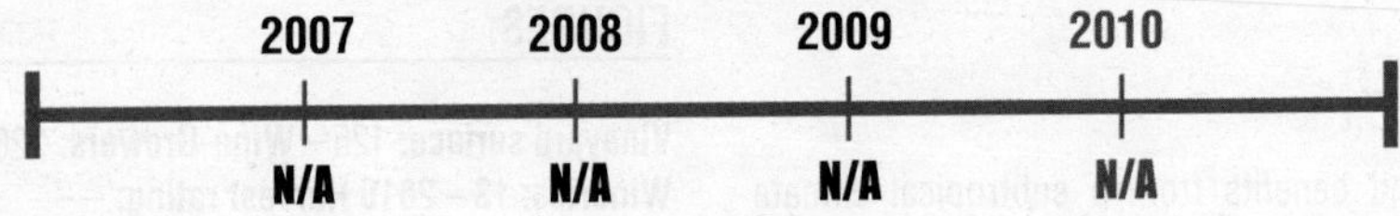

NEWS ABOUT THE VINTAGE:

The wines from La Mancha are not foreign to the deep changes that are happening in the market of wines of medium to low quality, a market niche where this giant wine region truly exerts a –at least– numeric hegemony. Changes come as a result of the investment in technology that most of the region's producers have undertaken in the last few years. Nevertheless, premium wines from La Mancha do not seem to be going places, probably because it might not be worth the while to produce a high-flying and expensive wine when the back label will betray its origin.

We have also been witness to how the local producers did not back their local white variety, *airén*, going instead for the available catalogue of foreign grapes, something slightly similar to what has happened with *cencibel* –the local clone or adaptation of the *tempranillo*– which is present on the labels but not in the vineyard; it seems the time has come for "white baits" for *verdejo* and *sauvignon blanc*, particularly attractive to producers with a foreign-market prospect set in their minds. The problem is that those plantings are still recent, and it is early to show greatness. Just the opposite happens with *macabeo*, whose old vines are able to render fruit and wines of real stature. As for the 2010 vintage, red wines show in better shape, given that the year was cooler than average, particularly in early grapes such as *tempranillo* and *syrah* that struggle to avoid overripeness in hotter vintages. We would like to mention the "Estola" type of wine, a traditional brand and, to our view, a model that –although still improvable– conveys a lot of singularity and "manchego" character. We even thing the region should think of using again the traditional "tinaja" (earthenware vessel) as a way to gain singularity, as long as the producers stick to more modern winemaking techniques for everything else.

The total vineyard surface of the DO has decreased 5,12 %, which means some 9.163 hectares less, mainly through subsidized uprooting in the last three years, and a serious decrease in the number of growers: the absence of exploitation profits and the ageing of the growers population are doing away with this traditional sector. *Airén* has been the grape variety most affected by subsidized uprooting, losing more than 8% of its total surface, although it is still the most planted variety in La Mancha with some 122.700 hectares. On the other hand, grape varieties foreign to this wine region like *pedro ximénez* or *gewürztraminer* have increased their plantings, with the prospect in mind of increasing exports.

LOCATION:

On the southern plateau in the provinces of Albacete, Ciudad Real, Cuenca and Toledo. It is the largest wine-growing region in Spain and in the world.

CLIMATE:

Extreme continental, with temperatures ranging between 40/45°C in summer and –10/12°C in winter. Rather low rainfall, with an average of about 375 mm per year.

SOIL:

The terrain is flat and the vineyards are situated at an altitude of about 700 m above sea level. The soil is generally sandy, limy and clayey.

GRAPE VARIETIES:

WHITE: *Airén* (majority), *Macabeo, Pardilla, Chardonnay, Sauvignon Blanc, Verdejo, Moscatel de Grano Menudo, Gewürztraminer, Parellada, Pero Ximénez, Riesling* and *Torrontés.*
RED: *Cencibel* (majority amongst red varieties), *Garnacha, Moravia, Cabernet Sauvignon, Merlot, Syrah, Cabernet Franc, Graciano, Malbec, Mencía, Monastrell, Pinot Noir, Petit Verdot* and *Bobal.*

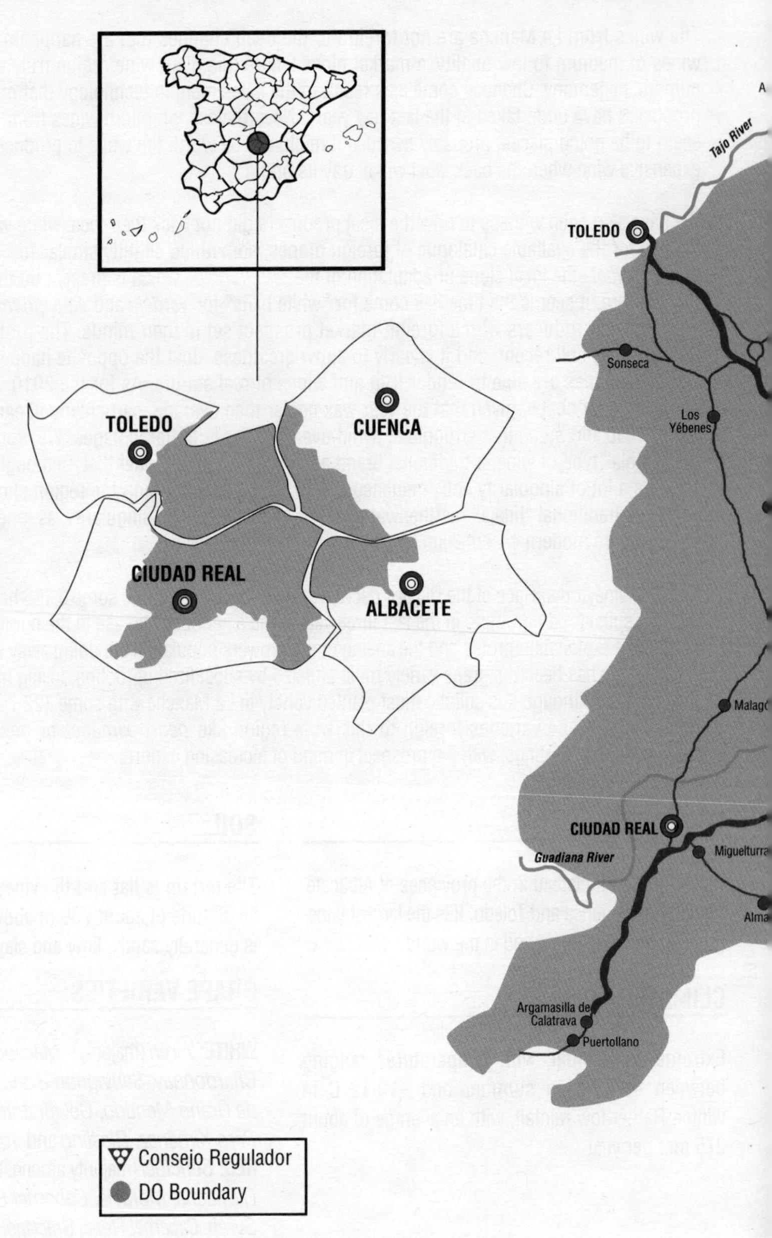
TOLEDO
CUENCA
CIUDAD REAL
ALBACETE
Consejo Regulador
DO Boundary
Tajo River
TOLEDO
Sonseca
Los Yébenes
Malagó
CIUDAD REAL
Guadiana River
Miguelturra
Alma
Argamasilla de Calatrava
Puertollano

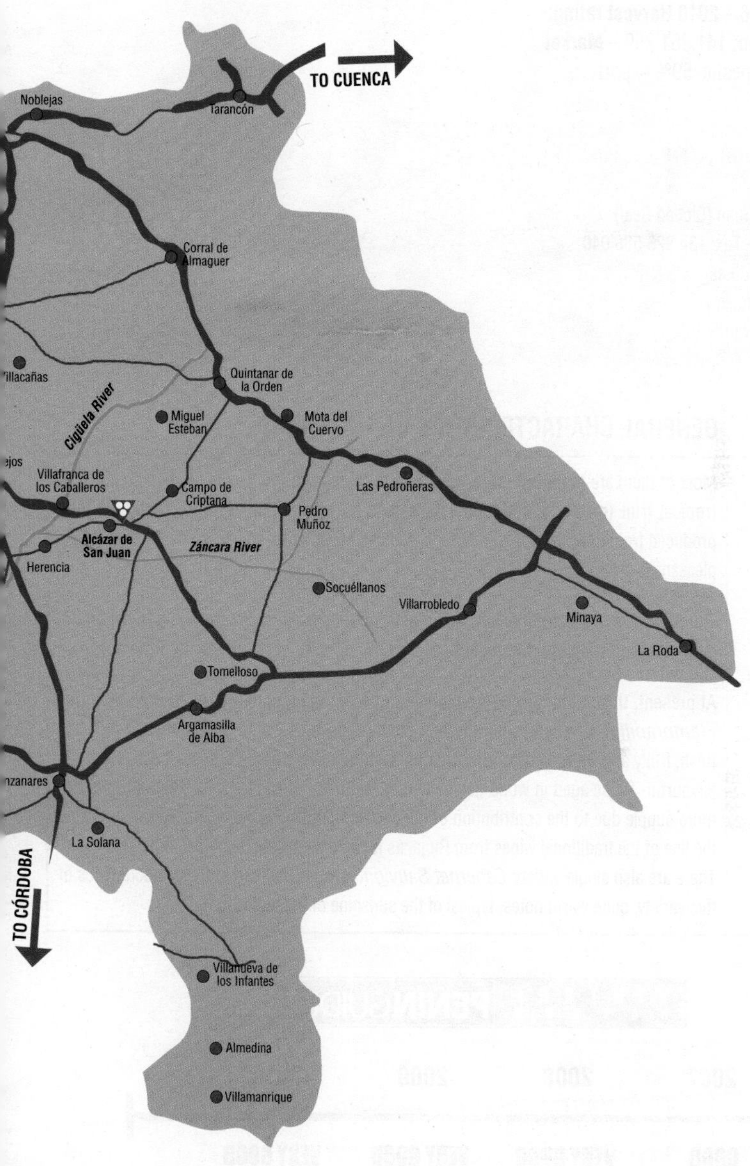
TO CUENCA
Noblejas
Tarancón
Corral de Almaguer
Quintanar de la Orden
Cigüela River
Miguel Esteban
Mota del Cuervo
Villafranca de los Caballeros
Campo de Criptana
Las Pedroñeras
Pedro Muñoz
Alcázar de San Juan
Herencia
Záncara River
Socuéllanos
Villarrobledo
Minaya
La Roda
Tomelloso
Argamasilla de Alba
La Solana
TO CÓRDOBA
Villanueva de los Infantes
Almedina
Villamanrique

FIGURES:

Vineyard surface: 169,900 – **Wine-Growers:** 18,067 – **Wineries:** 256 – **2010 Harvest rating:** Very Good – **Production:** 141,361,259 – **Market percentages:** 41% domestic. 59% export

CONSEJO REGULADOR
Avda. de Criptana, 73
13600 Alcázar de San Juan (Ciudad Real)
☎: +34 926 541 523 - Fax: +34 926 588 040
@ consejo@lamanchado.es
@ prensa@lamanchado.es
www.lamanchawines.com

GENERAL CHARACTERISTICS OF THE WINES

WHITES	Most of them are produced from Airén; they are fresh and fruity, sometimes with notes of tropical fruit (melon, banana, pineapple) and somewhat limited on the palate. Those produced from *Macabeo* are a bit more balanced and intense, and are fruity, fresh and very pleasant to drink.
ROSÉS	The colour can range from onion skin to pink; on the nose they are fresh and fruity; on the palate they are supple and very light.
REDS	At present, this is the type of the highest quality in the region. Based on the *Cencibel* (*Tempranillo*), one can especially find young red wines with a good colour, which are fresh, fruity and with a varietal character on the nose; on the palate they are meaty and quite flavourful. Those aged in wood generally maintain these characteristics, although they are more supple due to the contribution of the barrel. The Reservas and Gran Reservas follow the line of the traditional wines from Rioja, as far as the conception of their ageing. There are also single variety *Cabernet Sauvignon* wines that add to the characteristics of this variety, quite warm notes, typical of the sunshine of the region.

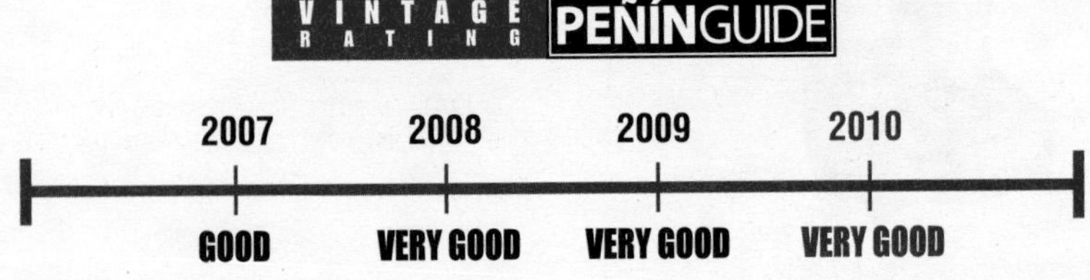

ALEJANDRO FERNÁNDEZ TINTO PESQUERA "EL VINCULO"

Avda. Juan Carlos, s/n
13610 Campo de Criptana (Ciudad Real)
☎: +34 926 563 709 - Fax: +34 926 563 709
elvinculo@elvinculo.com
www.grupopesquera.com

EL VÍNCULO 2005 TR
tempranillo.

89 Colour: dark-red cherry. Nose: powerfull, warm, toasty, cocoa bean, dark chocolate. Palate: powerful, spicy, fine bitter notes.

AMADIS DE YÉBENES

Jardín, 58
45830 Miguel Esteban (Toledo)
☎: +34 925 172 730 - Fax: +34 925 172 730
info@becay.es
www.becay.es

AMADIS DE YÉBENES 2007 TC
syrah, cencibel.

87 Colour: cherry, garnet rim. Nose: ripe fruit, spicy. Palate: powerful, flavourful, toasty, round tannins, great length.

BODEGA CENTRO ESPAÑOLAS

Ctra. Alcázar, s/n
13700 Tomelloso (Ciudad Real)
☎: +34 926 505 654 - Fax: +34 926 505 652
allozo@allozo.com
www.allozo.com

ALLOZO VERDEJO 2010 B
100% verdejo.

86 Colour: bright straw. Nose: balanced, fresh fruit, varietal, wild herbs. Palate: flavourful, fruity, great length, easy to drink.

ALLOZO MACABEO 2010 B
100% macabeo.

84 Colour: bright straw. Nose: fresh, citrus fruit, medium intensity. Palate: fresh, fruity, flavourful.

ALLOZO 2010 RD
100% tempranillo.

81 Colour: raspberry rose. Nose: ripe fruit, short. Palate: easy to drink, light-bodied, flavourful.

LADERO SELECCIÓN 2010 T
tempranillo.

87 Colour: very deep cherry, purple rim. Nose: fresh fruit, grassy. Palate: correct, fruity, flavourful.

ALLOZO FINCA LOS FRAILES CABERNET 2010 T
100% cabernet sauvignon.

86 Colour: cherry, purple rim. Nose: red berry notes, ripe fruit. Palate: round tannins, fruity, easy to drink.

ALLOZO FINCA DE LA FUENTE 2010 T
100% tempranillo.

86 Colour: deep cherry, garnet rim. Nose: ripe fruit, medium intensity. Palate: flavourful, fruity, round tannins.

ALLOZO SHYRAZ DE FINCA DE LA RAMA 2010 T
100% syrah.

83 Colour: cherry, purple rim. Nose: warm, herbaceous, fresh. Palate: fruity, light-bodied, easy to drink.

ALLOZO MERLOT DE FINCA LOMA DE LOS FRAILES 2010 T
100% merlot.

82 Colour: purple rim. Nose: fresh, slightly evolved, fresh fruit. Palate: light-bodied, flavourful, easy to drink.

ALLOZO 927 2008 T
tempranillo, merlot, syrah.

88 Colour: cherry, garnet rim. Nose: ripe fruit, balanced, spicy. Palate: good structure, fine bitter notes, round tannins.

LADERO MERLOT 2008 T
100% merlot.

84 Colour: deep cherry, garnet rim. Nose: ripe fruit, premature reduction notes, spicy. Palate: ripe fruit, powerful.

ALLOZO 2007 TC
100% tempranillo.

86 Colour: cherry, garnet rim. Nose: red berry notes, ripe fruit, spicy. Palate: flavourful, fruity, balanced.

ALLOZO 2004 TR
100% tempranillo.

86 Colour: cherry, garnet rim. Nose: ripe fruit, warm, powerfull, spicy. Palate: good structure, fruity, flavourful.

ALLOZO 2003 TGR
tempranillo.

86 Colour: light cherry, orangey edge. Nose: ripe fruit, old leather. Palate: flavourful, spicy, fine tannins.

BODEGA LA TERCIA-VINOS ECOLÓGICOS

Pl. Santa Quiteria, 12
13600 Alcázar de San Juan (Ciudad Real)
☎: +34 926 541 512 - Fax: +34 926 550 104
bodegalatercia@gmail.com
www.bodegalatercia.com

YEMANUEVA AIRÉN ECOLÓGICO 2010 B
100% airén.

78

YEMANUEVA TEMPRANILLO ECOLÓGICO 2009 T
100% tempranillo.

85 Colour: cherry, garnet rim. Nose: red berry notes, balanced, fresh. Palate: fruity, flavourful, easy to drink, good finish.

YEMASERENA TEMPRANILLO SELECCIÓN LIMITADA 2006 T
100% tempranillo.

86 Color bright cherry. Aroma ripe fruit, sweet spices, creamy oak, expressive. Taste flavourful, fruity, toasty, round tannins.

BODEGA Y VIÑAS ALDOBA

Ctra. Alcázar, s/n
13700 Tomelloso (Ciudad Real)
☎: +34 926 505 653 - Fax: +34 926 505 652
aldoba@allozo.com

ALDOBA 2010 B
100% macabeo.

79

ALDOBA 2010 T
100% tempranillo.

84 Colour: cherry, purple rim. Nose: fresh fruit, floral, fresh. Palate: fruity, good acidity, easy to drink.

ALDOBA 2006 TC
100% tempranillo.

86 Colour: cherry, garnet rim. Nose: ripe fruit, spicy. Palate: powerful, flavourful, toasty, round tannins, fruity aftestaste.

ALDOBA 2005 TR
100% tempranillo.

89 Color cherry, garnet rim. Aroma ripe fruit, spicy, creamy oak, toasty, complex. Taste powerful, flavourful, toasty, round tannins.

BODEGAS ALCARDET

Mayor, 130
45810 Villanueva de Alcardete (Toledo)
☎: +34 925 166 375 - Fax: +34 925 166 611
alcardet@terra.es
www.alcardet.com

GRUMIER 2010 T
syrah, tempranillo.

87 Colour: rose, purple rim. Nose: red berry notes, floral, lactic notes, fresh. Palate: powerful, flavourful, fruity, fresh.

ALCARDET ESP RESERVA

80 Colour: bright yellow. Nose: lees reduction notes, ripe fruit, faded flowers, sweet spices, aged wood nuances. Palate: flavourful, fleshy, thin.

BODEGAS AYUSO

Miguel Caro, 6
02600 Villarrobledo (Albacete)
☎: +34 967 140 458 - Fax: +34 967 144 925
comercial@bodegasayuso.es
www.bodegasayuso.es

ESTOLA VERDEJO 2010 B
100% verdejo.

86 Colour: bright straw. Nose: citrus fruit, tropical fruit, expressive. Palate: fresh, flavourful, fruity.

ARMIÑO 2010 B
100% airén.

84 Colour: bright straw. Nose: fresh, candied fruit, floral. Palate: easy to drink, sweetness, flavourful.

FINCA LOS AZARES SAUVIGNON BLANC 2010 B
100% sauvignon blanc.

84 Colour: bright straw. Nose: medium intensity, wild herbs, floral. Palate: balanced, correct.

CASTILLO DE BENIZAR MACABEO 2010 B
100% macabeo.

83 Colour: bright straw. Nose: floral, fresh, medium intensity. Palate: light-bodied, fresh.

ESTOLA 2009 BFB
80% airén, 20% chardonnay.

86 Colour: golden. Nose: ripe fruit, creamy oak, sweet spices. Palate: full, flavourful, fleshy.

CASTILLO DE BENIZAR CABERNET SAUVIGNON 2010 RD
100% cabernet sauvignon.

82 Colour: light cherry. Nose: medium intensity, grassy. Palate: correct, easy to drink.

CASTILLO DE BENIZAR TEMPRANILLO 2009 T JOVEN
100% tempranillo.

85 Colour: cherry, garnet rim. Nose: fresh fruit, red berry notes, neat. Palate: light-bodied, fruity, flavourful.

ESTOLA 2007 TC
100% tempranillo.

85 Colour: cherry, garnet rim. Nose: red berry notes, expressive, toasty. Palate: good acidity, fruity, flavourful, balsamic.

ESTOLA 2006 TR
75% tempranillo, 25% cabernet sauvignon.

85 Colour: cherry, garnet rim. Nose: ripe fruit, spicy, toasty, old leather. Palate: powerful, flavourful, toasty, round tannins.

FINCA LOS AZARES PETIT VERDOT 2005 T
100% petit verdot.

86 Colour: bright cherry, brick rim edge. Nose: spicy, aromatic coffee, creamy oak. Palate: round tannins, spicy, light-bodied, toasty.

FINCA LOS AZARES 2004 T
50% cabernet sauvignon, 50% merlot.

85 Colour: pale ruby, brick rim edge. Nose: tobacco, old leather, expressive, spicy. Palate: spicy, balsamic, toasty.

ESTOLA 1999 TGR
65% tempranillo, 35% cabernet sauvignon.

84 Colour: bright cherry, orangey edge. Nose: cocoa bean, sweet spices, toasty. Palate: light-bodied, long, round tannins.

BODEGAS BONJORNE

Ctra. La Roda Muntra, Km. 2.3
02630 La Roda (Albacete)
☎: +34 967 601 754 - Fax: +34 967 601 754
export@bonjorne.es
www.bonjorne.es

VIRIDIS BR
macabeo, sauvignon blanc.

84 Colour: bright golden. Nose: lees reduction notes, ripe fruit, sweet spices, pattiserie. Palate: ripe fruit, flavourful, thin.

BODEGAS CAMPOS REALES

Castilla La Mancha, 4
16670 El Provencio (Cuenca)
☎: +34 967 166 066 - Fax: +34 967 165 032
info@bodegascamposreales.com
www.bodegascamposreales.com

CANFORRALES ALMA VERDEJO 2010 B
verdejo.

85 Colour: bright straw. Nose: citrus fruit, tropical fruit, expressive. Palate: balanced, good acidity, fruity.

GLADIUM VIÑAS VIEJAS 2008 TC
tempranillo.

93 Colour: cherry, garnet rim. Nose: spicy, creamy oak, toasty, complex, powerfull, ripe fruit. Palate: powerful, flavourful, toasty, round tannins.

CANFORRALES CLÁSICO TEMPRANILLO 2010 T
tempranillo.

87 Color cherry, purple rim. Aroma expressive, fresh fruit, red berry notes, floral. Taste flavourful, fruity, good acidity, round tannins.

GLADIUM 2009 TC
tempranillo.

89 Color bright cherry. Aroma ripe fruit, sweet spices, creamy oak, expressive. Taste flavourful, fruity, toasty, round tannins.

CANFORRALES SYRAH 2009 T ROBLE
syrah.

86 Colour: cherry, purple rim. Nose: sweet spices, balsamic herbs, red berry notes. Palate: toasty, flavourful, correct.

CANFORRALES SELECCIÓN 2009 T
tempranillo.

85 Colour: cherry, garnet rim. Nose: toasty, spicy, ripe fruit. Palate: spicy, flavourful, long.

GLADIUM 2008 TC
tempranillo.

89 Colour: bright cherry. Nose: sweet spices, creamy oak, ripe fruit, red berry notes. Palate: flavourful, fruity, toasty, round tannins.

CÁNFORA 2006 T
tempranillo.

92 Colour: cherry, garnet rim. Nose: complex, ripe fruit, cocoa bean, sweet spices, expressive. Palate: powerful, fruity, concentrated, complex.

BODEGAS CASA ANTONETE

Barrio San José, s/n
02100 Tarazona de la Mancha (Albacete)
☎: +34 967 480 074 - Fax: +34 967 480 294
launion@casaantonete.com
www.casaantonete.com

NÉGORA CHARDONNAY 2010 B
100% chardonnay.

85 Colour: bright straw. Nose: tropical fruit, citrus fruit, fresh. Palate: light-bodied, fruity, fresh.

NÉGORA VERDEJO 2010 B
100% verdejo.

85 Colour: bright straw. Nose: floral, citrus fruit, expressive. Palate: good acidity, light-bodied, flavourful.

CASA ANTONETE MACABEO 2010 B
macabeo.

82 Colour: bright straw. Nose: slightly evolved, wild herbs. Palate: flavourful, fine bitter notes.

CASA ANTONETE 2010 RD
100% cencibel.

82 Colour: light cherry. Nose: slightly evolved. Palate: flavourful, fruity, good finish.

CASA ANTONETE TEMPRANILLO 2010 T
100% cencibel.

83 Colour: cherry, garnet rim. Nose: warm, fruit preserve. Palate: flavourful, fruity, great length.

NÉGORA CABERNET 2006 T
cabernet sauvignon.

85 Colour: cherry, garnet rim. Nose: spicy, warm, candied fruit. Palate: powerful, concentrated, toasty, round tannins.

CASA ANTONETE CENCIBEL 2005 TC
100% cencibel.

84 Colour: pale ruby, brick rim edge. Nose: tobacco, overripe fruit, roasted coffee. Palate: good acidity, slightly evolved, fresh.

NÉGORA MERLOT 2005 T
100% merlot.

78

CASA ANTONETE CENCIBEL 2004 TR
100% cencibel.

86 Colour: dark-red cherry, orangey edge. Nose: spicy, fine reductive notes, fruit liqueur notes. Palate: spicy, long.

BODEGAS CRISTO DE LA VEGA

General Goded, 6
13630 Socuéllamos (Ciudad Real)
☎: +34 926 530 388 - Fax: +34 926 530 024
comercial@bodegascrisve.com
www.bodegascrisve.com

EL YUGO AIRÉN 2010 B
airén.

84 Colour: bright straw. Nose: white flowers, fruit expression. Palate: flavourful, fruity, good acidity, good finish.

EL YUGO 2010 T
tempranillo, syrah, merlot.

87 Colour: cherry, purple rim. Nose: medium intensity, red berry notes, fresh. Palate: fruity, good structure, balanced, good acidity.

EL YUGO 2006 TC
100% tempranillo.

86 Colour: cherry, garnet rim. Nose: expressive, red berry notes, creamy oak. Palate: flavourful, fruity, good acidity, round tannins.

EL YUGO 2005 TR
tempranillo.

87 Colour: cherry, garnet rim. Nose: ripe fruit, toasty, complex, sweet spices. Palate: powerful, flavourful, toasty, round tannins, fleshy.

BODEGAS ENTREMONTES (NUESTRA SEÑORA DE LA PIEDAD)

Circunvalación, s/n
45800 Quintanar de la Orden (Toledo)
☎: +34 925 180 930 - Fax: +34 925 180 480
comercial@bodegasentremontes.com

CLAVELITO AIRÉN 2010 B
100% airén.

83 Colour: bright straw. Nose: grassy, fresh, medium intensity. Palate: easy to drink, flavourful.

CLAVELITO MACABEO 2010 B
100% macabeo.

81 Colour: bright straw. Nose: fresh, grassy, short. Palate: fresh, light-bodied, short.

CLAVELITO VERDEJO 2010 B
100% verdejo.

80 Colour: bright straw. Nose: fresh, grassy, medium intensity. Palate: light-bodied, fresh, lacks expression.

CLAVELITO SAUVIGNON BLANC 2010 B
100% sauvignon blanc.

76

CLAVELITO 2010 RD
100% tempranillo.

82 Colour: light cherry. Nose: medium intensity, red berry notes, ripe fruit. Palate: correct, fine bitter notes.

ENTREMONTES SYRAH 2010 T
100% syrah.

86 Colour: cherry, purple rim. Nose: balanced, medium intensity, fruit expression. Palate: easy to drink, good finish.

ENTREMONTES TEMPRANILLO 2010 T
100% tempranillo.

83 Colour: cherry, garnet rim. Nose: ripe fruit, medium intensity. Palate: fruity, good finish.

ENTREMONTES GARNACHA 2010 T
100% garnacha.

82 Colour: cherry, purple rim. Nose: ripe fruit, medium intensity. Palate: flavourful, good finish.

ENTREMONTES CABERNET SAUVIGNON 2010 T
100% cabernet sauvignon.

79

ENTREMONTES 2007 T ROBLE
100% tempranillo.

85 Colour: bright cherry. Nose: ripe fruit, sweet spices, creamy oak. Palate: flavourful, fruity, toasty, round tannins.

ENTREMONTES 2005 TC
100% tempranillo.

83 Colour: bright cherry, garnet rim. Nose: old leather, toasty, spicy. Palate: spicy, balsamic, flavourful.

ENTREMONTES 2002 TR
100% tempranillo.

86 Colour: cherry, garnet rim. Nose: fine reductive notes, old leather, candied fruit. Palate: flavourful, spicy, balanced.

ENTREMONTES 2002 TGR
100% tempranillo.

84 Colour: cherry, garnet rim. Nose: spicy, wet leather, fruit liqueur notes. Palate: spicy, long.

ENTREMONTES BN
60% macabeo, 40% verdejo.

82 Colour: bright yellow. Nose: ripe fruit, warm. Palate: light-bodied, easy to drink, good finish.

ENTREMONTES S/C SS
100% airén.

83 Colour: bright straw. Nose: pattiserie, sweet spices, fresh. Palate: sweetness, fruity, flavourful.

BODEGAS HERMANOS RUBIO

Ctra. de Villamuelas, s/n
45740 Villasequilla (Toledo)
☎: +34 925 310 284 - Fax: +34 925 325 133
info@bhrubio.com
www.bhrubio.com

ZOCODOVER SELECCIÓN SAUVIGNON BLANC 2010 B
100% sauvignon blanc.

89 Colour: bright straw. Nose: tropical fruit, white flowers, fresh. Palate: good acidity, balanced, fruity, fleshy.

SEÑORÍO DE ZOCODOVER 2007 TC
tempranillo.

85 Colour: cherry, purple rim. Nose: floral, red berry notes, expressive. Palate: good acidity, fruity, flavourful.

SEÑORÍO DE ZOCODOVER 2005 TR
tempranillo.

85 Colour: cherry, garnet rim. Nose: ripe fruit, spicy, balanced. Palate: powerful, ripe fruit.

ZOCODOVER SELECCIÓN 2002 TC
tempranillo, cabernet sauvignon.

84 Colour: cherry, garnet rim. Nose: sweet spices, creamy oak, expressive, red berry notes. Palate: flavourful, fleshy, balsamic.

VEGA CEDRON 2001 TR
tempranillo.

86 Colour: cherry, garnet rim. Nose: red berry notes, expressive, spicy. Palate: spicy, good acidity, flavourful, fleshy.

ZOCODOVER SELECCIÓN 2001 TR
tempranillo, cabernet sauvignon.

85 Colour: pale ruby, brick rim edge. Nose: balanced, red berry notes, creamy oak, toasty. Palate: fruity, flavourful, round tannins.

BODEGAS ISLA

Nuestra Señora de la Paz, 9
13210 Villarta San Juan (Ciudad Real)
☎: +34 926 640 004 - Fax: +34 926 640 062
b.isla@terra.es
www.bodegasisla.com

ISLA ORO AIRÉN 2010 B
100% airén.

77

ISLA ORO GARNACHA 2010 RD
100% garnacha.

75

ISLA ORO TEMPRANILLO SYRAH MERLOT 2010 T
33% tempranillo, 33% syrah, 33% merlot.

79

ISLA ORO TEMPRANILLO 2010 T
100% tempranillo.

78

ISLA ORO TEMPRANILLO 2007 TC
tempranillo.

81 Colour: cherry, garnet rim. Nose: toasty, spicy, tobacco. Palate: ripe fruit, correct.

BODEGAS LA REMEDIADORA

Alfredo Atieza, 149-151
02630 La Roda (Albacete)
☎: +34 967 440 600 - Fax: +34 967 441 465
export@laremediadora.com
www.laremediadora.com

LA VILLA REAL MACABEO 2010 B
100% macabeo.

85 Colour: bright straw. Nose: medium intensity, fresh, wild herbs. Palate: flavourful, correct.

LA VILLA REAL MOSCATEL 2009 B
100% moscatel.

82 Colour: straw. Nose: jasmine, ripe fruit, medium intensity. Palate: easy to drink, good finish.

LA VILLA REAL VENDIMIA SELECCIONADA 2010 RD
100% tempranillo.

86 Colour: raspberry rose. Nose: medium intensity, red berry notes, floral. Palate: flavourful, fruity, easy to drink.

LA VILLA REAL VENDIMIA SELECCIONADA 2010 T
50% tempranillo, 50% syrah.

87 Colour: deep cherry, purple rim. Nose: red berry notes, grassy, fresh. Palate: fruity, flavourful, great length.

LA VILLA REAL 2008 TC
50% merlot, 50% cabernet sauvignon.

89 Color cherry, garnet rim. Aroma ripe fruit, spicy, creamy oak, toasty, complex. Taste powerful, flavourful, toasty, round tannins.

BODEGAS LAHOZ

Ctra. N-310, km. 108,5
13630 Socuéllamos (Ciudad Real)
☎: +34 926 699 083 - Fax: +34 926 514 929
info@bodegaslahoz.com
www.bodegaslahoz.com

VEGA CÓRCOLES SAUVIGNON BLANC 2010 B
100% sauvignon blanc.

87 Colour: bright straw. Nose: white flowers, fruit expression, fresh. Palate: fruity, flavourful, easy to drink.

VEGA CÓRCOLES AIRÉN 2010 B
100% airén.

83 Colour: bright straw. Nose: floral, tropical fruit, short. Palate: light-bodied, fresh.

VEGA CÓRCOLES 2010 RD
100% tempranillo.

85 Colour: brilliant rose. Nose: fresh fruit, red berry notes, medium intensity, grassy. Palate: correct, balanced, flavourful.

VEGA CÓRCOLES TEMPRANILLO 2010 T
100% tempranillo.

86 Color cherry, purple rim. Aroma expressive, fresh fruit, red berry notes, floral. Taste flavourful, fruity, good acidity, round tannins.

VEGA CÓRCOLES TEMPRANILLO 2007 T ROBLE
100% tempranillo.

86 Colour: cherry, garnet rim. Nose: spicy, creamy oak, ripe fruit. Palate: flavourful, fruity, great length.

BODEGAS MARTÍNEZ SÁEZ

Finca San José - Ctra. Barrax, km. 14,8
02600 Villarrobledo (Albacete)
☎: +34 967 443 088 - Fax: +34 967 440 204
avidal@bodegasmartinezsaez.es
www.bodegasmartinezsaez.es

VIÑA ORCE MACABEO 2010 B
macabeo.

84 Colour: bright straw. Nose: fresh, citrus fruit, tropical fruit. Palate: light-bodied, fresh.

VIÑA ORCE 2010 RD
merlot.

85 Colour: raspberry rose. Nose: fresh fruit, wild herbs. Palate: fruity, flavourful, easy to drink.

VIÑA ORCE SYRAH 2010 T
syrah.

80 Colour: cherry, purple rim. Nose: expressive, floral, balsamic herbs. Palate: flavourful, fruity, good acidity.

VIÑA ORCE 2007 TC
60% tempranillo, 40% cabernet sauvignon.

85 Colour: deep cherry, garnet rim. Nose: ripe fruit, slightly evolved, wild herbs. Palate: powerful, spicy.

VIÑA ORCE 2002 TR
60% cabernet sauvignon, 40% merlot.

83 Colour: cherry, garnet rim. Nose: fruit preserve, wet leather. Palate: fruity, flavourful.

VIÑA ORCE TINTO MERLOT-MERLOT T ROBLE
merlot.

80 Colour: cherry, purple rim. Nose: fruit preserve, herbaceous, medium intensity. Palate: spicy, balsamic.

VIÑA ESCAMEL S/C ESP

83 Colour: bright straw. Nose: medium intensity, floral, aged wood nuances, toasty. Palate: fresh, fruity, flavourful, good acidity.

BODEGAS NARANJO

Felipe II, 5
13150 Carrión de Calatrava (Ciudad Real)
☎: +34 926 814 155 - Fax: +34 926 815 335
info@bodegasnaranjo.com
www.bodegasnaranjo.com

VIÑA CUERVA AIRÉN 2010 B
100% airén.

86 Colour: bright straw. Nose: fresh, fresh fruit, white flowers, expressive. Palate: fruity, good acidity, balanced.

VIÑA CUERVA 2010 RD
100% tempranillo.

81 Colour: rose, purple rim. Nose: fresh fruit, neat, expressive. Palate: light-bodied, flavourful.

VIÑA CUERVA 2008 TC
100% tempranillo.

88 Colour: cherry, garnet rim. Nose: red berry notes, complex, creamy oak. Palate: balanced, fleshy, flavourful.

BODEGAS SAN ISIDRO DE PEDRO MUÑOZ

Ctra. El Toboso, 1
13620 Pedro Muñoz (Ciudad Real)
☎: +34 926 586 057 - Fax: +34 926 568 380
administracion@viacotos.com
www.viacotos.com

LA HIJUELA TEMPRANILLO 2009 T
100% tempranillo.

80 Colour: cherry, garnet rim. Nose: wild herbs, fruit liqueur notes, slightly evolved. Palate: easy to drink, light-bodied.

GRAN AMIGO SANCHO 2007 TC
100% tempranillo.

86 Colour: cherry, garnet rim. Nose: ripe fruit, spicy, toasty. Palate: powerful, flavourful, toasty, round tannins.

BODEGAS VERDÚGUEZ

Los Hinojosos, 1
45810 Villanueva de Alcardete (Toledo)
☎: +34 925 167 493 - Fax: +34 925 166 148
verduguez@bodegasverduguez.com
www.bodegasverduguez.com

PALACIOS REALES VERDEJO 2010 B
100% verdejo.

83 Colour: bright straw. Nose: tropical fruit, fresh, floral. Palate: fleshy, fruity, light-bodied.

VEREDA MAYOR TEMPRANILLO 2010 T
100% tempranillo.

87 Colour: deep cherry, purple rim. Nose: red berry notes, balanced, fruit expression. Palate: flavourful, fruity, good acidity.

IMPERIAL TOLEDO CABERNET SAUVIGNON 2010 T
100% cabernet sauvignon.

80 Colour: bright cherry, purple rim. Nose: grassy, slightly evolved, medium intensity. Palate: easy to drink.

PALACIOS REALES OAKED SELECTION 2009 T ROBLE
60% tempranillo, 20% syrah, 20% merlot.

87 Colour: cherry, garnet rim. Nose: ripe fruit, sweet spices. Palate: fruity, good structure, spicy, great length.

IMPERIAL TOLEDO OLD VINE SELECTION 2007 T
100% tempranillo.

84 Colour: cherry, garnet rim. Nose: aromatic coffee, spicy, roasted coffee. Palate: fleshy, balsamic, correct.

IMPERIAL TOLEDO 2005 TR
100% tempranillo.

85 Colour: cherry, garnet rim. Nose: ripe fruit, spicy, toasty. Palate: powerful, flavourful, toasty, round tannins.

BODEGAS VERUM

Juan Antonio López Ramírez, 4
13700 Tomelloso (Ciudad Real)
☎: +34 926 511 404 - Fax: +34 926 515 047
administracion@bodegasverum.com
www.bodegasverum.com

VERUM GRAN CUEVA S/C BN ESPUMOSO
100% chardonnay.

87 Colour: bright straw. Nose: ripe fruit, dry nuts, candied fruit. Palate: ripe fruit, fruity, toasty.

BODEGAS VOLVER

Pza. de Grecia, 1
45005 Toledo (Toledo)
☎: +34 690 818 509 - Fax: +34 976 852 764
rafa@bodegasvolver.com
www.orowines.com

PASO A PASO VERDEJO 2010 B
verdejo.

87 Colour: bright straw. Nose: citrus fruit, tropical fruit, fragrant herbs, fresh. Palate: correct, fresh, fruity, easy to drink.

PASO A PASO TEMPRANILLO 2010 T
100% tempranillo.

91 Colour: cherry, purple rim. Nose: fresh fruit, red berry notes, fresh, expressive. Palate: good acidity, balanced, fruity, flavourful, fleshy.

VOLVER 2009 T
100% tempranillo.

92 Colour: cherry, purple rim. Nose: red berry notes, lactic notes, cocoa bean, creamy oak. Palate: good acidity, balanced, flavourful, fleshy, creamy, round tannins.

BODEGAS Y VIÑEDOS BRO VALERO

Ctra. Las Mesas, Km. 11
02600 Villarrobledo (Albacete)
☎: +34 649 985 103 - Fax: +34 914 454 675
bodegas@brovalero.es
www.brovalero.es

BRO VALERO SYRAH 2008 T
syrah.

87 Colour: cherry, purple rim. Nose: sweet spices, cocoa bean, balsamic herbs. Palate: good acidity, flavourful, fleshy.

BRO VALERO CABERNET SAUVIGNON 2007 TC
cabernet sauvignon.

84 Colour: cherry, garnet rim. Nose: fruit preserve, wet leather, toasty. Palate: powerful, fruity.

BODEGAS Y VIÑEDOS LADERO

Ctra. Alcázar, s/n
13700 Tomelloso (Ciudad Real)
☎: +34 926 505 653 - Fax: +34 926 505 652
ladero@allozo.com

LADERO 2010 B
verdejo.

80 Colour: bright straw. Nose: ripe fruit, medium intensity. Palate: flavourful, good finish.

LADERO CABERNET 2008 T
cabernet sauvignon.

86 Colour: cherry, garnet rim. Nose: expressive, red berry notes, balsamic herbs. Palate: flavourful, fruity, good acidity.

LADERO SYRAH 2008 T
syrah.

85 Colour: cherry, garnet rim. Nose: fruit preserve, spicy. Palate: flavourful, correct, great length.

LADERO TEMPRANILLO 2007 T ROBLE
tempranillo.

87 Colour: cherry, garnet rim. Nose: balanced, ripe fruit, spicy. Palate: flavourful, fruity, good structure, round tannins.

LADERO 2006 TC
tempranillo.

87 Colour: bright cherry. Nose: ripe fruit, sweet spices, creamy oak, expressive. Palate: flavourful, fruity, toasty, easy to drink.

LADERO 2005 TR
tempranillo.

85 Colour: bright cherry, orangey edge. Nose: ripe fruit, roasted coffee, balanced. Palate: balsamic, good acidity, flavourful.

BODEGAS YUNTERO

Pol. Ind. s/n, Ctra. Alcázar de San Juan
13200 Manzanares (Ciudad Real)
☎: +34 926 610 309 - Fax: +34 926 610 516
yuntero@yuntero.com
www.yuntero.com

YUNTERO 2010 B
85% macabeo, 10% sauvignon blanc, 5% moscatel.

84 Colour: bright straw. Nose: tropical fruit, citrus fruit, fresh. Palate: light-bodied, fresh, fruity.

YUNTERO VERDEJO SAUVIGNON BLANC 2010 B
verdejo, sauvignon blanc.

84 Colour: bright straw. Nose: medium intensity, white flowers. Palate: flavourful, fruity.

YUNTERO TEMPRANILLO SYRAH 2010 RD
tempranillo, syrah.

86 Colour: rose, purple rim. Nose: white flowers, red berry notes, fresh. Palate: fruity, fresh, flavourful, fleshy.

MUNDO DE YUNTERO 2009 T ROBLE
tempranillo, merlot.

86 Colour: cherry, garnet rim. Nose: balanced, medium intensity, red berry notes. Palate: fruity, easy to drink.

YUNTERO 2007 TC
tempranillo, cabernet sauvignon.

87 Colour: bright cherry, garnet rim. Nose: ripe fruit, sweet spices, creamy oak, expressive. Palate: flavourful, fruity, toasty.

YUNTERO 2006 TR
tempranillo.

86 Colour: cherry, garnet rim. Nose: red berry notes, cocoa bean, creamy oak. Palate: good acidity, balanced, correct, long.

YUNTERO SELECCIÓN 2003 TR
100% tempranillo.

84 Colour: cherry, garnet rim. Nose: spicy, roasted coffee, ripe fruit. Palate: toasty, round tannins, easy to drink.

CASA GUALDA

Tapias, 8
16708 Pozoamargo (Cuenca)
☎: +34 969 387 173 - Fax: +34 969 387 202
info@casagualda.com
www.casagualda.com

CASA GUALDA MACABEO 2010 B
macabeo.

86 Colour: bright straw. Nose: balanced, expressive, fruit expression, floral. Palate: flavourful, fruity, great length, balanced.

CASA GUALDA TEMPRANILLO 2010 T
90% tempranillo, 5% cabernet sauvignon, 5% merlot.

85 Colour: cherry, purple rim. Nose: expressive, ripe fruit. Palate: flavourful, fruity, good acidity.

CASA GUALDA 2008 TC
50% tempranillo, 50% cabernet sauvignon.

86 Colour: deep cherry, garnet rim. Nose: medium intensity, ripe fruit. Palate: powerful, spicy.

CASA GUALDA SELECCIÓN C&J 2008 T

86 Colour: very deep cherry, garnet rim. Nose: candied fruit, cocoa bean, sweet spices. Palate: good structure, spicy, round tannins.

CASA GUALDA SELECCIÓN L 50 ANIVERSARIO 2008 T
tempranillo, petit verdot, syrah.

85 Colour: cherry, garnet rim. Nose: roasted coffee, spicy, aromatic coffee. Palate: balsamic, toasty, roasted-coffee aftertaste.

COOPERATIVA LA UNIÓN

La Paz, s/n
13600 Alcazar de San Juan (Ciudad Real)
☎: +34 926 541 371 - Fax: +34 926 545 678
launion@ucaman.es

CAZ DE ALCAZAR AIRÉN 2010 B
100% airén.

82 Colour: bright straw. Nose: candied fruit, citrus fruit, slightly evolved. Palate: light-bodied, fresh, flavourful.

CAZ DE ALCAZAR ELÍTE 2009 T
100% cabernet sauvignon.

84 Colour: cherry, purple rim. Nose: expressive, floral, balsamic herbs, ripe fruit. Palate: good acidity, spicy, correct.

COOPERATIVA SAN ISIDRO - BODEGAS LATÚE

Camino Esperilla, s/n
45810 Villanueva de Alcardete (Toledo)
☎: +34 925 166 350 - Fax: +34 925 166 673
gerencia@latue.com
www.latue.com

PINGOROTE SAUVIGNON BLANC 2010 B JOVEN
sauvignon blanc.

88 Colour: bright straw. Nose: fresh, balanced, floral. Palate: flavourful, fresh, balanced, good acidity.

PINGOROTE 2010 T
tempranillo.

83 Colour: cherry, purple rim. Nose: slightly evolved, grassy, red berry notes. Palate: fruity, flavourful, great length.

PINGOROTE 2008 TC
tempranillo.

87 Colour: bright cherry. Nose: ripe fruit, creamy oak, expressive, spicy. Palate: flavourful, fruity, toasty, fleshy.

PINGOROTE 2004 TR
tempranillo.

86 Color cherry, garnet rim. Aroma ripe fruit, spicy, creamy oak, toasty, complex. Taste powerful, flavourful, toasty, round tannins.

LATÚE 2009 ESP
airén.

86 Colour: bright straw. Nose: medium intensity, dried herbs, dry nuts. Palate: flavourful, good structure, fine bitter notes.

COOPERATIVA SANTO NIÑO DE LA BOLA

Angel Moya, 24
16650 Las Mesas (Cuenca)
☎: +34 967 155 074 - Fax: +34 967 167 317
info@bodegastaray.es

TARAY AIRÉN 2010
airén.

85 Colour: bright straw, greenish rim. Nose: fresh fruit, medium intensity, grassy, tropical fruit. Palate: fruity.

EL PROGRESO SOCIEDAD COOP. CLM

Avda. de la Virgen, 89
13670 Villarubia de los Ojos (Ciudad Real)
☎: +34 926 896 088 - Fax: +34 926 896 135
elprogreso@cooprogres.com
www.bodegaselprogreso.com

OJOS DEL GUADIANA VERDEJO 2010 B
100% verdejo.

84 Colour: bright straw. Nose: medium intensity, ripe fruit. Palate: fruity, correct, good finish.

OJOS DEL GUADIANA AIRÉN JOVEN 2010 B
100% airén.

82 Colour: bright straw. Nose: fresh, tropical fruit, grassy. Palate: light-bodied, good acidity.

OJOS DEL GUADIANA SYRAH 2010 T ROBLE
100% syrah.

87 Colour: cherry, purple rim. Nose: expressive, red berry notes, sweet spices, aromatic coffee. Palate: fruity, flavourful, toasty.

OJOS DEL GUADIANA TEMPRANILLO 2010 T
tempranillo.

87 Colour: cherry, purple rim. Nose: fresh fruit, red berry notes, floral. Palate: flavourful, fruity, good acidity.

OJOS DEL GUADIANA 2008 TC
100% tempranillo.

84 Colour: deep cherry. Nose: woody, toasty. Palate: flavourful, fruity, spicy, great length.

OJOS DEL GUADIANA SELECCIÓN 2008 T
33,3% syrah, 33,3% merlot, 33,3% cabernet sauvignon.

84 Colour: cherry, garnet rim. Nose: sweet spices, creamy oak, ripe fruit. Palate: round tannins, spicy, balsamic.

OJOS DEL GUADIANA 2007 TR
100% tempranillo.

86 Colour: cherry, garnet rim. Nose: toasty, aromatic coffee, medium intensity. Palate: flavourful, fruity, great length, round tannins.

OJOS DEL GUADIANA 2005 TGR
100% tempranillo.

86 Color cherry, garnet rim. Aroma ripe fruit, spicy, creamy oak, toasty, complex. Taste powerful, flavourful, toasty, round tannins.

FINCA ANTIGUA

Ctra. Quintanar - Los Hinojosos, Km. 11,5
16417 Los Hinojosos (Cuenca)
☎: +34 969 129 700 - Fax: +34 969 129 496
info@fincaantigua.com
www.familiamartinezbujanda.com

FINCA ANTIGUA MOSCATEL 2010 B
100% moscatel.

88 Colour: bright yellow. Nose: varietal, expressive, balanced, honeyed notes, jasmine. Palate: flavourful, fruity, sweet.

FINCA ANTIGUA VIURA 2010 B
100% viura.

86 Colour: bright straw. Nose: wild herbs, tropical fruit, floral. Palate: balanced, good finish.

FINCA ANTIGUA SYRAH 2009 T
100% syrah.

91 Colour: bright cherry, garnet rim. Nose: ripe fruit, cocoa bean, sweet spices, complex. Palate: balanced, fine bitter notes, good acidity.

FINCA ANTIGUA PETIT VERDOT 2009 T
100% petit verdot.

89 Colour: bright cherry, purple rim. Nose: medium intensity, spicy, ripe fruit. Palate: good structure, fruity, flavourful.

FINCA ANTIGUA MERLOT 2009 T
100% merlot.

87 Colour: bright cherry. Nose: ripe fruit, sweet spices, medium intensity. Palate: flavourful, fruity, round tannins, fresh.

FINCA ANTIGUA 2008 TC
50% tempranillo, 20% cabernet sauvignon, 20% merlot, 10% syrah.

88 Colour: bright cherry, garnet rim. Nose: ripe fruit, spicy, cocoa bean, warm. Palate: ripe fruit, spicy, round tannins.

FINCA ANTIGUA GARNACHA 2008 T
100% garnacha.

88 Colour: bright cherry. Nose: ripe fruit, sweet spices, creamy oak, expressive, cocoa bean. Palate: flavourful, fruity, toasty, round tannins.

FINCA ANTIGUA CABERNET SAUVIGNON 2008 T
100% cabernet sauvignon.

87 Colour: deep cherry. Nose: ripe fruit, sweet spices, wild herbs. Palate: flavourful, fruity, round tannins.

FINCA ANTIGUA TEMPRANILLO 2008 T
100% tempranillo.

87 Colour: cherry, garnet rim. Nose: sweet spices, cocoa bean, toasty, ripe fruit. Palate: flavourful, fruity, round tannins.

CLAVIS VIÑEDO PICO GARBANZO 2006 TR
varias.

90 Colour: cherry, garnet rim. Nose: red berry notes, expressive, complex, cocoa bean, sweet spices, creamy oak. Palate: round tannins, good acidity, fleshy, flavourful, balanced.

FINCA ANTIGUA 2005 TR
50% merlot, 25% cabernet sauvignon, 25% syrah.

89 Colour: cherry, garnet rim. Nose: ripe fruit, spicy, creamy oak, toasty, complex. Palate: powerful, flavourful, toasty, round tannins, long.

FONTANA

Extramuros, s/n
16411 Fuente de Pedro Naharro (Cuenca)
☎: +34 969 125 433 - Fax: +34 969 125 387
gemag@bodegasfontana.com
www.bodegasfontana.com

FONTAL 2010 B
60% verdejo, 40% sauvignon blanc.

86 Colour: bright straw, greenish rim. Nose: wild herbs, balanced, white flowers. Palate: flavourful, fruity, fresh.

FONTAL TEMPRANILLO 2009 T ROBLE
100% tempranillo.

84 Colour: cherry, garnet rim. Nose: cocoa bean, spicy, creamy oak. Palate: round tannins, correct, balsamic.

FONTAL 2007 TC
85% tempranillo, 15% cabernet sauvignon.

86 Colour: cherry, garnet rim. Nose: candied fruit, spicy, warm. Palate: flavourful, great length, round tannins.

LA VID Y LA ESPIGA

San Antón, 30
16415 Villamayor de Santiago (Cuenca)
☎: +34 969 139 069 - Fax: +34 969 139 069
export@vidyespiga.es
www.bodegasvidyespiga.es

VEGABRISA SAUVIGNON/VERDEJO 2010 B
50% sauvignon blanc, 50% verdejo.

85 Colour: bright straw. Nose: balanced, white flowers. Palate: flavourful, fruity, ripe fruit.

VEGABRISA AIREN 2010 B
100% airén.

80 Colour: bright straw. Nose: herbaceous, fresh, grassy. Palate: fresh, easy to drink.

VEGABRISA 2010 RD
tempranillo.

84 Colour: light cherry. Nose: wild herbs, dried flowers. Palate: flavourful, fruity, easy to drink.

NUESTRA SEÑORA DE MANJAVACAS SOC. COOP.

Camino del Campo de Criptana, s/n
16630 Mota del Cuervo (Cuenca)
☎: +34 967 180 025 - Fax: +34 967 181 120
enologia@zagarron.com
www.zagarron.com

ZAGARRON SAUVIGNON BLANC 2010 B
100% sauvignon blanc.

85 Colour: bright straw. Nose: floral, citrus fruit, balanced, fresh fruit. Palate: fresh, easy to drink.

ZAGARRON VERDEJO 2010 B
100% verdejo.

82 Colour: bright straw. Nose: citrus fruit, grassy, fresh. Palate: fresh, light-bodied.

ZAGARRON TEMPRANILLO 2010 TC
100% tempranillo.

88 Colour: deep cherry, purple rim. Nose: red berry notes, balanced. Palate: fruity, flavourful, great length.

S.C.V. DE C-LM VIRGEN DE LAS VIÑAS

Ctra. Argamasilla de Alba, s/n
13700 Tomelloso (Ciudad Real)
☎: +34 926 510 865 - Fax: +34 926 512 130
atencion.cliente@vinostomillar.com
www.vinostomillar.com

TOMILLAR SAUVIGNON BLANC 2010 B
100% sauvignon blanc.

85 Colour: bright straw. Nose: fresh fruit, balanced, medium intensity. Palate: flavourful, easy to drink.

LORENZETE 2010 B
100% airén.

84 Colour: bright straw. Nose: medium intensity, fresh fruit, citrus fruit. Palate: fresh, light-bodied, easy to drink.

TOMILLAR 2008 TC
100% tempranillo.

83 Colour: cherry, garnet rim. Nose: spicy, wet leather, aged wood nuances, aromatic coffee, roasted coffee. Palate: spicy, long, harsh oak tannins.

TOMILLAR 2004 TR
80% cabernet sauvignon, 20% tempranillo.

83 Colour: cherry, garnet rim. Nose: spicy, fine reductive notes, wet leather, aged wood nuances, fruit liqueur notes. Palate: spicy, long, flavourful.

SAN ISIDRO LABRADOR SOC. COOP. CLM

Ramón y Cajal, 42
16640 Belmonte (Cuenca)
☎: +34 967 170 289 - Fax: +34 967 170 289
isbelmonte@ucaman.es
www.castibell.es

VISIBEL 2010 B
100% airén.

85 Colour: bright straw. Nose: ripe fruit, honeyed notes, fresh. Palate: easy to drink, light-bodied.

CASTIBELL 2009 T
100% tempranillo.

82 Colour: light cherry, garnet rim. Nose: medium intensity, red berry notes. Palate: fresh, fruity, easy to drink.

CASTIBELL 2005 TC
100% tempranillo.

84 Colour: dark-red cherry, brick rim edge. Nose: roasted coffee, overripe fruit. Palate: reductive nuances, flavourful.

SANTA CATALINA

Cooperativa, 2
13240 La Solana (Ciudad Real)
☎: +34 926 632 194 - Fax: +34 926 631 085
compras@santacatalina.es
www.santacatalina.es

LOS GALANES 2004 TC
100% tempranillo.

86 Colour: cherry, garnet rim. Nose: ripe fruit, medium intensity, spicy. Palate: good structure, flavourful, ripe fruit.

LOS GALANES AIRÉN 2010 B
100% airén.

85 Colour: bright straw. Nose: fresh, fresh fruit, medium intensity. Palate: flavourful, fruity, balanced.

LOS GALANES 2010 T
100% tempranillo.

85 Colour: cherry, purple rim. Nose: expressive, fresh fruit, floral. Palate: flavourful, fruity, easy to drink.

LOS GALANES 2004 TR
100% tempranillo.

86 Color cherry, garnet rim. Aroma ripe fruit, spicy, creamy oak, toasty, complex. Taste powerful, flavourful, toasty, round tannins.

VIHUCAS

Mayor, 3
45860 Villacañas (Toledo)
☎: +34 925 160 309 - Fax: +34 925 160 176
info@vihucas.com
www.vihucas.com

VIHUCAS CENCIBEL [TEMPRANILLO] 2010 T
tempranillo.

86 Colour: cherry, purple rim. Nose: red berry notes, raspberry, expressive, warm. Palate: fruity, flavourful, balanced, good acidity, easy to drink.

VIHUCAS COLECCIÓN FAMILIAR 2009 TR
100% merlot.

87 Colour: very deep cherry. Nose: fruit preserve, sweet spices, powerfull. Palate: powerful, toasty, great length, fleshy.

VIHUCAS FINCA DETRÉS 2009 T
merlot, tempranillo, graciano.

85 Colour: cherry, garnet rim. Nose: red berry notes, grassy, medium intensity. Palate: fresh, good finish, easy to drink.

VIHUCAS COLECCIÓN FAMILIAR 2008 T
100% merlot.

90 Colour: very deep cherry, garnet rim. Nose: ripe fruit, complex, balanced. Palate: balanced, good acidity, round tannins.

VIHUCAS QUINCE 2007 T ROBLE
100% tempranillo.

88 Colour: very deep cherry, garnet rim. Nose: ripe fruit, fruit preserve, spicy. Palate: powerful, spicy, fruity.

VIHUCAS DOBLE 08/09 T
merlot, tempranillo.

88 Colour: cherry, garnet rim. Nose: powerfull, balanced, ripe fruit, spicy. Palate: flavourful, good structure, round tannins.

VINÍCOLA DE CASTILLA

Pol. Ind. Calle I, s/n
13200 Manzanares (Ciudad Real)
☎: +34 926 647 800 - Fax: +34 926 610 466
nacional@vinicoladecastilla.com
www.vinicoladecastilla.com

SEÑORÍO DE GUADIANEJA CHARDONNAY 2010 B
100% chardonnay.

87 Colour: bright straw. Nose: white flowers, tropical fruit, expressive. Palate: light-bodied, flavourful, correct.

SEÑORÍO DE GUADIANEJA SAUVIGNON BLANC 2010 B
sauvignon blanc.

85 Colour: bright straw. Nose: grassy, fresh fruit, expressive. Palate: light-bodied, correct, easy to drink.

SEÑORÍO DE GUADIANEJA MACABEO 2010 B
macabeo.

82 Colour: bright straw. Nose: grassy, medium intensity, lacks fruit. Palate: light-bodied, good acidity, easy to drink.

SEÑORÍO DE GUADIANEJA VERDEJO 2010 B
verdejo.

81 Colour: bright straw. Nose: fresh, medium intensity, short. Palate: light-bodied, fine bitter notes, easy to drink.

SEÑORÍO DE GUADIANEJA PETIT VERDOT 2010 T
petit verdot.

87 Colour: cherry, purple rim. Nose: floral, fresh fruit, fresh. Palate: fleshy, fruity, easy to drink.

SEÑORÍO DE GUADIANEJA SYRAH 2010 T
syrah.

87 Colour: cherry, purple rim. Nose: fresh, fresh fruit, spicy. Palate: fruity, flavourful, easy to drink.

SEÑORÍO DE GUADIANEJA MERLOT 2010 T
100% merlot.

86 Colour: cherry, purple rim. Nose: fresh, fruit expression, floral. Palate: fleshy, fresh, flavourful.

SEÑORÍO DE GUADIANEJA TEMPRANILLO 2010 T
100% tempranillo.

85 Colour: cherry, purple rim. Nose: fresh, fresh fruit, medium intensity. Palate: light-bodied, flavourful, easy to drink.

SEÑORÍO DE GUADIANEJA CABERNET SAUVIGNON 2010 T
100% cabernet sauvignon.

85 Colour: cherry, purple rim. Nose: balsamic herbs, fruit expression, fresh. Palate: fresh, light-bodied, flavourful.

SEÑORÍO DE GUADIANEJA 2006 TC
tempranillo.

85 Colour: dark-red cherry. Nose: candied fruit, sweet spices, balanced. Palate: flavourful, correct, fine bitter notes.

SEÑORÍO DE GUADIANEJA CABERNET 2004 TGR
cabernet sauvignon.

85 Colour: light cherry, orangey edge. Nose: expressive, sweet spices, roasted coffee, cocoa bean. Palate: spicy, roasted-coffee aftertaste, lacks fruit.

GUADIANEJA RESERVA ESPECIAL 2003 TR
tempranillo.

84 Colour: cherry, purple rim. Nose: candied fruit, ripe fruit, expressive, medium intensity. Palate: good acidity, flavourful, sweetness, spicy.

GUADIANEJA 1995 TR
tempranillo.

86 Colour: light cherry, orangey edge. Nose: sweet spices, balsamic herbs, creamy oak, roasted coffee. Palate: round tannins, spicy, fleshy.

CANTARES ROSADO ESP

82 Colour: raspberry rose. Nose: ripe fruit, medium intensity, faded flowers. Palate: fruity, easy to drink, light-bodied.

VINÍCOLA DE TOMELLOSO

Ctra. Toledo - Albacete, Km. 130,8
13700 Tomelloso (Ciudad Real)
☎: +34 926 513 004 - Fax: +34 926 538 001
vinicola@vinicolatomelloso.com
www.vinicolatomelloso.com

GAZATE SAUVIGNON BLANC 2010 B
sauvignon blanc.

86 Colour: bright straw. Nose: balanced, varietal, floral. Palate: fresh, flavourful, fine bitter notes, great length.

GAZATE CHARDONNAY 2010 B
100% chardonnay.

86 Colour: bright straw. Nose: fresh fruit, expressive, fresh, neat. Palate: light-bodied, fruity, flavourful.

AÑIL 2010 B
100% macabeo.

87 Colour: bright straw, greenish rim. Nose: medium intensity, fresh fruit, floral. Palate: fresh, good finish, balanced.

GAZATE VERDEJO 2010 B
100% verdejo.

85 Colour: bright straw. Nose: grassy, tropical fruit, expressive. Palate: fruity, flavourful, fleshy.

TORRE DE GAZATE AIRÉN 2010 B
100% airén.

84 Colour: bright straw. Nose: floral, citrus fruit, expressive. Palate: fruity, light-bodied, easy to drink.

TORRE DE GAZATE 2010 RD
cabernet sauvignon.

86 Colour: rose, purple rim. Nose: raspberry, fresh fruit, fresh. Palate: easy to drink, light-bodied, flavourful.

TORRE DE GAZATE CENCIBEL 2010 T
100% tempranillo.

84 Colour: cherry, purple rim. Nose: fresh fruit, floral, balsamic herbs. Palate: flavourful, fruity, good acidity.

GAZATE MERLOT 2009 T
100% merlot.

86 Colour: cherry, purple rim. Nose: expressive, fresh fruit, floral, fresh. Palate: fruity, good acidity, fleshy.

FINCA CERRADA TEMPRANILLO 2009 T
tempranillo.

84 Colour: cherry, purple rim. Nose: red berry notes, floral. Palate: flavourful, fruity, good acidity, round tannins.

TORRE DE GAZATE 2006 TC
60% tempranillo, 40% cabernet sauvignon.

86 Colour: cherry, garnet rim. Nose: ripe fruit, balanced, expressive. Palate: round tannins, fruity, flavourful, fleshy.

GAZATE SYRAH 2009 T
100% syrah.

84 Colour: cherry, purple rim. Nose: grassy, red berry notes, medium intensity. Palate: fruity, flavourful.

GAZATE CABERNET SAUVIGNON 2009 T
100% cabernet sauvignon.

84 Colour: garnet rim. Nose: scrubland, ripe fruit, fresh. Palate: balsamic, spicy, easy to drink.

FINCA CERRADA 2006 TC
60% tempranillo, 30% cabernet sauvignon, 10% syrah. HHHHH3,91€

87 Colour: cherry, garnet rim. Nose: ripe fruit, spicy, creamy oak, toasty. Palate: powerful, flavourful, toasty, fruity.

TORRE DE GAZATE 2002 TR
50% tempranillo, 50% cabernet sauvignon.

85 Colour: cherry, garnet rim. Nose: ripe fruit, spicy, old leather. Palate: powerful, flavourful, toasty, round tannins.

TORRE DE GAZATE 2000 TGR
cabernet sauvignon.

83 Colour: light cherry, orangey edge. Nose: old leather, candied fruit. Palate: good structure, flavourful, fine tannins.

MANTOLÁN ESP
100% macabeo.

84 Colour: bright yellow. Nose: ripe fruit, fine lees, powerfull. Palate: flavourful, fruity.

VINNICO EXPORT

Muela, 16
03730 Jávea (Alicante)
☎: +34 965 791 967 - Fax: +34 966 461 471
info@vinnico.com
www.vinnico.com

FLOR DEL MONTGÓ TEMPRANILLO 2009 T
100% tempranillo.

86 Colour: very deep cherry, purple rim. Nose: sweet spices, grassy, red berry notes. Palate: flavourful, fruity, good structure.

VINOS COLOMAN

Goya, 17
13620 Pedro Muñoz (Ciudad Real)
☎: +34 926 586 410 - Fax: +34 926 586 656
coloman@satcoloman.com
www.satcoloman.com

BESANA REAL MACABEO 2010 B
100% macabeo.

77

BESANA REAL 2010 RD
100% tempranillo.

84 Colour: light cherry. Nose: medium intensity, citrus fruit. Palate: light-bodied, fruity, easy to drink.

BESANA REAL TEMPRANILLO 2010 T
100% tempranillo.

85 Colour: cherry, purple rim. Nose: fresh fruit, red berry notes, balanced. Palate: easy to drink, correct.

BESANA REAL SYRAH 2008 T ROBLE
100% syrah.

87 Colour: cherry, garnet rim. Nose: expressive, red berry notes, creamy oak, sweet spices. Palate: fruity, flavourful, fleshy, toasty.

BESANA REAL CABERNET SAUVIGNON 2007 T ROBLE
100% cabernet sauvignon.

86 Colour: deep cherry, garnet rim. Nose: medium intensity, ripe fruit, sweet spices. Palate: flavourful, fruity.

BESANA REAL 2007 TC
100% tempranillo.

86 Colour: cherry, garnet rim. Nose: powerfull, ripe fruit, cocoa bean, spicy. Palate: flavourful, fruity, great length.

VINOS Y BODEGAS

Ctra. de las Mesas, Km. 1
13630 Socuéllanos (Ciudad Real)
☎: +34 926 531 067 - Fax: +34 926 532 249
export@vinosybodegas.com
www.vinosybodegas.com

REAL BODEGA 2005 TC
tempranillo.

84 Colour: cherry, garnet rim. Nose: candied fruit, sweet spices, powerfull, warm. Palate: flavourful, fruity, spicy.

REAL BODEGA 2002 TR
tempranillo.

82 Colour: cherry, garnet rim. Nose: ripe fruit, spicy, toasty. Palate: powerful, flavourful, toasty, round tannins.

VIÑEDOS MEJORANTES

Ctra. de Villafranca, Km. 2
45860 Villacañas (Toledo)
☎: +34 925 201 036 - Fax: +34 925 200 023
portillejo@portillejo.com
www.portillejo.es

PORTILLEJO MERLOT 2009 T ROBLE
100% merlot.

83 Colour: cherry, garnet rim. Nose: toasty, spicy, medium intensity. Palate: flavourful, spicy, roasted-coffee aftertaste.

PORTILLEJO CABERNET SAUVIGNON 2009 T ROBLE
100% cabernet sauvignon.

81 Colour: pale ruby, brick rim edge. Nose: fruit preserve, roasted coffee, spicy.

PORTILLEJO CABERNET SAUVIGNON 2007 TC
100% cabernet sauvignon.

86 Colour: deep cherry, garnet rim. Nose: powerfull, varietal, fruit preserve, sweet spices. Palate: flavourful, round tannins.

PORTILLEJO 6675 2006 TC
100% cabernet sauvignon.

84 Colour: pale ruby, brick rim edge. Nose: creamy oak, spicy, toasty. Palate: fleshy, balsamic, dry wood.

PORTILLEJO CABERNET SAUVIGNON 2003 TR
100% cabernet sauvignon.

85 Colour: cherry, garnet rim. Nose: spicy, toasty, fruit preserve. Palate: powerful, flavourful, toasty, round tannins.

VIÑEDOS Y BODEGA LA CANDELARIA

San Clemente, 13
16612 Casas de Los Pinos (Cuenca)
☎: +34 969 383 291
info@lospinostempranillo.com
www.lospinostempranillo.com

SENDA 66 2009 T
tempranillo.

83 Colour: deep cherry, garnet rim. Nose: roasted coffee, fruit preserve, powerfull. Palate: powerful, toasty.

VIÑEDOS Y BODEGAS MUÑOZ

Ctra. Villarrubia, 11
45350 Noblejas (Toledo)
☎: +34 925 140 070 - Fax: +34 925 141 334
info@bodegasmunoz.com
www.bodegasmunoz.com

ARTERO MACABEO 2010 B
100% macabeo.

84 Colour: bright straw, greenish rim. Nose: wild herbs, medium intensity. Palate: flavourful, fruity, fine bitter notes.

BLAS MUÑOZ CHARDONNAY 2009 BFB
100% chardonnay.

90 Colour: bright golden. Nose: sweet spices, pattiserie, creamy oak, toasty, balanced, expressive. Palate: complex, rich, flavourful, fleshy, balanced. Personality.

ARTERO 2010 RD
100% tempranillo.

85 Colour: rose, purple rim. Nose: raspberry, red berry notes, fresh, floral. Palate: fruity, flavourful, light-bodied.

ARTERO TEMPRANILLO MERLOT 2008 TC
50% merlot, 50% tempranillo.

87 Colour: cherry, garnet rim. Nose: medium intensity, ripe fruit, spicy. Palate: spicy, ripe fruit, great length.

ARTERO MERLOT 2006 TR
100% merlot.

86 Colour: deep cherry, orangey edge. Nose: candied fruit, spicy. Palate: flavourful, fleshy, fruity aftestaste, great length.

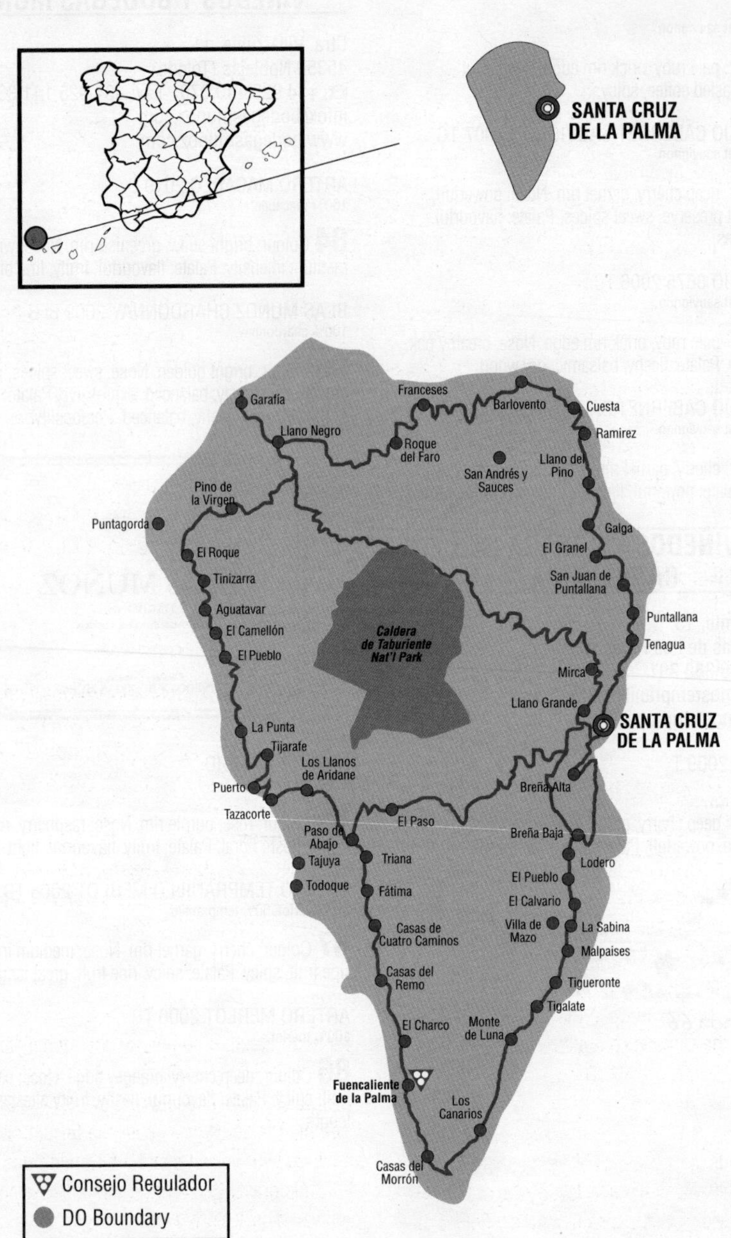
SANTA CRUZ
DE LA PALMA
Garafía
Franceses
Barlovento
Cuesta
Ramirez
Llano Negro
Roque
del Faro
San Andrés y
Sauces
Llano del
Pino
Pino de
la Virgen
Puntagorda
Galga
El Granel
El Roque
Tinizarra
San Juan de
Puntallana
Aguatavar
El Camellón
El Pueblo
Caldera
de Taburiente
Nat'l Park
Puntallana
Tenagua
Mirca
Llano Grande
SANTA CRUZ
DE LA PALMA
La Punta
Tijarafe
Los Llanos
de Aridane
Puerto
Tazacorte
Breña Alta
El Paso
Paso de
Abajo
Breña Baja
Tajuya
Triana
Lodero
Todoque
Fátima
El Pueblo
El Calvario
Casas de
Cuatro Caminos
Villa de
Mazo
La Sabina
Malpaises
Casas del
Remo
Tigueronte
Tigalate
El Charco
Monte
de Luna
Fuencaliente
de la Palma
Los
Canarios
Casas del
Morrón
Consejo Regulador
DO Boundary

NEWS ABOUT THE VINTAGE:

The wines from La Palma are suffering a sort of recession similar to that of 2007. This year, the DO has hardly harvested 700.000 kg. of grapes, 48% less than in 2009. The reasons behind this production decrease are two: the first one is a fortuitous circumstance, the fires that affected the southern part of the island in 2009; the second it is a deeper issue with a much more difficult solution, the fact that growers are progressively abandoning the vineyard, given the amount of vine diseases (mildew, powdery mildew, botrytis...) that have occurred in the last couple of years, as well as the almost impossible weather conditions that ever too often thwarts proper maturation of the grapes, or the delays in the payments of the grapes sold by growers to the local wineries.

All this horrid picture has not spoil the illusion of those producers who still believe in the quality of the local *malvasía*, surely the best in the whole of the Canary Islands and one of the best worldwide, the likes of Bodegas Carballo, whose Malvasía Dulce 2001 has reached 97 points, three more than its own 2008, included in both last and this year's edition. If we think "*malvasía*" in universal terms, we should for sure think of La Palma: all the local wines that have made it to our Podium are sweet wines made from this historic grape.

LOCATION:

The production area covers the whole island of San Miguel de La Palma, and is divided into three distinct sub-regions: Hoyo de Mazo, Fuencaliente and Northern La Palma.

CLIMATE:

Variable according to the altitude and the direction that the vineyards face. The relief is a fundamental aspect in La Palma, seeing as it gives rise to different climates and microclimates; one must not forget that it has the highest altitudes in relation to surface area of all the Canary Islands. Nevertheless, as it is situated in the Atlantic, it benefits from the effects of the trade winds (humid and from the northwest), which temper the temperatures and tone down the climatic contrasts.

SOIL:

The vineyards are situated at altitudes of between 200 m and 1,400 m above sea level in a coastal belt ranging in width which surrounds the whole island. Due to the ragged topography, the vineyards occupy the steep hillsides in the form of small terraces. The soil is mainly of volcanic origin.

GRAPE VARIETIES:

WHITE: *Malvasía, Güal and Verdello* (main); *Albillo, Bastardo Blanco, Bermejuela, Bujariego, Burra Blanca, Forastera Blanca, Listán Blanco, Moscatel, Pedro Ximénez, Sabro* and *Torrontés.*
RED: *Negramol* (main), *Listán Negro* (Almuñeco), *Bastardo Negro, Malvasía Rosada, Moscatel Negro, Tintilla, Castellana, Listán Prieto* and *Vijariego Negro.*

SUB-REGIONS:

Hoyo de Mazo: It comprises the municipal districts of Villa de Mazo, Breña Baja, Breña Alta and Santa Cruz de La Palma, at altitudes of between 200 m and 700 m. The vines grow over the terrain on hillsides covered with volcanic stone ('Empedrados') or with volcanic gravel ('Picón Granado'). White and mainly red varieties are grown.

Fuencaliente: It comprises the municipal districts of Fuencaliente, El Paso, Los Llanos de Aridane and Tazacorte. The vines grow over terrains of volcanic ash at altitudes of between 200 m and 1900 m. The white varieties and the sweet Malvasia stand out.

Northern La Palma: Situated at an altitude of between 100 m and 200 m, It comprises the municipal areas of Puntallana, San Andrés and Sauces, Barlovento, Garafía, Puntagorda and Tijarafe. The region is richer in vegetation and the vines grow on trellises and using the goblet system. The traditional 'Tea' wines are produced here.

FIGURES:

Vineyard surface: 737 – **Wine-Growers:** 1,246 – **Wineries:** 18 – **2010 Harvest rating:** N/A – **Production:** 518,000 – **Market percentages:** 99% domestic. 1% export

CONSEJO REGULADOR
Acosta Gómez, 7
38740 Fuencaliente (La Palma)
☎: +34 922 444 432 - Fax: +34 922 444 404
@ cr.vinoslapalma@terra.es
www.malvasiadelapalma.com

GENERAL CHARACTERISTICS OF THE WINES

WHITES	Produced mainly from *Bujariego* or combined with *Listán Blanco*. They are dry, fruity with certain rustic notes; on occasion they also display mineral and volcanic nuances. They are the most classic wines of the island; nevertheless, they are sweet wines from *Malvasía*, complex and original with notes that are reminiscent of fine herbs.
ROSÉS	The colour ranges from salmon to pink. The wines are light, fruity and delicate.
REDS	Produced mainly from *Negramol*, they usually have a deep cherry-red colour. As with the rosés, these wines are also fresh and light.
TEA WINE	A characteristic wine from La Palma, normally produced from *Negramol, Listán Prieto* and *Albillo*, and aged in tea (Canary oak), which gives it intense noses and palates of resin that combine with the fruity and herbaceous touches of the grape..

VINTAGE RATING PEÑÍNGUIDE

2007	2008	2009	2010
VERY GOOD	VERY GOOD	GOOD	GOOD

AGRÍCOLA VELHOCO

Juan Mayor, 32 Velhoco
38700 S/C de la Palma (Santa Cruz de Tenerife)
☎: +34 922 413 531
agricolavelhocos.l@hotmail.com

ORO DE RISCO 2008 T

70

BODEGA JOSÉ ALBERTO TABARES PÉREZ

Bellido Alto, s/n
38780 Tijarafe (Santa Cruz de Tenerife)
☎: +34 922 491 075 - Fax: +34 922 490 249

EL LAGAR 2010 T

78

BODEGA PERDOMO S.A.T.

Joaquina, 12 (Las Tricias)
38738 Garafia (La Palma)
☎: +34 922 400 089 - Fax: +34 922 400 689

PIEDRA JURADA ALBILLO 2010 B
albillo.

84 Colour: bright straw. Nose: citrus fruit, fresh fruit, balsamic herbs. Palate: flavourful, fruity.

PIEDRA JURADA 2010 B
albillo, listán blanco.

83 Colour: bright straw. Nose: candied fruit, citrus fruit, honeyed notes. Palate: flavourful, fruity, sweetness.

BODEGAS CARBALLO

Ctra. Las Indias, 74
38740 Fuencaliente de La Palma (Santa Cruz de Tenerife)
☎: +34 922 444 140 - Fax: +34 922 211 744
info@bodegascarballo.com
www.bodegascarballo.com

MALVASÍA DULCE CARBALLO 2008 B
malvasía.

94 Colour: bright golden. Nose: powerfull, varietal, candied fruit, citrus fruit, fruit liqueur notes. Palate: flavourful, powerful, fleshy, sweet, full.

MALVASÍA DULCE CARBALLO 2001 B
malvasía.

97 Colour: bright golden. Nose: candied fruit, citrus fruit, honeyed notes, white flowers, complex, varietal, sweet spices. Palate: flavourful, fleshy, complex, concentrated, good acidity, round.

BODEGAS NOROESTE DE LA PALMA

Bellido Alto, s/n
38780 Tijarafe (Santa Cruz de Tenerife)
☎: +34 922 491 075 - Fax: +34 922 491 075
administracion@vinosveganorte.com
www.vinosveganorte.com

VEGA NORTE 2010 B
listán blanco, albillo.

90 Colour: bright straw. Nose: fresh, fresh fruit, white flowers, tropical fruit, grassy. Palate: flavourful, fruity, good acidity, balanced.

VEGA NORTE ALBILLO 2010 B

89 Colour: bright straw. Nose: expressive, complex, mineral, fresh fruit. Palate: flavourful, fruity, fresh.

VEGA NORTE 2010 RD

83 Colour: rose, purple rim. Nose: candied fruit, medium intensity. Palate: fine bitter notes, ripe fruit.

VEGA NORTE "VINO DE TEA" 2010 T
negramoll.

88 Colour: bright cherry. Nose: fragrant herbs, balsamic herbs, fruit expression. Palate: fine bitter notes, light-bodied, spicy, long. Personality.

VEGA NORTE 2009 T FERMENTADO EN BARRICA

88 Colour: bright cherry. Nose: ripe fruit, sweet spices, creamy oak, balsamic herbs. Palate: flavourful, fruity, toasty, round tannins.

VEGA NORTE VENDIMIA SELECCIONADA X ANIVERSARIO 2009 T
prieto.

88 Colour: bright cherry. Nose: sweet spices, creamy oak, fruit expression, smoky. Palate: flavourful, fruity, toasty, round tannins, balsamic.

BODEGAS TAMANCA S.L.

Ctra. Gral. Tamanca, 75
38750 El Paso (Santa Cruz de Tenerife)
☎: +34 922 494 155 - Fax: +34 922 494 296
bioaad@telefonica.net

TAMANCA 2010 B
albillo, bujariego, malvasía, marmajuelo.

88 Colour: bright straw. Nose: fresh fruit, white flowers, grassy. Palate: flavourful, fruity, good acidity, balanced.

TAMANCA LISTÁN BLANCO 2010 B
listán blanco.

88 Colour: bright straw. Nose: powerfull, expressive, citrus fruit, ripe fruit. Palate: flavourful, fruity, fresh.

TAMANCA MALVASÍA 2008 B
malvasía.

90 Colour: bright yellow. Nose: powerfull, varietal, candied fruit, warm. Palate: flavourful, powerful, fine bitter notes, good acidity, long.

TAMANCA SABRO 2008 B
sabro.

88 Colour: bright yellow. Nose: candied fruit, citrus fruit, honeyed notes. Palate: flavourful, sweet, good acidity.

TAMANCA MALVASÍA DULCE 2005 B BARRICA
malvasía.

93 Colour: golden. Nose: powerfull, floral, honeyed notes, candied fruit, fragrant herbs, sweet spices, dark chocolate, petrol notes. Palate: flavourful, sweet, fruity, long.

TAMANCA PEDREGAL 2010 T BARRICA
negramoll, almuñeco, castellana, vijariego, baboso.

83 Colour: cherry, garnet rim. Nose: candied fruit, fruit expression, dark chocolate, sweet spices. Palate: flavourful, spicy, ripe fruit.

TAMANCA NEGRAMOLL 2010 T
negramoll.

80 Colour: bright cherry. Nose: medium intensity, fruit expression, warm. Palate: flavourful, light-bodied.

BODEGAS TENEGUÍA

Los Canarios, s/n
38740 Fuencaliente de La Palma (Santa Cruz de Tenerife)
☎: +34 922 444 078 - Fax: +34 922 444 394
enologia@vinosteneguia.com
www.vinosteneguia.com

TENEGUÍA LA GOTA 2010 B

88 Colour: bright straw. Nose: fresh, fresh fruit, white flowers, expressive, earthy notes. Palate: flavourful, fruity, good acidity, balanced.

TENEGUÍA ALBILLO 2010 B

87 Colour: bright straw. Nose: white flowers, ripe fruit, citrus fruit. Palate: flavourful, fruity, fresh.

TENEGUÍA MALVASÍA 2010 BFB

87 Colour: bright straw. Nose: ripe fruit, citrus fruit, white flowers. Palate: flavourful, fleshy, fine bitter notes.

ALBOR 2010 B

86 Colour: bright straw. Nose: fresh fruit, citrus fruit, floral. Palate: flavourful, fruity, fresh.

TENEGUÍA MALVASÍA B
malvasía.

90 Colour: bright golden. Nose: candied fruit, citrus fruit, faded flowers, honeyed notes. Palate: powerful, sweet, fine bitter notes.

TENEGUÍA 2009 RD

72

TENEGUÍA NEGRAMOLL 2010 T

76

CARLOS FERNÁNDEZ FELIPE

Las Ledas, 40
38710 Breña Baja (Santa Cruz de Tenerife)
☎: +34 922 434 439 - Fax: +34 922 434 439

AWARA 2010 B

87 Colour: pale. Nose: ripe fruit, fine lees, white flowers. Palate: flavourful, fruity, fresh.

VIÑA ETNA MALVASIA SABRO 2009 B

88 Colour: bright yellow. Nose: powerfull, tropical fruit, honeyed notes. Palate: flavourful, sweetness, concentrated.

AWARA 2010 RD

78

JUAN JESÚS PÉREZ Y ADRIÁN

Bajada al Puerto de Santo Domingo s/n
38787 Villa de Garafia (Santa Cruz de Tenerife)
☎: +34 649 924 348 - Fax: +34 649 924 348
tagalguen@hotmail.com

BLANCO 2010 B
listán blanco, malvasía.

86 Colour: pale. Nose: white flowers, fresh fruit, citrus fruit. Palate: flavourful, fresh, fruity.

TAGALQUÉN 2010 T

85 Colour: deep cherry. Nose: balsamic herbs, powerfull, ripe fruit, red berry notes. Palate: flavourful, fleshy, fruity.

JUAN MATÍAS TORRES PÉREZ

Ciudad Real, 10- Los Canarios
38740 Fuentecaliente de la Palma (Santa Cruz de Tenerife)
☎: +34 617 967 499
bodegasjuanmatias@lapalmaenred.com
www.lapalmaenred.com/bodegasjuanmatias

COLECCIÓN MINÚSCULA DE MATÍAS TORRES 2010 B
100% albillo.

90 Colour: bright straw. Nose: ripe fruit, citrus fruit, mineral, white flowers. Palate: flavourful, complex, fine bitter notes, long.

VID SUR DULCE 2008 B
100% malvasía.

93 Colour: golden. Nose: floral, honeyed notes, candied fruit, fragrant herbs, acetaldehyde. Palate: flavourful, sweet, fresh, fruity, good acidity, long.

VID SUR NEGRAMOLL 2010 T
90% negramoll, 10% listán negro.

68

LA CASA DEL VOLCÁN

Acceso Volcán San Antonio
38740 Fuencaliente de la Palma (Santa Cruz de Tenerife)
☎: +34 922 444 427 - Fax: +34 922 444 427
info@lacasadelvolcan.es
www.lacasadelvolcan.es

LA CASA DEL VOLCÁN 2010 B
albillo, bujariego, listán blanco.

86 Colour: bright straw. Nose: ripe fruit, citrus fruit, white flowers. Palate: flavourful, fruity, fine bitter notes.

ONÉSIMA PÉREZ RODRÍGUEZ

Las Tricias
38738 Garafia (La Palma)
☎: +34 922 463 481 - Fax: +34 922 463 481
vinosvitega@terra.es

VITEGA ALBILLO 2010 B
albillo.

87 Colour: bright straw. Nose: white flowers, ripe fruit, citrus fruit. Palate: flavourful, fruity, fresh.

VITEGA 2010 B
listán blanco.

84 Colour: straw. Nose: fresh fruit, citrus fruit, floral. Palate: flavourful, fruity, fresh.

VITEGA 2010 RD

83 Colour: rose, purple rim. Nose: ripe fruit, fruit expression. Palate: flavourful, fruity, fleshy.

VITEGA ALMUÑECO 2009 T
almuñeco.

83 Colour: deep cherry. Nose: powerfull, characterful, balsamic herbs, scrubland. Palate: flavourful, light-bodied, fine bitter notes. Personality.

VITEGA 2009 T BARRICA

83 Colour: pale ruby, brick rim edge. Nose: characterful, earthy notes, candied fruit. Palate: fine bitter notes, spicy.

VITEGA TEA 2009 T

81 Colour: bright cherry. Nose: candied fruit, warm, spicy. Palate: light-bodied, flavourful, long.

VITEGA 2006 TC
listán negro, prieto picudo.

70

VITEGA 2005 TR
50% tintilla, 50% castellana.

78

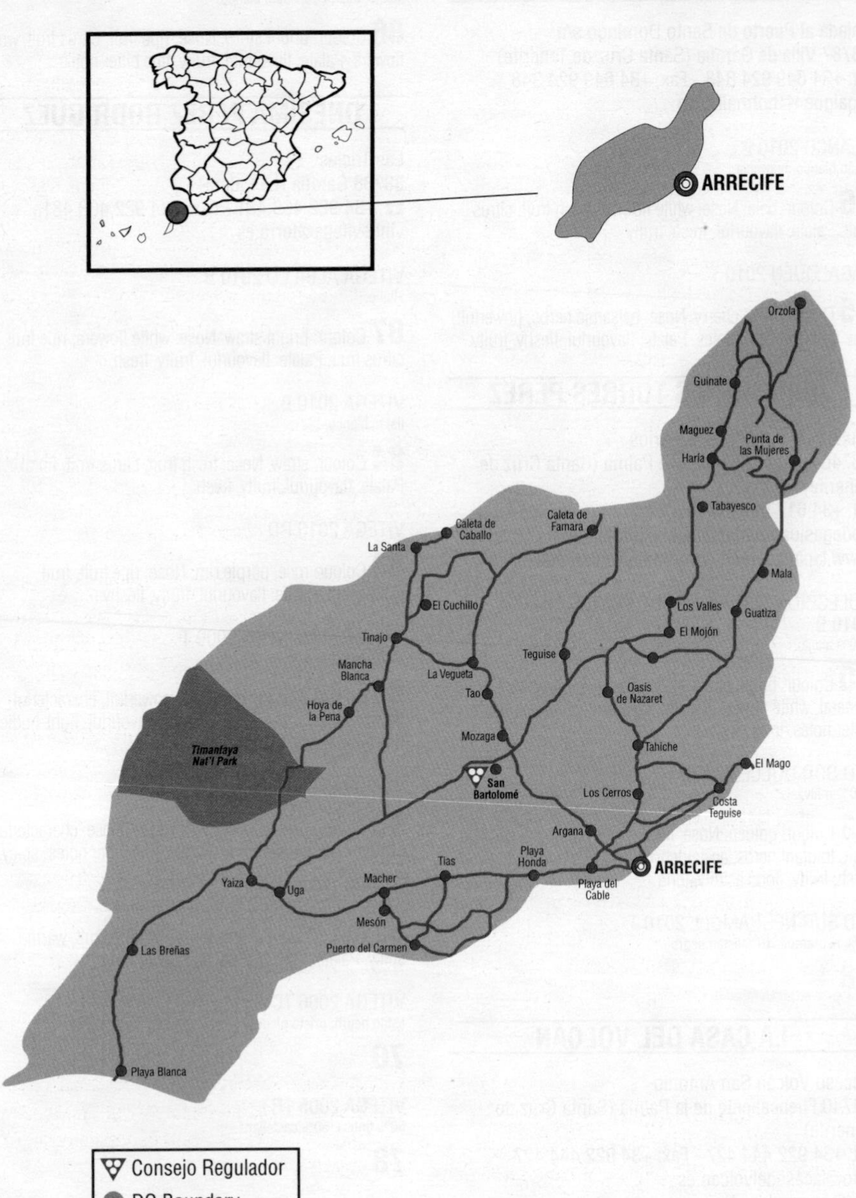
ARRECIFE
Orzola
Guinate
Maguez
Punta de
las Mujeres
Haría
Tabayesco
Caleta de
Famara
Caleta de
Caballo
La Santa
Mala
El Cuchillo
Los Valles
Guatiza
El Mojón
Tinajo
Mancha
Blanca
Teguise
La Vegueta
Oasis
de Nazaret
Hoya de
la Pena
Tao
Mozaga
Timanfaya
Nat'l Park
Tahiche
San
Bartolomé
El Mago
Los Cerros
Costa
Teguise
Argana
Playa
Honda
Tías
ARRECIFE
Yaiza
Uga
Macher
Playa del
Cable
Mesón
Puerto del Carmen
Las Breñas
Playa Blanca
Consejo Regulador
DO Boundary

NEWS ABOUT THE VINTAGE:

The 2010 vintage shows a high quality level, as befits a year with an excellent maturation cycle. As opposed to the hotter character of the 2009 vintage, 2010 enjoyed a more evident Atlantic influence that did away with the harmful effects of the torrid Saharan winds. Of all the 68 samples tasted, 18 reached our Podium, ten more than in last year's edition. Young white wines from Lanzarote made from *malvasía* show a lighter and fresher quality than those from La Palma, as well as a high varietal character. Regarding red wine renderings, those from El Grifo are the only ones that can compete with whites in terms of proper varietal expression. As for the sweet wines, Canari (the best rated in the whole of the island) keeps reigning; with its complex solera ageing, it has a sort of quality that reminds us of the great sweet wines from Madeira. Likewise, Arian 2010 (93 points), which has gained three points since last year's edition, tops the red wine ratings. The other rising star in the region, Bodegas Stratus –particularly with their sweet-wine catalogue– manages to get as many of his wines (5) as El Grifo at the top of the island's ranking.

It is quite telling that in an island where wine demand comes mainly from tourism (a less knowledgeable customer that buys wine as a souvenir in most cases), producers still try to improve their products and offer not only wines of the highest quality but also eco-friendly; their philosophy regards the vineyards as an important part of a natural system where things like water management become crucial, a serious approach which is now known and imitated all over the world.

LOCATION:

On the island of Lanzarote. The production area covers the municipal areas of Tinajo, Yaiza, San Bartolomé, Haría and Teguise.

CLIMATE:

Dry subtropical in nature, with low rainfall (about 200 mm per year) which is spread out irregularly throughout the year. On occasions, the Levante wind (easterly), characterised by its low humidity and which carries sand particles from the African continent, causes a considerable increase in the temperatures.

SOIL:

Volcanic in nature (locally known as 'Picón'). In fact, the cultivation of vines is made possible thanks to the ability of the volcanic sand to perfectly retain the water from dew and the scant rainfall. The island is relatively flat (the maximum altitude is 670 m) and the most characteristic form of cultivation is in 'hollows' surrounded by semicircular walls which protect the plants from the wind. This singular trainig system brings about an extremaly low density.

GRAPE VARIETIES:

WHITE: *Malvasía* (majority 75%), *Pedro Ximénez, Diego, Listán Blanco, Moscatel, Burrablanca, Breval.*
RED: *Listán Negra* (15%) and *Negramoll.*

FIGURES:

Vineyard surface: 1,958 – **Wine-Growers:** 1,754 – **Wineries:** 17 – **2010 Harvest rating:** Excellent – **Production:** 1,144,640 – **Market percentages:** 97% domestic. 3% export

CONSEJO REGULADOR
Arrecife, 9
35550 San Bartolomé (Las Palmas)
☎: +34 928 521 048 - Fax: +34 928 521 049
@ info@dolanzarote.com
www.dolanzarote.com

GENERAL CHARACTERISTICS OF THE WINES

WHITES	The most characteristic wines of the island are the white *Malvasía* wines. They have vegetative noses with volcanic and mineral nuances. There are more classical and traditional wines, which have a yellow amber colour, with almond and mellow noses; the young white wines, which have a golden yellow colour, great varietal noses, sometimes with noses of fennel or mint, and are flavourful on the palate; and the semi-sec, with similar characteristics, but sweeter on the palate.
ROSÉS	In general, they have a pink or raspberry pink colour and are quite fresh and fruity.
REDS	These are usually mid-tone, with a deep cherry-red colour; they are somewhat warm and have a good structure on the palate

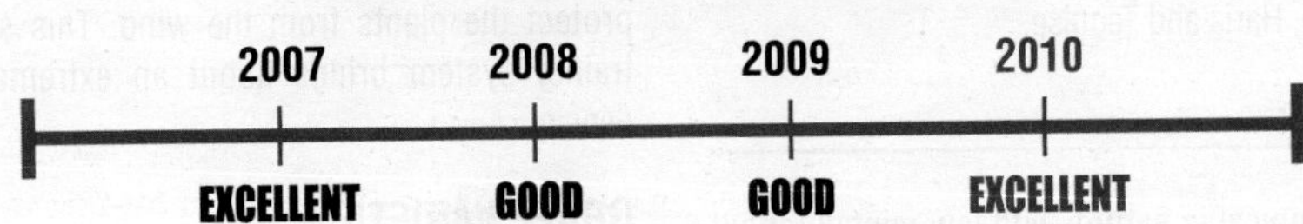

BODEGA LA GERIA

Ctra. de la Geria, Km. 19
35570 Yaiza-Lanzarote (Las Palmas de Gran Canaria)
☎: +34 928 173 178 - Fax: +34 928 511 370
bodega@lageria.com
www.lageria.com

MANTO 2010 B
malvasía.

88 Colour: pale. Nose: floral, ripe fruit, candied fruit, dried herbs. Palate: flavourful, fruity, sweetness, rich.

LA GERIA 2010 B
malvasía.

85 Colour: bright straw. Nose: white flowers, medium intensity, fresh fruit. Palate: flavourful, fruity, sweetness.

LA GERIA 2010 RD
listán negro.

83 Colour: raspberry rose. Nose: raspberry, candied fruit, grapey. Palate: powerful, flavourful, sweetness.

LA GERIA 2010 T
listán negro.

85 Colour: deep cherry. Nose: earthy notes, ripe fruit, smoky. Palate: fine bitter notes, flavourful, ripe fruit.

LA GERIA 2010 T MACERACIÓN CARBÓNICA
listán negro.

84 Colour: cherry, purple rim. Nose: powerfull, raspberry, fruit expression. Palate: flavourful, fruity, fresh.

LA GERIA MALVASÍA 2010 DULCE
malvasía.

84 Colour: bright straw. Nose: fresh fruit, citrus fruit, white flowers. Palate: flavourful, powerful, sweet.

LA GERIA MALVASÍA 2010 SEMIDULCE
malvasía.

81 Colour: bright straw. Nose: candied fruit, citrus fruit, faded flowers. Palate: powerful, sweetness, fine bitter notes.

LA GERIA MOSCATEL 2010 VINO DE LICOR
moscatel.

85 Colour: bright straw. Nose: white flowers, fresh fruit. Palate: flavourful, sweetness, fruity.

BODEGA LOS BERMEJOS

Camino a Los Bermejos, 7
35550 San Bartolomé de Lanzarote (Las Palmas)
☎: +34 928 522 463 - Fax: +34 928 522 641
bodega@losbermejos.com
www.losbermejos.com

BERMEJO MALVASIA NATURALMENTE DULCE 2010 B
100% malvasía.

92 Colour: bright yellow. Nose: candied fruit, fruit liqueur notes, dried flowers. Palate: flavourful, concentrated, sweet.

BERMEJO DIEGO ECOLÓGICO 2010 B
100% diego.

90 Colour: bright straw. Nose: ripe fruit, citrus fruit, white flowers, grassy. Palate: flavourful, fruity, good acidity, fine bitter notes.

BERMEJO MALVASÍA SEMIDULCE 2010 B
97% malvasía, 3% moscatel.

88 Colour: bright straw. Nose: white flowers, ripe fruit, candied fruit, citrus fruit. Palate: flavourful, fruity, fresh.

BERMEJO MALVASÍA SECO 2010 B
100% malvasía.

88 Colour: bright straw. Nose: white flowers, ripe fruit, citrus fruit. Palate: fruity, fresh, flavourful, mineral.

BERMEJO DIEGO 2010 B
100% diego.

88 Colour: bright straw. Nose: fresh fruit, fruit expression, citrus fruit, white flowers. Palate: fruity, fresh, light-bodied.

BERMEJO MOSCATEL NATURALMENTE DULCE 2010 B
100% moscatel.

88 Colour: bright straw. Nose: candied fruit, overripe fruit, honeyed notes. Palate: powerful, sweet, flavourful.

BERMEJO MALVASÍA 2010 BFB
100% malvasía.

87 Colour: bright straw. Nose: powerfull, smoky, earthy notes, ripe fruit, citrus fruit. Palate: powerful, flavourful, fine bitter notes.

ROSADO BERMEJO 2010 RD
100% listán negro.

86 Colour: light cherry. Nose: medium intensity, ripe fruit, fruit expression. Palate: flavourful, fruity, fresh.

BERMEJO TINTO MC 2010 T MACERACIÓN CARBÓNICA
100% listán negro.

88 Color cherry, purple rim. Aroma expressive, fresh fruit, red berry notes, floral. Taste flavourful, fruity, good acidity, round tannins.

BERMEJO 2009 T BARRICA
100% listán negro.

88 Colour: cherry, garnet rim. Nose: powerfull, ripe fruit, raspberry, creamy oak, sweet spices. Palate: flavourful, ripe fruit, spicy.

BERMEJO 2009 BN
100% malvasía.

88 Colour: bright straw. Nose: medium intensity, fresh fruit, dried herbs, fine lees, floral, expressive. Palate: fresh, fruity, flavourful, good acidity.

BODEGA MARTINON

Camino del Mentidero, 2
35572 Masdache Tías (Las Palmas)
☎: +34 928 834 160 - Fax: +34 928 834 160
info@bodegasmartinon.com
www.bodegasmartinon.com

MARTINÓN MALVASÍA SECO 2010 B
100% malvasía.

87 Colour: bright straw. Nose: white flowers, jasmine, fresh fruit, citrus fruit. Palate: flavourful, good acidity, ripe fruit.

BODEGA STRATVS

Ctra. La Geria, Km. 18
35570 Yaiza (Las Palmas)
☎: +34 928 809 977 - Fax: +34 928 524 651
bodega@stratvs.com
www.stratvs.com

STRATVS MALVASÍA NATURALMENTE DULCE 2010 B
100% malvasía.

94 Colour: bright yellow. Nose: floral, citrus fruit, candied fruit, honeyed notes. Palate: powerful, flavourful, ripe fruit, good acidity.

STRATVS MALVASÍA SECO 2010 B
100% malvasía.

91 Colour: bright straw. Nose: fresh fruit, fruit expression, dried herbs, white flowers. Palate: flavourful, fine bitter notes, good acidity, ripe fruit.

STRATVS DIEGO SEMIDULCE 2010 B
95% diego, 5% moscatel.

90 Colour: bright straw. Nose: white flowers, fresh fruit, candied fruit, dried herbs. Palate: flavourful, fruity, good acidity.

STRATVS MOSCATEL DULCE 2009 B
100% moscatel.

91 Colour: bright straw. Nose: white flowers, citrus fruit, spicy. Palate: flavourful, sweet, ripe fruit.

STRATVS MOSCATEL LICOR 2006 B
100% moscatel.

90 Colour: bright golden. Nose: overripe fruit, citrus fruit, cocoa bean, powerfull, varietal. Palate: flavourful, sweetness, good acidity.

STRATVS 2010 RD
100% tinta conejera.

89 Color rose, purple rim. Aroma powerfull, ripe fruit, red berry notes, floral, expressive. Taste fleshy, powerful, fruity, fresh.

STRATVS 2010 T
60% listán negro, 40% tinta conejera.

89 Colour: cherry, garnet rim. Nose: powerfull, expressive, complex, ripe fruit, spicy, smoky. Palate: powerful, fleshy, ripe fruit.

STRATVS 2007 TC
60% tinta conejera, 40% listán negro.

87 Colour: cherry, garnet rim. Nose: mineral, ripe fruit, earthy notes, wet leather. Palate: fine bitter notes, spicy, ripe fruit, toasty.

BODEGA VULCANO DE LANZAROTE

Victor Fernández Gopar, 5
35572 Tías (Las Palmas)
☎: +34 928 834 456 - Fax: +34 928 524 384
info@bodegavulcano.es
www.bodegavulcano.es

VULCANO DE LANZAROTE 2010 B
malvasía.

90 Colour: bright straw. Nose: white flowers, earthy notes, fresh fruit. Palate: flavourful, fruity, fresh, good acidity.

VULCANO DE LANZAROTE 2010 B
malvasía.

88 Colour: bright straw. Nose: candied fruit, citrus fruit, white flowers. Palate: flavourful, sweetness, fleshy, complex.

VULCANO DOLCE 2009 B
moscatel.

90 Color golden. Aroma powerfull, floral, honeyed notes, candied fruit, fragrant herbs. Taste flavourful, sweet, fresh, fruity, good acidity, long.

VULCANO DE LANZAROTE 2010 RD
50% negramoll, 50% listán negro.

84 Colour: light cherry. Nose: ripe fruit, raspberry, medium intensity. Palate: good acidity, flavourful, ripe fruit.

VULCANO DE LANZAROTE 2010 T
50% listán negro, 50% negramoll.

87 Colour: deep cherry. Nose: red berry notes, ripe fruit, toasty, spicy. Palate: flavourful, spicy, ripe fruit.

BODEGAS MALPAÍS DE MAGUEZ

Cueva de los Verdes, 5
35542 Punta Mujeres - Haria (Las Palmas)
☎: +34 616 908 484 - Fax: +34 928 848 110
bodegamalpais@gmail.com

LA GRIETA MALVASÍA SECO 2010 B
malvasía.

84 Colour: bright straw. Nose: jasmine, ripe fruit, citrus fruit, medium intensity. Palate: flavourful, fruity, fine bitter notes.

LA GRIETA 2010 T

81 Colour: cherry, garnet rim. Nose: powerfull, fruit preserve, raspberry, overripe fruit. Palate: flavourful, fine bitter notes, sweetness.

BODEGAS RUBICÓN

Ctra. Teguise - Yaiza, 2
35570 La Geria - Yaiza (Las Palmas)
☎: +34 928 173 708
bodegasrubicon@gmail.com
www.vinosrubicon.com

RUBICÓN MOSCATEL 2010 B
100% moscatel.

89 Colour: bright straw. Nose: ripe fruit, citrus fruit, fruit expression, honeyed notes. Palate: powerful, good acidity, flavourful.

RUBICÓN 2010 B
100% malvasía.

88 Colour: bright straw. Nose: powerfull, varietal, citrus fruit, white flowers. Palate: flavourful, fruity, fine bitter notes.

AMALIA 2010 B
100% malvasía.

87 Colour: bright straw. Nose: fresh fruit, citrus fruit, white flowers, dried herbs. Palate: flavourful, fruity, fresh.

RUBICÓN 2010 B
90% malvasía, 10% moscatel.

84 Colour: bright straw. Nose: white flowers, candied fruit, citrus fruit. Palate: fine bitter notes, good acidity, sweetness.

SWEET GOLD 2009 B
100% moscatel.

91 Colour: bright straw. Nose: citrus fruit, ripe fruit, honeyed notes. Palate: flavourful, powerful, sweet, good acidity.

EL GRIFO

Lugar de El Grifo, s/n
35550 San Bartolomé (Las Palmas)
☎: +34 928 524 036 - Fax: +34 928 832 634
malvasia@elgrifo.com
www.elgrifo.com

EL GRIFO MALVASÍA COLECCIÓN 2010 B
100% malvasía.

91 Colour: bright straw. Nose: fresh, fresh fruit, white flowers, varietal, expressive. Palate: flavourful, fruity, good acidity, balanced.

EL GRIFO CANARI DULCE DE LICOR B
100% malvasía.

95 Colour: light mahogany. Nose: powerfull, floral, honeyed notes, candied fruit, fragrant herbs, acetaldehyde, roasted almonds. Palate: flavourful, sweet, good acidity, long, concentrated.

ARIANA 2010 T
60% listán negro, 40% syrah.

93 Colour: black cherry. Nose: powerfull, characterful, raspberry, fruit expression, red berry notes, creamy oak, sweet spices. Palate: powerful, fleshy, fine bitter notes, round tannins.

EL GRIFO 2010 T BARRICA
100% listán negro.

91 Color bright cherry. Aroma ripe fruit, sweet spices, creamy oak, expressive. Taste flavourful, fruity, toasty, round tannins.

EL GRIFO 2010 T
100% listán negro.

90 Colour: cherry, purple rim. Nose: sweet spices, cocoa bean, red berry notes, ripe fruit. Palate: flavourful, good acidity, powerful, round tannins.

EL GRIFO MALVASÍA COLECCIÓN 2010 SEMIDULCE
100% malvasía.

89 Colour: bright straw. Nose: candied fruit, citrus fruit, dried flowers. Palate: flavourful, fruity, good acidity.

MOZAGA

Ctra. Arrecife a Tinajo, 78
35562 Mozaga (Lanzarote)
☎: +34 928 520 485 - Fax: +34 928 521 409
bodegasmozaga@hotmail.com

MOZAGA MALVASIA SEMIDULCE 2010 B
10% listán blanco, 90% malvasía.

85 Colour: bright straw. Nose: fruit expression, citrus fruit, white flowers. Palate: flavourful, fruity, sweetness.

MOZAGA MALVASIA SECO 2010 B
90% malvasía, 10% listán blanco.

84 Colour: bright straw. Nose: powerfull, citrus fruit, earthy notes. Palate: fine bitter notes, flavourful, spicy.

MOZAGA 75 VINO DE LICOR 2009 B
100% moscatel.

92 Colour: old gold. Nose: candied fruit, fruit liqueur notes, varnish, fruit liqueur notes. Palate: powerful, good acidity, fine bitter notes, sweet.

TEIGA 2008 BFB
100% malvasía.

86 Colour: bright golden. Nose: cocoa bean, roasted almonds, candied fruit, warm. Palate: flavourful, powerful, sweetness.

REYMAR

Pza. Virgen de Los Dolores, 19
35560 Tinajo (Las Palmas)
☎: +34 928 840 737 - Fax: +34 928 840 737
reymarmalvasia@terra.es

REYMAR MALVASÍA SECO 2010 B
malvasía.

88 Colour: bright straw. Nose: ripe fruit, citrus fruit, lactic notes, white flowers. Palate: flavourful, ripe fruit, long.

REYMAR MOSCATEL DIEGO 2010 BFB
85% diego, 15% moscatel.

88 Colour: bright yellow. Nose: ripe fruit, sweet spices, creamy oak, fragrant herbs. Palate: rich, smoky aftertaste, flavourful, fresh, good acidity.

REYMAR MALVASÍA MOSCATEL 2010 B
malvasía, moscatel.

86 Colour: bright straw. Nose: white flowers, citrus fruit, candied fruit. Palate: flavourful, fruity, good acidity.

REYMAR MOSCATEL DIEGO 2010 B
50% diego, 50% moscatel.

83 Colour: pale. Nose: powerfull, fresh fruit, fruit expression, honeyed notes. Palate: flavourful, sweetness, fine bitter notes.

REYMAR MOSCATEL DULCE 2006 B
moscatel.

92 Colour: bright golden. Nose: candied fruit, citrus fruit, sweet spices. Palate: powerful, confected, ripe fruit.

REYMAR MALVASÍA DULCE 2006 B
moscatel.

90 Colour: bright golden. Nose: fruit liqueur notes, dried fruit. Palate: powerful, sweetness, fine bitter notes.

REYMAR 2010 RD
listán negro.

80 Colour: onion pink. Nose: fruit liqueur notes, raspberry, macerated fruit. Palate: confected, ripe fruit.

REYMAR 2010 T

88 Colour: cherry, garnet rim. Nose: ripe fruit, fruit expression, creamy oak, sweet spices. Palate: spicy, ripe fruit, balsamic.

REYMAR VINO DE LICOR
listán negro.

85 Colour: cherry, garnet rim. Nose: powerfull, fruit liqueur notes, candied fruit. Palate: sweet, fruity, concentrated.

TIERRA DE VOLCANES

Las Vistas, 18
35570 Yaizas (Las Palmas)
☎: +34 630 889 454
stato@hotmail.es

TIERRA DE VOLCANES 2010 B
malvasía.

87 Colour: bright straw. Nose: powerfull, fresh fruit, citrus fruit, white flowers. Palate: flavourful, fruity, fresh.

TIERRA DE VOLCANES 2010 RD
malvasía, listán negro.

82 Colour: rose. Nose: powerfull, ripe fruit, candied fruit. Palate: powerful, fruity, sweetness.

VEGA DE YUCO

Camino del Cabezo s/n
35571 Tías (Las Palmas)
☎: +34 928 524 316 - Fax: +34 928 524 316
bodega@vegadeyuco.es
www.vegadeyuco.es

YAIZA 2010 B
malvasía.

88 Colour: bright straw. Nose: fresh fruit, citrus fruit, ripe fruit, white flowers. Palate: flavourful, fruity, fine bitter notes, good acidity.

VEGA DE YUCO 2010 B
100% malvasía.

85 Colour: pale. Nose: ripe fruit, citrus fruit, white flowers. Palate: flavourful, fruity, sweetness.

YAIZA SEMI 2010 B
100% malvasía.

85 Colour: bright straw. Nose: white flowers, fresh fruit, citrus fruit. Palate: flavourful, sweetness, good acidity.

PRINCESA ICO SEMIDULCE 2010 B
85% malvasía, 10% moscatel, 5% diego.

84 Colour: bright straw. Nose: candied fruit, fruit expression, honeyed notes. Palate: sweet, flavourful, fine bitter notes.

VEGA DE YUCO 2010 RD
listán negro.

87 Color rose, purple rim. Aroma powerfull, ripe fruit, red berry notes, floral, expressive. Taste fleshy, powerful, fruity, fresh.

VEGA DE YUCO 2010 T
listán negro.

82 Colour: deep cherry. Nose: candied fruit, warm, earthy notes. Palate: spicy, fine bitter notes.

YAIZA 2009 T
100% listán negro.

83 Colour: cherry, garnet rim. Nose: toasty, aromatic coffee, earthy notes. Palate: powerful, fine bitter notes, toasty.

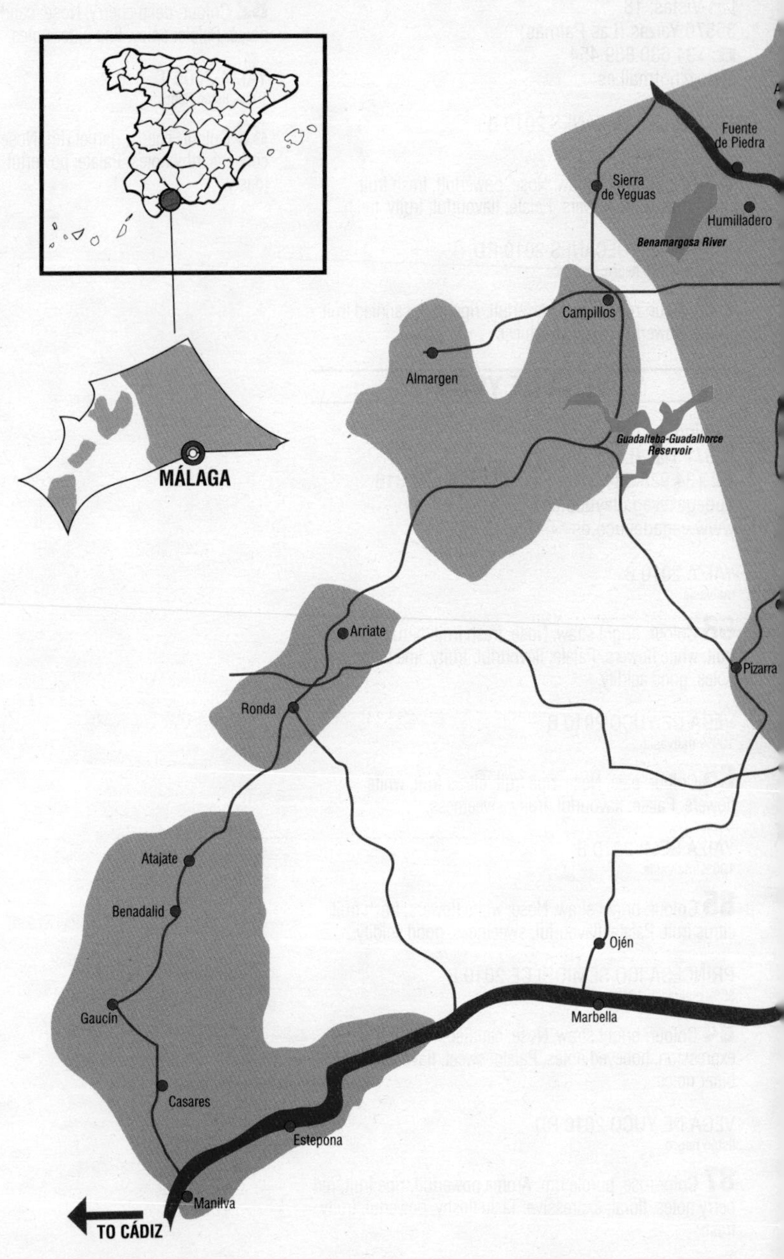
MÁLAGA
Fuente de Piedra
Sierra de Yeguas
Humilladero
Benamargosa River
Campillos
Almargen
Guadalteba-Guadalhorce Reservoir
Arriate
Pizarra
Ronda
Atajate
Benadalid
Ojén
Gaucín
Marbella
Casares
Estepona
Manilva
TO CÁDIZ

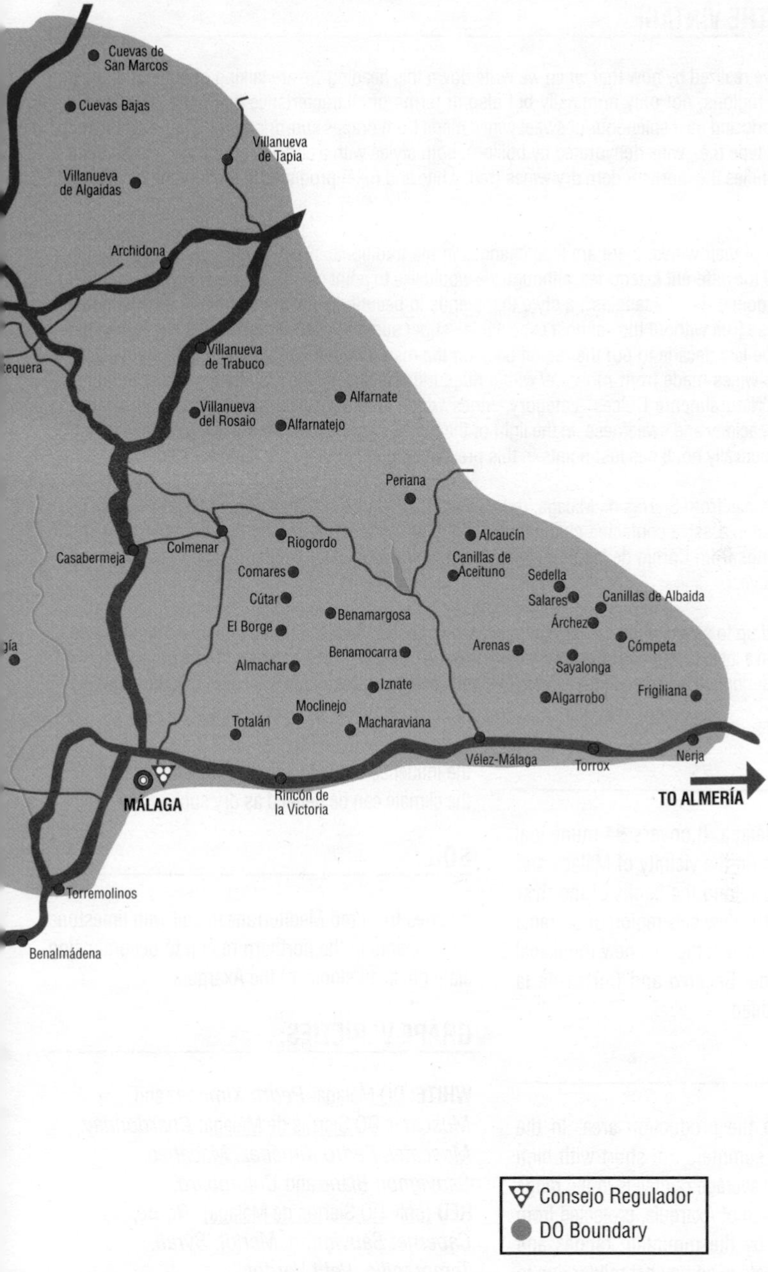

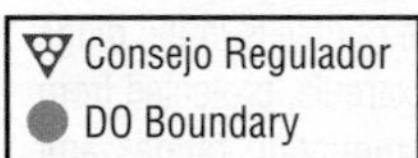
Cuevas de San Marcos
Cuevas Bajas
Villanueva de Tapia
Villanueva de Algaidas
Archidona
Villanueva de Trabuco
Alfarnate
Villanueva del Rosaio
Alfarnatejo
Periana
Colmenar
Riogordo
Casabermeja
Alcaucín
Canillas de Aceituno
Comares
Sedella
Salares
Canillas de Albaida
Cútar
Benamargosa
Árchez
El Borge
Benamocarra
Arenas
Cómpeta
Almachar
Sayalonga
Iznate
Frigiliana
Algarrobo
Moclinejo
Totalán
Macharaviana
Vélez-Málaga
Torrox
Nerja
MÁLAGA
Rincón de la Victoria
TO ALMERÍA
Torremolinos
Benalmádena
Consejo Regulador
DO Boundary

DO MÁLAGA Y SIERRAS DE MÁLAGA

NEWS ABOUT THE VINTAGE:

The reader may have realized by now that when we write down this heading we are talking of not just one but two different wine regions, not only nominally but also in terms of characteristics and style. The former represents the historic and past splendour of sweet wines made from grapes sun-dried on woven-grass mats, and the "arropado" type (i.e., wine dehydrated by boiling), both styles with a certain resemblance to Madeira wines; the latter signifies the more modern dry wines (red, white and rosé) produced in the mountains around the city of Ronda.

As for the typology of their wines, there are little changes in the traditional sweet renderings, except for the confusing names of the different categories, although we would like to point out it is praiseworthy the fact that they have not abandoned the "trasañejos", a style that blends in beautifully fine pungent and acetone notes with those of overripe fruit without the –almost expectable– super sugary palate. Nevertheless, the wines that have managed in the last decade to put the region back on the map (when it was about to fall into oblivion) are the sweet white wines made from *moscatel* with a huge mineral quality. Also, although to a –probably– lesser extent, the "Naturalmente Dulces" category, wines which year after year show wonderful balance between fruit notes, acidity and sweetness, in the light of the ratings that most of them have managed to get, and the fact that practically none has lost points in this present edition compared to last year's.

Regarding the dry wines from Sierras de Málaga, reds from the 2010 vintage show pretty irregular in quality, with fruit notes of an excessive confected character, although it was amazing to find that the *pinot noir* and *petit verdot* renderings from Cortijo de los Aguilares, within their (necessary) southern edge, have achieved a splendid level this year.

We have only tasted up to seven white samples and, even when currently they show a quality worth little else than a good "tapa" in a local tavern, we understand there is good potential in this category. There are also some well-made rosé renderings to be found in the region, but with such a vast catalogue within the DO, they logically get little attention.

LOCATION:

In the province of Málaga. It covers 54 municipal areas along the coast (in the vicinity of Málaga and Estepona) and inland (along the banks of the river Genil), together with the new sub-region of Serranía de Ronda, a region to which the two new municipal districts of Cuevas del Becerro and Cortes de la Frontera have been added.

CLIMATE:

Varies depending on the production area. In the northern region, the summers are short with high temperatures, and the average rainfall is in the range of 500 mm; in the region of Axarquía, protected from the northerly winds by the mountain ranges and facing south, the climate is somewhat milder due to the influence of the Mediterranean; whilst in the west, the climate can be defined as dry subhumid.

SOIL:

It varies from red Mediterranean soil with limestone components in the northern region to decomposing slate on steep slopes of the Axarquía.

GRAPE VARIETIES:

WHITE: DO Málaga: *Pedro Ximénez* and *Moscatel*; DO Sierras de Málaga: *Chardonnay, Moscatel, Pedro Ximénez, Macabeo, Sauvignon Blanc* and *Colombard.*
RED (only DO Sierras de Málaga): *Romé, Cabernet Sauvignon, Merlot, Syrah, Tempranillo, Petit Verdot.*

FIGURES:

Vineyard surface: 1,320 – **Wine-Growers:** 476 – **Wineries:** 39 – **2010 Harvest rating:** N/A – **Production:** 2,700,000 – **Market percentages:** --% domestic. --% export

TYPOLOGY OF CLASSIC WINES:

A) LIQUEUR WINES: from 15 to 22% vol.
B) NATURAL SWEET WINES: from 15 to 22 % vol. obtained from the *Moscatel* or *Pedro Ximénez* varieties, from musts with a minimum sugar content of 244 grams/litre.

c) NATURALLY SWEET WINES (with the same varieties, over 13% vol. and from musts with 300 grams of sugar/litre) and still wines (from 10 to 15% vol.).

Depending on their ageing:
- **Málaga Joven:** Unaged still wines.
- **Málaga Pálido:** Unaged non-still wines.
- **Málaga:** Wines aged for between 6 and 24 months.
- **Málaga Noble:** Wines aged for between 2 and 3 years.
- **Málaga Añejo:** Wines aged for between 3 and 5 years.
- **Málaga Trasañejo:** Wines aged for over 5 years.

CONSEJO REGULADOR
Plaza de los Viñeros,1
29008 Málaga
☎: +34 952 227 990 - Fax: +34 952 227 990
@ info@vinomalaga.com
www.vinomalaga.com

GENERAL CHARACTERISTICS OF THE WINES

TRADITIONAL WINES	Their personality is marked by the grape syrup, the must that is concentrated or dehydrated by the heat that caramelises the wine and gives it its characteristic colour, sweetness and mellowness. There is a distinction between the 'Málaga', a sweet wine produced from the first must of the grape, the *Pedro Ximénez* and the *Moscatel*, which are produced from the grapes of the same name.
MODERN WINES	Produced from autochtonous and foreign varieties, they are marked by the heat of the climate, especially in the case of the red wines, which are very sunny with 'scorched' notes. The new natural sweet whites offer pleasant soft, mellow aromas and are very fresh on the palate, and sweet at the same time.

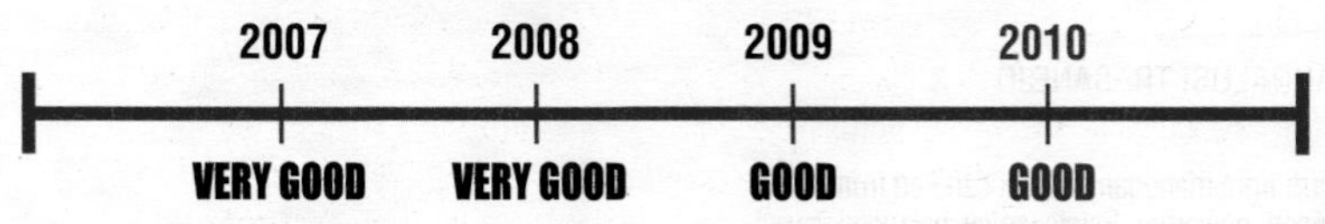

BODEGA A. MUÑOZ CABRERA

San Bartolomé, 5
29738 Moclinejo (Málaga)
☎: +34 952 400 594 - Fax: +34 952 400 743
bodega@dimobe.es
www.dimobe.es

PIAMATER 2010 B
moscatel.

88 Colour: yellow, greenish rim. Nose: candied fruit, fruit liqueur notes, dried herbs, medium intensity. Palate: balanced, sweet, fruity.

EL LAGAR DE CABRERA SYRAH 2009 T
syrah.

86 Colour: cherry, garnet rim. Nose: medium intensity, balanced, red berry notes, ripe fruit. Palate: flavourful, fruity, easy to drink.

EL LAGAR DE CABRERA 2008 TC
syrah.

86 Colour: cherry, garnet rim. Nose: toasty, sweet spices, medium intensity. Palate: ripe fruit, easy to drink, spicy.

SEÑORÍO DE BROCHES 2010 MOSCATEL
moscatel.

86 Colour: bright straw, greenish rim. Nose: medium intensity, balanced, faded flowers. Palate: rich, varietal, correct.

EL LAGAR DE CABRERA 2010 MOSCATEL
moscatel.

85 Colour: bright straw. Nose: white flowers, fruit expression, dried herbs. Palate: fleshy, flavourful, fresh.

ZUMBRAL CONARTE 2008 MOSCATEL
moscatel.

85 Colour: light mahogany. Nose: sweet spices, aged wood nuances, cocoa bean, toasty. Palate: rich, flavourful, toasty.

ARCOS DE MOCLINEJO DULCE PX
pedro ximénez.

87 Colour: light mahogany. Nose: toasty, sweet spices, dark chocolate. Palate: good structure, fruity, long, spicy, balanced.

RUJAQ ANDALUSI TRASAÑEJO
moscatel.

87 Colour: light mahogany. Nose: candied fruit, dried fruit, balanced, powerfull. Palate: spicy, balanced, sweet.

BODEGA ANTIGUA CASA DE GUARDIA

Ctra. Olias - Comares- El Romerillo
29197 (Málaga)
☎: +34 952 030 714 - Fax: +34 952 252 150
info@casadeguardia.com
www.casadeguardia.com

VERDIALES CR
100% pedro ximénez.

88 Colour: light mahogany. Nose: aromatic coffee, spicy, toasty, dried fruit. Palate: balanced, correct, full, spicy.

ISABEL II TRASAÑEJO
100% moscatel.

93 Colour: dark mahogany. Nose: dried fruit, cocoa bean, creamy oak, sweet spices, dark chocolate. Palate: creamy, powerful, flavourful, spirituous.

PAJARETE 1908 VINO DE LICOR
100% pedro ximénez.

87 Colour: light mahogany. Nose: dried fruit, aromatic coffee, caramel. Palate: good acidity, spirituous, unctuous.

VERDIALES SECO VINO DE LICOR
pedro ximénez.

86 Colour: old gold, amber rim. Nose: ripe fruit, expressive, cocoa bean, sweet spices. Palate: fine bitter notes, correct, spirituous, flavourful.

PEDRO XIMENEZ 1908 VINO DE LICOR
100% pedro ximénez.

85 Colour: dark mahogany. Nose: sweet spices, dark chocolate, aged wood nuances, creamy oak. Palate: full, rich, fleshy, toasty.

VERDIALES CONARTE VINO DE LICOR DULCE
70% pedro ximénez, 30% moscatel.

90 Colour: old gold, amber rim. Nose: fruit liqueur notes, varnish, dark chocolate, sweet spices, toasty. Palate: powerful, flavourful, fleshy, complex, round.

BODEGA CUESTA LA VIÑA

Antigua Ctra. Ronda-Sevilla, km. 21,6. A-2300
Montecorto
29400 Ronda (Málaga)
☎: +34 629 589 336 - Fax: +34 952 870 719
vinosjorgebonet@gmail.com

JORGE BONET 2010 T
syrah.

86 Colour: cherry, purple rim. Nose: fruit preserve, slightly evolved. Palate: fleshy, good structure, flavourful, round tannins.

JORGE BONET TSMC 2008 T
tempranillo, syrah, merlot, cabernet sauvignon.

87 Colour: cherry, garnet rim. Nose: ripe fruit, dark chocolate, sweet spices. Palate: flavourful, ripe fruit, long.

JORGE BONET 2007 T
tempranillo, syrah, merlot, cabernet sauvignon.

89 Colour: light cherry, orangey edge. Nose: ripe fruit, cocoa bean, caramel, toasty. Palate: powerful, flavourful, fleshy, toasty.

BODEGA DOÑA FELISA

Apartado 432
29400 Ronda (Málaga)
☎: +34 951 166 033 - Fax: +34 951 166 033
jlosantos@chinchillawine.com
www.chinchillawine.com

CHINCHILLA ALOQUE 2010 RD
tempranillo.

83 Colour: rose, purple rim. Nose: red berry notes, ripe fruit, slightly evolved. Palate: good acidity, correct, spicy.

CHINCHILLA NUEVO 2010 T ROBLE
tempranillo, cabernet sauvignon.

84 Colour: cherry, purple rim. Nose: red berry notes, warm, medium intensity. Palate: flavourful, fruity, light-bodied.

CHINCHILLA SEIS + SEIS 2007 T ROBLE
tempranillo, syrah.

82 Colour: cherry, garnet rim. Nose: overripe fruit, medium intensity, spicy. Palate: correct, fleshy.

CHINCHILLA CONARTE 2006 T
cabernet sauvignon, merlot.

88 Colour: bright cherry. Nose: ripe fruit, spicy, fruit liqueur notes. Palate: flavourful, fruity, toasty, round tannins.

CHINCHILLA 2006 T
cabernet sauvignon, merlot, syrah.

87 Colour: cherry, garnet rim. Nose: overripe fruit, spicy, powerfull. Palate: fleshy, full, flavourful, round tannins.

CHINCHILLA CABERNET 2005 T
cabernet sauvignon.

89 Colour: pale ruby, brick rim edge. Nose: ripe fruit, spicy, toasty, old leather. Palate: good acidity, balanced, spirituous.

BODEGA F. SCHATZ

Finca Sanguijuela, s/n Apdo. Correos 131
29400 Ronda (Málaga)
☎: +34 952 871 313 - Fax: +34 952 871 313
bodega@f-schatz.com
www.f-schatz.com

SCHATZ CHARDONNAY 2010 B
chardonnay.

83 Colour: bright yellow. Nose: citrus fruit, ripe fruit, spicy, creamy oak. Palate: lacks balance, fresh, light-bodied.

FINCA SANGUIJUELA 2007 TC
tempranillo, syrah, merlot, cabernet sauvignon.

89 Colour: cherry, garnet rim. Nose: ripe fruit, sweet spices, cocoa bean, toasty. Palate: spirituous, powerful, flavourful.

SCHATZ PETIT-VERDOT 2007 TC
petit verdot.

87 Colour: cherry, garnet rim. Nose: ripe fruit, fruit liqueur notes, aromatic coffee, roasted coffee. Palate: spirituous, good acidity, flavourful.

SCHATZ PINOT-NOIR 2007 TC
pinot noir.

86 Colour: pale ruby, brick rim edge. Nose: candied fruit, cocoa bean, aromatic coffee, toasty. Palate: good acidity, powerful, flavourful.

BODEGA JOAQUÍN FERNÁNDEZ

Finca Los Frutales Paraje de los Frontones
29400 Ronda (Málaga)
☎: +34 951 166 043 - Fax: +34 951 166 043
info@bodegajf.es
www.bodegajf.com

ROSADO LOS FRUTALES 2010 RD
merlot, syrah.

85 Colour: salmon. Nose: powerfull, ripe fruit, red berry notes, floral. Palate: fleshy, powerful, fruity, fresh.

FINCA LOS FRUTALES MERLOT SYRAH 2007 TC
merlot, syrah.

86 Colour: light cherry, orangey edge. Nose: slightly evolved, caramel, wet leather. Palate: good acidity, fine bitter notes, flavourful.

FINCA LOS FRUTALES IGUALADO 2007 T
garnacha, merlot, syrah, cabernet sauvignon.

82 Colour: pale ruby, brick rim edge. Nose: ripe fruit, aged wood nuances, spicy. Palate: slightly evolved, light-bodied, flavourful.

BODEGA KIENINGER

Los Frontones, 67 (Apdo. Correos 215)
29400 Ronda (Málaga)
☎: +34 952 879 554
martin@bodegakieninger.com
www.bodegakieninger.com

VINANA (13 MESES BARRICA) 2009 T
60% cabernet sauvignon, 30% cabernet franc, 10% merlot.

90 Colour: cherry, garnet rim. Nose: ripe fruit, spicy, toasty, complex. Palate: powerful, flavourful, toasty.

BODEGA LOS BUJEOS

Ctra. Ronda El Burgo, Km 1
29400 Ronda (Málaga)
☎: +34 610 269 422 - Fax: +34 952 161 160
bodegapasoslargos@gmail.com
www.bodegapasoslargos.com

A PASOS 2006 T
syrah, garnacha, merlot, cabernet sauvignon.

91 Colour: cherry, garnet rim. Nose: ripe fruit, expressive, balanced, sweet spices, creamy oak. Palate: powerful, flavourful, fleshy, complex.

PASOS LARGOS 2005 T ROBLE
cabernet sauvignon, petit verdot, merlot, syrah.

91 Colour: bright cherry, garnet rim. Nose: complex, balanced, ripe fruit, spicy. Palate: good structure, fruity, flavourful.

BODEGA VETAS

Camino Nador- Finca El Baco, s/n
29350 Arriate (Málaga)
☎: +34 647 177 620
info@bodegavetas.com
www.bodegavetas.com

VETAS SELECCIÓN 2005 T
40% cabernet franc, 40% cabernet sauvignon, 20% petit verdot.

93 Colour: cherry, garnet rim. Nose: ripe fruit, mineral, earthy notes, creamy oak. Palate: good acidity, spirituous, powerful, flavourful.

VETAS PETIT VERDOT 2004 T
100% petit verdot.

93 Colour: bright cherry. Nose: ripe fruit, sweet spices, creamy oak, expressive, mineral. Palate: flavourful, fruity, toasty, round tannins.

BODEGA Y VIÑEDOS DE LA CAPUCHINA

Cortijo La Capuchina, Apdo. Correos 26
29532 Mollina (Málaga)
☎: +34 952 111 565 - Fax: +34 952 031 583
info@bodegalacapuchina.es
www.bodegalacapuchina.es

CAPUCHINA VIEJA MOSCATEL SECO 2010 B
100% moscatel.

88 Colour: bright straw. Nose: ripe fruit, tropical fruit, white flowers. Palate: flavourful, fruity, fleshy, good acidity.

CAPUCHINA VIEJA 2007 T
40% cabernet franc, 40% syrah, 10% cabernet sauvignon, 10% merlot.

90 Colour: cherry, garnet rim. Nose: ripe fruit, earthy notes, spicy, creamy oak, balanced. Palate: concentrated, fleshy, complex, flavourful.

CAPUCHINA VIEJA CONARTE 2007 T
40% cabernet franc, 40% syrah, 10% cabernet sauvignon, 10% merlot.

88 Colour: cherry, garnet rim. Nose: ripe fruit, scrubland, mineral, spicy, toasty. Palate: flavourful, fleshy, spirituous, round.

CAPUCHINA VIEJA SOL 2010 BLANCO DULCE
100% moscatel.

89 Colour: bright golden. Nose: ripe fruit, tropical fruit, sweet spices, citrus fruit. Palate: unctuous, powerful, flavourful, rich.

BODEGAS ANTAKIRA

Sol, 9
29328 Sierra de Yeguas (Málaga)
☎: +34 952 746 474 - Fax: +34 952 721 000
info@narbonasolis.com
www.narbonasolis.com

REBALAJE 2010 B
85% doradilla, 10% moscatel, 5% pedro ximénez.

84 Colour: bright yellow. Nose: citrus fruit, fresh fruit, fragrant herbs. Palate: good acidity, powerful, fruity.

REBALAJE 2009 T
100% syrah.

83 Colour: cherry, garnet rim. Nose: ripe fruit, floral, grassy, sweet spices. Palate: good acidity, fleshy, green.

BODEGAS BENTOMIZ

Finca Almendro
Pago Cuesta Robano
29752 Sayalonga (Málaga)
☎: +34 952 115 939
info@bodegasbentomiz.com
www.bodegasbentomiz.com

ARIYANAS SECO SOBRE LÍAS 2010 B
100% moscatel.

89 Colour: bright straw. Nose: jasmine, white flowers, citrus fruit, balanced, elegant. Palate: fruity, good acidity, balanced.

ARIYANAS TERRUÑO PIZARROSO 2008 BC
100% moscatel.

94 Colour: bright golden. Nose: white flowers, mineral, fragrant herbs, citrus fruit. Palate: correct, unctuous, fleshy, complex.

ARIYANAS TINTO DE ENSAMBLAJE 2009 T
40% petit verdot, 35% tempranillo, romé.

90 Colour: cherry, garnet rim. Nose: ripe fruit, earthy notes, balsamic herbs. Palate: spicy, powerful, flavourful, fleshy.

ARIYANAS NATURALMENTE DULCE 2008 BLANCO DULCE
100% moscatel.

92 Colour: bright golden. Nose: fresh fruit, ripe fruit, sweet spices, honeyed notes. Palate: flavourful, rich, fleshy.

BODEGAS EXCELENCIA

Almendra, 40-42
29400 Ronda (Málaga)
☎: +34 952 236 622 - Fax: +34 952 244 718
jose.bravo@bodegasexcelencia.com
www.bodegasexcelencia.com

LOS FRONTONES 2008 TC

87 Colour: cherry, garnet rim. Nose: fruit preserve, sweet spices, dark chocolate, powerfull. Palate: flavourful, fleshy, round tannins.

BODEGAS GARCÍA HIDALGO

Partido Los Morales- LLano de la Cruz
29400 Ronda (Málaga)
☎: +34 670 940 693 - Fax: +34 951 920 675
info@bodegasgarciahidalgo.es
www.bodegasgarciahidalgo.es

ALCOBACÍN S/C T ROBLE
cabernet sauvignon, syrah, merlot.

83 Colour: cherry, purple rim. Nose: fruit preserve, sweet spices, dark chocolate. Palate: flavourful, fleshy, pruney.

BODEGAS GOMARA

Diseminado Maqueda Alto, 59
29590 Campanillas (Málaga)
☎: +34 952 434 195 - Fax: +34 952 626 312
bodegas@gomara.com
www.gomara.com

GOMARA CONARTE S/C B
pedro ximénez, moscatel.

87 Colour: light mahogany. Nose: candied fruit, spicy, pattiserie, acetaldehyde, dry nuts. Palate: sweet, spirituous, flavourful, creamy.

PAJARETE GOMARA
100% pedro ximénez.

85 Colour: dark mahogany. Nose: aromatic coffee, sweet spices, toasty, varnish. Palate: spirituous, flavourful, rich.

SECO AÑEJO GOMARA
100% pedro ximénez.

85 Colour: bright golden. Nose: warm, ripe fruit, dry nuts, creamy oak. Palate: powerful, flavourful, fleshy, spirituous.

MÁLAGA DULCE MÁLAGA
90% pedro ximénez, 10% moscatel.

84 Colour: dark mahogany. Nose: caramel, aromatic coffee, roasted coffee, varnish. Palate: creamy, long, flavourful.

GOMARA MOSCATEL
100% moscatel.

85 Colour: bright golden. Nose: candied fruit, honeyed notes, powerfull, floral. Palate: rich, flavourful, concentrated.

SECO GOMARA NOBLE
100% pedro ximénez.

82 Colour: bright yellow. Nose: pungent, candied fruit, dry nuts, white flowers. Palate: light-bodied, easy to drink, sweetness.

GOMARA PEDRO XIMÉNEZ PX
100% pedro ximénez.

82 Color dark mahogany. Aroma complex, fruit liqueur notes, dried fruit, pattiserie, toasty. Taste sweet, rich, unctuous, powerful.

MÁLAGA TRASAÑEJO GOMARA TRASAÑEJO
pedro ximénez.

90 Colour: dark mahogany. Nose: dried fruit, cocoa bean, aged wood nuances, caramel. Palate: good acidity, spirituous, flavourful, fleshy, toasty.

GRAN GOMARA TRASAÑEJO SOLERA
70% pedro ximénez, 30% moscatel.

90 Colour: mahogany. Nose: pungent, acetaldehyde, candied fruit, sweet spices, dry nuts. Palate: flavourful, sweet, spicy, long.

BODEGAS JORGE ORDÓÑEZ & CO

Bartolome Esteban Murillo, 11 Pol. Ind. La Pañoleta
29700 Velez-Málaga (Málaga)
☎: +34 952 504 706 - Fax: +34 951 284 796
office@jorge-ordonez.es
www.jorge-ordonez.es

JORGE ORDÓÑEZ & CO BOTANI 2010 B
moscatel.

91 Colour: bright straw. Nose: white flowers, jasmine, complex, expressive. Palate: flavourful, fruity, good acidity.

JORGE ORDÓÑEZ & CO Nº 1 SELECCIÓN ESPECIAL 2008 B
moscatel.

95 Colour: bright yellow. Nose: citrus fruit, candied fruit, white flowers, fragrant herbs. Palate: good acidity, balanced, elegant, round, unctuous.

ORDÓÑEZ & CO. Nº3 VIÑAS VIEJAS 2006 B
moscatel.

94 Colour: bright golden. Nose: balanced, expressive, complex, candied fruit, faded flowers. Palate: rich, flavourful, sweet, complex.

JORGE ORDÓÑEZ & CO Nº 2 VICTORIA 2008 BLANCO DULCE
moscatel.

96 Colour: bright yellow. Nose: powerfull, complex, citrus fruit, candied fruit, mineral, expressive. Palate: good acidity, balanced, elegant, flavourful, fruity, complex.

BODEGAS LUNARES DE RONDA

Almendra, 3
29400 Ronda (Málaga)
☎: +34 649 690 847
pmorales@bodegaslunares.com
www.bodegaslunares.com

ALTOCIELO 2009 T
syrah, cabernet sauvignon.

89 Colour: cherry, garnet rim. Nose: red berry notes, ripe fruit, sweet spices, creamy oak.

BODEGAS MÁLAGA VIRGEN

Autovía A-92, Málaga-Sevilla, Km. 132
29520 Fuente de Piedra (Málaga)
☎: +34 952 319 454 - Fax: +34 952 359 819
didier.bricout@bodegasmalagavirgen.com
www.bodegasmalagavirgen.com

TRES LEONES S/C B
moscatel.

86 Colour: bright yellow. Nose: varietal, balanced, jasmine. Palate: fruity, flavourful, good acidity, balanced, sweet, rich.

BARÓN DE RIVERO 2010 B
chardonnay, pedro ximénez.

85 Colour: pale. Nose: fresh fruit, white flowers, fresh. Palate: good acidity, fresh, fruity, flavourful.

SECO TRASAÑEJO B
pedro ximénez.

92 Colour: old gold, amber rim. Nose: fruit liqueur notes, roasted almonds, dry nuts, aged wood nuances. Palate: unctuous, rich, flavourful, long.

EL VIVILLO 2009 T
syrah.

82 Colour: cherry, garnet rim. Nose: fruit preserve, warm, balsamic herbs, sweet spices. Palate: good acidity, spirituous, round.

PERNALES SYRAH 2008 T
syrah.

88 Colour: cherry, garnet rim. Nose: medium intensity, balanced, red berry notes, ripe fruit. Palate: flavourful, fruity, round tannins.

SOL DE MÁLAGA
pedro ximénez, moscatel.

88 Colour: dark mahogany. Nose: dried fruit, aromatic coffee, aged wood nuances, sweet spices, varnish. Palate: concentrated, flavourful, powerful, fleshy, toasty.

CHORRERA CREAM AÑEJO
pedro ximénez.

91 Colour: dark mahogany. Nose: aged wood nuances, spicy, varnish, dry nuts, aromatic coffee, cocoa bean. Palate: fleshy, complex, powerful, flavourful.

TRAJINERO AÑEJO
pedro ximénez.

89 Colour: old gold, amber rim. Nose: dry nuts, aged wood nuances, spicy, pattiserie. Palate: powerful, flavourful, fleshy, complex.

MOSCATEL IBERIA MALAGA
moscatel.

87 Colour: light mahogany. Nose: dry nuts, caramel, pattiserie, sweet spices. Palate: fleshy, powerful, flavourful, long.

DON SALVADOR MOSCATEL
moscatel.

92 Colour: light mahogany. Nose: balanced, expressive, complex, acetaldehyde, varnish, sweet spices. Palate: sweet, flavourful, balanced.

MOSCATEL RESERVA DE FAMILIA MOSCATEL
moscatel.

90 Colour: old gold. Nose: dried fruit, caramel, aromatic coffee, sweet spices, toasty, complex. Palate: fleshy, complex, powerful, flavourful, toasty.

CARTOJAL PÁLIDO
moscatel, morisco.

87 Colour: bright yellow. Nose: white flowers, citrus fruit, medium intensity. Palate: good acidity, correct, flavourful.

PEDRO XIMÉNEZ RESERVA DE FAMILIA PX
pedro ximénez.

91 Colour: mahogany. Nose: candied fruit, dried fruit, honeyed notes, dry nuts. Palate: flavourful, unctuous, spicy, long.

MÁLAGA VIRGEN PX
pedro ximénez.

88 Color dark mahogany. Aroma complex, fruit liqueur notes, dried fruit, pattiserie, toasty. Taste sweet, rich, unctuous, powerful.

DON JUAN TRASAÑEJO
pedro ximénez.

93 Colour: dark mahogany. Nose: creamy oak, sweet spices, pattiserie, pungent, acetaldehyde, complex. Palate: sweet, good structure, rich, elegant, balanced.

DO MÁLAGA Y SIERRAS DE MÁLAGA

BODEGAS MOROSANTO

Cortijo Morosanto: La Cimada Ctra. Arriate - Setenil, Km. 1,6
29400 Ronda (Málaga)
☎: +34 952 216 566 - Fax: +34 952 216 566
info@bogasmorosanto.com
www.bodegasmorosanto.com

ROSADO 2010 RD
tempranillo.

86 Colour: salmon. Nose: fresh fruit, citrus fruit. Palate: flavourful, fruity, easy to drink, good acidity.

LUCIO 2010 T
syrah, tempranillo.

84 Colour: cherry, purple rim. Nose: candied fruit, toasty. Palate: fruity, easy to drink, good finish.

BODEGAS QUITAPENAS

Ctra. de Guadalmar, 12
29004 Málaga (Málaga)
☎: +34 952 247 595 - Fax: +34 952 105 138
ventas@quitapenas.es
www.quitapenas.es

QUITAPENAS MOSCATEL PLATA 2010 B
100% moscatel.

84 Colour: bright golden. Nose: candied fruit, sweet spices, citrus fruit, dried flowers. Palate: sweet, flavourful.

SOL SALERO B
100% pedro ximénez.

88 Colour: old gold. Nose: ripe fruit, dry nuts, sweet spices, pattiserie, varnish. Palate: powerful, flavourful, fleshy, toasty.

GUADALVIN 2010 T
syrah.

80 Colour: cherry, garnet rim. Nose: fruit preserve, boiled fruit notes, grassy. Palate: spirituous, lacks balance.

QUITAPENAS MÁLAGA DULCE 2010 MALAGA
100% pedro ximénez.

82 Colour: dark mahogany. Nose: roasted almonds, varnish, roasted coffee. Palate: powerful, spirituous, fleshy.

MÁLAGA VIÑA 2010 MÁLAGA
90% pedro ximénez, 10% moscatel.

80 Colour: dark mahogany. Nose: aromatic coffee, pattiserie, sweet spices, aged wood nuances. Palate: rich, flavourful, fleshy, complex.

MÁLAGA PX 2007 NOBLE
100% pedro ximénez.

87 Colour: light mahogany. Nose: dried fruit, sweet spices, pattiserie, dark chocolate. Palate: fleshy, concentrated, sweet, full.

MÁLAGA PAJARETE 2006 NOBLE
80% pedro ximénez, 15% moscatel, 5% rome.

86 Colour: light mahogany. Nose: pattiserie, creamy oak, dark chocolate, dried fruit, acetaldehyde. Palate: good structure, flavourful, correct.

QUITAPENAS MOSCATEL DORADO 2009 PÁLIDO
100% moscatel.

85 Colour: bright golden. Nose: candied fruit, fruit liqueur notes, dried flowers. Palate: unctuous, spirituous, sweet.

MÁLAGA VIEJO ABUELO 10 AÑOS TRASAÑEJO
90% pedro ximénez, 10% moscatel.

89 Colour: dark mahogany. Nose: dried fruit, cocoa bean, aromatic coffee, sweet spices, fruit liqueur notes. Palate: fleshy, complex, powerful, flavourful.

MÁLAGA ORO VIEJO 5 AÑOS TRASAÑEJO
90% pedro ximénez, 10% moscatel.

86 Colour: dark mahogany. Nose: caramel, pattiserie, creamy oak, dried fruit. Palate: good acidity, fleshy, rich, flavourful.

BODEGAS SÁNCHEZ ROSADO

Parcela 47- Polígono 14
29570 Cartama (Málaga)
☎: +34 600 504 302 - Fax: +34 952 213 644
info@bodegassanchezrosado.com
www.bodegassanchezrosado.com

CARTIMA CSXXI 2010 T ROBLE
syrah, merlot, cabernet sauvignon, tempranillo, garnacha.

84 Colour: cherry, purple rim. Nose: ripe fruit, balsamic herbs, toasty. Palate: good acidity, spirituous, flavourful.

BODEGAS VILORIA

Médico Luis Peralta, 2- Ofic.5
29400 Ronda (Málaga)
☎: +34 628 698 870 - Fax: +34 952 872 601
isidoro@sierrahidalga.com
www.bodegasviloria.com

LAGAREJO 2010 RD

87 Colour: ochre. Nose: ripe fruit, expressive, sweet spices, creamy oak. Palate: good acidity, round, powerful, flavourful.

LAGAREJO S/C T
tempranillo.

83 Colour: cherry, garnet rim. Nose: candied fruit, medium intensity. Palate: fleshy, powerful, fruity.

LAGAREJO 2006 T BARRICA
tempranillo, cabernet sauvignon, syrah, merlot, petit verdot.

86 Colour: cherry, garnet rim. Nose: medium intensity, balanced, fruit liqueur notes, spicy, fruit liqueur notes. Palate: fleshy, flavourful, round tannins.

BODEGAS Y VIÑEDOS CONRAD

Ctra. El Burgo, Km. 4,5
29400 Ronda (Málaga)
☎: +34 951 166 035 - Fax: +34 951 166 035
conrad@vinosconrad.com
www.vinosconrad.com

CREACIÓN CONRAD CRISTINA 2008 T
malbec, cabernet franc, petit verdot.

89 Colour: cherry, garnet rim. Nose: ripe fruit, scrubland, sweet spices. Palate: powerful, flavourful, spicy, long.

SOLEÓN 2008 T
cabernet sauvignon, cabernet franc, merlot.

88 Colour: cherry, garnet rim. Nose: powerfull, balanced, ripe fruit. Palate: flavourful, good structure, round tannins.

SAN LORENZO 2008 T
pinot noir, tempranillo.

87 Colour: cherry, garnet rim. Nose: candied fruit, spicy, toasty, mineral. Palate: good acidity, balanced, flavourful.

CEZAR VIÑEDOS Y BODEGA

Finca Buenavista- Pto. del Negro, Apdo. Correos 79 (Riacortax)
29480 Gaucín (Málaga)
☎: +34 672 073 495
re@enkvistwines.com
www.vinosdegaucin.com

SUEÑOS CABERNET SAUVIGNON 2007 T
cabernet sauvignon.

86 Colour: cherry, garnet rim. Nose: ripe fruit, sweet spices, caramel. Palate: fleshy, toasty, spirituous.

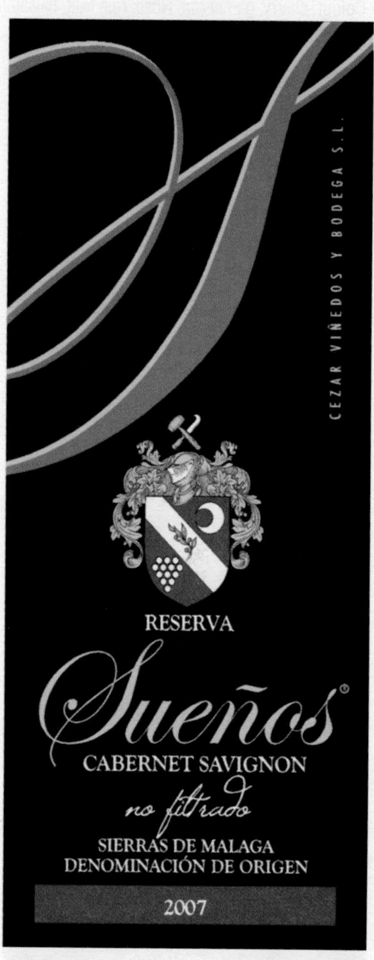

SUEÑOS INGA 2007 T
petit verdot, tempranillo, cabernet sauvignon.

81 Colour: cherry, garnet rim. Nose: slightly evolved, powerfull. Palate: fruity, spicy.

SUEÑOS PETIT VERDOT 2008 T
petit verdot.

80 Colour: cherry, garnet rim. Nose: faded flowers, fruit preserve, grassy, slightly evolved. Palate: good acidity, flavourful, spirituous.

SUEÑOS TEMPRANILLO 2007 TR
tempranillo.

84 Colour: cherry, garnet rim. Nose: ripe fruit, balsamic herbs, floral. Palate: ripe fruit, flavourful, fleshy.

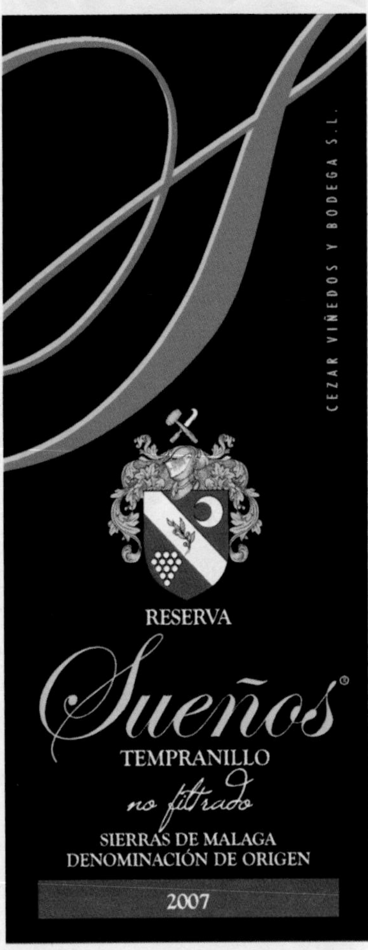

COMPAÑÍA DE VINOS TELMO RODRÍGUEZ

El Monte, s/n
01308 Lanciego (Álava)
☎: +34 945 628 315 - Fax: +34 945 628 314
contact@telmorodriguez.com
www.telmorodriguez.com

MR 2009 B
100% moscatel.

93 Colour: golden. Nose: powerfull, floral, candied fruit, fragrant herbs, citrus fruit. Palate: flavourful, sweet, fruity, good acidity.

MOLINO REAL 2007 B
100% moscatel.

96 Colour: bright yellow. Nose: white flowers, candied fruit, fragrant herbs, sweet spices, powerfull, expressive. Palate: flavourful, fruity, rich, fleshy, complex, good acidity, balanced, elegant.

CORTIJO LA FUENTE

Cortijo La Fuente, 10
29532 Mollina (Málaga)
☎: +34 663 045 906 - Fax: +34 952 740 513
cortijolafuente@terra.es

CORTIJO LA FUENTE NATURALMENTE DULCE (VENDIMIA TARDÍA) B
moscatel.

84 Colour: bright golden. Nose: candied fruit, fruit liqueur notes, faded flowers. Palate: fruity, good finish, sweet, spicy.

CORTIJO LA FUENTE S/C BLANCO AFRUTADO
moscatel.

87 Colour: bright yellow. Nose: white flowers, violets, wild herbs. Palate: flavourful, fruity, easy to drink.

CORTIJO LA FUENTE PX
pedro ximénez.

84 Colour: golden. Nose: candied fruit, pungent, faded flowers. Palate: fine bitter notes, correct, balanced.

CORTIJO LOS AGUILARES

Puente de la Ventilla. Ctra. a Campillo- Apdo. 119
29400 Ronda (Málaga)
☎: +34 952 874 457 - Fax: +34 951 166 000
info@cortijolosaguilares.com
www.cortijolosaguilares.com

CORTIJO LOS AGUILARES 2010 RD
30% merlot, 30% tempranillo, 30% syrah, 10% petit verdot.

88 Colour: rose, purple rim. Nose: powerfull, ripe fruit, red berry notes, floral, expressive. Palate: fleshy, powerful, fruity, fresh.

CORTIJO LOS AGUILARES PINOT NOIR 2010 T
100% pinot noir.

93 Colour: light cherry, garnet rim. Nose: elegant, balanced, expressive, red berry notes, ripe fruit, spicy. Palate: good structure, complex.

CORTIJO LOS AGUILARES 2010 T
50% tempranillo, 30% merlot, 20% syrah.

87 Colour: cherry, purple rim. Nose: red berry notes, balanced, medium intensity, wild herbs. Palate: flavourful, fleshy, good structure.

CORTIJO LOS AGUILARES TADEO 2008 T
100% petit verdot.

94 Colour: cherry, garnet rim. Nose: ripe fruit, red berry notes, expressive, sweet spices, mineral, creamy oak. Palate: balanced, round, unctuous, powerful, flavourful, fleshy.

CORTIJO LOS AGUILARES PAGO EL ESPINO 2008 T
25% tempranillo, 25% merlot, 21% cabernet sauvignon, 29% petit verdot.

90 Colour: cherry, garnet rim. Nose: candied fruit, cocoa bean, creamy oak. Palate: good structure, fleshy, balanced, fine bitter notes.

DESCALZOS VIEJOS

Finca Descalzos Viejos- Partido de los Molinos, s/n
29400 Ronda (Málaga)
☎: +34 952 874 696 - Fax: +34 952 874 696
info@descalzosviejos.com
www.descalzosviejos.com

DV CHARDONNAY 2010 B
chardonnay.

88 Colour: bright golden. Nose: ripe fruit, spicy, fine lees, dry nuts. Palate: powerful, flavourful, complex, fleshy, toasty.

DV DESCALZOS VIEJOS 2008 T
garnacha, syrah, merlot.

82 Colour: pale ruby, brick rim edge. Nose: fruit preserve, cocoa bean, sweet spices, toasty. Palate: good acidity, flavourful, spirituous.

DV CONARTE 2007 TC
petit verdot, cabernet sauvignon, syrah, merlot.

92 Colour: cherry, garnet rim. Nose: ripe fruit, powerfull, sweet spices, toasty, complex, earthy notes. Palate: good acidity, flavourful, spirituous, fleshy.

DV DESCALZOS VIEJOS (+) 2006 TC
cabernet sauvignon, merlot, syrah.

88 Colour: pale ruby, brick rim edge. Nose: ripe fruit, spicy, toasty, fine reductive notes. Palate: powerful, flavourful, toasty.

FINCA LA MELONERA

Paraje Los Frontones, Camino Ronda-Setenil s/n
29400 Ronda (Malaga)
info@lamelonera.com
www.lamelonera.com

PAYOYA NEGRA 2009 T
100% mediterraneas.

91 Colour: bright cherry. Nose: ripe fruit, sweet spices, creamy oak, expressive. Palate: flavourful, fruity, toasty, round tannins.

LA DONAIRA

Pza. Portugal, 23
29400 Ronda (Málaga)
☎: +34 951 705 965
info@mapa7g.com
www.mapa7g.com

LA DONAIRA 2010 RD

83 Colour: rose, purple rim. Nose: fruit preserve, powerfull. Palate: fruity, flavourful.

LA DONAIRA CABERNET SAUVIGNON 2008 T
cabernet sauvignon.

90 Color bright cherry. Aroma ripe fruit, sweet spices, creamy oak, expressive. Taste flavourful, fruity, toasty, round tannins.

LA DONAIRA CABERNET FRANC 2008 T
cabernet franc.

89 Colour: cherry, garnet rim. Nose: closed, medium intensity, toasty, spicy. Palate: fleshy, concentrated, good structure, round tannins.

LA DONAIRA SYRAH 2008 T
syrah.

88 Colour: deep cherry, garnet rim. Nose: spicy, dark chocolate, toasty, ripe fruit. Palate: flavourful, round tannins, fruity aftestaste.

TIERRAS DE MOLLINA

Avda. de las Américas, s/n- Cortijo Colarte
29532 Mollina (Málaga)
☎: +34 952 841 451 - Fax: +34 952 842 555
ajimena@hojiblanca.es
www.tierrasdemollina.net

MONTESPEJO 2010 B
70% doradilla, 30% moscatel.

87 Colour: yellow, straw. Nose: faded flowers, fresh fruit, citrus fruit. Palate: flavourful, fruity, good acidity, balanced.

CARPE DIEM DULCE NATURAL 2009 B
100% pedro ximénez.

87 Colour: bright yellow. Nose: candied fruit, faded flowers, tropical fruit, overripe fruit. Palate: spirituous, flavourful, powerful.

MONTESPEJO 2010 T
100% syrah.

85 Colour: cherry, purple rim. Nose: red berry notes, ripe fruit, floral, wild herbs. Palate: flavourful, fruity, fleshy.

MONTESPEJO 2009 T ROBLE
85% syrah, 15% merlot.

85 Colour: cherry, purple rim. Nose: red berry notes, ripe fruit, sweet spices, creamy oak. Palate: fleshy, flavourful, spicy.

CARPE DIEM MÁLAGA TRASAÑEJO MÁLAGA
90% pedro ximénez, 10% moscatel.

89 Colour: mahogany. Nose: candied fruit, fruit liqueur notes, pattiserie, spicy. Palate: good structure, flavourful, unctuous.

CARPE DIEM MÁLAGA AÑEJO
90% pedro ximénez, 10% moscatel.

87 Colour: mahogany. Nose: pungent, acetaldehyde, dried fruit, dry nuts. Palate: good structure, rich, spirituous.

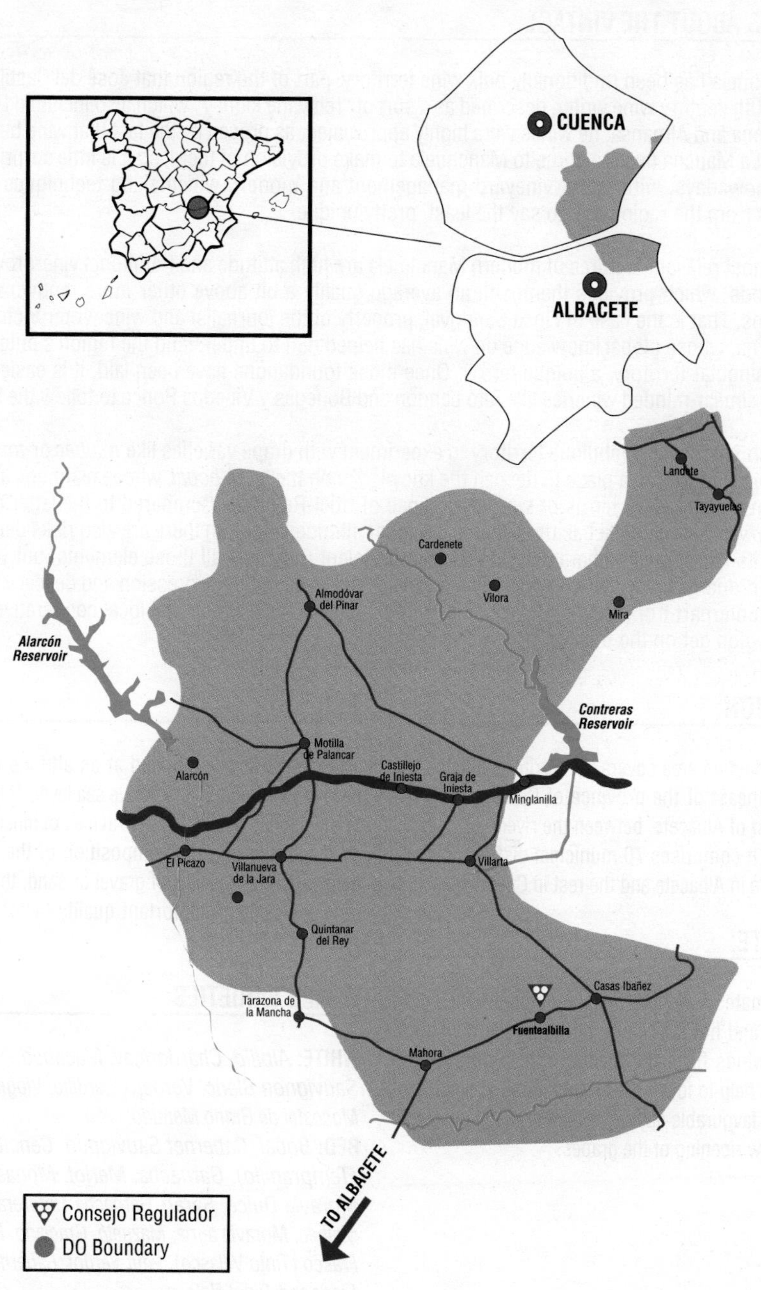
CUENCA
ALBACETE
Landete
Tayayuelas
Cardenete
Víllora
Mira
Almodóvar del Pinar
Alarcón Reservoir
Contreras Reservoir
Motilla de Palancar
Alarcón
Castillejo de Iniesta
Graja de Iniesta
Minglanilla
El Picazo
Villanueva de la Jara
Villarta
Quintanar del Rey
Casas Ibañez
Tarazona de la Mancha
Fuentealbilla
Mahora
TO ALBACETE
Consejo Regulador
DO Boundary

NEWS ABOUT THE VINTAGE:

Manchuela has been traditionally bulk wine territory, part of the region that José del Castillo, a late 20th century wine writer, described as a sort of "red wine kidney" which also included Utiel-Requena and Almansa. Its wines were highly appreciated, as proved by the fact that wine buyers from La Mancha used to come to Manchuela to make provision of them, so it is little surprising that nowadays, with better vineyard management and modern winemaking techniques, the wines from the region are, to say the least, pretty unique.

The most relevant features of modern Manchuela are high altitude and traditional vine-growing methods, which provides them with an average quality a bit above other more renown wine regions. That is the case of Finca Sandoval, property of the journalist and wine writer Víctor de la Serna, whose global knowledge on wine has helped him to understand the region's potential as a singular territory, a unique terroir. Once those foundations have been laid, it is easier for other similar-minded wineries like Alto Landón and Bodegas y Viñedos Ponce to follow the lead.

Manchuela is also a fabulous territory to experiment with grape varieties like *malbec* or *touriga nacional*, as well as a place to deepen the knowledge on the local *bobal*, whose plantings in the region are similar in terms of surface to those of Utiel-Requena. Compared to the latter area, the *bobal* in Manchuela has the benefits of higher altitude, although there are also risks derived from its late-ripening character. It takes a lot of talent to handle all those elements, but when done properly, the *bobal* from Manchuela can achieve even higher expression and delicacy than its counterpart from Valencia. We can only hope that the most traditional local cooperatives of the region get on the train of this "minor" revolution.

LOCATION:

The production area covers the territory situated in the southeast of the province of Cuenca and the northeast of Albacete, between the rivers Júcar and Cabriel. It comprises 70 municipal districts, 26 of which are in Albacete and the rest in Cuenca.

CLIMATE:

The climate is continental in nature, with cold winters and hot summers, although the cool and humid winds from the Mediterranean during the summer help to lower the temperatures at night, so creating favourable day-night temperature contrasts for a slow ripening of the grapes.

SOIL:

The vineyards are situated at an altitude ranging between 600 and 700 m above sea level. The terrain is mainly flat, except for the ravines outlined by the rivers. Regarding the composition of the terrain, below a clayey surface of gravel or sand, the soil is limy, which is an important quality factor for the region.

GRAPE VARIETIES:

WHITE: *Albillo, Chardonnay, Macabeo, Sauvignon Blanc, Verdejo, Pardillo, Viognier* and *Moscatel de Grano Menudo.*

RED: *Bobal, Cabernet Sauvignon, Cencibel (Tempranillo), Garnacha, Merlot, Monastrell, Moravia Dulce, Syrah, Garnacha Tintorera, Malbec, Moravia agria, Mazuelo, Graciano, Rojal, Frasco (Tinto Velasco), Petit Verdot, Cabernet Franc* and *Pinot Noir.*

FIGURES:

Vineyard surface: 4,139 – **Wine-Growers:** 900 – **Wineries:** 34 – **2010 Harvest rating:** Good – **Production:** 20,809,000 litres – **Market percentages:** --% domestic. --% export

CONSEJO REGULADOR
Matadero, 5
02260 Fuentealbilla (Albacete)
☎: +34 967 477 535 - Fax: +34 967 477 505
@ domanchuela@lamanchuela.es.
www.do-manchuela.com

GENERAL CHARACTERISTICS OF THE WINES

WHITES	Normally produced from *Macabeo*, they have a straw yellow colour, apple fruity aromas, and are pleasant and easy drinking.
ROSÉS	These have a raspberry colour; the *Bobal* variety gives intense fruity aromas to raspberry, and on occasion hints of herbs; on the palate they are flavourful, fresh and balanced
REDS	Cherry-coloured, they are very similar to the wines from La Mancha, with notes of blackberries and, on occasions, with an earthy background; they are supple, flavourful and warm on the palate. Those produced from *Bobal* have a better defined fruity expression (blackberry) and are very flavourful.

VINTAGE RATING PEÑÍNGUIDE

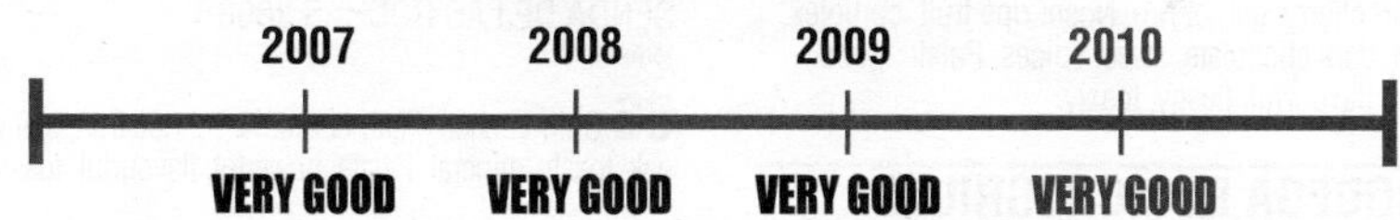

ALTOLANDÓN

Ctra. N-330, km. 242
16330 Landete (Cuenca)
☎: +34 677 228 974 - Fax: +34 962 300 662
altolandon@altolandon.com
www.altolandon.com

ALTOLANDÓN 2010 BFB
chardonnay.

90 Color bright yellow. Aroma powerfull, ripe fruit, sweet spices, creamy oak, fragrant herbs. Taste rich, smoky aftertaste, flavourful, fresh, good acidity.

RAYUELO 2008 T
bobal, monastrell, malbec.

92 Colour: cherry, garnet rim. Nose: red berry notes, ripe fruit, floral, mineral, balsamic herbs, creamy oak. Palate: concentrated, fleshy, complex, powerful, flavourful, mineral, elegant.

BODEGA CIEN Y PICO

San Francisco, 19
02240 Mahora (Albacete)
☎: +34 967 494 336 - Fax: +34 967 494 336
luisjimenez@gmail.com
www.cienypico.com

CIEN Y PICO KNIGHTS-ERRANT 2008 T
garnacha tintorera.

89 Colour: cherry, garnet rim. Nose: ripe fruit, cocoa bean, sweet spices, toasty. Palate: powerful, flavourful, ripe fruit.

CIEN Y PICO DOBLE PASTA 2008 T
garnacha tintorera.

87 Colour: cherry, garnet rim. Nose: ripe fruit, complex, cocoa bean, dark chocolate, sweet spices. Palate: good acidity, rich, flavourful, fleshy, toasty.

BODEGA EL MONEGRILLO

Finca El Monegrillo. Pol. Ind. 13- parcela 20
16235 Iniesta (Cuenca)
☎: +34 962 510 451 - Fax: +34 962 511 361
carlos.valsangiacomo@cherubino.es
www.cherubino.es

EL MONEGRILLO 2006 T
70% syrah, 30% cabernet sauvignon.

91 Colour: cherry, garnet rim. Nose: ripe fruit, spicy, complex, earthy notes, mineral. Palate: powerful, flavourful, toasty, round tannins.

BODEGA INIESTA

Andrés Iniesta, 2
02260 Fuentealbilla (Albacete)
☎: +34 628 163 189

FINCA EL CARRIL 2010 B
macabeo.

88 Colour: bright straw. Nose: fresh fruit, white flowers, expressive, fragrant herbs, tropical fruit. Palate: flavourful, fruity, good acidity, balanced.

FINCA EL CARRIL VALERIA 2010 BFB
macabeo.

90 Colour: bright yellow. Nose: ripe fruit, creamy oak, faded flowers, balsamic herbs. Palate: rich, flavourful, fresh, good acidity.

CORAZÓN LOCO 2010 B
verdejo, sauvignon blanc.

86 Color bright straw. Aroma fresh, fresh fruit, white flowers, expressive. Taste flavourful, fruity, good acidity, balanced.

BODEGA PARDO TOLOSA

Villatoya, 26
02215 Alborea (Albacete)
☎: +34 963 517 067 - Fax: +34 963 517 091
ventas@bodegapardotolosa.com
www.bodegapardotolosa.com

MIZARAN BOBAL 2010 RD
bobal.

86 Colour: rose, purple rim. Nose: red berry notes, floral, expressive. Palate: fleshy, powerful, fruity, fresh.

SENDA DE LAS ROCHAS 2008 T
tempranillo.

86 Colour: cherry, garnet rim. Nose: ripe fruit, spicy, creamy oak, toasty, mineral. Palate: powerful, flavourful, toasty.

BODEGAS RECIAL

Libertad, 1
02154 Pozo Lorente (Albacete)
☎: +34 606 835 131 - Fax: +34 967 572 063
gerencia@bodegasrecial.com
www.bodegasrecial.com

PÚRPURA POZO LORENTE 2008 TC

85 Colour: cherry, garnet rim. Nose: ripe fruit, scrubland, sweet spices, toasty. Palate: good acidity, ripe fruit, fleshy.

BODEGAS SAN GREGORIO MAGNO SOC. COOP. DE CLM

Ctra. de Ledaña, s/n
02246 Navas de Jorquera (Albacete)
☎: +34 967 482 134 - Fax: +34 967 482 134
sangregorio@amialbacete.com

MONTE MIRÓN 2006 T FERMENTADO EN BARRICA
100% bobal.

82 Colour: light cherry, orangey edge. Nose: ripe fruit, waxy notes, wet leather. Palate: ripe fruit, flavourful.

BODEGAS VILLAVID

Niño Jesús, 25
16280 Villarta (Cuenca)
☎: +34 962 189 006 - Fax: +34 962 189 125
info@villavid.com
www.villavid.com

VILLAVID MACABEO VERDEJO 2010 B
50% verdejo, 50% macabeo.

86 Colour: bright straw. Nose: expressive, citrus fruit, tropical fruit, floral. Palate: good acidity, fresh, fruity, flavourful.

VILLAVID 2010 RD
100% bobal.

84 Colour: rose, purple rim. Nose: raspberry, ripe fruit, floral, fresh. Palate: good acidity, fresh, fruity.

VILLAVID 2010 T
100% tempranillo.

86 Colour: cherry, purple rim. Nose: expressive, fresh fruit, red berry notes, floral, lactic notes. Palate: flavourful, fruity, correct.

BODEGAS Y VIÑEDOS PONCE

Ctra. San Clemente, s/n
16230 Villanueva de la Jara (Cuenca)
☎: +34 677 434 523 - Fax: +34 967 490 580
ponce@iniestahoy.com

CLOS LOJEN 2010 T
bobal.

92 Colour: cherry, garnet rim. Nose: red berry notes, ripe fruit, balsamic herbs, mineral. Palate: powerful, flavourful, fruity, fleshy, round tannins.

P.F. 2009 T
100% bobal.

93 Colour: cherry, purple rim. Nose: red berry notes, raspberry, mineral, cocoa bean, dark chocolate, creamy oak. Palate: balanced, elegant, powerful, flavourful, fruity, fleshy, slightly dry, soft tannins.

PINO 2009 T
100% bobal.

91 Colour: cherry, purple rim. Nose: red berry notes, ripe fruit, mineral, balanced, expressive. Palate: elegant, powerful, flavourful, fruity, fleshy, spicy.

LA CASILLA (ESTRECHA) 2009 T
100% bobal.

91 Colour: cherry, purple rim. Nose: red berry notes, floral, expressive, spicy, creamy oak. Palate: good acidity, elegant, flavourful, fruity, fleshy, round tannins.

LA CASILLA 2009 T

88 Colour: cherry, purple rim. Nose: red berry notes, raspberry, ripe fruit, dry stone. Palate: flavourful, fleshy, long, fruity aftestaste.

COOPERATIVA DEL CAMPO VÍRGEN DE LAS NIEVES

Paseo Virgen de las Nieves, 1
02247 Cenizate (Albacete)
☎: +34 967 482 006 - Fax: +34 967 482 805
cooperativa@virgendelasnieves.com
www.virgendelasnieves.com

ARTESONES DE CENIZATE 2010 B
100% macabeo.

84 Colour: bright straw. Nose: white flowers, ripe fruit, fresh. Palate: correct, fresh, fruity.

ARTESONES DE CENIZATE 2010 RD
100% bobal.

87 Colour: rose, purple rim. Nose: powerfull, ripe fruit, red berry notes, floral. Palate: fleshy, fruity, fresh.

ARTESONES DE CENIZATE SEMIDULCE 2010 RD
100% bobal.

84 Colour: rose, purple rim. Nose: ripe fruit, red berry notes, floral. Palate: fleshy, fruity, fresh, sweetness.

ARTESONES DE CENIZATE PETIT VERDOT 2010 T
100% petit verdot.

85 Colour: cherry, garnet rim. Nose: dried flowers, ripe fruit, balsamic herbs. Palate: good acidity, powerful, fruity, fresh.

ARTESONES DE CENIZATE TEMPRANILLO 2010 T
100% tempranillo.

84 Colour: cherry, purple rim. Nose: red berry notes, fruit liqueur notes, floral, fresh. Palate: fresh, fruity, easy to drink.

ARTESONES DE CENIZATE 2008 T
100% syrah.

84 Colour: cherry, garnet rim. Nose: ripe fruit, floral, spicy. Palate: good acidity, flavourful, easy to drink.

ARTESONES DE CENIZATE 2008 TC
100% tempranillo.

83 Colour: cherry, garnet rim. Nose: ripe fruit, warm, sweet spices, toasty. Palate: good acidity, flavourful, fleshy.

ARTESONES DE CENIZATE BOBAL 2007 TC
100% bobal.

84 Colour: cherry, garnet rim. Nose: ripe fruit, balsamic herbs, sweet spices, toasty. Palate: flavourful, fleshy, ripe fruit.

ARTESONES DE CENIZATE 2005 TR
100% tempranillo.

84 Colour: light cherry, garnet rim. Nose: ripe fruit, scrubland, spicy, toasty. Palate: warm, flavourful, fleshy.

COOPERATIVA UNIÓN CAMPESINA INIESTENSE

San Idefonso, 1
16235 Iniesta (Cuenca)
☎: +34 967 490 120 - Fax: +34 967 490 777
comercial@cooperativauci.com
www.cooperativauci.com

REALCE VIURA 2010 B
100% viura.

81 Colour: bright straw. Nose: ripe fruit, faded flowers, slightly evolved. Palate: warm, light-bodied, flavourful.

REALCE TEMPRANILLO 2010 T
100% tempranillo.

87 Colour: cherry, purple rim. Nose: floral, red berry notes, raspberry, expressive. Palate: fruity, fresh, flavourful, easy to drink.

REALCE TEMPRANILLO 2006 TC
100% tempranillo.

86 Colour: cherry, garnet rim. Nose: ripe fruit, spicy, creamy oak, toasty. Palate: powerful, flavourful, toasty, round tannins.

REALCE BOBAL 2010 RD
100% bobal.

85 Colour: rose, purple rim. Nose: candied fruit, red berry notes, expressive. Palate: creamy, ripe fruit, flavourful.

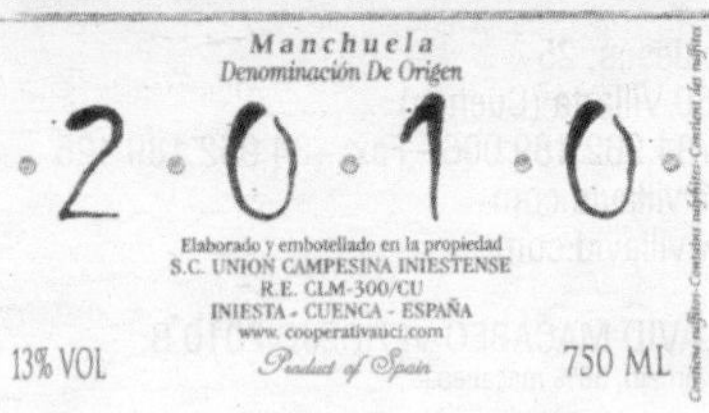

REALCE BOBAL 2004 TR
100% bobal.

83 Colour: light cherry, orangey edge. Nose: ripe fruit, aged wood nuances, toasty, slightly evolved. Palate: spicy, good acidity, flavourful.

FINCA SANDOVAL

Ctra. CM-3222, Km. 26,800
16237 Ledaña (Cuenca)
☎: +34 616 444 805
fincasandoval@gmail.com
www.grandespagos.com/sandoval.html

SIGNO GARNACHA 2009 T
90% garnacha tinta, 10% garnacha tintorera.

94 Colour: cherry, garnet rim. Nose: red berry notes, raspberry, expressive, sweet spices, creamy oak. Palate: good acidity, flavourful, fruity, fleshy, toasty, round tannins.

SIGNO BOBAL 2008 T
100% bobal.

93 Colour: cherry, garnet rim. Nose: powerfull, varietal, ripe fruit, red berry notes, earthy notes, cocoa bean, toasty. Palate: powerful, flavourful, fleshy, round tannins, balanced.

SALIA 2008 T
syrah, garnacha, garnacha tinta.

92 Colour: cherry, garnet rim. Nose: spicy, creamy oak, toasty, characterful, fruit expression. Palate: powerful, flavourful, toasty, round tannins.

FINCA SANDOVAL CUVEE TNS MAGNUM 2007 T
33% syrah, 67% touriga nacional.

95 Colour: black cherry, garnet rim. Nose: red berry notes, ripe fruit, earthy notes, scrubland, spicy, creamy oak. Palate: concentrated, flavourful, fruity, fleshy, complex, long, round tannins.

FINCA SANDOVAL 2007 T
syrah, monastrell, bobal.

92 Colour: cherry, garnet rim. Nose: mineral, creamy oak, sweet spices, fruit expression, red berry notes. Palate: powerful, fleshy, fine bitter notes, flavourful, concentrated.

NUESTRA SEÑORA DE LA CABEZA SOC. COOP.

Avda. del Vino, 10
02200 Casas Ibáñez (Albacete)
☎: +34 967 460 105 - Fax: +34 967 460 266
info@coop-cabeza.com
www.coop-cabeza.com

VIARIL 2009 BFB
macabeo.

87 Colour: bright straw. Nose: ripe fruit, faded flowers, spicy, creamy oak. Palate: rich, flavourful, fleshy, balanced.

VIARIL 2009 B
macabeo.

81 Colour: bright straw. Nose: ripe fruit, medium intensity, slightly evolved. Palate: lacks balance, fresh, flavourful.

VIARIL 2010 RD
bobal.

85 Colour: rose, purple rim. Nose: floral, raspberry, ripe fruit, lactic notes. Palate: correct, fruity, flavourful.

VIARIL 2010 T
syrah.

84 Colour: cherry, purple rim. Nose: grassy, ripe fruit, warm. Palate: good acidity, flavourful, green.

VIARIL 2009 T
cabernet sauvignon.

83 Colour: cherry, garnet rim. Nose: fruit preserve, balsamic herbs, green pepper. Palate: good acidity, powerful, flavourful.

VIARIL 2007 TC
tempranillo, syrah, cabernet sauvignon.

84 Colour: cherry, garnet rim. Nose: ripe fruit, grassy, spicy, toasty. Palate: powerful, flavourful, fleshy.

PAGOS DE FAMILIA VEGA TOLOSA

Correos, 6
02200 Casas Ibáñez (Albacete)
☎: +34 617 379 328 - Fax: +34 967 461 331
info@vegatolosa.com
www.vegatolosa.com

VEGA TOLOSA SELECCIÓN 2010 B
50% macabeo, 35% sauvignon blanc, 15% chardonnay.

85 Colour: bright straw. Nose: fresh, fresh fruit, white flowers, medium intensity. Palate: flavourful, fruity, good acidity.

VEGA TOLOSA LÁGRIMA DE SYRAH 2010 RD
100% syrah.

88 Color rose, purple rim. Aroma powerfull, ripe fruit, red berry notes, floral, expressive. Taste fleshy, powerful, fruity, fresh.

VEGA TOLOSA NATURE 2010 T
50% syrah, 50% tempranillo.

85 Colour: cherry, purple rim. Nose: red berry notes, ripe fruit, floral, balsamic herbs. Palate: light-bodied, fleshy, flavourful, spicy.

VEGA TOLOSA CURIUS 2009 T
85% bobal, 8% syrah, 7% merlot.

88 Colour: cherry, garnet rim. Nose: red berry notes, ripe fruit, aromatic coffee, cocoa bean, sweet spices, toasty, earthy notes. Palate: flavourful, fleshy, long, mineral.

VEGA TOLOSA BOBAL VIÑAS VIEJAS 2009 T
100% bobal.

87 Colour: cherry, garnet rim. Nose: ripe fruit, spicy, creamy oak, toasty. Palate: powerful, flavourful, toasty, round tannins.

SEÑORÍO DE MONTERRUIZ

La Plaza
16234 Casas de Santa Cruz (Cuenca)
☎: +34 967 493 828
reservas@monterruiz.com
www.señoriodemonterruiz.es

SEÑORIO DE MONTERRUIZ 2010 T
100% bobal.

86 Colour: cherry, purple rim. Nose: red berry notes, fresh fruit, floral, fresh, cocoa bean. Palate: light-bodied, fruity, easy to drink.

SEÑORIO DE MONTERRUIZ 2010 T MACERACIÓN CARBÓNICA
bobal.

86 Colour: cherry, purple rim. Nose: red berry notes, raspberry, ripe fruit, lactic notes, warm. Palate: good acidity, fruity, flavourful.

SOC. COOP. SAN ANTONIO ABAD

Valencia, 41
02270 Villamalea (Albacete)
☎: +34 967 483 023 - Fax: +34 967 483 536
gerencia@vinos-saac.com
www.vinos-saac.com

FLOR DEL PARAÍSO 2010 B
macabeo.

85 Colour: bright straw. Nose: tropical fruit, floral, fragrant herbs. Palate: fresh, fruity, easy to drink.

ALTOS DEL CABRIEL SELECCIÓN 2010 B
macabeo.

84 Colour: bright straw. Nose: ripe fruit, white flowers, dried herbs, fresh. Palate: light-bodied, flavourful, fruity.

ALTOS DEL CABRIEL 2010 RD
bobal.

88 Colour: rose, purple rim. Nose: floral, lactic notes, red berry notes, ripe fruit. Palate: fresh, fruity, powerful, flavourful, fleshy.

ALTOS DEL CABRIEL 2010 T
100% tempranillo.

82 Colour: cherry, purple rim. Nose: fruit preserve, ripe fruit, scrubland. Palate: powerful, flavourful, fruity.

GREDAS VIEJAS 2006 T ROBLE
syrah.

84 Colour: light cherry, orangey edge. Nose: ripe fruit, balsamic herbs, old leather, spicy, toasty. Palate: powerful, flavourful, fleshy.

VIÑAMALEA 2006 TC
tempranillo, syrah.

81 Colour: cherry, garnet rim. Nose: ripe fruit, grassy, wet leather, waxy notes, cigar, toasty. Palate: correct, flavourful, ripe fruit.

VITIVINOS ANUNCIACIÓN

Camino de Cabezuelas, s/n
02270 Villamalea (Albacete)
☎: +34 967 483 114 - Fax: +34 967 483 964
info@vitivinos.com
www.vitivinos.com

AZUA MACABEO 2010 B
macabeo.

86 Colour: bright straw. Nose: fresh fruit, tropical fruit, floral. Palate: good acidity, flavourful, fruity, good finish.

AZUA VERDEJO 2010 B
verdejo.

85 Colour: pale. Nose: citrus fruit, tropical fruit, white flowers. Palate: light-bodied, fresh, easy to drink.

AZUA BOBAL 2010 RD
bobal.

86 Colour: cherry, purple rim. Nose: lactic notes, floral, red berry notes, raspberry. Palate: good acidity, fruity, fresh, light-bodied.

AZUA SYRAH 2010 T ROBLE
syrah.

88 Colour: cherry, purple rim. Nose: raspberry, red berry notes, toasty, sweet spices. Palate: good acidity, powerful, flavourful, fleshy, toasty.

AZUA BOBAL 2010 T ROBLE
bobal.

87 Colour: cherry, garnet rim. Nose: red berry notes, floral, spicy, toasty. Palate: good acidity, powerful, flavourful.

AZUA CABERNET 2010 T ROBLE
cabernet sauvignon.

87 Colour: cherry, garnet rim. Nose: red berry notes, ripe fruit, balsamic herbs, creamy oak. Palate: good acidity, fruity, flavourful.

AZUA SELECCIÓN BOBAL VIEJO 2008 TC
bobal.

86 Colour: cherry, garnet rim. Nose: red berry notes, ripe fruit, floral, spicy, toasty. Palate: good acidity, powerful, flavourful, fleshy.

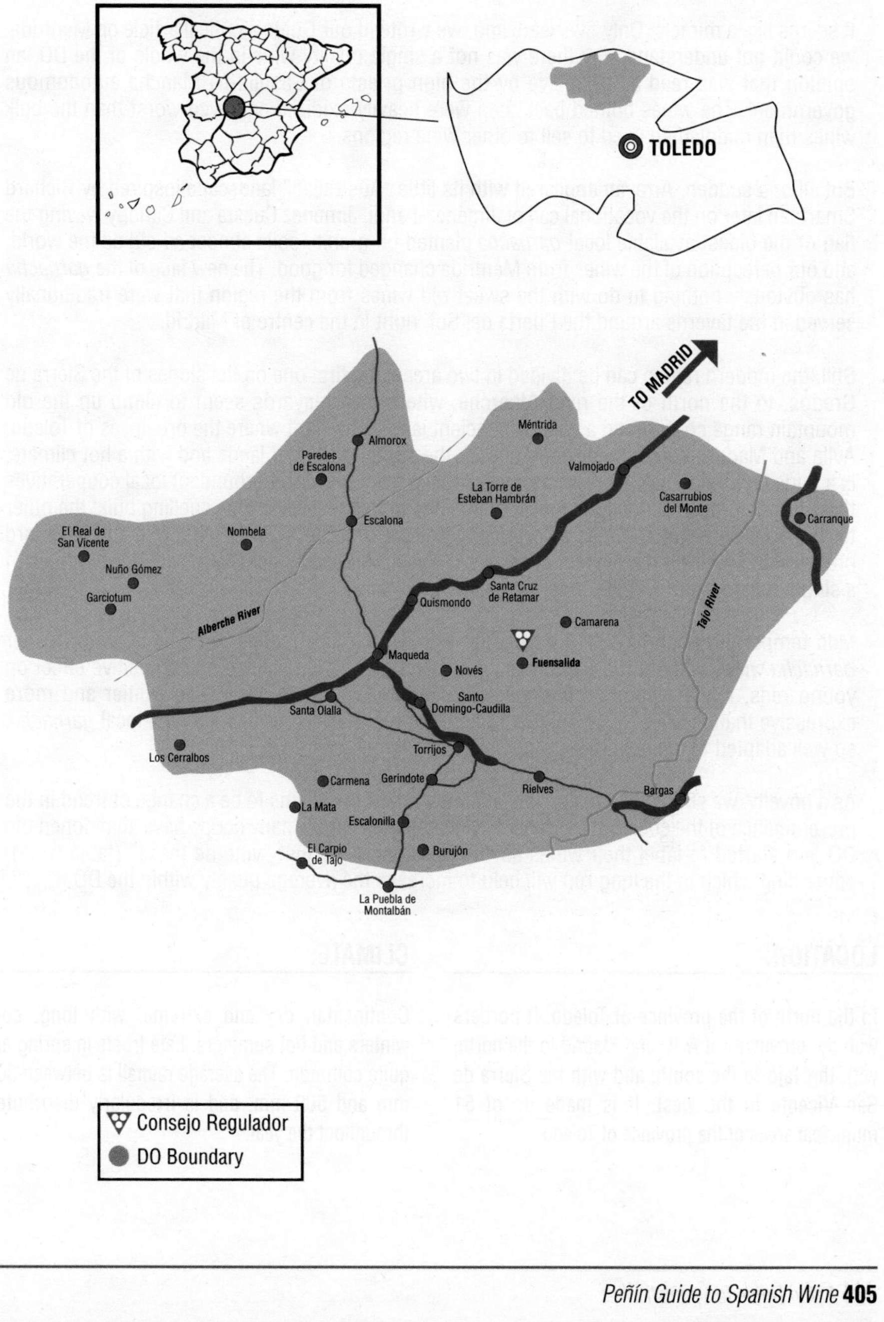

TOLEDO
TO MADRID
Méntrida
Almorox
Paredes de Escalona
Valmojado
La Torre de Esteban Hambrán
Casarrubios del Monte
Carranque
Escalona
El Real de San Vicente
Nombela
Nuño Gómez
Garciotum
Santa Cruz de Retamar
Quismondo
Alberche River
Tajo River
Camarena
Maqueda
Novés
Fuensalida
Santo Domingo-Caudilla
Santa Olalla
Los Cerralbos
Torrijos
Carmena
Gerindote
Rielves
Bargas
La Mata
Escalonilla
El Carpio de Tajo
Burujón
La Puebla de Montalbán

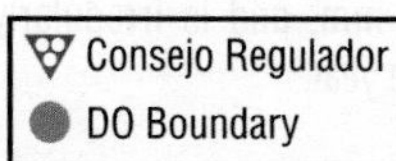
Consejo Regulador
DO Boundary

DO MÉNTRIDA

NEWS ABOUT THE VINTAGE:

It seems like a miracle. Only five years ago, we wrote in our Guide a critical article on Méntrida: we could not understand why there was not a single quality wine in the whole of the DO, an opinion that was read as offensive by the high priests of Castilla-La Mancha autonomous government. The wines bottled back then were heavily oxidized and even worst than the bulk wines than middlemen used to sell to other wine regions.

But all of a sudden, Arrayán appeared with its little "Australian" landscape inspired by Richard Smart, an later on the vocational call of Jiménez-Landi, Jiménez Cuesta and Canopy waving the flag of the oldest available local *garnacha* planted on granite soils almost as old as the world, and our perception of the wines from Méntrida changed for good. The new face of the *garnacha* has obviously nothing to do with the sweet red wines from the region that were traditionally served in the taverns around the Puerta del Sol, right in the centre of Madrid.

Still, the modern region can be divided in two areas: the first one on the slopes of the Sierra de Gredos, to the north of the river Alberche, where the vineyards seem to climb up the old mountain range conforming a wild and ancient landscape right where the provinces of Toledo, Ávila and Madrid merge; the second one, to the south, on flatter lands and with a hot climate, is a huge factory of bulk and overripe wines made from the all-too-abundant local cooperatives that still pay grapes by their alcohol content. Two opposite worlds: one spelling bulk, the other terroir, so it does not come as a surprise to see the differences in ratings, too, and to record precisely in Méntrida the biggest contrasts between the scores achieved by all the samples of a single region, from just 70 up to 97 points.

Mild temperatures during 2010 have allowed even the local coops to come up with fresher *garnacha* wines without the traditional confected notes, and has also had a positive effect on young reds, made mainly by the coops. Rosé and white wines are also fruitier and more expressive than in 2009. Even so, the potential of the DO lies inevitably on the local *garnacha*, so well adapted to the extremely hot climatic conditions of Toledo.

As a novelty, we should add that in the last few years there seems to be a change of trend in the pre-eminence of the cooperatives over private wineries, since many coops have abandoned the DO and started to label their wines as "VT de Castilla" or just "vino de mesa" (table wine), something which in the long run will help to increase the average quality within the DO.

LOCATION:

In the north of the province of Toledo. It borders with the provinces of Ávila and Madrid to the north, with the Tajo to the south, and with the Sierra de San Vicente to the west. It is made up of 51 municipal areas of the province of Toledo.

CLIMATE:

Continental, dry and extreme, with long, cold winters and hot summers. Late frosts in spring are quite common. The average rainfall is between 300 mm and 500 mm, and is irregularly distributed throughout the year.

SOIL:

The vineyards are at an altitude of between 400 m and 600 m, although some municipal districts of the Sierra de San Vicente reach an altitude of 800 m. The soil is mainly sandy-clayey, with a medium to loose texture.

GRAPE VARIETIES:

WHITE: *Albillo, Macabeo, Sauvignon Blanc, Chardonnay* and *Moscatel de Grano Menudo*.
RED: *Garnacha* (majority 85% of total), *Cencibel* (*Tempranillo*), *Cabernet Sauvignon, Merlot, Syrah, Petit Verdot, Cabernet Franc* and *Graciano*.

FIGURES:

Vineyard surface: 7,500 – **Wine-Growers:** 1,548 – **Wineries:** 28 – **2010 Harvest rating:** N/A – **Production:** 2,213,889 – **Market percentages:** 75% domestic. 25% export

CONSEJO REGULADOR
Avda. Cristo del Amparo, 16
45510 Fuensalida (Toledo)
☎: +34 925 785 185 - Fax: +34 925 784 154
@ administracion@domentrida.es
www.domentrida.es

GENERAL CHARACTERISTICS OF THE WINES

ROSÉS	Normally produced from *Garnacha*, they have a raspberry pink colour; they have a fruity aroma and are meaty and supple on the palate
REDS	These have a dark cherry colour; on the nose, they are noticeable for their hints of ripe fruit typical of long ripening periods; on the palate they are meaty, warm and supple.

VINTAGE RATING PEÑÍNGUIDE

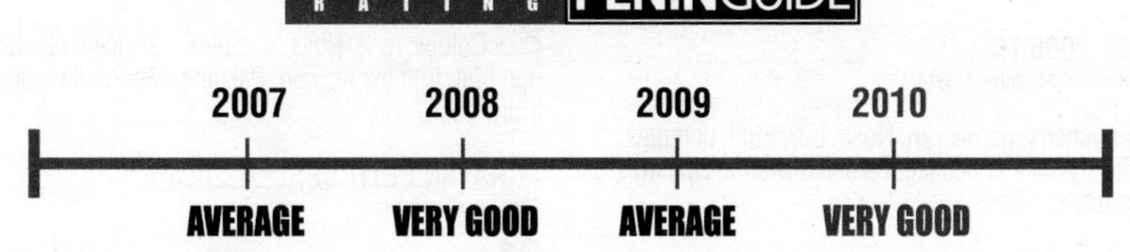

AGROVILLARTA

Ctra. Toledo-Ávila, Km. 48
45910 Escalona (Toledo)
☎: +34 913 441 990
comunicacion@haciendavillarta.com

YX 2010 B
chardonnay, sauvignon blanc.

86 Colour: bright straw. Nose: candied fruit, citrus fruit, faded flowers. Palate: fine bitter notes, spicy, ripe fruit.

ROSE 5 2010 RD

85 Colour: brilliant rose. Nose: medium intensity, red berry notes, fruit expression. Palate: flavourful, fruity, fresh.

BESANAS 2007 TC

87 Colour: cherry, garnet rim. Nose: candied fruit, sweet spices. Palate: powerful, spicy, ripe fruit, round tannins.

BESANAS 2006 TR

87 Colour: cherry, garnet rim. Nose: medium intensity, complex, creamy oak, dark chocolate. Palate: powerful, fine bitter notes, round tannins.

ALONSO CUESTA

Pza. de la Constitución, 4
45920 La Torre de Esteban Hambrán (Toledo)
☎: +34 925 795 742 - Fax: +34 925 795 742
administracion@alonsocuesta.com
www.alonsocuesta.com

ALONSO CUESTA 2010 B
verdejo, sauvignon blanc.

85 Colour: bright straw. Nose: ripe fruit, citrus fruit, white flowers. Palate: flavourful, fruity.

CAMARUS 2010 T
garnacha, syrah.

85 Colour: deep cherry. Nose: ripe fruit, fruit expression, scrubland. Palate: good acidity, flavourful, fleshy.

CAMARUS 2008 TC
garnacha, cabernet sauvignon, syrah.

88 Colour: cherry, garnet rim. Nose: powerfull, complex, ripe fruit, toasty, dark chocolate. Palate: powerful, ripe fruit, round tannins.

ALONSO CUESTA 2007 T
garnacha, tempranillo, cabernet sauvignon.

92 Colour: cherry, garnet rim. Nose: ripe fruit, spicy, creamy oak, toasty, complex, fruit expression. Palate: powerful, flavourful, toasty, round tannins.

BODEGAS ARRAYÁN

Finca La Verdosa, s/n
45513 Santa Cruz del Retamar (Toledo)
☎: +34 916 633 131 - Fax: +34 916 632 796
comercial@arrayan.es
www.arrayan.es

ESTELA DE ARRAYÁN 2007 T
syrah, merlot, petit verdot, cabernet sauvignon.

92 Colour: dark-red cherry. Nose: dry stone, ripe fruit, complex, expressive. Palate: flavourful, powerful, full, fruity, good structure, round tannins, smoky aftertaste.

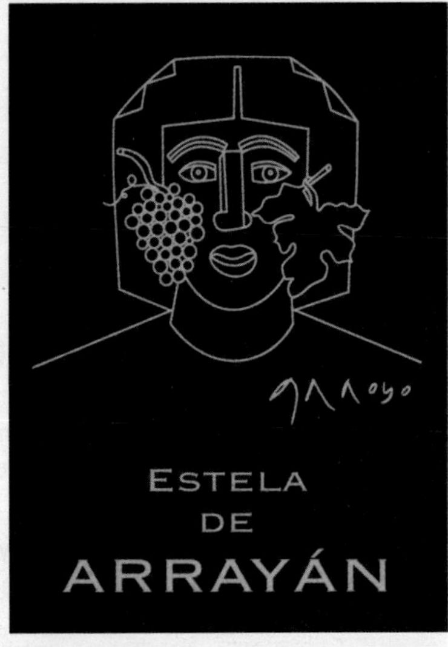

ARRAYÁN 2010 RD
merlot, syrah, cabernet sauvignon, petit verdot.

88 Colour: rose. Nose: complex, balanced, raspberry, ripe fruit, fruit expression. Palate: powerful, flavourful, fruity, fresh.

ARRAYÁN PETIT VERDOT 2008 T
100% petit verdot.

91 Colour: deep cherry. Nose: creamy oak, sweet spices, mineral, fruit expression. Palate: mineral, toasty, ripe fruit.

ARRAYÁN SYRAH 2008 T
syrah.

88 Colour: deep cherry. Nose: balanced, ripe fruit, fruit liqueur notes, wild herbs. Palate: spirituous, powerful, flavourful, fruity.

ARRAYÁN SELECCIÓN 2008 T
syrah, merlot, cabernet sauvignon, petit verdot.

87 Colour: deep cherry. Nose: sweet spices, toasty, mineral, ripe fruit. Palate: powerful, flavourful, fruity, varietal.

ARRAYÁN PREMIUM 2007 T
syrah, merlot, cabernet sauvignon, petit verdot.

91 Colour: dark-red cherry. Nose: undergrowth, ripe fruit, cocoa bean, toasty. Palate: fruity, powerful, flavourful, complex.

BODEGAS CANOPY

Avda. Barber, 71
45004 (Toledo)
☎: +34 619 244 878 - Fax: +34 925 283 681
achacon@masfuturo.com

MALPASO 2008 T
100% syrah.

95 Colour: cherry, garnet rim. Nose: balsamic herbs, scrubland, ripe fruit, creamy oak. Palate: flavourful, spicy, ripe fruit, fine bitter notes.

LA VIÑA ESCONDIDA 2008 T
100% garnacha.

94 Colour: cherry, garnet rim. Nose: mineral, creamy oak, sweet spices, ripe fruit, scrubland, balsamic herbs. Palate: flavourful, fine bitter notes, good acidity, long.

TRES PATAS 2008 T
80% garnacha, 20% syrah.

93 Colour: cherry, garnet rim. Nose: powerfull, ripe fruit, balsamic herbs, scrubland, sweet spices. Palate: flavourful, spicy, good acidity, round tannins.

CONGO 2008 T
100% garnacha.

92 Colour: cherry, garnet rim. Nose: mineral, powerfull, ripe fruit, sweet spices, creamy oak, scrubland. Palate: flavourful, fine bitter notes, balsamic, fruity.

BODEGAS JIMÉNEZ LANDI

Avda. Solana, 39-41
45930 Méntrida (Toledo)
☎: +34 918 178 213 - Fax: +34 918 178 213
jose@jimenezlandi.com
www.jimenezlandi.com

PIÉLAGO 2009 T
100% garnacha.

95 Colour: deep cherry. Nose: balsamic herbs, scrubland, raspberry, mineral. Palate: full, flavourful, fruity, complex.

ATAULFOS 2009 T
100% garnacha.

95 Colour: very deep cherry. Nose: red berry notes, fresh fruit, fruit expression, scrubland, balsamic herbs. Palate: long, spicy, easy to drink, ripe fruit, round, good acidity.

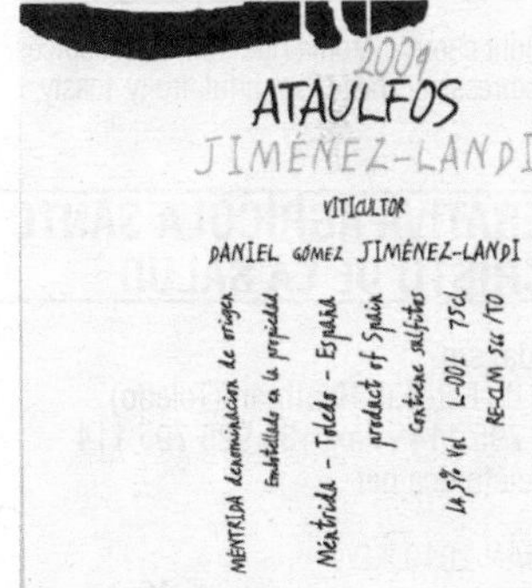

SOTORRONDERO 2009 T
60% syrah, 40% garnacha.

92 Colour: deep cherry. Nose: powerfull, varietal, warm, fruit preserve, ripe fruit. Palate: spicy, ripe fruit, fine bitter notes, elegant.

BODEGAS LA CERCA

Lepanto, 15
45950 Casarrubios del Monte (Toledo)
☎: +34 918 172 456 - Fax: +34 916 905 046
bodegaslacerca@yahoo.es

MOLINO VIEJO TEMPRANILLO 2010 T ROBLE
100% tempranillo.

87 Colour: cherry, purple rim. Nose: ripe fruit, warm, lactic notes. Palate: flavourful, fruity, fleshy.

MOLINO VIEJO 2007 TC

81 Colour: cherry, garnet rim. Nose: powerfull, warm, spicy, toasty. Palate: fine bitter notes, spicy.

BODEGAS Y VIÑEDOS TAVERA

Ctra. Valmojado - Toledo, Km. 22
45182 Arcicóllar (Toledo)
☎: +34 637 847 777 - Fax: +34 925 590 218
info@bodegastavera.com
www.bodegastavera.com

TAVERA 2010 T
garnacha.

87 Colour: cherry, purple rim. Nose: powerfull, characterful, ripe fruit, red berry notes. Palate: flavourful, fleshy, ripe fruit.

TAVERA 2009 T FERMENTADO EN BARRICA
100% syrah.

87 Color bright cherry. Aroma ripe fruit, sweet spices, creamy oak, expressive. Taste flavourful, fruity, toasty, round tannins.

COOPERATIVA AGRÍCOLA SANTO CRISTO DE LA SALUD

Ctra. Méntrida, s/n
45920 Torre de Esteban Hambrán (Toledo)
☎: +34 925 795 114 - Fax: +34 925 795 114
coopcrist@telefonica.net

TORRESTEBAN 2010 RD

80 Colour: brilliant rose. Nose: medium intensity, warm, ripe fruit. Palate: powerful, spicy, fine bitter notes.

REMURI TEMPRANILLO 2010 T
100% tempranillo.

83 Colour: deep cherry. Nose: fruit liqueur notes, characterful, powerfull. Palate: fleshy, concentrated, sweetness.

REMURI SYRAH 2010 T
100% syrah.

82 Colour: deep cherry. Nose: overripe fruit, warm, powerfull. Palate: powerful, sweetness, warm.

REMURI 2010 T ROBLE

81 Colour: very deep cherry. Nose: powerfull, warm, roasted coffee, aromatic coffee. Palate: powerful, fine bitter notes, harsh oak tannins.

SEÑORÍO DE ESTEBAN HAMBRÁN 2009 T
cencibel, garnacha.

77

TORRESTEBAN 2008 TC

80 Colour: bright cherry. Nose: spicy, ripe fruit, toasty. Palate: powerful, flavourful, sweetness.

TORRESTEBAN 2005 TC

80 Colour: pale ruby, brick rim edge. Nose: aromatic coffee, varnish, wet leather. Palate: fine bitter notes, spicy, ripe fruit.

TORRESTEBAN 2004 T

81 Colour: cherry, garnet rim. Nose: wet leather, fruit liqueur notes, spicy. Palate: fine bitter notes, spicy.

COOPERATIVA CONDES DE FUENSALIDA

Avda. San Crispín, 129
45510 Fuensalida (Toledo)
☎: +34 925 784 823 - Fax: +34 925 784 823
condesdefuensalida@hotmail.com
www.condesdefuensalida.iespana.es

CONDES DE FUENSALIDA 2010 RD
garnacha.

84 Colour: rose, purple rim. Nose: ripe fruit, red berry notes, floral. Palate: fleshy, powerful, fruity, fresh.

CONDES DE FUENSALIDA 2009 T

80 Colour: deep cherry. Nose: powerfull, warm, candied fruit. Palate: powerful, sweetness, slightly evolved.

CONDES DE FUENSALIDA 2007 TC

82 Colour: cherry, garnet rim. Nose: ripe fruit, sweet spices. Palate: flavourful, sweetness, round tannins.

COOPERATIVA NUESTRA SEÑORA DE LA NATIVIDAD

Puente San Roque, 1
45930 Méntrida (Toledo)
☎: +34 918 177 004 - Fax: +34 918 177 004
coopnatividad@gmail.com

VEGA BERCIANA 2010 RD
garnacha.

81 Colour: rose, purple rim. Nose: candied fruit, raspberry. Palate: flavourful, fruity, fresh.

VEGA BERCIANA 2010 T
garnacha.

78

VEGA BERCIANA 2007 TC

77

VALLE PEDROMORO 2006 T BARRICA
garnacha.

82 Colour: pale ruby, brick rim edge. Nose: medium intensity, elegant, fruit liqueur notes. Palate: spicy, fine bitter notes, good acidity.

LAS CAÑADAS DE CARTEMA

Mahonia, 2
28043 (Madrid)
☎: +34 913 433 026 - Fax: +34 913 433 090
info@cartema.es
www.cartema.com

CARTEMA 2007 B
sauvignon blanc, moscatel.

85 Colour: bright golden. Nose: candied fruit, dry nuts, honeyed notes. Palate: sweetness, good acidity, spirituous.

CARTEMA 2007 TC
syrah, tempranillo, cabernet sauvignon.

85 Colour: cherry, garnet rim. Nose: spicy, wet leather, ripe fruit. Palate: ripe fruit, spicy, fine bitter notes, fine tannins.

VIÑEDOS DE CAMARENA, SDAD. COOPERATIVA DE CLM

Ctra. Toledo - Valmojado, km. 24,6
45180 Camarena (Toledo)
☎: +34 918 174 347 - Fax: +34 918 174 632
vdecamarena@hotmail.com
www.vdecamarena.com

BASTIÓN DE CAMARENA 2010 RD
garnacha, tempranillo.

87 Colour: brilliant rose. Nose: faded flowers, fresh fruit, red berry notes. Palate: flavourful, fruity, fresh.

BASTIÓN DE CAMARENA 2010 T
95% garnacha, 5% syrah.

89 Color cherry, purple rim. Aroma expressive, fresh fruit, red berry notes, floral. Taste flavourful, fruity, good acidity, round tannins.

BASTIÓN DE CAMARENA 2008 T ROBLE
cabernet sauvignon, merlot, garnacha.

80 Colour: cherry, garnet rim. Nose: candied fruit, warm, spicy, dark chocolate. Palate: powerful, sweetness.

VIÑEDOS Y BODEGAS GONZÁLEZ

Real, 86
45180 Camarena (Toledo)
☎: +34 918 174 063 - Fax: +34 918 174 136
bodegasgonzalez@yahoo.es
www.vinobispo.com

VIÑA BISPO 2010 B
60% sauvignon blanc, 40% verdejo.

81 Colour: bright straw. Nose: dried flowers, candied fruit, citrus fruit. Palate: flavourful.

VIÑA BISPO 2010 RD
100% garnacha.

81 Colour: rose. Nose: ripe fruit, floral. Palate: flavourful, fruity, fleshy.

VIÑA BISPO 2008 T
60% cencibel, 30% syrah, 10% merlot.

70

VIÑA BISPO 2004 TC
80% cabernet sauvignon, 20% merlot.

83 Colour: pale ruby, brick rim edge. Nose: spicy, ripe fruit, wet leather. Palate: spicy, ripe fruit, fine tannins.

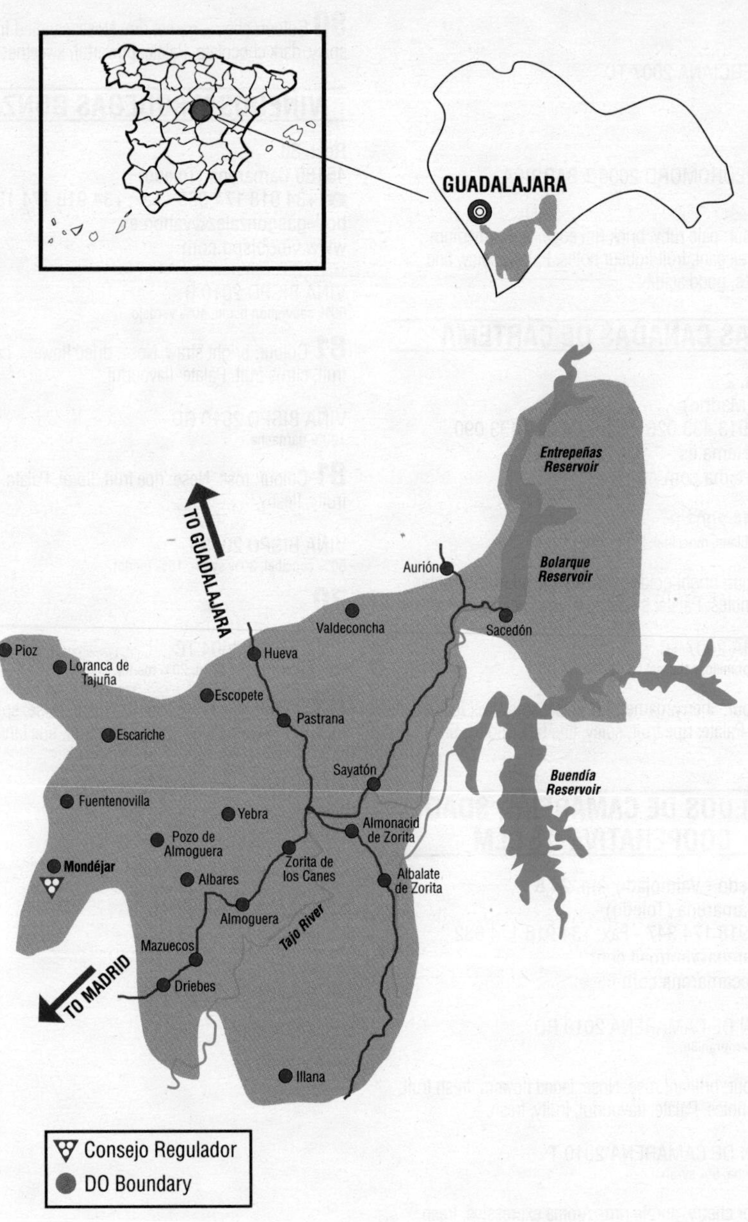
GUADALAJARA
TO GUADALAJARA
TO MADRID
Entrepeñas Reservoir
Bolarque Reservoir
Buendía Reservoir
Tajo River
Aurión
Sacedón
Valdeconcha
Pioz
Loranca de Tajuña
Hueva
Escopete
Pastrana
Escariche
Sayatón
Fuentenovilla
Yebra
Almonacid de Zorita
Pozo de Almoguera
Zorita de los Canes
Mondéjar
Albares
Albalate de Zorita
Almoguera
Mazuecos
Driebes
Illana
Consejo Regulador
DO Boundary

NEWS ABOUT THE VINTAGE:

In the light of the number of samples tasted from just one winery, the reader may think of Mondéjar as an elite designation of origin of just two wineries that survive in a strange fashion, or a territory ascribed to the "Vinos de Pago" status. But, alas! Mondéjar is a designation of origin with all what it takes to be one (regulations, president, vocals, et cetera) created soon after the original proposition of a single winery, Mariscal. What amazes us is the fact that they were actually given the right to become a DO in spite of the poor-to-average quality of their wines. The samples they sent for us to taste, a wine and a red, do not even manage to reach 85 points. We do not know for how long this situation is going to last, for how long the authorities are going to allow the DO to remain one. To make things even worst, just one of the two wineries sends us regularly samples for our Guide.

LOCATION:

In the southwest of the province of Guadalajara. It is made up of the municipal districts of Albalate de Zorita, Albares, Almoguera, Almonacid de Zorita, Driebes, Escariche, Escopete, Fuenteovilla, Illana, Loranca de Tajuña, Mazuecos, Mondéjar, Pastrana, Pioz, Pozo de Almoguera, Sacedón, Sayatón, Valdeconcha, Yebra and Zorita de los Canes.

CLIMATE:

Temperate Mediterranean. The average annual temperature is around 18°C and the average rainfall is 500 mm per year.

SOIL:

The south of the Denomination is characterized by red soil on lime-clayey sediments, and the north (the municipal districts of Anguix, Mondéjar, Sacedón, etc.) has brown limestone soil on lean sandstone and conglomerates.

GRAPE VARIETIES:

WHITE (40%): *Malvar* (majority 80% of white varieties), *Macabeo* and *Torrontés*.
RED (60%): *Cencibel* (*Tempranillo* – represents 95% of red varieties), *Cabernet Sauvignon* (5%) and *Syrah*.

FIGURES:

Vineyard surface: 600 – **Wine-Growers:** 400 – **Wineries:** 2 – **2010 Harvest rating:** Excellent – **Production:** 800,000 – **Market percentages:** 80% domestic. 20% export

CONSEJO REGULADOR
Pza. Mayor, 10
19110 Mondéjar (Guadalajara)
☎: 949 385 284 - Fax: 949 385 284
@ crdom@crdomondejar.com
www.crdomondejar.com

GENERAL CHARACTERISTICS OF THE WINES

WHITES	Those produced according to the more modern style tend to have a pale straw yellow colour; they have a fruity, fresh aroma and on the palate they are light and fruity; in the more traditional wines, however, there may appear notes of over-ripening.
ROSÉS	In general, they are light, supple and quite pleasant, although without excessive aromatic intensity..
REDS	These are probably the most interesting of the region. Produced mainly from *Cencibel*, their style resembles those from La Mancha: good aromatic intensity, with a presence of ripe fruit, supple and flavourful on the palate.

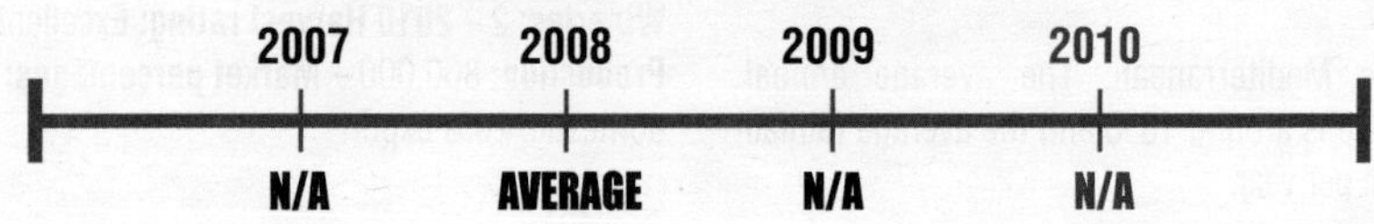

MARISCAL

Avda. Constitución, 37
19110 Mondéjar (Guadalajara)
☎: +34 949 385 138 - Fax: +34 949 387 740
comex@mariscal.es
www.mariscal.es

ARIS TORRONTÉS 2009 B
torrontés.

83 Colour: bright straw. Nose: medium intensity, citrus fruit, ripe fruit. Palate: flavourful, fruity, fresh.

TIERRA RUBIA SYRAH 2009 T
syrah.

84 Colour: cherry, purple rim. Nose: floral, ripe fruit, medium intensity. Palate: flavourful, fruity, lacks balance.

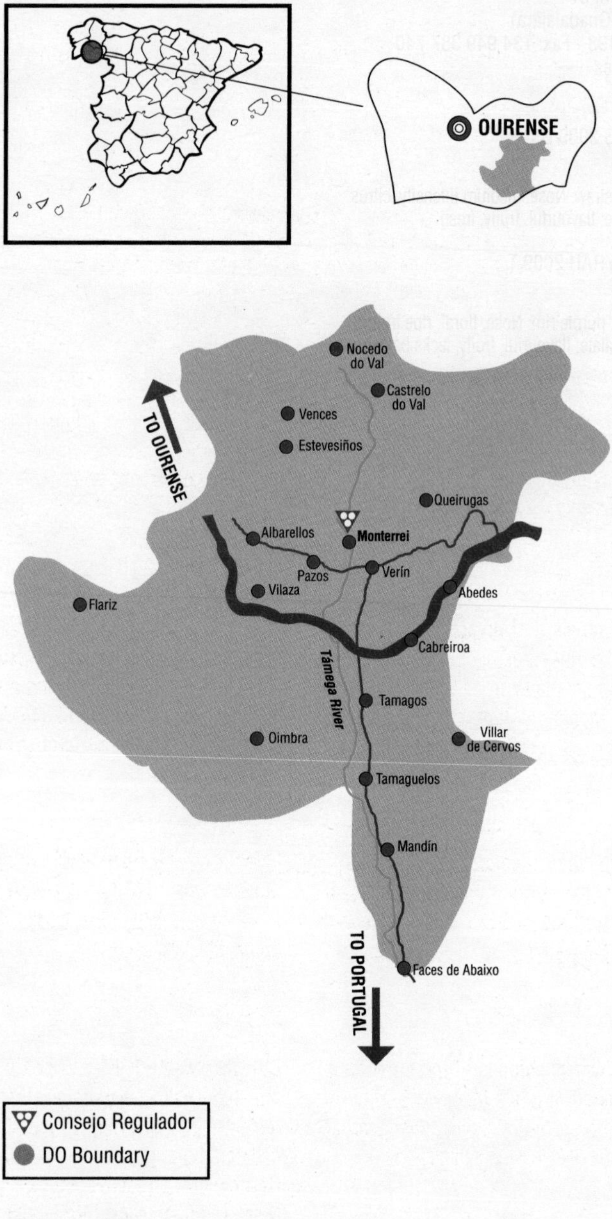

OURENSE
Nocedo do Val
Castrelo do Val
Vences
Estevesiños
TO OURENSE
Queirugas
Albarellos
Monterrei
Pazos
Verín
Vilaza
Abedes
Flariz
Cabreiroa
Támega River
Tamagos
Oimbra
Villar de Cervos
Tamaguelos
Mandín
Faces de Abaixo
TO PORTUGAL
Consejo Regulador
DO Boundary

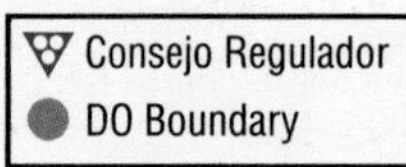

NEWS ABOUT THE VINTAGE:

Even in a hot year in the region like 2010 –particularly if we take into account that it enjoys a climate halfway between Atlantic and continental–, wines show good acidity levels, with good fruit weight, maybe just a little on the ripe side of things and therefore lacking the fine balsamic notes typical of the region. Red wines are correct, but considering that they still are something of novelty in the region, we can speak of a quality just a little above average.

This is a record year for us in terms of samples tasted from Monterrei, and we can assure the bet for quality the DO initiated a few years ago has surely paid off. The vintage hotter character has been benefitial to red wines, since it has done away with some herbaceous notes that might have –even slightly– lowered the scores in past editions. Ever since Raúl Pérez first got in contact with the region consulting for the winery Quinta da Muradella, we have learnt of the unique wild-herbs notes the dona blanca grape variety is able to achieve, in sheer contrast with the fruitier character of *godello*, or the wild red fruit notes of *merenzao* and *bastardo*, the latter planted in the hills bordering with Portugal. The wines made from grapes grown in the flatlands near the valley –where high yields are the norm– do not show as expressive, though. White wines have achieved over the years a well-defined character, with a high standard of quality for practically all the wines we have tasted, although in hotter vintages like 2010 we appreciate fruit notes of a riper quality; it is then and there that wines seem to switch to a different style, more unctuous and richer both in the nose and in the palate, a quality that seems to deepen its flavour, so can say that 2010 was a good vintage overall.

LOCATION:

In the east of the province of Orense, on the border with Portugal. The vineyards occupy the valley of Monterrei, and it is made up of the municipal districts of Verín, Monterrei, Oimbra and Castrelo do Vall.

CLIMATE:

Midway between the Atlantic and Continental influences. Drier than in the rest of Galicia, with maximum temperatures of 35°C in summer and minimum of –5°C in winter.

SOIL:

The vineyards cover the slopes of the mountains and valleys irrigated by the Támega river and its tributaries. The soil is quite clayey, deep, rather heavy and, in some places, somewhat sandy.

GRAPE VARIETIES:

WHITE: *Dona Blanca, Verdello* (*Godello*) and *Treixadura* (*Verdello Louro*), *Albariño, Caiño Blanco, Loureira* and *Blanca de Monterrei.*
RED: *Aranxa (Tempranillo), Caiño Tinto, Mencía, Bastardo* (or *María Ardoña*) and *Sousón.*

FIGURES:

Vineyard surface: 386 – **Wine-Growers:** 376 – **Wineries:** 25 – **2010 Harvest rating:** N/A – **Production:** 1,589,960 – **Market percentages:** 80% domestic. 20% export

SUB-REGIONS:

Val de Monterrei. Comprising the vineyards situated in the valley region (therefore, more level terrains) and covering the parishes and municipal districts belonging to the following city councils: Castrelo do Val (Castrelo do Val, Pepín and Nocedo); Monterrei (Albarellos, Infesta, Monterrei and Vilaza);

Oimbra (Oimbra, Rabal, O Rosal and San Cibrao); Verín (Abedes, Cabreiroa, Feces da Baixo, Feces de Cima, Mandín, Mourazos, Pazos, Queizás, A Rasela, Tamagos, Tamaguelos, Tintores, Verín, Vilela and Vilamaior do Val).

Ladeira de Monterrei. These vineyards occupy the hills. The parishes and municipal districts that make up this sub-region are: Castrelo do Val (Gondulfes and Servoi), Oimbra (As Chas and A Granxa), Monterrey (Flariz, Medeiros, Mixós, Estevesiños and Vences) and Verín (Queirugas).

CONSEJO REGULADOR
Mercado Comarcal, 1
32600 Verín (Ourense)
☎: +34 988 590 007 - Fax: +34 988 410 634
@ info@domonterrei.com
www.domonterrei.com

GENERAL CHARACTERISTICS OF THE WINES

WHITES	These have a straw yellow colour and are fresh and pleasant. Those produced from autochthonous grapes, as opposed to the flatter of the *Palomino* variety, are more intense and fruity, flavourful on the palate, with a good alcohol-acidity balance.
REDS	With a deep cherry-red colour, these are mainly young red wines which have a good fruity character, although, on occasions, there are herbaceous notes; on the palate they are light and fruity.

VINTAGE RATING PEÑÍNGUIDE

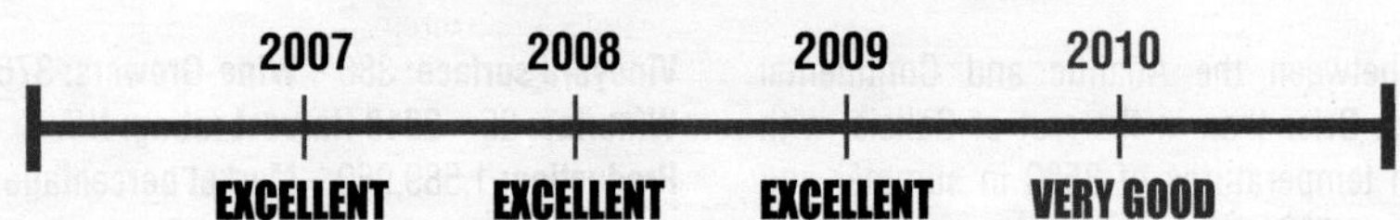

ADEGAS LADAIRO

Lg. O'Rosal, s/n
32613 Oimbra (Ourense)
☎: +34 988 422 757
info@bodegasladairo.com

LADAIRO GODELLO 2010 B
godello.

87 Colour: bright yellow, greenish rim. Nose: fruit expression, tropical fruit, powerfull, medium intensity. Palate: flavourful, fruity.

LADAIRO 2009 BFB
godello, treixadura.

90 Colour: bright yellow. Nose: candied fruit, jasmine, white flowers, honeyed notes. Palate: good structure, ripe fruit, spicy.

LADAIRO MENCÍA 2010 T
mencía.

87 Colour: deep cherry, purple rim. Nose: ripe fruit, medium intensity, wild herbs. Palate: flavourful, fruity, long.

LADAIRO 2009 T BARRICA
mencía, arauxa, bastardo.

90 Colour: bright cherry, garnet rim. Nose: sweet spices, creamy oak, cocoa bean, ripe fruit. Palate: flavourful, fruity, spicy, long.

ADEGAS TRIAY

Rua Ladairo, 36
32613 O'Rosal Oimbra (Ourense)
☎: +34 988 422 776 - Fax: +34 988 422 776
triayadegas@gmail.com
www.bodegastriay.com

TRIAY 2010 B
godello.

88 Colour: yellow, greenish rim. Nose: medium intensity, wild herbs. Palate: flavourful, fresh, good acidity, balanced, fine bitter notes.

TRIAY 2010 T
mencía.

87 Colour: cherry, purple rim. Nose: varietal, red berry notes, balsamic herbs. Palate: flavourful, good acidity.

ALMA ATLÁNTICA

Burgáns, 91
36633 Vilariño- Cambados (Pontevedra)
☎: +34 986 526 040 - Fax: +34 986 526 901
comercial@martincodax.com
www.martincodax.com

MARA MARTIN GODELLO 2010 B
godello.

87 Colour: bright straw, greenish rim. Nose: medium intensity, fresh fruit, wild herbs. Palate: flavourful, easy to drink, fine bitter notes.

BODEGA BOO-RIVERO

Touza, 22
32618 Villaza (Ourense)
☎: +34 988 425 950 - Fax: +34 988 425 950
bodegaboorivero@yahoo.es

FRAGAS DO LECER 2010 B
godello, treixadura.

90 Colour: bright yellow, greenish rim. Nose: ripe fruit, complex, medium intensity, balanced. Palate: rich, flavourful, fruity.

FRAGAS DO LECER 2010 T
mencía, bastardo, arauxa.

87 Colour: cherry, garnet rim. Nose: fruit expression, red berry notes, varietal, dried herbs. Palate: fruity, ripe fruit, good finish.

BODEGA COUTO MIXTO

Rua Principal, 46 Mandin
32698 Verin (Ourense)
☎: +34 636 762 200

COUTO MIXTO 2009 T
mencía.

89 Colour: very deep cherry, garnet rim. Nose: grassy, powerfull, balanced. Palate: good structure, fleshy, good acidity, round tannins.

BODEGA GARGALO

Rua Do Castelo, 59
32619 Pazos Verín (Ourense)
☎: +34 988 590 203 - Fax: +34 988 590 295
gargalo@verino.es
www.gargalo.es

TERRA DO GARGALO GODELLO 2010 B
godello, treixadura.

89 Colour: bright yellow, greenish rim. Nose: white flowers, medium intensity, expressive. Palate: fruity, balsamic, easy to drink.

TERRA DO GARGALO SOBRE LÍAS 2009 B
godello, treixadura.

90 Colour: bright yellow. Nose: candied fruit, dry nuts, balanced. Palate: good structure, fruity, fine bitter notes, good acidity.

TERRA DO GARGALO CARBALLO 2008 TC
tempranillo, mencía, bastardo.

87 Colour: bright cherry, garnet rim. Nose: toasty, spicy, powerfull. Palate: flavourful, spicy, toasty, ripe fruit.

BODEGA TABÚ

Praza A Carreira, 6 O Rosal
32613 Oimbra (Ourense)
☎: +34 665 644 500
bodegatabu@gmail.com

STIBADÍA 2010 B
godello, treixadura.

87 Colour: bright yellow, greenish rim. Nose: ripe fruit, dried herbs, tropical fruit. Palate: powerful, ripe fruit, long.

STIBADÍA 2009 B
godello, treixadura.

88 Colour: bright yellow. Nose: balanced, medium intensity, candied fruit, faded flowers. Palate: ripe fruit, rich.

STIBADÍA 2010 T
mencía, tempranillo.

87 Colour: bright cherry, purple rim. Nose: balanced, red berry notes. Palate: fleshy, ripe fruit, round tannins.

STIBADÍA 2009 T
mencía, tempranillo.

86 Colour: cherry, garnet rim. Nose: medium intensity, ripe fruit, neat. Palate: fruity, flavourful, ripe fruit, round tannins.

BODEGA VÍA ARXÉNTEA

Progreso, 61 Villaza
32618 Monterrei (Ourense)
☎: +34 687 409 618
viaarxentea@viaarxentea.com

VÍA ARXÉNTEA 2010 B
treixadura, godello.

91 Colour: bright straw. Nose: candied fruit, dried herbs, faded flowers, balanced, powerfull. Palate: flavourful, rich, fine bitter notes.

BODEGAS TAPIAS MARIÑÁN

Estr. Nacional 525, Km. 170,4
32619 Pazos Verín (Ourense)
☎: +34 988 411 693 - Fax: +34 988 411 693
info@tapiasmarinhan.com
www.tapiasmarinhan.es

PAZO DE MARIÑAN 2010 B
godello, treixadura, albariño.

89 Colour: bright yellow. Nose: candied fruit, wild herbs, citrus fruit. Palate: flavourful, ripe fruit, long.

QUINTAS DAS TAPIAS 2010 B
treixadura, godello, albariño.

89 Colour: bright yellow. Nose: medium intensity, ripe fruit, white flowers, jasmine. Palate: flavourful, fine bitter notes, good acidity.

QUINTAS DAS TAPIAS 2010 T
mencía.

87 Colour: cherry, purple rim. Nose: medium intensity, balanced, red berry notes, ripe fruit. Palate: fruity, easy to drink, good finish.

BODEGAS Y VIÑEDOS QUINTA DA MURADELLA

Avda. Luis Espada, 99- Entresuelo, dcha.
32600 Verín (Ourense)
☎: +34 988 411 724 - Fax: +34 988 590 427
muradella@verin.net

ALANDA 2010 B BARRICA
dona blanca, treixadura, monstruosa.

91 Colour: pale. Nose: dried flowers, citrus fruit, fragrant herbs, spicy, dry stone. Palate: flavourful, fleshy, complex, balanced.

MURADELLA 2009 B
treixadura, monstruosa.

92 Colour: bright yellow. Nose: faded flowers, ripe fruit, fragrant herbs, earthy notes, mineral. Palate: good acidity, flavourful, complex, fleshy.

GORVIA FERMENTADO EN BARRICA 2008 BFB
dona blanca.

93 Colour: bright straw. Nose: faded flowers, ripe fruit, fragrant herbs, earthy notes, creamy oak. Palate: rich, flavourful, fleshy, complex, fine bitter notes.

GORVIA 2008 T
mencía.

92 Colour: cherry, garnet rim. Nose: red berry notes, sweet spices, creamy oak, earthy notes. Palate: powerful, flavourful, ripe fruit, mineral, good acidity.

MURADELLA 2008 T
mencía, bastardo, sousón.

90 Colour: cherry, garnet rim. Nose: red berry notes, floral, balsamic herbs, spicy, mineral. Palate: flavourful, light-bodied, fresh, fruity, good acidity.

ALANDA 2008 T BARRICA
mencía, bastardo, garnacha tintorera.

87 Colour: cherry, garnet rim. Nose: fruit preserve, spicy, wild herbs, creamy oak. Palate: flavourful, fresh, ripe fruit, mineral.

CASTRO DE LOBARZÁN

Ctra. de Requeixo, 51- Villaza
32618 Monterrei (Ourense)
☎: +34 988 418 163 - Fax: +34 988 418 163
lobarzan@gmail.com

CASTRO DE LOBARZÁN 2010 B
godello, treixadura.

90 Colour: bright yellow, greenish rim. Nose: candied fruit, white flowers, powerfull, expressive. Palate: balanced, good acidity.

LOBARZÁN IS 2009 T
mencía, arauxa, bastardo.

91 Colour: cherry, purple rim. Nose: fruit expression, spicy, balanced, expressive. Palate: good structure, fruity, round tannins.

CASTRO DE LOBARZÁN MENCÍA 2009 T
mencía, arauxa.

89 Colour: deep cherry, garnet rim. Nose: fruit expression, wild herbs. Palate: good structure, flavourful, fleshy, long, spirituous.

CASTRO DE LOBARZÁN 2008 T
mencía, arauxa.

89 Colour: deep cherry, garnet rim. Nose: red berry notes, wild herbs, balanced, expressive. Palate: good structure, flavourful, round tannins.

CREGO E MONAGUILLO S.L.

Rua Nova, s/n
32618 Salgueira de Monterrei (Ourense)
☎: +34 988 418 164 - Fax: +34 988 418 164
tito@cregoemonaguillo.com
www.cregoemonaguillo.com

CREGO E MONAGUILLO 2010 B
godello, treixadura, dona blanca.

91 Color bright straw. Aroma fresh, fresh fruit, white flowers, expressive. Taste flavourful, fruity, good acidity, balanced.

CREGO E MONAGUILLO 2010 T
mencía.

88 Colour: deep cherry, purple rim. Nose: medium intensity, red berry notes, balanced. Palate: fruity, flavourful, good acidity.

FATHER 1943 2009 T
mencía, tempranillo.

92 Color bright cherry. Aroma ripe fruit, sweet spices, creamy oak, expressive. Taste flavourful, fruity, toasty, round tannins.

PAZO DAS TAPIAS

As Tapias - Pazos
32600 Verin (Ourense)
☎: +34 988 261 256 - Fax: +34 988 261 264
info@pazodomar.com
www.pazodastapias.com

ALMA DE BLANCO GODELLO 2010 B
100% godello.

88 Colour: bright straw, greenish rim. Nose: wild herbs, fresh, varietal, powerfull. Palate: flavourful, balsamic, long.

ALMA DE TINTO 2009 T
100% mencía.

86 Colour: deep cherry, garnet rim. Nose: medium intensity, dried herbs, red berry notes, ripe fruit. Palate: fruity, easy to drink.

PAZOS DEL REY

Carrero Blanco, 33- Albarellos
32618 Monterrei (Ourense)
☎: +34 988 425 959 - Fax: +34 988 425 949
info@pazosdelrey.com
www.pazosdelrey.com

PAZO DE MONTERREY 2010 B
100% godello.

91 Colour: bright straw, greenish rim. Nose: complex, balanced, varietal, expressive. Palate: flavourful, balanced, fine bitter notes.

SILA 2010 B
100% godello.

88 Colour: bright straw. Nose: white flowers, fresh fruit, fresh, expressive. Palate: flavourful, light-bodied, fresh, fruity.

SILA 2009 T BARRICA
100% mencía.

90 Colour: bright cherry. Nose: ripe fruit, expressive, spicy. Palate: fruity, toasty, round tannins.

QUINTA DO BUBLE

Casas dos Montes
32613 Oimbra (Ourense)
☎: +34 988 422 960 - Fax: +34 988 422 960
bodega@quintadobuble.com

QUINTA DO BUBLE 2010 B
godello.

89 Colour: bright yellow. Nose: candied fruit, dried herbs, balanced. Palate: long, fruity, flavourful, good acidity.

FINCA O RONCAL 2010 B
godello.

87 Colour: bright straw, greenish rim. Nose: wild herbs, fresh fruit, varietal, faded flowers. Palate: fruity, flavourful.

QUINTA DO BUBLE 2009 T BARRICA
mencía.

87 Colour: bright cherry. Nose: medium intensity, grassy, spicy. Palate: flavourful, fruity, toasty, round tannins.

VITIVINÍCOLA MENASA

Avda. de Sousas, 56 Bajos A - D
32600 Verin (Ourense)
☎: 988 414 802

VEGA DE LUCÍA 2010 B
godello.

86 Colour: bright straw. Nose: medium intensity, varietal, wild herbs. Palate: light-bodied, fruity, easy to drink.

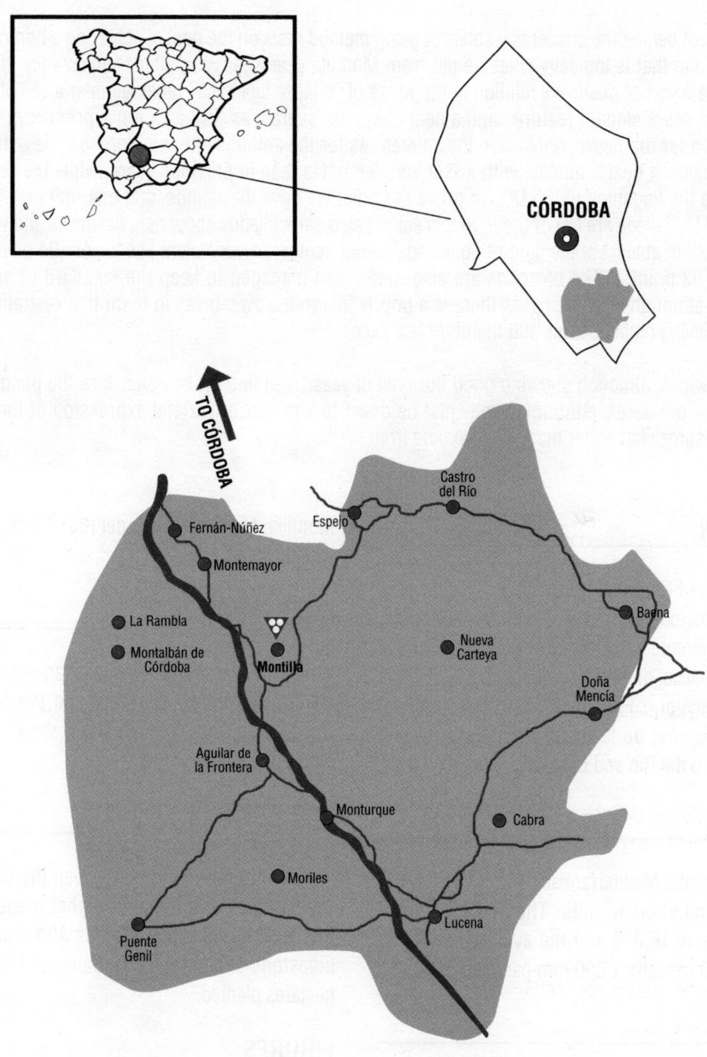
CÓRDOBA
TO CÓRDOBA
Castro del Río
Espejo
Fernán-Núñez
Montemayor
La Rambla
Montalbán de Córdoba
Montilla
Nueva Carteya
Baena
Doña Mencía
Aguilar de la Frontera
Monturque
Cabra
Moriles
Puente Genil
Lucena
Consejo Regulador
DO Boundary

DO MONTILLA-MORILES

NEWS ABOUT THE VINTAGE:

The concept behind the criaderas y soleras ageing method rests on the goal of achieving a homogenous product, and that is logically what we get from Montilla year after year, sheer consistency. It is also noticeable a sort of positive evolution in the wines of "crianza biológica" (ageing under a veil of yeast), with finer, more elegant features and a neat character overall, as well as a more prominent varietal expression for the *pedro ximénez* in the soleras. As for the amontillado and oloroso styles, they also seem to show a neater quality, with lesser wooden notes than in previous years, while the sweet PX wines are the flagships of the DO. To prove the point we have the ratings, and one more year Alvear 1830 and La Cañada are top of them. In this edition also amontillados show rich, flavourful and with lots of expression, at least in the light of –once again– our scores: Alvear Solera Fundación (94 points) and Boabdil (93 points). The olorosos are also made, and managed to keep the standard of previous editions, although in some cases there is a poorly integrated sweetness in them that restrains them from achieving higher scores and therefore real excellence.

The fino wines, although showing good flor (veil of yeast) and fine saline notes, lack the pungency of the finos from Jerez, although it may just be down to a matter of varietal expression of the *pedro ximénez*, somewhat softer than the *palomino* from Cádiz.

LOCATION:

To the south of Córdoba. It covers all the vineyards of the municipal districts of Montilla, Moriles, Montalbán, Puente Genil, Montruque, Nueva Carteya and Doña Mencía, and part of the municipal districts of Montemayor, Fernán-Núñez, La Rambla, Santaella, Aguilar de la Frontera, Lucena, Cabra, Baena, Castro del Río and Espejo.

CLIMATE:

Semi-continental Mediterranean, with long, hot, dry summers and short winters. The average annual temperature is 16.8°C and the average rainfall is between 500 mm and 1,000 mm per year.

SOIL:

The vineyards are situated at an altitude of between 125 m and 640 m. The soils are franc, franc-sandy and, in the higher regions, calcareous ('Albarizas'), which are precisely those of best quality, and which predominate in what is known as the Upper Sub-Region, which includes the municipal districts of Montilla, Moriles, Castro del Río, Cabra and Aguilar de la Frontera.

GRAPE VARIETIES:

WHITE: *Pedro Ximénez* (main variety), *Airén, Baladí, Moscatel, Torrontés* and *Verdejo.*
RED: *Tempranillo, Syrah* and *Cabernet Sauvignon.*

SUB-REGIONS:

We have to differentiate between the vineyards in the flatlands and those in higher areas –such as Sierra de Montilla and Moriles Alto–, prominently limestone soils of higher quality and hardly 2000 hectares planted.

FIGURES:

Vineyard surface: 6,001 – **Wine-Growers:** 2,895 – **Wineries:** 84 – **2010 Harvest rating:** Good – **Production:** 21,131,100 litres – **Market percentages:** 83% domestic. 17% export

CONSEJO REGULADOR
Rita Pérez, s/n
14550 Montilla (Córdoba)
☎: +34 957 699 957 - Fax: +34 957 652 866
@ consejo.montillamoriles@juntadeandalucia.es
www.montilla-moriles.org

GENERAL CHARACTERISTICS OF THE WINES

YOUNG WHITES	Created relatively recently, they are light and fruity wines for rapid consumption.
FINOS	Produced following the classical biological procedure of 'velo en flor'. With saline aromas of yeast and bitter almonds, they differ from the Jerezanos in being less dry on the palate.
OLOROSOS	These are mahogany coloured, with aromas of confectionery; they are sweet and flavourful on the palate.
AMONTILLADOS	Amber or old gold in colour. Nutty aroma (almonds and hazelnut); on the palate they have sweet notes with certain notes of biological ageing due to their origin as Finos.
PEDRO XIMÉNEZ	This is the Montilla-Moriles wine par excellence. Produced from sun-dried grapes, the colour may range from mahogany to very dark browns, thoroughly dense and concentrated. Unmistakable due to its aroma of raisins and dates, with a hint of toast; on the palate it is sweet, mellow and flavourful.

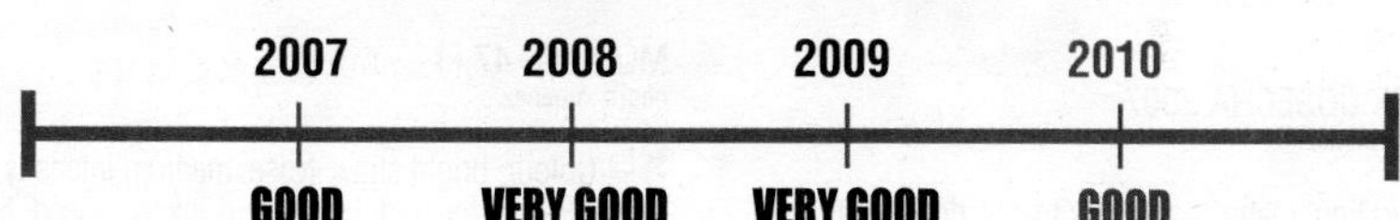

2007	2008	2009	2010
GOOD	VERY GOOD	VERY GOOD	GOOD

ALVEAR

María Auxiliadora, 1
14550 Montilla (Córdoba)
☎: +34 957 650 100 - Fax: +34 957 650 135
alvearsa@alvear.es
www.alvear.es

ALVEAR SOLERA FUNDACIÓN AM
100% pedro ximénez.

94 Colour: light mahogany. Nose: complex, expressive, elegant, spicy, pattiserie. Palate: flavourful, rich, good structure, great length, complex.

CARLOS VII AM
100% pedro ximénez.

90 Colour: old gold. Nose: powerfull, complex, elegant, dry nuts, toasty, varnish. Palate: rich, fine bitter notes, long, spicy.

C.B. FI
100% pedro ximénez.

90 Colour: bright straw. Nose: fresh, balanced, saline, pungent, faded flowers. Palate: flavourful, balanced, fine bitter notes.

ASUNCIÓN OL
100% pedro ximénez.

91 Colour: light mahogany. Nose: candied fruit, sweet spices, pattiserie, complex, dry nuts, roasted almonds. Palate: spirituous, fine bitter notes, sweetness.

ALVEAR PX DE AÑADA 2008
100% pedro ximénez.

90 Colour: old gold, amber rim. Nose: dried fruit, caramel, pattiserie. Palate: powerful, flavourful, complex, long.

ALVEAR PX COSECHA 2007
100% pedro ximénez.

91 Colour: light mahogany. Nose: toasty, dried fruit, sweet spices, cocoa bean, fruit liqueur notes. Palate: creamy, balanced, unctuous.

ALVEAR DULCE VIEJO 2000 PX RESERVA
100% pedro ximénez.

93 Colour: dark mahogany. Nose: balanced, complex, dried fruit, sun-drenched nuances, fruit liqueur notes, dark chocolate. Palate: balanced, elegant.

ALVEAR PX 1830 PX RESERVA
100% pedro ximénez.

98 Colour: dark mahogany. Nose: acetaldehyde, expressive, balanced, dried fruit, dark chocolate, cocoa bean. Palate: creamy, complex.

ALVEAR PX 1927
100% pedro ximénez.

90 Colour: mahogany. Nose: powerfull, candied fruit, tar, pattiserie, caramel. Palate: sweet, unctuous, toasty, balanced.

BODEGAS ARAGÓN Y CÍA.

Camino de la Estación, 11 Apdo. 534
14900 Lucena (Córdoba)
☎: +34 957 500 046 - Fax: +34 957 502 935
ventas@aragonycia.com
www.aragonycia.com

LAGAR DE CAMPOARAS B
pedro ximénez.

80 Colour: bright straw. Nose: medium intensity, dried herbs, short. Palate: sweetness, ripe fruit.

BOABDIL AM
pedro ximénez.

93 Colour: light mahogany. Nose: expressive, balanced, complex, acetaldehyde, spicy. Palate: full, flavourful, long, fine bitter notes, round.

PACORRITO AM
pedro ximénez.

86 Colour: old gold. Nose: pungent, dry nuts, acetaldehyde, sweet spices. Palate: flavourful, good structure, long.

MORILES 47 FI
pedro ximénez.

85 Colour: bright straw. Nose: medium intensity, dried herbs. Palate: flavourful, easy to drink, balanced, fine bitter notes.

PILYCRIM PCR
pedro ximénez.

84 Colour: bright yellow, greenish rim. Nose: powerfull, ripe fruit, dried herbs, candied fruit. Palate: rich, flavourful, sweet.

ARACELI PX
pedro ximénez.

86 Colour: mahogany. Nose: fruit preserve, candied fruit, pattiserie. Palate: sweet, flavourful, great length.

BODEGAS CRUZ CONDE

Ronda Canillo, 4
14550 Montilla (Córdoba)
☎: +34 957 651 250 - Fax: +34 957 653 619
info@bodegascruzconde.es
www.bodegascruzconde.es

CRUZ CONDE FI
100% pedro ximénez.

86 Colour: bright straw. Nose: saline, dried herbs, balanced. Palate: flavourful, rich, great length.

MERCEDES OL
100% pedro ximénez.

83 Colour: light mahogany. Nose: pattiserie, sweet spices, candied fruit. Palate: fruity, flavourful, sweetness.

CRUZ CONDE SOLERA FUNDACIÓN 1902 1995 PX
100% pedro ximénez.

92 Colour: dark mahogany. Nose: fruit liqueur notes, candied fruit, aged wood nuances, toasty, dark chocolate, aromatic coffee. Palate: creamy, balanced, unctuous.

CRUZ CONDE PX
100% pedro ximénez.

89 Colour: dark mahogany. Nose: complex, fruit liqueur notes, dried fruit, pattiserie, toasty. Palate: sweet, rich, unctuous, powerful.

BODEGAS DELGADO

Cosano, 2
14500 Puente Genil (Córdoba)
☎: +34 957 600 085 - Fax: +34 957 604 571
fino@bodegasdelgado.com
www.bodegasdelgado.com

LAGAR DE SAN ANTONIO 2010 B
pedro ximénez.

86 Colour: bright straw. Nose: elegant, balanced, ripe fruit. Palate: flavourful, fruity.

DELGADO 1874 AMONTILLADO NATURAL MUY VIEJO AM
100% pedro ximénez.

90 Colour: old gold, amber rim. Nose: complex, expressive, spicy, varnish, pungent. Palate: good structure, spicy, flavourful, great length.

SEGUNDA BOTA FI
palomino.

86 Colour: bright yellow. Nose: medium intensity, dry nuts, saline. Palate: correct, easy to drink.

MANOLO FI
palomino.

84 Colour: bright straw, greenish rim. Nose: medium intensity, dried herbs. Palate: correct, easy to drink, fine bitter notes.

F.E.O. FINO EXTRA OLOROSO OL
palomino.

86 Colour: bright yellow. Nose: saline, medium intensity, dry nuts. Palate: flavourful, correct, fine bitter notes.

DELGADO 1874 PX
pedro ximénez.

94 Colour: mahogany. Nose: expressive, dried fruit, fruit liqueur notes, complex, pattiserie, tobacco. Palate: complex, flavourful, toasty, long.

CALIFA PX
pedro ximénez.

89 Colour: dark mahogany. Nose: complex, fruit liqueur notes, dried fruit, pattiserie, toasty. Palate: sweet, rich, powerful, unctuous.

BODEGAS LA AURORA

Avda. de Europa, 7
14550 Montilla (Córdoba)
☎: +34 957 650 362 - Fax: +34 957 654 642
administracion@bodegaslaaurora.com
www.bodegaslaaurora.com

FINO AMANECER FI

84 Colour: bright straw, greenish rim. Nose: saline, medium intensity, dry nuts. Palate: fresh, easy to drink.

AMANECER PCR

84 Colour: bright yellow, greenish rim. Nose: macerated fruit, powerfull. Palate: correct, ripe fruit, sweet.

SOLERA 1981 PX
pedro ximénez.

90 Colour: mahogany. Nose: candied fruit, dried fruit, spicy, dark chocolate. Palate: flavourful, spirituous, sweet, toasty, great length.

AMANECER PX
pedro ximénez.

87 Colour: dark mahogany. Nose: complex, fruit liqueur notes, pattiserie, honeyed notes, caramel. Palate: sweet, rich, unctuous, powerful.

BODEGAS LUQUE

La Molinera, 3
14860 Doña Mencía (Córdoba)
☎: +34 957 676 029 - Fax: +34 957 676 029
bodegasluque@terra.es

EL ABUELO SOLERA 1888 AM
100% pedro ximénez.

87 Colour: light mahogany. Nose: powerfull, sweet spices, caramel. Palate: powerful, flavourful, rich, long.

LOS LUQUES (IMPERIAL) FI
100% pedro ximénez.

83 Colour: bright yellow. Nose: candied fruit, dry nuts, dried herbs. Palate: flavourful, rich.

FINO EL PATO FI
100% pedro ximénez.

82 Colour: bright yellow. Nose: medium intensity, varnish. Palate: correct, easy to drink.

BODEGAS MÁLAGA VIRGEN

Autovía A-92, Málaga-Sevilla, Km. 132
29520 Fuente de Piedra (Málaga)
☎: +34 952 319 454 - Fax: +34 952 359 819
didier.bricout@bodegasmalagavirgen.com
www.bodegasmalagavirgen.com

LAGAR DE BENAVIDES FI
pedro ximénez.

84 Colour: bright yellow. Nose: medium intensity, fresh, dried herbs. Palate: fine bitter notes, easy to drink.

BODEGAS MORENO

Fuente de la Salud, 2
14006 (Córdoba)
☎: +34 957 767 605 - Fax: +34 957 279 907
moreno@morenosa.com
www.morenosa.com

CABRIOLA AMONTILLADO VIEJO AM
100% pedro ximénez.

89 Colour: old gold, amber rim. Nose: balanced, elegant, sweet spices, acetaldehyde, dry nuts, toasty. Palate: full, flavourful, complex.

SIETE SABIOS AM
100% pedro ximénez.

89 Colour: old gold, amber rim. Nose: medium intensity, expressive, pattiserie, sweet spices, dry nuts. Palate: spicy, good structure.

MUSA AM
100% pedro ximénez.

84 Colour: old gold. Nose: toasty, sweet spices, aged wood nuances. Palate: flavourful, correct, easy to drink.

BENAVIDES FI
100% pedro ximénez.

84 Colour: bright straw, greenish rim. Nose: medium intensity, saline. Palate: flavourful, correct, easy to drink.

MUSA FI
100% pedro ximénez.

82 Colour: bright straw. Nose: candied fruit, medium intensity, saline. Palate: correct.

MUSA OL
100% pedro ximénez.

90 Colour: iodine, amber rim. Nose: candied fruit, dry nuts, spicy. Palate: powerful, rich, good structure, spicy, long.

PLATINO SOLERA OLOROSA OL
100% pedro ximénez.

90 Colour: iodine, amber rim. Nose: complex, balanced, powerfull, dry nuts, roasted almonds. Palate: flavourful, good structure, complex.

OLOROSO VIEJO FUNDACIÓN 1819 OL
100% pedro ximénez.

87 Colour: iodine, amber rim. Nose: roasted almonds, sweet spices, varnish. Palate: flavourful, spirituous, great length, fine bitter notes.

ALBOROQUE PC
100% pedro ximénez.

89 Colour: light mahogany. Nose: dry nuts, sweet spices, pattiserie. Palate: flavourful, fine bitter notes, balanced.

VIRGILIO PX
100% pedro ximénez.

90 Colour: dark mahogany. Nose: complex, fruit liqueur notes, dried fruit, pattiserie, toasty. Palate: sweet, rich, unctuous, powerful, toasty.

MUSA PX
100% pedro ximénez.

86 Colour: old gold, amber rim. Nose: varnish, acetaldehyde, candied fruit, sweet spices. Palate: rich, flavourful.

UNA VIDA PX
100% pedro ximénez.

85 Colour: mahogany. Nose: candied fruit, dried fruit, caramel. Palate: sweet, correct, good finish.

COMPAÑÍA VINÍCOLA DEL SUR - TOMÁS GARCÍA

Avda. Luis de Góngora y Argote, s/n
14550 Montilla (Córdoba)
☎: +34 957 650 204 - Fax: +34 957 652 335
info@vinicoladelsur.com
www.vinicoladelsur.com

MONTE CRISTO AM
100% pedro ximénez.

89 Colour: light mahogany. Nose: sweet spices, varnish, candied fruit, dry nuts. Palate: rich, flavourful, complex.

VERBENERA FI
pedro ximénez.

90 Colour: bright straw, greenish rim. Nose: balanced, elegant, faded flowers, saline. Palate: flavourful, full, fine bitter notes, fresh.

MONTE CRISTO FI
100% pedro ximénez.

88 Colour: bright yellow. Nose: pungent, saline, balanced, scrubland. Palate: flavourful, fresh, fine bitter notes.

MONTE CRISTO OL
100% pedro ximénez.

92 Colour: iodine, amber rim. Nose: expressive, complex, dry nuts. Palate: full, flavourful, elegant, spirituous.

TOMÁS GARCÍA PX
100% pedro ximénez.

89 Colour: dark mahogany. Nose: dried fruit, powerfull, pattiserie, sweet spices. Palate: flavourful, powerful, spirituous, sweet.

MONTE CRISTO PX
100% pedro ximénez.

87 Colour: mahogany. Nose: dark chocolate, caramel, pattiserie. Palate: concentrated, sweet, flavourful.

EQUIPO NAVAZOS

Cartuja, 1 - módulo 6
11401 Jerez de la Frontera (Cádiz)
☎: +34 649 435 979
equipo@navazos.com
www.equiponavazos.com

CASA DEL INCA 2010 PX
100% pedro ximénez.

96 Colour: dark mahogany. Nose: complex, dried fruit, pattiserie, toasty. Palate: sweet, rich, unctuous, powerful.

LA BOTA DE PEDRO XIMENEZ Nº25 BOTA NO PX
pedro ximénez.

96 Colour: dark mahogany. Nose: complex, fruit liqueur notes, dried fruit, pattiserie, toasty, powerfull. Palate: sweet, rich, unctuous, powerful, fine bitter notes.

GRACIA HERMANOS

Avda. Marqués de la Vega de Armijo, 103
14550 Montilla (Córdoba)
☎: +34 957 650 162 - Fax: +34 957 652 335
info@bodegasgracia.com
www.bodegasgracia.com

VIÑAVERDE 2010 B
pedro ximénez, verdejo, moscatel, macabeo, torrontés.

84 Colour: bright straw. Nose: faded flowers, fruit expression, medium intensity. Palate: light-bodied, easy to drink.

TAUROMAQUIA AMONTILLADO VIEJO AM
100% pedro ximénez.

88 Colour: old gold. Nose: expressive, candied fruit, sweet spices, acetaldehyde. Palate: flavourful, good structure, unctuous.

SOLERA FINA TAUROMAQUIA FI
100% pedro ximénez.

91 Colour: bright straw, greenish rim. Nose: balanced, elegant, complex, saline. Palate: good structure, flavourful, full, fine bitter notes.

SOLERA FINA MARÍA DEL VALLE FI
100% pedro ximénez.

89 Colour: bright straw, greenish rim. Nose: elegant, saline, pungent, balanced. Palate: flavourful, rich, fine bitter notes.

FINO CORREDERA FI
100% pedro ximénez.

87 Colour: bright yellow, greenish rim. Nose: saline, pungent, elegant, balanced, dried herbs. Palate: flavourful, rich.

TAUROMAQUIA OL
100% pedro ximénez.

86 Colour: light mahogany. Nose: candied fruit, sweet spices, caramel. Palate: fine bitter notes, flavourful, good structure.

TAUROMAQUIA PX
100% pedro ximénez.

90 Colour: mahogany. Nose: pattiserie, dark chocolate, powerfull, fruit liqueur notes. Palate: concentrated, flavourful, sweet, spicy, long.

GRACIA DULCE VIEJO PX
100% pedro ximénez.

89 Colour: dark mahogany. Nose: dark chocolate, toasty, sweet spices, candied fruit, sun-drenched nuances. Palate: good structure, flavourful, sweet, great length.

PÉREZ BARQUERO S.A.

Avda. Andalucía, 27
14550 Montilla (Córdoba)
☎: +34 957 650 500 - Fax: +34 957 650 208
info@perezbarquero.com
www.perezbarquero.com

VIÑA AMALIA 2010 B
pedro ximénez, moscatel, verdejo, torrontés.

83 Colour: bright straw, greenish rim. Nose: ripe fruit, tropical fruit, fragrant herbs. Palate: fruity, easy to drink.

GRAN BARQUERO AM
100% pedro ximénez.

91 Colour: old gold, amber rim. Nose: sweet spices, cocoa bean, saline, expressive. Palate: flavourful, balanced, long.

GRAN BARQUERO FI
100% pedro ximénez.

89 Colour: bright straw. Nose: dry nuts, faded flowers, saline, pungent. Palate: flavourful, fresh, fine bitter notes.

FINO LOS AMIGOS FI
100% pedro ximénez.

86 Colour: bright straw, greenish rim. Nose: pungent, saline, flor yeasts. Palate: flavourful, fresh, rich.

GRAN BARQUERO OL
100% pedro ximénez.

90 Colour: iodine, amber rim. Nose: powerfull, expressive, complex, spicy, dry nuts. Palate: elegant, rich, flavourful.

PÉREZ BARQUERO PEDRO XIMÉNEZ DE COSECHA 2009 PX
100% pedro ximénez.

88 Colour: old gold. Nose: sun-drenched nuances, dried fruit, complex, expressive, varietal. Palate: creamy, balanced, sweet, flavourful.

LA CAÑADA PX
100% pedro ximénez.

96 Colour: dark mahogany. Nose: complex, dried fruit, pattiserie, toasty, elegant, sun-drenched nuances. Palate: sweet, unctuous, powerful, long.

GRAN BARQUERO PX
100% pedro ximénez.

90 Colour: dark mahogany. Nose: dried fruit, complex, expressive, powerfull, pattiserie. Palate: good structure, unctuous, toasty.

TORO ALBALÁ

Avda. Antonio Sánchez Romero, 1
14920 Aguilar de la Frontera (Córdoba)
☎: +34 957 660 046 - Fax: +34 957 661 494
info@toroalbala.com
www.toroalbala.com

ELÉCTRICO FINO DEL LAGAR FI
100% pedro ximénez.

88 Colour: bright yellow. Nose: complex, pungent, saline. Palate: rich, powerful, fresh, fine bitter notes.

DON P.X. 2008 PX
100% pedro ximénez.

90 Colour: dark mahogany. Nose: fruit liqueur notes, dried fruit, pattiserie. Palate: sweet, rich, unctuous, powerful.

DON P.X. 1982 PX GRAN RESERVA
100% pedro ximénez.

94 Colour: dark mahogany. Nose: complex, fruit liqueur notes, dried fruit, pattiserie, roasted coffee, aromatic coffee. Palate: sweet, rich, unctuous, powerful.

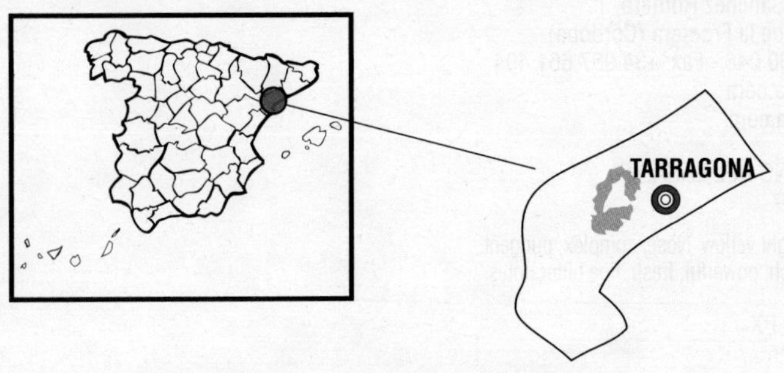

Consejo Regulador
DO Boundary

NEWS ABOUT THE VINTAGE:

It seems that Montsant is breathing hard on Priorat's neck, at least regarding the number of samples sent for our assessment. It is well known that some producers have interests in both designations of origin, and Montsant plays the role of a region of almost equal quality at just lower prices. Its varied soil structure, with more accessible vineyards, allows the DO to offer wines that bear the mark of singularity, as well as a more flexible use of the different varieties.

Red wines from the 2010 harvest show pretty ripe, although they have good fruit expression, considering that for Montsant's model the quality of the grapes is not as crucial as to other regions. Comparatively, they are fresher and more expressive than those from 2009, and even fresher (for the same year) than those from neighbouring Priorat where *licorella* (slate) soil is able to retain heat more easily than the clay and limestone soils –an even chalky– typical of Montsant, which allow a slower ripening cycle and and the preservation of primary features from the grape. The area of Cornudella is surely the coolest spot in the region, yielding the finest herbal notes. On the other hand, red wines from the 2008 vintage appear too ripe and even confected compared to those from 2007. Once again Espectacle and Trossos 2009 are amongst the best wines in the region.

LOCATION:

In the region of Priorat (Tarragona). It is made up of Baix Priorat, part of Alt Priorat and various municipal districts of Ribera d'Ebre that were already integrated into the Falset sub-region. In total, 16 municipal districts: La Bisbal de Falset, Cabaces, Capçanes, Cornudella de Montsant, La Figuera, Els Guiamets, Marçá, Margalef, El Masroig, Pradell, La Torre de Fontaubella, Ulldemolins, Falset, El Molar, Darmós and La Serra d'Almos. The vineyards are located at widely variable altitudes, ranging between 200 m to 700 m above sea level.

CLIMATE:

Although the vineyards are located in a Mediterranean region, the mountains that surround the region isolate it from the sea to a certain extent, resulting in a somewhat more Continental climate. Due to this, it benefits from the contrasts in day/night temperatures, which is an important factor in the ripening of the grapes. However, it also receives the sea winds, laden with humidity, which help to compensate for the lack of rainfall in the summer. The average rainfall is between 500 and 600 mm per year.

SOIL:

There are mainly three types of soil: compact calcareous soils with pebbles on the borders of the DO; granite sands in Falset; and siliceous slate (the same stony slaty soil as Priorat) in certain areas of Falset and Cornudella.

GRAPE VARIETIES:

WHITE: *Chardonnay, Garnacha Blanca, Macabeo, Moscatel, Pansal, Parellada.*
RED: *Cabernet Sauvignon, Cariñena, Garnacha Tinta, Garnacha Peluda, Merlot, Monastrell, Picapoll, Syrah, Tempranillo* and *Mazuela.*

FIGURES:

Vineyard surface: 1,970 – **Wine-Growers:** 800 – **Wineries:** 57 – **2010 Harvest rating:** Very Good – **Production:** 5,870,000 litres – **Market percentages:** 37% domestic. 63% export

CONSEJO REGULADOR
Plaça de la Quartera, 6
43730 Falset (Tarragona)
☎: +34 977 831 742 - Fax: +34 977 830 676
@ info@domontsant.com
www.domontsant.com

GENERAL CHARACTERISTICS OF THE WINES

WHITES	The most characteristic are the white wines based on *Garnacha Blanca*, which gives wines with body and a certain structure and the characteristic notes of herbs and hints of Mediterranean woodland, typical of the variety. The white wines from *Macabeo* are a little lighter and refined, fresh and fruity.
ROSÉS	There are not many examples, but in general they are produced from *Garnacha*. They are flavourful and fruity, maybe too full-bodied, but very pleasant with good red berry definition.
REDS	These are, without doubt, the most characteristic wines of the DO. They are produced almost exclusively from *Garnacha* or from a blend of this variety and *Mazuelo* with foreign varieties, especially *Cabernet Sauvignon* or *Syrah*. The young wines are fruity, meaty and flavourful. The best examples amongst those aged in barrels have high levels of fruitiness: they are powerful, meaty, with a high alcohol content. Mineral notes may also appear. They are reminiscent of Priorat wines, perhaps with less extraction and weight.
TRADITIONAL WINES	Liqueurs (sweet) are produced mainly from *Garnacha*. They are usually sticky and mellow on the palate, with aromas and a taste of raisins and preserved fruit.

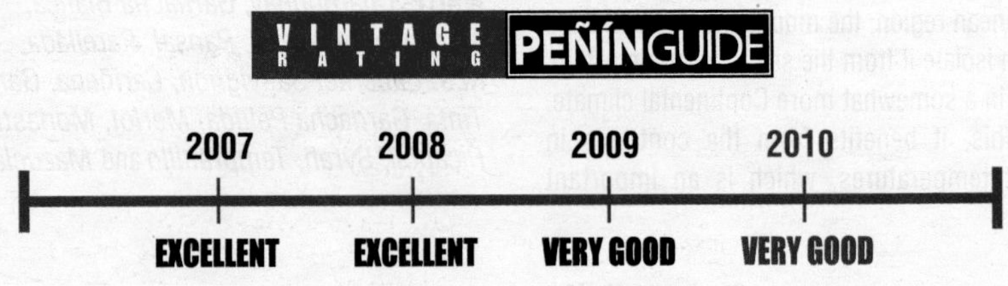

ACÚSTIC CELLER

St. Lluís, 12
43775 Marça (Tarragona)
☎: +34 629 472 988 - Fax: +34 977 678 149
acustic@acusticceller.com
www.acusticceller.com

ACÚSTIC 2010 B
garnacha blanca, garnacha roja, macabeo, pansal.

90 Colour: bright straw. Nose: complex, expressive, wild herbs, fresh fruit, white flowers. Palate: flavourful, complex, fruity.

AUDITORI 2009 T
100% garnacha.

94 Colour: very deep cherry, purple rim. Nose: balanced, expressive, mineral, sweet spices. Palate: good structure, good acidity, fine bitter notes.

BRAÓ 2009 T
garnacha, samsó.

93 Colour: bright cherry. Nose: ripe fruit, sweet spices, expressive, complex, elegant. Palate: flavourful, fruity, round tannins.

ACÚSTIC 2009 T
garnacha, samsó.

91 Colour: cherry, purple rim. Nose: red berry notes, violets, fragrant herbs, spicy. Palate: fruity, flavourful, full, complex.

AGRÍCOLA AUBACS I SOLANS

Carretera, 1
43736 La Figuera (Tarragona)
☎: +34 977 825 228 - Fax: +34 977 825 228
aubacs.i.solans@wanadoo.es

PROSIT 2009 TC
garnacha.

87 Colour: deep cherry, garnet rim. Nose: medium intensity, ripe fruit, spicy. Palate: fleshy, balsamic, ripe fruit.

AGRÍCOLA D'ULLDEMOLINS SANT JAUME

Saltadora, 17
43363 Ulldemolins (Tarragona)
☎: +34 977 561 613 - Fax: +34 977 561 613
coopulldemolins@omo.com
www.coopulldemolins.com

LES PEDRENYERES 2010 B
garnacha blanca.

87 Colour: bright straw. Nose: fresh, white flowers, ripe fruit. Palate: flavourful, fruity, good acidity, balanced.

ULLDEMOLINS 2009 T
garnacha.

85 Colour: cherry, garnet rim. Nose: medium intensity, red berry notes, wild herbs, warm. Palate: fruity, flavourful.

LES PEDRENYERES 2007 T
100% garnacha.

89 Colour: deep cherry. Nose: fruit liqueur notes, fruit liqueur notes, spicy, aromatic coffee. Palate: spicy, fine bitter notes, fine tannins.

AGRÍCOLA I SC DE LA SERRA D'ALMOS

Avinguda de la Cooperativa, s/n
43746 La Serra D'Almos (Tarragona)
☎: +34 977 418 125 - Fax: +34 977 418 399
coopserra@telefonica.net
www.serradalmos.com

MUSSEFRES 2009 B
macabeo, garnacha blanca, parellada.

86 Colour: bright yellow. Nose: balanced, medium intensity, white flowers. Palate: fruity, good finish, easy to drink.

MUSSEFRES 2009 T
cariñena, garnacha, cabernet sauvignon, ull de llebre.

80 Colour: very deep cherry, garnet rim. Nose: candied fruit, slightly evolved. Palate: flavourful, fruity.

MUSSEFRES 2008 TC
cariñena, garnacha.

88 Colour: cherry, garnet rim. Nose: powerfull, warm, fruit preserve, spicy, tobacco. Palate: flavourful, fruity, round tannins.

ANA I MOISÉS VITICULTORS

Finca "Clos Mesorah" Ctra. T-300 Falset Marça, Km. 1
43775 Marça Priorat (Tarragona)
☎: +34 935 343 026 - Fax: +34 936 750 316
moises@elviwines.com
www.elviwines.com

CLOS MESORAH 2009 TR
40% cariñena, 30% garnacha, 30% syrah.

91 Colour: dark-red cherry. Nose: ripe fruit, toasty, dark chocolate, fruit preserve. Palate: powerful, flavourful, fleshy.

ANGUERA DOMENECH

Sant Pere, 2
43743 Darmós (Tarragona)
☎: +34 977 405 857 - Fax: +34 977 404 106
angueradomenech@wanadoo.es
www.vianguera.com

RECLOT 2010 T
tempranillo, monastrell, garnacha.

86 Colour: cherry, garnet rim. Nose: balanced, ripe fruit, dried herbs. Palate: fruity, good structure, flavourful, fruity aftestaste.

VINYA GASÓ 2008 TC
garnacha, samsó, tempranillo.

87 Colour: bright cherry. Nose: ripe fruit, sweet spices, toasty, balsamic herbs. Palate: flavourful, fruity, toasty, round tannins.

BUIL & GINÉ

Ctra. de Gratallops - Vilella Baixa, Km. 11,5
43737 Gratallops (Tarragona)
☎: +34 977 839 810 - Fax: +34 977 839 811
info@builgine.com
www.builgine.com

17-XI 2008 T ROBLE
33% garnacha, 33% cariñena, 33% tempranillo.

86 Colour: cherry, garnet rim. Nose: powerfull, ripe fruit, fruit liqueur notes, spicy. Palate: flavourful, good structure, spicy.

BABOIX 2007 T
30% garnacha, 30% cariñena, 15% cabernet sauvignon, 15% merlot, 10% ull de llebre.

90 Colour: cherry, garnet rim. Nose: ripe fruit, fruit liqueur notes, dark chocolate, toasty. Palate: flavourful, powerful, spicy, long.

CASTELL D'OR

Mare Rafols, 3- 1r 4a
08720 Vilafranca del Penedès (Barcelona)
☎: +34 938 905 385 - Fax: +34 938 905 446
castelldor@castelldor.com
www.castelldor.com

TEMPLER 2007 TC
50% garnacha, 50% tempranillo.

87 Colour: cherry, purple rim. Nose: ripe fruit, red berry notes, sweet spices. Palate: flavourful, fruity, fleshy.

TEMPLER 2006 TR
40% cabernet sauvignon, 30% garnacha, 30% tempranillo.

87 Colour: cherry, garnet rim. Nose: ripe fruit, spicy, wild herbs. Palate: powerful, flavourful, round tannins.

CELLER CEDÓ ANGUERA

Ctra. La Serra d'Almos-Darmós, Km. 0,2
43746 La Serra d'Almos (Tarragona)
☎: +34 699 694 728 - Fax: +34 977 417 369
celler@cedoanguera.com
www.cedoanguera.com

ANEXE 2010 T
45% cariñena, 45% garnacha, 10% syrah.

86 Colour: cherry, garnet rim. Nose: powerfull, characterful, ripe fruit, balsamic herbs. Palate: flavourful, spicy, round tannins.

CLÒNIC 2008 T
60% cariñena, 20% cabernet sauvignon, 20% syrah.

90 Colour: deep cherry. Nose: powerfull, fruit preserve, sweet spices, dark chocolate. Palate: powerful, fine bitter notes, round tannins.

CLÒNIC SELECCIÓN 2007 T
60% cariñena, 20% cabernet sauvignon, 20% syrah.

88 Colour: deep cherry. Nose: powerfull, warm, ripe fruit, toasty, spicy. Palate: flavourful, spicy, ripe fruit.

CELLER COOPERATIU CORNUDELLA

Comte de Rius, 2
43360 Cornudella de Montsant (Tarragona)
☎: +34 977 821 329 - Fax: +34 977 821 329
info@cornudella.net
www.cornudella.net

CODOLAR 2010 RD
60% garnacha, 40% cariñena

82 Colour: salmon. Nose: balsamic herbs, floral, fresh fruit. Palate: flavourful, fruity, fresh.

CODOLAR 2009 T
50% garnacha, 50% cariñena.

87 Colour: cherry, garnet rim. Nose: ripe fruit, toasty, sweet spices. Palate: powerful, fleshy, fine bitter notes.

LES TROIES 2009 T
50% garnacha, 50% cariñena.

86 Colour: cherry, purple rim. Nose: red berry notes, violets, wild herbs. Palate: flavourful, fruity, good acidity.

CASTELL DE SIURANA GARNATXA DEL MONTSANT T
garnacha.

87 Colour: coppery red. Nose: candied fruit, red berry notes, floral. Palate: flavourful, sweetness, good acidity.

CASTELLA DE SIURANA MISTELA 2009 VINO DE LICOR
100% garnacha.

89 Colour: light cherry. Nose: candied fruit, powerfull, warm, spicy. Palate: ripe fruit, fine bitter notes, good acidity, long.

CELLER DE CAPÇANES

Llebaria, 4
43776 Capçanes (Tarragona)
☎: +34 977 178 319 - Fax: +34 977 178 319
cellercapcanes@cellercapcanes.com
www.cellercapcanes.com

MAS COLLET 2010 B
70% garnacha blanca, 30% macabeo.

86 Colour: bright yellow, greenish rim. Nose: balanced, fruit expression, white flowers. Palate: flavourful, ripe fruit, spicy, rich.

MAS DONÍS 2010 B
70% garnacha blanca, 30% macabeo.

86 Colour: bright yellow, greenish rim. Nose: medium intensity, floral, fragrant herbs. Palate: flavourful, fruity, good acidity.

MAS DONÍS 2010 RD
80% garnacha, 10% syrah, 10% merlot.

88 Colour: brilliant rose. Nose: balanced, fresh, red berry notes, dried flowers, dried herbs. Palate: fruity, flavourful, good acidity.

MAS DONÍS 2010 T
85% garnacha, 15% syrah.

87 Colour: cherry, garnet rim. Nose: scrubland, ripe fruit, powerfull. Palate: flavourful, fine bitter notes.

FLOR DE PRIMAVERA PERAJ HA'ABIB 2009 T
garnacha, samsó, cabernet sauvignon, tempranillo.

91 Colour: deep cherry, garnet rim. Nose: balanced, complex, sweet spices, wild herbs. Palate: rich, fruity, long, good acidity.

LASENDAL GARNATXA 2009 T BARRICA
85% garnacha, 15% syrah.

91 Colour: cherry, garnet rim. Nose: medium intensity, fragrant herbs, spicy, sweet spices. Palate: complex, good structure.

MAS TORTÓ 2009 TC
70% garnacha, 10% syrah, 10% merlot, 10% cabernet sauvignon.

90 Colour: bright cherry, garnet rim. Nose: sweet spices, ripe fruit, mineral. Palate: good structure, spicy, ripe fruit, round tannins.

MAS COLLET 2009 T BARRICA
garnacha, cariñena, tempranillo, cabernet sauvignon.

89 Colour: cherry, garnet rim. Nose: scrubland, red berry notes, ripe fruit, spicy. Palate: fleshy, ripe fruit, round tannins.

CABRIDA 2008 T
100% garnacha.

89 Colour: deep cherry, garnet rim. Nose: balanced, ripe fruit, fruit liqueur notes, spicy. Palate: fleshy, ripe fruit, long.

COSTERS DEL GRAVET 2007 T
cabernet sauvignon, garnacha, cariñena.

90 Colour: cherry, garnet rim. Nose: balanced, ripe fruit, spicy. Palate: good structure, flavourful, ripe fruit.

VALL DEL CALÀS 2007 T
merlot, tempranillo, garnacha.

89 Colour: very deep cherry, garnet rim. Nose: medium intensity, balanced, spicy, ripe fruit. Palate: flavourful, ripe fruit, spicy.

FLOR DE PRIMAVERA 2007 T
100% garnacha.

87 Colour: cherry, garnet rim. Nose: complex, ripe fruit, spicy, scrubland, warm. Palate: good structure, correct.

CELLER DOSTERRAS

Ctra. Falset a Marça, Km. 2
43775 Marça (Tarragona)
☎: +34 678 730 596
jgrau@dosterras.com
www.dosterras.com

VESPRES 2009 T
80% garnacha, 20% samsó.

89 Colour: very deep cherry, purple rim. Nose: powerfull, ripe fruit, fruit liqueur notes, violets. Palate: flavourful, fleshy, ripe fruit.

DOSTERRAS 2008 T
100% garnacha.

92 Colour: very deep cherry. Nose: medium intensity, ripe fruit, spicy. Palate: flavourful, mineral, long, round tannins.

CELLER EL MASROIG

Passeig de L'Arbre, 3
43736 El Masroig (Tarragona)
☎: +34 977 825 026
celler@cellermasroig.com
www.cellermasroig.com

ETNIC 2009 BFB
100% garnacha blanca.

90 Colour: bright yellow. Nose: fresh, expressive, floral, mineral. Palate: ripe fruit, spicy, fine bitter notes.

LES SORTS 2009 BFB
100% garnacha blanca.

89 Colour: bright straw. Nose: powerfull, ripe fruit, sweet spices, citrus fruit. Palate: flavourful, fruity, fresh.

LES SORTS ROSAT 2010 RD
90% garnacha, 10% mazuelo.

90 Colour: rose, purple rim. Nose: expressive, fresh, red berry notes. Palate: flavourful, fruity, fresh.

LES SORTS 2010 T MACERACIÓN CARBÓNICA
50% mazuelo, 30% garnacha, 20% syrah.

89 Colour: cherry, purple rim. Nose: balanced, fruit expression, floral, expressive. Palate: flavourful, fruity, easy to drink.

SOLÀ FRED 2010 T
90% mazuelo, 10% garnacha.

86 Colour: cherry, purple rim. Nose: red berry notes, floral, ripe fruit. Palate: flavourful, fruity, good acidity, round tannins.

ETNIC 2008 T
80% mazuelo, 20% garnacha.

92 Colour: cherry, garnet rim. Nose: powerfull, ripe fruit, warm, creamy oak, dark chocolate. Palate: powerful, spicy, ripe fruit.

CASTELL DE LES PINYERES 2008 T
40% garnacha, 40% mazuelo, 20% cabernet sauvignon, merlot, tempranillo.

91 Colour: cherry, garnet rim. Nose: earthy notes, ripe fruit, fruit expression, toasty. Palate: powerful, flavourful, spicy, long.

LES SORTS SYCAR 2008 T
60% mazuelo, 40% syrah.

90 Colour: cherry, garnet rim. Nose: powerfull, ripe fruit, toasty, creamy oak. Palate: flavourful, fine bitter notes, round tannins.

MAS ROIG 2007 TC
75% mazuelo, 15% garnacha, 10% cabernet sauvignon.

91 Colour: cherry, garnet rim. Nose: spicy, creamy oak, complex, roasted coffee, fruit preserve. Palate: powerful, flavourful, toasty, round tannins.

LES SORTS VINYES VELLES 2007 TC
50% mazuelo, 40% garnacha, 10% cabernet sauvignon.

89 Colour: cherry, garnet rim. Nose: sweet spices, toasty, cocoa bean. Palate: powerful, fleshy, spicy.

MISTELA NEGRA DEL MONTSANT T
100% mazuelo.

87 Colour: very deep cherry, garnet rim. Nose: overripe fruit, dried fruit, spicy. Palate: flavourful, rich.

CELLER ELS GUIAMETS

Avinguda Ctra., 23
43777 Els Guiamets (Tarragona)
☎: +34 977 413 018
eguasch@cellerelsguiamets.com
www.cellerelsguiamets.com

LOMETS 2010 B
garnacha blanca.

78

VALL SELLADA 2009 BFB
garnacha blanca.

72

GRAN METS 2007 TC
cabernet sauvignon, merlot, tempranillo.

88 Colour: cherry, garnet rim. Nose: powerfull, warm, dark chocolate, toasty. Palate: powerful, concentrated, sweetness.

GRAN METS 2006 TC
cabernet sauvignon, merlot, tempranillo.

92 Colour: cherry, garnet rim. Nose: toasty, spicy, dark chocolate, ripe fruit. Palate: flavourful, powerful, good acidity, fine bitter notes, round.

ISIS 2006 T
syrah, garnacha, cariñena.

89 Colour: dark-red cherry. Nose: powerfull, fruit preserve, fruit liqueur notes, toasty. Palate: powerful, flavourful, spicy, ripe fruit.

CELLER LAURONA S.A.

Ctra. Bellmunt - Sort dels Capellans, Pol. Ind. 21
43730 Falset (Tarragona)
☎: +34 977 831 712 - Fax: +34 977 831 797
laurona@cellerlaurona.com
www.cellerlaurona.com

LAURONA 2006 T
garnacha, cariñena, syrah, merlot.

90 Colour: deep cherry. Nose: cocoa bean, fruit expression, varietal, complex. Palate: powerful, flavourful, complex, sweetness, spirituous.

6 VINYES DE LAURONA 2005 T
60% garnacha, 40% cariñena.

92 Colour: cherry, garnet rim. Nose: ripe fruit, spicy, creamy oak, toasty, earthy notes, mineral. Palate: powerful, flavourful, toasty, round tannins.

CELLER LOS TROVADORES

Avda. de las Encinas, 25
28707 San Sebastián de los Reyes (Madrid)
☎: +34 679 459 074
cgomez@lostrovadores.com
www.lostrovadores.com

GALLICANT 2005 T
60% garnacha, 30% carignan, 10% syrah.

90 Colour: cherry, garnet rim. Nose: expressive, ripe fruit, toasty, spicy, cocoa bean, earthy notes. Palate: flavourful, balanced, toasty, round tannins, spicy.

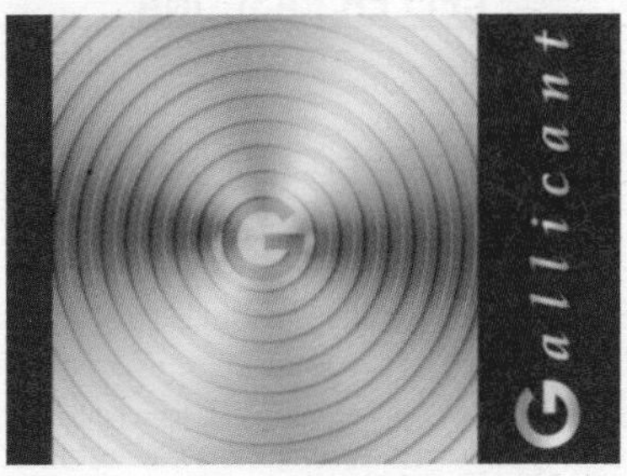

CELLER MALONDRO

Miranda, 27
43360 Cornudella del Montsant (Tarragona)
☎: +34 636 595 736 - Fax: +34 977 821 451
jcestivill@malondro.es
www.malondro.es

MALONDRO 2008 TC
50% garnacha, 50% cariñena.

92 Color cherry, garnet rim. Aroma ripe fruit, spicy, creamy oak, toasty, complex. Taste powerful, flavourful, toasty, round tannins.

LATRIA 2008 T
50% garnacha, 50% cariñena.

88 Colour: cherry, garnet rim. Nose: powerfull, ripe fruit, fruit expression, spicy, dark chocolate. Palate: flavourful, powerful, fleshy.

CELLER MAS DE LES VINYES

Mas de les Vinyes, s/n
43373 Cabacés (Tarragona)
☎: +34 652 568 848 - Fax: +34 977 719 690
josep@masdelesvinyes.com
www.masdelesvinyes.com

RACÓ D'ATANS 2006 TC
60% cabernet sauvignon, 20% garnacha, 20% merlot.

86 Colour: deep cherry, garnet rim. Nose: balanced, fruit preserve, spicy. Palate: ripe fruit, spicy, easy to drink.

CELLER PASCONA

Camí dels Fontals, s/n
43730 Falset (Tarragona)
☎: +34 609 291 770 - Fax: +34 977 117 098
info@pascona.com
www.pascona.com

PASCONA SELECCIÓ 2009 T ROBLE
50% merlot, 50% syrah.

89 Colour: deep cherry, garnet rim. Nose: complex, elegant, red berry notes, sweet spices. Palate: balanced, correct, good acidity, fruity.

PASCONA EVOLUCIÓ 2008 TC
50% garnacha, 50% cabernet sauvignon.

89 Colour: very deep cherry, garnet rim. Nose: complex, sweet spices, creamy oak, candied fruit, aromatic coffee. Palate: good structure, fleshy.

PASCONA TRADICIÓ 2007 TC
60% garnacha, 40% samsó.

87 Colour: cherry, garnet rim. Nose: spicy, aged wood nuances, toasty. Palate: flavourful, fruity.

CELLER SERRA MAJOR

Avda. Can Picañol, 43, 1º 3ª
08173 Sant Cugat Del Vallès (Barcelona)
☎: +34 689 952 891
victor@sarroges.com

TEIX 2009 T
garnacha, cabernet sauvignon, syrah.

89 Colour: very deep cherry, purple rim. Nose: fruit expression, floral, violets, scrubland. Palate: fruity, flavourful.

SARROGES 2009 T
garnacha, cabernet sauvignon, syrah.

80 Colour: very deep cherry, purple rim. Nose: fruit liqueur notes, slightly evolved. Palate: flavourful, fruity.

GRAN SARROGES 2008 TC
garnacha, cabernet sauvignon, syrah.

87 Colour: cherry, garnet rim. Nose: fruit preserve, creamy oak, sweet spices. Palate: powerful, concentrated, spirituous.

CELLER SUI GENERIS

Mas de l'Aleix
43886 Renau (Tarragona)
☎: +34 670 265 764 - Fax: +34 934 108 525
info@suigenerismontsant.com
www.suigenerismontsant.com

SUI GENERIS "VIN DE GARAGE" 2009 T
57% garnacha, 33% tempranillo, 10% cariñena.

86 Colour: cherry, garnet rim. Nose: fruit liqueur notes, fruit liqueur notes, powerfull, spicy. Palate: flavourful, spicy, long.

SUI GENERIS 2008 TC
36% garnacha, 24% cariñena, 16% tempranillo, 16% cabernet sauvignon, 8% merlot.

85 Colour: deep cherry, garnet rim. Nose: sweet spices, dark chocolate, candied fruit, fruit preserve. Palate: fruity, flavourful.

CELLERS BARONÍA DEL MONTSANT S.L.

Comte de Rius, 1
43360 Cornudella de Montsant (Tarragona)
☎: +34 977 821 483 - Fax: +34 977 821 483
englora@baronia-m.com
www.baronia-m.com

FLOR D'ENGLORA GARNATXA 2010 T
100% garnacha.

82 Colour: cherry, purple rim. Nose: medium intensity, red berry notes. Palate: light-bodied, fruity.

FLOR D'ENGLORA ROURE 2009 T
60% garnacha, 35% samsó, 2% merlot, 2% syrah, 1% ull de llebre.

90 Colour: deep cherry. Nose: powerfull, ripe fruit, spicy, mineral. Palate: ripe fruit, flavourful, fine bitter notes, round tannins.

ENGLORA 2008 TC
49% garnacha, 24% samsó, 19% cabernet sauvignon, 7% syrah, 1% ull de llebre.

90 Colour: cherry, garnet rim. Nose: powerfull, ripe fruit, toasty, sweet spices. Palate: flavourful, powerful, fine bitter notes, round tannins.

CLOS D'ENGLORA AV 14 2005 T
garnacha, samsó, cabernet sauvignon, cabernet franc, carmenere.

91 Colour: cherry, garnet rim. Nose: toasty, sweet spices, dark chocolate, ripe fruit. Palate: flavourful, powerful, spicy, ripe fruit, round tannins.

CELLERS CAN BLAU

Ctra. Bellmunt, s/n
43730 Falset (Tarragona)
☎: +34 629 261 379 - Fax: +34 968 716 051
info@orowines.com
www.orowines.com

CAN BLAU 2009 T
50% mazuelo, 30% garnacha, 20% syrah.

89 Colour: deep cherry, garnet rim. Nose: spicy, toasty, wild herbs, aged wood nuances. Palate: flavourful, fruity, good structure, long.

BLAU 2009 T
50% mazuelo, 30% garnacha, 20% syrah.

87 Colour: cherry, garnet rim. Nose: powerfull, spicy, aged wood nuances. Palate: flavourful, ripe fruit.

MAS DE CAN BLAU 2007 T
50% mazuelo, 30% garnacha, 20% syrah.

94 Colour: very deep cherry. Nose: complex, ripe fruit, sweet spices, cocoa bean. Palate: fleshy, good structure, good acidity, balanced, fine bitter notes, round tannins.

CELLERS SANT RAFEL

Ctra. La Torre, Km. 1,7
43774 Pradell de la Teixeta (Tarragona)
☎: +34 689 792 305 - Fax: +34 977 323 078
info@solpost.com
www.solpost.com

SOLPOST BLANC 2010 B ROBLE
100% garnacha blanca.

84 Colour: bright yellow. Nose: white flowers, balanced. Palate: fruity, flavourful, correct.

SOLPOST 2010 RD
50% garnacha, 50% syrah.

86 Colour: rose, purple rim. Nose: medium intensity, fresh fruit, red berry notes. Palate: flavourful, fruity, fresh.

SOLPOST FRESC 2009 TC
80% garnacha, 10% cabernet sauvignon, 10% syrah.

89 Colour: bright cherry. Nose: sweet spices, creamy oak, red berry notes. Palate: flavourful, fruity, toasty, round tannins.

SOLPOST 2007 T
50% garnacha, 35% cariñena, 15% cabernet sauvignon.

90 Colour: deep cherry, garnet rim. Nose: sweet spices, complex, cocoa bean, candied fruit. Palate: fruity, flavourful, complex.

CELLERS UNIÓ

Joan Oliver, 16-24
43206 Reus (Tarragona)
☎: +34 977 330 055 - Fax: +34 977 330 070
info@cellersunio.com
www.cellersunio.com

PERLAT 2009 T
40% garnacha, 40% mazuelo, 20% syrah.

88 Colour: cherry, garnet rim. Nose: red berry notes, ripe fruit, sweet spices, mineral. Palate: good structure, ripe fruit, spicy.

PERLAT SYRAH 2009 T
100% syrah.

88 Colour: deep cherry, garnet rim. Nose: wild herbs, ripe fruit, spicy. Palate: flavourful, full, round tannins.

DAIRO 2008 TC
40% garnacha, 40% mazuelo, 20% syrah.

87 Colour: cherry, purple rim. Nose: powerfull, toasty, sweet spices, ripe fruit. Palate: good structure, toasty, ripe fruit.

PERLAT GARNATXA 2007 T
100% garnacha.

87 Colour: cherry, garnet rim. Nose: fruit preserve, spicy. Palate: correct, balanced, spicy, ripe fruit.

CINGLES BLAUS

Finca Mas de les Moreres- Afueras de Cornudella, s/n
43360 Cornudella de Montsant (Tarragona)
☎: +34 977 326 080 - Fax: +34 977 323 928
info@cinglesblaus.com
www.cinglesblaus.com

OCTUBRE 2010 B

86 Color bright straw. Aroma fresh, fresh fruit, white flowers, expressive. Taste flavourful, fruity, good acidity, balanced.

OCTUBRE 2010 RD

85 Colour: rose, purple rim. Nose: powerfull, ripe fruit, fruit expression. Palate: flavourful, fine bitter notes, good acidity.

CINGLES BLAUS OCTUBRE 2009 T
mazuelo, garnacha, syrah.

89 Colour: deep cherry. Nose: mineral, fresh fruit, scrubland, balsamic herbs. Palate: flavourful, fruity, fresh.

CINGLES BLAUS MAS DE LES MORERES 2008 T
cabernet sauvignon, mazuelo, garnacha, merlot, syrah.

88 Colour: cherry, garnet rim. Nose: fruit preserve, warm, dark chocolate. Palate: powerful, flavourful, concentrated.

CINGLES BLAUS DOLÇ 2007 BLANCO DULCE

91 Colour: bright yellow. Nose: fruit preserve, citrus fruit, white flowers. Palate: powerful, spicy, ripe fruit.

COCA I FITÓ

11 de Setembre s/n
43736 Almoster (Tarragona)
☎: +34 619 776 948 - Fax: +34 935 457 092
info@cocaifito.cat
www.cocaifito.com

COCA I FITÓ ROSA 2010 RD
100% syrah.

90 Color rose, purple rim. Aroma powerfull, ripe fruit, red berry notes, floral, expressive. Taste fleshy, powerful, fruity, fresh.

JASPI NEGRE 2010 T
40% garnacha, 25% cabernet sauvignon, 30% cariñena, 5% syrah.

88 Colour: cherry, purple rim. Nose: powerfull, ripe fruit, red berry notes, sweet spices. Palate: flavourful, powerful, fruity.

JASPI MARAGDA 2009 T
45% garnacha, 25% cariñena, 25% syrah, 5% cabernet sauvignon.

90 Colour: cherry, garnet rim. Nose: ripe fruit, spicy, creamy oak, toasty, mineral. Palate: powerful, flavourful, toasty, round tannins.

JASPI NEGRE 2009 T
40% garnacha, 25% cabernet sauvignon, 30% cariñena, 5% syrah.

88 Colour: cherry, garnet rim. Nose: powerfull, ripe fruit, red berry notes, toasty, dark chocolate. Palate: powerful, flavourful, spicy.

COCA I FITÓ 2008 T
50% syrah, 30% garnacha, 20% cariñena.

93 Colour: cherry, garnet rim. Nose: ripe fruit, spicy, creamy oak, toasty, mineral, characterful. Palate: powerful, flavourful, toasty, round tannins.

DIT CELLER

Portal, 18
43393 Almoster (Tarragona)
☎: +34 636 406 939
tonicoca@gmail.com

SELENITA 2010 RD
60% syrah, 40% garnacha.

87 Colour: rose, purple rim. Nose: ripe fruit, red berry notes. Palate: flavourful, fleshy, sweetness.

CABIROL 2010 T
50% tempranillo, 50% garnacha.

88 Colour: cherry, purple rim. Nose: powerfull, ripe fruit, raspberry. Palate: flavourful, powerful, fleshy, sweetness.

SELENITA 2009 T
50% garnacha, 30% syrah, 20% cabernet sauvignon.

85 Colour: cherry, garnet rim. Nose: powerfull, fruit liqueur notes, warm. Palate: powerful, flavourful, fine bitter notes, round tannins.

ESPECTACLE VINS

Camí Manyetes, s/n
43737 Gratallops (Tarragona)
☎: +34 977 839 171 - Fax: +34 977 839 426
closmogador@closmogador.com
www.espectaclevins.com

ESPECTACLE 2008 T
100% garnacha.

96 Colour: cherry, purple rim. Nose: balsamic herbs, scrubland, fresh fruit, raspberry. Palate: flavourful, ripe fruit, good acidity, fine bitter notes.

ESPECTACLE 2007 T
garnacha.

96 Colour: cherry, garnet rim. Nose: mineral, ripe fruit, raspberry, scrubland. Palate: flavourful, fruity, fleshy, ripe fruit, good structure.

ÈTIM

Miquel Barceló, 31
43730 Falset (Tarragona)
☎: +34 977 830 105 - Fax: +34 977 830 363
info@etim.es
www.etim.es

ÈTIM 2010 B
100% garnacha blanca.

90 Colour: bright straw. Nose: fresh, fresh fruit, white flowers, expressive. Palate: flavourful, fruity, good acidity, balanced.

ÈTIM VEREMA TARDANA
2009 B
100% garnacha blanca.

90 Colour: bright straw. Nose: dried herbs, white flowers, fresh fruit. Palate: flavourful, sweetness, good acidity.

CASTELL DE FALSET 2009 B
100% garnacha blanca.

90 Color bright yellow. Aroma powerfull, ripe fruit, sweet spices, creamy oak, fragrant herbs. Taste rich, smoky aftertaste, flavourful, fresh, good acidity.

ÈTIM ROSAT 2010 RD
90% garnacha, 10% syrah.

86 Colour: rose. Nose: red berry notes, ripe fruit, floral. Palate: flavourful, fruity, fresh.

MARTIUS SELECTION 2010 T
40% garnacha, 40% cariñena, 20% merlot.

87 Colour: bright cherry. Nose: ripe fruit, fruit expression, sweet spices. Palate: flavourful, powerful, fleshy, fine bitter notes.

IMUS SELECCIÓ DE VINYES 2010 T
85% garnacha, 15% cariñena.

85 Colour: cherry, purple rim. Nose: powerfull, ripe fruit, spicy, scrubland. Palate: flavourful, powerful, fine bitter notes.

ÈTIM NEGRE 2009 T
60% garnacha, 30% cariñena, 10% syrah.

87 Colour: cherry, garnet rim. Nose: powerfull, ripe fruit, spicy, toasty. Palate: powerful, concentrated, fine bitter notes.

ÈTIM VEREMA TARDANA 2008 T
100% garnacha.

90 Colour: cherry, garnet rim. Nose: fruit preserve, candied fruit, spicy. Palate: flavourful, sweet, fine bitter notes, good acidity.

ÈTIM VEREMA SOBREMADURADA SELECCIÓ VINYES VELLES 2007 T
60% garnacha, 40% cariñena.

92 Colour: deep cherry, orangey edge. Nose: candied fruit, overripe fruit, sweet spices, cocoa bean. Palate: full, rich, flavourful.

ÈTIM VEREMA TARDANA 2007 T
100% garnacha.

91 Colour: cherry, garnet rim. Nose: powerfull, fruit liqueur notes, fruit liqueur notes, toasty. Palate: fine bitter notes, good acidity, unctuous, long.

ÈTIM GRENACHE 2007 T
85% garnacha, 15% cabernet sauvignon.

90 Color cherry, garnet rim. Aroma ripe fruit, spicy, creamy oak, toasty, complex. Taste powerful, flavourful, toasty, round tannins.

ÈTIM SELECTION SYRAH 2006 T
100% syrah.

90 Colour: cherry, garnet rim. Nose: powerfull, warm, fruit liqueur notes, toasty, aromatic coffee. Palate: flavourful, powerful, fine bitter notes.

CASTELL DE FALSET 2006 T
50% garnacha, 25% cariñena, 25% cabernet sauvignon.

88 Colour: cherry, garnet rim. Nose: powerfull, ripe fruit, toasty. Palate: flavourful, spicy, fine bitter notes.

ÈTIM L'ESPARVER 2006 T
garnacha, mazuelo, syrah, cabernet sauvignon.

88 Colour: cherry, garnet rim. Nose: powerfull, fruit liqueur notes, toasty, spicy, aromatic coffee. Palate: powerful, spicy, fine bitter notes.

ÈTIM RANCI
50% garnacha, 50% cariñena.

92 Colour: bright golden. Nose: powerfull, dry nuts, varnish, acetaldehyde. Palate: flavourful, powerful, sweetness, long.

JOAN D'ANGUERA

Mayor 34
43746 Darmós (Tarragona)
☎: +34 977 418 348 - Fax: +34 977 418 302
josep@cellersjoandanguera.com
www.cellersjoandanguera.com

JOAN D'ANGUERA 2010 T
syrah, garnacha.

89 Colour: bright cherry. Nose: expressive, violet drops, fruit expression. Palate: flavourful, fruity, fresh.

FINCA L'ARGATA 2009 T
60% garnacha, 40% syrah.

92 Colour: cherry, garnet rim. Nose: powerfull, characterful, mineral, earthy notes. Palate: flavourful, powerful, spicy, ripe fruit.

PLANELLA 2009 T
50% cariñena, 25% garnacha, 25% syrah.

87 Colour: cherry, garnet rim. Nose: powerfull, ripe fruit, fruit liqueur notes, warm, toasty, dark chocolate. Palate: powerful, flavourful, fine bitter notes.

FINCA L'ARGATA 2008 T
60% syrah, 40% garnacha.

91 Colour: cherry, garnet rim. Nose: ripe fruit, spicy, creamy oak, toasty, dark chocolate. Palate: powerful, flavourful, toasty, round tannins.

PLANELLA 2008 T
45% cariñena, 35% syrah, 20% garnacha.

91 Colour: cherry, garnet rim. Nose: ripe fruit, spicy, creamy oak, toasty, characterful. Palate: powerful, flavourful, toasty, round tannins.

BUGADER 2007 T
95% syrah, 5% garnacha.

92 Colour: bright cherry. Nose: fruit expression, dark chocolate, cocoa bean. Palate: flavourful, fruity, toasty, round tannins.

LA COVA DELS VINS

Bosquet, 5- àtic 4
43730 Falset (Tarragona)
☎: +34 977 831 148
covavins@wanadoo.es
www.lacovadelsvins.com

OMBRETA 2010 B
garnacha blanca.

86 Colour: bright yellow, greenish rim. Nose: white flowers, dried herbs, citrus fruit. Palate: flavourful, easy to drink.

DELER 2010 B
garnacha blanca, macabeo.

86 Colour: bright straw, greenish rim. Nose: balanced, fresh fruit, citrus fruit, white flowers. Palate: fresh, easy to drink, good acidity.

OMBRETA 2010 RD
garnacha.

88 Colour: rose, bright. Nose: fresh, medium intensity, wild herbs, dried flowers. Palate: flavourful, fruity, fruity aftestaste.

OMBRETA 2010 T
garnacha, syrah.

85 Colour: cherry, purple rim. Nose: powerfull, ripe fruit, fruit expression, grapey. Palate: flavourful, fruity, fresh, fleshy.

DELER 2010 T

85 Colour: cherry, purple rim. Nose: powerfull, characterful, toasty, dark chocolate, ripe fruit. Palate: powerful, fleshy, fine bitter notes.

OMBRA 2009 T BARRICA
garnacha, samsó, cabernet sauvignon.

88 Colour: deep cherry, purple rim. Nose: medium intensity, fruit expression, wild herbs. Palate: balanced, good acidity.

TERRÒS 2008 T
garnacha, samsó, syrah.

90 Colour: deep cherry, purple rim. Nose: medium intensity, balanced, ripe fruit, sweet spices. Palate: good structure, fleshy, round tannins.

MAS D'EN CANONGE

Pol. Ind. 7, Parc. 27
43775 Marça (Tarragona)
☎: +34 977 054 071 - Fax: +34 977 054 071
info@masdencanonge.com
www.masdencanonge.com

SOLEIES D'EN CANONGE 2010 B
garnacha blanca.

87 Colour: bright straw, greenish rim. Nose: medium intensity, white flowers, jasmine. Palate: flavourful, fine bitter notes, good acidity.

SORRES 2010 RD
garnacha, syrah.

82 Colour: salmon. Nose: medium intensity, red berry notes, fragrant herbs. Palate: flavourful, fruity, fresh.

SONS D'EN CANONGE 2008 T
60% garnacha, 30% cariñena, 10% tempranillo.

88 Colour: cherry, garnet rim. Nose: ripe fruit, spicy, toasty, complex. Palate: powerful, flavourful, toasty, round tannins.

RESSONS D'EN CANONGE 2008 T
60% garnacha, 40% syrah.

87 Colour: deep cherry, garnet rim. Nose: medium intensity, ripe fruit, spicy. Palate: flavourful, good structure, round tannins.

MAS PERINET

Finca Mas Perinet, s/n
43660 Cornudella de Montsant (Tarragona)
☎: +34 977 827 113 - Fax: +34 977 827 180
info@masperinet.com
www.masperinet.com

CLOS MARÍA 2007 B
63% garnacha blanca, 17% chenin blanc, 14% moscatel, 6% macabeo.

94 Colour: bright yellow. Nose: petrol notes, tobacco, ripe fruit, faded flowers, complex, fragrant herbs. Palate: rich, flavourful, fleshy, complex, balanced.

GOTIA 2006 T
36% garnacha, 33% merlot, 22% cabernet sauvignon, 9% syrah.

92 Colour: cherry, garnet rim. Nose: ripe fruit, expressive, mineral, spicy, scrubland. Palate: powerful, flavourful, fleshy, long, balanced.

GOTIA 2005 T
38% merlot, 35% garnacha, 16% cabernet sauvignon, 11% syrah.

93 Colour: cherry, garnet rim. Nose: ripe fruit, earthy notes, sweet spices, creamy oak. Palate: fleshy, ripe fruit, good acidity, flavourful, balanced.

NOGUERALS

Tou, 5
43360 Cornudella de Montsant (Tarragona)
☎: +34 650 033 546 - Fax: +34 934 419 879
noguerals@hotmail.com
www.noguerals.com

CORBATERA 2007 T
70% garnacha, 30% cabernet sauvignon.

91 Colour: cherry, garnet rim. Nose: spicy, creamy oak, toasty, complex, fruit expression, raspberry. Palate: powerful, flavourful, toasty, round tannins.

ORTO VINS

Major, 10
43736 El Masroig (Tarragona)
☎: +34 629 171 246
info@ortovins.com

BLANC D'ORTO 2010 B
garnacha blanca.

91 Colour: bright yellow. Nose: white flowers, ripe fruit, citrus fruit, spicy. Palate: flavourful, fruity, fine bitter notes, elegant.

LA CARRERADA 2009 T
samsó.

93 Colour: deep cherry. Nose: expressive, ripe fruit, raspberry, fragrant herbs, balsamic herbs, toasty. Palate: flavourful, powerful, fleshy, spicy, ripe fruit.

PALELL 2009 TC
garnacha peluda.

92 Colour: bright cherry. Nose: expressive, elegant, candied fruit, raspberry, spicy. Palate: flavourful, fruity, spicy, fine tannins.

LES PUJOLES 2009 TC
ull de llebre.

91 Colour: cherry, garnet rim. Nose: fruit expression, scrubland, balsamic herbs. Palate: flavourful, spicy, ripe fruit, good acidity.

LES COMES D'ORTO 2009 T
50% garnacha, 45% samsó, 5% ull de llebre.

90 Color bright cherry. Aroma ripe fruit, sweet spices, creamy oak, expressive. Taste flavourful, fruity, toasty, round tannins.

LES TALLADES DE CAL NICOLAU 2009 TC
picapoll negre.

90 Colour: cherry, garnet rim. Nose: expressive, ripe fruit, sweet spices. Palate: flavourful, spicy, ripe fruit.

ORTO 2009 T
55% samsó, 29% garnacha, 10% ull de llebre, 6% cabernet sauvignon.

89 Colour: cherry, purple rim. Nose: fresh fruit, red berry notes, floral. Palate: flavourful, fruity, good acidity, round tannins.

DOLÇ D'ORTO 2010 DULCE NATURAL
garnacha blanca, tripo de gat, marmella de monja, planta, trobat.

93 Colour: old gold, amber rim. Nose: fruit preserve, citrus fruit, honeyed notes, white flowers. Palate: flavourful, sweet, unctuous.

PORTAL DEL MONTSANT

Mas Parxet, Torren, 38
08391 Tiana (Barcelona)
☎: +34 933 950 811 - Fax: +34 933 955 500
info@parxet.com
www.parxet.es

SANTBRU 2009 B BARRICA
85% garnacha blanca, 15% garnacha gris.

90 Colour: bright yellow, greenish rim. Nose: candied fruit, sweet spices, warm. Palate: good structure, flavourful, long, spicy.

BRUNUS ROSÉ 2010 RD
100% garnacha.

90 Colour: rose, purple rim. Nose: medium intensity, fresh, red berry notes, fragrant herbs. Palate: flavourful, fruity, full.

BRUBERRY 2009 T
50% garnacha, 30% syrah, 20% cariñena.

89 Colour: very deep cherry, purple rim. Nose: powerfull, violets, balanced, ripe fruit, warm. Palate: flavourful, ripe fruit.

BRUNUS 2008 T
45% cariñena, 35% garnacha, 20% syrah.

90 Colour: bright cherry. Nose: ripe fruit, sweet spices, expressive, toasty. Palate: flavourful, fruity, round tannins, balsamic.

SANTBRU 2007 T
65% cariñena, 60% syrah, 15% garnacha.

92 Colour: deep cherry, purple rim. Nose: balanced, expressive, ripe fruit, sweet spices, cocoa bean. Palate: good structure, full, spicy, long.

PORTAL DEL PRIORAT

Sort dels Capellans, 5
43730 Falset, Priorat (Tarragona)
☎: +34 932 531 760 - Fax: +34 934 173 591
info@portaldelpriorat.com
www.portaldelpriorat.com

TROSSOS TROS 2009 B
garnacha blanca.

95 Colour: bright yellow. Nose: ripe fruit, mineral, sweet spices, creamy oak, scrubland. Palate: rich, fleshy, complex, flavourful, smoky aftertaste.

TROSSOS TROS 2008 T
garnacha.

95 Colour: light cherry. Nose: fruit liqueur notes, fruit liqueur notes, powerfull, spicy, creamy oak. Palate: powerful, flavourful, fleshy, complex.

RONADELLES

Finca La Plana, s/n
43360 Cornudella del Montsant (Tarragona)
☎: +34 977 821 104 - Fax: +34 977 274 913
info@ronadelles.com

CAP DE RUC 2009 T
garnacha.

88 Colour: bright cherry. Nose: ripe fruit, sweet spices, creamy oak. Palate: flavourful, fruity, toasty, round tannins.

PETIT 2008 T
garnacha, cariñena.

89 Color bright cherry. Aroma ripe fruit, sweet spices, creamy oak, expressive. Taste flavourful, fruity, toasty, round tannins.

GIRAL VINYES VELLES 2005 TC
garnacha, cariñena.

90 Colour: bright cherry, garnet rim. Nose: complex, expressive, sweet spices, cocoa bean, ripe fruit. Palate: balanced, fine bitter notes, spicy.

TERRASSES DEL MONTSANT

Major, 14
43746 La Serra d'Almos (Tarragona)
☎: +34 932 051 009 - Fax: +34 932 051 120
info@heretatnavas.com
www.heretatnavas.com

HERETAT NAVAS 2009 T
garnacha, cariñena, cabernet sauvignon, syrah.

85 Colour: cherry, garnet rim. Nose: ripe fruit, sweet spices, aromatic coffee. Palate: spicy, slightly overripe.

HERETAT NAVAS 2008 T
garnacha, cariñena, cabernet sauvignon, syrah.

87 Colour: deep cherry. Nose: spicy, ripe fruit, toasty. Palate: powerful, good acidity, fine bitter notes, round tannins.

VENDRELL RIVED

Bassa, 10
43775 Marçà (Tarragona)
☎: +34 977 263 053 - Fax: +34 977 263 053
celler@vendrellrived.com
www.vendrellrived.com

SERE 2010 T
garnacha, cariñena.

87 Colour: cherry, purple rim. Nose: medium intensity, wild herbs, red berry notes, violets. Palate: fruity, flavourful, good acidity.

L'ALLEU 2009 T
garnacha, cariñena.

87 Colour: cherry, purple rim. Nose: fragrant herbs, powerfull, ripe fruit, dark chocolate. Palate: powerful, fleshy, fine bitter notes.

L'ALLEU SELECCIÓ 2008 T
garnacha, cariñena.

89 Colour: bright cherry. Nose: sweet spices, creamy oak, fruit preserve, roasted coffee. Palate: flavourful, fruity, toasty, round tannins.

L'ALLEU SELECCIÓ 2007 T
garnacha, cariñena.

92 Colour: cherry, garnet rim. Nose: ripe fruit, spicy, creamy oak, toasty, earthy notes. Palate: powerful, flavourful, toasty, round tannins.

L'ALLEU SELECCIÓ 2006 T
garnacha, cariñena.

88 Colour: cherry, garnet rim. Nose: powerfull, ripe fruit, fruit liqueur notes, toasty, spicy, aromatic coffee. Palate: flavourful, spicy.

VENUS LA UNIVERSAL

Ctra. Porrera, s/n
43730 Falset (Tarragona)
☎: +34 699 435 154 - Fax: +34 639 121 244
info@venuslauniversal.com
www.venuslauniversal.com

DIDO 2010 B
macabeo, garnacha blanca.

90 Colour: bright straw. Nose: fragrant herbs, candied fruit, citrus fruit. Palate: flavourful, sweetness.

DIDO 2009 T
cariñena, syrah.

92 Colour: deep cherry, garnet rim. Nose: elegant, complex, powerfull, undergrowth, mineral. Palate: spirituous, good structure, powerful, flavourful, fruity, complex.

VENUS 2008 T

92 Colour: dark-red cherry, garnet rim. Nose: spicy, toasty, cocoa bean, ripe fruit, fruit liqueur notes, fruit expression, mineral. Palate: mineral, powerful tannins, flavourful, varietal, spirituous, ripe fruit.

VINATERRERS DEL COLL DE MORA

Pol. Ind. Sort dels Capellans Nau, 14
43730 Falset (Tarragona)
☎: +34 692 114 451
info@vinaterrers.com
www.vinaterrers.com

LLUNARA 2008 T
garnacha, cariñena, syrah, cabernet sauvignon.

90 Color cherry, garnet rim. Aroma ripe fruit, spicy, creamy oak, toasty, complex. Taste powerful, flavourful, toasty, round tannins.

VINS DE MAS SERSAL

President Companys- 4 1º 4ª
43470 La Selva del Camp (Tarragona)
☎: +34 666 415 735
vins@massersal.com
www.massersal.com

ESTONES 2009 T
garnacha, samsó.

87 Colour: cherry, garnet rim. Nose: creamy oak, toasty, fruit preserve. Palate: powerful, flavourful, round tannins.

VINYA B-CAN

Ctra. Bellmunt, s/n
43730 Falset (Tarragona)
☎: +34 682 471 916
ircata@avanteselecta.com

BULA 2009 T ROBLE
50% cariñena, 35% garnacha, 15% syrah.

92 Colour: cherry, garnet rim. Nose: powerfull, varietal, candied fruit, scrubland. Palate: flavourful, powerful, sweetness, fleshy, complex.

VINYES D'EN GABRIEL

Ctra. Darmós - La Serra, s/n
43746 Darmós (Tarragona)
☎: +34 609 989 345
info@vinyesdengabriel.com
www.vinyesdengabriel.com

L'HERAVI 2010 RD
50% garnacha, syrah.

78

L'HERAVI 2010 T
60% garnacha, 20% cariñena, 20% syrah.

88 Colour: cherry, purple rim. Nose: fruit expression, raspberry. Palate: powerful, flavourful, fruity.

L HERAVI SELECCIÓ 2009 TC
50% cariñena, 50% syrah.

91 Colour: black cherry. Nose: powerfull, fruit preserve, fruit expression, sweet spices, dark chocolate, cocoa bean. Palate: flavourful, powerful, concentrated.

L'HERAVI 2009 TC
50% cariñena, 50% garnacha.

88 Colour: bright cherry. Nose: ripe fruit, sweet spices, creamy oak. Palate: flavourful, fruity, toasty, round tannins.

MANS DE SAMSÓ 2009 T
100% cariñena.

87 Colour: black cherry. Nose: powerfull, fruit preserve, raspberry, sweet spices, dark chocolate. Palate: powerful, concentrated, fine bitter notes.

VINYES DOMÈNECH

Camí del Collet, 1
43776 Capçanes (Tarragona)
☎: +34 670 297 395
jidomenech@vinyesdomenech.com
www.vinyesdomenech.com

TEIXAR 2009 T
100% garnacha.

94 Colour: cherry, garnet rim. Nose: mineral, dry stone, red berry notes, ripe fruit, toasty, creamy oak. Palate: powerful, flavourful, fleshy, complex, spicy, ripe fruit.

FURVUS 2009 T
garnacha, merlot.

93 Colour: cherry, purple rim. Nose: red berry notes, fruit expression, lactic notes, creamy oak, sweet spices. Palate: flavourful, powerful, fleshy, ripe fruit.

TEIXAR 2008 T
100% garnacha.

94 Colour: cherry, garnet rim. Nose: powerfull, fruit liqueur notes, sweet spices, dark chocolate, mineral. Palate: powerful, flavourful, spicy, fine bitter notes.

FURVUS 2008 T
80% garnacha, 20% merlot.

92 Colour: bright cherry. Nose: sweet spices, creamy oak, expressive, fruit expression. Palate: flavourful, fruity, toasty, round tannins.

VIÑAS DEL MONTSANT

Partida Coll de Mora , s/n
43775 Marça (Tarragona)
☎: +34 977 831 309 - Fax: +34 977 831 356
fraguerau@fraguerau.com

FRA GUERAU 2010 RD
70% garnacha, 30% syrah.

86 Colour: light cherry, bright. Nose: red berry notes, fresh fruit, wild herbs. Palate: flavourful, fruity.

FRA GUERAU 2006 TC
garnacha, merlot, syrah, cabernet sauvignon.

88 Colour: deep cherry, garnet rim. Nose: fruit preserve, spicy. Palate: flavourful, round tannins, spicy.

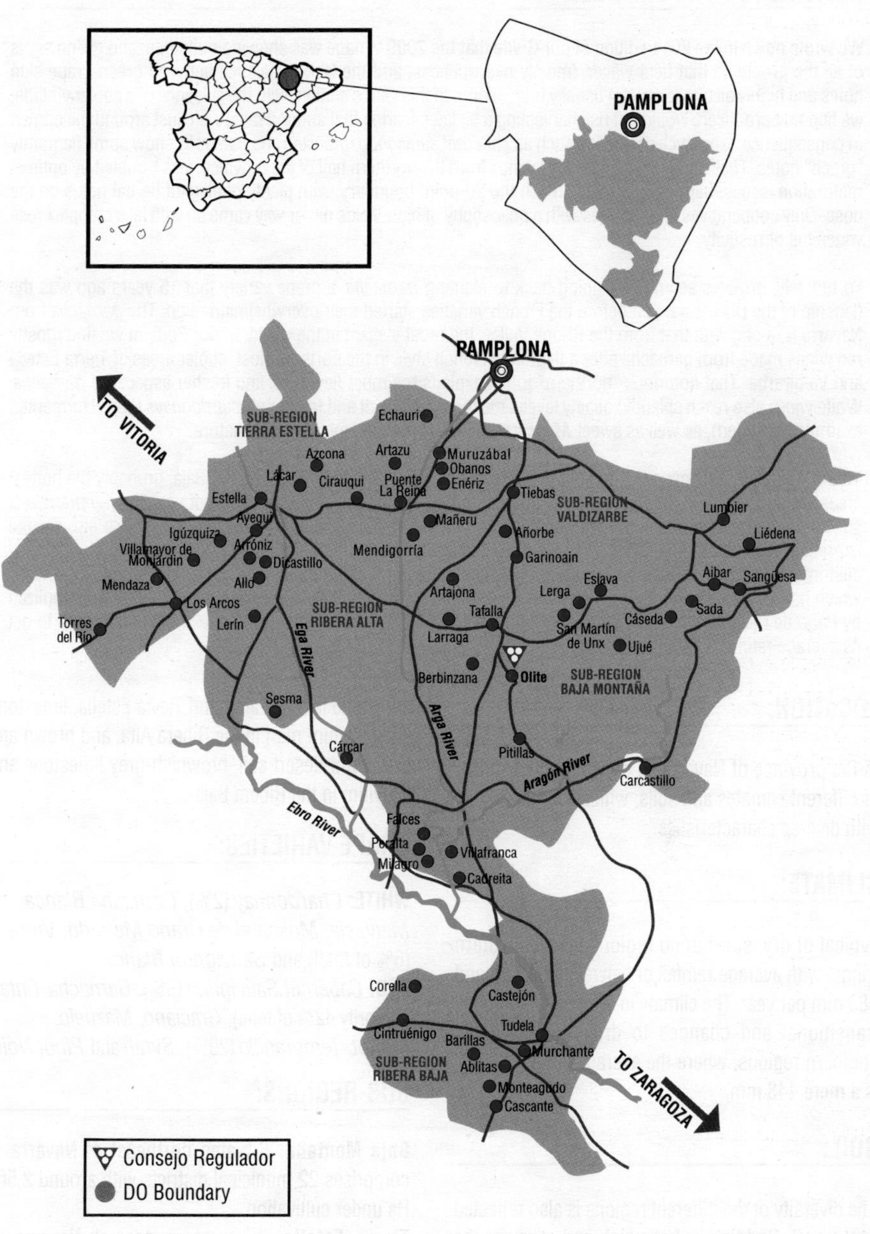
PAMPLONA
PAMPLONA
TO VITORIA
TO ZARAGOZA
SUB-REGION TIERRA ESTELLA
SUB-REGION VALDIZARBE
SUB-REGION RIBERA ALTA
SUB-REGION BAJA MONTAÑA
SUB-REGION RIBERA BAJA
Echauri
Azcona
Artazu
Muruzábal
Obanos
Enériz
Lácar
Cirauqui
Puente La Reina
Estella
Ayegui
Igúzquiza
Villamayor de Monjardín
Arróniz
Dicastillo
Allo
Mendaza
Los Arcos
Lerín
Torres del Río
Mañeru
Mendigorría
Tiebas
Añorbe
Garinoain
Artajona
Tafalla
Larraga
Berbinzana
Olite
Lerga
Eslava
San Martín de Unx
Ujué
Cáseda
Sada
Aibar
Sangüesa
Lumbier
Liédena
Sesma
Cárcar
Pitillas
Carcastillo
Ega River
Arga River
Aragón River
Ebro River
Falces
Peralta
Milagro
Villafranca
Cadreita
Corella
Cintruénigo
Castejón
Tudela
Barillas
Murchante
Ablitas
Monteagudo
Cascante
Consejo Regulador
DO Boundary

NEWS ABOUT THE VINTAGE:

We wrote down in the 2011 edition of our Guide that the 2009 vintage was showing quite ripe, and giving signs of all the problems that heat waves (mainly overripeness, and the lack of balance between green grape skin notes and highly alcoholic musts) usually bring along. In this year's edition, with the evidence of a cooler vintage, we find that producers would not risk harvesting a bit later, fearing that autumn rains were just around the corner. In consequence, long-cycled varieties such as *cabernet sauvignon*, *graciano* and *garnacha* show some flagrantly "green" notes. That is the reason why rosé wines from the northern half of the province, less troubled by optimal maturation issues, happened to easily reach the 90-point boundary, with plenty of elegant herbal notes on the nose. Only cooperatives and wineries with a philosophy of high-yields under way came up with less complex rosé wines full of rusticity.

Fortunately, growers seem to be going back to planting *garnacha*, a grape variety that 15 years ago was the flagship of the DO before, just before the French varieties started their overwhelming reign. The *garnacha* from Navarra is, along with that from the Rhône Valley, the most elegant in the world. In our Podium we find mostly red wines made from garnacha after a flagrantly French style in the northernmost, cooler areas of Tierra Estella and Valdizarbe. That notorious "northern" touch exploits the most flavourful and fresher aspects of *garnacha*. White wines also reach splendid quality levels: the most succulent and fresher of *chardonnays* (barrel fermented examples included), as well as sweet *Muscat* wines of an almost "meditational" nature.

Young wines are not apparently Navarra's strongest point, at least in 2010. In Ribera Baja, probably the hottest areas within the DO, young wines seem to reach a better balance. It was an excellent year for *tempranillo*, a shorter-cycled variety that thrives in cooler years, and we are sure than after ageing they will show quite expressive. One of the novelties within the DO, besides their commercial actions in restaurants and to final customers, is the proliferation of brand new wineries like Jardín de Lúculo, Domaines Lupier or La Calandria, which have manage to get their names within the vast catalogue of brands of the DO, apparently monopolized by Pago de Cirsus, with no less than seven wines in our Podium. Navarra, a land of extremes, manages to get its average ratings above 87 points.

LOCATION:

In the province of Navarra. It draws together areas of different climates and soils, which produce wines with diverse characteristics.

CLIMATE:

Typical of dry, sub-humid regions in the northern fringe, with average rainfall of between 593 mm and 683 mm per year. The climate in the central region is transitional and changes to drier conditions in southern regions, where the average annual rainfall is a mere 448 mm.

SOIL:

The diversity of the different regions is also reflected in the soil. Reddish or yellowish and stony in the Baja Montaña, brownish-grey limestone and limestone in Valdizarbe and Tierra Estella, limestone and alluvium marl in the Ribera Alta, and brown and grey semi-desert soil, brownish-grey limestone and alluvium in the Ribera Baja.

GRAPE VARIETIES:

WHITE: *Chardonnay* (2%), *Garnacha Blanca, Malvasía, Moscatel de Grano Menudo, Viura* (6% of total) and *Sauvignon Blanc.*
RED: *Cabernet Sauvignon* (9%), *Garnacha Tinta* (majority 42% of total), *Graciano, Mazuelo, Merlot, Tempranillo* (29%), *Syrah* and *Pinot Noir.*

SUB-REGIONS:

Baja Montaña. Situated northeast of Navarra, it comprises 22 municipal districts with around 2,500 Ha under cultivation.
Tierra Estella. In western central Navarra, it stretches along the Camino de Santiago. It has

1,800 Ha of vineyards in 38 municipal districts.

Valdizarbe. In central Navarra. It is the key centre of the Camino de Santiago. It comprises 25 municipal districts and has 1,100 Ha of vineyards.

Ribera Alta. In the area around Olite, it takes in part of central Navarra and the start of the southern region. There are 26 municipal districts and 3,300 Ha of vineyards.

Ribera Baja. In the south of the province, it is the most important in terms of size (4,600 Ha). It comprises 14 municipal districts.

FIGURES:

Vineyard surface: 13,360 – **Wine-Growers:** 3,300 – **Wineries:** 116 – **2010 Harvest rating:** Excellent – **Production:** 56,961,009 litres – **Market percentages:** 69% domestic. 31% export

CONSEJO REGULADOR

Rúa Romana, s/n
31690 Olite (Navarra)
☎: +34 948 741 812 - Fax: +34 948 741 776
@ consejoregulador@vinonavarra.com
info@navarrawine.com
www.vinonavarra.com

GENERAL CHARACTERISTICS OF THE WINES

WHITES	Although a minority product with respect to the red and rosé wines, young wines and wines fermented in barrels are also produced from the *Chardonnay* variety: golden yellow in colour, the best are characterised by their creamy and toasted aromas, which are well combined with fruit, and by their varietal character. Amongst the sweet wines, the whites from the *Moscatel de Grano Menudo*, a traditional variety which is slowly being recovered, stand out. There are few examples, although of high quality: grapey and honey aromas on the nose; flavourful, complex and fresh on the palate.
ROSÉS	Most are produced from *Garnacha*, although there are also examples from *Tempranillo* and *Cabernet Sauvignon*. Raspberry pink coloured, they are very fresh and fruity with a great character of red berries; on the palate they are balanced, flavourful and fruity.
REDS	These vary according to the varieties and the regions they are produced in. In the northern regions, where the Tempranillo predominates, the wines have a more Atlantic character; the aroma is more reminiscent of red berries; they are fresher with higher levels of acidity. In the south, the varietal character of the *Garnacha* stands out: the wines are warmer, with notes of ripe black fruit, round and supple on the palate. As well as these, there are the single variety wines from foreign varieties (mainly *Cabernet Sauvignon* and *Merlot*, with a marked varietal character), together with the red wines that combine autochthonous and foreign grape varieties.

VINTAGE RATING **PEÑÍNGUIDE**

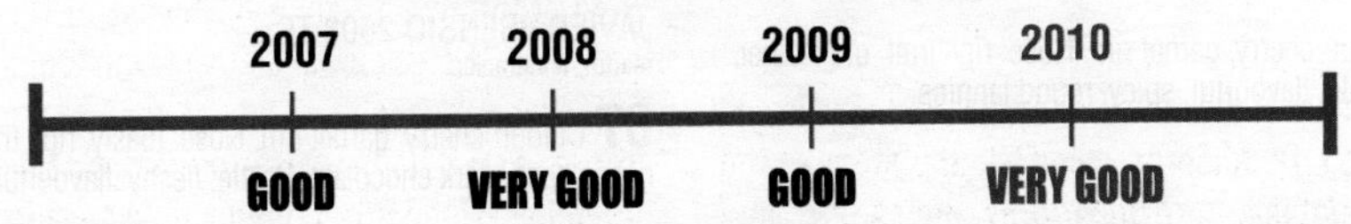

ARDOA

Las Mercedes, 31- 4º Depto. 4
48930 Las Arenas-Getxo (Bizkaia)
☎: +34 944 315 872 - Fax: +34 944 315 873
info@ardoa.com
www.ardoa.com

AGA 2009 T ROBLE
70% tempranillo, 30% cabernet sauvignon.

86 Colour: cherry, garnet rim. Nose: creamy oak, dark chocolate, spicy, ripe fruit. Palate: fruity, spicy.

AZCÚNAGA 2007 TC
60% tempranillo, 40% cabernet sauvignon.

84 Colour: bright cherry, orangey edge. Nose: fruit liqueur notes, medium intensity, toasty. Palate: spicy, ripe fruit, round tannins.

ARISTU

Ctra. N-240 Pamplona-Saca, Km. 35
31440 Lumbier (Navarra)
☎: +34 948 398 098 - Fax: +34 948 880 290
bodegasaristu@gmail.com

ARISTU 2010 B
garnacha blanca.

80 Colour: bright straw. Nose: faded flowers, ripe fruit, dried herbs. Palate: good acidity, flavourful, slightly evolved.

ARISTU GARNACHA 2009 RD
garnacha.

78

MAZTEGI GARNACHA 2010 T
garnacha.

82 Colour: cherry, purple rim. Nose: ripe fruit, balsamic herbs, herbaceous, fresh. Palate: fresh, light-bodied, flavourful.

ARISTU 2010 T
garnacha.

79

ARISTU 2004 TC
tempranillo, garnacha.

84 Colour: cherry, garnet rim. Nose: ripe fruit, old leather, spicy. Palate: flavourful, spicy, round tannins.

AROA BODEGAS

Apalaz, 13
31292 Gorozin-Zurukoain (Navarra)
☎: +34 948 921 867
info@aroawines.com
www.aroawines.com

AROA LARROSA 2010 RD
50% garnacha, 50% tempranillo.

90 Colour: rose, purple rim. Nose: powerfull, red berry notes, fruit expression. Palate: flavourful, powerful, fleshy.

AROA MUTIKO 2010 T
70% tempranillo, 30% garnacha.

90 Colour: bright cherry, purple rim. Nose: balanced, medium intensity, complex. Palate: fruity, long, good acidity.

AROA JAUNA 2006 TC
47% merlot, 40% cabernet sauvignon, 13% tempranillo.

89 Colour: cherry, garnet rim. Nose: spicy, creamy oak, toasty, earthy notes. Palate: powerful, flavourful, round tannins.

AROA GORENA 2005 TR
100% cabernet sauvignon.

90 Colour: bright cherry, garnet rim. Nose: varietal, ripe fruit, powerfull, spicy, warm. Palate: good structure, rich, fruity, round tannins, spicy.

ASENSIO VIÑEDOS Y BODEGAS

Mayor, 84
31293 Sesma (Navarra)
☎: +34 948 698 078 - Fax: +34 948 698 097
info@bodegasasensio.com

JAVIER ASENSIO 2010 B
sauvignon blanc, chardonnay.

87 Colour: bright straw. Nose: floral, wild herbs, medium intensity. Palate: flavourful, good acidity.

JAVIER ASENSIO 2010 RD
syrah.

85 Colour: rose, purple rim. Nose: floral, raspberry, ripe fruit. Palate: flavourful, powerful.

JAVIER ASENSIO 2008 TC
merlot, tempranillo.

87 Colour: cherry, garnet rim. Nose: toasty, ripe fruit, cocoa bean, dark chocolate. Palate: fleshy, flavourful, long.

JAVIER ASENSIO 2005 TR
cabernet sauvignon, merlot, tempranillo.

90 Colour: cherry, garnet rim. Nose: spicy, creamy oak, toasty, ripe fruit. Palate: powerful, flavourful, toasty, round tannins.

JAVIER ASENSIO MERLOT 2005 TR

88 Colour: cherry, garnet rim. Nose: ripe fruit, spicy, creamy oak. Palate: powerful, flavourful, toasty, round tannins.

JAVIER ASENSIO CABERNET SAUVIGNON 2005 TR
cabernet sauvignon.

88 Colour: cherry, garnet rim. Nose: ripe fruit, spicy, creamy oak, toasty. Palate: powerful, flavourful, toasty.

AZUL Y GARANZA BODEGAS

San Juan, 19
31310 Carcastillo (Navarra)
☎: +34 659 857 979 - Fax: +34 948 725 677
info@azulygaranza.com
www.azulygaranza.com

ROSA DE AZUL Y GARANZA 2010 RD
garnacha, tempranillo.

87 Colour: light cherry, bright. Nose: red berry notes, ripe fruit, wild herbs, elegant. Palate: light-bodied, easy to drink, good finish.

ABRIL DE AZUL Y GARANZA 2010 T
tempranillo, cabernet sauvignon.

90 Colour: cherry, purple rim. Nose: red berry notes, balanced, expressive, lactic notes. Palate: fruity, good structure, good acidity.

SEIS DE AZUL Y GARANZA 2009 T
merlot, cabernet sauvignon.

89 Colour: cherry, garnet rim. Nose: wild herbs, balsamic herbs, ripe fruit, earthy notes. Palate: spicy, complex, flavourful. Personality.

FIESTA DE AZUL Y GARANZA 2009 T JOVEN
tempranillo, garnacha.

88 Color cherry, purple rim. Aroma expressive, fresh fruit, red berry notes, floral. Taste flavourful, fruity, good acidity, round tannins.

DESIERTO DE AZUL Y GARANZA 2007 T
cabernet sauvignon.

91 Colour: deep cherry, garnet rim. Nose: earthy notes, dry stone, dried herbs, fruit liqueur notes. Palate: balanced, ripe fruit, spicy, long. Personality.

BODEGA DE SADA

Arrabal, 2
31491 Sada (Navarra)
☎: +34 948 877 013 - Fax: +34 948 877 433
bodega@bodegadesada.com
www.bodegadesada.com

PALACIO DE SADA 2010 RD
garnacha.

85 Colour: rose, purple rim. Nose: powerfull, ripe fruit, red berry notes, floral. Palate: fleshy, powerful, fruity, fresh.

PALACIO DE SADA GARNACHA 2009 T
garnacha.

84 Colour: cherry, purple rim. Nose: herbaceous, balsamic herbs, ripe fruit. Palate: powerful, flavourful, green.

PALACIO DE SADA 2008 TC
90% garnacha, 10% tempranillo, cabernet sauvignon.

89 Colour: cherry, garnet rim. Nose: fruit liqueur notes, toasty, sweet spices, warm. Palate: flavourful, spicy, ripe fruit.

PALACIO DE SADA 2005 TR
80% garnacha, 20% tempranillo, merlot, cabernet sauvignon.

85 Colour: cherry, garnet rim. Nose: ripe fruit, spicy, creamy oak, toasty. Palate: powerful, flavourful, toasty, round tannins.

PALACIO DE SADA GARNACHA 2002 TR
garnacha.

85 Colour: pale ruby, brick rim edge. Nose: spicy, fine reductive notes, wet leather, aged wood nuances, fruit liqueur notes. Palate: spicy, fine tannins, long.

BODEGA DE SARRÍA

Finca Señorío de Sarría, s/n
31100 Puente La Reina (Navarra)
☎: +34 948 202 200 - Fax: +34 948 202 202
info@taninia.com
www.bodegadesarria.com

SEÑORÍO DE SARRÍA CHARDONNAY 2010 B
chardonnay.

87 Colour: bright straw. Nose: fresh, white flowers, ripe fruit. Palate: flavourful, fruity, good acidity, balanced.

SEÑORÍO DE SARRÍA VIÑEDO Nº 3 2009 BFB
chardonnay.

90 Colour: bright yellow. Nose: powerfull, ripe fruit, sweet spices, fragrant herbs. Palate: rich, flavourful, fresh, good acidity.

SEÑORÍO DE SARRÍA 2010 RD
garnacha.

87 Colour: rose, purple rim. Nose: powerfull, ripe fruit, red berry notes, floral. Palate: fleshy, powerful, fruity, fresh.

SEÑORÍO DE SARRÍA VIÑEDO Nº 5 2010 RD
garnacha.

86 Colour: rose, purple rim. Nose: powerfull, ripe fruit, red berry notes, floral, expressive. Palate: fleshy, powerful, fruity, fresh, easy to drink.

SEÑORÍO DE SARRÍA 2008 TC
tempranillo, cabernet sauvignon.

85 Colour: cherry, garnet rim. Nose: old leather, cocoa bean, creamy oak, toasty. Palate: flavourful, fleshy, spicy.

SEÑORÍO DE SARRÍA 2005 TR
merlot, cabernet sauvignon.

88 Colour: cherry, garnet rim. Nose: varietal, balsamic herbs, spicy. Palate: balanced, round tannins.

SEÑORÍO DE SARRÍA VIÑEDO SOTÉS 2005 T
merlot, graciano, mazuelo, tempranillo, garnacha, cabernet sauvignon.

86 Colour: cherry, garnet rim. Nose: ripe fruit, old leather, spicy. Palate: good structure, long, spicy.

SEÑORÍO DE SARRÍA VIÑEDO Nº 8 2005 T
mazuelo.

85 Colour: cherry, garnet rim. Nose: ripe fruit, fine reductive notes, spicy. Palate: flavourful, spicy, ripe fruit.

SEÑORÍO DE SARRÍA RESERVA ESPECIAL 2004 TR
cabernet sauvignon.

89 Colour: bright cherry. Nose: expressive, elegant, mineral, red berry notes, ripe fruit, sweet spices. Palate: good structure, balanced.

SEÑORÍO DE SARRÍA MOSCATEL 2010 BLANCO DULCE
moscatel.

88 Colour: bright straw. Nose: varietal, white flowers, honeyed notes. Palate: flavourful, fruity, good acidity.

BODEGA INURRIETA

Ctra. Falces-Miranda de Arga, km. 30
31370 Falces (Navarra)
☎: +34 948 737 309 - Fax: +34 948 737 310
info@bodegainurrieta.com
www.bodegainurrieta.com

INURRIETA CUATROCIENTOS 2008 TC
50% cabernet sauvignon, 40% merlot, 10% graciano.

90 Colour: cherry, garnet rim. Nose: balanced, complex, ripe fruit, spicy. Palate: good structure, flavourful, round tannins.

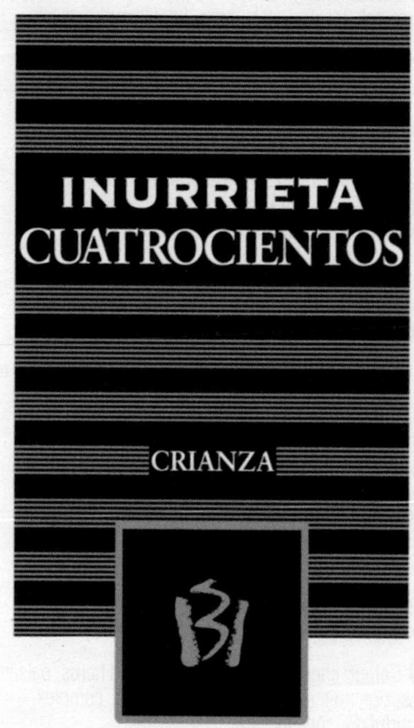

INURRIETA ORCHÍDEA 2010 B
100% sauvignon blanc.

92 Colour: bright straw. Nose: fresh fruit, white flowers, expressive, mineral. Palate: flavourful, fruity, good acidity, balanced.

INURRIETA MEDIODÍA 2010 RD
100% garnacha.

88 Colour: brilliant rose. Nose: wild herbs, medium intensity, red berry notes, floral, citrus fruit. Palate: fruity, flavourful, good acidity, balanced.

INURRIETA "SUR" 2009 T ROBLE
60% garnacha, 40% syrah.

89 Colour: cherry, purple rim. Nose: red berry notes, sweet spices, cocoa bean. Palate: fruity, good structure, round tannins.

INURRIETA NORTE 2009 T ROBLE
50% merlot, 50% cabernet sauvignon.

88 Colour: cherry, garnet rim. Nose: powerfull, ripe fruit, scrubland, balsamic herbs. Palate: powerful, flavourful, fleshy.

ALTOS DE INURRIETA 2007 TR
50% cabernet sauvignon, 50% garnacha.

90 Colour: cherry, garnet rim. Nose: ripe fruit, red berry notes, powerfull, expressive, balsamic herbs, creamy oak. Palate: fruity, flavourful, fleshy, toasty.

BODEGA MARQUÉS DE MONTECIERZO

San José, 62
31590 Castejón (Navarra)
☎: +34 948 814 414 - Fax: +34 948 814 420
info@marquesdemontecierzo.com
www.marquesdemontecierzo.com

EMERGENTE MOSCATEL 2010 B
moscatel.

88 Colour: golden. Nose: honeyed notes, candied fruit, fragrant herbs. Palate: flavourful, sweet, fresh, fruity, good acidity, long.

EMERGENTE 2010 B
chardonnay, moscatel.

88 Colour: bright straw. Nose: medium intensity, fresh fruit, white flowers. Palate: flavourful, fruity, fresh.

EMERGENTE 2010 B
chardonnay.

86 Colour: bright straw. Nose: fresh, fresh fruit, white flowers, expressive. Palate: flavourful, fruity, good acidity.

EMERGENTE ROSADO DE LÁGRIMA 2010 RD
garnacha, cabernet sauvignon, merlot.

85 Colour: rose, purple rim. Nose: medium intensity, red berry notes, wild herbs. Palate: powerful, fruity, fleshy.

GARNACHA 100 X 100 2010 T ROBLE
100% garnacha.

88 Colour: bright cherry, purple rim. Nose: powerfull, warm, red berry notes, spicy. Palate: fruity, good structure, flavourful.

EMERGENTE 2010 T
tempranillo, merlot, cabernet sauvignon.

79

EMERGENTE 2007 T ROBLE
tempranillo, cabernet sauvignon, merlot.

87 Colour: cherry, garnet rim. Nose: powerfull, ripe fruit, fruit preserve, toasty, sweet spices. Palate: powerful, fine bitter notes, ripe fruit.

EMERGENTE 2006 TC
tempranillo, cabernet sauvignon, merlot.

84 Colour: cherry, garnet rim. Nose: ripe fruit, spicy, creamy oak, toasty. Palate: powerful, flavourful, toasty, green, balsamic.

MARQUÉS DE MONTECIERZO MERLOT SELECCIÓN 2005 TC
100% merlot.

90 Colour: deep cherry, garnet rim. Nose: spicy, balsamic herbs, complex, varietal, ripe fruit. Palate: fruity, flavourful, complex.

EMERGENTE RESERVA NUMERADA 2005 TR
tempranillo, merlot, cabernet sauvignon.

87 Colour: cherry, garnet rim. Nose: balanced, spicy, old leather, wild herbs. Palate: spicy, ripe fruit, good structure, great length.

BODEGA MÁXIMO ABETE

Ctra. Estella-Sangüesa, Km. 43,5
31495 San Martín de Unx (Navarra)
☎: +34 948 738 120 - Fax: +34 948 738 120
info@bodegasmaximoabete.com
www.bodegasmaximoabete.com

GUERINDA 2010 RD
100% garnacha.

85 Colour: rose, purple rim. Nose: floral, ripe fruit, red berry notes. Palate: good acidity, flavourful, fruity, fresh.

GUERINDA 2009 T ROBLE
garnacha, graciano, tempranillo, merlot.

85 Colour: cherry, garnet rim. Nose: fruit preserve, toasty, creamy oak. Palate: powerful, flavourful, fine bitter notes.

GUERINDA 2006 TC
garnacha, merlot, graciano, cabernet sauvignon.

86 Colour: cherry, garnet rim. Nose: ripe fruit, warm, spicy. Palate: flavourful, fruity, rich, round tannins.

GUERINDA 2005 TR
garnacha, cabernet sauvignon, merlot.

89 Colour: cherry, garnet rim. Nose: ripe fruit, creamy oak, toasty, sweet spices. Palate: powerful, flavourful, toasty, round tannins.

BODEGA NUESTRA SEÑORA DEL ROMERO

Ctra. de Tarazona, 33- Apdo. Correos, 24
31520 Cascante (Navarra)
☎: +34 948 851 411 - Fax: +34 948 844 504
info@bodegasdelromero.com
www.bodegasdelromero.com

MALÓN DE ECHAIDE VIURA 2010 B
100% viura.

85 Colour: bright straw. Nose: fresh, fresh fruit, white flowers, expressive. Palate: flavourful, fruity, good acidity, fresh, light-bodied.

TORRECILLA 2010 B
100% viura.

85 Colour: bright golden. Nose: faded flowers, citrus fruit, dried herbs, fresh. Palate: flavourful, fresh, fruity, light-bodied.

MALÓN DE ECHAIDE 2010 RD
100% garnacha.

86 Colour: brilliant rose. Nose: wild herbs, fresh, dried flowers, citrus fruit. Palate: flavourful, fruity, fine bitter notes.

TORRECILLA 2010 RD
100% garnacha.

86 Colour: rose, purple rim. Nose: medium intensity, red berry notes, fresh fruit, dried flowers. Palate: easy to drink, fresh.

MALÓN DE ECHAIDE TEMPRANILLO 2010 T
100% tempranillo.

86 Colour: cherry, purple rim. Nose: powerfull, ripe fruit. Palate: flavourful, fleshy, fruity.

TORRECILLA 2010 T
100% tempranillo.

75

MALÓN DE ECHAIDE GARNACHA 2008 T ROBLE
100% garnacha.

88 Colour: cherry, garnet rim. Nose: powerfull, roasted coffee, cocoa bean, fruit expression. Palate: flavourful, powerful, fine bitter notes, toasty.

SEÑOR DE CASCANTE 2007 TC
85% tempranillo, 15% cabernet sauvignon.

88 Colour: cherry, garnet rim. Nose: toasty, spicy, ripe fruit. Palate: fruity, flavourful, great length, ripe fruit.

MALÓN DE ECHAIDE 2007 TC
80% tempranillo, 15% cabernet sauvignon, 5% merlot.

86 Colour: cherry, garnet rim. Nose: medium intensity, ripe fruit, spicy. Palate: easy to drink, ripe fruit.

TORRECILLA 2004 TC
100% tempranillo.

83 Colour: cherry, garnet rim. Nose: varietal, ripe fruit, old leather. Palate: fruity, easy to drink.

SEÑOR DE CASCANTE 2003 TGR
85% tempranillo, 15% cabernet sauvignon.

82 Colour: pale ruby, brick rim edge. Nose: spicy, fine reductive notes, wet leather, fruit liqueur notes. Palate: spicy, fine tannins, long, correct.

VIÑA PAROT 2003 TR
85% cabernet sauvignon, 15% tempranillo.

78

MALÓN DE ECHAIDE CABERNET SAUVIGNON 2001 TR
100% cabernet sauvignon.

87 Colour: cherry, garnet rim. Nose: ripe fruit, spicy, creamy oak, toasty. Palate: powerful, flavourful, toasty, balsamic.

MALÓN DE ECHAIDE MERLOT 2001 TR
100% merlot.

84 Colour: bright cherry. Nose: wild herbs, ripe fruit. Palate: flavourful, good structure, spicy, round tannins.

BODEGA OTAZU

Señorío de Otazu, s/n
31174 Etxauri (Navarra)
☎: +34 948 329 200 - Fax: +34 948 329 353
otazu@otazu.com
www.otazu.com

OTAZU CHARDONNAY 2009 B
chardonnay.

91 Colour: bright straw. Nose: fresh, white flowers, ripe fruit, neat. Palate: flavourful, fruity, good acidity, mineral.

OTAZU 2010 RD
merlot.

89 Colour: rose, purple rim. Nose: ripe fruit, red berry notes, floral, expressive. Palate: fleshy, powerful, fruity, fresh, easy to drink.

OTAZU 2007 TC
50% cabernet sauvignon, 35% tempranillo, 15% merlot.

92 Colour: deep cherry. Nose: mineral, powerfull, characterful, ripe fruit. Palate: creamy, fleshy, spicy, round tannins.

BODEGA PAGO DE CIRSUS

Ctra. de Ablitas a Ribaforada, Km. 5
31523 Ablitas (Navarra)
☎: +34 948 386 210 - Fax: +34 629 354 190
bodegasin@pagodecirsus.com
www.pagodecirsus.com

PAGO DE CIRSUS CHARDONNAY 2010 B
100% chardonnay.

90 Colour: bright yellow. Nose: powerfull, ripe fruit, sweet spices, fragrant herbs. Palate: rich, flavourful, fresh, good acidity.

PAGO DE CIRSUS SAUVIGNON BLANC 2010 B
100% sauvignon blanc.

88 Colour: bright straw. Nose: ripe fruit, citrus fruit, expressive. Palate: flavourful, fruity, fresh.

PAGO DE CIRSUS CHARDONNAY 2009 BFB
100% chardonnay.

91 Colour: bright yellow. Nose: varietal, balanced, expressive, spicy. Palate: fruity, rich, flavourful, good acidity, balanced, fine bitter notes.

PAGO DE CIRSUS MOSCATEL VENDIMIA TARDÍA 2007 BFB
moscatel.

91 Colour: golden. Nose: powerfull, floral, honeyed notes, candied fruit, overripe fruit. Palate: flavourful, sweet, fruity, good acidity, long.

PAGO DE CIRSUS DE IÑAKI NUÑEZ VENDIMIA SELECCIONADA 2008 TC
tempranillo, merlot, syrah.

90 Colour: cherry, garnet rim. Nose: ripe fruit, spicy, creamy oak, toasty, earthy notes. Palate: powerful, flavourful, toasty, round tannins.

PAGO DE CIRSUS OPUS II 2007 T
100% syrah.

93 Colour: cherry, purple rim. Nose: elegant, fruit expression, red berry notes, ripe fruit, mineral. Palate: rich, good structure, concentrated, complex, spicy, long.

PAGO DE CIRSUS DE IÑAKI NÚÑEZ SELECCIÓN DE FAMILIA 2007 T
tempranillo.

91 Colour: deep cherry, garnet rim. Nose: sweet spices, cocoa bean, ripe fruit, complex. Palate: good structure, complex, fleshy, round tannins.

PAGO DE CIRSUS DE IÑAKI NÚÑEZ CUVÉE ESPECIAL 2007 TR
tempranillo, merlot, syrah.

90 Colour: cherry, garnet rim. Nose: raspberry, fruit preserve, complex, expressive. Palate: good acidity, powerful, flavourful, fleshy.

BODEGA TÁNDEM

Ctra. Pamplona - Logroño Km. 35,9
31292 Lácar (Navarra)
☎: +34 948 536 031 - Fax: +34 948 536 068
bodega@tandem.es
www.tandem.es

ARS MÁCULA 2005 T
cabernet sauvignon, merlot.

89 Color bright cherry. Aroma ripe fruit, sweet spices, creamy oak, expressive. Taste flavourful, fruity, toasty, round tannins.

BODEGA Y VIÑAS VALDELARES

Ctra. Eje del Ebro, km. 60
31579 Carcar (Navarra)
☎: +34 656 849 602
valdelares@terra.es
www.valdelares.com

VALDELARES CHARDONNAY 2010 B
100% chardonnay.

84 Colour: bright straw. Nose: citrus fruit, dried flowers, ripe fruit. Palate: fresh, fruity, light-bodied.

VALDELARES 2010 T
50% merlot, 50% tempranillo.

85 Colour: bright cherry, purple rim. Nose: red berry notes, violets. Palate: fruity, light-bodied.

VALDELARES ALTA EXPRESIÓN 2008 TC
100% cabernet sauvignon.

90 Color cherry, garnet rim. Aroma ripe fruit, spicy, creamy oak, toasty, complex. Taste powerful, flavourful, toasty, round tannins.

VALDELARES 2008 TC
33% tempranillo, 33% cabernet sauvignon, 33% merlot.

88 Colour: cherry, garnet rim. Nose: raspberry, red berry notes, expressive, creamy oak. Palate: good acidity, flavourful, fruity, fleshy.

VALDELARES DULCE 2010 BLANCO DULCE
100% moscatel grano menudo.

86 Colour: bright straw. Nose: grapey, citrus fruit, tropical fruit, expressive. Palate: fresh, light-bodied, fruity, flavourful.

BODEGAS 1877

Brisol, 16 bis
28230 Las Rozas (Madrid)
☎: +34 917 104 880 - Fax: +34 917 104 881
anap@swd.es
www.swd.es

MARQUÉS DE LUZ 2007 TC
80% merlot, 20% cabernet sauvignon.

84 Colour: light cherry. Nose: fruit preserve, spicy, toasty. Palate: flavourful, round tannins.

BODEGAS AZPEA

Camino Itúrbero, s/n
31440 Lumbier (Navarra)
☎: +34 948 880 433 - Fax: +34 948 880 433
maite@bodegasazpea.com
www.bodegasazpea.com

AZPEA VINO DULCE DE MOSCATEL 2010 B
moscatel grano menudo.

87 Colour: bright straw. Nose: fresh, white flowers, expressive, honeyed notes. Palate: flavourful, fruity, good acidity, balanced.

AZPEA VIURA 2009 B
viura, moscatel.

83 Colour: bright straw. Nose: fresh, fresh fruit, white flowers. Palate: flavourful, fruity, good acidity, easy to drink.

AZPEA JOVEN 2009 T
tempranillo, cabernet sauvignon, garnacha.

87 Colour: cherry, garnet rim. Nose: ripe fruit, spicy, balsamic herbs, powerfull. Palate: flavourful, ripe fruit, correct, complex.

AZPEA SELECCIÓN 2007 T
merlot, garnacha, cabernet sauvignon.

84 Colour: bright cherry. Nose: ripe fruit, sweet spices, creamy oak, slightly evolved. Palate: flavourful, fruity, toasty, round tannins.

AZPEA GARNACHA 2006 T
garnacha.

85 Colour: cherry, garnet rim. Nose: powerfull, ripe fruit, sweet spices. Palate: spicy, powerful, round tannins.

BODEGAS BERAMENDI

Ctra. Tafalla, s/n
31495 San Martín de Unx (Navarra)
☎: +34 948 738 262 - Fax: +34 948 738 080
info@bodegasberamendi.com
www.bodegasberamendi.com

3F 2010 B
70% chardonnay, 30% moscatel.

87 Colour: bright straw. Nose: jasmine, fresh fruit, balanced. Palate: fruity, fresh, easy to drink, fine bitter notes.

3F 2010 RD
100% garnacha.

87 Colour: brilliant rose. Nose: red berry notes, wild herbs, dried flowers, expressive, fresh. Palate: fruity, flavourful, easy to drink.

BERAMENDI 2010 RD
100% garnacha.

85 Colour: brilliant rose. Nose: faded flowers, medium intensity, red berry notes. Palate: fruity, balanced, good acidity.

BERAMENDI 2010 T
80% tempranillo, 20% garnacha.

89 Colour: cherry, purple rim. Nose: expressive, fresh fruit, red berry notes, balsamic herbs. Palate: flavourful, fruity, good acidity, fleshy.

BERAMENDI TEMPRANILLO 2007 TC
100% tempranillo.

86 Colour: cherry, garnet rim. Nose: red berry notes, ripe fruit, balsamic herbs, sweet spices, toasty. Palate: flavourful, fleshy, spicy.

BERAMENDI MERLOT 2007 TC
80% merlot, 20% graciano.

84 Colour: cherry, garnet rim. Nose: sweet spices, toasty, ripe fruit. Palate: spicy, flavourful, fleshy.

BERAMENDI 2004 TR
60% merlot, 20% cabernet sauvignon, 20% tempranillo.

85 Colour: cherry, garnet rim. Nose: ripe fruit, spicy, toasty. Palate: powerful, flavourful, toasty, round tannins.

BODEGAS CAMILO CASTILLA

Santa Bárbara, 40
31591 Corella (Navarra)
☎: +34 948 780 006 - Fax: +34 948 780 515
info@bodegascamilocastilla.com
www.bodegascamilocastilla.com

MONTECRISTO 2010 B
100% moscatel.

86 Colour: bright straw, greenish rim. Nose: jasmine, white flowers, fruit expression. Palate: flavourful, fruity, easy to drink.

PINK 2010 RD
100% garnacha.

88 Colour: brilliant rose. Nose: powerfull, red berry notes, balsamic herbs. Palate: flavourful, good acidity, fine bitter notes.

MONTECRISTO 2010 RD
100% garnacha.

84 Colour: rose, purple rim. Nose: floral, red berry notes, ripe fruit, medium intensity. Palate: good acidity, flavourful, fresh.

MONTECRISTO 2008 TC
70% tempranillo, 30% cabernet sauvignon.

82 Colour: cherry, garnet rim. Nose: candied fruit, spicy. Palate: flavourful, good structure, sweetness.

MONTECRISTO MOSCATEL 2010 BLANCO DULCE
100% moscatel grano menudo.

90 Colour: bright yellow. Nose: tropical fruit, honeyed notes, grapey, elegant. Palate: good acidity, flavourful, fruity, fleshy.

CAPRICHO DE GOYA VINO DE LICOR
100% moscatel.

91 Colour: light mahogany. Nose: powerfull, dried fruit, fruit liqueur notes, expressive, acetaldehyde. Palate: powerful, concentrated, sweet.

BODEGAS CAMPOS DE ENANZO

Mayor, 189
31521 Murchante (Navarra)
☎: +34 948 838 030 - Fax: +34 948 838 677
export@camposenanzo.com
www.camposenanzo.com

ENANZO CHARDONNAY 2010 B BARRICA
chardonnay.

86 Colour: bright yellow. Nose: medium intensity, fruit expression, floral. Palate: fruity, flavourful, easy to drink.

BASIANO VIURA 2010 B
viura.

85 Colour: bright straw. Nose: medium intensity, fresh, dried herbs. Palate: fresh, light-bodied, easy to drink.

REMONTE CHARDONNAY 2010 B
chardonnay.

85 Colour: bright straw. Nose: floral, dried herbs, medium intensity. Palate: good acidity, light-bodied, fresh, easy to drink.

ENANZO 2010 RD
garnacha.

88 Colour: brilliant rose. Nose: fresh fruit, floral, wild herbs. Palate: fruity, flavourful, easy to drink, good acidity.

REMONTE 2010 RD
garnacha.

88 Colour: rose, purple rim. Nose: ripe fruit, red berry notes, floral, expressive. Palate: fleshy, powerful, fruity, fresh.

BASIANO GARNACHA 2010 RD
garnacha.

86 Colour: brilliant rose. Nose: candied fruit, fruit expression, floral. Palate: flavourful, fruity, fresh.

ENANZO TEMPRANILLO 2010 T
tempranillo.

87 Colour: cherry, purple rim. Nose: expressive, fresh fruit, red berry notes, floral. Palate: flavourful, fruity, good acidity.

BASIANO TEMPRANILLO 2010 T
tempranillo.

86 Colour: cherry, purple rim. Nose: medium intensity, balanced, fresh, red berry notes. Palate: flavourful, fruity.

REMONTE TEMPRANILLO 2009 T ROBLE
tempranillo.

85 Colour: bright cherry. Nose: ripe fruit, sweet spices, creamy oak, toasty. Palate: flavourful, fruity, toasty, round tannins.

ENANZO 2004 TR
tempranillo, cabernet sauvignon, merlot.

88 Colour: bright cherry, garnet rim. Nose: balanced, elegant, red berry notes, ripe fruit. Palate: fleshy, flavourful, good structure, fruity.

REMONTE 2004 TR
tempranillo, merlot, cabernet sauvignon.

86 Colour: cherry, garnet rim. Nose: expressive, balsamic herbs, fine reductive notes, cigar. Palate: powerful, flavourful, fresh, fleshy.

BODEGAS CAUDALIA

Rs. San Francisco, 7
26300 Nájera (La Rioja)
☎: +34 670 833 340 - Fax: +34 941 146 361
info@bodegascaudalia.com
www.bodegascaudalia.com

PAAL 100% SYRAH 01 2010 T
100% syrah.

88 Colour: cherry, purple rim. Nose: expressive, fresh fruit, red berry notes, floral, spicy. Palate: flavourful, fruity, good acidity, round tannins.

BODEGAS CHIVITE

Ribera, 34
31592 Cintruénigo (Navarra)
☎: +34 948 811 000 - Fax: +34 948 811 407
info@bodegaschivite.com
www.bodegaschivite.com

GRAN FEUDO EDICIÓN DULCE DE MOSCATEL 2010 B
moscatel grano menudo.

92 Colour: bright straw. Nose: white flowers, varietal, powerfull, candied fruit, fruit expression. Palate: flavourful, fruity, fresh, fleshy.

GRAN FEUDO CHARDONNAY 2010 B
chardonnay.

90 Colour: bright straw. Nose: fresh fruit, white flowers, fine lees, varietal. Palate: flavourful, fruity, good acidity, balanced.

GRAN FEUDO DULCE DE MOSCATEL 2010 B
moscatel.

89 Colour: bright straw. Nose: varietal, expressive, neat, fresh, citrus fruit. Palate: flavourful, fruity, fresh, fleshy.

GRAN FEUDO SUAVE 2010 B
chardonnay, moscatel grano menudo.

88 Colour: bright straw. Nose: fresh fruit, fruit expression, citrus fruit, dried herbs. Palate: flavourful, fruity, sweetness, good acidity.

CHIVITE COLECCIÓN 125 VENDIMIA TARDÍA 2008 B
moscatel.

95 Colour: golden. Nose: floral, honeyed notes, candied fruit, fragrant herbs, varietal, characterful, complex. Palate: flavourful, sweet, fresh, fruity, good acidity, long.

CHIVITE COLECCIÓN 125 2008 BFB
100% chardonnay.

93 Colour: bright yellow. Nose: powerfull, sweet spices, creamy oak, ripe fruit. Palate: rich, smoky aftertaste, flavourful, fresh, good acidity.

GRAN FEUDO EDICIÓN CHARDONNAY SOBRE LÍAS 2008 B
chardonnay.

90 Colour: bright straw. Nose: fresh, white flowers, fine lees, fruit expression. Palate: flavourful, good acidity, full, ripe fruit.

CHARDONNAY
2008
SOBRE LÍAS

NAVARRA
DENOMINACIÓN DE ORIGEN
PRODUCT OF SPAIN

GRAN FEUDO SOBRE LÍAS 2009 RD
tempranillo, garnacha, merlot.

90 Colour: brilliant rose. Nose: elegant, candied fruit, dried flowers, fragrant herbs, red berry notes. Palate: light-bodied, flavourful, good acidity, long, spicy.

ROSADO
2009
SOBRE LÍAS

TEMPRANILLO ·
GARNACHA ·
MERLOT

NAVARRA
DENOMINACIÓN DE ORIGEN
PRODUCT OF SPAIN

CHIVITE COLECCIÓN 125 2007 RD
tempranillo, merlot, cabernet sauvignon.

92 Colour: brilliant rose. Nose: fine lees, floral, red berry notes, scrubland. Palate: flavourful, fruity, fresh, fleshy, long, spicy.

GRAN FEUDO 2010 RD
garnacha.

89 Colour: rose, purple rim. Nose: ripe fruit, red berry notes, floral, varietal. Palate: fleshy, powerful, fruity, fresh.

CHIVITE BIOLÓGICO MERLOT 2007 T
merlot.

90 Colour: bright cherry. Nose: sweet spices, creamy oak, fruit preserve, neat. Palate: flavourful, fruity, toasty, round tannins.

CHIVITE EXPRESIÓN VARIETAL TEMPRANILLO 2007 T
tempranillo.

90 Colour: cherry, garnet rim. Nose: spicy, creamy oak, toasty, ripe fruit. Palate: powerful, flavourful, toasty, round tannins.

CHIVITE COLECCIÓN 125 2006 TR
71% tempranillo, 17% merlot, 12% cabernet sauvignon.

92 Colour: cherry, garnet rim. Nose: premature reduction notes, ripe fruit, toasty, dark chocolate. Palate: flavourful, powerful, fleshy, spicy, ripe fruit.

GRAN FEUDO EDICIÓN SELECCIÓN ESPECIAL 2007 TC
50% tempranillo, 30% cabernet sauvignon, 20% merlot.

90 Colour: cherry, garnet rim. Nose: powerfull, ripe fruit, creamy oak, aromatic coffee. Palate: powerful, fleshy, fine bitter notes, round tannins.

GRAN FEUDO EDICIÓN VIÑAS VIEJAS 2006 TR
tempranillo, garnacha, merlot.

90 Colour: cherry, garnet rim. Nose: powerfull, characterful, ripe fruit, aromatic coffee, dark chocolate. Palate: flavourful, powerful, fleshy, fine bitter notes.

GRAN FEUDO 2006 TR
tempranillo, merlot, cabernet sauvignon.

88 Colour: cherry, garnet rim. Nose: powerfull, ripe fruit, toasty, smoky. Palate: flavourful, powerful, fleshy, fine bitter notes.

GRAN FEUDO VIÑAS VIEJAS 2006 TR
tempranillo, garnacha, cabernet sauvignon, merlot.

88 Colour: cherry, garnet rim. Nose: sweet spices, creamy oak, ripe fruit, fruit expression. Palate: flavourful, powerful, fleshy, spicy.

GRAN FEUDO 2007 TC
tempranillo, garnacha, cabernet sauvignon.

88 Colour: cherry, garnet rim. Nose: earthy notes, ripe fruit, creamy oak. Palate: flavourful, fleshy, fine bitter notes, spicy.

BODEGAS CORELLANAS

Santa Bárbara, 29
31591 Corella (Navarra)
☎: +34 948 780 029 - Fax: +34 948 781 542
jdaniel@bodegascorellanas.com
www.bodegascorellanas.com

MOSCATEL SARASATE EXPRESIÓN 2010 B
100% moscatel.

88 Colour: bright straw. Nose: white flowers, ripe fruit, citrus fruit. Palate: flavourful, fruity, sweet.

VIÑA RUBICÁN 2010 B
60% moscatel grano menudo, 40% viura.

83 Colour: bright straw. Nose: fresh, floral, ripe fruit. Palate: flavourful, fruity, good acidity.

VIÑA RUBICÁN 2010 RD
100% garnacha.

82 Colour: rose, purple rim. Nose: ripe fruit, red berry notes, expressive. Palate: fleshy, fruity, fresh.

VIÑA RUBICÁN TEMPRANILLO 2010 T
100% tempranillo.

86 Colour: cherry, garnet rim. Nose: fresh, red berry notes, balanced. Palate: fruity, flavourful, easy to drink.

VIÑA RUBICÁN 2006 TC
85% tempranillo, 15% cabernet sauvignon.

83 Colour: cherry, garnet rim. Nose: dark chocolate, aromatic coffee, fruit liqueur notes. Palate: spicy, toasty.

VIÑA RUBICÁN 2005 TR
cabernet sauvignon, merlot, tempranillo.

86 Colour: cherry, garnet rim. Nose: medium intensity, spicy, ripe fruit. Palate: fruity, round tannins, good acidity.

BODEGAS DE LA CASA DE LÚCULO

Ctra. Larraga, s/n.
31150 Mendigorría (Navarra)
☎: +34 948 343 148 - Fax: +34 948 343 148
bodega@luculo.es
www.luculo.es

GADOL GARNACHA VIÑAS VIEJAS 2008 T
100% garnacha.

85 Colour: cherry, garnet rim. Nose: candied fruit, fruit liqueur notes, tar. Palate: fine bitter notes, spicy, ripe fruit.

JARDÍN DE LÚCULO 2007 T
100% garnacha.

93 Colour: cherry, garnet rim. Nose: red berry notes, varietal, fragrant herbs, spicy, elegant. Palate: good structure, complex, flavourful, good acidity, balanced.

CÁTULO 2007 T
100% garnacha.

88 Colour: cherry, garnet rim. Nose: spicy, toasty, ripe fruit. Palate: powerful, flavourful, toasty, round tannins.

BODEGAS FERNÁNDEZ DE ARCAYA

La Serna, 31
31210 Los Arcos (Navarra)
☎: +34 948 640 811 - Fax: +34 948 441 060
info@fernandezdearcaya.com
www.fernandezdearcaya.com

VIÑA PERGUITA 2010 T ROBLE
80% tempranillo, 15% cabernet sauvignon, 5% merlot.

84 Colour: bright cherry, garnet rim. Nose: ripe fruit, fruit preserve. Palate: flavourful, round tannins.

VIÑA PERGUITA 2008 TC
80% tempranillo, 15% cabernet sauvignon, 5% merlot.

87 Colour: cherry, garnet rim. Nose: ripe fruit, creamy oak, sweet spices. Palate: spicy, balanced, ripe fruit, round tannins.

FERNÁNDEZ DE ARCAYA 2007 TR
100% cabernet sauvignon.

90 Colour: bright cherry, garnet rim. Nose: medium intensity, red berry notes, ripe fruit, spicy. Palate: spicy, good acidity, round tannins.

BODEGAS ITURBIDE

Término la Torre, s/n
31350 Peralta (Navarra)
☎: +34 948 750 537 - Fax: +34 647 742 368
bodegasiturbide@bodegasiturbide.com
www.bodegasiturbide.com

NOVEM 2010 RD
100% garnacha.

85 Colour: rose, purple rim. Nose: raspberry, red berry notes, lactic notes, fresh. Palate: fresh, fruity, flavourful, fleshy.

9 NOVEM 2010 T
50% tempranillo, 50% garnacha.

78

BODEGAS LASIERPE

Ribera, s/n
31592 Cintruénigo (Navarra)
☎: +34 948 811 033 - Fax: +34 948 815 160
comercial@bodegacirbonera.com
www.dominiolasierpe.com

FINCA LASIERPE TEMPRANILLO GARNACHA 2010 T
60% tempranillo, 40% garnacha.

83 Colour: cherry, purple rim. Nose: fresh fruit, red berry notes, floral. Palate: flavourful, fruity, good acidity, round tannins.

FLOR DE LASIERPE GARNACHA VIÑAS VIEJAS 2008 T
100% garnacha.

88 Colour: bright cherry. Nose: sweet spices, creamy oak, expressive, fruit expression, red berry notes, earthy notes. Palate: flavourful, fruity, toasty.

DOMINIO LASIERPE 2007 TC
85% tempranillo, 15% cabernet sauvignon.

86 Colour: cherry, garnet rim. Nose: spicy, creamy oak, toasty, ripe fruit. Palate: powerful, flavourful, round tannins.

BODEGAS LEZAUN

Egiarte, 1
31292 Lakar (Navarra)
☎: +34 948 541 339 - Fax: +34 948 536 055
info@lezaun.com
www.lezaun.com

EGIARTE ROSADO 2010 RD
100% garnacha.

85 Colour: light cherry. Nose: medium intensity, fresh, floral. Palate: powerful, flavourful, fruity, good acidity, balanced.

LEZAUN TEMPRANILLO 2010 T MACERACIÓN CARBÓNICA
100% tempranillo.

90 Colour: cherry, purple rim. Nose: balanced, expressive, red berry notes, fresh fruit. Palate: fruity, flavourful, good acidity, balanced.

EGIARTE 2010 T
tempranillo, garnacha, merlot.

88 Colour: cherry, purple rim. Nose: red berry notes, ripe fruit, balanced. Palate: good structure, fruity, easy to drink, great length.

LEZAUN 2010 T
tempranillo.

85 Colour: deep cherry, purple rim. Nose: spicy, fruit preserve. Palate: fruity, flavourful, ripe fruit.

LEZAUN GAZAGA 2009 T ROBLE
50% tempranillo, 15% merlot, 35% cabernet sauvignon.

89 Color bright cherry. Aroma ripe fruit, sweet spices, creamy oak, expressive. Taste flavourful, fruity, toasty, round tannins.

LEZAUN 2007 TC
50% tempranillo, 35% cabernet sauvignon, 15% garnacha.

87 Colour: deep cherry, garnet rim. Nose: spicy, ripe fruit, balanced. Palate: flavourful, powerful, good structure.

LEZAUN 2007 TR
tempranillo, garnacha, graciano, cabernet sauvignon.

87 Colour: cherry, garnet rim. Nose: powerfull, warm, spicy. Palate: fleshy, spicy, toasty, great length, ripe fruit.

EGIARTE 2002 T
merlot, cabernet sauvignon, tempranillo.

89 Colour: cherry, garnet rim. Nose: ripe fruit, spicy, creamy oak, toasty, mineral. Palate: powerful, flavourful, toasty, round tannins.

EGIARTE 2002 TC
graciano, tempranillo.

86 Colour: cherry, garnet rim. Nose: creamy oak, sweet spices, old leather. Palate: good structure, flavourful, ripe fruit.

BODEGAS LOGOS

Avda. de los Fueros, 18
31522 Monteagudo (Navarra)
☎: +34 941 398 008 - Fax: +34 941 398 070

LOGOS 2010 RD
100% garnacha.

86 Colour: onion pink. Nose: candied fruit, red berry notes, floral. Palate: fine bitter notes, good acidity.

LOGOS II 2006 TC
40% garnacha, 40% cabernet sauvignon, 20% tempranillo.

87 Colour: bright cherry. Nose: sweet spices, creamy oak, candied fruit. Palate: flavourful, fruity, toasty, round tannins.

LOGOS I 2004 T
40% garnacha, 30% tempranillo, 30% cabernet sauvignon.

90 Colour: dark-red cherry. Nose: scrubland, toasty, sweet spices, ripe fruit. Palate: fine bitter notes, powerful, spicy, round tannins.

BODEGAS MACAYA

Ctra. Berbinzana, 74
31251 Larraga (Navarra)
☎: +34 948 711 549 - Fax: +34 948 711 788
info@bodegasmacaya.com
www.bodegasmacaya.com

CONDADO DE ALMARA FINCA LINTE 2009 T
100% tempranillo.

86 Colour: bright cherry. Nose: ripe fruit, sweet spices, creamy oak. Palate: flavourful, fruity, toasty.

CONDADO DE ALMARA SELECCIÓN 2008 T
100% tempranillo.

87 Colour: cherry, garnet rim. Nose: ripe fruit, spicy, creamy oak, toasty. Palate: powerful, flavourful, toasty, fleshy.

CONDADO DE ALMARA 2007 TR
70% tempranillo, 30% cabernet sauvignon.

88 Colour: cherry, garnet rim. Nose: sweet spices, creamy oak, ripe fruit. Palate: spicy, easy to drink.

CONDADO DE ALMARA 2007 TC
50% tempranillo, 50% cabernet sauvignon.

88 Colour: cherry, garnet rim. Nose: ripe fruit, creamy oak, toasty. Palate: powerful, flavourful, toasty, round tannins.

ALMARA CABERNET SAUVIGNON 2005 TR
100% cabernet sauvignon.

88 Colour: cherry, garnet rim. Nose: ripe fruit, spicy, creamy oak, toasty, wild herbs. Palate: powerful, flavourful, toasty, round tannins.

BODEGAS NAPARRALDE

Crtra. N 113, km 88,400
31591 Corella (Navarra)
☎: +34 948 782 255 - Fax: +34 948 401 182
administracion@naparralde.com
www.upain.es

UPAIN SYRAH SELECCIÓN PRIVADA 2010 T
100% syrah.

87 Colour: cherry, purple rim. Nose: red berry notes, sweet spices, creamy oak. Palate: spicy, easy to drink, fruity.

UPAIN SELECCIÓN PRIVADA GARNACHA 2009 T
100% garnacha.

87 Color bright cherry. Aroma ripe fruit, sweet spices, creamy oak, expressive. Taste flavourful, fruity, toasty, round tannins.

UPAIN SELECCIÓN PRIVADA TRES VARIEDADES 2008 T
33% tempranillo, 33% garnacha, 33% cabernet sauvignon.

87 Colour: bright cherry. Nose: ripe fruit, creamy oak, expressive, cocoa bean. Palate: flavourful, fruity, toasty, spicy.

UPAIN GARNACHA SELECCIÓN 2006 T
100% garnacha.

88 Colour: bright cherry, garnet rim. Nose: sweet spices, complex, cocoa bean, ripe fruit. Palate: good structure, fruity, flavourful.

BODEGAS OCHOA

Alcalde Maillata, 2
31390 Olite (Navarra)
☎: +34 948 740 006 - Fax: +34 948 740 048
info@bodegasochoa.com
www.bodegasochoa.com

OCHOA ROSADO DE LÁGRIMA FINCA EL BOSQUE 2010 RD

88 Colour: brilliant rose. Nose: fresh fruit, wild herbs, medium intensity, dried flowers, red berry notes. Palate: fruity, good acidity, flavourful.

OCHOA TEMPRANILLO 2007 TC

87 Colour: cherry, garnet rim. Nose: spicy, creamy oak, toasty. Palate: powerful, flavourful, toasty, round tannins.

OCHOA MIL GRACIAS GRACIANO 2007 TC
graciano.

86 Colour: bright cherry, garnet rim. Nose: toasty, spicy, ripe fruit. Palate: flavourful, fruity, long.

OCHOA 2005 TR

88 Colour: cherry, garnet rim. Nose: powerfull, fruit liqueur notes, roasted coffee, earthy notes, wet leather. Palate: ripe fruit, creamy, fine tannins.

OCHOA MOSCATEL 2010 BLANCO DULCE
moscatel.

90 Colour: bright yellow. Nose: white flowers, fresh fruit, citrus fruit, maceration notes, expressive. Palate: flavourful, fruity, fresh.

BODEGAS ORVALAIZ

Ctra. Pamplona-Logroño, s/n
31151 Óbanos (Navarra)
☎: +34 948 344 437 - Fax: +34 948 344 401
bodega@orvalaiz.es
www.orvalaiz.es

ORVALAIZ CHARDONNAY 2010 B
100% chardonnay.

86 Colour: bright yellow. Nose: grassy, fresh fruit, floral. Palate: fruity, balanced, good acidity, flavourful.

VIÑA ORVALAIZ 2010 B
90% viura, 10% malvar.

82 Colour: bright straw. Nose: floral, citrus fruit, dried herbs. Palate: good acidity, light-bodied, flavourful, fresh.

ORVALAIZ ROSADO DE LÁGRIMA 2010 RD
100% cabernet sauvignon.

85 Colour: rose, purple rim. Nose: powerfull, ripe fruit, red berry notes, floral, expressive. Palate: fleshy, fruity, fresh.

VIÑA ORVALAIZ ROSADO 2010 RD
90% garnacha, 10% tempranillo.

85 Colour: rose, purple rim. Nose: ripe fruit, red berry notes, floral. Palate: fleshy, fruity, fresh.

VIÑA ORVALAIZ 2010 T
75% tempranillo, 25% cabernet sauvignon.

83 Colour: cherry, purple rim. Nose: grassy, balsamic herbs, red berry notes. Palate: light-bodied, fresh, flavourful, fleshy.

ORVALAIZ CABERNET SAUVIGNON 2009 T ROBLE
100% cabernet sauvignon.

87 Colour: cherry, purple rim. Nose: powerfull, ripe fruit, toasty. Palate: flavourful, good acidity, fine bitter notes.

ORVALAIZ TEMPRANILLO 2009 T ROBLE
100% tempranillo.

86 Colour: cherry, garnet rim. Nose: medium intensity, balanced, ripe fruit, spicy. Palate: fruity, spicy, easy to drink.

ORVALAIZ MERLOT 2009 T ROBLE
100% merlot.

86 Colour: cherry, garnet rim. Nose: red berry notes, ripe fruit, grassy, toasty. Palate: good acidity, light-bodied, flavourful.

ORVALAIZ GARNACHA 2009 T ROBLE
100% garnacha.

84 Colour: cherry, garnet rim. Nose: balsamic herbs, spicy, new oak, fruit preserve. Palate: powerful, flavourful, fleshy.

ORVALAIZ 2007 TC
tempranillo, 30% cabernet sauvignon, 30% merlot.

85 Colour: cherry, garnet rim. Nose: ripe fruit, spicy, creamy oak, toasty. Palate: powerful, flavourful, toasty, fleshy.

SEPTENTRIÓN 2006 TC
85% tempranillo, 15% cabernet sauvignon.

88 Colour: cherry, garnet rim. Nose: ripe fruit, spicy, creamy oak, toasty, complex. Palate: powerful, flavourful, toasty.

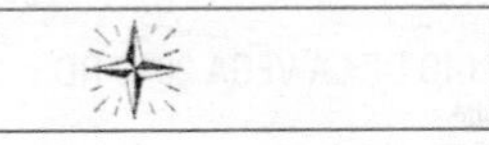

SEPTENTRION
NAVARRA
DENOMINACIÓN DE ORIGEN
crianza
2006

ORVALAIZ 2006 TR
50% tempranillo, 30% cabernet sauvignon, 20% merlot.

87 Colour: bright cherry, garnet rim. Nose: ripe fruit, balsamic herbs, spicy. Palate: good structure, fine bitter notes, powerful.

BODEGAS PAGO DE LARRÁINZAR S.L.

Camino de la Corona s/n
31240 Ayegui (Navarra)
☎: +34 948 550 421 - Fax: +34 948 556 120
info@pagodelarrainzar.com
www.pagodelarrainzar.com

RASO DE LARRAINZAR 2008 T
43% tempranillo, 31% merlot, 23% cabernet sauvignon, 3% garnacha.

90 Colour: cherry, garnet rim. Nose: spicy, creamy oak, toasty, complex, ripe fruit. Palate: powerful, flavourful, toasty, round tannins.

PAGO DE LARRAINZAR 2007 T
40% merlot, 40% cabernet sauvignon, 15% tempranillo, 5% garnacha.

91 Colour: cherry, garnet rim. Nose: ripe fruit, creamy oak, earthy notes, mineral. Palate: flavourful, powerful, fleshy, long.

BODEGAS PALACIO DE LA VEGA

Condesa de la Vega de Pozo, s/n
31263 Dicastillo (Navarra)
☎: +34 948 527 009 - Fax: +34 948 527 333
infopalaciodelavega@ambrosiovelasco.es
www.palaciodelavega.com

PALACIO DE LA VEGA CHARDONNAY 2010 BFB
chardonnay.

89 Colour: bright yellow. Nose: toasty, ripe fruit, spicy, balanced, varietal. Palate: flavourful, good acidity, fruity.

PALACIO DE LA VEGA 2010 RD
garnacha.

88 Color rose, purple rim. Aroma powerfull, ripe fruit, red berry notes, floral, expressive. Taste fleshy, powerful, fruity, fresh.

PALACIO DE LA VEGA CABERNET SAUVIGNON TEMPRANILLO 2008 TC
cabernet sauvignon, tempranillo.

87 Colour: cherry, garnet rim. Nose: ripe fruit, spicy, toasty, characterful, varietal. Palate: powerful, flavourful, toasty, round tannins.

CONDE DE LA VEGA DEL POZO 2004 TR
cabernet sauvignon, tempranillo, merlot.

86 Colour: cherry, garnet rim. Nose: old leather, tobacco, toasty. Palate: spicy, flavourful, fleshy.

BODEGAS PIEDEMONTE

Rua Romana, s/n
31390 Olite (Navarra)
☎: +34 948 712 406 - Fax: +34 948 740 090
bodega@piedemonte.com
www.piedemonte.com

PIEDEMONTE MOSCATEL 2010 B
100% moscatel grano menudo.

88 Colour: golden. Nose: powerfull, floral, honeyed notes, fragrant herbs. Palate: flavourful, sweet, fresh, fruity, good acidity.

PIEDEMONTE GAMMA 2010 B
chardonnay, viura, moscatel.

84 Colour: bright straw. Nose: medium intensity, white flowers, fresh. Palate: fruity, good acidity.

PIEDEMONTE 2010 RD
100% garnacha.

86 Colour: rose, purple rim. Nose: floral, red berry notes, citrus fruit, fresh. Palate: easy to drink, flavourful, fruity, fine bitter notes.

PIEDEMONTE GAMMA 2009 T
tempranillo, merlot, cabernet sauvignon.

86 Colour: bright cherry. Nose: ripe fruit, sweet spices, expressive. Palate: flavourful, fruity, toasty, good acidity.

PIEDEMONTE 2007 TC
34% tempranillo, 33% merlot, 33% cabernet sauvignon.

87 Colour: cherry, garnet rim. Nose: powerfull, ripe fruit, sweet spices. Palate: powerful, flavourful, fine bitter notes.

PIEDEMONTE CABERNET SAUVIGNON 2007 TC
100% cabernet sauvignon.

87 Colour: cherry, garnet rim. Nose: varietal, balsamic herbs, spicy. Palate: fleshy, flavourful, ripe fruit, great length.

PIEDEMONTE MERLOT 2007 TC
100% merlot.

86 Colour: bright cherry. Nose: ripe fruit, sweet spices, creamy oak, varietal. Palate: flavourful, fruity, toasty, round tannins.

PIEDEMONTE +DQUINCE 2006 T
100% merlot.

90 Color cherry, garnet rim. Aroma ripe fruit, spicy, creamy oak, toasty, complex. Taste powerful, flavourful, toasty, round tannins.

PIEDEMONTE 2006 TR
34% tempranillo, 33% merlot, 33% cabernet sauvignon.

89 Colour: bright cherry, garnet rim. Nose: balsamic herbs, spicy, mineral. Palate: good structure, flavourful, spicy, ripe fruit.

BODEGAS PRÍNCIPE DE VIANA

Mayor, 191
31521 Murchante (Navarra)
☎: +34 948 838 640 - Fax: +34 948 818 574
info@principedeviana.com
www.principedeviana.com

PRÍNCIPE DE VIANA CHARDONNAY 2010 B
100% chardonnay.

89 Colour: bright straw. Nose: fresh, fresh fruit, white flowers. Palate: flavourful, fruity, good acidity, balanced.

PRÍNCIPE DE VIANA VENDIMIA TARDÍA 2009 B
100% chardonnay.

90 Colour: golden. Nose: floral, honeyed notes, candied fruit, fragrant herbs. Palate: flavourful, sweet, fruity, good acidity, long.

PRÍNCIPE DE VIANA 2008 TC
40% tempranillo, 30% merlot, 30% cabernet sauvignon.

90 Colour: cherry, garnet rim. Nose: spicy, creamy oak, toasty, ripe fruit. Palate: powerful, flavourful, toasty, round tannins.

PRÍNCIPE DE VIANA GARNACHA 100% 2008 T ROBLE
garnacha.

90 Colour: bright cherry. Nose: sweet spices, creamy oak, expressive, red berry notes. Palate: flavourful, fruity, toasty, round tannins, complex.

PRÍNCIPE DE VIANA 1423 2005 TR
75% tempranillo, 10% merlot, 10% cabernet sauvignon, garnacha.

88 Colour: cherry, garnet rim. Nose: ripe fruit, spicy, complex. Palate: powerful, flavourful, toasty, round tannins.

BODEGAS SAN MARTÍN

Ctra. de Sanguesa, s/n
31495 San Martín de Unx (Navarra)
☎: +34 948 738 294 - Fax: +34 948 738 297
admon@bodegasanmartin.com
www.bodegasanmartin.com

ILAGARES 2010 B
100% viura.

87 Colour: bright straw. Nose: fresh fruit, grassy, white flowers, medium intensity. Palate: balanced, easy to drink, fresh.

ILAGARES 2010 RD
100% garnacha.

86 Colour: rose, purple rim. Nose: fresh, lactic notes, red berry notes, expressive. Palate: light-bodied, fresh, fruity, fleshy.

SEÑORÍO DE UNX GARNACHA 2010 T
garnacha.

84 Colour: cherry, purple rim. Nose: jasmine, ripe fruit, balsamic herbs. Palate: fleshy, flavourful, easy to drink.

ILAGARES 2010 T
70% tempranillo, garnacha, merlot, cabernet sauvignon.

83 Colour: cherry, garnet rim. Nose: scrubland, medium intensity, fruit expression. Palate: powerful, spicy, fine bitter notes.

ALMA DE UNX 2007 T
garnacha.

86 Colour: cherry, purple rim. Nose: red berry notes, cocoa bean, creamy oak. Palate: flavourful, harsh oak tannins, ripe fruit.

SEÑORÍO DE UNX 2007 TC
80% tempranillo, 20% garnacha.

84 Colour: bright cherry, garnet rim. Nose: spicy, powerfull, balsamic herbs, toasty. Palate: flavourful, fruity, spicy.

SEÑORÍO DE UNX 2004 TR
90% tempranillo, 10% garnacha.

89 Colour: cherry, garnet rim. Nose: ripe fruit, spicy, cocoa bean. Palate: good structure, flavourful, balanced, round tannins.

BODEGAS URABAIN

Ctra. Estella, 21
31262 Allo (Navarra)
☎: +34 948 523 011 - Fax: +34 948 523 409
vinos@bodegasurabain.com
www.bodegasurabain.com

URABAIN CHARDONNAY 2010 B
100% chardonnay.

88 Color bright straw. Aroma fresh, fresh fruit, white flowers, expressive. Taste flavourful, fruity, good acidity, balanced.

URABAIN ROSADO DE LÁGRIMA 2010 RD
100% merlot.

85 Colour: rose, purple rim. Nose: raspberry, floral, fresh. Palate: light-bodied, fresh, fruity, flavourful.

PRADO DE CHICA 2009 T
100% merlot.

88 Colour: cherry, garnet rim. Nose: ripe fruit, sweet spices, creamy oak, toasty. Palate: good structure, powerful, spicy.

BODEGAS VALCARLOS

Ctra. Circunvalación, s/n
31210 Los Arcos (Navarra)
☎: +34 948 640 806 - Fax: +34 948 640 866
info@bodegasvalcarlos.com
www.bodegasvalcarlos.com

FORTIUS CHARDONNAY 2010 B
100% chardonnay.

87 Colour: bright straw. Nose: fresh, white flowers, ripe fruit. Palate: flavourful, fruity, good acidity, balanced.

MARQUÉS DE VALCARLOS VIURA CHARDONNAY 2010 B
viura, chardonnay.

85 Colour: bright straw. Nose: grapey, dried herbs, ripe fruit. Palate: light-bodied, fresh, fruity.

FORTIUS 2010 B
viura, chardonnay.

84 Colour: bright straw. Nose: grassy, floral, fresh. Palate: fruity, easy to drink, good finish.

MARQUÉS DE VALCARLOS CHARDONNAY 2010 B
100% chardonnay.

83 Colour: bright straw. Nose: fragrant herbs, faded flowers, citrus fruit. Palate: light-bodied, flavourful, fresh, fruity.

FORTIUS 2010 RD
tempranillo, merlot.

86 Colour: rose, purple rim. Nose: red berry notes, floral, expressive. Palate: fleshy, fruity, fresh.

MARQUÉS DE VALCARLOS 2010 RD
tempranillo, merlot.

85 Colour: light cherry. Nose: medium intensity, fresh fruit. Palate: fruity, flavourful, good finish, good acidity.

FORTIUS TEMPRANILLO 2009 T
tempranillo.

87 Colour: cherry, purple rim. Nose: floral, red berry notes, powerfull, fresh. Palate: good acidity, fresh, fruity, flavourful.

MARQUÉS DE VALCARLOS TEMPRANILLO 2009 T
tempranillo.

86 Color cherry, purple rim. Aroma expressive, fresh fruit, red berry notes, floral. Taste flavourful, fruity, good acidity, round tannins.

FORTIUS MERLOT 2007 TC
100% merlot.

88 Colour: deep cherry, garnet rim. Nose: ripe fruit, powerfull, balanced, wild herbs. Palate: balanced, good structure, fruity.

MARQUÉS DE VALCARLOS 2007 TC
tempranillo, cabernet sauvignon.

86 Colour: cherry, garnet rim. Nose: ripe fruit, spicy, toasty, complex. Palate: flavourful, toasty, round tannins.

FORTIUS 2007 TC
tempranillo, cabernet sauvignon.

86 Colour: cherry, garnet rim. Nose: ripe fruit, spicy, creamy oak, toasty, fine reductive notes. Palate: powerful, flavourful, toasty.

FORTIUS 2005 TR
tempranillo, cabernet sauvignon.

87 Colour: pale ruby, brick rim edge. Nose: spicy, old leather, cigar, creamy oak, ripe fruit. Palate: good acidity, flavourful, fleshy.

MARQUÉS DE VALCARLOS 2005 TR
tempranillo, cabernet sauvignon.

86 Colour: cherry, garnet rim. Nose: ripe fruit, expressive, sweet spices, toasty. Palate: powerful, flavourful, rich, fleshy.

FORTIUS 2001 TGR
tempranillo, cabernet sauvignon.

88 Colour: pale ruby, brick rim edge. Nose: elegant, spicy, fine reductive notes, aged wood nuances, fruit liqueur notes. Palate: spicy, fine tannins, elegant, long, fleshy.

MARQUÉS DE VALCARLOS 1999 TGR
tempranillo, cabernet sauvignon.

87 Color pale ruby, brick rim edge. Aroma elegant, spicy, fine reductive notes, wet leather, aged wood nuances, fruit liqueur notes. Taste spicy, fine tannins, elegant, long.

BODEGAS VEGA DEL CASTILLO

Rua Romana, 7
31390 Olite (Navarra)
☎: +34 948 740 012 - Fax: +34 948 741 074
info@vegadelcastillo.com
www.vegadelcastillo.com

VEGA DEL CASTILLO ROSADO DE LÁGRIMA 2010 RD
garnacha.

86 Colour: rose, purple rim. Nose: red berry notes, raspberry. Palate: fruity, good structure, ripe fruit, good acidity.

MERAK VEGA DEL CASTILLO 2007 T
50% merlot, 25% cabernet sauvignon, 25% tempranillo.

88 Colour: cherry, garnet rim. Nose: spicy, dark chocolate, ripe fruit, toasty. Palate: powerful, flavourful, fleshy.

DUBHE 2007 T ROBLE
50% merlot, 25% cabernet sauvignon, 25% tempranillo.

88 Colour: bright cherry. Nose: ripe fruit, sweet spices, creamy oak, expressive. Palate: flavourful, fruity, toasty, fleshy.

AUZOLÁN LLAVERO ECOLÓGICO 2007 TC
cabernet sauvignon.

86 Colour: cherry, garnet rim. Nose: overripe fruit, balsamic herbs, spicy, toasty. Palate: good acidity, flavourful, fleshy.

VEGA DEL CASTILLO 2006 TR
50% tempranillo, 25% merlot, 25% cabernet sauvignon.

90 Color cherry, garnet rim. Aroma ripe fruit, spicy, creamy oak, toasty, complex. Taste powerful, flavourful, toasty, round tannins.

BODEGAS VIÑA MAGAÑA

San Miguel, 9
31523 Barillas (Navarra)
☎: +34 948 850 034 - Fax: +34 948 851 536
bodegas@vinamagana.com
www.vinamagana.com

VIÑA MAGAÑA MERLOT 2009 TR
100% merlot.

88 Colour: cherry, garnet rim. Nose: powerfull, toasty, aged wood nuances. Palate: powerful, flavourful, fine bitter notes.

MAGAÑA CALCHETAS 2008 T

92 Colour: cherry, garnet rim. Nose: powerfull, characterful, complex, mineral. Palate: powerful, flavourful, spicy, ripe fruit.

BARÓN DE MAGAÑA 2007 TC
merlot, cabernet sauvignon, syrah.

92 Colour: cherry, garnet rim. Nose: ripe fruit, spicy, creamy oak, toasty, characterful, aromatic coffee, dark chocolate. Palate: powerful, flavourful, toasty, round tannins.

DIGNUS 2007 TC
merlot, tempranillo, cabernet sauvignon.

90 Colour: cherry, garnet rim. Nose: powerfull, candied fruit, warm, toasty. Palate: flavourful, powerful, spicy, ripe fruit.

BODEGAS Y VIÑEDOS ARTAZU

Mayor, 3
31109 Artazu (Navarra)
☎: +34 945 600 119 - Fax: +34 945 600 850
artazu@artadi.com

SANTA CRUZ DE ARTAZU 2008 T
garnacha.

91 Colour: bright cherry. Nose: fruit expression, red berry notes, fragrant herbs, scrubland, balsamic herbs, creamy oak, sweet spices.

BODEGAS Y VIÑEDOS QUADERNA VIA

Ctra. Estella - Logroño, Km. 4
31241 Iguzquiza (Navarra)
☎: +34 948 554 083 - Fax: +34 948 556 540
comercial@quadernavia.com
www.quadernavia.com

QUADERNA VIA ESPECIAL 2009 T
tempranillo, cabernet sauvignon.

86 Colour: bright cherry, garnet rim. Nose: ripe fruit, balsamic herbs, wild herbs. Palate: good structure, fruity, spicy.

QV QUADERNA VIA 2008 T

87 Colour: deep cherry, garnet rim. Nose: creamy oak, dark chocolate, candied fruit. Palate: good structure, ripe fruit, spicy.

QUADERNA VIA 2006 RESERVA

89 Colour: cherry, garnet rim. Nose: toasty, ripe fruit, wild herbs, cocoa bean, sweet spices. Palate: balanced, fleshy, balsamic.

CAMINO DEL VILLAR

Camino del Villar. N-161, Km. 3
31591 Corella (Navarra)
☎: +34 948 401 321 - Fax: +34 948 781 414
sales@vinaaliaga.com
www.vinaaliaga.com

ALIAGA CARLANTONIO 2010 B
100% chardonnay.

88 Colour: bright yellow. Nose: powerfull, ripe fruit, creamy oak, fragrant herbs. Palate: rich, flavourful, fresh, good acidity.

ALIAGA DOSCARLOS 2010 B

87 Colour: bright yellow. Nose: dried flowers, ripe fruit, wild herbs. Palate: rich, powerful, flavourful, fleshy.

ALIAGA LÁGRIMA DE GARNACHA 2010 RD
garnacha.

86 Colour: rose, purple rim. Nose: lactic notes, floral, red berry notes, fresh fruit. Palate: fleshy, powerful, flavourful, rich, easy to drink.

ALIAGA TEMPRANILLO 2009 T
tempranillo.

80 Colour: cherry, garnet rim. Nose: ripe fruit, faded flowers, slightly evolved. Palate: green, light-bodied, slightly evolved.

VIÑA ALIAGA COLECCIÓN PRIVADA 2007 TC
85% tempranillo, 15% cabernet sauvignon.

87 Colour: cherry, garnet rim. Nose: ripe fruit, mineral, spicy, toasty. Palate: good acidity, powerful, flavourful, fleshy, long.

VIÑA ALIAGA GARNACHA VIEJA 2007 T
100% garnacha.

86 Colour: cherry, garnet rim. Nose: ripe fruit, balsamic herbs, spicy, toasty. Palate: light-bodied, flavourful, ripe fruit.

ALIAGA CUVÉE 2006 T
85% tempranillo, 15% cabernet sauvignon.

84 Colour: pale ruby, brick rim edge. Nose: ripe fruit, scrubland, fine reductive notes, toasty. Palate: powerful, flavourful, fleshy, toasty.

ALIAGA RESERVA DE LA FAMILIA 2005 TR
75% tempranillo, 25% cabernet sauvignon.

86 Colour: cherry, garnet rim. Nose: ripe fruit, spicy, creamy oak, toasty, old leather. Palate: powerful, flavourful, toasty.

VIÑA ALIAGA ANTONIO CORPUS 2002 T
100% garnacha.

87 Colour: pale ruby, brick rim edge. Nose: elegant, spicy, fine reductive notes, wet leather, aged wood nuances, fruit liqueur notes. Palate: spicy, fine tannins, long, round.

VIÑA ALIAGA VENDIMIA SELECCIONADA 2001 TR
70% tempranillo, 30% cabernet sauvignon.

87 Colour: pale ruby, brick rim edge. Nose: fine reductive notes, wet leather, aged wood nuances, fruit liqueur notes, toasty, smoky. Palate: spicy, elegant, long.

CASTILLO DE MONJARDÍN

Viña Rellanada, s/n
31242 Villamayor de Monjardín (Navarra)
☎: +34 948 537 412 - Fax: +34 948 537 436
sonia@monjardin.es
www.monjardin.es

CASTILLO DE MONJARDÍN CHARDONNAY 2010 B
chardonnay.

88 Colour: bright yellow. Nose: fruit expression, varietal, medium intensity, balanced, expressive, floral. Palate: fresh, fruity, good acidity.

CASTILLO DE MONJARDÍN CHARDONNAY 2008 BFB
chardonnay.

91 Colour: bright yellow. Nose: powerfull, sweet spices, creamy oak, fragrant herbs. Palate: rich, flavourful, fresh, good acidity.

CASTILLO DE MONJARDÍN CHARDONNAY 2007 B RESERVA
chardonnay.

90 Colour: bright straw. Nose: candied fruit, honeyed notes, white flowers. Palate: flavourful, fleshy, complex, good acidity.

CASTILLO DE MONJARDÍN MERLOT 2010 RD
merlot.

88 Colour: brilliant rose. Nose: citrus fruit, fresh fruit, red berry notes. Palate: fruity, fresh, easy to drink, flavourful, great length.

CASTILLO DE MONJARDÍN 2008 TC
cabernet sauvignon, merlot, tempranillo.

86 Colour: cherry, garnet rim. Nose: ripe fruit, spicy, creamy oak, toasty, old leather. Palate: powerful, flavourful, toasty.

CASTILLO DE MONJARDÍN DEYO 2007 TC
merlot.

89 Colour: cherry, garnet rim. Nose: spicy, creamy oak, toasty. Palate: powerful, flavourful, toasty, round tannins.

CASTILLO DE MONJARDÍN FINCA LOS CARASOLES 2005 TR
cabernet sauvignon, tempranillo.

86 Colour: cherry, garnet rim. Nose: ripe fruit, spicy, creamy oak, toasty. Palate: powerful, flavourful, toasty, balsamic.

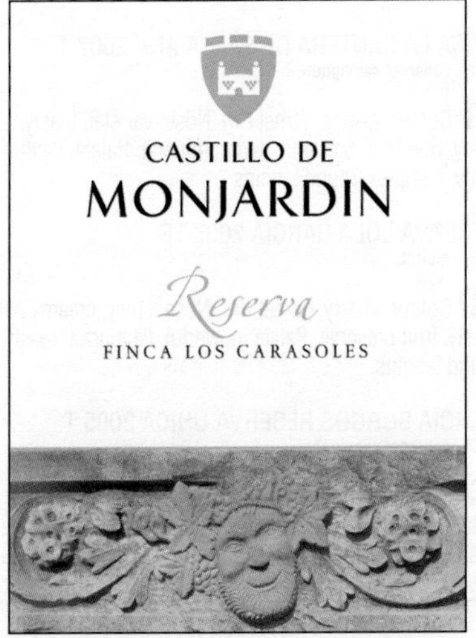

CRIANZAS Y VIÑEDOS R. REVERTE

Lejalde, 43
31593 Fitero (Navarra)
☎: +34 948 366 031 - Fax: +34 948 183 487
comercial@rafaelreverte.es
www.rafaelreverte.es

TIFERO 2010 B
chardonnay.

84 Colour: pale. Nose: medium intensity, fresh fruit, citrus fruit. Palate: flavourful, fruity, fresh.

TIFERO 2010 RD
garnacha.

86 Colour: raspberry rose. Nose: red berry notes, citrus fruit. Palate: fruity, fresh, good acidity, correct, fine bitter notes.

REVERTE 2010 T MACERACIÓN CARBÓNICA
tempranillo.

89 Colour: cherry, purple rim. Nose: red berry notes, raspberry, fresh, expressive, floral. Palate: light-bodied, flavourful, fruity, fleshy.

ODIPUS GRACIANO 2010 T
graciano.

86 Colour: bright cherry. Nose: ripe fruit, sweet spices, creamy oak. Palate: flavourful, fruity, toasty.

ODIPUS MAZUELO 2010 T
mazuelo.

86 Colour: cherry, purple rim. Nose: expressive, fresh fruit, red berry notes, floral. Palate: flavourful, fruity, good acidity, easy to drink.

ODIPUS GARNACHA 2009 T
garnacha.

88 Colour: cherry, purple rim. Nose: toasty, spicy, ripe fruit. Palate: good structure, ripe fruit, balanced, spicy.

CISTUM 2009 T
garnacha.

88 Colour: cherry, garnet rim. Nose: ripe fruit, fruit expression, smoky, roasted coffee. Palate: fine bitter notes, good acidity, ripe fruit.

SEPTO 2008 TC
garnacha, tempranillo, mazuelo, graciano, merlot, otras.

89 Color cherry, garnet rim. Aroma ripe fruit, spicy, creamy oak, toasty, complex. Taste powerful, flavourful, toasty, round tannins.

DOMAINES LUPIER

Monseñor Justo Goizueta, 4
31495 San Martín de Unx (Navarra)
☎: +34 639 622 111
info@domaineslupier.com
www.domaineslupier.com

DOMAINES LUPIER EL TERROIR 2008 T
100% garnacha.

94 Colour: dark-red cherry, garnet rim. Nose: candied fruit, balsamic herbs, scrubland, mineral, spicy, creamy oak. Palate: good acidity, flavourful, fleshy, complex.

DOMAINES LUPIER LA DAMA VIÑAS VIEJAS 2008 T
100% garnacha.

93 Colour: deep cherry. Nose: elegant, fresh, varietal, complex, fruit expression. Palate: elegant, balanced, fresh, fruity, mineral, spicy, fruity aftestaste.

FINCA ALBRET

Ctra. Cadreita-Villafranca, s/n
31515 Cadreita (Navarra)
☎: +34 948 406 806 - Fax: +34 948 406 699
info@fincaalbret.com
www.fincaalbret.com

ALBRET CHARDONNAY 2010 BFB
100% chardonnay.

89 Colour: bright yellow. Nose: powerfull, ripe fruit, sweet spices, fragrant herbs. Palate: rich, flavourful, fresh, good acidity.

ALBRET 2010 RD
100% garnacha.

88 Colour: rose, purple rim. Nose: powerfull, ripe fruit, red berry notes, floral. Palate: fleshy, powerful, fruity, fresh, rich.

ALBRET 2008 TC
50% tempranillo, 30% cabernet sauvignon, 20% merlot.

90 Colour: cherry, garnet rim. Nose: ripe fruit, spicy, creamy oak, toasty, complex. Palate: powerful, flavourful, toasty, fleshy.

ALBRET 2006 TR
70% tempranillo, 15% merlot, 15% cabernet sauvignon.

91 Colour: cherry, garnet rim. Nose: ripe fruit, spicy, creamy oak, toasty, complex. Palate: powerful, flavourful, toasty, fleshy, rich.

ALBRET LA VIÑA DE MI MADRE 2006 TR
95% cabernet sauvignon, 5% merlot.

89 Colour: bright cherry, garnet rim. Nose: medium intensity, ripe fruit, balsamic herbs. Palate: flavourful, good acidity, round tannins.

GARCÍA BURGOS

Finca Cantera de Santa Ana, s/n
31521 Murchante (Navarra)
☎: +34 948 847 734 - Fax: +34 948 847 734
info@bodegasgarciaburgos.com
www.bodegasgarciaburgos.com

GARCÍA BURGOS VENDIMIA SELECCIONADA 2009 T
60% cabernet sauvignon, 40% merlot.

91 Colour: cherry, garnet rim. Nose: mineral, varietal, spicy, toasty, balsamic herbs. Palate: flavourful, spicy, long, fine bitter notes.

SH 2009 T
100% syrah.

90 Colour: cherry, purple rim. Nose: powerfull, ripe fruit, sweet spices. Palate: powerful, fine bitter notes, long.

FINCA LA CANTERA DE SANTA ANA 2007 T
100% cabernet sauvignon.

91 Colour: cherry, garnet rim. Nose: varietal, toasty, spicy, ripe fruit, balsamic herbs, mineral. Palate: flavourful, fruity, complex, round tannins.

RESERVA LOLA GARCÍA 2006 TR
100% merlot.

90 Colour: cherry, garnet rim. Nose: spicy, creamy oak, toasty, fruit preserve. Palate: powerful, flavourful, toasty, round tannins.

GARCÍA BURGOS RESERVA UNICA 2005 T
100% cabernet sauvignon.

92 Colour: deep cherry, garnet rim. Nose: red berry notes, ripe fruit, mineral, spicy. Palate: good structure, fleshy, long.

IRACHE

Monasterio de Irache, 1
31240 Ayegui (Navarra)
☎: +34 948 551 932 - Fax: +34 948 554 954
irache@irache.com
www.irache.com

CASTILLO IRACHE GARNACHA ROSADO LÁGRIMA 2010 RD
100% garnacha.

85 Colour: rose, purple rim. Nose: fresh fruit, red berry notes, floral. Palate: good acidity, balanced, fruity.

CASTILLO IRACHE TEMPRANILLO 2010 T
100% tempranillo.

83 Colour: cherry, purple rim. Nose: ripe fruit, herbaceous, short. Palate: fresh, light-bodied, fine bitter notes.

IRACHE 2004 TR
60% tempranillo, 20% cabernet sauvignon, 20% merlot.

83 Colour: ruby red, garnet rim. Nose: tobacco, old leather, cocoa bean, sweet spices, ripe fruit. Palate: spirituous, good acidity, unctuous.

LA CALANDRIA (JAVIER CONTINENTE GAZTELAKUTO)

Camino de Aspra, s/n
31521 Murchante (Navarra)
☎: +34 630 904 327
luis@lacalandria.org
www.lacalandria.org

SONROJO 2010 RD
garnacha.

87 Colour: rose, purple rim. Nose: powerfull, ripe fruit, red berry notes, floral, expressive. Palate: fleshy, fruity, fresh, light-bodied, easy to drink.

VOLANDERA 2010 T MACERACIÓN CARBÓNICA
garnacha.

92 Colour: cherry, purple rim. Nose: red berry notes, floral, fresh fruit, mineral, grassy. Palate: flavourful, fruity, good acidity, round tannins.

CIENTRUENOS 2010 T BARRICA
garnacha.

92 Colour: bright cherry. Nose: sweet spices, creamy oak, expressive, red berry notes, mineral. Palate: flavourful, fruity, toasty, round tannins. Personality.

LADERAS DE MONTEJURRA

Paraje de Argonga, s/n
31263 Dicastillo (Navarra)
☎: +34 638 218 727
info@laderasdemontejurra.com
www.laderasdemontejurra.com

LA MERCED 2010 B
malvasía.

88 Colour: deep cherry. Nose: fresh fruit, citrus fruit, spicy, white flowers. Palate: flavourful, good acidity, long.

AMBURZA 2009 T
cabernet sauvignon, graciano, garnacha.

86 Colour: black cherry, garnet rim. Nose: earthy notes, ripe fruit, wild herbs, complex. Palate: spicy, flavourful, fruity.

LONG WINES

Avda. Monte, 46
28723 Algete (Madrid)
☎: +34 916 221 305 - Fax: +34 916 220 029
raquel@longwines.com
www.longwines.com

PUERTO DEL MONTE 2010 RD
100% garnacha.

90 Colour: rose, purple rim. Nose: powerfull, ripe fruit, red berry notes, floral, expressive. Palate: fleshy, powerful, fruity, fresh, fine bitter notes.

PUERTO DEL MONTE 2010 T
100% garnacha.

84 Colour: bright cherry, purple rim. Nose: red berry notes, balanced, grassy. Palate: flavourful, good acidity.

LUIS GURPEGUI MUGA

Ctra. Pamplona, s/n
31330 Villafranca (Navarra)
☎: +34 948 670 050 - Fax: +34 948 670 259
bodegas@gurpegui.es
www.gurpegui.es

MONTE ORY 2010 RD
garnacha.

87 Colour: raspberry rose. Nose: floral, red berry notes, expressive, raspberry. Palate: good acidity, fresh, fruity, flavourful.

MONTE ORY TEMPRANILLO-MERLOT 2010 T
tempranillo, merlot.

87 Colour: cherry, purple rim. Nose: red berry notes, ripe fruit, floral. Palate: flavourful, fruity, good acidity, easy to drink.

MONTE ORY TEMPRANILLO - CABERNET SAUVIGNON 2010 T
tempranillo, cabernet sauvignon.

83 Colour: cherry, purple rim. Nose: red berry notes, ripe fruit, dried flowers, balsamic herbs. Palate: fresh, light-bodied, flavourful, green.

MONTE ORY 2007 TC
tempranillo, garnacha, cabernet sauvignon.

85 Colour: cherry, garnet rim. Nose: ripe fruit, cocoa bean, sweet spices, toasty. Palate: good acidity, correct, flavourful, toasty.

MARCO REAL

Ctra. Pamplona-Zaragoza, Km. 38
31390 Olite (Navarra)
☎: +34 948 712 193 - Fax: +34 948 712 343
info@familiabelasco.com
www.familiabelasco.com

HOMENAJE 2010 B
viura, chardonnay.

86 Colour: bright straw. Nose: fresh, tropical fruit, white flowers. Palate: fruity, flavourful, balanced, easy to drink.

HOMENAJE 2010 RD
garnacha.

89 Colour: rose, purple rim. Nose: fresh fruit, raspberry, lactic notes, expressive. Palate: flavourful, fruity, fine bitter notes.

MARCO REAL COLECCIÓN PRIVADA 2008 TC
tempranillo, cabernet sauvignon, merlot, graciano.

90 Colour: cherry, garnet rim. Nose: ripe fruit, old leather, spicy, creamy oak. Palate: balanced, powerful, flavourful, complex.

MARCO REAL RESERVA DE FAMILIA 2007 TR
tempranillo, cabernet sauvignon, merlot, graciano.

91 Colour: black cherry. Nose: ripe fruit, complex, cocoa bean, sweet spices, toasty, mineral. Palate: good acidity, round, powerful, flavourful, fleshy, complex.

HOMENAJE 2007 TC
tempranillo, merlot.

89 Colour: cherry, garnet rim. Nose: red berry notes, ripe fruit, fine reductive notes, sweet spices, toasty. Palate: round, powerful, flavourful, round tannins.

MONASTIR

Gral. Vara del Rey, 7- 1º dcha.
26003 Logroño (La Rioja)
☎: +34 941 271 217 - Fax: +34 941 272 911
info@monastir.es
www.monastir.es

MONASTIR V 2008 T
tempranillo, cabernet sauvignon.

90 Colour: cherry, garnet rim. Nose: ripe fruit, spicy, creamy oak, toasty, balsamic herbs. Palate: powerful, flavourful, toasty.

NEKEAS

Las Huertas, s/n
31154 Añorbe (Navarra)
☎: +34 948 350 296 - Fax: +34 948 350 300
nekeas@nekeas.com
www.nekeas.com

NEKEAS CHARDONNAY "CUVÉE ALLIER" 2009 BFB
100% chardonnay.

90 Colour: bright straw. Nose: medium intensity, candied fruit, sweet spices, fragrant herbs. Palate: flavourful, ripe fruit, spicy.

NEKEAS CEPA X CEPA 2009 T
100% garnacha.

88 Colour: bright cherry. Nose: sweet spices, creamy oak, red berry notes. Palate: flavourful, fruity, toasty, round tannins.

EL CHAPARRAL DE VEGA SINDOA OLD VINE GARNACHA 2009 T
100% garnacha.

85 Colour: cherry, purple rim. Nose: red berry notes, ripe fruit, spicy, toasty. Palate: flavourful, good acidity, round tannins.

NEKEAS 2008 TC
60% cabernet sauvignon, 40% tempranillo.

88 Colour: bright cherry. Nose: ripe fruit, sweet spices, creamy oak. Palate: flavourful, fruity, toasty, round tannins.

NEKEAS CABERNET SAUVIGNON MERLOT 2007 TR
cabernet sauvignon, merlot.

88 Colour: cherry, garnet rim. Nose: ripe fruit, spicy, creamy oak, toasty, fine reductive notes. Palate: powerful, toasty, round tannins, fine bitter notes.

IZAR DE NEKEAS 2006 TR
40% cabernet sauvignon, 30% tempranillo, 30% merlot.

88 Colour: cherry, garnet rim. Nose: ripe fruit, spicy, cocoa bean. Palate: good structure, flavourful, round tannins, good acidity.

PAGO DE SAN GABRIEL

Paraje La Sarda. N-232, Km. 84,4
31590 Castejón (Navarra)
☎: +34 629 443 316 - Fax: +34 944 911 146
luisolarra@pagosangabriel.com
www.pagosangabriel.com

PRADOMAYOR DE ZUBIOLA 2008 T
80% cabernet sauvignon, 20% merlot.

89 Color bright cherry. Aroma ripe fruit, sweet spices, creamy oak, expressive. Taste flavourful, fruity, toasty, round tannins.

ZUBIOLA 2007 T
85% cabernet sauvignon, 15% merlot.

90 Colour: cherry, garnet rim. Nose: ripe fruit, spicy, creamy oak, toasty. Palate: powerful, flavourful, toasty, round tannins.

ZUBIOLA LOTE Nº 1 EDICIÓN LIMITADA 2007 T
90% cabernet sauvignon, 10% merlot.

89 Colour: deep cherry, garnet rim. Nose: sweet spices, ripe fruit, fine reductive notes, balanced. Palate: fleshy, flavourful, good structure.

SEÑORÍO DE ANDIÓN

Ctra. Pamplona-Zaragoza, Km. 38
31390 Olite (Navarra)
☎: +34 948 712 193 - Fax: +34 948 712 343
info@familiabelasco.com
www.familiabelasco.com

SEÑORÍO DE ANDIÓN MOSCATEL VENDIMIA TARDÍA 2007 B
moscatel.

93 Colour: golden. Nose: powerfull, floral, honeyed notes, candied fruit, fragrant herbs, citrus fruit. Palate: flavourful, sweet, fruity, good acidity, long.

SEÑORÍO DE ANDIÓN 2005 T
tempranillo, merlot, cabernet sauvignon.

92 Colour: cherry, garnet rim. Nose: ripe fruit, spicy, creamy oak, toasty, complex, fine reductive notes, cigar. Palate: powerful, flavourful, toasty, round tannins.

UNZU PROPIEDAD

Barón de la Torre, 4
31592 Cintruénigo (Navarra)
☎: +34 948 812 297 - Fax: +34 948 812 297
info@unzupropiedad.com
www.unzupropiedad.com

FINCAS DE UNZU 2010 RD
75% merlot, 25% garnacha.

90 Colour: rose, purple rim. Nose: powerfull, ripe fruit, red berry notes, floral. Palate: fleshy, powerful, fruity, fresh.

VINÍCOLA CORELLANA

Ctra. del Villar, s/n
31591 Corella (Navarra)
☎: +34 948 780 617 - Fax: +34 948 401 894
info@vinicolacorellana.com
www.vinicolacorellana.com

VIÑA ZORZAL GARNACHA 2010 RD
100% garnacha.

83 Colour: rose, purple rim. Nose: ripe fruit, red berry notes, floral, medium intensity. Palate: fleshy, fruity, fresh.

VIÑA ZORZAL GARNACHA 2010 T
100% garnacha.

87 Colour: cherry, purple rim. Nose: red berry notes, balanced, varietal, balsamic herbs. Palate: flavourful, fruity, good acidity.

VIÑA ZORZAL GRACIANO 2010 T
100% graciano.

77

REYNOBLE 2008 TC
garnacha, tempranillo.

87 Colour: bright cherry. Nose: ripe fruit, sweet spices. Palate: flavourful, fruity, toasty, round tannins.

VINÍCOLA NAVARRA

Avda. Pamplona, 25
31398 Tiebas (Navarra)
☎: +34 948 360 131 - Fax: +34 948 360 544
vinicolanavarra@domecqbodegas.com
www.vinicolanavarra.com

LAS CAMPANAS 2010 B
chardonnay, viura.

85 Colour: bright straw. Nose: medium intensity, white flowers, fresh fruit. Palate: flavourful, fruity, good acidity.

CASTILLO DE JAVIER 2010 RD
garnacha.

88 Colour: brilliant rose. Nose: red berry notes, wild herbs, fresh fruit, floral. Palate: flavourful, fruity, spicy, easy to drink.

LAS CAMPANAS 2010 RD
garnacha.

86 Colour: rose, purple rim. Nose: fresh fruit, red berry notes, expressive, floral. Palate: fleshy, powerful, flavourful, fresh.

LAS CAMPANAS 2010 T
tempranillo.

88 Colour: cherry, purple rim. Nose: ripe fruit, raspberry. Palate: flavourful, fruity, full.

VIÑA VALDORBA

Ctra. de la Estación, s/n
31395 Garinoain (Navarra)
☎: +34 948 720 505 - Fax: +34 948 720 505
bodegasvaldorba@bodegasvaldorba.com
www.bodegasvaldorba.com

EOLO CHARDONNAY 2010 B
100% chardonnay.

88 Colour: yellow. Nose: varietal, floral, fruit expression. Palate: powerful, flavourful, balanced, fine bitter notes, great length.

EOLO MOSCATEL 2009 B
100% moscatel.

88 Colour: bright yellow. Nose: fresh, fresh fruit, white flowers, expressive. Palate: flavourful, fruity, good acidity, balanced.

EOLO ROSADO SANGRADO 2010 RD
100% garnacha.

87 Colour: rose, purple rim. Nose: expressive, powerfull, red berry notes, violet drops, balsamic herbs. Palate: fresh, fruity, flavourful, fleshy.

EOLO 2010 RD
100% garnacha.

86 Colour: rose, purple rim. Nose: ripe fruit, red berry notes, floral, expressive. Palate: fleshy, fruity, fresh, easy to drink.

EOLO SYRAH 2009 T
100% syrah.

88 Colour: cherry, garnet rim. Nose: balanced, complex, spicy, red berry notes, ripe fruit. Palate: fleshy, spicy, ripe fruit.

EOLO GARNACHA 2009 T
100% garnacha.

84 Colour: cherry, garnet rim. Nose: ripe fruit, expressive, creamy oak, sweet spices. Palate: flavourful, fleshy, spicy, ripe fruit.

EOLO ROBLE 2009 T
50% garnacha, 50% cabernet sauvignon.

84 Colour: cherry, purple rim. Nose: red berry notes, ripe fruit, balsamic herbs. Palate: good acidity, fruity, light-bodied.

EOLO (5 VARIEDADES) 2008 TC
20% cabernet sauvignon, 20% merlot, 20% syrah, 20% tempranillo, 20% garnacha.

86 Colour: cherry, garnet rim. Nose: ripe fruit, fruit preserve, sweet spices, toasty. Palate: good acidity, flavourful, fleshy.

GRAN EOLO 2006 TR
30% tempranillo, 30% cabernet sauvignon, 40% merlot.

89 Colour: cherry, garnet rim. Nose: complex, balanced, ripe fruit, fragrant herbs. Palate: good structure, spicy, long, balsamic.

EOLO CRIANZA GARNACHA 2006 TC
100% garnacha.

86 Colour: cherry, garnet rim. Nose: red berry notes, ripe fruit, cocoa bean, dark chocolate, toasty. Palate: good acidity, powerful, flavourful.

CAURO GRAN EOLO 2002 TR
50% cabernet sauvignon, 50% graciano.

89 Colour: cherry, garnet rim. Nose: sweet spices, dark chocolate, ripe fruit, complex, balsamic herbs. Palate: spicy, ripe fruit.

VIÑEDOS DE CALIDAD

Ctra. Tudela, s/n
31591 Corella (Navarra)
☎: +34 948 782 014 - Fax: +34 948 782 164
info@vinosalex.com
www.vinosalex.com

ALEX VIURA 2010 B
viura.

84 Colour: bright straw. Nose: powerfull, ripe fruit, tropical fruit, floral. Palate: flavourful, fruity, ripe fruit.

ALEX GARNACHA 2010 RD
garnacha.

88 Colour: brilliant rose. Nose: red berry notes, fresh fruit, floral, violets, dried herbs. Palate: fruity, easy to drink, good acidity.

ALEX TEMPRANILLO 2010 T
tempranillo.

87 Colour: cherry, purple rim. Nose: red berry notes, fresh fruit, varietal. Palate: fruity, good structure, good acidity.

ONTINAR 14 BARRICAS 2008 T
50% tempranillo, 50% merlot.

89 Colour: bright cherry. Nose: ripe fruit, sweet spices, cocoa bean. Palate: flavourful, fruity, toasty, round tannins.

ALEX 2007 TC
70% tempranillo, 20% merlot, 10% graciano.

84 Colour: bright cherry, garnet rim. Nose: grassy, fresh fruit, spicy. Palate: light-bodied, easy to drink.

ALEX 2010 MOSCATEL
moscatel grano menudo.

89 Colour: bright straw. Nose: tropical fruit, honeyed notes, citrus fruit, balanced. Palate: good acidity, rich, ripe fruit, flavourful.

VIÑEDOS Y BODEGAS ALCONDE

Ctra. de Calahorra, s/n
31260 Lerín (Navarra)
☎: +34 948 530 058 - Fax: +34 948 530 589
info@bodegasalconde.com
www.bodegasalconde.com

VIÑA SARDASOL 2010 B
chardonnay.

88 Colour: bright straw. Nose: powerfull, fresh fruit, tropical fruit, fragrant herbs. Palate: good acidity, light-bodied, powerful, flavourful, fruity.

VIÑA SARDASOL 2010 RD
garnacha.

86 Colour: rose, purple rim. Nose: powerfull, red berry notes, floral, expressive. Palate: fruity, fresh.

BODEGAS ALCONDE SELECCIÓN "TINTO ROBLE" 2009 T ROBLE
60% garnacha, 40% merlot.

85 Colour: cherry, garnet rim. Nose: ripe fruit, expressive, balsamic herbs, toasty. Palate: powerful, flavourful, fleshy.

BODEGAS ALCONDE SELECCIÓN 2007 TC
tempranillo, garnacha, cabernet sauvignon.

87 Color cherry, garnet rim. Aroma ripe fruit, spicy, creamy oak, toasty, complex. Taste powerful, flavourful, toasty, round tannins.

BODEGAS ALCONDE SELECCIÓN TEMPRANILLO 2006 TR
tempranillo.

88 Colour: cherry, garnet rim. Nose: red berry notes, ripe fruit, sweet spices, toasty. Palate: powerful, flavourful, rich, round tannins.

BODEGAS ALCONDE SELECCIÓN GARNACHA 2006 TR
garnacha.

88 Colour: cherry, garnet rim. Nose: ripe fruit, spicy, creamy oak, toasty. Palate: powerful, flavourful, toasty, round tannins.

BODEGAS ALCONDE PREMIUM 2005 TR
tempranillo, garnacha, merlot.

89 Colour: cherry, garnet rim. Nose: old leather, tobacco, cocoa bean, creamy oak, sweet spices. Palate: good acidity, powerful, flavourful.

BARCELONA
TARRAGONA

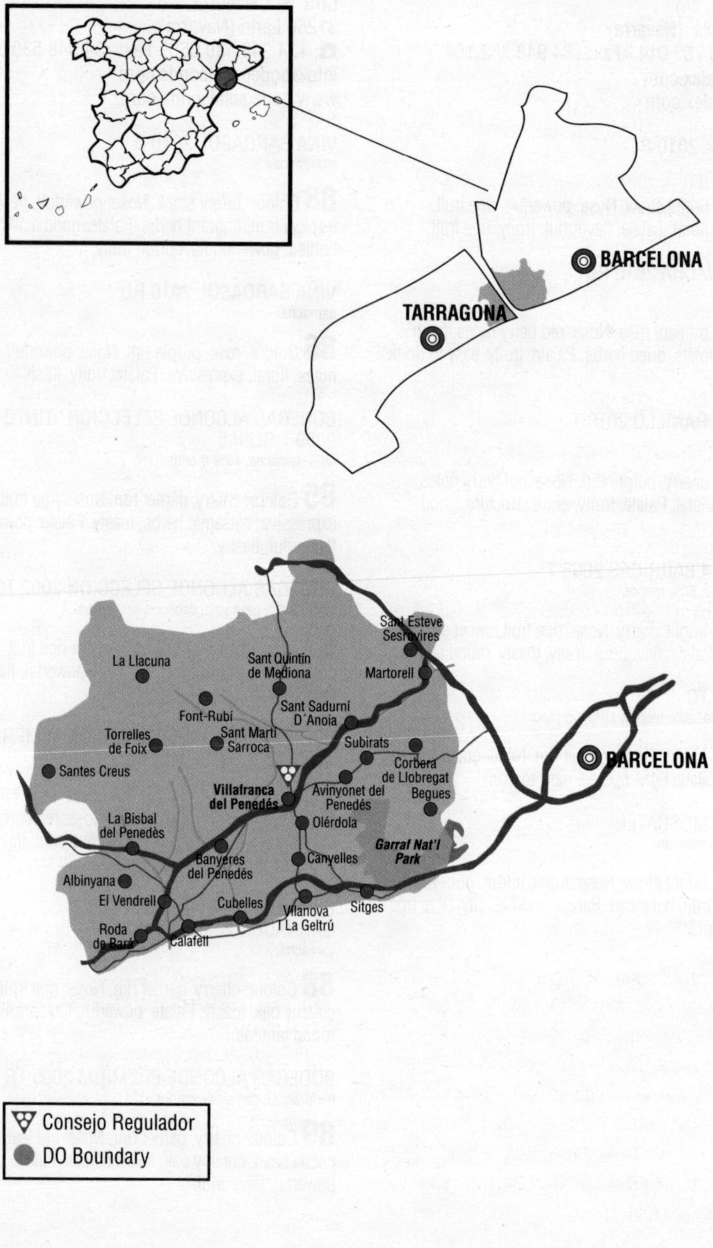

La Llacuna
Sant Quintín de Mediona
Sant Esteve Sesrovires
Martorell
Font-Rubí
Sant Sadurní D´Anoia
Torrelles de Foix
Sant Martí Sarroca
Subirats
Santes Creus
Corbera de Llobregat
BARCELONA
Villafranca del Penedés
Avinyonet del Penedés
Begues
La Bisbal del Penedès
Olérdola
Banyeres del Penedés
Canyelles
Garraf Nat'l Park
Albinyana
El Vendrell
Cubelles
Vilanova I La Geltrú
Sitges
Roda de Barà
Calafell

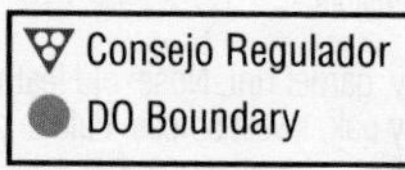

NEWS ABOUT THE VINTAGE:

Sad times for the DO Penedès seem to be coming to an end. The renewal the region initiated just three years ago is finally paying off. Its bet on the white *xarel.lo* grape variety has become a real power force for change. Now a reality, as we revealed in last year's edition of our Guide, *xarel.lo* continues its upward trend, hoping to drag along more and more producers in its wake and showing the clustering, fellowship effect that the region has been missing of late.

Although it is still too early to assess it, white wines from the region seem to be immersed in an upward trend; this year, we have tasted many more and better whites, a real example of how to get the best out a variety (*xarel.lo*) that has an evident potential beyond Cava production or in blends that can convey a truly Mediterranean character. The best samples are Gramona Xarel.lo Font Jui 2009 and Nun Vinya dels Taus, both with 93 points.

Regarding red winemaking we appreciate two different styles: on the one hand, those producers that resort to foreign (French) varieties like *merlot* and *cabernet sauvignon*, fully adapted to the region; an on the other a brave new world of producers interested in undertaking a sort of winemaking "turn of the screw" who have put their bets (and money) on local varieties. The former, the most numerous, have in wineries like Miguel Torres and Alemany i Corrío their best representatives, with wines like Mas la Plana 2008 and Sot Lefriec 2006, which even when made from grapes like *cabernet sauvignon*, manage to show a refined Mediterranean character, as long as they include in their blends even minimal percentages of the local varieties. On the other hand there is a smaller group, although a –maybe– more interesting one given its innovative character, which includes the likes of Jané Ventura Sumoll 2009 and Advent Sumoll 2008 from (respectively) Jané Ventura and Heretat Mont-Rubí.

LOCATION:

In the province of Barcelona, between the pre-coastal Catalonian mountain range and the plains that lead to the Mediterranean coast. There are three different areas: Penedès Superior, Penedès Central or Medio and Bajo Penedès.

CLIMATE:

Mediterranean, in general warm and mild; warmer in the Bajo Penedès region due to the influence of the Mediterranean Sea, with slightly lower temperatures in Medio Penedès and Penedès Superior, where the climate is typically pre-coastal (greater contrasts between maximum and minimum temperatures, more frequent frosts and annual rainfall which at some places can reach 990 litres per square metre).

SOIL:

There is deep soil, not too sandy or too clayey, permeable, which retains the rainwater well. The soil is poor in organic matter and not very fertile.

GRAPE VARIETIES:

WHITE: *Macabeo* (6,622 Ha), *Xarel·lo* (7,833 Ha), *Parellada* (6,045 Ha), *Chardonnay* (1,038 Ha), *Riesling, Gewürztraminer, Chenin Blanc, Moscatel de Alejandría* and *Garnacha Blanca.*
RED: *Garnacha, Merlot* (1,554 Ha), *Cariñena, Ull de Llebre* (*Tempranillo* – 1,507 Ha), *Pinot Noir, Monastrell, Cabernet Sauvignon* (11,487 Ha), *Syrah* and *Sumoll.*

DO PENEDÈS

SUB-REGIONS:

Penedès Superior. The vineyards reach an altitude of 800 m; the traditional, characteristic variety is the Parellada, which is better suited to the cooler regions.
Penedès Central or Medio. Cava makes up a large part of the production in this region; the most abundant traditional varieties are *Macabeo* and *Xarel-lo*.
Bajo Penedès. This is the closest region to the sea, with a lower altitude and wines with a markedly Mediterranean character.

FIGURES:

Vineyard surface: 24,248 – **Wine-Growers:** 3,786 – **Wineries:** 187 – **2010 Harvest rating:** N/A – **Production:** 19,295,282 litres – **Market percentages:** 75,2% domestic. 24,80% export

CONSEJO REGULADOR
Pol. Industrial Domenys II. Plaça Àgora. Apdo. 226
08720 Vilafranca del Penedès (Barcelona)
☎: +34 938 904 811 - Fax: +34 938 904 754
@ dopenedes@dopenedes.es
www.dopenedes.es

GENERAL CHARACTERISTICS OF THE WINES

WHITES	The classical wines of the region, produced with the *Macabeo, Xarel-lo, Parellada* varieties, which stand out for their fruity character and extreme lightness. They are fresh wines, and are pleasant to drink within the year. Barrel-fermented wines are also starting to appear, mainly single variety wines of *Xarel-lo* and *Macabeo*, with a greater capacity to age due to the contribution of the tannins of the wood. Another important group is the *Chardonnay* white wines, whether young (fruity, with lemony notes and fine varietal character) or fermented in barrels, which combine the fruity personality of *Chardonnay* with the creamy notes of the oak.
ROSÉS	Modern in style, raspberry pink coloured, powerful, aromatic and fresh. They are produced from varieties as diverse as *Tempranillo, Cabernet, Merlot* or *Pinot Noir*.
REDS	Those produced from autochthonous grapes, generally *Garnacha* and *Tempranillo*, are young red wines, and are pleasant and easy drinking, although, on occasions, they may be a bit light and have certain herbal notes due to overproduction in the vineyard. Regarding those aged in wood, they may come from foreign varieties (mainly *Cabernet* and *Merlot*) or combined with local grape varieties. They integrate the notes of fine wood with fruity aromas with a good intensity; on the palate they are concentrated and meaty.

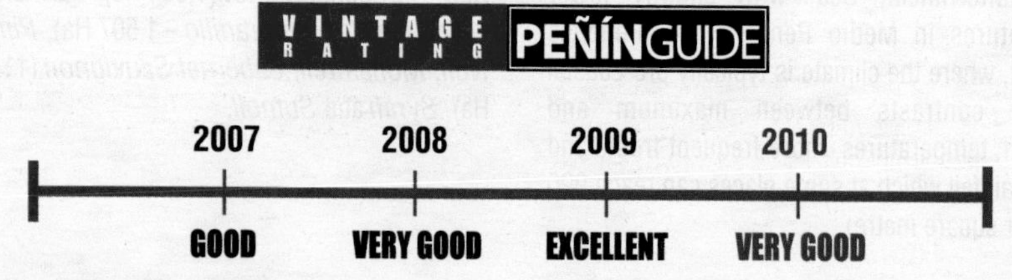

AGUSTÍ TORELLÓ MATA

La Serra, s/n
08770 Sant Sadurní D'Anoia (Barcelona)
☎: +34 938 911 173 - Fax: +34 938 912 616
info@agustitorellomata.com
www.agustitorellomata.com

XII SUBIRAT PARENT 2010 B
100% subirat parent.

90 Colour: bright straw. Nose: white flowers, fruit expression, fragrant herbs, mineral. Palate: powerful, fresh, fruity, complex, fleshy.

ALBET I NOYA

Can Vendrell de la Codina, s/n
08739 Sant Pau D'Ordal (Barcelona)
☎: +34 938 994 812 - Fax: +34 938 994 930
albetinoya@albetinoya.cat
www.albetinoya.cat

ALBET I NOYA COL.LECCIÓ CHARDONNAY 2010 B
chardonnay.

91 Colour: bright yellow, greenish rim. Nose: jasmine, medium intensity, fruit expression. Palate: flavourful, fruity, fine bitter notes.

ALBET I NOYA 3 MACABEUS 2010 B
macabeo.

90 Colour: bright straw, greenish rim. Nose: balanced, expressive, fragrant herbs, faded flowers, earthy notes. Palate: flavourful, fruity.

ALBET I NOYA EL FANIO 2010 B
xarel.lo.

90 Colour: bright yellow, greenish rim. Nose: elegant, balanced, white flowers, fragrant herbs. Palate: flavourful, rich, balanced, fine bitter notes.

ALBET I NOYA XAREL-LO CLÀSSIC 2010 B
xarel.lo.

88 Colour: bright straw, greenish rim. Nose: fresh fruit, white flowers, wild herbs, medium intensity. Palate: fresh, flavourful.

ALBET I NOYA PETIT ALBET 2010 B
chardonnay, xarel.lo.

86 Colour: bright straw. Nose: balanced, white flowers, wild herbs, powerfull, ripe fruit. Palate: flavourful, fruity, balanced.

ALBET I NOYA RESERVA MARTÍ 2007 T
tempranillo, syrah, cabernet sauvignon, merlot.

93 Colour: cherry, garnet rim. Nose: ripe fruit, spicy, toasty, dark chocolate, cocoa bean, elegant. Palate: powerful, flavourful, toasty, round tannins, round.

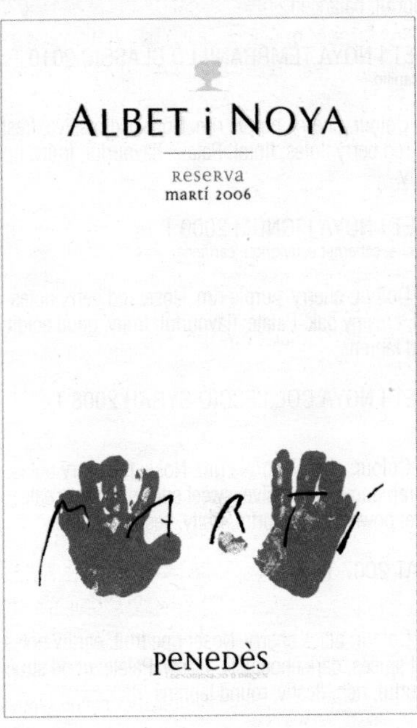

ALBET I NOYA DOLÇ LES TIMBES 2010 B
viognier.

86 Colour: bright straw. Nose: medium intensity, floral, dried herbs, citrus fruit. Palate: balanced, flavourful, sweetness.

ALBET I NOYA LIGNUM 2009 BFB
sauvignon blanc, chardonnay.

89 Colour: bright yellow, greenish rim. Nose: balanced, ripe fruit, white flowers. Palate: flavourful, correct, good finish.

ALBET I NOYA EL BLANC XXV "ECOLÓGICO" 2008 B
viognier, vidal, marina rion.

91 Colour: bright yellow. Nose: balanced, expressive, medium intensity, candied fruit, white flowers, spicy. Palate: flavourful, rich, balanced, fine bitter notes.

ALBET I NOYA PINOT NOIR MERLOT CLÀSSIC 2010 RD
pinot noir, merlot.

88 Colour: light cherry. Nose: medium intensity, fresh, faded flowers, wild herbs, red berry notes. Palate: fruity, flavourful, balanced.

ALBET I NOYA TEMPRANILLO CLÀSSIC 2010 T
tempranillo.

90 Colour: cherry, purple rim. Nose: expressive, fresh fruit, red berry notes, floral. Palate: flavourful, fruity, good acidity.

ALBET I NOYA LIGNUM 2009 T
garnacha, cabernet sauvignon, cariñena.

89 Colour: cherry, purple rim. Nose: red berry notes, floral, creamy oak. Palate: flavourful, fruity, good acidity, round tannins.

ALBET I NOYA COL.LECCIÓ SYRAH 2008 T
syrah.

92 Colour: cherry, purple rim. Nose: red berry notes, mineral, floral, expressive, sweet spices, creamy oak. Palate: powerful, flavourful, fruity, fleshy, complex.

BELAT 2007 T
belat.

92 Colour: black cherry. Nose: ripe fruit, earthy notes, sweet spices, dark chocolate, toasty. Palate: good structure, flavourful, rich, fleshy, round tannins.

FINCA LA MILANA 2006 T
caladoc, tempranillo, cabernet sauvignon, merlot.

91 Colour: cherry, garnet rim. Nose: ripe fruit, spicy, toasty, mineral. Palate: powerful, flavourful, toasty, fine tannins, elegant.

ALBET I NOYA DOLÇ ADRIÀ 2007 TINTO DULCE
syrah, merlot.

85 Colour: cherry, garnet rim. Nose: floral, red berry notes, ripe fruit, caramel. Palate: powerful, flavourful, complex, fleshy.

ALEMANY I CORRIO

Melió, 78
08720 Vilafranca del Penedès (Barcelona)
☎: +34 938 922 746 - Fax: +34 938 172 587
sotlefriec@soflefriec.com

PLOU I FA SOL 2010 B
xarel.lo, malvasía.

92 Colour: bright straw. Nose: white flowers, faded flowers, candied fruit, citrus fruit. Palate: flavourful, powerful, fleshy, fruity.

PRICIPIA MATHEMATICA 2010 B
xarel.lo.

91 Color bright straw. Aroma fresh, fresh fruit, white flowers, expressive. Taste flavourful, fruity, good acidity, balanced.

PAS CURTEI 2009 T
merlot, cabernet sauvignon, cariñena.

92 Colour: dark-red cherry. Nose: mineral, varietal, expressive, complex, powerfull, aromatic coffee, spicy, toasty, ripe fruit. Palate: powerful, flavourful, fruity, complex, mineral, toasty.

SOT LEFRIEC 2006 T
cabernet sauvignon, merlot, cariñena.

94 Colour: cherry, garnet rim. Nose: ripe fruit, fruit expression, toasty, dark chocolate. Palate: flavourful, fleshy, powerful, good acidity, fine bitter notes, spicy, long.

ALSINA & SARDÁ

Barrio Les Tarumbas, s/n
08733 Pla del Penedès (Barcelona)
☎: +34 938 988 132 - Fax: +34 938 988 671
alsina@alsinasarda.com
www.alsinasarda.com

ALSINA & SARDÁ FINCA LA BOLTANA 2010 B
100% xarel.lo.

89 Colour: bright straw. Nose: dried flowers, fruit expression, mineral, expressive. Palate: powerful, complex, fleshy, fruity.

ALSINA & SARDÁ CHARDONNAY XAREL.LO 2010 B
50% chardonnay, 50% xarel.lo.

87 Colour: bright yellow, greenish rim. Nose: fresh fruit, wild herbs, citrus fruit, white flowers. Palate: fresh, fruity.

ALSINA & SARDÁ BLANC DE BLANCS 2010 B
50% macabeo, 50% parellada.

86 Colour: coppery red. Nose: candied fruit, floral, complex. Palate: powerful, flavourful, fruity.

ALSINA & SARDÁ MERLOT LLÀGRIMA 2010 RD
100% merlot.

87 Colour: rose, purple rim. Nose: medium intensity, balanced, balsamic herbs, red berry notes. Palate: flavourful, fruity, good acidity.

ARNAU 2010 T
100% merlot.

86 Colour: cherry, purple rim. Nose: ripe fruit, balsamic herbs, spicy. Palate: good acidity, powerful, flavourful, fruity.

ALSINA & SARDÁ CAL JANES 2007 T
100% merlot.

85 Colour: cherry, garnet rim. Nose: ripe fruit, balsamic herbs, spicy, creamy oak. Palate: powerful, flavourful, fleshy.

ALSINA & SARDÁ RESERVA DE FAMILIA 2006 T
100% merlot.

88 Colour: pale ruby, brick rim edge. Nose: fragrant herbs, ripe fruit, expressive. Palate: powerful, flavourful, fleshy, easy to drink.

ALSINA & SARDÁ FINCA OLERDOLA 2006 TR
100% cabernet sauvignon.

86 Colour: cherry, garnet rim. Nose: ripe fruit, spicy, creamy oak. Palate: flavourful, toasty, round tannins.

ALSINA & SARDÁ MUSCAT LLÀGRIMA 2010
100% moscatel.

85 Colour: bright yellow. Nose: floral, fresh fruit, tropical fruit. Palate: flavourful, fruity, fresh, easy to drink.

AVINYÓ CAVAS

Masia Can Fontanals
08793 Avinyonet del Penedès (Barcelona)
☎: +34 938 970 055 - Fax: +34 938 970 691
avinyo@avinyo.com
www.avinyo.com

AVINYÓ MERLOT 2010 T
100% merlot.

84 Colour: cherry, purple rim. Nose: ripe fruit, balsamic herbs, scrubland. Palate: spicy, flavourful, fruity.

AVINYÓ CABERNET SAUVIGNON 2007 TC
100% cabernet sauvignon.

88 Colour: deep cherry, garnet rim. Nose: varietal, medium intensity, scrubland, ripe fruit. Palate: flavourful, fruity, good acidity, balanced.

BLANCHER-CAPDEVILA PUJOL

Plaça Pont Romà, Edificio Blancher
08770 Sant Sadurní D'Anoia (Barcelona)
☎: +34 938 183 286 - Fax: +34 938 911 961
blancher@blancher.es
www.blancher.es

BLANCHER BLANC SELECCIÓ 2010 B
xarel.lo, macabeo, parellada.

84 Colour: bright straw. Nose: floral, fruit expression, medium intensity. Palate: fine bitter notes, light-bodied, fruity.

BODEGA JAUME CASANELLAS

Camino Puigdàlber a las Cases Noves
08735 Guardiola de Font-Rubí (Barcelona)
☎: +34 938 988 185 - Fax: +34 938 988 185
rosmarina@rosmarina.com

ROS MARINA XAREL.LO 2010 BFB
100% xarel.lo.

89 Colour: bright straw. Nose: candied fruit, floral, fragrant herbs, mineral. Palate: powerful, flavourful, complex, good acidity.

MAS UBERNI CHARDONNAY 2010 B
100% chardonnay.

87 Colour: bright straw. Nose: white flowers, dried herbs, ripe fruit. Palate: light-bodied, fresh, flavourful, fleshy, complex.

ROS MARINA CABERNET MERLOT 2009 T ROBLE
70% cabernet sauvignon, 30% merlot.

87 Colour: light cherry, garnet rim. Nose: red berry notes, ripe fruit, toasty, sweet spices. Palate: good acidity, powerful, flavourful, fruity, fleshy.

ROS MARINA MERLOT 2008 T ROBLE
100% merlot.

87 Colour: light cherry, brick rim edge. Nose: ripe fruit, sweet spices, creamy oak, expressive. Palate: flavourful, fruity, toasty, fleshy.

MAS UBERNI ROSAT SELECCIÓ 2010 SC
75% cabernet sauvignon, 25% merlot.

83 Colour: rose, purple rim. Nose: ripe fruit, faded flowers, medium intensity. Palate: easy to drink, fresh, light-bodied.

BODEGAS CA N'ESTELLA

Masia Ca N'Estella, s/n
08635 Sant Esteve Sesrovires (Barcelona)
☎: +34 934 161 387 - Fax: +34 934 161 620
canestella@fincacanestella.com
www.fincacanestella.com

CLOT DELS OMS 2010 B
malvasía, chardonnay.

87 Colour: bright yellow, greenish rim. Nose: ripe fruit, white flowers, balanced. Palate: rich, flavourful, fruity.

PETIT CLOT DELS OMS 2010 B
20% macabeo, 40% xarel.lo, 30% chardonnay, 10% moscatel.

86 Colour: bright yellow, greenish rim. Nose: fragrant herbs, balanced, medium intensity. Palate: easy to drink, ripe fruit, flavourful.

GRAN CLOT DELS OMS XAREL.LO 2008 BFB
xarel.lo.

90 Colour: bright yellow. Nose: fragrant herbs, sweet spices, citrus fruit, ripe fruit. Palate: flavourful, ripe fruit, rich.

GRAN CLOT DELS OMS 2008 BFB
chardonnay.

88 Colour: bright yellow. Nose: powerfull, toasty, sweet spices, candied fruit. Palate: flavourful, spicy, fine bitter notes, ripe fruit.

CLOT DELS OMS BS B
malvasía, chardonnay.

85 Colour: straw. Nose: fresh fruit, white flowers, grassy. Palate: flavourful, fruity, fleshy.

CLOT DELS OMS 2010 RD
merlot.

86 Colour: rose, purple rim. Nose: red berry notes, white flowers, expressive. Palate: good acidity, fresh, flavourful.

PETIT CLOT DELS OMS 2010 RD
cabernet sauvignon.

86 Colour: raspberry rose. Nose: red berry notes, ripe fruit, floral, medium intensity. Palate: fruity, fresh, flavourful.

CLOT DELS OMS VI DOLÇ DE FRED 2008 RD
merlot.

85 Colour: cherry, garnet rim. Nose: medium intensity, candied fruit, floral. Palate: balanced, light-bodied, fruity, easy to drink.

PETIT CLOT DELS OMS 2009 T
20% merlot, 80% cabernet sauvignon.

88 Colour: cherry, purple rim. Nose: fresh fruit, red berry notes, floral, sweet spices. Palate: flavourful, fruity, good acidity.

CLOT DELS OMS 2008 TC
70% merlot, 30% cabernet sauvignon.

88 Colour: cherry, garnet rim. Nose: ripe fruit, sweet spices, dark chocolate, toasty. Palate: good finish, powerful, flavourful.

CLOT DELS OMS CABERNET SAUVIGNON 2005 T
cabernet sauvignon.

84 Colour: pale ruby, brick rim edge. Nose: ripe fruit, mineral, balsamic herbs.

GRAN CLOT DELS OMS 2005 TR
60% cabernet sauvignon, 40% merlot.

84 Colour: pale ruby, brick rim edge. Nose: elegant, spicy, wet leather, aged wood nuances, fruit liqueur notes, scrubland. Palate: spicy, fine tannins, elegant, long.

BODEGAS CAPITÀ VIDAL

Ctra. Villafranca-Igualada, Km. 30
08733 Pla del Penedès (Barcelona)
☎: +34 938 988 630 - Fax: +34 938 988 625
capitavidal@capitavidal.com
www.capitavidal.com

CLOS VIDAL BLANC DE BLANCS 2010 B
58% xarel.lo, 18% parellada, 14% macabeo, 10% moscatel.

86 Colour: pale. Nose: fruit expression, white flowers, fresh, medium intensity. Palate: light-bodied, fresh, fruity.

CLOS VIDAL ROSÉ CUVÉE 2010 RD
45% syrah, 30% merlot, 25% garnacha.

88 Colour: raspberry rose. Nose: floral, raspberry, candied fruit, expressive. Palate: fleshy, complex, powerful, fruity.

CLOS VIDAL MERLOT 2008 TC
85% merlot, 15% tempranillo.

83 Colour: cherry, garnet rim. Nose: ripe fruit, fragrant herbs, varietal, toasty. Palate: flavourful, fruity, lacks expression.

CLOS VIDAL CABERNET SAUVIGNON 2007 TROBLE
90% cabernet sauvignon, 10% tempranillo.

86 Colour: cherry, garnet rim. Nose: ripe fruit, balsamic herbs, toasty. Palate: flavourful, spicy, fleshy, green.

BODEGAS MUR BARCELONA

Rambla de la Generalitat, 1-9
08770 Sant Sadurni D'Anoia (Barcelona)
☎: +34 938 183 641 - Fax: +34 938 914 366
info@mur-barcelona.com
www.mur-barcelona.com

ROBERT MUR BLANCO SECO 2010 B
macabeo, xarel.lo, parellada.

86 Colour: bright straw. Nose: tropical fruit, white flowers, medium intensity. Palate: fresh, fruity, light-bodied.

MOST DORÉ 2010 B
xarel.lo, chardonnay.

84 Colour: bright straw. Nose: white flowers, citrus fruit, fresh fruit. Palate: flavourful, fresh, light-bodied.

ROBERT J. MUR ROSADO SECO 2010 RD
garnacha, monastrell, ull de llebre.

86 Colour: rose, purple rim. Nose: lactic notes, floral, balanced, red berry notes, ripe fruit. Palate: light-bodied, fresh, flavourful, good acidity.

MOST DORÉ 2010 RD
ull de llebre, garnacha tintorera.

84 Colour: light cherry. Nose: lactic notes, ripe fruit, dried flowers. Palate: flavourful, fruity, light-bodied, easy to drink.

ROBERT MUR 2010 T
ull de llebre, merlot, cabernet sauvignon.

86 Colour: cherry, garnet rim. Nose: red berry notes, ripe fruit, balsamic herbs. Palate: good acidity, flavourful, fruity.

MOST DORÉ 2009 T
ull de llebre.

87 Colour: cherry, garnet rim. Nose: cocoa bean, sweet spices, red berry notes, ripe fruit. Palate: good acidity, flavourful, rich, long.

BODEGAS PINORD

Doctor Pasteur, 6
08720 Vilafranca del Penedès (Barcelona)
☎: +34 938 903 066 - Fax: +34 938 170 979
pinord@pinord.es
www.pinord.es

PINORD DIORAMA CHARDONNAY 2010 B
chardonnay.

89 Colour: bright straw. Nose: fresh, white flowers, expressive, varietal. Palate: flavourful, fruity, good acidity.

PINORD VIÑA MIREIA 2010 B
moscatel, gewürztraminer.

86 Colour: bright straw. Nose: fresh fruit, floral, citrus fruit, expressive. Palate: good acidity, fresh, light-bodied, fruity.

PINORD CLOS DE TORRIBAS 2010 B
xarel.lo.

85 Colour: bright yellow, greenish rim. Nose: medium intensity, fresh, white flowers. Palate: fruity, easy to drink.

PINORD DIORAMA CABERNET SAUVIGNON 2010 RD
cabernet sauvignon.

85 Colour: rose, purple rim. Nose: powerfull, ripe fruit, floral. Palate: fleshy, powerful, fruity, fresh.

PINORD DIORAMA SYRAH 2009 T
syrah.

87 Colour: cherry, garnet rim. Nose: red berry notes, ripe fruit, balsamic herbs, toasty. Palate: spicy, flavourful, fruity.

PINORD DIORAMA MERLOT 2009 T
merlot.

85 Colour: cherry, garnet rim. Nose: red berry notes, ripe fruit, fragrant herbs, creamy oak. Palate: fleshy, good acidity, flavourful.

PINORD CLOS DE TORRIBAS 2007 TC
tempranillo, cabernet sauvignon.

88 Colour: bright cherry, orangey edge. Nose: spicy, tobacco, fruit liqueur notes. Palate: flavourful, full, ripe fruit, balanced, fine bitter notes.

PINORD CHATELDON 2004 TR
cabernet sauvignon, merlot.

87 Colour: cherry, garnet rim. Nose: medium intensity, spicy, balsamic herbs, old leather. Palate: flavourful, ripe fruit, spicy.

PINORD LA NANSA 2010 BLANCO DE AGUJA
macabeo, chardonnay.

83 Colour: bright straw. Nose: neat, fruit expression, medium intensity. Palate: fine bitter notes, sweetness, fruity.

BODEGAS TORRE DEL VEGUER

Urb. Torre de Veguer, s/n
08810 Sant Pere de Ribes (Barcelona)
☎: +34 938 963 190 - Fax: +34 938 962 967
torredelveguer@torredelveguer.com
www.torredelveguer.com

TORRE DEL VEGUER XAREL.LO 2010 B
xarel.lo.

90 Colour: bright straw. Nose: fresh, fresh fruit, white flowers, mineral. Palate: flavourful, fruity, good acidity, balanced.

TORRE DEL VEGUER MUSCAT 2010 B

88 Colour: bright straw. Nose: expressive, fresh fruit, citrus fruit, white flowers. Palate: flavourful, fruity, fresh.

TORRE DEL VEGUER DULCE VENDIMIA TARDÍA 2008 B
muscat.

91 Colour: bright golden. Nose: citrus fruit, honeyed notes, sweet spices, expressive. Palate: rich, powerful, flavourful, ripe fruit, creamy, balanced.

TORRE DEL VEGUER ROSAT DE LLÁGRIMA 2010 RD

84 Colour: rose, purple rim. Nose: powerfull, ripe fruit, red berry notes, floral. Palate: fleshy, powerful, fruity, fresh.

TORRE DEL VEGUER ECLECTIC 2008 T

83 Colour: bright cherry. Nose: ripe fruit, sweet spices, creamy oak. Palate: flavourful, fruity, toasty, round tannins.

TORRE DEL VEGUER RAÏMS DE LA INMORTALITAT 2 2000 TR

81 Colour: deep cherry, orangey edge. Nose: fruit liqueur notes, roasted coffee, aromatic coffee. Palate: fine bitter notes, toasty.

TORRE DEL VEGUER MARTA ESP

87 Colour: bright straw. Nose: medium intensity, fresh fruit, dried herbs, fine lees. Palate: fresh, fruity, flavourful, good acidity.

BODEGAS TORRES

Miguel Torres, 6
08720 Vilafranca del Penedès (Barcelona)
☎: +34 938 177 400 - Fax: +34 938 177 444
mailadmin@torres.es
www.torres.es

FRANSOLA 2010 B
95% sauvignon blanc, 5% parellada.

90 Colour: bright straw. Nose: citrus fruit, white flowers, fragrant herbs, expressive. Palate: powerful, fresh, fruity, flavourful.

WALTRAUD 2010 B
100% riesling.

90 Colour: bright yellow. Nose: varietal, ripe fruit, white flowers, medium intensity. Palate: easy to drink, rich, ripe fruit.

ATRIUM CHARDONNAY 2010 B
85% chardonnay, 15% parellada.

87 Colour: bright yellow. Nose: balanced, powerfull, varietal, ripe fruit. Palate: flavourful, fruity, rich.

ATRIUM MERLOT 2010 T
100% merlot.

87 Colour: cherry, purple rim. Nose: red berry notes, scrubland, balanced. Palate: fruity, flavourful, easy to drink.

MAS BORRÁS 2009 T
100% pinot noir.

89 Colour: cherry, garnet rim. Nose: ripe fruit, powerfull, roasted coffee, cocoa bean, toasty. Palate: good acidity, powerful, flavourful, fleshy, toasty.

CORONAS 2009 TC
86% tempranillo, 14% cabernet sauvignon.

88 Colour: deep cherry, garnet rim. Nose: sweet spices, creamy oak, ripe fruit, balanced. Palate: fleshy, fruity, spicy, round tannins.

ATRIUM CABERNET SAUVIGNON 2008 T
85% cabernet sauvignon, 15% tempranillo.

89 Colour: cherry, garnet rim. Nose: ripe fruit, scrubland, sweet spices. Palate: flavourful, fruity, easy to drink.

RESERVA REAL 2007 T
cabernet sauvignon, cabernet franc, merlot.

94 Colour: deep cherry, garnet rim. Nose: mineral, balanced, complex, expressive, creamy oak, sweet spices, varietal. Palate: fleshy, good structure, round tannins.

MAS LA PLANA CABERNET SAUVIGNON 2007 T
100% cabernet sauvignon.

93 Colour: cherry, garnet rim. Nose: ripe fruit, spicy, creamy oak, toasty, complex, wild herbs. Palate: powerful, flavourful, toasty, round tannins.

MAS LA PLANA CABERNET SAUVIGNON 1989 T
cabernet sauvignon.

91 Colour: pale ruby, brick rim edge. Nose: expressive, candied fruit, fruit liqueur notes, spicy, pattiserie, wet leather. Palate: flavourful, spicy, fine bitter notes, good acidity.

BODEGAS TRIAS BATLLE

Comerç, 6
08720 Vilafranca del Penedès (Barcelona)
☎: +34 938 902 627 - Fax: +34 938 901 724
bodegas@jtrias.com
www.jtrias.com

TRIAS BATLLE CHARDONNAY 2009 BC
chardonnay.

89 Colour: bright yellow. Nose: white flowers, faded flowers, ripe fruit, sweet spices. Palate: powerful, flavourful, fleshy, toasty.

TRIAS BATLLE 2007 TC
70% merlot, 15% cabernet sauvignon, 15% ull de llebre.

88 Colour: cherry, garnet rim. Nose: ripe fruit, expressive, mineral, sweet spices, toasty. Palate: good acidity, powerful, flavourful, easy to drink.

TRIAS BATLLE CABERNET SAUVIGNON 2007 TC
cabernet sauvignon.

84 Colour: dark-red cherry. Nose: fruit preserve, grassy, sweet spices. Palate: flavourful, fleshy, slightly evolved.

BODEGUES SUMARROCA

Barrio El Rebato, s/n
08739 Subirats (Barcelona)
☎: +34 938 911 092 - Fax: +34 938 911 778
tpuig@sumarroca.es
www.sumarroca.es

SUMARROCA SAUVIGNON BLANC 2010 B
100% sauvignon blanc.

88 Colour: yellow, greenish rim. Nose: balanced, medium intensity, fresh fruit, wild herbs. Palate: balanced, good acidity, long.

SUMARROCA TEMPS DE FLORS 2010 B

88 Colour: bright straw, greenish rim. Nose: balanced, white flowers, jasmine, citrus fruit, varietal. Palate: flavourful, fresh, fruity.

SUMARROCA MUSCAT 2010 B
moscatel.

87 Colour: bright straw. Nose: balanced, varietal, white flowers, fresh fruit. Palate: rich, fruity, balanced, good acidity.

SUMARROCA BLANC DE BLANCS 2010 B
macabeo, xarel.lo, parellada, moscatel, chardonnay.

87 Colour: bright yellow, greenish rim. Nose: powerfull, citrus fruit, jasmine, dried herbs. Palate: flavourful, easy to drink, correct.

SUMARROCA GEWÜRZTRAMINER 2010 B
100% gewürztraminer.

87 Colour: bright yellow, greenish rim. Nose: medium intensity, faded flowers, balanced. Palate: flavourful, fruity, full, good acidity.

SUMARROCA EL CODAL 2010 B
xarel.lo, macabeo, moscatel, parellada, chardonnay.

87 Colour: bright straw. Nose: white flowers, fruit expression. Palate: flavourful, fruity, good acidity, balanced.

SUMARROCA MINUET 2009 BFB
95% xarel.lo, 5% chardonnay.

87 Colour: bright yellow, greenish rim. Nose: candied fruit, sweet spices, dried herbs, creamy oak. Palate: good structure, flavourful, spicy.

SUMARROCA 2010 RD
tempranillo, cabernet sauvignon, merlot.

88 Colour: rose, bright. Nose: fruit expression, scrubland, faded flowers. Palate: flavourful, fleshy, long.

SUMARROCA PINOT NOIR 2010 RD
pinot noir.

87 Colour: rose, bright. Nose: medium intensity, red berry notes, ripe fruit, rose petals. Palate: fleshy, good structure.

SUMARROCA EL CODAL 2010 RD
garnacha, tempranillo, cabernet sauvignon.

86 Colour: rose. Nose: powerfull, ripe fruit, red berry notes, floral, expressive. Palate: fleshy, powerful, fruity, fresh.

SUMARROCA SIRIUS 2010 T
merlot, ull de llebre, cabernet sauvignon.

89 Colour: cherry, purple rim. Nose: fruit expression, wild herbs, violets. Palate: fruity, flavourful, long.

SUMARROCA EL CODAL 2010 T
tempranillo, syrah, merlot.

88 Colour: cherry, purple rim. Nose: medium intensity, red berry notes, wild herbs, violets. Palate: flavourful, balanced, good acidity.

SUMARROCA SANTA CREU DE CREIXÀ 2009 T
syrah, garnacha, cabernet franc, cabernet sauvignon.

89 Colour: cherry, garnet rim. Nose: ripe fruit, cocoa bean, dark chocolate, sweet spices, toasty. Palate: spirituous, powerful, flavourful, fleshy, toasty.

BÒRIA 2007 T
syrah, cabernet sauvignon.

91 Colour: black cherry, garnet rim. Nose: ripe fruit, dark chocolate, cocoa bean, creamy oak, complex. Palate: good acidity, round, powerful, flavourful, fleshy.

TERRAL 2007 T
syrah, cabernet sauvignon, merlot.

90 Color cherry, garnet rim. Aroma ripe fruit, spicy, creamy oak, toasty, complex. Taste powerful, flavourful, toasty, round tannins.

CAL RASPALLET VITICULTORS

Barri Sabanell, 11
08736 Font Rubí (Barcelona)
☎: +34 607 262 779
calraspallet@vinifera.cat

NUN VINYA DELS TAUS 2009 B
100% xarel.lo.

91 Colour: bright straw. Nose: ripe fruit, scrubland, fine lees, spicy. Palate: flavourful, fleshy, fresh, powerful.

IMPROVISACIÓ 2009 B
100% xarel.lo.

90 Colour: bright straw. Nose: scrubland, fresh fruit, fruit expression. Palate: complex, fruity, flavourful.

NUN VINYA DELS TAUS 2008 B
xarel.lo.

93 Colour: bright yellow. Nose: powerfull, ripe fruit, sweet spices, fragrant herbs. Palate: rich, smoky aftertaste, flavourful, good acidity.

CAN BONASTRE WINE RESORT

Ctra. B 224, Km. 13,2
08783 Masquefa (Barcelona)
☎: +34 937 726 167 - Fax: +34 937 727 929
bodega@canbonastre.com
www.canbonastre.com

MAUREL 2008 B
100% chardonnay.

90 Colour: bright golden. Nose: ripe fruit, dry nuts, powerfull, toasty, aged wood nuances, faded flowers. Palate: flavourful, fruity, spicy, toasty, long, fine bitter notes.

NARA 2007 TC
50% syrah, 40% cabernet sauvignon, 10% merlot.

92 Colour: cherry, garnet rim. Nose: ripe fruit, spicy, creamy oak, complex, dark chocolate. Palate: powerful, flavourful, toasty, round tannins.

ERUMIR 2006 TC
45% merlot, 45% tempranillo, 10% cabernet sauvignon.

88 Colour: cherry, garnet rim. Nose: powerfull, balanced, ripe fruit, toasty, spicy. Palate: fleshy, flavourful, long.

CAN BONASTRE 2006 TC
cabernet sauvignon, merlot, syrah.

86 Colour: cherry, garnet rim. Nose: toasty, spicy, ripe fruit, fruit liqueur notes. Palate: powerful, balsamic, warm.

CAN CAMPS

Cam Camps, s/n
08810 Olivella (Barcelona)
☎: +34 938 970 013

PEDRADURA 2005 TR
100% marcelant.

89 Colour: deep cherry. Nose: ripe fruit, toasty, spicy, wet leather, scrubland. Palate: flavourful, powerful, good structure, spicy.

CAN DESCREGUT

Masia Can Descregut s/n
08735 Vilobi del Penedès (Barcelona)
☎: +34 938 978 273 - Fax: +34 938 170 786
info@descregut.com
www.montdarac.com

DESCREGUT X 100 2010 B
100% xarel.lo.

88 Colour: bright straw, greenish rim. Nose: white flowers, citrus fruit, wild herbs, fresh. Palate: fruity, flavourful, balanced.

EQUILIBRI 2006 B
xarel.lo, chardonnay.

87 Colour: bright golden. Nose: sweet spices, dry nuts, creamy oak. Palate: rich, flavourful, spicy, ripe fruit.

DESCREGUT 100 MERLOT 2010 RD
100% merlot.

82 Colour: cherry, purple rim. Nose: ripe fruit, medium intensity, slightly evolved. Palate: fruity, easy to drink.

DESCREGUT 20/80 2005 T
merlot, syrah.

80 Colour: cherry, garnet rim. Nose: boiled fruit notes, herbaceous, short. Palate: spirituous, slightly evolved.

CAN FEIXES (HUGUET)

Finca Can Feixes, s/n
08718 Cabrera D'Anoia (Barcelona)
☎: +34 937 718 227 - Fax: +34 937 718 031
canfeixes@canfeixes.com
www.canfeixes.com

CAN FEIXES SELECCIÓ 2010 B
parellada, macabeo, chardonnay, malvasía.

87 Colour: bright yellow, greenish rim. Nose: fragrant herbs, citrus fruit, ripe fruit. Palate: easy to drink, balanced.

CAN FEIXES CHARDONNAY 2006 BFB
chardonnay.

90 Colour: bright yellow. Nose: powerfull, ripe fruit, sweet spices, creamy oak, fragrant herbs. Palate: rich, flavourful, fresh, good acidity.

CAN FEIXES SELECCIÓ 2006 TC
ull de llebre, cabernet sauvignon, merlot, petit verdot.

87 Color cherry, garnet rim. Aroma ripe fruit, spicy, creamy oak, toasty, complex. Taste powerful, flavourful, toasty, round tannins.

CAN FEIXES RESERVA ESPECIAL 2000ºººº TR
cabernet sauvignon, merlot.

89 Colour: pale ruby, brick rim edge. Nose: ripe fruit, toasty, complex, balsamic herbs, old leather. Palate: powerful, flavourful, toasty, round tannins.

CAN RÀFOLS DELS CAUS

Can Rafols del Caus s/n
08793 Avinyonet del Penedès (Barcelona)
☎: +34 938 970 013 - Fax: +34 938 970 370
canrafolsdelscaus@canrafolsdelscaus.com
www.canrafolsdelscaus.com

PETIT CAUS 2010 B
xarel.lo, macabeo, chardonnay, moscatel, chenin blanc, parellada.

87 Colour: bright straw. Nose: fresh, fresh fruit, white flowers, medium intensity. Palate: flavourful, fruity, easy to drink.

EL ROCALLÍS 2007 BFB
100% Incrozio manzoni.

91 Colour: bright yellow. Nose: powerfull, ripe fruit, sweet spices, creamy oak. Palate: rich, flavourful, fresh, balanced, elegant.

VINYA LA CALMA 2007 B
chenin blanc.

90 Color bright golden. Aroma ripe fruit, dry nuts, powerfull, toasty, aged wood nuances. Taste flavourful, fruity, spicy, toasty, long.

XAREL.LO PAIRAL 2007 B
xarel.lo.

87 Colour: bright yellow. Nose: dried flowers, ripe fruit, sweet spices, toasty. Palate: round, powerful, flavourful, fleshy.

PETIT CAUS 2010 RD
merlot, ull de llebre, syrah, cabernet sauvignon, cabernet franc.

87 Colour: raspberry rose. Nose: floral, candied fruit, balsamic herbs, expressive. Palate: flavourful, fresh, fleshy, good acidity.

PETIT CAUS 2010 T
merlot, syrah, cabernet franc.

87 Colour: cherry, purple rim. Nose: powerfull, ripe fruit, wild herbs. Palate: flavourful, fruity, fleshy.

GRAN CAUS 2006 TR
cabernet sauvignon, cabernet franc, merlot.

92 Colour: cherry, garnet rim. Nose: ripe fruit, spicy, creamy oak, toasty, complex, elegant. Palate: powerful, flavourful, toasty, round tannins.

CANALS & MUNNÉ

Pl. Pau Casals, 6
08770 Sant Sadurní D'Anoia (Barcelona)
☎: +34 938 910 318 - Fax: +34 938 911 945
info@canalsimunne.com
www.canalsimunne.com

BLANC PRÍNCEPS MUSCAT 2010 B
moscatel.

88 Colour: bright straw. Nose: fresh, white flowers, expressive, ripe fruit, honeyed notes. Palate: flavourful, fruity, good acidity, balanced.

GRAN BLANC PRÍNCEPS 2010 BFB
60% xarel.lo, 40% chardonnay.

88 Colour: bright straw. Nose: powerfull, ripe fruit, sweet spices, creamy oak, fragrant herbs. Palate: rich, flavourful, fresh, good acidity.

BLANC PRÍNCEPS SAUVIGNON 2010 B
80% sauvignon blanc, 20% xarel.lo.

87 Colour: bright straw. Nose: fruit expression, white flowers, balanced. Palate: light-bodied, fresh, fruity, flavourful.

BLANC PRÍNCEPS ECOLOGIC 2010 B
xarel.lo, chardonnay, sauvignon blanc.

85 Colour: bright straw. Nose: fresh, fresh fruit, white flowers, expressive. Palate: flavourful, fruity, good acidity.

ROSAT PRÍNCEPS MERLOT 2010 T
85% merlot, 15% tempranillo.

83 Colour: light cherry. Nose: medium intensity, floral, candied fruit. Palate: fruity, correct, good acidity, easy to drink.

NOIR PRÍNCEPS 2004 TC
50% cabernet sauvignon, 40% merlot, 10% tempranillo.

83 Colour: pale ruby, brick rim edge. Nose: spicy, fine reductive notes, wet leather, aged wood nuances, fruit liqueur notes. Palate: spicy, fine tannins, long.

CANALS NADAL

Ponent, 2
08733 El Pla del Penedès (Barcelona)
☎: +34 938 988 081 - Fax: +34 938 989 050
cava@canalsnadal.com
www.canalsnadal.com

CANALS NADAL GRAN XAREL.LO 2009 BFB
100% xarel.lo.

86 Colour: bright yellow, greenish rim. Nose: candied fruit, sweet spices, powerfull, creamy oak. Palate: rich, fruity, flavourful.

ANTONI CANALS NADAL CABERNET SAUVIGNON MERLOT 2006 TC
50% cabernet sauvignon, 50% merlot.

85 Colour: deep cherry, garnet rim. Nose: medium intensity, ripe fruit, spicy, dried herbs. Palate: fruity, good acidity.

CASA RAVELLA

Ravella, 1
08739 Ordal (Barcelona)
☎: +34 938 179 173 - Fax: +34 938 179 245
bodega@condedeolzinellas.com
www.casaravella.com

HEREDEROS DEL CONDE DE OLZINELLAS 2010 B
80% xarel.lo, 20% chardonnay.

88 Colour: bright straw. Nose: fresh, fresh fruit, white flowers, fragrant herbs. Palate: flavourful, fruity, balanced.

CASA RAVELLA 2009 BFB
70% xarel.lo, 30% chardonnay.

90 Colour: bright yellow. Nose: ripe fruit, faded flowers, sweet spices, creamy oak. Palate: elegant, powerful, rich, fleshy, flavourful.

CASA RAVELLA TINTO SELECCIÓN 2007 T
cabernet sauvignon.

90 Colour: dark-red cherry, garnet rim. Nose: ripe fruit, scrubland, earthy notes, mineral, complex. Palate: powerful, flavourful, fleshy, complex.

CASA RAVELLA TINTO SELECCIÓN 2006 T
100% cabernet sauvignon.

89 Colour: dark-red cherry, garnet rim. Nose: ripe fruit, scrubland, spicy, toasty. Palate: fine bitter notes, flavourful, fleshy.

CASTELL D'OR

Mare Rafols, 3- 1r 4a
08720 Vilafranca del Penedès (Barcelona)
☎: +34 938 905 385 - Fax: +34 938 905 446
castelldor@castelldor.com
www.castelldor.com

COSSETÀNIA 2010 B
50% xarel.lo, 30% macabeo, 20% parellada.

84 Colour: bright straw. Nose: white flowers, fragrant herbs, ripe fruit. Palate: powerful, fruity, fresh.

COSSETÀNIA CHARDONNAY B
100% chardonnay.

83 Colour: bright straw. Nose: dried flowers, citrus fruit, medium intensity. Palate: flavourful, fresh, light-bodied.

COSSETÀNIA 2010 RD
100% merlot.

85 Colour: rose, purple rim. Nose: red berry notes, ripe fruit, floral, expressive. Palate: powerful, flavourful, fresh, fruity.

COSSETÀNIA 2010 T
60% cabernet sauvignon, 40% merlot.

85 Colour: bright cherry. Nose: ripe fruit, sweet spices, creamy oak, expressive, balsamic herbs. Palate: flavourful, fruity, toasty.

COSSETÀNIA 2008 TC
80% tempranillo, 20% merlot.

86 Colour: light cherry, orangey edge. Nose: fruit preserve, fruit liqueur notes, toasty. Palate: good acidity.

COSSETÀNIA 2006 TR
100% cabernet sauvignon.

85 Colour: dark-red cherry, brick rim edge. Nose: overripe fruit, fruit preserve, wet leather, toasty. Palate: powerful, fleshy, round tannins.

CASTELLROIG FINCA SABATÉ I COCA

Ctra. Sant Sadurní d'Anoia a Vilafranca del Penedès, Km. 1
08739 Subirats (Barcelona)
☎: +34 938 911 927 - Fax: +34 938 914 055
info@castellroig.com
www.castellroig.com

CASTELLROIG XAREL.LO 2010 B
xarel.lo.

88 Colour: bright straw. Nose: white flowers, expressive, fragrant herbs, mineral. Palate: good acidity, fruity, flavourful.

CASTELLROIG XAREL.LO 2009 2009 B
xarel.lo.

88 Colour: bright straw. Nose: white flowers, macerated fruit, mineral, fragrant herbs. Palate: powerful, flavourful, fleshy.

CASTELLROIG SELECCIÓ NEGRE 2008 T
cabernet sauvignon, merlot.

87 Colour: very deep cherry, garnet rim. Nose: powerfull, ripe fruit, balsamic herbs, spicy. Palate: good structure, rich, long, spicy, round tannins.

CASTELLROIG ULL DE LLEBRE 2008 T
tempranillo.

87 Colour: deep cherry, garnet rim. Nose: fruit preserve, spicy. Palate: fruity, good acidity, round tannins.

CAVA RECAREDO

Tamarit, 10
08770 Sant Sadurní D'Anoia (Barcelona)
☎: +34 938 910 214 - Fax: +34 938 911 697
cava@recaredo.es
www.recaredo.com

CAN CREDO 2010 B
100% xarel.lo.

90 Colour: bright straw. Nose: fresh, neat, complex, earthy notes. Palate: mineral, flavourful, fleshy, complex.

ELS RAUSTALS 2007 T
75% cabernet sauvignon, 25% ull de llebre.

88 Colour: very deep cherry. Nose: powerfull, varietal, overripe fruit, candied fruit, creamy oak, roasted coffee, cedar wood. Palate: fleshy, complex, concentrated, fruity, powerful.

CAVAS BOLET

Finca Mas Lluet, s/n
08732 Castellvi de la Marca (Barcelona)
☎: +34 938 918 153
cavasbolet@cavasbolet.com
www.cavasbolet.com

BOLET VINYA SOTA BOSC 2010 B
75% moscatel, 25% gewürztraminer.

86 Colour: bright straw. Nose: fresh, fresh fruit, white flowers, expressive. Palate: flavourful, fruity, balanced, light-bodied, fresh.

BOLET 2010 B
95% xarel.lo, 5% macabeo.

84 Colour: bright straw. Nose: floral, ripe fruit, medium intensity. Palate: flavourful, fresh, fruity.

BOLET MERLOT 2010 RD
merlot.

83 Colour: rose, bright. Nose: medium intensity, ripe fruit, candied fruit. Palate: flavourful, fine bitter notes.

BOLET ULL DE LLEBRE 2010 T
tempranillo.

87 Colour: garnet rim. Nose: powerfull, ripe fruit, fruit preserve, dark chocolate, sweet spices. Palate: good structure, fleshy, flavourful.

BOLET NEGRE SELECCIÓ 2006 T
60% merlot, 40% cabernet sauvignon.

87 Colour: pale ruby, brick rim edge. Nose: ripe fruit, wet leather, tobacco, spicy, toasty. Palate: powerful, flavourful, fleshy, toasty.

BOLET MERLOT 2004 TC
merlot.

88 Colour: pale ruby, brick rim edge. Nose: elegant, spicy, fine reductive notes, wet leather, fruit liqueur notes. Palate: spicy, elegant, long, flavourful.

CAVAS FERRET

Avda. de Catalunya, 36
08736 Guardiola de Font-Rubí (Barcelona)
☎: +34 938 979 148 - Fax: +34 938 979 285
ferret@cavasferret.com
www.cavasferret.com

ABAC 2010 B
100% xarel.lo.

88 Colour: bright straw, greenish rim. Nose: fresh fruit, faded flowers, fragrant herbs, elegant. Palate: flavourful, fine bitter notes.

IGNEA DE FERRET 2010 B
40% parellada, 30% macabeo, 30% xarel.lo.

85 Colour: bright straw, greenish rim. Nose: white flowers, dried herbs, medium intensity. Palate: flavourful, correct, fruity.

FERRET BLANC SELECCIÓ DE BARRIQUES 2004 B
50% xarel.lo, 50% chardonnay.

82 Colour: bright golden. Nose: toasty, spicy, powerfull, dry nuts. Palate: oaky, spicy.

IGNEA DE FERRET 2010 RD
40% ull de llebre, 30% cabernet sauvignon, 30% merlot.

85 Colour: rose. Nose: powerfull, ripe fruit, faded flowers. Palate: flavourful, good acidity, fine bitter notes.

EZEQUIEL FERRET Nº 1 S/C T
ull de llebre, cabernet sauvignon, merlot.

87 Colour: dark-red cherry, orangey edge. Nose: powerfull, fruit preserve, tobacco, dark chocolate, spicy. Palate: good structure, spicy.

IGNEA DE FERRET 2009 T
40% cabernet sauvignon, 40% merlot, 20% ull de llebre.

85 Colour: deep cherry, garnet rim. Nose: fruit preserve, spicy, medium intensity. Palate: ripe fruit, correct.

FERRET NEGRE SELECCIÓ DE BARRIQUES 2004 T
46% cabernet sauvignon, 30% ull de llebre, 24% merlot.

84 Colour: bright cherry, orangey edge. Nose: medium intensity, spicy, fruit liqueur notes. Palate: fruity, fine bitter notes.

CAVES GRAMONA

Industria, 36
08770 Sant Sadurní D'Anoia (Barcelona)
☎: +34 938 910 113 - Fax: +34 938 183 284
comunicacion@gramona.com
www.gramona.com

GRAMONA MAS ESCORPÍ CHARDONNAY 2010 B
chardonnay.

93 Colour: bright straw. Nose: fresh, fresh fruit, white flowers, expressive, complex, mineral, elegant. Palate: flavourful, fruity, good acidity, balanced.

GRAMONA SAUVIGNON BLANC 2010 BFB
sauvignon blanc.

93 Colour: bright yellow. Nose: powerfull, ripe fruit, sweet spices, creamy oak, fragrant herbs, white flowers. Palate: rich, flavourful, fresh, good acidity, elegant.

GRAMONA GESSAMÍ 2010 B
moscatel de frontignan, moscatel alejandria, sauvignon blanc, gewürztraminer.

90 Colour: bright straw. Nose: white flowers, fresh fruit, tropical fruit, balanced. Palate: powerful, flavourful, fruity, easy to drink.

GRAMONA XAREL.LO FONT JUI 2009 B
xarel.lo.

93 Colour: bright yellow. Nose: ripe fruit, floral, expressive, complex, elegant, sweet spices, creamy oak. Palate: rich, powerful, flavourful, fleshy, complex.

VI DE GLASS GEWÜRZTRAMINER 2009 B
gewürztraminer.

90 Colour: bright golden. Nose: faded flowers, citrus fruit, candied fruit, balanced, powerfull. Palate: flavourful, fruity, complex, fleshy.

VI DE GLASS GEWÜRZTRAMINER 2006 B
gewürztraminer.

92 Colour: bright golden. Nose: candied fruit, white flowers, faded flowers, citrus fruit, medium intensity. Palate: flavourful, rich, complex.

PRIMEUR GRAMONA 2010 RD
syrah.

86 Colour: rose, bright. Nose: medium intensity, floral, red berry notes, rose petals. Palate: fruity, flavourful, balanced.

GRAMONA GRA A GRA PINOT NOIR 2009 T
pinot noir.

88 Colour: cherry, purple rim. Nose: red berry notes, ripe fruit, floral, powerfull, lactic notes, expressive. Palate: powerful, flavourful, rich, fleshy.

GRAMONA GRA A GRA 2006 BLANCO DULCE
riesling, chardonnay.

93 Colour: bright golden. Nose: candied fruit, petrol notes, jasmine, complex. Palate: rich, flavourful, fruity, balanced.

GRAMONA AGULLA ROSAT S/C DE AGUJA

85 Colour: light cherry. Nose: dry nuts, candied fruit, spicy. Palate: fruity, flavourful.

CAVES MUNGUST

San Josep, 10-12
08784 Sant Jaume Sesoliveres Piera (Barcelona)
☎: +34 937 763 016
info@cavesmungust.com
www.cavesmungust.com

PERE MUNNÉ DURÁN 2010 B
parellada, macabeo, xarel.lo.

81 Colour: bright straw. Nose: faded flowers, ripe fruit, candied fruit. Palate: slightly evolved, fresh, flavourful.

PERE MUNNÉ DURÁN S/C T
cabernet sauvignon, ull de llebre.

85 Colour: pale ruby, brick rim edge. Nose: fruit preserve, wild herbs, old leather. Palate: flavourful, fleshy, reductive nuances.

PERE MUNNÉ DURÁN 2010 T
ull de llebre, cabernet sauvignon.

84 Colour: bright cherry. Nose: sweet spices, fruit preserve, fine reductive notes. Palate: flavourful, toasty, round tannins.

CAVES NAVERÁN

Masia Can Parellada - Sant Martí Sadevesa - Ctra. Sitges a Igualada, Km. 25,1
08775 Torrelavit (Barcelona)
☎: +34 938 988 400 - Fax: +34 938 989 027
sadeve@naveran.com
www.naveran.com

MANUELA DE NAVERÁN 2010 B
100% chardonnay.

90 Colour: bright straw. Nose: fresh, fresh fruit, white flowers, expressive, citrus fruit. Palate: flavourful, fruity, good acidity, balanced.

CAVES ORIOL ROSSELL

Propietat Can Cassanyes, s/n
08732 St. Marçal (Barcelona)
☎: +34 977 671 061 - Fax: +34 977 671 050
oriolrossell@oriolrossell.com
www.oriolrossell.com

LES CERVERES XAREL.LO 2009 B
xarel.lo.

90 Colour: bright yellow. Nose: dried flowers, ripe fruit, expressive, sweet spices, creamy oak. Palate: powerful, flavourful, fleshy, toasty.

ROCAPLANA 2009 T
syrah.

86 Colour: cherry, purple rim. Nose: red berry notes, ripe fruit, floral, sweet spices. Palate: creamy, light-bodied, fresh, fruity.

CELLER JORDI LLUCH

Barrio Les Casetes, s/n
08777 Sant Quinti de Mediona (Barcelona)
☎: +34 938 988 138 - Fax: +34 938 988 138
vinyaescude@vinyaescude.com
www.vinyaescude.com

VINYA ESCUDÉ MAIOLES 2008 BFB
85% chardonnay, 15% xarel.lo.

87 Colour: bright golden. Nose: candied fruit, sweet spices, creamy oak, powerfull, varietal. Palate: flavourful, rich.

VINYA ESCUDÉ NOGUERA 2005 TC
85% cabernet sauvignon, 15% merlot.

88 Colour: cherry, garnet rim. Nose: ripe fruit, scrubland, dark chocolate. Palate: powerful, flavourful, toasty, round tannins.

CELLERS AVGVSTVS FORVM

Ctra. Sant Vicenç, s/n
43700 El Vendrell (Tarragona)
☎: +34 977 666 910 - Fax: +34 977 666 590
avgvstvs@avgvstvs.es
www.avgvstvs.es

AVGVSTVS CHARDONNAY 2010 BFB
100% chardonnay.

91 Colour: bright straw. Nose: creamy oak, smoky, ripe fruit, dried herbs. Palate: flavourful, complex, good acidity.

AVGVSTVS XAREL.LO 2010 BFB
100% xarel.lo.

90 Colour: bright straw. Nose: ripe fruit, fruit expression, spicy. Palate: flavourful, long, good acidity.

AVGVSTVS CHARDONNAY MAGNUM 2008 B
100% chardonnay.

91 Colour: bright golden. Nose: ripe fruit, sweet spices, creamy oak, balanced, fragrant herbs. Palate: fruity, rich, spicy.

AVGVSTVS CABERNET SAUVIGNON ROSÉ 2010 RD
100% cabernet sauvignon.

84 Colour: rose, purple rim. Nose: powerfull, ripe fruit, red berry notes, floral. Palate: fleshy, powerful, fruity, fresh.

AVGVSTVS CABERNET SAUVIGNON-MERLOT 2009 T ROBLE
50% cabernet sauvignon, 50% merlot.

89 Colour: dark-red cherry. Nose: toasty, spicy, fruit expression. Palate: fresh, fruity, powerful, flavourful, smoky aftertaste, spicy.

AVGVSTVS CABERNET FRANC 2009 T ROBLE
100% cabernet franc.

88 Colour: cherry, garnet rim. Nose: earthy notes, ripe fruit, warm. Palate: powerful, fleshy, sweetness, round tannins.

AVGVSTVS MERLOT SYRAH 2009 T
50% merlot, 50% syrah.

88 Colour: deep cherry. Nose: ripe fruit, spicy, creamy oak. Palate: powerful, flavourful, fruity.

AVGVSTVS TRAJANVS 2007 TR
40% cabernet sauvignon, 40% merlot, 20% cabernet franc.

91 Colour: deep cherry. Nose: ripe fruit, creamy oak, spicy, cocoa bean, scrubland. Palate: flavourful, fine bitter notes, spicy, round tannins, mineral.

AVGVSTVS VI VARIETALES MAGNUM 2007 TC
cabernet sauvignon, cabernet franc, tempranillo, garnacha, merlot, syrah.

90 Colour: very deep cherry, garnet rim. Nose: balanced, expressive, ripe fruit, spicy, earthy notes. Palate: good structure, complex, flavourful, spicy, round tannins.

CELLERS PLANAS ALBAREDA

Ctra. Guardiola, Km. 3
08735 Vilobí del Penedès (Barcelona)
☎: +34 938 922 143 - Fax: +34 938 922 143
planasalbareda@yahoo.es
www.planas-albareda.com

PLANAS ALBAREDA L'AVENC 2010 B
macabeo, xarel.lo, parellada, chardonnay.

85 Colour: bright straw. Nose: fruit expression, floral, fresh. Palate: powerful, flavourful, fruity.

PLANAS ALBAREDA ROSAT 2010 RD
merlot.

85 Colour: rose, purple rim. Nose: red berry notes, wild herbs, medium intensity. Palate: flavourful, fresh, fruity.

COLET VINOS

Cami del Salinar s/n
08739 Pacs del Penedès (Barcelona)
☎: +34 938 170 809 - Fax: +34 938 170 809
info@colet.cat
www.colet.cat

A POSTERIORI ROSAT BR
100% merlot.

89 Colour: raspberry rose. Nose: red berry notes, ripe fruit, floral. Palate: fresh, fruity, flavourful, fleshy, good acidity, fine bead.

A PRIORI BR
macabeo, chardonnay, riesling, gewürztraminer, moscatel.

88 Colour: bright straw. Nose: white flowers, fragrant herbs, fresh fruit, fresh, expressive. Palate: good acidity, fine bead, fresh, fruity.

COLET BLANC DE BLANC EXTRA BRUT TRADICIONNELLE ESP
xarel.lo, macabeo, parellada.

91 Colour: bright straw. Nose: fragrant herbs, white flowers, fine lees, expressive. Palate: good acidity, fine bead, light-bodied, fresh, fruity.

COLET ASSEMBLAGE S/C EXTRA BRUT
pinot noir, chardonnay.

91 Colour: onion pink. Nose: medium intensity, elegant, floral, complex, balsamic herbs. Palate: sweetness, fine bead, easy to drink, ripe fruit.

VATUA ! S/C EXTRA BRUT
50% moscatel, 40% parellada, 10% gewürztraminer.

88 Colour: bright straw. Nose: medium intensity, ripe fruit, fine lees, dry nuts. Palate: flavourful, spicy, easy to drink.

COLET NAVAZOS EXTRA BRUT 2008 EXTRA BRUT
xarel.lo.

93 Colour: bright straw. Nose: complex, saline, dry nuts, dried flowers. Palate: flavourful, good acidity, fine bitter notes, toasty, long.

COLET NAVAZOS EXTRA BRUT 2007 EXTRA BRUT RESERVA
chardonnay.

95 Colour: bright straw. Nose: fresh, powerfull, expressive, saline, flor yeasts, floral, fragrant herbs. Palate: fleshy, good acidity, fine bead, fine bitter notes, elegant. Personality.

COLET BLANC DE BLANC EXTRA BRUT GRAND CUVEÉ EXTRA BRUT
chardonnay, macabeo, xarel.lo.

92 Colour: bright golden. Nose: fine lees, white flowers, citrus fruit, fragrant herbs, dry nuts. Palate: fresh, powerful, flavourful, fleshy, good acidity, fine bead.

EMENDIS

Barrio de Sant Marçal, 67
08732 Castellet i La Gornal (Barcelona)
☎: +34 938 186 119 - Fax: +34 938 918 169
avalles@emendis.es
www.emendis.es

EMENDIS TRÍO VARIETAL 2010 B
macabeo, chardonnay, moscatel.

87 Colour: bright yellow, greenish rim. Nose: balanced, tropical fruit, white flowers. Palate: correct, easy to drink, fruity.

EMENDIS 2007 BFB
chardonnay, xarel.lo.

88 Colour: bright yellow. Nose: candied fruit, toasty, sweet spices. Palate: rich, flavourful, ripe fruit, spicy.

EMENDIS NOX 2010 RD
syrah, pinot noir.

84 Colour: light cherry. Nose: powerfull, warm, red berry notes, ripe fruit, dried flowers. Palate: good structure, fleshy, flavourful.

EMENDIS MATER 2006 TC
100% merlot.

88 Colour: cherry, garnet rim. Nose: ripe fruit, medium intensity, new oak, sweet spices. Palate: powerful, flavourful, toasty, round tannins, good structure.

EUDALD MASSANA NOYA

Finca El Maset, s/n
08739 Sant Pau D'Ordal (Subirats) (Barcelona)
☎: +34 938 994 124 - Fax: +34 938 994 139
bodega@massananoya.com
www.massananoya.com

CEPELL EUDALD MASSANA NOYA 2010 B
macabeo, xarel.lo, moscatel.

83 Colour: bright yellow, greenish rim. Nose: fresh fruit, wild herbs, citrus fruit. Palate: fruity, easy to drink, good finish.

EUDALD MASSANA NOYA CEPELL 2010 RD
merlot.

83 Colour: rose, purple rim. Nose: ripe fruit, floral, medium intensity. Palate: fleshy, light-bodied, fruity.

EUDALD MASSANA NOYA LA CREUETA 2009 T
cabernet sauvignon, merlot.

88 Color bright cherry. Aroma ripe fruit, sweet spices, creamy oak, expressive. Taste flavourful, fruity, toasty, round tannins.

FERRE I CATASUS

Ctra. de Sant Sadurní, Km. 8- Masía Can Gustems
08792 La Granada (Barcelona)
☎: +34 938 974 558 - Fax: +34 938 974 708
maracalvo@ferreicatasus.com
www.castelldelmirall.com

FERRÉ I CATASÚS SOMIATRUITES 2010 B
30% moscatel, 30% sauvignon blanc, 20% chenin blanc, 20% xarel.lo.

88 Colour: bright straw. Nose: fresh, fresh fruit, white flowers, expressive, dried herbs. Palate: flavourful, fruity, good acidity, balanced.

MAS SUAU 2010 B
30% xarel.lo, 30% sauvignon blanc, 20% macabeo, 20% parellada.

86 Colour: bright straw. Nose: floral, citrus fruit, fragrant herbs. Palate: good acidity, powerful, flavourful, fleshy.

FERRÉ I CATASÚS CHARDONNAY 2007 B
chardonnay.

88 Colour: bright golden. Nose: powerfull, ripe fruit, sweet spices, creamy oak, fragrant herbs. Palate: rich, smoky aftertaste, flavourful, fresh, good acidity.

CAP DE TRONS 2010 T
40% syrah, 30% cabernet sauvignon, 30% merlot.

88 Colour: bright cherry, purple rim. Nose: powerfull, balsamic herbs, fruit expression, balanced. Palate: fruity, easy to drink, good acidity.

MAS SUAU 2010 T
cabernet sauvignon, merlot, syrah, ull de llebre.

85 Colour: cherry, purple rim. Nose: fresh fruit, red berry notes, floral, balsamic herbs. Palate: flavourful, fruity, good acidity.

FERRÉ I CATASÚS CLÀSSIC 2007 T
cabernet sauvignon, merlot.

86 Colour: cherry, garnet rim. Nose: ripe fruit, spicy, creamy oak. Palate: toasty, flavourful, fleshy.

FINCA VALLDOSERA

Pol. Ind. Clot de Moja- Merlot, 11
08734 Moja (Barcelona)
☎: +34 938 904 353 - Fax: +34 938 904 334
euroseleccio@euroseleccio.com
www.fincavalldosera.com

VALLDOSERA 2010 B
100% xarel.lo.

88 Colour: pale. Nose: varietal, powerfull, expressive, fresh fruit. Palate: fruity, powerful, complex.

FINCA VALLDOSERA 2010 T
50% syrah, 35% merlot, 15% cabernet sauvignon.

88 Colour: deep cherry. Nose: raspberry, fruit expression, mineral. Palate: flavourful, fine bitter notes, good acidity.

GIRÓ DEL GORNER

Finca Giró del Gorner, s/n
08797 Puigdálber (Barcelona)
☎: +34 938 988 032 - Fax: +34 938 988 032
gorner@girodelgorner.com
www.girodelgorner.com

XAREL.LO GORNER 2010 B
100% xarel.lo.

87 Colour: bright yellow. Nose: ripe fruit, faded flowers, sweet spices, creamy oak. Palate: powerful, flavourful, fleshy, fine bitter notes.

BLANC GORNER 2010 B
macabeo, xarel.lo, parellada.

86 Colour: straw. Nose: dried flowers, ripe fruit, wild herbs. Palate: light-bodied, fresh, fruity.

ROSAT GORNER 2010 RD
100% merlot.

86 Colour: light cherry. Nose: wild herbs, ripe fruit, citrus fruit. Palate: flavourful, fruity, good acidity.

GIRÓ RIBOT

Finca El Pont, s/n
08792 Santa Fe del Penedès (Barcelona)
☎: +34 938 974 050 - Fax: +34 938 974 311
comercial@giroribot.es
www.giroribot.es

GIRO2 2010 B
100% giró.

89 Colour: bright straw. Nose: citrus fruit, floral, fragrant herbs, mineral. Palate: good acidity, balanced, flavourful, rich, fleshy.

GIRÓ RIBOT MUSCAT DE FRONTIGNAC 2010 B
100% moscatel grano menudo.

86 Colour: bright straw, greenish rim. Nose: varietal, balanced, floral. Palate: flavourful, fresh, correct, easy to drink.

GIRÓ RIBOT BLANC DE BLANCS 2010 B
50% xarel.lo, 30% macabeo, 20% parellada.

84 Colour: bright yellow. Nose: fresh fruit, wild herbs, citrus fruit. Palate: flavourful, good acidity, correct.

GRIMAU DE PUJADES

Castell de Les Pujades, s/n
08732 La Munia (Barcelona)
☎: +34 938 918 031 - Fax: +34 938 918 427
grimau@grimau.com
www.grimau.com

GRIMAU BLANC DE BLANCS 2010 B
macabeo, parellada, xarel.lo, chardonnay.

84 Colour: bright straw. Nose: floral, ripe fruit, medium intensity. Palate: light-bodied, fresh, fruity.

GRIMAU CHARDONNAY 2008 BC
chardonnay.

81 Colour: bright golden. Nose: overripe fruit, slightly evolved, roasted coffee. Palate: powerful, rich, oaky.

GRIMAU MERLOT 2010 RD
merlot.

82 Colour: light cherry. Nose: scrubland, balsamic herbs, ripe fruit. Palate: flavourful, good acidity, fine bitter notes.

RUBICUNDUS 2007 T
80% tempranillo, 20% cabernet sauvignon.

85 Colour: dark-red cherry, garnet rim. Nose: powerfull, fruit expression, scrubland. Palate: good structure, flavourful, long, fine bitter notes.

GRIMAU CABERNET SAUVIGNON 2005 TR
cabernet sauvignon.

76

HERETAT MAS TINELL

Ctra. de Vilafranca a St. Martí Sarroca, Km. 0,5
08720 Vilafranca del Penedès (Barcelona)
☎: +34 938 170 586 - Fax: +34 938 170 500
info@mastinell.com
www.mastinell.com

MAS TINELL CHARDONNAY 2010 B
100% chardonnay.

86 Colour: bright straw. Nose: white flowers, fragrant herbs, expressive, citrus fruit. Palate: fruity, rich, flavourful.

MAS TINELL ALBA BLANC DE LLUNA 2010 B
20% macabeo, 20% xarel.lo, 30% parellada, 30% moscatel.

86 Colour: bright straw. Nose: expressive, white flowers, tropical fruit. Palate: light-bodied, easy to drink, flavourful, fruity.

MAS TINELL GISELE 2009 BFB
100% xarel.lo.

90 Colour: bright golden. Nose: fragrant herbs, floral, creamy oak, citrus fruit. Palate: creamy, flavourful, fleshy.

MAS TINELL CLOS SANT PAU 2008 B
100% moscatel.

87 Colour: bright golden. Nose: fragrant herbs, floral, honeyed notes. Palate: fleshy, flavourful, fruity, sweetness.

MAS TINELL ARTE 2005 TR
34% cabernet sauvignon, 33% merlot, 33% garnacha.

84 Colour: cherry, garnet rim. Nose: tobacco, spicy, aromatic coffee. Palate: spicy, long, fleshy.

HERETAT MONT-RUBÍ

L'Avellà, 1
08736 Font- Rubí (Barcelona)
☎: +34 938 979 066 - Fax: +34 938 979 066
hmr@mont-rubi.com
www.mont-rubi.com

WHITE HMR 2010 B
100% xarel.lo.

90 Colour: bright straw. Nose: expressive, balanced, wild herbs, dried flowers, fresh. Palate: flavourful, good acidity, balanced, fine bitter notes.

ADVENT 2009 B
100% xarel.lo.

89 Colour: golden. Nose: powerfull, floral, honeyed notes, candied fruit, fragrant herbs, toasty. Palate: flavourful, sweet, fruity, good acidity, long.

ADVENT SUMOLL 2008 T
sumoll.

93 Colour: coppery red. Nose: powerfull, overripe fruit, petrol notes, pattiserie, sweet spices. Palate: flavourful, rich, toasty.

GAINTUS 2007 T
100% sumoll.

89 Colour: black cherry. Nose: ripe fruit, earthy notes, mineral, spicy, creamy oak. Palate: powerful, flavourful, good acidity, long.

DURONA 2005 T
30% sumoll, 20% garnacha, 20% cariñena, 10% merlot, 20% syrah.

89 Colour: pale ruby, brick rim edge. Nose: elegant, spicy, wet leather, aged wood nuances, fruit liqueur notes. Palate: spicy, fine tannins, long.

J. MIQUEL JANÉ

Masia Cal Costas, s/n
08736 Font- Rubí (Barcelona)
☎: +34 934 140 948 - Fax: +34 934 140 948
admin@jmigueljane.com
www.jmiqueljane.com

J. MIQUEL JANÉ SAUVIGNON BLANC 2010 B
100% sauvignon blanc.

88 Colour: bright straw. Nose: ripe fruit, dried flowers, fragrant herbs, expressive. Palate: powerful, flavourful, fruity, good acidity.

J. MIQUEL JANÉ BLANC BALTANA 2010 B
40% xarel.lo, 30% macabeo, 30% parellada.

85 Colour: bright straw. Nose: white flowers, fruit expression, medium intensity. Palate: light-bodied, fresh, fruity.

J. MIQUEL JANÉ CABERNET SAUVIGNON 2010 RD
100% cabernet sauvignon.

84 Colour: rose, purple rim. Nose: ripe fruit, faded flowers, powerfull. Palate: balanced, flavourful, fruity.

J. MIQUEL JANÉ 2010 T
merlot, cabernet sauvignon, garnacha.

83 Colour: dark-red cherry, purple rim. Nose: ripe fruit, balsamic herbs, spicy. Palate: powerful, flavourful, burning notes.

J. MIQUEL JANÉ 2005 TR
cabernet sauvignon, merlot, tempranillo.

86 Colour: deep cherry, garnet rim. Nose: medium intensity, ripe fruit, balsamic herbs, sweet spices. Palate: flavourful, correct.

JANÉ VENTURA

Ctra. Calafell, 2
43700 El Vendrell (Tarragona)
☎: +34 977 660 118 - Fax: +34 977 661 239
janeventura@janeventura.com
www.janeventura.com

JANÉ VENTURA "FINCA ELS CAMPS" MACABEU 2010 BFB
macabeo, malvasía.

93 Colour: bright yellow. Nose: powerfull, ripe fruit, sweet spices, creamy oak, fragrant herbs. Palate: rich, flavourful, fresh, good acidity.

JANÉ VENTURA SELECCIÓ 2010 B
xarel.lo, moscatel, sauvignon blanc, malvasía.

89 Colour: bright straw. Nose: mineral, fresh fruit, honeyed notes. Palate: flavourful, fruity, fresh.

JANÉ VENTURA SELECCIÓ 2010 RD
sumoll, syrah, tempranillo, merlot.

86 Colour: rose, purple rim. Nose: raspberry, fresh fruit, violet drops. Palate: flavourful, powerful, sweetness, fine bitter notes.

JANÉ VENTURA SUMOLL 2009 T
100% sumoll.

93 Colour: bright cherry. Nose: elegant, characterful, balsamic herbs, scrubland, fruit expression, red berry notes. Palate: flavourful, fruity, spicy, long, balsamic.

JANÉ VENTURA SELECCIÓ 12 VINYES 2009 T
40% tempranillo, 20% merlot, 20% cabernet sauvignon, 10% sumoll, 10% syrah.

91 Colour: cherry, purple rim. Nose: fruit expression, ripe fruit, sweet spices. Palate: flavourful, fruity, fleshy, round tannins.

JANÉ VENTURA "MAS VILELLA" COSTERS DEL ROTLLAN 2008 T
90% cabernet sauvignon, 5% sumoll, 5% tempranillo.

92 Colour: cherry, garnet rim. Nose: ripe fruit, fruit expression, scrubland, balsamic herbs. Palate: flavourful, spicy, ripe fruit, long.

JANÉ VENTURA "FINCA ELS CAMPS" ULL DE LLEBRE 2007 T
ull de llebre.

93 Colour: cherry, garnet rim. Nose: ripe fruit, spicy, creamy oak, complex, elegant, earthy notes, mineral. Palate: powerful, flavourful, toasty, round tannins.

JANÉ VENTURA "MAS VILELLA" COSTERS DEL ROTLLAN 2007 T
100% cabernet sauvignon.

91 Colour: cherry, garnet rim. Nose: ripe fruit, spicy, toasty, complex, scrubland, cocoa bean. Palate: powerful, flavourful, toasty, round tannins, fine bitter notes.

JAUME GIRÓ I GIRÓ

Montaner i Oller, 5
08770 Sant Sadurní D'Anoia (Barcelona)
☎: +34 938 910 165 - Fax: +34 938 911 271
cavagiro@cavagiro.com
www.cavagiro.com

JAUME GIRÓ I GIRÓ XAREL.LO CHARDONNAY 2010 B
90% xarel.lo, 10% chardonnay.

86 Colour: bright straw. Nose: ripe fruit, fragrant herbs. Palate: flavourful, correct, good acidity.

JAUME GIRÓ I GIRÓ CABERNET MERLOT 2008 T
cabernet sauvignon, merlot.

89 Colour: deep cherry, garnet rim. Nose: medium intensity, wild herbs, ripe fruit, varietal. Palate: flavourful, fine bitter notes, easy to drink.

JAUME LLOPART ALEMANY

Font Rubí, 9
08736 Font-Rubí (Barcelona)
☎: +34 938 979 133 - Fax: +34 938 979 133
info@jaumellopartalemany.com
www.jaumellopartalemany.com

JAUME LLOPART ALEMANY VINYA D'EN LLUC SAUVIGNON BLANC S/C B
100% sauvignon blanc.

86 Colour: bright straw. Nose: medium intensity, white flowers, faded flowers. Palate: correct, fine bitter notes, easy to drink.

JAUME LLOPART ALEMANY 2010 B
parellada, xarel.lo.

85 Colour: bright straw, greenish rim. Nose: wild herbs, medium intensity, faded flowers. Palate: flavourful, correct, good finish.

JAUME LLOPART ALEMANY 2010 RD
ull de llebre, merlot.

84 Colour: light cherry. Nose: balanced, ripe fruit, wild herbs, powerfull. Palate: flavourful, fleshy, ripe fruit, long.

JAUME LLOPART ALEMANY MERLOT 2010 T
100% merlot.

87 Colour: cherry, purple rim. Nose: expressive, fresh fruit, red berry notes, scrubland. Palate: flavourful, fruity, easy to drink.

JAUME SERRA

Ctra. de Vilanova, Km. 2,5
08800 Vilanova i la Geltru (Barcelona)
☎: +34 938 936 404 - Fax: +34 938 142 262
jaumeserra@jgc.es
www.garciacarrion.es

JAUME SERRA CHARDONNAY 2010 BFB
100% chardonnay.

87 Colour: bright yellow. Nose: ripe fruit, sweet spices, creamy oak, fragrant herbs, medium intensity. Palate: flavourful, fresh.

JAUME SERRA MACABEO 2010 B
100% macabeo.

83 Colour: bright yellow. Nose: ripe fruit, dried herbs. Palate: correct, easy to drink.

JAUME SERRA XAREL.LO 2010 B
100% xarel.lo.

83 Colour: bright yellow, greenish rim. Nose: balanced, faded flowers, fragrant herbs. Palate: flavourful, fruity, sweetness.

JAUME SERRA MERLOT 2010 RD
100% merlot.

85 Colour: rose, purple rim. Nose: floral, red berry notes, ripe fruit. Palate: flavourful, fruity, fleshy.

JAUME SERRA TEMPRANILLO 2009 T
100% tempranillo.

85 Colour: cherry, garnet rim. Nose: red berry notes, wild herbs, balanced. Palate: fruity, flavourful, good acidity.

JAUME SERRA 2007 TC
40% cabernet sauvignon, 40% merlot, 20% tempranillo.

82 Colour: cherry, garnet rim. Nose: fruit preserve, wild herbs, spicy. Palate: flavourful, spicy, easy to drink.

JAUME SERRA 2005 TR
40% cabernet sauvignon, 40% merlot, 20% tempranillo.

82 Colour: cherry, garnet rim. Nose: woody, spicy, fruit liqueur notes. Palate: correct, toasty, easy to drink.

JEAN LEÓN

Pago Jean León, s/n
08775 Torrelavit (Barcelona)
☎: +34 938 995 512 - Fax: +34 938 995 517
jeanleon@jeanleon.com
www.jeanleon.com

JEAN LEÓN PETIT CHARDONNAY 2010 B
100% chardonnay.

90 Colour: bright yellow. Nose: white flowers, fruit expression, mineral, fragrant herbs, expressive. Palate: powerful, complex, fruity, flavourful, elegant.

JEAN LEÓN VIÑA GIGI CHARDONNAY 2008 B
100% chardonnay.

94 Colour: bright golden. Nose: faded flowers, ripe fruit, powerfull, sweet spices, creamy oak. Palate: powerful, flavourful, complex, fleshy, toasty.

JEAN LEÓN PETIT MERLOT 2010 T ROBLE
100% merlot.

86 Colour: cherry, purple rim. Nose: medium intensity, spicy, red berry notes, scrubland. Palate: ripe fruit, easy to drink.

ZEMIS 2007 TR
50% cabernet sauvignon, 30% merlot, 20% cabernet franc.

92 Colour: deep cherry, garnet rim. Nose: dry stone, ripe fruit, sweet spices, creamy oak, elegant. Palate: long, spicy, balanced, fine bitter notes, good structure.

JEAN LEÓN VINYA PALAU MERLOT 2007 TC
100% merlot.

90 Colour: deep cherry, garnet rim. Nose: medium intensity, balanced, sweet spices, cocoa bean, ripe fruit. Palate: good structure, flavourful.

JEAN LEÓN CABERNET SAUVIGNON 2006 TR
85% cabernet sauvignon, 15% cabernet franc.

90 Colour: cherry, garnet rim. Nose: medium intensity, ripe fruit, sweet spices, scrubland. Palate: good structure, complex, spicy, ripe fruit, long.

JEAN LEÓN VINYA LA SCALA CABERNET SAUVIGNON 2001 TGR
100% cabernet sauvignon.

92 Color pale ruby, brick rim edge. Aroma elegant, spicy, fine reductive notes, wet leather, aged wood nuances, fruit liqueur notes. Taste spicy, fine tannins, elegant, long.

JORDI ALEMANY BONASTRE

Ctra. Gélida a St. Llorenç d'Hortons, km. 5,25
08790 Gelida (Barcelona)
☎: +34 933 713 279
jalemany@matadabello.com
www.matadabello.com

MATA D'ABELLO "TOIETES" 2010 B
xarel.lo.

84 Colour: bright yellow. Nose: ripe fruit, white flowers. Palate: flavourful, fine bitter notes, correct.

MATA D'ABELLO BALLÓ 2009 TC
merlot.

83 Colour: deep cherry, garnet rim. Nose: fruit preserve, toasty, fruit liqueur notes. Palate: fleshy, spicy, long.

FINCA ABELLO CINQUANTA-CINQUANTA 2010
merlot.

81 Colour: deep cherry, purple rim. Nose: powerfull, fruit preserve, sweet spices. Palate: flavourful, fine bitter notes.

JOSEP Mª RAVENTÓS BLANC

Plaça del Roure, s/n
08770 Sant Sadurní D'Anoia (Barcelona)
☎: +34 938 183 262 - Fax: +34 938 912 500
raventos@raventos.com
www.raventos.com

PERFUM DE VI BLANC 2010 B
moscatel, macabeo.

88 Colour: bright straw, greenish rim. Nose: varietal, jasmine, expressive, powerfull. Palate: flavourful, fruity, rich.

SILENCIS 2009 B
100% xarel.lo.

92 Colour: bright yellow. Nose: powerfull, sweet spices, fragrant herbs, medium intensity, candied fruit, citrus fruit. Palate: rich, smoky aftertaste, flavourful, fresh, good acidity.

LA ROSA DE RAVENTÓS I BLANC 2010 RD
pinot noir, merlot.

87 Colour: brilliant rose. Nose: medium intensity, red berry notes, citrus fruit, fragrant herbs. Palate: flavourful, fresh, fruity, good acidity.

11 DE ISABEL NEGRA 2008 T
100% monastrell.

93 Colour: cherry, garnet rim. Nose: spicy, creamy oak, toasty, complex, earthy notes, mineral, ripe fruit. Palate: powerful, flavourful, toasty, round tannins. Personality.

ISABEL NEGRA 2008 T
65% syrah, 20% cabernet sauvignon, 15% monastrell.

89 Colour: deep cherry, garnet rim. Nose: powerfull, mineral, warm, wild herbs, spicy. Palate: ripe fruit, balanced, flavourful.

JUVÉ Y CAMPS

Sant Venat, 1
08770 Sant Sadurní D'Anoia (Barcelona)
☎: +34 938 911 000 - Fax: +34 938 912 100
juveycamps@juveycamps.com
www.juveycamps.com

MIRANDA D'ESPIELLS 2010 B
100% chardonnay.

88 Colour: bright straw. Nose: dried flowers, fruit expression, balsamic herbs, mineral. Palate: powerful, flavourful, rich, fleshy.

ERMITA D'ESPIELLS 2010 B
36% xarel.lo, 32% macabeo, 12% parellada, 20% chardonnay.

87 Colour: bright straw. Nose: white flowers, fragrant herbs, fruit expression. Palate: light-bodied, fresh, fruity, complex.

FLOR D'ESPIELLS 2009 BFB
100% chardonnay.

88 Colour: bright golden. Nose: ripe fruit, dry nuts, powerfull, toasty. Palate: flavourful, fruity, spicy, toasty, long.

CASA VELLA D'ESPIELLS 2008 T
80% cabernet sauvignon, 20% merlot.

91 Colour: cherry, garnet rim. Nose: complex, ripe fruit, sweet spices, balanced. Palate: flavourful, spicy, long.

VIÑA ESCARLATA 2008 T
100% merlot.

90 Colour: cherry, garnet rim. Nose: balanced, complex, scrubland, ripe fruit. Palate: good structure, spicy, ripe fruit.

IOHANNES 2007 T
60% merlot, 40% cabernet sauvignon.

91 Colour: very deep cherry, garnet rim. Nose: balanced, powerfull, toasty, sweet spices, scrubland. Palate: good structure, flavourful, spicy, ripe fruit.

CASA VELLA D'ESPIELLS MAGNUM 2008 T ROBLE
80% cabernet sauvignon, 20% merlot.

90 Colour: deep cherry, garnet rim. Nose: powerfull, macerated fruit, spicy, scrubland, varietal. Palate: flavourful, good structure, spicy, good acidity.

LLOPART CAVA

Ctra. de Sant Sadurni - Ordal, Km. 4
08739 Subirats (Barcelona)
☎: +34 938 993 125 - Fax: +34 938 993 038
llopart@llopart.es
www.llopart.es

LLOPART CLOS DELS FÒSSILS CHARDONNAY 2010 B
85% chardonnay, 15% xarel.lo.

88 Colour: bright straw. Nose: fresh fruit, dried herbs. Palate: fruity, flavourful, balanced, fine bitter notes, good acidity.

LLOPART VITIS 2010 B
60% xarel.lo, 10% moscatel, 30% subirat parent.

86 Colour: bright straw. Nose: wild herbs, white flowers. Palate: correct, fruity, easy to drink.

LLOPART CASTELL DE SUBIRATS 2007 T ROBLE
40% merlot, 30% cabernet sauvignon, 30% tempranillo.

89 Color bright cherry. Aroma ripe fruit, sweet spices, creamy oak, expressive. Taste flavourful, fruity, toasty, round tannins.

LOXAREL

Masia Can Mayol, s/n
08735 Vilobí del Penedès (Barcelona)
☎: +34 938 978 001 - Fax: +34 938 978 111
loxarel@loxarel.com
www.loxarel.com

CORA DE LOXAREL 2010 B
xarel.lo, moscatel, chardonnay.

87 Colour: bright straw. Nose: fresh fruit, white flowers, expressive, powerfull, fragrant herbs. Palate: flavourful, fruity, good acidity, balanced.

GAIA DE LOXAREL 2010 B
100% sauvignon blanc.

87 Colour: bright yellow. Nose: tropical fruit, fresh fruit, floral, fragrant herbs. Palate: light-bodied, fresh, fruity, flavourful.

PETIT ARNAU DE LOXAREL 2010 RD
pinot noir, cabernet sauvignon, merlot.

83 Colour: light cherry. Nose: medium intensity, ripe fruit, lactic notes, red berry notes, dried flowers. Palate: flavourful, fruity.

GAL GRAN ARNAU DE LOXAREL 2009 RD
100% merlot.

86 Colour: light cherry, orangey edge. Nose: candied fruit, faded flowers, balsamic herbs. Palate: powerful, flavourful, fruity, spicy.

EOS DE LOXAREL SYRAH 2009 T
100% syrah.

89 Colour: cherry, garnet rim. Nose: ripe fruit, balsamic herbs, cocoa bean, toasty, expressive. Palate: complex, fleshy, powerful, flavourful.

OPS DE LOXAREL 2008 T
cabernet sauvignon, merlot, tempranillo.

88 Colour: cherry, garnet rim. Nose: red berry notes, ripe fruit, sweet spices, cocoa bean, toasty. Palate: good acidity, round, flavourful.

LOXAREL CABERNET 2007 TR
100% cabernet sauvignon.

87 Colour: cherry, garnet rim. Nose: ripe fruit, balsamic herbs, sweet spices, toasty. Palate: easy to drink, flavourful, fruity, fleshy.

MAS CARGOLS DE LOXAREL 2007 T
100% pinot noir.

86 Colour: light cherry, orangey edge. Nose: red berry notes, ripe fruit, sweet spices, wet leather. Palate: fleshy, complex, flavourful.

MARTÍ SERDÀ

Ctra. de Igualada a Vilafranca, Km. 31,300
08792 Santa Fe del Penedès (Barcelona)
☎: +34 938 974 411 - Fax: +34 938 974 405
info@martiserda.com
www.martiserda.com

VINYET 2010 B JOVEN
50% macabeo, 35% parellada, 15% xarel.lo.

85 Colour: bright straw, greenish rim. Nose: fresh fruit, wild herbs, faded flowers. Palate: flavourful, fruity, easy to drink.

MASÍA D'OR MEDIUM 2010 B
50% macabeo, 35% xarel.lo, 15% moscatel.

85 Colour: bright straw, greenish rim. Nose: varietal, white flowers, powerfull, candied fruit. Palate: sweetness, fruity.

MARE NOSTRUM VINO DE AGUJA 2010 B
40% macabeo, 35% xarel.lo, 25% parellada.

83 Colour: bright yellow. Nose: floral, medium intensity, fruit expression. Palate: flavourful, fresh, easy to drink.

VINYET 2010 RD JOVEN
40% merlot, 35% garnacha, 30% tempranillo.

84 Colour: rose. Nose: medium intensity, red berry notes, dried herbs. Palate: fruity, correct, easy to drink.

VINYET 2008 TC
75% tempranillo, 25% cabernet sauvignon.

86 Colour: cherry, garnet rim. Nose: fragrant herbs, spicy, ripe fruit. Palate: good structure, ripe fruit.

MARTÍ SERDÁ MERLOT 2005 TC
100% merlot.

83 Colour: cherry, garnet rim. Nose: balanced, toasty, spicy, scrubland. Palate: ripe fruit, easy to drink, spicy.

MARTÍ SERDÁ MAS FARRENY 2003 TR
80% merlot, 20% cabernet sauvignon.

85 Colour: bright cherry, garnet rim. Nose: fruit preserve, overripe fruit, sweet spices. Palate: pruney, long, flavourful.

MAS CAN COLOMÉ

Masies Sant Marçal s/n
08729 Castellet i La Gornal (Barcelona)
☎: +34 938 918 203 - Fax: +34 938 171 561
info@mascancolome.com
www.mascancolome.com

TURONET 2010 B
40% chardonnay, 30% xarel.lo, 10% sauvignon blanc.

90 Colour: bright straw, greenish rim. Nose: balanced, fresh fruit, wild herbs. Palate: correct, good acidity, balanced.

BLANC MEDITERRANI 2010 B
50% xarel.lo, 30% macabeo, 15% parellada, 15% moscatel.

86 Colour: bright straw. Nose: medium intensity, floral, dried herbs. Palate: flavourful, fine bitter notes, good acidity.

ROSADENC 2010 RD
40% garnacha, 40% syrah, 20% pinot noir.

86 Colour: light cherry. Nose: jasmine, wild herbs, faded flowers, ripe fruit. Palate: flavourful, fruity, good acidity.

TURO 2010 T
40% garnacha, 40% samsó, 20% syrah.

88 Colour: cherry, purple rim. Nose: balanced, expressive, scrubland, sweet spices, red berry notes. Palate: flavourful, fruity, good acidity.

MAS CANCOLOMÉ VITICULTORS 2009 BN
45% xarel.lo, 30% macabeo, 25% parellada.

86 Colour: bright straw, greenish rim. Nose: medium intensity, fresh fruit. Palate: fruity, correct, easy to drink.

SERENOR 2008 ESP
40% xarel.lo, 35% chardonnay, 15% macabeo, 10% parellada.

89 Colour: bright yellow, greenish rim. Nose: dry nuts, balanced, fresh, dried herbs. Palate: flavourful, fruity, fresh.

MAS CANDÍ

Ctra. de Les Gunyoles, s/n
08793 Les Gunyoles d'Avinyonet (Barcelona)
☎: +34 680 765 275
info@mascandi.com
www.mascandi.com

MAS CANDI PECAT NOBLE 2010 B
malvasía.

92 Colour: bright yellow. Nose: faded flowers, ripe fruit, citrus fruit, complex, expressive. Palate: rich, flavourful, fruity, fleshy, balanced.

MAS CANDI DESIG 2010 B
xarel.lo.

85 Colour: bright straw, greenish rim. Nose: medium intensity, white flowers, dried herbs. Palate: flavourful, fresh, fruity.

MAS CANDÍ QUATRE XAREL.LO QX 2009 BFB
xarel.lo.

89 Colour: bright yellow. Nose: medium intensity, ripe fruit, sweet spices, faded flowers. Palate: flavourful, rich, fruity.

MAS CANDÍ LES FORQUES 2008 T
cabernet sauvignon, sumoll.

90 Colour: black cherry, garnet rim. Nose: powerfull, ripe fruit, candied fruit, dark chocolate, sweet spices. Palate: ripe fruit, spicy, round tannins, good acidity.

MAS CANDÍ SOL+SOL 2007 T
cabernet sauvignon, sumoll, otras.

91 Colour: very deep cherry, garnet rim. Nose: powerfull, dark chocolate, sweet spices, scrubland, candied fruit. Palate: good structure, complex, powerful.

MAS CODINA

Barri El Gorner, s/n - Mas Codina
08797 Puigdalber (Barcelona)
☎: +34 938 988 166 - Fax: +34 938 988 166
info@mascodina.com
www.mascodina.com

MAS CODINA 2010 B
xarel.lo, macabeo, chardonnay, moscatel.

85 Colour: bright straw. Nose: white flowers, fragrant herbs, medium intensity. Palate: fine bitter notes, powerful, flavourful.

MAS CODINA 2010 RD
merlot, cabernet sauvignon.

83 Colour: light cherry. Nose: powerfull, ripe fruit, wild herbs. Palate: flavourful, fleshy, ripe fruit.

MAS CODINA VINYA MIQUEL 2007 T
syrah.

89 Colour: very deep cherry, garnet rim. Nose: macerated fruit, ripe fruit, sweet spices, cocoa bean. Palate: flavourful, sweet tannins.

MAS CODINA VINYA FERRER 2007 TC
cabernet sauvignon.

87 Colour: dark-red cherry, garnet rim. Nose: ripe fruit, balsamic herbs, spicy, creamy oak. Palate: good acidity, round, powerful, flavourful.

MAS COMTAL

Mas Comtal, 1
08793 Avinyonet del Penedès (Barcelona)
☎: +34 938 970 052 - Fax: +34 938 970 591
mascomtal@mascomtal.com
www.mascomtal.com

MAS COMTAL 2010 BFB
xarel.lo, chardonnay.

86 Colour: bright straw. Nose: faded flowers, dried herbs, ripe fruit. Palate: powerful, flavourful, fleshy, spicy, long.

MAS COMTAL JOAN MILA CUVÈE PRESTIGE 2006 B
50% xarel.lo, 50% chardonnay.

86 Colour: bright golden. Nose: ripe fruit, lees reduction notes, dry nuts, sweet spices. Palate: round, powerful, flavourful, fleshy.

PÉTREA 2005 BFB
85% chardonnay, 15% xarel.lo.

87 Colour: bright golden. Nose: powerfull, ripe fruit, sweet spices, creamy oak, fragrant herbs. Palate: rich, flavourful, fresh, fleshy.

ROSAT DE LLÀGRIMA 2010 RD
100% merlot.

85 Colour: light cherry. Nose: wild herbs, medium intensity, balanced. Palate: fruity, easy to drink.

MAS COMTAL 2010 T ROBLE
merlot, cabernet sauvignon, cabernet franc.

87 Colour: cherry, purple rim. Nose: medium intensity, red berry notes, ripe fruit, balsamic herbs, spicy. Palate: fruity, easy to drink, good finish.

ANTISTIANA 2008 T
85% merlot, 15% cabernet sauvignon.

88 Colour: cherry, garnet rim. Nose: ripe fruit, balsamic herbs, spicy, creamy oak. Palate: powerful, flavourful, fleshy, long.

PETREA 2005 TC
100% merlot.

88 Colour: light cherry, orangey edge. Nose: ripe fruit, fruit liqueur notes, spicy, creamy oak. Palate: powerful, flavourful, fleshy, complex.

LYRIC LICOROSO
merlot.

90 Colour: coppery red. Nose: fruit liqueur notes, cocoa bean, pattiserie, dark chocolate, toasty. Palate: balanced, powerful, flavourful, fleshy.

MAS FERRANT MARXANTS DE VINS

Córsega, 73- 1º
08029 (Barcelona)
☎: +34 934 191 000 - Fax: +34 934 193 170
jcivit@montferrant.com

MAS FERRANT SONATINA 2005 BFB
chardonnay.

93 Color bright golden. Aroma ripe fruit, dry nuts, powerfull, toasty, aged wood nuances. Taste flavourful, fruity, spicy, toasty, long.

MAS RODÓ VITIVINÍCOLA

km. 2 Ctra. Sant Pere Sacarrera a Sant Joan de Mediona
08773 Mediona (Barcelona)
☎: +34 932 385 780 - Fax: +34 932 174 356
info@masrodo.com
www.masrodo.com

MAS RODÓ MACABEO 2009 B
100% macabeo.

89 Colour: bright yellow. Nose: powerfull, ripe fruit, sweet spices, creamy oak. Palate: rich, flavourful, fresh, good acidity.

MAS RODÓ MONTONEGA 2009 B
100% montonega.

87 Colour: bright straw. Nose: white flowers, expressive, ripe fruit, fine lees. Palate: flavourful, fruity, good acidity, balanced.

MAS RODÓ CABERNET SAUVIGNON 2008 T
100% cabernet sauvignon.

84 Colour: dark-red cherry, garnet rim. Nose: powerfull, fruit preserve, toasty, sweet spices. Palate: powerful, ripe fruit, spicy.

MAS RODÓ MERLOT 2008 TC
100% merlot.

78

MASET DEL LLEÓ

C-244, Km. 32,5
08792 La Granada del Penedès (Barcelona)
☎: +34 902 200 250 - Fax: +34 938 921 333
info@maset.com
www.maset.com

MASET DEL LLEÓ CHARDONNAY FLOR DE MAR 2010 B
chardonnay.

87 Colour: bright yellow, greenish rim. Nose: fruit expression, faded flowers. Palate: flavourful, fruity, easy to drink, long.

MASET DEL LLEÓ XAREL.LO BLANC DE BLANCS 2010 B
xarel.lo.

86 Colour: bright straw, greenish rim. Nose: balanced, medium intensity, fresh fruit, floral. Palate: flavourful, good acidity, fine bitter notes.

MASET DEL LLEÓ MERLOT 2010 RD
merlot.

85 Color rose, purple rim. Aroma powerfull, ripe fruit, red berry notes, floral, expressive. Taste fleshy, powerful, fruity, fresh.

MASET DEL LLEÓ TEMPRANILLO SELECCIÓN 2009 T
tempranillo.

90 Color cherry, purple rim. Aroma expressive, fresh fruit, red berry notes, floral. Taste flavourful, fruity, good acidity, round tannins.

MASET DEL LLEÓ 2008 T ROBLE
tempranillo.

85 Color bright cherry. Aroma ripe fruit, sweet spices, creamy oak, expressive. Taste flavourful, fruity, toasty, round tannins.

MASET DEL LLEÓ MERLOT FOC 2007 TR
merlot.

88 Colour: light cherry, garnet rim. Nose: ripe fruit, fine reductive notes, spicy, toasty. Palate: powerful, spirituous, round.

MASET DEL LLEÓ CABERNET SAUVIGNON 2007 TR
cabernet sauvignon.

85 Colour: cherry, garnet rim. Nose: ripe fruit, spicy, toasty, complex. Palate: powerful, flavourful, toasty, round tannins.

MASIA VALLFORMOSA

La Sala, 45
08735 Vilobi del Penedès (Barcelona)
☎: +34 938 978 286 - Fax: +34 938 978 355
vallformosa@vallformosa.es
www.vallformosa.com

ANNA DE VALLFORMOSA 2010 B
xarel.lo, chardonnay.

88 Colour: bright straw. Nose: fresh, fresh fruit, white flowers, citrus fruit. Palate: flavourful, fruity, good acidity, balanced.

VALLFORMOSA VIÑA BLANCA 2010 B
macabeo, xarel.lo, parellada.

85 Colour: bright straw. Nose: dried flowers, fruit expression, citrus fruit. Palate: good acidity, flavourful, fruity.

MARINA DE VALLFORMOSA 2010 B
55% xarel.lo, 45% parellada.

83 Colour: pale. Nose: white flowers, citrus fruit, fresh. Palate: good acidity, correct.

CLAUDIA DE VALLFORMOSA 2010 B
70% parellada, 30% moscatel.

86 Colour: pale. Nose: white flowers, fresh fruit, expressive. Palate: fresh, fruity, flavourful, easy to drink.

VALLFORMOSA CLOS MASET 2006 T
100% cabernet sauvignon.

91 Colour: cherry, garnet rim. Nose: mineral, sweet spices, creamy oak, balsamic herbs. Palate: balanced, good acidity, flavourful, fleshy, round tannins.

GEMMA DE VALLFORMOSA 2010 RD
100% merlot.

87 Colour: rose, purple rim. Nose: red berry notes, fresh fruit, violet drops, raspberry. Palate: fruity, fresh, flavourful, fleshy.

VALLFORMOSA VIÑA ROSADA 2010 RD
garnacha, cariñena.

87 Colour: light cherry. Nose: floral, raspberry, ripe fruit, expressive. Palate: powerful, light-bodied, fresh, fruity.

MARINA DE VALLFORMOSA 2010 RD
70% tempranillo, 30% garnacha.

82 Colour: brilliant rose. Nose: fresh, fruit expression, floral. Palate: fresh, light-bodied, flavourful.

VALLFORMOSA VIÑA BRUNA 2009 T
tempranillo.

88 Colour: cherry, purple rim. Nose: expressive, fresh fruit, red berry notes, floral, sweet spices. Palate: flavourful, fruity, good acidity.

VALLFORMOSA SYRAH TEMPRANILLO 2009 T ROBLE
60% syrah, 40% tempranillo.

87 Colour: cherry, purple rim. Nose: red berry notes, creamy oak, floral. Palate: fruity, flavourful, fleshy, complex.

VALLFORMOSA 2006 TC
90% tempranillo, 10% garnacha.

87 Colour: cherry, garnet rim. Nose: wild herbs, ripe fruit, spicy, toasty. Palate: spirituous, flavourful, fleshy.

VALLFORMOSA TEMPRANILLO CABERNET SAUVIGNON 2005 TR
85% tempranillo, 15% cabernet sauvignon.

88 Colour: cherry, garnet rim. Nose: ripe fruit, creamy oak, toasty, fine reductive notes, balsamic herbs. Palate: powerful, flavourful, toasty.

VALLFORMOSA MASIA FREYÉ 2005 T
100% merlot.

87 Color cherry, garnet rim. Aroma ripe fruit, spicy, creamy oak, toasty, complex. Taste powerful, flavourful, toasty, round tannins.

MASIA FREYÉ MERLOT DE VALLFORMOSA 2005 T
100% merlot.

86 Colour: ruby red, garnet rim. Nose: ripe fruit, roasted coffee, varnish. Palate: fleshy, round tannins, balsamic.

VALLFORMOSA TEMPRANILLO CABERNET SAUVIGNON 2003 TGR
75% tempranillo, 25% cabernet sauvignon.

87 Colour: pale ruby, brick rim edge. Nose: spicy, fine reductive notes, wet leather, aged wood nuances, fruit liqueur notes. Palate: spicy, fine tannins, elegant, long.

VALLFORMOSA CABERNET SAUVIGNON 2003 T
cabernet sauvignon.

84 Colour: pale ruby, brick rim edge. Nose: elegant, spicy, wet leather, aged wood nuances, fruit liqueur notes, scrubland. Palate: spicy, fine tannins, elegant, long.

MATA D'ABELLÓ

Can Mata D'Abelló
08790 Gélida (Barcelona)
☎: +34 933 713 279 - Fax: +34 933 713 279
jalemany@matadabello.com
www.matadabello.com

TOTTÓ 2010 BFB
xarel.lo.

86 Colour: bright yellow, greenish rim. Nose: fresh fruit, wild herbs. Palate: correct, flavourful, fruity, easy to drink, spicy.

FINCA AVELLÓ XAREL.LO 2010 B
xarel.lo.

86 Colour: bright yellow, greenish rim. Nose: balanced, wild herbs, faded flowers. Palate: flavourful, fruity, easy to drink.

MONT MARÇAL

Finca Manlleu
08732 Castellví de la Marca (Barcelona)
☎: +34 938 918 281 - Fax: +34 938 919 045
mrivas@mont-marcal.com
www.mont-marcal.com

MONT MARÇAL 2010 B
50% xarel.lo, 30% sauvignon blanc, 20% chardonnay.

87 Colour: bright straw. Nose: white flowers, ripe fruit, expressive. Palate: powerful, flavourful, fleshy, fruity.

MONT MARÇAL 2010 RD
50% merlot, 35% cabernet sauvignon, 15% syrah.

84 Colour: rose, ochre. Nose: scrubland, medium intensity, dried flowers. Palate: flavourful, fleshy.

MONT MARÇAL 2010 T
merlot, tempranillo, syrah.

86 Colour: cherry, garnet rim. Nose: medium intensity, red berry notes, wild herbs, violets. Palate: flavourful, long.

MONT MARÇAL 2008 TC
50% merlot, 50% cabernet sauvignon.

85 Colour: light cherry, brick rim edge. Nose: ripe fruit, fruit preserve, toasty, creamy oak. Palate: spicy, flavourful, fleshy.

MONT MARÇAL 2007 TR
50% tempranillo, 50% cabernet sauvignon.

87 Colour: cherry, garnet rim. Nose: ripe fruit, spicy, toasty, complex, fine reductive notes. Palate: powerful, flavourful, toasty, round tannins.

PARATÓ

Can Respall de Renardes
08733 (Barcelona)
☎: +34 938 988 182 - Fax: +34 938 988 510
info@parato.es
www.parato.es

PARATÓ ÁTICA TRES X TRES 2010 B
5% macabeo, 62% xarel.lo, 33% chardonnay.

89 Colour: bright straw. Nose: faded flowers, ripe fruit, fragrant herbs, sweet spices, creamy oak. Palate: rich, flavourful, fleshy, complex.

FINCA RENARDES BLANC MACABEU + COUPAGE 2010 B
46% macabeo, 43% chardonnay, 11% xarel.lo.

88 Color bright straw. Aroma fresh, fresh fruit, white flowers, expressive. Taste flavourful, fruity, good acidity, balanced.

PARATÓ XAREL.LO 2010 B
100% xarel.lo.

87 Color bright straw. Aroma fresh, fresh fruit, white flowers, expressive. Taste flavourful, fruity, good acidity, balanced.

PARATÓ PINOT NOIR 2010 RD
100% pinot noir.

85 Colour: rose, purple rim. Nose: candied fruit, ripe fruit, expressive, floral. Palate: flavourful, fruity, fleshy.

FINCA RENARDES 2010 T ROBLE
tempranillo, cabernet sauvignon.

88 Colour: bright cherry, garnet rim. Nose: balanced, ripe fruit, cocoa bean, sweet spices. Palate: flavourful, ripe fruit, long.

PARATÓ ÁTICA PINOT NOIR 2007 TR
100% pinot noir.

90 Colour: cherry, garnet rim. Nose: ripe fruit, expressive, scrubland, spicy, creamy oak. Palate: good acidity, powerful, flavourful, fleshy.

PARATÓ SAMSÓ 2007 TR
100% cariñena.

89 Colour: cherry, garnet rim. Nose: complex, spicy, mineral. Palate: correct, round, light-bodied, flavourful, toasty.

PARATÓ NEGRE CLÀSSIC 2004 TR
70% cabernet sauvignon, 30% tempranillo.

87 Colour: pale ruby, brick rim edge. Nose: elegant, spicy, fine reductive notes, wet leather, aged wood nuances, fruit liqueur notes. Palate: spicy, fine tannins, long.

PARDAS

Finca Can Comas, s/n
08775 Torrelavit (Barcelona)
☎: +34 938 995 005
pardas@cancomas.com
www.pardas.net

PARDAS RUPESTRIS 2010 B
70% xarel.lo, 10% xarel.lo vermell, 10% malvasía, 10% macabeo.

88 Colour: bright straw. Nose: white flowers, ripe fruit, medium intensity. Palate: flavourful, ripe fruit, spicy.

PARDAS ASPRIU 2009 B
100% xarel.lo.

92 Colour: bright straw. Nose: powerfull, ripe fruit, citrus fruit, sweet spices, white flowers. Palate: flavourful, ripe fruit, fine bitter notes.

PARDAS XAREL.LO 2009 B
100% xarel.lo.

88 Colour: bright straw. Nose: citrus fruit, ripe fruit, floral. Palate: flavourful, fruity, fresh.

PARDAS ASPRIU 2007 T
15% cabernet sauvignon, 85% cabernet franc.

93 Colour: cherry, garnet rim. Nose: spicy, creamy oak, toasty, complex, mineral, ripe fruit. Palate: powerful, flavourful, toasty, round tannins.

PARDAS NEGRE FRANC 2007 T
20% cabernet sauvignon, 60% cabernet franc, 15% merlot, 5% sumoll.

91 Colour: dark-red cherry. Nose: varietal, powerfull, fresh, complex, ripe fruit. Palate: flavourful, powerful, fruity, fleshy, slightly dry, soft tannins.

PARÉS BALTÀ

Masía Can Baltá, s/n
08796 Pacs del Penedès (Barcelona)
☎: +34 938 901 399 - Fax: +34 938 901 143
paresbalta@paresbalta.com
www.paresbalta.com

CALCARI XAREL.LO 2010 B
xarel.lo.

91 Colour: bright yellow. Nose: medium intensity, balanced, wild herbs, faded flowers, varietal. Palate: flavourful, fruity, good acidity.

GINESTA 2010 B
gewürztraminer.

87 Colour: bright golden. Nose: balanced, ripe fruit, white flowers, jasmine, expressive. Palate: flavourful, rich.

BLANC DE PACS 2010 B
parellada, xarel.lo, macabeo.

86 Colour: bright yellow, greenish rim. Nose: balanced, dried flowers. Palate: fruity, correct, good acidity.

ELECTIO XAREL.LO 2009 B
xarel.lo.

89 Colour: bright yellow. Nose: balanced, ripe fruit, faded flowers. Palate: balanced, ripe fruit, long.

RADIX 2010 RD
syrah.

88 Colour: rose, purple rim. Nose: powerfull, ripe fruit, floral, expressive. Palate: fleshy, powerful, fruity, fresh.

ROS DE PACS 2010 RD
merlot, cabernet sauvignon, syrah.

84 Colour: light cherry. Nose: dried flowers, ripe fruit, medium intensity. Palate: flavourful, fleshy, slightly evolved.

INDÍGENA 2009 T
garnacha.

89 Colour: bright cherry, garnet rim. Nose: fruit preserve, sweet spices, cocoa bean. Palate: flavourful, fruity, sweet tannins.

PARÉS BALTÀ MAS PETIT 2009 T
cabernet sauvignon, garnacha.

87 Colour: cherry, garnet rim. Nose: warm, ripe fruit, balsamic herbs, spicy. Palate: fleshy, ripe fruit, round tannins, long.

HISENDA MIRET GARNATXA 2008 T
garnacha.

91 Colour: cherry, garnet rim. Nose: earthy notes, sweet spices, toasty, fruit liqueur notes. Palate: flavourful, ripe fruit, fine bitter notes, round tannins.

MAS ELENA 2008 T
merlot, cabernet sauvignon, cabernet franc.

90 Colour: cherry, garnet rim. Nose: balsamic herbs, ripe fruit, dry stone, spicy, toasty. Palate: flavourful, fruity, balanced.

ABSIS 2007 T
tempranillo, merlot, cabernet sauvignon, syrah.

93 Colour: black cherry, garnet rim. Nose: powerfull, dry stone, ripe fruit, dark chocolate, creamy oak, fruit preserve. Palate: fleshy, good structure, long, ripe fruit.

MAS IRENE 2006 T
merlot, cabernet franc.

92 Colour: very deep cherry, garnet rim. Nose: powerfull, spicy, creamy oak, ripe fruit. Palate: fleshy, ripe fruit, long.

MARTA DE BALTÀ 2006 T
syrah.

90 Colour: bright cherry, garnet rim. Nose: ripe fruit, fruit liqueur notes, cocoa bean, creamy oak. Palate: flavourful, good structure.

PUIG ROMEU

Barri Piscina, 5
08779 La Llacuna (Barcelona)
☎: +34 938 976 206 - Fax: +34 938 977 087
info@puig-romeu.com
www.puig-romeu.com

VINYA JORDINA 2010 B
50% viognier, 30% sauvignon blanc, 20% garnacha blanca.

91 Colour: bright straw. Nose: white flowers, fragrant herbs, fruit expression, sweet spices. Palate: flavourful, powerful, fleshy, complex, round.

3 NEGRES 2007 T
50% merlot, 30% syrah, 20% ull de llebre.

89 Color bright cherry. Aroma ripe fruit, sweet spices, creamy oak, expressive. Taste flavourful, fruity, toasty, round tannins.

HAUTE LA MASUCA 2008 BN
25% viognier, 25% pinot noir, 15% chenin blanc, 10% albariño, 15% parellada, 10% otras.

89 Colour: bright straw. Nose: white flowers, citrus fruit, fragrant herbs, fresh, expressive. Palate: good acidity, fine bead, fresh, fruity, flavourful.

BIEL.LO ESP RESERVA
pinot noir, parellada.

83 Colour: bright straw, greenish rim. Nose: medium intensity, dry nuts. Palate: fruity, easy to drink.

REFILAT

Agustí Manaut, 9
17539 Bolvir de Cerdanya (Girona)
☎: +34 972 895 003 - Fax: +34 972 883 156
refilat@telefonica.net

REFILAT XAREL.LO 2010 B
xarel.lo.

84 Colour: bright straw, greenish rim. Nose: fresh, medium intensity, wild herbs. Palate: flavourful, fresh, easy to drink.

REFILAT ROSAT MERLOT 2010 RD
merlot.

86 Colour: rose, purple rim. Nose: powerfull, ripe fruit, red berry notes, floral, expressive. Palate: fleshy, powerful, fruity.

REFILAT NEGRE S/C T
cabernet sauvignon, merlot.

87 Colour: cherry, purple rim. Nose: medium intensity, fruit expression, wild herbs. Palate: flavourful, fruity, easy to drink.

RENÉ BARBIER

Partida Torre del Gall, s/n
08739 St. Cugat de Sesgarrigues (Barcelona)
☎: +34 938 917 090 - Fax: +34 938 917 099
renebarbier@renebarbier.es
www.renebarbier.es

RENÉ BARBIER KRALINER 2010 B
40% xarel.lo, 30% macabeo, 30% parellada.

85 Colour: bright straw. Nose: fresh, fresh fruit, white flowers. Palate: flavourful, fruity, good acidity, balanced.

RENÉ BARBIER CHARDONNAY SELECCIÓN 2009 BFB
100% chardonnay.

87 Color bright yellow. Aroma powerfull, ripe fruit, sweet spices, creamy oak, fragrant herbs. Taste rich, smoky aftertaste, flavourful, fresh, good acidity.

RENÉ BARBIER 2010 RD
60% tempranillo, 20% garnacha, 20% cariñena.

86 Colour: light cherry. Nose: medium intensity, fragrant herbs, red berry notes, ripe fruit, faded flowers. Palate: flavourful, fruity.

RENÉ BARBIER SELECCIÓN CABERNET SAUVIGNON SELECCIÓN 2007 TC
100% cabernet sauvignon.

87 Colour: deep cherry, garnet rim. Nose: medium intensity, spicy, ripe fruit. Palate: flavourful, round tannins, spicy.

ROVELLATS

Finca Rovellats Bº La Bleda
08731 Sant Marti Sarroca (Barcelona)
☎: +34 934 880 575 - Fax: +34 934 880 819
rovellats@cavasrovellats.com
www.cavasrovellats.com

ROVELLATS BLANC PRIMAVERA 2010 B
45% macabeo, 35% xarel.lo, 20% chardonnay.

83 Colour: bright straw, greenish rim. Nose: medium intensity, dried flowers, fragrant herbs. Palate: flavourful, easy to drink, light-bodied.

ROVELLATS MERLOT 2010 RD
100% merlot.

81 Colour: light cherry. Nose: medium intensity, scrubland. Palate: correct, good finish.

ROVELLATS BRU DE TARDOR 2006 T
42% garnacha, 30% cabernet sauvignon, 23% merlot, 5% syrah.

88 Colour: light cherry, orangey edge. Nose: ripe fruit, fine reductive notes, earthy notes, scrubland. Palate: powerful, flavourful, complex.

SEGURA VIUDAS

Ctra. Sant Sadurní a St. Pere de Riudebitlles, Km. 5
08775 Torrelavit (Barcelona)
☎: +34 938 917 070 - Fax: +34 938 996 006
seguraviudas@seguraviudas.es
www.seguraviudas.com

VIÑA HEREDAD 2010 B
macabeo, xarel.lo, parellada.

86 Colour: bright straw. Nose: medium intensity, floral, wild herbs, fresh fruit. Palate: correct, balanced.

CREU DE LAVIT 2009 BFB
100% xarel.lo.

87 Colour: bright yellow. Nose: medium intensity, spicy, ripe fruit, faded flowers. Palate: fruity, balanced, fine bitter notes.

CLOS JUVÈNCIA 2010 RD
40% garnacha, 25% syrah, 20% tempranillo, 15% merlot.

86 Colour: light cherry. Nose: balanced, ripe fruit, floral, fragrant herbs. Palate: balanced, fine bitter notes, ripe fruit, flavourful.

MAS D'ARANYÓ 2005 TR
tempranillo, cabernet sauvignon, cariñena.

87 Colour: bright cherry. Nose: ripe fruit, sweet spices, creamy oak, expressive. Palate: flavourful, fruity, round tannins.

TERRAPRIMA

Can Ràfols dels Caus, s/n
08793 Avinyonet del Penedès (Barcelona)
☎: +34 938 970 013
info@terraprima.es
www.terraprima.es

TERRAPRIMA 2010 B
xarel.lo, riesling.

88 Colour: bright straw. Nose: white flowers, ripe fruit. Palate: flavourful, fruity, fresh, fleshy.

TERRAPRIMA 2007 T
cabernet franc, garnacha, syrah.

88 Colour: cherry, garnet rim. Nose: characterful, overripe fruit, aromatic coffee. Palate: powerful, fine bitter notes, ripe fruit.

TORELLÓ

Can Martí de Baix, Ctra. de Sant Sadurni a Gélida - Apdo. Correos 8
08770 Sant Sadurní D'Anoia (Barcelona)
☎: +34 938 910 793 - Fax: +34 938 910 877
torello@torello.es
www.torello.es

CRISALYS 2010 BFB
xarel.lo.

88 Colour: bright yellow. Nose: white flowers, ripe fruit, spicy, creamy oak. Palate: good acidity, rich, flavourful, fleshy.

VITTIOS VENDIMIA TARDÍA 2010 B
xarel.lo.

86 Colour: bright straw, greenish rim. Nose: candied fruit, white flowers, wild herbs. Palate: fruity, sweet, good finish.

PETJADES 2010 RD
merlot.

85 Colour: rose, purple rim. Nose: faded flowers, red berry notes, ripe fruit. Palate: powerful, flavourful, fruity, good acidity.

RAIMONDA 2005 TR
cabernet sauvignon, merlot.

88 Colour: light cherry, garnet rim. Nose: ripe fruit, spicy, creamy oak, fine reductive notes, complex. Palate: good acidity, powerful, flavourful, fleshy.

TORRENS MOLINER

Ctra Sant Sadurni - Piera BV-2242, - km 10,5
08784 La Fortesa (Barcelona)
☎: +34 938 911 033 - Fax: +34 938 911 761
tormol@torrensmoliner.com
www.torrensmoliner.com

TORRENS & MOLINER VINO BLANCO D'ANYADA XAREL.LO 2010 B
100% xarel.lo.

87 Colour: pale, greenish rim. Nose: white flowers, candied fruit, fragrant herbs. Palate: flavourful, fruity, fine bitter notes.

U MÉS U FAN TRES

Masía Navinés Bº Els Pujols
08736 Font-Rubí (Barcelona)
☎: +34 938 974 069 - Fax: +34 938 974 724
umesu@umesufan3.com
www.umesufan3.com

SOLITERRA 1+1=3 2010 B
xarel.lo.

88 Colour: bright straw, greenish rim. Nose: balanced, fresh, fragrant herbs. Palate: fresh, fruity, easy to drink, balsamic.

DAHLIA 1 + 1 = 3 2009 B
viognier, xarel.lo.

88 Colour: bright yellow. Nose: balanced, expressive, ripe fruit, white flowers. Palate: flavourful, fruity, balanced.

DÉFORA 1 + 1 = 3 2007 T
garnacha, cariñena.

90 Colour: cherry, garnet rim. Nose: expressive, complex, ripe fruit, spicy, balsamic herbs, dried flowers. Palate: flavourful, fruity, good structure.

VALL DOLINA

Plaça de la Creu, 1
08795 Olesa de Bonesvalls (Barcelona)
☎: +34 938 984 181 - Fax: +34 938 984 181
info@valldolina.com
www.valldolina.com

VALL DOLINA XAREL.LO "ECOLÓGICO" 2010 B
100% xarel.lo.

89 Colour: bright straw. Nose: fruit expression, white flowers, mineral, expressive. Palate: light-bodied, fresh, fruity, flavourful.

VALL DOLINA ECO 2010 RD
100% merlot.

85 Colour: rose, purple rim. Nose: powerfull, ripe fruit, red berry notes, floral. Palate: powerful, fruity, flavourful.

VALL DOLINA MERLOT ECO 2009 T
100% merlot.

87 Colour: cherry, garnet rim. Nose: red berry notes, ripe fruit, sweet spices, toasty. Palate: powerful, flavourful, fleshy, spicy.

VILADELLOPS VINÍCOLA

Celler Gran Viladellops
08734 Olérdola (Barcelona)
☎: +34 938 188 371 - Fax: +34 938 188 371
md@viladellops.com
www.viladellops.com

FINCA VILADELLOPS XAREL.LO 2009 BFB
100% xarel.lo.

90 Colour: bright golden. Nose: complex, elegant, floral, ripe fruit, sweet spices. Palate: spicy, ripe fruit, rich.

TURÓ DE LES ABELLES 2008 T
50% syrah, 50% garnacha.

91 Colour: black cherry, garnet rim. Nose: ripe fruit, spicy, roasted coffee, aromatic coffee. Palate: powerful, flavourful, toasty, ripe fruit.

FINCA VILADELLOPS 2008 T
60% garnacha, 40% syrah.

88 Color cherry, garnet rim. Aroma ripe fruit, spicy, creamy oak, toasty, complex. Taste powerful, flavourful, toasty, round tannins.

TURÓ DE LES ABELLES 2007 T
syrah, garnacha.

87 Colour: deep cherry. Nose: powerfull, overripe fruit, ripe fruit, dark chocolate, spicy. Palate: flavourful, powerful, warm, good acidity.

VINS EL CEP

Can Llopart de Les Alzines
08770 Sant Sadurní D'Anoia (Barcelona)
☎: +34 938 912 353 - Fax: +34 938 183 956
info@elcep.com
www.elcep.com

MARQUÉS DE GÉLIDA BLANC DE BLANCS 2010 B
35% xarel.lo, 30% macabeo, 25% parellada, 10% chardonnay.

85 Colour: pale. Nose: fresh fruit, white flowers, fragrant herbs. Palate: fruity, flavourful, fleshy.

L'ALZINAR ULL DE LLEBRE 2008 TC
100% tempranillo.

90 Colour: cherry, garnet rim. Nose: red berry notes, ripe fruit, creamy oak, cocoa bean. Palate: balanced, unctuous, powerful, flavourful, fleshy.

MARQUÉS DE GÉLIDA XAREL.LO 2010
xarel.lo.

86 Colour: bright straw. Nose: fragrant herbs, white flowers, faded flowers. Palate: flavourful, fruity, easy to drink.

VINS I CAVES CUSCÓ BERGA

Esplugues, 7
08793 Avinyonet del Penedès (Barcelona)
☎: +34 938 970 164
cuscoberga@cuscoberga.com
www.cuscoberga.com

CUSCÓ BERGA CHARDONNAY 2010 B
100% chardonnay.

84 Colour: bright straw. Nose: faded flowers, ripe fruit, grassy. Palate: light-bodied, fresh, flavourful.

CUSCÓ BERGA MUSCAT 2010 B
80% moscatel, 20% xarel.lo.

82 Colour: bright straw. Nose: white flowers, ripe fruit, medium intensity. Palate: light-bodied, flavourful, fresh, lacks balance.

CUSCÓ BERGA MERLOT SELECCIÓ 2010 RD
100% merlot.

83 Colour: rose, purple rim. Nose: ripe fruit, floral, balsamic herbs. Palate: fleshy, flavourful, fruity.

CUSCÓ BERGA ISAURA 2010 T
40% cabernet franc, 30% syrah, 20% merlot, 10% marcelan.

84 Colour: cherry, purple rim. Nose: ripe fruit, balsamic herbs, medium intensity. Palate: fleshy, fruity, green.

CUSCÓ BERGA CABERNET 2007 TC
80% cabernet sauvignon, 20% merlot.

86 Colour: pale ruby, brick rim edge. Nose: ripe fruit, wild herbs, tobacco, wet leather. Palate: good acidity, slightly evolved, flavourful, fleshy.

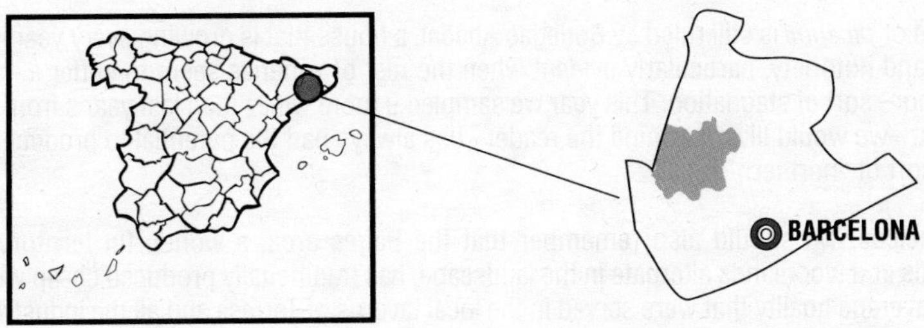

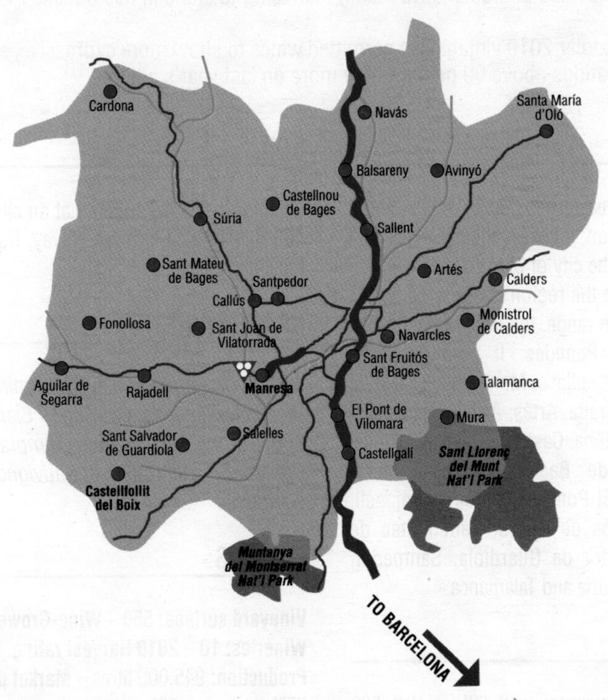

Consejo Regulador
DO Boundary

DO PLA DE BAGES

NEWS ABOUT THE VINTAGE:

The land of *picapoll* is still ruled by Bodegas Abadal, a house that is growing every year in both quality and notoriety, particularly evident when the rest of wineries seem to suffer a –maybe just minor– sort of stagnation. This year we sampled 9 more wines than last year's from a cool area that –we would like to remind the reader– has always had the potential to produce wines with a sort of "northern" touch.

Nevertheless, we should also remember that the Bages area, a wonderful territory were vineyards and woodlands alternate in the landscape, has traditionally produced cheap wines of just an average quality that were served in the local taverns of Terrasa and all the industrial belt around Barcelona. This fact has driven away possible investors, so it is difficult to think the region will ever become a sort of Catalonian Bordeaux. Even a winery like Abadal is property of Valentín Roquetas, a bulk-wine merchant who was able to bring his expertise in this sector to a more sophisticated and qualitative realm, managing to shine in this bucolic DO.

The somewhat cooler 2010 vintage has permitted wines to show more expressive, so we have 7 of them with ratings above 90 points, three more on last year's edition.

LOCATION:

Covering one of the eastern extremes of the Central Catalonian Depression; it covers the natural region of Bages, of which the city of Manresa is the urban centre. To the south the region is bordered by the Montserrat mountain range, the dividing line which separates it from Penedés. It comprises the municipal areas of Fonollosa, Monistrol de Caldres, Sant Joan de Vilatorrada, Artés, Avinyó, Balsareny, Calders, Callús, Cardona, Castellgalí, Castellfollit del Boix, Castellnou de Bages, Manresa, Mura, Navarcles, Navàs, El Pont de Vilomara, Rajadell, Sallent, Sant Fruitós de Bages, Sant Mateu de Bages, Sant Salvador de Guardiola, Santpedor, Santa María d'Oló, Súria and Talamanca.

CLIMATE:

Mid-mountain Mediterranean, with little rainfall (500 mm to 600 mm average annual rainfall) and greater temperature contrasts than in the Penedès.

SOIL:

The vineyards are situated at an altitude of about 400 m. The soil is franc-clayey, franc-sandy and franc-clayey-sandy.

GRAPE VARIETIES:

WHITE: *Chardonnay, Gewürztraminer, Macabeo, Picapoll, Parellada, Sauvignon Blanc.*
RED: *Sumoll, Ull de Llebre* (*Tempranillo*), *Merlot, Cabernet Franc, Cabernet Sauvignon, Syrah* and *Garnacha.*

FIGURES:

Vineyard surface: 550 – **Wine-Growers:** 96 – **Wineries:** 10 – **2010 Harvest rating:** Very Good – **Production:** 945,000 litres – **Market percentages:** 75% domestic. 25% export

CONSEJO REGULADOR
Casa de La Culla - La Culla, s/n
08240 Manresa (Barcelona)
☎: +34 938 748 236 - Fax: +34 938 748 094
@ info@dopladebages.com
www.dopladebages.com

GENERAL CHARACTERISTICS OF THE WINES

WHITES	These are of similar character to the Penedès white wines; they are young and fruity, and are the result of modern technology, both those that use autochtonous varieties and those based on *Chardonnay*.
ROSÉS	Produced mainly from *Merlot* and *Cabernet Sauvignon*, they have a raspberry pink colour and are clean and fruity on the nose with a good fruit expression of the grapes they are produced from.
REDS	Deep cherry-red coloured, fresh, with a pronounced character of the *viníferas* that they are based on. The fine varietal character of those produced from *Cabernet Sauvignon* stands out.

VINTAGE RATING PEÑÍNGUIDE

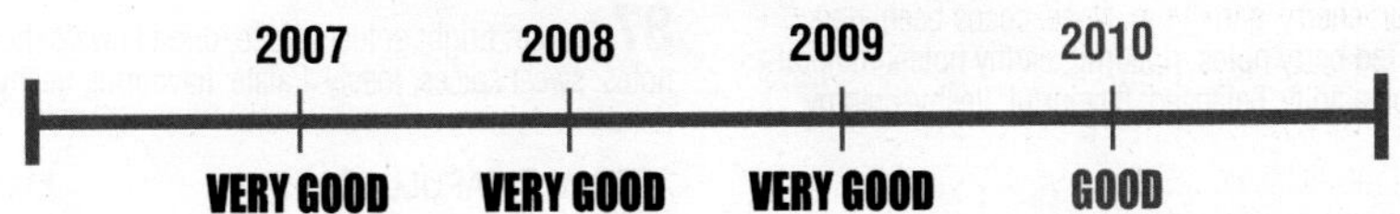

ABADAL

Santa María d'Horta d'Avinyó
08279 Santa María D'Horta D'Avinyó (Barcelona)
☎: +34 938 743 511 - Fax: +34 938 737 204
info@abadal.net
www.abadal.net

ABADAL PICAPOLL 2010 B
100% picapoll.

92 Colour: bright straw. Nose: fresh fruit, white flowers, fragrant herbs, mineral. Palate: fleshy, powerful, flavourful, rich, creamy, mineral.

NUAT 2008 B
100% picapoll.

89 Colour: bright golden. Nose: candied fruit, fruit liqueur notes, fragrant herbs, sweet spices. Palate: powerful, flavourful, fleshy, fine bitter notes. Personality.

ABADAL CABERNET SAUVIGNON 2010 RD
90% cabernet sauvignon, 10% sumoll.

88 Colour: rose, purple rim. Nose: raspberry, red berry notes, rose petals, expressive. Palate: fresh, powerful, flavourful, fruity.

ABADAL 3.9 2007 TR
85% cabernet sauvignon, 15% syrah.

91 Colour: cherry, garnet rim. Nose: cocoa bean, dark chocolate, red berry notes, ripe fruit, earthy notes, mineral. Palate: good acidity, balanced, flavourful, fleshy, creamy, mineral.

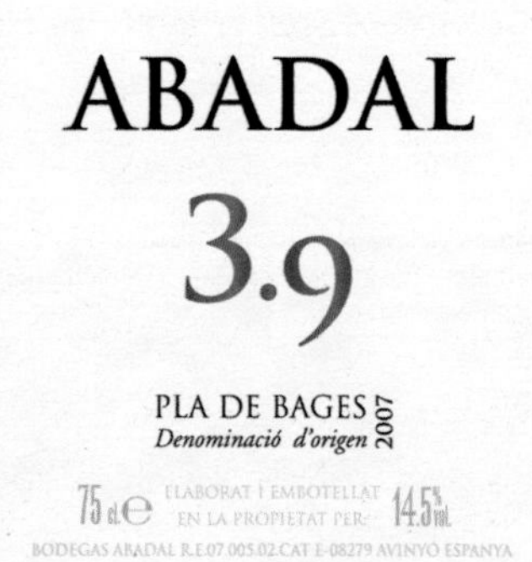

ABADAL EDICIÓN LIMITADA 2007 T
62% merlot, 18% cabernet sauvignon, 13% cabernet franc, 7% syrah.

91 Colour: cherry, garnet rim. Nose: balanced, ripe fruit, red berry notes, spicy, creamy oak, cocoa bean. Palate: good acidity, fruity, flavourful, ripe fruit, slightly dry, soft tannins.

ABADAL 5 MERLOT 2006 TR
100% merlot.

92 Colour: cherry, garnet rim. Nose: red berry notes, ripe fruit, earthy notes, mineral, creamy oak. Palate: fleshy, complex, flavourful, round tannins.

ABADAL SELECCIÓ 2006 T
40% cabernet franc, 40% cabernet sauvignon, 20% syrah.

91 Colour: cherry, garnet rim. Nose: ripe fruit, cocoa bean, aromatic coffee, balsamic herbs. Palate: flavourful, fleshy, mineral, balanced.

CELLER COOPERATIU D'ARTÉS SCCL - CAVES ARTIUM

Cr. Rocafort, 44
08271 Artés (Barcelona)
☎: +34 938 305 325 - Fax: +34 938 306 289
artium@cavesartium.com
www.cavesartium.com

ARTIUM PICAPOLL 2009 BFB
100% picapoll.

87 Colour: bright golden. Nose: dried flowers, honeyed notes, sweet spices, toasty. Palate: flavourful, fleshy, toasty, rich.

ARTIUM PICAPOLL 2009 B
100% picapoll.

85 Colour: bright golden. Nose: dried flowers, citrus fruit, fragrant herbs. Palate: light-bodied, fresh, fleshy.

ARTIUM MERLOT CAPRICI 2009 T
100% merlot.

86 Colour: cherry, garnet rim. Nose: ripe fruit, scrubland, floral, spicy. Palate: light-bodied, fresh, flavourful.

ARTIUM CABERNET SAUVIGNON 2007 TC
100% cabernet sauvignon.

85 Colour: deep cherry, orangey edge. Nose: wet leather, spicy, cocoa bean, ripe fruit. Palate: balsamic, light-bodied, flavourful.

ARTIUM VINYA ROCAS ALBAS 2006 TC
50% cabernet sauvignon, 50% merlot.

81 Colour: light cherry, brick rim edge. Nose: cocoa bean, toasty, medium intensity. Palate: pruney, light-bodied, lacks expression.

ARTIUM CABERNET SAUVIGNON 2005 TR
100% cabernet sauvignon.

86 Colour: pale ruby, brick rim edge. Nose: scrubland, cocoa bean, aromatic coffee, expressive. Palate: balsamic, spicy, flavourful, fleshy.

EL MOLI

Camí de Rajadell, Km. 3
08241 Manresa (Barcelona)
☎: +34 931 021 965 - Fax: +34 931 021 965
collbaix@cellerelmoli.com
www.cellerelmoli.com

COLLBAIX MACABEO PICAPOLL 2010 B
picapoll, macabeo.

86 Colour: bright straw. Nose: candied fruit, citrus fruit, dried flowers. Palate: fine bitter notes, sweetness, good acidity.

COLLBAIX SINGULAR 2007 T
100% cabernet sauvignon.

92 Colour: cherry, garnet rim. Nose: red berry notes, spicy, creamy oak, earthy notes, mineral. Palate: flavourful, fleshy, complex, mineral, round tannins.

COLLBAIX CUPATGE 2007 T
40% cabernet sauvignon, 30% merlot, 30% tempranillo.

88 Colour: cherry, garnet rim. Nose: ripe fruit, balsamic herbs, spicy, creamy oak, earthy notes. Palate: flavourful, toasty, round, mineral.

COLLBAIX LA LLOBETA 2007 T
60% cabernet sauvignon, 40% merlot.

88 Colour: cherry, garnet rim. Nose: balsamic herbs, spicy, creamy oak. Palate: powerful, flavourful, fleshy, mineral.

HERETAT OLLER DEL MAS

Ctra. de Igualada, Km. 3,4
08240 Manresa (Barcelona)
☎: +34 938 768 315
info@ollerdelmas.com
www.ollerdelmas.com

BERNAT OLLER BLANC DE PICAPOLLS 2010 B
50% picapoll blanc, 50% picapoll tinto.

87 Colour: bright yellow. Nose: floral, ripe fruit, fragrant herbs, powerfull. Palate: fleshy, complex, rich, flavourful.

PETIT BERNAT 2010 T
35% syrah, 35% cabernet franc, 20% merlot, 10% picapoll tinto.

85 Colour: cherry, purple rim. Nose: red berry notes, ripe fruit, sweet spices, balsamic herbs. Palate: good acidity, spirituous, flavourful.

ARNAU OLLER SELECCIÓ DE LA FAMILIA 2007 T
90% merlot, 10% picapoll tinto.

90 Colour: cherry, garnet rim. Nose: ripe fruit, mineral, spicy, creamy oak, elegant. Palate: good acidity, powerful, flavourful, fleshy.

BERNAT OLLER 2006 T
100% merlot.

88 Colour: cherry, garnet rim. Nose: red berry notes, ripe fruit, scrubland, fine reductive notes, toasty. Palate: good acidity, fleshy, complex, flavourful.

JAUMANDREU

Jaumandreu Canet de Fals
08259 Fonollosa (Barcelona)
☎: +34 938 369 579 - Fax: +34 938 369 505
info@jaumandreu.com
www.jaumandreu.com

MES QUE PARAULES 2010 B
85% sauvignon blanc, 10% chardonnay, 5% picapoll.

88 Colour: bright straw. Nose: fragrant herbs, white flowers, fruit expression, expressive. Palate: creamy, fruity, flavourful, fleshy.

MES QUE PARAULES 2009 RD
100% merlot.

84 Colour: light cherry. Nose: fragrant herbs, dried flowers, fruit expression. Palate: flavourful, fruity, fresh, easy to drink.

MES QUE PARAULES 2007 T
40% merlot, 35% cabernet sauvignon, 25% syrah.

86 Colour: cherry, garnet rim. Nose: ripe fruit, toasty, balsamic herbs. Palate: good acidity, unctuous, flavourful, fleshy, toasty.

CEDRUS 2007 T
55% merlot, 40% cabernet sauvignon, 5% syrah.

84 Colour: cherry, garnet rim. Nose: candied fruit, warm, medium intensity. Palate: light-bodied, toasty, correct.

IDAEUS 2006 T
65% syrah, 35% merlot.

86 Colour: cherry, garnet rim. Nose: ripe fruit, toasty, damp earth, mineral. Palate: flavourful, fleshy, toasty, round tannins.

JAUME GRAU - VINS GRAU

Ctra. C-37 de Igualada a Manresa, Km. 75,5
08255 Maians (Barcelona)
☎: +34 938 356 002 - Fax: +34 938 356 812
info@vinsgrau.com
www.vinsgrau.com

JAUME GRAU I GRAU AVRVM 2010 B
chardonnay, sauvignon blanc.

86 Colour: bright straw. Nose: fragrant herbs, floral, tropical fruit. Palate: unctuous, flavourful, fleshy.

JAUME GRAU I GRAU PICAPOLL 2010 B
picapoll.

85 Colour: pale. Nose: fresh, white flowers, citrus fruit, fine lees. Palate: fresh, light-bodied, easy to drink.

JAUME GRAU I GRAU MERLOT 2010 RD
merlot.

85 Colour: rose, purple rim. Nose: raspberry, fresh fruit, floral, fresh. Palate: fruity, flavourful, rich.

JAUME GRAU GRAU "GRATVS" 2006 TC
tempranillo, merlot.

86 Colour: cherry, garnet rim. Nose: ripe fruit, spicy, toasty, scrubland. Palate: powerful, flavourful, fleshy, balsamic.

JAUME GRAU GRAU "GRATVS" 2004 TR
100% merlot.

83 Colour: pale ruby, brick rim edge. Nose: spicy, roasted coffee, caramel. Palate: pruney, toasty, grainy tannins.

JAUME GRAU GRAU SENSVS 2000 TR
100% cabernet sauvignon.

84 Colour: pale ruby, brick rim edge. Nose: waxy notes, tobacco, balsamic herbs, earthy notes. Palate: light-bodied, sweetness, short.

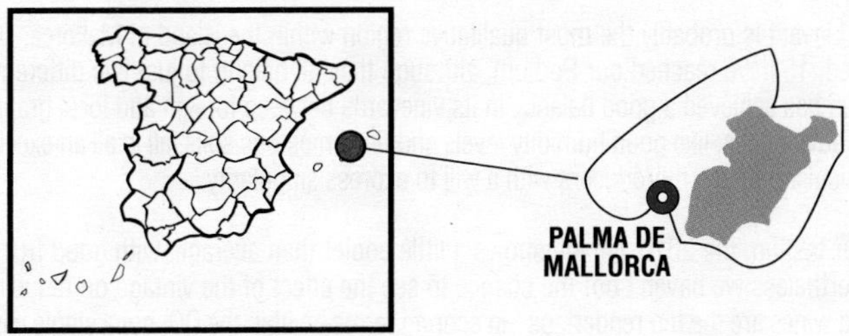
PALMA DE
MALLORCA

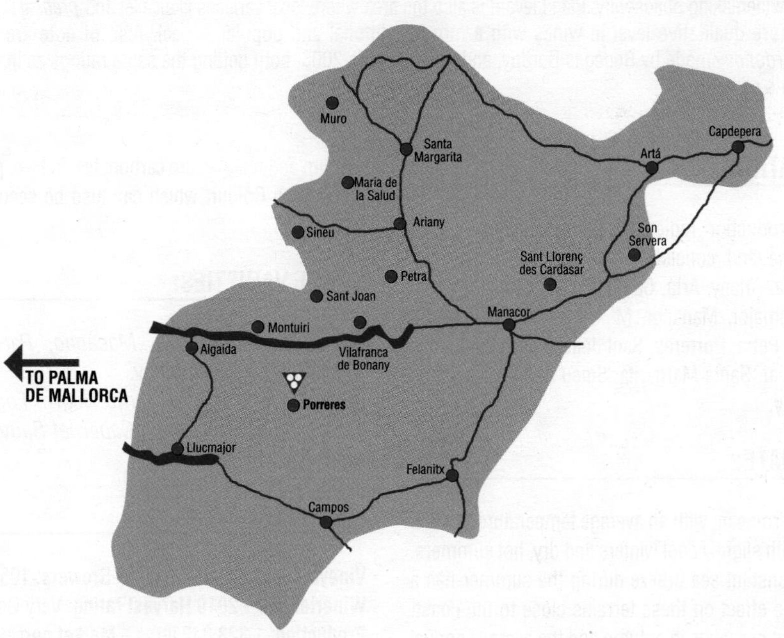
Muro
Santa
Margarita
Capdepera
Artá
Maria de
la Salud
Ariany
Sineu
Son
Servera
Sant Llorenç
des Cardasar
Petra
Sant Joan
Manacor
Montuiri
Algaida
Vilafranca
de Bonany
TO PALMA
DE MALLORCA
Porreres
Llucmajor
Felanitx
Campos

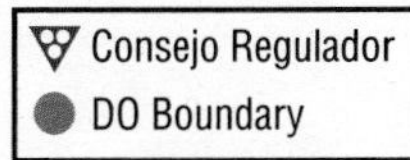
Consejo Regulador
DO Boundary

DO PLA I LLEVANT

NEWS ABOUT THE VINTAGE:

At present, Pla i Llevant is probably the most qualitative region within the island of Mallorca. Of a total of 52 samples tasted, 15 have reached our Podium, although they all belong to just five different wineries. Overall, the region has achieved a good balance in its vineyards between foreign and local grape varieties. It also has many advantages, like good humidity levels and fine limestone soils, all in all an excellent recipe for success, particularly for keen producers with a will to express singularity.

In the light of our tasting, the 2010 vintage shows a little cooler than average, with good fruit and floral expression. Nevertheless we haven't got the chance to see the effect of the vintage on red wines, since, even when young wines are the top renderings –in scoring terms– within the DO, not a single wine of them was sent for our assessment.

One more year, Jaume Mesquida has the best *cabernet sauvignon* wine of Mallorca. We have to keep in mind that Jaume, pioneered in the island the planting of foreign varieties; his sons have just followed suit his winemaking philosophy. Pla i Llevant is also the area where local varieties like callet and *prensal* reach a more qualitative level in wines with a more traditional and popular appeal. Also of note are the *chardonnay* made by Bodegas Bordoy, and Ses Ferritges 2006, both getting the same ratings as in last year's edition.

LOCATION:

The production region covers the eastern part of Majorca and consists of 18 municipal districts: Algaida, Ariany, Artá, Campos, Capdepera, Felanitx, Lluchamajor, Manacor, Mª de la Salud, Montuiri, Muro, Petra, Porreres, Sant Joan, Sant Llorens des Cardasar, Santa Margarita, Sineu and Vilafranca de Bonany.

CLIMATE:

Mediterranean, with an average temperature of 16°C and with slightly cool winters and dry, hot summers. The constant sea breeze during the summer has a notable effect on these terrains close to the coast. The wet season is in autumn and the average annual rainfall is between 450 mm and 500 mm.

SOIL:

The soil is made up of limestone rocks, which give limy-clayey soils. The reddish Colour: of the terrain is due to the presence of iron oxide. The clays and calcium and magnesium carbonates, in turn, provide the whitish Colour: which can also be seen in the vineyards.

GRAPE VARIETIES:

WHITE: *Prensal Blanc, Macabeo, Parellada, Moscatel* and *Chardonnay.*
RED: *Callet* (majority), *Manto Negro, Fogoneu, Tempranillo, Monastrell, Cabernet Sauvignon, Merlot* and *Syrah.*

FIGURES:

Vineyard surface: 347 – **Wine-Growers:** 105 – **Wineries:** 14 – **2010 Harvest rating:** Very Good – **Production:** 1,323,842 litres – **Market percentages:** 93% domestic. 7% export

CONSEJO REGULADOR
Molí de N'Amengual. Dusai, 3
07260 Porreres (Illes Balears)
☎: +34 971 168 569 - Fax: +34 971 168 569
@ info@plaillevantmallorca.es
www.plaillevantmallorca.es

GENERAL CHARACTERISTICS OF THE WINES

WHITES	The characteristics of the white wines are conditioned by the peculiarities of the foreign varieties. The *Prensal* grape gives wines that singularly express the 'terruño' character of the region.
ROSÉS	These follow in the line of the rosés of Binissalem, although the distinction comes from those produced from French grape varieties. The sensorial definition of these varieties does not prevent them, in certain cases, from being a little heavy on the nose.
REDS	These share the style that characterises the Mediterranean adaptation of the French varieties they are produced from. Thus, they give off balsamic hints in the nose; on the Palate: they offer supple and ripe tannins; they are flavourful and full bodied.

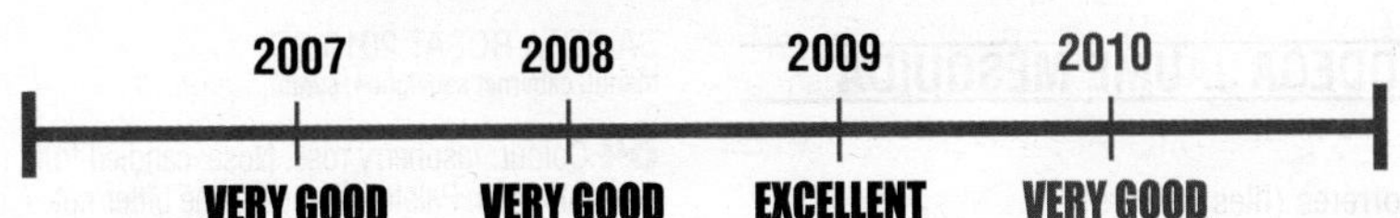

ARMERO I ADROVER

Camada Real s/n
07200 Mallorca (Illes Balears)
☎: +34 971 827 103 - Fax: +34 971 580 305
luisarmero@armeroiadrover.com
www.armeroiadrover.com

ARMERO ADROVER CHARDONNAY PRENSAL 2010 B

87 Colour: pale. Nose: ripe fruit, citrus fruit, white flowers. Palate: flavourful, fruity, fresh, good acidity.

ARMERO ADROVER CALLET-MERLOT 2007 T

87 Colour: cherry, garnet rim. Nose: powerfull, fruit expression, ripe fruit, creamy oak. Palate: fine bitter notes, good acidity, spicy.

ARMERO I ADROVER COLLITA DE FRUITS CALLET 2007 T
callet.

87 Colour: cherry, garnet rim. Nose: powerfull, fine reductive notes, aromatic coffee, warm. Palate: spicy, ripe fruit, easy to drink.

ARMERO I ADROVER COLLITA DE FRUITS 2005 T
callet, cabernet sauvignon, merlot.

89 Colour: cherry, garnet rim. Nose: ripe fruit, spicy, creamy oak, toasty, warm. Palate: powerful, flavourful, toasty, round tannins.

BODEGA JAUME MESQUIDA

Vileta, 7
07260 Porreres (Illes Balears)
☎: +34 971 647 106 - Fax: +34 971 168 205
info@jaumemesquida.com
www.jaumemesquida.com

CHARDONNAY BLANC ECOLÓGIC 2010 B
100% chardonnay.

85 Colour: bright straw. Nose: powerfull, ripe fruit, fruit preserve, citrus fruit. Palate: flavourful, fleshy, sweetness, full.

JAUME MESQUIDA NEGRE 2008 T
callet, manto negro, cabernet sauvignon, syrah.

88 Colour: cherry, garnet rim. Nose: scrubland, balsamic herbs, fruit liqueur notes, sweet spices. Palate: spicy, ripe fruit, fine bitter notes.

JAUME MESQUIDA CABERNET SAUVIGNON 2006 TC
100% cabernet sauvignon.

93 Colour: cherry, garnet rim. Nose: powerfull, warm, ripe fruit, sweet spices, toasty. Palate: flavourful, fleshy, spicy, ripe fruit, fine bitter notes.

BODEGAS BORDOY

Camí de Muntanya- Cala Blava - Lluc Mayor
07690 Lluchmajor (Illes Balears)
☎: +34 971 774 081 - Fax: +34 971 771 246
sarota@bodegasbordoy.es

SA ROTA BLANC CHARDONNAY 2010 B
chardonnay.

89 Colour: pale. Nose: balsamic herbs, ripe fruit, fruit expression, citrus fruit, creamy oak, sweet spices. Palate: flavourful, fruity, fresh.

SA ROTA BLANC CHARDONNAY 2010 B
chardonnay.

87 Colour: bright straw. Nose: fresh, fresh fruit, white flowers. Palate: flavourful, fruity, good acidity, balanced.

SA ROTA BLANC CHARDONNAY 2009 B
chardonnay.

92 Colour: bright yellow. Nose: sweet spices, creamy oak, fragrant herbs, fruit expression, varietal. Palate: rich, smoky aftertaste, flavourful, fresh, good acidity.

SA ROTA ROSAT 2010 RD
merlot, cabernet sauvignon, syrah.

84 Colour: raspberry rose. Nose: candied fruit, raspberry, fragrant herbs. Palate: balanced, fine bitter notes, good acidity.

SA ROTA 2009 T
cabernet sauvignon, merlot, syrah.

83 Colour: cherry, garnet rim. Nose: powerfull, varietal, ripe fruit, toasty. Palate: flavourful, powerful, fleshy, round tannins.

SA ROTA 2007 T

88 Colour: cherry, garnet rim. Nose: ripe fruit, sweet spices, toasty. Palate: fine bitter notes, flavourful, ripe fruit, round tannins.

SA ROTA MERLOT 2007 T
merlot.

88 Colour: cherry, garnet rim. Nose: powerfull, ripe fruit, toasty, new oak. Palate: ripe fruit, fine bitter notes, round tannins.

SA ROTA 2006 TR
cabernet sauvignon, merlot, syrah.

87 Colour: cherry, garnet rim. Nose: powerfull, fruit liqueur notes, toasty, spicy. Palate: flavourful, powerful, fine bitter notes, round tannins.

SA ROTA 2006 TC
cabernet sauvignon, merlot, syrah.

86 Colour: deep cherry. Nose: powerfull, warm, spicy, fruit liqueur notes. Palate: flavourful, powerful, fleshy.

SA ROTA SYRAH 2006 T
syrah.

86 Colour: cherry, garnet rim. Nose: spicy, smoky, toasty. Palate: good acidity, fine bitter notes, long.

SA ROTA MERLOT T
merlot.

85 Colour: cherry, purple rim. Nose: red berry notes, floral, fruit liqueur notes, dried fruit. Palate: flavourful, fruity, good acidity, round tannins, sweet.

BODEGAS PERE SEDA

Cid Campeador, 22
07500 Manacor (Illes Balears)
☎: +34 971 605 087 - Fax: +34 971 604 856
pereseda@pereseda.com
www.pereseda.com

CHARDONNAY PERE SEDA 2010 B
100% chardonnay.

88 Colour: bright straw. Nose: ripe fruit, citrus fruit, faded flowers. Palate: flavourful, fruity, fleshy.

PERE SEDA BLANC NOVELL 2010 B
prensal, macabeo, chardonnay.

87 Colour: bright straw. Nose: fresh, fresh fruit, expressive, white flowers. Palate: flavourful, fruity, good acidity, balanced.

L'ARXIDUC PERE SEDA 2010 B
parellada, moscatel, chardonnay.

85 Colour: bright straw. Nose: grassy, fresh fruit. Palate: flavourful, fruity, fleshy.

L'ARXIDUC PERE SEDA 2010 RD
70% merlot, 30% tempranillo.

83 Colour: brilliant rose. Nose: scrubland, medium intensity, warm, candied fruit. Palate: flavourful, spicy.

PERE SEDA NEGRE NOVELL 2009 T

88 Colour: cherry, garnet rim. Nose: powerfull, ripe fruit, balsamic herbs, earthy notes. Palate: powerful, spicy, ripe fruit.

GVIVM MERLOT-CALLET 2008 T
70% merlot, 30% callet.

87 Colour: cherry, garnet rim. Nose: spicy, aged wood nuances, ripe fruit. Palate: flavourful, spicy, ripe fruit.

PERE SEDA 2007 TC
merlot, syrah, cabernet sauvignon, callet.

91 Colour: cherry, garnet rim. Nose: powerfull, warm, ripe fruit, toasty. Palate: flavourful, spicy, ripe fruit, round tannins.

MOSSÈN ALCOVER 2007 T
60% callet, 40% cabernet sauvignon.

87 Colour: cherry, garnet rim. Nose: spicy, aromatic coffee, medium intensity, fruit liqueur notes. Palate: spicy, ripe fruit, fine bitter notes.

PERE SEDA 2005 TR
cabernet sauvignon, merlot, syrah, callet.

86 Colour: cherry, garnet rim. Nose: powerfull, ripe fruit, sweet spices. Palate: flavourful, powerful, fleshy, round tannins.

PERE SEDA 2009 BR
parellada, chardonnay.

84 Colour: bright straw. Nose: spicy, fragrant herbs, fresh fruit. Palate: fruity, fresh, good acidity.

VINS MIQUEL GELABERT

Carrer d'en Sales, 50
07500 Manacor (Illes Balears)
☎: +34 971 821 444 - Fax: +34 971 596 441
vinsmg@vinsmiquelgelabert.com
www.vinsmiquelgelabert.com

GOLÓS 2009 B
40% moscatel, 40% riesling, 20% giró.

88 Colour: bright straw. Nose: ripe fruit, citrus fruit, honeyed notes. Palate: flavourful, ripe fruit, good acidity.

SA VALL SELECCIÓ PRIVADA 2008 BFB
50% chardonnay, 25% prensal, 25% moscatel.

89 Colour: bright yellow. Nose: powerfull, ripe fruit, sweet spices, creamy oak. Palate: rich, smoky aftertaste, flavourful, fresh, good acidity.

GOLÓS 2008 T
60% callet, 25% manto negro, 15% fogoneu.

90 Colour: cherry, garnet rim. Nose: balsamic herbs, powerfull, warm, smoky, dark chocolate. Palate: flavourful, powerful, fine tannins.

VINYA DES MORÉ 2006 T
100% pinot noir.

87 Colour: cherry, garnet rim. Nose: wet leather, waxy notes, fruit liqueur notes, toasty. Palate: fine bitter notes, spirituous, light-bodied.

GRAN VINYA SON CAULES 2005 T
95% callet, 3% manto negro, 2% fogoneu.

91 Colour: cherry, garnet rim. Nose: ripe fruit, spicy, creamy oak, toasty, scrubland. Palate: powerful, flavourful, toasty, round tannins, mineral.

TORRENT NEGRE SELECCIÓ PRIVADA SYRAH 2005 T
100% syrah.

91 Colour: cherry, garnet rim. Nose: spicy, creamy oak, toasty, characterful, powerfull. Palate: powerful, flavourful, toasty, round tannins.

TORRENT NEGRE 2005 T
40% merlot, 30% cabernet sauvignon, 30% syrah.

88 Colour: deep cherry. Nose: characterful, warm, powerfull, fruit liqueur notes, fruit liqueur notes. Palate: fine bitter notes, spirituous, long.

TORRENT NEGRE CABERNET SELECCIÓ PRIVADA 2005 T
100% cabernet sauvignon.

87 Colour: very deep cherry. Nose: ripe fruit, spicy, characterful. Palate: powerful, flavourful, round tannins, fine bitter notes.

VINS TONI GELABERT

Camí dels Horts de Llodrá Km. 1,3
07500 Manacor (Illes Balears)
☎: +34 610 789 531
info@vinstonigelabert.com
www.vinstonigelabert.com

TONI GELABERT CHARDONNAY 2010 B
100% chardonnay.

91 Color bright yellow. Aroma powerfull, ripe fruit, sweet spices, creamy oak, fragrant herbs. Taste rich, smoky aftertaste, flavourful, fresh, good acidity.

VINYA MACABEU 2010 B
100% macabeo.

90 Colour: bright straw. Nose: fresh, fresh fruit, white flowers. Palate: flavourful, fruity, good acidity, balanced.

FANGOS BLANC 2010 B
70% prensal, 30% moscatel.

88 Colour: bright straw. Nose: varietal, grassy, floral. Palate: flavourful, fruity, fresh.

NEGRE DE SA COLONIA 2009 T
100% callet.

91 Colour: deep cherry. Nose: scrubland, candied fruit, sweet spices, creamy oak. Palate: flavourful, powerful, fleshy, long.

EQUILIBRI 2008 T
pinot noir.

88 Colour: cherry, garnet rim. Nose: ripe fruit, spicy, creamy oak, smoky, dark chocolate. Palate: powerful, flavourful, toasty, round tannins.

FANGOS NEGRE 2007 T
callet, cabernet sauvignon, merlot, syrah.

91 Colour: cherry, garnet rim. Nose: creamy oak, sweet spices, toasty. Palate: flavourful, spicy, ripe fruit.

TONI GELABERT COLONIA U 200 2007 TC
100% cabernet sauvignon.

90 Colour: bright cherry. Nose: sweet spices, fruit liqueur notes, warm, mineral. Palate: flavourful, fruity, toasty, round tannins.

TONI GELABERT MERLOT 2007 T
100% merlot.

88 Colour: cherry, garnet rim. Nose: spicy, creamy oak, toasty, expressive. Palate: powerful, flavourful, toasty, round tannins.

TONI GELABERT SYRAH 2006 T
100% syrah.

90 Colour: cherry, garnet rim. Nose: cocoa bean, aromatic coffee, powerfull, varietal, warm. Palate: flavourful, powerful, spicy.

SES HEREVES 2005 T
33% cabernet sauvignon, 33% merlot, 33% syrah.

91 Colour: cherry, garnet rim. Nose: mineral, fruit liqueur notes, fruit expression, sweet spices, creamy oak. Palate: balsamic, long, ripe fruit.

VINYES I BODEGUES MIQUEL OLIVER

Font, 26
07520 Petra-Mallorca
(Illes Balears)
☎: +34 971 561 117 -
Fax: +34 971 561 117
bodega@miqueloliver.com
www.miqueloliver.com

AIA 2008 T
merlot.

91 Colour: cherry, garnet rim. Nose: powerfull, ripe fruit, sweet spices. Palate: flavourful, fleshy, ripe fruit.

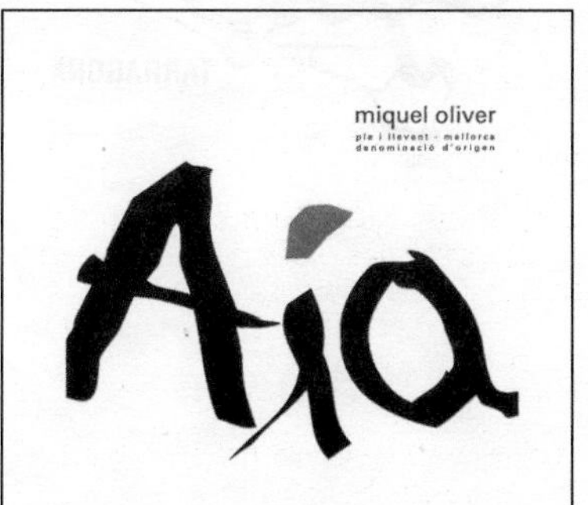

ORIGINAL MUSCAT MIQUEL OLIVER 2010 B
100% moscatel.

89 Colour: bright straw. Nose: fresh, white flowers, expressive, fresh fruit, citrus fruit. Palate: flavourful, fruity, good acidity.

ALEGRÍA 2010 RD
100% merlot.

86 Colour: coppery red. Nose: elegant, candied fruit, dried flowers, fragrant herbs, red berry notes. Palate: good acidity, long, spicy.

XPERIMENT 2008 T
100% callet.

89 Colour: cherry, garnet rim. Nose: powerfull, warm, fruit liqueur notes, spicy. Palate: flavourful, spicy, ripe fruit.

SES FERRITGES 2007 T
25% callet, 25% merlot, 25% cabernet sauvignon, 25% syrah.

92 Colour: cherry, garnet rim. Nose: powerfull, ripe fruit, creamy oak, sweet spices, complex. Palate: flavourful, powerful, ripe fruit, good acidity, fine bitter notes.

SYRAH NEGRE MIQUEL OLIVER 2007 T
100% syrah.

89 Colour: bright cherry. Nose: creamy oak, fruit expression, spicy. Palate: flavourful, fruity, toasty, round tannins.

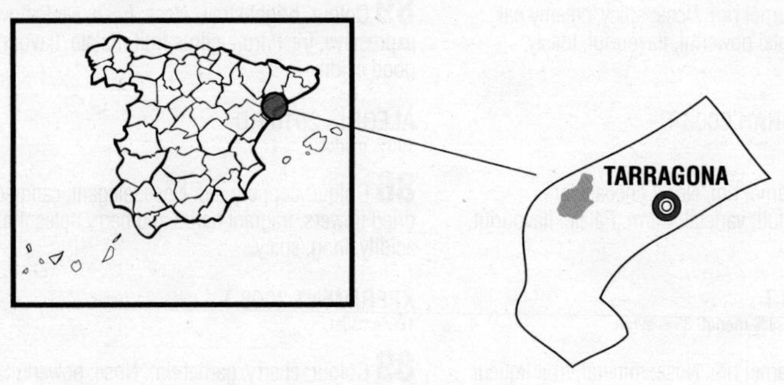
TARRAGONA

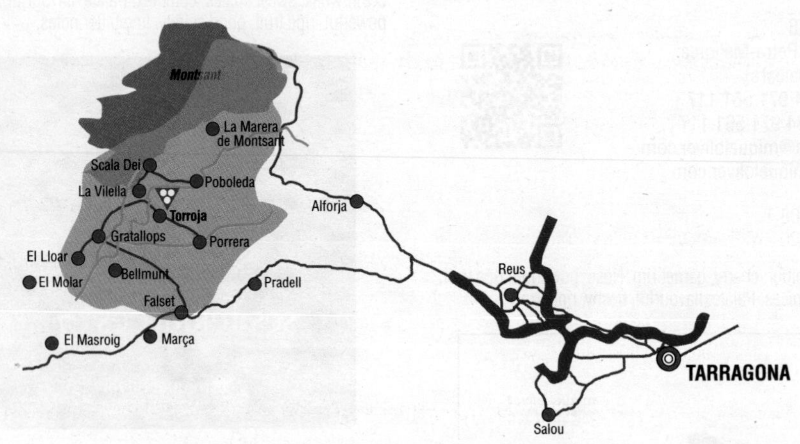
Montsant
La Marera de Montsant
Scala Dei
Poboleda
La Vilella
Torroja
Alforja
Gratallops
Porrera
El Lloar
Bellmunt
El Molar
Pradell
Reus
Falset
El Masroig
Marça
TARRAGONA
Salou

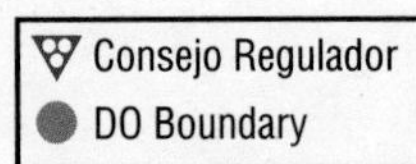
Consejo Regulador
DO Boundary

NEWS ABOUT THE VINTAGE:

The 2010 vintage was not a good one for white wines, which show little expression in the nose, surely a common trait of *garnacha blanca* renderings but particularly accentuated in cooler years. Red wines are still far more numerous than white, probably because most producers have not yet understood that this type should not only reflect a more Atlantic nature, easy to drink and with notes of herbs and green fruits, but to show also more body and a vigorous character, as well as terroir, a goal altogether easily achievable in this part of the Mediterranean. Currently, the wine wines from Priorat, although less in number, are much more expressive than the reds, probably due to the fact that the former are more sensitive to external elements like soil, weather and the age of the vines. The very few rosé samples of the 2010 vintage we have managed to taste were just average, or below, with a meaty quality and high alcohol. Also the 2010 reds are few and far between, as it happens every year; exploitation costs in the region being too high, producers cannot do anything but try and sell their young wines also at Priorat (i.e, high) prices. There is little way either to reassess red aged wines of 2008 and 2009. A big surprise was to see such a poor score for Vall Llach 2009, a wine with far too evident overripe notes.

LOCATION:

In the province of Tarragona. It is made up of the municipal districts of La Morera de Montsant, Scala Dei, La Vilella, Gratallops, Bellmunt, Porrera, Poboleda, Torroja, Lloá, Falset and Mola.

CLIMATE:

Although with Mediterranean influences, it is temperate and dry. One of the most important characteristics is the practical absence of rain during the summer, which ensures very healthy grapes. The average rainfall is between 500 and 600 mm per year.

SOIL:

This is probably the most distinctive characteristic of the region and precisely what has catapulted it to the top positions in terms of quality, not only in Spain, but around the world. The soil, thin and volcanic, is composed of small pieces of slate (llicorella), which give the wines a markedly mineral character. The vineyards are located on terraces and very steep slopes.

GRAPE VARIETIES:

WHITE: *Chenin Blanc, Macabeo, Garnacha Blanca, Pedro Ximénez.*
RED: *Cariñena, Garnacha, Garnacha Peluda, Cabernet Sauvignon, Merlot, Syrah.*

FIGURES:

Vineyard surface: 1,887 – **Wine-Growers:** 616 – **Wineries:** 92 – **2010 Harvest rating:** N/A – **Production:** 3,205,602 litres – **Market percentages:** 49% domestic. 51% export

CONSEJO REGULADOR
Major, 2
43737 Torroja del Priorat (Tarragona)
☎: +34 977 83 94 95 - Fax. +34 977 83 94 72
@ info@doqpriorat.org
www.doqpriorat.org

GENERAL CHARACTERISTICS OF THE WINES

WHITES	These are produced mainly from *Macabeo* and *Garnacha Blanca*. Straw yellow coloured, they have fruity noses and are reminiscent of mountain herbs; on the palate, they also show their Mediterranean character: they are somewhat warm with wild notes.
ROSÉS	These are maybe the least characteristic of the region. Due to the rather warm climate in which the grapes ripen, they are known for their ripe fruit notes; on the palate they are warm and flavourful.
REDS	The star product of the region. Produced from *Garnacha* and *Cariñena* combined in the high ranges with lesser percentages of foreign varieties; they are characterised by their very cloudy intense cherry colour. The best offer a nose with great complexity, with notes of very ripe fruit and the marked character of terruño (due to the effect of the slaty soil) that provide abundant mineral notes. On the palate, they have great character and structure; they are powerful, meaty, warm, and at the same time emphatically acidic, markedly tannic and very persistent.
RANCIOS AND SWEET WINES	The traditional Rancios of the region have noses of almonds and notes of mountain herbs; on the palate they are warm, flavourful with fine oxidative evolution. There is also a range of sweet wines produced according to more traditional criteria. They have a cloudy cherry colour; the nose is of black fruit, almost raisin-like and notes of toast due to their ageing in oak; on the palate they are sweet, sticky, very fruity and well-balanced due to their good acidity.

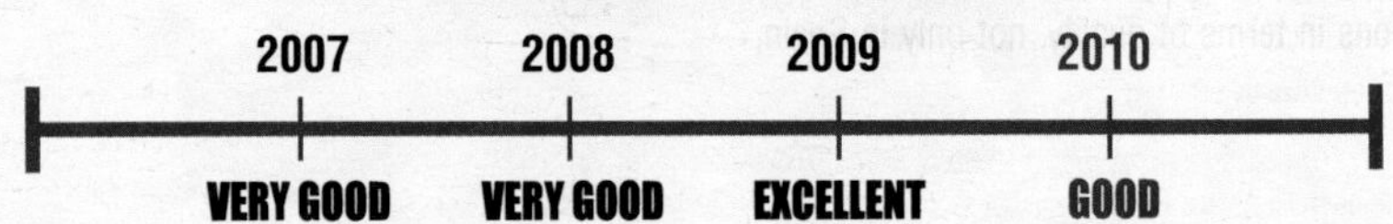

AGNÈS DE CERVERA

Ctra. El Molar - El Lloar, Km. 10
43736 El Molar (Tarragona)
☎: +34 977 054 851 - Fax: +34 977 054 851
enologia@agnesdecervera.com
www.agnesdecervera.com

LYTOS 2009 T
45% cariñena, 35% garnacha, 15% syrah, 5% cabernet sauvignon.

90 Colour: cherry, garnet rim. Nose: earthy notes, ripe fruit, fruit expression, creamy oak. Palate: flavourful, powerful, spicy.

ARGELES 2009 T
50% garnacha, 40% cariñena, 10% cabernet sauvignon.

88 Colour: deep cherry, garnet rim. Nose: ripe fruit, dark chocolate, creamy oak. Palate: flavourful, fruity, round tannins.

KALOS 2009 T
50% cariñena, 35% syrah, 15% cabernet sauvignon.

88 Colour: very deep cherry. Nose: ripe fruit, warm, fruit liqueur notes, dry stone. Palate: powerful, full, fruity, round tannins.

ALVARO PALACIOS

Afores, s/n
43737 Gratallops (Tarragona)
☎: +34 977 839 195 - Fax: +34 977 839 197
info@alvaropalacios.com

FINCA DOFÍ 2009 TC
70% garnacha, 15% cabernet sauvignon, 15% syrah.

94 Colour: cherry, garnet rim. Nose: ripe fruit, spicy, creamy oak, toasty, earthy notes, dry stone. Palate: powerful, flavourful, toasty, round tannins, good acidity.

LES TERRASSES VINYES VELLES 2009 TC
50% garnacha, 40% samsó, 5% cabernet sauvignon, 5% syrah.

92 Colour: cherry, garnet rim. Nose: powerfull, ripe fruit, fruit expression, sweet spices. Palate: mineral, long, balsamic, good structure.

GRATALLOPS VI DE LA VILA 2009 TC
45% garnacha, 45% samsó, 5% cabernet sauvignon, 5% syrah.

92 Colour: dark-red cherry. Nose: ripe fruit, cocoa bean, aromatic coffee, creamy oak. Palate: mineral, spicy, creamy, flavourful, full, powerful.

CAMINS DEL PRIORAT 2009 TC
45% samsó, 45% garnacha, 5% cabernet sauvignon, 5% syrah.

91 Colour: dark-red cherry. Nose: creamy oak, spicy, ripe fruit, dry stone, mineral. Palate: creamy, sweetness, fruity, powerful, flavourful, spirituous.

L'ERMITA 2008 TC
garnacha.

96 Colour: cherry, purple rim. Nose: spicy, fruit expression, raspberry, ripe fruit, scrubland. Palate: fruity, balsamic, spicy, good acidity, elegant.

AUTOR

Balandra, 6
43737 Torroja de Priorat (Tarragona)
☎: +34 977 838 285

AUTOR 2005 TC
garnacha, mazuelo, cabernet sauvignon.

88 Colour: deep cherry. Nose: mineral, spicy, dark chocolate, toasty, ripe fruit, fruit liqueur notes, fruit expression. Palate: complex, spirituous, good structure, powerful, flavourful.

AUTOR 2004 TR
garnacha, mazuelo, cabernet sauvignon.

90 Colour: deep cherry. Nose: cedar wood, creamy oak, fruit expression, ripe fruit, mineral. Palate: powerful, flavourful, spirituous, sweetness.

BLAI FERRÉ JUST

Piró, s/n
43737 Gratallops (Tarragona)
☎: +34 977 839 507 - Fax: +34 977 839 507
blai@cellercecilio.com

BILLO 2010 T
35% syrah, 35% garnacha, 20% cariñena, 10% cabernet sauvignon.

87 Colour: deep cherry. Nose: powerfull, varietal, stalky, red berry notes, smoky, balsamic herbs. Palate: warm, flavourful, powerful, spirituous.

BODEGA PARMI PRIORAT

Prat de la Riba, 20
43739 Porrera (Tarragona)
☎: +34 962 654 1368 - Fax: +34 977 828 209
info@parmipriorat.com
www.parmipriorat.com

L'INFANT 2007 T
garnacha, cariñena.

92 Colour: cherry, garnet rim. Nose: powerfull, ripe fruit, dark chocolate, creamy oak. Palate: powerful, flavourful, concentrated, fleshy, round tannins.

BODEGA SANTES GATES

Mas Borràs, s/n
43376 Poboleda (Tarragona)
☎: +34 977 340 029 - Fax: +34 977 340 046
info@tanevins.com
www.tanevins.com

TANE BN
40% pinot noir, 40% chardonnay, 20% otras.

89 Colour: bright straw. Nose: fresh fruit, dried herbs, fine lees, floral. Palate: fresh, flavourful, good acidity.

BODEGAS MAS ALTA

Ctra. T-702, Km. 16,8
43375 La Vilella Alta (Tarragona)
☎: +34 977 054 151 - Fax: +34 977 817 194
info@bodegasmasalta.com
www.bodegasmasalta.com

ARTIGAS 2010 BFB
50% garnacha blanca, 40% macabeo, 10% pedro ximénez.

92 Colour: bright straw. Nose: varietal, balanced, complex, powerfull, smoky, creamy oak, spicy. Palate: mineral, powerful, rich.

ELS PICS 2009 T
60% garnacha, 35% cariñena, 5% cabernet sauvignon.

90 Colour: cherry, garnet rim. Nose: overripe fruit, wild herbs, creamy oak. Palate: powerful, flavourful, sweetness, mineral, ripe fruit.

ARTIGAS 2008 T
70% garnacha, 20% cariñena, 10% cabernet sauvignon.

92 Colour: bright cherry. Nose: ripe fruit, sweet spices, creamy oak, earthy notes. Palate: flavourful, fruity, toasty, round tannins.

LA BASSETA 2008 T
40% garnacha, 40% cariñena, 20% syrah.

92 Colour: cherry, garnet rim. Nose: ripe fruit, spicy, creamy oak, toasty, fruit expression. Palate: powerful, flavourful, toasty, round tannins.

CIRERETS 2008 T
60% garnacha, 40% cariñena.

90 Colour: cherry, garnet rim. Nose: sweet spices, dark chocolate, ripe fruit, earthy notes. Palate: flavourful, fleshy, spicy, ripe fruit.

LA CREU ALTA 2007 T
55% cariñena, 45% garnacha.

92 Colour: cherry, garnet rim. Nose: powerfull, characterful, mineral, ripe fruit. Palate: powerful, sweetness, ripe fruit, long.

BUIL & GINÉ

Ctra. de Gratallops - Vilella Baixa, Km. 11,5
43737 Gratallops (Tarragona)
☎: +34 977 839 810 - Fax: +34 977 839 811
info@builgine.com
www.builgine.com

JOAN GINÉ 2009 B BARRICA
70% garnacha blanca, 28% macabeo, 2% pedro ximénez.

89 Colour: bright yellow, greenish rim. Nose: medium intensity, ripe fruit, spicy. Palate: flavourful, good structure, spicy, ripe fruit.

GINÉ GINÉ 2008 T
60% cariñena, 40% garnacha.

87 Colour: cherry, garnet rim. Nose: scrubland, toasty, spicy, dark chocolate. Palate: flavourful, powerful, fleshy, sweetness.

JOAN GINÉ 2007 T
45% garnacha, 45% cariñena, 10% cabernet sauvignon.

88 Colour: cherry, garnet rim. Nose: spicy, dark chocolate, ripe fruit. Palate: powerful, sweetness, ripe fruit.

PLERET 2005 T
45% cariñena, 25% garnacha, 10% cabernet sauvignon, 10% merlot, 10% syrah.

89 Colour: deep cherry. Nose: complex, powerfull, varietal, ripe fruit, earthy notes. Palate: complex, sweetness, spirituous, flavourful, fleshy.

BURGOS PORTA

Mas Sinén, s/n
43376 Poboleda (Tarragona)
☎: +34 696 094 509
burgos.porta@wanadoo.es
www.massinen.com

MAS SINÉN 2007 TC
48% garnacha, 15% samsó, 20% cabernet sauvignon, 17% syrah.

90 Colour: very deep cherry, purple rim. Nose: balanced, complex, mineral, dark chocolate. Palate: good structure, spicy, ripe fruit, long.

MAS SINÉN COSTER 2007 TC
50% garnacha, 40% cariñena, 10% cabernet sauvignon.

88 Colour: cherry, garnet rim. Nose: powerfull, warm, candied fruit. Palate: flavourful, powerful, fleshy, fine bitter notes.

CASA GRAN DEL SIURANA

Mayor, 3
43738 Bellmunt del Priorat (Tarragona)
☎: +34 932 233 022 - Fax: +34 932 231 370
perelada@castilloperelada.com
www.castilloperelada.com

GR-174 2010 T
35% garnacha, 30% cariñena, 35% cabernet sauvignon.

92 Colour: cherry, purple rim. Nose: expressive, fresh fruit, red berry notes, floral. Palate: flavourful, fruity, good acidity, fleshy, complex, rich.

GRAN CRUOR 2007 T
90% syrah, 10% cariñena.

94 Colour: cherry, garnet rim. Nose: red berry notes, ripe fruit, earthy notes, mineral, cocoa bean, spicy. Palate: complex, rich, powerful, flavourful, balanced, round, fleshy.

CRUOR 2007 T
30% garnacha, 30% cabernet sauvignon, 20% syrah, 10% merlot, cariñena.

90 Color bright cherry. Aroma ripe fruit, sweet spices, creamy oak, expressive. Taste flavourful, fruity, toasty, round tannins.

CELLER AIXALÀ I ALCAIT

Balandra, 8
43737 Torroja del Priorat (Tarragona)
☎: +34 629 507 807 - Fax: +34 977 839 516
pardelasses@gmail.com
www.pardelasses.com

DESTRANKIS 2009 T
80% garnacha, 20% cariñena.

90 Colour: deep cherry, garnet rim. Nose: powerfull, ripe fruit, fruit liqueur notes, sweet spices, creamy oak. Palate: good structure, flavourful, round tannins.

PARDELASSES 2009 T
100% cariñena.

88 Colour: cherry, garnet rim. Nose: powerfull, ripe fruit, raspberry, sweet spices. Palate: good acidity, round, powerful.

CELLER BARTOLOMÉ

Major
43738 Bellmunt del Priorat (Tarragona)
☎: +34 977 830 098 - Fax: +34 977 320 448
cellerbartolome@hotmail.com
www.primitiudebellmunt.com

PRIMITIU DE BELLMUNT 2009 T
50% garnacha, 50% samsó.

90 Colour: very deep cherry, garnet rim. Nose: balanced, expressive, mineral, sweet spices. Palate: flavourful, good structure, round tannins.

CLOS BARTOLOME 2009 T
garnacha, cariñena.

89 Colour: deep cherry, garnet rim. Nose: ripe fruit, aged wood nuances, varnish, balanced. Palate: good structure, fleshy, powerful.

CLOS BARTOLOME 2008 T
garnacha, cariñena.

90 Colour: bright cherry, garnet rim. Nose: complex, balanced, ripe fruit, mineral. Palate: fleshy, spicy, good structure.

PRIMITIU DE BELLMUNT 2007 T
50% garnacha, 50% samsó.

89 Colour: bright cherry, garnet rim. Nose: candied fruit, sweet spices. Palate: powerful, good structure, flavourful, round tannins, fine bitter notes.

CELLER BUJORN

Alt. de Sant Pere, 19
43374 La Vilella Baixa (Tarragona)
☎: +34 656 355 663
bujorn@tinet.cat
www.bujorn.cat

BUJORN 2009 T
66% cariñena, 17% garnacha, 17% cabernet sauvignon.

89 Colour: cherry, garnet rim. Nose: medium intensity, red berry notes, ripe fruit, dry stone. Palate: balanced, spicy, ripe fruit.

CELLER CAL PLA

Prat de la Riba, 1
43739 Porrera (Tarragona)
☎: +34 977 828 125 - Fax: +34 977 828 125
info@cellercalpla.com
www.cellercalpla.com

MAS D'EN COMPTE 2008 B
15% xarel.lo, 15% picapoll, 10% macabeo, 60% garnacha blanca.

90 Colour: bright yellow. Nose: varietal, powerfull, expressive, complex, smoky, sweet spices, fine reductive notes. Palate: powerful, spirituous, sweetness.

MAS D'EN COMPTE 2008 TC
50% garnacha, 40% cariñena, 10% cabernet sauvignon.

88 Colour: cherry, garnet rim. Nose: powerfull, warm, ripe fruit, creamy oak, toasty. Palate: powerful, flavourful, spicy, ripe fruit.

CELLER CAL PLA 2007 T
50% cariñena, 40% garnacha, 10% cabernet sauvignon.

84 Colour: cherry, garnet rim. Nose: medium intensity, premature reduction notes, old leather. Palate: flavourful, spicy.

CELLER CASTELLET

Font de Dalt, 11
43739 Porrera (Tarragona)
☎: +34 977 828 044
cellercastellet@yahoo.es

EMPIT 2008 TC
60% garnacha, 20% cariñena, 20% cabernet sauvignon.

89 Colour: cherry, garnet rim. Nose: spicy, complex, fruit preserve. Palate: powerful, flavourful, toasty, round tannins.

FERRAL 2008 T
60% garnacha, 20% syrah, 20% cabernet sauvignon.

85 Colour: deep cherry. Nose: powerfull, sulphur notes, candied fruit, toasty, spicy. Palate: powerful.

CELLER CECILIO

Piró, 28
43737 Gratallops (Tarragona)
☎: +34 977 839 181 - Fax: +34 977 839 507
celler@cellercecilio.com
www.cellercecilio.com

CELLER CECILIO BLANC 2010 B
100% garnacha blanca.

83 Colour: bright yellow. Nose: slightly evolved, ripe fruit, warm. Palate: fruity, easy to drink.

CELLER CECILIO NEGRE 2009 T
cariñena, garnacha, cabernet sauvignon, syrah.

86 Colour: deep cherry, garnet rim. Nose: ripe fruit, spicy, scrubland, dry stone. Palate: fleshy, spicy.

L'ESPILL 2007 TC
60% garnacha, 30% cariñena, 10% cabernet sauvignon.

87 Colour: dark-red cherry. Nose: fruit preserve, candied fruit, creamy oak, toasty. Palate: warm, sweetness, spirituous, spicy, ripe fruit.

L'ESPILL 2006 TC
60% garnacha, 30% cariñena, 10% cabernet sauvignon.

89 Colour: cherry, garnet rim. Nose: powerfull, candied fruit, fruit liqueur notes, toasty, sweet spices. Palate: powerful, fleshy, long.

CELLER DE L'ABADÍA

De la Font, 38
43737 Gratallops (Tarragona)
☎: +34 977 054 078 - Fax: +34 977 054 078
jeroni@cellerabadia.com
www.cellerabadia.com

SANT JERONI ROSAT 2010 RD
100% cariñena.

85 Colour: coppery red. Nose: candied fruit, smoky, balanced. Palate: powerful, flavourful, fruity, sweetness, spirituous.

SANT JERONI "GARNATXA DE L'HORT 2010 T
100% garnacha.

86 Colour: dark-red cherry. Nose: medium intensity, woody, creamy oak, spicy, ripe fruit. Palate: creamy, pruney, powerful, flavourful, spirituous, sweetness.

SANT JERONI 2009 T
80% cariñena, 20% cabernet sauvignon.

83 Colour: dark-red cherry. Nose: ripe fruit, aged wood nuances, short, powerfull. Palate: sweetness, spirituous, powerful.

ALICE 2007 T
50% cariñena, 25% garnacha, 15% syrah, 10% cabernet sauvignon.

90 Colour: cherry, garnet rim. Nose: ripe fruit, spicy, complex, earthy notes. Palate: powerful, flavourful, toasty, round tannins.

CLOS CLARA 2007 T
40% garnacha, 40% cariñena, 10% syrah, 10% cabernet sauvignon.

88 Colour: cherry, garnet rim. Nose: fruit preserve, fruit liqueur notes, toasty. Palate: flavourful, powerful, spicy, ripe fruit.

CELLER DE L'ENCASTELL

Castell, 13
43739 Porrera (Tarragona)
☎: +34 630 941 959
roquers@roquers.com
www.roquers.com

MARGE 2009 T
garnacha, cabernet sauvignon, merlot, syrah.

89 Colour: cherry, garnet rim. Nose: powerfull, characterful, ripe fruit, fruit liqueur notes. Palate: flavourful, fleshy, good acidity.

ROQUERS DE PORRERA 2008 TC
garnacha, merlot, cariñena, syrah.

90 Colour: cherry, garnet rim. Nose: powerfull, ripe fruit, fruit expression. Palate: powerful, flavourful, fleshy, concentrated.

ROQUERS DE SAMSÓ 2008 T
100% cariñena.

88 Colour: cherry, purple rim. Nose: powerfull, ripe fruit, sweet spices. Palate: powerful, spicy, ripe fruit, round tannins.

CELLER DELS PINS VERS

Afores, s/n
43736 El Molar (Tarragona)
☎: +34 977 825 458 - Fax: +34 977 825 458
info@lafuina.com
www.lafuina.com

LA FUINA 2008 T
cabernet sauvignon, garnacha, cariñena.

90 Colour: cherry, garnet rim. Nose: ripe fruit, spicy, toasty, balsamic herbs. Palate: powerful, flavourful, toasty, round tannins.

LA FUINA 2007 T
cabernet sauvignon, garnacha, cariñena.

88 Colour: black cherry. Nose: powerfull, ripe fruit, warm, fragrant herbs, spicy. Palate: fleshy, spicy, round tannins.

CELLER DEVINSSI

Masets, 1
43737 Gratallops (Tarragona)
☎: +34 977 839 523
devinssi@il-lia.com
www.devinssi.com

MAS DE LES VALLS 2008 T
garnacha, cariñena, cabernet sauvignon.

88 Colour: cherry, garnet rim. Nose: ripe fruit, toasty, sweet spices. Palate: powerful, spicy, ripe fruit.

IL.LIA 2007 T
garnacha, cariñena, cabernet sauvignon.

89 Colour: cherry, garnet rim. Nose: balanced, complex, dark chocolate, sweet spices, mineral. Palate: flavourful, spicy, ripe fruit, sweet tannins.

CELLER HIDALGO ALBERT

Pol. Ind. 14, Parc. 102
43376 Poboleda (Tarragona)
☎: +34 977 842 064 - Fax: +34 977 842 064
hialmi@yahoo.es

1270 A VUIT 2007 T
garnacha, syrah, cariñena, cabernet sauvignon, merlot.

92 Colour: cherry, purple rim. Nose: powerfull, warm, raspberry, creamy oak, sweet spices. Palate: flavourful, powerful, fleshy, ripe fruit.

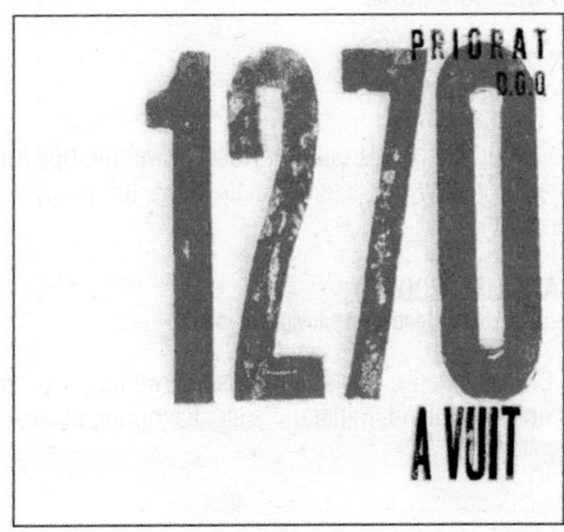

CELLER MAS BASTÉ

De la Font, 38
43737 Gratallops (Tarragona)
☎: +34 629 300 291 - Fax: +34 934 364 877
jacazurra@albagrup.com
www.cellerabadia.com

PEITES 2010 T
70% garnacha, 30% syrah.

87 Colour: deep cherry, purple rim. Nose: medium intensity, balsamic herbs, red berry notes, mineral. Palate: flavourful, fruity, round tannins.

PEITES 2009 TC
80% cariñena, 10% syrah, 10% cabernet sauvignon.

89 Colour: deep cherry, purple rim. Nose: balanced, ripe fruit, wild herbs, spicy, mineral. Palate: flavourful, fruity.

CLOS PEITES 2008 T
80% cariñena, 10% syrah, 10% cabernet sauvignon.

90 Colour: cherry, garnet rim. Nose: spicy, creamy oak, toasty, mineral. Palate: powerful, flavourful, toasty, round tannins.

PEITES 2008 T
cariñena, syrah, cabernet sauvignon.

87 Colour: cherry, garnet rim. Nose: powerfull, ripe fruit, warm, toasty. Palate: flavourful, powerful, fleshy.

CELLER MAS DOIX

Carme, 115
43376 Poboleda (Tarragona)
☎: +34 639 356 172 - Fax: +34 933 216 790
info@masdoix.com
www.masdoix.com

DOIX 2009 TC
garnacha, cariñena, merlot.

93 Colour: cherry, garnet rim. Nose: powerfull, ripe fruit, raspberry, creamy oak, toasty. Palate: powerful, fleshy, mineral, long.

SALANQUES 2009 T
cariñena, garnacha, cabernet sauvignon, merlot.

92 Colour: cherry, garnet rim. Nose: powerfull, ripe fruit, raspberry, scrubland, mineral. Palate: flavourful, powerful, fleshy, long.

LES CRESTES 2009 T
garnacha, cariñena, syrah.

90 Colour: deep cherry. Nose: earthy notes, ripe fruit, sweet spices, scrubland. Palate: powerful, flavourful, fleshy, fine bitter notes.

CELLER MAS GARRIAN

Mas del Camperol - Camí Rieres, s/n
43736 El Molar (Tarragona)
☎: +34 977 262 118 - Fax: +34 977 262 118
masgarrian@gmail.com
www.masgarrian.com

CLOS SEVERI JR 2009 T
cariñena, garnacha, cabernet sauvignon, syrah.

87 Colour: black cherry, garnet rim. Nose: balanced, balsamic herbs, spicy, earthy notes, fruit preserve. Palate: flavourful, ripe fruit, round tannins.

CLOS SEVERI 2006 T
cariñena, garnacha, cabernet sauvignon, syrah.

83 Colour: cherry, garnet rim. Nose: powerfull, characterful, fruit liqueur notes. Palate: powerful, concentrated.

MAS DEL CAMPEROL 2004 TC
cariñena, garnacha, cabernet sauvignon, syrah.

89 Colour: dark-red cherry. Nose: mineral, old leather, cigar, candied fruit, creamy oak, toasty. Palate: spirituous, powerful, flavourful.

CELLER PAHÍ

Carrer del Carme, 57
43376 Poboleda (Tarragona)
☎: +34 977 762 042 - Fax: +34 977 762 042
info@cellerpahi.com
www.celler-pahi.com

GAUBANÇA 2010 RD
cariñena, garnacha.

87 Colour: brilliant rose. Nose: medium intensity, red berry notes, scrubland. Palate: flavourful, good structure, fruity.

GAUBANÇA 2010 T
cariñena, garnacha, merlot, syrah.

87 Colour: very deep cherry. Nose: roasted coffee, spicy, ripe fruit. Palate: ripe fruit, mineral, flavourful, fleshy, toasty.

CELLER PRIOR PONS

Rey, 4
43375 La Vilella Alta (Tarragona)
☎: +34 606 547 865
info@priorpons.com
www.priorpons.com

PRIOR PONS 2008 T
40% garnacha, 45% mazuelo, 15% cabernet sauvignon.

90 Colour: deep cherry. Nose: fruit preserve, cedar wood, spicy, dark chocolate, powerfull, warm. Palate: flavourful, powerful, fruity, spirituous, fleshy.

PLANETS DE PRIOR PONS 2008 T
40% garnacha, 40% mazuelo, 10% cabernet sauvignon, 5% syrah, 5% merlot.

88 Colour: cherry, garnet rim. Nose: ripe fruit, spicy, creamy oak, toasty. Palate: powerful, flavourful, toasty, round tannins.

PLANETS DE PRIOR PONS 2007 T
40% garnacha, 40% mazuelo, 10% cabernet sauvignon, 5% syrah, 5% merlot.

89 Colour: cherry, purple rim. Nose: powerfull, ripe fruit, creamy oak, dark chocolate. Palate: powerful, fine bitter notes, toasty.

CELLER SABATÉ

Nou, 6
43374 La Vilella Baixa (Tarragona)
☎: +34 977 839 209 - Fax: +34 977 839 209
cellersabate@cellersabate.com
www.cellersabate.com

MAS PLANTADETA 2010 BFB
100% garnacha blanca.

88 Colour: bright yellow, greenish rim. Nose: medium intensity, fresh fruit, wild herbs. Palate: flavourful, fruity, long.

MAS D'EN BERNAT 2010 T
100% garnacha.

87 Colour: deep cherry. Nose: varietal, powerfull, fruit preserve, fruit liqueur notes. Palate: creamy, mineral, powerful, flavourful, sweetness, spirituous.

MAS PLANTADETA 2008 T ROBLE
100% garnacha.

88 Colour: cherry, garnet rim. Nose: powerfull, ripe fruit, toasty, sweet spices. Palate: spicy, flavourful, powerful.

MAS PLANTADETA 2006 TC
60% garnacha, 20% cariñena, 20% cabernet sauvignon.

84 Colour: cherry, garnet rim. Nose: powerfull, ripe fruit, toasty, sweet spices, dark chocolate. Palate: flavourful, powerful, fleshy, complex.

CELLER VALL-LLACH

Del Pont, 9
43739 Porrera (Tarragona)
☎: +34 977 828 244 - Fax: +34 977 828 325
celler@vallllach.com
www.vallllach.com

EMBRUIX DE VALL-LLACH 2009 T
31% cariñena, 29% garnacha, 17% syrah, 13% cabernet sauvignon, 10% merlot.

90 Colour: deep cherry. Nose: spicy, cedar wood, creamy oak, ripe fruit. Palate: spicy, long, mineral, powerful, flavourful, fleshy.

IDUS DE VALL-LLACH 2009 T
40% cariñena, 15% garnacha, 20% cabernet sauvignon, 15% merlot, syrah.

88 Colour: black cherry. Nose: fruit preserve, fruit liqueur notes, toasty. Palate: powerful, toasty, fine bitter notes.

VALL-LLACH 2009 T
50% cariñena, 10% garnacha, 15% cabernet sauvignon, 25% merlot.

86 Colour: dark-red cherry, garnet rim. Nose: powerfull, overripe fruit. Palate: flavourful, sweetness, sweet tannins.

CELLERS DE SCALA DEI

Rambla de la Cartoixa, s/n
43379 Scala Dei (Tarragona)
☎: +34 977 827 027 - Fax: +34 977 827 044
scaladei@codorniu.es
www.grupocodorniu.com

SCALA DEI 2010 T
90% garnacha, 5% syrah, 5% mazuelo.

89 Colour: dark-red cherry. Nose: dry stone, ripe fruit, varietal, powerfull, complex, balsamic herbs. Palate: spirituous, powerful, flavourful, sweetness.

SCALA DEI PRIOR 2009 TC
55% garnacha, 15% mazuelo, 20% cabernet sauvignon, 15% syrah.

88 Color cherry, garnet rim. Aroma ripe fruit, spicy, creamy oak, toasty, complex. Taste powerful, flavourful, toasty, round tannins.

CARTOIXA 2006 TR
40% garnacha, 25% mazuelo, 25% cabernet sauvignon, 10% syrah.

90 Colour: cherry, garnet rim. Nose: earthy notes, powerfull, expressive, ripe fruit, toasty, dark chocolate. Palate: spicy, ripe fruit, fine bitter notes, good acidity.

CELLERS UNIÓ

Joan Oliver, 16-24
43206 Reus (Tarragona)
☎: +34 977 330 055 - Fax: +34 977 330 070
info@cellersunio.com
www.cellersunio.com

ROUREDA LLICORELLA BLANC PEDRO XIMÉNEZ 2007 B
100% pedro ximénez.

89 Colour: bright yellow. Nose: medium intensity, balanced, expressive, wild herbs. Palate: flavourful, powerful, full, rich, spicy, smoky aftertaste.

TENDRAL SELECCIÓN 2008 T
40% cariñena, 60% garnacha.

88 Colour: cherry, garnet rim. Nose: powerfull, ripe fruit, toasty, sweet spices. Palate: flavourful, powerful, fleshy, long.

ROUREDA LLICORELLA 2007 T
45% garnacha, 40% cariñena, 10% cabernet sauvignon, 5% merlot.

87 Colour: cherry, garnet rim. Nose: powerfull, warm, fruit liqueur notes, dark chocolate. Palate: powerful, fine bitter notes, spicy.

ROUREDA LLICORELLA VITIS 60 2006 T
40% garnacha, 40% cariñena, 10% cabernet sauvignon, 10% syrah.

83 Colour: black cherry, purple rim. Nose: slightly evolved, powerfull, sweet spices. Palate: fleshy, flavourful.

CLOS BERENGUER

Ctra. T-734 del Masroig, km. 8,3
43735 El Molar (Tarragona)
☎: +34 977 361 390 - Fax: +34 977 361 390
info@closberenguer.com
www.closberenguer.com

CLOS BERENGUER BLANC 2007 B
garnacha blanca, pedro ximénez.

86 Colour: bright yellow. Nose: woody, aged wood nuances, ripe fruit, scrubland. Palate: slightly evolved, fleshy, powerful, spicy.

CLOS DE TAFALL "SELECCIO DE VINYES" 2009 T
garnacha, samsó, syrah, cabernet sauvignon.

89 Colour: deep cherry. Nose: ripe fruit, balanced, mineral, expressive, powerfull. Palate: good structure, fleshy, ripe fruit, long.

CLOS BERENGUER VINYA LES SORTS 2008 T
cabernet sauvignon.

88 Colour: black cherry. Nose: roasted coffee, dark chocolate, candied fruit. Palate: powerful, concentrated, sweetness.

CLOS BERENGUER SYRAH DE SELECCIÓ 2008 T
syrah, samsó.

87 Colour: black cherry. Nose: aromatic coffee, sweet spices, cedar wood, candied fruit. Palate: powerful, flavourful, full, fleshy, sweetness, spirituous.

CLOS BERENGUER SELECCIÓ 2008 T
garnacha, samsó, syrah, cabernet sauvignon.

87 Colour: cherry, garnet rim. Nose: earthy notes, overripe fruit, dark chocolate, aged wood nuances, aromatic coffee. Palate: powerful, flavourful, spicy, round tannins.

CLOS DE L'OBAC

Camí Manyetes, s/n
43737 Gratallops (Tarragona)
☎: +34 977 839 276 - Fax: +34 977 839 371
info@costersdelsiurana.com
www.costersdelsiurana.com

KYRIE 2007 BC
garnacha blanca, macabeo, xarel.lo, moscatel.

93 Colour: bright straw. Nose: candied fruit, citrus fruit, powerfull. Palate: flavourful, ripe fruit, fine bitter notes, good acidity.

MISERERE 2007 TC
garnacha, cabernet sauvignon, merlot, cariñena, tempranillo.

91 Colour: cherry, garnet rim. Nose: powerfull, warm, toasty, dark chocolate. Palate: flavourful, powerful, sweetness.

CLOS DE L'OBAC 2007 TC
garnacha, cabernet sauvignon.

90 Colour: cherry, garnet rim. Nose: earthy notes, powerfull, warm, ripe fruit, toasty. Palate: powerful, concentrated, sweetness, fine bitter notes.

CLOS FIGUERAS

Carrer La Font, 38
43737 Gratallops (Tarragona)
☎: +34 977 830 217 - Fax: +34 977 830 422
info@closfigueras.com
www.desfigueras.com

FONT DE LA FIGUERA 2010 B
viognier, chenin blanc, garnacha blanca.

90 Colour: bright yellow. Nose: varietal, powerfull, expressive, warm, scrubland, smoky. Palate: spirituous, fruity, rich, powerful, flavourful, complex.

CLOS FIGUERES 2009 T
garnacha, cariñena, cabernet sauvignon, monastrell, syrah.

90 Colour: cherry, garnet rim. Nose: ripe fruit, spicy, creamy oak, toasty, mineral. Palate: powerful, flavourful, toasty, round tannins.

SERRAS DEL PRIORAT 2009 T
garnacha, cariñena, syrah.

90 Colour: deep cherry. Nose: ripe fruit, raspberry, warm. Palate: powerful, spirituous, pruney, spicy, round tannins.

FONT DE LA FIGUERA 2009 T
garnacha, cariñena, syrah, cabernet sauvignon.

88 Colour: very deep cherry, purple rim. Nose: powerfull, ripe fruit, dark chocolate, sweet spices, dry stone. Palate: flavourful, fruity.

CLOS I TERRASSES

La Font, 1
43737 Gratallops (Tarragona)
☎: +34 977 839 022 - Fax: +34 977 839 179
info@closerasmus.com

CLOS ERASMUS 2009 T BARRICA
garnacha, syrah.

92 Colour: dark-red cherry. Nose: cocoa bean, sweet spices, smoky, fruit liqueur notes, ripe fruit. Palate: spirituous, sweetness, good structure, powerful, full, mineral, ripe fruit.

LAUREL 2008 T
garnacha, syrah, cabernet sauvignon.

86 Colour: cherry, garnet rim. Nose: fruit preserve, sweet spices. Palate: flavourful, fruity, round tannins.

CLOS MOGADOR

Camí Manyetes, s/n
43737 Gratallops (Tarragona)
☎: +34 977 839 171 - Fax: +34 977 839 426
closmogador@closmogador.com
www.closmogador.com

NELIN 2009 B

92 Colour: bright straw. Nose: candied fruit, citrus fruit, faded flowers, jasmine. Palate: flavourful, fruity, fine bitter notes, full.

CLOS MOGADOR 2008 T
garnacha, cariñena, merlot, syrah.

94 Colour: deep cherry. Nose: powerfull, ripe fruit, fruit expression, raspberry, mineral, earthy notes. Palate: flavourful, fleshy, round, long.

COSTERS DEL PRIORAT

Finca Sant Martí
43738 Bellmunt del Priorat (Tarragona)
☎: +34 618 203 473
info@costersdelpriorat.com
www.costersdelpriorat.com

CLOS CYPRES 2009 T
90% cariñena, 10% garnacha.

91 Colour: cherry, purple rim. Nose: powerfull, ripe fruit, red berry notes, creamy oak, toasty. Palate: flavourful, powerful, fleshy, round tannins.

ELIOS 2009 T
55% garnacha, 35% cariñena, 10% cabernet sauvignon, syrah.

90 Colour: cherry, purple rim. Nose: powerfull, fruit expression, raspberry, ripe fruit, dark chocolate, aromatic coffee. Palate: flavourful, powerful, good structure.

PISSARRES 2009 T
55% cariñena, 30% garnacha, 15% cabernet sauvignon, syrah.

87 Colour: cherry, garnet rim. Nose: fruit liqueur notes, toasty, spicy. Palate: flavourful, good acidity, fine bitter notes.

DE MULLER

Camí Pedra Estela, 34
43205 Reus (Tarragona)
☎: +34 977 757 473 - Fax: +34 977 771 129
lab@demuller.es
www.demuller.es

LEGITIM 2008 TC
50% garnacha, 35% merlot, 5% cariñena, 10% syrah.

87 Colour: very deep cherry. Nose: powerfull, fruit preserve, dark chocolate, sweet spices, warm, scrubland. Palate: good structure, fleshy, round tannins.

LES PUSSES DE MULLER 2006 TC
50% merlot, 50% syrah.

89 Colour: dark-red cherry. Nose: green pepper, ripe fruit, fruit expression, fragrant herbs. Palate: powerful, flavourful, fruity, fruity aftestaste.

LO CABALÓ 2006 TR
70% garnacha, 10% merlot, 10% syrah, 10% cariñena.

88 Colour: cherry, garnet rim. Nose: warm, fruit liqueur notes, spicy, toasty. Palate: sweetness, fine bitter notes, warm.

DOMINI DE LA CARTOIXA

Camino de la Solana, s/n
43736 El Molar (Tarragona)
☎: +34 606 443 736 - Fax: +34 977 771 737
info@closgalena.com
www.closgalena.com

CLOS GALENA 2009 TC
garnacha, cariñena, syrah, cabernet sauvignon.

90 Colour: dark-red cherry. Nose: fruit preserve, roasted coffee, woody. Palate: fleshy, powerful, flavourful, sweetness.

FORMIGA DE VELLUT 2009 T
garnacha, samsó, syrah.

89 Colour: cherry, purple rim. Nose: powerfull, sweet spices, ripe fruit. Palate: good structure, round tannins.

CROSSOS 2009 T
60% garnacha, 20% cabernet sauvignon, 20% cariñena.

86 Colour: deep cherry, purple rim. Nose: medium intensity, red berry notes, ripe fruit. Palate: fruity, spicy, correct.

GALENA 2007 T
garnacha, cariñena, merlot, cabernet sauvignon.

90 Color cherry, garnet rim. Aroma ripe fruit, spicy, creamy oak, toasty, complex. Taste powerful, flavourful, toasty, round tannins.

ELVIWINES

Finca "Clos Mesorah" Ctra. T-300 Falset Marça, Km. 1
43775 Marça Priorat (Tarragona)
☎: +34 935 343 026 - Fax: +34 936 750 316
moises@elviwines.com
www.elviwines.com

EL26 2008 T
40% cabernet sauvignon, 20% garnacha, 20% cariñena, 20% syrah.

92 Colour: cherry, garnet rim. Nose: powerfull, ripe fruit, toasty, dark chocolate. Palate: flavourful, powerful, fleshy, complex.

FERRER BOBET

Ctra. Falset a Porrera, Km. 6,5
43730 Falset (Tarragona)
☎: +34 609 945 532 - Fax: +34 935 044 265
eguerre@ferrerbobet.com
www.ferrerbobet.com

FERRER BOBET SELECCIÓ ESPECIAL 2008 T
95% cariñena, 5% garnacha.

94 Colour: very deep cherry. Nose: fruit liqueur notes, fruit expression, ripe fruit, mineral, spicy, smoky, cedar wood. Palate: mineral, spicy, flavourful, spirituous.

FERRER BOBET 2008 T
65% cariñena, 34% garnacha, 1% cabernet sauvignon.

93 Colour: deep cherry, garnet rim. Nose: powerfull, spicy, ripe fruit, fruit liqueur notes, earthy notes. Palate: flavourful, fruity, balanced.

GENIUM CELLER

Nou, 92- Bajos
43376 Poboleda (Tarragona)
☎: +34 977 827 146 - Fax: +34 977 827 146
genium@geniumceller.com
www.geniumceller.com

GENIUM XIMENIS 2009 BFB
90% pedro ximénez, 10% garnacha blanca.

88 Colour: bright yellow. Nose: candied fruit, scrubland, mineral, powerfull. Palate: flavourful, fruity, spicy.

GENIUM ROSER'S 2010 RD
100% garnacha.

87 Colour: raspberry rose. Nose: varietal, fresh, powerfull, complex, mineral. Palate: powerful, fruity, fresh.

GENIUM FRESC 2009 T ROBLE
80% garnacha, 20% cariñena.

87 Colour: very deep cherry, purple rim. Nose: powerfull, fruit preserve, sweet spices, dark chocolate. Palate: powerful, flavourful, spicy.

POBOLEDA VI DE VILA 2007 TR
70% garnacha, 20% cariñena, 10% merlot.

89 Colour: very deep cherry. Nose: fruit expression, candied fruit, ripe fruit, mineral, spicy, creamy oak, toasty. Palate: fleshy, spirituous, sweetness, fruity, powerful, flavourful.

GENIUM ECOLÒGIC 2007 T
50% garnacha, 30% merlot, 10% cariñena, 10% syrah.

86 Colour: deep cherry. Nose: slightly evolved, warm, fruit preserve, fruit liqueur notes. Palate: spirituous, sweetness, powerful, flavourful, fruity.

GENIUM CELLER 2006 TC
60% garnacha, 20% cariñena, 15% merlot, 5% syrah.

89 Colour: bright cherry. Nose: sweet spices, creamy oak, candied fruit. Palate: flavourful, fruity, toasty, round tannins.

GRAN CLOS

Montsant, 2
43738 Bellmunt del Priorat (Tarragona)
☎: +34 977 830 675 - Fax: +34 977 830 417
cellersfuentes@granclos.com
www.granclos.com

GRAN CLOS 2006 B
50% garnacha blanca, 50% macabeo.

89 Colour: bright yellow. Nose: spicy, aged wood nuances, smoky, dried herbs, ripe fruit. Palate: spirituous, powerful, flavourful, spicy, smoky aftertaste, oaky.

FINCA EL PUIG S.C. T
60% garnacha, 15% syrah, 15% cabernet sauvignon, 10% cariñena.

87 Colour: deep cherry. Nose: ripe fruit, creamy oak, toasty. Palate: flavourful, powerful, spirituous, sweetness, fleshy.

FINCA EL PUIG S.C. T
50% garnacha, 20% syrah, 20% cabernet sauvignon, 10% cariñena.

87 Colour: cherry, garnet rim. Nose: powerfull, ripe fruit, sweet spices. Palate: powerful, flavourful, fleshy, round tannins.

SOLLUNA 2008 T
75% garnacha, 15% cariñena, 10% merlot.

85 Colour: deep cherry, garnet rim. Nose: powerfull, scrubland, fruit preserve, overripe fruit. Palate: flavourful, good structure, round tannins.

CARTUS 2005 T
74% garnacha, 26% cariñena.

90 Colour: dark-red cherry. Nose: powerfull, ripe fruit, creamy oak, dark chocolate. Palate: flavourful, fine bitter notes, ripe fruit.

GRAN CLOS 2005 T
55% garnacha, 25% cariñena, 20% cabernet sauvignon.

88 Colour: cherry, garnet rim. Nose: powerfull, ripe fruit, toasty, sweet spices. Palate: powerful, spicy, mineral.

GRAN CLOS 2004 T
52% garnacha, 34% cariñena, 14% cabernet sauvignon.

90 Colour: cherry, garnet rim. Nose: sweet spices, ripe fruit, earthy notes. Palate: ripe fruit, flavourful, fine bitter notes.

CARTUS 2004 T
76% garnacha, 24% cariñena.

89 Colour: cherry, garnet rim. Nose: ripe fruit, spicy, creamy oak, toasty, earthy notes. Palate: powerful, flavourful, toasty, round tannins.

GRATAVINUM

Camí de la Vilella Baixa a El Lloar
Mas D'en Serres
43737 Gratallops (Tarragona)
☎: +34 938 901 399 - Fax: +34 938 901 143
gratavinum@gratavinum.com
www.gratavinum.com

GRATAVINUM 2 PI R 2008 T
60% garnacha, 25% cariñena, 10% cabernet sauvignon, 5% syrah.

91 Colour: cherry, garnet rim. Nose: earthy notes, powerfull, toasty. Palate: flavourful, powerful, spicy, ripe fruit.

GV5 2008 T
55% cariñena, 20% garnacha, 15% syrah, 10% cabernet sauvignon.

91 Colour: very deep cherry, garnet rim. Nose: powerfull, spicy, toasty, mineral, ripe fruit. Palate: good structure, fleshy.

HUELLAS

De la Mora de Sant Pere, 26- 2º
08880 Cubelles (Barcelona)
☎: +34 609 428 507
franckmassard@epicure-wines.com

MAS AMOR 2010 RD
garnacha, sumoll.

90 Colour: brilliant rose. Nose: varietal, powerfull, balanced, complex, fruit expression. Palate: fresh, fruity, flavourful, balsamic.

AMIC 2010 T

89 Colour: dark-red cherry. Nose: mineral, fruit expression, fresh fruit. Palate: flavourful, powerful, fresh.

HUMILITAT* 2009 T
60% garnacha, 40% cariñena.

89 Colour: cherry, garnet rim. Nose: mineral, ripe fruit, toasty, sweet spices. Palate: powerful, flavourful, fine bitter notes, full.

HUELLAS 2009 T
50% cariñena, 40% garnacha, 5% syrah, 5% cabernet sauvignon.

88 Colour: dark-red cherry. Nose: caramel, creamy oak, ripe fruit. Palate: complex, powerful, flavourful, fruity.

JOAN AMETLLER

Ctra. La Morera de Monsant - Cornudella, km. 3,2
43361 La Morera de Monsant (Tarragona)
☎: +34 933 208 439 - Fax: +34 933 208 437
ametller@ametller.com
www.ametller.com

CLOS CORRIOL 2010 B
60% garnacha blanca, 30% macabeo, 10% pedro ximénez, chardonnay.

88 Colour: bright yellow, greenish rim. Nose: balanced, expressive, scrubland, citrus fruit. Palate: flavourful, balanced, easy to drink.

CLOS MUSTARDÓ 2009 B
60% garnacha blanca, 30% macabeo, 10% chardonnay, pedro ximénez.

91 Colour: bright straw. Nose: ripe fruit, fruit liqueur notes, fruit expression, dried herbs, creamy oak, smoky. Palate: creamy, mineral, ripe fruit, flavourful, powerful, rich, smoky aftertaste.

CLOS CORRIOL 2010 RD
80% cabernet sauvignon, 20% garnacha.

86 Colour: rose, purple rim. Nose: powerfull, red berry notes, ripe fruit, fragrant herbs. Palate: fleshy, ripe fruit.

CLOS CORRIOL 2008 T
garnacha, cariñena.

86 Colour: deep cherry, garnet rim. Nose: powerfull, ripe fruit, spicy, warm, scrubland. Palate: good structure, fleshy.

CLOS MUSTARDÓ 2007 T
55% garnacha, 35% cariñena, 10% cabernet sauvignon, merlot.

87 Colour: cherry, garnet rim. Nose: ripe fruit, toasty. Palate: flavourful, spicy, fine bitter notes.

ELS IGOLS 2006 TR
30% cariñena, 60% garnacha, 10% merlot, cabernet sauvignon.

88 Colour: bright cherry, orangey edge. Nose: balanced, candied fruit, powerfull, spicy. Palate: spicy, ripe fruit.

JOAN SIMÓ

11 de Setembre, 7
43739 Porrera (Tarragona)
☎: +34 627 563 713 - Fax: +34 977 830 993
leseres@cellerjoansimo.com
www.cellerjoansimo.com

LES ERES 2007 T
50% cariñena, 35% garnacha, 15% cabernet sauvignon.

92 Colour: very deep cherry, garnet rim. Nose: balanced, scrubland, spicy, ripe fruit. Palate: good structure, rich, round tannins.

SENTIUS 2007 T
50% garnacha, 20% cabernet sauvignon, 10% merlot, 20% syrah, cariñena.

85 Colour: cherry, garnet rim. Nose: ripe fruit, spicy, slightly evolved. Palate: powerful, flavourful, toasty.

LA CONRERIA D'SCALA DEI

Carrer Mitja Galta, s/n - Finca Les Brugueres
43379 Scala Dei (Tarragona)
☎: +34 977 827 055 - Fax: +34 977 827 055
laconreria@vinslaconreria.com
www.vinslaconreria.com

LES BRUGUERES 2010 B
100% garnacha blanca.

88 Colour: bright straw. Nose: medium intensity, floral, scrubland. Palate: flavourful, fruity, balanced.

LA CONRERIA 2009 T
garnacha, syrah, merlot, cabernet sauvignon.

89 Colour: deep cherry. Nose: expressive, varietal, powerfull, fruit liqueur notes, candied fruit. Palate: balsamic, creamy, mineral, powerful, flavourful.

IUGITER 2008 T
garnacha, merlot, cabernet sauvignon, cariñena.

89 Colour: deep cherry, garnet rim. Nose: powerfull, ripe fruit, sweet spices, dry stone. Palate: good structure, spicy, ripe fruit, round tannins.

IUGITER SELECCIÓ VINYES VELLES 2007 TC
garnacha, cariñena, cabernet sauvignon.

88 Colour: dark-red cherry. Nose: fruit preserve, fruit liqueur notes, powerfull, warm, smoky, roasted coffee, sweet spices. Palate: fleshy, concentrated, flavourful.

MARCO ABELLA

Ctra. de Porrera a Cornudella del Montsant, Km. 0,7
43739 Porrera (Tarragona)
☎: +34 933 712 407 - Fax: +34 933 712 407
obayes@marcoabella.com
www.marcoabella.com

ÒLBIA 2008 B
macabeo, pedro ximénez, garnacha blanca.

88 Colour: bright yellow. Nose: dried flowers, candied fruit, mineral, medium intensity, spicy. Palate: powerful, flavourful, fleshy, spicy.

MAS MALLOLA 2007 T
40% garnacha, 40% cariñena, 10% cabernet sauvignon, 10% syrah.

90 Colour: cherry, garnet rim. Nose: red berry notes, ripe fruit, mineral, balanced, spicy, creamy oak. Palate: flavourful, fleshy, fine tannins.

CLOS ABELLA 2005 T
40% garnacha, 10% cabernet sauvignon, 40% cariñena, 10% syrah.

90 Colour: cherry, garnet rim. Nose: ripe fruit, mineral, spicy, creamy oak, varnish. Palate: powerful, fleshy, flavourful, balanced.

MAS IGNEUS

Ctra. Falset a Vilella Baixa T-710, Km. 11,1
43737 Gratallops (Tarragona)
☎: +34 977 262 259 - Fax: +34 977 054 027
celler@masigneus.com
www.masigneus.com

FA 206 2008 T
70% garnacha, 20% cariñena, 7% cabernet sauvignon, 3% syrah.

89 Colour: deep cherry. Nose: toasty, dark chocolate, powerfull, characterful, ripe fruit, fruit liqueur notes. Palate: spicy, ripe fruit, fine bitter notes.

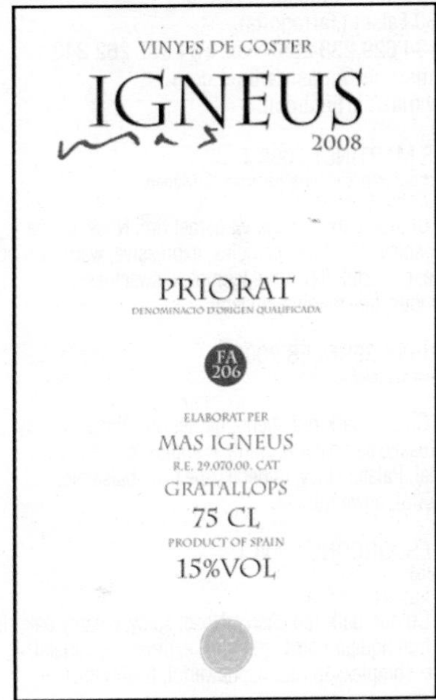

FA 104 2010 B
garnacha blanca.

91 Colour: bright yellow. Nose: balanced, white flowers, fresh fruit, complex, mineral. Palate: flavourful, fruity, rich.

BARRANC BLANC 2010 B
30% garnacha blanca, 50% macabeo, 15% pedro ximénez, 5% moscatel.

90 Colour: bright straw. Nose: fresh, fresh fruit, white flowers, expressive, mineral. Palate: flavourful, fruity, good acidity, balanced.

BARRANC NEGRE 2009 T
80% garnacha, 20% cariñena.

86 Colour: cherry, garnet rim. Nose: powerfull, ripe fruit, raspberry, toasty. Palate: flavourful, fine bitter notes, warm.

FA 112 2008 T
60% garnacha, 30% cariñena, 10% cabernet sauvignon.

88 Colour: deep cherry. Nose: powerfull, ripe fruit, sweet spices, dark chocolate. Palate: powerful, fine bitter notes, spicy, ripe fruit.

MAS MARTINET

Ctra. Falset - Gratallops, Km. 6
43730 Falset (Tarragona)
☎: +34 629 238 236 - Fax: +34 977 262 348
masmartinet@masmartinet.com
www.masmartinet.com

CLOS MARTINET 2008 T
garnacha, syrah, cariñena, cabernet sauvignon.

94 Colour: dark-red cherry, garnet rim. Nose: cocoa bean, spicy, dry stone, complex, expressive, warm, varietal. Palate: powerful, flavourful, complex, sweetness, spirituous, fine tannins, mineral.

CAMI PESSEROLES 2008 T
cariñena, garnacha.

94 Colour: dark-red cherry, garnet rim. Nose: creamy oak, toasty, damp earth, warm, complex, expressive, varietal. Palate: spicy, mineral, ripe fruit, balsamic, flavourful, powerful.

ELS ESCURÇONS 2008 T
garnacha.

92 Colour: dark-red cherry. Nose: spicy, creamy oak, ripe fruit, fruit liqueur notes, complex, expressive, varietal. Palate: complex, spirituous, powerful, flavourful.

MAS PERINET

Finca Mas Perinet, s/n - T-702, Km. 1,6
43361 La Morera de Montsant (Tarragona)
☎: +34 977 827 113 - Fax: +34 977 827 180
info@masperinet.com
www.masperinet.com

PERINET + PLUS 2006 T
51% cariñena, 41% garnacha, 8% syrah.

95 Colour: cherry, garnet rim. Nose: ripe fruit, expressive, mineral, cocoa bean, dark chocolate, creamy oak. Palate: powerful, flavourful, fleshy, complex, balanced.

PERINET 2006 T
36% mazuelo, 16% garnacha, 19% syrah, 15% cabernet sauvignon, 14% merlot.

92 Colour: cherry, garnet rim. Nose: ripe fruit, expressive, earthy notes, spicy, creamy oak. Palate: powerful, flavourful, fleshy, good acidity, round.

PETIT PERINET 2006 T
40% mazuelo, 40% garnacha, 20% cabernet sauvignon.

90 Colour: cherry, garnet rim. Nose: ripe fruit, scrubland, dry stone, spicy, toasty. Palate: powerful, flavourful, fleshy, complex.

PERINET 2005 T
40% mazuelo, 20% cabernet sauvignon, 20% syrah, 10% merlot, 10% garnacha.

92 Colour: cherry, garnet rim. Nose: complex, ripe fruit, mineral, spicy, fine reductive notes. Palate: flavourful, fleshy, ripe fruit, long.

MASET DEL LLEÓ

C-244, Km. 32,5
08792 La Granada del Penedès (Barcelona)
☎: +34 902 200 250 - Fax: +34 938 921 333
info@maset.com
www.maset.com

MAS VILÓ 2008 T
cariñena, garnacha.

89 Colour: cherry, purple rim. Nose: powerfull, ripe fruit, toasty, sweet spices. Palate: flavourful, fleshy, complex, spicy.

CLOS VILÓ 2007 T
cariñena, garnacha, cabernet sauvignon.

88 Colour: cherry, purple rim. Nose: powerfull, ripe fruit, raspberry, toasty, creamy oak. Palate: flavourful, powerful, good acidity, round tannins.

CLOS GRAN VILÓ 2006 T
cabernet sauvignon, cariñena, garnacha.

88 Colour: bright cherry, purple rim. Nose: sweet spices, creamy oak, candied fruit. Palate: good structure, fleshy.

MAYOL VITICULTORS

De la Bassa, 24
43737 Torroja del Priorat (Tarragona)
☎: +34 977 839 395 - Fax: +34 977 839 317
celler@mayol.eu
www.mayol.eu

ROSER 2010 BFB
90% macabeo, 10% garnacha blanca.

88 Colour: bright straw. Nose: short, fresh, ripe fruit. Palate: powerful, flavourful, fruity, spicy, creamy.

GLOP 2009 T
60% garnacha, 20% syrah, 10% cariñena, 10% cabernet sauvignon.

87 Colour: dark-red cherry. Nose: candied fruit, smoky, spicy, creamy oak. Palate: mineral, ripe fruit, powerful, flavourful, spirituous.

BROGIT 2008 TC
50% garnacha, 15% cariñena, 15% syrah, 15% cabernet sauvignon, 5% merlot.

89 Colour: very deep cherry. Nose: powerfull, sweet spices, dark chocolate, candied fruit. Palate: flavourful, good structure, mineral.

TORROJA DES DE DINS 2008 T
60% garnacha, 20% cariñena, 15% syrah, 5% cabernet sauvignon.

89 Colour: bright cherry, garnet rim. Nose: complex, mineral, ripe fruit, sweet spices, wild herbs. Palate: good structure, round tannins.

MELIS

Balandra, 54
43737 Torroja del Priorat (Tarragona)
☎: +34 937 313 021 - Fax: +34 937 312 371
javier@melispriorat.com
www.melispriorat.com

MELIS 2008 T
60% garnacha, 25% syrah, 15% cabernet sauvignon.

92 Colour: cherry, garnet rim. Nose: spicy, creamy oak, toasty, complex, fruit expression, ripe fruit. Palate: powerful, flavourful, toasty, round tannins.

ELIX 2008 T
45% garnacha, 25% cabernet sauvignon, 8% cariñena, 18% syrah, 4% merlot.

91 Colour: deep cherry, garnet rim. Nose: mineral, complex, expressive, warm, sweet spices. Palate: good structure, complex, balanced.

OBRADOR 2008 T
54% garnacha, 11% cariñena, 25% syrah, 8% cabernet sauvignon.

88 Colour: cherry, garnet rim. Nose: fruit liqueur notes, medium intensity, warm, toasty, spicy. Palate: flavourful, sweetness, fine bitter notes.

ELIX 2007 T
50% garnacha, 18% cabernet sauvignon, 10% cariñena, 16% syrah, 6% merlot.

92 Colour: dark-red cherry. Nose: mineral, spicy, creamy oak, ripe fruit, complex. Palate: fruity, powerful, flavourful, fleshy, full, complex.

ELIX 2006 T
34% garnacha, 24% cabernet sauvignon, 15% cariñena, 18% syrah, 9% merlot.

93 Colour: cherry, garnet rim. Nose: earthy notes, ripe fruit, toasty, spicy, wet leather. Palate: flavourful, powerful, fleshy, spicy, long.

MELIS 2006 T
63% garnacha, 15% syrah, 15% cariñena, 7% cabernet sauvignon.

93 Colour: cherry, garnet rim. Nose: ripe fruit, spicy, creamy oak, toasty, scrubland, mineral. Palate: powerful, flavourful, toasty, round tannins.

MERITXELL PALLEJÀ

Major, 32
43737 Gratallops (Tarragona)
☎: +34 670 960 735
info@nita.cat
www.nita.cat

NITA 2010 T
45% garnacha, 35% cariñena, 15% cabernet sauvignon, syrah.

85 Colour: dark-red cherry. Nose: slightly evolved, powerfull, varietal, fruit preserve. Palate: powerful, flavourful, fruity, sweetness.

MERUM PRIORATI S.L.

Ctra. de Falset, s/n
43739 Porrera (Tarragona)
☎: +34 977 828 307 - Fax: +34 977 828 324
info@merumpriorati.com
www.merumpriorati.com

ARDILES VIOGNIER 2009 B
100% viognier.

91 Colour: bright straw. Nose: varietal, powerfull, expressive, white flowers, fragrant herbs. Palate: spirituous, elegant, round, flavourful, powerful, complex.

OSMIN 2006 T
garnacha, cariñena, syrah, cabernet sauvignon.

90 Colour: cherry, garnet rim. Nose: powerfull, ripe fruit, toasty, spicy. Palate: powerful, flavourful, good acidity.

ARDILES 2006 T
garnacha, cariñena, syrah, cabernet sauvignon.

89 Colour: cherry, garnet rim. Nose: spicy, creamy oak, toasty, ripe fruit. Palate: powerful, flavourful, toasty, round tannins.

NOGUERALS

Tou, 5
43360 Cornudella de Montsant (Tarragona)
☎: +34 650 033 546 - Fax: +34 934 419 879
noguerals@hotmail.com
www.noguerals.com

ABELLARS 2007 T
50% garnacha, 25% cariñena, 15% cabernet sauvignon, 10% syrah.

87 Colour: cherry, garnet rim. Nose: dark chocolate, fruit preserve. Palate: sweetness, fine bitter notes, spicy.

PORTAL DEL PRIORAT

Clos del Portal - Pista del Lloar a Bellmunt s/n
43376 El Molar (Tarragona)
☎: +34 932 531 760 - Fax: +34 934 173 591
info@portaldelpriorat.com
www.portaldelpriorat.com

TROS DE CLOS 2009 T
cariñena.

94 Colour: cherry, garnet rim. Nose: red berry notes, ripe fruit, mineral, balanced, spicy, creamy oak, balsamic herbs. Palate: powerful, fleshy, complex, mineral, round, elegant.

NEGRE DE NEGRES 2009 T
garnacha, cariñena, cabernet sauvignon.

93 Colour: cherry, garnet rim. Nose: red berry notes, ripe fruit, mineral, sweet spices, creamy oak. Palate: balanced, powerful, flavourful, fleshy, complex.

SOMNI 2009 T
cariñena, syrah.

92 Colour: cherry, purple rim. Nose: ripe fruit, earthy notes, dark chocolate, creamy oak, expressive. Palate: complex, fleshy, mineral, flavourful, long.

GOTES DEL PRIORAT 2009 T
cariñena, garnacha, syrah.

89 Colour: cherry, garnet rim. Nose: mineral, cocoa bean, sweet spices, toasty, fruit expression. Palate: powerful, flavourful, toasty.

ROCA DE LES DOTZE

Turó, 5
08328 Alella (Barcelona)
☎: +34 662 302 214
info@rocadelesdotze.cat
www.rocadelesdotze.cat

NORAY 2007 T
garnacha, cabernet sauvignon, samsó, syrah.

90 Colour: cherry, garnet rim. Nose: complex, balanced, spicy. Palate: good structure, balanced, fine bitter notes, round tannins.

ROCA BRUIXA 2007 T
garnacha, syrah.

87 Colour: deep cherry, garnet rim. Nose: balanced, powerfull, candied fruit, sweet spices, dark chocolate. Palate: flavourful, good structure.

RODRÍGUEZ SANZO

Manuel Azaña, 9- Local 15
47014 Valladolid (Valladolid)
☎: +34 983 150 150 - Fax: +34 983 150 151
valsanzo@valsanzo.com
www.valsanzo.com

CANYERETS 2006 T
60% garnacha, 40% cariñena.

92 Colour: cherry, garnet rim. Nose: ripe fruit, powerfull, cocoa bean, dark chocolate, sweet spices, creamy oak, mineral. Palate: powerful, flavourful, complex, fleshy, balanced.

SABATÉ I MUR VINATERS

Major, 47
43737 Torroja del Priorat (Tarragona)
☎: +34 677 354 167
jsabateroig@eresmas.com

LES CLIVELLES DE TORROJA 2009 T
100% samsó.

88 Colour: very deep cherry, garnet rim. Nose: powerfull, balanced, fruit preserve, sweet spices. Palate: flavourful, ripe fruit, spicy.

SANGENÍS I VAQUÉ

Pl. Catalunya, 3
43739 Porrera (Tarragona)
☎: +34 977 828 238
celler@sangenisivaque.com
www.sangenisivaque.com

LO COSTER BLANC 2009 B
garnacha blanca, macabeo.

90 Colour: bright golden. Nose: complex, balanced, ripe fruit, sweet spices. Palate: flavourful, rich, balanced, spicy, mineral.

SANGENIS I VAQUÉ 2008 T
45% garnacha, 45% cariñena, 10% syrah.

88 Colour: deep cherry. Nose: powerfull, ripe fruit, toasty, sweet spices. Palate: flavourful, fine bitter notes, ripe fruit, round tannins.

SANGENIS I VAQUÉ 2007 T
45% garnacha, 45% mazuelo, 10% merlot.

88 Colour: deep cherry, garnet rim. Nose: warm, candied fruit, scrubland. Palate: good structure, ripe fruit, spicy.

CLOS MONLLEÓ 2005 T
50% garnacha, 50% cariñena.

87 Colour: cherry, garnet rim. Nose: powerfull, ripe fruit, sweet spices. Palate: flavourful, powerful, sweetness.

SOLA CLASSIC

Nou, 15
43738 Bellmunt del Priorat (Tarragona)
☎: +34 977 831 134
info@solaclassic.com
www.solaclassic.com

VINYES JOSEP 2008 T

86 Colour: cherry, garnet rim. Nose: spicy, complex, fruit preserve. Palate: powerful, flavourful, toasty, round tannins.

TERRA DE VEREMA

Baix de St. Pere, 1
43374 La Vilella Baixa (Tarragona)
☎: +34 656 607 867 - Fax: +34 934 159 698
admin@terradeverema.com
www.terradeverema.com

TRIUMVIRAT 2009 T
35% garnacha, 55% cariñena, 10% syrah.

87 Colour: bright cherry, garnet rim. Nose: scrubland, warm, powerfull, fruit liqueur notes. Palate: flavourful, ripe fruit, spicy.

CORELIUM 2007 T
90% cariñena, 10% garnacha.

91 Colour: very deep cherry. Nose: varietal, powerfull, complex, fruit preserve, fruit liqueur notes, cocoa bean, spicy, dark chocolate. Palate: powerful, fleshy, sweetness, spirituous, flavourful.

TERRA PERSONAS

Apartado 96
43730 Falset (Tarragona)
☎: +34 662 214 291
ruud.persoon@terrapersonas.com
www.terrapersonas.festis.cat

TERRAPERSONAS 2010 B
80% macabeo, 20% garnacha blanca.

89 Colour: bright straw. Nose: grassy, fresh fruit, fruit expression. Palate: flavourful, fruity, fleshy.

TERRAPERSONAS VERMELLA 2010 T
50% cariñena, 30% syrah, 20% garnacha.

87 Colour: cherry, garnet rim. Nose: powerfull, ripe fruit, floral, scrubland. Palate: flavourful, fine bitter notes, spicy.

TERRAPERSONAS 2009 T
50% cariñena, 30% garnacha, 20% syrah.

88 Colour: cherry, purple rim. Nose: ripe fruit, warm, powerfull, spicy. Palate: fleshy, fruity, round tannins.

TERRES DE VIDALBA

Terme de les Foreses
43376 Poboleda (Tarragona)
☎: +34 616 413 722
info@terresdevidalba.com

TOCS 2007 T
garnacha, cabernet sauvignon, syrah, merlot.

88 Colour: cherry, garnet rim. Nose: ripe fruit, spicy, creamy oak. Palate: powerful, flavourful, round tannins, fine bitter notes.

TERROIR AL LIMIT

Baixa Font, 12
43737 Torroja del Priorat (Tarragona)
☎: +34 977 828 057 - Fax: +34 977 828 380
dominik@terroir-al-limit.com
www.terroir-al-limit.com

PEDRA DE GUIX 2009 B
garnacha blanca, pedro ximénez.

90 Colour: bright yellow. Nose: medium intensity, complex, ripe fruit, scrubland, earthy notes. Palate: fleshy, complex, flavourful, powerful, spicy, mineral, creamy.

PEDRA DE GUIX 2008 B
garnacha blanca, pedro ximénez.

92 Colour: bright yellow. Nose: fragrant herbs, candied fruit, smoky. Palate: mineral, complex, fresh, powerful, flavourful, good acidity.

TORROJA VI DE LA VILA 2008 T
garnacha, cariñena.

95 Colour: cherry, garnet rim. Nose: powerfull, ripe fruit, warm, sweet spices, creamy oak, mineral. Palate: flavourful, powerful, fleshy, spicy, ripe fruit.

LES MANYES 2008 T
100% grenache.

95 Colour: dark-red cherry. Nose: varietal, elegant, expressive, complex, candied fruit, cocoa bean, cedar wood, balsamic herbs. Palate: balsamic, mineral, complex, spirituous, creamy.

ARBOSSAR 2008 T
100% cariñena.

92 Colour: deep cherry. Nose: varietal, expressive, elegant, fresh fruit, spicy, creamy oak. Palate: round, good acidity, powerful, flavourful, creamy, spicy.

LES TOSSES 2008 T
100% cariñena.

92 Colour: deep cherry. Nose: fruit liqueur notes, fruit preserve, powerfull, varietal, expressive. Palate: fleshy, concentrated, sweetness, spirituous, powerful, balsamic.

DITS DEL TERRA 2008 T
100% carignan.

91 Colour: dark-red cherry. Nose: ripe fruit, cedar wood, fruit liqueur notes, varietal, expressive, complex. Palate: mineral, spicy, creamy, flavourful, powerful, full, good acidity.

TORRES PRIORAT

Finca La Soleta, s/n
43737 El Lloar (Tarragona)
☎: +34 938 177 400 - Fax: +34 938 177 444
admin@torres.es
www.torres.es

SALMOS 2009 T
garnacha, syrah, cariñena.

88 Colour: dark-red cherry. Nose: spicy, toasty, ripe fruit, mineral. Palate: good acidity, sweetness, spirituous.

PERPETUAL 2008 TR
mazuelo, garnacha.

91 Nose: creamy oak, toasty, spicy, dark chocolate, ripe fruit, expressive, powerfull, fruit liqueur notes. Palate: complex, spirituous, powerful, flavourful.

TROSSOS DEL PRIORAT

Ctra. Gratallops a La Vilella Baixa, Km. 10,65
43737 Gratallops (Tarragona)
☎: +34 670 590 788
celler@trossosdelpriorat.com
www.trossosdelpriorat.com

ABRACADABRA 2009 B
70% garnacha blanca, 30% macabeo.

88 Colour: bright yellow, greenish rim. Nose: spicy, ripe fruit, mineral. Palate: flavourful, ripe fruit, good structure.

LO MÓN 2008 T
50% garnacha, 25% cariñena, 15% cabernet sauvignon, 10% syrah.

93 Colour: cherry, garnet rim. Nose: ripe fruit, spicy, creamy oak, toasty, mineral. Palate: powerful, flavourful, toasty, round tannins.

VINÍCOLA DEL PRIORAT

Piró, s/n
43737 Gratallops (Tarragona)
☎: +34 977 839 167 - Fax: +34 977 839 201
info@vinicoladelpriorat.com
www.vinicoladelpriorat.com

ÒNIX CLÀSSIC 2010 B
garnacha blanca, viura, pedro ximénez.

90 Colour: bright straw, greenish rim. Nose: medium intensity, wild herbs, dried flowers. Palate: fruity, flavourful, long.

MAS DELS FRARES 2010 T
garnacha, mazuelo, syrah, cabernet sauvignon, merlot.

89 Colour: dark-red cherry. Nose: fruit expression, fruit liqueur notes, ripe fruit, spicy, creamy oak, toasty. Palate: spirituous, complex, spirituous.

ÒNIX CLÁSSIC 2010 T
garnacha, mazuelo.

88 Colour: deep cherry. Nose: varietal, powerfull, fruit preserve, smoky, creamy oak. Palate: spirituous, powerful, flavourful.

ÒNIX FUSIÓ 2009 T
garnacha, syrah.

90 Colour: cherry, garnet rim. Nose: powerfull, ripe fruit, fruit expression, toasty. Palate: powerful, fine bitter notes, good acidity, spicy.

ÒNIX EVOLUCIÓ 2008 T
garnacha, mazuelo, cabernet sauvignon.

90 Colour: cherry, garnet rim. Nose: spicy, creamy oak, toasty, ripe fruit. Palate: powerful, flavourful, toasty, round tannins, long.

CLOS GEBRAT 2008 TC
35% garnacha, 30% cabernet sauvignon, 35% mazuelo.

86 Colour: very deep cherry. Nose: powerfull, fruit preserve, scrubland, spicy. Palate: good structure, round tannins.

ÒNIX SELECCIÓ 2006 TC
mazuelo.

88 Colour: cherry, garnet rim. Nose: ripe fruit, spicy, creamy oak, toasty, wet leather. Palate: powerful, flavourful, toasty, round tannins.

FRARES DOLÇ S.C. AÑEJO BARRICA
garnacha, mazuelo.

89 Colour: coppery red. Nose: expressive, powerfull, dry stone, fruit liqueur notes, fruit liqueur notes, candied fruit. Palate: unctuous, powerful, flavourful, sweet.

FRARES RANCI SC
garnacha, mazuelo.

90 Colour: light mahogany. Nose: toasty, spicy, dry nuts, honeyed notes, fruit liqueur notes. Palate: sweet, fine bitter notes, good acidity, spicy.

VINNICO EXPORT

Muela, 16
03730 Jávea (Alicante)
☎: +34 965 791 967 - Fax: +34 966 461 471
info@vinnico.com
www.vinnico.com

TOSALET 2009 T
50% garnacha, 20% cabernet sauvignon, 30% cariñena.

87 Colour: deep cherry. Nose: fruit preserve, fruit liqueur notes, spicy, creamy oak, toasty. Palate: spirituous, sweetness, ripe fruit, pruney.

VINYES ALTAIR

Consolacio, 26
43737 Gratallops (Tarragona)
☎: +34 646 748 500
alerany@telefonica.net

MASPERLA 2006 T
45% garnacha, 40% cariñena, 15% cabernet sauvignon, merlot, syrah.

91 Colour: deep cherry, garnet rim. Nose: complex, balanced, mineral, spicy. Palate: flavourful, fruity, round tannins.

IMAGINACIO 2005 T
45% garnacha, 40% cariñena, 15% cabernet sauvignon, merlot, syrah.

87 Colour: cherry, garnet rim. Nose: candied fruit, fruit liqueur notes, toasty, spicy. Palate: spirituous, fine bitter notes, spicy.

VINYES DE MANYETES

Camí Manyetes, s/n
43737 Gratallops (Tarragona)
☎: +34 977 839 171 - Fax: +34 977 839 426
euroseleccio@euroseleccio.com
www.vinyesdemanyetes.com

SOLERTIA 2009 T
41% garnacha, 29% cabernet sauvignon, 30% syrah.

86 Colour: cherry, garnet rim. Nose: powerfull, fruit preserve, aromatic coffee, caramel. Palate: sweetness, fine bitter notes, spirituous.

MANYETES 2008 T
65% cariñena, 25% garnacha, 6% cabernet sauvignon, 4% syrah.

94 Colour: deep cherry. Nose: cocoa bean, spicy, ripe fruit, fruit liqueur notes, violet drops, complex. Palate: flavourful.

VITICULTORS DEL PRIORAT

Partida Palells - Mas Subirat
43738 Bellmunt del Priorat (Tarragona)
☎: +34 977 262 268 - Fax: +34 977 262 268
morlanda@morlanda.com
www.morlanda.com

MORLANDA 2010 B
75% garnacha blanca, 25% macabeo.

89 Colour: bright straw. Nose: medium intensity, varietal, fresh fruit, scrubland, mineral. Palate: powerful, flavourful, fruity, fresh.

MAS DE SUBIRÁ 2008 TC
60% garnacha, 30% cariñena, 10% cabernet sauvignon.

88 Colour: cherry, garnet rim. Nose: medium intensity, candied fruit, aged wood nuances, dark chocolate. Palate: powerful, toasty, long.

MORLANDA 2007 TR
50% garnacha, 50% cariñena.

88 Colour: deep cherry. Nose: sweet spices, dark chocolate, creamy oak, fruit preserve. Palate: spicy, creamy, powerful, flavourful, sweetness, spirituous.

VITICULTORS MAS D'EN GIL

Finca Mas d'en Gil
43738 Bellmunt del Priorat (Tarragona)
☎: +34 977 830 192 - Fax: +34 977 830 152
mail@masdengil.com
www.masdengil.com

COMA ALTA 2010 B
70% garnacha blanca, 30% viognier.

88 Colour: bright straw. Nose: varietal, fresh, ripe fruit. Palate: fruity, powerful, flavourful, rich, spirituous.

COMA BLANCA 2009 BC
50% macabeo, 50% garnacha blanca.

89 Colour: bright straw. Nose: macerated fruit, scrubland, dry stone. Palate: powerful, flavourful, fruity, fresh.

CLOS FONTÀ 2008 TC
40% garnacha peluda, 20% garnacha pais, 10% cabernet sauvignon.

92 Colour: deep cherry. Nose: cedar wood, complex, expressive, varietal, spicy, cocoa bean, closed. Palate: spirituous, flavourful, complex.

COMA VELLA 2008 T
50% garnacha peluda, 20% garnacha pais, 20% cariñena, 10% syrah.

90 Colour: deep cherry. Nose: sweet spices, creamy oak, fruit expression, ripe fruit. Palate: creamy, spicy, ripe fruit, sweet tannins.

NUS 2009 DULCE NATURAL
80% garnacha, 15% syrah, 5% viognier.

92 Colour: very deep cherry. Nose: varietal, complex, candied fruit, fruit liqueur notes, fruit expression, earthy notes, dark chocolate, pattiserie, roasted almonds. Palate: flavourful, powerful, fruity, sweetness, spirituous.

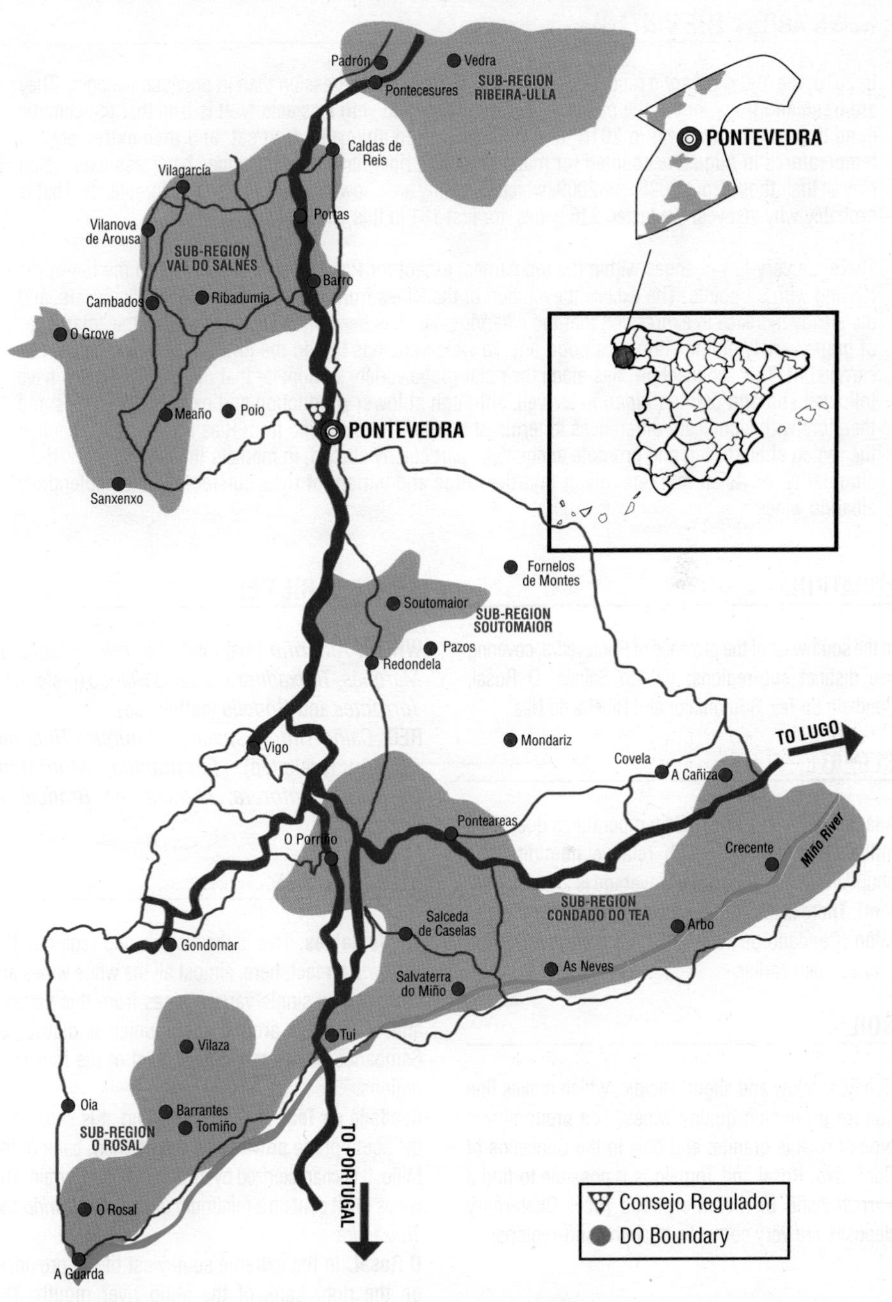
Padrón
Vedra
Pontecesures
SUB-REGION
RIBEIRA-ULLA
Caldas de
Reis
Vilagarcía
Vilanova
de Arousa
SUB-REGION
VAL DO SALNÉS
Portas
Barro
Cambados
Ribadumia
O Grove
Meaño
Poio
PONTEVEDRA
Sanxenxo
PONTEVEDRA
Fornelos
de Montes
Soutomaior
SUB-REGION
SOUTOMAIOR
Pazos
Redondela
Mondariz
TO LUGO
Covela
A Cañiza
Vigo
Ponteareas
O Porriño
Crecente
Miño River
SUB-REGION
CONDADO DO TEA
Salceda
de Caselas
Arbo
Gondomar
As Neves
Salvaterra
do Miño
Tui
Vilaza
Oia
Barrantes
Tomiño
SUB-REGION
O ROSAL
TO PORTUGAL
O Rosal
A Guarda
Consejo Regulador
DO Boundary

DO RÍAS BAIXAS

NEWS ABOUT THE VINTAGE:

In 2010, the 100% *albariño* renderings have a more subdued expression than in previous vintages. They are fresh and fruity, but in the palate they show richer and with less acidity. It is true that the climatic conditions were not great in 2010: first mildew caused abnormal fruit set, and then extremely hot temperatures in August accounted for made grapes to ripen faster, so the wines have less expression overall than those from 2008 and 2009, which currently are showing great power and complexity. That is probably why last year we tasted 216 wines, for just 181 in this year's edition.

There are very few changes within the top names, except for Pazo Piñeiro, which gets to the top of the ranking with 95 points. The excellent evolution of the wines from this region in the past five years, and the steady increase in expression that the *albariño* grape has been showing is a sign that the "marriage" of grape variety and territory is a good one, to which one has to add the formidable work the DO has carried out. This "connection" has made their star grape variety so popular that other wine regions have followed suit and planted *albariño* as well, although at lower production and exploitation prices and therefore with significant differences in terms of quality. The "Albariño from Rías Baixas" is a label that the region should keep and promote adequately, particularly abroad, in markets that appreciate varietal singularity, or Asian markets, given that the range and variety of their cuisine matches splendidly albariño wines.

LOCATION:

In the southwest of the province of Pontevedra, covering five distinct sub-regions: Val do Salnés, O Rosal, Condado do Tea, Soutomaior and Ribeira do Ulla.

CLIMATE:

Atlantic, with moderate, mild temperatures due to the influence of the sea, high relative humidity and abundant rainfall (the annual average is around 1600 mm). There is less rainfall further downstream of the Miño (Condado de Tea), and as a consequence the grapes ripen earlier.

SOIL:

Sandy, shallow and slightly acidic, which makes fine soil for producing quality wines. The predominant type of rock is granite, and only in the Concellos of Sanxenxo, Rosal and Tomillo is it possible to find a narrow band of metamorphous rock. Quaternary deposits are very common in all the sub-regions.

GRAPE VARIETIES:

WHITE: *Albariño* (majority), *Loureira Blanca* or *Marqués*, *Treixadura* and Caíño *Blanco* (preferred); *Torrontés* and *Godello* (authorized).

RED: *Caíño Tinto, Espadeiro, Loureira Tinta* and *Sousón* (preferred); *Tempranillo, Mouratón, Garnacha Tintorera, Mencía* and *Brancellao* (authorized).

SUB-REGIONS:

Val do Salnés. This is the historic sub-region of the *Albariño* (in fact, here, almost all the white wines are produced as single-variety wines from this variety) and is centred around the municipal district of Cambados. It has the flattest relief of the four sub-regions.

Condado do Tea. The furthest inland, it is situated in the south of the province on the northern bank of the Miño. It is characterized by its mountainous terrain. The wines must contain a minimum of 70% of *Albariño* and *Treixadura*.

O Rosal. In the extreme southwest of the province, on the right bank of the Miño river mouth. The warmest sub-region, where river terraces abound. The wines must contain a minimum of 70% of *Albariño* and *Loureira*.

Soutomaior. Situated on the banks of the Verdugo River, about 10 km from Pontevedra, it consists only of the municipal district of Soutomaior. It produces only single-varietals of *Albariño*.

Ribeira do Ulla. A new sub-region along the Ulla River, which forms the landscape of elevated valleys further inland. It comprises the municipal districts of Vedra and part of Padrón, Deo, Boquixon, Touro, Estrada, Silleda and Vila de Cruce. Red wines predominate.

FIGURES:

Vineyard surface: 3,698 – **Wine-Growers:** 6,596 – **Wineries:** 192 – **2010 Harvest rating:** Very Good – **Production:** 21,637,897 litres – **Market percentages:** 77,66% domestic. 22,40% export

CONSEJO REGULADOR

Centro de Apoyo de Cabanas

36143 Salcedo (Pontevedra)

☎: +34 986 854 850 / +34 864 530 -

Fax: +34 986 864 546

@ consejo@doriasbaixas.com

www.doriasbaixas.com

GENERAL CHARACTERISTICS OF THE WINES

WHITES	Marked by the personality of the *Albariño*. They have a colour that ranges from pale yellow to greenish yellow. The nose is of herbs and flowers with excellent intensity that may be reminiscent of rather ripe apples, apricot, fennel or mint. On the palate they stand out for their oily and glycerine-like mouthfeel, their fruity character and persistence (the best examples have good doses of complexity and elegance).
REDS	At present there is very limited production. The first examples reveal a marked Atlantic character; the wines are a very brilliant violet cherry colour; they stand out for their notes of red berries and herbs reminiscent of eucalyptus and, on the palate, for their high acidity.

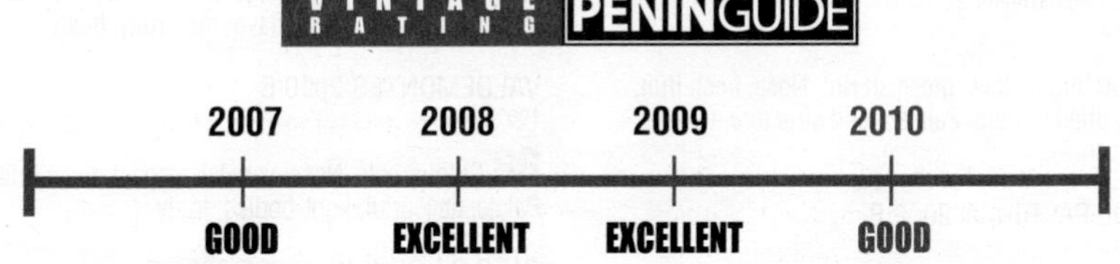

ADEGA CONDES DE ALBAREI

Camino a Bouza, 1 Castrelo
36639 Cambados (Pontevedra)
☎: +34 986 543 535 - Fax: +34 986 524 251
inf@condesdealbarei.com
www.condesdealbarei.com

CONDES DE ALBAREI 2010 B
100% albariño.

90 Colour: bright straw. Nose: white flowers, fresh fruit, ripe fruit, citrus fruit. Palate: powerful, flavourful, fleshy, fine bitter notes.

ENXEBRE VENDIMIA SELECCIONADA 2010 B
albariño.

89 Colour: bright straw. Nose: fresh, fresh fruit, white flowers, fragrant herbs. Palate: flavourful, fruity, good acidity, balanced.

CARBALLO GALEGO 2009 BFB
100% albariño.

93 Colour: bright straw. Nose: powerfull, varietal, ripe fruit, citrus fruit, cocoa bean. Palate: flavourful, powerful, long.

CONDES DE ALBAREI EN RAMA 2006 B
100% albariño.

91 Colour: bright straw. Nose: ripe fruit, grassy, varietal, sweet spices. Palate: spicy, ripe fruit, fine bitter notes.

ADEGA EIDOS

Padriñán, 65
36960 Sanxenxo (Pontevedra)
☎: +34 986 690 009 - Fax: +34 986 720 307
info@adegaeidos.com
www.adegaeidos.com

EIDOS DE PADRIÑÁN 2010 B
100% albariño.

90 Colour: bright straw, greenish rim. Nose: fresh fruit, wild herbs, dried flowers. Palate: good structure, fruity, flavourful, varietal.

VEIGAS DE PADRIÑÁN 2009 B
100% albariño.

92 Colour: yellow. Nose: candied fruit, jasmine, balanced, expressive, varietal. Palate: flavourful, fruity, rich, good structure, long.

CONTRAAPAREDE 2007 B
100% albariño.

91 Colour: bright yellow. Nose: candied fruit, floral, fragrant herbs. Palate: rich, fleshy, ripe fruit, good acidity.

ADEGA VALDÉS

Santa Cruz de Rivadulla, s/n
15885 Vedra (A Coruña)
☎: +34 981 512 439 - Fax: +34 981 509 226
comercial@gundian.com
www.adegavaldes.com

ALBARIÑO GUNDIAN 2010 B
100% albariño.

89 Colour: straw. Nose: ripe fruit, fruit expression, white flowers. Palate: flavourful, fruity, fresh.

XIRADELLA 2010 B
100% albariño.

89 Colour: pale. Nose: white flowers, fruit expression, scrubland. Palate: flavourful, fruity, fresh.

PAZO VILADOMAR 2010 B
80% treixadura, 20% albariño.

88 Colour: bright yellow. Nose: fresh fruit, balanced, varietal, floral. Palate: fruity, good finish.

ADEGAS AROUSA

Tirabao, 15 - Baión
36614 Vilanova de Arousa (Pontevedra)
☎: +34 986 506 113 - Fax: +34 986 715 454
grupoarousaboucina@gmail.com
www.adegasarousa.com

PAZO DA BOUCIÑA 2010 B
100% albariño.

90 Colour: pale. Nose: expressive, varietal, citrus fruit, fresh fruit, floral. Palate: flavourful, fruity, fresh.

VALDEMONXES 2010 B
100% albariño.

88 Colour: pale. Nose: varietal, elegant, fresh fruit. Palate: flavourful, light-bodied, fruity.

PAZO DA BOUCIÑA ARTE 2008 B
100% albariño.

90 Colour: bright yellow. Nose: candied fruit, white flowers, wild herbs. Palate: good structure, rich, ripe fruit.

ADEGAS CASTROBREY

Camanzo, s/n
36587 Vila de Cruces (Pontevedra)
☎: +34 986 583 643 - Fax: +34 986 583 722
bodegas@castrobrey.com
www.castrobrey.com

SIN PALABRAS CASTRO VALDÉS 2010 B
100% albariño.

88 Colour: yellow, greenish rim. Nose: balanced, fresh, grassy, faded flowers. Palate: flavourful, fruity, good acidity.

SEÑORÍO DA REGAS 2010 B
albariño, treixadura, godello, torrontés.

86 Colour: bright straw, greenish rim. Nose: medium intensity, grassy. Palate: easy to drink, good finish.

SEÑORÍO DE CRUCES 2010 B
100% albariño.

86 Colour: bright straw. Nose: medium intensity, white flowers, grassy. Palate: fruity, easy to drink.

ADEGAS D'ALTAMIRA

Altamira - Dena, s/n
36967 Meaño (Pontevedra)
☎: +34 986 746 046 - Fax: +34 986 745 725
oficina@adegasdaltamira.es
www.adegasdaltamira.es

ADEGAS D'ALTAMIRA SELECCIÓN 2009 B
100% albariño.

89 Colour: bright straw. Nose: fresh, fresh fruit, white flowers, expressive, varietal, fragrant herbs. Palate: flavourful, fruity, good acidity, balanced.

ADEGAS GRAN VINUM

Fermín Bouza Brei, 9 - 5ºB
36600 Vilagarcía de Arousa (Pontevedra)
☎: +34 986 555 742 - Fax: +34 986 555 742
info@adegasgranvinum.com
www.adegasgranvinum.com

ESENCIA DIVIÑA 2010 B
albariño.

91 Colour: bright straw. Nose: powerfull, ripe fruit, fruit expression. Palate: flavourful, powerful, fleshy.

GRAN VINUM 2010 B
albariño.

88 Colour: bright straw. Nose: fresh, fresh fruit, white flowers. Palate: flavourful, fruity, good acidity, balanced.

MAR DE VIÑAS 2010 B
albariño.

88 Colour: bright straw. Nose: fresh, fresh fruit, white flowers. Palate: flavourful, fruity, good acidity, balanced, fine bitter notes.

NESSA 2010 B
albariño.

88 Colour: bright straw. Nose: grassy, ripe fruit, sweet spices. Palate: flavourful, powerful, fleshy.

ADEGAS MORGADÍO

Albeos s/n
36429 Creciente (Pontevedra)
☎: +34 988 261 212 - Fax: +34 988 261 213
info@morgadio.com
www.morgadio.com

MORGADÍO 2010 B
100% albariño.

88 Colour: bright straw. Nose: fresh, fresh fruit, white flowers. Palate: flavourful, fruity, good acidity, balanced.

ADEGAS TOLLODOURO

Ctra. Tui-A Guarda, Km. 45
36760 O Rosal (Pontevedra)
☎: +34 986 609 810 - Fax: +34 986 609 811
bodega@tollodouro.com
www.tollodouro.com

PONTELLÓN ALBARIÑO 2010 B
albariño.

90 Colour: bright yellow, greenish rim. Nose: fresh fruit, grassy, varietal, elegant. Palate: flavourful, fruity, good acidity.

TOLLODOURO ROSAL 2010 B
albariño, loureiro, caiño blanco, treixadura.

88 Colour: bright straw. Nose: powerfull, ripe fruit, grassy. Palate: flavourful, fresh.

ADEGAS VALMIÑOR

A Portela, s/n - San Juan de Tabagón
36760 O'Rosal (Pontevedra)
☎: +34 986 609 060 - Fax: +34 986 609 313
valminor@valminorebano.com
www.adegasvalminor.com

DÁVILA 2010 B
albariño, loureiro, treixadura.

90 Colour: bright yellow. Nose: candied fruit, white flowers, varietal. Palate: flavourful, good acidity, fine bitter notes.

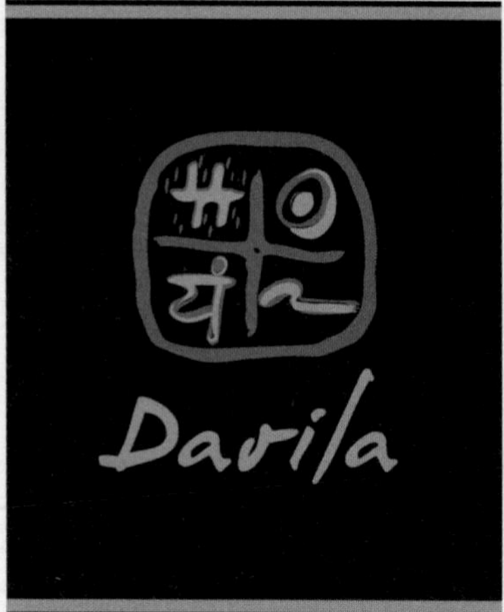

SERRA DA ESTRELA 2010 B
100% albariño.

88 Colour: bright straw. Nose: white flowers, fresh fruit, citrus fruit. Palate: flavourful, fruity, fresh.

TORROXAL 2010 B
albariño.

87 Colour: bright straw. Nose: fresh, fresh fruit, white flowers. Palate: flavourful, fruity, good acidity, balanced.

DÁVILA L100 2009 B
100% loureiro.

91 Colour: bright straw. Nose: powerfull, varietal, ripe fruit, citrus fruit. Palate: flavourful, fruity, fine bitter notes. Personality.

DÁVILA M.100 2007 B
albariño, loureiro, caiño blanco.

91 Colour: bright yellow. Nose: powerfull, ripe fruit, sweet spices, creamy oak, fragrant herbs, mineral. Palate: rich, flavourful, fresh, good acidity.

VALMIÑOR 2010 B
100% albariño.

90 Colour: bright yellow. Nose: medium intensity, white flowers, dried herbs. Palate: good structure, flavourful, rich.

ADEGAS VALTEA

Lg. Portela, 14
36429 Crecente (Pontevedra)
☎: +34 986 666 344 - Fax: +34 986 644 914
vilarvin@vilarvin.com
www.vilarvin.com

VALTEA 2010 B
100% albariño.

90 Colour: bright yellow. Nose: jasmine, fruit expression, varietal, balanced, wild herbs. Palate: flavourful, fruity, good acidity, fine bitter notes.

FINCA GARABATO 2009 B
100% albariño.

89 Colour: bright yellow. Nose: ripe fruit, dry nuts, faded flowers, lactic notes. Palate: flavourful, rich, fleshy.

PEDRAS RUBRAS 2007 B
100% albariño.

89 Colour: bright yellow. Nose: candied fruit, warm, sweet spices. Palate: flavourful, fine bitter notes, good acidity.

ALBARIÑO BAIÓN

Lg. Abelleira 4,5,6 - Baión
36614 Vilanova de Arousa (Pontevedra)
☎: +34 986 543 535 - Fax: +34 986 524 251
info@pazobaion.com
www.pazobaion.com

PAZO BAIÓN 2009 B
100% albariño.

91 Colour: bright straw. Nose: fresh, fresh fruit, white flowers, fine lees. Palate: flavourful, fruity, good acidity, balanced.

ALDEA DE ABAIXO

Novas, s/n
36778 O'Rosal (Pontevedra)
☎: +34 986 626 121 - Fax: +34 986 626 121
senoriodatorre@grannovas.com
www.grannovas.com

SEÑORÍO DA TORRE ROSAL 2010 B
70% albariño, 25% loureiro, 5% caiño blanco.

88 Colour: pale. Nose: fresh fruit, citrus fruit. Palate: flavourful, fruity, fresh.

GRAN NOVAS ALBARIÑO 2010 B
albariño.

88 Colour: pale. Nose: grassy, fresh fruit, citrus fruit. Palate: flavourful, fruity, fresh.

ALMA ATLÁNTICA

Burgáns, 91
36633 Vilariño- Cambados (Pontevedra)
☎: +34 986 526 040 - Fax: +34 986 526 901
comercial@martincodax.com
www.martincodax.com

ALBA MARTÍN 2010 B
albariño.

89 Colour: bright yellow. Nose: fresh, fresh fruit, white flowers. Palate: flavourful, fruity, good acidity, balanced.

ANXO MARTÍN 2010 B
85% albariño, 10% caiño blanco, 5% loureiro.

88 Colour: bright straw, greenish rim. Nose: medium intensity, dried herbs, balanced, varietal. Palate: flavourful, fruity.

ALTOS DE TORONA

Vilachán s/n
36740 Tomiño (Pontevedra)
☎: +34 986 288 212 - Fax: +34 986 401 185
hga@hgabodegas.com
www.reginaviarum.es

ALTOS DE TORONA 2010 B
85% albariño, 10% caiño blanco, 5% loureiro.

90 Colour: bright straw. Nose: mineral, fruit expression, citrus fruit. Palate: flavourful, fruity, fresh, fleshy.

TORRES DE ERMELO 2010 B
100% albariño.

88 Colour: bright straw. Nose: fresh, fresh fruit, white flowers. Palate: flavourful, fruity, good acidity, balanced.

ALBANTA 2010 B
100% albariño.

87 Colour: bright straw, greenish rim. Nose: fresh fruit, medium intensity, grassy. Palate: fresh, fruity, easy to drink.

BENJAMÍN MIGUEZ NOVAL

Porto de Abaixo, 10 - Porto
36458 Salvaterra de Miño (Pontevedra)
☎: +34 986 122 705
info@mariabargiela.com
www.mariabargiela.com

MARÍA BARGIELA 2010 B
90% albariño, 8% treixadura, 2% loureiro.

86 Colour: bright straw. Nose: floral, ripe fruit, medium intensity. Palate: good acidity, flavourful, fresh, fruity.

BODEGA CASTRO BAROÑA

Bristol 16 bis
28230 Las Rozas (Madrid)
☎: +34 917 104 880 - Fax: +34 917 104 881
anap@swd.es
www.swd.es

CASTRO BAROÑA 2010 B
100% albariño.

90 Colour: bright straw, greenish rim. Nose: grassy, medium intensity. Palate: flavourful, correct.

LAGAR DO CASTELO 2010 B
100% albariño.

89 Colour: bright straw, greenish rim. Nose: medium intensity, grassy, ripe fruit. Palate: flavourful, fruity, long.

BRUXA 2010 B
100% albariño.

87 Colour: bright straw, greenish rim. Nose: citrus fruit, fresh fruit, floral. Palate: good acidity, powerful, flavourful, fresh, fruity.

BODEGA FORJAS DEL SALNÉS

As Covas, 5
36968 Meaño (Pontevedra)
☎: +34 699 446 113 - Fax: +34 986 744 428
rodri@movistar.net

LEIRANA 2010 B
albariño.

92 Colour: bright straw. Nose: white flowers, fruit expression, ripe fruit, varietal. Palate: good acidity, flavourful, light-bodied, fruity, balanced.

LEIRANA BARRICA 2009 B
albariño.

93 Colour: bright yellow. Nose: dried flowers, ripe fruit, fruit expression, fragrant herbs, varietal, creamy oak. Palate: powerful, flavourful, complex, fleshy, long.

GOLIARDO ALBARIÑO 2009 B BARRICA
100% albariño.

93 Colour: bright yellow. Nose: ripe fruit, citrus fruit, white flowers, mineral, creamy oak, sweet spices. Palate: flavourful, fleshy, balanced, elegant.

GOLIARDO CAIÑO 2009 T
caiño.

93 Colour: light cherry, garnet rim. Nose: scrubland, undergrowth, mineral, creamy oak. Palate: light-bodied, good acidity, flavourful, fruity, elegant.

BASTIÓN DE LA LUNA 2009 T
loureiro, espadeiro, caiño, mencía.

92 Colour: cherry, garnet rim. Nose: ripe fruit, sweet spices, creamy oak, expressive, mineral. Palate: flavourful, fruity, fresh, fleshy.

GOLIARDO LOUREIRO 2009 T
loureiro.

91 Colour: black cherry, garnet rim. Nose: red berry notes, ripe fruit, varietal, mineral, toasty. Palate: powerful, flavourful, fleshy.

GOLIARDO ESPADEIRO 2009 T
espadeiro.

90 Colour: cherry, garnet rim. Nose: mineral, damp earth, ripe fruit, complex, varietal. Palate: slightly acidic, balsamic, fruity, flavourful.

BODEGA GRANBAZÁN

Tremoedo, 46
36628 Vilanova de Arousa (Pontevedra)
☎: +34 986 555 562 - Fax: +34 986 555 799
agrodebazan@agrodebazansa.es
www.agrodebazansa.es

GRANBAZÁN ETIQUETA ÁMBAR 2010 B
100% albariño.

91 Colour: bright straw. Nose: powerfull, ripe fruit, citrus fruit, fruit expression, grassy. Palate: flavourful, fruity, fresh.

GRANBAZÁN ETIQUETA VERDE 2010 B
100% albariño.

90 Colour: bright straw. Nose: fresh, white flowers, ripe fruit. Palate: flavourful, fruity, good acidity, balanced.

CONTRAPUNTO 2010 B
100% albariño.

86 Colour: bright straw, greenish rim. Nose: medium intensity, faded flowers. Palate: fruity, fine bitter notes, good acidity.

GRANBAZÁN LIMOUSIN 2009 B
100% albariño.

93 Colour: bright yellow. Nose: complex, balanced, candied fruit, white flowers, spicy. Palate: rich, flavourful, good structure.

BODEGA MARTINEZ SERANTES

Raul Alfonsin, 3 - Lugar Cruceiro Vello
36636 Ribadumia (Pontevedra)
☎: +34 941 454 050 - Fax: +34 941 454 529
bodega@bodegasriojanas.com
www.bodegasriojanas.com

CRUCEIRO VELLO 2010 B
100% albariño.

88 Colour: bright straw. Nose: fresh, white flowers, citrus fruit. Palate: flavourful, fruity, good acidity, balanced.

BODEGA ROSALÍA DE CASTRO

Valdamor, 18 - XII
36968 Meaño (Pontevedra)
☎: +34 986 747 779 - Fax: +34 986 748 940
www.pacolola.com

PACO & LOLA 2010 B
100% albariño.

92 Colour: bright straw. Nose: fresh, fresh fruit, white flowers, mineral. Palate: flavourful, fruity, good acidity, fresh.

ROSALÍA DE CASTRO 2010 B
100% albariño.

90 Colour: bright straw. Nose: white flowers, fresh fruit, citrus fruit. Palate: flavourful, fruity, fresh, fleshy.

LOLO 2010 B
100% albariño.

87 Colour: bright straw. Nose: white flowers, fruit expression, fragrant herbs, fresh, expressive. Palate: good acidity, powerful, rich, flavourful.

IWINE 2009 B
100% albariño.

90 Colour: bright straw. Nose: ripe fruit, expressive, floral. Palate: flavourful, good acidity, ripe fruit.

BODEGAS AGNUSDEI

Lugar de Axis - Simes, s/n
36968 Meaño (Pontevedra)
☎: +34 986 747 566 - Fax: +34 986 747 621
comercial@vinumterrae.com
www.vinumterrae.com

YOU & ME 2010 B
100% albariño.

91 Colour: bright straw. Nose: fresh, white flowers, fresh fruit. Palate: flavourful, fruity, good acidity, balanced.

AGNUSDEI ALBARIÑO 2010 B
100% albariño.

89 Colour: bright straw. Nose: fresh, white flowers. Palate: flavourful, fruity, good acidity, balanced.

BODEGAS AGUIUNCHO

Las Pedreiras, 1º A Villalonga
36990 Sanxenxo (Pontevedra)
☎: +34 986 720 980 - Fax: +34 986 727 063
info@aguiuncho.com
www.aguiuncho.com

AGUIUNCHO 2010 B
100% albariño.

89 Colour: pale. Nose: white flowers, ripe fruit, fruit expression. Palate: flavourful, powerful, fleshy, good acidity.

MAR DE ONS 2010 B
100% albariño.

88 Colour: bright straw. Nose: white flowers, ripe fruit, citrus fruit, grassy. Palate: flavourful, powerful, fleshy.

BODEGAS ALBAMAR

O Adro, 11 - Castrelo
36639 Cambados (Pontevedra)
☎: +34 660 292 750 - Fax: +34 986 520 048
info@bodegasalbamar.com

PEPE LUIS SOBRE LÍAS 2010 B
albariño.

90 Colour: bright yellow. Nose: ripe fruit, faded flowers, sweet spices. Palate: fleshy, complex, flavourful.

ALBAMAR 2010 B
albariño.

88 Colour: bright straw. Nose: expressive, ripe fruit, fragrant herbs. Palate: powerful, flavourful, easy to drink.

ALMA DE MAR SOBRE LÍAS 2010 B
albariño.

87 Colour: bright straw. Nose: candied fruit, white flowers, expressive. Palate: good acidity, fresh, fruity, flavourful.

BODEGAS AQUITANIA

Bauza, 17 Castrelo
36639 Cambados (Pontevedra)
☎: +34 986 520 895 - Fax: +34 986 520 895
info@bodegasaquitania.com
www.bodegasaquitania.com

BERNON 2010 B
100% albariño.

89 Colour: bright straw, greenish rim. Nose: medium intensity, fresh fruit, grassy. Palate: flavourful, easy to drink, fine bitter notes.

AQUITANIA 2010 B
100% albariño.

88 Colour: bright straw. Nose: white flowers, fresh fruit, citrus fruit, fresh. Palate: fresh, light-bodied, flavourful, easy to drink.

GOTA BUENA 2010 B
100% albariño.

87 Colour: bright straw, greenish rim. Nose: wild herbs, faded flowers, balanced. Palate: balanced, fruity, varietal.

BODEGAS AS LAXAS

As Laxas, 16
36430 Arbo (Pontevedra)
☎: +34 986 665 444 - Fax: +34 986 665 554
info@bodegasaslaxas.com
www.bodegasaslaxas.com

LAXAS 2010 B
100% albariño.

91 Colour: bright straw. Nose: ripe fruit, fresh fruit, citrus fruit. Palate: flavourful, fruity, fleshy.

BÁGOA DO MIÑO 2010 B
100% albariño.

90 Colour: bright straw. Nose: powerfull, ripe fruit, mineral, grassy. Palate: fruity, fresh, fine bitter notes.

VAL DO SOSEGO 2010 B
100% albariño.

90 Colour: bright straw. Nose: ripe fruit, citrus fruit, grassy. Palate: flavourful, fruity, fresh, fleshy.

CONDADO LAXAS 2010 B
60% albariño, 10% loureiro, 30% treixadura.

88 Colour: bright yellow. Nose: wild herbs, fresh fruit, floral. Palate: powerful, flavourful, long, good acidity.

ALVINTE 2010 B
100% albariño.

88 Colour: bright straw. Nose: fresh, fresh fruit, grassy. Palate: flavourful, fruity, good acidity, balanced, fine bitter notes.

BODEGAS COTO REDONDO

Bouza do Rato, s/n - Rubiós
36449 As Neves (Pontevedra)
☎: +34 986 667 212 - Fax: +34 986 648 279
info@bodegas-cotoredondo.com
www.bodegas-cotoredondo.com

SEÑORÍO DE RUBIÓS CONDADO BLANCO 2010 B
albariño, treixadura, loureiro, godello.

90 Colour: bright yellow. Nose: varietal, wild herbs, dried flowers, balanced. Palate: flavourful, fruity, good structure.

SEÑORÍO DE RUBIÓS ALBARIÑO 2010 B
100% albariño.

87 Colour: bright yellow. Nose: citrus fruit, fresh fruit, wild herbs. Palate: flavourful, fruity, fine bitter notes.

SEÑORÍO DE RUBIÓS CONDADO BLANCO 2007 B BARRICA
albariño, treixadura, loureiro, godello.

91 Colour: bright golden. Nose: powerfull, ripe fruit, sweet spices, cocoa bean. Palate: flavourful, powerful, fleshy, good acidity.

SEÑORÍO DE RUBIÓS VINO NOVO 2010 T MACERACIÓN CARBÓNICA
sousón, espadeiro, caiño, mencía, brancelado.

86 Colour: cherry, purple rim. Nose: fresh fruit, floral, fresh. Palate: fruity, light-bodied, fresh.

SEÑORÍO DE RUBIÓS CONDADO TINTO 2010 T
sousón, espadeiro, loureiro, mencía, caiño.

84 Colour: light cherry, purple rim. Nose: medium intensity, red berry notes. Palate: fruity, easy to drink, good finish.

SEÑORÍO DE RUBIÓS SOUSÓN 2010 T
100% sousón.

83 Colour: very deep cherry. Nose: fruit expression, balsamic herbs. Palate: spicy, fine bitter notes.

SEÑORÍO DE RUBIÓS MENCÍA 2009 T
100% mencía.

84 Colour: light cherry, garnet rim. Nose: red berry notes, balsamic herbs, grassy. Palate: flavourful, correct.

BODEGAS DEL PALACIO DE FEFIÑANES

Pza. de Fefiñanes
36630 Cambados (Pontevedra)
☎: +34 986 542 204 - Fax: +34 986 524 512
fefinanes@fefinanes.com
www.fefinanes.com

1583 ALBARIÑO DE FEFIÑANES 2010 BFB
albariño.

93 Colour: bright straw. Nose: powerfull, varietal, ripe fruit, fruit expression, white flowers. Palate: flavourful, powerful, fleshy, round tannins.

ALBARIÑO DE FEFIÑANES 2010 B
albariño.

92 Colour: bright straw. Nose: ripe fruit, citrus fruit, balsamic herbs, dried herbs. Palate: flavourful, powerful, fleshy.

ALBARIÑO DE FEFIÑANES III AÑO 2007 B
100% albariño.

94 Colour: bright yellow. Nose: powerfull, ripe fruit, sweet spices, fragrant herbs. Palate: rich, flavourful, fresh, good acidity.

BODEGAS EIDOSELA

Eidos de Abaixo, s/n - Sela
36494 Arbo (Pontevedra)
☎: +34 986 665 550 - Fax: +34 986 665 299
info@bodegaseidosela.com
www.bodegaseidosela.com

EIDOSELA 2010 B
albariño.

91 Colour: bright straw. Nose: powerfull, varietal, ripe fruit, mineral, fine lees. Palate: flavourful, powerful, complex.

EIDOSELA 2010 B
100% albariño.

90 Colour: bright straw, greenish rim. Nose: jasmine, citrus fruit, fresh fruit. Palate: flavourful, varietal, good acidity.

ETRA CONDADO 2010 B
albariño, loureiro, treixadura.

90 Colour: bright straw. Nose: fresh, fresh fruit, white flowers, expressive, mineral. Palate: flavourful, fruity, good acidity, balanced.

ARBASTRUM 2010 B
albariño, treixadura, otras.

89 Colour: bright straw. Nose: floral, fruit expression, balanced, wild herbs. Palate: flavourful, good structure, fruity.

ETRA ALBARIÑO 2010 B
100% albariño.

88 Colour: bright straw. Nose: grassy, ripe fruit, white flowers. Palate: flavourful, fruity, fresh.

BODEGAS FILLABOA

Lugar de Fillaboa, s/n
36450 Salvaterra do Miño (Pontevedra)
☎: +34 986 658 132 - Fax: +34 986 664 212
info@bodegasfillaboa.com
www.bodegasfillaboa.com

FILLABOA 2010 B
100% albariño.

91 Colour: bright straw. Nose: fresh, white flowers, expressive, citrus fruit. Palate: flavourful, fruity, good acidity, balanced, fine bitter notes.

FILLABOA SELECCIÓN FINCA MONTEALTO 2009 B
100% albariño.

93 Colour: bright straw. Nose: powerfull, varietal, ripe fruit, citrus fruit, grassy. Palate: flavourful, fleshy, complex.

BODEGAS LA CAÑA

Sestelo-Bayon s/n
36614 Sisan Ribadumia (Pontevedra)
☎: +34 952 504 706 - Fax: +34 951 284 796
office@jorge-ordonez.es
www.jorge-ordonez.es

LA CAÑA 2010 B
100% albariño.

92 Colour: bright yellow. Nose: complex, elegant, fresh fruit, wild herbs. Palate: light-bodied, flavourful, fruity, good acidity.

BODEGAS MAR DE FRADES

Lg. Arosa, 16 - Finca Valiñas
36637 Meis (Pontevedra)
☎: +34 986 680 911 - Fax: +34 986 680 926
info@mardefrades.com
www.mardefrades.com

MAR DE FRADES 2010 B
albariño.

88 Colour: bright golden. Nose: citrus fruit, white flowers, saline, dried herbs. Palate: fruity, flavourful, light-bodied, fresh.

FINCA VALIÑAS "CRIANZA SOBRE LÍAS" 2009 B
albariño.

87 Colour: bright golden. Nose: ripe fruit, faded flowers, dried herbs, sweet spices, toasty. Palate: rich, flavourful, fleshy, good acidity.

BODEGAS MARQUÉS DE VIZHOJA

Finca La Moreira s/n
36438 Arbo (Pontevedra)
☎: +34 986 665 825 - Fax: +34 986 665 960
marquesdevizhoja@marquesdevizhoja.com
www.marquesdevizhoja.com

SEÑOR DA FOLLA VERDE 2010 B
70% albariño, 15% treixadura, 15% loureiro.

89 Colour: bright straw. Nose: fresh, fresh fruit, white flowers, complex. Palate: flavourful, fruity, good acidity, balanced.

BODEGAS MARTÍN CÓDAX

Burgans, 91
36633 Vilariño-Cambados (Pontevedra)
☎: +34 986 526 040 - Fax: +34 986 526 901
comercial@martincodax.com
www.martincodax.com

BURGÁNS 2010 B
albariño.

89 Colour: bright straw. Nose: fresh, fresh fruit, white flowers. Palate: flavourful, fruity, good acidity, balanced, fine bitter notes.

MARTÍN CÓDAX 2010 B
albariño.

89 Colour: bright straw. Nose: fresh, white flowers, ripe fruit. Palate: flavourful, fruity, good acidity, balanced.

ORGANISTRUM 2009 B
albariño.

91 Colour: bright yellow. Nose: complex, expressive, varietal, candied fruit, white flowers. Palate: flavourful, full, fruity, long.

MARTIN CODAX LÍAS 2008 B
albariño.

90 Colour: bright golden. Nose: powerfull, expressive, balanced, varietal, lactic notes. Palate: flavourful, fruity, fleshy, sweetness.

GALLAECIA 2007 B
albariño.

90 Color bright golden. Aroma ripe fruit, dry nuts, powerfull, toasty, aged wood nuances. Taste flavourful, fruity, spicy, toasty, long.

BODEGAS NANCLARES

Castriño, 13 - Castrelo
36639 Cambados (Pontevedra)
☎: +34 986 520 763 - Fax: +34 986 524 958
bodega@bodegasnanclares.es
www.bodegasnanclares.com

ALBERTO NANCLARES ALBARIÑO 2010 B
100% albariño.

89 Colour: bright straw. Nose: ripe fruit, citrus fruit, fruit expression, grassy. Palate: flavourful, fruity, fleshy.

TEMPUS VIVENDI 2010 B
100% albariño.

87 Colour: bright yellow. Nose: dried herbs, faded flowers, medium intensity. Palate: flavourful, fruity.

SOVERRIBAS DE NANCLARES 2009 BFB
100% albariño.

88 Colour: bright straw. Nose: expressive, ripe fruit, spicy. Palate: flavourful, fleshy.

BODEGAS SANTIAGO ROMA

Catariño, 5 - Besomaño
36636 Ribadumia (Pontevedra)
☎: +34 986 718 477 - Fax: +34 986 718 477
bodega@santiagoroma.com
www.santiagoroma.com

ALBARIÑO SANTIAGO ROMA 2010 B
albariño.

89 Colour: bright straw, greenish rim. Nose: medium intensity, wild herbs. Palate: flavourful, fruity.

ALBARIÑO SANTIAGO ROMA SELECCIÓN 2009 B
100% albariño.

88 Colour: bright yellow. Nose: powerfull, ripe fruit, sweet spices, cocoa bean. Palate: fleshy, flavourful.

BODEGAS TERRAS GAUDA

Ctra. Tui - A Guarda, Km. 55
36760 O Rosal (Pontevedra)
☎: +34 986 621 001 - Fax: +34 986 621 084
terrasgauda@terrasgauda.com
www.terrasgauda.com

ABADÍA DE SAN CAMPIO 2010 B
100% albariño.

88 Colour: bright yellow. Nose: white flowers, balanced, wild herbs, candied fruit. Palate: flavourful, easy to drink, good acidity.

TERRAS GAUDA ETIQUETA NEGRA 2009 BFB
70% albariño, 20% loureiro, 10% caiño blanco.

91 Colour: bright straw. Nose: white flowers, ripe fruit, fruit expression, sweet spices, creamy oak. Palate: flavourful, powerful, fleshy, spicy.

LA MAR 2009 B
85% caiño blanco, 15% otras.

89 Colour: bright yellow. Nose: candied fruit, varietal, complex. Palate: flavourful, fruity, good structure, long.

TERRAS GAUDA 2010 B
70% albariño, 18% loureiro, caiño blanco.

90 Colour: bright straw. Nose: white flowers, citrus fruit, ripe fruit, varietal. Palate: powerful, fleshy, complex.

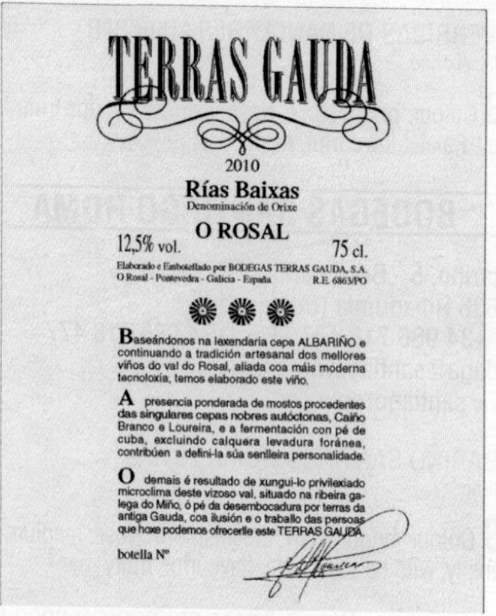

BODEGAS Y VIÑEDOS DON OLEGARIO

Refoxos, s/n - Corvillón
36634 Cambados (Pontevedra)
☎: +34 986 520 886 - Fax: +34 986 520 886
info@donolegario.com
www.donolegario.com

DON OLEGARIO ALBARIÑO 2010 B
albariño.

91 Colour: bright straw. Nose: powerfull, ripe fruit, citrus fruit, grassy. Palate: flavourful, fruity, easy to drink, good acidity.

DON OLEGARIO ALBARIÑO 2009 B
albariño.

91 Colour: bright yellow. Nose: powerfull, varietal, expressive, ripe fruit, fragrant herbs. Palate: flavourful, powerful, fleshy, complex, spicy.

BOUZA DO REI

Lugar de Puxafeita, s/n
36636 Ribadumia (Pontevedra)
☎: +34 986 710 257 - Fax: +34 986 718 393
bouzadorei@bouzadorei.com
www.bouzadorei.com

CASTEL DE BOUZA 2010 B
albariño.

90 Colour: bright straw. Nose: powerfull, fresh fruit, ripe fruit, balsamic herbs. Palate: flavourful, powerful, fruity, fresh.

BOUZA DO REI 2010 B
albariño.

89 Colour: bright straw. Nose: fresh, fresh fruit, white flowers, fine lees. Palate: flavourful, fruity, good acidity.

CODORNÍU

Avda. Jaume Codorníu, s/n
08770 Sant Sadurní D'Anoia (Barcelona)
☎: +34 938 183 232 - Fax: +34 938 910 822
s.martin@codorniu.es
www.codorniu.com

LEIRAS 2010 B
100% albariño.

88 Colour: bright straw. Nose: white flowers, balsamic herbs, mineral, expressive. Palate: fresh, powerful, flavourful, fleshy.

COMERCIAL GRUPO FREIXENET S.A.

Joan Sala, 2
08770 Sant Sadurní D'Anoia (Barcelona)
☎: +34 938 917 000 - Fax: +34 938 183 095
freixenet@freixenet.es
www.freixenet.es

VIONTA 2010 B
100% albariño.

87 Colour: bright straw, greenish rim. Nose: medium intensity, grassy, citrus fruit. Palate: flavourful, fruity, easy to drink.

CONSTANTINA SOTELO ARES

Castriño, 9-Castelo
36639 Cambados (Pontevedra)
☎: +34 986 524 704 - Fax: +34 986 524 704
adegasotelo@yahoo.es

ROSALÍA 2010 B
100% albariño.

90 Colour: bright yellow. Nose: fruit expression, wild herbs, floral. Palate: flavourful, powerful, good structure, good acidity, fine bitter notes.

ADEGA SOTELO 2010 B
100% albariño.

89 Colour: pale. Nose: expressive, varietal, fresh fruit. Palate: flavourful, fresh, fleshy.

DAVIDE

Serantes, 36 Balón
36614 Vilanova de Arousa (Pontevedra)
☎: +34 902 427 428 - Fax: +34 906 506 330
info@davide.es
www.davide.es

DAVIDE DUO 2009 B
70% albariño, 30% godello.

90 Colour: bright straw. Nose: white flowers, citrus fruit, fruit expression, fragrant herbs. Palate: good acidity, mineral, powerful, flavourful, elegant.

DAVIDE TRADICIÓN 2009 B
100% albariño.

89 Colour: bright yellow. Nose: ripe fruit, floral, fragrant herbs, expressive, mineral. Palate: good acidity, unctuous, flavourful, fruity.

ESCUDEIRO S.L.

Avda. Rosalia de Castro-Barrantes
36636 Ribadumia (Pontevedra)
☎: +34 986 710 777 - Fax: +34 986 710 777
bodegasescudeiro@yahoo.es

ALBARIÑO VIÑA ROEL 2010 B
albariño.

89 Colour: bright straw, greenish rim. Nose: expressive, varietal, elegant, fresh fruit, citrus fruit, grassy. Palate: flavourful, fruity, good acidity.

GERARDO MÉNDEZ

Galiñanes - Lores, 10
36968 Meaño (Pontevedra)
☎: +34 986 747 046 - Fax: +34 986 748 915
info@bodegasgerardomendez.com
www.bodegasgerardomendez.com

DO FERREIRO CEPAS VELLAS 2009 B
100% albariño.

93 Colour: bright yellow. Nose: complex, expressive, candied fruit, fragrant herbs, faded flowers. Palate: long, flavourful, good structure, complex, good acidity.

ALBARIÑO DO FERREIRO 2010 B
albariño.

93 Colour: bright straw. Nose: white flowers, ripe fruit, grassy, balsamic herbs. Palate: flavourful, fruity, fresh, fleshy.

JOSÉ CARLOS QUINTAS PÉREZ

Fonte, 20
36492 Quintela - Crecente (Pontevedra)
☎: +34 669 485 271 - Fax: +34 986 267 145
info@josecarlosquintasperez.es
www.oreidecampoverde.es

O REI DE CAMPOVERDE 2010 B
100% albariño.

88 Colour: bright straw. Nose: fresh, white flowers, candied fruit. Palate: flavourful, fruity, good acidity, balanced, rich.

DAINSUA 2010 B
75% albariño, 10% loureiro, 15% treixadura.

88 Colour: bright straw. Nose: fresh fruit, grassy, balanced. Palate: fresh, fruity, good acidity.

JULIÁN GONZÁLEZ AREAL

Finca Lavandeira - Rebordans, 1
36712 Tui (Pontevedra)
☎: +34 986 601 414 - Fax: +34 986 601 414
canonigoareal@canonigoareal.com

CANÓNIGO AREAL 2010 B
100% albariño.

86 Colour: bright yellow. Nose: medium intensity, grassy, dried flowers. Palate: flavourful, good acidity.

LA VAL

Lugar Muguiña, s/n - Arantei
36458 Salvaterra de Miño (Pontevedra)
☎: +34 986 610 728 - Fax: +34 986 611 635
laval@bodegaslaval.com
www.bodegaslaval.com

ORBALLO 2010 B
100% albariño.

90 Colour: bright straw. Nose: white flowers, fruit expression, fresh, expressive. Palate: complex, fleshy, powerful, flavourful, fruity.

LA VAL ALBARIÑO 2010 B
100% albariño.

89 Colour: bright straw. Nose: white flowers, fruit expression, fragrant herbs, elegant. Palate: complex, fleshy, powerful, flavourful.

FINCA DE ARANTEI 2010 B
100% albariño.

88 Colour: bright straw. Nose: dried flowers, citrus fruit, candied fruit, fresh. Palate: powerful, flavourful, fruity, good acidity.

TABOEXA 2010 B
100% albariño.

87 Colour: bright straw. Nose: citrus fruit, dried flowers, grassy. Palate: light-bodied, fresh, fruity, easy to drink.

LA VAL ALBARIÑO 2007 BFB
100% albariño.

88 Colour: bright yellow. Nose: ripe fruit, candied fruit, dried herbs, spicy, creamy oak. Palate: correct, spirituous, flavourful.

LA VAL CRIANZA SOBRE LÍAS 2005 BC
100% albariño.

91 Colour: bright golden. Nose: ripe fruit, faded flowers, fragrant herbs, expressive, elegant. Palate: powerful, rich, complex, fleshy, flavourful.

LAGAR DE BESADA

Pazo, 11
36968 Xil-Meaño (Pontevedra)
☎: +34 986 747 473 - Fax: +34 986 747 826
info@lagardebesada.com
www.lagardebesada.com

LAGAR DE BESADA 2010 B
100% albariño.

87 Colour: yellow, greenish rim. Nose: powerfull, grassy, dried herbs. Palate: powerful, long, good acidity.

BALADIÑA 2009 B
100% albariño.

90 Colour: bright yellow. Nose: scrubland, balanced, varietal. Palate: fruity, fresh, flavourful, good acidity. Personality.

AÑADA DE BALADIÑA 2004 B
100% albariño.

91 Colour: golden. Nose: candied fruit, expressive, balanced, powerfull, varietal. Palate: fleshy, flavourful, ripe fruit, fine bitter notes, long.

LAGAR DE COSTA

Sartaxes, 8 - Castrelo
36639 Cambados (Pontevedra)
☎: +34 986 543 526 - Fax: +34 986 543 526
contacto@lagardecosta.com
www.lagardecosta.com

LAGAR DE COSTA 2010 B
100% albariño.

89 Colour: bright straw, greenish rim. Nose: fresh, medium intensity, grassy. Palate: balanced, good acidity, fruity.

LAGAR DE COSTA 2009 B BARRICA
100% albariño.

90 Colour: bright yellow. Nose: powerfull, ripe fruit, sweet spices, creamy oak, fragrant herbs. Palate: rich, flavourful, fresh, good acidity.

MAIO5 2009 B
100% albariño.

90 Colour: bright straw. Nose: fresh, fresh fruit, white flowers, varietal. Palate: flavourful, fruity, good acidity, balanced.

LAGAR DE FORNELOS

Barrio de Cruces - Fornelos
36778La Guardia O Rosal (Pontevedra)
☎: +34 986 625 875 - Fax: +34 986 625 011
lagar@riojalta.com
www.riojalta.com

LAGAR DE CERVERA 2010 B
100% albariño.

92 Colour: bright straw. Nose: white flowers, ripe fruit, varietal, expressive. Palate: fleshy, good acidity, balanced, long, fine bitter notes.

LAGAR DO REI

Carballoso - Xil
36968 Meaño (Pontevedra)
☎: +34 986 743 189 - Fax: +34 986 745 287
correo@lagarderei.com
www.ecogalicia.com/lagarderei

LAGAR DE REI 2010 B
100% albariño.

86 Colour: bright yellow, greenish rim. Nose: white flowers, grassy. Palate: flavourful, fine bitter notes.

MAIOR DE MENDOZA

Rúa de Xiabre, 58
36613 Villagarcía (Pontevedra)
☎: +34 986 508 896 - Fax: +34 986 507 924
maiordemendoza@hotmail.es
www.maiordemendoza.com

FULGET 2010 B
100% albariño.

89 Colour: bright yellow. Nose: varietal, balanced, white flowers. Palate: fruity, flavourful, good acidity, fine bitter notes.

MAIOR DE MENDOZA "SOBRE LÍAS" 2010 B
100% albariño.

88 Colour: bright straw. Nose: fresh fruit, citrus fruit, grassy, balsamic herbs. Palate: flavourful, powerful, fruity, fresh.

MAIOR DE MENDOZA MACERACIÓN CARBÓNICA 2010 B MACERACIÓN CARBÓNICA
100% albariño.

85 Colour: bright straw. Nose: fresh fruit, white flowers, expressive. Palate: light-bodied, fresh, easy to drink.

MAIOR DE MENDOZA 3 CRIANZAS 2009 B
100% albariño.

89 Colour: bright yellow. Nose: complex, balanced, expressive, medium intensity, wild herbs. Palate: fresh, good acidity, fine bitter notes.

MAR DE ENVERO

Lugar Quintáns, 17
36638 Ribadumia (Pontevedra)
☎: +34 981 577 083 - Fax: +34 981 569 552
bodega@mardeenvero.es
www.mardeenvero.es

MAR DE ENVERO 2009 B
albariño.

90 Colour: bright straw. Nose: white flowers, ripe fruit, mineral. Palate: powerful, flavourful.

MARÍA VICTORIA DOVALO MÉNDEZ

Villarreis, 21 - Dena
36967 Meaño (Pontevedra)
☎: +34 941 454 050 - Fax: +34 941 454 529
bodega@bodegasriojanas.com
www.bodegasriojanas.com

VEIGA NAÚM 2010 B
100% albariño.

88 Colour: bright straw, greenish rim. Nose: fresh fruit, medium intensity, grassy. Palate: good structure, fruity, flavourful.

O AFORADO

As Eiras
36778 O'Rosal (Pontevedra)
☎: +34 627 558 188 - Fax: +34 986 565 339
dalonso@dalonga.com
www.aforado.com

AFORADO ROSAL 2010 B
80% albariño, caiño, loureiro.

91 Colour: bright straw. Nose: fresh fruit, ripe fruit, citrus fruit, dried herbs. Palate: flavourful, fruity, fresh, good acidity.

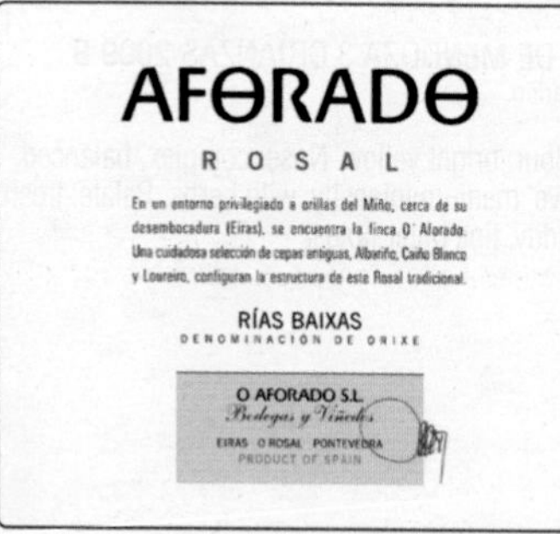

AFORADO 2010 B
100% albariño.

89 Colour: bright straw. Nose: white flowers, fresh fruit, citrus fruit. Palate: flavourful, fruity, fresh, spicy.

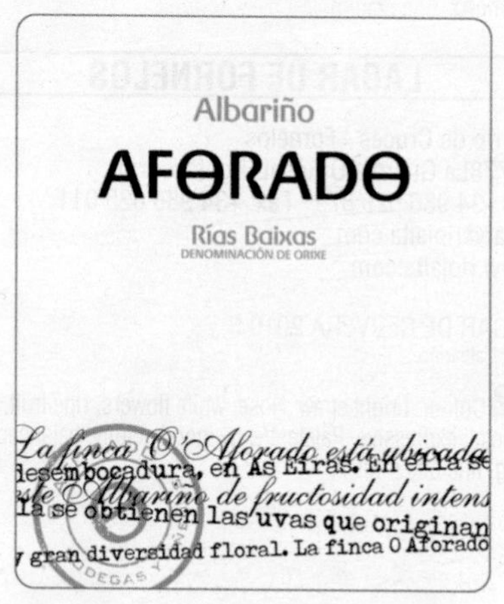

ORO WINES JUMILLA

Paraje de la Aragona
30520 Jumilla (Murcia)
☎: +34 968 435 022 - Fax: +34 968 716 051
info@orowines.com
www.orowines.com

KENTIA 2010 B
albariño.

88 Colour: bright straw. Nose: fresh, white flowers, varietal, citrus fruit, ripe fruit. Palate: flavourful, fruity, good acidity, balanced.

PAZO DE BARRANTES

Finca Pazo de Barrantes
36636 Barrantes (Pontevedra)
☎: +34 986 718 211 - Fax: +34 986 710 424
bodega@pazodebarrantes.com
www.pazodebarrantes.com

PAZO DE BARRANTES ALBARIÑO 2009 B
100% albariño.

94 Colour: bright yellow. Nose: dried flowers, ripe fruit, dried herbs, mineral. Palate: fresh, fleshy, complex, long, fine bitter notes, balanced.

PAZO DE BARRANTES ALBARIÑO 2010 B
100% albariño.

92 Colour: bright yellow. Nose: fragrant herbs, fruit expression, citrus fruit, ripe fruit, fine lees. Palate: flavourful, fine bitter notes, easy to drink.

PAZO DE SAN MAURO

Pombal, 3 - Porto
36458 Salvaterra de Miño (Pontevedra)
☎: +34 986 658 285 - Fax: +34 986 664 208
info@pazosanmauro.com
www.grupovinicolamarquesdevargas.com

PAZO SAN MAURO 2010 B
100% albariño.

89 Colour: bright straw. Nose: fresh fruit, white flowers. Palate: flavourful, fruity, good acidity, balanced.

SANAMARO 2009 B
95% albariño, 5% loureiro.

90 Colour: bright yellow, greenish rim. Nose: fresh fruit, wild herbs, balanced. Palate: flavourful, fruity, good acidity.

PAZO DE SEÑORANS

Vilanoviña, 50
36616 Meis (Pontevedra)
☎: +34 986 715 373 - Fax: +34 986 715 569
info@pazodesenorans.com
www.pazodesenorans.com

PAZO SEÑORANS. SELECCIÓN DE AÑADA 2004 B
100% albariño.

93 Colour: bright yellow. Nose: powerfull, ripe fruit, sweet spices, fragrant herbs, smoky. Palate: rich, smoky aftertaste, flavourful, fresh, good acidity.

SOL DE SEÑORANS 2006 B ROBLE
100% albariño.

94 Colour: bright straw. Nose: spicy, ripe fruit, citrus fruit, sweet spices, toasty. Palate: ripe fruit, good acidity, fine bitter notes, round.

PAZO SEÑORANS 2010 B
100% albariño.

92 Colour: bright straw. Nose: fresh, fresh fruit, white flowers. Palate: flavourful, fruity, good acidity, balanced.

PAZO DE VILLAREI

Vía Rápida do Salnés, Km. 5
36637 San Martiño de Meis (Pontevedra)
☎: +34 986 710 827 - Fax: +34 986 710 827
info@domecqbodegas.com
www.domecqbodegas.com

TERRA DOURO 2010 B
albariño.

90 Colour: bright yellow. Nose: ripe fruit, medium intensity, varietal, white flowers. Palate: flavourful, rich, ripe fruit, long.

PAZO DE VILLAREI 2010 B
albariño.

89 Colour: bright yellow. Nose: varietal, grassy, balanced, medium intensity. Palate: flavourful, fruity, good acidity.

PAZO PONDAL

Coto, s/n - Cabeiras
36436 Arbo (Pontevedra)
☎: +34 986 665 551 - Fax: +34 986 665 949
info@pazopondal.com
www.pazopondal.com

LEIRA 2010 B
100% albariño.

88 Colour: bright straw. Nose: ripe fruit, fresh fruit, citrus fruit. Palate: flavourful, fleshy, fruity.

PAZO PONDAL ALBARIÑO 2010 B
100% albariño.

88 Colour: bright yellow. Nose: citrus fruit, wild herbs, fresh fruit, dried flowers. Palate: flavourful, rich, long, fruity.

PAZOS DE LUSCO

Grixó - Alxén
36458 Salvaterra do Miño (Pontevedra)
☎: +34 987 514 550 - Fax: +34 987 514 570
info@dominiodetares.com
www.lusco.es

LUSCO 2010 B
100% albariño.

93 Colour: bright straw. Nose: fresh, fresh fruit, white flowers, fragrant herbs, powerfull. Palate: flavourful, fruity, good acidity, balanced.

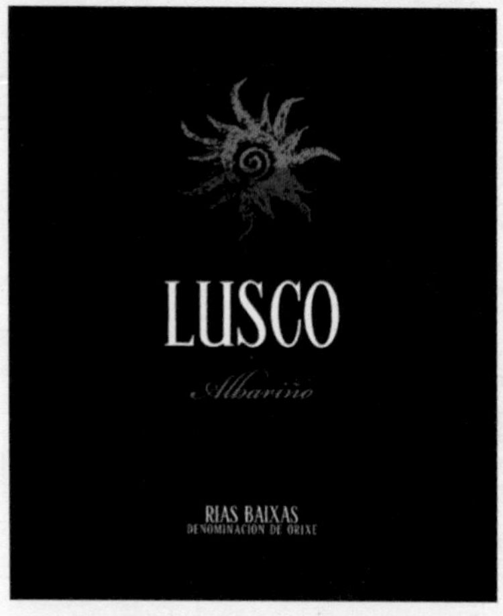

ZIOS DE LUSCO 2010 B
100% albariño.

91 Colour: bright straw. Nose: fresh fruit, white flowers, varietal, mineral. Palate: flavourful, fruity, good acidity, fleshy, fine bitter notes.

PAZO DE PIÑEIRO 2010 B
100% albariño.

95 Colour: bright straw. Nose: fresh, white flowers, expressive, mineral, floral. Palate: flavourful, fruity, good acidity, balanced, full.

QUINTA COUSELO

Barrio de Couselo, 13
36770 O'Rosal (Pontevedra)
☎: +34 986 625 051 - Fax: +34 986 625 051
quintacouselo@quintacouselo.com
www.quintacouselo.com

QUINTA DE COUSELO 2010 B
albariño, loureiro, treixadura, caiño blanco.

90 Colour: bright straw. Nose: powerfull, varietal, ripe fruit, citrus fruit. Palate: flavourful, fruity, spicy.

TURONIA 2010 B
albariño.

88 Colour: bright yellow. Nose: balanced, medium intensity, grassy. Palate: flavourful, fruity, good acidity.

QUINTA DE COUSELO 2009 B
albariño.

87 Color bright straw. Aroma fresh, fresh fruit, white flowers, expressive. Taste flavourful, fruity, good acidity, balanced.

RECTORAL DO UMIA

Plg. de Rua do Pan, 9
36636 Ribadumia (Pontevedra)
☎: +34 986 716 360 - Fax: +34 986 718 252
jmanuel@rectoraldoumia.com
www.rectoraldoumia.com

RECTORAL DO UMIA 2010 B
albariño.

88 Colour: bright straw. Nose: powerfull, ripe fruit, fruit expression, grassy. Palate: powerful, flavourful, fleshy.

MIUDIÑO 2010 B
albariño.

88 Colour: bright straw, greenish rim. Nose: medium intensity, varietal, fresh, fragrant herbs. Palate: flavourful, easy to drink, fine bitter notes.

PÓRTICO DA RIA 2010 B
albariño.

87 Colour: bright straw. Nose: medium intensity, wild herbs, fresh fruit. Palate: flavourful, fruity, fine bitter notes, good acidity.

RED BOTTLE INTERNATIONAL

Rosales, 6
09400 Aranda de Duero (Burgos)
☎: +34 947 515 884 - Fax: +34 947 515 886
rbi@redbottleint.com

ELAS 2010 B
100% albariño.

89 Colour: bright straw. Nose: fragrant herbs, fresh fruit, medium intensity. Palate: complex, flavourful, fruity, good structure.

SANTIAGO RUIZ

Rua do Vinicultor Santiago Ruiz
36760 San Miguel de Tabagón - O Rosal (Pontevedra)
☎: +34 986 614 083 - Fax: +34 986 614 142
info@bodegasantiagoruiz.com
www.bodegasantiagoruiz.com

SANTIAGO RUIZ 2010 B
70% albariño, 15% loureiro, 10% caiño blanco, 5% treixadura, godello.

88 Colour: bright straw, greenish rim. Nose: powerfull, grassy, dried flowers. Palate: fresh, fruity, easy to drink.

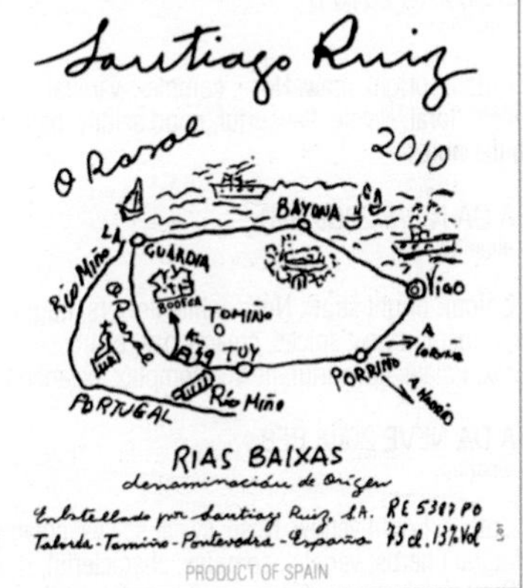

SEÑORÍO DE SOBRAL

Lg. Porto - Sobral
36458 Salvaterra do Miño (Pontevedra)
☎: +34 986 415 144 - Fax: +34 986 421 744
info@ssobral.net
www.ssobral.net

SEÑORÍO DE SOBRAL 2010 B
100% albariño.

88 Colour: bright straw. Nose: balanced, grassy, citrus fruit, fresh fruit. Palate: flavourful, fruity, long.

TERRA DE ASOREI

Rúa San Francisco, 2 - 1 Ofic. C-D
36630 Cambados (Pontevedra)
☎: +34 986 198 882 - Fax: +34 986 520 813
info@terradeasorei.com
www.terradeasorei.com

PAZO TORRADO 2010 B
100% albariño.

88 Colour: bright straw, greenish rim. Nose: fresh fruit, medium intensity, floral, varietal. Palate: flavourful, fruity, good acidity.

TERRA DE ASOREI 2010 B
100% albariño.

87 Colour: bright straw, greenish rim. Nose: balanced, medium intensity, white flowers. Palate: flavourful, full, good acidity.

UVAS FELICES

Agullers, 7
08003 Barcelona (Barcelona)
☎: +34 902 327 777
www.vilaviniteca.es

EL JARDÍN DE LUCIA 2010 B
albariño.

90 Colour: bright straw. Nose: varietal, fresh fruit, citrus fruit, mineral. Palate: fine bitter notes, good acidity, fleshy, long.

VALDAMOR

Valdamor, 8
36968 Xil - Meaño (Pontevedra)
☎: +34 986 747 111 - Fax: +34 986 747 743
clientes@valdamor.es
www.valdamor.es

VALDAMOR 2010 B
100% albariño.

89 Colour: bright straw. Nose: fresh, fresh fruit, white flowers, varietal. Palate: flavourful, fruity, good acidity, balanced.

NAMORÍO 2010 B
100% albariño.

89 Colour: bright straw. Nose: powerfull, fresh fruit, citrus fruit. Palate: flavourful, fruity, fresh, fleshy.

VALDAMOR SELECCIÓN 2009 B
100% albariño.

90 Colour: bright straw. Nose: fresh, fresh fruit, white flowers, varietal. Palate: flavourful, fruity, good acidity, balanced.

VALDAMOR BARRICA 2007 B
100% albariño.

88 Colour: bright straw. Nose: medium intensity, citrus fruit, ripe fruit. Palate: ripe fruit, fine bitter notes, spicy.

VIÑA ALMIRANTE

Peroxa, 5
36658 Portas (Pontevedra)
☎: +34 620 294 293 - Fax: +34 986 541 471
info@vinaalmirante.com
www.vinaalmirante.com

PIONERO MUNDI 2010 B
albariño.

91 Colour: bright yellow, greenish rim. Nose: fresh fruit, grassy. Palate: flavourful, fruity, rich, varietal.

PIONERO MACCERATO 2010 B
albariño.

89 Colour: bright straw. Nose: fresh, white flowers, varietal, ripe fruit. Palate: flavourful, fruity, good acidity.

VANIDADE 2010 B
albariño.

89 Colour: bright straw. Nose: powerfull, varietal, ripe fruit, citrus fruit, grassy. Palate: flavourful, fruity, fresh.

VIÑA CARTIN

Baceiro, 1 - Lantaño
36657 Portas (Pontevedra)
☎: +34 615 646 442 - Fax: +34 986 500 382
bodegas@montino.es
www.terrasdelantano.com

TERRAS DE LANTAÑO 2010 B
100% albariño.

90 Colour: bright yellow. Nose: expressive, fresh, neat, varietal. Palate: flavourful, fleshy, fruity.

VIÑA CARTIN 2010 B
albariño.

90 Color bright straw. Aroma fresh, fresh fruit, white flowers, expressive. Taste flavourful, fruity, good acidity, balanced.

VIÑA NORA

Bruñeiras, 7
36440 As Neves (Pontevedra)
☎: +34 986 667 210 - Fax: +34 986 664 610
info@vinanora.com
www.vinanora.com

NORA 2010 B
100% albariño.

89 Colour: bright yellow. Nose: candied fruit, dried flowers, elegant. Palate: balanced, fine bitter notes, good acidity.

VAL DE NORA 2010 B
100% albariño.

89 Colour: bright straw. Nose: complex, varietal, balanced, floral. Palate: flavourful, good acidity, balanced, fine bitter notes.

NORA DA NEVE 2009 BFB
100% albariño.

94 Colour: bright straw. Nose: white flowers, fragrant herbs, mineral, sweet spices, creamy oak, expressive, complex. Palate: flavourful, fleshy, complex, balanced, rich.

NORA DA NEVE 2008 BFB
100% albariño.

95 Colour: bright yellow. Nose: sweet spices, creamy oak, fragrant herbs, varietal, complex, characterful, ripe fruit. Palate: rich, smoky aftertaste, flavourful, fresh, good acidity

VIÑEDOS SINGULARES

Llorer, 31
08905 Hospitalet de Llobregat (Barcelona)
☎: +34 934 807 041 - Fax: +34 934 807 076
info@vinedossingulares.com
www.vinedossingulares.com

LUNA CRECIENTE 2010 B
albariño.

88 Colour: bright straw. Nose: white flowers, expressive, tropical fruit. Palate: flavourful, fruity, good acidity, balanced.

ZÁRATE

Bouza, 23
36668 Padrenda - Meaño (Pontevedra)
☎: +34 986 718 503 - Fax: +34 986 718 549
info@zarate.es
www.albarino-zarate.com

ZÁRATE 2010 B
100% albariño.

89 Colour: bright straw. Nose: ripe fruit, citrus fruit, white flowers. Palate: fine bitter notes, good acidity, ripe fruit.

ZÁRATE EL PALOMAR 2009 BFB
100% albariño.

92 Colour: bright straw. Nose: ripe fruit, citrus fruit, varietal, expressive. Palate: flavourful, fruity, good acidity.

ZÁRATE EL BALADO 2009 B
100% albariño.

90 Colour: bright yellow. Nose: smoky, creamy oak, fruit expression. Palate: slightly acidic, powerful, fruity, fresh.

ZÁRATE CAIÑO TINTO 2009 T
100% caiño.

90 Colour: cherry, garnet rim. Nose: varietal, expressive, powerfull, earthy notes, damp earth. Palate: astringent, light-bodied, fruity, fresh.

ZÁRATE LOUREIRO TINTO 2009 T
100% loureiro tinto.

87 Colour: cherry, purple rim. Nose: ripe fruit, balsamic herbs, scrubland. Palate: flavourful, fruity, fine bitter notes, slightly acidic, green.

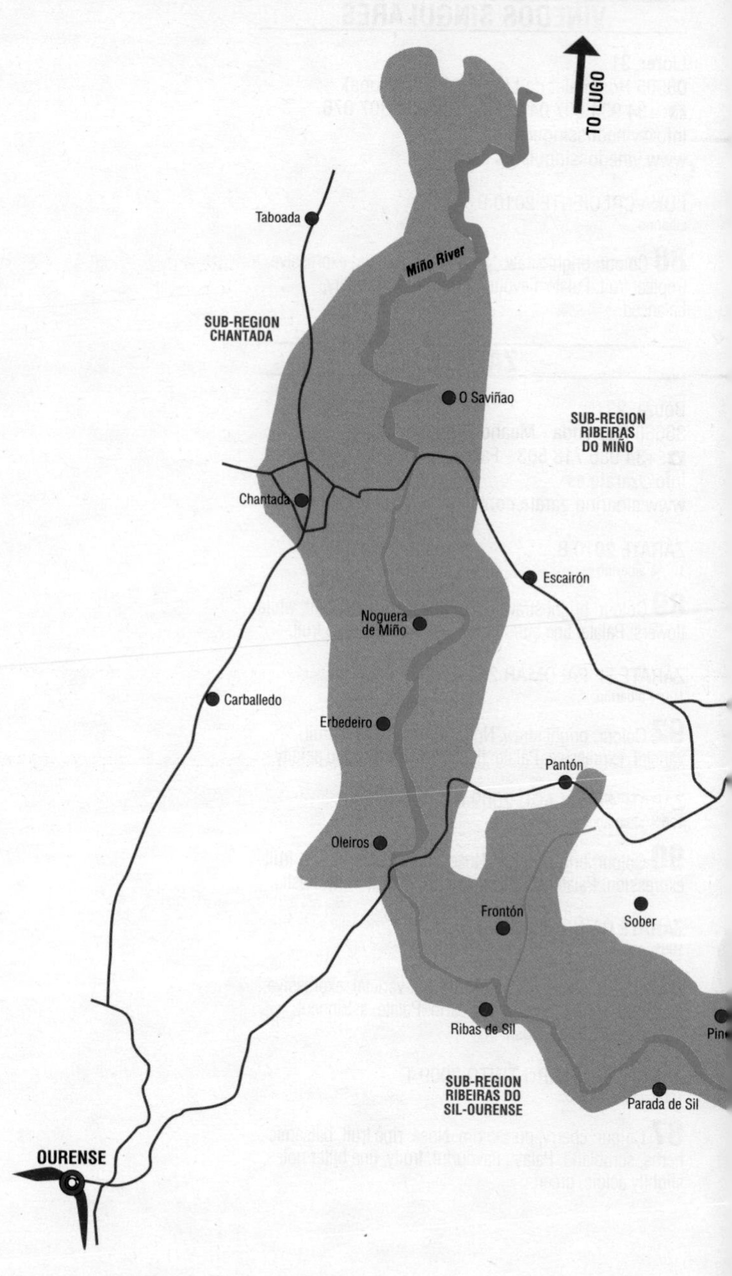
TO LUGO
Taboada
Miño River
SUB-REGION
CHANTADA
O Saviñao
SUB-REGION
RIBEIRAS
DO MIÑO
Chantada
Escairón
Noguera
de Miño
Carballedo
Erbedeiro
Pantón
Oleiros
Frontón
Sober
Ribas de Sil
SUB-REGION
RIBEIRAS DO
SIL-OURENSE
Parada de Sil
OURENSE

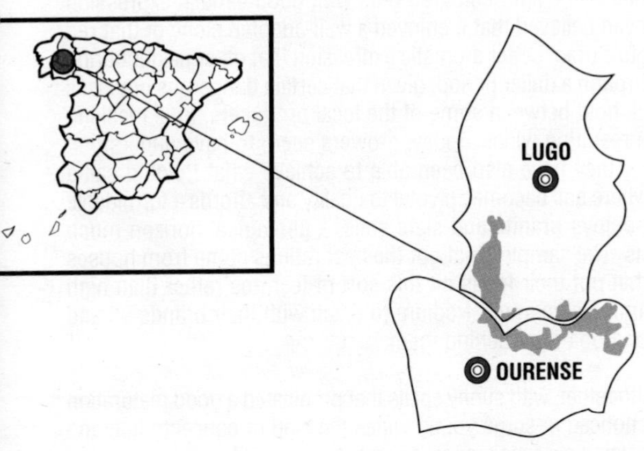
LUGO
OURENSE

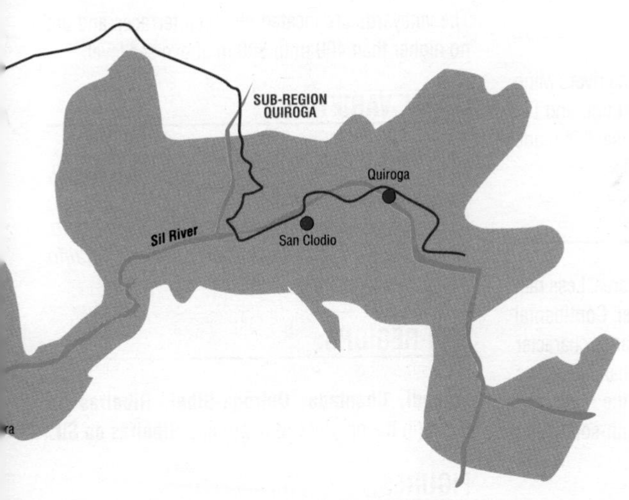
SUB-REGION
QUIROGA
Quiroga
Sil River
San Clodio

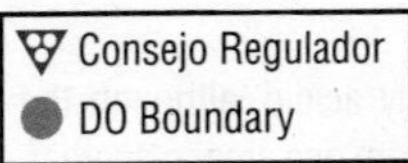
Consejo Regulador
DO Boundary

NEWS ABOUT THE VINTAGE:

The last few years have been crucial to the progress of the wines of this region. Back in the beginning, ten years ago, the DO had some light coloured reds with good varietal expression of *mencía*, to the point that it was even believed that it enjoyed a well-adapted clone of that red variety which allowed Ribeira Sacra to extract better aromatic expression that other neighbouring wine regions. Later, the area went through a duller period, given that certain dangerous practises like harvesting overripe grapes took hold between some of the local producers, thus masking any trace of varietal features in the resulting wines. Today, growers seem to have understood not only that this was no good, but they have also been able to achieve what I would call a "geological" quality in their wines, where soil becomes pivotal to quality and affords a formidable mineral character in a region that enjoys granite and slate soils, a geological horizon much envied in more renown wine regions. The samples that got the best ratings come from houses like Dominio de Bibei and Moure that put their focus on this sort of features rather than high yields. Both wineries manage to climb a step in our Podium to reach with their brands 96 and 95 wines respectively, with Ponte da Boga right behind them.

The 2010 vintage was an even one altogether, with sunny spells that propitiated a good maturation cycle for *mencía*. Nevertheless, we noticed in some young wines the kind of concentration and vinous character achieved only when using overripe grapes, a practise we have already condemned in the previous paragraph. This seems to happen mostly in wineries that do not set optimal maturation of the grapes as a goal, a crucial practise particularly with early variety such as *mencía*, houses that easily end up making wines with evident confected notes.

LOCATION:

The region extends along the banks of the rivers Miño and Sil in the south of the province of Lugo and the northern region of the province of Orense; it is made up of 17 municipal districts in this region.

CLIMATE:

Quite variable depending on the specific area. Less rain and slightly cooler climate and greater Continental influence in the Sil valley, and greater Atlantic character in the Miño valley. Altitude, on the other hand, also has an effect, with the vineyards closer to the rivers and with a more favourable orientation (south-southeast) being slightly warmer.

SOIL:

In general, the soil is highly acidic, although the composition varies greatly from one area to another. The vineyards are located on steep terraces and are no higher than 400 m to 500 m above sea level.

GRAPE VARIETIES:

WHITE: *Albariño, Loureira, Treixadura, Godello, Dona Blanca* and *Torrontés.*
RED: Main: *Mencía, Brancellao Merenzao, Garnacha Tintorera, Tempranillo, Sausón, Caiño Tinto* and *Mouratón.*

SUB-REGIONS:

Amandi, Chantada, Quiroga-Bibei, Ribeiras do Miño (in the province of Lugo) and **Ribeiras do Sil**.

FIGURES:

Vineyard surface: 1,271 – **Wine-Growers:** 2,842 – **Wineries:** 90 – **2010 Harvest rating:** Very Good – **Production:** 3,807,256 litres – **Market percentages:** 90% domestic. 10% export

CONSEJO REGULADOR
Rúa do Comercio, 6-8
27400 Monforte de Lemos (Lugo)
☎: +34 982 410 968 - Fax: +34 982 411 265
@ info@ribeirasacra.org
www.ribeirasacra.org

GENERAL CHARACTERISTICS OF THE WINES

WHITES	Single variety wines are produced from *Albariño* and *Godello*. The former have a greenish yellow colour with a fruity character and potency typical of *Albariño*; the latter are somewhat fresher than those of Valdeorras and less glycerine-like on the palate. There are also other white wines, the result of the blending of different varieties; these have a straw yellow colour and a fruity nose.
REDS	The single variety wines of *Mencía*, the most characteristic of the region, have a deep-red mid-tone colour; on the nose they are very fresh and roasted; on the palate, they are dry, fruity and without a pronounced structure.

VINTAGE RATING PEÑINGUIDE

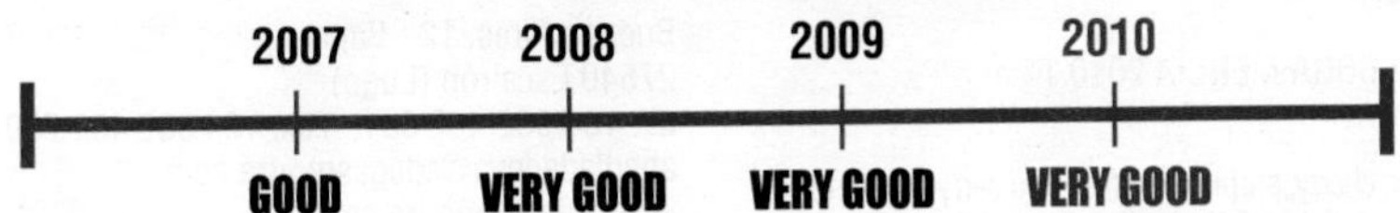

ADEGA DON RAMÓN

Rubín - Rozabales, 3
27413 Monforte de Lemos (Lugo)
☎: +34 982 155 770

DON RAMÓN MENCÍA 2010 T
mencía.

83 Colour: cherry, purple rim. Nose: ripe fruit, floral, grapey. Palate: good acidity, flavourful, easy to drink.

DON RAMÓN MENCÍA VENDIMIA SELECCIONADA 2008 T ROBLE
mencía.

86 Colour: bright cherry. Nose: ripe fruit, sweet spices, creamy oak, expressive. Palate: flavourful, fruity, toasty.

ADEGA PONTE DA BOGA

Couto Sampaio
32704 Castro Caldelas (Ourense)
☎: +34 988 203 306 - Fax: +34 988 203 299
ruben@pontedaboga.es

PONTE DA BOGA BLANCO DE BLANCOS 2010 B
62% godello, 33% albariño, 5% dona blanca.

90 Colour: bright straw. Nose: white flowers, citrus fruit, fruit expression, fragrant herbs. Palate: good acidity, rich, powerful, flavourful.

PONTE DA BOGA MENCÍA 2010 T
100% mencía.

87 Colour: cherry, purple rim. Nose: red berry notes, ripe fruit, scrubland. Palate: light-bodied, flavourful, fresh, fruity.

PONTE DA BOGA BANCALES OLVIDADOS MENCÍA 2009 T
mencía.

92 Colour: cherry, garnet rim. Nose: ripe fruit, floral, scrubland, mineral, spicy, creamy oak. Palate: fleshy, powerful, flavourful.

PONTE DA BOGA "CAPRICHO" 2009 T
85% merenzao, 5% sausón, 10% brancellao, mencía.

92 Colour: cherry, purple rim. Nose: red berry notes, ripe fruit, balsamic herbs, mineral, spicy. Palate: fleshy, complex, flavourful, ripe fruit, elegant.

ALAIS 2008 T
100% mencía.

88 Colour: cherry, garnet rim. Nose: ripe fruit, floral, balsamic herbs, spicy, toasty. Palate: complex, good acidity, powerful, flavourful

ADEGAS E VIÑEDOS VÍA ROMANA

A Ermida - Belesar
27500 Chantada (Lugo)
☎: +34 982 454 005 - Fax: +34 982 454 094
viaromana@viaromana.es
www.viaromana.es

VÍA ROMANA MENCÍA 2009 T
mencía.

88 Colour: cherry, purple rim. Nose: ripe fruit, mineral, sweet spices. Palate: flavourful, fruity, good acidity, toasty, round tannins.

VÍA ROMANA MENCÍA 2009 T BARRICA
mencía.

87 Colour: cherry, purple rim. Nose: red berry notes, ripe fruit, sweet spices, creamy oak. Palate: flavourful, fleshy, round tannins.

VÍA ROMANA SELECCIÓN DE AÑADA MAGNUM 2007 T
mencía.

88 Colour: light cherry, garnet rim. Nose: ripe fruit, mineral, sweet spices, creamy oak. Palate: powerful, flavourful, fleshy, complex.

ADEGAS MOURE

Buenos Aires, 12 - Bajo
27540 Escairón (Lugo)
☎: +34 982 452 031 - Fax: +34 982 452 700
abadiadacova@adegasmoure.com
www.adegasmoure.com

ABADÍA DA COVA ALBARIÑO 2010 B
albariño.

92 Colour: bright straw. Nose: fresh, white flowers, fine lees, ripe fruit, scrubland, balsamic herbs. Palate: flavourful, fruity, good acidity, balanced.

MOURE DE AUTOR 2010 T
85% mencía, 15% tempranillo.

95 Colour: bright cherry. Nose: ripe fruit, sweet spices, expressive, balsamic herbs, scrubland, spicy, cocoa bean. Palate: flavourful, toasty, round tannins, fleshy.

ABADÍA DA COVA MENCÍA 2010 T
100% mencía.

90 Colour: cherry, purple rim. Nose: red berry notes, fresh fruit, earthy notes. Palate: flavourful, fruity, good acidity, round tannins, fleshy, complex.

ABADÍA DA COVA ECOLOXICO 2010 T
mencía.

90 Colour: cherry, purple rim. Nose: red berry notes, fruit expression, floral, earthy notes. Palate: fleshy, complex, powerful, flavourful, mineral.

CEPA VELLA 2010 T
mencía.

85 Colour: cherry, purple rim. Nose: floral, red berry notes, ripe fruit, mineral. Palate: good acidity, flavourful, fleshy.

ABADÍA DA COVA 2009 T BARRICA
mencía.

91 Colour: cherry, garnet rim. Nose: red berry notes, ripe fruit, balsamic herbs, cocoa bean, sweet spices, creamy oak. Palate: powerful, flavourful, fleshy, round.

ADEGAS VALCAR

Lg. San Adrián Sacardebois
32747 Parada de Sil (Ourense)
☎: +34 988 208 245 - Fax: +34 988 208 246
adegasvalcar@adegasvalcar.com
www.adegasvalcar.com

VALCAR SELECCIÓN 2008 T
mencía.

87 Colour: cherry, garnet rim. Nose: ripe fruit, spicy, creamy oak, complex, balsamic herbs. Palate: powerful, flavourful, toasty.

ADEGAS VIÑA GAROÑA S.L.

Nogueira de Abaixo
27515 Chantada (Lugo)
☎: +34 982 171 636 - Fax: +34 982 162 373

VIÑA GAROÑA 2010 B
godello.

86 Colour: bright straw. Nose: white flowers, fresh fruit, fresh, expressive. Palate: flavourful, fresh, rich, fruity.

MARQUÉS DE GAROÑA MENCÍA 2010 T
mencía.

85 Colour: cherry, purple rim. Nose: floral, raspberry, ripe fruit, scrubland. Palate: fresh, flavourful, easy to drink.

ALGUEIRA

Doade, s/n
27460 Sober (Lugo)
☎: +34 629 208 917 - Fax: +34 982 410 299
info@adegaalgueira.com
www.adegaalgueira.com

ALGUEIRA PLURIVARIETAL 2010 B
40% godello, 40% albariño, 20% treixadura.

91 Colour: bright straw. Nose: white flowers, fragrant herbs, fresh fruit, balanced, mineral. Palate: good acidity, unctuous, powerful, flavourful, fruity, fleshy.

ALGUEIRA PLURIVARIETAL SOBRE LÍAS 2009 B ROBLE
40% godello, 40% albariño, 20% treixadura.

93 Colour: bright golden. Nose: floral, ripe fruit, sweet spices, creamy oak, expressive, elegant. Palate: good acidity, balanced, powerful, flavourful, fleshy, complex.

ALGUEIRA MENCÍA 2010 T
100% mencía.

87 Colour: bright cherry. Nose: floral, scrubland, ripe fruit, expressive. Palate: mineral, flavourful, fleshy, balsamic.

ALGUEIRA FINCAS 2009 T ROBLE
caiño, sousón.

91 Colour: cherry, garnet rim. Nose: ripe fruit, scrubland, sweet spices, toasty. Palate: good acidity, round, flavourful, good structure, fleshy.

ALGUEIRA MERENZAO 2009 T ROBLE
100% merenzao.

88 Nose: floral, ripe fruit, cocoa bean, dark chocolate, creamy oak, wild herbs. Palate: good acidity, powerful, flavourful, spicy, toasty.

ALGUEIRA PIZARRA 2008 T ROBLE
100% mencía.

90 Colour: cherry, garnet rim. Nose: ripe fruit, dark chocolate, sweet spices, toasty, complex, mineral. Palate: powerful, flavourful, long, round.

AMEDO

Tarrio, San Fiz
27516 Chantada (Lugo)
☎: +34 982 184 488 - Fax: +34 982 462 149
bodegasamedo@gmail.com
www.adegasamedo.com

AS GLORIAS GODELLO 2010 B
60% godello, 20% albariño, 20% treixadura.

88 Colour: bright straw. Nose: white flowers, tropical fruit, fragrant herbs. Palate: good acidity, unctuous, powerful, flavourful.

PERO BERNAL 2010 T
85% mencía, 15% tempranillo.

87 Colour: cherry, purple rim. Nose: ripe fruit, floral, earthy notes, complex. Palate: good acidity, powerful, flavourful, long.

AMEDO MENCÍA 2010 T
85% mencía, 15% garnacha.

86 Colour: cherry, purple rim. Nose: ripe fruit, floral, mineral, wild herbs. Palate: balsamic, flavourful, fleshy.

BODEGA SOUTELO

Compañía, 14
27400 Monforte de Lemos (Lugo)
☎: +34 982 410 778 - Fax: +34 982 410 529
info@bodegasoutelo.es
www.bodegasoutelo.com

CARDENAL RODRIGO DE CASTRO 2010 T
100% mencía.

84 Colour: cherry, purple rim. Nose: red berry notes, ripe fruit, floral, grassy. Palate: good acidity, flavourful, green.

BODEGA VICTORINO ÁLVAREZ

Luis Carballo, 74
32765 A Teixeira (Ourense)
☎: +34 988 207 418
adegasollio@yahoo.es

SOLLIO GODELLO 2010 B
100% godello.

90 Colour: bright straw. Nose: fresh, fresh fruit, white flowers, expressive, fragrant herbs. Palate: flavourful, fruity, good acidity, balanced.

SOLLÍO MENCÍA 2010 T
95% mencía, 5% brancellao.

88 Colour: cherry, purple rim. Nose: red berry notes, raspberry, floral, balsamic herbs. Palate: fleshy, complex, powerful, flavourful.

BODEGAS ALBAMAR

O Adro, 11 - Castrelo
36639 Cambados (Pontevedra)
☎: +34 660 292 750 - Fax: +34 986 520 048
info@bodegasalbamar.com

FUSCO 2010 T
mencía.

88 Colour: purple rim. Nose: raspberry, red berry notes, balsamic herbs, medium intensity. Palate: light-bodied, fresh, fruity.

BODEGAS COSTOYA

Boga, 26 - A Abeleda
32764 A Teixeira (Ourense)
☎: +34 600 417 273 - Fax: +34 988 601 332
carlos_costoya@temera.com

ALODIO 2010 T
85% mencía, 8% merenzao, 7% brancellao.

84 Colour: cherry, purple rim. Nose: red berry notes, ripe fruit, balsamic herbs. Palate: flavourful, fleshy, spicy.

BODEGAS RECTORAL DE AMANDI

Amandi
27423 Sober (Lugo)
☎: +34 988 384 200 - Fax: +34 988 384 068
vinos@bodegasgallegas.com
www.bodegasgallegas.com

RECTORAL DE AMANDI 2010 T
mencía.

88 Colour: cherry, purple rim. Nose: red berry notes, ripe fruit, mineral, earthy notes. Palate: good acidity, flavourful, fleshy, long, mineral.

CARLOS DÍAZ DIAZ

Vilachá - Doabe
27424 Sober (Lugo)
☎: +34 982 152 425

ESTRELA 2010 T
98% mencía, 2% garnacha.

83 Colour: cherry, purple rim. Nose: expressive, red berry notes, ripe fruit. Palate: flavourful, fruity, good acidity.

CASA MOREIRAS

San Martín de Siós, s/n
27430 Pantón (Lugo)
☎: +34 982 456 129 - Fax: +34 986 122 774
bodega@casamoreiras.com
www.casamoreiras.com

CASA MOREIRAS GODELLO 2010 B
75% godello, 15% treixadura, 10% albariño.

84 Colour: bright straw. Nose: faded flowers, dried herbs, ripe fruit. Palate: flavourful, fruity, good acidity.

CASA MOREIRAS MENCÍA 2010 T
85% mencía, 15% tempranillo.

88 Colour: cherry, purple rim. Nose: red berry notes, fresh fruit, fresh, expressive. Palate: good acidity, flavourful, fruity.

CHAO DO COUSO

O Cobo s/n Piñeiro
32780 Puebla de Trives (Ourense)
☎: +34 699 277 039
chaodocouso@hotmail.com
www.chaodecouso.com

ALCOUCE 2009 T ROBLE
100% mencía.

88 Colour: cherry, garnet rim. Nose: ripe fruit, wet leather, earthy notes, toasty. Palate: good acidity, powerful, flavourful, fleshy, toasty.

CONDADO DE SEQUEIRAS

Sequeiras - Camporramiro
27500 Chantada (Lugo)
☎: +34 944 732 516 - Fax: +34 944 120 227
condadodesequeiras@grupopeago.com

CONDADO DE SEQUEIRAS 2010 T
100% mencía.

87 Colour: cherry, purple rim. Nose: red berry notes, ripe fruit, earthy notes, scrubland. Palate: powerful, flavourful, fleshy, complex.

CONDADO DE SEQUEIRAS 2006 T ROBLE
100% mencía.

83 Colour: cherry, garnet rim. Nose: ripe fruit, balsamic herbs, cigar, old leather. Palate: correct, powerful, flavourful, fleshy.

DOMINIO DO BIBEI

Langullo, s/n
32781 Manzaneda (Ourense)
☎: +34 988 294 453 - Fax: +34 988 519 494
info@dominiodobibei.com
www.dominiodobibei.com

LAPOLA 2009 B
60% godello, 15% albariño, 25% dona blanca, loureiro, torrontés.

92 Colour: bright straw. Nose: white flowers, fresh fruit, citrus fruit, mineral. Palate: flavourful, fruity, fresh, spicy.

LAPENA 2008 B
godello, treixadura.

94 Colour: bright straw. Nose: candied fruit, citrus fruit, faded flowers, dry nuts. Palate: flavourful, ripe fruit, fine bitter notes.

LACIMA 2008 T
mencía.

95 Colour: cherry, garnet rim. Nose: red berry notes, mineral, elegant, spicy, creamy oak. Palate: good acidity, balanced, round, flavourful, fleshy.

LALAMA 2008 T
90% mencía, 7% garnacha, 3% mouraton.

91 Colour: cherry, garnet rim. Nose: mineral, expressive, creamy oak, ripe fruit. Palate: good acidity, powerful, flavourful, mineral.

DOMINIO DO BIBEI 2007 T
Brancellao.

95 Colour: cherry, garnet rim. Nose: fruit expression, expressive, balanced, complex, balsamic herbs, sweet spices, creamy oak. Palate: powerful, flavourful, elegant, long, mineral, fine tannins.

DON BERNARDINO

Santa Cruz de Brosmos, 9
27425 Sober (Lugo)
☎: +34 982 182 397 - Fax: +34 982 403 600
info@donbernardino.com
www.donbernardino.com

DON BERNARDINO 2010 T
mencía.

88 Colour: cherry, purple rim. Nose: expressive, fresh fruit, red berry notes, floral, mineral. Palate: flavourful, fruity, good acidity, round tannins.

DON BERNARDINO SELECCIÓN ESPECIAL 2009 T
mencía.

87 Colour: bright cherry. Nose: ripe fruit, sweet spices, creamy oak. Palate: flavourful, fruity, toasty, round tannins.

ERNESTO RODRÍGUEZ PÉREZ

Barrio, 13 Figueiroá
27460 Sober (Lugo)
☎: +34 982 152 410

VIÑA PEÓN 2010 T

85 Colour: cherry, garnet rim. Nose: medium intensity, overripe fruit, toasty, spicy. Palate: correct, flavourful, fruity, round tannins.

FINCA MILLARA BODEGAS Y VIÑEDOS

Millara Ribeiras do Miño
27439 Pantón (Lugo)
☎: +34 699 743 963
info@fincamillara.com

FINCA MILLARA 2008 T
100% mencía.

87 Colour: cherry, garnet rim. Nose: expressive, red berry notes, ripe fruit, scrubland. Palate: flavourful, fruity, good acidity.

JAVIER FERNÁNDEZ GONZÁLEZ

Pacios - Espasantes
27450 Pantón (Lugo)
☎: +34 982 456 228 - Fax: +34 982 456 228
javier.fdez@hotmail.com

SAIÑAS 2010 T
90% mencía, 10% garnacha.

90 Colour: cherry, purple rim. Nose: raspberry, red berry notes, floral, earthy notes. Palate: good acidity, powerful, flavourful, fruity, fleshy.

JAVIER FERNÁNDEZ VENDIMIA SELECCIONADA 2010 T
100% mencía.

87 Colour: cherry, purple rim. Nose: expressive, fresh fruit, red berry notes, floral. Palate: flavourful, fruity, good acidity.

SAIÑAS 2009 T BARRICA
98% mencía, 2% garnacha.

87 Colour: cherry, garnet rim. Nose: ripe fruit, spicy, creamy oak, toasty. Palate: powerful, flavourful, toasty, round tannins.

JORGE CARNERO FIUZA

Amandi- Pacio, 5
27423 Sober (Lugo)
☎: +34 661 644 952
cazoga@hotmail.com

VIÑA CAZOGA 2010 T
mencía.

83 Colour: cherry, purple rim. Nose: red berry notes, overripe fruit, medium intensity. Palate: fresh, fruity, flavourful.

DON DIEGO 2005 T
mencía.

88 Colour: cherry, garnet rim. Nose: ripe fruit, cocoa bean, sweet spices, fine reductive notes. Palate: good acidity, balanced, flavourful.

JOSÉ IGNACIO RODRÍGUEZ PÉREZ

Barantes de Arriba
27421 Sober (Lugo)
☎: +34 982 152 570
bodegasregueiral@gmail.com

VIÑA REGUEIRAL 2010 T
100% mencía.

84 Colour: deep cherry. Nose: ripe fruit, toasty, scrubland. Palate: flavourful, fruity, good acidity.

LAURA LÓPEZ LÓPEZ

Cantón - Amandi
27423 Sober (Lugo)
☎: +34 982 460 504

VAL DA LENDA 2010 T
mencía.

88 Colour: cherry, purple rim. Nose: expressive, fresh fruit, red berry notes, floral, mineral. Palate: flavourful, fruity, good acidity, round tannins.

LEIRABELLA

Leirabella - Sacardebois
32747 Parada do Sil (Ourense)
☎: +34 630 882 558 - Fax: +34 988 290 003
martin.lagaron@hotmal.es

BELLALEIRA 2010 T
85% mencía, 12% tempranillo, 3% garnacha.

86 Colour: cherry, purple rim. Nose: red berry notes, floral, wild herbs. Palate: good acidity, flavourful, fruity.

MANUEL FERNÁNDEZ RODRÍGUEZ

Lobios 54
27423 Sober (Lugo)
☎: +34 982 401 872

DOMINIO DE SANXIAO 2010 T
95% mencía, 5% otras.

86 Colour: cherry, purple rim. Nose: floral, red berry notes, ripe fruit, medium intensity. Palate: good acidity, correct, flavourful, fruity.

MARÍA JESÚS LÓPEZ CRISTÓBAL

Outeiro 20 - Bolmente
27425 Sober (Lugo)
☎: +34 982 152 981

CIVIDADE 2010 T
mencía.

86 Colour: cherry, purple rim. Nose: floral, red berry notes, ripe fruit, mineral. Palate: good acidity, fruity, powerful.

NAZ

Naz de Abaixo, 55 (Rosende)
27466 Sober (Lugo)
☎: +34 982 460 110
comercial@naz.es
www.naz.es

NAZ 2010 T
92% mencía, 3% garnacha, 5% tempranillo.

88 Colour: cherry, purple rim. Nose: floral, red berry notes, ripe fruit, scrubland, mineral. Palate: good acidity, powerful, flavourful, fruity.

PEDRO MANUEL RODRÍGUEZ PÉREZ

Sanmil, 41 - Santa Cruz de Brosmos
27425 Sober (Lugo)
☎: +34 982 152 508 - Fax: +34 982 402 000
adegasguimaro@gmail.com

GUIMARO MENCÍA 2010 T
mencía.

89 Colour: cherry, purple rim. Nose: ripe fruit, fresh, mineral, balsamic herbs. Palate: fresh, fruity, flavourful, balanced.

GUIMARO B1P 2009 T
mencía.

92 Colour: bright cherry. Nose: ripe fruit, fragrant herbs, mineral, spicy. Palate: light-bodied, flavourful, fleshy, complex, fine tannins.

GUIMARO B2M 2009 T
100% mencía.

92 Colour: cherry, purple rim. Nose: ripe fruit, earthy notes, scrubland, spicy, creamy oak. Palate: fleshy, complex, powerful, flavourful, round.

REGINA VIARUM

Doade, s/n
27424 Sober (Lugo)
☎: +34 619 009 777 - Fax: +34 986 227 129
info@reginaviarum.es
www.reginaviarum.es

REGINA VIARUM GODELLO 2010 B
70% godello, 15% treixadura, 15% loureiro.

84 Colour: bright straw. Nose: ripe fruit, fragrant herbs, faded flowers. Palate: spicy, light-bodied, flavourful.

REGINA VIARUM 2010 T
100% mencía.

89 Colour: dark-red cherry, purple rim. Nose: red berry notes, raspberry, ripe fruit. Palate: balanced, powerful, flavourful, fleshy, mineral.

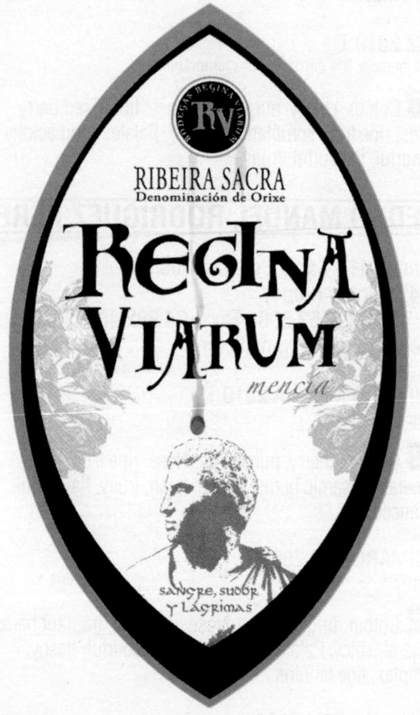

VÍA IMPERIAL 2010 T
100% mencía.

85 Colour: cherry, purple rim. Nose: red berry notes, ripe fruit, scrubland, mineral. Palate: fleshy, powerful, flavourful.

REGINA EXPRESIÓN 2008 T BARRICA
100% mencía.

86 Colour: bright cherry. Nose: ripe fruit, sweet spices, creamy oak, expressive. Palate: flavourful, fruity, toasty.

ROSA MARÍA PUMAR RODRÍGUEZ

Salgueiros, 8 Rozabales
27413 Monforte de Lemos (Lugo)
☎: +34 689 175 981
airapumar@gmail.com

SAN MAMED 2010 T
100% mencía.

88 Colour: cherry, purple rim. Nose: red berry notes, ripe fruit, mineral, expressive, floral. Palate: good acidity, balanced, fresh, fruity.

LINAXE D LVPIÁN MENCÍA 2010 T
100% mencía.

82 Colour: cherry, purple rim. Nose: overripe fruit, powerfull, floral. Palate: good acidity, flavourful, ripe fruit.

TERRAS DE LINCORA

Lincora Camporramiro
27514 Chantada (Lugo)
☎: +34 696 086 660

PORTELO MENCÍA 2010 T
mencía.

85 Colour: cherry, purple rim. Nose: red berry notes, ripe fruit, floral, scrubland. Palate: good acidity, balanced, flavourful.

VIÑA DOS SEIXAS MENCÍA 2010 T
mencía.

82 Colour: cherry, purple rim. Nose: overripe fruit, grassy, medium intensity. Palate: lacks balance, flavourful, fleshy.

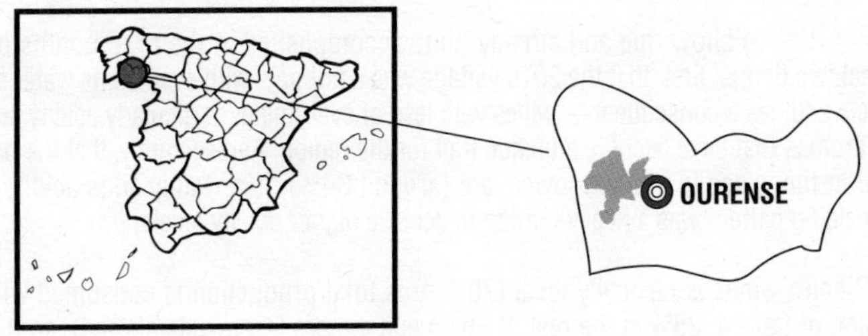

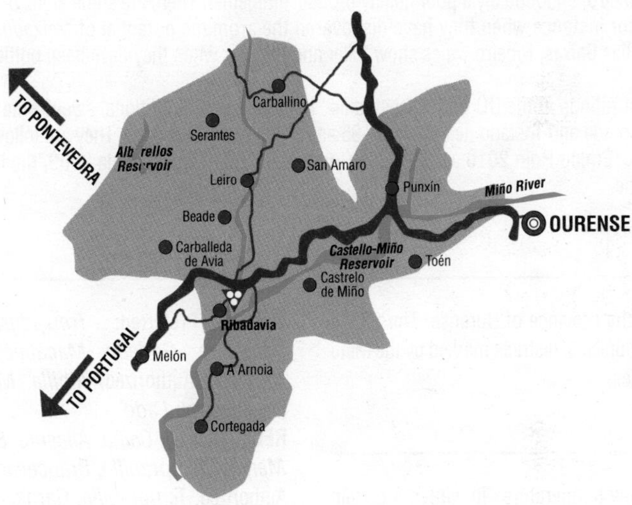

Consejo Regulador
DO Boundary

DO RIBEIRO

NEWS ABOUT THE VINTAGE:

The 2010 wines of Ribeiro show ripe and already quite accomplished in the first months of 2011, features that reveal two things: first, that the 2010 vintage was a hot one, with even some water stress at the end of the cycle and –as a consequence– wines with less of everything, particularly acidity and those herbal and floral aromas that have become a unique trait for the region. And secondly, that the *palomino* grape is blended in the wines in a much lower rate (around 30%); it certainly adds acidity, but its traditional high-yielding pattern was a heavy burden to achieve higher quality levels.

The market for Ribeiro wines is basically local (70% of is total production is consumed within the autonomous region of Galicia, 25% in the rest of Spain and a mere 5% travels abroad), so they have never felt necessary to try and open new markets beyond their regional borders. That is also probably why there are a considerable number of wineries (almost half a hundred) that do not send their samples for our assessment, for just around 25 of theme that do. It is also true that those that fail to do it are probably aware that they do not reach the standard of quality required for our Guide, and they remain faithful (I would dare saying it is mutual) to that most loyal local consumer used to the taste of the most traditional Ribeiro, undoubtedly a poor quality product altogether. There are some signs of change within the region, for instance when they have discovered the aromatic potential of *treixadura*. Same as it happens in Rías Baixas, Ribeiro wines show fuller and rounder when they have been bottled for a while.

Still, the best ratings in the DO go for "tostadillo" renderings, the traditional sweet wine of the region: Alma de Reboreda and Tostado de Teira, with 95 and 94 points respectively. They are followed closely by the dry wines Emilio Rojo 2010 and Coto de Gomariz Colleita Seleccionada 2009, the latter a barrel-fermented one.

LOCATION:

In the west of the province of Ourense. The region comprises 13 municipal districts marked by the Miño and its tributaries.

CLIMATE:

Atlantic, with low temperatures in winter, a certain risk of spring frosts, and high temperatures in the summer months. The average annual rainfall varies between 800 mm and 1,000 mm.

SOIL:

Predominantly granite, deep and rich in organic matter, although in some areas clayey soils predominate. The vineyards are on the slopes of the mountains (where higher quality wines are produced) and on the plains.

GRAPE VARIETIES :

WHITE: Preferred: *Treixadura, Torrontés, Palomino, Godello, Macabeo, Loureira* and *Albariño*. Authorized: *Albilla, Macabeo, Jerez*. Experimental: *Lado*.
RED: Preferred: *Caíño, Alicante, Sousón, Ferrón, Mencía, Tempranillo, Brancellao*.
Authorized: *Tempranillo, Garnacha*.

FIGURES:

Vineyard surface: 2,789 – **Wine-Growers:** 6,034 – **Wineries:** 116 – **2010 Harvest rating:** Very Good – **Production:** 9,600,000 litres – **Market percentages:** 95% domestic. 5% export

CONSEJO REGULADOR
Salgado Moscoso, 9
32400 Ribadavia (Ourense)
☎: +34 988 477 200 - Fax: +34 988 477 201
@ info@ribeiro.es
www.ribeiro.es

GENERAL CHARACTERISTICS OF THE WINES

WHITES	These are the most characteristic of the DO. The wines, produced from the autochtonous varieties (mainly *Treixadura* and *Torrontés*, although *Lairo*, *Loureira* and *Godello* are also used), are characterised by their fresh and fruity nose with notes of green apple, fennel and hints of flowers; on the palate they have good acidity, which makes them very fresh. Those produced from *Palomino*, however, are much more neutral, nosetically limited and less expressive on the palate.
REDS	The production is limited compared to the white wines. The most common are based on a non-local grape variety, the *Alicante*, exported after the phylloxera outbreak, which gives wines of medium quality and which are somewhat aggressive and acidic. Those of *Mencía*, on the other hand, have greater nosetic potency; they are fresh, light and pleasant to drink. Another line, still quite new, are the reds that experiment with other autochthonous grapes (*Brancellao, Caiño, Sousón* and *Ferrón*), which are more characteristic, but which, on some occasions, provide slight vegetative and herb sensations.

VINTAGE RATING PEÑÍNGUIDE

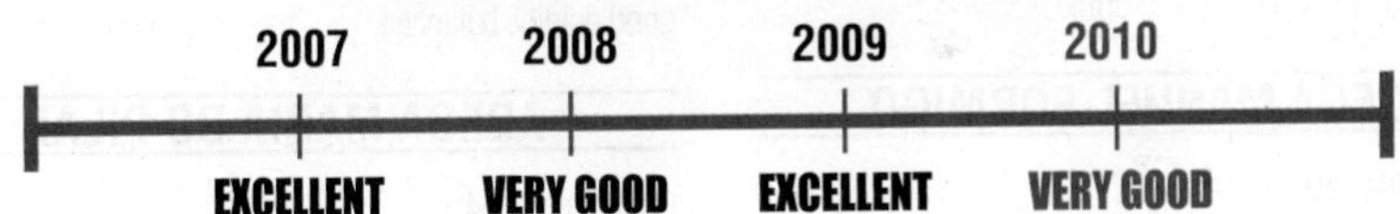

A PORTELA

Piñeiros, s/n
32431 Beade (Ourense)
☎: +34 988 480 050 - Fax: +34 988 480 050
beade@beadeprimacia.com
www.beadeprimacia.com

BEADE PRIMACÍA 2010 B
95% treixadura, 5% loureiro, albariño.

88 Colour: bright straw. Nose: powerfull, varietal, ripe fruit, white flowers. Palate: powerful, flavourful, fleshy.

SEÑORÍO DE BEADE 2010 B
treixadura, godello, torrontés, palomino.

88 Colour: bright straw. Nose: white flowers, ripe fruit, varietal. Palate: flavourful, fleshy, ripe fruit.

SEÑORÍO DE BEADE 2010 T
mencía, caiño, sousón.

88 Colour: deep cherry. Nose: raspberry, ripe fruit, balsamic herbs. Palate: flavourful, fruity, fleshy.

ADEGA DE ACINUS

Bº de Gomariz
32429 Leiro (Ourense)
☎: +34 636 766 791
alfredo.acinus@gmail.com

ACINUS S/C B
treixadura, loureiro, albariño.

84 Colour: yellow. Nose: grassy, medium intensity, fresh. Palate: fresh, balsamic, easy to drink.

ADEGA MANUEL FORMIGO

Cabo de Vila, 49
32431 Beade (Ourense)
☎: +34 627 569 885
info@fincateira.com
www.fincateira.com

FINCA TEIRA 2010 B
70% treixadura, 20% godello, 10% torrontés.

88 Colour: bright yellow. Nose: jasmine, ripe fruit, balanced. Palate: flavourful, easy to drink, good acidity, fruity.

FORMIGO 2010 B
treixadura, godello, palomino, otras.

88 Colour: bright straw. Nose: fresh, fresh fruit, white flowers. Palate: flavourful, fruity, good acidity, balanced.

TEIRA X 2010 B
treixadura, loureiro, albariño, alvilla.

87 Colour: bright yellow, greenish rim. Nose: wild herbs, citrus fruit, medium intensity. Palate: fresh, fruity, good acidity.

TEIRA X 2009 B
treixadura, loureiro, albariño, alvilla.

88 Colour: bright straw. Nose: white flowers, candied fruit, citrus fruit. Palate: flavourful, powerful, fruity.

TOSTADO DE TEIRA 2006 B
treixadura.

94 Colour: old gold, amber rim. Nose: candied fruit, honeyed notes, dry nuts, acetaldehyde, toasty. Palate: flavourful, powerful, spirituous, sweet.

FINCA TEIRA 2010 T
caiño, souson, brancellao, garnacha.

84 Colour: cherry, purple rim. Nose: powerfull, red berry notes, grassy. Palate: fresh, fruity, flavourful.

ADEGA MANUEL ROJO

Chaos s/n Arnoia
32417 Vigo (Pontevedra)
☎: +34 627 908 125
aroa@adegamanuelrojo.com
www.adegamanuelrojo.es

MANUEL ROJO 2010 B
treixadura, godello, lado, albariño.

91 Colour: bright straw. Nose: fresh, fresh fruit, white flowers, dry stone, balsamic herbs. Palate: flavourful, fruity, good acidity, balanced.

ADEGA MARÍA DO PILAR

Casardeita, 14
32430 Castrelo de Miño (Ourense)
☎: +34 988 475 236 - Fax: +34 988 475 236
adegasmariadopilar@hotmail.com
www.adegamariadopilar.com

SENLLEIRO SELECCIÓN 2010 B
60% godello, 30% treixadura, 10% albariño.

87 Colour: bright straw. Nose: scrubland, ripe fruit, citrus fruit, mineral. Palate: powerful, flavourful, fleshy, good acidity.

RECHAMANTE 2010 T
50% mencía, 50% tempranillo.

87 Colour: deep cherry. Nose: fruit expression, red berry notes. Palate: flavourful, fruity, fresh.

ADEGA PAZO DO MAR

Ctra. Ourense-Castrelo, Km. 12,5
32940 Toén (Ourense)
☎: +34 988 261 256 - Fax: +34 988 261 264
info@pazodomar.com
www.pazodomar.com

EXPRESIÓN DE PAZO DO MAR 2010 B
albariño.

88 Colour: bright straw, greenish rim. Nose: medium intensity, white flowers. Palate: fresh, fruity, fine bitter notes.

PAZO DO MAR 2010 B
treixadura, torrontés, godello.

87 Colour: bright straw. Nose: powerfull, ripe fruit, dried herbs. Palate: flavourful, fruity, fresh.

PAZO DO MAR 2010 T
mencía, garnacha.

83 Colour: cherry, garnet rim. Nose: ripe fruit, balsamic herbs. Palate: flavourful, fresh, fine bitter notes.

ADEGAS ÁUREA LUX

Rúa do Ribeiro, 29
32400 Ribadavia (Ourense)
☎: +34 655 393 673
info@aurealux.com
www.aurealux.com

PARADIGMA LEIVE 2010 B
50% treixadura, 35% albariño, 15% loureiro.

91 Colour: bright straw. Nose: powerfull, ripe fruit, citrus fruit, grassy, mineral. Palate: flavourful, fruity, fresh, fleshy.

LEIVE TREIXADURA 2010 B
100% treixadura.

84 Colour: bright straw. Nose: medium intensity, fruit expression, dried herbs. Palate: flavourful, ripe fruit.

LEIVE RELIQUIA 2009 BFB
50% treixadura, 35% albariño, 15% loureiro.

89 Colour: bright straw. Nose: ripe fruit, cocoa bean, sweet spices. Palate: flavourful, powerful, fleshy, spicy, ripe fruit.

LEIVA PRETO 2009 T
mencía, brancellao, sousón, caiño, multivarietales.

85 Colour: cherry, garnet rim. Nose: medium intensity, spicy, wet leather, ripe fruit. Palate: powerful, fleshy, flavourful.

ADEGAS DOMILLOR

San Clodio, s/n
32420 Leiro (Ourense)
☎: +34 682 471 916
ircata@avanteselecta.com

DOMILLOR 2010 B
70% treixadura, 5% lado, 5% loureiro, 10% godello, 5% albariño, 5% torrontés.

90 Colour: bright straw. Nose: fresh, fresh fruit, white flowers, fragrant herbs. Palate: flavourful, fruity, good acidity, balanced.

ADEGAS VALDAVIA

Lugar de Puzos, s/n - Cuñas
32454 Cenlle (Ourense)
☎: +34 669 892 681
comercial@adegasvaldavia.com
www.adegasvaldavia.com

CUÑAS DAVIA 2010 B
treixadura, albariño, godello, lado.

90 Colour: bright straw, greenish rim. Nose: fresh fruit, balanced, grassy. Palate: flavourful, fruity, good acidity, balanced, fine bitter notes.

CUÑAS DAVIA 2009 BFB
treixadura, albariño.

92 Colour: bright yellow, greenish rim. Nose: balanced, expressive, ripe fruit, dried herbs, spicy. Palate: powerful, flavourful, good structure, good acidity.

CUÑAS DAVIA 2009 T
caiño, sousón, mencía, brancellao.

84 Colour: bright cherry, garnet rim. Nose: balanced, red berry notes, spicy, fragrant herbs. Palate: fleshy, fruity.

ANTONIO MONTERO

Santa María
32430 Castrelo do Miño (Ourense)
☎: +34 607 856 002
antoniomontero@antoniomontero.com
www.antoniomontero.com

ANTONIO MONTERO "AUTOR" 2010 B
80% treixadura, 5% loureiro, 10% torrontés, 5% albariño.

86 Colour: bright straw, greenish rim. Nose: grassy, fresh, balanced. Palate: fruity, correct, easy to drink.

ALEJANDRVS 2009 B
treixadura.

89 Colour: bright yellow. Nose: candied fruit, citrus fruit, sweet spices. Palate: flavourful, fine bitter notes, good acidity, spicy.

ARCO DA VELLA A ADEGA DE ELADIO

Pza. de España, 1
32431 Beade (Ourense)
☎: +34 607 487 060 - Fax: +34 986 376 800
bodega@bodegaeladio.com
www.bodegaeladio.com

TORQUE DO CASTRO 2010 B
60% treixadura, 15% godello, 20% torrontés, 5% albariño.

84 Colour: bright straw. Nose: ripe fruit, medium intensity, fragrant herbs. Palate: flavourful, ripe fruit.

TARABELO 2009 TC
25% souson, 35% caiño, 15% garnacha tintorera, 15% brancellao, 10% tempranillo.

83 Colour: bright cherry. Nose: spicy, wet leather, ripe fruit, toasty. Palate: fine bitter notes, powerful.

BODEGA ALANÍS

Barbantes Estación
32450 Cenlle (Ourense)
☎: +34 988 384 200 - Fax: +34 988 384 068
vinos@bodegasgallegas.com
www.bodegasgallegas.com

GRAN CAMPIÑO 2010 B
treixadura, torrontés.

87 Colour: bright straw, greenish rim. Nose: fresh fruit, wild herbs, medium intensity. Palate: fleshy, flavourful, long.

GRAN ALANÍS 2009 B
palomino, treixadura, torrontés.

88 Colour: bright straw. Nose: powerfull, ripe fruit, citrus fruit. Palate: flavourful, fleshy, good acidity.

SAN TROCADO 2009 B
torrontés, treixadura.

87 Colour: bright straw, greenish rim. Nose: medium intensity, wild herbs, dried flowers. Palate: fresh, flavourful, good acidity.

BODEGA CASTRO REI

Lg. Sampaio s/n
32414 Ribadavia (Ourense)
☎: +34 615 323 221 - Fax: +34 988 472 069
maryjdd@hotmail.com
www.bodegacastrorei.com

DIVINO REI 2010 B
treixadura, albariño, loureiro.

88 Colour: bright straw. Nose: ripe fruit, fine lees, white flowers, tropical fruit. Palate: flavourful, powerful, fleshy.

BODEGA COOP. SAN ROQUE DE BEADE

Ctra. Ribadavia - Carballiño, Km. 4
32431 Beade (Ourense)
☎: +34 988 471 522 - Fax: +34 988 471 502
adegas@terradocastelo.com
www.terradocastelo.com

TERRA DO CASTELO GODELLO 2010 B
100% godello.

88 Colour: bright straw. Nose: ripe fruit, medium intensity, white flowers. Palate: flavourful, powerful, fleshy.

TERRA DO CASTELO TREIXADURA 2010 B
100% treixadura.

87 Colour: bright straw, greenish rim. Nose: medium intensity, dried herbs, citrus fruit. Palate: flavourful, correct, balanced.

TERRA DO CASTELO "SENSACIÓN" 2010 B
50% palomino, 30% treixadura, 15% torrontés, 5% godello.

87 Colour: bright straw. Nose: powerfull, varietal, ripe fruit, citrus fruit, grassy. Palate: flavourful, fruity, fleshy.

BODEGA MERLOT IBÉRICA

Rúa do Ribeiro, 75
32400 Ribadavia (Ourense)
☎: +34 988 471 508 - Fax: +34 988 471 508
info@veigadouro.com
www.veigadouro.com

VEIGA D'OURO 2010 B
treixadura, torrontés, albariño, godello.

88 Colour: bright yellow. Nose: ripe fruit, powerfull, balanced, warm. Palate: fleshy, flavourful, good acidity.

BODEGAS CAMPANTE

Finca Reboreda, s/n
32941 Puga (Ourense)
☎: +34 988 261 212 - Fax: +34 988 261 213
info@campante.com
www.campante.com

GRAN REBOREDA 2010 B
treixadura, godello, loureiro.

87 Colour: bright yellow, greenish rim. Nose: floral, fresh fruit, balanced. Palate: fleshy, fruity, good acidity.

ALMA DE REBOREDA TOSTADO 2005 B
100% treixadura.

95 Colour: iodine, amber rim. Nose: candied fruit, fruit preserve, honeyed notes, pattiserie, sweet spices, varnish. Palate: powerful, fleshy, sweet, fine bitter notes, full.

BODEGAS DOCAMPO

Lg. San Paio, s/n
32414 Ribadavia (Ourense)
☎: +34 988 470 436 - Fax: +34 988 470 421
sol@bodegasdocampo.com
www.bodegasdocampo.com

SEÑORÍO DA VILA 2010 B
100% treixadura.

89 Colour: bright yellow, greenish rim. Nose: balanced, complex, ripe fruit. Palate: fruity, flavourful, good acidity.

VIÑA DO CAMPO 2010 B
70% treixadura, 30% torrontés.

86 Colour: yellow, greenish rim. Nose: fresh fruit, citrus fruit, wild herbs. Palate: flavourful, fruity, easy to drink, good acidity.

VIÑA DO CAMPO GODELLO 2010 B
100% godello.

83 Colour: bright straw. Nose: powerfull, ripe fruit, citrus fruit. Palate: flavourful, spicy, fine bitter notes.

VIÑA DO CAMPO 2009 BFB
treixadura, torrontés.

86 Colour: bright yellow. Nose: candied fruit, sweet spices, wild herbs. Palate: flavourful, ripe fruit, balanced.

BODEGAS NAIROA

A Ponte, 2
32417 Arnoia (Ourense)
☎: +34 988 492 867 - Fax: +34 988 107 007
info@bodegasnairoa.com
www.bodegasnairoa.com

ALBERTE 2010 B
80% treixadura, 20% albariño.

89 Colour: bright straw. Nose: fragrant herbs, powerfull, ripe fruit. Palate: flavourful, fleshy.

VAL DE NAIROA 2010 B
80% treixadura, 10% albariño, 10% lado.

89 Colour: bright straw, greenish rim. Nose: white flowers, ripe fruit, balanced. Palate: fruity, good structure, flavourful, good acidity.

NAIROA 2010 B
30% treixadura, 40% torrontés, 30% palomino.

88 Colour: bright straw. Nose: ripe fruit, citrus fruit, complex, varietal. Palate: fleshy, flavourful, good acidity.

BODEGAS O'VENTOSELA

San Clodio
32574 Leiro (Ourense)
☎: +34 988 471 947
bodegasydestilerias@oventosela.com
www.oventosela.es

GRAN LEIRIÑA 2010 B
treixadura, godello, albariño, torrontés.

87 Colour: bright straw. Nose: ripe fruit, citrus fruit, grassy, dried flowers. Palate: flavourful, powerful, fleshy.

BODEGAS PEÑA

Rua da Igrexa, 4 - Vide
23430 Castrelo de Miño (Ourense)
☎: +34 988 489 094
info@lanceroribeiro.com
www.lancero.es

SEÑORÍO DO LANCERO 2010 B
70% treixadura, 10% torrontés, 15% godello, 4% lado, 1% otras.

84 Colour: bright yellow. Nose: ripe fruit, tropical fruit. Palate: flavourful, good finish.

VIÑA ENXIDO 2010 B
75% jerez, 25% variedades autóctona.

82 Colour: bright straw, greenish rim. Nose: medium intensity, fresh, grassy. Palate: fresh, easy to drink, fine bitter notes.

LANCERO 2010 T
40% garnacha, 60% mencía, sousón, caiño.

90 Colour: deep cherry. Nose: red berry notes, raspberry, balsamic herbs. Palate: flavourful, fruity, fresh. Personality.

CARMEN IGLESIAS QUINTELA

Toén
32940 Feá (Ourense)
☎: +34 629 587 571

GRAN GANDARELA 2010 B
treixadura, torrontés, loureiro.

87 Colour: bright straw. Nose: ripe fruit, citrus fruit, grassy. Palate: flavourful, fruity, fresh.

CASAL DE ARMÁN

Lugar O Cotiño, s/n. San Andrés de Camporredondo
32400 Ribadavia (Ourense)
☎: +34 699 060 464 - Fax: +34 988 491 809
bodega@casaldearman.net
www.casaldearman.net

CASAL DE ARMÁN 2010 B
90% treixadura, 5% albariño, 5% godello.

91 Colour: bright straw. Nose: powerfull, varietal, ripe fruit, mineral, balsamic herbs. Palate: flavourful, powerful, fleshy.

CASAL DE ARMÁN 2010 T
brancellao, sousón, caiño.

91 Colour: cherry, garnet rim. Nose: balsamic herbs, scrubland, floral, red berry notes, ripe fruit. Palate: flavourful, mineral, long, good acidity.

COTO DE GOMARIZ

Barrio de Gomariz
32429 Leiro (Ourense)
☎: +34 671 641 982 - Fax: +34 988 488 174
gomariz@cotodegomariz.com
www.cotodegomariz.com

COTO DE GOMARIZ 2010 B
treixadura, godello, torrontés, loureiro.

92 Colour: yellow, greenish rim. Nose: balsamic herbs, fruit expression, citrus fruit, balanced. Palate: fruity, flavourful, complex.

GOMARIZ X 2010 B
95% albariño, 5% treixadura.

91 Colour: bright yellow, greenish rim. Nose: ripe fruit, tropical fruit, powerfull. Palate: ripe fruit, long, fleshy, rich, good structure.

COTO DE GOMARIZ COLLEITA SELECCIONADA 2009 BFB
treixadura, godello, loureiro, albariño.

93 Colour: bright yellow. Nose: powerfull, ripe fruit, sweet spices, creamy oak, fragrant herbs. Palate: rich, smoky aftertaste, flavourful, fresh, good acidity.

ABADÍA DE GOMARIZ 2009 T
souson, brancellao, ferrol, mencía.

90 Colour: bright cherry. Nose: ripe fruit, sweet spices, creamy oak. Palate: flavourful, fruity, toasty, round tannins.

CUNQUEIRO

Prado de Miño, 4
32430 Castrelo de Miño (Ourense)
☎: +34 988 489 023 - Fax: +34 988 489 082
info@bodegascunqueiro.es
www.bodegascunqueiro.es

MAIS DE CUNQUEIRO 2010 B
torrontés.

89 Colour: bright straw, greenish rim. Nose: fresh, balsamic herbs, balanced. Palate: fruity, flavourful, fine bitter notes.

CUNQUEIRO III MILENIUM 2010 B
treixadura, loureiro, godello, albariño.

88 Colour: bright straw. Nose: ripe fruit, citrus fruit, white flowers. Palate: flavourful, fruity, fresh.

CUQUEIRA 2010 B
treixadura, torrontés, godello.

87 Colour: bright straw. Nose: white flowers, ripe fruit, citrus fruit. Palate: flavourful, fruity, good acidity, balanced.

EDUARDO PEÑA

Carrero Blanco, s/n - Barral
Castelo de Miño (Ourense)
☎: +34 629 872 130
bodega@bodegaeduardopenha.es
www.bodegaeduardopenha.es

EDUARDO PEÑA 2010 B
treixadura, godello, loureiro.

87 Colour: yellow, greenish rim. Nose: wild herbs, fresh fruit. Palate: flavourful, fine bitter notes, good acidity.

ELISA COLLARTE BERNÁRDEZ

San Andrés
32400 Ribadavia (Ourense)
☎: +34 986 473 266

CORDÓN DE SANTO ANDRÉ S/C B
treixadura, godello, albariño, loureiro.

87 Color bright straw. Aroma fresh, fresh fruit, white flowers, expressive. Taste flavourful, fruity, good acidity, balanced.

ELISA COLLARTE BARRICA 2010 T
mencía.

82 Colour: bright cherry, garnet rim. Nose: roasted coffee, sweet spices. Palate: flavourful, toasty.

EMILIO ROJO

Lugar de Remoiño, s/n
32233 Arnoia (Ourense)
☎: +34 988 488 050

EMILIO ROJO 2010 B
treixadura, lado, loureiro, albariño.

93 Colour: bright straw. Nose: scrubland, dry stone, damp undergrowth, complex, expressive. Palate: fresh, flavourful, fruity, varietal.

FRANCISCO FERNÁNDEZ SOUSA

Prado, 14
32430 Castrelo do Miño (Ourense)
☎: +34 988 489 077 - Fax: +34 986 272 148
info@terraminei.com
www.terraminei.com

TERRA MINEI 2010 B
100% treixadura.

87 Colour: bright straw. Nose: ripe fruit, citrus fruit, dried herbs. Palate: flavourful, fruity, good acidity.

HEREDEROS DE JESÚS FREIJIDO

Jose Antonio, 30-5º izq.
32400 Ribadavia (Ourense)
☎: +34 988 471 969 - Fax: +34 988 471 969
felienoavia@auna.com

AGAS DO TEMPO 2010 B

88 Colour: bright straw. Nose: grassy, ripe fruit, fruit expression, citrus fruit. Palate: flavourful, fruity, fresh.

JAVIER MONSALVE ALVAREZ

Villa Paz - A Ponte, s/n
32417 Arnoia (Ourense)
☎: +34 677 457 614
gerente@eloilorenzo.es
eloilorenzo.es

ELOI LORENZO 2010 B
treixadura, lado, loureiro, torrontés.

84 Colour: bright straw. Nose: powerfull, ripe fruit, white flowers. Palate: powerful, flavourful, fleshy.

JOSÉ ESTÉVEZ FERNÁNDEZ

Ponte
32417 Arnoia (Ourense)
☎: +34 696 402 970
joseestevezarnoia@gmail.com

MAURO ESTEVEZ 2010 B
65% treixadura, 20% lado, 10% albariño, 5% loureiro.

88 Colour: bright straw. Nose: ripe fruit, white flowers, grassy. Palate: flavourful, fruity, fresh, fleshy.

JOSÉ GONZÁLEZ ALVAREZ

32427 Gomariz - Leiro (Ourense)
☎: +34 988 488 233
eduardogonzalezbravo@gmail.com

EDUARDO BRAVO 2010 B
treixadura, albariño, torrontés.

88 Colour: bright yellow. Nose: fragrant herbs, powerfull, white flowers. Palate: fleshy, flavourful, rich, ripe fruit.

PAZO LALÓN 2010 B

84 Colour: pale. Nose: ripe fruit, fruit expression, citrus fruit. Palate: flavourful, fresh.

LAGAR DO MERENS

Chaos
32417 Arnoia (Ourense)
☎: +34 607 533 314
info@lagardomerens.com

LAGAR DO MERENS 2010 B
treixadura, lado, torrontés.

90 Colour: bright straw. Nose: ripe fruit, fruit expression, citrus fruit. Palate: flavourful, fruity, fleshy.

LAGAR DO MERENS 2009 BFB
treixadura, godello, albariño.

92 Colour: bright yellow. Nose: sweet spices, candied fruit, complex, expressive. Palate: good structure, flavourful, full, rich, spicy.

30 COPELOS 2009 T
caiño, sousón, ferrón, brancellao.

91 Colour: cherry, garnet rim. Nose: red berry notes, complex, balsamic herbs, balanced. Palate: flavourful, fruity, good structure, round tannins.

PAZO CASANOVA

Camiño Souto do Río, 1
Santa Cruz de Arrabaldo
32990 Ourense (Ourense)
☎: +34 988 384 196 - Fax: +34 988 384 196
casanova@pazocasanova.com
www.pazocasanova.com

CASANOVA 2010 B
80% treixadura, 20% godello, albariño, loureiro.

88 Colour: bright straw, greenish rim. Nose: dried herbs, citrus fruit, balanced. Palate: flavourful, fruity, easy to drink.

PAZO DE VIEITE

Ctra. Ribadavia a Carbadiño, Km. 6
32419 Vieite Leiro (Ourense)
☎: +34 988 488 229 - Fax: +34 988 488 229
info@pazodevieite.es
www.pazodevieite.es

1932 2010 B
100% treixadura.

89 Colour: bright straw, greenish rim. Nose: balanced, medium intensity, wild herbs, dried flowers, ripe fruit. Palate: fruity, flavourful.

PAZO LODEIRO (XULIO VÁZQUEZ QUINTELA)

O Barón Carvalliño
32500 (Ourense)
☎: +34 988 243 426

PAZO LODEIRO 2010 B
treixadura, torrontés, godello, loureiro.

88 Colour: bright straw. Nose: fresh, white flowers, ripe fruit, citrus fruit. Palate: flavourful, fruity, good acidity.

PAZO TIZÓN

Pol. Ind. Aimayor - Estaño, 4
28330 San Martín de la Vega (Madrid)
☎: +34 639 788 788
admon@pazotizon.com
www.pazotizon.com

EXTRAMUNDI 2010 B
treixadura, albariño.

88 Color bright straw. Aroma fresh, fresh fruit, white flowers, expressive. Taste flavourful, fruity, good acidity, balanced.

PRODUCCIONES A MODIÑO

Cubilledo-Gomariz
32420 Leiro (Ourense)
☎: +34 686 961 681
sanclodiovino@gmail.com
www.vinosanclodio.com

SANCLODIO 2010 B
treixadura, godello, loureiro, albariño, torrontés.

91 Colour: bright straw. Nose: powerfull, ripe fruit, citrus fruit, white flowers. Palate: flavourful, fleshy, powerful.

REY LAFUENTE

Prado Do Miño
32230 Castrelo do Miño (Ourense)
☎: +34 988 392 351 - Fax: +34 988 392 352
marcialreyrey@yahoo.es
www.vinarium.es

SUMUM 2010 B
treixadura, godello.

86 Colour: bright straw, greenish rim. Nose: grassy, balanced. Palate: fruity, flavourful.

SAMEIRÁS

San Andrés, 98
32415 Ribadavia (Ourense)
☎: +34 988 491 812 - Fax: +34 988 470 591
sameiras@terra.es

1040 SAMEIRÁS 2010 B
treixadura, lado, godello, albariño.

89 Colour: bright straw. Nose: white flowers, ripe fruit, tropical fruit. Palate: flavourful, fruity, good acidity, rich.

SAMEIRÁS 2010 B
treixadura, albariño, godello, lado, loureiro.

87 Colour: bright yellow, greenish rim. Nose: dried herbs, fresh fruit, white flowers. Palate: flavourful, fruity, ripe fruit.

VIÑA DO AVÓ 2010 B
treixadura, albariño, godello, torrontés.

87 Colour: bright straw, greenish rim. Nose: balanced, medium intensity, expressive, wild herbs. Palate: flavourful, fruity, good acidity.

SAMEIRÁS 2010 T
brancellao, caiño, mencía, sousón.

87 Colour: deep cherry. Nose: ripe fruit, raspberry, grassy. Palate: flavourful, fruity, fine bitter notes.

VIÑA DO AVÓ 2010 T
brancellao, souson, caiño, mencía.

83 Colour: bright cherry, garnet rim. Nose: medium intensity, red berry notes, sulphur notes. Palate: fruity, easy to drink.

VALDEPUGA S.L.

Ctra. Ourense a Cortegada, km 14
32940 Alongos -Toén (Ourense)
☎: +34 988 235 817 - Fax: +34 988 235 817
valdepuga@grupopuga.com
www.bodegasvaldepuga.com

VALDEPUGA 2010 B
treixadura, loureiro, godello, albariño.

88 Colour: bright straw. Nose: fresh, fresh fruit, white flowers. Palate: flavourful, fruity, good acidity, balanced.

TERRABOA 2010 B
treixadura, loureiro, godello, albariño.

87 Colour: bright straw, greenish rim. Nose: white flowers, fresh, balanced, wild herbs. Palate: flavourful, fruity, balanced.

VILERMA

Villerma - Gomariz
32429 Leiro (Ourense)
☎: +34 988 228 702 - Fax: +34 988 248 580

VILERMA 2010 B
treixadura, lado, torrontés, loureiro.

88 Colour: bright straw. Nose: fresh, white flowers, ripe fruit, dried herbs. Palate: flavourful, fruity, good acidity.

VIÑA MEIN S.L.

Mein, s/n
32420 Leiro (Ourense)
☎: +34 617 326 248 - Fax: +34 988 488 732
info.bodega@vinamein.com
www.vinamein.com

VIÑA MEIN 2010 B
treixadura, godello, loureiro, torrontés, albariño, otras.

90 Colour: bright straw, greenish rim. Nose: ripe fruit, tropical fruit, balanced, wild herbs. Palate: flavourful, rich.

VIÑA MEIN 2009 BFB
treixadura, godello, loureiro, torrontés, albariño, otras.

91 Colour: bright straw. Nose: powerfull, varietal, candied fruit, citrus fruit, white flowers. Palate: flavourful, fruity, fleshy.

VITIVINÍCOLA DEL RIBEIRO - VIÑA COSTEIRA

Valdepereira, s/n
32415 Ribadavia (Ourense)
☎: +34 988 477 210 - Fax: +34 988 470 330
info@pazoribeiro.com
www.vinoribeiro.com

COLECCIÓN COSTEIRA TREIXADURA DO RIBEIRO 2010 B
treixadura.

89 Colour: bright straw. Nose: fresh, fresh fruit, white flowers, expressive, scrubland, varietal. Palate: flavourful, fruity, good acidity, balanced.

VIÑA COSTEIRA 2010 B
treixadura, torrontés, otras.

88 Colour: bright straw, greenish rim. Nose: fresh fruit, balanced, expressive. Palate: flavourful, fruity, good acidity, balanced.

PAZO 2010 B
palomino, torrontés.

86 Colour: bright straw. Nose: floral, ripe fruit, citrus fruit. Palate: flavourful, fruity, good acidity.

COLECCIÓN COSTEIRA TREIXADURA BARRICA 2009 BFB
100% treixadura.

88 Colour: bright straw, greenish rim. Nose: ripe fruit, spicy, balanced. Palate: flavourful, fruity, good structure, spicy.

ALÉN DA ISTORIA 2009 T
caiño, brancellao, sousón, mencía.

82 Colour: bright cherry, purple rim. Nose: scrubland, balanced, red berry notes, ripe fruit. Palate: correct, lacks balance.

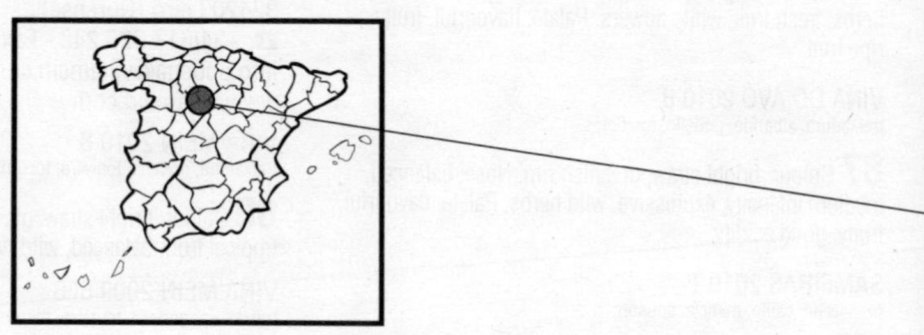

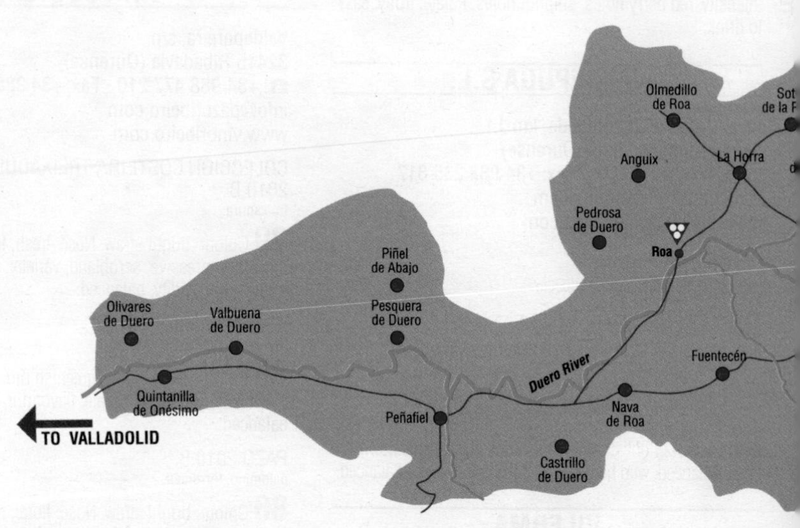
Olmedillo de Roa
Anguix
La Horra
Pedrosa de Duero
Roa
Piñel de Abajo
Pesquera de Duero
Olivares de Duero
Valbuena de Duero
Quintanilla de Onésimo
Duero River
Fuentecén
Nava de Roa
Peñafiel
Castrillo de Duero
TO VALLADOLID

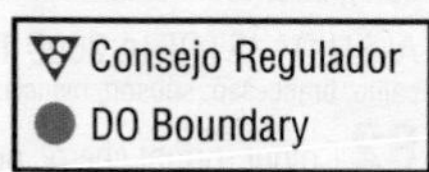
Consejo Regulador
DO Boundary

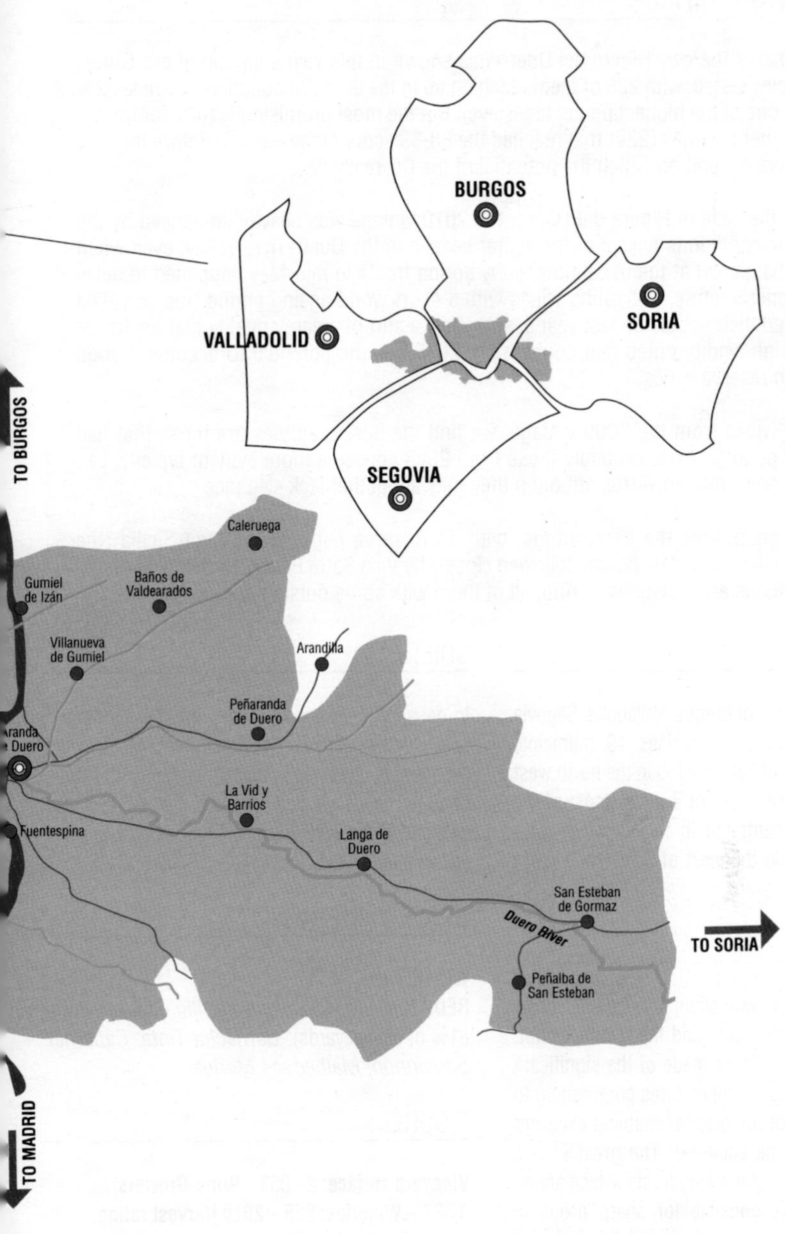
BURGOS
SORIA
VALLADOLID
SEGOVIA
TO BURGOS
TO MADRID
Caleruega
Gumiel de Izán
Baños de Valdearados
Villanueva de Gumiel
Arandilla
Peñaranda de Duero
Aranda de Duero
La Vid y Barrios
Fuentespina
Langa de Duero
San Esteban de Gormaz
Duero River
Peñalba de San Esteban
TO SORIA

DO RIBERA DEL DUERO

NEWS ABOUT THE VINTAGE:

Unstoppable, that is the way Ribera del Duero has shown in this year's edition of our Guide. Up to 652 samples tasted, with 225 of them reaching up to the 90-point boundary, a whole 32% of the total and one of the highest percentages ever. But the most promising feature for the DO is the great number of wines (220) that reached the 88-89 score range –and therefore the very doors of excellence–, and on which the potential of the DO really lies.

As it is usually the case in Ribera del Duero, the 2010 vintage was heavily influenced by the extreme climatic conditions typical of the winter season in the Duero river valley: even when the bud-break happened at the usual time, early spring frosts in mid-May happened to delay the cycle. In general terms, red young wines with a short wood-ageing period (the so-called robles) improved their scores on last year's, and show a sort of creamy quality that neutralize any green or high acidity notes that could arise. 2010 has the potential to become a good vintage for gran reserva wines.

Regarding red wines from the 2009 vintage, we find the best examples are those that had shorter ageing periods, while probably those from 2008 convey a more evident typicity, i.e., they are meaty and more powerful, although they may altogether lack elegance.

Vega Sicilia monopolizes the best ratings, with its Reserva Especial de Vega Sicilia (the "classic") top of the DO and 97 points, followed closely by Viña Satre Pesus, Dominio de Atauta Valdegatiles, Pingus and Valvuena 5º Año, all of them with some outstanding 96 points.

LOCATE:

Between the provinces of Burgos, Valladolid, Segovia and Soria. This region comprises 19 municipal districts in the east of Valladolid, 5 in the north west of Segovia, 59 in the south of Burgos (most of the vineyards are concentrated in this province with 10,000 Ha) and 6 in the west of Soria.en la parte occidental de Soria.

CLIMATE:

Continental in nature, with slight Atlantic influences. The winters are rather cold and the summers hot, although mention must be made of the significant difference in day-night temperatures contributing to the slow ripening of the grapes, enabling excellent acidity indexes to be achieved. The greatest risk factor in the region is the spring frosts, which are on many occasions responsible for sharp drops in production. The average annual rainfall is between 450 mm and 500 mm.

SOIL:

In general, the soils are loose, not very fertile and with a rather high limestone content. Most of the sediment is composed of layers of sandy limestone or clay. The vineyards are located on the interfluvial hills and in the valleys at an altitude of between 700 and 850 m.

GRAPE VARIETIES:

WHITE: *Albillo.*
RED: *Tinta del País* (*Tempranillo* – majority with 81% of all vineyards), *Garnacha Tinta, Cabernet Sauvignon, Malbec* and *Merlot.*

FIGURES:

Vineyard surface: 21,053 – **Wine-Growers:** 8,337 – **Wineries:** 255 – **2010 Harvest rating:** Excellent – **Production:** 72,549,642 litres – **Market percentages:** 68% domestic. 32% export

CONSEJO REGULADOR
Hospital, 6
09300 Roa (Burgos)
☎: +34 947 541 221 - Fax: +34 947 541 116
@ info@riberadelduero.es
www.riberadelduero.es

GENERAL CHARACTERISTICS OF THE WINES

ROSÉS	They are onion skin coloured, fruity and flavourful, although on occasions they may be a little alcoholic and heavy.
REDS	These are the top wines of the DO. Produced mainly from a red grape variety of the country (*Tempranillo*), they are an intense cherry colour. On the nose, they are characterised by their noses of very ripe fruit, with the great character of the skins which is normally reminiscent of the smell of ink, although there are also young wines with rustic notes. Ageing in barrels allows these powerful wines to mellow and to acquire greater elegance. Their solid tannins and fine structure make them exceptional products for ageing in wood and in the bottle. On the palate, the red wines from Ribera are powerful, with body and a good balance between alcohol and acidity.

VINTAGE RATING PEÑÍNGUIDE

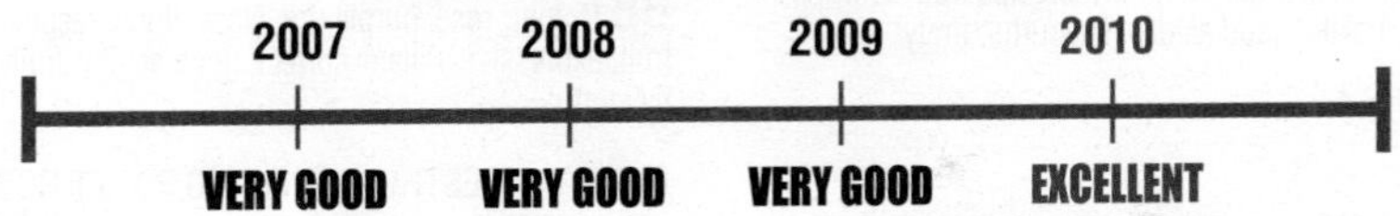

AALTO BODEGAS Y VIÑEDOS

Paraje Vallejo de Carril, s/n
47360 Quintanilla de Arriba (Valladolid)
☎: +34 620 351 182 - Fax: +34 983 036 949
aalto@aalto.es
www.aalto.es

AALTO 2008 T
100% tempranillo.

92 Colour: cherry, garnet rim. Nose: ripe fruit, dark chocolate, sweet spices, complex. Palate: fleshy, complex, flavourful, round tannins.

AALTO PS 2006 T
100% tempranillo.

93 Colour: deep cherry, garnet rim. Nose: characterful, complex, creamy oak, sweet spices, ripe fruit. Palate: good structure, fleshy, round tannins, long.

ABADÍA DE ACÓN

Ctra. Hontangas, Km. 0,4
09391 Castrillo de la Vega (Burgos)
☎: +34 947 509 292 - Fax: +34 947 508 586
abadiadeacon@abadiadeacon.com
www.abadiadeacon.com

ACÓN 2009 T ROBLE
tempranillo.

88 Colour: cherry, garnet rim. Nose: ripe fruit, overripe fruit, spicy. Palate: good acidity, flavourful, fruity.

ACÓN 2009 T
tempranillo.

85 Colour: cherry, garnet rim. Nose: overripe fruit, sweet spices. Palate: fruity, flavourful, roasted-coffee aftertaste, round tannins.

ACÓN 2007 TC
tempranillo.

90 Colour: cherry, garnet rim. Nose: ripe fruit, spicy, creamy oak, toasty, grassy. Palate: powerful, flavourful, toasty, round tannins.

ACÓN 2006 TR
85% tempranillo, 15% cabernet sauvignon.

92 Color cherry, garnet rim. Aroma ripe fruit, spicy, creamy oak, toasty, complex. Taste powerful, flavourful, toasty, round tannins.

ALEJANDRO FERNÁNDEZ TINTO PESQUERA

Real, 2
47315 Pesquera de Duero (Valladolid)
☎: +34 983 870 037 - Fax: +34 983 870 088
pesquera@pesqueraafernandez.com
www.grupopesquera.com

TINTO PESQUERA 2008 TC

89 Colour: cherry, garnet rim. Nose: ripe fruit, medium intensity, toasty, sweet spices. Palate: flavourful, fleshy, correct.

TINTO PESQUERA 2006 TR
tinto fino.

91 Colour: cherry, garnet rim. Nose: ripe fruit, spicy, aromatic coffee, fine reductive notes. Palate: easy to drink, ripe fruit, fine bitter notes.

ANTA BANDERAS

Ctra. Palencia-Aranda, Km. 68
09443 Villalba de Duero (Burgos)
☎: +34 947 613 050 - Fax: +34 947 613 051
info@antabanderas.com
www.antabodegas.com

ANTA BANDERA AR 2010 RD
80% tempranillo, 20% merlot.

88 Colour: rose, purple rim. Nose: floral, raspberry, fresh fruit, expressive. Palate: correct, good acidity, fruity, flavourful.

ANTA A4 NUESTRO EQUILIBRIO 2009 T ROBLE
100% tempranillo.

86 Colour: bright cherry. Nose: sweet spices, expressive, grassy. Palate: flavourful, fruity, toasty, round tannins.

ANTA A16 SELECCIÓN NUESTRA EXCELENCIA 2008 T
80% tempranillo, 15% cabernet sauvignon, 5% merlot.

87 Colour: cherry, garnet rim. Nose: overripe fruit, toasty, spicy. Palate: fruity, flavourful, fleshy, round tannins.

ANTA A10 BANDERAS NUESTRA PERFECCIÓN 2008 T
85% tempranillo, 15% cabernet sauvignon, 5% merlot.

85 Colour: cherry, garnet rim. Nose: overripe fruit, toasty, spicy. Palate: good acidity, flavourful, round tannins.

A DE ANTA MAGNUM 2004 T
80% tempranillo, 20% cabernet sauvignon.

88 Colour: cherry, garnet rim. Nose: ripe fruit, spicy, toasty, roasted coffee. Palate: powerful, flavourful, toasty, round tannins.

ARZUAGA NAVARRO

Ctra. N-122, Km. 325
47350 Quintanilla de Onésimo (Valladolid)
☎: +34 983 681 146 - Fax: +34 983 681 147
bodega@arzuaganavarro.com
www.arzuaganavarro.com

VIÑEDOS Y BODEGAS LA PLANTA 2010 T ROBLE
100% tinto fino.

89 Colour: bright cherry. Nose: sweet spices, fruit expression, roasted coffee. Palate: flavourful, fruity, toasty, round tannins.

ARZUAGA 2009 TC
90% tinto fino, 7% cabernet sauvignon, 3% merlot.

90 Colour: cherry, garnet rim. Nose: sweet spices, aromatic coffee, powerfull, fruit expression, roasted coffee. Palate: creamy, toasty, flavourful, fleshy.

VIÑEDOS Y BODEGAS LA PLANTA 2009 T
100% tinto fino.

88 Colour: deep cherry. Nose: powerfull, red berry notes, roasted coffee, dark chocolate. Palate: powerful, fleshy, smoky aftertaste.

GRAN ARZUAGA 2008 T
95% tinto fino, 5% blanca del pais.

94 Colour: bright cherry. Nose: sweet spices, creamy oak, expressive, fruit expression, red berry notes. Palate: flavourful, fruity, toasty, ripe fruit.

AMAYA ARZUAGA AUTOR 2007 T
100% tinto fino.

92 Colour: cherry, garnet rim. Nose: spicy, creamy oak, toasty, complex, earthy notes, mineral, fruit expression, red berry notes. Palate: powerful, flavourful, toasty, round tannins.

ARZUAGA 2008 TR
90% tinto fino, 10% cabernet sauvignon, merlot.

88 Colour: cherry, garnet rim. Nose: ripe fruit, cocoa bean, dark chocolate, sweet spices, toasty. Palate: powerful, flavourful, fleshy, toasty, round tannins.

ARZUAGA RESERVA ESPECIAL 2008 TR
100% tinto fino.

92 Colour: cherry, garnet rim. Nose: ripe fruit, spicy, creamy oak, toasty, complex, elegant, mineral. Palate: powerful, flavourful, toasty, round tannins.

ARZUAGA 2004 TGR
90% tinto fino, 5% cabernet sauvignon, 5% merlot.

91 Colour: cherry, garnet rim. Nose: creamy oak, toasty, fruit expression, red berry notes. Palate: flavourful, toasty, round tannins, fleshy.

ARZUAGA 2008 TC
90% tinto fino, 7% cabernet sauvignon, 3% merlot.

90 Colour: cherry, garnet rim. Nose: ripe fruit, spicy, creamy oak, toasty, elegant, fruit expression. Palate: powerful, flavourful, toasty, round tannins.

ASTRALES

Ctra. Olmedillo, Km. 7
09313 Anguix (Burgos)
☎: +34 947 554 222 - Fax: +34 947 554 085
administracion@astrales.es
www.astrales.es

ASTRALES 2008 T
tinto fino.

93 Colour: cherry, garnet rim. Nose: red berry notes, ripe fruit, expressive, dark chocolate, sweet spices, toasty. Palate: good acidity, rich, flavourful, fleshy, long.

ASTRALES 2007 T
tinto fino.

92 Colour: cherry, garnet rim. Nose: spicy, creamy oak, toasty, characterful, fruit expression, earthy notes. Palate: powerful, flavourful, round tannins, great length.

BADEN NUMEN

Carreterilla, s/n
47359 San Bernardo Valbuena de Duero (Valladolid)
☎: +34 615 995 552 - Fax: +34 983 683 041
bodega@badennumen.es
www.badennumen.es

BADEN NUMEN "B" 2010 T
100% tinto fino.

87 Colour: cherry, purple rim. Nose: red berry notes, ripe fruit, cocoa bean, dark chocolate, sweet spices. Palate: powerful, flavourful, fleshy, long.

BADEN NUMEN "N" 2008 TC
100% tinto fino.

91 Colour: dark-red cherry. Nose: fruit preserve, creamy oak, spicy, cocoa bean. Palate: good acidity, fleshy, sweetness, flavourful, full, toasty, round tannins.

BADEN NUMEN ORO "AU" 2008 T
100% tinto fino.

91 Colour: cherry, garnet rim. Nose: red berry notes, ripe fruit, complex, aromatic coffee, caramel. Palate: rich, flavourful, fleshy.

BODEGA CONVENTO SAN FRANCISCO

Calvario, 22
47300 Peñafiel (Valladolid)
☎: +34 983 878 052 - Fax: +34 983 873 052
bodega@bodegaconvento.com
www.bodegaconvento.com

CONVENTO SAN FRANCISCO 2006 T
92% tempranillo, 8% merlot.

85 Colour: cherry, garnet rim. Nose: ripe fruit, spicy, toasty, balsamic herbs. Palate: powerful, fleshy, flavourful.

CONVENTO SAN FRANCISCO SELECCIÓN ESPECIAL 2005 T BARRICA
90% tempranillo, 10% cabernet sauvignon.

91 Colour: dark-red cherry. Nose: ripe fruit, powerfull, toasty, earthy notes, creamy oak, spicy. Palate: good acidity, flavourful, round tannins, toasty.

BODEGA COOPERATIVA VIRGEN DE LA ASUNCIÓN

Las Afueras, s/n
09311 La Horra (Burgos)
☎: +34 947 542 057 - Fax: +34 947 542 057
info@virgendelaasuncion.com
www.virgendelaasuncion.com

VIÑA VALERA S/C RD
tempranillo.

70

ZARZUELA 6 MESES BARRICA 2010 T BARRICA
100% tinta del país.

86 Colour: bright cherry. Nose: ripe fruit, sweet spices, creamy oak. Palate: flavourful, fruity, toasty, round tannins.

VIÑA VALERA 2010 T JOVEN
100% tinta del país.

85 Colour: cherry, garnet rim. Nose: fruit expression, balsamic herbs. Palate: fruity, flavourful, spicy.

ZARZUELA 2010 T
tinta del país.

85 Colour: cherry, garnet rim. Nose: ripe fruit, balsamic herbs. Palate: fruity, flavourful, good acidity.

VIÑA VALERA 2009 T ROBLE
100% tinta del país.

86 Colour: cherry, purple rim. Nose: red berry notes, ripe fruit, sweet spices, creamy oak. Palate: creamy, fruity, flavourful, fleshy.

ZARZUELA 2007 TC
tinta del país.

87 Colour: cherry, garnet rim. Nose: fruit preserve, spicy. Palate: ripe fruit, easy to drink, slightly dry, soft tannins.

VIÑA VALERA 2007 TC
100% tinta del país.

85 Colour: cherry, garnet rim. Nose: ripe fruit, spicy. Palate: light-bodied, ripe fruit, good finish.

ZARZUELA 2006 TR
95% tempranillo, 5% cabernet sauvignon.

88 Colour: cherry, garnet rim. Nose: red berry notes, ripe fruit, powerfull, cocoa bean, sweet spices. Palate: good acidity, round, flavourful.

BODEGA CUESTAROA

Pol. Ind. de Janeiro, Tejera, 10
28110 Algete (Madrid)
☎: +34 916 289 162 - Fax: +34 916 289 291
cuestaroa@cuestaroa.es
www.cuestaroa.es

CUESTAROA 2008 T ROBLE
100% tinta del país.

88 Colour: bright cherry. Nose: sweet spices, creamy oak, red berry notes. Palate: flavourful, fruity, toasty, round tannins.

CUESTAROA 2007 TC
100% tinta del país.

90 Color cherry, garnet rim. Aroma ripe fruit, spicy, creamy oak, toasty, complex. Taste powerful, flavourful, toasty, round tannins.

BODEGA DE BLAS SERRANO

Ctra. Santa Cruz, s/n
09471 Fuentelcésped (Burgos)
☎: +34 606 338 632
dbs@bodegasdeblasserrano.com
www.bodegasdeblasserrano.com

PHYLOS 2008 T
100% tinta del país.

90 Nose: ripe fruit, creamy oak, balanced, powerfull, spicy, dark chocolate. Palate: flavourful, fleshy, round tannins, full, balanced.

MATHIS 2007 T
100% tinta del país.

91 Colour: cherry, garnet rim. Nose: ripe fruit, spicy, creamy oak, toasty, expressive, characterful, varietal. Palate: powerful, flavourful, toasty, round tannins.

DE BLAS SERRANO BODEGAS 2007 T
100% tinta del país.

88 Colour: cherry, garnet rim. Nose: fruit preserve, creamy oak, toasty, spicy. Palate: fleshy, flavourful, round tannins, full.

BODEGA HEMAR

La Iglesia, 31
09315 Fuentecén (Burgos)
☎: +34 947 532 718 - Fax: +34 947 532 768
info@bodegahemar.com
www.bodegahemar.com

HEMAR 7 MESES 2009 T
100% tempranillo.

88 Colour: cherry, garnet rim. Nose: ripe fruit, dark chocolate, sweet spices. Palate: fruity, good acidity, balanced.

HEMAR 12 MESES 2007 T
100% tempranillo.

85 Colour: cherry, garnet rim. Nose: candied fruit, spicy. Palate: correct, ripe fruit, spicy, easy to drink.

LLANUM 2006 T
100% tempranillo.

89 Colour: cherry, garnet rim. Nose: red berry notes, ripe fruit, expressive, dark chocolate, creamy oak. Palate: powerful, flavourful, fleshy.

BODEGA MATARROMERA

Ctra. Renedo-Pesquera, Km. 30
47359 Valbuena de Duero (Valladolid)
☎: +34 983 107 100 - Fax: +34 902 430 189
matarromera@matarromera.es
www.grupomatarromera.com

MELIOR 2010 T ROBLE
100% tinta del país.

85 Colour: cherry, purple rim. Nose: red berry notes, spicy, creamy oak. Palate: powerful, flavourful, fleshy.

MATARROMERA 2008 TC
100% tinta del país.

89 Colour: dark-red cherry. Nose: ripe fruit, powerfull, toasty, cocoa bean, dark chocolate. Palate: good acidity, fleshy, full, flavourful, round tannins.

MATARROMERA 2006 TR
100% tinta del país.

88 Colour: deep cherry, garnet rim. Nose: fruit liqueur notes, fruit preserve, toasty, sweet spices. Palate: fleshy, flavourful, spicy, round tannins.

MATARROMERA PRESTIGIO 2005 TR
100% tinta del país.

89 Colour: dark-red cherry. Nose: ripe fruit, sweet spices, cocoa bean, toasty. Palate: flavourful, fleshy, fine tannins, smoky aftertaste.

MATARROMERA 2004 TGR
100% tinta del país.

91 Colour: cherry, garnet rim. Nose: dark chocolate, sweet spices, fruit preserve. Palate: flavourful, fleshy, complex, round tannins.

MATARROMERA PRESTIGIO PAGO DE LAS SOLANAS 2001 T RESERVA ESPECIAL
100% tinta del país.

90 Colour: pale ruby, brick rim edge. Nose: spicy, fine reductive notes, wet leather, aged wood nuances, fruit liqueur notes. Palate: spicy, fine tannins, elegant, long.

BODEGA NOS RIQUEZA

Sánchez Calvo, 6
33402 Avilés (Asturias)
☎: +34 984 836 826 - Fax: +34 985 931 074
exportmanager@nosriqueza.com
www.nosriqueza.com

NOS RIQUEZA 2008 T
100% tempranillo.

88 Colour: dark-red cherry. Nose: ripe fruit, red berry notes, creamy oak, pattiserie, spicy. Palate: good acidity, flavourful, round tannins, fleshy, long.

BODEGA PAGO DE CIRSUS

Ctra. de Ablitas a Ribaforada, Km. 5
31523 Ablitas (Navarra)
☎: +34 948 386 210 - Fax: +34 629 354 190
bodegasin@pagodecirsus.com
www.pagodecirsus.com

SENDA DE LOS OLIVOS VENDIMIA SELECCIONADA 2008 T
tinto fino.

88 Colour: cherry, garnet rim. Nose: ripe fruit, toasty, spicy, creamy oak. Palate: good acidity, flavourful, fleshy, round tannins.

SENDA DE LOS OLIVOS FINCA LA CARRASCA 2007 T
100% tinto fino.

88 Colour: dark-red cherry. Nose: ripe fruit, powerfull, fruit preserve, dark chocolate, sweet spices. Palate: flavourful, fleshy, long, round tannins.

SENDA DE LOS OLIVOS EDICIÓN ESPECIAL 2006 T
tempranillo.

88 Colour: cherry, garnet rim. Nose: ripe fruit, fruit liqueur notes, spicy, toasty, wild herbs. Palate: good acidity, unctuous, flavourful, fleshy.

BODEGA PÁRAMO ARROYO

Ctra. de Roa Pedrosa, Km. 4
09314 Pedrosa de Duero (Burgos)
☎: +34 947 530 041 - Fax: +34 947 530 036
bodega@paramoarroyo.com
www.paramoarroyo.com

EREMUS 2010 T
100% tempranillo.

87 Colour: cherry, purple rim. Nose: wild herbs, fresh fruit. Palate: flavourful, fruity, good acidity.

VIÑA EREMOS 2009 T ROBLE
100% tempranillo.

87 Colour: cherry, garnet rim. Nose: balsamic herbs, red berry notes, ripe fruit, sweet spices. Palate: creamy, ripe fruit, flavourful.

EREMUS 2005 TR
100% tempranillo.

85 Colour: cherry, garnet rim. Nose: fruit preserve, toasty, sweet spices. Palate: flavourful, toasty, creamy, harsh oak tannins.

BODEGA RAUL CALVO BELTRÁN

Eras de Santa María, Parc. 3043
09400 Gumiel de Mercado (Burgos)
☎: +34 669 059 744
gestion@bodegasraulcalvo.com
www.bodegasraulcalvo.com

RAÚL CALVO 2009 T ROBLE
100% tempranillo.

86 Colour: cherry, garnet rim. Nose: red berry notes, ripe fruit, sweet spices, creamy oak. Palate: powerful, flavourful, fruity.

RAÚL CALVO 2008 TC
100% tempranillo.

86 Colour: cherry, garnet rim. Nose: ripe fruit, scrubland, spicy, toasty. Palate: correct, powerful, flavourful.

BODEGA RENTO

Santa María, 36
47359 Olivares de Duero (Valladolid)
☎: +34 902 430 170 - Fax: +34 902 430 189
emina@emina.es
www.bodegarento.es

RENTO 2005 TC
100% tinta del país.

90 Colour: dark-red cherry. Nose: ripe fruit, powerfull, toasty, sweet spices, dark chocolate. Palate: flavourful, fleshy, spicy, long, round tannins.

BODEGA S. ARROYO

Avda. del Cid, 99
09441 Sotillo de la Ribera (Burgos)
☎: +34 947 532 444 -
Fax: +34 947 532 444
info@tintoarroyo.com
www.tintoarroyo.com

VIÑARROYO 2010 RD
100% tempranillo.

86 Colour: rose, purple rim. Nose: powerfull, red berry notes, floral, expressive. Palate: powerful, fruity, flavourful.

TINTO ARROYO 2010 T
100% tempranillo.

87 Colour: cherry, purple rim. Nose: red berry notes, violets, wild herbs. Palate: fruity, fresh, good acidity, great length.

TINTO ARROYO 2009 T ROBLE
100% tempranillo.

85 Colour: bright cherry. Nose: ripe fruit, sweet spices, creamy oak, herbaceous. Palate: flavourful, fruity, toasty.

TINTO ARROYO VENDIMIA SELECCIONADA 2006 T
100% tempranillo.

92 Colour: cherry, garnet rim. Nose: red berry notes, ripe fruit, balanced, expressive, cocoa bean, dark chocolate, sweet spices, toasty. Palate: good acidity, fleshy, complex, flavourful.

TINTO ARROYO 2008 TC
100% tempranillo.

89 Colour: cherry, garnet rim. Nose: medium intensity, fruit expression, spicy. Palate: fruity, good structure, fine tannins.

TINTO ARROYO 2006 TR
100% tempranillo.

88 Colour: cherry, garnet rim. Nose: red berry notes, ripe fruit, powerfull, sweet spices. Palate: good acidity, flavourful, fleshy, complex.

TINTO ARROYO 2004 TGR
100% tempranillo.

88 Colour: deep cherry, garnet rim. Nose: balanced, ripe fruit, expressive. Palate: fruity, spicy, good acidity.

BODEGA SAN MAMÉS

Ctra. Valladolid, s/n
09315 Fuentecén (Burgos)
☎: +34 947 532 693 - Fax: +34 947 532 653
info@bodegassanmames.com
www.bodegasanmames.com

DOBLE R 2010 RD
tempranillo.

86 Colour: rose, purple rim. Nose: ripe fruit, red berry notes, floral. Palate: fleshy, powerful, fruity, fresh.

DOBLE R 2009 T
tempranillo.

88 Colour: cherry, purple rim. Nose: red berry notes, ripe fruit, spicy, wild herbs. Palate: flavourful, fruity, good acidity.

DOBLE R 2009 T ROBLE
tempranillo.

85 Colour: deep cherry, purple rim. Nose: cocoa bean, sweet spices, fruit preserve. Palate: toasty, roasted-coffee aftertaste.

DOBLE R 2008 TC
tempranillo.

88 Colour: deep cherry, garnet rim. Nose: toasty, sweet spices, powerfull, ripe fruit. Palate: good structure, fleshy, round tannins.

DOBLE R VENDIMIA SELECCIONADA 2007
tempranillo.

85 Colour: cherry, garnet rim. Nose: fruit preserve, roasted coffee. Palate: flavourful, toasty, round tannins.

BODEGA SAN ROQUE DE LA ENCINA, SDAD. COOP.

San Roque, 73
09391 Castrillo de la Vega (Burgos)
☎: +34 947 536 001 - Fax: +34 947 536 001
info@bodegasanroquedelaencina.com
www.bodegasanroquedelaencina.com

CERRO PIÑEL 2008 TC
tempranillo.

88 Colour: cherry, garnet rim. Nose: toasty, ripe fruit, sweet spices. Palate: powerful, flavourful, fleshy, concentrated.

MONTE PINADILLO 2008 TC
100% tinto fino.

87 Colour: cherry, garnet rim. Nose: candied fruit, fruit preserve, powerfull, characterful. Palate: powerful, flavourful, fleshy, ripe fruit.

MONTE DEL CONDE 2008 TC
tinto fino.

90 Colour: bright cherry. Nose: ripe fruit, sweet spices, creamy oak, varietal, characterful. Palate: flavourful, fruity, toasty, round tannins.

BODEGA VALLEBUENO

Ctra. Valbuena, 20
47315 Pesquera de Duero (Valladolid)
☎: +34 983 868 116 - Fax: +34 983 868 432
info@taninia.com
www.vallebueno.com

VALLEBUENO 2005 TC
100% tempranillo.

88 Colour: cherry, garnet rim. Nose: ripe fruit, powerfull, toasty, creamy oak. Palate: round tannins, fleshy, ripe fruit, spicy.

BODEGA VIÑA BUENA

Avda. Portugal, 96
09400 Aranda de Duero (Burgos)
☎: +34 947 546 414 - Fax: +34 947 506 694
vinabuena@vinabuena.com
www.vinabuena.com

FUERO REAL 2009 T
tempranillo.

83 Colour: cherry, garnet rim. Nose: ripe fruit, grassy, toasty. Palate: spicy, flavourful, fleshy.

VIÑA BUENA 2008 TC
tempranillo.

85 Colour: cherry, garnet rim. Nose: overripe fruit, creamy oak, spicy. Palate: good acidity, spicy, flavourful, round tannins.

FORO DE AUTOR 2005 T
tempranillo.

89 Colour: cherry, garnet rim. Nose: ripe fruit, spicy, creamy oak, toasty, complex. Palate: powerful, flavourful, toasty, fleshy.

BODEGA VIÑA VILANO S. COOP.

Ctra. de Anguix, 10
09314 Pedrosa de Duero (Burgos)
☎: +34 947 530 029 - Fax: +34 947 530 037
info@vinavilano.com
www.vinavilano.com

VIÑA VILANO 2010 RD
100% tempranillo.

85 Colour: rose, purple rim. Nose: floral, ripe fruit, balsamic herbs. Palate: fruity, fresh, flavourful.

VIÑA VILANO 2010 T
100% tempranillo.

85 Colour: cherry, garnet rim. Nose: fresh fruit, fresh, balsamic herbs. Palate: fruity, flavourful, fresh.

VIÑA VILANO 2010 T ROBLE
100% tempranillo.

82 Colour: cherry, garnet rim. Nose: fruit preserve, roasted coffee. Palate: slightly acidic, harsh oak tannins, smoky aftertaste.

VIÑA VILANO 2008 TC
100% tempranillo.

88 Color bright cherry. Aroma ripe fruit, sweet spices, creamy oak, expressive. Taste flavourful, fruity, toasty, round tannins.

VIÑA VILANO 2005 TR
100% tempranillo.

88 Colour: cherry, garnet rim. Nose: fruit preserve, spicy. Palate: fruity, round tannins.

TERRA INCÓGNITA 2004 T
100% tempranillo.

92 Colour: cherry, garnet rim. Nose: powerfull, ripe fruit, sweet spices, toasty, dark chocolate. Palate: powerful, flavourful, spicy, round tannins.

BODEGAS ABADÍA LA ARROYADA

La Tejera, s/n
09442 Terradillos de Esgueva (Burgos)
☎: +34 947 545 309 - Fax: +34 947 545 309
bodegas@abadialaarroyada.es
www.abadialaarroyada.es

ABADÍA LA ARROYADA 2009 T ROBLE
tempranillo.

85 Colour: bright cherry. Nose: ripe fruit, creamy oak, spicy. Palate: flavourful, toasty, round tannins.

ABADÍA LA ARROYADA 2007 TC
tempranillo.

90 Colour: cherry, garnet rim. Nose: floral, violets, ripe fruit, wild herbs, creamy oak. Palate: powerful, flavourful, fleshy, complex.

BODEGAS ALTO MIRALTARES

Ctra. La Aguilera, Pol. 4, Parcelas 124 y 126
09370 Quintana del Pidio (Burgos)
☎: +34 947 545 400 - Fax: +34 947 545 400
www.bodegasaltomiraltares.blogspot.com

ALTO MIRALTARES 6 MESES EN BARRICA 2008 T
100% tinta del país.

88 Colour: cherry, purple rim. Nose: red berry notes, raspberry, spicy, creamy oak. Palate: fruity, flavourful, fleshy, round tannins.

BODEGAS ARCO DE CURIEL

Calvario, s/n
47316 Curiel del Duero (Valladolid)
☎: +34 983 880 481 - Fax: +34 983 881 766
info@arcocuriel.com
www.arcocuriel.com

NEPTIS 2009 T
100% tempranillo.

85 Colour: cherry, garnet rim. Nose: ripe fruit, creamy oak. Palate: good acidity, fruity, round tannins.

ARCO DE CURIEL 2009 T ROBLE
100% tempranillo.

84 Colour: cherry, garnet rim. Nose: fruit expression, balsamic herbs. Palate: fruity, flavourful, round tannins, good acidity.

ARCO DE CURIEL 2009 T ROBLE
100% tempranillo.

82 Colour: cherry, garnet rim. Nose: ripe fruit, grassy, medium intensity. Palate: good acidity, flavourful, green.

ARCO DE CURIEL 2007 TC
100% tempranillo.

89 Colour: bright cherry, garnet rim. Nose: balanced, ripe fruit, creamy oak. Palate: flavourful, good structure, round tannins.

NEPTIS EXPRESION 2006 T
100% tempranillo.

88 Colour: cherry, garnet rim. Nose: spicy, creamy oak, toasty, complex, fruit liqueur notes. Palate: powerful, flavourful, toasty, round tannins.

BODEGAS ARROCAL S.L.

Eras de Santa María, s/n
09443 Gumiel de Mercado (Burgos)
☎: +34 947 561 290 - Fax: +34 947 561 290
arrocal@arrocal.com
www.arrocal.com

ROSA DE ARROCAL 2010 RD
50% tempranillo, 50% albillo.

87 Colour: rose, purple rim. Nose: powerfull, ripe fruit, red berry notes, floral, lactic notes. Palate: fleshy, powerful, fruity, fresh.

ARROCAL 2009 T
100% tempranillo.

86 Colour: bright cherry. Nose: ripe fruit, sweet spices, creamy oak, expressive. Palate: flavourful, fruity, toasty.

ARROCAL PASSIÓN 2008 T
100% tempranillo.

88 Colour: cherry, garnet rim. Nose: ripe fruit, powerfull, creamy oak, spicy. Palate: fruity, flavourful, fleshy, round tannins.

ARROCAL ANGEL 2007 T
100% tempranillo.

89 Colour: cherry, garnet rim. Nose: spicy, creamy oak, toasty, complex. Palate: powerful, flavourful, toasty, round tannins.

ARROCAL MÁXIMO 2006 T
100% tempranillo.

91 Colour: cherry, garnet rim. Nose: ripe fruit, spicy, creamy oak, toasty. Palate: powerful, flavourful, toasty, round tannins.

ARROCAL SELECCIÓN 2006 T
100% tempranillo.

90 Colour: cherry, garnet rim. Nose: ripe fruit, balsamic herbs, spicy. Palate: fruity, round tannins, balanced.

BODEGAS ASENJO & MANSO

Ctra. Palencia, Km. 58,200
09311 La Horra (Burgos)
☎: +34 947 505 269 - Fax: +34 947 505 269
info@asenjo-manso.com
www.asenjo-manso.com

SILVANUS 2007 TC
100% tempranillo.

90 Colour: cherry, garnet rim. Nose: ripe fruit, balanced, powerfull, creamy oak, spicy. Palate: flavourful, powerful, fleshy, spicy, round tannins.

CERES 2007 TC
100% tempranillo.

88 Colour: cherry, garnet rim. Nose: ripe fruit, creamy oak, spicy. Palate: flavourful, ripe fruit, round tannins, balanced.

CERES ECOLÓGICO 2007 T ROBLE
tempranillo.

88 Colour: cherry, garnet rim. Nose: powerfull, ripe fruit, aromatic coffee, spicy, creamy oak. Palate: flavourful, ripe fruit, round tannins, fleshy.

A&M 2006 TC
100% tempranillo.

92 Colour: cherry, garnet rim. Nose: red berry notes, ripe fruit, elegant, mineral, spicy, creamy oak. Palate: good acidity, round, flavourful, fleshy.

BODEGAS BALBÁS

La Majada, s/n
09311 La Horra (Burgos)
☎: +34 947 542 111 - Fax: +34 947 542 112
bodegas@balbas.es
www.balbas.es

BALBÁS 2007 TC
90% tempranillo, 10% cabernet sauvignon.

86 Colour: deep cherry, garnet rim. Nose: creamy oak, cocoa bean, fruit preserve. Palate: flavourful, good acidity, spicy.

RITUS 2006 T
75% tempranillo, 25% merlot.

89 Colour: dark-red cherry. Nose: ripe fruit, toasty, aromatic coffee, cocoa bean. Palate: flavourful, fleshy, creamy, round tannins.

BALBÁS 2006 TR
90% tempranillo, 10% cabernet sauvignon.

88 Colour: cherry, garnet rim. Nose: ripe fruit, creamy oak, spicy, powerfull. Palate: good acidity, flavourful, fleshy, round tannins.

ALITUS 2003 TR
75% tempranillo, 20% cabernet sauvignon, 5% merlot.

91 Colour: cherry, garnet rim. Nose: balanced, complex, elegant, ripe fruit, sweet spices. Palate: flavourful, fruity, good structure.

BODEGAS BOHÓRQUEZ

Ctra. Peñafiel, Km. 4
47315 Pesquera de Duero (Valladolid)
☎: +34 983 870 123 - Fax: +34 983 870 157
bodega@bodegasbohorquez.com
www.bodegasbohorquez.com

BOHÓRQUEZ 2006 TR
85% tempranillo, 12% cabernet sauvignon, 3% merlot.

90 Colour: cherry, garnet rim. Nose: powerfull, expressive, elegant, creamy oak, sweet spices. Palate: flavourful, ripe fruit, creamy, long, round tannins.

BODEGAS BRIEGO

Ctra. Cuellar, s/n
47311 Fompedraza (Valladolid)
☎: +34 983 892 156 - Fax: +34 983 892 156
info@bodegasbriego.com
www.bodegasbriego.com

SUPER NOVA 2009 T ROBLE
100% tempranillo.

88 Color bright cherry. Aroma ripe fruit, sweet spices, creamy oak, expressive. Taste flavourful, fruity, toasty, round tannins.

BRIEGO 2009 T ROBLE
100% tempranillo.

86 Colour: cherry, garnet rim. Nose: ripe fruit, scrubland, sweet spices, toasty. Palate: good acidity, flavourful, fleshy.

BRIEGO 2008 TC
100% tempranillo.

92 Colour: cherry, garnet rim. Nose: ripe fruit, fruit expression, complex, cocoa bean, creamy oak, spicy. Palate: good acidity, elegant, long, fine tannins.

SUPERNOVA 2008 TC
tinto fino.

88 Colour: cherry, garnet rim. Nose: overripe fruit, toasty, creamy oak. Palate: flavourful, fleshy, rich, spicy, slightly dry, soft tannins.

OYADA 2005 T
100% tempranillo.

89 Colour: very deep cherry, garnet rim. Nose: ripe fruit, sweet spices. Palate: good structure, concentrated, flavourful, ripe fruit, spicy, great length.

BODEGAS CASTILLO DE GUMIEL

Avda. de Extremadura, 55
09400 Aranda de Duero (Burgos)
☎: +34 947 510 839 - Fax: +34 947 510 839
castillodegumiel@hotmail.com
www.silenciovaldiruela.com

SILENCIO DE VALDIRUELA 2010 T
tinta del país.

86 Colour: cherry, purple rim. Nose: fresh fruit, red berry notes, balsamic herbs. Palate: flavourful, fruity, good acidity.

SILENCIO DE VALDIRUELA 2009 T ROBLE
tinta del país.

88 Colour: bright cherry. Nose: ripe fruit, sweet spices, creamy oak. Palate: flavourful, fruity, toasty, long.

SILENCIO DE VALDIRUELA 2007 TC
tinta del país.

83 Colour: cherry, garnet rim. Nose: medium intensity, creamy oak. Palate: fruity, round tannins, correct.

SILENCIO VIÑAS CENTENARIAS 2006 T BARRICA
tinta del país.

93 Colour: cherry, garnet rim. Nose: ripe fruit, spicy, creamy oak, toasty, complex, fruit expression, red berry notes. Palate: powerful, flavourful, round tannins, creamy.

SILENCIO DE VALDIRUELA 2006 TR
tinta del país.

90 Colour: cherry, garnet rim. Nose: spicy, creamy oak, toasty, red berry notes. Palate: powerful, flavourful, toasty, round tannins.

BODEGAS CEPA 21

Ctra. N-122, Km. 297
47318 Castrillo de Duero (Valladolid)
☎: +34 983 484 083 - Fax: +34 983 480 017
bodega@cepa21.com
www.cepa21.com

HITO 2010 RD
100% tinto fino.

88 Colour: rose, purple rim. Nose: red berry notes, wild herbs, balanced. Palate: fruity, flavourful, good acidity.

HITO 2009 T
100% tinto fino.

87 Colour: bright cherry. Nose: ripe fruit, sweet spices, expressive. Palate: flavourful, fruity, round tannins.

CEPA 21 2008 T
100% tinto fino.

92 Colour: cherry, garnet rim. Nose: ripe fruit, complex, elegant, cocoa bean, spicy. Palate: elegant, flavourful, rich, full, round tannins, toasty.

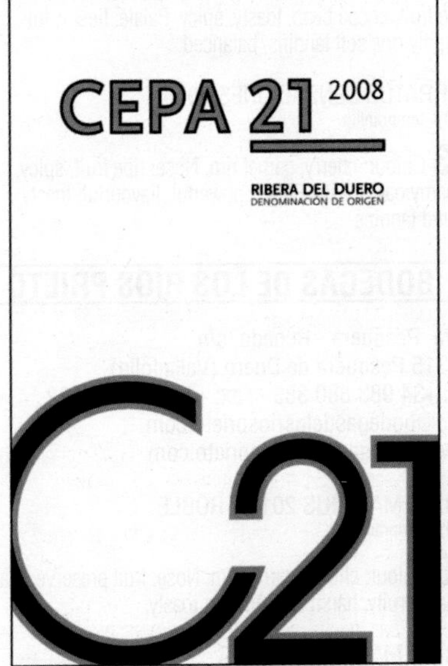

BODEGAS CHIVITE

Ribera, 34
31592 Cintruénigo (Navarra)
☎: +34 948 811 000 - Fax: +34 948 811 407
info@bodegaschivite.com
www.bodegaschivite.com

BALUARTE 2009 T ROBLE
tinta del país.

87 Colour: deep cherry. Nose: roasted coffee, smoky, ripe fruit. Palate: powerful, flavourful, fleshy.

BALUARTE 2008 TC
tinta del país.

89 Colour: cherry, garnet rim. Nose: spicy, creamy oak, toasty, characterful, ripe fruit. Palate: powerful, flavourful, toasty, round tannins.

BODEGAS CONDE SAN CRISTÓBAL

Ctra. Valladolid a Soria, Km. 303
47300 Peñafiel (Valladolid)
☎: +34 983 878 055 - Fax: +34 983 878 196
bodega@condesancristobal.com
www.condesancristobal.com

CONDE DE SAN CRISTÓBAL 2008 T
80% tinto fino, 10% merlot, 10% cabernet sauvignon.

88 Colour: deep cherry, garnet rim. Nose: ripe fruit, toasty, spicy, powerfull. Palate: flavourful, good acidity, great length.

BODEGAS CRUZ DE ALBA

Síndico, 4 y 5
47350 Quintanilla de Onésimo (Valladolid)
☎: +34 941 310 295 - Fax: +34 941 310 832
info@cruzdealba.es
www.cruzdealba.es

CRUZ DE ALBA 2008 TC
tempranillo.

91 Colour: cherry, garnet rim. Nose: ripe fruit, spicy, toasty, complex, sweet spices, cocoa bean, mineral. Palate: powerful, flavourful, toasty, round tannins, long.

BODEGAS CUEVAS JIMÉNEZ - FERRATUS

Ctra. Madrid-Irún, A-I km. 165
09370 Gumiel de Izán (Burgos)
☎: +34 638 007 140 - Fax: +34 638 010 311
bodega@ferratus.es
www.ferratus.es

FERRATUS 2007 T
100% tempranillo.

93 Colour: cherry, garnet rim. Nose: sweet spices, creamy oak, lactic notes, fruit expression, ripe fruit. Palate: flavourful, powerful, fleshy, long.

FERRATUS 2006 T
100% tempranillo.

94 Colour: cherry, garnet rim. Nose: spicy, toasty, complex, fruit expression, cocoa bean. Palate: powerful, flavourful, toasty, round tannins, long, mineral.

FERRATUS SENSACIONES 2006 T
100% tempranillo.

93 Colour: dark-red cherry. Nose: expressive, powerfull, ripe fruit, cocoa bean, toasty, spicy. Palate: fleshy, full, slightly dry, soft tannins, balanced.

FERRATUS SENSACIONES 2005 T
100% tempranillo.

93 Colour: cherry, garnet rim. Nose: ripe fruit, spicy, creamy oak, toasty. Palate: powerful, flavourful, toasty, round tannins.

BODEGAS DE LOS RÍOS PRIETO

Ctra. Pesquera - Renedo, s/n
47315 Pesquera de Duero (Valladolid)
☎: +34 983 880 383 - Fax: +34 983 878 032
info@bodegasdelosriosprieto.com
www.bodegasdelosriosprieto.com

PRIOS MAXIMUS 2010 T ROBLE
100% tempranillo.

86 Colour: cherry, garnet rim. Nose: fruit preserve, toasty. Palate: fruity, harsh oak tannins, toasty.

PRIOS MAXIMUS 2009 TC
95% tempranillo, 5% cabernet sauvignon.

87 Colour: cherry, garnet rim. Nose: overripe fruit, toasty, spicy. Palate: fruity, flavourful, round tannins, creamy.

LARA PRIOS MAXIMUS VINO DE AUTOR 2006 T
100% tempranillo.

90 Colour: cherry, garnet rim. Nose: red berry notes, fruit preserve, expressive, sweet spices, creamy oak. Palate: good acidity, powerful, fleshy, flavourful.

PRIOS MAXIMUS 2006 TR
100% tempranillo.

86 Colour: cherry, garnet rim. Nose: fruit preserve, toasty, aromatic coffee. Palate: toasty, flavourful, round tannins.

BODEGAS DEL CAMPO

Camino Fuentenavares, s/n
09370 Quintana del Pidío (Burgos)
☎: +34 947 561 034 - Fax: +34 947 561 038
bodegas@pagosdequintana.com
www.pagosdequintana.com

PAGOS DE QUINTANA ROBLE 2009 T
100% tinto fino.

88 Colour: cherry, garnet rim. Nose: ripe fruit, creamy oak, aromatic coffee, spicy. Palate: good acidity, flavourful, fruity, rich, round tannins.

PAGOS DE QUINTANA 2008 TC
100% tinto fino.

88 Colour: cherry, garnet rim. Nose: red berry notes, ripe fruit, powerfull, sweet spices, creamy oak. Palate: round, flavourful, fleshy.

PAGOS DE QUINTANA 2006 TR
100% tinto fino.

90 Colour: dark-red cherry. Nose: fruit expression, spicy, creamy oak, toasty. Palate: powerful, flavourful, round tannins, toasty, fleshy.

BODEGAS DOMINIO DE CAIR

Ctra. de Torresandino a Aranda de Duero
09370 La Aguilra (Burgos)
☎: +34 947 545 276
bodegas@dominiodecair.com
www.dominiodecair.com

CAIR 2008 T
100% tempranillo.

89 Colour: cherry, garnet rim. Nose: ripe fruit, spicy, creamy oak. Palate: powerful, flavourful, toasty, round tannins.

BODEGAS EMILIO MORO

Ctra. Peñafiel - Valoria, s/n
47315 Pesquera de Duero (Valladolid)
☎: +34 983 878 400 - Fax: +34 983 870 195
bodega@emiliomoro.com
www.emiliomoro.com

EMILIO MORO 2008 TC
100% tinto fino.

91 Colour: bright cherry, garnet rim. Nose: sweet spices, medium intensity, ripe fruit, creamy oak. Palate: good structure, fleshy, elegant, fine bitter notes.

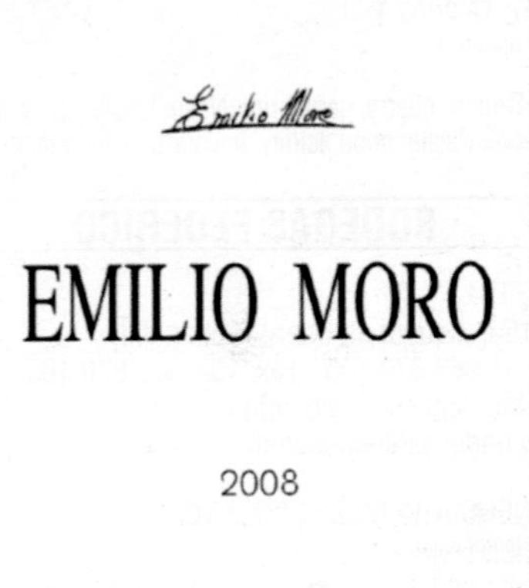

FINCA RESALSO 2010 T
tinto fino.

86 Colour: cherry, garnet rim. Nose: fruit preserve, toasty, spicy. Palate: fruity, good acidity, flavourful.

MALLEOLUS DE SANCHOMARTÍN 2008 T
100% tinta del país.

94 Colour: cherry, garnet rim. Nose: spicy, ripe fruit, red berry notes, dark chocolate, sweet spices, toasty. Palate: good acidity, round, flavourful, fleshy.

MALLEOLUS DE VALDERRAMIRO 2008 T
100% tinta del país.

94 Colour: cherry, garnet rim. Nose: ripe fruit, spicy, creamy oak, toasty, complex, mineral, expressive. Palate: powerful, flavourful, toasty, round tannins, fleshy, complex.

MALLEOLUS 2008 T
100% tinta del país.

93 Colour: cherry, garnet rim. Nose: balanced, red berry notes, ripe fruit, raspberry, cocoa bean, dark chocolate. Palate: powerful, flavourful, fleshy, complex, long.

BODEGAS EPIFANIO RIVERA

Onésimo Redondo, 1
47315 Pesquera de Duero (Valladolid)
☎: +34 983 870 109 - Fax: +34 983 870 109
comercial@epifaniorivera.com
www.epifaniorivera.com

ERIAL 2009 T
100% tinto fino.

88 Colour: cherry, garnet rim. Nose: overripe fruit, creamy oak, sweet spices. Palate: good acidity, fruity, flavourful, fleshy, round tannins.

ERIAL TF 2007 T
100% tinto fino.

88 Colour: cherry, garnet rim. Nose: toasty, spicy, fruit preserve. Palate: good acidity, flavourful, round tannins.

BODEGAS FEDERICO

Real, 154
47315 Pesquera de Duero (Valladolid)
☎: +34 983 870 105 - Fax: +34 983 870 105
info@bodegasfederico.com
www.bodegasfederico.com

AVENENCIA 12 MESES 2008 TC
100% tempranillo.

82 Colour: cherry, garnet rim. Nose: ripe fruit, premature reduction notes, toasty. Palate: lacks balance, slightly overripe.

AVENENCIA VENDIMIA SELECCIONADA 2005 TC
100% tempranillo.

82 Colour: cherry, garnet rim. Nose: fruit preserve, premature reduction notes, slightly evolved. Palate: slightly overripe, reductive nuances.

TERRACUM 2004 TR
100% tempranillo.

84 Colour: cherry, garnet rim. Nose: ripe fruit, sweet spices, toasty. Palate: lacks balance, flavourful, slightly evolved.

BODEGAS FÉLIX CALLEJO

Avda. del Cid, Km. 16
09441 Sotillo de la Ribera (Burgos)
☎: +34 947 532 312 - Fax: +34 947 532 304
callejo@bodegasfelixcallejo.com
www.bodegasfelixcallejo.com

VIÑA PILAR 2010 RD
tempranillo.

86 Colour: rose, purple rim. Nose: red berry notes, medium intensity, dried herbs. Palate: balanced, fruity, flavourful.

CALLEJO 6 MESES BARRICA 2009 T BARRICA
tempranillo.

89 Colour: deep cherry, garnet rim. Nose: ripe fruit, spicy, balanced. Palate: complex, fruity, round tannins.

CALLEJO 2008 TC
tempranillo.

89 Colour: bright cherry, garnet rim. Nose: medium intensity, ripe fruit, spicy. Palate: powerful, good structure, fruity.

CALLEJO 2007 TR
tempranillo.

91 Colour: cherry, garnet rim. Nose: ripe fruit, spicy, creamy oak, toasty. Palate: powerful, flavourful, toasty, round tannins.

FÉLIX CALLEJO SELECCIÓN 2006 TC
tempranillo.

90 Colour: cherry, garnet rim. Nose: aromatic coffee, sweet spices, ripe fruit, toasty, creamy oak, spicy. Palate: powerful, fleshy, long, round tannins.

GRAN CALLEJO 2005 TGR
tempranillo.

91 Colour: dark-red cherry, garnet rim. Nose: powerfull, expressive, ripe fruit, red berry notes, creamy oak, spicy. Palate: flavourful, fleshy, long, round tannins, ripe fruit.

BODEGAS FUENTESPINA

Camino Cascajo, s/n
09470 Fuentespina (Burgos)
☎: +34 921 596 002 - Fax: +34 921 596 035
ana@avelinovegas.com
www.avelinovegas.com

FUENTESPINA GRANATE 2010 T
tempranillo.

88 Colour: cherry, purple rim. Nose: red berry notes, ripe fruit, sweet spices, cocoa bean, toasty. Palate: powerful, flavourful, fruity.

FUENTESPINA 2010 T ROBLE
tempranillo.

87 Colour: bright cherry. Nose: ripe fruit, sweet spices, creamy oak. Palate: flavourful, fruity, toasty, round tannins.

FUENTESPINA SELECCIÓN 2007 T
tempranillo.

90 Colour: cherry, garnet rim. Nose: fruit expression, balanced, spicy, creamy oak. Palate: good acidity, unctuous, fleshy, complex.

FUENTESPINA 2007 TC
tempranillo.

87 Colour: cherry, garnet rim. Nose: ripe fruit, red berry notes, cocoa bean, creamy oak. Palate: good acidity, flavourful, fleshy.

FUENTESPINA 2005 TR
tempranillo.

89 Colour: cherry, garnet rim. Nose: balanced, ripe fruit, toasty, spicy. Palate: pruney, spicy, round tannins.

F DE FUENTESPINA 2004 TR
tempranillo.

91 Colour: very deep cherry. Nose: dark chocolate, sweet spices, creamy oak. Palate: balanced, fleshy, round tannins.

BODEGAS GARCÍA DE ARANDA

Ctra. de Soria, s/n
09400 Aranda de Duero (Burgos)
☎: +34 947 501 817 - Fax: +34 947 506 355
bodega@bodegasgarcia.com
www.bodegasgarcia.com

SEÑORÍO DE LOS BALDÍOS 2009 T ROBLE
100% tempranillo.

86 Colour: cherry, garnet rim. Nose: ripe fruit, creamy oak, spicy. Palate: fruity, round tannins, good acidity.

SEÑORÍO DE LOS BALDÍOS DON ANASTASIO GARCÍA 2010 RD
100% tempranillo.

87 Colour: rose, purple rim. Nose: expressive, fresh fruit, red berry notes. Palate: good acidity, fruity, light-bodied.

SEÑORÍO DE LOS BALDÍOS 2010 T
100% tempranillo.

86 Colour: cherry, purple rim. Nose: fresh fruit, medium intensity, fresh. Palate: flavourful, fruity, fresh.

SEÑORÍO DE LOS BALDÍOS 2008 TC
100% tempranillo.

87 Colour: deep cherry, purple rim. Nose: ripe fruit, creamy oak, toasty. Palate: correct, spicy, round tannins.

SEÑORÍO DE LOS BALDÍOS 2005 TR
100% tempranillo.

88 Colour: cherry, garnet rim. Nose: balanced, wet leather, spicy, ripe fruit. Palate: flavourful, good structure, round tannins.

BODEGAS HACIENDA MONASTERIO

Ctra. Pesquera - Valbuena, s/n
47315 Pesquera de Duero (Valladolid)
☎: +34 983 484 002 - Fax: +34 983 484 079
bmonasterio@haciendamonasterio.com
www.haciendamonasterio.com

HACIENDA MONASTERIO 2006 TR
tinto fino, cabernet sauvignon.

93 Colour: cherry, garnet rim. Nose: spicy, creamy oak, fruit expression, characterful, dark chocolate. Palate: powerful, flavourful, toasty, round tannins.

HACIENDA MONASTERIO 2008 T
tinta del país, cabernet sauvignon, merlot.

92 Colour: cherry, garnet rim. Nose: ripe fruit, dark chocolate, cocoa bean, creamy oak, earthy notes. Palate: spicy, powerful, fleshy, complex, long.

BODEGAS HERMANOS PÉREZ PASCUAS

Ctra. Roa, s/n
09314 Pedrosa de Duero (Burgos)
☎: +34 947 530 100 - Fax: +34 947 530 002
vinapedrosa@perezpascuas.com
www.perezpascuas.com

VIÑA PEDROSA 2009 TC
100% tinta del país.

88 Colour: cherry, garnet rim. Nose: ripe fruit, varietal, mineral, toasty, closed. Palate: powerful, flavourful, fleshy, toasty.

CEPA GAVILÁN 2009 T
100% tinta del país.

88 Colour: cherry, garnet rim. Nose: red berry notes, ripe fruit, cocoa bean, creamy oak. Palate: fresh, fruity, flavourful.

VIÑA PEDROSA 2007 TR
90% tinta del país, 10% cabernet sauvignon.

94 Colour: cherry, garnet rim. Nose: powerfull, ripe fruit, balsamic herbs, fine reductive notes, spicy, creamy oak. Palate: powerful, flavourful, complex, elegant, round tannins.

VIÑA PEDROSA LA NAVILLA 2007 T
100% tinta del país.

93 Colour: cherry, garnet rim. Nose: red berry notes, ripe fruit, mineral, spicy, creamy oak. Palate: powerful, good acidity, balanced, complex, fleshy, flavourful.

PÉREZ PASCUAS GRAN SELECCIÓN 2005 TGR
100% tinta del país.

94 Colour: cherry, garnet rim. Nose: ripe fruit, spicy, creamy oak, toasty, elegant, fine reductive notes. Palate: powerful, flavourful, toasty, round tannins.

VIÑA PEDROSA 2005 TGR
90% tinta del país, 10% cabernet sauvignon.

90 Colour: cherry, garnet rim. Nose: ripe fruit, balsamic herbs, fine reductive notes, spicy, toasty. Palate: powerful, flavourful, fleshy, complex.

BODEGAS HERMANOS SASTRE

San Pedro, s/n
09311 La Horra (Burgos)
☎: +34 947 542 108 - Fax: +34 947 542 108
sastre@vinasastre.com
www.vinasastre.com

REGINA VIDES 2006 T
100% tinta del país.

95 Colour: deep cherry. Nose: powerfull, warm, ripe fruit, toasty, aromatic coffee, dark chocolate. Palate: powerful, fleshy, flavourful, concentrated, round tannins.

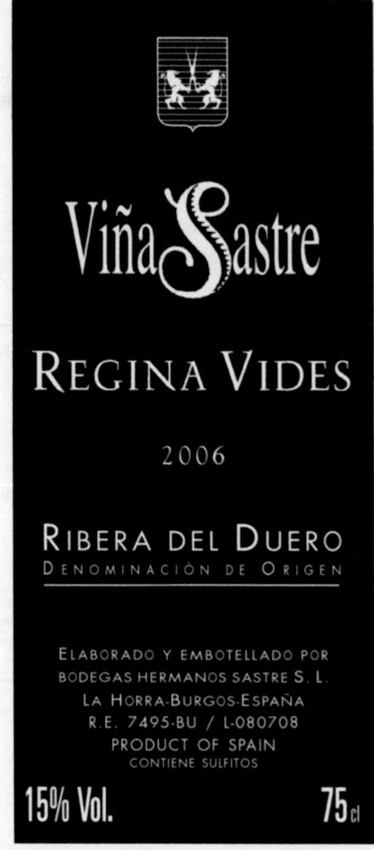

VIÑA SASTRE 2008 TC
100% tinta del país.

94 Colour: cherry, garnet rim. Nose: medium intensity, ripe fruit, complex. Palate: flavourful, good structure, spicy, round tannins, great length.

ACOS 2008 T
100% tinta del país.

93 Colour: cherry, garnet rim. Nose: complex, ripe fruit, powerfull, spicy, cocoa bean. Palate: flavourful, fleshy, complex.

VIÑA SASTRE PESUS 2007 T
80% tinta del país, 10% merlot, 10% cabernet sauvignon.

96 Colour: deep cherry. Nose: powerfull, balanced, expressive, mineral, creamy oak, sweet spices. Palate: powerful, fleshy, spicy, fine bitter notes, round.

BODEGAS HESVERA

Ctra. Peñafiel - Pesquera, Km. 5,5
47315 Pesquera de Duero (Valladolid)
☎: +34 983 870 137 - Fax: +34 983 870 201
hesvera@hesvera.es
www.hesvera.es

HESVERA 2009 T ROBLE
100% tinta del país.

86 Colour: cherry, garnet rim. Nose: medium intensity, grassy, spicy. Palate: correct, good acidity, easy to drink.

HESVERA 2008 TC
100% tinta del país.

87 Colour: cherry, garnet rim. Nose: fruit preserve, toasty, spicy. Palate: fruity, good acidity, fleshy, round tannins.

HESVERA COSECHA LIMITADA 2007 T
100% tinta del país.

86 Colour: cherry, garnet rim. Nose: fruit preserve, spicy, new oak. Palate: flavourful, powerful, round tannins.

BODEGAS IMPERIALES

Ctra. Madrid - Irun, Km. 171
09370 Gumiel de Izán (Burgos)
☎: +34 947 544 070 - Fax: +34 947 525 759
direccion@bodegasimperiales.com
www.bodegasimperiales.com

ABADÍA DE SAN QUIRCE NUEVE MESES EN BARRICA 2009 T
100% tempranillo.

90 Colour: cherry, garnet rim. Nose: ripe fruit, fruit expression, balanced, creamy oak, spicy, cocoa bean. Palate: good acidity, fleshy, fruity, full, round tannins.

ABADÍA DE SAN QUIRCE 2008 TC
100% tempranillo.

87 Color bright cherry. Aroma ripe fruit, sweet spices, creamy oak, expressive. Taste flavourful, fruity, toasty, round tannins.

ABADÍA DE SAN QUIRCE 2007 TC
100% tempranillo.

90 Color cherry, garnet rim. Aroma ripe fruit, spicy, creamy oak, toasty, complex. Taste powerful, flavourful, toasty, round tannins.

FINCA HELENA ALTA EXPRESIÓN 2006 T
100 % tempranillo.

92 Colour: cherry, garnet rim. Nose: ripe fruit, spicy, creamy oak, toasty, complex, mineral. Palate: flavourful, toasty, round tannins, complex, fleshy.

ABADÍA DE SAN QUIRCE 2005 TR
100% tempranillo.

91 Colour: deep cherry, garnet rim. Nose: balanced, cocoa bean, sweet spices, candied fruit. Palate: fleshy, great length, round tannins.

ABADÍA DE SAN QUIRCE 2004 TR
100% tempranillo.

91 Colour: very deep cherry. Nose: complex, overripe fruit, creamy oak, spicy, aged wood nuances. Palate: fleshy, flavourful, mineral, ripe fruit, balanced, round tannins.

ABADÍA DE SAN QUIRCE 2001 TGR
100% tempranillo.

90 Colour: deep cherry. Nose: elegant, spicy, fine reductive notes, wet leather, aged wood nuances, fruit liqueur notes. Palate: spicy, fine tannins, elegant, long.

BODEGAS ISMAEL ARROYO

Los Lagares, 71
09441 Sotillo de la Ribera (Burgos)
☎: +34 947 532 309 - Fax: +34 947 532 487
bodega@valsotillo.com
www.valsotillo.com

MESONEROS DE CASTILLA 2009 T ROBLE
100% tempranillo.

85 Colour: cherry, garnet rim. Nose: ripe fruit, toasty, sweet spices. Palate: good acidity, fruity, flavourful, round tannins.

VALSOTILLO 2006 TC
100% tinta del país.

91 Colour: cherry, garnet rim. Nose: ripe fruit, spicy, creamy oak, toasty, characterful. Palate: powerful, flavourful, toasty, round tannins.

VALSOTILLO 2005 TR
100% tinta del país.

89 Colour: dark-red cherry. Nose: ripe fruit, toasty, powerfull, dark chocolate. Palate: ripe fruit, flavourful, full, fleshy, round tannins.

VALSOTILLO VS 2004 TR
100% tinta del país.

92 Colour: cherry, garnet rim. Nose: ripe fruit, spicy, creamy oak, toasty, dark chocolate, earthy notes. Palate: powerful, flavourful, toasty, round tannins.

VALSOTILLO 2004 TGR
100% tinta del país.

92 Color pale ruby, brick rim edge. Aroma elegant, spicy, fine reductive notes, wet leather, aged wood nuances, fruit liqueur notes. Taste spicy, fine tannins, elegant, long.

VALSOTILLO 2004 TR
100% tinta del país.

87 Colour: cherry, garnet rim. Nose: ripe fruit, sweet spices, balanced. Palate: spicy, ripe fruit, easy to drink.

VALSOTILLO VS 2001 TR
100% tinta del país.

88 Colour: cherry, garnet rim. Nose: ripe fruit, warm, powerfull, toasty, aromatic coffee. Palate: powerful, spicy, ripe fruit.

BODEGAS LA CEPA ALTA

Ctra. de Quintanilla, 28
47359 Olivares de Duero (Valladolid)
☎: +34 983 294 381 - Fax: +34 983 681 010
laveguilla@gmail.com
www.vinoslaveguilla.com

CEPA ALTA 2010 T
100% tempranillo.

87 Colour: cherry, garnet rim. Nose: ripe fruit, balsamic herbs, red berry notes. Palate: flavourful, fruity, good acidity.

CEPA ALTA 2009 T ROBLE
100% tempranillo.

85 Colour: cherry, garnet rim. Nose: fruit preserve, toasty, spicy. Palate: fruity, easy to drink, smoky aftertaste, round tannins.

LAVEGUILLA 2009 T ROBLE
95% tempranillo, 5% cabernet sauvignon.

84 Colour: cherry, garnet rim. Nose: overripe fruit, spicy. Palate: warm, fruity, flavourful, round tannins.

LAVEGUILLA 2006 TR
95% tempranillo, 5% cabernet sauvignon.

87 Colour: cherry, garnet rim. Nose: ripe fruit, spicy, creamy oak. Palate: powerful, flavourful, toasty, round tannins.

LAVEGUILLA 2006 TC
95% tempranillo, 5% cabernet sauvignon.

87 Color cherry, garnet rim. Aroma ripe fruit, spicy, creamy oak, toasty, complex. Taste powerful, flavourful, toasty, round tannins.

CEPA ALTA 2006 TC
100% tempranillo.

85 Colour: cherry, garnet rim. Nose: ripe fruit, powerfull, spicy, toasty. Palate: powerful, flavourful, fleshy.

BODEGAS LA HORRA

Camino de Anguix s/n
09311 La Horra (Burgos)
☎: +34 947 613 963 - Fax: +34 947 613 963
rodarioja@roda.es

CORIMBO I 2009 T
100% tempranillo.

93 Colour: cherry, garnet rim. Nose: toasty, ripe fruit, mineral, powerfull, characterful, fruit expression. Palate: flavourful, toasty, round tannins.

CORIMBO 2009 T
100% tempranillo.

92 Colour: cherry, garnet rim. Nose: powerfull, creamy oak, cocoa bean, red berry notes. Palate: flavourful, fruity, fleshy, spicy, long.

BODEGAS LAMBUENA

Ctra. Fuentecén, s/n
09300 Roa (Burgos)
☎: +34 947 540 034 - Fax: +34 947 540 614
lambuena@bodegaslambuena.com
www.bodegaslambuena.com

LAMBUENA 2005 TR
100% tinto fino.

88 Colour: cherry, garnet rim. Nose: powerfull, warm, fruit liqueur notes, toasty, sweet spices. Palate: powerful, spicy, ripe fruit, round tannins.

BODEGAS LÓPEZ CRISTÓBAL

Barrio Estación, s/n
09300 Roa de Duero (Burgos)
☎: +34 947 561 139 - Fax: +34 947 540 606
info@lopezcristobal.com
www.lopezcristobal.com

LÓPEZ CRISTOBAL SELECCIÓN 2009 T
100% tinta del país.

86 Colour: cherry, garnet rim. Nose: ripe fruit, spicy, creamy oak, toasty. Palate: powerful, flavourful, toasty, round tannins.

LÓPEZ CRISTOBAL 2008 TC
95% tinta del país, 5% merlot.

91 Colour: very deep cherry, garnet rim. Nose: red berry notes, fresh, balanced, expressive. Palate: good structure, complex, round tannins, great length.

LÓPEZ CRISTOBAL 2010 T ROBLE

88 Colour: cherry, purple rim. Nose: red berry notes, sweet spices, balanced, violets. Palate: fruity, fresh, good acidity.

BAGÚS VENDIMIA SELECCIONADA 2008 T
tinta del país.

90 Colour: cherry, garnet rim. Nose: ripe fruit, balanced, spicy, toasty, cocoa bean. Palate: good acidity, fruity, flavourful, fine tannins.

LÓPEZ CRISTOBAL 2006 TR

89 Colour: dark-red cherry. Nose: ripe fruit, toasty, dark chocolate. Palate: spicy, flavourful, good acidity, fine tannins.

BODEGAS MUÑOZ Y MAZÓN

Avda. Valle Esgueva, 12
09310 Villatuelda (Burgos)
☎: +34 941 454 050 - Fax: +34 941 454 529
bodega@bodegasriojanas.com
www.bodegasriojanas.com

AZUEL ROBLE 2009 T
100% tempranillo.

87 Colour: cherry, garnet rim. Nose: mineral, varietal, fresh fruit. Palate: flavourful, fleshy, spicy, ripe fruit.

AZUEL 2008 TC
100% tempranillo.

86 Colour: cherry, garnet rim. Nose: ripe fruit, spicy. Palate: flavourful, fruity, good acidity.

BODEGAS MUSEO ONTAÑÓN

Avda. de Aragón, 3
26006 Logroño (La Rioja)
☎: +34 941 234 200 - Fax: +34 941 270 482
enoturismo@ontanon.es
www.ontanon.es

TEÓN DEL CONDADO 2009 T ROBLE

89 Colour: cherry, garnet rim. Nose: ripe fruit, red berry notes, powerfull, expressive, spicy. Palate: good acidity, fleshy, full, flavourful, round tannins.

TEÓN DEL CONDADO 2007 TC

89 Colour: cherry, garnet rim. Nose: powerfull, ripe fruit, red berry notes, creamy oak, spicy, cocoa bean. Palate: flavourful, ripe fruit, fleshy.

BODEGAS PAGOS DE MOGAR

Ctra. Pesquera, km. 0,2
47359 Valbuena de Duero (Valladolid)
☎: +34 983 683 011 - Fax: +34 983 683 011
comercial@bodegaspagosdemogar.com
www.bodegaspagosdemogar.com

MOGAR 2009 T ROBLE
100% tinta del país.

85 Colour: bright cherry. Nose: ripe fruit, sweet spices, creamy oak, expressive. Palate: flavourful, fruity, toasty, green.

MOGAR VENDIMIA SELECCIONADA 2007 TC
100% tinta del país.

88 Colour: cherry, garnet rim. Nose: sweet spices, fruit preserve, toasty. Palate: flavourful, ripe fruit, spicy, fine tannins.

BODEGAS PASCUAL

Ctra. de Aranda, Km. 5
09471 Fuentelcesped (Burgos)
☎: +34 947 557 351 - Fax: +34 947 557 312
tinto@bodegaspascual.com
www.bodegaspascual.com

HEREDAD DE PEÑALOSA 2010 T ROBLE
100% tempranillo.

84 Colour: cherry, garnet rim. Nose: fruit preserve, toasty, medium intensity. Palate: flavourful, fruity, round tannins.

BURÓ SELECCIÓN ESPECIAL 2009 T
100% tempranillo.

91 Colour: very deep cherry, garnet rim. Nose: complex, elegant, varietal, sweet spices, dry stone. Palate: good structure, fruity, good acidity, balanced.

BURÓ DE PEÑALOSA 2008 TC
100% tempranillo.

87 Colour: deep cherry, garnet rim. Nose: red berry notes, ripe fruit, floral. Palate: fruity, good structure, round tannins.

BURÓ DE PEÑALOSA 2006 TR
100% tempranillo.

89 Colour: cherry, garnet rim. Nose: fruit preserve, dark chocolate, sweet spices. Palate: good structure, complex, spicy, long, round tannins.

DIODORO AUTOR 2004 T
100% tempranillo.

89 Colour: cherry, garnet rim. Nose: powerfull, ripe fruit, creamy oak, sweet spices. Palate: flavourful, powerful, concentrated.

BODEGAS PEÑAFALCÓN

Pisuerga, 42
47300 Peñafiel (Valladolid)
☎: +34 625 184 871 - Fax: +34 983 882 156
info@bodegaspenafalcon.com
www.bodegaspenafalcon.com

PEÑAFALCÓN 2008 T ROBLE
100% tempranillo.

87 Colour: cherry, garnet rim. Nose: red berry notes, ripe fruit, sweet spices, aromatic coffee, toasty. Palate: good acidity, flavourful, spirituous, toasty.

PEÑAFALCÓN 2006 TC
tempranillo.

89 Colour: deep cherry, garnet rim. Nose: ripe fruit, fine reductive notes, sweet spices, toasty. Palate: powerful, complex, round, flavourful.

PEÑAFALCÓN VENDIMIA SELECCIÓN 2005 TC
tempranillo.

90 Colour: cherry, garnet rim. Nose: ripe fruit, spicy, creamy oak, toasty, mineral. Palate: powerful, flavourful, toasty, round tannins.

PEÑAFALCÓN 2005 TGR
tempranillo.

88 Colour: black cherry, orangey edge. Nose: spicy, fine reductive notes, aged wood nuances, fruit liqueur notes, dark chocolate. Palate: spicy, long, round.

PEÑAFALCÓN 2004 TR
100% tempranillo.

86 Colour: cherry, garnet rim. Nose: ripe fruit, toasty, old leather, sweet spices. Palate: powerful, flavourful, toasty.

PEÑAFALCÓN 2003 TGR
tempranillo.

89 Colour: pale ruby, brick rim edge. Nose: ripe fruit, expressive, cigar, cocoa bean, sweet spices. Palate: unctuous, flavourful, complex, toasty, roasted-coffee aftertaste.

BODEGAS PEÑALBA HERRAIZ

Sol de las Moreras, 3
09400 Aranda de Duero (Burgos)
☎: +34 947 508 249 - Fax: +34 947 511 145
miguelpma@ono.com

APTUS 2009 T ROBLE
100% tempranillo.

87 Colour: cherry, garnet rim. Nose: overripe fruit, powerfull, creamy oak, spicy. Palate: flavourful, powerful, round tannins, fleshy.

CARRAVID 2008 T
90% tempranillo, 10% garnacha.

87 Colour: cherry, garnet rim. Nose: ripe fruit, creamy oak, spicy. Palate: flavourful, good acidity, round tannins, fleshy.

BODEGAS PINGÓN

Ctra. N-122, Km. 311
47300 Peñafiel (Valladolid)
☎: +34 983 880 623 - Fax: +34 983 880 623
carramimbre@bodegaspingon.com
www.bodegaspingon.com

CARRAMIMBRE 2009 T ROBLE
95% tinto fino, 5% cabernet sauvignon.

88 Colour: cherry, garnet rim. Nose: ripe fruit, toasty, spicy, cocoa bean. Palate: fruity, flavourful, fleshy, round tannins.

ALTAMIMBRE 2008 T
100% tinto fino.

90 Color cherry, garnet rim. Aroma ripe fruit, spicy, creamy oak, toasty, complex. Taste powerful, flavourful, toasty, round tannins.

CARRAMIMBRE 2005 TR
95% tinto fino, 5% cabernet sauvignon.

88 Colour: cherry, garnet rim. Nose: powerfull, ripe fruit, toasty, spicy. Palate: flavourful, spicy, ripe fruit.

CARRAMIMBRE 2008 TC
95% tinto fino, 5% cabernet sauvignon.

88 Colour: cherry, garnet rim. Nose: red berry notes, ripe fruit, spicy, cocoa bean, toasty. Palate: good acidity, flavourful, fleshy.

BODEGAS PINNA FIDELIS

Camino Llanillos, s/n
47300 Peñafiel (Valladolid)
☎: +34 983 878 034 - Fax: +34 983 878 035
clientes@hotmail.com
www.pinnafidelis.com

PINNA FIDELIS 2009 T ROBLE
100% tinta del país.

88 Colour: bright cherry, purple rim. Nose: ripe fruit, varietal, creamy oak. Palate: ripe fruit, flavourful.

PINNA FIDELIS ROBLE ESPAÑOL 2007 T

89 Colour: cherry, garnet rim. Nose: creamy oak, toasty, complex, red berry notes, balsamic herbs. Palate: flavourful, fruity, round tannins.

PINNA FIDELIS 2006 TC
100% tinta del país.

86 Colour: cherry, garnet rim. Nose: ripe fruit, spicy, warm. Palate: flavourful, ripe fruit, spicy, easy to drink.

PINNA FIDELIS VENDIMIA SELECCIONADA 2005 T
100% tinta del país.

89 Colour: cherry, garnet rim. Nose: balanced, fruit expression, spicy. Palate: good structure, flavourful, ripe fruit, round tannins.

PINNA FIDELIS 2005 TR
100% tinta del país.

88 Colour: cherry, garnet rim. Nose: ripe fruit, fruit expression, powerfull, sweet spices. Palate: fruity, good structure, long.

BODEGAS PORTIA

Antigua Ctra. N-I, km. 170
09370 Gumiel de Izán (Burgos)
☎: +34 902 431 535
info@bodegasportia.com
www.bodegasportia.com

TRIENIA 2009 T
100% tinta del país.

93 Colour: cherry, garnet rim. Nose: overripe fruit, roasted coffee, dark chocolate, cocoa bean, aromatic coffee, earthy notes, dry stone. Palate: flavourful, powerful, concentrated, spicy, harsh oak tannins.

PORTIA PRIMA 2009 T
100% tempranillo.

91 Colour: cherry, garnet rim. Nose: spicy, creamy oak, toasty, mineral. Palate: powerful, flavourful, toasty, round tannins.

EBEIA DE PORTIA 2009 T ROBLE
100% tempranillo.

89 Colour: bright cherry. Nose: sweet spices, creamy oak, fruit expression, red berry notes. Palate: flavourful, fruity, toasty, round tannins.

PORTIA 2008 TC
100% tempranillo.

90 Colour: cherry, garnet rim. Nose: spicy, creamy oak, fruit expression. Palate: powerful, flavourful, round tannins.

BODEGAS RESALTE DE PEÑAFIEL

Ctra. N-122, Km. 312
47300 Peñafiel (Valladolid)
☎: +34 983 878 160 - Fax: +34 983 880 601
info@resalte.com
www.resalte.com

RESALTE VENDIMIA SELECCIONADA 2010 T
100% tempranillo.

88 Colour: cherry, purple rim. Nose: red berry notes, ripe fruit, sweet spices, toasty. Palate: powerful, flavourful, fleshy, fruity, toasty.

PEÑA ROBLE 2010 T
100% tempranillo.

86 Colour: cherry, purple rim. Nose: red berry notes, raspberry, floral, fresh, expressive. Palate: fresh, fruity, light-bodied, easy to drink.

RESALTE 2006 TC
100% tempranillo.

88 Colour: cherry, garnet rim. Nose: ripe fruit, sweet spices, creamy oak, fine reductive notes. Palate: round, flavourful, fleshy, round tannins.

RESALTE 2005 TR
100% tempranillo.

90 Colour: cherry, garnet rim. Nose: ripe fruit, spicy, creamy oak, toasty, fine reductive notes. Palate: powerful, flavourful, toasty, round tannins.

PEÑA ROBLE 2004 TC
100% tempranillo.

87 Colour: cherry, garnet rim. Nose: ripe fruit, cocoa bean, sweet spices, toasty. Palate: powerful, flavourful, fleshy, toasty.

PEÑA ROBLE 2003 TR
100% tempranillo.

88 Colour: cherry, garnet rim. Nose: ripe fruit, cigar, old leather, sweet spices, toasty. Palate: correct, spirituous, powerful, flavourful.

GRAN RESALTE 2001 T
100% tempranillo.

87 Colour: pale ruby, brick rim edge. Nose: ripe fruit, wet leather, tobacco, cocoa bean, toasty. Palate: good acidity, spirituous, flavourful, toasty.

BODEGAS REYES

Ctra. Valladolid - Soria, Km. 54
47300 Peñafiel (Valladolid)
☎: +34 983 873 015 - Fax: +34 983 873 017
info@teofiloreyes.com
www.bodegasreyes.com

TAMIZ 2009 T ROBLE
100% tempranillo.

87 Colour: cherry, garnet rim. Nose: red berry notes, spicy, wild herbs. Palate: flavourful, fruity, fresh, easy to drink.

TEÓFILO REYES 2008 TC
100% tempranillo.

88 Colour: cherry, garnet rim. Nose: red berry notes, raspberry, ripe fruit, creamy oak, expressive. Palate: powerful, flavourful, fleshy, complex.

TEÓFILO REYES VENDIMIA SELECCIONADA 2006 T

89 Colour: cherry, garnet rim. Nose: wild herbs, sweet spices, overripe fruit. Palate: good structure, balanced, round tannins.

BODEGAS RODERO

Ctra. Boada, s/n
09314 Pedrosa de Duero (Burgos)
☎: +34 947 530 046 - Fax: +34 947 530 097
rodero@bodegasrodero.com
www.bodegasrodero.com

CARMELO RODERO 9 MESES 2010 T
100% tempranillo.

89 Colour: cherry, garnet rim. Nose: ripe fruit, toasty, sweet spices. Palate: good acidity, flavourful, fruity, harsh oak tannins.

CARMELO RODERO 2010 T
100% tempranillo.

88 Colour: cherry, garnet rim. Nose: fresh fruit, floral, balsamic herbs. Palate: easy to drink, fruity, fresh, flavourful.

CARMELO RODERO 2009 T ROBLE
100% tempranillo.

89 Colour: cherry, garnet rim. Nose: ripe fruit, creamy oak, sweet spices. Palate: flavourful, good structure, round tannins, good acidity.

CARMELO RODERO 2008 TC
90% tempranillo, 10% cabernet sauvignon.

91 Colour: cherry, garnet rim. Nose: ripe fruit, spicy, creamy oak, toasty, complex. Palate: powerful, flavourful, toasty, round tannins, fleshy, complex.

CARMELO RODERO 2007 TR
90% tempranillo, 10% cabernet sauvignon.

91 Colour: cherry, garnet rim. Nose: spicy, dark chocolate, sweet spices, fruit preserve. Palate: powerful, flavourful, toasty, powerful tannins.

CARMELO RODERO TSM 2005 T
75% tempranillo, 15% merlot, 10% cabernet sauvignon.

94 Colour: bright cherry, garnet rim. Nose: elegant, balanced, complex, ripe fruit, spicy. Palate: good structure, rich, ripe fruit, round tannins.

PAGO DE VALTARREÑA 2005 T
75% tempranillo, 15% cabernet sauvignon, 10% merlot.

92 Colour: very deep cherry, garnet rim. Nose: characterful, complex, overripe fruit, mineral, sweet spices. Palate: complex, fleshy, fine bitter notes, round tannins, long.

BODEGAS SANTA EULALIA

Malpica, s/n
09311 La Horra (Burgos)
☎: +34 983 586 868 - Fax: +34 947 580 180
bodegasfrutosvillar@bodegasfrutosvillar.com
www.bodegasfrutosvillar.com

RIBERAL 2009 T ROBLE
100% tinta del país.

87 Colour: bright cherry. Nose: sweet spices, creamy oak, fruit expression. Palate: flavourful, fruity, toasty, round tannins.

CONDE DE SIRUELA 2009 T ROBLE
100% tinta del país.

86 Colour: cherry, garnet rim. Nose: ripe fruit, medium intensity, sweet spices, creamy oak. Palate: fresh, fruity, flavourful.

RIBERAL 2007 TC
100% tinta del país.

88 Colour: cherry, garnet rim. Nose: red berry notes, ripe fruit, fine reductive notes, cocoa bean, sweet spices, toasty. Palate: rich, flavourful, fleshy, good acidity.

CONDE DE SIRUELA 2006 TR
100% tinta del país.

88 Colour: deep cherry. Nose: ripe fruit, powerfull, sweet spices, cocoa bean, toasty. Palate: fleshy, complex, flavourful, fine tannins.

CONDE DE SIRUELA ELITE 2006 T ROBLE
100% tinta del país.

87 Colour: cherry, garnet rim. Nose: ripe fruit, spicy, creamy oak, toasty. Palate: powerful, flavourful, toasty, round tannins.

BODEGAS SEÑORIO DE NAVA

Ctra. Valladolid - Soria, 62
09318 Nava de Roa (Burgos)
☎: +34 987 209 790 - Fax: +34 987 209 808
c.puente@senoriodenava.es
www.senoriodenava.es

SEÑORÍO DE NAVA 2010 T
100% tinta del país.

86 Colour: cherry, purple rim. Nose: fruit expression, fresh. Palate: fresh, fruity, good acidity.

SEÑORÍO DE NAVA 2009 T ROBLE
85% tinto fino, 15% cabernet sauvignon.

86 Colour: cherry, garnet rim. Nose: wild herbs, spicy. Palate: fruity, easy to drink, correct.

VEGA CUBILLAS 2009 T ROBLE
85% tinta del país, 15% cabernet sauvignon.

84 Colour: cherry, garnet rim. Nose: fresh fruit, wild herbs, medium intensity. Palate: fruity, flavourful.

SEÑORÍO DE NAVA 2006 TR
100% tinta del país.

88 Colour: cherry, garnet rim. Nose: spicy, toasty, fruit preserve, old leather. Palate: powerful, flavourful, toasty, round tannins.

VEGA CUBILLAS 2006 TC
100% tinta del país.

86 Colour: cherry, garnet rim. Nose: ripe fruit, spicy, toasty, complex. Palate: powerful, flavourful, toasty.

BODEGAS TAMARAL

Ctra. N-122, Km. 310,6
47300 Peñafiel (Valladolid)
☎: +34 983 878 017 - Fax: +34 983 878 089
zarzuelo@tamaral.com
www.tamaral.com

TAMARAL FINCA LA MIRA 2009 T
100% tempranillo.

88 Colour: bright cherry. Nose: ripe fruit, sweet spices, creamy oak, expressive. Palate: flavourful, fruity, toasty, round tannins, fleshy.

TAMARAL 2009 T ROBLE
100% tempranillo.

87 Colour: cherry, garnet rim. Nose: red berry notes, balanced, expressive, sweet spices. Palate: ripe fruit, fruity, flavourful.

TAMARAL 2008 TC
tempranillo.

88 Colour: bright cherry. Nose: ripe fruit, sweet spices, creamy oak. Palate: flavourful, fruity, toasty, round tannins.

TAMARAL 2006 TR
100% tinto fino.

92 Colour: cherry, garnet rim. Nose: ripe fruit, spicy, creamy oak, toasty. Palate: powerful, flavourful, toasty, round tannins.

BODEGAS TARSUS

Ctra. de Roa - Anguix, Km. 3
09313 Anguix (Burgos)
☎: +34 947 554 218 - Fax: +34 947 541 804
tarsus@domecqbodegas.com
www.domecqbodegas.com

QUINTA DE TARSUS 2008 TC
tempranillo.

90 Colour: cherry, garnet rim. Nose: spicy, creamy oak, toasty, complex, red berry notes, ripe fruit. Palate: powerful, flavourful, toasty.

TARSUS 2005 TR
tempranillo, cabernet sauvignon.

90 Colour: cherry, garnet rim. Nose: ripe fruit, spicy, creamy oak, aromatic coffee. Palate: powerful, flavourful, toasty, round tannins.

TARSUS 2008 T BARRICA
98% tempranillo, 2% cabernet sauvignon.

90 Colour: cherry, garnet rim. Nose: red berry notes, ripe fruit, spicy, new oak. Palate: fleshy, powerful, flavourful, toasty, balsamic.

Ribera del Duero
Denominación de origen

Edición Limitada de 4.000 botellas | Botella Nº

BODEGAS THESAURUS

Ctra. Cuellar - Villafuerte, s/n
47359 Olivares de Duero (Valladolid)
☎: +34 983 250 319 - Fax: +34 983 250 329
exportacion@ciadevinos.com
www.bodegasthesaurus.com.com

DORIVM 2009 T ROBLE
100% tempranillo.

88 Colour: cherry, garnet rim. Nose: powerfull, ripe fruit, spicy, creamy oak, balsamic herbs. Palate: good acidity, ripe fruit, flavourful, round tannins.

CASTILLO DE PEÑAFIEL 2009 T ROBLE
100% tempranillo.

86 Colour: cherry, garnet rim. Nose: overripe fruit, creamy oak, sweet spices. Palate: fruity, flavourful, round tannins, good acidity.

VIÑA GOY 2009 T ROBLE
100% tempranillo.

86 Colour: bright cherry. Nose: ripe fruit, sweet spices, creamy oak. Palate: flavourful, fruity, toasty.

CASA CASTILLA 2009 T ROBLE
100% tempranillo.

86 Colour: cherry, garnet rim. Nose: red berry notes, ripe fruit, sweet spices, creamy oak. Palate: balanced, fruity, fleshy.

DORIVM 2009 T JOVEN
100% tempranillo.

84 Colour: cherry, garnet rim. Nose: medium intensity, fruit expression. Palate: fruity, fresh, flavourful, round tannins.

DORIVM 2008 TC
100% tempranillo.

88 Colour: cherry, garnet rim. Nose: sweet spices, creamy oak, ripe fruit. Palate: fruity, flavourful, good acidity, full, round tannins.

CASA CASTILLA 2007 TC
tempranillo.

87 Colour: cherry, garnet rim. Nose: red berry notes, ripe fruit, spicy, creamy oak. Palate: good acidity, fruity, flavourful.

CASTILLO DE PEÑAFIEL 2007 TC
100% tempranillo.

85 Colour: cherry, garnet rim. Nose: toasty, sweet spices, macerated fruit. Palate: fine bitter notes, fruity, flavourful, round tannins.

BODEGAS TIONIO

Ctra. de Valoria, Km. 7
47315 Pesquera de Duero (Valladolid)
☎: +34 933 950 811 - Fax: +34 983 870 185
info@parxet.es
www.parxet.es

AUSTUM 2009 T
tinta del país.

90 Colour: bright cherry. Nose: fresh fruit, spicy. Palate: fruity, toasty, round tannins, balanced, ripe fruit, long.

PAGO DE CASAR 2009 T
tannat, syrah, malbec.

89 Colour: cherry, garnet rim. Nose: red berry notes, fruit expression. Palate: fresh fruit tannins, good structure, flavourful.

PAGO DE CASAR 2008 T
cabernet sauvignon.

92 Colour: deep cherry, garnet rim. Nose: expressive, powerfull, sweet spices, balanced, complex, varietal, mineral. Palate: rich, powerful, flavourful, fruity, grainy tannins.

TIONIO 2006 TC
tempranillo.

90 Colour: cherry, garnet rim. Nose: ripe fruit, spicy, creamy oak, toasty. Palate: powerful, flavourful, toasty, round tannins.

TIONIO 2005 TR
tinta del país.

90 Colour: deep cherry. Nose: ripe fruit, balanced, spicy. Palate: good structure, ripe fruit, round tannins.

TIONIO 2005 TC
tinto fino.

89 Colour: cherry, garnet rim. Nose: medium intensity, balanced, ripe fruit. Palate: fruity, good structure, round tannins.

BODEGAS TORREDEROS

Ctra. Valladolid, Km. 289,300
09318 Fuentelisendo (Burgos)
☎: +34 947 532 627 - Fax: +34 947 532 731
administracion@torrederos.com
www.torrederos.com

TORREDEROS 2008 TC
100% tempranillo.

89 Colour: deep cherry, garnet rim. Nose: ripe fruit, spicy, balanced. Palate: correct, fine bitter notes, round tannins.

TORREDEROS 2005 TR
100% tempranillo.

89 Color cherry, garnet rim. Aroma ripe fruit, spicy, creamy oak, toasty, complex. Taste powerful, flavourful, toasty, round tannins.

BODEGAS TORREMORÓN

Ctra. Boada, s/n
09314 Quintanamanvirgo (Burgos)
☎: +34 947 554 075 - Fax: +34 947 554 036
torremoron@wanadoo.es
www.torremoron.com

TORREMORÓN 2010 RD
100% tempranillo.

86 Colour: rose, purple rim. Nose: wild herbs, fresh fruit. Palate: fresh, fruity, good acidity.

TORREMORÓN TEMPRANILLO 2010 T
100% tempranillo.

85 Colour: cherry, garnet rim. Nose: ripe fruit, red berry notes, balsamic herbs. Palate: ripe fruit, long, flavourful.

TORREMORÓN 2008 TC
100% tempranillo.

86 Colour: cherry, garnet rim. Nose: ripe fruit, spicy, toasty. Palate: powerful, flavourful, toasty, round tannins.

BODEGAS TRUS

Ctra. Pesquera Duero - Encinas, Km. 3
47316 Piñel de Abajo (Valladolid)
☎: +34 902 302 330 - Fax: +34 902 302 340
trus@bodegastrus.com
www.bodegastrus.com

KREL 2009 T ROBLE
100% tinto fino.

91 Colour: deep cherry, garnet rim. Nose: spicy, aged wood nuances, creamy oak, toasty, earthy notes, ripe fruit, fruit expression. Palate: fleshy, spicy, fruity.

KREL 2008 T ROBLE
100% tinto fino.

89 Colour: dark-red cherry, garnet rim. Nose: ripe fruit, spicy, toasty, aged wood nuances, earthy notes. Palate: flavourful, fleshy, toasty, round tannins.

TRUS 2005 TR
100% tinto fino.

91 Colour: cherry, garnet rim. Nose: ripe fruit, spicy, powerfull, expressive, toasty, cocoa bean, dark chocolate. Palate: flavourful, fleshy, balanced, round tannins.

BODEGAS VALDAYA

Ctra. de Burgos, s/n
09441 Sotillo de la Ribera (Burgos)
☎: +34 947 532 450 - Fax: +34 947 532 476
info@valdaya.com
www.bodegaspigon.com

VALDAYA 2009 T ROBLE
100% tinta del país.

87 Colour: deep cherry, garnet rim. Nose: red berry notes, ripe fruit, spicy, medium intensity. Palate: fruity, good acidity.

VALDAYA 2007 TC
100% tinta del país.

87 Colour: cherry, garnet rim. Nose: ripe fruit, spicy, creamy oak, toasty, complex. Palate: powerful, flavourful, toasty.

VALDAYA VENDIMIA SELECCIONADA 2007 TC
100% tinta del país.

87 Colour: cherry, garnet rim. Nose: overripe fruit, spicy, creamy oak. Palate: flavourful, fleshy, round tannins.

BODEGAS VALDEBILLA

Camino de Valdeande, s/n
09453 Tubilla del Lago (Burgos)
☎: +34 626 643 160 - Fax: +34 947 510 531
info@valdelago.com
www.valdelago.com

VALDELAGO 2008 T ROBLE
100% tempranillo.

86 Colour: cherry, garnet rim. Nose: red berry notes, ripe fruit, expressive, spicy, dark chocolate, toasty. Palate: good acidity, round, flavourful.

GAYUBAR 2008 T ROBLE
100% tempranillo.

84 Colour: cherry, garnet rim. Nose: fruit preserve, sweet spices, toasty. Palate: flavourful, round tannins, easy to drink.

VALDELAGO 2007 TR
100% tempranillo.

88 Colour: cherry, garnet rim. Nose: red berry notes, ripe fruit, balsamic herbs, spicy, creamy oak. Palate: good acidity, long, flavourful, fleshy.

VALDELAGO 2007 TC
100% tempranillo.

87 Colour: dark-red cherry. Nose: fruit preserve, toasty, powerfull. Palate: flavourful, powerful, round tannins, toasty.

BODEGAS VALDEVIÑAS

Ctra. Nacional 122, Km. 245
42320 Langa de Duero (Soria)
☎: +34 975 186 000 - Fax: +34 975 186 012
info@valdevinas.es
www.valdevinas.es

MIRAT 2004 TC
100% tempranillo.

89 Colour: cherry, garnet rim. Nose: spicy, toasty, ripe fruit, warm. Palate: flavourful, fleshy, spicy, ripe fruit.

TINAR DE MIRAT 2004 TC
100% tempranillo.

86 Colour: cherry, garnet rim. Nose: ripe fruit, candied fruit, spicy, wild herbs. Palate: fruity, round tannins.

MIRAT 2003 TR
100% tempranillo.

90 Colour: deep cherry. Nose: powerfull, fruit liqueur notes, ripe fruit, toasty, spicy, aged wood nuances, dark chocolate. Palate: flavourful, powerful, fleshy.

MIRAT 2003 TC
100% tempranillo.

87 Colour: deep cherry, garnet rim. Nose: powerfull, spicy, candied fruit, toasty. Palate: flavourful, fleshy.

BODEGAS VALDUBÓN

Antigua N-I, Km. 151
09460 Milagros (Burgos)
☎: +34 947 546 251 - Fax: +34 947 546 250
valdubon@valdubon.es
www.valdubon.es

VALDUBÓN DIEZ 2010 T
tinta del país.

91 Colour: cherry, garnet rim. Nose: ripe fruit, earthy notes, balanced, creamy oak, spicy, cocoa bean. Palate: balanced, fruity, long, spicy, fine tannins.

VALDUBÓN 2009 T
100% tinta del país.

88 Color cherry, purple rim. Aroma expressive, fresh fruit, red berry notes, floral. Taste flavourful, fruity, good acidity, round tannins.

VALDUBÓN 2009 T ROBLE
tempranillo.

86 Colour: cherry, garnet rim. Nose: overripe fruit, toasty, warm. Palate: good acidity, fleshy, fruity, flavourful, round tannins.

VALDUBÓN 2007 TC
tempranillo.

87 Colour: cherry, garnet rim. Nose: ripe fruit, spicy, toasty. Palate: powerful, flavourful, toasty, round tannins.

HONORIS DE VALDUBÓN 2006 T
tempranillo, cabernet sauvignon, merlot.

92 Colour: cherry, garnet rim. Nose: spicy, creamy oak, toasty, fragrant herbs. Palate: powerful, flavourful, toasty, round tannins.

VALDUBÓN 2005 TR
100% tinta del país.

87 Colour: cherry, garnet rim. Nose: ripe fruit, spicy, creamy oak, toasty, complex. Palate: powerful, flavourful, toasty.

BODEGAS VALLE DE MONZÓN

Paraje El Salegar, s/n
09370 Quintana del Pidío (Burgos)
☎: +34 947 545 694 - Fax: +34 947 545 694
bodega@vallemonzon.com
www.vallemonzon.com

HOYO DE LA VEGA 2010 RD
50% albillo, 50% tinta del país.

88 Color rose, purple rim. Aroma powerfull, ripe fruit, red berry notes, floral, expressive. Taste fleshy, powerful, fruity, fresh.

EL SALEGAR 2010 T
100% tinta del país.

87 Colour: cherry, purple rim. Nose: balsamic herbs, medium intensity, fresh. Palate: fruity, flavourful, easy to drink.

HOYO DE LA VEGA 2010 T
100% tinta del país.

86 Colour: deep cherry, purple rim. Nose: red berry notes, balanced, varietal. Palate: fruity, fresh, spicy.

GROMEJÓN 2010 T JOVEN
100% tinta del país.

86 Colour: cherry, garnet rim. Nose: ripe fruit, fresh, toasty, spicy. Palate: good acidity, flavourful, fruity, grainy tannins.

HOYO DE LA VEGA 2009 T BARRICA
100% tinta del país.

87 Colour: cherry, purple rim. Nose: medium intensity, red berry notes. Palate: fruity, good structure, round tannins, spicy.

EL SALEGAR 2007 TC
100% tinta del país.

91 Colour: cherry, garnet rim. Nose: red berry notes, ripe fruit, balanced, sweet spices, creamy oak. Palate: powerful, flavourful, fleshy, complex, soft tannins.

HOYO DE LA VEGA 2007 TC
100% tinta del país.

87 Colour: cherry, garnet rim. Nose: red berry notes, ripe fruit, spicy, creamy oak. Palate: powerful, flavourful, fleshy.

HOYO DE LA VEGA 2006 TR
100% tinta del país.

89 Colour: cherry, purple rim. Nose: ripe fruit, balanced, complex, wild herbs. Palate: good structure, fruity, flavourful, smoky aftertaste.

BODEGAS VALPINCIA

Ctra. de Melida, 3,5
47300 Peñafiel (Valladolid)
☎: +34 983 878 007 - Fax: +34 983 880 620
jbartolome@bodegasvalpincia.com
www.bodegasvalpincia.com

GLORIA MAYOR 2006 T

87 Colour: cherry, garnet rim. Nose: powerfull, fruit preserve, toasty, cocoa bean. Palate: fleshy, flavourful, spicy, round tannins.

PAGOS DE VALCERRACÍN 2010 T

86 Colour: cherry, garnet rim. Nose: fresh, ripe fruit, balsamic herbs. Palate: fruity, flavourful, good acidity, easy to drink.

VALPINCIA 2010 T
tinta del país.

85 Colour: cherry, purple rim. Nose: wild herbs, fresh fruit. Palate: fruity, easy to drink, good acidity.

PAGOS DE VALCERRACÍN 2009 T ROBLE

87 Colour: cherry, garnet rim. Nose: ripe fruit, powerfull, balsamic herbs, creamy oak, spicy. Palate: fleshy, fruity, flavourful, round tannins.

VALPINCIA 2009 T ROBLE

83 Colour: cherry, garnet rim. Nose: fruit preserve, toasty. Palate: spicy, flavourful, fruity, round tannins.

PAGOS DE VALCERRACÍN 2008 TC

87 Colour: cherry, garnet rim. Nose: red berry notes, wild herbs. Palate: fruity, good structure, easy to drink.

VALPINCIA 2008 TC
100% tinta del país.

83 Colour: cherry, garnet rim. Nose: red berry notes, ripe fruit, toasty, spicy. Palate: flavourful, fleshy, lacks balance.

VALPINCIA 2004 TR
100% tinta del país.

87 Colour: bright cherry, garnet rim. Nose: fruit preserve, tobacco, spicy. Palate: flavourful, fleshy, round tannins.

BODEGAS VEGA SICILIA

Ctra. N-122, Km. 323
47359 Valbuena de Duero (Valladolid)
☎: +34 983 680 147 - Fax: +34 983 680 263
vegasicilia@vega-sicilia.com
www.vega-sicilia.com

VEGA SICILIA RESERVA ESPECIAL 91/94/99 T
95% tinto fino, 5% cabernet sauvignon.

97 Colour: bright cherry, garnet rim. Nose: fruit preserve, warm, spicy, toasty, aromatic coffee, fine reductive notes. Palate: flavourful, good structure, toasty, long.

VALBUENA 5º 2007 T
90% tinto fino, 10% merlot, malbec.

96 Colour: cherry, garnet rim. Nose: ripe fruit, mineral, dry stone, creamy oak, sweet spices. Palate: flavourful, elegant, spicy, good acidity.

VALBUENA 5º 2006 T
tempranillo, merlot, cabernet sauvignon.

95 Colour: very deep cherry. Nose: earthy notes, powerfull, ripe fruit, creamy oak, sweet spices, aromatic coffee. Palate: flavourful, spicy, ripe fruit, fine bitter notes.

VEGA SICILIA ÚNICO 2002 T
95% tinto fino, 5% cabernet sauvignon.

95 Colour: deep cherry. Nose: ripe fruit, toasty, dark chocolate, aromatic coffee. Palate: flavourful, spicy, fine tannins, fine bitter notes.

BODEGAS VITULIA

Sendín, 49
09400 Aranda de Duero (Burgos)
☎: +34 947 515 051 - Fax: +34 947 515 051
vitulia@bodegasvitulia.com
www.bodegasvitulia.com

VITULIA 2008 T ROBLE
tempranillo.

83 Colour: light cherry, garnet rim. Nose: fruit preserve, spicy, toasty. Palate: correct, flavourful, toasty.

HACIENDA VITULIA VENDIMIA SELECCIONADAS 2007 T
tempranillo.

89 Colour: garnet rim. Nose: red berry notes, ripe fruit, fine reductive notes, cocoa bean, dark chocolate, toasty. Palate: balanced, flavourful, fleshy, round tannins.

VITULIA 2007 TC
98% tempranillo, 2% merlot.

85 Colour: cherry, garnet rim. Nose: fruit preserve, sweet spices, creamy oak. Palate: powerful, flavourful, fleshy.

BODEGAS VIYUELA

Ctra. de Quintanamanvirgo, s/n
09314 Boada de Roa (Burgos)
☎: +34 947 530 072 - Fax: +34 947 530 075
viyuela@bodegasviyuela.com
www.bodegasviyuela.com

VIYUELA MALOLÁCTICA EN BARRICA 2010 T

84 Colour: cherry, garnet rim. Nose: toasty, medium intensity, fruit preserve. Palate: fruity, smoky aftertaste, grainy tannins.

VIYUELA 3 + 3 2009 T
100% tempranillo.

85 Colour: cherry, garnet rim. Nose: fruit preserve, toasty, medium intensity. Palate: good acidity, fruity, round tannins.

VIYUELA 10 2006 T
100% tempranillo.

90 Colour: cherry, garnet rim. Nose: expressive, ripe fruit, creamy oak, spicy, cocoa bean. Palate: good acidity, balanced, fleshy, long, round tannins.

VIYUELA 2006 TC
100% tempranillo.

88 Colour: cherry, garnet rim. Nose: overripe fruit, spicy. Palate: fleshy, good structure, round tannins, fruity aftestaste.

VIYUELA SELECCIÓN 2005 T
100% tempranillo.

91 Colour: cherry, garnet rim. Nose: red berry notes, ripe fruit, complex, sweet spices. Palate: good acidity, powerful, flavourful, complex, fleshy.

VIYUELA 2004 TR
100% tempranillo.

88 Colour: very deep cherry, garnet rim. Nose: toasty, spicy, fruit preserve, old leather. Palate: flavourful, round tannins.

BODEGAS VIZCARRA

Finca Chirri, s/n
09317 Mambrilla de Castrejón (Burgos)
☎: +34 947 540 340 - Fax: +34 947 540 340
bodegas@vizcarra.es
www.vizcarra.es

VIZCARRA SENDA DEL ORO 2010 T
100% tinta del país.

90 Colour: cherry, purple rim. Nose: fresh fruit, red berry notes, floral, sweet spices, creamy oak. Palate: flavourful, fruity, good acidity, round tannins.

VIZCARRA TORRALVO 2009 T
tinto fino.

95 Colour: cherry, garnet rim. Nose: powerfull, complex, earthy notes, mineral, toasty. Palate: flavourful, powerful, fleshy, spicy, round tannins.

CELIA VIZCARRA 2009 T
90% tinto fino, 10% garnacha.

94 Colour: cherry, garnet rim. Nose: scrubland, ripe fruit, earthy notes, creamy oak, sweet spices. Palate: flavourful, powerful, fleshy, complex, long.

INÉS VIZCARRA 2009 T
90% tinto fino, 10% merlot.

93 Colour: cherry, garnet rim. Nose: powerfull, creamy oak, aromatic coffee, fruit preserve. Palate: flavourful, powerful, fleshy, mineral, ripe fruit, long.

VIZCARRA 2009 T
tinto fino.

92 Colour: cherry, garnet rim. Nose: ripe fruit, spicy, creamy oak, toasty. Palate: powerful, flavourful, toasty, round tannins.

BODEGAS Y VIÑEDOS ALIÓN

Ctra. N-122, Km. 312,4
Apdo. 73 Padilla de Duero
47300 Peñafiel (Valladolid)
☎: +34 983 881 236 - Fax: +34 983 881 246
alion@bodegasalion.com
www.bodegasalion.com

ALIÓN 2008 T
100% tinto fino.

92 Colour: deep cherry. Nose: sweet spices, dark chocolate, ripe fruit, expressive, new oak. Palate: flavourful, powerful, spicy, ripe fruit, fine bitter notes.

ALIÓN 2007 T
100% tinto fino.

94 Colour: cherry, garnet rim. Nose: ripe fruit, spicy, creamy oak, complex, fruit expression, dark chocolate. Palate: powerful, flavourful, toasty, round tannins.

BODEGAS Y VIÑEDOS DEL JARO

Ctra. Pesquera - Valbuena, s/n. Finca El Quiñón
47315 Pesquera de Duero (Valladolid)
☎: +34 900 505 855 - Fax: +34 956 852 339
vinos@gvitivinicola.com
www.grupohebe.com

SEMBRO 2009 T

85 Colour: cherry, garnet rim. Nose: fruit preserve, spicy, creamy oak. Palate: good acidity, flavourful, fruity, round tannins.

SED DE CANÁ 2008 T
tinto fino.

92 Colour: cherry, garnet rim. Nose: ripe fruit, creamy oak, toasty, complex, elegant, sweet spices. Palate: powerful, flavourful, toasty, round tannins, long.

CHAFANDÍN 2008 T
tinto fino.

91 Colour: cherry, garnet rim. Nose: red berry notes, ripe fruit, mineral, sweet spices, toasty. Palate: powerful, flavourful, complex, fleshy, long, round.

JAROS 2008 T
85% tempranillo, 12% cabernet sauvignon, 3% merlot.

88 Colour: cherry, garnet rim. Nose: red berry notes, ripe fruit, powerfull, sweet spices, toasty. Palate: powerful, flavourful, fruity.

BODEGAS Y VIÑEDOS ESCUDERO

Camino El Ramo, s/n
09311 Olmedillo de Roa (Burgos)
☎: +34 629 857 575 - Fax: +34 947 551 070
info@costaval.com
www.costaval.com

COSTAVAL 2009 T
100% tempranillo.

85 Colour: cherry, purple rim. Nose: expressive, fresh fruit, red berry notes, floral. Palate: flavourful, fruity, good acidity.

COSTAVAL 2009 T ROBLE
100% tempranillo.

85 Colour: cherry, garnet rim. Nose: medium intensity, wild herbs, cocoa bean. Palate: fruity, spicy, easy to drink.

ELOY ESCUDERO 2008 T
100% tempranillo.

86 Colour: bright cherry, garnet rim. Nose: creamy oak, toasty, ripe fruit. Palate: fleshy, ripe fruit.

COSTAVAL 2007 TC
100% tinto fino.

87 Colour: cherry, garnet rim. Nose: toasty, aromatic coffee, dark chocolate. Palate: flavourful, ripe fruit, fine bitter notes, round tannins.

COSTAVAL 2005 TR
100% tempranillo.

91 Colour: cherry, garnet rim. Nose: red berry notes, ripe fruit, mineral, sweet spices, creamy oak. Palate: elegant, powerful, flavourful, fleshy.

BODEGAS Y VIÑEDOS FRUTOS ARAGÓN

Paraje El Portillo, s/n
09300 Roa de Duero (Burgos)
☎: +34 947 541 901 - Fax: +34 947 540 730
carmen@frutosaragon.com
www.frutosaragon.com

DESAFÍO 06 2009 TC
tinta del país.

88 Colour: cherry, purple rim. Nose: red berry notes, ripe fruit, spicy, creamy oak. Palate: rich, flavourful, fleshy.

DESAFÍO 2008 TC

87 Colour: deep cherry, garnet rim. Nose: ripe fruit, sweet spices, creamy oak. Palate: flavourful, ripe fruit, spicy.

BODEGAS Y VIÑEDOS GALLEGO ZAPATERO

Segunda Travesía de la Olma, 4
09312 Anguix (Burgos)
☎: +34 648 180 777
info@bodegasgallegozapatero.com
www.bodegasgallegozapatero.com

YOTUEL 2008 T ROBLE
100% tinta del país.

87 Colour: cherry, garnet rim. Nose: powerfull, ripe fruit, creamy oak, sweet spices. Palate: flavourful, ripe fruit, round tannins.

YOTUEL SELECCIÓN 2007 T
100% tinta del país.

88 Colour: cherry, garnet rim. Nose: ripe fruit, creamy oak, powerfull, sweet spices. Palate: good acidity, flavourful, fleshy, round tannins.

BODEGAS Y VIÑEDOS JUAN MANUEL BURGOS

Aranda, 39
09471 Fuentelcesped (Burgos)
☎: +34 947 557 443 - Fax: +34 947 557 443
juanmanuelburgos@byvjuanmanuelburgos.com
www.byvjuanmanuelburgos.com

AVAN NACIMIENTO 2009 T
100% tinta del país.

88 Colour: cherry, purple rim. Nose: red berry notes, sweet spices, creamy oak, expressive, varietal. Palate: powerful, flavourful, fleshy, long.

AVAN CONCENTRACIÓN 2008 T
tinta del país.

90 Colour: cherry, purple rim. Nose: red berry notes, varietal, cocoa bean, dark chocolate, sweet spices, toasty. Palate: balanced, flavourful, fleshy, round tannins.

AVAN TERRUÑO DE VALDEHERNANDO 2007 T
100% tinta del país.

94 Colour: black cherry, garnet rim. Nose: red berry notes, ripe fruit, cocoa bean, aromatic coffee, sweet spices, creamy oak, expressive, balanced. Palate: powerful, flavourful, fleshy, complex, round, round tannins.

AVAN CEPAS CENTENARIAS 2007 T
100% tinta del país.

91 Colour: cherry, garnet rim. Nose: red berry notes, ripe fruit, dark chocolate, sweet spices, creamy oak. Palate: powerful, flavourful, fleshy, complex, balanced, round.

AVAN VIÑEDO DEL TORRUBIO 2007 T
100% tinta del país.

90 Colour: cherry, garnet rim. Nose: varietal, ripe fruit, red berry notes, mineral, spicy, creamy oak. Palate: powerful, flavourful, fruity, fleshy, harsh oak tannins.

BODEGAS Y VIÑEDOS LLEIROSO

Ctra. Monasterio, s/n
47359 Valbuena del Duero (Valladolid)
☎: +34 983 683 300
bodega@bodegaslleiroso.com
www.bodegaslleiroso.com

LVZMILLAR 2010 T ROBLE

86 Colour: deep cherry, purple rim. Nose: roasted coffee, creamy oak, dark chocolate. Palate: fruity, fresh, slightly dry, soft tannins.

LVZMILLAR 2009 T ROBLE
100% tempranillo.

88 Colour: cherry, garnet rim. Nose: ripe fruit, spicy, varietal. Palate: fruity, flavourful, great length, round tannins.

LLEIROSO LL 2007 T

89 Color cherry, garnet rim. Aroma ripe fruit, spicy, creamy oak, toasty, complex. Taste powerful, flavourful, toasty, round tannins.

LVZMILLAR 2007 TC
100% tempranillo.

88 Colour: cherry, garnet rim. Nose: ripe fruit, medium intensity. Palate: fleshy, flavourful, ripe fruit.

BODEGAS Y VIÑEDOS MARTÍN BERDUGO

Ctra. de la Colonia, s/n
09400 Aranda de Duero (Burgos)
☎: +34 947 506 331 - Fax: +34 947 506 602
jvelasco@martinberdugo.com
www.martinberdugo.com

MARTÍN BERDUGO 2010 T
tempranillo.

90 Colour: cherry, purple rim. Nose: expressive, fresh fruit, red berry notes, floral. Palate: flavourful, fruity, good acidity, fleshy.

MARTÍN BERDUGO 2009 T BARRICA
tempranillo.

88 Colour: cherry, garnet rim. Nose: ripe fruit, creamy oak, spicy, cocoa bean. Palate: good acidity, balanced, ripe fruit, round tannins.

MARTÍN BERDUGO 2008 TC
tempranillo.

88 Colour: cherry, garnet rim. Nose: ripe fruit, spicy, creamy oak, toasty, complex. Palate: powerful, flavourful, toasty, round tannins, fleshy.

MB MARTÍN BERDUGO 2006 T
tempranillo.

92 Colour: cherry, garnet rim. Nose: spicy, toasty, ripe fruit, dark chocolate. Palate: powerful, flavourful, toasty, round tannins.

BODEGAS Y VIÑEDOS MONTEABELLÓN

Calvario, s/n
09318 Nava de Roa (Burgos)
☎: +34 947 550 000 - Fax: +34 947 550 219
info@monteabellon.com
www.monteabellon.com

MONTEABELLÓN 5 MESES EN BARRICA 2009 T
100% tinta del país.

88 Colour: bright cherry. Nose: ripe fruit, sweet spices, expressive, roasted coffee. Palate: flavourful, fruity, toasty, fleshy, complex.

MONTEABELLÓN 14 MESES EN BARRICA 2008 T

88 Colour: cherry, garnet rim. Nose: ripe fruit, spicy, creamy oak, toasty, fine reductive notes. Palate: powerful, flavourful, toasty, round tannins.

MONTEABELLÓN FINCA LA BLANQUERA 2006 T
100% tempranillo.

92 Colour: cherry, garnet rim. Nose: ripe fruit, spicy, creamy oak, toasty, characterful. Palate: powerful, flavourful, toasty, round tannins.

MONTEABELLÓN 24 MESES EN BARRICA 2006 T

89 Colour: cherry, garnet rim. Nose: red berry notes, ripe fruit, spicy, creamy oak. Palate: balanced, flavourful, rich.

BODEGAS Y VIÑEDOS NEO

Ctra. N-122, Km. 274,5
09391 Castrillo de la Vega (Burgos)
☎: +34 947 514 393 - Fax: +34 947 515 445
info@bodegasconde.com
www.bodegasneo.com

NEO 2008 T
100% tempranillo.

89 Colour: cherry, garnet rim. Nose: raspberry, red berry notes, mineral, spicy, creamy oak, complex. Palate: balanced, powerful, flavourful, fruity, fleshy.

DISCO 2010 T
100% tempranillo.

90 Colour: bright cherry. Nose: ripe fruit, sweet spices, creamy oak, mineral. Palate: flavourful, fruity, toasty, fleshy, complex.

EL ARTE DE VIVIR 2010 T
100% tempranillo.

88 Colour: cherry, purple rim. Nose: red berry notes, raspberry, expressive, mineral. Palate: good acidity, spicy, powerful, flavourful.

SENTIDO 2009 T
100% tempranillo.

90 Colour: cherry, purple rim. Nose: ripe fruit, mineral, cocoa bean, sweet spices, toasty. Palate: powerful, flavourful, fruity, fleshy, balanced.

BODEGAS Y VIÑEDOS ORTEGA FOURNIER

Finca El Pinar, s/n
09316 Berlangas de Roa (Burgos)
☎: +34 947 533 006 - Fax: +34 947 533 010
jmortega@ofournier.com
www.ofournier.com

URBAN RIBERA 2008 T ROBLE
100% tinta del país.

89 Colour: cherry, garnet rim. Nose: raspberry, red berry notes, ripe fruit, wild herbs, mineral, creamy oak. Palate: good acidity, fruity, flavourful, toasty.

SPIGA 2006 T
100% tinta del país.

88 Colour: cherry, garnet rim. Nose: red berry notes, ripe fruit, sweet spices, creamy oak. Palate: ripe fruit, fleshy, flavourful.

ALFA SPIGA 2005 T
tinta del país.

92 Colour: cherry, garnet rim. Nose: ripe fruit, spicy, creamy oak, toasty, complex, mineral. Palate: powerful, flavourful, toasty, complex.

BODEGAS Y VIÑEDOS QUMRÁN

Pago de las Bodegas, s/n
47300 Padilla de Duero - Peñafiel (Valladolid)
☎: +34 983 882 103 - Fax: +34 983 881 514
info@bodegasqumran.es
www.bodegasqumran.es

QUMRÁN 2010 T ROBLE
100% tempranillo.

89 Colour: dark-red cherry. Nose: ripe fruit, red berry notes, spicy, creamy oak, balsamic herbs. Palate: fleshy, rich, slightly dry, soft tannins.

PROVENIUS 2008 T
100% tempranillo.

91 Colour: cherry, garnet rim. Nose: ripe fruit, balanced, expressive, creamy oak, cocoa bean. Palate: rich, flavourful, long, round tannins, good acidity.

QUMRÁN 2008 TC
100% tempranillo.

89 Colour: cherry, garnet rim. Nose: ripe fruit, fragrant herbs, creamy oak, dark chocolate. Palate: good acidity, fleshy, flavourful, round tannins.

BODEGAS Y VIÑEDOS RAUDA

Ctra. de Pedrosa, s/n
09300 Roa (Burgos)
☎: +34 947 540 224 - Fax: +34 947 541 811
informacion@vinosderauda.com
www.vinosderauda.com

TINTO ROA 2009 T ROBLE

82 Colour: cherry, garnet rim. Nose: overripe fruit, toasty. Palate: fruity, slightly acidic, grainy tannins.

MUSAI DE TINTO ROA 2008 TR

89 Color cherry, garnet rim. Aroma ripe fruit, spicy, creamy oak, toasty, complex. Taste powerful, flavourful, toasty, round tannins.

TINTO ROA 2008 TC

88 Colour: cherry, garnet rim. Nose: medium intensity, spicy, ripe fruit. Palate: correct, good acidity, round tannins.

TINTO ROA 2006 TR

88 Colour: cherry, garnet rim. Nose: powerfull, ripe fruit, creamy oak, spicy, aromatic coffee. Palate: flavourful, fleshy, creamy, round tannins.

BODEGAS Y VIÑEDOS RECOLETAS

Ctra. Quintanilla, s/n
47359 Olivares de Duero (Valladolid)
☎: +34 983 687 017 - Fax: +34 983 687 017
bodegas@gruporecoletas.com
www.bodegasrecoletas.com

RECOLETAS 2009 T ROBLE
100% tempranillo.

83 Colour: cherry, garnet rim. Nose: fruit preserve, toasty, slightly evolved. Palate: fruity.

RECOLETAS 2005 TC
100% tempranillo.

90 Colour: cherry, garnet rim. Nose: spicy, toasty, warm, sweet spices. Palate: powerful, flavourful, toasty, round tannins.

RECOLETAS 2005 TR
100% tempranillo.

89 Colour: cherry, garnet rim. Nose: fruit preserve, dark chocolate, creamy oak. Palate: fruity, fleshy, great length.

VALDECAMPAÑA 2005 TC
100% tempranillo.

85 Colour: cherry, garnet rim. Nose: ripe fruit, fine reductive notes, spicy, toasty. Palate: powerful, fleshy, flavourful.

RECOLETAS VENDIMIA SELECCIONADA 2004 T ROBLE
100% tempranillo.

90 Colour: deep cherry, garnet rim. Nose: complex, sweet spices, creamy oak, fragrant herbs. Palate: spicy, ripe fruit, great length.

BODEGAS Y VIÑEDOS ROBEAL

Ctra. Anguix, s/n
09300 Roa (Burgos)
☎: +34 947 484 706 - Fax: +34 947 482 817
info@bodegasrobeal.com
www.bodegasrobeal.com

BUEN MIÑÓN 2010 T
tempranillo.

89 Color cherry, purple rim. Aroma expressive, fresh fruit, red berry notes, floral. Taste flavourful, fruity, good acidity, round tannins.

VALNOGAL 2009 T ROBLE
100% tempranillo.

86 Colour: cherry, purple rim. Nose: medium intensity, ripe fruit. Palate: fruity, correct, easy to drink.

LA CAPILLA VENDIMIA SELECCIONADA 2008 T
tempranillo.

88 Color cherry, garnet rim. Aroma ripe fruit, spicy, creamy oak, toasty, complex. Taste powerful, flavourful, toasty, round tannins.

LA CAPILLA 2008 TC
tempranillo.

87 Colour: cherry, garnet rim. Nose: ripe fruit, spicy, creamy oak, toasty, mineral. Palate: powerful, flavourful, toasty.

VALNOGAL 16 MESES 2008 T BARRICA
tempranillo.

85 Colour: dark-red cherry. Nose: fruit expression, red berry notes, creamy oak. Palate: flavourful, fruity, round tannins, good acidity.

BODEGAS Y VIÑEDOS TÁBULA

Ctra. de Valbuena, km. 2
47359 Olivares de Duero (Valladolid)
☎: +34 608 219 019 - Fax: +34 983 395 472
armando@bodegastabula.es
www.bodegastabula.es

DAMANA 5 2010 T
100% tempranillo.

88 Colour: deep cherry. Nose: candied fruit, red berry notes, creamy oak, aromatic coffee. Palate: powerful, spicy, ripe fruit, round tannins.

CLAVE DE TÁBULA 2008 T
100% tempranillo.

93 Colour: cherry, garnet rim. Nose: ripe fruit, spicy, creamy oak, complex. Palate: powerful, flavourful, toasty, round tannins.

DAMANA 2008 TC
100% tempranillo.

90 Colour: cherry, garnet rim. Nose: ripe fruit, creamy oak, spicy, toasty, cocoa bean. Palate: good acidity, powerful, long, fine tannins.

TÁBULA 2007 T
100% tempranillo.

92 Colour: cherry, garnet rim. Nose: ripe fruit, spicy, creamy oak, toasty, varietal. Palate: powerful, flavourful, toasty, round tannins.

GRAN TÁBULA 2006 T
100% tempranillo.

93 Colour: cherry, garnet rim. Nose: spicy, creamy oak, toasty, fruit expression, mineral. Palate: powerful, flavourful, toasty, round tannins.

BODEGAS Y VIÑEDOS VALDERIZ

Ctra. Pedrosa, km 1
09300 Roa (Burgos)
☎: +34 947 540 460 - Fax: +34 947 541 032
bodega@valderiz.com
www.valderiz.com

VALDEHERMOSO 2010 T
tinto fino.

87 Colour: cherry, purple rim. Nose: red berry notes, raspberry, floral, expressive. Palate: good acidity, powerful, fruity, easy to drink.

VALDERIZ JUEGALOBOS 2009 T
tinto fino.

94 Colour: cherry, purple rim. Nose: red berry notes, mineral, sweet spices, creamy oak, elegant, complex. Palate: good acidity, round, unctuous, powerful, flavourful, fruity, complex.

VALDERIZ 2009 T
tinto fino.

91 Colour: cherry, garnet rim. Nose: red berry notes, mineral, cocoa bean, creamy oak. Palate: powerful, flavourful, fleshy, complex, toasty, harsh oak tannins.

VALDEHERMOSO 2009 T ROBLE
tinto fino.

89 Colour: cherry, garnet rim. Nose: ripe fruit, powerfull, creamy oak, spicy. Palate: good acidity, flavourful, powerful, fruity, round tannins.

VALDEHERMOSO 2008 TC
tinto fino.

89 Colour: cherry, garnet rim. Nose: ripe fruit, fruit expression, elegant, spicy, creamy oak. Palate: good acidity, fruity, flavourful, round tannins.

VALDERIZ TOMÁS ESTEBAN 2006 T
tinto fino.

93 Colour: cherry, garnet rim. Nose: balanced, elegant, ripe fruit, toasty, creamy oak, spicy, aromatic coffee. Palate: fleshy, fruity, powerful, elegant, balanced, fine tannins.

BODEGAS Y VIÑEDOS VALDUERO

Ctra. de Aranda, s/n
09443 Gumiel de Mercado (Burgos)
☎: +34 947 545 459 - Fax: +34 947 545 609
valduero@bodegasvalduero.com
www.bodegasvalduero.com

VALDUERO UNA CEPA 2009 T
tempranillo.

92 Colour: cherry, garnet rim. Nose: ripe fruit, cocoa bean, toasty, dark chocolate, expressive. Palate: creamy, long, fleshy, round tannins, elegant.

VALDUERO 2007 TC

88 Colour: cherry, garnet rim. Nose: candied fruit, fruit preserve, creamy oak, sweet spices. Palate: mineral, long, toasty, ripe fruit.

VALDUERO 6 AÑOS PREMIUM 2005 TR

89 Colour: dark-red cherry. Nose: ripe fruit, balanced, spicy, creamy oak, powerfull. Palate: flavourful, fleshy, round tannins, spicy.

BODEGAS Y VIÑEDOS VEGA DE YUSO S.L.

Basilón, 9 - Cañada Real, s/n
47350 Quintanilla de Onésimo (Valladolid)
☎: +34 983 680 054 - Fax: +34 983 680 294
bodega@vegadeyuso.com
www.vegadeyuso.com

VEGANTIGUA 10 MESES 2009 T BARRICA
100% tempranillo.

87 Colour: cherry, garnet rim. Nose: red berry notes, spicy, cocoa bean, expressive. Palate: good acidity, powerful, flavourful, fleshy.

TRES MATAS 2007 TC
100% tempranillo.

90 Colour: cherry, garnet rim. Nose: ripe fruit, expressive, sweet spices, toasty. Palate: balanced, flavourful, fleshy, round tannins.

BODEGAS Y VIÑEDOS VEGA REAL

Ctra. N-122, Km. 298,6
47318 Castrillo de Duero (Valladolid)
☎: +34 983 881 580 - Fax: +34 983 873 188
bodegas@vegareal.net
www.vegareal.net

VEGA REAL 2009 T ROBLE
100% tempranillo.

83 Colour: cherry, garnet rim. Nose: tobacco, medium intensity, slightly evolved. Palate: easy to drink, correct.

VEGA REAL 2007 TC
100% tempranillo.

87 Colour: cherry, garnet rim. Nose: ripe fruit, powerfull, toasty, spicy. Palate: good acidity, flavourful, round tannins, ripe fruit.

VEGA REAL 2004 TR
75% tempranillo, 25% cabernet sauvignon.

90 Colour: bright cherry, orangey edge. Nose: old leather, candied fruit, spicy. Palate: spicy, great length.

BODEGAS Y VIÑEDOS VIÑA MAYOR

Ctra. Valladolid - Soria, Km. 325,6
47350 Quintanilla de Onésimo (Valladolid)
☎: +34 983 680 461 - Fax: +34 983 027 217
gema.garcia.munoz@habarcelo.es
www.vina-mayor.es

VIÑA MAYOR 2010 T ROBLE
100% tempranillo.

88 Colour: cherry, purple rim. Nose: red berry notes, spicy, wild herbs. Palate: flavourful, easy to drink, good acidity, fresh.

SECRETO 2009 T ROBLE
100% tempranillo.

89 Colour: deep cherry, garnet rim. Nose: medium intensity, fruit expression. Palate: fruity, good structure, round tannins, spicy.

VIÑA MAYOR 2008 TC
100% tempranillo.

87 Colour: cherry, garnet rim. Nose: ripe fruit, spicy, creamy oak, toasty. Palate: flavourful, toasty, round tannins.

VIÑA MAYOR 2006 TR
100% tempranillo.

91 Colour: cherry, garnet rim. Nose: powerfull, ripe fruit, toasty, spicy. Palate: flavourful, balanced, good acidity, ripe fruit, fine tannins.

SECRETO 2005 TR
100% tempranillo.

92 Colour: cherry, garnet rim. Nose: ripe fruit, expressive, balanced, spicy, creamy oak. Palate: good acidity, flavourful, fleshy, complex.

VIÑA MAYOR 2003 TGR
100% tempranillo.

89 Colour: bright cherry, garnet rim. Nose: balanced, complex, ripe fruit. Palate: fruity, round tannins.

CEPAS Y BODEGAS

Paseo de Zorrilla, 77 - 3º D
47001 Valladolid (Valladolid)
☎: +34 983 355 543 - Fax: +34 983 340 824
info@cepasybodegas.com
www.cepasybodegas.com

ACONTIA 2009 T
100% tempranillo.

89 Colour: cherry, garnet rim. Nose: wild herbs, red berry notes, balanced, expressive. Palate: fruity, fresh, round tannins.

VILLACAMPA DEL MARQUÉS 2009 T ROBLE
100% tempranillo.

88 Colour: cherry, purple rim. Nose: fruit expression, spicy. Palate: good structure, complex, flavourful, spicy.

VILLACAMPA DEL MARQUÉS 2008 TR
tempranillo.

89 Colour: cherry, garnet rim. Nose: ripe fruit, spicy, creamy oak, toasty, medium intensity. Palate: powerful, flavourful, toasty, round tannins.

ACONTIA 2008 T
100% tempranillo.

87 Colour: cherry, garnet rim. Nose: red berry notes, ripe fruit, expressive, spicy, toasty. Palate: flavourful, fleshy, long.

CILLAR DE SILOS

Paraje El Soto, s/n
09370 Quintana del Pidio (Burgos)
☎: +34 947 545 126 - Fax: +34 947 545 605
bodega@cillardesilos.es
www.cillardesilos.es

CILLAR DE SILOS 2010 T
tempranillo.

89 Colour: rose, cherry, purple rim. Nose: medium intensity, red berry notes, wild herbs. Palate: fruity, flavourful, balanced.

TORRESILO 2008 T
tempranillo.

89 Colour: cherry, garnet rim. Nose: ripe fruit, powerfull, toasty, cocoa bean. Palate: good acidity, flavourful, full, fleshy, round tannins.

CILLAR DE SILOS 2008 T
tempranillo.

88 Colour: cherry, garnet rim. Nose: ripe fruit, creamy oak, spicy. Palate: flavourful, fleshy, full, round tannins.

CINEMA WINES

Felipe Gómez, 1
47140 Laguna de Duero (Valladolid)
☎: +34 983 545 539 - Fax: +34 983 545 539
www.cinemawines.es

CINEMA 2009 T
100% tempranillo.

85 Colour: bright cherry. Nose: ripe fruit, sweet spices, creamy oak. Palate: flavourful, fruity, toasty.

COMENGE BODEGAS Y VIÑEDOS

Camino del Castillo, s/n
47316 Curiel de Duero (Valladolid)
☎: +34 983 880 363 - Fax: +34 983 880 717
admin@comenge.com
www.comenge.com

COMENGE 2008 T
tempranillo.

89 Colour: cherry, garnet rim. Nose: ripe fruit, creamy oak, cocoa bean, spicy, balanced. Palate: good acidity, flavourful, fleshy, round tannins.

COMENGE 2007 T
tempranillo.

88 Colour: deep cherry, garnet rim. Nose: candied fruit, dark chocolate, sweet spices. Palate: fruity, flavourful, round tannins.

DON MIGUEL COMENGE 2006 T
tempranillo.

93 Colour: cherry, garnet rim. Nose: powerfull, expressive, ripe fruit, mineral, creamy oak, sweet spices. Palate: powerful, flavourful, concentrated, full.

COMENGE 2006 T
tempranillo.

88 Colour: cherry, garnet rim. Nose: ripe fruit, spicy, creamy oak, cocoa bean, dark chocolate. Palate: powerful, flavourful, round tannins, ripe fruit.

DON MIGUEL COMENGE 2005 T
90% tempranillo, 10% cabernet sauvignon.

93 Colour: cherry, garnet rim. Nose: ripe fruit, fruit expression, mineral, creamy oak, sweet spices. Palate: flavourful, powerful, fleshy.

COMPAÑÍA DE VINOS TELMO RODRÍGUEZ

El Monte, s/n
01308 Lanciego (Álava)
☎: +34 945 628 315 - Fax: +34 945 628 314
contact@telmorodriguez.com
www.telmorodriguez.com

M2 DE MATALLANA 2007 T
100% tinto fino.

90 Colour: dark-red cherry. Nose: earthy notes, ripe fruit, fruit liqueur notes, spicy, roasted almonds. Palate: ripe fruit, spicy, fleshy, powerful, spirituous.

MATALLANA 2006 T
tinto fino.

94 Colour: deep cherry. Nose: sweet spices, cedar wood, ripe fruit, fruit liqueur notes. Palate: spicy, mineral, roasted-coffee aftertaste, toasty.

CONVENTO DE OREJA

Avda. Palencia, 1
47010 (Valladolid)
☎: +34 685 990 596 - Fax: +34 913 710 098
convento@conventooreja.com
www.conventooreja.com

CONVENTO OREJA 2009 T ROBLE
100% tinta del país.

85 Colour: cherry, garnet rim. Nose: ripe fruit, spicy, cocoa bean. Palate: powerful, flavourful, fleshy.

CONVENTO OREJA 2008 TC
100% tinta del país.

87 Colour: cherry, garnet rim. Nose: overripe fruit, spicy, toasty, aromatic coffee. Palate: good acidity, rich, fleshy, round tannins.

CONVENTO OREJA 2007 TC
100% tinta del país.

88 Colour: cherry, garnet rim. Nose: red berry notes, ripe fruit, scrubland, spicy, toasty. Palate: good acidity, powerful, flavourful, fleshy.

CONVENTO OREJA MEMORIA 2006 TR
100% tinta del país.

90 Colour: cherry, garnet rim. Nose: ripe fruit, spicy, creamy oak, toasty. Palate: powerful, flavourful, toasty, round tannins.

DE BARDOS

Gral. Vara del Rey, 7- 1º dcha.
26003 Logroño (La Rioja)
☎: +34 941 271 217 - Fax: +34 941 272 911
info@debardos.com
www.debardos.com

ARS ROMANTICA 2008 T
100% tinta del país.

88 Colour: cherry, garnet rim. Nose: ripe fruit, candied fruit, sweet spices, creamy oak. Palate: light-bodied, fruity, flavourful, balanced.

ARS EPICA 2006 T
tinta del país.

89 Colour: cherry, garnet rim. Nose: ripe fruit, floral, balsamic herbs, mineral, spicy, creamy oak. Palate: powerful, flavourful, fleshy, complex, toasty.

ARS MÍTICA 2006 T
tempranillo, cabernet sauvignon.

88 Color cherry, garnet rim. Aroma ripe fruit, spicy, creamy oak, toasty, complex. Taste powerful, flavourful, toasty, round tannins.

ARS SUPREMA 2005 T
tempranillo.

88 Colour: cherry, garnet rim. Nose: ripe fruit, fine reductive notes, spicy, creamy oak. Palate: good acidity, fleshy, flavourful, toasty.

DEHESA DE LOS CANÓNIGOS S.A.

Ctra. Renedo - Pesquera, Km. 39
47315 Pesquera de Duero (Valladolid)
☎: +34 983 484 001 - Fax: +34 983 484 040
bodega@dehesacanonigos.com
www.bodegadehesadeloscanonigos.com

DEHESA DE LOS CANÓNIGOS 2005 TR
tinto fino, cabernet sauvignon, albillo.

89 Colour: cherry, garnet rim. Nose: ripe fruit, spicy, toasty, complex, powerfull, fruit preserve. Palate: powerful, flavourful, toasty, round tannins.

DEHESA DE LOS CANÓNIGOS MAGNUM SELECCIÓN ESPECIAL 2006 T
tinto fino, cabernet sauvignon.

88 Colour: pale ruby, brick rim edge. Nose: medium intensity, warm, fruit liqueur notes, spicy, toasty. Palate: spicy, fine bitter notes, long.

DEHESA DE LOS CANÓNIGOS 2007 TC
tinto fino, cabernet sauvignon.

88 Colour: cherry, garnet rim. Nose: ripe fruit, creamy oak, spicy. Palate: good acidity, flavourful, fine tannins, ripe fruit.

DEHESA VALDELAGUNA

Ctra. Valoria, Km. 16
Pesquera de Duero (Valladolid)
☎: +34 619 460 308 - Fax: +34 921 142 325
montelaguna@montelaguna.es
www.montelaguna.es

MONTELAGUNA 2009 TC
100% tempranillo.

87 Colour: bright cherry. Nose: ripe fruit, sweet spices, creamy oak, expressive. Palate: flavourful, fruity, toasty.

RA 2007 T
tempranillo.

90 Colour: bright cherry. Nose: ripe fruit, sweet spices, creamy oak, expressive, dark chocolate. Palate: flavourful, fruity, toasty, round tannins.

DÍAZ BAYO HERMANOS

Camino de los Anarinos, s/n
09471 Fuentelcésped (Burgos)
☎: +34 947 561 020 - Fax: +34 947 561 204
info@bodegadiazbayo.com
www.bodegadiazbayo.com

DARDANELOS 2010 T BARRICA
100% tempranillo.

88 Colour: cherry, purple rim. Nose: wild herbs, spicy, red berry notes. Palate: correct, fruity, round tannins.

NUESTRO 12 MESES 2009 T BARRICA
100% tempranillo.

92 Colour: cherry, garnet rim. Nose: red berry notes, ripe fruit, complex, balanced, sweet spices, creamy oak. Palate: elegant, powerful, flavourful, fleshy, long.

DIAZ BAYO POYATAS DE VALDEBRERO 2007 T BARRICA
90% tempranillo, 6% cabernet sauvignon, 4% garnacha.

92 Colour: cherry, garnet rim. Nose: ripe fruit, spicy, creamy oak, toasty, fragrant herbs. Palate: powerful, flavourful, toasty, round tannins.

DIAZ BAYO MAJUELO DE LA HOMBRÍA 2007 T BARRICA
100% tempranillo.

91 Colour: deep cherry. Nose: powerfull, ripe fruit, earthy notes, scrubland. Palate: flavourful, powerful, fleshy, complex.

NUESTRO CRIANZA 2007 TC
100% tempranillo.

90 Colour: cherry, garnet rim. Nose: ripe fruit, spicy, varietal, mineral. Palate: fruity, ripe fruit, great length.

NUESTRO 20 MESES 2006 T BARRICA
100% tempranillo.

93 Colour: very deep cherry, garnet rim. Nose: complex, fruit preserve, spicy, powerfull, earthy notes. Palate: good structure, full, round tannins.

FDB 2006 T BARRICA
100% tempranillo.

92 Colour: cherry, garnet rim. Nose: spicy, creamy oak, toasty, fruit expression. Palate: powerful, flavourful, toasty, long, good acidity.

DOMINIO BASCONCILLOS

Condado de Treviño, 55
09001 (Burgos)
☎: +34 947 473 300 - Fax: +34 947 473 360
info@dominiobasconcillos.com
www.dominiobasconcillos.com

DOMINIO BASCONCILLOS 12 MESES 2008 T ROBLE
100% tempranillo.

93 Colour: cherry, garnet rim. Nose: red berry notes, ripe fruit, characterful, dark chocolate, cocoa bean, creamy oak. Palate: good acidity, fleshy, powerful, flavourful, long.

VIÑA MAGNA 2008 TC
100% tempranillo.

90 Colour: cherry, garnet rim. Nose: ripe fruit, powerfull, expressive, cocoa bean, toasty. Palate: good acidity, elegant, spicy, fleshy, long, round tannins.

DOMINIO DE ATAUTA

Ctra. a Morcuera, s/n
42345 Atauta (Soria)
☎: +34 975 351 349
dominiodeatauta.ribera@arrakis.es
www.dominiodeatauta.com

PARADA DE ATAUTA 2009 T
tinto fino.

94 Colour: black cherry, garnet rim. Nose: red berry notes, ripe fruit, earthy notes, balanced, expressive, spicy, creamy oak. Palate: powerful, flavourful, fleshy, complex, fine tannins.

DOMINIO DE ATAUTA VALDEGATILES 2008 T
tinto fino.

96 Colour: dark-red cherry, garnet rim. Nose: ripe fruit, mineral, complex, elegant, cocoa bean, sweet spices, creamy oak. Palate: flavourful, fleshy, good acidity, balanced, long.

DOMINIO DE ATAUTA LA MALA 2008 TC
tinto fino.

94 Colour: bright cherry. Nose: powerfull, aromatic coffee, sweet spices, roasted coffee, fruit expression. Palate: flavourful, powerful, fleshy, good acidity, long.

DOMINIO DE ATAUTA 2008 TC
tinto fino.

92 Colour: cherry, garnet rim. Nose: spicy, creamy oak, toasty, fruit preserve. Palate: powerful, flavourful, toasty, round tannins.

TORRE DE GOLBAN 2007 TC
tinto fino.

90 Colour: black cherry, garnet rim. Nose: ripe fruit, varietal, spicy, creamy oak. Palate: flavourful, fruity, balanced, round tannins.

TORRE DE GOLBAN 2006 TR
tinto fino.

90 Colour: cherry, garnet rim. Nose: cigar, wet leather, toasty, cocoa bean. Palate: spicy, ripe fruit, long.

DOMINIO DE PINGUS S.L.

Hospital, s/n - Apdo. 93, Peñafiel
47350 Quintanilla de Onésimo (Valladolid)
☎: +34 639 833 854

PINGUS 2009 T
100% tempranillo.

96 Colour: very deep cherry. Nose: characterful, complex, expressive, red berry notes, creamy oak, new oak. Palate: flavourful, powerful, fleshy, good acidity, elegant, balanced.

FLOR DE PINGUS 2009 T
100% tempranillo.

94 Colour: very deep cherry. Nose: characterful, varietal, fruit expression, creamy oak, toasty. Palate: flavourful, fruity, fresh, fleshy, round tannins.

PSI 2009 T
100% tempranillo.

92 Colour: bright cherry, purple rim. Nose: raspberry, fruit expression, creamy oak, sweet spices. Palate: flavourful, powerful, spicy, ripe fruit, fine tannins.

DOMINIO ROMANO

Los Lagares, s/n
47319 Rábano (Valladolid)
☎: +34 983 871 661 - Fax: +34 938 901 143
dominioromano@dominioromano.es

CAMINO ROMANO 2008 T
100% tinto fino.

88 Colour: bright cherry. Nose: ripe fruit, sweet spices, roasted coffee. Palate: flavourful, fruity, toasty, round tannins.

DOMINIO ROMANO RDR 2007 T
100% tinto fino.

91 Colour: cherry, garnet rim. Nose: spicy, creamy oak, toasty, characterful, ripe fruit. Palate: powerful, flavourful, toasty, round tannins.

DOMINIO ROMANO 2007 T
100% tinto fino.

89 Colour: cherry, garnet rim. Nose: powerfull, ripe fruit, toasty, spicy. Palate: ripe fruit, powerful, fleshy.

DURÓN S.A.

Ctra. Roa - La Horra, km. 3,800
09300 Roa (Burgos)
☎: +34 902 227 700 - Fax: +34 902 227 701
bodega@cofradiasamaniego.com
www.bodegasduron.com

DURÓN 2007 TR
75% tinta del país, 15% cabernet sauvignon, 10% merlot.

85 Colour: cherry, garnet rim. Nose: ripe fruit, creamy oak, spicy. Palate: flavourful, spicy, slightly dry, soft tannins.

OPTIMO DE DURÓN 2005 TR
75% tinta del país, 15% cabernet sauvignon, 10% merlot.

88 Colour: cherry, garnet rim. Nose: ripe fruit, fine reductive notes, sweet spices, toasty. Palate: good acidity, powerful, flavourful, fleshy.

ÉBANO VIÑEDOS Y BODEGAS

Ctra. Nacional 122 Km., 299,6 Pol. Ind. 1 Parcela 32
47318 Castrillo de Duero (Valladolid)
☎: +34 986 609 060 - Fax: +34 986 609 313
ebano@valminorebano.com
www.ebanovinedosybodegas.com

ÉBANO 6 2008 T
100% tempranillo.

86 Colour: cherry, garnet rim. Nose: red berry notes, ripe fruit, sweet spices, creamy oak. Palate: powerful, flavourful, slightly evolved.

ÉBANO 2008 T
100% tempranillo.

92 Colour: cherry, garnet rim. Nose: ripe fruit, elegant, earthy notes, creamy oak, sweet spices. Palate: good acidity, flavourful, full, fleshy, long, fine tannins.

EL LAGAR DE ISILLA

Antigua Ctra. N-122, s/n
09471 La Vid (Burgos)
☎: +34 947 504 316 - Fax: +34 947 504 316
bodegas@lagarisilla.es
www.lagarisilla.es

EL LAGAR DE ISILLA 2010 RD
100% tempranillo.

88 Colour: rose, purple rim. Nose: powerfull, red berry notes, floral, expressive, lactic notes. Palate: fleshy, powerful, fruity, fresh.

EL LAGAR DE ISILLA 9 MESES GESTACIÓN 2009 T ROBLE
100% tempranillo.

88 Colour: bright cherry, garnet rim. Nose: powerfull, balanced, complex, ripe fruit, spicy, dark chocolate. Palate: good structure, fleshy.

EL LAGAR DE ISILLA 2009 T ROBLE
93% tempranillo, 7% cabernet sauvignon.

87 Colour: cherry, garnet rim. Nose: fresh, wild herbs. Palate: good structure, easy to drink, fruity.

EL LAGAR DE ISILLA 2007 TR
100% tempranillo.

88 Colour: cherry, garnet rim. Nose: red berry notes, ripe fruit, complex, spicy, toasty. Palate: good acidity, fleshy, flavourful.

EMINA

Ctra. San Bernardo, s/n
47359 Valbuena de Duero (Valladolid)
☎: +34 902 430 170 - Fax: +34 902 430 189
emina@emina.es
www.emina.es

EMINA PASIÓN 2010 T
100% tinta del país.

84 Colour: cherry, garnet rim. Nose: fruit preserve, grassy. Palate: fruity, flavourful.

EMINA 12 MESES 2009 T
100% tinta del país.

89 Colour: deep cherry, garnet rim. Nose: creamy oak, sweet spices, dark chocolate. Palate: flavourful, powerful, fruity, round tannins.

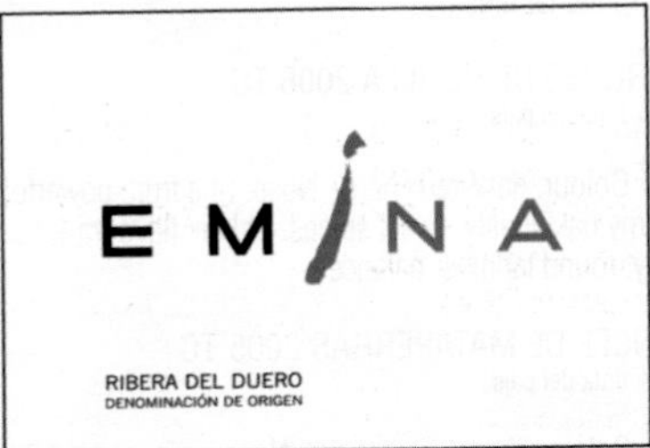

EMINA 2007 TC
100% tinta del país.

88 Colour: cherry, garnet rim. Nose: powerfull, toasty, spicy, ripe fruit. Palate: good acidity, flavourful, fleshy, round tannins.

EMINA PRESTIGIO 2006 TR
100% tinta del país.

89 Colour: very deep cherry. Nose: roasted coffee, dark chocolate, aromatic coffee, fruit liqueur notes. Palate: powerful, fine bitter notes, spicy, powerful tannins.

EMINA ATIO 2005 T RESERVA ESPECIAL
100% tinta del país.

90 Colour: dark-red cherry. Nose: powerfull, balanced, ripe fruit, toasty, dark chocolate, spicy. Palate: flavourful, ripe fruit, round tannins, full, fleshy.

EMINA 400 RESERVA ESPECIAL 2005 T
tinta del país.

88 Color bright cherry. Aroma ripe fruit, sweet spices, creamy oak, expressive. Taste flavourful, fruity, toasty, round tannins.

FINCA TORREMILANOS BODEGAS PEÑALBA LÓPEZ

Finca Torremilanos
09400 Aranda de Duero (Burgos)
☎: +34 947 512 852 - Fax:+34 947 508 044
nacional@torremilanos.com
www.torremilanos.com

MONTE CASTRILLO 2010 RD
100% tempranillo.

87 Colour: raspberry rose. Nose: red berry notes, ripe fruit, balsamic herbs, fresh. Palate: light-bodied, fresh, fruity, easy to drink.

MONTE CASTRILLO 7 MESES 2009 T ROBLE
100% tempranillo.

88 Colour: cherry, garnet rim. Nose: red berry notes, ripe fruit, mineral, creamy oak. Palate: good acidity, powerful, flavourful, fruity, toasty.

LOS CANTOS DE TORREMILANOS 2008 T
100% tempranillo.

91 Colour: cherry, garnet rim. Nose: red berry notes, fruit expression, mineral, expressive, creamy oak. Palate: powerful, flavourful, fruity, complex, fleshy.

TORREMILANOS 2008 T
100% tempranillo.

87 Colour: dark-red cherry, garnet rim. Nose: red berry notes, ripe fruit, sweet spices, creamy oak. Palate: good acidity, round, flavourful, fleshy.

CYCLO 2007 T
90% tempranillo, 5% garnacha, tempranillo blanco.

92 Colour: cherry, garnet rim. Nose: varietal, fruit expression, ripe fruit, spicy, creamy oak. Palate: powerful, flavourful, fleshy, complex.

TORREMILANOS 2007 TR
tempranillo.

88 Colour: cherry, garnet rim. Nose: ripe fruit, toasty, complex, sweet spices, caramel. Palate: powerful, flavourful, toasty, round tannins.

FINCA VILLACRECES, S.L.

Ctra. N-122 Km. 322
47350 Quintanilla de Onésimo (Valladolid)
☎: +34 983 680 437 - Fax: +34 983 683 314
villacreces@villacreces.com
www.villacreces.com

FINCA VILLACRECES NEBRO 2009 TC
100% tinto fino.

94 Colour: cherry, garnet rim. Nose: mineral, ripe fruit, creamy oak, sweet spices, white flowers. Palate: flavourful, spicy, good acidity, fine bitter notes, powerful tannins.

PRUNO 2009 T
90% tempranillo, 10% cabernet sauvignon.

92 Colour: bright cherry. Nose: ripe fruit, sweet spices, toasty. Palate: flavourful, fruity, toasty, round tannins.

FINCA VILLACRECES 2007 TC
tempranillo, merlot, cabernet sauvignon.

91 Colour: cherry, garnet rim. Nose: spicy, creamy oak, ripe fruit, new oak. Palate: powerful, flavourful, toasty, round tannins.

FUENTENARRO

Constitución, 32
09311 La Horra (Burgos)
☎: +34 947 542 092 - Fax: +34 947 542 083
bodegas@fuentenarro.com
www.fuentenarro.com

VIÑA FUENTENARRO VENDIMIA SELECCIONADA 2009 T
100% tempranillo.

90 Colour: cherry, garnet rim. Nose: ripe fruit, cocoa bean, creamy oak, spicy. Palate: good acidity, fruity, flavourful, balanced.

VIÑA FUENTENARRO 2009 T BARRICA
100% tempranillo.

87 Colour: cherry, garnet rim. Nose: overripe fruit, spicy, creamy oak. Palate: good acidity, fruity, flavourful, round tannins.

VIÑA FUENTENARRO 2008 TC
100% tempranillo.

89 Colour: cherry, garnet rim. Nose: ripe fruit, toasty, spicy. Palate: good acidity, flavourful, full, fleshy, round tannins.

VIÑA FUENTENARRO 2005 TR
100% tinta del país.

90 Colour: cherry, garnet rim. Nose: red berry notes, ripe fruit, complex, fine reductive notes, sweet spices, toasty. Palate: powerful, rich, flavourful, fleshy.

GRANDES BODEGAS

Ctra. de Sotillo de la Ribera, s/n
09311 La Horra (Burgos)
☎: +34 947 542 166 - Fax: +34 947 542 165
bodega@marquesdevelilla.com
www.marquesdevelilla.com

MARQUÉS DE VELILLA 2010 T
100% tinta del país.

87 Colour: cherry, purple rim. Nose: red berry notes, ripe fruit, balsamic herbs. Palate: good acidity, flavourful, ripe fruit, long.

MARQUÉS DE VELILLA FINCA LA MARÍA 2008 T
tinta del país.

88 Colour: cherry, garnet rim. Nose: powerfull, creamy oak, toasty, ripe fruit. Palate: powerful, fleshy, flavourful, full, round tannins.

MARQUÉS DE VELILLA 2006 TC
100% tinta del país.

90 Colour: dark-red cherry. Nose: ripe fruit, powerfull, creamy oak, toasty, sweet spices. Palate: flavourful, fleshy, spicy, round tannins, balanced.

DONCEL DE MATAPERRAS 2005 TC
100% tinta del país.

94 Colour: cherry, garnet rim. Nose: spicy, creamy oak, toasty, fragrant herbs, ripe fruit. Palate: powerful, flavourful, toasty, round tannins.

GREAT WINES FROM SPAIN

Camino de Santibáñez, s/n
47328 La Parrilla (Valladolid)
☎: +34 983 681 521 - Fax: +34 983 681 521
bodegas@altapavina.com
www.altapavina.es

VALDRINAL 6 2010 T ROBLE
tinto fino.

87 Colour: cherry, garnet rim. Nose: red berry notes, ripe fruit, spicy, creamy oak. Palate: balanced, flavourful, fleshy.

VALDRINAL 2008 TC
tinto fino.

88 Colour: cherry, garnet rim. Nose: ripe fruit, spicy, creamy oak. Palate: good acidity, fruity, flavourful, long.

VALDRINAL SQR2 2007 T ROBLE
tinto fino.

92 Colour: cherry, garnet rim. Nose: red berry notes, ripe fruit, elegant, earthy notes, cocoa bean, dark chocolate, creamy oak. Palate: good acidity, powerful, flavourful, fleshy, complex.

VALDRINAL 2006 TR
tinto fino.

89 Colour: light cherry, garnet rim. Nose: ripe fruit, elegant, sweet spices, toasty. Palate: balanced, unctuous, fleshy, complex, flavourful, fine tannins.

GRUPO ALGAR - ABILIA

Carpinteros, 13 P.I. Pinares Llanos
28670 Villaviciosa de Odón (Madrid)
☎: +34 916 169 122 - Fax: +34 916 166 724
info@grupoalgar.com
www.grupoalgar.com

ABILIA 2010 T
100% tempranillo.

87 Colour: cherry, purple rim. Nose: fresh fruit, red berry notes, floral, fresh. Palate: flavourful, fruity, good acidity.

ABILIA 2009 T ROBLE
100% tempranillo.

87 Colour: cherry, garnet rim. Nose: red berry notes, ripe fruit, earthy notes, creamy oak. Palate: good acidity, fleshy, flavourful.

ABILIA 2008 TC
tempranillo.

87 Colour: cherry, garnet rim. Nose: ripe fruit, creamy oak, spicy. Palate: good acidity, fruity, flavourful, round tannins.

ABILIA 2005 TR
tempranillo.

88 Colour: cherry, garnet rim. Nose: fruit expression, spicy. Palate: fruity, good acidity, round tannins.

GRUPO YLLERA

Autovía A-6, Km. 173, 5
47490 Rueda (Valladolid)
☎: +34 983 868 097 - Fax: +34 983 868 177
grupoyllera@grupoyllera.com
www.grupoyllera.com

VIÑA DEL VAL 2010 T
tempranillo.

88 Colour: cherry, purple rim. Nose: red berry notes, raspberry, expressive, balanced. Palate: fruity, powerful, flavourful, easy to drink.

BRACAMONTE 2009 T ROBLE
tempranillo.

88 Colour: cherry, garnet rim. Nose: ripe fruit, fruit expression, sweet spices. Palate: powerful, flavourful, fleshy, toasty, good finish.

BRACAMONTE 2006 TC
tempranillo.

90 Colour: cherry, garnet rim. Nose: red berry notes, ripe fruit, varietal, mineral, sweet spices, creamy oak. Palate: fresh, good acidity, round tannins, fleshy.

BRACAMONTE 2004 TR
100% tempranillo.

88 Colour: dark-red cherry, orangey edge. Nose: toasty, aromatic coffee, sweet spices, ripe fruit. Palate: creamy, long, powerful, flavourful, fleshy.

HACIENDA SOLANO

La Solana, 6
09370 La Aguilera (Burgos)
☎: +34 947 545 582 - Fax: +34 947 545 582
hacienda_solano@yahoo.es
www.haciendasolano.com

HACIENDA SOLANO 6 MESES 2009 T ROBLE
tempranillo.

86 Colour: dark-red cherry. Nose: fruit expression, powerfull, creamy oak, spicy. Palate: fleshy, flavourful, slightly dry, soft tannins.

HACIENDA SOLANO 12 MESES SELECCIÓN VIÑAS VIEJAS 2008 TC
tempranillo.

89 Colour: cherry, garnet rim. Nose: ripe fruit, balanced, powerfull, creamy oak, spicy. Palate: good acidity, flavourful, round tannins, fleshy.

LA COLECCIÓN DE VINOS

Domingo Martínez, 6- Bajo
47007 (Valladolid)
☎: +34 983 271 595 - Fax: +34 983 271 608
info@lacolecciondevinos.com
www.lacolecciondevinos.com

VALLIS 2009 T
100% tempranillo.

89 Colour: cherry, garnet rim. Nose: balanced, cocoa bean, creamy oak, ripe fruit. Palate: flavourful, fruity, spicy, round tannins.

PALACIO DE SANTA CRUZ VENDIMIA SELECCIONADA 2006 T
100% tempranillo.

89 Colour: cherry, garnet rim. Nose: fruit preserve, sweet spices, toasty, powerfull. Palate: fleshy, flavourful, round tannins.

1492 SANTAFÉ 2007 TC
100% tempranillo.

85 Colour: cherry, garnet rim. Nose: ripe fruit, spicy, toasty. Palate: powerful, flavourful, round tannins.

1492 SANTAFÉ 2006 TR
100% tempranillo.

86 Colour: cherry, garnet rim. Nose: ripe fruit, spicy, toasty, complex, fine reductive notes. Palate: powerful, flavourful, toasty.

LEGARIS

Ctra. Peñafiel - Encinas de Esgueva, km. 4,3
47316 Curiel de Duero (Valladolid)
☎: +34 983 878 088 - Fax: +34 983 881 034
info@legaris.es
www.legaris.es

LEGARIS 2009 T ROBLE
100% tinto fino.

89 Colour: cherry, garnet rim. Nose: ripe fruit, creamy oak, spicy, balsamic herbs. Palate: spicy, ripe fruit, fleshy, round tannins.

LEGARIS 2008 TC
100% tempranillo.

88 Colour: deep cherry, garnet rim. Nose: balanced, varietal, expressive, complex, mineral, spicy. Palate: balanced, ripe fruit, spicy.

LEGARIS 2005 TR
100% tempranillo.

91 Colour: cherry, garnet rim. Nose: ripe fruit, spicy, creamy oak, toasty. Palate: powerful, flavourful, toasty, round tannins.

LOESS

El Monte, 7- Bajo
47195 Arroyo de la Encomienda (Valladolid)
☎: +34 983 664 898 - Fax: +34 983 406 579
loess@loess.es
www.loess.es

LOESS COLLECTION 2008 T
tempranillo.

89 Color cherry, garnet rim. Aroma ripe fruit, spicy, creamy oak, toasty, complex. Taste powerful, flavourful, toasty, round tannins.

LOESS COLLECTION 2005 T
tempranillo.

90 Colour: bright cherry, garnet rim. Nose: balanced, elegant, creamy oak, sweet spices, ripe fruit. Palate: good structure, spicy, great length.

LYNUS VIÑEDOS Y BODEGAS

Camino de las Pozas, s/n
47350 Quintanilla de Onésimo (Valladolid)
☎: +34 983 680 224 - Fax: +34 983 680 224
info@lynus.es
www.lynus.es

PAGOS DEL INFANTE 2009 T ROBLE
100% tempranillo.

87 Colour: cherry, garnet rim. Nose: ripe fruit, balsamic herbs, cocoa bean, creamy oak. Palate: good acidity, correct, ripe fruit.

LYNUS 2008 TC
100% tempranillo.

90 Colour: cherry, garnet rim. Nose: ripe fruit, toasty, cocoa bean, spicy, powerfull. Palate: good acidity, round, flavourful, fruity, fine tannins.

PAGOS DEL INFANTE 2008 TC
100% tempranillo.

89 Color bright cherry. Aroma ripe fruit, sweet spices, creamy oak, expressive. Taste flavourful, fruity, toasty, round tannins.

LYNUS ÁUREA 2007 TR
100% tempranillo.

91 Colour: cherry, garnet rim. Nose: powerfull, ripe fruit, toasty, spicy, cocoa bean, aromatic coffee. Palate: good acidity, elegant, creamy, fleshy, round tannins.

MARQUÉS DE LA CONCORDIA FAMILY OF WINES

Hacienda Abascal, N-122, Km. 321,5
47360 Quintanilla de Onésimo (Valladolid)
☎: +34 914 365 924
comunicacion@arcoinvest-group.com
www.haciendas-espana.com

HACIENDA ABASCAL (MARQUÉS DE LA CONCORDIA) 2008 TC
100% tempranillo.

90 Colour: cherry, garnet rim. Nose: ripe fruit, spicy, toasty, expressive, balanced. Palate: good acidity, powerful, flavourful, fleshy.

HACIENDA ABASCAL PREMIUM (MARQUÉS DE LA CONCORDIA) 2008 T
100% tempranillo.

90 Colour: cherry, garnet rim. Nose: red berry notes, ripe fruit, mineral, cocoa bean, sweet spices, creamy oak. Palate: good acidity, round, powerful, flavourful, fleshy.

MARQUÉS DE VALPARAISO

Paraje los Llanillos, s/n
09370 Quintana del Pidío (Burgos)
☎: +34 947 545 286 - Fax: +34 947 545 163
m.valparaiso@fer.es
www.paternina.com

MARQUÉS DE VALPARAÍSO 2009 T ROBLE
tinto fino.

89 Colour: cherry, garnet rim. Nose: red berry notes, ripe fruit, cocoa bean, dark chocolate, sweet spices, toasty. Palate: powerful, flavourful, fruity, round tannins.

FINCA EL ENCINAL 2009 T ROBLE
tinto fino.

87 Colour: cherry, purple rim. Nose: red berry notes, ripe fruit, floral, spicy, creamy oak. Palate: flavourful, fresh, fruity.

FINCA EL ENCINAL 2008 TC
tinta del país.

88 Colour: bright cherry. Nose: sweet spices, creamy oak, expressive, red berry notes, ripe fruit. Palate: flavourful, fruity, toasty, round tannins.

MARQUÉS DE VALPARAÍSO 2008 TC
tinto fino.

87 Colour: cherry, purple rim. Nose: red berry notes, ripe fruit, dark chocolate, sweet spices, creamy oak. Palate: powerful, complex, flavourful, long, toasty.

MONTEBACO

Finca Montealto
47359 Valbuena de Duero (Valladolid)
☎: +34 983 485 128 - Fax: +34 983 485 033
montebaco@bodegasmontebaco.com
www.bodegasmontebaco.com

MONTEBACO 2009 TC
100% tempranillo.

90 Colour: cherry, garnet rim. Nose: ripe fruit, fruit expression, dry stone, creamy oak, spicy. Palate: ripe fruit, flavourful, powerful, fruity, round tannins.

SEMELE 2009 TC
90% tempranillo, 10% merlot.

87 Colour: deep cherry, garnet rim. Nose: balanced, medium intensity, red berry notes, ripe fruit, spicy. Palate: fruity, ripe fruit, long.

MONTEBACO 2008 TC
tempranillo.

91 Colour: cherry, garnet rim. Nose: expressive, ripe fruit, cocoa bean, creamy oak. Palate: powerful, flavourful, fleshy, round tannins.

MONTEBACO VENDIMIA SELECCIONADA 2006 T
100% tempranillo.

89 Colour: cherry, garnet rim. Nose: ripe fruit, spicy, creamy oak, toasty, complex. Palate: toasty, ripe fruit, good finish.

MONTEGAREDO

Ctra. Pedrosa,Km.. 1
09314 Boada de Roa (Burgos)
☎: +34 947 530 003 - Fax: +34 947 530 140
info@montegaredo.com
www.montegaredo.com

MONTEGAREDO 2010 T ROBLE
100% tinto fino.

88 Colour: cherry, purple rim. Nose: red berry notes, ripe fruit, sweet spices, creamy oak. Palate: powerful, flavourful, fleshy, round tannins, toasty.

PIRÁMIDE 2009 T
100% tinto fino.

89 Colour: cherry, garnet rim. Nose: ripe fruit, spicy, creamy oak, complex. Palate: powerful, flavourful, concentrated, fleshy, long, round tannins.

MONTEGAREDO 2009 TC
100% tinto fino.

87 Colour: cherry, garnet rim. Nose: ripe fruit, spicy, cocoa bean, creamy oak. Palate: good acidity, flavourful, fleshy, ripe fruit.

OSBORNE RIBERA DEL DUERO

Fernán Caballero, 7
11500 El Puerto de Santa María (Cádiz)
☎: +34 925 860 990 - Fax: +34 925 860 905
carolina.cerrato@osborne.es
www.osborne.es

SEÑORÍO DEL CID 2008 T ROBLE
tinto fino.

87 Colour: cherry, garnet rim. Nose: ripe fruit, powerfull, spicy, creamy oak. Palate: flavourful, fleshy, round tannins.

PAGO DE CARRAOVEJAS

Camino de Carraovejas, s/n
47300 Peñafiel (Valladolid)
☎: +34 983 878 020 - Fax: +34 983 878 022
administracion@pagodecarraovejas.com
www.pagodecarraovejas.com

PAGO DE CARRAOVEJAS 2009 TC
96% tinto fino, 4% cabernet sauvignon.

93 Colour: cherry, garnet rim. Nose: spicy, cocoa bean, toasty, red berry notes. Palate: good acidity, flavourful, fruity, fleshy, rich, complex.

PAGO DE CARRAOVEJAS 2007 TR
100% tinto fino.

93 Colour: cherry, garnet rim. Nose: creamy oak, toasty, complex, expressive, elegant, ripe fruit. Palate: powerful, flavourful, toasty, round tannins.

PAGO DE CARRAOVEJAS "CUESTA DE LAS LIEBRES" VENDIMIA SELECCIONADA 2007 TR
100% tinto fino.

95 Colour: cherry, garnet rim. Nose: ripe fruit, spicy, creamy oak, toasty, complex, earthy notes. Palate: powerful, flavourful, toasty, fleshy, complex, harsh oak tannins.

PAGO DE LOS CAPELLANES

Camino de la Ampudia, s/n
09314 Pedrosa de Duero (Burgos)
☎: +34 947 530 068 - Fax: +34 947 530 111
bodega@pagodeloscapellanes.com
www.pagodeloscapellanes.com

PAGO DE LOS CAPELLANES 2010 T ROBLE
100% tempranillo.

90 Colour: very deep cherry, purple rim. Nose: balanced, expressive, fruit expression, sweet spices. Palate: flavourful, good structure, good acidity.

PAGO DE LOS CAPELLANES 2008 TC
100% tempranillo.

91 Colour: cherry, garnet rim. Nose: red berry notes, ripe fruit, expressive, mineral, sweet spices, creamy oak. Palate: elegant, flavourful, fleshy, complex.

PAGO DE LOS CAPELLANES 2007 TR
100% tempranillo.

93 Colour: cherry, garnet rim. Nose: ripe fruit, spicy, creamy oak, toasty, expressive. Palate: powerful, flavourful, toasty, powerful tannins.

PAGO DE LOS CAPELLANES PARCELA EL PICÓN 2005 T
100% tempranillo.

95 Colour: cherry, garnet rim. Nose: powerfull, fruit expression, ripe fruit, earthy notes, mineral. Palate: powerful, balanced, fine bitter notes, good acidity, round tannins.

PAGO DE LOS CAPELLANES PARCELA EL NOGAL 2005 T
100% tempranillo.

92 Colour: cherry, garnet rim. Nose: powerfull, fruit preserve, warm, toasty, creamy oak. Palate: powerful, sweetness, fleshy.

PAGOS DE MATANEGRA

Pagos de Matanegra
09311 Olmedillo de Roa (Burgos)
☎: +34 947 551 310 - Fax: +34 947 551 309
info@pagosdematanegra.es
www.pagosdematanegra.es

MATANEGRA 2007 TC
100% tempranillo.

89 Colour: cherry, garnet rim. Nose: medium intensity, ripe fruit, sweet spices, earthy notes. Palate: good structure, flavourful.

MATANEGRA VENDIMIA SELECCIONADA 2007 T
100% tempranillo.

88 Colour: bright cherry, garnet rim. Nose: expressive, complex, cocoa bean, fruit preserve. Palate: good structure, flavourful, round tannins.

PAGOS DEL REY

Ctra. Palencia-Aranda, Km. 53
09311 Olmedillo de Roa (Burgos)
☎: +34 947 551 111 - Fax: +34 947 551 311
pdr@pagosdelrey.com
www.pagosdelrey.com

CONDADO DE ORIZA 2010 T ROBLE
tempranillo.

86 Colour: cherry, garnet rim. Nose: ripe fruit, red berry notes, medium intensity, creamy oak. Palate: good acidity, flavourful, fruity, slightly dry, soft tannins.

CONDADO DE ORIZA 2010 T JOVEN
tempranillo.

85 Colour: cherry, garnet rim. Nose: fruit preserve, spicy. Palate: good acidity, fruity, easy to drink.

ALTOS DE TAMARÓN 2010 T
tempranillo.

85 Colour: cherry, purple rim. Nose: balsamic herbs, red berry notes, powerfull. Palate: fruity, easy to drink.

ALTOS DE TAMARÓN 2010 T ROBLE
tempranillo.

84 Colour: bright cherry. Nose: sweet spices, creamy oak, red berry notes. Palate: flavourful, fruity, toasty.

CONDADO DE ORIZA 409 2008 T
tempranillo.

91 Colour: cherry, garnet rim. Nose: red berry notes, fruit expression, raspberry, expressive, sweet spices, creamy oak. Palate: rich, powerful, flavourful, fleshy, complex.

CONDADO DE ORIZA 2008 TC
tempranillo.

89 Colour: cherry, garnet rim. Nose: medium intensity, ripe fruit, spicy. Palate: fleshy, ripe fruit, round tannins.

ALTOS DE TAMARÓN 2008 TC
tempranillo.

87 Colour: cherry, garnet rim. Nose: ripe fruit, creamy oak, cocoa bean. Palate: good acidity, fleshy, flavourful, spicy, round tannins.

CONDADO DE ORIZA 2007 TR
tempranillo.

88 Color cherry, garnet rim. Aroma ripe fruit, spicy, creamy oak, toasty, complex. Taste powerful, flavourful, toasty, round tannins.

ALTOS DE TAMARÓN FUEGO Y HIELO 2007 T JOVEN
100% tempranillo.

87 Colour: cherry, garnet rim. Nose: ripe fruit, spicy, creamy oak, toasty, complex. Palate: powerful, flavourful, toasty.

ALTOS DE TAMARÓN 2006 TR
tempranillo.

90 Colour: cherry, garnet rim. Nose: ripe fruit, spicy, creamy oak, toasty, wet leather. Palate: powerful, flavourful, toasty, round tannins.

PÁRAMO DE GUZMÁN

Ctra. Circunvalación R-30, s/n
09300 Roa (Burgos)
☎: +34 947 541 191 - Fax: +34 947 541 192
esparamodeguzman@paramodeguzman.com
www.paramodeguzman.es

PÁRAMO DE GUZMÁN 2010 RD
100% tempranillo.

90 Colour: light cherry. Nose: dried flowers, fragrant herbs, fruit expression, fresh. Palate: light-bodied, flavourful, good acidity, long, spicy.

PÁRAMO DE GUZMÁN 2010 T BARRICA
100% tempranillo.

92 Colour: deep cherry. Nose: mineral, fruit expression, red berry notes, creamy oak. Palate: flavourful, powerful, fleshy, long, round tannins.

PÁRAMO DE GUZMÁN 2008 TR
100% tempranillo.

90 Colour: very deep cherry. Nose: powerfull, characterful, ripe fruit, raspberry, sweet spices. Palate: flavourful, powerful, fine bitter notes, good acidity, round tannins.

PÁRAMO DE GUZMÁN 2008 T
100% tempranillo.

90 Colour: deep cherry. Nose: creamy oak, sweet spices, cocoa bean, ripe fruit, fruit expression. Palate: flavourful, ripe fruit, spicy, round tannins.

RAÍZ DE GUZMÁN 2007 T
100% tempranillo.

93 Colour: cherry, garnet rim. Nose: mineral, earthy notes, ripe fruit, spicy, toasty, new oak. Palate: ripe fruit, flavourful, fruity, good acidity.

PÁRAMO DE GUZMÁN 2007 TC
100% tempranillo.

91 Colour: cherry, garnet rim. Nose: ripe fruit, spicy, toasty, dark chocolate, aromatic coffee. Palate: powerful, flavourful, toasty, round tannins.

RAÍZ DE GUZMÁN 2006 T
100% tempranillo.

94 Colour: cherry, garnet rim. Nose: powerfull, ripe fruit, creamy oak, cocoa bean, earthy notes. Palate: flavourful, powerful, fleshy, spicy, ripe fruit.

PARÍS TRIMIÑO BODEGA Y VIÑEDOS

Barrio San Roque, s/n
09300 Roa de Duero (Burgos)
☎: +34 947 540 033 - Fax: +34 947 540 033
bodegaparis@bodegaparis.com
www.bodegaparis.com

PARÍS 2009 T ROBLE
100% tempranillo.

86 Colour: bright cherry. Nose: ripe fruit, sweet spices, expressive. Palate: flavourful, fruity, toasty, round tannins.

PEPE LÓPEZ VINOS Y VIÑEDOS

Avda. Soria, 53 - Bajo
Buzón 136
47300 Peñafiel (Valladolid)
☎: +34 983 106 207 - Fax: +34 916 048 322
pepelopezvinos@yahoo.es
www.arrotos.es

ARROTOS 2010 T ROBLE
100% tempranillo.

85 Colour: bright cherry. Nose: ripe fruit, sweet spices, creamy oak. Palate: flavourful, fruity, toasty.

ARROTOS 2009 TC
95% tempranillo, 5% cabernet sauvignon.

85 Colour: cherry, garnet rim. Nose: red berry notes, ripe fruit, cocoa bean, sweet spices. Palate: fruity, correct.

ARROTOS 2006 TR
100% tempranillo.

87 Colour: cherry, garnet rim. Nose: red berry notes, fruit preserve, sweet spices, creamy oak. Palate: good acidity, balanced, fleshy.

PICO CUADRO

Del Río, 22
47350 Quintanilla de Onésimo (Valladolid)
☎: +34 983 680 113
picocuadro@picocuadro.com
www.picocuadro.com

PICO CUADRO 2008 T
100% tempranillo.

86 Colour: cherry, garnet rim. Nose: fruit preserve, toasty, spicy. Palate: good acidity, fine bitter notes, round tannins, flavourful.

PICO CUADRO VENDIMIA SELECCIONADA 2007 T
100% tempranillo.

91 Colour: cherry, garnet rim. Nose: red berry notes, ripe fruit, expressive, mineral, spicy, creamy oak. Palate: rich, flavourful, fleshy, spicy, toasty.

PROTOS BODEGAS RIBERA DUERO DE PEÑAFIEL

Bodegas Protos, 24-28
47300 Peñafiel (Valladolid)
☎: +34 983 878 011 - Fax: +34 983 878 012
bodega@bodegasprotos.com
www.bodegasprotos.com

PROTOS 2008 TC
100% tempranillo.

91 Colour: cherry, garnet rim. Nose: ripe fruit, spicy, creamy oak, complex, fine reductive notes, roasted coffee. Palate: powerful, flavourful, toasty, fleshy.

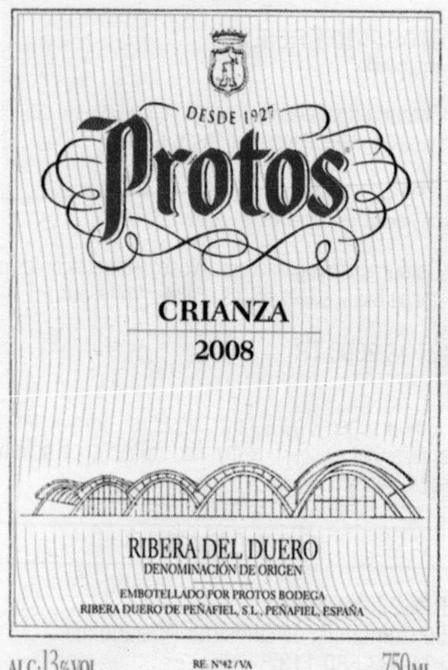

PROTOS SELECCIÓN FINCA EL GRAJO VIEJO 2009 T
tempranillo.

95 Colour: cherry, garnet rim. Nose: red berry notes, ripe fruit, sweet spices, cocoa bean, mineral. Palate: good acidity, powerful, flavourful, fleshy, toasty.

PROTOS 2009 T ROBLE
100% tempranillo.

90 Colour: cherry, purple rim. Nose: red berry notes, ripe fruit, sweet spices, cocoa bean, expressive. Palate: good acidity, powerful, flavourful, toasty.

PROTOS 2005 TR
100% tempranillo.

92 Colour: cherry, garnet rim. Nose: red berry notes, ripe fruit, sweet spices, toasty. Palate: balanced, elegant, flavourful, fleshy.

PROTOS 2004 TGR
100% tempranillo.

91 Colour: cherry, garnet rim. Nose: ripe fruit, old leather, sweet spices. Palate: unctuous, powerful, flavourful, fleshy, ripe fruit, round tannins.

SERIE PRIVADA CLUB DE VINOS PROTOS 2003 T
100% tempranillo.

90 Colour: light cherry, orangey edge. Nose: tobacco, old leather, spicy. Palate: fleshy, light-bodied, flavourful, slightly dry, soft tannins.

PROYECTOS SANCTVS

Monasterio de Silos 29 Boque C 4.C
28049 (Madrid)
☎: +34 617 331 411
info@sanctvs.com
www.sanctvs.com

ADAMÁ 2005 T
tinta del país.

87 Colour: dark-red cherry. Nose: overripe fruit, toasty, spicy, powerfull. Palate: flavourful, good acidity, round tannins, fruity.

QUINTA MILÚ

Camino El Val, s/n
La Aguilera (Burgos)
☎: +34 661 328 504
info@quintamilu.com
www.quintamilu.com

QUINTA MILÚ LA COMETA 2009 TC
tempranillo.

90 Colour: bright cherry, purple rim. Nose: fruit expression, sweet spices. Palate: fruity, flavourful, spicy, good acidity.

QUINTA MILÚ EL MALO 2009 TC
tempranillo.

88 Colour: very deep cherry. Nose: complex, balanced, dark chocolate, cocoa bean. Palate: fleshy, flavourful, round tannins.

MILÚ 2009 TC
tempranillo.

86 Colour: garnet rim. Nose: fruit preserve, balsamic herbs, dry stone, creamy oak. Palate: good acidity, powerful, flavourful.

REAL SITIO DE VENTOSILLA

Ctra. Magaz Aranda, Km. 66,1
09443 Gumiel del Mercado (Burgos)
☎: +34 947 546 900 - Fax: +34 947 546 999
bodega@pradorey.com
www.pradorey.com

PRADOREY 2010 RD FERMENTADO EN BARRICA
50% tempranillo, 50% merlot.

89 Colour: rose, purple rim. Nose: ripe fruit, powerfull, wild herbs. Palate: fruity, long, correct, easy to drink, spicy.

PRADOREY ÉLITE 2009 T
tempranillo.

94 Colour: very deep cherry. Nose: powerfull, characterful, complex, fruit expression, red berry notes, mineral, creamy oak, sweet spices. Palate: flavourful, fresh, good acidity, fruity, round tannins.

ADARO DE PRADOREY 2009 TC
100% tinto fino.

93 Colour: cherry, garnet rim. Nose: ripe fruit, red berry notes, creamy oak, mineral. Palate: creamy, spicy, ripe fruit, round tannins.

PRADOREY 2009 T ROBLE
95% tempranillo, 3% cabernet sauvignon, 2% merlot.

85 Colour: cherry, garnet rim. Nose: ripe fruit, sweet spices, creamy oak. Palate: good acidity, fruity, flavourful, round tannins.

PRADOREY FINCA VALDELAYEGUA 2008 TC
95% tempranillo, 3% cabernet sauvignon, 2% merlot.

88 Colour: cherry, garnet rim. Nose: toasty, spicy, ripe fruit, expressive. Palate: ripe fruit, balanced.

PRADOREY 2005 TR
95% tempranillo, 3% cabernet sauvignon, 2% merlot.

90 Colour: bright cherry, garnet rim. Nose: toasty, fruit preserve, spicy. Palate: long, round tannins.

PRADOREY 2004 TGR
95% tempranillo, 3% cabernet sauvignon, 2% merlot.

91 Colour: bright cherry, orangey edge. Nose: spicy, fine reductive notes, wet leather, fruit liqueur notes. Palate: spicy, fine tannins, elegant, long.

RED BOTTLE INTERNATIONAL

Rosales, 6
09400 Aranda de Duero (Burgos)
☎: +34 947 515 884 - Fax: +34 947 515 886
rbi@redbottleint.com

RIVENDEL 2009 T
100% tempranillo.

86 Colour: bright cherry. Nose: ripe fruit, creamy oak, spicy. Palate: flavourful, fruity, toasty, good acidity.

ADMIRACIÓN 2008 T
100% tempranillo.

88 Colour: cherry, garnet rim. Nose: ripe fruit, spicy, cocoa bean. Palate: ripe fruit, aged character, good acidity, fleshy, flavourful, long, round tannins.

REGOSTO

Camino Hormigueras, 163 Nave - 1 Discarlux
28031 (Madrid)
☎: +34 915 079 861 - Fax: +34 915 079 862
discarlux@discarlux.es

REGOSTO 2009 T ROBLE
tempranillo.

88 Colour: cherry, garnet rim. Nose: red berry notes, ripe fruit, powerfull, sweet spices, creamy oak. Palate: fleshy, powerful, flavourful, long.

REGOSTO 2006 TC
tempranillo.

87 Colour: cherry, garnet rim. Nose: spicy, fine reductive notes, aged wood nuances, sweet spices. Palate: spicy, long, creamy, flavourful.

RODRÍGUEZ SANZO

Manuel Azaña, 9- Local 15
47014 Valladolid (Valladolid)
☎: +34 983 150 150 - Fax: +34 983 150 151
valsanzo@valsanzo.com
www.valsanzo.com

VALSANZO 2008 TC
tempranillo.

88 Colour: cherry, garnet rim. Nose: red berry notes, ripe fruit, spicy, cocoa bean, toasty. Palate: good acidity, fleshy, flavourful, toasty.

PARAJES 2006 TR
100% tinto fino.

90 Colour: cherry, garnet rim. Nose: old leather, cocoa bean, dark chocolate, toasty, ripe fruit. Palate: fleshy, flavourful, toasty, easy to drink.

SANCIUS BODEGAS Y VIÑEDOS

Avda. San Gregorio, 18
47316 Piñel de Arriba (Valladolid)
☎: +34 608 698 597 - Fax: +34 983 872 119
info@sancius.com
www.sancius.com

SANCIUS 2008 T ROBLE
90% tinta del país, 10% cabernet sauvignon.

86 Colour: cherry, garnet rim. Nose: fruit preserve, toasty, warm. Palate: flavourful, fruity, good acidity, round tannins.

SANCIUS 2006 TC
tinta del país.

85 Colour: cherry, garnet rim. Nose: ripe fruit, creamy oak, toasty, complex, sweet spices. Palate: powerful, flavourful, toasty.

SELECCIÓN CÉSAR MUÑOZ

Acera de Recoletos, 14
47004 (Valladolid)
☎: +34 666 548 751
info@cesarmunoz.es
www.bodegasmagallanes.es

MAGALLANES 2007 TC
tempranillo.

91 Colour: cherry, garnet rim. Nose: ripe fruit, roasted coffee, dark chocolate. Palate: powerful, fine bitter notes, long.

SELECCIÓN TORRES

Del Rosario, 56
47311 Fompedraza (Valladolid)
☎: +34 938 177 400 - Fax: +34 938 177 444
mailadmin@torres.es
www.torres.es

CELESTE 2009 TC
tinto fino.

90 Colour: cherry, garnet rim. Nose: ripe fruit, red berry notes, spicy, balanced. Palate: good acidity, fleshy, flavourful, powerful, round tannins.

SEÑORIO DE BOCOS

Camino La Canaleja, s/n
47317 Bocos de Duero (Valladolid)
☎: +34 983 880 988 - Fax: +34 983 880 988
bodegas@senoriodebocos.com
www.senoriodebocos.com

AUTOR DE BOCOS 2009 T
100% tinta del país.

90 Colour: bright cherry. Nose: ripe fruit, sweet spices, creamy oak, expressive. Palate: flavourful, fruity, toasty, round tannins, fleshy, complex.

SEÑORIO DE BOCOS 2008 TC
100% tempranillo.

88 Colour: cherry, garnet rim. Nose: ripe fruit, powerfull, toasty. Palate: good acidity, fruity, long, creamy, fine tannins.

SOLTERRA COMPAÑÍA VINÍCOLA

Ctra. Pedrosa, Km. 1,5
09300 Roa (Burgos)
☎: +34 947 540 376
info@cvsolterra.com
www.cvsolterra.com

FUENTE NOGAL 2009 T ROBLE
100% tinto fino.

88 Colour: cherry, purple rim. Nose: ripe fruit, sweet spices, creamy oak, expressive. Palate: flavourful, fruity, toasty.

ALTO DE LOS ZORROS 2007 TC
100% tinto fino.

88 Colour: cherry, garnet rim. Nose: ripe fruit, earthy notes, cocoa bean, sweet spices, toasty. Palate: flavourful, fleshy, toasty, good acidity.

ALTO DE LOS ZORROS 2005 TR
100% tinto fino.

87 Colour: cherry, garnet rim. Nose: ripe fruit, spicy, creamy oak, toasty. Palate: powerful, flavourful, toasty.

TORRES DE ANGUIX

Camino La Tejera, s/n
09312 Anguix (Burgos)
☎: +34 947 554 008 - Fax: +34 947 554 129
enologia@torresdeanguix.com
www.torresdeanguix.com

R D'ANGUIX 2010 RD
100% tinta del país.

88 Colour: rose, purple rim. Nose: raspberry, red berry notes, floral, fresh, lactic notes. Palate: light-bodied, fresh, fruity, flavourful.

T D'ANGUIX 2010 T
100% tinta del país.

86 Colour: cherry, garnet rim. Nose: ripe fruit, red berry notes, powerfull. Palate: good acidity, ripe fruit, spicy.

GALLERY 101 2007 TC
100% tinta del país.

89 Colour: deep cherry, garnet rim. Nose: balanced, expressive, complex, spicy, balsamic herbs. Palate: fruity, ripe fruit, spicy.

T D'ANGUIX 2006 TC
100% tinta del país.

88 Colour: cherry, garnet rim. Nose: ripe fruit, creamy oak, toasty, sweet spices, expressive. Palate: powerful, flavourful, toasty.

D'ANGUIX 2005 T
100% tinta del país.

90 Colour: cherry, garnet rim. Nose: powerfull, toasty, candied fruit, sweet spices. Palate: fruity, spicy.

T D'ANGUIX 2004 TR
100% tinta del país.

90 Colour: pale ruby, brick rim edge. Nose: fruit liqueur notes, characterful, powerfull, toasty, spicy. Palate: powerful, fine bitter notes, flavourful.

GALLERY 101 2004 TR
100% tinta del país.

89 Colour: bright cherry, garnet rim. Nose: fruit preserve, creamy oak, sweet spices. Palate: ripe fruit, fleshy.

GALLERY 101 RESERVA VENDIMIA SELECCIONADA 2003 T
100% tinta del país.

88 Colour: cherry, garnet rim. Nose: ripe fruit, spicy, creamy oak. Palate: powerful, flavourful, toasty, round tannins.

T D'ANGUIX 2001 TGR
100% tinta del país.

89 Colour: pale ruby, brick rim edge. Nose: powerfull, ripe fruit, toasty, dark chocolate, aromatic coffee. Palate: spicy, ripe fruit, fine bitter notes, long.

UVAS FELICES

Agullers, 7
08003 Barcelona (Barcelona)
☎: +34 902 327 777
www.vilaviniteca.es

VENTA LAS VACAS 2009 T
tinto fino.

91 Colour: deep cherry. Nose: ripe fruit, expressive, spicy. Palate: complex, fleshy, fruity, powerful, slightly dry, soft tannins.

VALTRAVIESO

Finca La Revilla, s/n
47316 Piñel de Arriba (Valladolid)
☎: +34 983 484 030 - Fax: +34 983 484 037
valtravieso@valtravieso.com
www.valtravieso.com

VALTRAVIESO 2010 T
90% tinto fino, 5% cabernet sauvignon, 5% merlot.

87 Colour: cherry, garnet rim. Nose: ripe fruit, balsamic herbs, fresh. Palate: good acidity, fruity, flavourful, full.

VALTRAVIESO 2009 T ROBLE
90% tinto fino, 5% cabernet sauvignon, 5% merlot.

88 Colour: cherry, garnet rim. Nose: red berry notes, medium intensity, spicy. Palate: fleshy, ripe fruit, flavourful, round tannins.

VT VENDIMIA SELECCIONADA 2007 T
75% tinto fino, 15% cabernet sauvignon, 10% merlot.

90 Colour: cherry, garnet rim. Nose: creamy oak, sweet spices, ripe fruit. Palate: ripe fruit, fleshy, round tannins.

VT TINTA FINA 2007 T
100% tinto fino.

87 Colour: deep cherry, garnet rim. Nose: medium intensity, toasty, sweet spices, ripe fruit. Palate: fruity, spicy.

VALTRAVIESO 2007 TC
90% tinto fino, 5% cabernet sauvignon, 5% merlot.

86 Colour: cherry, garnet rim. Nose: ripe fruit, spicy, creamy oak, medium intensity. Palate: good acidity, flavourful, round tannins.

GRAN VALTRAVIESO 2006 TR
100% tinto fino.

93 Colour: cherry, garnet rim. Nose: dark chocolate, spicy, creamy oak, expressive, complex, fruit expression. Palate: spicy, long, mineral.

VALTRAVIESO 2006 TR
90% tinto fino, 5% cabernet sauvignon, 5% merlot.

91 Colour: cherry, garnet rim. Nose: spicy, creamy oak, toasty, earthy notes, fruit expression. Palate: flavourful, toasty, round tannins, spicy, balanced, fleshy.

VINCE JOHN

Ctra. Roa Peñafiel, Km. 8,3
09317 San Martín de Rubiales (Burgos)
☎: +34 947 550 121
bodega@vicentesanjuan.com
www.bodegavicentesanjuan.com

BLASÓN DE ROMERA 2010 RD
100% tempranillo.

88 Colour: rose. Nose: fruit expression, expressive, powerfull. Palate: good structure, flavourful, fruity, easy to drink, good acidity.

BLASÓN DE ROMERA TEMPRANILLO 2010 T
100% tempranillo.

84 Colour: cherry, garnet rim. Nose: ripe fruit, medium intensity. Palate: fruity, flavourful, good acidity.

BLASÓN DE ROMERA 2009 TC
100% tempranillo.

89 Color bright cherry. Aroma ripe fruit, sweet spices, creamy oak, expressive. Taste flavourful, fruity, toasty, round tannins.

BLASÓN DE ROMERA 2007 TR
100% tempranillo.

85 Colour: cherry, garnet rim. Nose: red berry notes, ripe fruit, sweet spices, toasty. Palate: powerful, flavourful, long.

VINOS HERCAL

Santo Domingo, 2
09400 Roa (Burgos)
☎: +34 947 541 281
ventas@somanilla.es
www.somanilla.es

BOCCA 2008 T ROBLE
tempranillo.

89 Colour: cherry, garnet rim. Nose: red berry notes, raspberry, dark chocolate, toasty. Palate: good finish, powerful, flavourful, toasty.

SOMANILLA VENDIMIA SELECCIONADA 2007 T
tempranillo.

90 Colour: bright cherry. Nose: ripe fruit, sweet spices, creamy oak, mineral. Palate: flavourful, fruity, toasty, round tannins.

VINOS SANTOS ARRANZ (LÁGRIMA NEGRA)

Ctra. de Valbuena, s/n
47315 Pesquera de Duero (Valladolid)
☎: +34 983 870 008 - Fax: +34 983 870 008
lagrimanegra82@hotmail.com
www.lagrima-negra.com

LÁGRIMA NEGRA 2009 T ROBLE
tinta del país.

84 Colour: cherry, garnet rim. Nose: fruit preserve, toasty. Palate: fruity, easy to drink.

LÁGRIMA NEGRA 2008 TC
tinta del país.

86 Colour: cherry, garnet rim. Nose: ripe fruit, spicy, balanced. Palate: fruity, flavourful, great length.

LÁGRIMA NEGRA 2006 TR
tinta del país, cabernet sauvignon.

88 Colour: cherry, garnet rim. Nose: ripe fruit, toasty, spicy. Palate: flavourful, round tannins, fleshy, long.

VIÑA ARNAIZ

Ctra. N-122, km. 281
09316 Haza (Burgos)
☎: +34 914 355 556 - Fax: +34 915 766 607
rarevalo@jgc.es
www.vinosdefamilia.com

MAYOR DE CASTILLA 2010 T
100% tempranillo.

85 Colour: cherry, garnet rim. Nose: ripe fruit, red berry notes, medium intensity. Palate: flavourful, fruity, fresh, good acidity.

VIÑA ARNÁIZ 2009 T ROBLE
95% tempranillo, 3% cabernet sauvignon, 2% merlot.

88 Color bright cherry. Aroma ripe fruit, sweet spices, creamy oak, expressive. Taste flavourful, fruity, toasty, round tannins.

MAYOR DE CASTILLA 2009 T ROBLE
100% tempranillo.

84 Colour: cherry, garnet rim. Nose: fruit preserve, toasty. Palate: fruity, round tannins, correct.

VIÑA ARNÁIZ 2008 TC
100% tempranillo.

86 Colour: cherry, garnet rim. Nose: ripe fruit, creamy oak, spicy. Palate: good acidity, fruity, round tannins.

VIÑA ARNÁIZ 2007 TR
85% tempranillo, 10% cabernet sauvignon, 5% merlot.

87 Colour: cherry, garnet rim. Nose: ripe fruit, creamy oak. Palate: good acidity, unctuous, ripe fruit, round tannins.

MAYOR DE CASTILLA 2007 TC
100% tempranillo.

87 Colour: cherry, garnet rim. Nose: red berry notes, ripe fruit, sweet spices, toasty. Palate: powerful, rich, flavourful, fleshy.

MAYOR DE CASTILLA 2007 TR
100% tempranillo.

86 Colour: cherry, garnet rim. Nose: ripe fruit, toasty, complex, sweet spices. Palate: powerful, flavourful, toasty.

MAYOR DE CASTILLA 2004 TGR
100% tempranillo.

88 Colour: cherry, garnet rim. Nose: ripe fruit, balanced, spicy. Palate: fruity, flavourful, spicy, ripe fruit.

VIÑA MAMBRILLA

Ctra. Pedrosa s/n
09318 Mambrilla de Castrejón (Burgos)
☎: +34 947 540 234 - Fax: +34 947 540 234
bodega@mambrilla.com
www.mambrilla.com

ALIDIS 2010 T
tinta del país.

86 Colour: cherry, purple rim. Nose: fresh fruit, red berry notes. Palate: flavourful, fruity, good acidity, round tannins.

ALIDIS 2009 T ROBLE
100% tinta del país.

88 Colour: bright cherry. Nose: ripe fruit, sweet spices, creamy oak. Palate: flavourful, fruity, toasty, long.

ALIDIS EXPRESIÓN 2008 TC
100% tinta del país.

89 Colour: cherry, garnet rim. Nose: ripe fruit, spicy, creamy oak, toasty. Palate: powerful, flavourful, toasty, round tannins, fleshy.

ALIDIS EXPRESIÓN 2007 TC
100% tinta del país.

90 Colour: cherry, garnet rim. Nose: ripe fruit, spicy, creamy oak, toasty, complex. Palate: powerful, flavourful, toasty, complex, fleshy, long.

ALIDIS 2007 TR
100% tinta del país.

88 Colour: cherry, garnet rim. Nose: sweet spices, toasty, fruit preserve. Palate: flavourful, spicy, great length.

ALIDIS VS 2006 T

92 Colour: cherry, garnet rim. Nose: powerfull, characterful, ripe fruit, fruit expression, sweet spices, toasty. Palate: powerful, sweetness, fleshy.

VIÑA SOLORCA

Ctra. Circunvalación, s/n
09300 Roa (Burgos)
☎: +34 947 541 823 - Fax: +34 947 540 035
info@bodegassolorca.com
www.bodegassolorca.com

BARÓN DEL VALLE 2009 T BARRICA
100% tempranillo.

86 Colour: cherry, garnet rim. Nose: ripe fruit, toasty, spicy. Palate: fruity, flavourful, round tannins, spicy.

VIÑA SOLORCA 2006 TC
100% tempranillo.

87 Colour: pale ruby, brick rim edge. Nose: medium intensity, cigar, fine reductive notes, ripe fruit, toasty. Palate: powerful, spicy, long.

GRAN SOLORCA 2005 TR
100% tempranillo.

91 Colour: bright cherry, garnet rim. Nose: complex, dark chocolate, sweet spices, ripe fruit. Palate: good structure, balanced, fine bitter notes, round tannins.

VIÑA VALDEMAZÓN

Pza. Sur, 3
47359 Olivares de Duero (Valladolid)
☎: +34 983 680 220
info@valdemazon.com
www.valdemazon.com

VIÑA VALDEMAZÓN VENDIMIA SELECCIONADA 2008 T
100% tempranillo.

92 Colour: cherry, garnet rim. Nose: ripe fruit, expressive, sweet spices, cocoa bean, aromatic coffee, toasty. Palate: good acidity, flavourful, full, spicy, round tannins.

VIÑAYTIA

Paraje El Soto, s/n
09370 Quintana del Pidio (Burgos)
☎: +34 947 545 126 - Fax: +34 947 545 605
bodega@cillardesilos.es

EL QUINTANAL 2010 T
tempranillo.

89 Colour: cherry, purple rim. Nose: expressive, fresh fruit, red berry notes, floral. Palate: flavourful, fruity, good acidity, round tannins, toasty.

VIÑEDOS ALONSO DEL YERRO

Finca Santa Marta - Ctra. Roa-Anguix, Km. 1,8
09300 Roa (Burgos)
☎: +34 913 160 121 - Fax: +34 913 160 121
mariadelyerro@vay.es
www.alonsodelyerro.com

"MARÍA" ALONSO DEL YERRO 2008 T
100% tempranillo.

94 Colour: cherry, garnet rim. Nose: spicy, creamy oak, toasty, complex, fruit expression, mineral. Palate: powerful, flavourful, toasty, round tannins.

ALONSO DEL YERRO 2008 T
tempranillo.

93 Colour: bright cherry. Nose: sweet spices, creamy oak, ripe fruit. Palate: flavourful, fruity, toasty, round tannins.

VIÑEDOS Y BODEGAS ÁSTER

Ctra. Palencia-Aranda, km. 55,1- Término El Caño
09312 Anguix (Burgos)
☎: +34 947 522 700 - Fax: +34 947 522 701
aster@riojalta.com
www.riojalta.com

ÁSTER FINCA EL OTERO 2009 T FERMENTADO EN BARRICA
100% tinta del país.

94 Colour: cherry, garnet rim. Nose: powerfull, fruit expression, red berry notes, sweet spices, cocoa bean, mineral. Palate: flavourful, powerful, fleshy, complex.

ÁSTER 2008 TC
100% tinta del país.

89 Colour: bright cherry, garnet rim. Nose: ripe fruit, dark chocolate, spicy, complex, old leather. Palate: good structure, fruity, round tannins.

ÁSTER 2005 TR
tinta del país.

90 Colour: bright cherry. Nose: ripe fruit, sweet spices, creamy oak, characterful, fine reductive notes. Palate: flavourful, fruity, toasty, round tannins.

VIÑEDOS Y BODEGAS GARCÍA FIGUERO

Ctra. La Horra - Roa, Km. 2,2
09311 La Horra (Burgos)
☎: +34 947 542 127 - Fax: +34 947 542 033
bodega@tintofiguero.com
www.tintofiguero.com

TINTO FIGUERO 4 2010 T ROBLE
100% tempranillo.

87 Colour: cherry, garnet rim. Nose: red berry notes, fresh fruit, undergrowth, sweet spices, toasty. Palate: spicy, powerful, flavourful.

FIGUERO NOBLE 2009 T
tempranillo.

88 Colour: dark-red cherry, garnet rim. Nose: ripe fruit, spicy, roasted coffee. Palate: powerful, fleshy, flavourful.

FIGUERO TINUS 2008 T
100% tempranillo.

91 Colour: cherry, garnet rim. Nose: red berry notes, ripe fruit, spicy, creamy oak, expressive, elegant. Palate: fleshy, complex, powerful, flavourful.

TINTO FIGUERO VENDIMIA SELECCIONADA 2008 T
100% tempranillo.

87 Colour: dark-red cherry, garnet rim. Nose: red berry notes, ripe fruit, mineral, spicy, creamy oak. Palate: round, unctuous, powerful, flavourful.

PAGO DE SANGARA 2007 TC
100% tempranillo.

87 Colour: cherry, garnet rim. Nose: overripe fruit, balsamic herbs, spicy. Palate: flavourful, fleshy, spicy, long.

TINTO FIGUERO 12 MESES BARRICA 2006 TC
tempranillo.

87 Colour: cherry, garnet rim. Nose: ripe fruit, spicy, creamy oak, toasty, complex, fine reductive notes. Palate: powerful, flavourful, toasty.

FIGUERO NOBLE 2005 T
tempranillo.

90 Colour: cherry, garnet rim. Nose: ripe fruit, cocoa bean, dark chocolate, sweet spices, creamy oak. Palate: powerful, flavourful, fleshy, ripe fruit, toasty.

TINTO FIGUERO VENDIMIA SELECCIONADA 2005 T
tempranillo.

90 Colour: cherry, garnet rim. Nose: ripe fruit, spicy, creamy oak, complex. Palate: powerful, flavourful, toasty, ripe fruit.

TINTO FIGUERO 15 MESES BARRICA 2005 TR
tempranillo.

87 Colour: cherry, garnet rim. Nose: ripe fruit, spicy, creamy oak, toasty. Palate: powerful, flavourful, toasty, round tannins.

VIÑEDOS Y BODEGAS GORMAZ

Ctra. de Soria, s/n
42330 San Esteban de Gormaz (Soria)
☎: +34 975 350 404 - Fax: +34 975 351 313
info@hispanobodegas.com
www.hispanobodegas.com

VIÑA GORMAZ 2010 T
tempranillo.

88 Colour: deep cherry, purple rim. Nose: balanced, fresh, red berry notes, wild herbs. Palate: balanced, fruity, good acidity.

CATANIA 2010 T JOVEN
tempranillo.

87 Colour: cherry, garnet rim. Nose: ripe fruit, red berry notes, fruit expression. Palate: good acidity, full, flavourful.

CATANIA 2009 T ROBLE
tempranillo.

87 Colour: cherry, garnet rim. Nose: spicy, balsamic herbs, ripe fruit, toasty. Palate: good acidity, flavourful, fleshy.

12 LINAJES 2009 T ROBLE
tempranillo.

84 Colour: cherry, garnet rim. Nose: overripe fruit, creamy oak. Palate: fruity, flavourful, round tannins.

VIÑA GORMAZ 2008 TC
tempranillo.

90 Colour: dark-red cherry. Nose: ripe fruit, creamy oak, spicy, cocoa bean. Palate: good acidity, flavourful, fleshy, long, fine tannins.

CATANIA 2008 TC
tempranillo.

86 Colour: cherry, garnet rim. Nose: fruit expression, spicy, toasty. Palate: good acidity, spicy, fruity, round tannins.

12 LINAJES 2008 TC
tempranillo.

84 Colour: cherry, garnet rim. Nose: red berry notes, ripe fruit, medium intensity. Palate: flavourful, fleshy.

12 LINAJES 2006 TR
tempranillo.

90 Colour: cherry, garnet rim. Nose: spicy, creamy oak, toasty, complex, red berry notes, ripe fruit. Palate: powerful, flavourful, toasty, round tannins.

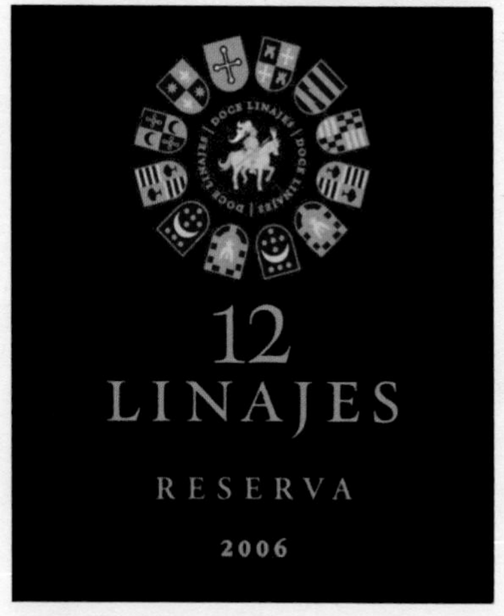

VIÑEDOS Y BODEGAS RIBÓN

Basilón, 15
47350 Quintanilla de Onésimo (Valladolid)
☎: +34 983 680 015 - Fax: +34 983 680 015
info@bodegasribon.com
www.bodegasribon.com

RIBÓN 2009 T ROBLE
tempranillo.

88 Colour: cherry, garnet rim. Nose: fruit expression, balsamic herbs, creamy oak, spicy. Palate: fruity, flavourful, full, fleshy, round tannins.

WINNER WINES

Avda. del Mediterráneo, 38
28007 Madrid (Madrid)
☎: +34 915 019 042 - Fax: +34 915 017 794
winnerwines@ibernoble.com
www.ibernoble.com

IBERNOBLE S/C TC
tempranillo, cabernet sauvignon.

87 Colour: bright cherry, garnet rim. Nose: ripe fruit, medium intensity, balanced. Palate: flavourful, spicy, easy to drink.

IBERNOBLE S.C. TR
tempranillo, cabernet sauvignon.

88 Colour: cherry, garnet rim. Nose: powerfull, creamy oak, toasty, aromatic coffee. Palate: flavourful, powerful, fleshy, fine bitter notes.

IBERNOBLE 2009 T ROBLE
tempranillo, cabernet sauvignon.

84 Colour: bright cherry. Nose: ripe fruit, creamy oak, spicy, balsamic herbs. Palate: flavourful, fruity, toasty.

IBERNOBLE COSECHA T
tempranillo, cabernet sauvignon.

85 Colour: cherry, garnet rim. Nose: ripe fruit, medium intensity, grassy. Palate: good acidity, flavourful, easy to drink.

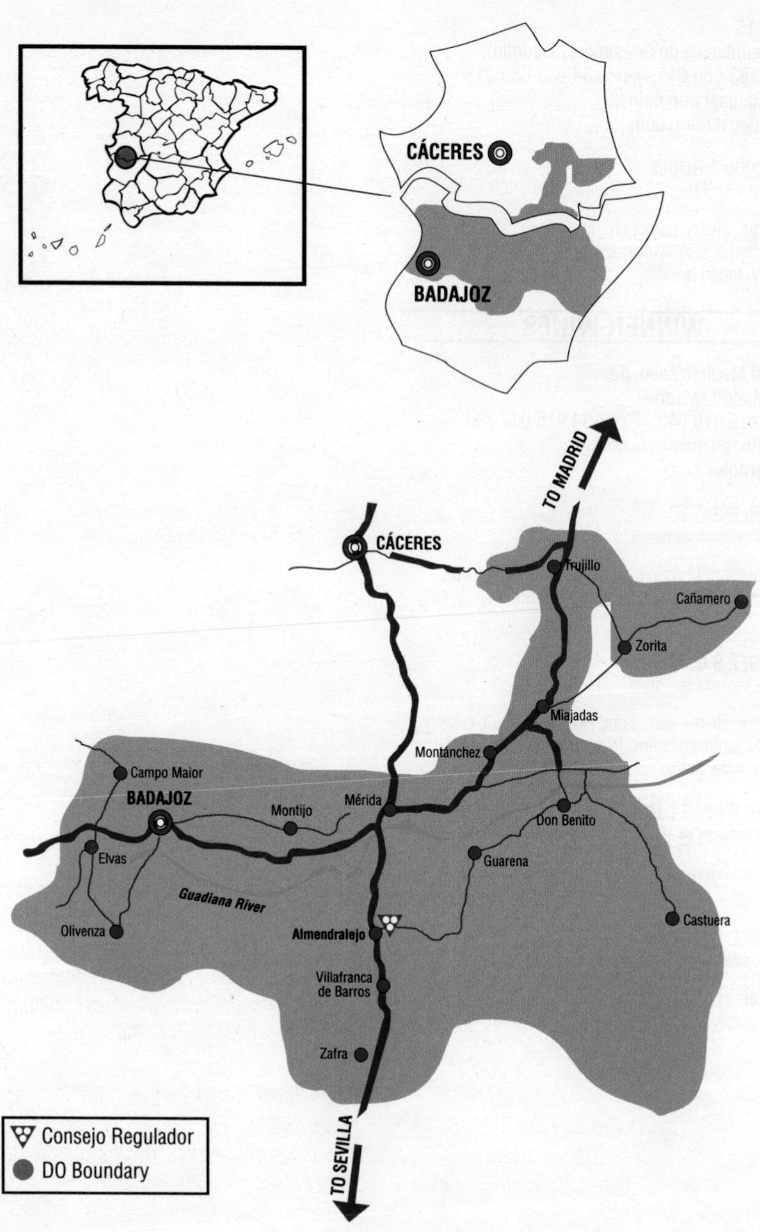
CÁCERES
BADAJOZ
TO MADRID
CÁCERES
Trujillo
Cañamero
Zorita
Miajadas
Montánchez
Campo Maior
BADAJOZ
Montijo
Mérida
Don Benito
Elvas
Guarena
Guadiana River
Olivenza
Almendralejo
Castuera
Villafranca de Barros
Zafra
Consejo Regulador
DO Boundary
TO SEVILLA

NEWS ABOUT THE VINTAGE:

Like day and night, that is the best way to describe the differences between the 2009 and the 2010 vintages in Ribera del Guadiana. Last year we pointed at the overtly overripe character and high alcohol levels of the 2009 wines, but in 2010 we have to talk of freshness and loads of expression. Young red renderings show a sort of freshness bordering in some cases with underripe, green notes, that regretfully has comes to characterize a small group of traditional produces who rather rely on high yields and care little for what is known as optimal ripeness, something particularly difficult to achieve in cooler years. Noteworthy are the young *tempranillo* and *syrah* wines from Señorío de Alange (Alvear), full of varietal character.

The worst face of the DO is represented by the wines from 2009, where overripe, confected notes are simply too evident. We have to remind that the region has very low altitude, and that means that day-night temperature differential is also low and heat waves a common feature, like those that happened in the summer of 2009 and eventually affected the quality of most young wines from that vintage. Another feature that renders vine growing in the region a pretty difficult business is their excessive reliance on short-cycled grape varieties like *tempranillo* and *syrah* instead of long-cycled ones (*garnacha tinta, monastrell, petit verdot, graciano* or *garnacha tintorera*) planted in the neighbouring province of Alentejo, in Portugal, which add fresher notes in hotter years.

Between the best wines of the DO we find the aged examples from Pago los Balancines, Bodegas Toribio Viña Puebla, Viñas de Alange or Viñedos y Bodegas Carabal, where we can easily appreciate the ageing potential of the local varieties. The following batch –in scoring terms– of aged wines shows on average dull, with excessive toasted notes and high alcohol.

The white wines of 2009 show just like the reds: fresh, fruity and floral, on the opposite side of the honey and liqueur-like character of previous vintages. In terms of varieties, white local grapes like *cayetana* or *pardina* are being progressively replaced by red varieties, mainly *tempranillo*.

LOCATION:

Covering the 6 wine-growing regions of Extremadura, with a total surface of more than 87,000 Ha as described below.

GRAPE VARIETIES:

WHITE: *Alarije, Borba, Cayetana Blanca, Pardina, Macabeo, Chardonnay, Chelva or Montua, Malvar, Parellada, Pedro Ximénez, Verdejo, Eva, Cigüente, Perruno, Moscatel de Alejandría, Moscatel de Grano Menudo, Sauvignon Blanc* and *Bobal Blanca.*
RED: *Garnacha Tinta, Tempranillo, Bobal, Cabernet Sauvignon, Garnacha Tintorera, Graciano, Mazuela, Merlot, Monastrell, Syrah, Pinot Noir* and *Jaén Tinto.*

SUB-REGIONS:

Cañamero. To the south east of the province of Cáceres, in the heart of the Sierra de Guadalupe. It comprises the municipal districts of Alia, Berzocana, Cañamero, Guadalupe and Valdecaballeros. The vineyards are located on the mountainside, at altitudes of between 600 m to 800 m. The terrain is rugged and the soil is slaty and loose. The climate is mild without great temperature contrasts, and the average annual rainfall is 750 mm to 800 mm. The main grape variety is the white *Alarije.*

Montánchez. Comprising 27 municipal districts. It is characterised by its complex terrain, with numerous hills and small valleys. The vineyards are located on brown acidic soil. The climate is Continental in nature and the average annual rainfall is between 500 mm and 600 mm. The white grape variety *Borba* occupies two thirds of the vineyards in the region.

Ribera Alta. This covers the Vegas del Guadiana and the plains of La Serena and Campo de Castuera and comprises 38 municipal districts. The soil is very sandy. The most common varieties are *Alarije*, *Borba* (white), *Tempranillo* and *Garnacha* (red).

Ribera Baja. Comprising 11 municipal districts. The vineyards are located on clayey-limy soil. The climate is Continental, with a moderate Atlantic influence and slight contrasts in temperature. The most common varieties are: *Cayetana Blanca* and *Pardina* among the whites, and *Tempranillo* among the reds.

Matanegra. Rather similar to Tierra de Barros, but with a milder climate. It comprises 8 municipal districts, and the most common grape varieties are *Beba*, *Montua* (whites), *Tempranillo*, *Garnacha* and *Cabernet Sauvignon* (reds).

Tierra de Barros. Situated in the centre of the province of Badajoz and the largest (4475 Ha and 37 municipal districts). It has flat plains with fertile soils which are rich in nutrients and have great water retention capacity (Rainfall is low: 350 mm to 450 mm per year). The most common varieties are the white *Cayetana Blanca* and *Pardina*, and the red *Tempranillo*, *Garnacha* and *Cabernet Sauvignon*.

FIGURES:

Vineyard surface: 29,000 – **Wine-Growers:** 3,832 – **Wineries:** 50 – **2010 Harvest rating:** Very Good – **Production:** 7,831,663 litres – **Market percentages:** --% domestic. --% export

CONSEJO REGULADOR

Ctra. Sevilla-Gijón, km. 114
06200 Almendralejo (Badajoz). Apdo. 299
☎: +34 924 671 302 - Fax: +34 924 664 703
@ informacion@riberadelguadiana.org
www.riberadelguadiana.eu

GENERAL CHARACTERISTICS OF THE WINES

WHITES	With the differences that may appear between the different sub-regions, the white wines are substantial, with a Mediterranean character (mountain herbs, undergrowth, supple on the palate, but at the same time, persistent and very flavourful).
ROSÉS	Except for some modern wine production with the usual raspberry flavour, they are, in general, warm, very fruity and with a point of sweetness produced by the high alcohol content.
REDS	The red wines are powerful, warm, supple, with sweet tannins and smoothness, even those based on the *Tempranillo*. Flavours of sunny vineyards with *Garnacha* that provide the ripe and fruity nuance characteristic of this grape variety.

BODEGA SAN MARCOS

Ctra. Aceuchal, s/n
06200 Almendralejo (Badajoz)
☎: +34 924 670 410 - Fax: +34 924 665 505
ventas@bodegasanmarcos.com
www.campobarro.com

CAMPOBARRO PARDINA 2010 B
100% pardina.

86 Colour: bright straw. Nose: fresh, fresh fruit, white flowers. Palate: flavourful, fruity, good acidity, balanced.

CAMPOBARRO MACABEO 2010 B
100% macabeo.

83 Colour: bright straw. Nose: white flowers, fresh fruit, tropical fruit. Palate: flavourful, fruity, good acidity.

CAMPOBARRO 2010 RD
100% tempranillo.

85 Colour: onion pink. Nose: elegant, candied fruit, dried flowers, red berry notes. Palate: light-bodied, flavourful, good acidity, long, spicy.

CAMPOBARRO SELECCIÓN 2009 T
50% mazuelo, 50% tempranillo.

83 Colour: cherry, garnet rim. Nose: cocoa bean, new oak, toasty, ripe fruit. Palate: fleshy, fine bitter notes, correct.

CAMPOBARRO TEMPRANILLO 2009 T
100% tempranillo.

81 Colour: cherry, garnet rim. Nose: candied fruit, fruit liqueur notes, warm. Palate: sweetness, fine bitter notes, warm.

HEREDAD DE BARROS 2007 TC
100% tempranillo.

84 Colour: cherry, garnet rim. Nose: ripe fruit, spicy, woody. Palate: powerful, flavourful, toasty, round tannins.

CAMPOBARRO CENCIBEL 2007 T ROBLE
100% tempranillo.

83 Colour: deep cherry. Nose: overripe fruit, fruit liqueur notes, smoky, caramel. Palate: spirituous, concentrated, grainy tannins.

CAMPOBARRO 2007 TC
100% tempranillo.

83 Colour: cherry, garnet rim. Nose: creamy oak, toasty, overripe fruit. Palate: powerful, flavourful, toasty, round tannins.

HEREDAD DE BARROS 2004 TR
100% tempranillo.

85 Color pale ruby, brick rim edge. Aroma elegant, spicy, fine reductive notes, wet leather, aged wood nuances, fruit liqueur notes. Taste spicy, fine tannins, elegant, long.

CAMPOBARRO 2004 TR
100% tempranillo.

85 Colour: pale ruby, brick rim edge. Nose: toasty, dark chocolate, aromatic coffee, overripe fruit, fruit liqueur notes. Palate: spicy, easy to drink, balsamic.

BODEGAS CAÑALVA

Coto, 54
10136 Cañamero (Cáceres)
☎: +34 927 369 405 - Fax: +34 927 369 405
info@bodegascanalva.com
www.bodegascañalva.com

FUENTE CORTIJO 2005 TC
100% tempranillo.

88 Colour: cherry, garnet rim. Nose: spicy, creamy oak, toasty, ripe fruit. Palate: powerful, flavourful, toasty, round tannins.

BODEGAS LAR DE BARROS INVIOSA

Apdo. Correos 291
06200 Almendralejo (Badajoz)
☎: +34 924 671 235 - Fax: +34 924 687 231
sophia@lardebarros.com
www.lardebarros.com

LAR DE BARROS 2010 B
90% macabeo, 10% chardonnay.

80 Colour: pale. Nose: medium intensity, short, fresh. Palate: flavourful, fruity, fresh.

LAR DE BARROS 2010 RD
100% syrah.

81 Colour: rose, purple rim. Nose: powerfull, ripe fruit, red berry notes. Palate: fleshy, powerful, fruity, fresh.

LAR DE BARROS TEMPRANILLO 2010 T
100% tempranillo.

80 Colour: deep cherry. Nose: medium intensity, ripe fruit, warm, grassy. Palate: powerful, fine bitter notes, slightly green tannins.

LAR DE BARROS 2009 T
100% tempranillo.

70

LAR DE BARROS 2006 TC
100% tempranillo.

76

LAR DE LARES 2004 TGR
100% tempranillo.

83 Colour: pale ruby, brick rim edge. Nose: fine reductive notes, wet leather, aged wood nuances, fruit liqueur notes, overripe fruit. Palate: spicy, fine tannins, long.

BODEGAS MARTÍNEZ PAIVA

Ctra. Gijón - Sevilla N-630, Km. 646
Apdo. Correos 87
06200 Almendralejo (Badajoz)
☎: +34 924 671 130 - Fax: +34 924 663 056
info@payva.es
www.payva.es

PAYVA MOSCATEL 2010 B
100% moscatel.

87 Colour: bright straw. Nose: fresh, white flowers, citrus fruit, varietal, fruit expression. Palate: flavourful, fruity, good acidity, balanced.

PAYVA CAYETANA BLANCA 2010 B
100% cayetana blanca.

85 Colour: bright straw. Nose: ripe fruit, citrus fruit, sweet spices, tropical fruit. Palate: flavourful, ripe fruit, fine bitter notes.

PAYVA MACABEO 2010 B
100% macabeo.

84 Colour: bright straw. Nose: ripe fruit, tropical fruit, citrus fruit. Palate: flavourful, fine bitter notes, good acidity.

PAYVA 2010 T
90% tempranillo, 10% graciano.

85 Colour: cherry, purple rim. Nose: red berry notes, floral, green pepper. Palate: flavourful, fruity, good acidity, round tannins.

DOÑA FRANCISQUITA 2010 T
80% tempranillo, 10% garnacha, 10% graciano.

82 Colour: cherry, purple rim. Nose: powerfull, aged wood nuances, red berry notes, woody. Palate: flavourful, fruity, fleshy.

PAYVA 2007 TC
80% tempranillo, 10% cabernet sauvignon, 10% graciano.

84 Colour: cherry, garnet rim. Nose: spicy, toasty, overripe fruit. Palate: powerful, toasty, round tannins.

PAYVA SELECCIÓN 2006 TC
100% tempranillo.

87 Colour: cherry, garnet rim. Nose: spicy, toasty, overripe fruit. Palate: powerful, flavourful, toasty, round tannins.

PAYVA 2005 TR
80% tempranillo, 20% graciano.

88 Colour: pale ruby, brick rim edge. Nose: balsamic herbs, wet leather, cigar, ripe fruit, toasty, spicy. Palate: flavourful, spicy, long.

BODEGAS MEDINA

Ctra. N-432, Km. 76
06310 Puebla de Sancho Pérez (Badajoz)
☎: +34 924 575 060 - Fax: +34 924 575 076
info@bodegasmedina.net
www.bodegasmedina.net

JALOCO 2010 RD
cabernet sauvignon.

82 Colour: rose, purple rim. Nose: ripe fruit, red berry notes, medium intensity. Palate: fleshy, powerful, fruity, fresh.

JALOCO 2009 T ROBLE
cabernet sauvignon.

80 Colour: cherry, garnet rim. Nose: roasted coffee, dark chocolate, caramel, overripe fruit. Palate: powerful, fleshy, concentrated.

JALOCO 2008 TC
cabernet sauvignon.

78

BODEGAS ORAN

Ctra de Sevilla 34
06200 Almendralejo (Badajoz)
☎: +34 662 952 800 - Fax: +34 924 665 406
www.bodegasoran.com

SEÑORÍO DE ORÁN 2009 B
pardina.

85 Colour: bright straw. Nose: white flowers, expressive, ripe fruit. Palate: flavourful, fruity, good acidity, balanced.

VIÑA ROJA TEMPRANILLO 2009 T
tempranillo.

84 Colour: cherry, garnet rim. Nose: ripe fruit, red berry notes, balanced. Palate: flavourful, fine bitter notes, correct.

CASTILLO DE FERIA 2007 TC
tempranillo.

76

BODEGAS PARADELLS

Finca El Charro
06002 Badajoz (Badajoz)
☎: +34 924 105 006 - Fax: +34 924 105 007
bodega@bodegasparadells.com
www.bodegasparadells.com

ZAOS VENDIMIA SELECCIONADA 2008 TC
tempranillo.

83 Colour: cherry, garnet rim. Nose: fruit preserve, sweet spices, toasty. Palate: warm, fleshy, flavourful.

ZAOS VENDIMIA SELECCIONADA 2008 T ROBLE
tempranillo.

82 Colour: cherry, garnet rim. Nose: fruit preserve, roasted coffee, scrubland. Palate: correct, fresh, toasty.

ZAOS VENDIMIA SELECCIONADA 2008 T
tempranillo.

78

BODEGAS ROMALE

Pol. Ind. Parc. 6, Manz. D
06200 Almendralejo (Badajoz)
☎: +34 924 667 255 - Fax: +34 924 665 877
romale@romale.com
www.romale.com

PRIVILEGIO DE ROMALE 2006 TR
100% tempranillo.

85 Colour: cherry, garnet rim. Nose: ripe fruit, spicy, creamy oak, toasty. Palate: powerful, flavourful, toasty, round tannins.

BODEGAS RUIZ TORRES

Ctra. EX 116, km.33,8
10136 Cañamero (Cáceres)
☎: +34 927 369 024 - Fax: +34 927 369 302
info@ruiztorres.com
www.ruiztorres.com

ATTELEA 2010 B
100% macabeo.

82 Colour: bright straw. Nose: ripe fruit, tropical fruit. Palate: flavourful, fresh.

ATTELEA 2009 T ROBLE
tempranillo.

79

ATTELEA 2006 TC
tempranillo, cabernet sauvignon.

82 Colour: bright cherry. Nose: sweet spices, caramel, fruit preserve, warm. Palate: flavourful, fruity, toasty, round tannins.

BODEGAS TORIBIO VIÑA PUEBLA

Luis Chamizo, 12-21
06310 Puebla de Sancho Pérez (Badajoz)
☎: +34 924 551 449 - Fax: +34 924 551 449
info@bodegastoribio.com
www.bodegastoribio.com

VIÑA PUEBLA 2010 BFB
macabeo.

90 Colour: bright yellow. Nose: powerfull, sweet spices, creamy oak, fragrant herbs. Palate: rich, smoky aftertaste, flavourful, fresh, good acidity.

VIÑA PUEBLA MACABEO 2010 B
macabeo.

85 Colour: bright straw. Nose: white flowers, jasmine, fresh fruit. Palate: good acidity, fine bitter notes.

VIÑA PUEBLA VERDEJO 2010 B
verdejo.

85 Colour: bright straw. Nose: fresh, white flowers, tropical fruit, ripe fruit. Palate: flavourful, fruity, balanced.

VIÑA PUEBLA CHARDONNAY 2009 BFB
chardonnay.

90 Colour: bright yellow. Nose: powerfull, ripe fruit, sweet spices, creamy oak, tropical fruit. Palate: rich, smoky aftertaste, flavourful, good acidity.

VIÑA PUEBLA GOLOSINA 2010 RD
garnacha.

87 Colour: rose, purple rim. Nose: ripe fruit, red berry notes, floral. Palate: fleshy, powerful, fruity, fresh.

VIÑA PUEBLA TEMPRANILLO 2010 T
tempranillo.

83 Colour: cherry, garnet rim. Nose: powerfull, warm, overripe fruit. Palate: powerful, sweetness, warm.

MADRE DEL AGUA 2009 T
garnacha tintorera, tempranillo, cabernet sauvignon, garnacha.

93 Colour: cherry, garnet rim. Nose: spicy, creamy oak, toasty, complex, raspberry, violet drops. Palate: powerful, flavourful, toasty, round tannins.

VIÑA PUEBLA SELECCIÓN 2009 T
tempranillo, cabernet sauvignon, syrah, garnacha.

88 Colour: bright cherry. Nose: sweet spices, creamy oak, ripe fruit. Palate: flavourful, fruity, toasty, round tannins.

VIÑA PUEBLA ESENZIA 2008 TC
coupage.

89 Colour: cherry, garnet rim. Nose: ripe fruit, spicy, creamy oak, roasted coffee. Palate: powerful, flavourful, toasty, round tannins.

VIÑA PUEBLA 2007 TC
tempranillo.

85 Colour: cherry, garnet rim. Nose: spicy, creamy oak, toasty. Palate: powerful, flavourful, toasty, round tannins.

BODEGAS VITICULTORES DE BARROS

Ctra. de Badajoz, s/n
06200 Almendralejo (Badajoz)
☎: +34 924 664 852 - Fax: +34 924 664 852
export@vbarros.com
www.viticultoresdebarros.com

EMPERADOR DE BARROS CAYETANA 2010 B
cayetana blanca.

87 Color bright straw. Aroma fresh, fresh fruit, white flowers, expressive. Taste flavourful, fruity, good acidity, balanced.

CAYETANA FRESH 2010 B
cayetana blanca.

85 Colour: bright straw. Nose: fresh, fresh fruit, white flowers. Palate: flavourful, fruity, good acidity, balanced.

ROSÉ 2010 RD

86 Colour: rose, purple rim. Nose: powerfull, ripe fruit, red berry notes, floral. Palate: fleshy, powerful, fruity, fresh.

EMPERADOR DE BARROS TEMPRANILLO 2010 T
tempranillo.

87 Colour: cherry, purple rim. Nose: red berry notes, floral, medium intensity, ripe fruit. Palate: flavourful, fruity, round tannins, fine bitter notes.

VIZANA 2008 TC
tempranillo.

87 Colour: cherry, garnet rim. Nose: ripe fruit, spicy, creamy oak, toasty. Palate: powerful, flavourful, toasty, round tannins.

HIJOS DE FRANCISCO ESCASO

Ctra. Villafranca, 15
06360 Fuente del Maestre (Badajoz)
☎: +34 924 530 012 - Fax: +34 924 531 703
bodegasescaso@infonegocio.com
www.vallarcal.com

VALLARCAL 2009 B
cayetana blanca.

85 Colour: bright straw. Nose: fresh fruit, white flowers, medium intensity. Palate: flavourful, fruity, good acidity.

VALLARCAL 2009 T ROBLE
100% tempranillo.

85 Colour: cherry, garnet rim. Nose: creamy oak, dark chocolate, overripe fruit, warm. Palate: powerful, fleshy, round tannins.

VALLARCAL 2008 TC
100% tempranillo.

83 Colour: cherry, garnet rim. Nose: powerfull, ripe fruit, creamy oak. Palate: flavourful, ripe fruit, round tannins.

VALLARCAL 2006 TR
100% tempranillo.

81 Colour: cherry, garnet rim. Nose: ripe fruit, spicy, toasty, balsamic herbs. Palate: powerful, flavourful, toasty, round tannins.

MARCELINO DÍAZ

Mecánica, s/n
06200 Almendralejo (Badajoz)
☎: +34 924 677 548 - Fax: +34 924 660 977
bodega@madiaz.com
www.madiaz.com

PUERTA PALMA 2010 B
pardina.

82 Colour: bright straw. Nose: white flowers, medium intensity, candied fruit. Palate: flavourful, good acidity, balanced.

PUERTA PALMA 2010 T
tempranillo, cabernet sauvignon, graciano.

82 Colour: cherry, purple rim. Nose: red berry notes, raspberry, grassy. Palate: flavourful, fine bitter notes.

PUERTA PALMA FINCA LAS TENDERAS 2008 TC
tempranillo, cabernet sauvignon.

84 Colour: bright cherry. Nose: ripe fruit, sweet spices, toasty. Palate: flavourful, fruity, toasty, round tannins.

PAGO LOS BALANCINES

Paraje la Agraria, s/n
06475 Oliva de Mérida (Badajoz)
☎: +34 616 534 537
alunado@pagolosbalancines.com
www.pagolosbalancines.com

ALUNADO 2009 BFB
100% chardonnay.

92 Colour: bright yellow. Nose: powerfull, sweet spices, creamy oak, balsamic herbs, fruit expression, citrus fruit, mineral. Palate: rich, smoky aftertaste, flavourful, good acidity.

SALITRE 2009 T
100% garnacha tintorera.

95 Colour: bright cherry. Nose: sweet spices, creamy oak, expressive, mineral, fruit preserve, fruit expression, violet drops. Palate: flavourful, fruity, toasty, round tannins.

HUNO MATANEGRA 2009 TC
33% cabernet sauvignon, 33% tempranillo, 33% garnacha tintorera.

94 Colour: cherry, garnet rim. Nose: creamy oak, toasty, characterful, ripe fruit, mineral. Palate: powerful, flavourful, toasty, round tannins.

HUNO 2008 T
25% tempranillo, 55% cabernet sauvignon, 10% merlot, 10% garnacha.

93 Colour: cherry, garnet rim. Nose: ripe fruit, spicy, creamy oak, toasty, mineral. Palate: powerful, flavourful, toasty, round tannins.

S. COOP. DEL CAMPO SAN ISIDRO

El Mirador, s/n
06197 Entrín Bajo (Badajoz)
☎: +34 924 481 105 - Fax: +34 924 481 017
info@coopsanisidroentrin.es
www.coopsanisidroentrin.es

VEGA HERRERA 2010 T
tempranillo.

81 Colour: cherry, garnet rim. Nose: overripe fruit, warm, medium intensity, grassy. Palate: sweetness, spirituous, fruity.

SOCIEDAD COOPERATIVA NUESTRA SEÑORA DE LA SOLEDAD

Santa Marta, s/n
06207 Aceuchal (Badajoz)
☎: +34 924 680 228 - Fax: +34 924 687 052
mduran@bodegaslasoledad.com

ORGULLO DE BARROS TEMPRANILLO 2010 T
tempranillo.

77

ORGULLO DE BARROS 2008 TC
tempranillo.

78

SEÑORÍO DE PEDRAZA 2006 TC
tempranillo.

83 Colour: cherry, garnet rim. Nose: powerfull, ripe fruit, toasty, spicy. Palate: powerful, ripe fruit, round tannins.

SOCIEDAD COOPERATIVA SAN ISIDRO DE VILLAFRANCA DE LOS BARROS

Ctra. Fuente del Mestre, 12
06220 Villafranca de los Barros (Badajoz)
☎: +34 924 524 136 - Fax: +34 924 524 020
info@cooperativasanisidro.com
www.cooperativasanisidro.com

VALDEQUEMAO MACABEO 2010 B
macabeo.

84 Colour: bright straw. Nose: fresh, fresh fruit, white flowers. Palate: flavourful, fruity, good acidity, balanced.

VALDEQUEMAO TEMPRANILLO 2010 T
tempranillo.

85 Colour: cherry, purple rim. Nose: powerfull, red berry notes, ripe fruit, grassy. Palate: flavourful, fruity, fine bitter notes.

VALDEQUEMAO 2008 TC
tempranillo.

81 Colour: cherry, garnet rim. Nose: creamy oak, caramel, candied fruit, fruit liqueur notes. Palate: powerful, spicy, fine bitter notes.

VALDEQUEMAO 2008 T ROBLE
tempranillo.

81 Colour: cherry, garnet rim. Nose: overripe fruit, warm, dark chocolate, caramel. Palate: fine bitter notes, spirituous, round tannins.

VALDEQUEMAO 2004 TR
tempranillo.

87 Colour: cherry, garnet rim. Nose: ripe fruit, spicy, creamy oak, toasty. Palate: powerful, flavourful, toasty, round tannins.

SOCIEDAD COOPERATIVA VIÑAOLIVA

Pol. Ind., Parcela 4-17
06200 Almendralejo (Badajoz)
☎: +34 924 677 321
acoex@bme.es
www.vinaoliva.com

ZALEO PARDINA 2010 B
100% pardina.

85 Colour: bright straw. Nose: fresh, fresh fruit, white flowers. Palate: flavourful, fruity, good acidity, balanced.

ZALEO 2010 RD
100% tempranillo.

84 Colour: rose, purple rim. Nose: ripe fruit, red berry notes, floral. Palate: fleshy, powerful, fruity, fresh.

ZALEO TEMPRANILLO 2010 T
100% tempranillo.

85 Colour: cherry, purple rim. Nose: red berry notes, floral, ripe fruit. Palate: flavourful, fruity, good acidity, round tannins.

ZALEO PREMIUM 2009 T
100% tempranillo.

87 Colour: bright cherry. Nose: sweet spices, creamy oak, overripe fruit. Palate: flavourful, fruity, toasty, round tannins.

ZALEO SELECCIÓN 2009 T
100% tempranillo.

85 Colour: cherry, garnet rim. Nose: overripe fruit, warm, toasty, dark chocolate. Palate: powerful, sweetness, spicy.

VINÍCOLA GUADIANA

Barjola, 15
06200 Almendralejo (Badajoz)
☎: +34 924 661 080 - Fax: +34 924 671 413
vigua@vinicolaguadiana.com
www.vinicolaguadiana.com

VIGUA 2010 T
100% tempranillo.

87 Colour: cherry, purple rim. Nose: fresh fruit, red berry notes, floral. Palate: flavourful, fruity, good acidity, round tannins.

BASANGUS 2008 TC
100% tempranillo.

85 Colour: cherry, garnet rim. Nose: ripe fruit, spicy, toasty. Palate: powerful, flavourful, toasty, round tannins.

VIÑA SANTA MARINA

Ctra. N-630, Km. 634 - Apdo. Correos 714
06800 Mérida (Badajoz)
☎: +34 902 506 364 - Fax: +34 924 027 675
bodega@vsantamarina.com
www.vsantamarina.com

TORREMAYOR 2008 TC
100% tempranillo.

84 Colour: pale ruby, brick rim edge. Nose: ripe fruit, spicy, toasty, caramel. Palate: powerful, flavourful, toasty, round tannins.

TORREMAYOR 2005 TR
100% tempranillo.

85 Colour: deep cherry. Nose: medium intensity, toasty, spicy, aromatic coffee, overripe fruit. Palate: spicy, balsamic, toasty.

VIÑAS DE ALANGE S.A.

Ctra. Almendralejo - Palomas, km 6,900 - Apdo. 231
06200 Almendralejo (Badajoz)
☎: +34 924 120 082 - Fax: +34 924 120 028
palacioquemado@alvear.es
www.palacioquemado.com

SEÑORÍO DE ALANGE TEMPRANILLO 2010 T
100% tempranillo.

88 Colour: cherry, purple rim. Nose: red berry notes, floral, ripe fruit. Palate: flavourful, fruity, good acidity, round tannins, long.

SEÑORÍO DE ALANGE SYRAH 2010 T
100% syrah.

88 Colour: cherry, purple rim. Nose: red berry notes, floral, powerfull, ripe fruit. Palate: flavourful, fruity, round tannins, fine bitter notes.

"PQ" PRIMICIA 2009 T
tempranillo, garnacha, syrah.

90 Colour: bright cherry. Nose: sweet spices, creamy oak, new oak, red berry notes, raspberry. Palate: flavourful, fruity, toasty, round tannins.

SEÑORÍO DE ALANGE ENSAMBLAJE 2009 T
40% tempranillo, 30% garnacha, 30% syrah.

85 Colour: cherry, garnet rim. Nose: powerfull, characterful, toasty, new oak, aged wood nuances, ripe fruit. Palate: powerful, fleshy, fruity, grainy tannins.

PALACIO QUEMADO 2007 TC
100% tempranillo.

81 Colour: bright cherry. Nose: sweet spices, fruit liqueur notes, roasted coffee. Palate: toasty, round tannins, fine bitter notes.

PALACIO QUEMADO 2005 TR
100% tempranillo.

88 Colour: cherry, garnet rim. Nose: ripe fruit, spicy, creamy oak, toasty. Palate: powerful, flavourful, toasty, round tannins.

VIÑEDOS Y BODEGA CARABAL

Ctra. Alía - Castilblanco, Km. 10
10137 Alía (Cáceres)
☎: +34 917 346 152 - Fax: +34 913 720 440
info@carabal.es
www.carabal.es

CARABAL 2007 TC
syrah, cabernet sauvignon, tempranillo, graciano.

90 Colour: cherry, garnet rim. Nose: spicy, creamy oak, toasty, red berry notes. Palate: powerful, flavourful, toasty, round tannins.

RASGO 2007 T ROBLE
syrah, tempranillo.

87 Colour: cherry, garnet rim. Nose: spicy, toasty, overripe fruit, warm, dark chocolate. Palate: powerful, flavourful, toasty, round tannins.

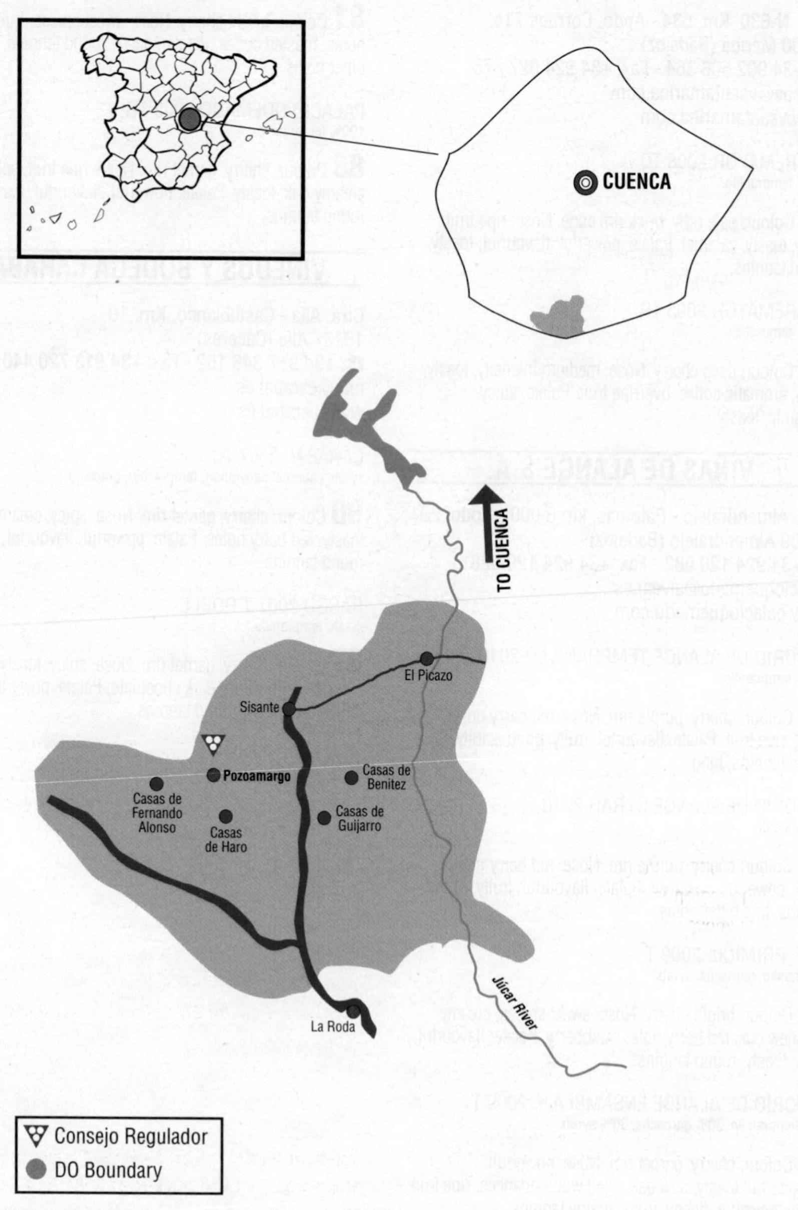
CUENCA
TO CUENCA
El Picazo
Sisante
Pozoamargo
Casas de Benitez
Casas de Fernando Alonso
Casas de Haro
Casas de Guijarro
La Roda
Júcar River
Consejo Regulador
DO Boundary

NEWS ABOUT THE VINTAGE:

Ribera del Júcar remains unchanged in every aspect: the number of its wineries and the quality of its wines. We will never be able to fathom on which geo-climatic conditions was decided that it could become a DO in its own right. Of all the wine regions that surround La Mancha (Uclés, Manchuela, Almansa…) Ribera del Júcar is the only one that does not have any singular features to single it out from its huge mother-designation, La Mancha, unless politicians decided its "independence" just to avoid the sort of bad reputation that such label used to have a few years ago. In the beginning, the dynamism of Casa Gualda seemed to harbour good expectations, but a whole decade has passed and the leading role now belongs to Elviwines and its kosher renderings, under the consultancy of José Luis Pérez. But we should remember that its excellence rests mainly on the genuine talent of a man, and has probably less to do with the region's geo-climatic conditions.

Only two wines have managed to reach 90 points, and they are both from the above-mentioned Elviwines, a 100% *petit verdot* and a blend of this variety with *cabernet sauvignon* and *syrah.* Almost 70% of the samples tasted fall below the 88-point mark, which means the quality still remains just a little below average.

What Ribera del Júcar is probably missing is a genuine identity, and the producers should get down to work on it if they do not want to loose market share. To start with, the region enjoys both climate and soils suitable for quality winemaking, as long as they get the right choice of grape varieties considering that it has the type of high average temperatures typical of La Mancha. In this sense, probably *cabernet sauvignon* and *petit verdot* can achieve good results, along with bobal and *garnacha tintorera.* A good starting point for it all would be to make the local producers understand that a higher average quality of the wines of the DO will benefit them all.

LOCATION:

The 7 wine producing municipal districts that make up the DO are located on the banks of the Júcar, in the south of the province of Cuenca. They are: Casas de Benítez, Casas de Guijarro, Casas de Haro, Casas de Fernando Alonso, Pozoamargo, Sisante and El Picazo. The region is at an altitude of between 650 and 750 m above sea level.

CLIMATE:

Continental in nature, dry, and with very cold winters and very hot summers. The main factor contributing to the quality of the wine is the day-night temperature contrasts during the ripening season of the grapes, which causes the process to be carried out slowly.

SOIL:

The most common type of soil consists of pebbles on the surface and a clayey subsoil, which provides good water retention capacity in the deeper levels.

GRAPE VARIETIES:

RED: *Cencibel* or *Tempranillo, Cabernet Sauvignon, Merlot, Syrah, Bobal, Cabernet Franc* and *Petit Verdot.*
WHITE: *Moscatel de Grano Menudo* and *Sauvignon Blanc.*

FIGURES:

Vineyard surface: 9,200 – **Wine-Growers:** 988 – **Wineries:** 9 – **2010 Harvest rating:** Very Good – **Production:** 537,715 litres – **Market percentages:** 40% domestic. 60% export

CONSEJO REGULADOR
Pza. del Ayuntamiento, s/n
16708 Pozoamargo (Cuenca)
☎: +34 969 387 182 - Fax: +34 969 387 208
@ do@vinosriberadeljucar.com
www.vinosriberadeljucar.com

GENERAL CHARACTERISTICS OF THE WINES

REDS	With an intense cherry colour and violet edge when they are young, they resemble the wines of the peripheral regions of La Mancha, characterised by less rusticity. On the nose, the notes of blackberries, red berries and earthy nuances stand out. On the palate, they are expressive, with tannins which are flavourful and liverly; freshly acidic with varietal reminders of the principal grape variety, the *Cencibel*.

VINTAGE RATING PEÑÍNGUIDE

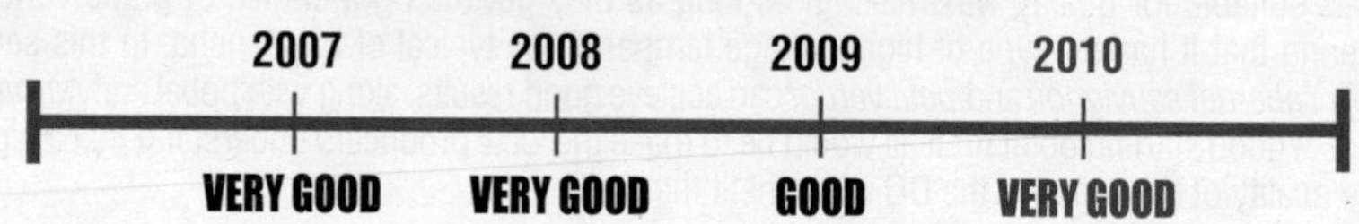

BODEGA SAN GINÉS

Virgen del Carmen, 6
16707 Casas de Benítez (Cuenca)
☎: +34 969 382 037 - Fax: +34 969 382 449
laboratorio@cincoalmudes.es
www.cincoalmudes.es

CINCO ALMUDES TEMPRANILLO 2010 T
tempranillo.

86 Colour: cherry, purple rim. Nose: red berry notes, ripe fruit, scrubland, dried flowers. Palate: flavourful, fleshy, fruity.

LAS ERAS TRADICIÓN 2009 T
bobal.

87 Colour: cherry, purple rim. Nose: red berry notes, ripe fruit, wild herbs, creamy oak. Palate: good acidity, flavourful, balsamic, fleshy.

CINCO ALMUDES 2008 TC
tempranillo.

83 Colour: cherry, garnet rim. Nose: ripe fruit, grassy, old leather, toasty. Palate: correct, flavourful, easy to drink.

CINCO ALMUDES TRADICIÓN 2008
tempranillo.

85 Colour: cherry, garnet rim. Nose: red berry notes, ripe fruit, balsamic herbs, spicy, toasty. Palate: fleshy, powerful, flavourful.

BODEGAS Y VIÑEDOS ILLANA

Finca Buenavista, s/n
16708 Pozoamargo (Cuenca)
☎: +34 969 147 039 - Fax: +34 969 147 057
info@bodegasillana.com
www.bodegasillana.com

CASA DE ILLANA 2010 B
moscatel, sauvignon blanc.

84 Colour: bright straw. Nose: citrus fruit, ripe fruit, fragrant herbs, mineral. Palate: powerful, flavourful, fresh, fruity.

CASA DE ILLANA 2010 T
tempranillo.

84 Colour: cherry, purple rim. Nose: red berry notes, ripe fruit, grassy. Palate: powerful, flavourful, fruity.

CASA DE ILLANA SELECCIÓN 2008 T
petit verdot, syrah.

86 Colour: dark-red cherry, garnet rim. Nose: spicy, ripe fruit, balsamic herbs, toasty. Palate: rich, flavourful, fruity.

CASA DE ILLANA TRADICIÓN 2007 T
tempranillo, bobal, merlot.

85 Colour: cherry, garnet rim. Nose: ripe fruit, fine reductive notes, old leather, spicy. Palate: flavourful, toasty, ripe fruit.

CASA DE ILLANA TRESDECINCO 2006 TC

85 Colour: cherry, garnet rim. Nose: ripe fruit, toasty, tobacco, old leather. Palate: powerful, flavourful, toasty, round tannins.

CASA GUALDA

Tapias, 8
16708 Pozoamargo (Cuenca)
☎: +34 969 387 173 - Fax: +34 969 387 202
info@casagualda.com
www.casagualda.com

CASA GUALDA SAUVIGNON BLANC 2010 B
sauvignon blanc.

84 Colour: bright straw. Nose: ripe fruit, faded flowers, warm. Palate: flavourful, fruity, good acidity.

CASA GUALDA SYRAH 2009 T
syrah.

84 Colour: cherry, garnet rim. Nose: herbaceous, fruit preserve, grassy. Palate: good acidity, flavourful, green.

COOPERATIVA PURÍSIMA CONCEPCIÓN

Ctra. Minaya - San Clemente, Km. 10
16610 Casas de Fernando Alonso (Cuenca)
☎: +34 969 383 043 - Fax: +34 969 383 153
info@vinoteatinos.com
www.vinoteatino.com

TEATINOS SYRAH 2010 T
100% syrah.

88 Colour: cherry, purple rim. Nose: raspberry, floral, red berry notes, balanced. Palate: good acidity, light-bodied, fresh, flavourful, round.

TEATINOS TEMPRANILLO 2010 T
100% tempranillo.

87 Colour: cherry, purple rim. Nose: red berry notes, raspberry, fresh. Palate: good acidity, fruity, flavourful, fleshy.

TEATINOS CLAROS DE CUBA 2006 TR
100% tempranillo.

88 Colour: cherry, garnet rim. Nose: candied fruit, cocoa bean, dark chocolate, sweet spices, toasty. Palate: good acidity, powerful, flavourful, fleshy, round tannins.

TEATINOS 40 BARRICAS SIGNVM 2006 TC
100% tempranillo.

85 Colour: cherry, garnet rim. Nose: ripe fruit, mineral, creamy oak. Palate: powerful, flavourful, fleshy, toasty.

TEATINOS SELECCIÓN 40 BARRICAS TEMPRANILLO 2005 TR
100% tempranillo.

87 Colour: cherry, garnet rim. Nose: ripe fruit, earthy notes, spicy, toasty. Palate: balanced, flavourful, fleshy, round tannins.

TEATINOS DULCE MOSCATEL 2010 BLANCO DULCE
100% moscatel grano menudo.

88 Colour: bright straw. Nose: white flowers, citrus fruit, tropical fruit, fresh, expressive. Palate: flavourful, fruity, good acidity.

ELVIWINES

Finca "Clos Mesorah" Ctra. T-300 Falset Marça, Km. 1
43775 Marça Priorat (Tarragona)
☎: +34 935 343 026 - Fax: +34 936 750 316
moises@elviwines.com
www.elviwines.com

NESS 2009 B
50% sauvignon blanc, 50% moscatel.

85 Colour: bright yellow. Nose: faded flowers, ripe fruit, tropical fruit. Palate: flavourful, fruity, rich.

ADAR 2008 T
37% cabernet sauvignon, 35% petit verdot, 28% syrah.

90 Colour: cherry, garnet rim. Nose: ripe fruit, mineral, warm, creamy oak, spicy, cocoa bean, expressive. Palate: balanced, fleshy, flavourful, full, ripe fruit, round tannins.

ADAR PETIT VERDOT 2008 T
100% petit verdot.

90 Colour: cherry, garnet rim. Nose: powerfull, ripe fruit, fragrant herbs, earthy notes, creamy oak, spicy. Palate: balanced, round, flavourful, fleshy, round tannins.

NESS 2008 T
merlot, syrah, tempranillo, cabernet sauvignon.

88 Colour: cherry, garnet rim. Nose: earthy notes, powerfull, fruit preserve, creamy oak, cocoa bean, dark chocolate. Palate: sweetness, fleshy, toasty, warm.

VIÑA ENCINA DE ELVIWINES 2007 T
bobal, tempranillo, cabernet sauvignon, merlot.

87 Colour: cherry, garnet rim. Nose: powerfull, ripe fruit, spicy, creamy oak, warm. Palate: fine bitter notes, fruity, fleshy, flavourful, round tannins.

LA MAGDALENA SOCIEDAD COOPERATIVA

Ctra. de la Roda, s/n
16611 Casas de Haro (Cuenca)
☎: +34 969 380 722 - Fax: +34 969 380 722
vinos@vegamoragona.com
www.vegamoragona.com

VEGA MORAGONA 2010 B
moscatel.

86 Colour: bright straw. Nose: fresh fruit, citrus fruit, tropical fruit, floral. Palate: fresh, fruity, good acidity, flavourful.

VEGA MORAGONA MOSCATEL DE GRANO MENUDO 2010 B
moscatel grano menudo.

84 Colour: golden. Nose: powerfull, floral, honeyed notes, candied fruit. Palate: flavourful, sweet, fresh, fruity, good acidity.

VEGA MORAGONA TEMPRANILLO 2010 T JOVEN
tempranillo.

88 Colour: cherry, purple rim. Nose: red berry notes, lactic notes, floral, fresh fruit, mineral. Palate: fresh, fruity, flavourful, easy to drink.

VEGA MORAGONA CABERNET SAUVIGNON 2008 T
cabernet sauvignon.

88 Colour: cherry, garnet rim. Nose: red berry notes, ripe fruit, scrubland, balsamic herbs, mineral, creamy oak. Palate: fleshy, powerful, flavourful.

VEGA MORAGONA 2008 TC
tempranillo, cabernet sauvignon.

87 Colour: cherry, garnet rim. Nose: ripe fruit, balsamic herbs, sweet spices, toasty. Palate: good acidity, flavourful, toasty.

VEGA MORAGONA SYRAH 2008 T
syrah.

87 Colour: cherry, purple rim. Nose: red berry notes, floral, mineral, sweet spices, creamy oak. Palate: good acidity, flavourful, fruity, fleshy.

VEGA MORAGONA ALTA SELECCIÓN 2005 TR
tempranillo, cabernet sauvignon.

89 Colour: cherry, garnet rim. Nose: ripe fruit, fragrant herbs, earthy notes, spicy, toasty. Palate: balanced, powerful, flavourful, long.

NEWS ABOUT THE VINTAGE:

Yet another year we have broken every previous record and managed to taste almost 1200 samples from La Rioja alone. 2010 is probably one of the best vintages in the DO ever, a cool year that has provided their young wines with an excellent red fruit character and a vivid varietal expression. Nevertheless, the real measure to assess the quality of the vintage and determine whether it will go down in history as one of the best ever will come with aged (mainly crianza) wines. The best two examples –although different in style– of young wines this year are LZ 2010, from Telmo Rodríguez, and Artuke Maceración Carbónica 2010.

White wines are progressively getting more and more specific weight within the DO, and it is more common to see them high in the rankings. Up to 38 of them have hit the 90-point mark, even when they resort to *viura* exclusively, as in Mártires 2010, or blending that variety with *garnacha blanca* and *malvasía*, as it is the case of Qué Bonito Cacareaba 2010. They are also some interesting examples of wines made from the unusual *tempranillo blanco*, like Ad Libitum Tempranillo Blanco 2010.

As for the crianza category, the best example is Óbalo 2008 (93 points), while the reserva renderings from 2007 are showing overall quite balanced and expressive, like the refined Dalmau 2007, from Marqués de Murrieta, a house that also leads the ratings for the gran reserva category with two different vintages (2001 and 2004) of its Castillo Ygay Gran Reserva Especial.

The commercialization of its wines has known an important increase thanks to a general fall in price, something which logically favours bigger and more flexible regions like Rioja.

LOCATION:

Occupying the Ebro valley. To the north it borders with the Sierra de Cantabria and to the south with the Sierra de la Demanda, and is made up of different municipal districts of La Rioja, the Basque Country and Navarra. The most western region is Haro and the easternmost, Alfaro, with a distance of 100 km between the two. The region is 40 km wide.es de 40 kilómetros.

CLIMATE:

Quite variable depending on the different sub-regions. In general, there is a combination of Atlantic and Mediterranean influences, the latter becoming more dominant as the terrain descends from west to east, becoming drier and hotter. The average annual rainfall is slightly over 400 mm.

SOIL:

Various types: the clayey calcareous soil arranged in terraces and small plots which are located especially in Rioja Alavesa, la Sonsierra and some regions of Rioja Alta; the clayey ferrous soil, scattered throughout the region, with vineyards located on reddish, strong soil with hard, deep rock; and the alluvial soil in the area close to the rivers; these are the most level vineyards with larger plots; here the soil is deeper and has pebbles.

GRAPE VARIETIES:

WHITE: *Viura* (7,045 Ha), *Malvasía* and *Garnacha Blanca, Chardonnay, Sauvignon Blanc, Verdejo, Maturana Blanca, Tempranillo Blanco* and *Torrontés.*
RED: *Tempranillo* (majority with 38,476 Ha), *Garnacha, Graciano, Mazuelo, Maturana Tinta, Maturano* and *Monastrell.*

SUB-REGIONS:

Rioja Alta. This has Atlantic influences; it is the most extensive with some 20,500 Ha and produces wines well suited for ageing.

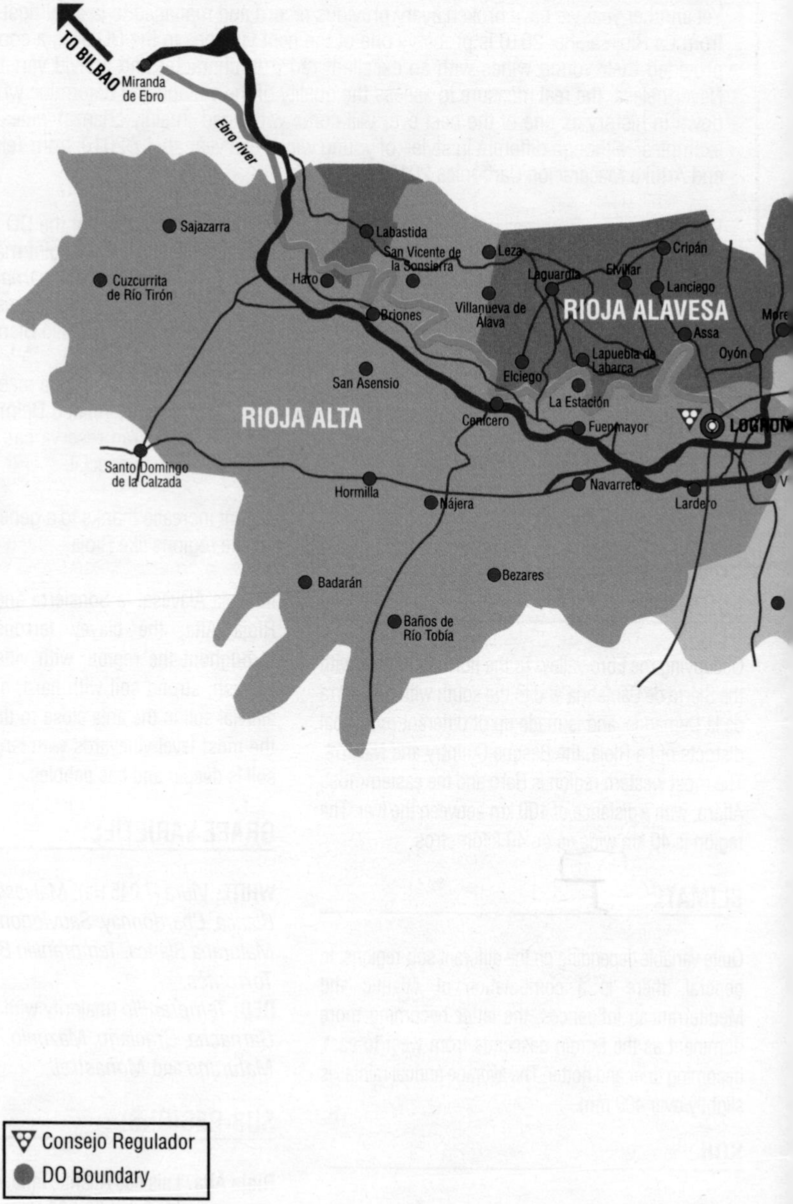

TO BILBAO
Miranda de Ebro
Ebro river
Sajazarra
Cuzcurrita de Río Tirón
Labastida
San Vicente de la Sonsierra
Leza
Cripán
Laguardia
Elvillar
Lanciego
Haro
RIOJA ALAVESA
Villanueva de Álava
Briones
Assa
Oyón
Lapuebla de Labarca
Elciego
San Asensio
La Estación
RIOJA ALTA
Cenicero
Fuenmayor
LOGROÑ
Santo Domingo de la Calzada
Hormilla
Navarrete
Lardero
Nájera
Bezares
Badarán
Baños de Río Tobía
Consejo Regulador
DO Boundary

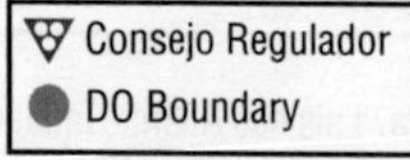

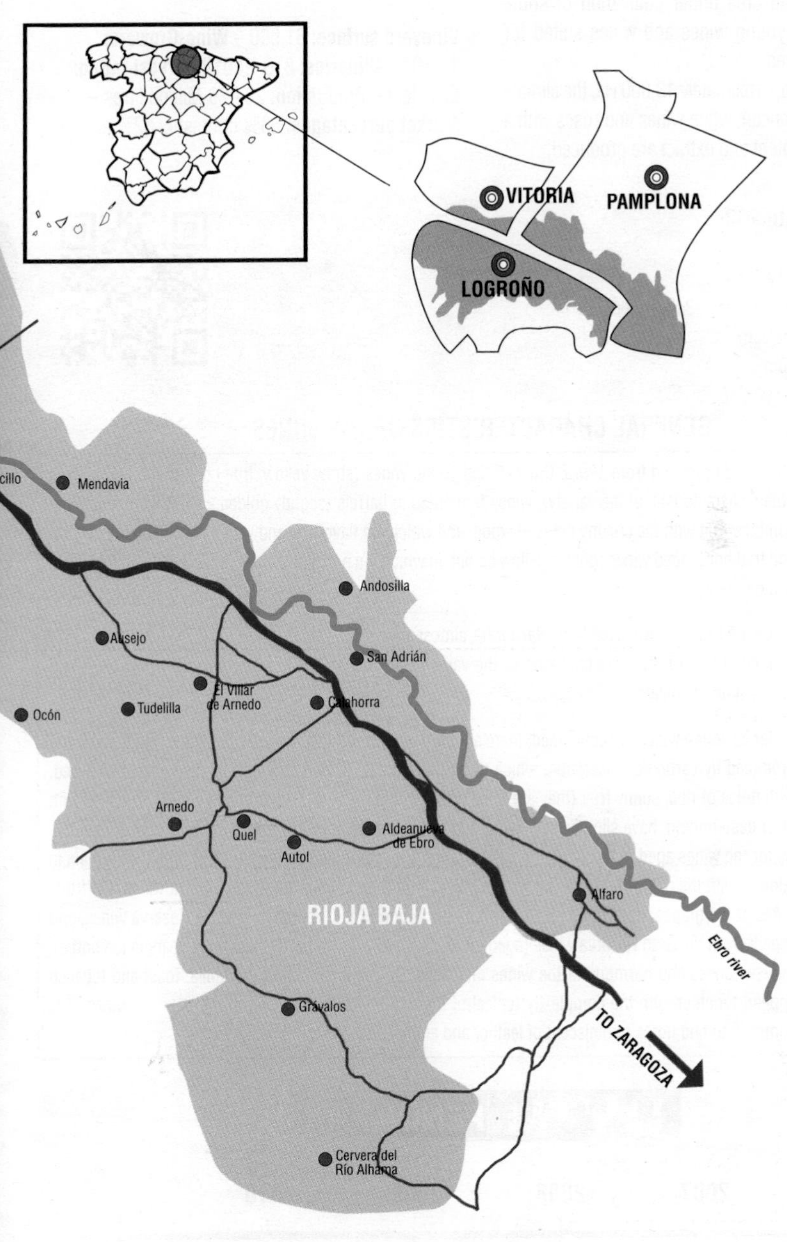

VITORIA
PAMPLONA
LOGROÑO
ncillo
Mendavia
Andosilla
Ausejo
San Adrián
El Villar de Arnedo
Calahorra
Ocón
Tudelilla
Arnedo
Quel
Autol
Aldeanueva de Ebro
Alfaro
RIOJA BAJA
Ebro river
TO ZARAGOZA
Grávalos
Cervera del Río Alhama

Rioja Alavesa. A mixture of Atlantic and Mediterranean influences, with an area under cultivation of some 11,500 Ha; both young wines and wines suited for ageing are produced.
Rioja Baja. With approximately 18,000 Ha, the climate is purely Mediterranean; white wines and rosés with a higher alcohol content and extract are produced.

FIGURES:

Vineyard surface: 61,960 – **Wine-Growers:** 17,607 – **Wineries:** 810 – **2010 Harvest rating:** Excellent – **Production:** 284,29 Million litres – **Market percentages:** 68% domestic. 32% export

CONSEJO REGULADOR
Estambrera, 52
26006 Logroño (La Rioja)
☎: +34 941 500 400 - Fax: +34 941 500 672
@ info@riojawine.com
www.riojawine.com

GENERAL CHARACTERISTICS OF THE WINES

WHITES	These are produced from *Viura.* One can find young wines (straw yellow, fruity noses and herbaceous notes, characteristic of the variety), wines fermented in barrels (slightly golden yellow, with noses that combine fruit with the creamy notes of wood, and which are flavourful and well-balanced on the palate), and traditional aged wines (golden yellow colour, in which the notes of the oak predominate on the palate and on the nose).
ROSÉS	These are basically produced from *Garnacha*, almost always cultivated in Rioja Baja. The have a raspberry pink colour and reflect the character of the variety they are produced from they are fruity, fresh and pleasant on the palate.
REDS	As far as young wines are concerned, there are the wines from Rioja Alavesa, harvested traditionally and produced by carbonic maceration, which gives them great roasted strength: intense cherry coloured, with notes of ripe, sunny fruit (they are to be drunk within the year). Other young wines, produced with prior destemming, have slightly less colour and fruit intensity: they are light, fresh and easy drinking. As for the wines aged in wood, their characteristics are determined by the length of time they remain in contact with the oak, which determines the intensity of their colour. So, in the Crianza wines, the fruity notes of the grapes are slightly toned down by the action of the wood, while in the Reserva wines, and especially in the Gran Reserva wines (aged for at least two years in barrels and three years in the bottle), the roundness and harmony of the wines increases. On the nose, noses of vanilla, toast and tobacco appear, together with the complexity typical of the reduction in the bottle. In the younger wines, it is common to find notes reminiscent of leather and animal noses.

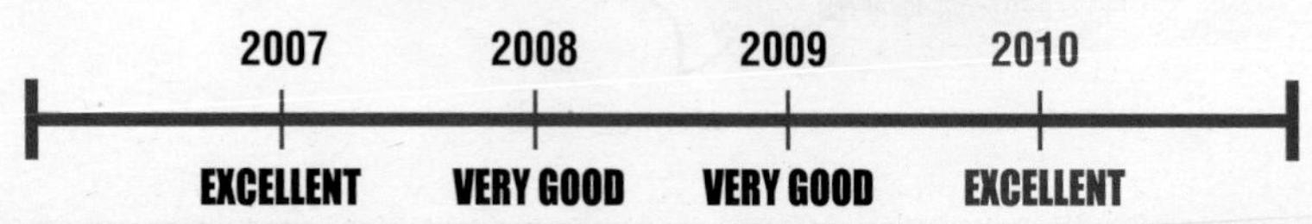

AGRÍCOLA LABASTIDA TIERRA

El Olmo, 8
01330 Labastida (Álava)
☎: +34 945 331 230 - Fax: +34 945 331 257
info@tierryvino.com
www.tierrayvino.com

TIERRA DE FIDEL 2010 B
20% garnacha blanca, 20% viura, 20% malvasía, 40% otras.

89 Color bright straw. Aroma fresh, fresh fruit, white flowers, expressive. Taste flavourful, fruity, good acidity, balanced.

TIERRA DE FERNÁNDEZ GÓMEZ 2010 B
70% viura, 20% garnacha blanca, 10% malvasía.

88 Color bright straw. Aroma fresh, fresh fruit, white flowers, expressive. Taste flavourful, fruity, good acidity, balanced.

TIERRA DE FIDEL 2009 B
20% garnacha blanca, 20% viura, 20% malvasía, 40% otras.

90 Colour: bright straw. Nose: faded flowers, ripe fruit, scrubland, fragrant herbs, expressive, complex. Palate: rich, flavourful, fleshy, complex.

TIERRA DE FERNÁNDEZ GÓMEZ 2010 RD
70% tempranillo, 30% garnacha.

88 Color rose, purple rim. Aroma powerfull, ripe fruit, red berry notes, floral, expressive. Taste fleshy, powerful, fruity, fresh.

EL PRIMAVERA 2010 T
100% tempranillo.

89 Colour: deep cherry, purple rim. Nose: red berry notes, ripe fruit, powerfull. Palate: good structure, flavourful, round tannins.

FERNÁNDEZ GÓMEZ 2010 T
80% tempranillo, 10% viura, 10% garnacha.

88 Colour: cherry, purple rim. Nose: ripe fruit, floral, balsamic herbs, medium intensity. Palate: light-bodied, flavourful, fruity.

EL BELISARIO 2008 T
100% tempranillo.

93 Colour: black cherry, garnet rim. Nose: red berry notes, ripe fruit, earthy notes, sweet spices, toasty. Palate: good acidity, elegant, balanced, powerful, flavourful, complex, round tannins.

TIERRA FIDEL 2008 T
50% garnacha, 50% graciano.

90 Colour: cherry, garnet rim. Nose: ripe fruit, spicy, creamy oak, toasty, complex. Palate: powerful, flavourful, toasty, spicy, fleshy, complex.

TIERRA 2008 TC
100% tempranillo.

90 Colour: cherry, garnet rim. Nose: red berry notes, ripe fruit, balanced, complex, sweet spices, earthy notes, toasty. Palate: powerful, flavourful, fleshy, complex.

EL BELISARIO 2006 T
100% tempranillo.

92 Colour: deep cherry, garnet rim. Nose: complex, ripe fruit, spicy, powerfull, candied fruit. Palate: good structure, flavourful, rich, round tannins.

ALTOS DE RIOJA VITICULTORES Y BODEGUEROS

Ctra. Logroño, s/n
01300 Laguardia (Alava)
☎: +34 945 600 693 - Fax: +34 945 600 692
altosderioja@altosderioja.com

ALTOS R 2010 B
60% viura, 40% malvasía.

90 Colour: bright straw. Nose: fresh fruit, white flowers, neat, fine lees. Palate: flavourful, fruity, good acidity, balanced.

ALTOS R PIGEAGE 2007 T
90% tempranillo, 10% graciano.

91 Colour: cherry, garnet rim. Nose: ripe fruit, spicy, creamy oak, sweet spices. Palate: powerful, flavourful, toasty, round tannins.

ALTOS R 2007 TC
100% tempranillo.

88 Colour: bright cherry. Nose: ripe fruit, sweet spices, dark chocolate. Palate: flavourful, fruity, sweet tannins.

ALTOS R 2005 TR
100% tempranillo.

90 Colour: cherry, garnet rim. Nose: ripe fruit, spicy, creamy oak, toasty. Palate: powerful, flavourful, toasty, round tannins.

AMADOR GARCÍA CHAVARRI

Avda. Río Ebro, 68 - 70
01307 Baños de Ebro (Álava)
☎: +34 945 290 385 - Fax: +34 975 290 373
bodegasamadorgarcia@gmail.com
www.bodegasamadorgarcia.com

AMADOR GARCÍA 2005 TC
tempranillo, garnacha, mazuelo.

88 Colour: cherry, garnet rim. Nose: ripe fruit, balsamic herbs, fine reductive notes, cocoa bean, sweet spices, toasty. Palate: fleshy, toasty, flavourful.

AMADOR GARCÍA 2010 BFB
viura.

87 Colour: bright straw. Nose: ripe fruit, floral, sweet spices, creamy oak. Palate: rich, fruity, flavourful, toasty.

PEÑAGUDO 2007 T
tempranillo, garnacha, graciano.

85 Colour: light cherry, garnet rim. Nose: ripe fruit, scrubland, spicy, creamy oak. Palate: powerful, flavourful, fleshy.

ANTIGUAS VIÑAS DE RIOJA

Camino de Murillo, 22
26141 Alberite (La Rioja)
☎: +34 941 436 729 - Fax: +34 941 436 588
rrpp@antiguasvinasderioja.es
www.antiguasvinasderioja.es

CALAVIA 2010 T
80% tempranillo, 20% mazuelo.

83 Colour: cherry, purple rim. Nose: grassy, red berry notes. Palate: fruity, easy to drink.

CALAVIA COLECCIÓN PRIVADA 2008 T
80% tempranillo, 20% mazuelo.

90 Colour: bright cherry. Nose: sweet spices, creamy oak, fruit expression, scrubland. Palate: flavourful, fruity, toasty, round tannins.

CALAVIA 2008 TC
90% tempranillo, 10% graciano.

87 Colour: cherry, garnet rim. Nose: varietal, ripe fruit, spicy. Palate: good structure, flavourful, good acidity.

AUDIUS 2007 T
100% tempranillo.

87 Colour: bright cherry, garnet rim. Nose: toasty, ripe fruit, wild herbs. Palate: fruity, flavourful, good acidity.

HACIENDA CALAVIA 2005 TR
90% tempranillo, 10% graciano.

87 Colour: pale ruby, brick rim edge. Nose: smoky, aromatic coffee, fine reductive notes. Palate: powerful, flavourful, spicy.

ANTONIO ALCARAZ

Ctra. Vitoria-Logroño, Km. 57
01300 Laguardia (Álava)
☎: +34 658 959 745 - Fax: +34 965 888 359
rioja@antonio-alcaraz.es
www.antonio-alcaraz.es

ANTONIO ALCARAZ 2008 TC
80% tempranillo, 10% mazuelo.

90 Colour: cherry, garnet rim. Nose: powerfull, ripe fruit, toasty, aromatic coffee. Palate: powerful, spicy, round tannins.

GLORIA ANTONIO ALCARAZ 2008 TC
100% tempranillo.

90 Colour: black cherry, garnet rim. Nose: red berry notes, ripe fruit, sweet spices, cocoa bean, toasty, expressive. Palate: powerful, flavourful, fruity, toasty.

ANTONIO ALCARAZ 2007 TR
90% tempranillo, 10% graciano, mazuelo.

90 Colour: cherry, garnet rim. Nose: red berry notes, ripe fruit, balanced, expressive, spicy, toasty. Palate: good acidity, powerful, flavourful, toasty.

ARACO

Ctra. Lapuebla, s/n
01300 Laguardia (Álava)
☎: +34 945 600 209 - Fax: +34 945 600 067
araco@bodegasaraco.com
www.bodegasaraco.com

ARACO 2010 B
viura.

87 Color bright straw. Aroma fresh, fresh fruit, white flowers, expressive. Taste flavourful, fruity, good acidity, balanced.

ARACO 2010 T
tempranillo.

86 Colour: cherry, purple rim. Nose: fresh fruit, wild herbs, balanced. Palate: fruity, good finish.

ARACO 2008 TC
tempranillo.

85 Colour: cherry, garnet rim. Nose: fine reductive notes, ripe fruit, spicy, toasty. Palate: correct, flavourful, toasty.

ARACO 2005 TR
tempranillo.

87 Colour: cherry, garnet rim. Nose: red berry notes, ripe fruit, balsamic herbs, toasty. Palate: good acidity, flavourful, fleshy.

ARRIAGA Y MIMÉNDEZ COMPAÑIA DE VINOS

Capitán Cortés, 6. Piso 4 - Puerta 3
26003 Logroño (La Rioja)
☎: +34 687 421 306 - Fax: +34 941 287 072
info@arriagaymimendez.com
www.arriagaymimendez.com

LA INVIERNA 2007 TC
100% tempranillo.

88 Colour: bright cherry. Nose: ripe fruit, sweet spices, creamy oak. Palate: flavourful, fruity, toasty, round tannins.

ARTUKE BODEGAS Y VIÑEDOS

La Serna, 24
01307 Baños de Ebro (Álava)
☎: +34 945 623 323 - Fax: +34 945 623 323
artuke@artuke.com
www.artuke.com

ARTUKE 2010 T MACERACIÓN CARBÓNICA
95% tempranillo, 5% viura.

92 Colour: cherry, purple rim. Nose: floral, mineral, violet drops, fresh fruit. Palate: good acidity, fruity, flavourful, fleshy, round tannins.

ARTUKE SELECCIÓN 2010 T
90% tempranillo, 10% graciano.

89 Colour: cherry, purple rim. Nose: floral, red berry notes, ripe fruit, spicy, toasty. Palate: fleshy, complex, powerful, flavourful.

ARTUKE K4 2009 T
80% tempranillo, 20% graciano.

96 Colour: bright cherry. Nose: red berry notes, raspberry, sweet spices, cocoa bean, earthy notes. Palate: flavourful, fruity, toasty, round tannins.

ARTUKE FINCA DE LOS LOCOS 2009 T
75% tempranillo, 25% graciano.

95 Colour: bright cherry. Nose: creamy oak, expressive, mineral, red berry notes, ripe fruit. Palate: flavourful, fruity, toasty, round tannins.

ARTUKE 2008 TC
90% tempranillo, 10% graciano.

92 Colour: cherry, garnet rim. Nose: creamy oak, toasty, fruit expression. Palate: powerful, toasty, round tannins.

BAIGORRI

Ctra. Vitoria-Logroño, Km. 53
01307 Samaniego (Álava)
☎: +34 945 609 420 - Fax: +34 945 609 407
mail@bodegasbaigorri.com
www.bodegasbaigorri.com

BAIGORRI 2006 BFB
90% viura, 10% malvasía.

91 Color bright yellow. Aroma powerfull, ripe fruit, sweet spices, creamy oak, fragrant herbs. Taste rich, smoky aftertaste, flavourful, fresh, good acidity.

BAIGORRI 2010 RD
50% tempranillo, 50% garnacha.

85 Colour: rose, purple rim. Nose: powerfull, ripe fruit, raspberry. Palate: flavourful, powerful, fleshy.

BAIGORRI 2010 T MACERACIÓN CARBÓNICA
100% tempranillo.

87 Colour: cherry, purple rim. Nose: floral, red berry notes. Palate: flavourful, fruity, good acidity, round tannins.

BAIGORRI GARNACHA 2009 T
100% garnacha.

93 Colour: very deep cherry, purple rim. Nose: expressive, ripe fruit, cocoa bean, sweet spices, mineral. Palate: good structure, flavourful, round tannins.

BAIGORRI 2007 TC
90% tempranillo, 10% otras.

91 Colour: cherry, garnet rim. Nose: red berry notes, ripe fruit, sweet spices, creamy oak, balanced. Palate: good acidity, complex, flavourful, fleshy, elegant.

BAIGORRI BELUS 2008 T
70% tempranillo, 20% mazuelo, 10% garnacha.

90 Colour: very deep cherry, purple rim. Nose: ripe fruit, fruit preserve, creamy oak. Palate: good structure, ripe fruit, spicy.

BAIGORRI DE GARAGE 2007 T
100% tempranillo.

91 Colour: deep cherry, garnet rim. Nose: ripe fruit, balanced, sweet spices. Palate: good structure, fruity, round tannins.

BAIGORRI 2006 TR
100% tempranillo.

92 Colour: cherry, garnet rim. Nose: red berry notes, ripe fruit, sweet spices, creamy oak, complex, expressive. Palate: good acidity, round, rich, flavourful, long.

BARÓN DE LEY

Ctra. Mendavia - Lodosa, Km. 5,5
31587 Mendavia (Navarra)
☎: +34 948 694 303 - Fax: +34 948 694 304
info@barondeley.com
www.barondeley.com

BARÓN DE LEY FINCA MONASTERIO 2008 T
80% tempranillo, 20% otras.

91 Colour: cherry, garnet rim. Nose: ripe fruit, spicy, toasty, new oak. Palate: powerful, flavourful, toasty, round tannins.

BARÓN DE LEY 2006 TR
100% tempranillo.

87 Colour: cherry, garnet rim. Nose: ripe fruit, spicy, creamy oak. Palate: powerful, flavourful, toasty, round tannins.

BARÓN DE LEY 2001 TGR
100% tempranillo.

87 Colour: pale ruby, brick rim edge. Nose: spicy, toasty, cocoa bean. Palate: easy to drink, light-bodied, classic aged character.

BODEGA ABEL MENDOZA MONGE

Ctra. Peñacerrada, 7
26338 San Vicente de la Sonsierra (La Rioja)
☎: +34 941 308 010 - Fax: +34 941 308 010
jarrarte.abelmendoza@gmail.com

ABEL MENDOZA VIURA 2010 BFB
100% viura.

87 Colour: bright straw. Nose: ripe fruit, faded flowers, complex, creamy oak. Palate: rich, powerful, fleshy, complex, long.

JARRARTE 2010 T
100% tempranillo.

89 Colour: cherry, purple rim. Nose: red berry notes, floral, expressive. Palate: flavourful, fruity, good acidity, round tannins.

ABEL MENDOZA TEMPRANILLO GRANO A GRANO 2008 T
100% tempranillo.

93 Colour: cherry, garnet rim. Nose: red berry notes, fruit expression, mineral, sweet spices, creamy oak, elegant. Palate: elegant, balanced, powerful, flavourful, round tannins.

ABEL MENDOZA SELECCIÓN PERSONAL 2008 T
100% tempranillo.

91 Colour: cherry, garnet rim. Nose: red berry notes, raspberry, cocoa bean, sweet spices, creamy oak. Palate: good acidity, fruity, flavourful, round.

JARRARTE 2007 T
tempranillo.

87 Colour: cherry, garnet rim. Nose: ripe fruit, spicy, toasty. Palate: powerful, flavourful, toasty, round tannins.

BODEGA ANTIGUA USANZA

Camino Garugele, s/n
26338 San Vicente de la Sonsierra (La Rioja)
☎: +34 941 334 156 - Fax: +34 941 334 254
antiguausanza@antiguausanza.com
www.antiguausanza.com

BALTHUS 2008 T
100% tempranillo.

89 Colour: cherry, garnet rim. Nose: ripe fruit, spicy, creamy oak, toasty. Palate: powerful, flavourful, toasty, round tannins.

BAU 2008 TC
90% tempranillo, 5% graciano, 5% garnacha.

86 Colour: deep cherry, garnet rim. Nose: fruit preserve, spicy. Palate: fruity, spicy, easy to drink.

BAU 2005 TR
90% tempranillo, 5% graciano, 5% garnacha.

88 Colour: cherry, garnet rim. Nose: ripe fruit, spicy. Palate: flavourful, round tannins, correct.

BODEGA CLÁSSICA

Camino del Campo Santo s/n
26338 San Vicente de la Sonsierra (La Rioja)
☎: +34 941 271 217 - Fax: +34 941 272 911
info@bodegaclassica.com
www.bodegaclassica.com

HACIENDA LÓPEZ DE HARO 2007 TC
tempranillo, garnacha, graciano.

86 Colour: cherry, garnet rim. Nose: ripe fruit, fine reductive notes, cocoa bean, toasty. Palate: powerful, fleshy, complex, toasty.

QP "VINTAGE" 2006 T
tempranillo, graciano.

90 Colour: cherry, garnet rim. Nose: spicy, creamy oak, toasty, complex, fruit preserve. Palate: powerful, flavourful, toasty, round tannins.

QP 2006 T

88 Colour: cherry, garnet rim. Nose: ripe fruit, toasty, cocoa bean, dark chocolate. Palate: powerful, flavourful, toasty, ripe fruit.

BODEGA CONTADOR

Ctra. Baños de Ebro, Km. 1
26338 San Vicente de la Sonsierra (La Rioja)
☎: 941 334 228 - Fax: 941 334 537
info@bodegacontador.com
www.bodegacontador.com

QUÉ BONITO CACAREABA 2010 B
viura, garnacha blanca, malvasía.

94 Colour: bright yellow. Nose: powerfull, citrus fruit, ripe fruit, fragrant herbs, sweet spices, creamy oak, elegant. Palate: balanced, unctuous, rich, flavourful, fleshy, complex.

PREDICADOR 2010 B
garnacha blanca, malvasía, viura.

92 Colour: bright straw. Nose: floral, ripe fruit, sweet spices, creamy oak, expressive, mineral. Palate: good acidity, round, unctuous, flavourful, complex, fresh.

CONTADOR 2009 T
tempranillo, garnacha.

98 Colour: dark-red cherry, garnet rim. Nose: red berry notes, fruit expression, complex, earthy notes, mineral, powerfull, new oak, toasty. Palate: fleshy, powerful, flavourful, fruity, harsh oak tannins, fine bitter notes.

LA VIÑA DE ANDRÉS ROMEO 2009 T
tempranillo.

95 Colour: cherry, garnet rim. Nose: ripe fruit, mineral, spicy, new oak, toasty, cocoa bean. Palate: round, flavourful, fleshy, complex, round tannins.

LA CUEVA DEL CONTADOR 2009 T
tempranillo.

94 Colour: black cherry, garnet rim. Nose: fruit expression, mineral, sweet spices, cocoa bean, new oak, elegant. Palate: flavourful, fleshy, ripe fruit, balanced, elegant, round tannins.

PREDICADOR 2009 T
tempranillo, garnacha, viura.

92 Colour: cherry, garnet rim. Nose: powerfull, ripe fruit, complex, spicy, creamy oak. Palate: balanced, flavourful, fleshy, good acidity, round tannins.

BODEGA ENTRECEPAS

Avda. de Mendavia, 29
26006 Logroño (La Rioja)
☎: +34 917 104 880 - Fax: +34 917 104 881
anap@swd.es
www.swd.es

ENTRECEPAS 2005 TC
57% tempranillo, 20% graciano, 13% garnacha, 10% mazuelo.

85 Colour: cherry, garnet rim. Nose: ripe fruit, spicy, toasty. Palate: powerful, flavourful, toasty, ripe fruit.

ENTRECEPAS 2003 TR
65% tempranillo, 28% mazuelo, 7% garnacha.

86 Colour: cherry, garnet rim. Nose: spicy, fruit liqueur notes, old leather. Palate: flavourful, fine bitter notes, ripe fruit
.

BODEGA NOS RIQUEZA

Sánchez Calvo, 6
33402 Avilés (Asturias)
☎: +34 984 836 826 - Fax: +34 985 931 074
exportmanager@nosriqueza.com
www.nosriqueza.com

NOEGA 2008 T
75% tempranillo, 25% garnacha.

87 Colour: deep cherry, garnet rim. Nose: ripe fruit, spicy, wild herbs. Palate: balanced, ripe fruit, round tannins.

BODEGA SAN PRUDENCIO

Ctra. Viana, Km. 1
01322 Moreda (Álava)
☎: +34 945 601 034 - Fax: +34 945 622 451
saenzbe@gmail.com
www.bodegasanprudencio.com

ENVITE SEDUCCIÓN 2010 B
90% viura, 10% malvasía.

85 Colour: golden. Nose: floral, candied fruit, medium intensity. Palate: flavourful, sweet, fresh, fruity, good acidity.

ENVITE 2010 B
90% viura, 10% malvasía.

83 Colour: bright straw. Nose: white flowers, citrus fruit, dried herbs. Palate: good acidity, flavourful, fresh, fruity.

CUETO 2010 B
viura, malvasía.

81 Colour: bright straw. Nose: fresh, fresh fruit, white flowers, expressive. Palate: flavourful, fruity.

CONCLAVE ESENCIA 2008 B
90% viura, 10% malvasía.

91 Colour: bright yellow. Nose: white flowers, fruit expression, sweet spices, creamy oak. Palate: round, unctuous, powerful, flavourful, fruity.

ENVITE 2010 RD
garnacha, viura.

86 Colour: raspberry rose. Nose: red berry notes, ripe fruit, white flowers, expressive. Palate: powerful, fresh, fruity.

CUETO RD
garnacha, viura.

85 Colour: brilliant rose. Nose: ripe fruit, floral, powerfull, balanced. Palate: flavourful, fleshy, fruity, easy to drink.

ENVITE 2010 T
70% tempranillo, 25% garnacha.

85 Colour: cherry, purple rim. Nose: red berry notes, raspberry, balsamic herbs, floral. Palate: light-bodied, fresh, fruity, easy to drink.

CUETO 2010 T
60% tempranillo, 25% garnacha, 10% mazuelo, 5% graciano.

84 Colour: cherry, garnet rim. Nose: red berry notes, ripe fruit, scrubland. Palate: spirituous, flavourful, fleshy.

CUETO TENDENCIA 2009 T
tempranillo, mazuelo, garnacha, graciano.

88 Colour: cherry, garnet rim. Nose: red berry notes, ripe fruit, wild herbs, sweet spices. Palate: fleshy, powerful, flavourful, round.

DEPADRE 2008 T
50% tempranillo, 50% garnacha.

88 Colour: cherry, garnet rim. Nose: powerfull, red berry notes, ripe fruit, spicy, creamy oak. Palate: powerful, flavourful, fleshy, toasty.

ENVITE 2008 TC
60% tempranillo, 25% garnacha, 15% mazuelo.

85 Colour: cherry, garnet rim. Nose: ripe fruit, cigar, old leather, spicy, toasty. Palate: light-bodied, flavourful, spirituous.

CUETO 2007 TC
60% tempranillo, 25% garnacha, 10% mazuelo, 5% graciano.

88 Colour: cherry, garnet rim. Nose: ripe fruit, wild herbs, fine reductive notes, spicy. Palate: flavourful, fleshy, ripe fruit, toasty.

CONCLAVE 2005 TR
60% tempranillo, 35% garnacha.

87 Color cherry, garnet rim. Aroma ripe fruit, spicy, creamy oak, toasty, complex. Taste powerful, flavourful, toasty, round tannins.

CUETO 2005 TR
65% tempranillo, 20% garnacha, 15% mazuelo.

85 Colour: cherry, garnet rim. Nose: ripe fruit, old leather, tobacco, spicy, toasty. Palate: good acidity, powerful, flavourful.

BODEGA SOLABAL

Camino San Bartolomé, 6
26339 Abalos (La Rioja)
☎: +34 941 334 492 - Fax: +34 941 308 164
solabal@solabal.es
www.solabal.es

MUÑARRATE 2010 B
100% viura.

88 Colour: bright straw. Nose: ripe fruit, grassy, balsamic herbs. Palate: flavourful, fruity, fresh.

MUÑARRATE 2010 RD
100% garnacha.

87 Colour: raspberry rose. Nose: wild herbs, faded flowers, fresh. Palate: fruity, flavourful.

MUÑARRATE 2010 T
100% tempranillo.

88 Colour: deep cherry, purple rim. Nose: medium intensity, wild herbs. Palate: fleshy, flavourful, fruity, full.

SOLABAL 2008 TC
100% tempranillo.

90 Colour: cherry, garnet rim. Nose: ripe fruit, red berry notes, spicy. Palate: flavourful, powerful, fleshy, round tannins.

SOLABAL 2007 TR
100% tempranillo.

90 Colour: cherry, garnet rim. Nose: powerfull, ripe fruit, toasty, sweet spices. Palate: flavourful, powerful, fleshy, round tannins.

ESCULLE DE SOLABAL 2006 TC
100% tempranillo.

87 Colour: cherry, garnet rim. Nose: powerfull, fruit liqueur notes, toasty, sweet spices. Palate: flavourful, spicy, ripe fruit.

VALA DE SOLABAL 2006 TC
100% tempranillo.

87 Colour: cherry, garnet rim. Nose: spicy, creamy oak, toasty, characterful. Palate: powerful, toasty, round tannins.

BODEGA VIÑA EGUILUZ

Camino de San Bartolomé, 10
26339 Abalos (La Rioja)
☎: +34 941 334 064 - Fax: +34 941 583 022
info@bodegaseguiluz.es
www.bodegaseguiluz.es

EGUILUZ 2010 T
100% tempranillo.

86 Colour: deep cherry, purple rim. Nose: balsamic herbs, grassy, fruit expression. Palate: fruity, easy to drink.

EGUILUZ 2006 TC
tempranillo.

87 Colour: bright cherry. Nose: fine reductive notes, fruit preserve, toasty, aromatic coffee. Palate: flavourful, ripe fruit, spicy.

BODEGAS 1808

Ctra. El Villar Polígono 7 Biribil, 33
01300 Laguardia (Alava)
☎: +34 945 293 450 - Fax: +34 945 293 450
1808@rioja1808.com
www.rioja1808.com

1808 VIURA 2008 B
100% viura.

87 Colour: bright golden. Nose: candied fruit, ripe fruit, dried herbs, creamy oak. Palate: powerful, flavourful, rich.

1808 2007 TC
100% tempranillo.

87 Colour: cherry, garnet rim. Nose: spicy, creamy oak, toasty, complex, fruit preserve. Palate: powerful, flavourful, toasty.

1808 2006 TR
100% tempranillo.

87 Colour: cherry, garnet rim. Nose: medium intensity, balanced, ripe fruit, fruit liqueur notes, dark chocolate. Palate: flavourful, spicy, fine tannins.

BODEGAS AGE

Barrio de la Estación, s/n
26360 Fuenmayor (La Rioja)
☎: +34 941 293 500 - Fax: +34 941 293 501
bodegasage@pernod-ricard.com
www.bodegasage.com

SIGLO SACO 2007 TC
85% tempranillo, 10% mazuelo, 5% garnacha.

87 Colour: bright cherry, garnet rim. Nose: medium intensity, balanced, ripe fruit, spicy. Palate: easy to drink, ripe fruit, spicy.

SIGLO 2005 TR
85% tempranillo, 10% mazuelo, 5% graciano.

87 Colour: cherry, garnet rim. Nose: ripe fruit, spicy. Palate: flavourful, fruity, correct, good acidity.

SIGLO 2004 TGR
85% tempranillo, 10% mazuelo, 5% graciano.

85 Colour: cherry, garnet rim. Nose: fruit liqueur notes, spicy, old leather. Palate: flavourful, light-bodied, correct, easy to drink.

BODEGAS ALABANZA

Pol. Ind. El Sequero , Avda. Cameros, 27
26150 Agoncillo (La Rioja)
☎: +34 941 437 051 - Fax: +34 941 437 077
bodegasalabanza@bodegasalabanza.com
www.bodegasalabanza.com

ALABANZA 2010 T
tempranillo.

85 Colour: cherry, purple rim. Nose: ripe fruit, red berry notes. Palate: powerful, flavourful, fleshy, round tannins.

ALABANZA 2006 TC
tempranillo, garnacha.

87 Colour: cherry, garnet rim. Nose: ripe fruit, creamy oak, toasty, complex. Palate: powerful, flavourful, toasty.

ALABANZA 2006 TR
tempranillo, garnacha, mazuelo, graciano.

85 Colour: cherry, garnet rim. Nose: spicy, creamy oak, toasty, complex. Palate: powerful, flavourful, toasty.

ALABANZA SELECCIÓN 2005 T
tempranillo, mazuelo, graciano.

86 Colour: cherry, garnet rim. Nose: ripe fruit, spicy, creamy oak, fine reductive notes. Palate: powerful, flavourful, toasty.

BODEGAS ALADRO

Barco, 23
01340 Elciego (Álava)
☎: +34 679 822 754
aladro@aladro.es
www.aladro.es

ALADRO 2010 B
viura.

84 Colour: bright straw. Nose: floral, fresh fruit, citrus fruit. Palate: flavourful, fruity, fine bitter notes, correct.

ALADRO 2010 T
tempranillo.

88 Colour: cherry, purple rim. Nose: fresh fruit, red berry notes, floral. Palate: flavourful, fruity, good acidity, round tannins.

BODEGAS ALICIA ROJAS

Ctra. Nacional 232, Km. 376 - 377
26513 Ausejo (La Rioja)
☎: +34 941 430 010 - Fax: +34 941 430 286
info@bodegasaliciarojas.com
www.bodegasaliciarojas.es

FINCA ALICIA ROJAS MALVASÍA 2007 BFB
100% malvasía.

86 Colour: bright golden. Nose: powerfull, candied fruit, dried flowers, toasty. Palate: flavourful, fleshy, ripe fruit.

ALICIA ROJAS COLECCIÓN PRIVADA GARNACHA 2007 TR
100% garnacha.

89 Colour: bright cherry, garnet rim. Nose: spicy, balsamic herbs, ripe fruit. Palate: good structure, flavourful, complex, round tannins.

ALICIA ROJAS COLECCIÓN PRIVADA TEMPRANILLO 2007 TR
100% tempranillo.

88 Colour: cherry, garnet rim. Nose: varietal, ripe fruit, cocoa bean, sweet spices. Palate: balanced, good acidity, round tannins.

FINCA ALICIA ROJAS 2007 TC
95% tempranillo, 5% graciano.

86 Colour: cherry, garnet rim. Nose: ripe fruit, spicy, toasty, fruit preserve. Palate: powerful, flavourful, toasty, round tannins.

SOLARCE 2007 TC
80% tempranillo, 15% garnacha, 5% graciano.

85 Colour: cherry, garnet rim. Nose: fruit preserve, medium intensity, spicy. Palate: flavourful, spicy, easy to drink.

FINCA ALICIA ROJAS 2004 TR
80% tempranillo, 10% graciano, 10% mazuelo.

85 Colour: bright cherry, orangey edge. Nose: old leather, spicy. Palate: spicy, ripe fruit, easy to drink.

BODEGAS ALTANZA

Ctra. Nacional 232, Km. 419,5
26360 Fuenmayor (Rioja)
☎: +34 941 450 860 - Fax: +34 941 450 804
altanza@bodegasaltanza.com
www.bodegasaltanza.com

LEALTANZA 2010 B
60% viura, 40% sauvignon blanc.

90 Colour: bright straw. Nose: fresh, fresh fruit, white flowers, expressive, citrus fruit. Palate: flavourful, fruity, good acidity, balanced.

LEALTANZA 2010 RD
100% tempranillo.

85 Colour: rose, purple rim. Nose: red berry notes, slightly evolved. Palate: flavourful, fruity, fresh, good acidity.

HACIENDA VALVARÉS 2008 TC
tempranillo.

86 Colour: bright cherry. Nose: ripe fruit, sweet spices, creamy oak, slightly evolved. Palate: flavourful, fruity, toasty, round tannins.

EDULIS 2007 TC
100% tempranillo.

87 Colour: cherry, garnet rim. Nose: red berry notes, ripe fruit, fine reductive notes, cocoa bean, sweet spices, toasty. Palate: good acidity, flavourful, fleshy, ripe fruit.

LEALTANZA AUTOR 2005 T
100% tempranillo.

91 Colour: black cherry, orangey edge. Nose: ripe fruit, cocoa bean, dark chocolate, toasty, expressive. Palate: balanced, powerful, flavourful, fleshy, toasty.

LEALTANZA 2005 TR
100% tempranillo.

89 Colour: black cherry, orangey edge. Nose: ripe fruit, expressive, complex, sweet spices, cocoa bean, toasty. Palate: ripe fruit, flavourful, fleshy, toasty.

LEALTANZA CLUB 2005 TR
100% tempranillo.

89 Colour: cherry, garnet rim. Nose: ripe fruit, spicy, toasty, complex. Palate: powerful, flavourful, toasty, spicy.

LEALTANZA ARTISTAS ESPAÑOLES DALÍ 2004 TR
100% tempranillo.

90 Colour: pale ruby, brick rim edge. Nose: ripe fruit, tobacco, cigar, old leather, aged wood nuances, toasty. Palate: good finish, long, fleshy.

LEALTANZA SELECCIÓN 2004 TR
tempranillo.

88 Colour: light cherry, garnet rim. Nose: ripe fruit, complex, spicy, toasty, mineral, fine reductive notes. Palate: balanced, powerful, complex, fleshy, toasty.

LEALTANZA SELECCIÓN 2001 TR
100% tempranillo.

88 Color pale ruby, brick rim edge. Aroma elegant, spicy, fine reductive notes, wet leather, aged wood nuances, fruit liqueur notes. Taste spicy, fine tannins, elegant, long.

LEALTANZA 2001 TGR
100% tempranillo.

88 Colour: pale ruby, brick rim edge. Nose: fruit liqueur notes, ripe fruit, waxy notes, wet leather, toasty. Palate: slightly evolved, powerful, flavourful.

LEALTANZA ARTISTAS ESPAÑOLES GAUDÍ 2005 RESERVA
100% tempranillo.

93 Colour: pale ruby, brick rim edge. Nose: ripe fruit, fine reductive notes, fruit liqueur notes, dark chocolate, sweet spices, toasty. Palate: good acidity, balanced, powerful, flavourful.

BODEGAS ALTOS DEL MARQUÉS

Ctra. Navarrete, 1
26372 Hornos de Moncalvillo (La Rioja)
☎: +34 941 286 728 - Fax: +34 941 286 729
info@altosdelmarques.com
www.altosdelmarques.com

ALTOS DEL MARQUÉS 2008 T
85% tempranillo, 10% garnacha, 5% mazuelo.

87 Colour: cherry, garnet rim. Nose: powerfull, fruit expression, raspberry, creamy oak. Palate: powerful, flavourful, spicy, ripe fruit.

ALTOS DEL MARQUÉS 2008 TC
100% tempranillo.

87 Colour: bright cherry. Nose: ripe fruit, sweet spices, smoky. Palate: flavourful, fruity, toasty, round tannins.

BODEGAS ALTÚN

Las Piscinas, 30
01307 Baños de Ebro (Álava)
☎: +34 945 609 317 - Fax: +34 945 609 309
altun@bodegasaltun.com
www.bodegasaltun.com

ALBIKER 2010 T MACERACIÓN CARBÓNICA
95% tempranillo, 5% viura.

91 Colour: cherry, purple rim. Nose: floral, violet drops, raspberry, red berry notes, expressive. Palate: good acidity, balanced, fruity, flavourful, fleshy.

ANA DE ALTÚN 2010 B
75% viura, 25% malvasía.

88 Colour: bright straw, greenish rim. Nose: floral, citrus fruit, wild herbs. Palate: fresh, flavourful, good acidity.

ALTÚN 2008 TC
100% tempranillo.

90 Colour: bright cherry. Nose: ripe fruit, sweet spices, creamy oak, lactic notes. Palate: flavourful, toasty, round tannins.

SECRETO DE ALTÚN 2008 T
100% tempranillo.

91 Colour: cherry, garnet rim. Nose: ripe fruit, spicy, creamy oak, mineral. Palate: powerful, toasty, round tannins, fleshy.

EVEREST 2007 T
100% tempranillo.

93 Colour: cherry, garnet rim. Nose: creamy oak, toasty, expressive, raspberry, lactic notes. Palate: powerful, flavourful, toasty, round tannins.

ALTÚN 2006 TR
100% tempranillo.

90 Colour: cherry, garnet rim. Nose: spicy, characterful, creamy oak. Palate: powerful, flavourful, round tannins.

BODEGAS AMAREN

Ctra. Baños de Ebro, s/n,
01307 Villabuena (Álava)
☎: +34 945 175 240 - Fax: +34 945 174 566
bodegas@bodegasamaren.com
www.bodegasamaren.com

ANGELES DE AMAREN 2007 T
85% tempranillo, 15% graciano.

92 Colour: cherry, garnet rim. Nose: spicy, creamy oak, toasty, characterful, red berry notes. Palate: powerful, flavourful, round tannins, mineral.

AMAREN TEMPRANILLO 2005 TR
100% tempranillo.

92 Colour: cherry, garnet rim. Nose: spicy, creamy oak, toasty, scrubland. Palate: flavourful, toasty, round tannins.

AMAREN 2009 BFB
85% viura, 15% malvasía.

91 Colour: bright yellow. Nose: ripe fruit, sweet spices, creamy oak, fragrant herbs. Palate: rich, smoky aftertaste, flavourful, fresh, good acidity.

BODEGAS ANTIÓN

Manuel Iradier, 13
01340 Elciego (Álava)
☎: +34 902 122 211 - Fax: +34 945 622 229
marketing@grupoproconsol.com
www.bodegantion.com

ANTIÓN VARIETAL TEMPRANILLO 2008 T
100% tempranillo.

92 Colour: cherry, garnet rim. Nose: spicy, creamy oak, toasty, red berry notes, fruit expression. Palate: powerful, flavourful, toasty, round tannins, spicy.

ANTIÓN GRACIANO 2008 T
100% graciano.

90 Colour: cherry, garnet rim. Nose: powerfull, characterful, ripe fruit, toasty, dark chocolate. Palate: powerful, fleshy, spicy, ripe fruit.

ANTIÓN PREMIUM 2007 T
100% tempranillo.

92 Colour: dark-red cherry. Nose: powerfull, characterful, fruit preserve, creamy oak, sweet spices, cocoa bean. Palate: powerful, fleshy, concentrated, good acidity.

BARÓN DE OJA 2007 TC
100% tempranillo.

91 Colour: cherry, garnet rim. Nose: ripe fruit, powerfull, characterful, roasted coffee. Palate: powerful, flavourful, fleshy, round tannins.

ANTIÓN SELECCIÓN 2007 T
100% tempranillo.

90 Colour: cherry, garnet rim. Nose: spicy, creamy oak, complex, fruit preserve. Palate: powerful, toasty, round tannins.

BODEGAS BAGORDI

Ctra. de Estella, Km. 32
31261 Andosilla (Navarra)
☎: +34 948 674 860 - Fax: +34 948 674 238
info@bagordi.com
www.bagordi.com

BAGORDI GRACIANO 2009 TR
100% graciano.

86 Colour: cherry, purple rim. Nose: spicy, fruit preserve, creamy oak, sweet spices. Palate: powerful, flavourful, fleshy.

BAGORDI 2004 TR
80% tempranillo, 20% garnacha.

83 Colour: pale ruby, brick rim edge. Nose: powerfull, fruit liqueur notes, pattiserie, aged wood nuances. Palate: flavourful, spirituous, ripe fruit, round tannins.

BAGORDI GARNACHA 2000 TR
100% garnacha.

84 Colour: cherry, garnet rim. Nose: powerfull, fruit liqueur notes, toasty. Palate: flavourful, powerful, spicy.

BODEGAS BERBERANA

Ctra. El Ciego s/n
26350 Cenicero (La Rioja)
☎: +34 914 365 924
gromero@arcoinvest-group.com
www.berberana.com

BERBERANA VIÑA ALARDE 2007 TC
100% tempranillo.

87 Colour: cherry, garnet rim. Nose: balanced, ripe fruit, spicy. Palate: flavourful, fruity, good structure, easy to drink.

BERBERANA VIÑA ALARDE 2006 TR
80% tempranillo, 20% garnacha.

87 Colour: cherry, garnet rim. Nose: medium intensity, spicy, old leather. Palate: flavourful, balanced, round tannins.

BERBERANA CARTA DE ORO 2006 TR
80% tempranillo, 20% garnacha.

85 Colour: pale ruby, brick rim edge. Nose: ripe fruit, old leather, waxy notes, tobacco, spicy, toasty. Palate: flavourful, ripe fruit, spicy.

BODEGAS BERCEO

Cuevas, 32-34-36
26200 Haro (La Rioja)
☎: +34 941 310 744 - Fax: +34 941 310 744
bodegas@gurpegui.es
www.gurpegui.es

VIÑA BERCEO 2008 TC
tempranillo, garnacha, graciano.

90 Colour: dark-red cherry. Nose: spicy, aged wood nuances, fresh fruit, closed. Palate: fruity, powerful, flavourful, creamy, spicy.

VIÑA BERCEO 2010 RD
garnacha, tempranillo, viura.

84 Colour: rose, purple rim. Nose: ripe fruit, red berry notes, floral, expressive. Palate: fleshy, powerful, fruity.

PRIMI 2010 T
tempranillo, graciano, garnacha.

87 Colour: cherry, purple rim. Nose: powerfull, red berry notes, floral, spicy. Palate: good acidity, round, flavourful, fruity.

VIÑADRIÁN 2010 T
tempranillo, garnacha.

87 Colour: cherry, purple rim. Nose: fresh fruit, red berry notes, floral. Palate: flavourful, fruity, good acidity, round tannins.

LOS DOMINIOS DE BERCEO 2007 TC
tempranillo.

91 Colour: cherry, garnet rim. Nose: ripe fruit, mineral, spicy, creamy oak. Palate: complex, round, unctuous, flavourful.

BERCEO "NUEVA GENERACIÓN" 2007 TC
tempranillo, garnacha, graciano.

90 Colour: dark-red cherry. Nose: fruit expression, varietal, powerfull, fresh, balanced, cocoa bean, creamy oak. Palate: fruity, powerful, flavourful, balsamic.

LOS DOMINIOS DE BERCEO "RESERVA 36" 2006 TR
tempranillo.

90 Colour: black cherry, garnet rim. Nose: ripe fruit, complex, spicy, toasty. Palate: good acidity, powerful, flavourful, fleshy, complex.

GONZALO DE BERCEO 2001 TGR
tempranillo, graciano, mazuelo.

90 Colour: cherry, garnet rim. Nose: ripe fruit, complex, balanced, sweet spices, toasty. Palate: round, unctuous, flavourful, complex, toasty.

VIÑA BERCEO 2010 BFB
viura, malvasía, garnacha blanca.

85 Colour: bright yellow. Nose: powerfull, ripe fruit, sweet spices, creamy oak. Palate: rich, smoky aftertaste, flavourful, good acidity.

GONZALO DE BERCEO 2006 TR
tempranillo, graciano, mazuelo, garnacha.

89 Colour: cherry, garnet rim. Nose: ripe fruit, expressive, scrubland, sweet spices, toasty. Palate: powerful, flavourful, fleshy, ripe fruit.

BODEGAS BERONIA

Ctra. Ollauri - Nájera, Km. 1,8
26220 Ollauri (La Rioja)
☎: +34 941 338 000 - Fax: +34 941 338 266
beronia@beronia.es
www.beronia.es

BERONIA VIURA 2010 BFB
100% viura.

86 Colour: bright straw, greenish rim. Nose: medium intensity, fresh, fragrant herbs. Palate: fruity, good acidity.

BERONIA VIURA 2010 B
100% viura.

83 Colour: bright straw, greenish rim. Nose: medium intensity, wild herbs, fresh. Palate: fresh, light-bodied, easy to drink.

BERONIA 2010 RD
100% tempranillo.

86 Colour: brilliant rose. Nose: fresh fruit, citrus fruit. Palate: fruity, fresh, flavourful, easy to drink.

BERONIA TEMPRANILLO ELABORACIÓN ESPECIAL 2009 T
100% tempranillo.

90 Colour: cherry, garnet rim. Nose: ripe fruit, fruit expression, cocoa bean, creamy oak. Palate: ripe fruit, powerful, fleshy.

III A.C., BERONIA 2008 T
92% tempranillo, 4% graciano, 4% mazuelo.

91 Colour: very deep cherry. Nose: cocoa bean, creamy oak, mineral, ripe fruit. Palate: powerful, fine bitter notes, round tannins.

BERONIA 2008 TC
83% tempranillo, 15% garnacha, 2% mazuelo.

87 Colour: deep cherry. Nose: powerfull, ripe fruit, toasty, scrubland. Palate: ripe fruit, balsamic, round tannins.

BERONIA GRACIANO 2007 T
100% graciano.

88 Colour: cherry, garnet rim. Nose: spicy, cocoa bean, characterful, varietal, grassy. Palate: flavourful, spicy, ripe fruit.

BERONIA 2006 TR
90% tempranillo, 5% graciano, 5% mazuelo.

89 Colour: pale ruby, brick rim edge. Nose: ripe fruit, wet leather, creamy oak, spicy. Palate: flavourful, fine bitter notes, spicy.

BERONIA MAZUELO 2006 TR
100% mazuelo.

86 Colour: cherry, garnet rim. Nose: ripe fruit, floral, creamy oak, toasty. Palate: flavourful, fine bitter notes, round tannins.

BERONIA 2003 TGR
92% tempranillo, 4% mazuelo, 4% mazuelo.

90 Colour: pale ruby, brick rim edge. Nose: wet leather, tobacco, fruit liqueur notes, toasty, spicy. Palate: flavourful, fleshy, spicy.

BERONIA SELECCIÓN 198 BARRICAS 2001 TR
87% tempranillo, 7% mazuelo, 6% graciano.

89 Colour: cherry, garnet rim. Nose: spicy, creamy oak, toasty, fruit liqueur notes. Palate: powerful, toasty, round tannins, fine bitter notes.

BODEGAS BILBAÍNAS

Estación, 3
26200 Haro (La Rioja)
☎: +34 941 310 147 - Fax: +34 935 051 567
m.oyono@bodegasbilbainas.com
www.bodegasbilbainas.com

VIÑA ZACO 2008 T
100% tempranillo.

90 Colour: cherry, garnet rim. Nose: powerfull, ripe fruit, sweet spices. Palate: flavourful, powerful, fleshy.

VIÑA POMAL 2008 TC
100% tempranillo.

88 Colour: cherry, garnet rim. Nose: powerfull, ripe fruit, sweet spices, dark chocolate. Palate: flavourful, fine bitter notes, good acidity.

VIÑA POMAL "ALTO DE LA CASETA" 2007 T
100% tempranillo.

93 Colour: bright cherry. Nose: ripe fruit, sweet spices, earthy notes, characterful. Palate: flavourful, toasty, round tannins.

LA VICALANDA 2006 TR
100% tempranillo.

94 Colour: cherry, garnet rim. Nose: creamy oak, complex, earthy notes, expressive. Palate: powerful, flavourful, toasty, round tannins.

VIÑA POMAL 2006 TR
100% tempranillo.

90 Colour: deep cherry, orangey edge. Nose: ripe fruit, spicy, varietal, toasty. Palate: flavourful, good acidity, elegant.

LA VICALANDA 2004 TGR
100% tempranillo.

95 Colour: cherry, garnet rim. Nose: powerfull, fruit liqueur notes, toasty, aromatic coffee, sweet spices. Palate: powerful, flavourful, ripe fruit, long, round tannins.

BODEGAS BRETÓN CRIADORES

Ctra. de Fuenmayor, Km. 1,5
26370 Navarrete (La Rioja)
☎: +34 941 440 840 - Fax: +34 941 440 812
info@bodegasbreton.com
www.bodegasbreton.com

LORIÑÓN 2008 TC
100% tempranillo.

89 Colour: deep cherry. Nose: expressive, varietal, ripe fruit, sweet spices, creamy oak. Palate: powerful, spicy, round tannins.

L 5 LORIÑÓN 2008 TC
85% tempranillo, 15% graciano.

88 Color cherry, garnet rim. Aroma ripe fruit, spicy, creamy oak, toasty, complex. Taste powerful, flavourful, toasty, round tannins.

LORIÑÓN 2006 TR
90% tempranillo, 10% graciano.

88 Colour: cherry, garnet rim. Nose: spicy, smoky, wet leather. Palate: powerful, fleshy, good acidity, fine bitter notes.

ALBA DE BRETÓN 2005 TR
85% tempranillo, 15% graciano.

92 Colour: deep cherry. Nose: fruit expression, powerfull, characterful, spicy, cocoa bean. Palate: powerful, flavourful, fine bitter notes.

DOMINIO DE CONTE 2005 TR
90% tempranillo, 10% graciano.

91 Colour: deep cherry. Nose: fruit liqueur notes, sweet spices, earthy notes. Palate: powerful, spicy, ripe fruit.

LORIÑÓN 2005 TGR
80% tempranillo, 15% graciano, 5% mazuelo.

90 Colour: deep cherry. Nose: powerfull, fruit liqueur notes, spicy, toasty. Palate: powerful, spirituous, long.

BODEGAS CAMPILLO

Ctra. de Logroño, s/n
01300 Laguardia (Álava)
☎: +34 945 600 826 - Fax: +34 945 600 837
info@bodegascampillo.es
www.bodegascampillo.es

CAMPILLO 2010 BFB
85% viura, 10% malvasia, 5% chardonnay.

91 Colour: bright yellow. Nose: powerfull, ripe fruit, sweet spices, creamy oak. Palate: rich, flavourful, fresh, good acidity.

CAMPILLO 2010 RD
100% tempranillo.

89 Colour: rose, purple rim. Nose: red berry notes, fresh fruit, floral, lactic notes, wild herbs, fresh, expressive. Palate: fleshy, powerful, flavourful, fruity, elegant.

CAMPILLO 2007 TC
100% tempranillo.

90 Colour: cherry, garnet rim. Nose: ripe fruit, balanced, spicy, cigar, fine reductive notes. Palate: fleshy, classic aged character, long.

CAMPILLO FINCA CUESTA CLARA 2005 TR
100% tempranillo.

93 Colour: bright cherry, garnet rim. Nose: complex, balanced, varietal, creamy oak, sweet spices. Palate: concentrated, ripe fruit.

CAMPILLO 2004 TR
tempranillo.

91 Colour: deep cherry, garnet rim. Nose: balanced, spicy, complex, ripe fruit, creamy oak. Palate: flavourful, round tannins.

CAMPILLO RESERVA ESPECIAL 2004 TR
85% tempranillo, 10% graciano, 5% cabernet sauvignon.

90 Colour: deep cherry, garnet rim. Nose: medium intensity, ripe fruit, spicy. Palate: fruity, flavourful, good acidity.

CAMPILLO 2001 TGR
95% tempranillo, 5% graciano.

89 Colour: very deep cherry, garnet rim. Nose: dark chocolate, creamy oak, tobacco, fruit expression. Palate: good structure, flavourful, spicy, round tannins.

BODEGAS CAMPO VIEJO

Camino de la Puebla, 50
26006 Logroño (La Rioja)
☎: +34 941 279 951 - Fax: +34 941 279 901
campoviejo@domecqbodegas.com
www.campoviejo.com

CAMPO VIEJO 2010 B
viura.

84 Colour: bright straw. Nose: grassy, fruit expression, white flowers. Palate: flavourful, fruity.

CV DE CAMPO VIEJO 2010 RD
100% tempranillo.

86 Colour: brilliant rose. Nose: red berry notes, fresh, lactic notes, citrus fruit. Palate: fruity, light-bodied, easy to drink.

COLECCIÓN PRIVADA FÉLIX AZPILICUETA 2007 T
tempranillo, graciano, cariñena.

93 Colour: cherry, garnet rim. Nose: elegant, characterful, ripe fruit, toasty, creamy oak, new oak, sweet spices. Palate: flavourful, powerful, fleshy, complex, long.

CAMPO VIEJO 2007 TC
tempranillo, garnacha tinta, graciano.

88 Colour: cherry, garnet rim. Nose: medium intensity, spicy, ripe fruit. Palate: fruity, good acidity, balanced.

AZPILICUETA 2007 TC
tempranillo, graciano, mazuelo.

91 Colour: cherry, garnet rim. Nose: creamy oak, toasty, complex, fruit expression. Palate: powerful, flavourful, toasty, round tannins.

ALCORTA CARMEN RUSCADELLA 2007 T

89 Colour: deep cherry, garnet rim. Nose: ripe fruit, balanced, sweet spices, creamy oak. Palate: fruity, good structure, round tannins.

AZPILICUETA 2006 TR
85% tempranillo, 10% graciano, 5% mazuelo.

91 Colour: bright cherry, orangey edge. Nose: spicy, balsamic herbs, expressive, cedar wood, ripe fruit. Palate: toasty, round, unctuous, flavourful, fleshy.

ALCORTA 2006 TR
tempranillo.

87 Colour: deep cherry, garnet rim. Nose: dark chocolate, spicy, fruit preserve. Palate: ripe fruit, spicy, slightly dry, soft tannins.

DOMINIO CAMPO VIEJO 2006 T
tempranillo, graciano, mazuelo.

91 Colour: cherry, garnet rim. Nose: ripe fruit, spicy, creamy oak, toasty. Palate: powerful, flavourful, toasty, round tannins.

CV DE CAMPO VIEJO 2007 TC
tempranillo, garnacha, graciano.

88 Colour: cherry, garnet rim. Nose: roasted coffee, sweet spices, cocoa bean, aromatic coffee, ripe fruit. Palate: balsamic, powerful, flavourful, fleshy.

ALCORTA 2007 TC
tempranillo.

87 Colour: cherry, garnet rim. Nose: ripe fruit, balanced, spicy. Palate: fruity, flavourful.

CAMPO VIEJO 2005 TR
tempranillo, graciano, mazuelo.

89 Colour: cherry, garnet rim. Nose: ripe fruit, spicy, toasty, medium intensity. Palate: powerful, flavourful, toasty, round tannins.

CAMPO VIEJO 2002 TGR
tempranillo, graciano, mazuelo.

88 Colour: deep cherry, garnet rim. Nose: tobacco, old leather, ripe fruit. Palate: good structure, flavourful, spicy.

CAMPO VIEJO SEMIDULCE
viura.

80 Colour: bright yellow. Nose: ripe fruit, dried herbs, medium intensity. Palate: good acidity, fine bitter notes, sweetness.

BODEGAS CASA PRIMICIA

Camino de la Hoya, 1
01300 Laguardia (Álava)
☎: +34 945 600 296 - Fax: +34 945 621 252
info@bodegascasaprimicia.com
www.bodegasprimicia.com

VIÑA DIEZMO 2008 TC
100% tempranillo.

85 Colour: cherry, garnet rim. Nose: ripe fruit, toasty, old leather, tobacco. Palate: flavourful, toasty, fleshy.

JULIÁN MADRID 2006 TR
80% tempranillo, 20% otras.

86 Colour: cherry, garnet rim. Nose: ripe fruit, balsamic herbs, spicy, toasty. Palate: powerful, fleshy, long.

COFRADÍA 2005 TR
100% tempranillo.

88 Colour: cherry, garnet rim. Nose: ripe fruit, toasty, balsamic herbs. Palate: powerful, flavourful, toasty, round tannins.

BODEGAS CASTILLO DE SAJAZARRA

Del Río, s/n
26212 Sajazarra (La Rioja)
☎: +34 941 320 066 -
Fax: +34 941 320 251
bodega@castillo-de-sajazarra.com
www.castillo-de-sajazarra.com

CASTILLO DE SAJAZARRA 2005 TR
100% tempranillo.

90 Colour: bright cherry, orangey edge. Nose: complex, expressive, varietal, pattiserie, creamy oak. Palate: flavourful, spicy, ripe fruit.

HERENZA KOSHER CRIANZA 2008
ELVIWINES 2008 TC
100% tempranillo.

92 Colour: bright cherry. Nose: creamy oak, spicy, fruit expression, fresh fruit. Palate: fruity, toasty, round tannins, light-bodied, powerful, flavourful, full, complex.

SOLAR DE LÍBANO 2008 TC
97% tempranillo, 3% graciano.

91 Colour: cherry, garnet rim. Nose: spicy, creamy oak, fruit expression. Palate: powerful, toasty, round tannins, good acidity.

DIGMA AUTOR 2006 TR
100% tempranillo.

93 Colour: cherry, garnet rim. Nose: expressive, complex, creamy oak, sweet spices. Palate: flavourful, spicy, mineral, fleshy, concentrated.

SOLAR DE LÍBANO 2004 TR
97% tempranillo, 2% graciano, 1% garnacha.

89 Colour: cherry, garnet rim. Nose: spicy, creamy oak, toasty, fine reductive notes. Palate: powerful, flavourful, toasty, round tannins, spicy.

MATI KOSHER ELVIWINES 2009 T
100% tempranillo.

91 Colour: cherry, purple rim. Nose: fruit expression, balsamic herbs, scrubland, mineral. Palate: light-bodied, flavourful, fruity, complex, mineral.

BODEGAS CERROLAZA

Ctra. Nacional 232-Salida 10 vía servicio
26006 Logroño (La Rioja)
☎: +34 941 286 728 - Fax: +34 941 286 729
info@bodegascerrolaza.com
www.bodegascerrolaza.com

ATICUS VENDIMIA SELECCIONADA 2008 T
100% tempranillo.

90 Colour: cherry, garnet rim. Nose: ripe fruit, spicy, toasty, complex, sweet spices. Palate: powerful, flavourful, toasty, round tannins.

ATICUS 2007 TC
100% tempranillo.

87 Colour: cherry, garnet rim. Nose: creamy oak, toasty, ripe fruit. Palate: powerful, flavourful, toasty, round tannins.

ATICUS 2005 TR
100% tempranillo.

87 Colour: cherry, garnet rim. Nose: powerfull, ripe fruit, spicy, smoky. Palate: spicy, fine bitter notes.

BODEGAS CORRAL

Ctra. de Logroño, Km. 10
26370 Navarrete (La Rioja)
☎: +34 941 440 193 - Fax: +34 941 440 195
info@donjacobo.es
www.donjacobo.es

DON JACOBO 2010 B
100% viura.

83 Colour: bright straw. Nose: ripe fruit, citrus fruit. Palate: flavourful, powerful, fleshy.

DON JACOBO 2010 RD
50% garnacha, 50% tempranillo.

85 Colour: brilliant rose. Nose: ripe fruit, candied fruit. Palate: flavourful, ripe fruit.

DON JACOBO ECOLÓGICO 2008 T
50% mazuelo, 50% tempranillo.

90 Colour: bright cherry. Nose: sweet spices, creamy oak, dark chocolate. Palate: flavourful, fruity, toasty, round tannins.

DON JACOBO 2008 TR
85% tempranillo, 10% garnacha, mazuelo.

87 Colour: cherry, garnet rim. Nose: ripe fruit, spicy, creamy oak, wet leather. Palate: powerful, flavourful, toasty, round tannins.

DON JACOBO 2006 TC
85% tempranillo, 10% garnacha, 5% mazuelo, graciano.

87 Colour: cherry, garnet rim. Nose: fruit liqueur notes, toasty, spicy. Palate: flavourful, spicy, round tannins.

ALTOS DE CORRAL 2005 T FERMENTADO EN BARRICA
100% tempranillo.

88 Colour: pale ruby, brick rim edge. Nose: elegant, ripe fruit, creamy oak, dark chocolate, aromatic coffee. Palate: spicy, elegant, good acidity, fine bitter notes.

ALTOS DE CORRAL 2002 TR
100% tempranillo.

90 Colour: pale ruby, brick rim edge. Nose: elegant, spicy, fine reductive notes, wet leather, aged wood nuances. Palate: spicy, fine tannins, elegant, long.

DON JACOBO 1995 TGR
85% tempranillo, 15% garnacha.

90 Colour: pale ruby, brick rim edge. Nose: elegant, spicy, fine reductive notes, wet leather, aged wood nuances. Palate: spicy, fine tannins, elegant, long.

BODEGAS COVILA

Camino del Soto, 26
01306 La Puebla de Labarca (Álava)
☎: +34 945 627 232 - Fax: +34 945 627 295
comercial@covila.es
www.covila.es

COVILA 2005 TR
100% tempranillo.

87 Colour: cherry, garnet rim. Nose: ripe fruit, spicy, toasty, fine reductive notes. Palate: flavourful, toasty, round tannins.

COVILA 2010 T MACERACIÓN CARBÓNICA
100% tempranillo.

89 Colour: cherry, purple rim. Nose: expressive, fresh fruit, red berry notes, floral, lactic notes. Palate: flavourful, fruity, good acidity.

BODEGAS CUNA DE REYES

Ctra. de Uruñuela, s/n
26300 Najera (La Rioja)
☎: +34 941 360 280 - Fax: +34 941 410 423
bodegas@cunadereyes.es
www.cunadereyes.es

CUNA DE REYES 2008 TC
85% tempranillo, garnacha, mazuelo.

87 Colour: cherry, garnet rim. Nose: ripe fruit, woody, wild herbs. Palate: ripe fruit, correct, fine bitter notes, toasty.

CUNA DE REYES EDICCIÓN LIMITADA 2007 T
100% tempranillo.

88 Colour: very deep cherry, garnet rim. Nose: expressive, ripe fruit, spicy, cocoa bean. Palate: flavourful, fruity.

CUNA DE REYES 2005 TR
tempranillo, garnacha, mazuelo.

87 Colour: cherry, garnet rim. Nose: ripe fruit, spicy, creamy oak, toasty. Palate: powerful, flavourful, toasty, round tannins.

BODEGAS DARIEN

Ctra. Logroño-Zaragoza, Km. 7
26006 Logroño (La Rioja)
☎: +34 941 258 130 - Fax: +34 941 265 285
info@darien.es
www.darien.es

DARIEN 2010 T
100% tempranillo.

88 Colour: cherry, purple rim. Nose: red berry notes, floral, ripe fruit. Palate: flavourful, fruity, good acidity, round tannins.

DARIEN 2007 TC
85% tempranillo, 12% graciano, 3% mazuelo.

88 Colour: bright cherry, garnet rim. Nose: red berry notes, spicy, dried herbs, balanced. Palate: ripe fruit, long, round tannins.

DARIEN 2006 TR
85% tempranillo, 8% graciano, 7% garnacha.

88 Colour: bright cherry, garnet rim. Nose: complex, balanced, sweet spices, creamy oak. Palate: flavourful, ripe fruit, spicy.

DELIUS 2004 TR
80% tempranillo, 20% graciano.

89 Colour: very deep cherry, garnet rim. Nose: medium intensity, sweet spices, cocoa bean. Palate: good structure, ripe fruit, spicy, round tannins.

DARIEN SELECCIÓN 2003 T
68% tempranillo, 32% mazuelo.

89 Colour: deep cherry, garnet rim. Nose: balanced, ripe fruit, spicy, dark chocolate. Palate: flavourful, fruity, good structure.

BODEGAS DE LOS HEREDEROS DEL MARQUÉS DE RISCAL

Torrea, 1
01340 Elciego (Álava)
☎: +34 945 606 000 - Fax: +34 945 606 023
marquesderiscal@marquesderiscal.com
www.marquesderiscal.com

MARQUÉS DE RISCAL 2010 RD
tempranillo.

87 Colour: brilliant rose. Nose: red berry notes, grassy, fresh. Palate: fruity, correct, good acidity.

FINCA TORREA 2007 TR
tempranillo, graciano.

95 Colour: cherry, garnet rim. Nose: fruit liqueur notes, sweet spices, varnish, dark chocolate, aromatic coffee. Palate: fine bitter notes, ripe fruit, powerful tannins.

MARQUÉS DE RISCAL 2007 TR
90% tempranillo, 10% graciano, mazuelo.

91 Colour: cherry, garnet rim. Nose: powerfull, ripe fruit, creamy oak, sweet spices. Palate: flavourful, powerful, fleshy, round tannins, long.

MARQUÉS DE ARIENZO 2007 TC
tempranillo, graciano, mazuelo.

86 Colour: cherry, garnet rim. Nose: ripe fruit, spicy, wet leather. Palate: spicy, ripe fruit, round tannins.

MARQUÉS DE RISCAL 2004 TGR
tempranillo, graciano, mazuelo.

93 Colour: deep cherry, orangey edge. Nose: aromatic coffee, sweet spices, toasty. Palate: flavourful, spicy, ripe fruit, long.

MARQUÉS DE RISCAL 150 ANIVERSARIO 2001 TGR
tempranillo, graciano, otras.

92 Colour: pale ruby, brick rim edge. Nose: elegant, spicy, fine reductive notes, wet leather, aged wood nuances. Palate: spicy, fine tannins, elegant, long.

BARÓN DE CHIREL 2005 T
tempranillo, otras.

93 Colour: deep cherry, garnet rim. Nose: fruit liqueur notes, sweet spices, dark chocolate, aromatic coffee. Palate: flavourful, fine bitter notes, ripe fruit, round tannins.

BODEGAS DE SANTIAGO

Avda. del Ebro, 50
01307 Baños de Ebro (Álava)
☎: +34 945 609 201 - Fax: +34 945 609 201
b.desantiago@telefonica.net

LAGAR DE SANTIAGO 2010 B
100% viura.

88 Colour: bright yellow. Nose: balanced, fresh, wild herbs, citrus fruit. Palate: flavourful, fruity, long, good acidity.

LAGAR DE SANTIAGO 2009 BFB
100% viura.

86 Colour: bright straw. Nose: ripe fruit, sweet spices, cocoa bean. Palate: flavourful, fine bitter notes, good acidity.

LAGAR DE SANTIAGO 2010 T
85% tempranillo, 15% viura.

90 Colour: cherry, purple rim. Nose: expressive, red berry notes, floral, fruit expression. Palate: flavourful, fruity, good acidity, round tannins.

LAGAR DE SANTIAGO 2008 TC
100% tempranillo.

89 Colour: very deep cherry, purple rim. Nose: ripe fruit, creamy oak, sweet spices. Palate: fleshy, flavourful, round tannins.

BODEGAS DEL MEDIEVO

Circunvalación San Roque, s/n
26559 Aldeanueva de Ebro (La Rioja)
☎: +34 941 163 141 - Fax: +34 941 144 204
info@bodegasdelmedievo.com
www.bodegasdelmedievo.com

COFRADE 2010 B
100% viura.

88 Colour: bright straw, greenish rim. Nose: fragrant herbs, medium intensity, fresh. Palate: flavourful, balsamic, easy to drink.

MEDIEVO 2009 BFB
100% viura.

85 Colour: yellow, greenish rim. Nose: toasty, spicy. Palate: easy to drink, good finish.

COFRADE 2010 RD
100% garnacha.

87 Colour: brilliant rose. Nose: fresh, medium intensity, wild herbs, red berry notes. Palate: fresh, fruity, easy to drink.

COFRADE 2010 T MACERACIÓN CARBÓNICA
100% tempranillo.

88 Colour: cherry, purple rim. Nose: fresh fruit, red berry notes, floral, expressive. Palate: correct, fruity, flavourful.

MEDIEVO 2008 TC
80% tempranillo, 10% garnacha, 5% mazuelo, 5% graciano.

87 Colour: deep cherry, purple rim. Nose: ripe fruit, spicy. Palate: fruity, easy to drink, good finish.

MDV 2007 T
100% graciano.

88 Colour: deep cherry, garnet rim. Nose: balanced, ripe fruit, spicy, fruit preserve, toasty, dark chocolate. Palate: flavourful.

MEDIEVO 2006 TR
80% tempranillo, 10% garnacha, 10% mazuelo, graciano.

87 Colour: bright cherry, garnet rim. Nose: medium intensity, red berry notes, ripe fruit, spicy. Palate: flavourful, round tannins.

BODEGAS DINASTÍA VIVANCO

Ctra. Nacional 232, s/n
26330 Briones (La Rioja)
☎: +34 941 322 013 - Fax: +34 941 322 316
infobodega@dinastiavivanco.es
www.dinastiavivanco.es

VIVANCO VIURA MALVASÍA TEMPRANILLO 2010 B
70% viura, 20% malvasía, 10% tempranillo blanco.

88 Colour: bright straw. Nose: fragrant herbs, citrus fruit, white flowers. Palate: flavourful, fruity, fleshy.

VIVANCO TEMPRANILLO GARNACHA 2010 RD
85% tempranillo, 15% graciano.

90 Colour: rose, purple rim. Nose: powerfull, ripe fruit, red berry notes, floral, lactic notes. Palate: fleshy, powerful, fruity, fresh.

COLECCIÓN VIVANCO PARCELAS DE GARNACHA 2008 T
100% garnacha.

94 Colour: bright cherry. Nose: sweet spices, creamy oak, ripe fruit, balsamic herbs, scrubland. Palate: flavourful, fruity, toasty, round tannins, fleshy.

COLECCIÓN VIVANCO 4 VARIETALES 2008 TC
70% tempranillo, 15% graciano, 10% garnacha, 5% mazuelo.

89 Colour: dark-red cherry, purple rim. Nose: candied fruit, sweet spices, creamy oak, toasty. Palate: fleshy, spicy.

COLECCIÓN VIVANCO PARCELAS DE MAZUELO 2008 T
100% mazuelo.

88 Colour: bright cherry, purple rim. Nose: powerfull, varietal, spicy, ripe fruit. Palate: fleshy, flavourful, spicy, round tannins.

DINASTÍA VIVANCO 2008 TC
100% tempranillo.

87 Colour: cherry, garnet rim. Nose: medium intensity, balanced, spicy, ripe fruit. Palate: flavourful, correct, fine bitter notes.

COLECCIÓN VIVANCO PARCELAS DE GRACIANO 2007 T
100% graciano.

91 Colour: black cherry. Nose: powerfull, dark chocolate, creamy oak, sweet spices. Palate: concentrated, good structure, round tannins.

DINASTÍA VIVANCO 2005 TR
90% tempranillo, 10% graciano.

87 Colour: bright cherry, garnet rim. Nose: powerfull, dark chocolate, sweet spices. Palate: good structure, fleshy, round tannins.

BODEGAS DOMECO DE JARAUTA

Camino Sendero Royal, 5
26559 Aldeanueva de Ebro (La Rioja)
☎: +34 941 163 078 - Fax: +34 941 163 078
luis@bodegasdomecodejarauta.com
www.bodegasdomecodejarauta.com

VIÑA MARRO 2010 T
100% tempranillo.

86 Colour: cherry, purple rim. Nose: red berry notes, raspberry, fresh. Palate: fleshy, good acidity, easy to drink.

SANCHO BARÓN 2009 T
100% garnacha.

84 Colour: cherry, garnet rim. Nose: ripe fruit, fruit liqueur notes, grassy. Palate: light-bodied, flavourful, spirituous.

VIÑA MARRO 2008 TC
90% tempranillo, 10% graciano.

86 Colour: cherry, garnet rim. Nose: spicy, creamy oak, red berry notes, ripe fruit. Palate: powerful, flavourful, toasty, fleshy.

VIÑA MARRO VENDIMIA SELECCIONADA 2008 T
100% tempranillo.

85 Colour: cherry, garnet rim. Nose: ripe fruit, spicy, grassy. Palate: fruity, good finish, spicy.

LAR DE SOTOMAYOR ECOLÓGICO 2008 T
100% tempranillo.

85 Colour: cherry, purple rim. Nose: red berry notes, fruit preserve, toasty, spicy. Palate: good acidity, flavourful, fruity.

DOMECO DE JARAUTA 2007 T
100% tempranillo.

90 Colour: cherry, garnet rim. Nose: ripe fruit, spicy, toasty, fine reductive notes. Palate: powerful, flavourful, toasty, ripe fruit.

VIÑA MARRO 2005 TR
100% tempranillo.

87 Colour: cherry, garnet rim. Nose: ripe fruit, spicy, toasty, fine reductive notes. Palate: flavourful, toasty, fleshy.

BODEGAS EDUARDO GARRIDO

Pza. de la Constitución, 2
26339 Abalos (La Rioja)
☎: +34 941 334 187 - Fax: +34 941 334 010

EDUARDO GARRIDO GARCÍA 2009 T JOVEN
tempranillo, mazuelo, garnacha.

88 Colour: cherry, purple rim. Nose: expressive, fresh fruit, red berry notes, floral. Palate: flavourful, fruity, good acidity.

EDUARDO GARRIDO GARCÍA 2007 TC

88 Colour: cherry, garnet rim. Nose: red berry notes, expressive, balsamic herbs, spicy, creamy oak. Palate: powerful, flavourful, fleshy, easy to drink.

BODEGAS EL CIDACOS

Ctra. de Carbonera, s/n
26512 Tudelilla (La Rioja)
☎: +34 941 152 058 - Fax: +34 941 152 303
info@bodegaselcidacos.com
www.bodegaselcidacos.com

CONDE OTIÑANO 2008 TC
80% tempranillo, 20% garnacha.

84 Colour: pale ruby, brick rim edge. Nose: ripe fruit, medium intensity, fine reductive notes, toasty. Palate: good acidity, balanced, flavourful.

CONDE OTIÑANO 2005 TR
80% tempranillo, 15% garnacha, 5% graciano.

82 Colour: pale ruby, brick rim edge. Nose: fruit liqueur notes, wet leather, toasty, sweet spices. Palate: good acidity, flavourful, toasty.

BODEGAS EL CONVENTO

Las Cocinillas, s/n
01330 Labastida (Rioja)
☎: +34 628 833 065
info@fincadelarica.com
www.fincadelarica.com

EL GUÍA DE FINCA DE LA RICA 2010 T
tempranillo.

86 Color cherry, purple rim. Aroma expressive, fresh fruit, red berry notes, floral. Taste flavourful, fruity, good acidity, round tannins.

EL BUSCADOR DE FINCA DE LA RICA 2009 T ROBLE
tempranillo.

88 Colour: bright cherry. Nose: ripe fruit, creamy oak, spicy. Palate: flavourful, fruity, toasty, round tannins.

BODEGAS ESCUDERO

Ctra. de Arnedo, s/n
26587 Grávalos (La Rioja)
☎: +34 941 398 008 - Fax: +34 941 398 070
bodega@bodegasescudero.com
www.bodegasescudero.com

BECQUER 2009 BFB
60% chardonnay, 40% viura.

83 Colour: bright straw. Nose: slightly evolved, candied fruit, medium intensity. Palate: fine bitter notes, good acidity.

SOLAR DE BECQUER 2010 T
60% garnacha, 40% tempranillo.

87 Colour: light cherry. Nose: medium intensity, red berry notes, fruit expression. Palate: flavourful, fruity, fresh.

BECQUER 2008 T
70% tempranillo, 30% garnacha.

91 Colour: cherry, garnet rim. Nose: ripe fruit, dark chocolate, cocoa bean, sweet spices, toasty. Palate: round, powerful, flavourful, fleshy.

VIDAU 2005 T
75% tempranillo, 25% garnacha.

91 Colour: cherry, garnet rim. Nose: ripe fruit, spicy, creamy oak, toasty, characterful. Palate: powerful, flavourful, toasty, round tannins.

ARVUM 2005 T
100% vidau.

90 Colour: dark-red cherry. Nose: powerfull, characterful, ripe fruit, toasty, sweet spices. Palate: powerful, good acidity, fine bitter notes.

SOLAR DE BECQUER 2004 TR
70% tempranillo, 20% mazuelo, 10% garnacha.

85 Colour: pale ruby, brick rim edge. Nose: dry nuts, ripe fruit, spicy, wet leather. Palate: powerful, spicy, round tannins.

BODEGAS ESTRAUNZA

Avda. La Poveda, 25
01306 Lapuebla de Labarca (Álava)
☎: +34 945 627 245 - Fax: +34 945 627 293
bodegasestraunza@euskalnet.net
www.bodegasestraunza.com

SOLAR DE ESTRAUNZA 2010 B
100% viura.

87 Colour: bright straw. Nose: white flowers, fresh fruit, fragrant herbs, expressive. Palate: balanced, fresh, fruity, flavourful.

SOLAR DE ESTRAUNZA 2010 RD
50% viura, 50% tempranillo.

89 Colour: raspberry rose. Nose: fresh, citrus fruit, wild herbs, complex, elegant. Palate: correct, fresh, fruity, balanced.

SOLAR DE ESTRAUNZA 2010 T
100% tempranillo.

88 Colour: cherry, purple rim. Nose: balanced, fruit expression, violets. Palate: flavourful, fruity, good acidity, round tannins.

SOLAR DE ESTRAUNZA 2008 TC
100% tempranillo.

86 Colour: cherry, garnet rim. Nose: red berry notes, ripe fruit, aged wood nuances, toasty. Palate: good acidity, flavourful, ripe fruit.

SOLAR DE ESTRAUNZA 2005 TR
100% tempranillo.

87 Colour: cherry, garnet rim. Nose: ripe fruit, old leather, spicy, toasty. Palate: good acidity, rich, flavourful.

SOLAR DE ESTRAUNZA 2005 TGR
100% tempranillo.

87 Colour: cherry, garnet rim. Nose: ripe fruit, cigar, old leather, sweet spices, toasty. Palate: powerful, flavourful, fleshy, ripe fruit.

BODEGAS EXEO

Costanilla del Hospital s/n
01330 Labastida (Álava)
☎: +34 649 940 040
carlos@bodegasexeo.com
www.bodegasexeo.com

CIFRAS 2010 B
100% garnacha blanca.

88 Colour: bright straw. Nose: white flowers, scrubland, fresh, fruit expression. Palate: powerful, flavourful, rich, fleshy, complex.

CIFRAS 2010 T
100% garnacha.

91 Colour: cherry, purple rim. Nose: violet drops, raspberry, red berry notes, balsamic herbs, complex, expressive. Palate: good acidity, elegant, fruity, flavourful, fleshy.

LETRAS MINÚSCULAS 2010 T
70% tempranillo, 30% garnacha.

88 Colour: cherry, purple rim. Nose: floral, red berry notes, balanced, expressive. Palate: good acidity, fresh, fruity, flavourful.

CIFRAS 2009 T
100% garnacha.

88 Colour: bright cherry. Nose: sweet spices, creamy oak, fruit expression. Palate: flavourful, fruity, toasty, round tannins.

CIFRAS 2008 T
garnacha.

89 Colour: cherry, garnet rim. Nose: ripe fruit, spicy, creamy oak, toasty, mineral. Palate: powerful, flavourful, toasty, round tannins.

BODEGAS EXOPTO

Ctra. de Elvillar, 26
01300 Laguardia (Álava)
☎: +34 650 213 993
info@exopto.net
www.exopto.net

HORIZONTE DE EXOPTO 2009 B
80% viura, 10% garnacha blanca, 10% malvasía.

90 Color bright yellow. Aroma powerfull, ripe fruit, sweet spices, creamy oak, fragrant herbs. Taste rich, smoky aftertaste, flavourful, fresh, good acidity.

BOZETO DE EXOPTO 2010 T
50% garnacha, 40% tempranillo, 10% graciano.

86 Colour: bright cherry, purple rim. Nose: medium intensity, fresh fruit, balsamic herbs. Palate: easy to drink, fruity, good acidity.

HORIZONTE DE EXOPTO 2008 T
80% tempranillo, 10% garnacha, 10% graciano.

91 Colour: cherry, garnet rim. Nose: expressive, red berry notes, ripe fruit, dark chocolate, sweet spices. Palate: good acidity, fleshy, powerful, flavourful.

BODEGAS FAUSTINO

Ctra. de Logroño, s/n
01320 Oyón (Álava)
☎: +34 945 622 500 - Fax: +34 945 622 511
info@bodegasfaustino.es
www.bodegasfaustino.es

FAUSTINO V 2010 B
100% viura.

88 Colour: bright straw. Nose: ripe fruit, citrus fruit, expressive. Palate: flavourful, fruity, fresh, good acidity.

FAUSTINO V 2010 RD
100% tempranillo.

87 Colour: rose, purple rim. Nose: floral, lactic notes, raspberry, fresh fruit. Palate: good acidity, balanced, powerful, flavourful.

FAUSTINO 2009 TC
100% tempranillo.

87 Colour: bright cherry. Nose: sweet spices, creamy oak, fruit expression. Palate: flavourful, fruity, toasty, round tannins.

FAUSTINO V 2006 TR
92% tempranillo, 8% mazuelo.

88 Colour: cherry, garnet rim. Nose: spicy, creamy oak, complex. Palate: powerful, flavourful, toasty, round tannins.

FAUSTINO DE AUTOR RESERVA ESPECIAL 2004 TR
86% tempranillo, 14% graciano.

92 Colour: cherry, garnet rim. Nose: ripe fruit, spicy, creamy oak, characterful. Palate: powerful, flavourful, toasty, round tannins.

FAUSTINO I 75 ANIVERSARIO 2004 TGR
92% tempranillo, 8% graciano.

92 Colour: deep cherry. Nose: wet leather, fruit liqueur notes, cigar, dark chocolate, aromatic coffee. Palate: spicy, ripe fruit, fine bitter notes.

FAUSTINO EDICIÓN ESPECIAL 2001 T
100% tempranillo.

91 Colour: bright cherry. Nose: elegant, spicy, fine reductive notes, earthy notes. Palate: spicy, fine tannins, elegant, long.

FAUSTINO I 1999 TGR
85% tempranillo, 10% graciano, 5% mazuelo.

90 Colour: pale ruby, brick rim edge. Nose: elegant, spicy, fine reductive notes, wet leather, fruit liqueur notes. Palate: spicy, fine tannins, elegant, long.

BODEGAS FERNÁNDEZ EGUILUZ

Los Morales, 7 bajo
26339 Abalos (La Rioja)
☎: +34 941 334 166 - Fax: +34 941 308 055
p.larosa@hotmail.es
www.penalarosa.com

PEÑA LA ROSA 2010 B
viura.

84 Colour: bright straw. Nose: citrus fruit, ripe fruit, fragrant herbs. Palate: fleshy, flavourful, fruity, light-bodied.

PEÑA LA ROSA 2010 T
tempranillo.

87 Colour: cherry, purple rim. Nose: expressive, fresh fruit, red berry notes, floral. Palate: flavourful, fruity, good acidity, easy to drink.

PEÑA LA ROSA VENDIMIA SELECCIONADA 2006 T
tempranillo.

88 Colour: cherry, garnet rim. Nose: red berry notes, ripe fruit, violets, spicy. Palate: fruity, flavourful, round tannins.

BODEGAS FIN DE SIGLO

Camino Arenzana de Arriba, 16
26311 Arenzana de Abajo (La Rioja)
☎: +34 941 410 042 - Fax: +34 941 410 043
bfs@bodegasfindesiglo.com
www.bodegasfindesiglo.com

RIBAGUDA 2008 BFB
100% viura.

88 Colour: bright yellow. Nose: powerfull, ripe fruit, sweet spices, creamy oak, fragrant herbs. Palate: rich, flavourful, fresh, good acidity, easy to drink.

RIBAGUDA 2006 TC
100% tempranillo.

87 Colour: cherry, garnet rim. Nose: ripe fruit, spicy, creamy oak, toasty. Palate: powerful, flavourful, toasty, round tannins.

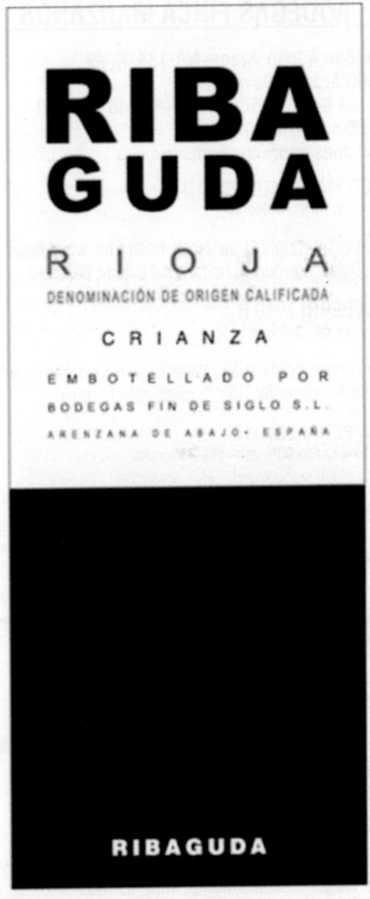

RIBAGUDA CEPAS VIEJAS 2006 TC
tempranillo, garnacha.

83 Colour: bright cherry, garnet rim. Nose: spicy, medium intensity, balanced. Palate: fruity, correct.

RIBAGUDA CEPAS VIEJAS 2005 TR
70% tempranillo, 25% garnacha, 5% mazuelo.

87 Colour: cherry, garnet rim. Nose: medium intensity, ripe fruit, spicy. Palate: fruity, good acidity, spicy.

RIBAGUDA CEPAS VIEJAS GARNACHA 2004 TC
100% garnacha.

87 Colour: cherry, garnet rim. Nose: old leather, ripe fruit, spicy. Palate: flavourful, ripe fruit, good acidity.

BODEGAS FINCA MANZANOS

Ctra. San Adrián-Azagra NA-134, K. 49
31560 Azagra (Navarra)
☎: +34 948 692 500 - Fax: +34 948 692 700
info@fincamanzanos.com
www.fincamanzanos.com

FINCA MANZANOS 2010 B
85% viura, 15% chardonnay.

88 Colour: bright straw. Nose: fresh fruit, white flowers, neat. Palate: flavourful, fruity, good acidity, balanced.

VIÑA BERRI 2010 B
95% viura, 5% chardonnay.

86 Colour: bright straw. Nose: fresh fruit, tropical fruit, grassy. Palate: fruity, light-bodied, easy to drink.

VIÑA BERRI 2010 RD
34% tempranillo, 33% garnacha, 33% viura.

85 Colour: raspberry rose. Nose: floral, ripe fruit, fresh. Palate: correct, light-bodied, flavourful.

VIÑA BERRI 2009 T
95% tempranillo, 5% garnacha.

83 Colour: cherry, purple rim. Nose: stalky, fruit preserve. Palate: fruity, flavourful.

FINCA MANZANOS 2007 TC
90% tempranillo, 5% garnacha, 5% mazuelo.

87 Colour: cherry, garnet rim. Nose: dark chocolate, ripe fruit, sweet spices. Palate: flavourful, fleshy.

SEÑORIO DE ARNEDO 2007 TC
90% tempranillo, 10% garnacha.

86 Colour: deep cherry, purple rim. Nose: fruit preserve, sweet spices. Palate: powerful, fruity, correct.

FINCA MANZANOS 2005 TR
85% tempranillo, 10% graciano, 5% garnacha.

88 Colour: pale ruby, brick rim edge. Nose: fruit liqueur notes, aromatic coffee, spicy, wet leather. Palate: powerful, spicy, round tannins.

V. FERNÁNDEZ DE MANZANOS 2005 TR
85% tempranillo, 15% graciano.

87 Colour: cherry, garnet rim. Nose: ripe fruit, creamy oak, toasty, sweet spices. Palate: powerful, flavourful, toasty, round tannins.

SEÑORIO DE ARNEDO 2005 TR
90% tempranillo, 5% garnacha, 5% graciano.

86 Colour: cherry, garnet rim. Nose: toasty, spicy, ripe fruit. Palate: fruity, flavourful, easy to drink.

VIÑA MARICHALAR 2005 T
85% tempranillo, 10% graciano, 5% garnacha.

84 Colour: cherry, garnet rim. Nose: medium intensity, fruit liqueur notes, aromatic coffee, wet leather. Palate: fine bitter notes, spicy, ripe fruit.

BODEGAS FOS

Término de Vialba, s/n
01340 Elciego (Álava)
☎: +34 945 606 681 - Fax: +34 945 606 608
fos@bodegasfos.com
www.bodegasfos.com

FOS 2010 B
100% viura.

88 Colour: yellow, greenish rim. Nose: balanced, medium intensity, wild herbs. Palate: balanced, fine bitter notes, good acidity.

FOS 2008 TC
95% tempranillo, 5% graciano.

88 Colour: cherry, garnet rim. Nose: ripe fruit, spicy, dark chocolate, sweet spices. Palate: fruity, fleshy, round tannins.

FOS BARANDA 2007 T
100% tempranillo.

87 Colour: bright cherry, garnet rim. Nose: dark chocolate, sweet spices, roasted coffee. Palate: toasty, fine bitter notes.

FOS 2006 TR
80% tempranillo, 20% graciano.

89 Colour: cherry, garnet rim. Nose: ripe fruit, spicy, creamy oak. Palate: powerful, flavourful, toasty, round tannins.

BODEGAS FUENMAYOR S.A.

Buicio, 5 - 6
26360 Fuenmayor (La Rioja)
☎: +34 941 450 935 - Fax: +34 941 450 936
bodegasfuenmayor@bodegasfuenmayor.com
www.bodegasfuenmayor.com

NOCEDAL 2008 TC
tempranillo.

78

NOCEDAL 2005 TR
tempranillo.

84 Colour: cherry, garnet rim. Nose: spicy, toasty, fruit liqueur notes, fine reductive notes. Palate: flavourful, toasty, ripe fruit.

BODEGAS GÓMEZ CRUZADO

Avda. Vizcaya, 6 "Barrio de la Estación"
26200 Haro (La Rioja)
☎: +34 941 312 502 - Fax: +34 941 303 567
bodega@gomezcruzado.com
www.gomezcruzado.com

GÓMEZ CRUZADO SELECCIÓN 2007 T
100% tempranillo.

88 Colour: cherry, garnet rim. Nose: medium intensity, cocoa bean, ripe fruit. Palate: ripe fruit, flavourful.

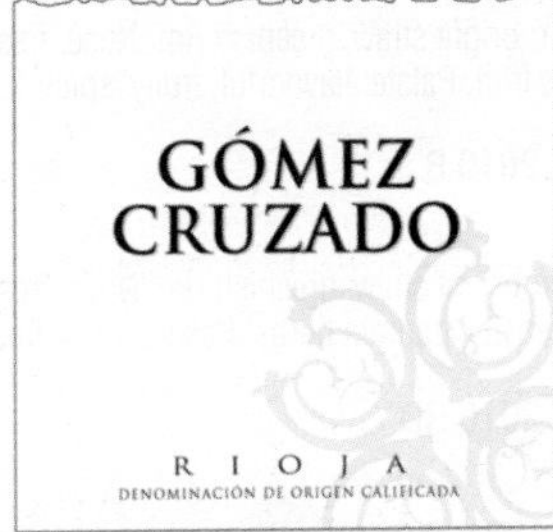

HONORABLE GÓMEZ CRUZADO 2007 T
tempranillo.

91 Colour: bright cherry. Nose: ripe fruit, sweet spices, creamy oak, expressive. Palate: flavourful, fruity, round tannins.

GÓMEZ CRUZADO "GC" 2008 T
tempranillo.

91 Colour: cherry, purple rim. Nose: red berry notes, fruit expression, balanced, expressive. Palate: fruity, flavourful, good acidity.

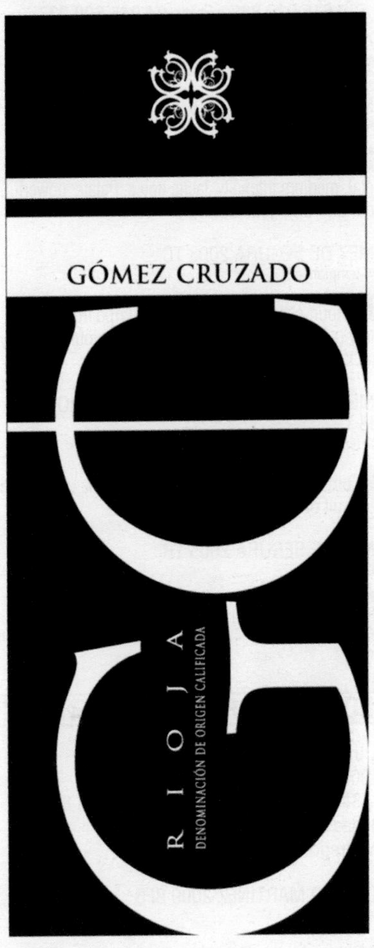

VIÑA ANDREA 2001 TGR
85% tempranillo, 10% mazuelo.

88 Color pale ruby, brick rim edge. Aroma elegant, spicy, fine reductive notes, wet leather, aged wood nuances, fruit liqueur notes. Taste spicy, fine tannins, elegant, long.

BODEGAS GÓMEZ DE SEGURA IBÁÑEZ

Barrio El Campillar, 7
01300 Laguardia (Álava)
☎: +34 615 929 828 - Fax: +34 945 600 227
info@gomezdesegura.com
www.gomezdesegura.com

GÓMEZ DE SEGURA 2010 T
100% tempranillo.

88 Colour: cherry, purple rim. Nose: red berry notes, varietal, medium intensity, lactic notes. Palate: powerful, flavourful, fruity, good acidity.

GÓMEZ DE SEGURA 2008 TC
100% tempranillo.

89 Colour: cherry, garnet rim. Nose: ripe fruit, spicy, creamy oak, complex. Palate: powerful, flavourful, toasty, round tannins, fruity.

GÓMEZ DE SEGURA VENDIMIA SELECCIONADA 2008 T
100% tempranillo.

84 Colour: cherry, garnet rim. Nose: premature reduction notes, fruit preserve. Palate: fruity, correct.

GÓMEZ DE SEGURA 2005 TR
100% tempranillo.

87 Colour: deep cherry, garnet rim. Nose: medium intensity, ripe fruit, spicy. Palate: fruity, good acidity, round tannins.

BODEGAS GREGORIO MARTÍNEZ

Pol. Ind. 1- Parcela 12
26190 Nalda (La Rioja)
☎: +34 941 220 266 - Fax: +34 941 203 849
bodegas@gregoriomartinez.com
www.gregoriomartinez.com

GREGORIO MARTÍNEZ 2009 BFB
100% viura.

85 Colour: bright straw. Nose: lactic notes, ripe fruit, fruit expression, sweet spices, cocoa bean. Palate: flavourful, fruity, fleshy.

GREGORIO MARTÍNEZ VENDIMIA SELECCIONADA 2005 TC
100% tempranillo.

88 Colour: cherry, garnet rim. Nose: spicy, creamy oak, toasty, complex. Palate: powerful, flavourful, round tannins, toasty.

GREGORIO MARTÍNEZ 2005 TC
100% tempranillo.

87 Colour: cherry, garnet rim. Nose: spicy, creamy oak, toasty, dark chocolate. Palate: powerful, flavourful, toasty, round tannins.

GREGORIO MARTÍNEZ 2001 TR
100% tempranillo.

86 Colour: pale ruby, brick rim edge. Nose: fruit liqueur notes, toasty, sweet spices. Palate: powerful, flavourful, spicy, fine bitter notes.

BODEGAS HEREDAD BAÑOS BEZARES S.L.

Solana, s/n
26290 Briñas (La Rioja)
☎: +34 941 312 423 - Fax: +34 941 303 020
bodega@banosbezares.com
www.banosbezares.com

GRAN BOHEDAL 2010 BFB
100% viura.

89 Colour: bright straw, greenish rim. Nose: fresh fruit, spicy, citrus fruit. Palate: flavourful, fruity, spicy.

BOHEDAL 2010 B
100% viura.

84 Colour: bright straw, greenish rim. Nose: fresh, medium intensity, fragrant herbs. Palate: fruity, fresh.

BOHEDAL 2010 RD
100% tempranillo.

84 Colour: rose, purple rim. Nose: medium intensity, wild herbs. Palate: sweetness, flavourful.

BOHEDAL 2010 T
100% tempranillo.

88 Colour: cherry, purple rim. Nose: floral, ripe fruit, sweet spices. Palate: flavourful, powerful, fleshy.

BOHEDAL 2010 T MACERACIÓN CARBÓNICA
100% tempranillo.

87 Colour: cherry, purple rim. Nose: powerfull, ripe fruit, fruit expression, violet drops. Palate: flavourful, fruity, fresh.

GRAN BOHEDAL 2008 TC
100% tempranillo.

85 Colour: dark-red cherry, orangey edge. Nose: ripe fruit, premature reduction notes, waxy notes, tobacco, spicy. Palate: good acidity, flavourful, fleshy, complex.

HEBABE 2007 T
100% graciano.

88 Colour: cherry, garnet rim. Nose: red berry notes, citrus fruit, ripe fruit, scrubland, wild herbs, creamy oak. Palate: spicy, flavourful, fleshy.

GRAN BOHEDAL 2002 TR
100% tempranillo.

86 Colour: light cherry, orangey edge. Nose: ripe fruit, wet leather, waxy notes, spicy. Palate: correct, fleshy, complex, reductive nuances.

GRAN BOHEDAL 2001 TGR
100% tempranillo.

85 Colour: light cherry, orangey edge. Nose: ripe fruit, wet leather, tobacco, spicy. Palate: good acidity, flavourful, fleshy.

BODEGAS HERMANOS PECIÑA

Ctra. de Vitoria, Km. 47
26338 San Vicente de la Sonsierra (La Rioja)
☎: +34 941 334 366 - Fax: +34 941 334 180
info@bodegashermanospecina.com
www.bodegashermanospecina.com

CHOBEO DE PECIÑA 2009 BFB
100% viura.

88 Colour: bright straw. Nose: ripe fruit, white flowers, creamy oak. Palate: flavourful, fleshy, powerful.

SEÑORÍO DE P. PECIÑA 2010 T
95% tempranillo, 3% graciano, 2% garnacha.

87 Colour: deep cherry. Nose: fruit preserve, floral. Palate: powerful, sweetness, fleshy.

GRAN CHOBEO DE PECIÑA 2008 T
100% tempranillo.

90 Colour: deep cherry, garnet rim. Nose: toasty, spicy, ripe fruit. Palate: good structure, fruity, fine bitter notes, round tannins.

SEÑORÍO DE P. PECIÑA 2006 TC
95% tempranillo, 3% graciano.

87 Colour: cherry, garnet rim. Nose: ripe fruit, cocoa bean, sweet spices. Palate: ripe fruit, spicy.

CHOBEO DE PECIÑA 2005 T
100% tempranillo.

89 Colour: cherry, garnet rim. Nose: ripe fruit, spicy, toasty, complex, fine reductive notes. Palate: powerful, flavourful, toasty, round tannins.

SEÑORÍO DE P. PECIÑA 2001 TGR
95% tempranillo, 3% graciano, 2% garnacha.

88 Colour: light cherry, orangey edge. Nose: medium intensity, ripe fruit, fine reductive notes, wild herbs. Palate: flavourful, balanced.

PECIÑA VENDIMIA SELECCIONADA 2001 TR
95% tempranillo, 3% graciano, 2% garnacha.

86 Colour: light cherry, orangey edge. Nose: spicy, toasty, tobacco. Palate: flavourful, ripe fruit, round tannins.

SEÑORÍO DE P. PECIÑA 2001 TR
tempranillo, garnacha, graciano.

84 Colour: light cherry, orangey edge. Nose: fine reductive notes, spicy, fruit liqueur notes. Palate: light-bodied, spicy.

BODEGAS IZADI

Herrería Travesía II, 5
01307 Villabuena de Álava (Álava)
☎: +34 945 609 086 - Fax: +34 945 609 261
club@grupoartevino.com
www.grupoartevino.com

IZADI 2010 BFB
viura, malvasía.

89 Colour: bright yellow. Nose: sweet spices, creamy oak, fragrant herbs, fruit expression. Palate: rich, smoky aftertaste, flavourful, fresh, good acidity.

IZADI EXPRESIÓN 2009 T
tempranillo, graciano.

93 Colour: cherry, garnet rim. Nose: fruit expression, red berry notes, sweet spices, cocoa bean, creamy oak. Palate: flavourful, good acidity, fine bitter notes, grainy tannins.

IZADI 2007 TC
tempranillo.

88 Colour: black cherry. Nose: creamy oak, toasty, dark chocolate, ripe fruit, warm. Palate: toasty, spicy, ripe fruit.

IZADI EL REGALO 2005 TR
tempranillo, graciano, mazuelo, garnacha.

91 Colour: cherry, garnet rim. Nose: sweet spices, toasty, dark chocolate, aromatic coffee. Palate: powerful, flavourful, fleshy, spicy.

BODEGAS LA CATEDRAL - BODEGAS OLARRA

Avda. de Mendavia, 30
26009 Logroño (La Rioja)
☎: +34 941 235 299 - Fax: +34 941 253 703

GRAN EPULUM 2010 T
85% tempranillo, 10% garnacha, 5% mazuelo, graciano.

89 Colour: cherry, purple rim. Nose: expressive, red berry notes, floral. Palate: flavourful, fruity, good acidity, round tannins.

GRAN EPULUM 2008 TC
80% tempranillo, 10% garnacha, 10% mazuelo, graciano.

86 Colour: cherry, garnet rim. Nose: ripe fruit, wet leather, spicy. Palate: fruity, flavourful.

GRAN EPULUM 2005 TR
90% tempranillo, 5% garnacha, 5% mazuelo, graciano.

88 Colour: cherry, garnet rim. Nose: ripe fruit, spicy, creamy oak, toasty. Palate: flavourful, toasty, fleshy.

BODEGAS LA EMPERATRIZ

Ctra. Santo Domingo - Haro, Km. 31,500
26241 Baños de Rioja (La Rioja)
☎: +34 941 300 105 - Fax: +34 941 300 231
correo@bodegaslaemperatriz.com
www.bodegaslaemperatriz.com

FINCA LA EMPERATRIZ VIURA 2010 B
100% viura.

89 Colour: bright straw. Nose: fresh, fresh fruit, white flowers. Palate: flavourful, fruity, good acidity, balanced.

FINCA LA EMPERATRIZ VIURA CEPAS VIEJAS 2008 B
100% viura.

91 Color bright yellow. Aroma powerfull, ripe fruit, sweet spices, creamy oak, fragrant herbs. Taste rich, smoky aftertaste, flavourful, fresh, good acidity.

FINCA LA EMPERATRIZ TEMPRANILLO 2010 T
100% tempranillo.

86 Colour: bright cherry, purple rim. Nose: red berry notes, balanced, powerfull. Palate: fruity, flavourful, good finish, easy to drink.

FINCA LA EMPERATRIZ GARNACHA CEPAS VIEJAS 2009 T
100% garnacha.

92 Colour: cherry, garnet rim. Nose: complex, elegant, expressive, creamy oak. Palate: spicy, ripe fruit, long, balsamic.

FINCA LA EMPERATRIZ 2008 TC
95% tempranillo, 3% garnacha, 2% viura.

91 Colour: cherry, garnet rim. Nose: creamy oak, cocoa bean, fruit expression, raspberry. Palate: powerful, flavourful, fleshy, complex.

FINCA LA EMPERATRIZ PARCELA Nº 1 2009 T
100% tempranillo.

92 Colour: bright cherry. Nose: ripe fruit, sweet spices, creamy oak, earthy notes, lactic notes. Palate: flavourful, fruity, toasty, round tannins, mineral.

FINCA LA EMPERATRIZ TERRUÑO 2008 T
100% tempranillo.

90 Colour: cherry, garnet rim. Nose: ripe fruit, spicy, creamy oak, toasty. Palate: powerful, flavourful, toasty.

FINCA LA EMPERATRIZ 2005 TR
90% tempranillo, 10% garnacha, graciano, viura.

87 Colour: cherry, garnet rim. Nose: powerfull, complex, characterful, ripe fruit. Palate: powerful, fleshy, complex.

BODEGAS LACUS

Cervantes, 18- 1º
26559 Aldeanueva de Ebro (La Rioja)
☎: +34 649 331 799
inedito@bodegaslacus.com
www.bodegaslacus.com

INÉDITO 2009 BFB
garnacha blanca.

90 Colour: bright yellow. Nose: powerfull, ripe fruit, sweet spices, fragrant herbs, balsamic herbs. Palate: rich, smoky aftertaste, flavourful, fresh, good acidity, fleshy.

INÉDITO 3/3 2009 T
50% tempranillo, 30% garnacha, 20% graciano.

90 Color cherry, purple rim. Aroma expressive, fresh fruit, red berry notes, floral. Taste flavourful, fruity, good acidity, round tannins.

INÉDITO S 2008 T
50% graciano, 40% tempranillo, 10% garnacha.

90 Colour: cherry, garnet rim. Nose: red berry notes, balsamic herbs, wild herbs, spicy. Palate: good acidity, balanced, flavourful, fleshy.

INÉDITO H12 2008 T
75% graciano, 25% garnacha.

90 Colour: cherry, garnet rim. Nose: red berry notes, fruit preserve, balsamic herbs, scrubland, wild herbs. Palate: good acidity, flavourful, fruity, balsamic.

BODEGAS LAGUNILLA

Ctra. de Elciego, s/n
26350 Cenicero (La Rioja)
☎: +34 914 365 924 - Fax: +34 941 453 114
gromero@arcoinvest-group.com
www.berberana.com

LAGUNILLA CASA DEL COMENDADOR 2007 TC
80% tempranillo, 20% garnacha.

89 Colour: cherry, garnet rim. Nose: powerfull, warm, ripe fruit, toasty, sweet spices. Palate: spicy, long, flavourful, fleshy.

LAGUNILLA 2007 TC
80% tempranillo, 20% garnacha.

86 Colour: cherry, garnet rim. Nose: ripe fruit, old leather, spicy, toasty. Palate: good acidity, flavourful, toasty.

LAGUNILLA CASA DEL COMENDADOR 2006 TR
80% tempranillo, 20% garnacha.

89 Colour: cherry, garnet rim. Nose: ripe fruit, spicy, balanced. Palate: ripe fruit, spicy, flavourful, good structure.

LAGUNILLA 2006 TR
80% tempranillo, 20% garnacha.

87 Colour: cherry, garnet rim. Nose: ripe fruit, spicy, old leather. Palate: flavourful, fine bitter notes, ripe fruit.

LAGUNILLA OPTIMUS 2005 T
100% tempranillo.

87 Colour: cherry, garnet rim. Nose: smoky, ripe fruit, old leather, roasted coffee. Palate: flavourful, fleshy, toasty.

BODEGAS LAR DE PAULA

Coscojal, s/n
01309 Elvillar (Álava)
☎: +34 945 604 068 - Fax: +34 945 604 105
info@lardepaula.com
www.lardepaula.com

LAR DE PAULA MADURADO 2009 T
tempranillo.

87 Colour: cherry, purple rim. Nose: red berry notes, raspberry, floral. Palate: powerful, flavourful, fruity, easy to drink.

MERUS.4 2007 T
tempranillo.

91 Colour: cherry, garnet rim. Nose: ripe fruit, powerfull, sweet spices, creamy oak. Palate: round, flavourful, fleshy, complex, toasty.

LAR DE PAULA 2007 TC
tempranillo.

88 Colour: cherry, garnet rim. Nose: ripe fruit, spicy, creamy oak, expressive. Palate: good acidity, flavourful, fleshy, toasty.

4 BESOS TEMPRANILLO 2006 T
tempranillo.

88 Colour: cherry, garnet rim. Nose: ripe fruit, dark chocolate, cocoa bean, toasty, old leather. Palate: good acidity, powerful, flavourful, toasty.

LAR DE PAULA AÑADA 2005 T
tempranillo.

89 Colour: light cherry, garnet rim. Nose: ripe fruit, cocoa bean, creamy oak. Palate: ripe fruit, flavourful, round tannins.

LAR DE PAULA 2005 TR
tempranillo.

88 Colour: light cherry, garnet rim. Nose: ripe fruit, spicy, toasty, fine reductive notes. Palate: powerful, flavourful, fleshy.

BODEGAS LARRAZ

Paraje Ribarrey. Pol. 12- Parcela 50
26350 Cenicero (La Rioja)
☎: +34 639 728 581
info@bodegaslarraz.com
www.bodegaslarraz.com

CAUDUM BODEGAS LARRAZ 2008 T
tempranillo.

86 Colour: cherry, garnet rim. Nose: smoky, new oak, aromatic coffee, ripe fruit. Palate: powerful, fleshy, ripe fruit.

CAUDUM BODEGAS LARRAZ SELECCIÓN ESPECIAL 2007 T
tempranillo.

88 Colour: cherry, garnet rim. Nose: spicy, creamy oak, toasty, fruit preserve, characterful. Palate: powerful, flavourful, round tannins.

CAUDUM BODEGAS LARRAZ 2007 T
tempranillo.

88 Colour: bright cherry. Nose: sweet spices, creamy oak, fruit expression. Palate: flavourful, fruity, toasty, round tannins.

BODEGAS LEZA GARCÍA

San Ignacio, 26
26313 Uruñuela (La Rioja)
☎: +34 941 371 142 - Fax: +34 941 371 035
bodegasleza@bodegasleza.com
www.bodegasleza.com

BARÓN DE VILLACAMPA 2010 T
85% tempranillo, 10% garnacha, 5% mazuelo.

87 Colour: bright cherry, purple rim. Nose: wild herbs, red berry notes. Palate: flavourful, fruity, easy to drink.

VALDEPALACIOS 2010 T
85% tempranillo, 10% garnacha, 5% mazuelo.

87 Colour: cherry, purple rim. Nose: medium intensity, balanced, red berry notes. Palate: fruity, flavourful, good acidity.

LEZA GARCÍA 2009 T
100% tempranillo.

87 Colour: cherry, garnet rim. Nose: ripe fruit, red berry notes, fine reductive notes, toasty. Palate: round, flavourful, long.

LEZA GARCÍA VENDIMIA SELECCIONADA 2009 T
85% tempranillo, 10% garnacha, 5% mazuelo.

86 Colour: cherry, purple rim. Nose: red berry notes, raspberry, expressive. Palate: balanced, good acidity, fruity.

VALDEPALACIOS VENDIMIA SELECCIONADA 2009 T
95% tempranillo, 5% garnacha.

85 Colour: cherry, garnet rim. Nose: red berry notes, raspberry, floral, fresh. Palate: light-bodied, fresh, fruity.

LG DE LEZA GARCÍA 2008 T
100% tempranillo.

88 Colour: cherry, garnet rim. Nose: red berry notes, ripe fruit, spicy, creamy oak. Palate: flavourful, fleshy, toasty.

VALDEPALACIOS 2007 TC
90% tempranillo, 10% garnacha.

86 Colour: pale ruby, brick rim edge. Nose: ripe fruit, fruit liqueur notes, sweet spices, toasty. Palate: warm, flavourful, toasty.

BARÓN DE VILLACAMPA 2007 TC
tempranillo, garnacha.

86 Colour: cherry, garnet rim. Nose: ripe fruit, spicy, toasty, fine reductive notes. Palate: powerful, flavourful, toasty.

LEZA GARCÍA 2005 TR
90% tempranillo, 10% garnacha.

87 Colour: pale ruby, brick rim edge. Nose: ripe fruit, fruit liqueur notes, old leather, cigar. Palate: good acidity, round, flavourful.

LEZA GARCÍA 2004 TGR
90% tempranillo, 10% garnacha.

87 Colour: pale ruby, brick rim edge. Nose: fruit liqueur notes, cigar, wet leather, smoky, toasty. Palate: good acidity, flavourful, fine tannins.

BARÓN DE VILLACAMPA 2004 TR
90% tempranillo, 10% garnacha.

85 Colour: cherry, garnet rim. Nose: ripe fruit, toasty, wet leather. Palate: powerful, flavourful, toasty, fleshy.

BODEGAS LOLI CASADO

Avda. de la Poveda, 46
01306 Lapuebla de Labarca (Álava)
☎: +34 945 607 096 - Fax: +34 945 607 412
loli@bodegaslolicasado.com
www.bodegaslolicasado.com

POLUS 2010 B
100% viura.

85 Colour: bright straw, greenish rim. Nose: fresh fruit, wild herbs, medium intensity. Palate: fresh, fruity.

POLUS 2009 BFB
100% viura.

88 Colour: bright yellow. Nose: powerfull, ripe fruit, sweet spices, creamy oak. Palate: rich, flavourful, fresh, good acidity.

POLUS 2007 BC
100% viura.

87 Colour: bright straw, greenish rim. Nose: balanced, medium intensity, ripe fruit, sweet spices. Palate: rich, powerful, flavourful.

JAUN DE ALZATE 2010 T JOVEN

86 Colour: cherry, purple rim. Nose: red berry notes, ripe fruit, fresh, floral. Palate: good acidity, flavourful, fruity.

POLUS TEMPRANILLO 2009 T
100% tempranillo.

88 Colour: cherry, purple rim. Nose: roasted coffee, spicy. Palate: fruity, flavourful, round tannins.

JAUN DE ALZATE 2008 TC
90% tempranillo, 5% graciano, 5% mazuelo.

87 Colour: cherry, garnet rim. Nose: sweet spices, cocoa bean, fruit preserve. Palate: flavourful, correct, good acidity.

POLUS GRACIANO 2007 T
85% graciano, 15% tempranillo.

85 Colour: cherry, garnet rim. Nose: ripe fruit, dark chocolate, reduction off-odours. Palate: ripe fruit, balanced.

JAUN DE ALZATE 2005 TR
90% tempranillo, 5% graciano, 5% mazuelo.

87 Colour: cherry, garnet rim. Nose: fruit preserve, sweet spices. Palate: light-bodied, fruity, good finish.

POLUS 2005 TR
100% tempranillo.

86 Colour: deep cherry, purple rim. Nose: sweet spices, creamy oak, cocoa bean. Palate: good acidity, correct.

JAUN DE ALZATE 2004 TGR
90% tempranillo, 5% graciano, 5% mazuelo.

87 Colour: cherry, garnet rim. Nose: ripe fruit, cocoa bean, medium intensity, balanced. Palate: flavourful, fruity, round tannins.

POLUS VENDIMIA SELECCIONADA 2004 TGR
75% tempranillo, 25% graciano.

86 Colour: cherry, garnet rim. Nose: old leather, tobacco, spicy. Palate: flavourful, ripe fruit, round tannins.

BODEGAS LUIS ALEGRE

Ctra. Navaridas, s/n
01300 Laguardia (Álava)
☎: +34 945 600 089 - Fax: +34 945 600 729
luisalegre@bodegasluisalegre.com
www.luisalegre.com

LUIS ALEGRE SELECCIÓN DE ROBLES EUROPA 2009 BFB
90% viura, 10% malvasía.

89 Colour: bright yellow. Nose: ripe fruit, faded flowers, elegant, fragrant herbs. Palate: good acidity, rich, powerful, flavourful, fleshy.

LUIS ALEGRE 2010 T MACERACIÓN CARBÓNICA
90% tempranillo, 5% garnacha, 5% viura.

88 Colour: deep cherry, purple rim. Nose: balanced, red berry notes, floral, fruit expression. Palate: fruity, balanced, good acidity.

KODEN DE LUIS ALEGRE 2009 T
100% tempranillo.

90 Colour: cherry, purple rim. Nose: expressive, red berry notes, ripe fruit, balsamic herbs, wild herbs. Palate: powerful, flavourful, spicy.

PONTAC DE PORTILES 2008 T
90% tempranillo, 10% garnacha.

92 Colour: cherry, garnet rim. Nose: ripe fruit, creamy oak, toasty, complex, sweet spices, cocoa bean, dark chocolate. Palate: flavourful, toasty, balsamic, fleshy, complex.

GRAN VINO PONTAC 2007 T
95% tempranillo, 5% graciano.

91 Colour: cherry, garnet rim. Nose: red berry notes, raspberry, ripe fruit, expressive, complex, balsamic herbs, sweet spices, creamy oak. Palate: powerful, flavourful, fleshy, complex.

LUIS ALEGRE PARCELA Nº 5 2007 TR
100% tempranillo.

89 Colour: cherry, garnet rim. Nose: red berry notes, ripe fruit, cocoa bean, dark chocolate, sweet spices. Palate: good acidity, powerful, flavourful, creamy.

LUIS ALEGRE 2007 TC
85% tempranillo, 5% mazuelo, 5% graciano, 5% garnacha.

86 Colour: cherry, garnet rim. Nose: ripe fruit, balsamic herbs, spicy, creamy oak. Palate: good acidity, round, flavourful, fleshy.

LUIS ALEGRE SELECCIÓN ESPECIAL 2006 TR
95% tempranillo, 2,5% graciano, 2,5% mazuelo.

89 Color cherry, garnet rim. Aroma ripe fruit, spicy, creamy oak, toasty, complex. Taste powerful, flavourful, toasty, round tannins.

BODEGAS LUIS CAÑAS

Ctra. Samaniego, 10
01307 Villabuena (Álava)
☎: +34 945 623 373 - Fax: +34 945 609 289
bodegas@luiscanas.com
www.luiscanas.com

HIRU 3 RACIMOS 2006 T
100% tempranillo.

93 Colour: cherry, garnet rim. Nose: powerfull, ripe fruit, creamy oak, sweet spices, cocoa bean. Palate: powerful, concentrated, good acidity, round tannins.

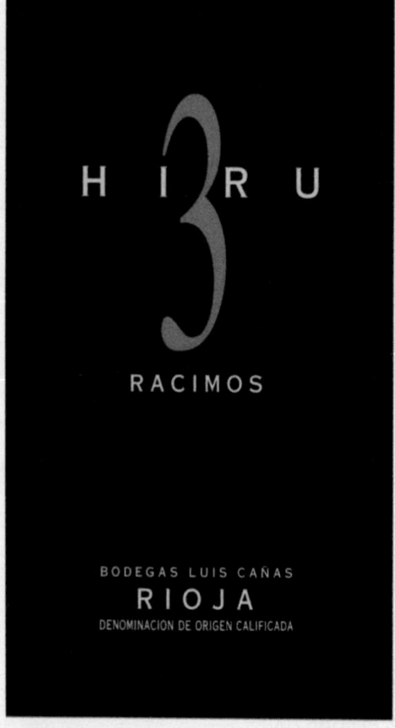

LUIS CAÑAS 2005 TR
95% tempranillo, 5% graciano.

90 Colour: light cherry, garnet rim. Nose: ripe fruit, fine reductive notes, spicy, toasty. Palate: good acidity, balanced, flavourful.

LUIS CAÑAS 2004 TGR
95% tempranillo, 5% graciano.

91 Colour: ruby red, orangey edge. Nose: ripe fruit, expressive, spicy, toasty, complex. Palate: good acidity, elegant, flavourful, complex.

LUIS CAÑAS SELECCIÓN DE FAMILIA 2004 TR
85% tempranillo, 15% otras.

91 Colour: ruby red, orangey edge. Nose: ripe fruit, old leather, spicy, toasty. Palate: good acidity, flavourful, ripe fruit, elegant.

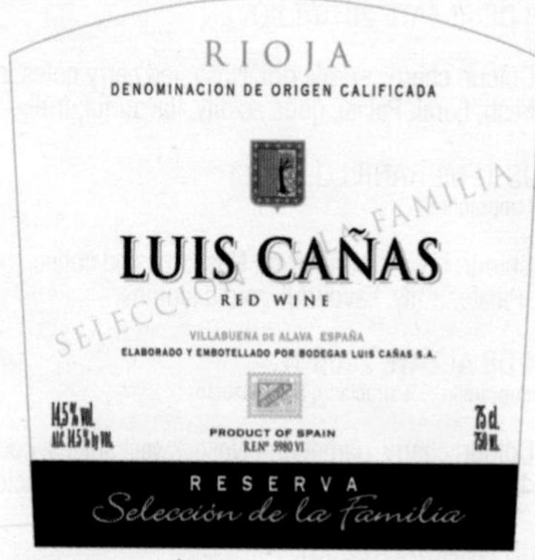

LUIS CAÑAS 2010 BFB
85% viura, 15% malvasía.

88 Colour: bright straw. Nose: spicy, ripe fruit, faded flowers, creamy oak. Palate: good acidity, elegant, flavourful.

LUIS CAÑAS 2008 TC
95% tempranillo, 5% garnacha.

88 Colour: bright cherry. Nose: sweet spices, creamy oak, red berry notes. Palate: flavourful, fruity, toasty, round tannins.

BODEGAS MARQUÉS DE VITORIA

Camino de Santa Lucía, s/n
01320 Oyón (Álava)
☎: +34 945 622 134 - Fax: +34 945 601 496
info@bodegasmarquesdevitoria.es
www.marquesdevitoria.com

MARQUÉS DE VITORIA 2010 B
100% viura.

87 Colour: bright straw. Nose: fresh fruit, wild herbs, fresh. Palate: fruity, fresh, easy to drink.

MARQUÉS DE VITORIA 2010 RD
100% tempranillo.

87 Colour: brilliant rose. Nose: medium intensity, red berry notes, lactic notes, dried flowers. Palate: balanced, fine bitter notes, good acidity.

ECCO DE MARQUÉS DE VITORIA 2010 T
100% tempranillo.

86 Colour: cherry, purple rim. Nose: red berry notes, ripe fruit, floral, expressive. Palate: fresh, fruity, flavourful, fleshy.

MARQUÉS DE VITORIA 2008 TC
100% tempranillo.

90 Colour: cherry, garnet rim. Nose: ripe fruit, balanced, varietal, spicy, balsamic herbs. Palate: ripe fruit, flavourful, round tannins.

MARQUÉS DE VITORIA 2007 TR
100% tempranillo.

88 Colour: cherry, garnet rim. Nose: ripe fruit, spicy, toasty. Palate: powerful, flavourful, toasty, round tannins.

MARQUÉS DE VITORIA 2004 TGR
100% tempranillo.

88 Colour: cherry, garnet rim. Nose: ripe fruit, spicy, toasty. Palate: powerful, flavourful, toasty, round tannins.

BODEGAS MARTÍNEZ CORTA

Ctra. Cenicero, s/n
20313 Uruñuela (La Rioja)
☎: +34 670 937 520 - Fax: +34 941 362 120
administracion@bodegasmartinezcorta.com
www.bodegasmartinezcorta.com

MARTÍNEZ CORTA CEPAS ANTIGUAS 2010 B
70% viura, 30% malvasía.

87 Colour: bright straw. Nose: medium intensity, sulphur notes, floral. Palate: flavourful, fine bitter notes, good acidity.

MARTÍNEZ CORTA CEPAS ANTIGUAS 2010 T
100% tempranillo.

88 Colour: deep cherry, purple rim. Nose: red berry notes, balanced, medium intensity, varietal. Palate: fruity, flavourful.

SOROS 2010 T
100% tempranillo.

87 Colour: cherry, purple rim. Nose: expressive, fresh fruit, red berry notes, floral. Palate: flavourful, fruity, good acidity.

MARTÍNEZ CORTA 2008 TC
100% tempranillo.

88 Colour: dark-red cherry. Nose: powerfull, smoky, toasty, dark chocolate, fruit preserve. Palate: powerful, spicy, ripe fruit.

SOROS 2008 TC
100% tempranillo.

88 Colour: cherry, garnet rim. Nose: spicy, creamy oak, toasty, fruit expression. Palate: powerful, flavourful, toasty, round tannins.

MARTÍNEZ CORTA 33 MAGNUM 2007 T
100% tempranillo.

89 Colour: cherry, garnet rim. Nose: dark chocolate, cocoa bean, ripe fruit, toasty, creamy oak. Palate: flavourful, powerful, fleshy, spicy, round tannins.

SOROS 2007 T
100% tempranillo.

88 Colour: deep cherry. Nose: creamy oak, dark chocolate, ripe fruit, sweet spices. Palate: powerful, spicy, ripe fruit, round tannins.

MARTÍNEZ CORTA SELECCIÓN ESPECIAL 2007 T
100% tempranillo.

88 Colour: dark-red cherry. Nose: powerfull, fruit preserve, dark chocolate, toasty. Palate: spicy, ripe fruit, fine bitter notes.

BODEGAS MARTÍNEZ PALACIOS

Real, 22
26220 Ollauri (Rioja)
☎: +34 941 338 023 - Fax: +34 941 338 023
bodegasmtzpalacios@yahoo.es
www.bodegasmartinezpalacios.com

ORMAEGUI 2010 BFB
90% viura, 10% garnacha blanca.

80 Colour: bright straw, greenish rim. Nose: slightly evolved, grassy. Palate: flavourful, easy to drink.

MARTÍNEZ PALACIOS 2010 T JOVEN
tempranillo.

85 Colour: cherry, purple rim. Nose: floral, red berry notes, medium intensity. Palate: good acidity, flavourful, fruity, fleshy.

MARTÍNEZ PALACIOS 2007 TC
100% tempranillo.

84 Colour: cherry, garnet rim. Nose: spicy, ripe fruit, fine reductive notes. Palate: good acidity, slightly evolved, easy to drink.

MARTÍNEZ PALACIOS PAGO CANDELA 2005 T
90% tempranillo, 10% graciano.

85 Colour: cherry, garnet rim. Nose: ripe fruit, balsamic herbs, spicy, toasty. Palate: good acidity, flavourful, fleshy, green.

BODEGAS MEDRANO IRAZU S.L.

San Pedro, 14
01309 Elvillar (Álava)
☎: +34 945 604 066 - Fax: +34 945 604 126
amador@bodegasmedranoirazu.com
www.bodegasmedranoirazu.com

MAS DE MEDRANO - FINCA LAS AGUZADERAS 2008 T

89 Colour: cherry, garnet rim. Nose: powerfull, ripe fruit, creamy oak, sweet spices, new oak. Palate: flavourful, powerful, fleshy, complex.

MEDRANO IRAZU 2010 BFB
100% viura.

81 Colour: bright straw. Nose: fresh, wild herbs. Palate: fruity, light-bodied.

MEDRANO-IRAZU SELECCIÓN 2010 T
100% tempranillo.

88 Colour: cherry, purple rim. Nose: fresh, varietal, red berry notes, medium intensity. Palate: flavourful, powerful, fruity.

LUIS MEDRANO 2008 T
tempranillo.

92 Colour: black cherry. Nose: powerfull, ripe fruit, fruit preserve, creamy oak. Palate: powerful, concentrated, fleshy, powerful tannins.

MEDRANO IRAZU 2008 TC
tempranillo.

88 Colour: cherry, garnet rim. Nose: red berry notes, ripe fruit, sweet spices, creamy oak. Palate: good acidity, powerful, flavourful.

MEDRANO IRAZU 2006 TR
tempranillo.

89 Colour: cherry, garnet rim. Nose: ripe fruit, toasty, complex, cocoa bean, sweet spices. Palate: powerful, flavourful, elegant, fleshy.

BODEGAS MENTOR

San Antón, 4-Entpta. dcha.
26002 Logroño (La Rioja)
☎: +34 941 270 795 - Fax: +34 941 244 577
info@puertagotica.es
www.puertagotica.es

MENTOR 2007 TC
100% tempranillo.

91 Colour: cherry, garnet rim. Nose: sweet spices, creamy oak, dark chocolate, ripe fruit, warm. Palate: flavourful, fleshy, spicy, round tannins.

MENTOR ROBERTO TORRETTA 2005 T
100% tempranillo.

94 Colour: cherry, garnet rim. Nose: ripe fruit, spicy, creamy oak, toasty, powerfull, mineral. Palate: powerful, flavourful, toasty, round tannins.

MENTOR 2005 TR
100% tempranillo.

92 Colour: cherry, garnet rim. Nose: spicy, dark chocolate, aromatic coffee, ripe fruit, creamy oak, toasty. Palate: ripe fruit, long, fine bitter notes.

BODEGAS MITARTE

Avda. Rioja, 5
01330 Labastida (Álava)
☎: +34 945 331 069 - Fax: +34 945 331 069
bodegas@mitarte.com
www.mitarte.com

MITARTE 2010 B
100% viura.

89 Colour: bright straw, greenish rim. Nose: fruit expression, candied fruit. Palate: flavourful, rich, fruity, good acidity.

S Y C (SANTIAGO Y CARMEN) DE MITARTE 2009 BFB

89 Colour: bright yellow. Nose: faded flowers, candied fruit, expressive, creamy oak. Palate: good acidity, powerful, flavourful, fruity, toasty.

MITARTE 2010 RD
50% tempranillo, 50% garnacha.

87 Colour: brilliant rose. Nose: red berry notes, lactic notes, raspberry. Palate: fruity, good acidity, correct, fresh, flavourful.

MITARTE 2010 T MACERACIÓN CARBÓNICA
80% tempranillo, 12% garnacha, 8% viura.

87 Colour: cherry, purple rim. Nose: floral, red berry notes, fresh fruit. Palate: correct, light-bodied, fresh, flavourful.

MITARTE 3 HOJA 2010 T
100% tempranillo.

86 Colour: deep cherry, purple rim. Nose: medium intensity, red berry notes. Palate: flavourful, fruity, balanced.

MITARTE VENDIMIA SELECCIONADA 2008 TC
100% tempranillo.

85 Colour: cherry, garnet rim. Nose: ripe fruit, complex, balanced, medium intensity, sweet spices. Palate: good acidity, fruity, flavourful.

MITARTE 2006 TR
100% tempranillo.

88 Colour: cherry, garnet rim. Nose: fruit preserve, balsamic herbs, sweet spices, toasty. Palate: good acidity, powerful, fleshy, flavourful.

MITARTE MAZUELO 2006 T
100% mazuelo.

85 Colour: light cherry, orangey edge. Nose: citrus fruit, ripe fruit, slightly evolved, fine reductive notes. Palate: ripe fruit, flavourful, reductive nuances.

S Y C (SANTIAGO Y CARMEN) DE MITARTE 2005 T
100% tempranillo.

88 Colour: cherry, garnet rim. Nose: sweet spices, red berry notes, ripe fruit, creamy oak. Palate: ripe fruit, powerful, flavourful, fleshy, fine tannins.

DE FAULA 2005 TR

87 Colour: cherry, garnet rim. Nose: ripe fruit, spicy, creamy oak, toasty, warm. Palate: powerful, flavourful, toasty.

BODEGAS MONTEALTO

Las Piscinas, s/n
01307 Baños del Ebro (Alava)
☎: +34 918 427 013 - Fax: +34 918 427 013
contacta@meddissl.com

ROBATIE 2010 T JOVEN

89 Colour: cherry, purple rim. Nose: fresh, red berry notes, raspberry, floral, lactic notes. Palate: fleshy, powerful, flavourful, fruity.

ROBATIE VENDIMIA SELECCIONADA 2007 T
100% tempranillo.

92 Colour: cherry, garnet rim. Nose: spicy, creamy oak, toasty, red berry notes. Palate: powerful, flavourful, toasty, round tannins.

ROBATIE 2007 TC

88 Colour: cherry, garnet rim. Nose: creamy oak, sweet spices, cocoa bean, fruit expression. Palate: flavourful, ripe fruit, spicy.

ROBATIE 2005 TR

86 Colour: deep cherry. Nose: powerfull, warm, ripe fruit, toasty, spicy. Palate: flavourful, fleshy, complex.

BODEGAS MORAZA

Ctra. Peñacerrada, s/n
26338 San Vicente de la Sonsierra (La Rioja)
☎: +34 941 334 473 - Fax: +34 941 334 473
bodega@bodegasmoraza.com
www.bodegasmoraza.com

MORAZA 2010 B
100% viura.

82 Colour: bright straw. Nose: wild herbs, candied fruit. Palate: light-bodied, fresh, easy to drink, fine bitter notes.

ALESAGO 2010 T
100% tempranillo.

88 Colour: cherry, purple rim. Nose: fresh fruit, red berry notes, floral. Palate: flavourful, fruity, good acidity, round tannins.

MORAZA 2010 T
96% tempranillo, 3% viura, 1% garnacha.

87 Colour: cherry, purple rim. Nose: ripe fruit, scrubland, floral. Palate: flavourful, fruity, fresh.

MORAZA VENDIMIA SELECCIONADA 2008 T BARRICA
100% tempranillo.

88 Colour: very deep cherry. Nose: roasted coffee, sweet spices. Palate: powerful, fine bitter notes, good structure.

MORAZA 2007 TC
100% tempranillo.

82 Colour: cherry, garnet rim. Nose: fruit preserve, characterful. Palate: powerful, fleshy, round tannins.

BODEGAS MUGA

Barrio de la Estación, s/n
26200 Haro (La Rioja)
☎: +34 941 310 498 - Fax: +34 941 312 867
info@bodegasmuga.com
www.bodegasmuga.com

MUGA 2010 BFB
90% viura, 10% malvasía.

90 Colour: bright straw. Nose: powerfull, ripe fruit, spicy, white flowers. Palate: flavourful, fruity, fleshy.

MUGA 2010 RD
60% garnacha, 30% viura, 10% tempranillo.

87 Colour: onion pink. Nose: floral, fruit expression, expressive, elegant. Palate: correct, fleshy, fruity, powerful, flavourful.

MUGA SELECCIÓN ESPECIAL 2006 TR
70% tempranillo, 20% garnacha, 10% mazuelo, graciano.

91 Colour: cherry, garnet rim. Nose: creamy oak, toasty, complex, fruit liqueur notes. Palate: flavourful, toasty, round tannins, concentrated.

PRADO ENEA 2004 TGR
80% tempranillo, 20% garnacha, mazuelo, graciano.

94 Colour: pale ruby, brick rim edge. Nose: spicy, fine reductive notes, wet leather, aged wood nuances, fruit liqueur notes. Palate: spicy, fine tannins, elegant, long.

MUGA 2008 TC
70% tempranillo, 20% garnacha, 10% mazuelo, graciano.

89 Colour: cherry, garnet rim. Nose: sweet spices, aromatic coffee, ripe fruit. Palate: flavourful, powerful, fleshy, spicy, round tannins.

BODEGAS MURÚA

Ctra. Laguardia, s/n
01340 Elciego (Álava)
☎: +34 945 606 260 - Fax: +34 945 606 326
info@bodegasmurua.com
www.bodegasmurua.com

MURÚA 2007 BFB
viura, garnacha blanca, malvasía.

89 Colour: bright yellow. Nose: ripe fruit, faded flowers, fragrant herbs, creamy oak, petrol notes. Palate: fleshy, complex, powerful, flavourful.

MURÚA 2004 TR
tempranillo, graciano.

87 Colour: deep cherry. Nose: dark chocolate, sweet spices, toasty. Palate: flavourful, powerful, spicy, easy to drink.

BODEGAS MUSEO ONTAÑÓN

Avda. de Aragón, 3
26006 Logroño (La Rioja)
☎: +34 941 234 200 - Fax: +34 941 270 482
enoturismo@ontanon.es
www.ontanon.es

VETIVER 2009 B
viura.

88 Colour: bright straw. Nose: medium intensity, dried flowers. Palate: flavourful, fruity, good acidity.

ONTAÑÓN 2008 TC
tempranillo, garnacha.

88 Colour: cherry, garnet rim. Nose: spicy, toasty, complex, fruit preserve. Palate: powerful, flavourful, toasty, round tannins.

ARTESO 2007 TC
tempranillo, garnacha, graciano.

90 Colour: very deep cherry, garnet rim. Nose: balanced, complex, ripe fruit, spicy. Palate: flavourful, good structure.

ONTAÑÓN 2005 TR
tempranillo, graciano.

89 Colour: very deep cherry. Nose: powerfull, fruit preserve, sweet spices, cocoa bean. Palate: flavourful, fleshy, long, round tannins.

BODEGAS NAVA-RIOJA S.A.T.

Ctra. Eje del Ebro, s/n
31261 Andosilla (Navarra)
☎: +34 948 690 454 - Fax: +34 948 674 491
info@bodegasnavarioja.com
www.bodegasnavarioja.com

OTIS TARDA 2010 T

88 Colour: cherry, purple rim. Nose: floral, red berry notes, violet drops. Palate: flavourful, fruity, good acidity, round tannins.

PARDOÑO 2010 T

85 Colour: cherry, purple rim. Nose: red berry notes, floral, slightly evolved, ripe fruit. Palate: flavourful, fruity, good acidity, round tannins.

PARDOÑO 2007 TC

85 Colour: cherry, garnet rim. Nose: medium intensity, ripe fruit, spicy. Palate: fruity, easy to drink.

BODEGAS NAVAJAS

Camino Balgarauz, 2
26370 Navarrete (La Rioja)
☎: +34 941 440 140 - Fax: +34 941 440 657
bodegasnavajas@terra.es
www.bodegasnavajas.com

NAVAJAS 2007 TC

86 Colour: light cherry. Nose: medium intensity, ripe fruit, toasty, sweet spices. Palate: good acidity, toasty, easy to drink.

BODEGAS NESTARES EGUIZÁBAL

Alberto Villanueva 82-84
26144 Galilea (La Rioja)
☎: +34 941 480 351 - Fax: +34 941 480 351
info@nestareseguizabal.com
www.nestareseguizabal.com

SEGARES LAS LLECAS 2009 T
100% tempranillo.

88 Colour: cherry, garnet rim. Nose: balsamic herbs, sweet spices, fresh fruit. Palate: spicy, fruity, long.

SEGARES 2007 TC
100% tempranillo.

88 Colour: cherry, garnet rim. Nose: complex, balanced, cocoa bean, ripe fruit. Palate: fruity, good structure, easy to drink, good acidity.

SEGARES 2006 TR
100% tempranillo.

88 Colour: cherry, garnet rim. Nose: ripe fruit, dark chocolate, creamy oak, fine reductive notes. Palate: good structure, fruity, flavourful.

ARZOBISPO DIEGO DE TEJADA 2005 T
100% tempranillo.

88 Colour: cherry, garnet rim. Nose: medium intensity, balanced, sweet spices, cocoa bean. Palate: good structure, fruity.

BODEGAS OBALO

Ctra. 232 A, Km. 26
26339 Abalos (Rioja)
☎: +34 941 744 056 - Fax: +34 941 744 165
malvarez@avpositivo.com
www.bodegasmilcientodos.com

OBALO 2010 T
tempranillo.

91 Colour: cherry, purple rim. Nose: fruit expression, varietal, earthy notes, lactic notes. Palate: powerful, flavourful, fleshy, ripe fruit, fine bitter notes, balanced.

ALTINO 2009 TC
100% tempranillo.

93 Colour: cherry, purple rim. Nose: red berry notes, ripe fruit, mineral, dark chocolate, sweet spices, creamy oak. Palate: complex, fleshy, flavourful, fruity, toasty.

OBALO 2008 TC
100% tempranillo.

93 Colour: cherry, garnet rim. Nose: ripe fruit, spicy, creamy oak, toasty, mineral, cocoa bean. Palate: powerful, flavourful, toasty, round tannins.

ALTINO 2008 TC
100% tempranillo.

92 Colour: cherry, garnet rim. Nose: red berry notes, ripe fruit, earthy notes, cocoa bean, dark chocolate, sweet spices, creamy oak. Palate: good acidity, flavourful, fleshy, toasty.

BODEGAS OLARRA

Avda. de Mendavia, 30
26009 Logroño (La Rioja)
☎: +34 941 235 299 - Fax: +34 941 253 703
bodegasolarra@bodegasolarra.es
www.bodegasolarra.es

CERRO AÑÓN 2008 TC
80% tempranillo, 10% garnacha, 10% mazuelo, graciano.

88 Colour: cherry, garnet rim. Nose: ripe fruit, spicy, creamy oak, toasty. Palate: powerful, flavourful, toasty, round tannins.

CERRO AÑÓN 2005 TR
80% tempranillo, 10% garnacha, 10% mazuelo, graciano.

90 Colour: cherry, garnet rim. Nose: ripe fruit, spicy, creamy oak, expressive, aromatic coffee. Palate: powerful, flavourful, toasty, round tannins.

SUMMA 2005 TR
75% tempranillo, 15% mazuelo, 10% graciano.

88 Colour: cherry, garnet rim. Nose: medium intensity, varietal, ripe fruit, toasty. Palate: round, fine bitter notes, good acidity.

BODEGAS OLARTIA

Pza. Asunción, 8
26222 Rodezno (La Rioja)
☎: +34 941 338 296 - Fax: +34 941 338 360
contacto@bodegasolartiaa.com
www.bodegasolartia.com

VIÑA OLARTIA 2007 TC
100% tempranillo.

88 Colour: cherry, garnet rim. Nose: ripe fruit, candied fruit, spicy. Palate: flavourful, fruity, spicy, good acidity.

SEÑORÍO DE OLARTIA 2004 TR
100% tempranillo.

88 Colour: cherry, garnet rim. Nose: medium intensity, balanced, ripe fruit. Palate: good structure, fruity, round tannins.

SEÑORIO DE OLARTIA 2001 TGR
80% tempranillo, 10% graciano, 10% mazuelo.

88 Colour: cherry, garnet rim. Nose: ripe fruit, spicy, creamy oak, complex, dark chocolate. Palate: powerful, flavourful, toasty, round tannins.

BODEGAS ONDALÁN

Ctra. de Logroño, nº 22
01320 Oyón (Álava)
☎: +34 945 622 537 - Fax: +34 945 622 538
ondalan@ondalan.es
www.ondalan.es

ONDALÁN 2010 B
100% viura.

87 Colour: bright straw, greenish rim. Nose: fresh fruit, citrus fruit, balanced, varietal. Palate: fruity, flavourful.

ONDALÁN 2010 T
100% tempranillo.

87 Colour: cherry, purple rim. Nose: red berry notes, floral. Palate: flavourful, fruity, good acidity, round tannins.

ONDALÁN 2008 TC
80% tempranillo, 20% graciano.

86 Colour: cherry, garnet rim. Nose: ripe fruit, spicy, balsamic herbs. Palate: fruity, spicy.

100 ABADES GRACIANO SELECCIÓN 2007 T
100% graciano.

88 Colour: deep cherry, garnet rim. Nose: spicy, ripe fruit, balanced. Palate: fruity, flavourful, round tannins.

ONDALÁN 2007 TR
70% tempranillo, 30% graciano.

88 Colour: bright cherry. Nose: medium intensity, ripe fruit, balanced, balsamic herbs. Palate: fruity, flavourful, round tannins.

BODEGAS ONDARRE

Ctra. de Aras, s/n
31230 Viana (Navarra)
☎: +34 948 645 300 - Fax: +34 948 646 002
bodegasondarre@bodegasondarre.es
www.bodegasondarre.es

MAYOR DE ONDARRE 2005 TR
tempranillo, mazuelo.

88 Colour: cherry, garnet rim. Nose: ripe fruit, spicy, creamy oak, toasty. Palate: powerful, flavourful, toasty, ripe fruit.

ONDARRE 2005 TR
75% tempranillo, 10% garnacha, 15% mazuelo.

88 Colour: cherry, garnet rim. Nose: balanced, varietal, ripe fruit, spicy. Palate: spicy, ripe fruit, round tannins.

BODEGAS ORBEN

Ctra. Laguardia, Km. 60
01340 Laguardia (Álava)
☎: +34 945 609 086 - Fax: +34 945 609 261
club@grupoartevino.com
www.grupoartevino.com

MALPUESTO 2009 T
tempranillo.

95 Colour: cherry, purple rim. Nose: earthy notes, mineral, fruit expression, raspberry, creamy oak, sweet spices. Palate: flavourful, powerful, fleshy, complex, spicy, round tannins.

ORBEN 2007 T
tempranillo, graciano.

91 Colour: cherry, garnet rim. Nose: ripe fruit, spicy, characterful. Palate: powerful, toasty, round tannins, long.

BODEGAS ORTUBIA

Camino de Uriso, s/n
26292 Villalba de Rioja (La Rioja)
☎: +34 660 975 323 - Fax: +34 941 310 842
ortubia@bodegasortubia.com
www.bodegasortubia.com

ORTUBIA 2009 B
100% viura.

80 Colour: bright straw. Nose: ripe fruit, spicy, roasted coffee. Palate: slightly evolved, rich, flavourful.

ORTUBIA 2007 T
100% tempranillo.

87 Colour: bright cherry. Nose: ripe fruit, sweet spices, creamy oak. Palate: flavourful, toasty, round tannins.

1958 DE ORTUBIA 2006 TR
100% tempranillo.

90 Colour: cherry, garnet rim. Nose: creamy oak, sweet spices, aromatic coffee, ripe fruit, fine reductive notes. Palate: flavourful, powerful, fleshy, complex.

BODEGAS OSTATU

Ctra. Vitoria, 1
01307 Samaniego (Álava)
☎: +34 945 609 133 - Fax: +34 945 623 338
ostatu@ostatu.com
www.ostatu.com

OSTATU 2010 B
85% viura, 15% malvasía.

88 Colour: bright straw. Nose: fresh, fresh fruit, white flowers. Palate: flavourful, fruity, good acidity, balanced.

GLORIA DE OSTATU 2006 T
100% tempranillo.

94 Colour: cherry, garnet rim. Nose: spicy, creamy oak, toasty, complex, red berry notes, fruit expression, earthy notes. Palate: powerful, flavourful, toasty, round tannins, fleshy.

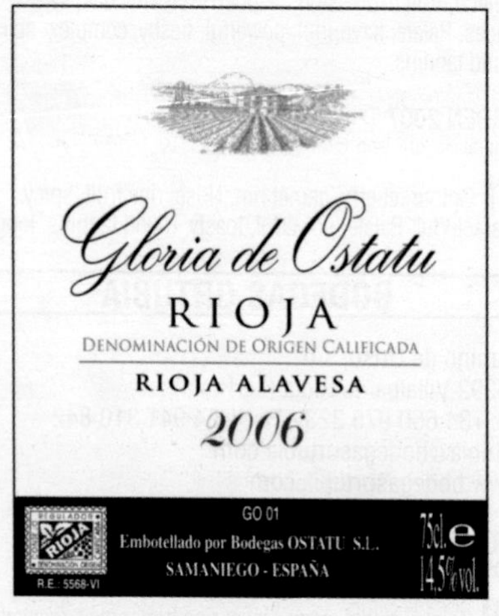

OSTATU 2010 T MACERACIÓN CARBÓNICA
95% tempranillo, 5% viura, graciano, mazuelo, garnacha.

88 Colour: bright cherry, purple rim. Nose: red berry notes, wild herbs, powerfull, expressive. Palate: flavourful, fruity, great length, fleshy.

MAZARREDO DE OSTATU 2008 T
90% tempranillo, 10% graciano, mazuelo, garnacha.

90 Colour: cherry, purple rim. Nose: fresh fruit, red berry notes, floral, creamy oak. Palate: flavourful, fruity, good acidity, round tannins.

OSTATU LADERAS DEL PORTILLO 2007 T
98% tempranillo, 2% viura.

91 Colour: deep cherry. Nose: fruit expression, raspberry, sweet spices, creamy oak. Palate: flavourful, fleshy, fruity, fine bitter notes.

OSTATU SELECCIÓN 2007 T
95% tempranillo, 5% graciano.

90 Colour: dark-red cherry. Nose: balsamic herbs, neat, fruit expression, red berry notes, creamy oak, dark chocolate. Palate: long, mineral, good finish.

OSTATU 2006 TR
100% tempranillo.

92 Colour: cherry, garnet rim. Nose: spicy, creamy oak, toasty, fruit expression, mineral. Palate: powerful, flavourful, toasty, round tannins.

BODEGAS PALACIO

San Lázaro, 1
01300 Laguardia (Álava)
☎: +34 945 600 151 - Fax: +34 945 600 297
cosme@bodegaspalacio.com
www.bodegaspalacio.es

COSME PALACIO 1984 2008 B
malvasía, viura.

91 Colour: bright golden. Nose: ripe fruit, powerfull, sweet spices, toasty. Palate: creamy, ripe fruit, powerful, flavourful.

COSME PALACIO VENDIMIA SELECCIONADA 2008 B
viura.

88 Colour: bright straw. Nose: candied fruit, citrus fruit, faded flowers. Palate: flavourful, fleshy, complex.

MILFLORES 2010 T
100% tempranillo.

89 Colour: bright cherry, purple rim. Nose: fresh fruit, wild herbs, faded flowers. Palate: good structure, fruity, rich.

COSME PALACIO "1894" 2008 T
90% tempranillo, 10% graciano.

89 Colour: deep cherry, garnet rim. Nose: balanced, spicy, ripe fruit. Palate: flavourful, balanced.

GLORIOSO 2008 TC
100% tempranillo.

87 Colour: black cherry, garnet rim. Nose: ripe fruit, spicy, cocoa bean, fruit preserve. Palate: flavourful, ripe fruit, fruity aftestaste.

COSME PALACIO VENDIMIA SELECCIONADA 2008 TC
tempranillo.

87 Colour: cherry, garnet rim. Nose: powerfull, varietal, spicy, ripe fruit. Palate: fruity, spicy, good acidity.

GLORIOSO RESERVA ESPECIAL 2006 T
100% tempranillo.

87 Colour: cherry, garnet rim. Nose: powerfull, balsamic herbs, spicy. Palate: flavourful, spicy, easy to drink.

COSME PALACIO 2006 TR
100% tempranillo.

87 Colour: cherry, garnet rim. Nose: medium intensity, varietal, ripe fruit, spicy. Palate: fruity, good acidity.

GLORIOSO 2004 TGR
100% tempranillo.

90 Colour: cherry, garnet rim. Nose: ripe fruit, wild herbs, complex. Palate: good structure, flavourful, ripe fruit, complex.

BODEGAS PALACIOS REMONDO

Avda. Zaragoza, 8
26540 Alfaro (La Rioja)
☎: +34 941 180 207 - Fax: +34 941 181 628
info@palaciosremondo.com

PLÁCET VALTOMELLOSO 2009 B
viura.

93 Colour: bright yellow. Nose: balanced, medium intensity, fresh fruit, complex. Palate: fruity, fresh, good acidity, fine bitter notes.

PLÁCET VALTOMELLOSO 2008 B
viura.

91 Colour: bright yellow. Nose: powerfull, ripe fruit, fine lees, jasmine. Palate: fleshy, rich, fruity, ripe fruit, balanced.

LA VENDIMIA 2010 T
50% tempranillo, 50% garnacha.

87 Colour: cherry, purple rim. Nose: ripe fruit, expressive, sweet spices. Palate: flavourful, ripe fruit, fine bitter notes.

LA MONTESA 2009 TC
70% garnacha, 25% tempranillo, 5% mazuelo.

91 Colour: cherry, garnet rim. Nose: creamy oak, dark chocolate, aromatic coffee, fruit preserve, fruit expression. Palate: spicy, ripe fruit, long.

PROPIEDAD VIÑAS TRADICIONALES 2008 T
60% garnacha, 40% tempranillo.

93 Colour: cherry, garnet rim. Nose: ripe fruit, spicy, creamy oak, toasty, characterful, earthy notes. Palate: powerful, flavourful, toasty, round tannins.

LA MONTESA 2008 TC
55% garnacha, 35% tempranillo, 10% mazuelo.

92 Colour: cherry, garnet rim. Nose: expressive, ripe fruit, fruit expression, sweet spices, creamy oak. Palate: balsamic, spicy, round tannins.

BODEGAS PATROCINIO

Ctra. Cenicero
26313 Uruñuela (La Rioja)
☎: +34 941 371 319 - Fax: +34 941 371 435
info@bodegaspatrocinio.com

SEÑORÍO DE UÑUELA 2010 B
viura.

88 Colour: bright straw, greenish rim. Nose: medium intensity, wild herbs. Palate: fresh, fruity, flavourful.

LÁGRIMAS DE MARÍA 2010 B
100% viura.

85 Colour: bright straw. Nose: faded flowers, ripe fruit, dried herbs, fresh. Palate: good acidity, fresh, fruity.

SEÑORÍO DE UÑUELA 2007 BFB
100% viura.

84 Colour: bright yellow. Nose: creamy oak, ripe fruit, spicy. Palate: rich, toasty, roasted-coffee aftertaste.

LÁGRIMAS DE MARÍA 2010 RD
100% tempranillo.

87 Colour: salmon. Nose: raspberry, red berry notes, floral, fresh. Palate: fleshy, powerful, flavourful, fruity, easy to drink.

SEÑORÍO DE UÑUELA 2010 RD
100% tempranillo.

86 Colour: light cherry. Nose: raspberry, violet drops. Palate: ripe fruit, good acidity.

SEÑORÍO DE UÑUELA 2010 T
100% tempranillo.

89 Colour: cherry, purple rim. Nose: fresh fruit, red berry notes, floral. Palate: flavourful, fruity, good acidity, round tannins.

LÁGRIMAS DE MARÍA 2010 T
100% tempranillo.

87 Colour: cherry, purple rim. Nose: expressive, ripe fruit, raspberry. Palate: flavourful, spicy, round tannins.

SANCHO GARCÉS 2010 T
100% tempranillo.

86 Colour: cherry, purple rim. Nose: fresh fruit, red berry notes, floral. Palate: flavourful, fruity, good acidity, easy to drink.

ZINIO GARNACHA 2010 T
100% garnacha.

82 Colour: cherry, purple rim. Nose: fruit liqueur notes, unripe grapeskin notes, floral. Palate: fresh, light-bodied, flavourful.

LÁGRIMAS DE MARÍA 2009 T
tempranillo.

89 Colour: bright cherry. Nose: ripe fruit, sweet spices, creamy oak, expressive, fruit expression. Palate: flavourful, fruity, toasty, round tannins.

LÁGRIMAS DE MARÍA 2008 TC

89 Colour: cherry, garnet rim. Nose: ripe fruit, creamy oak, cocoa bean. Palate: good structure, ripe fruit, long, fruity aftestaste.

ZINIO VENDIMIA SELECCIONADA 2008 TR
85% tempranillo, 15% graciano.

88 Colour: dark-red cherry, garnet rim. Nose: sweet spices, ripe fruit. Palate: good structure, fleshy, flavourful, round tannins.

ZINIO 2008 T
tempranillo, garnacha.

88 Colour: deep cherry, garnet rim. Nose: powerfull, balanced, ripe fruit, spicy. Palate: good structure, ripe fruit.

SEÑORÍO DE UÑUELA 2008 TC
100% tempranillo.

87 Colour: cherry, garnet rim. Nose: ripe fruit, creamy oak, toasty, characterful. Palate: powerful, toasty, round tannins.

SANCHO GARCÉS 2008 TC
100% tempranillo.

87 Colour: deep cherry. Nose: fruit expression, red berry notes, spicy. Palate: fruity, balanced, good acidity, round tannins.

ZINIO VENDIMIA SELECCIONADA 2007 TC
100% tempranillo.

88 Colour: cherry, garnet rim. Nose: spicy, dark chocolate, ripe fruit. Palate: fleshy, ripe fruit, long.

SEÑORÍO DE UÑUELA 2006 TR
100% tempranillo.

88 Colour: deep cherry, garnet rim. Nose: powerfull, balanced, ripe fruit. Palate: good structure, flavourful, ripe fruit, good acidity.

SANCHO GARCÉS 2006 TR
100% tempranillo.

88 Colour: bright cherry. Nose: sweet spices, creamy oak, fruit preserve. Palate: flavourful, fruity, toasty, round tannins.

LÁGRIMAS DE MARÍA 2006 TR

88 Colour: very deep cherry, garnet rim. Nose: dark chocolate, creamy oak. Palate: fleshy, powerful, round tannins.

ZINIO 2008 T
tempranillo, graciano.

87 Colour: cherry, garnet rim. Nose: toasty, spicy, ripe fruit. Palate: fruity, fleshy, round tannins.

BODEGAS PEDRO MARTÍNEZ ALESANCO

José García, 20
26310 Badarán (La Rioja)
☎: +34 941 367 075 - Fax: +34 941 367 075
info@bodegasmartinezalesanco.com
www.bodegasmartinezalesanco.com

PEDRO MARTÍNEZ ALESANCO 2010 BFB
100% viura.

85 Colour: bright straw. Nose: ripe fruit, citrus fruit, fragrant herbs. Palate: good acidity, flavourful, rich.

PEDRO MARTÍNEZ ALESANCO 2010 T
100% tempranillo.

87 Colour: cherry, purple rim. Nose: expressive, fresh fruit, floral, violet drops. Palate: flavourful, fruity, good acidity.

PEDRO MARTÍNEZ ALESANCO 2008 TC
80% tempranillo, 20% garnacha.

88 Colour: cherry, garnet rim. Nose: ripe fruit, spicy, creamy oak, toasty, fine reductive notes. Palate: flavourful, toasty, round tannins.

PEDRO MARTÍNEZ ALESANCO 2006 TR
90% tempranillo, 10% garnacha.

87 Colour: cherry, garnet rim. Nose: red berry notes, ripe fruit, powerfull, spicy, fine reductive notes. Palate: balanced, fleshy, flavourful.

PEDRO MARTÍNEZ ALESANCO SELECCIÓN 2006 TR
40% maturana tinta, 30% tempranillo, 30% garnacha.

87 Colour: cherry, garnet rim. Nose: ripe fruit, toasty, complex, sweet spices. Palate: powerful, flavourful, toasty, round tannins, easy to drink.

PEDRO MARTÍNEZ ALESANCO 2005 TGR
50% tempranillo, 50% garnacha.

87 Colour: cherry, garnet rim. Nose: red berry notes, ripe fruit, expressive, creamy oak. Palate: powerful, fleshy, flavourful, round tannins.

BODEGAS PERICA

Avda. de la Rioja, 59
26340 San Asensio (La Rioja)
☎: +34 941 457 152 - Fax: +34 941 457 240
correo@bodegasperica.com
www.bodegasperica.com

OLAGOSA 2010 BFB
95% viura, 5% malvasía.

86 Colour: bright straw. Nose: sweet spices, ripe fruit, fruit expression, fresh, expressive. Palate: powerful, flavourful, rich, fleshy.

6 CEPAS 6 2010 T
100% tempranillo.

90 Colour: cherry, purple rim. Nose: fresh fruit, red berry notes, floral, varietal. Palate: flavourful, fruity, good acidity, round tannins.

MI VILLA 2010 T
85% tempranillo, 15% garnacha.

88 Colour: cherry, purple rim. Nose: red berry notes, violet drops, balanced. Palate: flavourful, fruity, balanced.

OLAGOSA 2008 TC
90% tempranillo, 5% garnacha, 5% mazuelo.

90 Colour: deep cherry, garnet rim. Nose: ripe fruit, expressive, balanced. Palate: balanced, good acidity.

PERICA ORO RESERVA ESPECIAL 2006 TR
95% tempranillo, 5% graciano.

93 Colour: cherry, garnet rim. Nose: fruit expression, balanced, sweet spices. Palate: fruity, flavourful, good acidity.

OLAGOSA 2006 TR
90% tempranillo, 5% garnacha, 5% mazuelo.

89 Colour: cherry, garnet rim. Nose: ripe fruit, spicy, toasty, cocoa bean. Palate: powerful, flavourful, toasty, round tannins.

OLAGOSA 2004 TGR
90% tempranillo, 5% garnacha, 5% mazuelo.

90 Colour: cherry, garnet rim. Nose: fruit liqueur notes, spicy, balanced. Palate: good structure, complex, good acidity.

BODEGAS PUELLES

Camino de los Molinos, s/n
26339 Ábalos (La Rioja)
☎: +34 941 334 415 - Fax: +34 941 334 132
informacion@bodegaspuelles.com
www.bodegaspuelles.com

PUELLES 2009 B
80% viura, 20% garnacha blanca, malvasía, chenin blanc.

85 Colour: bright straw. Nose: faded flowers, ripe fruit, grassy. Palate: good acidity, fruity, fresh.

PUELLES 2008 TC
tempranillo.

85 Colour: cherry, garnet rim. Nose: ripe fruit, medium intensity, balanced, spicy. Palate: flavourful, spicy, easy to drink.

MOLINO DE PUELLES ECOLÓGICO 2006 T
tempranillo.

87 Colour: cherry, garnet rim. Nose: red berry notes, ripe fruit, scrubland, spicy, toasty. Palate: good acidity, flavourful, long.

PUELLES 2005 TR
tempranillo.

87 Color cherry, garnet rim. Aroma ripe fruit, spicy, creamy oak, toasty, complex. Taste powerful, flavourful, toasty, round tannins.

PUELLES ZENUS 2004 T
tempranillo.

87 Colour: cherry, garnet rim. Nose: spicy, ripe fruit, tobacco. Palate: fleshy, round tannins, long.

BODEGAS RAMÍREZ DE LA PISCINA

Ctra. Vitoria-Laguardia, s/n
26338 San Vicente de la Sonsierra (La Rioja)
☎: +34 941 334 505 - Fax: +34 941 334 506
rampiscina@euskalnet.net
www.ramirezdelapiscina.com

RAMÍREZ DE LA PISCINA 2010 B
100% viura.

83 Colour: bright straw. Nose: fragrant herbs, citrus fruit, candied fruit. Palate: powerful, fine bitter notes.

RAMÍREZ DE LA PISCINA 2010 RD
50% viura, 50% garnacha.

82 Colour: raspberry rose. Nose: medium intensity, fresh, fresh fruit. Palate: lacks expression, light-bodied.

RAMÍREZ DE LA PISCINA 2010 T
100% tempranillo.

88 Colour: cherry, purple rim. Nose: powerfull, ripe fruit, floral, raspberry. Palate: flavourful, fruity, fleshy.

RAMÍREZ DE LA PISCINA SELECCIÓN 2008 TC
100% tempranillo.

89 Colour: cherry, garnet rim. Nose: ripe fruit, fruit expression, sweet spices, creamy oak. Palate: powerful, concentrated, fleshy.

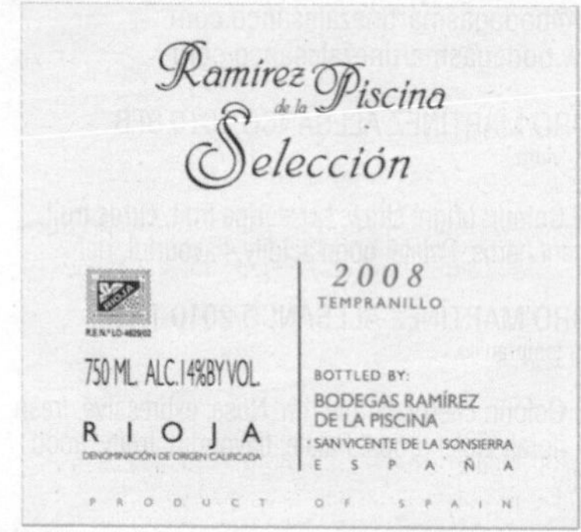

RAMÍREZ DE LA PISCINA 2008 TC
tempranillo.

86 Colour: deep cherry. Nose: powerfull, characterful, ripe fruit, toasty, new oak. Palate: fine bitter notes, good acidity, flavourful.

RAMÍREZ DE LA PISCINA 2006 T
100% tempranillo.

88 Colour: cherry, garnet rim. Nose: powerfull, ripe fruit, toasty, aromatic coffee. Palate: powerful, flavourful, fine bitter notes.

RAMÍREZ DE LA PISCINA SELECCIÓN 2005 TR
100% tempranillo.

88 Colour: cherry, garnet rim. Nose: powerfull, ripe fruit, fruit liqueur notes, toasty, spicy. Palate: powerful, spicy, round tannins.

RAMÍREZ DE LA PISCINA 2005 TR
100% tempranillo.

86 Colour: deep cherry. Nose: powerfull, characterful, ripe fruit, toasty, spicy. Palate: flavourful, powerful, fleshy.

SANTA MARÍA DE LA PISCINA 2001 TGR
100% tempranillo.

87 Colour: pale ruby, brick rim edge. Nose: powerfull, ripe fruit, toasty, spicy. Palate: flavourful, spicy, fine bitter notes.

BODEGAS RAMÓN BILBAO

Avda. Santo Domingo, 34
26200 Haro (La Rioja)
☎: +34 941 310 295 - Fax: +34 941 310 832
info@bodegasramonbilbao.es
www.bodegasramonbilbao.es

RAMÓN BILBAO TEMPRANILLO EDICIÓN LIMITADA 2008 TC
tempranillo.

92 Colour: cherry, garnet rim. Nose: spicy, creamy oak, toasty, characterful, red berry notes. Palate: powerful, flavourful, toasty, round tannins.

RAMÓN BILBAO 2008 TC
tempranillo.

89 Color cherry, garnet rim. Aroma ripe fruit, spicy, creamy oak, toasty, complex. Taste powerful, flavourful, toasty, round tannins.

MIRTO DE RAMÓN BILBAO 2006 T
tempranillo.

92 Colour: deep cherry. Nose: creamy oak, toasty, ripe fruit, fruit expression. Palate: ripe fruit, toasty, spicy, round tannins, good acidity.

RAMÓN BILBAO 2006 TR
tempranillo, graciano, mazuelo.

90 Colour: cherry, garnet rim. Nose: powerfull, ripe fruit, raspberry, creamy oak, sweet spices. Palate: powerful, flavourful, fleshy, complex.

RAMÓN BILBAO 2004 TGR
tempranillo, mazuelo, graciano.

90 Colour: deep cherry. Nose: wet leather, ripe fruit, toasty, spicy. Palate: powerful, spicy, ripe fruit, round tannins.

VIÑA TURZABALLA 2001 TGR
tempranillo.

89 Colour: pale ruby, brick rim edge. Nose: spicy, fine reductive notes, wet leather, aged wood nuances, fruit liqueur notes. Palate: spicy, fine tannins, elegant, long.

BODEGAS REMÍREZ DE GANUZA

Constitución, 1
01307 Samaniego (Álava)
☎: +34 945 609 022 - Fax: +34 945 623 335
fernando@remirezdeganuza.com
www.remirezdeganuza.com

REMÍREZ DE GANUZA 2006 TR
tempranillo, graciano.

95 Colour: cherry, garnet rim. Nose: ripe fruit, creamy oak, sweet spices, cocoa bean, earthy notes, mineral. Palate: powerful, flavourful, fleshy, round tannins.

ERRE PUNTO B

89 Colour: bright straw. Nose: fresh, white flowers, expressive, ripe fruit, sweet spices. Palate: flavourful, fruity, balanced.

ERRE PUNTO 2010 T MACERACIÓN CARBÓNICA
tempranillo, graciano, viura, malvasía.

91 Colour: cherry, purple rim. Nose: expressive, fresh fruit, red berry notes, floral. Palate: fruity, powerful, flavourful, fleshy.

TRASNOCHO 2007 T
tempranillo, graciano, viura.

94 Colour: cherry, garnet rim. Nose: powerfull, ripe fruit, creamy oak, toasty, earthy notes, fruit expression. Palate: flavourful, powerful, fleshy, round tannins.

VIÑA COQUETA 2006 T
90% tempranillo, 10% graciano.

92 Colour: bright cherry. Nose: fruit expression, cocoa bean, creamy oak. Palate: flavourful, fruity, toasty, round tannins.

FINCAS DE GANUZA 2005 TR
tempranillo, graciano, viura.

91 Colour: deep cherry. Nose: powerfull, ripe fruit, fruit expression, creamy oak, new oak. Palate: spicy, creamy, round tannins.

BODEGAS RIOJANAS

Estación, 1 - 21
26350 Cenicero (La Rioja)
☎: +34 941 454 050 - Fax: +34 941 454 529
bodega@bodegasriojanas.com
www.bodegasriojanas.com

PUERTA VIEJA 2010 B
100% viura.

84 Colour: bright straw. Nose: fresh, expressive, dried flowers, citrus fruit. Palate: flavourful, fruity, good acidity.

VIÑA ALBINA 2010 BFB
100% viura.

82 Colour: bright yellow. Nose: slightly evolved, fresh, creamy oak, ripe fruit. Palate: flavourful, rich, fruity.

VIÑA ALBINA SEMIDULCE 2001 B RESERVA
90% viura, 10% malvasía.

92 Color golden. Aroma powerfull, floral, honeyed notes, candied fruit, fragrant herbs. Taste flavourful, sweet, fresh, fruity, good acidity, long.

ARTACHO 4M 2010 T
100% tempranillo.

88 Colour: cherry, garnet rim. Nose: mineral, fruit expression, raspberry, ripe fruit. Palate: flavourful, ripe fruit, fine bitter notes.

CANCHALES 2010 T
100% tempranillo.

87 Colour: cherry, purple rim. Nose: red berry notes, balanced, fresh. Palate: fruity, easy to drink, round tannins.

MONTE REAL 2008 TC
100% tempranillo.

88 Colour: cherry, garnet rim. Nose: powerfull, ripe fruit, sweet spices, toasty, aromatic coffee. Palate: flavourful, fleshy, good acidity.

PUERTA VIEJA 2008 TC
80% tempranillo, 15% mazuelo, 5% graciano.

85 Colour: cherry, garnet rim. Nose: ripe fruit, spicy, toasty, aromatic coffee, wet leather. Palate: powerful, flavourful, toasty, round tannins.

GRAN ALBINA VENDIMIA 2006 T
34% tempranillo, 33% mazuelo, 33% graciano.

89 Colour: cherry, garnet rim. Nose: fruit liqueur notes, sweet spices, aromatic coffee, fine reductive notes. Palate: flavourful, spicy, ripe fruit.

GRAN ALBINA 2005 TR
34% tempranillo, 33% mazuelo, 33% graciano.

90 Colour: pale ruby, brick rim edge. Nose: powerfull, warm, fruit liqueur notes, toasty, spicy. Palate: powerful, fleshy, spicy, ripe fruit.

VIÑA ALBINA 2005 TR
80% tempranillo, 15% mazuelo, 5% graciano.

90 Colour: cherry, garnet rim. Nose: spicy, creamy oak, toasty. Palate: powerful, flavourful, toasty, round tannins.

MONTE REAL 2005 TR
100% tempranillo.

88 Colour: pale ruby, brick rim edge. Nose: wet leather, fruit preserve, toasty, spicy. Palate: spicy, ripe fruit, fine bitter notes.

MONTE REAL 2004 TGR
100% tempranillo.

88 Colour: cherry, garnet rim. Nose: powerfull, fruit liqueur notes, spicy, wet leather. Palate: powerful, spirituous, spicy.

VIÑA ALBINA 2004 TGR
80% tempranillo, 15% mazuelo, 5% graciano.

87 Colour: cherry, garnet rim. Nose: fruit liqueur notes, warm, spicy, toasty. Palate: spicy, ripe fruit, round tannins.

VIÑA ALBINA 2010 SEMIDULCE
95% viura, 5% malvasía.

83 Colour: bright yellow. Nose: candied fruit, medium intensity, spicy. Palate: fresh, flavourful, fruity, sweetness.

BODEGAS RIOLANC

Curillos, 36
01308 Lanciego (Álava)
☎: +34 945 608 140 - Fax: +34 945 608 140
riolanc@riolanc.com
www.riolanc.com

RIOLANC VENDIMIA SELECCIONADA 2010 T
85% tempranillo, 15% mazuelo.

85 Colour: cherry, purple rim. Nose: ripe fruit, floral, medium intensity. Palate: fleshy, fresh, easy to drink.

RIOLANC VENDIMIA SELECCIONADA 2008 T
100% tempranillo.

84 Colour: bright cherry. Nose: ripe fruit, sweet spices, creamy oak, expressive. Palate: flavourful, fruity, toasty, fleshy.

PULPO PAUL 2008 CRIANZA
100% tempranillo.

85 Colour: cherry, garnet rim. Nose: fruit preserve, spicy, toasty. Palate: fruity, powerful.

BODEGAS RODA

Avda. de Vizcaya, 5
26200 Haro (La Rioja)
☎: +34 941 303 001 - Fax: +34 941 312 703
rodarioja@roda.es
www.roda.es

CIRSION 2009 T
100% tempranillo.

96 Colour: cherry, purple rim. Nose: powerfull, complex, fruit expression, ripe fruit, creamy oak. Palate: powerful, fleshy, good acidity, round, round tannins.

SELA 2009 T
89% tempranillo, 8% graciano.

89 Colour: cherry, purple rim. Nose: fragrant herbs, ripe fruit, spicy, toasty. Palate: flavourful, fruity, fleshy.

RODA 2007 TR
89% tempranillo, 8% garnacha, 3% graciano.

91 Colour: cherry, garnet rim. Nose: ripe fruit, spicy, creamy oak, earthy notes. Palate: powerful, flavourful, round tannins.

RODA I 2006 TR
100% tempranillo.

95 Colour: cherry, garnet rim. Nose: ripe fruit, cocoa bean, toasty, spicy, earthy notes. Palate: flavourful, powerful, fleshy, long, round tannins.

BODEGAS RUIZ GÓMEZ

Las Cueva, s/n
26340 San Asensio (La Rioja)
☎: +34 629 533 550 - Fax: +34 941 457 129
bodegasruizgomez@ya.com

CABEZALGO 2010 T
tempranillo.

86 Colour: cherry, purple rim. Nose: fresh, red berry notes, ripe fruit, raspberry, powerfull. Palate: fresh, fruity, flavourful.

CABEZALGO 2007 TC
tempranillo.

85 Colour: cherry, garnet rim. Nose: ripe fruit, toasty, balanced. Palate: powerful, flavourful, spicy, ripe fruit.

CABEZALGO 2005 TR
tempranillo.

86 Colour: bright cherry. Nose: ripe fruit, sweet spices, creamy oak. Palate: flavourful, fruity, toasty, round tannins.

BODEGAS SEÑORÍO DE YERGA

Barrio Bodegas, s/n
26142 Villamediana (La Rioja)
☎: +34 941 435 003 - Fax: +34 941 435 003
info@senoriodeyerga.com

MONTE YERGA 2010 B
viura.

85 Colour: bright straw. Nose: white flowers, grassy, ripe fruit. Palate: flavourful, fruity, good acidity.

MONTE YERGA 2010 RD

82 Colour: rose, purple rim. Nose: medium intensity, candied fruit, faded flowers. Palate: flavourful, fine bitter notes.

MONTE YERGA 2010 T

88 Colour: cherry, purple rim. Nose: fresh fruit, red berry notes, floral. Palate: flavourful, fruity, good acidity, round tannins.

CASTILLO DE YERGA 2007 TC
90% tempranillo, 10% garnacha.

87 Colour: cherry, garnet rim. Nose: ripe fruit, spicy, toasty, complex, powerfull, balsamic herbs. Palate: powerful, toasty, round tannins.

CASTILLO YERGA 2006 TR
90% tempranillo, 10% mazuelo.

85 Colour: cherry, garnet rim. Nose: ripe fruit, creamy oak, complex, sweet spices. Palate: powerful, flavourful, toasty, round tannins.

CASTILLO YERGA 2001 TGR
85% tempranillo, 10% graciano, 5% mazuelo.

88 Colour: pale ruby, brick rim edge. Nose: elegant, spicy, fine reductive notes, old leather. Palate: spicy, fine tannins, elegant, round.

BODEGAS SOLANA DE RAMÍREZ RUIZ

Arana, 24
26339 Abalos (La Rioja)
☎: +34 941 334 354 - Fax: +34 941 308 049
solramirez@infonegocio.com
www.valsarte.com

SOLANA DE RAMÍREZ 2010 B
100% viura.

87 Colour: bright straw. Nose: medium intensity, dried flowers, ripe fruit. Palate: flavourful, fruity, fleshy.

SOLANA DE RAMÍREZ 2010 T
90% tempranillo, 5% garnacha, 5% viura.

87 Colour: cherry, purple rim. Nose: fresh fruit, red berry notes, floral. Palate: flavourful, fruity, good acidity, round tannins.

VALSARTE VENDIMIA SELECCIONADA 2009 TC
60% tempranillo, 40% otras.

85 Colour: cherry, garnet rim. Nose: powerfull, warm, fruit liqueur notes, toasty, spicy. Palate: powerful, spicy, round tannins.

SOLANA DE RAMÍREZ 2008 TC
100% tempranillo.

83 Colour: pale ruby, brick rim edge. Nose: varnish, aromatic coffee, fruit liqueur notes. Palate: fine bitter notes, fine tannins, spicy.

VALSARTE 2007 TC
100% tempranillo.

84 Colour: deep cherry. Nose: spicy, toasty, ripe fruit, fruit liqueur notes. Palate: flavourful, spirituous, spicy.

VALSARTE 2004 TR
85% tempranillo, 10% graciano, 5% otras.

87 Colour: cherry, garnet rim. Nose: powerfull, characterful, fruit liqueur notes, pattiserie. Palate: spicy, easy to drink, fine bitter notes.

BODEGAS SOLAR DE SAMANIEGO

Ctra. De Elciego s/n
01300 Laguardia (Álava)
☎: +34 902 227 700 - Fax: +34 902 227 701
bodega@cofradiasamaniego.com
www.solardesamaniego.com

SOLAR DE SAMANIEGO 2007 TC
95% tempranillo, 5% graciano.

86 Colour: cherry, garnet rim. Nose: ripe fruit, spicy, characterful. Palate: flavourful, good structure, spicy.

VALCAVADA 2005 TR
80% tempranillo, 20% graciano.

90 Colour: deep cherry, garnet rim. Nose: complex, balanced, cocoa bean, sweet spices. Palate: good structure, ripe fruit, round tannins.

SOLAR DE SAMANIEGO 2004 TR
92% tempranillo, 8% graciano.

87 Colour: very deep cherry, garnet rim. Nose: complex, balanced, spicy. Palate: flavourful, fruity.

BODEGAS SOLAR VIEJO

Camino de la Hoya, s/n
01300 Laguardia (Álava)
☎: +34 945 600 113 - Fax: +34 945 600 600
solarviejo@solarviejo.com
www.solarviejo.com

SOLAR VIEJO 2010 T
tempranillo.

87 Colour: deep cherry, purple rim. Nose: red berry notes, violets, balanced. Palate: fruity, good acidity, balsamic.

SOLAR VIEJO VENDIMIA SELECCIONADA 2008 T
tempranillo.

87 Colour: cherry, garnet rim. Nose: ripe fruit, spicy, creamy oak, toasty, medium intensity. Palate: powerful, flavourful, toasty, fleshy.

SOLAR VIEJO 2008 TC
tempranillo.

85 Colour: cherry, garnet rim. Nose: ripe fruit, spicy, toasty, sweet spices, fine reductive notes. Palate: powerful, flavourful, toasty.

SOLAR VIEJO 2005 TR
90% tempranillo, 10% graciano.

88 Colour: pale ruby, brick rim edge. Nose: ripe fruit, cocoa bean, dark chocolate, sweet spices, toasty. Palate: good acidity, balanced, flavourful, fleshy.

BODEGAS SONSIERRA

El Remedio, s/n
26338 San Vicente de la Sonsierra (La Rioja)
☎: +34 941 334 031 - Fax: +34 941 334 245
administracion@sonsierra.com
www.sonsierra.com

SONSIERRA 2010 B
100% viura.

87 Colour: bright straw, greenish rim. Nose: fresh fruit, floral, balanced. Palate: flavourful, fruity, good acidity.

SONSIERRA 2010 RD
100% tempranillo.

86 Colour: rose, purple rim. Nose: ripe fruit, red berry notes, floral, complex. Palate: powerful, flavourful, fruity, fresh.

SONSIERRA TEMPRANILLO 2010 T
100% tempranillo.

88 Colour: cherry, purple rim. Nose: fresh fruit, red berry notes, floral. Palate: flavourful, fruity, easy to drink.

SONSIERRA VENDIMIA SELECCIONADA 2008 TC
100% tempranillo.

90 Colour: cherry, garnet rim. Nose: ripe fruit, toasty, complex, balsamic herbs. Palate: flavourful, toasty, good finish, fleshy, round tannins, long.

SONSIERRA 2008 TC
100% tempranillo.

87 Colour: cherry, purple rim. Nose: floral, ripe fruit, complex, expressive, creamy oak, spicy. Palate: balanced, flavourful, fruity, fleshy.

PERFUME DE SONSIERRA DAVID DELFÍN 2007 T
100% tempranillo.

92 Colour: cherry, garnet rim. Nose: red berry notes, expressive, spicy, creamy oak, mineral. Palate: good acidity, balanced, fruity, flavourful.

PAGOS DE LA SONSIERRA EDICIÓN ESPECIAL DAVID DELFÍN 2006 T
100% tempranillo.

90 Colour: cherry, garnet rim. Nose: ripe fruit, toasty, sweet spices. Palate: powerful, flavourful, fleshy, spicy.

SONSIERRA 2006 TR
100% tempranillo.

89 Colour: cherry, garnet rim. Nose: balanced, ripe fruit, fine reductive notes, sweet spices. Palate: good acidity, round, fleshy, flavourful.

PAGOS DE LA SONSIERRA 2004 TR
100% tempranillo.

89 Colour: cherry, garnet rim. Nose: ripe fruit, creamy oak, toasty, complex, sweet spices. Palate: powerful, flavourful, toasty, fleshy, mineral.

SONSIERRA 2001 TGR
100% tempranillo.

86 Colour: pale ruby, brick rim edge. Nose: spicy, fine reductive notes, wet leather, aged wood nuances, fruit liqueur notes. Palate: spicy, fine tannins, long.

BODEGAS TARÓN

Ctra. de Miranda, s/n
26211 Tirgo (La Rioja)
☎: +34 941 301 650 - Fax: +34 941 301 817
info@bodegastaron.com
www.bodegastaron.com

TARÓN 2010 B
100% viura.

86 Colour: bright straw. Nose: ripe fruit, floral, wild herbs. Palate: good acidity, fruity, easy to drink.

TARÓN 2010 RD
50% tempranillo, 50% garnacha.

87 Colour: rose, purple rim. Nose: powerfull, ripe fruit, red berry notes, floral. Palate: fleshy, powerful, fruity, fresh.

TARÓN TEMPRANILLO 2010 T
100% tempranillo.

87 Colour: cherry, purple rim. Nose: fresh fruit, red berry notes, floral. Palate: flavourful, fruity, good acidity, round tannins.

TARÓN 4MB 2008 T
100% tempranillo.

90 Colour: cherry, garnet rim. Nose: floral, red berry notes, raspberry, sweet spices. Palate: good acidity, powerful, flavourful, fleshy.

TARÓN 2005 TR
tempranillo.

88 Colour: light cherry, orangey edge. Nose: red berry notes, fruit liqueur notes, medium intensity, fine reductive notes, toasty. Palate: balanced, flavourful, spicy, toasty.

TARÓN 2008 TC
90% tempranillo, 10% mazuelo.

87 Colour: cherry, garnet rim. Nose: ripe fruit, spicy, toasty. Palate: flavourful, toasty, round tannins.

BODEGAS TOBÍA

Paraje Senda Rutia, s/n
26214 Cuzcurrita de Río Tirón (La Rioja)
☎: +34 941 301 780 - Fax: +34 941 328 045
tobia@bodegastobia.com
www.bodegastobia.com

DAIMON 2010 BFB
56% malvasía, 44% viura.

91 Colour: bright straw. Nose: powerfull, ripe fruit, sweet spices, creamy oak, fragrant herbs. Palate: rich, flavourful, fresh, good acidity.

VIÑA TOBÍA 2010 B
95% viura, 5% malvasía.

90 Colour: bright straw. Nose: white flowers, fresh fruit, fragrant herbs, expressive. Palate: good acidity, complex, fleshy, flavourful, fruity.

DAIMON 2010 B

88 Colour: bright straw. Nose: ripe fruit, lactic notes, sweet spices. Palate: flavourful, powerful, fleshy.

ALMA DE TOBÍA 2010 RD FERMENTADO EN BARRICA
60% tempranillo, 25% graciano, 15% otras.

90 Colour: rose, purple rim. Nose: powerfull, ripe fruit, red berry notes, floral, expressive, sweet spices, creamy oak. Palate: fleshy, powerful, fruity, fresh, elegant.

DAIMON 2010 RD FERMENTADO EN BARRICA
45% tempranillo, 30% graciano, 15% garnacha, 10% merlot.

90 Colour: rose, purple rim. Nose: fruit expression, raspberry, creamy oak. Palate: powerful, fleshy, good structure.

VIÑA TOBÍA 2010 RD
100% garnacha.

87 Colour: rose, purple rim. Nose: powerfull, ripe fruit, red berry notes, floral. Palate: fleshy, powerful, fruity, fresh.

VIÑA TOBÍA 2010 T
100% tempranillo.

90 Colour: cherry, garnet rim. Nose: powerfull, fruit expression, fragrant herbs. Palate: ripe fruit, flavourful, fruity.

DAIMON 2009 T
37% tempranillo, 25% garnacha, 24% graciano, 13% merlot.

90 Colour: bright cherry. Nose: sweet spices, creamy oak, fruit expression. Palate: flavourful, fruity, toasty, powerful tannins.

TOBÍA GRACIANO 2008 TC
100% graciano.

88 Colour: deep cherry, garnet rim. Nose: powerfull, spicy, fruit preserve, fruit liqueur notes. Palate: good structure, fleshy, round tannins.

TOBÍA SELECCIÓN 2007 TC
80% tempranillo, 10% graciano, 10% garnacha.

89 Colour: cherry, garnet rim. Nose: wild herbs, ripe fruit, balanced, complex. Palate: fruity, powerful, round tannins.

OSCAR TOBÍA 2006 T
90% tempranillo, 10% graciano.

89 Colour: deep cherry, garnet rim. Nose: ripe fruit, spicy, balanced. Palate: ripe fruit, long, round tannins.

BODEGAS URBINA

Campillo, 33
26214 Cuzcurrita de Río Tirón (La Rioja)
☎: +34 941 224 271 - Fax: +34 941 224 271
urbina@fer.es
www.urbinavinos.com

URBINA 2009 B
100% viura.

78

URBINA GARNACHA 2009 T
100% garnacha.

85 Colour: cherry, purple rim. Nose: ripe fruit, floral. Palate: flavourful, fruity.

URBINA TEMPRANILLO 2009 T
100% tempranillo.

82 Colour: pale ruby, brick rim edge. Nose: slightly evolved, fruit liqueur notes. Palate: spicy, fine bitter notes.

URBINA 2006 TC
95% tempranillo, 2,5% mazuelo, 2,5% graciano.

82 Colour: pale ruby, brick rim edge. Nose: fine reductive notes, fruit liqueur notes, aromatic coffee. Palate: classic aged character, long.

URBINA RESERVA ESPECIAL 2004 TR
95% tempranillo, 2,5% mazuelo, 2,5% graciano.

87 Colour: cherry, garnet rim. Nose: ripe fruit, spicy, creamy oak. Palate: flavourful, toasty, round tannins.

URBINA RESERVA ESPECIAL 2001 TR
tempranillo, 2,5% mazuelo, 2,5% graciano.

89 Colour: pale ruby, brick rim edge. Nose: spicy, fine reductive notes, wet leather, aged wood nuances, fruit liqueur notes. Palate: spicy, fine tannins, elegant, long.

URBINA SELECCIÓN 1999 TC
95% tempranillo, 2,5% mazuelo, 2,5% graciano.

82 Colour: pale ruby, brick rim edge. Nose: roasted almonds, slightly evolved, reduction off-odours. Palate: easy to drink, classic aged character.

URBINA RESERVA ESPECIAL 1998 TR
95% tempranillo, 2,5% mazuelo, 2,5% graciano.

85 Colour: pale ruby, brick rim edge. Nose: elegant, spicy, wet leather, fruit liqueur notes. Palate: spicy, fine tannins, long.

URBINA 1996 TGR
95% tempranillo, 2,5% mazuelo, 2,5% graciano.

85 Colour: pale ruby, brick rim edge. Nose: wet leather, tobacco, fruit liqueur notes. Palate: spirituous, spicy, classic aged character.

URBINA ESPECIAL 1995 TGR
95% tempranillo, 2,5% mazuelo, 2,5% graciano.

86 Colour: light cherry, orangey edge. Nose: medium intensity, spicy. Palate: good structure, fine bitter notes.

URBINA ESPECIAL 1994 TGR
95% tempranillo, 2,5% mazuelo, 2,5% graciano.

87 Colour: light cherry, orangey edge. Nose: tobacco, wet leather. Palate: light-bodied, spicy, fine tannins.

URBINA ESPECIAL 1991 TGR
95% tempranillo, 2,5% mazuelo, 2,5% graciano.

88 Colour: pale ruby, brick rim edge. Nose: elegant, spicy, wet leather, aged wood nuances. Palate: spicy, fine tannins, elegant, long.

BODEGAS VALDELACIERVA

Ctra. Burgos, Km. 13
26370 Navarrete (La Rioja)
☎: +34 941 440 620 - Fax: +34 941 440 787
info@hispanobodegas.com
www.hispanobodegas.com

VALDELAMILLO 2010 T
tempranillo.

85 Colour: cherry, purple rim. Nose: expressive, red berry notes, floral. Palate: flavourful, fruity, good acidity, fresh, easy to drink.

CAMPO ALTO 2010 T
tempranillo.

82 Colour: cherry, purple rim. Nose: red berry notes, fruit liqueur notes, floral, medium intensity. Palate: light-bodied, fresh, fruity.

VALDELAMILLO 2008 TC
tempranillo.

85 Colour: cherry, garnet rim. Nose: ripe fruit, spicy, toasty, fine reductive notes. Palate: flavourful, toasty, fleshy, ripe fruit.

CAMPO ALTO 2008 TC
tempranillo.

84 Colour: cherry, garnet rim. Nose: ripe fruit, aged wood nuances, toasty. Palate: flavourful, ripe fruit, good acidity.

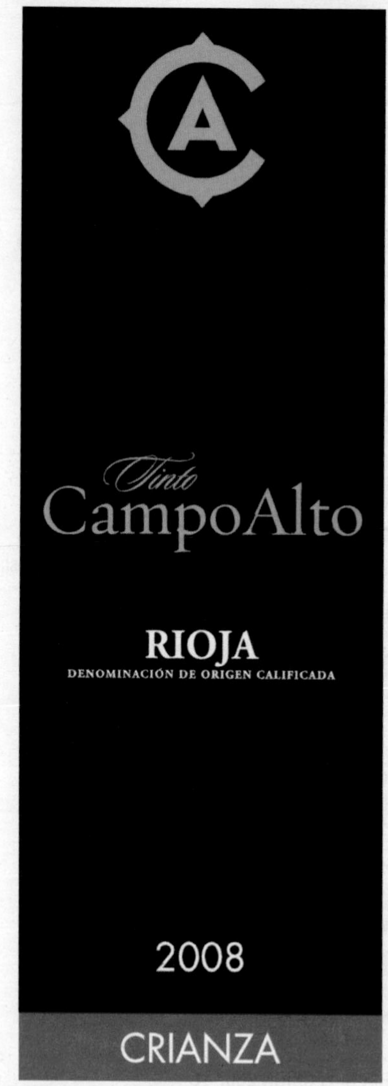

CAMPO ALTO 2007 TR
tempranillo.

82 Colour: cherry, garnet rim. Nose: ripe fruit, fine reductive notes, toasty, short. Palate: good acidity, correct, slightly evolved.

VALDELAMILLO 2007 TR
tempranillo.

81 Colour: cherry, garnet rim. Nose: ripe fruit, spicy, toasty, medium intensity. Palate: good acidity, flavourful, fleshy.

BODEGAS VALDELANA

Puente Barricuelo, 67-69
01340 Elciego (Álava)
☎: +34 945 606 055 - Fax: +34 945 606 587
info@bodegasvaldelana.com
www.bodegasvaldelana.com

VALDELANA 2010 T
95% tempranillo, 5% viura.

90 Colour: deep cherry, purple rim. Nose: red berry notes, powerfull, varietal. Palate: balanced, ripe fruit, long, round tannins.

LADRÓN DE GUEVARA DE AUTOR 2010 T
95% tempranillo, 5% graciano.

90 Colour: cherry, purple rim. Nose: raspberry, red berry notes, fresh, powerfull, lactic notes, dark chocolate, cocoa bean, creamy oak. Palate: good acidity, correct, unctuous, powerful, flavourful, fleshy.

LADRÓN DE GUEVARA 2010 T
95% tempranillo, 5% viura.

89 Colour: cherry, garnet rim. Nose: powerfull, characterful, ripe fruit. Palate: flavourful, powerful, fleshy.

AGNUS DE VALDELANA DE AUTOR 2010 T
95% tempranillo, 5% graciano.

87 Colour: cherry, purple rim. Nose: red berry notes, ripe fruit, expressive, fresh, roasted coffee, cocoa bean. Palate: good acidity, flavourful, fruity, fleshy.

LADRÓN DE GUEVARA DE AUTOR 2008 TC
95% tempranillo, 5% graciano.

91 Colour: cherry, garnet rim. Nose: ripe fruit, raspberry, dark chocolate, cocoa bean, sweet spices, expressive. Palate: good acidity, balanced, powerful, fleshy, complex.

AGNUS D VALDELANA 2008 TC
95% tempranillo, graciano.

88 Colour: cherry, garnet rim. Nose: ripe fruit, raspberry, complex, aromatic coffee, roasted coffee. Palate: ripe fruit, spicy, flavourful, toasty.

VALDELANA 2008 TC
95% tempranillo, 5% mazuelo.

88 Colour: black cherry, garnet rim. Nose: red berry notes, raspberry, ripe fruit, cocoa bean, sweet spices, roasted coffee. Palate: fleshy, rich, flavourful.

LADRÓN DE GUEVARA 2008 TC
95% tempranillo, 5% mazuelo.

88 Colour: cherry, garnet rim. Nose: sweet spices, red berry notes, ripe fruit, creamy oak. Palate: powerful, rich, fruity.

LADRÓN DE GUEVARA 2005 TR
95% tempranillo, 5% graciano.

91 Colour: cherry, garnet rim. Nose: ripe fruit, spicy, creamy oak, red berry notes. Palate: powerful, flavourful, toasty, round tannins, rich, fleshy.

VALDELANA 2005 TR
95% tempranillo, 5% graciano.

89 Colour: cherry, garnet rim. Nose: ripe fruit, cocoa bean, aromatic coffee, toasty. Palate: good acidity, powerful, flavourful, fleshy.

BODEGAS VALDEMAR

Camino Viejo, s/n
01320 Oyón (Álava)
☎: +34 945 622 188 - Fax: +34 945 622 111
info@valdemar.es
www.valdemar.es

CONDE DE VALDEMAR FINCA ALTO CANTABRIA 2010 BFB
100% viura.

87 Colour: bright yellow. Nose: balanced, slightly evolved, spicy, citrus fruit. Palate: fruity, flavourful, good acidity.

INSPIRACIÓN VALDEMAR 2010 B

86 Colour: bright yellow. Nose: varietal, balanced, fruit expression, white flowers. Palate: fruity, correct, good acidity, easy to drink.

CONDE DE VALDEMAR 2010 B
100% viura.

84 Colour: bright straw, greenish rim. Nose: fragrant herbs, fresh fruit. Palate: fruity, flavourful.

CONDE DE VALDEMAR 2010 RD
85% garnacha, 15% tempranillo.

85 Colour: rose, purple rim. Nose: medium intensity, ripe fruit, raspberry. Palate: flavourful, powerful, fine bitter notes.

VALDEMAR TEMPRANILLO 2010 T
100% tempranillo.

90 Colour: cherry, purple rim. Nose: scrubland, fruit expression, raspberry. Palate: flavourful, fleshy, spicy.

CONDE DE VALDEMAR 2008 TC
90% tempranillo, 10% mazuelo.

89 Colour: cherry, garnet rim. Nose: powerfull, ripe fruit, creamy oak. Palate: flavourful, ripe fruit, spicy.

CONDE DE VALDEMAR GARNACHA 2008 T
100% garnacha.

88 Colour: deep cherry. Nose: powerfull, warm, toasty, aromatic coffee. Palate: flavourful, powerful, fleshy, sweetness.

INSPIRACIÓN VALDEMAR 2007 T
90% tempranillo, 10% graciano.

91 Colour: bright cherry. Nose: creamy oak, ripe fruit, spicy, earthy notes. Palate: flavourful, fruity, toasty, round tannins.

INSPIRACIÓN VALDEMAR EDICIÓN LIMITADA 2005 T
70% tempranillo, 20% experimental, 10% graciano.

93 Colour: cherry, garnet rim. Nose: toasty, ripe fruit, cocoa bean, dark chocolate. Palate: powerful, flavourful, toasty, round tannins.

INSPIRACIÓN VALDEMAR MATURANA 2005 T
100% maturana.

92 Colour: black cherry. Nose: powerfull, varietal, characterful, ripe fruit, toasty, sweet spices, dark chocolate. Palate: powerful, fleshy, concentrated, round tannins.

CONDE DE VALDEMAR 2005 TR
90% tempranillo, 10% mazuelo.

90 Colour: cherry, garnet rim. Nose: ripe fruit, spicy, creamy oak, toasty. Palate: powerful, flavourful, toasty, round tannins.

INSPIRACIÓN VALDEMAR GRACIANO 2005 T
100% graciano.

90 Colour: cherry, garnet rim. Nose: ripe fruit, fragrant herbs, earthy notes, creamy oak. Palate: spicy, round, balanced, powerful, flavourful, fleshy.

CONDE DE VALDEMAR 2004 TGR
85% tempranillo, 10% mazuelo, 5% graciano.

88 Colour: cherry, garnet rim. Nose: ripe fruit, spicy, dark chocolate, aged wood nuances. Palate: powerful, toasty, round tannins.

BODEGAS VALLEMAYOR

Ctra. Logroño-Vitoria, 38
26360 Fuenmayor (La Rioja)
☎: +34 941 450 142 - Fax: +34 941 450 376
comercial@vallemayor.com
www.vallemayor.com

VALLE MAYOR WHITE RIOJA 2010 B
100% viura.

85 Colour: bright straw. Nose: fresh fruit, dried herbs. Palate: flavourful, fine bitter notes, easy to drink.

VALLE MAYOR WHITE RIOJA OAK 2008 B
100% viura.

85 Colour: bright golden. Nose: medium intensity, candied fruit, dry nuts, sweet spices. Palate: fleshy, fine bitter notes.

VALLE MAYOR 2010 RD

84 Colour: brilliant rose. Nose: expressive, elegant, fruit expression, red berry notes. Palate: good acidity, fine bitter notes, fruity.

SEÑORÍO DE LA LUZ 2010 T
100% tempranillo.

83 Colour: cherry, purple rim. Nose: fruit preserve, slightly evolved, grassy. Palate: fine bitter notes, good acidity.

COLECCIÓN VALLE MAYOR VIÑA ENCINEDA VENDIMIA SELECCIONADA 2009 T
100% tempranillo.

85 Colour: bright cherry. Nose: ripe fruit, sweet spices, creamy oak, premature reduction notes. Palate: flavourful, fruity, toasty.

VALLEMAYOR 2007 TC
90% tempranillo, 5% mazuelo, 5% graciano.

83 Colour: cherry, garnet rim. Nose: ripe fruit, fruit liqueur notes, toasty, fine reductive notes. Palate: good acidity, unctuous, fleshy.

COLECCIÓN VALLE MAYOR VIÑA CERRADILLA VENDIMIA SELECCIONADA 2005 TC
90% tempranillo, 10% mazuelo.

88 Colour: cherry, garnet rim. Nose: fruit liqueur notes, aged wood nuances, toasty, old leather. Palate: ripe fruit, long, flavourful.

VALLEMAYOR 2005 TR
85% tempranillo, 10% mazuelo, 5% graciano.

85 Colour: light cherry, orangey edge. Nose: ripe fruit, wet leather, cigar, toasty. Palate: good acidity, fleshy, reductive nuances.

VALLEMAYOR 2001 TGR
85% tempranillo, 10% mazuelo, 5% graciano.

86 Colour: pale ruby, brick rim edge. Nose: elegant, spicy, fine reductive notes, wet leather, aged wood nuances, fruit liqueur notes. Palate: spicy, fine tannins, flavourful.

BODEGAS VALLOBERA S.L.

Camino de la Hoya, s/n
01300 Laguardia (Álava)
☎: +34 945 621 204 - Fax: +34 945 600 040
bsanpedro@vallobera.com
www.vallobera.com

CAUDALIA 2010 B

87 Colour: pale. Nose: expressive, ripe fruit, citrus fruit, lactic notes. Palate: flavourful, fruity, fleshy.

VALLOBERA 2010 B

86 Colour: bright straw. Nose: fresh, fresh fruit, white flowers, tropical fruit. Palate: flavourful, fruity, good acidity, balanced.

VALLOBERA 2008 TC
tempranillo.

91 Colour: cherry, garnet rim. Nose: ripe fruit, creamy oak, sweet spices. Palate: powerful, flavourful, toasty, round tannins.

FINCA VALLOBERA 2007 T

88 Color bright cherry. Aroma ripe fruit, sweet spices, creamy oak, expressive. Taste flavourful, fruity, toasty, round tannins.

TERRAN 2007 T

87 Colour: cherry, garnet rim. Nose: red berry notes, ripe fruit, earthy notes, creamy oak. Palate: good acidity, balanced, flavourful.

BODEGAS VALSACRO

Ctra. N-232, Km. 364
26510 Pradejón (La Rioja)
☎: +34 941 145 105 - Fax: +34 941 145 869
ventas@valsacro.com
www.valsacro.com

VALSACRO DIORO 2005 T
vidau.

90 Colour: very deep cherry. Nose: overripe fruit, toasty, smoky. Palate: flavourful, powerful, ripe fruit, round tannins.

VALSACRO 2005 T
40% vidau, 50% tempranillo, 10% mazuelo.

89 Colour: cherry, garnet rim. Nose: dark chocolate, aromatic coffee, ripe fruit. Palate: powerful, concentrated, spicy.

BODEGAS VARAL

San Vicente, 40
01307 Baños de Ebro (Álava)
☎: +34 945 623 321 - Fax: +34 945 623 321
bodegasvaral@bodegasvaral.com
www.bodegasvaral.com

ESENCIAS DE VARAL 2010 B

87 Colour: bright straw. Nose: fresh, white flowers. Palate: flavourful, fruity, good acidity, balanced.

JOVEN DE VARAL 2010 T
95% tempranillo, 5% viura.

87 Colour: cherry, purple rim. Nose: red berry notes, fresh fruit, balanced, expressive. Palate: fruity, fresh, easy to drink, flavourful.

ESENCIAS DE VARAL 2007 T
100% tempranillo.

90 Colour: cherry, garnet rim. Nose: ripe fruit, spicy, creamy oak, toasty. Palate: powerful, toasty, round tannins.

VARAL VENDIMIA SELECCIONADA 2007 T
100% tempranillo.

90 Colour: cherry, garnet rim. Nose: ripe fruit, spicy, creamy oak, characterful, dark chocolate. Palate: powerful, flavourful, toasty, round tannins.

CRIANZA DE VARAL 2007 T
tempranillo.

90 Colour: bright cherry. Nose: sweet spices, expressive, raspberry, fruit expression. Palate: flavourful, fruity, toasty, round tannins.

RESERVA DE VARAL 2006 TR

88 Color cherry, garnet rim. Aroma ripe fruit, spicy, creamy oak, toasty, complex. Taste powerful, flavourful, toasty, round tannins.

BODEGAS VÉLEZ

Camino de la Llana s/n (Finca El Rincón)
26380 El Cortijo, Logroño (La Rioja)
☎: +34 941 217 038 - Fax: +34 941 217 037
info@bodegasvelez.com
www.bodegasvelez.com

CORTIJO ICONO 2010 BFB
100% viura.

91 Colour: bright yellow. Nose: ripe fruit, sweet spices, creamy oak, fragrant herbs, complex. Palate: rich, smoky aftertaste, flavourful, fresh, good acidity, complex.

CORTIJO ICONO 2006 TR
100% tempranillo.

87 Colour: bright cherry. Nose: sweet spices, creamy oak, ripe fruit. Palate: flavourful, fruity, toasty, round tannins.

BODEGAS VILLADAVALILLO

Pza. Mayor, 2
26338 San Vicente de la Sonsierra (La Rioja)
☎: +34 941 334 435 - Fax: +34 941 334 435
bodegaslagardezabala@hotmail.com
www.bodegaslagardezabala.com

LAGAR DE ZABALA 2008 TC
95% tempranillo, 5% garnacha.

88 Colour: cherry, garnet rim. Nose: caramel, dark chocolate, aromatic coffee, ripe fruit. Palate: powerful, flavourful, spicy.

LAGAR DE ZABALA 2006 TC
95% tempranillo, 5% garnacha.

86 Colour: cherry, garnet rim. Nose: powerfull, ripe fruit, sweet spices. Palate: ripe fruit, classic aged character.

LAGAR DE ZABALA 2005 TR
95% tempranillo, 5% garnacha.

86 Colour: cherry, garnet rim. Nose: wet leather, powerfull, characterful, fruit liqueur notes, dark chocolate, aromatic coffee. Palate: spicy, classic aged character, round tannins.

BODEGAS VINÍCOLA REAL

Ctra. Nalda, km- 9
26120 Albelda de Iregua (La Rioja)
☎: +34 941 444 233 - Fax: +34 941 444 427
info@vinicolareal.com
www.vinicolareal.com

CUEVA DEL MONGE 2008 BFB
70% viura, 20% malvasía, 5% moscatel, 5% garnacha blanca.

88 Colour: bright straw. Nose: floral, candied fruit, ripe fruit, dried herbs, sweet spices. Palate: fleshy, rich, flavourful, balanced.

VIÑA LOS VALLES ECOLÓGICO 2009 TC
70% tempranillo, 15% garnacha, 15% graciano.

90 Colour: cherry, garnet rim. Nose: red berry notes, ripe fruit, balsamic herbs, sweet spices, toasty. Palate: good acidity, balanced, flavourful, fruity, toasty.

CUEVA DEL MONGE 2008 T FERMENTADO EN BARRICA
100% tempranillo.

86 Colour: cherry, garnet rim. Nose: red berry notes, ripe fruit, fine reductive notes, dark chocolate, sweet spices. Palate: flavourful, fleshy, toasty.

VIÑA LOS VALLES 50 & 50 2007 TC
50% graciano, 50% garnacha.

90 Color cherry, garnet rim. Aroma ripe fruit, spicy, creamy oak, toasty, complex. Taste powerful, flavourful, toasty, round tannins.

VIÑA LOS VALLES 70 & 30 2007 TC
70% tempranillo, 30% graciano.

88 Colour: cherry, garnet rim. Nose: red berry notes, ripe fruit, fine reductive notes, sweet spices, toasty. Palate: rich, powerful, flavourful, fleshy.

VIÑA LOS VALLES 80 & 20 2007 TC
80% tempranillo, 20% mazuelo.

87 Colour: cherry, garnet rim. Nose: ripe fruit, wild herbs, spicy, toasty. Palate: long, powerful, flavourful.

CONFESOR 2005 T
85% tempranillo, 10% graciano, mazuelo, 5% garnacha.

91 Colour: cherry, garnet rim. Nose: red berry notes, ripe fruit, balanced, expressive, sweet spices, toasty, complex. Palate: round, unctuous, flavourful, fleshy.

200 MONGES 2005 TR
85% tempranillo, 10% mazuelo, 5% graciano.

89 Colour: cherry, garnet rim. Nose: red berry notes, ripe fruit, old leather, spicy, toasty. Palate: balanced, flavourful, round tannins.

200 MONGES SELECCIÓN ESPECIAL 2004 TR
100% tempranillo.

92 Colour: cherry, garnet rim. Nose: red berry notes, ripe fruit, old leather, tobacco, spicy, toasty. Palate: powerful, flavourful, spirituous, complex.

200 MONGES 1999 TGR
85% tempranillo, 15% mazuelo, 10% graciano.

89 Colour: pale ruby, brick rim edge. Nose: elegant, fine reductive notes, wet leather, aged wood nuances, fruit liqueur notes. Palate: spicy, fine tannins, elegant, long.

BODEGAS VIÑA LAGUARDIA

Ctra. Laguardia s/n
01309 Elvillar (Álava)
☎: +34 945 604 143 - Fax: +34 945 604 150
ivan.mingo@yahoo.es
www.vinalaguardia.es

URTEKO 2010 T MACERACIÓN CARBÓNICA
100% tempranillo.

87 Colour: cherry, purple rim. Nose: floral, red berry notes, raspberry, fresh. Palate: powerful, fruity, light-bodied, easy to drink.

ECANIA 2005 TC
100% tempranillo.

87 Colour: pale ruby, brick rim edge. Nose: ripe fruit, fruit liqueur notes, powerfull, fine reductive notes, spicy, toasty. Palate: good acidity, flavourful, fleshy, toasty.

ECANIA VENDIMIA SELECCIÓN 2005 T
100% tempranillo.

87 Colour: cherry, garnet rim. Nose: ripe fruit, spicy, creamy oak, toasty. Palate: powerful, flavourful, toasty.

ECANIA 2004 TR
100% tempranillo.

85 Colour: pale ruby, brick rim edge. Nose: ripe fruit, spicy, toasty, smoky, expressive. Palate: powerful, flavourful, complex, fleshy, toasty.

BODEGAS VIRGEN DEL VALLE

Ctra. a Villabuena, 3
01307 Samaniego (Álava)
☎: +34 945 609 033 - Fax: +34 945 609 106
cincel@cincel.net
www.cincel.net

CINCEL 2004 TR
95% tempranillo, 5% graciano, mazuelo.

85 Colour: cherry, garnet rim. Nose: ripe fruit, old leather, woody. Palate: flavourful, spicy.

CINCEL 2001 TR
90% tempranillo, 10% graciano, mazuelo.

84 Colour: cherry, garnet rim. Nose: ripe fruit, spicy, toasty. Palate: powerful, flavourful, toasty, round tannins.

CINCEL 2000 TGR

86 Nose: tobacco, old leather, fruit preserve. Palate: ripe fruit, aged character, spicy.

BODEGAS Y VIÑAS SENDA GALIANA

Barrio Bodegas, s/n
26142 Villamediana (La Rioja)
☎: +34 941 435 375 - Fax: +34 941 436 072
info@sendagaliana.com

SENDA GALIANA 2010 B

80 Colour: bright straw. Nose: ripe fruit, citrus fruit, medium intensity. Palate: fresh, fruity, light-bodied.

GALIANA 2010 RD

87 Colour: rose. Nose: powerfull, violet drops, ripe fruit. Palate: flavourful, fruity.

SENDA GALIANA 2010 T

83 Colour: deep cherry. Nose: powerfull, ripe fruit, fruit expression, violet drops. Palate: flavourful, fruity.

SENDA GALIANA 2007 TC

78

SENDA GALIANA 2006 TR

83 Colour: cherry, garnet rim. Nose: ripe fruit, spicy, woody. Palate: powerful, flavourful, toasty.

SENDA GALIANA 2001 TGR
tempranillo, mazuelo, graciano.

85 Colour: cherry, garnet rim. Nose: tobacco, old leather, ripe fruit, dry nuts. Palate: good acidity, good finish.

BODEGAS Y VIÑEDOS ALUÉN

Robledal, 18
26320 Baños de Río Tobia (La Rioja)
☎: +34 607 166 152 - Fax: +34 941 374 851
info@bodegasaluen.com
www.bodegasaluen.com

ALUÉN + 2008 T
100% tempranillo.

89 Colour: cherry, garnet rim. Nose: fruit preserve, expressive, cocoa bean, creamy oak. Palate: fleshy, rich, flavourful.

ALUÉN 2006 TC
92% tempranillo, 8% graciano.

85 Colour: cherry, garnet rim. Nose: overripe fruit, warm, sweet spices, toasty. Palate: good acidity, balanced, flavourful.

BODEGAS Y VIÑEDOS ALVAR

Camino de Ventosa, s/n
26371 Ventosa (La Rioja)
☎: +34 941 441 905 - Fax: +34 941 441 917
alvar@bodegasalvar.com
www.bodegasalvar.com

MILETO EDICIÓN LIMITADA 2007 T
80% tempranillo, 10% garnacha, 10% graciano.

89 Colour: bright cherry. Nose: ripe fruit, wild herbs, spicy. Palate: spicy, easy to drink, ripe fruit.

LIVIUS GRACIANO 2006 T
graciano.

90 Colour: cherry, garnet rim. Nose: powerfull, ripe fruit, spicy. Palate: flavourful, balsamic, aged character.

LIVIUS TEMPRANILLO 2006 T
tempranillo.

87 Colour: bright cherry, garnet rim. Nose: spicy, ripe fruit, cocoa bean. Palate: flavourful, ripe fruit, round tannins.

BODEGAS Y VIÑEDOS ALVAREZ ALFARO

Ctra. Comarcal 384, Km. 0,850
26559 Aldeanueva de Ebro (La Rioja)
☎: +34 686 944 243 - Fax: +34 941 144 210
info@bodegasalvarezalfaro.com
www.bodegasalvarezalfaro.com

ALVAREZ ALFARO 2008 TC
80% tempranillo, 10% mazuelo, 8% garnacha, 2% graciano.

88 Colour: dark-red cherry, garnet rim. Nose: red berry notes, ripe fruit, cocoa bean, sweet spices, toasty. Palate: powerful, flavourful, fleshy, balanced.

BODEGAS Y VIÑEDOS ARTADI

Ctra. de Logroño, s/n
01300 Laguardia (Álava)
☎: +34 945 600 119 - Fax: +34 945 600 850
info@artadi.com
www.artadi.com

ARTADI VIÑAS DE GAIN 2010 B
viura.

91 Colour: bright straw. Nose: scrubland, fresh fruit, citrus fruit, dried herbs. Palate: flavourful, fruity, fresh, fleshy.

ARTADI 2010 T MACERACIÓN CARBÓNICA

89 Colour: cherry, purple rim. Nose: fresh fruit, red berry notes, floral, expressive. Palate: flavourful, fruity, good acidity, round tannins.

VIÑA EL PISÓN 2009 T
100% tempranillo.

97 Colour: deep cherry, purple rim. Nose: mineral, ripe fruit, red berry notes, creamy oak, sweet spices, cocoa bean. Palate: flavourful, powerful, fleshy, fruity, fresh, fine tannins.

ARTADI PAGOS VIEJOS 2009 T
100% tempranillo.

96 Colour: dark-red cherry. Nose: sweet spices, creamy oak, aromatic coffee, dark chocolate, ripe fruit. Palate: flavourful, powerful, fleshy, complex, long, mineral.

ARTADI VALDEGINÉS 2009 T
100% tempranillo.

95 Colour: cherry, garnet rim. Nose: fruit expression, raspberry, floral, creamy oak. Palate: spicy, ripe fruit, good acidity, fine tannins.

ARTADI LA POZA DE BALLESTEROS 2009 T
100% tempranillo.

95 Colour: very deep cherry. Nose: cocoa bean, sweet spices, creamy oak, ripe fruit, dark chocolate. Palate: powerful, flavourful, fleshy, creamy, spicy.

ARTADI EL CARRETIL 2009 T
100% tempranillo.

95 Colour: very deep cherry, purple rim. Nose: dark chocolate, sweet spices, creamy oak, fruit expression, raspberry, mineral. Palate: flavourful, powerful, fleshy, spicy, ripe fruit.

ARTADI VIÑAS DE GAIN 2008 T
100% tempranillo.

91 Colour: bright cherry. Nose: ripe fruit, sweet spices, creamy oak, mineral, scrubland. Palate: flavourful, fruity, toasty, round tannins.

BODEGAS Y VIÑEDOS ILURCE

Avda. de Logroño, 7
26540 Alfaro (La Rioja)
☎: +34 941 180 829 - Fax: +34 941 183 897
info@ilurce.com
www.ilurce.com

ILURCE 2010 RD
100% garnacha.

85 Colour: rose, purple rim. Nose: fruit expression, raspberry. Palate: flavourful, fruity, spicy.

ILURCE 2009 T
100% tempranillo.

84 Colour: cherry, purple rim. Nose: fruit preserve, medium intensity. Palate: fruity, flavourful, correct.

ILURCE GRACIANO 2006 TC
100% graciano.

85 Colour: deep cherry. Nose: powerfull, ripe fruit, toasty, spicy. Palate: powerful, fleshy, mineral, balsamic.

ILURCE VENDIMIA SELECCIONADA 2005 TC
60% garnacha, 40% tempranillo.

89 Colour: cherry, garnet rim. Nose: powerfull, characterful, fruit liqueur notes, toasty. Palate: powerful, fleshy, warm.

ILURCE 2004 TC
70% tempranillo, 15% garnacha, 15% graciano.

84 Colour: pale ruby, brick rim edge. Nose: spicy, varnish, aromatic coffee. Palate: spicy, fine bitter notes.

ILURCE VENDIMIA SELECCIONADA 2001 TR
60% tempranillo, 40% garnacha.

87 Colour: deep cherry, orangey edge. Nose: powerfull, ripe fruit, sweet spices, aromatic coffee. Palate: good finish, fine bitter notes.

BODEGAS Y VIÑEDOS LABASTIDA

Avda. Diputación, 22
01330 Labastida (Álava)
☎: +34 945 331 161 - Fax: +34 945 331 118
info@bodegaslabastida.com
www.bodegaslabastida.com

SOLAGÜEN CEPAS VIEJAS 2009 T
50% tempranillo, 50% garnacha.

90 Colour: cherry, garnet rim. Nose: sweet spices, creamy oak, fruit expression, red berry notes. Palate: flavourful, powerful, fleshy.

SOLAGÜEN 2008 TC
100% tempranillo.

89 Colour: deep cherry. Nose: raspberry, fruit expression, sweet spices, creamy oak. Palate: flavourful, good acidity, ripe fruit.

SOLAGÜEN SELECCIÓN ANIVERSARIO 2006 TC
100% tempranillo.

88 Colour: cherry, garnet rim. Nose: ripe fruit, spicy, creamy oak, smoky. Palate: powerful, flavourful, toasty, round tannins.

SOLAGÜEN 2006 TR
100% tempranillo.

87 Colour: bright cherry, garnet rim. Nose: powerfull, varietal, ripe fruit, spicy. Palate: fleshy, fruity, flavourful.

MANUEL QUINTANO 2005 TR
75% tempranillo, 25% garnacha.

88 Colour: cherry, garnet rim. Nose: spicy, creamy oak, toasty, fruit preserve. Palate: powerful, toasty, round tannins.

SOLAGÜEN 2004 TGR
100% tempranillo.

86 Colour: bright cherry, orangey edge. Nose: varnish, aromatic coffee, ripe fruit, toasty. Palate: warm, fine bitter notes, spicy.

BODEGAS Y VIÑEDOS MARQUÉS DE CARRIÓN

Ctra. Logroño, s/n
01330 Labastida (Álava)
☎: +34 945 331 643 - Fax: +34 945 331 694
eromero@jgc.es
www.vinosdefamilia.com

ANTAÑO 2010 B
100% viura.

83 Colour: bright straw. Nose: citrus fruit, dried herbs, faded flowers, medium intensity. Palate: fresh, fruity, flavourful.

ANTAÑO TEMPRANILLO 2010 T
90% tempranillo, 5% garnacha, 5% graciano.

83 Colour: cherry, purple rim. Nose: medium intensity, dried herbs. Palate: fruity, light-bodied, easy to drink.

MARQUÉS DE CARRIÓN 2008 TC
80% tempranillo, 15% graciano, 5% mazuelo.

87 Colour: cherry, garnet rim. Nose: powerfull, ripe fruit, creamy oak. Palate: flavourful, fruity.

ANTAÑO 2008 TC
85% tempranillo, 5% garnacha, 5% mazuelo, 5% graciano.

84 Colour: cherry, garnet rim. Nose: smoky, spicy, ripe fruit, fine reductive notes. Palate: spicy, fine bitter notes, fine tannins.

ANTAÑO 2005 TR
85% tempranillo, 5% garnacha, 5% mazuelo, 5% graciano.

85 Colour: cherry, garnet rim. Nose: old leather, spicy, ripe fruit, fruit liqueur notes. Palate: flavourful, ripe fruit.

MARQUÉS DE CARRIÓN 2005 TR
80% tempranillo, 15% graciano, 5% mazuelo.

84 Colour: deep cherry. Nose: fruit liqueur notes, spicy, fine reductive notes, toasty. Palate: powerful, fleshy, spicy.

BODEGAS Y VIÑEDOS MORAL

Camino del Carmen, s/n
26311 Arenzana de Abajo (La Rioja)
☎: +34 941 243 053 - Fax: +34 941 243 053
info@bodegasmoral.es
www.bodegasmoral.es

TOLUACHE 2009 T
100% garnacha.

78

TOLUACHE 2006 TC
tempranillo, garnacha.

81 Colour: cherry, garnet rim. Nose: powerfull, candied fruit, slightly evolved. Palate: good acidity, fine bitter notes.

TOLUACHE 2005 TR
tempranillo, garnacha.

85 Colour: cherry, garnet rim. Nose: ripe fruit, spicy, creamy oak, dark chocolate. Palate: powerful, flavourful, round tannins.

BODEGAS Y VIÑEDOS PUENTE DEL EA

Camino Aguachal s/n
26212 Sajazarra (La Rioja)
☎: +34 941 320 405 - Fax: +34 941 320 406
puentedelea@gmail.com
www.puentedelea.com

PUENTE DEL EA 2010 BFB
viura.

90 Colour: bright straw. Nose: expressive, elegant, ripe fruit, citrus fruit, spicy. Palate: flavourful, fleshy, spicy, ripe fruit.

ERIDANO VIURA SOBRE LÍAS 2010 B
viura.

86 Colour: bright straw. Nose: grassy, white flowers, ripe fruit. Palate: flavourful, fruity, fine bitter notes.

PUENTE DEL EA 2010 RD
garnacha, tempranillo.

87 Colour: brilliant rose. Nose: red berry notes, lactic notes, powerfull. Palate: fruity, flavourful, balanced, ripe fruit, good acidity.

PUENTE DEL EA AUTOR 2009 T

91 Colour: bright cherry, purple rim. Nose: red berry notes, ripe fruit, balanced, powerfull. Palate: good structure, fruity, round tannins.

ERIDANO VENDIMIA SELECCIONADA 2009 T JOVEN

89 Color cherry, purple rim. Aroma expressive, fresh fruit, red berry notes, floral. Taste flavourful, fruity, good acidity, round tannins.

ERIDANO CRIANZA PLATA 2008 TC
tempranillo.

92 Colour: cherry, garnet rim. Nose: ripe fruit, spicy, creamy oak, toasty, complex. Palate: flavourful, toasty, round tannins.

PUENTE DEL EA 2008 TC
tempranillo.

89 Colour: bright cherry. Nose: sweet spices, creamy oak, expressive. Palate: flavourful, fruity, toasty, round tannins.

BODEGAS Y VIÑEDOS PUJANZA

Ctra. del Villar, s/n
01300 Laguardia (Álava)
☎: +34 945 600 548 - Fax: +34 945 600 522
gerencia@bodegaspujanza.com
www.bodegaspujanza.com

PUJANZA NORTE 2008 T
100% tempranillo.

93 Colour: cherry, garnet rim. Nose: spicy, creamy oak, toasty, mineral, characterful, ripe fruit. Palate: powerful, flavourful, toasty, round tannins.

PUJANZA 2008 T
100% tempranillo.

92 Colour: cherry, garnet rim. Nose: powerfull, ripe fruit, new oak, cocoa bean, mineral. Palate: flavourful, powerful, good acidity, fine bitter notes, round tannins.

BODEGAS Y VIÑEDOS TRITIUM

Dr. Estanislao del Campo, 28
26350 Cenicero (La Rioja)
☎: +34 627 410 801
bodegastritium@gmail.com
www.tritium.es

TRITIUM TEMPRANILLO 2009 T
tempranillo.

87 Colour: cherry, garnet rim. Nose: ripe fruit, floral, balsamic herbs, spicy, toasty. Palate: good acidity, flavourful, fleshy.

TRITIUM 6MB 2008 T
tempranillo.

87 Colour: cherry, garnet rim. Nose: ripe fruit, aromatic coffee, roasted coffee. Palate: powerful, fleshy, good acidity.

TRITIUM VENDIMIA SELECCIONADA 2007 TC
tempranillo.

89 Colour: cherry, garnet rim. Nose: red berry notes, ripe fruit, spicy, toasty. Palate: good acidity, flavourful, fleshy, toasty.

BODEGAS Y VIÑEDOS ZUAZO GASTÓN

Las Norias, 2
01320 Oyón (Álava)
☎: +34 945 601 526 - Fax: +34 945 622 917
zuazogaston@zuazogaston.com
www.zuazogaston.com

ZUAZO GASTÓN 2010 B

88 Colour: bright straw. Nose: fresh, fresh fruit, white flowers, lactic notes. Palate: flavourful, fruity, good acidity, balanced.

FINCA COSTANILLAS 2009 T

87 Colour: cherry, garnet rim. Nose: fruit preserve, sweet spices. Palate: powerful, concentrated, toasty.

ZUAZO GASTÓN 2008 TC

87 Colour: cherry, garnet rim. Nose: powerfull, ripe fruit, spicy. Palate: flavourful, toasty.

ZUAZO GASTÓN 2006 TR

88 Colour: deep cherry. Nose: fruit preserve, sweet spices, creamy oak, dark chocolate. Palate: fine bitter notes, good acidity, powerful.

BODEGAS YSIOS

Camino de la Hoya, s/n
01300 Laguardia (Álava)
☎: +34 945 600 640 - Fax: +34 945 600 520
ysios@pernod-ricard.com
www.ysios.com

YSIOS EDICIÓN LIMITADA 2007 TR
100% tempranillo.

94 Colour: cherry, garnet rim. Nose: red berry notes, ripe fruit, complex, spicy, toasty. Palate: good acidity, powerful, flavourful, fleshy, complex, toasty.

YSIOS 2006 TR
100% tempranillo.

90 Colour: deep cherry. Nose: toasty, sweet spices, balanced, ripe fruit. Palate: flavourful, good structure, round tannins.

YSIOS 2007 TR
100% tempranillo.

92 Colour: very deep cherry, garnet rim. Nose: ripe fruit, balanced, complex. Palate: flavourful, fleshy, good acidity.

BODEGAS ZUGOBER

Tejerías, 13-15
01306 Lapuebla de Labarca (Álava)
☎: +34 945 627 228 - Fax: +34 945 627 281
contacto@belezos.com
www.zugober.com

BELEZOS 2008 BFB

86 Colour: bright golden. Nose: candied fruit, sweet spices, cocoa bean. Palate: powerful, concentrated, fleshy.

BELEZOS ACUARELA 2010 T

86 Colour: cherry, purple rim. Nose: red berry notes, ripe fruit, fresh, balsamic herbs. Palate: powerful, flavourful, fresh, fruity.

BELEZOS VENDIMIA SELECCIONADA 2007 T

88 Colour: cherry, garnet rim. Nose: powerfull, characterful, warm, toasty, aromatic coffee. Palate: spicy, ripe fruit, fine bitter notes.

BELEZOS 2007 TC

87 Colour: cherry, garnet rim. Nose: ripe fruit, spicy, creamy oak. Palate: powerful, flavourful, toasty.

BELEZOS 2004 TR

88 Colour: cherry, garnet rim. Nose: ripe fruit, spicy, toasty, dark chocolate. Palate: powerful, flavourful, toasty, round tannins.

CARLOS SAMPEDRO PÉREZ DE VIÑASPRE

Páganos, 44- Bajo
01300 Laguardia (Álava)
☎: +34 945 600 146 - Fax: +34 945 600 146
info@bodegascarlossampedro.com
www.bodegascarlossampedro.com

PEÑALTA 2010 B
100% viura.

82 Colour: bright yellow. Nose: medium intensity, ripe fruit, citrus fruit. Palate: flavourful, fleshy.

BRILLADOR 2010 T MACERACIÓN CARBÓNICA
tempranillo.

86 Colour: cherry, purple rim. Nose: raspberry, fruit preserve, expressive. Palate: good acidity, fruity, flavourful.

CARLOS SAN PEDRO PÉREZ DE VIÑASPRE 2008 T
100% tempranillo.

90 Colour: bright cherry. Nose: fruit preserve, creamy oak, dark chocolate. Palate: flavourful, fruity, toasty, round tannins.

VIÑASPERI 2007 TC
100% tempranillo.

85 Colour: cherry, garnet rim. Nose: spicy, creamy oak, toasty. Palate: powerful, flavourful, round tannins.

CARLOS SERRES

Avda. Santo Domingo, 40
26200 Haro (La Rioja)
☎: +34 941 310 294 - Fax: +34 941 310 418
info@carlosserres.com
www.carlosserres.com

SERRES VIURA 2010 B
100% viura.

88 Colour: bright straw. Nose: fresh, fresh fruit, white flowers. Palate: flavourful, fruity, good acidity, fine bitter notes.

ONOMÁSTICA 2008 B RESERVA
100% viura.

88 Colour: bright golden. Nose: powerfull, candied fruit, fruit preserve, sweet spices, cocoa bean. Palate: powerful, ripe fruit, good finish, pruney.

SERRES 2010 RD
tempranillo.

87 Colour: rose, purple rim. Nose: powerfull, ripe fruit, red berry notes, floral. Palate: fleshy, powerful, fruity, fresh.

SERRES TEMPRANILLO 2010 T
100% tempranillo.

83 Colour: cherry, purple rim. Nose: fresh fruit, red berry notes, floral. Palate: flavourful, fruity, good acidity, easy to drink.

CARLOS SERRES 2008 TC
85% tempranillo, 15% garnacha.

88 Colour: cherry, purple rim. Nose: powerfull, balanced, spicy, ripe fruit. Palate: flavourful, good structure, round tannins.

CARLOS SERRES 2005 TR
90% tempranillo, 10% graciano.

87 Colour: cherry, garnet rim. Nose: medium intensity, ripe fruit, spicy. Palate: flavourful, ripe fruit, round tannins.

CARLOS SERRES 2004 TGR
85% tempranillo, 10% graciano, 5% mazuelo.

88 Colour: dark-red cherry, garnet rim. Nose: ripe fruit, spicy, aromatic coffee. Palate: flavourful, balanced, good acidity, round tannins.

ONOMÁSTICA 2004 TR
80% tempranillo, 10% graciano, 10% mazuelo.

88 Colour: cherry, garnet rim. Nose: balanced, powerfull, ripe fruit, sweet spices. Palate: balanced, flavourful.

CASTILLO DE CUZCURRITA

San Sebastián, 1
26214 Cuzcurrita del Río Tirón (La Rioja)
☎: +34 941 328 022 - Fax: +34 941 301 620
info@castillodecuzcurrita.com
www.castillodecuzcurrita.com

SEÑORÍO DE CUZCURRITA 2006 T
100% tempranillo.

92 Colour: cherry, garnet rim. Nose: spicy, creamy oak, toasty, ripe fruit. Palate: powerful, flavourful, toasty, round tannins.

COMPAÑÍA DE VINOS TELMO RODRÍGUEZ

El Monte, s/n
01308 Lanciego (Álava)
☎: +34 945 628 315 - Fax: +34 945 628 314
contact@telmorodriguez.com
www.telmorodriguez.com

LZ 2010 T
tempranillo, graciano, garnacha.

92 Colour: cherry, garnet rim. Nose: complex, balsamic herbs, red berry notes, fruit expression. Palate: fresh, fruity, powerful, flavourful.

LANZAGA 2008 T
tempranillo, graciano, garnacha.

92 Colour: deep cherry. Nose: expressive, raspberry, red berry notes, creamy oak, sweet spices. Palate: flavourful, fruity, fine bitter notes, ripe fruit, round tannins.

ALTOS DE LANZAGA 2007 T
tempranillo, graciano, garnacha.

93 Colour: deep cherry. Nose: powerfull, ripe fruit, fruit expression, sweet spices, creamy oak. Palate: flavourful, fruity, elegant, long.

CÓRDOBA MARTÍNEZ S.C.

La Poveda, 64
01306 Lapuebla de Labarca (Álava)
☎: +34 945 627 212 - Fax: +34 945 607 364
info@bodegasjosecordoba.com
www.bodegasjosecordoba.com

JOSÉ CÓRDOBA 2010 B
90% viura, 10% malvasía.

85 Colour: bright straw. Nose: fresh, fresh fruit, white flowers. Palate: flavourful, fruity, good acidity, balanced.

JOSÉ CÓRDOBA 2010 T
100% tempranillo.

88 Colour: bright cherry, purple rim. Nose: fresh, red berry notes, wild herbs. Palate: fruity, easy to drink, round tannins.

CRIADORES DE RIOJA

Ctra. de Clavijo, s/n
26141 Alberite (La Rioja)
☎: +34 941 436 702 - Fax: +34 941 436 430
info@criadoresderioja.com
www.criadoresderioja.com

CASTILLO DE CLAVIJO 2010 BFB
100% viura.

87 Colour: bright yellow. Nose: ripe fruit, white flowers, medium intensity. Palate: fruity, flavourful.

CASTILLO DE CLAVIJO 2007 TC
90% tempranillo, 10% garnacha.

86 Colour: cherry, garnet rim. Nose: ripe fruit, powerfull, spicy. Palate: flavourful, fruity, balanced.

CASTILLO DE CLAVIJO 2006 TR
90% tempranillo, 10% mazuelo.

88 Colour: cherry, garnet rim. Nose: ripe fruit, balanced, fine reductive notes, spicy. Palate: flavourful, complex, ripe fruit, round tannins.

CASTILLO DE CLAVIJO 2004 TGR
80% tempranillo, 10% mazuelo, 10% graciano.

87 Colour: bright cherry, orangey edge. Nose: fruit liqueur notes, tobacco, fine reductive notes. Palate: fruity, spicy, balanced.

CVNE - COMPAÑÍA VINÍCOLA DEL NORTE DE ESPAÑA

Barrio de la Estación, s/n
26200 Haro (La Rioja)
☎: +34 941 304 800 - Fax: +34 941 304 815
marketing@cvne.com
www.cvne.com

CUNE 2010 B
100% viura.

88 Colour: bright straw. Nose: fresh fruit, citrus fruit, grassy. Palate: flavourful, fruity, fresh.

MONOPOLE 2010 B
100% viura.

88 Colour: bright straw. Nose: white flowers, fresh fruit, scrubland, expressive, fresh. Palate: good acidity, fresh, fruity, flavourful.

CORONA SEMIDULCE 2008 B
85% viura, 15% malvasía, garnacha blanca.

92 Colour: golden. Nose: powerfull, floral, honeyed notes, fragrant herbs, petrol notes. Palate: flavourful, sweet, fresh, fruity, good acidity, long.

CUNE 2010 RD
100% tempranillo.

87 Colour: rose, purple rim. Nose: floral, fruit expression, fresh, medium intensity. Palate: light-bodied, fresh, fruity.

CUNE 2009 TC
80% tempranillo, 20% garnacha.

89 Colour: cherry, garnet rim. Nose: spicy, fruit expression, sweet spices, cocoa bean. Palate: flavourful, spicy, ripe fruit, round tannins.

CUNE 2008 TR
85% tempranillo, 15% mazuelo, garnacha, graciano.

90 Colour: cherry, garnet rim. Nose: spicy, creamy oak, toasty, ripe fruit. Palate: powerful, toasty, round tannins.

IMPERIAL 2007 TR
85% tempranillo, 10% graciano, 5% mazuelo.

94 Colour: cherry, garnet rim. Nose: spicy, creamy oak, toasty, earthy notes. Palate: powerful, flavourful, toasty, round tannins.

DIEZ-CABALLERO

Barrihuelo, 73
01340 Elciego (Álava)
☎: +34 944 807 295 - Fax: +34 944 630 938
diez-caballero@diez-caballero.es
www.diez-caballero.es

DÍEZ-CABALLERO 2010 BFB
100% viura.

82 Colour: bright straw. Nose: overripe fruit, dried herbs, slightly evolved. Palate: good acidity, spirituous, green.

DÍEZ-CABALLERO VICTORIA 2008 T
100% tempranillo.

91 Colour: cherry, garnet rim. Nose: ripe fruit, creamy oak, toasty, sweet spices. Palate: powerful, flavourful, toasty, round tannins.

DÍEZ-CABALLERO 2008 TC
100% tempranillo.

88 Colour: cherry, garnet rim. Nose: medium intensity, ripe fruit, dark chocolate. Palate: flavourful, fruity, good finish, spicy.

DÍEZ-CABALLERO 2005 TR
100% tempranillo.

89 Colour: cherry, garnet rim. Nose: ripe fruit, complex, balanced, varietal. Palate: flavourful, fruity, good structure.

DÍEZ-CABALLERO VENDIMIA SELECCIONADA 2004 TR
100% tempranillo.

88 Colour: deep cherry, garnet rim. Nose: complex, spicy, ripe fruit. Palate: good structure, flavourful, complex, fruity.

DIOS ARES

Ctra. de Navaridas s/n
01300 Laguardia (Alava)
☎: +34 945 600 678 - Fax: +34 945 600 619
export@bodegasdiosares.com

ARES 2010 B
viura.

88 Colour: straw. Nose: fresh fruit, varietal, powerfull, fresh, neat. Palate: elegant, balanced, fruity, light-bodied, powerful, flavourful.

ARES 2009 TC
100% tempranillo.

90 Colour: cherry, garnet rim. Nose: powerfull, varietal, spicy, cedar wood, fresh fruit, fruit expression. Palate: good structure, fruity, powerful, flavourful.

ARES 2008 TR
tempranillo.

91 Colour: cherry, garnet rim. Nose: ripe fruit, creamy oak, sweet spices, cocoa bean. Palate: flavourful, ripe fruit, spicy, round tannins.

DOMINIO DE BERZAL

Término Río Salado, s/n
01307 Baños de Ebro (Álava)
☎: +34 945 623 368 - Fax: +34 945 623 368
info@dominioberzal.com
www.dominioberzal.com

DOMINIO DE BERZAL 2010 B
90% viura, 10% malvasía.

88 Colour: bright straw. Nose: fresh, white flowers, ripe fruit. Palate: flavourful, fruity, good acidity, balanced.

DOMINIO DE BERZAL 2010 T
90% tempranillo, 10% viura.

88 Colour: cherry, purple rim. Nose: raspberry, red berry notes, powerfull, fruit expression. Palate: flavourful, fruity, fleshy.

DOMINIO DE BERZAL 2008 TC
95% tempranillo, 5% graciano.

89 Colour: cherry, garnet rim. Nose: red berry notes, fresh fruit, cocoa bean, sweet spices, toasty. Palate: good acidity, fresh, fruity, easy to drink.

DOMINIO DE BERZAL SELECCIÓN PRIVADA 2008 T
100% tempranillo.

88 Colour: cherry, garnet rim. Nose: ripe fruit, spicy, roasted coffee. Palate: powerful, flavourful, toasty, round tannins.

DUNVIRO S.C.

Ctra. Logroño, Km. 362
26500 Calahorra (La Rioja)
☎: +34 941 130 626 - Fax: +34 941 130 626
dunviro@bodegasdunviro.com
www.bodegasdunviro.com

DUNVIRO 2008 TC
90% tempranillo, 5% mazuelo, 5% graciano.

83 Colour: cherry, garnet rim. Nose: ripe fruit, spicy, fine reductive notes. Palate: powerful, flavourful, toasty.

DUNVIRO 2005 TR
90% ttempranillo, 5% graciano, 5% mazuelo.

84 Colour: cherry, garnet rim. Nose: ripe fruit, toasty, sweet spices. Palate: toasty, fleshy, correct.

DUNVIRO 2001 TGR
tempranillo.

87 Colour: pale ruby, brick rim edge. Nose: ripe fruit, wet leather, waxy notes, aged wood nuances. Palate: powerful, light-bodied, flavourful.

EL COTO DE RIOJA

Camino Viejo de Logroño, 26
01320 Oyón (Álava)
☎: +34 945 622 216 - Fax: +34 945 622 315
cotorioja@elcoto.com
www.elcoto.com

EL COTO 2010 B
100% viura.

84 Colour: pale, greenish rim. Nose: tropical fruit, white flowers. Palate: fresh, flavourful, easy to drink.

EL COTO 2010 RD
80% garnacha, 20% tempranillo.

88 Colour: onion pink. Nose: elegant, candied fruit, dried flowers, red berry notes. Palate: light-bodied, flavourful, good acidity, long, spicy.

COTO MAYOR 2007 TC
90% tempranillo, 10% graciano.

90 Colour: cherry, garnet rim. Nose: ripe fruit, spicy, creamy oak, toasty. Palate: powerful, flavourful, toasty, round tannins.

COTO REAL 2005 TR
80% tempranillo, 10% garnacha, 10% graciano.

90 Colour: cherry, garnet rim. Nose: ripe fruit, spicy, toasty, complex. Palate: powerful, flavourful, toasty, round tannins.

EL COTO DE IMAZ 2005 TR
100% tempranillo.

89 Colour: deep cherry, garnet rim. Nose: ripe fruit, sweet spices, cocoa bean. Palate: balanced, good acidity, unctuous.

EL COTO 2008 TC
100% tempranillo.

88 Colour: cherry, garnet rim. Nose: ripe fruit, sweet spices, cocoa bean, aromatic coffee, dark chocolate. Palate: powerful, fleshy, spicy, good acidity.

EL COTO DE IMAZ SELECCIÓN ANIVERSARIO 2004 TR
100% tempranillo.

89 Colour: deep cherry, orangey edge. Nose: elegant, spicy. Palate: spicy, fine tannins, elegant, long.

EL COTO DE IMAZ 2001 TGR
100% tempranillo.

89 Colour: deep cherry, garnet rim. Nose: cocoa bean, sweet spices, ripe fruit. Palate: fruity, fleshy, round tannins.

EMPATÍA

Pza. Fermín Gurbindo, 2
26339 Abalos (La Rioja)
☎: +34 941 334 302 - Fax: +34 941 308 023
direccion@hotelvilladeabalos.com
www.hotelvilladeabalos.com

EMPATÍA 2009 BFB
70% viura, 15% malvasía, 15% garnacha blanca.

87 Colour: bright straw, greenish rim. Nose: spicy, toasty, ripe fruit, fragrant herbs. Palate: correct, spicy.

EMPATÍA VENDIMIA SELECCIONADA 2008 T
90% tempranillo, 10% garnacha.

86 Colour: cherry, garnet rim. Nose: ripe fruit, fine reductive notes, sweet spices, toasty, balsamic herbs. Palate: fleshy, flavourful, toasty, good finish.

EMPATÍA VENDIMIA SELECCIONADA 2007 T
90% tempranillo, 10% garnacha.

87 Colour: cherry, garnet rim. Nose: ripe fruit, creamy oak, sweet spices. Palate: flavourful, toasty, concentrated.

FINCA ALLENDE

Pza. Ibarra, 1
26330 Briones (La Rioja)
☎: +34 941 322 301 - Fax: +34 941 322 302
info@finca-allende.com
www.finca-allende.com

MÁRTIRES 2010 B
100% viura.

95 Colour: bright yellow. Nose: ripe fruit, sweet spices, mineral, fragrant herbs, creamy oak. Palate: good acidity, powerful, flavourful, fleshy, complex, balanced.

ALLENDE 2009 B
viura, malvasía.

92 Colour: bright yellow. Nose: candied fruit, floral, sweet spices, mineral, elegant. Palate: rich, flavourful, fruity, fleshy, complex, good acidity.

AVRVS 2008 T
85% tempranillo, 15% graciano.

95 Colour: cherry, garnet rim. Nose: characterful, creamy oak, sweet spices, mineral. Palate: flavourful, fruity, long, mineral, round tannins, spicy.

CALVARIO 2008 T
90% tempranillo, 2% graciano, 8% garnacha.

93 Colour: black cherry, garnet rim. Nose: ripe fruit, fruit expression, cocoa bean, dark chocolate, sweet spices, creamy oak. Palate: flavourful, fleshy, complex, balanced, fine tannins.

ALLENDE 2008 T
100% tempranillo.

91 Color bright cherry. Aroma ripe fruit, sweet spices, creamy oak, expressive. Taste flavourful, fruity, toasty, round tannins.

FINCA EGOMEI

Ctra. Corella, s/n
26240 Alfaro (La Rioja)
☎: +34 948 781 021 - Fax: +34 948 780 515
info@egomei.es
www.bodegasab.com

EGOMEI 2008 T
85% tempranillo, 15% graciano.

91 Colour: cherry, garnet rim. Nose: spicy, creamy oak, toasty, ripe fruit, balsamic herbs. Palate: powerful, flavourful, round tannins.

EGOMEI ALMA 2007 T
75% tempranillo, 25% graciano.

92 Colour: cherry, garnet rim. Nose: spicy, creamy oak, fruit preserve, roasted coffee. Palate: powerful, flavourful, toasty, round tannins.

FINCA NUEVA

Las Eras, 14
26330 Briones (La Rioja)
☎: +34 941 322 301
fincanuevabriones@gmail.com

FINCA NUEVA 2010 BFB
100% viura.

90 Colour: bright yellow. Nose: ripe fruit, sweet spices, creamy oak, fragrant herbs. Palate: rich, flavourful, fresh, good acidity.

FINCA NUEVA 2010 T
tempranillo.

89 Colour: cherry, garnet rim. Nose: fresh, medium intensity, red berry notes, floral, raspberry. Palate: fruity, fresh, good acidity, fleshy, round tannins.

FINCA NUEVA 2007 TC
tempranillo.

89 Colour: cherry, garnet rim. Nose: medium intensity, ripe fruit, dry nuts, toasty, spicy. Palate: good acidity, fleshy, round, round tannins.

FINCA NUEVA 2005 TR
100% tempranillo.

90 Colour: cherry, garnet rim. Nose: medium intensity, ripe fruit, expressive, creamy oak, cocoa bean, spicy. Palate: balanced, flavourful, full, fleshy, ripe fruit, round tannins.

FINCA VALPIEDRA

El Montecillo, s/n
26360 Fuenmayor (La Rioja)
☎: +34 941 450 876 - Fax: +34 941 450 875
info@bujanda.com
www.familiamartinezbujanda.com

CANTOS DE VALPIEDRA 2008 T
100% tempranillo.

91 Colour: deep cherry, garnet rim. Nose: expressive, complex, ripe fruit, spicy. Palate: flavourful, fruity, complex.

FINCA VALPIEDRA 2007 TR
92% tempranillo, 6% graciano, 2% experimental.

91 Colour: bright cherry, garnet rim. Nose: mineral, complex, expressive. Palate: good structure, ripe fruit, long, round tannins.

FLORENTINO DE LECANDA

Cuevas, 36
26200 Haro (La Rioja)
☎: +34 941 303 477 - Fax: +34 941 312 707
florentinodelecanda@fer.es
www.bodegaslecanda.com

FLORENTINO DE LECANDA 2008 TC
80% tempranillo, 20% garnacha.

84 Colour: cherry, garnet rim. Nose: powerfull, ripe fruit, cocoa bean. Palate: flavourful, powerful, fine bitter notes.

CASUNE 2005 TC
100% tempranillo.

88 Colour: cherry, garnet rim. Nose: powerfull, varietal, aromatic coffee, dark chocolate. Palate: spirituous, fleshy, round tannins.

FLORENTINO DE LECANDA 2003 TR
80% tempranillo, 20% garnacha.

87 Colour: bright cherry. Nose: characterful, fruit liqueur notes, dark chocolate. Palate: spirituous, fine bitter notes.

FRANCO ESPAÑOLAS

Cabo Noval, 2
26009 Logroño (La Rioja)
☎: +34 941 251 300 - Fax: +34 941 262 948
francoespanolas@francoespanolas.com
www.francoespanolas.com

VIÑA SOLEDAD 2010 B
viura.

85 Colour: bright straw. Nose: citrus fruit, white flowers, dried herbs, powerfull. Palate: good acidity, fresh, fruity.

DIAMANTE 2010 B
viura, malvasía.

84 Colour: bright yellow. Nose: white flowers, ripe fruit, tropical fruit. Palate: fresh, fruity, sweetness.

RIOJA BORDÓN 2010 RD
garnacha, viura.

87 Colour: rose, purple rim. Nose: powerfull, ripe fruit, lactic notes. Palate: powerful, fleshy, complex.

RIOJA BORDÓN 2007 TC
tempranillo, garnacha.

87 Colour: cherry, garnet rim. Nose: ripe fruit, spicy, old leather. Palate: fruity, balanced, easy to drink, fine tannins.

RIOJA BORDÓN 2006 TR
tempranillo, garnacha, mazuelo.

87 Colour: cherry, garnet rim. Nose: powerfull, ripe fruit, spicy, aromatic coffee. Palate: spicy, classic aged character, fine bitter notes.

BARON D'ANGLADE 2005 TR
tempranillo, mazuelo, graciano.

92 Colour: cherry, garnet rim. Nose: ripe fruit, spicy, creamy oak, toasty, wet leather, elegant. Palate: powerful, flavourful, toasty, round tannins.

RIOJA BORDÓN 2004 TGR
tempranillo, garnacha, mazuelo, graciano.

88 Colour: bright cherry. Nose: ripe fruit, sweet spices, elegant. Palate: flavourful, fruity, toasty, round tannins.

GAILUR

Avda. Puente del Ebro, 76
01307 Baños del Ebro (Álava)
☎: +34 945 609 158 - Fax: +34 943 835 952
exportgailur@euskalnet.net
www.bodegasgailur.com

SOLAR GAILUR 2010 B
100% viura.

84 Colour: bright straw. Nose: dried flowers, citrus fruit, grassy. Palate: light-bodied, fresh, fruity.

SOLAR GAILUR 2010 RD
40% tempranillo, 60% viura.

85 Colour: brilliant rose. Nose: expressive, red berry notes, floral. Palate: flavourful, fruity, fresh.

GAILUR GARNACHA 2008 TC
100% garnacha.

86 Colour: cherry, garnet rim. Nose: powerfull, ripe fruit, spicy. Palate: fine bitter notes, good acidity.

GONZÁLEZ TESO

El Olmo, 34-36
01330 Labastida (Álava)
☎: +34 656 745 954 - Fax: +34 945 331 321
j.gontes@hotmail.com
www.bodegasgonzalezteso.com

GONTÉS 2010 B
85% viura, 15% maturana blanca.

87 Colour: bright straw. Nose: lactic notes, floral, fruit expression. Palate: flavourful, fresh, fruity, good acidity.

GONTÉS 2010 T
80% tempranillo, 10% garnacha, 5% graciano, 5% mazuelo.

86 Colour: cherry, purple rim. Nose: red berry notes, floral, balsamic herbs, fresh. Palate: light-bodied, fresh, fruity, easy to drink.

GONTÉS 2009 T FERMENTADO EN BARRICA
tempranillo.

86 Colour: cherry, garnet rim. Nose: red berry notes, ripe fruit, sweet spices, creamy oak. Palate: good acidity, flavourful, fruity.

OLMO 34 2008 T
50% tempranillo, 30% garnacha, 20% graciano.

88 Colour: cherry, garnet rim. Nose: wild herbs, red berry notes, ripe fruit, creamy oak. Palate: full, flavourful, fruity, round tannins.

GONTÉS EXPRESIÓN 2007 T
100% tempranillo.

88 Colour: cherry, garnet rim. Nose: overripe fruit, spicy, cocoa bean, toasty. Palate: balanced, flavourful, fruity, round tannins.

GONTÉS 2007 TC
90% tempranillo, 10% garnacha.

87 Colour: cherry, garnet rim. Nose: ripe fruit, spicy, cocoa bean, creamy oak. Palate: flavourful, fleshy, good acidity.

GONTÉS EXPRESIÓN 2005 T
100% tempranillo.

88 Colour: black cherry, garnet rim. Nose: ripe fruit, fine reductive notes, spicy, creamy oak. Palate: powerful, flavourful, fleshy, good acidity, harsh oak tannins.

GRANJA NUESTRA SEÑORA DE REMELLURI

Ctra. Rivas, s/n
01330 Labastida (Álava)
☎: +34 945 331 801 - Fax: +34 945 331 802
info@remelluri.com
www.remelluri.com

REMELLURI 2008 B
8 variedades, 2 autóctonas, 6 del valle del ródano.

92 Colour: bright straw. Nose: elegant, candied fruit, citrus fruit, sweet spices. Palate: flavourful, fruity, good acidity.

REMELLURI 2007 B
8 variedades, 2 autóctonas, 6 del valle del ródano.

93 Colour: bright straw. Nose: expressive, characterful, candied fruit, fresh fruit, citrus fruit. Palate: flavourful, fleshy, complex.

REMELLURI 2007 TR
90% tempranillo, 5% garnacha, 5% graciano.

93 Colour: very deep cherry, garnet rim. Nose: complex, elegant, balanced, ripe fruit, dark chocolate. Palate: fleshy, ripe fruit, round tannins.

REMELLURI 2006 TR
90% tempranillo, 5% garnacha, 5% graciano.

92 Colour: cherry, garnet rim. Nose: ripe fruit, spicy, toasty, complex. Palate: powerful, flavourful, toasty, round tannins.

REMELLURI COLECCIÓN JAIME RODRÍGUEZ 2004 T
70% tempranillo, 25% garnacha, 5% graciano.

93 Colour: black cherry, garnet rim. Nose: ripe fruit, sweet spices, cocoa bean, complex. Palate: powerful, flavourful, fleshy, full.

LA GRANJA REMELLURI 1999 TGR
86% tempranillo, 12% garnacha, 2% graciano.

93 Colour: cherry, garnet rim. Nose: complex, fine reductive notes, spicy, ripe fruit, fruit liqueur notes. Palate: balanced, fine tannins.

GRUPO VINÍCOLA MARQUÉS DE VARGAS

Ctra. Zaragoza, Km. 6
26006 Logroño (La Rioja)
☎: +34 941 261 401 - Fax: +34 941 238 696
bodega@marquesdevargas.com
www.marquesdevargas.com

MARQUÉS DE VARGAS 2006 TR
75% tempranillo, 10% mazuelo, 5% garnacha, 10% otras.

89 Colour: cherry, garnet rim. Nose: elegant, complex, ripe fruit, sweet spices. Palate: flavourful, ripe fruit, round tannins.

MARQUÉS DE VARGAS HACIENDA PRADOLAGAR 2005 TR
60% tempranillo, 10% mazuelo, 10% garnacha, 20% otras.

93 Colour: deep cherry, garnet rim. Nose: ripe fruit, balanced, expressive, spicy. Palate: good structure, round tannins.

MARQUÉS DE VARGAS RESERVA PRIVADA 2005 TR
40% tempranillo, 10% mazuelo, 10% garnacha, 40% otras.

93 Colour: very deep cherry, garnet rim. Nose: complex, balanced, spicy, elegant. Palate: good structure, fine bitter notes, balanced, ripe fruit, round tannins.

GRUPO YLLERA

Autovía A-6, Km. 173, 5
47490 Rueda (Valladolid)
☎: +34 983 868 097 - Fax: +34 983 868 177
grupoyllera@grupoyllera.com
www.grupoyllera.com

COELUS JOVEN 2010 T
tempranillo.

85 Colour: cherry, purple rim. Nose: fruit expression, varietal, balsamic herbs. Palate: flavourful, fresh, easy to drink.

COELUS 2007 TC
tempranillo.

83 Colour: cherry, garnet rim. Nose: ripe fruit, medium intensity, spicy, premature reduction notes. Palate: light-bodied, fine bitter notes, reductive nuances.

COELUS 2004 TR
tempranillo.

84 Colour: cherry, garnet rim. Nose: ripe fruit, expressive, cocoa bean, spicy, toasty, fine reductive notes. Palate: flavourful, fleshy, ripe fruit.

HACIENDA GRIMÓN

Galera, 6
26131 Ventas Blancas (La Rioja)
☎: +34 629 787 525 - Fax: +34 941 482 184
hacienda.grimon@gmail.com
www.haciendagrimon.com

HACIENDA GRIMÓN 2008 TC
85% tempranillo, 10% garnacha, 56% graciano.

90 Colour: cherry, garnet rim. Nose: powerfull, ripe fruit, sweet spices. Palate: spicy, ripe fruit, fine tannins.

LABARONA 2005 TR
85% tempranillo, 10% garnacha, 5% graciano.

90 Colour: cherry, garnet rim. Nose: ripe fruit, spicy, creamy oak. Palate: powerful, flavourful, toasty.

FINCA LA ORACIÓN 2008 T
100% tempranillo.

86 Colour: cherry, garnet rim. Nose: spicy, creamy oak, ripe fruit. Palate: powerful, toasty, round tannins, flavourful, spicy.

FINCA
LA ORACION

ESTE VINO HA SIDO ELABORADO CON LAS MEJORES UVAS DE LA VARIEDAD TEMPRANILLO: BAYAS PEQUEÑAS Y UVAS SUELTAS.

SU MADURACIÓN EN BODEGA Y SU POSTERIOR AFINAMIENTO EN BOTELLA, CONFIEREN A ESTE VINO UNAS CARACTERÍSTICAS SINGULARES.

ES POSIBLE QUE CON EL PASO DEL TIEMPO PUEDA APARECER ALGÚN EXTRACTO NATURAL (BITALTRATOS), POR LO QUE EN ESTE CASO LE ACONSEJAMOS DECANTAR.

LA PRIMERA COSECHA DE ESTE VINO HA SIDO DE 8.432 BOTELLAS.

LE FELICITAMOS POR SER UNA DE LAS POCAS PERSONAS QUE VA A TENER LA OPORTUNIDAD DE DISFRUTAR DE ESTE VINO ÚNICO.

BOTELLA Nº

VIÑEDOS PROPIOS

RIOJA
DENOMINACION DE ORIGEN CALIFICADA

HACIENDA URBIÓN

Santiago Aldaz, s/n
26120 Albelda de Iregua (Rioja)
☎: +34 941 444 233 - Fax: +34 941 444 427
info@vinicolareal.com

URBIÓN CUVEE 2009 T
90% tempranillo, 10% garnacha.

86 Colour: cherry, purple rim. Nose: red berry notes, floral, sweet spices, toasty. Palate: powerful, flavourful, fruity.

URBIÓN 2007 TC
90% tempranillo, 10% garnacha.

87 Colour: cherry, garnet rim. Nose: red berry notes, ripe fruit, spicy, toasty. Palate: powerful, flavourful, fleshy, complex.

HEREDAD UGARTE

Ctra. A-124, Km. 61
01309 Paganos (Álava)
☎: +34 945 282 844 - Fax: +34 945 271 319
info@heredadugarte.com
www.egurenugarte.com

MARTÍN CENDOYA 2007 TR
80% tempranillo, 15% graciano, mazuelo.

91 Colour: cherry, garnet rim. Nose: spicy, creamy oak, toasty, fruit expression, raspberry. Palate: powerful, flavourful, toasty, round tannins.

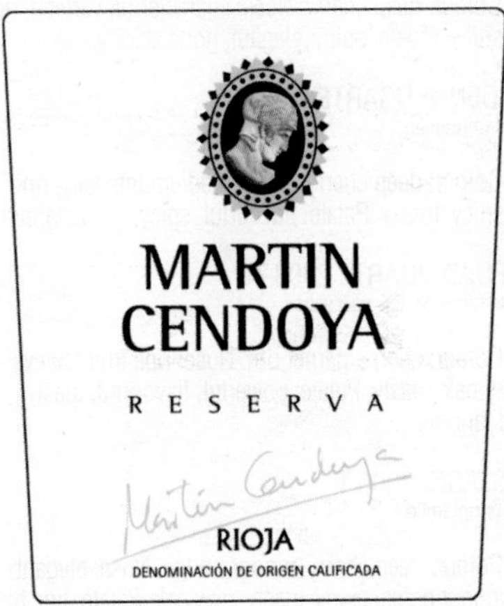

DOMINIO DE UGARTE 2007 TR
95% tempranillo, 5% graciano.

88 Colour: deep cherry. Nose: expressive, balanced, ripe fruit. Palate: flavourful, fine bitter notes, spicy.

MARTÍN CENDOYA MALVASÍA 2010 B
100% malvasía.

88 Colour: bright straw, greenish rim. Nose: wild herbs, fresh fruit, elegant, complex. Palate: fruity, fresh, balanced.

TÉRMINO DE UGARTE 2010 T
100% tempranillo.

89 Colour: cherry, purple rim. Nose: fresh fruit, red berry notes, floral. Palate: flavourful, fruity, good acidity, round tannins.

UGARTE 2009 T
100% tempranillo.

87 Colour: deep cherry. Nose: characterful, varietal, ripe fruit, spicy. Palate: spicy, elegant, good acidity.

CINCUENTA UGARTE 2009 T
100% tempranillo.

85 Colour: deep cherry. Nose: medium intensity, ripe fruit, spicy, toasty. Palate: flavourful, spicy, round tannins.

HEREDAD UGARTE 2008 TC
92% tempranillo, 8% garnacha.

88 Colour: cherry, garnet rim. Nose: ripe fruit, spicy, creamy oak, toasty. Palate: powerful, flavourful, toasty, round tannins.

ANASTASIO 2006 T
100% tempranillo.

91 Colour: deep cherry, orangey edge. Nose: elegant, fruit liqueur notes, spicy, toasty, new oak. Palate: fine bitter notes, flavourful, fine bitter notes.

CEDULA REAL 2003 TGR
90% tempranillo, 10% mazuelo.

89 Colour: cherry, garnet rim. Nose: fruit expression, ripe fruit, sweet spices, creamy oak. Palate: ripe fruit, spicy.

HERMANOS CASTILLO PÉREZ

Camino de la Estación, 15
26330 Briones (La Rioja)
☎: +34 667 730 651 - Fax: +34 941 301 006
info@bodegaszurbal.com
www.bodegaszurbal.com

ZURBAL 2010 B
viura.

87 Colour: pale. Nose: medium intensity, candied fruit, citrus fruit, white flowers. Palate: flavourful, fruity, sweetness.

ZURBAL 2010 RD

88 Colour: cherry, purple rim. Nose: lactic notes, floral, red berry notes, expressive, fresh. Palate: good acidity, complex, flavourful, light-bodied, fleshy.

ZURBAL 2010 T
95% tempranillo, 5% garnacha, mazuelo.

86 Colour: cherry, purple rim. Nose: floral, ripe fruit, raspberry. Palate: flavourful, light-bodied, full.

ZURBAL 2008 TC
95% tempranillo, 5% garnacha, mazuelo.

87 Colour: cherry, garnet rim. Nose: powerfull, ripe fruit, toasty, spicy. Palate: flavourful, spicy, ripe fruit.

HERMANOS FRÍAS DEL VAL

Herrerías, 13
01307 Villabuena (Álava)
☎: +34 945 609 172 - Fax: +34 945 609 172
info@friasdelval.com
www.friasdelval.com

HERMANOS FRÍAS DEL VAL 2010 B
100% viura.

84 Colour: bright yellow. Nose: dried herbs, faded flowers, ripe fruit. Palate: good acidity, correct, flavourful, fruity.

HERMANOS FRÍAS DEL VAL 2009 BFB
100% viura.

86 Colour: bright straw. Nose: ripe fruit, citrus fruit, white flowers. Palate: flavourful, fruity, fresh.

DON PEDUZ 2010 T
100% tempranillo.

90 Colour: cherry, purple rim. Nose: powerfull, red berry notes, raspberry, scrubland. Palate: flavourful, powerful, fleshy.

HERMANOS FRÍAS DEL VAL 2010 T MACERACIÓN CARBÓNICA
90% tempranillo, 10% viura.

86 Colour: bright cherry, purple rim. Nose: red berry notes, balanced, powerfull. Palate: fleshy, ripe fruit, fruity aftestaste.

HERMANOS FRÍAS DEL VAL 2008 TC
100% tempranillo.

88 Colour: deep cherry, garnet rim. Nose: fruit expression, violets. Palate: fruity, flavourful, round tannins.

HERMANOS LAREDO VILLANUEVA C.B.

Mayor, 18
01309 Leza (Álava)
☎: +34 945 605 018 - Fax: +34 945 605 178
bodegaslaredo@telefonica.net
www.bodegaslaredo.com

LAREDO ANAIAK 2010 B
80% viura, 20% malvasía.

82 Colour: bright straw, greenish rim. Nose: medium intensity, fresh. Palate: fresh, easy to drink.

SEÑORÍO DE LAREDO 2003 B RESERVA
50% viura, 50% malvasía.

85 Color bright golden. Aroma ripe fruit, dry nuts, powerfull, toasty, aged wood nuances. Taste flavourful, fruity, spicy, toasty, long.

LAREDO ANAIAK 2009 RD
50% garnacha, 50% tempranillo.

78

LAREDO ANAIAK 2009 T
95% tempranillo, 5% otras.

80 Colour: cherry, purple rim. Nose: floral, ripe fruit, grassy. Palate: flavourful, fruity, good acidity.

EXPRESIÓN DE LAREDO 2006 T
80% tempranillo, 10% graciano, 10% mazuelo.

85 Colour: light cherry, orangey edge. Nose: ripe fruit, cigar, fine reductive notes, spicy, toasty. Palate: good acidity, flavourful, toasty.

SEÑORÍO DE LAREDO 2005 TC
90% tempranillo, 5% graciano, 5% mazuelo.

82 Colour: cherry, garnet rim. Nose: ripe fruit, spicy, toasty, wet leather. Palate: toasty, reductive nuances.

SEÑORÍO DE LAREDO 2004 TR
90% tempranillo, 5% mazuelo, 5% graciano.

83 Colour: pale ruby, brick rim edge. Nose: ripe fruit, wet leather, waxy notes, toasty. Palate: round, flavourful, ripe fruit.

SEÑORÍO DE LAREDO 19988 TGR
80% tempranillo, 10% graciano, 10% mazuelo.

89 Colour: pale ruby, brick rim edge. Nose: fruit liqueur notes, ripe fruit, fine reductive notes, aged wood nuances. Palate: light-bodied, flavourful, long, elegant, spirituous.

JON ZAMALLOA, S.C.

Camino Los Linares, 7
01330 Labastida (Álava)
☎: +34 944 575 091 - Fax: +34 944 575 135
jagoba@zamalloa.net

VIÑA URGOITI 2008 TC
90% tempranillo, 10% graciano.

86 Colour: cherry, purple rim. Nose: sweet spices, creamy oak. Palate: flavourful, fine bitter notes, good acidity.

JUAN CARLOS SANCHA

Finca Fuentelacazuela
C° de Las Barreras, s/n
26320 BAños de Río Tobía (La Rioja)
☎: +34 639 216 011
juancarlossancha@yahoo.es

AD LIBITUM TEMPRANILLO BLANCO 2009 B
tempranillo blanco.

88 Colour: bright straw. Nose: macerated fruit, balsamic herbs, scrubland. Palate: fruity, spicy, fine bitter notes.

AD LIBITUM MATURANA TINTA 2009 T
maturana.

92 Colour: cherry, garnet rim. Nose: ripe fruit, spicy, creamy oak, grassy, balsamic herbs. Palate: powerful, flavourful, toasty, round tannins.

PEÑA EL GATO GARNACHA 2009 T
garnacha.

90 Colour: bright cherry. Nose: ripe fruit, sweet spices, creamy oak. Palate: flavourful, fruity, toasty, round tannins.

LA RIOJA ALTA

Avda. Vizcaya, 8
26200 Haro (La Rioja)
☎: +34 941 310 346 -
Fax: +34 941 312 854
riojalta@riojalta.com
www.riojalta.com

VIÑA ALBERDI 2006 TC
tempranillo.

89 Colour: deep cherry, orangey edge. Nose: aromatic coffee, spicy, toasty, ripe fruit. Palate: toasty, flavourful, fine bitter notes.

VIÑA ARDANZA 2004 TR
80% tempranillo, 20% garnacha.

94 Colour: pale ruby, brick rim edge. Nose: fruit liqueur notes, aromatic coffee, dark chocolate, characterful, expressive. Palate: flavourful, easy to drink, spicy, long.

VIÑA ARANA 2004 TR
95% tempranillo, 95% mazuelo.

92 Colour: pale ruby, brick rim edge. Nose: spicy, fine reductive notes, wet leather, aged wood nuances, fruit liqueur notes. Palate: spicy, fine tannins, elegant, long.

GRAN RESERVA 904 RIOJA ALTA 1998 TGR
90% tempranillo, 10% graciano.

95 Colour: pale ruby, brick rim edge. Nose: aromatic coffee, aged wood nuances, spicy, wet leather, tobacco. Palate: spicy, long, good finish, fine tannins.

LA RIOJA ALTA GRAN RESERVA 890 1995 TGR
95% tempranillo, 3% graciano, 2% mazuelo.

90 Colour: pale ruby, brick rim edge. Nose: elegant, fruit liqueur notes, tobacco, wet leather. Palate: spicy, long, easy to drink.

LAN

Paraje del Buicio, s/n
26360 Fuenmayor (La Rioja)
☎: +34 941 450 950 - Fax: +34 941 450 567
info@bodegaslan.com
www.bodegaslan.com

LAN D-12 2008 T
100% tempranillo.

91 Colour: deep cherry, purple rim. Nose: fruit expression, varietal, balanced. Palate: fruity, flavourful, good acidity, balanced.

LAN A MANO 2007 T
80% tempranillo, 10% mazuelo, 10% graciano.

92 Colour: very deep cherry. Nose: roasted coffee, tobacco, fruit preserve, complex, expressive. Palate: good structure, flavourful, spicy, long.

CULMEN 2005 TR
90% tempranillo, 10% graciano.

94 Colour: black cherry, garnet rim. Nose: complex, expressive, elegant, mineral, cocoa bean. Palate: good structure, complex, fleshy, round tannins, full.

LAN 2005 TR
90% tempranillo, 10% mazuelo.

89 Colour: very deep cherry, garnet rim. Nose: sweet spices, creamy oak, ripe fruit. Palate: flavourful, fruity, round tannins.

VIÑA LANCIANO 2005 TR
85% tempranillo, 15% mazuelo.

89 Colour: deep cherry, garnet rim. Nose: powerfull, characterful, ripe fruit, dark chocolate, sweet spices. Palate: flavourful, fleshy.

LAN 2007 TC
100% tempranillo.

87 Colour: cherry, garnet rim. Nose: spicy, ripe fruit, medium intensity. Palate: flavourful, ripe fruit, easy to drink.

LAN 2003 TGR
85% tempranillo, 10% mazuelo, 5% garnacha.

90 Colour: cherry, garnet rim. Nose: balanced, tobacco, spicy, creamy oak. Palate: ripe fruit, spicy, fruity aftestaste.

LAUNA

Ctra. Vitoria-Logroño, Km. 57
01300 Laguardia (Alava)
☎: +34 605 718 150 - Fax: +34 956 824 108
info@bodegaslauna.com
www.bodegaslauna.com

TEO'S 2008 T
100% tempranillo.

90 Colour: cherry, garnet rim. Nose: red berry notes, ripe fruit, balsamic herbs, cocoa bean, sweet spices, toasty. Palate: good acidity, powerful, flavourful, fleshy, toasty.

LAUNA PLUS 2008 TC
100% tempranillo.

88 Colour: cherry, garnet rim. Nose: powerfull, roasted coffee, fruit expression. Palate: concentrated, harsh oak tannins.

LAUNA PLUS 2007 TR
90% tempranillo, 10% graciano, mazuelo.

90 Colour: cherry, garnet rim. Nose: powerfull, ripe fruit, fruit liqueur notes, roasted coffee. Palate: powerful, concentrated, fine bitter notes.

LAVALLE

Mayor, 51
01309 Navaridas (Álava)
☎: +34 945 605 032 - Fax: +34 945 605 032

LAVALLE 2010 T
95% tempranillo, 5% otras.

86 Colour: deep cherry, purple rim. Nose: ripe fruit, spicy, medium intensity. Palate: fruity, light-bodied, easy to drink.

LONG WINES

Avda. Monte, 46
28723 Algete (Madrid)
☎: +34 916 221 305 - Fax: +34 916 220 029
raquel@longwines.com
www.longwines.com

FINCA MÓNICA 2009 T
100% tempranillo.

88 Colour: cherry, purple rim. Nose: expressive, fresh fruit, red berry notes, floral. Palate: flavourful, fruity, good acidity.

FINCA AMALIA 2007 TC
75% tempranillo, 25% garnacha.

89 Colour: cherry, garnet rim. Nose: fruit liqueur notes, red berry notes, expressive, sweet spices. Palate: fruity, flavourful, toasty.

FINCA AMALIA 2006 TR
75% tempranillo, 25% garnacha, mazuelo.

87 Colour: cherry, garnet rim. Nose: ripe fruit, red berry notes, fine reductive notes, toasty. Palate: good acidity, round, flavourful, fleshy.

FINCA AMALIA T ROBLE
tempranillo.

87 Colour: cherry, garnet rim. Nose: red berry notes, ripe fruit, expressive, cocoa bean, sweet spices, toasty. Palate: good acidity, powerful, flavourful, fleshy.

LUBERRI MONJE AMESTOY

Camino de Rehoyos, s/n
01340 Elciego (Álava)
☎: +34 945 606 010 - Fax: +34 945 606 482
luberri@luberri.com
www.luberri.com

LUBERRI 2010 T MACERACIÓN CARBÓNICA
95% tempranillo, 5% viura.

90 Colour: bright cherry, purple rim. Nose: red berry notes, violets, lactic notes, expressive. Palate: fruity, fresh, good acidity.

BIGA DE LUBERRI 2008 TC
tempranillo.

90 Colour: cherry, garnet rim. Nose: red berry notes, raspberry, ripe fruit, balanced, expressive, cocoa bean, sweet spices. Palate: rich, powerful, flavourful, toasty.

SEIS DE LUBERRI 2008 T
tempranillo.

90 Colour: cherry, purple rim. Nose: red berry notes, floral, balsamic herbs, cocoa bean, sweet spices, toasty. Palate: good acidity, powerful, flavourful, fleshy, long.

LUBERRI CEPAS VIEJAS 2006 TC
tempranillo.

87 Colour: black cherry, garnet rim. Nose: fruit preserve, powerfull, roasted coffee, sweet spices. Palate: good acidity, powerful, flavourful, fleshy.

MONJE AMESTOY 2006 T
95% tempranillo, 5% cabernet sauvignon.

87 Colour: cherry, garnet rim. Nose: ripe fruit, fruit preserve, spicy, toasty, aromatic coffee. Palate: rich, flavourful, long, fleshy, complex.

MAETIERRA DOMINUM

Vara de Rey, 7- 1º dcha.
26003 Logroño (La Rioja)
☎: +34 941 271 217 - Fax: +34 941 272 911
info@maetierradominum.com
www.maetierradominum.com

GAVANZA 2007 T
tempranillo, graciano, garnacha.

87 Colour: cherry, garnet rim. Nose: red berry notes, ripe fruit, scrubland, sweet spices, toasty. Palate: good acidity, powerful, flavourful, fleshy.

MARQUÉS CAMPO NUBLE

Avda. del Ebro, s/n
26540 Alfaro (La Rioja)
☎: +34 941 183 502 - Fax: +34 941 183 157
camponuble@camponuble.com
www.bodegasgarvey.com

CAMPO BURGO 2008 TC
100% tempranillo.

88 Colour: cherry, garnet rim. Nose: ripe fruit, red berry notes, cocoa bean, sweet spices, creamy oak. Palate: ripe fruit, good acidity, spicy.

CONDE DE ROMANONES 2007 TR
tempranillo.

86 Colour: cherry, garnet rim. Nose: ripe fruit, red berry notes, spicy, toasty. Palate: balanced, good acidity, fleshy.

MARQUÉS DE CAMPO NUBLE 2007 TC
90% tempranillo, 10% garnacha.

84 Colour: pale ruby, brick rim edge. Nose: ripe fruit, wet leather, tobacco, toasty. Palate: ripe fruit, flavourful, fleshy.

MARQUÉS DE CAMPO NUBLE 2006 TR
100% tempranillo.

87 Colour: pale ruby, brick rim edge. Nose: fruit liqueur notes, aged wood nuances, sweet spices, toasty, old leather. Palate: good acidity, round, spirituous.

CAMPO BURGO 2006 TR
100% tempranillo.

84 Colour: pale ruby, brick rim edge. Nose: aged wood nuances, fruit liqueur notes, wet leather, medium intensity. Palate: good acidity, unctuous, flavourful.

MARQUÉS DE ARVIZA

Bodegas San Cristóbal, 34 A
26360 Fuenmayor (La Rioja)
☎: +34 941 451 245 - Fax: +34 941 451 246
info@marquesdearviza.es
www.bodegasmarquesdearviza.com

EL TRACTOR VENDIMIA SELECCIONADA 2007 T
75% tempranillo, 25% graciano.

90 Colour: cherry, garnet rim. Nose: red berry notes, ripe fruit, mineral, sweet spices, creamy oak. Palate: good acidity, powerful, flavourful, toasty.

MARQUÉS DE ARVIZA 2006 TC
90% tempranillo, 5% graciano, 5% garnacha.

85 Colour: bright cherry, garnet rim. Nose: sweet spices, balsamic herbs, ripe fruit, toasty. Palate: balanced, powerful, flavourful.

MARQUÉS DE ARVIZA 2005 TR
90% tempranillo, 10% garnacha.

83 Colour: deep cherry, orangey edge. Nose: ripe fruit, scrubland, sweet spices, cocoa bean. Palate: good acidity, complex, flavourful, spicy.

MARQUÉS DE CÁCERES

Ctra. Logroño, s/n
26350 Cenicero (La Rioja)
☎: +34 941 454 000
- Fax: +34 941 454 400
marquesdecaceres@fer.es
www.marquesdecaceres.com

MARQUÉS DE CÁCERES 2010 B
100% viura.

86 Colour: bright straw. Nose: white flowers, citrus fruit, fresh fruit. Palate: fresh, fruity, light-bodied, flavourful.

SATINELA SEMI-DULCE 2010 B
93% viura, 7% malvasía.

86 Colour: bright straw. Nose: fruit preserve, fruit expression, citrus fruit. Palate: flavourful, fruity, fresh.

MARQUÉS DE CÁCERES ANTEA 2009 BFB
93% viura, 7% malvasía.

87 Colour: bright straw. Nose: fresh fruit, citrus fruit, grassy, faded flowers, sweet spices. Palate: flavourful, fruity, fleshy.

MARQUÉS DE CÁCERES 2010 RD
85% tempranillo, 15% garnacha.

88 Colour: brilliant rose. Nose: elegant, candied fruit, dried flowers, fragrant herbs. Palate: light-bodied, flavourful, good acidity, long, spicy.

MC MARQUÉS DE CÁCERES 2009 T
100% tempranillo.

93 Colour: cherry, garnet rim. Nose: spicy, toasty, complex, fruit preserve. Palate: powerful, toasty, round tannins, fine bitter notes.

MARQUÉS DE CÁCERES 2008 TC
85% tempranillo, 10% garnacha, 5% graciano.

90 Colour: cherry, garnet rim. Nose: ripe fruit, fruit expression, toasty, spicy. Palate: flavourful, fleshy, spicy, ripe fruit.

MARQUÉS DE CÁCERES 2007 TC
85% tempranillo, 10% garnacha, 5% graciano.

89 Colour: cherry, garnet rim. Nose: ripe fruit, spicy, creamy oak, toasty. Palate: powerful, flavourful, toasty, round tannins.

MARQUÉS DE CÁCERES 2005 TR
85% tempranillo, 10% garnacha, 5% graciano.

92 Colour: cherry, garnet rim. Nose: spicy, creamy oak, toasty, ripe fruit, mineral. Palate: powerful, flavourful, toasty, round tannins.

MARQUÉS DE CÁCERES 2004 TGR
85% tempranillo, 10% garnacha, 5% graciano.

93 Colour: deep cherry. Nose: powerfull, dark chocolate, cocoa bean, new oak, ripe fruit. Palate: flavourful, powerful, fleshy, balanced.

MARQUÉS DE GRIÑÓN

Ctra. de El Ciego, s/n
26350 Cenicero (La Rioja)
☎: +34 914 365 924
gromero@arcoinvest-group.com
www.marquesdegrinon.com

MARQUÉS DE GRIÑÓN ALEA 2009 T
100% tempranillo.

86 Colour: cherry, garnet rim. Nose: ripe fruit, toasty, cedar wood. Palate: flavourful, fruity, fleshy.

MARQUÉS DE GRIÑÓN ALEA 2007 T
100% tempranillo.

89 Colour: cherry, garnet rim. Nose: powerfull, varietal, ripe fruit. Palate: ripe fruit, long, fleshy, full, round tannins.

MARQUÉS DE GRIÑÓN COLECCIÓN PRIVADA 2007 TC
100% tempranillo.

88 Colour: deep cherry, garnet rim. Nose: balanced, expressive, ripe fruit, sweet spices. Palate: flavourful, fruity, spicy.

MARQUÉS DE LA CONCORDIA FAMILY OF WINES

Ctra. El Ciego, s/n
26350 Cenicero (La Rioja)
☎: +34 914 365 924
gromero@arcoinvest-group.com
www.haciendas-espana.com

HACIENDA SUSAR 2007 T
100% tempranillo.

90 Colour: black cherry, purple rim. Nose: toasty, spicy, ripe fruit. Palate: fleshy, good structure, powerful, ripe fruit.

MARQUÉS DE LA CONCORDIA 2007 TC
100% tempranillo.

88 Colour: cherry, garnet rim. Nose: creamy oak, toasty, expressive, ripe fruit. Palate: powerful, flavourful, toasty, round tannins.

MARQUÉS DE LA CONCORDIA 2005 TR
100% tempranillo.

87 Colour: cherry, garnet rim. Nose: ripe fruit, old leather, spicy, varietal. Palate: flavourful, good structure, round tannins.

MARQUÉS DE MURRIETA

Finca Ygay- Ctra. N-232 Logroño-Zaragoza, PK 403
26006 Logroño (La Rioja)
☎: +34 941 271 374 - Fax: +34 941 251 606
rrpp@marquesdemurrieta.com
www.marquesdemurrieta.com

CAPELLANIA 2006 B
100% viura.

93 Colour: bright straw. Nose: sweet spices, cocoa bean, ripe fruit. Palate: spicy, ripe fruit, round tannins, long.

CAPELLANIA 2005 B
100% viura.

94 Colour: bright golden. Nose: ripe fruit, dry nuts, powerfull, toasty, aged wood nuances, acetaldehyde. Palate: flavourful, fruity, spicy, toasty, long.

MARQUÉS DE MURRIETA 2007 TR
85% tempranillo, 8% garnacha, 6% mazuelo, 1% graciano.

92 Colour: cherry, garnet rim. Nose: fruit expression, expressive, elegant, sweet spices, creamy oak. Palate: flavourful, fruity, fleshy, complex, harsh oak tannins.

MARQUÉS DE MURRIETA 2005 TR
84% tempranillo, 13% garnacha, 3% mazuelo.

93 Colour: cherry, garnet rim. Nose: complex, elegant, fruit expression, earthy notes, sweet spices, creamy oak. Palate: flavourful, ripe fruit, long, fine tannins.

DALMAU 2005 TR
92% tempranillo, 4% cabernet sauvignon, 4% graciano.

96 Colour: deep cherry. Nose: powerfull, characterful, ripe fruit, dark chocolate, sweet spices, new oak. Palate: flavourful, powerful, fleshy, round, round tannins.

DALMAU 2007 TR
85% tempranillo, 8% cabernet sauvignon, 7% graciano.

97 Colour: very deep cherry. Nose: mineral, fruit expression, creamy oak, sweet spices, dark chocolate. Palate: flavourful, powerful, fine bitter notes, round tannins.

MARQUÉS DE MURRIETA 2006 TR
88% tempranillo, 7% mazuelo, 3% garnacha, 2% graciano.

91 Colour: cherry, garnet rim. Nose: spicy, creamy oak, fruit preserve, ripe fruit. Palate: flavourful, fleshy, ripe fruit, round tannins.

CASTILLO YGAY 2001 TGR
93% tempranillo, 7% mazuelo.

97 Colour: pale ruby, brick rim edge. Nose: elegant, spicy, fine reductive notes, wet leather, aged wood nuances, fruit liqueur notes, aromatic coffee. Palate: spicy, fine tannins, elegant, long.

CASTILLO YGAY 2004 TGR
93% tempranillo, 7% mazuelo.

95 Colour: cherry, garnet rim. Nose: wet leather, ripe fruit, candied fruit, sweet spices, aromatic coffee. Palate: fine bitter notes, ripe fruit, spicy, long, good acidity.

MARQUÉS DE REINOSA

Ctra. Rincón de Soto, s/n
26560 Autol (La Rioja)
☎: +34 941 401 327 - Fax: +34 941 390 065
bodegas@marquesdereinosa.com
www.marquesdereinosa.com

MARQUÉS DE REINOSA 2010 B
95% viura, 5% verdejo.

86 Colour: bright straw. Nose: dried flowers, fresh, medium intensity, wild herbs. Palate: balanced, good acidity, correct.

MARQUÉS DE REINOSA 2010 RD
100% garnacha.

83 Colour: rose, purple rim. Nose: ripe fruit, faded flowers, dried herbs. Palate: fleshy, short, light-bodied.

MARQUÉS DE REINOSA TEMPRANILLO 2010 T
100% tempranillo.

89 Colour: cherry, purple rim. Nose: medium intensity, red berry notes, balanced. Palate: fruity, round tannins, good acidity.

MARQUÉS DE REINOSA 2008 TC
100% tempranillo.

87 Colour: cherry, garnet rim. Nose: medium intensity, ripe fruit, spicy, toasty. Palate: flavourful, fleshy, long.

MARQUÉS DE REINOSA 2004 TGR
tempranillo.

88 Colour: cherry, garnet rim. Nose: ripe fruit, spicy, creamy oak, complex. Palate: powerful, flavourful, toasty, round tannins.

MARQUÉS DE TOMARES, UNIÓN DE VITICULTORES RIOJANOS

Ctra. de Cenicero, s/n- Apdo. Correos, 3
26360 Fuenmayor (La Rioja)
☎: +34 941 451 129 - Fax: +34 941 450 297
info@marquesdetomares.com
www.marquesdetomares.es

MARQUÉS DE TOMARES EXCELLENCE 3F 2009 T
90% tempranillo, 10% graciano.

90 Colour: bright cherry. Nose: ripe fruit, sweet spices, creamy oak. Palate: flavourful, fruity, toasty, round tannins.

MARQUÉS DE TOMARES 2008 TC
90% tempranillo, 7% mazuelo, 3% graciano.

87 Colour: cherry, garnet rim. Nose: ripe fruit, spicy, creamy oak. Palate: powerful, flavourful, toasty, round tannins.

MARQUÉS DE TOMARES DOÑA CARMEN 2005 TR
90% graciano, 10% tempranillo.

88 Colour: bright cherry. Nose: ripe fruit, sweet spices, creamy oak. Palate: flavourful, fruity, toasty, round tannins.

MARQUÉS DEL PUERTO

Ctra. de Logroño, s/n
26360 Fuenmayor (La Rioja)
☎: +34 941 450 001 - Fax: +34 941 450 051
bmp@mbrizard.com
www.mariebrizard.com

MARQUÉS DEL PUERTO 2010 B JOVEN
100% viura.

84 Colour: bright straw, greenish rim. Nose: fresh fruit, white flowers, medium intensity. Palate: fruity, fresh.

MARQUÉS DEL PUERTO 2009 BFB
100% viura.

85 Colour: bright yellow. Nose: ripe fruit, sweet spices, creamy oak. Palate: rich, flavourful, fresh, good acidity.

MARQUÉS DEL PUERTO 2010 RD
50% tempranillo, 50% garnacha.

86 Colour: rose, purple rim. Nose: lactic notes, red berry notes, fresh fruit, floral. Palate: fleshy, fresh, fruity, light-bodied, flavourful.

MARQUÉS DEL PUERTO 2008 TC
90% tempranillo, 10% mazuelo.

83 Colour: light cherry, orangey edge. Nose: ripe fruit, wet leather, fine reductive notes. Palate: powerful, round, long.

BENTUS 2005 TR
80% tempranillo, 20% mazuelo, graciano, garnacha.

85 Colour: cherry, garnet rim. Nose: ripe fruit, spicy, toasty, old leather. Palate: powerful, flavourful, toasty, ripe fruit.

MARQUÉS DEL PUERTO 2005 TR
90% tempranillo, 10% mazuelo.

84 Colour: pale ruby, brick rim edge. Nose: ripe fruit, fruit liqueur notes, fruit liqueur notes, fine reductive notes. Palate: good acidity, balanced, flavourful.

MARQUÉS DEL PUERTO 2001 TGR
92% tempranillo, 6% mazuelo, 2% graciano.

86 Colour: pale ruby, brick rim edge. Nose: fruit liqueur notes, aged wood nuances, spicy, toasty. Palate: good acidity, correct, flavourful, fleshy.

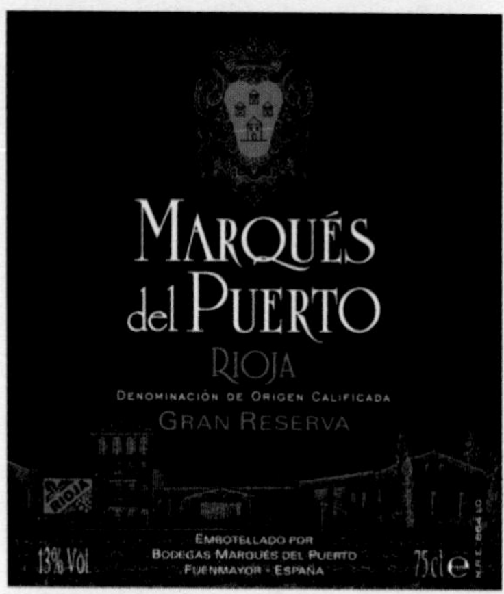

ROMÁN PALADINO 1995 TGR
88% tempranillo, 7% mazuelo, 5% graciano.

87 Color pale ruby, brick rim edge. Aroma elegant, spicy, fine reductive notes, wet leather, aged wood nuances, fruit liqueur notes. Taste spicy, fine tannins, elegant, long.

MARTÍNEZ LACUESTA

Paraje de Ubieta, s/n
26200 Haro (La Rioja)
☎: +34 941 310 050 - Fax: +34 941 303 748
bodega@martinezlacuesta.com
www.martinezlacuesta.com

HINIA 2009 T
100% tempranillo.

92 Colour: cherry, garnet rim. Nose: spicy, creamy oak, toasty, complex, fruit expression, mineral. Palate: powerful, flavourful, toasty, round tannins.

MARTÍNEZ LACUESTA 2008 TC
80% tempranillo, 15% graciano, 5% mazuelo.

90 Colour: cherry, garnet rim. Nose: ripe fruit, fine reductive notes, cocoa bean, sweet spices. Palate: spicy, flavourful, fleshy, ripe fruit.

CAMPEADOR 2005 TR
tempranillo, garnacha.

88 Colour: deep cherry. Nose: ripe fruit, fruit expression, aromatic coffee, sweet spices. Palate: flavourful, spicy, ripe fruit.

MAYORAZGO ZACARÍAS DE BIVIAN

Plazuela Campillo, 1
26214 Cuzcurrita de Río Tirón (La Rioja)
☎: +34 941 301 625 - Fax: +34 941 311 866
info@zacariasbivian.com
www.zacariasbivian.com

ZACARIAS DE BIVIAN 2005 TR
tempranillo, garnacha.

84 Colour: cherry, garnet rim. Nose: aged wood nuances, spicy, ripe fruit, expressive. Palate: powerful, flavourful, reductive nuances.

MIGUEL ÁNGEL MURO

Avda. Gasteiz, 29
01306 Lapuebla de Labarca (Álava)
☎: +34 945 607 081 - Fax: +34 945 607 081
info@bodegasmiguelangelmuro.com
www.bodegasmuro.com

MIGUEL ÁNGEL MURO 2010 T
85% tempranillo, 15% viura.

82 Colour: cherry, purple rim. Nose: red berry notes, medium intensity. Palate: fruity, light-bodied, good acidity.

AMENITAL 2009 TC
40% tempranillo, 40% graciano, 20% maturana.

91 Colour: cherry, purple rim. Nose: red berry notes, raspberry, complex, powerfull, cocoa bean, sweet spices, toasty. Palate: fruity, powerful, flavourful, toasty.

MURO BUJANDA 2007 TC
100% tempranillo.

90 Colour: cherry, garnet rim. Nose: ripe fruit, balsamic herbs, dark chocolate, cocoa bean, toasty. Palate: good acidity, flavourful, round tannins.

AMENITAL 2007 TC
70% tempranillo, 30% graciano.

88 Colour: cherry, garnet rim. Nose: ripe fruit, fragrant herbs, caramel, toasty. Palate: balanced, powerful, fleshy, round tannins.

MURO 2006 TR
80% tempranillo, 20% graciano.

88 Colour: cherry, garnet rim. Nose: red berry notes, ripe fruit, sweet spices, toasty. Palate: fleshy, complex, toasty, round.

MONTECILLO

Ctra. Navarrete-Fuenmayor, Km. 2
26360 Fuenmayor (La Rioja)
☎: +34 956 869 000 - Fax: +34 956 869 026
comunicaciones@osborne.es
www.osborne.es

VIÑA MONTY 2008 TC
tempranillo.

87 Colour: light cherry, garnet rim. Nose: ripe fruit, sweet spices, toasty. Palate: powerful, flavourful, toasty.

MONTECILLO 2007 TC
tempranillo.

88 Colour: light cherry, garnet rim. Nose: ripe fruit, old leather, spicy. Palate: flavourful, fleshy, toasty.

CUMBRE MONTECILLO 2006 TR
tempranillo.

91 Colour: dark-red cherry, garnet rim. Nose: ripe fruit, elegant, spicy, creamy oak. Palate: powerful, flavourful, fleshy, complex, round tannins.

VIÑA MONTY 2006 TR
tempranillo.

90 Colour: cherry, garnet rim. Nose: ripe fruit, balsamic herbs, sweet spices, fine reductive notes. Palate: good acidity, round, flavourful, toasty.

MONTECILLO 2006 TR
tempranillo.

87 Colour: light cherry, garnet rim. Nose: ripe fruit, toasty, sweet spices. Palate: powerful, flavourful, toasty, round tannins.

MONTECILLO SELECCIÓN ESPECIAL 2003 TGR
tempranillo.

89 Colour: light cherry, orangey edge. Nose: ripe fruit, old leather, spicy, toasty, expressive. Palate: round, fleshy, round tannins.

OLIVIER RIVIÈRE VINOS

Pepe Blanco, 6
26140 Lardero (La Rioja)
☎: +34 690 733 541 - Fax: +34 941 452 476
olive_riviere@yahoo.fr

JEQUITIBÁ 2010 B
viura, garnacha blanca, malvasía.

90 Colour: bright straw. Nose: fresh, fresh fruit, white flowers. Palate: flavourful, fruity, good acidity, fine bitter notes.

RAYOS UVA 2010 T
tempranillo, graciano.

90 Colour: cherry, purple rim. Nose: fresh fruit, red berry notes, floral, expressive, lactic notes, mineral. Palate: flavourful, fruity, good acidity, round tannins, light-bodied.

GANKO 2009 T
tempranillo, garnacha, mazuelo, graciano.

91 Colour: cherry, purple rim. Nose: red berry notes, raspberry, mineral, spicy, balanced, expressive. Palate: fresh, fruity, powerful, flavourful, complex.

PAGO DE LARREA

Ctra. Elciego-Cenicero, Km. 1,2
01340 Elciego (Álava)
☎: +34 945 606 063 - Fax: +34 945 606 697
bodega@pagodelarrea.com
www.pagodelarrea.com

CAECUS VERDERÓN 2010 BFB
95% viura, 5% malvasía.

88 Colour: bright straw. Nose: powerfull, candied fruit, toasty. Palate: flavourful, spicy, ripe fruit.

CAECUS 2010 T
90% tempranillo, 10% garnacha.

88 Colour: cherry, purple rim. Nose: varietal, ripe fruit. Palate: flavourful, fleshy, powerful.

CAECUS 2008 TC
100% tempranillo.

86 Colour: deep cherry, garnet rim. Nose: cocoa bean, creamy oak, sweet spices. Palate: fleshy, spicy, ripe fruit.

CAECUS 2006 TR
100% tempranillo.

87 Colour: deep cherry, purple rim. Nose: spicy, old leather, balanced, varietal. Palate: flavourful, ripe fruit, long.

PAGOS DEL REY S.L.

Ctra. N-232, PK 422,7
26360 Fuenmayor (La Rioja)
☎: +34 941 450 818 - Fax: +34 941 450 818
pdr@pagosdelrey.com
www.pagosdelrey.com

ARNEGUI 2010 B
100% viura.

86 Nose: fresh, fresh fruit, white flowers, candied fruit. Palate: flavourful, fruity, correct, easy to drink.

ARNEGUI 2010 RD
garnacha.

85 Colour: brilliant rose. Nose: fresh, medium intensity, dried herbs. Palate: fruity, flavourful, correct, good acidity.

ARNEGUI 2010 T
tempranillo.

87 Colour: cherry, purple rim. Nose: red berry notes, grapey, floral, expressive. Palate: fleshy, light-bodied, fruity.

CASTILLO DE ALBAI 2010 T
tempranillo.

87 Colour: cherry, purple rim. Nose: balsamic herbs, red berry notes, expressive. Palate: good acidity, fresh, fruity.

CASTILLO DE ALBAI 2008 TC
tempranillo.

88 Colour: cherry, garnet rim. Nose: ripe fruit, powerfull, expressive, toasty. Palate: good acidity, flavourful, fleshy.

ARNEGUI 2008 TC
tempranillo.

87 Colour: cherry, garnet rim. Nose: ripe fruit, balsamic herbs, fine reductive notes, spicy, toasty. Palate: powerful, flavourful, complex, toasty.

CASTILLO DE ALBAI 2006 TR
tempranillo.

86 Colour: pale ruby, brick rim edge. Nose: ripe fruit, sweet spices, creamy oak, expressive. Palate: flavourful, fruity, toasty, round tannins.

ARNEGUI 2006 TR
tempranillo.

84 Colour: cherry, garnet rim. Nose: ripe fruit, spicy, creamy oak. Palate: powerful, flavourful, toasty, round tannins.

PAISAJES Y VIÑEDOS

Pza. Ibarra, 1
26330 Briones (La Rioja)
☎: +34 941 322 301 - Fax: +34 941 322 302
comunicacio@vilaviniteca.es

PAISAJES VIII LA PASADA 2008 T
100% tempranillo.

91 Colour: bright cherry. Nose: sweet spices, creamy oak, expressive, fruit preserve. Palate: flavourful, fruity, toasty, round tannins.

PAISAJES V VALSALADO 2008 T
tempranillo, garnacha, mazuelo, graciano.

89 Colour: deep cherry. Nose: dark chocolate, sweet spices, ripe fruit, earthy notes. Palate: flavourful, powerful, fleshy, fine bitter notes.

PAISAJES CECIAS T
garnacha.

86 Colour: very deep cherry. Nose: overripe fruit, spicy, toasty. Palate: concentrated, sweetness.

PATERNINA

Avda. Santo Domingo, 11
26200 Haro (La Rioja)
☎: +34 941 310 550 - Fax: +34 941 312 778
paternina@paternina.com
www.paternina.com

BANDA DORADA 2010 B
viura.

85 Colour: bright straw. Nose: ripe fruit, white flowers, wild herbs. Palate: fleshy, flavourful, fruity.

CONDE DE LOS ANDES 2001 B
viura, malvasía.

90 Colour: bright golden. Nose: ripe fruit, dry nuts, powerfull, toasty, aged wood nuances, petrol notes. Palate: flavourful, fruity, spicy, toasty, long.

BANDA ROSA 2010 RD
garnacha, viura.

85 Colour: rose, purple rim. Nose: powerfull, ripe fruit, red berry notes, floral. Palate: fleshy, fruity, fresh.

MONTE HARO "TEMPRANILLO" 2009 T
tempranillo.

87 Colour: cherry, garnet rim. Nose: powerfull, ripe fruit, roasted coffee. Palate: long, spicy, ripe fruit.

PATERNINA SELECCIÓN ESPECIAL 2008 T

88 Colour: cherry, garnet rim. Nose: ripe fruit, wet leather, spicy, toasty. Palate: flavourful, fleshy, round.

PATERNINA BANDA ORO 2007 TC
tempranillo, garnacha, mazuelo.

88 Colour: cherry, garnet rim. Nose: spicy, toasty, fruit liqueur notes. Palate: powerful, flavourful, toasty, round tannins.

PATERNINA BANDA AZUL 2007 TC
tempranillo, garnacha, mazuelo.

86 Colour: cherry, garnet rim. Nose: spicy, creamy oak, toasty, fruit liqueur notes. Palate: powerful, toasty, round tannins.

CONDES DE LOS ANDES 2005 TR
tempranillo, garnacha, mazuelo.

90 Colour: cherry, garnet rim. Nose: ripe fruit, spicy, fine reductive notes. Palate: complex, flavourful, aged character, ripe fruit.

PATERNINA BANDA ROJA 2005 TR
tempranillo, garnacha, mazuelo.

88 Colour: cherry, garnet rim. Nose: ripe fruit, spicy, creamy oak, toasty. Palate: flavourful, toasty, round tannins.

CONDES DE LOS ANDES 2004 TGR
tempranillo, mazuelo, graciano.

91 Colour: cherry, garnet rim. Nose: complex, tobacco, fine reductive notes. Palate: balanced, complex, fine tannins, spicy.

GRACIELA BLANCO DULCE RESERVA
viura, malvasía.

83 Colour: bright golden. Nose: ripe fruit, grapey, fruit liqueur notes. Palate: balanced, good acidity, sweetness.

R. LÓPEZ DE HEREDIA VIÑA TONDONIA

Avda. Vizcaya, 3
26200 Haro (La Rioja)
☎: +34 941 310 244 - Fax: +34 941 310 788
bodega@lopezdeheredia.com
www.tondonia.com

VIÑA TONDONIA 1997 B RESERVA
90% viura, 10% malvasía.

90 Colour: bright golden. Nose: ripe fruit, dry nuts, powerfull, toasty, aged wood nuances. Palate: flavourful, spicy, toasty, long, ripe fruit.

VIÑA TONDONIA 2001 TR
75% tempranillo, 15% garnacha, 10% graciano, mazuelo.

92 Colour: pale ruby, brick rim edge. Nose: cedar wood, sweet spices, ripe fruit, wild herbs, waxy notes. Palate: powerful, flavourful, spicy, smoky aftertaste.

RAMÓN DE AYALA LETE E HIJOS

Fuentecilla, s/n
26290 Briñas (La Rioja)
☎: +34 941 310 575 - Fax: +34 941 312 544
bodegas@rayalaehijos.com

VIÑA SANTURNIA 2010 B
90% viura, 10% garnacha blanca.

85 Colour: bright straw. Nose: fragrant herbs, fresh, medium intensity. Palate: light-bodied, fresh, easy to drink.

VIÑA SANTURNIA 2010 T
100% tempranillo.

87 Colour: cherry, purple rim. Nose: powerfull, ripe fruit. Palate: flavourful, good acidity, fine bitter notes.

VIÑA SANTURNIA 2007 TC
100% tempranillo.

88 Colour: bright cherry. Nose: ripe fruit, sweet spices. Palate: flavourful, fruity, toasty, round tannins.

DEÓBRIGA COLECCIÓN PRIVADA 2007 T
60% tempranillo, 40% graciano.

88 Colour: cherry, garnet rim. Nose: ripe fruit, toasty, dark chocolate. Palate: spicy, ripe fruit, round tannins.

DEÓBRIGA SELECCIÓN FAMILIAR 2005 T
tempranillo, graciano.

87 Colour: deep cherry. Nose: ripe fruit, toasty, spicy, dark chocolate. Palate: powerful, fleshy, spicy, round tannins.

VIÑA SANTURNIA 2005 TR
90% tempranillo, 5% graciano, 5% mazuelo.

87 Colour: deep cherry. Nose: powerfull, ripe fruit, sweet spices, toasty. Palate: flavourful, powerful, fleshy.

RIOJA VEGA

Ctra. Logroño-Mendavia, Km. 92
31230 Viana (Navarra)
☎: +34 948 646 263 - Fax: +34 948 645 612
info@riojavega.com
www.riojavega.com

RIOJA VEGA G Y G 2010 T
50% garnacha, 50% graciano.

88 Colour: cherry, purple rim. Nose: red berry notes, dried flowers, balsamic herbs, expressive, complex. Palate: good acidity, correct, fruity, fresh, flavourful.

RIOJA VEGA 9 BARRICAS 2008 T
50% tempranillo, 25% mazuelo, 25% graciano.

88 Colour: cherry, garnet rim. Nose: ripe fruit, spicy, creamy oak, roasted coffee. Palate: powerful, flavourful, toasty, round tannins.

RIOJA VEGA 2008 TC
80% tempranillo, 15% garnacha, 5% mazuelo.

87 Colour: cherry, garnet rim. Nose: ripe fruit, spicy, toasty. Palate: powerful, flavourful, toasty, round tannins.

RIOJA VEGA 2006 TR
85% tempranillo, 10% graciano, 5% mazuelo.

87 Colour: cherry, garnet rim. Nose: toasty, spicy, aromatic coffee, ripe fruit. Palate: spicy, ripe fruit, round tannins.

RIOJA VEGA 2001 TGR
75% tempranillo, 20% graciano, 5% mazuelo.

87 Colour: cherry, garnet rim. Nose: powerfull, ripe fruit, sweet spices, cigar. Palate: flavourful, powerful, spicy, ripe fruit.

RODRÍGUEZ SANZO

Manuel Azaña, 9- Local 15
47014 Valladolid (Valladolid)
☎: +34 983 150 150 - Fax: +34 983 150 151
valsanzo@valsanzo.com
www.valsanzo.com

LACRIMUS 2008 TC
85% tempranillo, 15% graciano.

91 Colour: cherry, garnet rim. Nose: ripe fruit, spicy, creamy oak, roasted coffee. Palate: powerful, flavourful, toasty, round tannins.

LA SENOBA 2008 T
50% tempranillo, 50% graciano.

90 Colour: cherry, garnet rim. Nose: powerfull, ripe fruit, scrubland, spicy, toasty. Palate: balanced, flavourful, fruity aftestaste, long.

SANTAMARÍA LÓPEZ

Ctra. Elvillar, s/n
01300 Laguardia (Álava)
☎: +34 945 621 212 - Fax: +34 945 621 222
santamaria@santamarialopez.com
www.santamarialopez.com

ANGEL SANTAMARÍA 2008 BFB
viura, malvasía.

86 Colour: bright straw. Nose: citrus fruit, slightly evolved, spicy. Palate: powerful, fine bitter notes, sweetness.

EDITOR 2010 T
tempranillo.

85 Colour: cherry, purple rim. Nose: medium intensity, characterful, ripe fruit, grassy. Palate: flavourful, fleshy, good acidity.

EDITOR 2008 TC
tempranillo.

88 Colour: cherry, garnet rim. Nose: powerfull, ripe fruit, cedar wood, sweet spices. Palate: powerful, spicy, ripe fruit.

ANGEL SANTAMARÍA VENDIMIA SELECCIONADA 2006 T
tempranillo.

87 Colour: deep cherry. Nose: fruit preserve, creamy oak, varnish. Palate: powerful, fine bitter notes, spicy.

ANGEL SANTAMARÍA VENDIMIA SELECCIONADA 2005 TR
tempranillo.

89 Colour: cherry, garnet rim. Nose: spicy, creamy oak, toasty, fruit preserve. Palate: powerful, toasty, round tannins.

SDAD. COOP. BODEGA SAN MIGUEL

Ctra. de Zaragoza, 7
26513 Ausejo (La Rioja)
☎: +34 941 430 005 - Fax: +34 941 430 209
robertomonfor@hotmail.com

CAMPOLOSA 2010 T
100% tempranillo.

88 Colour: cherry, purple rim. Nose: fresh fruit, floral, varietal, fruit expression. Palate: flavourful, fruity, good acidity, round tannins.

CAMPOLOSA 2008 TC
90% tempranillo, 10% garnacha.

86 Colour: cherry, garnet rim. Nose: ripe fruit, spicy, creamy oak, toasty, complex. Palate: powerful, flavourful, toasty.

HEBE 2007 TC
100% tempranillo.

86 Colour: cherry, purple rim. Nose: ripe fruit, red berry notes, balsamic herbs, sweet spices. Palate: good acidity, fruity, powerful, flavourful.

CAMPOLOSA 2004 TR
100% tempranillo.

88 Color cherry, garnet rim. Aroma ripe fruit, spicy, creamy oak, toasty, complex. Taste powerful, flavourful, toasty, round tannins.

SEÑORÍO DE ARANA

La Cadena, 20
01330 Labastida (Álava)
☎: +34 945 331 150 - Fax: +34 944 212 738
info@senoriodearana.com
www.senoriodearana.com

VIÑA DEL OJA 2010 T
100% tempranillo.

87 Colour: cherry, purple rim. Nose: ripe fruit, fruit expression, red berry notes. Palate: powerful, flavourful, fine bitter notes.

VIÑA DEL OJA 2007 TC
90% tempranillo, 10% mazuelo.

86 Colour: cherry, garnet rim. Nose: ripe fruit, spicy, toasty. Palate: powerful, flavourful, toasty, round tannins.

VIÑA DEL OJA 2004 TR
90% tempranillo, 5% mazuelo, 5% graciano.

89 Colour: deep cherry, garnet rim. Nose: complex, powerfull, ripe fruit, sweet spices, dark chocolate. Palate: concentrated, flavourful, round tannins.

SEÑORÍO DE SAN VICENTE

Los Remedios, 27
26338 San Vicente de la Sonsierra (La Rioja)
☎: +34 902 334 080 - Fax: +34 945 600 885
info@eguren.com
www.eguren.com

SAN VICENTE 2008 T
100% tempranillo.

96 Colour: dark-red cherry. Nose: cocoa bean, sweet spices, characterful, complex, mineral, elegant, ripe fruit. Palate: flavourful, powerful, good acidity, spicy.

SAN VICENTE 2007 T
100% tempranillo.

95 Colour: cherry, garnet rim. Nose: ripe fruit, spicy, toasty, complex, medium intensity, fine reductive notes, new oak. Palate: powerful, flavourful, toasty, round tannins.

SEÑORÍO DE ULÍA

Paraje del Buicio, s/n
26360 Fuenmayor (La Rioja)
☎: +34 941 450 567 - Fax: +34 941 450 567
info@marquesdeulia.com

MARQUÉS DE ULÍA 2007 TC
100% tempranillo.

88 Color cherry, garnet rim. Aroma ripe fruit, spicy, creamy oak, toasty, complex. Taste powerful, flavourful, toasty, round tannins.

MARQUÉS DE ULÍA 2005 TR
tempranillo, mazuelo.

89 Colour: cherry, garnet rim. Nose: medium intensity, sweet spices, cocoa bean, ripe fruit. Palate: flavourful, good acidity, spicy.

LA VENDIMIA MARQUÉS DE ULÍA 2005 T
tempranillo, graciano.

88 Colour: cherry, garnet rim. Nose: spicy, ripe fruit, balanced, complex. Palate: ripe fruit, long, round tannins.

SIERRA CANTABRIA

Amorebieta, 3
26338 San Vicente de la Sonsierra (La Rioja)
☎: +34 902 334 080 - Fax: +34 941 334 371
info@eguren.com
www.eguren.com

SIERRA CANTABRIA ORGANZA 2010 B
viura, malvasía, garnacha.

93 Colour: bright straw. Nose: powerfull, expressive, white flowers, ripe fruit, wild herbs. Palate: long, fruity, complex, powerful.

SIERRA CANTABRIA ORGANZA 2009 B
viura, malvasía, garnacha blanca.

93 Colour: bright straw. Nose: powerfull, ripe fruit, scrubland, mineral, dried flowers. Palate: flavourful, fruity, balanced.

MURMURÓN 2010 T
100% tempranillo.

89 Colour: bright cherry, purple rim. Nose: fruit expression, wild herbs, violets. Palate: fruity, good acidity, balanced.

SIERRA CANTABRIA COLECCIÓN PRIVADA 2009 T
100% tempranillo.

95 Colour: black cherry. Nose: fruit expression, raspberry, toasty, new oak. Palate: flavourful, powerful, fleshy, complex, harsh oak tannins.

FINCA EL BOSQUE 2009 T
100% tempranillo.

93 Colour: deep cherry. Nose: aged wood nuances, roasted coffee, creamy oak, ripe fruit. Palate: fleshy, complex, toasty, mineral, creamy.

SIERRA CANTABRIA COLECCIÓN PRIVADA 2008 T
100% tempranillo.

96 Colour: bright cherry. Nose: ripe fruit, sweet spices, creamy oak, neat, varietal, mineral. Palate: flavourful, fruity, toasty, round tannins.

FINCA EL BOSQUE 2008 T
100% tempranillo.

95 Colour: cherry, garnet rim. Nose: ripe fruit, spicy, creamy oak, toasty, elegant, complex, mineral. Palate: powerful, flavourful, toasty, round tannins.

AMANCIO 2008 T
100% tempranillo.

93 Colour: bright cherry, garnet rim. Nose: roasted coffee, sweet spices, dark chocolate. Palate: powerful, concentrated, good structure.

AMANCIO 2007 T
100% tempranillo.

94 Colour: bright cherry, garnet rim. Nose: roasted coffee, sweet spices, creamy oak, ripe fruit. Palate: fruity, good structure, long, elegant, round.

SIERRA CANTABRIA CUVÈE ESPECIAL 2007 T
tempranillo.

92 Colour: bright cherry, garnet rim. Nose: creamy oak, cocoa bean, sweet spices, toasty, ripe fruit. Palate: ripe fruit, long, flavourful, round tannins.

SIERRA CANTABRIA 2007 TC
100% tempranillo.

91 Colour: bright cherry, garnet rim. Nose: elegant, red berry notes, spicy. Palate: balanced, fine bitter notes, fruity, long.

SIERRA CANTABRIA 2006 TR
tempranillo.

92 Colour: cherry, garnet rim. Nose: medium intensity, expressive, fruit expression, sweet spices, cocoa bean. Palate: flavourful, good structure, fruity aftestaste, long.

SIERRA CANTABRIA 2005 TGR
97% tempranillo, 3% graciano.

93 Colour: cherry, garnet rim. Nose: ripe fruit, spicy, creamy oak, toasty, characterful, varietal, tobacco, mineral. Palate: powerful, flavourful, toasty, round tannins.

SIERRA CANTABRIA 2004 TGR
97% tempranillo, 3% graciano.

94 Colour: cherry, garnet rim. Nose: mineral, powerfull, spicy, cocoa bean. Palate: flavourful, fine bitter notes, round, ripe fruit, round tannins.

SOTO DE TORRES

Camino Los Arenales, s/n
01330 Labastida (Álava)
☎: +34 938 177 400 - Fax: +34 938 177 444
mailadmin@torres.es
www.torres.es

IBÉRICOS 2009 TC
100% tempranillo.

88 Colour: deep cherry, purple rim. Nose: red berry notes, varietal, fresh. Palate: fruity, spicy, good acidity.

TIERRA ANTIGUA

Urb. Monje Vigilia, 7
26120 Albelda de Iregua (La Rioja)
☎: +34 941 444 233 - Fax: +34 941 444 427
info@tierrantigua.com
www.tierrantigua.com

TIERRA ANTIGUA 2005 TR
85% tempranillo, 15% graciano, garnacha.

92 Colour: cherry, garnet rim. Nose: ripe fruit, spicy, expressive, powerfull, sweet spices, toasty. Palate: powerful, flavourful, complex, long.

ETHOS VENDIMIA SELECCIONADA 2005 T
100% tempranillo.

88 Colour: black cherry, cherry, garnet rim. Nose: red berry notes, ripe fruit, aromatic coffee, sweet spices, toasty. Palate: powerful, flavourful, toasty, spirituous, round.

TOBELOS BODEGAS Y VIÑEDOS

Ctra. N 124, Km. 45
26290 Briñas (La Rioja)
☎: +34 941 305 630 - Fax: +34 941 313 028
tobelos@tobelos.com
www.tobelos.com

TOBELOS 2010 BFB
90% viura, 10% garnacha blanca.

88 Colour: bright straw, greenish rim. Nose: medium intensity, fresh, fragrant herbs. Palate: fruity, flavourful, spicy.

TOBELOS GARNACHA 2009 T
100% garnacha.

89 Colour: cherry, garnet rim. Nose: ripe fruit, spicy, creamy oak, characterful. Palate: powerful, toasty, fruity.

LEUKADE AUTOR 2008 T
100% tempranillo.

88 Colour: cherry, garnet rim. Nose: roasted coffee, dark chocolate, aromatic coffee, ripe fruit. Palate: flavourful, spicy, good acidity, fine bitter notes.

TOBELOS 2007 T
100% tempranillo.

87 Colour: cherry, garnet rim. Nose: powerfull, ripe fruit, toasty. Palate: flavourful, fleshy, round tannins.

TAHÓN DE TOBELOS 2006 TR
100% tempranillo.

91 Colour: cherry, garnet rim. Nose: powerfull, ripe fruit, creamy oak, dark chocolate. Palate: powerful, flavourful, fleshy, round tannins.

TORRE DE OÑA

Finca San Martín
01309 Páganos - Laguardia (Álava)
☎: +34 945 621 154 - Fax: +34 945 621 171
info@torredeona.com
www.torredeona.com

FINCA SAN MARTÍN 2008 T
tempranillo.

88 Colour: deep cherry. Nose: spicy, fruit liqueur notes, creamy oak, aromatic coffee. Palate: spicy, fine bitter notes, round tannins.

TORRE DE OÑA 2007 TR
90% tempranillo, mazuelo.

92 Colour: cherry, garnet rim. Nose: creamy oak, toasty, complex, fruit expression, mineral. Palate: toasty, round tannins, fleshy, long.

VALORIA

Ctra. de Burgos, Km. 5
26006 Logroño (La Rioja)
☎: +34 941 204 059 - Fax: +34 941 204 155
bodega@bvaloria.com
www.vina-valoria.es

VIÑA VALORIA VENDIMIA SELECCIONADA 2010 B
100% viura.

81 Colour: bright straw, greenish rim. Nose: fresh, medium intensity. Palate: light-bodied, easy to drink.

VIÑA VALORIA VENDIMIA SELECCIONADA 2010 RD
70% tempranillo, 20% garnacha, 10% graciano.

84 Colour: raspberry rose. Nose: floral, fruit expression, fresh, medium intensity. Palate: light-bodied, fruity, flavourful.

VIÑA VALORIA 2005 TR
70% tempranillo, 20% mazuelo, 10% graciano.

85 Colour: cherry, garnet rim. Nose: ripe fruit, spicy, roasted coffee. Palate: powerful, flavourful, toasty, smoky aftertaste.

VIÑA VALORIA VENDIMIA SELECCIONADA 2010 T
100% tempranillo.

88 Colour: deep cherry, purple rim. Nose: fresh fruit, medium intensity, wild herbs. Palate: slightly acidic, fresh.

VIÑA VALORIA 2008 TC
70% tempranillo, 20% mazuelo, 10% graciano.

85 Colour: cherry, garnet rim. Nose: ripe fruit, spicy, creamy oak, roasted coffee. Palate: powerful, flavourful, toasty, ripe fruit.

VIÑA VALORIA 1992 TGR
70% tempranillo, 20% garnacha, 10% graciano.

88 Colour: pale ruby, brick rim edge. Nose: smoky, spicy, fruit liqueur notes, aged wood nuances, expressive. Palate: good acidity, elegant, spirituous, flavourful, fine tannins.

VINÍCOLA RIOJANA DE ALCANADRE S.C.

San Isidro, 46
26509 Alcanadre (La Rioja)
☎: +34 941 165 036 - Fax: +34 941 165 289
g.elvira@riojanadealcanadre.com
www.vinicolariojanadealcanadre.com

ARADÓN 2010 B
100% viura.

87 Colour: bright straw. Nose: white flowers, tropical fruit, fragrant herbs. Palate: fresh, light-bodied, fruity, flavourful.

ARADÓN 2010 RD
garnacha.

85 Colour: brilliant rose. Nose: balanced, red berry notes. Palate: flavourful, fruity, correct, good acidity.

ARADÓN GARNACHA 2010 T
100% garnacha.

85 Colour: cherry, purple rim. Nose: grapey, red berry notes, ripe fruit, grassy. Palate: light-bodied, fresh, fruity.

ARADÓN 2008 TC
90% tempranillo, 5% mazuelo, 5% garnacha.

87 Colour: cherry, garnet rim. Nose: red berry notes, ripe fruit, fresh, medium intensity, toasty, sweet spices. Palate: good acidity, flavourful, toasty.

ARADÓN 2005 TR
90% tempranillo, 5% mazuelo, 5% garnacha.

87 Colour: cherry, garnet rim. Nose: ripe fruit, floral, balsamic herbs, toasty, fine reductive notes. Palate: good acidity, creamy, spicy, toasty.

VIÑA BUJANDA

Diputación, s/n
01320 Oyón (Alava)
☎: +34 941 450 876 - Fax: +34 941 450 875
info@bujanda.com
www.familiamartinezbujanda.com

VIÑA BUJANDA 2010 B
100% viura.

86 Colour: bright straw, greenish rim. Nose: fresh fruit, tropical fruit, white flowers. Palate: fruity, flavourful, fresh.

VIÑA BUJANDA 2010 RD
100% tempranillo.

83 Colour: light cherry. Nose: ripe fruit, characterful, powerfull. Palate: fine bitter notes, concentrated.

VIÑA BUJANDA 2010 T
100% tempranillo.

87 Colour: bright cherry, purple rim. Nose: balsamic herbs, ripe fruit, powerfull. Palate: fleshy, ripe fruit, good acidity.

VIÑA BUJANDA 2008 TC
100% tempranillo.

89 Color cherry, garnet rim. Aroma ripe fruit, spicy, creamy oak, toasty, complex. Taste powerful, flavourful, toasty, round tannins.

VIÑA BUJANDA 2006 TR
100% tempranillo.

88 Colour: cherry, garnet rim. Nose: medium intensity, ripe fruit, spicy. Palate: ripe fruit, good acidity.

VIÑA EIZAGA

Camino de la Hoya s/n
01300 Laguardia (Alava)
☎: +34 675 154 279
contacto@vinoseizaga.com
www.vinoseizaga.com

VIÑA EIZAGA 2010 T
100% tempranillo.

86 Colour: cherry, purple rim. Nose: red berry notes, wild herbs, powerfull, varietal. Palate: light-bodied, fruity, easy to drink.

LAGAR DE EIZAGA 2008 TC
100% tempranillo.

88 Colour: cherry, garnet rim. Nose: powerfull, ripe fruit, sweet spices. Palate: flavourful, powerful, concentrated, round tannins.

VIÑA EIZAGA 2007 T
100% tempranillo.

87 Colour: cherry, garnet rim. Nose: spicy, creamy oak, toasty, characterful. Palate: flavourful, toasty, round tannins.

VIÑA EIZAGA 2004 TR
100% tempranillo.

87 Colour: cherry, garnet rim. Nose: toasty, spicy, aged wood nuances, aromatic coffee. Palate: powerful, toasty, round tannins.

VIÑA HERMINIA

Camino de los Agudos, s/n
26559 Aldeanueva de Ebro (La Rioja)
☎: +34 941 142 305 - Fax: +34 941 142 303
marketing@caballero.es
www.vherminia.es

VIÑA HERMINIA EXCELSUS 2009 T
50% garnacha, 50% tempranillo.

90 Colour: cherry, purple rim. Nose: red berry notes, ripe fruit, complex, expressive, sweet spices. Palate: creamy, fruity, flavourful.

DOMINIA HERMINIA 2009 T
garnacha.

88 Colour: black cherry, purple rim. Nose: red berry notes, raspberry, sweet spices, complex. Palate: good acidity, fruity, fleshy.

DOMINIA HERMINIA 2009 T
graciano.

88 Colour: cherry, garnet rim. Nose: powerfull, ripe fruit, fragrant herbs. Palate: rich, powerful, fleshy, balsamic.

VIÑA HERMINIA 2008 TC
85% tempranillo, 15% garnacha.

86 Colour: cherry, garnet rim. Nose: ripe fruit, toasty, sweet spices. Palate: powerful, flavourful, toasty, round tannins.

VIÑA HERMINIA 2006 TR
85% tempranillo, 15% garnacha.

88 Colour: cherry, garnet rim. Nose: ripe fruit, complex, balanced, sweet spices, cocoa bean. Palate: correct, elegant, unctuous, fleshy.

VIÑA HERMOSA

Avda. de la Rioja, s/n
26221 Gimileo (La Rioja)
☎: +34 941 304 231 - Fax: +34 941 304 326
santalba@santalba.com
www.santiagoijalba.com

ABANDO 2010 BFB
viura.

87 Colour: yellow, greenish rim. Nose: fresh fruit, wild herbs, varietal. Palate: fresh, flavourful, good acidity.

ABANDO 2010 RD

87 Colour: rose. Nose: powerfull, floral, rose petals, lactic notes, expressive, sweet spices. Palate: good acidity, flavourful, fruity, fleshy.

SANTALBA ECOLÓGICO 2009 T

90 Colour: cherry, purple rim. Nose: balsamic herbs, scrubland, ripe fruit. Palate: flavourful, fruity, fresh.

VIÑA HERMOSA 2007 T

85 Colour: bright cherry. Nose: sweet spices, creamy oak, ripe fruit. Palate: flavourful, fruity, round tannins.

OGGA 2005 TR
tempranillo.

88 Colour: cherry, garnet rim. Nose: spicy, ripe fruit, earthy notes. Palate: ripe fruit, spicy, fine tannins.

ABANDO VENDIMIA SELECCIONADA 2005 T

88 Colour: cherry, garnet rim. Nose: creamy oak, toasty. Palate: powerful, flavourful, toasty, round tannins.

VIÑA HERMOSA 2005 TR

85 Colour: cherry, garnet rim. Nose: ripe fruit, dark chocolate, aromatic coffee. Palate: spicy, fine bitter notes, good acidity.

ABANDO VENDIMIA SELECCIONADA 2004 TR

90 Colour: cherry, garnet rim. Nose: ripe fruit, sweet spices, earthy notes. Palate: powerful, flavourful, fleshy, spicy.

VIÑA IJALBA

Ctra. Pamplona, Km. 1
26006 Logroño (La Rioja)
☎: +34 941 261 100 - Fax: +34 941 261 128
vinaijalba@ijalba.com
www.ijalba.com

IJALBA MATURANA 2010 B
100% maturana blanca.

90 Colour: bright straw. Nose: white flowers, candied fruit, fruit expression, faded flowers. Palate: flavourful, spicy, ripe fruit.

GENOLI 2010 B
100% viura.

87 Colour: straw. Nose: ripe fruit, faded flowers, grassy. Palate: flavourful, fruity, fresh.

ALOQUE 2010 RD JOVEN
50% tempranillo, 50% garnacha.

88 Colour: brilliant rose. Nose: red berry notes, fresh, medium intensity, elegant. Palate: fruity, flavourful, good acidity, balanced.

LIVOR 2010 T JOVEN
100% tempranillo.

88 Colour: cherry, purple rim. Nose: expressive, red berry notes, floral, wild herbs, mineral. Palate: flavourful, fruity, good acidity, round tannins, powerful.

DIONISIO RUIZ IJALBA 2009 T
100% maturana.

90 Colour: cherry, garnet rim. Nose: creamy oak, toasty, characterful, fruit preserve, sweet spices, balsamic herbs. Palate: powerful, flavourful, toasty, round tannins.

IJALBA 2007 TC
90% tempranillo, 10% graciano.

88 Colour: cherry, garnet rim. Nose: powerfull, ripe fruit, spicy, toasty. Palate: powerful, fine bitter notes, ripe fruit.

MÚRICE 2007 TC
90% tempranillo, 10% graciano.

87 Colour: cherry, garnet rim. Nose: creamy oak, toasty, ripe fruit, aromatic coffee. Palate: powerful, flavourful, toasty, round tannins.

IJALBA 2006 TR
80% tempranillo, 20% graciano.

90 Colour: bright cherry. Nose: sweet spices, creamy oak, ripe fruit. Palate: flavourful, fruity, round tannins, toasty.

IJALBA GRACIANO 2009 TC
100% graciano.

88 Colour: cherry, garnet rim. Nose: powerfull, ripe fruit, balsamic herbs, scrubland, sweet spices. Palate: powerful, fleshy, ripe fruit.

IJALBA SELECCIÓN ESPECIAL 2001 TR
50% tempranillo, 50% graciano.

91 Colour: cherry, garnet rim. Nose: ripe fruit, sweet spices, toasty. Palate: ripe fruit, spicy, fine bitter notes.

VIÑA OLABARRI

Ctra. Anguciana, s/n
26200 Haro (La Rioja)
☎: +34 941 310 937 - Fax: +34 941 311 602
info@bodegasolabarri.com
www.bodegasolabarri.com

VIÑA OLABARRI 2009 TC
100% tempranillo.

88 Colour: bright cherry, purple rim. Nose: red berry notes, spicy, varietal. Palate: fruity, good structure, flavourful.

BIKANDI VENDIMIA SELECCIONADA 2009 TC
100% tempranillo.

88 Colour: deep cherry, garnet rim. Nose: red berry notes, spicy, cocoa bean. Palate: correct, balanced, fruity, round tannins.

VIÑA OLABARRI 2007 TR
90% tempranillo, 10% graciano.

88 Colour: deep cherry, garnet rim. Nose: complex, balanced, sweet spices, fruit preserve. Palate: good structure, fruity, flavourful.

BIKANDI VENDIMIA SELECCIONADA 2005 TR
100% tempranillo.

88 Colour: bright cherry, garnet rim. Nose: spicy, fine reductive notes, fruit preserve. Palate: fruity, good structure, round tannins.

VIÑA OLABARRI 2004 TGR
80% tempranillo, 20% graciano, mazuelo.

86 Colour: deep cherry, garnet rim. Nose: ripe fruit, sweet spices, cocoa bean. Palate: good structure, spicy, long.

VIÑA REAL

Ctra. Logroño - Laguardia, Km. 4,8
01300 Laguardia (Álava)
☎: +34 945 625 255 - Fax: +34 945 625 211
marketing@cvne.com
www.cvne.com

VIÑA REAL 2010 BFB
100% viura.

91 Color bright yellow. Aroma powerfull, ripe fruit, sweet spices, creamy oak, fragrant herbs. Taste rich, smoky aftertaste, flavourful, fresh, good acidity.

VIÑA REAL 2009 TC
90% tempranillo, 10% garnacha, mazuelo, graciano.

92 Colour: cherry, purple rim. Nose: powerfull, characterful, complex, fruit expression. Palate: flavourful, powerful, fleshy, long.

VIÑA REAL 2004 TGR
95% tempranillo, 5% graciano.

92 Colour: deep cherry. Nose: expressive, fruit liqueur notes, aromatic coffee, sweet spices, creamy oak. Palate: flavourful, spicy, ripe fruit, round tannins.

VIÑA REAL 2006 TR
90% tempranillo, 10% graciano, garnacha, mazuelo.

92 Colour: deep cherry. Nose: ripe fruit, fruit liqueur notes, expressive, aromatic coffee, aged wood nuances. Palate: flavourful, fine bitter notes, spicy, long.

VIÑA SALCEDA

Ctra. Cenicero, Km. 3
01340 Elciego (Álava)
☎: +34 945 606 125 - Fax: +34 945 606 069
info@vinasalceda.com
www.vinasalceda.com

VIÑA SALCEDA 2007 TR
90% tempranillo, 10% graciano.

92 Colour: cherry, garnet rim. Nose: powerfull, ripe fruit, new oak, sweet spices, cocoa bean. Palate: flavourful, powerful, fleshy, spicy, ripe fruit.

VIÑA SALCEDA 2008 TC
85% tempranillo, 15% mazuelo, graciano.

89 Colour: cherry, garnet rim. Nose: ripe fruit, spicy, creamy oak, toasty, varietal. Palate: powerful, flavourful, toasty, round tannins.

CONDE DE LA SALCEDA 2005 TR
100% tempranillo.

92 Colour: cherry, garnet rim. Nose: ripe fruit, spicy, creamy oak, toasty, characterful, fine reductive notes. Palate: powerful, flavourful, toasty, round tannins.

VIÑEDOS DE ALDEANUEVA S. COOP.

Avda. Juan Carlos I, 100
26559 Aldeanueva de Ebro (La Rioja)
☎: +34 941 163 039 - Fax: +34 941 163 585
va@aldeanueva.com
www.aldeanueva.com

CULTO 2007 T
60% graciano, 40% tempranillo.

89 Colour: bright cherry, garnet rim. Nose: ripe fruit, sweet spices, balanced. Palate: flavourful, fruity, good acidity.

AZABACHE VENDIMIA SELECCIONADA 2007 TC
60% tempranillo, 30% garnacha, 10% graciano.

85 Colour: deep cherry, garnet rim. Nose: powerfull, slightly evolved. Palate: fruity, flavourful.

AZABACHE 2010 RD
garnacha.

89 Color rose, purple rim. Aroma powerfull, ripe fruit, red berry notes, floral, expressive. Taste fleshy, powerful, fruity, fresh.

AZABACHE TEMPRANILLO 2010 T
tempranillo.

86 Colour: very deep cherry. Nose: red berry notes, ripe fruit. Palate: flavourful, ripe fruit.

AZABACHE GRACIANO 2006 TR
graciano.

86 Colour: bright cherry, garnet rim. Nose: ripe fruit, spicy. Palate: good structure, ripe fruit.

VIÑEDOS DE ALFARO

Camino de los Agudos s/n
26559 Aldeanueva de Ebro (La Rioja)
☎: +34 941 142 389 - Fax: +34 941 142 386
info@vinedosdealfaro.com
www.vinedosdealfaro.com

REAL AGRADO 2010 B
viura, garnacha blanca.

82 Colour: bright straw, greenish rim. Nose: fresh, medium intensity, floral. Palate: flavourful, fresh, easy to drink.

REAL AGRADO 2010 RD
garnacha.

86 Colour: brilliant rose. Nose: red berry notes, fresh fruit, medium intensity. Palate: fruity, fresh, flavourful, easy to drink.

REAL AGRADO 2008 T
garnacha, tempranillo.

86 Colour: cherry, purple rim. Nose: expressive, fresh fruit, red berry notes, floral. Palate: flavourful, fruity, good acidity, complex, fleshy.

CONDE DEL REAL AGRADO 2007 TC
60% garnacha, 25% tempranillo, 10% mazuelo, 5% graciano.

88 Colour: cherry, garnet rim. Nose: ripe fruit, spicy, creamy oak, toasty. Palate: powerful, flavourful, toasty, round tannins.

RODILES VENDIMIA SELECCIONADA 2005 T
100% graciano.

92 Nose: ripe fruit, spicy, creamy oak, toasty, complex, sweet spices. Palate: powerful, flavourful, toasty, round tannins, balanced.

RODILES 2005 T
25% tempranillo, 25% mazuelo, 25% garnacha, 25% graciano.

87 Colour: cherry, garnet rim. Nose: ripe fruit, sweet spices, cocoa bean, toasty. Palate: good acidity, flavourful, roasted-coffee aftertaste.

CONDE DEL REAL AGRADO 2005 TR
40% garnacha, 45% tempranillo, 5% mazuelo, 10% graciano.

86 Colour: light cherry, orangey edge. Nose: fruit preserve, sweet spices, dark chocolate, toasty. Palate: unctuous, correct, easy to drink.

VIÑEDOS DE PÁGANOS

Ctra. Navaridas, s/n
01309 Páganos (Álava)
☎: +34 945 600 590 - Fax: +34 945 600 885
info@eguren.com
www.eguren.com

LA NIETA 2009 T
100% tempranillo.

95 Colour: cherry, garnet rim. Nose: ripe fruit, spicy, toasty, complex, aged wood nuances, dark chocolate, aromatic coffee, mineral. Palate: powerful, flavourful, toasty, harsh oak tannins.

LA NIETA 2008 T
100% tempranillo.

96 Colour: black cherry. Nose: powerfull, complex, ripe fruit, fruit expression, raspberry, dry stone, mineral. Palate: flavourful, powerful, fleshy, complex, spicy.

EL PUNTIDO 2008 T
100% tempranillo.

95 Colour: cherry, garnet rim. Nose: spicy, creamy oak, toasty, complex, powerfull, varietal, ripe fruit, red berry notes. Palate: powerful, flavourful, toasty, powerful tannins.

EL PUNTÍDO 2007 T
100% tempranillo.

94 Colour: cherry, garnet rim. Nose: ripe fruit, spicy, creamy oak, toasty, complex, fruit expression, mineral. Palate: powerful, flavourful, toasty, round tannins.

VIÑEDOS DEL CONTINO

Finca San Rafael, s/n
01321 Laserna (Álava)
☎: +34 945 600 201 - Fax: +34 945 621 114
laserna@contino.es
www.cvne.com

CONTINO 2010 B
malvasía, garnacha blanca, viura.

91 Colour: bright straw. Nose: fresh, fresh fruit, white flowers, neat, fine lees. Palate: flavourful, fruity, good acidity, balanced.

CONTINO VIÑA DEL OLIVO 2008 T
90% tempranillo, 10% graciano.

93 Colour: cherry, garnet rim. Nose: powerfull, complex, characterful, fruit expression, sweet spices, creamy oak, toasty. Palate: flavourful, powerful, fleshy, concentrated, round tannins.

CONTINO GARNACHA 2008 T
garnacha.

92 Colour: cherry, garnet rim. Nose: ripe fruit, sweet spices, creamy oak. Palate: powerful, flavourful, round tannins.

CONTINO GRACIANO 2007 T
100% graciano.

94 Colour: cherry, garnet rim. Nose: fragrant herbs, balsamic herbs, ripe fruit, creamy oak, sweet spices, cocoa bean. Palate: powerful, flavourful, fleshy, concentrated, long.

CONTINO 2007 TR
85% tempranillo, 10% graciano, 5% garnacha, mazuelo.

91 Colour: cherry, garnet rim. Nose: sweet spices, creamy oak, ripe fruit, fruit expression. Palate: flavourful, fine bitter notes, good acidity.

CONTINO 2006 TR
85% tempranillo, 10% graciano, 5% mazuelo, garnacha.

91 Colour: deep cherry. Nose: aromatic coffee, dark chocolate, toasty, ripe fruit. Palate: spicy, ripe fruit, long.

CONTINO "MAGNUM" 2005 TGR
70% tempranillo, 15% garnacha, 15% graciano.

93 Colour: cherry, garnet rim. Nose: ripe fruit, complex, expressive, cocoa bean, dark chocolate, sweet spices, creamy oak. Palate: balanced, elegant, powerful, flavourful, fleshy.

VIÑEDOS DEL TERNERO

Finca El Ternero
09200 Miranda de Ebro (Burgos)
☎: +34 941 320 021 - Fax: +34 941 302 729
ana@vinedosdelternero.com
www.vinedosdelternero.com

MIRANDA 2008 TC
95% tempranillo, 5% mazuelo.

91 Colour: cherry, garnet rim. Nose: ripe fruit, fragrant herbs, fine reductive notes, spicy. Palate: complex, powerful, flavourful, fleshy.

PICEA 650 2006 T
95% tempranillo, 5% mazuelo.

93 Colour: cherry, garnet rim. Nose: powerfull, balanced, red berry notes, ripe fruit, balsamic herbs, spicy, earthy notes. Palate: good acidity, elegant, round, powerful, complex, fleshy.

PICEA 650 2006 T
95% tempranillo, 5% mazuelo.

92 Colour: cherry, garnet rim. Nose: red berry notes, ripe fruit, wild herbs, mineral, spicy, creamy oak. Palate: spicy, flavourful, fleshy.

SEL DE SU MERCED 2006 TR
95% tempranillo, 5% mazuelo.

90 Colour: cherry, garnet rim. Nose: red berry notes, ripe fruit, fragrant herbs, mineral, cocoa bean, sweet spices. Palate: spicy, flavourful, correct, good acidity.

MIRANDA 2006 T
95% tempranillo, 5% mazuelo.

89 Colour: cherry, garnet rim. Nose: floral, red berry notes, ripe fruit, aromatic coffee, sweet spices. Palate: flavourful, fleshy, easy to drink.

MIRANDA 2006 TC
95% tempranillo, 5% mazuelo.

89 Colour: cherry, garnet rim. Nose: ripe fruit, red berry notes, expressive, spicy, toasty. Palate: rich, powerful, flavourful.

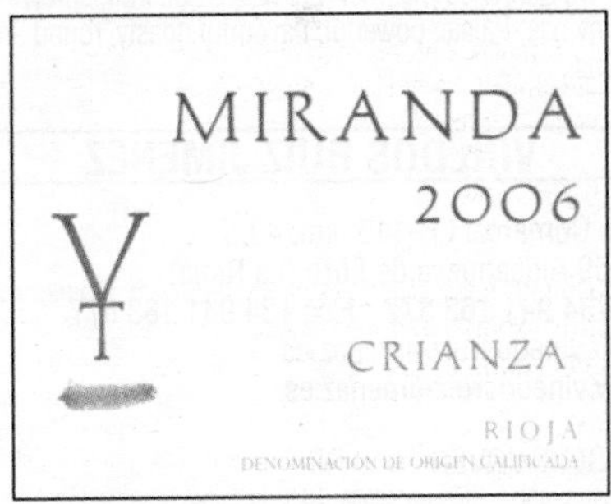

SEL DE SU MERCED 2005 TR
95% tempranillo, 5% mazuelo.

91 Colour: cherry, garnet rim. Nose: ripe fruit, cocoa bean, aromatic coffee, sweet spices, creamy oak. Palate: flavourful, fleshy, complex, balanced.

VIÑEDOS REAL RUBIO

Avda. La Rioja s/n
26559 Aldeanueva de Ebro (La Rioja)
☎: +34 941 163 672 - Fax: +34 941 163 672
mariluz@bodegasrealrubio.com
www.bodegasrealrubio.com

REAL RUBIO 2010 B
viura, verdejo.

89 Colour: bright straw. Nose: fresh, white flowers, expressive, wild herbs, balsamic herbs. Palate: flavourful, fruity, good acidity, balanced. Personality.

REAL RUBIO FINCA EL TORDILLO 2010 T
tempranillo, graciano.

88 Colour: cherry, purple rim. Nose: fresh fruit, red berry notes, floral, lactic notes. Palate: flavourful, fruity, good acidity, round tannins.

REAL RUBIO 2008 TC
tempranillo, graciano.

91 Colour: cherry, garnet rim. Nose: ripe fruit, spicy, creamy oak. Palate: powerful, flavourful, toasty, round tannins.

VIÑEDOS RUIZ JIMÉNEZ

Ctra. Comarcal LR-115, km. 43,5
26559 Aldeanueva de Ebro (La Rioja)
☎: +34 941 163 577 - Fax: +34 941 163 577
info@vinedosruiz-jimenez.es
www.vinedosruiz-jimenez.es

PERSEUS JOVEN 2010 RD
45% tempranillo, 45% garnacha, 10% graciano.

82 Colour: rose, purple rim. Nose: ripe fruit, faded flowers, powerfull, medium intensity. Palate: slightly evolved, fleshy, flavourful.

PERSEUS JOVEN 2010 T
85% tempranillo, 15% garnacha.

88 Colour: cherry, purple rim. Nose: expressive, fresh fruit, red berry notes, floral. Palate: flavourful, fruity, good acidity.

VALCALIENTE GARNACHA 2008 TC
100% garnacha.

89 Colour: cherry, garnet rim. Nose: red berry notes, ripe fruit, fragrant herbs, cocoa bean, creamy oak. Palate: good acidity, flavourful, fruity, fleshy.

VALCALIENTE 2006 TR
85% tempranillo, 15% graciano.

86 Colour: dark-red cherry, orangey edge. Nose: ripe fruit, balsamic herbs, toasty, wet leather. Palate: good acidity, powerful, flavourful.

VIÑEDOS SINGULARES

Llorer, 31
08905 Hospitalet de Llobregat (Barcelona)
☎: +34 934 807 041 - Fax: +34 934 807 076
info@vinedossingulares.com
www.vinedossingulares.com

JARDÍN ROJO 2010 T
tempranillo.

89 Colour: cherry, purple rim. Nose: red berry notes, raspberry, floral, expressive. Palate: good acidity, flavourful, fresh, fruity.

VIÑEDOS Y BODEGAS DE LA MARQUESA

Herrería, 76
01307 Villabuena de Álava (Álava)
☎: +34 945 609 085 - Fax: +34 945 623 304
info@valserrano.com
www.valserrano.com

VALSERRANO PREMIUM 2000 B GRAN RESERVA
95% viura, 5% malvasía.

92 Color bright golden. Aroma ripe fruit, dry nuts, powerfull, toasty, aged wood nuances. Taste flavourful, fruity, spicy, toasty, long.

VALSERRANO MAZUELO 2008 T
100% mazuelo.

89 Colour: very deep cherry, garnet rim. Nose: ripe fruit, powerfull, spicy. Palate: fruity, flavourful, fleshy, long, round tannins.

VALSERRANO 2008 TC
90% tempranillo, 10% mazuelo.

88 Colour: cherry, garnet rim. Nose: ripe fruit, spicy, toasty. Palate: powerful, flavourful, toasty, round tannins.

VALSERRANO 2006 TR
90% tempranillo, 10% graciano.

90 Colour: deep cherry, garnet rim. Nose: balanced, complex, cocoa bean, sweet spices. Palate: good structure, spicy, round tannins.

VALSERRANO 2010 BFB
95% viura, 5% malvasía.

89 Colour: bright golden. Nose: ripe fruit, faded flowers, dried herbs, spicy, creamy oak. Palate: elegant, rich, flavourful, fleshy.

VALSERRANO 2004 TGR
90% tempranillo, 10% graciano.

87 Colour: cherry, garnet rim. Nose: spicy, medium intensity, balanced, ripe fruit. Palate: flavourful, ripe fruit, spicy.

WINNER WINES

Avda. del Mediterráneo, 38
28007 Madrid (Madrid)
☎: +34 915 019 042 - Fax: +34 915 017 794
winnerwines@ibernoble.com
www.ibernoble.com

VIÑA SASETA 2010 T
100% tempranillo.

87 Colour: cherry, purple rim. Nose: red berry notes, raspberry, floral, wild herbs. Palate: powerful, flavourful, fruity.

VIÑA SASETA 2007 TC
90% tempranillo, 5% graciano, 5% mazuelo.

87 Colour: cherry, garnet rim. Nose: red berry notes, ripe fruit, spicy, fine reductive notes, toasty. Palate: flavourful, fleshy, toasty.

VIÑA SASETA 2004 TR
tempranillo, mazuelo, graciano.

88 Colour: cherry, garnet rim. Nose: ripe fruit, scrubland, fine reductive notes, spicy, creamy oak. Palate: fleshy, flavourful, long, balanced.

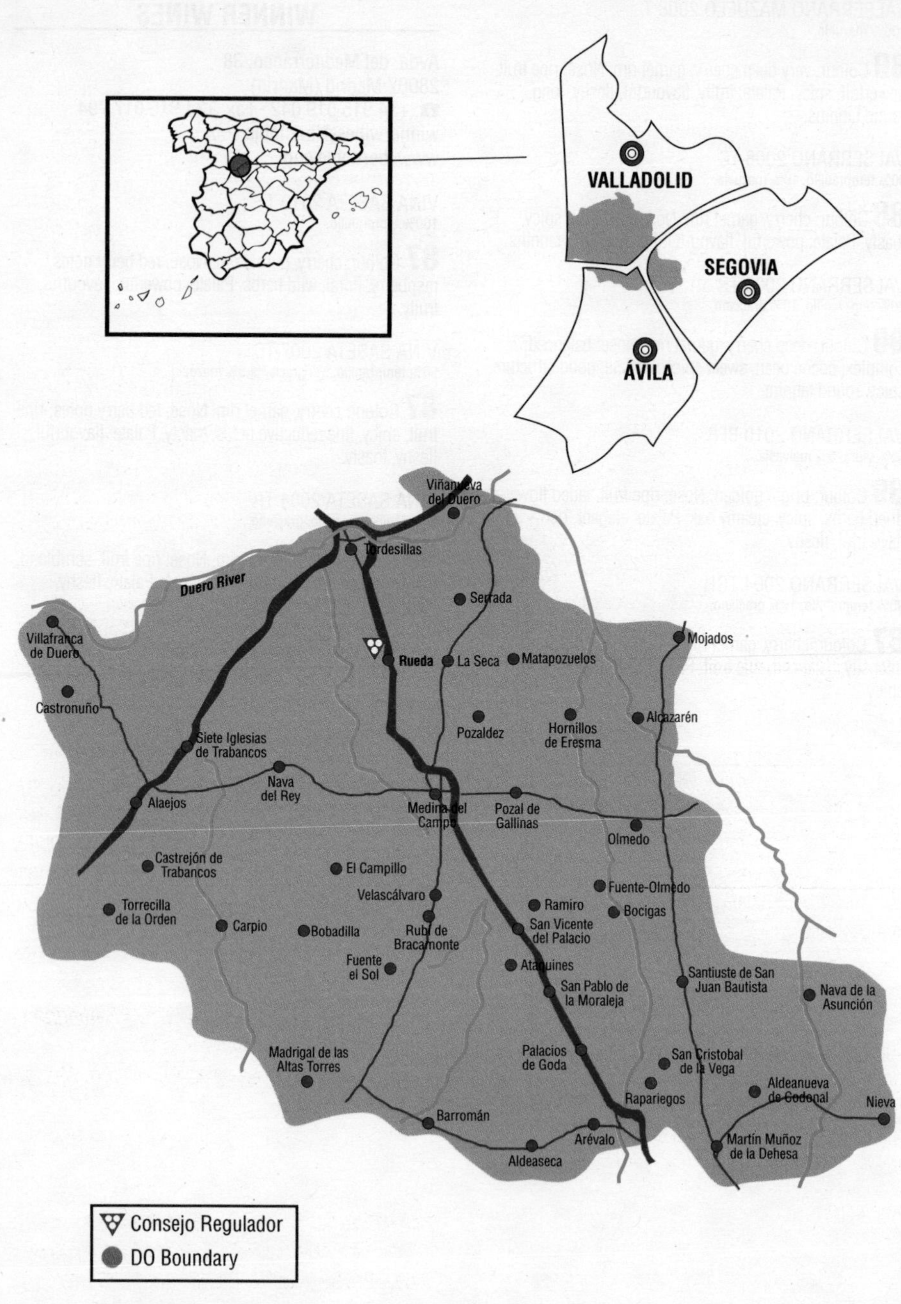
VALLADOLID
SEGOVIA
ÁVILA
Viñanueva del Duero
Tordesillas
Duero River
Serrada
Villafranca de Duero
Rueda
La Seca
Matapozuelos
Mojados
Castronuño
Pozaldez
Hornillos de Eresma
Alcazarén
Siete Iglesias de Trabancos
Nava del Rey
Alaejos
Medina del Campo
Pozal de Gallinas
Olmedo
Castrejón de Trabancos
El Campillo
Velascálvaro
Fuente-Olmedo
Torrecilla de la Orden
Carpio
Bobadilla
Rubí de Bracamonte
Ramiro
San Vicente del Palacio
Bocigas
Fuente el Sol
Ataquines
San Pablo de la Moraleja
Santiuste de San Juan Bautista
Nava de la Asunción
Madrigal de las Altas Torres
Palacios de Goda
San Cristobal de la Vega
Rapariegos
Aldeanueva de Codonal
Nieva
Barromán
Arévalo
Aldeaseca
Martín Muñoz de la Dehesa
Consejo Regulador
DO Boundary

NEWS ABOUT THE VINTAGE:

Rueda's success has started to be worrying. In the last few years this designation of origin has grown and multiplied itself in every direction: the number of hectares, wineries and bottle sold, production figures... But this success can be read under a bothering light, too. When La Mancha "adopted" Rueda's star variety, *verdejo*, and started to make wines sold at bargain prices, Rueda's answer was to low both price and quality in a way that, in the long run, will surely hurt the region's steady progress. The DO has increased its sales, but at rock-bottom prices. New plantings in their first year of production have witnessed how the kilogram of grapes has gone from 1 euro at the time they were planted to a mere 30 cents now.

The *verdejo* from the region cannot be compared in typicity or varietal expression to that of any other region. Besides, the 2010 vintage was both cooler and more humid than 2009; mildew affected the vines during flowering, although it did not manage to negatively spoil the overall quality. In tasting terms the wines appear fresher and with more fruit expression, but the way some wines are being bottled far to early to sell them as quickly as possible is causing that even in cooler vintages they show occasionally ripe and even overripe notes. The current *sauvignon blanc* renderings are not as expressive as those from previous vintages: the variety's adaptation to the region is making it loose part of its varietal character, undoubtedly a most unwelcome side-effect.

The top wines in Rueda's ranking are three classic wines within the DO, Naiades 2008, Belondrade y Lurton 2009 and El Transistor 2009, all of them showing the finest balance between fruit and alcohol, as well as great complexity and depth.

LOCATION:

In the provinces of Valladolid (53 municipal districts), Segovia (17 municipal districts) and Ávila (2 municipal districts). The vineyards are situated on the undulating terrain of a plateau and are conditioned by the influence of the river Duero that runs through the northern part of the region.

CLIMATE:

Continental in nature, with cold winters and short hot summers. Rainfall is concentrated in spring and autumn. The average altitude of the region is between 600 m and 700 m, and only in the province of Segovia does it exceed 800 m.

SOIL:

Many pebbles on the surface. The terrain is stony, poor in organic matter, with good aeration and drainage. The texture of the soil is variable although, in general, sandy limestone and limestone predominate.

GRAPE VARIETIES:

WHITE: *Verdejo* (52%), *Viura* (22%), *Sauvignon Blanc* (7%) and *Palomino Fino* (19%).
RED: *Tempranillo, Cabernet Sauvignon, Merlot* and *Garnacha.*

FIGURES:

Vineyard surface: 11,739 – **Wine-Growers:** 1,700 – **Wineries:** 58 – **2010 Harvest rating:** Very Good – **Production:** 55,124,027 litres – **Market percentages:** 85% domestic. 15% export

CONSEJO REGULADOR
Real, 8
47490 Rueda (Valladolid)
☎: +34 983 868 248 - Fax: +34 983 868 135
@ crdo.rueda@dorueda.com
www.dorueda.com

GENERAL CHARACTERISTICS OF THE WINES

WHITES	These are produced mainly from *Verdejo*. As the percentage of this grape variety increases (from Rueda to Rueda Verdejo), a more characteristic style is obtained. Greenish straw coloured, they offer fine and elegant noses, fruity, with hints of fennel, mint and apple. On the palate they are fresh, fruity and with a characteristic bitter aftertaste, which contrasts with the sensation of ripe grapes, sweetness and freshness. Those produced from *Sauvignon Blanc* offer good roasted potency, with floral notes and, in most cases, notes of tropical fruit. They are flavourful with a certain oily character.
SPARKLING	These are produced according to the traditional method of a second fermentation in the bottle. They are fresh with hints of yeast, although, in general, they are slightly heavier than the Cavas.
REDS	These are based mainly on the *Tempranillo*, with the participation of especially *Cabernet Sauvignon*. They have a quite intense cherry colour and are fruity, meaty and flavourful; they may be reminiscent of the red wines of Cigales.
CLASSIC WHITES	The so-called 'Dorado' fits the pattern of the traditional Generoso wines. Produced from a minimum of 40% Verdejo and an alcohol content not less than 15°, they have a golden colour and a slightly toasted palate due to the long oxidation process they are subjected to in the wooden barrels. There is also a 'Palido' labelling for wines of this style with shorter ageing in wood.

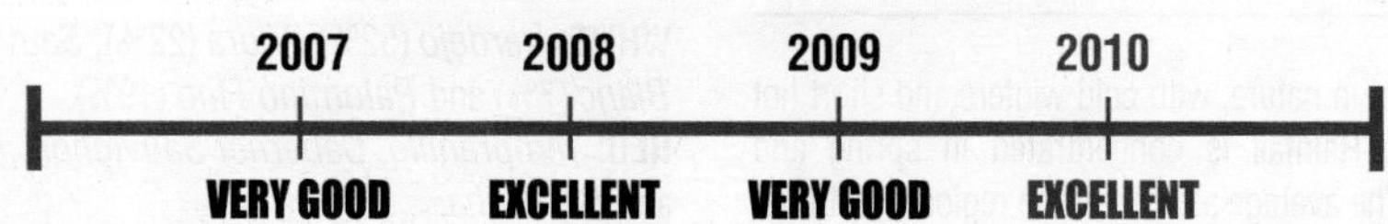

ALTAENCINA GLOBAL

Cañada Real, 30
47008 (Valladolid)
☎: +34 639 780 716 - Fax: +34 983 868 905
altaencina@altaencina.com
www.altaencina.com

QUIVIRA VERDEJO 2010 B
100% verdejo.

88 Colour: bright straw. Nose: fresh, fresh fruit, jasmine, varietal. Palate: flavourful, fruity, good acidity, balanced.

ÁLVAREZ Y DÍEZ

Juan Antonio Carmona, 12
47500 Nava del Rey (Valladolid)
☎: +34 983 850 136 - Fax: +34 983 850 761
bodegas@alvarezydiez.com
www.alvarezydiez.com

MONTE ALINA 2010 B
verdejo, viura.

85 Colour: pale. Nose: fruit expression, citrus fruit, faded flowers. Palate: flavourful, fine bitter notes, easy to drink.

MANTEL BLANCO RUEDA VERDEJO 2010 B
verdejo.

90 Colour: bright straw. Nose: fresh, fresh fruit, white flowers, grassy. Palate: flavourful, fruity, good acidity, balanced.

MANTEL BLANCO SAUVIGNON BLANC 2010 B
sauvignon blanc.

87 Colour: bright straw. Nose: fresh, white flowers, expressive, candied fruit. Palate: flavourful, fruity, balanced.

MANTEL BLANCO 2008 BFB
verdejo.

88 Colour: bright yellow. Nose: sweet spices, creamy oak, overripe fruit, medium intensity. Palate: good acidity, unctuous, flavourful.

ÁNGEL RODRÍGUEZ VIDAL

Torcido, 1
47491 La Seca (Valladolid)
☎: +34 983 816 302 - Fax: +34 983 816 302
martinsancho@martinsancho.com

MARTÍNSANCHO VERDEJO 2010 B
100% verdejo.

91 Colour: bright straw. Nose: fresh, white flowers, ripe fruit, complex, varietal. Palate: flavourful, fruity, good acidity, balanced.

AURA (DOMECQ BODEGAS)

Autovía del Noroeste, Km. 175
47490 Rueda (Valladolid)
☎: +34 983 868 286 - Fax: +34 983 868 168
mcarreir@domecqbodegas.com
www.domecqbodegas.com

AURA VERDEJO 2010 B
91% verdejo, 9% sauvignon blanc.

89 Colour: bright straw. Nose: fresh, white flowers, varietal. Palate: flavourful, fruity, good acidity, balanced.

AVELINO VEGAS

Real del Pino, 36
40460 Santiuste (Segovia)
☎: +34 921 596 002 - Fax: +34 921 596 035
ana@avelinovegas.com
www.avelinovegas.com

MONTESPINA SAUVIGNON 2010 B JOVEN
sauvignon blanc.

90 Colour: bright straw, greenish rim. Nose: powerfull, tropical fruit, balanced. Palate: flavourful, fruity, fine bitter notes.

CIRCE 2010 B
verdejo.

90 Colour: bright straw. Nose: fresh, fresh fruit, white flowers, expressive, varietal. Palate: flavourful, fruity, good acidity, balanced, rich.

MONTESPINA VERDEJO 2010 B JOVEN
verdejo.

89 Colour: bright yellow, greenish rim. Nose: balanced, ripe fruit, varietal. Palate: rich, flavourful, great length.

CASA DE LA VEGA VERDEJO 2010 B JOVEN
verdejo.

88 Colour: bright straw. Nose: tropical fruit, citrus fruit, fragrant herbs, fresh. Palate: light-bodied, fruity, fresh, flavourful.

BELLORIVINOS

Cobalto, 37
47012 (Valladolid)
☎: +34 619 708 546
juan@bellorivinos.com

BELLORI 2009 BFB
verdejo.

92 Colour: bright yellow. Nose: ripe fruit, sweet spices, creamy oak, fragrant herbs. Palate: rich, flavourful, good acidity.

BELONDRADE

Quinta San Diego - Camino del Puerto, s/n
47491 La Seca (Valladolid)
☎: +34 983 481 001 - Fax: +34 600 590 024
info@belondrade.com
www.belondrade.com

BELONDRADE Y LURTON 2009 BFB
100% verdejo.

95 Colour: bright straw. Nose: expressive, ripe fruit, fruit expression, citrus fruit, creamy oak, sweet spices. Palate: flavourful, fleshy, spicy, ripe fruit.

BODEGA COOPERATIVA VIRGEN DE LA ASUNCIÓN

Las Afueras, s/n
09311 La Horra (Burgos)
☎: +34 947 542 057 - Fax: +34 947 542 057
info@virgendelaasuncion.com
www.virgendelaasuncion.com

ZARZUELA 2010 B
verdejo.

88 Colour: bright straw. Nose: fresh, fresh fruit, white flowers. Palate: flavourful, fruity, good acidity, balanced.

BODEGA CUATRO RAYAS AGRÍCOLA CASTELLANA

Ctra. Rodilana, s/n
47491 La Seca (Valladolid)
☎: +34 983 816 320 - Fax: +34 983 816 562
info@cuatrorayas.org
www.cuatrorayas.org

CUATRO RAYAS VERDEJO 2010 B
verdejo.

90 Colour: bright straw. Nose: fresh, white flowers, candied fruit. Palate: flavourful, fruity, good acidity, balanced.

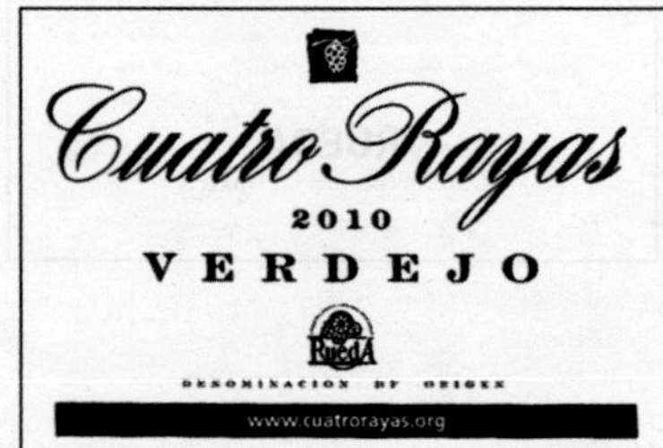

PALACIO DE VIVERO 2010 B
100% verdejo.

89 Colour: bright straw. Nose: fresh, white flowers, balsamic herbs, ripe fruit. Palate: flavourful, fruity, good acidity.

CUATRO RAYAS SAUVIGNON 2010 B
sauvignon blanc.

87 Colour: bright straw. Nose: tropical fruit, candied fruit, medium intensity. Palate: light-bodied, fresh, fruity.

BITÁCORA VERDEJO 2010 B
100% verdejo.

87 Colour: bright straw. Nose: ripe fruit, tropical fruit, floral. Palate: varietal, sweetness, full.

APOTEOSIS 2010 B
100% verdejo.

87 Colour: pale. Nose: candied fruit, citrus fruit, white flowers. Palate: flavourful, fruity, fresh.

VISIGODO VERDEJO 2010 B
100% verdejo.

91 Colour: bright straw. Nose: fresh, white flowers, grassy. Palate: flavourful, fruity, good acidity, spicy, long.

VELITERRA 2010 B
verdejo.

85 Colour: bright straw. Nose: ripe fruit, citrus fruit, dried herbs. Palate: flavourful, fruity, fresh.

AZUMBRE VERDEJO VIÑEDOS CENTENARIOS 2010 B
100% verdejo.

88 Colour: bright straw. Nose: fresh, white flowers, ripe fruit. Palate: flavourful, fruity, good acidity, balanced.

CUATRO RAYAS VIÑEDOS CENTENARIOS 2010 B
100% verdejo.

92 Colour: bright straw. Nose: fresh fruit, white flowers, varietal, mineral. Palate: flavourful, fruity, good acidity, fine bitter notes.

CUATRO RAYAS 2008 BFB
100% verdejo.

90 Colour: bright yellow. Nose: powerfull, ripe fruit, sweet spices. Palate: rich, smoky aftertaste, flavourful, fresh, good acidity.

VACCEOS RD
tempranillo.

82 Colour: brilliant rose. Nose: candied fruit, red berry notes, floral. Palate: fruity, fresh.

VACCEOS TEMPRANILLO 2009 T ROBLE
100% tempranillo.

88 Colour: bright cherry. Nose: sweet spices, creamy oak, expressive, red berry notes. Palate: flavourful, fruity, round tannins.

VACCEOS 2007 TC
100% tempranillo.

88 Color cherry, garnet rim. Aroma ripe fruit, spicy, creamy oak, toasty, complex. Taste powerful, flavourful, toasty, round tannins.

DOLCE BIANCO VERDEJO 2010 SEMIDULCE
100% verdejo.

85 Colour: pale. Nose: white flowers, tropical fruit, fresh fruit, fresh. Palate: flavourful, fresh, fruity.

PÁMPANO SEMIDULCE
100% verdejo.

83 Colour: bright straw. Nose: floral, medium intensity, candied fruit, citrus fruit. Palate: flavourful, sweetness, fine bitter notes.

BODEGA EL ALBAR LURTON

Camino Magarin s/n
47529 Villafranca del Duero (Valladolid)
☎: +34 983 034 030 - Fax: +34 983 034 040
bodega@jflurton.es
www.francoislurton.com

HERMANOS LURTON VERDEJO 2010 B
verdejo.

87 Colour: bright straw. Nose: medium intensity, fresh fruit, floral. Palate: good acidity, flavourful, fruity, fresh.

HERMANOS LURTON SAUVIGNON BLANC 2010 B
sauvignon blanc.

86 Colour: bright straw. Nose: white flowers, fruit expression, fragrant herbs. Palate: flavourful, fruity, easy to drink.

HERMANOS LURTON CUESTA DE ORO 2008 BFB
verdejo.

90 Colour: bright golden. Nose: fine lees, faded flowers, ripe fruit, dried herbs, creamy oak. Palate: rich, spicy, balanced, fleshy.

BODEGA EMINA MEDINA DEL CAMPO

Ctra. Medina del Campo - Olmedo, Km. 1,5
47400 Medina del Campo (Valladolid)
☎: +34 983 800 001 - Fax: +34 902 430 189
eminarueda@emina.es
www.eminarueda.es

MELIOR VERDEJO 2010 B
100% verdejo.

90 Colour: bright straw. Nose: floral, citrus fruit, expressive, fragrant herbs. Palate: fleshy, fruity, rich, flavourful.

EMINA RUEDA 2010 B
90% verdejo, 10% viura.

86 Colour: bright straw. Nose: fresh fruit, tropical fruit, medium intensity. Palate: good acidity, fresh, easy to drink.

EMINA VERDEJO 2010 B
100% verdejo.

88 Colour: bright straw. Nose: fresh fruit, white flowers, varietal. Palate: flavourful, fruity, good acidity, balanced.

EMINA SAUVIGNON 2010 B
100% sauvignon blanc.

86 Colour: bright straw. Nose: tropical fruit, fresh, floral. Palate: fruity, light-bodied, fresh, easy to drink.

SELECCIÓN PERSONAL CARLOS MORO EMINA VERDEJO 2009 BFB
100% verdejo.

93 Colour: bright yellow. Nose: powerfull, ripe fruit, sweet spices, creamy oak, fragrant herbs. Palate: rich, flavourful, fresh, good acidity.

EMINA ROSADO BR
100% tempranillo.

78

EMINA BN
100% verdejo.

84 Colour: bright straw. Nose: medium intensity, dried herbs, fine lees, floral. Palate: fresh, fruity, flavourful, good acidity.

EMINA SS
100% verdejo.

86 Colour: bright straw. Nose: medium intensity, fresh fruit, dried herbs, fine lees, floral. Palate: flavourful, good acidity, sweetness.

BODEGA GÓTICA

Ctra. Rueda - La Seca, Km. 1,2
47490 Rueda (Valladolid)
☎: +34 983 868 387 - Fax: +34 983 868 387
mjhmonsalve@ya.com
www.trascampanas.com

TRASCAMPANAS VERDEJO 2010 B
100% verdejo.

92 Colour: bright straw. Nose: fresh, white flowers, ripe fruit, expressive, varietal. Palate: flavourful, fruity, good acidity, balanced.

TRASCAMPANAS SAUVIGNON 2010 B
100% sauvignon blanc.

90 Colour: bright straw. Nose: candied fruit, dried herbs, faded flowers. Palate: flavourful, long, sweetness.

MONSALVE VERDEJO 2010 B
100% verdejo.

89 Colour: bright straw. Nose: fresh, fresh fruit, white flowers, ripe fruit. Palate: flavourful, fruity, good acidity.

POLÍGONO 10 SAUVIGNON 2010 B
100% sauvignon blanc.

88 Colour: bright straw. Nose: white flowers, expressive, ripe fruit. Palate: flavourful, fruity, good acidity, fine bitter notes.

POLÍGONO 10 VERDEJO 2010 B
100% verdejo.

89 Colour: bright straw. Nose: fresh, white flowers, ripe fruit. Palate: flavourful, fruity, good acidity, balanced.

BADAJO RUEDA 2010 B
100% verdejo.

88 Colour: bright straw. Nose: fresh, fresh fruit, expressive, citrus fruit, fragrant herbs. Palate: flavourful, fruity, fleshy, fresh.

MOYORIDO VERDEJO 2010 B
100% verdejo.

88 Colour: bright straw. Nose: candied fruit, citrus fruit, white flowers. Palate: flavourful, powerful, sweetness.

CAMINO LA FARA VERDEJO 2010 B
100% verdejo.

88 Colour: bright straw. Nose: fresh, fresh fruit, varietal. Palate: flavourful, fruity, good acidity, balanced.

BODEGA HERMANOS DEL VILLAR

Zarcillo, s/n
47490 Rueda (Valladolid)
☎: +34 983 868 904 - Fax: +34 983 868 905
info@orodecastilla.com
www.orodecastilla.com

ORO DE CASTILLA VERDEJO 2010 B
100% verdejo.

88 Color bright straw. Aroma fresh, fresh fruit, white flowers, expressive. Taste flavourful, fruity, good acidity, balanced.

ORO DE CASTILLA SAUVIGNON BLANC 2010 B
100% sauvignon blanc.

86 Colour: bright straw. Nose: fresh fruit, expressive, citrus fruit. Palate: flavourful, fruity, good acidity.

BODEGA LA SOTERRAÑA

Ctra. Valladolid - Madrid N-601, Km. 151
47410 Olmedo (Valladolid)
☎: +34 983 601 026 - Fax: +34 983 601 026
edominguez@bodegaslasoterrana.com
www.bodegaslasoterrana.com

ERESMA SAUVIGNON 2010 B
100% sauvignon blanc.

90 Colour: bright straw. Nose: fresh, fresh fruit, white flowers, expressive, mineral. Palate: flavourful, fruity, good acidity, balanced, fleshy.

ERESMA 2010 B
verdejo.

88 Colour: bright straw. Nose: candied fruit, citrus fruit, white flowers. Palate: flavourful, fruity, fleshy.

ERESMA VERDEJO 2010 B
100% verdejo.

87 Colour: bright straw. Nose: fresh, white flowers, expressive, fragrant herbs. Palate: flavourful, fruity, balanced, easy to drink.

77 RUEDA 2010 B
80% verdejo, 20% viura.

86 Colour: bright straw. Nose: fresh, fresh fruit, white flowers, expressive, fragrant herbs. Palate: flavourful, fruity, good acidity, fresh.

BODEGA MONTE BLANCO

Ctra. Valladolid, Km. 24,5
Serrada (Valladolid)
☎: +34 941 310 295 - Fax: +34 941 310 832
info@bodegas-monteblanco.es
www.bodegas-monteblanco.es

MONTE BLANCO DE RAMÓN BILBAO VERDEJO 2010 B
verdejo.

90 Colour: bright straw. Nose: white flowers, fragrant herbs, citrus fruit, powerfull, expressive. Palate: good acidity, powerful, flavourful, fleshy.

BODEGA NOS RIQUEZA

Sánchez Calvo, 6
33402 Avilés (Asturias)
☎: +34 984 836 826 - Fax: +34 985 931 074
exportmanager@nosriqueza.com
www.nosriqueza.com

NOS RIQUEZA 2010 B
100% verdejo.

89 Colour: bright straw. Nose: candied fruit, citrus fruit, grassy. Palate: good structure, fleshy, fruity.

BODEGA PALACIO DE BORNOS

Ctra. Madrid - Coruña, km. 170,6
47490 Rueda (Valladolid)
☎: +34 983 868 116 - Fax: +34 983 868 432
info@taninia.com
www.palaciodeborno.com

PALACIOS DE BORNOS LA CAPRICHOSA 2010 B
verdejo.

91 Colour: bright straw. Nose: fresh fruit, white flowers, mineral, varietal. Palate: flavourful, fruity, good acidity.

PALACIOS DE BORNOS VERDEJO 2010 B
100% verdejo.

88 Colour: bright straw. Nose: fresh, white flowers, grassy, ripe fruit. Palate: flavourful, fruity, good acidity, balanced.

PALACIO DE BORNOS SAUVIGNON BLANC 2010 B
100% sauvignon blanc.

88 Colour: bright straw. Nose: fresh, white flowers, varietal, ripe fruit. Palate: flavourful, fruity, good acidity, fine bitter notes.

PALACIO DE BORNOS SEMIDULCE 2010 B
100% sauvignon blanc.

84 Colour: bright straw. Nose: powerfull, floral, honeyed notes, fragrant herbs. Palate: flavourful, sweet, fresh, fruity, good acidity.

PALACIO DE BORNOS VERDEJO VENDIMIA SELECCIONADA 2009 BFB
verdejo.

92 Colour: bright yellow. Nose: powerfull, ripe fruit, sweet spices, creamy oak, fragrant herbs, citrus fruit. Palate: rich, smoky aftertaste, flavourful, fresh, good acidity.

PALACIOS DE BORNOS VERDEJO 2009 BFB
verdejo.

90 Colour: bright yellow. Nose: powerfull, ripe fruit, sweet spices, creamy oak, fragrant herbs. Palate: rich, smoky aftertaste, flavourful, fleshy.

PALACIOS DE BORNOS BR
verdejo.

83 Color bright straw. Aroma medium intensity, fresh fruit, dried herbs, fine lees, floral. Taste fresh, fruity, flavourful, good acidity.

PALACIOS DE BORNOS BN
verdejo.

84 Colour: bright straw. Nose: medium intensity, fresh fruit, fine lees, floral, fragrant herbs. Palate: fresh, fruity, flavourful, fine bead.

PALACIOS DE BORNOS SS
verdejo.

84 Colour: bright straw. Nose: medium intensity, fresh fruit, floral, fragrant herbs. Palate: fresh, fruity, flavourful, good acidity.

BODEGA REINA DE CASTILLA

Ctra. Serrada - La Seca. La Moya, s/n
47491 La Seca (Valladolid)
☎: +34 983 816 667 - Fax: +34 983 816 663
bodega@reinadecastilla.es
www.reinadecastilla.es

EL BUFÓN VERDEJO 2010 B
100% verdejo.

92 Colour: bright straw. Nose: expressive, citrus fruit, fragrant herbs, mineral. Palate: flavourful, fruity, good acidity, balanced, fleshy.

REINA DE CASTILLA VERDEJO 2010 B
100% verdejo.

91 Colour: bright straw. Nose: fresh, white flowers, expressive, mineral, citrus fruit. Palate: flavourful, fruity, good acidity, balanced, fleshy, complex.

REINA DE CASTILLA SAUVIGNON BLANC 2010 B
100% sauvignon blanc.

91 Colour: bright straw. Nose: fresh, fresh fruit, white flowers, mineral. Palate: flavourful, fruity, good acidity, balanced.

ISABELINO 2010 B
70% verdejo, 30% viura.

89 Colour: bright straw. Nose: fresh, white flowers, tropical fruit. Palate: flavourful, fruity, good acidity, balanced.

VASALLO VERDEJO 2010 B
100% verdejo.

86 Colour: bright straw. Nose: fresh, fresh fruit, white flowers, expressive, grassy. Palate: flavourful, fruity, good acidity.

BODEGA VALDEHERMOSO

Pasión, 13 - 4ºD
47001 (Valladolid)
☎: +34 651 993 680
valdehermoso@valdehermoso.com
www.valdehermoso.com

LAGAR DEL REY 2010 B
verdejo.

89 Colour: bright straw. Nose: fresh, white flowers, ripe fruit. Palate: flavourful, fruity, good acidity, fine bitter notes.

BODEGA VALDELOSFRAILES

Camino de Cubillas, s/n
47290 Cubillas de Santa Marta (Valladolid)
☎: +34 983 485 028 - Fax: +34 983 485 028
valdelosfrailes@matarromera.es
www.valdelosfrailes.es

VALDELOSFRAILES 2010 B
verdejo.

88 Colour: bright straw. Nose: fresh, jasmine, ripe fruit. Palate: flavourful, fruity, good acidity, balanced.

BODEGA VIÑA VILANO S. COOP.

Ctra. de Anguix, 10
09314 Pedrosa de Duero (Burgos)
☎: +34 947 530 029 - Fax: +34 947 530 037
info@vinavilano.com
www.vinavilano.com

VIÑA VILANO VERDEJO 2010 B
100% verdejo.

88 Colour: bright straw. Nose: fresh, white flowers, citrus fruit, ripe fruit. Palate: flavourful, fruity, good acidity, fine bitter notes.

BODEGAS CASTELO DE MEDINA

Ctra. CL-602, Km. 48
47465 Villaverde de Medina (Valladolid)
☎: +34 983 831 932 - Fax: +34 983 831 857
comercial@castelodemedina.es
www.castelodemedina.es

CASTELO NOBLE 2008 BFB
85% verdejo, 15% sauvignon blanc.

88 Colour: bright golden. Nose: ripe fruit, dry nuts, powerfull, toasty. Palate: flavourful, fruity, spicy, toasty, long.

CASTELO DE MEDINA VERDEJO 2010 B
100% verdejo.

90 Color bright straw. Aroma fresh, fresh fruit, white flowers, expressive. Taste flavourful, fruity, good acidity, balanced.

REAL CASTELO 2010 B
85% verdejo, 15% sauvignon blanc.

89 Colour: bright straw. Nose: fresh, fresh fruit, expressive, dried flowers, grassy. Palate: flavourful, fruity, good acidity, green.

CASTELO DE LA DEHESA 2010 B
50% verdejo, 30% viura, 20% sauvignon blanc.

87 Colour: bright straw. Nose: fresh, expressive, tropical fruit. Palate: flavourful, fruity, good acidity, easy to drink.

CASTELO ÁMBAR SEMIDULCE 2009 B
100% sauvignon blanc.

86 Colour: golden. Nose: powerfull, floral, candied fruit. Palate: flavourful, sweet, fresh, fruity, good acidity, long.

CASTEL BURGO BN
85% verdejo, 15% sauvignon blanc.

83 Colour: bright straw. Nose: dried herbs, candied fruit, fresh. Palate: light-bodied, fruity, fresh.

CASTELO DE MEDINA SAUVIGNON BLANC 2010 B
100% sauvignon blanc.

91 Colour: bright straw. Nose: grassy, balsamic herbs, citrus fruit. Palate: light-bodied, fresh, ripe fruit.

BODEGAS CHIVITE

Ribera, 34
31592 Cintruénigo (Navarra)
☎: +34 948 811 000 - Fax: +34 948 811 407
info@bodegaschivite.com
www.bodegaschivite.com

BALUARTE 2010 B
100% verdejo.

91 Color bright straw. Aroma fresh, fresh fruit, white flowers, expressive. Taste flavourful, fruity, good acidity, balanced.

BODEGAS COPABOCA

N-122, Km. 407
47114 Tordesillas (Valladolid)
☎: +34 983 395 655 - Fax: +34 983 307 729
santiago@copaboca.com
www.copaboca.com

COPABOCA VERDEJO 2010 B
100% verdejo.

88 Colour: bright straw. Nose: fresh, white flowers, expressive, tropical fruit. Palate: flavourful, fruity, good acidity, balanced, fleshy.

GORGORITO VERDEJO 2010 B
100% verdejo.

88 Colour: bright straw. Nose: fresh, white flowers, ripe fruit. Palate: flavourful, fruity, good acidity.

EMILIO GIMENO 2010 B
verdejo.

86 Colour: bright straw. Nose: white flowers, candied fruit, medium intensity. Palate: flavourful, fruity, good acidity, fine bitter notes.

BODEGAS DE LOS HEREDEROS DEL MARQUÉS DE RISCAL

Torrea, 1
01340 Elciego (Álava)
☎: +34 945 606 000 - Fax: +34 945 606 023
marquesderiscal@marquesderiscal.com
www.marquesderiscal.com

MARQUÉS DE RISCAL SAUVIGNON BLANC 2010 B
100% sauvignon blanc.

92 Colour: bright straw. Nose: fresh, white flowers, expressive, grassy, balsamic herbs, ripe fruit. Palate: flavourful, fruity, good acidity, balanced.

FINCA MONTICO 2009 B
verdejo.

91 Colour: bright yellow. Nose: powerfull, candied fruit, sweet spices, fragrant herbs. Palate: flavourful, fine bitter notes, balanced.

MARQUÉS DE RISCAL LIMOUSIN 2008 B
100% verdejo.

91 Colour: bright yellow. Nose: powerfull, ripe fruit, creamy oak. Palate: rich, smoky aftertaste, flavourful, fresh, good acidity.

FINCA MONTICO 2010 B
100% verdejo.

92 Colour: bright straw. Nose: white flowers, ripe fruit, neat, varietal, mineral. Palate: flavourful, fruity, good acidity, balanced.

MARQUÉS DE RISCAL RUEDA VERDEJO 2010 B
100% verdejo.

91 Colour: bright straw. Nose: fresh fruit, white flowers, characterful, varietal, mineral. Palate: flavourful, fruity, good acidity, balanced.

BODEGAS DE LOS RÍOS PRIETO

Ctra. Pesquera - Renedo, s/n
47315 Pesquera de Duero (Valladolid)
☎: +34 983 880 383 - Fax: +34 983 878 032
info@bodegasdelosriosprieto.com
www.bodegasdelosriosprieto.com

PRIOS MAXIMUS VERDEJO 2010 B
100% verdejo.

88 Colour: bright straw. Nose: fresh, white flowers, grassy, ripe fruit. Palate: flavourful, fruity, good acidity, balanced.

BODEGAS FÉLIX LORENZO CACHAZO S.L.

Ctra. Medina del Campo, Km. 9
47220 Pozáldez (Valladolid)
☎: +34 983 822 176 - Fax: +34 983 822 008
bodegas@cachazo.com
www.cachazo.com

MANIA RUEDA VERDEJO 2010 B
100% verdejo.

90 Colour: bright straw. Nose: fresh, fresh fruit, white flowers, expressive, elegant. Palate: flavourful, fruity, good acidity, balanced.

GRAN CARDIEL RUEDA VERDEJO 2010 B
100% verdejo.

89 Colour: bright straw. Nose: fresh, white flowers, ripe fruit. Palate: flavourful, fruity, good acidity.

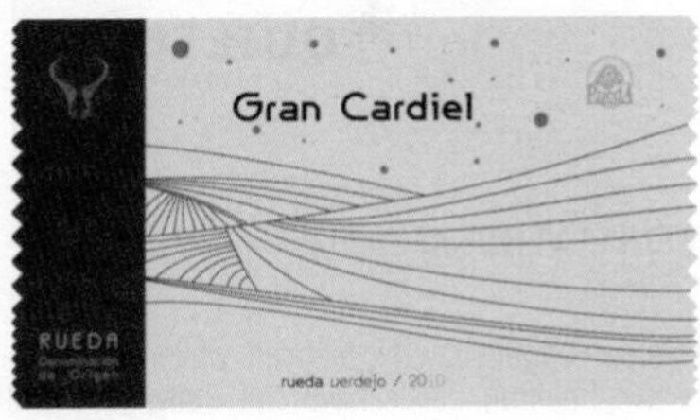

CARRASVIÑAS VERDEJO 2010 B
100% verdejo.

89 Colour: bright straw. Nose: fresh fruit, white flowers, grassy. Palate: flavourful, fruity, good acidity, balanced, fleshy.

QUIETUS VERDEJO 2010 B
100% verdejo.

88 Colour: bright straw. Nose: fresh, tropical fruit, white flowers, balanced. Palate: light-bodied, fresh, fruity, fleshy.

AVENENCIA VERDEJO 2009 B
100% verdejo.

86 Colour: bright straw. Nose: fresh, white flowers, expressive, ripe fruit. Palate: flavourful, fruity, good acidity.

CARRASVIÑAS ESPUMOSO BR
100% verdejo.

89 Color bright straw. Aroma medium intensity, fresh fruit, dried herbs, fine lees, floral. Taste fresh, fruity, flavourful, good acidity.

BODEGAS FÉLIX SANZ S.L.

Ronda Aradillas, s/n
47490 Rueda (Valladolid)
☎: +34 983 868 044 - Fax: +34 983 868 133
info@bodegasfelixsanz.es
www.bodegasfelixsanz.es

VIÑA CIMBRÓN VERDEJO SELECCIÓN 2010 B
100% verdejo.

90 Colour: bright straw. Nose: fresh, fresh fruit, white flowers, lactic notes. Palate: flavourful, fruity, good acidity, balanced.

VIÑA CIMBRÓN RUEDA SAUVIGNON 2010 B
100% sauvignon blanc.

89 Colour: bright straw. Nose: fresh, fresh fruit, white flowers, fragrant herbs. Palate: flavourful, fruity, balanced, fleshy.

VIÑA CIMBRÓN 2010 BFB
100% verdejo.

88 Colour: bright yellow. Nose: ripe fruit, sweet spices, creamy oak. Palate: rich, smoky aftertaste, flavourful, fresh, good acidity.

VIÑA CIMBRÓN RUEDA 2010 B
70% verdejo, 25% viura, 5% sauvignon blanc.

87 Colour: bright straw. Nose: fresh, fresh fruit, white flowers, expressive, citrus fruit. Palate: flavourful, fruity, easy to drink.

VIÑA CIMBRÓN VERDEJO 2010 B
100% verdejo.

86 Colour: bright straw. Nose: fresh, fresh fruit, white flowers, grassy. Palate: flavourful, fruity, good acidity, balanced.

VIÑA CIMBRÓN 2010 RD
63% tempranillo, 37% garnacha.

90 Colour: rose, purple rim. Nose: powerfull, ripe fruit, red berry notes, floral. Palate: fleshy, powerful, fruity, fresh.

BODEGAS GARCÍA DE ARANDA

Ctra. de Soria, s/n
09400 Aranda de Duero (Burgos)
☎: +34 947 501 817 - Fax: +34 947 506 355
bodega@bodegasgarcia.com
www.bodegasgarcia.com

SEÑORÍO DE LOS BALDÍOS VERDEJO 2010 B
100% verdejo.

89 Colour: bright straw. Nose: citrus fruit, fresh fruit, floral, fragrant herbs, varietal. Palate: fresh, fruity, flavourful, fleshy, balanced.

ORO BLANCO VERDEJO 2010 B
100% verdejo.

87 Colour: bright straw. Nose: white flowers, ripe fruit, fragrant herbs. Palate: flavourful, fruity, good acidity, balanced.

ORO BLANCO RUEDA 2010 B
50% verdejo, 50% viura.

85 Colour: bright straw. Nose: fresh, fresh fruit, white flowers, expressive. Palate: flavourful, fruity, good acidity.

BODEGAS GARCÍAREVALO

Pza. San Juan, 4
47230 Matapozuelos (Valladolid)
☎: +34 983 832 914 - Fax: +34 983 832 986
enologo@garciarevalo.com
www.garciarevalo.com

TRES OLMOS LÍAS 2010 B
100% verdejo.

90 Colour: bright straw. Nose: grassy, powerfull, varietal, white flowers. Palate: flavourful, fruity, good acidity.

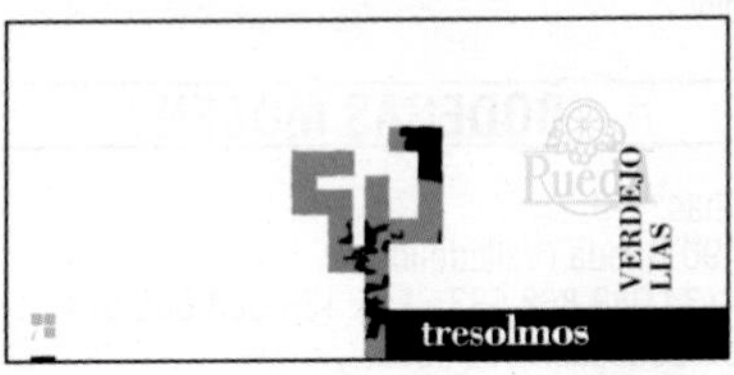

VIÑA ADAJA VERDEJO 2010 B
100% verdejo.

89 Colour: bright straw. Nose: fresh, white flowers, ripe fruit, citrus fruit. Palate: flavourful, fruity, good acidity, balanced.

BODEGAS GARCIGRANDE

Aradillas, s/n
57490 Rueda (Valladolid)
☎: +34 983 868 561 - Fax: +34 983 868 449
info@hispanobodegas.com
www.hispanobodegas.com

SEÑORÍO DE GARCI GRANDE VERDEJO 2010 B
100% verdejo.

90 Color bright straw. Aroma fresh, fresh fruit, white flowers, expressive. Taste flavourful, fruity, good acidity, balanced.

12 LINAJES VERDEJO 2010 B
100% verdejo.

90 Colour: bright straw. Nose: fresh, white flowers, varietal, neat, fresh fruit. Palate: flavourful, fruity, good acidity, balanced.

SEÑORÍO DE GARCI GRANDE 2010 B
verdejo, viura.

87 Colour: bright straw. Nose: fresh, fresh fruit, white flowers, expressive, tropical fruit. Palate: flavourful, fruity, good acidity, balanced.

BODEGAS IMPERIALES

Ctra. Madrid - Irun, Km. 171
09370 Gumiel de Izán (Burgos)
☎: +34 947 544 070 - Fax: +34 947 525 759
direccion@bodegasimperiales.com
www.bodegasimperiales.com

ABADÍA DE SAN QUIRCE VERDEJO 2010 B
100% verdejo.

90 Colour: bright straw. Nose: fresh fruit, white flowers, varietal. Palate: flavourful, fruity, good acidity, balanced.

BODEGAS JOSÉ PARIENTE

Ctra. Rueda - La Seca, km. 2.5
47491 La Seca (Valladolid)
☎: +34 983 816 600 - Fax: +34 983 816 620
info@josepariente.com
www.josepariente.com

JOSÉ PARIENTE VERDEJO 2010 B
100% verdejo.

91 Colour: bright straw. Nose: fresh, fresh fruit, white flowers, varietal, grassy, complex. Palate: flavourful, fruity, good acidity, balanced.

JOSÉ PARIENTE SAUVIGNON BLANC 2010 B
100% sauvignon blanc.

88 Colour: bright straw. Nose: fresh, white flowers, expressive, tropical fruit. Palate: flavourful, fruity, balanced.

JOSÉ PARIENTE 2009 BFB
100% verdejo.

88 Colour: bright yellow. Nose: powerfull, ripe fruit, sweet spices, creamy oak. Palate: rich, smoky aftertaste, flavourful, fresh, good acidity.

BODEGAS LA ESPERANZA

Brisol, 16 bis
28230 Las Rozas (Madrid)
☎: +34 917 104 880 - Fax: +34 917 104 881
anap@swd.es
www.swd.es

PÍA 2010 B
100% verdejo.

88 Colour: bright straw. Nose: fresh, fresh fruit, white flowers, balsamic herbs. Palate: flavourful, fruity, good acidity.

BODEGAS MOCEN

Arribas, 7-9
47490 Rueda (Valladolid)
☎: +34 983 868 533 - Fax: +34 983 868 514
info@bodegasmocen.com
www.bodegasantano.com

ALTA PLATA VERDEJO 2010 B
100% verdejo.

91 Colour: bright straw. Nose: fresh, white flowers, ripe fruit. Palate: flavourful, fruity, good acidity, balanced.

AÑ SAUVIGNON SEMIDULCE 2010 B
100% sauvignon blanc.

87 Colour: bright straw. Nose: candied fruit, fruit preserve, citrus fruit. Palate: flavourful, sweetness.

VIÑA PATI 2010 B

87 Colour: bright straw. Nose: fresh, white flowers, ripe fruit. Palate: flavourful, fruity, good acidity, balanced.

LEGUILLÓN VERDEJO 2010 B
100% verdejo.

91 Colour: bright straw. Nose: fresh, white flowers, ripe fruit. Palate: flavourful, fruity, good acidity, balanced.

MOCÉN SAUVIGNON 2010 B
100% sauvignon blanc.

89 Colour: bright straw. Nose: fresh, fresh fruit, fragrant herbs, expressive. Palate: flavourful, fruity, good acidity, balanced.

MOCÉN VERDEJO 2008 BFB
100% verdejo.

90 Colour: bright yellow. Nose: powerfull, sweet spices, creamy oak, overripe fruit. Palate: rich, smoky aftertaste, flavourful, fresh, good acidity.

AÑ BN ESPUMOSO
100% verdejo.

84 Color bright straw. Aroma medium intensity, fresh fruit, dried herbs, fine lees, floral. Taste fresh, fruity, flavourful, good acidity.

MOCÉN VERDEJO 2010 B
100% verdejo.

89 Colour: bright straw. Nose: fresh, white flowers, ripe fruit, citrus fruit. Palate: flavourful, fruity, good acidity, balanced.

BODEGAS NAIA

Camino San Martín, s/n
47491 La Seca (Valladolid)
☎: +34 628 434 933
info@bodegasnaia.com
www.bodegasnaia.com

NAIA 2010 B
100% verdejo.

92 Colour: bright straw. Nose: white flowers, varietal, complex, ripe fruit. Palate: flavourful, fruity, good acidity, balanced.

LAS BRISAS 2010 B
verdejo.

90 Colour: bright straw. Nose: fresh, white flowers, ripe fruit. Palate: flavourful, fruity, good acidity.

K-NAIA 2010 B
85% verdejo, 15% sauvignon blanc.

90 Colour: bright straw. Nose: fresh, fresh fruit, white flowers, balsamic herbs. Palate: flavourful, fruity, good acidity, balanced.

NAIADES 2008 BFB
100% verdejo.

97 Colour: bright yellow. Nose: faded flowers, ripe fruit, fragrant herbs, sweet spices, creamy oak, balanced, expressive. Palate: powerful, flavourful, fleshy, complex, mineral.

BODEGAS NILO

Federico García Lorca, 7
47490 Rueda (Valladolid)
☎: +34 690 068 682 - Fax: +34 983 868 366
info@bodegasnilo.com
www.bodegasnilo.com

BIANCA 2010 B
100% verdejo.

87 Colour: bright straw. Nose: white flowers, citrus fruit, fragrant herbs. Palate: balanced, fresh, fruity, flavourful.

BODEGAS PEÑAFIEL

Ctra. N-122, Km. 311
47300 Peñafiel (Valladolid)
☎: +34 983 881 622 - Fax: +34 983 881 944
bodegaspenafiel@bodegaspenafiel.com
www.bodegaspenafiel.com

ALBA MIROS 2010 B
verdejo.

90 Colour: bright straw. Nose: fresh, white flowers, ripe fruit. Palate: flavourful, fruity, good acidity, balanced.

BODEGAS PRADOREY

Ctra. Nacional VI, Km. 172,5
47490 Gumiel Mercado (Burgos)
☎: +34 983 444 048 - Fax: +34 983 868 564
bodeg@pradorey.com
www.pradorey.com

PRADOREY SAUVIGNON BLANC 2010 B
100% sauvignon blanc.

91 Colour: bright straw. Nose: fresh, fresh fruit, expressive, fragrant herbs. Palate: flavourful, fruity, good acidity, complex.

PR 3 BARRICAS 2008 BFB
100% verdejo.

93 Colour: bright yellow. Nose: powerfull, ripe fruit, sweet spices, creamy oak, fragrant herbs, citrus fruit. Palate: rich, smoky aftertaste, flavourful, fresh, good acidity, fleshy.

PRADOREY VERDEJO 2010 B
100% verdejo.

90 Colour: bright straw. Nose: fragrant herbs, citrus fruit, fresh, expressive. Palate: fresh, flavourful, fleshy, balanced.

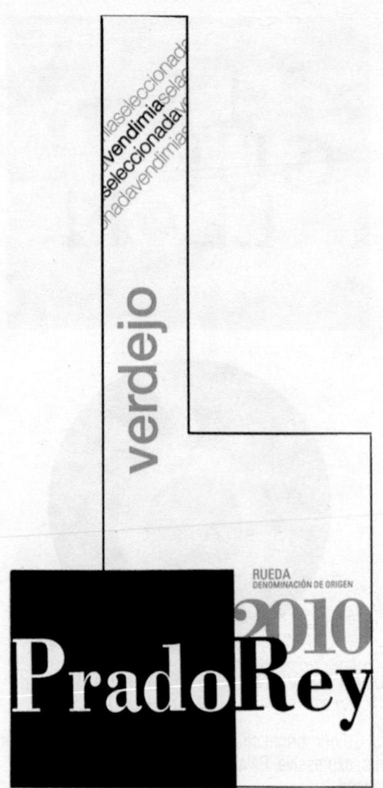

BODEGAS PROTOS

Ctra. CL 610, Medina - La Seca Km. 32,5
47491 La Seca (Valladolid)
☎: +34 983 816 608
bodega@bodegasprotos.com
www.bodegasprotos.com

PROTOS 2009 B BARRICA
100% verdejo.

93 Colour: bright yellow. Nose: ripe fruit, dry nuts, fine lees, spicy, creamy oak. Palate: elegant, balanced, powerful, flavourful, fleshy, toasty.

PROTOS VERDEJO 2010 B
100% verdejo.

91 Colour: bright straw. Nose: white flowers, tropical fruit, citrus fruit, balsamic herbs. Palate: good acidity, rich, flavourful, fruity, long.

BODEGAS RUEDA PÉREZ

Boyón
47220 Pozáldez (Valladolid)
☎: +34 650 454 657 - Fax: +34 983 822 049
satruedaperez@terra.es
www.bodegasruedaperez.es

VIÑA BURÓN VERDEJO 2010 B
100% verdejo.

91 Colour: bright straw. Nose: white flowers, grassy. Palate: flavourful, fruity, good acidity, balanced.

JOSÉ GALO VERDEJO SELECCIÓN 2010 B
100% verdejo.

89 Color bright straw. Aroma fresh, fresh fruit, white flowers, expressive. Taste flavourful, fruity, good acidity, balanced.

ZAPADORADO VERDEJO 2010 B
100% verdejo.

87 Color bright straw. Aroma fresh, fresh fruit, white flowers, expressive. Taste flavourful, fruity, good acidity, balanced.

BODEGAS SEÑORÍO DE NAVA

Ctra. Valladolid - Soria, 62
09318 Nava de Roa (Burgos)
☎: +34 987 209 790 - Fax: +34 987 209 808
c.puente@senoriodenava.es
www.senoriodenava.es

VAL DE LAMAS VERDEJO 2010 B
100% verdejo.

86 Color bright straw. Aroma fresh, fresh fruit, white flowers, expressive. Taste flavourful, fruity, good acidity, balanced.

SEÑORÍO DE NAVA VERDEJO 2010 B
100% verdejo.

84 Colour: bright straw. Nose: overripe fruit, warm, medium intensity. Palate: fresh, light-bodied, fruity.

BODEGAS TAMARAL

Ctra. N-122, Km. 310,6
47300 Peñafiel (Valladolid)
☎: +34 983 878 017 - Fax: +34 983 878 089
zarzuelo@tamaral.com
www.tamaral.com

TAMARAL VERDEJO 2010 B
100% verdejo.

88 Colour: bright straw. Nose: fresh, white flowers, powerfull, varietal, ripe fruit. Palate: flavourful, fruity, good acidity.

BODEGAS TIONIO

Ctra. de Valoria, Km. 7
47315 Pesquera de Duero (Valladolid)
☎: +34 933 950 811 - Fax: +34 983 870 185
info@parxet.es
www.parxet.es

AUSTUM VERDEJO 2010 B
100% verdejo.

88 Colour: bright yellow. Nose: candied fruit, citrus fruit, tropical fruit, balsamic herbs. Palate: flavourful, fruity, full.

BODEGAS TORRES

Miguel Torres, 6
08720 Vilafranca del Penedès (Barcelona)
☎: +34 938 177 400 - Fax: +34 938 177 444
mailadmin@torres.es
www.torres.es

VERDEO 2010 B
verdejo.

88 Colour: bright straw. Nose: citrus fruit, white flowers, fragrant herbs, expressive. Palate: good acidity, flavourful, fruity.

BODEGAS VAL DE VID

Ctra. Valladolid - Medina, Km. 23,6
47239 Serrada (Valladolid)
☎: +34 983 559 914 - Fax: +34 983 559 914
esther.vega@avintec.es

CONDESA EYLO 2010 B
100% verdejo.

90 Colour: bright straw. Nose: fresh, fresh fruit, white flowers, tropical fruit, grassy. Palate: flavourful, fruity, good acidity, balanced.

VAL DE VID VERDEJO 2010 B
100% verdejo.

90 Colour: pale. Nose: white flowers, powerfull, characterful, complex. Palate: flavourful, powerful, sweetness.

VAL DE VID 2010 B
70% verdejo, 30% viura.

90 Colour: bright straw. Nose: fresh, fresh fruit, white flowers, expressive, mineral. Palate: flavourful, fruity, good acidity, balanced.

EYLO RUEDA 2010 B
70% verdejo, 30% viura.

88 Colour: bright straw. Nose: white flowers, grassy, ripe fruit. Palate: flavourful, fruity, good acidity, balanced.

BODEGAS VALPINCIA

Ctra. de Melida, 3,5
47300 Peñafiel (Valladolid)
☎: +34 983 878 007 - Fax: +34 983 880 620
jbartolome@bodegasvalpincia.com
www.bodegasvalpincia.com

VALPINCIA VERDEJO 2010 B
verdejo.

89 Colour: bright straw. Nose: fresh, fresh fruit, white flowers, grassy. Palate: flavourful, fruity, good acidity, fine bitter notes.

VALPINCIA 2010 B
verdejo, viura.

86 Colour: bright straw. Nose: white flowers, candied fruit, citrus fruit. Palate: flavourful, fruity, good acidity.

BODEGAS VERACRUZ S.L.

Juan A. Carmona, 1
47500 Nava del Rey (Valladolid)
☎: +34 983 850 136 - Fax: +34 983 850 761
j.benito@alvarezydiez.com

ERMITA VERACRUZ VERDEJO 2010 B
verdejo.

92 Colour: bright straw. Nose: fresh, fresh fruit, white flowers, varietal, mineral, neat. Palate: flavourful, fruity, good acidity.

BODEGAS VERDEAL

Nueva, 8
40200 Cuéllar (Segovia)
☎: +34 921 140 125 - Fax: +34 921 142 421
info@bodegasverdeal.com
www.bodegasverdeal.com

VERDEAL 2010 B
100% verdejo.

90 Colour: bright straw. Nose: fresh, fresh fruit, white flowers, expressive, mineral, scrubland. Palate: flavourful, fruity, good acidity, balanced.

BODEGAS VIORE

Camino de la Moy, s/n
47491 La Seca (Valladolid)
☎: +34 941 454 050 - Fax: +34 941 454 529
bodega@bodegasriojanas.com
www.bodegasriojanas.com

VIORE VERDEJO 2010 B
100% verdejo.

90 Colour: bright straw. Nose: fresh, fresh fruit, white flowers. Palate: flavourful, fruity, good acidity, balanced.

VIORE RUEDA 2010 B
70% verdejo, 30% viura.

89 Colour: bright straw. Nose: medium intensity, ripe fruit, tropical fruit. Palate: fleshy, fruity, flavourful.

BODEGAS VITULIA

Sendín, 49
09400 Aranda de Duero (Burgos)
☎: +34 947 515 051 - Fax: +34 947 515 051
vitulia@bodegasvitulia.com
www.bodegasvitulia.com

VITULIA VERDEJO 2010 B
100% verdejo.

87 Colour: bright yellow. Nose: ripe fruit, sweet spices, creamy oak, fragrant herbs. Palate: rich, flavourful, fresh, good acidity.

BODEGAS Y VIÑEDOS ÁNGEL LORENZO CACHAZO S.L.

Estación, 53
47220 Pozaldez (Valladolid)
☎: +34 983 822 481 - Fax: +34 983 822 012
bodegamartivilli@jet.es
www.martivilli.com

LORENZO CACHAZO 2010 B
verdejo, viura.

88 Colour: straw. Nose: ripe fruit, citrus fruit, floral. Palate: flavourful, fruity, good acidity.

MARTIVILLÍ VERDEJO 2010 B
100% verdejo.

91 Colour: bright straw. Nose: fresh, fresh fruit, white flowers. Palate: flavourful, fruity, good acidity, balanced.

MARTIVILLÍ SAUVIGNON BLANC 2010 B
sauvignon blanc.

88 Colour: bright straw. Nose: citrus fruit, tropical fruit, fresh. Palate: good acidity, flavourful, fruity, easy to drink.

BODEGAS Y VIÑEDOS MARTÍN BERDUGO

Ctra. de la Colonia, s/n
09400 Aranda de Duero (Burgos)
☎: +34 947 506 331 - Fax: +34 947 506 602
jvelasco@martinberdugo.com
www.martinberdugo.com

MARTÍN BERDUGO VERDEJO 2010 B
verdejo.

89 Colour: bright straw. Nose: fresh, fresh fruit, white flowers. Palate: flavourful, fruity, fine bitter notes, fresh.

BODEGAS Y VIÑEDOS MONTEABELLÓN

Calvario, s/n
09318 Nava de Roa (Burgos)
☎: +34 947 550 000 - Fax: +34 947 550 219
info@monteabellon.com
www.monteabellon.com

MONTEABELLÓN VERDEJO 2010 B
100% verdejo.

88 Colour: bright straw. Nose: fresh, fresh fruit, white flowers, neat, varietal. Palate: flavourful, fruity, good acidity.

BODEGAS Y VIÑEDOS NEO

Ctra. N-122, Km. 274,5
09391 Castrillo de la Vega (Burgos)
☎: +34 947 514 393 - Fax: +34 947 515 445
info@bodegasconde.com
www.bodegasneo.com

PRIMER MOTIVO VERDEJO 2010 B
100% verdejo.

88 Colour: bright straw. Nose: white flowers, varietal, fruit expression, mineral. Palate: light-bodied, fruity, fresh, flavourful, easy to drink, fine bitter notes.

BODEGAS Y VIÑEDOS SHAYA

Ctra. Aldeanueva del Codonal s/n
40462 Aldeanueva del Codonal (Segovia)
☎: +34 968 435 022
info@orowines.com
www.orowines.com

SHAYA 2010 B
100% verdejo.

90 Colour: pale. Nose: fruit expression, fresh fruit, fragrant herbs. Palate: fruity, flavourful, light-bodied, easy to drink.

SHAYA HABIS 2009 BFB
100% verdejo.

93 Colour: bright yellow. Nose: powerfull, ripe fruit, sweet spices, creamy oak, fragrant herbs, elegant. Palate: rich, smoky aftertaste, flavourful, fresh, good acidity.

CAMPOS GÓTICOS

Parcela 622
09312 Anguix (Burgos)
☎: +34 979 165 121 - Fax: +34 979 712 343
clientedirecto@camposgoticos.es
www.camposgoticos.es

CAMPOS GÓTICOS VERDEJO VENDIMIA TARDÍA 2009 B
100% verdejo.

88 Colour: bright yellow. Nose: powerfull, candied fruit, citrus fruit, spicy. Palate: powerful, fleshy, sweetness, fine bitter notes.

COMERCIAL GRUPO FREIXENET S.A.

Joan Sala, 2
08770 Sant Sadurní D'Anoia (Barcelona)
☎: +34 938 917 000 - Fax: +34 938 183 095
freixenet@freixenet.es
www.freixenet.es

FRAY GERMÁN VERDEJO 2010 B
85% verdejo, 15% viura.

87 Colour: bright straw. Nose: white flowers, citrus fruit, fragrant herbs. Palate: fresh, fruity, flavourful, light-bodied.

ETCÉTERA 2010 B
50% verdejo, 50% viura.

86 Colour: bright straw. Nose: floral, fresh fruit, medium intensity. Palate: light-bodied, fresh, good acidity, easy to drink.

FRAY GERMÁN SAUVIGNON BLANC 2010 B
100% sauvignon blanc.

84 Colour: bright straw. Nose: faded flowers, ripe fruit, grassy, citrus fruit. Palate: correct, flavourful, light-bodied.

COMPAÑÍA DE VINOS TELMO RODRÍGUEZ

El Monte, s/n
01308 Lanciego (Álava)
☎: +34 945 628 315 - Fax: +34 945 628 314
contact@telmorodriguez.com
www.telmorodriguez.com

EL TRANSISTOR 2009 B
100% verdejo.

95 Colour: bright straw. Nose: white flowers, ripe fruit, fruit expression, citrus fruit, creamy oak, lactic notes. Palate: flavourful, fruity, ripe fruit, long.

COMPAÑÍA DE VINOS MIGUEL MARTÍN

Ctra. Burgos - Portugal, Km. 101
47290 Cubillas de Santa María (Valladolid)
☎: +34 983 250 319 - Fax: +34 983 250 329
exportacion@ciadevinos.com
www.ciadevinos.com

CASTICAL VERDEJO 2010 B
verdejo.

87 Colour: bright straw. Nose: fresh, fresh fruit, white flowers, expressive. Palate: flavourful, fruity, good acidity.

DÒMINE VERDEJO 2010 B
verdejo, sauvignon blanc.

86 Colour: bright straw. Nose: citrus fruit, tropical fruit, white flowers. Palate: fresh, fruity, flavourful.

VIÑA GOY RUEDA 2010 B
verdejo, viura.

84 Colour: bright straw. Nose: dried herbs, ripe fruit, floral. Palate: fleshy, flavourful, fruity.

CASA CASTILLA 2010 RD
tempranillo.

86 Colour: rose, purple rim. Nose: red berry notes, ripe fruit, powerfull, floral. Palate: light-bodied, fresh, fruity, flavourful.

COMPAÑÍA DE VIÑEDOS IBERIAN

Camino Viejo de Rota s/n
11500 El Puerto de Santa María (Cádiz)
☎: +34 956 854 204 - Fax: +34 956 852 339
pedidos@vinosiberian.com
www.vinosiberian.com

VIÑA OROPÉNDOLA 2010 B
verdejo.

91 Colour: bright straw. Nose: fresh, expressive, ripe fruit, white flowers, grassy. Palate: flavourful, fruity, good acidity, fine bitter notes.

CUEVAS DE CASTILLA

Ctra. Madrid - Coruña, Km. 170,6
47490 Rueda (Valladolid)
☎: +34 983 686 116 - Fax: +34 983 868 432
info@taninia.com
www.taninia.com

ESPADAÑA VERDEJO 2010 B
100% verdejo.

87 Colour: bright straw. Nose: fresh, fresh fruit, white flowers. Palate: flavourful, fruity, good acidity, easy to drink.

HUERTA DEL REY 2010 RD
tempranillo.

87 Colour: rose, purple rim. Nose: powerfull, ripe fruit, red berry notes, floral. Palate: fleshy, powerful, fruity, fresh.

SEÑORÍO DE ILLESCAS 2004 TC
tempranillo.

85 Colour: cherry, garnet rim. Nose: ripe fruit, spicy, creamy oak, toasty, complex. Palate: powerful, flavourful, toasty, round tannins, fleshy.

CVNE - COMPAÑÍA VINÍCOLA DEL NORTE DE ESPAÑA

Barrio de la Estación, s/n
26200 Haro (La Rioja)
☎: +34 941 304 800 - Fax: +34 941 304 815
marketing@cvne.com
www.cvne.com

MONOPOLE S. XXI 2010 B
verdejo.

88 Colour: bright straw. Nose: fresh, white flowers, varietal. Palate: flavourful, fruity, good acidity, balanced.

DE ALBERTO

Ctra. de Valdestillas, 2
47239 Serrada (Valladolid)
☎: +34 983 559 107 - Fax: +34 983 559 084
info@dealberto.com
www.dealberto.com

DE ALBERTO VERDEJO SELECCIÓN 2010 B
verdejo.

90 Colour: bright straw. Nose: fresh, fresh fruit, white flowers, expressive, fragrant herbs. Palate: flavourful, fruity, elegant.

MONASTERIO DE PALAZUELOS 2010 B
70% verdejo, 30% viura.

88 Colour: bright straw. Nose: white flowers, fragrant herbs, fresh fruit, medium intensity. Palate: good acidity, correct, powerful, flavourful.

MONASTERIO DE PALAZUELOS VERDEJO 2010 B
verdejo.

88 Colour: bright straw. Nose: fresh, fresh fruit, white flowers, fragrant herbs. Palate: flavourful, fruity, good acidity, balanced.

DIEZ SIGLOS DE VERDEJO

Ctra. Valladolid Km. 24,5
47231 Serrada (Valladolid)
☎: +34 983 660 888 - Fax: +34 983 660 888
comercial1@diezsiglos.es
www.diezsiglos.es

DIEZ SIGLOS 2010 B
verdejo.

88 Colour: bright straw. Nose: fresh, fruit expression, jasmine. Palate: flavourful, fruity, good acidity, balanced.

CANTO REAL 2010 B
100% verdejo.

88 Colour: bright straw. Nose: fresh, white flowers, ripe fruit, varietal. Palate: flavourful, fruity, good acidity.

ESTANCIA PIEDRA S.L.

Ctra. Toro a Salamanca, km. 5

49800 Toro (Zamora)
☎: +34 980 693 900 - Fax: +34 980 693 901
info@estanciapiedra.com
www.estanciapiedra.com

PIEDRA VERDEJO 2010 B
100% verdejo.

90 Colour: bright straw. Nose: fresh, fresh fruit, white flowers, grassy. Palate: flavourful, fruity, good acidity.

FINCA CASERÍO DE DUEÑAS

Ctra. Cl. 602, km. 50,2
47465 Villaverde de Medina (Valladolid)
☎: +34 915 006 000 - Fax: +34 915 006 006
pzumft@habarcelo.es
www.habarcelo.es

VIÑA MAYOR VERDEJO 2010 B
100% verdejo.

89 Colour: bright straw. Nose: fresh fruit, white flowers, floral. Palate: flavourful, fruity, balanced.

VIÑA MAYOR 2009 BFB
100% verdejo.

90 Colour: bright yellow. Nose: ripe fruit, sweet spices, creamy oak, fragrant herbs, lactic notes. Palate: rich, flavourful, fresh, good acidity.

FINCA MONTEPEDROSO

Término La Morejona, s/n
47490 Rueda (Valladolid)
☎: +34 941 450 876 - Fax: +34 941 450 876
info@bujanda.com
www.familiamartinezbujanda.com

FINCA MONTEPEDROSO 2010 B
verdejo.

90 Colour: bright straw. Nose: white flowers, fresh fruit, tropical fruit, fragrant herbs, expressive. Palate: good acidity, fruity, flavourful, fleshy.

FRANCISCO JAVIER SANZ CANTALAPIEDRA

San Judas, 2
47491 La Seca (Valladolid)
☎: +34 983 816 669 - Fax: +34 983 816 639
bodega@ordentercera.com
www.ordentercera.com

ORDEN TERCERA VERDEJO 2010 B JOVEN
100% verdejo.

91 Colour: bright straw. Nose: fresh, white flowers, ripe fruit, citrus fruit, grassy. Palate: flavourful, fruity, good acidity.

GREAT WINES FROM SPAIN

Camino de Santibáñez, s/n
47328 La Parrilla (Valladolid)
☎: +34 983 681 521 - Fax: +34 983 681 521
bodegas@altapavina.com
www.altapavina.es

VALDRINAL DE SANTAMARÍA 2010 B
verdejo.

89 Colour: bright straw. Nose: white flowers, dried herbs, citrus fruit, tropical fruit. Palate: powerful, fleshy, flavourful, fine bitter notes.

GRUPO ALGAR - ABILIA

Carpinteros, 13 P.I. Pinares Llanos
28670 Villaviciosa de Odón (Madrid)
☎: +34 916 169 122 - Fax: +34 916 166 724
info@grupoalgar.com
www.grupoalgar.com

ABILIA VERDEJO VIURA 2010 B
verdejo, viura.

87 Colour: bright straw. Nose: fresh, fresh fruit, white flowers, expressive. Palate: flavourful, fruity, good acidity, fresh, light-bodied.

ABILIA VERDEJO 2010 B
100% verdejo.

84 Colour: bright straw. Nose: faded flowers, ripe fruit, balsamic herbs. Palate: good acidity, light-bodied, fresh, fruity.

GRUPO YLLERA

Autovía A-6, Km. 173, 5
47490 Rueda (Valladolid)
☎: +34 983 868 097 - Fax: +34 983 868 177
grupoyllera@grupoyllera.com
www.grupoyllera.com

VIÑA CANTOSÁN VARIETAL VERDEJO 2010 B
verdejo.

90 Colour: bright straw. Nose: fresh, varietal, expressive, white flowers, fresh fruit, fine lees. Palate: flavourful, fruity, fresh, fleshy, good acidity.

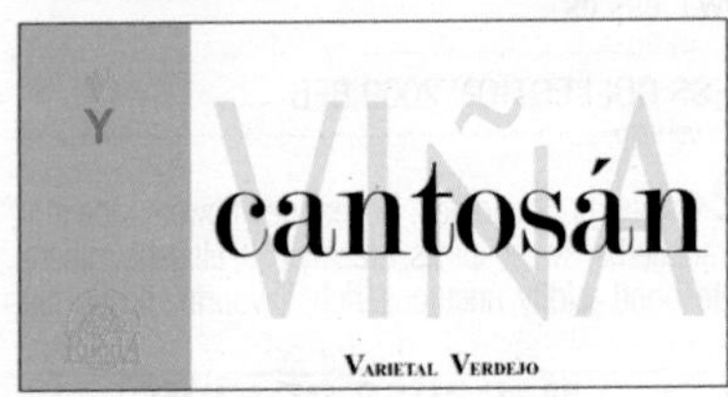

TIERRA BUENA 2010 B
verdejo.

88 Colour: bright straw. Nose: fresh fruit, tropical fruit, fresh, expressive. Palate: fresh, fruity, flavourful, good acidity.

BRACAMONTE VERDEJO 2010 B
verdejo.

87 Colour: bright straw. Nose: dried flowers, fresh, expressive, candied fruit. Palate: correct, fresh, flavourful, easy to drink.

BRACAMONTE VERDEJO VIURA SAUVIGNON BLANC 2010 B JOVEN
verdejo, viura, sauvignon blanc.

85 Colour: bright straw. Nose: fresh, fresh fruit, white flowers, expressive. Palate: flavourful, fruity, good acidity.

CANTOSÁN BR
verdejo.

85 Colour: bright yellow. Nose: white flowers, fresh fruit, citrus fruit, fragrant herbs. Palate: powerful, flavourful, fruity, easy to drink.

CANTOSÁN BN
verdejo.

82 Colour: bright yellow. Nose: fine lees, candied fruit, white flowers. Palate: good acidity, fine bead, ripe fruit.

CANTOSÁN RESERVA ESPECIAL ESP
verdejo.

86 Color bright straw. Aroma medium intensity, fresh fruit, dried herbs, fine lees, floral. Taste fresh, fruity, flavourful, good acidity.

JAVIER SANZ VITICULTOR

San Judas, 2
47491 La Seca (Valladolid)
☎: +34 983 816 669 - Fax: +34 983 816 639
bodega@jsviticultor.com
www.jsviticultor.com

REY SANTO VERDEJO 2010 B
100% verdejo.

90 Colour: bright straw. Nose: fresh, white flowers, ripe fruit, varietal. Palate: flavourful, fruity, good acidity, balanced.

VILLA NARCISA RUEDA VERDEJO 2010 B
100% verdejo.

89 Colour: bright straw. Nose: fresh fruit, floral, fragrant herbs. Palate: powerful, flavourful, fruity, fleshy.

VILLA NARCISA SAUVIGNON BLANC 2010 B
100% sauvignon blanc.

88 Colour: bright straw. Nose: medium intensity, varietal, candied fruit. Palate: sweetness, ripe fruit, fine bitter notes.

LA COLECCIÓN DE VINOS

Domingo Martínez, 6- Bajo
47007 (Valladolid)
☎: +34 983 271 595 - Fax: +34 983 271 608
info@lacolecciondevinos.com
www.lacolecciondevinos.com

OTER DE CILLAS VERDEJO 2010 B
100% verdejo.

89 Colour: bright straw. Nose: fresh, fresh fruit, white flowers, varietal. Palate: flavourful, fruity, good acidity, fine bitter notes.

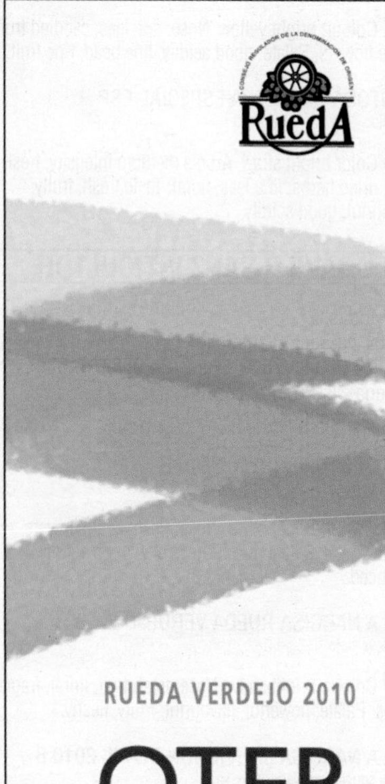

LEGARIS

Ctra. Peñafiel - Encinas de Esgueva, km. 4,3
47316 Curiel de Duero (Valladolid)
☎: +34 983 878 088 - Fax: +34 983 881 034
info@legaris.es
www.legaris.es

LEGARIS VERDEJO 2010 B
93% verdejo, 7% sauvignon blanc.

88 Colour: bright straw. Nose: candied fruit, citrus fruit, tropical fruit. Palate: fresh, easy to drink, ripe fruit.

LIBERALIA ENOLÓGICA

Camino del Palo, s/n
49800 Toro (Zamora)
☎: +34 980 692 571 - Fax: +34 980 692 571
byvliberalia@hotmail.com
www.liberalia.es

ENEBRAL 2010 B
100% verdejo.

91 Colour: bright straw. Nose: fresh, white flowers, varietal, mineral, grassy. Palate: flavourful, fruity, good acidity.

LOESS

El Monte, 7- Bajo
47195 Arroyo de la Encomienda (Valladolid)
☎: +34 983 664 898 - Fax: +34 983 406 579
loess@loess.es
www.loess.es

LOESS COLLECTION 2009 BFB
100% verdejo.

92 Colour: bright golden. Nose: dried flowers, ripe fruit, fragrant herbs, sweet spices, creamy oak, elegant, mineral. Palate: good acidity, unctuous, rich, flavourful, fleshy, toasty.

MARQUÉS DE IRÚN

Nueva, 7-9
47491 La Seca (Valladolid)
☎: +34 956 851 751 - Fax: +34 956 859 204
marketing@caballero.es
www.marquesdeirun.es

MARQUÉS DE IRÚN VERDEJO 2010 B
100% verdejo.

87 Colour: bright straw. Nose: fresh, floral, ripe fruit. Palate: flavourful, fruity, balanced.

MONTEBACO

Finca Montealto
47359 Valbuena de Duero (Valladolid)
☎: +34 983 485 128 - Fax: +34 983 485 033
montebaco@bodegasmontebaco.com
www.bodegasmontebaco.com

MONTEBACO VERDEJO SOBRE LÍAS 2010 B
100% verdejo.

90 Colour: bright straw. Nose: fresh, white flowers, grassy, mineral. Palate: flavourful, fruity, good acidity.

OSBORNE RIBERA DEL DUERO

Fernán Caballero, 7
11500 El Puerto de Santa María (Cádiz)
☎: +34 925 860 990 - Fax: +34 925 860 905
carolina.cerrato@osborne.es
www.osborne.es

SEÑORIO DEL CID 2010 B
verdejo.

90 Colour: bright straw. Nose: fresh fruit, white flowers, neat, medium intensity. Palate: flavourful, fruity, good acidity.

OSSIAN VIDES Y VINOS

San Marcos, 5
40447 Nieva (Segovia)
☎: +34 696 159 121 - Fax: +34 921 594 207
ossian@ossian.es
www.ossian.es

QUINTALUNA 2010 B
100% verdejo.

87 Colour: bright straw. Nose: fresh fruit, citrus fruit, tropical fruit. Palate: flavourful, fruity, fresh.

PAGOS DEL REY RUEDA

Avda. Morejona, 6
47490 Rueda (Valladolid)
☎: +34 983 868 182 - Fax: +34 983 868 182
rueda@pagosdelrey.com
www.pagosdelrey.com

ANALIVIA SAUVIGNON BLANC 2010 B
sauvignon blanc.

92 Colour: bright straw. Nose: fresh, fresh fruit, white flowers, mineral. Palate: flavourful, fruity, good acidity, balanced.

BLUME SAUVIGNON BLANC 2010 B
sauvignon blanc.

90 Colour: bright straw. Nose: fresh, white flowers, grassy, varietal, ripe fruit. Palate: flavourful, fruity, good acidity, balanced.

BLUME VERDEJO 2010 B
verdejo.

89 Colour: bright straw. Nose: fresh, fresh fruit, expressive, mineral, dried flowers. Palate: flavourful, fruity, complex.

ANALIVIA VERDEJO 2010 B
verdejo.

88 Colour: bright straw. Nose: fragrant herbs, citrus fruit, fresh. Palate: light-bodied, fresh, fruity, flavourful.

ANALIVIA RUEDA 2010 B
verdejo, sauvignon blanc.

87 Colour: bright straw. Nose: white flowers, ripe fruit, grassy. Palate: flavourful, fruity, good acidity, balanced.

BLUME RUEDA 2010 B
verdejo, sauvignon blanc.

87 Colour: bright straw. Nose: fresh, white flowers, ripe fruit. Palate: flavourful, fruity, good acidity, balanced.

PALACIO DE VILLACHICA

Ctra. Nacional 122, Km. 433
49800 Toro (Zamora)
☎: +34 983 372 289 - Fax: +34 983 381 356
admin@palaciodevillachica.com
www.palaciodevillachica.com

ABSIDE VERDEJO 2010 B
100% verdejo.

88 Colour: bright straw. Nose: floral, fresh fruit, citrus fruit, tropical fruit. Palate: good acidity, fine bitter notes, fruity.

PREDIO DE VASCARLÓN

Ctra. Rueda, s/n
47491 La Seca (Valladolid)
☎: +34 983 816 325 - Fax: +34 983 816 326
vascarlon@prediodevascarlon.com
www.prediodevascarlon.com

ATELIER VERDEJO 2010 B
verdejo.

90 Colour: bright straw. Nose: fresh fruit, white flowers, fragrant herbs, mineral. Palate: flavourful, fruity, good acidity, balanced, fleshy.

TARDEVIENES 2010 B
verdejo, viura.

87 Colour: bright straw. Nose: fresh fruit, white flowers, expressive, tropical fruit. Palate: flavourful, fruity, good acidity, light-bodied.

RODRÍGUEZ SANZO

Manuel Azaña, 9- Local 15
47014 Valladolid (Valladolid)
☎: +34 983 150 150 - Fax: +34 983 150 151
valsanzo@valsanzo.com
www.valsanzo.com

VIÑA SANZO VERDEJO 2010 B
100% verdejo.

91 Colour: bright straw, greenish rim. Nose: varietal, fresh, fresh fruit, tropical fruit, mineral. Palate: fleshy, good acidity, fine bitter notes, ripe fruit.

VIÑA SANZO SOBRE LÍAS 2009 B
verdejo.

90 Colour: bright golden. Nose: ripe fruit, citrus fruit, dried flowers, fine lees, expressive, sweet spices. Palate: rich, fleshy, good acidity, flavourful.

SEÑORITA MALAUVA "MARIDAJE BOUTIQUE"

Esquina Catedral Cascajares s/n
47002 (Valladolid)
☎: +34 983 394 955 - Fax: +34 983 394 955
info@vinotecamalauva.es
www.vinotecamalauva.es

SEÑORITA MALAUVA "EXPRESIÓN TERROIR" ARMONÍA 1 2009 B
100% verdejo.

89 Colour: bright straw. Nose: white flowers, expressive, ripe fruit. Palate: flavourful, fruity, good acidity, balanced.

SITIOS DE BODEGA

Cuatro Calles, s/n
47491 La Seca (Valladolid)
☎: +34 983 103 223 - Fax: +34 983 816 561
info@sitiosdebodega.com
www.sitiosdebodega.com

PALACIO DE MENADE SAUVIGNON BLANC 2010 B
sauvignon blanc.

92 Colour: bright straw. Nose: fresh, white flowers, varietal, ripe fruit. Palate: flavourful, fruity, good acidity, balanced.

PALACIO DE MENADE VERDEJO 2010 B
verdejo.

89 Colour: bright straw. Nose: dried flowers, citrus fruit, fresh. Palate: fleshy, fresh, fruity.

MENADE SAUVIGNON BLANC 2010 B
sauvignon blanc.

86 Colour: bright straw. Nose: ripe fruit, grassy, white flowers. Palate: flavourful, sweetness, fruity.

TERA Y CASTRO

Oruro, 9 - Bajo izda.
28016 Madrid (Madrid)
☎: +34 915 902 529 - Fax: +34 915 644 431
info@teraycastro.com
www.teraycastro.com

PENTIO 2010 B
100% verdejo.

91 Colour: bright straw. Nose: fresh, white flowers, ripe fruit, varietal. Palate: flavourful, fruity, good acidity.

DILECTUM 2007 BFB
100% verdejo.

91 Colour: bright yellow. Nose: powerfull, ripe fruit, sweet spices, creamy oak, fragrant herbs. Palate: rich, flavourful, fresh, good acidity.

TERNA BODEGAS

Cuatro Calles, s/n
47491 La Seca (Valladolid)
☎: +34 983 103 223 - Fax: +34 983 816 561
info@sitiosdebodega.com
www.sitiosdebodega.com

V3 VIÑAS VIEJAS VERDEJO 2009 BFB
verdejo.

92 Colour: bright yellow. Nose: powerfull, sweet spices, creamy oak, earthy notes. Palate: rich, smoky aftertaste, flavourful, fresh, good acidity.

SAXUM (TERRENOS PEDREGOSOS) SAUVIGNON BLANC 2008 BFB
sauvignon blanc.

92 Colour: bright yellow. Nose: sweet spices, creamy oak, fragrant herbs, candied fruit. Palate: rich, smoky aftertaste, flavourful, fresh, good acidity.

TOMÁS POSTIGO SASTRE

Estación,12
47300 (Valladolid)
☎: +34 983 873 019 - Fax: +34 983 873 019
administracion@tomaspostigo.es
www.tomaspostigo.es

TOMÁS POSTIGO 2010 B
verdejo.

88 Colour: bright straw. Nose: fresh, ripe fruit, grassy, faded flowers. Palate: flavourful, fruity, good acidity.

TOMÁS POSTIGO 2008 BFB
verdejo.

91 Colour: bright golden. Nose: sweet spices, new oak, fruit expression. Palate: balanced, unctuous, round, rich, flavourful, powerful.

UNZU PROPIEDAD

Barón de la Torre, 4
31592 Cintruénigo (Navarra)
☎: +34 948 812 297 - Fax: +34 948 812 297
info@unzupropiedad.com
www.unzupropiedad.com

LABORES DE UNZU VERDEJO 2010 B
100% verdejo.

91 Colour: bright straw. Nose: fresh, fresh fruit, white flowers, expressive. Palate: flavourful, fruity, good acidity.

UVAS FELICES

Agullers, 7
08003 Barcelona (Barcelona)
☎: +34 902 327 777
www.vilaviniteca.es

EL PERRO VERDE 2010 B
verdejo.

91 Colour: bright straw. Nose: fresh, fresh fruit, white flowers, expressive, grassy. Palate: flavourful, fruity, good acidity, balanced.

VEGA DE LA REINA (HACIENDA MARQUÉS DE LA CONCORDIA FAMILY OF WINES))

Avenida Nava del Rey 8
47490 Rueda (Valladolid)
☎: +34 914 365 924
comunicacion@arcoinvest-group.com
www.haciendas-espana.com

VEGA DE LA REINA VERDEJO 2010 B
80% verdejo, 20% viura.

91 Colour: bright straw. Nose: fresh, white flowers, neat, ripe fruit. Palate: flavourful, fruity, good acidity, balanced.

VEGA DE LA REINA 2010 B
85% verdejo, 15% sauvignon blanc.

91 Colour: bright straw. Nose: fragrant herbs, tropical fruit, fresh, complex. Palate: flavourful, fruity, light-bodied, fleshy.

VEGA MURILLO BODEGAS Y VIÑEDOS

Santiago, 9
47001 Valladolid (Valladolid)
☎: +34 983 360 284 - Fax: +34 983 345 546

VEGA MURILLO 2010 B
verdejo.

88 Colour: bright straw. Nose: fresh, white flowers, ripe fruit. Palate: flavourful, fruity, good acidity, balanced.

VINOS SANZ

Ctra. Madrid - La Coruña, Km. 170,5
47490 Rueda (Valladolid)
☎: +34 983 868 100 - Fax: +34 983 868 117
vinossanz@vinossanz.com
www.vinossanz.com

SANZ VERDEJO 2010 B
100% verdejo.

92 Colour: bright straw. Nose: fresh, fresh fruit, white flowers, expressive, fragrant herbs. Palate: flavourful, fruity, good acidity, balanced, mineral.

FINCA LA COLINA SAUVIGNON BLANC 2010 B
100% sauvignon blanc.

92 Colour: bright straw. Nose: fresh, fresh fruit, faded flowers, grassy, ripe fruit. Palate: flavourful, fruity, good acidity, balanced.

FINCA LA COLINA VERDEJO CIEN X CIEN 2010 B
100% verdejo.

93 Colour: bright straw. Nose: fresh, white flowers, mineral, varietal, ripe fruit. Palate: flavourful, fruity, good acidity, balanced.

SANZ CLÁSICO 2010 B
70% verdejo, 30% viura.

90 Colour: bright straw. Nose: fresh, fresh fruit, dried flowers. Palate: flavourful, fruity, good acidity, balanced.

SANZ SAUVIGNON BLANC 2010 B
100% sauvignon blanc.

90 Colour: bright straw. Nose: fresh, white flowers, varietal, tropical fruit. Palate: flavourful, good acidity, balanced.

VINOS TERRIBLES

Paseo Marques de Zafra, 35
28028 (Madrid)
☎: +34 910 005 834
flequi@ziries.es

TERRIBLE 2010 B
100% verdejo.

88 Colour: bright straw. Nose: fresh, fresh fruit, white flowers, expressive, tropical fruit. Palate: flavourful, fruity, good acidity, balanced.

TERRIBLE 2009 T
100% tinta del país.

89 Colour: cherry, garnet rim. Nose: red berry notes, ripe fruit, earthy notes, cocoa bean, spicy, toasty. Palate: good acidity, powerful, flavourful, fleshy, complex.

VIÑA DEL SOPIÉ

Pol. Ind. La Alberquería, s/n
31230 Viana (Navarra)
☎: +34 948 645 008 - Fax: +34 948 645 166
info@familiabelasco.com
www.familiabelasco.com

VIÑA DEL SOPIÉ VERDEJO 2010 B
verdejo.

88 Colour: bright straw. Nose: fresh, white flowers, ripe fruit. Palate: flavourful, fruity, good acidity.

VIÑA DEL SOPIÉ RUEDA 2010 B
verdejo.

86 Colour: bright yellow. Nose: ripe fruit, citrus fruit, tropical fruit. Palate: fine bitter notes, fruity.

VIÑAYTIA

Paraje El Soto, s/n
09370 Quintana del Pidio (Burgos)
☎: +34 947 545 126 - Fax: +34 947 545 605
bodega@cillardesilos.es

EL QUINTANAL 2010 B
verdejo.

88 Colour: bright straw. Nose: expressive, varietal, fresh fruit, citrus fruit. Palate: flavourful, fruity, good acidity.

VIÑEDOS DE NIEVA

Camino Real, s/n
40447 Nieva (Segovia)
☎: +34 921 594 628 - Fax: +34 921 595 409
info@vinedosdenieva.com
www.vinedosdenieva.com

BLANCO NIEVA PIE FRANCO 2010 B
100% verdejo.

93 Colour: bright straw. Nose: fresh, fresh fruit, white flowers, expressive, fragrant herbs. Palate: flavourful, fruity, good acidity, balanced, mineral.

BLANCO NIEVA 2010 B
100% verdejo.

91 Colour: bright straw. Nose: fresh, fresh fruit, white flowers, expressive, fragrant herbs. Palate: flavourful, fruity, good acidity, balanced, fleshy.

BLANCO NIEVA SAUVIGNON 2010 B
100% sauvignon blanc.

91 Colour: bright straw. Nose: fresh, fresh fruit, white flowers, expressive, tropical fruit, mineral. Palate: flavourful, fruity, good acidity, balanced.

LOS NAVALES VERDEJO 2010 B
100% verdejo.

89 Colour: bright straw. Nose: fresh, fresh fruit, white flowers, expressive, fragrant herbs. Palate: flavourful, fruity, balanced.

BLANCO NIEVA 2007 BFB
100% verdejo.

88 Colour: bright yellow. Nose: powerfull, sweet spices, creamy oak, fragrant herbs, candied fruit. Palate: rich, flavourful, fresh, good acidity.

VIÑEDOS SECA S.L.

Pozobueno, 3
47491 La Seca (Valladolid)
☎: +34 620 212 111 - Fax: +34 913 294 950
vlaseca2@gmail.com

VIÑA PRETEL VERDEJO 2010 B
verdejo.

86 Colour: bright straw. Nose: citrus fruit, dried flowers, fragrant herbs. Palate: powerful, fresh, fruity.

VIÑA PRETEL 2010 B
verdejo, viura.

84 Colour: bright straw. Nose: fresh, fresh fruit, white flowers, expressive. Palate: flavourful, fruity, good acidity.

VIÑEDOS SINGULARES

Llorer, 31
08905 Hospitalet de Llobregat (Barcelona)
☎: +34 934 807 041 - Fax: +34 934 807 076
info@vinedossingulares.com
www.vinedossingulares.com

AFORTUNADO 2010 B
verdejo.

89 Colour: bright straw. Nose: powerfull, ripe fruit, fruit expression, tropical fruit, white flowers. Palate: flavourful, fruity, fresh, fleshy, good acidity.

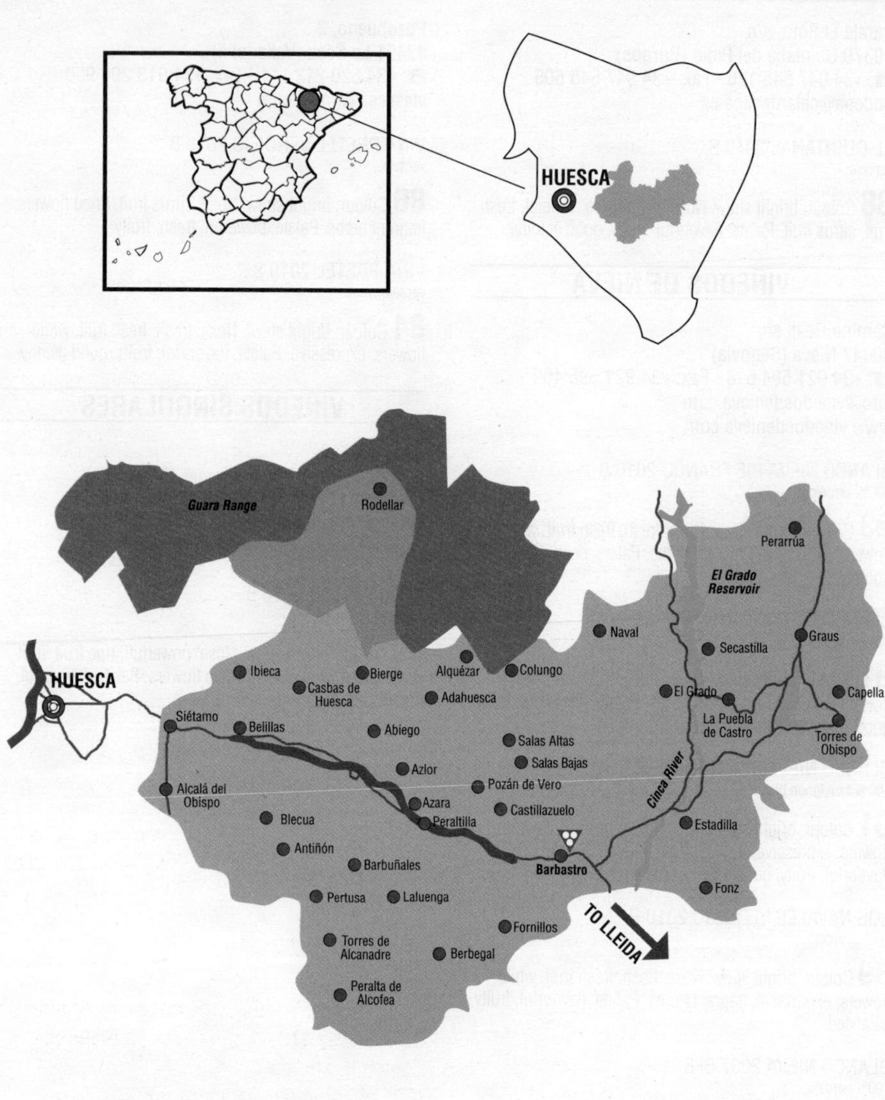
HUESCA
Guara Range
Rodellar
Perarrúa
El Grado Reservoir
Naval
Graus
Secastilla
Ibieca
Bierge
Alquézar
Colungo
HUESCA
Casbas de Huesca
Adahuesca
El Grado
Capella
Siétamo
Belillas
Abiego
La Puebla de Castro
Torres de Obispo
Salas Altas
Salas Bajas
Azlor
Alcalá del Obispo
Pozán de Vero
Cinca River
Azara
Castillazuelo
Blecua
Peraltilla
Estadilla
Antiñón
Barbuñales
Barbastro
Fonz
Pertusa
Laluenga
TO LLEIDA
Fornillos
Torres de Alcanadre
Berbegal
Peralta de Alcofea
Consejo Regulador
DO Boundary

NEWS ABOUT THE VINTAGE:

Somontano is one of the few examples within the Spanish wine regions where great winemaking is matched by an equally exceeding marketing approach. And that is probably where the origin of its success lies. This 25-year-old DO has been able to unify the different personal criteria of the local producers –all of them with at least a top wine in their portfolios– and create an excellent international image for its wines, something that undoubtedly benefits everybody there. Under its guidance, wine tourism has known a great development in the region and has taken the brand name "Somontano" to even higher peaks. In spite of the abysmal differences in terms of size between the wineries, the small producers are not just mere onlookers; rather on the contrary, they show a highly pro-active attitude in the development of the DO as a whole.

While all this is taking place, the wines, the real ambassadors of the region, continue to grow in quality. We have hardly sampled any wines from the 2010 vintage, what leads us to believe that winemakers have decided to put aside those wines for wood-ageing purposes, so we will have to wait to assess their quality. Regarding white wines, made from –mainly– *chardonnay* and *gewürztraminer*, they are improving every year in both single-variety renderings and blends. In these latter examples, the *chardonnay* adds structure and a richer palate, while *gewürztraminer* jazz up the whole concoction with its typical floral aromas.

For the third year in a row, Enate Uno Chardonnay 2006 gets the highest score (95 points) within the DO, so it becomes a true Nº 1, as its name anticipated. We will keep a close eye on it to see whether next year is able to reach 97 points (or more), the score it got four years ago in the 2008 edition of our Guide.

As for the aged red wines, we deem the best names are Irius Premium 2007, Blecua 2001 and Enate Reserva Especial 2006, all of them blends of different varieties in an almost miraculous balance that have reached some well-deserved 94 points.

LOCATION:

In the province of Huesca, around the town of Barbastro. The region comprises 43 municipal districts, mainly centred round the region of Somontano and the rest of the neighbouring regions of Ribagorza and Monegros.

CLIMATE:

Characterised by cold winters and hot summers, with sharp contrasts in temperature at the end of spring and autumn. The average annual rainfall is 500 mm, although the rains are scarcer in the south and east

SOIL:

The soil is mainly brownish limestone, not very fertile, with a good level of limestone and good permeability.

GRAPE VARIETIES:

WHITE: *Macabeo, Garnacha Blanca, Alcañón, Chardonnay, Riesling, Sauvignon Blanc* and *Gewürztraminer.*
RED: *Tempranillo, Garnacha Tinta, Cabernet Sauvignon, Merlot, Moristel, Parraleta, Pinot Noir* and *Syrah.*

FIGURES:

Vineyard surface: 4,888 – **Wine-Growers:** 498 – **Wineries:** 34 – **2010 Harvest rating:** Excellent – **Production:** 13,989,600 litres – **Market percentages:** 80% domestic. 20% export

CONSEJO REGULADOR
Avda. de la Merced, 64
22300 Barbastro (Huesca)
☎: +34 974 313 031 - Fax: +34 974 315 132
@ erio@dosomontano.com
www.dosomontano.com

GENERAL CHARACTERISTICS OF THE WINES

WHITES	The traditional wines of the region, they are based on the *Macabeo* variety, giving young wines with a straw yellow colour, which are fresh and easy drinking (worthy of mention is the only existing example of late harvest *Macabeo*, which has revealed a complexity uncommon to this variety). Although of higher quality, they are generally produced from *Chardonnay*, whether for young wines or wines fermented in barrels, which gives white wines with powerful aromas, with good varietal definition, oily and flavourful on the palate.
ROSÉS	Produced from autochthonous or foreign grapes, they follow the line of the modern rosés: raspberry pink in colour, good fruit intensity, light, fresh and easy drinking.
REDS	The traditional red wine of the region, produced from *Moristel* and *Tempranillo*, is notably fruity and intense. There have also been very interesting experiences with single variety wines produced from local grapes, specifically *Moristel* and *Parraleta*, of notable quality; both produced as young wines and characterised by an excellent fruity character and a certain complexity of notes. In the rest of the red wines the foreign varieties impose themselves, blended with the local grapes or presented separately. The aged *Cabernet* and *Merlot* wines stand out for their Atlantic influence, varietal character, aromatic potency and fine blend with the wood due to not excessive ageing periods; they have a good structure on the palate.

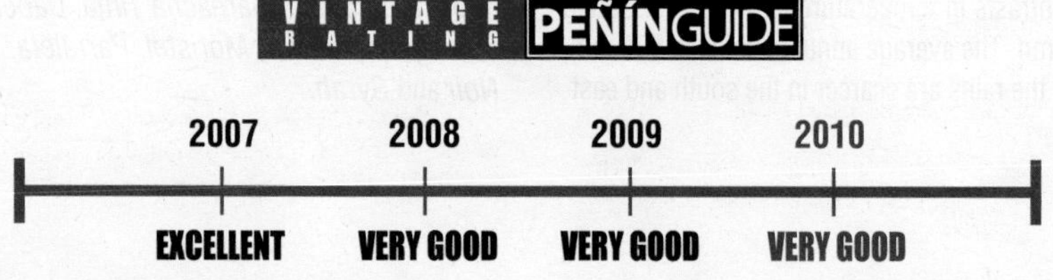

BAL D'ISABENA BODEGAS

Ctra. A-1605, Km. 11,2
22587 Laguarres (Huesca)
☎: +34 974 544 302 - Fax: +34 974 310 151
info@baldisabena.com
www.baldisabena.com

COJÓN DE GATO GEWÜRZTRAMINER 2010 B
gewürztraminer, otras.

91 Colour: bright straw. Nose: floral, fresh fruit, citrus fruit, fragrant herbs, expressive. Palate: good acidity, correct, light-bodied, fruity, flavourful.

REIS D'ISABENA 2010 B
chardonnay, gewürztraminer.

90 Colour: bright straw. Nose: fresh fruit, white flowers, grassy. Palate: flavourful, fruity, good acidity, balanced.

ISÁBENA 2010 RD
merlot.

86 Colour: rose, purple rim. Nose: floral, fresh fruit, fresh. Palate: light-bodied, fresh, fruity, easy to drink.

COJÓN DE GATO 2009 T
merlot, syrah, otras.

92 Colour: cherry, garnet rim. Nose: mineral, expressive, ripe fruit. Palate: flavourful, fruity, spicy, round tannins.

ISÁBENA 2009 T
garnacha, merlot, syrah.

87 Colour: bright cherry. Nose: ripe fruit, sweet spices, creamy oak. Palate: flavourful, fruity, toasty, round tannins.

REIS D'ISABENA 2006 T
merlot, cabernet sauvignon.

85 Colour: cherry, garnet rim. Nose: ripe fruit, spicy, toasty. Palate: powerful, flavourful, toasty, round tannins.

BLECUA

Ctra. Naval, Km. 3,7
22300 Barbastro (Huesca)
☎: +34 974 302 216 - Fax: +34 974 302 098
marketing@vinasdelvero.es
www.bodegablecua.com

BLECUA 2005 T
garnacha, tempranillo, merlot, cabernet sauvignon.

92 Colour: cherry, garnet rim. Nose: creamy oak, toasty, complex, mineral, ripe fruit. Palate: powerful, flavourful, toasty, round tannins.

BLECUA 2001 TR
garnacha, tempranillo, merlot, cabernet sauvignon.

94 Colour: cherry, garnet rim. Nose: elegant, spicy, fine reductive notes, wet leather, aged wood nuances, fruit liqueur notes. Palate: spicy, fine tannins, elegant, long.

BODEGA OTTO BESTUÉ

Ctra. A-138, Km. 0,5
22312 Enate (Huesca)
☎: +34 974 305 157 - Fax: +34 974 305 157
info@bodega-ottobestue.com
www.bodega-ottobestue.com

OTTO BESTUÉ CHARDONNAY ABUELA JOAQUINA 2010 B
chardonnay.

88 Colour: bright straw. Nose: fragrant herbs, citrus fruit, floral, powerfull. Palate: flavourful, fleshy, creamy, good acidity.

OTTO BESTUÉ 2010 RD
100% cabernet sauvignon.

89 Colour: rose, purple rim. Nose: powerfull, ripe fruit, red berry notes, floral. Palate: fleshy, powerful, fruity, fresh.

OTTO BESTUÉ FINCA RABLEROS 2008 T
50% tempranillo, 50% cabernet sauvignon.

87 Colour: pale ruby, brick rim edge. Nose: ripe fruit, balsamic herbs, cocoa bean, dark chocolate. Palate: good acidity, flavourful, fleshy.

OTTO BESTUÉ FINCA SANTA SABINA 2008 TC
80% cabernet sauvignon, 20% tempranillo.

86 Colour: cherry, garnet rim. Nose: ripe fruit, cocoa bean, dark chocolate, creamy oak. Palate: powerful, flavourful, fleshy, long.

BODEGA PIRINEOS

Ctra. Barbastro - Naval, Km. 3,5
22300 Barbastro (Huesca)
☎: +34 974 311 289 - Fax: +34 974 306 688
info@bodegapirineos.com
www.bodegapirineos.com

PIRINEOS GEWÜRZTRAMINER 2010 B
gewürztraminer.

90 Colour: bright straw. Nose: fresh fruit, white flowers, varietal. Palate: flavourful, fruity, good acidity, balanced.

PIRINEOS MESACHE 2010 B
macabeo, chardonnay, gewürztraminer.

87 Colour: bright straw. Nose: white flowers, fresh fruit, expressive. Palate: good acidity, light-bodied, fruity, easy to drink.

MONTESIERRA 2010 B
macabeo, chardonnay.

85 Colour: bright yellow. Nose: fragrant herbs, floral, fresh fruit. Palate: fruity, flavourful, fleshy.

PIRINEOS SELECCIÓN MARBORÉ 2009 B
viognier.

91 Colour: bright straw. Nose: fresh, fresh fruit, white flowers, sweet spices. Palate: flavourful, fruity, good acidity, balanced.

MONTESIERRA 2010 RD
tempranillo, garnacha.

89 Colour: rose, purple rim. Nose: floral, fresh fruit, violet drops. Palate: flavourful, fruity, fleshy.

PIRINEOS 2010 RD
merlot, cabernet sauvignon.

88 Colour: rose, purple rim. Nose: fresh, expressive, ripe fruit. Palate: flavourful, fruity, fleshy.

ALQUÉZAR 2010 RD
tempranillo, garnacha.

88 Colour: raspberry rose. Nose: elegant, dried flowers, fragrant herbs, red berry notes. Palate: light-bodied, flavourful, good acidity, long, spicy.

PIRINEOS MESACHE 2010 T
garnacha, parraleta, syrah, cabernet sauvignon.

88 Colour: cherry, purple rim. Nose: red berry notes, fresh, expressive. Palate: powerful, fruity, flavourful, fleshy.

PIRINEOS SELECCIÓN 2008 T
syrah, garnacha.

88 Colour: deep cherry, orangey edge. Nose: candied fruit, ripe fruit, earthy notes, creamy oak, spicy. Palate: flavourful, powerful, round tannins, ripe fruit.

PIRINEOS MERLOT- CABERNET 2007 TC
merlot, cabernet sauvignon.

90 Colour: cherry, garnet rim. Nose: mineral, ripe fruit, spicy, toasty, balsamic herbs. Palate: powerful, flavourful, fleshy, toasty.

SEÑORÍO DE LAZÁN 2006 TR
tempranillo, cabernet sauvignon, moristel.

88 Colour: dark-red cherry, orangey edge. Nose: spicy, cocoa bean, dark chocolate, toasty. Palate: fleshy, powerful, flavourful, rich, long.

MARBORÉ 2004 T
tempranillo, merlot, cabernet sauvignon, moristel, parraleta.

92 Colour: cherry, garnet rim. Nose: ripe fruit, creamy oak, toasty, expressive, characterful. Palate: powerful, flavourful, toasty, round tannins.

BODEGAS ABINASA

Ctra. Tarragona a San Sebastián, Km. 180
22124 Lascellas (Huesca)
☎: +34 974 319 156 - Fax: +34 974 319 156
info@bodegasabinasa.com
www.bodegasabinasa.com

ANA CHARDONNAY MACABEO 2010 B
chardonnay, macabeo.

86 Colour: bright straw. Nose: fresh fruit, citrus fruit, medium intensity. Palate: flavourful, light-bodied, easy to drink.

ANA 2009 T ROBLE
merlot, cabernet sauvignon.

87 Colour: cherry, garnet rim. Nose: ripe fruit, expressive, aromatic coffee, cocoa bean. Palate: powerful, flavourful, fleshy, toasty.

ANA 2006 TC
merlot, cabernet sauvignon.

87 Colour: dark-red cherry, orangey edge. Nose: expressive, creamy oak, spicy, old leather. Palate: flavourful, fleshy, balanced.

ANA SERIES LIMITADAS 2005 T
merlot, cabernet sauvignon.

87 Colour: bright cherry, orangey edge. Nose: ripe fruit, cigar, tobacco, toasty. Palate: good acidity, flavourful, good structure.

ANA 2004 T
cabernet sauvignon, merlot.

88 Colour: cherry, garnet rim. Nose: spicy, creamy oak, toasty, ripe fruit. Palate: powerful, flavourful, toasty, round tannins.

BODEGAS ALODIA

Ctra. de Colungo, s/n
22147 Adahuesca (Huesca)
☎: +34 974 318 265
info@alodia.es
www.alodia.es

ALODIA ALCAÑÓN 2010 B
100% alcañón.

87 Colour: bright straw. Nose: floral, grassy, powerfull. Palate: flavourful, light-bodied, fruity, fine bitter notes.

ALODIA PARRALETA 2010 RD
100% parraleta.

88 Colour: rose, purple rim. Nose: floral, red berry notes, raspberry, expressive. Palate: balanced, flavourful, fruity, fleshy.

ALODIA GARNACHA 2009 T
100% garnacha.

86 Colour: cherry, purple rim. Nose: mineral, red berry notes, medium intensity. Palate: fleshy, spicy, mineral.

ALODIA SYRAH 2008 T
100% syrah.

87 Colour: cherry, garnet rim. Nose: ripe fruit, raspberry, spicy, creamy oak. Palate: good acidity, correct, flavourful.

ORACHE ECOLÓGICO 2008 T
cabernet sauvignon, garnacha.

87 Colour: cherry, garnet rim. Nose: ripe fruit, balsamic herbs, creamy oak. Palate: balsamic, fleshy, flavourful.

ALODIA MORISTEL 2008 T
100% moristel.

86 Colour: cherry, garnet rim. Nose: ripe fruit, balsamic herbs, spicy, toasty. Palate: powerful, flavourful, balsamic.

ALODIA TINTO SEDUCCIÓN 2006 T
syrah, parraleta.

88 Colour: cherry, garnet rim. Nose: spicy, toasty, complex, ripe fruit. Palate: powerful, flavourful, toasty, round tannins.

ALODIA CRUZ DE LOS 2006 T
cabernet sauvignon, garnacha.

88 Colour: cherry, garnet rim. Nose: spicy, creamy oak, toasty, fruit liqueur notes. Palate: powerful, flavourful, toasty, round tannins.

ALODIA LUXURIA 2007 ESP
cabernet sauvignon, garnacha.

84 Colour: salmon. Nose: faded flowers, candied fruit, fruit liqueur notes. Palate: ripe fruit, sweetness.

BODEGAS BALLABRIGA

Ctra. de Cregenzán, Km. 3
22300 Barbastro (Huesca)
☎: +34 974 310 216 - Fax: +34 974 306 163
info@bodegasballabriga.com
www.bodegasballabriga.com

PETRET 2010 B
gewürztraminer, chardonnay.

88 Colour: bright straw. Nose: floral, citrus fruit, fresh. Palate: light-bodied, flavourful, fruity, easy to drink.

NUNC 2010 B
chardonnay, gewürztraminer, alcañón.

88 Colour: bright straw. Nose: white flowers, powerfull, fragrant herbs, citrus fruit. Palate: creamy, light-bodied, fruity.

PETRET 2010 RD
cabernet sauvignon, garnacha.

87 Colour: cherry, purple rim. Nose: raspberry, red berry notes, white flowers, fresh, balanced. Palate: powerful, flavourful, fruity, fresh.

EL SEÑOR JOSÉ 2010 T
syrah.

87 Colour: cherry, purple rim. Nose: fresh fruit, red berry notes, floral. Palate: flavourful, fruity, good acidity.

NUNC 2007 T
merlot, syrah, cabernet sauvignon, otras.

92 Colour: cherry, garnet rim. Nose: ripe fruit, spicy, balsamic herbs, scrubland, earthy notes. Palate: flavourful, ripe fruit, round tannins.

PARRALETA EMOTION 2007 T
parraleta.

91 Colour: cherry, garnet rim. Nose: ripe fruit, creamy oak, toasty, complex, scrubland. Palate: powerful, flavourful, toasty, round tannins. Personality.

AUCTOR SELECCIÓN FINCA ROSELLAS 2007 T
cabernet sauvignon, merlot, garnacha.

84 Colour: pale ruby, brick rim edge. Nose: dark chocolate, aromatic coffee, ripe fruit, old leather. Palate: flavourful, light-bodied, good structure.

BODEGAS ESTADA

Ctra. A-1232, Km. 6,4
22313 Castillazuelo (Huesca)
☎: +34 637 741 214
info@bodegasestada.com
www.bodegasestada.es

ESTADA SAN CARBÁS 2010 B
chardonnay.

87 Colour: bright straw. Nose: white flowers, citrus fruit, fragrant herbs, expressive. Palate: flavourful, light-bodied, fresh, fruity.

ESTADA 2010 RD
50% tempranillo, 50% syrah.

90 Colour: rose, purple rim. Nose: ripe fruit, red berry notes, floral, expressive. Palate: fleshy, powerful, fruity, fresh.

VILLA ESTATA 2006 T
45% cabernet sauvignon, 35% tempranillo, 20% garnacha.

88 Colour: dark-red cherry, orangey edge. Nose: cocoa bean, aromatic coffee, ripe fruit. Palate: flavourful, fleshy, long.

ESTADA 2006 TR
50% cabernet sauvignon, 32% tempranillo, 15% garnacha, 3% merlot.

87 Colour: cherry, garnet rim. Nose: spicy, creamy oak, toasty. Palate: powerful, flavourful, toasty, round tannins.

BODEGAS FÁBREGAS

Cerler, s/n
22300 Barbastro (Huesca)
☎: +34 974 310 498 - Fax: +34 974 310 498
info@bodegasfabregas.com
www.bodegasfabregas.com

MINGUA 2010 B
chardonnay, garnacha blanca.

85 Colour: bright straw. Nose: dried herbs, floral, fresh fruit. Palate: flavourful, fruity, good acidity.

FÁBREGAS PURO MERLOT 2007 T
merlot.

88 Colour: cherry, garnet rim. Nose: aromatic coffee, spicy, toasty, expressive. Palate: good acidity, fleshy, complex.

FÁBREGAS PURO SYRAH 2007 T
syrah.

86 Colour: cherry, garnet rim. Nose: ripe fruit, complex, creamy oak. Palate: fruity, flavourful, fleshy, round tannins.

MINGUA 2006 TC
cabernet sauvignon, merlot.

87 Colour: cherry, garnet rim. Nose: spicy, creamy oak, toasty, fruit liqueur notes. Palate: powerful, flavourful, toasty, round tannins.

VEGA FERRERA 2006 TC
40% cabernet sauvignon, 30% merlot, 30% syrah.

85 Colour: cherry, garnet rim. Nose: ripe fruit, balsamic herbs, spicy. Palate: balanced, flavourful, fleshy.

BODEGAS IRIUS

Ctra. N-240, Km. 154,5
22300 Barbastro (Huesca)
☎: +34 974 269 900
visitairius@bodegairius.com
www.bodegairius.com

ALBAT ELIT 2010 B
80% chardonnay, 20% gewürztraminer.

87 Color bright straw. Aroma fresh, fresh fruit, white flowers, expressive. Taste flavourful, fruity, good acidity, balanced.

ALBAT ELIT GEWÜRZTRAMINER 2010 B
100% gewürztraminer.

86 Colour: pale. Nose: fresh fruit, floral, balsamic herbs. Palate: flavourful, fruity, fresh.

ABSUM VARIETALES 2009 B
60% chardonnay, 25% gewürztraminer, 15% pinot noir.

90 Colour: bright straw. Nose: ripe fruit, aged wood nuances, pattiserie, creamy oak. Palate: rich, flavourful, powerful, fleshy.

ABSUM COLECCIÓN GEWÜRZTRAMINER 2009 B
100% gewürztraminer.

89 Colour: bright golden. Nose: powerfull, citrus fruit, candied fruit, white flowers, sweet spices. Palate: flavourful, fruity, fine bitter notes, good acidity.

ABSUM VARIETALES 2009 T
50% tempranillo, 35% merlot, 15% cabernet sauvignon, 5% syrah.

91 Colour: bright cherry. Nose: sweet spices, creamy oak, red berry notes, ripe fruit. Palate: flavourful, fruity, round tannins.

ALBAT ELIT 2009 T
45% tempranillo, 30% merlot, 25% cabernet sauvignon.

88 Colour: cherry, purple rim. Nose: red berry notes, powerfull, expressive, creamy oak. Palate: fresh, fruity, flavourful, fleshy, long.

ABSUM COLECCIÓN SYRAH 2008 T
100% syrah.

93 Colour: cherry, garnet rim. Nose: toasty, complex, fruit expression, red berry notes, new oak, sweet spices. Palate: powerful, flavourful, toasty, round tannins.

ABSUM COLECCIÓN MERLOT 2008 T
100% merlot.

91 Colour: cherry, garnet rim. Nose: ripe fruit, creamy oak, cocoa bean. Palate: flavourful, spicy, ripe fruit, fine bitter notes.

ABSUM COLECCIÓN TEMPRANILLO 2008 T
100% tempranillo.

91 Colour: bright cherry. Nose: sweet spices, creamy oak, mineral, ripe fruit, red berry notes. Palate: flavourful, fruity, toasty, round tannins.

IRIUS PREMIUM 2007 T
tempranillo, merlot, cabernet sauvignon, syrah.

94 Colour: cherry, garnet rim. Nose: fruit expression, raspberry, ripe fruit, earthy notes, toasty, new oak, cocoa bean. Palate: flavourful, fleshy, complex, concentrated, ripe fruit, round tannins.

IRIUS SELECCIÓN 2007 T
tempranillo, merlot, cabernet sauvignon, syrah.

92 Colour: bright cherry. Nose: ripe fruit, sweet spices, creamy oak, red berry notes, characterful, mineral. Palate: flavourful, fruity, toasty, round tannins.

ALBAT ELIT 2007 TC
60% merlot, 20% tempranillo, 20% cabernet sauvignon.

88 Colour: cherry, garnet rim. Nose: red berry notes, expressive, aromatic coffee, cocoa bean. Palate: fruity, rich, flavourful, fleshy.

ALBAT ELIT 2006 TR
75% tempranillo, 15% merlot, 10% cabernet sauvignon.

89 Colour: cherry, garnet rim. Nose: ripe fruit, balanced, expressive, aromatic coffee, cocoa bean, dark chocolate.

BODEGAS LALANNE

Castillo San Marcos, s/n
22300 Barbastro (Huesca)
☎: +34 974 310 689 - Fax: +34 974 310 689
lalanne@bodegaslalanne.com
www.bodegaslalanne.com

LALANNE GRAN VINO LATASTE 2008 TC
cabernet sauvignon, tempranillo, merlot, syrah, pinot noir.

87 Colour: cherry, garnet rim. Nose: spicy, creamy oak, overripe fruit, dark chocolate. Palate: powerful, flavourful, toasty, round tannins.

LALANNE CLASSIC 2008 TC
70% cabernet sauvignon, 30% merlot.

84 Colour: cherry, garnet rim. Nose: ripe fruit, old leather, roasted coffee. Palate: powerful, flavourful, toasty.

BODEGAS LASIERRA

Baja, 12
22133 Bespén (Huesca)
☎: +34 974 260 365 - Fax: +34 974 260 365
info@bodegaslasierra.es
www.bodegaslasierra.es

BESPÉN CHARDONNAY MACABEO 2010 B
80% chardonnay, 20% macabeo.

86 Colour: bright straw. Nose: dried flowers, wild herbs, citrus fruit. Palate: creamy, light-bodied, fruity, fresh.

BESPÉN 2010 RD
tempranillo.

84 Colour: rose, purple rim. Nose: overripe fruit, fresh, medium intensity. Palate: fresh, light-bodied, flavourful.

BESPÉN 2010 T
tempranillo, merlot.

83 Colour: cherry, purple rim. Nose: fresh, medium intensity, fruit preserve. Palate: flavourful, fleshy, light-bodied, sweetness.

BESPÉN VENDIMIA SELECCIONADA MERLOT 2008 T
merlot.

88 Colour: cherry, garnet rim. Nose: ripe fruit, spicy, creamy oak, fragrant herbs. Palate: powerful, flavourful, toasty.

BESPÉN 2008 TC
cabernet sauvignon.

86 Colour: cherry, garnet rim. Nose: earthy notes, ripe fruit, cocoa bean, balsamic herbs. Palate: flavourful, fleshy, fruity, toasty.

BESPÉN VENDIMIA SELECCIONADA SYRAH 2008 T
syrah.

85 Colour: cherry, garnet rim. Nose: ripe fruit, spicy, toasty, balsamic herbs. Palate: good acidity, flavourful, fleshy.

BODEGAS LAUS

Ctra. N-240, km 154,8
22300 Barbastro (Huesca)
☎: +34 974 269 708 - Fax: +34 974 269 715
info@bodegaslaus.com
www.bodegaslaus.com

LAUS FLOR DE GEWÜRZTRAMINER 2010 B
100% gewürztraminer.

91 Colour: bright straw. Nose: white flowers, citrus fruit, fragrant herbs, varietal. Palate: good acidity, balanced, round, unctuous, fruity, fleshy.

LAUS FLOR DE CHARDONNAY 2010 B
100% chardonnay.

89 Color bright straw. Aroma fresh, fresh fruit, white flowers, expressive. Taste flavourful, fruity, good acidity, balanced.

LAUS 700 ALT 2007 B
65% chardonnay, 35% gewürztraminer.

90 Colour: bright golden. Nose: ripe fruit, expressive, fragrant herbs, sweet spices, toasty.

LAUS FLOR DE MERLOT 2010 RD
85% merlot, 15% cabernet sauvignon.

88 Colour: rose, purple rim. Nose: powerfull, red berry notes. Palate: fleshy, powerful, fruity, fresh.

LAUS 2008 T ROBLE
40% merlot, 30% cabernet sauvignon, 30% tempranillo.

88 Colour: bright cherry. Nose: sweet spices, creamy oak, scrubland. Palate: flavourful, fruity, toasty, round tannins.

LAUS 2007 TC
50% cabernet sauvignon, 50% merlot.

88 Colour: cherry, garnet rim. Nose: spicy, cocoa bean, dark chocolate, ripe fruit. Palate: good acidity, balanced, flavourful.

LAUS 700 ALT 2005 TC
40% syrah, 35% cabernet sauvignon, 25% merlot.

89 Colour: cherry, garnet rim. Nose: creamy oak, toasty, ripe fruit. Palate: powerful, flavourful, toasty, round tannins.

LAUS 2005 TR
100% cabernet sauvignon.

88 Colour: cherry, garnet rim. Nose: spicy, creamy oak, toasty, ripe fruit. Palate: powerful, flavourful, toasty, round tannins.

BODEGAS MELER

Luis Buñuel, 15 - 4ª A
22300 Barbastro (Huesca)
☎: +34 609 833 756 - Fax: +34 974 306 871
bodegasmeler@yahoo.es
www.bodegasmeler.com

MELER CHARDONNAY EDICIÓN LIMITADA 2010 B
100% chardonnay.

88 Colour: bright straw. Nose: white flowers, varietal, ripe fruit. Palate: flavourful, fruity, good acidity, balanced.

MELER 95 SOBRE ALJEZ 2007 B
100% chardonnay.

91 Colour: bright golden. Nose: spicy, creamy oak, pattiserie, ripe fruit. Palate: rich, powerful, flavourful, fleshy.

MELER CABERNET 2010 RD
100% cabernet sauvignon.

87 Colour: rose, purple rim. Nose: powerfull, red berry notes, floral. Palate: fleshy, powerful, fruity, fresh.

MELER SYRAH 2010 T
100% syrah.

88 Colour: cherry, garnet rim. Nose: powerfull, fresh, ripe fruit, red berry notes. Palate: good acidity, flavourful, fruity, ripe fruit.

MELER LUMBRETA 2008 T ROBLE
cabernet sauvignon, garnacha, tempranillo.

88 Colour: cherry, garnet rim. Nose: red berry notes, mineral, fine reductive notes, creamy oak, violet drops. Palate: unctuous, powerful, flavourful, fleshy, long, toasty.

ANDRES MELER 2006 T
100% cabernet sauvignon.

91 Colour: cherry, garnet rim. Nose: spicy, creamy oak, toasty, complex, overripe fruit. Palate: powerful, flavourful, toasty, round tannins.

MELER 2005 TC
50% merlot, 50% cabernet sauvignon.

90 Colour: dark-red cherry, orangey edge. Nose: balsamic herbs, cocoa bean, spicy, cigar. Palate: flavourful, powerful, fleshy, complex.

BODEGAS MONTE ODINA

Monte Odina, s/n
22415 Ilche (Huesca)
☎: +34 974 343 480 - Fax: +34 974 343 484
bodega@monteodina.com
www.monteodina.com

MONTE ODINA GEWURZTRAMINER 2010 B
100% gewürztraminer.

87 Nose: white flowers, dried herbs, citrus fruit. Palate: flavourful, fruity, fleshy, light-bodied, fresh.

MONTE ODINA RD
cabernet sauvignon.

88 Colour: rose, purple rim. Nose: raspberry, red berry notes, expressive, floral. Palate: good acidity, fruity, fresh, rich, flavourful.

MONTE ODINA 2010 T
50% merlot, 50% cabernet sauvignon.

85 Colour: cherry, purple rim. Nose: red berry notes, fresh, expressive. Palate: correct, flavourful, easy to drink.

MONTE ODINA MERLOT 2007 T
merlot.

87 Colour: cherry, garnet rim. Nose: ripe fruit, spicy, creamy oak, expressive. Palate: powerful, fleshy, rich.

MONTE ODINA 2006 TC
cabernet sauvignon, merlot.

87 Colour: dark-red cherry, orangey edge. Nose: old leather, ripe fruit, spicy, toasty. Palate: unctuous, powerful, flavourful, fleshy.

MONTE ODINA CABERNET 2008
cabernet sauvignon.

84 Colour: pale ruby, brick rim edge. Nose: balsamic herbs, overripe fruit, spicy. Palate: flavourful, rich, fleshy.

BODEGAS OBERGO

Ctra. La Puebla, Km. 0,6
22439 Ubiergo (Huesca)
☎: +34 669 357 866
bodegasobergo@obergo.es
www.obergo.es

LÁGRIMAS DE OBERGO 2010 RD
garnacha, syrah.

87 Colour: rose, purple rim. Nose: red berry notes, raspberry, expressive, medium intensity. Palate: powerful, flavourful, fleshy, fruity.

OBERGO CARAMELOS 2010 T
garnacha.

90 Colour: bright cherry. Nose: ripe fruit, sweet spices, creamy oak, warm. Palate: flavourful, fruity, round tannins, roasted-coffee aftertaste.

OBERGO SYRAH 2009 T
syrah.

91 Colour: bright cherry. Nose: sweet spices, creamy oak, expressive, tar, dark chocolate, overripe fruit. Palate: flavourful, toasty, round tannins, powerful.

OBERGO VARIETALES 2008 T
cabernet sauvignon.

91 Color cherry, garnet rim. Aroma ripe fruit, spicy, creamy oak, toasty, complex. Taste powerful, flavourful, toasty, round tannins.

OBERGO "FINCA LA MATA" 2008 T
merlot, cabernet sauvignon, garnacha.

90 Color cherry, garnet rim. Aroma ripe fruit, spicy, creamy oak, toasty, complex. Taste powerful, flavourful, toasty, round tannins.

BODEGAS OLVENA

Paraje El Ariño, s/n
Ctra. Nacional 123, Km. 5
22300 Barbastro (Huesca)
☎: +34 974 308 481 - Fax: +34 974 308 482
info@bodegasolvena.com
www.bodegasolvena.com

OLVENA CHARDONNAY 2010 B
chardonnay.

86 Colour: bright straw. Nose: faded flowers, candied fruit, medium intensity. Palate: flavourful, fruity, fresh.

OLVENA 2010 RD
merlot.

83 Colour: brilliant rose. Nose: candied fruit, medium intensity, slightly evolved. Palate: spicy, easy to drink.

OLVENA CUATRO O EL PAGO DE LA LIBÉLULA 2007 T
cabernet sauvignon, merlot, syrah, tempranillo.

90 Color bright cherry. Aroma ripe fruit, sweet spices, creamy oak, expressive. Taste flavourful, fruity, toasty, round tannins.

OLVENA HACHE 2006 T
garnacha, syrah.

88 Colour: cherry, garnet rim. Nose: ripe fruit, spicy, toasty, dark chocolate. Palate: powerful, flavourful, toasty, round tannins.

BODEGAS OSCA

La Iglesia, 1
22124 Ponzano (Huesca)
☎: +34 974 319 017 - Fax: +34 974 319 175
bodega@bodegasosca.com
www.bodegasosca.com

OSCA GARNACHA BLANCA 2010 B
garnacha blanca.

85 Colour: bright straw. Nose: fresh fruit, white flowers. Palate: flavourful, fruity, good acidity.

OSCA 2010 B
macabeo, garnacha blanca.

85 Colour: bright straw. Nose: white flowers, citrus fruit, grassy. Palate: good acidity, unctuous, fruity.

OSCA 2010 RD
tempranillo, moristel.

87 Colour: rose, purple rim. Nose: floral, red berry notes, powerfull, fresh, expressive. Palate: flavourful, light-bodied, fresh, fleshy, easy to drink.

OSCA 2009 T
tempranillo, moristel.

86 Nose: ripe fruit, toasty, spicy, balsamic herbs, cocoa bean. Palate: powerful, flavourful, fleshy, spicy.

OSCA 2006 TC
tempranillo, cabernet sauvignon.

87 Colour: cherry, garnet rim. Nose: overripe fruit, spicy. Palate: ripe fruit, fine bitter notes, good acidity.

MASCÚN SYRAH 2006 T
syrah.

87 Colour: cherry, garnet rim. Nose: ripe fruit, spicy, roasted coffee. Palate: unctuous, flavourful.

OSCA GRAN EROLES 2006 TR
cabernet sauvignon, tempranillo.

86 Colour: cherry, garnet rim. Nose: fruit liqueur notes, balsamic herbs, spicy, toasty. Palate: flavourful, rich, fleshy.

MASCÚN MERLOT 2004 T
merlot.

87 Colour: cherry, garnet rim. Nose: spicy, toasty, fruit preserve. Palate: powerful, flavourful, toasty, round tannins.

BODEGAS RASO HUETE

Joaquín Costa, 23
22423 Estadilla (Huesca)
☎: +34 974 305 357 - Fax: +34 974 305 357
info@bodegasrasohuete.com
www.bodegasrasohuete.com

ARNAZAS MERLOT 2006 T ROBLE
merlot.

87 Colour: pale ruby, brick rim edge. Nose: elegant, spicy, wet leather, aged wood nuances, fruit liqueur notes. Palate: spicy, fine tannins, elegant, long.

ARNAZAS CABERNET-MERLOT 2005 TC
cabernet sauvignon, merlot.

89 Colour: bright cherry, orangey edge. Nose: spicy, cocoa bean, dark chocolate, creamy oak, ripe fruit. Palate: flavourful, powerful.

TRASHUMANTE 2005 T

86 Colour: light cherry, brick rim edge. Nose: spicy, cigar, old leather, tobacco. Palate: balanced, flavourful, fleshy.

PARTIDA ARNAZAS CABERNET-MERLOT 2004 T

87 Colour: cherry, garnet rim. Nose: ripe fruit, sweet spices, toasty, wet leather. Palate: flavourful, powerful, spicy, ripe fruit.

BODEGAS SERS

Pza. Mayor, 7
22417 Cofita (Huesca)
☎: +34 667 596 155
info@bodegassers.com
www.bodegassers.com

SÈRS BLANQUÉ 2010 B
100% chardonnay.

88 Colour: bright straw. Nose: fresh fruit, white flowers, varietal. Palate: flavourful, fruity, good acidity, balanced.

SÈRS PRIMER 2010 T
100% syrah.

86 Colour: cherry, purple rim. Nose: ripe fruit, raspberry, expressive. Palate: creamy, fruity, light-bodied, fresh.

SÈRS SINGULAR 2009 T
100% parraleta.

88 Colour: cherry, purple rim. Nose: ripe fruit, toasty, cocoa bean, spicy. Palate: good acidity, balanced, flavourful, fleshy.

SÈRS TEMPLE 2008 TC
60% cabernet sauvignon, 40% merlot.

88 Colour: cherry, garnet rim. Nose: ripe fruit, dark chocolate, cocoa bean, creamy oak. Palate: good acidity, flavourful, rich, fleshy.

SÈRS TEMPLE 2006 TR
cabernet sauvignon, merlot, syrah.

87 Colour: cherry, garnet rim. Nose: ripe fruit, spicy, creamy oak, toasty. Palate: powerful, flavourful, toasty, round tannins.

BODEGAS SIERRA DE GUARA

Ctra. A-1 1229, Km. 0,2
22124 Las Cellas (Huesca)
☎: +34 974 340 671 - Fax: +34 974 319 363
ventas@bodegassierradeguara.es
www.bodegassierradeguara.es

DRIAS SEVIL 2007 T
50% cabernet sauvignon, 50% merlot.

88 Colour: cherry, garnet rim. Nose: balsamic herbs, dark chocolate, cocoa bean, spicy. Palate: powerful, fleshy, rich, flavourful.

IDRIAS CHARDONNAY 2010 B
100% chardonnay.

86 Colour: bright golden. Nose: white flowers, candied fruit. Palate: flavourful, fruity, good acidity, balanced.

IDRIAS CHARDONNAY EDICIÓN ESPECIAL 2007 BFB
chardonnay.

89 Colour: bright golden. Nose: dried flowers, fragrant herbs, pattiserie, creamy oak. Palate: good acidity, balanced, powerful, flavourful.

IDRIAS MERLOT 2010 RD
100% merlot.

87 Colour: rose, purple rim. Nose: fresh fruit, floral, dried herbs. Palate: light-bodied, fresh, flavourful.

IDRIAS TEMPRANILLO 2010 T
100% tempranillo.

87 Colour: cherry, purple rim. Nose: fresh fruit, red berry notes. Palate: flavourful, fruity, good acidity, round tannins.

IDRIAS ABIEGO 2008 T
50% cabernet sauvignon, 50% merlot.

90 Colour: cherry, garnet rim. Nose: ripe fruit, spicy, creamy oak, toasty. Palate: powerful, flavourful, toasty, round tannins.

CHESA

Autovía A-22, km. 57
22300 Barbastro (Huesca)
☎: +34 649 870 637 - Fax: +34 974 313 552
bodegaschesa@hotmail.com
www.bodegaschesa.com

CHESA GEWÜRZTRAMINER 2010 B
100% gewürztraminer.

86 Colour: bright straw. Nose: fragrant herbs, white flowers, medium intensity. Palate: good acidity, unctuous, flavourful, fruity.

CHESA 2010 RD
100% cabernet sauvignon.

89 Colour: cherry, purple rim. Nose: red berry notes, raspberry, floral, fresh, expressive. Palate: creamy, fruity, powerful, flavourful.

CHESA MERLOT CABERNET 2010 T
65% merlot, 35% cabernet sauvignon.

87 Colour: cherry, purple rim. Nose: red berry notes, fresh fruit, expressive. Palate: fruity, powerful, flavourful, fleshy.

CHESA 2009 T ROBLE
65% merlot, 35% cabernet sauvignon.

87 Colour: cherry, garnet rim. Nose: ripe fruit, warm, spicy, cocoa bean, toasty. Palate: flavourful, fleshy, rich.

DALCAMP

Constitución, 4
22415 Monesma de San Juan (Huesca)
☎: +34 973 760 018 - Fax: +34 973 760 523
rdalfo@mixmail.com
www.castillodemonesma.com

CASTILLO DE MONESMA 2010 RD
cabernet sauvignon.

86 Colour: rose, purple rim. Nose: floral, fresh fruit, medium intensity. Palate: powerful, flavourful, light-bodied, fresh.

CASTILLO DE MONESMA 2010 T
70% merlot, 30% cabernet sauvignon.

86 Colour: cherry, purple rim. Nose: ripe fruit, balsamic herbs, earthy notes. Palate: flavourful, fresh, light-bodied, fleshy, powerful.

CASTILLO DE MONESMA 2008 TC
80% cabernet sauvignon, 20% merlot.

88 Colour: pale ruby, brick rim edge. Nose: cocoa bean, dark chocolate, spicy, red berry notes, ripe fruit. Palate: flavourful, fleshy, balsamic, easy to drink, round.

CASTILLO DE MONESMA
CRIANZA
CABERNET SAUVIGNON - MERLOT

EMBOTELLADO EN LA PROPIEDAD POR DALCAMP S.L.
22415 MONESMA DE SAN JUAN - ILCHE - ESPAÑA
PRODUCT OF SPAIN
14%vol R.E. 40817 - HU 75cl.
CONTIENE SULFITOS
SOMONTANO
DENOMINACIÓN DE ORIGEN

CASTILLO DE MONESMA CABERNET SAUVIGNON 2006 TR
cabernet sauvignon.

88 Colour: cherry, garnet rim. Nose: ripe fruit, spicy, creamy oak, toasty, complex, balsamic herbs. Palate: powerful, flavourful, toasty, round tannins.

CASTILLO DE MONESMA 2006 TR
90% cabernet sauvignon, 10% merlot.

88 Colour: cherry, garnet rim. Nose: spicy, creamy oak, toasty, complex, fruit liqueur notes. Palate: powerful, flavourful, toasty, round tannins.

CASTILLO DE MONESMA 2005 TC
cabernet sauvignon, merlot.

88 Colour: bright cherry, orangey edge. Nose: spicy, dark chocolate, cocoa bean, toasty. Palate: spicy, good acidity, flavourful, fleshy.

CASTILLO DE MONESMA 2004 T RESERVA ESPECIAL
cabernet sauvignon, merlot.

88 Color cherry, garnet rim. Aroma ripe fruit, spicy, creamy oak, toasty, complex. Taste powerful, flavourful, toasty, round tannins.

DE BEROZ

Pol. Valle del Cinca - Calle B- 26-24
22300 Barbastro (Huesca)
☎: +34 974 269 921 - Fax: +34 974 269 921
bodega@deberoz.com
www.deberoz.com

DE BEROZ ESENCIA DE BLANCOS 2010 B
85% chardonnay, 15% gewürztraminer.

89 Colour: bright straw. Nose: powerfull, citrus fruit, candied fruit. Palate: flavourful, fine bitter notes, good acidity.

DE BEROZ ESENCIA DE TINTOS 2010 RD
50% cabernet sauvignon, 20% merlot, 20% syrah, 10% garnacha.

88 Colour: rose, purple rim. Nose: powerfull, ripe fruit, red berry notes, scrubland. Palate: fleshy, powerful, fruity, flavourful.

DE BEROZ NUESTRO ROBLE 2008 T
40% cabernet sauvignon, 40% merlot, 10% tempranillo, 10% moristel.

87 Colour: cherry, garnet rim. Nose: ripe fruit, spicy, cocoa bean, dark chocolate. Palate: powerful, flavourful, fleshy, balsamic.

DE BEROZ CRIANZA ESPECIAL 2007 T
50% cabernet sauvignon, 30% merlot, 20% syrah.

90 Colour: cherry, garnet rim. Nose: ripe fruit, expressive, cocoa bean. Palate: powerful, flavourful, fleshy.

LAR DE BEROZ 2006 T
50% cabernet sauvignon, 30% syrah, 10% garnacha, 10% parraleta.

91 Colour: cherry, garnet rim. Nose: ripe fruit, toasty, sweet spices. Palate: flavourful, fleshy, toasty.

DE BEROZ RESERVA FAMILIA 2006 T
70% cabernet sauvignon, 10% merlot, 10% syrah, 10% tempranillo.

90 Colour: dark-red cherry, orangey edge. Nose: balsamic herbs, spicy, toasty. Palate: round, rich, flavourful, fleshy.

ENATE

Avda. de las Artes, 1
22314 Salas Bajas (Huesca)
☎: +34 974 302 580 - Fax: +34 974 300 046
bodega@enate.es
www.enate.es

ENATE CHARDONNAY-234 2010 B
100% chardonnay.

90 Colour: bright straw. Nose: fresh, varietal, ripe fruit, floral. Palate: flavourful, fruity, good acidity, balanced.

ENATE GEWÜRZTRAMINER 2010 B
100% gewürztraminer.

90 Colour: bright straw. Nose: fresh, fresh fruit, white flowers, varietal. Palate: flavourful, fruity, good acidity, balanced.

ENATE CHARDONNAY 2008 BFB
100% chardonnay.

94 Color bright yellow. Aroma powerfull, ripe fruit, sweet spices, creamy oak, fragrant herbs. Taste rich, smoky aftertaste, flavourful, fresh, good acidity.

ENATE UNO CHARDONNAY 2006 BFB
chardonnay.

96 Colour: bright yellow. Nose: powerfull, ripe fruit, creamy oak, mineral, pattiserie. Palate: rich, smoky aftertaste, flavourful, fresh, good acidity.

ENATE 2010 RD
100% cabernet sauvignon.

89 Colour: rose, purple rim. Nose: floral, fresh fruit, red berry notes. Palate: fleshy, powerful, fruity, fresh, round tannins.

ENATE TAPAS 2010 T
tempranillo.

87 Colour: cherry, purple rim. Nose: powerfull, ripe fruit, raspberry. Palate: flavourful, powerful, fleshy.

ENATE MERLOT-MERLOT 2007 T
100% merlot.

91 Colour: cherry, garnet rim. Nose: spicy, creamy oak, aromatic coffee. Palate: powerful, flavourful, toasty, round tannins.

ENATE RESERVA ESPECIAL 2006 TR
cabernet sauvignon, merlot.

93 Colour: cherry, garnet rim. Nose: spicy, creamy oak, toasty, characterful, fruit expression, elegant. Palate: powerful, flavourful, toasty, round tannins, fine bitter notes.

ENATE VARIETALES 2006 T
tempranillo, cabernet sauvignon, merlot, syrah.

90 Colour: cherry, garnet rim. Nose: ripe fruit, spicy, creamy oak, toasty, powerfull, characterful. Palate: powerful, flavourful, toasty, round tannins, fine bitter notes.

ENATE TEMPRANILLO CABERNET SAUVIGNON 2006 TC
70% tempranillo, 30% cabernet sauvignon.

88 Colour: cherry, garnet rim. Nose: spicy, creamy oak, toasty. Palate: powerful, flavourful, toasty, round tannins.

ENATE
CRIANZA
TEMPRANILLO - CABERNET SAUVIGNON
2006
SOMONTANO
DENOMINACIÓN DE ORIGEN

ENATE UNO 2005 T
cabernet sauvignon, merlot.

94 Colour: light cherry. Nose: powerfull, characterful, ripe fruit, fruit liqueur notes, toasty, aromatic coffee. Palate: flavourful, ripe fruit, spicy, long.

ENATE CABERNET SAUVIGNON 2005 TR
100% cabernet sauvignon.

92 Colour: cherry, garnet rim. Nose: spicy, creamy oak, toasty, complex, mineral, elegant, varietal. Palate: powerful, flavourful, toasty, round tannins.

ENATE CABERNET MERLOT 2008 T
50% cabernet sauvignon, 50% merlot.

88 Colour: cherry, garnet rim. Nose: scrubland, ripe fruit, toasty, spicy. Palate: flavourful, ripe fruit, easy to drink, round tannins.

ENATE SYRAH-SHIRAZ 2007 T
100% syrah.

92 Colour: cherry, garnet rim. Nose: creamy oak, toasty, sweet spices. Palate: powerful, flavourful, toasty, round tannins.

VINSOM

Ctra. Berbegal, Km. 2,5
22300 Barbastro (Huesca)
☎: +34 974 269 188 - Fax: +34 974 269 188
info@lafirmadevinos.com
www.docelunas.es

12 LUNAS 2010 B
chardonnay, gewürztraminer.

90 Colour: bright straw. Nose: fresh, fresh fruit, white flowers, spicy. Palate: flavourful, fruity, good acidity, balanced.

12 LUNAS 2010 RD
syrah.

90 Color rose, purple rim. Aroma powerfull, ripe fruit, red berry notes, floral, expressive. Taste fleshy, powerful, fruity, fresh.

12 LUNAS 2007 T
tempranillo, merlot, syrah.

91 Colour: cherry, garnet rim. Nose: ripe fruit, spicy, creamy oak, toasty, scrubland. Palate: powerful, flavourful, toasty, round tannins.

12 LUNAS (MÁS UNA) 2007 T
tempranillo, syrah, cabernet sauvignon.

90 Colour: bright cherry. Nose: sweet spices, creamy oak, spicy. Palate: flavourful, fruity, toasty, round tannins.

VIÑAS DEL VERO

Ctra. Naval, Km. 3,7
22300 Barbastro (Huesca)
☎: +34 974 302 216 - Fax: +34 974 302 098
marketing@vinasdelvero.es
www.vinasdelvero.es

VIÑAS DEL VERO CHARDONNAY 2010 B
100% chardonnay.

94 Colour: bright straw. Nose: white flowers, ripe fruit, varietal, expressive. Palate: flavourful, fruity, good acidity, balanced.

VIÑAS DEL VERO GEWÜRZTRAMINER COLECCIÓN 2010 B
100% gewürztraminer.

90 Colour: bright straw. Nose: white flowers, citrus fruit, fragrant herbs, varietal. Palate: good acidity, fruity, flavourful, easy to drink.

VIÑAS DEL VERO MACABEO CHARDONNAY 2010 B
macabeo, chardonnay.

89 Colour: bright straw. Nose: fresh, fresh fruit, white flowers. Palate: flavourful, fruity, good acidity, balanced.

VIÑAS DEL VERO CLARIÓN 2009 B
chardonnay, garnacha blanca.

92 Colour: bright straw. Nose: fresh, fresh fruit, white flowers, spicy. Palate: flavourful, fruity, good acidity, balanced.

VIÑAS DEL VERO CHARDONNAY COLECCIÓN 2008 B
100% chardonnay.

93 Colour: bright yellow. Nose: powerfull, ripe fruit, sweet spices, fragrant herbs. Palate: rich, smoky aftertaste, flavourful, fresh, good acidity.

VIÑAS DEL VERO PINOT NOIR COLECCIÓN 2009 T
100% pinot noir.

92 Colour: cherry, garnet rim. Nose: fruit expression, ripe fruit, balsamic herbs, scrubland. Palate: flavourful, fruity, ripe fruit, easy to drink.

VIÑAS DEL VERO LA MIRANDA DE SECASTILLA 2008 T
garnacha, parraleta, syrah.

91 Colour: cherry, garnet rim. Nose: ripe fruit, spicy, toasty, earthy notes. Palate: powerful, flavourful, toasty, round tannins.

VIÑAS DEL VERO SECASTILLA 2007 T
garnacha.

93 Colour: cherry, garnet rim. Nose: ripe fruit, spicy, complex, earthy notes, aromatic coffee, toasty. Palate: powerful, flavourful, toasty, round tannins.

VIÑAS DEL VERO SYRAH COLECCIÓN 2007 T
100% syrah.

90 Colour: cherry, garnet rim. Nose: ripe fruit, spicy, creamy oak, characterful. Palate: powerful, flavourful, toasty, round tannins.

VIÑAS DEL VERO GRAN VOS 2005 TR
cabernet sauvignon, mencía.

90 Color cherry, garnet rim. Aroma ripe fruit, spicy, creamy oak, toasty, complex. Taste powerful, flavourful, toasty, round tannins.

DO TACORONTE-ACENTEJO

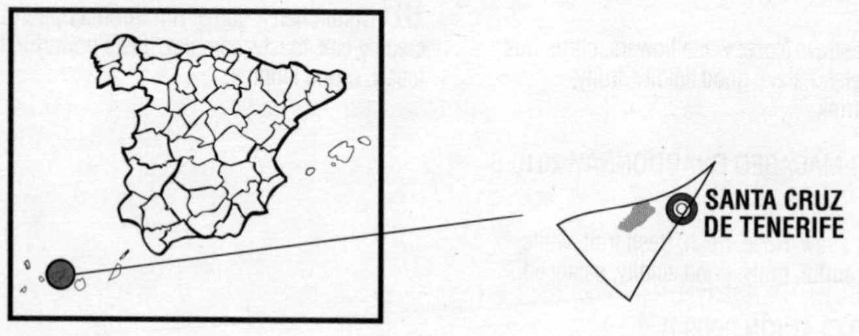

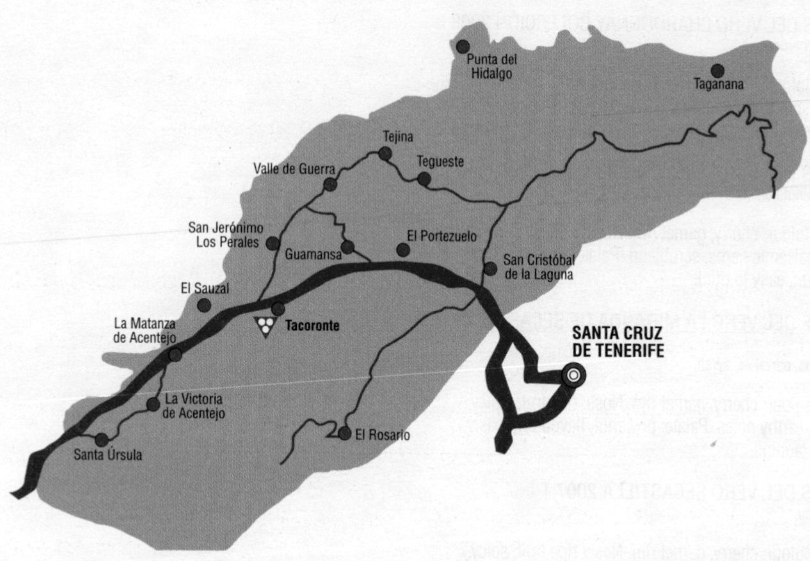

Consejo Regulador

DO Boundary

NEWS ABOUT THE VINTAGE:

As it happened last year between 2008 and 2009, 2010 shows pretty similar to its preceding vintage, given that climatic conditions very much of the same, with the trade winds bringing to the island good humidity levels to counteract the torrid influence of the African winds that so often alter the ripening cycle, and thus allowing the opportunity of a cooler, fresher vintage only slightly affected at harvest time by some late rains that forced growers to pick up grapes in several tries.

Young red wines made by the method of carbonic maceration have a plus of ripe fruit notes that seems to make them much more drinkable. Viña Norte 2010 (89 points) and Marba 2010 (88 points) are the best of this type of wines.

In general terms, all the young wines have improved their ratings this year, although it was not the best one in the DO, something that leads us to believe that good winemaking practices are becoming more common, affording for the region's wines a more homogenous quality within the segment of truly Atlantic wines.

As in every edition of our Guide, sweet wines from Bodegas Insulares, with their brand name of Humboldt, show the true winemaking potential of the island. Also this year Magma de Cráter Crianza 2006, from Bodegas Buten, manages to go up the rankings to share the Podium of the region with Bodegas Insulares.

LOCATION:

Situated in the north of Tenerife, stretching for 23 km and is composed of 9 municipal districts: Tegueste, Tacoronte, El Sauzal, La Matanza de Acentejo, La Victoria de Acentejo, Santa Úrsula, La Laguna, Santa Cruz de Tenerife and El Rosario.

CLIMATE:

Typically Atlantic, affected by the orientation of the island and the relief which give rise to a great variety of microclimates. The temperatures are in general mild, thanks to the influence of the trade winds, which provide high levels of humidity, around 60%, although the rains are scarce.

SOIL:

The soil is volcanic, reddish, and is made up of organic matter and trace elements. The vines are cultivated both in the valleys next to the sea and higher up at altitudes of up to 1,000 m.

GRAPE VARIETIES:

WHITE: PREFERRED: *Güal, Malvasía, Listán Blanco* and *Marmajuelo.*
AUTHORIZED: *Pedro Ximénez, Moscatel, Verdello, Vijariego, Forastera Blanca, Albillo, Sabro, Bastardo Blanco, Breval, Burra Blanca* and *Torrontés.*
RED: PREFERRED: *Listán Negra* and *Negramoll.*
AUTHORIZED: *Tintilla, Moscatel Negro, Castellana Negra, Cabernet Sauvignon, Merlot, Pinot Noir, Ruby Cabernet, Syrah, Tempranillo, Bastardo Negro, Listán Prieto, Vijariego Negro* and *Malvasía Rosada.*

SUB-REGIONS:

Anaga (covering the municipal areas of La Laguna, Santa Cruz de Tenerife and Tegueste) which falls within the limits of the Anaga Rural Park.

DO TACORONTE-ACENTEJO

FIGURES:

Vineyard surface: 1,174 – **Wine-Growers:** 1,816 – **Wineries:** 48 – **2010 Harvest rating:** Very Good – **Production:** 717,807 litres – **Market percentages:** --% domestic. --% export

CONSEJO REGULADOR
Ctra. General del Norte, 97
38350 Tacoronte (Santa Cruz de Tenerife)
☎: +34 922 560 107 - Fax: +34 922 561 155
@ consejo@tacovin.com
www.tacovin.com

GENERAL CHARACTERISTICS OF THE WINES

WHITES	These are light and fruity; they are produced in small quantities.
ROSÉS	Produced mainly from *Listán Negro*, they maintain the varietal character of this stock and are fresh and pleasant to drink.
REDS	These are the most characteristic wines of the DO. The young red wines have a deep cherry-red or deep red ruby colour; on the nose they develop aromas with a good intensity; they are fresh and fruity and transmit a somewhat wild character, but are original from the *Listán* grape. Recently, Crianza wines aged in barrels have also been produced.

VINTAGE RATING PEÑÍNGUIDE

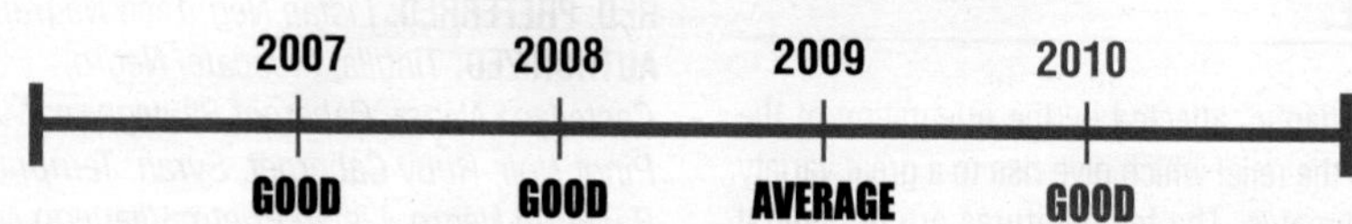

BODEGA ACEVEDO

Camino El Guincho, 140
38270 Valle de Guerra (Santa Cruz de Tenerife)
☎: +34 922 538 023 - Fax: +34 922 545 212
antace@bodegaacevedo.com
www.bodegaacevedo.com

ACEVEDOPAGOS DE ROMA 2010 B
100% marmajuelo.

86 Colour: bright straw. Nose: ripe fruit, fresh fruit, expressive. Palate: flavourful, fruity, fresh.

ACEVEDO VIDUEÑO 2010 B
30% moscatel, 5% listán blanco, 65% otras.

82 Colour: bright straw. Nose: candied fruit, citrus fruit, medium intensity. Palate: flavourful, fine bitter notes, spicy.

ACEVEDO ROSA 2010 RD
100% listán negro.

75

ACEVEDO ROJO 2010 T
70% listán negro, 20% negramoll, 10% castellana.

85 Colour: bright cherry. Nose: red berry notes, wild herbs, balanced, medium intensity. Palate: flavourful, fruity, balanced.

ACEVEDO VERIJADIEGO 2010 T
100% vijariego.

68

BODEGA DOMÍNGUEZ IV GENERACIÓN

Calvario, 79
38350 Tacoronte (Santa Cruz de Tenerife)
☎: +34 922 572 435 - Fax: +34 922 572 435
administracion@bodegadominguez.es
www.bodegadominguez.com

DOMÍNGUEZ BLANCO DE UVA TINTA 2010 B
negramoll.

84 Colour: bright straw. Nose: white flowers, ripe fruit, fragrant herbs. Palate: flavourful, fine bitter notes, good acidity.

DOMÍNGUEZ MALVASÍA CLÁSICO 2009 B
malvasía.

92 Colour: golden. Nose: powerfull, floral, honeyed notes, candied fruit, fragrant herbs, acetaldehyde, pungent. Palate: flavourful, sweet, fresh, fruity, good acidity, long.

DOMÍNGUEZ CLÁSICO 2010 T
listán negro, negramoll, tintilla.

84 Colour: deep cherry. Nose: spicy, scrubland, balsamic herbs, ripe fruit. Palate: spicy, fine bitter notes.

DOMÍNGUEZ SELECCIÓN NEGRAMOLL 2008 T
negramoll.

85 Colour: bright cherry, garnet rim. Nose: ripe fruit, spicy. Palate: fruity, balanced.

DOMÍNGUEZ SELECCIÓN NEGRAMOLL 2006 T
negramoll.

84 Colour: bright cherry. Nose: fruit liqueur notes, spicy, dark chocolate. Palate: fine bitter notes, good acidity.

BODEGA EL LOMO

Ctra. El Lomo, 18
38280 Tegueste (Santa Cruz de Tenerife)
☎: +34 922 545 254 - Fax: +34 922 546 453
oficina@bodegaellomo.com
www.bodegaellomo.com

EL LOMO 2010 B
listán blanco, gual, malvasía.

85 Colour: bright yellow, greenish rim. Nose: ripe fruit, tropical fruit, white flowers. Palate: flavourful, fruity, easy to drink.

EL LOMO 2010 T MACERACIÓN CARBÓNICA
100% listán negro.

84 Colour: bright cherry. Nose: balanced, red berry notes, balsamic herbs. Palate: flavourful, fruity, easy to drink.

EL LOMO 2010 T
listán negro, negramoll, listán blanco.

82 Colour: deep cherry. Nose: ripe fruit, spicy, toasty. Palate: flavourful, good acidity, fine bitter notes.

EL LOMO 2009 T BARRICA
listán negro, negramoll.

85 Colour: deep cherry. Nose: expressive, ripe fruit, dark chocolate. Palate: spicy, ripe fruit, round tannins.

EL LOMO 2008 TC
listán negro.

86 Colour: cherry, garnet rim. Nose: ripe fruit, spicy, creamy oak, toasty. Palate: powerful, flavourful, toasty, round tannins.

BODEGA EL MOCANERO

Ctra. General, 347
38350 Tacoronte (Santa Cruz de Tenerife)
☎: +34 922 560 762 - Fax: +34 922 564 452
elmocanerosl@hotmail.com

EL MOCANERO 2010 B
listán blanco.

84 Colour: bright straw. Nose: powerfull, candied fruit, earthy notes. Palate: powerful, fine bitter notes, good acidity.

EL MOCANERO 2010 RD
listán negro, negramoll.

86 Colour: rose, purple rim. Nose: ripe fruit, red berry notes, floral, expressive. Palate: fleshy, powerful, fruity, fresh.

EL MOCANERO 2010 T
listán negro, listán blanco, negramoll.

84 Colour: bright cherry, purple rim. Nose: wild herbs, red berry notes, ripe fruit. Palate: correct, fruity.

EL MOCANERO NEGRAMOLL 2010 T
negramoll.

82 Colour: cherry, garnet rim. Nose: balsamic herbs, scrubland, powerfull. Palate: fruity, easy to drink, flavourful.

EL MOCANERO 2010 T MACERACIÓN CARBÓNICA
listán negro.

80 Colour: bright cherry, cherry, purple rim. Nose: dried herbs, medium intensity. Palate: light-bodied, good finish.

BODEGA EL RETIRO

La Resbala s/n
38370 La Matanza de Acentejo (Santa Cruz de Tenerife)
☎: +34 658 827 047 - Fax: +34 922 503 246
terellalu@hotmail.com

RETIRO 2010 T

82 Colour: bright cherry. Nose: fruit preserve, scrubland. Palate: fine bitter notes, spicy, round tannins.

BODEGA INSERCASA

Finca El Fresal - Camino Juan Fernandez, Valle Guerra
38270 La Laguna (Santa Cruz de Tenerife)
☎: +34 680 446 868 - Fax: +34 922 270 626
info@vinobronce.com
www.vinobronce.com

BRONCE ECOLÓGICO 2010 T

87 Colour: bright cherry, garnet rim. Nose: red berry notes, sweet spices, scrubland. Palate: good structure, flavourful, spicy.

BRONCE SYRAH 2010 T
syrah.

87 Colour: bright cherry. Nose: sweet spices, cocoa bean, wild herbs. Palate: fruity, flavourful, spicy.

BODEGA LA ISLETA

Camino de La Cairosa, 24
38280 Teguste (Santa Cruz de Tenerife)
☎: +34 678 760 156
bodega@laisleta.es
www.laisleta.es

LA ISLETA 2010 T
listán negro, negramoll.

82 Colour: bright cherry, purple rim. Nose: medium intensity, red berry notes, wild herbs. Palate: fruity, correct.

BODEGA LA PALMERA

Camino La Herrera, 83
38350 El Sauzal (Santa Cruz de Tenerife)
☎: +34 922 573 485 - Fax: +34 922 652 566
info@bodegalapalmera.com
www.bodegalapalmera.com

LA PALMERA 2010 T
95% listán negro, 3% moll, 1% castellana, 1% syrah.

84 Colour: cherry, purple rim. Nose: medium intensity, red berry notes, balsamic herbs. Palate: fruity, flavourful, easy to drink.

BODEGAS BUTEN

San Nicolás, 122
38360 El Sauzal (Santa Cruz de Tenerife)
☎: +34 922 573 272 - Fax: +34 922 573 272
crater@bodegasbuten.com
www.craterbodegas.com

CRÁTER 2007 T BARRICA
listán negro, negramoll.

92 Colour: deep cherry. Nose: powerfull, elegant, aromatic coffee, ripe fruit, earthy notes. Palate: flavourful, fine bitter notes, spicy, long.

MAGMA DE CRÁTER 2006 TC
negramoll, syrah.

95 Colour: very deep cherry. Nose: expressive, elegant, ripe fruit, spicy, cocoa bean, earthy notes. Palate: flavourful, spicy, long, fine tannins.

BODEGAS INSULARES TENERIFE

Vereda del Medio, 48
38350 Tacoronte (Santa Cruz de Tenerife)
☎: +34 922 570 617 - Fax: +34 922 570 043
bitsa@bodegasinsularestenerife.es
www.bodegasinsularestenerife.es

VIÑA NORTE 2010 B
listán blanco.

84 Colour: bright straw. Nose: medium intensity, white flowers, balanced. Palate: flavourful, good acidity.

HUMBOLDT MALVASÍA 2006 B
malvasía.

93 Colour: golden. Nose: powerfull, floral, honeyed notes, candied fruit, fragrant herbs, petrol notes, lactic notes. Palate: flavourful, sweet, good acidity, long.

HUMBOLDT VENDIMIA TARDÍA 2005 B
listán blanco.

92 Color golden. Aroma powerfull, floral, honeyed notes, candied fruit, fragrant herbs. Taste flavourful, sweet, fresh, fruity, good acidity, long.

VIÑA NORTE 2010 T MACERACIÓN CARBÓNICA
95% listán negro, 5% negramoll.

89 Colour: cherry, purple rim. Nose: fresh fruit, floral, fresh, expressive. Palate: light-bodied, fruity, fresh, easy to drink.

VIÑA NORTE 2010 T
listán negro, negramoll.

89 Colour: cherry, purple rim. Nose: medium intensity, balanced, red berry notes, balsamic herbs. Palate: flavourful, fruity, good structure.

VIÑA NORTE 2010 T BARRICA
listán negro, negramoll.

88 Colour: bright cherry, garnet rim. Nose: balanced, red berry notes, spicy, balsamic herbs. Palate: good structure, flavourful, fruity.

VIÑA NORTE 2008 T
listán negro, negramoll.

90 Color bright cherry. Aroma ripe fruit, sweet spices, creamy oak, expressive. Taste flavourful, fruity, toasty, round tannins.

VIÑA NORTE 2007 TC
listán negro, otras.

89 Colour: cherry, garnet rim. Nose: ripe fruit, cocoa bean, creamy oak, sweet spices. Palate: good structure, fleshy.

HUMBOLDT VERDELLO 2005 BLANCO DULCE
verdello.

94 Colour: bright golden. Nose: candied fruit, citrus fruit, dry nuts, faded flowers, petrol notes. Palate: flavourful, sweetness, full.

HUMBOLDT 1997 BLANCO DULCE
listán blanco.

95 Colour: bright golden. Nose: balsamic herbs, powerfull, candied fruit, citrus fruit, honeyed notes, petrol notes. Palate: powerful, flavourful, sweet, complex, concentrated, full.

HUMBOLDT 2001 TINTO DULCE
listán negro.

95 Colour: black cherry. Nose: powerfull, fruit liqueur notes, overripe fruit, varnish, dark chocolate, acetaldehyde. Palate: powerful, sweet, fine bitter notes, long, sweet tannins.

CALDOS DE ANAGA

Cruz de Candelaria, 20
38203 La Laguna (Santa Cruz de Tenerife)
☎: +34 922 255 478 - Fax: +34 922 255 478
caldos@caldosdeanaga.com
www.caldosdeanagas.com

CUEVAS DE LINO 2010 T
90% listán negro, 10% vijariego negro.

84 Colour: bright cherry, purple rim. Nose: red berry notes, wild herbs. Palate: easy to drink.

CÁNDIDO HERNÁNDEZ PÍO

Limeras con Avda. Tinguaro
38370 La Matanza de Acenjo (Santa Cruz de Tenerife)
☎: +34 922 577 270 - Fax: +34 922 577 390
candher2@teleline.es

CALIUS S/C B

85 Colour: bright straw. Nose: medium intensity, ripe fruit, tropical fruit. Palate: fruity, easy to drink.

VIÑA RIQUELAS GUAL 2009 B

88 Colour: bright straw, greenish rim. Nose: medium intensity, ripe fruit, citrus fruit, fine lees. Palate: flavourful, good acidity.

PUNTA DEL SOL 2001 B

85 Colour: bright straw. Nose: ripe fruit, citrus fruit, scrubland, balsamic herbs. Palate: flavourful, fine bitter notes, good acidity.

CALIUS 2010 T

85 Colour: cherry, garnet rim. Nose: medium intensity, ripe fruit, scrubland. Palate: fine bitter notes, spicy, ripe fruit.

BALCÓN CANARIO 2006 T

80 Colour: pale ruby, brick rim edge. Nose: fruit liqueur notes, aromatic coffee, sweet spices. Palate: flavourful, fine bitter notes, good acidity.

CARBAJALES

Barranco de San Juan, s/n
38350 Tacoronte (Santa Cruz de Tenerife)
☎: +34 922 275 763 - Fax: +34 922 275 763
loscarbajales@gmail.com
www.carbajales.es

CARBAJALES 2010 T
90% listán negro, 10% cabernet sauvignon, syrah.

85 Colour: cherry, purple rim. Nose: red berry notes, balanced, expressive, sweet spices, floral. Palate: fruity, flavourful.

EL GRANILETE

Calvario, 140
38350 Tacoronte (Santa Cruz de Tenerife)
☎: +34 922 211 414 - Fax: +34 922 209 945
jgescuela@terra.es

EL GRANILETE 2010 T
90% listán negro, 10% tintilla.

80 Colour: bright cherry, garnet rim. Nose: medium intensity, fresh fruit, balsamic herbs. Palate: easy to drink, balsamic.

FINCA LA HORNACA

Camino Hacienda el Pino, 42
38350 Tacoronte (Santa Cruz de Tenerife)
☎: +34 922 560 676
info@hoyadelnavio.com
www.hoyadelnavio.com

HOYA DEL NAVÍO 2010 T
50% listán negro, 50% negramoll.

82 Colour: bright cherry. Nose: fruit preserve, dark chocolate, sweet spices. Palate: flavourful, ripe fruit.

HOYA DEL NAVÍO 2009 T
50% listán negro, 50% negramoll.

83 Colour: deep cherry. Nose: medium intensity, ripe fruit, balsamic herbs. Palate: spicy, fine bitter notes.

HIMACOPASA

Avda. Reyes Católicos, 23
38005 Santa Cruz de Tenerife (Santa Cruz de Tenerife)
☎: +34 922 218 155 - Fax: +34 922 215 666
sofusa@gruposocas.com

SANSOFÉ 2010 T

84 Colour: light cherry. Nose: medium intensity, red berry notes. Palate: fruity, light-bodied, easy to drink.

J.A. FLORES

Cuchareras Bajas, 2
38370 La Matanza de Acentejo (Tenerife)
☎: +34 922 577 194 - Fax: +34 922 577 194

VIÑA FLORES 2010 T

79

JUAN GUTIERREZ LEÓN

Pérez Díaz, 44
38380 La Victoria (Santa Cruz de Tenerife)
☎: +34 922 581 003 - Fax: +34 922 581 831

HACIENDA ACENTEJO 2010 T

83 Colour: deep cherry. Nose: ripe fruit, spicy, sweet spices. Palate: flavourful, good acidity.

JUAN J. FUENTES TABARES

Camino El Boquerón, s/n
38270 La Laguna (Santa Cruz de Tenerife)
☎: +34 922 541 500 - Fax: +34 922 541 000
info@orquidariolycaste.com

VIÑA EL DRAGO 2009 T
listán negro, merlot, rubi, cabernet sauvignon.

88 Colour: cherry, garnet rim. Nose: powerfull, expressive, ripe fruit, sweet spices. Palate: powerful, fleshy, round tannins.

MARBA

Ctra. del Socorro, 253 - Portezuelo
38280 Tegueste (Santa Cruz de Tenerife)
☎: +34 639 065 015 - Fax: +34 922 638 400
marba@bodegasmarba.es
www.bodegasmarba.es

MARBA BLANCO BARRICA 2010 B
80% listán blanco, 20% otras.

88 Colour: bright straw. Nose: wild herbs, dried flowers, balanced, medium intensity. Palate: fruity, flavourful.

MARBA AFRUTADO 2010 B
60% listán blanco, 40% otras.

88 Colour: bright straw. Nose: fresh fruit, citrus fruit, dried flowers. Palate: flavourful, fruity, fresh, sweetness.

MARBA 2010 B
80% listán blanco, 20% otras.

84 Colour: bright straw, greenish rim. Nose: wild herbs, tropical fruit, powerfull. Palate: flavourful, fruity, good acidity.

MARBA 2010 RD
80% listán negro, 20% otras.

87 Colour: rose, purple rim. Nose: powerfull, ripe fruit, red berry notes, floral. Palate: fleshy, powerful, fruity, fresh.

MARBA TRADICIONAL 2010 T
80% listán negro, 20% otras.

88 Colour: bright cherry. Nose: red berry notes, balsamic herbs, powerfull, balanced. Palate: fruity, flavourful, balanced.

MARBA 2010 T MACERACIÓN CARBÓNICA
90% listán negro, 10% otras.

88 Colour: cherry, purple rim. Nose: fresh fruit, red berry notes, fresh. Palate: flavourful, fruity.

MONJE

Camino Cruz de Leandro, 36
38359 El Sauzal (Santa Cruz de Tenerife)
☎: +34 922 585 027 - Fax: +34 922 585 027
monje@bodegasmonje.com
www.bodegasmonje.com

HOLLERA MONJE 2010 T MACERACIÓN CARBÓNICA
listán negro.

86 Colour: cherry, garnet rim. Nose: wild herbs, red berry notes, medium intensity. Palate: fruity, flavourful.

VERIJADIEGO MONJE 2008 T
vijariego.

90 Colour: deep cherry. Nose: sweet spices, toasty, ripe fruit. Palate: powerful, spicy, fine bitter notes, mineral. Personality.

TINTILLA MONJE 2008 T FERMENTADO EN BARRICA
tintilla.

83 Colour: deep cherry. Nose: powerfull, ripe fruit, dark chocolate, toasty. Palate: flavourful, fine bitter notes, round tannins.

PRESAS OCAMPO

Los Alamos de San Juan, 5
38350 Tacoronte (Santa Cruz de Tenerife)
☎: +34 922 571 689 - Fax: +34 922 561 700
comercial@presasocampo.com
www.presasocampo.com

PRESAS OCAMPO 2010 T
listán negro, negramoll, castellana.

85 Colour: cherry, garnet rim. Nose: sweet spices, red berry notes, grassy. Palate: flavourful, powerful, fruity, spicy.

PRESAS OCAMPO 2010 T MACERACIÓN CARBÓNICA
80% listán negro, 20% negramoll.

83 Colour: cherry, purple rim. Nose: red berry notes, medium intensity, balsamic herbs. Palate: light-bodied, fruity, easy to drink.

ALYSIUS 2010 T
listán negro, negramoll, castellana, vijariego.

82 Colour: bright cherry. Nose: grassy, stalky. Palate: flavourful, balsamic.

TROPICAL MAR

Ctra. Los Angeles, 69
38360 Sauzal (Santa Cruz de Tenerife)
☎: +34 922 575 184
info@dongustavo.eu

DON GUSTAVO 2010 B

84 Colour: bright straw, greenish rim. Nose: medium intensity, wild herbs, spicy, faded flowers. Palate: light-bodied, easy to drink.

DON GUSTAVO 2010 RD

75

DON GUSTAVO 2010 T

82 Colour: cherry, garnet rim. Nose: ripe fruit, balanced, spicy. Palate: good structure, flavourful.

VIÑA EL MATO

Calvario, 270
38350 Tacoronte (Santa Cruz de Tenerife)
☎: +34 625 148 774 - Fax: +34 922 561 752
josesarabia@hotmail.com

VIÑA EL MATÓ 2010 T
90% listán negro, 10% listán blanco.

81 Colour: bright cherry, garnet rim. Nose: medium intensity, wild herbs. Palate: light-bodied, fruity.

VIÑA EL MATÓ 2010 T MACERACIÓN CARBÓNICA
100% listán negro.

80 Colour: bright cherry, purple rim. Nose: scrubland, grassy, powerfull. Palate: light-bodied, good finish.

NEWS ABOUT THE VINTAGE:

The DO Tarragona has evolved quite well in the last few years to become a sort of "transitional region", passing from a situation where not a single wine seemed to shine to a territory where some producers can come up with renderings that can convey the producer's personality, which is something of a big step, all things considered. Tarragona has been a sort o supply region for Cava and other provincial designations of origin that fattened the market with cheap, popular wines, and has managed a relatively easy passage to modern times. Nevertheless, once that huge step was over, most of the producers seemed to run out of steam and did not manage to go ahead and keep perfecting their wines, which has a reflect on the few number of samples that hit the 90-point mark. Just the most conscientious of the region's producers have been able to keep their wines up in the rankings year after year, regardless of the quality of the vintage.

Regarding white wine productions, producers seem to be strictly focused on trying to extract maximum freshness rather than achieving the degree of complexity and finesse that could take them to the "most sacred" rankings of our Podium. The exceptions are two barrel-fermented renderings, Muller Chardonnay and Adernats, both from the 2010 vintage.

As for the current vintage, it seems again to follow the same quality pattern as in 2009, with better overall results for red wines. In general terms, wines are fresher, with good red fruit notes and an easy and occasionally long palate. Probably it is in red winemaking where the truest identity of the DO lies, thanks to wines with a solid Mediterranean and balsamic edge easily assimilable to this region's identity. Terrer d'Aubert 2008 is the best red wine from Tarragona, thanks to a judicious and utterly balanced work with *cabernet sauvignon*.

We must pay special attention to the traditional "vinos de licor" (liquor wines), which are amongst the top of the region's rankings, particularly those made by De Muller.

Alongside the significant work of the local producers, the DO is focusing its efforts in knowing a little deeper about the red variety sumoll, present in the whole of Catalunya. Thanks to the effort of forward-thinking winemakers, we now know that sumoll, broadly despised in the recent past given its propensity to high yields, can produce wines of finesse as long as per vine production levels are closely watched. The best example within the DO is Sumoi Capvespre, from Agrícola y Secció de Crédit de Rodonya.

LOCATION:

The region is situated in the province of Tarragona. It comprises two different wine-growing regions: El Camp and Ribera d'Ebre, with a total of 72 municipal areas.

CLIMATE:

Mediterranean in the region of El Camp, with an average annual rainfall of 500 mm. The region of the Ribera has a rather harsh climate with cold winters and hot summers; it also has the lowest rainfall in the region (385 mm per year).

SOIL:

El Camp is characterized by its calcareous, light terrain, and the Ribera has calcareous terrain and also some alluvial terrain.

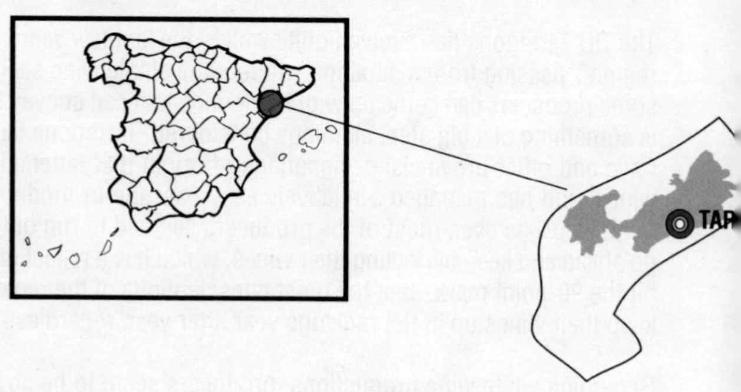
TAR

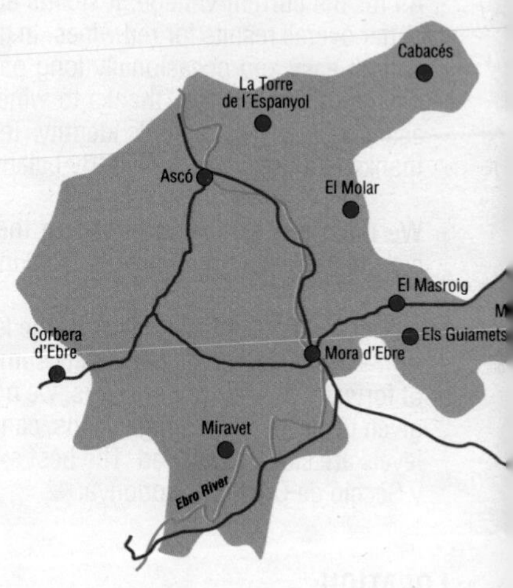
Cabacés
La Torre de l´Espanyol
Ascó
El Molar
El Masroig
Els Guiamets
Corbera d'Ebre
Mora d'Ebre
Miravet
Ebro River

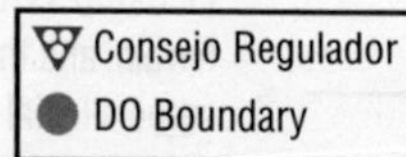
Consejo Regulador
DO Boundary

Cabra
del Camp
SUB-REGION
ALT CAMP
Vila-Rodona
Valls
Alcover
Cornudella
de Montsant
SUB-REGION
TARRAGONÉS
La Secuita
Alforja
L´Aleixar
La Nou de Gala
Riudecols
Reus
Les Borges
del Camp
Torredembarra
iudecanyes
Vila-Seca
TARRAGONA
SUB-REGION
BAIX CAMP
Mont-Roig
del Camp
Salou
Cambrils

DO TARRAGONA

GRAPE VARIETIES:

WHITE: *Chardonnay, Macabeo, Xarel·lo, Garnacha Blanca, Parellada, Moscatel de Alejandría, Moscatel de Frontignan, Sauvignon Blanc, Malvasía.*
RED: *Samsó* (*Cariñena*), *Garnacha, Ull de Llebre* (*Tempranillo*), *Cabernet Sauvignon, Merlot, Monastrell, Pinot Noir, Syrah.*

SUB-REGIONS:

El Camp and Ribera d'Ebre
(See specific characteristics in previous sections).

FIGURES:

Vineyard surface: 6,600 – **Wine-Growers:** 1,800 – **Wineries:** 33 – **2010 Harvest rating:** Very Good – **Production:** 4,000,000 litres – **Market percentages:** 50% domestic. 50% export

CONSEJO REGULADOR
Avda. Catalunya, 50
43002 Tarragona
☎: +34 977 217 931 - Fax: +34 977 229 102
@ dotarragona@ctmail.net

GENERAL CHARACTERISTICS OF THE WINES

WHITES	These have a markedly Mediterranean character, with notes reminiscent of mountain herbs. Yellow straw in colour, they are fresh, fruity and flavourful on the palate.
ROSÉS	Most of these have a colour that ranges from salmon to raspberry. They are fresh, fruity, light and pleasant to drink.
REDS	The young wines are the most characteristic. They have a cherry colour and are fruity, flavourful, with a slightly warm hint due to the Mediterranean influence, although much less meaty and powerful than those of Montsant.
TRADITIONAL WINES	These are the Licorosos (sweet) and the so-called Rancios Secos, with an alcohol content of between 13.5° and 23°, and the Generosos (dry), with an alcohol content of between 14° and 23°. Some also undergo the traditional processes.

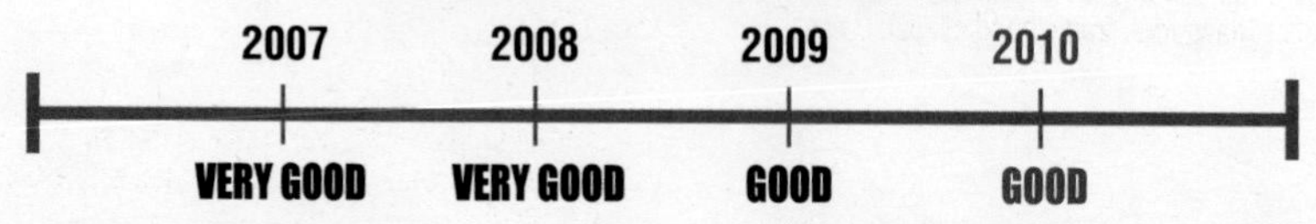

AGRÍCOLA I CAIXA AGRÀRIA I SECCIÓ DE CREDIT DE BRAFIM S.C.C.L.

Major, 50
43812 Brafim (Tarragona)
☎: +34 977 620 061 - Fax: +34 977 620 061
oficina@agricolabrafim.com
www.agricolabrafim.com

PUIG RODÓ MACABEU 2010 B
macabeo.

83 Colour: bright yellow. Nose: ripe fruit, dried flowers, grassy. Palate: full, fresh, flavourful.

PUIG RODÓ XAREL.LO 2010 B
xarel.lo.

80 Colour: bright straw. Nose: faded flowers, grassy, slightly evolved. Palate: green, flavourful.

PUIG RODÓ 2010 RD
ull de llebre.

86 Colour: rose, purple rim. Nose: powerfull, red berry notes, floral, expressive. Palate: flavourful, fruity, light-bodied, easy to drink.

PUIG RODÓ NEGRA 2010 T
ull de llebre, merlot.

84 Colour: cherry, purple rim. Nose: ripe fruit, floral, medium intensity. Palate: flavourful, fleshy, fruity.

PUIG RODÓ NEGRA 2008 T
ull de llebre, merlot.

87 Colour: cherry, garnet rim. Nose: ripe fruit, sweet spices, creamy oak. Palate: powerful, flavourful, fleshy.

AGRÍCOLA Y SECCIÓ DE CRÉDIT DE RODONYA

St. Sebastia, 3
43812 Rodonya (Tarragona)
☎: +34 977 608 010
crodonya@telefonica.net

SOL IXENT 2010 B
60% macabeo, 30% parellada, 10% xarel.lo.

84 Colour: bright straw. Nose: fresh, fresh fruit, white flowers. Palate: flavourful, fruity, good acidity, correct.

MIGJORN 2010 RD
100% tempranillo.

87 Colour: rose, purple rim. Nose: medium intensity, red berry notes. Palate: fruity, fresh, good acidity, balanced.

SUMOI CAPVESPRE S/C T
100% sumol.

92 Colour: cherry, garnet rim. Nose: expressive, balanced, ripe fruit, candied fruit, floral. Palate: balanced, ripe fruit, complex.

CAPVESPRE 2010 T
100% tempranillo.

88 Colour: cherry, purple rim. Nose: expressive, fresh fruit, red berry notes, floral. Palate: flavourful, fruity, good acidity, light-bodied.

IOMUS BLANC DE NOIRES 2009 ESP
100% sumol.

87 Colour: bright straw. Nose: fresh fruit, dried herbs, faded flowers. Palate: flavourful, fruity, good acidity. Personality.

IOMUS CLAS 2009 ESP
100% sumol.

86 Colour: rose, bright. Nose: fresh fruit, medium intensity, dried herbs. Palate: fresh, fruity, long.

IOMUSCRYO 2009 ESP
100% sumol.

86 Colour: rose, bright. Nose: balanced, fresh, dried flowers, medium intensity. Palate: flavourful, good acidity, easy to drink.

IOMUS ANCESTRAL 2009 ESP
100% sumol.

86 Colour: light cherry, bright. Nose: medium intensity, fragrant herbs, red berry notes. Palate: correct, fine bitter notes, good acidity.

BODEGA COOPERATIVA VILA-RODONA

Ctra. Santes Creus, s/n
43814 Vila-Rodona (Tarragona)
☎: +34 977 638 004 - Fax: +34 977 639 075
copvilar@copvilar.e.telefonica.net
www.coopvila-rodona.com

FLAMA ROJA 2004 TR
merlot, tempranillo.

83 Colour: pale ruby, brick rim edge. Nose: ripe fruit, old leather, spicy, toasty. Palate: flavourful, fleshy, balanced.

BODEGAS J. M. BACH I FILLS

Camí Vell de Cambrils 180
43480 Vilaseca (Tarragona)
☎: +34 977 353 099 - Fax: +34 977 353 154
closbarenys@closbarenys.com
www.closbarenys.com

CLOS BARENYS MUSCAT 2010 B
moscatel.

72

CLOS BARENYS MERLOT/SYRAH 2007 T
merlot, syrah.

86 Colour: cherry, garnet rim. Nose: fruit preserve, balsamic herbs, dark chocolate. Palate: fleshy, spicy, round tannins.

CLOS BARENYS 2004 TC
merlot, cabernet sauvignon.

86 Colour: cherry, garnet rim. Nose: ripe fruit, spicy, toasty, old leather. Palate: powerful, flavourful, toasty, round tannins.

CASTELL D'OR

Mare Rafols, 3- 1r 4a
08720 Vilafranca del Penedès (Barcelona)
☎: +34 938 905 385 - Fax: +34 938 905 446
castelldor@castelldor.com
www.castelldor.com

FLAMA ROJA 2010 B
50% macabeo, 50% xarel.lo.

85 Colour: bright straw. Nose: fresh, fresh fruit, white flowers, expressive. Palate: flavourful, fruity, good acidity.

FLAMA ROJA 2010 RD
100% tempranillo.

87 Colour: rose, purple rim. Nose: powerfull, red berry notes, floral, expressive, lactic notes. Palate: fleshy, powerful, fruity, fresh.

FLAMA ROJA 2008 T
85% tempranillo, 15% garnacha.

85 Colour: cherry, garnet rim. Nose: ripe fruit, balsamic herbs, spicy, creamy oak. Palate: good acidity, flavourful, fleshy.

CELLER LA BOELLA

Autovía Reus - Tarragona, km. 12
43110 La Canonja (Tarragona)
☎: +34 977 771 515 - Fax: +34 977 300 306
celler@laboella.com
www.laboella.com

MAS LA BOELLA 2010 RD
75% merlot, 25% monastrell.

83 Colour: brilliant rose. Nose: ripe fruit, grassy, dried flowers. Palate: light-bodied, fresh, fruity.

MAS LA BOELLA 2010 T
60% monastrell, 20% cabernet sauvignon, 20% merlot.

86 Colour: deep cherry, purple rim. Nose: ripe fruit, fruit preserve, powerfull. Palate: fleshy, correct.

MAS LA BOELLA VI DE GUARDA 2008 T
100% cabernet sauvignon.

90 Colour: bright cherry, garnet rim. Nose: balanced, balsamic herbs, ripe fruit, spicy. Palate: balanced, fleshy, ripe fruit.

CELLER MAS BELLA

Sant Roc, 8 - Masmolets
43813 Valls (Tarragona)
☎: +34 600 269 786 - Fax: +34 977 613 092
cellermasbella@gmail.com

BELLA 2010 B
macabeo, parellada.

86 Colour: bright yellow. Nose: balanced, expressive, white flowers, dried herbs. Palate: fruity, good acidity, easy to drink.

BELLA 2010 RD
ull de llebre.

82 Colour: rose, purple rim. Nose: floral, ripe fruit, slightly evolved. Palate: good acidity, fine bitter notes, flavourful.

BELLA 2010 T
ull de llebre.

87 Colour: cherry, purple rim. Nose: fresh fruit, red berry notes, floral. Palate: flavourful, fruity, balanced.

CELLERS UNIÓ

Joan Oliver, 16-24
43206 Reus (Tarragona)
☎: +34 977 330 055 - Fax: +34 977 330 070
info@cellersunio.com
www.cellersunio.com

ROUREDA BLANC DE BLANCS 2010 B
50% macabeo, 40% xarel.lo, 10% chardonnay.

86 Colour: bright straw. Nose: fresh fruit, white flowers. Palate: flavourful, fruity, good acidity, fine bitter notes.

ROUREDA RUBÍ 2010 RD
40% merlot, 40% tempranillo, 20% sumoll.

86 Colour: rose, purple rim. Nose: fresh fruit, red berry notes, raspberry, floral. Palate: flavourful, fruity, fresh, easy to drink.

ROUREDA NEGRE 2010 T
50% garnacha, 30% mazuelo, 20% syrah.

86 Colour: cherry, purple rim. Nose: fruit expression, violets, wild herbs. Palate: flavourful, fruity, fruity aftestaste.

ROUREDA 2007 TC
40% garnacha, 40% ull de llebre, 20% cabernet sauvignon.

86 Colour: cherry, garnet rim. Nose: ripe fruit, spicy, creamy oak, complex. Palate: powerful, flavourful, toasty.

DE MULLER

Camí Pedra Estela, 34
43205 Reus (Tarragona)
☎: +34 977 757 473 - Fax: +34 977 771 129
lab@demuller.es
www.demuller.es

SOLIMAR 2010 B
50% macabeo, 35% moscatel, 15% sauvignon blanc.

87 Colour: bright straw. Nose: balanced, white flowers, ripe fruit. Palate: flavourful, fruity, good acidity, fine bitter notes.

DE MULLER MUSCAT 2010 B
100% moscatel.

87 Colour: bright straw. Nose: white flowers, fruit expression, expressive. Palate: powerful, flavourful, fresh, fruity.

MISA DULCE SUPERIOR B
60% garnacha blanca, 40% macabeo.

87 Colour: bright golden. Nose: toasty, spicy, wild herbs, acetaldehyde. Palate: correct, rich, spicy.

DE MULLER CHARDONNAY 2010 BFB
chardonnay.

91 Colour: bright yellow. Nose: ripe fruit, dried flowers, fragrant herbs, sweet spices, creamy oak. Palate: good acidity, powerful, flavourful, fleshy.

SOLIMAR 2010 RD
70% tempranillo, 15% syrah, 15% cabernet sauvignon.

85 Colour: rose. Nose: balanced, ripe fruit, dried flowers, balsamic herbs. Palate: flavourful, good acidity.

DE MULLER SYRAH 2010 T ROBLE
100% syrah.

88 Colour: bright cherry, garnet rim. Nose: ripe fruit, sweet spices, complex, cocoa bean.

DE MULLER CABERNET SAUVIGNON 2008 TC
100% cabernet sauvignon.

88 Colour: cherry, garnet rim. Nose: ripe fruit, balsamic herbs, sweet spices, creamy oak, toasty. Palate: good acidity, powerful, flavourful, fleshy.

DE MULLER MERLOT 2008 T BARRICA
100% merlot.

88 Colour: cherry, garnet rim. Nose: ripe fruit, fragrant herbs, spicy, creamy oak. Palate: flavourful, fleshy, good acidity, balanced.

SOLIMAR 2008 TC
60% cabernet sauvignon, 40% merlot.

83 Colour: cherry, garnet rim. Nose: ripe fruit, grassy, medium intensity, creamy oak. Palate: flavourful, fleshy, good acidity.

PORPORES DE MULLER 2005 TR
cabernet sauvignon, merlot, tempranillo.

88 Colour: cherry, garnet rim. Nose: fruit preserve, spicy, balsamic herbs, complex. Palate: flavourful, fruity, fine bitter notes, balanced.

DE MULLER AVREO SEMIDULCE S/C AÑEJO
70% garnacha, 30% garnacha blanca.

91 Colour: light mahogany. Nose: ripe fruit, honeyed notes, acetaldehyde, caramel, sweet spices, toasty. Palate: spirituous, fleshy, complex, flavourful.

DE MULLER AVREO SECO S/C AÑEJO
70% garnacha, 30% garnacha blanca.

89 Colour: light mahogany. Nose: acetaldehyde, dry nuts, aged wood nuances, roasted almonds, spicy, toasty. Palate: rich, fleshy, complex, balanced.

MAS DE VALLS 2009 BN
55% macabeo, 35% chardonnay, 10% parellada.

87 Colour: bright straw. Nose: fine lees, dried flowers, ripe fruit, fragrant herbs. Palate: powerful, flavourful, good acidity, fine bead.

RESERVA REINA VIOLANT 2007 ESP
50% chardonnay, 50% pinot noir.

89 Colour: bright straw. Nose: dried herbs, fine lees, floral, ripe fruit, complex. Palate: fresh, fruity, flavourful, good acidity, fine bead, elegant.

DE MULLER GARNACHA SOLERA 1926 SOLERA
100% garnacha.

94 Colour: light mahogany. Nose: fruit liqueur notes, ripe fruit, sweet spices, cocoa bean, pattiserie, toasty, expressive. Palate: good acidity, round, unctuous, powerful, flavourful, fleshy, complex. Personality.

PAJARETE SOLERA 1851 VINO DE LICOR
moscatel, garnacha, garnacha blanca.

93 Colour: dark mahogany. Nose: acetaldehyde, candied fruit, caramel, sweet spices, pattiserie. Palate: rich, flavourful, long, spirituous.

DE MULLER RANCIO SECO VINO DE LICOR
garnacha tinta, garnacha blanca.

91 Colour: light mahogany. Nose: powerfull, complex, expressive, pungent, rancio notes, aged wood nuances, sweet spices, wild herbs. Palate: burning notes, confected, spirituous, fine bitter notes.

DE MULLER MOSCATEL AÑEJO VINO DE LICOR
100% moscatel.

90 Colour: old gold. Nose: candied fruit, fruit liqueur notes, honeyed notes, powerfull. Palate: flavourful, rich, sweet, balanced.

EL VI A PUNT

☎: +34 625 408 974
comercial@elviapunt.com
www.elviapunt.com

NON BAG IN BOX (3 LITROS) S/C RD
tempranillo.

76

MAS DEL BOTÓ

Bon Recer, 13
43007 (Tarragona)
☎: +34 630 982 747 - Fax: +34 977 236 396
pep@masdelboto.cat
www.masdelboto.cat

GANAGOT 2007 T
60% garnacha, 25% cabernet sauvignon, 15% samsó.

85 Colour: cherry, garnet rim. Nose: ripe fruit, warm, sweet spices, toasty. Palate: good acidity, powerful, flavourful.

GANAGOT 2006 T
85% garnacha, 10% samsó, 5% cabernet sauvignon.

84 Colour: dark-red cherry. Nose: ripe fruit, wild herbs, expressive, spicy, creamy oak. Palate: good acidity, flavourful, fleshy, toasty.

GANAGOT 2005 T
85% garnacha, 10% samsó, 5% cabernet sauvignon.

88 Colour: cherry, garnet rim. Nose: spicy, ripe fruit, balsamic herbs, creamy oak, balanced. Palate: powerful, flavourful, fleshy, complex, round tannins.

MAS DELS FRARES (FACULTAT D'ENOLOGIA DE TARRAGONA)

Ctra. TV-7211, Km. 7,2
43120 Constantí (Tarragona)
☎: +34 977 520 197 - Fax: +34 977 522 156
fincafe@urv.cat

URV AROMATIC 2010 B

84 Colour: bright straw, greenish rim. Nose: medium intensity, fresh, dried herbs, citrus fruit. Palate: fresh, easy to drink, correct.

URV 2010 B

83 Colour: bright straw. Nose: fresh, fragrant herbs. Palate: flavourful, fine bitter notes.

URV 2010 T

84 Colour: cherry, purple rim. Nose: floral, ripe fruit, scrubland. Palate: flavourful, fleshy, green.

URV 2008 TC

86 Colour: cherry, garnet rim. Nose: ripe fruit, scrubland, toasty. Palate: good acidity, balanced, flavourful, fleshy.

URV 2007 TR

86 Colour: cherry, garnet rim. Nose: ripe fruit, spicy, toasty, complex, scrubland. Palate: powerful, flavourful, toasty, round tannins.

URV BLANC DE BLANCS BR

88 Colour: bright straw. Nose: fresh fruit, dried herbs, fine lees, white flowers. Palate: fresh, fruity, flavourful, good acidity.

MAS VICENÇ

Mas Vicenç, s/n
43811 Cabra de Camp (Tarragona)
☎: +34 977 630 024 - Fax: +34 977 630 134
masvicens@masvicens.com
www.masvicenç.com

MAS VICENÇ 2010 B
90% macabeo, 10% moscatel.

87 Colour: pale. Nose: fresh, fresh fruit, white flowers, expressive, fragrant herbs. Palate: flavourful, fruity, balanced.

MAS VICENÇ DOLÇ 2010 B
100% moscatel.

87 Color golden. Aroma powerfull, floral, honeyed notes, candied fruit, fragrant herbs. Taste flavourful, sweet, fresh, fruity, good acidity, long.

MAS VICENÇ 2010 T
100% ull de llebre.

89 Colour: cherry, purple rim. Nose: red berry notes, floral, complex, expressive. Palate: powerful, flavourful, fleshy, balanced.

MAS VICENÇ 2009 TC
80% ull de llebre, 20% syrah.

86 Colour: deep cherry, garnet rim. Nose: medium intensity, ripe fruit, dark chocolate, sweet spices. Palate: fleshy, spicy, long.

MAS VICENÇ 2008 TC
60% ull de llebre, 40% cabernet sauvignon.

88 Colour: bright cherry, garnet rim. Nose: balanced, ripe fruit, sweet spices, cocoa bean, scrubland. Palate: fleshy, good structure.

SERRA DE LLABERIA

Avda. Vidal i Barraquer, 12, 8º- 4ª
43005 Tarragona (Tarragona)
☎: +34 977 824 122 - Fax: +34 977 824 122
info@serradellaberia.com
www.serradellaberia.com

SERRA DE LLABERIA ELISABETH 2007 B
80% garnacha blanca, 20% chardonnay.

75

SERRA DE LLABERIA ELISABETH 2005 TR
60% cabernet sauvignon, 30% merlot, 10% garnacha.

86 Colour: cherry, garnet rim. Nose: spicy, creamy oak, fruit preserve, medium intensity, warm. Palate: powerful, flavourful, toasty.

SERRA DE LLABERIA ELISABETH 2004 TR
60% cabernet sauvignon, 30% merlot, 10% garnacha.

88 Colour: cherry, garnet rim. Nose: fruit preserve, tobacco, spicy, balsamic herbs. Palate: ripe fruit, spicy, long.

SERRA DE LLABERIA ELISABETH 2003 T
60% cabernet sauvignon, 30% merlot, 10% garnacha.

88 Color cherry, garnet rim. Aroma ripe fruit, spicy, creamy oak, toasty, complex. Taste powerful, flavourful, toasty, round tannins.

VINÍCOLA I SECCIÓ DE CRÉDIT SANT ISIDRE DE NULLES

Estació, s/n
43887 Nulles (Tarragona)
☎: +34 977 614 965 - Fax: +34 977 602 622
casinulles@casinulles.com
www.vinicoladenulles.com

ADERNATS 2010 BFB
100% xarel.lo.

90 Colour: bright yellow, greenish rim. Nose: balanced, ripe fruit, floral. Palate: flavourful, correct, good acidity, spicy.

ADERNATS SEDUCCIÓ 2010 B
40% moscatel, 25% xarel.lo, 20% chardonnay, 15% parellada.

86 Colour: bright straw. Nose: medium intensity, white flowers, citrus fruit. Palate: fruity, good finish.

ADERNATS BLANC 2010 B
65% macabeo, 25% xarel.lo, 15% parellada.

85 Colour: bright straw. Nose: medium intensity, wild herbs, fresh fruit, faded flowers. Palate: fresh, fruity.

ADERNATS ROSAT 2010 RD
60% ull de llebre, 35% merlot, 5% cabernet sauvignon.

89 Colour: light cherry. Nose: fresh, red berry notes, white flowers, expressive. Palate: fruity, good acidity, balanced, fine bitter notes.

ADERNATS ANGELUS 2010 T
50% ull de llebre, 36% cabernet sauvignon, 14% merlot.

85 Colour: cherry, garnet rim. Nose: powerfull, ripe fruit, scrubland, fruit preserve. Palate: flavourful, good structure.

ADERNATS NEGRE JOVE 2010 T
50% ull de llebre, 35% merlot, 15% cabernet sauvignon.

83 Colour: cherry, purple rim. Nose: ripe fruit, grassy, medium intensity. Palate: fresh, fruity, flavourful.

ADERNATS 2008 TC
50% ull de llebre, 25% cabernet sauvignon, 25% merlot.

87 Colour: cherry, garnet rim. Nose: sweet spices, cocoa bean, pattiserie, candied fruit. Palate: flavourful, fruity, toasty.

VINOS PADRÓ

Avda. Catalunya, 64-70
43812 Brafim (Tarragona)
☎: +34 977 620 012 - Fax: +34 977 620 486
info@vinspadro.com
www.vinspadro.com

IPSIS 2009 TC
tempranillo, merlot.

90 Colour: cherry, garnet rim. Nose: toasty, sweet spices, ripe fruit. Palate: flavourful, good structure, spicy, round tannins, fleshy.

IPSIS BLANCO FLOR 2010 B
macabeo, xarel.lo, parellada, moscatel.

86 Colour: bright straw, greenish rim. Nose: medium intensity, wild herbs, fresh fruit. Palate: flavourful, correct.

IPSIS XAREL.LO 2010 B
xarel.lo.

86 Colour: bright straw. Nose: fresh fruit, white flowers, expressive. Palate: fruity, good acidity, thin.

IPSIS CHARDONNAY 2010 B
chardonnay.

80 Colour: pale. Nose: dried flowers, ripe fruit, fragrant herbs. Palate: powerful, flavourful, green.

IPSIS 2010 RD
tempranillo, merlot.

85 Colour: rose, bright. Nose: medium intensity, fragrant herbs, balanced. Palate: correct, good finish.

IPSIS 2010 T
tempranillo, merlot.

88 Colour: cherry, purple rim. Nose: expressive, fresh fruit, red berry notes, floral. Palate: flavourful, fruity, fleshy.

CRINEL 2008 TC
tempranillo, garnacha.

88 Colour: cherry, garnet rim. Nose: toasty, aromatic coffee, caramel, balsamic herbs. Palate: flavourful, spicy, ripe fruit.

VINS ECOLÒGICS HELGA HARBIG CEREZO

Plaça St. Joan, 3
43515 Resquera (Tarragona)
☎: +34 977 404 711

ERIKA DE PAUMERA 2010 RD

84 Colour: rose, purple rim. Nose: powerfull, fruit liqueur notes, overripe fruit. Palate: flavourful, fleshy, correct.

VINYES DEL TERRER

Camí del Terrer, s/n
43480 Vila-Seca (Tarragona)
☎: +34 977 269 229 - Fax: +34 977 269 229
info@terrer.net
www.terrer.net

BLANC DEL TERRER 2010 B
sauvignon blanc.

88 Colour: bright straw. Nose: powerfull, complex, burnt matches, spicy. Palate: flavourful, fruity, fleshy, fine bitter notes.

NUS DEL TERRER 2009 T
cabernet sauvignon, garnacha.

93 Colour: cherry, garnet rim. Nose: ripe fruit, spicy, creamy oak, toasty, characterful, mineral, expressive. Palate: powerful, flavourful, toasty, good acidity.

TERRER D'AUBERT 2009 T
cabernet sauvignon.

92 Colour: cherry, garnet rim. Nose: powerfull, characterful, creamy oak, toasty, sweet spices. Palate: powerful, flavourful, fleshy, round tannins.

TERRER D'AUBERT 2008 T
100% cabernet sauvignon.

92 Colour: cherry, garnet rim. Nose: ripe fruit, creamy oak, toasty, earthy notes. Palate: powerful, flavourful, toasty, round tannins.

NUS DEL TERRER 2008 T
garnacha, cabernet sauvignon.

91 Colour: cherry, garnet rim. Nose: ripe fruit, spicy, expressive, neat, fine reductive notes. Palate: powerful, flavourful, toasty, round tannins.

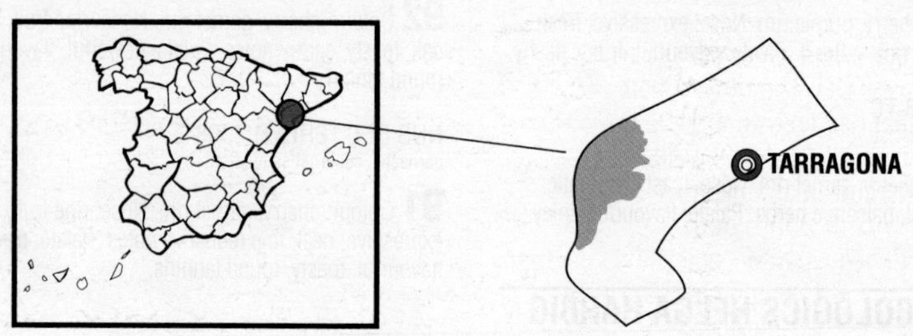

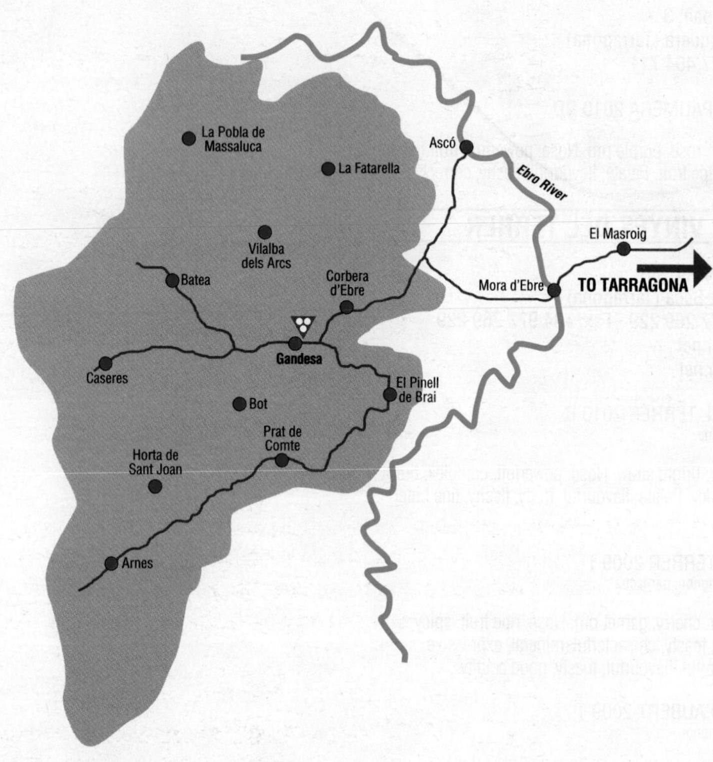

Consejo Regulador
DO Boundary

NEWS ABOUT THE VINTAGE:

In Terra Alta, white wines are the real power engine and the only –almost exclusive– foreseeable future for the DO. The region's bet on *garnacha blanca* and the DO's decision to come up with a back label destined to defend the singularity of this grape variety –a novelty we announced in last year's edition– are a good evidence of the possibilities of this recent move, although there are already a couple of wines that bear evidence of its potential, Llàgrimes de Tardor 2009 and L'Avi Arrufí 2009, both with 92 points. We have to follow their progress as closely as possible to see whether their makers are getting more involved in the goal of achieving higher quality wines. So far, the number of 100% *garnacha blanca* wines sampled do not reach but a-bit-above-the-average level, something that once again bears evidence of the need to keep working on it to achieve it as soon as possible.

But since "man does not live by garnacha blanca alone" in this region, as proved by the best-rated white wines in the DO (those of Bodega Edetària), we should have a closer look at the way this winery's bet is on the best association of foreign and local –say Mediterranean– varieties, along with the region's amazing terroir expression that shines through in its Edetària 2005, a wine that faithfully represents the ageing potential of garnacha blanca when blended with other varieties like *macabeo* or *viognier*, which add acidity and aromatic intensity.

The 2010 vintage was a much better one for red wine renderings, thanks to higher fruit weight and freshness. The best wines are –again– Edetària 2007 and L'Aví Arrufí 2007, with 93 and 92 points respectively.

The cooperative sector is still quite powerful in the region; it has a highly productive sense and cares little about the universe of unique, singular wines, something that impedes to a certain extent consistent quality and therefore the possibility for small producers to climb up steps in terms of reputation.

LOCATION:

In the southeast of Catalonia, in the province of Tarragona. It covers the municipal districts of Arnes, Batea, Bot, Caseres, Corbera d Ebre, La Fatarella, Gandesa, Horta de Sant Joan, Pinell de Brai, La Pobla de Massaluca, Prat de Comte and Vilalba dels Arcs.

CLIMATE:

Mediterranean, with continental influences. It is characterized by its hot, dry summers and very cold winters, especially in the higher regions in the east. The average annual rainfall is 400 mm. Another vital aspect is the wind: the 'Cierzo' and the 'Garbi' (Ábrego) winds.

SOIL:

The vineyards are located on an extensive plateau at an altitude of slightly over 400 m. The soil is calcareous and the texture mainly clayey, poor in organic matter and with many pebbles.

GRAPE VARIETIES:

WHITE: *Chardonnay, Garnacha Blanca, Parellada, Macabeo, Moscatel, Sauvignon Blanc, Chenin, Pedro Ximénez.* Experimental: *Viognier.*
RED: *Cabernet Sauvigon, Cariñena, Garnacha Tinta, Garnacha Peluda, Syrah, Tempranillo, Merlot, Samsó, Cabernet Franc.* Experimental: *Petit Verdot, Marselane, Caladoc.*

DO TERRA ALTA

FIGURES:

Vineyard surface: 5,755 – **Wine-Growers:** 1,473 – **Wineries:** 45 – **2010 Harvest rating:** Very Good – **Production:** 16,619 litres – **Market percentages:** 30% domestic. 70% export

CONSEJO REGULADOR
Avinguda Catalunya, 31
43780 Gandesa (Tarragona)
☎: +34 977 421 278 - Fax: +34 977 421 623
@ info@doterraalta.com
www.doterraalta.com

GENERAL CHARACTERISTICS OF THE WINES

WHITES	These are the most interesting products of the region. They are produced from the *Garnacha Blanca* variety, and have a purely Mediterranean character. With yellowish nuances, they have moses of ripe fruit and mountain herbs; they are supple, warm, complex and very expressive on the palate.
ROSÉS	Mainly produced from *Garnacha*, they offer all the fruitiness and tastiness on the palate, that one expects from this variety.
REDS	Cherry-coloured, they are characterised by their ripe fruit nose; they are quite flavourful on the palate.
GENEROSOS	This is another of the traditional wines of the region, whether in its Rancio or Mistela versions.

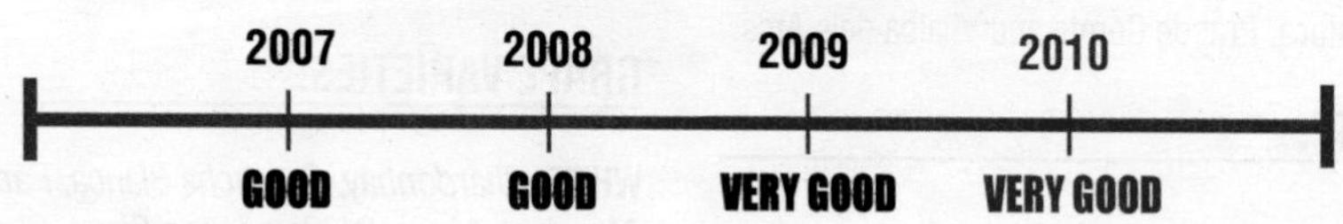

AGRARIA SANT SALVADOR D'HORTA

Navarra, 53
43596 Horta de Sant Joan (Tarragona)
☎: +34 977 422 000 - Fax: +34 977 422 001
coop.horta@tinet.cat

AIXABIGUES 2010 B
garnacha blanca.

82 Colour: bright straw, greenish rim. Nose: fruit expression, slightly evolved. Palate: flavourful, fine bitter notes.

AIXABIGUES 2010 RD
garnacha.

78

RACO DEL CONVENT ESP
macabeo, garnacha blanca.

84 Colour: bright straw. Nose: grassy, balsamic herbs, ripe fruit. Palate: fruity, fresh.

AGRÍCOLA DE CORBERA D'EBRE

Ponent, 21
43784 Corbera d'Ebre (Tarragona)
☎: +34 977 420 432 - Fax: +34 977 420 304
coop@corbera.tinet.org

MIRMIL-LÓ S/C B
garnacha blanca.

87 Colour: bright straw. Nose: medium intensity, white flowers, dried herbs. Palate: fresh, flavourful, good acidity.

MIRMIL-LÓ PARELLADA 2010 B
parellada.

85 Colour: bright straw. Nose: white flowers, expressive, fruit expression. Palate: flavourful, fruity, good acidity.

MIRMIL-LÓ ROSAT 2010 RD
80% garnacha, 20% syrah.

83 Colour: light cherry. Nose: red berry notes, violet drops, floral. Palate: fruity, easy to drink, fine bitter notes.

MIRMIL-LÓ NEGRE 2010 T
40% garnacha, 25% cariñena, 25% tempranillo, 10% syrah.

80 Colour: cherry, garnet rim. Nose: medium intensity. Palate: light-bodied, good finish, easy to drink.

VALL EXCELS 2007 TC
40% garnacha, 40% cariñena, 20% tempranillo.

87 Colour: cherry, garnet rim. Nose: red berry notes, ripe fruit, cocoa bean, sweet spices, mineral. Palate: ripe fruit, spicy.

NAKENS ESCUMÓS ESP
parellada.

83 Colour: bright straw. Nose: candied fruit, citrus fruit, medium intensity. Palate: fine bitter notes, sweetness.

POBLE VELL BLANCO VINO DE LICOR BLANCO
50% garnacha blanca, 50% pedro ximénez.

88 Colour: light mahogany. Nose: candied fruit, fruit liqueur notes, fruit liqueur notes, toasty, sweet spices. Palate: powerful, sweet, fine bitter notes, spirituous.

POBLE VELL TINTO VINO DE LICOR TINTO
garnacha blanca.

87 Colour: pale ruby, brick rim edge. Nose: powerfull, warm, spicy, fruit liqueur notes. Palate: sweetness, spirituous, fine bitter notes.

AGRICOLA ST JOSEP

Estació, 2
43785 Bot (Tarragona)
☎: +34 977 428 035 - Fax: +34 977 428 192
info@coopbot.com
www.coopbot.com

CLOT D'ENCÍS 2010 B
garnacha blanca, sauvignon blanc, chenin blanc, macabeo, chardonnay, moscatel.

86 Colour: bright straw. Nose: dried flowers, medium intensity, wild herbs. Palate: balanced, fine bitter notes, good acidity.

BRAU DE BOT 2010 B
garnacha blanca, sauvignon blanc, chenin blanc, macabeo, chardonnay, moscatel.

84 Colour: bright straw. Nose: white flowers, wild herbs. Palate: fruity, easy to drink, good acidity.

LLÀGRIMES DE TARDOR 2009 BFB
100% garnacha blanca.

92 Colour: bright yellow. Nose: powerfull, ripe fruit, sweet spices, creamy oak, fragrant herbs. Palate: rich, flavourful, fresh, good acidity.

CLOT D'ENCIS 2010 RD
100% syrah.

84 Colour: rose. Nose: medium intensity, floral, red berry notes, powerfull. Palate: flavourful, fruity, easy to drink.

CLOT D'ENCÍS 2010 T
garnacha, cabernet sauvignon, cariñena, syrah.

87 Colour: bright cherry, purple rim. Nose: medium intensity, red berry notes, violets. Palate: flavourful, fruity, good structure.

BRAU DE BOT 2010 T
garnacha, ull de llebre, cariñena.

84 Colour: bright cherry, purple rim. Nose: medium intensity, red berry notes, dried flowers. Palate: flavourful, fruity, correct.

LA PLANA D'EN FONOLL 2009 T
garnacha, cabernet sauvignon, syrah, cariñena, merlot.

87 Colour: cherry, garnet rim. Nose: dark chocolate, sweet spices, ripe fruit, powerfull. Palate: fleshy, fruity, round tannins.

LLÀGRIMES DE TARDOR 2007 TC
45% garnacha, 20% syrah, 15% cabernet sauvignon, 15% cariñena, 5% merlot.

89 Colour: cherry, garnet rim. Nose: medium intensity, spicy, ripe fruit, scrubland. Palate: flavourful, fruity, round tannins.

LLÀGRIMES DE TARDOR SELECCIÓ 2006 TC
cariñena, syrah, garnacha, cabernet sauvignon, merlot.

90 Colour: cherry, garnet rim. Nose: ripe fruit, creamy oak, complex, sweet spices. Palate: powerful, flavourful, toasty, round tannins.

LLÀGRIMES DE TARDOR MISTELA NEGRA 2009 VINO DE LICOR
100% garnacha.

88 Colour: black cherry. Nose: powerfull, warm, fruit preserve. Palate: powerful, flavourful, concentrated.

LLÀGRIMES DE TARDOR MISTELA BLANCA VINO DE LICOR
100% garnacha blanca.

89 Colour: bright golden. Nose: powerfull, expressive, warm, candied fruit, citrus fruit. Palate: powerful, flavourful, sweet.

ALGRAMAR

Major, 12
43782 Vilalba dels Arcs (Tarragona)
☎: +34 977 438 007
xalvarezsatue@gmail.com
www.algramar.com

VN ALGRAMAR S/C B
sauvignon blanc, garnacha blanca, chenin blanc.

86 Colour: bright yellow. Nose: medium intensity, wild herbs, floral. Palate: flavourful, fruity, easy to drink.

VALL NOVENES 2009 T
60% garnacha, 40% syrah.

86 Colour: cherry, garnet rim. Nose: powerfull, warm, varietal, scrubland. Palate: flavourful, fleshy, round tannins.

GRAN VN ALGRAMAR 2006 TC
garnacha, syrah, cabernet sauvignon.

88 Colour: cherry, garnet rim. Nose: sweet spices, creamy oak, dark chocolate, fruit liqueur notes. Palate: flavourful, fleshy, ripe fruit, warm.

VALL NOVENES 2006 TC
garnacha, syrah, cabernet sauvignon.

86 Colour: cherry, garnet rim. Nose: medium intensity, ripe fruit, spicy. Palate: fruity, balanced, good acidity.

ALTAVINS VITICULTORS

Tarragona, 42
43786 Batea (Tarragona)
☎: +34 977 430 596 - Fax: +34 977 430 371
altavins@altavins.com
www.altavins.com

ILERCAVONIA 2010 B
100% garnacha blanca.

87 Colour: straw, pale. Nose: wild herbs, faded flowers, fresh. Palate: balanced, fine bitter notes, good acidity.

ALMODÍ PETIT BLANC 2010 B
65% garnacha blanca, 30% chardonnay, 5% moscatel.

82 Colour: bright straw. Nose: slightly evolved, candied fruit. Palate: fruity, good finish, easy to drink.

ALMODÍ 2010 T ROBLE
50% garnacha, 40% syrah, 10% merlot.

88 Colour: deep cherry, purple rim. Nose: ripe fruit, sweet spices, powerfull. Palate: fleshy, ripe fruit, spicy, round tannins.

ALMODÍ PETIT NEGREG 2010 T
65% garnacha, 30% syrah, 5% cariñena.

87 Colour: cherry, purple rim. Nose: medium intensity, red berry notes, balanced, floral, balsamic herbs. Palate: flavourful, fruity, good structure.

TEMPUS 2008 T ROBLE
36% syrah, 24% garnacha, 18% merlot, 12% cariñena, 10% cabernet sauvignon.

87 Colour: cherry, garnet rim. Nose: sweet spices, dark chocolate, candied fruit. Palate: flavourful, fruity, good structure, round tannins.

EL COFÍ 2008 T
55% cabernet sauvignon, garnacha.

85 Colour: deep cherry, garnet rim. Nose: ripe fruit, candied fruit, sweet spices, slightly evolved. Palate: good structure, flavourful, good acidity.

DOMUS PENSI 2006 TC
35% cabernet sauvignon, 30% garnacha, 15% syrah, 10% merlot, 10% tempranillo.

87 Colour: very deep cherry. Nose: tobacco, candied fruit, fruit liqueur notes, fruit liqueur notes, spicy. Palate: flavourful, fleshy.

ANDREU ROCA VAQUE

Avda. Terra Alta, 67
43786 Batea (Tarragona)
☎: +34 610 254 964 - Fax: +34 977 705 773
roca.andreu@gmail.com

VALL DE VINYES 2010 B
garnacha blanca, macabeo.

86 Colour: bright straw. Nose: fresh, white flowers, expressive. Palate: flavourful, fruity, good acidity, balanced.

VALL DE VINYES 2010 T
garnacha, syrah.

86 Colour: cherry, purple rim. Nose: ripe fruit, powerfull, wild herbs. Palate: fruity, fleshy, round tannins, long.

VALL DE VINYES 2005 T BARRICA
garnacha, syrah.

87 Colour: bright cherry. Nose: ripe fruit, sweet spices, creamy oak, fruit liqueur notes. Palate: fruity, toasty, round tannins, fleshy.

BODEGAS PINORD

Doctor Pasteur, 6
08720 Vilafranca del Penedès (Barcelona)
☎: +34 938 903 066 - Fax: +34 938 170 979
pinord@pinord.es
www.pinord.es

PINORD DIORAMA GARNACHA BLANCA 2010 B
garnacha blanca.

88 Colour: bright straw. Nose: white flowers, fruit expression, mineral, fragrant herbs. Palate: good acidity, powerful, flavourful.

PINORD DIORAMA GARNACHA NEGRA 2010 T
garnacha negra.

86 Colour: cherry, garnet rim. Nose: red berry notes, ripe fruit, floral, sweet spices. Palate: fresh, fruity, flavourful.

CATERRA

Glorieta, s/n
43783 La Pobla de Massaluca (Tarragona)
☎: +34 977 439 765 - Fax: +34 977 439 765
catapoma@telefonica.net
www.caterra.es

FONT CALENTA 2010 B
macabeo, garnacha blanca.

86 Colour: bright straw. Nose: medium intensity, white flowers. Palate: flavourful, good structure, long, good acidity.

HEREUS CATERRA 2010 B
100% garnacha blanca.

85 Colour: yellow, pale. Nose: medium intensity, faded flowers, wild herbs. Palate: fruity, flavourful, easy to drink.

FONT CALENTA BRISAT 2009 B
20% garnacha blanca, 80% macabeo.

81 Colour: bright golden. Nose: toasty, powerfull, candied fruit, warm. Palate: powerful, fine bitter notes.

FONT CALENTA NEGRO 2010 T
60% garnacha, 40% cariñena.

85 Colour: deep cherry, purple rim. Nose: medium intensity, violets, red berry notes. Palate: flavourful, fruity, easy to drink.

HEREUS CATERRA 2009 T
70% garnacha, 20% cariñena, 10% syrah.

84 Colour: cherry, garnet rim. Nose: sweet spices, powerfull, warm, ripe fruit. Palate: good structure, fruity, flavourful.

L'ESPERIT DEL CERÇ 2008 TC
80% garnacha, 20% samsó.

85 Colour: deep cherry, garnet rim. Nose: fruit preserve, sweet spices. Palate: flavourful, fleshy, sweet tannins.

CELLER AGRÍCOLA FUSTER

Finca Coma Dén Bonet
43780 Gandesa (Tarragona)
☎: +34 977 232 671 - Fax: +34 977 234 665
dardell@dardell.es
www.dardell.es

PROHOM 2010 B
garnacha blanca, viognier, roussane.

88 Colour: bright yellow, greenish rim. Nose: balanced, expressive, jasmine. Palate: ripe fruit, flavourful, balanced.

DARDELL GARNACHA & VIOGNIER 2010 B
garnacha blanca, viognier.

87 Colour: bright straw, greenish rim. Nose: medium intensity, fresh fruit, wild herbs. Palate: fruity, easy to drink.

DARDELL GARNACHA Y SYRAH 2010 T
garnacha, syrah.

85 Colour: cherry, purple rim. Nose: varietal, balanced, balsamic herbs, red berry notes. Palate: flavourful, fruity, balanced.

CELLER BÁRBARA FORÉS

Santa Anna, 28
43780 Gandesa (Tarragona)
☎: +34 977 420 160 - Fax: +34 977 421 399
info@cellerbarbarafores.com
www.cellerbarbarafores.com

EL QUINTÀ BÁRBARA FORÉS 2010 BFB
garnacha blanca.

91 Colour: bright yellow. Nose: ripe fruit, faded flowers, sweet spices, fragrant herbs. Palate: long, flavourful, fruity.

BÁRBARA FORÉS 2010 B
95% garnacha blanca, 5% viognier.

89 Colour: bright yellow. Nose: varietal, fresh, balanced, expressive, scrubland. Palate: flavourful, full, fruity, good structure, good acidity.

VI DOLÇ NATURAL BÁRBARA FORÉS 2008 B
garnacha blanca.

89 Colour: bright golden. Nose: candied fruit, dry nuts, honeyed notes. Palate: flavourful, sweet, good acidity.

BÁRBARA FORÉS 2010 RD
56% garnacha, 37% syrah, 8% samsó.

86 Colour: rose. Nose: expressive, balanced, red berry notes, violets. Palate: ripe fruit, easy to drink, balanced.

EL TEMPLARI 2009 T
55% garnacha, 45% morenillo.

89 Colour: cherry, garnet rim. Nose: balanced, powerfull, ripe fruit, sweet spices. Palate: flavourful, fruity, round tannins, long.

BÁRBARA FORÉS NEGRE 2009 T
70% garnacha, 20% syrah, 10% cariñena.

88 Color bright cherry. Aroma ripe fruit, sweet spices, creamy oak, expressive. Taste flavourful, fruity, toasty, round tannins.

COMA D'EN POU BÀRBARA FORÉS 2006 T
35% garnacha, 38% syrah, 27% cabernet sauvignon.

91 Colour: bright cherry, garnet rim. Nose: complex, mineral, sweet spices, creamy oak. Palate: flavourful, complex, fine bitter notes, balanced, round tannins.

CELLER BATEA

Moli, 30
43786 Batea (Tarragona)
☎: +34 977 430 056 - Fax: +34 977 430 589
enolegs@cellerbatea.com
www.cellerbatea.com

LAS COLINAS DEL EBRO 2010 B
garnacha blanca.

87 Colour: bright straw. Nose: medium intensity, white flowers, wild herbs, tropical fruit. Palate: flavourful, fruity, good acidity.

VALL MAJOR 2010 B
garnacha blanca.

86 Colour: bright straw, greenish rim. Nose: medium intensity, varietal, wild herbs, dried flowers. Palate: flavourful, easy to drink, fresh.

PRIMICIA CHARDONNAY 2010 B
chardonnay.

86 Colour: bright yellow. Nose: jasmine, white flowers, wild herbs. Palate: flavourful, fruity, rich.

LAS COLINAS DEL EBRO 2010 T
syrah, garnacha.

88 Colour: bright cherry, purple rim. Nose: ripe fruit, violets, powerfull, varietal, spicy. Palate: flavourful, fruity, round tannins.

VALL MAJOR NEGRE 2010 T
garnacha, syrah.

87 Colour: cherry, purple rim. Nose: red berry notes, ripe fruit, scrubland. Palate: flavourful, spicy, fruity, fruity aftestaste.

TIPICITAT 2007 T
garnacha, carignan.

90 Color cherry, garnet rim. Aroma ripe fruit, spicy, creamy oak, toasty, complex. Taste powerful, flavourful, toasty, round tannins.

VIVERTELL 2007 TC
garnacha, tempranillo, syrah, cabernet sauvignon.

87 Colour: cherry, garnet rim. Nose: grassy, wild herbs, ripe fruit, spicy. Palate: flavourful, good structure, round tannins.

LAS COLINAS DEL EBRO SELECCION 2007 T
garnacha, syrah.

87 Colour: cherry, garnet rim. Nose: ripe fruit, sweet spices, balanced, medium intensity. Palate: flavourful, fruity, round tannins.

L'AUBE "SELECCIO DE VINYES VELLES" 2006 TC
merlot, garnacha, cabernet sauvignon, syrah, tempranillo.

88 Colour: cherry, garnet rim. Nose: balanced, medium intensity, ripe fruit. Palate: flavourful, spirituous, balsamic.

EQUINOX MOSCATEL
moscatel.

90 Colour: light mahogany. Nose: powerfull, characterful, warm, candied fruit. Palate: sweet, unctuous, warm.

CELLER COOPERATIU GANDESA

Avda. Catalunya, 28
43780 Gandesa (Tarragona)
☎: +34 977 420 017 - Fax: +34 977 420 403
perefiguereo@coopgandesa.com
www.coopgandesa.com

GANDESOLA 2010 B
100% garnacha blanca.

86 Colour: bright straw, greenish rim. Nose: medium intensity, fragrant herbs, dried flowers. Palate: flavourful, good acidity.

ANTIC CASTELL 2010 B ROBLE
100% garnacha blanca.

83 Colour: bright yellow, greenish rim. Nose: medium intensity, dried flowers. Palate: flavourful, fruity, easy to drink, good acidity.

CÉSAR MARTINELL 2007 BFB
100% garnacha blanca.

84 Colour: bright straw. Nose: powerfull, varietal, aged wood nuances. Palate: spicy, ripe fruit.

SOMDINOU 19 2010 RD
100% garnacha.

86 Colour: brilliant rose. Nose: medium intensity, balanced, red berry notes, wild herbs, dried flowers. Palate: fruity, good acidity, fine bitter notes.

GANDESOLA 2010 RD
80% garnacha, 15% cabernet sauvignon, 5% syrah.

82 Colour: brilliant rose. Nose: dried herbs, medium intensity, candied fruit. Palate: fruity, correct.

GANDESOLA 2010 T
20% garnacha, 80% tempranillo.

86 Colour: cherry, purple rim. Nose: medium intensity, red berry notes, balanced, violets. Palate: flavourful, fruity, easy to drink.

ANTIC CASTELL 2009 T
70% garnacha, 20% cariñena, 10% syrah.

84 Colour: cherry, garnet rim. Nose: toasty, spicy, ripe fruit. Palate: flavourful, fruity.

GANDESOLA 2008 TC
40% garnacha, 40% samsó, 20% syrah.

86 Colour: cherry, garnet rim. Nose: balanced, ripe fruit, sweet spices, dried herbs. Palate: flavourful, good structure, fleshy, good acidity.

VARVALL 2006 TC
16% cabernet sauvignon, 33% garnacha, 33% cariñena, 18% syrah.

89 Colour: cherry, garnet rim. Nose: balanced, expressive, ripe fruit, cocoa bean, sweet spices. Palate: flavourful, good structure, good acidity.

SOMDINOU 19 2006 T
samsó, garnacha.

85 Colour: light cherry, garnet rim. Nose: medium intensity, fruit preserve, spicy. Palate: fruity, easy to drink.

GANDESA MISTELA TINTA 2008
100% garnacha.

85 Colour: cherry, garnet rim. Nose: aromatic coffee, candied fruit, dried fruit. Palate: sweet, concentrated, spirituous.

VI DE LICOR 1919 VINO DE LICOR
100% garnacha blanca.

90 Colour: bright golden. Nose: sweet spices, aromatic coffee, fruit liqueur notes, candied fruit. Palate: fine bitter notes, warm, powerful.

GANDESA MISTELA BLANCA VINO DE LICOR
100% garnacha blanca.

82 Colour: bright straw. Nose: powerfull, candied fruit, citrus fruit, honeyed notes. Palate: flavourful, sweet, ripe fruit.

CELLER JORDI MIRÓ

Sant Marc, 96
43784 Corbera d'Ebre (Tarragona)
☎: +34 629 602 354
jordi@ennak.com
www.cellerjordimiro.com

JORDI MIRÓ MP 2010 B
garnacha blanca.

85 Colour: yellow, greenish rim. Nose: medium intensity, white flowers, faded flowers, honeyed notes. Palate: fruity, easy to drink, good finish.

JORDI MIRÓ MC 2010 T
garnacha, syrah.

87 Colour: cherry, purple rim. Nose: fruit expression, floral, expressive, scrubland. Palate: flavourful, fruity, easy to drink.

ENNAK 2010 T
garnacha, tempranillo, cabernet sauvignon, merlot.

86 Colour: bright cherry, purple rim. Nose: powerfull, ripe fruit, balsamic herbs. Palate: ripe fruit, flavourful.

CELLER LA BOLLIDORA

Carrer Tacons, 8
43782 Vilalba dels Arcs (Tarragona)
☎: +34 620 267 536 - Fax: +34 977 438 020
info@cellerlabollidora.com
www.cellerlabollidora.com

SAÓ 2010 B
garnacha, syrah, samsó.

87 Colour: bright straw. Nose: ripe fruit, citrus fruit, sweet spices. Palate: flavourful, fruity, ripe fruit.

FLOR DE GARNATXA 2008 BFB
garnacha blanca.

88 Colour: bright straw. Nose: scrubland, powerfull, warm, toasty, cocoa bean. Palate: fine bitter notes, good acidity, spicy.

SAÓ 2009 T
garnacha, syrah, samsó.

84 Colour: cherry, garnet rim. Nose: dark chocolate, sweet spices, ripe fruit. Palate: fleshy, flavourful.

PLAN B 2008 T
garnacha, morenillo, syrah, samsó.

82 Colour: cherry, garnet rim. Nose: fruit preserve, premature reduction notes. Palate: flavourful, spicy, ripe fruit.

PUNTO G 2006 T
samsó, morenillo, syrah, garnacha.

87 Colour: cherry, garnet rim. Nose: powerfull, dark chocolate, sweet spices, candied fruit, fruit preserve. Palate: flavourful, good structure, powerful.

CELLER MARIOL

Rosselló, 442 - Bajos
08025 (Barcelona)
☎: +34 934 367 628 - Fax: +34 934 500 281
celler@cellermariol.es
www.cellermariol.es

CASA MARIOL CUPATGE DINÀMIC CHARDONNAY 2010 B
90% chardonnay, 10% moscatel.

86 Colour: bright yellow. Nose: fresh fruit, jasmine, balanced. Palate: flavourful, fruity, rich.

CASA MARIOL ULL DE LLEBRE (TEMPRANILLO) 2009 TC
100% ull de llebre.

87 Color cherry, garnet rim. Aroma ripe fruit, spicy, creamy oak, toasty, complex. Taste powerful, flavourful, toasty, round tannins.

CASA MARIOL MERLOT 2009 TC
100% merlot.

86 Colour: cherry, garnet rim. Nose: ripe fruit, scrubland, balanced. Palate: flavourful, good acidity, round tannins.

CASA MARIOL CABERNET SAUVIGNON 2008 TR
100% cabernet sauvignon.

84 Colour: cherry, garnet rim. Nose: warm, powerfull, fruit liqueur notes, spicy, fruit preserve. Palate: flavourful, spicy, ripe fruit.

CASA MARIOL SAMSÓ 2007 TC
100% samsó.

86 Colour: cherry, garnet rim. Nose: candied fruit, spicy, dried herbs. Palate: fruity, long, good acidity.

CASA MARIOL MERLOT 2007 TR
merlot.

86 Colour: very deep cherry. Nose: slightly evolved, candied fruit, dark chocolate. Palate: good structure, fleshy.

CASA MARIOL SYRAH 2005 TR
100% syrah.

88 Colour: deep cherry, garnet rim. Nose: ripe fruit, powerfull, balanced, spicy. Palate: flavourful, ripe fruit, round tannins.

CASA MARIOL CABERNET SAUVIGNON 2005 TR
cabernet sauvignon.

87 Colour: deep cherry, bright ochre rim. Nose: fruit preserve, balanced, ripe fruit, warm. Palate: flavourful, fleshy, round tannins.

CELLER MENESCAL

Avda. Catalunya, s/n
43785 Bot (Tarragona)
☎: +34 977 428 095 - Fax: +34 977 428 261
info@cellermenescal.com
www.cellermenescal.com

AVUS 2010 BFB
garnacha blanca.

83 Colour: bright yellow. Nose: slightly evolved, faded flowers. Palate: flavourful, fruity, easy to drink, spicy.

AVUS 2009 T ROBLE
garnacha, syrah, merlot, tempranillo.

86 Colour: very deep cherry. Nose: medium intensity, spicy, varnish, candied fruit. Palate: flavourful, slightly dry, soft tannins.

AVUS DOLÇ 2008 T
garnacha.

88 Colour: cherry, garnet rim. Nose: ripe fruit, spicy, creamy oak, toasty, complex. Palate: powerful, toasty, sweet.

CELLER PIÑOL

Avda. Aragón, 9
43786 Batea (Tarragona)
☎: +34 977 430 505 - Fax: +34 977 430 498
info@cellerpinol.com
www.vinospinol.com

PORTAL N. SRA. PORTAL 2010 B
garnacha blanca, sauvignon blanc, viognier, moscatel, macabeo.

90 Colour: yellow. Nose: powerfull, balanced, expressive, white flowers, wild herbs. Palate: flavourful, fruity, fresh.

L'AVI ARRUFÍ 2009 BFB
100% garnacha blanca.

92 Color bright yellow. Aroma powerfull, ripe fruit, sweet spices, creamy oak, fragrant herbs. Taste rich, smoky aftertaste, flavourful, fresh, good acidity.

JOSEFINA PIÑOL 2009 B
100% garnacha blanca.

88 Colour: light mahogany. Nose: candied fruit, fruit liqueur notes, toasty. Palate: powerful, sweet, warm, spirituous.

RAIG DE RAIM 2010 T ROBLE
garnacha, syrah, cariñena, tempranillo, merlot.

87 Colour: cherry, purple rim. Nose: ripe fruit, balsamic herbs, powerfull, spicy. Palate: fleshy, concentrated, fruity, long.

FINCA MORENILLO 2009 T
morenillo.

90 Colour: cherry, garnet rim. Nose: balanced, ripe fruit, spicy, complex. Palate: balanced, complex, flavourful.

PORTAL N. SRA. PORTAL 2009 T ROBLE
garnacha, cariñena, merlot, syrah, tempranillo.

89 Colour: cherry, garnet rim. Nose: ripe fruit, creamy oak, sweet spices, balanced, powerfull. Palate: good structure, ripe fruit, round tannins.

MATHER TERESINA SELECCIÓN DE VIÑAS VIEJAS 2008 T
morenillo, garnacha, cariñena.

91 Color cherry, garnet rim. Aroma ripe fruit, spicy, creamy oak, toasty, complex. Taste powerful, flavourful, toasty, round tannins.

SA NATURA 2008 T
cariñena, merlot, syrah, petit verdot.

88 Colour: deep cherry, garnet rim. Nose: powerfull, ripe fruit, sweet spices, dark chocolate. Palate: fleshy, fruity, balsamic, spicy.

L'AVI ARRUFÍ 2007 T
garnacha, cariñena, merlot, syrah.

92 Colour: cherry, garnet rim. Nose: complex, balanced, ripe fruit, sweet spices. Palate: good structure, flavourful, good acidity, fine bitter notes, round tannins.

JOSEFINA PIÑOL 2009 TINTO DULCE
garnacha, syrah.

90 Colour: very deep cherry. Nose: powerfull, raspberry, overripe fruit, fruit liqueur notes. Palate: powerful, spirituous.

CELLER TERN

Ctra. Vilalba, s/n
43786 Batea (Tarragona)
☎: +34 977 430 939 - Fax: +34 977 430 433
ternobradordevi@gmail.com
www.ternobradordevi.com

TERN 2010 B
100% garnacha blanca.

87 Colour: bright straw. Nose: fresh, fresh fruit, white flowers. Palate: flavourful, fruity, good acidity, balanced.

CELLER XAVIER CLUA

Vall de Sant Isidre, 41
43782 Vilalba dels Arcs (Tarragona)
☎: +34 977 263 069 - Fax: +34 977 439 003
info@cellerclua.com
www.cellerclua.com

MAS D'EN POL 2010 B
60% garnacha blanca, 20% chardonnay, 15% sauvignon blanc, 5% moscatel.

86 Colour: bright straw. Nose: white flowers, medium intensity. Palate: flavourful, fruity, good acidity.

MAS D'EN POL 2010 T
50% garnacha, 20% syrah, 15% merlot, 15% cabernet sauvignon.

86 Colour: bright cherry, purple rim. Nose: medium intensity, red berry notes, scrubland. Palate: fruity, easy to drink.

SPLET 2010 T
70% cariñena, 30% cabernet sauvignon.

84 Colour: deep cherry, purple rim. Nose: powerfull, warm, ripe fruit. Palate: flavourful, ripe fruit.

CLUA MIL.LENNIUM 2007 TC
garnacha, cabernet sauvignon, syrah, merlot.

88 Colour: bright cherry, garnet rim. Nose: candied fruit, fruit preserve, warm, powerfull. Palate: flavourful, fleshy, spicy.

MAS D'EN POL 2007 T BARRICA
garnacha, cabernet sauvignon, syrah, merlot.

88 Colour: bright cherry. Nose: ripe fruit, sweet spices, expressive. Palate: flavourful, fruity, round tannins, spicy.

CLUA MIL.LENNIUM 2006 TC
60% garnacha, 20% cabernet sauvignon, 15% syrah, 5% merlot.

88 Colour: cherry, garnet rim. Nose: balanced, expressive, ripe fruit, tobacco, spicy. Palate: flavourful, fruity, spicy, ripe fruit, long.

MAS D'EN POL 2006 T BARRICA
garnacha, cabernet sauvignon, syrah, merlot.

87 Colour: deep cherry, garnet rim. Nose: medium intensity, balanced, ripe fruit, wild herbs. Palate: ripe fruit, long, good acidity.

CELLERS TARRONÉ

Calvari, 22
43786 Batea (Tarragona)
☎: +34 977 430 109 - Fax: +34 977 430 183
info@cellerstarrone.com
www.cellerstarrone.com

MERIAN 2010 B
100% garnacha blanca.

87 Colour: bright yellow. Nose: medium intensity, fresh fruit, dried herbs. Palate: balanced, fine bitter notes, varietal, flavourful.

MERIAN DULCE NATURAL 2010 T
100% garnacha.

90 Colour: black cherry. Nose: powerfull, dried fruit, raspberry. Palate: flavourful, sweet, fine bitter notes.

MERIAN 2010 T
70% garnacha, 10% syrah, 10% cabernet sauvignon, 10% merlot.

86 Colour: black cherry, purple rim. Nose: ripe fruit, candied fruit, powerfull. Palate: powerful, flavourful.

TORREMADRINA ROBLE 2009 T
60% garnacha, 10% cabernet sauvignon, 20% merlot, 10% ull de llebre.

87 Colour: very deep cherry. Nose: balanced, spicy, toasty, ripe fruit. Palate: good structure, flavourful, full, round tannins.

TORREMADRINA 2007 TC
60% garnacha, 20% syrah, 10% merlot, 10% cabernet sauvignon.

87 Colour: deep cherry, garnet rim. Nose: toasty, spicy, powerfull, balsamic herbs. Palate: fleshy, powerful, round tannins.

TORREMADRINA SELECCIÓN 2005 TC
70% garnacha, 10% merlot, 10% syrah, 10% cabernet sauvignon.

89 Colour: cherry, garnet rim. Nose: balanced, mineral, ripe fruit, spicy, warm. Palate: balanced, spicy.

CELLERS UNIÓ

Joan Oliver, 16-24
43206 Reus (Tarragona)
☎: +34 977 330 055 - Fax: +34 977 330 070
info@cellersunio.com
www.cellersunio.com

GRAN COPOS 2010 B
100% garnacha blanca.

87 Colour: bright yellow. Nose: fresh fruit, jasmine, balanced. Palate: correct, fine bitter notes, good acidity.

CLOS DEL PINELL 2010 B
100% garnacha blanca.

86 Colour: bright straw. Nose: medium intensity, fresh fruit, dried flowers. Palate: fresh, fruity, easy to drink.

COPOS NATURE 2010 B
50% garnacha blanca, 50% macabeo.

84 Colour: yellow, pale. Nose: faded flowers, medium intensity. Palate: flavourful, easy to drink.

CLOS DEL PINELL 2010 RD
70% garnacha, 30% cabernet sauvignon.

83 Colour: light cherry. Nose: wild herbs, floral, balanced. Palate: easy to drink, fruity, sweetness.

COPOS NATURE 2010 T
40% cabernet sauvignon, 20% mazuelo, 40% tempranillo.

86 Colour: cherry, purple rim. Nose: medium intensity, red berry notes. Palate: flavourful, fruity, good acidity, balanced.

CLOS DEL PINELL 2010 T
50% garnacha, 40% cariñena, 10% syrah.

85 Colour: cherry, purple rim. Nose: medium intensity, scrubland, fresh fruit. Palate: fruity, easy to drink, good finish.

CLOS DEL PINELL 2007 TC
50% garnacha, 45% cariñena, 5% morenillo.

86 Colour: deep cherry, garnet rim. Nose: old leather, spicy, ripe fruit. Palate: flavourful, balanced, round tannins.

REINA ELIONOR 2006 TR
40% garnacha, 40% tempranillo, 20% cabernet sauvignon.

85 Colour: deep cherry, garnet rim. Nose: toasty, spicy, creamy oak, ripe fruit. Palate: flavourful, ripe fruit, fine bitter notes.

GRAN COPOS 2005 TR
40% garnacha, 30% cariñena, 20% cabernet sauvignon, 10% syrah.

87 Colour: cherry, garnet rim. Nose: ripe fruit, spicy, toasty. Palate: powerful, flavourful, toasty, round tannins.

COVIALBA

Cervantes, 1-5
43782 Vilalba dels Arcs (Tarragona)
☎: +34 977 438 010 - Fax: +34 977 438 294
covilalba@covilalba.com
www.covilalba.com

SUPREM 2010 B
macabeo, garnacha blanca.

85 Colour: bright straw, greenish rim. Nose: medium intensity, wild herbs, dried flowers. Palate: fruity, easy to drink, good acidity.

SUPREM 2010 T
garnacha, merlot, cariñena.

87 Colour: cherry, purple rim. Nose: floral, violets, red berry notes, balanced. Palate: fruity, flavourful, balanced, easy to drink.

DAVID GWYN JONES

Carrer Pilonet, 8
43594 El Pinell de Brai (Tarragona)
☎: +34 681 163 663
spain@donferrantwine.com

DON FERRANTI 2010 B
garnacha blanca, macabeo.

83 Colour: golden. Nose: medium intensity, dried flowers. Palate: flavourful, ripe fruit, easy to drink.

DON FERRANTI GARNACHA BLANCA 2010 BFB
garnacha blanca.

80 Colour: bright yellow. Nose: slightly evolved, faded flowers, short. Palate: ripe fruit, good finish.

DON FERRANTI 2010 T
garnacha, samsó.

81 Colour: cherry, purple rim. Nose: slightly evolved, red berry notes. Palate: fruity, light-bodied, easy to drink.

DON FERRANTI SYRAH 2009 T
syrah.

84 Colour: very deep cherry, purple rim. Nose: macerated fruit, warm. Palate: flavourful, powerful, ripe fruit.

DON FERRANTI 2009 T FERMENTADO EN BARRICA
garnacha, samsó.

84 Colour: cherry, purple rim. Nose: ripe fruit, medium intensity. Palate: flavourful, fruity, good finish.

ECOVITRES

La Verge, 6
43470 Vilalba dels Arcs (Tarragona)
☎: +34 977 438 196
info@ecovitres.com
www.ecovitres.com

ASPIRALL 2010 T
garnacha.

86 Colour: cherry, purple rim. Nose: medium intensity, red berry notes, wild herbs. Palate: fruity, easy to drink.

GRAN GOTANYA 2007 TC
garnacha, morenillo, merlot.

88 Colour: cherry, garnet rim. Nose: ripe fruit, spicy, toasty, complex. Palate: powerful, flavourful, toasty, round tannins.

EDETÀRIA

Finca El Mas - Ctra. Gandesa a Villalba, s/n
43780 Gandesa (Tarragona)
☎: 977 421 534 - Fax: 977 421 534
info@edetaria.com
www.edetaria.com

EDETANA 2010 B
70% garnacha blanca, 30% viognier.

90 Colour: bright straw, greenish rim. Nose: elegant, varietal, expressive, fragrant herbs. Palate: fruity, flavourful, good acidity, balanced.

VÍA TERRA 2010 B
garnacha blanca.

90 Color bright straw. Aroma fresh, fresh fruit, white flowers, expressive. Taste flavourful, fruity, good acidity, balanced.

VINYA D'IRTO 2010 B
garnacha blanca, macabeo.

89 Colour: bright straw. Nose: fruit expression, fresh, floral, fragrant herbs. Palate: flavourful, fresh, fruity.

EDETÀRIA 2009 BFB
85% garnacha blanca, 15% macabeo.

91 Colour: bright straw. Nose: grassy, citrus fruit, sweet spices, cocoa bean, candied fruit. Palate: fine bitter notes, flavourful, fleshy, long.

EDETÀRIA 2008 BFB
85% garnacha blanca, 15% macabeo.

92 Colour: bright yellow. Nose: faded flowers, ripe fruit, sweet spices, creamy oak. Palate: flavourful, fleshy, good acidity, toasty.

EDETÀRIA 2005 BFB
85% garnacha blanca, 15% macabeo.

95 Colour: bright golden. Nose: petrol notes, aged wood nuances, smoky, dry nuts, waxy notes. Palate: powerful, flavourful, rich, fleshy, complex, balanced, spirituous.

VÍA TERRA 2010 T
garnacha.

90 Colour: deep cherry, garnet rim. Nose: red berry notes, scrubland, balanced. Palate: flavourful, good structure, round tannins.

VINYA D'IRTO 2010 T JOVEN
garnacha, syrah.

87 Colour: cherry, garnet rim. Nose: ripe fruit, earthy notes, scrubland. Palate: flavourful, fruity, good acidity.

EDETÀRIA DOLÇ 2009 TC
70% garnacha, 30% cabernet sauvignon.

91 Colour: black cherry. Nose: powerfull, characterful, warm, fruit expression, raspberry. Palate: powerful, concentrated, sweet.

EDETANA 2009 T
60% garnacha fina, 30% garnacha peluda, 10% samsó.

89 Colour: cherry, garnet rim. Nose: fruit expression, mineral, spicy, scrubland. Palate: good acidity, flavourful, fleshy, complex.

EDETÀRIA 2008 T
60% garnacha peluda, 30% syrah, 5% cabernet sauvignon, 5% cariñena.

91 Colour: cherry, garnet rim. Nose: powerfull, ripe fruit, dry stone, earthy notes, sweet spices, creamy oak. Palate: flavourful, fruity, fleshy, toasty.

EDETÀRIA 2007 T
60% garnacha peluda, 25% syrah, 15% samsó.

92 Colour: very deep cherry, garnet rim. Nose: ripe fruit, candied fruit, cocoa bean, sweet spices. Palate: good structure, fleshy, round tannins.

EL VI A PUNT

☎: +34 625 408 974
comercial@elviapunt.com
www.elviapunt.com

SINE BAG IN BOX (3 LITROS) S/C B
garnacha blanca.

81 Colour: bright straw, greenish rim. Nose: powerfull, wild herbs. Palate: easy to drink, correct.

JOSE SANTIAGO VICENS VALLESPÍ

Avda. Aragó, 20
43780 Gandesa (Tarragona)
☎: +34 977 421 080 - Fax: +34 977 421 080
josepvicensv@wanadoo.es
www.vinsjosepvicens.com

VINYES DEL GRAU 2010 B
100% garnacha blanca.

84 Colour: bright straw. Nose: medium intensity, tropical fruit, balanced. Palate: flavourful, easy to drink, good acidity.

VINYES DEL GRAU SYRAH 2010 T
syrah.

89 Colour: cherry, purple rim. Nose: red berry notes, violets, balanced, expressive. Palate: balanced, fine bitter notes, good acidity, flavourful, fruity.

VINYES DEL GRAU NEGRO 2009 T
65% garnacha, 25% cariñena, 10% syrah.

83 Colour: cherry, garnet rim. Nose: red berry notes, ripe fruit. Palate: powerful, fruity, round tannins.

VINYES DEL GRAU SYRAH 2008 TC
100% syrah.

88 Colour: deep cherry, garnet rim. Nose: creamy oak, sweet spices, pattiserie, candied fruit. Palate: good structure, flavourful, round tannins.

VINYES DEL GRAU 2007 TC
65% garnacha, 25% cariñena, 10% syrah.

88 Colour: very deep cherry. Nose: balanced, complex, ripe fruit, spicy, scrubland. Palate: good structure, fleshy, fruity, round tannins.

LAFOU CELLER

Mas Gabrielet
43786 Batea (Tarragona)
☎: +34 938 743 511 - Fax: +34 938 737 204
info@lafou.net
www.lafou.net

LAFOU 2008 T
garnacha, syrah, cabernet sauvignon.

90 Colour: cherry, garnet rim. Nose: powerfull, ripe fruit, toasty, spicy. Palate: powerful, fine bitter notes, spicy, round tannins.

LAFOU 2007 T
60% garnacha, 25% syrah, 15% cabernet sauvignon.

91 Colour: cherry, garnet rim. Nose: ripe fruit, spicy, toasty, complex, mineral. Palate: powerful, flavourful, toasty, round tannins.

SERRA DE CAVALLS

Bonaire, 1
43594 El Pinell de Brai (Tarragona)
☎: +34 977 426 049 - Fax: +34 977 426 049
sat@serradecavalls.com
www.serradecavalls.com

SERRA DE CAVALLS 2010 B
50% chardonnay, 50% garnacha blanca.

87 Colour: bright yellow. Nose: fresh fruit, wild herbs, floral. Palate: flavourful, fruity, good acidity.

SERRA DE CAVALLS 2008 BFB
100% garnacha blanca.

86 Colour: bright straw. Nose: powerfull, warm, toasty. Palate: fine bitter notes, powerful, spicy.

SERRA DE CAVALLS 2008 B BARRICA
70% chardonnay, 30% garnacha blanca.

86 Colour: bright straw. Nose: expressive, sweet spices, cocoa bean, ripe fruit. Palate: spicy, fleshy, flavourful.

SERRA DE CAVALLS 2010 T
50% tempranillo, 50% garnacha.

86 Colour: cherry, purple rim. Nose: sweet spices, dark chocolate, ripe fruit, candied fruit. Palate: fleshy, ripe fruit.

SERRA DE CAVALLS 1938 2008 T FERMENTADO EN BARRICA
30% cabernet sauvignon, 60% merlot, 10% syrah.

84 Colour: cherry, garnet rim. Nose: fruit preserve, spicy, scrubland. Palate: fleshy, concentrated, balsamic.

SERRA DE CAVALLS 2008 TC
60% merlot, 30% cabernet sauvignon, 10% tempranillo.

84 Colour: cherry, garnet rim. Nose: fruit preserve, old leather, spicy. Palate: flavourful, spicy.

SOMDINOU

Avda. Catalunya, 28
43780 Gandesa (Tarragona)
☎: +34 977 420 017 - Fax: +34 977 420 403
joanmariariera@hotmail.com
www.somdinou.cat

SOM 19 2007 BC
garnacha blanca.

88 Colour: bright straw. Nose: sweet spices, cocoa bean, candied fruit, citrus fruit. Palate: fine bitter notes, fleshy, powerful.

PURESA 2007 T
100% cariñena.

89 Colour: deep cherry, garnet rim. Nose: balanced, complex, spicy, cocoa bean, creamy oak. Palate: fleshy, flavourful, good acidity, round tannins.

VINS ALGARS

Algars, 68
43786 Batea (Tarragona)
☎: +34 645 159 066
laarma85@gmail.com

DE NICANOR 2010 T
garnacha, syrah, merlot.

86 Colour: deep cherry, purple rim. Nose: medium intensity, ripe fruit, balanced. Palate: flavourful, ripe fruit.

VINS DEL TROS

Major, 13
43782 Vilalba dels Arcs (Tarragona)
☎: +34 605 096 447 - Fax: +34 977 438 042
info@vinsdeltros.com
www.vinsdeltros.com

CENT X CENT 2010 BC
100% garnacha blanca.

86 Color bright straw. Aroma fresh, fresh fruit, white flowers, expressive. Taste flavourful, fruity, good acidity, balanced.

AY DE MÍ 2009 T
70% garnacha, 30% syrah.

87 Color bright cherry. Aroma ripe fruit, sweet spices, creamy oak, expressive. Taste flavourful, fruity, toasty, round tannins.

VINS SAT LA BOTERA

Sant Roc, 26
43786 Batea (Tarragona)
☎: +34 977 430 009 - Fax: +34 977 430 801
labotera@labotera.com
www.labotera.com

VILA-CLOSA 2010 B
100% garnacha blanca.

86 Colour: bright yellow. Nose: fresh fruit, white flowers. Palate: varietal, flavourful, fruity, good acidity.

BRUNA DOLÇ 2010 T
50% garnacha, 50% syrah.

92 Colour: black cherry. Nose: powerfull, characterful, warm, fruit liqueur notes. Palate: fine bitter notes, sweet, ripe fruit.

L'ARNOT 2010 T
garnacha, syrah, samsó.

86 Colour: very deep cherry. Nose: ripe fruit, powerfull, violets. Palate: balanced, good acidity, ripe fruit.

VILA-CLOSA 2009 T
70% syrah, 30% garnacha.

86 Colour: cherry, garnet rim. Nose: ripe fruit, sweet spices, cocoa bean, medium intensity. Palate: spicy, ripe fruit, round tannins.

MUDÈFER 2007 T
garnacha, syrah, samsó.

86 Colour: cherry, garnet rim. Nose: ripe fruit, tobacco, spicy. Palate: good structure, ripe fruit, long, good acidity.

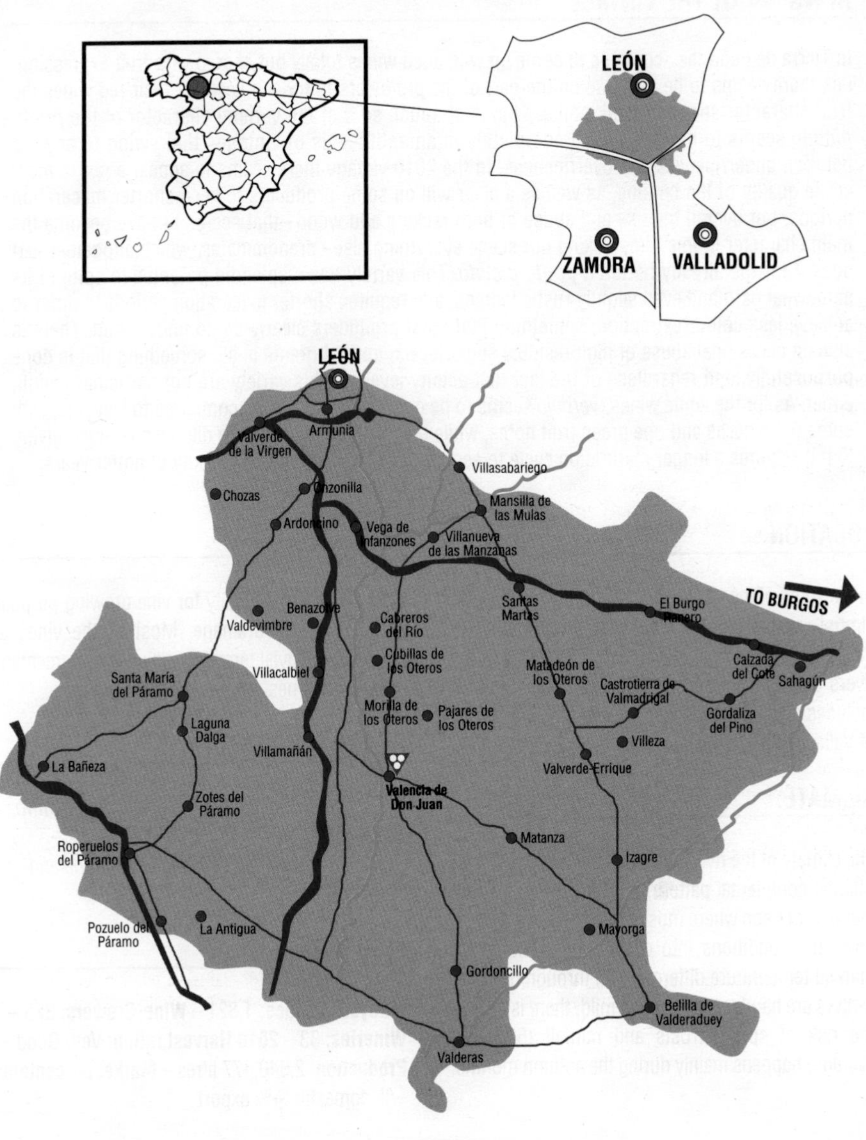
LEÓN
ZAMORA
VALLADOLID
LEÓN
Armunia
Valverde de la Virgen
Villasabariego
Chozas
Onzonilla
Mansilla de las Mulas
Ardoncino
Vega de Infanzones
Villanueva de las Manzanas
Santas Martas
El Burgo Ranero
TO BURGOS
Benazolve
Valdevimbre
Cabreros del Río
Cubillas de los Oteros
Villacalbiel
Matadeón de los Oteros
Calzada del Coto
Sahagún
Santa María del Páramo
Castrotierra de Valmadrigal
Morilla de los Oteros
Pajares de los Oteros
Gordaliza del Pino
Laguna Dalga
Villeza
Villamañán
La Bañeza
Valverde-Enrique
Valencia de Don Juan
Zotes del Páramo
Matanza
Roperuelos del Páramo
Izagre
Pozuelo del Páramo
La Antigua
Mayorga
Gordoncillo
Belilla de Valderaduey
Valderas
Consejo Regulador
DO Boundary

DO TIERRA DE LEÓN

NEWS ABOUT THE VINTAGE:

In Tierra de León they continue to come up with aged wines totally out of step with fruit expression, i.e., there seems to be little will on the part of the producers to try and keep for their red wines the fruit character above the oak notes. This is so much so that the varietal character of the *prieto picudo* seems to have vanished completely in an apotheosis of vintages that swing to and fro between underripeness and overripeness. In the 2010 vintage there seems to appear a raw, almost crude quality of the tannins, as well as a clear will on some producers to keep shorter maceration periods, but overall the use and abuse of both racking and wood –that seems to have become the main character in this film, kicking out scene everything else– predominates, which altogether just does it for the already battered *prieto picudo*. This variety has a splendid potential in spite of its somewhat hard and even slightly rustic tannins, and requires shorter maceration periods in order to achieve less colour extraction, something that most producers clearly do no understand. There is also an occasional abuse of high residual sugar levels, up to 4 grams in all, something that is done purposefully, and regardless of the fact that acidity levels of this variety are not particularly high, either. As for the white wines, *verdejo* seems to be gaining on singularity compared to last year, with some fresh herbs and ripe green fruit notes, while the albarín shows a more diluted character, giving that it requires a longer maturation cycle to acquire the structure and complexity of hotter years.

LOCATION

In the south of the province of León with the vineyard almost exclusively around the municipality of Valencia de Don Juan in a sort of triangle with the rivers Cea and Esla taking the other two corners. It includes also 19 municipal districts of the province of Valladolid.

CLIMATE:

The climate of the river valleys would follow a milder Atlantic continental pattern, but the high plateau of that part of León where most of the vines are planted turns the conditions into cooler ones. There is a marked temperature differential all through the year, winters are harsh and summers mild, there is always the risk of spring frosts and rainfall (500 mm average) happens mainly during the autumn months.

SOIL:

They are of great quality for vine growing purposes and have good drainage. Most of the vines are planted on alluvial terraces with varying percentages of clay and limestone and a rocky subsoil.

GRAPE VARIETIES:

WHITE: *Albarín, Verdejo, Godello, Palomino, Malvasía.*
RED: *Prieto picudo, Mencía, Garnacha* and *Tempranillo.*

FIGURES:

Vineyard surface: 1,321 – **Wine-Growers:** 375 – **Wineries:** 33 – **2010 Harvest rating:** Very Good – **Production:** 2,540,477 litres – **Market percentages:** --% domestic. --% export

CONSEJO REGULADOR
Alonso Castrillo, 29.
24200 Valencia de Don Juan (León)
☎: +34 987 751 089 - Fax: +34 987 750 012
@ vinotierradeleon@yahoo.es /
directortecnico@dotierradeleon.es
www.dotierradeleon.es

GENERAL CHARACTERISTICS OF THE WINES

WHITES	Fully ripe local *Albarín* is the grape used to make some fine toasty wines which feature white fruit notes, roasted herbs and a fairly high alcohol content.
ROSÉS	The traditional and slightly carbonic –de aguja– rosé wines from the region are still made, although they have improved their quality with the best varietal values of the *Prieto Picudo* grape.
REDS	The majority are made from *Prieto Picudo* and are similar to those made from *Mencía* but an altogether fuller body and marked tannins. They are also very intense in colour, with a nose of fresh fruit and herbal nuances.

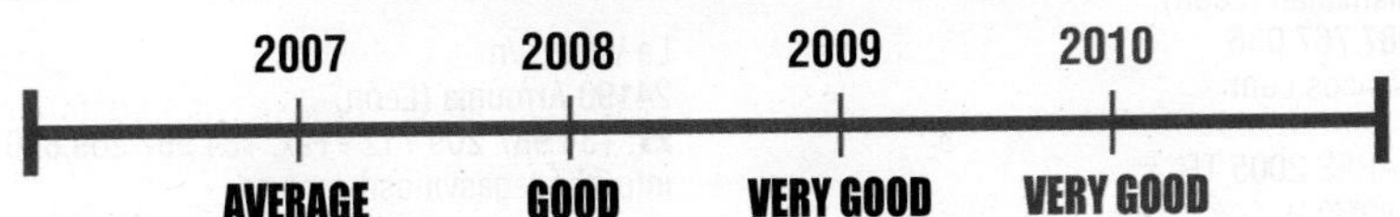

2007	2008	2009	2010
AVERAGE	GOOD	VERY GOOD	VERY GOOD

BODEGA GORDALIZA DEL PINO

Ctra. Sahagún, s/n
24325 Gordaliza del Pino (León)
☎: +34 987 784 057 - Fax: +34 987 784 057
info@bodegagordaliza.es
www.bodegagordaliza.es

EL TESORO DEL PÁRAMO 2005 TC
mencía, prieto picudo.

85 Colour: cherry, garnet rim. Nose: fruit liqueur notes, cedar wood, sweet spices. Palate: fresh, fruity, light-bodied, balsamic.

BODEGA NOS RIQUEZA

Sánchez Calvo, 6
33402 Avilés (Asturias)
☎: +34 984 836 826 - Fax: +34 985 931 074
exportmanager@nosriqueza.com
www.nosriqueza.com

NOS RIQUEZA 2010 RD
100% prieto picudo.

85 Colour: rose, purple rim. Nose: varietal, powerfull, fresh, balanced, fresh fruit. Palate: sweetness, fruity, light-bodied.

BODEGAS MARCOS MIÑAMBRES

Camino de Pobladura, s/n
24234 Villamañán (León)
☎: +34 987 767 038
satvined@picos.com

LOS SILVARES 2005 TR
100% prieto picudo.

86 Colour: cherry, garnet rim. Nose: ripe fruit, spicy, cedar wood, creamy oak, sweet spices.

BODEGAS MARGÓN

Isaac García de Quirós, 6 - 1
24200 Valencia de Don Juan (León)
☎: +34 987 750 800 - Fax: +34 987 750 481
bodegasmargon@gmail.com
www.bodegasmargon.com

PRICUM ALBARÍN VALDEMUZ 2009 B BARRICA

89 Colour: bright yellow. Nose: ripe fruit, sweet spices, creamy oak, fragrant herbs. Palate: rich, smoky aftertaste, flavourful, fresh, good acidity.

PRICUM ALBARÍN VALDEMUZ 2008 B BARRICA

84 Colour: bright golden. Nose: candied fruit, scrubland, creamy oak, slightly evolved. Palate: ripe fruit, spicy, creamy.

PRICUM PRIMEUR 2010 T

89 Colour: dark-red cherry. Nose: damp earth, fruit expression, fresh fruit, wild herbs, characterful. Palate: fresh, light-bodied, powerful, flavourful, easy to drink, balsamic.

PRICUM VALDEMUZ 2008 T
100% prieto picudo.

91 Colour: dark-red cherry. Nose: complex, varietal, expressive, aged wood nuances, cedar wood, fresh fruit. Palate: fresh.

PRICUM PRIETO PICUDO 2008 T
prieto picudo.

90 Colour: cherry, garnet rim. Nose: mineral, ripe fruit, fruit expression, sweet spices. Palate: powerful, fleshy, toasty, round tannins.

PRICUM PARAJE DE EL SANTO 2008 T
100% prieto picudo.

90 Colour: cherry, garnet rim. Nose: balsamic herbs, scrubland, ripe fruit, toasty, aromatic coffee. Palate: powerful, fleshy, spicy.

BODEGAS VINOS DE LEÓN

La Vega, s/n
24190 Armunia (León)
☎: +34 987 209 712 - Fax: +34 987 209 800
info@bodegasvinosdeleon.es
www.bodegasvinosdeleon.es

VALJUNCO 2010 B
100% verdejo.

80 Colour: bright straw. Nose: candied fruit, citrus fruit. Palate: flavourful, light-bodied.

VALJUNCO 2010 RD
100% prieto picudo.

82 Colour: rose, purple rim. Nose: ripe fruit, grassy, medium intensity. Palate: powerful, flavourful, fresh.

VALJUNCO 2010 T
prieto picudo.

85 Colour: deep cherry. Nose: ripe fruit, fruit expression, grassy, balsamic herbs. Palate: flavourful, fruity, full.

VALJUNCO 2008 TC

85 Colour: cherry, garnet rim. Nose: powerfull, fruit liqueur notes, aromatic coffee, roasted coffee. Palate: spicy, fine bitter notes, round tannins.

VALJUNCO 2007 TC
100% prieto picudo.

87 Colour: cherry, garnet rim. Nose: ripe fruit, balsamic herbs, spicy, creamy oak. Palate: flavourful, fleshy, balsamic.

DON SUERO 2004 TR
100% prieto picudo.

87 Colour: dark-red cherry, orangey edge. Nose: old leather, ripe fruit, spicy, toasty. Palate: spicy, flavourful, slightly evolved.

BODEGAS Y VIÑEDOS LA SILVERA

Ctra. de Pajares, s/n
24209 Pajares de los Oteros (León)
☎: +34 618 174 176
gregory@mengoba.com
www.mengoba.com

PRETO 2010 RD
prieto picudo.

87 Colour: rose, purple rim. Nose: powerfull, red berry notes, floral, fruit preserve. Palate: fleshy, powerful, fruity, fresh.

PRETO 2009 T JOVEN
prieto picudo.

86 Colour: bright cherry. Nose: powerfull, fruit preserve, fruit liqueur notes, maceration notes. Palate: fleshy, fruity, fresh fruit tannins, mineral.

FINCA LA SILVERA 2007 T
prieto picudo.

90 Colour: cherry, garnet rim. Nose: ripe fruit, fruit expression, toasty, balsamic herbs. Palate: flavourful, toasty, round tannins.

BODEGAS Y VIÑEDOS PEDRO CASIS

Las Bodegas, s/n
24325 Gordaliza del Pino (León)
☎: +34 987 699 618 - Fax: +34 987 699 618
bodegascasis@gmail.com
www.bodegascasis.com

CASIS GODELLO 2010 B
95% godello, 5% albarín.

82 Colour: bright straw. Nose: powerfull, ripe fruit, citrus fruit, white flowers. Palate: flavourful, light-bodied, good acidity.

CASIS PRIETO PICUDO 2010 T
100% prieto picudo.

81 Colour: dark-red cherry. Nose: varietal, powerfull, fresh. Palate: sweetness, fruity, flavourful, stalky, fruity aftestaste.

CASIS PRIETO PICUDO 2009 T
95% prieto picudo, 5% tempranillo, mencía.

86 Colour: cherry, garnet rim. Nose: powerfull, characterful, ripe fruit, fruit expression. Palate: flavourful, powerful, fleshy.

CASIS PRIETO PICUDO 2005 TC
90% prieto picudo, 10% mencía, tempranillo.

87 Colour: cherry, garnet rim. Nose: ripe fruit, dark chocolate, sweet spices. Palate: flavourful, powerful, toasty.

FRANCISCO GONZÁLEZ

La Fragua, s/n
24324 Villeza (León)
☎: +34 987 263 710 - Fax: +34 987 263 710
info@villeza.com
www.villeza.com

LÁGRIMA DE VILLEZA 2010 B
90% albarín, 10% godello.

85 Colour: bright straw. Nose: fresh, fresh fruit, white flowers. Palate: flavourful, fruity, good acidity.

LÁGRIMA DE VILLEZA 2010 RD
prieto picudo, mencía, tempranillo, garnacha.

85 Colour: onion pink. Nose: candied fruit, dried flowers, fragrant herbs, red berry notes. Palate: light-bodied, flavourful, good acidity, long, spicy.

TINTO VILLEZA 6 MESES 2009 T
70% prieto picudo, 30% mencía.

86 Colour: cherry, garnet rim. Nose: powerfull, fruit liqueur notes, toasty. Palate: powerful, fleshy, fine bitter notes.

TINTO VILLEZA 12 MESES 2008 TC
100% prieto picudo.

87 Colour: cherry, garnet rim. Nose: fresh, varietal, balanced, cedar wood, creamy oak, undergrowth. Palate: powerful, flavourful, fruity, mineral.

GORDONZELLO

Alto de Santa Marina, s/n
24294 Gordoncillo (León)
☎: +34 987 758 030 - Fax: +34 987 757 201
info@gordonzello.com
www.gordonzello.com

PEREGRINO VERDEJO 2010 B
100% verdejo.

88 Colour: bright golden. Nose: ripe fruit, white flowers, fragrant herbs, fresh, expressive. Palate: fruity, fresh, flavourful, good acidity.

PEREGRINO ALBARÍN 2010 B
100% albarín.

88 Colour: bright straw. Nose: fresh, fresh fruit, white flowers, expressive, tropical fruit. Palate: flavourful, fruity, good acidity, balanced.

PEREGRINO CUVÈE 2009 B
100% albarín.

81 Colour: bright yellow. Nose: woody, spicy, slightly evolved. Palate: powerful, slightly evolved, good structure.

PEREGRINO 2010 RD
100% prieto picudo.

88 Colour: rose, purple rim. Nose: ripe fruit, raspberry, expressive. Palate: good acidity, fresh, fruity, flavourful.

GURDOS 2010 RD
100% prieto picudo.

87 Colour: rose, purple rim. Nose: powerfull, red berry notes, raspberry, floral. Palate: fleshy, powerful, fruity, easy to drink.

PEREGRINO MACERACIÓN PELICULAR 2010 T
100% prieto picudo.

88 Colour: cherry, purple rim. Nose: red berry notes, floral, fruit expression. Palate: fruity, good acidity.

PEREGRINO 2008 T ROBLE
100% prieto picudo.

85 Colour: dark-red cherry. Nose: fresh fruit, balsamic herbs, damp undergrowth. Palate: good acidity, grainy tannins, flavourful.

PEREGRINO TINTO 14 2007 TC
100% prieto picudo.

88 Colour: deep cherry. Nose: powerfull, expressive, ripe fruit, fruit liqueur notes, roasted coffee, dark chocolate. Palate: spicy, powerful, long.

PEREGRINO 2006 TC
100% prieto picudo.

86 Colour: cherry, garnet rim. Nose: fruit liqueur notes, aromatic coffee, dark chocolate, toasty. Palate: powerful, good acidity, fine bitter notes.

PEREGRINO 2006 TR
100% prieto picudo.

86 Colour: cherry, garnet rim. Nose: earthy notes, undergrowth, characterful, varietal, spicy, cedar wood. Palate: good structure, powerful, flavourful, spicy, roasted-coffee aftertaste.

LOS PALOMARES

Los Palomares, 6
24230 Valdevimbre (León)
☎: +34 987 304 218 - Fax: +34 987 304 193
lospalomares@bodegalospalomares.com
www.bodegalospalomares.com

3 PALOMARES 2010 B
100% verdejo.

90 Colour: straw. Nose: fragrant herbs, damp earth, candied fruit, fruit expression. Palate: sweetness, powerful, flavourful, fruity, fresh.

3 PALOMARES 2010 RD
prieto picudo.

86 Colour: rose, purple rim. Nose: fruit expression, red clay notes, dry stone. Palate: balsamic, easy to drink, sweetness, fruity.

3 PALOMARES 2009 T
prieto picudo.

89 Colour: cherry, garnet rim. Nose: powerfull, candied fruit, fruit preserve. Palate: powerful, fleshy, round.

3 PALOMARES 2007 TC
prieto picudo.

86 Colour: cherry, garnet rim. Nose: ripe fruit, toasty, dark chocolate, smoky. Palate: flavourful, fleshy, spicy, ripe frui

MEORIGA BODEGAS & VIÑEDOS

Ctra. de Alberite s/n
47680 Mayorga (Valladolid)
☎: +34 983 751 182 - Fax: +34 983 751 182
bodegas@meoriga.com
www.meoriga.com

SEÑORÍO DE MOGROVEJO 2010 B
100% verdejo.

86 Colour: bright straw. Nose: scrubland, white flowers. Palate: flavourful, fine bitter notes, good acidity.

SEÑORÍO DE MOGROVEJO 2010 RD
prieto picudo.

89 Colour: rose, purple rim. Nose: powerfull, ripe fruit, red berry notes, floral. Palate: fleshy, powerful, fruity, fresh.

SEÑORÍO DE MOGROVEJO 2009 T ROBLE
prieto picudo.

85 Colour: dark-red cherry. Nose: fresh fruit, red berry notes, wild herbs, spicy, cedar wood. Palate: fruity, fresh, powerful, flavourful, balsamic, fresh fruit tannins.

SEÑORÍO DE MOGROVEJO 2008 TC
prieto picudo.

87 Colour: cherry, garnet rim. Nose: spicy, creamy oak, toasty, fruit expression. Palate: powerful, flavourful, toasty, round tannins.

SDAD. COOP. VINÍCOLA COMARCAL VALDEVIMBRE

Ctra. de León, s/n
24230 Valdevimbre (León)
☎: +34 987 304 195 - Fax: +34 987 304 195
valdevim@hotmail.com

ABADÍA DE BALDEREDO 2010 RD
prieto picudo.

80 Colour: brilliant rose. Nose: ripe fruit, floral. Palate: flavourful, fruity, fresh.

ABADÍA DE BALDEREDO 2007 TC
prieto picudo.

76

SDAD. COOP. VINOS DE LA RIBERA DEL CEA

Avda. Panduro y Villafañe, 15
24220 Valderas (León)
☎: +34 987 762 191 - Fax: +34 987 762 191
info@riberacea.e.telefonica.net

VIÑA TRASDERREY 2010 RD
100% prieto picudo.

86 Colour: rose, purple rim. Nose: elegant, dried flowers, fragrant herbs, red berry notes. Palate: light-bodied, flavourful, good acidity, long, spicy.

VILLACEZÁN

San Juan, 10
24294 Gordoncillo (León)
☎: +34 987 758 031 - Fax: +34 987 758 031
villacezan@villacezan.com
www.villacezan.com

VILLACEZÁN ALBARÍN 2010 B
albarín.

90 Colour: bright straw. Nose: fresh, fresh fruit, white flowers. Palate: flavourful, fruity, balanced, fleshy.

MOLENDORES 2010 RD
prieto picudo.

86 Colour: brilliant rose. Nose: powerfull, ripe fruit, fruit expression, red berry notes. Palate: fine bitter notes, flavourful, good acidity.

VILLACEZÁN 12 MESES 2009 T
prieto picudo.

86 Colour: cherry, garnet rim. Nose: powerfull, ripe fruit, warm. Palate: powerful, fleshy, sweetness, round tannins.

GALIO 2009 T
prieto picudo.

86 Colour: bright cherry. Nose: sweet spices, creamy oak, overripe fruit. Palate: flavourful, fruity, toasty, round tannins.

DEHESA DE VILLACEZÁN 2009 T
prieto picudo, mencía.

82 Colour: cherry, garnet rim. Nose: powerfull, candied fruit, fruit preserve. Palate: fleshy, sweetness, fruity.

GALIO 2008 T
prieto picudo.

89 Colour: cherry, garnet rim, deep cherry. Nose: sweet spices, toasty, dark chocolate. Palate: powerful, flavourful, spicy, ripe fruit.

VIÑEDOS Y BODEGA PARDEVALLES

Ctra. de León, s/n
24230 Valdevimbre (León)
☎: +34 987 304 222 - Fax: +34 987 304 222
info@pardevalles.es
www.pardevalles.com

PARDEVALLES ALBARÍN 2010 B
100% albarín.

88 Colour: bright straw. Nose: citrus fruit, fruit expression, fragrant herbs. Palate: good acidity, flavourful, powerful, fruity.

PARDEVALLES 2010 RD
100% prieto picudo.

88 Colour: rose, purple rim. Nose: elegant, red berry notes, floral, lactic notes. Palate: fruity, fresh, flavourful.

PARDEVALLES 2010 T
100% prieto picudo.

83 Colour: cherry, garnet rim. Nose: fresh, medium intensity, varietal. Palate: fresh fruit tannins, flavourful, powerful, fruity.

PARDEVALLES GAMONAL 2009 T
100% prieto picudo.

91 Colour: dark-red cherry. Nose: fruit liqueur notes, candied fruit, aromatic coffee, fruit expression. Palate: fine bitter notes, fresh fruit tannins, fruity, flavourful.

PARDEVALLES CARROLEÓN 2008 T
100% prieto picudo.

92 Colour: cherry, garnet rim. Nose: powerfull, ripe fruit, sweet spices, toasty, creamy oak. Palate: powerful, fleshy, sweetness, round tannins.

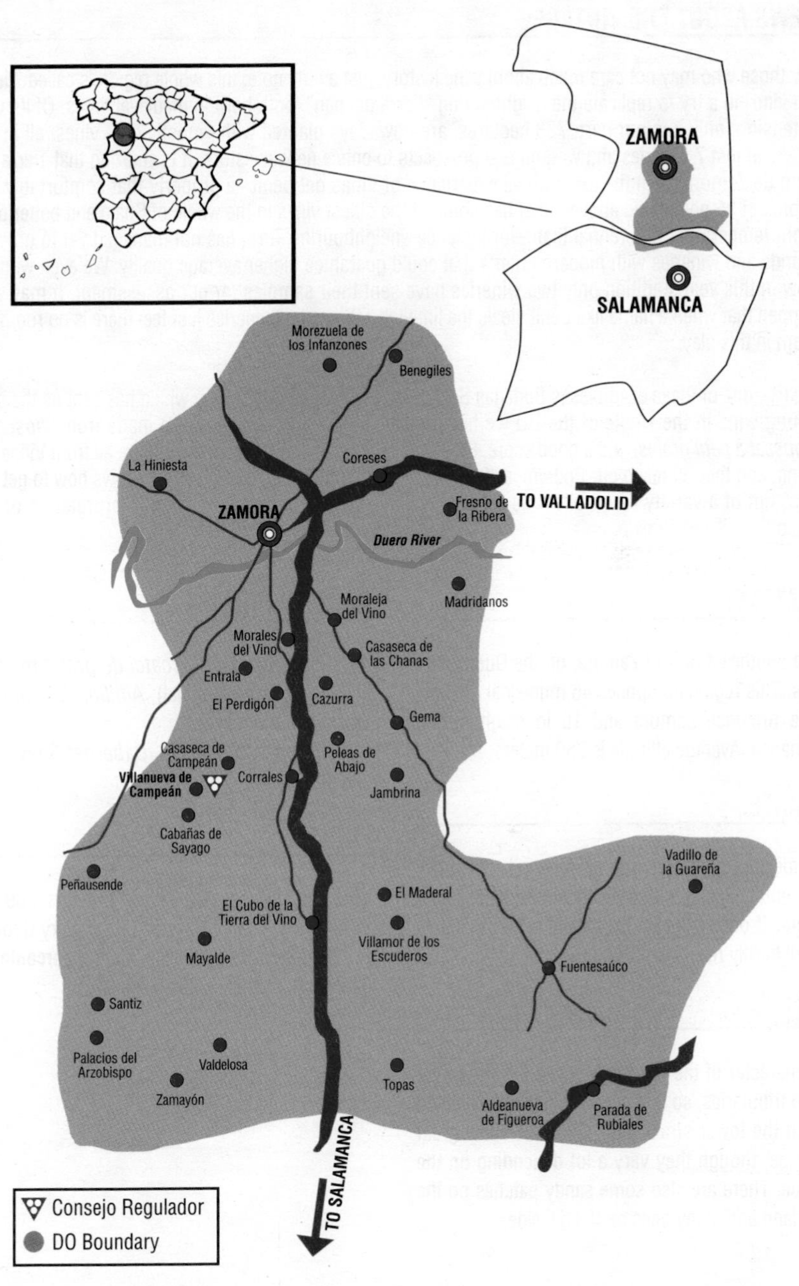
ZAMORA
SALAMANCA
Morezuela de los Infanzones
Benegiles
La Hiniesta
Coreses
ZAMORA
Fresno de la Ribera
TO VALLADOLID
Duero River
Madridanos
Moraleja del Vino
Morales del Vino
Casaseca de las Chanas
Entrala
Cazurra
El Perdigón
Gema
Casaseca de Campeán
Peleas de Abajo
Villanueva de Campeán
Corrales
Jambrina
Cabañas de Sayago
Vadillo de la Guareña
Peñausende
El Maderal
El Cubo de la Tierra del Vino
Villamor de los Escuderos
Mayalde
Fuentesaúco
Santiz
Palacios del Arzobispo
Valdelosa
Topas
Zamayón
Aldeanueva de Figueroa
Parada de Rubiales
TO SALAMANCA
Consejo Regulador
DO Boundary

DO TIERRA DEL VINO DE ZAMORA

NEWS ABOUT THE VINTAGE:

For those who may not care much about wine history, just a little note: this whole region is called "tierra del vino" in a try to replicate the neighbouring "tierra del pan", both born in medieval times. Of its vast extension, only a minor part, 738 hectares, are nowadays planted with –mostly old– vines, all in the hands of just 7 wineries and with no real prospects to entice new investors. It is amazing that Tierra del Vino de Zamora, with the exceptional experience of Viñas del Cénit –a property that comfortably got scores of 95 points and above–, that has some of the oldest vines in the whole of Spain and better day-night temperature differential than –for instance– neighbouring Toro, has not managed yet to grow in brands and wineries with modern criteria that could guarantee higher average quality. We even witness how in this year's edition only two wineries have sent their samples for our assessment. It may well happen that when a name like Cénit steals the limelight, the rest of wineries just feel there is no room for them in this play.

Clearly, one of these examples is Bodegas Seleccionadas Armando, a winery which has sent us the only young wine in the whole of the DO we have managed to taste, a white wine made from *moscatel* (*muscat à petit grains*) and a good score, 88 points. The rest of samples tasted (4) are all from Viñas del Cénit, and they all reach our Podium, a "four out of four" triumph for a winery that knows how to get the best out of a variety as excellent as the *tempranillo*, with an equally excellent interpretation of the region's soil and climate.

LOCATION:

In the southeast part of Zamora, on the Duero river banks. This region comprises 46 municipal districts in the province Zamora and 10 in neighbouring Salamanca. Average altitude is 750 meters.

CLIMATE:

Extreme temperatures as correspond to a dry continental pattern, with very hot summers and cold winters. It does not rain much and average annual rainfall hardly reaches 400 mm.

SOIL:

The character of the territory derives from the river Duero tributaries, so it is predominantly alluvial and clay in the lower strata that might not allow great drainage, though they vary a lot depending on the altitude. There are also some sandy patches on the plain land and stony ones on the hill side.

GRAPE VARIETIES:

WHITE: *Malvasía, Moscatel de grano menudo* and *Verdejo* (preferential); *Albillo, Palomino* and *Godello* (authorized).
RED: *Tempranillo* (main), *Cabernet Sauvignon* and *Garnacha.*

FIGURES:

Vineyard surface: 707 – **Wine-Growers:** 209 – **Wineries:** 9 – **2010 Harvest rating:** Very Good – **Production:** 527,700 litres – **Market percentages:** 62,77% domestic. 37,23% export

CONSEJO REGULADOR
Plaza Mayor, 1
49708 Villanueva de Campeán (Zamora)
☎: +34 980 560 055 - Fax: +34 980 560 055
@ info@tierradelvino.net
www.tierradelvino.net

GENERAL CHARACTERISTICS OF THE WINES

WHITES	They are fresh wines wines a slight herbal *Malvasía* character, full, flavoursome, with good alcohol content and a refreshing acidity.
REDS	They are very intense in colour, with a powerful nose and some complexity given by the great percentage of old vines found in the region. They also have higher acidity levels compared to Toro, thanks to the likewise higher altitude and the retention properties of the soil..

VINTAGE RATING PEÑÍNGUIDE

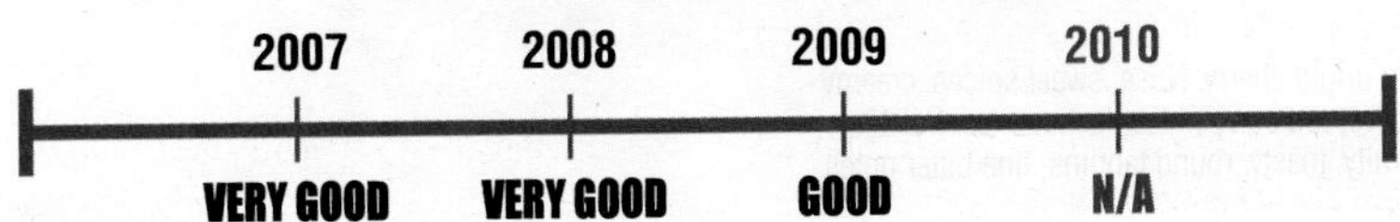

BODEGAS SELECCIONADAS ARMANDO

"Viña Concita y Adilen" Ctra. N-630, Km. 270
49192 Zamora (Zamora)
☎: +34 980 538 683 - Fax: +34 980 538 683
bodegas.armando@gmail.com
www.bodegas-armando.com

CATEDRAL DE ZAMORA 2010 B
100% moscatel grano menudo.

88 Color golden. Aroma powerfull, floral, honeyed notes, candied fruit, fragrant herbs. Taste flavourful, sweet, fresh, fruity, good acidity, long.

VIÑAS DEL CÉNIT

Ctra. de Circunvalación, s/n
49708 Villanueva de Campeán (Zamora)
☎: +34 609 119 248 - Fax: +34 976 852 764
info@bodegascenit.com
www.bodegascenit.com

VIA CENIT 2009 T
tempranillo.

94 Colour: bright cherry. Nose: sweet spices, creamy oak, expressive, red berry notes, lactic notes. Palate: flavourful, fruity, toasty, round tannins, fine bitter notes.

VENTA MAZARRÓN 2009 T
100% tempranillo.

93 Colour: bright cherry. Nose: ripe fruit, sweet spices, creamy oak, expressive, mineral. Palate: flavourful, fruity, toasty, round tannins.

ALEO 2009 T ROBLE
100% tempranillo.

90 Colour: bright cherry. Nose: ripe fruit, sweet spices, roasted coffee. Palate: flavourful, fleshy, toasty.

CENIT 2007 T
100% tempranillo.

96 Colour: cherry, garnet rim. Nose: ripe fruit, fruit expression, mineral, creamy oak, new oak, complex. Palate: flavourful, fleshy, complex, ripe fruit, round.

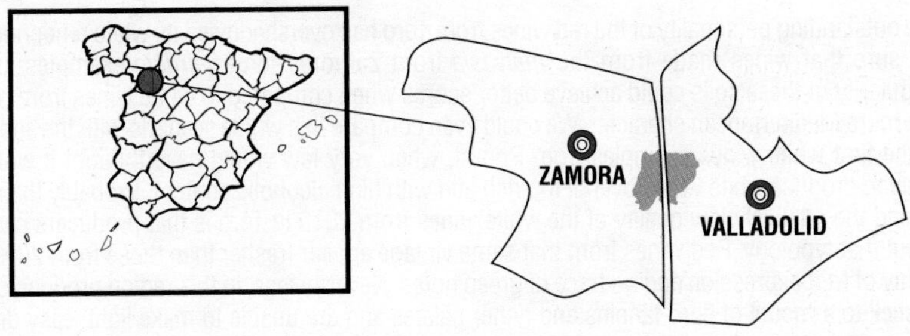

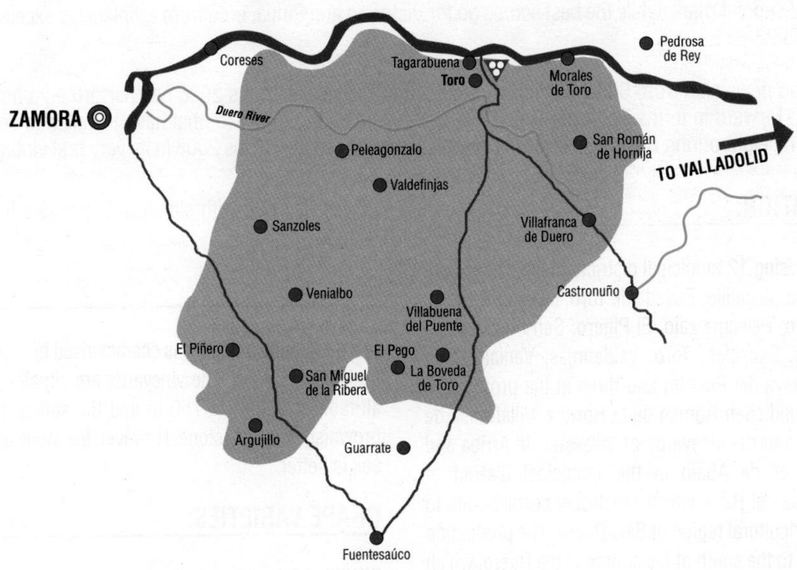

Consejo Regulador

DO Boundary

NEWS ABOUT THE VINTAGE:

The outstanding personality of the red wines from Toro has overshadowed its white renderings. We are sure that wines made from the *malvasía* from Zamora, some *verdejo* examples and the singularity of these soils could achieve better scores when compared to white wines from regions of a more Mediterranean character. We could even compare this whole scenario with the apparition of the first white wines examples from Priorat, when very few would have thought it worth the while to produce white wines overall too rich and with high alcoholic content. Probably the reason behind the relatively low quality of the white wines from 2010 in Toro is that producers care little about that typology. Red wines from that same vintage appear fresher than those from 2009, with plenty of fruit expression and no trace of green notes. Nevertheless, in this region producers seem to stick to a model of hard tannins and richer palates and are unable to make light, easy drinking wines. As for the red examples of 2009, a hot year by any standard, aged wines have taken in all the toasted elements from the oak to try and neutralize the confected character of that vintage.

The hot wagon in Toro carries big names like Teso la Monja, Pintia, Numanthia or Dominio de Bendito, all of them a real blessing in terms of reputation for the region. Up to 67 samples have hit the 90-point mark, while the best scores go for Victorino and Pintia, both from a vintage as excellent as 2008.

Good news also from Bodegas Fariña –their Gran Colegiata Campus 2006 has performed a huge step forward in terms of quality– and from Bodegas Alonso del Hierro, that have travelled to Toro from neighbouring Ribera del Duero to get 93 points for its red Paydos 2008 in its very first vintage.

LOCATION:

Comprising 12 municipal districts of the province of Zamora (Argujillo, Boveda de Toro, Morales de Toro, El Pego, Peleagonzalo, El Piñero, San Miguel de la Ribera, Sanzoles, Toro, Valdefinjas, Venialbo and Villanueva del Puente) and three in the province of Valladolid (San Román de la Hornija, Villafranca de Duero and the vineyards of Villaester de Arriba and Villaester de Abajo in the municipal district of Pedrosa del Rey), which practically corresponds to the agricultural region of Bajo Duero. The production area is to the south of the course of the Duero, which crosses the region from east to west.

CLIMATE:

Extreme continental, with Atlantic influences and quite arid, with an average annual rainfall of between 350 mm and 400 mm. The winters are harsh (which means extremely low temperatures and long periods of frosts) and the summers short, although not excessively hot, with significant contrasts in day-night temperatures.

SOIL:

The geography of the DO is characterised by a gently-undulating terrain. The vineyards are situated at an altitude of 620 m to 750 m and the soil is mainly brownish-grey limestone. However, the stony alluvial soil is better.

GRAPE VARIETIES:

WHITE: *Malvasía* and *Verdejo.*
RED: *Tinta de Toro* (majority) and *Garnacha.*

FIGURES:

Vineyard surface: 5,783 – **Wine-Growers:** 1,312 – **Wineries:** 51 – **2010 Harvest rating:** Excellent – **Production:** 11,597,747 litres – **Market percentages:** 50% domestic. 50% export

CONSEJO REGULADOR
De la Concepción, 3
Palacio de los Condes de Requena
49800 Toro (Zamora)
☎:+34 980 690 335 - Fax: +34 980 693 201
@ consejo@dotoro.es
www.dotoro.es

GENERAL CHARACTERISTICS OF THE WINES

WHITES	Produced mainly from the *Malvasía* variety, they have a colour ranging from pale yellow to greenish yellow; on the nose, rustic notes may appear, and on the palate, they have a slightly bitter aftertaste.
ROSÉS	The *Tinta de Toro* and *Garnacha* varieties are used, and are blended or used alone to produce single variety wines. Rosy coloured, they have notes of ripe red berries; they are meaty and fruity on the palate.
REDS	These are the most characteristic of the region. They have an astringency typical of the *Tinta de Toro* variety, and a high alcohol content (13° or more) and good acidity levels. When the wines are young, they have a dark cherry colour with violet nuances; on the nose they have good intensity with notes reminiscent of blackberries and black berry fruit in general; on the palate, they are powerful, flavourful, meaty, slightly overripe and have a good persistency. Those aged in wood maintain the notes of ripe fruit together with the contribution of the oak and the meatiness on the palate

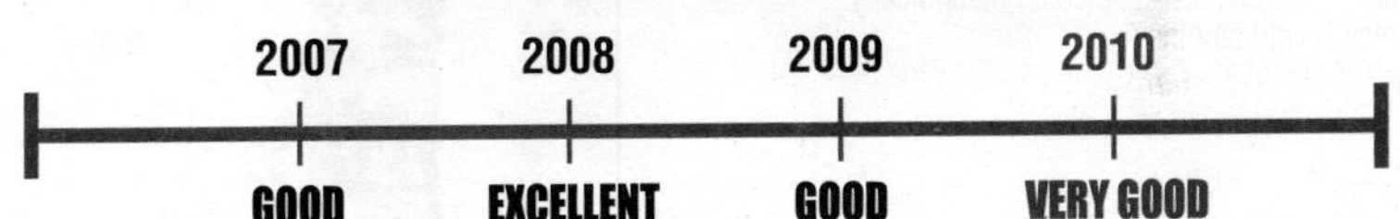

2007	2008	2009	2010
GOOD	EXCELLENT	GOOD	VERY GOOD

ÁLVAREZ Y DÍEZ

Juan Antonio Carmona, 12
47500 Nava del Rey (Valladolid)
☎: +34 983 850 136 - Fax: +34 983 850 761
bodegas@alvarezydiez.com
www.alvarezydiez.com

VALMORO 2007 T
tinta de Toro.

91 Colour: cherry, garnet rim. Nose: ripe fruit, powerfull, mineral, spicy, toasty. Palate: powerful, fleshy, complex, flavourful, toasty.

BODEGA BURDIGALA (F. LURTON & M. ROLLAND)

Camino Magarín, s/n
47529 Villafranca del Duero (Valladolid)
☎: +34 980 692 100 - Fax: +34 983 034 040
bodega@burdigala.es
www.francoislurton.com

CAMPO ALEGRE 2008 T
100% tinta de Toro.

90 Colour: dark-red cherry. Nose: ripe fruit, medium intensity, dark chocolate, sweet spices. Palate: fleshy, complex, spicy, round tannins.

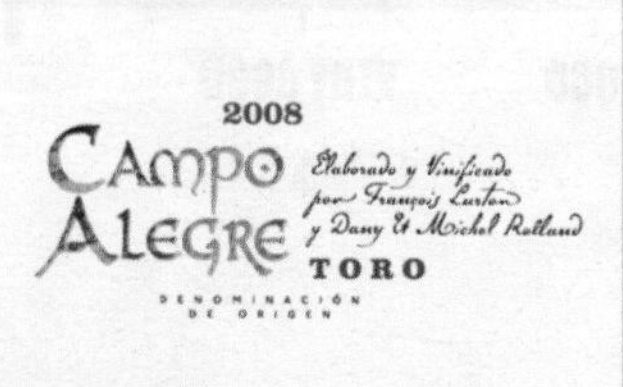

CAMPO ELISEO 2005 T
100% tinta de Toro.

92 Colour: cherry, garnet rim. Nose: ripe fruit, spicy, creamy oak. Palate: powerful, flavourful, toasty, round tannins.

BODEGA CYAN

Ctra. Valdefinjas - Venialbo, Km. 9,2, Finca La Calera
49800 Toro (Zamora)
☎: +34 980 568 029 - Fax: +34 980 568 036
cyan@matarromera.es
www.bodegacyan.es

SELECCIÓN PERSONAL CARLOS MORO CYAN 2005 T RESERVA ESPECIAL
100% tinta de Toro.

91 Colour: very deep cherry, garnet rim. Nose: toasty, spicy, ripe fruit. Palate: ripe fruit, round tannins, spicy.

CYAN PRESTIGIO 2005 TC
100% tinta de Toro.

90 Colour: cherry, garnet rim. Nose: spicy, creamy oak, toasty, fruit expression. Palate: powerful, flavourful, round tannins.

CYAN 12 MESES 2005 TC
100% tinta de Toro.

88 Colour: cherry, garnet rim. Nose: fruit preserve, spicy. Palate: good structure, fruity, flavourful.

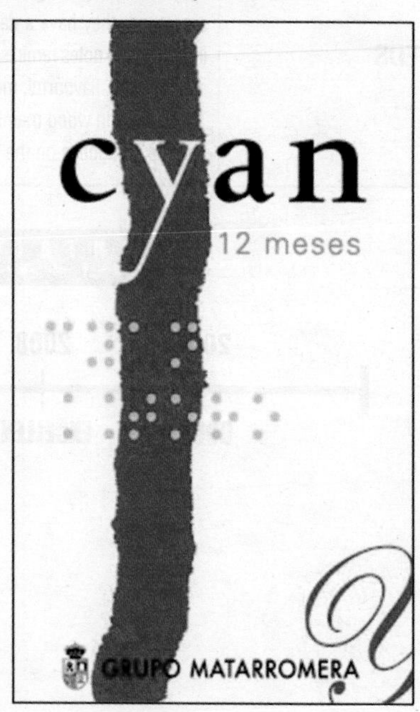

CYAN PAGO DE LA CALERA 2004 T
100% tinta de Toro.

90 Colour: cherry, garnet rim. Nose: spicy, creamy oak, toasty. Palate: powerful, flavourful, toasty, round tannins.

BODEGA DEL PALACIO DE LOS FRONTAURA Y VICTORIA

Santiago, 17 - 4º
47001 (Valladolid)
☎: +34 983 360 284 - Fax: +34 983 345 546
cpardo@bodegasfrontaura.es
www.bodegasfrontaura.es

DOMINIO DE VALDELACASA 2008 T
tinta de Toro.

92 Colour: cherry, garnet rim. Nose: red berry notes, ripe fruit, mineral, spicy, creamy oak. Palate: fleshy, complex, powerful, flavourful, round tannins.

FRONTAURA 2006 TC
tinta de Toro.

91 Colour: cherry, garnet rim. Nose: ripe fruit, dark chocolate, cocoa bean, sweet spices, toasty. Palate: good acidity, unctuous, rich, flavourful, fleshy, round tannins.

BODEGA ELÍAS MORA

Juan Mora, s/n
47530 San Román de Hornija (Valladolid)
☎: +34 983 784 029 - Fax: +34 983 784 190
info@bodegaseliasmora.com
www.bodegaseliasmora.com

VIÑAS ELÍAS MORA 2009 T ROBLE
100% tinta de Toro.

90 Colour: cherry, garnet rim. Nose: powerfull, ripe fruit, fruit preserve. Palate: powerful, fleshy, good acidity, fine bitter notes.

ELÍAS MORA 2008 TC
100% tinta de Toro.

91 Colour: cherry, garnet rim. Nose: warm, spicy, roasted coffee. Palate: ripe fruit, fleshy, powerful.

ELÍAS MORA 2005 TR
100% tinta de Toro.

92 Colour: cherry, garnet rim. Nose: spicy, creamy oak, toasty, characterful, varietal. Palate: powerful, flavourful, toasty, round tannins.

BODEGA FLORENCIO SALGADO NARROS

Ctra. Toro - Salamanca, Km. 3,20
49800 Toro (Zamora)
☎: +34 649 761 324
bodega.salgadonarros@yahoo.com

PICO ROYO 2009 T
tinta de Toro.

82 Colour: black cherry. Nose: powerfull, overripe fruit, warm. Palate: powerful, fine bitter notes, spicy.

PICO ROYO 2007 T
tinta de Toro.

87 Colour: cherry, garnet rim. Nose: powerfull, ripe fruit, toasty. Palate: powerful, flavourful, fine bitter notes.

BODEGA NOS RIQUEZA

Sánchez Calvo, 6
33402 Avilés (Asturias)
☎: +34 984 836 826 - Fax: +34 985 931 074
exportmanager@nosriqueza.com
www.nosriqueza.com

NOS RIQUEZA 16 MESES 2008 T
100% tinta de Toro.

91 Colour: cherry, garnet rim. Nose: ripe fruit, spicy, creamy oak, toasty. Palate: powerful, flavourful, toasty, round tannins.

NOS RIQUEZA 2005 TC
100% tinta de Toro.

87 Colour: deep cherry. Nose: creamy oak, spicy, ripe fruit. Palate: flavourful, spicy, ripe fruit.

BODEGA NUMANTHIA

Real, s/n
49882 Valdefinjas (Zamora)
☎: +34 980 699 147 - Fax: +34 980 699 164
www.numanthia.com

TERMANTHIA 2008 T
100% tinta de Toro.

95 Colour: cherry, garnet rim. Nose: spicy, creamy oak, toasty, complex, fruit expression, red berry notes, scrubland. Palate: powerful, flavourful, toasty, round tannins.

TERMANTHIA

TERMANTHIA 2009 T
100% tinta de Toro.

95 Colour: dark-red cherry. Nose: powerfull, varietal, characterful, creamy oak, new oak, sweet spices, red berry notes. Palate: fleshy, flavourful, concentrated, fruity, round tannins.

NUMANTHIA 2008 T
100% tinta de Toro.

95 Colour: bright cherry. Nose: ripe fruit, sweet spices, creamy oak, fresh, varietal. Palate: flavourful, fruity, toasty, round tannins.

NUMANTHIA 2009 T
100% tinta de Toro.

94 Colour: bright cherry. Nose: sweet spices, creamy oak, expressive, red berry notes, fruit expression. Palate: flavourful, fruity, toasty, round tannins.

TERMES 2008 T
tinta de Toro.

94 Colour: bright cherry. Nose: sweet spices, creamy oak, expressive, powerfull, ripe fruit, red berry notes, lactic notes. Palate: flavourful, fruity, toasty, round tannins.

TERMES 2009 T
100% tinta de Toro.

93 Color bright cherry. Aroma ripe fruit, sweet spices, creamy oak, expressive. Taste flavourful, fruity, toasty, round tannins.

BODEGA PAGO DE CUBAS

Ctra. Toro Valdefinjas, Km. 6,9
49882 Valdefinjas (Zamora)
☎: +34 980 568 125 - Fax: +34 980 059 965

INCRÉDULO 2009 T
tinta de Toro.

88 Colour: bright cherry. Nose: ripe fruit, sweet spices, creamy oak, aged wood nuances. Palate: flavourful, fruity, toasty, round tannins.

BODEGA TAURINO

Finca Los Prados, s/n
47529 Villafranca de Duero (Valladolid)
☎: +34 983 481 076 - Fax: +34 983 481 076
info@taurino.es
www.taurino.es

TAURINO 2007 T

88 Color cherry, garnet rim. Aroma ripe fruit, spicy, creamy oak, toasty, complex. Taste powerful, flavourful, toasty, round tannins.

BODEGAS A. VELASCO E HIJOS S.L.

Ctra. Tordesillas. Pol. Ind. Norte - Parc. 17-18
49800 Toro (Zamora)
☎: +34 980 692 455 - Fax: +34 980 692 455
tecnico@bodegasvelascoehijos.com
www.bodegasvelascoehijos.com

GARABITAS SELECCIÓN 2009 TC
100% tinta de Toro.

88 Colour: cherry, garnet rim. Nose: powerfull, ripe fruit, roasted coffee, cocoa bean. Palate: powerful, fine bitter notes, fleshy, round tannins.

PEÑA REJAS 2009 T ROBLE
100% tinta de Toro.

88 Colour: bright cherry. Nose: ripe fruit, sweet spices, expressive. Palate: flavourful, fruity, toasty, round tannins.

PEÑA REJAS 2008 TC
100% tinta de Toro.

89 Colour: cherry, garnet rim. Nose: ripe fruit, spicy, creamy oak, toasty, characterful, varietal. Palate: powerful, flavourful, toasty, round tannins.

GARABITAS SELECCIÓN VIÑAS VIEJAS 2008 T
100% tinta de Toro.

86 Colour: cherry, garnet rim. Nose: creamy oak, aromatic coffee, dark chocolate, ripe fruit. Palate: powerful, spicy, ripe fruit.

BODEGAS CAMPIÑA S. COOP. CYL.

Ctra. Toro-Veniablo, Km. 6,9
49882 Valdefinjas (Zamora)
☎: +34 980 568 125 - Fax: +34 980 059 965
info@bodegascampina.com
www.bodegascampina.com

CAMPIÑA 2010 T
100% tinta de Toro.

86 Colour: cherry, garnet rim. Nose: fruit preserve, powerfull. Palate: fruity, fleshy, balanced, round tannins.

CAMPIÑA 2009 T ROBLE
tinta de Toro.

86 Colour: cherry, garnet rim. Nose: powerfull, ripe fruit, warm. Palate: powerful, fine bitter notes.

CAMPIÑA 2008 TC
100% tinta de Toro.

86 Colour: cherry, garnet rim. Nose: powerfull, fruit preserve, dark chocolate, spicy. Palate: flavourful, fleshy, spicy.

BODEGAS CARMEN RODRÍGUEZ

Ctra. Salamanca, ZA 605, Km. 1,6
49800 Toro (Zamora)
☎: +34 980 568 005
crcarodorum@yahoo.es

CARODORUM SELECCIÓN 2008 TC
tinta de Toro.

92 Colour: cherry, garnet rim. Nose: earthy notes, ripe fruit, creamy oak, sweet spices. Palate: flavourful, powerful, fleshy.

CARODORUM 2008 TC
tinta de Toro.

89 Colour: bright cherry. Nose: sweet spices, creamy oak, fruit expression. Palate: flavourful, toasty, round tannins.

CARODORUM 2007 TC
tinta de Toro.

88 Colour: deep cherry, garnet rim. Nose: balanced, toasty, spicy, warm. Palate: flavourful, good structure, long.

BODEGAS COPABOCA

N-122, Km. 407
47114 Tordesillas (Valladolid)
☎: +34 983 395 655 - Fax: +34 983 307 729
santiago@copaboca.com
www.copaboca.com

GORGORITO 2010 T
100% tinta de Toro.

88 Colour: cherry, garnet rim. Nose: powerfull, fruit expression, red berry notes. Palate: flavourful, powerful, fleshy, grainy tannins.

GORGORITO SELECCIÓN 2010 T ROBLE
100% tinta de Toro.

87 Colour: bright cherry. Nose: ripe fruit, red berry notes, balsamic herbs. Palate: flavourful, fruity, fine bitter notes.

BODEGAS COVITORO

Ctra. de Tordesillas, 13
49800 Toro (Zamora)
☎: +34 980 690 347 - Fax: +34 980 690 143
santiago@covitoro.com
www.covitoro.com

CERMEÑO 2010 B
95% malvasía, 5% verdejo.

87 Colour: bright straw, greenish rim. Nose: white flowers, medium intensity, tropical fruit. Palate: flavourful, easy to drink.

CERMEÑO 2010 RD
100% tinta de Toro.

85 Colour: brilliant rose. Nose: powerfull, candied fruit, red berry notes. Palate: powerful, flavourful, fleshy.

CERMEÑO VENDIMIA SELECCIONADA 2010 T
100% tinta de Toro.

89 Colour: cherry, purple rim. Nose: fresh fruit, red berry notes, floral. Palate: flavourful, fruity, good acidity, round tannins.

BACO DE COVITORO 2009 T ROBLE
100% tinta de Toro.

86 Colour: bright cherry, garnet rim. Nose: sweet spices, cocoa bean, ripe fruit. Palate: fruity, round tannins, spicy.

ARCO DEL RELOJ 2008 T
100% tinta de Toro.

92 Colour: bright cherry. Nose: sweet spices, creamy oak, fruit expression, mineral. Palate: flavourful, fruity, toasty, round tannins.

CAÑUS VERUS 2007 T
100% tinta de Toro.

90 Colour: cherry, garnet rim. Nose: powerfull, ripe fruit, spicy, cocoa bean. Palate: spicy, ripe fruit.

GRAN CERMEÑO 2007 TC
100% tinta de Toro.

87 Colour: garnet rim. Nose: warm, toasty, ripe fruit. Palate: flavourful, fruity.

MARQUÉS DE LA VILLA 2004 TR
100% tinta de Toro.

88 Colour: cherry, garnet rim. Nose: ripe fruit, spicy, toasty, smoky. Palate: powerful, flavourful, toasty, round tannins.

BODEGAS FARIÑA

Camino del Palo, s/n
49800 Toro (Zamora)
☎: +34 980 577 673 - Fax: +34 980 577 720
comercial@bodegasfarina.com
www.bodegasfarina.com

COLEGIATA 2010 RD
100% tinta de Toro.

89 Colour: brilliant rose. Nose: elegant, candied fruit, dried flowers, fragrant herbs, red berry notes. Palate: light-bodied, flavourful, good acidity, long, spicy.

PRIMERO 2010 T MACERACIÓN CARBÓNICA
tinta de Toro.

88 Colour: deep cherry. Nose: fresh fruit, red berry notes, floral. Palate: flavourful, fruity, fresh, fleshy.

GRAN COLEGIATA CAMPUS 2006 TC
100% tinta de Toro.

94 Colour: cherry, garnet rim. Nose: spicy, creamy oak, toasty, complex, balsamic herbs. Palate: powerful, flavourful, round tannins, mineral.

GRAN COLEGIATA ROBLE FRANCÉS 2006 TC
100% tinta de Toro.

91 Colour: cherry, garnet rim. Nose: ripe fruit, spicy, creamy oak. Palate: powerful, flavourful, toasty, round tannins.

GRAN COLEGIATA VINO DE LÁGRIMA 2009 T ROBLE
tinta de Toro.

87 Color bright cherry. Aroma ripe fruit, sweet spices, creamy oak, expressive. Taste flavourful, fruity, toasty, round tannins.

GRAN COLEGIATA 2004 TC
100% tinta de Toro.

87 Colour: cherry, garnet rim. Nose: ripe fruit, spicy, creamy oak, toasty. Palate: powerful, toasty, round tannins.

BODEGAS FRANCISCO CASAS

Paseo de San Cosme, 6
28600 Navalcarnero (Madrid)
☎: +34 918 110 207 - Fax: +34 918 110 798
f.casas@bodegascasas.com
www.bodegascasas.com

CAMPARRÓN 2010 B
100% malvasía.

83 Colour: bright straw. Nose: medium intensity, ripe fruit, grassy. Palate: flavourful, fruity, fleshy.

CAMPARRÓN SELECCION 2010 T
tinta de Toro.

89 Colour: cherry, purple rim. Nose: fresh fruit, red berry notes, floral, toasty. Palate: flavourful, fruity, good acidity, round tannins.

CAMPARRÓN NOVUM 2010 T
tinta de Toro.

87 Colour: cherry, purple rim. Nose: medium intensity, red berry notes, balanced. Palate: fruity, good structure, fleshy.

ABBA 2008 T
100% tinta de Toro.

88 Colour: bright cherry. Nose: ripe fruit, sweet spices, creamy oak. Palate: flavourful, fruity, toasty, round tannins.

CAMPARRÓN 2008 TC
100% tinta de Toro.

86 Colour: cherry, garnet rim. Nose: ripe fruit, toasty, sweet spices. Palate: flavourful, ripe fruit, long.

CAMPARRÓN 2006 TR
100% tinta de Toro.

87 Colour: cherry, garnet rim. Nose: spicy, creamy oak, toasty, ripe fruit. Palate: powerful, flavourful, round tannins.

BODEGAS GIL LUNA

Ctra. Toro - Salamanca, Km. 2
49800 Toro (Zamora)
☎: +34 980 698 509 - Fax: +34 980 698 294
pbgiluna@giluna.com
www.giluna.com

TRES LUNAS ECOLÓGICO 2009 T
95% tinta de Toro, 5% garnacha.

83 Colour: deep cherry. Nose: fruit preserve, toasty, spicy, woody. Palate: fleshy, toasty.

TRES LUNAS 2008 T
95% tinta de Toro, 5% garnacha.

89 Colour: bright cherry, garnet rim. Nose: medium intensity, complex, ripe fruit, spicy. Palate: flavourful, fruity, long.

GIL LUNA 2006 T
95% tinta de Toro, 5% garnacha.

87 Colour: bright cherry. Nose: ripe fruit, sweet spices, creamy oak, fine reductive notes. Palate: flavourful, fruity, toasty, round tannins.

BODEGAS MONTE LA REINA

Ctra. Toro - Zamora, Km. 436,7
49881 Toro (Zamora)
☎: +34 980 082 011 - Fax: +34 980 082 012
bodega@montelareina.es
www.montelareina.es

CASTILLO MONTE LA REINA 2009 T ROBLE
100% tempranillo.

89 Colour: cherry, garnet rim. Nose: red berry notes, ripe fruit, dark chocolate, cocoa bean, sweet spices, toasty. Palate: good acidity, flavourful, fleshy, toasty.

TERTIUS 2009 T ROBLE
100% tempranillo.

88 Colour: cherry, garnet rim. Nose: red berry notes, ripe fruit, spicy, cocoa bean, dark chocolate, creamy oak. Palate: powerful, flavourful, fleshy, long.

CASTILLO MONTE LA REINA 2008 T FERMENTADO EN BARRICA
100% tempranillo.

89 Colour: cherry, garnet rim. Nose: balsamic herbs, red berry notes, ripe fruit, sweet spices, creamy oak. Palate: powerful, complex, fleshy, flavourful.

CASTILLO MONTE LA REINA VERDEJO 2010 B
100% verdejo.

86 Colour: bright straw. Nose: fragrant herbs, citrus fruit, tropical fruit. Palate: light-bodied, fresh, fruity, flavourful.

INARAJA 2005 T
100% tempranillo.

92 Colour: cherry, garnet rim. Nose: complex, powerfull, creamy oak, sweet spices, cocoa bean, ripe fruit. Palate: fleshy, powerful, flavourful, round tannins, good structure.

CASTILLO MONTE LA REINA VENDIMIA SELECCIONADA 2005 T
100% tempranillo.

91 Colour: pale ruby, brick rim edge. Nose: ripe fruit, powerfull, aromatic coffee, sweet spices. Palate: powerful, complex, fleshy, balanced.

BODEGAS REJADORADA S.L.

Rejadorada, 11
49800 Toro (Zamora)
☎: +34 980 693 089 - Fax: +34 980 693 089
rejadorada@rejadorada.com
www.rejadorada.com

BRAVO DE REJADORADA 2008 T
100% tinta de Toro.

91 Colour: cherry, garnet rim. Nose: toasty, dark chocolate, ripe fruit, powerfull. Palate: powerful, fleshy, spicy, ripe fruit.

NOVELLUM REJADORADA 2007 TC
tinta de Toro.

90 Colour: cherry, garnet rim. Nose: ripe fruit, spicy, creamy oak, toasty, characterful, varietal. Palate: powerful, flavourful, round tannins.

SANGO DE REJADORADA 2006 TR
100% tinta de Toro.

90 Colour: cherry, garnet rim. Nose: roasted coffee, aromatic coffee, fruit preserve. Palate: spicy, ripe fruit, fine bitter notes.

REJADORADA ROBLE 2009 T ROBLE
100% tinta de Toro.

87 Colour: cherry, garnet rim. Nose: ripe fruit, toasty, aromatic coffee. Palate: powerful, concentrated, fine bitter notes.

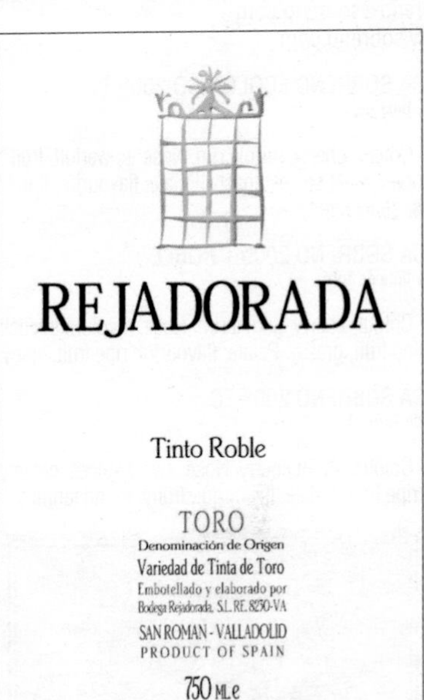

BODEGAS SIETECERROS

Finca Villaester -Villaester de Arriba
47540 Pedrosa del Rey (Valladolid)
☎: +34 983 784 083 - Fax: +34 983 784 142
sietecerros@bodegasietecerros.com
www.bodegasietecerros.com

QUEBRANTARREJAS 2009 T
100% tinta de Toro.

85 Colour: cherry, garnet rim. Nose: powerfull, warm, fruit liqueur notes, toasty, spicy. Palate: powerful, spicy, ripe fruit.

VALDELAZARZA 2006 TC
100% tinta de Toro.

86 Colour: cherry, garnet rim. Nose: spicy, wild herbs, ripe fruit. Palate: flavourful, fruity.

BODEGAS SOBREÑO

Ctra. N-122, Km. 423
49800 Toro (Zamora)
☎: +34 980 693 417 - Fax: +34 980 693 416
sobreno@sobreno.com
www.sobreno.com

FINCA SOBREÑO ECOLÓGICO 2009 T
100% tinta de Toro.

87 Colour: cherry, purple rim. Nose: powerfull, fruit preserve, sweet spices, toasty. Palate: flavourful, fine bitter notes, good acidity.

FINCA SOBREÑO 2009 T ROBLE
100% tinta de Toro.

86 Colour: cherry, garnet rim. Nose: medium intensity, candied fruit, grassy. Palate: flavourful, ripe fruit, spicy.

FINCA SOBREÑO 2008 TC
tinta de Toro.

87 Colour: bright cherry. Nose: sweet spices, creamy oak, ripe fruit. Palate: flavourful, fruity, round tannins.

BODEGAS TORESANAS

Ctra. Tordesillas, s/n
49800 Toro (Zamora)
☎: +34 983 868 116 - Fax: +34 983 868 432
info@taninia.com
www.toresanas.com

AMANT NOVILLO 2010 T
100% tinta de Toro.

88 Colour: deep cherry, purple rim. Nose: red berry notes, balanced, varietal. Palate: fruity, balanced, long.

AMANT 2009 T ROBLE
100% tinta de Toro.

87 Colour: bright cherry. Nose: ripe fruit, sweet spices, creamy oak. Palate: flavourful, fruity, toasty, round tannins.

OROT 2005 TC
100% tinta de Toro.

88 Colour: cherry, garnet rim. Nose: creamy oak, sweet spices, ripe fruit. Palate: powerful, concentrated, fleshy.

BODEGAS TORREDUERO

Pol. Ind. Norte - Parcela 5
49800 Toro (Zamora)
☎: +34 980 693 421 - Fax: +34 980 693 422
bodega@bodegastorreduero.com
www.bodegastorreduero.com

PEÑAMONTE 2010 B
100% verdejo.

83 Colour: bright straw. Nose: floral, candied fruit, citrus fruit. Palate: fleshy, fine bitter notes, good acidity.

PEÑAMONTE 2010 RD
85% tinta de Toro, 15% garnacha.

85 Colour: rose, purple rim. Nose: red berry notes, ripe fruit. Palate: flavourful, fruity, easy to drink, fine bitter notes.

PEÑAMONTE 2010 T
100% tinta de Toro.

80 Colour: bright cherry, purple rim. Nose: medium intensity, dried herbs. Palate: light-bodied, lacks expression.

PEÑAMONTE 2009 T BARRICA
100% tinta de Toro.

88 Colour: bright cherry. Nose: ripe fruit, sweet spices. Palate: flavourful, fruity, toasty, round tannins.

MARQUÉS DE PEÑAMONTE 2008 T ROBLE
100% tinta de Toro.

88 Colour: cherry, garnet rim. Nose: red berry notes, ripe fruit, powerfull, spicy, roasted coffee. Palate: balanced, flavourful, powerful, fleshy.

PEÑAMONTE 2007 TC
tinta de Toro.

87 Colour: cherry, garnet rim. Nose: ripe fruit, spicy, cocoa bean, expressive. Palate: powerful, flavourful, fleshy, toasty.

MARQUÉS DE PEÑAMONTE 2006 TR
100% tinta de Toro.

88 Colour: cherry, garnet rim. Nose: powerfull, ripe fruit, creamy oak, sweet spices. Palate: spicy, ripe fruit, round tannins.

PEÑAMONTE 2006 TC
100% tinta de Toro.

87 Colour: cherry, garnet rim. Nose: cocoa bean, spicy, toasty, ripe fruit. Palate: flavourful, fleshy, balsamic, light-bodied.

BODEGAS VEGA SAUCO

Avda. Comuneros, 108
49810 Morales de Toro (Zamora)
☎: +34 980 698 294 - Fax: +34 980 698 294
vegasauco@vegasauco.com
www.vegasauco.com

VEGA SAÚCO EL BEYBI 2009 T ROBLE
100% tinta de Toro.

84 Colour: cherry, garnet rim. Nose: fruit preserve, toasty, spicy. Palate: ripe fruit, flavourful.

VEGA SAÚCO "TO" 2008 TC
100% tinta de Toro.

86 Colour: cherry, garnet rim. Nose: spicy, creamy oak, toasty, complex. Palate: powerful, toasty, round tannins.

ADOREMUS 2005 TR
100% tinta de Toro.

91 Colour: cherry, garnet rim. Nose: complex, sweet spices, ripe fruit, creamy oak. Palate: good structure, fleshy, round tannins.

ADOREMUS 2001 TGR
100% tinta de Toro.

90 Colour: cherry, garnet rim. Nose: powerfull, wet leather, ripe fruit, sweet spices. Palate: powerful, fleshy, toasty.

BODEGAS Y PAGOS MATARREDONDA

Ctra. Toro - Valdefinjas, km. 2,5
49800 Toro (Zamora)
☎: +34 980 059 981 - Fax: +34 980 059 981
libranza@vinolibranza.com
www.vinolibranza.com

JUAN ROJO 2006 T
tinta de Toro.

92 Colour: black cherry, cherry, garnet rim. Nose: red berry notes, ripe fruit, mineral, sweet spices, creamy oak. Palate: good acidity, round, powerful, flavourful, round tannins.

LIBRANZA 2006 T RESERVA ESPECIAL
tinta de Toro.

90 Colour: cherry, garnet rim. Nose: ripe fruit, spicy, creamy oak, toasty, complex. Palate: powerful, flavourful, toasty.

LIBRANZA 2006 T
tinta de Toro.

88 Colour: dark-red cherry, garnet rim. Nose: powerfull, complex, ripe fruit, spicy, toasty. Palate: flavourful, powerful, fleshy, long.

BODEGAS Y VIÑEDOS ANZIL

Avda. Europa 20, Bajo Parque Empresarial La Moraleja
28108 Alcobendas (Madrid)
☎: +34 915 006 000 - Fax: +34 915 006 006
rrpp@vina-mayor.es
wwwbodegasanzil.es

VIÑA MAYOR TORO 2008 T
tinta de Toro.

90 Colour: deep cherry, garnet rim. Nose: ripe fruit, spicy, balanced, varietal. Palate: ripe fruit, flavourful, good structure.

FINCA ANZIL VENDIMIA SELECCIONADA 2007 T
tinta de Toro.

88 Colour: bright cherry, garnet rim. Nose: medium intensity, ripe fruit, sweet spices. Palate: powerful, toasty.

BODEGAS Y VIÑEDOS BURLÓN

Perú, 10 - 4º dcha.
47004 Valladolid (Valladolid)
☎: +34 983 302 245 - Fax: +34 983 308 553
info@bodegasburlon.com
www.bodegasburlon.com

VIÑA EL TORILÓN 2008 TC

88 Colour: cherry, garnet rim. Nose: balanced, ripe fruit, cocoa bean, sweet spices. Palate: long, balanced, good acidity.

VIÑA TORILÓN 2006 TR

88 Colour: very deep cherry. Nose: dark chocolate, toasty, ripe fruit. Palate: spicy, ripe fruit.

BODEGAS Y VIÑEDOS MAURODOS

Ctra. N-122, Km. 412 - Villaester
47112 Pedrosa del Rey (Valladolid)
☎: +34 983 784 418 - Fax: +34 983 784 018
comunicacion@bodegasmauro.com
www.bodegasanroman.com

PRIMA 2009 TC
90% tinta de Toro, 10% garnacha.

88 Colour: bright cherry. Nose: sweet spices, fruit preserve, toasty, roasted coffee. Palate: flavourful, fruity, toasty, round tannins.

SAN ROMÁN 2008 T
100% tinta de Toro.

93 Colour: bright cherry. Nose: creamy oak, expressive, fruit expression, cocoa bean. Palate: flavourful, fruity, toasty, round tannins.

BODEGAS Y VIÑEDOS PINTIA

Ctra. de Morales, s/n
47530 San Román de Hornija (Valladolid)
☎: +34 983 680 147 - Fax: +34 983 680 263
vegasicilia@vega-sicilia.com
www.vega-sicilia.com

PINTIA 2008 T
100% tinta de Toro.

96 Colour: very deep cherry. Nose: powerfull, ripe fruit, fruit expression, raspberry, cocoa bean. Palate: flavourful, spicy, ripe fruit, fine bitter notes, good acidity.

BODEGAS Y VIÑEDOS VALDUERO

Ctra. de Aranda, s/n
09443 Gumiel de Mercado (Burgos)
☎: +34 947 545 459 - Fax: +34 947 545 609
valduero@bodegasvalduero.com
www.bodegasvalduero.com

ARBUCALA 2008 T

88 Colour: very deep cherry, garnet rim. Nose: toasty, dark chocolate, fruit preserve. Palate: fleshy, powerful, toasty, spicy, long.

BODEGUEROS QUINTA ESENCIA

Eras, 37
47520 Castronuño (Valladolid)
☎: +34 605 887 100 - Fax: +34 983 866 391
ferrin@bodeguerosquintaesencia.com
www.bodeguerosquintaesencia.com

SOFROS 2009 T
100% tinta de Toro.

89 Colour: bright cherry. Nose: ripe fruit, sweet spices, roasted coffee. Palate: flavourful, fruity, toasty, round tannins.

CAÑADA DEL PINO

Pol. Ind. 6 - Parcela 83
49810 Morales de Toro (Zamora)
☎: +34 676 701 918 - Fax: +34 980 698 318
fincayerro@terra.es

CIRIO 2009 T

85 Colour: cherry, purple rim. Nose: ripe fruit, warm. Palate: fruity, fleshy, flavourful, great length.

FINCA YERRO 2008 T ROBLE

88 Color bright cherry. Aroma ripe fruit, sweet spices, creamy oak, expressive. Taste flavourful, fruity, toasty, round tannins.

CEPAS Y BODEGAS

Paseo de Zorrilla, 77 - 3º D
47001 Valladolid (Valladolid)
☎: +34 983 355 543 - Fax: +34 983 340 824
info@cepasybodegas.com
www.cepasybodegas.com

ACONTIA 2009 T
100% tinta de Toro.

88 Colour: cherry, garnet rim. Nose: ripe fruit, spicy, creamy oak, toasty. Palate: powerful, flavourful, toasty, round tannins.

VIÑALCASTA 2009 T ROBLE
100% tinta de Toro.

87 Colour: cherry, garnet rim. Nose: balanced, ripe fruit, sweet spices. Palate: powerful, fruity, spicy, round tannins.

VIÑALCASTA 2007 TC
100% tinta de Toro.

89 Colour: bright cherry. Nose: ripe fruit, sweet spices, creamy oak. Palate: flavourful, fruity, toasty, round tannins.

COMPAÑÍA DE VINOS TELMO RODRÍGUEZ

El Monte, s/n
01308 Lanciego (Álava)
☎: +34 945 628 315 - Fax: +34 945 628 314
contact@telmorodriguez.com
www.telmorodriguez.com

GAGO 2008 T
100% tinta de Toro.

91 Colour: cherry, garnet rim. Nose: red berry notes, dark chocolate, aromatic coffee, toasty, balsamic herbs. Palate: ripe fruit, powerful, flavourful, complex, fleshy.

PAGO LA JARA 2007 T
100% tinta de Toro.

92 Colour: cherry, garnet rim. Nose: red berry notes, ripe fruit, expressive, mineral, dark chocolate, sweet spices, toasty. Palate: powerful, rich, flavourful, balanced.

CORAL DUERO

Ascensión, s/n
49154 El Pego (Zamora)
☎: +34 980 606 333 - Fax: +34 980 606 333
rompesedas@rompesedas.com
www.rompesedas.com

ROMPESEDAS FINCA LAS PARVAS 2006 T
tinta de Toro.

92 Colour: cherry, garnet rim. Nose: ripe fruit, spicy, creamy oak, toasty, expressive, varietal. Palate: flavourful, toasty, round tannins.

ROMPESEDAS 2006 T
100% tinta de Toro.

90 Colour: cherry, garnet rim. Nose: spicy, creamy oak, toasty. Palate: powerful, flavourful, toasty, round tannins.

DOMINIO DEL BENDITO

Pza. Santo Domingo, 8
49800 Toro (Zamora)
☎: +34 980 693 306 - Fax: +34 980 694 991
info@bodegadominiodelbendito.es

DOMINIO DEL BENDITO EL PRIMER PASO 2009 T ROBLE
100% tinta de Toro.

91 Colour: cherry, garnet rim. Nose: powerfull, ripe fruit, creamy oak, dark chocolate. Palate: powerful, flavourful, fleshy, toasty, long.

EL TITÁN DEL BENDITO 2008 T
100% tinta de Toro.

95 Colour: cherry, garnet rim. Nose: ripe fruit, creamy oak, toasty, complex, expressive, characterful. Palate: powerful, flavourful, toasty, round tannins, mineral.

EL TITÁN DEL BENDITO 2007 T
100% tinta de Toro.

93 Colour: deep cherry, garnet rim. Nose: powerfull, cocoa bean, warm, expressive. Palate: good structure, flavourful, full.

DOMINIO DEL BENDITO LAS SABIAS 16 MESES 2007 T
100% tinta de Toro.

91 Colour: cherry, garnet rim. Nose: spicy, creamy oak, toasty, complex. Palate: powerful, flavourful, toasty, round tannins.

ESTANCIA PIEDRA S.L.

Ctra. Toro a Salamanca, km. 5
49800 Toro (Zamora)
☎: +34 980 693 900 - Fax: +34 980 693 901
info@estanciapiedra.com
www.estanciapiedra.com

PIEDRA 2010 RD
100% tinta de Toro.

88 Color rose, purple rim. Aroma powerfull, ripe fruit, red berry notes, floral, expressive. Taste fleshy, powerful, fruity, fresh.

PIEDRA ROJA 2007 TC
100% tinta de Toro.

90 Color cherry, garnet rim. Aroma ripe fruit, spicy, creamy oak, toasty, complex. Taste powerful, flavourful, toasty, round tannins.

LA GARONA 2006 T
75% tinta de Toro, 25% garnacha.

88 Colour: cherry, garnet rim. Nose: spicy, creamy oak, roasted coffee. Palate: powerful, flavourful, toasty, round tannins.

PIEDRA PAREDINAS 2005 T
100% tinta de Toro.

93 Colour: cherry, garnet rim. Nose: spicy, creamy oak, toasty, complex, fruit expression. Palate: powerful, flavourful, toasty, round tannins.

PIEDRA PLATINO SELECCIÓN 2005 TR
100% tinta de Toro.

91 Colour: cherry, garnet rim. Nose: spicy, toasty, complex, sweet spices. Palate: powerful, flavourful, round tannins.

FRUTOS VILLAR

Eras de Santa Catalina, s/n
49800 Toro (Zamora)
☎: +34 983 586 868 - Fax: +34 983 580 180
bodegasfrutosvillar@bodegasfrutosvillar.com
www.bodegasfrutosvillar.com

MURUVE 2010 T
tinta de Toro.

88 Colour: cherry, purple rim. Nose: fresh fruit, red berry notes. Palate: flavourful, fruity, good acidity, round tannins.

MURUVE ÉLITE 2008 T
100% tinta de Toro.

89 Colour: deep cherry, garnet rim. Nose: spicy, balanced, complex, cocoa bean, toasty. Palate: good structure, fruity, flavourful.

MURUVE 2008 TC
100% tinta de Toro.

88 Colour: cherry, garnet rim. Nose: powerfull, toasty, spicy, smoky. Palate: powerful, fleshy, fine bitter notes.

MURUVE 2008 T ROBLE
tinta de Toro.

87 Colour: cherry, purple rim. Nose: ripe fruit, medium intensity, spicy. Palate: flavourful, good structure, fleshy.

MURUVE 2007 TR
100% tinta de Toro.

88 Colour: cherry, garnet rim. Nose: spicy, creamy oak, toasty, warm. Palate: powerful, toasty, round tannins.

HACIENDA TERRA D'URO

Campanas, 4
47001 (Valladolid)
☎: +34 983 362 591
haciendaterraduro@yahoo.es

TERRA D'URO 2009 T
tinta de Toro.

90 Color bright cherry. Aroma ripe fruit, sweet spices, creamy oak, expressive. Taste flavourful, fruity, toasty, round tannins.

URO 2008 T
tinta de Toro.

93 Colour: cherry, garnet rim. Nose: ripe fruit, spicy, creamy oak, earthy notes. Palate: powerful, flavourful, toasty, round tannins.

TERRA D'URO SELECCIÓN 2008 T
tinta de Toro.

92 Colour: cherry, garnet rim. Nose: ripe fruit, spicy, creamy oak, toasty. Palate: powerful, flavourful, toasty, round tannins.

LIBERALIA ENOLÓGICA

Camino del Palo, s/n
49800 Toro (Zamora)
☎: +34 980 692 571 - Fax: +34 980 692 571
byvliberalia@hotmail.com
www.liberalia.es

LIBERALIA CERO 2010 T FERMENTADO EN BARRICA
100% tinta de Toro.

90 Colour: bright cherry. Nose: ripe fruit, sweet spices, creamy oak. Palate: flavourful, fruity, toasty, round tannins.

LIBERALIA TRES 2010 T ROBLE
100% tinta de Toro.

89 Colour: cherry, purple rim. Nose: fruit expression, red berry notes, sweet spices. Palate: flavourful, fruity, good structure.

LIBERALIA CABEZA DE CUBA 2007 TC
100% tinta de Toro.

92 Colour: bright cherry. Nose: ripe fruit, sweet spices, creamy oak, earthy notes. Palate: flavourful, toasty, round tannins.

LIBERALIA CUATRO 2007 TC
100% tinta de Toro.

88 Colour: cherry, garnet rim. Nose: ripe fruit, spicy, cocoa bean. Palate: flavourful, powerful, round tannins.

ANCESTROS 2006 TR
100% tinta de Toro.

92 Colour: deep cherry. Nose: complex, expressive, spicy, mineral, ripe fruit. Palate: good structure, fleshy, round tannins.

LIBERALIA CINCO 2005 TR
100% tinta de Toro.

92 Colour: bright cherry, garnet rim. Nose: balanced, expressive, varietal, ripe fruit. Palate: flavourful, good structure, fleshy, ripe fruit.

LIBER 2004 TGR
100% tinta de Toro.

92 Colour: deep cherry, garnet rim. Nose: ripe fruit, spicy, complex. Palate: good structure, spicy, ripe fruit.

MARQUÉS DE OLIVARA

Eras de Santa Catalina, s/n
49800 Toro (Zamora)
☎: +34 980 693 425 - Fax: +34 980 693 409
marquesdeolivara@marquesdeolivara.com
www.marquesdeolivara.com

VIÑAS DE OLIVARA 2010 T
tinta de Toro.

87 Colour: bright cherry. Nose: ripe fruit, sweet spices, expressive. Palate: flavourful, fruity, round tannins.

MARQUÉS DE OLIVARA VENDIMIA SELECCIONADA 2008 T
100% tinta de Toro.

88 Color cherry, garnet rim. Aroma ripe fruit, spicy, creamy oak, toasty, complex. Taste powerful, flavourful, toasty, round tannins.

MARQUÉS DE OLIVARA 2008 TC
tinta de Toro.

87 Colour: cherry, garnet rim. Nose: powerfull, warm, ripe fruit, toasty, aromatic coffee. Palate: powerful, spicy, toasty.

MATSU

Gral. Vara del Rey, 7 1º Dcha.
26003 Logroño (La Rioja)
☎: +34 941 271 217 - Fax: +34 941 272 911
info@bodegamatsu.com
www.bodegamatsu.com

MATSU EL PÍCARO 2010 T
100% tinta de Toro.

89 Colour: cherry, purple rim. Nose: red berry notes, raspberry, floral, mineral. Palate: round, unctuous, good acidity, fruity, fleshy.

MATSU EL RECIO 2009 T
100% tinta de Toro.

90 Colour: cherry, garnet rim. Nose: red berry notes, ripe fruit, spicy, creamy oak, powerfull, expressive, mineral. Palate: powerful, flavourful, fleshy, complex.

MATSU EL VIEJO 2008 T
tinta de Toro.

92 Colour: cherry, garnet rim. Nose: ripe fruit, earthy notes, cocoa bean, sweet spices, toasty. Palate: unctuous, powerful, fleshy, flavourful.

PAGOS DEL REY

Avda. de los Comuneros, 90
49810 Morales de Toro (Zamora)
☎: +34 980 698 023 - Fax: +34 980 698 020
pdr@pagosdelrey.com
www.pagosdelrey.com

FINCA LA MEDA 2010 B
malvasía.

83 Colour: bright straw. Nose: powerfull, candied fruit, medium intensity. Palate: fine bitter notes, varietal, flavourful.

BAJOZ MALVASÍA 2010 B
malvasía.

82 Colour: bright straw. Nose: white flowers, candied fruit. Palate: flavourful, powerful, fine bitter notes.

BAJOZ 2010 RD
tinta de Toro.

86 Colour: rose, purple rim. Nose: ripe fruit, raspberry. Palate: flavourful, fruity, fresh, fleshy.

FINCA LA MEDA 2010 RD
tinta de Toro.

82 Colour: rose, purple rim. Nose: medium intensity, dried herbs. Palate: fine bitter notes, slightly acidic.

OUNO 2010 T
tinta de Toro.

88 Colour: cherry, garnet rim. Nose: powerfull, ripe fruit, violet drops. Palate: flavourful, powerful, fine bitter notes.

CAÑO TEMPRANILLO 2010 T
tinta de Toro.

87 Colour: cherry, purple rim. Nose: fresh fruit, grassy, medium intensity. Palate: correct, easy to drink, fruity, balsamic.

BAJOZ 2010 T JOVEN
tinta de Toro.

86 Colour: cherry, purple rim. Nose: balsamic herbs, fruit expression, spicy. Palate: flavourful, fruity, fleshy.

FINCA LA MEDA 2010 T
tinta de Toro.

86 Colour: deep cherry, purple rim. Nose: fresh fruit, grassy. Palate: fruity, easy to drink.

CAÑO TEMPRANILLO GARNACHA 2010 T
tempranillo, garnacha.

86 Colour: cherry, purple rim. Nose: fresh fruit, grassy, spicy. Palate: flavourful, fruity, fleshy.

FINCA LA MEDA 2007 TC
tinta de Toro.

90 Colour: cherry, garnet rim. Nose: spicy, creamy oak, toasty, characterful. Palate: powerful, flavourful, toasty, round tannins.

BAJOZ 2007 TC
tinta de Toro.

87 Colour: cherry, garnet rim. Nose: powerfull, warm, ripe fruit. Palate: spicy, good acidity.

CAÑO 2007 TC
tinta de Toro.

87 Colour: deep cherry, garnet rim. Nose: aromatic coffee, spicy, ripe fruit. Palate: good structure, flavourful, toasty.

FINCA LA MEDA ALTA EXPRESIÓN 2006 T
tinta de Toro.

92 Colour: cherry, garnet rim. Nose: spicy, creamy oak, toasty, mineral, ripe fruit. Palate: powerful, flavourful, toasty, round tannins.

GRAN BAJOZ DE AUTOR 2006 TC
tinta de Toro.

91 Colour: cherry, garnet rim. Nose: ripe fruit, spicy, creamy oak, toasty. Palate: powerful, flavourful, round tannins.

PALACIO DE VILLACHICA

Ctra. Nacional 122, Km. 433
49800 Toro (Zamora)
☎: +34 983 372 289 - Fax: +34 983 381 356
admin@palaciodevillachica.com
www.palaciodevillachica.com

PALACIO DE VILLACHICA 2010 T
100% tinta de Toro.

87 Colour: deep cherry, purple rim. Nose: medium intensity, red berry notes. Palate: fruity, good structure.

PALACIO DE VILLACHICA 2009 T ROBLE
tinta de Toro.

86 Colour: bright cherry, garnet rim. Nose: fruit preserve, sweet spices, cocoa bean. Palate: fleshy, flavourful.

PALACIO DE VILLACHICA 2008 TC
tinta de Toro.

87 Colour: deep cherry, garnet rim. Nose: red berry notes, ripe fruit, balanced, spicy. Palate: flavourful, fruity.

PALACIO DE VILLACHICA SELECCIÓN 2005 T
100% tinta de Toro.

89 Colour: cherry, garnet rim. Nose: spicy, creamy oak, toasty, characterful. Palate: toasty, round tannins, spicy.

QUINOLA SUÁREZ

Paseo de Zorrilla, 11- 4 izq.
47007 Valladolid (Valladolid)
☎: +34 625 227 321
garagewine@quinola.es
www.quinola.es

QUINOLA GARAGE WINE 2008 T ROBLE
100% tinta de Toro.

90 Colour: black cherry, garnet rim. Nose: powerfull, ripe fruit, cocoa bean, toasty, mineral. Palate: powerful, flavourful, fleshy, toasty.

QUINTA DE LA QUIETUD

Tomás Bayón, 56
47491 La Seca (Valladolid)
☎: +34 983 034 995 - Fax: +34 983 034 995
maritesacris@hotmail.com
www.quintaquietud.com

CORRAL DE CAMPANAS 2009 T
100% tinta de Toro.

92 Colour: cherry, garnet rim. Nose: powerfull, ripe fruit, creamy oak, spicy. Palate: ripe fruit, balsamic, complex.

LA MULA DE LA QUIETUD 2007 T
100% tinta de Toro.

88 Colour: black cherry. Nose: powerfull, fruit liqueur notes, fruit preserve, roasted coffee. Palate: powerful, sweetness, fleshy.

ACTITUD DE LA QUIETUD 2006 T
tinta de Toro.

92 Colour: bright cherry. Nose: sweet spices, creamy oak, expressive, ripe fruit, red berry notes, lactic notes. Palate: flavourful, fruity, toasty, round tannins.

QUINTA QUIETUD 2006 T
100% tinta de Toro.

90 Colour: cherry, garnet rim. Nose: spicy, dried herbs, fruit liqueur notes. Palate: complex, fruity, good structure, spicy.

RODRÍGUEZ SANZO

Manuel Azaña, 9- Local 15
47014 Valladolid (Valladolid)
☎: +34 983 150 150 - Fax: +34 983 150 151
valsanzo@valsanzo.com
www.valsanzo.com

TERRAS DE JAVIER RODRÍGUEZ 2009 T
tinta de Toro.

92 Colour: bright cherry. Nose: sweet spices, creamy oak, red clay notes, ripe fruit, fruit expression. Palate: flavourful, fruity, toasty, round tannins, long.

SEÑORITA MALAUVA "MARIDAJE BOUTIQUE"

Esquina Catedral Cascajares s/n
47002 (Valladolid)
☎: +34 983 394 955 - Fax: +34 983 394 955
info@vinotecamalauva.es
www.vinotecamalauva.es

SEÑORITA MALAUVA "EXPRESIÓN TERROIR" ARMONÍA 3 2008 T
tinta de Toro.

88 Colour: bright cherry. Nose: sweet spices, creamy oak, ripe fruit. Palate: flavourful, fruity, toasty, round tannins.

SEÑORITA MALAUVA "EXPRESIÓN TERROIR" ARMONÍA 5 2007 T
tinta de Toro.

87 Colour: cherry, garnet rim. Nose: creamy oak, overripe fruit, roasted coffee. Palate: powerful, flavourful, toasty, round tannins.

TERNA BODEGAS

Cuatro Calles, s/n
47491 La Seca (Valladolid)
☎: +34 983 103 223 - Fax: +34 983 816 561
info@sitiosdebodega.com
www.sitiosdebodega.com

MORFEO "CEPAS VIEJAS" 2009 T
tinta de Toro.

90 Colour: bright cherry. Nose: sweet spices, creamy oak, expressive, red berry notes, ripe fruit. Palate: flavourful, fruity, toasty, round tannins, fleshy.

MORFEO 2008 T
100% tinta de Toro.

89 Colour: black cherry. Nose: balanced, complex, ripe fruit, spicy. Palate: flavourful, fleshy, round tannins.

TESO LA MONJA

Paraje Valdebuey- Ctra. ZA-611, Km. 6,3
49882 Valdefinjas (Zamora)
☎: +34 980 568 143 - Fax: +34 980 508 144
info@eguren.com
www.eguren.com

VICTORINO 2009 T
tinta de Toro.

96 Colour: bright cherry. Nose: ripe fruit, sweet spices, creamy oak, expressive, scrubland, earthy notes, mineral. Palate: flavourful, fruity, mineral, roasted-coffee aftertaste, round tannins.

ALABASTER 2009 T
100% tinta de Toro.

96 Colour: black cherry. Nose: spicy, creamy oak, toasty, complex, fruit expression, raspberry, ripe fruit, mineral, dry stone. Palate: powerful, flavourful, toasty, round tannins.

ALMIREZ 2009 T
100% tinta de Toro.

94 Colour: deep cherry. Nose: balanced, varietal, ripe fruit, red berry notes, creamy oak. Palate: creamy, ripe fruit, long.

VICTORINO 2008 T
100% tinta de Toro.

97 Colour: deep cherry. Nose: fruit expression, raspberry, powerfull, characterful, sweet spices, creamy oak. Palate: ripe fruit, long, fleshy, powerful, flavourful.

ALABASTER 2008 T
100% tinta de Toro.

96 Colour: cherry, garnet rim. Nose: ripe fruit, spicy, creamy oak, complex, powerfull, aged wood nuances, new oak. Palate: powerful, flavourful, toasty, round tannins.

ALMIREZ 2008 T
tinta de Toro.

93 Colour: dark-red cherry. Nose: powerfull, varietal, characterful, fruit expression, mineral. Palate: flavourful, powerful, fleshy, fruity.

VALBUSENDA

Ctra. Peleagonzalo - Zamora, s/n
49800 Toro (Zamora)
☎: +34 980 699 560 - Fax: +34 980 699 566
comercial@valbusenda.com
www.valbusenda.com

VALBUSENDA CEPAS VIEJAS 2008 T
100% tinta de Toro.

87 Colour: cherry, garnet rim. Nose: balanced, ripe fruit, sweet spices, powerfull. Palate: ripe fruit, spicy, fleshy, round tannins.

VALBUSENDA 2007 TC
tinta de Toro.

88 Colour: very deep cherry, garnet rim. Nose: spicy, toasty, ripe fruit. Palate: fruity, flavourful, round tannins.

VALBUSENDA 2007 T ROBLE
100% tinta de Toro.

87 Colour: bright cherry. Nose: ripe fruit, sweet spices, creamy oak. Palate: flavourful, toasty, round tannins.

VALBUSENDA 2004 TR

87 Colour: cherry, garnet rim. Nose: ripe fruit, spicy, creamy oak. Palate: powerful, flavourful, round tannins.

VETUS

Ctra. Toro a Salamanca, Km. 9,5
49800 Toro (Zamora)
☎: +34 945 609 086 - Fax: +34 980 056 012
vetus@bodegasvetus.com
www.bodegasvetus.com

CELSUS 2009 T
tinta de Toro.

93 Colour: cherry, garnet rim. Nose: powerfull, varietal, mineral, earthy notes, ripe fruit. Palate: flavourful, powerful, fleshy, spicy, ripe fruit, balanced.

FLOR DE VETUS 2009 T
100% tinta de Toro.

91 Colour: bright cherry. Nose: ripe fruit, sweet spices, creamy oak, mineral, varietal. Palate: fruity, toasty, round tannins.

VETUS 2007 T
tinta de Toro.

94 Colour: cherry, garnet rim. Nose: ripe fruit, spicy, creamy oak, toasty, complex. Palate: powerful, flavourful, toasty, round tannins, full.

VIÑAGUAREÑA

Ctra. Toro a Salamanca, Km. 12,5
49800 Toro (Zamora)
☎: +34 980 568 013 - Fax: +34 980 568 134
info@vinotoro.com
www.vinotoro.com

IDUNA 2010 B
100% verdejo.

88 Colour: bright yellow. Nose: sweet spices, creamy oak, ripe fruit. Palate: fruity, flavourful.

MUNIA 2009 T ROBLE
100% tinta de Toro.

85 Colour: cherry, purple rim. Nose: sweet spices, overripe fruit. Palate: warm, flavourful, ripe fruit, round tannins.

MUNIA 2008 TC
100% tinta de Toro.

87 Colour: cherry, garnet rim. Nose: powerfull, ripe fruit, sweet spices. Palate: powerful, fleshy, spicy.

MUNIA ESPECIAL 2008 T ROBLE
100% tinta de Toro.

86 Colour: cherry, garnet rim. Nose: powerfull, ripe fruit, fruit expression, dark chocolate, aromatic coffee. Palate: spicy, fine bitter notes.

VIÑEDOS ALONSO DEL YERRO

Finca Santa Marta - Ctra. Roa-Anguix, Km. 1,8
09300 Roa (Burgos)
☎: +34 913 160 121 - Fax: +34 913 160 121
mariadelyerro@vay.es
www.alonsodelyerro.com

PAYDOS 2008 T
100% tinta de Toro.

93 Colour: cherry, garnet rim. Nose: spicy, creamy oak, toasty, elegant, ripe fruit. Palate: powerful, flavourful, toasty, round tannins.

VIÑEDOS DE VILLAESTER

Villaester de Arriba
47540 Pedrosa del Rey (Valladolid)
☎: +34 948 645 008 - Fax: +34 948 645 166
info@familiabelasco.com
www.familiabelasco.com

VILLAESTER 2004 T
tinta de Toro.

91 Colour: deep cherry. Nose: ripe fruit, creamy oak, dark chocolate. Palate: fleshy, toasty, ripe fruit.

VOCARRAJE

Ctra. San Román, s/n
49810 Moral de Toro (Zamora)
☎: +34 980 698 172 - Fax: +34 980 698 172
info@vocarraje.es
www.vocarraje.es

ABDÓN SEGOVIA 2009 T ROBLE
100% tinta de Toro.

81 Colour: cherry, garnet rim. Nose: overripe fruit, powerfull, warm. Palate: powerful, ripe fruit.

ABDÓN SEGOVIA 2008 TC
100% tinta de Toro.

91 Colour: cherry, garnet rim. Nose: ripe fruit, spicy, creamy oak, mineral. Palate: powerful, flavourful, toasty, round tannins.

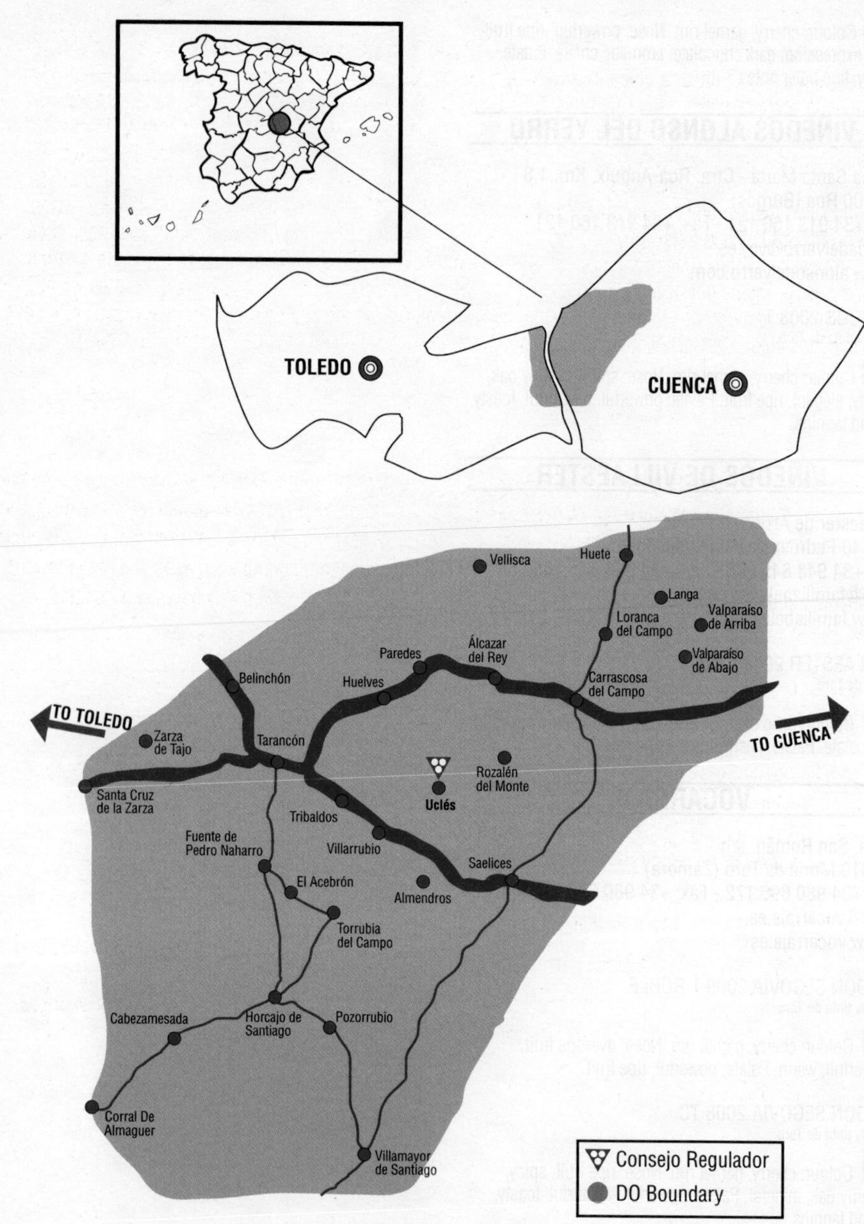
TOLEDO
CUENCA
Vellisca
Huete
Langa
Loranca del Campo
Valparaíso de Arriba
Paredes
Álcazar del Rey
Valparaíso de Abajo
Belinchón
Huelves
Carrascosa del Campo
TO TOLEDO
TO CUENCA
Zarza de Tajo
Tarancón
Rozalén del Monte
Santa Cruz de la Zarza
Uclés
Tribaldos
Fuente de Pedro Naharro
Villarrubio
Saelices
El Acebrón
Almendros
Torrubia del Campo
Cabezamesada
Horcajo de Santiago
Pozorrubio
Corral De Almaguer
Villamayor de Santiago
Consejo Regulador
DO Boundary

NEWS ABOUT THE VINTAGE:

Uclés is yet another wine region around the infinite territory of La Mancha. Its main city is Tarancón, in the province of Cuenca, a place that was historically a centre for the storage and distribution of bulk wines. A few years ago, the region decided to part with its mother-region, under the consideration that Uclés had a kind of geo-climatic singularity that had little to do with that of La Mancha. To start with, Uclés vines are planted mainly in higher and more diverse soils than those from La Mancha, a fact that seemed to rush its independence. The 2010 vintage in the region was a cool one, so there is a little increase in the average scores for the young wines of that year. The most veteran wineries in the region, Fontana and Finca la Estacada, also get the best scores, although it is perhaps difficult to assess their true position within Uclés ranking, considering that 120! wineries have decided not to send us their samples, probably out of fear of a critical score, of just because their main business is on bulk wine, a badly paid product that somehow keeps the region alive; also we should bear in mind that many of those wineries included in Uclés list may be labelling their products as VT Castilla or even DO La Mancha.

LOCATION:

Midway between Cuenca (to the west) and Toledo (to the northwest), this DO is made up of 25 towns from the first province and three from the second. However, the majority of vineyards are situated in Tarancón and the neighbouring towns of Cuenca, as far as Huete - where La Alcarria starts - the largest stretch of border in the DO.

CLIMATE:

The Altamira sierra forms gentle undulations that rise from an average of 600 metres in La Mancha, reaching 1,200 metres. These ups and downs produce variations in the continental climate, which is less extreme, milder and has a Mediterranean touch. As such, rain is scarce, more akin to a semi-dry climate.

SOIL:

Despite spreading over two provinces with different soil components, the communal soils are deep and not very productive, of a sandy and consistent texture, becoming more clayey as you move towards the banks of the rivers Riansares and Bendija.

GRAPE VARIETIES:

RED: *Tempranillo, Merlot, Cabernet Sauvignon, Garnacha* and *Syrah.*
WHITE: *Verdejo, Moscatel de Grano Menudo, Chardonnay, Sauvignon Blanc* and *Viura (macabeo).*

FIGURES:

Vineyard surface: 1,700 – **Wine-Growers:** 122 – **Wineries:** 5 – **2010 Harvest rating:** Good – **Production:** 180,000 litres – **Market percentages:** 30% domestic. 70% export

CONSEJO REGULADOR
Avda. Miguel Cervantes, 93
16400 Tarancón (Cuenca)
☎: +34 969 135 056 - Fax: +34 969 135 421
@ gerente@vinosdeucles.com
www.vinosdeucles.com

GENERAL CHARACTERISTICS OF THE WINES

REDS	The majority are *Cencibel*, producing young and also slightly aged wines, defined by aromas of very fresh grape skins, a very flavoursome and rounded body, and fruit with an alcohol content/acidity balance better controlled than in other nearby areas of La Mancha. Far removed from those more rustic wines, a hint of terroir and extra minerals is detected in these, due to the presence of minerals dissolved in the soils.

VINTAGE RATING PEÑINGUIDE

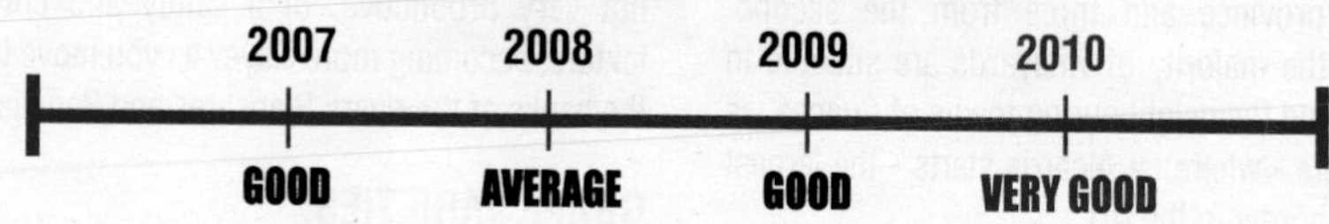

CAMPOS DE VIENTO

Avda. Diagonal, 590 - 5º 1ª
08021 Barcelona (Barcelona)
☎: +34 660 445 464
info@vinergia.com
www.vinergia.com

CAMPOS DE VIENTO 2010 T
100% tempranillo.

86 Colour: cherry, purple rim. Nose: floral, red berry notes, raspberry, lactic notes. Palate: good acidity, light-bodied, fresh, fruity.

COOPERATIVA NUESTRA SEÑORA DE LA SOLEDAD

Ctra. Tarancón, s/n
16411 Fuente de Pedro Naharro (Cuenca)
☎: +34 969 125 039 - Fax: +34 969 125 907
info@bodegasoledad.com
www.bodegasoledad.com

SOLMAYOR 2010 B
chardonnay, sauvignon blanc.

83 Colour: bright straw. Nose: tropical fruit, grapey, white flowers. Palate: powerful, fresh, fruity.

SOLMAYOR 2010 T
tempranillo.

84 Colour: cherry, purple rim. Nose: red berry notes, ripe fruit, warm, medium intensity. Palate: good acidity, powerful, flavourful, fleshy.

SOLMAYOR 2010 T ROBLE
tempranillo.

84 Colour: cherry, garnet rim. Nose: red berry notes, ripe fruit, spicy, creamy oak. Palate: flavourful, fleshy, thin.

SOLMAYOR 2007 TC
tempranillo.

86 Colour: cherry, garnet rim. Nose: red berry notes, ripe fruit, warm, spicy, toasty. Palate: spicy, toasty, powerful, flavourful.

FINCA LA ESTACADA

Ctra. N-400, Km. 103
16400 Tarancón (Cuenca)
☎: +34 969 327 099 - Fax: +34 969 327 199
enologia@fincalaestacada.com
www.fincalaestacada.com

FINCA LA ESTACADA 2010 B
chardonnay, sauvignon blanc.

84 Colour: bright straw. Nose: fresh fruit, powerfull, tropical fruit. Palate: flavourful, fruity, sweetness, slightly acidic.

LA ESTACADA 2009 TC
syrah, merlot.

91 Colour: bright cherry. Nose: sweet spices, creamy oak, earthy notes, ripe fruit. Palate: flavourful, fruity, toasty, round tannins.

FINCA LA ESTACADA 6 MESES BARRICA 2009 T ROBLE
tempranillo.

88 Colour: deep cherry. Nose: expressive, ripe fruit, sweet spices, creamy oak. Palate: flavourful, fleshy, good acidity, fine tannins.

FONTANA

Extramuros, s/n
16411 Fuente de Pedro Naharro (Cuenca)
☎: +34 969 125 433 - Fax: +34 969 125 387
gemag@bodegasfontana.com
www.bodegasfontana.com

ESENCIA DE FONTANA 2008 T
100% tempranillo.

90 Colour: cherry, garnet rim. Nose: red berry notes, ripe fruit, cocoa bean, dark chocolate, sweet spices, creamy oak. Palate: good acidity, powerful, flavourful, fleshy.

LA VID Y LA ESPIGA

San Antón, 30
16415 Villamayor de Santiago (Cuenca)
☎: +34 969 139 069 - Fax: +34 969 139 069
export@vidyespiga.es
www.bodegasvidyespiga.es

CAÑADA REAL 2010 B
50% sauvignon blanc, 50% verdejo.

84 Colour: bright straw. Nose: dried flowers, citrus fruit, ripe fruit. Palate: fresh, fruity, flavourful, easy to drink.

CAÑADA REAL 2010 RD
tempranillo.

84 Colour: onion pink, bright. Nose: grapey, ripe fruit, dried flowers. Palate: good acidity, balanced, flavourful, fleshy.

CAÑADA REAL 2010 T
tempranillo.

85 Colour: cherry, purple rim. Nose: red berry notes, raspberry, fruit preserve, sweet spices. Palate: good acidity, unctuous, flavourful.

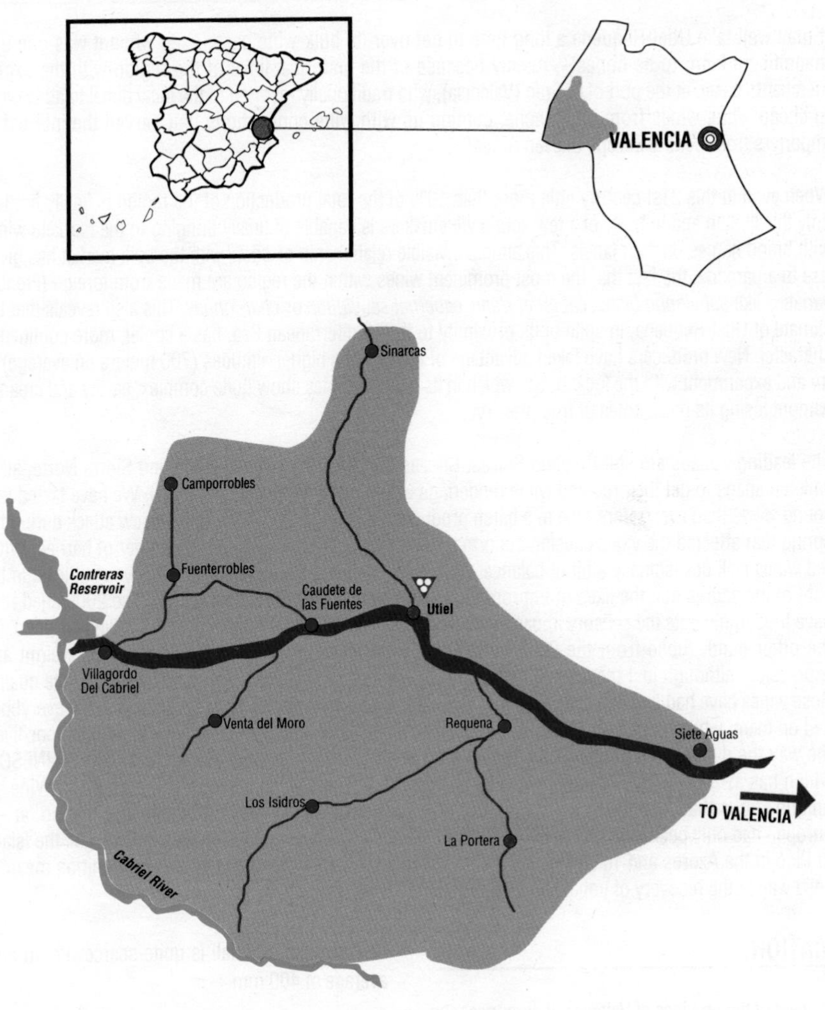

Consejo Regulador
DO Boundary

NEWS ABOUT THE VINTAGE:

It may well take Utiel-Requena a long time to get over its bulk-wine past –even when it was one of a magnificent kind, to be honest–, mainly because of the historical links of the region with the export merchants based at the port of El Grao (Valencia), who traditionally resorted to the local bobal to add colour to cheap white wines from La Mancha, coming up with wine concoctions that served the interest of importers from Central Europe of even Africa!.

When even in this 21st century little more than 10% of the total production of the region is finally bottled, only the illusion and tenacity of a few young winemakers is capable of finally bringing to the markets wines with brand names on their labels. This almost invisible relationship of *bobal* with the bulk market has given rise to a paradox, the fact that the most prominent wines within the region are made from foreign (French) varieties like *sauvignon blanc*, *cabernet franc*, *cabernet sauvignon* or *chardonnay*. This also reveals that the climate of Utiel-Requena, in spite of its proximity to the Mediterranean Sea, has a cooler, more continental character. New producers have taken advantage of the region's higher altitudes (700 meters on average) to try and experiment with the local bobal, which in its best examples show quite complex, earthy and creamy, without losing its basic notes of fruit preserve.

The leading houses are still Hispano Suizas, Chozas Carrascal, Vera de Estenas and Sierra Norte, all of which manage to get their red and white renderings within the top rankings of the DO. We have tasted less young wines than ever before, due to a harsh production decrease (20%) due to a mildew attack during the spring that affected the vines causing abnormal fruit set and a serious fall in the number of berries. While red wines lack occasionally a bit of balance, white wine samples were exceptional this year, at least in the light of the scores that the likes of Impromptu, Las Tres and Cerro Bercial finally got. The 2009 aged reds have tried to mitigate the sensory impact of overripeness with an equal excess of wood, failing all along. On the other hand, those from the 2008 vintage are exemplary in terms of freshness, fruit weight and expression, although just the leading names, for the rest of wineries show a much lower average quality. Rosé wines have had two bad years in a row that have done away with the high expectations that everybody had on them, when made from *bobal*. Leaving aside the quality of the wines, we have to mention positively the way the dynamic character of the region's wineries has been recognised this year by the UNESCO, which has awarded Utiel-Requena with the first Spanish "Cultural Landscape of the Vine and Wine", a unique status that recognizes a wine history that goes back more than 2500 years and that so far –in Europe– had only been awarded to Saint-Émilion in France, the river Douro terraces in Portugal, the Island of Pico in the Azores and Tokaj-Hegyalja region in Hungary. We only hope that this recognition means a solid way to the recovery of bobal and its promotion to wine stardom.

LOCATION:

In thewest of the province of Valencia. It comprises the municipal districts of Camporrobles, Caudete de las Fuentes, Fuenterrobles, Requena, Siete Aguas, Sinarcas, Utiel, Venta del Moro and Villagordo de Cabriel.

CLIMATE:

Continental,with Mediterranean influences, coldwinters and slightly milder summers than in other regions of the province. Rainfall is quite scarcewith an annual average of 400 mm.

SOIL:

Mainly brownish-grey, almost red limestone, poor in organic matter andwith good permeability. The horizon of the vineyards are broken by the silhouette of the odd tree planted in the middle of the vineyards,which, bordered bywoods, offer a very attractive landscape.

GRAPE VARIETIES:

RED: *Bobal, Tempranillo, Garnacha, Cabernet Sauvignon, Merlot, Syrah, Pinot Noir, Garnacha Tintorera, Petit Verdot* and *Cabernet Franc.*
WHITE: *Tardana, Macabeo, Merseguera, Chardonnay, Sauvignon Blanc, Parellada, Xarel.lo, Verdejo, Moscatel de Grano Menudo, Viognier* and *Albariño.*

FIGURES:

Vineyard surface: 36,633 – **Wine-Growers:** 6,297 – **Wineries:** 108 – **2010 Harvest rating:** Very Good – **Production:** 28,406,000 litres – **Market percentages:** 29% domestic. 71% export

CONSEJO REGULADOR
Sevilla, 12. Apdo. 61
46300 Utiel (Valencia)
☎: +34 962 171 062 - Fax: +34 962 172 185
@ info@utielrequena.org
www.utielrequena.org

GENERAL CHARACTERISTICS OF THE WINES

WHITES	Firstly, there are the most traditional from *Merseguera*, fresh with wild notes; secondly, the more modern variety from *Macabeo*, with greater aromatic potency, fresh and light; and finally, single variety wines from *Chardonnay*, some fermented in barrels.
ROSÉS	Produced from *Bobal*, they have a pink to salmon colour; their aromas are fresh and fruity,with some what wild and vegetative aromas; on the palate they are fresh and pleasant.
REDS	As opposed to the traditional wines from *Bobal*, with a lot of colour but with some what rustic notes, the *Garnacha* variety gives rise to young, fresh, fruity and very correct red wines. For the Crianza wines some *Bobal* is included. Those of this type are flavourful, rounded and, on occasion, some what warm.
SPARKLING	Cavas and Espumosos are produced according to the traditional methods not included in the DO Cava.

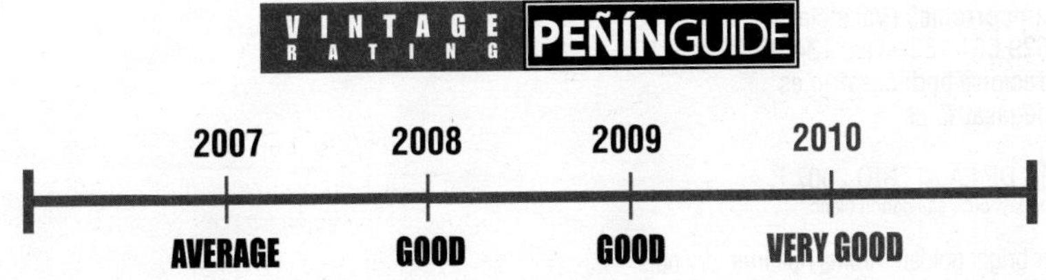

BODEGA Y VIÑEDOS CARRES

Francho, 1
46352 Casas de Eufema (Valencia)
☎: +34 675 515 729
contacto@bodegacarres.com
www.bodegacarres.com

EL OLIVASTRO 2009 T
bobal.

90 Colour: cherry, garnet rim. Nose: powerfull, ripe fruit, sweet spices, toasty, earthy notes. Palate: powerful, concentrated, fleshy.

BODEGAS ARANLEÓN

Ctra. Caudete, 3
46310 Los Marcos - Caudete de las Fuentes (Valencia)
☎: +34 963 631 640 - Fax: +34 962 185 150
maria@aranleon.com
www.aranleon.com

AHORA ARANLEÓN 2009 TC
bobal, merlot, cabernet sauvignon, tempranillo, syrah.

85 Colour: cherry, purple rim. Nose: warm, overripe fruit, creamy oak. Palate: fresh, fruity, good finish.

ARANLEÓN SÓLO 2007 T
30% bobal, 40% tempranillo, 30% syrah.

87 Colour: cherry, garnet rim. Nose: ripe fruit, cocoa bean, caramel. Palate: correct, flavourful, toasty.

ARANLEÓN HELIX 2005 T ROBLE
10% bobal, 20% merlot, 30% tempranillo, 40% cabernet sauvignon.

89 Colour: cherry, garnet rim. Nose: ripe fruit, spicy, creamy oak, toasty, characterful. Palate: powerful, flavourful, toasty, round tannins.

BODEGAS ATRIO

Apóstol Santiago, 42
46330 Camporrobles (Valencia)
☎: +34 629 661 183 - Fax: +34 962 181 518
administracion@bodegasatrio.es
www.bodegasatrio.es

MATTICES DE LA ATTRIO 2007 B
50% chardonnay, 50% sauvignon blanc.

89 Color bright golden. Aroma ripe fruit, dry nuts, powerfull, toasty, aged wood nuances. Taste flavourful, fruity, spicy, toasty, long.

PASSION DE LA BODEGA 2005 T ROBLE
75% bobal, 20% cabernet sauvignon, 5% merlot.

91 Colour: cherry, garnet rim. Nose: ripe fruit, spicy, creamy oak, toasty, characterful. Palate: powerful, flavourful, toasty, round tannins.

SEDUCCIÓN DE LA BODEGA 2005 T
75% bobal, 15% syrah, 10% tempranillo.

88 Colour: cherry, garnet rim. Nose: spicy, toasty, fruit preserve, candied fruit. Palate: powerful, flavourful, toasty, round tannins.

BODEGAS FINCA ARDAL

Ctra. N-322, Km. 452
46340 Requena (Valencia)
☎: +34 962 302 835 - Fax: +34 962 302 835
bodega@fincaardal.com
www.fincaardal.com

TANUS 2007 TC
70% tempranillo, 20% syrah, 10% bobal.

88 Colour: cherry, garnet rim. Nose: fruit liqueur notes, fruit liqueur notes, toasty, varnish, old leather. Palate: spicy, ripe fruit, fine bitter notes.

OCHO CUERDAS 2006 TC
40% cabernet sauvignon, 40% syrah, 20% merlot.

88 Colour: cherry, garnet rim. Nose: spicy, creamy oak, toasty. Palate: powerful, flavourful, toasty, round tannins.

LAGAR DE LAR 2005 TC
60% tempranillo, 25% cabernet sauvignon, 15% merlot.

91 Colour: black cherry, brick rim edge. Nose: spicy, mineral, balsamic herbs, expressive, elegant. Palate: balanced, round, flavourful, fleshy.

OCHO CUERDAS BOBAL 2005 TC
100% bobal.

87 Colour: bright cherry. Nose: sweet spices, ripe fruit, toasty. Palate: flavourful, fruity, toasty, round tannins.

BODEGAS HISPANO SUIZAS

Ctra. N-322, Km. 451,7
46357 El Pontón (Valencia)
☎: +34 962 138 318 - Fax: +34 962 138 318
info@bodegashispanosuizas.com
www.bodegashispanosuizas.com

IMPROMPTU 2010 B
100% sauvignon blanc.

94 Colour: bright yellow. Nose: powerfull, ripe fruit, sweet spices, fragrant herbs. Palate: rich, smoky aftertaste, flavourful, fresh, good acidity.

BASSUS DULCE BOBAL-PINOT NOIR RD
bobal, pinot noir.

90 Colour: coppery red. Nose: caramel, aged wood nuances, sweet spices, candied fruit. Palate: powerful, fruity, flavourful.

BASSUS PREMIUM 2008 T
bobal, cabernet franc, syrah, merlot, petit verdot.

91 Colour: cherry, garnet rim. Nose: spicy, creamy oak, toasty, dark chocolate, aromatic coffee. Palate: powerful, flavourful, toasty, round tannins.

BASSUS PINOT NOIR 2008 T
100% pinot noir.

90 Colour: cherry, garnet rim. Nose: expressive, elegant, ripe fruit, spicy. Palate: flavourful, sweetness, fleshy.

QUOD SUPERIUS 2007 T
bobal, cabernet franc, syrah, merlot.

91 Colour: cherry, garnet rim. Nose: spicy, creamy oak, toasty, fruit liqueur notes, earthy notes. Palate: powerful, flavourful, toasty, round tannins.

BODEGAS MURVIEDRO

Ampliación Pol. El Romeral, s/n
46340 Requena (Valencia)
☎: +34 962 329 003 - Fax: +34 962 329 002
murviedro@murviedro.es
www.murviedro.es

CUEVA DE LA ESPERA 2010 B
80% chardonnay, 20% pinot noir.

88 Colour: bright straw. Nose: fresh, fresh fruit, white flowers, expressive, honeyed notes. Palate: flavourful, fruity, good acidity, balanced.

COROLILLA VERDEJO 2010 B
100% verdejo.

83 Colour: bright golden. Nose: candied fruit, citrus fruit. Palate: flavourful, fleshy.

MURVIEDRO COLECCIÓN TEMPRANILLO 2010 T
100% tempranillo.

85 Colour: cherry, garnet rim. Nose: powerfull, ripe fruit, fruit liqueur notes. Palate: powerful, concentrated, warm.

COROLILLA 2008 TC
100% bobal.

91 Colour: cherry, garnet rim. Nose: red berry notes, ripe fruit, expressive, earthy notes, toasty. Palate: unctuous, flavourful, fleshy, mineral, spicy.

CUEVA DE LA CULPA 2008 T
60% bobal, 40% merlot.

91 Colour: cherry, garnet rim. Nose: creamy oak, toasty, characterful, balsamic herbs, scrubland. Palate: powerful, flavourful, toasty, round tannins.

COROLILLA 2007 TR
100% bobal.

89 Colour: cherry, garnet rim. Nose: spicy, creamy oak, toasty, fruit expression, red berry notes. Palate: powerful, flavourful, toasty, round tannins.

BODEGAS PALMERA

Paraje Corral Charco de Agut
46300 Utiel (Valencia)
☎: +34 626 706 394
klauslauerbach@hotmail.com
www.bodegas-palmera.com

VIÑA CABRIEL SUPERIOR 2009 T
56% tempranillo, 21% merlot, 23% cabernet sauvignon.

88 Colour: cherry, garnet rim. Nose: red berry notes, ripe fruit, expressive, balsamic herbs, mineral, toasty. Palate: good acidity, flavourful, fleshy.

CAPRICHO 2009 T
55% cabernet sauvignon, 30% merlot, 15% tempranillo.

88 Colour: cherry, garnet rim. Nose: red berry notes, ripe fruit, expressive, balsamic herbs, mineral. Palate: flavourful, fleshy, round tannins.

BOBAL Y TEMPRANILLO SUPERIOR 2008 T
bobal, tempranillo.

90 Colour: cherry, garnet rim. Nose: powerfull, ripe fruit, red berry notes, creamy oak. Palate: powerful, fleshy, spicy.

L'ANGELET 2007 TC
tempranillo, cabernet sauvignon.

90 Colour: cherry, garnet rim. Nose: ripe fruit, earthy notes, mineral, spicy, creamy oak. Palate: good acidity, balanced, fleshy, complex.

BODEGAS SIERRA NORTE

Pol. Ind. El Romeral. Transporte- Parc. C2
46340 Requena (Valencia)
☎: +34 962 323 099 - Fax: +34 962 323 048
info@bodegasierranorte.com
www.bodegasierranorte.com

CERRO BERCIAL SELECCIÓN 2010 B
40% chardonnay, 30% sauvignon blanc, 30% macabeo.

91 Colour: bright straw. Nose: fresh, fresh fruit, white flowers, sweet spices. Palate: flavourful, fruity, good acidity, balanced.

FUENTESECA 2010 B
80% macabeo, 20% sauvignon blanc.

87 Colour: bright straw. Nose: ripe fruit, citrus fruit, white flowers. Palate: flavourful, fruity, fresh.

FUENTESECA 2010 RD
80% bobal, 20% cabernet sauvignon.

86 Colour: rose, purple rim. Nose: ripe fruit, red berry notes, floral, expressive, balsamic herbs. Palate: powerful, fruity, fresh, flavourful.

CERRO BERCIAL 2010 RD
100% bobal.

84 Colour: rose, purple rim. Nose: red berry notes, floral, fruit preserve. Palate: fleshy, powerful, fruity, fresh.

CERRO BERCIAL "EL ROSADO" 2009 RD
40% merlot, 40% bobal, 20% garnacha.

85 Colour: light cherry. Nose: powerfull, warm, candied fruit. Palate: powerful, fleshy, fine bitter notes.

TEMPERAMENTO DE BOBAL 2010 T
100% bobal.

88 Colour: bright cherry. Nose: ripe fruit, sweet spices, creamy oak, expressive, lactic notes. Palate: flavourful, fruity, toasty, round tannins.

FUENTESECA 2010 T
60% bobal, 40% cabernet sauvignon.

84 Colour: cherry, purple rim. Nose: red berry notes, ripe fruit, balsamic herbs. Palate: flavourful, fruity, easy to drink.

PASION DE BOBAL 2009 T
100% bobal.

90 Colour: cherry, garnet rim. Nose: spicy, creamy oak, toasty, ripe fruit, lactic notes, red berry notes. Palate: powerful, flavourful, toasty, round tannins.

CERRO BERCIAL 2008 T BARRICA
65% tempranillo, 35% bobal.

91 Colour: bright cherry. Nose: sweet spices, creamy oak, expressive, lactic notes, raspberry. Palate: flavourful, fruity, toasty, round tannins.

FUENTESECA 2008 TC
100% tempranillo.

88 Colour: bright cherry. Nose: ripe fruit, sweet spices, creamy oak. Palate: flavourful, fruity, toasty, round tannins.

CERRO BERCIAL PARCELA "LADERA LOS CANTOS" 2006 T
63% bobal, 37% cabernet sauvignon.

91 Colour: cherry, garnet rim. Nose: ripe fruit, spicy, creamy oak, toasty, earthy notes. Palate: powerful, flavourful, toasty, round tannins.

CERRO BERCIAL 2006 TC
43% bobal, 57% tempranillo.

88 Colour: cherry, garnet rim. Nose: ripe fruit, spicy, creamy oak, dark chocolate. Palate: powerful, toasty, round tannins.

CERRO BERCIAL 2004 TR
65% tempranillo, 20% bobal, 15% cabernet sauvignon.

90 Colour: cherry, garnet rim. Nose: creamy oak, toasty, complex, sweet spices, wet leather. Palate: powerful, flavourful, toasty, round tannins.

BODEGAS TORRES LUNA

Finca "Los Señoritos"
46352 Campo Arcis - Requena (Valencia)
☎: +34 699 917 543
info@bodegastorresluna.es
www.bodegastorresluna.es

IZÁN DE LUNA 2009 T
cabernet sauvignon, merlot, syrah.

83 Colour: cherry, garnet rim. Nose: ripe fruit, grassy, balsamic herbs. Palate: warm, flavourful, lacks expression.

PREDIO NOAH 2007 TC
cabernet sauvignon, merlot, syrah.

83 Colour: pale ruby, brick rim edge. Nose: overripe fruit, scrubland, short. Palate: good acidity, fleshy, slightly evolved.

PREDIO NOAH SYRAH 2007 T
100% syrah.

82 Colour: pale ruby, brick rim edge. Nose: overripe fruit, scrubland, premature reduction notes. Palate: good acidity, flavourful, thin.

BODEGAS TORROJA

Nogueral, 3
46357 Azagador (Valencia)
☎: +34 962 304 232 - Fax: +34 962 303 833
herve@bodegastorroja.com
www.bodegastorroja.com

CAÑADA MAZÁN TARDANA 2010 B
100% tardana.

87 Colour: bright straw. Nose: fresh, white flowers, expressive, citrus fruit. Palate: flavourful, fruity, good acidity, rich.

SYBARUS TARDANA 2010 B
100% tardana.

87 Colour: bright straw. Nose: fresh, fresh fruit, white flowers. Palate: flavourful, fruity, good acidity, balanced.

CAÑADA MAZÁN BOBAL 2010 RD
100% bobal.

85 Colour: rose, purple rim. Nose: ripe fruit, red berry notes, floral, expressive. Palate: fleshy, powerful, fruity, fresh.

CAÑADA MAZÁN 2007 TC
70% tempranillo, 30% cabernet sauvignon.

87 Colour: cherry, garnet rim. Nose: powerfull, candied fruit, fruit liqueur notes, toasty. Palate: powerful, fleshy, spicy.

SYBARUS BOBAL 2007 T
100% bobal.

86 Colour: cherry, garnet rim. Nose: candied fruit, fruit preserve, warm, creamy oak. Palate: spicy, ripe fruit, fleshy.

SYBARUS SYRAH 2006 TC
100% syrah.

87 Colour: cherry, garnet rim. Nose: aged wood nuances, varnish, fruit liqueur notes, candied fruit. Palate: powerful, concentrated, fruity, round tannins.

SYBARUS RESERVA DE FAMILIA 2003 TR
cabernet sauvignon, merlot, syrah, bobal, pinot noir.

85 Colour: cherry, garnet rim. Nose: spicy, creamy oak, toasty, ripe fruit. Palate: powerful, flavourful, toasty, round tannins.

SYBARUS 2002 TR
80% tempranillo, 15% cabernet sauvignon, 5% merlot.

83 Colour: pale ruby, brick rim edge. Nose: elegant, fine reductive notes, wet leather, aged wood nuances, fruit liqueur notes. Palate: spicy, fine tannins, elegant.

BODEGAS UTIELANAS

San Fernando, 18
46300 Utiel (Valencia)
☎: +34 962 171 157 - Fax: +34 962 170 801
info@bodegasutielanas.com
www.bodegasutielanas.com

VEGA INFANTE 2010 BFB
macabeo.

88 Colour: bright yellow. Nose: powerfull, ripe fruit, sweet spices, fragrant herbs. Palate: rich, smoky aftertaste, flavourful, fresh, good acidity.

VEGA INFANTE 2010 B
macabeo.

87 Colour: bright straw. Nose: fresh, white flowers, expressive, citrus fruit. Palate: flavourful, fruity, good acidity, balanced.

VEGA INFANTE 2010 RD
bobal.

83 Colour: rose. Nose: ripe fruit, medium intensity. Palate: sweetness, ripe fruit.

VEGA INFANTE MADURADO EN BARRICA 2010 T
bobal, tempranillo.

90 Colour: cherry, purple rim. Nose: fruit preserve, lactic notes, creamy oak. Palate: fresh, flavourful, fleshy, toasty.

VEGA INFANTE 2010 T

83 Colour: cherry, purple rim. Nose: ripe fruit, red berry notes. Palate: flavourful, spicy, long.

VEGA INFANTE 2006 TC

87 Colour: cherry, garnet rim. Nose: spicy, creamy oak, toasty, candied fruit. Palate: powerful, flavourful, toasty, round tannins.

VEGA INFANTE 2004 TR
bobal.

88 Color cherry, garnet rim. Aroma ripe fruit, spicy, creamy oak, toasty, complex. Taste powerful, flavourful, toasty, round tannins.

BODEGAS VEREDA REAL

San Sebastián, 85
46340 Requena (Valencia)
☎: +34 962 304 340 - Fax: +34 962 304 340
tecnico@bodegasveredareal.com
www.bodegasveredareal.com

BROTE MACABEO 2010 B
macabeo.

83 Colour: bright straw. Nose: medium intensity, white flowers. Palate: fruity, fresh, flavourful.

BOBALIA 2006 T ROBLE
bobal.

86 Colour: cherry, garnet rim. Nose: ripe fruit, roasted coffee, balsamic herbs. Palate: powerful, toasty, round tannins.

TESORO DE REQUENA 2005 T
bobal.

85 Colour: pale ruby, brick rim edge. Nose: ripe fruit, old leather, spicy, toasty. Palate: powerful, fleshy, flavourful, good acidity.

SELECTTO 2004 TC
tempranillo, bobal, syrah, merlot.

86 Colour: cherry, garnet rim. Nose: spicy, fine reductive notes, toasty, medium intensity. Palate: good acidity, flavourful, round tannins.

ETTNOS 2003 TR
65% bobal, 25% syrah, 10% cabernet sauvignon.

85 Colour: light cherry. Nose: ripe fruit, scrubland, old leather, toasty. Palate: fleshy, flavourful, spicy.

VEREDA REAL BOBAL TGR
bobal.

82 Colour: pale ruby, brick rim edge. Nose: ripe fruit, balsamic herbs, wet leather, spicy. Palate: flavourful, spicy, green.

BODEGAS VICENTE GANDÍA PLA

Ctra. Cheste a Godelleta, s/n
46370 Chiva (Valencia)
☎: +34 962 524 242 - Fax: +34 962 524 243
sgandia@vicentegandia.com
www.vicentegandia.com

FINCA DEL MAR CHARDONNAY 2010 B
100% chardonnay.

87 Colour: bright straw. Nose: fresh, fresh fruit, white flowers, expressive. Palate: flavourful, fruity, good acidity.

HOYA DE CADENAS 2010 B
50% chardonnay, 30% sauvignon blanc, 20% viura.

85 Colour: bright yellow. Nose: white flowers, fruit expression, balsamic herbs, balanced. Palate: good acidity, fresh, fruity.

HOYA DE CADENAS 2010 RD
100% bobal.

83 Colour: rose, purple rim. Nose: balsamic herbs, ripe fruit, floral, fresh. Palate: fresh, fruity, flavourful.

FINCA DEL MAR CABERNET SAUVIGNON 2010 T
100% cabernet sauvignon.

87 Colour: cherry, purple rim. Nose: ripe fruit, balsamic herbs, scrubland. Palate: powerful, flavourful, fleshy.

HOYA DE CADENAS CABERNET SAUVIGNON 2010 T
100% cabernet sauvignon.

85 Colour: cherry, purple rim. Nose: ripe fruit, floral, grassy, warm. Palate: fleshy, powerful, flavourful.

HOYA DE CADENAS SHIRAZ 2010 T
syrah.

85 Colour: cherry, purple rim. Nose: expressive, fresh fruit, red berry notes, floral. Palate: flavourful, fruity, good acidity.

FINCA DEL MAR MERLOT 2010 T
100% merlot.

84 Colour: cherry, purple rim. Nose: red berry notes, ripe fruit, sweet spices. Palate: spicy, light-bodied, fresh, fruity.

HOYA DE CADENAS MERLOT 2009 T
100% merlot.

85 Colour: bright cherry. Nose: sweet spices, creamy oak, expressive, warm. Palate: flavourful, toasty, round tannins.

FINCA DEL MAR TEMPRANILLO 2009 T
100% tempranillo.

84 Colour: cherry, garnet rim. Nose: ripe fruit, balsamic herbs, spicy, creamy oak. Palate: thin, flavourful, fruity.

BO - BOBAL ÚNICO 2008 T
100% bobal.

89 Colour: cherry, garnet rim. Nose: red berry notes, ripe fruit, wild herbs, sweet spices. Palate: fleshy, complex, flavourful.

CEREMONIA 2007 TR
60% tempranillo, 30% cabernet sauvignon, 10% bobal.

88 Colour: cherry, garnet rim. Nose: red berry notes, ripe fruit, balsamic herbs, spicy, toasty. Palate: flavourful, rich, round tannins.

HOYA DE CADENAS RESERVA PRIVADA 2007 TR
85% tempranillo, 15% cabernet sauvignon.

87 Colour: cherry, purple rim. Nose: red berry notes, ripe fruit, violet drops, sweet spices. Palate: powerful, flavourful, fruity, fleshy.

HOYA DE CADENAS TEMPRANILLO 2007 TR
100% tempranillo.

85 Colour: light cherry, orangey edge. Nose: ripe fruit, wild herbs, old leather. Palate: powerful, flavourful, toasty.

GENERACIÓN 1 2006 T
70% bobal, 15% syrah, 15% cabernet sauvignon.

90 Colour: cherry, garnet rim. Nose: ripe fruit, earthy notes, spicy, toasty, expressive. Palate: balanced, unctuous, flavourful, round tannins.

BODEGAS Y VIÑEDOS DE UTIEL

Finca El Renegado, s/n
46315 Caudete de las Fuentes (Valencia)
☎: +34 962 174 029 - Fax: +34 962 171 432
info@bodegasdeutiel.com
www.bodegasdeutiel.com

ACTUM COLECCIÓN MACABEO CHARDONNAY 2010 B
50% macabeo, 50% chardonnay.

86 Color bright straw. Aroma fresh, fresh fruit, white flowers, expressive. Taste flavourful, fruity, good acidity, balanced.

ACTUM SAUVIGNON BLANC 2010 B
100% sauvignon blanc.

85 Colour: bright straw. Nose: fresh, expressive, ripe fruit, faded flowers. Palate: flavourful, fruity, good acidity.

NODUS CHARDONNAY 2010 B
100% chardonnay.

84 Colour: bright straw. Nose: fresh, white flowers, expressive, fragrant herbs. Palate: flavourful, fruity, good acidity, fleshy.

ACTUM COLECCIÓN SYRAH TEMPRANILLO 2010 T
50% syrah, 50% tempranillo.

88 Colour: cherry, garnet rim. Nose: red berry notes, ripe fruit, scrubland, creamy oak. Palate: flavourful, fleshy, spicy.

NODUS TINTO DE AUTOR 2009 TC
25% merlot, 25% cabernet sauvignon, 15% syrah, 15% bobal.

89 Colour: cherry, garnet rim. Nose: cocoa bean, aromatic coffee, sweet spices, ripe fruit. Palate: powerful, flavourful, fleshy, mineral.

CAPELLANA TINTO DE AUTOR 2009 TC
50% cabernet sauvignon, 50% tempranillo.

89 Color bright cherry. Aroma ripe fruit, sweet spices, creamy oak, expressive. Taste flavourful, fruity, toasty, round tannins.

NODUS MERLOT DELIRIUM 2009 T
100% merlot.

87 Colour: cherry, garnet rim. Nose: powerfull, ripe fruit, spicy, toasty. Palate: flavourful, powerful, fleshy, long.

ACTUM VARIETAL 2008 T
80% merlot, 20% cabernet sauvignon.

88 Colour: cherry, garnet rim. Nose: spicy, creamy oak, toasty. Palate: powerful, flavourful, toasty, round tannins.

ACTUM 2007 TC
80% merlot, 20% cabernet sauvignon.

88 Colour: cherry, garnet rim. Nose: ripe fruit, creamy oak, toasty. Palate: powerful, flavourful, toasty, round tannins.

CERRO GALLINA

Artana, 22
12540 Villareal de los Infantes (Castellón)
☎: +34 676 897 251 - Fax: +34 964 920 877
info@cerrogallina.com
www.cerrogallina.com

CERROGALLINA 2008 T
100% bobal.

91 Colour: bright cherry, garnet rim. Nose: medium intensity, red berry notes, ripe fruit, mineral. Palate: fruity, flavourful, round tannins.

CHERUBINO VALSANGIACOMO

Ctra. Cheste - Godelleta, Km. 1
46370 Chiva (Valencia)
☎: +34 962 510 451 - Fax: +34 962 511 361
carlos.valsangiacomo@cherubino.es
www.cherubino.es

MARQUÉS DE CARO 2010 RD
100% bobal.

84 Colour: rose, purple rim. Nose: ripe fruit, red berry notes, floral. Palate: fleshy, powerful, fruity, easy to drink.

DRASSANES 2008 T
60% syrah, 40% cabernet sauvignon.

88 Colour: bright cherry. Nose: sweet spices, creamy oak, candied fruit. Palate: flavourful, fruity, toasty, round tannins.

CHOZAS CARRASCAL

Vereda San Antonio Pol. Ind. Catastral, 16 Parcelas 136-138
46340 San Antonio de Requena (Valencia)
☎: +34 963 410 395 - Fax: +34 963 168 067
chozas@chozascarrascal.es
www.chozascarrascal.es

LAS TRES 2010 BFB
chardonnay, sauvignon blanc, macabeo.

92 Color bright yellow. Aroma powerfull, ripe fruit, sweet spices, creamy oak, fragrant herbs. Taste rich, smoky aftertaste, flavourful, fresh, good acidity.

LAS DOS CES 2010 B
sauvignon blanc.

88 Colour: bright straw. Nose: white flowers, expressive, ripe fruit. Palate: flavourful, fruity, good acidity, balanced.

LAS CUATRO 2010 RD
tempranillo, garnacha, syrah, merlot.

88 Colour: light cherry. Nose: candied fruit, fruit liqueur notes, balsamic herbs, sweet spices, toasty. Palate: fine bitter notes, powerful, fleshy.

LAS DOS CES 2010 T
bobal, tempranillo, syrah.

88 Colour: cherry, purple rim. Nose: red berry notes, ripe fruit, raspberry, balsamic herbs, creamy oak. Palate: good acidity, fruity, flavourful.

EL CF DE CHOZAS CARRASCAL 2008 T
cabernet franc.

94 Colour: cherry, garnet rim. Nose: candied fruit, fruit expression, creamy oak, sweet spices, balsamic herbs, mineral, earthy notes. Palate: flavourful, fleshy, long.

LAS OCHO 2008 T
bobal, monastrell, garnacha, tempranillo, cabernet sauvignon, otras.

92 Colour: cherry, garnet rim. Nose: scrubland, spicy, toasty, ripe fruit, mineral. Palate: good acidity, balanced, flavourful, fleshy.

JUANPEDRÓS 2008 T
bobal.

90 Colour: cherry, garnet rim. Nose: ripe fruit, old leather, tobacco, earthy notes. Palate: good acidity, balanced, fleshy, toasty.

COMERCIAL GRUPO FREIXENET S.A.

Joan Sala, 2
08770 Sant Sadurní D'Anoia (Barcelona)
☎: +34 938 917 000 - Fax: +34 938 183 095
freixenet@freixenet.es
www.freixenet.es

BESO DE REQUENA 2007 TC
bobal.

91 Colour: cherry, garnet rim. Nose: red berry notes, floral, expressive, cocoa bean, creamy oak. Palate: good acidity, balanced, fruity, powerful, flavourful.

COVIÑAS COOP. V.

Avda. Rafael Duyos, s/n
46340 Requena (Valencia)
☎: +34 962 300 680 - Fax: +34 962 302 651
covinas@covinas.com
www.covinas.com

VIÑA ENTERIZO MACABEO 2010 B
macabeo.

85 Colour: bright straw. Nose: fresh, white flowers, expressive. Palate: flavourful, fruity, good acidity, balanced.

AULA MACABEO BLANCO DE LÁGRIMA 2010 B
macabeo.

84 Colour: bright straw. Nose: expressive, dried herbs, ripe fruit. Palate: flavourful, fruity, good acidity, correct.

AULA 2009 BFB
100% macabeo.

85 Colour: bright golden. Nose: ripe fruit, candied fruit, sweet spices, creamy oak. Palate: good acidity, fleshy, flavourful.

AULA BOBAL ROSADO DE LÁGRIMA 2010 RD
bobal.

88 Colour: rose, purple rim. Nose: powerfull, ripe fruit, red berry notes, floral. Palate: fleshy, powerful, fruity, fresh.

AL VENT BOBAL 2010 RD
100% bobal.

86 Colour: brilliant rose. Nose: dried flowers, fragrant herbs, red berry notes. Palate: light-bodied, flavourful, good acidity, long, spicy.

VIÑA ENTERIZO BOBAL 2010 RD
bobal.

85 Color rose, purple rim. Aroma powerfull, ripe fruit, red berry notes, floral, expressive. Taste fleshy, powerful, fruity, fresh.

VIÑA ENTERIZO TEMPRANILLO 2010 T
tempranillo.

84 Colour: cherry, purple rim. Nose: floral, expressive, fruit liqueur notes. Palate: good acidity, fruity, flavourful, creamy.

AULA MERLOT 2008 TC
merlot.

90 Colour: cherry, garnet rim. Nose: red berry notes, ripe fruit, balsamic herbs, cocoa bean, toasty. Palate: fleshy, correct, round tannins.

VIÑA ENTERIZO 2008 TC
garnacha, bobal, tempranillo.

87 Colour: cherry, garnet rim. Nose: powerfull, characterful, fruit liqueur notes, toasty, dark chocolate. Palate: fine bitter notes, round tannins.

AULA SYRAH 2007 TC
100% syrah.

90 Nose: ripe fruit, expressive, sweet spices, creamy oak. Palate: good acidity, powerful, flavourful, fleshy.

DOMINIO DE LA VEGA

Ctra. Madrid - Valencia, Km. 270,6
46390 San Antonio. (Valencia)
☎: +34 962 320 570 - Fax: +34 962 320 330
info@dominiodelavega.com
www.dominiodelavega.com

DOMINIO DE LA VEGA ICE WINE 2010 B
sauvignon blanc, chardonnay, macabeo.

88 Colour: bright straw. Nose: powerfull, floral, honeyed notes, candied fruit, fragrant herbs. Palate: flavourful, sweet, fresh, fruity, good acidity, long.

SAUVIGNON BLANC DOMINIO DE LA VEGA 2010 BFB
sauvignon blanc.

87 Colour: bright yellow. Nose: ripe fruit, sweet spices, creamy oak, fragrant herbs. Palate: rich, smoky aftertaste, flavourful, fresh, good acidity.

AÑACAL DOMINIO DE LA VEGA 2010 B
macabeo.

86 Colour: bright straw. Nose: fresh, fresh fruit, white flowers, expressive, citrus fruit. Palate: flavourful, fruity, good acidity, balanced.

AÑACAL DOMINIO DE LA VEGA 2010 RD
100% bobal.

87 Colour: rose, purple rim. Nose: lactic notes, floral, red berry notes, raspberry. Palate: good acidity, flavourful, fleshy, fruity.

DOMINIO DE LA VEGA BOBAL 2010 T
bobal.

87 Colour: bright cherry. Nose: ripe fruit, sweet spices, creamy oak. Palate: flavourful, fruity, toasty, round tannins.

DOMINIO DE LA VEGA 2008 T ROBLE
bobal, cabernet sauvignon, syrah.

87 Colour: bright cherry. Nose: ripe fruit, sweet spices, creamy oak. Palate: flavourful, fruity, toasty, round tannins.

DOMINIO DE LA VEGA 2006 TC
bobal, cabernet sauvignon, syrah.

86 Colour: deep cherry. Nose: powerfull, spicy, toasty, ripe fruit. Palate: easy to drink, ripe fruit, creamy.

DOMINIO DE LA VEGA 2004 TR
bobal, cabernet sauvignon, tempranillo.

85 Colour: cherry, garnet rim. Nose: powerfull, ripe fruit, toasty. Palate: flavourful, spirituous, ripe fruit.

ARTE MAYOR III T
bobal.

91 Colour: cherry, garnet rim. Nose: spicy, creamy oak, toasty, candied fruit. Palate: powerful, flavourful, toasty, round tannins.

EMILIO CLEMENTE

Camino de San Blas, s/n
46340 Requena (Valencia)
☎: +34 661 563 041
info@eclemente.es
www.eclemente.es

FLORANTE 2010 B
75% macabeo, 25% tardana.

88 Color bright straw. Aroma fresh, fresh fruit, white flowers, expressive. Taste flavourful, fruity, good acidity, balanced.

PEÑAS NEGRAS MADURADO 2009 T
50% cabernet sauvignon, 50% merlot.

83 Colour: cherry, garnet rim. Nose: ripe fruit, balsamic herbs, grassy. Palate: flavourful, good acidity, green.

PEÑAS NEGRAS 2009 T
66% cabernet sauvignon, 34% merlot.

78

EXCELENCIA 2008 T
51% cabernet sauvignon, 49% merlot.

88 Colour: cherry, garnet rim. Nose: powerfull, toasty, smoky. Palate: powerful, concentrated, toasty.

EMILIO CLEMENTE 2006 TC
45% tempranillo, 25% cabernet sauvignon, 25% merlot, 5% bobal.

86 Colour: pale ruby, brick rim edge. Nose: toasty, spicy, aromatic coffee, candied fruit. Palate: spicy, ripe fruit, fine bitter notes.

FINCA CASA LO ALTO

Ctra. Caudete - Los Isidros
46310 Venta del Moro (Valencia)
☎: +34 962 139 381
info@casa-lo-alto.es
www.casa-lo-alto.es

FINCA CASA LO ALTO DON MATIN 2009 T
73% bobal, 27% garnacha.

80 Colour: cherry, garnet rim. Nose: unripe grapeskin notes, overripe fruit, medium intensity. Palate: flavourful, lacks expression.

FINCA CASA LO ALTO 2008 TR
42% syrah, 26% garnacha, 22% cabernet sauvignon, 10% cabernet franc.

85 Colour: cherry, garnet rim. Nose: aromatic coffee, dark chocolate, sweet spices, toasty. Palate: good acidity, flavourful, fleshy.

FINCA CASA LO ALTO 2008 TC
63% tempranillo, 18% garnacha, 13% syrah, 6% cabernet sauvignon.

83 Colour: cherry, garnet rim. Nose: overripe fruit, herbaceous, slightly evolved. Palate: green, lacks expression.

FINCA CASA LO ALTO CHARDONNAY 2009
90% chardonnay, 10% sauvignon blanc, verdejo.

84 Colour: bright golden. Nose: ripe fruit, faded flowers, sweet spices, toasty. Palate: ripe fruit, sweet, flavourful.

FINCA SAN BLAS

Partida de San Blas, s/n
46340 Requena (Valencia)
☎: +34 963 375 617 - Fax: +34 963 370 707
info@fincasanblas.com
www.fincasanblas.com

FINCA SAN BLAS 2009 B
mersenguera, chardonnay, chenin blanc.

87 Colour: bright straw. Nose: white flowers, expressive, fragrant herbs. Palate: flavourful, fruity, good acidity, balanced.

LOMALTA M&S 2009 T
merlot, syrah.

87 Colour: cherry, purple rim. Nose: ripe fruit, red berry notes, grassy, creamy oak. Palate: good acidity, fruity, flavourful.

INCA SAN BLAS 2007 T
bobal, cabernet sauvignon, tempranillo.

86 Colour: pale ruby, brick rim edge. Nose: ripe fruit, balsamic herbs, spicy, tobacco. Palate: powerful, flavourful, fleshy.

LABOR DEL ALMADEQUE MERLOT MAGNUM 2007 TC
merlot.

84 Colour: cherry, garnet rim. Nose: spicy, roasted coffee, aromatic coffee, fruit liqueur notes. Palate: spicy, ripe fruit, fine bitter notes.

LABOR DEL ALMADEQUE RESERVA DE LA FAMILIA 2003 TR
cabernet sauvignon, tempranillo.

85 Colour: pale ruby, brick rim edge. Nose: roasted coffee, aromatic coffee, wet leather. Palate: spirituous, fine bitter notes.

LATORRE AGROVINÍCOLA

Ctra. Requena, 2
46310 Venta del Moro (Valencia)
☎: +34 962 185 028 - Fax: +34 962 185 422
luismiguel@latorreagrovinicola.com
www.latorreagrovinicola.com

PARREÑO 2010 B
viura, verdejo.

81 Colour: bright golden. Nose: fruit liqueur notes, fruit liqueur notes. Palate: fine bitter notes, lacks expression.

CATAMARÁN 2009 BFB
viura, verdejo.

83 Colour: bright yellow. Nose: ripe fruit, sweet spices, creamy oak, fragrant herbs. Palate: rich, flavourful, good acidity.

PARREÑO 2010 RD
bobal.

82 Colour: rose, purple rim. Nose: ripe fruit, floral, expressive. Palate: fleshy, fruity, fresh.

PARREÑO 2010 T
tempranillo, cabernet sauvignon.

82 Colour: cherry, purple rim. Nose: ripe fruit, balsamic herbs, medium intensity. Palate: light-bodied, fresh, warm.

DUQUE DE ARCAS 2010 T
tempranillo, cabernet sauvignon.

82 Colour: cherry, purple rim. Nose: fruit liqueur notes, fresh, medium intensity. Palate: warm, fruity, green.

DUQUE DE ARCAS 2007 TC
tempranillo, bobal, cabernet sauvignon.

80 Colour: pale ruby, brick rim edge. Nose: smoky, cigar, premature reduction notes. Palate: good acidity, warm, slightly evolved.

DUQUE DE ARCAS TEMPRANILLO 2003 TR
tempranillo.

83 Colour: pale ruby, brick rim edge. Nose: spicy, fine reductive notes, wet leather, aged wood nuances, fruit liqueur notes. Palate: spicy, fine tannins, long.

DUQUE DE ARCAS 2001 TGR
bobal.

84 Colour: pale ruby, brick rim edge. Nose: spicy, fine reductive notes, wet leather, aged wood nuances, fruit liqueur notes. Palate: spicy, fine tannins, elegant.

DUQUE DE ARCAS BOBAL 2001 TR
bobal.

82 Colour: pale ruby, brick rim edge. Nose: aromatic coffee, fruit liqueur notes, toasty. Palate: spirituous, fine bitter notes.

DUQUE DE ARCAS 1999 TGR
bobal, tempranillo.

83 Colour: pale ruby, brick rim edge. Nose: spicy, fine reductive notes, wet leather, aged wood nuances, fruit liqueur notes. Palate: spicy, fine tannins, elegant, long.

MAS DE BAZÁN

Ctra. Villar de Olmos, Km. 2
46340 Requena (Valencia)
☎: +34 962 303 586
masdebazan@agrodebazansa.es
www.agrodebazansa.es

BOSQUE REAL MERLOT 2010 RD
70% bobal, 15% merlot, 15% garnacha.

86 Color rose, purple rim. Aroma powerfull, ripe fruit, red berry notes, floral, expressive. Taste fleshy, powerful, fruity, fresh.

MAS DE BAZÁN BOBAL 2007 TC
100% bobal.

85 Colour: pale ruby, brick rim edge. Nose: overripe fruit, cocoa bean, spicy. Palate: flavourful, fleshy, good finish.

MAS DE BAZÁN COUPAGE 2007 TC
bobal, tempranillo, garnacha, merlot, syrah.

85 Colour: cherry, garnet rim. Nose: ripe fruit, tobacco, spicy, toasty. Palate: good acidity, flavourful, fleshy.

MAS DE BAZÁN 2006 TR
50% merlot, 25% bobal, 10% cabernet sauvignon, 10% garnacha, 5% syrah.

89 Colour: light cherry, orangey edge. Nose: ripe fruit, old leather, cocoa bean, toasty. Palate: round, good acidity, fleshy.

MAS DE BAZÁN TEMPRANILLO 2006 TC
100% tempranillo.

87 Colour: cherry, garnet rim. Nose: ripe fruit, spicy, cocoa bean, creamy oak. Palate: rich, flavourful, fleshy.

MAS DE BAZÁN MERLOT 2006 TC
100% merlot.

85 Colour: pale ruby, brick rim edge. Nose: old leather, tobacco, ripe fruit, toasty. Palate: rich, powerful, flavourful, fleshy.

MAS DE BAZÁN SYRAH 2006 TC
100% syrah.

85 Colour: pale ruby, brick rim edge. Nose: ripe fruit, expressive, warm, cigar, creamy oak. Palate: good acidity, flavourful, fleshy, slightly evolved.

MAS DE BAZÁN CABERNET SAUVIGNON 2006 TC
100% cabernet sauvignon.

83 Colour: deep cherry, orangey edge. Nose: scrubland, ripe fruit, old leather. Palate: warm, correct, flavourful.

ROMERAL VINÍCOLA

Pol. Ind. "El Romeral" Parcela 1-2
46340 Requena (Valencia)
☎: +34 962 303 665 - Fax: +34 962 304 991
romeralvinicola@romeralvinicola.com
www.romeralvinicola.com

CASTILLO DE REQUENA 2010 RD
100% bobal.

84 Colour: rose, purple rim. Nose: powerfull, red berry notes, expressive, overripe fruit. Palate: fleshy, powerful, fruity.

ARDILLA MERLOT 2010 T
100% merlot.

87 Colour: cherry, purple rim. Nose: expressive, red berry notes, floral. Palate: flavourful, fruity, good acidity, round tannins.

ARDILLA SYRAH 2010 T
100% syrah.

85 Colour: cherry, purple rim. Nose: powerfull, ripe fruit, red berry notes. Palate: flavourful, fruity, concentrated.

ARDILLA CABERNET SAUVIGNON 2010 T
100% cabernet sauvignon.

84 Colour: cherry, purple rim. Nose: powerfull, varietal, ripe fruit, herbaceous. Palate: flavourful, good acidity, round tannins.

ARDILLA TEMPRANILLO 2010 T
100% tempranillo.

82 Colour: cherry, garnet rim. Nose: powerfull, ripe fruit, sweet spices. Palate: fruity, spicy.

TORRE ORIA

Ctra. Pontón - Utiel, Km. 3
46390 El Derramador (Valencia)
☎: +34 962 320 289 - Fax: +34 962 320 311
santiago.sancho@natra.es
www.torreoria.com

MARQUÉS DE REQUENA 2010 B
100% macabeo.

85 Colour: bright straw. Nose: fresh, fresh fruit, expressive. Palate: flavourful, fruity, good acidity, fine bitter notes.

MARQUÉS DE REQUENA 2010 RD JOVEN
100% bobal.

87 Colour: rose, purple rim. Nose: powerfull, ripe fruit, red berry notes, floral. Palate: fleshy, powerful, fruity, fresh.

VERA DE ESTENAS

Junto N-III, km. 266 - Paraje La Cabezuela
46300 Utiel (Valencia)
☎: +34 962 171 141 - Fax: +34 962 174 352
estenas@estenas.es
www.estenas.es

VIÑA LIDÓN 2010 BFB
chardonnay, macabeo.

91 Colour: bright straw. Nose: fresh, ripe fruit, citrus fruit, fragrant herbs. Palate: flavourful, fruity, good acidity, balanced.

VERA DE ESTENAS 2010 B
macabeo, chardonnay.

88 Colour: pale. Nose: tropical fruit, expressive, ripe fruit, floral. Palate: good acidity, powerful, flavourful, fruity.

VERA DE ESTENAS BOBAL 2010 RD
bobal.

87 Colour: rose, purple rim. Nose: floral, raspberry, red berry notes. Palate: light-bodied, fresh, fruity, easy to drink.

VERA DE ESTENAS 2010 T BARRICA
bobal, merlot, cabernet sauvignon, tempranillo.

88 Colour: cherry, garnet rim. Nose: red berry notes, expressive, spicy, creamy oak. Palate: good acidity, light-bodied, fresh, fruity.

MARTÍNEZ BERMELL MERLOT 2009 T FERMENTADO EN BARRICA
100% merlot.

90 Colour: bright cherry. Nose: ripe fruit, sweet spices, creamy oak. Palate: flavourful, fruity, toasty, round tannins.

VERA DE ESTENAS 2009 T BARRICA
bobal, cabernet sauvignon, merlot, tempranillo, syrah.

85 Colour: bright cherry. Nose: ripe fruit, sweet spices, new oak, toasty, dark chocolate. Palate: flavourful, fruity, toasty, round tannins.

VIÑA MARIOL 2009 T
100% bobal.

85 Colour: cherry, purple rim. Nose: red berry notes, ripe fruit, spicy. Palate: flavourful, fruity, good acidity, round tannins.

VERA DE ESTENAS 2007 TC
tempranillo, bobal, cabernet sauvignon, merlot.

89 Colour: cherry, garnet rim. Nose: spicy, creamy oak, toasty, characterful, fruit preserve. Palate: powerful, flavourful, toasty, round tannins.

CASA DON ÁNGEL BOBAL 2006 T
100% bobal.

93 Colour: cherry, garnet rim. Nose: spicy, creamy oak, toasty, characterful, earthy notes, mineral. Palate: powerful, flavourful, toasty, round tannins.

VERA DE ESTENAS 2006 TR
bobal, cabernet sauvignon, tempranillo, merlot.

88 Color cherry, garnet rim. Aroma ripe fruit, spicy, creamy oak, toasty, complex. Taste powerful, flavourful, toasty, round tannins.

CASA DON ÁNGEL MALBEC 7-8 T
malbec.

91 Colour: cherry, garnet rim. Nose: ripe fruit, spicy, creamy oak, toasty, characterful, earthy notes, varietal. Palate: powerful, flavourful, toasty, round tannins.

VINÍCOLA DEL OESTE S.A.

Ctra. N-III, Km. 271
46390 San Antonio Requena (Valencia)
☎: +34 962 320 002 - Fax: +34 962 320 533
info@castaro.com
www.castaro.com

VIÑA CASTARO SELECCIÓN 2005 TR
100% cabernet sauvignon.

90 Colour: cherry, garnet rim. Nose: ripe fruit, spicy, creamy oak, toasty, characterful. Palate: powerful, flavourful, toasty, round tannins.

VIÑA CASTARO 2005 TR
52% cabernet sauvignon, 48% tempranillo.

86 Colour: pale ruby, brick rim edge. Nose: spicy, fine reductive notes, wet leather, aged wood nuances, fruit liqueur notes. Palate: spicy, fine tannins, long.

VIÑA CASTARO 2005 TC
52% cabernet sauvignon, 48% tempranillo.

85 Colour: pale ruby, brick rim edge. Nose: old leather, ripe fruit, spicy, toasty. Palate: good acidity, rich, flavourful, fleshy.

VINOS PASIEGO

Avda. Virgen de Tejeda, 28
46320 Sinarcas (Valencia)
☎: +34 962 306 175 - Fax: +34 962 306 175
bodega@vinospasiego.com
www.vinospasiego.com

PASIEGO LAS SUERTES 2010 B
60% chardonnay, 40% sauvignon blanc.

90 Colour: bright yellow. Nose: powerfull, ripe fruit, sweet spices, creamy oak, fragrant herbs. Palate: rich, flavourful, fresh, good acidity.

PASIEGO LA BLASCA 2008 TC
39% cabernet sauvignon, 31% tempranillo, 27% merlot, 3% bobal.

87 Colour: cherry, garnet rim. Nose: powerfull, fruit preserve, toasty, spicy. Palate: spicy, toasty.

PASIEGO DE AUTOR 2005 TC
47% cabernet sauvignon, 33% bobal, 20% tempranillo.

92 Colour: cherry, garnet rim. Nose: ripe fruit, spicy, creamy oak, toasty, characterful, mineral. Palate: powerful, flavourful, toasty, round tannins.

VIÑEDOS Y BODEGAS VEGALFARO

Ctra. Pontón - Utiel, Km. 3
46340 Requena (Valencia)
☎: +34 962 320 680 - Fax: +34 962 321 126
rodolfo@vegalfaro.com
www.vegalfaro.com

VEGALFARO 2010 B
80% chardonnay, 20% sauvignon blanc.

90 Colour: bright straw. Nose: fresh, fresh fruit, white flowers, expressive, mineral. Palate: flavourful, fruity, good acidity, balanced.

VEGALFARO 2010 T
50% bobal, 50% merlot.

88 Colour: cherry, purple rim. Nose: red berry notes, floral, balsamic herbs, mineral. Palate: fleshy, powerful, flavourful, fruity.

VEGALFARO 2008 TC
40% tempranillo, 40% merlot, 20% syrah.

89 Colour: cherry, garnet rim. Nose: red berry notes, ripe fruit, earthy notes, sweet spices, creamy oak. Palate: rich, powerful, fleshy.

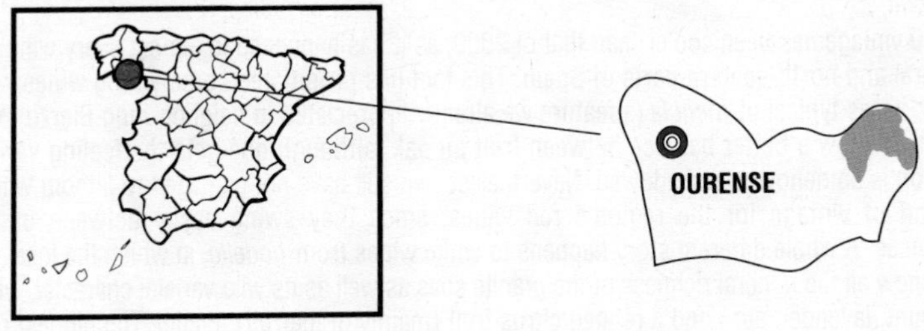
OURENSE

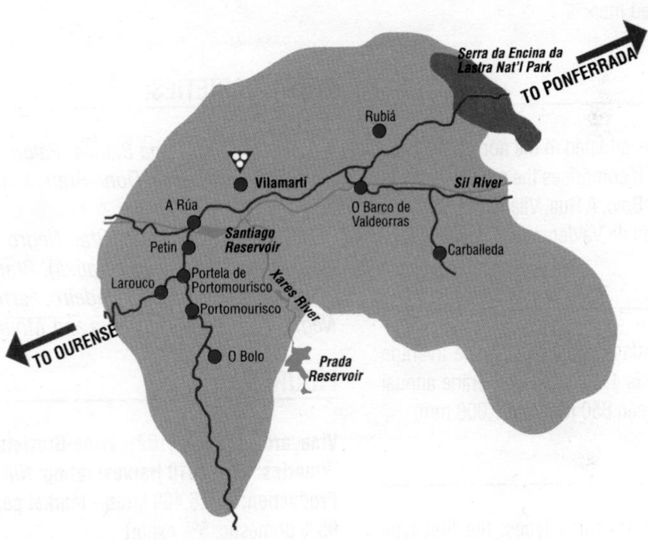
Serra da Encina da Lastra Nat'l Park
TO PONFERRADA
Rubiá
Vilamartí
O Barco de Valdeorras
Sil River
A Rúa
Santiago Reservoir
Petin
Carballeda
Portela de Portomourisco
Larouco
Xares River
Portomourisco
TO OURENSE
O Bolo
Prada Reservoir

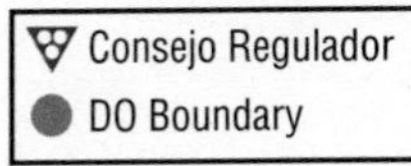
Consejo Regulador
DO Boundary

DO VALDEORRAS

NEWS ABOUT THE VINTAGE:

The 2010 vintage has been cooler than that of 2009, as it has happened in almost every wine region in the central and north-eastern parts of Spain. This fact has propitiated some young wines with fresh balsamic notes typical of *mencía* (a feature we already appreciated in neighbouring Bierzo), while the aged wines show a better balance between fruit an oak, although one gets the feeling varietal fruit expression is somehow overshadowed. Nevertheless, we still have not managed to fathom which is the ideal kind of vintage for the region's red wines, since they swing easily between under– and overripeness. A whole different story happens to white wines from *godello*, in which the local variety is able to show all the mineral richness of the granite soils as well as its wild varietal character, with herbal notes (mint, lavender, etc.) and a refined citrus fruit (mainly grapefruit) quality. The biggest revelation this year has been Pedrouzos Magnum 2008, from Valdesil, than in its first appearance in our Guide gets 96 points, even above the always complex and mineral As Sortes, which in its 2009 vintage has reached 95 points. Wines all that broaden up a qualitative catalogue that for a long time was led exclusively by Guitián and Godeval. In the last couple of years, though, some new alternatives have also appeared, the likes of Bodegas Avanthia (Grupo Ordoñez) and the ineffable Telmo Rodríguez with his Gaba do Xil (white) and his red mencía.

LOCATION:

The DO Valdeorras is situated in the northeast of the province of Orense. It comprises the municipal areas of Larouco, Petín, O Bolo, A Rua, Vilamartín, O Barco, Rubiá and Carballeda de Valdeorras.

CLIMATE:

Continental, with Atlantic influences. The average annual temperature is 11°C and the average annual rainfall ranges between 850 mm and 1,000 mm.

SOIL:

Quite varied. There are three types: the first type which is settled on shallow slate with many stones and a medium texture; the second type on deeper granite with a lot of sand and finally the type that lies on sediments and terraces, where there are usually a lot of pebbles.

GRAPE VARIETIES:

WHITE: *Godello, Dona Blanca, Palomino, Loureira, Treixadura, Dona Branca, Albariño, Torrontes* and *Lado.*
RED: *Mencía, Merenzao, Grao Negro, Garnacha, Tempranillo (Araúxa), Brancellao, Sousón, Caíño Tinto, Espadeiro, Ferrón, Gran Negro, Garnacha Tintureira* and *Mouratón.*

FIGURES:

Vineyard surface: 1,157 – **Wine-Growers:** 1,514 – **Wineries:** 47 – **2010 Harvest rating:** N/A – **Production:** 3,025,469 litres – **Market percentages:** 95% domestic. 5% export

CONSEJO REGULADOR
Ctra. Nacional 120, km. 463
32340 Vilamartín de Valdeorras (Ourense)
☎: +34 988 300 295 - Fax: +34 988 336 887
@ consello@dovaldeorras.com
www.dovaldeorras.com

GENERAL CHARACTERISTICS OF THE WINES

WHITES	Produced from the *Godello* variety, they offer high quality. They are straw yellow or pale yellow in colour. Aromatically, they are not excessively intense, although fine and delicate, with pleasant floral notes. On the palate, they are characterised by their tastiness, excellent acidity and, often, by their oily essence.
REDS	The *Mencía* variety is used, with which mainly young red wines are produced with a markedly Atlantic character, defined aromas of blackberries; they are dry and fruity on the palate.

VINTAGE RATING PEÑÍNGUIDE

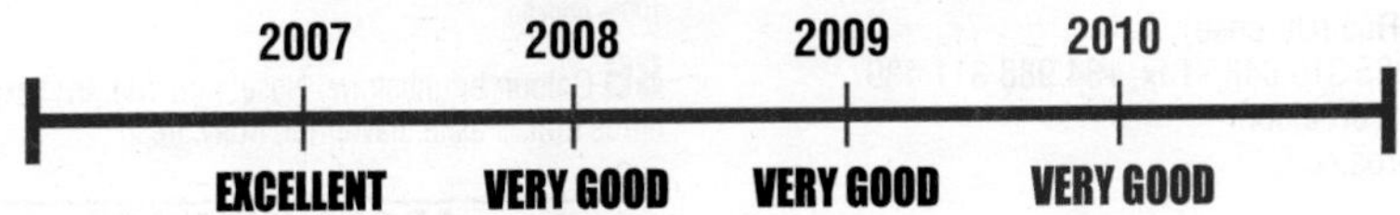

A TAPADA S.A.T.

Finca A Tapada
32310 Rubiá (Ourense)
☎: +34 988 324 197 - Fax: +34 988 324 197

GUITIÁN GODELLO SOBRE LÍAS 2010 B
godello.

92 Colour: bright straw. Nose: fresh, fresh fruit, white flowers, fine lees. Palate: flavourful, fruity, good acidity, balanced.

GUITIÁN GODELLO 2009 BFB
godello.

93 Colour: bright yellow. Nose: powerfull, sweet spices, creamy oak, fragrant herbs, candied fruit. Palate: rich, smoky aftertaste, flavourful, fresh, good acidity.

GUITIÁN GODELLO 2009 B
100% godello.

89 Colour: straw. Nose: powerfull, candied fruit, citrus fruit. Palate: fleshy, powerful, flavourful.

ADEGA A COROA

A Coroa, s/n
32350 A Rúa (Ourense)
☎: +34 988 310 648 - Fax: +34 988 311 439
acoroa@acoroa.com
www.acoroa.com

A COROA 2010 B
100% godello.

89 Colour: bright yellow. Nose: fresh, balanced, varietal, citrus fruit, wild herbs. Palate: balanced, good acidity, fruity, flavourful.

ADEGA ALAN

San Roque, 36
32350 A Rúa (Ourense)
☎: +34 988 311 457
alandeval@alandeval.com
www.alandeval.com

ALAN DE VAL GODELLO 2010 B
100% godello.

86 Colour: bright straw. Nose: medium intensity, dried herbs, fresh, candied fruit. Palate: fresh, ripe fruit.

ALAN DE VAL PEDRAZAIS 2010 BFB
100% godello.

86 Colour: bright straw. Nose: ripe fruit, candied fruit. Palate: good structure, flavourful, long.

ALAN DE VAL PEDRAZAIS MENCÍA 2010 T BARRICA
100% mencía.

88 Colour: dark-red cherry, purple rim. Nose: sweet spices, ripe fruit, balsamic herbs. Palate: fleshy, fruity, spicy, good acidity.

ALAN DE VAL MENCÍA 2010 T
100% mencía.

85 Colour: cherry, purple rim. Nose: medium intensity, wild herbs. Palate: flavourful, easy to drink.

ADEGA DA PINGUELA

Camino del Disco, 18 - 1B
32350 A Rúa (Ourense)
☎: +34 654 704 753
adega@adegadapinguela.com
www.adegadapinguela.com

MEMORIA DE VENTURA 2010 B
100% godello.

86 Colour: bright straw. Nose: ripe fruit, fruit expression, citrus fruit. Palate: flavourful, fruity, fresh.

ADEGA MELILLAS

A Coroa, s/n
32350 A Rúa (Ourense)
☎: +34 988 310 510
info@adegamelillas.com
www.adegamelillas.com

LAGAR DO CIGUR 2010 B
100% godello.

88 Colour: bright straw. Nose: fresh fruit, white flowers, varietal. Palate: flavourful, fruity, good acidity, balanced.

LAGAR DO CIGUR 2010 T
80% mencía, 20% tempranillo.

91 Colour: cherry, purple rim. Nose: red berry notes, balanced, spicy, lactic notes, violets. Palate: flavourful, fruity, round tannins.

LAGAR DO CIGUR 2008 T BARRICA
80% mencía, 10% tempranillo, 10% merenzao.

87 Colour: bright cherry. Nose: ripe fruit, sweet spices, creamy oak, smoky. Palate: flavourful, fruity, toasty, round tannins.

ADEGA O CASAL

Malladín, s/n
32310 Rubiá (Ourense)
☎: +34 689 675 800 - Fax: +34 988 324 286
casalnovo@casalnovo.es
www.casalnovo.es

CASAL NOVO GODELLO 2010 B
100% godello.

89 Colour: bright straw, greenish rim. Nose: medium intensity, dried herbs, faded flowers. Palate: fruity, flavourful, good acidity.

CASAL NOVO MENCÍA 2010 T
100% mencía.

88 Colour: light cherry, purple rim. Nose: dried flowers, red berry notes, wild herbs. Palate: fruity, flavourful, easy to drink, balsamic.

ADEGA O CEPADO

Patal, 11
32310 Rubia de valdeorras (Ourense)
☎: +34 666 186 128
info@cepado.com
www.cepado.com

CEPADO GODELLO 2010 B
100% godello.

90 Colour: bright straw, greenish rim. Nose: varietal, expressive, balanced, dried herbs. Palate: good structure, fruity, complex.

CEPADO MENCÍA 2010 T
100% mencía.

88 Colour: cherry, purple rim. Nose: fresh fruit, red berry notes. Palate: flavourful, fruity, good acidity, round tannins.

ADEGA QUINTA DA PEZA

Ctra. Nacional 120, km.467
32350 A Rua de Valdeorras (Ourense)
☎: +34 988 311 537 - Fax: +34 981 232 642
quintadapeza@gmail.com
www.quintadapeza.es

QUINTA DA PEZA GODELLO 2010 B
100% godello.

90 Colour: bright straw. Nose: fresh, fresh fruit, white flowers, varietal. Palate: flavourful, fruity, good acidity, balanced.

QUINTA DA PEZA 2010 T
100% mencía.

85 Colour: cherry, garnet rim. Nose: fruit expression, balsamic herbs, balanced. Palate: fruity, easy to drink, long.

QUINTA DA PEZA ORO MENCÍA BARRICA 2009 TC
100% mencía.

88 Colour: cherry, garnet rim. Nose: balanced, cocoa bean, spicy. Palate: good structure, fleshy, fruity, balsamic.

BODEGA ELADIO SANTALLA PARADELO

Conde Fenosa, 36
32300 O Barco de Valdeorras (Ourense)
☎: +34 630 762 607
eladio@bodegaseladiosantalla.com

HACIENDA UCEDIÑOS 2010 B
100% godello.

92 Colour: bright straw. Nose: powerfull, ripe fruit, spicy, scrubland. Palate: flavourful, fruity, fleshy.

HACIENDA UCEDIÑOS 2009 T
100% mencía.

88 Colour: cherry, purple rim. Nose: wild herbs, medium intensity, balanced, fresh fruit, red berry notes. Palate: flavourful, good structure.

BODEGAS AVANTHIA

Avda. Galicia, 20
32300 O Barco de Valdeorras (Ourense)
☎: +34 988 108 282 - Fax: +34 988 325 309
godeval@godeval.com
www.godeval.com

AVANTHIA GODELLO 2010 B
godello.

93 Colour: bright straw. Nose: powerfull, ripe fruit, citrus fruit, cocoa bean, spicy. Palate: flavourful, fleshy, long, fine bitter notes.

AVANTHIA CUVEE MOSTEIRO 2009 T
mencía.

93 Colour: garnet rim. Nose: red berry notes, ripe fruit, powerfull, expressive, mineral, dark chocolate, creamy oak. Palate: elegant, round, unctuous, powerful, flavourful, fleshy.

AVANTHIA MENCÍA 2009 T
mencía.

90 Colour: garnet rim. Nose: red berry notes, ripe fruit, mineral, cocoa bean, sweet spices, creamy oak. Palate: powerful, flavourful, fleshy, toasty.

BODEGAS D'BERNA

Villamartín de Valdeorras s/n
32340 Córgomo ()
☎: +34 988 324 557 - Fax: +34 988 324 557
www.bodegasdberna.com

D'BERNA 2010 B
godello.

91 Colour: bright straw. Nose: grassy, white flowers, varietal. Palate: flavourful, fine bitter notes, good acidity.

D'BERNA 2010 T
mencía.

87 Colour: cherry, purple rim. Nose: raspberry, red berry notes, balsamic herbs. Palate: flavourful, fruity, fresh.

BODEGAS GODEVAL

Avda. de Galicia, 20
32300 El Barco de Valdeorras (Ourense)
☎: +34 988 108 282 - Fax: +34 988 325 309
godeval@godeval.com
www.godeval.com

GODEVAL CEPAS VELLAS 2010 B
godello.

91 Colour: bright straw. Nose: fresh, fresh fruit, mineral, white flowers, citrus fruit. Palate: flavourful, fruity, good acidity, balanced.

GODEVAL 2010 B
godello.

89 Colour: bright straw. Nose: fresh, fresh fruit, white flowers. Palate: flavourful, fruity, good acidity, balanced.

BODEGAS RUCHEL

Ctra. de Cernego, s/n
32340 Vilamartín de Valdeorras (Ourense)
☎: +34 986 253 345 - Fax: +34 986 253 345
info@vinosruchel.com
www.vinosruchel.com

RUCHEL GODELLO 2010 B
100% godello.

86 Colour: bright straw, greenish rim. Nose: candied fruit, balanced, dried herbs. Palate: fruity, easy to drink, good finish.

GRAN RUCHEL GODELLO 2006 B
100% godello.

82 Colour: yellow, greenish rim. Nose: candied fruit, ripe fruit, citrus fruit, white flowers, slightly evolved. Palate: ripe fruit, long.

RUCHEL MENCÍA 2009 T
85% mencía, 15% tempranillo.

85 Colour: cherry, garnet rim. Nose: powerfull, ripe fruit, sweet spices. Palate: powerful, fleshy, fine bitter notes.

DON AMADEO MENCÍA 2008 T
85% mencía, 15% tempranillo.

81 Colour: light cherry. Nose: woody, varnish, warm. Palate: fine bitter notes, spicy.

BODEGAS SAMPAYOLO

Ctra. de Barxela, s/n
32358 Petín de Valdeorras (Ourense)
☎: +34 679 157 977
info@sampayolo.com
www.sampayolo.com

SAMPAYOLO GODELLO 2010 B
godello.

88 Colour: bright straw. Nose: wild herbs, varietal, medium intensity, candied fruit. Palate: flavourful, good acidity, balanced.

SAMPAYOLO GODELLO 2010 B BARRICA
godello.

88 Colour: bright yellow. Nose: candied fruit, spicy, wild herbs. Palate: fruity, good structure, long.

GARNACHA VELLA DA CHAIRA DO RAMIRIÑO 2010 T
100% garnacha.

87 Colour: deep cherry. Nose: balsamic herbs, powerfull, varietal, ripe fruit. Palate: powerful, good acidity, fine bitter notes.

SAMPAYOLO MENCÍA 2010 T
mencía.

85 Colour: cherry, purple rim. Nose: medium intensity, red berry notes, faded flowers. Palate: flavourful, fruity.

SAMPAYOLO LAGAR DE BRIMEDA 2010 T BARRICA
33% mencía, 33% garnacha, 33% tempranillo.

85 Colour: cherry, garnet rim. Nose: wild herbs, spicy. Palate: flavourful, balanced, good acidity, good finish.

BODEGAS VALDESIL

Córgomo, s/n
32348 Córgomo (Ourense)
☎: +34 988 337 900 - Fax: +34 988 337 901
valdesil@valdesil.com
www.valdesil.com

VALDESIL GODELLO SOBRE LÍAS 2010 B
godello.

91 Colour: bright straw. Nose: fresh, fresh fruit, white flowers. Palate: flavourful, fruity, good acidity, balanced.

MONTENOVO GODELLO 2010 B
godello.

88 Colour: bright straw. Nose: fresh fruit, varietal, expressive. Palate: flavourful, fruity, fleshy.

PEDROUZOS MAGNUM 2009 B
100% godello.

95 Colour: bright straw. Nose: mineral, fresh fruit, fruit expression, grassy, sweet spices. Palate: flavourful, fruity, good acidity, fine bitter notes.

PEZAS DA PORTELA 2009 BFB
godello.

93 Colour: bright yellow. Nose: powerfull, sweet spices, fragrant herbs, cocoa bean. Palate: rich, flavourful, fresh, good acidity.

VALDESIL GODELLO SOBRE LÍAS 2009 B
godello.

90 Colour: bright straw. Nose: fresh, fresh fruit, white flowers, expressive. Palate: flavourful, fruity, balanced, fleshy, complex.

PEDROUZOS MAGNUM 2008 B
100% godello.

96 Colour: bright straw. Nose: varietal, elegant, expressive, fresh fruit, scrubland, mineral. Palate: flavourful, fruity, spicy, ripe fruit, fine bitter notes.

PEZAS DA PORTELA 2008 BFB
100% godello.

94 Colour: bright yellow. Nose: powerfull, sweet spices, creamy oak, fragrant herbs, varietal. Palate: rich, flavourful, fresh, good acidity.

CARBALLAL

Ctra. de Carballal, km 2,2
32356 Petín de Valdeorras (Ourense)
☎: +34 988 311 281 - Fax: +34 988 311 281
bodegascarballal@hotmail.com

EREBO GODELLO 2010 B
100% godello.

90 Colour: bright straw, greenish rim. Nose: fresh fruit, wild herbs, dried herbs. Palate: fruity, flavourful, varietal.

EREBO MENCÍA 2010 T
100% mencía.

90 Colour: cherry, purple rim. Nose: ripe fruit, scrubland, floral. Palate: flavourful, fleshy.

EREBO MENCÍA 2008 T BARRICA
100% mencía.

91 Colour: bright cherry. Nose: ripe fruit, sweet spices, creamy oak, expressive, balsamic herbs. Palate: flavourful, fruity, toasty, round tannins.

COMPAÑÍA DE VINOS TELMO RODRÍGUEZ

El Monte, s/n
01308 Lanciego (Álava)
☎: +34 945 628 315 - Fax: +34 945 628 314
contact@telmorodriguez.com
www.telmorodriguez.com

GABA DO XIL GODELLO 2010 B
godello.

92 Colour: bright straw. Nose: fresh, fresh fruit, white flowers. Palate: flavourful, fruity, good acidity, balanced.

JOAQUÍN REBOLLEDO

San Roque, 11
32350 A Rúa (Ourense)
☎: +34 988 372 307 - Fax: +34 988 371 427
info@joaquinrebolledo.com
www.joaquinrebolledo.com

JOAQUÍN REBOLLEDO GODELLO 2010 B
100% godello.

90 Colour: bright straw. Nose: fresh, fresh fruit, white flowers, citrus fruit. Palate: flavourful, fruity, good acidity, balanced.

JOAQUÍN REBOLLEDO MENCÍA 2010 T
100% mencía.

90 Colour: cherry, purple rim. Nose: fresh fruit, red berry notes, floral, varietal, balsamic herbs. Palate: flavourful, fruity, good acidity, round tannins.

JOAQUÍN REBOLLEDO 2009 T BARRICA
50% mencía, 30% tempranillo, 20% otras.

88 Colour: cherry, garnet rim. Nose: powerfull, ripe fruit, balsamic herbs, sweet spices. Palate: flavourful, fruity, fleshy.

MANUEL CORZO MACÍAS

Chandoiro, s/n
32372 O Bolo (Ourense)
☎: +34 690 842 772

VIÑA CORZO GODELLO 2010 B
100% godello.

89 Colour: pale. Nose: powerfull, ripe fruit. Palate: fruity, light-bodied, fresh.

VIÑA CORZO MENCÍA 2010 T
100% mencía.

83 Colour: cherry, garnet rim. Nose: powerfull, ripe fruit, spicy. Palate: powerful, good acidity, fine bitter notes.

MARÍA TERESA NÚÑEZ VEGA

Barxela s/n
32356 Petín ()
☎: +34 988 311 251 - Fax: +34 988 311 251
biocaarroyo@yahoo.es
www.bioca.es

BIOCA GODELLO 2010 B
100% godello.

91 Colour: bright straw. Nose: powerfull, varietal, fresh fruit, citrus fruit. Palate: powerful, flavourful, fleshy.

MENCÍAS DE DOS

Cuatro Calles, s/n
47491 La Seca (Valladolid)
☎: +34 983 103 223 - Fax: +34 983 816 561
info@sitiosdebodega.com
www.sitiosdebodega.com

OLLO DE GALO LÍAS 2010 B
godello.

91 Color bright straw. Aroma fresh, fresh fruit, white flowers, expressive. Taste flavourful, fruity, good acidity, balanced.

RAFAEL PALACIOS

Avda. de Somoza, 81
32350 A Rúa de Valdeorras (Ourense)
☎: +34 988 310 162 - Fax: +34 988 310 162
bodega@rafaelpalacios.com
www.rafaelpalacios.com

LOURO DO BOLO 2010 B
94% godello, 6% treixadura.

93 Colour: bright yellow. Nose: candied fruit, citrus fruit, dried flowers, sweet spices. Palate: flavourful, fruity, fleshy, fine bitter notes, good acidity, complex.

AS SORTES 2009 B
100% godello.

94 Colour: bright yellow. Nose: ripe fruit, mineral, dry stone, complex, sweet spices, creamy oak. Palate: powerful, flavourful, fleshy, complex, spicy, balanced.

SANTA MARTA

Córgomo, s/n
32340 Villamartín de Ourense (Ourense)
☎: +34 988 324 559 - Fax: +34 988 324 559
info@vinaredo.com
www.vinaredo.com

VIÑAREDO GODELLO 2010 B
100% godello.

91 Colour: yellow, greenish rim. Nose: fresh fruit, grassy, varietal, balanced. Palate: rich, fruity, good acidity.

VIÑAREDO GODELLO BARRICA 2009 BFB
100% godello.

88 Color bright yellow. Aroma powerfull, ripe fruit, sweet spices, creamy oak, fragrant herbs. Taste rich, smoky aftertaste, flavourful, fresh, good acidity.

VIÑAREDO MENCÍA 2010 T
100% mencía.

86 Colour: cherry, purple rim. Nose: balanced, red berry notes, wild herbs. Palate: fruity, flavourful, easy to drink.

VIÑAREDO SOUSÓN 2009 T
100% souson.

88 Colour: cherry, garnet rim. Nose: expressive, violet drops, fresh fruit, floral. Palate: flavourful, fruity, fleshy.

VIÑAREDO MENCÍA BARRICA 2007 T
100% mencía.

82 Colour: cherry, garnet rim. Nose: ripe fruit, old leather, premature reduction notes. Palate: fleshy, good structure.

VIÑA SOMOZA BODEGAS Y VIÑEDOS

Avda. Somoza, s/n
32350 A Rúa (Ourense)
☎: +34 656 407 857 - Fax: +34 988 310 918
bodega@vinosomoza.com
www.vinosomoza.com

VIÑA SOMOZA GODELLO SOBRE LIAS 2010 B
100% godello.

89 Colour: bright straw. Nose: fresh, white flowers, varietal. Palate: flavourful, fruity, good acidity, balanced.

VIÑA SOMOZA GODELLO SELECCIÓN 2009 B ROBLE
100% godello.

90 Colour: bright yellow. Nose: candied fruit, citrus fruit, complex, balanced, spicy, balsamic herbs. Palate: good structure, full, rich, long.

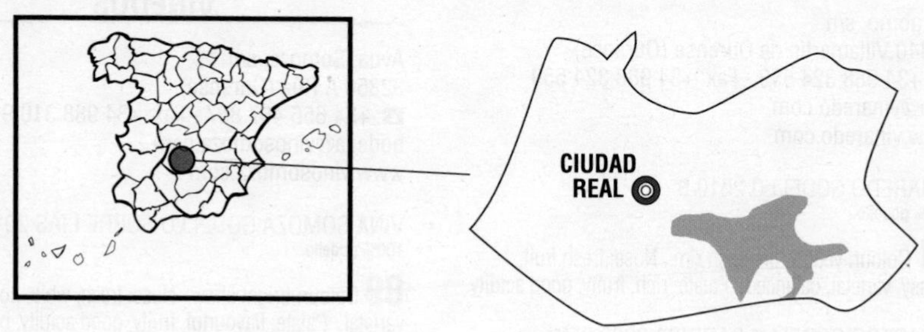
CIUDAD
REAL

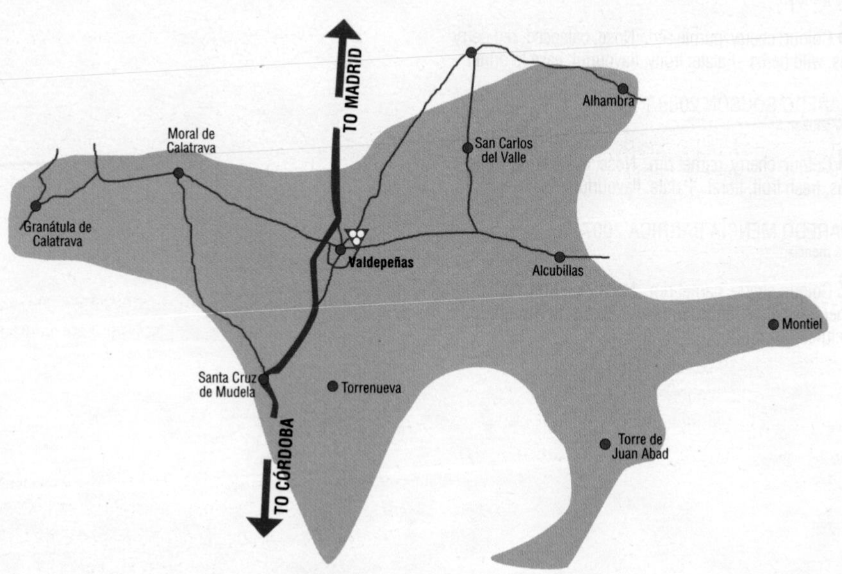
TO MADRID
Alhambra
San Carlos
del Valle
Moral de
Calatrava
Granátula de
Calatrava
Valdepeñas
Alcubillas
Montiel
Santa Cruz
de Mudela
Torrenueva
Torre de
Juan Abad
TO CÓRDOBA

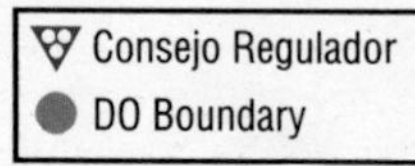
Consejo Regulador
DO Boundary

NEWS ABOUT THE VINTAGE:

Valdepeñas continues to belong to the model of low-price, correct, just average Spanish wine mainly red in typology. That is the way the DO started, the way it had kept itself for years and also the way it has progressively lost its past splendour. The "Valdepeñas"our grandfathers knew, with wines that ruled this whole country, has dwindled over the years from the almost 229 bodegas it had in the Seventies to hardly forty registered nowadays in the DO. It is true that in former times the portrait of Valdepeñas had a sort of Burgundian feel about it, given the high percentages of white wines that were mixed with red. Today, they still are soft, easy drinking wines that just occasionally show certain notes derived from the concrete vats in which they are usually kept. Probably this old-fashioned material could –along with the most modern winemaking techniques– add to the region's wines a singularity (i.e, the identification of a unique territory) capable of turning around their image in the contemporary wine context.

This year, same as it has happened in neighbouring La Mancha, young wines show a little fresher and fruitier than in 2009. In this DO differences between vintages are easy to spot in young wines and get progressively more difficult as the wines age in oak, the main reason behind it being the high yields common in the region –which causes a sort of homogenization of the vintages while diluting any sort of singularity– and the also common use of older oak to age the wines.

All these features are much more noticeable in wines with shorter ageing periods, given the softening effect in these wines of long "in the bottle" crianzas.

The very few samples of rosé wines we have been able to sample show quite balanced in terms of freshness and fruit expression, which is good news in a region with high average summer temperatures. White wines are also correct, pretty much in line with previous vintages.

LOCATION:

On the southern border of the southern plateau, in the province of Ciudad Real. It comprises the municipal districts of Alcubillas, Moral de Calatrava, San Carlos del Valle, Santa Cruz de Mudela, Torrenueva and Valdepeñas and part of Alhambra, Granátula de Calatrava, Montiel and Torre de Juan Abad.

CLIMATE:

Continental in nature, with cold winters, very hot summers and little rainfall, which is usually around 250 and 400 mm per year.

SOIL:

Mainly brownish-red and brownish-grey limestone soil with a high lime content and quite poor in organic matter.

GRAPE VARIETIES:

WHITE: *Airén, Macabeo, Chardonnay, Sauvignon Blanc, Moscatel de Grano Menudo* and *Verdejo.*
RED: *Cencibel (Tempranillo), Garnacha, Cabernet Sauvignon, Merlot, Syrah* and *Petit Verdot.*

FIGURES:

Vineyard surface: 25,430 – **Wine-Growers:** 3,109 – **Wineries:** 42 – **2010 Harvest rating:** N/A – **Production:** -- litres – **Market percentages:** 61% domestic. 39% export

CONSEJO REGULADOR
Constitución, 23
13300 Valdepeñas (Ciudad Real)
☎: +34 926 322 788 - Fax: +34 926 321 054
@ consejo@dovaldepenas.es
www.dovaldepenas.es

GENERAL CHARACTERISTICS OF THE WINES

WHITES	These are produced from *Airén*. They have a pale or straw yellow colour; on the nose they are fresh and fruity and may develop aromas reminiscent of banana or pineapple; on the palate, they are fresh and pleasant, although they have slightly low acidity.
ROSÉS	Raspberry pink or salmon pink in colour, they are fresh, fruity, pleasant and easy drinking.
REDS	The young wines from *Cencibel* have a deep cherry-red colour with violet nuances; the aroma is fresh and fruity, almost always with good intensity; on the palate, the freshness and the fruity nuances that make them so pleasant to drink are very noticeable. Those aged in wood start to benefit from the cleaner aromas of oak due to the use of newer barrels. They are supple and quite flavourful on the palate.

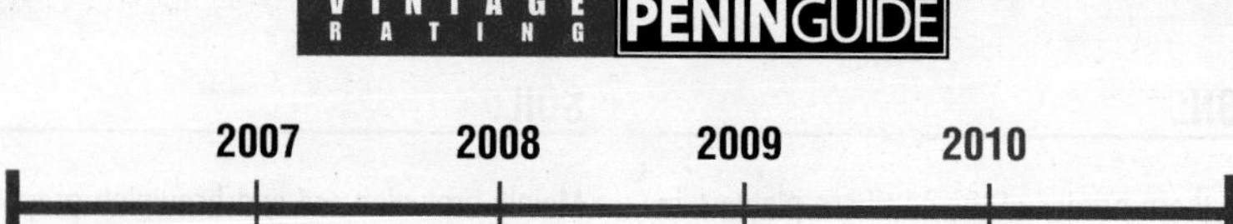

2007	2008	2009	2010
VERY GOOD	EXCELLENT	GOOD	GOOD

BODEGA HACIENDA LA PRINCESA

Ctra. San Carlos del Valle, km. 8 - Apdo. Correos 281
13300 Valdepeñas (Ciudad Real)
☎: +34 638 335 185
haciendalaprincesa@telefonica.net
www.haciendalaprincesa.com

HACIENDA LA PRINCESA DEBIR 2009 BFB
100% chardonnay.

86 Colour: old gold, amber rim. Nose: ripe fruit, pattiserie, creamy oak. Palate: good acidity, flavourful, fleshy.

BODEGAS FERNANDO CASTRO

Paseo Castelar, 70
13730 Santa Cruz de Mudela (Ciudad Real)
☎: +34 926 342 168 - Fax: +34 926 349 029
fernando@bodegasfernandocastro.com
www.bodegasfernandocastro.com

VALDEMONTE S/C T
tempranillo.

83 Colour: cherry, purple rim. Nose: red berry notes, fresh, medium intensity. Palate: lacks balance, light-bodied, easy to drink.

CASTILLO SANTA BÁRBARA 2008 T
50% syrah, 50% merlot.

85 Colour: cherry, garnet rim. Nose: ripe fruit, creamy oak, medium intensity. Palate: easy to drink, flavourful, light-bodied.

RAÍCES SYRAH SELECCIÓN 2006 T
100% syrah.

81 Colour: cherry, garnet rim. Nose: roasted coffee, woody, smoky. Palate: dry wood, fleshy.

RAÍCES 2005 TC
tempranillo.

84 Colour: black cherry. Nose: medium intensity, ripe fruit, old leather. Palate: good finish, ripe fruit.

RAÍCES 2004 TR
tempranillo.

87 Colour: cherry, garnet rim. Nose: cocoa bean, sweet spices, creamy oak, expressive. Palate: spicy, flavourful, fleshy, toasty.

BODEGAS JUAN RAMÍREZ

Torrecilla, 138
13300 Valdepeñas (Ciudad Real)
☎: +34 926 322 021 - Fax: +34 926 320 495
info@bodegasjuanramirez.com
www.bodegasjuanramirez.com

ALBA DE LOS INFANTES 2009 BFB
100% airén.

82 Colour: bright yellow. Nose: toasty, spicy. Palate: lacks balance, toasty.

ALBA DE LOS INFANTES 2006 TC
100% tempranillo.

82 Colour: deep cherry, garnet rim. Nose: fruit preserve, fruit liqueur notes. Palate: fruity, good finish.

ALBA DE LOS INFANTES 2001 TR
100% tempranillo.

85 Colour: cherry, garnet rim. Nose: spicy, creamy oak, candied fruit. Palate: powerful, flavourful, toasty.

BODEGAS MARÍN PERONA

Castellanos, 99
13300 Valdepeñas (Ciudad Real)
☎: +34 926 313 192 - Fax: +34 926 313 347
bodegas@merxi.com
www.tejeruelas.com

VIÑA ALDANTE 2010 B
100% airén.

85 Colour: bright straw. Nose: white flowers, fruit expression, fresh. Palate: fresh, easy to drink, flavourful.

MARÍN PERONA VERDEJO 2010 B
100% verdejo.

84 Color bright straw. Aroma fresh, fresh fruit, white flowers, expressive. Taste flavourful, fruity, good acidity, balanced.

TEJERUELAS 2010 B
100% airén.

81 Colour: bright straw. Nose: medium intensity, citrus fruit, short. Palate: light-bodied, fruity.

TEJERUELAS SEMI 2010 B
100% airén.

80 Colour: bright straw. Nose: dried herbs, short. Palate: easy to drink, good finish, sweetness.

TEJERUELAS 2010 T
100% tempranillo.

86 Colour: black cherry, purple rim. Nose: expressive, powerfull, fruit expression. Palate: fleshy, fruity, great length.

VIÑA ALDANTE 2010 T
60% tempranillo, 40% airén.

82 Colour: cherry, garnet rim. Nose: short, fresh, balsamic herbs. Palate: light-bodied, easy to drink.

CALAR VIEJO 2007 TC
100% tempranillo.

86 Colour: cherry, garnet rim. Nose: toasty, sweet spices, cocoa bean, candied fruit. Palate: powerful, flavourful, toasty.

MARÍN PERONA 2004 TR
100% tempranillo.

86 Colour: cherry, garnet rim. Nose: ripe fruit, spicy, toasty. Palate: flavourful, soft tannins, balsamic, balanced.

MARÍN PERONA 2000 TGR
100% tempranillo.

87 Colour: cherry, garnet rim. Nose: ripe fruit, spicy, toasty, complex. Palate: powerful, flavourful, toasty, round tannins.

BODEGAS MEGIA E HIJOS - CORCOVO-

Magdalena, 33
13300 Valdepeñas (Ciudad Real)
☎: +34 926 347 828 - Fax: +34 926 347 829
jamegia@corcovo.com
www.corcovo.com

CORCOVO VERDEJO 2010 B
100% verdejo.

87 Colour: bright yellow. Nose: fresh fruit, citrus fruit, wild herbs, varietal. Palate: balanced, fine bitter notes, flavourful.

CORCOVO AIREN 2010 B
100% airén.

85 Colour: bright golden. Nose: white flowers, fresh fruit, citrus fruit, expressive. Palate: good acidity, fruity, flavourful.

CORCOVO TEMPRANILLO 2010 T
100% tempranillo.

87 Colour: very deep cherry, purple rim. Nose: balanced, expressive, red berry notes. Palate: correct, fruity, great length, flavourful.

CORCOVO SYRAH 24 BARRICAS 2009 T
100% syrah.

88 Colour: cherry, purple rim. Nose: fresh fruit, floral, expressive, complex, creamy oak. Palate: good acidity, fruity, fleshy, round tannins.

CORCOVO TEMPRANILLO 2009 T ROBLE
100% tempranillo.

86 Colour: cherry, garnet rim. Nose: ripe fruit, sweet spices, toasty. Palate: harsh oak tannins, long, flavourful.

CORCOVO 2007 TC
100% tempranillo.

87 Colour: bright cherry, garnet rim. Nose: ripe fruit, balanced, expressive, sweet spices. Palate: fruity, flavourful, good structure.

CORCOVO 2005 TR
100% tempranillo.

86 Colour: cherry, garnet rim. Nose: spicy, cocoa bean, creamy oak. Palate: soft tannins, fleshy, good acidity.

BODEGAS MUREDA

Ctra. N-IV, Km. 184,1
13300 Valdepeñas (Ciudad Real)
☎: +34 926 318 058 - Fax: +34 926 318 058
administracion@mureda.es
www.mureda.es

MUREDA CUVÉE BRUT 2008 ESP
60% sauvignon blanc, 20% airén, 20% macabeo.

85 Colour: bright straw. Nose: fresh fruit, fine lees, floral, sweet spices, pattiserie. Palate: fresh, fruity, flavourful, good acidity.

MUREDA CUVÉE BRUT ROSÉ 2008 ESP
100% garnacha.

82 Colour: light cherry. Nose: candied fruit, sweet spices. Palate: ripe fruit, easy to drink.

MUREDA GRAN CUVÉE 2007 ESP RESERVA
60% chardonnay, 20% airén, 20% macabeo.

84 Colour: yellow. Nose: ripe fruit, spicy, dry nuts. Palate: correct, good finish, easy to drink.

BODEGAS NAVARRO LÓPEZ

Autovía Madrid - Cádiz, Km. 193
13300 Valdepeñas (Ciudad Real)
☎: +34 902 193 431 - Fax: +34 902 193 432
laboratorio@navarrolopez.com
www.navarrolopez.com

DON AURELIO 2008 TC
cencibel.

87 Colour: black cherry, garnet rim. Nose: balanced, ripe fruit, spicy. Palate: flavourful, good structure, ripe fruit.

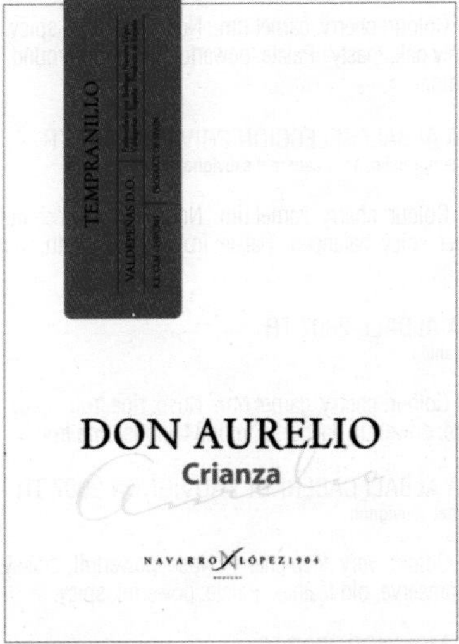

DON AURELIO MACABEO VERDEJO 2010 B
macabeo, verdejo.

85 Colour: bright straw. Nose: fresh, white flowers, tropical fruit. Palate: flavourful, fruity, good acidity, balanced.

DON AURELIO 2010 RD
tempranillo.

88 Colour: raspberry rose. Nose: white flowers, fresh fruit, red berry notes, complex, expressive. Palate: balanced, fruity, flavourful, fleshy.

DON AURELIO TEMPRANILLO 2010 T

87 Colour: cherry, purple rim. Nose: fresh fruit, red berry notes, floral. Palate: flavourful, fruity, good acidity, round tannins.

DON AURELIO GARNACHA 2010 T
garnacha.

86 Colour: very deep cherry. Nose: wild herbs, red berry notes, medium intensity. Palate: fleshy, good structure, fruity, fruity aftestaste.

DON AURELIO 2009 T BARRICA
100% tempranillo.

86 Colour: cherry, purple rim. Nose: red berry notes, fresh, expressive. Palate: easy to drink, fruity, flavourful.

DON AURELIO 2006 TR
tempranillo.

86 Colour: cherry, garnet rim. Nose: candied fruit, fruit preserve, spicy. Palate: fruity, fleshy, good structure.

DON AURELIO 2005 TGR
tempranillo.

86 Colour: bright cherry, garnet rim. Nose: candied fruit, spicy. Palate: flavourful, fruity, balanced.

BODEGAS REAL

Finca Marisánchez - Ctra. de Valdepeñas a Cózar, Km. 12,8
13300 Valdepeñas (Ciudad Real)
☎: +34 914 577 588 - Fax: +34 914 577 210
comercial@bodegas-real.com
www.bodegas-real.com

BONAL TEMPRANILLO 2010 T
100% tempranillo.

87 Colour: cherry, purple rim. Nose: ripe fruit, red berry notes, scrubland. Palate: good acidity, powerful, flavourful.

PALACIO DE IBOR 2004 TR
80% tempranillo, 20% cabernet sauvignon.

85 Colour: pale ruby, brick rim edge. Nose: ripe fruit, old leather, cigar, sweet spices. Palate: good acidity, flavourful, harsh oak tannins.

FÉLIX SOLÍS

Autovía del Sur, Km. 199
13300 Valdepeñas (Ciudad Real)
☎: +34 926 322 400 - Fax: +34 926 322 417
fsa@felixsolisavantis.com
www.felixsolisavantis.com

VIÑA ALBALI SEMIDULCE 2010 B
airén.

84 Colour: bright yellow. Nose: dried herbs, dried flowers. Palate: correct, sweetness.

ALBALI ARIUM VERDEJO 2010 B
verdejo.

84 Colour: bright golden. Nose: white flowers, citrus fruit, tropical fruit, expressive. Palate: fruity, flavourful, fresh, fleshy.

VIÑA ALBALI VERDEJO 2010 B
verdejo.

83 Colour: bright straw. Nose: tropical fruit, fragrant herbs, neat. Palate: fresh, light-bodied.

LOS MOLINOS VIURA AIREN 2010 B
viura, airén.

82 Colour: bright straw. Nose: expressive, floral, fresh. Palate: easy to drink, light-bodied.

VIÑA ALBALI TEMPRANILLO 2010 RD
tempranillo.

86 Colour: rose, purple rim. Nose: red berry notes, floral, expressive. Palate: fleshy, fruity, fresh.

ALBALI ARIUM 2010 RD
tempranillo.

86 Color rose, purple rim. Aroma powerfull, ripe fruit, red berry notes, floral, expressive. Taste fleshy, powerful, fruity, fresh.

LOS MOLINOS 2010 RD
tempranillo.

84 Colour: salmon. Nose: wild herbs, floral, medium intensity. Palate: fresh, light-bodied, easy to drink.

ALBALI ARIUM TEMPRANILLO 2010 T
100% tempranillo.

87 Colour: bright cherry, cherry, purple rim. Nose: red berry notes, lactic notes, balanced. Palate: fruity, full.

VIÑA ALBALI TEMPRANILLO 2010 T
tempranillo.

85 Colour: black cherry, purple rim. Nose: medium intensity, wild herbs. Palate: powerful, ripe fruit, great length.

LOS MOLINOS 2010 T
100% tempranillo.

82 Colour: cherry, purple rim. Nose: floral, ripe fruit, fresh. Palate: fleshy, light-bodied, fresh.

ALBALI ARIUM 2008 TC
100% tempranillo.

88 Colour: bright cherry, garnet rim. Nose: ripe fruit, wet leather, spicy. Palate: flavourful, fruity, round tannins.

LOS MOLINOS 2008 TC
tempranillo.

84 Colour: bright cherry, garnet rim. Nose: ripe fruit, spicy, old leather. Palate: ripe fruit, easy to drink.

VIÑA ALBALI 2008 TC
tempranillo.

84 Colour: cherry, garnet rim. Nose: wet leather, animal reductive notes, spicy. Palate: flavourful, correct, great length.

ALBALI ARIUM 2007 TR
100% tempranillo.

87 Colour: cherry, garnet rim. Nose: ripe fruit, spicy, creamy oak, toasty. Palate: powerful, flavourful, round tannins.

VIÑA ALBALI SELECCIÓN PRIVADA 2007 TR
85% tempranillo, 15% cabernet sauvignon.

87 Colour: cherry, garnet rim. Nose: cedar wood, wet leather, spicy, balanced. Palate: fruity, great length, round tannins.

VIÑA ALBALI 2007 TR
tempranillo.

86 Colour: cherry, garnet rim. Nose: ripe fruit, spicy. Palate: powerful, flavourful, round tannins, ripe fruit.

VIÑA ALBALI CABERNET SAUVIGNON 2007 TR
cabernet sauvignon.

84 Colour: very deep cherry. Nose: powerfull, grassy, fruit preserve, old leather. Palate: powerful, spicy.

LOS MOLINOS 2007 TR
tempranillo.

83 Colour: light cherry, orangey edge. Nose: medium intensity, aromatic coffee, sweet spices. Palate: correct, flavourful.

ALBALI ARIUM 2005 TGR
100% tempranillo.

89 Colour: pale ruby, brick rim edge. Nose: ripe fruit, complex, spicy, toasty. Palate: balsamic, long, flavourful, fleshy, soft tannins.

LOS MOLINOS 2005 TGR
tempranillo.

87 Colour: pale ruby, brick rim edge. Nose: elegant, spicy, fine reductive notes, wet leather. Palate: spicy, fine tannins, long.

VIÑA ALBALI SELECCIÓN PRIVADA 2005 TGR
tempranillo.

87 Colour: pale ruby, brick rim edge. Nose: scrubland, spicy, dark chocolate. Palate: spicy, toasty, soft tannins.

VIÑA ALBALI 2005 TGR
tempranillo.

85 Colour: bright cherry, brick rim edge. Nose: wet leather, cigar, cocoa bean, expressive. Palate: fleshy, balsamic, toasty.

VIÑA ALBALI GRAN RESERVA DE LA FAMILIA 2003 TGR
tempranillo, cabernet sauvignon.

88 Colour: dark-red cherry, garnet rim. Nose: spicy, fine reductive notes, fruit liqueur notes. Palate: spicy, fine tannins, long.

GRUPO DE BODEGAS VINARTIS

Ctra. A-IV, Km. 200,5
13300 Valdepeñas (Ciudad Real)
☎: +34 926 347 860 - Fax: +34 926 322 742
www.grupodebodegasvinartis.com

PATA NEGRA 2009 T ROBLE
100% tempranillo.

84 Colour: cherry, garnet rim. Nose: ripe fruit, spicy, roasted coffee. Palate: balsamic, toasty.

SEÑORÍO DE LOS LLANOS 2009 T
tempranillo, cabernet sauvignon.

80 Colour: cherry, garnet rim. Nose: fruit liqueur notes, medium intensity, short. Palate: spicy, flavourful.

SEÑORÍO DE LOS LLANOS 2008 TC
tempranillo.

84 Colour: cherry, garnet rim. Nose: sweet spices, toasty. Palate: fresh, easy to drink, light-bodied.

SEÑORÍO DE LOS LLANOS 2007 TR
tempranillo.

85 Colour: bright cherry, orangey edge. Nose: cocoa bean, spicy, wet leather. Palate: good acidity, fleshy, flavourful.

PATA NEGRA 2005 TR
100% tempranillo.

83 Colour: cherry, garnet rim. Nose: spicy, aromatic coffee, toasty. Palate: light-bodied, flavourful.

SEÑORÍO DE LOS LLANOS 2005 TGR
tempranillo.

83 Colour: bright cherry, orangey edge. Nose: wet leather, sweet spices, toasty. Palate: flavourful, fleshy.

PATA NEGRA 2004 TGR
100% tempranillo.

86 Colour: cherry, garnet rim. Nose: cocoa bean, sweet spices, red berry notes. Palate: soft tannins, toasty, fleshy.

LOS MARCOS

Cristo, 2
13730 Santa Cruz de Mudela (Ciudad Real)
☎: +34 926 349 028 - Fax: +34 926 349 030
fernando@bodegasfernandocastro.com
www.bodegaslosmarcos.com

MONTECRUZ TEMPRANILLO S/C T
tempranillo.

83 Colour: cherry, purple rim. Nose: ripe fruit, fresh, medium intensity. Palate: light-bodied, fresh, flavourful.

MONTECRUZ 2004 TR
tempranillo.

85 Colour: light cherry, orangey edge. Nose: ripe fruit, cocoa bean, spicy. Palate: flavourful, spicy.

MONTECRUZ SELECCIÓN 2002 TGR

84 Colour: black cherry, garnet rim. Nose: fruit preserve, slightly evolved, spicy. Palate: fleshy, flavourful, round tannins.

MIGUEL CALATAYUD S.A.

Postas, 20
13300 Valdepeñas (Ciudad Real)
☎: +34 926 348 070 - Fax: +34 926 322 150
vegaval@vegaval.com
www.vegaval.com

VEGAVAL PLATA VERDEJO 2010 B
100% verdejo.

84 Colour: bright golden. Nose: tropical fruit, floral, fresh. Palate: light-bodied, fresh, fruity.

VEGAVAL PLATA TEMPRANILLO 2010 T
100% tempranillo.

85 Colour: cherry, purple rim. Nose: red berry notes, fresh, balanced. Palate: fruity, flavourful, fleshy.

VEGAVAL PLATA GARNACHA 2010 T
100% garnacha.

84 Colour: cherry, purple rim. Nose: wild herbs, balsamic herbs, medium intensity. Palate: fresh, flavourful, easy to drink.

VEGAVAL PLATA MERLOT 2010 T
100% merlot.

83 Colour: cherry, purple rim. Nose: fresh, expressive, red berry notes. Palate: light-bodied, fresh, fruity.

VEGAVAL PLATA CABERNET SAUVIGNON 2010 T
100% cabernet sauvignon.

83 Colour: cherry, purple rim. Nose: balsamic herbs, fragrant herbs, fresh. Palate: easy to drink, balsamic.

VEGAVAL PLATA SYRAH 2010 T
100% syrah.

82 Colour: cherry, purple rim. Nose: fresh, red berry notes, short. Palate: lacks fruit, stalky.

VEGAVAL PLATA 2008 TC
100% tempranillo.

85 Colour: cherry, garnet rim. Nose: ripe fruit, spicy, toasty. Palate: correct, fresh, flavourful.

VEGAVAL PLATA 2006 TR
100% tempranillo.

83 Colour: cherry, garnet rim. Nose: medium intensity, spicy, ripe fruit. Palate: correct, easy to drink, good finish.

VEGAVAL PLATA 2004 TGR
100% tempranillo.

75

VEGAVAL PLATA AIRÉN 2010 SS
95% airén, 5% verdejo.

83 Colour: bright golden. Nose: dried herbs, grassy, fresh. Palate: light-bodied, fresh, easy to drink.

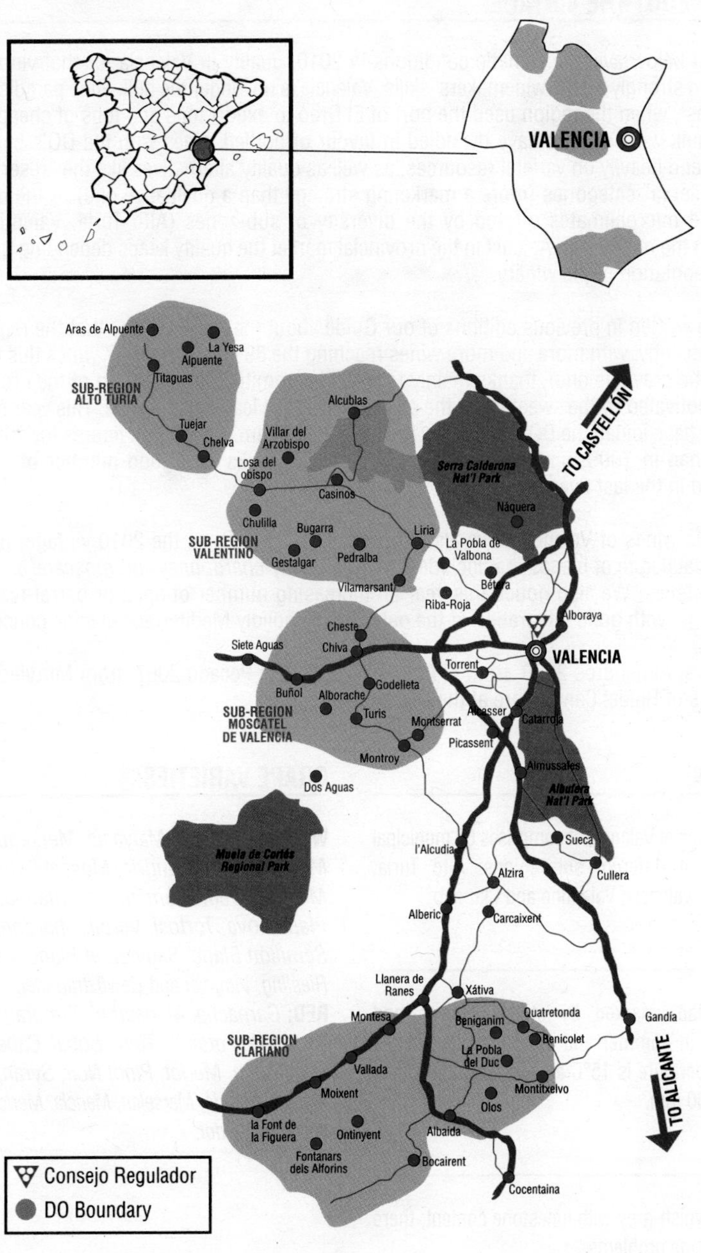
VALENCIA
Aras de Alpuente
La Yesa
Alpuente
Titaguas
SUB-REGION ALTO TURIA
Tuejar
Chelva
Alcublas
Villar del Arzobispo
Losa del obispo
Casinos
Chulilla
Bugarra
Pedralba
Gestalgar
SUB-REGION VALENTINO
Serra Calderona Nat'l Park
Náquera
TO CASTELLÓN
Liria
La Pobla de Valbona
Bétera
Vilamarsant
Riba-Roja
Alboraya
Cheste
Siete Aguas
Chiva
VALENCIA
Torrent
Buñol
Alborache
Godelleta
Turis
SUB-REGION MOSCATEL DE VALENCIA
Montserrat
Alcasser
Catarroja
Picassent
Montroy
Almussafes
Dos Aguas
Albufera Nat'l Park
Muela de Cortés Regional Park
Sueca
l'Alcudia
Cullera
Alzira
Alberic
Carcaixent
Llanera de Ranes
Xátiva
Montesa
Quatretonda
Beniganim
Benicolet
Gandía
SUB-REGION CLARIANO
La Pobla del Duc
Vallada
Montixelvo
Moixent
Olos
TO ALICANTE
la Font de la Figuera
Ontinyent
Albaida
Fontanars dels Alforins
Bocairent
Cocentaina
Consejo Regulador
DO Boundary

NEWS ABOUT THE VINTAGE:

With just below-average climatic conditions in 2010, quality in Valencia for that vintage has depended strongly on the winemakers' skills. Valencia is no longer the bulk-wine paradise it was in the past, when the region used the port of El Grao to export tons and tons of cheap wines. Today, bulk-wine exports have dwindled in favour of bottled wines with the DO's back label that depend heavily on varietal resources, as well as quality alternatives like the "reserva" and "gran reserva" categories (more a marketing strategy than a qualitative one) or the different soils and microclimates offered by the diversity of sub-zones (Alto Turia, Valentino and Clariano) the region has. At least in the provincial market the quality keeps depending primarily on the reputation of the winery.

We have written in previous editions of our Guide about the meteoric rise that the region has known recently, with more and more wines reaching the 89-point mark (37 wines this year for just 29 the previous one), thanks mainly to a solid commitment on the part of the producers, highly motivated by the sweet times the sector is living, at least quality-wise. This year two new wineries have joined the DO, which now includes 84 of them. Production figures for 2010 were higher than in 2009, up to 2,5 million litres more, thanks to a good number of hectares replanted in the last five years.

The white wines of Valencia have also improved their quality in the 2010 vintage, thanks a diverse catalogue of blends that includes predominantly *chardonnay* and *moscatel* along with other varieties. We also notice this year an increasing number of aged or barrel-fermented renderings, with good integration of the oak within a solidly Mediterranean wine concept.

As always, Almendros 2009, from El Angosto, Cueva del Pecado 2007, from Murviedro, and the wines of Rafael Cambra are at the top of the ratings

LOCATION:

In the province of Valencia. It comprises 66 municipal districts in 4 different sub-regions: Alto Turia, Moscatel de Valencia, Valentino and Clariano.

CLIMATE:

Mediterranean, marked by strong storms and downpours in summer and autumn. The average annual temperature is 15°C and the average annual rainfall is 500 mm.

SOIL:

Mostly brownish-grey with limestone content; there are no drainage problems.

GRAPE VARIETIES:

WHITE: *Macabeo, Malvasía, Merseguera, Moscatel de Alejandría, Moscatel de Grano Menudo, Pedro Ximénez, Plantafina, Plantanova, Tortosí, Verdil, Chardonnay, Semillon Blanc, Sauvignon Blanc, Verdejo, Riesling, Viognier* and *Gewüztraminer.*
RED: *Garnacha, Monastrell, Tempranillo, Tintorera, Forcallat Tinta, Bobal, Cabernet Cauvignon, Merlot, Pinot Noir, Syrah, Graciano, Malbec, Mandó, Marselan, Mencía, Merlot, Mazuelo* and *Petit Verdot.*

SUB-REGIONS:

There are four in total: **Alto Turia,** the highest sub-region (700 to 800 m above sea level) comprising 6 municipal districts; **Valentino** (23 municipal districts), in the centre of the province; the altitude varies between 250 m and 650 m; **Moscatel de Valencia** (9 municipal districts), also in the central region where the historical wine from the region is produced; and **Clariano** (33 municipal districts), to the south, at an altitude of between 400 m and 650 m.

FIGURES:

Vineyard surface: 13,079 – **Wine-Growers:** 11,000 – **Wineries:** 84 – **2010 Harvest rating:** Very Good – **Production:** 64,479,053 litres – **Market percentages:** 32% domestic. 68% export

CONSEJO REGULADOR
Quart, 22
46001 Valencia
☎: +34 963 910 096 - Fax: +34 963 910 029
@ info@vinovalencia.org
www.vinovalencia.org

GENERAL CHARACTERISTICS OF THE WINES

WHITES	The most classic, young and fresh with pleasant wild nuances, are produced from *Merseguera*. Also typical are those made from *Moscatel* (the historic variety of the region), and are used both for dry white wines, very aromatic and light, and for the characteristic Mistelas of the region, which have a pale colour when they are from the latest harvest and golden yellow if they are older. They are all characterised by their musky and grapy aromas.
ROSÉS	The current trend is towards raspberry pink coloured rosés, which are fresh and light, with a good fruity and aromatic potency.
REDS	The most characteristic wines are produced from *Monastrell* and *Garnacha*; the wines are slightly warm with notes of ripe fruit, although with less vigour than those from Utiel-Requena and lighter than those from Alicante. Wines from other varieties have begun to be produced recently, mainly *Tempranillo* and *Cabernet Sauvignon*, which give supple, flavourful red wines with a Mediterranean character.

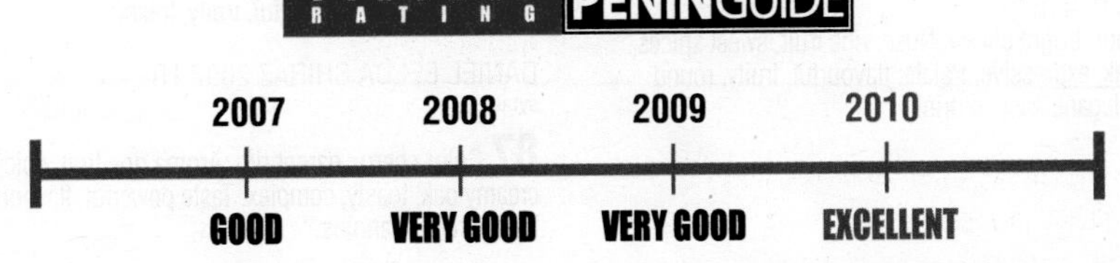

ALVAREZ NÖLTING

Colón 7, 21
46004 Valencia (Valencia)
☎: +34 963 290 696 - Fax: +34 963 445 463
info@alvareznolting.com
www.alvareznolting.com

ALVAREZ NÖLTING CHARDONNAY 2010 B BARRICA
100% chardonnay.

90 Colour: bright yellow. Nose: powerfull, candied fruit, citrus fruit. Palate: spicy, ripe fruit, fine bitter notes, long.

ALVAREZ NÖLTING SYRAH 2008 T
100% syrah.

91 Colour: cherry, garnet rim. Nose: roasted coffee, earthy notes. Palate: flavourful, powerful, spicy, ripe fruit.

ALVAREZ NÖLTING 2006 T
70% tempranillo, 30% cabernet sauvignon.

91 Colour: cherry, garnet rim. Nose: ripe fruit, spicy, creamy oak, toasty, characterful. Palate: powerful, flavourful, toasty, round tannins.

ANTONIO ARRAEZ

Arcediano Ros, 35
46630 Fuente La Higuera (Valencia)
☎: +34 962 290 031 - Fax: +34 962 290 339
info@bodegasarraez.com
www.antonioarraez.com

A2 VERDIL 2010 B
verdil.

88 Color bright straw. Aroma fresh, fresh fruit, white flowers, expressive. Taste flavourful, fruity, good acidity, balanced.

MALA VIDA 2009 T ROBLE
cabernet sauvignon, monastrell, garnacha tintorera, syrah.

89 Color bright cherry. Aroma ripe fruit, sweet spices, creamy oak, expressive. Taste flavourful, fruity, toasty, round tannins.

A2 MONASTRELL 2009 T ROBLE
100% monastrell.

88 Colour: bright cherry. Nose: ripe fruit, sweet spices, creamy oak, expressive. Palate: flavourful, fruity, round tannins, elegant, easy to drink.

A2 SYRAH 2009 T ROBLE
100% syrah.

84 Colour: light cherry, orangey edge. Nose: fruit preserve, sweet spices, toasty. Palate: unctuous, flavourful, fleshy.

LAGARES 2009 TC
100% cabernet sauvignon.

83 Colour: cherry, garnet rim. Nose: ripe fruit, spicy, creamy oak, toasty, slightly evolved. Palate: powerful, flavourful, toasty.

LAGARES 2006 TR
cabernet sauvignon, syrah, monastrell.

85 Colour: deep cherry, orangey edge. Nose: red berry notes, ripe fruit, old leather. Palate: good acidity, long, spicy.

BODEGA J. BELDA

Ctra. Benirrama s/n
46635 Fontanars dels Alforins (Valencia)
☎: +34 962 222 278 - Fax: +34 962 222 245
info@danielbelda.com
www.danielbelda.com

DANIEL BELDA CHARDONNAY 2010 B
chardonnay.

88 Colour: bright yellow. Nose: powerfull, ripe fruit, creamy oak, cocoa bean. Palate: rich, smoky aftertaste, flavourful, fresh, good acidity.

DANIEL BELDA VERDIL 2010 B
verdil.

83 Colour: bright straw. Nose: grassy, sulphur notes. Palate: fruity, fresh.

DANIEL BELDA ROSAT 2010 RD
merlot.

87 Colour: rose, purple rim. Nose: powerfull, ripe fruit, red berry notes. Palate: fleshy, powerful, fruity, fresh.

DANIEL BELDA PINOT NOIR 2010 T
pinot noir.

88 Colour: bright cherry. Nose: expressive, ripe fruit, raspberry. Palate: flavourful, fruity, fresh.

DANIEL BELDA SHIRAZ 2007 TR
syrah.

87 Color cherry, garnet rim. Aroma ripe fruit, spicy, creamy oak, toasty, complex. Taste powerful, flavourful, toasty, round tannins.

DANIEL BELDA MERLOT 2007 TR
merlot.

85 Colour: cherry, garnet rim. Nose: ripe fruit, cocoa bean, dark chocolate, spicy. Palate: good acidity, flavourful, fleshy.

CA'BELDA 2006 T FERMENTADO EN BARRICA
monastrell, tintorera.

91 Colour: cherry, garnet rim. Nose: ripe fruit, spicy, complex. Palate: powerful, flavourful, toasty, round tannins.

BODEGA LA VIÑA

Portal de Valencia, 52
46630 La Font de la Figuera (Valencia)
☎: +34 962 290 078 - Fax: +34 962 232 039
info@vinosdelavina.com
www.vinosdelavina.com

ICONO CHARDONNAY 2010 B
chardonnay.

85 Colour: bright straw. Nose: fresh, fresh fruit, white flowers. Palate: flavourful, fruity, good acidity, balanced.

ICONO SYRAH 2010 T
syrah.

87 Color cherry, purple rim. Aroma expressive, fresh fruit, red berry notes, floral. Taste flavourful, fruity, good acidity, round tannins.

ICONO TEMPRANILLO 2010 T
tempranillo.

87 Colour: cherry, purple rim. Nose: red berry notes, floral, ripe fruit. Palate: flavourful, fruity, good acidity, round tannins.

CASA L'ANGEL CABERNET 2010 T
cabernet sauvignon.

86 Colour: cherry, garnet rim. Nose: fruit preserve, warm, scrubland. Palate: powerful, spicy, ripe fruit.

ICONO MERLOT 2010 T
merlot.

85 Colour: black cherry. Nose: ripe fruit, sweet spices, warm. Palate: flavourful, fruity, round tannins.

ICONO CABERNET SAUVIGNON 2010 T
cabernet sauvignon.

84 Colour: cherry, purple rim. Nose: ripe fruit, grassy, green pepper. Palate: flavourful, fleshy, light-bodied.

CASA L'ANGEL 2010 T
tempranillo, cabernet sauvignon.

83 Colour: cherry, garnet rim. Nose: fruit preserve, characterful. Palate: powerful, concentrated, sweetness.

CASA L'ANGEL CEPAS VIEJAS 2009 T
tempranillo, cabernet sauvignon.

88 Colour: deep cherry. Nose: powerfull, fruit preserve, warm. Palate: powerful, fleshy, good structure.

VENTA DEL PUERTO 12 2008 T
cabernet sauvignon, merlot, syrah, tempranillo.

91 Colour: bright cherry. Nose: sweet spices, creamy oak, ripe fruit. Palate: flavourful, toasty, round tannins, spicy.

VENTA DEL PUERTO 18 VENDIMIA SELECCIONADA 2007 T BARRICA
tempranillo, cabernet sauvignon, merlot, syrah.

90 Colour: cherry, garnet rim. Nose: ripe fruit, spicy, toasty, characterful, roasted coffee. Palate: powerful, flavourful, toasty, ripe fruit.

BODEGAS ARANLEÓN

Ctra. Caudete, 3
46310 Los Marcos - Caudete de las Fuentes (Valencia)
☎: +34 963 631 640 - Fax: +34 962 185 150
maria@aranleon.com
www.aranleon.com

BLÉS CRIANZA DE ARANLEÓN 2008 TC
50% tempranillo, 30% monastrell, 20% cabernet sauvignon.

88 Colour: cherry, garnet rim. Nose: red berry notes, ripe fruit, expressive, creamy oak. Palate: powerful, flavourful, fleshy, toasty.

EL ÁRBOL DE ARANLEÓN 2007 TC
monastrell, tempranillo, syrah, merlot, cabernet sauvignon.

91 Colour: cherry, garnet rim. Nose: spicy, creamy oak, toasty, characterful. Palate: powerful, flavourful, toasty.

BODEGAS 40 GRADOS NORTE

Fontanares
(Valencia)
☎: +34 615 167 272
dmocholi@40gradosnorte.com
www.40gradosnorte.com

MAR DE SAÓ 2008 T
55% syrah, 20% bobal, 25% tempranillo.

88 Colour: cherry, garnet rim. Nose: spicy, toasty, complex, ripe fruit. Palate: powerful, flavourful, toasty, round tannins.

COTA 8 30 2007 T
40% bobal, 40% tempranillo, 20% cabernet sauvignon.

90 Colour: cherry, garnet rim. Nose: spicy, toasty, complex, ripe fruit, mineral. Palate: powerful, toasty, round tannins.

BODEGAS BATALLER

Camí Real, 94-96
46841 Castelló de Rugat (Valencia)
☎: +34 962 813 017 - Fax: +34 962 813 017
vinosbenicadell@telepolis.com

D'ALBA VARIETAL MOSCATEL 2010 B
100% moscatel.

85 Colour: pale. Nose: fresh fruit, citrus fruit, varietal. Palate: flavourful, fruity, fresh.

BENICADELL TEMPRANILLO 2010 T
100% tempranillo.

83 Colour: cherry, purple rim. Nose: fresh, ripe fruit, medium intensity. Palate: flavourful, fruity, correct.

BENICADELL 2008 TC
100% tempranillo.

78

BODEGAS EL ANGOSTO

Martínez Valls, 41
46870 Ontinyent (Valencia)
☎: +34 962 380 638 - Fax: +34 962 911 349
info@bodegaelangosto.com
www.bodegaelangosto.com

ALMENDROS 2010 B
verdejo, chardonnay, riesling.

92 Colour: bright yellow. Nose: powerfull, ripe fruit, sweet spices, creamy oak, fragrant herbs. Palate: rich, flavourful, fresh, good acidity.

LA TRIBU 2010 T
monastrell, syrah, garnacha tintorera.

89 Colour: cherry, purple rim. Nose: fresh fruit, red berry notes. Palate: flavourful, fruity, good acidity, round tannins.

ANGOSTO NEGRE 2009 T
garnacha tintorera, syrah, cabernet franc.

92 Colour: cherry, garnet rim. Nose: ripe fruit, spicy, toasty, complex, sweet spices, balsamic herbs, scrubland. Palate: flavourful, toasty, round tannins.

ANGOSTO 2010 B
verdejo, moscatel grano menudo, chardonnay.

91 Colour: bright straw. Nose: faded flowers, ripe fruit, citrus fruit, grassy. Palate: flavourful, fleshy, complex.

ALMENDROS 2009 T
34% garnacha tintorera, 33% syrah, 33% marselan.

95 Colour: cherry, garnet rim. Nose: spicy, creamy oak, toasty, complex, mineral, dry stone, fruit expression. Palate: powerful, flavourful, toasty, round tannins.

BODEGAS EL VILLAR S.C.V.

Avda. del Agricultor, 1- P.I. San Vicente
46170 Villar de Arzobispo (Valencia)
☎: +34 962 720 050 - Fax: +34 961 646 060
coopvillar@elvillar.com
www.elvillar.com

LADERAS 2010 B
macabeo.

83 Colour: bright straw. Nose: floral, fresh fruit. Palate: flavourful, fruity, fresh.

LADERAS 2010 T
tempranillo.

81 Colour: cherry, garnet rim. Nose: ripe fruit, warm, spicy. Palate: easy to drink, slightly evolved.

TAPIAS 2005 TC
merlot.

82 Colour: pale ruby, brick rim edge. Nose: pattiserie, spicy, aromatic coffee, wet leather. Palate: fine bitter notes, spicy, ripe fruit.

VIÑA VILLAR 2004 TR
tempranillo.

83 Colour: pale ruby, brick rim edge. Nose: ripe fruit, tobacco, wet leather, waxy notes. Palate: correct, good acidity, flavourful.

BODEGAS ENGUERA

Ctra. CV - 590, Km. 51,5
46810 Enguera (Valencia)
☎: +34 962 224 318 - Fax: +34 961 364 167
bodega@cessa.es
www.bodegasenguera.com

BLANC D'ENGUERA 2010 B
verdil.

88 Colour: bright yellow. Nose: powerfull, ripe fruit, sweet spices, creamy oak, fragrant herbs. Palate: rich, flavourful, fresh, good acidity.

MEGALA 2009 T
monastrell, syrah.

92 Colour: cherry, garnet rim. Nose: ripe fruit, spicy, creamy oak, toasty, mineral. Palate: powerful, flavourful, toasty, round tannins.

ANGELICAL 2007 T
tempranillo, monastrell, syrah.

89 Colour: bright cherry. Nose: ripe fruit, sweet spices, creamy oak, lactic notes. Palate: flavourful, fruity, toasty, round tannins.

SUEÑO DE MEGALA 2006 T
tempranillo, monastrell, merlot.

91 Colour: cherry, garnet rim. Nose: elegant, candied fruit, fine reductive notes, spicy. Palate: flavourful, spicy, ripe fruit.

BODEGAS LOS FRAILES

Casa Los Frailes, s/n
46635 Fontanaresdels Alforins (Valencia)
☎: +34 962 222 220 - Fax: +34 963 363 153
info@bodegaslosfrailes.com
www.bodegaslosfrailes.com

TRILOGÍA 2010 B
33% sauvignon blanc, 33% moscatel, 33% verdil.

90 Colour: bright yellow. Nose: powerfull, ripe fruit, sweet spices, creamy oak, fragrant herbs. Palate: rich, flavourful, fresh, good acidity.

EFE MONASTRELL 2010 RD BARRICA
100% monastrell.

86 Colour: brilliant rose. Nose: powerfull, raspberry, red berry notes, spicy, fragrant herbs. Palate: flavourful, ripe fruit, good acidity.

BILOGÍA 2010 T
50% monastrell, 50% tempranillo.

89 Colour: bright cherry. Nose: ripe fruit, sweet spices, creamy oak, varietal. Palate: flavourful, toasty, round tannins, long.

EFE MONASTRELL 2010 T
100% monastrell.

88 Colour: cherry, garnet rim. Nose: powerfull, ripe fruit, fruit expression. Palate: flavourful, ripe fruit, spicy.

TRILOGÍA 2008 T
70% monastrell, 20% cabernet sauvignon, 10% tempranillo.

92 Colour: cherry, garnet rim. Nose: ripe fruit, spicy, creamy oak, toasty, characterful, mineral. Palate: powerful, flavourful, toasty, spicy, ripe fruit.

MOMA DELS FRADES 2008 T BARRICA
50% monastrell, 50% marselan.

90 Color bright cherry. Aroma ripe fruit, sweet spices, creamy oak, expressive. Taste flavourful, fruity, toasty, round tannins.

LOS FRAILES 2008 T
monastrell, cabernet sauvignon.

90 Colour: cherry, garnet rim. Nose: complex, red berry notes, creamy oak. Palate: powerful, flavourful, toasty, fleshy, fruity.

AFTER 3 VENDIMIA TARDÍA 2005 T
100% monastrell.

87 Colour: cherry, garnet rim. Nose: ripe fruit, spicy, roasted coffee, cocoa bean. Palate: powerful, flavourful, toasty.

BODEGAS LOS PINOS

Casa Los Pinos
46635 Fontanars dels Alforins (Valencia)
☎: +34 962 222 090 - Fax: +34 962 222 086
bodegaslospinos@bodegaslospinos.com
www.bodegaslospinos.com

BROTE 2010 BFB
70% verdil, 30% viognier.

88 Colour: bright straw. Nose: fresh, fresh fruit, white flowers, sweet spices. Palate: flavourful, fruity, good acidity, balanced.

DOMINIO LOS PINOS SALVATGE 2010 B
33% moscatel, 33% sauvignon blanc, 33% verdil.

84 Colour: bright straw. Nose: citrus fruit, fragrant herbs, fresh. Palate: good acidity, fruity, flavourful.

DOMINIO LOS PINOS SALVATGE 2010 RD
50% monastrell, 50% garnacha.

81 Colour: rose, purple rim. Nose: candied fruit, red berry notes. Palate: sweetness, powerful.

DOMINIO LOS PINOS 2010 T BARRICA
40% tempranillo, 40% syrah, 20% cabernet sauvignon.

89 Colour: bright cherry. Nose: expressive, red berry notes, lactic notes, creamy oak. Palate: flavourful, fruity, round tannins.

LOS PINOS 0 % 2010 T
40% monastrell, 30% syrah, 30% garnacha.

88 Colour: cherry, purple rim. Nose: expressive, floral, ripe fruit, earthy notes. Palate: flavourful, fruity, good acidity.

DOMINIO LOS PINOS SALVATGE 2010 T
60% monastrell, 40% cabernet franc.

87 Colour: cherry, purple rim. Nose: expressive, fresh fruit, red berry notes. Palate: flavourful, fruity, good acidity, long, round.

DOMINIO LOS PINOS 2009 TC
50% cabernet sauvignon, 30% monastrell, 20% merlot.

90 Colour: cherry, garnet rim. Nose: creamy oak, toasty, complex, red berry notes. Palate: powerful, flavourful, toasty, round tannins.

BROTE 2008 TC
40% garnacha, 40% merlot, 20% monastrell.

88 Colour: black cherry. Nose: ripe fruit, creamy oak, toasty, dark chocolate. Palate: powerful, ripe fruit, fine bitter notes.

BODEGAS MURVIEDRO

Ampliación Pol. El Romeral, s/n
46340 Requena (Valencia)
☎: +34 962 329 003 - Fax: +34 962 329 002
murviedro@murviedro.es
www.murviedro.es

ALBA DE MURVIEDRO 2010 B
60% sauvignon blanc, 40% moscatel.

88 Colour: bright straw. Nose: fresh, white flowers, varietal. Palate: flavourful, fruity, good acidity, balanced.

LOS MONTEROS 2010 B
50% merseguera, 50% moscatel.

88 Colour: bright straw. Nose: fresh, fresh fruit, white flowers, varietal, citrus fruit. Palate: flavourful, fruity, good acidity, balanced.

ESTRELLA 10 2010 B
moscatel.

87 Color golden. Aroma powerfull, floral, honeyed notes, candied fruit, fragrant herbs. Taste flavourful, sweet, fresh, fruity, good acidity, long.

ROSA DE MURVIEDRO 2010 RD

86 Colour: rose, purple rim. Nose: powerfull, ripe fruit, red berry notes, floral. Palate: fleshy, fruity, fresh.

ESTRELLA 10 2010 RD
75% moscatel, 25% garnacha.

84 Colour: rose, purple rim. Nose: candied fruit, fresh, expressive, balanced. Palate: powerful, flavourful, fruity, fresh.

MURVIEDRO COLECCIÓN PETIT VERDOT 2010 T
petit verdot.

90 Colour: cherry, garnet rim. Nose: powerfull, ripe fruit, raspberry, fruit expression. Palate: flavourful, ripe fruit, spicy, long.

MURVIEDRO COLECCIÓN SYRAH 2010 T
syrah.

88 Colour: bright cherry. Nose: ripe fruit, sweet spices, lactic notes. Palate: flavourful, fruity, round tannins.

MURVIEDRO EXPRESIÓN 2008 TC
55% monastrell, 45% garnacha.

92 Colour: bright cherry. Nose: sweet spices, expressive, roasted coffee, powerfull, fruit expression. Palate: flavourful, fruity, toasty, round tannins.

MURVIEDRO 2008 TC
50% tempranillo, 30% monastrell, 20% syrah.

90 Colour: cherry, garnet rim. Nose: spicy, toasty, cocoa bean. Palate: powerful, spicy, easy to drink.

LOS MONTEROS 2008 TC

88 Colour: bright cherry. Nose: ripe fruit, sweet spices, creamy oak, toasty. Palate: flavourful, fruity, toasty, round tannins.

CUEVA DEL PECADO 2007 T
60% tempranillo, 40% cabernet sauvignon.

93 Colour: cherry, garnet rim. Nose: ripe fruit, fruit expression, scrubland, balsamic herbs. Palate: flavourful, fleshy, spicy, balsamic.

BODEGAS ONTINIUM

Avda. Almansa, 17
46870 Ontinyent (Valencia)
☎: +34 962 380 849 - Fax: +34 962 384 419
info@coopontinyent.com
www.coopontinyent.com

ONTINIUM 2010 B
80% macabeo, 20% merseguera.

78

ONTINIUM SYRAH 2010 T
100% syrah.

88 Colour: cherry, purple rim. Nose: expressive, fresh fruit, red berry notes, floral, lactic notes. Palate: flavourful, fruity, good acidity, fleshy.

ONTINIUM TEMPRANILLO 2010 T
100% tempranillo.

84 Colour: cherry, purple rim. Nose: expressive, fresh fruit, red berry notes. Palate: flavourful, fruity, good acidity, round tannins.

ONTINIUM 2008 T BARRICA
60% syrah, 30% tempranillo, 10% monastrell.

83 Colour: cherry, garnet rim. Nose: ripe fruit, spicy, complex, old leather. Palate: powerful, flavourful, toasty, round tannins.

BODEGAS POLO MONLEÓN

Ctra. Valencia - Ademuz, Km. 86
46178 Titaguas (Valencia)
☎: +34 961 634 148 - Fax: +34 961 634 148
info@hoyadelcastillo.com
www.hoyadelcastillo.com

HOYA DEL CASTILLO ALTO TURIA 2010 B
70% mersenguera, 30% macabeo.

89 Colour: bright yellow. Nose: powerfull, ripe fruit, sweet spices, creamy oak, fragrant herbs. Palate: rich, flavourful, fresh, good acidity.

HOYA DEL CASTILLO ALTO TURIA 2010 RD
100% bobal.

84 Colour: brilliant rose. Nose: elegant, fresh fruit, red berry notes. Palate: flavourful, fruity, fresh.

HOYA DEL CASTILLO ALTO TURIA 2010 T
80% tempranillo, 20% bobal.

86 Colour: cherry, purple rim. Nose: fresh fruit, red berry notes, floral. Palate: flavourful, fruity, good acidity.

HOYA DEL CASTILLO 2006 TC
80% tempranillo, 10% bobal, 10% garnacha.

86 Colour: cherry, garnet rim. Nose: ripe fruit, spicy, creamy oak, toasty. Palate: powerful, flavourful, toasty, round tannins.

BODEGAS SÁNCHEZ ZAHONERO

Ricardo Serrano, 13
46392 Siete Aguas (Valencia)
☎: +34 962 340 052
bodega@sanchezzahonero.com
www.sanchezzahonero.com

CAPRICHO 2008 T
tempranillo, syrah, garnacha.

88 Colour: bright cherry. Nose: sweet spices, creamy oak, red berry notes. Palate: flavourful, fruity, toasty, round tannins.

LÉSSÈNCIA 2008 T
syrah, tempranillo.

84 Colour: cherry, garnet rim. Nose: ripe fruit, spicy, toasty, complex, expressive. Palate: powerful, flavourful, toasty, round tannins.

LÉSSÈNCIA 2007 T
tempranillo, syrah.

82 Colour: cherry, garnet rim. Nose: ripe fruit, spicy, toasty, rancio notes. Palate: powerful, flavourful, toasty.

BODEGAS UTIELANAS

San Fernando, 18
46300 Utiel (Valencia)
☎: +34 962 171 157 - Fax: +34 962 170 801
info@bodegasutielanas.com
www.bodegasutielanas.com

SUEÑOS DEL MEDITERRÁNEO 2010 B
macabeo.

84 Colour: bright straw. Nose: fresh, fresh fruit, white flowers, expressive. Palate: flavourful, fruity, good acidity.

SUEÑOS DEL MEDITERRÁNEO 2010 RD
bobal.

83 Colour: brilliant rose. Nose: powerfull, ripe fruit, red berry notes, fragrant herbs. Palate: flavourful, fresh.

SUEÑOS DEL MEDITERRÁNEO 2010 T
bobal.

85 Colour: cherry, purple rim. Nose: red berry notes, floral, ripe fruit. Palate: flavourful, fruity, good acidity, round tannins.

SUEÑOS DEL MEDITERRÁNEO 2010 T FERMENTADO EN BARRICA
100% bobal.

83 Colour: bright cherry. Nose: ripe fruit, sweet spices, creamy oak. Palate: flavourful, fruity, toasty.

SUEÑOS DEL MEDITERRÁNEO 2008 TC

83 Colour: pale ruby, brick rim edge. Nose: ripe fruit, old leather, spicy. Palate: good acidity, unctuous, slightly evolved.

BODEGAS ÚVULA

Doctor J.J. Domine, 3 - 16
46011 (Valencia)
☎: +34 657 982 696
info@cuinare.com

ÚVULA PLATTUM S/C S/C T

84 Colour: pale ruby, brick rim edge. Nose: ripe fruit, cocoa bean, spicy, slightly evolved. Palate: flavourful, fleshy, ripe fruit.

BODEGAS VEGALFARO

Ctra. Pontón - Utiel, Km. 3
46430 El Derramador - Requena (Valencia)
☎: +34 962 320 680 - Fax: +34 962 321 126
info@vegalfaro.com
www.vegalfaro.com

PASAMONTE 2010 B
sauvignon blanc.

88 Colour: bright yellow. Nose: ripe fruit, creamy oak, fragrant herbs. Palate: rich, flavourful, fresh, good acidity.

PASAMONTE 2009 T
garnacha tintorera.

91 Colour: bright cherry. Nose: ripe fruit, sweet spices, creamy oak, expressive, complex. Palate: flavourful, fruity, toasty, round tannins.

REBEL.LIA 2009 T
40% bobal, 40% garnacha tintorera, 20% tempranillo.

88 Colour: cherry, garnet rim. Nose: red berry notes, ripe fruit, cocoa bean, aromatic coffee, toasty. Palate: good acidity, flavourful, fleshy.

BODEGAS VEGAMAR S.L.

Garcesa, s/n
46175 Calles (Valencia)
☎: +34 962 109 813 - Fax: +34 962 100 320
comercial@bodegasvegamar.com
www.bodegasvegamar.com

VIÑA COSTOSA 2010 B
60% macabeo, 40% sauvignon blanc.

84 Colour: bright straw. Nose: fresh, fresh fruit, expressive. Palate: flavourful, fruity, good acidity.

VIÑA CARRASSES 2006 TC
50% tempranillo, 30% merlot, 10% cabernet sauvignon.

84 Colour: cherry, garnet rim. Nose: ripe fruit, spicy, toasty. Palate: flavourful, toasty, round tannins.

VEGAMAR 2005 TR
80% tempranillo, 20% cabernet sauvignon.

85 Colour: cherry, garnet rim. Nose: ripe fruit, spicy, creamy oak, toasty. Palate: powerful, flavourful, toasty, round tannins.

BODEGAS VICENTE GANDÍA PLA

Ctra. Cheste a Godelleta, s/n
46370 Chiva (Valencia)
☎: +34 962 524 242 - Fax: +34 962 524 243
sgandia@vicentegandia.com
www.vicentegandia.com

EL MIRACLE CHARDONNAY-SAUVIGNON BLANC 2010 B
60% chardonnay, 40% sauvignon blanc.

85 Color bright straw. Aroma fresh, fresh fruit, white flowers, expressive. Taste flavourful, fruity, good acidity, balanced.

FUSTA NOVA BLANC 2010 B
moscatel.

85 Colour: bright straw. Nose: white flowers, fragrant herbs, mineral. Palate: light-bodied, fresh, fruity.

CASTILLO DE LIRIA 2010 B
80% viura, 20% sauvignon blanc.

83 Colour: bright straw. Nose: overripe fruit, floral, balsamic herbs. Palate: flavourful, good acidity, correct.

FUSTA NOVA MOSCATEL 2008 B
100% moscatel.

87 Colour: golden. Nose: powerfull, floral, honeyed notes, candied fruit. Palate: flavourful, sweet, fresh, fruity, long.

EL MIRACLE 120 ANIVERSARIO 2009 T
65% tempranillo, 35% syrah.

86 Colour: bright cherry. Nose: ripe fruit, sweet spices, creamy oak. Palate: flavourful, fruity, toasty.

CASTILLO DE LIRIA 2007 TC
100% tempranillo.

83 Colour: cherry, garnet rim. Nose: ripe fruit, spicy, creamy oak, toasty. Palate: powerful, flavourful, toasty.

CASTILLO DE LIRIA 2007 TR
100% tempranillo.

83 Colour: cherry, garnet rim. Nose: ripe fruit, creamy oak, toasty, balsamic herbs. Palate: powerful, flavourful, toasty.

CASTILLO DE LIRIA 2010 MOSCATEL
moscatel.

86 Colour: bright straw. Nose: ripe fruit, candied fruit, floral. Palate: fresh, fruity, flavourful, spirituous.

BODEGAS VICENTE RIBERA E HIJO

Pol. Ind. L'Ombria - P5
46635 Fontanares (Valencia)
☎: +34 609 867 777 - Fax: +34 962 222 168
bodegas.ribera@terra.es

CLAUS DE CELLER 2007 TR
syrah, tempranillo, merlot.

88 Colour: cherry, garnet rim. Nose: ripe fruit, spicy, aromatic coffee, balsamic herbs, scrubland. Palate: flavourful, spicy.

ATUELL 2007 T
tempranillo, merlot, garnacha tintorera.

86 Colour: cherry, garnet rim. Nose: ripe fruit, spicy, creamy oak, toasty. Palate: powerful, flavourful, toasty.

VICENTE RIBERA CABERNET SHYRAZ 2006 TC
cabernet sauvignon, syrah.

82 Colour: cherry, garnet rim. Nose: ripe fruit, spicy, creamy oak, toasty, fine reductive notes. Palate: powerful, flavourful, toasty, round tannins.

BODEGAS VIDAL

Valencia, 16
12550 Almazora (Castellón)
☎: +34 964 503 300 - Fax: +34 964 560 604
info@bodegasvidal.com
www.bodegasvidal.com

UVA D'OR MOSCATEL MISTELA
moscatel.

91 Color golden. Aroma powerfull, floral, honeyed notes, candied fruit, fragrant herbs. Taste flavourful, sweet, fresh, fruity, good acidity, long.

CELLER DEL ROURE

Ctra. de Les Alcusses, Km. 2,5
46640 Moixent (Valencia)
☎: +34 962 295 020
info@cellerdelroure.es

CULLEROT 2010 B
25% macabeo, 25% malvasía, 10% pedro ximénez, 5% verdil, 35% chardonnay.

89 Colour: bright straw. Nose: fresh, fresh fruit, white flowers. Palate: flavourful, fruity, good acidity, fine bitter notes.

CULLEROT 2009 B
macabeo, malvasía, pedro ximénez, verdil, chardonnay.

88 Colour: bright straw. Nose: floral, fragrant herbs, expressive, complex. Palate: long, good acidity, balanced, unctuous.

LES ALCUSSES 2008 T
60% monastrell, 10% garnacha tintorera, 10% cabernet sauvignon, 15% merlot.

91 Colour: cherry, garnet rim. Nose: powerfull, complex, earthy notes, ripe fruit. Palate: ripe fruit, spicy, good acidity.

MADURESA 2007 T
20% mandó, 20% cabernet sauvignon, 20% syrah, 10% petit verdot, 10% monastrell, 20% otras.

92 Colour: cherry, garnet rim. Nose: spicy, creamy oak, toasty, complex, mineral, dry stone, ripe fruit. Palate: powerful, flavourful, toasty, round tannins.

CHERUBINO VALSANGIACOMO

Ctra. Cheste - Godelleta, Km. 1
46370 Chiva (Valencia)
☎: +34 962 510 451 - Fax: +34 962 511 361
carlos.valsangiacomo@cherubino.es
www.cherubino.es

MARQUÉS DE CARO 2010 B
70% merseguera, 30% moscatel.

86 Color bright straw. Aroma fresh, fresh fruit, white flowers, expressive. Taste flavourful, fruity, good acidity, balanced.

MARQUÉS DE CARO MOSCATEL 2010 B
100% moscatel.

85 Colour: bright straw. Nose: candied fruit, citrus fruit, floral. Palate: flavourful, sweet, fine bitter notes.

MARQUÉS DE CARO TEMPRANILLO 2010 T
100% tempranillo.

87 Colour: cherry, purple rim. Nose: red berry notes, floral, ripe fruit. Palate: flavourful, fruity, good acidity, round tannins.

MARQUÉS DE CARO SHIRAZ 2010 T
100% syrah.

85 Colour: cherry, garnet rim. Nose: powerfull, scrubland. Palate: fine bitter notes, ripe fruit, slightly green tannins.

MARQUÉS DE CARO 2006 TC
60% cabernet sauvignon, 30% syrah, 10% bobal.

83 Colour: cherry, garnet rim. Nose: ripe fruit, spicy, creamy oak, toasty. Palate: powerful, flavourful, toasty, round tannins.

MARQUÉS DE CARO 2005 TR
50% tempranillo, 50% cabernet sauvignon.

83 Colour: pale ruby, brick rim edge. Nose: ripe fruit, old leather, spicy. Palate: flavourful, fleshy, long.

VITTORE 2010 MOSCATEL
100% moscatel.

87 Colour: bright straw. Nose: white flowers, candied fruit, honeyed notes. Palate: flavourful, sweetness.

CHESTE AGRARIA COOP. V. ANECOOP BODEGAS

La Estación, 5
46380 Cheste (Valencia)
☎: +34 962 511 671 - Fax: +34 962 511 732
bodega@chesteagraria.com
www.reymos.es

AMATISTA 2010 ESP
100% moscatel.

87 Colour: pale. Nose: white flowers, fresh fruit, citrus fruit, expressive. Palate: flavourful, fruity, fresh.

REYMOS 2010 ESP
100% moscatel.

76

COOP. V. SAN PEDRO APÓSTOL. MOIXENT

Pza. de la Hispanidad, 4
46640 Moixent (Valencia)
☎: +34 962 260 020 - Fax: +34 962 260 560
info@closdelavall.com
www.closdelavall.com

CLOS DE LA VALL PX 2010 BFB
pedro ximénez.

90 Color bright yellow. Aroma powerfull, ripe fruit, sweet spices, creamy oak, fragrant herbs. Taste rich, smoky aftertaste, flavourful, fresh, good acidity.

CLOS DE LA VALL 2010 B
macabeo, moscatel.

86 Colour: bright straw. Nose: fresh, fresh fruit, white flowers. Palate: flavourful, fruity, good acidity, balanced.

CLOS DE LA VALL 2009 T
monastrell, cabernet sauvignon, tempranillo.

86 Colour: cherry, purple rim. Nose: expressive, red berry notes, floral. Palate: flavourful, fruity, fleshy, ripe fruit.

CLOS DE LA VALL 2007 TC
monastrell, cabernet sauvignon, tempranillo.

88 Colour: cherry, garnet rim. Nose: candied fruit, fruit liqueur notes, toasty, spicy. Palate: powerful, spicy, long.

CLOS DE LA VALL 2006 TR
monastrell, cabernet sauvignon, tempranillo.

87 Color cherry, garnet rim. Aroma ripe fruit, spicy, creamy oak, toasty, complex. Taste powerful, flavourful, toasty, round tannins.

HERETAT DE TAVERNERS

Ctra. Fontanars - Moixent, Km. 1,8
46635 Fontanars dels Alforins (Valencia)
☎: +34 962 132 437 - Fax: +34 962 222 298
info@heretatdetaverners.com
www.heretatdetaverners.com

HERETAT DE TAVERNERS REIXIU 2010 BC
chardonnay, sauvignon blanc.

90 Colour: bright yellow. Nose: ripe fruit, sweet spices, creamy oak, fragrant herbs, elegant. Palate: rich, smoky aftertaste, flavourful, fresh, good acidity.

HERETAT DE TAVERNERS BEN VIU S/C T
graciano, otras.

87 Colour: cherry, garnet rim. Nose: ripe fruit, spicy, creamy oak, toasty, complex, earthy notes. Palate: powerful, flavourful, toasty, long.

HERETAT DE TAVERNERS GRACIANO 2008 TR
graciano.

91 Colour: cherry, garnet rim. Nose: ripe fruit, spicy, creamy oak, complex, mineral. Palate: powerful, flavourful, toasty, fleshy.

HERETAT DE TAVERNERS EL VERN 2007 TC
tempranillo, garnacha tintorera, cabernet sauvignon, merlot.

88 Color bright cherry. Aroma ripe fruit, sweet spices, creamy oak, expressive. Taste flavourful, fruity, toasty, round tannins.

HERETAT DE TAVERNERS MALLAURA 2006 TR
cabernet sauvignon, monastrell, tempranillo, garnacha tintorera.

87 Color cherry, garnet rim. Aroma ripe fruit, spicy, creamy oak, toasty, complex. Taste powerful, flavourful, toasty, round tannins.

PUNT DOLÇ T
monastrell, garnacha tintorera.

91 Colour: cherry, garnet rim. Nose: ripe fruit, spicy, creamy oak, toasty, complex. Palate: powerful, flavourful, toasty, sweet.

LA BARONÍA DE TURIS

Ctra. de Godelleta, 22
46389 Turis (Valencia)
☎: +34 962 526 011 - Fax: +34 962 527 282
baronia@baroniadeturis.es
www.baroniadeturis.es

DOMINIO DEL MAGRO 2010 B
semillón blanc.

85 Colour: bright straw. Nose: fresh fruit, white flowers, varietal. Palate: flavourful, fruity, good acidity.

1920 2008 T
cabernet sauvignon, merlot, syrah.

89 Colour: cherry, garnet rim. Nose: ripe fruit, spicy, creamy oak, toasty, earthy notes. Palate: powerful, flavourful, toasty, round tannins.

LA LUNA DE MAR 2008 T
tempranillo, cabernet sauvignon, merlot, syrah.

88 Colour: bright cherry. Nose: sweet spices, creamy oak, fruit expression. Palate: flavourful, fruity, toasty, round tannins.

DONA DOLÇA 2010 MISTELA
moscatel.

82 Colour: bright straw. Nose: citrus fruit, grapey, expressive. Palate: good acidity, fresh, fruity.

MISTELA MOSCATEL TURÍS 2010 VINO DE LICOR
moscatel.

88 Colour: bright straw. Nose: powerfull, candied fruit, citrus fruit, honeyed notes. Palate: powerful, sweet, fleshy.

LA CASA DE LAS VIDES BODEGUES I VINYES

Corral el Galtero, s/n
46890 Agullent (Valencia)
☎: +34 962 135 003 - Fax: +34 962 135 494
bodega@lacasadelasvides.com
www.lacasadelasvides.com

ACVLIVS 2008 T
70% monastrell, 20% tempranillo, 10% syrah.

90 Colour: cherry, garnet rim. Nose: ripe fruit, spicy, toasty, fine reductive notes. Palate: powerful, flavourful, toasty.

CVP 2008 T
50% tempranillo, 40% syrah, 10% otras.

84 Colour: cherry, garnet rim. Nose: ripe fruit, spicy, creamy oak, toasty. Palate: powerful, flavourful, toasty, round tannins.

PAGO CASA GRAN

Ctra. Mogente Fontanares, km. 9,5
46640 Mogente (Valencia)
☎: +34 962 261 004 - Fax: +34 962 261 004
comercial@pagocasagran.com
www.pagocasagran.com

REPOSO 2010 B
70% gewürztraminer, 30% moscatel.

88 Colour: straw. Nose: scrubland, fresh fruit, citrus fruit, mineral. Palate: fruity, fresh, light-bodied, sweetness.

CASA BENASAL 2010 T
syrah, monastrell, merlot.

88 Colour: cherry, purple rim. Nose: ripe fruit, scrubland, spicy, toasty. Palate: flavourful, fleshy, fruity.

CASA BENASAL ELEGANT 2008 T
monastrell, syrah, garnacha tintorera.

90 Colour: bright cherry. Nose: ripe fruit, sweet spices, creamy oak. Palate: flavourful, fruity, toasty, round tannins.

CASA BENASAL CRUX 2008 T
garnacha tintorera, monastrell, syrah.

90 Colour: cherry, garnet rim. Nose: characterful, ripe fruit, fruit expression, creamy oak. Palate: flavourful, powerful, fleshy.

CASA BENASAL 2008 T
merlot, syrah, cabernet sauvignon, monastrell.

85 Colour: cherry, garnet rim. Nose: medium intensity, slightly evolved, fruit preserve, candied fruit. Palate: powerful, fleshy, ripe fruit.

FALCATA ARENAL 2007 T
garnacha, monastrell.

91 Colour: cherry, garnet rim. Nose: ripe fruit, spicy, creamy oak, complex, earthy notes, mineral. Palate: powerful, flavourful, toasty, round tannins.

FALCATA CASA GRAN 2007 T
garnacha tintorera, monastrell.

90 Colour: cherry, garnet rim. Nose: ripe fruit, fruit expression, mineral, spicy, creamy oak. Palate: good acidity, flavourful, fleshy, round tannins.

FALCATA BIO 2009
merlot, syrah, monastrell.

88 Colour: cherry, garnet rim. Nose: red berry notes, ripe fruit, fragrant herbs, sweet spices. Palate: light-bodied, fruity, flavourful, easy to drink.

RAFAEL CAMBRA

Pza. Concepción, 13 - 19
46870 Ontinyent (Valencia)
☎: +34 616 463 245 - Fax: +34 962 383 855
rafael@rafaelcambra.es
www.rafaelcambra.es

EL BON HOMME 2010 T
50% monastrell, cabernet sauvignon.

90 Colour: cherry, purple rim. Nose: red berry notes, ripe fruit. Palate: flavourful, fruity, good acidity, round tannins.

MINIMUM 2009 T
70% monastrell, 30% cabernet franc.

93 Colour: cherry, garnet rim. Nose: spicy, toasty, complex, fruit expression, red berry notes, new oak. Palate: powerful, flavourful, round tannins, mineral.

RAFAEL CAMBRA DOS 2009 T
50% cabernet sauvignon, 50% cabernet franc.

91 Colour: bright cherry. Nose: sweet spices, creamy oak, expressive, red berry notes, ripe fruit. Palate: flavourful, fruity, toasty, round tannins, elegant.

RAFAEL CAMBRA UNO 2008 T
100% monastrell.

90 Colour: bright cherry. Nose: sweet spices, creamy oak, candied fruit, ripe fruit. Palate: flavourful, fruity, toasty.

TORRE ORIA

Ctra. Pontón - Utiel, Km. 3
46390 El Derramador (Valencia)
☎: +34 962 320 289 - Fax: +34 962 320 311
santiago.sancho@natra.es
www.torreoria.com

NU 2009 T
syrah.

88 Colour: cherry, garnet rim. Nose: ripe fruit, fruit preserve, creamy oak, sweet spices. Palate: fleshy, spicy, ripe fruit.

VIÑAS DEL PORTILLO S.L.

P.I. El Llano F2 P4 Apdo. 130
46360 Buñol (Valencia)
☎: +34 962 504 827 - Fax: +34 962 500 937
vinasdelportillo@vinasdelportillo.es

ALTURIA 2010 B

88 Colour: bright straw. Nose: fresh, fresh fruit, white flowers. Palate: flavourful, fruity, good acidity, balanced.

CASTILLO DE BUÑOL 2010 B
moscatel, macabeo, merseguera.

86 Color bright straw. Aroma fresh, fresh fruit, white flowers, expressive. Taste flavourful, fruity, good acidity, balanced.

CASTILLO DE BUÑOL 2010 T

78

CASTILLO DEL LLANO 2007 TC

84 Colour: pale ruby, brick rim edge. Nose: medium intensity, spicy, aromatic coffee. Palate: flavourful, spicy, easy to drink.

VITICULTORES LO NECESARIO

Casas del Rey
46310 Casas del Rey (Valencia)
☎: +34 636 172 417
diego@fernandezpons.es
www.lonecesario.es

LONECESARIO 2007 T
bobal.

92 Colour: deep cherry. Nose: powerfull, complex, warm, mineral, cocoa bean, creamy oak. Palate: complex, powerful, flavourful, round, mineral, creamy, toasty.

ZAGROMONTE

Ctra. L'Ombria, Km. 1
46635 Fontanars dels Alforins (Valencia)
☎: +34 962 222 261 - Fax: +34 962 222 257
info@bodegas-torrevellisca.es
www.bodegas-torrevellisca.com

PALACIO DE TORREVELLISCA 2010 B
25% verdejo, 50% macabeo, 25% verdil.

84 Colour: bright straw. Nose: fresh, fresh fruit, white flowers, expressive. Palate: flavourful, fruity, good acidity.

TORREVELLISCA MERLOT 2005 TC
merlot.

85 Colour: pale ruby, brick rim edge. Nose: ripe fruit, cigar, wet leather, spicy. Palate: correct, flavourful, spicy.

TORREVELLISCA 2001 TR
100% cabernet sauvignon.

84 Colour: pale ruby, brick rim edge. Nose: spicy, fine reductive notes, wet leather, fruit liqueur notes. Palate: spicy, fine tannins, elegant, long, spirituous.

PALACIO DE TORREVELLISCA 2010 T
50% tempranillo, 50% syrah.

83 Colour: cherry, purple rim. Nose: expressive, fresh fruit, red berry notes, floral. Palate: flavourful, fruity, good acidity.

ARGENTUM 2009 TC
50% tempranillo, 50% cabernet sauvignon.

84 Colour: pale ruby, brick rim edge. Nose: slightly evolved, old leather, ripe fruit. Palate: correct, flavourful, reductive nuances.

AURUM DE ZAGROMONTE 2009 TC
50% merlot, 50% cabernet sauvignon.

86 Colour: cherry, garnet rim. Nose: ripe fruit, roasted coffee, dark chocolate. Palate: powerful, toasty, ripe fruit.

BRUNDISIUM 2008 TC
50% tempranillo, 25% cabernet franc, 25% cabernet sauvignon.

87 Colour: pale ruby, brick rim edge. Nose: red berry notes, ripe fruit, old leather, tobacco, cocoa bean, sweet spices. Palate: balsamic, flavourful, fleshy.

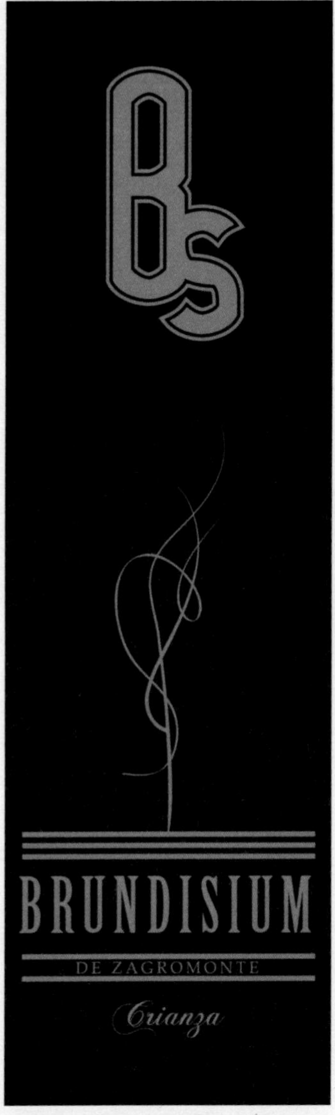

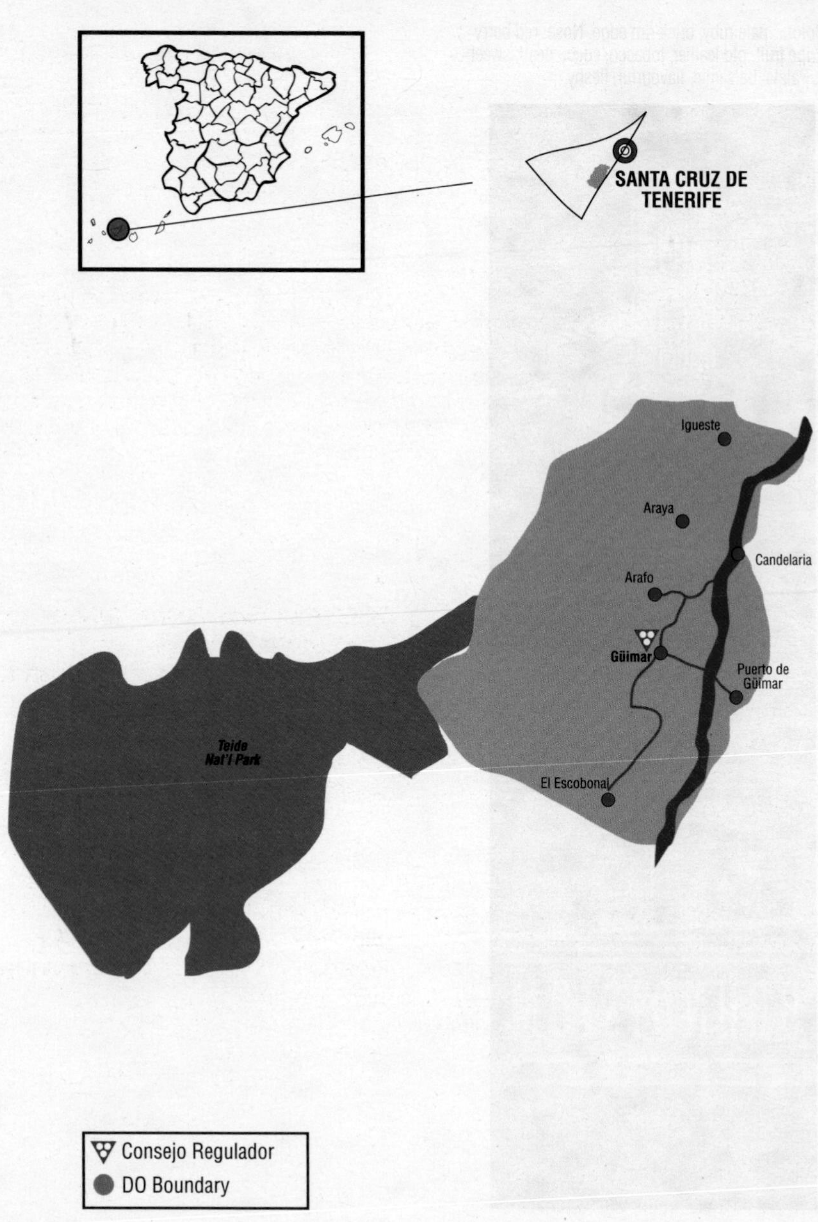
SANTA CRUZ DE TENERIFE
Igueste
Araya
Candelaria
Arafo
Güímar
Puerto de Güímar
Teide Nat'l Park
El Escobonal
Consejo Regulador
DO Boundary

NEWS ABOUT THE VINTAGE:

If last year the harvest was a little below average in terms of quality given an excess on the influence of the trade winds and the difficulty the grapes found to ripen properly, in this occasion, with just average climatic conditions, wines show more expressive, with lesser green notes and even excellent fruit expression in some red examples. We do not remember ever having as many wines (9) from this region reaching the 90-point mark. The white wine Gran Virtud gets again 92 points, pretty much in line with the best the region has to offer in that category. We understand producers have been far more careful and rigorous at picking time in order to achieve that sort of quality.

The diversity of soils (volcanic in the highlands, slate in the middle levels and with a more clay content in the flatlands) could provide forward-minded –if they were any– with an equally diverse catalogue of flavours, from white wines of the richest sweetness made from *listán* planted in the lowlands, to the more mineral and herbal renderings that might eventually be made from grapes grown in the middle and higher areas. In this sense it would also be possible to take advantage of the more subdued insolation levels of late afternoon on the west side of Teide to achieve wines that could surely become the most expressive examples in the whole of the island. It is a pity, though, that the Magi of winemaking do not exist here, just yet. The best wines are white *malvasía* renderings, with no oak whatsoever, or as little as possible.

LOCATION:

On the island of Tenerife. It practically constitutes a prolongation of the Valle de la Orotava region to the southeast, forming a valley open to the sea, with the Las Dehesas region situated in the mountains and surrounded by pine forests where the vines grow in an almost Alpine environment. It covers the municipal districts of Arafo, Candelaria and Güímar.

CLIMATE:

Although the influence of the trade winds is more marked than in Abona, the significant difference in altitude in a much reduced space must be pointed out, which gives rise to different microclimates, and pronounced contrasts in day-night temperatures, which delays the harvest until 1st November.

SOIL:

Volcanic at high altitudes, there is a black tongue of lava crossing the area where the vines are cultivated on a hostile terrain with wooden frames to raise the long vine shoots.

GRAPE VARIETIES:

WHITE: *Gual, Listán Blanco, Malvasía, Moscatel, Verdello* and *Vijariego.*
RED: *Bastardo Negro, Listán Negro* (15% of total), *Malvasía Tinta, Moscatel Negro, Negramoll, Vijariego Negro, Cabernet Sauvignon, Merlot, Pinot Noir, Ruby Cabernet, Syrah* and *Tempranillo.*

FIGURES:

Vineyard surface: 560 – **Wine-Growers:** 564 – **Wineries:** 21 – **2010 Harvest rating:** N/A – **Production:** 210,000 litres – **Market percentages:** 100% domestic

CONSEJO REGULADOR
Tafetana, 14
38500 Güímar (Santa Cruz de Tenerife)
☎: +34 922 514 709 - Fax: +34 922 514 485
@ consejo@vinosvalleguimar.com
www.vinosvalleguimar.com

GENERAL CHARACTERISTICS OF THE WINES

WHITES	These are the most characteristic product of the area, with more than 80% of the production. They are produced from *Listán Blanco*, and the best stand out for their expressivity, refinement and complexity. They have a pale yellow colour; delicate aromas of flowers and fruit; on the palate they are complex, flavourful and persistent.
REDS	These play a minor role in the overall production. Deep cherry-red coloured, they tend to be fruity with wild nuances; on the palate they are dry, fruity and light.

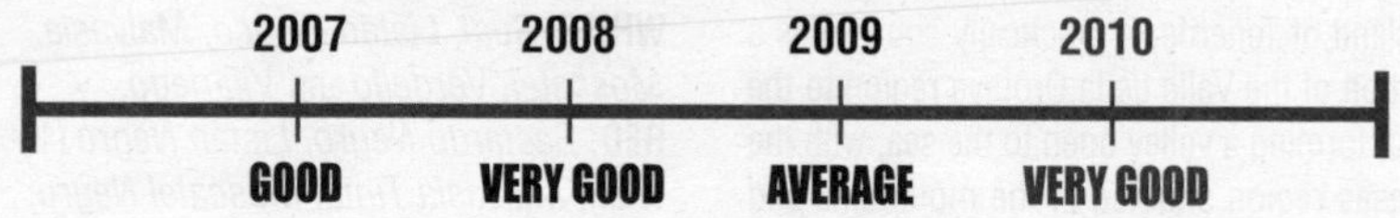

ARCA DE VITIS

Chinguaro, 26-B - San Francisco Javier
38500 Güímar (Santa Cruz de Tenerife)
☎: +34 922 512 552 - Fax: +34 922 512 552
arcadevitis@arcadevitis.com
www.arcadevitis.com

CONTIEMPO VIDUEÑOS SECO 2010 B
marmajuelo, malvasía, moscatel, verdejo, gual.

88 Colour: yellow, greenish rim. Nose: wild herbs, faded flowers, fresh. Palate: balanced, fine bitter notes, flavourful.

CONTIEMPO MOSCATEL AFRUTADO 2010 B
moscatel.

88 Colour: bright straw. Nose: powerfull, ripe fruit, citrus fruit, white flowers. Palate: ripe fruit, flavourful, good acidity.

CONTIEMPO MALVASÍA SECO 2010 B
malvasía.

84 Colour: bright straw, greenish rim. Nose: citrus fruit, wild herbs, fresh, medium intensity. Palate: fruity, light-bodied, good finish.

CONTIEMPO MALVASÍA 2008 B
malvasía.

88 Colour: bright yellow. Nose: candied fruit, spicy, balanced, powerfull. Palate: good structure, powerful, flavourful.

CONTIEMPO 2010 RD
listán negro, merlot.

84 Colour: brilliant rose. Nose: ripe fruit, raspberry, floral. Palate: fine bitter notes, fruity, fresh.

CONTIEMPO TINTO DE POSTRE 2010 T
baboso negro.

87 Colour: cherry, garnet rim. Nose: candied fruit, overripe fruit, raspberry. Palate: powerful, sweet, fruity.

CONTIEMPO VENDIMIA SELECCIONADA 2010 T
syrah.

85 Colour: deep cherry. Nose: balsamic herbs, powerfull, red berry notes, sweet spices. Palate: powerful, fine bitter notes, ripe fruit.

BODEGA COMARCAL VALLE DE GÜIMAR

Subida a Los Loros, Km. 4
38550 Arafo (Santa Cruz de Tenerife)
☎: +34 922 510 437 - Fax: +34 922 510 437
info@bodegacomarcalguimar.com
www.bodegacomarcalguimar.com

BRUMAS DE AYOSA 2010 B
listán blanco.

85 Colour: bright straw. Nose: white flowers, fresh fruit, dried herbs. Palate: flavourful, easy to drink.

BRUMAS DE AYOSA AFRUTADO 2010 B
listán blanco, marmajuelo, moscatel.

84 Colour: bright straw. Nose: white flowers, ripe fruit, citrus fruit. Palate: flavourful, fruity, sweetness.

BRUMAS DE AYOSA 2010 RD
listán negro.

82 Colour: rose, purple rim. Nose: medium intensity, floral, raspberry. Palate: flavourful, fruity.

BRUMAS DE AYOSA 2010 T
60% listán negro, tempranillo, ruby, cabernet sauvignon, merlot.

82 Colour: cherry, garnet rim. Nose: ripe fruit, medium intensity, balsamic herbs. Palate: flavourful, fruity.

BRUMAS DE AYOSA 2007 ESP RESERVA
listán blanco.

80 Colour: bright straw. Nose: powerfull, candied fruit, citrus fruit, lees reduction notes. Palate: sweetness, slightly acidic.

BRUMAS DE AYOSA 2007 ESP
listán blanco.

77

BODEGA PICO ARGUAMA

Lomo la Arena, 9
38530 Igueste Candelaria (Santa Cruz de Tenerife)
☎: +34 922 501 110

PICO ARGUAMA 2010 T
70% listán negro, 25% negramoll, 5% tintilla.

70

BODEGA VIÑA CHAGUA

Barranco Badajoz s/n
38500 Güimar (Santa Cruz de Tenerife)
☎: +34 922 514 289 - Fax: +34 922 511 168
bodegachagua@hotmail.es

CHAGUA AFRUTADO 2010 B
listán blanco, moscatel.

87 Colour: bright straw. Nose: white flowers, ripe fruit. Palate: flavourful, fruity, fresh.

BLANCO CHAGUA 2010 B
listán blanco.

80 Colour: bright straw. Nose: short, faded flowers. Palate: easy to drink, fresh.

TINTO CHAGUA 2010 T
listán negro.

80 Colour: deep cherry. Nose: ripe fruit, floral, medium intensity. Palate: flavourful, light-bodied.

BODEGAS VIÑA DEL MACHADO

Avda. Santa Cruz, 27
38500 Güimar (Santa Cruz de Tenerife)
☎: +34 922 512 544 - Fax: +34 922 514 651
ferreol@melosar.com
www.melosar.com

MELOSAR NATURALMENTE DULCE MALVASÍA 2008 B
malvasía.

90 Colour: bright golden. Nose: dry nuts, dried fruit, citrus fruit. Palate: powerful, sweet, good acidity.

VIÑA MELOSAR 2009 T BARRICA

84 Colour: cherry, garnet rim. Nose: fruit liqueur notes, fruit expression, dark chocolate, sweet spices. Palate: round tannins, ripe fruit.

MELOSAR NATURALMENTE DULCE 2008 T
listán negro, tempranillo, cabernet sauvignon.

84 Colour: black cherry. Nose: powerfull, warm, overripe fruit. Palate: sweet, concentrated, fine bitter notes.

EL BORUJO

Ctra. a la Cumbre, Km. 4,2
38550 Arafo (Santa Cruz de Tenerife)
☎: +34 636 824 919
el_borujo@hotmail.com
www.elborujo.es

EL BORUJO 2010 B BARRICA
gual, malvasía, moscatel, listán blanco.

91 Colour: bright yellow. Nose: candied fruit, sweet spices, balanced. Palate: flavourful, rich, fruity, spicy.

EL BORUJO 2010 B
listán blanco, moscatel, marmajuelo.

90 Colour: yellow, greenish rim. Nose: floral, jasmine, ripe fruit, tropical fruit, fine lees. Palate: balanced, fine bitter notes, easy to drink.

EL BORUJO 2009 B BARRICA
gual, malvasía, moscatel, listán blanco.

90 Colour: bright straw. Nose: powerfull, fine lees, fruit expression, tropical fruit. Palate: flavourful, powerful, fleshy.

EL BORUJO 2010 T
listán negro, tempranillo.

82 Colour: deep cherry. Nose: ripe fruit, fruit expression, dark chocolate. Palate: flavourful, ripe fruit, good acidity.

FERRERA

Calvo Sotelo, 44
38550 Arafo (Santa Cruz de Tenerife)
☎: +34 649 487 835 - Fax: +34 922 237 359
carmengloria@bodegaferrera.com

FERRERA 2010 B
albillo, listán blanco, moscatel.

86 Colour: bright straw. Nose: white flowers, balanced, expressive, tropical fruit. Palate: flavourful, fruity, ripe fruit.

FERRERA 2010 T

87 Colour: cherry, purple rim. Nose: fresh fruit, red berry notes, floral, sweet spices. Palate: flavourful, fruity, good acidity, round tannins.

LOS PELADOS

Hoya Cartaya, 32 - Chacona
38500 Güimar (Santa Cruz de Tenerife)
☎: +34 922 512 786 - Fax: +34 922 514 485
bodegaslospelados@hotmail.com

LOS PELADOS 2010 B
listán blanco.

84 Colour: bright straw, greenish rim. Nose: medium intensity, white flowers, citrus fruit, wild herbs. Palate: fruity, flavourful, easy to drink.

LOS PELADOS 2010 T
listán negro, negramoll.

88 Colour: deep cherry. Nose: fragrant herbs, ripe fruit, raspberry. Palate: flavourful, fine bitter notes, good acidity, fleshy.

MIGUEL ANGEL HERNÁNDEZ

Morras del Tanque
38550 Arafo (Santa Cruz de Tenerife)
☎: +34 922 511 405 - Fax: +34 922 290 064
mangel3@comtf.es

VIÑAS HERZAS 2010 T

78

VIÑAS HERZAS 2010 B
listán blanco, moscatel, gual.

87 Colour: bright straw, greenish rim. Nose: white flowers, wild herbs, citrus fruit. Palate: flavourful, fruity, easy to drink.

SAT VIÑA LAS CAÑAS

Barranco Badajoz, s/n
38500 Güimar (Santa Cruz de Tenerife)
☎: +34 637 592 759 - Fax: +34 922 512 716
vegalascanas@hotmail.com

GRAN VIRTUD LISTÁN BLANCO 2010 B
listán blanco.

91 Colour: bright straw, greenish rim. Nose: candied fruit, white flowers, complex, balanced. Palate: fruity, flavourful, spicy.

VEGA LAS CAÑAS AFRUTADO 2010 B
listán blanco, moscatel.

84 Colour: bright straw. Nose: powerfull, fruit expression, white flowers. Palate: fruity, fresh, sweetness.

VEGA LAS CAÑAS 2010 B
listán blanco.

83 Colour: bright straw. Nose: ripe fruit, citrus fruit, dried flowers. Palate: flavourful, fruity, fine bitter notes.

GRAN VIRTUD MALVASÍA 2009 B
malvasía.

90 Color bright straw. Aroma fresh, fresh fruit, white flowers, expressive. Taste flavourful, fruity, good acidity, balanced.

GRAN VIRTUD B
vijariego.

92 Colour: light mahogany. Nose: powerfull, floral, honeyed notes, candied fruit, fragrant herbs. Palate: flavourful, sweet, fresh, fruity, good acidity, long.

AMOR ALMA & ORIGEN 2010 RD

83 Colour: raspberry rose. Nose: floral, fresh fruit, raspberry. Palate: flavourful, fruity, fresh.

GRAN VIRTUD 2010 T

91 Color bright cherry. Aroma ripe fruit, sweet spices, creamy oak, expressive. Taste flavourful, fruity, toasty, round tannins.

GRAN VIRTUD 2010 T DULCE

90 Colour: cherry, purple rim. Nose: balsamic herbs, fruit expression, raspberry. Palate: flavourful, fruity, fleshy.

VEGA LAS CAÑAS 2010 T
listán negro, tintilla, syrah.

84 Colour: deep cherry. Nose: powerfull, ripe fruit, red berry notes. Palate: powerful, spicy.

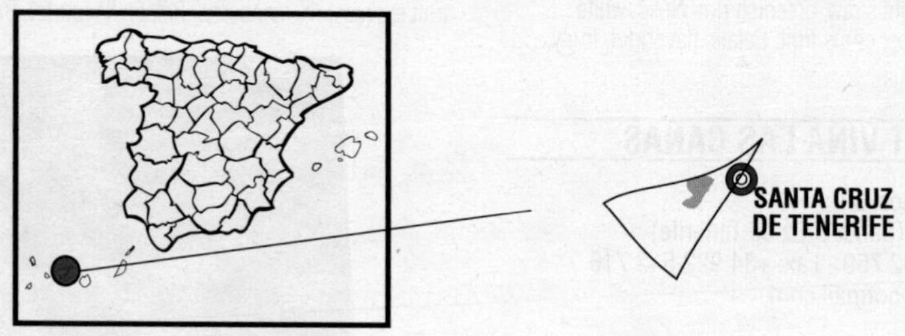
SANTA CRUZ
DE TENERIFE

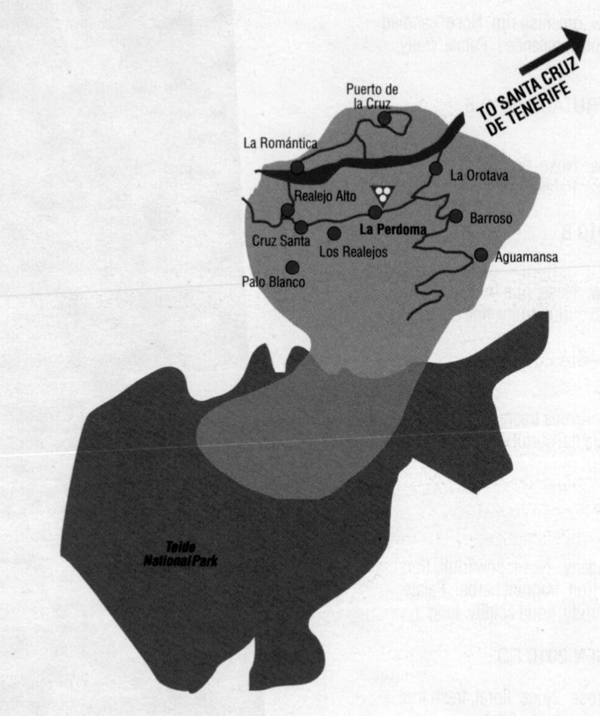
TO SANTA CRUZ
DE TENERIFE
Puerto de
la Cruz
La Romántica
La Orotava
Realejo Alto
La Perdoma
Barroso
Cruz Santa
Los Realejos
Aguamansa
Palo Blanco
Teide
National Park

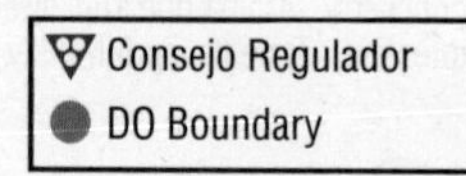
Consejo Regulador
DO Boundary

NEWS ABOUT THE VINTAGE:

It is not by chance that the marvellous landscape of La Orotava, beyond the banana plantings and the British "*malvasía*", amazed both Humboldt and Jules Verne. The banana still occupies the lowlands, and *malvasía* remained planted until the late 19th century, while today vineyards climb up the upper territories (thus exposed to the effects of the trade winds) that lead us to the Teide National Park. That is the reason why it is difficult to find a perfect vintage in this wine region. 2010 has been no exception to the rule, with abundant and occasional rains that delayed the cycle and made maturation an almost impossible goal. Thus, although they are more difficult to notice in white wines made from *listán*, some red wines show blatant herbaceous notes –on the verge of green–, caused by underripe grapes.

As a novelty, the region has a new winery, Suertes del Marqués, a project based on grape selection and vineyard partitioning. Suerte del Marqués Candio 2008 gets 90 points. Also in that sort of score range we find a sweet *malvasía*, Arautava Malvasía 2008, which gets 92 points. Not much, but something to mitigate the region's lack of bigger names.

LOCATION:

In the north of the island of Tenerife. It borders to the west with the DO Ycoden-Daute-Isora and to the east with the DO Tacoronte-Acentejo. It extends from the sea to the foot of the Teide, and comprises the municipal districts of La Orotava, Los Realejos and El Puerto de la Cruz.

CLIMATE:

As with the other regions on the islands, the weather is conditioned by the trade winds, which in this region result in wines with a moderate alcohol content and a truly Atlantic character. The influence of the Atlantic is also very important, in that it moderates the temperature of the costal areas and provides a lot of humidity. Lastly, the rainfall is rather low, but is generally more abundant on the north face and at higher altitudes.

SOIL:

Light, permeable, rich in mineral nutrients and with a slightly acidic pH due to the volcanic nature of the island. The vineyards are at an altitude of between 250 mm and 700 m.

GRAPE VARIETIES:

WHITE:
MAIN: *Güal, Malvasía, Verdello, Vijariego, Albillo, Forastera Blanca* o *Doradilla, Sabro, Breval* and *Burrablanca.*
AUTHORIZED: *Bastardo Blanco, Forastera Blanca* (*Gomera*), *Listán Blanco, Marmajuelo, Moscatel, Pedro Ximénez* and *Torrontés.*
RED:
MAIN: *Listán Negro, Malvasía Rosada, Negramoll, Castellana Negra, Mulata, Tintilla, Cabernet Sauvignon, Listán Prieto, Merlot, Pinot Noir, Ruby Cabernet, Syrah* and *Tempranillo.*
AUTHORIZED: *Bastardo Negro, Moscatel Negra, Tintilla* and *Vijariego Negra.*

FIGURES:

Vineyard surface: 519 – **Wine-Growers:** 776 – **Wineries:** 18 – **2010 Harvest rating:** Excellent – **Production:** 330,000 litres – **Market percentages:** 90% domestic. 10% export

CONSEJO REGULADOR
Parque Recreativo El Bosquito, nº1
Urb. La Marzagana II - La Perdona
38315 La Orotava (Santa Cruz de Tenerife)
☎: +34 922 309 923 - Fax: +34 922 309 924
@ do-valleorotava@terra.es
www.dovalleorotava.com

GENERAL CHARACTERISTICS OF THE WINES

WHITES	These are similar to those from Tacoronte in that they share the same Atlantic character. They have a straw yellow colour and are fresh and fruity with somewhat herbaceous notes, and in the best of the examples can reproduce the refinement of fennel or mint.
ROSÉS	Although the production is much lower, there are some fine examples of modern rosés with a raspberry colour, very fruity aromas, which are fresh and pleasant on the palate.
REDS	These are young wines, with a deep cherry-red colour, good aromatic intensity and notes of red berries in line with their Atlantic character; on the palate they are light, flavourful and pleasant.

VINTAGE RATING PEÑÍNGUIDE

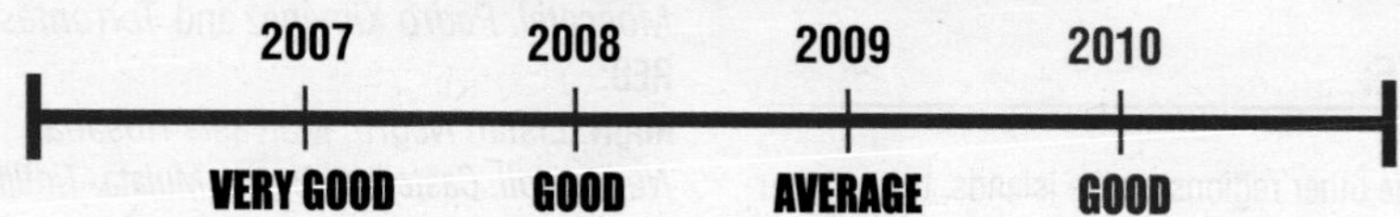

BODEGA LA SUERTITA

La Cruz Santa - Los Realejos
38410 (Santa Cruz de tenerife)
☎: +34 669 408 761
informacion@lasuertita.com
www.lasuertita.com

LA SUERTITA 2010 B
100% listán blanco.

85 Colour: straw. Nose: fresh fruit, grassy, white flowers. Palate: flavourful, fruity, fresh.

LA SUERTITA 2010 B
listán blanco.

85 Colour: bright straw. Nose: white flowers, fresh fruit, citrus fruit. Palate: flavourful, fruity, fresh.

LA SUERTITA 2009 B BARRICA
listán blanco.

88 Colour: bright straw. Nose: powerfull, candied fruit, fruit preserve, citrus fruit, creamy oak, sweet spices. Palate: powerful, fleshy, fine bitter notes.

LA SUERTITA VIJARIEGO 2009 B BARRICA
vijariego.

82 Colour: bright straw. Nose: faded flowers, warm, slightly evolved, candied fruit. Palate: flavourful, powerful, fleshy.

BODEGA SECADERO

San Benito
38410 Los Realejos (Santa Cruz de Tenerife)
☎: +34 665 807 966
info@bodegasecadero.com
www.bodegasecadero.com

CUPRUM 2010 T
listán negro, tintilla.

85 Colour: cherry, garnet rim. Nose: fruit expression, raspberry. Palate: flavourful, powerful, fleshy, fine bitter notes.

BODEGA TAFURIASTE

Las Candias Altas, 11
38312 La Orotava (Santa Cruz de Tenerife)
☎: +34 922 336 027 - Fax: +34 922 336 027
vinos@bodegatafuriaste.com
www.bodegatafuriaste.com

TAFURIASTE AFRUTADO 2010 B
97% listán blanco, 3% moscatel.

84 Colour: bright straw. Nose: characterful, candied fruit, citrus fruit. Palate: flavourful, good acidity, fine bitter notes.

TAFURIASTE 2010 RD
listán negro.

82 Colour: rose, purple rim. Nose: powerfull, red berry notes, floral. Palate: fleshy, fresh, easy to drink.

TAFURIASTE 2010 T
100% listán negro.

85 Colour: deep cherry. Nose: powerfull, smoky, earthy notes, stalky. Palate: fine bitter notes, powerful, spicy.

VINOS TAFURIASTE VENDIMIA SELECCIONADA 4 MESES 2010 T
100% listán negro.

85 Colour: cherry, garnet rim. Nose: powerfull, aromatic coffee, raspberry. Palate: flavourful, powerful, fleshy, fine bitter notes.

BODEGA TAJINASTE

El Ratiño, 5
38315 La Orotava (Santa Cruz de Tenerife)
☎: +34 696 030 347 - Fax: +34 922 308 720
bodega@tajinaste.net
www.tajinaste.net

TAJINASTE 2010 B
100% listán blanco.

84 Colour: bright yellow, greenish rim. Nose: medium intensity, citrus fruit, fresh fruit. Palate: light-bodied, good finish.

TAJINASTE AFRUTADO 2010 B
100% listán blanco.

83 Colour: bright straw. Nose: fresh fruit, citrus fruit, white flowers. Palate: flavourful, fruity, fresh.

TAJINASTE 2010 RD
listán negro.

81 Colour: brilliant rose. Nose: medium intensity, candied fruit, warm. Palate: fine bitter notes, good acidity.

CAN 2010 T
listán negro, vijariego.

88 Colour: deep cherry. Nose: fresh fruit, spicy. Palate: fine bitter notes, balsamic, ripe fruit.

TAJINASTE 2010 T BARRICA
100% listán negro.

87 Colour: bright cherry, purple rim. Nose: balsamic herbs, wild herbs, spicy. Palate: fruity, balsamic.

TAJINASTE TRADICIONAL 2010 T
100% listán negro.

86 Colour: bright cherry. Nose: balsamic herbs, grassy, red berry notes. Palate: fine bitter notes, good acidity, slightly green tannins.

TAJINASTE VENDIMIA SELECCIONADA 2009 T
100% listán negro.

86 Colour: bright cherry, garnet rim. Nose: sweet spices, woody, ripe fruit, balsamic herbs. Palate: fruity, flavourful, spicy.

BODEGA VALLEORO

Ctra. General La Oratova - Los Realejos, Km. 4,5
38315 La Orotava (Santa Cruz de Tenerife)
☎: +34 922 308 031 - Fax: +34 922 308 233
info@bodegavalleoro.com
www.bodegavalleoro.com

GRAN TEHYDA AFRUTADO 2010 B
listán blanco.

85 Colour: bright straw. Nose: white flowers, candied fruit. Palate: flavourful, powerful, sweetness.

GRAN TEHYDA 2010 RD
listán negro.

84 Colour: rose. Nose: ripe fruit, raspberry, floral. Palate: flavourful, fruity, fresh.

GRAN TEHYDA 2010 T
listán negro.

85 Colour: deep cherry. Nose: powerfull, ripe fruit, scrubland, spicy. Palate: powerful, fine bitter notes.

BODEGAS EL PENITENTE

Camino La Habanera, 286
38300 La Orotava (Santa Cruz de Tenerife)
☎: +34 922 331 646 - Fax: +34 922 309 024
bodegas@elpenitentesl.es
www.bodegaselpenitente.es

ARAUTAVA FINCA LA HABANERA 2010 B
albillo.

88 Colour: bright straw. Nose: balsamic herbs, ripe fruit, citrus fruit, creamy oak. Palate: powerful, flavourful, fine bitter notes.

ARAUTAVA 2010 B
listán blanco.

87 Colour: bright straw. Nose: powerfull, fresh fruit, citrus fruit, dried herbs. Palate: flavourful, fruity, fresh.

ARAUTAVA 2009 B
albillo.

82 Colour: bright straw. Nose: acetaldehyde, slightly evolved, overripe fruit, dry nuts. Palate: concentrated, sweet, fine bitter notes.

ARAUTAVA MALAVASÍA DULCE 2008 B
malvasía.

92 Color golden. Aroma powerfull, floral, honeyed notes, candied fruit, fragrant herbs. Taste flavourful, sweet, fresh, fruity, good acidity, long.

ARAUTAVA 2002 B
listán blanco.

88 Colour: light mahogany. Nose: powerfull, warm, candied fruit, acetaldehyde, pungent. Palate: sweet, fine bitter notes, long.

ARAUTAVA KRYOS 2010 T
listán negro.

88 Colour: deep cherry. Nose: fruit expression, red berry notes, earthy notes, mineral. Palate: powerful, fine bitter notes, good acidity.

ARAUTAVA 2010 T FERMENTADO EN BARRICA
listán negro.

87 Colour: bright cherry, purple rim. Nose: red berry notes, balsamic herbs, balanced, spicy. Palate: fruity, fine bitter notes, slightly dry, soft tannins.

ARAUTAVA 2009 T
listán negro.

83 Colour: dark-red cherry. Nose: overripe fruit, dried fruit, warm. Palate: powerful, concentrated.

LA HAYA

Calzadillas, s/n La Cruz Santa
38415 Los Realejos (Santa Cruz de Tenerife)
☎: +34 629 051 413 - Fax: +34 922 345 313
jaghcatire@telefonica.net

LA HAYA AFRUTADO 2010 B
listán blanco, otras.

81 Colour: bright straw, greenish rim. Nose: citrus fruit, short. Palate: fresh, light-bodied, good acidity.

LA HAYA 2009 B BARRICA
listán blanco, otras.

85 Colour: bright straw. Nose: powerfull, ripe fruit, fruit expression, citrus fruit, toasty. Palate: flavourful, easy to drink.

LOS GÜINES

Pista Los Guines, s/n El Horno
38410 Los Realejos (Santa Cruz de Tenerife)
☎: +34 922 343 320 - Fax: +34 922 353 855
www.bodegalosguines.com

LOS GÜINES 2010 B

85 Colour: bright straw. Nose: fresh fruit, citrus fruit, floral. Palate: flavourful, fleshy, complex, fine bitter notes.

LOS GÜINES 2010 T

70

PROPIEDAD VITICOLA SUERTES DEL MARQUÉS

Tomás Zerolo, 15
38300 La Orotava (Santa Cruz de Tenerife)
☎: +34 922 501 300 - Fax: +34 922 503 462
ventas@suertesdelmarques.com
www.suertesdelmarques.com

SUERTES DEL MARQUÉS 2010 B BARRICA
75% listán blanco, 25% vidueño.

88 Colour: bright straw. Nose: candied fruit, citrus fruit, toasty, cocoa bean. Palate: powerful, flavourful, fleshy.

SUERTES DEL MARQUÉS SECO 2010 B MACERACIÓN CARBÓNICA
80% listán blanco, 10% pedro ximénez, 10% moscatel.

87 Colour: bright straw. Nose: floral, fresh fruit, fresh, expressive. Palate: fruity, flavourful, light-bodied, mineral.

7 FUENTES AFRUTADO 2010 B
100% listán blanco.

83 Colour: bright straw. Nose: fresh fruit, citrus fruit, white flowers. Palate: flavourful, fruity, fresh.

SUERTES DEL MARQUÉS AFRUTADO 2010 B
100% listán blanco.

80 Colour: bright straw. Nose: balsamic herbs, candied fruit, citrus fruit, floral, slightly evolved. Palate: flavourful, ripe fruit, good acidity.

SUERTES DEL MARQUÉS 2009 B BARRICA
75% listán blanco, 25% vidueño.

87 Colour: bright straw. Nose: creamy oak, aromatic coffee, sweet spices, candied fruit. Palate: powerful, spicy, fine bitter notes.

SUERTES DEL MARQUÉS LA SOLANA 2010 T
100% listán negro.

84 Colour: bright cherry, garnet rim. Nose: scrubland, wild herbs, woody. Palate: flavourful, spicy, balsamic.

SUERTES DEL MARQUÉS LA SOLANA 2009 T
100% listán negro.

88 Colour: cherry, garnet rim. Nose: powerfull, warm, ripe fruit, fruit liqueur notes. Palate: powerful, fine bitter notes, good acidity.

SUERTES DEL MARQUÉS EL ESQUILÓN 2009 T
70% listán negro, 30% tintilla.

87 Colour: bright cherry, garnet rim. Nose: balanced, wild herbs, scrubland, spicy. Palate: fruity, spicy.

7 FUENTES 2009 T
90% listán negro, 10% tintilla.

86 Colour: bright cherry, garnet rim. Nose: red berry notes, wild herbs, spicy. Palate: flavourful, good structure, spicy.

SUERTES DEL MARQUÉS CANDIO 2008 T
100% listán negro.

90 Colour: bright cherry, garnet rim. Nose: ripe fruit, balsamic herbs, spicy, balanced. Palate: flavourful, spicy, ripe fruit.

7 FUENTES 2008 TC
85% listán negro, 15% tintilla.

85 Colour: cherry, garnet rim. Nose: toasty, spicy, ripe fruit, balsamic herbs. Palate: fruity, balsamic.

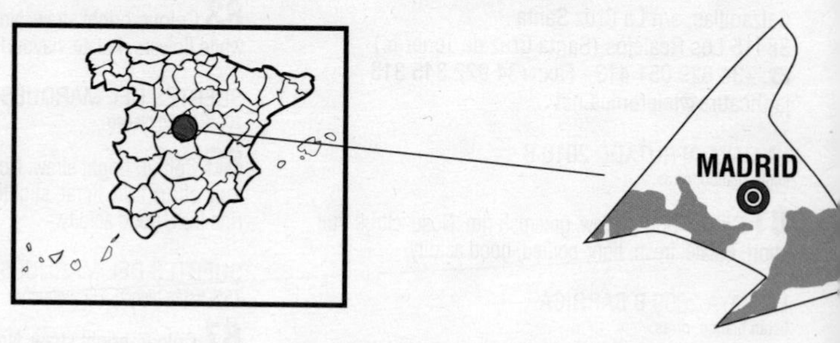

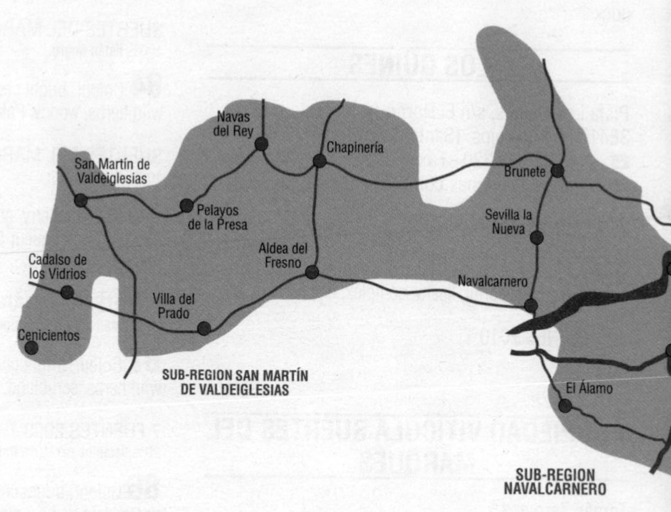

Consejo Regulador

DO Boundary

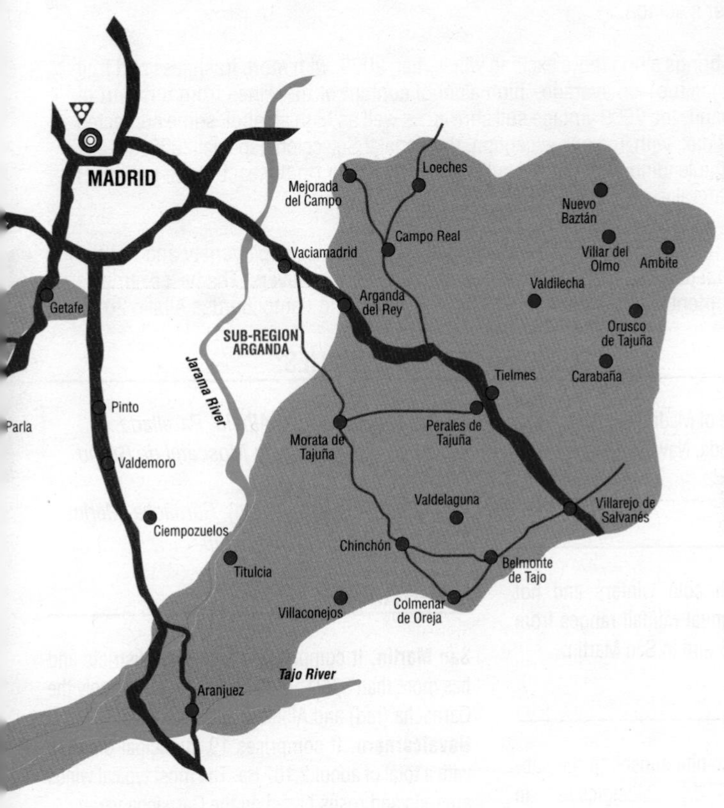
MADRID
Mejorada
del Campo
Loeches
Campo Real
Nuevo
Baztán
Vilar del
Olmo
Ambite
Vaciamadrid
Getafe
Arganda
del Rey
Valdilecha
Orusco
de Tajuña
SUB-REGION
ARGANDA
Jarama River
Carabaña
Tielmes
Pinto
Parla
Perales de
Tajuña
Morata de
Tajuña
Valdemoro
Valdelaguna
Villarejo de
Salvanés
Ciempozuelos
Chinchón
Titulcia
Belmonte
de Tajo
Colmenar
de Oreja
Villaconejos
Tajo River
Aranjuez

NEWS ABOUT THE VINTAGE:

A few years ago nobody could have predicted the capacity of Madrid to produce great wines, and least of all in the western part of the province, that most rugged and bucolic territory with the historical burden of the cooperatives.

The core of this new forward "movement" is the town of San Martín de Valdeiglesias, pretty close to Méntrida (Toledo) and Cebreros (Ávila), an area with granite and slate soils where Telmo Rodríguez, already 15 years ago, put his keen eyes, and where we now find some new stars like Bodegas Bernabeleva and more recently Marañones. Even the road-runner of Quim Vila has shown an interest in this area joining forces with Comando G (Daniel Jiménez-Landi, Marc Isart and Fernando García) to create a wine with the name of El Hombre Bala ("The bullet man") that in its first vintage has got 94 points. Good news also from Carlos Falcó, Marqués de Griñón, whose El Rincón Garnacha 2007 climbs up the rankings from just 88 points the previous vintage to 94 points in this year's edition.

The 2010 vintage also brings along more exciting wines than 2009, with more freshness and fruit weight to counterbalance the –on average– high alcohol content of the wines from this part of the DO. On the other hand, the 2009 vintage still shows, as well as high alcohol, some confected notes and an excess of oak, with just one exception, the Regajal Selección Especial 2009, already a classic wine that is the leading name in the sub-zone of Arganda (to the east of the province) thanks to its highly mineral expression.

As for the white wine renderings and curiously enough, is the *albillo* grape variety and not the local *malvar* the one that has awaken the interest of the Anglo-Saxon buyers. The best examples of its expression and potential are to be found in Picarana 2010 and Cantocuerdas Albillo 2010.

LOCATION:

In the south of the province of Madrid, it covers three distinct sub-regions: Arganda, Navalcarnero and San Martín de Valdeiglesias.

CLIMATE:

Extreme continental, with cold winters and hot summers. The average annual rainfall ranges from 461 mm in Arganda to 658 mm in San Martín.

SOIL:

Rather unfertile soil and granite subsoil in the sub-region of San Martín de Valdeiglesias; in Navalcarnero the soil is brownish-grey, poor, with a subsoil of coarse sand and clay; in the sub-region of Arganda the soil is brownish-grey, with an acidic pH and granite subsoil.

GRAPE VARIETIES:

WHITE: *Malvar, Airén, Albillo, Parellada, Macabeo, Torrontés* and *Moscatel de Grano Menudo.*
RED: *Tinto Fino* (Tempranillo), *Garnacha, Merlot, Cabernet Sauvignon* and *Syrah.*

SUB-REGIONS:

San Martín. It comprises 9 municipal districts and has more than 3,821 Ha of vineyards, with mainly the Garnacha (red) and Albillo (white) varieties.
Navalcarnero. It comprises 19 municipal districts with a total of about 2,107 Ha. The most typical wines are reds and rosés based on the Garnacha variety.
Arganda. With 5,830 Ha and 26 municipal districts, it is the largest sub-region of the DO. The main varieties are the white Malvar and the red Tempranillo or Tinto Fino.

FIGURES:

Vineyard surface: 8,152 – **Wine-Growers:** 2,808 – **Wineries:** 46 – **2010 Harvest rating:** N/A – **Production:** 5,209,924 litres – **Market percentages:** 76% domestic. 24% export

CONSEJO REGULADOR
Ronda de Atocha, 7
28012 Madrid
☎: +34 915 348 511 / +34 915 347 240 - +34 Fax: 915 538 574
@ aprovim@vinosdemadrid.es
www.vinosdemadrid.es

GENERAL CHARACTERISTICS OF THE WINES

WHITES	The most characteristic are those produced from *Malvar* in the sub-region of Arganda. Fruity and pleasant, on occasion they have wild notes; on the palate they are fresh, flavourful and supple. They are also produced from traditional 'sobremadre' wines (they follow a barrelling process with the skins lasting about three months) and, in line with more modern trends, white wines fermented in barrels.
ROSÉS	Mainly produced from *Garnacha*, they have a pink colour; on the nose they are fresh, powerful and fruity; on the palate, they have the tastiness typical of this variety.
REDS	Firstly, there are those produced from *Tinto Fino*, mainly from Arganda. They are mostly young wines, light and fruity, in line with the wines from La Mancha. In Navalcarnero and San Martín, the *Garnacha* variety is used. In the latter area, the aromas and flavours of the red wines are concentrated, with a character of ripe fruit, earthy notes, meaty and flavourful on the palate.

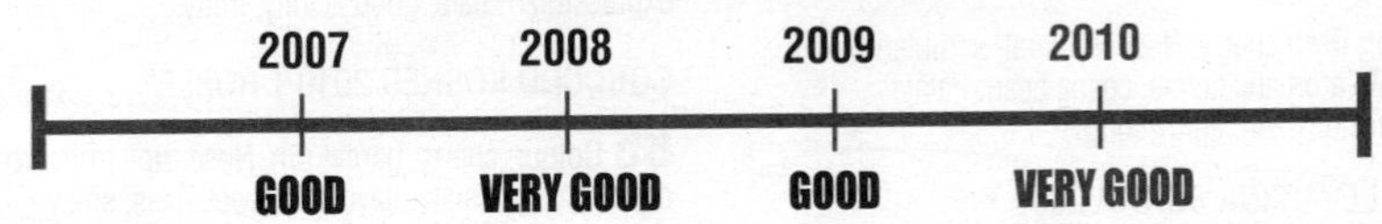

BERNABELEVA

Ctra. Avila Toledo (N-403), Km. 81,600
28680 San Martín de Valdeiglesias (Madrid)
☎: +34 915 091 909
bodega@bernabeleva.com
www.bernabeleva.com

CANTOCUERDAS MOSCATEL DE BERNABELEVA 2009 B
moscatel.

94 Colour: bright straw. Nose: expressive, varietal, fruit preserve, citrus fruit. Palate: powerful, sweet, fine bitter notes, balanced.

NAVAHERREROS 2009 T
garnacha.

92 Colour: bright cherry. Nose: candied fruit, raspberry, mineral, balsamic herbs, scrubland. Palate: flavourful, spicy, good acidity.

CANTOCUERDAS ALBILLO 2009 B
albillo.

93 Colour: bright straw. Nose: fresh, balanced, varietal, mineral, candied fruit, citrus fruit. Palate: flavourful, fruity, good acidity, fine tannins.

NAVAHERREROS BLANCO DE BERNABELEVA 2009 B
albillo, macabeo.

92 Colour: bright straw. Nose: mineral, ripe fruit, citrus fruit, balsamic herbs, dried herbs. Palate: flavourful, powerful, fleshy, sweetness.

BERNABELEVA "ARROYO DE TÓRTOLAS" 2009 T
garnacha.

94 Colour: deep cherry. Nose: mineral, scrubland, candied fruit, aromatic coffee, cocoa bean. Palate: flavourful, fruity, fresh, spicy, long.

BERNABELEVA VIÑA BONITA 2009 T
garnacha.

93 Colour: bright cherry. Nose: expressive, scrubland, ripe fruit, red berry notes, sweet spices. Palate: flavourful, fruity, fresh, fleshy.

BERNABELEVA "CARRIL DEL REY" 2009 T
garnacha.

90 Colour: deep cherry. Nose: powerfull, fruit preserve, scrubland, balsamic herbs, mineral. Palate: flavourful, powerful, fleshy, complex.

BODEGA DEL REAL CORTIJO

Cortijo de San Isidro
28300 Aranjuez (Madrid)
☎: +34 915 357 735 - Fax: +34 915 547 027
clientes@realcortijo.com
www.realcortijo.com

HOMET 2006 TR
70% tempranillo, 10% cabernet sauvignon, 10% merlot, 10% syrah.

86 Colour: black cherry, garnet rim. Nose: ripe fruit, earthy notes, old leather, toasty. Palate: flavourful, fleshy, spirituous.

HOMET 2005 TR
70% tempranillo, 10% cabernet sauvignon, 10% merlot, 10% syrah.

86 Colour: cherry, garnet rim. Nose: cocoa bean, sweet spices, toasty, ripe fruit. Palate: powerful, flavourful, fleshy, toasty.

BODEGA ECOLÓGICA LUIS SAAVEDRA

Ctra. de Escalona, 5
28650 Cenicientos (Madrid)
☎: +34 914 606 053 - Fax: +34 914 606 053
info@bodegasaavedra.com
www.bodegasaavedra.com

CORUCHO ALBILLO MOSCATEL 2010 B
albillo, moscatel.

85 Colour: bright golden. Nose: candied fruit, citrus fruit, dried flowers. Palate: powerful, sweetness, good acidity.

CORUCHO 2010 RD
garnacha.

83 Colour: rose, purple rim. Nose: raspberry, fruit expression. Palate: good acidity, fruity.

CORUCHO KOSHER 2010 T ROBLE

85 Colour: cherry, garnet rim. Nose: ripe fruit, aromatic coffee, spicy. Palate: flavourful, sweetness, spicy.

CORUCHO 2009 T

88 Colour: cherry, garnet rim. Nose: candied fruit, spicy, toasty. Palate: flavourful, spicy, ripe fruit, good acidity.

CORUCHO GARNACHA CEPAS VIEJAS 2008 T
garnacha.

91 Colour: bright cherry. Nose: expressive, fruit expression, ripe fruit, earthy notes. Palate: ripe fruit, fine bitter notes, long.

LUIS SAAVEDRA 2008 T

90 Colour: deep cherry. Nose: sweet spices, powerfull, fruit liqueur notes, earthy notes. Palate: flavourful, spicy, ripe fruit, fine tannins.

BODEGA MARAÑONES

Hilero, 7 - Nave 9
28696 Pelayos de la Presa (Madrid)
☎: +34 918 647 702
fernandogarcia@bodegamaranones.com
www.bodegamaranones.com

PICARANA 2010 B
albillo.

94 Colour: bright straw. Nose: jasmine, white flowers, earthy notes, mineral. Palate: flavourful, fruity, fresh, sweetness, good acidity, fine bitter notes.

PIESDESCALZOS 2010 B
100% albillo.

93 Colour: bright yellow. Nose: spicy, toasty, aromatic coffee, ripe fruit. Palate: spicy, ripe fruit, long, toasty.

PEÑA CABALLERA 2009 T
100% garnacha.

94 Colour: deep cherry. Nose: powerfull, varietal, ripe fruit, mineral, dry stone. Palate: flavourful, fruity, good acidity, fine bitter notes.

LABROS 2009 T
100% garnacha.

92 Colour: deep cherry. Nose: scrubland, balsamic herbs, ripe fruit. Palate: flavourful, powerful, fine bitter notes.

TREINTA MIL MARAVEDÍES 2009 T
60% garnacha, 40% syrah.

90 Colour: cherry, garnet rim. Nose: candied fruit, fruit expression, powerfull, scrubland, earthy notes, spicy. Palate: flavourful, fruity, fleshy, sweetness.

BODEGA Y VIÑEDOS GOSÁLBEZ ORTI

Real, 14
28813 Pozuelo del Rey (Madrid)
☎: +34 918 725 399 - Fax: +34 918 725 399
bodega@qubel.com
www.qubel.com

MAYRIT S/C B
albillo.

82 Colour: pale. Nose: ripe fruit, dried flowers, fragrant herbs. Palate: flavourful, fine bitter notes, fruity.

QUBÉL REVELACIÓN 2010 T
65% tempranillo, 20% syrah, 5% cabernet sauvignon, 5% merlot, 5% malvar.

88 Colour: cherry, garnet rim. Nose: ripe fruit, spicy, creamy oak, toasty. Palate: powerful, flavourful, toasty, round tannins.

MAYRIT BARRICA 2009 T
80% tempranillo, 20% syrah.

85 Colour: deep cherry. Nose: scrubland, red berry notes, fruit expression. Palate: flavourful, fleshy, fruity.

QUBÉL EXCEPCIÓN 2006 T
100% garnacha.

90 Colour: cherry, garnet rim. Nose: expressive, fruit liqueur notes, spicy, scrubland. Palate: flavourful, spicy, fine tannins.

QUBÉL NATURE 2004 T
70% tempranillo, 20% syrah, 10% cabernet sauvignon.

91 Colour: deep cherry. Nose: powerfull, warm, fruit liqueur notes, toasty, wet leather. Palate: flavourful, spicy, ripe fruit, long.

QUBÉL PACIENCIA 2004 TR
tempranillo, syrah, cabernet sauvignon.

88 Colour: bright cherry. Nose: ripe fruit, sweet spices, creamy oak, scrubland. Palate: flavourful, fruity, toasty, round tannins.

BODEGAS ANDRÉS DÍAZ

Palencia, 32
28600 Navalcarnero (Madrid)
☎: +34 918 111 391
info@bodegasandresdiaz.es
www.bodegasandresdiaz.es

DÓRIO TEMPRANILLO 2010 T
tempranillo.

88 Colour: bright cherry. Nose: ripe fruit, sweet spices, creamy oak, varietal. Palate: flavourful, fruity, toasty, round tannins.

BODEGAS LICINIA

Carrera de Poniente, 10
28530 Morata de Tajuña (Madrid)
☎: +34 918 731 579 - Fax: +34 918 731 579
o.fernandez@licinia.es
www.bodegaslicinia.es

LICINIA 2008 T
60% tempranillo, 40% syrah.

93 Colour: cherry, garnet rim. Nose: spicy, creamy oak, toasty, characterful, ripe fruit. Palate: powerful, flavourful, toasty, round tannins.

BODEGAS NUEVA VALVERDE

Santo Domingo de Silos, 6 - bajo dcha.
28036 (Madrid)
☎: +34 915 640 191
info@bodegasnuevavalverde.com
www.bodegasnuevavalverde.com

TEJONERAS ALTA SELECCIÓN 2007 T
40% cabernet sauvignon, 20% merlot, 20% syrah, 20% tempranillo.

88 Colour: bright cherry. Nose: ripe fruit, sweet spices, creamy oak. Palate: flavourful, fruity, toasty, round tannins.

750 2006 T
40% merlot, 30% cabernet sauvignon, 20% syrah, 10% garnacha.

88 Colour: cherry, garnet rim. Nose: powerfull, fruit liqueur notes, toasty, sweet spices. Palate: ripe fruit, fine bitter notes, round tannins.

BODEGAS ORUSCO

Alcalá, 54
28511 Valdilecha (Madrid)
☎: +34 918 738 006 - Fax: +34 918 738 336
esther@bodegasorusco.com
www.bodegasorusco.com

MAÍN TEMPRANILLO 2010 T
90% tempranillo, 10% syrah.

83 Colour: cherry, garnet rim. Nose: powerfull, warm, fruit preserve. Palate: flavourful, powerful, sweetness.

ARMONIUM 2008 T
70% merlot, 30% cabernet sauvignon.

87 Colour: cherry, garnet rim. Nose: ripe fruit, toasty, dark chocolate. Palate: powerful, fleshy, sweetness.

MAÍN 2008 TC
90% tempranillo, 10% cabernet sauvignon.

85 Colour: cherry, garnet rim. Nose: ripe fruit, spicy, creamy oak, toasty. Palate: powerful, flavourful, toasty, round tannins.

BODEGAS Y VIÑEDOS PEDRO GARCÍA

Soledad, 10
28380 Colmenar de Oreja (Madrid)
☎: +34 918 943 278 - Fax: +34 918 942 589
byv_pedrogarcia@telefonica.net

PEDRO GARCÍA MALVAR 2010 B
100% malvar.

84 Color bright straw. Aroma fresh, fresh fruit, white flowers, expressive. Taste flavourful, fruity, good acidity, balanced.

LA ROMERA 2010 T JOVEN
50% tempranillo, 25% syrah, 25% merlot.

84 Colour: cherry, garnet rim. Nose: powerfull, ripe fruit, scrubland. Palate: powerful, fine bitter notes, round tannins, ripe fruit.

ISLA DE SAN PEDRO BARRICA SELECCIÓN 2008 T
80% syrah, 20% tempranillo.

85 Colour: very deep cherry. Nose: powerfull, characterful, overripe fruit, toasty, dark chocolate. Palate: powerful, concentrated, spirituous.

ISLA DE SAN PEDRO 2008 TC

83 Colour: bright cherry. Nose: ripe fruit, sweet spices, creamy oak, powerfull. Palate: flavourful, fruity, toasty, round tannins.

COMANDO G

Villamanin, 27 - 4º E
28011 (Madrid)
☎: +34 696 366 555
daniel@jimenezlandi.com

LA BRUJA AVERÍA 2010 T
garnacha.

94 Colour: cherry, garnet rim. Nose: balsamic herbs, scrubland, spicy. Palate: flavourful, fruity, good acidity, fine bitter notes.

LAS UMBRÍAS 2009 T
garnacha.

94 Colour: deep cherry. Nose: balsamic herbs, red berry notes, sweet spices, warm. Palate: flavourful, fruity, spicy, ripe fruit, fine tannins.

COMERCIAL GRUPO FREIXENET S.A.

Joan Sala, 2
08770 Sant Sadurní D'Anoia (Barcelona)
☎: +34 938 917 000 - Fax: +34 938 183 095
freixenet@freixenet.es
www.freixenet.es

HEREDAD TORRESANO CUEVA DE TORRESANO 2007 TC
100% tempranillo.

87 Colour: cherry, garnet rim. Nose: ripe fruit, spicy, creamy oak, toasty. Palate: powerful, flavourful, toasty, spicy.

HEREDAD TORRESANO 2007 T ROBLE
100% tempranillo.

86 Colour: light cherry, cherry, garnet rim. Nose: ripe fruit, spicy, toasty. Palate: flavourful, fleshy, ripe fruit, toasty.

HEREDAD TORRESANO 2007 TC
100% tempranillo.

86 Colour: cherry, garnet rim. Nose: ripe fruit, cocoa bean, spicy, toasty. Palate: flavourful, fruity, toasty.

EL REGAJAL

Antigua Ctra. Andalucía, Km. 50,5
28300 Aranjuez (Madrid)
☎: +34 913 078 903 - Fax: +34 913 576 312
isabel@garip.es

EL REGAJAL SELECCIÓN ESPECIAL 2009 T
merlot, cabernet sauvignon, syrah, tempranillo.

93 Colour: cherry, garnet rim. Nose: spicy, creamy oak, toasty, complex, overripe fruit. Palate: powerful, flavourful, toasty, round tannins.

LAS RETAMAS DE EL REGAJAL 2009 T
merlot, cabernet sauvignon, syrah, tempranillo.

91 Colour: cherry, garnet rim. Nose: characterful, ripe fruit, raspberry. Palate: flavourful, powerful, fleshy, long.

FIGUEROA

Convento, 19
28380 Colmenar de Oreja (Madrid)
☎: +34 918 944 859 - Fax: +34 918 944 859
bodegasjesusfigueroa@hotmail.com

FIGUEROA 2010 B
moscatel, macabeo, malvar.

86 Colour: bright straw. Nose: fresh, white flowers, ripe fruit. Palate: flavourful, fruity, good acidity, balanced.

FIGUEROA 2009 T ROBLE
tempranillo, merlot.

84 Colour: very deep cherry. Nose: powerfull, roasted coffee, dark chocolate. Palate: powerful, concentrated, fine bitter notes.

FIGUEROA 2007 TC
100% tempranillo.

87 Colour: bright cherry. Nose: ripe fruit, roasted coffee. Palate: flavourful, fruity, toasty, round tannins.

FIGUEROA 2006 TR
100% tempranillo.

84 Colour: black cherry. Nose: powerfull, warm, ripe fruit, toasty, spicy. Palate: flavourful, powerful, fleshy.

LA CASA DE MONROY

José Moya, 12
45940 Valmojado (Toledo)
☎: +34 918 170 102
info@bodegasmonroy.es
www.bodegasmonroy.es

LA CASA DE MONROY SELECCIÓN VIÑAS VIEJAS 2008 T
90% garnacha, 5% garnacha tintorera, 5% syrah.

91 Colour: bright cherry. Nose: sweet spices, expressive, overripe fruit, fruit liqueur notes, balsamic herbs, scrubland, toasty. Palate: flavourful, fruity, toasty, round tannins.

LAS MORADAS DE SAN MARTÍN

Pago de Los Catillejos - Ctra. M-541, Km. 4,7. Apdo. Correos 25
28680 San Martín de Valdeiglesias (Madrid)
☎: +34 691 676 570 - Fax: +34 915 417 590
bodega@lasmoradasdesanmartin.es
www.lasmoradasdesanmartin.es

LAS MORADAS DE SAN MARTÍN INITIO 2007 T
92% garnacha, 8% cabernet sauvignon, syrah.

90 Colour: cherry, garnet rim. Nose: candied fruit, fruit expression, toasty, spicy. Palate: ripe fruit, long, mineral, spicy.

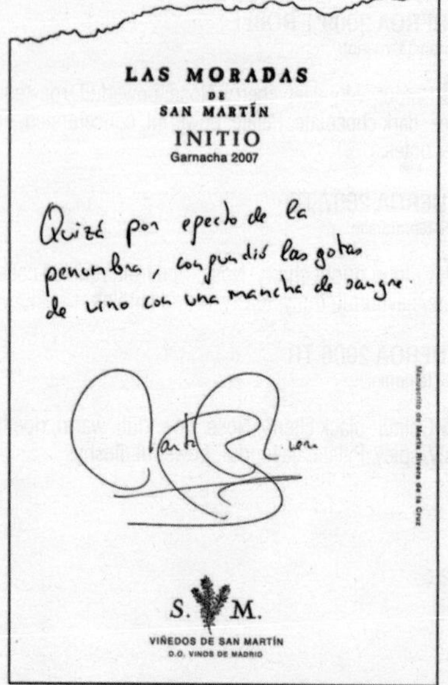

LAS MORADAS DE SAN MARTÍN LIBRO VII LAS LUCES 2007 T
100% garnacha.

91 Colour: very deep cherry. Nose: powerfull, warm, ripe fruit, sweet spices, new oak. Palate: powerful, sweetness, fleshy, fine bitter notes.

LAS MORADAS DE SAN MARTÍN INITIO 2006 T
garnacha.

89 Colour: cherry, garnet rim. Nose: powerfull, warm, fruit liqueur notes, spicy. Palate: spicy, ripe fruit, fine bitter notes.

PAGOS DE FAMILIA MARQUÉS DE GRIÑÓN

Finca Casa de Vacas - Ctra. CM-4015, Km. 23
45692 Malpica de Tajo (Toledo)
☎: +34 925 597 222 - Fax: +34 925 789 416
info@pagosdefamilia.com
www.pagosdefamilia.com

EL RINCÓN GARNACHA 2007 T
garnacha.

94 Colour: cherry, purple rim. Nose: red berry notes, raspberry, fresh fruit, expressive, mineral, creamy oak. Palate: flavourful, fleshy, complex, fruity, balanced, round tannins.

EL RINCÓN 2006 T
syrah, garnacha.

90 Color bright cherry. Aroma ripe fruit, sweet spices, creamy oak, expressive. Taste flavourful, fruity, toasty, round tannins.

RICARDO BENITO

Las Eras, 5
28600 Navalcarnero (Madrid)
☎: +34 918 110 097 - Fax: +34 918 112 663
bodega@ricardobenito.com
www.ricardobenito.com

TAPÓN DE ORO 2010 B
malvar, moscatel.

88 Colour: bright straw. Nose: fresh, fresh fruit, white flowers. Palate: flavourful, fruity, good acidity, balanced.

MADRILEÑO DE RICARDO BENITO 2009 T
tempranillo.

84 Colour: cherry, garnet rim. Nose: overripe fruit, spicy, warm. Palate: flavourful, spicy, good acidity.

DIVIDIVO 2008 T
tinto fino, otras.

92 Colour: cherry, garnet rim. Nose: ripe fruit, spicy, creamy oak, toasty, complex, powerfull. Palate: powerful, flavourful, toasty, round tannins.

ASIDO 2007 T
tinto fino, otras.

90 Colour: bright cherry. Nose: sweet spices, creamy oak, fruit expression, ripe fruit. Palate: flavourful, fruity, toasty, round tannins.

TAPÓN DE ORO 2007 T
tempranillo, garnacha.

89 Colour: cherry, garnet rim. Nose: candied fruit, warm, spicy, toasty, aromatic coffee. Palate: flavourful, spicy, ripe fruit, fine bitter notes.

DUÁN 2007 T
tempranillo, syrah, garnacha, merlot, cabernet sauvignon.

86 Colour: deep cherry. Nose: powerfull, spicy, aromatic coffee. Palate: flavourful, spicy, ripe fruit, round tannins.

SEÑORÍO DE VAL AZUL

Urb. Valgrande, 37
28370 Chinchón (Madrid)
☎: +34 616 005 565
evaayuso@arrakis.es
www.senoriodevalazul.es

FABIO 2007 T
syrah, merlot, tempranillo.

86 Colour: cherry, garnet rim. Nose: aromatic coffee, dark chocolate, toasty. Palate: flavourful, powerful, fine bitter notes.

VAL AZUL 2007 T
cabernet sauvignon, syrah, merlot, tempranillo.

86 Colour: deep cherry. Nose: medium intensity, fruit preserve, toasty, spicy. Palate: powerful, spicy, warm.

TAGONIUS

Ctra. Ambite, Km. 4,4
28550 Tielmes (Madrid)
☎: +34 918 737 505 - Fax: +34 918 746 161
comercial@tagonius.com
www.tagonius.com

TAGONIUS 2007 T ROBLE
merlot, syrah, cabernet sauvignon, tempranillo.

89 Colour: cherry, garnet rim. Nose: ripe fruit, creamy oak, spicy, balsamic herbs. Palate: flavourful, fruity, toasty, round tannins.

TAGONIUS 2006 TC
syrah, cabernet sauvignon, merlot, tempranillo.

88 Colour: cherry, garnet rim. Nose: ripe fruit, expressive, balsamic herbs, toasty. Palate: powerful, flavourful, fleshy, smoky aftertaste.

TAGONIUS MERLOT 2006 T
100% merlot.

88 Colour: light cherry. Nose: ripe fruit, expressive, fragrant herbs, toasty, warm. Palate: powerful, flavourful, ripe fruit.

TAGONIUS MARIAGE 2005 T
merlot, cabernet sauvignon.

90 Colour: light cherry. Nose: ripe fruit, old leather, mineral, spicy, creamy oak. Palate: good acidity, balanced, spirituous, flavourful.

TAGONIUS GRAN VINO 2004 TR
cabernet sauvignon, merlot, syrah, tempranillo.

91 Colour: cherry, garnet rim. Nose: ripe fruit, mineral, sweet spices, creamy oak. Palate: good acidity, powerful, flavourful, fleshy.

TAGONIUS 2004 TR
cabernet sauvignon, merlot, syrah, tempranillo.

88 Colour: black cherry, garnet rim. Nose: fruit preserve, scrubland, sweet spices, toasty. Palate: flavourful, fleshy, toasty.

UVAS FELICES

Agullers, 7
08003 Barcelona (Barcelona)
☎: +34 902 327 777
www.vilaviniteca.es

HOMBRE BALA 2010 T
garnacha.

94 Colour: cherry, purple rim. Nose: scrubland, balsamic herbs, ripe fruit, red berry notes, spicy. Palate: flavourful, ripe fruit, spicy, good acidity.

VALLE DEL SOL S.A.T. 4478

Ctra. de Cadalso de los Vidrios, Km. 0,3
28600 Navalcarnero (Madrid)
☎: +34 918 101 075 - Fax: +34 918 110 926
valledelsol@bodegasvalledelsol.com

ANTÏNOS MALVAR 2010 B
malvar.

86 Colour: bright straw. Nose: ripe fruit, floral, fragrant herbs. Palate: flavourful, fruity, fresh, good acidity.

ANTÏNOS 2010 RD
garnacha, tempranillo.

88 Colour: rose, purple rim. Nose: red berry notes, raspberry, floral, lactic notes. Palate: light-bodied, fresh, fruity, flavourful, easy to drink.

ANTÏNOS 2010 T ROBLE
cabernet sauvignon.

87 Colour: cherry, purple rim. Nose: red berry notes, floral, balsamic herbs, varietal, sweet spices, toasty. Palate: good acidity, flavourful, fleshy.

LOS CASTINES 2010 T
garnacha.

86 Colour: cherry, purple rim. Nose: fresh fruit, red berry notes, floral. Palate: flavourful, fruity, good acidity, easy to drink.

VALDECEPA 2010 T JOVEN
tempranillo, garnacha, syrah.

85 Colour: cherry, purple rim. Nose: red berry notes, ripe fruit, medium intensity. Palate: light-bodied, flavourful, fruity, easy to drink.

ANTÏNOS 2009 T ROBLE
cabernet sauvignon.

88 Colour: cherry, garnet rim. Nose: red berry notes, ripe fruit, spicy, creamy oak. Palate: good acidity, flavourful, fruity, round tannins.

VINÍCOLA DE ARGANDA SOCIEDAD COOPERATIVA MADRILEÑA

Camino de San Martín de la Vega, 16
28500 Arganda del Rey (Madrid)
☎: +34 918 710 201 - Fax: +34 918 710 201
vinicola@cvarganda.e.telefonica.net
www.vinicoladearganda.com

PAGO VILCHES 2010 B
100% malvar.

83 Colour: bright straw. Nose: faded flowers, ripe fruit, dried herbs. Palate: flavourful, powerful, fleshy.

BALADÍ 2008 BFB
100% malvar.

85 Colour: bright straw. Nose: ripe fruit, white flowers. Palate: flavourful, fruity, fine bitter notes.

PAGO VILCHES 2010 RD
tempranillo.

77

PERUCO 2006 TR
100% tempranillo.

87 Colour: cherry, garnet rim. Nose: ripe fruit, scrubland. Palate: flavourful, ripe fruit, spicy.

VIÑA RENDERO C.V.C. T
100% tempranillo.

84 Colour: deep cherry. Nose: characterful, ripe fruit, fruit expression. Palate: flavourful, fruity, round tannins.

PAGO VILCHES 2010 T
100% tempranillo.

86 Colour: cherry, garnet rim. Nose: red berry notes, sweet spices, cocoa bean. Palate: flavourful, fruity, fleshy.

VIÑA RENDERO SELECCIÓN ESPECIAL 2008 T ROBLE
100% tempranillo.

86 Colour: cherry, garnet rim. Nose: ripe fruit, spicy, creamy oak, toasty. Palate: powerful, flavourful, toasty, round tannins.

VIÑA RENDERO 2007 TC
100% tempranillo.

84 Colour: cherry, garnet rim. Nose: powerfull, ripe fruit, spicy. Palate: flavourful, sweetness.

VINOS JEROMÍN

San José, 8
28590 Villarejo de Salvanés (Madrid)
☎: +34 918 742 030 - Fax: +34 918 744 139
comercial@vinosjeromin.com
www.vinosjeromin.com

PUERTA DEL SOL MALVAR 2010 BFB
malvar.

84 Colour: bright straw. Nose: powerfull, ripe fruit, sweet spices, white flowers. Palate: flavourful, fruity, fleshy.

PUERTA DE ALCALÁ 2010 B
malvar.

84 Colour: bright straw. Nose: fresh, fresh fruit, white flowers. Palate: flavourful, fruity, good acidity, balanced.

PUERTA CERRADA 2010 B
malvar, airén.

83 Colour: bright straw. Nose: powerfull, citrus fruit, white flowers. Palate: flavourful, fruity, fresh.

PUERTA CERRADA 2010 RD
tempranillo, garnacha, malvar.

84 Colour: rose. Nose: candied fruit, medium intensity. Palate: flavourful, fruity, fresh.

PUERTA DE ALCALÁ 2010 RD
tempranillo, garnacha.

83 Colour: rose. Nose: medium intensity, red berry notes. Palate: flavourful, light-bodied, fruity.

PUERTA DE ALCALÁ 2010 T
tempranillo, syrah.

86 Colour: cherry, purple rim. Nose: red berry notes, fruit expression, scrubland. Palate: flavourful, fruity, fine bitter notes.

PUERTA CERRADA 2010 T
tempranillo, garnacha.

82 Colour: cherry, garnet rim. Nose: powerfull, ripe fruit, warm. Palate: powerful, fine bitter notes, sweetness.

GREGO 2009 T ROBLE
tempranillo, syrah.

88 Colour: cherry, garnet rim. Nose: powerfull, warm, ripe fruit. Palate: flavourful, powerful, spicy.

GREGO GARNACHA CENTENARIAS 2009 T ROBLE
garnacha.

85 Colour: deep cherry. Nose: powerfull, ripe fruit, spicy, scrubland. Palate: flavourful, powerful, spicy, round tannins.

MADRILEÑO DE JEROMÍN 2009 T
tempranillo.

82 Colour: cherry, garnet rim. Nose: powerfull, overripe fruit, spicy. Palate: powerful, ripe fruit, fine bitter notes.

PUERTA DE ALCALÁ 2008 TC
tempranillo.

90 Colour: cherry, garnet rim. Nose: ripe fruit, spicy, creamy oak, toasty, new oak. Palate: powerful, flavourful, toasty, round tannins.

PUERTA DEL SOL VARIETALES 2007 TC
cabernet sauvignon, merlot, tempranillo.

85 Color bright cherry. Aroma ripe fruit, sweet spices, creamy oak, expressive. Taste flavourful, fruity, toasty, round tannins.

PUERTA DE ALCALÁ 2007 TR
tempranillo.

84 Colour: deep cherry. Nose: toasty, spicy, dark chocolate, ripe fruit. Palate: flavourful, powerful, fleshy, ripe fruit.

PUERTA DEL SOL TEMPRANILLO 2007 TC
tempranillo.

84 Colour: cherry, garnet rim. Nose: powerfull, characterful, fruit liqueur notes, ripe fruit, aromatic coffee. Palate: fine bitter notes, warm, ripe fruit.

FÉLIX MARTÍNEZ CEPAS VIEJAS 2006 TR
tempranillo, syrah.

90 Colour: cherry, garnet rim. Nose: aged wood nuances, creamy oak, ripe fruit. Palate: powerful, spicy, ripe fruit.

GREGO 2006 TC
tempranillo, syrah, garnacha.

88 Colour: very deep cherry. Nose: powerfull, fruit liqueur notes, ripe fruit, spicy, dark chocolate. Palate: powerful, ripe fruit, long.

DOS DE MAYO EDICIÓN LIMITADA 2006 TC
tempranillo.

87 Colour: bright cherry. Nose: ripe fruit, sweet spices, creamy oak. Palate: flavourful, fruity, toasty, round tannins.

MANU VINO DE AUTOR 2005 TC
tempranillo, syrah, merlot, garnacha, cabernet sauvignon.

91 Colour: cherry, garnet rim. Nose: ripe fruit, spicy, creamy oak, toasty. Palate: powerful, flavourful, toasty, round tannins.

VINOS Y ACEITES LAGUNA

Illescas, 5
28360 Villaconejos (Madrid)
☎: +34 918 938 196 - Fax: +34 918 938 344
info@lagunamadrid.com
www.lagunamadrid.com

ALMA DE VALDEGUERRA 2010 B
malvar.

84 Colour: bright straw. Nose: fresh, fresh fruit, white flowers, expressive. Palate: flavourful, fruity, good acidity, sweetness.

ALMA DE VALDEGUERRA 2010 RD
tempranillo.

84 Colour: rose. Nose: candied fruit, red berry notes, characterful. Palate: flavourful, sweetness, fruity.

ALMA DE VALDEGUERRA 2010 T
tempranillo.

87 Colour: cherry, purple rim. Nose: powerfull, fruit expression, red berry notes. Palate: flavourful, powerful, fleshy.

VALDEGUERRA LACUNA 2008 TC
tempranillo.

87 Colour: black cherry. Nose: candied fruit, roasted coffee, spicy, cocoa bean. Palate: powerful, concentrated, fine bitter notes.

EXUN PASIÓN 2006 T
60% tempranillo, 30% cabernet sauvignon, 10% merlot.

88 Colour: cherry, garnet rim. Nose: overripe fruit, toasty, spicy. Palate: sweetness, fine bitter notes, round tannins.

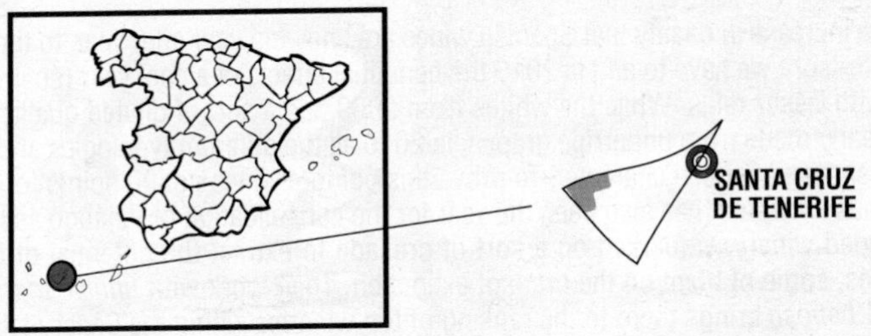

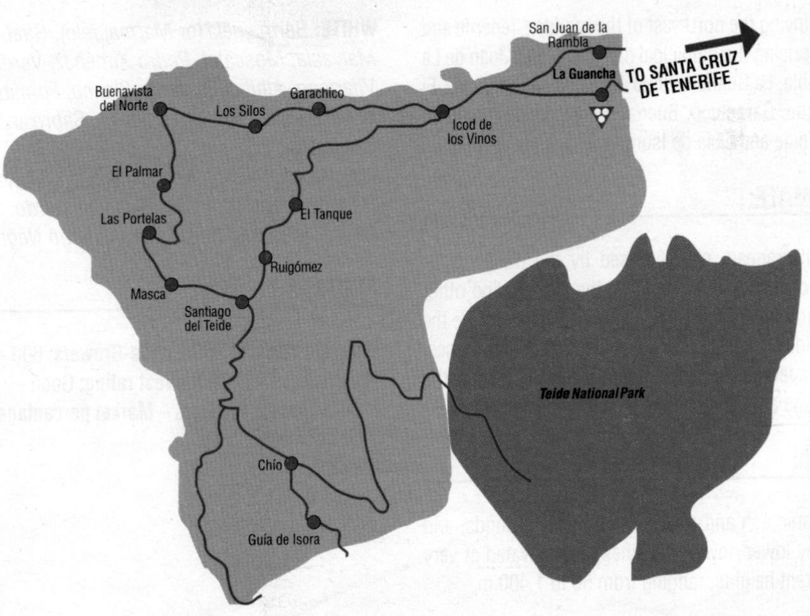

Consejo Regulador

DO Boundary

DO YCODEN-DAUTE-ISORA

NEWS ABOUT THE VINTAGE:

As well as the increase in quality that Spanish wines are knowing year after year, to those from Ycoden-Daute-Isora we have to add in 2010 the benefitial effects of a cool year (so it was also 2009), but with lesser rains. While the whites from 2009 had a sort of diluted quality and the reds were clearly made from underripe grapes, in 2010 all the different typologies show much more expression and varietal character. To prove this point, 4 wines got 90 points for just two on the previous vintage. It has also been the year for the consolidation of Viñátigo as the most forward-minded winery, embarked on a sort of crusade to extract the potential of the local grape varieties, some of them on the brink of extinction. Their work with *tintilla*, *marmajuelo*, *vijariego* and *baboso* brings them to the ranking of top wineries within the Canary Islands.

LOCATION:

Occupying the northeast of the island of Tenerife and comprising the municipal districts of San Juan de La Rambla, La Guancha, Icod de los Vinos, Los Silos, El Tanque, Garachico, Buenavista del Norte, Santiago del Teide and Guía de Isora.

CLIMATE:

Mediterranean, characterised by the multitude of microclimates depending on the altitude and other geographical conditions. The trade winds provide the humidity necessary for the development of the vines. The average annual temperature is 19°C and the average annual rainfall is around 540 mm.

SOIL:

Volcanic ash and rock on the higher grounds, and clayey lower down. The vines are cultivated at very different heights, ranging from 50 to 1,400 m.

GRAPE VARIETIES:

WHITE: *Bermejuela* (or *Marmajuelo*), *Güal, Malvasía, Moscatel, Pedro Ximénez, Verdello, Vijariego, Albillo, Bastardo Blanco, Forastera Blanca, Listán Blanco* (majority), *Sabro* and *Torrontés.*

RED: *Tintilla, Listán Negro* (majority), *Malvasía Rosada, Negramoll Castellana, Bastardo Negra, Moscatel Negra* and *Vijariego Negra.*

FIGURES:

Vineyard surface: 250 – **Wine-Growers:** 600 – **Wineries:** 19 – **2010 Harvest rating:** Good – **Production:** 29,400 litres – **Market percentages:** 100% domestic

CONSEJO REGULADOR
La Palmita, 10
38440 La Guancha (Sta. Cruz de Tenerife)
☎: +34 922 130 246 - Fax: +34 922 828 159
@ ycoden@ycoden.com / promocion@ycoden.com
www.ycoden.com

GENERAL CHARACTERISTICS OF THE WINES

WHITES	The most characteristic wines of the DO are the white wines produced from *Listán*, which are fresh, flavourful and quite expressive. They are produced as dry, semi sec and sweet wines and there are also examples of wines fermented in barrels.
ROSÉS	These have a strawberry colour, good fruit expression and are pleasantly herbaceous.
REDS	These have a deep cherry-red colour; they are fruity and fresh; on occasion they develop soothing aromas: eucalyptus and autumn leaves.

VINTAGE RATING PEÑÍNGUIDE

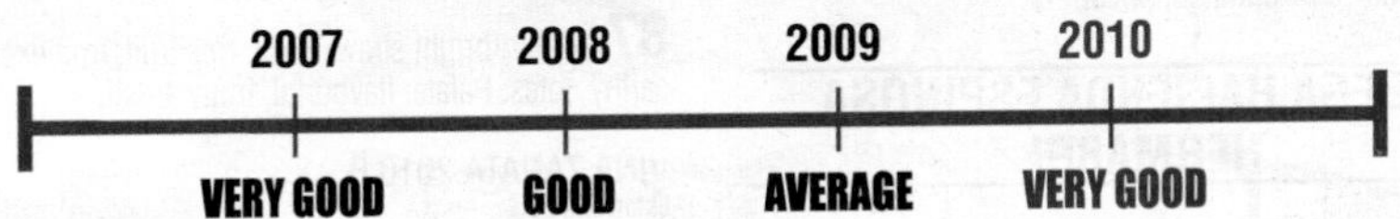

BODEGA COMARCAL DE ICOD

Camino Cuevas del Rey, 1
38430 Icod de los Vinos (Santa Cruz de Tenerife)
☎: +34 922 122 395 - Fax: +34 922 814 688
icod@bodegasinsularestenerife.es
www.bodegasinsularestenerife.es

EL ANCÓN 2010 T
listán negro.

85 Colour: cherry, purple rim. Nose: red berry notes, fruit expression, balsamic herbs. Palate: flavourful, good acidity.

MIRADERO 2010 BLANCO AFRUTADO
listán blanco.

87 Colour: bright straw. Nose: ripe fruit, citrus fruit, dried herbs. Palate: flavourful, fruity, sweetness.

MIRADERO 2010 ROSADO AFRUTADO
listán negro, listán blanco.

84 Colour: rose, purple rim. Nose: ripe fruit, raspberry, expressive. Palate: flavourful, powerful, fleshy.

EL ANCÓN NEGRAMOLL 2006 TINTO DULCE
negramoll.

90 Colour: black cherry. Nose: overripe fruit, dried fruit, smoky. Palate: concentrated, sweet.

BODEGA HACIENDA ESPINOSA HERMABRI

Finca Espinosa - Bº La Caleta de Interian
38450 Garachico (Santa Cruz de Tenerife)
☎: +34 922 830 247 - Fax: +34 922 241 047

VIÑA HERMABRI 2010 B

81 Colour: bright straw, greenish rim. Nose: fruit expression, white flowers, stalky. Palate: fine bitter notes, light-bodied.

VIÑA HERMABRI 2010 T

75

BODEGA VIÑA ENGRACIA

Paseo La Centinela, 53
38430 Icod de los Vinos (Santa Cruz de Tenerife)
☎: +34 922 810 857 - Fax: +34 922 860 895
vinosengracia@hotmail.com

VIÑA ENGRACIA 2010 B
100% listán blanco.

84 Colour: bright straw. Nose: fresh fruit, citrus fruit, white flowers. Palate: flavourful, fruity, fresh, fine bitter notes.

VIÑA ENGRACIA 2010 T
65% listán negro, 30% negramoll, 5% tintilla.

65

BODEGA VIÑA ZANATA

El Sol, 3
38440 La Guancha (Santa Cruz de Tenerife)
☎: +34 922 288 166 - Fax: +34 922 828 166
zanata@zanata.net
www.zanata.net

VIÑA ZANATA 2010 B
listán blanco.

87 Colour: bright straw. Nose: ripe fruit, fruit expression, earthy notes. Palate: flavourful, fruity, fresh.

VIÑA ZANATA 2010 B
listán blanco.

83 Colour: bright straw. Nose: dried flowers, ripe fruit, fruit expression, citrus fruit. Palate: flavourful, fresh, fruity.

VIÑA ZANATA 2010 T
listán blanco, listán negro, negramoll.

81 Colour: deep cherry. Nose: violet drops, medium intensity, balsamic herbs. Palate: fine bitter notes, spicy, easy to drink.

TARA TINTILLA 2009 T
tintilla.

85 Colour: deep cherry. Nose: expressive, ripe fruit, smoky, spicy, earthy notes. Palate: flavourful, fine bitter notes, spicy.

VIÑA ZANATA MALVASÍA 2009 BLANCO DULCE
malvasía.

84 Colour: bright golden. Nose: sweet spices, overripe fruit, slightly evolved. Palate: sweet, rich, fruity.

BODEGAS ACEVIÑO

La Patita, 63
38430 Icod de los Vinos (Santa Cruz de Tenerife)
☎: +34 922 810 237 - Fax: +34 922 810 237
bodegasacevino@yahoo.es

ACEVIÑO 2010 B
listán blanco.

84 Colour: bright straw. Nose: grassy, citrus fruit, ripe fruit. Palate: flavourful, fruity, fine bitter notes.

ACEVIÑO SEMIDULCE 2010 B
listán blanco.

84 Colour: bright straw. Nose: expressive, fruit preserve, citrus fruit, white flowers. Palate: flavourful, fine bitter notes, good acidity.

ACEVIÑO 2010 RD
listán negro.

83 Colour: rose, purple rim. Nose: floral, candied fruit, violet drops. Palate: powerful, sweetness, spicy.

ACEVIÑO 2010 T
listán negro.

77

BODEGAS VIÑAMONTE

Avda. Villanueva, 34
35440 La Guancha (Santa Cruz de Tenerife)
☎: +34 922 130 037 - Fax: +34 922 130 037
bodegasvmonte@hotmail.com

VIÑAMONTE DULCE 2010 B
70% listán blanco, 30% otras.

86 Colour: bright straw. Nose: candied fruit, white flowers, powerfull. Palate: powerful, sweetness, good acidity.

VIÑAMONTE AFRUTADO 2010 B
100% listán blanco.

82 Colour: bright straw. Nose: medium intensity, candied fruit, white flowers. Palate: flavourful, sweetness, fruity.

VIÑAMONTE 2009 B
100% listán blanco.

84 Colour: bright straw. Nose: candied fruit, citrus fruit, tropical fruit, sweet spices. Palate: flavourful, sweetness, fine bitter notes.

VIÑAMONTE 2010 RD
80% listán negro, 20% listán blanco.

77

VIÑAMONTE 2010 T
100% listán negro.

70

VIÑAMONTE DULCE 2006 T
60% listán negro, 40% otras.

87 Colour: pale ruby, brick rim edge. Nose: powerfull, candied fruit, balsamic herbs. Palate: fine bitter notes, good acidity, spirituous.

BODEGAS VIÑÁTIGO

Cabo Verde, s/n
38440 La Guancha (Santa Cruz de Tenerife)
☎: +34 922 828 768 - Fax: +34 922 829 936
vinatigo@vinatigo.com
www.vinatigo.com

VIÑÁTIGO MARMAJUELO 2010 B
marmajuelo.

90 Colour: bright straw. Nose: ripe fruit, citrus fruit, fruit expression. Palate: flavourful, powerful, fleshy. Personality.

VIÑÁTIGO MALVASÍA 2010 B
malvasía.

87 Colour: bright straw. Nose: fresh fruit, citrus fruit, dried herbs. Palate: flavourful, fruity, fresh, sweetness.

VIÑÁTIGO GUAL 2008 B

89 Colour: bright yellow, greenish rim. Nose: candied fruit, honeyed notes, jasmine. Palate: fruity, rich, flavourful, good acidity, balanced.

VIÑÁTIGO VIJARIEGO 2007 BFB

86 Colour: bright yellow. Nose: toasty, sweet spices. Palate: flavourful, rich, roasted-coffee aftertaste.

VIÑÁTIGO TINTILLA 2008 T ROBLE
tintilla.

87 Colour: cherry, garnet rim. Nose: powerfull, ripe fruit, spicy. Palate: fine bitter notes, spicy, grainy tannins.

VIÑÁTIGO BABOSO 2008 T

82 Colour: deep cherry. Nose: powerfull, warm, slightly evolved, smoky. Palate: powerful, fine bitter notes.

C.B. LUIS I., ANTONIO Y JAVIER LÓPEZ DE AYALA

El Majuelos, 2
38450 Garachico (Santa Cruz de Tenerife)
☎: +34 922 133 079 - Fax: +34 922 830 066
jlopezaz@wanadoo.es

HACIENDA SAN JUAN 2010 B
malvasía.

83 Colour: bright straw. Nose: candied fruit, citrus fruit, dried herbs. Palate: powerful, fleshy, sweetness.

HACIENDA SAN JUAN BN
malvasía.

78

CUEVA DEL REY

Camino Cuevas del Rey, 8
38430 Icod de los Vinos (Santa Cruz de Tenerife)
☎: +34 922 121 414 - Fax: +34 922 121 414

CUEVA DEL REY 2010 B

76

CUEVA DEL REY 2010 RD

70

CUEVA DEL REY 2010 T

82 Colour: cherry, purple rim. Nose: powerfull, red berry notes, fruit expression, scrubland. Palate: flavourful, fine bitter notes, good acidity.

M. ELISA VICTORIA LÓPEZ DE AYALA LEÓN-HUERTA

Finca Malpaís, 11 El Guincho
38458 Garachico (Santa Cruz de Tenerife)
☎: +34 922 830 016

CANALES DEL PALMAR 2010 T

85 Colour: deep cherry. Nose: powerfull, raspberry, balsamic herbs. Palate: powerful, fine bitter notes, good acidity.

TINOCA

Camino Las Suertes, 18
38430 Icod de los Vinos (Santa Cruz de Tenerife)
☎: +34 658 992 743 - Fax: +34 922 335 002
vinotinoca@gmail.com
www.vinotinoca.com

TINOCA MALVASÍA 2009 BLANCO DULCE
100% malvasía.

88 Colour: bright golden. Nose: powerfull, candied fruit, citrus fruit. Palate: ripe fruit, good finish, spicy.

VIÑA SPINOLA

Camino Esparragal, s/n
38470 Los Silos (Santa Cruz de Tenerife)
☎: +34 922 840 977 - Fax: +34 922 840 977

VIÑA SPINOLA 2010 B

72

VIÑA SPINOLA MALVASÍA SECO 2009 B

82 Colour: bright golden. Nose: citrus fruit, slightly evolved, fruit preserve, spicy. Palate: flavourful, powerful, fleshy.

VIÑA SPINOLA MALVASÍA SECO 2008 B

87 Colour: bright straw. Nose: candied fruit, citrus fruit, dry nuts. Palate: flavourful, sweetness, good acidity.

VIÑA SPINOLA MALVASÍA SECO 2004 B

88 Colour: bright golden. Nose: citrus fruit, candied fruit, white flowers. Palate: flavourful, sweetness, good acidity.

VIÑA SPINOLA MALVASÍA SECO 2003 B

88 Colour: golden. Nose: floral, honeyed notes, candied fruit. Palate: flavourful, sweet, fresh, fruity, good acidity, long.

VIÑA SPINOLA MALVASÍA SECO 2002 B

85 Colour: bright straw. Nose: powerfull, candied fruit, citrus fruit. Palate: fruity, sweetness, fine bitter notes.

VIÑA SPINOLA MALVASÍA SECO 1996 B

88 Colour: bright straw. Nose: candied fruit, citrus fruit, dry nuts, fruit preserve. Palate: powerful, sweetness, fine bitter notes.

VIÑA SPINOLA 2010 RD

72

VIÑA SPINOLA 2010 T

72

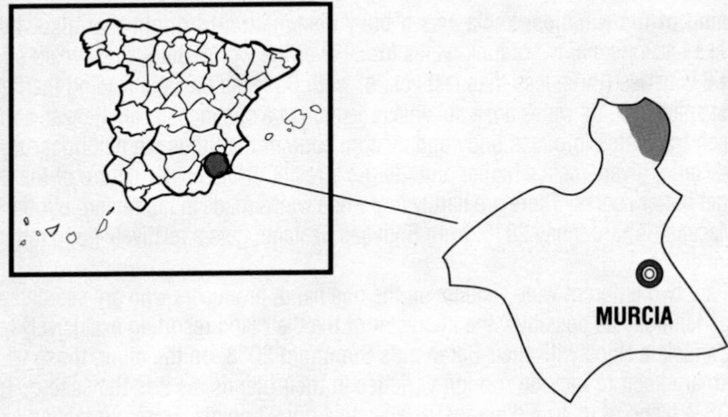

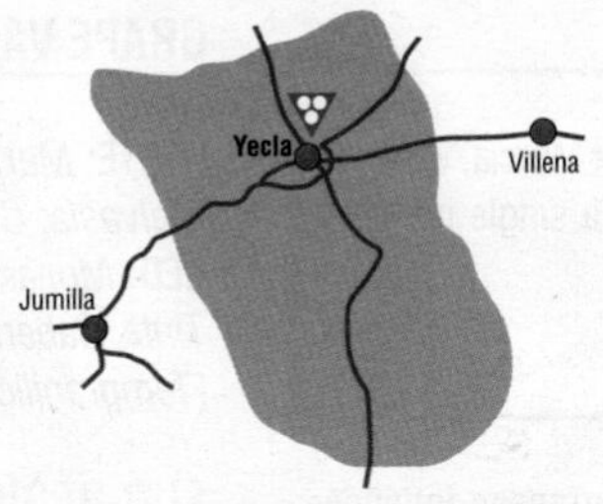

Consejo Regulador
DO Boundary

NEWS ABOUT THE VINTAGE:

At the beginning of the Nineties, Yecla was a busy designation of origin that also, through some cooperatives like La Purísima, made bulk-wines for all over the world. But just 20 years after, Yecla has shrunk to just 8 wineries (three less than last year's), with Bodegas Castaño leading the fight to bring it back to its past splendour. Its wines are a suitable reflection of a continental climate with a mediterranean influence, which translates into less body and alcohol content than those in neighbouring regions like Jumilla and Alicante, given Yecla's higher altitude. As a result of the cooler nature of the 2010 vintage, young wines get better scores. There are hardly any white wines made in the region, but the best of them all, Castaño Macabeo-Chardonnay 2010, from Bodegas Castaño, gets a relatively good rating: 88 points.

In Yecla there are two different wine visions: on the one hand, producers who are searching to reflect in their wines –as faithfully as possible– the character of the their land resorting exclusively to *monastrell*, like Antonio Candela e Hijos with their Barahonda Summum 2008; on the other, those who, in a more tolerant mood, are keen to include foreign varieties in their blends, as it is the case of Trenza Family Collection 2008, a blend of up to 5 different varieties that got 93 points. From our tasting experience, we clearly see that the most interesting wines are not those made from just a single variety, but whenever we find a good example of them, like Viña Detrás de la Casa Syrah 2007 (92 points), we rejoice it even more. Regarding the presence of Yecla's wines abroad, the wineries themselves have worked a lot on it and eventually managed to increase their export figures from 80% up to 92%, leaving a mere 8% for the Spanish market, heavily affected in any case by a big economical crisis.

LOCATION:

In the northeast of the province of Murcia, within the plateau region, and comprising a single municipal district, Yecla.

CLIMATE:

Continental, with a slight Mediterranean influence, with hot summers and cold winters, and little rainfall, which is usually around 300 mm per annum.

SOIL:

Fundamentally deep limestone, with good permeability. The vineyards are on undulating terrain at a height of between 400 m and 800 m above sea level.

GRAPE VARIETIES:

WHITE: *Merseguera, Airén, Macabeo, Malvasía, Chardonnay.*
RED: *Monastrell* (majority 85% of total), *Garnacha Tinta, Cabernet Sauvignon, Cencibel* (*Tempranillo*), *Merlot, Tintorera, Syrah.*

SUB-REGIONS:

Yecla Campo Arriba, with Monastrell as the most common variety and alcohol contents of up to 14°, and **Yecla Campo Abajo,** whose grapes produce a lower alcohol content (around 12° for reds and 11.5° for whites).

FIGURES:

Vineyard surface: 6,150 – **Wine-Growers:** 570 – **Wineries:** 8 – **2010 Harvest rating:** N/A – **Production:** 7,297,000 litres – **Market percentages:** 8% domestic. 92% export

CONSEJO REGULADOR
Centro de Desarrollo Local
Poeta Francisco A. Jiménez, s/n - P.I. Urbayecla II
30510 Yecla (Murcia)
☎: +34 968 792 352 - Fax: +34 968 792 352
@ indo@yeclavino.com
www.yeclavino.com

GENERAL CHARACTERISTICS OF THE WINES

WHITES	These have a straw yellow colour; they are fruity and have quite a good aromatic intensity, although on the palate their acidity is somewhat low.
ROSÉS	Although they are not the most representative wines of the region, the best wines are produced according to modern techniques for this type of wine and they are therefore quite fruity, fresh and pleasant.
REDS	Thes are the most characteristic wines of the region and also the most abundant. Produced mainly from *Monastrell*, they have either a violet cherry or deep cherry-red colour. Their aroma is of ripe fruit and there may sometimes be hints of raisining, due to the strong sunshine of the region. They are meaty, warm and supple on the palate.

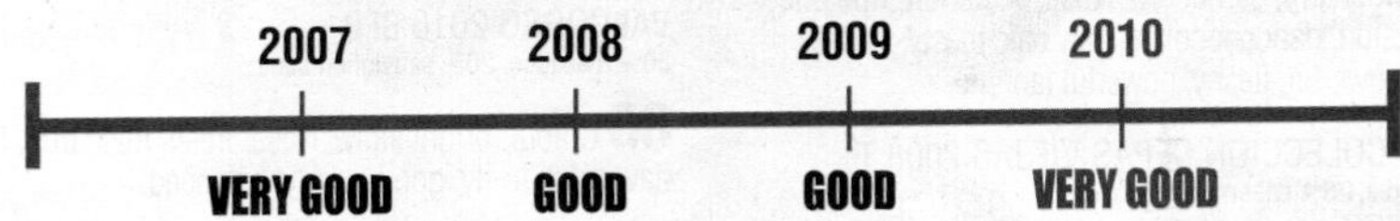

BODEGAS CASTAÑO

Ctra. Fuenteálamo, 3 - Apdo. 120
30510 Yecla (Murcia)
☎: +34 968 791 115 - Fax: +34 968 791 900
info@bodegascastano.com
www.bodegascastano.com

CASTAÑO MACABEO CHARDONNAY 2010 B
50% macabeo, 50% chardonnay.

88 Colour: bright straw. Nose: fresh, white flowers, expressive. Palate: flavourful, fruity, good acidity, balanced.

CASTAÑO MONASTRELL 2010 RD JOVEN
100% monastrell.

83 Colour: coppery red. Nose: candied fruit, spicy, scrubland. Palate: flavourful, fruity, fleshy.

CASTAÑO MONASTRELL 2010 T
100% monastrell.

90 Colour: cherry, purple rim. Nose: expressive, fresh fruit, red berry notes, floral, complex. Palate: flavourful, fruity, good acidity, round tannins.

HÉCULA 2009 T
100% monastrell.

88 Colour: bright cherry. Nose: sweet spices, creamy oak, ripe fruit, red berry notes. Palate: flavourful, fruity, toasty, round tannins.

CASA CISCA 2008 T
100% monastrell.

94 Colour: cherry, garnet rim. Nose: powerfull, ripe fruit, fruit expression, dark chocolate, new oak, toasty. Palate: flavourful, powerful, fleshy, powerful tannins.

CASTAÑO COLECCIÓN CEPAS VIEJAS 2008 T
80% monastrell, 20% cabernet sauvignon.

92 Colour: cherry, garnet rim. Nose: spicy, creamy oak, toasty, complex, mineral, ripe fruit, red berry notes. Palate: powerful, flavourful, toasty, round tannins.

POZUELO 2008 TC
65% monastrell, 10% syrah, 20% cabernet sauvignon, 5% garnacha tintorera.

87 Colour: bright cherry. Nose: sweet spices, creamy oak, ripe fruit. Palate: flavourful, fruity, toasty, round tannins.

VIÑA DETRÁS DE LA CASA SYRAH 2007 T
100% syrah.

92 Colour: cherry, garnet rim. Nose: ripe fruit, spicy, creamy oak, toasty, mineral. Palate: powerful, flavourful, toasty, round tannins.

VIÑA DETRÁS DE LA CASA CABERNET SAUVIGNON-TINTORERA 2007 TC
37% garnacha tintorera, 63% cabernet sauvignon.

92 Colour: cherry, garnet rim. Nose: ripe fruit, creamy oak, toasty, complex, sweet spices, wet leather. Palate: powerful, flavourful, toasty, round tannins.

VIÑA AL LADO DE LA CASA 2007 T
75% monastrell, 10% syrah, 10% cabernet sauvignon, 5% garnacha tintorera.

90 Colour: bright cherry. Nose: ripe fruit, creamy oak, mineral. Palate: flavourful, fruity, toasty, round tannins.

POZUELO 2007 TR
70% monastrell, 10% cabernet sauvignon, 10% merlot, 10% syrah.

88 Colour: cherry, garnet rim. Nose: aged wood nuances, aromatic coffee, ripe fruit, toasty, sweet spices. Palate: flavourful, powerful, fleshy, spicy, ripe fruit.

CASTAÑO MONASTRELL DULCE T
100% monastrell.

89 Colour: bright cherry. Nose: expressive, overripe fruit, dried fruit, dark chocolate. Palate: flavourful, fruity, toasty, sweet, concentrated.

BODEGAS LA PURÍSIMA

Ctra. de Pinoso, 3
30510 Yecla (Murcia)
☎: +34 968 751 257 - Fax: +34 968 795 116
info@bodegaslapurisima.com
www.bodegaslapurisima.com

VALCORSO 2010 BFB
80% macabeo, 20% sauvignon blanc.

86 Colour: bright straw. Nose: fresh, fresh fruit. Palate: flavourful, fruity, good acidity, balanced.

ESTÍO MACABEO 2010 B
80% macabeo, 20% sauvignon blanc.

82 Colour: bright straw. Nose: fresh, fresh fruit, white flowers. Palate: flavourful, fruity, easy to drink.

ESTÍO 2010 RD
50% monastrell, 30% syrah, 20% tempranillo.

86 Colour: rose, purple rim. Nose: powerfull, ripe fruit, red berry notes, expressive. Palate: fleshy, powerful, fruity, fresh.

VALCORSO SYRAH 2010 T
100% syrah.

88 Color cherry, purple rim. Aroma expressive, fresh fruit, red berry notes, floral. Taste flavourful, fruity, good acidity, round tannins.

ESTÍO 2010 T
70% monastrell, 20% syrah, 10% tempranillo.

87 Colour: cherry, purple rim. Nose: fresh fruit, red berry notes, floral. Palate: flavourful, fruity, good acidity, round tannins.

VALCORSO ECOLÓGICO 2010 T
80% monastrell, 20% syrah.

87 Colour: cherry, purple rim. Nose: fresh fruit, red berry notes, floral, balanced. Palate: flavourful, fruity, good acidity, round tannins.

VALCORSO MONASTRELL 2009 T BARRICA
95% monastrell, 5% syrah.

86 Colour: cherry, purple rim. Nose: sweet spices, creamy oak, ripe fruit. Palate: spicy, round tannins, balanced.

ESTÍO MONASTRELL ECOLÓGICO 2009 T BARRICA
90% monastrell, 10% syrah.

85 Colour: cherry, garnet rim. Nose: fresh, ripe fruit, balanced. Palate: fruity, flavourful.

TRAPÍO 2008 T
100% monastrell.

88 Colour: bright cherry. Nose: sweet spices, creamy oak, overripe fruit, wet leather. Palate: flavourful, fruity, toasty, round tannins.

IV EXPRESIÓN 2007 T
85% monastrell, 10% syrah, 5% garnacha.

88 Colour: bright cherry. Nose: sweet spices, creamy oak, ripe fruit. Palate: flavourful, fruity, toasty, round tannins.

IGLESIA VIEJA 2006 TC
70% monastrell, 15% syrah, 15% tempranillo.

84 Colour: cherry, garnet rim. Nose: ripe fruit, spicy, aged wood nuances. Palate: flavourful, toasty, correct.

IGLESIA VIEJA 2004 TR
85% monastrell, 15% cabernet sauvignon.

84 Colour: ruby red, orangey edge. Nose: spicy, overripe fruit. Palate: toasty, round tannins, slightly overripe.

BODEGAS SEÑORÍO DE BARAHONDA

Ctra. de Pinoso, km. 3
30510 Yecla (Murcia)
☎: +34 968 718 696 - Fax: +34 968 790 928
info@barahonda.com
www.barahonda.com

BARAHONDA 2010 B
macabeo, airén.

85 Colour: bright straw. Nose: candied fruit, citrus fruit, medium intensity. Palate: flavourful, fruity, fleshy.

BARAHONDA 2010 RD
monastrell.

82 Colour: rose, purple rim. Nose: ripe fruit, red berry notes, expressive. Palate: fleshy, fresh.

BARAHONDA MONASTRELL 2010 T
monastrell.

88 Colour: cherry, purple rim. Nose: expressive, red berry notes, floral, fresh. Palate: flavourful, fruity, powerful, round.

NABUKO 2010 T
monastrell, syrah.

87 Colour: cherry, purple rim. Nose: fresh fruit, red berry notes, sweet spices. Palate: flavourful, fruity, good acidity, round tannins.

CARRO 2010 T
monastrell, syrah, tempranillo, merlot.

85 Colour: cherry, purple rim. Nose: expressive, red berry notes, floral. Palate: flavourful, fruity, light-bodied.

BARAHONDA BARRICA 2009 T BARRICA
monastrell, syrah.

89 Colour: cherry, purple rim. Nose: powerfull, ripe fruit, dark chocolate, sweet spices, creamy oak. Palate: flavourful, powerful, fleshy.

NIREA 2009 T
monastrell, garnacha, syrah.

87 Colour: cherry, garnet rim. Nose: spicy, creamy oak, toasty, overripe fruit. Palate: powerful, flavourful, toasty, round tannins.

HEREDAD CANDELA MONASTRELL 2009 T
monastrell.

86 Colour: bright cherry. Nose: sweet spices, creamy oak, expressive, ripe fruit. Palate: flavourful, fruity, toasty, round tannins.

BARAHONDA SUMMUM 2008 T
100% monastrell.

91 Colour: cherry, garnet rim. Nose: ripe fruit, sweet spices, creamy oak, expressive. Palate: flavourful, fruity, toasty, round tannins.

NIREA MONASTRELL 2008 T
monastrell.

89 Colour: cherry, garnet rim. Nose: ripe fruit, spicy, creamy oak, toasty, dark chocolate. Palate: powerful, flavourful, toasty, round tannins.

BARAHONDA 2008 TC
monastrell, syrah.

87 Colour: cherry, garnet rim. Nose: ripe fruit, creamy oak, toasty, sweet spices. Palate: powerful, flavourful, toasty, round tannins.

BELLUM EL PRINCIPIO 2006 T BARRICA
monastrell.

89 Colour: ruby red, orangey edge. Nose: sweet spices, aged wood nuances, ripe fruit. Palate: fleshy, flavourful, round tannins.

BELLUM EL REMATE 2006 T
monastrell.

88 Colour: cherry, garnet rim. Nose: sweet spices, aromatic coffee, dark chocolate. Palate: spirituous, flavourful, long.

BARAHONDA MO 5 T
monastrell.

88 Colour: cherry, purple rim. Nose: fresh fruit, red berry notes, floral, sweet spices. Palate: flavourful, fruity, round tannins, spicy.

DANIEL ALBA BODEGAS

Pintor Juan Albert, 7 Piso 3A
30510 Yecla (Murcia)
☎: +34 628 687 673
info@danielalbabodegas.com
www.danielalbabodegas.com

LA MÁQUINA MONASTRELL 2008 T
86% monastrell, 8% syrah, 6% garnacha.

91 Colour: cherry, garnet rim. Nose: ripe fruit, spicy, creamy oak, toasty. Palate: powerful, flavourful, toasty, round tannins.

LONG WINES

Avda. Monte, 46
28723 Algete (Madrid)
☎: +34 916 221 305 - Fax: +34 916 220 029
raquel@longwines.com
www.longwines.com

CASA DEL CANTO 2008 T ROBLE
60% monastrell, 20% cabernet sauvignon, 20% syrah.

90 Colour: bright cherry. Nose: creamy oak, earthy notes, candied fruit. Palate: flavourful, fruity, toasty, round tannins.

CASA DEL CANTO 2007 TR
55% monastrell, 30% cabernet sauvignon, 15% syrah.

89 Colour: cherry, garnet rim. Nose: spicy, creamy oak, toasty, fruit liqueur notes. Palate: powerful, flavourful, toasty, round tannins.

TRENZA WINES S.L.

Avda. Matías Saenz Tejada, s/n. Edif. Fuengirola Center - Local 1
29640 Fuengirola (Málaga)
☎: +34 615 343 320 - Fax: +34 952 588 467
david@vinnico.com
www.trenzawines.com

TRENZA Z-STRAND 2008 T
87% syrah, 8% monastrell, 5% cabernet sauvignon.

89 Colour: cherry, garnet rim. Nose: powerfull, warm, overripe fruit, new oak, toasty. Palate: flavourful, powerful, fleshy, round tannins.

TRENZA FAMILY COLLECTION 2008 T
50% monastrell, 22% cabernet sauvignon, 13% syrah, 9% merlot, 6% garnacha.

93 Colour: cherry, garnet rim. Nose: spicy, creamy oak, toasty, complex, ripe fruit, mineral. Palate: powerful, flavourful, toasty, round tannins.

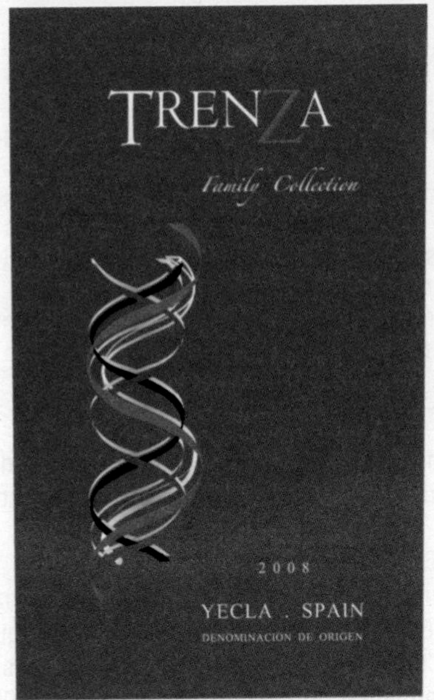

VALLE DE SALINAS

Ctra. El Carche, Km. 11,5
30520 Jumilla (Murcia)
☎: +34 968 781 812 - Fax: +34 968 716 063
info@valledesalinas.com
www.valledesalinas.com

CARACOL SERRANO 2010 T
monastrell, cabernet sauvignon, syrah.

86 Colour: cherry, garnet rim. Nose: expressive, floral, ripe fruit. Palate: flavourful, fruity, good acidity, round tannins.

ALTOS DEL CUCO T

85 Color cherry, purple rim. Aroma expressive, fresh fruit, red berry notes, floral. Taste flavourful, fruity, good acidity, round tannins.

VINNICO EXPORT

Muela, 16
03730 Jávea (Alicante)
☎: +34 965 791 967 - Fax: +34 966 461 471
info@vinnico.com
www.vinnico.com

PAU 2010 B
macabeo, sauvignon blanc.

84 Colour: bright straw. Nose: faded flowers, candied fruit, citrus fruit. Palate: flavourful, spicy, ripe fruit.

FLOR DEL MONTGÓ OLD VINES MONASTRELL 2010 T
100% monastrell.

85 Colour: cherry, purple rim. Nose: expressive, red berry notes. Palate: flavourful, fruity, good acidity.

FLOR DEL MONTGÓ MONASTRELL ORGANIC 2010 T
100% monastrell.

85 Colour: cherry, purple rim. Nose: expressive, floral, fruit expression. Palate: fruity, good acidity, easy to drink.

PAU 2009 T
monastrell, syrah, tempranillo.

87 Colour: bright cherry. Nose: sweet spices, creamy oak, overripe fruit. Palate: flavourful, fruity, toasty, round tannins.

MONTGÓ MONASTRELL SHIRAZ 2009 T
70% monastrell, 20% syrah, 10% cabernet sauvignon.

86 Colour: cherry, purple rim. Nose: expressive, red berry notes, balanced. Palate: flavourful, fruity, good acidity.

PICOS DEL MONTGÓ BARREL SELECT 2008 T
50% monastrell, 20% syrah, 15% garnacha, 10% merlot, 5% cabernet sauvignon.

86 Colour: cherry, garnet rim. Nose: sweet spices, fruit preserve, creamy oak. Palate: round tannins, correct, creamy.

VINOS DE PAGO

The "Vinos de Pago" are linked to a single winery, and it is a status given to that winery on the grounds of unique micro-climatic features and proven evidence of consistent high quality over the years, with the goal to produce wines of sheer singularity. So far, only 13 "Vinos de Pago" labels have been granted for three different autonomous regions (La Mancha, Navarra and Comunidad Valenciana). The "Vinos de Pago" category has the same status as a DO. This "pago" should not be confused with the other "pago" term used in the wine realm, which refers to a plot, a smaller vineyard within a bigger property. The "Pagos de España" association was formed in 2000 when a group of small producers of single estate wines got together to defend the singularity of their wines. In 2003, the association became Grandes Pagos de España, responding to the request of many colleagues in other parts of the country who wished to make the single-growth concept better known, and to seek excellence through the direct relationship between wines and their places of origin.

PAGO CALZADILLA: Located in the Mayor river valley, in the part of the Alcarria region that belongs to the province of Cuenca, it enjoys altitude levels ranging between 845 and 1005 meters. The vines are mostly planted on limestone soils with pronounced slopes (with up to a 40% incline), so terraces and slant plots have become the most common feature, following the altitude gradients. The grape varieties planted are tempranillo, cabernet-sauvignon, garnacha and syrah.

PAGO CAMPO DE LA GUARDIA: The vineyards are in the town of La Guardia, to the northeast of the province of Toledo, on a high plateau known as Mesa de Ocaña. Soils are deep and with varying degrees of loam, clay and sand. The climate follows a continental pattern, with hot and dry summers and particularly dry and cold winters. The presence of the Tajo River to the north and the Montes de Toledo to the south promote lower rainfall levels than in neighbouring areas, and thus more concentration of aromas and phenolic compounds.

PAGO CASA DEL BLANCO: Its vineyards are located at an altitude of 617 metres in Campo de Calatrava, in the town of Manzanares, right in the centre of the province of Ciudad Real, and therefore with a mediterranean/continental climate. Soils have varying degrees of loam and sand, and are abundant in lithium, surely due to the ancient volcanic character of the region.

PAGO DEHESA DEL CARRIZAL: Property of Marcial Gómez Sequeira, Dehesa del Carrizal is located in the town of Retuerta de Bullaque, to the north of Ciudad Real. It enjoys a continental climate and high altitude (900 metres). The winemaker, Ignacio de Miguel, uses primarily foreign (French) varieties such as *cabernet sauvignon.*

PAGO DOMINIO DE VALDEPUSA: Located in the town of Malpica de Tajo (Toledo), its owner, Carlos Falcó (Marqués de Griñón) pioneered the introduction in Spain of foreign grape varieties such as *cabernet sauvignon* and *chardonnay* as well as the wire training techniques for warm climates designed by Richard Smart. Using long-cycled grape varieties, its wines are meaty, succulent, and with elegant tannins.

PAGO EL TERRERAZO: El Terrerazo, property of Bodegas Mustiguilo, is the first "Vinos de Pago" label granted within the autonomous region of Valencia. It comprises 62 hectares at an altitude of 800 meters between Utiel and Sinarcas where an excellent clone of *bobal* – that yields small and loose berries– is grown. It enjoys a mediterranean-continental climate and the vineyard gets the influence of humid winds blowing from the sea, which is just 80 kilometres away from the property. Soils are characterized limestone and clay in nature, with abundant sand and stones.

PAGO FINCA ÉLEZ: It became the first of all Vino de Pago designations of origin. Its owner is Manuel Manzaneque, and it is located at an altitude of 1000 metres in El Bonillo, in the province of Albacete. The winery became renown by its splendid *chardonnay*, but today also make a single-varietal *syrah* and some other red renderings.

PAGO FLORENTINO: Located in the municipality of Malagón (Ciudad Real), between natural lagoons to the south and the Sierra de Malagón to the north, at an altitude of some 630-670 metres. Soils are mainly siliceous with limestone and stones on the surface and a subsoil of slate and limestone. The climate is milder and dryer than that of neighbouring towns.

PAGO GUIJOSO: Finca El Guijoso is property of Bodegas Sánchez Muliterno, located in El Bonillo, between the provinces of Albacete and Ciudad Real. Surrounded by bitch and juniper woods, the vines are planted on stone (guijo in Spanish, from which it takes its name) soils at an altitude of 1000 metres. Wines are all made from French varieties, and have a clear French lean also in terms of style.

PAGO LOS BALAGUESES: The "Pago de los Balagueses" is located to the south west of the Utiel-Requena wine region, just 20 kilometres away from Requena. At approximately 700 metres over the sea level, it enjoys a continental type of climate with mediterranean influence and an average annual rainfall of around 450 mm. The vines are planted on low hills –a feature that favours water drainage– surrounded by pines, almond and olive trees, thus giving shape to a unique landscape.

PAGO PRADO DE IRACHE: Its vineyard is located in the municipality of Ayegui (Navarra) at an altitude of 450 metres. Climate is continental with strong Atlantic influence and soils are mainly of a loamy nature.

PAGO DE OTAZU: Its vineyards are located in Navarra, between two mountain ranges (Sierra del Perdón and Sierra de Echauri), and is probably the most northerly of all Spanish wine regions. It is a cool area with Atlantic climate and a high day-night temperature contrast. Soils in that part of the country, near the city of Pamplona, are limestone-based with abundant clay and stones, therefore with good drainage that allows vines to sink their roots deeper into the soil.

PAGO SEÑORÍO DE ARÍNZANO: Located in the city of Estella, in Navarra, to the northeast of Spain, the vineyard is in a valley near the Pyrenees and crossed by the Ega river, which moderates the temperatures. Climate has here a strong Atlantic influence with high day-night temperature contrast. Soils are complex in nature, with varying levels of loam, marl, clay and highly degraded limestone rock.

PAGO CALZADILLA

PAGO CALZADILLA

Ctra. Huete a Cuenca, Km. 3
16500 Huete (Cuenca)
☎: +34 969 143 020 - Fax: +34 969 147 047
info@pagodecalzadilla.com
www.pagodecalzadilla.net

CALZADILLA CS 1000 2008 T
cabernet sauvignon.

92 Colour: cherry, garnet rim. Nose: mineral, earthy notes, red berry notes, ripe fruit, expressive. Palate: mineral, flavourful, powerful, fleshy, round tannins.

OPTA CALZADILLA 2008 T
tempranillo, garnacha, syrah.

88 Colour: cherry, purple rim. Nose: red berry notes, ripe fruit, cocoa bean, aromatic coffee, creamy oak. Palate: round, fruity, flavourful, toasty.

CALZADILLA CLASSIC 2007 T
tempranillo, cabernet sauvignon, garnacha, syrah.

90 Colour: cherry, garnet rim. Nose: red berry notes, ripe fruit, complex, mineral, sweet spices, creamy oak. Palate: flavourful, powerful, fleshy, balanced.

GRAN CALZADILLA 2006 T
70% tempranillo, 30% cabernet sauvignon.

91 Colour: cherry, garnet rim. Nose: ripe fruit, expressive, powerfull, complex, mineral. Palate: long, spicy, flavourful, fleshy.

PAGO CAMPO DE LA GUARDIA

BODEGAS MARTÚE LA GUARDIA

Campo de la Guardia, s/n
45760 La Guardia (Toledo)
☎: +34 925 123 333 - Fax: +34 925 123 332
bodegasenlaguardia@martue.com
www.martue.com

MARTÚE SYRAH 2008 T
syrah.

89 Colour: cherry, garnet rim. Nose: cocoa bean, dark chocolate, ripe fruit, expressive. Palate: powerful, flavourful, fleshy.

MARTÚE 2008 T

88 Colour: cherry, garnet rim. Nose: red berry notes, ripe fruit, balsamic herbs, creamy oak, warm. Palate: fruity, flavourful, powerful, fleshy.

MARTÚE ESPECIAL 2007 T

88 Colour: cherry, garnet rim. Nose: spicy, toasty, ripe fruit. Palate: powerful, flavourful, balsamic, fleshy.

PAGO CASA DEL BLANCO

PAGO CASA DEL BLANCO

Ctra. Manzanares a Moral de Calatrava, Km. 23,2
13200 Manzanares (Ciudad Real)
☎: +34 917 480 606 - Fax: +34 913 290 266
quixote@pagocasadelblanco.com
www.pagocasadelblanco.com

QUIXOTE MERLOT TEMPRANILLO PETIT VERDOT 2006 T
merlot, tempranillo, petit verdot.

86 Colour: cherry, garnet rim. Nose: ripe fruit, red berry notes, scrubland, balsamic herbs, spicy. Palate: fruity, flavourful, fleshy.

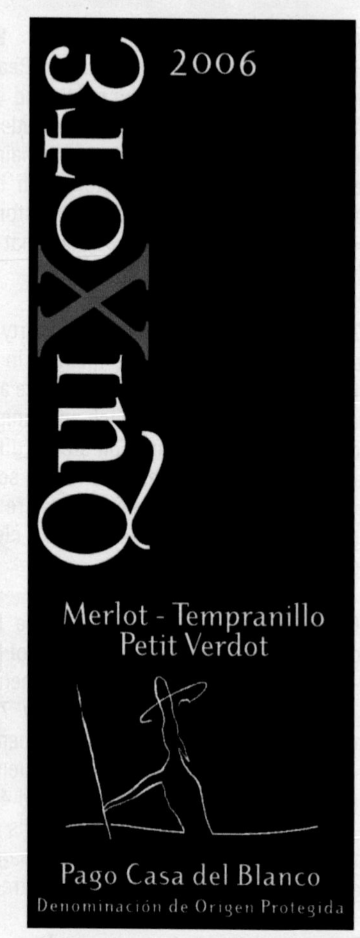

QUIXOTE PETIT VERDOT 2006 T
petit verdot.

85 Colour: cherry, garnet rim. Nose: red berry notes, ripe fruit, scrubland, balsamic herbs. Palate: flavourful, fleshy, toasty.

QUIXOTE CABERNET SAUVIGNON SYRAH 2005 T
cabernet sauvignon, syrah.

86 Colour: cherry, garnet rim. Nose: spicy, dark chocolate, cocoa bean, toasty. Palate: balsamic, fleshy, powerful, flavourfult.

PAGO DEHESA DEL CARRIZAL

DEHESA DEL CARRIZAL

Ctra. Navas de Estena, Km. 5,000
13194 Retuerta del Bullaque (Ciudad Real)
☎: +34 925 421 773 - Fax: +34 925 421 761
bodega@dehesadelcarrizal.com
www.dehesadelcarrizal.com

DEHESA DEL CARRIZAL CHARDONNAY 2010 B
chardonnay.

89 Colour: bright straw. Nose: white flowers, ripe fruit, citrus fruit, toasty. Palate: powerful, fine bitter notes, round tannins.

DEHESA DEL CARRIZAL CHARDONNAY 2009 B
chardonnay.

90 Colour: bright straw. Nose: ripe fruit, citrus fruit, white flowers. Palate: flavourful, powerful, fleshy, sweetness.

DEHESA DEL CARRIZAL CHARDONNAY 2008 B
chardonnay.

91 Color bright yellow. Aroma powerfull, ripe fruit, sweet spices, creamy oak, fragrant herbs. Taste rich, smoky aftertaste, flavourful, fresh, good acidity.

DEHESA DEL CARRIZAL SYRAH 2008 T
syrah.

91 Colour: cherry, garnet rim. Nose: spicy, creamy oak, toasty, characterful. Palate: powerful, flavourful, toasty, round tannins.

DEHESA DEL CARRIZAL MV ROJO 2007 T
tempranillo, merlot, syrah, cabernet sauvignon.

88 Colour: cherry, garnet rim. Nose: powerfull, ripe fruit, creamy oak, sweet spices. Palate: flavourful, powerful, fleshy, fine bitter notes.

DEHESA DEL CARRIZAL CABERNET SAUVIGNON 2006 T
cabernet sauvignon.

91 Colour: deep cherry. Nose: sweet spices, varietal, expressive, characterful, ripe fruit. Palate: flavourful, spicy, ripe fruit, long.

PAGO DOMINIO DE VALDEPUSA

PAGOS DE FAMILIA MARQUÉS DE GRIÑÓN

Finca Casa de Vacas - Ctra. CM-4015, Km. 23
45692 Malpica de Tajo (Toledo)
☎: +34 925 597 222 - Fax: +34 925 789 416
info@pagosdefamilia.com
www.pagosdefamilia.com

CALIZA 2007 T
syrah, petit verdot.

89 Colour: cherry, garnet rim. Nose: ripe fruit, earthy notes, spicy, creamy oak. Palate: balanced, flavourful, fleshy, long.

MARQUÉS DE GRIÑÓN CABERNET SAUVIGNON 2006 T
cabernet sauvignon.

92 Colour: cherry, garnet rim. Nose: ripe fruit, expressive, balsamic herbs, spicy, creamy oak. Palate: powerful, flavourful, fleshy, creamy, balsamic.

MARQUÉS DE GRIÑÓN PETIT VERDOT 2006 T
petit verdot.

91 Colour: cherry, garnet rim. Nose: complex, red berry notes, ripe fruit, earthy notes, mineral, scrubland. Palate: fruity, powerful, flavourful, fleshy, round tannins.

SVMMA VARIETALIS 2006 T
cabernet sauvignon, petit verdot, syrah.

91 Colour: cherry, garnet rim. Nose: red berry notes, complex, spicy, mineral. Palate: flavourful, powerful, fleshy, balanced.

MARQUÉS DE GRIÑÓN SYRAH 2006 T
syrah.

90 Colour: cherry, garnet rim. Nose: red berry notes, ripe fruit, balsamic herbs, creamy oak. Palate: flavourful, fleshy, balsamic, mineral.

MARQUÉS DE GRIÑÓN EMERITVS 2005 TR
cabernet sauvignon, petit verdot, syrah.

93 Colour: cherry, garnet rim. Nose: ripe fruit, balsamic herbs, warm, spicy, creamy oak. Palate: powerful, flavourful, fleshy, complex, mineral.

PAGO EL TERRERAZO

MUSTIGUILLO VIÑEDOS Y BODEGA

Ctra. N-330, km 196,5 El Terrerazo
46300 Utiel (Valencia)
☎: +34 962 168 260 - Fax: +34 962 168 259
info@bodegamustiguillo.com
www.bodegamustiguillo.com

QUINCHA CORRAL 2009 T
bobal.

95 Colour: deep cherry. Nose: spicy, creamy oak, fruit expression, balsamic herbs, damp undergrowth. Palate: good acidity, elegant, flavourful, powerful, fruity, complex.

FINCA TERRERAZO 2009 T
100% bobal.

94 Colour: deep cherry. Nose: expressive, balanced, complex, varietal, fruit expression. Palate: fresh, fruity, complex, creamy, balsamic, mineral.

PAGO FINCA ÉLEZ

VIÑEDOS Y BODEGA MANUEL MANZANEQUE

Ctra. Ossa de Montiel a El Bonillo, Km. 11,500
02610 El Bonillo (Albacete)
☎: +34 967 585 003 - Fax: +34 967 370 649
info@manuelmanzaneque.com
www.manuelmanzaneque.com

MANUEL MANZANEQUE CHARDONNAY 2008 BFB
chardonnay.

89 Colour: bright yellow. Nose: candied fruit, citrus fruit, sweet spices. Palate: flavourful, powerful, fine bitter notes, varietal.

MANUEL MANZANEQUE NUESTRA SELECCIÓN 2007 T
20% cabernet sauvignon, 70% tempranillo, 10% merlot.

91 Colour: cherry, garnet rim. Nose: earthy notes, powerfull, ripe fruit, toasty, dark chocolate. Palate: flavourful, fleshy, complex, concentrated.

MANUEL MANZANEQUE NUESTRO SYRAH 2007 T
syrah.

89 Colour: deep cherry. Nose: ripe fruit, sweet spices, aromatic coffee. Palate: spicy, ripe fruit, flavourful.

MANUEL MANZANEQUE FINCA ÉLEZ 2007 TC
50% cabernet sauvignon, 40% tempranillo, 10% merlot.

87 Colour: black cherry. Nose: earthy notes, powerfull, warm, toasty. Palate: flavourful, powerful, sweetness.

PAGO FLORENTINO

BODEGAS Y VIÑEDOS LA SOLANA

Ctra. Porzuna - Camino Cristo del Humilladero, km. 3
13420 Malagón (Ciudad Real)
☎: +34 983 681 146 - Fax: +34 983 681 147
bodega@pagoflorentino.com
www.pagoflorentino.com

PAGO FLORENTINO 2009 T
100% cencibel.

87 Colour: cherry, purple rim. Nose: ripe fruit, dark chocolate, cocoa bean, earthy notes. Palate: flavourful, fleshy, toasty.

PAGO FLORENTINO 2008 T
100% cencibel.

89 Colour: dark-red cherry. Nose: roasted coffee, powerfull, ripe fruit, sweet spices. Palate: flavourful, powerful, fleshy, roasted-coffee aftertaste.

PAGO GUIJOSO

BODEGAS Y VIÑEDOS SÁNCHEZ MULITERNO

Tesifonte Gallego, 5
02002 (Albacete)
☎: +34 967 193 222 - Fax: +34 967 193 292
bodegas@sanchez-muliterno.com
www.sanchez-muliterno.com

DIVINUS 2008 BFB
chardonnay.

88 Colour: bright yellow. Nose: ripe fruit, dried flowers, wild herbs, creamy oak. Palate: rich, flavourful, fleshy.

VEGA GUIJOSO 2009 T
63% merlot, 30% syrah, 7% cabernet sauvignon.

87 Colour: cherry, garnet rim. Nose: ripe fruit, scrubland, earthy notes, complex, pattiserie. Palate: powerful, flavourful, fleshy.

MAGNIFICUS 2008 T
85,1% syrah, 14,9% cabernet sauvignon.

89 Colour: cherry, garnet rim. Nose: spicy, creamy oak, toasty, candied fruit, fruit preserve. Palate: powerful, flavourful, toasty, round tannins, warm.

VIÑA CONSOLACIÓN 2006 TR
cabernet sauvignon.

88 Colour: cherry, garnet rim. Nose: warm, ripe fruit, earthy notes, spicy, toasty. Palate: correct, flavourful, fleshy.

PAGO LOS BALAGUESES

VIÑEDOS Y BODEGAS VEGALFARO

Ctra. Pontón - Utiel, Km. 3
46340 Requena (Valencia)
☎: +34 962 320 680 - Fax: +34 962 321 126
rodolfo@vegalfaro.com
www.vegalfaro.com

PAGO DE LOS BALAGUESES 2008 TC
100% merlot.

91 Colour: cherry, garnet rim. Nose: red berry notes, ripe fruit, earthy notes, fragrant herbs, cocoa bean, sweet spices, creamy oak. Palate: rich, powerful, flavourful, fleshy.

PAGO PRADO DE IRACHE

IRACHE

Monasterio de Irache, 1
31240 Ayegui (Navarra)
☎: +34 948 551 932 - Fax: +34 948 554 954
irache@irache.com
www.irache.com

PRADO IRACHE VINO DE PAGO 2006 T
tempranillo, cabernet sauvignon, merlot.

90 Colour: bright cherry, orangey edge. Nose: red berry notes, ripe fruit, fragrant herbs, mineral. Palate: good acidity, flavourful, fleshy, mineral, long.

PAGO DE OTAZU

BODEGA OTAZU

Señorío de Otazu, s/n
31174 Etxauri (Navarra)
☎: +34 948 329 200 - Fax: +34 948 329 353
otazu@otazu.com
www.otazu.com

SEÑORÍO DE OTAZU 2007 T
cabernet sauvignon, tempranillo, merlot.

95 Colour: deep cherry. Nose: mineral, ripe fruit, creamy oak, sweet spices, cocoa bean. Palate: flavourful, fleshy, spicy, long, round.

SEÑORÍO DE OTAZU ALTAR 2006 T
90% cabernet sauvignon, 10% tempranillo.

95 Colour: black cherry. Nose: powerfull, ripe fruit, creamy oak, toasty, spicy, cocoa bean. Palate: balsamic, spicy, long, elegant.

SEÑORIO DE OTAZU VITRAL 2005 TC
95% cabernet sauvignon, 5% tempranillo.

94 Colour: very deep cherry. Nose: powerfull, ripe fruit, red berry notes, creamy oak, dark chocolate. Palate: powerful, fleshy, good acidity, round tannins, long.

All the wines included in this section are made by the so-called traditional method of a second fermentation in the bottle, the same one used in Cava –and Champagne– production, but in areas outside those ascribed to Cava or any other Spanish DO. They represent a tiny part of all the sparkling wines made in Spain and their figures and quality are understandably far away from those of Cava.

AGROALIMENTARIA VIRGEN DEL ROCÍO

Avda. de Cabezudos, s/n
21730 Almonte (Huelva)
☎: +34 959 406 146 - Fax: +34 959 407 052
administracion@raigal.com
www.raigal.com

RAIGAL BR

83 Colour: bright yellow. Nose: toasty, roasted almonds, dry nuts. Palate: flavourful, great length.

BODEGAS BARBADILLO

Luis de Eguilaz, 11
11540 Sanlúcar de Barrameda (Cádiz)
☎: +34 956 385 500 - Fax: +34 956 385 501
barbadillo@barbadillo.com
www.barbadillo.com

BARBADILLO BETA 2010 BR
70% palomino, 30% chardonnay.

86 Color bright straw. Aroma medium intensity, fresh fruit, dried herbs, fine lees, floral. Taste fresh, fruity, flavourful, good acidity.

BODEGAS ROMERO

Avda. Magaz, s/n
06392 El Raposo (Badajoz)
☎: +34 924 570 448 - Fax: +34 924 570 448
romero@bodegasromero.com
www.bodegasromero.com

BURBUJA DE EVA-BEBA 2010 ESP
90% eva-beba, 10% gewürztraminer.

80 Colour: pale. Nose: candied fruit, citrus fruit, fragrant herbs. Palate: flavourful, fruity, fresh.

LA MAGDALENA SOCIEDAD COOPERATIVA

Ctra. de la Roda, s/n
16611 Casas de Haro (Cuenca)
☎: +34 969 380 722 - Fax: +34 969 380 722
vinos@vegamoragona.com
www.vegamoragona.com

VEGA MORAGONA 2010 RD
bobal.

87 Colour: rose, purple rim. Nose: red berry notes, ripe fruit, fresh, expressive. Palate: good acidity, fresh, light-bodied.

LIBERALIA ENOLÓGICA

Camino del Palo, s/n
49800 Toro (Zamora)
☎: +34 980 692 571 - Fax: +34 980 692 571
byvliberalia@hotmail.com
www.liberalia.es

ARIANE 2009 ESP
92% verdejo, 8% moscatel.

85 Colour: bright straw. Nose: floral, citrus fruit, dried herbs, lees reduction notes. Palate: good acidity, light-bodied, fresh, fine bitter notes.

PRADA A TOPE

La Iglesia, s/n
24546 Canedo (León)
☎: +34 902 400 101 - Fax: +34 987 567 000
info@pradaatope.es
www.pradaatope.es

XAMPRADA EXTRA BRUT 2007 RD
godello, mencía.

78

XAMPRADA EXTRA BRUT 2008 EXTRA BRUT
godello, chardonnay.

81 Colour: bright straw. Nose: powerfull, candied fruit, faded flowers. Palate: fine bitter notes, fruity.

SERRANO

Finca La Cabaña, 30
30594 Pozo Estrecho (Murcia)
☎: +34 968 556 298 - Fax: +34 968 556 298
vinos@bodegaserrano.es
www.bodegaserrano.com

GALTEA S/C BN
40% chardonnay, 30% moscatel, 30% malvasía.

82 Colour: bright golden. Nose: faded flowers, honeyed notes, pattiserie. Palate: unctuous, fresh, flavourful.

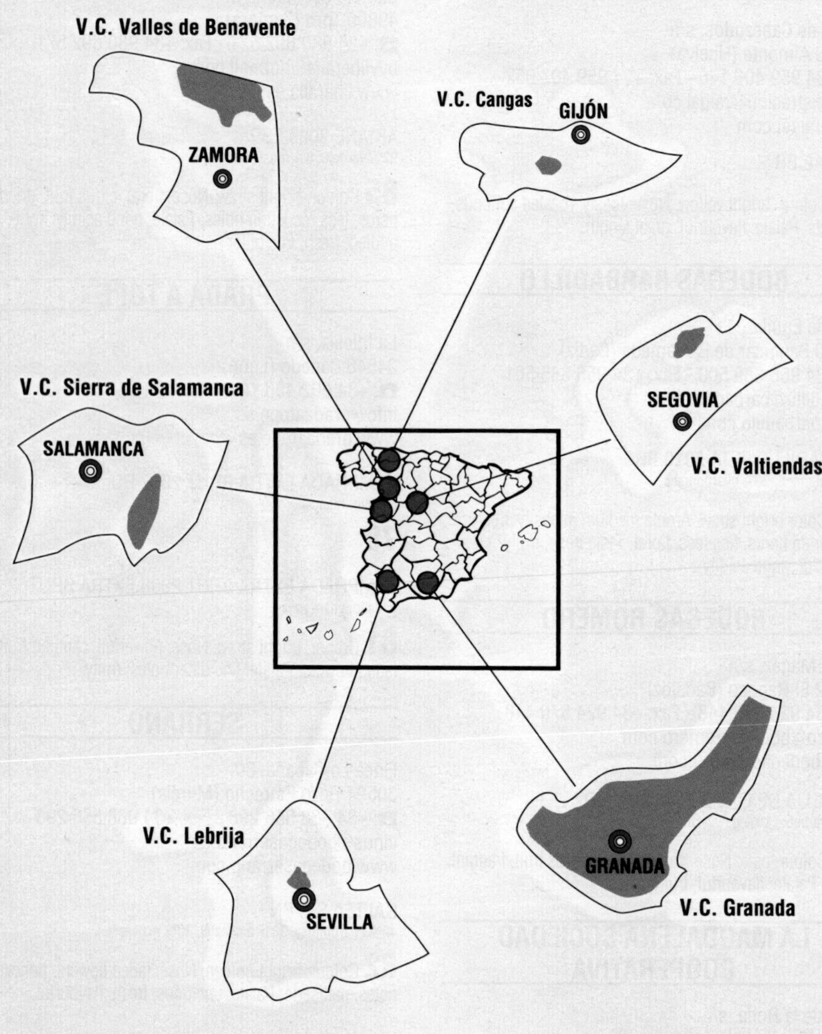

V.C. Valles de Benavente
ZAMORA
V.C. Cangas
GIJÓN
V.C. Sierra de Salamanca
SALAMANCA
SEGOVIA
V.C. Valtiendas
V.C. Lebrija
SEVILLA
GRANADA
V.C. Granada
DO Boundary

So far, there are only five wine regions that have achieved the status "Vino de Calidad" ("Quality Wine Produced in Specified Regions"): Lebrija, Valtiendas, Granada, Sierra de Salamanca and Valles de Benavente, regions that are allowed to label their wines with the VCPRD seal. This quality seal works as a sort of "training" session for the DO category, although it is still quite unknown for the average consumer.

VINO DE CALIDAD DE CANGAS

Located to the south-eastern part of the province of Asturias, bordering with León, Cangas del Narcea has unique climatic conditions, completely different to the rest of the municipalities of Asturias; therefore, its wines have sheer singularity. With lower rainfall levels and more sunshine hours than the rest the province, vines are planted on slate, siliceous and sandy soils. The main varieties are albarín blanco and albillo (white), along with *garnacha tintorera*, *mencía* and *verdejo negro* (red).

VINO DE CALIDAD DE LEBRIJA

Recognized by the Junta de Andalucía on March the 11th 2009. The production area includes the towns of Lebrija and El Cuervo, in the province of Sevilla.

The wines ascribed to the "Vino de Calidad de Lebrija" designation of quality will be made solely from the following grape varieties:

– **White varieties:** *moscatel de Alejandría*, *palomino*, *palomino fino*, *sauvignon blanc* and that traditionally known as *vidueño* (*montúo de pilas*, *mollar cano*, *moscatel morisco*, *perruno*).

– **Red varieties:** *cabernet sauvignon*, *syrah*, *tempranillo*, *merlot* and *tintilla de Rota*.

Types of wines: white, red, generosos (fortified) and generosos de licor, naturally sweet and mistelas.

VINO DE CALIDAD DE GRANADA

Wines that come from anywhere within the provincial limits of Granada, it includes nearly 20 wineries and a hundred growers. It enjoys a mediterranean climate with Atlantic influence. Characterized by a rugged topography, the vineyards occupy mostly the highest areas, with an average altitude of around 1200 meters, a feature that provides this territory with an ample day-night temperature differential. The region is promoting white grape varieties such as *vijiriega*, *moscatel* and *pedro ximénez*, as well as red (*tempranillo*, *garnacha*, *monastrell*) and even some French ones, widely planted in the province. Soil structure, although diverse, is based mainly on clay and slate.

VINO DE CALIDAD DE LOS VALLES DE BENAVENTE

Recognized by the Junta de Castilla y León in September 2000, the VCPRD comprises nowadays more than 50 municipalities and three wineries in Benavente, Santibáñez de Vidriales and San Pedro de Ceque. The production areas within the region are five (Valle Vidriales, Valle del Tera, Valle Valverde, La Vega and Tierra de Campos) around the city of Benavente, the core of the region. Four rivers (Tera, Esla, Órbigo and Valderadey, all of them tributary to the Duero river) give the region its natural borders.

VINO DE CALIDAD SIERRA DE SALAMANCA

The "Vino de Calidad" status was ratified to Sierra de Salamanca by the Junta de Castilla y León (Castilla y León autonomous government) in June 2010, becoming the third one to be granted within the region. Sierra de Salamanca lies in the south of the province of Salamanca, and includes 26 towns, all within the same province. Vines are planted mostly on terraces at the top of the hills and on clay soils based on limestone. Authorized varieties are *viura*, *moscatel de grano menudo* and *palomino* (white), as well as *rufete*, *garnacha* and *tempranillo* (red).

VINO DE CALIDAD VALTIENDAS

An area to the north of the province of Segovia relatively known thanks to the brand name Duratón, also the name of the river that crosses a region that has mainly *tempranillo* planted, a grape variety known there also as *tinta del país*. The wines are fruitier and more acidic than those from Ribera del Duero, thanks to an altitude of some 900 metres and clay soils with plenty of stones.

CANGAS

BODEGA MONASTERIO DE CORIAS

Monasterio de Corias, s/n
33800 Cangas del Narcea (Asturias)
☎: +34 985 810 493
monasteriodecorias@narcea.es
www.monasteriodecorias.com

MONASTERIO DE CORIAS VIÑA GRANDIELLA 2010 B
90% albarín, 2% moscatel, 8% albillo.

84 Colour: bright straw. Nose: dried flowers, citrus fruit, ripe fruit, balsamic herbs. Palate: powerful, flavourful, good finish.

MONASTERIO DE CORIAS SEIS OCTAVOS 2010 T BARRICA
40% mencía, 60% albarín negro.

89 Colour: cherry, purple rim. Nose: ripe fruit, wild herbs, sweet spices. Palate: good acidity, powerful, flavourful, mineral, complex.

CORIAS GUILFA 2009 T
60% verdejo tinto, 40% carrasquín.

90 Colour: cherry, garnet rim. Nose: red berry notes, earthy notes, spicy, creamy oak, expressive. Palate: good acidity, complex, fleshy, powerful, flavourful, long, mineral.

MONASTERIO DE CORIAS 2009 T BARRICA
40% mencía, 40% albarín negro, 10% carrasquín, 10% verdejo tinto.

87 Colour: cherry, garnet rim. Nose: red berry notes, ripe fruit, sweet spices, earthy notes. Palate: light-bodied, fresh, flavourful, complex.

BODEGAS ANTÓN CHICOTE

La Galiana, 88 Limés
33800 Cangas de Narcea (Asturias)
☎: +34 985 810 934
bodegachicote@hotmail.com

VIÑA GALIANA 2009 T
50% mencía, 20% verdejo negro, 20% albarin negro, 10% carrasquin.

88 Colour: cherry, garnet rim. Nose: red berry notes, ripe fruit, scrubland, balsamic herbs, earthy notes. Palate: good acidity, balanced, flavourful, fruity.

PENDERUYOS SELECCIÓN 2009 T
33% verdejo negro, 33% carrasquin, 34% albarin negro.

87 Colour: cherry, garnet rim. Nose: red berry notes, ripe fruit, balanced. Palate: good acidity, fruity, flavourful, fleshy.

BODEGAS DEL NARCEA

Las Barzaniellas
33817 Cangas del Narcea (Oviedo)
☎: +34 985 813 103 - Fax: +34 985 813 103
bodegadelnarcea@hotmail.com
www.bodeganarcea.com

PESGOS 2009 T ROBLE
albarin tinto, verdejo tinto, carrasquin.

88 Colour: cherry, garnet rim. Nose: ripe fruit, expressive, earthy notes, scrubland, creamy oak. Palate: powerful, flavourful, complex, fruity.

BODEGAS OBANCA

Obanca, 12
33800 Cangas del Narcea (Asturias)
☎: +34 626 956 571 - Fax: +34 985 811 539
informacion@obanca.com
www.obanca.com

DESCARGA 2009 T
albariño tinto, mencía, verdejo tinto.

91 Colour: cherry, purple rim. Nose: floral, red berry notes, ripe fruit, balsamic herbs. Palate: elegant, balanced, powerful, flavourful, fruity.

CASTRO DE LIMÉS 2009 T
carrasquín.

88 Colour: cherry, purple rim. Nose: red berry notes, ripe fruit, wild herbs, dry stone, creamy oak. Palate: good acidity, powerful, flavourful, complex.

DOMINIO DEL UROGALLO

Pol. Obanca, C. Empresas, nave 2
33819 Cangas de Narcea (Asturias)
☎: +34 626 568 238
info@dominiodelurogallo.com
www.dominiodelurogallo.com

PESICO 2010 B
100% albarín.

92 Colour: pale, greenish rim. Nose: white flowers, fruit expression, fragrant herbs, mineral, elegant. Palate: good acidity, powerful, flavourful, rich, fruity.

GRANADA

BODEGA ANCHURÓN

Isaac Albeniz, 10 2º
18012 (Granada)
☎: +34 958 277 764 - Fax: +34 958 277 764
info@anchuron.es
www.anchuron.com

ANCHURÓN 2010 B
90% sauvignon blanc, 10% chardonnay.

85 Colour: bright straw. Nose: citrus fruit, ripe fruit, dried herbs, balsamic herbs, earthy notes. Palate: good acidity, rich, flavourful, fleshy.

ANCHURÓN 2009 RD
50% syrah, 50% cabernet sauvignon.

80 Colour: raspberry rose. Nose: ripe fruit, floral, slightly evolved. Palate: good acidity, correct, easy to drink.

MARQUÉS DE CASA PARDIÑAS C.B.

Finca San Torcuato
18540 Huélago (Granada)
☎: +34 630 901 094 - Fax: +34 958 252 297
info@spiracp.es
www.marquesdecasapardiñas.com

SPIRA VENDIMIA SELECCIONADA 2010 T
60% tempranillo, 35% cabernet sauvignon, 5% merlot.

90 Colour: cherry, garnet rim. Nose: red berry notes, ripe fruit, spicy, creamy oak, earthy notes. Palate: powerful, flavourful, fleshy, fruity.

SIERRA DE SALAMANCA

BODEGA CÁMBRICO

Paraje El Guijarral, s/n
37658 Villanueva del Conde (Salamanca)
☎: +34 923 281 006 - Fax: +34 923 213 605
info@cambrico.com
www.cambrico.com

575 UVAS DE CÁMBRICO 2008 T
64% tempranillo, 32% rufete, 4% calabrés.

90 Colour: cherry, garnet rim. Nose: red berry notes, ripe fruit, earthy notes, mineral, creamy oak, complex. Palate: balanced, elegant, powerful, flavourful, fleshy.

ROCHAL

Salas Pombo, 17
37670 Santibáñez de la Sierra (Salamanca)
☎: +34 923 435 260 - Fax: +34 923 435 260
info@bodegasrochal.com
www.bodegasrochal.com

ZAMAYÓN 2010 T
rufete.

88 Colour: cherry, purple rim. Nose: red berry notes, cocoa bean, dark chocolate, sweet spices, expressive. Palate: fruity, flavourful, fleshy, toasty.

ZAMAYÓN OSIRIS 2009 T
rufete, tempranillo.

88 Colour: cherry, garnet rim. Nose: red berry notes, ripe fruit, spicy, creamy oak. Palate: powerful, flavourful, rich, fleshy.

VINOS LA ZORRA

San Pedro s/n
37610 Mogarraz (Salamanca)
☎: +34 923 418 042
estanverdes@vinoslazorra.es
www.vinoslazorra.es

LA ZORRA 2010 T
80% rufete, 20% tempranillo.

90 Colour: bright cherry. Nose: sweet spices, creamy oak, expressive, red berry notes. Palate: flavourful, fruity, toasty, round tannins.

VALLES DE BENAVENTE

BODEGA EL TESORO SOC. COOP.

Pol. La Mata - Camino Viñas, s/n
4962 Brime de Urz (Zamora)
☎: +34 636 982 233
bodega_el_tesoro@terra.com

PETAVONIUM 2007 TC
100% prieto picudo.

86 Colour: dark-red cherry, garnet rim. Nose: cocoa bean, ripe fruit, toasty. Palate: round tannins, flavourful, fleshy.

BODEGAS OTERO

Avda. El Ferial, 22
49600 Benavente (Zamora)
☎: +34 980 631 600 - Fax: +34 980 631 722
info@bodegasotero.es
www.bodegasotero.es

VALLEOSCURO PRIETO PICUDO 2010 RD
100% prieto picudo.

86 Colour: rose, purple rim. Nose: fresh fruit, lactic notes, floral. Palate: flavourful, light-bodied, fresh, fruity.

VALLEOSCURO 2010 B
100% verdejo.

83 Colour: bright straw. Nose: citrus fruit, tropical fruit, fresh. Palate: fresh, light-bodied, fruity.

VALLEOSCURO 2010 RD
prieto picudo, tempranillo.

88 Colour: rose, purple rim. Nose: fresh fruit, lactic notes, white flowers. Palate: light-bodied, fresh, fruity, flavourful, fleshy.

VALLEOSCURO PRIETO PICUDO TEMPRANILLO 2010 T
prieto picudo, tempranillo.

88 Colour: cherry, purple rim. Nose: red berry notes, fresh fruit, floral. Palate: flavourful, fresh, fruity, light-bodied, easy to drink.

OTERO 2006 TC
100% prieto picudo.

85 Colour: cherry, garnet rim. Nose: spicy, toasty, earthy notes. Palate: fleshy, flavourful, fruity.

OTERO 2004 TR
prieto picudo.

86 Colour: black cherry, orangey edge. Nose: cocoa bean, spicy, toasty, old leather. Palate: rich, powerful, flavourful, fleshy.

VALTIENDAS

BODEGAS VAGAL

La Fuente, 19
40314 Valtiendas (Segovia)
☎: +34 921 527 331 - Fax: +34 921 527 332
jose.vagal@gmail.com
www.vagal.com

VAGAL CUVÉE JOANA 2009 T

88 Colour: black cherry, garnet rim. Nose: red berry notes, ripe fruit, balsamic herbs, spicy, creamy oak. Palate: light-bodied, fruity, flavourful, round tannins.

VAGAL PAGO ARDALEJOS 2006 T
100% tinta del país.

90 Colour: cherry, garnet rim. Nose: ripe fruit, varietal, mineral, cocoa bean, spicy. Palate: balanced, powerful, fleshy, complex, flavourful.

BODEGAS ZARRAGUILLA

Iglesia, 14
40237 Sacramenia (Segovia)
☎: +34 921 527 270
informacion@bodegaszarraguilla.es
www.bodegaszarraguilla.es

ZARRAGUILLA 2008 T ROBLE
tempranillo.

88 Colour: cherry, garnet rim. Nose: red berry notes, ripe fruit, earthy notes, spicy, creamy oak. Palate: light-bodied, fruity, flavourful, good acidity.

VENNUR 2007 TC
100% tempranillo.

89 Colour: cherry, garnet rim. Nose: red berry notes, earthy notes, cocoa bean, dark chocolate, sweet spices, creamy oak. Palate: flavourful, fruity, fleshy, toasty, round tannins.

ZETA 37 2007 T
100% tempranillo.

86 Colour: cherry, garnet rim. Nose: ripe fruit, sweet spices, toasty, warm. Palate: powerful, flavourful, fleshy.

VINOS DE LA TIERRA

The number of "Vino de la Tierra" categories granted so far, 45, means the status is growing in importance, given that growers are only required to specify geographical origin, grape variety and alcohol content. For some, it means an easy way forward for their more experimental projects, difficult to be contemplated by the stern regulations of the designations of origin, as it is the case of vast autonomous regions such as La Mancha, Castilla y León or Extremadura. For the great majority, it is a category able to fostering vineyards with high quality potential, a broader varietal catalogue and therefore the opportunity to come up with truly singular wines, a sort of sideway entrance to the DO status.

The different "Vino de la Tierra" designations have been listed in alphabetical order.

In theory, the "Vino de la Tierra" status is one step below that of the DO, and it is the Spanish equivalent to the French "Vins de Pays", which pioneered worldwide this sort of category. In Spain, however, it has some unique characteristics. For example, the fact that the designation "Vino de la Tierra" is not always the ultimate goal, but it is rather used as a springboard to achieve the highly desired DO category. In addition, as it has happened in other countries, many producers have opted for this type of association with less stringent regulations that allow them greater freedom to produce wine. Therefore, in this section there is a bit of everything: from great wines to more simple and ordinary examples, a broad catalogue that works as a sort of testing (and tasting!) field for singularity as well as for new flavours and styles derived from the use of local, autochthonous varieties.

The new Spanish Ley del Vino (Wine Law) maintains the former status of "Vino de la Tierra", but establishes an intermediate step between this and the DO one. They are the so-called 'Vinos de Calidad con Indicación Geográfica' (Quality Wines with Geographical Indication), under which the region in question must remain for a minimum of five years.

In the light of the tasting carried out for this section, there is a steady improvement in the quality of these wines, as well as fewer misgivings on the part of the wineries about the idea of joining these associations.

VT 3 RIBERAS

Granted by the administration at the end of 2008 for the wines produced and within the "3 Riberas" geographical indication. The different typologies are: rosé, white, red and noble wines.

VT ABANILLA

This small wine region comprises the municipalities of Abanilla and Fortuna –in the eastern part of the province of Murcia– and some 1500 hectares, although most of its production is sold to the neighbouring DO Alicante. The region enjoys a hot, dry climate, limestone soils and low rainfall, features all that account for good quality prospects, although there are some differences to be found between the northern and the southern areas within it, given the different altitudes. The grape varieties allowed in the region for red winemaking are: *bonicaire, cabernet sauvignon, forcallat tinta, garnacha tintorera, merlot, petit verdot, crujidera* and *syrah*. For white wines, we find *chardonnay, malvasía, moravia dulce, moscatel de grano menudo* and *sauvignon blanc.*

VT ALTIPLANO DE SIERRA NEVADA
VT NORTE DE GRANADA

With the goal to free Granada's geographical indication exclusively for the "Vino de Calidad" category, in 2009 the VT Norte de Granada changed its name to VT Altiplano de Sierra Nevada. The new geographical indication comprises 43 municipalities in the north of the province of Granada. The authorized grape varieties for white wine production in the region are *chardonnay, baladí verdejo, airen, torrontés, palomino, pedro ximénez, macabeo and sauvignon blanc*; also *tempranillo, monastrell, garnacha tinta, cabernet franc, cabernet sauvignon, pinot noir, merlot*, and *syrah* for red wines.

VT BAILÉN

Bailén wine region comprises 350 hectares in some municipal districts within the province of Jaén but fairly close to La Mancha. Wines are made mainly from the grape variety known as "*molinera de Bailén*", that cannot be found anywhere else in the world, but also from other red grape varieties such as *garnacha tinta, tempranillo* and *cabernet sauvignon*, as well as the white *pedro ximénez*.

VT BAJO ARAGÓN

The most "mediterranean" region within Aragón autonomous community, it borders three different provinces (Tarragona, Castellón and Teruel) and is divided in four areas: Campo de Belchite, Bajo Martín, Bajo Aragón and Matarraña. Soils are mainly clay and limestone in nature, very rich in minerals with high potash content. The climate is suitable for the right maturation of the grapes, with the added cooling effect of the 'Cierzo' (northerly wind), together with the day-night temperature contrast, just the perfect combination for the vines. The main varieties are *garnacha* (both red and white), although foreign grapes like *syrah, cabernet sauvignon, merlot* and *chardonnay* are also present, as well as *tempranillo* and *cariñena*.

www.vinodelatierradelbajoaragon.com

VT BARBANZA E IRIA

The last geographical indication to be granted to the autonomous region of Galicia back in 2007, Barbanza e Iria is located within the Ribera de la Ría de Arosa wine region, in the north of the province of Pontevedra. They make both red an white wines from with varieties such as *albariño, caíño blanco, godello, loureiro blanco* (also known as *marqués*), *treixadura* and *torrontés* (white); and *brancellao, caíño tinto, espadeiro, loureiro tinto, mencía* and *susón* (red).

VT BETANZOS

Betanzos, in the province of La Coruña, became the second VT designation to be granted in Galicia. The vineyards is planted with local white varieties like *blanco legítimo, Agudelo* (*godello*) and *jerez*, as well as red grapes like *garnacha, mencía* and *tempranillo*.

VT CÁDIZ

Located in the south of the province of Cádiz, a vast region with a long history of wine production, the "Vinos de la Tierra de Cádiz" comprises 15 municipalities still under the regulations of the DO regarding grape production, but not winemaking. The authorised white varieties are: *garrido, palomino, chardonnay, moscatel, mantúa, perruno, macabeo, sauvignon blanc* y *pedro ximénez*, as well as the red *tempranillo, syrah, cabernet sauvignon, garnacha tinta, monastrel, merlot, tintilla de rota, petit verdot* and *cabernet franc*.

VT CAMPO DE CARTAGENA

Campo de Cartagena is a flatland region close to the Mediterranean Sea and surrounded by mountains of a moderate height. The vineyard surface ascribed to the VT is just 8 hectares. The climate is mediterranean bordering on an arid, desert type, with very hot summers, mild temperatures for the rest of the year, and low and occasional rainfall. The main varieties in the region are *bonicaire, forcallat tinta, petit verdot, tempranillo, garnacha tintorera, crujidera, merlot, syrah* and *cabernet sauvignon* (red); and *chardonnay, malvasía, moravia dulce, moscatel de grano menudo* and *sauvignon blanc* (white).

VT CASTELLÓ

Located in the eastern part of Spain, on the Mediterranean coast, the geographical indication Vinos de la Tierra de Castelló is divided in two different areas: Alto Palancia –Alto Mijares, Sant Mateu and Les Useres–, and Vilafamés. The climatic conditions in this wine region are good to grow varieties such as *tempranillo, monastrell, garnacha, garnacha tintorera, cabernet sauvignon, merlot* and *syrah* (red), along with *macabeo* and *merseguera* (white).

www.vinosdecastellon.com

VT CASTILLA Y LEÓN

Another one of the regional 'macro-designations' for the wines produced in up to 317 municipalities within the autonomous region of Castilla y León. A continental climate with little rainfall, together with diverse soil patterns, are the most distinctive features of a region that can be divided into the Duero basin (part of the Spanish central high plateau) and the mountainous perimeter that surrounds it.

www.asovintcal.com

VT CASTILLA

Castilla-La Mancha, a region that has the largest vineyard surface in the planet (600.000 hectares, equivalent to 6% of the world's total vineyard surface, and to half of Spain's) has been using this Vino de la Tierra label since 1999 (the year the status was granted) for wines produced outside its designations of origin. The main grape varieties are *airén, albillo, chardonnay, macabeo* (*viura*), *malvar, sauvignon blanc, merseguera, moscatel de grano menudo, pardillo* (marisancho), *Pedro Ximénez* and *torrontés* (white);and *bobal, cabernet sauvignon, garnacha tinta, merlot, monastrell, petit verdot, syrah, tempranillo, cencibel* (*jacivera*), *coloraíllo, frasco, garnacha tintorera, moravia agria, moravia dulce* (*crujidera*), *negral* (tinto basto) and *tinto velasco* (red).

VT CÓRDOBA

It includes the wines produced in the province of Córdoba, with the exception of those bottled within the DO Montilla-Moriles label. All in all, we are talking of some 300 hectares and red and rosé wines made from *cabernet sauvignon, merlot, syrah, tempranillo, pinot noir* and *tintilla de Rota* grape varieties.

VT COSTA DE CANTABRIA

Wines produced in the Costa de Cantabria wine region as well as some inland valleys up to an altitude of 600 meters. The grape varieties used for white winemaking are *godello, albillo, chardonnay, malvasía, ondarribi zuri, picapoll blanco* and *verdejo blanco*; and just two for red wines: *ondarribi beltza* and *verdejo negro*. The region comprises some 8 hectares of vineyards.

VT CUMBRES DE GUADALFEO
VT CONTRAVIESA-ALPUJARRA

Formerly known as "Vino de la Tierra de Contraviesa-Alpujarra", this geographical indication is used for wines made in the wine region located in the western part of the Alpujarras, in a border territory between two provinces (Granada and Almería), two rivers (Guadalfeo and Andarax), and very close to the Mediterranean Sea. The grape varieties used for white wine production are *montúa, chardonnay, sauvignon blanc, moscatel, jaén blanca, Pedro Ximénez, vijirego* y *perruno*; for red wines, they have *garnacha tinta*, *tempranillo*, *cabernet sauvignon*, *cabernet franc*, *merlot*, *pinot noir* and *syrah*.

VT DESIERTO DE ALMERÍA

Granted in the summer of 2003, the wine region comprises a diverse territory in the north of the province of Almería that includes the Tabernas Dessert as well as parts of the Sierra de Alhamilla, Sierra de Cabrera and the Cabo de Gata Natural Park. Harsh, climatic desert conditions follow a regular pattern of hot days and cooler nights that influence heavily the character of the resulting wines. The vineyard's average altitude is 525 meters. The varieties planted are *chardonnay*, *moscatel*, *macabeo* and *sauvignon blanc* (white); as well as *tempranillo*, *cabernet sauvignon*, *monastrell*, *merlot*, *syrah* and *garnacha tinta* (red).
www.vinosdealmeria.es/zonas-viticolas/desierto-de-almeria

VT EIVISSA

The production area includes the entire island of Ibiza (Eivissa), with the vineyards located in small valleys amongst the mountains –which are never higher than 500 meters– on clay-reddish soil covered by a thin limestone crust. Low rainfall levels and hot, humid summers are the most interesting climatic features. The authorized red varieties are *monastrell*, *tempranillo*, *cabernet sauvignon*, *merlot* and *syrah*; *macabeo*, *parellada*, *malvasía*, *chardonnay* and *moscatel* make up the white-grape catalogue.

VT EXTREMADURA

It comprises all the municipalities within the provinces of Cáceres and Badajoz, made up of six different wine regions. In December 1990, the regional government approved the regulations submitted by the Comisión Interprofesional de Vinos de la Tierra de Extremadura, and approved its creation. The varieties used for the production of white wines are *alarije*, *borba*, *cayetana blanca*, *chardonnay*, *chelva*, *malvar*, *viura*, *parellada*, *Pedro Ximénez* and *verdejo*; for red wines, they have *bobal*, *mazuela*, *monastrell*, *tempranillo*, *garnacha*, *graciano*, *merlot*, *syrah* and *cabernet sauvignon*.

VT FORMENTERA

This geographical indication comprises the wines produced in the island of Formentera. The dry, subtropical mediterranean climate, characterised by abundant sunshine hours and summers with high temperatures and humidity levels but little rainfall, evidently requires grape varieties well adapted to this type of weather. Red varieties are *monastrell*, *fogoneu*, *tempranillo*, *cabernet sauvignon* and *merlot*; *malvasía*, *premsal blanco*, *chardonnay* and *viognier* make up its white-grape catalogue.

VT GÁLVEZ

Gálvez wine region, located in the province of Toledo, comprises nine municipalities: Cuerva, Gálvez, Guadamur, Menasalvas, Mazambraz, Polán, Pulgar, San Martín de Montalbán and Totanes. The authorized grape varieties are *tempranillo* and *garnacha tinta*.

VT ILLA DE MENORCA

The island of Menorca, a Biosphere Reserve, has a singular topography of gentle slopes; marl soils with a complex substratum of limestone, sandstone and slate, a mediterranean climate and northerly winter winds are the most significant features from a viticultural point of view. The wines produces in the island should be made exclusively from white grape varieties like *chardonnay*, *macabeo*, *malvasía*, *moscatel*, *parellada* or *moll*; as for the red renderings, *cabernet sauvignon*, *merlot*, *monastrell*, *tempranillo* and *syrah* get clearly the upper hand.

VT LADERAS DE GENIL
VT GRANADA SUROESTE

Formerly known (up to 2009) as VT Granada Suroeste, the label includes some 53 municipalities in the province of Granada. The region enjoys a unique microclimate very suitable for grape growing, given its low rainfall and the softening effect of the Mediterranean Sea. The white grape varieties used for wine production are *vijiriego*, *macabeo*, *Pedro Ximénez*, *palomino*, *moscatel de Alejandría*, *chardonnay* and *sauvignon blanc*; as well as the red *garnacha tinta*, *perruna*, *tempranillo*, *cabernet sauvignon*, *merlot*, *syrah* and *pinot noir*, predominantly.

VT LAUJAR-ALPUJARRA

This wine region is located at an altitude of 800 to 1500 meters between the Sierra de Gádor and the Sierra Nevada Natural Park. It has some 800 hectares of vines grown on terraces. Soils are chalk soils poor in organic matter, rocky and with little depth. The climate is moderately continental, given the sea influence and its high night-day temperature differential. The predominant grape varieties are *jaén blanco*, *macabeo*, *vijiriego*, *Pedro Ximénez*, *chardonay* and *moscatel de grano menudo* (white); and *cabernet sauvignon*, *merlot*, monastrell, *tempranillo*, *garnachas tinta* and *syrah* (red).
www.vinosdealmeria.es/bodegas/vino-de-la-tierra-laujar-alpujarra

VT LIÉBANA

VT Liébana includes the municipalities of Potes, Pesagüero, Cabezón de Liébana, Camaleño, Castro Cillorigo y Vega de Liébana, all of them within the area of Liébana, located in the southwest of the Cantabria bordering with Asturias, León and Palencia. The authorized varieties are *mencía*, *tempranillo*, *garnacha*, *garciano*, *merlot*, *syrah*, *pinot noir*, *albarín negro* and *cabernet sauvignon* (red); and *palomino*, *godello*, *verdejo*, *albillo*, *chardonnay* and *albarín blanco* (white).

VT LOS PALACIOS

Los Palacios is located in the south-western part of the province of Sevilla, by the lower area of the Guadalquivir river valley. The wines included in this VT are white wines made from *airén*, *chardonnay*, *colombard* and *sauvignon blanc*.

VT MALLORCA

The production area of VT Mallorca includes all the municipalities within the island, which has predominantly limestone soils with abundant clay and sandstone, and a mediterranean climate with mild temperatures all-year-round. Red varieties present in the island are *callet*, *manto negro*, *cabernet sauvignon*, *fogoneu*, *merlot*, *monastrell*, *syrah*, *tempranillo* and *pinot noir*, along with the white *prensal* (*moll*), *chardonnay*, *macabeo*, *malvasía*, *moscatel de Alejandría*, *moscatel de grano menudo*, *parellada*, *riesling* and *sauvignon blanc*.

VT NORTE DE ALMERÍA

The Vinos de la Tierra Norte de Almería label comprises four municipalities in the Norte de Almería area, right in the north of the province. They produce white, red and rosé wines from grape varieties such as *airén*, *chardonnay*, *macabeo* and *sauvignon blanc* (white); as well as *cabernet sauvignon*, *merlot*, *monastrell*, *tempranillo* and *syrah* for red winemaking and *tempranillo* and *monastrell* for rosé.

VT POZOHONDO

The regulations for VT Pozoblanco were approved by the autonomous government of Castilla-La Mancha in the year 2000. It comprises the municipalities of Alcadozo, Peñas de San Pedro and Pozohondo, all of them in the province of Albacete.

VT RIBERA DEL ANDARAX

The Ribera del Andarax wine region is located in the middle area of the Andarax river valley at an altitude of 700 to 900 meters. Soils are varied in structure, with abundant slate, clay and sand. It enjoys an extreme mediterranean climate, with low occasional rainfall and high average temperatures. The grape varieties present in the region are predominantly *macabeo*, *chardonnay* and *sauvignon blanc* (white); and *cabernet sauvignon*, *merlot*, *syrah*, *garnacha*, *tempranillo*, *monastrell* and *pinot noir* (red).

www.vinosdealmeria.es/zonas-viticolas/ribera-de-andarax

VT RIBERA DEL GÁLLEGO-CINCO VILLAS

Ribera del Gállego-Cinco Villas wine region is located in the territory along the Gállego river valley until it almost reaches the city of Zaragoza. Although small, its vineyards are shared between the provinces of Huesca and Zaragoza. Soils are mostly gravel in structure, which affords good drainage. The grape varieties used for wine production are *garnacha*, *tempranillo*, *carbernet sauvignon* and *merlot* (red), and mostly *macabeo* for white wines.

www.vinosdelatierradearagon.es

VT RIBERA DEL JILOCA

Ribera del Jiloca, located in the south-eastern part of Aragón along the Jiloca river valley, is a wine region with a great winemaking potential, given its geo-climatic conditions. Vines are mostly planted on slate terraces perched on the slopes of the Sistema Ibérico mountain range, at high altitude, something that affords wines of great quality and singularity. Vines are planted mostly on alluvial limestone terraces of ancient river beds. *Garnacha* is the predominant grape, followed by *macabeo*. A dry climate, abundant sunlight hours and cold winters are the features that account for the excellent quality of the local grapes.

www.vinosdelatierradearagon.es/empresas/ribera_del_jiloca.php

VT RIBERA DEL QUEILES

Up to sixteen municipalities from two different provinces (seven from Navarra and nine from Zaragoza) are part of the VT Ribera del Queiles. Wines are exclusively red, made from *cabernet sauvignon*, *graciano*, *garnacha tinta*, *merlot*, *tempranillo* and *syrah*. It has a regulating and controlling body (Comité Regulador de Control y Certificación) and so far just one winery.

www.vinosdelatierradearagon.es

VT SERRA DE TRAMUNTANA-COSTA NORD

Currently, this VT comprises 41,14 hectares an up to eighteen municipal districts in the island of Mallorca, between the cape of Formentor and the southwest coast of Andratx, with mainly brownish-grey and limestone soils. Single-variety wines from *malvasía*, *moscatel*, *moll*, *parellada*, *macabeo*, *chardonnay* and *sauvignon blanc* (white), as well as *cabernet sauvignon*, *merlot*, *syrah*, *monastrell*, *tempranillo*, *callet* and *manto negro* (red) stand out.

VT SIERRA DE ALCARAZ

The Sierra del Alcaraz wine region comprises the municipal districts of Alcaraz, El Ballestero, El Bonillo, Povedilla, Robledo, and Viveros, located in the western part of the province of Albacete, bordering with Ciudad Real. The VT status was granted by the autonomous government of Castilla-La Mancha in the year 2000. The red varieties planted in the region are *cabernet sauvignon*, *merlot*, *bobal*, *monastrell*, *garnacha tinta* and *garnacha tintorera*; along with white *moravia dulce*, *chardonnay*, *chelva*, *eva*, *alarije*, *malvar*, *borba*, *parellada*, *cayetana blanca* and *Pedro Ximénez*.

VT SIERRA DE LAS ESTANCIAS Y LOS FILABRES

Located in the namesake mountain region in the province of Almería, this VT was approved along with its regulations in 2008. The grape varieties planted in the region are *airén*, *chardonnay*, *macabeo*, *sauvignon blanc* and *moscatel de grano menudo* –also known as morisco–, all of them white; and red *cabernet sauvignon*, *merlot*, *monastrell*, *tempranillo*, *syrah*, *garnacha tinta*, *pinot noir* and *petit verdot*.

VT SIERRA NORTE DE SEVILLA

This region, located in the north of the province of Sevilla at the foothills of Sierra Morena, has a landscape of gentle hills and altitudes that range from 250 to almost 1000 metres. The climate in the region is mediterranean, with hot, dry summers, mild winters and a fairly high average rainfall. Since 1998, grape varieties such as *tempranillo*, *garnacha tinta*, *cabernet sauvignon*, *cabernet franc*, *merlot*, *pinot noir*, *petit verdot* and *syrah* (red); and *chardonnay*, *Pedro Ximénez*, *colombard*, *sauvignon blanc*, *palomino* and *moscatel de Alejandría* (white) have been planted in the region.

VT SIERRA SUR DE JAÉN

In this VT there are some 400 hectares planted with vines, although a minor percentage are table grapes. The label includes wines made in the Sierra Sur de Jaén wine region. White wines are made from *jaén blanca* and *chardonnay*, and red from *garnacha tinta*, *tempranillo*, *cabernet sauvignon*, *merlot*, *syrah* and *pinot noir*.

VT TORREPEROGIL

This geographical indication in the province of Jaén, whose regulations were approved in 2006, comprises 300 hectares in the area of La Loma, right in the centre of the province. The climate is mediterranean with continental influence, with cold winters and dry and hot summers. The wines are made mainly from *garnacha tinta*, *syrah*, *cabernet sauvignon* and *tempranillo* (red); and *jaén blanco* and *Pedro Ximénez* (white).

VT VALDEJALÓN

Established in 1998, it comprises 36 municipal districts in the mid- and lower-Jalón river valley. The vines are planted on alluvial, brownish-grey limestone soils, with low annual average rainfall of some 350 mm. They grape varieties planted are white (*macabeo*, *garnacha blanca*, *moscatel* and *airén*) and red (*garnacha*, *tempranillo*, *cabernet sauvignon*, *syrah*, *monastrell* and *merlot*).

www.vinodelatierravaldejalon.com

VT VALLE DEL CINCA

Located in the southeast of the province of Huesca, almost bordering with Catalunya, Valle del Cinca is a traditional wine region that enjoys favourable climatic and soil conditions for vine growing: soils are mainly limestone and clay, and the average annual rainfall barely reaches 300 mm (irrigation is usually required). Grape varieties predominantly planted in the region are *macabeo* and *chardonnay* (white), along with *garnacha tinta*, *tempranillo*, *cabernet sauvignon* and *merlot* (red).

www.vinosdelatierradearagon.es

VT VALLE DEL MIÑO-OURENSE

This wine region is located in the north of the province of Ourense, along the Miño river valley. The authorized grape varieties are *treixadura*, *torrontés*, *godello*, *albariño*, *loureira* and *palomino* –also known as *xerez*– for white wines, and *mencía*, *brancellao*, *mouratón*, *sousón*, *caíño* and *garnacha* for reds.

VT VALLES DE SADACIA

A designation created to include the wines made from the grape variety known as *moscatel riojana*, which was practically lost with the phylloxera bug and has been recuperated to produce both "vino de licor" and normal white *moscatel*. Depending on winemaking, the latter may either be dry, semi-dry or sweet. The vineyards that belong to this VT are mainly located in the south-western part of the region, in the Sadacia and Cidacos river valleys, overall a very suitable territory for vine growing purposes.

VT VILLAVICIOSA DE CÓRDOBA

One of the most recent geographical indications granted by the autonomous government of Andalucía back in 2008, it includes white and sweet wines made in the Villaviciosa wine region. The authorized varieties are *baladí verdejo*, *moscatel de Alejandría*, *palomino fino*, *palomino*, *Pedro Ximénez*, *airén*, *calagraño Jaén*, *torrontés* and *verdejo*.

3 RIBERAS

ABADÍA DE LA OLIVA VIÑEDOS Y BODEGAS

Ctra. Caparroso-Carcastillo, Km. 17,5
31310 Carcastillo (Navarra)
☎: +34 948 725 285 - Fax: +34 948 725 285
bodega@abadiadelaoliva.com
www.bodegaabadiadelaoliva.com

ABADÍA DE LA OLIVA 2010 B
garnacha blanca.

88 Colour: bright straw. Nose: fresh fruit, citrus fruit, white flowers, fragrant herbs. Palate: good acidity, fleshy, powerful, flavourful, fruity.

ABADÍA DE LA OLIVA CHARDONNAY 2010 BFB
chardonnay.

86 Colour: bright yellow. Nose: ripe fruit, creamy oak, medium intensity. Palate: rich, flavourful, fresh, good acidity.

ABADÍA DE LA OLIVA CHARDONNAY B
chardonnay.

85 Colour: bright golden. Nose: ripe fruit, dried flowers, medium intensity, wild herbs. Palate: correct, fresh, powerful.

ABADÍA DE LA OLIVA LACRIMA ROSA 2010 RD
garnacha.

84 Colour: rose, purple rim. Nose: red berry notes, floral, fruit liqueur notes. Palate: fleshy, powerful, fruity, fresh.

ABADÍA DE LA OLIVA ORACIÓN VINO DE MISA 2010 RD
garnacha.

83 Colour: brilliant rose. Nose: ripe fruit, candied fruit, fresh. Palate: good acidity, sweet, easy to drink.

ABADÍA DE LA OLIVA 2010 T
tempranillo.

87 Colour: cherry, purple rim. Nose: red berry notes, ripe fruit, floral, balsamic herbs. Palate: slightly acidic, unctuous, powerful, flavourful.

ABADÍA DE LA OLIVA 2009 T ROBLE
cabernet sauvignon, merlot, tempranillo.

86 Colour: cherry, garnet rim. Nose: red berry notes, ripe fruit, warm, scrubland. Palate: good acidity, fleshy, complex, flavourful.

ALMA DE ABADÍA DE LA OLIVA NATURALMENTE DULCE 2010 MOSCATEL
moscatel grano menudo.

88 Colour: bright golden. Nose: tropical fruit, honeyed notes, candied fruit, expressive. Palate: good acidity, rich, flavourful, fruity.

ALTIPLANO DE SIERRA NEVADA NORTE DE GRANADA

BODEGA ANCHURÓN

Isaac Albeniz, 10 2º
18012 (Granada)
☎: +34 958 277 764 - Fax: +34 958 277 764
info@anchuron.es
www.anchuron.com

CORTIJO EL ANCHURÓN 2008 T ROBLE
40% syrah, 30% cabernet sauvignon, 30% tempranillo.

88 Colour: cherry, garnet rim. Nose: ripe fruit, aged wood nuances, toasty, earthy notes. Palate: good acidity, powerful, flavourful, fleshy.

ANCHURÓN PLUS MERLOT SYRAH 2007 T ROBLE
50% merlot, 50% syrah.

89 Colour: deep cherry, garnet rim. Nose: powerfull, ripe fruit, toasty, spicy, mineral. Palate: fleshy, spicy, slightly dry, soft tannins, balanced.

ANCHURÓN PLUS TEMPRANILLO CABERNET 2007 T
50% tempranillo, 50% cabernet sauvignon.

88 Colour: cherry, garnet rim. Nose: ripe fruit, aged wood nuances, spicy, toasty. Palate: balanced, round, flavourful, fleshy.

CORTIJO EL ANCHURÓN 2006 T BARRICA
50% syrah, 50% cabernet sauvignon.

86 Colour: cherry, garnet rim. Nose: powerfull, wild herbs, fruit preserve, earthy notes. Palate: powerful, fleshy, toasty, spirituous.

BODEGAS MUÑANA

Ctra. Graena a La Peza, s/n
18517 Cortes y Graena (Granada)
☎: +34 958 670 715 - Fax: +34 958 670 715
bodegasmunana@gmail.com
www.bodegasmunana.com

MUÑANA Ñ 2008 T
60% tempranillo, 30% cabernet sauvignon, 10% monastrell.

88 Color bright cherry. Aroma ripe fruit, sweet spices, creamy oak, expressive. Taste flavourful, fruity, toasty, round tannins.

MUÑANA Ñ 3 CEPAS 2008 T
65% syrah, 30% cabernet sauvignon, 5% merlot.

88 Colour: black cherry, garnet rim. Nose: ripe fruit, scrubland, spicy, mineral. Palate: spirituous, unctuous, powerful, flavourful.

BAJO ARAGÓN

BODEGA COOP. NTRA. SRA. DEL OLIVAR

Avda. José Antonio s/n
50131 Lecera (Zaragoza)
☎: +34 976 835 016 - Fax: +34 976 835 016
valssira@hotmail.com
www.bodegasvalssira.es

VALSSIRA 2010 B
macabeo.

82 Colour: bright straw. Nose: overripe fruit, floral, wild herbs. Palate: correct, flavourful, fine bitter notes.

VALSSIRA 2010 RD
garnacha.

87 Color rose, purple rim. Aroma powerfull, ripe fruit, red berry notes, floral, expressive. Taste fleshy, powerful, fruity, fresh.

VALSSIRA 2010 T
garnacha.

86 Colour: cherry, purple rim. Nose: expressive, red berry notes, floral, ripe fruit. Palate: flavourful, fruity, good acidity.

VALSSIRA 2009 T
garnacha.

85 Colour: cherry, garnet rim. Nose: red berry notes, ripe fruit, balsamic herbs, toasty. Palate: powerful, flavourful, fleshy.

VALSSIRA 2007 T
garnacha.

86 Colour: cherry, garnet rim. Nose: ripe fruit, old leather, tobacco, spicy. Palate: rich, flavourful, long.

VALSSIRA 24 MESES BARRICA T
garnacha.

87 Colour: pale ruby, brick rim edge. Nose: elegant, spicy, fine reductive notes, wet leather, aged wood nuances. Palate: spicy, fine tannins, long, powerful, flavourful.

BODEGAS LECERANAS

Ignacio de Ara, 3
50002 Zaragoza (Zaragoza)
☎: +34 976 461 056 - Fax: +34 976 461 558
bodegasevohe@terra.es

EVOHÉ 2010 T
100% garnacha.

90 Colour: cherry, purple rim. Nose: red berry notes, floral, expressive, complex. Palate: fruity, powerful, flavourful.

COOPERATIVA DEL CAMPO SAN PEDRO DE CRETAS

Avda. Reino de Aragón, 10
44623 Cretas (Teruel)
☎: +34 978 850 309 - Fax: +34 978 850 309
coop.cretas@telefonica.net

BELVÍ 2010 B
100% garnacha blanca.

80 Colour: pale. Nose: white flowers, citrus fruit, medium intensity. Palate: fresh, light-bodied, easy to drink.

BELVÍ 2010 RD
90% garnacha, 10% syrah.

85 Color rose, purple rim. Aroma powerfull, ripe fruit, red berry notes, floral, expressive. Taste fleshy, powerful, fruity, fresh.

BELVÍ 2009 T
60% garnacha, 30% tempranillo, 10% syrah.

83 Colour: cherry, garnet rim. Nose: new oak, toasty, overripe fruit. Palate: fresh, light-bodied, flavourful.

DOMINIO MAESTRAZGO

Royal, 13
44550 Alcorisa (Teruel)
☎: +34 978 840 642 - Fax: +34 978 841 054
bodega@dominiomaestrazgo.com
www.dominiomaestrazgo.com

SANTOLEA 2009 T
85% garnacha, 15% tempranillo.

86 Colour: cherry, garnet rim. Nose: powerfull, red berry notes, candied fruit, scrubland. Palate: round tannins, correct, flavourful.

DOMINIO MAESTRAZGO 2008 T BARRICA
65% garnacha, 20% tempranillo, 15% syrah.

91 Colour: cherry, garnet rim. Nose: earthy notes, mineral, red berry notes, ripe fruit, creamy oak. Palate: flavourful, powerful, fleshy, long.

DOMINIO MAESTRAZGO SYRAH 2008 T BARRICA
100% syrah.

87 Colour: cherry, purple rim. Nose: spicy, creamy oak, ripe fruit. Palate: good acidity, light-bodied, flavourful.

DOMINIO MAESTRAZGO 2007 T
garnacha, tempranillo, syrah.

88 Colour: cherry, garnet rim. Nose: red berry notes, ripe fruit, old leather, spicy, toasty. Palate: fruity, flavourful, fleshy, correct.

REX DEUS 2005 T
85% garnacha, 10% syrah, 5% cabernet sauvignon.

90 Colour: cherry, garnet rim. Nose: ripe fruit, spicy, creamy oak, toasty. Palate: powerful, flavourful, toasty, round tannins.

FANBAR

Camino del Descanso, s/n
44520 Samper de Calanda (Teruel)
☎: +34 978 822 778 - Fax: +34 978 822 778
fanbar@fanbar.es
www.fanbar.es

FANDOS Y BARRIUSO TECA DE VAL DE CERÍN 2009 B
100% teca.

84 Colour: coppery red. Nose: powerfull, fruit expression, citrus fruit, balsamic herbs, fragrant herbs. Palate: flavourful, fruity, fresh, balsamic.

FANDOS Y BARRIUSO ROYAL DE ALLOZA DE VALDE LA MARGA 2004 T BARRICA
royal de alloza.

90 Colour: deep cherry, orangey edge. Nose: red berry notes, wild herbs, complex. Palate: balsamic, mineral, fruity, flavourful.

FANDOS Y BARRIUSO ROMERO DE HIJAR 2004 T BARRICA
romero de hijar.

86 Colour: bright cherry, orangey edge. Nose: candied fruit, balsamic herbs, medium intensity. Palate: spicy, balsamic, flavourful.

GRUPO MAGALIA

Avda. de Aragón 110
50710 Maella (Zaragoza)
☎: +34 976 638 004 - Fax: +34 976 639 215
gerencia@magalia.org
www.magalia.org

CASTILLO DE MAGALIA S/C B
100% macabeo.

78

MAGALIA 2009 BFB
80% garnacha blanca, 20% macabeo.

84 Colour: bright golden. Nose: citrus fruit, fragrant herbs, pattiserie. Palate: fleshy, flavourful, easy to drink.

MAGALIA SELECCIÓN 2009 T
50% garnacha, 30% syrah, 10% cabernet sauvignon, 10% cariñena.

90 Colour: cherry, purple rim. Nose: spicy, red berry notes, powerfull, mineral. Palate: fruity, powerful, complex, mineral.

MAGALIA 2009 T
80% garnacha, 20% syrah.

86 Colour: cherry, purple rim. Nose: fruit expression, expressive, fresh. Palate: good structure, fruity, easy to drink.

VENTA D'AUBERT S.L.

Ctra. Valderrobres a Arnes, Km. 28
44580 Cretas (Teruel)
☎: +34 978 769 021 - Fax: +34 978 769 031
ventadaubert@gmx.net
www.ventadaubert.com

VENTA D'AUBERT VIOGNIER 2010 B
100% viognier.

92 Colour: bright yellow. Nose: sweet spices, creamy oak, fragrant herbs, ripe fruit, white flowers. Palate: rich, smoky aftertaste, flavourful, fresh, good acidity.

VENTUS 2008 TC
41% cabernet sauvignon, 33% garnacha, 8% cabernet franc, 5% merlot, 5% syrah.

88 Colour: cherry, garnet rim. Nose: spicy, ripe fruit, expressive. Palate: balsamic, correct, fleshy.

VENTA D'AUBERT MERLOT 2007 T
100% merlot.

87 Colour: cherry, garnet rim. Nose: ripe fruit, toasty, sweet spices, creamy oak. Palate: flavourful, fleshy, toasty.

DIONUS 2005 TR
60% cabernet sauvignon, 20% merlot, 20% cabernet franc.

86 Colour: cherry, garnet rim. Nose: sweet spices, cocoa bean, ripe fruit. Palate: round tannins, flavourful, fleshy.

VINOS MONTANER

Avda. Aragón 85
50710 Maella (Zaragoza)
☎: +34 976 638 748 - Fax: +34 976 638 384
vinosmontaner@telefonica.net

BARONO GARNACHA BLANCA 2010 B
100% garnacha blanca.

84 Colour: bright golden. Nose: faded flowers, fruit expression, fresh. Palate: creamy, fresh, flavourful.

BARONO GARNACHA BLANCA 2009 B
100% garnacha blanca.

84 Colour: bright golden. Nose: slightly evolved, fragrant herbs, short. Palate: rich, fleshy.

BARONO 2010 RD
100% garnacha.

83 Colour: rose, purple rim. Nose: powerfull, ripe fruit, red berry notes, floral. Palate: fleshy, fruity, fresh.

FINCA MAS NOU BARONO 2010 T
cabernet sauvignon, syrah, garnacha.

88 Colour: cherry, purple rim. Nose: expressive, fresh fruit, red berry notes, floral. Palate: flavourful, fruity, round tannins, easy to drink.

BARONO 2009 T
cabernet sauvignon, syrah, garnacha.

87 Colour: cherry, purple rim. Nose: red berry notes, ripe fruit, creamy oak, spicy. Palate: balsamic, fruity, flavourful.

BARONO 2 ANGEL & JAVIER 2008 T
cabernet sauvignon, garnacha, syrah.

87 Colour: cherry, garnet rim. Nose: spicy, roasted coffee. Palate: correct, fleshy, flavourful, slightly dry, soft tannins.

BARONO 2008 T
cabernet sauvignon, syrah, garnacha.

86 Colour: cherry, garnet rim. Nose: ripe fruit, cocoa bean, spicy, creamy oak. Palate: balsamic, fruity, flavourful.

CÁDIZ

BODEGA REGANTÍO

Ctra. CA-6105 Km. 8
11630 Arcos de la Frontera (Cádiz)
☎: +34 956 231 193
info@bodegaregantio.com
www.bodegaregantio.com

REGANTÍO 2010 B
75% palomino, 35% moscatel.

84 Colour: bright golden. Nose: floral, smoky, honeyed notes. Palate: balanced, rich, fleshy.

EXPRESIÓN DE REGANTÍO 2010 T
50% syrah, 25% cabernet sauvignon, 25% merlot.

85 Colour: cherry, purple rim. Nose: floral, fruit liqueur notes, fresh. Palate: fresh, fruity, flavourful.

FINE TEMPO 2009 T
50% syrah, 50% petit verdot.

88 Colour: cherry, garnet rim. Nose: ripe fruit, aromatic coffee, new oak, toasty. Palate: unctuous, flavourful, fleshy, complex.

REGANTÍO CUVÉE 2009 T ROBLE
40% syrah, 35% cabernet sauvignon, 15% merlot, 10% tempranillo.

84 Colour: cherry, garnet rim. Nose: ripe fruit, sweet spices, toasty. Palate: correct, fleshy, toasty.

ALBERITE 2009 T
25% syrah, 25% tempranillo, 25% merlot, 25% cabernet sauvignon.

82 Colour: cherry, garnet rim. Nose: sweet spices, pattiserie, dried fruit, warm. Palate: burning notes, lacks balance, spicy.

BODEGAS BARBADILLO

Luis de Eguilaz, 11
11540 Sanlúcar de Barrameda (Cádiz)
☎: +34 956 385 500 - Fax: +34 956 385 501
barbadillo@barbadillo.com
www.barbadillo.com

MAESTRANTE 2010 B
palomino.

87 Colour: bright straw. Nose: fresh, fresh fruit, white flowers, expressive. Palate: flavourful, fruity, good acidity, sweetness.

CASTILLO DE SAN DIEGO 2010 B
100% palomino.

85 Colour: straw, pale. Nose: medium intensity, ripe fruit, tropical fruit, warm. Palate: fine bitter notes, light-bodied, lacks fruit.

GIBALBÍN 2009 T
tempranillo, syrah, merlot, cabernet sauvignon, tintilla.

87 Colour: cherry, purple rim. Nose: red berry notes, candied fruit, grassy. Palate: flavourful, fruity, fleshy.

GIBALBÍN 2008 T
tempranillo, tintilla, syrah, cabernet sauvignon.

84 Colour: bright cherry. Nose: ripe fruit, sweet spices, creamy oak. Palate: flavourful, fruity, toasty, round tannins.

BODEGAS OSBORNE

Fernán Caballero, 7
11500 El Puerto de Santa María (Cádiz)
☎: +34 925 860 990 - Fax: +34 925 860 905
carolina.cerrato@osborne.es
www.osborne.es

GADIR 2010 B
60% palomino, 40% chardonnay.

82 Colour: bright straw. Nose: white flowers, grassy, fresh. Palate: light-bodied, easy to drink.

BODEGAS VALDIVIA

Zoilo Ruiz Mateo Camacho, s/n
11408 Jerez de la Frontera (Cádiz)
☎: +34 956 314 358 - Fax: +34 956 169 657
info@bodegasvaldivia.com
www.bodegasvaldivia.com

PASO DE LA PLATA B
palomino.

88 Color bright straw. Aroma fresh, fresh fruit, white flowers, expressive. Taste flavourful, fruity, good acidity, balanced.

CORTIJO DE JARA

Cortijo de Jara, Ctra. de Gibalbin, Km. 5
11407 Jerez de la Frontera (Cádiz)
☎: +34 956 338 163 - Fax: +34 956 338 163
puerta.nueva@terra.es
www.cortijodejara.com

CORTIJO DE JARA 2009 T ROBLE
tempranillo, merlot, syrah.

84 Colour: cherry, purple rim. Nose: red berry notes, expressive, creamy oak. Palate: fruity, flavourful, easy to drink.

FINCA MONCLOA

Manuel María González, 12
11403 Jerez de la Frontera (Cádiz)
☎: +34 956 357 000 - Fax: +34 956 357 043
nacional@gonzalezbyass.es
www.gonzalezbyass.com

FINCA MONCLOA 11 BARRICAS 2008 T
64% cabernet sauvignon, 36% syrah.

90 Colour: cherry, garnet rim. Nose: sweet spices, red berry notes, balanced, expressive. Palate: round tannins, good structure, flavourful, complex.

FINCA MONCLOA 2008 T
65% syrah, 32% cabernet sauvignon, 3% tintilla de rota.

87 Colour: cherry, garnet rim. Nose: ripe fruit, spicy, creamy oak, neat. Palate: correct, flavourful, round tannins, long.

HEREDEROS DE ARGÜESO S.A.

Mar, 8
11540 Sanlúcar de Barrameda (Cádiz)
☎: +34 956 385 116 - Fax: +34 956 368 169
argueso@argueso.es
www.argueso.es

BLANCO ARGÜESO B
100% palomino.

84 Colour: bright straw. Nose: flor yeasts, candied fruit, fragrant herbs. Palate: flavourful, fruity, fine bitter notes.

HUERTA DE ALBALÁ

Ctra. CA - 6105, Km. 4
11630 Arcos de la Frontera (Cádiz)
☎: +34 647 746 048 - Fax: +34 856 023 053
bodega@huertadealbala.com
www.huertadealbala.com

BARBAROSA 2010 RD
100% syrah.

85 Colour: rose, purple rim. Nose: powerfull, ripe fruit, floral, expressive. Palate: fleshy, powerful, fruity.

BARBAZUL 2009 T
80% syrah, 10% merlot, 10% cabernet sauvignon.

87 Colour: cherry, garnet rim. Nose: ripe fruit, balsamic herbs, spicy. Palate: light-bodied, fresh, round tannins, easy to drink.

TABERNER Nº 1 2007 T
60% syrah, 37% merlot, 3% cabernet sauvignon.

90 Colour: deep cherry, brick rim edge. Nose: mineral, balsamic herbs, toasty, cocoa bean. Palate: round tannins, balanced, spicy, long.

TABERNER 2007 T
60% syrah, 26% merlot, 14% cabernet sauvignon.

87 Colour: cherry, garnet rim. Nose: roasted coffee, fruit preserve, balsamic herbs, expressive. Palate: flavourful, round tannins, spicy.

LOS ENTRECHUELOS

Finca Torrecera Ctra. Jerez - La Ina, Km. 14,5
11595 Torrecera (Cádiz)
☎: +34 856 030 073 - Fax: +34 856 030 033
comercial@entrechuelos.com

ENTRECHUELOS 2010 B
chardonnay.

83 Colour: bright straw. Nose: candied fruit, citrus fruit, faded flowers. Palate: flavourful, fine bitter notes, good acidity.

ENTRECHUELOS 2008 T
tempranillo, syrah, merlot, cabernet sauvignon.

84 Colour: cherry, garnet rim. Nose: fruit preserve, scrubland, toasty. Palate: flavourful, fleshy, spicy.

MANUEL ARAGÓN

Olivo, 1
11130 Chiclana de la Frontera (Cádiz)
☎: +34 956 400 756 - Fax: +34 956 532 907
administracion@bodegamanuelaragon.com
www.bodegamanuelaragon.com

MANUEL ARAGÓN SAUVIGNON BLANC 2010 B
sauvignon blanc.

85 Colour: bright straw. Nose: spicy, acetaldehyde, pungent. Palate: rich, flavourful, fleshy.

MANUEL ARAGÓN 2008 TC
tempranillo, syrah.

85 Colour: cherry, garnet rim. Nose: aged wood nuances, roasted coffee, fruit preserve. Palate: light-bodied, fresh, easy to drink.

MIGUEL DOMECQ

Finca Torrecera, Ctra. Jerez - La Ina, Km. 14,5
11595 Torrecera (Cádiz)
☎: +34 856 030 073 - Fax: +34 856 030 033
comercial@entrechuelos.com

ALHOCEN 2010 B
chardonnay.

84 Colour: bright straw. Nose: fresh, fresh fruit, white flowers, expressive. Palate: flavourful, fruity, good acidity.

ALHOCEN SELECCIÓN PERSONAL 2008 T ROBLE
syrah, merlot, tempranillo, cabernet sauvignon.

88 Colour: cherry, garnet rim. Nose: red berry notes, ripe fruit, complex, spicy, creamy oak. Palate: good acidity, unctuous, flavourful.

ALHOCEN 2008 T ROBLE
syrah, merlot.

87 Colour: cherry, garnet rim. Nose: ripe fruit, cocoa bean, sweet spices, toasty. Palate: powerful, flavourful, fleshy.

CAMPO DE CARTAGENA

SERRANO

Finca La Cabaña, 30
30594 Pozo Estrecho (Murcia)
☎: +34 968 556 298 - Fax: +34 968 556 298
vinos@bodegaserrano.es
www.bodegaserrano.com

VIÑA GALTEA SEMIDULCE 2010 B
40% chardonnay, 30% moscatel, 30% malvasía.

82 Colour: pale. Nose: grapey, white flowers, fragrant herbs. Palate: sweetness, fruity, fleshy.

DARIMUS CABERNET SYRAH 2008 T BARRICA
80% cabernet sauvignon, 20% syrah.

80 Colour: cherry, garnet rim. Nose: woody, spicy, fresh. Palate: slightly tart, flavourful, balsamic.

DARIMUS SYRAH DULCE 2010 TINTO DULCE
100% syrah.

88 Nose: sweet spices, ripe fruit, floral, expressive. Palate: creamy, flavourful, fruity, complex.

CASTELLÓ

BODEGAS Y VIÑEDOS BARÓN D'ALBA

Partida Vilar la Call, 10
12118 Les Useres (Castellón)
☎: +34 608 032 884 - Fax: +34 964 767 306
info@barondalba.com
www.barondalba.com

CLOS D'ESGARRACORDES 2010 B
100% macabeo.

85 Colour: bright straw. Nose: fresh, expressive, dried herbs, faded flowers. Palate: flavourful, fruity, good acidity.

CLOS D' ESGARRACORDES 2010 RD
50% garnacha, 50% cabernet sauvignon.

70

CLOS D'ESGARRACORDES 2008 T BARRICA
60% tempranillo, 30% merlot, 10% monastrell.

89 Colour: bright cherry. Nose: ripe fruit, creamy oak, expressive, spicy. Palate: flavourful, fruity, toasty, round tannins, fleshy.

CLOS D'ESGARRACORDES SELECCIÓN ESPECIAL 2007 TC
40% merlot, 30% cabernet sauvignon, 20% tempranillo, 10% syrah.

87 Colour: cherry, garnet rim. Nose: ripe fruit, spicy, toasty, fine reductive notes. Palate: powerful, flavourful, toasty, round tannins.

MASÍA DE LA HOYA

Avda. Navarro Reverter, 1
12400 Segorbe (Castellón)
☎: +34 964 710 050 - Fax: +34 964 713 484
masiadelahoya@masiadelahoya.com
www.masiadelahoya.com

MASÍA DE LA HOYA SYRAH 2009 T
100% syrah.

85 Colour: cherry, garnet rim. Nose: toasty, spicy, ripe fruit, neat. Palate: harsh oak tannins, spicy, creamy, flavourful.

CASTILLA

ALTOLANDÓN

Ctra. N-330, km. 242
16330 Landete (Cuenca)
☎: +34 677 228 974 - Fax: +34 962 300 662
altolandon@altolandon.com
www.altolandon.com

L AME MALBEC 2008 T
malbec.

91 Colour: cherry, garnet rim. Nose: red berry notes, ripe fruit, raspberry, cocoa bean, dark chocolate, creamy oak. Palate: spicy, powerful, flavourful, fleshy.

AMADIS DE GAULA

Geronimo Ceballos, 2
13270 Almagro (Ciudad Real)
☎: +34 926 562 424
www.amadisdegaula.com

REQUIEBRO VERDEJO 2010 B
100% verdejo.

85 Colour: bright straw. Nose: grassy, floral, candied fruit. Palate: good acidity, fruity, flavourful.

REQUIEBRO FRISANTE B
100% moscatel.

82 Colour: bright straw. Nose: grapey, white flowers, medium intensity. Palate: fresh, fruity, sweetness.

Nº5 REQUIEBRO 2010 RD
100% merlot.

86 Colour: rose, purple rim. Nose: raspberry, red berry notes, floral, expressive. Palate: good acidity, fresh, fruity, fleshy.

REQUIEBRO 2009 T
100% syrah.

86 Colour: cherry, purple rim. Nose: red berry notes, ripe fruit, balsamic herbs, expressive. Palate: fresh, fruity, green.

REQUIEBRO SYRAH CABERNET SAUVIGNON 2008 T
60% syrah, 40% cabernet sauvignon.

86 Colour: cherry, garnet rim. Nose: red berry notes, ripe fruit, floral, expressive, creamy oak. Palate: good acidity, fresh, fruity, flavourful.

REQUIEBRO SELECCIÓN 2006 T
100% tempranillo.

87 Colour: cherry, garnet rim. Nose: red berry notes, ripe fruit, sweet spices, cocoa bean, toasty. Palate: fleshy, complex, powerful, flavourful, round tannins.

GRIAL DE AMADIS 2005 T
100% syrah.

89 Colour: cherry, garnet rim. Nose: red berry notes, ripe fruit, sweet spices, cocoa bean, dark chocolate. Palate: balanced, powerful, flavourful, fleshy.

BODEGA ABAXTERRA

Ctra. CMM 3200, Km. 27,500
13343 Villamanrique (Ciudad Real)
☎: +34 669 822 950 - Fax: +34 912 480 616
ebilbao@bodegas-abaxterra.com

ABAXTERRA 2009 T ROBLE
70% tempranillo, 30% syrah.

88 Colour: deep cherry, garnet rim. Nose: red berry notes, ripe fruit, sweet spices, cocoa bean, toasty. Palate: balanced, round, powerful, flavourful.

BODEGA DEHESA DE LUNA

Cristo, 15 2ºD
02630 La Roda (Albacete)
☎: +34 967 548 508 - Fax: +34 967 548 022
contacto@dehesadeluna.com
www.dehesadeluna.com

DEHESA DE LUNA 2008 T
tempranillo, syrah, cabernet sauvignon.

87 Colour: cherry, garnet rim. Nose: ripe fruit, warm, balsamic herbs, mineral, toasty. Palate: balanced, powerful, flavourful.

DEHESA DE LUNA TEMPRANILLO 2008 T
tempranillo.

87 Colour: cherry, garnet rim. Nose: red berry notes, ripe fruit, earthy notes, cocoa bean, dark chocolate, sweet spices, toasty. Palate: elegant, unctuous, flavourful, complex.

BODEGA FINCA EL RETAMAR

Ctra. CM-4022, km. 2,5
45100 Sonseca (Toledo)
☎: +34 687 765 400 - Fax: +34 925 380 950
info@fincaelretamar.com
www.peces-barba.com

ROSADO BARBAROSA 2010 RD
garnacha, tempranillo.

85 Colour: rose, purple rim. Nose: floral, red berry notes, fresh. Palate: fruity, light-bodied, easy to drink.

BODEGA GARCÍA DE LA ROSA (AGROCONGOSTO S.L.)

Podadores, 12
45350 Noblejas (Toledo)
☎: +34 925 140 605 - Fax: +34 925 140 605
carlosgarciarosa@bodegagarciadelarosa.es
www.bodegagarciadelarosa.es

CASTILLO PALOMARES 2010 B
airén.

84 Colour: bright straw. Nose: expressive, candied fruit, citrus fruit. Palate: flavourful, sweetness, full.

NÓBRIGA 2009 T
tempranillo, syrah.

90 Colour: bright cherry. Nose: ripe fruit, sweet spices, creamy oak, expressive, raspberry, red berry notes. Palate: flavourful, fruity, toasty, round tannins.

BODEGA HACIENDA LA PRINCESA

Ctra. San Carlos del Valle, km. 8 - Apdo. Correos 281
13300 Valdepeñas (Ciudad Real)
☎: +34 638 335 185
haciendalaprincesa@telefonica.net
www.haciendalaprincesa.com

HACIENDA LA PRINCESA DEBIR DE GALA 2008 T ROBLE
100% tempranillo.

87 Colour: cherry, garnet rim. Nose: ripe fruit, warm, spicy, creamy oak. Palate: powerful, flavourful, fleshy, fruity.

HACIENDA LA PRINCESA DEBIR DE JAKUE 2008 T
100% tempranillo.

86 Colour: cherry, garnet rim. Nose: ripe fruit, old leather, spicy, toasty. Palate: powerful, flavourful, fleshy.

HACIENDA LA PRINCESA DEBIR DE SUCUNZA 2008 T
50% tempranillo, 50% merlot.

85 Colour: cherry, garnet rim. Nose: ripe fruit, spicy, roasted coffee. Palate: good acidity, flavourful, fleshy.

BODEGA LOS ALJIBES

Finca Los Aljibes
02520 Chinchilla de Montearagón (Albacete)
☎: +34 918 843 472 - Fax: +34 918 844 324
info@fincalosaljibes.com
www.fincalosaljibes.com

VIÑA ALJIBES 2010 B
80% sauvignon blanc, 20% chardonnay.

87 Colour: bright yellow. Nose: fruit expression, medium intensity, fresh fruit. Palate: rich, fruity, good acidity.

VIÑA ALJIBES 2010 RD
100% syrah.

86 Colour: rose. Nose: fruit expression, balanced, faded flowers. Palate: easy to drink, flavourful, fruity.

VIÑA ALJIBES 2009 T
38% petit verdot, 38% cabernet sauvignon, 24% tempranillo.

83 Colour: cherry, garnet rim. Nose: varietal, grassy, ripe fruit. Palate: fruity, spicy, good finish.

ALJIBES 2007 T
merlot, cabernet franc, cabernet sauvignon.

90 Colour: cherry, garnet rim. Nose: medium intensity, complex, balanced, elegant, red berry notes, spicy. Palate: flavourful, fruity, spicy, easy to drink.

SELECTUS 2007 T
merlot, syrah, cabernet sauvignon, cabernet franc.

90 Colour: cherry, garnet rim. Nose: toasty, sweet spices, candied fruit, ripe fruit. Palate: fleshy, round tannins, long.

ALJIBES CABERNET FRANC 2007 T
100% cabernet franc.

90 Colour: cherry, garnet rim. Nose: scrubland, red berry notes, spicy, complex. Palate: fruity, good structure, good acidity, round tannins.

ALJIBES SYRAH 2005 T
100% syrah.

91 Colour: cherry, garnet rim. Nose: red berry notes, fresh fruit, spicy, mineral. Palate: flavourful, complex, ripe fruit, great length, good acidity.

BODEGA MATEOS HIGUERA

Ctra. CM-3127 P.k. 7,100
13240 La Solana (Ciudad Real)
☎: +34 676 920 905 - Fax: +34 926 633 826
ventas@vegamara.es
www.vegamara.es

VEGA DEMARA 2010 B
90% verdejo, 10% airén.

82 Colour: cherry, garnet rim. Nose: fruit liqueur notes, medium intensity, toasty. Palate: flavourful, fleshy, toasty.

VEGA DEMARA 2010 T
100% tempranillo.

80 Colour: cherry, purple rim. Nose: fruit liqueur notes, fresh, medium intensity. Palate: light-bodied, fresh, fruity.

VEGA DEMARA SELECCIÓN 2006 T
100% tempranillo.

82 Colour: cherry, garnet rim. Nose: ripe fruit, scrubland, creamy oak. Palate: powerful, flavourful, fleshy.

BODEGA PALAREA

Paraje Hondo del Cerro Cuadrado
02260 Chinchilla de Montearagón (Albacete)
☎: +34 967 619 619 - Fax: +34 967 619 620
fincamanzanares@gmail.com
www.vinospalarea.com

PALAREA MERLOT 2006 T
100% merlot.

87 Colour: bright cherry, orangey edge. Nose: fruit preserve, cocoa bean, dark chocolate, old leather, tobacco. Palate: creamy, powerful, flavourful, fleshy.

PALAREA EXPRESSION 2005 T
33% cabernet sauvignon, 33% merlot, 33% syrah.

89 Colour: pale ruby, brick rim edge. Nose: elegant, spicy, fine reductive notes, wet leather, aged wood nuances. Palate: spicy, fine tannins, long, round, unctuous.

PALAREA 2005 T
33% cabernet sauvignon, 33% merlot, 33% syrah.

87 Colour: light cherry, orangey edge. Nose: ripe fruit, fruit liqueur notes, sweet spices, cigar, fine reductive notes. Palate: warm, powerful, flavourful, fleshy.

PALAREA 2004 TR
33% cabernet sauvignon, 33% merlot, 33% syrah.

87 Colour: light cherry, orangey edge. Nose: ripe fruit, tobacco, old leather, spicy, toasty. Palate: flavourful, fleshy, round tannins.

BODEGA PARDO TOLOSA

Villatoya, 26
02215 Alborea (Albacete)
☎: +34 963 517 067 - Fax: +34 963 517 091
ventas@bodegapardotolosa.com
www.bodegapardotolosa.com

MIZARAN TEMPRANILLO 2007 T
tempranillo.

84 Colour: cherry, garnet rim. Nose: fruit preserve, grassy, spicy, roasted coffee. Palate: good acidity, flavourful, fleshy.

BODEGA TIKALO

Finca Guadianeja - Ctra. de Catellar de Santiago a Torre de Juan Abad, Km. 28,800
13343 Villamanrique (Ciudad Real)
☎: +34 926 694 091
info@bodegatikalo.com
www.bodegatikalo.com

ALBALIZA 2010 RD
tempranillo, cabernet sauvignon, garnacha.

82 Colour: rose, purple rim. Nose: red berry notes, ripe fruit, lactic notes. Palate: ripe fruit, green, flavourful.

RUBENS 2009 T
tempranillo.

87 Colour: cherry, purple rim. Nose: red berry notes, floral, powerfull, expressive. Palate: powerful, flavourful, fruity, fresh.

ALBALIZA 2009 T
tempranillo, garnacha.

85 Colour: cherry, purple rim. Nose: red berry notes, candied fruit, fresh, lactic notes. Palate: good acidity, flavourful, fruity.

KIOS 2005 T
tempranillo.

87 Colour: cherry, garnet rim. Nose: red berry notes, ripe fruit, spicy, toasty. Palate: good acidity, flavourful, toasty, round tannins.

KIOS ÉLITE 2004 T
tempranillo.

89 Colour: cherry, garnet rim. Nose: ripe fruit, fine reductive notes, earthy notes, creamy oak. Palate: powerful, flavourful, fleshy, rich, long.

BODEGA Y VIÑEDO TINEDO

Ctra. CM 3102, Km. 30
13630 Socuéllamos (Ciudad Real)
☎: +34 926 118 999
info@tinedo.com
www.tinedo.com

CALA N 1 2009 T
75% tempranillo, 20% syrah, 5% cabernet sauvignon.

88 Colour: cherry, garnet rim. Nose: red berry notes, ripe fruit, balsamic herbs, cocoa bean, dark chocolate. Palate: concentrated, powerful, flavourful, fleshy.

BODEGAS ALCARDET

Mayor, 130
45810 Villanueva de Alcardete (Toledo)
☎: +34 925 166 375 - Fax: +34 925 166 611
alcardet@terra.es
www.alcardet.com

FINCA ALMEDO 2009 T
syrah, tempranillo.

83 Colour: cherry, purple rim. Nose: red berry notes, ripe fruit, floral. Palate: flavourful, fruity, round tannins.

BODEGAS ARÚSPIDE

Ciriaco Cruz, 2
13300 Valdepeñas (Ciudad Real)
☎: +34 926 347 075 - Fax: +34 926 347 875
info@aruspide.com
www.aruspide.com

ÁGORA 2010 B MACERACIÓN CARBÓNICA
viognier.

87 Colour: bright golden. Nose: fresh fruit, tropical fruit, fragrant herbs, expressive. Palate: fruity, fresh, flavourful, easy to drink.

ÁGORA VERDEJO 2010 BFB
verdejo.

82 Colour: bright straw, greenish rim. Nose: ripe fruit, tropical fruit, spicy. Palate: easy to drink, light-bodied.

ÁGORA TEMPRANILLO 2010 T MACERACIÓN CARBÓNICA
tempranillo.

87 Colour: cherry, purple rim. Nose: fresh fruit, red berry notes, floral. Palate: flavourful, fruity, good acidity, round tannins.

AUTOR DE ARÚSPIDE TEMPRANILLO 2007 T
tempranillo.

89 Colour: cherry, garnet rim. Nose: ripe fruit, fine reductive notes, spicy, toasty. Palate: good acidity, round, powerful, flavourful, fleshy, long.

ÁGORA TEMPRANILLO 2007 T ROBLE
tempranillo.

82 Colour: bright cherry. Nose: ripe fruit, sweet spices, creamy oak, cigar, fine reductive notes. Palate: warm, flavourful, slightly evolved.

BODEGAS BARREDA

Ramalazo, 2
45880 Corral de Almaguer (Toledo)
☎: +34 925 207 223 - Fax: +34 925 207 223
nacional@bodegas-barreda.com
www.bodegas-barreda.com

TORRE DE BARREDA SYRAH 2009 T
100% syrah.

86 Colour: bright cherry. Nose: ripe fruit, sweet spices, expressive. Palate: flavourful, fruity, toasty, round tannins.

TORRE DE BARREDA TEMPRANILLO 2009 T
100% tempranillo.

85 Colour: cherry, garnet rim. Nose: red berry notes, ripe fruit, floral, expressive. Palate: fleshy, light-bodied, flavourful.

TORRE DE BARREDA PAÑOFINO 2008 T ROBLE
100% tempranillo.

91 Colour: cherry, garnet rim. Nose: ripe fruit, creamy oak, toasty, sweet spices. Palate: powerful, flavourful, toasty, ripe fruit, round tannins.

TORRE DE BARREDA AMIGOS 2007 T
65% tempranillo, 25% syrah, 10% cabernet sauvignon.

88 Colour: cherry, garnet rim. Nose: cocoa bean, dark chocolate, red berry notes, ripe fruit. Palate: good acidity, fruity, powerful, flavourful, toasty.

BODEGAS BONJORNE

Ctra. La Roda Muntra, Km. 2.3
02630 La Roda (Albacete)
☎: +34 967 601 754 - Fax: +34 967 601 754
export@bonjorne.es
www.bonjorne.es

BONJORNE 3 MESES BARRICA 2009 T
tempranillo, cabernet sauvignon, syrah.

83 Colour: cherry, garnet rim. Nose: grassy, red berry notes, fruit preserve. Palate: spicy, green, flavourful.

BONJORNE SELECCIÓN 6 MESES BARRICA 2008 T
merlot, cabernet sauvignon, syrah.

84 Colour: bright cherry. Nose: ripe fruit, creamy oak, balsamic herbs. Palate: flavourful, toasty, fleshy.

BONJORNE 2007 T
merlot, cabernet sauvignon, syrah.

85 Colour: light cherry, brick rim edge. Nose: old leather, tobacco, spicy, toasty. Palate: powerful, flavourful, spicy.

BODEGAS CASAQUEMADA

Ctra. Ruidera, Km. 5,5
13710 Argamasilla de Alba (Ciudad Real)
☎: +34 628 621 187 - Fax: +34 926 511 515
casaquemada@casaquemada.es
www.casaquemada.es

BRINCHO KOSHER 2007 T
100% tempranillo.

90 Colour: cherry, garnet rim. Nose: macerated fruit, scrubland, violet drops, sweet spices, toasty. Palate: balanced, powerful, flavourful, toasty.

HACIENDA CASAQUEMADA 2007 T
100% tempranillo.

89 Colour: cherry, garnet rim. Nose: red berry notes, ripe fruit, expressive, earthy notes, spicy, creamy oak. Palate: good acidity, powerful, flavourful, fleshy.

ANEA DE CASAQUEMADA 2005 T
100% syrah.

89 Colour: cherry, garnet rim. Nose: ripe fruit, sweet spices, toasty, cocoa bean. Palate: powerful, flavourful, fleshy, complex, round tannins.

BODEGAS CORONADO

Ctra. San Isidro, s/n
16620 La Alberca de Záncara (Cuenca)
☎: +34 676 463 483 - Fax: +34 967 150 107
informacion@bodegascoronado.com
www.bodegascoronado.com

CHARCÓN SAUVIGNON BLANC 2010 B
100% sauvignon blanc.

87 Colour: straw. Nose: fresh fruit, varietal, dried flowers, fragrant herbs. Palate: fruity, flavourful, fleshy, fresh, good acidity.

VIÑA CHARCÓN SYRAH 2010 T ROBLE
100% syrah.

85 Colour: cherry, purple rim. Nose: candied fruit, aromatic coffee, spicy, toasty. Palate: good acidity, flavourful, thin.

CHARCÓN 2010 T
40% petit verdot, 30% syrah, 30% cencibel.

78

VIÑA CHARCÓN SELECCIÓN 2007 T ROBLE
50% merlot, 50% cencibel.

86 Colour: cherry, garnet rim. Nose: ripe fruit, cocoa bean, dark chocolate, spicy. Palate: powerful, flavourful, fleshy.

VIÑA CHARCÓN 2007 T ROBLE
50% cencibel, 50% cabernet sauvignon.

83 Colour: cherry, garnet rim. Nose: ripe fruit, spicy, toasty. Palate: powerful, toasty, good finish.

BODEGAS DEL MUNI

Ctra. de Lillo, 48
45310 Villatobas (Toledo)
☎: +34 925 152 511 - Fax: +34 925 152 511
info@bodegasdelmuni.com
www.bodegasdelmuni.com

CORPUS DEL MUNI 2010 B
verdejo, riesling.

87 Colour: bright straw. Nose: grapey, candied fruit, floral. Palate: good acidity, sweetness, fruity, flavourful.

CORPUS DEL MUNI (ETIQUETA NARANJA) 2010 B
verdejo, sauvignon blanc, chardonnay.

86 Nose: white flowers, citrus fruit, fragrant herbs, balanced. Palate: good acidity, rich, flavourful, fleshy.

CORPUS DEL MUNI (ETIQUETA AMARILLA) 2010 B
macabeo, riesling.

84 Colour: bright straw. Nose: fragrant herbs, white flowers, fresh, expressive. Palate: good acidity, fresh, fruity.

CORPUS DEL MUNI (ETIQUETA VERDE) 2009 BFB
chardonnay, sauvignon blanc.

87 Colour: bright golden. Nose: dried herbs, faded flowers, ripe fruit, sweet spices, creamy oak. Palate: rich, powerful, flavourful, toasty.

CORPUS DEL MUNI 2010 RD
100% petit verdot.

85 Colour: cherry, purple rim. Nose: red berry notes, ripe fruit, floral, fresh, expressive. Palate: good acidity, fruity, flavourful.

CORPUS DEL MUNI 2009 T ROBLE
80% tempranillo, 12% syrah, 5% petit verdot, 3% garnacha.

87 Colour: cherry, purple rim. Nose: red berry notes, spicy, creamy oak, expressive. Palate: good acidity, powerful, flavourful, fruity.

CORPUS DEL MUNI "VIÑA LUCÍA" 2005 TC
100% tempranillo.

88 Colour: light cherry, brick rim edge. Nose: ripe fruit, cocoa bean, dark chocolate, toasty, fine reductive notes. Palate: flavourful, fleshy, toasty, long.

CORPUS DEL MUNI "SELECCIÓN ESPECIAL" 2002 T
tempranillo.

88 Nose: ripe fruit, old leather, cigar, spicy, cocoa bean, toasty. Palate: fleshy, light-bodied, flavourful, fine tannins.

BODEGAS EGUREN

Avda. del Cantábrico, s/n
01013 Vitoria (Álava)
☎: +34 945 282 844 - Fax: +34 945 271 319
info@heredadugarte.com
www.heredadugarte.com

REINARES 2010 B
100% viura.

84 Colour: bright straw. Nose: white flowers, tropical fruit, medium intensity. Palate: good acidity, light-bodied, fresh.

MERCEDES EGUREN SAUVIGNON BLANC 2010 B
100% sauvignon blanc.

82 Colour: bright straw. Nose: floral, ripe fruit, warm. Palate: fresh, light-bodied, thin.

REINARES 2010 RD
50% tempranillo, 50% garnacha.

85 Colour: rose, purple rim. Nose: floral, raspberry, red berry notes. Palate: fresh, fruity, flavourful.

MERCEDES EGUREN
CABERNET SAUVIGNON 2010 RD
100% cabernet sauvignon.

81 Colour: rose, purple rim. Nose: ripe fruit, red berry notes, medium intensity. Palate: fleshy, fruity, fresh.

PAZOS DE EGUREN TEMPRANILLO 2010 T
100% tempranillo.

87 Colour: cherry, purple rim. Nose: red berry notes, raspberry, fresh, expressive. Palate: fresh, fruity, light-bodied, flavourful.

REINARES TEMPRANILLO 2010 T
100% tempranillo.

80 Colour: light cherry. Nose: fruit preserve, grassy, warm. Palate: light-bodied, fresh, fruity.

MERCEDES EGUREN SHIRAZ TEMPRANILLO 2009 T
50% syrah, 50% tempranillo.

87 Colour: cherry, purple rim. Nose: red berry notes, cocoa bean, sweet spices, toasty. Palate: good acidity, fruity, flavourful.

MERCEDES EGUREN CABERNET SAUVIGNON 2009 T
100% cabernet sauvignon.

86 Colour: cherry, purple rim. Nose: red berry notes, ripe fruit, scrubland, balsamic herbs. Palate: warm, flavourful, balsamic.

CONDADO DE EGUREN TEMPRANILLO 2009 T
100% tempranillo.

85 Colour: cherry, garnet rim. Nose: red berry notes, ripe fruit, warm, balsamic herbs. Palate: good acidity, flavourful, toasty.

BODEGAS EL LINZE

Duque de Liria, 9
28015 Madrid (Madrid)
info@ellinze.com
www.ellinze.com

EL LINZE VIOGNIER 2010 B
viognier.

88 Colour: bright straw. Nose: fragrant herbs, sweet spices, creamy oak, ripe fruit. Palate: rich, flavourful, fleshy, long.

EL LINZE 2008 T
syrah.

90 Colour: cherry, garnet rim. Nose: red berry notes, ripe fruit, floral, sweet spices, creamy oak. Palate: good acidity, round, powerful, flavourful, fleshy.

BODEGAS ERCAVIO

Camino de los Molinos, s/n
45312 Cabañas de Yepes (Toledo)
☎: +34 925 122 281 - Fax: +34 925 137 033
masquevinos@fer.es
www.bodegasercavio.com

ERCAVIO 2010 B BARRICA
100% malvar.

91 Colour: bright straw. Nose: medium intensity, balanced, closed, spicy, creamy oak. Palate: complex, sweetness, powerful, flavourful, varietal, fresh, fruity, mineral, ripe fruit.

ERCAVIO 2010 B
95% airén, 5% sauvignon blanc.

89 Colour: bright straw. Nose: undergrowth, red clay notes, scrubland, fresh fruit. Palate: good acidity, fruity, flavourful, sweetness.

ERCAVIO 2010 RD
100% tempranillo.

89 Colour: bright, rose, purple rim. Nose: powerfull, varietal, expressive, raspberry, rose petals. Palate: powerful, flavourful, fresh, fruity, fruity aftestaste.

ERCAVIO TEMPRANILLO 2009 T ROBLE
100% tempranillo.

90 Nose: complex, expressive, powerfull, cocoa bean, spicy, fruit expression, ripe fruit. Palate: spirituous, fleshy, fruity, spicy, soft tannins.

ERCAVIO SELECCIÓN LIMITADA 2008 T
90% tempranillo, 10% merlot.

89 Colour: dark-red cherry. Nose: fruit liqueur notes, fruit preserve, new oak, toasty. Palate: ripe fruit, spicy, powerful, sweetness.

LA MESETA 2007 T
50% tempranillo, 50% syrah.

89 Colour: deep cherry. Nose: spicy, fruit liqueur notes, fruit preserve, sweet spices, aged wood nuances, toasty. Palate: warm, spirituous, powerful, flavourful, ripe fruit, round tannins.

LA PLAZUELA 2005 T
80% cencibel, 20% garnacha.

91 Colour: bright cherry. Nose: ripe fruit, sweet spices, creamy oak, characterful. Palate: flavourful, fruity, round tannins, varietal.

ERCAVIO CENCIBEL DULCE NATURAL T
cencibel.

87 Colour: cherry, garnet rim. Nose: fruit liqueur notes, red berry notes, ripe fruit, sweet spices. Palate: powerful, flavourful, fruity.

BODEGAS ESCUDERO

Ctra. de Arnedo, s/n
26587 Grávalos (La Rioja)
☎: +34 941 398 008 - Fax: +34 941 398 070
bodega@bodegasescudero.com
www.bodegasescudero.com

TUDEJEM 2009 T
100% cencibel.

85 Colour: black cherry. Nose: ripe fruit, sweet spices, characterful. Palate: powerful, concentrated, sweetness.

BODEGAS GAZULES

Ríos Rosas, 44A - 7G
28003 Madrid (Madrid)
☎: +34 915 985 465 - Fax: +34 915 339 698
jcamacho.martinez@yahoo.es
wwww.bodegasgazules.com

PRIVILEGIO DE GAZULES 2007 T
70% syrah, 30% cabernet sauvignon.

88 Colour: cherry, garnet rim. Nose: ripe fruit, spicy, creamy oak, characterful. Palate: powerful, flavourful, toasty, round tannins.

BODEGAS HACIENDA ALBAE

Malecón de Santiago, 7
13710 Argamasilla de Alba (Ciudad Real)
☎: +34 917 756 330 - Fax: +34 913 132 135
info@haciendaalbae.com
www.haciendaalbae.com

ALBAE ESENCIA CHARDONNAY 2010 B
100% chardonnay.

87 Colour: bright straw. Nose: tropical fruit, citrus fruit, fragrant herbs, expressive. Palate: rich, fruity, flavourful, fleshy.

HACIENDA ALBAE CHARDONNAY 2009 BFB
100% chardonnay.

90 Colour: bright golden. Nose: sweet spices, creamy oak, citrus fruit. Palate: creamy, flavourful, complex, fleshy.

ALBAE ESENCIA 2009 T
70% syrah, 30% merlot.

85 Colour: cherry, purple rim. Nose: red berry notes, spicy, expressive. Palate: fruity, flavourful, fleshy, round tannins.

HACIENDA ALBAE SELECCIÓN 60/40 2007 T
60% cabernet sauvignon, 40% merlot.

87 Colour: cherry, garnet rim. Nose: fruit preserve, sweet spices, creamy oak. Palate: balsamic, flavourful, balanced.

HACIENDA ALBAE SELECCIÓN 2006 T BARRICA
100% tempranillo.

90 Colour: cherry, garnet rim. Nose: cocoa bean, sweet spices, creamy oak, expressive, mineral. Palate: balsamic, balanced, good acidity.

HACIENDA ALBAE TEMPRANILLO 2006 T
100% tempranillo.

87 Colour: cherry, garnet rim. Nose: creamy oak, sweet spices, ripe fruit. Palate: powerful, flavourful, fleshy.

HACIENDA ALBAE 888 T

91 Colour: cherry, garnet rim. Nose: creamy oak, cocoa bean, expressive, complex, ripe fruit, fine reductive notes. Palate: powerful, flavourful, complex, fleshy, spicy, soft tannins.

BODEGAS JUAN RAMÍREZ

Torrecilla, 138
13300 Valdepeñas (Ciudad Real)
☎: +34 926 322 021 - Fax: +34 926 320 495
info@bodegasjuanramirez.com
www.bodegasjuanramirez.com

AMPELO SYRAH 2010 T ROBLE
100% syrah.

85 Colour: cherry, purple rim. Nose: red berry notes, ripe fruit, balanced. Palate: fruity, easy to drink.

BODEGAS LAHOZ

Ctra. N-310, km. 108,5
13630 Socuéllamos (Ciudad Real)
☎: +34 926 699 083 - Fax: +34 926 514 929
info@bodegaslahoz.com
www.bodegaslahoz.com

RECATO SAUVIGNON BLANC 2009 BFB
100% sauvignon blanc.

87 Colour: bright golden. Nose: citrus fruit, ripe fruit, fragrant herbs, creamy oak. Palate: flavourful, fleshy, ripe fruit.

RECATO TEMPRANILLO 9 MESES 2007 T BARRICA
100% tempranillo.

87 Colour: cherry, garnet rim. Nose: red berry notes, spicy, creamy oak. Palate: good acidity, fruity, flavourful.

ABAD DE SOTO 2007 T
100% tempranillo.

85 Colour: cherry, garnet rim. Nose: red berry notes, ripe fruit, creamy oak. Palate: good acidity, flavourful, thin.

BODEGAS LÓPEZ PANACH

Finca El Calaverón, Apdo. 336
02600 Villarrobledo (Albacete)
☎: +34 967 573 140 - Fax: +34 967 573 297
bodegas@lopezpanach.com
www.lopezpanach.com

LÓPEZ PANACH VERDEJO 2010 B
100% verdejo.

84 Colour: straw. Nose: fresh fruit, white flowers. Palate: fruity, flavourful, easy to drink.

LÓPEZ PANACH COUPAGE 2006 T
50% tempranillo, 25% merlot, 12,5% syrah, 12,5% cabernet sauvignon.

84 Colour: cherry, garnet rim. Nose: spicy, cigar, cocoa bean, toasty. Palate: good acidity, flavourful, fleshy, toasty.

LÓPEZ PANACH TEMPRANILLO 2010 T
100% tempranillo.

82 Colour: cherry, purple rim. Nose: herbaceous, ripe fruit, medium intensity. Palate: light-bodied, fresh, green.

LÓPEZ PANACH TEMPRANILLO CABERNET 2008 T ROBLE
50% tempranillo, 50% cabernet sauvignon.

84 Colour: cherry, garnet rim. Nose: fruit preserve, warm, balsamic herbs, toasty. Palate: light-bodied, fleshy, balsamic, toasty.

LÓPEZ PANACH TEMPRANILLO 2004 T
100% tempranillo.

83 Colour: ruby red, orangey edge. Nose: ripe fruit, spicy, wet leather. Palate: warm, powerful, flavourful, toasty.

BODEGAS MANO A MANO

Ctra. CM-412, Km. 100
13248 Alhambra (Ciudad Real)
☎: +34 619 349 394 - Fax: +34 926 691 162
info@bodegamanoamano.com
www.bodegamanoamano.com

MANO A MANO 2010 T
100% tempranillo.

89 Colour: cherry, purple rim. Nose: fruit preserve, sweet spices, cocoa bean. Palate: powerful, flavourful, fruity, fleshy.

VENTA LA OSSA TNT 2009 T
75% tempranillo, 25% touriga nacional.

95 Colour: cherry, purple rim. Nose: red berry notes, floral, balanced, elegant, cocoa bean, dark chocolate, sweet spices, creamy oak. Palate: fleshy, complex, flavourful, fruity, toasty.

VENTA LA OSSA SYRAH 2009 T
100% syrah.

94 Colour: cherry, purple rim. Nose: red berry notes, ripe fruit, complex, expressive, balanced, sweet spices, toasty. Palate: powerful, flavourful, fleshy, complex, balanced.

VENTA LA OSSA 2009 TC
100% tempranillo.

93 Colour: cherry, garnet rim. Nose: red berry notes, ripe fruit, floral, spicy, cocoa bean, dark chocolate, toasty. Palate: rich, flavourful, fleshy, fine bitter notes.

BODEGAS MARTÍNEZ SÁEZ

Finca San José - Ctra. Barrax, km. 14,8
02600 Villarrobledo (Albacete)
☎: +34 967 443 088 - Fax: +34 967 440 204
avidal@bodegasmartinezsaez.es
www.bodegasmartinezsaez.es

MARTÍNEZ SAEZ ROSA ROSARUM 2010 RD
syrah.

85 Colour: rose, purple rim. Nose: lactic notes, floral, red berry notes. Palate: good acidity, fresh, flavourful.

MARTÍNEZ SAEZ SELECCIÓN 2008 TR
cabernet sauvignon, syrah, merlot.

86 Colour: cherry, garnet rim. Nose: red berry notes, spicy, toasty, grassy. Palate: flavourful, fleshy, balanced, toasty.

MARTÍNEZ SAEZ DÚO 2006 TR
cabernet sauvignon, syrah.

85 Colour: pale ruby, brick rim edge. Nose: fruit preserve, caramel, cocoa bean. Palate: powerful, flavourful, fleshy, long.

BODEGAS MONTALVO WILMOT

Ctra. Ruidera, km. 10,2 Finca Los Cerrillos
13710 Argamasilla de Alba (Ciudad Real)
☎: +34 926 699 069 - Fax: +34 926 699 069
silvia@montalvowilmot.com
www.montalvowilmot.com

MONTALVO WILMOT VERDEJO COLECCIÓN 2010 B
100% verdejo.

83 Colour: bright straw. Nose: floral, ripe fruit, grassy, medium intensity. Palate: light-bodied, fresh, easy to drink.

MONTALVO WILMOT SYRAH 2009 T ROBLE
100% syrah.

89 Colour: cherry, garnet rim. Nose: red berry notes, raspberry, lactic notes, fruit expression, creamy oak. Palate: good acidity, flavourful, fruity.

MONTALVO WILMOT TEMPRANILLO-CABERNET 2008 T ROBLE
75% tempranillo, 25% cabernet sauvignon.

87 Colour: cherry, garnet rim. Nose: ripe fruit, toasty, sweet spices, cocoa bean. Palate: fleshy, flavourful, round tannins.

MONTALVO WILMOT CABERNET DE FAMILIA 2006 T
100% cabernet sauvignon.

88 Colour: cherry, garnet rim. Nose: ripe fruit, sweet spices, cocoa bean, scrubland. Palate: flavourful, toasty, fleshy.

MONTALVO WILMOT COLECCIÓN PRIVADA 2006 T ROBLE
75% tempranillo, 25% cabernet sauvignon.

87 Colour: cherry, garnet rim. Nose: fruit preserve, scrubland, aged wood nuances. Palate: flavourful, spirituous, confected.

BODEGAS MORALIA

Avda. de la Vendimia, 1
13350 Moral de Calatrava (Ciudad Real)
☎: +34 926 330 910 - Fax: +34 926 319 523
bodegasmoralia@telefonica.net
www.bodegasmoralia.es

MORALIA 2010 B
100% verdejo.

87 Colour: yellow, greenish rim. Nose: balanced, fruit expression, dried herbs, medium intensity. Palate: rich, flavourful, fruity, ripe fruit.

MORALIA 2007 T ROBLE
100% merlot.

87 Colour: bright cherry, garnet rim. Nose: medium intensity, ripe fruit, complex. Palate: fruity, flavourful, round tannins.

MORALIA TRONCAL 2006 T ROBLE
100% tempranillo.

89 Colour: cherry, garnet rim. Nose: toasty, creamy oak, cocoa bean, ripe fruit. Palate: flavourful, fleshy, ripe fruit.

BODEGAS MUREDA

Ctra. N-IV, Km. 184,1
13300 Valdepeñas (Ciudad Real)
☎: +34 926 318 058 - Fax: +34 926 318 058
administracion@mureda.es
www.mureda.es

MUREDA SAUVIGNON BLANC 2010 B
100% sauvignon blanc.

84 Colour: bright straw. Nose: ripe fruit, warm, fragrant herbs. Palate: good acidity, fresh, fruity.

MUREDA CHARDONNAY 2010 B
100% chardonnay.

84 Colour: bright straw. Nose: white flowers, fresh fruit, fragrant herbs. Palate: fresh, flavourful, light-bodied, thin.

MUREDA MERLOT 2010 T
100% merlot.

88 Colour: cherry, purple rim. Nose: fresh, raspberry, red berry notes, floral. Palate: powerful, flavourful, fruity, fresh, easy to drink.

MUREDA TEMPRANILLO 2010 T
100% tempranillo.

87 Colour: cherry, purple rim. Nose: red berry notes, ripe fruit, fresh, floral. Palate: fruity, flavourful, fleshy, easy to drink.

MUREDA SYRAH 2010 T
100% syrah.

87 Colour: bright cherry, purple rim. Nose: red berry notes, balanced, medium intensity. Palate: flavourful, fruity, correct.

BODEGAS NAVARRO LÓPEZ

Autovía Madrid - Cádiz, Km. 193
13300 Valdepeñas (Ciudad Real)
☎: +34 902 193 431 - Fax: +34 902 193 432
laboratorio@navarrolopez.com
www.navarrolopez.com

PREMIUM 1904 2008 T
tempranillo, graciano.

88 Colour: cherry, purple rim. Nose: balsamic herbs, red berry notes, creamy oak, expressive. Palate: balanced, complex, fruity, fleshy.

TREBOLAR 2007 T
tempranillo, garnacha, cabernet sauvignon, petit verdot.

87 Colour: cherry, garnet rim. Nose: ripe fruit, spicy, toasty, old leather. Palate: powerful, flavourful, toasty, round tannins.

BODEGAS REAL

Finca Marisánchez - Ctra. de Valdepeñas a Cózar, Km. 12,8
13300 Valdepeñas (Ciudad Real)
☎: +34 914 577 588 - Fax: +34 914 577 210
comercial@bodegas-real.com
www.bodegas-real.com

FINCA MARISÁNCHEZ CHARDONNAY 2010 B
100% chardonnay.

85 Colour: pale. Nose: white flowers, ripe fruit, fragrant herbs. Palate: rich, fresh, flavourful.

FINCA MARISÁNCHEZ 2006 T ROBLE
80% tempranillo, 10% merlot, 10% syrah.

88 Colour: cherry, garnet rim. Nose: red berry notes, ripe fruit, floral, spicy, toasty. Palate: correct, powerful, flavourful, toasty.

VEGA IBOR TEMPRANILLO 2007 T BARRICA
100% tempranillo.

88 Colour: cherry, garnet rim. Nose: red berry notes, raspberry, ripe fruit, cocoa bean, sweet spices, toasty. Palate: flavourful, fruity, fleshy, toasty.

BODEGAS RÍO NEGRO

Ctra. CM 1001, Km. 37,400
19230 Cogolludo (Guadalajara)
☎: +34 639 301 817 - Fax: +34 913 026 750
info@fincarionegro.es
www.fincarionegro.com

FINCA RÍO NEGRO 2008 T
80% tempranillo, 20% syrah.

92 Colour: bright cherry. Nose: sweet spices, creamy oak, balsamic herbs, scrubland, red berry notes. Palate: flavourful, fruity, toasty, round tannins.

FINCA RÍO NEGRO 2009 T
tempranillo, syrah, cabernet sauvignon, merlot.

92 Colour: bright cherry. Nose: ripe fruit, sweet spices, creamy oak, mineral. Palate: flavourful, fruity, toasty, round tannins.

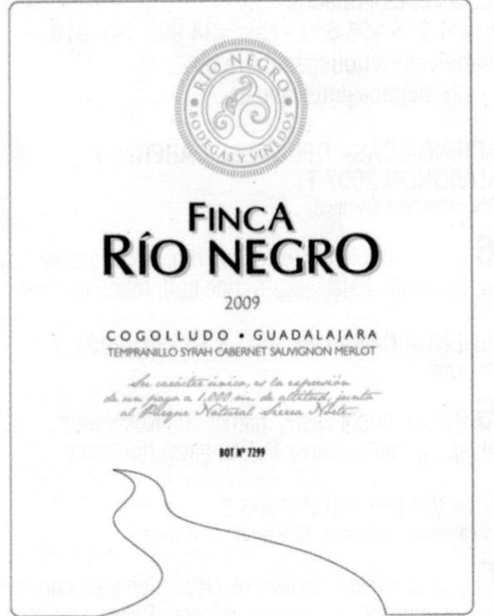

BODEGAS TIERRAS DE ORGAZ

Orgaz, 12
45460 Manzaneque (Toledo)
☎: +34 666 417 377
jcserrano@btor.es
www.bodegastierrasdeorgaz.com

MERNAT 2009 T
merlot, syrah, cabernet sauvignon, petit verdot, tempranillo.

84 Colour: cherry, garnet rim. Nose: fruit preserve, grassy, warm, sweet spices. Palate: powerful, fleshy, flavourful.

BODEGAS VERUM

Juan Antonio López Ramírez, 4
13700 Tomelloso (Ciudad Real)
☎: +34 926 511 404 - Fax: +34 926 515 047
administracion@bodegasverum.com
www.bodegasverum.com

VERUM 2009 T
merlot, tempranillo, cabernet sauvignon.

87 Colour: cherry, garnet rim. Nose: red berry notes, mineral, expressive. Palate: fleshy, fruity, flavourful, round tannins.

VERUM 2010 B
75% sauvignon blanc, 25% gewürztraminer.

88 Colour: bright straw. Nose: white flowers, fresh fruit, tropical fruit. Palate: good acidity, light-bodied, fresh, flavourful.

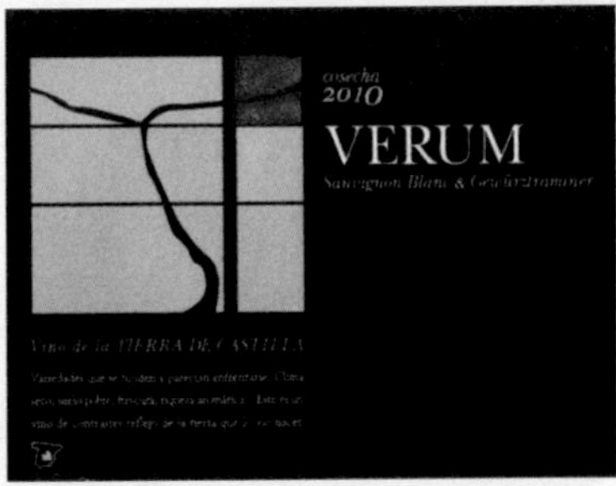

VERUM TERRA 2010 B
100% airén.

85 Colour: straw. Nose: fresh fruit, varietal, white flowers, fragrant herbs. Palate: good acidity, fruity, fleshy, fresh.

VERUM 2010 RD
60% tempranillo, 40% cabernet franc.

84 Colour: rose, purple rim. Nose: lactic notes, red berry notes, ripe fruit, medium intensity. Palate: fresh, fruity, fleshy.

VERUM 2008 T
60% merlot, 30% tempranillo, 10% cabernet sauvignon.

88 Colour: cherry, garnet rim. Nose: ripe fruit, expressive, complex, mineral, creamy oak. Palate: flavourful, fleshy, spicy, long.

BODEGAS VILLAVID

Niño Jesús, 25
16280 Villarta (Cuenca)
☎: +34 962 189 006 - Fax: +34 962 189 125
info@villavid.com
www.villavid.com

WOMAN SOUL OF VILLAVID 2010 B
70% verdejo, 30% macabeo.

84 Colour: bright straw. Nose: candied fruit, grapey, fresh. Palate: good acidity, sweet, flavourful.

VILLAVID 2008 T
50% tempranillo, 50% syrah.

87 Colour: cherry, garnet rim. Nose: raspberry, candied fruit, spicy, creamy oak. Palate: good acidity, flavourful, fruity, sweetness.

BODEGAS Y VIÑEDOS ALCARREÑOS

Cº Viejo de las Navas s/n
19162 Pioz (Guadalajara)
☎: +34 949 820 812 - Fax: +34 949 310 985
bovial@bovial.es
www.bovial.es

BOVIAL CAMINO BLANCO 2010 B
sauvignon blanc.

85 Colour: bright straw. Nose: fresh, fresh fruit, white flowers. Palate: flavourful, fruity, good acidity, balanced.

BOVIAL CAMINO ROSADO 2009 RD
tempranillo.

84 Colour: rose, purple rim. Nose: floral, red berry notes, ripe fruit. Palate: good acidity, sweetness, flavourful.

BOVIAL MONTE ALCARRIA 2009 T
tempranillo.

87 Colour: bright cherry. Nose: sweet spices, creamy oak, red berry notes, ripe fruit. Palate: flavourful, fruity, toasty.

BODEGAS Y VIÑEDOS CASA DEL VALLE

Ctra. de Yepes - Añover de Tajo, Km. 47,700 - Finca Valdelagua
45313 Yepes (Toledo)
☎: +34 925 155 533 - Fax: +34 925 147 019
casadelvalle@bodegasolarra.es
www.bodegacasadelvalle.es

HACIENDA CASA DEL VALLE CABERNET SAUVIGNON 2007 T
100% cabernet sauvignon.

86 Colour: bright cherry, garnet rim. Nose: grassy, ripe fruit, powerfull. Palate: fleshy, ripe fruit, round tannins.

HACIENDA CASA DEL VALLE SYRAH 2007 T
100% syrah.

86 Colour: bright cherry, garnet rim. Nose: warm, ripe fruit, spicy, fruit preserve. Palate: flavourful, fruity.

FINCA VALDELAGUA 2006 T
40% cabernet sauvignon, 40% syrah, 20% merlot.

88 Colour: cherry, garnet rim. Nose: ripe fruit, complex, spicy, creamy oak, wild herbs, mineral. Palate: balanced, round tannins.

BODEGAS Y VIÑEDOS CASTIBLANQUE

Isaac Peral, 19
13610 Campo de Criptana (Ciudad Real)
☎: +34 926 589 147 - Fax: +34 926 589 148
info@bodegascastiblanque.com
www.bodegascastiblanque.com

BALDOR TRADICIÓN CHARDONNAY 2010 BFB
100% chardonnay.

87 Colour: bright golden. Nose: ripe fruit, tropical fruit, sweet spices, creamy oak. Palate: elegant, powerful, flavourful, fleshy.

BALDOR CHARDONNAY DOWN 2010 B
100% chardonnay.

86 Colour: bright yellow. Nose: ripe fruit, sweet spices, creamy oak, fragrant herbs. Palate: rich, flavourful, fresh, good acidity.

ILEX AIRÉN 2010 B
100% airén.

80 Colour: pale, greenish rim. Nose: grapey, faded flowers, medium intensity. Palate: light-bodied, fresh, thin.

ILEX 2010 RD
100% syrah.

82 Colour: rose, purple rim. Nose: red berry notes, ripe fruit, dried flowers. Palate: fresh, flavourful, balsamic.

ILEX 2010 T
80% syrah, 10% garnacha, tempranillo.

87 Colour: cherry, purple rim. Nose: red berry notes, raspberry, lactic notes, floral, expressive, powerfull. Palate: good acidity, flavourful, fleshy.

ILEX DOWN 2010 T
80% syrah, 10% tempranillo, 10% garnacha.

86 Colour: cherry, purple rim. Nose: fresh fruit, red berry notes, floral. Palate: flavourful, fruity, good acidity.

DOWN CABERNET SAUVIGNON 2009 T
cabernet sauvignon.

89 Colour: cherry, garnet rim. Nose: red berry notes, ripe fruit, scrubland, mineral, new oak. Palate: good acidity, flavourful, fleshy, toasty.

BALDOR OLD VINES 2009 T
100% cabernet sauvignon.

85 Colour: cherry, garnet rim. Nose: red berry notes, dried fruit, expressive, new oak, balsamic herbs. Palate: toasty, flavourful, spicy.

ILEX COUPAGE 2008 T
50% syrah, 30% tempranillo, 10% garnacha, 10% cabernet sauvignon.

87 Colour: cherry, garnet rim. Nose: red berry notes, ripe fruit, sweet spices, toasty. Palate: good acidity, unctuous, flavourful, fleshy.

ILEX COUPAGE DOWN 2008 T
50% syrah, 10% garnacha, 30% tempranillo, 10% cabernet sauvignon.

87 Colour: cherry, garnet rim. Nose: red berry notes, ripe fruit, raspberry, cocoa bean, sweet spices. Palate: good acidity, powerful, flavourful.

BALDOR TRADICIÓN TEMPRANILLO 2007 T
100% tempranillo.

84 Nose: fruit preserve, toasty, spicy, warm. Palate: good acidity, flavourful, fleshy.

BODEGAS Y VIÑEDOS SÁNCHEZ MULITERNO

Tesifonte Gallego, 5
02002 (Albacete)
☎: +34 967 193 222 - Fax: +34 967 193 292
bodegas@sanchez-muliterno.com
www.sanchez-muliterno.com

FINCA LA SABINA 2009 T
70% tempranillo, syrah.

89 Colour: cherry, garnet rim. Nose: ripe fruit, fruit expression, scrubland. Palate: flavourful, fruity, fleshy.

BODEGAS Y VIÑEDOS TAVERA

Ctra. Valmojado - Toledo, Km. 22
45182 Arcicóllar (Toledo)
☎: +34 637 847 777 - Fax: +34 925 590 218
info@bodegastavera.com
www.bodegastavera.com

TAVERA ANTIGUOS VIÑEDOS 2010 RD

84 Colour: brilliant rose. Nose: red berry notes, fruit expression. Palate: flavourful, fruity, fresh.

TAVERA 2010 T MACERACIÓN CARBÓNICA

85 Colour: cherry, purple rim. Nose: red berry notes, ripe fruit, violet drops, fresh. Palate: light-bodied, fresh, fruity, fleshy.

TAVERA ANTIGUOS VIÑEDOS 2008 T
100% garnacha.

84 Colour: cherry, garnet rim. Nose: fruit liqueur notes, medium intensity, fresh. Palate: light-bodied, fresh, flavourful.

TAVERA SYRAH TEMPRANILLO 2008 T
tempranillo, syrah.

83 Colour: cherry, garnet rim. Nose: overripe fruit, balsamic herbs, fresh. Palate: fresh, light-bodied, flavourful.

TAVERA VENDIMIA SELECCIONADA 2007 T
tempranillo, syrah, garnacha.

84 Colour: cherry, garnet rim. Nose: spicy, overripe fruit, expressive. Palate: spicy, flavourful, fleshy.

BODEGAS ZIRIES

Menasalbas, 18
45120 San Pablo de los Montes (Toledo)
☎: +34 679 443 792
flequi@ziries.es
www.lobecasope.com

NAVALEGUA 2010 T BARRICA
garnacha.

87 Colour: cherry, garnet rim. Nose: caramel, candied fruit, raspberry, warm. Palate: fine bitter notes, spicy, balsamic.

ZIRIES 2009 T
garnacha.

89 Colour: cherry, garnet rim. Nose: floral, red berry notes, ripe fruit, earthy notes, creamy oak. Palate: balanced, powerful, flavourful, fleshy.

CAMINO ALTO

Polillo, 4
45860 Villacañas (Toledo)
☎: +34 925 200 878
julioraboso@bodegascaminoalto.com
www.bodegascaminoalto.com

CAMINO ALTO 2010 B
chardonnay, sauvignon blanc.

84 Colour: bright straw. Nose: white flowers, candied fruit, fresh. Palate: good acidity, powerful, flavourful.

CAMINO ALTO SELECCIÓN 2009 T
100% tempranillo.

88 Colour: cherry, garnet rim. Nose: red berry notes, floral, mineral, cocoa bean, creamy oak. Palate: good acidity, round, fruity, powerful, flavourful.

CAMINO ALTO 2009 T ROBLE
100% tempranillo.

86 Colour: bright cherry. Nose: ripe fruit, sweet spices, creamy oak. Palate: flavourful, fruity, toasty.

CASA CARRIL CRUZADO

Casa Carril Cruzado
16236 Villagarcía del Llano (Cuenca)
☎: +34 967 571 154 - Fax: +34 967 571 155
bodega@casacarrilcruzado.com
www.casacarrilcruzado.com

CASA CARRIL CRUZADO CHARDONNAY SAUVIGNON BLANC 2010 B
chardonnay, sauvignon blanc.

82 Colour: golden. Nose: spicy, citrus fruit, ripe fruit, faded flowers. Palate: light-bodied, fresh, flavourful, easy to drink.

CASA CARRIL CRUZADO PETIT VERDOT 2010 RD
petit verdot.

85 Colour: rose, purple rim. Nose: ripe fruit, red berry notes, floral, medium intensity. Palate: fleshy, fruity, fresh.

CASA CARRIL CRUZADO 2010 T
cabernet sauvignon, syrah, tempranillo, merlot, petit verdot.

82 Colour: cherry, garnet rim. Nose: grassy, herbaceous, fruit preserve. Palate: powerful, fleshy, balsamic.

CASA CARRIL CRUZADO 2009 T ROBLE
cabernet sauvignon, syrah, tempranillo, petit verdot.

84 Colour: bright cherry. Nose: ripe fruit, sweet spices, toasty. Palate: flavourful, fruity, toasty, round tannins.

CASA GUALDA

Tapias, 8
16708 Pozoamargo (Cuenca)
☎: +34 969 387 173 - Fax: +34 969 387 202
info@casagualda.com
www.casagualda.com

CASA GUALDA UNICO 2010 B
sauvignon blanc, moscatel.

84 Colour: bright straw. Nose: medium intensity, ripe fruit, citrus fruit, white flowers. Palate: flavourful, fruity, fresh.

CASA GUALDA NATURA 2010 T
tempranillo.

86 Colour: cherry, purple rim. Nose: fruit expression, ripe fruit, fragrant herbs. Palate: ripe fruit, flavourful.

CASA GUALDA SINGULAR 2008 T
syrah, bobal, tempranillo.

86 Colour: cherry, garnet rim. Nose: candied fruit, warm, toasty, spicy. Palate: powerful, flavourful, spicy, ripe fruit.

CASA GUALDA NATURA 2008 T ROBLE
tempranillo.

84 Colour: bright cherry. Nose: candied fruit, scrubland, sweet spices, cocoa bean. Palate: flavourful, powerful, sweetness.

CASA GUALDA PLUS ULTRA 2007 T
bobal, petit verdot.

85 Colour: deep cherry. Nose: dark chocolate, overripe fruit, warm. Palate: flavourful, concentrated, sweetness.

CASALOBOS

Ctra. Porzuna CM-412, Km. 6,5
13196 Picón (Ciudad Real)
☎: +34 926 600 002
bodega@casalobos.es
www.casalobos.es

CASALOBOS 2007 T
40% cabernet sauvignon, 35% syrah, 17% petit verdot, 8% tempranillo.

91 Colour: cherry, garnet rim. Nose: creamy oak, toasty, complex, scrubland, fruit preserve. Palate: powerful, flavourful, toasty, round tannins.

CLUNIA

Camino Torre 1
09410 Coruña del Conde (Burgos)
☎: +34 607 185 951 - Fax: +34 948 818 574
pavez@principedeviana.com

CLUNIA SYRAH 2009 T
100% syrah.

92 Colour: cherry, purple rim. Nose: red berry notes, raspberry, floral, sweet spices, creamy oak. Palate: good acidity, round, unctuous, flavourful, fruity, fleshy, complex.

CLUNIA TEMPRANILLO 2009 T
100% tempranillo.

90 Colour: cherry, garnet rim. Nose: red berry notes, expressive, mineral, spicy, toasty. Palate: good acidity, elegant, creamy, spicy, flavourful.

COOPERATIVA PURÍSIMA CONCEPCIÓN

Ctra. Minaya - San Clemente, Km. 10
16610 Casas de Fernando Alonso (Cuenca)
☎: +34 969 383 043 - Fax: +34 969 383 153
info@vinoteatinos.com
www.vinoteatino.com

AIRAZ VIURA 2010 B
100% viura.

82 Colour: bright yellow. Nose: ripe fruit, floral, medium intensity. Palate: green, light-bodied, fresh.

GARNACHA AIRAZ 2010 RD
100% garnacha.

84 Colour: raspberry rose. Nose: lactic notes, floral, candied fruit. Palate: sweet, fruity, flavourful.

AIRAZ COLECCIÓN 2010 T
100% tempranillo.

89 Colour: cherry, purple rim. Nose: expressive, balanced, red berry notes, fresh fruit. Palate: powerful, flavourful, fleshy, fruity, fresh, unctuous.

COOPERATIVA UNIÓN CAMPESINA INIESTENSE

San Idefonso, 1
16235 Iniesta (Cuenca)
☎: +34 967 490 120 - Fax: +34 967 490 777
comercial@cooperativauci.com
www.cooperativauci.com

SEÑORÍO DE INIESTA SAUVIGNON BLANC 2010 B
100% sauvignon blanc.

83 Colour: bright straw. Nose: white flowers, fragrant herbs, tropical fruit. Palate: good acidity, fresh, flavourful.

SEÑORÍO DE INIESTA BOBAL 2010 RD
100% bobal.

87 Colour: rose, purple rim. Nose: raspberry, red berry notes, fresh, expressive. Palate: fleshy, powerful, flavourful, fresh, fruity.

SEÑORÍO DE INIESTA TEMPRANILLO 2010 T
100% tempranillo.

84 Colour: cherry, purple rim. Nose: red berry notes, fruit liqueur notes, floral, balsamic herbs. Palate: powerful, flavourful, fruity, great length.

SEÑORÍO DE INIESTA CABERNET SAUVIGNON 2010 T
100% cabernet sauvignon.

82 Colour: cherry, purple rim. Nose: dried flowers, grassy, ripe fruit. Palate: flavourful, fruity, balsamic.

COSECHEROS Y CRIADORES

Diputación, s/n
01320 Oyón (Álava)
☎: +34 945 601 944 - Fax: +34 945 601 412
nacional@cosecherosycriadores.com
www.familiamartinezbujanda.com

INFINITUS GEWÜRZTRAMINER 2010 B
gewürztraminer.

89 Colour: bright straw. Nose: white flowers, fresh fruit, fragrant herbs, fresh. Palate: fresh, fruity, light-bodied, flavourful.

INFINITUS ORGÁNICO 2010 B
airén, viura.

84 Colour: bright straw. Nose: tropical fruit, grassy, medium intensity. Palate: light-bodied, fresh, fruity.

INFINITUS VIURA CHARDONNAY 2010 B
viura, chardonnay.

82 Colour: bright straw. Nose: ripe fruit, citrus fruit, fragrant herbs. Palate: light-bodied, easy to drink, thin.

INFINITUS TEMPRANILLO CABERNET FRANC 2010 RD
cabernet franc, tempranillo.

86 Colour: rose, purple rim. Nose: lactic notes, floral, red berry notes, raspberry. Palate: light-bodied, good acidity, fruity.

INFINITUS MALBEC 2010 T
malbec.

88 Colour: cherry, purple rim. Nose: expressive, red berry notes, ripe fruit, balsamic herbs. Palate: fresh, fruity, fleshy, flavourful.

INFINITUS ORGÁNICO 2010 T
tempranillo, merlot, syrah.

88 Colour: cherry, purple rim. Nose: red berry notes, ripe fruit, floral, fresh, expressive. Palate: fruity, powerful, flavourful, balsamic.

INFINITUS MERLOT 2010 T
merlot.

87 Colour: cherry, purple rim. Nose: fresh, red berry notes, ripe fruit, floral. Palate: fresh, fruity, light-bodied, flavourful.

INFINITUS SYRAH 2010 T
syrah.

87 Colour: cherry, purple rim. Nose: red berry notes, raspberry, floral, fresh. Palate: balanced, fruity, flavourful, fleshy.

INFINITUS TEMPRANILLO 2010 T
tempranillo.

87 Color cherry, purple rim. Aroma expressive, fresh fruit, red berry notes, floral. Taste flavourful, fruity, good acidity, round tannins.

INFINITUS CABERNET SAUVIGNON 2010 T
cabernet sauvignon.

86 Colour: cherry, purple rim. Nose: ripe fruit, balsamic herbs, balanced. Palate: good acidity, flavourful, balsamic, fruity.

INFINITUS TEMPRANILLO CABERNET SAUVIGNON 2009 T
cabernet sauvignon, tempranillo.

86 Colour: bright cherry, garnet rim. Nose: ripe fruit, creamy oak, cocoa bean, spicy. Palate: fruity, spicy.

DEHESA DE LOS LLANOS

Ctra. Peñas de San Pedro, Km. 5,5
02006 Albacete (Albacete)
☎: +34 967 243 100 - Fax: +34 967 243 093
info@dehesadelosllanos.es
www.dehesadelosllanos.com

MAZACRUZ CIMA 2010 B
verdejo.

89 Colour: bright golden. Nose: white flowers, citrus fruit, ripe fruit, fragrant herbs. Palate: rich, flavourful, fleshy.

MAZACRUZ 2010 B
sauvignon blanc, verdejo.

87 Colour: bright straw. Nose: fresh, white flowers, expressive, tropical fruit. Palate: fruity, good acidity, easy to drink.

MAZACRUZ 2009 T
syrah, graciano, tempranillo, petit verdot.

86 Colour: cherry, purple rim. Nose: red berry notes, ripe fruit, aromatic coffee, toasty. Palate: good acidity, powerful, flavourful, fleshy.

MAZACRUZ CIMA 2008 TC
cabernet sauvignon, syrah, merlot, petit verdot.

90 Colour: cherry, garnet rim. Nose: red berry notes, ripe fruit, spicy, earthy notes, creamy oak. Palate: good acidity, powerful, flavourful, fleshy.

DEHESA Y VIÑEDOS DE NAVAMARÍN

Ctra. Comarcal 313, Km. 1
02160 Lezuza (Albacete)
☎: +34 967 376 005 - Fax: +34 967 376 003
pedrojnavarro@aldonzavinos.com
www.aldonzavinos.com

ALDONZA ALBO 2010 B
79% sauvignon blanc, 21% macabeo.

87 Colour: bright straw. Nose: white flowers, citrus fruit, fragrant herbs. Palate: balanced, fruity, fresh, flavourful.

ALDONZA NAVAMARÍN 2006 T
cabernet sauvignon, merlot, syrah, tempranillo.

85 Colour: cherry, garnet rim. Nose: ripe fruit, balsamic herbs, cocoa bean, spicy. Palate: fleshy, spicy, round tannins.

ALDONZA SELECCIÓN 2006 TR
cabernet sauvignon, tempranillo, merlot, syrah.

84 Colour: dark-red cherry, orangey edge. Nose: ripe fruit, warm, balsamic herbs, old leather. Palate: good acidity, flavourful, fleshy, toasty.

ALDONZA PISCES 2006 T
tempranillo, syrah, cabernet sauvignon, merlot.

82 Colour: bright cherry, orangey edge. Nose: fruit preserve, spicy, toasty, old leather. Palate: flavourful, thin, toasty.

DIONISOS

Unión, 82
13300 Valdepeñas (Ciudad Real)
☎: +34 926 313 248 - Fax: +34 926 322 813
info@labodegadelasestrellas.com
www.labodegadelasestrellas.com

PAGOS DEL CONUCO 2006 T
100% tempranillo.

87 Colour: cherry, garnet rim. Nose: ripe fruit, spicy, creamy oak, warm. Palate: long, round, flavourful, round tannins.

VINUM VITAE 2005 TC
100% tempranillo.

90 Colour: cherry, garnet rim. Nose: ripe fruit, cocoa bean, aromatic coffee, dark chocolate, toasty, sweet spices. Palate: powerful, flavourful, fleshy, toasty, spicy.

EGO PRIMUS 2003 TC
70% tempranillo, 15% cabernet sauvignon, 15% syrah.

86 Colour: ruby red, orangey edge. Nose: ripe fruit, warm, spicy, toasty. Palate: flavourful, fleshy, round tannins.<

DOMINIO DE EGUREN

San Pedro, s/n
01309 Páganos (Álava)
☎: +34 945 600 117 - Fax: +34 945 600 554
info@eguren.com
www.eguren.com

CÓDICE 2009 T
100% tempranillo.

90 Colour: bright cherry. Nose: ripe fruit, sweet spices, creamy oak, powerfull, earthy notes. Palate: flavourful, fruity, toasty, round tannins.

DOMINIO DE PUNCTUM

Ctra. N-301, Km. 162
16660 Las Pedroñeras (Cuenca)
☎: +34 912 959 998 - Fax: +34 912 959 997
comercial@dominiodepunctum.com
www.dominiodepunctum.com

LOBETIA CHARDONNAY 2010 B
100% chardonnay.

87 Colour: bright straw. Nose: floral, citrus fruit, fragrant herbs. Palate: fruity, powerful, flavourful, fleshy.

PUNCTUM VIOGNIER 2010 B
viognier.

86 Colour: bright straw. Nose: expressive, dried flowers, tropical fruit. Palate: flavourful, fruity, good acidity, balanced.

PUNCTUM SAUVIGNON BLANC 2010 B
sauvignon blanc.

83 Colour: bright yellow. Nose: faded flowers, dried herbs, ripe fruit. Palate: rich, flavourful, fleshy.

LOBETIA TEMPRANILLO 2010 T
tempranillo.

87 Colour: cherry, purple rim. Nose: red berry notes, ripe fruit, mineral, spicy. Palate: powerful, rich, fruity, flavourful, fleshy.

PUNCTUM TEMPRANILLO PETIT VERDOT 2010 T
tempranillo, petit verdot.

86 Colour: cherry, purple rim. Nose: red berry notes, floral, medium intensity. Palate: flavourful, fruity, good acidity, round tannins.

PUNCTUM TEMPRANILLO PETIT VERDOT 2010 T ROBLE
tempranillo, petit verdot.

86 Colour: cherry, purple rim. Nose: red berry notes, ripe fruit, balsamic herbs, creamy oak. Palate: fleshy, flavourful, good acidity.

PUNCTUM SYRAH 2010 T
syrah.

86 Colour: cherry, purple rim. Nose: red berry notes, raspberry, floral, expressive. Palate: warm, powerful, flavourful, fruity.

PUNCTUM CABERNET SAUVIGNON GRACIANO 2010 T ROBLE
cabernet sauvignon, graciano.

84 Colour: bright cherry. Nose: ripe fruit, creamy oak, grassy, spicy. Palate: flavourful, toasty, green.

PUNCTUM CABERNET SAUVIGNON MERLOT 2010 T
cabernet sauvignon, merlot.

80 Colour: cherry, purple rim. Nose: fruit preserve, boiled fruit notes, grassy. Palate: spicy, flavourful, fleshy.

EL PROGRESO SOCIEDAD COOP. CLM

Avda. de la Virgen, 89
13670 Villarubia de los Ojos (Ciudad Real)
☎: +34 926 896 088 - Fax: +34 926 896 135
elprogreso@cooprogres.com
www.bodegaselprogreso.com

MI CHUPITO 2010 B
100% airén.

80 Colour: bright straw. Nose: grassy, fresh. Palate: easy to drink, lacks expression.

ENCOMIENDA DE CERVERA

Finca Encomienda de Cervera
13270 Almagro (Ciudad Real)
☎: +34 926 102 099 - Fax: +34 926 106 098
info@ecervera.com
www.encomiendadecervera.com

POKER DE TEMPRANILLOS 2009 TC
tempranillo.

89 Colour: cherry, garnet rim. Nose: red berry notes, ripe fruit, sweet spices, cocoa bean, dark chocolate. Palate: good acidity, flavourful, fleshy, toasty.

VULCANUS TEMPRANILLO 2009 TC
tempranillo.

86 Colour: cherry, garnet rim. Nose: floral, warm, ripe fruit, spicy, creamy oak. Palate: good acidity, flavourful, fleshy.

1758 SELECCIÓN 2009 TC
petit verdot.

84 Colour: cherry, garnet rim. Nose: floral, red berry notes, ripe fruit, balsamic herbs. Palate: powerful, flavourful, fleshy, rich.

...De una tierra viva, de origen volcánico, nace un vino único...
...From vivid volcanic lands, arises a unique wine...

VINO DE LA TIERRA DE CASTILLA
BODEGAS ENCOMIENDA DE CERVERA

MAAR DE CERVERA SYRAH 2008 TC
syrah.

86 Colour: cherry, garnet rim. Nose: floral, red berry notes, ripe fruit, expressive. Palate: good acidity, fruity, flavourful, fleshy.

FÉLIX SOLÍS

Autovía del Sur, Km. 199
13300 Valdepeñas (Ciudad Real)
☎: +34 926 322 400 - Fax: +34 926 322 417
fsa@felixsolisavantis.com
www.felixsolisavantis.com

CONSIGNA CHARDONNAY 2010 B
chardonnay.

86 Colour: bright straw. Nose: white flowers, fresh fruit, fragrant herbs. Palate: fruity, flavourful, fresh, fleshy.

ORQUESTRA CHARDONNAY 2010 B
chardonnay.

83 Colour: bright straw. Nose: ripe fruit, citrus fruit, fragrant herbs. Palate: correct, easy to drink, lacks expression.

CONSIGNA TEMPRANILLO 2010 RD
tempranillo.

83 Colour: rose, purple rim. Nose: fresh, red berry notes, floral. Palate: fruity, fresh, lacks expression.

ORQUESTA TEMPRANILLO 2010 T
tempranillo.

87 Colour: cherry, purple rim. Nose: red berry notes, fresh, expressive. Palate: flavourful, fleshy, fruity, good acidity.

CONSIGNA TEMPRANILLO 2010 T
tempranillo.

86 Colour: cherry, purple rim. Nose: red berry notes, fresh, medium intensity. Palate: good acidity, unctuous, light-bodied, fresh.

CONSIGNA MERLOT 2010 T
merlot.

86 Colour: cherry, purple rim. Nose: red berry notes, scrubland, expressive. Palate: fruity, flavourful, easy to drink.

ORQUESTRA MERLOT 2010 T
merlot.

85 Colour: cherry, purple rim. Nose: ripe fruit, fresh, balsamic herbs. Palate: good acidity, fruity, thin.

CONSIGNA SHIRAZ 2010 T
syrah.

84 Colour: cherry, purple rim. Nose: floral, fresh fruit, expressive. Palate: correct, fresh, thin.

CONSIGNA CABERNET SAUVIGNON 2010 T
cabernet sauvignon.

84 Colour: cherry, purple rim. Nose: red berry notes, fresh fruit, fragrant herbs. Palate: good acidity, fruity, flavourful.

ORQUESTRA CABERNET SAUVIGNON 2010 T
cabernet sauvignon.

82 Colour: cherry, purple rim. Nose: ripe fruit, warm, medium intensity. Palate: good acidity, light-bodied, thin.

FINCA CASA ALARCÓN

Ctra. Montealegre, km 4,5
02660 Caudete (Albacete)
☎: +34 965 828 266 - Fax: +34 965 825 717
beatriz.andres@anara.es
www.casalarcon.com

CASA ALARCÓN VIOGNIER 2010 B
viognier.

86 Colour: bright straw. Nose: citrus fruit, white flowers, medium intensity. Palate: fresh, light-bodied, flavourful.

CASA ALARCÓN 2010 RD
petit verdot, syrah.

84 Colour: rose, purple rim. Nose: fresh fruit, red berry notes, floral, medium intensity. Palate: light-bodied, fresh, easy to drink.

DON JAIME DE CASA ALARCÓN 2009 T
70% tempranillo, 20% cabernet sauvignon, 10% syrah.

89 Colour: cherry, garnet rim. Nose: ripe fruit, warm, earthy notes, spicy, creamy oak. Palate: light-bodied, flavourful, fleshy, long.

BLAU 2008 T
60% monastrell, 40% merlot.

87 Colour: cherry, garnet rim. Nose: ripe fruit, cocoa bean, dark chocolate, toasty, balsamic herbs. Palate: great length, flavourful, fleshy.

TRIA ROBLE AMERICANO 2008 T
90% syrah, 5% merlot, 5% petit verdot.

86 Colour: cherry, garnet rim. Nose: ripe fruit, spicy, aromatic coffee, toasty. Palate: flavourful, fleshy, creamy.

NEA 2008 T
petit verdot.

85 Colour: cherry, garnet rim. Nose: ripe fruit, balsamic herbs, spicy, creamy oak. Palate: flavourful, fleshy, good acidity, toasty.

TRÍA ROBLE FRANCÉS 2007 T
90% syrah, 5% merlot, 5% petit verdot.

87 Colour: cherry, garnet rim. Nose: ripe fruit, aromatic coffee, spicy, creamy oak. Palate: long, good acidity, fleshy, flavourful.

FINCA CONSTANCIA

Camino del Bravo, s/n
45543 Otero (Toledo)
☎: +34 914 903 700 - Fax: +34 916 612 124
lslara@gonzalezbyass.es
www.gonzalezbyass.es

FINCA CONSTANCIA TEMPRANILLO P23 2009 T
tempranillo.

90 Colour: cherry, purple rim. Nose: fresh fruit, red berry notes, floral, expressive. Palate: complex, fruity, flavourful, fleshy.

FINCA CONSTANCIA 2009 T
syrah, cabernet sauvignon, petit verdot, tempranillo, graciano, cabernet franc.

88 Colour: cherry, purple rim. Nose: red berry notes, fresh, expressive. Palate: round tannins, fruity, flavourful.

FINCA CORONADO

Sevilla, s/n
13440 Argamasilla de Calatrava (Ciudad Real)
☎: +34 618 614 888
info@fincacoronado.com
www.fincacoronado.com

FINCA CORONADO 2007 T
30% tempranillo, 30% cabernet sauvignon, 20% syrah, 10% petit verdot, 5% merlot, 5% graciano.

87 Colour: cherry, garnet rim. Nose: fruit preserve, warm, sweet spices, toasty. Palate: powerful, flavourful, fleshy, complex, balanced.

FINCA EL REFUGIO BODEGAS Y VIÑEDOS

Romeral, 1A
28250 Torrelodones (Madrid)
☎: +34 629 512 478
info@fincaelrefugio.es
www.fincaelrefugio.es

LEGADO FINCA EL REFUGIO VERDEJO 2010 B
100% verdejo.

85 Colour: bright straw. Nose: floral, tropical fruit, citrus fruit, fresh. Palate: fruity, flavourful, fleshy.

LEGADO FINCA EL REFUGIO 3 MESES 2010 T ROBLE
100% tempranillo.

87 Colour: bright cherry. Nose: sweet spices, creamy oak, red berry notes. Palate: flavourful, fruity, toasty, easy to drink.

LEGADO FINCA EL REFUGIO 15 MESES 2009 T ROBLE
100% petit verdot.

86 Colour: cherry, garnet rim. Nose: ripe fruit, spicy, creamy oak, toasty. Palate: powerful, flavourful, toasty, round tannins.

LEGADO FINCA EL REFUGIO 14 MESES 2007 T ROBLE
60% cabernet sauvignon, 40% merlot.

85 Colour: cherry, garnet rim. Nose: red berry notes, ripe fruit, grassy, sweet spices, toasty. Palate: green, flavourful, fleshy.

FINCA LA ESTACADA

Ctra. N-400, Km. 103
16400 Tarancón (Cuenca)
☎: +34 969 327 099 - Fax: +34 969 327 199
enologia@fincalaestacada.com
www.fincalaestacada.com

SECUA DULCE 2010 B
chardonnay.

83 Colour: yellow. Nose: candied fruit, warm, fruit liqueur notes, citrus fruit. Palate: flavourful, fleshy, sweetness, good acidity.

FINCA LA ESTACADA 2010 RD
tempranillo.

85 Colour: raspberry rose. Nose: powerfull, ripe fruit, red berry notes, expressive. Palate: fleshy, powerful, fruity, fresh, sweet.

SECUA CABERNET-SYRAH 2008 T
cabernet sauvignon, syrah.

90 Colour: cherry, garnet rim. Nose: red berry notes, ripe fruit, floral, scrubland, earthy notes, sweet spices, toasty. Palate: good acidity, powerful, flavourful, fleshy, toasty.

FINCA LA ESTACADA 12 MESES BARRICA 2008 T BARRICA
tempranillo, cabernet sauvignon, syrah, merlot.

86 Colour: cherry, garnet rim. Nose: fruit preserve, spicy, toasty, dark chocolate, fine reductive notes. Palate: flavourful, spicy, fine bitter notes.

FINCA LA ESTACADA 18 MESES BARRICA 2007 T
tempranillo, cabernet sauvignon, syrah, merlot.

90 Colour: ruby red, orangey edge. Nose: red berry notes, ripe fruit, balsamic herbs, scrubland, sweet spices, cocoa bean. Palate: powerful, flavourful, complex, fleshy, round.

SECUA CABERNET-SYRAH 2006 T
80% cabernet sauvignon, 20% syrah.

91 Colour: bright cherry, garnet rim. Nose: mineral, complex, ripe fruit, cocoa bean. Palate: flavourful, light-bodied, easy to drink, fine bitter notes, fine tannins.

FINCA LA ESTACADA SELECCIÓN VARIETALES 2006 T BARRICA
tempranillo, cabernet sauvignon, merlot, syrah.

89 Colour: cherry, garnet rim. Nose: powerfull, smoky, roasted coffee, ripe fruit, earthy notes. Palate: flavourful, fleshy, powerful.

FINCA LA VALONA VIÑEDOS Y BODEGAS

D. Victoriano González, 39
16220 Quintanar del Rey (Cuenca)
☎: +34 967 496 600 - Fax: +34 967 495 495
info@fincalavalona.com
www.fincalavalona.com

LA VALONA 2010 B
verdejo, sauvignon blanc, viognier, viura.

85 Colour: bright straw. Nose: fine lees, citrus fruit, ripe fruit, warm. Palate: powerful, flavourful, rich, fleshy.

LA VALONA SELECCIÓN 2007 T
100% tempranillo.

91 Colour: cherry, garnet rim. Nose: red berry notes, ripe fruit, mineral, cocoa bean, dark chocolate, sweet spices. Palate: good acidity, round, powerful, flavourful.

LA VALONA 4 MESES EN BARRICA 2007 T
100% tempranillo.

88 Colour: cherry, garnet rim. Nose: ripe fruit, fine reductive notes, spicy, creamy oak. Palate: good acidity, flavourful, round tannins.

LA VALONA 12 MESES EN BARRICA 2007 T
100% tempranillo.

88 Colour: cherry, garnet rim. Nose: red berry notes, ripe fruit, spicy, toasty. Palate: long, rich, flavourful, fleshy, mineral.

FINCA LORANQUE

Finca Loranque, s/n
45593 Bargas (Toledo)
☎: +34 669 476 849 - Fax: +34 925 512 450
fincaloranque@fincaloranque.com
www.fincaloranque.com

LACRUZ FINCA LORANQUE TEMPRANILLO SYRAH 2009 T
tempranillo.

86 Colour: cherry, purple rim. Nose: red berry notes, fruit expression, sweet spices, creamy oak. Palate: flavourful, fleshy, round tannins.

LORANQUE EL GRANDE 2007 T
100% syrah.

88 Colour: cherry, purple rim. Nose: fruit preserve, powerfull, spicy, cocoa bean, toasty. Palate: rich, full, flavourful, mineral, balanced.

LACRUZ DE FINCA LORANQUE SYRAH 2006 T
100% syrah.

86 Colour: cherry, garnet rim. Nose: ripe fruit, spicy, creamy oak. Palate: flavourful, toasty, round tannins.

LACRUZ DE FINCA LORANQUE CABERNET SAUVIGNON 2006 T
cabernet sauvignon.

86 Color cherry, garnet rim. Aroma ripe fruit, spicy, creamy oak, toasty, complex. Taste powerful, flavourful, toasty, round tannins.

FINCA LORANQUE SYRAH-TEMPRANILLO 2006 T
50% syrah, 50% tempranillo.

84 Colour: cherry, garnet rim. Nose: ripe fruit, warm, waxy notes, old leather. Palate: powerful, flavourful, fleshy.

FINCA LOS ALIJARES BODEGA Y VIÑEDOS

Avda. de la Paz, 5
45180 Camarena (Toledo)
☎: +34 918 174 364 - Fax: +34 918 174 364
gerencia@fincalosalijares.com
www.fincalosalijares.com

FINCA LOS ALIJARES VIOGNIER 2010 B
100% viognier.

85 Colour: bright straw. Nose: fragrant herbs, white flowers, citrus fruit. Palate: good acidity, fruity, fresh, flavourful.

FINCA LOS ALIJARES GRACIANO 2009 TC
100% graciano.

87 Colour: dark-red cherry. Nose: ripe fruit, powerfull, creamy oak, spicy, balsamic herbs. Palate: flavourful, fruity, round tannins.

FINCA LOS ALIJARES PETIT VERDOT SYRAH 2009 TC
50% petit verdot, 50% syrah.

87 Colour: dark-red cherry. Nose: powerfull, overripe fruit, toasty, dark chocolate, creamy oak. Palate: flavourful, round tannins, good acidity, fruity.

FINCA LOS ALIJARES OLD VINEYARS GARNACHA 2009 T
100% garnacha.

87 Colour: light cherry. Nose: ripe fruit, spicy, creamy oak, fruit expression. Palate: good acidity, spicy, fruity, round tannins.

FINCA LOS ALIJARES SYRAH 2009 T
syrah.

85 Colour: dark-red cherry. Nose: overripe fruit, toasty, spicy. Palate: fruity, flavourful.

FINCA LOS ALIJARES 2007
merlot, syrah, graciano.

85 Colour: cherry, garnet rim. Nose: fruit preserve, toasty, spicy. Palate: fruity, flavourful, smoky aftertaste, harsh oak tannins.

FONTANA

Extramuros, s/n
16411 Fuente de Pedro Naharro (Cuenca)
☎: +34 969 125 433 - Fax: +34 969 125 387
gemag@bodegasfontana.com
www.bodegasfontana.com

GRAN FONTAL VENDIMIA SELECCIONADA 2007 TR
100% tempranillo.

89 Colour: bright cherry. Nose: ripe fruit, sweet spices, creamy oak, expressive. Palate: flavourful, fruity, toasty, round tannins, aged character.

QUERCUS 2006 T
100% tempranillo.

92 Colour: cherry, garnet rim. Nose: mineral, ripe fruit, sweet spices, cocoa bean, complex. Palate: powerful, flavourful, complex, fleshy, round tannins.

DUETO DE FONTANA 2004 T
50% cabernet sauvignon, 50% merlot.

90 Colour: pale ruby, brick rim edge. Nose: elegant, spicy, fine reductive notes, aged wood nuances. Palate: spicy, fine tannins, elegant, long, flavourful, fleshy.

MONT REAGA

Ctra. N-420, Km. 333,2 Apdo. Correos 6
16649 Monreal del Llano (Cuenca)
☎: +34 645 769 801 - Fax: +34 967 182 518
mont-reaga@mont-reaga.com
www.mont-reaga.com

BLANCO DE MONTREAGA 2008 BFB
100% sauvignon blanc.

88 Colour: bright yellow. Nose: ripe fruit, dried flowers, sweet spices, creamy oak. Palate: good acidity, rich, powerful, flavourful.

ISOLA DE MONTREAGA 2010 RD
merlot.

82 Colour: rose, purple rim. Nose: ripe fruit, slightly evolved, short. Palate: green, ripe fruit.

ISOLA DE MONTREAGA 2010 T
50% syrah, 50% tempranillo.

84 Colour: cherry, purple rim. Nose: red berry notes, ripe fruit, balsamic herbs. Palate: flavourful, fruity, good acidity.

TEMPO DE MONTREAGA 2008 T
50% cabernet sauvignon, 50% merlot.

85 Colour: cherry, garnet rim. Nose: red berry notes, ripe fruit, spicy, creamy oak. Palate: good acidity, flavourful, spicy.

LA ESENCIA DE MONTREAGA 2006 T
100% syrah.

89 Colour: cherry, garnet rim. Nose: red berry notes, violet drops, ripe fruit, cocoa bean, toasty. Palate: powerful, flavourful, good structure, complex.

TEMPO DE MONTREAGA LA ESPERA 2005 T
70% cabernet sauvignon, 30% merlot.

85 Colour: cherry, garnet rim. Nose: red berry notes, boiled fruit notes, balsamic herbs, creamy oak. Palate: powerful, flavourful, warm.

MONTREAGA CLÁSICO 2004 T
100% syrah.

89 Colour: cherry, garnet rim. Nose: ripe fruit, dark chocolate, cocoa bean, sweet spices, toasty. Palate: rich, balanced, flavourful, fleshy, complex.

LAS LIRAS 2004 T
cabernet sauvignon.

87 Colour: cherry, garnet rim. Nose: ripe fruit, fruit preserve, powerfull, warm, wild herbs, toasty. Palate: good acidity, flavourful, fleshy.

FATA MORGANA 2006 TINTO DULCE
100% merlot.

89 Colour: pale ruby, brick rim edge. Nose: ripe fruit, dried fruit, cocoa bean, dark chocolate, sweet spices. Palate: good acidity, unctuous, powerful, flavourful, fruity.

ORGANIC SIGNATURE WINES

Extramuros, s/n
02260 Fuentealbilla (Albacete)
☎: +34 967 472 503 - Fax: +34 967 472 516
info@organicsignaturewines.es
www.organicsignaturewines.es

FRANCHETE ECOLÓGICO ASSEMBLAGE 2010 T
cabernet sauvignon, bobal, tempranillo, garnacha.

84 Colour: cherry, garnet rim. Nose: overripe fruit, herbaceous, warm. Palate: light-bodied, fresh, short.

FRANCHETE SYRAH PETIT VERDOT ECOLÓGICO 2010 T JOVEN
syrah, petit verdot.

82 Colour: cherry, purple rim. Nose: red berry notes, ripe fruit, fresh, medium intensity. Palate: light-bodied, fresh, flavourful, slightly acidic.

FRANCHETE CABERNET SAUVIGNON ECOLÓGICO 2010 T JOVEN
100% cabernet sauvignon.

80 Colour: cherry, purple rim. Nose: overripe fruit, balsamic herbs, short. Palate: light-bodied, fresh, ripe fruit, green.

FRANCHETE TINTO 2005 T BARRICA

82 Colour: cherry, garnet rim. Nose: fruit liqueur notes, herbaceous, slightly evolved. Palate: lacks balance, short, stalky, dry wood.

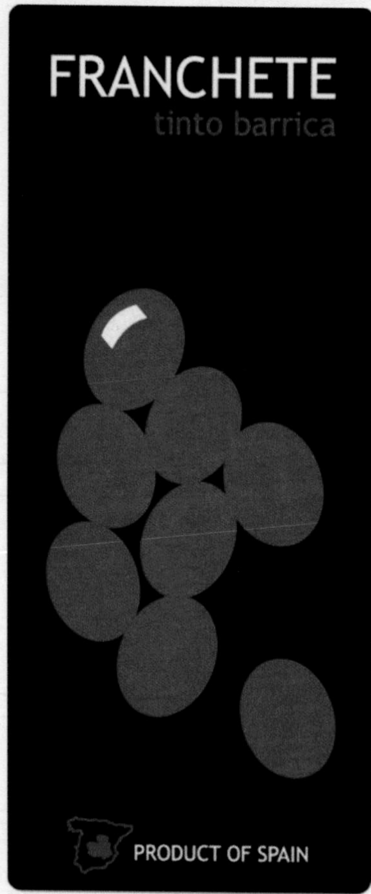

FINCA LASTONAR T BARRICA

80 Colour: cherry, garnet rim. Nose: ripe fruit, warm, short. Palate: slightly acidic, light-bodied, short.

FRANCHETE CABERNET SAUVIGNON ECOLÓGICO 2007 TC
100% cabernet sauvignon.

80 Colour: cherry, garnet rim. Nose: fruit preserve, wet leather, premature reduction notes. Palate: light-bodied, balsamic, thin.

OSBORNE MALPICA DE TAJO

Ctra. Malpica - Pueblanueva, km 6
45692 Malpica de Tajo (Toledo)
☎: +34 925 860 990 - Fax: +34 925 860 905
comunicacion@osborne.es
www.osborne.es

SOLAZ SHIRAZ-TEMPRANILLO 2008 T
50% syrah, 50% tempranillo.

86 Colour: cherry, garnet rim. Nose: red berry notes, expressive, creamy oak. Palate: easy to drink, flavourful, spicy.

SOLAZ MERLOT 2008 T
65% merlot, 35% tempranillo.

86 Colour: cherry, garnet rim. Nose: red berry notes, fresh, creamy oak. Palate: correct, fresh, light-bodied, easy to drink.

SOLAZ CABERNET SELECCIÓN FAMILIAR 2008 T
80% cabernet sauvignon, 20% syrah.

86 Colour: cherry, purple rim. Nose: red berry notes, sweet spices, expressive. Palate: creamy, ripe fruit, flavourful.

SOLAZ TEMPRANILLO-CABERNET SAUVIGNON 2008 T
tempranillo.

83 Colour: cherry, garnet rim. Nose: medium intensity, ripe fruit, wild herbs, fresh. Palate: green, light-bodied, unctuous.

DOMINIO DE MALPICA VENDIMIA SELECCIONADA T
cabernet sauvignon.

87 Colour: ruby red, orangey edge. Nose: fresh fruit, balsamic herbs, expressive. Palate: correct, fresh, fruity.

PAGO DE GUZQUE

Marqués de Molins, 7- 7º
02001 (Albacete)
☎: +34 967 219 076 - Fax: +34 967 214 709
info@pagodeguzque.com
www.pagodeguzque.com

GRACIANO DE GUZQUE 2008 T
graciano.

88 Colour: cherry, garnet rim. Nose: ripe fruit, spicy, toasty, scrubland. Palate: warm, flavourful, fleshy.

EL PASO DE GUZQUE 2007 T
tempranillo, graciano.

86 Colour: cherry, garnet rim. Nose: fruit preserve, old leather, spicy, toasty. Palate: good acidity, flavourful, toasty.

PAGO DE MONTAL

Paraje Mainetes
02651 Fuenteálamo (Albacete)
☎: +34 938 743 511 - Fax: +34 938 737 204
info@pagodemontal.com
www.pagodemontal.com

MONTAL MACABEO AIRÉN 2010 B
70% macabeo, 30% airén.

84 Colour: bright straw. Nose: ripe fruit, citrus fruit, white flowers. Palate: flavourful, fruity, sweetness.

MONTAL MONASTRELL-SYRAH 2010 T
85% monastrell, 15% syrah.

88 Colour: cherry, purple rim. Nose: powerfull, varietal, red berry notes, sweet spices, creamy oak. Palate: rich, flavourful, fruity.

MONTAL GARNACHA 2008 T
100% garnacha.

87 Colour: cherry, garnet rim. Nose: ripe fruit, mineral, balsamic herbs, toasty. Palate: powerful, good acidity, spicy, flavourful.

PAGO DE VALLEGARCÍA

Claudio Coello, 35 Bajo C
28001 Madrid (Madrid)
☎: +34 925 421 407 - Fax: +34 925 421 822
comercial@vallegarcia.com
www.vallegarcia.com

VALLEGARCÍA VIOGNIER 2009 BFB
100% viognier.

94 Colour: bright yellow. Nose: medium intensity, ripe fruit, spicy, smoky, fragrant herbs, mineral. Palate: rich, fruity, spicy, ripe fruit, fleshy, complex.

VALLEGARCÍA SYRAH 2008 T
100% syrah.

92 Colour: black cherry. Nose: expressive, balanced, ripe fruit, sweet spices, creamy oak, cocoa bean. Palate: fruity, flavourful, complex, fine tannins, spicy.

HIPPERIA 2007 T
47% cabernet sauvignon, 47% merlot, 5% petit verdot, 1% cabernet franc.

91 Colour: cherry, garnet rim. Nose: red berry notes, ripe fruit, mineral, cocoa bean, scrubland. Palate: powerful, flavourful, fleshy, long, round tannins.

PAGO DEL VICARIO

Ctra. Ciudad Real - Porzuna, (CM-412) Km. 16
13196 Ciudad Real (Ciudad Real)
☎: +34 926 666 027 - Fax: +34 670 099 520
info@pagodelvicario.com
www.pagodelvicario.com

PAGO DEL VICARIO BLANCO DE TEMPRANILLO 2010 B
tempranillo.

87 Colour: bright straw. Nose: wild herbs, dried herbs, fresh fruit, citrus fruit. Palate: flavourful, correct.

TALVA 2007 BFB
chardonnay, sauvignon blanc.

85 Colour: yellow. Nose: ripe fruit, toasty, spicy. Palate: ripe fruit, spicy, good finish, easy to drink.

PAGO DEL VICARIO CORTE DULCE 2007 B
50% chardonnay, 50% sauvignon blanc.

80 Colour: bright golden. Nose: candied fruit, slightly evolved, sweet spices. Palate: fruity, easy to drink.

PAGO DEL VICARIO PETIT VERDOT 2010 RD
petit verdot.

86 Colour: light cherry, bright. Nose: balanced, red berry notes, ripe fruit, citrus fruit. Palate: fleshy, flavourful, great length.

PAGO DEL VICARIO MERLOT DULCE 2008 T
merlot.

85 Colour: bright cherry, garnet rim. Nose: expressive, powerfull, overripe fruit, raspberry. Palate: sweet, flavourful.

PAGO DEL VICARIO 50-50 2007 T
tempranillo, cabernet sauvignon.

89 Colour: cherry, garnet rim. Nose: ripe fruit, scrubland, spicy. Palate: balanced, ripe fruit, spicy, round tannins.

PAGO DEL VICARIO MONAGÓS 2007 T
syrah, garnacha.

87 Colour: bright cherry, garnet rim. Nose: premature reduction notes, animal reductive notes, ripe fruit, spicy. Palate: concentrated, complex, flavourful.

PENTA 2007 T
merlot, petit verdot, tempranillo, cabernet sauvignon, syrah.

87 Colour: cherry, garnet rim. Nose: ripe fruit, spicy, dried herbs. Palate: fruity, flavourful, round tannins, balanced.

PAGO DEL VICARIO AGIOS 2007 T
tempranillo, garnacha.

85 Colour: deep cherry, garnet rim. Nose: ripe fruit, spicy, creamy oak, old leather. Palate: ripe fruit, flavourful.

QUINTA DE AVES

Ctra. CR-P-5222, Km. 11,200
13350 Moral de Calatrava (Ciudad Real)
☎: +34 915 716 514 - Fax: +34 915 711 151
qda@grupomaresa.com
www.quintadeaves.es

QUINTA DE AVES ALAUDA 2010 B
80% sauvignon blanc, 20% chardonnay.

87 Color bright straw. Aroma fresh, fresh fruit, white flowers, expressive. Taste flavourful, fruity, good acidity, balanced.

QUINTA DE AVES AIRÉN 2010 B
100% airén.

85 Colour: bright straw. Nose: white flowers, fresh fruit, medium intensity. Palate: correct, light-bodied, easy to drink.

QUINTA DE AVES OTUS 2009 T
42% merlot, 42% syrah, 16% graciano.

88 Colour: cherry, garnet rim. Nose: ripe fruit, sweet spices, toasty, cocoa bean. Palate: good acidity, powerful, flavourful, fleshy.

QUINTA DE AVES NOCTUA 2008 T BARRICA
100% tempranillo.

88 Colour: cherry, garnet rim. Nose: ripe fruit, spicy, creamy oak, toasty, earthy notes. Palate: powerful, flavourful, toasty, round tannins.

SELEENTE VIÑEDOS Y BODEGAS

Ctra. Toledo - Talavera, Km. 56,500
45685 Montearagón (Toledo)
☎: +34 628 935 890 - Fax: +34 925 865 435
info@seleente.com
www.seleente.com

SELEENTE VINTAGE 2008 T
46% cabernet sauvignon, 33% petit verdot, 6,5% merlot, 14,5% syrah.

87 Colour: deep cherry, garnet rim. Nose: sweet spices, ripe fruit, fruit expression. Palate: fleshy, rich, round tannins.

SELEENTE 2007 T
34,5% merlot, 22% petit verdot, 16,5% syrah, 18% tempranillo, 9% cabernet sauvignon.

88 Colour: deep cherry, garnet rim. Nose: ripe fruit, sweet spices, cocoa bean. Palate: fruity, flavourful, round tannins.

VINÍCOLA DE CASTILLA

Pol. Ind. Calle I, s/n
13200 Manzanares (Ciudad Real)
☎: +34 926 647 800 - Fax: +34 926 610 466
nacional@vinicoladecastilla.com
www.vinicoladecastilla.com

OLIMPO PRIVILEGIO 2009 B BARRICA
moscatel, chardonnay, sauvignon blanc.

84 Colour: bright yellow. Nose: powerfull, fragrant herbs, fruit preserve, petrol notes. Palate: rich, smoky aftertaste, flavourful, fresh.

OLIMPO PRIVILEGIO 2009 T BARRICA
syrah, cabernet sauvignon, merlot.

87 Colour: cherry, garnet rim. Nose: red berry notes, ripe fruit, sweet spices, creamy oak. Palate: flavourful, fleshy, toasty, roasted-coffee aftertaste, powerful.

VINNICO EXPORT

Muela, 16
03730 Jávea (Alicante)
☎: +34 965 791 967 - Fax: +34 966 461 471
info@vinnico.com
www.vinnico.com

EL PASO DE LAZO 2010 B
viura, verdejo.

86 Colour: bright straw. Nose: fresh, citrus fruit, ripe fruit, dried herbs. Palate: good acidity, fresh, fruity.

VANESA 2010 B
viura, verdejo.

85 Colour: bright straw. Nose: fresh, fresh fruit, white flowers, expressive. Palate: flavourful, fruity, good acidity.

LA NIÑA DE COLUMBUS 2010 B
sauvignon blanc.

83 Colour: bright straw. Nose: medium intensity, floral, fresh fruit. Palate: fruity, easy to drink.

CAPA VERDEJO 2010 B
verdejo.

82 Colour: bright straw. Nose: fresh fruit, medium intensity. Palate: fruity, easy to drink, fine bitter notes.

DOS PUNTOS 2010 T
85% tempranillo, 15% syrah.

89 Colour: cherry, purple rim. Nose: lactic notes, floral, red berry notes, expressive. Palate: fruity, flavourful, easy to drink.

EL PASO DE LAZO 2010 T
90% tempranillo, 10% syrah.

87 Colour: cherry, purple rim. Nose: floral, red berry notes, fresh, expressive. Palate: good acidity, round, flavourful, fruity.

VANESA 2010 T
100% tempranillo.

87 Color cherry, purple rim. Aroma expressive, fresh fruit, red berry notes, floral. Taste flavourful, fruity, good acidity, round tannins.

CAPA TEMPRANILLO 2010 T
tempranillo, teca.

86 Colour: cherry, purple rim. Nose: red berry notes, ripe fruit, wild herbs. Palate: good acidity, powerful, flavourful, fleshy.

LA NIÑA DE COLUMBUS 2010 T
100% cabernet sauvignon.

86 Colour: cherry, purple rim. Nose: red berry notes, ripe fruit, balsamic herbs, fresh. Palate: light-bodied, fresh, fruity, easy to drink.

LA NIÑA DE COLUMBUS SHIRAZ 2010 T
100% syrah.

85 Colour: cherry, purple rim. Nose: red berry notes, ripe fruit, warm, expressive. Palate: powerful, fruity, flavourful, fleshy.

DOS PUNTOS ORGANIC 2010 T
100% tempranillo.

85 Colour: cherry, purple rim. Nose: red berry notes, ripe fruit, fresh, scrubland. Palate: creamy, fleshy, balsamic.

VINOS COLOMAN

Goya, 17
13620 Pedro Muñoz (Ciudad Real)
☎: +34 926 586 410 - Fax: +34 926 586 656
coloman@satcoloman.com
www.satcoloman.com

PEDROTEÑO AIRÉN 2010 B
100% airén.

81 Colour: straw. Nose: fresh, white flowers, fresh fruit. Palate: fresh, lacks expression.

PEDROTEÑO 2010 T
100% tempranillo.

81 Colour: cherry, garnet rim. Nose: candied fruit, fresh. Palate: lacks expression, easy to drink.

VIÑEDOS CIGARRAL SANTA MARÍA

Cerro del Emperador, s/n
45002 Toledo (Toledo)
☎: +34 925 252 496 - Fax: +34 925 253 523
adolfo@adolfo-toledo.com
www.cigarralsantamaria.com

PAGO DEL AMA SYRAH 2008 T BARRICA
syrah.

91 Colour: bright cherry. Nose: sweet spices, creamy oak, red berry notes, earthy notes, mineral. Palate: flavourful, toasty, ripe fruit, round.

PAGO DEL AMA MERLOT 2008 T
merlot.

89 Colour: dark-red cherry. Nose: powerfull, candied fruit, warm, toasty, cocoa bean. Palate: powerful, flavourful, fleshy, round tannins.

VIÑEDOS MEJORANTES

Ctra. de Villafranca, Km. 2
45860 Villacañas (Toledo)
☎: +34 925 201 036 - Fax: +34 925 200 023
portillejo@portillejo.com
www.portillejo.es

VALDEPORT 2008 T ROBLE
70% cabernet sauvignon, 10% tempranillo, 15% merlot, 5% petit verdot.

84 Colour: cherry, garnet rim. Nose: fruit preserve, grassy, balsamic herbs. Palate: toasty, good acidity, flavourful, fleshy.

VIÑEDOS Y BODEGAS EL CASTILLO

Ctra. Ossa de Montiel, Km. 1,2
02600 Villarrobledo (Albacete)
☎: +34 967 573 230 - Fax: +34 967 573 048
manolovic13@hotmail.com
www.bodegaselcastillo.com

ARGUM SAUVIGNON BLANC 2010 B
100% sauvignon blanc.

84 Colour: bright straw, greenish rim. Nose: medium intensity, dried herbs. Palate: light-bodied, easy to drink, good finish.

ARGUM TEMPRANILLO CABERNET 2010 T
85% tempranillo, 15% cabernet sauvignon.

85 Colour: cherry, purple rim. Nose: red berry notes, expressive, warm, balsamic herbs. Palate: powerful, flavourful, fleshy.

ARGUM SYRAH 2010 T
100% syrah.

84 Colour: cherry, purple rim. Nose: ripe fruit, warm, medium intensity. Palate: good acidity, flavourful, good finish.

ARGUM 2009 T ROBLE
50% tempranillo, 35% merlot, 15% cabernet sauvignon.

86 Colour: cherry, garnet rim. Nose: ripe fruit, balsamic herbs, spicy, toasty. Palate: powerful, flavourful, fleshy, lacks expression, toasty.

ROBLE PARRA 2008 T
100% tempranillo.

89 Colour: cherry, garnet rim. Nose: ripe fruit, old leather, spicy, toasty. Palate: balanced, flavourful, fleshy.

ARGUM SAUVIGNON BLANC 2010 SS
100% sauvignon blanc.

84 Colour: bright straw. Nose: balanced, wild herbs. Palate: ripe fruit, easy to drink.

VIÑEDOS Y BODEGAS MUÑOZ

Ctra. Villarrubia, 11
45350 Noblejas (Toledo)
☎: +34 925 140 070 - Fax: +34 925 141 334
info@bodegasmunoz.com
www.bodegasmunoz.com

LEGADO MUÑOZ CHARDONNAY 2010 B
100% macabeo.

88 Colour: bright yellow. Nose: citrus fruit, tropical fruit, expressive, fragrant herbs. Palate: good acidity, fleshy, powerful, fruity.

FINCA MUÑOZ CEPAS VIEJAS 2008 T ROBLE
100% tempranillo.

90 Colour: cherry, garnet rim. Nose: red berry notes, ripe fruit, raspberry, cocoa bean, dark chocolate, creamy oak. Palate: correct, flavourful, fleshy, complex.

LEGADO MUÑOZ TEMPRANILLO 2010 T
100% tempranillo.

86 Colour: cherry, purple rim. Nose: red berry notes, raspberry, wild herbs, floral. Palate: fresh, fruity, flavourful, easy to drink.

LEGADO MUÑOZ GARNACHA 2009 T
100% garnacha.

86 Color bright cherry. Aroma ripe fruit, sweet spices, creamy oak, expressive. Taste flavourful, fruity, toasty, round tannins.

LEGADO MUÑOZ MERLOT 2009 T
100% merlot.

86 Colour: cherry, garnet rim. Nose: ripe fruit, creamy oak, toasty, sweet spices. Palate: flavourful, toasty, round tannins.

LEGADO MUÑOZ CABERNET SAUVIGNON 2009 T
100% cabernet sauvignon.

85 Colour: cherry, garnet rim. Nose: red berry notes, ripe fruit, grassy, spicy, toasty. Palate: correct, flavourful, fleshy.

LEGADO MUÑOZ PETIT VERDOT 2009 T
petit verdot.

85 Colour: cherry, garnet rim. Nose: red berry notes, ripe fruit, balsamic herbs, sweet spices, toasty. Palate: fleshy, flavourful, good acidity.

FINCA MUÑOZ BARREL AGED 2008 T ROBLE
100% tempranillo.

87 Colour: cherry, garnet rim. Nose: ripe fruit, wild herbs, spicy, creamy oak. Palate: fleshy, flavourful, spicy, toasty.

VITIVINOS ANUNCIACIÓN

Camino de Cabezuelas, s/n
02270 Villamalea (Albacete)
☎: +34 967 483 114 - Fax: +34 967 483 964
info@vitivinos.com
www.vitivinos.com

LLANOS DEL MARQUÉS BOBAL ECOLÓGICO 2010 T
bobal.

85 Colour: cherry, purple rim. Nose: red berry notes, grassy, floral. Palate: correct, fresh, fruity.

LLANOS DEL MARQUÉS BOBAL 2009 T
bobal.

87 Colour: cherry, garnet rim. Nose: red berry notes, ripe fruit, balsamic herbs, spicy, creamy oak. Palate: correct, round, flavourful.

CASTILLA-CAMPO DE CALATRAVA

AMANCIO MENCHERO MÁRQUEZ

Legión, 27
13260 Bolaños de Calatrava (Ciudad Real)
☎: +34 926 870 076 - Fax: +34 926 871 558
amanciomenchero@hotmail.com

CUBA 38 2010 T
tempranillo.

86 Colour: cherry, garnet rim. Nose: fruit liqueur notes, ripe fruit, scrubland, medium intensity. Palate: good acidity, flavourful, fruity.

CASTILLA Y LEÓN

ABADÍA RETUERTA

Ctra. N-122, km. 332,5
47340 Sardón de Duero (Valladolid)
☎: +34 983 680 314 - Fax: +34 983 680 286
info@abadia-retuerta.es
www.abadia-retuerta.es

ABADÍA RETUERTA 2010 B

91 Colour: bright straw. Nose: fresh fruit, white flowers, expressive, sweet spices. Palate: flavourful, fruity, good acidity, balanced.

ABADÍA RETUERTA PETIT VERDOT PV 2009 T
petit verdot.

95 Colour: black cherry, garnet rim. Nose: ripe fruit, fruit expression, cocoa bean, sweet spices, creamy oak, expressive. Palate: powerful, flavourful, fleshy, complex, balanced, round tannins.

ABADÍA RETUERTA PAGO NEGRALADA 2009 T BARRICA
tempranillo.

94 Colour: cherry, garnet rim. Nose: ripe fruit, varietal, spicy, cocoa bean, toasty, expressive. Palate: good acidity, powerful, flavourful, fleshy, balanced.

ABADÍA RETUERTA PAGO VALDEBELLÓN 2009 T BARRICA
cabernet sauvignon.

94 Colour: cherry, garnet rim. Nose: powerfull, varietal, creamy oak, dark chocolate, ripe fruit, fruit expression. Palate: powerful, fleshy, flavourful, ripe fruit, round tannins.

PAGO LA GARDUÑA SYRAH 2009 T
syrah.

93 Colour: cherry, garnet rim. Nose: ripe fruit, violet drops, dark chocolate, sweet spices, creamy oak. Palate: powerful, flavourful, fleshy, complex, fruity aftestaste, fine tannins.

ABADÍA RETUERTA SELECCIÓN ESPECIAL 2009 T
75% tempranillo, 25% cabernet sauvignon.

92 Colour: cherry, garnet rim. Nose: ripe fruit, fruit expression, red berry notes, creamy oak, sweet spices. Palate: powerful, flavourful, ripe fruit, round tannins.

ALTOS DE SAN ESTEBAN

Ildefonso Sánchez del Río, 4 - 3ºB
33001 Oviedo (Asturias)
☎: +34 660 145 313
mamarques@telecable.es

ALTOS DE SAN ESTEBAN VIÑAS DE MONTE 2009 TC
mencía, cabernet sauvignon, merlot.

90 Colour: cherry, garnet rim. Nose: red berry notes, mineral, cocoa bean, balsamic herbs, toasty. Palate: powerful, flavourful, fleshy, long, mineral.

ALTOS DE SAN ESTEBAN 2009 TC
35% mencía, 33% cabernet sauvignon, 32% merlot.

88 Colour: cherry, purple rim. Nose: red berry notes, ripe fruit, scrubland, creamy oak, spicy. Palate: powerful, flavourful, toasty.

ALTOS DE SAN ESTEBAN LA MENDAÑONA 2008 TC
100% mencía.

92 Colour: cherry, purple rim. Nose: red berry notes, expressive, mineral, cocoa bean, sweet spices, creamy oak. Palate: powerful, flavourful, fruity, complex, balanced.

ARRIAGA Y MIMÉNDEZ COMPAÑIA DE VINOS

Capitán Cortés, 6. Piso 4 - Puerta 3
26003 Logroño (La Rioja)
☎: +34 687 421 306 - Fax: +34 941 287 072
info@arriagaymimendez.com
www.arriagaymimendez.com

MITERNA CORTE UNO 2006 T BARRICA
100% prieto picudo.

90 Colour: cherry, garnet rim. Nose: ripe fruit, complex, earthy notes, toasty. Palate: powerful, flavourful, toasty, round tannins.

MITERNA CORTE DOS 2006 T BARRICA
100% prieto picudo.

86 Colour: cherry, garnet rim. Nose: ripe fruit, fine reductive notes, toasty, sweet spices. Palate: good acidity, powerful, flavourful, fleshy.

AVELINO VEGAS

Real del Pino, 36
40460 Santiuste (Segovia)
☎: +34 921 596 002 - Fax: +34 921 596 035
ana@avelinovegas.com
www.avelinovegas.com

CONDADO REAL 2010 RD
tempranillo.

87 Colour: raspberry rose. Nose: lactic notes, red berry notes, raspberry, floral, expressive. Palate: light-bodied, fruity, fresh, flavourful, good finish.

VEGAS 3 2009 T
40% tempranillo, 30% cabernet sauvignon, 30% merlot.

88 Colour: cherry, garnet rim. Nose: ripe fruit, expressive, earthy notes, cocoa bean, aromatic coffee, toasty. Palate: powerful, flavourful, fleshy, toasty.

BELONDRADE

Quinta San Diego - Camino del Puerto, s/n
47491 La Seca (Valladolid)
☎: +34 983 481 001 - Fax: +34 600 590 024
info@belondrade.com
www.belondrade.com

QUINTA APOLONIA BELONDRADE 2010 B
100% verdejo.

92 Colour: bright straw. Nose: scrubland, fresh fruit, fruit expression, varietal, expressive, elegant. Palate: powerful, complex, fruity, ripe fruit.

QUINTA CLARISA BELONDRADE 2010 RD
tempranillo.

88 Colour: light cherry. Nose: faded flowers, candied fruit. Palate: spicy, fine bitter notes, fleshy, good acidity.

BODEGA ALISTE

Pza. de España, 4
49520 Figueruela de Abajo (Zamora)
☎: +34 676 986 570 - Fax: +34 944 231 816
javier@hacedordevino.com
www.vinosdealiste.com

GEIJO 2008 BFB
40% viura, 30% verdejo, 30% chardonnay.

87 Colour: bright golden. Nose: faded flowers, ripe fruit, creamy oak, slightly evolved. Palate: creamy, long, rich.

MARINA DE ALISTE 2009 T
90% tempranillo, 10% syrah.

88 Colour: cherry, garnet rim. Nose: red berry notes, fruit liqueur notes, spicy, creamy oak. Palate: powerful, flavourful, fruity, fleshy, complex.

MARINA DE ALISTE 2008 TC
90% tempranillo, 10% syrah.

91 Colour: cherry, garnet rim. Nose: powerfull, fruit expression, red berry notes, mineral, earthy notes. Palate: flavourful, fleshy, spicy, creamy.

BODEGA CÁMBRICO

Paraje El Guijarral, s/n
37658 Villanueva del Conde (Salamanca)
☎: +34 923 281 006 - Fax: +34 923 213 605
info@cambrico.com
www.cambrico.com

CÁMBRICO RUFETE 2006 T
100% rufete.

92 Colour: bright cherry, orangey edge. Nose: ripe fruit, dried flowers, complex, expressive, sweet spices, cocoa bean. Palate: balanced, unctuous, powerful, flavourful, fleshy.

CÁMBRICO TEMPRANILLO 2006 T
100% tempranillo.

90 Colour: bright cherry, orangey edge. Nose: ripe fruit, complex, scrubland, mineral, fine reductive notes. Palate: powerful, flavourful, mineral.

BODEGA CASTO PEQUEÑO

Calvario s/n
24220 Valderas (León)
☎: +34 987 762 426 - Fax: +34 987 763 147
bodega@castopequeno.com
www.castopequeno.com

QUINTA HINOJAL 2010 B
100% verdejo.

83 Colour: straw. Nose: fresh fruit, white flowers. Palate: fresh, easy to drink.

QUINTA HINOJAL 2010 RD
100% tempranillo.

84 Colour: brilliant rose. Nose: candied fruit, fresh. Palate: fruity, flavourful, easy to drink.

QUINTA HINOJAL 2006 T
100% tempranillo.

87 Colour: cherry, garnet rim. Nose: ripe fruit, cocoa bean, aromatic coffee, creamy oak. Palate: powerful, flavourful, fleshy, toasty.

BODEGA CUATRO RAYAS AGRÍCOLA CASTELLANA

Ctra. Rodilana, s/n
47491 La Seca (Valladolid)
☎: +34 983 816 320 - Fax: +34 983 816 562
info@cuatrorayas.org
www.cuatrorayas.org

CABALLERO DE CASTILLA TEMPRANILLO 2009 T ROBLE
tempranillo.

86 Colour: cherry, purple rim. Nose: red berry notes, cocoa bean, dark chocolate, toasty. Palate: fruity, flavourful, spicy, easy to drink.

CASA MARÍA TEMPRANILLO 2009 T
100% tempranillo.

84 Colour: cherry, garnet rim. Nose: ripe fruit, cocoa bean, dark chocolate, sweet spices, warm. Palate: flavourful, fleshy, fruity.

BODEGA DON JUAN DEL AGUILA

Real de Abajo, 100
05110 El Barraco (Ávila)
☎: +34 920 281 032
bodegadonjuandelaguila@gmail.com
www.donjuandelaguila.es

GAZNATA 2010 RD
garnacha.

80 Colour: rose, purple rim. Nose: floral, lactic notes, ripe fruit. Palate: burning notes, correct, fleshy.

GAZNATA 2010 T
garnacha.

75

GAZNATA CONCRETE 2009 T
garnacha.

88 Colour: cherry, garnet rim. Nose: floral, ripe fruit, earthy notes, expressive. Palate: good acidity, fleshy, flavourful, rich.

GAZNATA EXTRA 2008 T
garnacha.

90 Colour: cherry, garnet rim. Nose: ripe fruit, spicy, creamy oak, earthy notes. Palate: flavourful, toasty, fleshy, complex, mineral.

BODEGA EL ALBAR LURTON

Camino Magarin s/n
47529 Villafranca del Duero (Valladolid)
☎: +34 983 034 030 - Fax: +34 983 034 040
bodega@jflurton.es
www.francoislurton.com

EL ALBAR LURTON EXCELENCIA 2008 T
tempranillo.

93 Color cherry, garnet rim. Aroma ripe fruit, spicy, creamy oak, toasty, complex. Taste powerful, flavourful, toasty, round tannins.

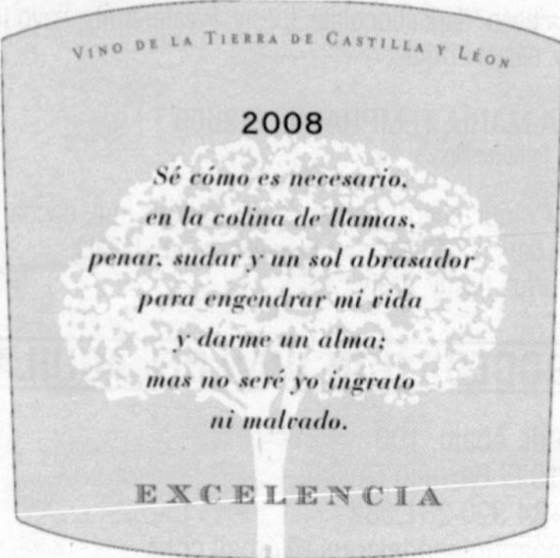

BODEGA EL TESORO SOC. COOP.

Pol. La Mata - Camino Viñas, s/n
4962 Brime de Urz (Zamora)
☎: +34 636 982 233
bodega_el_tesoro@terra.com

URZ 2008 T ROBLE
100% tempranillo.

82 Colour: cherry, garnet rim. Nose: fruit preserve, dried flowers, short. Palate: fresh, light-bodied, lacks expression.

BODEGA EMINA MEDINA DEL CAMPO

Ctra. Medina del Campo - Olmedo, Km. 1,5
47400 Medina del Campo (Valladolid)
☎: +34 983 800 001 - Fax: +34 902 430 189
eminarueda@emina.es
www.eminarueda.es

HEREDAD DE EMINA GEWÜRZTRAMINER 2009 B
100% gewürztraminer.

87 Colour: bright yellow. Nose: ripe fruit, tropical fruit, balanced. Palate: flavourful, rich, good acidity.

EMINA CHARDONNAY 2009 B
100% chardonnay.

87 Colour: bright yellow. Nose: toasty, spicy, ripe fruit, dried herbs. Palate: flavourful, good structure, spicy, good acidity.

BODEGAS ALDEASOÑA

Apdo. Correos 34
47300 Peñafiel (Valladolid)
☎: +34 983 878 052 - Fax: +34 983 873 052
cpitarch@bodegaconvento.com

ALDEASOÑA 2005 T
aragones.

92 Colour: black cherry. Nose: balanced, expressive, ripe fruit, toasty, spicy, dark chocolate. Palate: fleshy, balanced, ripe fruit, round tannins.

BODEGAS ARET

Agustín Vázquez, 30
49600 Benavente (Zamora)
☎: +34 680 398 262
pedrocasasm@terra.es

ARET 2009 T
100% prieto picudo.

87 Colour: bright cherry, orangey edge. Nose: candied fruit, dark chocolate, cocoa bean. Palate: fruity, flavourful, fleshy, round tannins.

BODEGAS CANOPY

Avda. Barber, 71
45004 (Toledo)
☎: +34 619 244 878 - Fax: +34 925 283 681
achacon@masfuturo.com

K OS 2008 T
100% garnacha.

93 Colour: deep cherry. Nose: mineral, overripe fruit, creamy oak, warm, balsamic herbs. Palate: flavourful, ripe fruit, balsamic, fine bitter notes, long.

BODEGAS CASTELO DE MEDINA

Ctra. CL-602, Km. 48
47465 Villaverde de Medina (Valladolid)
☎: +34 983 831 932 - Fax: +34 983 831 857
comercial@castelodemedina.es
www.castelodemedina.es

VALPASO 2009 B
chardonnay.

86 Colour: bright yellow. Nose: citrus fruit, fragrant herbs, expressive, balanced. Palate: balanced, powerful, flavourful.

VIÑA CASTELO 2010 RD
garnacha.

86 Colour: salmon. Nose: white flowers, raspberry, fresh fruit. Palate: good acidity, flavourful, fruity, easy to drink.

VEGA BUSIEL 2009 T
60% syrah, 40% tempranillo.

81 Colour: deep cherry, brick rim edge. Nose: fruit preserve, balsamic herbs, old leather. Palate: light-bodied, correct, easy to drink.

SYTÉ 2008 T
60% syrah, 40% tempranillo.

91 Colour: cherry, garnet rim. Nose: aromatic coffee, dark chocolate, cocoa bean, ripe fruit. Palate: flavourful, fleshy, good acidity, round.

BODEGAS COPABOCA

N-122, Km. 407
47114 Tordesillas (Valladolid)
☎: +34 983 395 655 - Fax: +34 983 307 729
santiago@copaboca.com
www.copaboca.com

ALVA MATER VERDEJO 2010 B
100% verdejo.

82 Colour: bright straw. Nose: citrus fruit, ripe fruit, faded flowers. Palate: fresh, light-bodied, lacks balance, easy to drink.

ALVA MATER 2010 RD
100% tempranillo.

84 Colour: rose, purple rim. Nose: fresh fruit, red berry notes, floral. Palate: powerful, flavourful, fruity, fresh.

ALVA MATER 2010 T
100% tempranillo.

86 Colour: cherry, purple rim. Nose: expressive, floral, ripe fruit, raspberry. Palate: powerful, flavourful, fruity.

BODEGAS ESCUDERO

Ctra. de Arnedo, s/n
26587 Grávalos (La Rioja)
☎: +34 941 398 008 - Fax: +34 941 398 070
bodega@bodegasescudero.com
www.bodegasescudero.com

CREPÚSCULO 2007 T
100% tinta del país.

84 Colour: dark-red cherry. Nose: fruit preserve, overripe fruit, roasted coffee. Palate: powerful, fine bitter notes.

BODEGAS FÉLIX CALLEJO

Avda. del Cid, Km. 16
09441 Sotillo de la Ribera (Burgos)
☎: +34 947 532 312 - Fax: +34 947 532 304
callejo@bodegasfelixcallejo.com
www.bodegasfelixcallejo.com

FINCA VALDELROBLE 2008 T
tempranillo, merlot, syrah.

89 Colour: bright cherry. Nose: ripe fruit, sweet spices, creamy oak, expressive, complex. Palate: flavourful, fruity, toasty, fleshy, complex.

BODEGAS GARCÍA NIÑO

Avda. Julio, s/n
09410 Arandilla (Burgos)
☎: +34 916 192 294 - Fax: +34 916 126 072
fernando@bodegasgarcianino.es
www.altorredondo.es

ALTORREDONDO 14 MESES 2007 T
100% tempranillo.

88 Colour: cherry, garnet rim. Nose: ripe fruit, cocoa bean, dark chocolate, spicy, creamy oak. Palate: flavourful, fleshy, toasty, long.

PAGO DE COSTALAO 24 MESES 2006 TC
100% tempranillo.

91 Colour: cherry, garnet rim. Nose: ripe fruit, earthy notes, cocoa bean, dark chocolate, spicy, creamy oak. Palate: powerful, flavourful, fleshy, balanced.

BODEGAS LEDA

Mayor, 48
47320 Tudela de Duero (Valladolid)
☎: +34 983 520 682 - Fax: +34 983 520 682
info@bodegasleda.com
www.bodegasleda.com

MÁS DE LEDA 2008 TC
100% tinto fino.

91 Colour: cherry, garnet rim. Nose: red berry notes, ripe fruit, sweet spices, creamy oak. Palate: good acidity, powerful, flavourful, toasty, round.

LEDA VIÑAS VIEJAS 2005 T
tinto fino.

92 Colour: cherry, garnet rim. Nose: red berry notes, ripe fruit, mineral, sweet spices, toasty, elegant. Palate: balanced, round, unctuous, powerful, flavourful.

BODEGAS MAURO

Cervantes, 12
47320 Tudela de Duero (Valladolid)
☎: +34 983 521 972 - Fax: +34 983 521 439
comunicacion@bodegasmauro.com
www.bodegasmauro.com

MAURO 2008 TC
86% tempranillo, 14% syrah.

88 Colour: cherry, garnet rim. Nose: ripe fruit, aromatic coffee, spicy, toasty, overripe fruit. Palate: powerful, flavourful, fleshy, toasty, round.

TERREUS 2006 TC
100% tempranillo.

94 Colour: bright cherry. Nose: sweet spices, ripe fruit, red berry notes, cocoa bean, roasted coffee, lactic notes. Palate: flavourful, fruity, toasty, round tannins, full.

BODEGAS MOCEN

Arribas, 7-9
47490 Rueda (Valladolid)
☎: +34 983 868 533 - Fax: +34 983 868 514
info@bodegasmocen.com
www.bodegasantano.com

BRAVÍA 2009 T ROBLE
100% tempranillo.

84 Colour: cherry, purple rim. Nose: red berry notes, ripe fruit, floral, balsamic herbs. Palate: good acidity, powerful, flavourful, fleshy.

COBRANZA 2008 T
100% tempranillo.

85 Colour: cherry, garnet rim. Nose: ripe fruit, candied fruit, sweet spices, toasty. Palate: fleshy, flavourful, balanced.

COBRANZA VENDIMIA SELECCIONADA 2005 T ROBLE
100% tempranillo.

88 Colour: cherry, garnet rim. Nose: red berry notes, ripe fruit, earthy notes, spicy, toasty. Palate: flavourful, fleshy, round.

BODEGAS MONTE LA REINA

Ctra. Toro - Zamora, Km. 436,7
49881 Toro (Zamora)
☎: +34 980 082 011 - Fax: +34 980 082 012
bodega@montelareina.es
www.montelareina.es

VIZORRO 2010 T
100% tempranillo.

86 Colour: cherry, purple rim. Nose: red berry notes, ripe fruit, expressive, floral. Palate: fruity, fleshy, flavourful.

VIZORRO 2010 B
100% verdejo.

85 Colour: bright straw. Nose: wild herbs, fruit expression. Palate: easy to drink, correct, good acidity.

VIZORRO 2010 RD
100% tempranillo.

83 Colour: brilliant rose. Nose: fruit expression, medium intensity. Palate: fresh, fruity, good acidity.

BODEGAS PEÑASCAL

Ctra. Valladolid - Segovia N-60,1 km. 7,3
47140 Laguna de Duero (Valladolid)
☎: +34 983 546 080 - Fax: +34 983 546 081
pzumft@habarcelo.es
www.barceloestates.es

PEÑASCAL S.C. RD

83 Colour: brilliant rose. Nose: fresh fruit, red berry notes, medium intensity. Palate: flavourful, fruity, fresh.

CUESTA DEL AIRE TEMPRANILLO SHIRAZ 2007 T
tempranillo, syrah.

85 Colour: cherry, garnet rim. Nose: ripe fruit, spicy, creamy oak, toasty, earthy notes. Palate: powerful, flavourful, toasty, round tannins.

BODEGAS SANTA RUFINA

Pago Fuente La Teja. Pol. Ind. 3 - Parcela 102
47290 Cubillas de Santa Marta (Valladolid)
☎: +34 983 585 202 - Fax: +34 983 585 202
info@bodegassantarufina.com
www.bodegassantarufina.com

BOSQUE REAL VERDEJO 2010 B
100% verdejo.

86 Colour: bright straw, greenish rim. Nose: scrubland, powerfull, varietal. Palate: flavourful, fruity.

BOSQUE REAL CABERNET 2009 T
100% cabernet sauvignon.

83 Colour: pale ruby, brick rim edge. Nose: red berry notes, ripe fruit, balsamic herbs, grassy. Palate: balsamic, flavourful, fleshy.

BOSQUE REAL MERLOT 2009 T
100% merlot.

78

BODEGAS TRITÓN

Pol. Parc. 146/148 Paraje Cantagrillos
49708 Villanueva de Campeán (Zamora)
☎: +34 968 435 022 - Fax: +34 968 716 051
info@orowines.com
www.orowines.com

TRIDENTE MENCÍA 2010 T
100% mencía.

89 Colour: bright cherry. Nose: ripe fruit, sweet spices, aromatic coffee, roasted coffee. Palate: flavourful, fruity, toasty, round tannins.

TRIDENTE PRIETO PICUDO 2009 T
100% prieto picudo.

94 Colour: cherry, garnet rim. Nose: red berry notes, ripe fruit, fragrant herbs, mineral, cocoa bean, dark chocolate, sweet spices. Palate: full, fruity, flavourful, long, creamy, toasty.

TRIDENTE TEMPRANILLO 2009 T
100% tempranillo.

91 Colour: bright cherry. Nose: sweet spices, aromatic coffee, cocoa bean, dark chocolate, toasty, red berry notes. Palate: flavourful, fruity, toasty, fleshy, complex.

BODEGAS VALDEÁGUILA

Avda. de la Paz, 26
37658 Garcibuey (Salamanca)
☎: +34 923 437 168 - Fax: +34 923 437 168
info@valdeaguila.com
www.valdeaguila.com

VIÑA SALAMANCA 2010 B
malvasía, verdejo.

84 Colour: bright straw. Nose: tropical fruit, grassy, faded flowers. Palate: light-bodied, flavourful, fresh.

VIÑA SALAMANCA RUFETE-TEMPRANILLO 2010 RD
rufete, tempranillo.

83 Colour: rose, purple rim. Nose: fresh, candied fruit, short. Palate: light-bodied, fresh, fruity.

VIÑA SALAMANCA RUFETE-TEMPRANILLO 2010 T
rufete, tempranillo.

86 Colour: cherry, purple rim. Nose: red berry notes, ripe fruit, expressive. Palate: fruity, flavourful, easy to drink.

ALAGÓN 2008 T ROBLE
tempranillo, rufete.

87 Colour: cherry, garnet rim. Nose: red berry notes, lactic notes, cocoa bean, medium intensity. Palate: good acidity, flavourful, fleshy.

BODEGAS VINOS DE LEÓN

La Vega, s/n
24190 Armunia (León)
☎: +34 987 209 712 - Fax: +34 987 209 800
info@bodegasvinosdeleon.es
www.bodegasvinosdeleon.es

PALACIO DE LEÓN CUVÉE 2008 T
100% tempranillo.

86 Colour: cherry, garnet rim. Nose: red berry notes, spicy, creamy oak. Palate: powerful, flavourful, fruity.

BODEGAS Y VIÑEDOS LA MEJORADA

Monasterio de La Mejorada
47410 Olmedo (Valladolid)
☎: +34 606 707 041 - Fax: +34 983 483 061
contacto@lamejorada.es
www.lamejorada.es

LA MEJORADA LAS CERCAS 2008 T ROBLE
60% tempranillo, 40% syrah.

90 Colour: bright cherry, garnet rim. Nose: fruit expression, expressive, complex, spicy. Palate: flavourful, fruity, easy to drink.

LA MEJORADA LAS NORIAS 2008 T ROBLE
100% tempranillo.

88 Colour: bright cherry, garnet rim. Nose: spicy, ripe fruit, balanced. Palate: spicy, fruity, flavourful.

VILLALAR 2008 T ROBLE
90% cabernet sauvignon, 10% tempranillo.

87 Colour: bright cherry, garnet rim. Nose: spicy, fresh, red berry notes, ripe fruit. Palate: flavourful, fruity, balanced.

VILLALAR ORO 2007 T ROBLE
tempranillo.

88 Colour: bright cherry, garnet rim. Nose: balanced, complex, elegant, red berry notes, spicy, creamy oak. Palate: flavourful, toasty, spicy.

LA MEJORADA LAS CERCAS 2006 T ROBLE
60% tempranillo, 40% syrah.

92 Colour: deep cherry, garnet rim. Nose: complex, ripe fruit, macerated fruit, spicy, mineral. Palate: full, fleshy, round tannins.

BODEGAS Y VIÑEDOS VALDUERO

Ctra. de Aranda, s/n
09443 Gumiel de Mercado (Burgos)
☎: +34 947 545 459 - Fax: +34 947 545 609
valduero@bodegasvalduero.com
www.bodegasvalduero.com

GARCÍA VIADERO ALBILLO 2010 B
albillo.

89 Colour: bright straw. Nose: ripe fruit, citrus fruit, varietal. Palate: flavourful, fruity, fleshy.

COMANDO G

Villamanin, 27 - 4º E
28011 (Madrid)
☎: +34 696 366 555
daniel@jimenezlandi.com

RUMBO AL NORTE 2010 T
100% garnacha.

96 Colour: deep cherry. Nose: expressive, red berry notes, fruit expression, spicy, mineral. Palate: flavourful, fruity, good acidity, fine bitter notes, easy to drink. Personality.

COMPAÑÍA DE VINOS TELMO RODRÍGUEZ

El Monte, s/n
01308 Lanciego (Álava)
☎: +34 945 628 315 - Fax: +34 945 628 314
contact@telmorodriguez.com
www.telmorodriguez.com

PEGASO "GRANITO" 2008 T
100% garnacha.

95 Colour: deep cherry. Nose: varietal, powerfull, raspberry, fruit expression, balsamic herbs, mineral. Palate: flavourful, good acidity, fine bitter notes, long.

PEGASO "BARRANCOS DE PIZARRA" 2008 T
100% garnacha.

92 Colour: bright cherry. Nose: fruit liqueur notes, candied fruit, fruit expression, sweet spices. Palate: flavourful, spicy, fine bitter notes, round tannins.

COMPAÑÍA DE VINOS MIGUEL MARTÍN

Ctra. Burgos - Portugal, Km. 101
47290 Cubillas de Santa María (Valladolid)
☎: +34 983 250 319 - Fax: +34 983 250 329
exportacion@ciadevinos.com
www.ciadevinos.com

RETOLA VERDEJO 2010 B
verdejo.

84 Colour: bright straw. Nose: fresh, faded flowers, ripe fruit. Palate: fruity, good acidity, fine bitter notes.

MARTÍN VERÁSTEGUI VENDIMIA SELECCIONADA 2010 B
verdejo.

84 Colour: bright straw. Nose: white flowers, candied fruit, tropical fruit. Palate: light-bodied, fresh, fruity.

MARTÍN VERÁSTEGUI 2008 BFB
verdejo.

87 Colour: bright golden. Nose: ripe fruit, dry nuts, sweet spices, toasty. Palate: rich, flavourful, fleshy.

MARTÍN VERÁSTEGUI P.X. B
pedro ximénez.

88 Colour: light mahogany. Nose: ripe fruit, dry nuts, aromatic coffee, caramel. Palate: spirituous, powerful, flavourful, fleshy.

RETOLA 2010 RD
12,5% tempranillo.

82 Colour: rose, purple rim. Nose: ripe fruit, balsamic herbs, short. Palate: spirituous, fresh, light-bodied.

MARTÍN VERÁSTEGUI VENDIMIA SELECCIONADA 2009 RD

85 Colour: raspberry rose. Nose: red berry notes, ripe fruit, faded flowers, medium intensity. Palate: flavourful, fruity, fresh.

RETOLA TEMPRANILLO 2010 T
tempranillo.

85 Colour: dark-red cherry. Nose: ripe fruit, powerfull, fruit expression. Palate: fruity, flavourful, easy to drink, round tannins.

RETOLA 6 MESES 2008 T

86 Colour: cherry, garnet rim. Nose: ripe fruit, powerfull, creamy oak, spicy. Palate: good acidity, round tannins, flavourful.

RETOLA 12 MESES 2006 T BARRICA
tempranillo.

86 Colour: cherry, garnet rim. Nose: creamy oak, spicy, fruit preserve. Palate: good acidity, fruity, flavourful, round tannins.

DANIEL EL TRAVIESO S.L.

Cuesta de las Descargas, 11 bis
28005 (Madrid)
☎: +34 696 366 555
daniel@jimenezlandi.com

EL REVENTÓN 2009 T
100% garnacha.

95 Colour: cherry, garnet rim. Nose: elegant, expressive, red berry notes, spicy. Palate: flavourful, fresh, fruity, complex, good acidity.

DANIEL V. RAMOS (ZERBEROS FINCA)

Real de Abajo, 100
05110 El Barraco (Ávila)
☎: +34 687 410 952
dvrcru@gmail.com
winesdanielramosvinos.blogspot.com

ZERBEROS PIZARRA 2008 T ROBLE
98% garnacha, 2% jaen.

92 Colour: cherry, garnet rim. Nose: red berry notes, fruit preserve, sweet spices, cocoa bean, complex. Palate: spicy, flavourful, complex, fleshy, mineral.

ZERBEROS "ARENA PIZARRA" 2008 T ROBLE
100% garnacha.

91 Colour: cherry, garnet rim. Nose: ripe fruit, expressive, spicy, cocoa bean, earthy notes, dry stone. Palate: creamy, fleshy, complex, flavourful.

ZERBEROS ARENA 2008 T ROBLE
100% garnacha.

90 Colour: cherry, garnet rim. Nose: fruit liqueur notes, red berry notes, acetaldehyde, spicy, varnish, toasty, earthy notes. Palate: warm, rich, flavourful, fleshy.

DE ALBERTO

Ctra. de Valdestillas, 2
47239 Serrada (Valladolid)
☎: +34 983 559 107 - Fax: +34 983 559 084
info@dealberto.com
www.dealberto.com

FINCA VALDEMOYA 2010 RD
100% tempranillo.

85 Colour: rose, purple rim. Nose: raspberry, fresh fruit, floral. Palate: fleshy, powerful, flavourful, fresh.

FINCA VALDEMOYA 2007 T
80% tempranillo, 20% cabernet sauvignon.

88 Colour: cherry, garnet rim. Nose: ripe fruit, spicy, creamy oak, toasty, balsamic herbs. Palate: powerful, flavourful, toasty, round tannins.

CCCL 2007 T BARRICA
80% tempranillo, 20% cabernet sauvignon.

87 Colour: cherry, garnet rim. Nose: ripe fruit, wild herbs, spicy, creamy oak. Palate: powerful, full, fleshy, flavourful.

DEHESA DE CADOZOS

Ctra. de Bermillo de Sayago a Almeida, Km. 21
49211 Villamor de Cadozos (Zamora)
☎: +34 914 550 253 - Fax: +34 915 448 142
nmaranon@cadozos.com
www.cadozos.com

CADOZOS PINOT NOIR 2008 T
100% pinot noir.

91 Colour: black cherry, cherry, garnet rim. Nose: red berry notes, ripe fruit, mineral, sweet spices, creamy oak. Palate: good acidity, round, powerful, flavourful, fleshy, long.

SAYAGO 830 2007 T
tinto fino, pinot noir.

85 Colour: very deep cherry. Nose: powerfull, ripe fruit, toasty, creamy oak, new oak. Palate: powerful, flavourful, good acidity, grainy tannins.

CADOZOS 2005 T
tinto fino, pinot noir.

90 Colour: cherry, garnet rim. Nose: elegant, expressive, fine reductive notes, creamy oak, toasty, earthy notes. Palate: flavourful, spicy, creamy, round tannins.

ENOLÓGICA WAMBA

El Puente, 7
09220 Pampliega (Burgos)
☎: +34 662 073 038 - Fax: +34 947 423 048
contacto@enologicawamba.es
www.enologicawamba.es

AMBISNA VERDEJO 2010 B
verdejo.

89 Colour: bright straw. Nose: varietal, citrus fruit, tropical fruit, grassy. Palate: good acidity, balanced, flavourful, fruity, fleshy, rich.

LYNA 2010 RD
100% tempranillo.

85 Colour: rose, purple rim. Nose: lactic notes, floral, red berry notes. Palate: fresh, light-bodied, fruity, flavourful.

ZARZANAS 2008 T
tempranillo, syrah, merlot.

87 Colour: cherry, garnet rim. Nose: ripe fruit, spicy, creamy oak, warm. Palate: flavourful, fleshy, fruity, good finish.

LYNA 2008 T
tempranillo.

86 Colour: cherry, garnet rim. Nose: candied fruit, warm, creamy oak. Palate: good acidity, spicy, flavourful.

AMBISNA TEMPRANILLO 2007 T
100% tempranillo.

89 Colour: cherry, garnet rim. Nose: red berry notes, ripe fruit, balsamic herbs, sweet spices, toasty. Palate: flavourful, fruity, fleshy.

ZARZANAS 2007 T
100% tempranillo.

87 Colour: cherry, garnet rim. Nose: red berry notes, ripe fruit, cocoa bean, dark chocolate, creamy oak. Palate: good acidity, fruity, fleshy.

ERMITA DEL CONDE

Camino de la Torre, 1
09410 Coruña del Conde (Burgos)
☎: +34 627 464 468
bodega@ermitadelconde.com
www.ermitadelconde.com

VIÑA SULPICIA ALBILLO CENTENARIO 2009 B
100% albillo.

87 Colour: bright straw. Nose: fragrant herbs, white flowers, citrus fruit. Palate: flavourful, fresh, easy to drink.

ERMITA DEL CONDE 2008 T
90% tempranillo, 10% merlot.

91 Colour: cherry, garnet rim. Nose: ripe fruit, expressive, spicy, creamy oak. Palate: fleshy, balanced, powerful, flavourful, long.

FINCA FUENTEGALANA

Ctra. Comarcal M-501, Km. 65
05429 Navahondilla (Ávila)
☎: +34 628 775 926
info@fuentegalana.com
www.fuentegalana.com

TOROS DE GUISANDO 2010 RD
syrah.

84 Colour: rose, purple rim. Nose: floral, red berry notes, ripe fruit. Palate: flavourful, fresh, fruity, easy to drink.

TOROS DE GUISANDO 2008 T
80% syrah, 15% merlot, 5% cabernet sauvignon.

88 Colour: dark-red cherry, garnet rim. Nose: red berry notes, ripe fruit, cocoa bean, sweet spices, toasty. Palate: powerful, flavourful, long, good acidity.

TOROS DE GUISANDO SYRAH 2008 T
syrah.

87 Colour: cherry, garnet rim. Nose: floral, red berry notes, spicy, creamy oak. Palate: good acidity, round, flavourful, fleshy.

TOROS DE GUISANDO CABERNET SAUVIGNON 2008 T
cabernet sauvignon.

86 Colour: dark-red cherry, garnet rim. Nose: red berry notes, ripe fruit, balsamic herbs, spicy. Palate: good acidity, powerful, flavourful.

FINCA LA RINCONADA

Finca La Rinconada
47520 Castronuño (Valladolid)
☎: +34 914 901 871 - Fax: +34 916 620 430
fincalarinconada@fincalarinconada.es
www.fincalarinconada.es

BARCOLOBO BARRICA SELECCIÓN 2010 T
95% tempranillo, 3% syrah, 2% cabernet sauvignon.

88 Colour: cherry, purple rim. Nose: fresh fruit, expressive, spicy. Palate: light-bodied, flavourful, fruity, round tannins.

BARCOLOBO 12 MESES BARRICA 2009 T
75% tempranillo, 20% syrah, 5% cabernet sauvignon.

89 Colour: cherry, garnet rim. Nose: powerfull, red berry notes, cocoa bean, sweet spices, creamy oak. Palate: good acidity, round, unctuous, powerful, flavourful.

FINCA TORREMILANOS BODEGAS PEÑALBA LÓPEZ

Finca Torremilanos
09400 Aranda de Duero (Burgos)
☎: +34 947 512 852 - Fax: +34 947 508 044
nacional@torremilanos.com
www.torremilanos.com

PEÑALBA-LÓPEZ 2009 B
50% sauvignon blanc, 50% tempranillo blanco.

89 Colour: bright yellow. Nose: ripe fruit, aged wood nuances, sweet spices, roasted coffee. Palate: powerful, flavourful, fleshy, toasty.

GARMENDIA VIÑEDOS Y BODEGA

Finca Santa Rosalia, s/n
34260 Vizmalo (Burgos)
☎: +34 947 166 171 - Fax: +34 947 166 147
info@bodegasgarmendia.com
www.bodegasgarmendia.com

GARMENDIA GRAN SELECCIÓN 2010 BFB
100% verdejo.

91 Colour: bright straw. Nose: white flowers, citrus fruit, fragrant herbs, creamy oak. Palate: good acidity, flavourful, fleshy, creamy.

GARMENDIA 2010 B
verdejo, viura.

88 Colour: bright straw. Nose: white flowers, tropical fruit, fragrant herbs. Palate: balanced, unctuous, fruity, flavourful.

GARMENDIA SELECCIÓN 2005 T
tempranillo, merlot.

88 Colour: black cherry, garnet rim. Nose: ripe fruit, spicy, cocoa bean, toasty. Palate: good acidity, balanced, toasty, fleshy, full.

GARMENDIA 2005 T FERMENTADO EN BARRICA
tempranillo, garnacha, graciano.

86 Colour: black cherry, orangey edge. Nose: spicy, caramel, toasty, ripe fruit. Palate: correct, round, flavourful, fleshy.

GARNACHA ALTO ALBERCHE

Camino del Pimpollar, s/n
05100 Navaluenga (Ávila)
☎: +34 616 416 542
info@altoalberche.es
www.altoalberche.es

7 NAVAS 2010 T
garnacha.

91 Colour: cherry, purple rim. Nose: candied fruit, raspberry, warm, balsamic herbs. Palate: flavourful, fruity, fresh, fleshy.

7 NAVAS 2009 T ROBLE
garnacha.

92 Colour: cherry, garnet rim. Nose: elegant, characterful, ripe fruit, red berry notes, sweet spices, scrubland, balsamic herbs. Palate: flavourful, spicy, easy to drink.

7 NAVAS SELECCIÓN 2008 T
garnacha.

92 Colour: deep cherry. Nose: spicy, ripe fruit, fruit expression, balsamic herbs, scrubland. Palate: flavourful, fruity, long, good acidity, fine bitter notes.

GODELIA

Antigua Ctra. N-VI, Km. 403,5
24547 Pieros Cacabelos (León)
☎: +34 987 546 279 - Fax: +34 987 548 026
export@godelia.es
www.godelia.es

LIBAMUS T
100% mencía.

91 Colour: bright cherry. Nose: ripe fruit, sweet spices, creamy oak, raspberry, red berry notes. Palate: flavourful, fruity, sweetness, spicy.

GORDONZELLO

Alto de Santa Marina, s/n
24294 Gordoncillo (León)
☎: +34 987 758 030 - Fax: +34 987 757 201
info@gordonzello.com
www.gordonzello.com

CANDIDUS 2010 B
100% verdejo.

82 Colour: bright straw. Nose: candied fruit, white flowers, tropical fruit. Palate: good acidity, fresh, fruity.

GREAT WINES FROM SPAIN

Camino de Santibáñez, s/n
47328 La Parrilla (Valladolid)
☎: +34 983 681 521 - Fax: +34 983 681 521
bodegas@altapavina.com
www.altapavina.es

ALTA PAVINA PINOT NOIR CITIUS 2008 TC
pinot noir.

87 Colour: pale ruby, brick rim edge. Nose: ripe fruit, balsamic herbs, spicy, toasty, fine reductive notes. Palate: good acidity, powerful, flavourful, round tannins.

ALTA PAVINA SELECTO 2008 T
tempranillo, pinot noir.

80 Colour: light cherry, garnet rim. Nose: fruit preserve, old leather, spicy. Palate: warm, slightly evolved, flavourful.

GRUPO YLLERA

Autovía A-6, Km. 173, 5
47490 Rueda (Valladolid)
☎: +34 983 868 097 - Fax: +34 983 868 177
grupoyllera@grupoyllera.com
www.grupoyllera.com

OLIVANTE DE LAURA SEMIDULCE 2010 B
moscatel grano menudo.

84 Colour: golden. Nose: floral, honeyed notes, candied fruit. Palate: flavourful, sweet, fresh, fruity, good acidity.

CUVI 2009 T ROBLE
tempranillo.

83 Colour: cherry, garnet rim. Nose: overripe fruit, balsamic herbs, warm, spicy, toasty. Palate: fleshy, toasty, good acidity.

YLLERA 2006 TC
tempranillo.

89 Colour: cherry, garnet rim. Nose: red berry notes, ripe fruit, cocoa bean, toasty. Palate: powerful, flavourful, long, toasty, balanced.

YLLERA 25 ANIVERSARIO 2005 T
tempranillo.

92 Colour: cherry, garnet rim. Nose: ripe fruit, sweet spices, cocoa bean, toasty, mineral. Palate: good acidity, powerful, flavourful, fleshy, round tannins.

YLLERA DOMINUS 2005 TR
tempranillo.

91 Colour: cherry, garnet rim. Nose: creamy oak, ripe fruit, expressive, sweet spices, elegant. Palate: flavourful, unctuous, toasty, round tannins.

YLLERA 5.5 ESP
verdejo.

85 Color bright straw. Aroma medium intensity, fresh fruit, dried herbs, fine lees, floral. Taste fresh, fruity, flavourful, good acidity.

YLLERA VENDIMIA SELECCIONADA 2003 TR
tempranillo.

90 Colour: cherry, garnet rim. Nose: creamy oak, cocoa bean, ripe fruit, spicy. Palate: round tannins, complex, flavourful, spicy.

LEYENDA DEL PÁRAMO

Rañadero, 32
24400 Ponferrada (León)
☎: +34 626 194 347
info@bodegasdelparamo.com
www.bodegasdelparamo.com

MITTEL 2010 B
100% albarín.

87 Colour: bright straw. Nose: dried flowers, tropical fruit, ripe fruit, scrubland. Palate: good acidity, light-bodied, fresh, flavourful.

MITTEL 2010 RD
100% prieto picudo.

88 Colour: rose, purple rim. Nose: floral, red berry notes, ripe fruit, raspberry. Palate: good acidity, fresh, light-bodied, fruity.

FLOR DEL PÁRAMO 2010 RD
prieto picudo.

87 Colour: brilliant rose. Nose: powerfull, ripe fruit, red berry notes, floral, expressive. Palate: fleshy, powerful, fruity, fresh.

FLOR DEL PÁRAMO 2010 T
prieto picudo.

90 Colour: cherry, purple rim. Nose: floral, raspberry, red berry notes, mineral, expressive. Palate: fruity, flavourful, fleshy, good acidity.

EL MÉDICO 2009 T ROBLE
100% prieto picudo.

92 Colour: cherry, garnet rim. Nose: red berry notes, ripe fruit, cocoa bean, aromatic coffee, sweet spices, creamy oak. Palate: good acidity, powerful, flavourful, fleshy, complex.

LIBERALIA ENOLÓGICA

Camino del Palo, s/n
49800 Toro (Zamora)
☎: +34 980 692 571 - Fax: +34 980 692 571
byvliberalia@hotmail.com
www.liberalia.es

LIBERALIA UNO 2010 BLANCO DULCE
90% moscatel, 10% albillo.

88 Colour: bright straw. Nose: ripe fruit, citrus fruit, honeyed notes, white flowers. Palate: fleshy, fruity, fresh, flavourful, easy to drink.

MALDIVINAS VIÑA Y VINO

Los Pinillas, 1
28032 (Madrid)
☎: +34 913 710 587
carlos@maldivinas.es
www.maldivinas.es

LA MOVIDA 2009 T
100% garnacha.

92 Colour: light cherry, garnet rim. Nose: ripe fruit, fruit liqueur notes, earthy notes, mineral, spicy, creamy oak. Palate: good acidity, powerful, flavourful, complex.

OSSIAN VIDES Y VINOS

San Marcos, 5
40447 Nieva (Segovia)
☎: +34 696 159 121 - Fax: +34 921 594 207
ossian@ossian.es
www.ossian.es

OSSIAN 2009 BFB
100% verdejo.

94 Colour: bright straw. Nose: dried flowers, fragrant herbs, spicy, creamy oak, fruit expression, mineral. Palate: good acidity, unctuous, powerful, flavourful, fleshy.

PEÑALBA LA VERDE BODEGAS VIZAR

Ctra. N 122, Km. 341
47329 Villabáñez (Valladolid)
☎: +34 983 682 690 - Fax: +34 983 682 125
info@bodegasvizar.es
www.bodegasvizar.es

VIZAR SYRAH 2009 T
100% syrah.

92 Colour: cherry, garnet rim. Nose: red berry notes, powerfull, cocoa bean, dark chocolate, spicy, creamy oak, earthy notes. Palate: powerful, fruity, flavourful, fleshy, complex.

VIZAR SELECCIÓN ESPECIAL 2009 T
50% tinto fino, 50% syrah.

88 Colour: cherry, garnet rim. Nose: red berry notes, fruit preserve, dark chocolate, cocoa bean, spicy. Palate: good acidity, flavourful, fleshy, complex.

VIZAR 12 MESES 2008 T
85% tinto fino, 15% cabernet sauvignon.

89 Colour: cherry, garnet rim. Nose: red berry notes, ripe fruit, balsamic herbs, sweet spices, toasty. Palate: good acidity, powerful, flavourful, fruity, round tannins.

QUINTA DE LA QUIETUD

Tomás Bayón, 56
47491 La Seca (Valladolid)
☎: +34 983 034 995 - Fax: +34 983 034 995
maritesacris@hotmail.com
www.quintaquietud.com

ABABOL VERDEJO SOBRE LÍAS 2009 B
100% verdejo.

86 Colour: bright golden. Nose: lees reduction notes, faded flowers, ripe fruit, fine reductive notes. Palate: spicy, fleshy, flavourful.

EL GRAN ABABOL 2008 B
100% verdejo.

89 Colour: bright golden. Nose: ripe fruit, dried herbs, faded flowers, spicy, toasty. Palate: good acidity, flavourful, fleshy, creamy, toasty.

ABABOL EL TINTO 2009 T
95% tempranillo, 5% cabernet sauvignon.

84 Colour: cherry, purple rim. Nose: fruit preserve, fruit liqueur notes, scrubland. Palate: good acidity, fruity, flavourful.

QUINTA SARDONIA

Casa, s/n - Granja Sardón
47340 Sardón de Duero (Valladolid)
☎: +34 650 498 353 - Fax: +34 983 032 884
jbougnaud@quintasardonia.com
www.quintasardania.es

QUINTA SARDONIA QS 2008 T
57% tinto fino, 29,5% cabernet sauvignon, 4,5% syrah, 4% merlot, 5% otras.

92 Colour: cherry, garnet rim. Nose: red berry notes, ripe fruit, earthy notes, mineral, sweet spices. Palate: concentrated, powerful, flavourful, fleshy, complex.

RAMIRO WINE CELLAR

Camino Viejo de Simancas, km. 3,5
47008 Valladolid (Valladolid)
☎: +34 983 274 202 - Fax: +34 983 274 202
bodega@ramirowinecellar.com
www.ramirowinecellar.com

CÓNDITA 2008 T ROBLE
100% tempranillo.

88 Colour: cherry, garnet rim. Nose: red berry notes, fresh fruit, expressive, creamy oak. Palate: fruity, flavourful, fleshy.

RAMIRO'S 2007 T
100% tempranillo.

88 Colour: cherry, garnet rim. Nose: red berry notes, ripe fruit, cocoa bean, creamy oak. Palate: powerful, flavourful, fleshy, long.

ROCHAL

Salas Pombo, 17
37670 Santibáñez de la Sierra (Salamanca)
☎: +34 923 435 260 - Fax: +34 923 435 260
info@bodegasrochal.com
www.bodegasrochal.com

CALIXTO 2007 T
rufete, tempranillo.

91 Colour: cherry, garnet rim. Nose: red berry notes, expressive, spicy, balsamic herbs, creamy oak. Palate: good acidity, powerful, flavourful, fleshy.

SELECCIÓN CÉSAR MUÑOZ

Acera de Recoletos, 14
47004 (Valladolid)
☎: +34 666 548 751
info@cesarmunoz.es
www.bodegasmagallanes.es

ALTER ENOS 2007 BFB
verdejo.

91 Colour: bright yellow. Nose: dried flowers, citrus fruit, tropical fruit, creamy oak, elegant. Palate: rich, flavourful, complex, fleshy, creamy.

TERA Y CASTRO

Oruro, 9 - Bajo izda.
28016 Madrid (Madrid)
☎: +34 915 902 529 - Fax: +34 915 644 431
info@teraycastro.com
www.teraycastro.com

EILUN 2010 B
100% gewürztraminer.

88 Colour: bright straw. Nose: dried flowers, ripe fruit, fragrant herbs. Palate: fleshy, powerful, flavourful, rich.

EILUN VERDEJO 2009 B
100% verdejo.

92 Colour: bright yellow. Nose: white flowers, fragrant herbs, ripe fruit, creamy oak, expressive, elegant. Palate: good acidity, balanced, flavourful, fleshy.

TERNA BODEGAS

Cuatro Calles, s/n
47491 La Seca (Valladolid)
☎: +34 983 103 223 - Fax: +34 983 816 561
info@sitiosdebodega.com
www.sitiosdebodega.com

E TERNA PRIETO PICUDO 2009 T
100% prieto picudo.

90 Colour: cherry, garnet rim. Nose: red berry notes, ripe fruit, balsamic herbs, mineral. Palate: good acidity, powerful, flavourful, fleshy, complex.

E TERNA GARNACHA 2007 T
100% garnacha.

88 Colour: cherry, garnet rim. Nose: red berry notes, ripe fruit, powerfull, mineral, spicy, creamy oak. Palate: fleshy, powerful, flavourful, long.

VILLA MARÍA

Ctra. Sanabria, Km. 3,800
24750 La Bañeza (León)
☎: +34 987 605 918 - Fax: +34 987 632 020
gaspar@legumbresluengo.es

VILLA MARÍA 2006 T ROBLE
85% cabernet sauvignon, 15% merlot.

86 Colour: pale ruby, brick rim edge. Nose: red berry notes, ripe fruit, balsamic herbs, dark chocolate, toasty. Palate: flavourful, fleshy, long.

VILLACEZÁN

San Juan, 10
24294 Gordoncillo (León)
☎: +34 987 758 031 - Fax: +34 987 758 031
villacezan@villacezan.com
www.villacezan.com

MAR DE CASTILLA 2008 T ROBLE
78% prieto picudo, 15% mencía, 12% tempranillo.

85 Colour: cherry, garnet rim. Nose: ripe fruit, dark chocolate, cocoa bean, sweet spices, warm. Palate: flavourful, fleshy, good finish.

VINOS MALAPARTE

Ctra. del Henar, km. 3,5
40200 Cuéllar (Segovia)
☎: +34 921 105 204
info@vinosmalaparte.es
www.vinosmalaparte.es

MALAPARTE 2008 T
tinto fino.

88 Colour: cherry, garnet rim. Nose: red berry notes, ripe fruit, aromatic coffee, caramel, sweet spices. Palate: good acidity, flavourful, fleshy.

VIÑA ALBARES

Camino Rea,l s/n
24310 Albares de la Ribera (León)
☎: +34 987 519 147 - Fax: +34 987 519 152
info@vinaalbareswine.com
www.vinaalbareswine.com

V A GEWÜRZTRAMINER 2010 B
gewürztraminer.

87 Colour: bright straw. Nose: floral, expressive, ripe fruit. Palate: good acidity, sweetness, rich, flavourful.

V A SAUVIGNON BLANC 2010 B
sauvignon blanc.

86 Colour: bright straw. Nose: dried herbs, white flowers, fresh. Palate: fresh, flavourful, fleshy, good acidity.

V A CHARDONNAY - GEWÜRZTRAMINER 2010 B
chardonnay, gewürztraminer.

86 Colour: bright straw. Nose: fragrant herbs, citrus fruit, floral. Palate: light-bodied, fresh, flavourful, good acidity.

V A ROSADO 2010 RD
syrah, merlot.

87 Colour: rose, purple rim. Nose: floral, red berry notes, fresh. Palate: powerful, flavourful, fresh, fruity.

VIÑEDOS DE VILLAESTER

Villaester de Arriba
47540 Pedrosa del Rey (Valladolid)
☎: +34 948 645 008 - Fax: +34 948 645 166
info@familiabelasco.com
www.familiabelasco.com

AVUTARDA 2009 T
tempranillo, cabernet sauvignon.

88 Colour: cherry, purple rim. Nose: red berry notes, ripe fruit, expressive, spicy, dark chocolate. Palate: good acidity, flavourful, fleshy, toasty.

VIÑEDOS Y BODEGAS CUMAL

P.I. Bierzo Alto, Los Barredos, 4
24318 San Román de Bembibre (León)
☎: +34 987 514 550 - Fax: +34 987 514 570
info@dominiodetares.com
www.dominiodetares.com

TOMBÚ RD
100% prieto picudo.

88 Colour: brilliant rose. Nose: elegant, candied fruit, dried flowers, fragrant herbs, red berry notes. Palate: light-bodied, flavourful, good acidity, long, spicy.

LLANOS DE CUMAL 2008 T
100% prieto picudo.

90 Colour: dark-red cherry. Nose: ripe fruit, fresh, warm, sweet spices. Palate: flavourful, fruity, toasty, round tannins.

CUMAL 2007 T
100% prieto picudo.

91 Colour: cherry, garnet rim. Nose: spicy, creamy oak, toasty, ripe fruit. Palate: powerful, flavourful, toasty, round tannins.

CUMBRES DE GUADALFEO CONTRAVIESA-ALPUJARRA

BODEGA GARCÍA DE VERDEVIQUE

Los García de Verdevique
18439 Castaras (Granada)
☎: +34 958 957 025
info@bodegasgarciadeverdevique.com
www.bodegasgarciadeverdevique.com

LOS GARCÍA DE VERDEVIQUE 2009 B BARRICA
100% vijariego.

87 Colour: bright golden. Nose: candied fruit, honeyed notes, sweet spices. Palate: creamy, long, flavourful.

LOS GARCÍA DE VERDEVIQUE 2005 T BARRICA
80% tempranillo, 20% cabernet sauvignon.

90 Colour: cherry, garnet rim. Nose: fruit preserve, fruit liqueur notes, spicy, creamy oak, earthy notes. Palate: good acidity, flavourful, fleshy, balanced.

GARCÍA DE VERDEVIQUE ESP
100% vijariego.

76

DOMINIO BUENAVISTA

Ctra. de Almería, s/n
18480 Ugíjar (Granada)
☎: +34 958 767 254 - Fax: +34 958 767 254
info@dominiobuenavista.com
www.dominiobuenavista.com

VELETA VIJIRIEGA 2010 B
90% vijariego, 10% chardonnay.

85 Colour: bright straw. Nose: fresh, expressive, faded flowers, ripe fruit. Palate: flavourful, fruity, good acidity.

VELETA CHARDONNAY 2010 B
chardonnay.

84 Colour: bright straw. Nose: ripe fruit, faded flowers, short. Palate: powerful, flavourful, slightly overripe.

VELETA NOLADOS 2008 T
40% cabernet sauvignon, 40% cabernet franc, 20% tempranillo.

91 Colour: dark-red cherry. Nose: dry stone, ripe fruit, fruit liqueur notes, complex, expressive, varietal, sweet spices, fruit expression. Palate: powerful, flavourful, complex, fruity, mineral, creamy.

VELETA CABERNET SAUVIGNON 2008 T
cabernet sauvignon.

89 Colour: deep cherry. Nose: fruit liqueur notes, fruit expression, ripe fruit. Palate: spirituous, fruity, powerful, flavourful, spicy.

VELETA TEMPRANILLO 2008 T
tempranillo.

89 Colour: dark-red cherry. Nose: varietal, powerfull, neat, ripe fruit, fruit liqueur notes. Palate: fruity, flavourful, powerful, good acidity, balsamic, mineral.

LOS BARRANCOS

Ctra. Cádiar - Albuñol, km. 9,4
18449 Lobras (Granada)
☎: +34 958 343 218 - Fax: +34 958 343 412
info@los-barrancos.es
www.losbarrancos.es

CERRO DE LA RETAMA 2008 T
40% tempranillo, 40% cabernet sauvignon, 20% merlot.

89 Colour: cherry, garnet rim. Nose: ripe fruit, balsamic herbs, earthy notes, mineral, spicy, creamy oak. Palate: balanced, flavourful, fleshy, toasty.

CORRAL DE CASTRO 2008 T ROBLE
80% tempranillo, 20% cabernet sauvignon.

88 Colour: cherry, garnet rim. Nose: ripe fruit, mineral, spicy, creamy oak. Palate: good acidity, flavourful, mineral, round tannins.

CÓRDOBA

BODEGAS JESÚS NAZARENO

Avda. Cañete de las Torres, 33
14850 Baena (Córdoba)
☎: +34 957 670 225 - Fax: +34 957 690 873
bodejenaza@bodejenaza.com

CASTILLO DE BAENA 2008 T
60% tempranillo, 40% syrah.

82 Colour: bright cherry. Nose: ripe fruit, sweet spices, roasted coffee. Palate: flavourful, fruity, toasty.

BODEGAS LA AURORA

Avda. de Europa, 7
14550 Montilla (Córdoba)
☎: +34 957 650 362 - Fax: +34 957 654 642
administracion@bodegaslaaurora.com
www.bodegaslaaurora.com

LLANOS DE PALACIO 2005 T ROBLE
cabernet sauvignon.

85 Colour: bright cherry, garnet rim. Nose: sweet spices, ripe fruit, balanced. Palate: flavourful, spicy, ripe fruit.

LLANOS DE PALACIO VENDIMIA SELECCIONADA T
syrah.

84 Colour: bright cherry, purple rim. Nose: fruit expression, candied fruit. Palate: flavourful, fruity.

COSTA CANTABRIA

BODEGAS VIDULAR

Barrio Río Lastra, 264
39761 Junta de Voto (Cantabria)
☎: +34 619 710 302 - Fax: +34 942 631 324
info@riberadelason.com
www.riberadelason.com

RIBERA DEL ASÓN 2010 B
60% albariño, 40% chardonnay.

87 Colour: bright straw. Nose: fresh fruit, tropical fruit, white flowers, fragrant herbs, expressive. Palate: powerful, flavourful, fruity, fresh, fleshy.

LANCINA VIÑEDOS Y BODEGA

B. Tuebre, 31
39790 Bárcena de Cicero (Cantabria)
☎: +34 942 642 205
lancina@lancina.es

LANCINA 2010 B
50% riesling, 50% godello.

90 Colour: bright straw. Nose: fresh fruit, fruit expression, citrus fruit, floral. Palate: flavourful, fruity, fresh, good acidity.

EIVISSA

CAN RICH DE BUSCATELL

Camí de Sa Vorera, s/n
07820 San Antonio (Illes Ballears)
☎: +34 971 803 377 - Fax: +34 971 803 377
info@bodegascanrich.com
www.bodegascanrich.com

CAN RICH 2010 B
60% chardonnay, 40% malvasía.

91 Colour: bright straw. Nose: fresh, fresh fruit, white flowers, complex, mineral. Palate: flavourful, fruity, good acidity.

CAN RICH ERESO 2010 BFB
80% chardonnay, 20% malvasía.

88 Colour: bright straw. Nose: ripe fruit, citrus fruit, spicy. Palate: flavourful, fruity, fresh, fleshy.

CAN RICH 2010 RD
60% syrah, 40% tempranillo.

82 Colour: coppery red. Nose: floral, candied fruit, medium intensity. Palate: sweetness, spicy.

CAN RICH VI NEGRE 2008 T
60% merlot, 20% cabernet sauvignon, 20% tempranillo.

87 Colour: cherry, garnet rim. Nose: earthy notes, fruit liqueur notes, ripe fruit. Palate: spirituous, fine bitter notes, good acidity.

CAN RICH SELECCIÓN 2007 T
60% cabernet sauvignon, 30% merlot, 10% tempranillo.

88 Colour: deep cherry. Nose: fruit liqueur notes, spicy, creamy oak, balsamic herbs, scrubland. Palate: flavourful, spicy, ripe fruit.

LAUSOS CABERNET SAUVIGNON 2006 T
100% cabernet sauvignon.

91 Colour: deep cherry. Nose: scrubland, balsamic herbs, toasty. Palate: ripe fruit, spicy, fine tannins.

CAN RICH DULCE VINO DE LICOR
100% malvasía.

84 Colour: bright straw. Nose: fruit liqueur notes, citrus fruit, warm. Palate: flavourful, ripe fruit.

VINOS CAN MAYMÓ

Casa Can Maymó
07816 Sant Mateu d'Albarca (Illes Ballears)
☎: +34 971 805 100 - Fax: +34 971 805 100
info@bodegascanmaymo.com

CAN MAYMÓ 2010 B
70% malvasía, 30% moscatel.

87 Colour: bright straw. Nose: scrubland, ripe fruit, citrus fruit. Palate: flavourful, fruity, fresh, fine bitter notes.

CAN MAYMÓ 2010 RD
100% syrah.

90 Colour: brilliant rose. Nose: candied fruit, dried flowers, fragrant herbs, red berry notes. Palate: light-bodied, flavourful, good acidity, long, spicy.

CAN MAYMÓ MERLOT 2009 T
100% merlot.

89 Colour: light cherry. Nose: expressive, fresh, balsamic herbs, scrubland. Palate: flavourful, fruity, spicy.

CAN MAYMÓ 2009 T BARRICA
60% syrah, 40% merlot.

87 Colour: light cherry. Nose: expressive, medium intensity, balsamic herbs. Palate: flavourful, light-bodied, fresh.

CAN MAYMÓ TRADICIÓN 2009 T
50% monastrell, 50% syrah.

86 Colour: bright cherry. Nose: ripe fruit, sweet spices, creamy oak. Palate: flavourful, fruity, toasty, round tannins.

EL TERRERAZO

MUSTIGUILLO VIÑEDOS Y BODEGA

Ctra. N-330, km 196,5 El Terrerazo
46300 Utiel (Valencia)
☎: +34 962 168 260 - Fax: +34 962 168 259
info@bodegamustiguillo.com
www.bodegamustiguillo.com

MESTIZAJE 2010 T
65% bobal, 35% tempranillo, cabernet sauvignon, merlot, syrah.

91 Colour: dark-red cherry. Nose: undergrowth, mineral, fruit expression, rose petals, violet drops. Palate: complex, fresh, fruity, spicy, mineral, fruity aftestaste.

EXTREMADURA

BODEGA DE MIRABEL

Buenavista, 31
10220 Pago de San Clemente (Cáceres)
☎: +34 927 323 154 - Fax: +34 927 323 154
bodegademirabel@hotmail.com

TRIBEL DE MIRABEL 2009 T
55% cabernet sauvignon, 45% syrah.

91 Colour: bright cherry. Nose: sweet spices, creamy oak, overripe fruit. Palate: flavourful, toasty, round tannins.

MIRABEL 2007 T
85% tempranillo, 15% cabernet sauvignon.

92 Colour: bright cherry. Nose: ripe fruit, sweet spices, creamy oak. Palate: fruity, toasty, round tannins.

BODEGA SAN MARCOS

Ctra. Aceuchal, s/n
06200 Almendralejo (Badajoz)
☎: +34 924 670 410 - Fax: +34 924 665 505
ventas@bodegasanmarcos.com
www.campobarro.com

CAMPOBRAVO 2010 B
92% cayetana blanca, 8% moscatel.

85 Colour: bright straw. Nose: fresh, fresh fruit, white flowers. Palate: flavourful, fruity, good acidity, sweetness.

CAMPOBRAVO SYRAH 2010 RD
100% syrah.

87 Colour: rose, purple rim. Nose: ripe fruit, red berry notes. Palate: fleshy, powerful, fruity, fresh.

BODEGAS ALAUDE

Semillero de Empresas, N-2
06120 Oliva de la Frontera (Badajoz)
☎: +34 924 740 174
info@bodegasalaude.com
www.bodegasalaude.com

QVINTA ALAVDE 2008 T ROBLE
80% tempranillo, 20% cabernet sauvignon.

86 Colour: bright cherry. Nose: ripe fruit, sweet spices. Palate: flavourful, fruity, toasty, round tannins.

ALIVS 2007 T
60% tempranillo, 40% cabernet sauvignon.

83 Colour: bright cherry. Nose: sweet spices, creamy oak, medium intensity. Palate: flavourful, fruity, toasty, round tannins.

BODEGAS CAÑALVA

Coto, 54
10136 Cañamero (Cáceres)
☎: +34 927 369 405 - Fax: +34 927 369 405
info@bodegascanalva.com
www.bodegascañalva.com

CAÑALVA CABERNET SAUVIGNON MERLOT 2010 T
75% cabernet sauvignon, 25% merlot.

85 Colour: cherry, purple rim. Nose: red berry notes, floral, warm. Palate: fresh, fruity, flavourful, fleshy.

CAÑALVA 2010 T
100% tempranillo.

83 Colour: cherry, purple rim. Nose: overripe fruit, fresh, medium intensity. Palate: flavourful, fruity, fleshy.

CAÑALVA COUPAGE ESPECIAL 2009 TC
25% cabernet sauvignon, 25% merlot, 25% syrah, 25% tempranillo.

88 Colour: cherry, garnet rim. Nose: red berry notes, ripe fruit, cocoa bean, dark chocolate, creamy oak. Palate: powerful, flavourful, fleshy, round.

CAÑALVA TINTO FINO 2006 TR
100% tempranillo.

83 Colour: pale ruby, brick rim edge. Nose: old leather, overripe fruit, roasted coffee. Palate: rich, flavourful, spicy.

CAÑALVA SYRAH 2006 T ROBLE
100% syrah.

82 Colour: cherry, garnet rim. Nose: fruit preserve, scrubland, spicy. Palate: flavourful, ripe fruit, toasty.

LUZ 2009 SEMIDULCE
80% macabeo, 20% moscatel.

85 Colour: bright straw. Nose: fresh fruit, citrus fruit, tropical fruit. Palate: light-bodied, fresh, fruity, easy to drink.

BODEGAS CARLOS PLAZA

Sol s/n
06196 Cartagena (Badajoz)
☎: +34 924 687 932 - Fax: +34 924 687 932
export@bodegascarlosplaza.com
www.carlosplaza.com

CARLOS PLAZA 2010 T
90% tempranillo, 10% syrah.

88 Colour: cherry, purple rim. Nose: ripe fruit, scrubland. Palate: flavourful, fine bitter notes, good acidity.

CARLOS PLAZA 2009 T
70% tempranillo, 15% syrah, 15% merlot.

85 Colour: bright cherry. Nose: sweet spices, creamy oak, fruit preserve. Palate: flavourful, fruity, toasty, round tannins.

BODEGAS DE AGUILAR

P.I. N-430 La Radio, 10
06760 Navalvillar de Pela (Badajoz)
☎: +34 924 861 257 - Fax: +34 924 861 257
bodegasdeaguilar@gmail.com
www.bodegasdeaguilar.es

AGUILAR 2010 B
alarije.

74

AGUILAR 6 MESES 2006 T
tempranillo, graciano.

80 Colour: pale ruby, brick rim edge. Nose: aromatic coffee, fruit liqueur notes, slightly evolved. Palate: warm, fine bitter notes.

AGUILAR 12 MESES 2006 T
cabernet sauvignon, graciano.

77

BODEGAS HABLA

Ctra. A-V, km. 259
10200 Trujillo (Cáceres)
☎: +34 927 659 180 - Fax: +34 927 659 180
habla@bodegashabla.com
www.bodegashabla.com

HABLA DEL SILENCIO 2009 T
syrah, cabernet sauvignon, tempranillo.

88 Colour: cherry, garnet rim. Nose: fruit preserve, fruit liqueur notes, creamy oak. Palate: powerful, fleshy, sweetness, fine bitter notes.

HABLA Nº 7 2007 T
cabernet sauvignon, tempranillo, petit verdot.

93 Colour: cherry, garnet rim. Nose: spicy, creamy oak, toasty, ripe fruit, mineral. Palate: powerful, flavourful, toasty, ripe fruit.

HABLA Nº 6 2007 T
syrah.

92 Colour: bright cherry. Nose: sweet spices, creamy oak, red berry notes, lactic notes. Palate: flavourful, toasty, round tannins, ripe fruit.

BODEGAS JOSÉ OTERO VAQUERA

Ctra. Azuaga - Maguilla, Km. 11,5
06920 Azuaga (Badajoz)
☎: +34 924 144 078 - Fax: +34 924 144 079
info@vinosbureo.com
www.vinosbureo.com

BUREO CABERNET 2008 T
100% cabernet sauvignon.

85 Colour: bright cherry. Nose: sweet spices, creamy oak, ripe fruit. Palate: flavourful, fruity, toasty, round tannins, balsamic.

730 DÍAS 2006 T
100% tempranillo.

87 Colour: cherry, garnet rim. Nose: ripe fruit, spicy, creamy oak, toasty. Palate: powerful, flavourful, toasty, round tannins.

BODEGAS LAR DE BARROS INVIOSA

Apdo. Correos 291
06200 Almendralejo (Badajoz)
☎: +34 924 671 235 - Fax: +34 924 687 231
sophia@lardebarros.com
www.lardebarros.com

LAR DE ORO 2010 B
100% chardonnay.

81 Colour: bright straw. Nose: ripe fruit, citrus fruit. Palate: flavourful, light-bodied.

LAR DE ORO 2010 T
100% cabernet sauvignon.

87 Colour: bright cherry. Nose: sweet spices, creamy oak, red berry notes. Palate: flavourful, fruity, toasty, round tannins.

BODEGAS ORAN

Ctra de Sevilla 34
06200 Almendralejo (Badajoz)
☎: +34 662 952 800 - Fax: +34 924 665 406
www.bodegasoran.com

SEÑORÍO DE ORÁN 2007 TC
tempranillo.

84 Colour: bright cherry. Nose: sweet spices, creamy oak, ripe fruit. Palate: flavourful, fruity, toasty, round tannins.

BODEGAS ROMERO

Avda. Magaz, s/n
06392 El Raposo (Badajoz)
☎: +34 924 570 448 - Fax: +34 924 570 448
romero@bodegasromero.com
www.bodegasromero.com

PRADOMAYO 2009 B
100% gewürztraminer.

80 Colour: bright straw. Nose: ripe fruit, honeyed notes, citrus fruit. Palate: flavourful, fruity, sweetness.

ALMONAZAR 2010 RD
60% tempranillo, 40% garnacha.

84 Colour: rose, purple rim. Nose: ripe fruit, red berry notes. Palate: fleshy, fruity, fresh.

PRADOMAYO 2009 T ROBLE
60% tempranillo, 20% cabernet sauvignon, 20% otras.

83 Colour: cherry, garnet rim. Nose: ripe fruit, creamy oak, toasty. Palate: powerful, toasty, round tannins.

BODEGAS RUIZ TORRES

Ctra. EX 116, km.33,8
10136 Cañamero (Cáceres)
☎: +34 927 369 024 - Fax: +34 927 369 302
info@ruiztorres.com
www.ruiztorres.com

TRAMPAL 2010 B
macabeo.

83 Colour: bright straw. Nose: white flowers, ripe fruit. Palate: flavourful, fruity.

ANTEROS 2010 B
pardina.

76

ANTEROS 2010 RD
tempranillo.

80 Colour: rose. Nose: tropical fruit, red berry notes. Palate: flavourful, fruity, fresh.

TRAMPAL 2009 RD
tempranillo.

83 Colour: rose, purple rim. Nose: ripe fruit, red berry notes, expressive. Palate: fleshy, powerful, fruity, fresh.

ANTEROS 2010 T
tempranillo.

87 Colour: cherry, purple rim. Nose: red berry notes, ripe fruit. Palate: flavourful, fruity, good acidity, round tannins.

TRAMPAL 2007 TC
tempranillo, garnacha.

77

SIERRA DE GUADALUPE BR
macabeo, chardonnay.

76

EX DE EXTREMADURA BN
chardonnay, macabeo.

80 Colour: bright straw. Nose: ripe fruit, grassy. Palate: flavourful, fruity, fresh.

SIERRA DE GUADALUPE SS
macabeo, chardonnay.

78

EX DE EXTREMADURA SS
chardonnay, macabeo.

77

BODEGAS TORIBIO VIÑA PUEBLA

Luis Chamizo, 12-21
06310 Puebla de Sancho Pérez (Badajoz)
☎: +34 924 551 449 - Fax: +34 924 551 449
info@bodegastoribio.com
www.bodegastoribio.com

TORIBIO ECOLÓGICO 2010 B
macabeo.

83 Colour: bright straw. Nose: fresh fruit, white flowers, expressive. Palate: flavourful, good acidity, lacks expression.

TORIBIO ECOLÓGICO 2010 T
tempranillo.

90 Colour: cherry, purple rim. Nose: fresh fruit, red berry notes, sweet spices. Palate: flavourful, fruity, good acidity, round tannins.

BODEGAS VIÑA EXTREMEÑA

Ctra. de Alange, s/n
06200 Almendralejo (Badajoz)
☎: +34 924 670 158 - Fax: +34 924 670 159
info@vinexsa.com
www.vinexsa.com

MONASTERIO DE TENTUDIA 2008 T
tempranillo.

83 Colour: pale ruby, brick rim edge. Nose: powerfull, candied fruit, fruit liqueur notes, spicy. Palate: spicy, spirituous, fine bitter notes.

TENTUDIA PREMIUM 2007 T
syrah, cabernet sauvignon.

85 Colour: cherry, garnet rim. Nose: ripe fruit, spicy, toasty. Palate: powerful, flavourful, toasty, round tannins.

CORTE REAL PLATINUM 2006 T
cabernet sauvignon, merlot.

88 Colour: pale ruby, brick rim edge. Nose: fine reductive notes, wet leather, aged wood nuances, fruit liqueur notes. Palate: spicy, fine tannins, elegant, long.

CORTE REAL 2005 T
cabernet sauvignon, tempranillo.

86 Colour: pale ruby, brick rim edge. Nose: spicy, wet leather, aged wood nuances, fruit liqueur notes. Palate: spicy, fine tannins, elegant, long.

BODEGAS Y VIÑEDOS ÁNGEL SÁNCHEZ REDONDO

Circunvalación Sur de Plasencia, Urb. Haza del Obispo 500m. (Finca Pago de Los Angeles)
10006 Plasencia (Cáceres)
☎: +34 927 116 250
ana@vinaplacentina.com
www.fincaelpalomar.com

VIÑA PLACENTINA CABERNET SAUVIGNON 2007 T
cabernet sauvignon.

83 Colour: bright cherry. Nose: spicy, tobacco, aged wood nuances, toasty. Palate: easy to drink, ripe fruit, spicy.

VIÑA PLACENTINA ECOLÓGICO CABERNET SAUVIGNON 2004 T
cabernet sauvignon.

85 Colour: ruby red, orangey edge. Nose: ripe fruit, old leather, powerfull, medium intensity. Palate: good acidity, flavourful, fleshy.

CATALINA ARROYO

Ctra. Don Benito - Miajadas, Km. 1.900
06400 Don Benito (Badajoz)
☎: +34 924 147 192 - Fax: +34 924 841 852
catalina.arroyo@terra.es
www.bodegascatalinaarroyo.com

CATALINA ARROYO CABERNET SAUVIGNON 2008 T ROBLE
cabernet sauvignon.

82 Colour: pale ruby, brick rim edge. Nose: pattiserie, caramel, fruit liqueur notes, spicy. Palate: light-bodied, spicy, easy to drink.

MISINO 2008 T
cabernet sauvignon.

82 Colour: bright cherry. Nose: sweet spices, creamy oak, overripe fruit, warm. Palate: flavourful, toasty, round tannins.

CATALINA ARROYO MERLOT 2008 T
merlot.

76

MARCELINO DÍAZ

Mecánica, s/n
06200 Almendralejo (Badajoz)
☎: +34 924 677 548 - Fax: +34 924 660 977
bodega@madiaz.com
www.madiaz.com

THEODOSIUS 2008 TC
tempranillo, graciano.

85 Colour: bright cherry. Nose: sweet spices, creamy oak, fruit liqueur notes. Palate: flavourful, fruity, toasty, round tannins.

MARQUÉS DE VALDUEZA

Autovía de Extremadura A-5 Km. 360
06800 Mérida (Badajoz)
☎: +34 913 191 508 - Fax: +34 913 084 034
contact@marquesdevaldueza.com
www.marquesdevaldueza.com

MARQUÉS DE VALDUEZA ETIQUETA ROJA 2009 T
53,2% cabernet sauvignon, 44,9% syrah, 1,9% merlot.

92 Colour: bright cherry. Nose: creamy oak, expressive, red berry notes, fruit expression. Palate: flavourful, toasty, round tannins, ripe fruit.

VALDUEZA 2009 T
53,4% syrah, 29,2% cabernet sauvignon, 17,4% merlot.

91 Colour: bright cherry. Nose: sweet spices, fruit preserve, new oak, toasty. Palate: flavourful, fruity, toasty, round tannins.

MARQUÉS DE VALDUEZA 2008 T
91% syrah, 9% cabernet sauvignon.

94 Colour: bright cherry. Nose: fruit expression, raspberry, new oak, characterful, mineral. Palate: flavourful, fruity, toasty, round tannins.

MARQUÉS DE VALDUEZA ETIQUETA ROJA 2008 T
61% cabernet sauvignon, 37% syrah, 2% merlot.

90 Colour: bright cherry. Nose: ripe fruit, sweet spices, creamy oak. Palate: flavourful, fruity, toasty, round tannins.

VALDUEZA 2008 T
syrah, cabernet sauvignon, merlot.

88 Colour: dark-red cherry. Nose: overripe fruit, powerfull, creamy oak, spicy. Palate: good acidity, flavourful, round tannins, fleshy.

MARQUÉS DE VALDUEZA 2007 T
47% syrah, 38% cabernet sauvignon, 21% merlot.

92 Colour: bright cherry. Nose: sweet spices, ripe fruit, creamy oak, mineral, earthy notes. Palate: flavourful, fruity, toasty, round tannins.

VIÑA SANTA MARINA

Ctra. N-630, Km. 634 - Apdo. Correos 714
06800 Mérida (Badajoz)
☎: +34 902 506 364 - Fax: +34 924 027 675
bodega@vsantamarina.com
www.vsantamarina.com

ALTARA 2010 B
montúa, cayetana blanca, pardina.

84 Colour: bright straw. Nose: fresh fruit, white flowers, grassy. Palate: flavourful, fruity, good acidity.

VIÑA SANTA MARINA VIOGNIER SECO 2010 B
100% viognier.

83 Colour: bright golden. Nose: candied fruit, citrus fruit, medium intensity. Palate: flavourful, fruity, fleshy.

ALTARA AURUM 2010 B
80% montúa, 20% viognier.

81 Colour: bright golden. Nose: candied fruit, citrus fruit, fragrant herbs. Palate: flavourful, fruity, fine bitter notes.

VIÑA SANTA MARINA VIOGNIER VENDIMIA TARDÍA 2006 B
100% viognier.

87 Colour: bright golden. Nose: medium intensity, candied fruit, fruit preserve, citrus fruit, fruit liqueur notes. Palate: sweetness, ripe fruit, spicy, long.

CELTUS TEMPRANILLO 2008 T
100% tempranillo.

86 Colour: cherry, purple rim. Nose: fresh fruit, red berry notes, sweet spices. Palate: flavourful, fruity, good acidity, round tannins.

GLADIATOR 2008 T
60% syrah, 30% cabernet sauvignon, 10% petit verdot.

84 Color cherry, garnet rim. Aroma ripe fruit, spicy, creamy oak, toasty, complex. Taste powerful, flavourful, toasty, round tannins.

EQUUS 2008 TC
tempranillo, cabernet sauvignon, syrah.

82 Colour: bright cherry. Nose: sweet spices, fruit liqueur notes, aromatic coffee. Palate: flavourful, fruity, toasty, round tannins.

VIÑA SANTA MARINA CABERNET SAUVIGNON-SYRAH 2007 TR
cabernet sauvignon, syrah.

85 Colour: cherry, garnet rim. Nose: medium intensity, expressive, fruit liqueur notes, spicy. Palate: spicy, balsamic, fine bitter notes.

MIRACULUS 2005 T
merlot, cabernet sauvignon, syrah.

86 Colour: cherry, garnet rim. Nose: ripe fruit, spicy, toasty. Palate: powerful, flavourful, toasty, round tannins.

FORMENTERA

CAP DE BARBARIA

Elisenda de Pinos, 1 Casa A
08034 (Barcelona)
☎: +34 609 855 556
info@capdebarbaria.com
www.capdebarbaria.com

CAP DE BARBARIA 2008 T
45% cabernet sauvignon, 30% merlot, 20% monastrell, 5% fogoneu.

93 Colour: cherry, garnet rim. Nose: aged wood nuances, dark chocolate, balsamic herbs, scrubland, fruit liqueur notes. Palate: flavourful, spicy, balsamic, fine tannins.

TERRAMOLL

Ctra. de La Mola, Km. 15,5
07872 El Pilar de la Mola (Illes Ballears)
☎: +34 971 327 257 - Fax: +34 971 327 293
info@terramoll.es
www.terramoll.es

SAVINA 2010 B
47% viognier, 34% moscatel, 14% malvasía, 5% garnacha blanca.

90 Colour: bright straw. Nose: fresh fruit, white flowers, expressive, grassy. Palate: flavourful, fruity, good acidity, balanced. Personality.

TERRAMOLL 2010 RD
46% merlot, 36% cabernet sauvignon, 18% monastrell.

89 Colour: brilliant rose. Nose: elegant, candied fruit, dried flowers, fragrant herbs, red berry notes. Palate: light-bodied, flavourful, good acidity, long, spicy.

TERRAMOLL ES MONESTIR 2008 T
monastrell.

91 Colour: cherry, garnet rim. Nose: ripe fruit, spicy, creamy oak, toasty, mineral, earthy notes. Palate: powerful, flavourful, toasty, round tannins.

ILLA DE MENORCA

VINYA SA CUDIA

Cos de Gracia, 7
07702 Mahón (Illes Balears)
☎: +34 686 361 445 - Fax: +34 971 353 607
info@vinyasacudia.com
www.vinyasacudia.com

VINYA SA CUDÍA 2010 B
100% malvasía.

85 Colour: bright straw. Nose: medium intensity, grapey, fruit expression, grassy. Palate: flavourful, fleshy, ripe fruit.

VINYES BINITORD DE MENORCA

Camino Lloc de Monges 39º 57'21"; 3º 51'16"
07760 Ciutadella de Menorca (Illes Balears)
☎: +34 654 909 714
asalord@infotelecom.es
www.binitord.com

BINITORD BLANC 2010 B
chardonnay, merlot, macabeo.

91 Colour: bright straw. Nose: ripe fruit, white flowers, fragrant herbs, mineral, expressive. Palate: good acidity, flavourful, light-bodied, fresh, fleshy, elegant.

BINITORD 2009 B
chardonnay, merlot, macabeo.

92 Colour: bright straw. Nose: saline, dried flowers, ripe fruit, wild herbs, mineral, balanced, expressive. Palate: rich, powerful, flavourful, fleshy, complex.

BINITORD BLANC 2008 B
chardonnay, macabeo, merlot.

90 Colour: bright straw. Nose: floral, ripe fruit, dry nuts, balsamic herbs, spicy. Palate: good acidity, round, unctuous, flavourful.

BINITORD ROSAT 2010 RD
tempranillo.

85 Colour: rose, purple rim. Nose: red berry notes, raspberry, floral, lactic notes. Palate: fleshy, flavourful, fruity, good structure.

BINITORD NEGRE 2009 T
cabernet sauvignon, merlot.

88 Colour: cherry, garnet rim. Nose: ripe fruit, balsamic herbs, fragrant herbs, mineral, spicy. Palate: powerful, flavourful, fleshy.

BINITORD ROURE 2008 T
tempranillo, cabernet sauvignon, syrah.

89 Colour: cherry, garnet rim. Nose: ripe fruit, expressive, spicy, creamy oak, mineral. Palate: good acidity, flavourful, round tannins.

LAUJAR-ALPUJARRA

BODEGA EL CORTIJO DE LA VIEJA

Paraje de la Vieja, s/n Ctra. A-348 Km. 75
04480 Alcolea (Almería)
☎: +34 950 343 919 - Fax: +34 950 343 919
comercial@iniza.net
www.iniza.net

INIZA MACABEO 2010 B
macabeo, sauvignon blanc.

81 Colour: bright straw. Nose: dried flowers, ripe fruit, fragrant herbs. Palate: fresh, light-bodied, flavourful.

INIZA 2010 T MACERACIÓN CARBÓNICA
75% garnacha, 25% tempranillo.

89 Colour: cherry, purple rim. Nose: floral, red berry notes, fresh fruit. Palate: fruity, flavourful, fleshy.

INIZA CABERNET SAUVIGNON 2009 T
cabernet sauvignon.

87 Colour: cherry, garnet rim. Nose: ripe fruit, floral, balsamic herbs, earthy notes. Palate: good acidity, fleshy, powerful, flavourful.

INIZA 4 CEPAS 2009 T
40% syrah, 30% tempranillo, 20% merlot, 10% petit verdot.

83 Colour: cherry, purple rim. Nose: fruit preserve, earthy notes, grassy, expressive. Palate: good acidity, powerful, flavourful.

INIZA 2008 T BARRICA
tempranillo, syrah, merlot.

84 Colour: cherry, garnet rim. Nose: ripe fruit, earthy notes, balsamic herbs, toasty. Palate: astringent, powerful, complex, fleshy.

VALLE DE LAUJAR

Ctra. de Laujar a Berja, Km. 2,2
04470 Laujar de Andarax (Almería)
☎: +34 950 514 200 - Fax: +34 950 608 001

VIÑA LAUJAR S.C. B

88 Colour: bright golden. Nose: fruit preserve, fruit expression, earthy notes. Palate: spirituous, powerful, flavourful, sweet, full, good acidity, unctuous, fruity.

VIÑA LAUJAR MACABEO 2010 B
macabeo.

80 Colour: bright straw. Nose: expressive, ripe fruit, faded flowers. Palate: flavourful, fruity.

VIÑA LAUJAR COTA 950 2009 B
sauvignon blanc, chardonnay.

85 Colour: bright straw. Nose: slightly evolved, fresh, short, fruit liqueur notes, earthy notes. Palate: spirituous, flavourful, powerful, fruity, sweetness.

FINCA MATAGALLO 2009 T
60% syrah, 40% merlot.

79

VIÑA LAUJAR 2007 T
100% syrah.

78

VIÑA LAUJAR ESPUMOSO BN
100% macabeo.

82 Colour: straw. Nose: fine reductive notes, dry nuts, fresh, neat. Palate: correct, good acidity, sweetness, flavourful, fresh, classic aged character, creamy.

LIÉBANA

RÍO SANTO

Cillorigo de Liébana
39584 Esanos (Cantabria)
☎: +34 652 286 474
info@riosanto.es
www.riosanto.es

LUSIA 2009 T ROBLE
85% mencía, 15% tempranillo.

92 Colour: cherry, purple rim. Nose: floral, mineral, cocoa bean, creamy oak, red berry notes, ripe fruit, balsamic herbs. Palate: mineral, powerful, flavourful, fleshy, complex.

MALLORCA

4 KILOS VINÍCOLA

1ª Volta, 168 Puigverd
07200 Felanitx (Illes Balears)
☎: +34 660 226 641 - Fax: +34 971 580 523
fgrimalt@4kilos.com
www.4kilos.com

GALLINAS & FOCAS 2009 T
50% manto negro, 50% syrah.

94 Colour: cherry, garnet rim. Nose: red berry notes, earthy notes, mineral, spicy, creamy oak, complex. Palate: powerful, flavourful, fleshy, complex, balanced.

4 KILOS 2009 T
callet, cabernet sauvignon, merlot.

93 Colour: cherry, garnet rim. Nose: ripe fruit, expressive, powerfull, spicy, mineral. Palate: powerful, flavourful, fleshy, complex, round tannins.

12 VOLTS 2009 T
syrah, merlot, cabernet sauvignon, callet, fogonneu.

93 Colour: light cherry, garnet rim. Nose: fruit expression, ripe fruit, sweet spices. Palate: flavourful, fruity, balanced.

BINIGRAU

Fiol, 33
07143 Biniali (Illes Ballears)
☎: +34 971 512 023 - Fax: +34 971 886 495
info@binigrau.es
www.binigrau.es

NOU NAT 2010 B
prensal blanc, chardonnay.

93 Colour: bright straw. Nose: powerfull, expressive, fruit expression, citrus fruit, sweet spices. Palate: flavourful, fleshy, long, mineral.

OBAC DE BINIGRAU 2008 TC
manto negro, callet, merlot, cabernet sauvignon, syrah.

89 Colour: cherry, garnet rim. Nose: scrubland, ripe fruit, smoky. Palate: flavourful, toasty, ripe fruit.

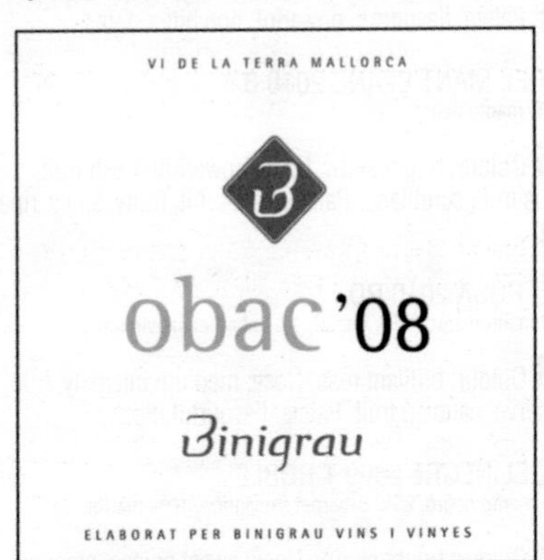

BINIGRAU CHARDONNAY 2010 BFB
chardonnay.

91 Colour: bright straw. Nose: white flowers, ripe fruit, fruit expression, citrus fruit. Palate: flavourful, fruity, fleshy, full.

E BINIGRAU 2010 RD
manto negro, merlot.

89 Color rose, purple rim. Aroma powerfull, ripe fruit, red berry notes, floral, expressive. Taste fleshy, powerful, fruity, fresh.

E NEGRE DE BINIGRAU 2010 T
manto negro, merlot.

92 Colour: cherry, garnet rim. Nose: ripe fruit, spicy, earthy notes, characterful. Palate: powerful, flavourful, round tannins.

BINIGRAU SELECCIÓ 2008 T
manto negro, callet, merlot.

94 Colour: cherry, garnet rim. Nose: ripe fruit, spicy, creamy oak, toasty, complex, earthy notes, mineral. Palate: powerful, flavourful, toasty, round tannins.

BODEGAS ÁNGEL

Ctra. Sta María - Sencelles, km. 4,8
07320 Santa María del Camí (Illes Ballears)
☎: +34 971 621 638
info@bodegasangel.com
www.bodegasangel.com

ÁNGEL BLANCA DE BLANCA 2010 B
60% prensal, 40% chardonnay.

89 Colour: bright straw. Nose: grassy, fresh fruit, ripe fruit. Palate: flavourful, powerful, fine bitter notes.

ÁNGEL MANT BLANC 2010 B
100% manto negro.

86 Colour: bright straw. Nose: powerfull, fresh fruit, citrus fruit, scrubland. Palate: flavourful, fruity, spicy, ripe fruit.

LAU ROSA 2010 RD
75% manto negro, 24% merlot, 1% cabernet sauvignon.

83 Colour: brilliant rose. Nose: medium intensity, fruit preserve, candied fruit. Palate: flavourful, fleshy.

ÁNGEL NEGRE 2009 T ROBLE
55% manto negro, 35% cabernet sauvignon, 10% merlot.

91 Colour: bright cherry. Nose: sweet spices, creamy oak, expressive, fruit expression, violet drops. Palate: flavourful, toasty, round tannins.

BODEGAS CA'N VIDALET

Ctra. Alcudia - Pollença PMV 220-1, Km. 4,85
07460 Pollença (Illes Ballears)
☎: +34 971 531 719 - Fax: +34 971 535 395
info@canvidalet.com
www.canvidalet.com

CA'N VIDALET SES PEDRES 2010 B
100% chardonnay.

90 Colour: bright straw. Nose: floral, fragrant herbs, varietal, neat. Palate: good acidity, light-bodied, flavourful.

CA'N VIDALET BLANC DE BLANCS 2010 B
40% chardonnay, 40% sauvignon blanc, 20% moscatel.

85 Colour: bright straw. Nose: white flowers, tropical fruit, fresh. Palate: fresh, light-bodied, flavourful, easy to drink.

CA'N VIDALET BLANC DE NEGRES 2010 RD
60% merlot, 20% cabernet sauvignon, 20% syrah.

86 Colour: onion pink. Nose: white flowers, tropical fruit, fresh. Palate: creamy, light-bodied, flavourful, fresh.

CA'N VIDALET TERRA FUSCA 2008 T
100% syrah.

91 Colour: cherry, garnet rim. Nose: ripe fruit, cocoa bean, creamy oak, sweet spices, roasted coffee. Palate: unctuous, good acidity, powerful, flavourful, fleshy.

CA'N VIDALET SO DEL XIPRER-GRAN SELECCIÓN 2008 T
80% cabernet sauvignon, 20% merlot.

91 Colour: cherry, garnet rim. Nose: red berry notes, ripe fruit, spicy, old leather, mineral. Palate: fruity, fleshy, spicy.

CA'N VIDALET SO DEL XIPRER 2008 T
70% merlot, 30% cabernet sauvignon.

90 Colour: cherry, garnet rim. Nose: ripe fruit, balsamic herbs, spicy, creamy oak. Palate: flavourful, fleshy, easy to drink.

BODEGAS RIBAS

Montanya, 2
07330 Consell (Illes Ballears)
☎: +34 971 622 673 - Fax: +34 971 622 746
info@bodegaribas.com
www.bodegaribas.com

SIONETA OLIVER LOMA 2010 B

90 Colour: bright straw. Nose: fresh fruit, white flowers. Palate: flavourful, fruity, good acidity, balanced.

SIÓ 300 ANIVERSARIO 2009 T
70% manto negro, 30% syrah.

95 Colour: cherry, garnet rim. Nose: mineral, ripe fruit, toasty. Palate: flavourful, ripe fruit, spicy, round tannins.

BODEGAS SON PUIG

Finca Son Puig, s/n
07194 Puigpunyent Mallorca (Illes Balears)
☎: +34 971 614 184 - Fax: +34 971 614 184
info@sonpuig.com
www.sonpuig.com

SONPUIG 2010 BFB
64% chardonnay, 36% moll.

86 Colour: bright straw. Nose: powerfull, characterful, candied fruit, honeyed notes. Palate: fine bitter notes, ripe fruit, spicy.

SONPUIG ESTIU 2010 T
31% tempranillo, 28% merlot, 26% callet, 15% cabernet sauvignon.

87 Colour: cherry, garnet rim. Nose: powerfull, warm, candied fruit, earthy notes. Palate: powerful, fleshy, fine bitter notes.

GRAN SONPUIG 2007 T
69% merlot, 31% cabernet sauvignon.

90 Colour: bright cherry. Nose: smoky, dark chocolate, fruit liqueur notes, fruit preserve. Palate: fine bitter notes, warm, powerful.

SONPUIG 2007 T
47% tempranillo, 33% merlot, 20% cabernet sauvignon.

88 Colour: cherry, garnet rim. Nose: ripe fruit, spicy, creamy oak, toasty. Palate: powerful, flavourful, toasty, round tannins.

FINCA SON BORDILS

Ctra. Inca - Sineu, Km. 4,1
07300 Inca (Illes Ballears)
☎: +34 971 182 200 - Fax: +34 971 182 202
info@sonbordils.es
www.sonbordils.es

SON BORDILS BLANC DE RAÏM BLANC 2010 B
prensal.

90 Colour: bright yellow. Nose: ripe fruit, tropical fruit, floral, mineral. Palate: fresh, fruity, light-bodied, flavourful, complex.

FINCA SON BORDILS CHARDONNAY 2010 B
chardonnay.

89 Colour: bright golden. Nose: fruit expression, ripe fruit, powerfull, dried herbs. Palate: flavourful, fruity, fleshy, unctuous.

SON BORDILS MUSCAT 2010 B
moscatel.

88 Colour: bright straw. Nose: fresh, fresh fruit, white flowers, expressive, citrus fruit. Palate: flavourful, fruity, good acidity.

FINCA SON BORDILS CHARDONNAY 2008 BFB
chardonnay.

91 Colour: bright yellow. Nose: powerfull, ripe fruit, sweet spices, creamy oak. Palate: rich, smoky aftertaste, flavourful, fleshy, toasty.

SON BORDILS ROSAT DE MONASTRELL 2010 RD
monastrell.

90 Colour: rose, purple rim. Nose: powerfull, ripe fruit, red berry notes, floral, expressive. Palate: fleshy, powerful, fruity, fresh, long.

FINCA SON BORDILS MERLOT 2005 T
merlot.

90 Colour: pale ruby, brick rim edge. Nose: ripe fruit, complex, cigar, old leather, sweet spices. Palate: good acidity, spirituous, unctuous, flavourful.

FINCA SON BORDILS SYRAH 2005 T
syrah.

88 Colour: cherry, garnet rim. Nose: ripe fruit, earthy notes, spicy, creamy oak. Palate: powerful, flavourful, fleshy, complex.

SON BORDILS NEGRE 2005 T
manto negro, callet, cabernet sauvignon.

88 Colour: deep cherry, orangey edge. Nose: ripe fruit, old leather, tobacco, cocoa bean, sweet spices, toasty. Palate: good acidity, balanced, spirituous.

FINCA SON BORDILS CABERNET SAUVIGNON 2005 T
cabernet sauvignon.

86 Colour: cherry, garnet rim. Nose: complex, ripe fruit, old leather, cigar, toasty. Palate: powerful, flavourful, fleshy, complex.

JAUME DE PUNTIRÓ

Pza. Nova, 23
07320 Santa María del Camí (Illes Balears)
☎: +34 971 620 023 - Fax: +34 971 620 023
pere@vinsjaumedepuntiro.com
www.vinsjaumedepuntiro.com

PORPRAT 2008 T
100% merlot.

85 Color bright cherry. Aroma ripe fruit, sweet spices, creamy oak, expressive. Taste flavourful, fruity, toasty, round tannins.

JOSÉ L. FERRER

Conquistador, 103
07350 Binissalem (Illes Baleas)
☎: +34 971 511 050 - Fax: +34 971 870 084
info@vinosferrer.com
www.vinosferrer.com

JOSÉ L. FERRER D2UES MOLL CHARDONNAY MOLL 2010 B
50% chardonnay, 50% moll.

85 Color bright straw. Aroma fresh, fresh fruit, white flowers, expressive. Taste flavourful, fruity, good acidity, balanced.

VINS MIQUEL GELABERT

Carrer d'en Sales, 50
07500 Manacor (Illes Ballears)
☎: +34 971 821 444 - Fax: +34 971 596 441
vinsmg@vinsmiquelgelabert.com
www.vinsmiquelgelabert.com

AUTÓCTON 2008 T
40% callet, 20% manto negro, 20% fogoneu, 20% otras.

91 Colour: cherry, garnet rim. Nose: mineral, fruit expression, raspberry, toasty, sweet spices. Palate: flavourful, spicy, ripe fruit.

VINS NADAL

Ramón Llull, 2
07350 Binissalem (Illes Balears)
☎: +34 971 511 058 - Fax: +34 971 870 150
albaflor@vinsnadal.com
www.vinsnadal.com

COUPAGE 110 VINS NADAL 2008 T
34% manto negro, 27% cabernet sauvignon, 21% syrah, 18% merlot.

89 Colour: cherry, garnet rim. Nose: ripe fruit, spicy, toasty, characterful. Palate: powerful, flavourful, toasty, round tannins.

SYRAH 110 VINS NADAL 2007 T BARRICA
100% syrah.

90 Colour: cherry, garnet rim. Nose: spicy, cocoa bean, ripe fruit, fruit expression, aged wood nuances, aromatic coffee. Palate: flavourful, fleshy, spirituous, long.

MERLOT 110 VINS NADAL 2006 T BARRICA
100% merlot.

87 Colour: cherry, garnet rim. Nose: powerfull, varietal, fruit preserve, toasty. Palate: flavourful, powerful, concentrated.

VINYES MORTITX

Ctra. Pollensa Lluc, Km. 10,9
07315 Escorca (Illes Ballears)
☎: +34 971 182 339 - Fax: +34 971 531 914
info@vinyesmortitx.com
www.vinyesmortitx.com

L'U BLANC MORTITX 2009 B
75% malvasía, 25% moscatel.

87 Colour: bright straw. Nose: powerfull, fruit liqueur notes, citrus fruit, warm. Palate: flavourful, powerful, fleshy, sweetness.

L'ERGULL DE MORTITX 2009 BC
60% malvasía, 30% chardonnay, 10% riesling.

85 Colour: bright straw. Nose: candied fruit, warm, spicy, creamy oak. Palate: fine bitter notes, flavourful, spirituous.

FLAIRES DE MORTITX 2010 RD
80% monastrell, 20% cabernet sauvignon.

78

L'U DE MORTITX 2007 TC
64% syrah, 24% merlot, 12% cabernet sauvignon.

90 Colour: cherry, garnet rim. Nose: ripe fruit, spicy, creamy oak, toasty, characterful, smoky. Palate: powerful, toasty, round tannins.

RODAL PLA DE MORTITX 2007 T
70% merlot, 15% syrah, 15% cabernet sauvignon.

88 Colour: bright cherry. Nose: ripe fruit, sweet spices, creamy oak, balsamic herbs, scrubland. Palate: flavourful, fruity, toasty, round tannins.

MURCIA

LONG WINES

Avda. Monte, 46
28723 Algete (Madrid)
☎: +34 916 221 305 - Fax: +34 916 220 029
raquel@longwines.com
www.longwines.com

ESTANCIA DEL SILENCIO 2010 T
80% monastrell, 20% syrah.

87 Colour: cherry, garnet rim. Nose: ripe fruit, balsamic herbs, balanced, expressive. Palate: powerful, flavourful, fleshy.

NORTE DE GRANADA

BODEGA VERTIJANA

Paseo de Sierra Nevada, 18
18516 Policar (Granada)
☎: +34 605 074 459
vertijana@hotmail.com

VERTIJANA 1 2008 T BARRICA
tempranillo.

87 Colour: cherry, garnet rim. Nose: red berry notes, ripe fruit, wild herbs, sweet spices, creamy oak. Palate: powerful, flavourful, spicy.

VERTIJANA 3 2008 T
tempranillo, cabernet sauvignon, merlot.

78

IRVING

Finca el Duque Ctra. de Huéscar a Santiago de la Espada. km 13,500
18830 Huéscar (Granada)
☎: +34 653 527 560 - Fax: +34 917 150 632
pedidos@irving.es
www.irving.es

IRVING 2010 T
tempranillo, cabernet sauvignon.

75

IRVING COLECCIÓN FAMILIAR 2007 T
tempranillo, merlot, syrah, cabernet sauvignon.

87 Colour: cherry, garnet rim. Nose: ripe fruit, warm, fruit liqueur notes, sweet spices, toasty. Palate: powerful, flavourful, fleshy.

NARANJUEZ

Fuente Vieja, 26
18516 Marchal (Granada)
☎: +34 637 222 326
naranjuez@gmail.com
www.vinossingulares.wordpress.com

NARANJUEZ PINOT NEGRA 2008 T
100% pinot noir.

89 Colour: light cherry, orangey edge. Nose: wet leather, cigar, fruit preserve, wild herbs. Palate: spicy, mineral, powerful, flavourful.

RIBERA DEL ANDARAX

EL MARCHAR BAJO ANDARAX

Isla Cies, 42 - 1ºC
04720 Agua Dulce (Almería)
☎: +34 620 292 921 - Fax: +34 950 342 434
juliquif@hotmail.com

EL MARCHAR BAJO ANDARAX 2004 TR
tempranillo, merlot.

75

FINCA ÁNFORA

Paraje Barranco del Obispo, s/n.
04729 Enix (Almeria)
☎: +34 950 520 336 - Fax: +34 950 341 614
info@vegaenix.com
www.vegaenix.com

VEGA ENIX CALIDÓN 2008 T
cabernet sauvignon, garnacha, merlot, syrah, monastrell.

88 Colour: cherry, garnet rim. Nose: red berry notes, ripe fruit, scrubland, earthy notes, creamy oak. Palate: flavourful, fleshy, spicy.

VEGA ENIX UNO MÁS 2008 T
garnacha, monastrell, merlot.

85 Colour: cherry, garnet rim. Nose: ripe fruit, mineral, wild herbs. Palate: correct, flavourful, fleshy.

VEGA ENIX CALIDÓN 2007 T
cabernet sauvignon, garnacha, merlot, syrah, monastrell.

89 Colour: cherry, garnet rim. Nose: ripe fruit, wild herbs, earthy notes, complex, creamy oak. Palate: unctuous, complex, fleshy, flavourful.

VEGA ENIX ARISTEO 2007 T
cabernet sauvignon, syrah, merlot.

89 Colour: cherry, garnet rim. Nose: ripe fruit, scrubland, earthy notes, sweet spices. Palate: ripe fruit, powerful, mineral, flavourful.

VEGA ENIX LAURENTI 2006 T
cabernet sauvignon.

92 Colour: cherry, garnet rim. Nose: red berry notes, ripe fruit, mineral, spicy, toasty. Palate: good acidity, powerful, flavourful, fleshy, complex.

VEGA ENIX XOLAIR 2006 T
merlot.

91 Colour: cherry, garnet rim. Nose: ripe fruit, wild herbs, earthy notes, sweet spices. Palate: good acidity, powerful, flavourful, fleshy.

VEGA ENIX DAMARIS 2006 T
syrah.

90 Colour: cherry, garnet rim. Nose: red berry notes, ripe fruit, aromatic coffee, toasty. Palate: balanced, unctuous, powerful, flavourful, smoky aftertaste.

VEGA ENIX SANTYS 2005 T
syrah, garnacha.

88 Colour: cherry, garnet rim. Nose: ripe fruit, fine reductive notes, sweet spices, toasty. Palate: powerful, flavourful, ripe fruit.

RIBERA DEL GÁLLEGO CINCO VILLAS

BODEGA PEGALAZ

Ctra. A-1202, Km. 7 Desvío Ermita Santa Quiteria
22806 Santa Eulalia de Gállego (Zaragoza)
☎: +34 625 643 440
www.pegalaz.com

FIRÉ 2009 B
macabeo.

92 Colour: bright yellow. Nose: powerfull, ripe fruit, creamy oak, fragrant herbs, elegant, expressive. Palate: rich, smoky aftertaste, flavourful, fresh, good acidity.

FIRÉ 2007 T
cabernet sauvignon, merlot, tempranillo.

91 Colour: cherry, garnet rim. Nose: mineral, fruit expression, toasty, aromatic coffee. Palate: flavourful, fine bitter notes, good acidity, fine tannins.

FIRÉ 2006 T
cabernet sauvignon, merlot, tempranillo.

92 Colour: bright cherry. Nose: sweet spices, creamy oak, overripe fruit, earthy notes. Palate: flavourful, fruity, toasty, round tannins.

BODEGAS EJEANAS

Avda. Cosculluela, 23
50600 Ejea de los Caballeros (Zaragoza)
☎: +34 976 663 770 - Fax: +34 976 663 770
export@bodegasejeanas.com
www.bodegasejeanas.com

UVA NOCTURNA 2010 B
verdejo, moscatel, chardonnay.

88 Colour: bright straw. Nose: medium intensity, white flowers, ripe fruit. Palate: flavourful, fruity, fresh, sweetness.

VEGA DE LUCHÁN MOSCATEL 2009 B
85% moscatel, 15% verdejo.

87 Colour: golden. Nose: powerfull, floral, candied fruit, fragrant herbs. Palate: flavourful, sweet, fresh, fruity, good acidity, long.

VEGA DE LUCHÁN RD
60% garnacha, 40% cabernet sauvignon.

90 Colour: rose, purple rim. Nose: powerfull, ripe fruit, red berry notes, floral, expressive. Palate: fleshy, powerful, fruity, fresh, complex.

UVA NOCTURNA MERLOT 2010 T
100% merlot.

86 Colour: cherry, purple rim. Nose: red berry notes, fresh fruit, floral, fresh. Palate: powerful, flavourful, fresh, fruity.

UVA NOCTURNA GARNACHAS VIEJAS 2007 T
100% garnacha.

89 Colour: light cherry, garnet rim. Nose: red berry notes, ripe fruit, expressive, mineral, sweet spices, toasty. Palate: good acidity, powerful, flavourful, round tannins.

VEGA DE LUCHÁN CABERNET SAUVIGNON 2006 T
100% cabernet sauvignon.

89 Colour: cherry, garnet rim. Nose: ripe fruit, fruit liqueur notes, earthy notes, sweet spices, toasty. Palate: good acidity, powerful, flavourful, complex.

VEGA DE LUCHÁN 2005 T BARRICA
80% tempranillo, 20% cabernet sauvignon.

86 Colour: light cherry, garnet rim. Nose: ripe fruit, warm, fine reductive notes, earthy notes. Palate: good acidity, powerful, flavourful, spicy.

BODEGAS UNCASTELLUM S.L.

Ctra. Uncastillo - Sos del Rey Católico, s/n
50678 Uncastillo (Zaragoza)
☎: +34 976 679 110 - Fax: +34 976 679 110
uncastellum@umcastellum.com
www.uncastellum.com

UNCASTELLUM REX 2007 T
tempranillo, garnacha, merlot, cabernet sauvignon.

88 Colour: cherry, garnet rim. Nose: ripe fruit, scrubland, earthy notes, spicy. Palate: complex, fleshy, powerful, flavourful, toasty.

UNCASTELLUM AUREUM 2007 T

87 Colour: cherry, garnet rim. Nose: ripe fruit, earthy notes, mineral, wild herbs. Palate: fleshy, flavourful, ripe fruit, toasty.

UNCASTELLUM 2007 T BARRICA
tempranillo, garnacha.

86 Colour: cherry, garnet rim. Nose: fruit preserve, wild herbs, earthy notes, fine reductive notes, spicy, toasty. Palate: flavourful, fleshy, toasty.

FLORAL DE UNCASTELLUM T
tempranillo, garnacha.

88 Colour: cherry, purple rim. Nose: red berry notes, violet drops, dried flowers, fragrant herbs. Palate: complex, light-bodied, fresh, fruity.

EDRA

Ctra A - 132, km 26
22800 Ayerbe (Huesca)
☎: +34 679 420 455 - Fax: +34 974 380 829
edra@bodega-edra.com
www.bodega-edra.com

EDRA GRULLAS DE PASO 2008 T
tempranillo, garnacha, merlot, cabernet sauvignon.

87 Colour: cherry, garnet rim. Nose: ripe fruit, balsamic herbs, spicy, mineral. Palate: balanced, flavourful, fleshy.

EDRA XTRA SYRAH 2007 T
syrah.

87 Colour: cherry, garnet rim. Nose: ripe fruit, expressive, cocoa bean, spicy, warm. Palate: good acidity, balanced, flavourful, fleshy, round tannins.

EDRA MERLOT SYRAH 2006 T
syrah, merlot.

89 Colour: cherry, garnet rim. Nose: ripe fruit, sweet spices, creamy oak, expressive. Palate: good acidity, light-bodied, flavourful, fleshy, round tannins.

RIBERA DEL JILOCA

BODEGA VINAE MURERI

Ctra. Murero-Atea - Finca La Moratilla
50366 Murero (Zaragoza)
☎: +34 976 808 033 - Fax: +34 976 808 034
info@vinaemureri.com
www.vinaemureri.com

MURET ORO 2010 T
garnacha.

89 Colour: cherry, garnet rim. Nose: ripe fruit, spicy, creamy oak. Palate: powerful, flavourful, toasty, round tannins.

XILOCA 2010 T
garnacha.

88 Colour: bright cherry. Nose: earthy notes, ripe fruit, fruit expression, sweet spices. Palate: flavourful, fine bitter notes, good acidity, round tannins.

MURET VIDADILLO 2009 T
80% vidadillo, 20% bobal.

90 Colour: bright cherry. Nose: ripe fruit, sweet spices, creamy oak, red berry notes, expressive. Palate: flavourful, fruity, toasty, round tannins.

MURET ORO 2009 T
garnacha.

89 Color bright cherry. Aroma ripe fruit, sweet spices, creamy oak, expressive. Taste flavourful, fruity, toasty, round tannins.

MURET AZUL 2008 T
garnacha.

87 Colour: deep cherry. Nose: fruit preserve, fruit liqueur notes, toasty, smoky. Palate: powerful, concentrated, round tannins.

MURERO 2005 T
100% garnacha.

88 Colour: deep cherry. Nose: powerfull, ripe fruit, creamy oak, sweet spices. Palate: powerful, concentrated, sweetness.

RIBERA DEL QUEILES

GUELBENZU

Paraje La Lombana
50513 Vierlas (Zaragoza)
☎: +34 948 202 200 - Fax: +34 948 202 202
j.oteiza@bodegadesarria.com
www.guelbenzu.com

GUELBENZU RED 2010 T
merlot.

89 Colour: cherry, purple rim. Nose: red berry notes, raspberry, expressive, mineral. Palate: balanced, unctuous, good acidity, fruity, flavourful.

GUELBENZU VIERLAS 2009 T
syrah.

88 Colour: cherry, garnet rim. Nose: ripe fruit, warm, spicy, medium intensity. Palate: flavourful, fleshy, good finish.

GUELBENZU AZUL 2008 T
tempranillo.

88 Colour: cherry, garnet rim. Nose: ripe fruit, balsamic herbs, spicy, toasty. Palate: powerful, flavourful, fleshy, round.

GUELBENZU EVO 2007 T
cabernet sauvignon.

87 Colour: cherry, garnet rim. Nose: ripe fruit, sweet spices, cocoa bean, dark chocolate, toasty. Palate: good acidity, flavourful, balsamic, fleshy.

GUELBENZU LOMBANA 2006 T
graciano.

86 Colour: cherry, garnet rim. Nose: ripe fruit, warm, spicy, creamy oak. Palate: good acidity, unctuous, flavourful, round tannins.

GUELBENZU LAUTUS 2005 T
coupage multivarietal.

88 Colour: pale ruby, brick rim edge. Nose: ripe fruit, old leather, sweet spices, dark chocolate, cocoa bean. Palate: good structure, flavourful, fleshy, long.

PROYECTO GARNACHAS DE ESPAÑA

Gral. Vara del Rey, 7 1º Dcha.
26003 Logroño (La Rioja)
☎: +34 941 271 217 - Fax: +34 941 272 911
info@garnachasdeespana.com
www.garnachasdeespana.com

LA GARNACHA SALVAJE DEL MONCAYO 2009 T
100% garnacha.

88 Colour: cherry, purple rim. Nose: ripe fruit, floral, mineral, overripe fruit. Palate: good acidity, unctuous, powerful, flavourful, fruity.

WINERY ARTS

Gral. Vara del Rey 7, 1º dcha.
26003 Logroño (La Rioja)
☎: +34 941 271 217 - Fax: +34 941 272 911
info@wineryarts.com
www.wineryarts.com

NUEVE (EDICIÓN ESPECIAL 9/9/9 2009 T
tempranillo, merlot.

88 Colour: cherry, purple rim. Nose: red berry notes, ripe fruit, mineral, balsamic herbs, sweet spices. Palate: good acidity, flavourful, fleshy.

NUEVE 2007 T
tempranillo, cabernet franc.

90 Colour: black cherry, cherry, garnet rim. Nose: red berry notes, ripe fruit, spicy, toasty. Palate: powerful, flavourful, concentrated, long, toasty.

SEIS AL REVÉS 2007 T
tempranillo, merlot.

89 Colour: cherry, garnet rim. Nose: red berry notes, ripe fruit, fragrant herbs, sweet spices, creamy oak. Palate: round, unctuous, flavourful, fruity.

TRES AL CUADRADO 2007 T
garnacha, merlot, tempranillo.

88 Colour: cherry, garnet rim. Nose: ripe fruit, earthy notes, cocoa bean, dark chocolate, toasty. Palate: mineral, fleshy, flavourful.

SIERRA NORTE DE SEVILLA

COLONIAS DE GALEÓN

Plazuela, 39
41370 Cazalla de la Sierra (Sevilla)
☎: +34 955 710 092 - Fax: +34 955 710 093
info@coloniasdegaleon.com
www.coloniasdegaleon.com

PETIT OCNOS 2009 B
100% chardonnay.

86 Colour: bright golden. Nose: faded flowers, ripe fruit, dried herbs, creamy oak. Palate: good acidity, unctuous, flavourful.

OCNOS 2009 BFB
80% chardonnay, 20% viognier.

85 Colour: bright golden. Nose: citrus fruit, dried flowers, fragrant herbs, medium intensity. Palate: rich, flavourful, thin.

COLONIAS DE GALEÓN 2010 T MACERACIÓN CARBÓNICA
50% cabernet franc, 30% tempranillo, 20% syrah.

85 Colour: cherry, purple rim. Nose: expressive, ripe fruit, red berry notes, medium intensity. Palate: good acidity, balanced, fleshy.

SILENTE SELECCIÓN 2006 T ROBLE
50% cabernet franc, 30% merlot, 10% tempranillo, 10% syrah.

88 Colour: cherry, garnet rim. Nose: caramel, sweet spices, candied fruit. Palate: flavourful, fleshy, toasty.

VALDEJALÓN

LATIDOS DE VINO (EPILENSE DE VINOS Y VIÑEDOS)

La Quimera del oro 30 n3ºD
50019 (Zaragoza)
☎: +34 669 148 771
fmora@latidosdevino.com
www.latidosdevino.com

LATIDOS I LOVE MOSCATEL 2010 B
100% moscatel.

88 Colour: bright golden. Nose: candied fruit, honeyed notes, citrus fruit, expressive. Palate: balanced, fleshy, flavourful, fruity.

LATIDOS I LOVE 2010 B
80% macabeo, 20% garnacha blanca.

83 Colour: bright straw. Nose: floral, citrus fruit, fragrant herbs. Palate: fruity, flavourful, easy to drink.

LATIDOS I LOVE 2010 RD
garnacha.

86 Colour: rose, purple rim. Nose: raspberry, fresh fruit, expressive. Palate: fruity, fresh, light-bodied, fleshy.

LATIDOS I LOVE 2010 T
garnacha.

88 Colour: cherry, purple rim. Nose: floral, spicy, red berry notes, complex, expressive. Palate: balanced, fruity, fleshy.

LATIDOS I LOVE LATIDOS 2008 T FERMENTADO EN BARRICA
garnacha.

90 Colour: cherry, garnet rim. Nose: red berry notes, fragrant herbs, creamy oak, spicy, expressive. Palate: balanced, good acidity, flavourful, fleshy, soft tannins.

LATIDOS I LOVE 2008 T BARRICA
90% garnacha, 10% syrah.

88 Colour: cherry, garnet rim. Nose: toasty, spicy, red berry notes. Palate: flavourful, fruity, fleshy, round tannins.

VALLE DEL CINCA

BODEGAS VALONGA

Monte Valonga, s/n
22500 Belver de Cinca (Huesca)
☎: +34 974 435 127 - Fax: +34 974 339 101
bodegas@valonga.com
www.valonga.com

VALONGA CHARDONNAY 2010 B
chardonnay.

86 Colour: bright straw. Nose: fresh, expressive, dried flowers, balsamic herbs. Palate: flavourful, fruity, good acidity.

VALONGA 2010 RD
syrah, cabernet sauvignon, tempranillo.

86 Colour: rose, purple rim. Nose: ripe fruit, red berry notes, floral, expressive. Palate: fleshy, powerful, fruity, fresh.

VALONGA SASO ALTO 2007 T
garnacha, syrah.

87 Colour: cherry, garnet rim. Nose: red berry notes, ripe fruit, aromatic coffee, dark chocolate. Palate: good acidity, flavourful, fleshy, toasty.

VALLE DE SADACIA

CASTILLO DE MAETIERRA

Ctra. de Murillo, s/n
26500 Calahorra (La Rioja)
☎: +34 941 271 217 - Fax: +34 941 272 911
info@castillodemaetierra.com
www.castillodemaetierra.com

SPANISH WHITE GUERRILLA SAUVIGNON BLANC 2010 B
6,5% sauvignon blanc.

89 Colour: bright straw. Nose: citrus fruit, wild herbs, dried flowers, expressive. Palate: fleshy, complex, powerful, fruity, long.

SPANISH WHITE GUERRILLA CHARDONNAY 2010 B
100% chardonnay.

89 Colour: bright yellow. Nose: dried flowers, fruit expression, fragrant herbs. Palate: powerful, flavourful, fresh, fruity, round, unctuous.

SPANISH WHITE GUERRILLA GEWÜRZTRAMINER 2010 B
100% gewürztraminer.

88 Colour: bright straw. Nose: floral, tropical fruit, scrubland, expressive. Palate: powerful, flavourful, good acidity.

DRY LIBALIS 2010 B
moscatel grano menudo, viura, chardonnay.

88 Colour: bright yellow. Nose: white flowers, fruit expression, expressive, fresh. Palate: powerful, flavourful, fruity, fleshy.

LIBALIS 2010 B
moscatel grano menudo, viura, malvasía.

87 Colour: bright yellow. Nose: floral, candied fruit, expressive. Palate: good acidity, fresh, fruity, easy to drink.

SPANISH WHITE GUERRILLA ALBARIÑO 2010 B
100% albariño.

86 Colour: bright straw. Nose: dried flowers, fruit expression, balsamic herbs. Palate: good acidity, fresh, light-bodied, fruity.

SPANISH WHITE GUERRILLA RIESLING 2010 B
100% riesling.

86 Colour: bright yellow. Nose: ripe fruit, dried herbs, balanced. Palate: good acidity, correct, flavourful.

SPANISH WHITE GUERRILLA VERDEJO 2010 B
100% verdejo.

84 Colour: bright straw. Nose: ripe fruit, floral, fragrant herbs. Palate: spicy, light-bodied, fresh.

SPANISH WHITE GUERRILLA VIOGNIER 2009 B
100% viognier.

86 Colour: bright yellow. Nose: powerfull, ripe fruit, sweet spices, creamy oak. Palate: rich, flavourful, fresh, good acidity.

SPANISH WHITE GUERRILLA CHARDONNAY 2009 B BARRICA
100% chardonnay.

82 Colour: bright golden. Nose: ripe fruit, caramel, roasted coffee. Palate: powerful, rich, toasty.

MELANTE 2008 B
100% moscatel grano menudo.

93 Colour: golden. Nose: powerfull, honeyed notes, candied fruit, floral. Palate: flavourful, sweet, fresh, fruity, good acidity, long.

VIÑEDOS DE ESPAÑA

BODEGA EL MONEGRILLO

Finca El Monegrillo. Pol. Ind. 13- parcela 20
16235 Iniesta (Cuenca)
☎: +34 962 510 451 - Fax: +34 962 511 361
carlos.valsangiacomo@cherubino.es
www.cherubino.es

NOVIEMBRE DE FINCA EL MONEGRILLO 2006 T
60% syrah, 40% cabernet sauvignon.

93 Colour: very deep cherry. Nose: sweet spices, cocoa bean, dark chocolate, earthy notes, damp earth, ripe fruit. Palate: powerful, fleshy, complex, concentrated, long.

VINYES MORTITX

Ctra. Pollensa Lluc, Km. 10,9
07315 Escorca (Illes Balears)
☎: +34 971 182 339 - Fax: +34 971 531 914
info@vinyesmortitx.com
www.vinyesmortitx.com

DOLÇ DE GEL MORTITX 2010 B
50% riesling, 50% moscatel.

88 Color golden. Aroma powerfull, floral, honeyed notes, candied fruit, fragrant herbs. Taste flavourful, sweet, fresh, fruity, good acidity, long.

Just outside the "Vino de Calidad" status, we find the "Vino de Mesa" ("Table Wine") category, which are those not included in any of the other categories (not even in the "Vino de la Tierra" one, regarded as "Vino de Mesa" by the Ley del Vino ("Wine Law"). The present editions of our Guide has up to 41 table wines rated as excellent, something which is quite telling, and force us to a change of mind in regard to the popular prejudice against this category, traditionally related –almost exclusively– to bulk, cheap wines.

In this section we include wines made in geographical areas that do not belong to any designation of origin (DO as such) or association of Vino de la Tierra, although most of them come indeed from wines regions with some vine growing and winemaking tradition.

We do not pretend to come up with a comprehensive account of the usually overlooked vinos de mesa (table wines), but to enumerate here some Spanish wines that were bottled with no geographic label whatsoever.

The wineries are listed alphabetically within their Autonomous regions. The reader will discover some singular wines of –in some cases– excellent quality that could be of interest to those on the look out for novelties or alternative products to bring onto their tables.

ANDALUCÍA

BARRANCO OSCURO

Cortijo Barranco Oscuro
18440 Cádiar (Granada)
☎: +34 615 380 910
bodega@barrancooscuro.com
www.barrancooscuro.com

GARNATA 2009 T
garnacha.

88 Colour: cherry, purple rim. Nose: ripe fruit, earthy notes, wild herbs, cocoa bean. Palate: burning notes, spirituous, flavourful, fleshy.

RUBAIYAT BARRANCO OSCURO 2008 T
syrah.

87 Colour: cherry, garnet rim. Nose: aged wood nuances, ripe fruit, warm, spicy, new oak. Palate: flavourful, powerful, fleshy, complex.

BO2 BARRANCO OSCURO 2007 T
tempranillo.

87 Colour: cherry, garnet rim. Nose: ripe fruit, earthy notes, spicy, creamy oak, fresh, varietal. Palate: warm, fruity, flavourful, toasty.

BORGOÑON GRANATE 2006 TC
pinot noir.

82 Colour: cherry, garnet rim. Nose: ripe fruit, earthy notes, spicy, toasty. Palate: good acidity, powerful, flavourful, fleshy, complex.

TEMPRANILLO Y MÁS 2006 T
tempranillo, garnacha, cabernet sauvignon, cabernet franc, merlot.

78

1368 PAGO CERRO LAS MONJAS 2004 TC
garnacha, syrah, cabernet franc, cabernet sauvignon, merlot.

84 Colour: cherry, garnet rim. Nose: ripe fruit, sweet spices, creamy oak. Palate: flavourful, fruity, toasty, round tannins.

BODEGA CAUZÓN

Avda. Andalucía, 20
18517 Graena (Granada)
☎: +34 676 856 164
bodegacauzon@gmail.com
www.bodegacauzon.blogspot.com

IRADEI CAUZÓN 2009 T
30% cabernet sauvignon, 30% tempranillo, 30% merlot, 10% garnacha.

89 Colour: cherry, garnet rim. Nose: red berry notes, ripe fruit, raspberry, spicy, sweet spices, creamy oak. Palate: good acidity, flavourful, fleshy, mineral.

CAUZÓN PINOT NOIR 2009 T
100% pinot noir.

87 Colour: cherry, garnet rim. Nose: fruit preserve, earthy notes, mineral, expressive, sweet spices. Palate: good acidity, elegant, flavourful, fleshy, complex.

CAUZÓN 2009 T
50% merlot, 50% tempranillo.

86 Colour: cherry, garnet rim. Nose: ripe fruit, fruit preserve, scrubland, spicy. Palate: powerful, flavourful, fruity, fleshy.

IRADEI CAUZÓN 2008 T
30% cabernet sauvignon, 30% tempranillo, 30% merlot, 10% garnacha.

87 Colour: cherry, garnet rim. Nose: red berry notes, ripe fruit, earthy notes, dry stone, spicy, creamy oak. Palate: good acidity, powerful, flavourful, fleshy, complex.

BODEGA F. SCHATZ

Finca Sanguijuela, s/n Apdo. Correos 131
29400 Ronda (Málaga)
☎: +34 952 871 313 - Fax: +34 952 871 313
bodega@f-schatz.com
www.f-schatz.com

SCHATZ 2010 RD
muskattrollinger.

86 Colour: rose, purple rim. Nose: powerfull, ripe fruit, red berry notes, floral. Palate: fleshy, powerful, fruity, fresh.

ACINIPO 2005 TC
lemberger.

88 Colour: deep cherry, garnet rim. Nose: candied fruit, balanced, expressive, medium intensity, spicy, wild herbs. Palate: fruity, correct.

BODEGA KIENINGER

Los Frontones, 67 (Apdo. Correos 215)
29400 Ronda (Málaga)
☎: +34 952 879 554
martin@bodegakieninger.com
www.bodegakieninger.com

7 VIN (13 MESES BARRICA) 2009 T
50% blaufraenkisch, 50% zweigelt.

93 Colour: cherry, garnet rim. Nose: ripe fruit, citrus fruit, cocoa bean, spicy, creamy oak, mineral. Palate: complex, flavourful, fleshy, balanced. Personality.

BODEGAS BENTOMIZ

Finca Almendro
Pago Cuesta Robano
29752 Sayalonga (Málaga)
☎: +34 952 115 939
info@bodegasbentomiz.com
www.bodegasbentomiz.com

ARIYANAS DAVID 2010 T
100% merlot.

87

BODEGAS JORGE ORDÓÑEZ & CO

Bartolome Esteban Murillo, 11 Pol. Ind. La Pañoleta
29700 Velez-Málaga (Málaga)
☎: +34 952 504 706 - Fax: +34 951 284 796
office@jorge-ordonez.es
www.jorge-ordonez.es

ORDÓÑEZ & CO. Nº4 ESENCIA 2005 B
moscatel.

94 Colour: old gold. Nose: ripe fruit, honeyed notes, sweet spices, toasty, expressive. Palate: powerful, rich, fleshy, flavourful, good acidity, round, unctuous.

BODEGAS MÁLAGA VIRGEN

Autovía A-92, Málaga-Sevilla, Km. 132
29520 Fuente de Piedra (Málaga)
☎: +34 952 319 454 - Fax: +34 952 359 819
didier.bricout@bodegasmalagavirgen.com
www.bodegasmalagavirgen.com

MOSCATEL NARANJA B
moscatel.

84 Colour: bright golden. Nose: citrus fruit, fruit expression, candied fruit, complex. Palate: powerful, flavourful, fruity.

BODEGAS Y VIÑEDOS MONTES DE MÁLAGA

Nicolás Gogol, 12
29004 Málaga (Málaga)
☎: +34 952 303 081 - Fax: +34 952 320 571
byvmontesdemalaga@hotmail.com
www.bodegasyviñedosmontesdemalaga.es

LISTON 2009 TINTO DULCE
100% garnacha.

90 Colour: cherry, garnet rim. Nose: red berry notes, ripe fruit, fruit liqueur notes, varnish, sweet spices. Palate: good acidity, sweetness, fruity, fleshy.

EQUIPO NAVAZOS

Cartuja, 1 - módulo 6
11401 Jerez de la Frontera (Cádiz)
☎: +34 649 435 979
equipo@navazos.com
www.equiponavazos.com

NAVAZOS NIEPOORT 2010 B
palomino.

93 Colour: bright straw. Nose: white flowers, flor yeasts, saline, dry nuts, grassy. Palate: flavourful, fruity, fine bitter notes.

MARQUÉS DE LA CONCORDIA FAMILY OF WINES

Estación de Parchite, 104
29400 Ronda (Málaga)
☎: +34 914 365 900
gromero@arcoinvest-group.com
www.haciendas-espana.com

ÁNDALUS PETIT VERDOT 2005 T
petit verdot.

92 Colour: cherry, garnet rim. Nose: red berry notes, ripe fruit, sweet spices, dark chocolate, toasty. Palate: balanced, powerful, flavourful, complex, toasty.

NARANJUEZ

Fuente Vieja, 26
18516 Marchal (Granada)
☎: +34 637 222 326
naranjuez@gmail.com
www.vinossingulares.wordpress.com

NARANJUEZ PRISA MATA 2008 T
40% tempranillo, 20% cabernet sauvignon, 15% cabernet franc, 10% merlot, 10% pinot noir, 5% garnacha.

88 Colour: cherry, garnet rim. Nose: earthy notes, ripe fruit, scrubland. Palate: good acidity, fleshy, flavourful.

NARANJUEZ PRISA MATA 2007 T
45% tempranillo, 15% cabernet sauvignon, 10% pinot noir, 5% garnacha.

87 Colour: pale ruby, brick rim edge. Nose: damp earth, spicy, toasty, old leather. Palate: powerful, spirituous, flavourful, mineral.

NESTARES RINCÓN VINOS Y BODEGAS

Finca Juan de Reyes, s/n
18430 Torvizcon (Granada)
☎: +34 655 959 500 - Fax: +34 958 272 125
info@alpujarride.com
www.alpujarride.com

IN 1.0 2010 T
tempranillo, merlot, syrah.

92 Color cherry, purple rim. Aroma expressive, fresh fruit, red berry notes, floral. Taste flavourful, fruity, good acidity, round tannins.

PAGO DEL MARENOSTRUM

Ctra. A-348, Km. 85-86
04460 Fondón (Almería)
☎: +34 926 666 027 - Fax: +34 670 099 520
info@pagodelvicario.com

1500 H PINOT NOIR 2007 T
100% pinot noir.

90 Colour: deep cherry, orangey edge. Nose: ripe fruit, scrubland, mineral, expressive. Palate: correct, round, flavourful, fleshy.

1500 H 2007 T
merlot, tempranillo, cabernet sauvignon, pinot noir.

88 Colour: cherry, garnet rim. Nose: scrubland, ripe fruit, sweet spices, closed. Palate: ripe fruit, flavourful, fleshy, long.

SEDELLA VINOS

Término Las Viñuelas s/n
29715 Sedella (Málaga)
☎: +34 687 463 082 - Fax: +34 967 140 723
info@sedellavinos.com
www.sedellavinos.com

SEDELLA 2008 T
romé, garnacha, otras.

91 Colour: cherry, garnet rim. Nose: saline, fruit expression, scrubland, spicy, creamy oak. Palate: good acidity, flavourful, fleshy, spicy, balsamic

VIÑAS DE PURULIO

San Bonifacio, 42
18516 Marchal (Granada)
☎: +34 958 690 226

PURULIO T
cabernet sauvignon, merlot, pinot noir, syrah.

84 Colour: cherry, garnet rim. Nose: red berry notes, ripe fruit, earthy notes, mineral, grassy. Palate: powerful, flavourful, fleshy.

ARAGÓN

EDRA

Ctra A - 132, km 26
22800 Ayerbe (Huesca)
☎: +34 679 420 455 - Fax: +34 974 380 829
edra@bodega-edra.com
www.bodega-edra.com

EDRA BLANCOLUZ 2010 B
viognier.

87 Colour: bright straw. Nose: citrus fruit, wild herbs, floral, expressive. Palate: unctuous, flavourful, powerful, fleshy.

VINOS DIVERTIDOS

Avda. de la Ilustración 21 C48
50012 Zaragoza (Zaragoza)
☎: +34 976 551 514 - Fax: +34 976 566 362
josemarcomolinero@yahoo.es
www.vinosdivertidos.es

MARÍA DE LA O 2009 T
100% garnacha.

85 Colour: cherry, garnet rim. Nose: ripe fruit, faded flowers, wild herbs, creamy oak. Palate: good acidity, flavourful, fleshy.

BALEARS

BINIGRAU

Fiol, 33
07143 Biniali (Illes Balears)
☎: +34 971 512 023 - Fax: +34 971 886 495
info@binigrau.es
www.binigrau.es

BINIGRAU DOLÇ T
manto negro, merlot.

87 Colour: bright cherry. Nose: ripe fruit, sweet spices, creamy oak, expressive. Palate: fruity, toasty, round tannins, sweet.

VINS TONI GELABERT

Camí dels Horts de Llodrá Km. 1,3
07500 Manacor (Illes Balears)
☎: +34 610 789 531
info@vinstonigelabert.com
www.vinstonigelabert.com

TORRE DES CANONGE 2008 T
cabernet sauvignon, syrah, pinot noir.

92 Colour: cherry, garnet rim. Nose: spicy, smoky. Palate: flavourful, powerful, fleshy, long.

CANARIAS

BODEGAS VIÑÁTIGO

Cabo Verde, s/n
38440 La Guancha (Santa Cruz de Tenerife)
☎: +34 922 828 768 - Fax: +34 922 829 936
vinatigo@vinatigo.com
www.vinatigo.com

TACANDE 2006 T

86 Colour: deep cherry. Nose: warm, fruit liqueur notes, toasty, aged wood nuances. Palate: sweetness, fine bitter notes, ripe fruit.

CASTILLA Y LEÓN

ARZUAGA NAVARRO

Ctra. N-122, Km. 325
47350 Quintanilla de Onésimo (Valladolid)
☎: +34 983 681 146 - Fax: +34 983 681 147
bodega@arzuaganavarro.com
www.arzuaganavarro.com

FAN D. ORO 2009 BFB
100% chardonnay.

87 Colour: bright yellow. Nose: powerfull, characterful, candied fruit, citrus fruit. Palate: flavourful, powerful, spicy, fine bitter notes.

BODEGA ELÍAS MORA

Juan Mora, s/n
47530 San Román de Hornija (Valladolid)
☎: +34 983 784 029 - Fax: +34 983 784 190
info@bodegaseliasmora.com
www.bodegaseliasmora.com

DULCE BENAVIDES
uvas pasas, tinta de Toro.

88 Colour: cherry, purple rim. Nose: red berry notes, raspberry, fruit liqueur notes, sweet spices. Palate: good acidity, powerful, flavourful.

BODEGAS MARCOS MIÑAMBRES

Camino de Pobladura, s/n
24234 Villamañán (León)
☎: +34 987 767 038
satvined@picos.com

M. MIÑAMBRES ALBARÍN S.C. B
100% albarín.

86 Colour: bright yellow. Nose: mineral, ripe fruit, scrubland. Palate: powerful, smoky aftertaste, rich.

M. MIÑAMBRES 2010 RD
prieto picudo, cencibel.

68

M. MIÑAMBRES 2007 T
prieto picudo, cencibel.

86 Colour: cherry, garnet rim. Nose: fruit expression, wild herbs. Palate: fresh, flavourful, powerful, creamy.

BODEGAS SELECCIONADAS ARMANDO

"Viña Concita y Adilen" Ctra. N-630, Km. 270
49192 Zamora (Zamora)
☎: +34 980 538 683 - Fax: +34 980 538 683
bodegas.armando@gmail.com
www.bodegas-armando.com

GRAN QUINTA DURI VINO DE AUTOR 2006 T
juan garcía.

90 Colour: cherry, garnet rim. Nose: red berry notes, ripe fruit, cocoa bean, dark chocolate, creamy oak, earthy notes. Palate: rich, powerful, flavourful, fruity, fleshy, toasty, balanced.

CATHEDRAL DE ZAMORA 2004 TR
juan garcía.

85 Colour: cherry, garnet rim. Nose: overripe fruit, slightly evolved, roasted coffee, warm. Palate: fruity, sweetness, flavourful.

DANIEL V. RAMOS (ZERBEROS FINCA)

Real de Abajo, 100
05110 El Barraco (Ávila)
☎: +34 687 410 952
dvrcru@gmail.com
winesdanielramosvinos.blogspot.com

ZERBEROS VINO PRECIOSO 2009 B
100% albillo.

92 Colour: bright yellow. Nose: mineral, dry stone, complex, expressive, powerfull, varietal, wild herbs, spicy. Palate: creamy, powerful, flavourful, full, complex.

ZERBEROS VIENTO ZEPHYROS 2009 B ROBLE
60% albillo, 40% sauvignon blanc.

91 Colour: yellow, greenish rim. Nose: powerfull, varietal, complex, fruit liqueur notes, fruit expression, earthy notes, dry stone. Palate: complex, fleshy, rich, full, powerful, spirituous.

PÉREZ CARAMÉS

Peña Picón, s/n
24500 Villafranca del Bierzo (León)
☎: +34 987 540 197 - Fax: +34 987 540 314
info@perezcarames.com
www.perezcarames.com

CASAR DE SANTA INÉS 2-9 2009 T
84% merlot, 9% pinot noir, 7% tempranillo.

84 Colour: cherry, purple rim. Nose: red berry notes, floral, grassy. Palate: flavourful, fruity, good acidity, round tannins.

CASAR DE SANTA INÉS 2008 T
49% merlot, 20% mencía, 18% pinot noir, 8% tempranillo, 5% cabernet sauvignon.

85 Colour: cherry, garnet rim. Nose: ripe fruit, spicy, creamy oak, toasty. Palate: powerful, flavourful, toasty

VINOS MALAPARTE

Ctra. del Henar, km. 3,5
40200 Cuéllar (Segovia)
☎: +34 921 105 204
info@vinosmalaparte.es
www.vinosmalaparte.es

DOLCE FAR NIENTE 2009 T
tinto fino.

91 Colour: light mahogany, orangey edge. Nose: ripe fruit, pattiserie, sweet spices, aged wood nuances. Palate: good acidity, fruity, flavourful, toasty.

CASTILLA LA MANCHA

BODEGAS Y VIÑEDOS CASTIBLANQUE

Isaac Peral, 19
13610 Campo de Criptana (Ciudad Real)
☎: +34 926 589 147 - Fax: +34 926 589 148
info@bodegascastiblanque.com
www.bodegascastiblanque.com

SOLAMENTE 2010 B
100% airén.

82 Colour: bright straw. Nose: white flowers, ripe fruit. Palate: flavourful, fruity, good acidity.

SOLAMENTE 2010 RD
100% syrah.

85 Colour: rose, purple rim. Nose: ripe fruit, floral, warm. Palate: fleshy, powerful, fruity, fresh.

SOLAMENTE 2010 T
60% tempranillo, 25% garnacha, 15% syrah.

85 Colour: cherry, purple rim. Nose: red berry notes, ripe fruit, balsamic herbs. Palate: flavourful, fruity, good acidity.

LA COMPAÑIA BODEGUERA DE UCLÉS

Cortés de Castillala Mancha, 3
13240 La Solana (Ciudad Real)
☎: +34 649 849 287
info@parfan.es
www.parfan.es

PARFÁN 2005 T
cabernet sauvignon.

91 Colour: cherry, garnet rim. Nose: ripe fruit, earthy notes, mineral, spicy, toasty. Palate: good acidity, balanced, powerful, flavourful.

PARFÁN 2004 T
cabernet sauvignon.

93 Colour: cherry, garnet rim. Nose: red berry notes, ripe fruit, elegant, balanced, complex, mineral, creamy oak. Palate: powerful, flavourful, fleshy, complex, long, round tannins.

CATALUNYA

BLAU NOU

Ctra. de San Martí Vell a Madremanya, km. 4
17462 San Martí Vell (Girona)
☎: +34 609 324 049 - Fax: +34 972 304 000
dambois@hotmail.com
www.eccocciwine.com

ECCOCI TINTO PREMIUM 2008 T
merlot, cabernet franc, marselan.

89 Colour: cherry, garnet rim. Nose: ripe fruit, cigar, cocoa bean, dark chocolate, mineral. Palate: flavourful, fleshy, balanced, toasty.

ECCOCI BLANCO 2010 B
viognier, roussanne, petit menseng.

88 Colour: bright golden. Nose: white flowers, citrus fruit, candied fruit. Palate: rich, flavourful, fleshy, good acidity.

ECCOMI SUPER PREMIUM 2009 T
marselan, cabernet franc.

92 Colour: cherry, garnet rim. Nose: ripe fruit, creamy oak, toasty, complex. Palate: powerful, flavourful, toasty, round tannins.

ECCOCI TINTO PREMIUM 2009 T
merlot, petit verdot, cabernet franc, marselan.

88 Colour: cherry, purple rim. Nose: raspberry, cocoa bean, dark chocolate, expressive, ripe fruit. Palate: light-bodied, fresh, fruity, flavourful.

ECCOMI SUPER PREMIUM 2008 TC
merlot, cabernet franc, marselan.

92 Colour: cherry, garnet rim. Nose: ripe fruit, powerfull, cocoa bean, dark chocolate, sweet spices, creamy oak. Palate: powerful, flavourful, fleshy, complex, toasty.

CARRIEL DELS VILARS

Mas Can Carriel Els Vilars
17753 Espolla (Girona)
☎: +34 972 563 335
carrieldelsvilars@hotmail.com

CARRIEL DELS VILARS 2009 T
40% garnacha, 35% syrah, 15% cabernet sauvignon, 10% cariñena.

87 Colour: dark-red cherry. Nose: ripe fruit, mineral, earthy notes, cigar, fine reductive notes. Palate: powerful, flavourful, fleshy, complex, mineral.

CARRIEL DELS VILARS 2008 T
50% garnacha, 35% syrah, 10% cabernet sauvignon, 5% cariñena.

90 Colour: dark-red cherry, orangey edge. Nose: powerfull, expressive, earthy notes, mineral, spicy, animal reductive notes. Palate: spirituous, complex, powerful, flavourful, full.

CARRIEL DELS VILARS 2007 T
40% garnacha, 35% syrah, 20% cabernet sauvignon, 5% cariñena.

86 Colour: dark-red cherry, black cherry, orangey edge. Nose: fruit preserve, wild herbs, damp earth, mineral, fine reductive notes. Palate: unctuous, powerful, flavourful.

ROSAT ESCUMÒS 2007 ESP
macabeo, xarel.lo, garnacha tinta, garnacha blanca, parellada.

84 Colour: ochre. Nose: ripe fruit, dried fruit, faded flowers, fine reductive notes. Palate: flavourful, sweetness, ripe fruit.

MISTELA DE CHARDONNAY 2009 MISTELA ROBLE
100% chardonnay.

88 Colour: bright golden. Nose: fruit liqueur notes, ripe fruit, grapey, sweet spices, honeyed notes. Palate: good acidity, rich, flavourful, spirituous.

CELLER RAMÓN SADURNI

Can Sadurní
08799 Sant Pere Molanta (Barcelona)
☎: +34 666 771 308
auladelvi@hotmail.com

RR SADURNÍ 2010 B
xarel.lo.

85 Colour: bright straw. Nose: white flowers, citrus fruit, fragrant herbs. Palate: fruity, flavourful, easy to drink.

RR SADURNÍ 2010 RD
merlot.

84 Colour: rose, purple rim. Nose: lactic notes, floral, red berry notes, ripe fruit. Palate: good acidity, fresh, fruity, flavourful.

JOAN SARDÀ

Ctra. Vilafranca a St. Jaume dels Domenys, Km. 8,1
08732 Castellvi de la Marca (Barcelona)
☎: +34 937 720 900 - Fax: +34 937 721 495
joansarda@joansarda.com
www.joansarda.com

BLANC DE SALOBRE BLANCO DULCE
garnacha, moscatel, macabeo, pedro ximénez.

88 Colour: light mahogany. Nose: honeyed notes, ripe fruit, cocoa bean, dark chocolate, aged wood nuances, sweet spices, toasty. Palate: spirituous, powerful, flavourful, fleshy.

KAIROS

Dels Nostris, 26
08185 Lliça de Vall (Barcelona)
☎: +34 938 436 061 - Fax: +34 938 439 671
kairos@vinodegaraje.com
www.kairosvino.com

KAIROS 2010 T
100% tempranillo.

90 Colour: cherry, garnet rim. Nose: powerfull, characterful, ripe fruit, spicy, smoky, earthy notes. Palate: powerful, concentrated, fleshy.

LAUREANO SERRES MONTAGUT

Gaudí, 1
43594 El Pinell de Brai (Tarragona)
☎: +34 977 426 356 - Fax: +34 977 426 192
laureano@serres.net
www.serres.net

MENDALL BB ESCOLLADES DEL 5 2005 B
100% bernatxa blanca.

91 Colour: golden. Nose: expressive, complex, wild herbs, spicy, petrol notes. Palate: flavourful, good structure, complex.

MENDALL MIAH MACAMIAU DEL 5 2005 B
100% macabeo.

89 Colour: golden. Nose: medium intensity, wild herbs, balanced, dried flowers. Palate: good structure, flavourful, balanced, rich.

MAS CANDÍ

Ctra. de Les Gunyoles, s/n
08793 Les Gunyoles d'Avinyonet (Barcelona)
☎: +34 680 765 275
info@mascandi.com
www.mascandi.com

MAS CANDI CAN28 2009 T
100% mandó.

90 Colour: bright cherry, purple rim. Nose: medium intensity, red berry notes, fragrant herbs. Palate: flavourful, good acidity, balanced, fruity.

MAS COMTAL

Mas Comtal, 1
08793 Avinyonet del Penedès (Barcelona)
☎: +34 938 970 052 - Fax: +34 938 970 591
mascomtal@mascomtal.com
www.mascomtal.com

GRAN ANGULAR - IN.M 100% 2010 B
incrocio manzoni.

87 Color bright straw. Aroma fresh, fresh fruit, white flowers, expressive. Taste flavourful, fruity, good acidity, balanced.

PIZZICATO 2010 RD
muscato de Hamburgo.

86 Colour: onion pink. Nose: candied fruit, red berry notes, floral. Palate: light-bodied, flavourful, good acidity, fruity.

PARDAS

Finca Can Comas, s/n
08775 Torrelavit (Barcelona)
☎: +34 938 995 005
pardas@cancomas.com
www.pardas.net

PARDAS SUMOLL ROSAT 2010 RD
sumoll.

89 Colour: brilliant rose. Nose: varietal, powerfull, fresh, fresh fruit, red berry notes. Palate: balanced, powerful, fresh, complex.

VINS DE TALLER

Nou, 5
17469 Siurana d'Empordà (Girona)
☎: +34 972 525 578 - Fax: +34 934 816 434
info@vinsdetaller.com
www.vinsdetaller.com

VINS DE TALLER PHLOX 2010 B
chardonnay, marsanne, roussanne.

91 Colour: bright straw. Nose: white flowers, expressive, ripe fruit, fragrant herbs, mineral. Palate: flavourful, fruity, good acidity, balanced, elegant.

VINS DE TALLER GRIS 2010 RD
100% marselan.

90 Colour: raspberry rose. Nose: ripe fruit, faded flowers, earthy notes, dry stone. Palate: good acidity, fleshy, powerful, flavourful.

VINS DE TALLER GEUM 2010 T
100% merlot.

90 Colour: cherry, purple rim. Nose: red berry notes, ripe fruit, balsamic herbs, mineral, expressive. Palate: good acidity, flavourful, fleshy, easy to drink.

VINS DE TALLER MM 2008 TC
merlot, marselan.

92 Colour: cherry, garnet rim. Nose: ripe fruit, fragrant herbs, earthy notes, spicy, creamy oak. Palate: elegant, flavourful, powerful, complex, fleshy, round tannins.

VINS DE TALLER MLOT 2007 TC
merlot.

90 Colour: cherry, garnet rim. Nose: ripe fruit, balsamic herbs, earthy notes, fine reductive notes, spicy, toasty. Palate: complex, fleshy, flavourful, long, mineral, balanced.

COMUNIDAD VALENCIANA

BODEGA MAS L'ALTET

Mas L'Altet Partida de la Creu s/n
03838 Alfafara (Alicante)
☎: +34 609 759 708
nina@bodegamaslaltet.com
www.bodegamaslaltet.com

AVI DE MAS L'ALTET 2009 T
72% syrah, 20% cabernet sauvignon, 8% merlot.

91 Colour: black cherry. Nose: powerfull, warm, toasty, expressive, ripe fruit. Palate: powerful, flavourful, concentrated, fleshy, round tannins.

BODEGAS LADRÓN DE LUNAS

Pintor Peiró, 10 - bajo izq.
46010 Valencia (Valencia)
☎: +34 660 958 980
administracion@ladrondelunas.es
www.ladrondelunas.es

LADRÓN DE LUNAS 2006 T
bobal, tempranillo, cabernet sauvignon.

88 Color cherry, garnet rim. Aroma ripe fruit, spicy, creamy oak, toasty, complex. Taste powerful, flavourful, toasty, round tannins.

BODEGAS SIERRA DE CABRERAS

Mollenta, 27
03638 Salinas (Alicante)
☎: +34 647 515 590
info@carabibas.com
www.carabibas.com

CARABIBAS VS 2009 T
cabernet sauvignon, merlot, monastrell.

90 Colour: bright cherry. Nose: sweet spices, ripe fruit, toasty. Palate: flavourful, fruity, toasty, round tannins.

CELLER LA MUNTANYA

Compositor Paco Esteve, 13
03830 Muro de l'Alcoi (Alicante)
☎: +34 607 902 235 - Fax: +34 965 531 248
info@cellerlamuntanya.com
www.cellerlamuntanya.com

ALBIR 2010 B
50% malvasía, 25% merseguera, 15% macabeo.

90 Colour: bright straw. Nose: white flowers, fresh fruit, dried herbs, mineral. Palate: good acidity, rich, fruity, flavourful.

LLIURE ALBIR 2009 B
garnacha blanca, malvasía.

93 Colour: bright yellow. Nose: powerfull, dry nuts, candied fruit, sweet spices, cocoa bean. Palate: flavourful, powerful, fruity, fleshy, complex, long.

CELLER LA MUNTANYA DOLÇ NATURAL 2009 B
malvasía.

92 Colour: golden. Nose: floral, honeyed notes, fragrant herbs, expressive, balanced. Palate: flavourful, sweet, fresh, fruity, good acidity, long.

CELLER LA MUNTANYA NEGRE 2009 T
monastrell, garnacha, garnacha tinta, bobal, bonicaire.

93 Colour: cherry, garnet rim. Nose: expressive, elegant, sweet spices, fragrant herbs, scrubland. Palate: flavourful, fruity, fresh, complex, balsamic. Personality.

PAQUITO EL CHOCOLATERO 2009 T
50% monastrell, 25% giró, 25% garnacha.

88 Colour: cherry, garnet rim. Nose: floral, red berry notes, ripe fruit, balsamic herbs, sweet spices, toasty. Palate: fleshy, flavourful, good acidity, toasty.

ALMOROIG 2007 T
69% monastrell, 16% giró, 15% garnacha.

91 Colour: cherry, garnet rim. Nose: red berry notes, ripe fruit, floral, spicy, toasty. Palate: balanced, powerful, flavourful, fleshy, round tannins.

SALVADOR POVEDA

CV 830 Ctra. Salinas, Km. 3
03640 Monóvar (Alicante)
☎: +34 966 960 180 - Fax: +34 965 473 389
salvadorpoveda@salvadorpoveda.com
www.salvadorpoveda.com

ROSELLA 2010 RD
monastrell.

78

VINS DEL COMTAT

Turballos, 1 - 3
03820 Cocentaina (Alicante)
☎: +34 965 593 194 - Fax: +34 965 593 590
vinsdelcomtat@gmail.com
www.vinsdelcomtat.com

VIOGNIER DE VINS DEL COMTAT 2010 B
100% viognier.

88 Colour: bright straw. Nose: fresh, fresh fruit, white flowers, expressive. Palate: flavourful, fruity, good acidity.

VIÑEDOS CULTURALES

Purísima, 15 Bajo
03380 Bigastro (Alicante)
☎: +34 966 770 353 - Fax: +34 966 770 353
vinedosculturales@gmail.com

PARQUE NATURAL "LA VIÑA DE SIMÓN" 2010 B
100% merseguera.

94 Colour: bright yellow. Nose: powerfull, ripe fruit, sweet spices, fragrant herbs. Palate: rich, smoky aftertaste, flavourful, fresh, good acidity.

PARQUE NATURAL "EL CARRO" 2010 B
100% moscatel.

92 Colour: bright straw. Nose: ripe fruit, fruit expression, mineral. Palate: flavourful, fruity, ripe fruit, good acidity, fine bitter notes.

EXTREMADURA

VINOS DE ÁNGEL DOMÍNGUEZ

Colón, 1
06220 Villafranca de los Barros (Badajoz)
☎: +34 669 568 565
angeldominguez@terra.es
www.bodegassofos.tk

SOFOS 2009 B
pardina.

92 Colour: bright golden. Nose: dried flowers, ripe fruit, sweet spices, creamy oak. Palate: rich, powerful, flavourful, fleshy, complex.

GALICIA

BODEGAS MARQUÉS DE VIZHOJA

Finca La Moreira s/n
36438 Arbo (Pontevedra)
☎: +34 986 665 825 - Fax: +34 986 665 960
marquesdevizhoja@marquesdevizhoja.com
www.marquesdevizhoja.com

MARQUÉS DE VIZHOJA 2010 B

85 Colour: bright straw. Nose: tropical fruit, floral, medium intensity. Palate: fresh, light-bodied, flavourful, easy to drink.

COTO DE GOMARIZ

Barrio de Gomariz
32429 Leiro (Ourense)
☎: +34 671 641 982 - Fax: +34 988 488 174
gomariz@cotodegomariz.com
www.cotodegomariz.com

VX CUVÉE CACO 2007 T
souson, caiño, carabuñeira, mencía.

91 Colour: cherry, garnet rim. Nose: red berry notes, ripe fruit, elegant, sweet spices, creamy oak, mineral. Palate: flavourful, fruity, fleshy, complex.

ENVINATE

Gran Vía, 2 - 1ºC
27600 Sarria (Lugo)
☎: +34 686 461 301
asesoria.envinate@gmail.com

PUZZLE 2010 T
tempranillo, garnacha.

92 Colour: black cherry. Nose: expressive, balanced, ripe fruit, creamy oak, sweet spices, cocoa bean. Palate: flavourful, fruity, full, ripe fruit, fine tannins.

DAS LOUSAS MENCÍA 2009 T
mencía.

88 Colour: dark-red cherry. Nose: overripe fruit, toasty, spicy, powerfull. Palate: good acidity, flavourful, fruity, round tannins.

LA RIOJA

CASTILLO DE MAETIERRA

Ctra. de Murillo, s/n
26500 Calahorra (La Rioja)
☎: +34 941 271 217 - Fax: +34 941 272 911
info@castillodemaetierra.com
www.castillodemaetierra.com

LIBALIS 2010 RD
moscatel grano menudo, syrah.

84 Colour: rose. Nose: red berry notes, candied fruit, floral, fresh. Palate: light-bodied, fresh, fruity, easy to drink.

MADRID

VALQUEJIGOSO

Ctra, Villamanta - Méntrida, s/n
28610 Villamanta (Madrid)
☎: +34 650 492 390
aureliogarcia@valquejigoso.com
www.valquejigoso.com

DEHESA DE VALQUEJIGOSO 2008 T
40% cabernet sauvignon, 20% syrah, 20% negral, 10% cabernet franc, 5% garnacha, 5% petit verdot.

92 Colour: cherry, garnet rim. Nose: powerfull, warm, ripe fruit, creamy oak, spicy. Palate: flavourful, powerful, fleshy, round tannins.

VALQUEJIGOSO V2 2007 T
45% cabernet sauvignon, 18% syrah, 17% petit verdot, 5% negral, 5% cabernet franc, 5% merlot.

94 Colour: cherry, garnet rim. Nose: spicy, creamy oak, toasty, ripe fruit, characterful, complex, scrubland. Palate: powerful, flavourful, toasty, round tannins.

NAVARRA

LA CALANDRIA (JAVIER CONTINENTE GAZTELAKUTO)

Camino de Aspra, s/n
31521 Murchante (Navarra)
☎: +34 630 904 327
luis@lacalandria.org
www.lacalandria.org

TIERGA 2008 T
garnacha.

93 Colour: cherry, garnet rim. Nose: ripe fruit, floral, wild herbs, spicy, creamy oak. Palate: fleshy, complex, spicy, good acidity.

GLOSARY and INDEXES

TERMINOLOGY RELATED TO COLOUR

AMBER. The first step in the oxidative ageing of sherry generoso wines, brandies, whiskies and rum, somewhere between yellow and coppery red.

BEADS. The slow rising string of bubbles in a sparkling wine.

BRICK RED. An orangey hue, similar to that of a brick, used to describe reds aged in bottle for more than 10 years or in barrel for longer than six.

BRILLIANT. Related to a young and neat wine.

CANDY CHERRY. This is used to define a colour lighter than a red but darker than a rosé.

CLEAN. Utterly clean, immaculate.

CLOUDY. Lacking clarity.

COPPERY. A reddish nuance that can be appreciated in whites aged in wood for a long period, generally amontillados and some palo cortados.

CHERRY. Commonly used to express red colour. It can take all sort of degrees from 'light' all the way to 'very dark' or almost 'black cherry'.

DARK. This often refers to a tone slightly lighter than 'deep' and synonymous to "medium-intensity".

DEEP. A red with a very dark colour, which hardly lets us see the bottom of the glass.

DULL. A wine lacking in liveliness, usually with an ochre hue.

GARNET RED. A common nuance in medium to light reds. If the wine is an intense cherry red it could have a garnet rim only if it comes from cooler regions; if it is more luminous and open than the violet rim of a dark wine, it generally would be a young wine.

GOLDEN. Gold in colour with yellow –predominantly– to reddish tones.

GLIMMER. A vague brilliance.

IODINE. A tone similar to iodine tincture stains (old gold and brownish) displayed by rancio and generoso wines have after their long oxidative ageing.

LIVELY. A reflection of the youth of a wine through bright, brilliant colours.

MAHOGANY. Describes the second stage of ageing in brandies, rum and generoso sherry (fortified) wines. A hue between brown and yellow displayed by wines when long aged.

OCHRE. Yellow-orangey hue, the last colour phase of a table wine, generally found in wines with a long oxidative ageing; it is a sign of their decline.

OILY. A wine that appears dense to the eye, usually sweet and with high alcohol content.

OLD GOLD. Gold colour with the brownish tones found in amontillados and a bit lighter than the mahogany nuance predominant in oloroso sherry.

ONION SKIN. A touch lighter than salmon colour.

OPAQUE. A wine with such depth of colour we cannot see the bottom of the glass. Generally found in very old pedro ximénez and therefore akin to caramelised notes.

OPEN. Very pale, not at all intense.

ORANGEY EDGE. Intermediate phase between a deep red and brick red found towards the rim in red wines of a medium age. It generally appears sooner in wines with higher alcohol content and it is also typical of wines made from pinot noir.

RASPBERRY. Sort of pinkish colour with a bluish rim, it is the optimal colour for rosé wines since it denotes freshness, youth and a good acidity.

RIM. Also known as 'edge', it refers to the lighter colour the wine displays at the edge of the oval when we hold the glass at 45°, as opposed to the 'core' or main body of colour right in the centre. If it is a young red, it will show normally violet or raspberry nuances; when slightly older, it will be a deeper red or garnet, and if has been in the bottle for more than five years it might be anything from ruby to tawny through brick red and orangey.

RUBY. Slightly orangey hue with a yellow nuance found in old wines that have lost part of their original cherry colour.

SALMON. A tone slightly redder than pink found in rosé wines with less acidity and more alcohol.

STEELY. Pale colour with metallic reflections (reminiscent of those from steel) found in some whites.

STRAW-COLOURED. This term should be understood as straw yellow, the colour found in the majority of young white wines, halfway between yellow and green. It can also be described as "lemony".

TERMINOLOGY RELATED TO AROMA

ACETONE. Very close notes to those of nail varnish, typical of very old eau de vie.

ALCOHOL. It is not a pejorative term for an excess of alcohol –in which case we would refer to it as burning–, but just a predominant, non-aggressive note.

ALDEHYDE. A sensory note of oxidized, slightly rancid alcohol, typical of old wines with high alcohol content that have undergone oxidative ageing.

ANIMAL. Not a positive note, generally the result of long storage in bottle, also referred to as 'wet dog' or 'wet hide' and normally associated with a lack of hygiene. If it is found in younger vintages, then it could be a symptom of "brett" (see brett).

ATTIC. An aroma associated with that of old dry wood and dust typical of attics, mainly found in fortified wines aged in wood and in very old wines aged for a long period in old barrels which happen to have also been bottled for more than ten years.

BALSAMIC. A trait usually associated to wood-aged wines in hot regions, where high temperatures accelerate their evolution. It also refers to the aroma of dry herbs such as eucalyptus and bay leaf, as well as incense and tar.

BLACK FRUIT. It refers to the sort of toasted aromas of very ripe grapes, those almost 'burnt skin' notes found in reds that have undergone a long vatting period in contact with the skins.

"BRETT". This is the abbreviation for a new term (brettanomyces) to describe an old problem: the aroma of stables, henhouse, and wet new leather generally found along with reductive off-odours in wines that have been in the bottle for more than ten years. These aromas were considered part of the sensory complexity of old wines and therefore tolerated. Nowadays, due to better olfactory research and more hygienic working conditions in the wineries, they are easily detected and considered more a defect. In addition, today brett is often found in younger wines as this particular bacteria or yeast usually develops better in wines with higher ph levels. The increase in the ph of wines is quite common these days due to global warming, riper grapes and the use of fertilizers over the past thirty-five years.

BROOM. An aroma reminiscent of Mediterranean shrubs, only a bit dryer.

CANDIED FRUIT. This is a sweet nuance, somewhere between toasted and jammy, which is found in whites with a long oxidative ageing and in some sweet white wines.

CAROB. Anybody who has chewed or smelt one of those beans cannot would easily recall its typical blend of sweetness and toasted notes, as well as the slightly rustic nuance. It is usually found in old brandy aged in soleras of pedro ximénez and in deep, concentrated wines made from very ripe grapes.

CEDAR. The somewhat perfumed aroma of cedar, a soft wood commonly found in Morocco.

CHARACTERFUL. Used to express the singularity of a wine above the rest. It may refer to winemaking, terroir or the peculiarities of its ageing.

CITRUS. An aroma reminiscent of lemon, orange and grapefruit.

CLASSIC RIOJA. A note named after the more traditional and popular style of Rioja, with predominantly woody notes (normally from very old wood) along with a typical character of sweet spices and occasionally candle wax nuances instead of fruit, given the oxidative character provided by long ageing periods.

CLEAR. A wine with no defects, neither in the nose nor in the palate.

CLOSED. A term to describe a faint or not properly developed nose. Almost always found in concentrated wines from a good vintage, which evolve very slowly in the bottle, but it can also be found in wines recently bottled.

COCOA. Delicate, slightly toasted aroma found in wines aged in wood for a moderately long time that have evolved very well in the bottle.

COMPLEX. A wine abundant in aromas and flavours related either to grape variety, soil or ageing, although none of those features is particularly prominent.

CREAMY. Aroma of finely toasted oak (usually French) with notes of caramelised vanilla.

DATES. A sweet aroma with hints of dates and a raisiny nuance.

EARTHY. An aroma somewhere between clay and dust typical of red wines made from ripe grapes and with high alcohol content. It can also refer in some wines to a mineral nuance.

ELEGANT. A harmonious combination of fine, somewhat restrained aromatic notes related to perfumed wood, and a light, pleasantly balanced richness or complexity (see complex).

ETHEREAL. This is used to describe spirits, fortified wines and wines with a certain intensity of alcohol in their oxidative evolution; the strength of the alcohol reveals the rancid-type aromas. It has a lot to do with age.

EVOLUTION NOTES. Generally used to describe wines aged prematurely by either oxygen or heat, e.g., a wine that has been left in a glass for several hours.

FINE. A synonym for elegant.

FINE LEES. This is an aroma between herbaceous and slightly toasty that is produced by the contact of the wine with the lees (dead yeasts cells) after the fermentation has taken place, a process called autolysis that helps to make the wine more complex and to give it a richer aroma.

FLOR. This is a pungent, saline aroma typically found in sherry wines, particularly fino, manzanilla and, to a lesser degree, amontillado. It is caused by a film-forming yeast known as 'flor' in Spanish (literally flower), which transfers to the wine its singular smell and flavour.

FLORAL. Reminiscent of the petals of certain flowers –such as roses and jasmine– noticeable in certain northern withes or in quality reds after a bottle-ageing spell that also delivers some spicy notes.

FRAGRANT HERBS. An aroma similar to soaps and perfumes made from lavender, rosemary, lemon, orange blossom or jasmine. It is found in white wines that undergo pre-fermentative cold skin maceration.

FRESH. A wine with lively aroma and hardly any alcohol expression.

FRESH FRUIT. These are fruity notes produced by a slow grape-ripening cycle typical of mild climates.

FRUIT EXPRESSION. Related to different flavours and aromas reminiscent of various fruits and fine herbs.

FRUITY. Fruit notes with a fine herbal character and even hints of green grass.

HERBACEOUS. A vague note of vine shoots, scrub and geranium leaf caused by an incomplete maturation of the grape skin.

INTENSE. A powerful aroma that can be immediately referred to as such when first nosing the wine.

IODINE. This refers to iodine tincture, a combination of the sweetish smell of alcohol, toasted notes, liniment and varnish or lacquer.

JAM. Typical notes of very ripe black fruit slightly caramelised by a slow oxidative ageing in oak barrels. Very similar to forest fruit jam (prunes, blackberries, blueberries, redcurrants, cherries…). Found in red wines –generally from southern regions– with a high concentration of fruit notes giving that they are made resorting to long vatting periods, which provide longer contact with the skins.

MACERATION. These are aromas similar to those produced during fermentation and that –logically– found in young wines.

MEDITERRANEAN. An aroma where various prominent notes (sweetness, alcohol, burning and raisiny notes, caramel…) produced by grapes grown in hot regions blend in to characterize the wines.

MINERAL NOTES. Used to describe wines that have a subtle nose with plenty of notes reminiscent of flint, slate, hot stones or dry sand.

MUSK. A term to describe the sweet and grapey notes typical of highly aromatic varieties such as moscatel, riesling and gewürztraminer.

ROASTED COFFEE. (See terms of taste).

SUBDUED FRUIT. It generally refers to aromas produced by a fast ripening of the grapes typical of warm climates.

NUTS. Notes generally found in white wines with oxidative ageing; the oxygen in the air gives rise to aromas and flavours reminiscent of nuts (bitter almond, hazelnut, walnut…). When ageing spells are longer and –most importantly– take place in older casks, there will appear notes that are closer to fruits like figs, dates and raisins.

ORANGE PEEL. Typical fruity aroma found in certain white wines with, above all, a vibrant spicy character.

ORGANIC NOTES. A way to define the fermentative aromas –essentially related to yeast– and typical of young white wines and also fortified generoso wines from the sherry region.

OVERRIPE FRUIT. An aroma typical of young wines that are already slightly oxidized and reminiscent of grape bunches with some signs of rot –noble or not–, or simply bruised or recently pressed grapes.

OXIDATIVE EVOLUTION. Notes related to the tendency of a wine to age by the action of oxygen that passes through the pores of the cask or barrel (micro-oxidation), or during racking.

PATISSERIE. An aroma between sweet and toasted with hints of caramelised sugar and vanilla typical of freshly baked cakes. It is found in wines –generally sweet– that have been aged in oak for a long time and it is caused by both oxidative evolution and the aromatic elements (mainly vanillin) found in oak.

PEAT. A slightly burnt aroma that occurs when the notes of ripe grapes blend in with the toasted aromas of new oak in wines with a high alcohol content.

PHENOLIC. A short and derivative way to describe polyphenols (a combination of the tannins and anthocyanins, vegetal elements of the grape), it describes aromas of grape skins macerated for a long time that yield notes somewhere between ink and a pressed bunch of grapes.

PORT. This is the sweet aroma of wine made from somewhat raisiny or overripe grapes and reminiscent of the vintage Ports made with a short oxidative ageing.

PUNGENT. A prominent aromatic note produced by the combination of alcohol, wood and flor notes and typical of –particularly– fino sherry wines.

RANCIO. This is not a defect but a note better known as "sherryfied" and brought about by oxidative ageing.

RED FRUIT. An aromatic note that refers to forest red fruits (blackberries, redcurrants, mulberries) as well as slightly unripe cherries and plums.

REDUCTION. A wine aroma caused by the lack of oxygen during long bottle ageing, which gives rise to notes like tobacco, old leather, vanilla, cinnamon, cocoa, attic, dust, etc.

REDUCTION OFF-ODOURS. This is a negative set of aromas, halfway between boiled cabbage and boiled eggs, produced by the lees in wines that have not been properly aerated or racked.

REDUCTIVE TANK OFF-ODOURS. A smell between metal and boiled fruit typical of wines stored in large vats at high temperatures. The sulphur added –probably in excess– combines with the wine and reduces its freshness and the expression of fruit notes. This phenomenon is largely found in the production of bulk wines.

RIPE GRAPE SKIN. The aroma that a very ripe grape gives off when squeezed, similar to that of ink or of ripe grape bunches just pressed.

SALINE. This is the note acquired by a fino that has aged in soleras under flor yeast.

SEASONED WOOD. It refers to notes that may appear in wines aged in barrel for a long period –more than four or five years– which have lost the fine toasted aromas and flavours of new oak.

SHRUB. An aroma typically herbal found in Mediterranean regions, a mixture of rosemary, thyme and other typically semi-arid herbs. It refers to the dry, herbaceous note found generally in white and red wines from warmer regions.

SOLERA. An aroma close to the damp, seasoned, aged aroma of an old bodega for oloroso wines.

SPICY. It refers to the most common household spices (pepper, cloves, cinnamon) that appear in wines that undergo long and slow oxidative ageing in oak casks or barrels.

SPIRITUOUS. Both a flavour and an olfactory feature related to high alcohol content but without burning sensations. It is an almost 'intellectual' term to define alcohol, since that product is nothing else but the "spirit of wine".

STEWED FRUIT. Notes of stewed or 'cooked' fruit appear in wines made from well-ripened –not overripe– grapes and are similar to those of jam.

TAR. The pitchy, petrolly aromas of very toasted wood, associated with concentrated red wines with lots of colour, structure and alcohol.

TERROIR. An aromatic note determined by the soil and climate and therefore with various nuances: mountain herbs, minerals, stones, etc.

TOASTED SUGAR. Sweet caramelised aromas.

TOFFEE. A note typical of the milk coffee creams (lactic and toasted nuances mixed together) and present in some crianza red wines.

TROPICAL NOTES. The sweet white fruit aromas present in white wines made from grapes that have ripened very quickly and lack acidity.

TRUFFLE. Similar note to that of a mixture of damp earth and mushrooms.

UNDERGROWTH. This is the aromatic nuance between damp earth, grass and fallen leaves found in well-assembled, wood-aged reds that have a certain fruity expression and good phenolic concentration.

VANILLA. A typical trait of wines –also fortified– aged in oak, thanks to the vanillin, an element contained in that type of wood.

VARIETAL EXPRESSION. This is the taste and aroma of the variety or varieties used to make the wine.

VARNISH. A typical smell found in very old or fortified wines due to the oxidation of the alcohol after a long wood-ageing period. The varnished-wood note is similar to the aroma of eau de vie or spirits aged in wood.

VARNISHED WOOD. A sharp note typical of wines aged in wood for a long period, during which the alcohol oxidises and gives off an aroma of acetone, wood or nail varnish.

VISCOUS. The sweet taste and aromatic expression of wines with high alcohol content.

VOLATILE. A note characteristic of wines with high volatile acidity, i.e., just the first sign of them turning into vinegar. It is typical of poorly stabilized young wines or aged wines either with a high alcohol content or that have taken on this note during the slow oxidative wood-ageing phase, although we should remember it is a positive trait in the case of generoso wines.

WINE PRESS. The aroma of the vegetal parts of the grape after fermentation, vaguely reminiscent of pomace brandy, grapeskins and ink.

WITHERED FLOWERS. This is a sort of 'toasty' nuance typical of good champagnes made with a high percentage of pinot noir and some cavas which have aged perfectly in the bottle and on their lees for a long time.

WOODY. It describes an excess of notes of wood in a wine. The reason could be either a too long ageing period or the wine's lack of structure.

YEASTY. The dry aroma of bread yeast that can be perceived in young cavas or champagnes, or wines that have just been bottled.

TERMINOLOGY RELATED TO THE PALATE

ALCOHOL. A gentle, even sweet note of fine spirits; it is not a defect.

ALCOHOLIC EDGES. A slight excess of alcohol perceived on the tongue, but which does not affect the overall appreciation of the wine.

AMPLE. A term used to describe richness. It is a sensation generally experienced on the attack.

BITTER. A slight, non-aggressive note of bitterness, often found in some sherry wines (finos, amontillados) and the white wines from Rueda; it should not be regarded as a negative feature, quite on the contrary, it helps to counterbalance soft or slightly sweet notes.

CARAMELISED. A very sweet and toasted note typical of some unctuous wines aged in oloroso or pedro ximénez casks.

DENSE. This is related to the body of the wine, a thick sensation on the palate.

FATNESS. "Gordo" (fat) is the adjective used in Jerez to describe a wine with good body; it is the antonym of "fino" (light).

FLABBY. Used to describe a wine low in acidity that lacks freshness.

FLAVOURFUL. A pronounced and pleasant sensation on the palate produced by the combination of various sweet nuances.

FULL. A term used to describe volume, richness, some sweetness and round tannins; that is, a wine with a fleshy character and an almost fat palate.

LIGHT. The opposite of meaty, dense or concentrated; i.e., a wine with little body.

LONG. This refers to the persistence of the flavour after the wine has been swallowed.

MEATY. A wine that has body, structure and which can almost literally be "chewed".

NOTES OF WOOD. Well-defined notes somewhere between woody and resin generally found in wines matured in younger casks.

OILY. This is the supple, pleasantly fat sensation produced by glycerine. It is more prominent in older wines –thanks to the decrease in acidity– or in certain varieties such as riesling, gewürztraminer, chardonnay, albariño and godello.

OXIDATIVE AGEING. It refers to the influence of the air in the evolution of wine. Depending on the level of oxygen in the air, oxidation will take place in wine to a greater or lesser extent. Oxidative ageing happens when the air comes in contact with the wine either during racking –which ages the wine faster– or through the pores of the wood.

PASTY. This is not a pejorative term, simply a very sweet and dense taste.

ROASTED COFFEE. The sweet and toasted note of caramelised sugar typically found in wines aged in oak barrels –generally burnt inside–, or else the taste of very ripe (sometimes even overripe) grapes.

ROUGH TANNINS. Just unripe tannins either from the wood or the grape skins.

ROUND. This is an expression commonly used to describe a wine without edges, supple, with volume and body.

SWEETENED. Related to sweetness, only with an artificial nuance.

SWEETNESS. A slightly sweet note that stands out in a wine with an overall dry or tannic character.

SOFT TANNINS. Both alcohol and adequately ripened grapes help to balance out the natural bitter character of the tannins. They are also referred to as fat or oily tannins.

TANNIC. This is term derived from tannin, a substance generally found in the skin of the grape and in the wood that yields a somewhat harsh, vegetal note. In wines, it displays a slightly harsh, sometimes even grainy texture.

UNCTUOUS. This refers to the fat, pleasant note found in sweet wines along with their somewhat sticky sweetness.

VELVETY. A smooth, pleasant note on the palate typical of great wines where the tannins and the alcohol have softened down during ageing.

VIGOROUS. A wine with high alcohol content.

WARM. The term speaks of alcohol in a more positive way.

WELL-BALANCED. A term that helps to define a good wine: none of the elements that are part of it (alcohol, acidity, dry extract, oak) is more prominent than the other, just pure balance.

ABONA

91	Flor de Chasna 2010 T Barrica	58
90	Testamento Malvasía Esencia 2008 B	58
90	Testamento Malvasía 2009 BFB	58
89	Testamento Malvasía 2010 BFB	58
89	Frontos 2010 T Barrica	59
89	Flor de Chasna Naturalmente Dulce 2010 B	58
88	Frontos 2010 T	59
88	Testamento Malvasía Dulce 2010 Blanco dulce	59
88	Pagos Reverón B	60
87	Cumbres de Abona 2010 T	58
87	Frontos Semiseco Ecológico 2010 B	59
87	Los Tableros 2010 B Barrica	59
87	Marqués de Fuente 2009 T Barrica	58
87	Testamento Malvasía Dry 2010 B	58
87	Viña Arese 2010 B	60
87	Testamento Malvasía 2008 BFB	58
86	Frontos 2010 B	59
86	Pagos Reverón 2009 T Barrica	60
86	Flor de Chasna 2010 T Maceración Carbónica	59
86	Chasnero Acacia 2010 B	58
86	Viña Arese T Barrica	60
86	Mencey de Chasna Afrutado 2010 B	59

ALELLA

93	Marfil Mot dolç 2003 B	64
92	Marqués de Alella Allier 2009 BFB	66
92	In Vita 2010 B	65
91	Marfil Generoso Semi 1976 B	64
91	Marfil Violeta 2003 T	64
91	In Vita 2009 B	65
90	Alta Alella Dolç Mataró 2009 Tinto dulce	65
90	Alta Alella Lanius 2009 BFB	65
90	Marfil Moscatel 2008 ESP	64
90	Alta Alella Blanc de Neu 2009 BFB	65
90	Perfum de Pansa 2009 B	66
89	Marfil Generoso Sec 1976 B	64
89	Alta Alella Parvus Chardonnay 2010 BFB	64
89	Alta Alella Parvus Syrah 2009 T	65
89	Marqués de Alella 2010 B	66
89	Alta Alella Pansa Blanca 2010 B	65
89	Alta Alella Syrah 2008 T	65
88	Marfil Blanc de Noirs 2008 BR	64
88	Acot 2009 RD	66
87	Marqués de Alella Pansa Blanca 2009 B	66
87	Roura Crianza Tres Ceps 2007 TC	66
87	Roura Xarel.lo 2010 B	66
87	Marfil Rosat 2008 BR Espumoso	64
87	Roura Merlot 2007 T	66
87	Marqués de Alella VGR 2009 B	66

ALICANTE

95	VC Madera 2009 T	84
95	VC Metal 2009 T	84
95	Curro 2009 T	74
94	Casta Diva Reserva Real 2002 B Reserva	77
94	Estrecho Monastrell 2006 T	76
94	Salinas 1237 2007 T	79
94	El Sequé 2009 T	80
94	Beryna 10º Aniversario 2009 T	74
94	VC Tierra 2009 T	84
93	Furtiva Lágrima 2010 B	77
93	Enrique Mendoza Moscatel de Mendoza 2008 B	76
93	Enrique Mendoza Santa Rosa 2006 TR	76
93	Enrique Mendoza Shiraz 2008 TC	76
93	Mira Salinas 2007 T	79
92	Gran Imperial GE Reserva Especial	82
92	La Diva 2010 BC	77
92	VC Fuego 2009 T	84
92	VC Agua 2009 T	84
92	VC Fusión 2009 T	84
91	Miguel Navarro 2010 B	79
91	Enrique Mendoza Cabernet Sauvignon 2007 TC	76
91	Cristal.li 2009 B	83
91	Penya Cadiella Selecció 2006 T	83
91	Casta Diva Recóndita Armonía T	77
91	Puerto Salinas 2007 T	79
91	Casa Balaguer 2007 T	74
91	Sein 2009 T	73
91	Essens 2010 B	73
91	Los Cipreses de Usaldón 2010 T	84
90	Terra Natura Clásico 2006 TC	79
90	Enrique Mendoza Cabernet Sauvignon - Shiraz 2007 TR	76
90	Fondillón 1987 S/C Fondillón Gran Reserva	83
90	Bahía de Denia 2010 B Joven	73
90	Boca Negra 2007 TC	77
90	Agulló 2007 T	78
90	Quo Vadis S/C Fondillón	77
90	Miguel Navarro Monastrell Tempranillo 2010 T Barrica	79
90	Tarima Monastrel 2010 T	80
90	Tarima Hill 2009 T	80

ALMANSA

92	La Atalaya 2009 T	89
92	Adaras 2006 T	89
91	Alaya 2009 T	89
90	La Huella de Adaras 2008 T	89
90	Calizo de Adaras 2010 T	89
90	Santa Cruz 2010 T	88
90	Laya 2009 T	89
89	Higueruela 2010 T	88
89	La Vega de Adaras 2008 T	89
89	Santa Cruz 2010 B	88
89	Rupestre 2009 T Roble	88
88	Adaras Selección 2010 BFB	88
88	Aldea de Adaras 2010 T	89
88	Tintoralba Selección 2008 T Roble	88
88	Matamangos Syrah 2007 T	89

ARABAKO TXAKOLINA

89	Malkoa Txakoli 2009 B	93
87	Señorío de Astobiza 2010 B	93

ARLANZA

92	Buezo Nattan 2004 TR	100
91	Buezo Petit Verdot Tempranillo 2004 T	100
90	Cascajuelo 2009 T Roble	99
90	Garmendia 2010 T	100
90	Pagos de Negredo Magnum 2006 TC	100
90	Buezo Tempranillo 2004 TC	100
90	Buezo Nattan 2005 TC	99
90	Dominio de Manciles 2010 RD Barrica	98
89	Buezo Petit Verdot Tempranillo 2005 TC	99
89	Buezo Varietales 2004 TC	99
89	Nabal 2008 TC	98
88	Garmendia 2010 RD	100
87	Dominio de Manciles 2004 TR	98
87	Monte Amán Pago de Valdeágueda Viñas Viejas 2004 T	99
87	Tinto Lerma 2008 TC	98
87	Garmendia 2009 T Roble	100
87	Lerma Selección 2007 TR	98
87	Castillo de Ura 2010 B	99

ARRIBES

92 La Setera 2008 T Roble 105
91 Gran Abadengo 2005 TR 104
91 Transitium Durii 2007 T 105
90 Condado de Fermosel Vendimia Seleccionada 2006 TC ..105
89 Bruñal 2005 T 104
89 Arribes de Vettonia 2004 TR....104
88 Arribes de Vettonia 2008 TC....104
88 La Setera 2008 TC 105
88 Abadengo 2010 B 104
88 Abadengo 2006 TC....104
87 Abadengo 2004 TR....105
87 La Setera 2010 T 105
87 Abadengo Malvasía 2009 B Barrica 104

BIERZO

96 La Faraona 2008 T 114
95 Villa de Corullón 2008 T 114
95 Moncerbal 2008 T 114
95 Ultreia 2009 T 116
94 Pétalos del Bierzo 2009 T 114
94 Valtuille Cepas Centenarias 2007 T Roble....113
94 Pittacum Aurea 2007 TC....120
94 Hombros 2008 T 114
94 Herencia del Capricho 2008 BFB 113
94 Las Lamas 2008 T 114
93 Xestal 2007 T 113
93 Mencía Luna Beberide 2009 T 111
93 Peique Selección Familiar 2006 T 112
93 Pittacum 2007 TC....120
93 Paixar Mencía 2008 T 113
93 Altos de Losada 2007 T 115
93 Godelia 12 meses 2009 T Roble....115
92 Val de Paxariñas "Capricho" 2010 B 113
92 Casar de Burbia 2009 T 113
92 Peique Viñedos Viejos 2007 T Roble 112
92 Tares P. 3 2007 T Roble 119
92 Mengoba de Espanillo 2009 T 112
92 Soto del Vicario Go de Godello 2009 BFB....117
92 Ledo. 8 2007 T 110
92 Luna Beberide Art 2009 T 111
92 Gancedo 2006 TR....113
91 Tilenus Pagos de Posada 2003 TR 115
91 El Castro de Valtuille Joven 2009 T 113
91 Dominio de Tares Godello 2010 BFB 119
91 Campo Redondo Godello 2010 B 109
91 Tebaida 2009 T 113
91 Martín Sarmiento 2006 T 112
91 Dominio de Tares Cepas Viejas 2008 TC....120
91 Tilenus Pieros 2002 T 115
91 Mengoba Godello sobre lías 2009 B 112
91 El Castro de Valtuille 2008 T 113
91 Soto del Vicario Men Selección 2008 T 117
91 Demasiado Corazón 2009 BFB 111
91 Caneiros 2007 T Roble....118
91 La Bienquerida 2007 T 115
91 Flavium 2009 T Roble....117
90 Baloiro 2008 TC 110
90 Carracedo 2007 T 110
90 Tilenus 2005 TC 114
90 Tilenus Envejecido en Roble 2007 T Roble....114
90 Prada a Tope 2006 TR 116
90 Ambos Mencía 2007 T 115
90 Bembibre 2007 T 120
90 Campo Redondo 2009 T Roble....110
90 Gotín del Risc Essencia 2007 T Roble 110
90 Hacienda Sael Godello 2010 B 109
90 Solar de Sael 2007 TC 109
90 Losada 2008 T 115
90 Castro Ventosa"Vintage" 2008 T 113
90 Flavium 2008 TC....117
90 Soto del Vicario Men 2008 T 117
90 Tierras de Albares 2007 TC....119
90 Brezo Mencía 2009 T 112
90 Palacio de Canedo 2007 TR 116
90 Don Osmundo 2008 T 114
90 Godelia Blanco sobre lías 2010 B 115
90 Godelia Blanco Selección 2009 B 115
90 Ledo Club de Barricas 2007 T 110
90 Valdaiga X 2010 T 116
90 Vega Montán VM Velvet 2008 T 111
90 Picantal 2008 T 116
90 Pago de Valdoneje Viñas Viejas 2008 T 118

BINISSALEM MALLORCA

93 P. de Maria 2008 T 124
93 Tianna Negre "Bocchoris" 2009 T 125
91 Macià Batle Reserva Privada 2007 TR 124
90 Buc 2006 TC....125
90 Daurat 2010 BFB 125
90 José L. Ferrer 2008 TC 126
90 José L. Ferrer 2005 TR 126
90 Mollet González Suñer 2010 B Joven 127
90 Tianna Negre 2009 T 125
90 El Vino del Llaüt 2010 B 124
89 Vinya Taujana Blanc de Blanc 2010 B 127
89 J.P. 2006 TC 125
89 Ses Nines Negre 2010 T 125
89 LLum 2010 B 124
89 Dos Marias 2010 T 124
88 Torrent Fals 2007 TC 127
88 Macià Batle 2008 TC....124
88 Macià Batle Blanc de Blancs 2010 B 124
88 Albaflor 2010 RD 127
88 Ses Nines Selecció 07/9 2009 T 124
88 José L. Ferrer D2UES Syrah Callet 2009 T 126
88 José L. Ferrer Pedra de Binissalem 2009 T 126

BIZKAIKO TXAKOLINA

92 Doniene 2010 BFB 132
91 Marko 2010 B 133
91 Señorío de Otxaran 2010 B 135
91 Itsas Mendi Urezti 2008 B 133
91 Uriondo 2009 BFB....135
90 Doniene 2010 B 132
90 Uixar 2010 B 133
90 Gorka Izagirre Arima 2009 B 133
90 Artxanda 2010 B 132
90 Artzai 2009 B 134
89 Itsas Mendi 2010 B 133
89 Otxanduri 2010 B 134
89 Saratsu 2010 B 133
88 Nekesolo 2010 B 133
88 Itsasmendi nº 7 2008 B 133
88 Aretxaga 2010 B 135
88 Erdikoetxe 2010 B 132
88 Aguirrebeko 2010 B 131
88 Gorka Izagirre 2010 B 133
88 Magalarte Jabi Aretxabaleta 2010 B 134
88 Magalarte Iñaki Aretxabaleta 2010 B 133
88 Oxinbaltza 2010 B 134
88 Bikandi Txacolina 2010 B 131
88 Abio Txacolina 2010 B 131
88 Sagastibeltza Karrantza 2010 B 133
88 Amunategi 2010 B 131
88 Artzai 2008 B 134

BULLAS

93 Lavia+ Monastrell Viña Vieja 2006 TC....141
92 3000 Años 2006 T....140
92 Valche 2006 TC....139
92 Lavia Monastrell Syrah 2007 TC....141
92 Lavia+ Monastrell Viña Vieja 2007 TC....141
90 Las Reñas Monastrell 2010 T....140
90 Sortius Syrah 2009 T Roble....140
90 Valche 2007 TC....139
89 Carrascalejo 2010 T....141
89 Siscar T....140
89 Chaveo 2006 TC....139
88 Las Reñas 2008 T Barrica....140
88 Partal de Autor 2006 T....139
88 Almudí Uno 2007 TC....139
88 Almudí Tres 2007 TC....139
88 Chaveo 2007 TC....139
88 Tercia de Ulea 2008 TC....139

CALATAYUD

93 Las Rocas de San Alejandro 2009 T....147
93 Las Rocas Viñas Viejas 2009 T....148
93 Lajas 2008 T....150
92 Atteca Armas 2007 T....146
92 Real de Aragón Centenaria 2008 T....147
92 Lajas 2007 T....150
91 Alto Las Pizarras 2008 T....148
91 Baltasar Gracián Garnacha Viñas Viejas 2009 T....148
91 El Puño Garnacha 2007 T....149
91 Filón 2010 T Roble....150
90 Unus 2009 T....145
90 Baltasar Gracián Vendimia Seleccionada 2010 T....147
90 Baltasar Gracián 2007 TC....148
90 Baltasar Gracián 2006 TR....148
90 Armantes Selección Especial 2008 T....146
90 Langa Emoción 2009 T....147
90 Honoro Vera Garnacha 2010 T....146
90 Atteca 2009 T....146
90 Teorema 2009 T....148
90 Muzares 2010 T....146
90 Manga del Brujo 2009 T....149
90 Fabla Garnacha Especial 2008 T....148
90 Stylo 2009 T....145
90 La Garnacha Olvidada de Aragón 2009 T....150

CAMPO DE BORJA

97 Aquilón 2008 T....154
95 Alto Moncayo 2008 T....154
93 Alto Moncayo Veratón 2008 T....154
93 Oxia 2006 TC....155
93 Pagos del Moncayo Garnacha 2009 T....156
92 Fagus de Coto de Hayas 2009 T....154
92 Borsao Tres Picos 2009 T....155
92 Moscatel Ainzón 90 días 2010 B Barrica....156
92 Pagos del Moncayo Syrah 2009 T....156
92 Coto de Hayas Solo 10 2010 T....154
92 Borsao Berola 2007 T....156
91 Borsao Selección 2010 T....155
91 Coto de Hayas Garnacha Centenaria 2010 T....154
91 Terrazas del Moncayo Garnacha 2008 T Roble....156
91 Cayus Selección 2009 T....156
91 Pagos del Moncayo 2010 T....156
91 Aragus Ecológico 2010 T....154
90 Coto de Hayas 2007 TR....155
90 Coto de Hayas Tempranillo Cabernet 2010 T Roble....154
90 Borsao Bole 2008 T....155

CARIÑENA

94 Aylés "Tres de 3000" 2007 T....169
92 Anayón Garnacha 2008 T....168
92 Prinur Moscatel 2009 B....163
92 Sierra de Viento Moscatel Vendimia Tardía B....164
91 Longus 2006 T....164
91 Jabalí Garnacha-Syrah 2010 T....165
91 Prinur Viñas Viejas 2005 T....163
91 Torrelongares Licor de Garnacha 2006 Vino de Licor....166
91 Sierra de Viento Garnacha Gran Selección 2006 T....164
91 Altius 2008 TC....170
90 Care XCLNT 2008 T....160
90 Altius Garnacha 2010 T....170
90 Urbezo Chardonnay 2010 B....170
90 Viña Urbezo 2010 T Maceración Carbónica....170
90 Dominio de Longaz Premium 2006 T....165
90 Anayón 2006 T Barrica....167
90 Barón de Lajoyosa Moscatel Mistela....162
90 Gran Víu Selección 2008 T....172
90 Pulchrum Crespiello 2006 T....160
90 Urbezo Garnacha 2010 T....171
90 Jabalí Tempranillo - Cabernet 2010 T....165
90 Care 2010 T Roble....160
90 Anayón Chardonnay 2010 BFB....166
90 Menguante Garnacha Blanca 2010 B....172
90 Prinur Selección Calar 2005 T....163
90 Sierra de Viento Garnacha 2008 T....164
90 GHM Garnacha Hacienda Molleda 2006 T Roble....168
90 Menguante Vidadillo 2008 T....172
90 Care Garnacha Cabernet Sauvignon 2008 TR....160
90 GHM Gran Hacienda Molleda 2009 TC....168
90 Beso de Vino Selección 2009 T....167

CATALUNYA

94 Clos D'Agon 2009 T....180
94 L'Equilibrista 2010 B....177
93 Clos Valmaña 2009 TC....180
93 Idoia Blanc 2009 BFB....177
93 Alcor 2007 T....181
93 Alcor 2008 T....181
93 L'Equilibrista 2009 T....177
92 Clos D'Agon 2010 B....180
92 Maset del LLeó Syrah 2006 TR....182
92 L'Equilibrista Garnatxa 2009 T....177
91 Sentits Negres 2009 T....176
91 Macizo 2010 B....183
91 Signes 2009 T....176
91 Sentits Blancs 2010 B....176
90 Santes 2009 RD....182
89 Ca N'Estruc 2010 T....177
89 Idoia 2009 T....177
89 Proyecto Cu4tro 2007 T....180
89 Fermí de Fermí Bohigas 2008 TR....180
89 Nerola 2009 T....177
89 Amic de Clos D'Agon 2010 T....179

CAVA

97 Gramona Celler Batlle 2000 BR Gran Reserva....218
96 Raventós i Blanc GR Personal M.R.N. 1999 BN....222
95 Recaredo Reserva Particular 2002 BN Gran Reserva....204
95 Castell Sant Antoni Torre de L'Homenatge 1999 BN GR....200
94 Reserva Real BR Reserva....217
94 Castell Sant Antoni Gran Reserva Magnum 2005 BN....200
94 Núria Claverol 2007 BR Reserva....195
94 Gramona Celler Batlle 2001 BR Gran Reserva....218
94 Jeroboam Torelló 2005 BN Gran Reserva....232
93 Gramona Imperial 2006 BR Gran Reserva....218

93 Castell Sant Antoni GR 2005 BN Gran Reserva..............200
93 Magnum La Finca BN Gran Reserva 222
93 Sumarroca Gran Brut Allier 2006 BR 195
93 Juvé & Camps R de la Familia Magnum 2008 BN R 223
93 Tantum Ergo Chardonnay Pinot Noir 2008 BN 191
93 Chozas Carrascal BN Reserva 213
92 Jaume Codorníu BR 213
92 Gramona Argent 2007 BR Reserva..............218
92 Gran Juvé Camps 2007 BR Gran Reserva 222
92 Albet i Noya 2007 BN Gran Reserva 188
92 Albert de Vilarnau 2007 BR Fermentado en Barrica 235
92 Castillo Perelada Cuvée Especial 2008 BN 201
92 Recaredo Brut de Bruts 2004 BN Gran Reserva 204
92 Llopart Leopardi 2006 BN Gran Reserva 223
92 Recaredo 2007 BN Gran Reserva 204
92 Parxet Aniversario BN 229
92 Blanca Cusiné 2008 BR 229
92 Artemayor IV Cava BN 214
92 Agustí Torelló Mata Gran Reserva Barrica 2007 BN 187
92 Castell Sant Antoni Gran Brut Magnum BR Reserva 199
92 Turo d'en Mota 2000 BN Reserva..............204
92 Castell Sant Antoni Gran Brut BR Gran Reserva 199
92 Tantum Ergo Pinot Noir Rosé 2009 BN 191
92 Adernats XC 2006 Gran Reserva 235
92 Jaume Llopart Alemany Vinya d'en Ferran 2006 BN GR ..221
92 Jané Ventura de L'Orgue BN 220
92 Parisad 2003 Brut Extra Gran Reserva 196
92 Torelló by Custo Barcelona 2006 BR Gran Reserva 232
92 Castell Sant Antoni Camí del Sot BN Reserva 200
91 Albert de Vilarnau Chardonnay 2007 BN Gran Reserva 235
91 Gran Reserva María Cabane Extra Brut Gran Reserva ..229
91 Berta Bouzy 2007 BR Reserva 203
91 Reina Mª Cristina Blanc de Noirs 2008 BR Reserva 212
91 Mestres Cupage Barcelona 2006 BR Reserva..............207
91 Gramona III Lustros 2004 BN Gran Reserva 218
91 Juvé & Camps Milesimé Chardonnay 2007 BR Reserva ..222
91 Juvé & Camps Reserva de la Familia 2008 BN GR 223
91 Colomer Costa BN Reserva 202
91 Segura Viudas Reserva Heredad BR Gran Reserva 231
91 Albet i Noya Brut 21 Barrica 2006 BR 187
91 Lácrima Baccus Summum 2007 BN Gran Reserva..............207
91 Vidal i Ferré 2006 BN Gran Reserva 205
91 L'O de L'Origan Magnum BN 223
91 Privat Opus Evolutium BN Gran Reserva 189
91 Kripta 2006 BN Gran Reserva..............187
91 Marrugat Rosado 2007 BR Reserva 225
91 Llopart Ex-Vite 2005 BR Gran Reserva 223
91 Signat 5 Estrellas BR Reserva 208
91 Giró Ribot Avant BR Reserva..............217
91 Giró Ribot Mare 2006 BN Gran Reserva 217
91 Sumarroca Gran Brut 2007 BR Gran Reserva..............195
91 Torelló 225 2007 BN Gran Reserva 232
91 Gran Plus Ultra BN 213
91 Castell Sant Antoni 37.5 Brut BR 199
91 Cava Naveran Perles Blanques 2007 BR 209
91 Hillium 2005 BN Gran Reserva 206
91 Gran Torelló 2007 BN Gran Reserva 232
91 Castell Sant Antoni Gran Rosat Pinot Noir BN 200
91 Odisea Naverán BN 209
91 Recaredo Subtil 2006 BN Gran Reserva 204
91 Canals Canals 2006 BN Gran Reserva 197
91 Castell Sant Antoni Camí del Sot Magnum BN Reserva ..200
90 Agustí Vilaret 2006 Gran Reserva 203
90 Mestres Mas Vía 2000 BR Gran Reserva 207
90 Rimarts 2007 BN Gran Reserva 230
90 Gramona Allegro BR 217
90 Loxarel Reserva Familia 2006 BN 224
90 Brut Barroco BR Reserva..............216
90 Jaume Llopart Alemany 2006 BN Gran Reserva 221
90 Castell Sant Antoni Gran Barrica 2006 BN GR 200
90 L'Hereu BR 222
90 Elias i Terns 2004 BN 228
90 Ferret BR Reserva 206
90 Ferret 2006 BN Gran Reserva..............206
90 Torre Galimany 2007 BN Gran Reserva 232
90 Jaume Giró i Giró Selecte 2006 BN Gran Reserva 220
90 Cava Sumarroca Cuvée 2007 BN Gran Reserva 195
90 Sumarroca 2008 BR Reserva 195
90 Albet i Noya Brut 21 BR 188
90 Lácrima Baccus Heretat 2009 BR 207
90 Avinyó Selecció La Ticota 2006 BN Gran Reserva 189
90 Jané Ventura Vintage 2007 BN Gran Reserva..............220
90 María Casanovas 2008 BN Gran Reserva 203
90 Torelló Magnum 2007 BN Gran Reserva..............232
90 Marqués de Gelida 2004 BN Gran Reserva..............236
90 Conde de Caralt Blanc de Blancs BR 208
90 Vidal i Ferré BR Reserva 205
90 Vilarnau Vintage 2007 BR Gran Reserva..............235
90 Agustí Torelló Mata 2007 BN Gran Reserva 187
90 Agustí Torelló Mata Magnum 2005 BN Gran Reserva....187
90 Mas Tinell Brut Rosé 2007 BR Reserva 219
90 Canals Nadal Gran Vintage 2008 BR Reserva 197
90 1 + 1 = 3 Gran Reserva Especial 2005 BN 233
90 Canals & Munné Magnum 2004 BN Gran Reserva........196
90 Canals & Munné Gran Duc XXI 2006 BN Gran Reserva......196
90 Vall Dolina 2008 BN Reserva 234
90 Colomer Prestige 2006 BN Gran Reserva..............202
90 Rosa Cusine 2007 RD 229
90 Castell Sant Antoni 37.5 Brut Nature BN 200
90 Cava Reserva Barrica Brut Nature Carles Andreu 2008 209
90 Dominio de la Vega BN Reserva 214
90 Ferré i Catasús 2007 BN Reserva 215
90 Sumarroca 2006 BN Gran Reserva 195
90 MM Premium Cuvée Millesime 2007 BR 224
90 Gran Claustro Cuvée Esp. de Castillo Perelada 2006 BN GR..201
90 Cava Rosado Reserva Barrica Brut Carles Andreu 2008 209
90 Bayanus 375ml 2008 BN Reserva 187
90 Mestres Cupage 80 Aniversario 2004 BR Reserva 207
90 Marrugat Rima 32 BN Reserva 225
90 Meritum BR Gran Reserva..............216
90 Trepat 2006 BR 216
90 Emendis Imum BN Reserva..............214
90 Raventós i Blanc De Nit BR 222
90 Parés Baltà Selectio BR 229
90 Nasol de Rechenna BR 234
90 Salvatge Rosé 2008 RD Reserva 209
90 Mont Marçal Gran Cuvée BR 227
90 Juvé & Camps Blanc de Noirs 2008 222
90 Canals Nadal Magnum 2007 BN Reserva 197
90 Torelló 2007 BN 233
90 Ferret Rosado BR Reserva..............206
90 Alsina & Sardá Mas D'Alsina BN Reserva 188
90 El Xamfrà Magnum 2006 BN Reserva..............214
90 Aire de L'O de L'Origan BN 223
90 Alta Alella Mirgin Blanc 2007 BN Gran Reserva 188
90 Parxet Pansa Blanca Barrica 2008 BR 229
90 Ãngel Cupatge 2010 BN 210
90 Rovellats Magnum 2006 BN 231
90 Rovellats Col.lecció 2006 Brut Extra Gran Reserva........231
90 Canals & Munné Reserva de L'Avi 2004 BN GR 197
90 Ferré i Catasús Clàssic 2007 BN Reserva 215
90 Fuchs de Vidal Cuvée BN Reserva 190
90 Non Plus Ultra BR 213
90 Pago de Tharsys Millésime Rosé Reserva 2007 BR 228
90 Pago de Tharsys Millésime 2005 BN Gran Reserva 228
90 Martí Serdà Cuvée Real BN Gran Reserva 225
90 Mestres Cupage 50 años de "Cava" 2006 BR Reserva ..207
90 Aureum de Mont Marçal BN Reserva..............228
90 Jané Ventura Reserva de la Música 2008 BR Reserva ..219

CIGALES

93 César Príncipe 2008 TC 241
92 Balvinar Pagos Seleccionados 2006 TC 243
91 Valdelosfrailes Vendimia Seleccionada 2006 T 243
91 Lezcano-Lacalle Dú 2004 T 243
91 La Legua Capricho 2007 T 247
91 Sinforiano 2008 TC....244
91 Selección Personal Carlos Moro Valdelosfrailes 2006 T ..242
90 Valdelosfrailes Prestigio 2006 TR....243
90 Ovidio García Esencia 2006 TC....247
90 Calderona 2005 TR....246
90 Traslanzas 2008 T 248
90 Trascasas 2007 TR....244
90 Hiriart Lágrima 2010 RD 242
90 Ovidio García 2005 TR 247
90 Hiriart 2008 TC....242
90 Carredueñas 2010 RD Fermentado en Barrica 245
90 Balvinar Pagos Seleccionados 2007 TC 243
90 Las Luceras 2010 RD 244
89 Lezcano-Lacalle 2004 TR 243
89 Carredueñas 2010 RD 245
89 Museum Real 2005 TR....246
89 Sinforiano 2006 TR 244
89 Hiriart 2010 T Roble 242

CONCA DE BARBERÀ

94 Grans Muralles 2007 TGR 252
94 Grans Muralles 2008 T 252
92 Gatzara 2010 T 256
91 Torre del Moro 2009 T 254
90 Vino Tinto Trepat Carles Andreu 2009 T 254
90 Milmanda 2009 B 252
90 Clos Montblanc Masía Les Comes 2006 TR 256
90 Clos Montblanc Xipella Blanc 2010 B 256
90 La Llopetera 2008 TC 254
90 Espurna 2008 T 257
90 Gatzara 2008 TC....257
90 Manuela Ventosa 2008 T 257
90 Espurna 2007 T 257
89 Josep Foraster Selecció 2006 TR....255
89 Clos Montblanc Merlot Premium 2006 TC 256
89 Les Paradetes 2006 TC....254
89 Carles Andreu Parellada 2010 B 254
89 Rendé Masdeu 2006 TR 257
89 Els Bassots 2008 B 254
88 Josep Foraster 2008 TC 255
88 Castillo de Montblanc Macabeo/Chardonnay 2010 B 256
88 Clos Montblanc Syrah Premium 2009 T 256
88 Rendé Masdeu 2010 RD 257
88 Portell 2005 TR 258
88 Vinya Plans 2008 TC....258
88 Clos Montblanc Xipella Premium 2009 T 256
88 Carlania 2007 T 253
88 Molí dels Capellans 2010 B 255
88 Francoli 2006 TR 253
88 Guspi Embigats de la María 2008 T 255
88 Mas del Nen 2009 T 252
88 Sanstravé Finca Gasset Moscatel 2009 BFB 253
88 Castell de la Comanda 2004 TR 253
88 Mas de la Sabatera 2008 T 257
88 Gatzara 2010 B 256

CONDADO DE HUELVA

91 S' Px Solera 1989 Vino de licor 264
90 Oliveros Pedro Ximénez PX 263
90 Convento PX 265
89 Misterio Oloroso Seco OL 265
89 S' Naranja Vino de licor 264
88 Doceañero CR 262
88 Par Vino Naranja Vino de licor 263
88 VDM Orange 265
88 S' Px Dulce Natural Vino de licor 264
88 Convento Naranja 2008 Semidulce 265
87 Doceañero Oloroso Condado Viejo 262
87 M.F. La Nuez Condado Pálido 264
87 Avellanero Cream GE 264
87 Marqués de Villalúa Colección 2009 B 265
87 Amaranto Generoso de Licor Dulce 264
87 Viña Doñana Vino Naranja B 263
86 Mioro Gran Selección 2009 B 265
86 Marqués de Villalúa 2010 B 265
86 1955 Condado Pálido Condado Pálido 262
86 Naranja de Oro Vino naranja 263
86 Onubis GE 262
86 1955 GE 263
86 Ricahembra Solera 1980 GE 263
86 Espinapura Condado Pálido 264
86 Vado del Quema S/C B 262
86 Torreumbría 2008 T 266
86 Melquiades Saenz "Vino de Naranja" B 262
86 Convento de Morañina 2010 B 264
86 Viña Doñana 2008 B Roble 263
86 Torrecanales Naranja OL 266

COSTERS DEL SEGRE

94 Taleia 2010 B 271
94 Thalarn 2009 T 271
93 Cérvoles Estrats 2006 T 274
93 Auzells 2010 B 276
92 Cérvoles 2010 BFB....274
92 Geol 2007 T 277
92 Vilosell 2008 T 277
92 Saó Expressiu 2007 T 275
92 Vallisbona 89 2009 B 275
92 FInca Racons 2010 B 277
91 Missenyora 2009 BFB....276
91 Castell del Remei Oda Blanc 2010 BFB....272
91 Acusp 2009 T 271
91 Ónra Molta Honra 2009 T 273
90 Raimat Gran Brut BR 276
90 Eixaders 2008 BFB 276
90 Castell del Remei 1780 2006 T 272
90 Castell del Remei Oda 2008 T 272
90 Saó Blanc 2009 B 275
90 Saó Abrivat 2008 T 275
90 Siós Selección 2008 T 271
90 Cérvoles Negre 2007 T 274
90 Alto Siós 2007 T 271
90 Quest 2009 T 271
90 Clos Pons Roc Nu 2008 TC 275
90 Ekam Essència 2010 B 271
90 Cérvoles Colors 2010 B 274

EL HIERRO

90 Viña Frontera 2010 T Maceración Carbónica....281
86 Viña Frontera 2010 B 281
83 Viña Frontera Baboso 2009 T 281
82 Viña Frontera Afrutado 2010 B 281
80 Viña Frontera 2008 T Barrica....281
79 Viña Frontera Verijadiego 2009 T 281
79 Viña Frontera 2010 RD 281
68 Viña Frontera 2009 T 281

EMPORDÀ

94 Castillo de Perelada Ex Ex 8 2006 T 287
93 Gresa 2007 T 296
93 Mas Oller Plus 2008 T 294
92 Castillo de Perelada 5 Fincas 2006 TR 287
92 Castillo Perelada Garnatxa de l'Empordà B 287
92 Mas Oller 2010 B 293
92 Finca Garbet 2006 T 288
92 Vd'O 1.07 2007 T 296
92 Vd'O 3.08 2008 T 296
91 Castillo Perelada Chardonnay 2010 B 286
91 Castillo Perelada Gran Claustro 2005 T 288
91 Ctònia 2010 BFB 294
91 Oliver Conti Carlota 2009 T 295
91 Mas Oller Pur 2010 T 293
91 Heus 2010 T 292
91 Celler Marià Pagès Garnacha S/C B 289
91 Dolç de Gerisena 2005 Vino de licor 285
90 Anubis Garnatxa de l'Empordà 1996 Dulce Natural GR 291
90 Masía Carreras 2009 BFB 290
90 Finca Garbet 2005 T 288
90 Oliver Conti 2007 TR 295
90 Castillo Perelada La Garriga 2010 B 287
90 Rhodes 2007 T 293
90 Bonfill 2006 T 288
90 Castillo Perelada Finca Malaveïna 2007 T 288
90 Castillo Perelada Finca Espolla 2008 T 287
90 Castillo Perelada Finca Malaveïna 2008 T 287
90 Mas Oller Blau 2010 T 293
90 Blanc de Gresa 2010 BFB 296
90 Sota els Àngels 2009 B 296

GETARIAKO TXAKOLINA

89 Aialle 2009 B 302
89 Txomín Etxaníz Berezia 2010 B 303
89 K5 Argiñano 2010 B 302
88 Txakoli Rezabal 2010 B 301
88 Txomín Etxaníz 2010 B 303
88 Talai Berri 2010 B 303
88 Mokoroa 2010 B 303
88 Eugenia Txomín Etxaníz 2009 ESP 303
87 Aizpurua. B 2010 B 302
87 Akarregi Txiki 2010 B 301
87 Ameztoi 2010 B 301
87 Gañeta Berezia 2009 B 302
87 Urki 2010 B 304
87 Txomín Etxaníz White Wine 2010 B 303
87 Upaingoa 2010 B 301

GRAN CANARIA

90 Los Berrazales Semiseco 2010 B 308
90 Viña Amable 2010 T 308
90 Los Berrazales Dulce Natural 2010 B 308
88 Agala Dulcelena dulce 2010 B 308
88 Nubia 2010 B 308
88 Los Berrazales Dulce 2009 B Barrica 308
87 Agala Vendimia Nocturna 2010 Blanco Semidulce 308
87 Los Berrazales Seco 2010 B 308
86 Agala 2010 B 308
85 El Convento de la Vega 2009 T 308
84 La Higuera Mayor 2008 T 308

JEREZ

99 La Bota de Fino (Bota nº 27) FI 321
99 La Bota de Manzanilla Pasada (Bota nº 30 "Capataz Rivas") MZ 322
98 La Bota de Amontillado (Bota nº 31) AM 321
97 Venerable VORS PX 317
97 Osborne Rare Sherry Solera BC 200 OL 317
97 Moscatel Viejísimo Toneles Moscatel 327
96 La Ina FI 321
96 Manzanilla en Rama Saca de Invierno MZ 312
96 Reliquia PX 313
96 Osborne Rare Sherry AOS AM 317
96 La Bota de Manzanilla (Bota nª 32) MZ 322
96 Cardenal VORS PC 327
96 Don Gonzalo VOS OL 327
96 Solera Su Majestad VORS OL 327
96 Colección Roberto Amillo Palo Cortado PC 322
96 La Bota de Oloroso "Bota punta Nº 28" OL 322
95 Sibarita V.O.R.S. OL 317
95 La Panesa Especial Fino S/C FI 325
95 Pastrana Manzanilla Pasada MZ 316
95 Barbadillo Amontillado VORS AM 312
95 Reliquia AM 312
95 Fernando de Castilla "P.X. Antique" PX 323
95 Gonzalez Byass Añada 1982 1982 PC 324
95 Colección Roberto Amillo Amontillado AM 322
95 Colección Roberto Amillo Oloroso OL 322
95 Colección Roberto Amillo Pedro Ximénez PX 322
94 Papirusa MZ Solera 321
94 Old & Plus Amontillado VORS AM 326
94 Villapanés S/C OL 325
94 Napoleón 30 años VORS 50 cl. AM 316
94 Reliquia PC 313
94 Gran Orden PX 314
94 Noé PX 324
94 San León Reserva de Familia MZ 324
94 Fernando de Castilla "Palo Cortado Antique" PC 323
94 Fino Quinta FI 317
94 Osborne Solera India OL 317
94 Coliseo VORS AM 327
94 Solera 1842 VOS OL 327
94 El Tresillo Amontillado Viejo S/C AM 325
94 Harveys VORS Rich Old OL 315
94 Manzanilla en Rama Saca de primavera MZ 313
93 Royal Ambrosante 20 años PX 327
93 Amontillado 51-1ª V.O.R.S AM 317
93 Capuchino V.O.R.S PC 317
93 Old & Plus Oloroso OL 326
93 Old & Plus P.X. PX 326
93 Ynocente FI 327
93 Tío Mateo FI 326
93 Barbadillo Palo Cortado VORS PC 313
93 Oñana AM 313
93 Apóstoles VORS PC 324
93 Amontillado del Duque VORS AM 323
93 Tío Pepe FI 323
93 San León "Clásica" MZ 324
93 Sacromonte 15 años OL 319
93 Osborne Rare Sherry Solera PAP PC 317
93 Oloroso Tradición VORS OL 319
93 Harveys VORS PC 315
93 San Emilio PX 321
93 Osborne Rare Sherry PX PX 317
92 La Cigarrera Moscatel 316
92 Río Viejo OL 321
92 NPU AM 326
92 Triana 30 años VORS PX 316
92 Obispo Gascón PC 313
92 Príncipe AM 312
92 Garvey 1780 VOS PX 314
92 San Patricio FI 314
92 Matusalem VORS CR 323
92 1730 PX 312
92 Fernando de Castilla "Amontillado Antique" AM 323
92 Fernando de Castilla "Oloroso Antique" OL 323

92	Bertola FI	322
92	Fino Imperial 30 años VORS AM	322
92	Royal Esmeralda VOS Amontillado 20 años AM	327
92	Coquinero AM	317
92	Amontillado Tradición VORS AM	318
92	Vieja Solera 30 años VORS PX	323
92	Garvey 1780 VORS OL	314
92	Alfaraz PX	312
92	Fernando de Castilla "PX Premium" PX	323
92	Harveys VORS AM	315
92	Gutiérrez Colosía Solera Familiar OL	315
92	Añada 1997 Oloroso Abocado OL	321
92	Quo Vadis AM	320
92	Gutiérrez Colosía Fino en Rama FI	315
92	El Maestro Sierra Oloroso Extraviejo 1/7 OL	321
92	Manzanilla I think S/C MZ	322
91	Emilín Moscatel	321
91	El Maestro Sierra FI	321
91	El Maestro Sierra Viejísimo PX	321
91	Royal Corregidor 20 años VOS OL	327
91	Don José OL	326
91	La Gitana MZ	316
91	Jerez Cortado Wellington 20 años VOS PC	316
91	Jauna PC	314
91	Don José María FI	328
91	Don José María OL	328
91	Las Medallas de Argüeso MZ	324
91	Fernando de Castilla "Fino Antique" FI	323
91	Bertola 12 años AM	322
91	Sacromonte 15 años PX	319
91	La Goya MZ	320
91	Oxford 1970 PX	320
91	Gutiérrez Colosía FI	315
91	Osborne 1827 PX	317
91	Pedro Ximénez Tradición VOS PX	319
91	Faraón 30 años VORS 50 cl. OL	316
91	Garvey 1780 VORS PX	314
91	Valdivia Sun Pale Cream PCR	319
91	Terry Fino FI	318
91	Harveys FI	315
91	Viña AB AM	323
91	Pedro Romero MZ	318
91	Cardenal Cisneros PX	326
91	Gutiérrez Colosía MZ	315
91	La Cigarrera AM	316
90	East India CR	321
90	Lustau Escuadrilla AM	321
90	Regente PC	326
90	César Florido Moscatel Especial Moscatel	319
90	Gobernador S/C OL	325
90	Marqués de Rodil S/C PC	325
90	Eva Cream CR	312
90	Barbadillo Oloroso Seco VORS OL	313
90	Reliquia OL	313
90	Solear MZ	313
90	Asalto Amoroso B	313
90	Don José María MZ	328
90	Don José María CR	328
90	Argüeso Amontillado Viejo VORS AM	324
90	Alburejo OL	312
90	La Guita MZ	325
90	Wellington 30 años VORS PC	316
90	Sacromonte 15 años AM	319
90	Valdivia Atrum CR	319
90	Valdivia Prune OL	319
90	Gutiérrez Colosía Solera Familiar AM	315
90	Palo Cortado Tradición VORS PC	319
90	Baco de Élite Medium Dry OL	320
90	Fernando de Castilla Fino Classic FI	323
90	Argüeso AM	324
90	Mira la Mar MZ	312
90	Terry Amontillado AM	318
90	Terry Pedro Ximénez PX	318
90	Triana PX	316
90	Harveys VORS PX	316
90	Gutiérrez Colosía Solera Familiar PC	315
90	La Sanluqueña MZ	318
90	Flor del Museo CR	314
90	Cruz del Mar OL	320
90	Leonor PC	324
90	La Cigarrera OL	317
90	Ambrosía Moscatel	326

JUMILLA

95	Casa Castillo Pie Franco 2008 T	342
95	El Nido 2008 T	335
94	Valtosca 2009 T	342
94	Clío 2008 T	335
93	Las Gravas 2008 T	343
93	Alma de Luzón 2007 T	337
93	Portú 2008 T	336
93	Gorgocil Tempranillo 2008 T	343
93	Portú 2007 T	337
92	Luzón 2010 T	336
92	Alceño Syrah Premium 2009 T	342
92	Barón del Solar Manos Colección Privada 2008 T	332
92	Juan Gil 12 meses 2009 T	335
91	Altico Syrah 2008 T	334
91	Divus 2009 T	332
91	Juan Gil 4 meses 2010 T	335
91	Alceño Dulce 2007 T	342
91	Tavs Selección 2009 T	335
91	Casa Castillo Monastrell 2010 T	342
91	Cármine 2009 T	341
91	Juan Gil 18 meses 2009 T	336
91	Gorgocil Monastrell 2008 T	343
91	Familia Pacheco Selección 2008 T	339
91	Alceño 4 meses 2009 T Roble	342
90	Canalizo 2007 TC	334
90	Altos de Luzón 2007 T	337
90	Luzón 2008 TC	337
90	Silvano García Moscatel 2009 B	339
90	Casa de la Ermita 2008 TC	340
90	Chardonnay Pío del Ramo 2009 B Barrica	337
90	Crápula 2009 T	341
90	Sierva 2008 TC	334
90	Animic 2010 B	341
90	Pacheco 2010 T	339
90	Alceño 12 meses Autor 2006 T	342
90	Omblancas Denuño Syrah 2010 T	341

LA MANCHA

93	Gladium Viñas Viejas 2008 TC	353
92	Volver 2009 T	358
92	Cánfora 2006 T	354
91	Finca Antigua Syrah 2009 T	361
91	Paso a Paso Tempranillo 2010 T	358
90	Blas Muñoz Chardonnay 2009 BFB	367
90	Clavis Viñedo Pico Garbanzo 2006 TR	361
90	Vihucas Colección Familiar 2008 T	363
89	Finca Antigua 2005 TR	361
89	La Villa Real 2008 TC	356
89	Aldoba 2005 TR	352
89	Zocodover Selección Sauvignon Blanc 2010 B	355
89	Finca Antigua Petit Verdot 2009 T	361
89	El Vínculo 2005 TR	351
89	Gladium 2008 TC	354
89	Gladium 2009 TC	354

MONTILLA MORILES

98 Alvear PX 1830 PX Reserva....426
96 La Cañada PX 430
96 Casa del Inca 2010 PX 429
96 La Bota de Pedro Ximenez nº25 Bota NO PX 429
94 Alvear Solera Fundación AM 426
94 Don P.X. 1982 PX Gran Reserva 431
94 Delgado 1874 PX 427
93 Alvear Dulce Viejo 2000 PX Reserva....426
93 Boabdil AM 426
92 Monte Cristo OL 429
92 Cruz Conde Solera Fundación 1902 1995 PX 427
91 Asunción OL 426
91 Alvear PX Cosecha 2007 PX 426
91 Solera Fina Tauromaquia FI 430
91 Gran Barquero AM 430
90 Alvear PX 1927 PX 426
90 Carlos VII AM 426
90 C.B. FI 426
90 Alvear PX de Añada 2008 PX 426
90 Verbenera FI 429
90 Tauromaquia PX 430
90 Musa OL 428
90 Platino Solera Olorosa OL 428
90 Virgilio PX 429
90 Gran Barquero OL 430
90 Gran Barquero PX 430
90 Delgado 1874 Amontillado Natural muy Viejo AM 427
90 Don P.X. 2008 PX 431
90 Solera 1981 PX 427

MONTSANT

96 Espectacle 2007 T 443
96 Espectacle 2008 T 442
95 Trossos Tros 2009 B 446
95 Trossos Tros 2008 T 446
94 Teixar 2008 T 448
94 Mas de Can Blau 2007 T 441
94 Clos María 2007 B 445
94 Auditori 2009 T 435
94 Teixar 2009 T 448
93 Gotia 2005 T 445
93 Braó 2009 T 435
93 Coca i Fitó 2008 T 442
93 Dolç D'Orto 2010 Dulce Natural 446
93 Furvus 2009 T 448
93 La Carrerada 2009 T 445
92 Bugader 2007 T 444
92 Ètim Verema Sobremadurada Sele. Vinyes Velles 2007 T ..443
92 6 Vinyes de Laurona 2005 T 439
92 Malondro 2008 TC 439
92 Dosterras 2008 T 438
92 Etnic 2008 T 438
92 Furvus 2008 T 448
92 Santbru 2007 T 446
92 Dido 2009 T 447
92 Palell 2009 TC 445
92 Venus 2008 T 447
92 Gran Mets 2006 TC 439
92 Finca L'Argata 2009 T 444
92 Ètim Ranci 443
92 L'Alleu Selecció 2007 T 447
92 Gotia 2006 T 445
92 Bula 2009 T Roble 448
91 Flor de Primavera Peraj Ha'Abib 2009 T 437
91 Lasendal Garnatxa 2009 T Barrica 437
91 Finca L'Argata 2008 T 444
91 Planella 2008 T 444
91 Corbatera 2007 T 445
91 Castell de les Pinyeres 2008 T 438
91 Mas Roig 2007 TC 438
91 Clos D'Englora AV 14 2005 T 441
91 Ètim Verema Tardana 2007 T 443
91 Cingles Blaus Dolç 2007 Blanco Dulce 442
91 L´Heravi Selecció 2009 TC 448
91 Acústic 2009 T 435
91 Blanc D'Orto 2010 B 445
91 Les Pujoles 2009 TC....445
91 Clos Mesorah 2009 TR....436
90 Terròs 2008 T 444
90 Costers del Gravet 2007 T 437
90 Mas Tortó 2009 TC....437
90 Baboix 2007 T 436
90 Les Sorts Rosat 2010 RD 438
90 Englora 2008 TC....441
90 Ètim Grenache 2007 T 443
90 Ètim Verema Tardana 2009 B 443
90 Ètim 2010 B 443
90 Laurona 2006 T 439
90 Ètim Selection Syrah 2006 T 443
90 Brunus 2008 T 446
90 Santbru 2009 B Barrica 446
90 Brunus Rosé 2010 RD 446
90 Giral Vinyes Velles 2005 TC 446
90 Gallicant 2005 T 439
90 Dido 2010 B 447
90 Les Sorts Sycar 2008 T 438
90 Clònic 2008 T 436
90 Acústic 2010 B 435
90 Castell de Falset 2009 B 443
90 Solpost 2007 T 441
90 Coca i Fitó Rosa 2010 RD 442
90 Jaspi Maragda 2009 T 442
90 Les Comes D'Orto 2009 T 446
90 Les Tallades de Cal Nicolau 2009 TC 446
90 Llunara 2008 T 447
90 Ètim Verema Tardana 2008 T 443
90 Flor D'Englora Roure 2009 T 440
90 Etnic 2009 BFB....438

NAVARRA

95 Chivite Colección 125 Vendimia Tardía 2008 B 460
94 Domaines Lupier El Terroir 2008 T 473
93 Chivite Colección 125 2008 BFB....460
93 Señorío de Andión moscatel Vendimia Tardía 2007 B ..477
93 Jardín de Lúculo 2007 T 464
93 Domaines Lupier La Dama Viñas Viejas 2008 T 474
93 Pago de Cirsus Opus II 2007 T 457
92 Chivite Colección 125 2006 TR....462
92 Gran Feudo Edición Dulce de Moscatel 2010 B 460
92 Inurrieta Orchídea 2010 B 454
92 Señorío de Andión 2005 T 477
92 Barón de Magaña 2007 TC 471
92 Magaña Calchetas 2008 T 471
92 García Burgos Reserva Unica 2005 T 474
92 Chivite Colección 125 2007 RD 462
92 Otazu 2007 TC 457
92 Volandera 2010 T Maceración Carbónica 475
92 Cientruenos 2010 T Barrica 475
91 Marco Real Reserva de Familia 2007 TR 476
91 Otazu Chardonnay 2009 B 456
91 Capricho de Goya Vino de Licor 459
91 Santa Cruz de Artazu 2008 T 471
91 Castillo de Monjardín Chardonnay 2008 BFB 472
91 Pago de Cirsus Chardonnay 2009 BFB....457
91 Pago de Cirsus de Iñaki Núñez Sel. de Familia 2007 T 457
91 García Burgos Vendimia Seleccionada 2009 T 474

91 Finca La Cantera de Santa Ana 2007 T 474
91 Pago de Larrainzar 2007 T 468
91 Desierto de Azul y Garanza 2007 T 453
91 Albret 2006 TR 474
91 Pago de Cirsus Moscatel Vendimia Tardía 2007 BFB 457
90 Gran Feudo Chardonnay 2010 B 460
90 Ochoa Moscatel 2010 Blanco dulce 466
90 Señorío de Sarría Viñedo Nº 3 2009 BFB 453
90 Altos de Inurrieta 2007 TR 455
90 Inurrieta Cuatrocientos 2008 TC 454
90 Valdelares Alta Expresión 2008 TC 458
90 Príncipe de Viana Vendimia Tardía 2009 B 469
90 Marco Real Colección Privada 2008 TC 476
90 Montecristo Moscatel 2010 Blanco Dulce 459
90 Javier Asensio 2005 TR 453
90 Castillo de Monjardín Chardonnay 2007 B Reserva 472
90 Logos I 2004 T 465
90 Pago de Cirsus de Iñaki Núñez Cuvée Especial 2007 TR ..457
90 Pago de Cirsus Chardonnay 2010 B 457
90 Nekeas Chardonnay "Cuvée Allier" 2009 BFB 476
90 Fernández de Arcaya 2007 TR 464
90 Dignus 2007 TC 471
90 Reserva Lola García 2006 TR 474
90 Príncipe de Viana 2008 TC 469
90 Vega del Castillo 2006 TR 471
90 Pago de Cirsus de Iñaki Nuñez Vendimia Selec. 2008 TC 457
90 Sh 2009 T 474
90 Lezaun Tempranillo 2010 T Maceración Carbónica........465
90 Albret 2008 TC 474
90 Marques de Montecierzo Merlot Selección 2005 TC 455
90 Puerto del Monte 2010 RD 475
90 Monastir V 2008 T 476
90 Gran Feudo Sobre Lías 2009 RD 461
90 Piedemonte +dQuince 2006 T 468
90 Abril de Azul y Garanza 2010 T 453
90 Zubiola 2007 T 477
90 Aroa Gorena 2005 TR 452
90 Fincas de Unzu 2010 RD 477
90 Chivite Biológico Merlot 2007 T 462
90 Chivite Expresión Varietal Tempranillo 2007 T 462
90 Gran Feudo Edición Viñas Viejas 2006 TR 463
90 Gran Feudo Edición Selección Especial 2007 TC 462
90 Gran Feudo Edición Chardonnay Sobre Lías 2008 B 461
90 Raso de Larrainzar 2008 T 467
90 Aroa Mutiko 2010 T 452
90 Aroa Larrosa 2010 RD 452
90 Príncipe de Viana Garnacha 100% 2008 T Roble 469

PAGO CALZADILLA

92 Calzadilla Cs 1000 2008 T 994
91 Gran Calzadilla 2006 T 994
90 Calzadilla Classic 2007 T 994
88 Opta Calzadilla 2008 T 994

PAGO CAMPO DE LA GUARDIA

89 Martúe Syrah 2008 T 994
88 Martúe Especial 2007 T 994
88 Martúe 2008 T 994

PAGO CASA DEL BLANCO

86 Quixote Cabernet Sauvignon Syrah 2005 T 995
86 Quixote Merlot Tempranillo Petit Verdot 2006 T 994
85 Quixote Petit Verdot 2006 T 995

PAGO DEHESA DEL CARRIZAL

91 Dehesa del Carrizal Cabernet Sauvignon 2006 T 995
91 Dehesa del Carrizal Chardonnay 2008 B 995
91 Dehesa del Carrizal Syrah 2008 T 995
90 Dehesa del Carrizal Chardonnay 2009 B 995
89 Dehesa del Carrizal Chardonnay 2010 B 995
88 Dehesa del Carrizal MV Rojo 2007 T 995

PAGO DOMINIO DE VALDEPUSA

93 Marqués de Griñón Emeritvs 2005 TR 995
92 Marqués de Griñón Cabernet Sauvignon 2006 T 995
91 Marqués de Griñón Petit Verdot 2006 T 995
91 Svmma Varietalis 2006 T 995
90 Marqués de Griñón Syrah 2006 T 995
89 Caliza 2007 T 995

PAGO EL TERRERAZO

95 Quincha Corral 2009 T 996
94 Finca Terrerazo 2009 T 996

PAGO FINCA ÉLEZ

91 Manuel Manzaneque Nuestra Selección 2007 T 996
89 Manuel Manzaneque Chardonnay 2008 BFB....................996
89 Manuel Manzaneque Nuestro Syrah 2007 T 996
87 Manuel Manzaneque Finca Élez 2007 TC 996

PAGO FLORENTINO

89 Pago Florentino 2008 T 996
87 Pago Florentino 2009 T 996

PAGO GUIJOSO

89 Magnificus 2008 T 996
88 Viña Consolación 2006 TR 996
88 Divinus 2008 BFB 996
87 Vega Guijoso 2009 T 996

PAGO LOS BALAGUESES

91 Pago de Los Balagueses 2008 TC 997

PAGO PRADO DE IRACHE

90 Prado Irache Vino de Pago 2006 T 997

PAGO SEÑORÍO DE OTAZU

95 Señorío de Otazu 2007 T 997
95 Señorío de Otazu Altar 2006 T 997
94 Señorío de Otazu vitral 2005 TC 997

PENEDÈS

95 Colet Navazos Extra Brut 2007 Extra Brut Reserva........497
94 Reserva Real 2007 T 488
94 Sot Lefriec 2006 T 484
94 Jean León Viña Gigi Chardonnay 2008 B 502
93 Gramona Gra a Gra 2006 Blanco dulce 495
93 Gramona Mas Escorpí Chardonnay 2010 B 494
93 Albet i Noya Reserva Martí 2007 T 483
93 Jané Ventura "Finca Els Camps" Macabeu 2010 BFB 500
93 Jané Ventura "Finca Els Camps" Ull de llebre 2007 T ..500
93 Mas La Plana Cabernet Sauvignon 2007 T 489
93 Absis 2007 T 510
93 Gramona Xarel.lo Font Jui 2009 B 494
93 Pardas Aspriu 2007 T 509
93 Nun Vinya dels Taus 2008 B 490
93 11 de Isabel Negra 2008 T 503

93 Gramona Sauvignon Blanc 2010 BFB 494
93 Colet Navazos Extra Brut 2008 Extra Brut 497
93 Jané Ventura Sumoll 2009 T 500
93 Mas Ferrant Sonatina 2005 BFB 506
93 Advent Sumoll 2008 T 499
92 Nara 2007 TC 490
92 Vi de Glass Gewürztraminer 2006 B 494
92 Albet i Noya Col.lecció Syrah 2008 T 484
92 Pas Curtei 2009 T 484
92 Gran Caus 2006 TR 491
92 Jané Ventura "Mas Vilella" Costers del Rotllan 2008 T 501
92 Jean León Vinya La Scala Cabernet Sauvignon 2001 TGR..502
92 Zemis 2007 TR 502
92 Mas Irene 2006 T 510
92 Silencis 2009 B 502
92 Plou i Fa Sol 2010 B 484
92 Belat 2007 T 484
92 Colet Blanc de Blanc Extra Brut Grand Cuveé Extra Brut ..497
92 Pardas Aspriu 2009 B 509
92 Mas Candi Pecat Noble 2010 B 505
91 Avgvstvs Chardonnay 2010 BFB 496
91 Avgvstvs Trajanvs 2007 TR 496
91 Vallformosa Clos Maset 2006 T 507
91 Bòria 2007 T 490
91 Albet i Noya Col.lecció Chardonnay 2010 B 483
91 Albet i Noya El Blanc XXV "ecológico" 2008 B 483
91 El Rocallís 2007 BFB 491
91 Hisenda Miret Garnatxa 2008 T 510
91 Calcari Xarel.lo 2010 B 510
91 Pardas Negre Franc 2007 T 509
91 Finca La Milana 2006 T 484
91 Torre del Veguer Dulce Vendimia Tardía 2008 B 488
91 Vinya Jordina 2010 B 510
91 Jané Ventura Selecció 12 Vinyes 2009 T 500
91 Iohannes 2007 T 503
91 Casa Vella D'Espiells 2008 T 503
91 Avgvstvs Chardonnay Magnum 2008 B 496
91 Mas Candí Sol+Sol 2007 T 505
91 Colet Assemblage S/C Extra Brut 497
91 Colet Blanc de Blanc Extra Brut Tradicionnelle ESP 496
91 Jané Ventura "Mas Vilella" Costers del Rotllan 2007 T 500
91 Pricipia Mathematica 2010 B 484
91 Nun Vinya dels Taus 2009 B 490
91 Turó de les Abelles 2008 T 513
91 Mas La Plana Cabernet Sauvignon 1989 T 489
90 Maurel 2008 B 490
90 Gramona Gessamí 2010 B 494
90 Parató Ática Pinot Noir 2007 TR 509
90 Albet i Noya Tempranillo Clàssic 2010 T 484
90 Can Feixes Chardonnay 2006 BFB 491
90 Vinya La Calma 2007 B 491
90 Jean León Petit Chardonnay 2010 B 502
90 Fransola 2010 B 488
90 Waltraud 2010 B 488
90 Marta de Baltà 2006 T 510
90 L'Alzinar Ull de Llebre 2008 TC 513
90 Finca Viladellops Xarel.lo 2009 BFB 513
90 Manuela de Naverán 2010 B 495
90 Mas Tinell Gisele 2009 BFB 499
90 Les Cerveres Xarel.lo 2009 B 495
90 Casa Vella D'Espiells Magnum 2008 T Roble 503
90 Viña Escarlata 2008 T 503
90 Gran Clot dels Oms Xarel.lo 2008 BFB 486
90 Mas Elena 2008 T 510
90 Jean León Cabernet Sauvignon 2006 TR 502
90 Avgvstvs Xarel.lo 2010 BFB 496
90 Torre del Veguer Xarel.lo 2010 B 488
90 Lyric Licoroso 506
90 Improvisació 2009 B 490
90 Terral 2007 T 490
90 Albet i Noya 3 Macabeus 2010 B 483
90 Mas Candí Les Forques 2008 T 505
90 Casa Ravella 2009 BFB 492
90 Avgvstvs VI Varietales Magnum 2007 TC 496
90 Défora 1 + 1 = 3 2007 T 513
90 Turonet 2010 B 504
90 Albet i Noya EL Fanio 2010 B 483
90 XII Subirat Parent 2010 B 483
90 Maset del Lleó Tempranillo Selección 2009 T 507
90 Casa Ravella Tinto Selección 2007 T 492
90 Can Credo 2010 B 493
90 White Hmr 2010 B 499
90 Jean León Vinya Palau Merlot 2007 TC 502
90 Vi de Glass Gewürztraminer 2009 B 494

PLA DE BAGES

92 Abadal 5 Merlot 2006 TR 518
92 Abadal Picapoll 2010 B 518
92 Collbaix Singular 2007 T 519
91 Abadal 3.9 2007 TR 518
91 Abadal Selecció 2006 T 518
91 Abadal Edición Limitada 2007 T 518
90 Arnau Oller Selecció de la Familia 2007 T 519
89 Nuat 2008 B 518
88 Abadal Cabernet Sauvignon 2010 RD 518
88 Bernat Oller 2006 T 519
88 Collbaix Cupatge 2007 T 519
88 Collbaix La Llobeta 2007 T 519
88 Mes Que Paraules 2010 B 519

PLA I LLEVANT

93 Jaume Mesquida Cabernet Sauvignon 2006 TC 524
92 Ses Ferritges 2007 T 527
92 Sa Rota Blanc Chardonnay 2009 B 524
91 Ses Hereves 2005 T 527
91 Toni Gelabert Chardonnay 2010 B 526
91 Pere Seda 2007 TC 525
91 Aia 2008 T 527
91 Gran Vinya Son Caules 2005 T 526
91 Torrent Negre Selecció Privada Syrah 2005 T 526
91 Fangos Negre 2007 T 526
91 Negre de Sa Colonia 2009 T 526
90 Toni Gelabert Colonia U 200 2007 TC 526
90 Toni Gelabert Syrah 2006 T 527
90 Vinya Macabeu 2010 B 526
90 Golós 2008 T 526

PRIORAT

96 L'Ermita 2008 TC 531
95 Perinet + Plus 2006 T 544
95 Torroja Vi de la Vila 2008 T 548
95 Les Manyes 2008 T 548
94 Finca Dofí 2009 TC 531
94 Clos Mogador 2008 T 539
94 Clos Martinet 2008 T 544
94 Gran Cruor 2007 T 533
94 Ferrer Bobet Selecció Especial 2008 T 540
94 Manyetes 2008 T 550
94 Cami Pesseroles 2008 T 544
94 Tros de Clos 2009 T 546
93 Doix 2009 TC 536
93 Kyrie 2007 BC 538
93 Elix 2006 T 545
93 Melis 2006 T 545
93 Ferrer Bobet 2008 T 540
93 Lo Món 2008 T 548
93 Negre de Negres 2009 T 546

92 Les Eres 2007 T 542
92 Les Terrasses Vinyes Velles 2009 TC 531
92 Salanques 2009 T 536
92 Clos Fontà 2008 TC 550
92 Clos Erasmus 2009 T Barrica 539
92 Artigas 2008 T 532
92 La Basseta 2008 T 532
92 La Creu Alta 2007 T 532
92 Nelin 2009 B 539
92 Perinet 2005 T 544
92 Artigas 2010 BFB 532
92 EL26 2008 T 540
92 Canyerets 2006 T 546
92 Somni 2009 T 546
92 Arbossar 2008 T 548
92 Gratallops Vi de la Vila 2009 TC 531
92 L'Infant 2007 T 532
92 Elix 2007 T 545
92 Melis 2008 T 545
92 Els Escurçons 2008 T 544
92 Les Tosses 2008 T 548
92 Nus 2009 Dulce Natural 550
92 GR-174 2010 T 533
92 1270 a Vuit 2007 T 535
92 Pedra de Guix 2008 B 548
92 Perinet 2006 T 544
91 Gratavinum 2 Pi R 2008 T 541
91 GV5 2008 T 541
91 Miserere 2007 TC 538
91 Clos Mustardó 2009 B 542
91 Perpetual 2008 TR 548
91 Corelium 2007 T 547
91 Camins del Priorat 2009 TC 531
91 Clos Cypres 2009 T 539
91 Dits del Terra 2008 T 548
91 Elix 2008 T 545
91 Ardiles Viognier 2009 B 545
91 FA 104 2010 B 543
91 Masperla 2006 T 549
90 Embruix de Vall-Llach 2009 T 537
90 Cartoixa 2006 TR 538
90 Roquers de Porrera 2008 TC 535
90 Barranc Blanc 2010 B 543
90 Gran Clos 2004 T 541
90 Clos Figueres 2009 T 539
90 Mas D'en Compte 2008 B 534
90 Ònix Evolució 2008 T 549
90 Coma Vella 2008 T 550
90 Clos Galena 2009 TC 540
90 Galena 2007 T 540
90 Clos de L'Obac 2007 TC 538
90 Osmin 2006 T 546
90 Clos Abella 2005 T 543
90 Mas Sinén 2007 TC 533
90 Prior Pons 2008 T 537
90 Alice 2007 T 535
90 Ònix Fusió 2009 T 549
90 Primitiu de Bellmunt 2009 T 533
90 Cruor 2007 T 533
90 Lo Coster Blanc 2009 B 546
90 Mas Mallola 2007 T 543
90 Petit Perinet 2006 T 544
90 Cirerets 2008 T 532
90 Lytos 2009 T 531
90 Elios 2009 T 539
90 Frares Ranci SC 549
90 Ònix Clàssic 2010 B 548
90 Serras del Priorat 2009 T 539
90 Font de la Figuera 2010 B 539
90 Clos Peites 2008 T 536
90 Mas Amor 2010 RD 542
90 Els Pics 2009 T 532
90 Les Crestes 2009 T 536
90 Pedra de Guix 2009 B 548
90 Destrankis 2009 T 533
90 La Fuina 2008 T 535
90 Cartus 2005 T 541
90 Clos Bartolome 2008 T 533
90 Autor 2004 TR 531
90 Noray 2007 T 546

RÍAS BAIXAS

95 Pazo de Piñeiro 2010 B 570
95 Nora da Neve 2008 BFB 572
94 Nora da Neve 2009 BFB 572
94 Albariño de Fefiñanes III año 2007 B 561
94 Sol de Señorans 2006 B Roble 569
94 Pazo de Barrantes Albariño 2009 B 568
93 Fillaboa Selección Finca Montealto 2009 B 562
93 Pazo Señorans. Selección de Añada 2004 B 569
93 Lusco 2010 B 570
93 Albariño Do Ferreiro 2010 B 565
93 Do Ferreiro Cepas Vellas 2009 B 565
93 Carballo Galego 2009 BFB 554
93 Granbazán Limousin 2009 B 559
93 1583 Albariño de Fefiñanes 2010 BFB 561
93 Leirana Barrica 2009 B 558
93 Goliardo Caiño 2009 T 558
93 Goliardo Albariño 2009 B Barrica 558
92 Pazo Señorans 2010 B 569
92 Veigas de Padriñán 2009 B 554
92 Lagar de Cervera 2010 B 567
92 Zárate El Palomar 2009 BFB 573
92 Pazo de Barrantes Albariño 2010 B 569
92 Albariño de Fefiñanes 2010 B 561
92 Leirana 2010 B 558
92 Paco & Lola 2010 B 559
92 La Caña 2010 B 562
92 Bastión de la Luna 2009 T 558
91 Fillaboa 2010 B 562
91 Laxas 2010 B 560
91 Esencia Diviña 2010 B 555
91 Granbazán Etiqueta Ámbar 2010 B 559
91 Organistrum 2009 B 563
91 Aforado Rosal 2010 B 568
91 Don Olegario Albariño 2009 B 564
91 Terras Gauda Etiqueta Negra 2009 BFB 563
91 Añada de Baladiña 2004 B 566
91 Pionero Mundi 2010 B 572
91 Dávila L100 2009 B 556
91 La Val Crianza sobre Lías 2005 BC 566
91 Señorío de Rubiós Condado Blanco 2007 B Barrica 561
91 Goliardo Loureiro 2009 T 558
91 Zios de Lusco 2010 B 570
91 Contraaparede 2007 B 554
91 Dávila M.100 2007 B 556
91 Pazo Baión 2009 B 557
91 Condes de Albarei En Rama 2006 B 554
91 You & Me 2010 B 560
91 Eidosela 2010 B 562
91 Don Olegario Albariño 2010 B 564
90 Orballo 2010 B 566
90 Bágoa do Miño 2010 B 560
90 Pontellón Albariño 2010 B 555
90 Eidos de Padriñán 2010 B 554
90 Sanamaro 2009 B 569
90 Condes de Albarei 2010 B 554
90 Granbazán Etiqueta Verde 2010 B 559
90 Castel de Bouza 2010 B 564

RIBEIRA SACRA

RIBEIRO

RIBERA DEL DUERO

93 Gran Valtravieso 2006 TR 656
93 Don Miguel Comenge 2006 T 638
93 Trienia 2009 T 622
93 Raíz de Guzmán 2007 T 651
93 Adaro de PradoRey 2009 TC 653
92 Secreto 2005 TR 637
92 Arzuaga Reserva Especial 2008 TR 602
92 Tinto Arroyo Vendimia Seleccionada 2006 T 605
92 Aalto 2008 T 600
92 Sed de Caná 2008 T 630
92 Monteabellón Finca La Blanquera 2006 T 633
92 Páramo de Guzmán 2010 T Barrica 651
92 Alión 2008 T 630
92 ValSotillo VS 2004 TR 618
92 Valdrinal SQR2 2007 T Roble 645
92 Finca Helena Alta Expresión 2006 T 617
92 Briego 2008 TC 610
92 Hacienda Monasterio 2008 T 615
92 Vizcarra 2009 T 630
92 Cepa 21 2008 T 611
92 Ébano 2008 T 642
92 Tábula 2007 T 635
92 Tamaral 2006 TR 624
92 Protos 2005 TR 652
92 Dominio de Atauta 2008 TC 641
92 Cyclo 2007 T 644
92 Pago de los Capellanes Parcela El Nogal 2005 T 650
92 Terra Incógnita 2004 T 608
92 Honoris de Valdubón 2006 T 627
92 Valduero Una Cepa 2009 T 636
92 Acón 2006 TR 600
92 A&M 2006 TC 609
92 Nuestro 12 meses 2009 T Barrica 640
92 Alfa Spiga 2005 T 633
92 MB Martín Berdugo 2006 T 632
92 Pruno 2009 T 644
92 FDB 2006 T Barrica 640
92 Amaya Arzuaga Autor 2007 T 601
92 Viña Valdemazón Vendimia Seleccionada 2008 T 658
92 Pago de Casar 2008 T 625
92 Corimbo 2009 T 619
92 Pago de Valtarreña 2005 T 623
92 Diaz Bayo Poyatas de Valdebrero 2007 T Barrica 640
92 Astrales 2007 T 602
92 ValSotillo 2004 TGR 618
92 Alidis VS 2006 T 658
92 PSI 2009 T 641
91 Viña Mayor 2006 TR 637
91 Gran Solorca 2005 TR 658
91 Pago de los Capellanes 2008 TC 649
91 Chafandín 2008 T 631
91 Condado de Oriza 409 2008 T 650
91 Legaris 2005 TR 646
91 Páramo de Guzmán 2007 TC 651
91 Emilio Moro 2008 TC 613
91 Costaval 2005 TR 631
91 Lynus Áurea 2007 TR 647
91 Alitus 2003 TR 610
91 López Cristobal 2008 TC 619
91 ValSotillo 2006 TC 617
91 Finca Villacreces 2007 TC 644
91 Valderiz 2009 T 636
91 Abadía de San Quirce 2004 TR 617
91 Avan Cepas Centenarias 2007 T 632
91 Carmelo Rodero 2008 TC 623
91 Viyuela Selección 2005 T 630
91 Trus 2005 TR 626
91 Matarromera 2004 TGR 604
91 Callejo 2007 TR 614
91 Gran Callejo 2005 TGR 614
91 Montebaco 2008 TC 648
91 Protos 2004 TGR 652
91 Protos 2008 TC 652
91 PradoRey 2004 TGR 653
91 Convento San Francisco Sel. Especial 2005 T Barrica 602
91 Carmelo Rodero 2007 TR 623
91 Valtravieso 2006 TR 656
91 Portia Prima 2009 T 622
91 Baden Numen "N" 2008 TC 602
91 Cruz de Alba 2008 TC 612
91 Arzuaga 2004 TGR 602
91 Mathis 2007 T 603
91 Baden Numen Oro "AU" 2008 T 602
91 El Salegar 2007 TC 628
91 F de Fuentespina 2004 TR 615
91 Arrocal Máximo 2006 T 609
91 Dominio Romano RDR 2007 T 641
91 Magallanes 2007 TC 654
91 Figuero Tinus 2008 T 659
91 Valdubón Diez 2010 T 627
91 Venta Las Vacas 2009 T 656
91 Los Cantos de Torremilanos 2008 T 643
91 Tinto Pesquera 2006 TR 600
91 Krel 2009 T Roble 626
91 Buró Selección Especial 2009 T 620
91 Abadía de San Quirce 2005 TR 617
91 Diaz Bayo Majuelo de la Hombría 2007 T Barrica 640
91 Pico Cuadro Vendimia Seleccionada 2007 T 652
91 Provenius 2008 T 633
90 T D'Anguix 2004 TR 655
90 Arzuaga 2008 TC 602
90 Altos de Tamarón 2006 TR 650
90 Quinta de Tarsus 2008 TC 624
90 Tarsus 2005 TR 624
90 M2 de Matallana 2007 T 638
90 Lara Prios Maximus Vino de Autor 2006 T 613
90 Austum 2009 T 625
90 Tionio 2006 TC 626
90 Lynus 2008 TC 647
90 VT Vendimia Seleccionada 2007 T 656
90 Celeste 2009 TC 654
90 Martín Berdugo 2010 T 632
90 Bagús Vendimia Seleccionada 2008 T 619
90 Arrocal Selección 2006 T 609
90 Sentido 2009 T 633
90 Pagos de Quintana 2006 TR 613
90 Abadía de San Quirce 2007 TC 617
90 Avan Concentración 2008 T 632
90 12 Linajes 2006 TR 660
90 Bracamonte 2006 TC 646
90 Figuero Noble 2005 T 660
90 Vizcarra Senda del Oro 2010 T 630
90 Abadía la Arroyada 2007 TC 608
90 Bohórquez 2006 TR 610
90 Portia 2008 TC 622
90 Matarromera Prestigio
Pago de las Solanas 2001 T Reserva Especial 604
90 Emina Atio 2005 T Reserva Especial 643
90 Rento 2005 TC 605
90 Protos 2009 T Roble 652
90 PradoRey 2005 TR 653
90 Marqués de Velilla 2006 TC 644
90 Vega Real 2004 TR 636
90 Viña Magna 2008 TC 641
90 Altamimbre 2008 T 621
90 Áster 2005 TR 659
90 Viña Fuentenarro Vendimia Seleccionada 2009 T 644
90 Recoletas Vendimia Seleccionada 2004 T Roble 634
90 Mirat 2003 TR 627
90 Viña Gormaz 2008 TC 660

90 Recoletas 2005 TC 634
90 Silvanus 2007 TC 609
90 Páramo de Guzmán 2008 TR 651
90 Abadía de San Quirce 2001 TGR 617
90 Somanilla Vendimia Seleccionada 2007 T 657
90 Félix Callejo Selección 2006 TC 614
90 Pago de los Capellanes 2010 T Roble 649
90 Viña Pedrosa 2005 TGR 616
90 Acón 2007 TC 600
90 Phylos 2008 T 603
90 Viña Fuentenarro 2005 TR 644
90 Silencio de Valdiruela 2006 TR 610
90 Damana 2008 TC 635
90 Nuestro Crianza 2007 TC 640
90 Autor de Bocos 2009 T 655
90 Peñafalcón Vendimia Selección 2005 TC 620
90 Serie Privada Club de Vinos Protos 2003 T 652
90 Ra 2007 T 640
90 Disco 2010 T 633
90 Convento Oreja Memoria 2006 TR 639
90 Páramo de Guzmán 2010 RD 651
90 Tres Matas 2007 TC 636
90 Avan Viñedo del Torrubio 2007 T 632
90 Hacienda Abascal (Marqués de la Concordia) 2008 TC 647
90 Viyuela 10 2006 T 630
90 Parajes 2006 TR 654
90 Hacienda Abascal Premium (Marqués de la Concordia) 2008 T 647
90 D'Anguix 2005 T 655
90 Resalte 2005 TR 622
90 Loess Collection 2005 T 647
90 Arzuaga 2009 TC 601
90 Fuentespina Selección 2007 T 615
90 Quinta Milú La Cometa 2009 TC 652
90 Monte del Conde 2008 TC 607
90 Tarsus 2008 T Barrica 625
90 Abadía de San Quirce Nueve Meses en Barrica 2009 T 617
90 Montebaco 2009 TC 648
90 Alidis Expresión 2007 TC 658
90 Tionio 2005 TR 626
90 CuestaRoa 2007 TC 603
90 Tinto Figuero Vendimia Seleccionada 2005 T 660
90 Páramo de Guzmán 2008 TR 651
90 Torre de Golban 2007 TC 641
90 Torre de Golban 2006 TR 641

RIBERA DEL GUADIANA

95 Salitre 2009 T 669
94 Huno Matanegra 2009 TC 669
93 Huno 2008 T 669
93 Madre del Agua 2009 T 668
92 Alunado 2009 BFB 669
90 Viña Puebla 2010 BFB 667
90 Viña Puebla Chardonnay 2009 BFB 667
90 Carabal 2007 TC 671
90 "PQ" Primicia 2009 T 671
89 Viña Puebla Esenzia 2008 TC 668
88 Viña Puebla Selección 2009 T 668
88 Payva 2005 TR 666
88 Palacio Quemado 2005 TR 671
88 Fuente Cortijo 2005 TC 665
88 Señorío de Alange Tempranillo 2010 T 671
88 Señorío de Alange Syrah 2010 T 671

RIBERA DEL JÚCAR

90 Adar 2008 T 676
90 Adar Petit Verdot 2008 T 676
89 Vega Moragona Alta Selección 2005 TR 676
88 Vega Moragona Tempranillo 2010 T Joven 676
88 Ness 2008 T 676
88 Teatinos Dulce Moscatel 2010 Blanco dulce 676
88 Teatinos Syrah 2010 T 675
88 Vega Moragona Cabernet Sauvignon 2008 T 676
88 Teatinos Claros de Cuba 2006 TR 675
87 Teatinos Selección 40 Barricas Tempranillo 2005 TR 676
87 Teatinos Tempranillo 2010 T 675
87 Viña Encina de Elviwines 2007 T 676
87 Vega Moragona 2008 TC 676
87 Vega Moragona Syrah 2008 T 676
87 Las Eras Tradición 2009 T 675

RIOJA

98 Contador 2009 T 686
97 Viña El Pisón 2009 T 743
97 Dalmau 2007 TR 762
97 Castillo Ygay 2001 TGR 762
96 Cirsion 2009 T 731
96 Artadi Pagos Viejos 2009 T 743
96 Sierra Cantabria Colección Privada 2008 T 770
96 La Nieta 2008 T 778
96 Artuke K4 2009 T 684
96 San Vicente 2008 T 769
96 Dalmau 2005 TR 762
95 Castillo Ygay 2004 TGR 763
95 La Vicalanda 2004 TGR 695
95 Gran Reserva 904 Rioja Alta 1998 TGR 758
95 Avrvs 2008 T 751
95 San Vicente 2007 T 769
95 La Viña de Andrés Romeo 2009 T 686
95 Finca El Bosque 2008 T 770
95 Malpuesto 2009 T 723
95 Roda I 2006 TR 731
95 El Puntido 2008 T 778
95 La Nieta 2009 T 778
95 Remírez de Ganuza 2006 TR 729
95 Mártires 2010 B 751
95 Finca Torrea 2007 TR 702
95 Sierra Cantabria Colección Privada 2009 T 770
95 Artuke Finca de los Locos 2009 T 684
95 Artadi Valdeginés 2009 T 743
95 Artadi La Poza de Ballesteros 2009 T 743
95 Artadi El Carretil 2009 T 743
94 Imperial 2007 TR 748
94 La Vicalanda 2006 TR 695
94 Contino Graciano 2007 T 778
94 Viña Ardanza 2004 TR 758
94 Culmen 2005 TR 758
94 Gloria de Ostatu 2006 T 724
94 Prado Enea 2004 TGR 720
94 La Cueva del Contador 2009 T 686
94 El Puntido 2007 T 778
94 Qué Bonito Cacareaba 2010 B 686
94 Amancio 2007 T 770
94 Ysios Edición Limitada 2007 TR 745
94 Colección Vivanco Parcelas de Garnacha 2008 T 703
94 Trasnocho 2007 T 730
94 Mentor Roberto Torretta 2005 T 718
94 Capellania 2005 B 762
94 Sierra Cantabria 2004 TGR 770
93 Altos de Lanzaga 2007 T 747
93 Plácet Valtomelloso 2009 B 725
93 Propiedad Viñas Tradicionales 2008 T 725
93 Remelluri Colección Jaime Rodríguez 2004 T 754
93 Contino Viña del Olivo 2008 T 778
93 Contino "Magnum" 2005 TGR 779
93 Abel Mendoza Tempranillo Grano a Grano 2008 T 685
93 Barón de Chirel 2005 T 702

Score	Wine	Page
91	Cortijo Icono 2010 BFB	740
91	Sel de Su Merced 2005 TR	779
91	Egomei 2008 T	751
91	Inspiración Valdemar 2007 T	738
91	Confesor 2005 T	741
91	Campillo 2010 BFB	696
91	La Montesa 2009 TC	725
91	Anastasio 2006 T	756
91	Faustino Edición Especial 2001 T	707
91	Barón de Oja 2007 TC	692
91	Izadi El Regalo 2005 TR	711
91	Díez-Caballero Victoria 2008 T	749
91	Solar de Líbano 2008 TC	699
91	Cumbre Montecillo 2006 TR	765
91	Dominio Campo Viejo 2006 T	698
91	Sierra Cantabria 2007 TC	770
91	Secreto de Altún 2008 T	691
91	Amaren 2009 BFB	692
91	Finca La Emperatriz 2008 TC	712
91	Cosme Palacio 1984 2008 B	725
91	Ganko 2009 T	765
91	Los Dominios de Berceo 2007 TC	693
91	Altos R Pigeage 2007 T	681
91	Obalo 2010 T	722
91	Lan D-12 2008 T	758
91	Contino 2010 B	778
91	Artadi Viñas de Gain 2010 B	742
91	Mati Kosher Elviwines 2009 T	699
91	Horizonte de Exopto 2008 T	706
91	Miranda 2008 TC	779
91	Contino 2006 TR	779
91	Puente del Ea Autor 2009 T	745
91	Honorable Gómez Cruzado 2007 T	709
91	Plácet Valtomelloso 2008 B	725
91	Daimon 2010 BFB	735
91	Cifras 2010 T	706
91	Conclave Esencia 2008 B	687
91	Mentor 2007 TC	718
91	Ares 2008 TR	749
90	Alma de Tobía 2010 RD Fermentado en Barrica	735
90	Viña Tobía 2010 T	735
90	Arteso 2007 TC	721
90	Dionisio Ruiz Ijalba 2009 T	774
90	Ijalba 2006 TR	774
90	Ijalba Maturana 2010 B	774
90	Sonsierra Vendimia Seleccionada 2008 TC	733
90	Beronia 2003 TGR	695
90	Beronia Tempranillo Elaboración Especial 2009 T	695
90	Cune 2008 TR	748
90	Viña Pomal 2006 TR	695
90	Viña Los Valles 50 & 50 2007 TC	740
90	Lealtanza Artistas Españoles Dalí 2004 TR	690
90	Faustino I 1999 TGR	707
90	Gonzalo de Berceo 2001 TGR	694
90	Los Dominios de Berceo "Reserva 36" 2006 TR	694
90	Viña Berceo 2008 TC	693
90	Conde de Valdemar 2005 TR	738
90	Valdemar Tempranillo 2010 T	738
90	Inspiración Valdemar Graciano 2005 T	738
90	Valsacro Dioro 2005 T	739
90	Don Jacobo 1995 TGR	700
90	Hacienda Susar 2007 T	761
90	Viña Tondonia 1997 B Reserva	767
90	Luis Cañas 2005 TR	716
90	La Rioja Alta Gran Reserva 890 1995 TGR	758
90	Lan 2003 TGR	759
90	Ramón Bilbao 2006 TR	729
90	Coto Real 2005 TR	750
90	Valserrano 2006 TR	781
90	Solabal 2008 TC	688
90	Solabal 2007 TR	688
90	Marqués de Cáceres 2008 TC	761
90	Ostatu Selección 2007 T	724
90	Martínez Lacuesta 2008 TC	764
90	Tierra Fidel 2008 T	681
90	Campillo 2007 TC	696
90	Campillo Reserva Especial 2004 TR	696
90	Muro Bujanda 2007 TC	765
90	Muga 2010 BFB	720
90	Valdelana 2010 T	737
90	Conde de los Andes 2001 B	766
90	Altos de Corral 2002 TR	700
90	Altún 2008 TC	691
90	Gran Albina 2005 TR	730
90	Viña Albina 2005 TR	730
90	Loriñón 2005 TGR	696
90	Biga de Luberri 2008 TC	760
90	Luberri 2010 T Maceración Carbónica	760
90	Don Peduz 2010 T	756
90	Olagosa 2008 TC	727
90	6 Cepas 6 2010 T	727
90	Seis de Luberri 2008 T	760
90	Cerro Añón 2005 TR	722
90	Olagosa 2004 TGR	728
90	Altún 2006 TR	691
90	Ysios 2006 TR	746
90	Finca La Emperatriz Terruño 2008 T	712
90	Coto Mayor 2007 TC	750
90	Esencias de Varal 2007 T	739
90	Tierra 2008 TC	681
90	Marqués de Vitoria 2008 TC	717
90	Aticus Vendimia Seleccionada 2008 T	700
90	Valcavada 2005 TR	733
90	Viña Monty 2006 TR	765
90	Antión Selección 2007 T	692
90	Antonio Alcaraz 2008 TC	683
90	Antonio Alcaraz 2007 TR	683
90	Arvum 2005 T	705
90	Mazarredo de Ostatu 2008 T	724
90	Tarón 4MB 2008 T	734
90	Vivanco Tempranillo Garnacha 2010 RD	703
90	Carlos San Pedro Pérez de Viñaspre 2008 T	746
90	Castillo de Sajazarra 2005 TR	698
90	Varal Vendimia Seleccionada 2007 T	740
90	Viña Zaco 2008 T	695
90	Gloria Antonio Alcaraz 2008 TC	683
90	Pagos de la Sonsierra Ed. Espec. David Delfín 2006 T	733
90	Livius Graciano 2006 T	742
90	Condes de los Andes 2005 TR	767
90	Viña Los Valles Ecológico 2009 TC	740
90	Finca Nueva 2005 TR	752
90	Puente del Ea 2010 BFB	744
90	Ramón Bilbao 2004 TGR	729
90	La Senoba 2008 T	768
90	Lealtanza 2010 B	689
90	Domeco de Jarauta 2007 T	704
90	Don Jacobo Ecológico 2008 T	700
90	Baigorri Belus 2008 T	685
90	Horizonte de Exopto 2009 B	706
90	Labarona 2005 TR	754
90	Antión Graciano 2008 T	692
90	Gran Chobeo de Peciña 2008 T	711
90	Crianza de Varal 2007 T	740
90	Viña Herminia Excelsus 2009 T	773
90	Marqués de Tomares Excellence 3F 2009 T	763
90	Lagar de Santiago 2010 T	702
90	Inédito 3/3 2009 T	712
90	Inédito S 2008 T	713
90	Hacienda Grimón 2008 TC	754
90	Berceo "Nueva Generación" 2007 TC	693

90 Koden de Luis Alegre 2009 T ...715
90 Rayos Uva 2010 T ...765
90 Jequitibá 2010 B ...765
90 Altos R 2005 TR ...681
90 Finca Nueva 2010 BFB ...751
90 QP "Vintage" 2006 T ...686
90 Glorioso 2004 TGR ...725
90 Calavia Colección Privada 2008 T ...682
90 El Tractor Vendimia Seleccionada 2007 T ...760
90 Peña El Gato Garnacha 2009 T ...757
90 Ladrón de Guevara de Autor 2010 T ...737
90 1958 de Ortubia 2006 TR ...724
90 Sel de Su Merced 2006 TR ...779
90 Inédito 2009 BFB ...712
90 Inédito H12 2008 T ...713
90 Launa Plus 2007 TR ...759
90 Teo's 2008 T ...759
90 Santalba Ecológico 2009 T ...774
90 Abando Vendimia Seleccionada 2004 TR ...774
90 Daimon 2009 T ...735
90 Altos R 2010 B ...681
90 Viña Tobía 2010 B ...735
90 Tierra de Fidel 2009 B ...681
90 Daimon 2010 RD Fermentado en Barrica ...734
90 Solagüen Cepas Viejas 2009 T ...743
90 Ares 2009 TC ...749

RUEDA

97 Naiades 2008 BFB ...799
95 Belondrade y Lurton 2009 BFB ...786
95 El Transistor 2009 B ...804
93 Finca La Colina Verdejo Cien x Cien 2010 B ...812
93 Blanco Nieva Pie Franco 2010 B ...813
93 Sel. Personal Carlos Moro Emina Verdejo 2009 BFB ...789
93 PR 3 Barricas 2008 BFB ...800
93 Protos 2009 B Barrica ...800
93 Shaya Habis 2009 BFB ...804
92 Sanz Verdejo 2010 B ...811
92 Marqués de Riscal Sauvignon Blanc 2010 B ...794
92 Naia 2010 B ...799
92 Ermita Veracruz Verdejo 2010 B ...802
92 Trascampanas Verdejo 2010 B ...789
92 Saxum (Terrenos Pedregosos) Sauvignon Blanc 2008 BFB ...810
92 V3 Viñas Viejas Verdejo 2009 BFB ...810
92 Palacio de Bornos Verdejo Vendimia Sel. 2009 BFB ...792
92 Analivia Sauvignon Blanc 2010 B ...809
92 Finca La Colina Sauvignon Blanc 2010 B ...811
92 EL Bufón Verdejo 2010 B ...792
92 Finca Montico 2010 B ...795
92 Palacio de Menade Sauvignon Blanc 2010 B ...810
92 Cuatro Rayas Viñedos Centenarios 2010 B ...786
92 Bellori 2009 BFB ...786
92 Loess Collection 2009 BFB ...808
91 Martínsancho Verdejo 2010 B ...785
91 Martivillí Verdejo 2010 B ...803
91 Viña Sanzo Verdejo 2010 B ...810
91 Marqués de Riscal Rueda Verdejo 2010 B ...795
91 Marqués de Riscal Limousin 2008 B ...794
91 Blanco Nieva 2010 B ...813
91 Blanco Nieva Sauvignon 2010 B ...813
91 Vega de la Reina Verdejo 2010 B ...811
91 Vega de la Reina 2010 B ...811
91 Alta Plata Verdejo 2010 B ...798
91 Leguillón Verdejo 2010 B ...799
91 Castelo de Medina Sauvignon Blanc 2010 B ...794
91 Orden Tercera Verdejo 2010 B Joven ...806
91 El Perro Verde 2010 B ...811
91 Protos Verdejo 2010 B ...801
91 Pentio 2010 B ...810
91 Dilectum 2007 BFB ...810
91 Enebral 2010 B ...808
91 Pradorey Sauvignon Blanc 2010 B ...800
91 Viña Burón Verdejo 2010 B ...801
91 José Pariente Verdejo 2010 B ...798
91 Reina de Castilla Verdejo 2010 B ...792
91 Reina de Castilla Sauvignon Blanc 2010 B ...792
91 Visigodo Verdejo 2010 B ...787
91 Labores de Unzu Verdejo 2010 B ...811
91 Baluarte 2010 B ...794
91 Tomás Postigo 2008 BFB ...811
91 Viña Oropéndola 2010 B ...805
91 Palacios de Bornos La Caprichosa 2010 B ...791
91 Finca Montico 2009 B ...794
90 Sanz Clásico 2010 B ...812
90 Sanz Sauvignon Blanc 2010 B ...812
90 Tres Olmos Lías 2010 B ...797
90 Cuatro Rayas Verdejo 2010 B ...786
90 Castelo de Medina Verdejo 2010 B ...793
90 Monte Blanco de Ramón Bilbao Verdejo 2010 B ...791
90 Señorío de Garci Grande Verdejo 2010 B ...797
90 Atelier Verdejo 2010 B ...809
90 Viña Cantosán Varietal Verdejo 2010 B ...807
90 Mantel Blanco Rueda Verdejo 2010 B ...785
90 Condesa Eylo 2010 B ...802
90 Las Brisas 2010 B ...799
90 Palacios de Bornos Verdejo 2009 BFB ...792
90 Trascampanas Sauvignon 2010 B ...789
90 Alba Miros 2010 B ...800
90 Hermanos Lurton Cuesta de Oro 2008 BFB ...788
90 Mania Rueda Verdejo 2010 B ...795
90 Pradorey Verdejo 2010 B ...800
90 Señorio del Cid 2010 B ...809
90 Montebaco Verdejo sobre Lías 2010 B ...809
90 Montespina Sauvignon 2010 B Joven ...786
90 Melior Verdejo 2010 B ...788
90 Eresma Sauvignon 2010 B ...791
90 Val de Vid Verdejo 2010 B ...802
90 Verdeal 2010 B ...802
90 Piedra Verdejo 2010 B ...806
90 Shaya 2010 B ...804
90 De Alberto Verdejo Selección 2010 B ...805
90 Viore Verdejo 2010 B ...803
90 12 Linajes Verdejo 2010 B ...797
90 K-Naia 2010 B ...799
90 Viña Sanzo sobre Lías 2009 B ...810
90 Val de Vid 2010 B ...802
90 Cuatro Rayas 2008 BFB ...787
90 Viña Mayor 2009 BFB ...806
90 Viña Cimbrón 2010 RD ...796
90 Finca Montepedroso 2010 B ...806
90 Blume Sauvignon Blanc 2010 B ...809
90 Circe 2010 B ...786
90 Rey Santo Verdejo 2010 B ...807
90 Mocén Verdejo 2008 BFB ...799
90 Viña Cimbrón Verdejo Selección 2010 B ...796
90 Abadía de San Quirce Verdejo 2010 B ...797

SOMONTANO

96 Enate Uno Chardonnay 2006 BFB ...827
94 Enate Chardonnay 2008 BFB ...827
94 Viñas del Vero Chardonnay 2010 B ...828
94 Irius Premium 2007 T ...821
94 Blecua 2001 TR ...817
94 Enate Uno 2005 T ...828
93 Viñas del Vero Chardonnay Colección 2008 B ...829
93 Viñas del Vero Secastilla 2007 T ...829
93 Enate Reserva Especial 2006 TR ...827
93 Absum Colección Syrah 2008 T ...821

Score	Wine	Page
92	Marboré 2004 T	818
92	Blecua 2005 T	817
92	Viñas del Vero Pinot Noir Colección 2009 T	829
92	Viñas del Vero Clarión 2009 B	829
92	Enate Cabernet Sauvignon 2005 TR	828
92	Irius Selección 2007 T	821
92	Enate Syrah-Shiraz 2007 T	828
92	Cojón de Gato 2009 T	817
92	Nunc 2007 T	819
91	Absum Colección Merlot 2008 T	821
91	Parraleta Emotion 2007 T	819
91	Andres Meler 2006 T	822
91	Laus Flor de Gewürztraminer 2010 B	822
91	Absum Varietales 2009 T	820
91	Absum Colección Tempranillo 2008 T	821
91	Obergo Varietales 2008 T	823
91	Enate Merlot-Merlot 2007 T	827
91	Viñas del Vero La Miranda de Secastilla 2008 T	829
91	Meler 95 sobre Aljez 2007 B	822
91	Lar de Beroz 2006 T	826
91	Cojón de Gato Gewürztraminer 2010 B	817
91	Obergo Syrah 2009 T	823
91	12 Lunas 2007 T	828
91	Pirineos Selección Marboré 2009 B	818
90	Pirineos Gewürztraminer 2010 B	817
90	Pirineos Merlot- Cabernet 2007 TC	818
90	Viñas del Vero Gewürztraminer Colección 2010 B	829
90	Viñas del Vero Gran Vos 2005 TR	829
90	Viñas del Vero Syrah Colección 2007 T	829
90	Enate Chardonnay-234 2010 B	827
90	Enate Gewürztraminer 2010 B	827
90	Enate Varietales 2006 T	828
90	Olvena Cuatro o El Pago de la Libélula 2007 T	823
90	Meler 2005 TC	822
90	Idrias Abiego 2008 T	825
90	Absum Varietales 2009 B	820
90	Estada 2010 RD	820
90	Laus 700 Alt 2007 B	822
90	Obergo "Finca la Mata" 2008 T	823
90	Obergo Caramelos 2010 T	823
90	12 Lunas 2010 B	828
90	12 Lunas (Más Una) 2007 T	828
90	De Beroz Crianza Especial 2007 T	826
90	De Beroz Reserva Familia 2006 T	827
90	Reis d'Isabena 2010 B	817
90	12 Lunas 2010 RD	828

TACORONTE-ACENTEJO

Score	Wine	Page
95	Humboldt 1997 Blanco dulce	835
95	Humboldt 2001 Tinto dulce	835
95	Magma de Cráter 2006 TC	835
94	Humboldt Verdello 2005 Blanco dulce	835
93	Humboldt Malvasía 2006 B	835
92	Cráter 2007 T Barrica	835
92	Humboldt Vendimia Tardía 2005 B	835
92	Domínguez Malvasía Clásico 2009 B	833
90	Viña Norte 2008 T	835
90	Verijadiego Monje 2008 T	838
89	Viña Norte 2010 T Maceración Carbónica	835
89	Viña Norte 2007 TC	835
89	Viña Norte 2010 T	835

TARRAGONA

Score	Wine	Page
94	De Muller Garnacha Solera 1926 Solera	846
93	Pajarete Solera 1851 Vino de licor	846
93	Nus del Terrer 2009 T	849
92	Terrer d'Aubert 2008 T	849
92	Sumoi Capvespre S/C T	843
92	Terrer d'Aubert 2009 T	849
91	De Muller Chardonnay 2010 BFB	845
91	De Muller Rancio Seco Vino de licor	846
91	Nus del Terrer 2008 T	849
91	De Muller Avreo Semidulce s/c Añejo	846
90	De Muller Moscatel Añejo Vino de licor	846
90	Adernats 2010 BFB	848
90	Ipsis 2009 TC	848
90	Mas la Boella Vi de Guarda 2008 T	844

TERRA ALTA

Score	Wine	Page
95	Edetària 2005 BFB	862
92	L'Avi Arrufí 2007 T	859
92	Llàgrimes de Tardor 2009 BFB	853
92	Edetària 2007 T	862
92	Edetària 2008 BFB	862
92	L'Avi Arrufí 2009 BFB	859
92	Bruna Dolç 2010 T	864
91	Coma d'En Pou Bàrbara Forés 2006 T	856
91	El Quintà Bárbara Forés 2010 BFB	856
91	Mather Teresina Selección de Viñas Viejas 2008 T	859
91	Edetària Dolç 2009 TC	862
91	Edetària 2009 BFB	862
91	Lafou 2007 T	863
91	Edetària 2008 T	862
90	Llàgrimes de Tardor Selecció 2006 TC	854
90	Vi de Licor 1919 Vino de licor	858
90	Josefina Piñol 2009 Tinto Dulce	860
90	Edetana 2010 B	862
90	Merian Dulce Natural 2010 T	860
90	Portal N. Sra. Portal 2010 B	859
90	Equinox Moscatel	857
90	Vía Terra 2010 B	862
90	Vía Terra 2010 T	862
90	Lafou 2008 T	863
90	Finca Morenillo 2009 T	859
90	Tipicitat 2007 T	857

TIERRA DE LEÓN

Score	Wine	Page
92	Pardevalles Carroleón 2008 T	872
91	Pardevalles Gamonal 2009 T	872
91	Pricum Valdemuz 2008 T	868
90	Pricum Prieto Picudo 2008 T	868
90	Pricum Paraje de El Santo 2008 T	868
90	3 Palomares 2010 B	870
90	Finca La Silvera 2007 T	869
90	Villacezán Albarín 2010 B	871
89	Señorío de Mogrovejo 2010 RD	871
89	Galio 2008 T	872
89	Pricum Albarín Valdemuz 2009 B Barrica	868
89	Pricum Primeur 2010 T	868
89	3 Palomares 2009 T	870

TIERRA DEL VINO DE ZAMORA

Score	Wine	Page
96	Cenit 2007 T	876
94	Via Cenit 2009 T	876
93	Venta Mazarrón 2009 T	876
90	Aleo 2009 T Roble	876
88	Catedral de Zamora 2010 B	876

TORO

Score	Wine	Page
97	Victorino 2008 T	896
96	Pintia 2008 T	890
96	Victorino 2009 T	895
96	Alabaster 2008 T	896
96	Alabaster 2009 T	895

95 Termanthia 2008 T 882
95 Numanthia 2008 T 882
95 El Titán del Bendito 2008 T 891
95 Termanthia 2009 T 882
94 Vetus 2007 T 896
94 Gran Colegiata Campus 2006 TC 884
94 Almirez 2009 T 895
94 Termes 2008 T 883
94 Numanthia 2009 T 882
93 San Román 2008 T 890
93 Piedra Paredinas 2005 T 891
93 El Titán del Bendito 2007 T 891
93 Almirez 2008 T 896
93 Celsus 2009 T 896
93 Uro 2008 T 892
93 Paydos 2008 T 897
93 Termes 2009 T 883
92 Liberalia Cabeza de Cuba 2007 TC 892
92 Liberalia Cinco 2005 TR 892
92 Finca La Meda Alta Expresión 2006 T 894
92 Pago La Jara 2007 T 891
92 Corral de Campanas 2009 T 894
92 Carodorum Selección 2008 TC 883
92 Campo Eliseo 2005 T 880
92 Inaraja 2005 T 887
92 Liber 2004 TGR 893
92 Juan Rojo 2006 T 889
92 Dominio de Valdelacasa 2008 T 881
92 Matsu El Viejo 2008 T 893
92 Rompesedas Finca las Parvas 2006 T 891
92 Elías Mora 2005 TR 881
92 Actitud de la Quietud 2006 T 894
92 Terras de Javier Rodríguez 2009 T 895
92 Ancestros 2006 TR 892
92 Arco del Reloj 2008 T 884
92 Terra D'uro Selección 2008 T 892
91 Gran Bajoz de Autor 2006 TC 894
91 Gran Colegiata Roble Francés 2006 TC 884
91 Villaester 2004 T 897
91 Valmoro 2007 T 880
91 Piedra Platino Selección 2005 TR 892
91 Dominio del Bendito El Primer Paso 2009 T Roble 891
91 Elías Mora 2008 TC 881
91 Adoremus 2005 TR 889
91 Castillo Monte la Reina Vendimia Seleccionada 2005 T 887
91 Frontaura 2006 TC 881
91 Gago 2008 T 891
91 Dominio del Bendito Las Sabias 16 meses 2007 T 891
91 Selección Personal Carlos Moro Cyan 2005 T R Esp. 880
91 Abdón Segovia 2008 TC 897
91 Nos Riqueza 16 meses 2008 T 882
91 Flor de Vetus 2009 T 896
91 Bravo de Rejadorada 2008 T 887
90 Liberalia Cero 2010 T Fermentado en Barrica 892
90 Novellum Rejadorada 2007 TC 887
90 Sango de Rejadorada 2006 TR 887
90 Cyan Prestigio 2005 TC 880
90 Cañus Verus 2007 T 884
90 Piedra Roja 2007 TC 891
90 Viñas Elías Mora 2009 T Roble 881
90 Quinta Quietud 2006 T 895
90 Cyan Pago de la Calera 2004 T 881
90 Quinola Garage Wine 2008 T Roble 894
90 Viña Mayor Toro 2008 T 889
90 Rompesedas 2006 T 891
90 Finca La Meda 2007 TC 894
90 Morfeo "Cepas Viejas" 2009 T 895
90 Matsu El Recio 2009 T 893
90 Campo Alegre 2008 T 880
90 Libranza 2006 T Reserva Especial 889
90 Adoremus 2001 TGR 889
90 Terra D'uro 2009 T 892

UCÉS

91 La Estacada 2009 TC 901
90 Esencia de Fontana 2008 T 901
88 Finca la Estacada 6 meses barrica 2009 T Roble 901
86 Campos de Viento 2010 T 901
86 Solmayor 2007 TC 901
85 Cañada Real 2010 T 902

UTIEL-REQUENA

94 Impromptu 2010 B 907
94 El Cf de Chozas Carrascal 2008 T 912
93 Casa Don Ángel Bobal 2006 T 917
92 Las Ocho 2008 T 912
92 Las Tres 2010 BFB 912
92 Pasiego de Autor 2005 TC 918
91 Corolilla 2008 TC 907
91 Cerro Bercial Parcela "Ladera los Cantos" 2006 T 908
91 Cerro Bercial 2008 T Barrica 908
91 Arte Mayor III T 914
91 Cerro Bercial Selección 2010 B 908
91 Viña Lidón 2010 BFB 917
91 Cueva de la Culpa 2008 T 907
91 Bassus Premium 2008 T 907
91 Quod Superius 2007 T 907
91 Beso de Requena 2007 TC 913
91 Lagar de Lar 2005 TC 906
91 Passion de la bodega 2005 T Roble 906
91 Cerrogallina 2008 T 912
91 Casa Don Ángel Malbec 7-8 T 917
90 Martínez Bermell Merlot 2009 T Fermentado en Barrica 917
90 Aula Syrah 2007 TC 913
90 Aula Merlot 2008 TC 913
90 Generación 1 2006 T 910
90 Vega Infante Madurado en Barrica 2010 T 909
90 Vegalfaro 2010 B 918
90 Pasiego Las Suertes 2010 B 918
90 Cerro Bercial 2004 TR 908
90 L'Angelet 2007 TC 908
90 Bassus Pinot Noir 2008 T 907
90 Juanpedrós 2008 T 912
90 El Olivastro 2009 T 906
90 Bassus Dulce Bobal-Pinot Noir RD 907
90 Pasion de Bobal 2009 T 908
90 Bobal y Tempranillo Superior 2008 T 907
90 Viña Castaro Selección 2005 TR 918

VALDEORRAS

96 Pedrouzos Magnum 2008 B 925
95 Pedrouzos Magnum 2009 B 925
94 As Sortes 2009 B 926
94 Pezas da Portela 2008 BFB 925
93 Guitián Godello 2009 BFB 922
93 Louro do Bolo 2010 B 926
93 Avanthia Godello 2010 B 924
93 Pezas da Portela 2009 BFB 925
93 Avanthia Cuvee Mosteiro 2009 T 924
92 Gaba do Xil Godello 2010 B 926
92 Guitián Godello sobre lías 2010 B 922
92 Hacienda Ucediños 2010 B 923
91 Viñaredo Godello 2010 B 927
91 Godeval Cepas Vellas 2010 B 924
91 Lagar do Cigur 2010 T 922
91 Erebo Mencía 2008 T Barrica 925
91 Ollo de Galo Lías 2010 B 926

91 Bioca Godello 2010 B 926
91 D'Berna 2010 B 924
91 Valdesil Godello sobre Lías 2010 B 925
90 Erebo Godello 2010 B 925
90 Erebo Mencía 2010 T 925
90 Joaquín Rebolledo Godello 2010 B 926
90 Valdesil Godello sobre Lías 2009 B 925
90 Viña Somoza Godello Selección 2009 B Roble 927
90 Joaquín Rebolledo Mencía 2010 T 926
90 Cepado Godello 2010 B 923
90 Quinta da Peza Godello 2010 B 923
90 Avanthia Mencía 2009 T 924

VALDEPEÑAS

89 Albali Arium 2005 TGR 934
88 Viña Albali Gran Reserva de la Familia 2003 TGR 935
88 Corcovo Syrah 24 Barricas 2009 T 932
88 Don Aurelio 2010 RD 933
88 Albali Arium 2008 TC 934
87 Bonal Tempranillo 2010 T 933
87 Los Molinos 2005 TGR 934
87 Don Aurelio 2008 TC 933
87 Don Aurelio Tempranillo 2010 T 933
87 Corcovo Verdejo 2010 B 932
87 Marín Perona 2000 TGR 932
87 Albali Arium 2007 TR 934
87 Albali Arium Tempranillo 2010 T 934
87 Viña Albali Selección Privada 2005 TGR 935
87 Corcovo 2007 TC 932
87 Corcovo Tempranillo 2010 T 932
87 Viña Albali Selección Privada 2007 TR 934
87 Raíces 2004 TR 931

VALENCIA

95 Almendros 2009 T 942
93 Cueva del Pecado 2007 T 945
93 Minimum 2009 T 951
92 Megala 2009 T 943
92 Maduresa 2007 T 948
92 Trilogía 2008 T 943
92 Angosto Negre 2009 T 942
92 Murviedro Expresión 2008 TC 945
92 Almendros 2010 B 942
92 Lonecesario 2007 T 951
91 Venta del Puerto 12 2008 T 941
91 Les Alcusses 2008 T 948
91 Rafael Cambra Dos 2009 T 951
91 El Árbol de Aranleón 2007 TC 941
91 Alvarez Nölting 2006 T 940
91 Heretat de Taverners Graciano 2008 TR 949
91 Uva D'Or Moscatel Mistela 948
91 Angosto 2010 B 942
91 Pasamonte 2009 T 946
91 Sueño de Megala 2006 T 943
91 Falcata Arenal 2007 T 950
91 Ca'Belda 2006 T Fermentado en Barrica 941
91 Punt Dolç T 949
91 Alvarez Nölting Syrah 2008 T 940
90 Rafael Cambra Uno 2008 T 951
90 Dominio Los Pinos 2009 TC 944
90 Venta del Puerto 18 Vendimia Sel. 2007 T Barrica 941
90 Falcata Casa Gran 2007 T 950
90 Heretat de Taverners Reixiu 2010 BC 949
90 Alvarez Nölting Chardonnay 2010 B Barrica 940
90 MoMa dels Frades 2008 T Barrica 943
90 Clos de la Vall PX 2010 BFB 949
90 Murviedro 2008 TC 945
90 El Bon Homme 2010 T 951
90 Casa Benasal Elegant 2008 T 950
90 Acvlivs 2008 T 950
90 Cota 8 30 2007 T 942
90 Murviedro Colección Petit Verdot 2010 T 944
90 Los Frailes 2008 T 944
90 Trilogía 2010 B 943
90 Casa Benasal Crux 2008 T 950

VALLE DE GÜIMAR

92 Gran Virtud B 959
91 Gran Virtud Listán Blanco 2010 B 959
91 El Borujo 2010 B Barrica 958
91 Gran Virtud 2010 T 959
90 El Borujo 2010 B 958
90 Melosar Naturalmente Dulce Malvasía 2008 B 958
90 El Borujo 2009 B Barrica 958
90 Gran Virtud Malvasía 2009 B 959
90 Gran Virtud 2010 T 959
88 Los Pelados 2010 T 958
88 Contiempo Vidueños Seco 2010 B 957
88 Contiempo Moscatel Afrutado 2010 B 957
88 Contiempo Malvasía 2008 B 957

VALLE DE LA OROTAVA

92 Arautava Malavasía Dulce 2008 B 964
90 Suertes del Marqués Candio 2008 T 965
88 Arautava Kryos 2010 T 964
88 Suertes del Marqués La Solana 2009 T 965
88 La Suertita 2009 B Barrica 963
88 Can 2010 T 964
88 Suertes del Marqués 2010 B Barrica 965
88 Arautava Finca la Habanera 2010 B 964
88 Arautava 2002 B 964
87 Arautava 2010 T Fermentado en Barrica 964
87 Tajinaste 2010 T Barrica 964
87 Suertes del Marqués 2009 B Barrica 965
87 Suertes del Marqués El Esquilón 2009 T 965
87 Suertes del Marqués Seco 2010 B Maceración Carbónica ..965
87 Arautava 2010 B 964

VINO DE CALIDAD DE CANGAS

92 Pesico 2010 B 1002
91 Descarga 2009 T 1002
90 Corias Guilfa 2009 T 1002
89 Monasterio de Corias Seis Octavos 2010 T Barrica 1002
88 Pesgos 2009 T Roble 1002
88 Castro de Limés 2009 T 1002
88 Viña Galiana 2009 T 1002

VINO DE CALIDAD DE GRANADA

90 Spira Vendimia Seleccionada 2010 T 1003
85 Anchurón 2010 B 1003
80 Anchurón 2009 RD 1003

VINO DE CALIDAD DE LOS VALLES DE BENAVENTE

88 Valleoscuro 2010 RD 1004
88 Valleoscuro Prieto Picudo Tempranillo 2010 T 1004
86 Otero 2004 TR 1004
86 Petavonium 2007 TC 1003
86 Valleoscuro Prieto Picudo 2010 RD 1004

VINO DE CALIDAD DE SIERRA DE SALAMANCA

90 575 Uvas de Cámbrico 2008 T 1003
90 La Zorra 2010 T 1003
88 Zamayón 2010 T 1003

88 Zamayón Osiris 2009 T 1003

VINOS DE MESA

94 Ordóñez & Co. Nº4 Esencia 2005 B 1091
94 Parque Natural "La Viña de Simón" 2010 B 1099
94 Valquejigoso V2 2007 T 1101
93 Parfán 2004 T 1095
93 7 Vin (13 meses Barrica) 2009 T 1091
93 Navazos Niepoort 2010 B 1091
93 Celler La Muntanya Negre 2009 T 1099
93 Lliure Albir 2009 B 1098
93 Tierga 2008 T 1101
92 Ándalus Petit Verdot 2005 T 1091
92 Vins de Taller MM 2008 TC....1098
92 Puzzle 2010 T 1100
92 Celler La Muntanya Dolç Natural 2009 B 1098
92 Torre Des Canonge 2008 T 1093
92 Eccomi Super Premium 2008 TC 1096
92 Parque Natural "El Carro" 2010 B 1099
92 Eccomi Super Premium 2009 T 1095
92 Zerberos Vino Precioso 2009 B 1094
92 Dehesa de Valquejigoso 2008 T 1100
92 Sofos 2009 B 1099
92 IN 1.0 2010 T 1092
91 Almoroig 2007 T 1099
91 VX Cuvée Caco 2007 T 1100
91 Zerberos Viento Zephyros 2009 B Roble 1094
91 Mendall BB Escollades del 5 2005 B 1097
91 Sedella 2008 T 1092
91 Dolce Far Niente 2009 T 1094
91 Vins de Taller Phlox 2010 B 1098
91 Parfán 2005 T 1095
91 Avi de Mas L'Altet 2009 T 1098
90 Gran Quinta Duri Vino de Autor 2006 T 1093
90 Albir 2010 B 1098
90 Vins de Taller MLOT 2007 TC 1098
90 1500 H Pinot Noir 2007 T 1092
90 Liston 2009 Tinto Dulce 1091
90 Carabibas VS 2009 T 1098
90 Carriel dels Vilars 2008 T 1096
90 Vins de Taller Gris 2010 RD 1098
90 Vins de Taller Geum 2010 T 1098
90 Mas Candi Can28 2009 T 1097
90 Kairos 2010 T 1097
68 M. Miñambres 2010 RD 1093

VINO DE PAGO DE OTAZU

95 Señorío de Otazu Altar 2006 T 997
95 Señorío de Otazu 2007 T 997
94 Señorio de Otazu Vitral 2005 TC....997

VINO DE PAGO EL TERRERAZO

95 Quincha Corral 2009 T 996
94 Finca Terrerazo 2009 T 996

VINO DE PAGO LOS BALAGUESES

91 Pago de los Balagueses 2008 TC....997

VINOS DE CALIDAD VALTIENDAS V.C.P.R.D.

90 Vagal Pago Ardalejos 2006 T 1005
89 Vennur 2007 TC 1005
88 Zarraguilla 2008 T Roble 1005
88 Vagal Cuvée Joana 2009 T 1005
86 Zeta 37 2007 T ....

VINOS DE MADRID

94 Bernabeleva "Arroyo de Tórtolas" 2009 T 970
94 Picarana 2010 B 971
94 Cantocuerdas Moscatel de Bernabeleva 2009 B 970
94 Peña Caballera 2009 T 971
94 La Bruja Avería 2010 T 973
94 Las Umbrías 2009 T 973
94 El Rincón Garnacha 2007 T 974
94 Hombre Bala 2010 T 975
93 El Regajal Selección Especial 2009 T 973
93 Licinia 2008 T 972
93 Bernabeleva Viña Bonita 2009 T 970
93 Piesdescalzos 2010 B 971
93 Cantocuerdas Albillo 2009 B 970
92 Dividivo 2008 T 975
92 Navaherreros 2009 T 970
92 Labros 2009 T 971
92 Navaherreros Blanco de Bernabeleva 2009 B 970
91 Tagonius Gran Vino 2004 TR 975
91 Corucho Garnacha Cepas Viejas 2008 T 971
91 Qubél Nature 2004 T 971
91 Manu Vino de Autor 2005 TC 978
91 La Casa de Monroy Selección Viñas Viejas 2008 T 974
91 Las Retamas del Regajal 2009 T 973
91 Las Moradas de San Martín Libro VII Las Luces 2007 T ..974
90 Félix Martínez Cepas Viejas 2006 TR 977
90 Puerta de Alcalá 2008 TC 977
90 Asido 2007 T 975
90 El Rincón 2006 T 974
90 Qubél Excepción 2006 T 971
90 Bernabeleva "Carril del Rey" 2009 T 970
90 Treinta Mil Maravedíes 2009 T 971
90 Luis Saavedra 2008 T 971
90 Las Moradas de San Martín Initio 2007 T 974
90 Tagonius Mariage 2005 T 975

VINOS ESPUMOSOS

87 Vega Moragona 2010 RD 999
86 Barbadillo Beta 2010 BR 999
85 Ariane 2009 ESP 999

VIÑEDOS DE ESPAÑA

93 Noviembre de Finca El Monegrillo 2006 T 1088
88 Dolç de Gel Mortitx 2010 B 1088

VT 3 RIBERAS

88 Abadía de la Oliva 2010 B 1014
88 Alma de Abadía de la Oliva Naturalmente Dulce 2010 Moscatel 1014
87 Abadía de la Oliva 2010 T 1014
86 Abadía de la Oliva Chardonnay 2010 BFB....1014
86 Abadía de la Oliva 2009 T Roble....1014

VT ALTIPLANO DE SIERRA NEVADA

89 Anchurón Plus Merlot Syrah 2007 T Roble 1014
88 Muñana Ñ 2008 T 1014
88 Muñana Ñ 3 Cepas 2008 T 1015
88 Cortijo El Anchurón 2008 T Roble 1014
88 Anchurón Plus Tempranillo Cabernet 2007 T 1014
86 Cortijo El Anchurón 2006 T Barrica 1014

VT BAJO ARAGÓN

92 Venta d'Aubert Viognier 2010 B 1016
91 Dominio Maestrazgo 2008 T Barrica 1016

90 Rex Deus 2005 T ... 1016
90 Fandos y Barriuso Royal de Alloza de Valde la Marga 2004 T Barrica ... 1016
90 Evohé 2010 T ... 1015
90 Magalia Selección 2009 T ... 1016
88 Ventus 2008 TC ... 1017
88 Finca Mas Nou Barono 2010 T ... 1017
88 Dominio Maestrazgo 2007 T ... 1016
87 Barono 2 Angel & Javier 2008 T ... 1017
87 Dominio Maestrazgo Syrah 2008 T Barrica ... 1016
87 Barono 2009 T ... 1017
87 Venta D'Aubert Merlot 2007 T ... 1017
87 Valssira 2010 RD ... 1015
87 Valssira 24 meses barrica T ... 1015

VT CÁDIZ

90 Taberner nº 1 2007 T ... 1019
90 Finca Moncloa 11 Barricas 2008 T ... 1018
88 Paso de La Plata B ... 1018
88 Fine Tempo 2009 T ... 1017
88 Alhocen Selección personal 2008 T Roble ... 1019
87 Gibalbín 2009 T ... 1018
87 Maestrante 2010 B ... 1017
87 Taberner 2007 T ... 1019
87 Finca Moncloa 2008 T ... 1018
87 Barbazul 2009 T ... 1018
87 Alhocen 2008 T Roble ... 1019
85 Castillo de San Diego 2010 B ... 1018
85 Manuel Aragón 2008 TC ... 1019
85 Manuel Aragón Sauvignon Blanc 2010 B ... 1019
85 Barbarosa 2010 RD ... 1018
85 Expresión de Regantío 2010 T ... 1017

VT CAMPO DE CARTAGENA

88 Darimus Syrah Dulce 2010 Tinto Dulce ... 1019
82 Viña Galtea Semidulce 2010 B ... 1019
80 Darimus Cabernet Syrah 2008 T Barrica ... 1019

VT CASTELLÓ

89 Clos D'Esgarracordes 2008 T Barrica ... 1020
87 Clos D'Esgarracordes Selección Especial 2007 TC ... 1020

VT CASTILLA

95 Venta la Ossa TNT 2009 T ... 1030
94 Vallegarcía Viognier 2009 BFB ... 1049
94 Venta la Ossa Syrah 2009 T ... 1030
93 Venta la Ossa 2009 TC ... 1030
92 Quercus 2006 T ... 1047
92 Vallegarcía Syrah 2008 T ... 1049
92 Finca Río Negro 2008 T ... 1032
92 Clunia Syrah 2009 T ... 1037
92 Finca Río Negro 2009 T ... 1033
91 La Plazuela 2005 T ... 1028
91 Aljibes Syrah 2005 T ... 1022
91 Pago del Ama Syrah 2008 T Barrica ... 1051
91 Torre de Barreda PañoFino 2008 T Roble ... 1026
91 Casalobos 2007 T ... 1037
91 Secua Cabernet-Syrah 2006 T ... 1045
91 L´Ame Malbec 2008 T ... 1020
91 Hipperia 2007 T ... 1049
91 Hacienda Albae 888 T ... 1029
91 La Valona Selección 2007 T ... 1046
91 Ercavio 2010 B Barrica ... 1028
90 Dueto de Fontana 2004 T ... 1047
90 Ercavio Tempranillo 2009 T Roble ... 1028
90 Hacienda Albae Selección 2006 T Barrica ... 1029
90 Vinum Vitae 2005 TC ... 1039
90 Aljibes 2007 T ... 1022
90 Selectus 2007 T ... 1022
90 Finca Muñoz Cepas Viejas 2008 T Roble ... 1052
90 Códice 2009 T ... 1039
90 El Linze 2008 T ... 1028
90 Finca Constancia Tempranillo P23 2009 T ... 1043
90 Aljibes Cabernet Franc 2007 T ... 1022
90 Brincho Kosher 2007 T ... 1026
90 Mazacruz Cima 2008 TC ... 1038
90 Hacienda Albae Chardonnay 2009 BFB ... 1029
90 Clunia Tempranillo 2009 T ... 1037
90 Secua Cabernet-Syrah 2008 T ... 1045
90 Finca la Estacada 18 meses barrica 2007 T ... 1045
90 Nóbriga 2009 T ... 1022

VT CASTILLA-CAMPO DE CALATRAVA

86 Cuba 38 2010 T ... 1053

VT CASTYLE

96 Rumbo al Norte 2010 T ... 1061
95 Pegaso "Granito" 2008 T ... 1061
95 Abadía Retuerta Petit Verdot PV 2009 T ... 1053
95 El Reventón 2009 T ... 1062
94 Terreus 2006 TC ... 1058
94 Abadía Retuerta Pago Negralada 2009 T Barrica ... 1053
94 Abadía Retuerta Pago Valdebellón 2009 T Barrica ... 1053
94 Ossian 2009 BFB ... 1066
94 Tridente Prieto Picudo 2009 T ... 1060
93 Pago la Garduña Syrah 2009 T ... 1053
93 K OS 2008 T ... 1057
93 El Albar Lurton Excelencia 2008 T ... 1056
92 Quinta Apolonia Belondrade 2010 B ... 1054
92 Leda Viñas Viejas 2005 T ... 1058
92 Yllera 25 Aniversario 2005 T ... 1065
92 Abadía Retuerta Selección Especial 2009 T ... 1053
92 Quinta Sardonia QS 2008 T ... 1067
92 Cámbrico Rufete 2006 T ... 1055
92 Aldeasoña 2005 T ... 1056
92 Zerberos Pizarra 2008 T Roble ... 1062
92 La Mejorada Las Cercas 2006 T Roble ... 1061
92 Eilun Verdejo 2009 B ... 1068
92 Vizar Syrah 2009 T ... 1067
92 7 Navas Selección 2008 T ... 1064
92 7 Navas 2009 T Roble ... 1064
92 Pegaso "Barrancos de Pizarra" 2008 T ... 1061
92 La Movida 2009 T ... 1066
92 El Médico 2009 T Roble ... 1066
92 Altos de San Esteban La Mendañona 2008 TC ... 1054
91 Yllera Dominus 2005 TR ... 1065
91 Más de Leda 2008 TC ... 1058
91 Cumal 2007 T ... 1069
91 Marina de Aliste 2008 TC ... 1055
91 Pago de Costalao 24 meses 2006 TC ... 1058
91 Ermita del Conde 2008 T ... 1063
91 Zerberos "Arena Pizarra" 2008 T Roble ... 1062
91 Alter Enos 2007 BFB ... 1068
91 Calixto 2007 T ... 1068
91 Syté 2008 T ... 1057
91 7 Navas 2010 T ... 1064
91 Libamus T ... 1064
91 Garmendia Gran Selección 2010 BFB ... 1064
91 Tridente Tempranillo 2009 T ... 1060
91 Cadozos Pinot Noir 2008 T ... 1062
91 Abadía Retuerta 2010 B ... 1053
90 Yllera Vendimia Seleccionada 2003 TR ... 1066
90 Cadozos 2005 T ... 1062
90 Cámbrico Tempranillo 2006 T ... 1055

90 Miterna Corte Uno 2006 T Barrica 1054
90 E Terna Prieto Picudo 2009 T 1068
90 Zerberos Arena 2008 T Roble 1062
90 La Mejorada Las Cercas 2008 T Roble 1060
90 Altos de San Esteban Viñas de Monte 2009 TC 1054
90 Flor del Páramo 2010 T 1066
90 Gaznata Extra 2008 T 1056
90 LLanos de Cumal 2008 T ....

VT CONTRAVIESA-ALPUJARRA

91 Veleta Nolados 2008 T 1070
90 Los García de Verdevique 2005 T Barrica 1070
89 Veleta Cabernet Sauvignon 2008 T 1070
89 Cerro de la Retama 2008 T 1070
89 Veleta Tempranillo 2008 T 1070
88 Corral de Castro 2008 T Roble 1070

VT CÓRDOBA

85 Llanos de Palacio 2005 T Roble 1071
84 Llanos de Palacio Vendimia Seleccionada T 1070
82 Castillo de Baena 2008 T 1070

VT COSTA DE CANTABRIA

90 Lancina 2010 B 1071
87 Ribera del Asón 2010 B 1071

VT EIVISSA

91 Can Rich 2010 B 1071
91 Lausos Cabernet Sauvignon 2006 T 1071
90 Can Maymó 2010 RD 1071
89 Can Maymó Merlot 2009 T 1071
88 Can Rich Ereso 2010 BFB 1071
88 Can Rich Selección 2007 T 1071

VT EL TERRERAZO

91 Mestizaje 2010 T 1072

VT EXTREMADURA

94 Marqués de Valdueza 2008 T 1076
93 Habla nº 7 2007 T 1073
92 Marqués de Valdueza 2007 T 1076
92 Mirabel 2007 T 1072
92 Habla nº 6 2007 T 1073
92 Marqués de Valdueza Etiqueta Roja 2009 T 1076
91 Valdueza 2009 T 1076
91 Tribel de Mirabel 2009 T 1072
90 Toribio Ecológico 2010 T 1075
90 Marqués de Valdueza Etiqueta Roja 2008 T 1076
88 Corte Real Platinum 2006 T 1075
88 Cañalva Coupage Especial 2009 TC 1073
88 Habla del Silencio 2009 T 1073
88 Valdueza 2008 T 1076
88 Carlos Plaza 2010 T 1073

VT FORMENTERA

93 Cap de Barbaria 2008 T 1077
91 Terramoll Es Monestir 2008 T 1077
90 Savina 2010 B 1077
89 Terramoll 2010 RD 1077

VT ILLA DE MENORCA

92 Binitord 2009 B 1077
91 Binitord Blanc 2010 B 1077
90 Binitord Blanc 2008 B 1077

VT LAUJAR-ALPUJARRA

89 Iniza 2010 T Maceración Carbónica 1078
88 Viña Laujar s.c. B 1078
87 Iniza Cabernet Sauvignon 2009 T 1078
85 Viña Laujar Cota 950 2009 B 1078

VT LIÉBANA

92 Lusia 2009 T Roble 1079

VT MALLORCA

95 Sió 300 Aniversario 2009 T 1081
94 Binigrau Selecció 2008 T 1080
94 Gallinas & Focas 2009 T 1079
93 Nou Nat 2010 B 1079
93 4 Kilos 2009 T 1079
93 12 volts 2009 T 1079
92 E Negre de Binigrau 2010 T 1080
91 Binigrau Chardonnay 2010 BFB 1080
91 Ángel Negre 2009 T Roble 1080
91 Ca'n Vidalet Terra Fusca 2008 T 1080
91 Ca'n Vidalet So del Xiprer-Gran Selección 2008 T 1080
91 Autócton 2008 T 1082
91 Finca Son Bordils Chardonnay 2008 BFB 1081
90 Son Bordils Blanc de raïm Blanc 2010 B 1081
90 Syrah 110 Vins Nadal 2007 T Barrica 1082
90 Finca Son Bordils Merlot 2005 T 1081
90 L'U de Mortitx 2007 TC 1082
90 Gran Sonpuig 2007 T 1081
90 Ca'n Vidalet Ses Pedres 2010 B 1080
90 Son Bordils Rosat de Monastrell 2010 RD 1081
90 Ca'n Vidalet So del Xiprer 2008 T 1080
90 Sioneta Oliver Loma 2010 B 1081

VT MURCIA

87 Estancia del Silencio 2010 T 1083

VT NORTE DE GRANADA

89 Naranjuez Pinot Negra 2008 T 1083
87 Estancia del Silencio 2010 T 1083
87 Vertijana 1 2008 T Barrica 1083
87 Irving Colección Familiar 2007 T 1083

VT RIBERA DEL ANDARAX

92 Vega Enix Laurenti 2006 T 1084
91 Vega Enix Xolair 2006 T 1084
90 Vega Enix Damaris 2006 T 1084
89 Vega Enix Calidón 2007 T 1084
89 Vega Enix Aristeo 2007 T 1084

VT RIBERA DEL GÁLLEGO-CINCO VILLAS

92 Firé 2009 B 1084
92 Firé 2006 T 1084
91 Firé 2007 T 1084
90 Vega de Luchán RD 1084
89 Vega de Luchán Cabernet Sauvignon 2006 T 1085
89 Uva Nocturna Garnachas Viejas 2007 T 1085
89 Edra Merlot Syrah 2006 T 1085
88 Floral de Uncastellum T 1085
88 Uncastellum Rex 2007 T 1085
88 Uva Nocturna 2010 B 1084

87 Uncastellum Aureum 2007 T 1085
87 Edra Xtra Syrah 2007 T 1085
87 Edra Grullas de Paso 2008 T 1085
87 Vega de Luchán Moscatel 2009 B 1084
86 Uncastellum 2007 T Barrica 1085
86 Vega de Luchán 2005 T Barrica 1085
86 Uva Nocturna Merlot 2010 T 1085

VT RIBERA DEL JILOCA

90 Muret Vidadillo 2009 T 1085
89 Muret Oro 2009 T 1086
89 Muret Oro 2010 T 1085
88 Murero 2005 T 1086
88 Xiloca 2010 T 1085
87 Muret Azul 2008 T 1086

VT RIBERA DEL QUEILES

90 Nueve 2007 T 1086
89 Seis al Revés 2007 T 1086
89 Guelbenzu Red 2010 T 1086
88 Guelbenzu Azul 2008 T 1086
88 Guelbenzu Lautus 2005 T 1086
88 Guelbenzu Vierlas 2009 T 1086
88 Tres al Cuadrado 2007 T 1087
88 Nueve (Edición Especial 9/9/9 2009 T 1086
88 La Garnacha Salvaje del Moncayo 2009 T 1086
87 Guelbenzu Evo 2007 T 1086
86 Guelbenzu Lombana 2006 T 1086

VT SIERRA NORTE DE SEVILLA

88 Silente Selección 2006 T Roble 1087
86 Petit Ocnos 2009 B 1087
85 Ocnos 2009 BFB 1087
85 Colonias de Galeón 2010 T Maceración Carbónica....1087

VT VALDEJALÓN

90 Latidos I Love Latidos 2008 T Fermentado en Barrica....1087
88 Latidos I Love 2010 T 1087
88 Latidos I Love 2008 T Barrica....1087
88 Latidos I Love Moscatel 2010 B 1087
86 Latidos I Love 2010 RD 1087
83 Latidos I Love 2010 B 1087

VT VALLE DEL CINCA

87 Valonga Saso Alto 2007 T 1087
86 Valonga 2010 RD 1087
86 Valonga Chardonnay 2010 B 1087

VT VALLES DE SADACIA

93 Melante 2008 B 1088
89 Spanish White Guerrilla Sauvignon Blanc 2010 B 1088
89 Spanish White Guerrilla Chardonnay 2010 B 1088
88 Spanish White Guerrilla Gewürztraminer 2010 B 1088
88 Dry Libalis 2010 B 1088
87 Libalis 2010 B 1088
86 Spanish White Guerrilla Albariño 2010 B 1088
86 Spanish White Guerrilla Riesling 2010 B 1088
86 Spanish White Guerrilla Viognier 2009 B 1088

YCODEN-DAUTE-ISORA

90 Viñátigo Marmajuelo 2010 B 983
90 El Ancón Negramoll 2006 Tinto Dulce 982
89 Viñátigo Gual 2008 B 983
88 Viña Spinola Malvasía Seco 1996 B 984
88 Tinoca Malvasía 2009 Blanco Dulce 984
88 Viña Spinola Malvasía Seco 2003 B 984
88 Viña Spinola Malvasía Seco 2004 B 984
87 Viñátigo Tintilla 2008 T Roble....983
87 Viña Zanata 2010 B 982
87 Miradero 2010 Blanco Afrutado 982
87 Viñamonte Dulce 2006 T 983
87 Viña Spinola Malvasía Seco 2008 B 984
87 Viñátigo Malvasía 2010 B 983

YECLA

94 Casa Cisca 2008 T 988
93 Trenza Family Collection 2008 T 990
92 Castaño Colección Cepas Viejas 2008 T 988
92 Viña Detrás de la Casa Syrah 2007 T 988
92 Viña Detrás de la Casa
Cabernet Sauvignon-Tintorera 2007 TC 988
91 Barahonda Summum 2008 T 989
91 La Máquina Monastrell 2008 T 990
90 Castaño Monastrell 2010 T 988
90 Viña al lado de la Casa 2007 T 988
90 Casa del Canto 2008 T Roble 990
89 Castaño Monastrell Dulce T 988
89 Barahonda Barrica 2009 T Barrica 989
89 Casa del Canto 2007 TR 990
89 Trenza Z-Strand 2008 T 990
89 Nirea Monastrell 2008 T 989
89 Bellum El Principio 2006 T Barrica 990

C

D

E

F

G

H

I

J

K

L

M

N

O

P

Q

R

W

X

Z

A

C

D

F

G

H

I

M

P

T

U

V

W

X

MAP OF THE DO´S IN SPAIN AND VINOS DE PAGO

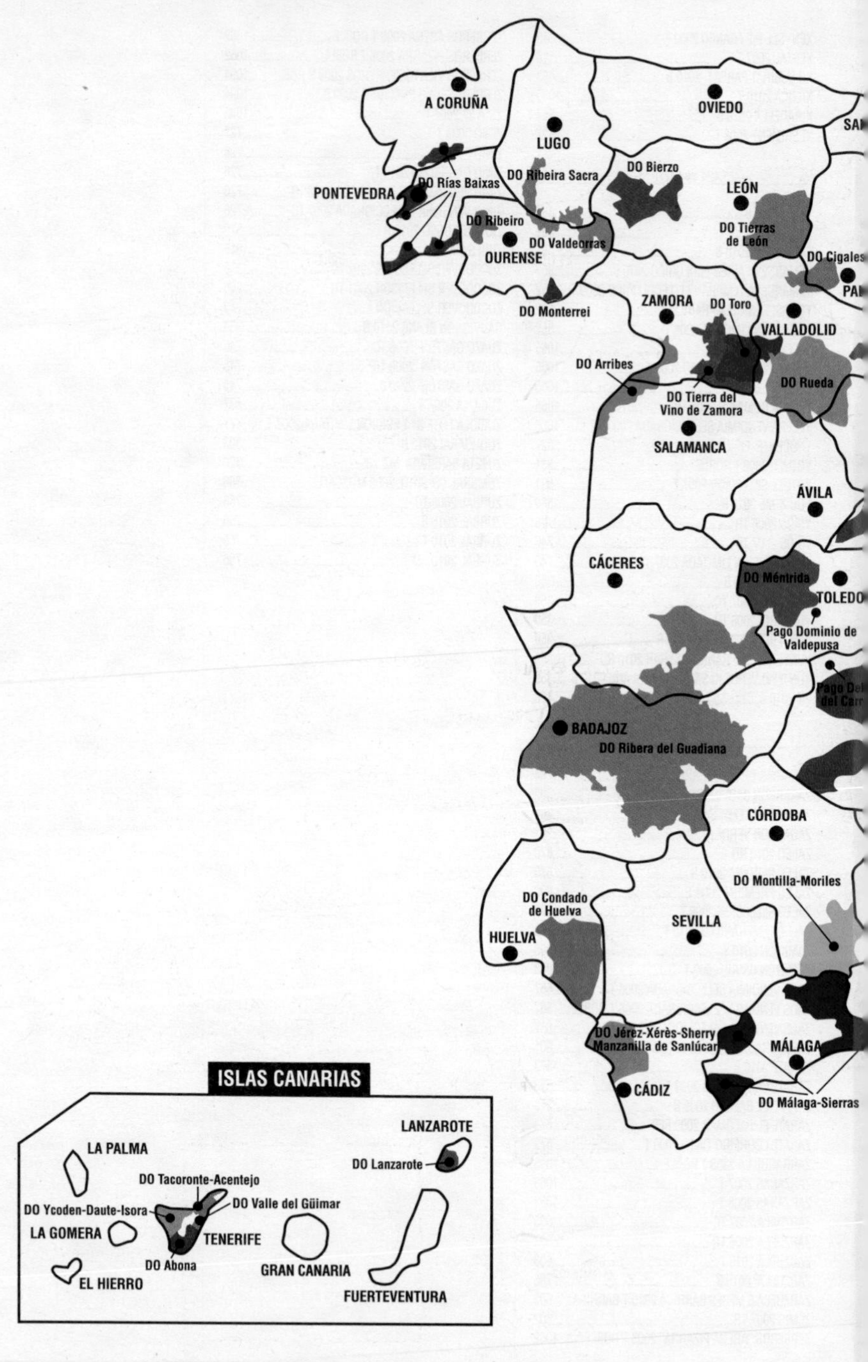

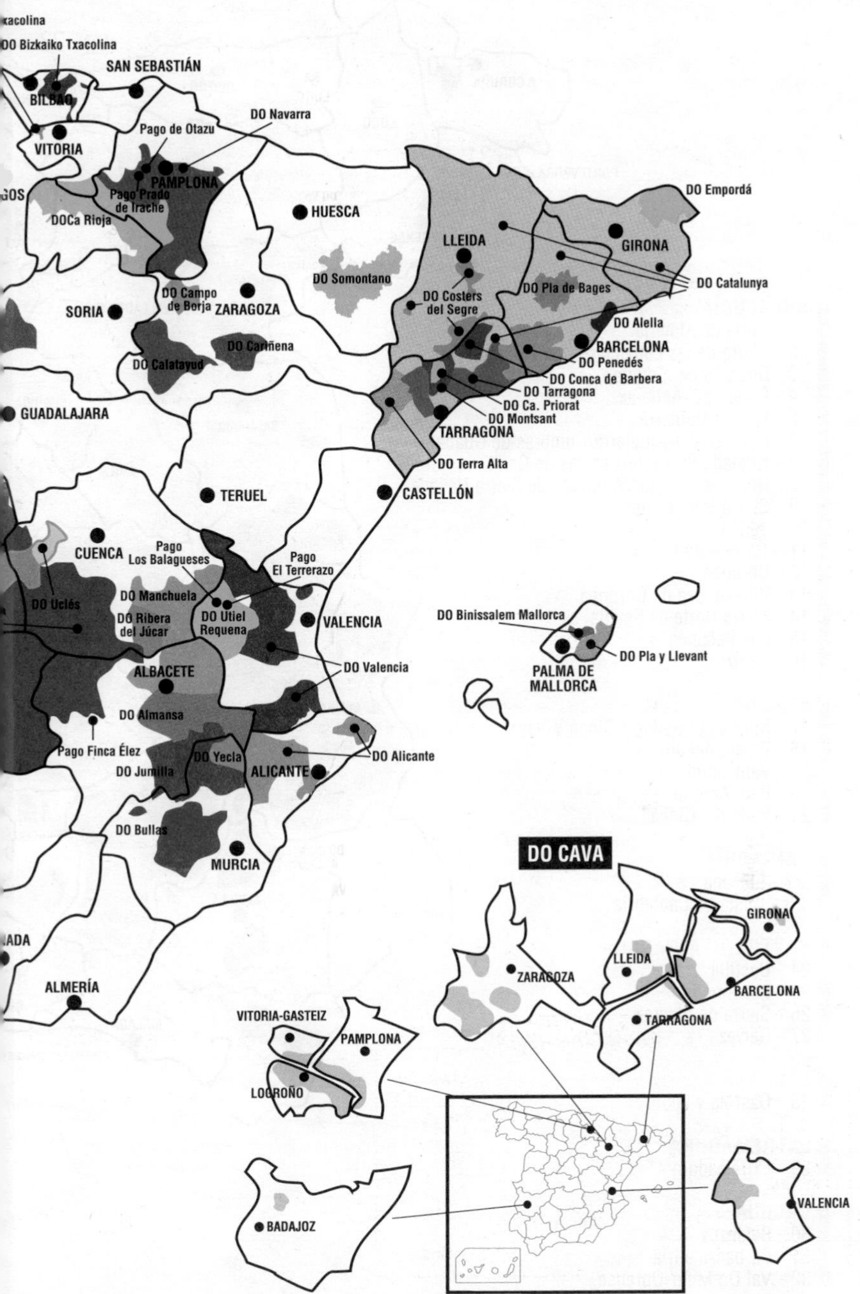

xacolina
DO Bizkaiko Txacolina
SAN SEBASTIÁN
BILBAO
VITORIA
Pago de Otazu
DO Navarra
PAMPLONA
Pago Prado de Irache
DOCa Rioja
HUESCA
DO Somontano
LLEIDA
DO Costers del Segre
DO Empordá
GIRONA
DO Catalunya
DO Pla de Bages
DO Alella
BARCELONA
DO Penedés
DO Conca de Barbera
DO Tarragona
DO Ca. Priorat
DO Montsant
TARRAGONA
DO Terra Alta
DO Campo de Borja
ZARAGOZA
SORIA
DO Cariñena
DO Calatayud
GUADALAJARA
TERUEL
CASTELLÓN
CUENCA
Pago Los Balagueses
Pago El Terrerazo
DO Uclés
DO Manchuela
DO Ribera del Júcar
DO Utiel Requena
VALENCIA
DO Valencia
ALBACETE
DO Almansa
Pago Finca Élez
DO Jumilla
DO Yecla
ALICANTE
DO Alicante
DO Bullas
MURCIA
ADA
ALMERÍA
DO Binissalem Mallorca
DO Pla y Llevant
PALMA DE MALLORCA
DO CAVA
ZARAGOZA
LLEIDA
GIRONA
BARCELONA
TARRAGONA
VITORIA-GASTEIZ
PAMPLONA
LOGROÑO
BADAJOZ
VALENCIA

MAP OF VINOS DE LA TIERRA

ANDALUCÍA
1 - Norte de Almería
2 - Sierra de las Estancias y los Filabres
3 - Desierto de Almería
4 - Ribera del Andarax
5 - Laujar-Alpujarra
6 - Contraviesa-Alpujarra/Cumbres de Guadalfeo
7 - Granada Suroeste/Laderas de Genil
8 - Norte de Granada/Altiplano de Sierra Nevada
9 - Sierra Sur de Jaén
10 - Bailén
11 - Torreperogil
12 - Córdoba
13 - Villaviciosa de Córdoba
14 - Sierra Norte de Sevilla
15 - Los Palacios
16 - Cádiz

ARAGÓN
17 - Ribera del Gállego-Cinco Villas
18 - Ribera del Jiloca
19 - Valdejalón
20 - Bajo Aragón
21 - Valle del Cinca

CANTABRIA
22 - Liébana
23 - Costa de Cantabria

CASTILLA-LA MANCHA
24 - Castilla
25 - Pozohondo
26 - Sierra de Alcaraz
27 - Gálvez

CASTILLA Y LEÓN
28 - Castilla y León

EXTREMADURA
29 - Extremadura

GALICIA
30 - Betanzos
31 - Barbanza e Iria
32 - Val Do Miño-Ourense

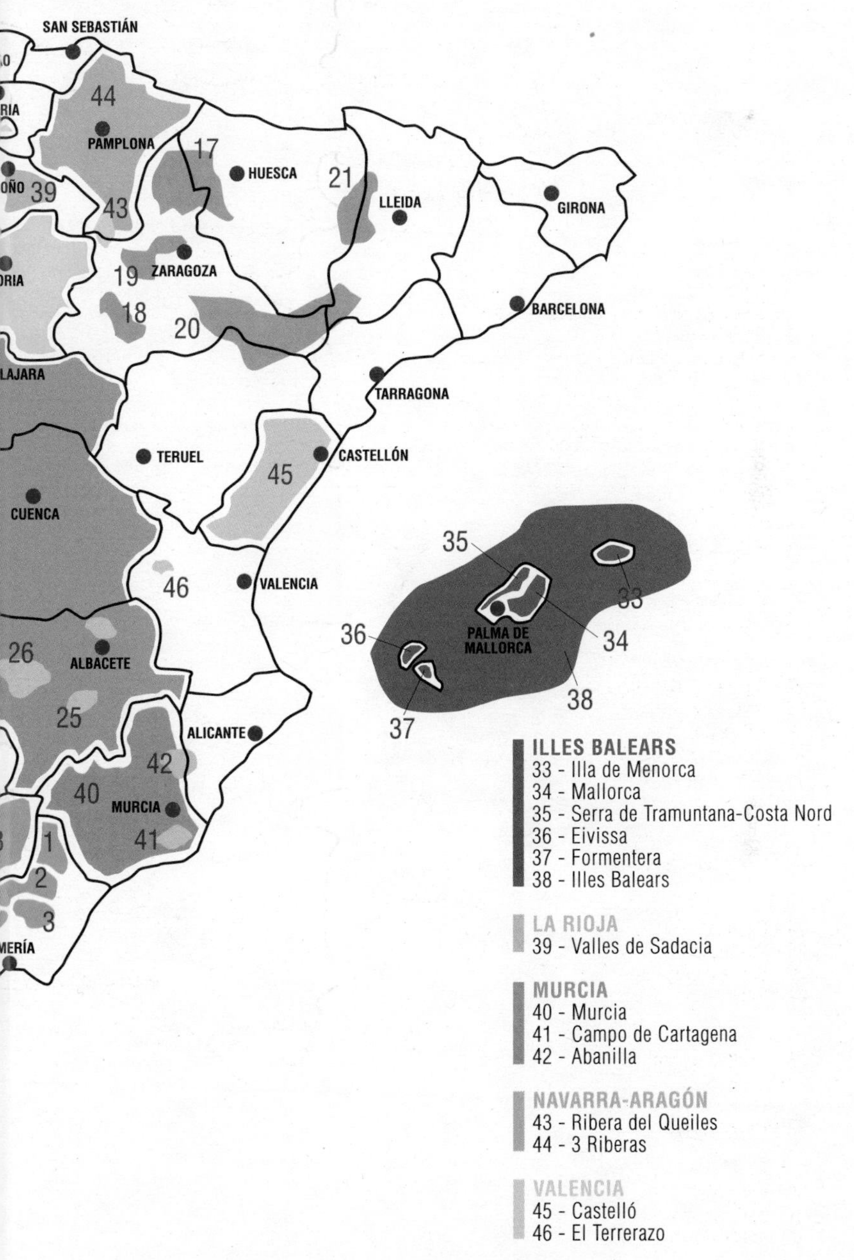

SAN SEBASTIÁN
44
PAMPLONA
17
HUESCA
21
LLEIDA
GIRONA
39
43
19
ZARAGOZA
18
20
BARCELONA
TARRAGONA
TERUEL
CASTELLÓN
45
CUENCA
35
33
46
VALENCIA
36
PALMA DE MALLORCA
34
37
38
26
ALBACETE
25
ALICANTE
42
40
MURCIA
41
1
2
3
ILLES BALEARS
33 - Illa de Menorca
34 - Mallorca
35 - Serra de Tramuntana-Costa Nord
36 - Eivissa
37 - Formentera
38 - Illes Balears
LA RIOJA
39 - Valles de Sadacia
MURCIA
40 - Murcia
41 - Campo de Cartagena
42 - Abanilla
NAVARRA-ARAGÓN
43 - Ribera del Queiles
44 - 3 Riberas
VALENCIA
45 - Castelló
46 - El Terrerazo